New York EXTRA

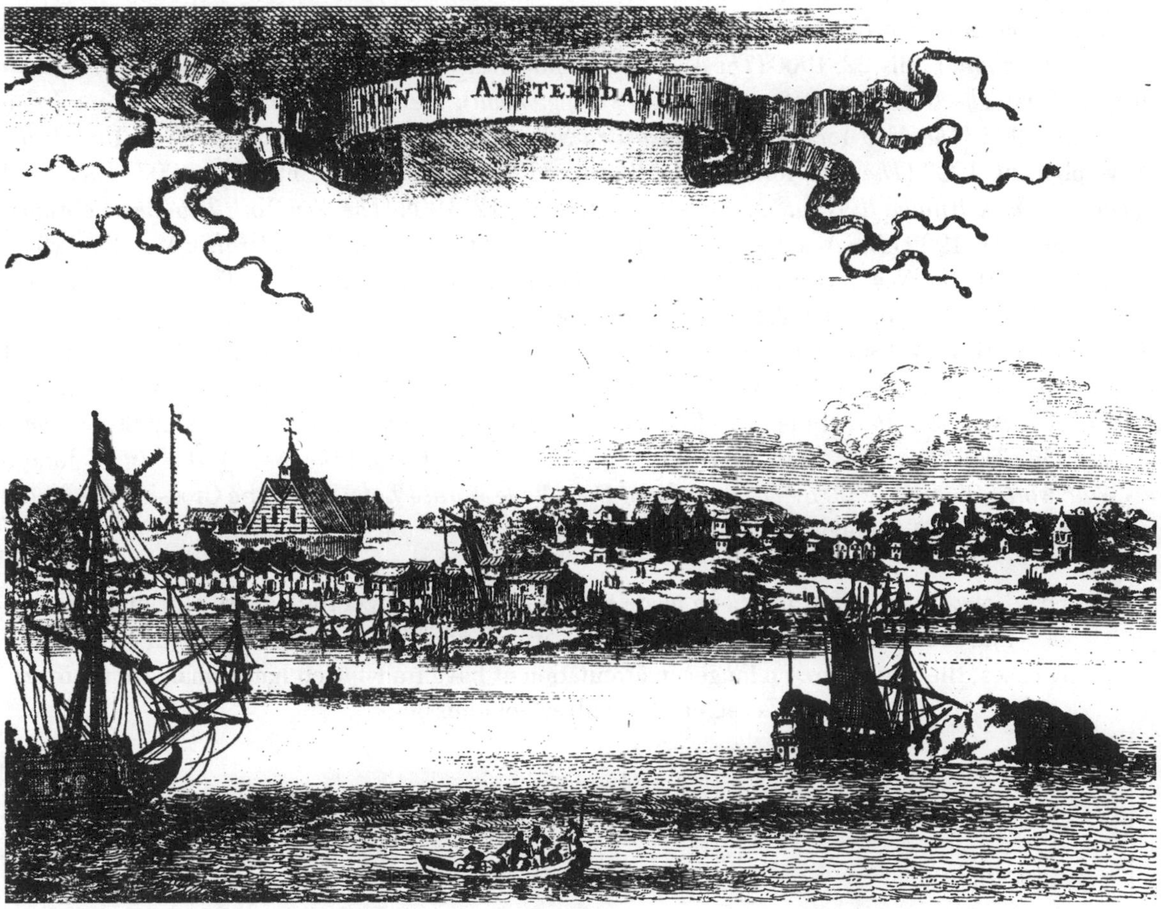

A Newspaper History of the Greatest City in the World from 1671 to the 1939 World's Fair

From the Collection of Eric C. Caren

CASTLE BOOKS

I would like to dedicate *New York Extra* to my favorite New Yorker, my wife Eydie.

Publisher's Note: Every effort has been made to contact the owners of the papers reprinted herein, and to obtain permissions where necessary, all of which are acknowledged. In many cases, the papers are no longer in circulation or have transferred hands many times over. We regret any inadvertent omissions.

The materials in this book have been reproduced from old and exceedingly rare and valuable newspapers. We believe that the articles and photographs herein are of such historic importance that an occasional lapse in the quality of reproduction is justified.

Published by Castle Books,
a division of Book Sales, Inc.
114 Northfield Avenue
Edison, NJ 08837, USA

Compiled by Eric C. Caren

ISBN 0-7858-1138-9
Printed in the United States of America

CONTENTS

NOTE: All papers are from New York City unless otherwise indicated in the title or in parentheses
Publications are presented chronologically except where adjustments have been made to accommodate spreads.

PAGE	DATE	PUBLICATION	ARTICLES OF INTEREST
37	December 21, 1782	THE ROYAL GAZETTE	As the title and coat of arms suggest, the British controlled NY at this point of the Revolution. Note ads for a "Livery Stable Keeper" and "Furrier from London".
38-39	May 5, 1783	NEW YORK GAZETTE AND WEEKLY MERCURY	American Revolution— New Yorkers read about the cessation of hostilities, P. 2, col. 2.
40-43	November 28, 1783	NEW YORK MORNING POST	New Yorkers read the Treaty of Paris ending the American Revolution! Plus, the British troops leave the city, American troops march in, and Washington and his officers dine at Fraunces Tavern (still open today in NY).
44	December 18, 1783	SALEM GAZETTE (Salem, MA)	Washington's farewell to his officers at "Frances" (sic) Tavern, see Col. 1.
45-46	September 30, 1784	NEW YORK PACKET	A post-Revolution NY newspaper. Note the illustrated slave ad (slavery would not be abolished in NY for another fifty years).
47	July 1, 1786	THE DAILY ADVERTISER	Early issue of NY's first successful daily newspaper.
48	August 11, 1788	BOSTON GAZETTE	NY ratifies the U. S. Constitution
49-50	April 15, 1789	GAZETTE OF THE UNITED STATES	Vol. I, # 1 issue of what would become the mouthpiece of Washington's Federalist Party. It contains the earliest report of the election of Washington as our first President.
51-52	May 2, 1789	GAZETTE OF THE UNITED STATES	George Washington is inaugurated as First President of the United States. He takes the oath in NYC (first capital of the country).
53	September 30, 1789	GAZETTE OF THE UNITED STATES	John Jay is appointed the first Chief Justice of the United States, col. 2.
54	October 7, 1789	GAZETTE OF THE UNITED STATES	First National Thanksgiving Day proclaimed by George Washington in NYC.
55	January 9, 1790	GAZETTE OF THE UNITED STATES	New Yorkers read the text of President Washington's first State of the Union Address and are told of his fashion statement to the Congress (see col. 3).
56-57	April 25, 1794	AMERICAN MINERVA	Rare, short-lived newspaper edited by Noah Webster and filled with ads placed by the creator of the famous dictionary which bears his name.
58	April 2, 1802	AMERICAN CITIZEN AND GENERAL ADVERTISER	"Dentist to the late President Washington", Dr. Greenwood places an ad for his dental practice.
59-62	July 13, 1804	NEW YORK EVENING POST	The Burr-Hamilton duel resulting in the death of the latter is reported here in the newspaper that Alexander Hamilton founded in 1801, the longest running newspaper in NY.
63-64	August 22, 1807	AMERICAN CITIZEN	Robert Fulton writes to the editor of this NY newspaper announcing completion of his first famous steam boat trip from Albany to NY, col. 4.
65	January 5, 1808	L'ORACLE AND DAILY ADVERTISER	Very early bi-lingual (English-French) NY newspaper. Perhaps the first foreign daily newspaper in the city.
66-67	July 11, 1812	THE WAR	Unusual NY paper that came out to report the events of the War of 1812 as they unfolded. Includes the 4th of July celebration in the City.
68-70	July 11, 1822	LONG ISLAND FARMER (Jamaica, Queens County)	An early Queens County newspaper.
71-72	August 4, 1825	AMERICAN EAGLE (Huntington, NY)	Very early Long Island newspaper typical of the period. The front page is filled with a miscellany including poetry, piracy, and one piece headed, "Conjugal Affection". Local ads fill the back page.
73	April 7, 1826	NEW YORK AMERICAN	Many New Yorkers get their first look at a train. A far cry from the NYC subway!
74	July 18, 1827	THE MASSACHUSETTS SPY (Worcester, MA)	New York State abolishes slavery and blacks in NYC take to the streets to celebrate.
75-76	July 8, 1831	NEW YORK SPECTATOR	Ex-President James Monroe dies in NYC. This newspaper drapes its columns in black mourning rules.
77-78	April 4, 1834	THE MAN	Organized labor at the start of the Industrial Revolution—"Great Meeting of Mechanics and the Working Men of the City of New York". This is the earliest pro-labor penny paper.
79	December 23, 1835	POUGHKEEPSIE JOURNAL (Poughkeepsie, NY)	Map of the destructive NYC fire of 1835, followed by an all-too-lengthy list of buildings which were burned down.
80	March 15, 1838	THE EMANCIPATOR	NYC played host to a number of early abolitionist movements. This paper was the organ of the American Anti-Slavery Society.
81	August 3, 1839	THE SUN	"Arrival of the Steam Ship British Queen" An unusually large wood engraving on *The Sun's* front page to commemorate the ships landing on Sandy Hook.

PAGE	DATE	PUBLICATION	ARTICLES OF INTEREST
82-84	October 9, 1839	EVENING PALLADIUM (New Haven, CT)	The Amistad—A very detailed account of the affair ending in the capture of the ship by American authorities in New York.
85	c. mid-January 1840	EXTRA SUN	Incredible spot news production combined the reporting of the explosion of the steamship Lexington with a lithographic print of the drama. This was done by a young N. Currier, later of Currier & Ives fame. This broadside extra was said to be printed within days of the disaster in the Long Island Sound.
86	November 14, 1840	NEW YORK OBSERVER	A look at "New York Railroads".
87-88	August 18, 1844	LADIES' MAN AND EVERYBODY'S BEAU, Vol. 1, #1.	Even in the middle of the 19th century there were New Yorkers looking for lighter and more entertaining newspapers (apparently not enough though, since we can find no record that this paper survived to Vol. 1 #2).
89-91	January 1, 1845	ANNUAL PICTORIAL NY HERALD	People and places around NYC are featured in this special New Year's annual edition of the Herald.
92-94	June 8, 1848	NEW YORK PATHFINDER	To help you find your way— early transportation paper "Devoted to steamers, railroads, omnibuses, stages . . . "
95	August 18, 1849	NEW YORK DAY-BOOK	NYC entertainment in 1849: Christy Minstrels, opera, and ballet. See first column.
96-97	September 18, 1851	THE NEW YORK TIMES	The beginning of a legend in print journalism—the first issue of The New York Times.
98-99	February 23, 1852	TAYLOR'S BULLETIN	This "saloon" newspaper, with a menu on the back, gives us an idea of what dishes New York restaurants offered their patrons in the mid-19th century. Get the news, train schedules, entertainment, drink, and have dinner without ever leaving the bar.
100	November 12, 1853	NEW YORK ILLUSTRATED NEWS	"Firemen's Celebration—The Procession In Broadway". Also note Brady's (Photographic) Gallery building with camera above the sign.
101	January 7, 1854	GLEASON'S PICTORIAL (Boston, MA)	"New Regulation Uniform of the New York Police"
102-3	March 18, 1854	GLEASON'S PICTORIAL (Boston, MA)	"Panoramic Views of Broadway"
104	March 6, 1858	HARPER'S WEEKLY	"Sleighing In Broadway"
105	August 28, 1858	HARPER'S WEEKLY	"The Burning of the City Hall, New York, August 18, 1858"
106	September 2, 1858	NEW YORK EVENING EXPRESS	Celebration of the completion of the Atlantic Telegraph Cable.
107	October 9, 1858	NEW YORK CLIPPER	One of the City's first sporting journals. The front page shows early use of gloves in a boxing bout.
108	October 16, 1858	HARPER'S WEEKLY	"Destruction of the New York Crystal Palace By Fire..."
109	November 13, 1858	HARPER'S WEEKLY	A front page look at "The New Brick Church In Fifth Avenue, New York"
110	August 13, 1859	FRANK LESLIE'S ILLUSTRATED NEWS	"The Great War on the New York Piggeries"
111	October 22, 1859	GLEASON'S PICTORIAL LINE OF BATTLE SHIP (Boston, MA)	A front page "View of the Fulton Ferry Buildings, Brooklyn, Long Island, N.Y."
112-3	September 1, 1860	NEW YORK ILLUSTRATED NEWS	"Our Marble Palaces—The New Store of Messrs. Lord & Taylor..." Note that the back page mistakenly prints the year as 1880. Plus the "New York Yacht Club sailing in two squadrons".
114	March 2, 1861	FRANK LESLIE'S ILLUSTRATED NEWS	President Elect-Lincoln meets NY Mayor at City Hall on his way to begin duties in Washington, D.C.
115	May 28, 1861	NEW YORK SEMI WEEKLY TRIBUNE	"The Murder of Col. Ellsworth" This New York Zouave was murdered while trying to remove the "Rebel Flag" from the Marshall House in Alexandria, VA. To many in the North, he became known as the first Union martyr of the Civil War.
116	November 19, 1861	THE SUN	The Civil War—"Organization of the Irish Brigade" from New York, including an illustrated biography of one of its members.
117	January 1, 1862	NY HERALD NEWSMAN'S NEW YEARS ADDRESS	Union patriotic New Years Address by the newsmen of the Herald.
118	July 16, 1863	NY DAILY NEWS	Civil War Draft Riots in NYC.
119	February 25, 1864	THE DRUM BEAT (Brooklyn, NY)	Sanitary Fair newspaper. Its purpose was to raise money for hospitals and other needs related to the young men fighting for the union cause. Also note the front page description of Long Island.
120-1	August 27, 1864	HARPER'S WEEKLY	Famed illustrator Thomas Nast gives us a woodcut view of Central Park in summer.

PAGE	DATE	PUBLICATION	ARTICLES OF INTEREST
122-3	March 11, 1865	FRANK LESLIE'S ILLUSTRATED NEWS	"Our Volunteer Fire Department"
124-5	May 13, 1865	FRANK LESLIE'S ILLUSTRATED NEWS	President Lincoln's funeral procession along Broadway.
126	May 2, 1864	THE WORLD	A very early view of the proposed Brooklyn Bridge.
127	July 14, 1865	NEW YORK HERALD	P. T. Barnum's museum is destroyed by fire. He would go on to make a national sensation with his circus.
128-9	November 4, 1865	FRANK LESLIE'S ILLUSTRATED NEWS	Brooklyn Atlantics vs. Brooklyn Eckfords surrounded by "the leading players of the principal clubs of New York, Brooklyn, and Newark".
130	February 3, 1866	FRANK LESLIE'S ILLUSTRATED NEWS	NYC Policemen in the Baton Exercise at Police Headquarters.
131	October 17, 1867	BALL PLAYERS CHRONICLE	Edited by Henry Chadwick, this is the first periodical devoted to the game of baseball. "The Championship Pennant Leaves Brooklyn for the First Time".
132	February 13, 1869	HARPER'S WEEKLY	"The Horse Market, Bull's Head, New York City"
133	August 19, 1869	THE REVOLUTION	The first women's suffrage paper edited by Elizabeth Cady Stanton and owned by Susan B. Anthony.
134	December 23, 1869	STREET AND SMITH'S NY WEEKLY	New York meets Buffalo Bill! This picture and story by Ned Buntline introduces New Yorkers to a living legend.
135-6	April 1, 1870	THE JEWISH TIMES	Early Jewish newspaper discusses "Mount Sinai Hospital".
137-8	September 18, 1870	THE WORLD	The good old days? Not according to this "Murder Map of New York" with its "Blood-Red Record".
139	July 22, 1871	THE NEW YORK TIMES	First installment of the *Times* expose. Boss Tweed and his Tammany Ring—$44,000+ for carpets on June 6th alone.
140	October 21, 1871	THE DAY'S DOINGS	"What are We Coming To? — Female Tramway-car conductors".
141	November 25, 1871	HARPER'S WEEKLY	Victoria Woodhull and four other "adventurous women of this city" go to the polls and demand to be allowed to vote.
142-3	c. January 10, 1872	THE LIFE AND DEATH OF JAMES FISK, JR.	A special "one shot" newspaper devoted to the killing of James Fisk, Jr., the Robber Baron of the Erie Railroad. The murderer is pictured below a portrait of the mistress who came between them. The grand funeral spilled out of the opera house Fisk had purchased.
144	January 13, 1872	HARPER'S BAZAR	The latest fashions is "Ladies and Children's Dresses".
145	c. Fall 1872	GREELEY CAMPAIGN BUDGET	Vol. 1 # 1 issue of this rare campaign newspaper supporting Horace Greeley, editor of the NY Tribune, for President. He would die before the votes were counted (and he would still have lost).
146-9	February 18, 1873	WOODHULL AND CLAFLIN'S WEEKLY	Free Love and Free Press in NY. This newspaper was published by a radical proponent of free thought and free love. Victoria Woodhull was an editor and a candidate for President. Much of this issue includes her recent arrest for "circulating obscene literature".
150	June 23, 1873	THE NEW SENSATION	"The Fastest Girl in New York"—A look at what a wild NY party girl might have worn in 1873.
151-2	November 21, 1873	THE DAILY GRAPHIC	Boss Tweed in prison, "At Last". Plus, "Tweed's Romantic Life".
153	November 9, 1874	NEW YORK HERALD	"Awful Calamity"? Wild animals "Broken loose from Central Park"— including bison, tigers, lions, bears, and a rhinoceros—attack and kill people on the streets of the city. No, this was a newspaper hoax!
154	December 2, 1874	THE DAILY GRAPHIC	Christmas season ads, including Santa Claus at Lord & Taylor.
155	c. late January 1875	PICTORIAL HISTORY OF THE BEECHER -TILTON SCANDAL	A "one shot" news journal deals with the Beecher-Tilton scandal. Reverend Henry Ward Beecher was having an affair with the wife of Theodore Tilton—a huge scandal in Brooklyn.
156	c. late January 1875	THE HUMORS OF THE BROOKLYN SCANDAL or THE FUNNY SIDE OF A SERIOUS SUBJECT	(see comment above).
157	July 15, 1875	THE DAILY GRAPHIC	NY millionaires Vanderbilt (NY Central Railroad) and Gould (Union Pacific) are satirized here.
158	January 1, 1876	FRANK LESLIE'S ILLUSTRATED NEWS	"Holiday Exhibition of Dolls in a Window at Macy's"
159-60	February 1876	FIRE RECORD	Fire Department newspaper features the NY Tribune building on front page and fire fighting equipment ads on the back page.
161	August 19, 1876	THE ILLUSTRATED WEEKLY	A front page look at Cornelius Vanderbilt "New York's Railroad King and Millionaire".

PAGE	DATE	PUBLICATION	ARTICLES OF INTEREST
162	c. October 1876	HAYES CAMPAIGN COMIC PICTORIAL	This pro-Hayes campaign newspaper arouses fear that if Tilden is elected, he will embrace the old Ring including Boss Tweed.
163	November 8, 1876	THE SUN	Dewey Defeats Truman! *No*, Tilden Defeats Hayes! Anxious to announce that NY Governor Samuel Tilden, a hero in the Tweed Ring expose, was elected president, The Sun jumps the gun.
164	April 7, 1877	SPIRIT OF THE TIMES	A front page look at "Delmonico's Cafe".
165	November 24, 1877	HARPER'S WEEKLY	Illustrations showing "How the Streets of New York are Cleaned".
166-7	August 10, 1878	HARPER'S WEEKLY	"Scenes and Incidents on Coney Island"
168	February 21, 1880	ILLUSTRATED POLICE NEWS (Boston, MA)	The recently invented telephone (1876) is employed by enterprising NY "Call Girls".
169-70	September 10, 1881	HARPER'S WEEKLY	"The New York Stock Exchange"
171	September 24, 1881	HARPER'S WEEKLY	"A Game of Lawn Tennis, Staten Island Club Grounds"
172	October 8, 1881	HARPER'S WEEKLY	Opium was the big drug problem in late 19th century New York. This illustration shows the infamous opium den.
173-4	November 19, 1881	HARPER'S WEEKLY	"The Grand Street Tenement-House Disaster"
175	June 24, 1882	HARPER'S WEEKLY	The electric light comes to NYC.
176	May 24, 1883	BROOKLYN DAILY EAGLE	The opening of the great and famous Brooklyn Bridge uniting Manhattan and Brooklyn.
177	January 3, 1885	NATIONAL POLICE GAZETTE	A humorous look at "Joys of Travel on the Elevated".
178	June 13, 1885	FRANK LESLIE'S ILLUSTRATED NEWS	The Statue of Liberty—"The Gift of the French Republic to the United States"
179	c. 1885	PUCK	Cover the Statue of Liberty with ads? A sarcastic suggestion from famed comic illustrator F. Opper regarding raising the additional funds to complete the installation of the Statue of Liberty.
180	October 29, 1886	THE WORLD	The Statue of Liberty is dedicated.
181	July 29, 1886	THE DAILY GRAPHIC	"The Camp of Buffalo Bill's Wild West, Staten Island". Note Annie Oakley firing her pistol at bottom center.
182	March 19, 1887	COHEN'S SATURDAY BUDGET	The death of Rev. Henry Ward Beecher plus, "The Metropolitan Museum—How the Sunday Opening Plan is Progressing".
183-5	March 24, 1888	FRANK LESLIE'S ILLUSTRATED NEWS	The great Blizzard of 1888 illustrated.
186	March 13, 1888	THE SUN	The famous Blizzard of 1888.
187-8	May 11, 1889	FRANK LESLIE'S ILLUSTRATED NEWS	The Washington Centennial— Huge celebration in NYC for the 100th anniversary of the inauguration of our first President.
189	July 8, 1889	THE DAILY GRAPHIC	"The New Polo Grounds"
190	July 27, 1889	NEW YORK ILLUSTRATED NEWS	Boxing champion John L. Sullivan toots his own horn as editor of this illustrated sporting journal. He has reason to be proud—he has just defeated Kilrain in a 75-round bout. It is also the last professional bare-knuckle fight in the U.S.
191	February 2, 1890	NEW YORK WORLD-SUPPLEMENT	New York World correspondent outdoes the fictional hero in Jules Verne's "Around the World in 80 Days". The World issues this special poster to celebrate.
192	April 19, 1890	THE EVENING SUN	A look at the local stars in both the National League as well as the short-lived Players League.
193	March 7, 1891	HARPER'S WEEKLY	"The New York Hotels on the Plaza, New York"
194	March 14, 1891	HARPER'S WEEKLY	"The Waldorf" Hotel
195	November 30, 1892	NEW YORK ADVOCATE	Illustrated and priced Bloomingdales advertisement includes toys and dolls.
196	December 8, 1892	NEW YORK ADVOCATE	Full page Bloomingdales advertisement with prices.
197	May 21, 1893	THE WORLD	The humorous side of late 19th century city streets, with traffic jams even then.
198	February 3, 1894	HARPER'S WEEKLY	"A Performance of 'Carmen' In the Remodeled Metropolitan Opera House, New York"
199	January 5, 1896	THE WORLD	NY is treated to the first comic strip—The Yellow Kid by R. F. Outcault. Soon this figure lead to the term, "Yellow Journalism" to define the sensationalistic newspapers of the era.

PAGE	DATE	PUBLICATION	ARTICLES OF INTEREST
200	April 24, 1896	THE SUN	The first publicly shown motion picture on "Thomas A. Edison's Vitascope", is described in the first column.
201	October 11, 1896	NEW YORK JOURNAL	"Has Public Taste Sunk to this Degrading Level?" Apparently so, since the paper uses detailed illustrations to describe the performance of "a vulgar young woman" who undresses on the stage.
202	September 21, 1897	THE SUN	"Yes, Virginia", there is a Santa Claus. Here is where it all started with the answer by The Sun's editor to little Virginia's fabled question, creating one of the most famous editorials ever.
203	February 17, 1898	THE WORLD	Explosion of the battleship Maine—New York Yellow Journalism at its zenith.
204-5	c. November 1897	THE MAIL AND EXPRESS MAGAZINE SUPPLEMENT	A view of the New York skyline in the 1890's.
206-7	January 13, 1898	LESLIE'S WEEKLY	"The Greater New York—Born, January 1st, 1898" New York at this point contained all five of its boroughs.
208	April 30, 1898	THE NORTH SIDE NEWS	"Buildings and Grounds of The New York University, University Heights"
209	May 29, 1898	NEW YORK JOURNAL	The "New York Letter Carrier's Band" take part in "Decoration Day in Aid of Maine Fund".
210	June 25, 1898	NEW YORK JOURNAL	Spanish-American War—A front page look at Roosevelt's Rough Riders and a report of the death of many NY society youth on the way to Santiago.
211	July 10, 1898	THE WORLD	"Col. 'Teddy' Roosevelt Leading the Charge of the Rough Riders" during the Spanish-American War.
212	August 13, 1898	THE NORTH SIDE NEWS	Bikes fill the Bronx—a favorite leisure activity of the period as seen in this organized "Bicycle Parade".
213	September 10, 1898	THE NORTH SIDE NEWS	"Bronx Borough's First Synagogue"
214	October 1898	THE HORSELESS AGE	Wealthy New Yorkers are seen in their early automobile.
215-6	November 5, 1898	THE NORTH SIDE NEWS	Teddy Roosevelt comes to the Bronx as reported in a Bronx Borough newspaper.
217	July 29, 1899	HARPER'S WEEKLY	"The Strike of the Trolley Employees in New York City"
218-9	November 20, 1898	NEW YORK TRIBUNE ILLUSTRATED SUPPLEMENT	"The Newest County"—Nassau County, Long Island.
220	September 30, 1899	NEW YORK TRIBUNE	A front page look at the celebration on the Hudson River in honor of Admiral Dewey, hero of the Spanish-American War.
221-2	March 25, 1900	NEW YORK JOURNAL	Ground is broken for the "Rapid Transit Tunnel".
223	July 7, 1900	HARPER'S WEEKLY	"The Harlem River Speedway, New York City"
224	July 22, 1900	NEW YORK TRIBUNE ILLUSTRATED SUPPLEMENT	"The Tenement Child in the City"
225	July 7, 1901	NEW YORK DAILY TRIBUNE	"Types of Street Merchants"
226	August 4, 1901	NEW YORK TRIBUNE ILLUSTRATED SUPPLEMENT	"The Barrel of Love at Coney Island"
227	September 2, 1901	THE NEW YORK PRESS	"Carrie Nation (famous for taking hatchets to liquor establishments) Sweeps Through City and is Arrested, But Soon Released"
228	March 23, 1902	NEW YORK TRIBUNE ILLUSTRATED SUPPLEMENT	A look at Ellis Island.
229	June 29, 1902	NEW YORK TRIBUNE ILLUSTRATED SUPPLEMENT	The Flatiron Building, "The Remarkable New Skyscraper at Twenty-third St., Fifth Ave. and Broadway".
230	July 12, 1903	NEW YORK TRIBUNE ILLUSTRATED SUPPLEMENT	"Some of the Nine New Theatres that will Greet Manhattan Pleasure Seekers Next Season"
231	November 29, 1903	NEW YORK TRIBUNE ILLUSTRATED SUPPLEMENT	Houses are cleared to make room "On the Site of the New, Grand Central Railway Terminal".
232	December 20, 1903	NEW YORK TRIBUNE	The Williamsburg Bridge opens.
233	June 15, 1904	THE EVENING SUN—EXTRA	"The General Slocum Burned in East River"
234	July 17, 1904	NEW YORK TRIBUNE ILLUSTRATED SUPPLEMENT	Plans for the New Pennsylvania Station.
235	July 24, 1904	NEW YORK PRESS ILLUSTRATED SUPPLEMENT	"When the Multitudes Flee the City"

PAGE	DATE	PUBLICATION	ARTICLES OF INTEREST
236	October 13, 1905	THE EVENING SUN	Auto racing on Long Island.
237	June 26, 1906	THE GLOBE	"Millionaire Murderer and Woman who was the Cause of His Crime". The murder of Stanford White by Harry Thaw.
238	January 12, 1908	NEW YORK TRIBUNE	The New York Public Library nears completion.
239	February 2, 1908	NEW YORK TRIBUNE	The more things change, the more they stay the same!
240	March 21, 1909	NEW YORK TRIBUNE	"1909 Spring Fashions"
241	April 12, 1909	NEW YORK HERALD Paris edition	"New Queensboro Bridge Costs New York City $20,000,000"
242	May 12, 1909	NEW YORK HERALD Paris edition	The Wright Brothers " . . . Get Rousing Reception from New Yorkers".
243	November 27, 1910	NEW YORK TRIBUNE ILLUSTRATED SUPPLEMENT	"Where to put the Titanic?" Over a year before its tragic maiden voyage, this paper ponders the question of where the oversized ship will dock once it reaches New York. The illustration gives an unusual sense of scale by placing Henry Hudson's Half Moon sideways within the Titanic's walls.
244	March 26, 1911	THE TRIBUNE	The Triangle Shirtwaist Factory fire.
245	October 30, 1911	THE WORLD	*The World* announces that its proprietor, Joseph Pulitzer, has died.
246	January 26, 1913	THE BROOKLYN DAILY EAGLE	"John D. Rockefeller's $100,000,000 Foundation"
247	April 9, 1913	THE BROOKLYN DAILY EAGLE	The Brooklyn team that played the first game at the new Ebbets Field.
248-9	April 6, 1913	THE BROOKLYN DAILY EAGLE	The local newspaper celebrates the first game ever at Ebbets Field.
250	April 20, 1913	THE BROOKLYN DAILY EAGLE	"New Subways Mean Prosperity for Brooklyn"
251	May 8, 1915	THE NEW YORK PRESS	The Lusitania—The German warning "Notice" is superimposed over the front page. This notice had appeared several days before the Lusitania left New York.
252-3	July 4, 1915	THE NEW YORK PRESS	J. P. Morgan is shot at his home near Glen Cove, Long Island.
254	August 30, 1917	THE EVENING WORLD	Troops parade down Fifth Avenue in this tremendous send-off before going to fight in the First World War.
255	January 7, 1919	NEW YORK TRIBUNE	Teddy Roosevelt dies at his home in Oyster Bay, Long Island.
256	January 6, 1920	THE BOSTON POST	The local Boston newspaper announces, "Babe Ruth Sold to the Yankees".
257	September 16, 1920	THE WISCONSIN NEWS	Anarchist bomb on Wall Street.
258	October 11, 1923	LOS ANGELES EXAMINER	"Casey at the Bat!" Casey Stengel helps the NY Giants win the first game of this "Subway Series" against the Yankees with a dramatic ninth inning home run.
259	October 15, 1923	THE EVENING BULLETIN (Providence, RI)	"Yanks Win World's Baseball Championship". Yanks defeat Giants in the Subway Series.
260	December 21, 1924	THE WORLD	"Red Magic Section"—Harry Houdini edited this unusual Sunday supplement. He is shown here in his handcuffs.
261-2	April 8, 1927	THE WORLD	New Yorkers get their first look at a television in operation.
263	June 14, 1927	DAILY MIRROR	Charles Lindbergh welcomed back to the City after his famed NY to Paris hop.
264	July 21, 1927	THE BALTIMORE NEWS (Baltimore, MD)	Jack Dempsey defeats Jack Sharkey at Yankee Stadium.
265	September 30, 1927	LOS ANGELES EVENING HERALD	"Ruth Hits 60th Home Run"
266	October 8, 1927	THE SAN FRANCISCO CALL	Yankees win the 1927 World Series in 4 straight. Some say this was the greatest team in the history of the game.
267	October 20, 1928	PANORAMA—NEW YORK'S ILLUSTRATED NEWS WEEKLY	It's a bird. It's a plane, no, it's the Dirigible over Manhattan.
268	April 15, 1929	DAILY NEWS	A headline that sums up the Roaring 20s perfectly with sex, booze, music, wealth, and scandal: "Park Ave. Gin-Jazz Love Drama Bared in Millionaire's Death Duel".
269-70	October 29, 1929	THE SUN	The stock market crashes.
271-2	May 1, 1931	BROOKLYN DAILY EAGLE	The Empire State Building opens.

PAGE	DATE	PUBLICATION	ARTICLES OF INTEREST
273-4	October 24, 1931	THE SUN	The George Washington Bridge opens.
275-6	December 18, 1931	BROOKLYN DAILY EAGLE	Infamous gangster Legs Diamond is slain.
277	September 2, 1932	NEW YORK HERALD TRIBUNE	Mayor Jimmy Walker resigns his office.
278-9	October 2, 1932	NEW YORK HERALD TRIBUNE	A rare report on "the called shot", the World Series home run which Ruth predicted with a point of his finger.
280-1	June 3, 1935	NEW YORK POST	"Normandie Sets Record—100,000 Here Cheer Arrival"
282	October 24, 1935	DAILY RECORD (Boston, MA)	Big time NYC gangster killed. "Dutch Schultz Shot Down!" in Newark as another gang member is killed in Manhattan.
283	May 4, 1936	SAN FRANCISCO CHRONICLE	Joe DiMaggio gets three hits in his debut appearance on the Yankee team (also, his first major league game).
284	June 23, 1938	DAILY RECORD (Boston, MA)	Joe Louis knocks out Max Schmeling in the first round at Yankee Stadium.
285-6	July 14, 1938	EVENING PUBLIC LEDGER (Philadelphia, PA)	Howard Hughes welcomed in NYC after his around-the-world flight.
287-9	October 31, 1938	DAILY NEWS	The "War of the Worlds" broadcast frightens many New Yorkers as it does citizens throughout the nation.
290-3	April 30, 1939	THE NEW YORK TIMES	The Fair and the City—Special Supplement announces events at the 1939 World's Fair, plus an incredible roster of stars grace the Broadway stage in the theater listings of the day.
294	June 23, 1939	DAILY NEWS	Entertainment page featuring ads for the Cotton Club and the Apollo Theater.

A SPEECH made by His Excellency

BENJAMIN FLETCHER,

Captain General, & Governour in Chief of Their Majesties

Province of New-York,

And the Territories depending thereon, Vice-Admiral of the same,

To the REPRESENTATIVES Assembled together for that Province at the City of *NEW-YORK* October the 24th 1692.

Gentlemen,

YOu are Convened here by *Their Majesties Writ*, to Consult and Advise for such *Proper Methods* as may be *Effectual* for Their *Majesties Service* in the *Common Defence* of this *Province*, in which the *Security* of your own *Persons & Properties* being equally concern'd, I shall need but few Arguments to prevail upon you in a *speedy Dispatch* of those things which may conduce to Both. The Season of the Year, & your own Desires of spending the sharpness of the Winter in your Families, I hope will quicken you to a *Dispatch* of such things as are laid before you.

And *First*, That we may the better hope for a *Blessing* from *Almighty God*, I Recommend to your Care, *That Provision be made for the Support and Incouragement of an Able Ministry, and for the strict & due Observation of the Lords Day.*

In the *Next* place, I desire you'l look into the *Debts of the Government*, & consider of a *Fund* for the *Payment of them*, which being done, I shall take care to prevent any futher Incumbrance during my Administration.

The Necessary Support of the Government I Reco[illegible] this *Time of War*, *none* of you being *Ignorant*, that the *Indians* in our *Alliance* must be *supplyed* with *Arms*, *Ammunition*, and *other Presents*.

I have visited the *Frontieers*, and put them in some *Posture of Defence* for this *present Winter*, & am required by *Their Majesties* to build *Forts* at *Albany*, *Schenectady*, & such other places as I shall see *Convenient*, which being once *well done*, will ease the *Annual Charge* of *Posting Militia* there.

I am informed, the *Revenue* settled on *Their Present Majesties*, determines in *April* next; I hope you'l not be wanting in the *Expression* of your *Loyalty & Affections* to *Their Majesties*, who are of the *same Religion* with our Selves, but rather Out-do what *former Assemblies* have done.

The *Settlement of our Court of Judicature*, with the *Sallaryes of the Judges*, do also shortly expire: *Justice*, and the *due Administration* of the *Laws* is the *Life of Government*. You'l consider the *Continuation* of that *Act*, in relation to *Courts of Justice*, with a *proper Support* for the *Judges*, as an *Advantage to your Selves*, and all the *Subjects* of this *Province*.

I will not Question your *True Zeal* for *Their Majesties Service* and *Your own Well-fare*. I cannot think of *more Effectual ways to answer both those Ends* than by *Unity & Concord* amongst us, *Burying all Heats & Annamosities in the Grave of Oblivion*. And if you can think of any Act by which *Your Properties & Liberties may be better Secured*, you shall find a *ready Concurrence in me for your Satisfaction* & the *Publick Good*, in which I shall never mix my *own private Interest*. And so *Gentlemen* I wish a *Happy Agreement* amongst you for *Their Majesties Service*, *Your own Prosperity* and the *Common Safety*.

Printed by *William Bradford*, Anno Dom. 1693.

Numb. LV.

THE

New-York Weekly JOURNAL.

Containing the freshest Advices, Foreign, and Domestick.

MUNDAY November 25*th*, 1734.

To all my Subscribers and Benefactors who take my weekly Journall.

Gentlemen, Ladies and Others;

AS you last week were Disappointed of my Journall, I think it Incumbent upon me, to publish my Apoligy which is this. On the Lords Day, the Seventeenth of this Instant, I was Arrested, taken and Imprisoned in the common Goal of this Citty, by Virtue of a Warrant from the *Governour*, and the Honorable *Francis Harrison*, Esq; and others in Councill of which (God willing) yo'l have a Coppy, whereupon I was put under such Restraint that I had not the Liberty of Pen, Ink, or Paper, or to see, or speak with People, till upon my Complaint to the Honourable the Chief Justice, at my appearing before him upon my *Habias Corpus* on the *Wednesday* following. Who discountenanced that Proceeding, and therefore I have had since that Time, the Liberty of Speaking through the Hole of the Door, to my Wife and Servants by which I doubt not yo'l think me sufficiently Excused for not sending my last weeks *Journall*, and I hope for the future by the Liberty of Speaking to my Servants thro' the Hole of the Door of the Prison, to entertain you with my weekly *Journal* as formerly.

And am your obliged
Humble Servant,
J. Peter Zenger.

Mr. Zenger;

AS the Liberty of the Press is justly esteemed and universally acknowledged by Englishmen, to be the grand Paladium of all their Liberties, which Liberty of the Press, I have rejoyced to see well defended in Sundry of your Papers, and particularly by your No. 2. 3. 10. 11. 15. 16. 17. 18. 24. & 54. and by an annoninous Authors Observations on the chief Justices Charge of *January* last; now, for as much as it may not only be of present Use, but of future Advantage, that such Matters of Fact, that concern the Liberty of the Press, may be faithfully recorded and transmitted to Posterity, therefore I have sent you a Detail of such particulars that concern the Liberty of the Press within this Colony, and because I would not have you or my self charged with the Publication of a Libel, I shall confine my self to a plain Narration of Facts without any comments.

On Tuesday *the* 15*th of* Octo. 1734. *The supream Court of* New-York, *began, when the Honourable* James De Lancey, Esq; *Cheif Justie charged the Grand Jury. The Conclusion of which Charge was as follows.*

Gentlemen, I shall conclude with reading a Paragraph or two out of the same Book, † concerning Libels; they are arrived to that height, that they call

THE
New-York Weekly JOURNAL.

Containing the freshest Advices, Foreign, and Domestick.

MUNDAY August 18th, 1735.

To my Subscribers and Benefactors.

Gentlemen ;

I Think my self in Duty bound to to make publick Acknowledgment for the many Favours received at your Hands, which I do in this Manner return you my hearty Thanks for. I very soon intend to print my Tryal at Length, that the World may see how unjust my Sufferings have been, so will only at this Time give this short Account of it.

On *Munday* the 4*th* Instant my Tryal for Printing Parts of my Journal *No.* 13. and 23. came on, in the Supreme Court of this Province, before the most numerous Auditory of People, I may with Justice say, that ever were seen in that Place at once; my Jury sworn were,

1 *Harmanus Rutgers*,
2 *Stanley Holms*,
3 *Edward Man*,
4 *John Bell*,
5 *Samuel Weaver*,
6 *Andrew Marschalk*,
7 *Egbert Van Borsen*,
8 *Thomas Hunt*,
9 *Benjamin Hildrith*,
10 *Abraham Kiteltass*,
11 *John Goelet*,
12 *Hercules Wendover*,

John Chambers, Esq; had been appointed the Term before by the Court as my Council, in the Place of *James Alexander* and *William Smith*, who were then silenced on my Account, and to Mr. *Chambers*'s Assistance came *Andrew Hamilton*, Esq; of *Philadelphia* Barrester at Law; when Mr Attorney offered the Information and the Proofs, Mr. *Hamilton* told him, he would acknowledge my Printing and Publishing the Papers in the Information, and save him the Trouble of that Proof, and offered to prove the Facts of those Papers true, and had Witnesses ready to prove every Fact; he long insisted on the Liberty of Making Proof thereof, but was over-ruled therein. Mr. Attorney offered no Proofs of my Papers being *false*, *malicious* and *seditious*, as they were charged to be, but insisted that they were Lybels tho' true. There were many Arguments and Authorities on this point, and the Court were of Opinion with Mr. Attorney on that Head: But the Jury having taken the Information out with them, they returned in about Ten Minutes, and found me *Not Guilty*; upon which there were immediately three Hurra's of many Hundreds of People in the presence of the Court, before the Verdict was returned. The next Morning my Discharge was moved for and granted, and sufficient was subscribed by my fellow Citizens for payment of sundry Debts, for which I was also charged in Custody, and about Noon I had my Liberty from my long Imprisonment above eight Months. Above Forty of the Citizens entertained Mr. *Hamilton* at the black Horse that Day at Dinner, to express their Acknowledment of his Generosity on this Occasion, and at his Departure next Day he was saluted with the great Guns of several Ships in the Harbour, as a public Testimony of the glorious Defence he made in the Cause of Liberty in this Province.

March 16. 1746-7. THE *NUMB.* 217

NEW-YORK GAZETTE, REVIVED IN THE WEEKLY POST-BOY.

With the freshest Advices Foreign and Domestick.

Mr. *Parker*. *From my House near Wesel, Feb.* 28.

I HAVE waited with a great deal of Patience, to see whether any of our Commissioners would answer Mr. *Alexander Miles*'s Letter, in your *Postboy*, N°213, as I am a true Friend to one of them, I could not bear to see such gross Reflections cast, without *proper* Animadversions; upon which, for the Benefit of of your Readers, I take the Liberty to make in the following Manner.

The Man that's steady to his Trust,
Sincerely good as well as just,
Prefers the Publick, far before
The adding Riches to his Store.

The great Number of Commissioners appointed, may be a wrong Thing in those who appointed them, but surely can be no Reflection no the Commissioners; neither do I think it any Reflection on those that appointed them; and for this Reason, that if £. 1000 of the Country's Money was to be given away, surely it was more prudent to oblige *twelve* People by it, than *two*.

But to the Point; The Commissioners are grosly reflected upon for sending 300 *Guns, or Things in the Shape of Guns, which were condemned by the Gunsmiths at* Albany, *as not of the Value of old Iron*: This may be true; but in what are the Commissioners to blame, if Mr. *Miles* would have considered that thoseCommissioners were appointed by an Assembly that were of the People called *Quakers*, and those that were governed by them? Can it be imagined then, that any Commissioner so appointed, would have gone against the Bent and Inclination of his Constituents, as to have purchased such Arms as would have killed the Enemy? No; that would be a Justification of Friends going to War, so contrary to their pacifick Principles; besides, the Commissioners knew very well that those very Arms had been in *Oliver Cromwell*'s Army; and they were not so ignorant, or unacquainted with the *English* History, but that they also knew, that *Oliver Cromwell*'s Arms and Name struck the greatest Terror into the *French* Nation; therefore if they could purchase such Things as would terrify the *French*, without killing them, would not the Commissioners have been wrong to have acted otherways, when such Actions must have interfered with their Friends avowed Principles.

I must further observe, that all the Commissioners were not equally concerned in purchasing these Guns and Swords; and what makes me thinks so, is what a Commissioner, one of my Friends, say (who often makes my House his Home) when the Affair was mentioned to him, he was told those Guns were good for nothing; he answered, *Aye, perhaps you think I am a Fool; don't you think I can see what one of the Designs was, of raising these Forces? why aye, I will tell you; when this Expedition is over, these very Men will be employed to quell the Rioters, and then if their Arms are no better than Clubs, we shall stand a good Chance.* It is plain, that some of the Commissioners are known to every Body to have opposed the Rioters, their Abettors and Ring-leaders; therefore that Number never would have consented to put useless Arms in their future Protectors Hands.

The price of the Guns and Swords I believe may be right; but then the Swords were manufactured in the Country; they are properly *Country Produce*, and the Manufacturers were such as never make use of those Instruments, so could not be so good Judges as your fighting Men: But Mr.*Miles* must be a Novice, not to know, that Commissioners are appointed to get Money; the very Name implies it; a Commissioner that can't make it worth his While, is not fit for his Office. As for that sly Rub, of the Commissioners Frugality, in purchasing *stinking Beef*, to say no more of it than it deserves, it is a Falshood: The Case is this; if a Commissioner has Beef of his own that he can't sell, having been a little too sparing in his Salt, pray which is most reasonable, that one Man should *lose* 20 Barrils of Beef, or the Country *pay* for them? the Answer is plain; besides, I am told that Beef won't keep so well on a fresh River, as it will when sent to Sea: It would be unreasonable the Commissioners should attempt to alter the Laws of Nature, or be censured for natural Consequences. But without making a Joke of the Thing, I appeal to all the World, Whether there are not a thousand Instances to be given, where Beef has stunk after it was purchased. So much for your stinking Beef, Mr. *Miles*.

I shall just touch upon your fine *Court of Judicature*, as you are pleased to call it, and then conclude. Mr. *Miles* must know, if he knows any Thing, that it is a peculiar Priviledge of an *Englishman* to be tried by God and his Country, and Noblemen for the greatest of Crimes, by their Peers, which are also their Country; to be tried by God, is to appeal to him who knows our Conduct, to put it into the Hearts of good Men, to acquit the Innocent and punish the Guilty: To be tried by our Country, is to be taken in a very extensive Sense; by 12 Men upon their Oaths, or the Representatives of the People in General Assembly, which in this Province (if I may be allowed to compare great Things with small) is something like the Trials of the House of Lords in *Britain*; because the Members do it upon their Honours, being not under any Oath; and the Members here only under the political Tye of an Affirmation; but to pretend to say, when a Man is tried by his Country, he is not tried by the Laws of *England*, but by his Friends, is such a Reflection upon our Representatives, that I think they ought to resent it in the most publick Manner, by their Resolves: In my poor Opinion, the Reflection would not have been so great, if they had even said, that the Majority of the Assembly had joined in supporting the Rioters in their Invasion of private Property and Obstruction of publick Justice; for to take a Person out of Goal, that is in Debt or under Prosecution, shews a longing Desire to relieve the Distressed at any Rate, and may be esteemed an Act of Charity. But let the people petition for a Dissolution of the present Assembly when they think fit, and if it should be granted them, I can tell the Petitioners, there are sufficient Numbers, that depend upon being protected with Impunity for past Crimes, that will make their getting into the Assembly necessary, as well as their Election sure.

It gives me great Comfort, to think that my Friend, who is one of the principal Heads and Directors of these same Rioters, will get clear: Upon my asking him, What would be the Case when the new Governor came? *Aye*, says he, *I will consent to make as much Paper-Money as he wants, and let him have the sole Management of it; and if it be found necessary, for the Peace of the Government, to hang some of those Rioters, I will shrink my Neck out of the Collar, and give in the Names of those that are proper Sacrifices, to the injured Owners of the Land, and then will retire and become your Neighbour.* — Now Mr. *Alexander Miles*, if I find this is not a full Answer to your Letter, the next Time the Commissioner or his Son comes to my House, I will get them to answer it; and in the mean time, am my Friend's and the People's

Most obedient humble Servant,

M. VRELANDT.

Custom-House, New-York, Inward Entries.

Brig. King George, Ch. Dickinson from Barbados. Snow York, J. Wilson from the Orknies. Outward Entries. *Sloop Lydia, J. Milliken for Boston. Sloop Jane, Th. Alston, Sloop Don Lopez, Ralph Thurmond for Cape Breton. Sloop Brother & Sister, J. Bailey for Anguila. Ship Jacob, J. Anderson for Coracoa.* Cleared. *Th. Alston to Cape Breton. Ship Caledonia, P. Campbell to Lewis on Delaware. Ship Anne, Wm. Robinson to W-Indies. Sloop Anne, Sol. Frith to Jamaica. Sloop Stork, Th. Witter, Sloop Griffin, Wm. Brown to Coracoa. Sloop Polly, Asa King to Madera.*

Just Imported in the Snow *Somerset*, Capt. *John Butler* Commander, from *Liverpool*, the following Goods, and are to be Sold by ROBERT HALIBURTON, at the Store of Mr. *Friend Lucas*, near the Meal-Market.

DELFT Ware,	*White Jeans,*	*Bunts of different sizes*
Hatts,	*Nonsoprettics,*	*Beds and bolsters,*
Checks of different	*Woollen Stockings,*	*Kendal cottons,*
Osnabrigs. (breadths	*Woollen Caps,*	*Broad Cloth. Kerseys,*
Irish Linnens.	*Cordage, diffrent sizes*	*Large & small Bar-Lead,*
Thread, coloured and (stitching.	*Men's Shoes,*	*Shot, sorted.*
Nails of different sorts.	*Women's callimanco & worsted damask Shoes*	*Cheshire Cheese,*
Sheeting Linnen,	*Woollen gloves,*	*Hard-ware, a fine assortment.*
Linnen handkerchiefs,	*Mohair buttons,*	
Grogram,	*Silk twist buttons,*	*Earthen Ware,*
Tufted Fustian,	*Mohair, Cotton laces,*	*Fine Salt,*
Bolster Tick.	*Counterpains of different sorts,*	*Grindstones, with several other Goods.*
White Stripes,		

NOTICE is hereby given, that a good School-Master is very much wanted at the Landing, *near* New-Brunswick, *where a full School may be had as soon as a Master will settle there, as there is not one in all that Place.*

STOLEN on Sunday Night the 8th March, out of the Stable of John Ryder, *at* Philipse's borough *in the County of* Westchester, *a large brown Horse about 15 Hands high, has a small Star on his Forehead, and goes narrow with his Hams behind, he is branded in several Places, but not very plain, on his Fore-Shoulder with* I H. *and on his Left Thigh with* I R. *Whoever takes up the said Horse, and brings him to his said Owner, shall have* Five Pounds *Reward, and all reasonable Charges, paid by*

JOHN RYDER.

For LONDON,

The Snow Sally, Ferdinando Clark, *Master,*

HAving Two Thirds of her Lading already engaged, will sail with all possible Expedition.

For Freight or Passage, agree with the said Master, or Daniel Shatford.

Deserted the 24th February, *from the* Virginia *Company quarter'd in the Fort at* New-York, *the three following Soldiers, viz.*

George Malcolm, *an Irishman, about 6 Feet high, aged 36 Years. short black Hair, very much mark'd with the Small Pox and freckled, a stoop in his Shoulders, knock-keed, has a drolling Speech; a Labourer.*

Archibald Hanna, *an Irishman, about 5 Feet 6 Inches high, aged about 22 Years, brown Complexion, a Scar over the left Eye, an upright Walk; a Sawyer by Trade.*

James Row, *an Irishman, about 5 Feet 5 Inches high, aged 25 Years, a Weaver by Trade, of a brown Complexion, smooth-faced, a small Stoop in his Shoulder; they carried off their Regimentals.*

Whoever apprehends the said Deserters, or either of them, that he or they be brought to their Quarters, shall receive Two Pistoles *Reward for each, paid by* Beverly Robinson.

Treasury-Office, New-York, 2d February, 1746-7.

Pursuant to an Act of the General Assembly, passed the last Sessions, I do hereby give Notice to all Persons who are indebted and in arrear on Account of the Excise laid by former Acts of this Colony, that unless they pay the same within two Months after the Date hereof, their Recognizances will be immediately thereafter put in Suit; and the Farmers of the Excise for this present Year, are desired to be punctual in their Payments; there being by the said Act, a Penalty of Fifty Pounds laid upon me, in case I shall neglect or omit to put all the before-mentioned Recognizances in Suit, if Failure be made in the Payments thereof. And all those indebted to His Majesty for Duties, are also desired to pay the same forthwith, as they would avoid further Trouble.

ABRAHAM DE PEYSTER, *Treasurer.*

To be SOLD,

TWO Likely Negro Men, one of them a Ship-Carpenter by Trade, and the other understands a Team or Plantation-Work: Also a Negro Wench with two small Children; the Wench understands House-work. Any Person inclining to purchase, may apply to Susannah Marsh, *Widow, at* Perth-Amboy, *who will dispose of them on reasonable Terms.*

A Good Horse about six Years old, Albany *breed, and a handsome Chair almost new, to be Sold; enquire of* John Brazier, *near the Hon.* Rip Van Dam's, *Esq;*

BY a Law passed the last Sessions, a Publick Lottery is directed, to consist of 10,000 Tickets, at 30 s. each. 1665 of which to be fortunate, viz.

Number of Prizes.		Value of each.	Total Value.
1	of	£. 500,	£. 500,
1	of	300,	300,
1	of	200,	200,
10	of	100,	1000,
30	of	50,	1500,
40	of	25,	1000,
59	of	15,	885,
400	of	10,	4000,
1123	of	5,	5615,

1665 Prizes. } 8335 Blanks. } *10,000 Tickets, at 30 s. makes £. 15,000.*

15 per Cent. to be deducted from the Prizes. The Profits will be employed towards founding a College within this Colony, for the regular Education of Youth; And as such a laudable Design will greatly tend to the Welfare and Reputation of this Colony; it is expected the Inhabitants will readily be excited to become Adventurers. Publick Notice will be given of the precise Time for putting the Tickets into the Boxes, that such Adventurers as shall be minded to see the same don, may be present at the doing thereof. The Drawing to commence on or before the first Day of June *next, at the* City-Hall *of* New-York, *under the Inspection of the Corporation, who are impowered to appoint two or more of their Body to inspect all and every Transaction of the said Lottery; and two Justices of the Peace, or other reputable Freeholders or Inhabitants of every County in this Colony, if they see Cause to depute the same at their next or any subsequent general Sessions of the Peace. Notice will be given in the* New-York Post Boy *fourteen Days before the Drawing. The Managers are sworn faithfully to execute the Trust reposed in them, and have given Security for the faithful Discharge of the same. As the late Lottery has given general Satisfaction, the same Care will be taken, and the same Regulations observed in this, with respect to the Tickets, the Drawing, keeping the Books, and other Particulars, as near as possible. The Blanks as well as Prizes will be published weekly in the* New-York Post Boy. *Such as forge or counterfeit any Ticket, or alter the Number, and are thereof convicted, by the said Act are to suffer Death as in Cases of Felony. The Money will be paid to the Possessors of the Benefit Tickets as soon as the Drawing is finished.*

Tickets are to be had at the Dwelling-houses of Messrs. Peter Vallete *and* Peter Van Brugh Livingston, *who are appointed Managers.*

To be SOLD or LET from the first of *May* next, For a Term of Years,

TWO good and well finished Houses, Stable, Garden and Lot of Ground in New-Brunswick, *containing in Breadth, fronting to* Burnet-Street *and to* Peace-Street, *each Sixty-three Feet; and in Length from the one Street to the other, Eighty-six Feet; and lies adjoining to the House and Lot of Mr.* Jacob Ouke, *situated in the most publick Part of the said Town, and exceedingly convenient for a Merchant or Tradesman. Whoever inclines to purchase the said Term, may apply to* Thomas Harding *living on the Premises, or to Mr.* Joseph Royal, *Merchant in* New-York, *to be informed further.*

Lately published, and Sold by Wm. Bradford *in* Philadelphia; Wm. Merieyer *in* New-York, & D. Schuyler, *Esq; in* New-Brunswick,

Mirabilia Dei inter Indicos: Or, *The Rise and Progress of a remarkable* Work of Grace *amongst a Number of the Indians in the Provinces of New Jersey and Pensilvania. Justly represented in a Journal kept by Order of the* Honourable Society in Scotland for promoting Christian Knowledge. *With some general Remarks. By* David Brainerd, *Minister of the Gospel, and Missionary from the said Society. Published by the Reverend and Worthy Correspondents of the said Society; with a Preface by them.* (Price 3 s)

GOOD Bonnet-Papers, Cartridge Paper and Press-Papers, to be Sold by the Printer hereof, wholesale & retail.

NEW-YORK: *Printed by* James Parker, *at the New Printing-Office in* Beaver-Street, *Where Advertisements are taken in, and all Persons may be supplied with this Paper.*

July 20. 1749. NUMB. 1075.

The Pennſylvania GAZETTE.

Containing the freſheſt Advices, Foreign and Domeſtick.

To his Excellency the honourable GEORGE CLINTON, *Captain general and governor in chief of the colony of* New-York, *and territories thereon depending in* America, *vice admiral of the ſame, and admiral of the white ſquadron of his majeſty's fleet;*

The humble Addreſs *of the General Aſſembly of the ſaid colony.*

May it pleaſe your Excellency,

WE his majeſty's moſt dutiful and loyal ſubjects, the general aſſembly of the colony of *New-York*, return your excellency our thanks, for your congratulations upon the re-eſtabliſhment of peace; and moſt ſincerely and heartily wiſh, that this, and his majeſty's other colonies on the continent, may be entirely freed from thoſe calamaties to which they have been expos'd during the war; and that your excellency may be more ſucceſsful in cultivating among us, the arts of peace, as well for the future ſecurity, as preſent proſperity, of the people of this colony.

We muſt acknowledge, *Sir*, with all mankind, that it can be of no ſervice, or rather that it would be in vain to make laws, if they with whom the executive powers of government are intruſted, be diſabled from putting them in execution: but we are not ſenſible that we have been acceſſary to any ſuch diſability ~~in this government; the general aſſemblies~~ having always (as we humbly conceive) manifeſted their duty to the crown, in making ample and honourable proviſion for the ſupport of this his majeſty's government; though they may ſometimes have differed with governors, as to modes and forms in the method of doing it; and yet have had a proper regard to the royal intention, in the commiſſion and inſtructions to governors, by taking care that the money given by them, ſhould be duly applied to the reſpective uſes for which they gave it.

We hope your excellency will excuſe us, if in our conſiderations on the extracts of his majeſty's inſtructions, we happen to differ in ſentiments on the conſtruction; though your excellency has not indulg'd us with communicating yours: We preſume your excellency has not juſt now receiv'd them (tho' it ſhould ſeem the ſpeech inſinuates as much) but that they have been ſtanding inſtructions to all your excellency's predeceſſors (ſome alterations in the ſtyle only of your excellency's copy excepted:) And though there be no royal injunction apparent in them, for the practice ſo much exploded for many years paſt, for the miſchiefs of which the grant of a five years ſupport was productive, and of which your excellency ſeem'd at firſt to be made ſenſible upon ample conſiderations; yet we find governors, upon more mature deliberation, would willingly engroſs the ſweets of that method to themſelves, of which the people neither ever had, or ever can expect any benefit.

We muſt beg leave to obſerve to your excellency, that the general aſſembly do not perceive any eſſential difference with reſpect to his majeſty's ſervice, and the royal intention concerning the ſupport of the government of this colony, whether the governor, and other officers in the government, have their ſalaries provided annually, or for the term of five years; which laſt your excellency demanded by your ſpeech on the fourteenth of *October* laſt; and the ſame claim (as we take it) your excellency now renews, by your reference to it.

It muſt be obvious to every one, that the time of our preſent meeting is moſt inconvenient to much the greater part of the members, for the very reaſon mentioned by your excellency: And though we ſhall at all times chearfully poſtpone our private intereſt to the attendance on the publick exigency; yet we are conſtrained to declare, that from the experience we have had of the unhappy influence which has for ſome time paſt, and ſtill does direct your excellency's adminiſtration, we have but little hopes of indulgence from your excellency at any time, however conſiſtent it may be with the publick welfare.

And as your excellency is pleas'd to tell us, you cou'd not think it proper to meet us, till you knew the ſentiments of his majeſty's miniſters in reſpect to our refuſing to grant the ſupport of government in the manner you aſked it laſt fall; ſo as we are not further enlightened in the matter at this time, we cannot but continue in the ſame opinion we then were.

Whatever juſt demands there may be due for ſervices done the publick, beſides the ordinary occurrences; that they have remain'd ſo long unpaid, cannot with juſtice be aſcrib'd to any default in the general aſſembly, who have ever been careful to provide for ſuch, and did paſs a bill wherein proviſion was made, as may be ſeen in the printed journal of our proceedings; and therefore, their remaining ſtill undiſcharg'd, is ſolely to be imputed to the unſeaſonable prorogation of the general aſſembly on the twelfth of *November* laſt, whereby that bill, with ſeveral others, was defeated.

We ſincerely lament the hardſhips which ſome of our poor brethren, priſoners in *Canada*, have, and ſtill do ſuffer, by their long confinement there; and are fully perſuaded they might long ſince have been releaſed, had proper meaſures been taken by thoſe whoſe province it is: And here we beg leave to remind your excellency, of the aſſurances we gave you on that head, in our addreſs of the nineteenth of *October* laſt, that we would chearfully provide for all reaſonable expence attending ſuch ſervice.

We muſt conclude upon the whole, with declaring to your excellency, that we can give no other or better anſwer to the preſent ſpeech, than we did towards the concluſion of our addreſs, in anſwer to your excellency's ſpeech of the fourteenth of *October* laſt, which was (among other things) in ſubſtance, that we were confirm'd in our opinion, that the faithful repreſentatives of the people, could never recede from the method of an annual ſupport.

By order of the general aſſembly,
City of New-York, DAVID JONES, *Speaker.*
Aſſembly chamber, 5th of July, 1749.

HAMBURGH, April 5.

WE are told, that all military preparations in his Pruſſian majeſty's dominions are very much ſlackened of late, from whence it is hoped, that ſome method will be found for calming the troubles in the North, before they riſe ſo high as an open rupture; and it is ſtill rendered the more likely by the handing about the following paper, which is ſaid to be the copy of a letter to his Britannick majeſty, from his nephew the king of Pruſſia.

Sir, and Brother,

YOUR majeſty's intereſt and mine are the ſame with regard to the tranquility of the North. Reports are ſpread all over Europe, that this tranquility may be diſturbed. For my part, I ſee no likelihood of it in the main; and it ſeems, that nothing but reciprocal diſtruſt and ill-grounded ſuſpicions can hitherto have gained thoſe rumours any credit.

But as the ſmalleſt objects may, by encreaſing, become material, as one ought to neglect nothing for the maintenance of peace, and that every thing becomes important to thoſe who are fond of preſerving it, I apply to your majeſty, whom I know to be in the ſame ſentiments, to the end that, by our joint endeavours, we may ſo much the more effectually contribute thereto. The ſuſpicions which Sweden's neighbours entertain of her, can reſt only on two objects.

The *firſt*, which is manifeſtly frivolous, regards the dangerous projects which they ſeem reſolved to impute to that power againſt her neighbours. Your majeſty's diſcernment is too quick not to perceive the falſity of it at the firſt glance. The *other* falls on the change of the preſent form of government in Sweden; a project which they father on the prince ſucceſſor. Methinks the declaration which the prince and the ſenate made very lately to the court of Ruſſia upon this ſubject, is ſo perſpicuous, ſo poſitive, and ſo prudent, that it leaves nothing farther to be wiſhed by ſuch powers as intereſt themſelves in maintaining the preſent government of that kingdom.

The defenſive alliance that I made with Sweden, to which France acceded, and the original of which was ſhewn to the count de Keyſerling, the Ruſſian miniſter at my court, and a copy of which was communicated in due time to your majeſty's miniſtry at London, hath no relation to any new meaſures; but is, nevertheleſs, binding on France and myſelf to maintain the ſucceſſion, actually eſtabliſhed in Sweden, and mutually to defend each other, in caſe any ſhould attack us.

God forbid that I ſhould ſuppoſe any powers in friendſhip with us capable of ſo black deſigns, or that I ſhould ſo much as ſuſpect them of ſuch dangerous projects! But I entreat your majeſty to join your endeavours with mine, to engage both parties to proper explications, which will be found equally ſalutary for them. I muſt intreat your attention to all the points that I have been explaining, and that your majeſty would employ your credit and good offices to extinguiſh that fire which glows at preſent under the embers, and which if it once break out, will ſpread into flames thro' all Europe.

I am very ready, and offer, with great pleaſure, to enter into all the meaſures which your majeſty ſhall think requiſite for the preſerving of peace, perſwaded that his moſt chriſtian majeſty, who has no leſs at heart than we, the maintenance of the peace in Europe, and the tranquility of the North, will join his efforts to ours, to contribute the more powerfully thereto.

The preſent occaſion which offers itſelf to your majeſty, is one of the moſt favourable for augmenting the glory of your reign, for ſupporting

T H E

INDEPENDENT REFLECTOR.

NUMBER VII.

Thurſday, January 11. 1753.

A Propoſal of ſome farther Regulations, for the ſpeedier and more effectual Extinguiſhing of FIRES, *that may happen in this City.*

--- Vaga per veterem dilapſo flamma culinam
Vulcano, ſummum properabat lambere Tectum. HOR.

IT is a common Obſervation, that the Inhabitants of this City are remarkable for their Agility in extinguiſhing Fires: And ſince ſo judicious a Poet as *Virgil*, hath compared the Induſtry of the *Tyrians*, to the Labours of the Bee; I think the amazing Celerity, with which my Fellow-Citizens cluſter together, at the Ringing of the FIRE-BELL, may fitly be reſembled, to the Swarming of thoſe curious Inſects, at the Sound of the Inſtrument uſed for that Purpoſe. To purſue the Simile, there is not a Drone amongſt them; but the Rich and the Poor, are alike indefatigable in preſerving their Neighbour's Property, from the devouring Flames. It is one univerſal Hurry, and inceſſant Activity: Nay, they have often expoſed themſelves to the Peril of their Lives, and performed Feats almoſt ſurpaſſing Comprehenſion or Belief. They toil with unwearied Diligence, and ſeem inſenſible of the Danger which threatens them. In a Word, they ſtand in the Midſt of the Flames, as unconcerned as Salamanders, mocking at Fear, and ſtriving to out-vie each other, in ſuppreſſing the general Calamity. A noble Emulation, and worthy the higheſt Eulogium!

NOR ought the Companies, lately formed for the Preſervation of Goods at Fires, be paſſed over, without that Share of Applauſe, which is due to ſo laudable an Undertaking. An Undertaking, that deſerves to be commemorated with Gratitude and Honour, as it exhibits a glaring Atteſtation of their public Spirit, and exemplary Devotion to their Country. They have been at a conſiderable Expence, in furniſhing themſelves with a proper Apparatus; and given undeniable Proofs, of the extenſive Utility, of their reſpective Societies. Animated by their Example, may others project Expedients, equally tending to the public Benefit; and reap for their Reward, an equal Share of public Gratitude!

FOR my own Part, as my future Speculations will, on the one Hand, evince my Reluctance, at ſparing the Rod, where Correction is neceſſary; ſo they will, on the other, ſhew my Readineſs, to beſtow all due Honour, upon whatever deſerves the Approbation of the Public. Would to Heaven, I never had an Opportunity but to praiſe, with an abſolute Privation of the leaſt Neceſſity, for the Exerciſe of my Chaſtiſements! From this diſintereſted Impartiality, I cannot refrain from paying to Merit, its juſt Tribute of Commendation and Renown. I ſhall therefore, take the Liberty, ſtill a Moment to detain the Reader, in order to expreſs my own, and my Countrymen's grateful Senſe of the Corporation's Liberality, in making ſuch ample

H Proviſion

Proviſion for the Extinguiſhing of Fires, that we are in Want of but few Things requiſite to that End. As moſt Inventions, however, arrive at Perfection, by gradual Improvements, there is, I conceive, a Poſſibility of ſuper-adding ſundry Regulations, for the ſpeedier controuling the Rage, of that terrible Element.

IT hath more than once been obſerved, that our Engines are incapable of throwing Water, to ſuch a Height as is ſometimes neceſſary. Of this we had a dreadful Inſtance, when the Steeple of *Trinity Church* took Fire. On that Occaſion, we obſerved, with univerſal Terror, that the Engines could ſcarce deliver the Water, to the Top of the Roof. The Spire, however, was far beyond its Reach; and had not Providence ſmiled upon the aſtoniſhing Dexterity and Reſolution of a few Men, who aſcended the Steeple within, that ſplendid and ſuperb Edifice, had, in all Probability, been reduced to Aſhes.

WE are, therefore, in Want of at leaſt one Engine of the largeſt Size, which throws Water about One Hundred and Seventy Feet high, diſcharges two Hundred Gallons in a Minute, and coſts about Sixty Five Pounds Sterling. Such an Engine would have another Advantage, beſides carrying the Water to ſo great a Height. The prodigious Quantity it deliver'd, would be of unſpeakable Service at all Fires.

ANOTHER Thing, in which our preſent Method of extinguiſhing Fires, is capable of farther Improvement, is this: It is uſual for People, in Caſes of Fire, to form themſelves into two Lines, the One to convey the full Buckets to the Engine, and the Other to return the empty Ones. Now it frequently happens, that when the Engine is full, Word is given, to *ſtop Water*. This occaſions a total Ceſſation in the Conveyance of more Water to the Engine, as well as the greateſt Confuſion in the Ranks; the Conſequence of which is, that the Engine is empty, before the Ranks regain their former Regularity, which creates a conſiderable Intermiſſion in its playing. The miſchievous Effects of this are apparent, on the leaſt Reflection; for theſe Interruptions, be they ever ſo ſmall, give the Fire Time to reſume its Fury, and which, if often repeated, requires a much greater Quantity of Water for its total Suppreſſion, than would be neceſſary, was the Engine continued in one regular and uninterrupted Exerciſe. This Inconvenience might, I conceive, be eaſily remedied, by ſupplying each Engine with a large Tub, of at leaſt the Size of an Hogſhead; which being made of Cedar, might be ſufficiently ſtrong, and at the ſame Time light enough, to be portable by two Men: This Veſſel ought to be placed near the Engine, and all the full Buckets to be emptied into it. From this capacious Tub, three or four Men might conſtantly and equally keep the Engine repleniſhed; which would enable it to play an equable and uniform Stream. The happy Effects reſulting from ſuch an Expedient, would, I am perſuaded, be immediately viſible: And indeed, the Truth of the Propoſition is evident, and conſtantly exemplified in Life: For a Pail of Water, ſprinkled by Degrees on a common Fire, will very little affect it: In reality, all the Water may be waſted without extinguiſhing it; which nevertheleſs, thrown on it together, would be ſufficient entirely to quench it.

AGAIN, Fires often happen ſo remote from Water, as to occaſion a Want of People, and in Places where the Paſſage is too narrow, to admit of a ſufficient Number of double Lines, to ſupply the Engines. In ſuch Caſes, I would propoſe, that People ſhould form themſelves into three ſingle Lines, inſtead of two double Ones; the two exterior Ones for the full Buckets; which, as they are emptied into the great Tub, ſhould be laid at the Feet of the firſt Man of the inner Line, to be reconveyed to the Water. This Line would be ſufficient, to return the empty Buckets of the other two. And by that Method, three Men might do the uſual Buſineſs of four, and in three Quarters of the Space of Ground.

THIS Œconomy is well worthy our Conſideration; nor can we, on theſe Occaſions, be too well ſupplied with Water. With reſpect to the Tubs before-mentioned, I muſt take the Liberty, to entreat our Magiſtrates, that we remain no longer without them. For could they be applied to no other Uſe, than what I have already pointed out, that alone would render them extremely ſerviceable: But they will alſo, be of ſignal Advantage in other Reſpects: They will, in a great Meaſure, ſecure the Engines againſt being clogged and choaked with the Sand and Pebbles ſcoop'd into the Buckets at the River Side: For the Buckets being emptied into them, the Sand and Pebbles will ſink to the Bottom, and the Water only be thrown into the Engines.

ANOTHER Advantage that would ariſe from the Uſe of ſuch Tubs, is, that no Movement or Change of Situation in the Engine, nor any other Accident that might impede its playing, need occaſion any Interruption to the Ranks, in conveying Water; to which, they are at preſent greatly ſubject, on every ſuch Emergency: For there being no Reſervoir to receive the Water, when the Engine is full, or changing Place, the Lines muſt, during that Interval, either ceaſe conveying it, or ſet the full Buckets on the Ground, where they are generally overſet, and the Water loſt.

IT is further to be remarked, that many Parts of the City, too remote from the River, to be ſupplied with Water from thence, are very deficient in public Wells. I am ſenſible, that when this has been mentioned, it hath often been eſteemed a full Reply, that the People have Wells enough in their Yards. But the Inconveniences generally attending the bringing Water from thence, are ſufficient Reaſons, for making more public Wells in the Streets: For, without aſſigning any other, the Opportunity it affords for robbing the Houſes, thro' which the Water is brought, is an Evil almoſt as bad as the Fire itſelf.

To what hath already been propoſed, the Reader will give me Leave to add, that ſome of my Countrymen, whom Nature hath bleſſed with better Lungs, than Underſtandings, are often, on theſe melancholy Occaſions, very loud and vociferous; and others as fond of being Directors, and exerciſing a kind of Superintendency over the Reſt. Thro' this Confuſion and Vociferation, the Inſtructions given by the proper Directors, are often neglected, and generally incapable of being heard. It would therefore be of great Uſe, if People would make it a Rule not to ſpeak, but when it is abſolutely neceſſary. In a Word, let them reſerve their Loquacity, till they Return to their Spouſes, when probably they will be relieved from the Pain, of ſo long a Silence, by ſundry pertinent and momentous Queries.

ADD to all this, that it ought invariably to be obſerved, at great Fires, that all the large Engines play nearly on the ſame Part of the Fire. The Advantage of this may not, perhaps, appear at firſt Sight; but on the leaſt Conſideration, it will eaſily be obſerved, that the Heat of a great Fire, will drink up a ſingle Stream of Water, without any perceptible Diminution; and in like Manner, the ſeveral different Parts of it, will bear ſeveral different Streams of Water, without being ſenſibly affected; but let them all be directed to the ſame Part of the Fire, and they will effectually extinguiſh it there; which done, the Streams may be directed to ſome other Part, till the Whole be ſuppreſſed. The ſmall Engines may, in the mean Time, be kept employed, in preventing the Communication of the Fire, to the neighbouring Buildings.

THE preceeding Propoſals are only intended as rude Suggeſtions, ſo far to engage the Attention of the Curious, as either to improve theſe imperfect Hints, or to ſubſtitute in their Room, more effectual Expedients, for the readier Extinguiſhing of Fire: For I am not ſo attached to my own Notions, as to prefer them, to what may appear more likely to anſwer the Purpoſe; but ſhould chearfully inſert in this Paper, any more plauſible Project, with proper Reſpect to the ingenious Correſpondent.

X.

THO'

THO' the following Reſolves contain a greater Encomium on the Author, than he thinks himſelf intitled to; yet as they were drawn up by a venerable Club of Widow'd-Matrons, he thinks himſelf obliged, in Complaiſance to ſuch reſpectable Correſpondents, to publiſh ſo precious a Memorial of their well-meant Gratitude: A Memorial which, to a Perſon of his independent Principles, will be a ſufficient Recompence for a Thouſand Obloquies of the commiſſion'd Malefactor, or dignified Criminal, who calumniates him, only becauſe he dreads to have his Conduct, ſcrutiniz'd and expos'd.

To the INDEPENDENT REFLECTOR.

S I R,

'LAST Monday Night, we, the Subſcribers met at the Room of the Widow *M. K.* 'according to Summons reſpectively received in the Morning, in order to join 'with her, in a Letter of Thanks to the *Reflector*, for publiſhing her Letter concerning 'the Road and City-Watch, with ſo much Honour. As ſoon as we were ſeated, the 'Company deſired *Mrs. Threadneedle* to read your Paper, with an audible Voice '(during all which Time there actually was, however incredible it may ſeem, a profound 'Silence,) after which we came to the following Reſolves.

'*Reſolved*,

'THAT the Thanks of this Club, be preſented to the *Independent Reflector*, for 'engaging ſo heartily, in the Defence of poor Widows, and pointing out the Defects of 'a Law, which, in our feminine Opinion, hath neither Rhime nor Reaſon, but opens 'a Door for enormous Roguery, and Oppreſſion triumphant.

'*Reſolved*,

'THAT he be preſented with our humble Petition, to reſume the ſame Subject, by 'the Firſt of *May* next; unleſs in the mean Time, there appears convincing Evidence, 'of the Contrition and Amendment, of our common Oppreſſor.

'*Reſolved*,

'THAT for the Future, *Mrs. Threadneedle* and *M. K.* be a Committee of the whole 'Club, to conſider of Grievances, to be laid before the *Reflector*.

'*Reſolved*,

'THAT the ſaid *Mrs. Threadneedle*, do preſent the Author of the *Reflector*, with a 'Pair of fringed party-colour'd Mittens, at our joint Expence, as ſoon as he is diſcovered, 'in Memorial of our Gratitude, for his pathetic Repreſentation of our Calamity. In 'Witneſs whereof, wiſhing him a *Happy New-Year*, we have hereunto ſet our Hands, 'the Firſt Day of *January*, 1753.

M. K.
Alice Threadneedle.
Rebecca Nettletop.
Biddy Loveleſs.
Martha Froſt.
Sarah Ridinghood.
Deborah Wrinkle.

Z.

THE Author takes this Opportunity, for returning his Thanks, to the Reverend Gentleman, who did him ſuch ſignal Honour, laſt Sunday, as to make him the Subject of his Sermon; and greatly admires his Ingenuity, in proving him to be the Gog *and* Magog *of the* Apocalypſe, *who have, hitherto, puzzled all the Divines in the World. Nor doth he diſpair of the further Honour, to ſupply this ardent Preacher, in the Courſe of his Papers, with freſh Materials, to diſplay his Talents, in unravelling Prophecies; in diſcovering the Accompliſhment of many of the Old Teſtament Types, in the* Independent Reflector, *and exerting his Zeal, againſt all Sects but his own.*

The Author has the higheſt Deteſtation of that Perfidy to the young Lady, mentioned in the Letter ſigned Philogamus, *from* Newark; *and tho' the Villain that abuſed her, juſtly deſerves to be ſtigmatized, yet ſhe, and our Correſpondent, muſt excuſe him from any Reflections on a Subject that is not within the Deſign of this Paper.*

The Letter ſigned Amicus, *relating to a Light-Houſe, ſhall not eſcape my Attention.*

N E W - Y O R K:
Printed by JAMES PARKER, *at the* NEW-PRINTING-OFFICE, *in* Beaver-Street, *by whom Letters to the Author are taken in.*

Engr for the London Ma
The South Prospect the City
1
2
3
4
6
9
10
12

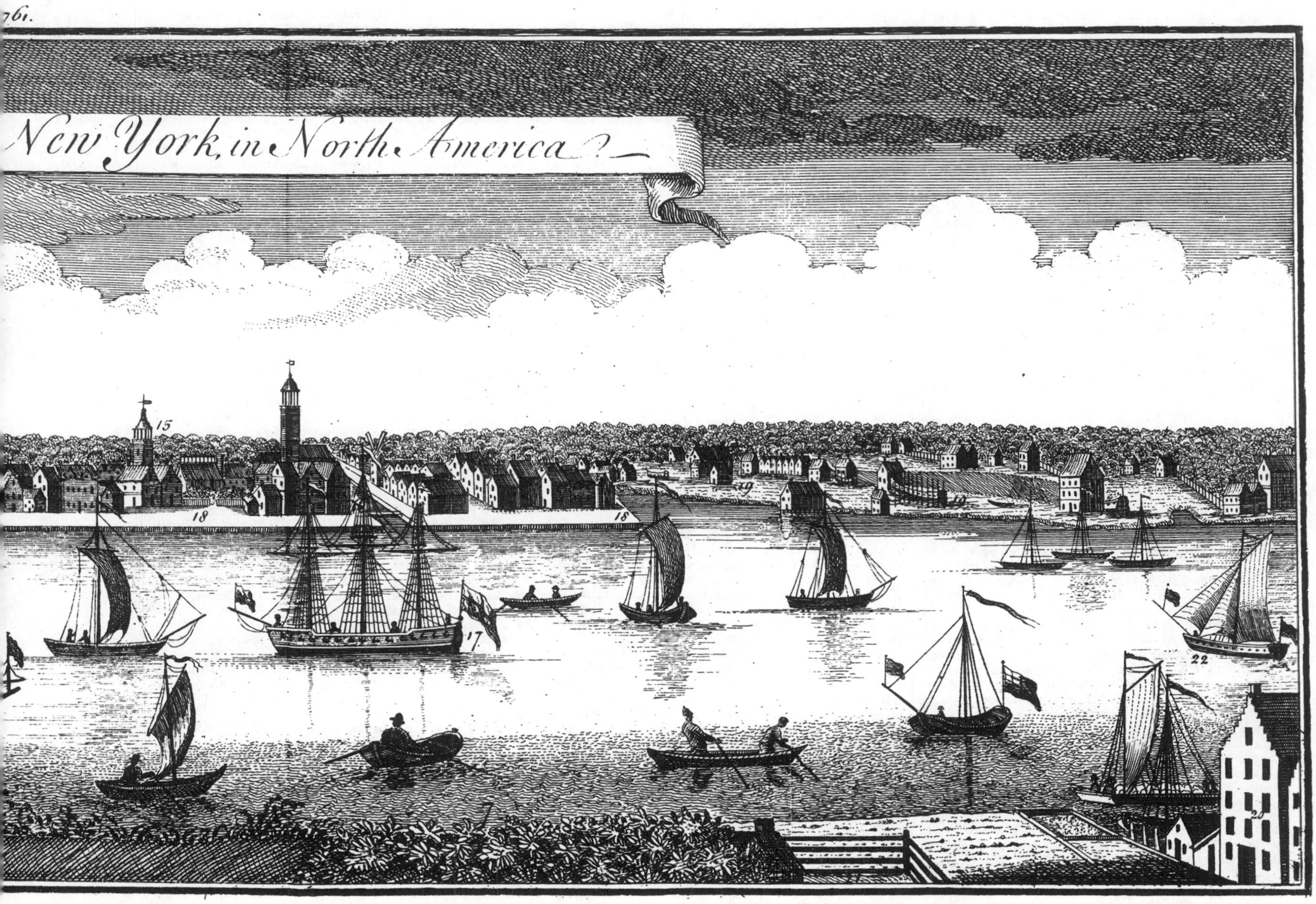
761.
New York, in North America.
15
18
18
19
17.
22
20

THE [*Numb.* 747.]

MARYLAND GAZETTE,

Containing the freſheſt Advices foreign and domeſtic.

THURSDAY, *Auguſt* 30, 1759.

NEW-YORK, *Auguſt* 20.

Journal of the Siege of Niagara, tranſlated from the French.

July 6, 1759.

ABOUT Seven at Night a Soldier, who was hunting, came with all Diligence to acquaint Monſieur Pouchot, that he had diſcovered, at the Entrance of the Wood, a Party of Savages, and that they had even fired on ſome other Hunters. Monſieur Pouchot immediately ſent M. Selviert, Captain in the Regiment of Rouſillon, at the Head of one Picquet, a Dozen Canadian Voluntiers preceded them, and on their coming to the Edge of the Woods, a Number of Indians fired upon them, which they returned, and were obliged to retire: They took Meſſieurs Furnace and Aloque, Interpreters of the Iroquois, two Canadians, and two other Gentlemen. They made another Diſcharge and retired. Monſieur Pouchot fired ſome Cannon upon them. Monſieur Selviert lay all Night, with 100 Men, in the Demilune, and the reſt of the Garriſon was under Arms on the Ramparts till Midnight.

Saturday, 7th July. We perceived 7 Barges on the Lake, a League and a Half Diſtance from the Fort; we judged by that it was the Engliſh come to beſiege us: Monſieur Pouchot ordered the General to be beat, and employed all Hands to work on the Batteries, to erect Embraſures, all being En Barbet before. He immediately diſpatched a Courier to Monſieur Chevert, to give him Notice of what happened; he alſo ſent out Monſieur Laforce, Captain of the Schooner Iroquoiſe, to deſtroy the Engliſh Barges where he could find them. All that Day ſeveral Savages ſhewed themſelves on the Edge of the Deſarts. Monſieur Laforce fired ſeveral Cannon Shot at them; and perceived they were working at an Entrenchment at the Little Swamp, which is a League and a Half from the Fort. The Guards this Night as the Night before.

Sunday, 8th July. The Schooner continued to cruize and fire on the Engliſh Camp. About 9 in the Morning an Engliſh Officer brought a Letter from Brigadier Prideaux, to Monſieur Pouchot, to ſummons him, propoſing him all Advantages and good Treatment; all which he very politely refuſed, and even ſeemed to be unwilling to receive the Engliſh General's Letter. The Remainder of this Day the Engliſh made no Motions.

Tueſday 10th. At 2 o'Clock all our Men were on the Ramparts, and at Day-break we perceived they had opened their Trenches, at the Entrance of the Wilderneſs, at about 300 Toiſes from the Fort; we made a very hot Fire upon them all Day. M. Chabourt arrived with the Garriſon of the Little Fort, and ſeven or eight Savage Iroquoiſe and Miſſagoes. Monſieur Pouchot went to palliſade the Ditches: The Service as uſual, only the Addition of two Officers to lie in the covered Way. About 11 o'Clock at Night Orders were given to make all the Picquets fire from the covered Way, to hinder the Workmen of the Enemy. M. Laforce ſent his Boat on Shore for Monſieur Pouchot's Orders.

Wedneſday, 11th July. The Works continue on both Sides. At Noon a Party of about 15 *M*en, Soldiers and Militia, went very nigh the Trenches of the Enemy, and perceived them ſally out between 4 and 500, who came towards them at a quick Pace, but they were ſtopped by our Cannon. They began on the other Side of the Swamp, which is to the Left of their Trench, another about twenty Yards; and at 5 o'Clock they began to play two Grenadoe Royal *M*ortars. At 6 o'Clock two Savages of the Five Nations, who were invited by one Cayendeſſe, of their Nation, came to ſpeak to *M.* Pouchot; the Firing ceaſed on both Sides during this Parley. At 10 o'Clock we began to fire again, and then we found the Engliſh had 8 *M*ortars.

Night between the 11th and 12th. The Enemy ran their Parallel from their firſt Trench to the Lake Side, where it ſeemed they intended to eſtabliſh a Battery. At two in the Afternoon, four Chiefs of the Five Nations came to us on Paſole, and ſaid they were going to retire to Belle Famille. The Enemy wrought the reſt of that Day, and perfected their Night's Work. *M.* Laforce had Orders to proceed to Frontenac, and to return immediately: In the Night between the 12th and 13th they fired many Bombs: I went with 30 *M*en to obſerve where the Enemy wrought.

Friday, 13th July. A Canoe arrived from *M*onſieur de Ville, to hear how we ſtood at this Poſt (or rather for the Canada Poſt.)

The Enemy threw a great many Bombs all this Day, and continued to work to perfect their Trenches: We fired a great many Cannon Shot. *M*any of their Savages croſſed the River, and deſired to ſpeak with us; there were but two of thoſe Nations with us. I went out with five Voluntiers, to act as the Night before. The Enemy fired no Bombs till about midnight.

Saturday, 14th July. At Day-break we found they had prolong'd their Trenches to the Lake Side, in ſpite of the great Fire from our Cannon and muſquetry, during the Night, and perfected it during the Day Time; they have placed four mortars and thrown many Bombs. All our Garriſon lay in the covered Way, and on the Ramparts.

Sunday, 15th July. In the morning we perceived they had finiſh'd their Works begun the Night before: During the Night they threw about 30 Bombs; the reſt of the Day and Night they threw a great many, but did not incommode us in any Shape.

Monday, 16th July. At Dawn of Day we ſpied, about half a League off, two Barges, at which we diſcharged ſome Cannon, on which they retired: In the Courſe of the Day they continued to throw ſome Bombs. They have already diſabled us about 20 Men. All our Men lie on Beaver, or in their Clothes, and armed. We do what we can to incommode them with our Cannon.

Tueſday, 17th July. Until ſix this Morning we had a thick Fog, ſo that we could not diſcern the Works of the Enemy; but it clearing a little up, we ſaw they had raiſed a Battery of three Pieces of Cannon, and four Mortars on the other Side of the River; they began to fire about 7 A. M. and M. Pouchot placed all the Guns he could againſt them: The Fire was briſk on both Sides all Day, they ſeemed moſt inclined to batter the Houſe where the Commandant lodges. The Service as uſual for the Night.

Wedneſday, 18th July. There was as great Firing as on the preceding Day; we had one Soldier diſmembered, and four wounded by their Bombs.

Thurſday, 19th July. At the Dawn of Day we found the Enemy had begun a Parallel about 80 Yards long in Front of the Fort. The Fire was very great on both Sides. At 2 P. M. arrived the Schooner Iroquoiſe, from Frontenac, and laid a-breaſt of the Fort, waiting for a Calm, not being able to get in, the Enemy having a Battery on the other Side of the River. Monſieur Pouchot will have the Boat on Shore as ſoon as the Wind falls.

Friday 20th. The Engliſh have made a third Parallel, towards the Lake; they are To-day about 160 Yards from the Fort: They cannot have worked quietly at the Sappe, having had a great Fire of Muſquetry all Night long, which they were obliged to bear. During the Day they made a great Firing with their Mortars, and they perfected their Works begun the Night of the 19th to the 20th. We had one Man killed, and four wounded. The Fire of the Muſquetry was very hot on both Sides till Eleven at Night, when the Enemy left off, and we continued ours all Night. Two Canoes were ſent on board the Schooner, who are to go to Montreal and Tironto.

Saturday 21ſt. During the Night the Enemy made a 4th Parallel, which is about 100 Yards from the Fort, in which it appears they will erect a Battery for a Breach in the Flag Baſtion. They have hardly fired any Cannon or Bombs in the Day, which gives Room to think they are tranſporting their Cannon and Artillery from their old Battery to their new one. The Service as uſual.

Their Battery on the other Side, fired but little in the Day. The Schooner went off to ſee two Canoes over to Tironto, one of which is to poſt to Montreal, and from thence ſhe is to cruize off Oſwego, to try to ſtop the Enemy's Convoys when on their Way. The Company of Voluntiers are always to paſs the Night in the covered Way.

Sunday 22d. All the Night was a ſtrong Conflict on both Sides. We had one Man killed by them and by our own Cannon. We fired almoſt all our Cannon with Cartridges. They worked in the Night to perfect all their Works begun the Night before. The Enemy began to fire red hot Balls in the Night; they alſo fired Fire-Poles. All Day they continued at Work to eſtabliſh their Batteries. They fired as uſual, Bombs and Cannon. The Service as uſual for the Night of the 22d and 23d. They worked hard to perfect their Batteries, being ardently ſuſtained by their Muſquetry.

Monday 23d. We added two Pieces of Cannon to the Baſtion of the Lake, to oppoſe thoſe of the Enemy's Side. At 8 A. M. four Savages brought a Letter from Monſieur Aubrey to Monſieur Pouchot, by which we learn, that he was arrived at the great Iſland, before the little Fort, at the Head of 2500 Men, half French, and half Savages: Monſieur Pouchot immediately ſent back four Savages with the Anſwer to M. Aubrey's Letter, informing him of the Enemy's Situation. Theſe Savages, before they came in, ſpoke to the Five Nations, and gave them five Belts to engage them to retire from the Enemy: They ſaw Part of the Enemy's Camp, and told us the firſt or ſecond in Command was killed by one of our Bullets, and two of their Guns broken, and one Mortar: We have Room to hope, that with ſuch Succours we may oblige the Enemy to raiſe the Siege, with the Loſs of Men, and as they take up much Ground, they muſt be beat, not being able to rally quick enough.

At 2 P. M. They unmaſked another Battery of — Pieces of Cannon, three of which were 18 Pounders, the others 12 and 6. They began with a briſk Fire, which continued two Hours, then ſlackened. About Five P. M. we ſaw a Barge go over to Belle Famille, on the other Side of the River, and ſome Motions made there: One of the four Savages which went off this Morning, returned his Porcelain (i. e. Wampum) he had nothing new. The Service of the Night as uſual. We worked hard to place two Pieces, 12 Pounders, on the middle of the Curtains, to bear upon their Battery.

Tueſday, 24th July. The Enemy began their Fire about 4 o'Clock this Morning, and continued to fire with the ſame Vivacity the reſt of the Day. At 8 A. M. we perceived our Army was approaching, having made ſeveral Diſcharges of Muſquetry at Belle Famille.

At 9 the Fire began on both Sides, and laſted Half an Hour: We wait to know who has the Advantage of thoſe two: At 2 P. M. we heard by a Savage, that our Army was routed, and almoſt all made Priſoners, by the Treachery of our Savages: When immediately the Engliſh Army had the Pleaſure to inform us of it, by ſummoning us to ſurrender.

The above, with ſome Letters, were found in an Embraſure, after we were in Poſſeſſion of the Fort; ſince which tranſlated, and the Original given to Sir William Johnſon.

Extract of a Letter from Ticondoroga, Auguſt 2, 1759.

"*General Gage and his Aid de Camp left this Place for Niagara, laſt Sunday—Part of the City of Quebeck is burnt by General Wolfe (this from Head-Quarters) I hope by this Time we are in Poſſeſſion of it.*"

Camp, at Ticonderoga, Auguſt 2, 1759.

"*The French retired from Crown-Point, to St. John's, at the End of the Lake.—Our next Movement will be to St. John's, from which acroſs to Montreal, is but* 15 *Miles.—We hear Quebeck is two thirds deſtroy'd by General Wolfe.*"

Extract of a Letter from Albany, dated Auguſt 6.

I congratulate you on the extraordinary Succeſs of our Armies at Ticonderoga, Niagara and Crown-Point, which Places are (thro' God's Bleſſing) in Poſſeſſion of our Troops. Ticonderoga and Crown-Point the Enemy abandon'd. Niagara they defended bravely, in Expectation of a Reinforcement from Venango, which came the Day they ſurrender'd, and made a bold Attack upon our Army. It is ſaid all the Indians, except the brave Mohawks, ſtood Neuter the firſt Onſet the Enemy made, to ſee, it is thought, which Way the Scale would turn; for I believe it was imprinted in their Minds the French were invincible. As ſoon as they found to the contrary, and that the French gave Way, it is ſaid but a Yard of Ground, they fell on them like ſo many Butchers, with their Tomahawks and long Knives, whooping and ſhouting, as if Heaven and Earth were coming together, and kill'd Abundance of the Enemy; the Number of Priſoners exceed 700. *Whether the Barbarities at Fort William-Henry, and Ohio, has influenc'd any of our Troops to encourage the Savages is uncertain; but ſure it is, that moſt of the French that came from Venango are Encouragers of ſuch Cruelties, and I hope at this Time they have Satisfaction.*

Extract of another Letter from Albany, dated Auguſt 8.

"*A new Fort is immediately to be conſtructed near the Place where Crown-Point formerly ſtood. It is exceeding good Land about it. Our People have found three large Fields of green Peaſe, which was ſufficient for the whole Army two Days, and are looking out for more.*"

Extract of a third Letter from Albany, dated Auguſt 12.

"*By an Expreſs arrived this Day from Crown Point, we learn, that Lieut. Hamilton, of the Royal, with ſome other Officers, and a few Indians, were gone upon a Scout, and intended to proceed as far as Quebec. This Day arrived here from Schenectady about* 640 *French Priſoners, amongſt which are about* 12 *Officers, and as many Women: The Men look well; and in particular the late Governor of Niagara, is a ſoldierly looking Man. Eight French Priſoners, and* 4 *Yorkers, were drowned at Schenectady by the Sinking of a Scow.*"

Letters from Albany, by laſt Thurſday's Mail, ſay, That General AMHERST is making all poſſible Preparations to proceed to St. John's, and will be ready in a few Days, having ordered a ſufficient Number of Men to garriſon the conquered Forts, &c.—That the Fort at Ticonderoga is eſteemed by our Engineers to be the ſtrongeſt and neateſt in America, being founded on a Rock, the Ditch round it dug in a Rock, and the Caſemates made in a Rock alſo.—And that Capt. Jacobs, who was ſome Time ago taken, upon a Scouting-Party, and carried to Crown-Point, eſcaped from the Enemy in the Confuſion of their Retreat from that Place; and is returned to our Camp.

Since our laſt ſeven Sloops arrived here from Albany, with about 640 French Priſoners, Officers included, being the whole of the Garriſon of Niagara: Among the Officers are, Monſ. Pouchot, who was Commander in Chief of the Fort, and Monſ. Villars, both Captains, and Knights of the Order of St. Lewis: There are ten other Officers, one of which is the famous Monſ. Joncœur, a very noted Man among the Seneca Indians, and whoſe Father was the firſt that hoiſted French Colours in that Country: His Brother, alſo a Priſoner, is now here, and has been very humane to many Engliſhmen, having purchaſed ſeveral of them from the Savages. Monſ. Larmenau, with two Privates, made their Eſcape near Fort Harkamer, and are ſuppoſed to be gone to Canada.

The Officers and Men in general, both Canadians and Regulars, look well, and do not appear as if they had fed for ſome Time on Horſe-Fleſh; on the contrary they are very robuſt, fat, and ſpry-looking Men.

Among the Priſoners taken the Day the Fort ſurrendered, is the infamous Monſ. Morang, who commanded at Monongahela when General Braddock was defeated, where ſo many of our brave Countrymen were cruelly maſſacreed, not one of the Wounded being ever heard of ſince, of which there were many Hundreds: However we hear the Mohawks inſiſt on having their Share of all the Priſoners taken in the Party that he commanded.

There were ſeveral Engliſh Priſoners found in the Fort at Niagara, when it ſurrendered, among which were the following, viz. John Peter, who was taken the 23d *of May laſt in Company with Robinſon and Bell (who were left among the Indians) that belonged to Captain Bullet's Company of Virginians, on their Way to Fort Ligonier from Ray's Town. Margaret Painter, taken* 18 *Months ſince, in Pennſylvania Government. Edward Hoſkins, taken* 10 *Years ſince, on the Borders of New-England. Nathaniel Sullivan, taken at Patowmack, in Virginia, the* 25*th of September laſt. Iſabel Stockton, a Dutch Girl, taken October* 1, 1757, *at Wincheſter. Chriſtopher and Michael Franks, Brothers, born at Tulpehoken, County of Berks, in Pennſylvania. John M'Daniel, taken the* 12*th of July,* 1758, *near Halifax, in Nova-Scotia. Molly Heyſham, taken four Years ſince at the Blue-Mountain, ſhe was twice condemned by the Indians to be burnt, but ranſomed by her Maſter. Alſo two or three young Children, Names unknown, whoſe Parents were killed by the Indians when taken.*

Many of the above Priſoners have been at Niagara, one or two Years paſt, and had their Liberty to walk about, as the Captives made to the Southward muſt paſs that Way in their Rout to Canada: They ſay that they had an Account there of Quebec being inveſted by General Wolfe, that Monſ. *M*ontcalm was there, but did no command, as *M*onſ. Vaudreuil was Generaliſſimo of all the Troops in Canada.

Saturday laſt arrived the Privateer Sloop Catharine, Capt. Kennedy, from an unſucceſsful Cruize; who about a Week ago met the Privateer Ship Royal Hunter, of this Port, then going to South-Carolina to heave down.

Yeſterday Captain Oldfield arrived here from Rhode-Iſland, which Place he left laſt Friday Afternoon: A Gentleman there writes on the Back of his Letter to his Correſpondent here, dated the 17th,

"We have juſt now an Account that QUEBEC is
"actually taken."

Captain Oldfield ſays, That juſt as he came away, Colonel Hubbard came into Town from Boſton, and informed, That they were Rejoicing there for the taking of QUEBEC when he left it.

The 29th of July laſt, General Amherſt appointed as a Day of Public Thankſgiving throughout his whole Army.

Monday laſt Capt. Jones arrived here in 31 Days from the Muſqueto Shore, by whom we are informed, that the Engliſh People, who fled from the Bay of Honduras ſome Time ago, for Fear of the Spaniards, had all returned back, their Apprehenſions being ill grounded.

General Amherſt, according to the lateſt Accounts that could be received from Crown-Point, ſtill continued at that Place, and was forwarding the Works of the new Fort with all imaginable Expedition. But it was ſaid he ſoon intended to ſet off from thence to attack St. John's.

A Liſt of Men of War, &c. in the River St. Lawrence, under the Command of Admiral Saunders.

Ship Neptune of 90 Guns, Princeſs Amelia 84, Royal William 86, Dublin 74, Shrewſbury 74, Warſpite 74, Terrible 74, Northumberland 70, Somerſet 70, Devonſhire 70, Vanguard 70, Captain 70, Centurion 70, Prince of Orange 70, Bedford 66, Prince Frederick 66, Medway 64, Intrepid 64, Windſor 64, Orford 64, Alcide 64, Stirling-Caſtle 64, Tryton 64, Pembroke 60, Sutherland 50.——In all 25 Ships of the Line.

Frigates. Diana 36 Guns, Richmond 32, Leoſtoffe 32, Trent 32, Lizard 32, Echo 32, Euris 28, Fowey 28, Hind 24, Nightingale 20, Squirrel 20, Seahorſe 20, Scarborough 20.

Fire-ſhips. Race-Horſe 20 Guns, Cornet 18, Strombolo 18.

Bombs. Pelican 18 Guns, Baltimore 18.

Sloops. Scorpion 18, Porcupine 16, Zephyr 16, Rodney Cutter 8.

In all 47 Sail of Men of War.

Extract of a Letter from Crown-Point, Auguſt 10, 1759.

"*Captain Kennedy, with a few Indians, has taken in Hand to go from hence, thro' the Woods, to Quebec. They went off Yeſterday, and in their Way going down the Side of the Lake, they ſaw two Sloops and a Schooner about* 20 *Miles from this Place, one of the Sloops carrying* 24 *Guns; whereupon Capt.*

March THE No. 500.

NEW-YORK MERCURY.

Containing the freshest* ADVICES, *Foreign and Domestic.

Printed by HUGH GAINE, Bookseller, Printer and Stationer, at the *Bible & Crown*, in *Hanover-Square*.

Where may be had, a neat Assortment of Books and Stationary Ware; and where Country Merchants may be supplied with Bibles, Testaments, Primers, Spelling-Books, &c. on the best Terms; and Seafaring Men with Waggoners, Compasses, Kalanders, Journal Books, Paper and Quills, &c.

☞ All Sorts of Printing Work done with Care and Dispatch.

MONDAY, MARCH 1, 1762.

Price Current in NEW-YORK,

Wheat, per Bushel,	6s 9d	Beef per Barrel,	2l	10s od
Flour, -	18s od	Pork, -	4l	5s od
Brown Bread, -	18s od	Salt, -		2s 6d
West-India Rum,	5s od	Bohea Tea, - -		7s od
New England ditto,	3s 2d	Bees Wax, - -		1s 8d
Muscovado Sugar,	50s od	Chocolate, p.Doz.	2l	os. d.
Single refin'd ditto,	1s 3d	Nut Wood, -	2l	10s od
Molasses, —	2s 9d	Oak ditto, -	1l	10s od

High-Water at NEW-YORK, to Monday next.

MONDAY	53 min. after 1	FRIDAY	21 min. after 5
TUESDAY	40 min. after 2	SATUR.	7 min. after 6
WEDNES.	26 min. after 3	SUNDAY	46 min. after 6
THURS.	14 min. after 4	☽'s First Quar. Wednes.	

HUGH GAINE,

Bookseller, Printer and Stationer, at the Bible *and* Crown, *in* Hanover-Square, *has imported in the last Vessels from* London, *a very good Assortment of Books and Stationary, among which are the following*, viz.

1. BEAUTIFUL Folio Bibles, with Cuts, the Common Prayer, and Concordance.
2. Quarto Bibles of different Sizes, with or without the Common Prayer; and a great Variety of School Bibles, for Children, and large and small Common Prayers very neatly bound and gilt.
3. Watts's Works compleat, in 6 Vols. Quarto.
4. Watts's Psalms, Hymns, and Lyric Poems.
5. The Rational Foundation of a Christian Church, and the Terms of Christian Communion. To which are added, three Discourses, viz. The Pattern of a Deflenting Preacher; 2d, The Office of Deacons; 3d, Invitations to Church Fellowship. By Isaac Watts, D. D.
6. The Glory of Christ as God-Man displayed in three Discourses. By Isaac Watts, D. D.
7. The World to Come: Or, Discourses on the Joys and Sorrows of departed Souls at Death, and the Glory or Terror of the Resurrection. In 2 Vols. By Isaac Watts.
8. Orthodoxy and Charity. By Isaac Watts.
9. Devout Exercises on the Heart, in Meditation and Soliloquy, Prayers and Praise. By the late pious and ingenious Mrs. Rowe. Revised and published at her Request, by Isaac Watts, D. D.
10. Discourses of the Love of God, and its Influence on all the Passions. By Isaac Watts.
11. The Redeemer and the Sanctifier, of the Sacrifice of Christ, and the Operations of the Spirit Vindicated. By Isaac Watts.
12. Sermons on various Subjects, divine and moral, with a sacred Hymn suited to each Subject. In 2 Vols. By Isaac Watts.
13. Twelve Discourses upon some practical Parts of Solomon's Song. By William Romaine.
14. Twelve Discourses upon the Law and Gospel. By William Romaine, M. A.
15. A Practical Comment on the 107th Psalm. By William Romaine.
16. The Works of the Rev. Mr. John Flavel, late Minister of the Gospel, at Dartmouth, in Devon. In 2 Vols. Folio, a very good Edition, printed in Glasgow, and sold much cheaper than the London Edition.
17. Expository Notes, with practical Observations, on the New Testament of our Lord and Saviour Jesus Christ. By William Burkitt, M. A. late Vicar and Lecturer of Dedham in Essex. The 15th Edition, carefully corrected.
18. A complete Concordance to the Holy Scriptures of the Old and New Testament: In two Parts. By Alexander Cruden, M. A.
19. The Works of the truly pious and learned Mr. Joseph Allen, some time Minister of the Gospel at Taunton, in Somersetshire. In 2 Vols.
20. The Scriptures made Easy. Being a complete History of the Holy Bible, by Question and Answer: By the Rev. George Reves, M. A. Illustrated with Copper Plates.
21. A Guide to eternal Glory: Or, brief Directions to all Christians how to attain everlasting Life.
22. The Royal Psalter: Or, King David's Meditations, selected for the Use of Children and young Persons. To which are added, the useful Proverbs and wise Sayings of King Solomon, with Meditations moral and divine.
23. Spiritual Songs: Or, Songs of Praise with Penetential Cries to Almighty God upon several Occasions. By Mr. Mason.
24. The Confession of Faith, the larger and shorter Catechism, with the Scripture Proofs at large. Together, with the Sum of Saving Knowledge, &c. of publick Authority in the Church of Scotland. With Acts of Assembly and Parliament, relative to, and approbative of, the same.
25. The same in a small Edition.
26. An Explanatory Catechism: Or, an Explanation of the Assembly's Shorter Catechism: By Thomas Vincent.
27. The New Practice of Piety: Containing the necessary Duties of a Christian Life, or the Means of acquiring every Virtue, the Remedies against every Vice, and Directions how to resist all Temptations: Adapted to the Genius of the present Age.
28. Several Discourses concerning the Terms of Acceptance with God. By Benjamin Hoadly. M. A. Rector of St. Peter's Poor, now Lord Bishop of Winchester.

LIKEWISE,

Imperial, Royal, Demoy, Foolscap and Pot Paper, the two last Sorts gilt or plain, Counting House Files, Ledgers, Day Books and Journals; Quills, Pounce, Sealing Wax, Wafers, Clark's best Leather Ink Pots, Snuff and Tobacco Boxes, beautiful red and blue MOROCCO POCKET BOOKS, and,

PLAYING CARDS.

Likewise, This Day is published, by said H. Gaine,

LETTERS and Dialogues, between *THERON, PAULINUS*, and *ASPASIO*. Upon the Nature of Love to GOD. Faith in CHRIST, and Assurance of a Title to Eternal Life. With some Remarks on the Sentiments of the Rev. Messrs. HERVEY and MARSHALL, on these Subjects.

Published at the Request of many.

By JOSEPH BELLAMY, *A. M. of Bethlem in New-England.*

HAGUE, (in Holland) Nov. 27.

THE last accounts from the Army of Prince Ferdinand, are of the 22d ult. to which day there had happened nothing new in those parts.

Every thing continued in the same situation in Silesia on the 16th ult. and in Saxony on the 20th.

Letters from Hamburgh of the 24th of November, say, that the day before, an estafette had passed through that town going to Copenhagen, dispatched by the Prince of Wirtemburgh to the Prussian Minister there, with advice, that after having reinforced the garrison of Colberg, he had quitted his intrenchments before that place; and that, on the 16th instant, he had joined General Platen at Griffenberg, without having sustained any loss on his march through the enemy.

Rouen, (a City of France, capital of the Province of Normandy) Novem. 22. On the 8th a motion was made in our parliament, to examine the book entitled the *Constitutions of the Jesuits*. A second motion was made by another member, to enquire into the principles of morality taught by the Jesuits. The debate was adjourned till the next day, when one of the members having complained to the chambers against nine different tracts of Jesuits, and delivered them in at the table, it was ordered, "That the Attorney-General should examine the said pieces, and make a report to the chambers. It was also ordered, that the superiors of the three houses of the Jesuits in this city, should, within the space of three days, deliver to the clerk of the parliament a copy of the *Constitutions of the Jesuits*, printed at Prague in 1757.

Paris, (the Capital of France) Nov. 23. The thirty members of the parliament of Besancon, whom the King sent into exile about two years ago, are recalled to resume their functions.

Constantinople, (the Metropolis of the Turkish Empire) Oct. 20. The Pestilence still makes great havock in this City, and likewise in the suburbs of Pera and Galathea; but as winter is coming on, we hope to be soon delivered from this dreadful scourge.

Hildesheim, (a Bishoprick in Germany) Nov. 20. It appears that the plan of the Allies is to keep their head-quarters at Eimbeck all the winter: That place was not any longer tenable for the French, for want of provisions; but it will be so to the Allies, if it is not disputed with them, because they can draw provisions from Hanover, which abounds with magazines.

Paris, Nov. 24. The small-pox makes great ravages, and has cut down several of our warriors, whom the rage of war had spared. The Viscount de Crussol is just now attacked with that disease on his return from the army. The Marquis de Laval, son of the Duke, died the 13th of this month, in a post which the army had abandoned. His chagrin at seeing himself in the enemy's power struck the pox in.

The regiment of Montmorin is gone from Bourdeaux to Rochfort, in order to embark there.

Genoa, (a Republic in Italy) Nov. 18. The French privateers have taken four English ships in sight of Carthagena; two of whom were richly laden, and near the entrance of the port.

London, December 4.

An exact List of the number of Merchant Ships taken and ransomed, for nine Months, ending with September.

Total of ships taken.		Total of ships ransomed.	Total of ransom money.	
83	January	16	£.11,150	
83	February	12	6,970	10
51	March	3	930	
54	April	7	2,484	
70	May	22	28,457	15
103	June	31	19,872	10
83	July	27	20,802	5
77	August	11	8,522	10
80	September	15	11,090	10
684		144 ransomed for	110,280	

If 144 *ships paid in nine months* 110,280*l. for their ransom, how much would* 683 *ships have paid?*

The answer is — £.523,064 *nine months*
130,766 *three months*
200,000 *Ajax Indiaman*

Total of one year's captures. 853,830

Deduct for North American ships given up to privateers belonging to the Fr. sugar islands 53,830

Total of neat captures one year 800,000

Ships.

1 *East Indies, from thence to London.*

54 *Virginia and Maryland, viz.* 43 *from thence to sundry ports of England, Scotland, &c. and* 10 *to ditto, from sundry ports of England, Scotland, and* 1 *from Cadiz.*

44 *Newfoundland, viz.* 30 *from thence to sundry ports of England, Scotland, Straits, &c. and* 14 *to ditto, from Ireland, Jersey, and sundry other English ports.*

30 *Carolina, from thence to sundry British and Irish ports, &c. and to ditto, from sundry other British ports, &c.*

27 *Jamaica, viz.* 23 *from thence to ditto, and* 4 *to ditto, from ditto.*

8 *Barbadoes, from thence to ditto, and to ditto, from ditto.*

80 *Leeward Islands, from thence to ditto, and to ditto, from ditto.*

42 *North America, from thence to ditto, and to ditto, from ditto.*

86 *North America, from thence to sugar islands, and to ditto (only some few) from sugar islands to ports of North America.*

6 *North America, from thence to other ports of the same.*

24 *Africa, from thence to America. and to ditto, from sundry British and Irish ports, &c.*

74 *Straits, Portugal, &c. from thence to sundry British, Irish, and other ports, and to ditto, including Turkey, Gibraltar, Portugal, Madeira, Belleisle, &c.*

46 *Baltic, from thence to ditto, and to ditto, including Denmark, Hamburgh, Bremen, &c.*

69 *From sundry British and Irish ports, isles and ports adjacent, and to other ports of the same.*

93 *Sundry ships and voyages, not particularly distinguished.*

684 *Total.*

The following sums, besides those formerly mentioned, have been granted by the Irish Parliament: To the Trustees of the linnen manufacture to encourage the raising hemp and flax in that kingdom, 2000l. per annum for two years. Towards inclosing, fixing, and deepening the channel of the River Boyne below the bridge of Drogheda to the bar of the said river, 2000l. For widening and repairing Baal's Bridge, in the city of Limerick, and for continuing a new quay, &c. 4500l. For finiſhing the harbour of Wicklow, 1850l. 8s. 9d. For continuing the Ballaſt-office wall to the Eaſt end of the piles, 5000l. For making the river Lagan navigable from Loughneagh to Belfaſt, 4000l.

Beſides the 2000l. given to the Dublin Society for the improvement of Huſbandry, and other uſeful arts, as formerly mentioned, 10,000l. is granted to them to be diſtributed to ſo many of the ſeveral perſons who petitioned the Houſe of Commons this Seſſion for præmiums or rewards, upon which Reports have been made.

Decem. 7. The States of Franconia have at length conſented to the two Millions of rations, &c. demanded of them by the French; but have reſolved to make remonſtrances on this matter to the Courts of Vienna and Verſailles.

M. de Vrintz, late Agent or Reſident of the Court of Vienna at Bremen, and his wife, who were apprehended by order of Prince Ferdinand of Brunſwick, and carried to Stade, are releaſed from their confinement; but they are enjoined to reſide at Oldenburg, and appear no more at Bremen during the preſent war.

The following are the Heads of the Act for repealing the Compulſive Clauſe:

" By an Act 1 George III. for Relief of Inſolvent Debtors, any Creditor of any Priſoner charged in Execution is empowered to compel ſuch Priſoner to deliver up his eſtate and effects in order to his being diſcharged; as by the ſaid Act is directed; and many inconveniences having ariſen from ſuch power being given to Creditors;

" From the 19th of November, 1761, the Compulſive Clauſe in the above-mentioned act ſhall be repealed to all intents and purpoſes.

" Nevertheleſs, Offences committed againſt the ſaid Act before the ſaid 19th of November, may be ſued for; and the offenders ſhall be liable to the penalties and forfeitures thereby incurred."

December 10. A few days ago ſailed for the Weſt Indies Mr. Harriſon, jun. of Red Lion-ſtreet, Holborn, with ſome mathematical machines, invented and made by his father and him, towards the diſcovering the longitude at ſea.

Dec. 11. *An account of the ſums raiſed by the* LAND-TAX *ſince the* REVOLUTION.

Years.	Tax per Pound.	Produce.
1688	1s.	500,000
89	2	1,000,000
90	2	1,000,000
91	2	1,000,000
92	3	1,500,000
93	3	1,500,000
94	3	1,500,000
95, 96, 97	4	6,000,000
98, 99	3	3,000,000
1700	2s. 6d.	1,250,000
1701 to 12	4	24,000,000
13 to 15	2	3,000,000
16	4	2,000,000
17 to 21	2	5,000,000
22 to 26	4	10,000,000
27	3	1,500,000
28, 29	2	2,000,000
30, 31	3	3,000,000
32, 33	1	1,000,000
34 to 39	2	6,000,000
40 to 49	4	20,000,000
50 to 52	3	4,500,000
53 to 55	2	3,000,000
56 to 60 inclusive	4	10,000,000
	Total £.	113,250,000

To the PRINTER.

SIR,

HAVING lately read the French Memorial relative to a peace, without regarding any thing further than the articles themſelves, the following thoughts upon them readily occured to me. I have made my calculations very low. Some gentlemen perhaps will ſet them at a truer, that is, a higher rate.

On the terms propoſed, the Engliſh would get, Canada, 1800 miles long, 1260 broad.

Nova Scotia, 1500 miles long, 400 broad.

And weſt of the Carolina's, ſeveral hundred miles; all which being near four times as big as England, Scotland, and Ireland, put together, if valued at one fourth of what England is worth, per ann. ſterling, £.	5,000,000
Fiſheries on all the coaſts, iſles, River St. Lawrence, &c. — —	2,000,000
Neutral Iſles, if only Dominico and Tobago	1,000,000
Advantages in the Eaſt-Indies, ſuppoſe the Eaſt India Company give up half their conqueſts - -	1,000,000
Senegal and Goree - -	500,000
Total of the Engliſh profit per ann. -	9,500,000
The difference to the French by this, and their loſs, would be yearly - -	19,000,000
A peace for 10 years at 9,500,000 l. would be	95,000,000
A peace for 20 years - -	190,000,000

Which would well reimburſe us for all the expence of this war; and ſink the French as low in trade, riches, or power.

Minorca affords good watering for ſhips; gives you power and reſpect among the States in the Mediterranean: And thus is worth ſomething.

I obſerve, Louiſiana was to be ſo limited, that it could propoſe to itſelf no great things. Beſides that, the navigation to it is much impeded by ſhallows, rocks, falls, &c. and the mouth of the Miſſiſippi, the only way to it, may, at any time, in a few Hours be blocked up by us.

The Iſle of St. Peter only for their fiſheries, ſo little, and ſo reſtrained, to be defenceleſs, and an Engliſh officer to inſpect their behaviour; this could not promiſe itſelf mighty things neither.

A place in Africa for them for their ſlaves would never hurt us.

And Belleiſle, a poor barren place, is worth little or nothing to any body, eſpecially to us.

Dunkirk is almoſt choaked up with ſand.

What could induce our Patriot to give up Guadaloupe, the ballance of trade in ſugars, &c. I know not, unleſs for the ſake of peace; which this next year, will be worth twelve millions, or more; beſides the lives of many thouſand of brave men, and wounds in abundance.

Venice, (a republic of Italy) *November* 10. *The politicia ns of this city conſider the alliance between the Ottoman Porte and the King of Pruſſia, as a treaty of great conſequence. They pretend, that the ſcope of it, is to ballance the quadruple alliance between the Courts of Vienna, Peterſburgh, Varſaw, and Venice; by which the power of the Turks has been effectually kept within bounds. The object of this, if they are to be believed, is to reſtrain the power of the Roman and Ruſſian Empires, and to preſerve not only the Crown of Pruſſia, but alſo other Princes and States, who are invited to accede thereto, in the quiet poſſeſſion of their reſpective dominions, conſtitution, and independency; in conſequence of which, the Ottoman Porte will be at all times at liberty to interfere with the affairs of Europe, in caſe any of the contracting parties are attacked by either or by both thoſe Empires.*

Rome, (the capital of the Pope's territories, and of Italy) *Nov.* 12. *The Bookſeller Pagliarini who has been impriſoned a year for publiſhing a libel, intitled, The Wolves in Sheep's cloathing, is condemned (by the Congregation of Good Government at Rome) to the galleys for ſeven years.*

Rouen, (E. lon. 1. 6. lat. 49. 30. a city of France, capital of the prince of Normandy) *November* 23. *The 21ſt inſt. at the firſt ſitting of our Parliament after the long vacation, information was given of divers abuſes committed in the Province, relative to the adminiſtration of juſtice; then one of the members obſerved, that the regiſtering of the Twentieths had been agreed to with this modification, that no reſearches ſhould be made concerning the increaſe of the ſubjects eſtates or effects; an that the levies or collections then extent, ſhould ſerve as a ſtandard for the new aſſeſſments to be made, that nevertheleſs, the Comptrollers has made immenſe reſearches, and conſiderably augmented the taxes, which augmentations were always confirmed by the Commiſſaries appointed; and that in ſuch circumſtances it was neceſſary to provide for the relief of the oppreſſed province.*

After deliberating on the affair, it was reſolved, that the Attorney General ſhould be charged to write to all his ſubſtitutes, that they muſt ſend him memorials, and make enquiries into the augmentations impoſed by the Comptrollers, whoſe names they are to tranſmit to the ſaid Attorney General. The Commiſſion was of a very delicate nature, and yet it has been executed.

New-York, March 1.

The Vendue, of the Houſe next Door to the Croſs Key's, near the Fly Market, was obliged to be poſtponed laſt Thurſday, but it will commence at the Coffee-Houſe To-morrow, at Eleven o'Clock in the Forenoon.

We are credibly informed, That a ſmart Shock of an Earthquake, was felt about 4 o'Clock in the Morning of the 21ſt ultimo, at Middletown, (New-Jerſey) and other Parts adjacent.

Thurſday Morning laſt, John Likens, and Mary his Wife, with Elizabeth Ridgeway, were committed to our Goal, for attempting to rob a Man the Night before, near the Freſh Water: The two Women cut the Man in ſeveral Places with Knives, he having knock'd down Likens and another of their Aſſociates before their Faces as ſoon as they attempted to rob him.

Next Day one Joſeph Wholeſtock was committed to Goal alſo, for going into the Houſe of James Livingſton, Eſq; and taking therefrom ſeveral Articles that were found upon him a few Minutes after he took them, having been ſeen by ſome of the Neighbours, was purſued and taken.

And on Saturday, Samuel Playford, received 39 Laſhes at the Whipping Poſt, for making free with a Piece of Handkerchiefs in the Shop of Doctor Milligan, in Beaver-Street, a few Days before: He arrived here from London with his Wife, only 4 Weeks ago.

The Ship Mancheſter Capt. Chambers, is expected to Sail for London the firſt fair Wind.

We hear that the Price of Beaver Furr is much fallen in London, and of Logwood much raiſed.

The ingenious Doctor Eliot, of Killingſworth in Connecticut, has wrote a Treatiſe on making of Iron from ſea Sand, a moſt curious and uſeful Diſcovery. The Iron proves to be of the beſt and pureſt Kind.

To the Honourable

Major General Thomas Gage, *Governor of* Montreal, *and its Dependences, &c. &c.*

The Humble Addreſs *of the Trading People of the City and Government of* Montreal.

WE His Majeſty's moſt dutiful and loyal Subjects, the Trading People of the City and Government of *Montreal*, inſpired with Sentiments of the moſt affectionate Loyalty to the beſt of Sovereigns, beg Leave, upon the Commencement of the Year, to preſent our moſt unfeigned Tribute of Duty and Reſpect to You, His Majeſty's Repreſentative in this Government.

With Hearts full of moſt ſincere Joy, we congratulate your Excellency, upon the rapid and uninterrupted Series of Victories and Succeſſes, which, under the Divine Bleſſing, have attended His Majeſty's Arms by Sea and Land, during the preſent War; and offer up our moſt ardent Vows, and Prayers, to the ſupreme Director of the Univerſe, for a Continuance of the ſame.

We beg Leave to aſſure you, that we are unable---extremely unable, to expreſs the grateful Senſe we have, of the Moderation and Juſtice of your Adminiſtration; and the great Encouragement and Protection you have, upon all Occaſions, given to Trade and Commerce; the Eaſineſs of Acceſs to your Perſon; the polite and condeſcending Manner with which we are received; the expeditious Adminiſtration of Juſtice, and the late Appointment of an Engliſh Council, to hear and redreſs the Complaints of His Majeſty's Subjects, are convincing Proofs, that you have the higheſt Senſe of, and ſtricteſt Regard to, the Liberties and Privileges of a *Britiſh* Subject. And it gives us infinite Pleaſure, that we can, with ſtrict Regard to Truth, ſay, That we find ourſelves in the full and free Enjoyment of thoſe ineſtimable Privileges, which, as Subjects of one of the beſt Governments in the World, we are intitled to. No Encroachments upon our Properties, or Inſults upon our Perſons, but what are redreſſed, with the utmoſt Juſtice and Humanity.

From the great Benevolence and Candour, which among the many other Virtues that conſtitute your Character, we promiſe ourſelves the fulleſt Security of our Rights and Liberties. And we humbly hope, that whilſt we continue to manifeſt the ſincereſt Loyalty and Attachment to our moſt gracious Sovereign, and cheerful Obedience to the Government of His Repreſentative, we ſhall not fail of the Continuance of your Excellency's Countenance and Protection.

We therefore with Sentiments of the moſt dutiful Reſpect, and cordial eſteem, do unanimouſly wiſh your Excellency a happy Year, in the moſt extenſive Senſe of that Expreſſion, by the Acceſſion of every Thing that can any Way contribute to the Happineſs of yourſelf and Family.

We are, May it pleaſe your Excellency,
Moſt reſpectfully,
Your Dutiful and Obedient Servants,

The Trading People of the City and Government of Montreal.

Montreal, Jan. 1, 1762.

To which His Excellency was pleaſed to give the following Anſwer.

To the Trading People of the City and Government of Montreal.
Gentlemen,

" *I Thank you for your very kind Addreſs; and heartily rejoice with you, in the ſignal Succeſſes of His Majeſty's Arms, during the Courſe of this War. I flatter myſelf that the new Branch of Commerce opened to His Majeſty's Subjects, by the Conqueſt of this Country, will, thro' your Integrity, Care, and Induſtry, be improved to the higheſt Advantage.*

" *You will find a Readineſs in me to encourage your Endeavours, and ſecond your Attempts; and will ever meet with that Protection, for your Perſons and Properties, which every Perſon, born under the benign Influence of a Britiſh Government, has a Right to expect and demand.*

" I am Gentlemen,
" Your Moſt Obedient Humble Servant,

Thomas Gage.

To all Perſons intereſted in the Lands herein after mentioned.

WHEREAS his late Majeſty King George the Second, by Letters Patent under the great Seal of the Colony of New-York, bearing Date the Eighteenth Day of July, one Thouſand ſeven Hundred and Forty; did grant and confirm, unto John Schuyler, jun. Philip Schuyler, Stephen Bayard, Samuel Bayard, jun. James Stephenſon and John Livingſton; all that certain Tract or Parcel of Land, ſituate, lying and being on the Eaſt Side of Hudſon's River above Saraghtoga, in the County of Albany, beginning on the Eaſt Bank of the ſaid River, at the Northweſt Corner of the Land, formerly granted to William Kettlehuyn, at the Mouth of a ſmall Brook, which falls into the ſaid River, oppoſite to a ſmall Iſland in the River, and runs thence Eaſt one Hundred and Ninety-three Chains, then North nine Degrees, Eaſt ſix Hundred and Fifty-one Chains, then Weſt Thirty-three Chains, then South ſixty Degrees, Weſt two Hundred and five Chains, to Hudſon's River, then down the Stream of the ſaid River (including ſix Iſlands lying in the ſaid River, oppoſite to this Tract) to the Place where this ſame Tract of Land firſt began; containing in the whole Twelve Thouſand Acres of Land, and the uſual Allowance for Highways; of which ſaid Lands we the Subſcribers are part Owners and Proprietors; and as they are undivided, and we are inclined to have Partition thereof, purſuant to an Act of the Lieutenant-Governor, the Council, and the General Aſſembly, paſſed the Eighth Day of January laſt, entitled, " An Act for the more effectual collecting of his Majeſty's Quit Rents in the Colony of New-York, and for Partition of Lands in order thereto." We do hereby give Notice, that John Winne, of the City of Albany, Gentleman, Abraham Jacob Lanſing, of Stone Rabie, in the County of Albany, Gentleman, and Killian De Ridder, of Saraghtoga, in the ſaid County, Gentleman, are appointed to make Partition of the ſaid Lands ſo undivided; and that they the ſaid Commiſſioners will meet on the Twenty Eighth Day of May next, at the Court Houſe in the ſaid City of Albany, to proceed to the Partition of the ſaid Lands, and all Perſons intereſted therein, are hereby required to attend then and there for that Purpoſe, either by themſelves or their Attornies. Given under our Hands this Twenty-fifth Day of February, in the Year of our Lord one Thouſand ſeven Hundred and Sixty-two.

WILLIAM BAYARD,
PHILIP LIVINGSTON.

Custom-House, New-York, Inward-Entries.
NONE.
Outward-Entries.
Sloop Little Sally, James Prince, for Monto Christo.
Cleared for Departure.
Schooner Betsey, John Amonet, to Virginia.
Sloop Susanna, Andrew Langworthy, to R. Island.
Brigantine Polly, Isaac Winn, to London.
Fariholm, James Johnson, to Monto Christo.
Snow John and Matty, J. Moat, to Belfast and Newry.
Sloop Cornelius, Daniel Lawrence, to St. Augustine.
Sea Nymph, David Youngs;
Philadelphia, Francis Fearis; And,
Elisabeth, Richard Allen, to Jamaica.
Ship Nancy, Charles M'Kinzie, to Londonderry.
Brigt. Charming Beckey, Luke Troy, to St. Croix.

By Permission of His Honour the Lieutenant Governor.
FOR THE BENEFIT OF
Mr. QUELCH.
By a Company of COMEDIANS.
At the New Theatre in *Chaple-Street*, on *Thursday* next, being the 4th of *March*, will be presented, a *Tragedy*, written by *Shakespear*, and alter'd by Mr. *Garrick*, call'd,
ROMEO and JULIET.
The Part of ROMEO, to be perform'd by
Mr. *H A L L A M*,
Prince, by Mr. *Douglass*; *Paris*, by Mr. *Tomlinson*; *Montague*, by Mr. *Sturt*; *Capulet*, by Mr. *Morris*; *Mercutio*, by Mr. *Douglass*; *Benvolio*, by Mr. *A. Hallam*; *Tibalt*, by Mr. *Reed*; Friar *Lawrence*, by Mr. *Allyn*; Friar *John*, by Mr. *Tremain*.
The Part of JULIET, to be perform'd by
Mrs. *D O U G L A S S*.
Lady *Capulet*, by Mrs. *Allyn*; *Nurse*, by Mrs. *Morris*.
In the MASQUERADE SCENE,
Mr. *A. Hallam* will perform a COMIC DANCE.
With an additional SCENE, and the
FUNERAL PROCESSION
OF JULIET
To the MONUMENT of the CAPULETS.
In which will be Sung,
A SOLEMN DIRGE.
The Vocal Parts by Mrs. *Morris*, Mr. *Quelch*, Mr. *Sturt* Mr. *Tremain*, and Mrs. *Allyn*, &c.
To begin exactly at 6 o'Clock.
TICKETS to be had of H. GAINE, Printer, Bookseller and Stationer, at the *Bible & Crown*, in *Hanover-Square*, and of Mr. *Quelch*, at his Lodgings, at Captain *Crew's*, next Door but one to the *Theatre*.
BOXES 8s. PIT 5s. GALLERY 3s.
*** The Ceremony of waiting on Ladies and Gentlemen at their Houses with Bills, has been for some Time left off in this Company; the frequent Solicitations on these Occasions, having been found rather an Inconvenience to the Persons so waited on, than a Compliment; for which Reason, Mr. *Quelch* hopes the Town will dispense with a personal Application, and Favour him with their Company.

SOLD for no Fault,
A Likely Negro Girl, between 9 and 10 Years of Age, has had the Small Pox and Meazels, and Country born. Enquire of H. GAINE.

To be Sold,
By Christopher Heysham,
At his Store, in King-Street, next Door below Mr. William Proctor's, Vendue-Master; the following Kinds of European Goods, for Cash, or short Credit, viz.
WORSTED Stuffs, Silk Dresdens, ditto, Venetians, Calimancoes, figur'd Lastings, Tammies, Durants, Camblets, Cambletees, Linnen and Cotton Checks, *wooling Cloaths and Coatings*, Gartering, Tapes, Qualities, sewing Silks, and Ribbons, Thread, Pins, Men's and Boy's Hats of divers Sorts, Ladies Riding ditto, Worsted, Thread, Cotton and Silk Stockings, Breeches Patterns, of most Colours, Men's and Women's Worsted Gloves, Women's Black Mitts, *Manchester Velvets*, *Thicksetts*, *Jeans*, Cambrick, Poplins, Barcelona, Taffety and Spitlefields *Handkerchiefs*, *Silk Caps*, Women's neat Shoes and Goloshoes, Men's single Channel Pumps and Boots, and a few ready made Men's Suits of Ratteen, at 4 l. 10s. per Suit.
Also, Jamaica and Barbados Rum, Cheshire Cheese, and good old Claret in Hogsheads, or in Bottles.

To be Sold, at public Vendue,
On Monday *the* 22d *of* March,
A Very good House with 5 Fire Places, 4 good Rooms, 2 good Bed Rooms, a good Kitchen and Cellar; and three Lots of Ground, on the Church Ground; stands well for a Publick House, and is now a Tavern. Whoever inclines to purchase the same any Time before, may apply to C. E. Colvill, or Henry Grigg, now on the Premisses.

T O B E S O L D,
At Prince Town, New-Jersey, *upon* Thursday *the* 25th *of* March *inst.*
FOUR Lots of Land lately belonging to *Muir* and *Crawford*, lying to the South of the Main Road, leading to *New-York*, and East of the College in said Town; there is a good new dwelling House upon one of the Lots, a Store upon another, and a small new House upon a Third; all the Lots are divided, and well fenced in. Any Person having a Mind to purchase the Whole, or any Part before the Day of Sale, may apply to *Robert Ritchie*, Merchant, in *Philadelphia*, or Mr. *Yard*, Vintner, in *Prince Town*.

J O H N A B E E L,
At Coenties's Market, has to sell
CHOICE West-India Rum, by the Hogshead; and excellent Muscovado Sugar by the Hogshead or Barrell.

To be Sold, by
J A M E S A B E E L,
At Coenties's-Market;
A Parcel of very good *Irish* Mess Pork.

Mr. Gaine, Feb. 23, 1762.
The Corporation of this City desire you'll insert in your next Mercury, *the last Clause in a Law of this Province, entitled,* An Act for the more effectual Prevention of Fires, and for regulating of Buildings in the City of *New York*, *made and published the* 8th *of January last, being in the Words following, viz.*
AND whereas the Storing of Pitch, Tar, Turpentine, or Shingles in any Houses, Store-houses, Cellars, or other Places within this City, may be of very bad Consequences, in Case of Fire breaking out at, or near the Place, where any such Commodities are stored: *Be it therefore Enacted by the Authority aforesaid,* That from and after the first Day of *May* next, no Pitch, Tar, Turpentine, or Shingles, shall, or may, be put in any Place to the Southward of *Fresh-Water*, other than in such proper Place or Places, to be appointed and approved of by the Mayor, Aldermen and Commonalty in Common Council convened; under the Penalty of *Ten Pounds* for every Offence, or refusal to remove the same, to be recovered and levied of, and from any Person or Persons storing or owing such Pitch, Tar, Turpentine, or Shingles, in Manner and Form as the Fines on Buildings in this Act are recoverable, for the Use of the Poor of the said City.

New York, February 25, 1762.
We the Subscribers being this Day appointed in Common-Council, a Committee, to treat with such Persons as shall incline to Watch this City, and take Charge of the City Lamps for the ensuing Year, DO, in Obedience to said Appointment, hereby give Notice, that on Wednesday, the Third Day of March next, at Two o'Clock in the Afternoon of the same Day, shall attend at the Common Council Chamber, in the City-Hall of the said City, in order to receive Proposals from such as may then incline to offer for the Purpose abovesaid.
JOHN BOGERT, jun.
PETER MESIER,
NICHOLAS ROOSEVELT,
THOMAS RANDLE,
GEORGE BREWERTON.

To be Sold,
A Plantation, containing 420 Acres of Land, neatly situated on a public Road near *King's Town*, within about 4 Miles of *Prince Town* College, in the Corporation of *New Brunswick*, in *East New-Jersey*; 250 Acres of which is cleared and fit for the Plow, it being extraordinary good for both Wheat and Pasture; 20 Acres of choice good Meadows, and more may be made, it being extraordinary well Timber'd and Water'd, and in good repair of Fences; has on it two good dwelling Houses and two Barns, with several Conveniencies of other Buildings; likewise two good Orchards, with Variety of choice grafted Fruits; and is convenient to both Mills and Markets; the Purchaser may be suited with the Whole, or Part of the same. For further Particulars enquire of the Owner, living on the Premisses, who will give an indisputable Title for the same.
JOHN BAYLES.

To be Sold,
THE House and Lot of Ground in Broad-Street, near the Watch House, lately belonging to Henry Plea, deceased; the Lot is 26 Feet Front. Whoever inclines to purchase the same, may apply to Andrew Barclay, in Wall Street, who will agree for the same on reasonable Terms.

To be LETT,
ON *a lease of two years to come from May next, a genteel dwelling house, situated in Newtown, with a large garden, and 12 acres of land, together with a stable, chair house, hen house, and other privileges. For particulars enquire of Isaac Isaacs on the premisses.*

STRAYED or stolen on *Saturday* night, the 16th instant, from the premises of *Nathan Haines*, in *Evesham*, in the county of *Burlington*, *West-New-Jersey*, A young black Mare, with some white hairs in her forehead, one white hind foot; about 14 hands and an half high, trots and gallops; a new leather saddle with an *English* tree and no housings, supposed to be taken by a man who has lately come in these parts, and has called himself by several names, as *John*, *James* and *William Green*, thought to be about 25 years of age, about 5 feet 7 inches high, fresh complexion, wears his own brown hair, says he is an *Englishman*, but thought to be an *Irishman*: Hand on when he went away, a halfworn hat, brown cloath coat full trimmed, a black flowered velvet jacket, and drab coloured cloth breeches, white shirt, brown snuff coloured stockings, halfworn shoes; took with him a brown camblet coat, brown holland jacket, and a dark coloured bearskin great-coat with metal buttons. Whoever secures the said Mare and Saddle, so that the owner may have them again, shall have *Fifty Shillings*, and if the mare and thief both secured, so that the thief may be brought to justice, they shall receive the above reward of *Five Pounds* with reasonable charges paid by me
Phila. Jan. 19, 1762. SAMUEL HEWLINGS.

WORKING OXEN,
TO be sold, by Edward Antill, at his Seat near New-Brunswick, in New-Jersey, four or five Yoke of working Cattle, of different Ages, from 8 to three Years old; they are now fit for Service, being in good Heart, and full Flesh'd; they are fed upon good Hay and Corn.

DRUGS & MEDICINES
IN GENERAL,
A very large quantity, fresh imported in the last vessels from London, and sold at the very lowest prices wholesale or retail, by
EDWARD AGAR,
Chymist and druggist, in Beaver-Street, New-York, late from London; where likewise is fitted up on the shortest notice, in the neatest and cheapest manner, (with fresh medicines; the preparations being chiefly made by himself, with the utmost care and punctuality) all sorts of medicine chests, either for land or sea service, and small ones for family use, with directions for the use of each particular therein contained, if required.
A Large quantity of lint, tow, pill boxes, vials, lancets and cases; cases of pocket instruments; setts of teeth instruments; artery needles; marble morters and pestles; wafer paper; gold and silver leaf; small pewter syringes; glyster pipes; French and Scotch barley; verdigrese, flour of brimstone, allum, copperas, scales and weights in bozes; Dr. James's fever powders; Lockyer's universal pill, being an efficacious remedy for the scurvey and all cutaneous eruptions; Anderson's Scotch pi[illegible]; Dr. Hooper's female pills, these are particularly adapted to disorders incident to the female sex, and have met with great success for the purposes for which they are administred; saloop; Greenhough's tincture for the teeth, the best remedy hitherto discovered for the scurvey in the gums, and cleaning and preserving the teeth; Bateman's drops, an excellent remedy for all rhumatic complaints, surprizingly eases that most racking pain of the gout, on once or twice taking; Godfrey's cordial; Daffy's elixir, very useful in all families; it is a cordial aromatic purging elixir, is very serviceable in all cholicky disorders, and gripings in the stomach or bowels, proceeding frequently from wind, which this elixir surprizingly dispels, and gives immediate ease to the patent; Stoughton's bitters; the original balsom of health, being of the same quality, and equal in all respects to that sold under the title of Turlington's balsam of life, and at half the price; Æther, a new invented remedy for the head ach, which it instantly removes on the first or second application; spicery of all sorts, viz. cinamon, nutmegs, mace, cloves, ginger, cardamoms, &c. Likewise perfumery of all sorts, wholesale or retail, cheaper than can be imported from London, viz. fine hard and soft pomatum, hungary, lavender, honey water, essences of lavender, rosemary, lemons, burgamot, and ambergrese, the best hair powder, both plain and perfum'd, likewise grey powder; shaving boxes and brushes; the best marble wash balls and boxes, shaving powder, castile soap, the court or ladies black sticking plaister, fine lip save, cold cream, the many excellences of it, as a costmetick above all other lotions and washes whatsoever, are too numerous to be repeated, all that is necessary to say in its behalf is, that its own merit has recommended its use among all the ladies of the first quality and rank in England; fine Italan red and white cosmetick powders, lavender flowers, tooth powders and brushes, fine Italian scouring drops for taking out spots from silk and cloth; oil skin; ink powders; eau de luce; a variety of other articles, too numerous to repeat in an advertisement.
N. B. A fresh parcel of Stratsbourgh rappe snuff, likewise fine Spermeciti oil, for burning in lamps.

T W O H O U S E S,
To be sold, one fronting Broad-Street, in which Mr. Eustace now lives, 26 Feet Front and Rear, and 96 Feet deep. Also the House immediately in the Rear, and fronting New-Street, now occupied by Capt. Smith, 27 Feet Front, 26 Feet Rear, and 6 Rod in depth, all Dutch Measure. The Houses will be sold together or separate, at publick Vendue, on the Premisses, on Wednesday the 3d of March, at 11 o'Clock, or any Time before at private Sale, by Stephen Callow, at the Crown and Cushion in Wall-Street.

JARVIS ROEBUCK,
Cork-Cutter, from LONDON,
Living at the Foot of Pot-Baker's-Hill, between the Fly-Market, and the New-Dutch-Church;
CUTS, and has to sell, all Sorts and Sizes of the best Velvet Corks, wholesale and retail: Has also, an Assortment of Shop Goods, which he will sell on the lowest Terms for Cash. Also, Violins, Scates, Fiddle Strings, Powder Blue by the Dozen, Nuremberg Salve, and Harlem Oyl by the Bottle, Box, or Quantity.

T W O H O U S E S,
To be Let, one with 3 Rooms on a Floor, 2 Story high, with a Cellar, and 6 Fire-Places. The other has three Rooms, and three Fire-Places, a Cellar Kitchen, and a good Well in the Yard, that serves both Houses. Enquire of James Lowey, at the Ship-Yards.

To be Sold,
BY the Widow Hays, living in New-Street, next Door to Col. Thody, All Sorts of Pickles, consisting of Peaches, Cucumbers, Beans, Peppers, &c.

TWO *Houses, and the Lots of Ground, in Crown-Street, now in the Occupation of Mr. Van Bura, and the Miss Lawrence's. For further Particulars enquire of Robert Griffiths, near Peck's Slip.*

To be Sold,
A Lot of Wood Land upon Staten-Island, in Richmond County, in the Province of New-York, containing 23 Acres and a Quarter, near Mr. Watson's. Enquire of Denyse Denyse, at the Narrows, on Nassau-Island, or Mr. Garrit Rapalje, in New-York, who will agree on reasonable Terms, and give a good Title for the same.

London, October 10, 1761.

This Day were publiſhed, and given gratis, Propoſals for Printing by Subſcription, In Eight Volumes in Quarto,

A NEW EDITION of the

STATUTES AT LARGE,

From MAGNA CHARTA to the End of the laſt PARLIAMENT, 1761.

Printed by Mark Baſkett, and the Aſſigns of Robert Baſkett; and H. Woodfall and W. Strahan, Statute and Law Printers to the King's moſt excellent Majeſty.

CONDITIONS.

1. The Work ſhall be printed on a fine large Demy Paper; the Letter and Page the ſame as the Specimen annexed to the Propoſals.

2. The Price to Subſcribers will be only 5 l. a Sett, or 12s. 6d. each Volume in Sheets.

3. No Books will be ſold to thoſe who do not Subſcribe, under 6l. a Sett.

4. Half a Guinea only is deſired to be paid at Subſcribing, that the Patentees may be able to aſcertain the Number it will be neceſſary to print, in order to give the propoſed Advantage to Subſcribers. This Half Guinea to be made up 12 s. 6 d. on the Receipt of the Firſt Volume; and 12 s. 6 d. more to be paid at the Delivery of every ſucceeding Volume.

5. The Volumes ſhall be delivered, either ſingle or otherwiſe, as faſt as they can be printed, according to the above Terms; and the Whole is intended to be finiſhed by Michaelmas Term 1762.

Subſcriptions are taken in, and Receipts given, by J. Worral in Bell-yard, Temple-Bar; Mr. Waller, Mrs. Shuckburgh, and Mrs. Whithers, in Fleet-ſtreet.

Subſcriptions are likewiſe taken in by DAVID HALL, at the NEW PRINTING-OFFICE, in Market-ſtreet, PHILADELPHIA.

To all Perſons intereſted in the Lands herein after mentioned.

WHEREAS his late Majeſty King William the Third, by Letters Patent under the Great Seal of the Colony of New-York, bearing Date the Fourteenth Day of February 1701-2, and the Thirteenth Year of his Reign, did grant and confirm unto Robert Walters, Leigh Atwood, Cornelius De Peyſter, Caleb Heathcote, Matthew Clarkſon, John Cholwell, Richard Slater, Lancaſter Simes, Robert Lurting and Barne Coſens; a certain Tract of Land in the County of Weſtcheſter, bounded Northerly by the Manor of Cortlandt, Eaſterly with Bedford Line of Three Miles ſquare, the White Fields and Byram River; Southerly by the Land of John Hariſon, Rye Line ſtretching to Byram River aforeſaid, and the White Plains; and Weſterly by Bronkx River and the Manor of Philipſburg, excepting out of the Bounds aforeſaid, all the Lands within Richbell's Patent, according to the Lines of the ſaid Patent now in the Tenure and Occupation of Colonel Caleb Heathcote, which firſt above named Tract of Land was purchaſed by Colonel Caleb Heathcote and others, with whom he has agreed, excepting James Mott and Henry Diſbrow, whom he hath undertaken to ſatisfy; within which Bounds, there are by Eſtimation about five thouſand Acres of profitable Land, beſides Waſtes and Woodlands, of which ſaid Lands or ſuch particular Parts thereof, as have not been legally ſold, we the Subſcribers are part Owner or Proprietors; and as they are undivided, and we are inclined to have Partition thereof, purſuant to an Act of the Lieutenant Governor, the Council, and General Aſſembly, paſſed on the Eighth Day of January laſt, entitled, An Act for the more effectual Collecting of his Majeſty's Quit Rents, in the Colony of New-York; and for Partition of Lands in Order thereto; we do hereby give Notice, that Charles Clinton, Eſq; of Little-Britain, in Ulſter County, Jonathan Brown, Gentleman, of Rye, in Weſt Cheſter County, and Eliſha Budd, of the White-Plains, in Weſtcheſter County, aforeſaid, are appointed to make Partition of the ſaid Lands ſo divided: And that they the ſaid Commiſſioners will meet on Thurſday the 27th Day of May next, at the Court Houſe at the White Plains, in the County of Weſtcheſter, to proceed to the Partition of the ſaid Lands. And all Perſons intereſted therein, are hereby required to attend then and there for that Purpoſe, either by themſelves, or their Attornies.

Given under our Hands, this 23d Day of February, in the Year of our Lord 1762.

A. DE PEYSTER,
ANNE DELANCEY.
LEWIS JOHNSTON.
MATTHEW CLARKSON.

The Partnerſhip of Moriſon and

Miligan, diſſolved the 13th Inſt. and the Accounts due on ſaid Partnerſhip, will be paid, when due, by

DAVID MILLIGAN,

At his Store near the Ferry-Stairs, who will ſettle all Accounts relative to that Partnerſhip.

NOTICE is hereby given, to all

Perſons, who have any Demands on the Snow Mary and Sarah, lately belonging to Benjamin Hawxhurſt, that they are deſired to make the ſame known to the Subſcribers on or before the firſt Day of April.

WILLIAM HAWXHUTST,
JACOB TOWNSEND.

A Quantity of choice Iriſh Butter,

(juſt imported) to be ſold, at James M'Evers's Store, Alſo, Bobea Tea by the Cheſt, and beſt Connecticut barreled Beef and Pork.

To be Sold at Publick Vendue on the Premiſſes, on Monday the 5th of April next,

A Large and convenient Dwelling

Houſe, two and a half Story high, between the Fly-Market and Beekman's Slip, in Queen-Street; having ſix Fire Places; three Rooms on a Floor, a good Cellar under the whole Houſe, lately floor'd, with a Cellar Kitchen, a Yard and Garden, the Yard paved with flat Stone, a good Pump and Ciſtern in it, and a Gang Way four Feet wide, the middle Parlour wainſcoted with Mahogany, neatly carv'd; the back Parlour wainſcoted all over, the Houſe inſide lately neatly painted; any Perſon inclining to purchaſe before the Day of Sale, may apply to WILLIAM RICHARDS on the Premiſſes, who will give a good Title for the ſame.

To be Sold, at Private Sale,

A Lot of Land lying in the Town

of Weſtcheſter, within a Call of the Landing, near the Church, the Place is well ſituated, a good Houſe with 3 Fire places on one Floor, with a Cellar and Kitchen, a good Barn and Well; the Place is fit for a Store or a Tavern, or a private Gentleman, being near the Publick Road; there being belonging to the Eſtate 10 or 12 Acres of Ground more or leſs, with a half Right to the Commons of Weſt Cheſter; the Ground belonging to the Eſtate, is all a Garden or mowing Ground, very commodious.. Any Perſon inclining to Buy, enquire at Mr. Duncan Reed, at the Sign of the Royal Sovereign on one Side, and the Scotch Arms on the other; oppoſite to the New Chapel in New-York.

VITRIOLICK ÆTHER.

For the certain and ſpeedy Cure of the Head-ach.

THE Head-ach is a Complaint

which few People think much of (or give very little Pity to thoſe afflicted therewith) except the Perſons feeling the Pain, than which I think none can be more exquiſite and diſagreeable, and the uſual Remedies, ſuch as ſmelling Salts, Hungary and Lavender Water, and the like, being found inefficatious, and very ſeldom giving immediate Eaſe to the Perſon afflicted, induced me to offer this to the Publick, by way of Advertiſement; being the moſt effectual Remedy ever yet diſcovered, and has been uſed with the greateſt Succeſs by ſeveral eminent Perſons in England, ſeldom or never failing to remove the Pain, on the firſt or ſecond Application; which is chiefly external, by pouring a few Drops into the Palm of the Hand, and holding it immediately to the Forehead, preſſing the Hand tight, on which cauſes a pretty great Heat in the Head ſeemingly, but it intirely vaniſhes on the Hand being remov'd, and the Head-ach tho' before ever ſo violent is generally cur'd; its Succeſs is principally owing to its ſurpriſing Subtilty and Elaſticity, (thereby exhilerating the Motion of the Animal Spirits, and removing any Obſtructions in the Nervous fluids, which is principally the Cauſe of the Diſorder) which it poſſeſſes beyond any other known fluid, and from whence it is juſtly call'd Æther, being ſo extreamly light and volatile, that a drop or two let fall on the back of the Hand, diſſipates itſelf into the Air immediately, leaving the Hand quite dry; therefore the Perſons uſing it muſt obſerve to be very quick in they Application. It is likewiſe of great Service in Rheumatick Pains, and all Paralytick Complaints and Numbneſs, or Pains in any Part of the Body, in which Caſes the Perſon ſhould take about half a Tea Spoonful at Night going to Bed in a little Wine, apply it outwardly to the Part affected once or twice a Day, beſides keeping the Part warm with Flannel, and its Succeſs will be ſurpriſing.

This Æther is prepared, and ſold only, by EDWARD AGAR, Chymiſt, in Beaver Street, New-York.

Who has likewiſe to ſell, a large Quantity of Starch, either in ſmall Caſks of about 40lb. each, at 6d. per lb. or by the Dozen at 7d. Likewiſe Straſbourgh and Rapee Snuff, and all Sorts of Spices very Cheap, freſh imported.

ENNIS GRAHAM, Taylor,

Is removed from Broad-Street, to the Corner of Wall-Street, facing the Meal-Market, near the Coffee-Houſe, where he continues the Taylors buſineſs as uſual, and ſells by wholeſale or Retail.

A Neat Aſſortment of ſuperfine

and coarſe Cloths, of the neweſt colours, fine Hair Shags of various colours, Black and Crimſon Geneva Velvets, Mancheſter Velvets of different colours, feddered Pluſh and Velvets, Worſted Breeches pieces, Gold and Silver lace, Vellum, Thread, Cord, chain Garters, Buttons and Buttonhole binding, Mancheſter and Geneva Velvet ſhapes, fine and coarſe Iriſh Linnens, Doulaſs and Garlix, ſuperfine and coarſe Shalloons, white and brown Fuſtians, Shamoy ſkins, Buckrams and glazed Linnens, ſewing Silks and Threads of the beſt ſorts, a variety of Silk and Twiſt buttons, Scarf and all Silk twiſt, Knee Garters, Gilt and plated Buttons, Collar Velvets, Taylor's caſt Irons and Shears of different ſizes, Braſs lined Thimbles, Penknives, White Chapel Needles, Knotch and Sleeve Boards, &c. &c. N. B. Good Encouragement is given to Journeymen Taylors.

For South-Carolina, or the Fleet,

The *SLOOP*

TYGER,

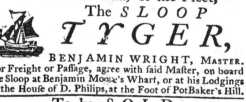

BENJAMIN WRIGHT, MASTER.

For Freight or Paſſage, agree with ſaid Maſter, on board the Sloop at Benjamin Moore's Wharf, or at his Lodgings at the Houſe of D. Philips, at the Foot of PotBaker's Hill.

To be SOLD,

A Healthy, Strong, likely Negro Wench, about 21 Years of Age, has had the Small-Pox and Meaſels, and can do all manner of Houſe Work: For farther particulars, Enquire of H. Gaine, at the Bible and Crown, in Hanover-Square.

Taken up in the River, Two BOATS,

GOING adrift; any Perſon proving their property, and paying the charge of this Advertiſement, and a ſmall Conſideration to the Perſon that found them, may have them again, by applying to William Woods, in the Bowery-Lane.

To be Sold, at public Vendue,

On Friday the Nineteenth Day of March Inſt. on the Premiſſes, or at private Sale any Time before,

THE Farm or Plantation that David

Seaman, late of Oyſter Bay, in Queens County, died ſiezed of, lying within the Townſhip of Oyſter Bay aforeſaid, and about Two Miles from Jericho, containing about Two Hundred and Fifty Acres of very good Land, with very good Buildings, Two Orchards, One in its prime, the other is young and chiefly grafted with choice good Fruit, and plenty of good Timber on ſaid Farm, and likewiſe about Three Hundred Acres of plain Land, lying about Three Miles diſtant, to be ſold either with the Farm or not, at the Election of the Purchaſer.

By us
Richard Willets,
William Seaman,
David Seaman,
Zebulun Seaman,
Executors.

To be ſold, in the Townſhip of Bergan, and Province of New-Jerſey, a FARM,

CONTAINING about 400 Acres of choice Land and Meadow, with a Right in Bergan Commons, vaſtly convenient for raiſing Stock: There may be mowed off ſaid Farm yearly, not leſs than 300 Loads of choice Hay: There is a pretty good Houſe on the Premiſſes, a good Barn, and a young Orchard: 'Tis not more than 7 Miles from New-York. Whoever inclines to purchaſe the ſame, may apply to Andrew Teed, at Secacus, in the Townſhip of Bergan, aforeſaid, who will agree for the ſame on reaſonable Terms, and give a good Title.

To be SOLD,

A Tract of Land at the Nine-Partners, near Filkin-Town,

CONTAINING, Eleven Hundred Acres, it hath plenty of Swamps and fine Timber, there are ſeveral cleared fields in the ſaid Tract, in good Fence: Any Perſon inclining to purchaſe the whole, or part, may apply to Joſeph Sacket, Jun. living in New-York, who intends to be at Filkin Town the Second Week in April next.

To be LETT, and entered upon the firſt Day of May next, at Elizabeth-Town, in the Province of New-Jerſey;

A Large commodious Dwelling-Houſe, in which Cornelius Hetfield, Eſq; now lives: Said Houſe is two Story high, has ſix Rooms on a Floor, with 7 Fire-places, and a very good Cellar under the whole Houſe, with a large Kitchen, and a good Garden, about ſix Acres of good Land, a young Orchard on the ſame, and an excellent good living Spring near the Houſe, and is very pleaſantly ſituated in the Town.

Said Hetfield has to diſpoſe of, a good Aſſortment of Dry Goods, Ironmongery and Cutlery Ware, which he will ſell at prime Coſt, for Caſh; and all Perſons that are indebted to him, are deſired to diſcharge their reſpective Accounts in a ſhort Time. N. B. He has likewiſe to diſpoſe of, a Quantity of choice ſeaſoned two Inch Plank.

JAMES BYERS,

Braſs-Founder, next Door to Mr. Heyman Levy's, In Bayard-Street,

MAKES all ſorts of Braſs Work, viz. Andirons, Tongs, Shovels, Fenders, Candleſticks, and caſts all Sorts of Braſs for Mills: He alſo makes beautiful Wier Cages for Parots, hangs Bells in the beſt Manner, with Care and Expedition.

If *Martin Huber*, Native of *Ba-*

zil, in *Switzerland*, who has been abſent from his Family about 10 or 12 Years, and thought to be in ſome part of *America*, will apply to *William Bayard*, and Company, in *New-York*, he may hear of ſomething very conſiderable to his Advantage. N. B. He ſet out from *Bazil* for *America*, and enter'd as a Soldier, but was afterwards diſcharged. Any Perſon who can give Intelligence of him, whether dead or alive, will be thankfully rewarded.

Imported by the laſt Ship from London, a very large Aſſortment of choice Drugs, chemical and galenical Medicines, and are ſold Wholeſale and Retail, at the loweſt Prices, by

JAMES MURRAY,

Druggiſt and Wholeſale Apothecary from London, at the Sign of the Bell, oppoſite the Meal-Market, New York: Medicine Cheſts for Plantations, Sea Surgeons, and Commanders of Ships, carefully fitted out.

Alſo Boxes, with proper Directions, of all Prices, very uſeful for Families that live diſtant from a Surgeon; alſo Captains of Ships who do not carry a Doctor.

PEPPER Mint Water, *Bateman's* Pectoral Drops, *Stoughton's* Stomach Elixir, *Godfrey's* Cordial, *Scot's* Pills, *Daffy's* Elixir, Dr. *Pitcairn's* Pectoral Pills, *Squire's* Grand Elixir, Spirits of Scurvy Graſs, *Boſtock's* Elixir, *Lockyer's* Pills, *Britiſh* Oil, Dr. *Sinclair's* Aſtmatic Drops, Surgeon's Capital Inſtruments, Rupture Bandages, Ivory Syringes, Pocket Caſes of ditto, Caſes with ſix Lancets, Common Lancets, Caſes of Artery Needles, Teeth Inſtruments, Bolus Knives, Morters of all Sizes, Box Scales and Weights, *Hooper's* Pills, Dr. *France's* Female Elixir, *Greenough's* famous Tincture for cleanſing and preſerving the Teeth, Ditto, Tincture for the Tooth-Ache, Cupping Glaſſes, Dr. *James's* Fever Powder, Cinnamon, Cloves, Nutmegs, and Mace; Fine Cyprus Searches, *Turlington's* Balſam of Life, Iſinglaſs, beſt Sago and Saloop, Oil of Lavender and Burgamont, Hungary Water, Beſt Damaſk Roſe Water, Shavings of Hartſhorn. Regimental Medecine Cheſts, to be ſold at a very low Advance, on the Sterling Coſt.

The above, and all other advertiſed Medicines, from the original Warehouſes in London.

New-York RACES,

To be Run for, on Monday the

17th of May, on the New Courſe, at Harlem, A PURSE OF ONE HUNDRED POUNDS, free for any Horſe, Mare or Gelding, carrying Ten Stone, the beſt of three Four Mile Heats, paying three Piſtoles Entrance, or double at the Poſt.

On Tueſday the 18th, a Give and Take Purſe, of FORTY POUNDS, free for any Horſe, Mare or Gelding, Fourteen Hands, to carry Nine Stone, higher or lower, Weight in Proportion, the beſt of three Four Mile Heats, paying Five Dollars Entrance, or double at the Poſt.

On Wedneſday the 19th, the Entrance of the two firſt Days to be Run for by Four and Five Years Old only; Four Years Old to carry Eight Stone, and Five Years Old Nine Stone, the beſt of three Two Mile Heats, paying Two Dollars Entrance, or double at the Poſt; the Entrance of this Day to go to the Second Horſe.

No leſs than Three reputed Running Horſes to Start for either of theſe Purſes, and to Run according to His Majeſty's Articles.

All Horſes, &c. that Run for either of theſe PURSES, to be entered with Mr. John Leary, in New-York, on Saturday the 15th of May, and proper Certificates under the Hands of the Breeders, to be then produced of the Ages of the Four and Five Years Old. All Diſputes will be determined by proper Judges, to be appointed for that Purpoſe

N°. 558.

THE Boston-Gazette, AND COUNTRY JOURNAL.

Containing the freshest Advices, Foreign and Domestic.

MONDAY, DECEMBER 9, 1765.

Boston, December 6, 1765.

To the PRINTERS,

AMIDST the Multiplicity of excellent Pieces which your Press has handed to the Publick, I do not recollect that any great Notice has been taken of the very popular Argument, which has been much insisted on by the ministerial Writers, to justify the present hard Treatment, the Colonies so unanimously and justly complain of. This is, that as Great-Britain has expended large Sums to preserve us from Destruction, it is highly fit and reasonable she should be reimbursed the Expence contracted on *our* Account. Mighty plausible this, no Doubt, but at the same Time most wretchedly fallacious. It may be demanded of these Reasoners, whether Great-Britain was not securing her own Existence by the Expence incurred (if they will have it so) on our Behalf. No one can contest that her Grandeur, if not her very Being, depends on these Colonies continuing subject to her Dominion. And it is I think very evident that she was as much interested in every Battle fought in America, as if it had been fought on Hounslow Heath. It is true, the Consequences were more remote than they would have been on that Supposition, but not the less certain, or the less fatal. Besides, did not these Colonies do their utmost, nay, did they not exert themselves beyond their Ability in the common Cause. If so, and we did every Thing we had Power to do, shall we be punished for not doing, what it was impossible we should perform?

If any one doubts the Importance and Value of the Colonies to Great-Britain, I would beg Leave to recommend the following Extract from the ingenious Mr. Postlethwayt, who with Regard to the very great Benefit resulting from the Colonies, observes, "That in order to set the Affair in a true Light, it should be considered what the Condition of the Kingdom was before we had any Plantations, and this certainly was very low and despicable. In the victorious Reign of Edward the 3d, there was a Balance of Trade struck, and delivered into the Exchequer, by which it appeared, that the Exports of one Year exceeded the Imports by £.255,224 13s 8d, which for that Time was a large Sum. At the Time Queen Elizabeth entered upon the Government, the Customs procured £ 36000 a Year. At the Restoration they were let to Farm for £ 400,000. and produced considerably above double that Sum before the Revolution.

"The People of London before we had any Plantations, and but very little Trade, were computed at about 100,000. At the Death of Queen Elizabeth they were increased to 150,000, and are now (1755) about six Times that Number. In those Days, we had not only our naval Stores, but our Ships from our Neighbours. Germany furnished us with all Things made of Metal, even to Nails; Wine, Paper, Linnen, and a Thousand other Things came from France. Portugal furnished us with Sugar; and all the Products of America were poured into us from Spain. In short, the legal Interest of Money was 12 per Cent. and the common Price of our Lands ten or twelve Years Purchase. We may add, that our Manufactures were few, and those but indifferent, the Number of English Merchants very small, and the whole Shipping of the Nation much inferior to what now belongs to the Northern Colonies only."

Mr. Postlethwayt next examines the Condition of the Kingdom since Colonies and Plantations have been established, which he asserts is altered for the better, to a Degree almost beyond Credibility. Our Manufactures are prodigiously increased, chiefly by the Demand for them in the Plantations, where they at least take off one Half, and supply us with many valuable Commodities for Exportation, which is as great Emolument to the Mother Kingdom, as to the Plantations themselves.

"Instead also of taking off the Quantities of foreign Commodities, from other Nations, that we were wont to do, we actually, by Means of our Plantations, export those very Goods, and sometimes to the very same Nations, from whence we formerly imported them: Sugar, Rum, Tobacco, are the Sources of private Wealth, and public Revenue, which would have proved so many Drains to impoverish us, had they not been raised in our Colonies. It is now no longer in the Power of the Russians to make us pay what they please for Hemp and Flax. The Swedes cannot, as they have heretofore done, compel us to pay their own Price, and that too in ready Money, for Pitch and Tar; nor would it be in their Power to distress us should they attempt it, by raising the Price of Copper and Iron. Logwood and other dying Woods are sunk 75 per Cent. Indigo, &c. other Materials for dying, are in our own Power, and at moderate Prices. In fine, the Advantages are infinite that redound to us from our American Empire; where we have at least a Million of British Subjects, and between 1500 and 2000 Sail of Shipping constantly employed. Such have been the Fruits, such is the Condition of our Plantations; and let any Man doubt of the Benefits resulting from them to this Nation, if he can.

"When our Colonies were in their Infancy, they were some Burden to this Nation; and this must ever be the Case of all Plantations at their first Settlement. But the National Benefit has proved so *unspeakably greater*, when compared with the first Expence, *or any other since to protect them*, that it bears no Manner of Proportion, and is almost beyond the Power of Computation. Past Experience therefore shews, how impolitic it is to desert infant Colonies, whose Establishment has been undertaken on well grounded Motives, for the Sake of a few Thousand Pounds beyond what might be expected, when they are likely to repay their Mother Country in a ten-fold Degree."

Mr. Postlethwayt is mistaken here, as the Expence of most of the Colonies were borne *wholly* by the first Planters.

Upon this View of Things, must we not determine ourselves under infinite Obligations to Great Britain, for the Aid and Assistance she so kindly afforded these Colonies, when surrounded by *their* French and Indian Enemies? Is it not the highest Ingratitude, to refuse to sacrifice the most invaluable Rights and Privileges, at the Call of those, who so generously took up Arms in *our* Defence? So generously, I say, as no possible Advantage could accrue to themselves. Amazing Generosity! disinterested Friendship! which these degenerate Days can scarcely parallel. Let us no longer refuse to submit to the Stamp Act, no longer grumble at what is usually stiled the Sugar Act; such Refusal, and such Discontent, being totally repugnant to that grateful Spirit by which it surely becomes us to be animated towards our tender Mother Country.

But to be serious. If Great Britain reaps such immense Advantages from the Colonies, why are we so often told, that the late War was undertaken *solely* on *our* Account? Can this be realized?

—— Credat Judæus Apella;
Non Ego.

What becomes of the Charge of Ingratitude which the Ministerial Writers are so very fond of exhibiting against us? This Charge might certainly be urged with a much better Grace by the Colonists; since tho' it is allowed that the War might be undertaken in Part from a *Concern* for the Colonies, (I hope this will be thought a generous Concession) yet if the Colonies exerted themselves to the utmost in the common Cause, what must be thought of the present oppressive Measures, when they had before been of such very great Service to the Nation, and had contributed so largely to her Grandeur and Opulence? This to be sure is like the Currency of the Kingdom it comes from, true Sterling Gratitude. According to these Measures, it should seem, that whoever does another a Favour, by which he promotes his own Interest, *more* than his Neighbours, has nevertheless, ever after, a Right to deprive him of his Liberty, Property, and every Convenience and Comfort of Life. Most admirable Doctrine this! not more absurd however, than are those Arguments by which the Vindication of a justly detested Act is *attempted*. *Your humble Servant*, A. B.

NEW-YORK, NOVEMBER 28.

In the Hope, Captain Jacobson, lately arrived, came Passenger PETER DE LANCEY, junr. Esq; from London, where he had been appointed one of the Inspectors of Stamps for America.——As soon as he was properly inform'd how disagreeable it was to his Countrymen that he should hold that Office, he readily offered to resign it, and Yesterday, according to his Promise and appointment the Evening before, a Number of Gentlemen assembled for the Purpose, and he publickly declared his Resignation, and sign'd and deliver'd a Paper, of which the following is a true Copy.

This Resignation has gain'd him great Applause and entirely restored him to the Esteem of the Public.

WHEREAS since my late Return to this my native Land, I have found the *Office of Inspector of STAMPS*, to which I was appointed in *England*, and which I accepted, to be extremely disagreeable and odious to all Ranks and Conditions of my Countrymen—And having maturely considered the just Causes of their Aversion to the *Stamp Act*, and the Consequences of being by them detested as an Enemy to *American* and *English* Liberty, and deserted by my Friends;---and being sincerely desirous to promote the real Interest of my Country, and recover its Good-Will and Opinion,.....I do hereby, with the utmost Chearfulness and Willingness, promise to resign the said Office;....and DO, without any Equivocation or mental Reservation, solemnly declare, upon my Honour, that I never will, directly or indirectly, either by myself or any other Person, serve in the said Office, nor in any Way or Manner contribute to the Execution of the *Stamp Act* in *America*.

Given under my Hand, in the City of New-York, *this 27th Day of* November, 1765, *before a Number of Gentlemen Inhabitants of this City.*

PETER DE LANCEY, jun.

Extract of a Letter from Philadelphia, dated Nov. 26.

"In my last I informed you Capt. Gregory was below from St. Kitts. I believe you will rejoice to see the spirit of liberty arising in the West-Indies, which you have an account of in the following letter from St. Kitts. Besides which I can with certainty inform you, that at Nevis, liberty reigns, where they also burnt the horrible stamps; but they having but few of them, and thinking it would not make a fire large enough, they seized a man of war's boat, hauled her up, put the stamps in her, and set the whole on fire."

Capt. Gregory cleared out at St Kitts, the 4th November, without Stamped Paper—Coming up the river, Capt. Hawker's boat boarded him, asked, why he had not stamped paper, was told there was none to be had. The stamp master for Barbados died the 27th October, at Barbados, where people begin to grumble much."

'ST. CHRISTOPHERS, 4th Nov. 1765.

On thursday night the 31st October last, a vast number of People gathered at the tavern of Mr. Noland's, and about 8 o'clock, proceeded to the house of Mr. John Hopkins, who was deputized by Mr. Tuchett, distributor of the stamp paper; in whose house was the chest which contained the stamps; at their arrival there were three huzzas, and the papers demanded which was delivered by a woman, and were committed to the flames, which was made before the deputy's door, and upon the conclusion of the burning, Mr. Hopkins was made to swear never to be concerned with stamp paper any more, nor never to suffer them to be kept in his house; yet the mob was not satisfied with that, but entered his house, and searched it through, until they were well convinced they were all delivered up to be burnt; Mr. Hopkins was also made to conduct the mob about 3 4ths of a mile in the country where Tuchett was concealed, and he delivered himself to the mob and was brought to the market, with drums beating, and was there made to swear never to have any further connection with stamp paper, and that he had no commission; for that was most wanted to be burnt, and submitted to do any thing that the mob chose to make him do. When they had finished with him, they went to the secretary's office, where about 4 or 5 quires were, but the keys of the office not being ready to open the door, Mr. Smith, the secretary, made the mob break it open, and he delivered up the stamp-paper, which was burnt before his office; Mr. Smith was then conducted home with great acclamations of huzzas, they then marched to the marshal's office, where one quire of the stamps was, which the mob demanded, and was delivered up by the marshal very honorably and burnt before his door; they afterwards marched to the custom house, having suspicion that great quantities of the stamps were there, but upon the collector's declaring, over and over, upon his word and honor, that not one stamp was in his office, they were reconciled and went their tour thro' the town for the whole night, to morrow night will be burnt the effigies of the distributor of the stamps and his deputy, on a gallows... The deputy received no other damage but having his door pulled down, and a few shingles ripp'd off his house.'

BOSTON, *December* 9.

ON Tuesday last was held a Meeting of the Merchants and Traders in this Town, at the British Coffee House, when they came to sundry Resolutions, a Copy of which not being prepared for the Press we cannot give them to our Readers this Week.

In general,—they have agreed, That in all Orders they may send to Great-Britain for Goods, they will direct their Correspondents not to ship them, unless the *Stamp-Act* is repealed, excepting what is absolutely necessary for carrying on the Fishery, and for carrying on Manufactures.——That they will (without Delay) countermand any Orders they may have already sent to Great-Britain for Goods.——And further that they will not purchase any Goods that may be imported into the Province, by any Persons whatever for Sale, contrary to the Spirit of their Agreement, but that they will take every prudent Measure in their Power to discourage the Sale of such Goods.

We learn, that above 220 of the principal Merchants have already signed the above Agreement.

The Gentlemen in Trade are

desired to be punctual in their Attendance this Evening at 5 o'Clock, at the British Coffee House, as Matters of Importance will be before them.

Captain Clark, arrived at New-York in 7 Weeks from Bristol; and Captain Watts, arrived here from Liverpool, have both bro't public Prints to the 1st of October, but they contain nothing very material.

At a Meeting of about Twelve Hundred of the Freemen and Freeholders in this City of New-York, on the 26th of November, Instructions were agreed upon to be given their Representatives in General Assembly and accordingly were delivered them the Day following.

We hear a Ship from the Grenades bound to Piscataqua, got ashore on Plumb Island, but received little or no Damage.

Captain Jarvis arrived at the Vineyard last Week in 30 Days from Surrinam: On his Passage, the 15th of November in Lat. 34 Long 70: 00: he spoke a Sloop in Distress, bound from Rhode Island to the Bay of Honduras, —— Miller, Master, who had been overset, had his Hold full of Water, but had freed his Vessel: Capt. Miller lost his Mast, Bowsprit & Boom, was then standing for South-Carolina, and had been out 13 Days.

Tuesday Night last we had a severe Storm, the Wind blowing hard at N. E. In which a Brig, Capt. Watts, that Day arrived from Liverpool, was drove on the Ferry Ways at Charlestown, and received so much Damage, that her Cargo, consisting of Salt, was destroyed.

The same Night being exceeding dark, a Man belonging to the Country coming to Roxbury, with Provisions, lost his Way about four Miles from Town, and was found dead the next Morning.

The Custom-House Officers have taken the Molasses Bond, and given Certificates; and we hear they are now about clearing out Vessels.

What follows is wrote on a thin Piece of Bark, and was sent to us, with a Desire of having it inserted.

"Boston, November 1st, 1765. Sir. *This is neither Paper, Parchment, nor Vellum;— Query, May not all Instruments be wrote on Bark, and so avoid the Stamp-duties, and yet be Valid? If so, I am ready to supply with good Writing-Bark, all those whose Conscicences are bound by the late Act——* A B".

MR. H—— presents his respectful Compliments to Mr. *Gloria Mundi*, and acquaints him, that from a sincere Regard to his Wife and Children, he should readily furnish him with a Recipe for turning Cyder into Wine, provided any essential Service would be thereby done them; but as the Ingredients therefor require *Cash*, and the Process *a little Care and Labour*, as well as *Continence*, he thinks him the *most improper* Person to take up the Vintner's Business.— At the same Time, he cannot but express his Surprize that one who can write Treatises upon the Efficacy of Cane and Apple-Juice, upon the human Eye and Skin, and has indeed dealt so long with *Familiar Spirits*, as to be tho't capable of doing any Thing, should yet condescend to ask the Secret of an Art, which may be easily investigated by the meanest Capacity.

PHILADELPHIA, November 28.

The Merchants and Traders of this City, have prepared, and signed, a Memorial, addressed to the Merchants and Manufacturers of Great Britain, requesting their Interest with the Parliament, for the Repeal of that most unconstitutional Law (the Stamp-Act) and for removing the Restrictions laid on the Trade of the Colonies; in which is very clearly, and strongly, represented, the great Loss it must be to the People of England, as well as to the Colonists, in case the Grievances complained of are not speedily redressed,—The above mentioned Memorial is to be forwarded by Captain Smith, now ready to sail for Liverpo

Capt. Gregory from St. Kitts, is the first vessel arrived here from any port, that has been cleared out after the first of November; he having been cleared out on unstamped paper the 4th instant at St. Kitts, and arrived here without molestation, those papers being deemed sufficient.—Captain Gregory informs us, that all public business goes on at St. Kitts as usual, nor was it stopped in the least for want of stamped paper. The collector told capt. Gregory a few days before the paper was destroyed, that he would not use any of the stamped paper, as he had not received any orders concerning it from home, but he would go on as usual.

Yesterday arrived Captain Bennet from New Providence, who informs us, that there was no stamp nor stamp master there, they went on with business as usual. Captain Bennet was cleared out about the 10th Inst. without stamped paper.

The same day arrived Captain Lyon from Antigua, who informs us, that he was cleared out the 1st Inst. but that many others were cleared out afterwards, and business went on as before, there being neither stamp nor stamp master as yet arrived at that island.

By the above accounts, we find the OFFICES in general are opened in the West-Indies. But alas! what is doing in America? where is now your *Freedom*? all locked up in the offices of each province.

NEW YORK, December 2.

On Thursday last about Ten o'Clock, a Party of about 200 of the Citizens, crossed to Long Island in Pursuit of Zechariah Hood Stamp-Master of Maryland, who a few Weeks ago was too warmly pursued in his own Country to stay for their Resentment, and came hither for Protection; but had little Rest here, therefore went to Flushing; and our Party getting Scent, went to his Lodgings, where they were joined by others from the City who went up by Water, and a Committee entering the House, he appeared, when being interrogated about his Name and Commission, he generously confessed. Thus obtaining the Prize, they politely required his Resignation, but some stumbling Blocks on his Part coming in the Way, it soon came to a downright INSIST; here he yielded, and after signing a proper Instrument for the Purpose, the Company at Ten at Night convey'd him in a Chair to Jamaica, (4 Miles Distant) where he swore before a Magistrate to abide by it.

On this he received three hearty Cheers, and had their Assurance of his being civilly treated in the City for the future; after which, at Midnight, he was conducted back to his Lodgings:——But before parting, Mr. Hood signify'd, that had he been used with half the Civility in Maryland as by them, he would not have come so far to resign so disagreeable an Office to the Publick;——and he thank'd them kindly.

In the Minerva, Captain Tillet, came Passenger, a young Gentleman, named Simon Metcalf, who, it was reported, held some Office in the Stamp Way, but he last Saturday Noon satisfied the Publick by the following Affidavit, viz.

City of New York, ss.

SIMON METCALF, maketh Oath, that he is not appointed Distributor or Inspector, of the Stamp Paper, Parchment or Velum, appointed by a late Act of Parliament, to take Place, and to be issued in America; neither is he directly or indirectly to his Knowledge, concerned in either of the said Offices, of Distributor or Inspector. SIMON METCALF.

Sworn 30th Novem. 1765, before me
WHITEHEAD HICKS.

As no Licenses for Marriage could be obtained since the first of November, for Want of stamped Paper, we can assure the Publick several genteel Couple were published in the different Churches of this City last Week; and we hear that the young Ladies of this Place are determined to join Hands with none but such as will to the utmost endeavour to abolish the Custom of marrying with Licence, which amounts to many Hundreds per Annum that might as well be saved.

Captain James Chambers, of this Port, is arrived at London, from the Musqueto Shore; and Captain Hawthorn, from this Place, at Bristol; and we are told that Doctor Moffat, and Mr. Howard, from Rhode Island, are arrived in England.

PORTSMOUMH, December 6.

In Consequence of a Resolution of the General Assembly of this Province forwarded; the Proceedings of the General Congress at New York, were sent by special Order to the Speaker, and laid before the House, unanimously approved the 22d of November, and a Committee appointed to sign and forward the several Petitions to *Barlow Trecothick* and *John Wentworth*, Esq's: who are appointed special Agents to present them, &c.

CUSTOM-HOUSE, *BOSTON.* ENTERD IN.
Bray from Antigua; Phillips & Watts from Liverpool.

Buried in the Town of Boston, since our last
Eight Whites. Three Blacks.
Baptiz'd in the several Churches. Seven.

High Water at Boston, for this present Week.

Monday, 55 m. aft.	8	Friday, 0 m. aft.	12
Tuesday, 44 m. aft.	9	Saturday 49 m. aft.	12
Wednesday, 29 m. aft.	10	Lord's-day, 33 m. aft.	1
Thursday, 12 m. aft.	11	New ☽ 12 Day 2 Aft.	

The Maſſachuſetts Gazette. No. 8.

THURSDAY, January [illegible]. 1766.

PHILADELPHIA, Dec. 19.

FRIDAY laſt arrived here the ſchooner Charming Nancy, Capt. Mullowney, from Halifax. About noon it was reported, at the coffee-houſe, that a gentleman in this city had received a ream of ſtamped paper from Halifax, and that Capt. Mullowney had brought ſome to clear out his own veſſel; whereupon a deputation of 10 or 12 gentlemen was ſent from the Coffee-Houſe to demand the papers, but the ream proved only to be half a Sheet, with eighteen pence worth of oppreſſion, which was a cover to that gentleman's letter, and he delivered up as ſoon as demanded; they then waited on Capt. Mullowney, & aſked if he had any ſtamped paper, to which he anſwered in the negative; they then deſired him to go with them to the Coffee-Houſe, which he conſented to, and there made oath as is inſerted below; the half ſheet was then ſuſpended and burnt amidſt the the acclamations of a great number of gentlemen. In the afternoon a ſtamped news-paper from Halifax, was hung up in the Coffee-Houſe, with theſe labels, on one ſide, *Liberty, Property, and no Stamps. May this be the fate of every enemy to Liberty.* On the other ſide, *Liberty triumphant, and Oppreſſion in chains,* And in the evening, Capt. Mullowney's oath being read, the paper was ſet on fire, accompanied with loud huzzas.

Philadelphia, ſſ. WHEREAS it is this Day reported, that I brought in with me, and have now on board my Veſſel, the Schooner Charming Nancy, from Halifax, ſundry ſtamped Papers, as well for clearing out my ſaid Veſſel in this Port of Philadelphia, as for other Purpoſes; now I do hereby declare, that I have not brought with me any ſtamped Papers, of any Kind for the Purpoſes aforeſaid, or for any other Purpoſe whatever (the Stamped Papers neceſſary for clearing out the ſaid Veſſel from Halifax excepted) and that, to my Knowledge, there are not any ſtamped Papers, of any Kind (except as before excepted) on board the ſaid Veſſel. JOHN MALONY.

Sworn before me, Philadelphia,
December 13, 1765.
GEORGE BRYAN.

From Quebec we learn, that the Inhabitants of that Place are alſo very uneaſy on Account of the Stamp Act; and that the Printers of the Gazette there have been obliged to drop printing it, their Cuſtomers all refuſing to receive it, if ſtamped.

From St Chriſtophers we have received the News-Papers without Stamps, as uſual; and we have the Pleaſure of informing our Readers, that the patriotic Spirit increaſes among theſe free People; that there is hardly a Man among them, from the higheſt to the loweſt, who does not openly ſhow his hearty Abhorrence of the Stamp Law; and that, on the Fifth of November, the Inhabitants had a grand Entertainment there, when the Effigies of ſeveral Perſons were hung up and burnt, who were ſuppoſed to be the principal Contrivers and Promoters of that moſt oppreſſive Act.

[illegible] ſtamp paper is driſtributed at Halifax, by one [illegible]elwood, who is a priſoner in his own Houſe, & [illegible]ded by a party of ſoldiers night and day, leſt [illegible]ld fall a victim to the juſtly enraged people, [illegible]reaten his life, and have conveyed letters to him, deſiring him to prepare for another world, for he ſhould ſoon quit this.

At a meeting of the Heart and Hand fire company,
Philadelphia, the 5th of December, 1765.

WE the members of ſaid company taking into our ſerious conſideration the late unconſtitutional and oppreſſive STAMP-ACT, and further conſidering that John Hughes, Eſq; a member of this company, is the perſon appointed to diſtribute the DETESTABLE STAMPS in this province (and ſtill continues to hold the ſaid commiſſion, in contempt of the general voice of his country and fellow citizens) have unanimouſly agreed, that unleſs Mr. Hughes do immediately reſign his ſaid odious commiſſion, without any equivocation, evaſion or mental reſervation, he ſhall be no longer continued a member of this company, but be held in the utmoſt contempt by each of us. And at the ſame time we think it our duty to declare, that this our reſolution does not proceed from any diſlike to Mr. Hughes's perſon or private character, but purely againſt his diſgraceful office. Signed, by order of the company,

DAVID HALL, Clk.

A copy of the above was left at Mr. Hughes's houſe, by four of the members, he being from home; and after his return, the Clerk waited on him for his anſwer, which was in the following terms, viz. That he had no anſwer to give the gentlemen; that they had done what they thought proper in the affair; and that he would take his own time to do what he thought proper.

London-Coffee-Houſe, Baltimore-Town, Maryland,
December 10. 1765.

To the SONS OF LIBERTY, in NEW-YORK,
GREETING:

WE your Brethren on Behalf of ourſelves and many more, HEARTILY return you our moſt grateful and ſincere Thanks for your Vigilance in apprehending and bringing Zachariah Hood, Eſq; Stamp Maſter for this Province to a Senſe of his Treachery to his Country, and for cauſing him before a Magiſtrate on his Oath, to renounce the deſpicable Employment. per Order,

MARYLANDER.

Extract from the Votes of the General Aſſembly of the Colony of New-York.

Die Martis, 3 ho. P. M. 17th Dec. 1765.

THE General Aſſembly of the Colony of New-York, taking into their ſerious Conſideration ſeveral Acts of Parliament lately paſſed, granting Stamp and other Duties to his Majeſty, and reſtricting the Trade of this Colony, apprehending an Abolition of that Conſtitution under which they have ſo long and happily enjoyed the Rights and Liberties of Engliſhmen, and being clearly of Opinion that it is the Intereſt of Great-Britain, a Dependence on which they eſteem their Felicity, to confirm them in the Enjoyment of thoſe Rights; think it their indiſpenſible Duty to make a Declaration of their Faith and Allegiance to His Majeſty King GEORGE the Third, of their ſubmiſſion to the Supreme Legiſlative Power; and at the ſame Time to ſhew that the Rights claimed by them are in no Manner inconſiſtent with either: For which Purpoſe they are come to the following Reſolutions, that is to ſay:

Reſolved, Nemine Contradicente, *That the People of this Colony owe the ſame Faith and Allegiance to his Majeſty King George the Third, that are due to him from his Subjects in Great-Britain.*

Reſolved, N. C. *That they owe Obedience to all Acts of Parliament not inconſiſtent with the eſſential Rights and Liberties of Engliſhmen, and are intituled to the ſame Rights and Liberties which his Majeſty's Engliſh Subjects both within and without the Realm have ever enjoyed.*

Reſolved, N. C. *That his Majeſty's Subjects in England, are ſecured in the ſuperior Advantages they enjoy principally by the Privilege of an Exemption from Taxes not of their own Grant, and their Right to Trials by their Peers---The firſt ſecures the People collectively from unreaſonable Impoſitions; and without the Second, Individuals are at the arbitrary Diſpoſition of the executive Power.*

Reſolved, N. C. *That the Coloniſts did not forfeit theſe eſſential Rights by their Emigration; becauſe this was by the Permiſſion and Encouragement of the Crown; and that they rather merit Favour, than a Deprivation of thoſe Rights, by giving an almoſt boundleſs Extent to the Britiſh Empire, expanding its Trade, increaſing its Wealth, and augmenting that Power which renders it ſo formidable to all Europe.*

Reſolved, N. C. *That the Acts of Trade giving a Right of Juriſdiction to the Admiralty Courts, in Proſecutions for Penalties and Forfeitures, manifeſtly infringes the Right of Trials by Jury; and that the late Act for granting Stamp Duties, not only expoſes the American Subjects to an intolerable Inconvenience and Expence, by compelling them to a Defence at a great Diſtance from Home; but, by impoſing a Tax, utterly deprives them of the eſſential Right of being the ſole Diſpoſers of their own Property.*

Reſolved, N. C. *That all Aids to the Crown, in Great-Britain, are Gifts of the People by their Repreſentatives in Parliament, as appears from the Preamble of every Money Bill, in which the Commons are ſaid to Give and Grant to his Majeſty.*

Reſolved, N. C. *That it involves the greateſt Inconſiſtency with the known Principles of the Engliſh Conſtitution, to ſuppoſe that the Honourable Houſe of Commons of Great-Britain can, without diveſting the Inhabitants of this Colony of their moſt eſſential Rights, grant to the Crown their or any Part of their Eſtates for any Purpoſe whatſoever.*

Reſolved, N. C. *That from the firſt Settlement of the Colonies, it has been the Senſe of the Government at Home, that ſuch Grants could not be conſtitutionally made; and therefore Applications for the Support of Government, and other public Exigences, have always been made to the Repreſentatives of the People of this Colony; and frequently during the late War by immediate orders from the Crown, upon which they exerted themſelves with ſo much Liberality, that the Parliament thought proper to contribute to their Reimburſement.*

Reſolved, N. C. *That if the People of this Colony ſhould be deprived of the ſole Right of Taxing themſelves, or preſenting ſuch Sums as the public Exigencies require, they would be laid under the greateſt Diſadvantages, as the united Intereſt of the Electors, or Elected, which conſtitute the Security of His Majeſty's Subjects in Great-Britain, will opperate ſtrongly againſt them.*

Reſolved, N. C. *That the Impracticability of inducing the Colonies to grant Aids in equal Manner, proportioned to their ſeveral Abilities, does by no Means induce a Neceſſity of diveſting the Colonies of their eſſential Rights.*

Reſolved, N. C. *That it is the Duty of every Friend to Great-Britain, and this Colony, to cultivate a hearty Union between them.*

Reſolved, N. C. *That if the Honourable Houſe of Commons inſiſt on their Power of Taxing this Colony, and by that Means deprive its Inhabitants of what they have always looked upon as an undoubted Right, tho' this Power ſhould be exerted in the mildeſt Manner, it will teach them to conſider the People of Great-Britain, as veſted with abſolute Power to diſpoſe of all their Property, and tend to weaken that Affection for the Mother Country, which this Colony ever had, and is extremely deſirous of retaining.*

Reſolved, N. C. *That in order to keep the Colonies in due Subjection to, and Dependence upon Great-Britain, it is not neceſſary to deprive them of the Right they have long enjoyed, of Taxing themſelves; ſince the ſame Right has been enjoyed by the Clergy within the Realm, and by all the Subjects of Great-Britain without the Realm, until the late Innovation.*

Reſolved, N. C. *That the Duties lately impoſed by Act of Parliament on the Trade of this Colony, are very grievious and burthenſome; and in the Apprehenſion of this Houſe, impoſſible to be paid: Have already greatly diminiſhed the advantageous Traffic heretofore carried on with the foreign Iſlands in the Weſt Indies; and in conſequence muſt render us unable to purchaſe the Manufactures of Great-Britain.*

New-York, Dec. 23.

On Tueſday Evening, a great Multitude of People appeared and paſſed through moſt of the Streets in this City, attending and carrying a Gallows, on which hung the Effigies of three Men, ſaid to be intended to repreſent Mr. G. G-----le, Lord C---vill, and Gen. M-rr-y; the Firſt for being one of the principal Authors of the Stamp Act, the Second for having endeavoured to enforce it by ordering our Veſſels to be ſtopped and the Third for having executed the firſt ſtamp'd Inſtrument that has appear'd in this Place, and for having uttered (as was repored) many opprobrious Speeches againſt the Inhabitants for oppoſing the Act.

The two other Figures were dreſſed in laced Cloaths and Hats, Labels were affixed to all of them to ſignify their Character and Offences. They were at laſt carried into the Fields, where a Fire was kindled, and they with the Gallows, were all conſumed together.

It was obſerved upon this Occaſion, that there appeared two Parties, who oppoſed each other, though each of them were profeſſed Enemies to the Stamps; but it was fear'd that ſuch a Diviſion, at a Time when the Stamp Act really operates ſo far towards our Deſtruction, as to ſtop all Buſineſs, would be the moſt likely Means to complete the Matter, and bring it to have its full Effect.

Extract of a Letter from an eminent Houſe in London, two of which are Members of Parliament, to a Merchant in this City, dated September 10, 1765.

"The Account you ſend us of the State of Affairs with you, gives us a very ſenſible Concern, and we hope the preſent Miniſtry will, at the Meeting of Parliament, take the neceſſary Steps for your Relief.

Friday laſt the Gentlemen of the Law in this City, had a Meeting, when they came to a Reſolution to carry on Buſineſs as uſual, without paying any Regard to the STAMP ACT; and we hope the Gentlemen of the Faculty in the neighbouring Provinces will follow ſo laudable an Example.

NEWPORT, December 23.

We hear from New-York, that laſt Tueſday the Effigies of Lord B——te, Lord C-l—lle, and ——————, were exhibited in that City on a Gallows, and in that Manner carried through the Place, attended by a very numerous Concourſe of People of all Ranks, and afterwards burnt, amidſt the united Acclamations of theſe true Sons of Liberty. The Populace afterwards proceeded to the City-Hall, and demanded the Stamped Papers, in order to deſtroy thoſe Inſtruments of Oppreſſion and Slavery; but by the Interceſſion of the Civil Officers, and Merchants, were diſſuaded from executing their Deſigns. Theſe Proceedings were occaſioned by ſome freſh Orders concerning the Stamps.

Laſt Friday Capt. Battar arrived here in 42 Days from Jamaica. He was cleared out at Port-Royal, with a Stamped Clearance, the Inhabitants of that Place, we are ſorry to ſay, having permitted the Uſe of Stamps: But at Kingſton, Veſſels were cleared out as heretofore, without any Regard to the Stamp Act, and the Inhabitants were determined to oppoſe it.

Laſt Week arrived here from England, viz New-York, Philip Durell, Eſq; in order to take the Command of his Majeſty's Ship Cygnet, now in this Harbour, in the Room of Charles Leſlie, Eſq; promoted.

We hear from Providence, that the Inferior Court for that County was held there laſt Monday, and proceeded in Buſineſs as uſual.

Extract of a Letter from St. Kitts.

"We the Inhabitants of St. Kitts have followed the true loyal Spirit of the North-Americans, by burning and totally deſtroying the Stamps: You never ſaw People more ſpirited than what we were on that Occaſion: The North-American Sailors that belonged to Sloops and Schooners in the Road, behaved like young Lions. The People in the Iſland of Nevis followed our Example, and were ſo enraged that they burnt two Houſes, and went ſo far as to burn the King's Boat that was lying upon the Bay: This laſt Step, I think, was too daring. And on the 5th of November, being Gunpowder Plot, the Stamp-maſter and his Deputy, were carried in Effigy through the Town, and in the Evening burnt in the Common Paſture. The Evening concluded with an elegant Supper, Drums beating, and French Horns playing; and the laſt Toaſt given was, LIBERTY, PROPERTY, AND NO STAMPS.'

We hear from Connecticut, That there is to be a GENERAL MEETING of the Reſpectable *Populace* of ſaid Colony, at *Hartford*, on Wedneſday the 8th Day *January* next: Wherefore thoſe that are ſo diſpoſed in the ſeveral Counties will doubtleſs attend.——

BOSTON, December 30.

We hear the Great and General Court of this Province is to meet at the Court-Houſe in this Town, on Wedneſday the 15th of January, being the Day they were prorogued to.

taws blame a white man, a trader, for betraying them to the Creeks. Letters from the country of Greeks say, that they were a hundred in number, that they killed 30 out of 40 Choctaws, and brought one prisoner home, whom they burnt; they declared the Choctaws behaved with great bravery, for when they had fought till their amunition was expended, they rushed in amongst the thickest of their enemies, knocking them down with their Tomahawks and the but ends of their muskets. The Creeks own the loss of 12 men, among whom were Molton, another good friend of ours, his son, and the Oakfuskee king. The victors delivered the gorget, medal and commission of the Red Captain, who was a great medal chief, to Mr. Hewit, a trader, in order to be returned to the commissary, or the superintendant.

Decem. 1. Last Wednesday arrived here from England, his Majesty's ship Martin, Thomas Heyward Esq; commander, who is appointed for the North Carolina station. The Bonetta, Capt. Wallace, appointed for the East Florida station, sailed with the Marten, and was to touch at the Bahamas.

New-York, December 14.

Friday last arrived here from South-Carolina, with Captain Schermerhorn, the famous Attakullakulla, or the Little Carpenter, Oucconnostota, or the Great-Warior, and the Raven King of Toogoloo, with six other chiefs and warriors of the Cherokee nation, accompanied by an interpreter; and next day they had an audiance of his excellency General Gage, the commander in chief.

All the field and staff-officers, at head quarters, and those of the corps in this garrison, together with several other gentlemen, attended the general on this occasion.

The chiefs, after being introduced, delivered the letters of recommendation they brought to his excellency from the southward; and the Little-Carpenter and Great Warior alternately addressed him, implored his interposition and good offices, in directing Sir William Johnson, the superintendant of Indian affairs, to mediate a peace between their nation, the Cherokees, and the six nations of Iroquois, they being deputed here on an embassy for that purpose.

They met with a gracious reception from the general, and his excellency has been pleased to give orders, they shall be properly entertained, and attended while they remain here.

He promised them his protection in the business they are employed in; and informed them he would give the necessary orders, for their proceeding to-morrow on board a sloop for Albany.

The chiefs having been informed that there was a theatre in this city, expressed a desire of seeing a play acted; and the general has thought proper to gratify their curiosity, and has given directions that proper places shall be got for them in the house this evening.

Portsmouth, in New-Hampshire, Dec. 18.

One Josiah Prescot of Deerfield, in the south west part of Nottingham, being out a hunting on the 26th day of November last, about three miles from his house he spy'd a Moose at a hundred yards distance; he immediately fir'd at her, and shot her down dead; upon that there arose up two more at a little farther distance; he immediately charg'd his gun again, and shot down the second; and while the other was smelling of his mate, he charg'd again, and shot down the third; and while he was charging his gun again a fourth came up toward the others, he shot her dead also: two of them were old ones, the other two young ones; one of the old ones was ten feet high and ten long, the other eight feet high and ten feet long; the other two were about six feet high and eight feet long: After this extraordinary exploit was over, he was joined by a partner, who being at a little distance and hearing the guns, came up to his assistance, and in going home, he got help to dress the moose; a wild cat they killed on their return.—This is fact.

Last Monday evening came on here a severe snow storm, and about 11o'clock it rained very hard, attended with a high wind for several hours, then shifting cleared off, and blew a meer hurricane, which forced six topsail vessels from the Long Wharf to Kittery Side of the river: several of them were ready to sail for the West Indies; five of them were got off yesterday, and we hear they have received no great damage.

Tuesday last died at Kittery, after a short illness, Capt. William Wentworth.

BOSTON.

The church-clergy of New York and New-Jersey, being assembled together in a *voluntary convention*, and assisted by some of their brethern from the neighbouring provinces, took into consideration the propriety and expediency of addressing the public, on the subject of an American Episcopate. After a thorough discussion of the point, they were unanimously of opinion, that fairly to explain the plan on which American Bishops had been requested, to lay before the public the reasons of this request, to answer the objections that have been made, and to obviate those that might otherwise be conceived against it, was both a matter of necessity and duty. It was accordingly voted, that something to this purpose should be published, and the Rev. Thomas Bradbury Chandler D. D. Rector of St. John's church in Elizabeth-town, New-Jersey, was appointed to this service.—This work is just published entitled, *An Appeal to the Public in behalf of the Church of England in America.* Application had been previously made in Britain, requesting one or more Bishops to be sent to America.

Dr. Chandler mentions in his introduction that should any objections continue, which shall be thought to deserve notice, the objectors are invited to propose them that they may be fairly and candidly debated before the tribunal of the public; and if none shall be offered, it will be taken for granted, that all parties acquiesce and are satisfied.

Extract of a letter from MontiChristi, Nov. 6.

"New disputes have arisen between the French and Spaniards; within these ten days the French have not suffered the Spanish small craft to bring any Molasses, and the Spaniards drive away all the French craft, so that the trade is in a manner stoped for the present. We have just heard that Cape Nicolas Mole is opened for the English, but do not know upon what regulation.

At three o'clock last Thursday morning a fire broke out in the shop of Mr. Mark Fitz, chaise-maker of Newburyport, which soon consumed that and two other buildings contiguous thereto, together with six new chaises. The weather was so extreme cold, that the engines was with great difficulty managed, but the inhabitants exerted themselves in an extrordinary manner, and saved two dwelling-houses which were in imminent danger.

The meeting of this town stands adjourned 'till to-morrow 3 o'clock, P M. at which time 'tis expected there will be a general attendance.

On the 11th inst. arrived here the Nova-Scotia packet, Capt. Cavenaugh from Halifax. Richard Reeves, Esq; register of seizures, and first clerk to the honourable board of commissioners of his majesty's customs *&c.* came passenger in the said packet.

The honourable the commissioners of the customs have appointed Samuel Fitch Esq; their Solicitor.

And George Lyde Esq; surveyor and searcher of the customs for the port of Boston, until the arrival of Robert Chamier Esq; the present surveyor, *&c.* who is now in England.

We hear that a number of trading men at Providence have petitioned the honourable board of commissioners here, that a collector of his majesty's customs may be appointed to reside at that place.

We hear the towns of Roxbury, Eastham and Ashburnham, have unanimously concurred with this town in the regulation respecting œconomy, &c.

We hear the Senegal man of war is stationed at New-port, Rhode-island, for three years, and is soon to sail from Halifax for her station.

As the Post arrived just as we had finished the paper, we printed this Supplement on purpose to oblige our Customers.

MONDAY *July* 3, 1769. THE NUMB. 1383.

NEW-YORK GAZETTE; OR, THE WEEKLY POST-BOY.

With the freſheſt Advices, Foreign and Domeſtick.

From the NEWPORT MERCURY, *of June* 17, 1769.
(*re-publiſhed by deſire.*)

SATURDAY the 3d inſtant, in the afternoon, the Planet Venus, agreeable to the prediction of aſtronomers, made her tranſit under the Sun:—People in general, big with expectation, impatiently waited the arrival of this extraordinary phenomenon; and the ſky being very clear had a fine opportunity of having their curioſity gratified.

To behold the univerſal attention turned from earth to Heaven; to ſee the eager inſpection of the obſervers, the various inſtruments employed; and to hear the converſation, on that occaſion, gave me the higheſt pleaſure. The obſervatory was ſurrounded by people of all ranks, ages, ſexes and colours, ſome furniſhed with quadrants, and ſome with perſpective glaſſes; others with ſmoked ſpectacles and ſmoked window glaſs, and a few with perforated boots and pig-yokes, and all were ambitiouſly attentive to catch the very inſtant of the external and internal contact of the Planet. After an obſervation of the total immerſion, the obſervatory was thrown open, and every one, who had an inclination, had an opportunity to ſee Venus on the Sun's diſk, through a reflecting or refracting teleſcope. It was, if poſſible, an addition to my pleaſure, to ſee how inquiſitive ſome people were, after taking a ſatisfactory view of the phenomenon, to know what aſtronomical uſe might be made of the obſervation, and how fond they, who had the leaſt acquaintance with aſtronomy, were to give them information. Of the few who pretended to any knowledge in that noble ſcience, I enjoyed the greateſt triumph; for, beſides an equal acquaintance with aſtronomy, I could boaſt a ſkill in aſtrology paramount to them all; and this drew about me by far the greateſt number of the ſpectators.

I would not pretend to ſay any thing in my own praiſe, for, as ſomebody well obſerves, the leaſt that a man ſays in his own praiſe is ſtill too much; but the publick cannot wonder at my being an adept, when they conſider, that I ſprang from an Arabian family famous for aſtrology, and that a right line drawn from the father of aſtrology through my great progenitor, and through Raimundus Lullius, and continued down to the preſent time, would more certainly hit me, than a *Jure-divino* right line, if there were any ſuch line, would, drawn from St. Peter, paſs through A-b-p Laud, and ſtrike B-p would-be Seabury; and as certainly as a line drawn from the center of the earth through the Planet Venus, at the time of the tranſit, would, continued far enough, paſs through the Sun; but not to ſay too much in my own praiſe, I ſhall only add, that, by the many inſtances I had given of my aſtrological ſkill, I had ſuch reputation, that, as was before obſerved, the bulk of the crowd throng'd about me.

There can be no occaſion for aſſigning a reaſon why the principal attention ſhould, on that account, be paid to me, for the maſs of mankind, it is well known, in all ages of the world, have believed in the influence of the celeſtial luminaries, on human affairs, as well as the vegetable kingdom.

I was ſurrounded by a mixed multitude, all impatient to know, from *me*, what was portended by this rare appearance; but from the ſpirit of pride, which is predominant in human nature, each one, imagining that he knew the true indications, was ſo ſtrongly urged to give his ſentiments, that, before I had time to declare the prognoſtication, they all burſt upon me with ſuch a confuſed vociferation, that finding it was impoſſible for me to hear them diſtinctly, or to be-heard myſelf, I thought beſt to retreat to my houſe; accordingly I went home; but I was ſoon followed, and my houſe ſurrounded.

After attending ſome time to the crowd from my chamber window, I catch'd their general ſentiments, and attempted ſeveral times to utter the prognoſtication, but finding it impoſſible to ſilence them, I deſired them to retire, promiſing them that I would publiſh my ſentiments on this important point in your paper of this day. Wherefore give me leave, Sir, by your Mercury, to inform them, that they are *toto Cælo*,—intirely miſtaken That neither earthquake, peſtilence, famine or war, neither a long continuance of the preſent miniſtry, and perſecution of John Wilkes, Eſq;—neither a long duration of the impoſitions on America, of the board of commiſſioners of the cuſtoms, and the arbitrary government of Verres, nor the introduction of a Biſhop among us, as ſome few imagined,——that neither theſe nor any other calamities, which their fears ſuggeſted, were portended by the extraordinary phenomenon.——But, on the contrary, on the word of an aſtrologer, I do aver,—that the late tranſit was not only harmleſs and innocent; but in conſequence thereof, the earth and the cattle on a thouſand hills, will yield an abundant increaſe:——The iron period of oppreſſion will ſoon paſs off, and ſaturnian times return:——That our civil liberties will be reſtored, and our religious liberties continued:——That, as at the time of that glorous tranſit, the Sun was in *Gemini*, in the *Twins*, and it was, properly ſpeaking, a tranſit of Venus *under* the Sun; propagation eſpecially, for about fifty years to come (till half the time before another tranſit ſhall have run out) will be carried on with ſuch rapidity, that inſtead of the number of people on this continent doubling every 30 or 40 years, they will double every 15 or 20 years, (the increaſe of the inhabitants in Britiſh America will be in that proportion during that period) ſo that, reckoning the preſent number of people to be three millions, and aſſuming that they will double in ſixteen years and one third of a year, which is nearly a third part of the prolifick period, at the cloſe thereof there will be in Britiſh America twenty-four millions, which is at leaſt three times the number of the inhabitants in Great Britain.—If this prognoſtication prove true, which the particular ſituation of the Sun in the eclíptick, and Venus tranſit being *under* the Sun, as above hinted, fully warrants, in fifty years our numbers alone will protect us in the enjoyment of our liberties againſt the efforts of any power on earth.

Newport, June 12, 1769. ASTROLOGUS.

A Kick *for the* WHIPPER. Nº LII.

By Sir ISAAC FOOT.

—which ſay they are APOSTLES *and are not.*——
ST. JOHN.

THAT the "patrons of the *Independent ſchiſm*" (as Sq. *T.* Nº 51. impudently calls us) are "oblig'd to deny that the APOSTLES had any ſucceſſors in *their* office," is very true; but that, not becauſe they have ever been "preſſed with the force of thoſe arguments that have been brought againſt them" by *epiſcopalians*,—no; but becauſe they have been *preſs'd with* the united *force* of SCRIPTURE and *reaſon*. We therefore need not apprehend that our ſentiments on this ſubject will ſuffer in the leaſt even from the *truly* "RUDE breath of Sq. *T*'s. examination."

The *W.* blames Dr. *C.* (whether juſtly or not, let the reader judge) for that, while he wou'd have us believe that *Biſhops* ſucceed the APOSTLES, he did not give us a "SCRIPTURAL deſcription of the *apoſtolic-office*," that we might thereby judge whether modern *Biſhops* are really *Apoſtles* or not.—Inſtead of ſupplying Dr. *C*'s deficiency, the moſt intrepid Sq. *T.* only "AFFIRMS, in direct oppoſition to the *W.* that the diſtinguiſhing characteriſtics of the apoſtolic office are *government, ordination* and *confirmation*; and that without the leaſt ſcriptural proof imaginable After feebly endeavouring to diſprove the *W*'s deſcription of the apoſtolate, he infers indeed as a conſequence, what he had before magnanimouſly AFFIRM'D, and wou'd have us believe, "it appears after the moſt candid examination," (*candid!* ha! ha! ha!) that, if the *W*'s. ſentiments are *wrong*, his own obſervations are certainly *right*: But I beg leave to inform Sq. *T.* that tho' we ſhou'd ſuppoſe the *W.* to be *wrong*, we are not therefore, in ſuch a caſe as this, oblig'd to conclude, that HE is certainly *right*. Two men may in ſuch a caſe differ in opinion, and yet both be miſtaken.——Let us however *candidly examine* the RUDE *breath* of Sq. *T*'s *candid examination.*

1. The *W.* had ſaid, that the APOSTLES were "CHOSEN *witneſſes of* CHRIST *to the world*. Here Sq. *T.* endeavours to raiſe a duſt, to blind the eyes of the reader, ſtarts fancied difficulties with the view of embarraſſing the argument, and uſing the word *choſen—Witneſſes of Chriſt*, &c. in a ſenſe different from that in which the *W.* did, wou'd fain betray the reader into an opinion, that the "women who conſtantly attended our Saviour's miniſtry, &c.—*Philip* and *Stephen*, and even the *Deacons* (tho' the loweſt *miniſterial* order) of the Church of England, were or are as really CHOSEN witneſſes of CHRIST's *reſurrection*, as thoſe whom we excluſively call APOSTLES. Fully to expoſe Sq. *T*'s unfair dealing on this occaſion, wou'd of itſelf require an whole *Kick*; I wiſh I had time and room to do it: But if the reader will only be ſo impartial, as *candidly* and carefully to conſider, with that reverence every *Chriſtian* owes to the SCRIPTURES, the following texts, viz. *Acts* i. 2, 8, 21—26.——ii. 14, 32.——iii. 15.——iv. 33.——v. 18, 32.——ix. 15.——x. 41.——xxii. 14, 15.——xxvi. 16, &c. I'm poſitive he will be convinc'd by ſuch a *cloud of witneſſes*, that the APOSTLES were in ſuch a ſenſe *choſen witneſſes of* CHRIST, as no man beſides ever *has been*, or propably ever *will be*.

2. The *W.* mention'd as a characteriſtic of the APOSTLES, that they were "*Sent forth to publiſh* CHRIST's *goſpel*, AND *erect his church among all mankind.*" Now 'tis plain, that the *W* never ſuppoſ'd, that none but the APOSTLES were in any ſenſe "*ſent forth* to publiſh the goſpel of CHRIST;"—he believes, I dare ſay, that, even in our day, thoſe, whom Sq. *T.* (in a manner quite unbecoming an *American ſchiſmatic*) calls *ſchiſmatical diſſenters*, are as properly SENT FORTH *to publiſh the goſpel*, as any modern *Biſhops* whatever, (the Biſhop of O-----g not excepted) tho' they may fondly *dream* themſelves *Apoſtles*. He probably meant that the APOSTLES were peculiarly *ſent forth*, i. e. with more ample credentials than any others cou'd pretend to;—however, he certainly did not mean to diſjoin (as Sq. *T.* unfairly does) founding of churches from preaching, i. e. the *ultimate* from the *immediate* deſign of their miſſion, but evidently conſiders both together as a characteriſtic of their office. Shou'd Sq. *T.* make it a characteriſtic of his own office, that he *publiſhes* periodical papers, and *Whips* the *W.* he wou'd ſurely think himſelf miſrepreſented, if any body ſhou'd object that others publiſh'd periodical papers as well as he. That, in the firſt age of the church, others beſides the APOSTLES preach'd the goſpel, nobody doubts; but if any *others* were properly qualify'd to *erect churches* among *Jews* and *Pagans*, in ſpite of their prejudices; and if any ſuch churches were by them actually erected, I muſt confeſs I'm at a loſs to find out who were the *founders*. That the APOSTLES had power to *ordain* officers in, and *govern* the church, all allow, and nobody, I dare ſay, ever dreamt of maintaining the contrary; and yet as tho' the *W.* had deny'd it, Sq. *T* ſeriouſly undertakes to prove it, and that (forſooth!) out of the *W*'s. own mouth, who had very juſtly ſaid, that the APOSTLES were ſent forth—*to erect* CHRIST's *church among all mankind*. Sq. *T*'s. inference is certainly juſt; but then, as tho' it were diſputed, he triumphantly declares, that "there is no getting over this concluſion, without abſurdly ſuppoſing, &c."——'Tis indeed truly *abſurd* to ſuppoſe (to uſe Sq. *T*'s words) "that a few men, 13 only "with St. *Paul*, cou'd PERSONALLY ſuperintend and ad "miniſter in this church which was erected among all "mankind." But what is the conſequence? Why, that they muſt have *ſuperintended* and *adminiſtred* (according to Sq. *T*'s. notions) *by proxy*;—(and indeed even Dr. *C.* does not deny but "*that preſbyters may have a ſubordinate authority to govern*) and that others therefore muſt have been employ'd to *govern* and *ordain* in the church before the APOSTLES. From the whole it appears, that Sq. *T.* has himſelf inadvertently diſprov'd what he had before ſo ſtoutly AFFIRM'D. *viz.* "that *government, ordination* &c. were the diſtinguiſhing characteriſtics of the apoſtolic office." If *preſbyters* can in any caſe *govern* as well as *publiſh the goſpel*, 'tis plain, that (even according to Sq. *T.*) *government* is no characteriſtic of an *Apoſtle* Thus poor fellow! while he thought he was *whipping* the *W.* he has been *whipping* Dr. *C.* and *himſelf*.

3. The next and the laſt article which the *W.* mentions is,—that *the* APOSTLES *were furniſh'd for their work by the infallible guidance and miraculous gift of the holy ſpirit*, TOGETHER WITH *a power of conveying ſuch gifts of the ſpirit, as the Holy Ghoſt* (not the Apoſtles themſelves) thought proper, *to the converts to chriſtianity*, *by the laying on of their hands*. Here, as before, what the *W* had join'd together Sq. *T.* puts aſunder. Artfully to divide an enemy's forces ſo as to combat the two diviſions ſeparately, is no ſmall piece of generalſhip;—Sq. *T* awkwardly attempts it; but every ſpectator ſees that the *W.* never ſuppos'd that either the *infalliable guidance* or the *miraculous gifts* of the Holy Spirit were *of themſelves* characteriſtic of an APOSTLE.—The one, the other, or both of theſe were ſometimes at leaſt, enjoy'd by *Moſes*, *David*, *Elijah*, *Eliſha*, and the reſt of the Prophets; and yet nobody ever thought of calling *them* APOSTLES: Other things beſides theſe are certainly neceſſary to the *apoſtolic* character.—A man may have the *infallible guidance* and *miraculous gifts* of the holy ſpirit himſelf, and yet not be able to communicate them to others.—This was evidently the caſe of the ſeven deacons, and tho' "*Stephen* in particular was full of the holy ghoſt, and did great *wonders and miracles* among the people;" yet we do not find, that either he or *Philip* (*Acts* viii. 6, 7, &c.) ever communicated to others "the gifts of the ſpirit," any more than SIMON MAGUS, who after the impoſition of the hands of St. *Peter* and St. *John*, probably wrought miracles, and yet would fain have purchaſed with *money*, (as doubtleſs many biſhopricks have been purchaſed) the ſame faculty of communication. Communicating the *gifts of the holy ghoſt, by impoſition of hands*, was certainly peculiar to the APOSTLES, and Sq. *T.* indeed owns it was ſo; but then he ſuppoſes this *extraordinary* branch of the apoſtolic office, was nothing more than a modern *Je ne ſcay quoi* kind of mimickry, call'd *comfirmation*, which exhibits no extraordinary phænomena whatſoever. Communicating to others the gift of tongues, the power of working miracles, &c which St. *Paul*, 2 *Cor.* xii. 12, calls *the ſigns of an apoſtle*, was, no doubt, a great *confirmation* of the faith of the firſt proſelytes to chriſtianity; but that in our day any real *confirmation* is to be expected from the ſolemn farce exhibited by the impoſition of the hands of a Biſhop, who is ſo far from being able to communicate miraculous powers, that he has not any even of his own, is one of the moſt ridiculous opinions, that perhaps ever entered into the heart of man. In ſhort, 'tis not more evident, that *Biſhops* are really true miniſters of the goſpel, than that they have no right (for want of miraculous powers) to imitate the *Apoſtles* in what they call *confirmation*. "But here, *venerable Whipper*, flinch not," (for the *W.* even while you *whip* him, does not) "but ſpeak full to the caſe. Will you aſſert," that your *Biſhops* can convey the GIFTS as well as the *graces* of the ſpirit?—The laſt of which (ſo far as I've hitherto underſtood you) was all you ever before ſuppos'd *the* HOLY GHOST thought proper a *Biſhop* ſhould convey. *Gifts* and *graces* are ſurely very different things, and if *Biſhops* pretend to convey the *firſt*, as well as the *laſt*, we certainly have a right to expect miracles from them, as a proof and a *confirmation* of their apoſtleſhip. "It appears therefore after the moſt candid examination," that neither *government*, *ordination* nor *confirmation*, are "diſtinguiſhing marks of the apoſtolic office," and conſequently that no *Biſhop* whatever can be conſider'd as an APOSTLE. E.

ERRATA. Nº L. par. 1. line 8. for *national*, read *natural* No. LI. par. 4. line 16. for *conſtitution*, read *continuation*.

The NEW-YORK Preacher, Nº VI.

ECCLESIAST. XVI. 20.

The PREACHER *ſought to find out acceptable words, and that which was written was* UPRIGHT, *even words of* TRUTH.

WHOEVER publiſhes any thing to the world, ſhould be careful that what he delivers is truth, and that it is done in a manner as inoffenſive as poſſible; but, tho' he ſhould not be ſo happy as to pleaſe every reader, he ought to deliver only the *truth*, or drop his pen; as no zeal how great ſoever, for the beſt cauſe, can alter the nature of things, to juſtify the publiſhing of *falſehoods*. I have therefore in my SERMONS, endeavour'd, as far as I knew, to keep TRUTH on my ſide, and have publiſh'd my thoughts in the open, free, declamatory manner, I have lately obſerved frequently us'd in our PULPITS.---A manner, I confeſs, excellently adapted to my purpoſe, as I can bring in, or leave out things at pleaſure; or

WHEREAS GERARDUS GROESBECK and ABRAHAM TEN BROECK, did make, and with their Hands subscribe, a certain Writing bearing Date the Twentieth Day of February, Anno Domini One Thousand Seven Hundred and Sixty-nine, and publish'd the same Twelve Weeks successively in Hugh Gaine's News-Paper, entitled, the New-York Gazette, and Weekly Mercury; and in James Parker's News Paper, entitled, the New-York Gazette, or the Weekly Post-Boy, two of the Public News-Papers of this Colony; which said Writing was, and is directed by the Tenor thereof, to all Persons interested in the Lots therein after mentioned; and recites, "That whereas His late Majesty King GEORGE the Second, by his Letters Patent, under the Great Seal of the Province of New-York, bearing Date the Fifteenth Day of June, in the Thirteenth Year of his Majesty's Reign, Annoque Domini One Thousand Seven Hundred and Thirty-nine, DID grant and confirm, unto *Edward Collins*, *James De Lancey*, *Gerardus Stuyvesant*, *Stephen Van Renselaer*, *Charles Williams* and *Frederick Morris*, a certain Tract of Land in the County of *Albany*, called *Walumscback*, to the Eastward of a Place called *Hojack*, beginning at a certain marked Tree, which is 147 Chains distant from the late Dwelling House of *Garret Cornelius Van Ness*, measured on a Line running South 75 Degrees East, from the South East Corner of the said House, to the said Tree; and running from the said marked Tree, North 13 Degrees and 30 Minutes West, 90 Chains and 40 Links: Then North 40 Degrees and 45 Minutes East, 220 Chains; then North 77 Degrees East, 90 Chains; then South 31 Degrees and 40 Minutes East, 604 Chains; then South 65 Degrees West, 92 Chains; then North 44 Degrees and 30 Minutes West, 150 Chains; then North 75 Degrees West, 129 Chains; then North 20 Degrees West, 146 Chains; then South 60 Degrees West, 173 Chains; and then North 4 Degrees West, 76 Chains, to the Place where this Tract of Land first begun; containing 12000 Acres of Land, and the usual Allowance for Highways. And whereas Partition of the said Tract of Land has been made by the said original Proprietors abovenamed, on the 31st Day of May, Annoque Domini 1742, that by the said Partition, the Lots No. 5, 14, 21 and 28, fell to the Share of, and on the same Day was conveyed to *Stephen Groesbeck*: And that whereas they the Subscribers are Part-Owners and Proprietors of all the four Lots beforementioned, and are inclined to have Partition made of the same, pursuant to two Acts of the Governor, Council and General Assembly of the Colony of New-York, the one entitled, "An Act for the more effectual collecting his Majesty's Quit Rents in the Colony of New York, and for Partition of Lands in order thereto," passed on the 8th Day of January, in the Year of our Lord 1762: The other, entitled An "Act to continue an Act, entitled, An Act for the more effectual collecting of his Majesty's Quit Rents in the Colony of New-York, and for Partition of Lands in order thereto," and also to continue one other Act, entitled, "An Act to explain Part of an Act, entitled, An Act for the more effectual collecting of his Majesty's Quit Rents in the Colony of New-York, and for Partition of Lands in order thereto," passed the 31st of December, 1768. And did therefore pursuant to the said Acts, thereby give Notice, That *John R. Bleecker* and *Peter Lansing*, Esqrs. and *Thomas Hun*, Gent. all of the City of *Albany*, were appointed Commissioners to make Partition of the said Lots; and that we the said Commissioners would meet on Tuesday the 30th Day of May next ensuing the Day of the Date thereof, at the House of Mr. *Richard Cartwright*, Innholder, in the City of *Albany*, to proceed to the Partition of the same; and did, then and there desire all Persons interested therein, to attend then and there for that Purpose. NOW therefore we the said *John R. Bleecker*, *Peter Lansing* and *Thomas Hun*, Commissioners so appointed as aforesaid, DO hereby signify our said Appointment: And do hereby give Notice, that we will meet at the House of *Richard Cartwright*, in the City of *Albany*, on Monday the 31st of July next, to proceed to the said Partition; and we desire all Persons interested or concerned to attend accordingly. Given under our Hands at *Albany*, this 6th Day of June, in the Year of our Lord, One Thousand Seven Hundred Sixty-nine.

JOHN R. BLEECKER,
PETER LANSING,
THOMAS HUN.

New York, June 15, 1769.

NOTICE is hereby given, That I the Subscriber, being this Day appointed Chairman of a Committee of the Corporation of the City of *New-York*, for causing their Water Lot, on the West Side of *Peck's* Slip, to be filled up, and a Pier of Eighteen Feet laid contiguous to said Slip; Do in behalf of said Committee, notify to all Persons who shall be desirous to contract for filling up said Water Lot, and making the aforesaid Pier, that they send in their Names with their Proposals, to me at my House as soon as possible, that the same may be laid before the said Committee for their Approbation, in order to have the same carried on, and compleated without Delay.

BENJAMIN BLAGGE.

New York, June 5, 1769.

TO BE SOLD.
ON EASY TERMS.

EIGHTEEN Thousand Acres of Land, divided into Ninety Farms, of 200 Acres each, situated on the South Side of the *Mohocks* River, in the County of *Albany*, in the Center of a well inhabited Country, having the Settlements along the *Mohocks* River, for the North Bounds; on the South or Rear, the Settlements of *Cherry Valley*; the Patents of *Groesbeck* and *Wagenaer*; of *Theobalds*, *Young*, and of *Peter Schuyler*, and others, on each of which are considerable Settlements: On the West they are bounded by the Villages known by the Names of *Hartman's Dorp*, *Wagenear's Dorp*, and *Contreman's Dorp*; on the South are the Settlements of *Cobus Kill*, *New-Dorlach*, and *Schoharie*. As they lay between *Cherry Valley* and the *Mohocks* River, it is needless to mention, that they are convenient to Settlers. The Lands are in general very rich; they are covered with Linden, Butter-Nut, Sugar Maple, and Oak: Several Streams proper for Mills, run through them, and some Parts are plenty of Lime-Stone. For further Particulars, enquire of *James Duane*, Esq; Attorney at Law in *New York*; of *Peter Sylvester*, Esq; at *Albany*; of Col. *Henry Frey*, at *Conejoharie*, who lives within four Miles of the said Lands; or of *Peter Du Bois*, the Owner thereof, at the *Wall-Kill*, in *Ulster* County.

N. B. These Farms will be sold singly, or in Lots of 100 Acres each, or a Number of Farms together, as may best suit Purchasers: And such of them as shall remain unsold by the 20th of *September* next, will then be sold at Public Vendue, at the Court-House at *Albany*.---One Half of the Purchase Money will be required at the Execution of the Deeds; for the Remainder, Bonds with Security, will be taken.

TO BE SOLD,

LOT N° 46, in the Oblong, County of Dutchess, and Province of New York; containing 500 Acres, esteemed as good Land as any in that Part of the Country. For further Particulars, enquire of DAVID VAN HORNE, in Wall-Street, New York.

TO BE SOLD,

THREE Years and five Months Time of a Servant Man and his Wife,--both High Germans:--The Man is a Nail-Smith, and a Black-Smith by Trade, but can do any sort of Farming Work: The Woman can spin and sew, but has been chiefly used to Country-Work of all kinds, and even working in the Field,--and can cook for common Families.---They are sold for no Fault, but want of Employment: For further Particulars, Enquire of the Printer hereof.

WHEREAS several of the Owners or Claimers of the Common Lands allotted to the Patent of *Secaukus*, in the County of *Bergen*, in the Province of *New-Jersey* have made frequent Applications to the General-Assembly of the said Province, for a Law appointing Commissioners to make Partition of said Common Lands; These are therefore to certify, that a Number of the said Owners, or Claimers of said Common Lands, will at the next Sessions of General Assembly of said Province renew their Application for the above said Law; of which intended Application, all Persons laying Claim to the whole, or any Part of said Commons, or otherwise concerned therein, are desired to take Notice, and make their Objections, if any they have, to said Law. Of which Application frequent Notice has been heretofore given;--
Dated May 18, 1769.

TO BE SOLD

At public Vendue on Tuesday the 11th Day of July next, or at private Sale any Time before.

A Good convenient Dwelling House, with the Lot whereon it stands, situate in *Montgomeries* Ward in the City of *New-York*, a little to the Eastward of Mr. *Des Brosses*, and now in the Possession of *Abraham Anthony*------The House is two Stories high; has a Parlour Kitchen adjoining, and a Cellar under that. There are six Fire-places:---The Lot is 24 Feet front and 100 Feet back:---The House is the whole Breadth of the Lot, and 34 feet back, exclusive of the Kitchen which is 24 Feet.--Any Person inclining to purchase before the Day of Sale, may apply to *John Anthony*, near the *Exchange*.

PUBLIC notice is hereby given, that we the subscribers, trustees for all the creditors of Garret Sp. Dewint, of the island of St. Thomas, in the West-Indies, merchant; are ready to make a dividend of the estate of the said Garrat Sp. Dewint, among his creditors, and we hereby desire all the said creditors, to meet on the 10th day of July next, at ten of the clock in the forenoon, of the same day, at the dwelling house of Walter Brock, in Wall-street, in the city of New-York, for that purpose. Dated the 4th day of May, 1769.

BENJAMIN BLAGGE,
ISAAC CORSA,
JOSEPH BULL,

THE Honourable the Commissioners of his Majesty's Customs, observing that Ships and Vessels frequently incur Forfeitures, and their Owners become subject to heavy Penalties, thro' the Misconduct or Negligence of the Masters and Seamen; and particularly by the Masters not making true Reports of their Cargoes, which they sometimes pretend they are not able to do, from the Manner that they take in their Loading at Foreign Ports: And at other Times they pretend that the Seamen take on board private Ventures, and secrete the same from their Knowledge so as to be landed clandestinely upon their arrival without payment of Duty.

And several Ships and Vessels seized for the Commission of Offences of this Kind having been released in Consequence of such Representations from the Owners; the Commissioners think it necessary to advertise for the Information of all Persons whom it may concern, That upon the Detection and Discovery of any such Offences in future, the same will be prosecuted as the Law directs; so that it behoves the Owners to suppress the Custom of suffering the Seamen to take in private Ventures; and also to admonish the Masters to be punctual in taking an Account of their Cargoes, and to pay a strict Regard to their Oaths in reporting the same, as well at the Ports of their first arrival, as the Ports of Entry in *North-America*. By Order of the Commissioners,
Boston, April 14, 1769. RICHARD REEVE, Sec'y.

SELLING off at prime cost, a fresh and general assortment of drugs and medicines, patented medicines, shop furniture, surgeons instruments &c. by Thomas Bridgen Attwood, who is remov'd from Broad-Street, to a house the corner of Nassau Street, opposite to the house formerly in the possession of General Amherst, now occupied by Mr. Le Roy---where country orders will be punctually executed, physicians and family prescriptions faithfully made up, and all favours duly acknowleged.

TO BE SOLD,
By JOHN LONG *in* Pearl-Street, *near the* Battery.

GOOD Lisbon Wine, by the Quarter Cask, Hogshead, or larger Quantity, for Cash or short Credit.

THOMAS WILLIAM MOORE, and Co.

Have to sell at their Store in Hanover-Square, opposite Mr. Charles McEvers, the following goods, which they will sell on the lowest terms for cash or short credit;

CALLICOES,	Cotton romals,
Fustians,	Cotton handkerchiefs,
Jeans,	Brown and white thread hose,
Dimities,	Silk and worsted breeches
Diaper,	pieces,
Plain and flowered lawns,	Irish dowlass,
Cambricks,	A large assortment of linens,
6 4 book muslin,	11 8, 3 4, 7-8, 4 4 checks,
Sprig'd and check muslins,	Striped hollands,
Muslin handkerchiefs,	Bed bunts. Broad cloths,
Swiss lawns,	Druggits, shage,
Taffeties,	Shalloons,
Persians,	Buckram,
Painted silks,	Worsted damask,
Ribbons,	Cross barr'd stuffs,
Childrens thread hose,	Scotch plaid, &c.

Teneriff WINE,

In Pipes, Hogsheads, and Quarter Casks, to be SOLD,
By ELEAZER MILLER, jun.
ALSO,
An Assortment of East-India and European Goods; imported last Fall, at his Store in Hanover-Square.

A complete Assortment, at the
UNIVERSAL STORE, OR

At the Sign of the
Looking Glass & Druggist Pot,
At the Corner of the Old Slip-Market,
NEW-YORK;

A variety of Pictures, Looking-Glasses and Paper Hanging.
With Flint Glasses of all Kinds.
London and Bristol Crown Window Glass of all Sizes, as large as 27 by 22 Inches.
Coach and Plate Glass.
Painters and Limners Colours, mix'd or unmix'd.
Varnishes of all Kinds.—Japanners Articles, Gold and Silver Leaf, &c.
Dying Colours, with every Article belonging to dying.
Fullers Articles,———Founders and Smelters ditto.—Hatters Trimmings.
—Foil and Stones, &c. for Jewellers.
—London and hard Metal Pewter.—
Brass and Copper Ware.—Carpeting of all Kinds.—China ditto.—Spicery.
DRUGS and MEDICINES.
With a general Assortment of genuine patented Medicines, warranted, and Shop Furnitures.

*** N. B. *The above Advertisement, being only the Heads, which consists of a Variety of Articles, almost every particular in each Branch can be commanded at the above Store.*

ALSO: English Sail Cloth, No. 1, to 6.—Nails and Brads of all Sizes. Tin Sheets in Boxes; Sheet Iron; Sheet and Bar Lead; Shot of all Sizes; English and German Steel,—Variety of Chimney Tiles,—Allum, Copperas, Brimstone, Salt Petre; Borax.—Seeds, &c. for Distillers.

SOLD WHOLESALE and RETAIL.

Just published, and to be sold by HUGH GAINE, *at the Bible and Crown, in Hanover-Square,* (*Price* 5s. 6d.)

THE
APPEAL DEFENDED:
OR
The proposed AMERICAN EPISCOPATE
VINDICATED.

IN ANSWER to the Objections and Misrepresentations of Dr. Chauncey, and others.
By THOMAS BRADBURY CHANDLER, D. D.

"There are some Spirits in the World, who, unless they are in actual Possession of Despotism themselves, are daily haunted with the Apprehension of being subject to it in others; and who seem to speak and act under the strange Persuasion, that every Thing short of Persecution against what they dislike, must terminate in the Persecution of themselves."

FOR SALE,
At GARRAT NOEL's,
Next Door to the Merchant's Coffee-House,

A GREAT Variety of the most elegant
PICTURES,

Framed and glazed in AMERICA, which in Neatness of Workmanship, equal any imported from *England*, and will be SOLD at a much lower Price.

LIQUID TRUE BLUE, and ULTRAMARINE INK, sold by the Printer hereof.

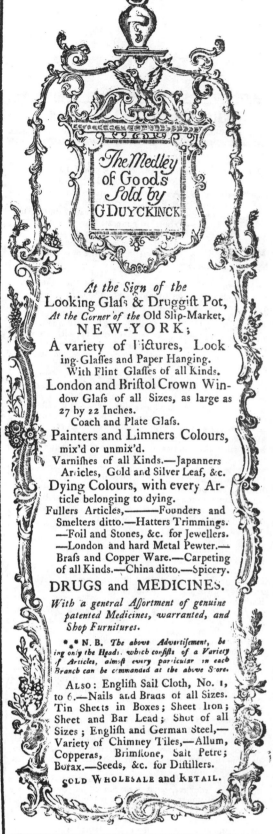

NEW-YORK: Printed by JAMES PARKER, at the NEW PRINTING-OFFICE in *Beaver-Street*, where Subscriptions, and Advertisements, &c. for this Paper are taken in.

THURSDAY, Dec. 23, 1773. [No. 36.]

RIVINGTON's

NEW-YORK GAZETTEER: OR, THE Connecticut, Hudson's River, New-Jersey, and Quebec WEEKLY ADVERTISER.

PRINTED by JAMES RIVINGTON, facing the COFFEE-HOUSE BRIDGE.

Assize of BREAD,——*Flour* at 21s. *per Cent.*

A White Loaf of the finest Flour, to weigh 1lb. 7 oz. and a half for 4 Coppers.

Published the 8th of November 1773.

HIGH-WATER at NEW YORK, this Week.

Thursday,	45 min. after 11	Monday,	57 min. after 2
Friday,	38 min. after 12	Tuesday,	37 min. after 3
Saturday,	27 min. after 1	Wednes.	22 min. after 4
Sunday,	12 min. after 2		

PRICE CURRENT, in NEW-YORK.

Wheat per Bushel,	7s. 8d.	Muscovado Sugar,	58s.	Fine Salt, 2s. 6d. Coarse	do. 2s.
Flour,	20s. od.	Single refind, do.	1s. od.	Indian Corn per Bushel,	4s. od.
Brown Bread,	17s. 6d.	Molasses,	2s. od.	Bills of Exchange,	£. 80-0
West-India Rum,	3s. 8d.	Beef per Barrel,	48s. od.	Do. at Philadel.	£. 67½
New-England, do.	2s. 8d.	Pork,	74s. od.	Do. at Boston.	par.

Debates in the House of Commons continued.

Mr. CHARLES FOX. I rejoice, Sir, to find that we are at last got into a debate, from which I was afraid we were altogether departing. As the matter has been managed, the question before this House is, whether it be at all expedient for the legislative power to interpose in an affair of this kind?

I was exceedingly young, Sir, when I went to the University; not, however, so young, but that the matter of subscription struck me. At the age of *twelve*, youth, when matriculated, are required to subscribe *articuli fidea* PUNTAXAU; but, at sixteen, they are to subscribe the oaths of *allegiance* and *supremacy*. Now, Sir, whether it be supposed that their *political* is of more importance than their *religious* Creed, I will not take upon me to determine; but it should seem that the institution supposes them not capable of understanding the sublime mysteries of politicks until *sixteen*, though at *twelve* it is apprehended they can both understand, relish, and swallow down the sublimer mysteries of religion! As to the distinction which hath been laid down by a Right Honourable Gentleman who spoke some time since (Welbore Ellis) that "it is only subscribing to what they are hereafter to be instructed in, and means no more than a repetition of a Creed;" Sir, this subscription as well as repetition is a solemn thing; it is a serious *attestation of the truth of propositions*, not a syllable of which, according to the Gentleman's own confession, the youth who subscribes can understand. Why therefore attest the truth of what he is ignorant? Is not this to teach our youth to prevaricate; and will not an habit of prevarication lead to the destruction of all that prompt ingenuous frankness, which ought to be the glory and the pride of youth?

This House, Sir, is accustomed to accept of the *single affirmation* of witnesses; and is it not a dangerous doctrine to teach, that because an oath is *not* administered, a person may solemnly bear attestation to the truth of what, being entirely ignorant of, may, for aught he can tell, be entire *falsehood*! I relish not such doctrine, Sir; I think it has a dangerous tendency; and I should therefore wish that the chair might be quitted, in order that we may discuss the vast importance which can redound to the state, as well as the infinite benefit which accrues to individuals, from their being trained most solemnly to attest and subscribe to the truth of a string of propositions, all of which they are as entirely ignorant of as they are of the face of the country said to be in the moon!

Mr. Fuller. I pretend not, for my part, to be conversant in these matters; but I think, Sir, the question exceedingly short. The competency of the House to take cognizance of the affair is, I presume, on all hands agreed; those therefore who think that all is *right* with respect to the articles, will be for your *not* quitting the chair; those, on the other hand, who may think some things *wrong*, will be *for* your leaving the chair, in order that the errors may be inquired into and amended.

A Member. I confess myself, Sir, exceedingly sorry that the honourable Gentleman who made this motion did not last year move the House on the occasion. From the complexion of the House at *that* time, it is more than probable success might have crowned his well-meant endeavours.—However, Sir, as I entirely concur with him in opinion, I shall speak in defence of a measure I so ardently wish may be adopted.

Sir, the inclination of this House was known during the last session; hints were dropped sufficient to alarm the two Universities: Yet how, Sir, did they act upon the occasion? *Oxford*, grown old in errors, persisted with an obstinacy scarcely to be parallelled; she would no nothing: *Cambridge*, indeed, to save appearances, did—what? why as good as nothing. We are still, Sir, to be shackled in the same manner, as in the superstitious days of Monkish darkness; the all-cheering sun of reformation hath indeed arisen, but we prevent its reflecting rays from enlightening our minds in the manner to be wished. The tyranny of a LAUD is pleaded for; his accursed farrago is to be crammed down the throats of our youth; and it is not enough that we have shaken off the Roman yoke, but our necks are still to be burthened with the Calvinistic mill-stone invented by a despicable Ecclesiastic. Men seem, Sir, to have an aversion to every kind of reformation until the evils complained of are past enduring. Rome tyrannized for ages uncontrouled; she lorded it over men's consciences with impunity; she fomented discords, promoted assassinations; but till, intoxicated with success, she proceeded to dethrone potentates, till she wrested the sword out of the hands of the civil magistrate, she was not resisted; then, Sir, men felt, and redressed their wrongs; and shall not we feel, and redress the remnants of her superstition? Forbid it, Toleration! Forbid it, Religious Liberty! No, Sir, we will persevere, certain that, in the end, truth will prevail; common sense will triumph over mysticism, reason over superstition, and a rational system of faith and manners over the relicks of Monkish spirituality: I therefore, Sir, am for your instantly quitting the chair.

Mr. Charles Jenkinson. A cursory view of the times would convince any man of the honourable Gentleman's mistake who spoke last, accusing Laud as the principal promoter of that farrago, as the Gentleman was pleased to term it. [Here he referred to an act passed in the reign of Edward VI. and also quoted several particulars relative to Professor Cheek, Queen Elizabeth, and James I.]

From the passages, Sir, here alluded to, it is manifest, that what the honourable Gentleman hath attributed to Laud, is the work of other hands. But granting it, Sir, as the Gentleman says; yet candour must allow that Laud, with all his faults, was a very great man. With respect, Sir, to the matter of subscription, I profess myself an advocate for the measure, a convert to its utility. I know, Sir, with men of lively parts and a brilliancy of genius, there is nothing so easy as to place an object in such a light, as that the by-standers cannot refrain from beholding it with ridicule: I know, Sir, that the hacknied term *superstition* may be called in with great dexterity, as a bugbear to alarm weak minds, by suggesting groundless terrors: But, surely, Sir, this cannot be called a *superstitious age*; it is rather an age of *scepticism*; under the notion of religious liberty, the solemn truths of religion itself are treated with contempt, and sceptical infidelity abounds.

Some men, Sir, are for laying our youth under no restraint; others go farther; they argue for the natural excellence of the passions; and urge, that they should be left to indulge them at will. But, Sir, if the *passions* are *early* felt, sad experience proves, that *reason* is a guest which takes not up her residence in our breasts till a *late*, very *late* period of life. One man, who calls himself a philosopher, hath contended that man, as he comes into the world, should be left entirely to himself; at random to receive each impression from without, at random to follow each suggestion from within. I do confess, Sir, I should have a great curiosity to try the experiment; but certain I am, a person trained in such a manner would be a man quite unfit to live in society. This, Sir, is the mode of education contended for by *Rousseau*, whom I always looked upon as an *ingenious madman*. With respect, therefore, Sir, to an exemption from human ties, in matters of religion, I am against it. So much depends upon the right education of youth, that every innovation on an established mode, which for ages hath been found to answer the end, should be avoided. That the present mode, adopted at our Universities, has answered the end, the past and present experience may determine. Whence the man, who explored the unfrequented paths of science, unlocked the secret stores of knowledge, and laid open the hidden treasures of learning and of wisdom? whence, Sir, *Bacon*? From an University. Whence, Sir, he who, by the most geometric proofs, sought out the laws of matter and of motion? whence *Newton*? From an University. On the other hand, whence all that scepticism, that froth of words, that puerile stuff, so much the taste of the present times: I will answer you, Sir, NOT from an University; but from your Hume's, your Bolingbroke's, your Rousseau's, and others of this despicable tribe.

Since then, Sir, the custom of our Universities, *for ages*, hath answered every end the state could require in the education of its youth, I am not for substituting another mode; I am not for making an innovation upon their establishment.

Nor is it, Sir, an establishment peculiar to *English* Universities; all foreign ones have their tests. At the University of Paris I know a test is established, and the members are required to testify their strict adherence to such doctrines as characterize the religion of the country. By the edict of Nantz, also, provision is made, that Protestants, the *Dissenters* of that country, shall, nevertheless, declare their assent to a certain form prescribed. What, therefore, hath been so universally adopted, I should suppose adopted, because found to be of national utility; and I shall not, Sir, give my voice for England to be exempt from what hath been found, by foreigners, necessary for the maintenance of the religion of the country; by consequence, I strenuously oppose the motion, and your quitting the chair.

Mr. Montague. A Gentleman some time since congratulated a noble Lord opposite me, on his election to the Chancellorship of an University; and seemed to intimate, that his Lordship might use his weight with the University in behalf of that side the Gentleman espoused. I am afraid the noble Lord has *too much weight* with some bodies, and *too little* with others; however, his Lordship has, I am informed, given his *opinion* on the subject. As to the education of youth, it cannot be deemed more important than I think it; but, with respect to requiring subscription from *all* indiscriminately, I confess, I think it absurd; for the very knowledge of those articles our youth subscribe would be of no manner of advantage in civil life. I know a noble youth (the young Marquis of Granby) who has all the goodness of his much-lamented father's heart, is possessed of infinite genius, and, as a classick, few, I believe, surpass him; yet, with respect to the articles, I don't know that ever he professed himself a *supra* or a *sub-lapsarian*; and, though a tolerable Grecian, he may yet not know whether the so much contested Greek word should be *Omousia* or *Omoiousia*. The knowledge of these matters is unnecessary, and, therefore, no attestation of their truth or falshood is required.

Mr. Townshend. It is so seldom I differ from the honourable Gentleman who spoke last, that I am sure it would give me infinite concern, did I not think, that the difference so observable among particular friends, during the course of this debate, evinced that it was carried on with the greatest freedom and impartiality. I do not, Sir, rise warmly to espouse *either* side of the question. I am rather *neuter*; a situation in which I am not accustomed often to stand. I think the honourable Gentleman's motion reaches *too far*, and yet I think it ought not to be entirely opposed. I am not displeased with the Gentleman who sits below me (Sir Roger Newdigate) nor should I censure any Gentleman who now does, or proposes hereafter to represent the University of Oxford, for warmly opposing the motion; but I flatter myself, that, if the University should hereafter, in its wisdom, think fit to desist from requiring subscription, the Gentleman, who now so strenuously argues *against* the measure, may then be induced to change his opinion, and be the first to extol the reformation made by the University.

As to the Humes, the Bolingbrokes, and the Rousseaus, I verily think them, Sir, the *worst pests* to society: But, Sir, don't let us go into the opposite extreme; let something be done, and, if we cannot comply with all, let us shew a willingness to comply with such part as cannot injure the cause of truth, of religion, of virtue.

[Here the Hon. Mr. Fitzmaurice and Lord North being up, the House was, for a long time, divided who should speak first; at length the speaker decided in favour of the Hon. Thomas Fitzmaurice, and he began as follows:]

Hon. Thomas Fitzmaurice,—elder brother to the Earl of Shelburne. This young Gentleman was chosen, since the general election, Member for Calne in Wiltshire; he has generally divided with the minority; but as Lord Shelburne has of late been reconciled to Administration, he now generally votes with the Treasury Bench.] Upon a subject of this kind, it is possible, Sir, that a person as obscure as myself may throw some light. The question before us seems to be, Whether it is at all expedient for this House to interfere in the matter of subscription, and, if expedient, whether *this* be the time it should interfere? For my part, Sir, I cannot divest myself of the idea, that the motion the honourable Gentleman hath this day made, is, some how or other, connected with or involved in the motion which was made last year. The petitioners, seeing it impossible to gain their point in a *direct* manner, have endeavoured obliquely to obtain the prayer of the petition. Beginning with the youth of the Universities, they thought, would be a step towards ending with themselves. The stratagem was artful, yet easily to be seen through; and as, Sir, I believe this to be the case, I do not think it expedient for this House to interfere *at all*.

But, Sir, a[illegible] consider the state of religion amongst us. Such is the degeneracy of the age, that, if we give way in one instance, we shall be pestered with petitions to grant many unwarrantable things. Has not this been the case, Sir, already? First come the *Dissenters*; next comes an allegation, that the degrees of consanguinity, prohibited from intermarrying with each other, should be abolished, and that leave should be given for a man to marry his *grandmother*. Dr. *Kennicott*, of *Oxford*, tells the publick, that we have a *spurious Bible*, to which no credit should be given; he hath, therefore, received *ten thousand pounds* for collecting manuscripts, and will not, I suppose, have finished before he receives another *ten thousand pounds*. Mr. *Foote*, the comedian, had the shameless effrontery from his theatre to tell us, that the *ten commandments* might be divided into *two* parts, and that he would make a *comedy* of each part. Now, Sir, when such licentiousness, such sacrilegious assertions, are daily propagated, I think, instead of relaxing, we should keep a stricter hand. Besides, Sir, was the subscription at matriculation such a grievance as is pretended, why do foreigners flock in such multitudes to Oxford in preference to Cambridge? I know many there at present who think the complaint frivolous. In short, Sir, I wish the House not on any account to interfere, and if it does determine to interfere, I am clearly of opinion that this is not the *proper time*.

[*To be continued.*]

The following Piece was deferred, for want of Room in our last.

MR. RIVINGTON, DEC. 11, 1773.

I FIND that an *impudent fellow*, in your last paper, has assumed to himself the honour of the four *patriotic* lines against POP-LI-COLA, and in favour of *smuggling*,---or *something else*,--which you printed some time ago; and which must be *allowed* to contain more true *spirit of brains*, than any four lines that were ever before *retorted*. He intimates also, that the "*Continuation* was by ANOTHER HAND,"--not nearly equal, sooth to say, to the *great original*.---Such *bare-faced* impositions upon the public, I am convinced, cannot long pass undetected, nor go unpunished. 'Tis evident to all the world---if the world will but open its eyes, (and it's a blind puppy, if it will not)---that the *Continuator* is the *original* HIMSELF; no *other* person on earth being qualified to *imitate* HIS *inimitable* style so *inimitably*. In proof of what I assert, I here present you with

A SECOND CONTINUATION OF THE LIBERTY SONG.

V.

Troddle, troddle, 'tis got in my *noddle*,
I feel all my SPIRITS *arising*,
And if POP-LI-COLA I *now* should meet, O *la*!
I sure should do something *surprizing*.
CHORUS. What *stuff* is for a *Hero* fitter,
Than that which makes a *Comet-Splitter*?

VI.

A dog in a doublet, I'm not out of trouble yet,
He still *clings* his *tail* like a *hoop-pole*;
With *scurrilous froth* he attacks me, and *doth*
Refuse *for* to leave me a *loop-hole*.
CHORUS. But O! what feats my fame shall swell,
When once I've learn'd to *spe--ell*, spell!

VII.

Leave, ladies, your *tea-things*, my WATERS are *the* [things;
And *they* too will bring me some pelf in;
Your wants you must alter; so *Lags* * is a halter,
So's POP too---to *string up himself in*.
CHORUS. And who can fitter be to *swing*,
Than he who will not *cheat* the K---g?

VIII.

Such *clinging*, & *swinging*, & *ringing*, & *stringing*,
With so many *puny* PRETENCES;
I swear by old *Juppy*, I'll *poison* the *puppy*,
If ever--I *come* to my *senses*:
CHORUS. For that I'm mad's as plain a *case*,
As is the nose upon my face.

IX.

The TORIES are *rogues*, and *deceitful* sad *dogs*,
But it ne'er has been *said* that the WHIGS *lie*;
They're *chaste* and *discreet*, and their *words* are as *sweet*,
And as free from HOGOO, as--a *pig-stye*.
CHORUS. And *they* and I will do fine things,
'Ere yet the *whistling* BLACKBIRD *sings*.

X.

There are *blockheads* & *sots*, aye, and MACULÆ SPOTS,
As sure as the sun is *above* us:
Mundungus, and RHOMBUS, and *rascals* among us,
And SOME who *pretend* that they *love* us.
CHORUS. Sing *guns* and *sons*, and *sons* of guns,
And mark how *glib* my language runs.

XI.

I think I shall *match* him--I'll *kill* him, & *scratch* him,
With *blunderbuss*, CANNON, or *pistol*;
And as I'm a sinner, I'll *then* turn a SKINNER,
And *flay* him---*as clean as a whistle*. [sinner:
CHORUS. Sing sinner and SKINNER, & SKINNER and
Good *night*, gentle reader, I'm going to *dinner*.
GRAND CHORUS. HUZZA, HUZZA, HUZZA!
TO DINNER, to DINNER, to [DINNER.

☞ To be *continued*, as the *Tea occasion* may require.

* For the *tautological nonsense* of this elegant word, which, it seems, signifies a *string* in *French*, where it has *no existence*, and in *English*, where it was never used *before*, nor ever will be used again, a *halter*,---for *Poplicola*; so that this wonderful Being is a *Tory*, the *halter* of a Tory, and even a halter for that *very* Tory to *hang himself in*; see SKINNER's *Etymologicon*; a work highly esteemed by all *learned antiquaries*, amongst whom this *wonderful author* cuts so *conspicuous* a figure.

TO THE WORTHY INHABITANTS of the CITY of NEW-YORK.

THE cause, Fellow Citizens, which I espouse, asks nothing but an impartial judgment; and this impartial judgment, I have now hopes to obtain. Violent rage soon dissipates its own strength. The partizans of the *Dutch Company* have fired their vollies of obloquy, threats, and abuse: This was their whole amunition; and they must be therefore now quite harmless. I have ventured to lance the *imposthume*, and have allowed their *purulence* a free discharge; it may therefore be expected that they will not be quite so *restless* for the future. I am sorry, however that even the *name* of *liberty* should be disgraced by being subservient to indecencies of language unbecoming the characters of men; and could pity the authors themselves, was I not convinced that their callous insensibility will secure them from confusion on this occasion.*

I mean not to censure the persons in opposition. Many of them are undoubtedly lovers of their country; and many, with honest purposes, have been deluded by passionate exclamations for liberty. To such as these I address myself; and while I speak the language of candour and simplicity, I flatter myself I shall be heard, and heard not in vain.

That, if we purchase the Tea, our money will be taken from us *without our consent*, is, I believe, a position too ridiculous to be any longer imposed on the most credulous. Common sense will inform every man, that when he can buy an article, or reject it at his pleasure, his money, if he chuses to purchase, cannot be said, without the grossest absurdity, to *be forced* from him. If my opponents mean no more, when they say that "the money is forced out of our pockets," than that *the people will consent to buy the tea*, I will no more dispute with them, than I would, if they contended, that *smuggling* is for the good of the *community*, and a *Weasel* as large as a *Capon*; and afterwards informed me that they meant by "the good of the *community*," the *gain* of the traders to *Holland*; and by a *Weasel*, nothing else but a GREY GOOSE.

"But if we take the tea, say they, we *pay* the duty." In no other sense, say I, than as you may be said to pay the charges of manufacturing, storing, and shipping any commodity which you buy, whether it has been exported from *Holland* or *Great-Britain*. These expences are blended in the *value* of the commodity; and you may, with as much justice be said to pay *duties* to the *States of Holland*, when you purchase any articles of the *Dutch*, the price of which has been augmented by *customs*, or *fees* exacted by that government, as when you buy the teas of the East-India Company. The only difference in the latter case is a favourable one. That the price will not, on account of the duty, be raised, but the teas disposed of at AUCTION to the higest bidder.

"But our acceptance of the tea, it is urged, will be "construed into a *consent* that the Parliament may *may tax* "*us as they please*."

As this objection seems to have weight with many honest men, and as it is the only one that bears the least plausibility, we will carefully consider it in all its parts, and enquire,——

1st. Whether the tea exported by the India Company cannot be admitted without establishing a precedent against us.

2d. Whether a toleration of the Parliament's exercise of a power to impose duties on *their own exports*, can give them a claim to impose duties on the *exports* of the Americans, and to lay taxes on our goods, houses, lands, &c. &c.

1st. There is no necessary connection between our *receiving the tea*, and an *admission of their claim to impose duties*. For such an acceptance will give them a *claim*, neither by our IMMEDIATE *consent*, nor by PRESCRIPTION. By spirited resolves and declarations of our rights, we can hold up our *denial* of their *claim*, at the same time that we recieve the *teas* merely on the footing of their being of *convenience and advantage* to us. On the same ground we admit the *imposts* on *letters*, and import MOLASSES, tho' subject to a duty. Public protestations of our *denial* of their claim will bar them from founding their right on IMMEDIATE *consent*; and, for the same reason also, from pleading PRESCRIPTION. For *prescriptive* right, arising only from presumption of *tacit* consent, can never be urged where there has been a *publick* and *constant denial* of the claim.

But assuming (what has now been disproved) that their claim could originate from this root; I urge——

* The Reader is here presented with a Sample of the decent Epithets, which have been bestowed on POPLICOLA by his Antagonists:

Poplicola "is a Curse to the Community, and a Disgrace to Human Nature." "The *lying*, infamous, and sophistical Poplicola—Fye Poplicola, fye, you are a *Disgrace* to *Human* "*Nature*; and though I do not believe you have *Courage* to *rob* on the *High Way*, yet I doubt not your Baseness "would induce you to *pick Pockets*." A STUDENT OF THE LAW."

One would imagine he had *studied* at the *Forum* of *Billingsgate*. He says, "If *Poplicola* does not yield the Palm, "he must be hissed off the Stage." I cry his Mercy, give up the Palm, and confess that I have no more Stomach to contest with *him*, than with a *Bargeman* on the Thames. Had this Writer lived in the Time of *Scriblerus*, his Performance would have made no inconsiderable Figure in the *Bathos*. Reader, accept the following Specimen in the second Sentence of his Address, where he honours my PEN by making it in the same Breath, first a *Guide* leading its Neighbours into the *Dark* Mazes of Error, and then a *Wand* to *lull* their virtuous Apprehensions asleep: "He who *prostitutes* his PEN to deceive his Neighbours into the *dark Mazes* of Error, or to LULL their virtuous Apprehensions asleep."

— Peace and gentle Oblivion rest over the Ashes of such a *harmless* Composition!

—— But, poor Poplicola! how will you be able to resist, when not only *manly* PROSE, but those fair *Virgins*, the MUSES, appear against you!

Alas! what Perils do inviron
The Man that meddles with *cold Iron*. HUDIBRAS.

'Twould be a Pity, however, that so *sweet* a *Babe* of the Muses should *be born but to die*. I will therefore protract its Existence, at least for a Moment, by presenting it to my Readers.

A Hint, as a *Song*, to be improved, as the *Tea Occasion* may require.

There's POP—LI—COLA, that *Lags* of a TORY,
He came with *Scholastick-Pretence*,
By ingemination, 'twas inculcation,
'Twas *Tauto*—LOGICAL—NONSENSE.
Tolde—Roddle, Toroddle, toroll;
Tolde—Roddle, Toroddle, toroll, &c.

I confess, however, that tho' this PROOF might pass with some for the *true* SPIRITS of *Helicon*, yet it has a little of the *deadly* HOGOO of New England: And tho' I am no Poet (*nascitur enim, non fit*, and *Apollo* never smiled over my Cradle) yet I may answer in the Words of Shakespeare, That our Author may be a *well-meaning* Man, "But his "*Meaning* is like a Grain of *Wheat* hid in a *Bushel of Chaff*; "[illegible] search all Day for it, and when you have found it, "[illegible] *your Labour*."

CHARLESTOWN, *Nov.* 26.

Reports prevail that the office of Brigadier General is to be abolifhed, and that a Major General, on the American Staff, is to refide with the Commander in Chief at New-York. Several other new arrangements are likewife talked of.

The Eagle tranfport, with a company of the Royal Regiment of Artillery, under the command of Capt. Johnfton, from New-York, for Peufacola, is put into Jamaica.

BOSTON, Dedember 16.

It being underftood that Mr. Rotch, owner of the fhip Dartmouth, rather lingered in his preparations to return her to London with the Eaft-India Company's tea on board, there was on Monday laft a meeting of the Committee of feveral of the neighbouring towns, in Bofton, and Mr. Rotch was fent for, and enquired of whether he continued his refolution to comply with the injunctions of the body affembled, at the Old South Meeting-houfe, on Monday and Tuefday preceding. Mr. Rotch anfwered, that in the interim, he had taken the advice of the beft council, and found that in cafe he went on of his own motion to fend that fhip to fea, in the condition fhe was then in, it muft inevitably ruin him, and therefore he muft beg them to confider what he had faid at the faid meetings, to be the effect of compulfion and unadvifed, and in confequence that he was not holden to abide by it, when he was now affured that he muft be utterly ruined in cafe he did. Mr. Rotch was then afked whether he would demand a clearance for his fhip in the Cuftom-houfe, and in cafe of a refufal, enter a proteft, and then apply in like manner for a pafs, and order her to fea. To all which he anfwered in the negative; the Committees, doubtlefs, informing their conftituents of what had paffed, a very full meeting of the body was again affembled at the Old South Meeting-houfe, on Tuefday afternoon, and Mr. Rotch being again prefent, was enquired of as before, and a motion was made and feconded, that Mr. Rotch be enjoined forthwith to repair to the Collector of the Cuftoms, and demand a clearance of the fhip; and ten Gentlemen were appointed to accompany him as witneffes of the demand. Mr. Rotch then proceeded with the Committee to Mr. Harrifon's lodgings, and made the demand. Mr. Harrifon obferved, he could not give anfwer till he confulted the Comptroller, but would at office hours, next morning, give a decifive anfwer. On the return of Mr. Rotch and the Committee, to the body with this report, the meeting was adjourned to Thurfday morning at ten o'clock.

We are pofitively informed, that the patriotic inhabitants of Lexington, at a late meeting, unanimoufly refolved againft the ufe of Bohea tea of all forts, Dutch or Englifh importation; and to manifeft the fincerity of their refolution, they brought together every ounce contained in the town, and committed it to one common bonfire.

We are alfo informed, Charleftown is in motion to follow their illuftrious example.

fumed; the fourth fhip is caft away, and it is fuppofed the people of Sandwich have before now confumed the tea in their own way.

Tuefday night an exprefs arrived here from Bofton, who left it laft Friday, and brings fundry letters, among which is the following, viz.

Bofton, December 17, 1773.

Gentlemen,

" Yefterday we had a greater meeting of the body than ever. The country coming in from twenty miles round, and every ftep was taken that was practicable for returning the Teas. The moment it was known out of doors, that Mr. Rotch could not obtain a pafs for his fhip, by the Caftle, a number of people huzza'd in the ftreet, and in a very little time, every ounce of the tea on board of Capt. Hall, Bruce, and Coffin, was immerfed in the Bay, without the leaft injury to private property.

" The fpirit of the people on this occafion furprifed all parties, who view'd the fcene.

" We conceiv'd it our duty to afford you the moft early advice of this interefting event, by exprefs, which, departing immediately, obliges us to conclude.

By order of the Committee.

" P. S. The other veffel, viz. Capt. Loring, belonging to Meffrs. Clarkes, with 48 chefts, was, by the act of God, caft on fhore, on the back of Cape Cod.——[This was the 4th and laft veffel freighted for Bofton with tea from the Eaft-India Company.]

Further accounts of the proceedings of the people of Bofton, on the 17th of December.

About five in the evening fixty perfons in difguife went on board Capt. Hall's veffel, feized the chefts, and poured every ounce of tea into the water, after which they proceeded on board the veffels commanded by Captains Bruce and Coffin, took into their poffeffion all the tea they found on board, and caft the whole overboard, and to fatisfy the inhabitants that the deftruction was total and perfect, an exact account was taken by the acting parties, of every cheft fhipped by the honourable Eaft-India company, which was compared with the manifeft of the cargoes, and found to tally moft exactly with each of them. This execution was completed before ten o'clock at night, in the prefence of feven thoufand people, great numbers of whom were affembled from many of the neighbouring towns.

A certain Racoon named Connor, one of the fpectators, tempted by the exquifite flavour of the fineft hyfon, greedily filled his pockets, and the lining of his doublet with tea, which fo enraged the people, that after every grain of it was taken from him, and difcharged into the water, he underwent a horrible difcipline which threatened his life.

We have inexpreffible fatisfaction in acquainting our readers, that it is determined, on the arrival of the fhip Nancy, Capt. Lockyer, with the tea from the honourable Eaft-India company, the commander will be made acquainted with the fentiments of the inhabitants refpecting the fhipping that

Extract of a letter from Bofton, *Dec.* 17.

" Yefterday there were, in my opinion, 8000 people met at the South Meeting Houfe, and after trying all poffible means to fave the Company's property, in vain, the people (who had been fitting upon thorns for above an hour and a half) were by fix o'clock, on the Governor's peremptory refufal to give a let-pafs, fo enraged, that, as one man, they went to the wharf, and by nine all the three fhips were unloaded, and the tea effectually, and in the fulleft fenfe of the word, utterly deftroyed.

Bofton, December 17, 1773.

Gentlemen,

" Yefterday we had a greater meeting of the body than ever. The country coming in from twenty miles round, and every ftep was taken that was practicable for returning the Teas. The moment it was known out of doors, that Mr. Rotch could not obtain a pafs for his fhip, by the Caftle, a number of people huzza'd in the ftreet, and in a very little time, every ounce of the tea on board of Capt. Hall, Bruce, and Coffin, was immerfed in the Bay, without the leaft injury to private property.

" The fpirit of the people on this occafion furprifed all parties, who view'd the fcene.

" We conceiv'd it our duty to afford you the moft early advice of this interefting event, by exprefs, which, departing immediately, obliges us to conclude.

By order of the Committee.

" P. S. The other veffel, viz. Capt. Loring, belonging to Meffrs. Clarkes, with 48 chefts, was, by the act of God, caft on fhore, on the back of Cape Cod.——[This was the 4th and laft veffel freighted for Bofton with tea from the Eaft-India Company.]

Further accounts of the proceedings of the people of Bofton, on the 17th of December.

About five in the evening fixty perfons in difguife went on board Capt. Hall's veffel, feized the chefts, and poured every ounce of tea into the water, after which they proceeded on board the veffels commanded by Captains Bruce and Coffin, took into their poffeffion all the tea they found on board, and caft the whole overboard, and to fatisfy the inhabitants that the deftruction was total and perfect, an exact account was taken by the acting parties, of every cheft fhipped by the honourable Eaft-India company, which was compared with the manifeft of the cargoes, and found to tally moft exactly with each of them. This execution was completed before ten o'clock at night, in the prefence of feven thoufand people, great numbers of whom were affembled from many of the neighbouring towns.

A certain Racoon named Connor, one of the fpectators, tempted by the exquifite flavour of the fineft hyfon, greedily filled his pockets, and the lining of his doublet with tea, which fo enraged the people, that after every grain of it was taken from him, and difcharged into the water, he underwent a horrible difcipline which threatened his life.

PURSUANT to an order made by the Hon. Daniel Horsemanden and Thomas Jones, Esqrs; two of the judges of the supreme court of judicature for the province of New-York, upon the petition of James Seaman, of the city of New-York, shipwright, and several of his creditors. Notice is hereby given to all the creditors of the said James Seaman, to shew cause (if any they have) on the 31st day of December instant, before the said judges, at eleven o'clock in the forenoon of the same day, at the chambers of the Hon. Daniel Horsmanden, Esq; in Smith-Street, in the city of New-York, why an assignment of the estate of the said James Seaman should not be made to Messrs. Walter and Thomas Buchanan, and Comfort Sands, of the said city, merchants, pursuant to the prayer of the said petition, and he the said James Seaman be thereupon discharged, agreeable to the directions of the several acts of the legislature of the colony of New-York, for the relief of insolvent debtors, which were by an act of the Governor, the Council and General Assembly of the said colony, made and passed on the 8th day of March, 1773, entitled, "an act for the relief of insolvent debtors within this colony," allowed to the said James Seaman, and other persons therein named. Dated at New-York, the 14th day of December 1773.

New-York, December 14, 1773.

PROPOSALS

FOR PRINTING BY SUBSCRIPTION,

The Memoirs of the Life of the Rev. GEORGE WHITEFIELD, A. M. *late Chaplain to the Countess of Huntingdon,*

IN which every circumstance worthy of notice, both in his private and public character is recorded. Faithfully selected from his original papers, journals and letters.--Illustrated by a variety of interesting and entertaining anecdotes, from the best authorities.

To which are added,

A particular account of his death and funeral; and extracts from the sermons which were preached on that occasion. Compiled by the Rev. JOHN GILLIES, D. D.

CONDITIONS,

I. It shall be printed in large twelves, on good paper, and with new and neat types.

II. It will consist of about 300 pages, and the price to subscribers will be no more than Six Shillings, *neatly bound and lettered, although the London edition is near double that price.*

III. It shall be put to the press as soon as 300 have subscribed; and the names of the subscribers shall be printed at the beginning.

IV. The book as soon as finished, will be delivered to the subscribers, upon paying Six Shillings.

V. Those who subscribe for twelve books, to have a thirteenth gratis.

☞ *The universal esteem and applause which Mr. Whitefield received from people of all ranks and denominations on the extensive continent of British America, which he visited seven different times, encourage the subscribers to hope, that this book (compiled by a learned Divine) which gives a particular account of the life, travels, &c. of so worthy and eminent a minister of the gospel, will meet with that encouragement which it so justly deserves.*

HODGE and SHOBER.

Subscriptions are thankfully received by Hodge and Shober, the publishers, at the Newest Printing-Office, in Maiden-Lane, near the Fly-Market, and by all the printers and booksellers on the continent.

Just published, price 2s. 6d.

AND TO BE SOLD BY

Noel & Hazard,

THE SECURITY OF ENGLISHMEN's LIVES OR THE TRUST, POWER & DUTY OF THE GRAND JURIES OF ENGLAND,

EXPLAINED according to the fundamentals of the English government, and the declarations of the same made in parliament by many statutes.

By the celebrated John *Lord* Somers,

Who was eminently distinguished for his zeal in the glorious Revolution by King WILLIAM the third, and of whom Mr. WALPOLE gives this elegant encomium; That he was

"One of those divine men, who like a chapel in a palace, remain unprofaned, while all the rest is tyranny, corruption, and folly. All the traditional accounts of him, the historians of the last age, and its best authors represent him, as the most incorrupt lawyer, and the honestest statesman, as a master orator, a genius of the finest taste, and as a patriot of the noblest and most extensive views; as a man, who dispersed blessings by his life, and planned them for posterity."

† This work was composed to correct the sanguinary spirit of the STEUART reigns, by refuting the pernicious principle, that Grand Juries as accusers are not to enquire into all the evidence they can obtain. It was never answered, and is the only book that gives real light and instruction for the due discharge of the important office of a Grand Juror.

It is reprinted in a very convenient size for the pocket.

A new Edition of

LYON's URANIA,

The best collection of psalm tunes, hymns, and anthems extant, on thick paper, is just published. Price 12s.

To be sold at private Sale,

On reasonable Terms,

THE house and farm whereon the widow Comes now lives, being part of the estate of the late John Comes, situated in the town-spot of Jamaica on Long-Island, a most remarkable good stand for either a tavern or a merchant, being occupied in the former with credit, for many years. The house has six fire places, and the whole in good repair; in the yard is a new stone well, two barns and barracks, two corn cribs, with many other conveniences; the farm contains about 53 acres, part of which is excellent timber. The purchaser may have more land, either arable or wood, lying contiguous, if wanted; and likewise some stock. For terms apply to the subscribers, executors to the estate of John Comes, deceased.

KEZIA COMES, Executrix,
HENRY DAWSON, Executor.

Morris Town, October 18, 1773.

AT a meeting of some of the Iron-Masters of the province of New-Jersey, at Morris-Town, this day, it was agreed to adjourn the business of the said meeting to Wednesday the 29th day of December next, and to give a general and public invitation to all proprietors and managers of iron works in this province, and in the provinces of New-York and Pennsylvania, to attend in person, or by their proxies on the said 29th day of December, in order to assist [illegible] framing some regulations which seem absolutely necessary [illegible] carrying on iron works in this part of America, and will [illegible] the end be conducive to the advantage of the labourer, as [illegible] as to the proprietors.

PETER MACKIE, Secretary.

To be LET, and may be entered on immediately,

[illegible] VINE CELLAR,

[illegible] able to with[illegible] and uniform for [illegible] on which the [illegible]

Choice Spermaceti

CANDLES,

JUST ARRIVED,

AND TO BE SOLD BY

Samuel Burling,

At his Store between Beekman & Burling's Slip,

Also a choice Parcel of St. Vincent's

RUM, &c.

A CHIMNEY SWEEPER

For SALE.

TO be sold, a likely hearty Negro man, about thirty-three years of age, a CHIMNEY SWEEPER by trade, having served four years to that business, and is esteemed an expert hand:——He has also been used to attend on Gentlemen, take care of horses, &c. and is a handy active fellow. Inquire of the Printer.

BY order of Robert R. Livingston, jun. Esq; Recorder for the city and county of New-York, notice is hereby given, that on application made to him by Thomas Pearsall, one of the creditors of Henry Snelling, of London, in Great Britain, watch-maker, a non-resident, he did, in pursuance of an act of the Governor, Council, and General Assembly, of the province of New-York, entitled, "An act to prevent frauds in debtors," direct all the estate of the said Henry Snelling to be seized, and that unless he does discharge his debts within one year and a day from the time of such seizure made, all his estate, real and personal, so seized and taken, will be sold for the satisfaction of his creditors, provided the same be not within that time redeemed, and sufficient security given to the creditors of the said Henry Snelling to answer the value thereof, with the costs. Given under my hand, at New-York, the 15th day of December, in the year of our Lord 1773.

TO BE SOLD,

A CHOICE NEW

CLARICHORD,

Having four Stops,

Likewise a few Hogsheads of OLD JAMAICA SPIRITS; Also, a few Hogsheads of OLD ANTIGUA RUM,

By David Phillips,

At the Horse and Cart, in Horse and Cart Street.

For CORK and DUBLIN,

THE SHIP COUNTESS OF DONEGAL, ANDREW REED, Master.

FOR Freight or Passage, apply to GREG, CUNNINGHAM, and Co. or said Master on board, at Mr. VAN ZANDTS WHARF.

OFFICER's RIGHTS

To LANDS in AMERICA.

A PERSON ready to treat for the Purchase of them, may be heard of at JAMES RIVINGTON's.

BY virtue of an act of assembly of the province of New-Jersey, for the better enabling creditors to recover their just debts from persons who abscond themselves: Two fifth parts of a certain tract or parcel of land, situate near Perth-Amboy, between the roads leading to Woodbridge and New-Brunswick; containing in the whole about ninety acres, on which is a good dwelling-house, two barns, an orchard, and other out-houses; very pleasant for a gentleman, and convenient for any tradesman: Likewise, two fifth parts of two lots of very good salt meadow, lying upon the house lot creek in Rariton meadow, and distinguished by the inside and outside lots; the inside lot containing about five, and the outside eight acres. And also two fifth parts of another six acre lot of salt meadow, lying below Nathaniel Lufborough's, adjoining the Sound from Perth-Amboy to Woodbridge. The premises were late in the possession of Thomas Carryl, and attached in an action brought in the court of Common Pleas, for the county of Middlesex, in the province aforesaid, at the suit of Walter Livington, Esq; against the aforesaid Thomas Carryl. In pursuance of the act of assembly aforesaid, and by virtue of an order and rule of the said court of Common Pleas; we the Auditors, appointed by a rule of the said court, do give notice, that on Tuesday the 18th day of January next, at the house of Elijah Dunham, Inn-Holder in Perth-Amboy, the two fifths of said house, tracts of land, and lots of salt meadow aforesaid, will be sold at public vendue. The terms of sale will be made known at the time and place aforesaid. Dated November 2, 1773.

JOHN JOHNSON,
SAM. SERJANT, } AUDITORS.
WM. BURNET.

S. SP. SKINNER,

Near King's College,

IN NEW-YORK.

MAKES *the best of* RUM;—he makes it of a wholesome clean flavour, quite free from *offensive* DEADLY *stinking* HOGOO, and of substantial *natural proof,* and sells either for cash, or the usual credit, or for melasses.

FOR DOMINICA, ST. KITT's, ST. EUSTATIA, and the BAY of HONDURAS,

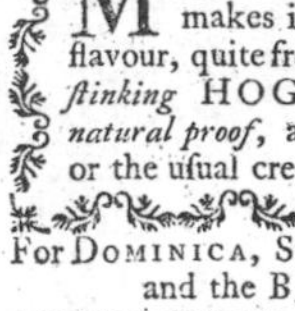

To sail in Ten Days

The Sloop SALLY,

JOSEPH CRAIG, MASTER;

FOR freight or passage apply to the Master on board the vessel at Garrison's wharf, or to William Malcom.

New-York, Dec. 8. 1773.

To be Sold,

At Public Auction, at the Merchant's Coffee-House in this city, on Tuesday the 18th day of January next, if not in the [illegible] disposed of.

A HOUSE and lot of ground in Smith-Street in the tenure of Dr. Chovet; the house is two stories high; consists of four rooms with fire-places; three bed rooms, cellar, cellar kitchen, an out kitchen with bed rooms for servants; a large yard, pump, cistern, gangway and grass plat; front and rear 24 feet in length, on one side 134 feet 6 inches; on the other side 130 feet. The title is indisputable. Any person inclined to purchase the same im[illegible] to John [illegible]

To be Sold immediately,

Or LET from the first day of May next,

THE valuable and improved farm, now in the possession of Mr. Samuel Brunson, lying in Smith's Clove, in the north part of Orange county, containing upwards of 1000 acres of upland and meadow ground of the best sort, situate about 55 miles distant from New-York, on the post road to Albany, and four miles from Hudson's River, where there is a water lot belonging to this tract: It is one mile from Bethlehem meeting-house, in which there is a ground right to three pews, reserved for the owner of the land. There is on the farm a house not quite finished, containing six rooms, one story and a half high, with cellars underneath, a barn, an orchard of about 100 apple-trees, and a cyder-mill; a fine living stream runs through the whole tract, and abounds with trout; a grist mill and saw mill, each about a mile distant from the house, adjoining this farm. There is also on the tract plenty of pure marl-lime stone, clay for bricks, and building stone; contiguous to this tract there is a large range for cattle, and many other advantages rarely to be met with; deer and plenty of game in their season. For conditions of sale, or terms of lease, apply to John W. Smith, attorney at law, in New-York.

Also to be sold, on very easy terms,

A number of farms or lots of land in the patent of Cheesecocks, Orange county, in Aquasan Hook patent, adjoining Batten Kill; in Deforrest's patent, lying on White Creek; in David Schuyler's patent, on the South side of the Mohawk's river, all in Albany, Tryon, and Charlotte counties. In Minisink patent, Ulster county; in the oblong patent, Westchester county; in Wilkin's patent, Orange county; in Col. Glen's patent, Albany county; in Dean's patent, Lake Champlain; in Garrat Slover's patent, Albany county. Also farms in the townships of Kingsberry, Queensberry, and Galway, &c. all laid out in lots and divided. For particulars, apply as before directed.

WE the Subscribers take this Method to forewarn all persons without Exception, not to gun, fish, or otherwise commit any Trespass on the Manor of Queen's Village, alias Lloyd's or Horse Neck, as every offender from the date hereof, may depend on being prosecuted as the law directs, by

Queen's Village,
Dec. 10. 1773.

HENRY LLOYD.
JOSEPH LLOYD.
JOHN LLOYD.
JAMES LLOYD.

RICHARD DEANE,

DISTILLER,

TAKES this method to return his sincere thanks to all his friends and customers for their past favours, and to acquaint them, he has now ready for sale, at his distillery, between the College and the North River, in Murray's Street, near Vauxhall,

A quantity of neat brandy,	Red ratifia,
Rasberry brandy,	Cinnamon water,
Cherry brandy,	Clove do.
Cherry rum,	Orange do.
Brandy shrub,	Annifeed, do.
Shrub of Jamaica Spirits,	All-fours,
Geneva,	Doctor Stevens,
Spirits of wine,	West-India and New-York rum,
Jamaica Spirits,	Madeira and Teneriffe wines, &c. &c.
Royal Usquebaugh,	

The good quality of said Deane's liquors has, for several years past, been well experienced, but in a more particular manner this last year; as the demand for them have exceeded his expectations tenfold.

☞ And still he is determined, if possible, to make better.

Being fully convinced, by long experience, that the surest means to acquire a speedy sale of the above articles, is to make them of full quality; at a moderate charge; as he is determined to sell on as reasonable terms as any one else. And good attendance, which, with every other endeavour to give general satisfaction, will be the constant study of the publick's Very obliged,

And very humble servant,

R. DEANE.

TO BE SOLD

By Public Vendue, to the highest bidder on Monday the 10th day of January next,

THE grist mill, saw mill, and plantation, late the property of John Brainbridge, situate upon Rocky Brook, in the township of Windsor, county of Middlesex, and province of New-Jersey. The plantation contains about 56 acres of excellent land, on which are erected, besides the mills, two good frame dwelling-houses, a blacksmith's shop, store-houses, &c. The grist mill is in good order, has two pair of stones, one of them French Burr, and stands upon as fine a stream as any in the province, for in the driest season, it was never known to fail; and being in the heart of a fine wheat country, it has every advantage for carrying on the business extensively. The saw mill is likewise in good order. This stand is also one of the best in the Province for a store, one having been kept there for many years past; and as it lies about midway between Philadelphia and New-York, the communication to both these places (the Stages from Burlington and Bordentown going twice a week) renders the transportation of goods to and from either of them extremely convenient, and at a small expence.

The purchaser, upon paying down one third of the purchase money, may have a reasonable time for the payment of the remainder with interest, giving security if required.

The sale to begin at twelve o'clock in the afternoon on the premises, where the subscribers purpose to attend and will give a good title to the purchaser, and immediate possession.

December 3, 1773.

JOHN IMLAY,
ISAAC WIKOFF, and
CURTIS CLAY.

TO BE SOLD,

By Christopher Bancker,

AT his Store near the Royal Exchange, formerly occupied by Flores Bancker, *who is now opening a fresh and general assortment of*

GLASS, CHINA,

AND

EARTHEN WARE,

All which he will sell cheap for Cash, or the usual Credit, wholesale and retail.

TO be hired out for a term of years, the owner having no use for him at present; a likely, healthy, handy,

Negro Boy,

About nine years of age. Enquire of the [illegible]

John J. Roosevelt

HAS FOR SALE,

At his Store in MAIDEN-LANE,

The following articles, just imported in the last Vessels from EUROPE.

THE most elegant and extensive variety of pictures ever imported into this place, one in particular with a very handsome frame and glass, of Regulus, opposing the entreaties of the Roman Senate, importuning him not to return to Carthage, price 14l.

- A large assortment of looking glasses, sconces and dressing glasses,
- A large assortment of japan'd tea boards, from 1l. 9s. to 6l. each,
- Japan'd tea chests,
- Tea urns, bread baskets,
- Plate warmers,
- Sugar tongs,
- Bottle stands,
- Plated do. paper do.
- Iron chests,
- Variety of paper hangings, writing paper,
- Sealing wax, wafers,
- Ink powder,
- Pocket books, with & without instruments,
- Inlaid mahogany tea chests, the cannisters lin'd with lead,
- Enamel'd do.
- Enamel'd sugar boxes,
- Plated, enamel'd, and brass candlesticks,
- Enamel'd tooth pick cases,
- Plated bread baskets,
- Plated snuffers & stands,
- Plated dish crosses,
- Plated milk pails,
- Plated tea urns,
- Plated coffee pots,
- Enamel'd ink stands,
- Enamel'd & paper snuff boxes,
- Paper dressing boxes, at 9l. each.
- Japan'd do.
- Corks with silver tops,
- Plated, japan'd, and ebony crewet frames,
- Glasses neatly cut, with silver tops,
- Silver'd labels for decanters,
- Japan'd quadrille pools,
- Silver hilted swords,
- Polished steel do.
- Maps,
- Dissected do. in boxes,
- Brass branches,
- A variety of cut and plain decanters,
- Wine glasses,
- Ale glasses,
- Salts, fruit plates,
- Sallad bowls,
- Jelly glasses,
- Toy crewets,
- Goggles,
- Wine and water glasses,
- An elegant assortment of burnt china jars and beakers,
- Fruit baskets,
- Butter tubs,
- Sauce boats,
- Pickle leaves,
- Milk pots,
- Plates,
- Kite's foot tobacco,
- 6 by 7, 7 by 9, 8 by 10, 11 by 9, 10 by 12, 10 by 14, 12 by 14, 11 by 13, 12 by 16, 13 by 16, 14 by 20, best crown window glass,
- Coach glass,
- Powder blue,
- White lead, ground in oil, dry do.
- Spanish brown, ground in oil, dry do.
- Yellow oaker, ground in oil, dry do.
- Verdigrise, ground in oil,
- Red lead,
- Vermillion,
- Prussian blue,
- White vitriol,
- Litharge,
- Amber,
- Gold leaf,
- Whiting,
- Painting brushes,
- Best pencils,
- Linseed oil,
- Spirits of turpentine,
- Harlem oil,
- Double and single refin'd loaf sugar,
- Lump do.
- Chocolate,
- Spices, &c. &c.

To be Sold,

Sundry very valuable TRACTS of

LAND,

Situated in the County of HUNTERDON, and Province of NEW-JERSEY, *viz.*

THE farm whereon John Tinney now lives, containing 187 acres, with a good house and barn; one half of the land cleared is extraordinary for wheat, and the rest good timber land. The farm is well water'd, and lies within three miles of New German Town, where there is a good market for all kinds of produce.

Also another farm, now in the possession of the aforesaid John Tinney, containing 218 acres, on which is a very good bearing orchard, a large quantity of very good meadow, and more may be made at a small expence. There is a sufficient quantity of the land cleared, and on the rest is extraordinary timber, which is much wanted in that neighbourhood.

A very valuable farm now in the possession of Matthias Cranmer, containing 287 acres, situated within one mile of New German Town, 150 acres of which are cleared, and is excellent wheat land; about 20 acres are meadow in good English grass, and much more may be made with very little trouble. There is a young orchard, a good house, and a very large Dutch framed barn, on the same.

A valuable farm in possession of Peter Blooms, containing 209 acres, situated in the township of Alexandria, about two miles from the river Delaware, and three from Alexandria whereon is a good house, barn, &c. 100 acres of the land are cleared, and extraordinary wheat land; about 20 acres of it are meadow, and more may be easily made.

A farm in possession of Joseph Fishbrough, containing 284 acres, adjoining Peter Bloom's farm; there are 100 acres cleared, which are very good wheat land, and a sufficient quantity of meadow, in good English grass, with a good house, barn, &c. thereon.

A farm in possession of Richard Reid, containing 146 acres, situated in the township of Bethlehem, five miles from the Union Iron Works, where there is a good market for all kinds of produce. It is extraordinary wheat land, 70 acres are cleared, with 15 acres of meadow, and a good house, barn, &c.

Also a farm, or tract of land, situated at New Windsor, in the county of Middlesex, and province of New-Jersey, within two miles of Hides Town, containing 134 acres, chiefly very good, and adjoins the farm whereon Richard Hutchinson now lives.

A farm, or tract of land, situated in the county of Monmouth, whereon Thomas Story now lives, containing 330 acres of excellent wheat land and meadow; it lies in a thick settled part of the county, and there is a ready market at hand for the produce. It is but at small distances from places of worship and mills, and there is a large young orchard, a new framed house, &c. on the same.

A tract of 180 acres, nearly adjoining the aforesaid tract very good wheat land and meadow.

A tract of land situated at Tom's river, in the county of Monmouth aforesaid, containing 813 acres.

About thirty farms in the county of Sussex, all in good repair, with good tenantable houses and barns.

Possession will be given by the first of March, and an indisputable title for the same, by Henry Cuyler at New-York, and John Smith, Esq; at Perth Amboy, of whom the terms and conditions may be known. (tf)

TO BE SOLD,

TWO stocking frames or looms, both in good order for working; one almost new, of twenty-three gage, the other of twenty-one; also, another frame of twenty three gage, somewhat older than the above, may be had, if wanted; enquire of Aaron Clark, living at the Fulling-Mills, in Elizabeth-Town Raway, where fulling, dying and dressing of cloth, is now carried on by approved workmen, who will endeavour to serve such as favour them with their custom, in such a manner, as they with reason hope will give satisfaction; they having every requisite for carrying on said works, they think at least equal to any in America.

TO BE LET, and entered upon the first day of May next, the dwelling-house and lot, in which Mr. Cornelius Clopper now lives, opposite Dr. William Browne[illegible]'s in Hanover-Square. Enquire of [illegible]

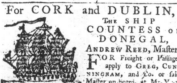

MONDAY, *June* 6. 1774. (NUMB. 2019)

The BOSTON Evening-Poſt.

Containing the freſheſt & moſt important Advices, Foreign and Domeſtick.

Printed by THOMAS and JOHN FLEET, at the HEART and CROWN in Cornhill.

Meſſ'rs PRINTERS,

Better is the End of a Thing than the Beginning thereof.

SOLOMON.

THIS obſervation of Solomon's I believe will be verified with reſpect to the tyranny which this country now ſuffers. The act for blocking up the harbour of Boſton is ſuch a violation of all the principles of juſtice and humanity, the laws of GOD and of reaſon, as will render it odious in the ſight of all rational and virtuous beings; and the wiſe and good through the world will unite in their ſupplications to the merciful LORD of the univerſe, that He would deliver this people from ſuch unparallelled oppreſſion! Human nature is ſhocked with ſuch barbarity, and every man of religion and honour will exert all his powers for the ſalvation of this highly injured Country. We are informed here, that the people of Boſton and other ſea port towns are greatly diſtreſſed with the tyranny which is coming upon them; but be not diſcouraged my countrymen, we have yet a glorious proſpect for Liberty before us, and I truſt we ſhall ſoon ſee the SALVATION OF GOD.—All the godly are ardent in their cries to HIM who has all tyrants in his hands and *is higher than the higheſt*, for your help—and he will hear and anſwer!

My countrymen, if the tyranny ſhould not ſpeedily be removed, we who live in the back country, intend to ſtop payment of the quit rents which we have heretofore given the King. This will be an act of juſtice and patriotiſm, for until our Rights are reſtored we muſt for our own defence keep all the money we can in the Country.

Many other things we have under conſideration, but before we make many important moves, we want to have the grand Congreſs or States-General, choſen by the whole Continent, meet and form the union and the plans for operation. When this is done, we ſhall not fear what man can do unto us; by the help of GOD we can do all things, and preſerve our Liberties unſullied to the lateſt generation. When once the ſtandard of Freedom is erected by the States General, Americans will flock to it in thouſands and tens of thouſands and millions! with a courage and ardour which nothing *human* can withſtand——Let no one deſpair, our cauſe is righteous, all good men will be for us, and none but the *vileſt* will be againſt us. We have every thing to animate our exertions, perhaps a more important cauſe never was ſuſpended upon human conduct, the fate of millions and unborn generations may depend upon our ſucceſs in this great concern——There is not a nobler, more moving and glorious ſight under the ſun, than a brave people ſtruggling for their Liberties! Heaven itſelf is moved with ſuch a ſcene! and the eternal GOD will look down with pleaſure to behold HIS offspring contending for thoſe ſacred rights which HE hath given them!

A COUNTRYMAN.

Green Mountains, May 19, 1774.

Meſſ'rs PRINTERS,

The following was received from Above.

"THE tyranny of the Britiſh Miniſters againſt America (I make no diſtinction between Boſton and other parts of the Continent, becauſe the tyranny is deſigned for them ALL) ſtands alone and unequalled in the records of Time! It will ſtain Britain with eternal infamy—but prove the Salvation of this Weſtern World."——

A PROPHET.

NEW-YORK, *May* 30.

Tueſday laſt the Grand Committee met according to Adjournment, and the Committee appointed to draw the Anſwer to the Boſton Letters, reported a Draught, which was unanimouſly agreed to, and ordered to be engroſſed and forwarded with the utmoſt Diſpatch: A copy of it was ordered to be tranſmitted by the Chairman, to the Committee of Correſpondence for the City of Philadelphia.

We are informed this Letter propoſes to the People of Boſton, that a Congreſs of the Colonies ſhould be convoked without Delay, to determine and direct the Meaſures to be purſued for Relief of the Town of Boſton, and the Redreſs of all the American Grievances.

We hear from Dublin, that moſt of the ſoldiers of the regiments, expecting orders to go from Ireland to America, who know and know not the country, openly beſpeak themſelves the happineſs of handſome wives, comfortable lots of land, and habitations on that continent, by a full exerciſe of their induſtry, and a removal from their preſent ſtations, firſt cauſed by a decay of encouragement in their native country, by the oppreſſions of their maſters and landlords.

BOSTON, June 6, 1774.

We hear the Corporation of Harvard College have voted that conſidering the preſent dark Aſpect of our public Affairs—There be no public Commencement this Year—and that the Candidates for the firſt and ſecond Degrees, ſhall receive their Degrees in a general Diploma. Which Vote hath been concurred by the Overſeers of the College.

The Meeting of the Overſeers is adjourned to the 14th of July, ſo that they who do not apply before that Time, cannot have their Names inſerted in the general Diploma, nor be admitted to their Degree this Year.

His Majeſty's Ships, Frigates and Schooners, are now placed in ſuch a manner in our Harbour, as will prevent any Veſſels from coming in or going out, ſo that the Act of Parliament for blocking up the Port of Boſton, is now in all its Parts carrying into Execution with the greateſt Severity, many Veſſels being already prevented from coming in, and Fiſhing Boats and other ſmall Craft ſtrictly ſearch'd; ſo that we have reaſon to expect, that in a little time this Town will be in a truly diſtreſſed and melancholy Situation.

Saturday laſt being the anniverſary of his Majeſty's Birth-Day, when he entered the 37th Year of his Age; the ſame was obſerved here by firing the Cannon of the Batteries in this Town; alſo at Caſtle William, and aboard the Men of War in the Harbour.

Wedneſday laſt arrived here three Tranſports in 5 Weeks from Portſmouth, having on board the 43d Regiment; which, with the 4th Regiment, that had embarked from Plymouth, is is ſaid are to be quartered in this Town; the 5th and 37th Regiments from Ireland, are alſo daily expected.

NEW-YORK, April 26.

A Congreſs of Deputies from the ſeveral Colonies is thought to be abſolutely neceſſary to deviſe means of reſtoring harmony between Great Britain and the Colonies, and prevent matters from coming to extremities.

all Trade with the Weſt Indies, we can ſtarve them and ruin their Plantations by withholding our Proviſions and Lumber in ſix Months, which will ſtop the 4 & an half per Cent to the Crown, ruin a great number of Merchants in London who are concerned in the Weſt Indies, & deliver us from the ſlow Poiſon we uſually import from thence. 3d, By witholding Flax Seed from Ireland can ruin the Linen Manufactury in twelve Months; this will reduce about 300,000 People to a want of employ, which with near an equal number of Britiſh Manufacturers in Great Britain reduced to the ſame ſtate, will ſoon muſter Tumults enough to fill their Hands and Hearts at Home, there is no ſatisfying ſtarving People but by killing or feeding them. Theſe are the means we are cooly deliberating, we have other things in contemplation, as ſtopping our Ports intirely and laying up all our ſhipping and ſome other things, ſhall try to convene a General Congreſs of all the Colonies as ſoon as may be. May *God* give Wiſdom and Firmneſs, Prudence and Patience, in this time of Trial."

One Day laſt Week, a Son of Mr. Iſrael Loring, Houſewright, near 8 Years of Age, accidentally fell from a Pile of Boards in his Father's Yard, by which he was ſo much hurt, that he died the next Day.

Yeſterday Afternoon died here Mr. *Richard Draper*, Printer, aged 47 Years, after a long and tedious Indiſpoſition, which he bore with the Patience of a Chriſtian and the Fortitude of a good Man.——His Funeral is to be on Wedneſday next.

The ſame Evening died Mrs. *Meriam Maſon*, aged 50, Conſort of Mr. *Jonathan Maſon*, Merchant. Her Remains are to be interred next Wedneſday Afternoon at 6 o'Clock.

DIED.] Mrs. *Hannah Robinſon*.—Mrs. *Mary Dillaway*, Wife of Mr. *John Dillaway*, Cooper.—Mrs. *Shaw*, aged 36.—Mrs. *Hayden*, Wife of Mr. *Hayden*, Shoemaker.——

Meſſrs. FLEETS,

AS ſome of my worthy Friends have thought (not a little to my diſadvantage) that I was a Signer to the Addreſs to the late Governor Hutchinſon; I beg leave thro' the Channel of your Paper, to acquaint them, that it is a miſtake, and eaſily to be accounted for, when the Reſentment is allowed for which the reading of this Liſt raiſes in the Breaſt of every Friend to the Commnnity, together with the near Sound Nathaniel Greenwood *bears with that of* Nathaniel Greenough; *but his Friends may be aſſured he never ſaw the Addreſs, till it was in the Paper of the 30th Inſtant, and conſequently never ſigned it.* The ſaid

---

Whereas Publick Notice has been given to the Proprietors of a Townſhip lying on both Sides *Amaraſcoggin* River, in the County of *Cumberland*, in the late Province of *Main*, granted by the Great and General Court, on the 11th Day of *June* A. D. 1771, to *David Phipps*, Eſq; and others, of the Taxes that have been aſſeſſed on the Rights of ſaid Proprietors; ſeveral of which are delinquent in the Payment of ſaid Taxes:—Said Delinquents are therefore hereby notified, that unleſs they pay their Taxes to *Seth Haſtings* of *Cambridge*, or *Samuel Harrington* of *Waltham*, Collectors of Taxes for ſaid Proprietors, by 7 o'Clock in the Morning of the 29th Day of *June* next, their Rights will be ſold (as the Law directs) for the Payment of their Taxes and incidental Charges. The Sale begin to at 8 o'Clock in ſaid Morning, at the Dwelling-Houſe of Capt. *Jonathan Brewer*, Innholder in *Waltham*, and continue by Adjournment (if need be) till the whole be ſold. To which Time and Place ſaid Proprietors Meeting ſtands adjourned.

May 29th, 2774.

Braddyll Smith, *Alex. Shepard*, *Nathaniel Bridge*, } Committee for Sale.

To the Honorable JEREMIAH POWELL, Eſq; one of His Majeſty's Juſtices of the Peace throughout the Province of the *Maſſachuſetts-Bay*, humbly ſhew,

The Subſcribers, more than five of the Proprietors of a Tract of Land lying in the County of *York*, ſituate between the Rivers *Great-Oſſipee* and *Little-Oſſipee*, within the County aforeſaid, containing the Breadth of all that Space between the ſaid Rivers, and ſo running Southweſterly from *Saco* River, more than Twelve Miles, which ſame Tract was purchaſed of one Captain *Sunday*, an Indian Sagamore, by *Francis Small*, who lived on the ſame Land a long Time, and had a quiet Poſſeſſion thereof, and the ſaid Petitioners being now in the Poſſeſſion of the ſame, and being deſirous of being an acting Propriety, according to the Law in that Caſe made and provided; do requeſt your Worſhip to call a Meeting to be held at the Houſe of Mr. *Samuel March*, Innholder in *Scarborough*, in the County of *Cumberland*, on the firſt Monday of *Auguſt* next, at Ten of the Clock in the Forenoon, to act on the following Articles, to wit:

1ſt, To chooſe a Moderator.

2dly, To chooſe a Proprietors Clerk.

3dly, To chooſe a Committee to tranſact the prudential Affairs of ſaid Proprietors.

4thly, To chooſe Agents to proſecute and defend Suits in behalf of ſaid Proprietors.

5thly, To agree on any Method for raiſing Money or ſettling the ſame Land, as alſo to agree on any Method for calling future Meetings.

May 17th, 1774.

Samuel Small,
Samuel Small, jun.
Samuel March,
Joſhua Small,
Benjamin Small,
Nathaniel Milliken,
John Wright,
Nathan Chicke,
Joſeph Small,
James Small,
Benjamin Mead Lord.

Province of the Maſſachuſetts Bay.

L. S.

To SAMUEL MARCH of *Scarborough*, in the County of *Cumberland*, in ſaid Province, Gentleman, one of ſaid Proprietors, Greeting.

In purſuance of the foregoing Application and Requeſt, you are hereby required to give Notice (in Time and Manner as the Law directs) to the ſaid Proprietors, that a Meeting of ſaid Proprietors is to be holden at the Time and Place, and for the Purpoſes mentioned in the afore-written Petition.

Given under my Hand and Seal, this 28th Day of *May*, A. D. 1774.

JERE. POWELL, Juſtice of the Peace throughout the Province aforeſaid.

May the 28th, 1774.

By Virtue of the afore-written Warrant to me directed, I do hereby notify and warn the Proprietors of the aforeſaid Lands, to meet at the Dwelling-Houſe of *Samuel March*, Innholder in *Scarborough* aforeſaid, on the firſt Monday of *Auguſt* next, at Ten of the Clock in the Forenoon, for the Purpoſes therein mentioned.

SAMUEL MARCH.

Lately broke out of Bridewell, a ſturdy well ſet Negro Fellow, about 27 Years of Age, well known in Town by the Name of *Pomp Fleet*:—He has had the Small Pox, the Marks of which appear very diſtinct in his Face, being much darker than the other Parts of his Skin; is about 5 Feet 6 Inches high; had with him a good dark brown Coat, white Breeches and Stockings, alſo black ditto, and often has his Wool dreſſed in the Maccaroni Taſte:—He is ſuppoſed to be lurking about with an Indian Wench, whom he calls his Wife.——Whoever will take him up and commit him to Bridewell, or to any of his Majeſty's Goals, ſhall be rewarded for their Trouble by the Printers hereof.

All Maſters of Veſſels and others, who ſhall harbour, conceal, or carry off ſaid Fellow, (who is a Servan) may depend on being proſecuted to the extent of the Law. June 4 1774.

No CUSTOM-HOUSE, Boſton, June 4, 1774.

THURSDAY, FEBRUARY 16, 1775. [No. 96.]

RIVINGTON's

NEW-YORK GAZETTEER; OR, THE Connecticut, Hudſon's River, New-Jerſey, and Quebec WEEKLY ADVERTISER.

PRINTED at his OPEN and UNINFLUENCED PRESS, fronting HANOVER-SQUARE.

Aſſize of BREAD,——*Flour at* 20s. *per Cwt.*

A Wheaten Loaf of the fineſt Flour, to weigh 1 lb. 8 oz. and a half, for 4 Coppers.

Publiſhed the 8th of December, 1774.

HIGH-WATER at NEW-YORK, this Week.

Thurſday,	46 min. after 9	Monday,	40 min. after 12
Friday,	30 min. after 10	Tueſday,	27 min. after 1
Saturday,	14 min. after 11	Wedneſ.	20 min. after 2
Sunday,	57 min. after 11		

PRICE CURRENT, in NEW-YORK.

Wheat, per Buſhel,	7s. 0d.	Muſcovado Sugar,	50 to 60s.	Fine Salt, 2s. 6d.	Coarſe do.
Flour,	19s. 6d.	Single refined do.	1s. 2d.	Indian Corn, per Buſhel,	3s. to 3s 6
Brown Bread,	13s. 6d.	Molaſſes,	2s. 0d.	Bills of Exchange,	£. 170
Weſt-India Rum,	3s. 4d.	Beef, per Barrel,	45s. 0d.	Do. at Philadelphia,	162-½
New-England do.	2s. 6d.	Pork,	60 to 65s.	Do. at Boſton,	

To the Americans.

Friends and Countrymen,

MUCH time and treaſure have been ſpent, to accommodate the conteſts between Britain and her colonies; though the affair has been very ſerious, yet not one juſt or proper ſtep has been taken to accompliſh it. Every one, who can ſee the length of his noſe, muſt ſee the folly of all irritating meaſures; ſuch ludicrous attempts have, and forever will widen the breaches between Great-Britain and her colonies. The temperate, diſcreet coloniſts, have been too indolent; whilſt reſtleſs ſpirits, by ignis fatuus, led the inconſiderate into the deep gulphs of ſedition, where they loſt virtue, loyalty, and good manners.

The mode of accommodation, or oppoſition, call it which you pleaſe, adopted by the congreſs, was borrowed from the ſeditious Boſtonians, who formed the plan, before the congreſs had a being, and was vigorouſly oppoſed, by the virtuous among themſelves, by the name of a ſolemn league and covenant; which the ſeditious entered into, in the manner, and enforced by the penalties, the aſſociation is eſtabliſhed by.

Had the congreſs checked the ſeditious then; had they ſupported the loyaliſts, who had long, bitterly complained; had they oppoſed the anarchy and tumultuous tyranny then prevalent; had they laid the Boſtonians under firm obligations to do juſtice to the India Company; and to make decent acknowledgments to their ſovereign, for their violence and inſults; had this been the preamble to the aſſociation, the port might have been opened, the three-penny duties and petty complaints removed, their loyalty and our liberty ſecured.

Something like this would have laid a foundation to have built upon; the congreſs might then have merited the praiſe of the Boſtonians forever, and of the colonies during good behaviour: This was the way to have entered into an accommodation; and it was ſo plain and obvious, that nothing but a peculiar inchantment could have led them from it: However, they joined the factious, and by that junction, the virtuous were and are perſecuted, all government trampled upon, the King's officers civil and military inſulted, and his property invaded: They alſo wantonly adopted, "approved, recommended," the ſeditious reſolves of Suffolk county. This imprudent, ill-timed conduct, threw the province into an irregular fit; out of which it is not likely to recover; confirmed the ſeditious, and gave too much countenance to ſedition in the colonies.

Now, ſeeing we can entertain no hopes of peace with our parent ſtate, from the mediation of the congreſs, let us conſider the proviſion made for the peace of the colonies. The aſſociation, which, with ſome, is every thing, is calculated for the meridian of a Spaniſh inquiſition; it is ſubverſive of, inconſiſtent with, the wholeſome laws of our happy conſtitution; it abrogates or ſuſpends many of them, eſſential to the peace and order of government; it takes the goverment out of the hands of the governor, council, and general aſſembly; and the execution of the laws out of the hands of the civil magiſtrates and juries. The congreſs exerciſes the legiſlative, the committees, the executive powers: The injuſtice and oppreſſion of the one and the other, are ſelf-evident: But as it is of the Boſtonian manufactory, a new edition, fitted to the neceſſities of his Majeſties moſt loyal ſubjects, at home and abroad, will ſoon appear in both worlds, with a pacific, patriotic addreſs, agreeable to the old, catholic, generous principles of the colony.

In the mean time, we muſt learn the humiliating doctrine of a blind implicit faith, and of paſſive obedience, and nonreſiſtance; for a committorial court of inquiſition, is introduced throughout the deluded colonies; with all its horrid appendixes; our lives, liberties, and properties are ſubmitted to it. Theſe inquiſitors and ſpies, are to inſpect, and watch the motions of the coloniſts, and to inforce a due obedience to the rules of the congreſs.

Their power is arbitrary and unlimited, they may judge by appearances, and condemn unſeen and unheard; they are under no check, there is no appeal to another court, they are not accountable to any power: Willing, or unwilling, we muſt be willing to obey the mandates of the congreſs; we, though unwilling, muſt will all the profits of our late importations to the ſeditious ſaints at Boſton. The charitable congreſs have given a title to them; the committees by, and with the authority of lawleſs mobs, claim them; the very leaſt theſe pious ſaints can do, for ſuch unheard of favours, is, to ſtir up ſedition, and pray for the continuance of ſuch charitable donations.

But, as the power is tyrannous, ſo, the puniſhment is horrible; they are authoriſed to proclaim his Majeſty's beſt ſubjects, foes to America! to paſs an act of outlawry againſt them! to caſt them out of all civil ſociety? deprive them of the benefit of law, and civil commerce! For the ſame reaſon, they might have proclaimed them traitors! ---Foes to America! Why are the beſt ſubjects ſo wantonly abuſed? Are they foes to the King? no, but you want they ſhould be. Are they foes to the laws of the empire or province? no, but the aſſociation is? Are they foes to the intereſt of America? no, but their perſecutors are. Why are the beſt men out-lawed, who obey the laws of God, of nature, of the province, and of the empire. Where there is no law, there can be no tranſgreſſion. How will the loyal Canadians reliſh your inſiduous, inſnaring addreſſes, when they hear of a tyranny that exceeds all they had ever heard of?

The Canadian act, which occaſioned ſo much canting on the one hand, and diſloyal invectives on the other, has no ſuch hoſtile appearance as this: This however, reminds me of a remark, that the late uſurper's finger was heavier than King, lords, and commons: He uſed theſe engines to cover and forward his rebellious pranks; and as he gained ground, he built upon them, until, at length, he and his tools paſſed an edict, that it was high treaſon againſt the common wealth, for any perſon, in any caſe, to aid and aſſiſt the King, the Queen even not excepted! By theſe wicked, arbitrary engines, the rebels were increaſed there, as they have been here; and a pretext given to murder the beſt people in the nation, and to ſeize their eſtates, the King not excepted!

Send back, we pray you, theſe inſidious engines of perſecution and cuelty from whence they came; for you have no reaſon, no right, no power to uſe them: How ſimilar your ends and deſigns are to his, your next edition may with horror inform us: Fie, fie, Americans, fie! Are theſe proofs of your love and gratitude to your good King, and happy country? Are theſe the effects of your feigned patriotiſm and liberty? You ſee who went before you, with all your ſpecious pretexts of patriotiſm and every thing elſe; and you know how they all ended. Review the tyranny, the horrors, and havock of thoſe days, and how long they laſted, even until all things returned unto the old channel again.

But it is time to think of terms of accommodation with our King and his parliament; and who are proper perſons to undertake this? The congreſs have adopted ſuch irritating meaſures, as diſqualify them for this pacific office; and we pray, that love and duty to their King and country may induce them forever to decline that very great undertaking.

After the hoſtile combinations entered into by the colonies, we can expect nothing of this nature from the throne; for our King cannot diſpence with the rebellion of the Boſtonians, without ſubmiſſion, and proper acknowledgments: He cannot repeal the acts of parliament in a lump; nor yet declare that they have not a lawful authority over us. If then, we go on, as we have begun, he muſt either attack us, ſword in hand; or, as he is averſe to ſhed human blood, he may lawfully ſell his colonies to ſuch as can, and will govern them. We cannot exiſt without government and we are not in a capacity to unite among ourſelves, nor to govern one another. And then like the miſerable Corſicans, we ſhall pay very dear, for our paſt rebellion and ingratitude.

It is then our duty and intereſt to offer terms of reconciliation, to our parent ſtate; and they ought to be reaſonable ones.—Such as may be made with ſafety on our ſide; and accepted with dignity on theirs. I can think of no example, ſo worthy of our imitation, as the Prodigal Son's. Let us then ariſe, and jointly, by and with the influence of our worthy Repreſentatives, go, and addreſs our moſt gracious King and the Parliament, ſaying, Fathers, we have ſinned againſt Heaven, and before you; and we are not worthy to be called your loyal ſubjects.—Such filial love, duty, and obedience, will aſſuredly meet with a kind, and welcome reception; and be indulged with all that we can reaſonably want here, or juſtly hope for hereafter.

By America's Real Friend.

Suffolk County, February 4, 1775.

An Addreſs to the Inhabitants of Cortlandt's Manor.

I am one amongſt you, tho' yet a ſtranger, an inhabitant of Cortlandt's manor; I have nothing to dread or fear from the reſentment of any perſon or perſons, as I mean to give no offence to any individual; only wiſhing, that reaſon and common prudence may take place of preſent bickerings, and the deteſtable poiſon of party faction. It is a matter no longer to be hid under a cloud, whether we are in reality, his Majeſty's loyal ſubjects or not; I have all the reaſon in the world to believe, that the worthy people of this Manor are ſo to all intents and purpoſes; I mean as to their private ſentiments; but alas! my friends, the time is at hand, when thoſe ſentiments alone will not be of ſufficient validity to juſtify the loyalty of your hearts. It requires no great penetration to aſſign reaſons for your ſilence in matters of ſo great importance; your conduct, my friends in this laſt point, is not to be blamed; it rather redounds to your credit in the eyes of every one that knows the life of a farmer. The farmer is brought up to peace and tranquility: politics, and the deſigns of crafty men are ſtrangers to his honeſt minds; his care and toil, with the ſweat of his brow, is to turn the furrows which give us ſubſiſtence: It is from induſtry, that worthy merchants are enabled to extend their commerce,—commerce! the vitals of a nation, every country has its ſhare in different commodities, deſigned by the will of an omnipotent Being to depend on each other, linked in a chain of civil ſociety. I preſume it will not be improper to ſee what part of this advantage providence has allotted us; the queſtion may be eaſily ſolved; we are placed in a fertile land, teeming forth, in abundance, the neceſſaries of life for ourſelves, and a ſuperfluity, which brings the wealth of other nations to our own coffers.-Every individual enjoys his ſhare according to his induſtry and ſituation in life; he is protected in his poſſeſſions, by what? 'Tis by the paternal care, the penetrating eye, and the mighty arm of his mother country; who like a hen, when the hawk is near, hovers round her chickens, takes them under her wings, and preſerves them from the enemy. I think I have accounted for your inattention to political matters, as not being within the ſphere of your occupations, but confined to the laudable purſuit of your own buſineſs; and, I ſincerely wiſh it to continue without interruption; to effect which, there is only one method left.—I have already obſerved, that our good intentions, kept in ſilence, are not ſufficient to diſtinguiſh our loyalty; It may do amongſt ourſelves; but let us conſider facts which we know to be true; they are recent in our memories, and need not recapitulation; it is ſufficient that we are informed of the conſequences in England, where they are conſidered as actions founded on rebellious principles, ſubverſive of all law and government, and abuſive, in the higheſt degree, to his Majeſty's crown and dignity. I have ſaid, I am one amongſt you, my ſituation has given me opportunity to form ideas of your behaviour and ſentiments, I believe you, in a general ſenſe, firmly attached to loyalty and our admirable conſtitution; that you wiſh to live and die ſubjects only to the Britiſh empire; but how is this to be manifeſted, and that it ſhould be declared, there is an abſolute neceſſity, without delay, for the following reaſons: That the coloniſts of New-York are under the ſame dilemma with the other provinces and the continent throughout, conſidered as combinants in a general plan, which gives ſo much offence to the ſupreme authority, whoſe dignity cannot, nor will not, be inſulted. Let us of Cortlandt's manor, clear ourſelves of the general imputation; we do not deſerve it, then, why ſhould we ſuffer it? We never conſented to congreſſes nor committees, we deteſt the deſtruction of private property, we abhor the proceedings of riotous and diſorderly people, and finally, we wiſh to live and die, the ſame loyal ſubjects we have ever been, to his moſt ſacred Majeſty GEORGE the THIRD. Let us my friends, declare, and acknowledge this, our indiſpenſible duty, by ſigning our names to the paper now circulating in this manor, wrote and adapted for the ſubſcription of none but ROYALISTS.---It is not enough for a man to ſay, that I am a loyal ſubject, no more than to ſay I am a pious and true chriſtian, it muſt be his work, his dependance on, his energy, his indefatigable effort; to promote honor and glory to the true ſyſtem of his preſervation. As charity, my friends, is a characteriſtic of a good man and a chriſtian, I wiſh by no means it ſhould be impaired, in this our manor of Cortlandt; permit me, my neighbours, to inſtance one point in particular to which I hope you will pay ſtrict adherence, viz. If you ſhould diſagreeably find any one, or more amongſt you who are blind to their own happineſs, let me intreat you to take no advantage of their weakneſs, rather uſe lenient and mild perſuaſions; tell them their true intereſt; uſe all your endeavours that if poſſible they may return to their right ſenſes:---In this you will ſhine in triple capacity, you recover the loſt man, you draw together the bands of unity, and are an honor to your King and country.

Form of an Aſſociation in Cortlandt's Manor.

WHEN the minds of people are agitated, ſome with juſt, and ſome with falſe ideas of their rights and privileges, when anarchy and confuſion are ſpreading their baneful wings over this once happy and flouriſhing Continent: At this moſt intereſting period, it is the duty of every individual, for the good of himſelf and poſterity, to purſue that courſe which conſcience dictates to be right. No one, if impartial, can be at a loſs for the clue of direction, the object is plain to every honeſt, tho' ever ſo illiterate capacity: The loyalty we owe to the beſt of Kings is the grand magnetic point, that will infallibly fix us on a ſolid baſis. There are none amongſt us (if we cooly reflect) but what will find themſelves bound by the ſtrongeſt ties of gratitude, to acknowledge that we have been, and ſtill may be, the happieſt people on earth, under the glorious and unparalelled conſtitution of Great-Britain! And if prejudice, popular declamations, and the hateful current of party faction, are not too ſtrong for truth and matters of fact; we muſt allow that the grand pitch of commerce we have arrived at, the progreſs we have made in arts and ſciences; the amazing rapadity in extending, ſettling and improving our land eſtates; the magnificent appearance and flouriſhing condition of our towering cities; the opulence of the inhabitants, and every other bleſſing under GOD which we *do*, and ſtill *may* enjoy derived their origin from, and have their exiſtence in the laws, the lenity, and the unlimited indulgence of our parent ſtate; which has hitherto protected us, is ever able, and would be ready, if we deſerve it, to defend us againſt all invaders of our peace and tranquility, by ſending to our ſupport the terror of the univerſe, the BRITISH ARMS!—For a proof of this let us revert to the late war, when the French and Savages with fire and ſword, were ravaging the country; when the cries of murder and ſcalping were echoed from every quarter of the woods; the infants brains daſhed out before the eyes of its afflicted parents; the parents tortured to death by the horrid and ſhocking barbarities of the Indians; and numbers flying from their habitations, expoſed to famine, and every ſpecies of diſtreſs. Let us reflect on thoſe direful calamities: Let us be grateful to the power which preſerved us, which ſent forth her INVINCIBLE VETERANS, vanquiſhed our enemies, and finally reinſtated us in quiet poſſeſſion of our own.—If we have a right to complain of the Britiſh acts of parliament, we have a Governor, Council and Aſſembly, to repreſent our grievances to the KING, LORDS and COMMONS; we are aſſured that we ſhall be heard: We have no buſineſs with *Congreſſes* and *Committees*. Such methods only ſerve to irritate our beſt friends Let us proceed in the direct line of our duty: We are contending with a mighty nation, of great mercy and long forbearance, ever ſparing of the effuſion of blood; but when rouzed to reſentment, we may feel the weight of her indignation.—Therefore we, the ſubſcribers, freeholders, and inhabitants of Cortlandt's Manor, in the county of Weſtcheſter, being actuated by no other motives than the dictates of conſcience and common ſenſe, are led to declare our firm and indiſſoluble attachment to our moſt gracious Sovereign GEORGE the THIRD, his crown and dignity; and with grateful hearts to acknowledge, that we are indebted to his paternal care, for the preſervation of our lives and fortunes: And as we have ever been a happy and free people, ſubject only to the laws and government of Great-Britain, we will pay no regard to any reſolves, or reſtrictions, but ſuch as are enjoined us by our CONSTITUTIONAL DELEGATES. Every thing to the contrary, WE deem ILLEGAL.

The above is ſubſcribed by ſeveral hundreds of the inhabitants.

To all perſons intereſted in the tract of land hereafter mentioned, containing 3000 acres.

WHEREAS Abraham Haſbrook, Jacobus Bruyn, and Richard Eſdall, purſuant to a law of the colony of New-York, did divide a certain tract of land commonly called the Wawayanda patent, in the county of Orange. AND WHEREAS the ſaid commiſſioners did ſet apart to the perſons holding the undivided rights of the town of Goſhen, (commonly called the Goſhen town rights) a certain tract of land of about three thouſand acres, ſituate in the ſaid patent, on the weſt ſide of the drowned lands, and bounded as follows; beginning at a heap of ſtones in the line of the Jerſey claim, ſix miles from the Miniſinck mountains; thence ſouth fifty four degrees, weſt ſixty four chains, to a white oak tree marked; thence north forty five degrees and fifteen minutes, weſt four hundred and fifty-four chains, to a traverſe line run along the foot of ſaid mountains; thence along the ſaid line north-eaſterly, as it runs to the aforeſaid Jerſey claim; thence ſouth forty five degrees and fifteen minutes, eaſt four hundred and eighty chains to the place of beginning, containing three thouſand acres of land, as by the proceedings of the ſaid commiſſioners, filed in the ſecretary's office of the ſaid colony, and in the clerk's office of the ſaid county of Orange, will fully appear. We the ſubſcribers being part owners of the ſaid tract of three thouſand acres, and being deſirous of having partition made of the ſame, purſuant to an act of the lieutenant Governor, the Council, and the General Aſſembly of the colony of New York, entitled, "An act for the more effectual collecting his Majeſty's quit-rents in the colony of New-York, and for partition of lands in order thereto," paſſed the eighth day of January, one thouſand ſeven hundred and ſixty-two and of other certain act of the Governor, the Council, and General Aſſembly of New-York, entitled, "An act to continue an act, entitled, an act for the more effectual collecting his Majeſty's quit-rents in the colony of New-York, and for partition of lands in order thereto; and alſo to continue one other act, entitled, "An act to explain part of an act, entitled, an act for the more effectual collecting his Majeſty's quit-rents in the colony of New York, and for partition of lands in order thereto," paſſed the thirtieth day of December, one thouſand ſeven hundred and ſixty-eight.

We do therefore, hereby give Notice, that Joſhua Davis, Elnathan Corey, and James Dolſon, all of the Precinct of Goſhen, perſons not intereſted in the ſaid lands, are appointed commiſſioners for the partition of the ſaid lands, and that they, the ſaid commiſſioners will meet on Monday the 15th day of May next, at the houſe of Samuel Gale, in the town of Goſhen, in the ſaid county of Orange, Inn keeper, to proceed to the partition of the ſaid lands, and all perſons intereſted in the ſaid lands, are hereby required to attend on the day and at the place aforeſaid, for the purpoſe abovementioned. AND WHEREAS it may be inconvenient for ſome of the Proprietors to attend at Goſhen, with their title deeds; we the ſubſcribers deſire all ſuch perſons to apply to William Beekman, of the city of New-York, Merchant, or William Wickham, of the ſame city, Attorney at Law, as ſoon as conveniently may be, and acquaint them with the proportions they reſpectively hold in the ſaid three thouſand acres of land, and produce to them their deeds: And it is further deſired, that all proprietors in and about Goſhen, would, previous to the above mentioned meeting, produce their title deeds to Daniel Everitt, Henry Wiſner, or Peter Clowes, in order that their reſpective proportions in the ſaid three thouſand acres may be particularly known.

Given under our hands the ninth day of February, one thouſand ſeven hundred and ſeventy five.

WILLIAM WICKHAM,
WILLIAM BECKMAN.

3m. 95

At a special meeting of the ... General Proprietors of the Western Division of New-Jersey, at the city of Burlington, on Thursday and Friday the 10th and 11th days of November,

PRESENT, &c.

IT WAS RESOLVED,

THAT as it is evident the Eastern Proprietors are not disposed to come into the equitable measures proposed by this Board, for settling a true line of partition between them, this Board will assert and maintain their right to the lands lying to the westward of a line to be run from the mouth of Machackamack, lately established as the northern boundary of this province, to the station point at Little Egg-Harbour, and to the eastward of the exparte line run by Mr. John Lawrence.

Also resolved and ordered,

That every proprietor or others holding under them, who have a right to locate lands within any of the first four dividends, may be allowed to survey the same on any part of the lands within the angle lying to the westward and eastward of the lines before mentioned, subject to the resolutions of this Board already agreed upon; and provided also, that those who have warrants now to locate, shall locate and return the same to the Surveyor General, within six months from this time; and all others who may obtain warrants hereafter, within six months from the date of such warrants. *Resolved also*, That a sixth dividend be granted, to be located within the angle only, at the rate of fifteen hundred acres to each propriety, the warrants therefore to be granted by the Council of Proprietors at their meeting in February next, or any subsequent meeting.

At another special meeting of said Board, on the fifth of December, 1774.

This Board having understood, that very ungenerous and undue means have been taken by the Eastern Proprietors or their agents, to induce such persons living within the angle, and who are actually, bona fide, purchasers under the said Eastern Proprietors, to believe that the Western Proprietors mean and intend to disturb their possessions and improvements, and to take their lands from them: This Board do resolve and agree, that they have no such sinister intention, but mean to give to every such purchaser, or those under whom they hold, the full opportunity of covering such their possessions and improvements with West-Jersey rights, at a reasonable and moderate price; and that in the mean time such possessions and improvements be secured to them without interruption or disturbance, or until an act of Assembly can be obtained to regulate the same, and finally obtain all matters in controversy between the said Proprietors: But that it is nevertheless to be understood, that no such favour is intended or can be shewn to any person whatever, who may hereafter chuse to run the risk of making any future purchases of the Eastern Proprietors, of any of the lands that are contained within the said angle,—this Board protesting against any sales of the Eastern Proprietors, which they may hereafter think proper to make.

The above resolves are directed to be published for the information of the General Proprietors, and all others who may be concerned. By order of the Board,

88 DANIEL ELLIS, Register.

New-York, Jan. 27, 1775.

By Order of the Common-Council.

Notice is hereby given,

THAT on Monday the 20th Day of March next, at three o'Clock in the Afternoon, at the Common Council Chamber, in the City Hall of this City, will be let to farm, by public Out-cry, to the highest Bidder,

The FERRY,

From Peck's Slip, to the new Landing-place or Wharf at Brooklyn-Ferry, for one Year, to commence on the first Day of May next. The Terms and Conditions may be known, by enquiring at the Town Clerk's Office.

Augustus Van Cortlandt, Clerk.

SAMUEL LOUDON,

HAS added to the CIRCULATING LIBRARY, since the catalogue was printed, more than two hundred volumes, and still continues to add to it: In the spring he intends to publish a supplement to the catalogue. The proprietor is ambitious of enriching his library, with an extensive variety of useful and entertaining books. Should any possess a superfluity of such books, they may have ready sale for them at the library.

AITKIN'S new edition of DILWORTH's spelling books is just come to hand; being one of the best ever published in America or elsewhere; printed with a new type, on good paper, well bound; with the addition of two elegant copper plates. Country stores, school masters and others, are supplied with these and other school books at the lowest prices.

Also to be sold by S. LOUDON,

Clark's martyrology, Willison's works, essay on the character, manners and genius of women, Smollet's works, Buchan's family physician, Crookshank's history church of Scotland, Hervey's works, Henry's commentary on the bible, Clark's family bible, with a variety of family and common bibles, psalm books; Walker's sermons, Bunyan's works, with a large variety of divinity books, history books, &c. Writing paper, sealing wax, wafers and Holland quills; also a pair 12 inch globes, pictures, perspective views, maps. He takes in subscriptions for printing Haweis's evangelical sermons, and communicants spiritual companion, in one octavo volume; Thomson's travels through Asia, the holy land, &c.

JUST PUBLISHED price 6d. a pamphlet containing an account of the surprizing deliverance of the Rev. John Rodgers, from a threatned imprisonment,---the conversion of a very young lady,---the wonderful goodness of God in the relief of the Rev. David Anderson and his family, when reduced to great distress,---the conversion of John Earl of Rochester, &c. &c.

The Vestry of the City of New-York,

Acquaint the Public,

THAT in, and by order of the court of general quarter sessions of the peace, now holding for the city and county of New-York, they were appointed overseers of the several public wells and pumps within the said city, for one year; and will, in consequence of said appointment, meet at the tavern of John Simmons, near the City-Hall, on Tuesday the 14th day of February instant, at 5 o'clock in the afternoon, to treat with any person or persons, that shall then incline to offer to take charge of the wells and pumps, during the time aforesaid. Dated the 7th Day of February, 1775.

By order of the Vestry,

Peter Berton, *Foreman.*

To be SOLD,

A Pair of Dappled Grey Horses,

FIFTEEN Hands and an Inch high, eight Years old next Grass, one got by Young Sterling, three Quarters Blood; the other got by Frederick, a well-bred Horse, imported from England, fit for Saddle or Carriage, they may be seen by applying to Mr. Leary, at his Stables.

Wool and Cotton Cards,

A Large Parcel,

To be sold by RICHARD SHARPE.

To be Let,

THE very commodious House and Store, in the Occupation of Mess. Greg, Cunningham and Co. The Situation for Business is the best in the City. Apply to Thomas Randal, or Theophilact Bache.

To be LET,

The HOUSE now occupied by Robert Alexander, and Co.

On Hunter's Quay.

For Particulars apply to John Miller, living in said House.

For Falmouth, in Old England,

The BRIGANTINE, CHARMING PEGGY,

JOHN LAWRANCE Commander

SHE is a prime sailor, has excellent Accommodations for Passengers, and will sail on Thursday next. For Passage enquire of the Commander on board, at Hallett's Wharf.

To all persons interested in the Lands hereafter mentioned.

WHEREAS Andries Coeyemans, the son and heir of Barent Pieterse Coeyemans, after the decease of the said Barent, by his humble petition presented to Robert Hunter, Esq; then Captain-General and Governor in Chief of the province of New-York, did set forth, that his said father, in his life-time, and at his death, stood seized of a certain tract of land, tenements, griftmill, and saw mills, and other inheritances, with their appurtenances, situated, lying, and being in and near the manor of Rensselaerwyck, in the county of Albany, as of an estate in fee-simple to him, his heirs and assigns for ever, by the grants or patents of former Governors of this same province, and other mean conveyances in the law, and prayed to have the same granted and confirmed to him, his heirs, and assigns for ever, by the boundaries hereafter mentioned, and confirmed within the bounds and limits of his father's said patents and deeds, for greater certainty and plainness, that is to say, beginning at a certain creek, called Peter Brouk's Creek, or the Creek of Coxhaxki, including the same creek on the west side of Hudson's river; thence up along the said river, as it runs to a brook over against the middle of Jan Ryersen's island, to a certain small run of water, thence from the said river backwards up into the woods west and by north, half a point more northerly, twelve miles English measure, being the northern bounds of said land; and the southern bounds beginning at the mouth of the said Peter Brouk his Creek, and thence up the same, including the same, as is aforesaid, until it comes to Coxhaxki; thence up into the woods by a due west course, until it is twelve English miles distant from the mouth of the said creek; from the west end of which distance last mentioned a straight line, drawn northerly until it meets and closes with the west end aforesaid northerly bounds, makes the westerly bounds thereof, and the easterly bounds thereof is the said Hudson's river.

AND WHEREAS her late Majesty Queen Anne, in consequence of and pursuant to the prayer of the said petition, by her letters patent, under the Great Seal of the province of New-York, bearing date the twenty-sixth day of August, in the thirteenth year of her reign, and in the year of our Lord One thousand seven hundred and fourteen, did give, grant, ratify, and confirm, unto the said Andries Coeyemans, his heirs and assigns, for ever, ALL that the said certain tract or parcel of land within the limits and bounds last beforementioned and described, together with all and singular dwelling-houses, grist mills, saw mills, barns, stables, gardens, orchards, buildings, edifices, and appurtenances.

AND WHEREAS the said Andries Coeyemans, did on the first day of October, in the year of our Lord 1716, for a valuable consideration, grant, bargain, sell, release, enfeof and confirm unto Samuel Coeyemans and Aryaantie Coeyemans, and to their heirs and assigns for ever, ALL those lands, tenements, hereditaments, houses, water, grist mills and saw mills, situate, lying and being in the county of Albany, in and near the manor of Rensselaerwyck, by such metes and bounds as are particularly mentioned and described in the said letters patent last above in part recited.

AND WHEREAS the said Andries Coeyemans afterwards intermarried with David Ver Planck of the county of Albany, and the said Aryaantie and David, or one of them, and the said Samuel Coeyemans have divided some part of the said lands and premises between them, and have sold and leased other parts thereof, on certain yearly ground rents.

AND WHEREAS the said Samuel Coeyemans, by his indentures of lease and release, the lease bearing date the fourth, and the release the fifth day of September, in the year of our Lord 1739, for the consideration therein mentioned, did grant, bargain, sell, alien, enfeof, remise, release, and confirm unto Coenradt Ten Eyck, and his heirs and assigns for ever, ALL his the said Samuel Coeyemans's estate, right, title, interest, property, possession claim and demand whatsoever, both in law and equity, of or into all such parts, purparts, shares, proportions and parcels of all and singular the said lands, tenements, hereditaments, rights, privileges, waters and streams of water, and appurtenances, herein before, and in the said indenture from the said Andries Coeyemans to the said Samuel and Aryaantie Coeyemans, particularly mentioned and expressed, and as then were in common and then as yet remained to be divided between the said Samuel, Aryaantie and David.

AND WHEREAS we the subscribers are part owners of all the lands contained in the boundaries last above particularly mentioned and described (excepting such parts thereof as have been heretofore divided, sold and leased as abovementioned) and are inclined to have partition made of the same, pursuant to one certain act of the Lieutenant-Governor, the Council, and General Assembly of the colony of New-York, entitled, "An act for the more effectually "collecting his Majesty's quit-rents in the colony of New-"York, and for partition of lands in order thereto," passed the eighth day of January, 1762, and of one other certain act of the Governor, the Council, and General Assembly of the colony of New-York, entitled, "An act to continue "an act entitled, an act for the more effectually collecting "his Majesty's quit-rents in the colony of New-York, and "for partition of lands in order thereto," and also to continue an act, entitled, "An act to explain part of an "act, entitled, an act for the more effectually collecting his "Majesty's quit-rents in the colony of New-York, and for "partition of lands in order thereto," passed the thirtieth day of December, 1768.

We do therefore hereby give notice, that Robert Yates, of the city of Albany, Esq; Thomas Palmer, of the county of Ulster, surveyor, and Caspar M. Halenbeck, of Coxhaxki, yeoman (persons not interested in the said lands) are appointed commissioners for the partition thereof, pursuant to the aforesaid acts, and that they, the aforesaid commissioners, will meet on Tuesday the twenty-first day of March next, at the house of Richard Cartwright, in the city of Albany, vintner, to proceed to the partition of the lands aforesaid (excepting as above-said) and all persons interested in the said lands are hereby required to attend on the day, and at the place aforesaid, for the purposes above-mentioned. Given under our hands, the ninth day of December, in the year of our Lord 1774. And we Jacob C. Ten Eyck, and Anthony Ten Eyck, two of the said subscribers, do hereby countermand an advertisement by us published in this paper, to notify the appointment of commissioners for the partition of the lands abovementioned.

JACOB C. TEN EYCK,
ANTHONY TEN EYCK,
DANIEL G. VAN ANTWERP.

To [all] persons interested in the Tract of Land last herein-after mentioned.

WHEREAS Edmund Andross, Esq; Lieutenant and Governor General under his Royal Highness James Duke of York and Albany, &c. of all his territories in America, did give and grant to Jan Hendricks Van Solsbergh and Gerrit Slichlenhorst, and to their heirs and assigns forever, all that certain parcel of land near unto Albany, lying on the eastern side of Hudson's river, and stretching along the river north north-east from a certain small creek or kill running from the second Claver to the creek or kill of Major Abraham Staats, in length twelve hundred rods, then stretching east south east, is in breadth five hundred and ten rod, then south south-west to the creek or kill called Keesywey's Kill, twelve hundred rod; and thence west north-west to the second Claver afore-mentioned, five hundred and ten rod, together with the drowned or sunken meadow adjoining, wherein are some small islands. The aforesaid parcel of land containing one thousand and twenty morgan.

AND WHEREAS partition of the said tract of land was afterwards made between the proprietors thereof, and the following tract was laid out as one distinct, separate and divided part thereof, and is bounded as follows: That is to say, "BEGINNING on the east side of Hudson's river, at a mark'd Eyper tree, standing by the mouth of Major Abraham's creek, on the banks of Hudson's river, and runs from thence south sixty-seven degrees and thirty minutes east, five hundred and ten rods, then south twenty two degrees and thirty minutes west, six hundred rods; thence north sixty seven degrees and thirty minutes west, five hundred and nineteen rods to the said river, by a small run of water; from thence along the said Hudson's river to the place of beginning, containing four hundred and eighty-four morgans, one hundred and fifty-two rods; also a segment of a circle of low meadow or drowned land on said river, containing about forty acres, together with a small island near the said premises."

AND WHEREAS I the subscriber am part owner and proprietor of the last mentioned tract of land: NOW THEREFORE, by virtue of a certain act of the Lieutenant Governor, the Council and the General Assembly of the colony of New-York, passed the 8th day of January 1762, entitled, "An Act for the more effectual collecting of his Majesty's quit rents in the colony of New-York, and for partition of lands in order thereto;" And also by virtue of another act, entitled, "An Act to continue an Act, entitled an Act for the more effectual collecting his Majesty's quit rents in the colony of New-York, and for the partition of lands in order thereto," and also to continue one other act, entitled "An Act to explain part of an act, entitled, an act for the more effectual collecting his Majesty's quit rents in the colony of New-York, and for partition of lands in order thereto," passed the 31st day of December, 1768. I DO HEREBY GIVE NOTICE, That *Henry Van Schaack*, of Kinderhook, in the county of *Albany*, Esq; and *Henry Glen* and *Hermanus H. Wendel*, of *Schenectady*; in the said county Esquires, not interested in the said last mentioned tract of land, are appointed Commissioners to make partition thereof, and that they the said Commissioners will meet at the Dwelling House of *Richard Cartwright*, tavern keeper, in the city of Albany, aforesaid, on Tuesday the 30th day of May next, to proceed to the partition of the said land; and all persons interested therein are hereby required to attend then and there for that purpose, either by themselves or their attornies. Given under my hand, the 7th of February, in the year of our Lord 1775.

JOHN DUNCAN.

WHEREAS we the Commissioners appointed pursuant to several acts of the legislature of this colony, for the survey and partition of the twenty-one following lots of land, (to wit)

Lot No. 2, in the general allotment, No. 3; lot No. 12. in the general allotment, No. 4; lot No. 12. in the general allotment, No. 5; lot No. 10, in the general allotment, No. 6; lot No. 5, in the general allotment, No 7; lot No. 7, in the general allotment, No. 8; lot No. 4, in the general allotment, No. 9; lot No. 2, in the general allotment, No. 10; lot No. 6, in the general allotment, No. 13; lot No. 4, in the general allotment, No. 14; lot No. 5, in the general allotment, No. 15; lot No. 9, in the general allotment, No. 16; lot No. 2, in the general allotment, No. 17; lot No. 10, in the general allotment, No. 18; lot No. 12, in the general allotment, No. 19; lot No. 6, in the general allotment, No. 20; lot No. 3, in the general allotment, No. 21; lot No. 11, in the general allotment, No. 22; lot No. 10, in the general allotment, No. 23; lot No. 2, in the general allotment, No. 24; and lot No. 8, in the general allotment, No. 25: which lots upon the general partition of a certain tract of land, in the county of Albany, called Kayaderosseres, alias Queensborough, fell to the share of Johannes Fisher, one of the patentees of the same, have proceeded to the survey, partition, and balloting for the said lots; but previous to the said partition and balloting, have, pursuant to the said acts set apart for defraying the expence of the said survey and partition, part of the said premises, to wit, all that 1000 acres of land, being part of lot No. 6, in the said thirteenth allotment of the genral partition of the said patent, bounded as follows, viz. beginning on the north bounds of the fourth general alotment, at a beech sapling, marked No. 5, and 6, being the south-east corner of lot No. 5 of said allotment, No. 13; thence along the same, north 83 chains and 66 links; thence east 85 chains and 76 links, to the west bounds of lot No. 7 of said allotment, No. 13; thence along the same, south 175 chains and 66 links, to a hemlock sapling, marked No. 6 and 7, in the north bounds of the fourth allotment aforesaid; thence along the same, north 57 degrees, west 50 chains and 56 links; and thence north 57 degrees west, 43 chains, to the place where it first began, containing 1000 acres of land. Now therefore, we the said Commissioners do hereby give notice, that on Monday the 13th day of March, next ensuing the date hereof, at the house of Robert Clenches, inholder in the town of Schenectady, will expose to sale at public vendue, the said premises to the highest bidder; and such title will be given to such purchaser, as is described in and by the said acts, by us,

THOMAS PALMER,
CHRISTOPHER YATES, } Commissioners.
BERIAH PALMER,

Dated at Albany, January 2, 1775.

To be SOLD,

A Valuable FARM,

(Late Major Bayard's)

LYING in Flushing, adjoining the King's-Road leading to Jamaica, and about half a mile from Flushing town; containing 235 acres of clear land, the greatest part of which is exceeding good meadow, where can be cut 30 or 40 loads of good English hay; about 20 acres of good wood land, 28 or 30 acres of very good salt meadow adjoining the up-land, which produces 60 or 70 loads of hay yearly, besides a quantity of sedge; a very good house two stories high, with four rooms on a floor, all in the best repair; a good barn, three barracks, waggon house, chair house, coach house, smoak house, fowl house, and other out-houses too tedious to mention; five large orchards, which produces between 60 and 70 hogsheads a year; a good cyder mill, adjoining a large store house, all under shingle roofs; with a variety of all kind of fruit trees. The whole is well watered, and a good well and spring near the house. Said farm is all in good fence, and in very good order either for a gentleman or farmer. Any person inclining to purchase the same, may apply to John Van Dyck, at Red hook, in King's County, or to Matthias Van Dyck, now living on the premises, and agree on reasonable terms. An indisputable title will be given

---

Spermaceti Candles,

Of the first Quality,

To be SOLD,

By DANIEL LUDLOW.

THE PARTNERSHIP

Of George Folliott and Company, is dissolved,

THEREFORE all those who are indebted to them are requested to make immediate Payment to George Folliott or John Moore; and all those who have any Accounts against said Partnership, are desired to send them in, that they may be adjusted and paid.

To William M'Donald, Esq; late High Sheriff of the county of Sommerset, in the Eastern Division of the province of New-Jersey, and to such persons as may be inclined to purchase the Farm and Lands, late of Cornelius Van Horne, of the said county, Esq; deceased, and to all others whom the subject of this notification may concern.

WHEREAS the said Cornelius Van Horne, was at the time of his death, indebted among other persons to John Chambers, of the city of New-York, since deceased, (whose Representative one of the subscribers Augustus Van Cortlandt is) in eleven hundred and seventy pounds, besides a considerable arrear of interest, and was also largely indebted to divers other persons, and being seized of a dwelling-house, barn, farm and tract of land, in Sommerset county aforesaid, containing upwards of 1000 acres, whereon he lived at the time of his decease, and which hath since been occupied by his widow Elizabeth Van Horne, and his son John Van Horne; he the said Cornelius Van Horne made his Will, and devised the same subject to the payment of his debts, to his said widow during her life, and the remainder to his son Philip Van Horne, Esq; and the said John Van Horne lately deceased. AND WHEREAS the said widow and children of the said Cornelius Van Horne, in order to satisfy the creditors of the said Cornelius, as well as their own creditors, did by indenture of release duly executed, and proved, dated the 26th of February, 1774; grant and release the said farm, plantation, and tract of land to the subscribers, Charles M'Evers and Augustus Van Cortlandt, in fee simple; in trust nevertheless, to sell and dispose of the same, and in the first place to apply the monies arising therefrom towards payment and satisfaction of the debts, due from the said Cornelius Van Horne, at the time of his decease, and then one moiety of the remaining money towards payment and satisfaction of the debts of the said Philip Van Horne, and the other moiety towards satisfaction of the debts of the said John Van Horne: AND WHEREAS we are informed that you, the said late Sheriff of the county of Sommerset, on pretext of Judgments entered against the Executors of the said Cornelius Van Horne, and against the said Philip Van Horne and John Van Horne, since the transfer of the said estate to us in trust as aforesaid, have seized and taken into your hands the said farm and plantation, and do mean to proceed to sell the same, at public Vendue; now therefore, to prevent all impositions upon purchasers, we have thought fit to give this public notice of our title to the said farm and plantation, that we intend to sell the same in execution of our trust, and to apply the money arising therefrom in the manner which the said Deed as well as the principles of Law and Equity direct. And we do hereby prohibit you, the said Sheriff from *selling*, and caution all persons against *purchasing* the said farm or plantation, under such Judgments or Executions as they would wish to avoid litigation and expence; we do further advertise, that we stand ready to agree with any persons for the sale of the said farm and plantation, at a reasonable price, either *all together* or in *parcels*; being advised by Council that our title, (which we are willing to produce to an Enquirer) will be good and sufficient to the purchasers.

Dated this 30th January, 1775.

Charles M'Evers,

94 Augustus Van Cortlandt.

Four Dollars Reward.

LOST,

A Ship's LONG BOAT,

COuntry built, twenty-one feet long, seven feet broad, with a black bottom, and bright sides, not painted, from Mr. Vanzant's wharf. Whoever will bring the said boat to Mess. Greg, Cunningham, and Co. shall have the above reward.

To be Sold,

ALL that certain Messuage or Dwelling-House, and the Store-House, adjoining, as also the Lot of Ground whereon the Dwel-House doth stand; and which is thereunto belonging, situate and being in Wall-Street, and in the South Ward of this City, belonging to Andrew Barclay, containing in front to Wall-street forty-two feet, more or less, in length on the South-East Side, 108 Feet, on the North-West Side, sevent-two feet six Inches; from thence westerly, nine Feet, nine Inches, thence South-westerly forty-two Feet three Inches in Breadth, in the Rear, 48 Feet six Inches.

For Particulars enquire of Andrew Barclay. If not disposed of at private Sale, by the 20th of April, it will be sold at public Vendue.

JOHN DAVAN,

LEATHER DRESSER and BREECHES MAKER, at the sign of the Crown and Breeches, next Door to Messrs. Robert aud John Murray, in Queen-Street, near the Fly-Market, NEW-YORK;

COntinues to carry on that Business as usual, in all its Branches, wholesale and retail: He has at this Time a great Variety of Buck and Doe Skin Breeches; Indian and oyl dressed Deer Skin for Traders or country Stores; the best of Shamoy for Linings, and Wool for Clothiers or Hatters to be had at all Times; and a considerable Abatement will be made to those who purchase a Quantity of any of those Articles.

N. B. Likewise a few very neat Caraboo Skins for Sale.

ROBERT R. LIVINGSTON, Esquire, one of the Judges of the Province of New-York, does hereby order notice to be given in all the public news-papers within this colony of New-York, that on application made to him by James Dole, of the city of Albany, merchant, a creditor of John M'Lean, of the county of Charlotte, in pursuance of four several acts of the legislature of the colony of New-York, one entitled, "An act to prevent frauds in debtors;" one other entitled, "An act to continue an act, entitled, an act to prevent frauds in debtors, with an addition thereto;" one other, entitled, "An act further to continue an act, entitled an act to prevent frauds in debtors, with the act therein mentioned;" and one other act, entitled "An act to amend and make valid the acts therein mentioned." I have directed the whole estate, real and personal, of the said John M'Lean to be seized, and that unless he does return and discharge his debts within three mouths after such public notice given, that all his estate, real and personal, so seized and taken, will be sold for the satisfaction of his creditors. Given under my hand this 24th day of December, in the year of our Lord 1774.

ROBERT R. LIVINGSTON.

The above order is published as the notice hereby directed, and all persons concerned are hereby notified accordingly.

WATERTOWN, June 17.

Last Thursday the inhabitants of the town of Boston were made acquainted, by the beat of drum, that an expedition was to be undertaken, against our enemy's ships in Nantasket road, and for erecting proper fortifications in the lower harbor. Accordingly detachments from the colonial regiments, commanded by the Colonels Marshal and Whitney, and a battalion of train commanded by Lieut. Col. Crafts, were embarked on board boats at the Long-wharf, together with cannon, ammunition, provisions, intrenching tools, and every necessary implement, and proceeded for Pettick's-island and Hull, where they were joined by some Continental troops, and sea coast companies, so as to make near six hundred men at each place; a like number of the militia from the towns in the vicinity of Boston harbor, with a detachment from the train, and some field pieces, took post at Moon-island, Hoff's-neck, and Point Alderton.—At the same time a detachment from the Continental army under the command of Col. Whitcomb, with two eighteen pounders, one thirteen inch mortar, with the necessary apparatus, intrenching tools, &c. were embarked for Long-island, to take post there; the troops did not arrive at their several places of distination till near morning, occasioned by a flat calm; notwithstanding, such was the activity and alertness of our men, that they had the cannon planted, and a line of defence hove up on Long-island and Nantasket-hill in a few hours, when a cannon shot from Long-island announced to the enemy our design. Upon which a signal was immediately made for the whole fleet, consisting of eight ships, two snows, two brigs and one schooner, to remove and get under way. The Commodore (Banks) bore our fire, and returned it with spirit, till a shot from Long-island pierced the upper works of his ship, when he immediately unmoored or cut his cables and got under sail, and happy for him that he did so, for in a small space of time afterward a shell from our works fell in the very spot he had just before quitted. Unhappily our cannon did not arrive at Pettick's-island and Nantasket, as soon as might have been wished, but the fire from the latter place being properly pointed against the Commodore's ship, who came too in the Light-House channel, is apprehended to have done considerable execution.—In short, the enemy were compelled once more to make a disgraceful precipitate flight; and we have it now in our power to congratulate our readers on our being in full possession of the lower harbor of Boston; and had the wind have been to the eastward, we are confident we should have had the much greater pleasure of giving them joy on our being in the possession of many of their ships. Through divine providence, not one of our men were hurt.

The ministerial fleet on Friday last, before they quitted the harbor of Boston, blew up the Light-House, which entirely destroyed the same.

We can assure the public, that there is not a ministerial troop in all New-England, except what are prisoners; nor is there a ministerial ship in any harbor in New-England.

Yesterday se'nnight the Highlanders taken in the Scotchman mentioned in our last, were conducted to the Provost prison in Boston, by a strong guard from Col. Glover's at Marblehead,—The officers are sent to Concord, and we hear the soldiers are going to Worcester.

It was reported yesterday at Salem that two large ships were taken the night preceding.

NEW-YORK, June 24.

Extract of a letter from St. Eustatia, dated May 31.

"By a vessel that arrived here this moment from Antigua, ... had arrived there from London, who brought an account that the grand fleet of foreigners were not to leave England till the middle of April, their sailing orders being postponed till that time."

Last Friday morning the two Philadelphia battalions, commanded by the Colonels Shee and Magaw, marched from this city for King's Bridge, where, we hear, they are to be encamped.

PHILADELPHIA, June 25.

Accounts, received this day from Canada, say that Gen. Thompson, with two thousand men, has been defeated by four thousand, and that the General was accidentally taken prisoner. But it is hoped that Gen. Sullivan, who appears to be in high spirits, will soon be able to give a better account of our affairs in Canada.

By letters from Boston received this day, we learn that soon after the men of war and transports were drove from Nantasket road, two more transports arrived there with upwards of two hundred Highlanders on board, which were both made prizes after some resistance.

Extract of a letter from New-York, dated June 24, 1776.

"Since my letter on Friday last, a most barbarous and infernal plot has been discovered amongst the Tories. The particulars I cannot give you, as the Committee of Examination consists of but three, who are sworn to secrecy, two of Washington's guards are concerned, and a third, who they tempted to join them, made the first discovery. The general report of their design is as follows: Upon the arrival of the troops, they were to murder all the Staff Officers, blow up the magazines, and secure the passes of the town. Gilbert Forbes, gunsmith, in the Broadway, was taken between two and three o'clock Saturday morning, and carried before our Congress, who were then sitting. He refused to make any discovery, upon which he was sent to jail, and put in irons. Young Livingston went to see him early in the morning, told him he was sorry to find he had been concerned, and, as his time was very short, not having above three days to live, advised him to prepare himself. This had the desired effect. He asked to be carried before the Congress again, and he would discover all he knew; several have been since taken, between twenty and thirty, among them our Mayor, who are all now under confinement. It is said their party consisted of about five hundred.

"On Saturday afternoon our men returned from the Hook, without being able to effect their design; not having heavy cannon sufficient to make any breach in the light-house, they made the attack Friday morning twenty minutes after three and continued firing till about six; no lives are lost on our side, only two men very slightly wounded.

"I have just heard the Mayor has confessed bringing money from Tryon, to pay for rifle guns that Forbes had made. A large party goes off his morning to the Hook again with heavy cannon, &c. the men of war there I am afraid will hurt them, as they can command the pass.—Burgoyne is arrived at Quebec with his fleet. No account of ours. I expect to go to Long Island this day, in a party of about two hundred, in quest of Tories."

September 7, 1776. THE PENNSYLVANIA LEDGER: Numb. LXXXV.
Or the Virginia, Maryland, Pennsylvania, and New-Jersey
WEEKLY ADVERTISER.
SATURDAY, September 7, 1776.
Philadelphia: Printed by JAMES HUMPHREYS, junr. in *Front-street*, at the Corner of *Black-horse* Alley:—Where Essays, Articles of News, Advertisements, &c. are gratefully received and impartially inserted. And Where Subscriptions are taken in for this Paper, at *Ten Shillings* per Year.

them through the Creek to the Chickasaw nation, where five hundred warriors from each nation are to join them, and then come by Chote, who have promised their assistance, and then to take possession of the frontiers of North Carolina and Virginia; at the same time that his Majesty's forces make a diversion on the sea coast of those provinces. If any of the inhabitants have any beef, cattle, flour, pork or horses to spare, they shall have a good price for them, by applying to us as soon as his Majesty's troops are embodied. I am, yours, &c.

HENRY STUART."

Wattaga.

This day Nathan Read came before me one of the Justices of Wattaga, and made oath on the Holy Evangelists of Almighty God, that a stranger came up to Charles Roberson's gate yesterday evening, who he was he did not know, and delivered a letter, a true copy of which is above.

JOHN CARTER.

Sworn before me the 19th May, 1776.
Attest. JAMES SMITH.

Extract of a letter from Charlestown, South-Carolina, July 21, 1776.

"You are undoubtedly informed before this that that detestable villain, Steuart, has prevailed upon the Cherokees to take up the hatchet against our countrymen, this however does not in the least intimidate us. Our people march forth against the savages with all the alacrity and cheerfulness you conceive, and with a full determined resolution to extirpate the whole tribe. The damage done to us by them is yet trifling. A number of the heads of the Tories in this province, when they heard of the breaking out of the Indians, wrote to our Governor, and told him that they never dreamt the King would descend to such low and diabolical designs, that they were now willing to do every thing in their power to assist their brethren in America.—These are men of influence on the frontiers, and will be very useful against the Indians.

July 27. "In a little brush with the Indians the other day, our people were succesful, killed, wounded and took prisoners a considerable number. Col. M'Intosh, of Georgia, with a party of his regiment, went out a few days ago to reconnoitre the situation of the two young Wright's, who are posted on St. Mary's river, which seperate Florida from Georgia. When he came within two miles of their fort, he was fired on from an out post of theirs, our Colonel returned the fire, killed one and took nine prisoners, upon which the fort fired an alarm gun; the man of war below hearing this, immediately detached a barge with a Lieutenant and nine men, all these the Colonel thought proper to seize upon.—In the brig lately taken here with Highlanders on board was found about £ 600 sterling worth of goods.

July 31. "There is now an expedition determined on to Florida, where the enemy have about 1000 men posted at St. Augustine."

WILLIAMSBURG, *August* 24.

Extract of a letter from Charlestown, July 29, 1776.

"Now at anchor off Charlestown bar, the Bristol of 50 guns, Experiment of 50, with a small sloop supposed to be armed, acting as a tender; the Palliser transport ship, still having part of the Experiment's cannon or stores on board: another transport ship and a brigantine, which have discharged the Bristol's cannon and stores they had on board.

"Within the bar, at anchor, the Active of 32 guns, Spyhnx of 20 guns, and the Pigot hospital ship, late an Indiaman.

"Sailed from the bar, on Wednesday last, a frigate of 20 or more guns, which arrived the day before, and steered to the Southward. The Syren of 28 guns yesterday morning steered the same course."

A letter from Hilesborough, north Carolina, dated August 1, informs us, that the Indians have committed some outrages on the frontiers of that province, have put to death many individuals, and murdered several families; but we hope their career is before this time stopped by some thousands of the militia that were marching against them.

WATERTOWN, *August* 26.

Last Wednesday arrived at Portsmouth, a prize ship of about two hundred tons burthen, mounting twenty guns, twelve of which wood. She was bound from the Bay of Hunduras for London, laden with mahogany and logwood, and taken by the Hancock and Franklin privateers.

By the eastern post we are informed, that on Monday last arrived at Portsmouth, New-Hampshire, a vessel from Holland, with dry goods, drugs, spices, &c.

The post from No. Four informs us of a gondola, with about twenty-five men, being taken by the enemy in Lake Champlain.

Yesterday morning a prize ship arrived safe in Marblehead, from Jamaica, laden with sugar, cotton, &c. She was chased in by the Milford frigate, and another cruiser, so near that one of the forts hulled one of the enemy's vessels. We have not heard by whom she was taken.

NEW-PORT, *August* 22.

By a gentleman from Dartmouth we are assured, that a privateer belonging to Fair-Haven had taken a very large Jamaica ship, with seven hundred hogsheads of sugar, two hundred hogsheads of rum, and a large quantity of cotton; this ship was so valuable, that the Captain of the privateer, who was the best pilot for the eastern shore of any on board went on board the ship to carry her in, and was parted with by the privateer last Sunday week. The privateer is arrived with more prisoners than men belonging to her.

NEW-HAVEN, *August* 28.

Last Monday passed our harbour, standing to the westward, two frigates, the Niger of thirty-two guns, Capt. Talbot, the other is said to carry twenty-eight guns, also a large brig of sixteen or eighteen guns, who had in company two small vessels supposed to be prizes. They left the English fleet, near New-York last Friday sevenight, and it is probable will remain in the Sound, to interrupt our communication with the army at New-York.

PHILADELPHIA.

Extract of a letter from New-York, dated Sept. 1.

"Last Monday morning we went over to Long-Island, and about midnight we were alarmed by the return of some of our scouting parties, who advised us that the English were in motion, and coming up the island with several field pieces. It was generally thought not to be the main body, but only a detachment, with a view to possess themselves of some advantageous heights. Upon which near 3000 men were ordered out, consisting chiefly of the Pennsylvania and Maryland troops, to attack them on their march. About sunrise we came up with a very large body of them. The Delaware and Maryland battalions made one party. Col. Atlee, with his battalion a little before us, had taken post in an orchard and behind a barn, and on the approach of the enemy he gave them a very severe fire, which he bravely kept up for a considerable time, until they were near surrounding him, when he retreated to the woods. The enemy then advanced towards us, upon which Lord Sterling, who commanded, immediately drew us up in a line, and offered them battle in the true English taste. The British army then advanced within about three hundred yards of us, and began a very heavy fire from their cannon and mortars, for both the balls and shells flew very fast, now and then taking off a head. Our men stood it amazingly well, not even one of them shewed a disposition to shrink.

"Our orders were not to fire until the enemy came within fifty yards of us, but when they perceived we stood their fire so coolly and resolutely, they declined coming any nearer, although treble our number. In this situation we stood from sunrise to twelve o'clock, the enemy firing upon us the chief part of the time, when the main body of their army, by a rout we never dreamed of, had entirely surrounded us, and drove within the lines, or scattered in the woods, all our men, except the Delaware and Maryland battalions, who were standing at bay with double their number. Thus situated, we were ordered to attempt a retreat, by fighting our way through the enemy, who had posted themselves, and nearly filled every field and road between us and our lines. We had not retreated a quarter of a mile before we were fired upon by an advanced party of the enemy, and those upon our rear were playing upon us, with their artillery. Our men fought with more than Roman virtue, and, I am convinced, would have stood until they were shot down to a man. We forced the advanced party, which first attacked us, to give way, thro' which opening we got a passage down to the side of a marsh, seldom before waded over, which we passed, and then swam a narrow river; all the time exposed to the fire of the enemy. The companies commanded by Captains Ramsey and Scot were in the front, and sustained the first fire of the enemy, when hardly a man fell.

"The whole of the right wing of our battalion, thinking it impossible to pass through the marsh, attempted to force their way through the woods, where they were almost to a man killed or taken. The Maryland battalion has lost two hundred and fifty-nine men, amongst whom are twelve officers. Capts. Veazy and Bowey, the first certainly killed; Lieuts. Butler, Sterrett, Dent, Coursey, Muse, Prawl; Ensigns, Coats and Fernandes; who of them are killed, or who prisoners, is yet uncertain. Many of the officers lost their swords and guns. We have since intirely abandoned Long-Island, bringing off all our military stores.

"Generals Sullivan and Sterling are both prisoners. Col. Atlee, Miles and Piper, are also taken. There are about a thousand men missing in all, We took a few prisoners. By a Lieutenant we took, we understand they had about 23,000 men on the island that morning. Most of our Generals were on a high hill in our lines, viewing us with glasses. When we began our retreat, they could see the enemy we had to pass through, though we could not. Many of them thought we would surrender in a body, without firing. When we began the attack, General Washington wrung his hands, and cried out, *Good God, what brave fellows I must this day lose!* Major Guest commanded the Maryland batalion, the Col. and Lieut. Col. being both at York. Capts. Adams and Lucas were sick. The Major, Capt. Ramsey, and Lieut. Plunkett, were foremost, and within 40 yards of the enemy's muzzles, when they were fired upon by the enemy, who were chiefly under cover of an orchard, save a few that shewed themselves and pretended to give up, clubbing their firelocks until we came within that distance, when they immediately presented and blazed in our faces; they intirely overshot us, and killed some men away behind in the rear. I had the satisfaction of dropping one of them the first fire I made. I was so near I could not miss. I discharged my rifle seven times that day as deliberately as I ever did at a mark, and with as little perturbation."

WAR OFFICE, *Philadelphia, September* 5.

CONGRESS having directed the Board of "War "to call in the several recruiting parties of "the German battalion, and that they have them "formed and armed with all possible expedition and "forwarded to New-York, taking measures and "giving proper directions to have the battalion re-"cruited to the full complement so soon as the same "can be done." The officers of the said battalion are hereby enjoined immediately to repair with their men to the city of Philadelphia, that the Board may take the necessary steps to fulfil the directions of Congress. RICHARD PETERS, Secretary.

time the conversation passed, and in Capt. Smithers's presence, as they were then employed together in paying for fire arms they had collected; on view of the receipts there appeared three of them with the figures plainly altered to the ninth, with different ink, which surprised the whole company. Randolph then strenuously insisted on a reference to Mr. Nixon's receipt, to prove his innocence of the forgery, which he said would appear the same day as his own, or the day before at farthest, when he received the money for the aforesaid purpose. Some of the referrees told Mr. Randolph, he appeared to be the reporter of the story to Mr. Williams; whereupon he grew so impertinent and noisy, that Mr. Meredith, after giving him several reproofs, genteelly shewed him the door. The company then parted.

On the 24th inst. Mr. Randolph being gone out of town, Mr. Williams went with me, and called on Mr. Maurice Rogers at Mr. Nesbit's store, for a sight of Mr. Nixon's receipt, which Mr. Randolph had referred to, Mr. Nesbit advised that some of the referrees should be present, on which Mr. Reese Meredith and Mr. Boyle were called in, and on examination found the receipt dated the sixth of July, agreeable to Mr. Williams's evidence.

Soon after my arrival in Philadelphia, being informed of this report of Reed's, I applied to the Council of Safery. As they had recommended me to his Excellency General Washington, I thought the report not only injured me but them also, as it cast a reflection on their judgment; they gave me a letter to Col. Thomas M'Kean, Esq; Chairman of the Committee of Inspection, referring the examination of this aspersion on my character to the Committee. The letter is as follows:

"Sir, In Committee of Safhty, July 10, 1776.

"Mr. Arthur Donaldson having informed this Committee, that in his late absence at New-York, the end and intention of his journey there have been maliciously and wickedly misrepresented, and his family made extremely unhappy by it; this Committee declare that he went there at the request of Gen. Washington, to assist in a defensive work of great importance, in which his skill and abilities, it was thought, might be usefully employed.

"Next to the duty of detecting and punishing those who are engaged in practices injurious to the cause of liberty, is that of acquitting the innocent of false and unjust accusations, and Mr. Donaldson looks for, and expects a public enquiry aud justification. This Committee, to whom he applied to set on foot such enquiry, have their time at present too much employed in many public services to enter into it, even if it was thought a proper object for them; but they are of opinion they cannot do better than to recommend it to the City Committee, who will, no doubt, chearfully take any trouble which so just and necessary business may occasion.

"By order of the Board, I am your humble servant,

OWEN BIDDLE, Chairman.

To Thomas M'Kean, Esq;
Chairman of the City Committee.

On my application to Col. M'Kean, he advised me not to pursue the matter; for the militia of this city, being then in motion for the camp, neither the Committee, the parties or evidences, could attend; the matter was therefore suspended. Mr. Randolph being at present engaged under Gen. Mercer, and staying but one day in Philadelphia, made it necessary for me to take this short method to vindicate my character, which, I hope, will satisfy the public of the innocence of their humble servant, ARTHUR DONALDSON.

Philadelphia, August 27, 1776.

In COUNCIL of SAFETY, Philadelphia, Oct. 1, 1776.

Resolved, That this Board will on Saturday next appoint twelve recruiting sergeants, to raise the more expeditious the quota of men to be furnished by this state to the continent, agreeable to a late resolve of Congress.

Ordered, That the above resolve be published, that persons willing to engage in that service, who can be well recommended, may send in their applications.

Extract from the minutes, JACOB S. HOWELL, Sec.

WILLIAMSBURG, Sept. 20.

Since our last, another vessel has arrived at Hampton, with twelve hundred bushels of salt; and on Thursday one came up to Burwell's ferry, with a quantity of that useful article, besides rum, sugar, linens, &c. She came from Cape Nicola Mole, and brings advice of an insurrection of the Negroes in Jamaica, on account of the scarcity of provisions. Between sixty and seventy white people had been killed, numbers of the Negroes taken and gibbeted, and martial law proclaimed through the island.

His Excellency General LEE is expected here daily, from the southward.

Last Thursday Capt. Theodorick Bland's troop of lighthorse arrived in town, from Petersburg. And yesterday arrived from Gloucester the seventh regiment of foot (late Daingerfield's, now Crawford's) in place of the fifth, who, as well as the fourth and sixth, are under orders to proceed to New-York.

BALTIMORE, Sept. 25.

Extract of a letter from a gentleman in Martinico, to his friend in this town, dated St. Pierre's, August 16, 1776.

"Every thing seems to indicate an approaching rupture between France and England, and you need not be surprised, if in my next letter, I inform you that hostilities are commenced. By a frigate, that arrived a few days ago from France, the General of this island has received instructions to protect all American vessels:—The like instructions were sent to Guadalope and St. Domingo, by two frigates that sailed at the same time, from France; in consequence of which, several guarda coasts are ordered to be immediately fitted out here, to cruise about the island, and afford protection to such American vessels as are bound here. Four ships of the line, and five frigates, are hourly expected from France, for the same purpose."

On Monday night, the 23d. inst. arrived here from Philadelphia, on her way to Virginia, the lady of his Excellency Gen. Washington, accompanied by Thomas Nelson, junr. Esq; (a Delegate from Virginia) and his lady, John Custis, George Washington Lewis, Nathaniel Nelson, and Robert Gates Esqrs. of Virginia; and this morning they proceeded for Alexandria.

NEWARK, (East New-Jersey) Sept. 21.

Since our last, printed in New-York the ninth instant, we have collected the following intelligence relative to the fleet and armies of our enemies, viz. That a battery was opened on a point of land on Long-Island, opposite the east end of Blackwell's-Island, which cannonaded our fort at Hoorn's-Hook for several days, but to little purpose, we having no more than two men killed and four wounded.—Wednesday the eleventh, a number of the enemy took possession of Bahanna and Montresour's islands, from whence it was imagined they intended to land either at Harlem or Morrissania.—Thursday the 12th, two ships of war made their appearance at Hellgate, having come through the Sound.—Friday the 13th, a signal gun was fired from the Admiral's ship at three o'clock,

P. M. when the Phœnix and Roebuck of forty four guns each, the Orpheus of thirty, and another frigate, got under way, and went up the East river, through a very hot fire from all our batteries.—Saturday the 14th, in the evening, four other frigates and two transports run up the East river, to join those that went the day before.—Sunday the 15th, the Asia, and two other ships of war proceeded up the North river, but were roughly handled by our battery at Powles hook; and the next morning, by daylight, the Asia came down much faster than she went up, three ships of war being nearly all destroyed by four of our fire ships that run in among them, and nothing prevented their total destruction but a gale of wind, that sprung up at that instant. The same day, about eleven o'clock, the enemy effected the landing of a number of men near Mr. Stuyvesant's house in the Bowery, about two miles from the city, under cover of a most tremendous fire from eight or ten ships of war, and in a few hours after took possession of the city of New-York.

We hear that the English troops attacked part of our army near the Blue Ball, last Monday, about four o'clock in the afternoon; that the enemy was twice repulsed, and beat back near two miles, leaving behind them many killed and taken prisoners, with three field pieces, some baggage, &c. &c. More authentic accounts of these affairs are hourly expected, when they shall be published in due season.

Wednesday last the Asia went up the North river again.

The same day there was a smart firing from Bergen point, at two tenders, a sloop and a schooner, that lay near Shutter's island, at the mouth of Newark bay.

Yesterday morning, a very heavy firing was heard on York island, at Bergen town.

We hear there are no more than one thousand of the King's troops now in New-York, and those principally Englishmen.

SEPTEMBER 28.

In our last, we informed our readers that the city of New-York was in flames on Saturday morning, the twenty-first inst. since which we had many and different reports concerning that melancholy affair, the most authentic of which, we believe, is as follows, viz. That the fire originated at or near Whitehall, soon extended to the Exchange, took its course up the west side of Broad-street, as far as Verlattenberg-hill, consuming all the blocks from the Whitehall up. The flames extended across the Broadway from the house of Mr. David Johnston to Beaver-lane, or Fincher's-alley, on the west, and carried all before it, a few buildings excepted, to the house at the corner of Bercley-street, wherein the late Mr. Adam Vandenberg lived, sweeping all the cross streets in the way. The buildings left standing on the west-side of the Broadway, are supposed to be, Capt. Thomas Randall's, Capt. Kennedy's, Dr. Mallat's, Mr. John Cortlandt's sugar house and dwelling house, Dr. Jones's, Hull's tavern, St. Paul's, Mr. Axtell's and Mr. Rutherford's. The cause of the fire is not known. We imagine about a sixth part of the whole city is destroyed, and many families have lost their all.

Wednesday last Brigadier General Sullivan, who was lately taken by the King's troops on Long-island, was exchanged for Gen. Prescot, who commanded at Chamble. General M'Donald would not be accepted for Lord Stirling.

Sunday last a number of the regulars embarked in boats from New-York island, near Greenwich, and it was supposed intended to attack Powles-Hook, but in the afternoon they disembarked, and gave over the attempt for that time. Monday the Roebuck, with three other ships, came too opposite our battery at that post, and after discharging about one hundred cannon, landed near five hundred men, our people having evacuated the place some hours before, and carried off their artillery, &c. They are now advantageously posted on the heights at the mill, about one mile from the enemy, and are busy throwing up entrenchments, having been reinforced with about four thousand men.

TO BE SOLD, a two story BRICK HOUSE in Front-street, and STORE in Water-street, next door to Mr. Benjamin Towne's printing-office, and nearly opposite the London Coffee-House. Apply to

WILLIAM HENRY.

KEYSER's genuine PILLS.

SO well known all over Europe, and in this and the neighbouring colonies, for their superior efficacy, and peculiar mildness, in perfectly eradicating every degree of a CERTAIN DISEASE, without the least trouble or confinement, are now selling, with particular directions for using them, at ten, twenty, and forty shillings a box, by NICHOLAS BROOKS, at his Dry Goods, Picture and Jeweller shop in Second-street, the fourth door above Black-horse-alley, at which place may be had Meredant's Drops.

Keyser's famous pills also cure the RHEUMATISM.

N. B. Good allowance is made to those who sell again.

Philad. October 1, 1776.

TAKEN out of the subscriber's bake-house, a METAL WATCH, with a China face, maker's name Dowdim, London, No. 1770. Whoever brings said Watch to the printer hereof, or to the subscriber, shall have TWO DOLLARS reward, and no questions asked.

ROBERT CRAFTS, baker,
in Second-street, near New-Market.

N. B. If offered for sale, please to stop it.

Baltimore, September 27, 1776.

TWENTY POUNDS Reward.

RAN away from the Northampton furnace, Baltimore county, the two following convict servant men, viz. WILLIAM ORTON (on the 24th of August last) an Englishman, about twenty-nine years of age, round visage, of a swarthy complexion, pitted with the smallpox, dark brown hair, a well set fellow, five feet nine inches high. He had on an iron collar with horns to it, a white kersey jacket, a sailor's green ditto, old striped Holland shirt, crocus trousers, and an old felt hat.

ROBERT BROWN (the 16th instant) an Englishman, a stout well made fellow, twenty-three years of age, five feet nine or ten inches high, long visage, dark complexion, dark brown hair, black eyes, by trade a collar and harness maker, had on an old kersey jacket, oznabrug shirt, a small round hat, and crocus trousers.

Whoever takes up said servants, and brings them home, shall have, if thirty miles from home, thirty shillings; if forty miles, forty shillings; if fifty miles, fifty shillings; if sixty miles, three pounds; if one hundred miles, five pounds; if two hundred miles, ten pounds for each, including what the law allows.

HENRY HOWARD.

N. B. Said William Orton has been a soldier, and has had severe whippings. Robert Brown writes a good hand, and may probably forge a pass.

Boston-Gazette, AND COUNTRY JOURNAL.

Containing the freshest Advices, Foreign and Domestic.

Printed by BENJAMIN EDES, in WATERTOWN.

MONDAY, October 7, 1776.

That though his Lordship had at present no power to treat with them as Independant States, he might, if there was the same good disposition in Britain, much sooner obtain fresh powers from thence for that purpose, than powers could be obtained by Congress from the several colonies, to consent to a submission. His Lordship then, saying he was sorry to find that no accommodation was like to take place, put an end to the conference.

"Upon the whole, it did not appear to your Committee that his Lordship's commission contained any other authority of importance than what is expressed in the act of parliament, viz. that of granting pardons with such exceptions as the Commissioners shall think proper to make, and of declaring America, or any part of it to be in the King's peace upon submission. For as to the power of inquiring into the state of America, which his Lordship mentioned to us, and of conferring and consulting with any persons the Commissioners might think proper, and representing the result of such conversations to the Ministry, who (provided the colonies would subject themselves) might after all or might not, at their pleasure, make any alterations in the former instructions to governors, or propose in Parliament any amendment of the acts complained of, we apprehended any expectation from the effect of such a power would have been too uncertain and precarious to be relied on by America, had she still continued in her state of dependance."

—— —— ——

In CONGRESS, *September* 16, 1776.

Resolved, That eighty-eight battalions be enlisted as soon as possible, to serve during the present war, and that each State furnish their respective quotas in the following proportion, viz.

	Battalions
New Hampshire	3
Massachusetts Bay	15
Rhode Island	2
Connecticut	8
New York	4
New Jersey	4
Pennsylvania	12
Delaware	1
Maryland	8
Virginia	15
North Carolina	9
South Carolina	6
Georgia	1

That Twenty Dollars be given as a bounty to each non commissioned officer and private soldier, who shall enlist to serve during the present war, unless sooner discharged by Congress.

That Congress make provision for granting lands in the following proportions to the officers and soldiers who shall so engage in the service and continue therein to the close of the war, or until discharged by Congress, and to the representatives of such officers and soldiers as shall be slain by the enemy; such lands to be provided by the United States, and whatever expence shall be necessary to procure such land, the said expence shall be paid and borne by the States in the same proportion as the other expences of the war, viz

To a Colonel	500 acres.
a Lieutenant Colonel	450
a Major	400
a Captain	300
a Lieutenant	200
an Ensign	150

Each non commissioned officer and soldier 100 acres.

That the appointment of all officers and filling up all vacancies, (except general officers) be left to the governments of the several States, and that every State provide arms, cloathing, and every necessary for its quota of troops, according to the foregoing estimate; the expence of the cloathing to be deducted from the pay of the soldiers as usual.

That all officers be commissioned by Congress.

That it be recommended to the several States that they take the most speedy and effectual measures for enlisting their several quotas. That the money to be given for bounties be paid by the Pay Master in the department where the soldier shall enlist.

That each soldier receive pay and subsistance from the time of their enlistment.

September 18, 1776.

Resolved, That if rations be received by the officers or privates in the Continental army in money, they be paid at the rate of eight ninetieth parts of a dollar per ration.

That the bounty and grants of land, offered by Congress by a resolution of the 16th instant as an encouragement to the officers and soldiers to engage to serve in the army of the United States during the war, shall extend to all who are or shall be enlisted for that term, the bounty of Ten Dollars which any of the soldiers have received from the Continent on account of a former enlistment, to be deducted from the Twenty Dollars offered by said resolution.

That no officer in [illegible] Continental army is allowed to hold more [illegible] one commission, or to receive pay but in one capacity.

September [illegible].

That the Adjutants of regiments in the Continental army be allowed the pay and rations of Captains, and have the rank of First Lieutenants.

In order to prevent the officers and soldiers who shall be entitled to the lands hereafter to be granted, by the resolution of Congress of the 16th, from disposing of the same during the war.

Resolved, That this Congress will not grant lands to any person or persons claiming under the assignment of an officer or soldier.

By order of Congress.

JOHN HANCOCK, President.

PHILADELPHIA, Sept. 18.

On Friday last Major General Prescot and Brigadier General M'Donald set off from this city to New York, in order to be exchanged for Major General Sullivan and Brigadier General Lord Sterling.

Several letters from France mention the very friendly disposition of the court and people of that kingdom towards the United States.

On Friday last arrived here from Martinico, the Continental ship of war the reprisal, Lambert Weeks, Esq; commander. On board of said ship came passengers several French Officers, who we hear are strongly recommended to the honorable the Congress by the Governor of Martinico. One of them it is said is an accomplished Engineer.

Extract of a letter from the West Indies, Aug. 2.

"Capt. Weeks of the Continental ship Reprisal, arrived off St. Pierre's, Martinique, on Saturday evening last, at which time the Shark sloop of war, Capt. John Chapman, of 16 9-pounders, just come from England, was at anchor there, slipped his cables in pursuit of the ship with provincial colours, and coming pretty near, ordered them to strike, giving her several shot, which were bravely returned by Capt Weeks, and an engagement ensued, which lasted near an hour, when the Shark bore away, and the provincial ship took the advantage of getting safe into harbour. Capt. Weeks had only one man wounded in the arm, by the bursting of a gun on board his ship—The loss of the enemy is not yet known. Capt Weeks, on landing, met with a joyful reception, from the Commander in Chief to the poorest inhabitant, the concourse of all ranks of people being very great on the occasion.

"Captain Chapman has since waited on the General to demand the ship for the King his master, as belonging to rebels and traitors. He was answered that he had no orders of this kind, but on the contrary to protect them, which he would abide by. Captain Chapman replied, if the ship was not given up, it would be considered by his Majesty as a full declaration of war on the part of France; and an express is sent home by the Admiral, at Antigua in consequence of this transaction.

"Captain Weeks, on his passage from America took three very valuable prizes, bound home from the West Indies; and as he put several men on board, to carry them into port, he had only 126 men in his ship, at the time of the action.

"The 29th ult. a frigate arrived express from Brest at Port Royal, with dispatches to the General, to have every Port in the French Islands put into the best posture of defence, and to protect, support defend and give every assistance to the American vessels, also to oppose his Britannick Majesty's ships that shall offer to commit hostilities on their coast. What they mean by this you may easily conceive.

"We have the happiness to acquaint you that from every account we have seen, Captain Weeks behaved extremely well, and has acquired much honor and reputation with the French at Martinique, many of whom were spectators of the whole affair."

HARTFORD, September 30.

Since our last many companies from the State of Massachusetts Bay have passed thro' this town on their way to join the American army near New York.

Last Thursday His Excellency General Washington was pleased to grant a dismission to the several regiments of Militia who lately went from the western part of this State, their place having been previously supplied by the arrival of the Militia from the Eastward.

Mr. Hugh Gaine, late Printer in New York, and who left that place when it was evacuated by our army, has opened his Office in Newark New Jersey, where he continues the Publication of the New-York Gazette, one of which we have received, dated the 21st instant, from which the following is extracted, viz.

NEWARK, September 21.

Since our last printed in New York, the 9th instant, we have collected the following intelligence That a battery was opened on [illegible] Long-Island opposite the end of Blackwell's Island which cannonaded our fort on Horn's Hook for several days, but to little purpose, we having no more than two men killed and four wounded.— Wednesday the 11th, a number of the enemy took possession of Bahanna and Montresure's islands, from whence it was imagined they intended to land either at Harlem or Morrissania. Thursday the 12th, two ships of war made their appearance at Hell Gate, having come thro' the Sound. Friday the 13th, a signal gun was fired from the admiral's ship at 3 o'clock, P. M. when the Phoenix and Roebuck of 44 guns, the Orpheus of 30, and another frigate, got under way, and went up the East River, through a very hot fire from all our batteries. Saturday the 14th, in the evening 4 other frigates and 2 transports run up the East-River, to join those that went the day before.— Sunday the 15th, the Asia, and 2 other ships of war proceed up the North River, but were roughly handled by our battery at Powles Hook; and the next morning by day light, the Asia came down much faster than she went up, the 2 ships of war being nearly all destroyed by 4 of our fire ships that run in among them, and nothing prevented their total destruction but a gale of wind that sprung up at that instant. On Sunday the 15th, about 11 o'clock, the enemy effected the landing of a number of men near Mr. Stuyvesant's house in the Bowrey, about two miles from the city, under cover of a most tremendous fire from 8 or 10 ships of war, and in a few hours after took possession of the city of New-York.

— — — — —

NEW-LONDON, Sept. 27.

Extract of a letter from an officer in the army, to his friend in this town, dated New Harlem, September 21, 1776.

"Last Monday the enemy landed at New-York, under cover of their shipping, when our whole army retreated to this place. As for myself I was out on a scouting party as far as Hunt's point—and on hearing the cannon I immediately returned to the regiment of rangers, but too late to go into the city—Well, on Monday morning the General ordered us to go and take the enemy's advanced guard; accordingly we set out just before day, and found where they were; at day-brake we were discovered by the enemy, who were 400 strong, and we were 120—they marched up within six Rods of us, and there form'd to give us battle, which we were ready for; and Colonel Knowlton gave Orders to fire, which we did, and stood theirs 'till we perceived they were getting their flank-guards round us. After giving them eight rounds a piece the Colonel gave orders for retreating, which we performed very well, without the loss of a man while retreating, though we lost about 10 while in action. We retreated two miles and a half and then made a stand, and sent off for a reinforcement, which we soon received, and drove the dogs near three miles.—My poor Colonel, in the second attack, was shot just by my side, the ball entered the small of his back—I took hold of him, asked him if he was badly woundly? he told me he was; but, says he, I do not value my life if we do but get the day: I then ordered two men to carry him off. He desired me by all means to keep up this flank. He seemed as unconcerned and calm as tho' nothing had happened to him. In the spot where the Colonel was wounded, at least within 4 rods round him, lay 15 or 16 of the Enemy dead, with 5 or 6 of our people. Several deserters say we made great havock among them. The next day we went to bury our dead, and found near a dozen with their heads split open by the Hessians."

Extract of a Letter from a Gentleman in our Army near New York, dated September 23, 1776.

"Some say part of the fleet are sailed—if they are going off, it is most likely they are going on the last part of their Ordert, to burn and destroy the Sea Ports—In the Action of last Monday, we killed 300 of the Enemy, and wounded 500."

— — — — —

PORTSMOUTH, September 28.

On Thurday last arrived here the Prize ship *Royal Exchange*, Lawrence Bowden late master, she was taken by the Continental ship Columbus, Abraham Whipple, Esq; commander, on the 29th ult. on her passage from Grenada to London, having on board a valuable cargo, consisting of two hundred and eighty four hogsheads and 2 tierces of Sugar, fifty five hogsheads of Rum, 11 hhds Coffee, 2 bales Cotton, and some Madeira Wine. The Prize master (Mr. Olney) informs of two other prizes being taken by the Columbus, just before this, on their passage to Europe from the West Indies; and in his passage hither spoke with the Providence Brigantine belonging to the United States, who informed him of her taking two valuable prizes, and sent into Providence.

15th, that he is going to break up Eaſt Florida. Preſident Rutledge in a letter to the Council writes, that the South Carolinians had deſtroyed five Indian towns in the lower ſettlements, and laid waſte their fields of corn. They have had two ſkirmiſhes, in which the Carolinians have been ſucceſsful. They ſuppoſe they killed between 60 and 70 men.

Another veſſel is arrived at Hampton with 1400 buſhels of ſalt, and a ſmall quantity of rum. The captain informs, that he ſpoke a French ſhip, one of a fleet of 14 ſail, laden with goods, and bound for Delaware. A number of French officers were likewiſe on board, who intended to offer their ſervices to the United States of America.

BOSTON, October 3.

Saturday laſt arrived at Cape Ann from a ſhort cruiſe, Capt. Coos, and carried in with him another fine prize ſhip from the Weſt Indies, with 394 hogſheads ſugar, 180 puncheons rum, 50 bags cotton, 20 caſks indigo, 20 caſks turtleſhell, 70 turtle, a quantity of mehogany ſome plate & caſh.

WATERTOWN, October 7.

Wedneſday laſt arrived at Boſton, a prize brig, taken by the Continental ſhip Columbus, Abraham Whipple, Eſq; Commander, bound from Antigua to Ireland, laden with Rum.

Laſt Wedneſday returned to Salem, after a ſhort Cruiſe, the Brigantine Maſſachuſetts, of this State, commanded by Capt. Souther He informs that a few Days after he ſailed he fell in with and took a Brigantine of about 250 Tons, from Falmouth in England, mounting ſix 3 pounders, and having on board a Captain and about 20 Privates of the 16th Regiment of Dragoons with their Horſes and Accoutrements, alſo the Chaplain of ſaid Regiment, and ſome Dry Goods, which the Captain ſays is his own Property. The whole Number of Priſoners 35. This Veſſel ſailed from Falmouth the 27th of July, juſt a month after they embarked, in Company with 12 others, under Convoy of the Daphne of 32 Guns, from whom they parted but a Day or two before they were taken; they all had the ſame Kind of Cargo, making in the whole 230 Horſes. A Fleet of about 70 Sail ſailed about three Days before them under a ſtrong Convoy having on board the Remainder of the 16th Regiment of Dragoons, and the laſt Diviſion of Hanoverians, conſiſting 'tis ſaid, of 5000 men, bound to New York; they were ſhort of Horſe Proviſions, ſome of the Horſes died of the Staggers, and 'tis ſuppoſed the late Gales have deſtroyed many more. The People in England, we hear, began to be very uneaſy.

The Prize above mentioned we learn arrived at Townſend at the Eaſtward the middle of laſt week

A Privateer belonging to Salem which arrived there laſt Thurſday fell in with the Fleet of twelve Sail, and was ſo cloſely purſued by the Daphne that the Enemy fired muſket balls into her; but by heaving over all her Guns, Water and Proviſions, and by ſawing down her upper Works they (barely) eſcaped.

We alſo hear that three more prizes have arrived at the Eaſtward, 2 laden with Fiſh, the other with Molaſſes.

Extract of a letter from Mount Waſhington, dated September 26, 1776

" Since the affair of laſt Monday week the enemy hazard nothing great.—We have ſince that time abandoned Powles Hook—Moutreſour the engineer came out the other day as a flag, and ſays they have hung up conſiderable numbers—We are now ſtrongly poſted, and I think in a much better ſituation than we have ever been yet to make a ſtand; in a few days more we ſhall be invincible.—There is a Committee from Congreſs to form a new army."

Extract of a letter from Harlem, (New York,) September 26 1776.

" Friday laſt was diſcovered a vaſt cloud of ſmoke ariſing from the North part of the city, which continued 'till Saturday evening——The conſequence was that the bread way from the new city hall down to white hall is laid in aſhes. Our friends were immediately ſuſpected, and according to the report of a flag of truce who came to our lines ſoon after, thoſe that were found on or near the ſpot were pitched into the conflagation; ſome hanged by the heels and others by their necks, with their throats cut. Inhuman barbarity!—One Hale in New York, on ſuſpicion of being a ſpy was taken up and dragg'd without ceremony to the execution poſt, and hung up. —Gen Waſhington has ſince ſent in a flag, ſuppoſed to be on that account.—The 22d inſtant, was tried for cowardice, diſobedience of orders, and daring to preſent his firelock at a ſuperior officer in time of the late ſkirmiſh, one Leffingwell of Norwich for which he was condemned to be ſhot, accordingly all preparations were made, himſelf brought to the field, was fixed on his knees, and while the guards was marching to execute the decree, the General ſent a pardon, declaring never to forgive another."

ters, preparing boats to croſs the Lake."

Extract of a letter from Mount Waſhington, dated September 26, 1776

" In a ſkirmiſh on Montreſour's iſland on the morning of the 23 of September, was kill'd Major *Thomas Henley*, aid de camp to Major General *Heath*———This young hero was a native of Charleſtown near Boſton, of an ancient and reputable family.

We hear that Capt. Greely in a Privateer belonging to Boſton who ſaid from thence laſt Monday afternoon ſent into Marblehead laſt Friday a Prize Brig, laden with Pork and Beef.

Saturday laſt a Sloop laden with Lumber, was ſent into Boſton by Captain Waters. She was bound to New York from the Eaſtward—Is it not aſtoniſhing that there ſhould ſtill be ſuch People among us, who would ſupply our Enemies to cut their own throats?

Saturday laſt a Ship and a Sloop were ſeen ſtanding in for Boſton; but we have not heard who they are.

By an extract from a letter from a young man to his Father in this town, dated Ticonderoga Sept. 29th, we are informed, That the worthy Capt. *Edward Harrington*, of this town, Died Sept. 23d, after about three weeks ſickneſs who is much lamented by all the officers and men under his command.

Two Gentlemen who paſſed thro' this Town Yeſterday from New York which they left laſt Tueſday inform, that nothing material had then happened.

*** *The Town of Boſton being now clear of the Small-Pox, the Publiſher of this Paper propoſes to remove there ſoon—therefore requeſts thoſe of his Cuſtomers who are deſirous of continuing ſuch, to make it known—and all that are indebted for the ſame, to diſcharge their Arrears.——Notice of the Time of Removal, will be given in our next.*

TAKEN up at Sea near Miſperkey and ſent into Narroquaguar by Capt. John Lambert Commander of the armed Schooner Diligent, a Sloop about twenty four tuns, in ballaſt, all Sails ſet, no Perſon on board; the right Owner paying Expences, may apply to the Printer, where he may have an order for ſaid ſloop.

Sept 2 1776 JOHN LAMBERT.

TEN DOLLARS REWARD.

LAST Friday night the ſhop of the ſubſcriber was broke open, and the following articles ſtolen, viz Eleven ſtone rings, ſome very valuable; a number of ſilver ſhoe and knee buckles, ſome odd ones; a number of plated buckles; ſome plated ſtock buckles; ſeveral pair ſtone buttons; a number of ſilver ear rings, and one odd gold ear-ring;—alſo a handſome blue ſurtout, with a wide red cape.—Whoever ſhall apprehend the thief or thieves ſo that the owner may have his goods again ſhall receive *TEN DOLLARS* reward from

Medford Oct 7. *WILLIAM COWEN*

LEFT at the houſe of the ſubſcriber in Cambridge, ſome time ſince, a Surtout, and an old Ridinghood. The owners may have them again, paying charges.

SAM'L WHITTEMORE.

TO BE SOLD

A SLOOP, well found, with ſails, rigging, &c. lately caulk'd and grav'd, and is fitted for immadiate ſervice. Inquire of *Samuel Barrett*, at whoſe wharff ſhe now lies——A few excellent English Cod Hooks, Sail Needles of different ſorts and Palms, to be Sold by the ſaid Barret.

DEſerted from my Company on his march from No 4 or Charleſtown New Hampſhire to Ticonderoga, in Sept. 1776; *Edward Norton*, a well built man about 27 years of age, 5 feet 3 inches high [illegible] ſword Whoever ſh

old, 14 hands high, long dock, has a white face, paces and trots Whoever will ſend ſaid Horſe to Major Ruggles, in Roxbury, ſhall have a handſome reward for their trouble

STray'd or ſtolen from Proſpect Hill, the laſt of Auguſt, a brown Horſe, about 7 years old, loſt one eye, has a ſwell face—Alſo a black Horſe Colt, about 4 years old, has a thick neck—Likewiſe a red Horſe Colt, loſt laſt May, about 3 years old black mane and tail, off hind foot white. Whoever ſhall bring them to William Kettle, at Concord, Baker, or Samuel Ireland, at Proſpect Hill, ſhall have Three Dollars Reward for each, and all neceſſary Charges paid. WILLIAM KETTLE.

mouth, the following Goods juſt imported from France.

150 dozen Thread Stockings.
400lb. black and cloth coloured ſewing Silks.
300 dozen printed Linnen Handkerchiefs.
700 Rheams Writing Paper.
a quantity of white Thread, and about
50 pieces Corded Dimothy.

J. RUSSELL Auctioneer.

On *FRIDAY* the 11th of *October*, at Ten in the Morning, will be ſold by public Vendue, at *Bedford*, in *Dartmouth*,

THE Cargoes of the ſhip *Charming Sally*,
Snow *Ann*, and
Brig *John*, conſiſting of,

634 Hogſheads 31 Tierces, and 61 Barrels of Sugar; 118 Bales of Cotton; 90 Hogſheads of Rum; 40 Bags of Ginger, and 25 Tons Fuſtick.

☞ The ſales will begin preciſely at Ten, on each of the above Days.—Thoſe who intend to be Purchaſers, are requeſted to attend in Time, leſt they meet with the ſame Diſappointment that ſome others did at *Bedford*, not long ſince.——Pleaſe to obſerve, That the above Veſſels will be put up at at One o'Clock, on the Day of Sale.

J RUSSELL, Auctioneer.

Caſh given for POT and PEARL ASH by *ENOCH BROWN*, oppoſite Roxbury Meeting.

TAKEN up in Waltham laſt Week a black Mare, about 12 Years old. The Owner paying Charges, may have her again. Inquire at the Printing Office in Watertown.

STRAYED or Stolen out of the Paſture of Richard Trumball of Charleſtown on the Night following the 29th of September ult, a pale red Mare, 8 Years old, flaxen Mane and Tail, 14 & half or 15 Hands high; 'tis ſuppos'd ſhe is gone toward Connecticut Whoever will take up ſaid Mare and return her to the Subſcriber, ſhall have Six Dollars Reward, and all neceſſary Charges paid by me.

BENJAMIN PIPER.

Charleſtown, October 7 1776.

JOSHUA BLANCHARD,

Sells by Wholeſale or Retail, at his Store & Wine Cellar, Dock Square, *Boſton*;

MADEIRA, Teneriffe Fyal, Liſbon. Caccaville, Claret, old Red Port and ſweet Wines, fine old French Brandy, Weſt India and New-England Rum, Jamaica Rum and old Jamaica Spirits Porter, Vinegar Brandy, Holland's Geneva. Brown Sugar by the Hogſhead or Barrel, Loaf Sugar, Coffee, Chocolate, Alſpice, Cotton Wool, Ginger with a general Aſſortment of Groceries.

Weſt India and New England Rum, Brown Sugars in Barrels at Watertown Bridge enquire of Mr. John Clark, or at Mr. Ezekiel Hall's Diſtill Houſe, Hollands Gin in Caſes.

INOCULATING HOSPITAL.

Wm. Aſpinwall & Leml Hayward

TAKES this method to acquaint the Publick that they have under their Care, at Sewall's Point in Brooklyn, an Inoculating Hoſpital for the Small Pox with very large and ſuitable Accommodations, and a large and convenient Dwelling Houſe, at a Diſtance from the Infection of ſaid Hoſpital, in which their patients may tarry until it is certain they have receiv'd the Infection: More than 100 Perſons are now Patients in ſaid Hoſpital and as good accommodations remain for as many more.

THE Regiſter of Deeds for the County of Suffolk, notifies all whom it may concern, that he has opened an Office near the Rev. Mr. Haven's Meeting Houſe in Dedham.

Sept. 16, 1776

STRAYED from the paſture of Mr. Eleazer Baker, at the Punch Bowl, in Brookline, on Monday the 2d. of this inſt. September, a coal black Mare, about three years old, with a grey

At Sudbury, next door to John Noyes, Eſq; near Barker's (formerly Bryam's) Tavern.

A Variety of ENGLISH GOODS,

Alſo,—At the ſame place is to be Sold, by

GREENLEAF and FIELD,

New-England and Weſt India rum, brandy, Malaga & other wines, loaf & brown ſugars, with moſt kinds of Weſt India goods, as low as the times will admit of.—*Alſo*,—barr iron, hallow ware, grindſtones, &c.

N. B. All perſons indebted to the late company of *Amory* and *Greenleaf*, are requeſted immediately to pay their balances to ſaid Greenleaf.

Boſton, July 8, 1776.

—One Hale in New York, on ſuſpicion of being a ſpy was taken up and dragg'd without ceremony to the execution poſt, and hung up.

THE
ESSEX
OR
New-Hampſhire
AND
WEEKLY
(No. 148.)
JOURNAL:
THE
PACKET,
THE
ADVERTISER.

VOL. III. FRIDAY, NOVEMBER 1, 1776.

This will teach them the great political virtues of humility, patience and moderation, without which, every man in power, becomes a ravenous beaſt of prey.

This mode of conſtituting the great offices of ſtate will anſwer very well for the preſent, but if, by experiment, it ſhould be found inconvenient, the legiſlature may at its leiſure deviſe other methods of creating them by elections of the people at large, as in Connecticut, or it may enlarge the term for which they ſhall be choſen, to ſeven years, or three years, or life, or make any other alterations which the ſociety ſhall find productive of its eaſe, its ſafety, its freedom, or in one word, its happineſs.

A rotation of all offices, as well as of Repreſentatives and Counſellors, has many advocates, and is contended for with many plauſible arguments. It would be attended, no doubt, with many advantages, and if the ſociety has a ſufficient number of ſuitable characters, to ſupply the great number of vacancies, which would be made by ſuch a rotation, I can ſee no objection to it. Theſe perſons may be allowed to ſerve for three years, and then be excluded three years, or for any longer or ſhorter term.

Any ſeven or nine of the legiſlative Council, may be made a quorum, for doing buſineſs as a Privy Council, to adviſe the Governor, in the exerciſe of the executive branch of power, and in all acts of State.

The Governor ſhould have the command of the militia, and of all your armies. The power of pardons ſhould be with the Governor and Council.

Judges, Juſtices, and all other officers, civil and military, ſhould be nominated and appointed by the Governor, with the advice and conſent of council, unleſs you chooſe to have a government more popular; if you do, all officers, civil and military, may be choſen by joint ballot of both Houſes, or in order to preſerve the independence and importance of each Houſe, by ballot of one Houſe, concurred by the other. Sheriffs ſhould be choſen by the freeholders of counties—ſo ſhould Regiſters of Deeds, and Clerks of Counties.

All officers ſhould have commiſſions, under the hand of the Governor, and ſeal of the Colony.

The dignity and ſtability of government in all its branches, the morals of the people, and every bleſſing of ſociety, depends ſo much upon an upright and ſkilful adminiſtration of juſtice, that the judicial power ought to be diſtinct from both the legiſlative and executive, and independent upon both, that ſo it may be a check upon both, as both ſhould be checks upon that. The Judges therefore, ſhould always be men of learning and experience in the laws, of exemplary morals, great patience, calmneſs, coolneſs and attention. Their minds ſhould not be diſtracted with jarring intereſts; they ſhould not be dependant upon any men or body of men. To theſe ends they ſhould hold eſtates for life in their offices, or in other words, their commiſſions ſhould be during their good behavior, and their ſalaries aſcertained and eſtabliſhed by law. For miſbehaviour, the grand inqueſt of the Colony, the Houſe of Repreſentatives, ſhould impeach them before the Governor and Council, where they ſhould have time and opportunity to make their defence, but if convicted, ſhould be removed from their offices, and ſubjected to ſuch other puniſhment as ſhall be thought proper.

A militia law requiring all men, or with very few exceptions, beſides caſes of conſcience, to be provided with arms and ammunition, to be trained at certain ſeaſons, and requiring counties, towns, or other ſmall diſtricts to be provided with public ſtocks of ammunition and entrenching utenſils, and with ſome ſettled plans for tranſporting proviſions after the militia, when marched to defend their country againſt ſudden invaſions, and requiring certain diſtricts to be provided with field-pieces, companies of matroſſes and perhaps ſome regiments of light horſe, is always a wiſe inſtitution, and in the preſent circumſtances of our country indiſpenſible.

Laws for the liberal education of youth, eſpecially of the lower claſs of people, are ſo extremely wiſe and uſeful, that to a humane and generous mind, no expence for this purpoſe would be thought extravagant.

The very mention of ſumptuary laws will excite a ſmile. Whether our countrymen have wiſdom or virtue enough to ſubmit to them I know not. But the happineſs of the people might be greatly promoted by them, and a revenue ſaved, ſufficient to carry on this war for ever. Frugality is a great revenue, beſides curing us of vanities, levities and fopperies which are real antidotes to all great, manly and warlike virtues.

But muſt not all commiſſions run in the name of a king? No. Why may they not as well run thus, "The Colony of   to A. B. greeting, and be teſted by the Governor?

Why may not writs, inſtead of running in the name of king, run thus, "The Colony of   to the Sheriff, &c. and be teſted by the chief Juſtice.

Why may not indictments conclude, "againſt the peace of the Colony of   and the dignity of the ſame?

A Conſtitution, founded on theſe principles, introduces knowledge among the people, and inſpires them with a conſcious dignity, becoming Freemen. A general emulation takes place, which cauſes good humour, ſociability, good manners, and good morals to be general. That elevation of ſentiment, inſpired by ſuch a government, makes the common people brave and enterprizing. That ambition which is inſpired by it makes them ſober, induſtrious and frugal. You will find among them ſome elegance, perhaps, but more ſolidity; a little pleaſure, but a great deal of buſineſs—ſome politeneſs, but more civility. If you compare ſuch a country with the regions of domination, whether Monarchical or Ariſtocratical, you will fancy yourſelf in Arcadia or Eliſium.

If the Colonies ſhould aſſume governments ſeparately, they ſhould be left entirely to their own choice of the forms, and if a Continental conſtitution ſhould be formed, it ſhould be a Congreſs, containing a fair and adequate repreſentation of the Colonies, and its authority ſhould ſacredly be confined to theſe caſes, viz. war, trade, diſputes between Colony and Colony, the Poſt-Office, and the unappropriated lands of the Crown, as they uſed to be called.

Theſe Colonies, under ſuch forms of government, and in ſuch a union, would be unconquerable by all the Monarchies of Europe.

You and I, my dear friend, have been ſent into life, at a time when the greateſt law givers of antiquity would have wiſhed to have lived.—How few of the human race have ever enjoyed an opportunity of making an election of government more than of air, ſoil, or climate, for themſelves or their children.—When! Before the preſent epocha, had three millions of people full power and a fair opportunity to form and eſtabliſh the wiſeſt and happieſt government that human wiſdom can contrive? I hope you will avail yourſelf and your country of that extenſive learning and indefatigable induſtry which you poſſeſs, to aſſiſt her in the information of the happieſt governments, and the beſt character of a great people.—For myſelf, I muſt beg you to keep my name out of ſight, for this feeble attempt, if it ſhould be known to be mine, would oblige me to apply to myſelf thoſe lines of the immortal John Milton, in one of his ſonnets.

"*I did but teach the age to quit their clogs*
"*By the plain rules of ancient Liberty,*
"*When lo! a barbarious noiſe ſurrounded me,*
"*Of owls and cuckoos, aſſes, apes and dogs.*"

NEW-HAVEN, October 2.

Extract of a letter from an Officer at fort Stanwix, dated Auguſt 17.

"Part of the third battalion of New-Jerſey troops being ſtationed here about three weeks ago it was thought proper to ſend a ſerjeant and four men to reconnoitre towards Oſwego; but Enſign Iſaiah Younglove, being deſirous to go, went in the room of the ſerjeant; having travelled about 60 miles, were fired on early one morning, by a party of ten Indians, but their guns being wet (it having rained the preceeding night) could not return the fire, the Enſign, and another, who after repeatedly priming, at length diſcharged their pieces. They were then directed by the Enſign, to fix their bayonets, who, at that inſtant, received a ball in his lungs, and fell; notwithſtanding, he ordered his men to advance, and lying on his back, loaded, and ſhot one of the Indians dead; but two of his men being killed, he deſired the others to flee, telling them that he could not live more than five minutes, and ſaid, "that it was a pity they ſhould expoſe their own lives: The ſurviving two came off, and gave us the above accounts."

NEW-LONDON October 18.

The following paper was lately ſent through Suffolk County on Long-Iſland, by order of Gov. Tryon.

THE Governor of the Province recommends to the Inhabitants of Suffolk County, the following meaſures, as the beſt means for thoſe who have been active in the Rebellion, to preſeve their lives and ſave their Eſtates, viz. That all offenſive arms, indiſcriminately, be forthwith collected in each reſpective Manor, Townſhip, and Precinct, as ſoon as poſſible, to deliver them up at Head-Quarters, to the Commander in chief of the kings troops. That thoſe who have been active in the rebellion, if fit to bear arms, forthwith wait on the General, and inliſt in the regular ſervice, for the term of the preſent war; if not fit to bear arms to ſend one of their ſons to inliſt in their ſtead; if no ſons, to perform ſome unaſked ſignal ſervice that may merit the protection of government. The inhabitants of each town to aſſociate to prevent any perſon going to the Main and ſecure thoſe coming from thence, and to ſecure and deliver up all perſons known to be active enemies to the rights of the Conſtitution.

And the ſeveral townſhips to furniſh as many men as poſſible, fit to bear arms, to invite thoſe back who have fled from the country, to inliſt in General Dalancy's brigade.

And laſtly, The Inhabitants to ſend what wood, forage and proviſions they can ſpare, to New-York market, or to ſuch place as the General ſhall order.

The following copy of a letter was lately brought from Long-Iſland.

New-York, 27th Sept. 1776.

SIR,

You are to deſire the Juſtices of the Peace to ſummon the farmers in their diſtrict to attend at their houſe or [illegible]ther centrial place, if more convenient, to [illegible] of each farmer what grain and ſtraw they [illegible]pare——as to hay we muſt have the whole, for which you will give them a proper certificate for me to pay them by. All the rebels that are in arms, the whole of their grain and forage to be ſeized for the uſe of the king, &c.

To Mr. *Punderſon.* Sir,
Your humble [illegible]
JOHN MOR[illegible]
Com[illegible]
Fo[illegible]

He alſo inſerted, that all which had removed off were deemed rebels and dealt with accordingly.

October 1, 1776. A true [illegible]
EBENEZER PUN[illegible]

The following paragraphs were extracted from the New-York Mercury, printed in the City of New-York, which has been received by the way of Long-Iſland.

NEW-YORK, *October* 7.

We are informed by a gentleman juſt eſcaped from New-England, that the rebels have lately carried many hundred head of cattle from the Eaſt end of Long-Iſland, to New-London, in Connecticut, and that their privateers are very buſy in negociating this kind of buſineſs, and have moreover committed ſome of their uſual tyrannical and oppreſſive acts, upon ſeveral loyal ſubjects in thoſe parts.

His majeſty's forces are in poſſeſſion of the city of New-York, with all the Sound of Long and Staten-Iſlands, and nearly of New-York Iſland. They are alſo in poſſeſſion of Powles-Hook, and command the Eaſt River and Connecticut Sound. All this has been obtained with very little difficulty and loſs on the part of the troops; the rebels, after the battle, or rather rout of the 27th of Auguſt, having never attempted to face the ſoldiers, but fled every way with the utmoſt precipitation. They quitted works, which they had been labouring upon during the whole ſummer without ſcarce the conflict of a day.

The king's troops have not ſuſtained the loſs of one hundred men; while the rebels by the beſt accounts, cannot have loſt fewer than between four and five thouſand, in killed, wounded and taken priſoners; to mention nothing of deſerters, who leave them daily.

[*Our readers will very much queſtion the truth of the above account, when they are aſſured, that a letter from a perſon of diſtinction in New-York, has been intercepted, the writer of which informs his friend that the regular army in the late encounters have loſt 1200 men, and 100 officers killed.*]

From the LONDON GAZETTE.

WHITEHALL, *August* 24*th*, 1776.

Captain Hope arrived on Wednesday evening last, from South-Carolina, with dispatches from Commodore Sir Peter Parker, and Lieutenant-General Clinton.

Extract of a letter from Sir Peter Parker, to Mr. Stevens, Secretary of the Admiralty, dated within Charlestown-Bar, July 9, 1776.

"It having been judged adviſable to make an attempt upon Charleſtown in South-Carolina, the Fleet ſailed from Cape Fear on the 1ſt of June, and on the 4th, anchored off Charleſtown Bar. The 5th, ſounded the bar, and laid down Buoys preparatory to the intended entrance of the Harbor. The 7th, all the Frigates, and moſt of the tranſports, got over the bar, into Five-Fathom-Hole. The 9th, General Clinton landed on Long-Iſland with about [illegible]or 500 men. The 10th, the Briſtol got over the Bar with ſome difficulty. The 15th, gave the Captains of the Squadron my arrangement for the attack of the Batteries on Sullivan's Iſland, and the next day acquainted General Clinton that the Ships were ready. The General fixed on the 23d, for our joint attack, but the wind proving unfavorable prevented its taking effect. The 25th, the Experiment arrived, and next day came over the Bar, when a new arrangement was made for the attack. The 28th, at half an hour after nine in the morning, informed General Clinton by ſignal, that I ſhould go on the attack.. At half an hour after ten, I made the ſignal to weigh; and about a quarter after eleven, the Briſtol, Experiment, Active, and Solebay, brought up againſt the Fort. The Thunder-Bomb, covered by the Friendſhip armed veſſel, brought the Saliant angle of the Eaſt baſtion, to bear N. W[illegible] by N. and Colonel James (who has ever ſi[illegible] arrival been very anxious to give the be[illegible]ce) threw ſeveral Shells a little before an[illegible]g the engagement, in [illegible]y good d[illegible]on. The Sphinx, Acteon, an[illegible]en, were to have been to the Weſtward, to prevent Fire-ſhips, or other Veſſels from annoying the ſhips engaged, to enfilade the works, and, if the Rebels ſhould be driven from them, to cut of their retreat, if poſſible. This laſt ſervice was not performed, owing to the ignorance of the pilot, who run the three Frigates aground. The Sphynx and Syren got off in a few hours, but the Actæon remained faſt until the next morning, when the Captain and other Officers thought proper to ſcuttle and ſet her on fire. I ordered a Court Martial on the Captain, Officers, and Company, and they have been honourably acquited. Captain Hope made his armed Ship as uſeful as he could on this occaſion, and he merits every thing that can be ſaid in his favour. During the time of our being a-breſt of the Fort, which was near ten hours, a briſk fire was kept up by the ſhips, with intervals, and we had the ſatisfaction, after being engaged two hours, to oblige the Rebels to ſlacken their Fire very much. We drove large parties ſeveral times out of the Fort, which were replaced by others from the Main. About half an hour after three, a conſiderable reinforcement from Mount Pleaſant, hung a man on a tree, at the back of the Fort, and we imagine the ſame party ran away about an hour after, for the Fort was then totally ſilenced, and evacuated near an hour and an half, but the Rebels finding that our army could not take poſſeſſion, about ſix o' clock, a conſiderable body of people re-entered the Fort, and renewed the firing from 2 or 3 guns, the reſt being, I ſuppoſe, diſmounted. About nine o'clock, it being very dark, great part of our ammunition expended, the people fatigued, the tide of ebb almoſt done, no proſpect from the Eaſtward, and no poſſibility of our being of any further ſervice, I ordered the ſhips to withdraw to their former moorings. Their Lordſhips will ſee plainly by this account, that if the troops could have co-operated on this attack, his majeſty would have been in poſſeſſion of Sullivan's Iſland. But I muſt beg leave here to be fully underſtood, leſt it ſhould be imagined that I mean to throw the moſt diſtant reflection on our army: I ſhould not diſcharge my conſcience, were I not to acknowledge, that ſuch was my opinion of his majeſty's troops, from the General, down to the private ſoldier, that after I had been engaged ſome hours, and perceived that the troops had not got footing on the North end of Sullivan's Iſland, I was perfectly ſatisfied that the landing was impracticable, and that the attempt would have been the deſtruction of many brave men, without the leaſt probability of ſucceſs; and this, I am certain will appear to be the caſe, when General Clinton repreſents his ſituation——The Briſtol had 40 men killed, and 71 wounded; the Experiment 23 killed and 56 wounded, both of them ſuffered much in their hulls, maſts and rigging; the Active had Lieutenant Pike killed, and 6 men wounded; and the Solebay 8 wounded. Not one man who was quartered at the beginning of the action on the Briſtol's quarter-deck eſcaped being killed or wounded. Capt. Morris loſt his right arm, and received other wounds, and is ſince dead; the Maſter is wounded in his right arm, but will recover the uſe of it. I received ſeveral contuſions at different times, but as none of them are on any part where the leaſt danger can be apprehended, they are not worth mentioning. Lieutenants Caufield, Molloy, and Nugent, were the Lieutenants of the Briſtol in the action; they behaved ſo remarkably well, that it is impoſſible to ſay to whom the preference is due; and ſo indeed I may ſay of all the petty Officers, Ship's company, and Volunteers. At the head of the latter, I muſt place Lord William Campbell, who was ſo condeſcending as to accept of the direction of ſome guns on the lower gun deck. His Lordſhip received a contuſion on his left ſide, but I have the happineſs to inform their Lordſhips that it has not proved of much conſequence. Capt. Scott, of the Experiment, loſt his left arm, and is otherwiſe ſo much wounded, that I fear he will not recover. I cannot conclude this letter without remarking, that when it was known that we had many men too weak to come to quarters, almoſt all the ſeamen belonging to the tranſports offered their ſervice with a truly Britiſh ſpirit, and a juſt ſenſe of the cauſe we are engaged in. I accepted of upwards of fifty to ſupply the place of our ſick. The maſters of many tranſports attended with their boats, but particular thanks are due to Mr. Chambers, the maſter of the Mercury.

All the regiments will be embarked in a few days. The firſt brigade, conſiſting of four regiments, will ſail in a day or two, under convoy, for New-York; and the Briſtol and Experiment will, I hope, ſoon follow with the remainder.

Sir Peter Parker's Squadron conſiſted of the following ſhips and veſſels:

Ships, &c.	*Guns,*	*Commanders.*
Briſtol - - -	50	{ Sir Peter Parker. { Capt. J. Morris.
Experiment - -	50	Alexander Scott.
Active - - -	28	William Williams.
Solebay - - -	28	Thomas Symonds.
Actæon - - -	28	Criſtopher Atkins.
Syren - - -	28	Tobias Furneaux.
Sphynx - - -	20	Anthony Hunt.
Friendſhip arm'd veſſel	22	Charles Hope.
Ranger ſloop - -	8	Roger Wills.
Thunder Bomb -	8	James Reid.
St. Laurence ſchooner	-	Lieut John Graves.

NEW-HAVEN, *October* 23.

The enemy have extended this way, as far as new-Rochel, ſmall parties of them, have advanced as far as Marrineck. In one of the churches at New-Rochel, was ſtored more than two thouſand buſhels of ſalt, which has fallen into the hands of the enemy. It was owned by the State of New York.

Laſt Friday there was a ſmart ſkirmiſh near the above church, between a detatched party of the enemy, and one from our army, in which we loſt eight or ten men, and ſome wounded, among the latter, was Col, Shepard, of the Maſſachuſetts Bay, who was ſlighly wounded in his throat, and who commanded the party---- the enemy's loſs is not known.

We hear that near two hundred ſail of the enemy's fleet, are on this ſide Hell-Gate, the chief of them lying near Hart-Iſland.

HARTFORD, *October* 28.

Gen. Waterbury, with about 100 *of our people who were taken priſoners in our late unſucceſsful engagement on Lake Champlain, were ſoon after releaſed, on giving their paroles, not to take up arms againſt government till an exchange takes place, and are all returned home.*

By the Southern poſt we have the following particulars from our lines near New-York, in addition to what is contained under New-Heven head viz. That on Monday laſt a party of Tories (about 100 *in number) ſome of whom came from Long-Iſland, under the command of the infamous Major Rogers, made an attack upon an advanced party of our men, when a ſmart engagement enſued, which laſted a conſiderable time, in which the enemy were totally routed, about* 20 *killed on the ſpot, and* 36 *taken priſoners, who are ſafely lodged in the goal at the White-Plains, that the gallant commander, with his uſual bravery, left his men* in time of action, *and made his eſcape;——That on Thurſday morning another engagement commenced between a body of the Britiſh troops and a party of our men, under the command of General Lee, near the houſe of Mr. Stephen Ward, about ſix miles from the White-Plains, which had not terminated when our informant left that place.——We hear the enemy have left their lines at Harlem.*

BOSTON, OCTOBER 31.

Extract of a letter from Eaſt-Cheſter, October 23:

"The enemy have landed their main body at Eaſt-Cheſter where we had a ſmall engagement, we loſt 12 men. but we had the advantage of them, we have had authentic intelligence of their loſing 500 killed and wounded. The enemy lay on the Eaſt-river, and we on the North, two miles diſtant from each other. We have New-York Iſland ſtill in our poſſeſſion, with a garriſon of 1800 men, commanded by Gen. Putnam. The main body of our army lay at the above place, waiting for the enemy to attack us; it is my opinion if they ſhould not do it ſoon, we ſhall attack them; we have gained the advantage of them the two laſt engagements, there is no diſpute but what a general attack will commence very ſoon: I think the ſalvation of America depends upon our conduct in the next engagement; it will either be the deſtruction of the Britiſh Army, or ours; the two armies are ſo near together, that they muſt be both engaged at one time. I have juſt received intelligence of a battle that was fought laſt night at Merrinick, about ſeven miles from this. The enemy had a number killed and wounded, we took thirty priſoners. We cannot learn what loſs our army ſuſtained, but we came off victorious."

PORTSMOUTH, *October*, 29.

Arrived here laſt Sunday a prize ſhip called the SUCCESS, *Eleazer Ball late Maſter, taken by the Retaliation privateer from Salem, in lat.* 42. *long.* 47. *She ſailed from Jamaica the 9th of Auguſt, was taken the 6th of October. Her cargo conſiſts of* 244 *Hogſheads and* 12 *Tierces of Suga*, 156 *Puncheons of Rum,* 4 *bags of Cotton, Mahogany, fuſtic, &c. The ſaid privateer had alſo taken a brig and ſhip, and the prize ſaw her engage another ſhip.*

NEWBURY-PORT, *November* 1.

Laſt Monday ſailed from this Port for Boſton one of the Continental Frigates of 28 *guns, built here, commanded by* HECTOR M'NEIL, Eſq; *and the ſame evening arrived in Boſton Harbour.*

Several prizes with valuable cargoes of rum and Sugar, have arrived at Portſmouth, this week, the particulars of their cargoes we have not yet received.

By letters from Ticonderoga we learn, that the enemy are in poſſeſſion of Crown-Point, and daily expected to attack that place.

Extract of a letter from a Gentleman in Spain, dated September 12.

"*We have no novelty this way, only that the king of Portugal has comply'd with Britain's mean requeſt viz, to drive all American veſſels out of Liſbon, and other his ports. When I left Cadiz (which was the* 15*th of Auguſt) there were* 12 *ſail of the Line, all* 70 *gun ſhips, and* 4 *frigates with* 2 *bombs, almoſt fit for the ſea, ſix of which ſailed the day after me, and are off Liſbon cruizing, ſuppoſed to prevent any ſuccour going to Liſbon, and to watch the motion of the Portugueſe; there were alſo in Cadiz, great numbers of tranſports, and more, with ſhips of war, daily expected, their preparation never was greater in time of war; their deſtination is a profound ſecret, ſome ſay they are bound to Benizaris, others to Liſbon, I am of opinion, to both, for this reaſon, they have all their beſt officers and ſoldiers about Cadiz and Port St. Mary's, and have a greater armament than they ever had before, and daily preſſing for their Ships, and recruiting at every place, both within and without the Streights; there are letters in town that mention that there were officers at Hanover, recruiting for the American ſervice, when a large body of men got together and ſwore no more ſhould go in that ſervice, and carried their point that time. Whether other attempts will be made or not, they cannot ſay.*"

On Wedneſday the 6*th inſtant, at ten in the morning, will be ſold, at Public Auction, on the wharf of* Capt. DANIEL MARQUAND,

THE Snow *Millham* and her Cargo, conſiſting of Bread, Beef, Pork, Peaſe, Rice, Flour, Rum, Oatmeal, Butter, Empty Water Caſks, Soldiers Beds and Blankets, two Carriage Guns, two new Cables, and ſundry other articles.——Alſo at the ſame place, at three in the afternoon, the Schooner *Eagle* and Cargo, conſiſting of 50 hogſheads Cod-Fiſh, and 10,000 feet of Lumber.

Newbury Port, November 1*ſt*, 1776.

DIED.] The 2.th of October of a Fever, the Reverend Mr. WILLIAM EMERSON of Concord, in the 34th year of his age, he was on his return home from the army at Ticonderoga, where he had been Chaplain.

MONDAY, January 20, 1777. THE NUMBER 628.

CONNECTICUT COURANT, AND HARTFORD WEEKLY INTELLIGENCER.

Containing the Freshest ADVICES, Both FOREIGN and DOMESTIC.

PRINTED AND PUBLISHED BY EBENEZER WATSON, NEAR THE GREAT BRIDGE.

PHILADELPHIA, January 4.

Last Monday morning the prisoners taken at Trenton, with a number of women and children, amounting in the whole to near one thousand, were brought to this city. The wretched condition of these unhappy men, most of whom were dragged from their wives and families by a despotic and avaricious Prince, must sensibly affect every generous mind with the dreadful effects of arbitrary power.

Col. Rohl died at Trenton on Thursday the 26th of December, of the wounds he received in the engagement that morning.

PROVIDENCE, January 4.

We learn that the enemy have sent a number of women and children from Newport to Narraganset.

Capt. Jones, in the Retaliation Privateer, of this port, and Capt. Dennis, in a privateer belonging to Newport, have taken a brig from Scotland, bound to New-York via Antigua, and sent her into a safe harbour. Her cargo, we hear, consists of dry-goods, &c. to the amount of 8000l. sterling.

Undoubted Intelligence is received from Newport, that the enemy consider the Inhabitants on the island as prisoners of war, and have absolutely refused to grant the benefit of their boaste pardons to a number who made application for the same.

It is said that the enemy's troops at Newport have received orders to hold themselves in readiness for embarkation at a moment's notice, but whether on board transports or their flat-bottomed boats is not mentioned: A number of carpenters have been busily employed in repairing the latter.

HARTFORD, Jan. 20.

Last Friday the General Assembly of this State ended their adjourned Session at Middletown.

We have various Reports of Successes attending our Arms in New-Jersey, but nothing particular has been received from that Quarter since our last.

Last Saturday about twenty British officers and soldiers came to town from the Westward; about 160 more are on their Way to this place; they are part of the 500 who were lately taken prisoners at Princetown, as mentioned in our last.

To the melancholly picture already exhibited of the brutal behaviour of the Britons, (who vainly boast being ever pre-eminent in Mercy) aided by Hessian and Waldeck Mercenaries, in New-York and New-Jersey, it gives us pain to add, that they have not only outraged the Feelings of Humanity to many people, who were so unhappy as to fall into their Hands, particularly the Fair Sex, but have degraded themselves beyound the Power of Language to express, by wantonly destroying the curious Water Works at New-York, an elegant public Library at Trenton, and the grand Orrery, made by the celebrated Rittenhouse, which was placed in the College at Princeton---a Piece of Mechanism, which the most untutored Savage, staying the Hand of Violence, would have beheld with Wonder, Reverence and Delight!---Thus are our cruel Enemies warring against Liberty, Virtue, and the Arts and Sciences.---" *How are the mighty fallen!*"

At a General Assembly of the Governor and Company of the State of Connecticut, holden at Middletown, by Adjournment, on the 18th Day of December, Anno Domini 1776.

An ACT for securing Boats and other small Craft, and for preventing any Persons going out of any Harbour, River or Creek without Licence.

BE it enacted by the Governor, Council and Representatives in General Court assembled, and by the Authority of the same, That no Person or Persons shall, under any Pretences whatever, depart from any Port, Harbour, Bay, Creek, River, or any other Place whatever within this State, in any Boat, Skiff, Canoe, or any other small Craft without Liberty in Writing, first had and obtained from one or more of the Select-Men of the Town from whence such Person or Persons would depart.

And it is further enacted and resolved, That the Select-Men belonging to the several Towns on the Sea Coast within this State be, and they are hereby empowered and directed to cause said small Craft belonging to their respective Towns to be drawn up in same convenient Place or Places as to them shall seem meet, who are to take such Measures properly to secure them, as the Circumstances of the Case may require.

And it is further enacted by the Authority aforesaid, That if any Person or Persons whatever shall presume, contrary to the true Intent and Meaning of this Act, to depart from any Part, Harbour, Bay, Creek, River, or any other Place whatever on the Sea Coast, in any such Boat, Skiff, Canoe or other small Craft as aforesaid, without such Liberty first had and obtained of the Select-Men, or any one of them as aforesaid, such Person or Persons shall, on Conviction thereof, before any one Assistant or Justice of the Peace, pay a Fine to the Treasury of the Town where such Conviction shall be had, according to the Nature and Circumstances of the Offence, not exceeding Forty Shillings.

A true Copy of Record,
Examin'd, by
GEORGE WYLLYS, *Sec'ry.*

At a General Assembly of the Governor and Company of the State of Connecticut, in New-England, holden at Middletown, in said State, by Adjournment, on the 18th Day of December, A.D. 1776.

WHEREAS the sick and impotent Soldiers of other States, as they pass and re-pass through this State, while in the Service of the United States, do often stand in need of Support and Relief.

RESOLVED by this Assembly, that the Select-Men of the several Towns, shall, and they are hereby ordered, to afford proper and necessary Support and Relief to such sick and impotent Soldier or Soldiers, belonging to any other State, as may be passing or re-passing through this State, in the Service of the United States, and not able to Provide for themselves, and Exhibit an Account of the Expence that hath or shall Accrue therein, to the Committee of the Pay-Table, which for the Future shall be acknowledged by such Soldier or Soldiers, under his or their Hand, also signifying to what State he or they belong, and what Regiment and Company he or they are of within such State, provided he or they are capable of giving such information and subscribing such Acknowledgment, and the Committee of Pay-Table are thereupon directed to adjust said Account of Expence, and give an Order for the Payment thereof upon the Treasurer, and Charge the same to the State to which he belongs, or the United States of America, in Order that it may be re-paid.

A true Copy of Record
Examined by
GEORGE WYLLYS, *Sec'ry.*

Mr. WATSON,

The cause of justice obliges us the committee of the town of Pittsfield, in conjunction with said town, to desire you to give the following declaration and resolves a place in your public papers, in order that the public may not be misled by an enemy.

AS every man's principles are best known by their conduct, so it appears that Capt. Charles Goodrich, who was advertised by the committee of safety, in Sept. 2, 1776; in order to exculpate himself from the charge of being an enemy to his country, has endeavoured to turn the charge of inimical conduct on the committee, and has carried his unlimited satire, even against the council of the State of the Massachusetts Bay: He tells the public in Sept. 16 1776, that the council had judged him to be a friend to his country, & condemned the committee, as being entirely ignorant of the line of their duty, and guilty of great indecency towards the constitutional authority of this State. If there was any such resolve, it must be judging *expartie*; for the committee were neither cited nor called upon by the council, nor any body else, to answer for their conduct---So that it appears said Goodrich has represented the council to be the most partial, arbitrary body of men that ever existed, not giving the committee the priviledge of a hearing or any trial in the case: In this light said Goodrich has set forth the constitutional authority of this State, as he calls it.

But that there is no such constitutional authority in this State, is evident, for in Sept. 1776, the house of representatives, have sent out their hand bills to each town in this State, to see if they would give leave to the present house to form the modele of a new constitution, and weather they, the people, choose to have it sent abroad to the people at large, to be inspected, before its ratification; by all which it appears said Goodrich has set the honourable council in the most odious and contemptable light possible. If any should be so bold as to say we have a constitution; we ask what is it? we never had but one constitution, which was that of our charter, which we have some time ago rejected, and now we are to seek for another.

The committee being thus injuriously treated, refered the matter to the town, to whom they are responsible, who has taken the matter into hand, and passed the following resolves.

First, The question being put, whether the town will adopt the above declaration?

Voted in the affirmative.

Second, The question being put whether the town is satisfied, respecting the facts charged against Capt. Charles Goodrich, in an advertisement, bearing date, Sept. 21, 1776, and whether the town will justify the committee in publishing said Goodrich?

Voted in the affirmative.

Third, The question being put whether Captain Charles Goodrich has acted as an enemy to the union of the people and the cause of justice, in publishing the committee in an advertisement bearing date September 16th, 1776?

Voted in the affirmative.

Fourth, The question being put whether the town will order the above declaration and resolves to be published in the *Connecticut Courant*, for the restoration of the character of their committee?

Voted in the affirmative.

By order of the town of Pittsfield,
ELI ROOT, Moderator.

A true copy. ISRAEL DICKENSON, Town-Clerk.

NEW LONDON, Jan. 17.

Last Monday Capt. Tobaoda arrived here in a sloop from Curracoa, which place he left the 22d of November, and 13 days after having sprung a leak he put in to Ocouy; eight days before he left Ocouy a ship arrived there from Havre de Grace, the master of which informed him that a declaration of war had taken place between Spain and Portugal, and that the same was daily expected between France and Great Britain. The cargo of the above sloop is very valuable, consisting of blankets, duck, some Powder, &c. The sloop run into Newport harbour last Saturday, and narrowly escaped being taken by the enemy before they perceived the harbour was in their possession.

The following is an Extract of a Letter from a Gentleman of Honor and Distinction, a Prisoner in New-York, dated 26th December, 1776.

"The distress of the prisoners cannot be communicated by words, 20 or 30 die every day, they lie in heaps unburied, what numbers of my countrymen have died by cold and hunger, perished for want of the common necessaries of life, I have seen it. This sir is the boasted *British clemency*, (I myself had well night perished under it.) The New-England people can have no idea of such barbarous policy, nothing can stop such treatment but retaliation. I ever despised *private* revenge, but that of the *public* must be in this case just and necessary, it is due to the manes of our murdered countrymen, and that alone can protect the survivors, in the like situation, rather than experience again their barbarity and insults, may I fall by the sword of the Hessians."

I am, &c.

FISH-KILL.

By a gentleman just arrived from Philadelphia, we are informed, that shortly after the battle at Trenton, a party of 120 of the troops under Gen. Washington, fell in with about 200 of Gen. Howe's *Tory* soldiers, defeated them, took 23 prisoners, 7 baggage waggons, and 12 horses:---The gentleman says the prisoners arrived in Philadelphia before he left it.

On Sunday the 5th instant one of our scouting parties met with a party of the enemy, at Connecticut Farms, in New-Jersey, killed 17, and took 57 prisoners.

TUESDAY, October 24, 1780. THE NUMBER 822.

CONNECTICUT COURANT,

AND THE

WEEKLY INTELLIGENCER.

HARTFORD: Printed by HUDSON and GOODWIN, near the Great-Bridge.

About the middle of August a victualing fleet sailed from Corke, together with a number of loaded ships from England bound to New York; on board of the former were about 3000 German recruits, under convoy of a 50 gun ship and two frigates. We received this account by a ship, one of the fleet, safe moored in Newport harbour. From London prints, down to the 7th of August, we have taken the following articles, viz

PARIS, July 27.

IT seems the rendezvous of the ships that have not joined will be at Corunna, where Monsieur D'Estaing is to take the command of the fleet.

There are great movements among the troops. Upwards of 40 000 men are already on the coasts of Britanny, and several other regiments both foot and dragoons are filing off on that side. It is suspected some grand project is on foot, that will come to light in the course of next month. Every thing is quiet as yet, but it is like the stillness of the air before the storm. We can say nothing more; we must wait.

The moment our Court received the courier extraordinary from Madrid respecting the sailing of the combined fleet, orders were sent to Brest to hasten the sailing of every ship in the road. The ships wait only for the signal to sail, which will probably not be until the arrival of the Spanish fleet.

The Rochfort squadron is at last arrived at Brest. It was laden with warlike stores, particularly cannon, which have already served to arm the Northumberland.

LONDON, July 4.

We learn from Lisbon that a large body of Spanish forces have marched upon the frontiers of that kingdom, and a peremptory answer has been at the same time demanded from the Court of Portugal by the Spanish minister there, to the request made by the Court of Madrid, that English ships of war of every denomination shall be refused admittance into the Portuguese habours. A copy of the late Spanish declaration, which is dated May 23, 1780, has been delivered by the Court of Portugal to our Envoy at Lisbon, and was immediately sent home by the Milford frigate.

August 3. Letters now in town, dated from Paris, are written by persons whose situation in public life must have given them opportunities of authentic intelligence relative to some late proceedings in America. Amongst other particulars, they remark (extraordinary as the circumstance may appear) that the Colonists have actually reduced their enormous debt of two hundred millions of dollars to five million sterling; and that this manoeuvre, so far from occasioning the least alarm, had given general satisfation. Admitting the fact, such a circumstance must certainly furnish our opponents on the other side the Atlantic with fresh force to continue the war. The victory gained at Charlestown is important; but its advantages must gradually lesson if they retard the peace.

August 7. It was some time the determination of Ministers to have raised again the apprehensions of an invasion, for the purpose of procuring if possible, fresh subscriptions, and diverting the public attention from prospects of more immediate and eminent danger. But it was suggested, soon after the instructions had been given to Lord N—— and the rest of their runners, that this alarm would give an absolute sanction to the armed associations in the several towns and counties of Britain, and add to the phalanx of opposition, which was already but too powerful and threatening. Owing to this diffidence of their strength, they have spared this delusion; and as the tumults happily intervened, to give them a temporary recess, and a new ground for imposition, they say they have never felt the want of this never failing expedient.

The grand fleet under Admiral Geary, now out on a cruize, consists of 29 sail of the line, and is shortly to be reinforced by 11 more, which will make 40 capital ships.

In consequence of the great want of seamen, no more protections will be granted till his Majesty's ships are properly manned.

Orders are sent to Ireland, to impress into his Majesty's service all the useful hands they could, and send them to England as soon as possible.

It is reported that the Parliament will, soon after the next prorogation, which is the 24th instant, be dissolved by a royal proclamation, and new writs will be issued out for electing Members for counties, cities, and boroughs, throughout the kingdom.

Notwithstanding the vigilance of Admiral Geary, the combined fleet of France and Spain, have at last effected a junction off Ferrol, and consists of not less than fifty-two ships of the line and eighteen frigates.

ANNAPOLIS, September.

The following is a true copy of a second original letter found in a Major Rugley's house, 13 miles from Cambden, South Carolina; the Major having departed, on the approach of our troops, in such haste, as not to have time to secure his papers; the originals have been compared with several letters from Lord Rawdon to the Baron de Kalb and Gen. Gates, and are exactly and clearly the same hand writing.

[Secret.] Cambden, July 7, 1780.

SIR,

I SEND you the names of some of the field officers who are at present under Gen. Sumpter's command. Perhaps you may have such acquaintance with some of them, at least with their characters, that you may tempt them with proposals, without fear of betraying you. The service which I would have them perform, is, to advise Sumpter to advance and fix his encampment behind Berkley's Creek, where there is a very specious position.

I will promise five hundred guineas to any of them who will prevail upon him to take that step; will give you notice of it; will particularise the enemy's force, and mark what detachments are made to secure their camp from surprize. Whoever undertakes it, may depend upon the strictest secrecy being observed; for, upon that head, I am sure I may rely upon you. Very plausible arguments may be used for counselling Sumpter, to take that position; it may particularly be represented, that he would thereby cover the Waxhaws from the incursions of our cavalry, and secure all the grain of that district: That Mecan's detachment from its halting at Hanging-Rock, is evidently weak, and acting on the defensive; and, as we can support our light troops much more readily from Hanging Rock, than he can sustain his present position, his advanced parties will always be circumscribed in their range, and must always suffer when they fall in with ours. To prevent their having any apprehensions from me, reports may be propagated in their camp, that Caswell had defeated M'Arthur, and was pressing forward against me, their credulity would ardently embrace a tale so consonant to their wishes; and the asserter might, in spreading it, make a parade of his zeal. The difficulty will be to procure a proper emissary; if he conducts the business well, he shall be rewarded in proportion to the importance of the service. There is in their camp, a Lieutenant-Colonel Lacey, a prisoner on parole to us, who, endeavouring to persude Patten to follow his example, has been confined, and injuriously treated by Sumpter; possibly that may be a good channel for the business. No evil can arise from a discovery of the proposal. Sumpter might, indeed, pretend to give into the snare, and might lay an ambuscade for us, but, as I should march prepared for every occurrence, I might probably draw as much advantage from meeting him in that manner, as if I had been the assailant. We must only take care not to be duped; for if the person whom we try, reveals the affair to Sumpter, the latter may go halves with him; and to entitle him to the money, may encamp at Berkley's-creek, one afternoon, and go off next morning. The terms must be clear and bonna fide towards us at least. Should Sumpter be reinforced, I think him likely to take the step without instigation. Shew this letter to Major Mecan, and believe me, Sir,

Your very humble servant,

RAWDON.

Major Rugley.

Such are the mean arts the enemy now use in hopes of subduing this country.

September 29.

A genuine copy of a letter to Generals Smallwood and Gist, from the Chevalier Dubuyson.

Charlotte, August 26, 1780.

"Dear Generals,

"Having received several wounds in the action of the 16th instant, I was made a prisoner with the Honorable Major General the Baron de Kalb, with whom I served as Aid-de-Camp and friend, and had an opportunity of attending that great and good officer during the short time he languished with eleven wounds, which proved mortal on the third day.

"It is with pleasure I obey the Baron's last commands, in presenting his most affectionate compliments to all the officers and men of his division: expressed the greatest satisfaction in the testimony given by the British army of the bravery of his troops; and he was charmed with the firm opposition they made to superior force, when abandoned by the rest of the army. The gallant behaviour of the Delaware regiment and the companies of artillery attached to the brigades, afforded him infinite pleasure, and the examplary conduct of the whole division gave him an endearing sense of the merit of the troops he had the honor to command.

I am, dear Generals,
With regard and respect,
Your most obedient,
humble servant,

Le CHEVALIER DUBUYSON."

To Brigadier Generals Smallwood and Gist.

PHILADELPHIA, October 7.

Extract of a letter from Pittsburgh, dated Sept. 1.

"Since my last, the Savages have killed and scalped ten men, about 60 miles up the Monongohela; and Capt. Bird, with a few regulars and Canadians, and they report 700 Savages, hath entirely broke up one of the Kentucky settlements, having made prisoners 400 men, women and children. But this stroke may prove serviceable to us, as it will, I hope, if not finally stopped, give a check to the emigrations to the Ohio, which is prodigious, and which must weaken the country below. The grasping hand of the covetous and avaracious monopolizer, not only of American money, but of American lands, has in a manner put arms into the hands of our enemies. The former practice is now I hope, effectually abolished, and I wish the latter was."

Extract of a letter from the Eastern Shore of Maryland, to a gentleman in this city, dated Sept. 30.

"Since writing the inclosed letter we have certain advices by Mr. Goldsborough, that the enemy had plundered the town of Vienna, and burnt a new brig; and on their way down called at Col. John Henry's, and destroyed his house and furniture. All the Colonel's family was in Somerset, except himself, who, on the approach of the enemy, had retired to a house in the neighbourhood, where he had removed his plate and papers. This was a very fortunate circumstance for him, as they intended to take away his life, had they found him at home. They took away one negro man from Mr. Henry, and another from Mr. Steele, a near neighbour.

October 11.

Extract of a letter from camp, Tappan, October 2.

"You have had the particulars of traitor Arnold's conduct, before his getting on board the Vulture sloop of war, which lay near Stoney Point; but his conduct since he went into New York, is still a greater proof of his villainy (if greater villainy was possible.) At his arrival with the British, he had upwards of 50 of our warmest friends in New York taken up, and put into dungeons and other places of confinement. But there is a providence attending the unhappy friends to their country, that puts it out of his power to injure them, other than imprisonment. Such was the precipitate flight he made, to save his neck from the halter, that he had no time to move off a single paper, or any other matter which can be a testimony against those he would otherwise ruin in person and estate. Gen. Robertson came up yesterday to Dobb's Ferry, with a flag, which was soon dismissed, it being of so trifling a nature, viz. to intreat His Excellency General Washington, at the request of Sir Harry Clinton, to use lenity to Major Andre. It had the effect to respite him for some hours, as the flag did not return till five o'clock, which was the hour fixed in general orders for his execution; This day at 12 o'clock it took place, by hanging him by the neck. Perhaps no person (on like occasion) ever suffered the ignominious death, that was more regretted by officers and soldiers of every rank in our army; or did I ever see any person meet his fate with more fortitude and equal conduct. When he was ordered to mount the waggon under the gallows, he replied, "He was ready to die, but wished the mode to have been in some more elligible way, prefering to be shot*". After he opened his shirt collar, fixed the rope, and tied his handkerchief over his eyes, he was asked by the officer commanding the troops, If he wished to say any thing? He replied, "I have said all I had to say before, and have only to request the gentlemen present, to bear testimony that I met death as a brave man."

"The flag mentioned to have come out with General Robertson, was received by General Green and Colonel Hamilton; and what is curious, Arnold sent his resignation, by desire, that General Washington should forward it to Congress; with an insolent letter, intimating he never would serve Congress any more, nor need they expect it. And moreover, that if Major Andre should be executed by order of General Washington, that he would strike a blow on some of his friends on the Continent that should sufficiently retaliate, for his loss to his Prince. General Green, when he read the letter, treated it with contempt, and threw it on the

* He was dressed in full uniform; and after his execution, his servant demanding his cloaths, which he received. His body was buried near the gallows

SATURDAY, DECEMBER 21, 1782. THE ROYAL GAZETTE. No. 651.

NEW-YORK, *Published by* JAMES RIVINGTON, *Printer to the King's Most Excellent Majesty.*

HIGH-WATER at NEW-YORK, this WEEK.
SAT. 57 m. after 4 | Wed 49 m. after 7
Sun. 34 m. after 5 | Thu. 40 m. after 8
Mond. 14 m. after 6 | Frid. 35 m. after 9
Tuesd. 59 m. after 6

Sugar House Paper,
To be sold, enquire of the Printer.

Swords, Cutteaux, and Pistols of various kinds.

☞ The most beautiful CANES in great Variety for Gentlemen and Ladies.

Commissary-General's Office, Maiden-Lane, Dec. 16, 1782.

ALL Persons having Demands against the Commissary-General's Department, for Forage, Fuel, Provisions, or any other Thing whatever, are hereby desired to bring their Accounts for settlement to this Office on or before the 31st Instant.

Barrack Master General's Office.
Water Street, 17th December, 1782.

ALL PERSONS having demands against the BARRACK MASTER-GENERAL'S DEPARTMENT, between the 5th and 26th of May, 1782, are desired to bring in their ACCOUNTS to this Office immediately that they may be settled.

For SALE, by the PIECE,
At the MANUFACTORY STORE,
No. 50, Water-Street, between the Fly-Market and Burling-Slip, *cheap as usual*,

A Large and fresh importation of the following GOODS: Twilled Bath Coatings, Superfine, and Second Broad Cloths, London Brown, blue, Scarlet, Drabs of the newest colours; some twill'd for over Coats (water proof) Super and Second white Cloth, &c. A few very fine Carpets, a large quantity of Men's fine Shoes, with many other articles too tedious to mention.

A few Pieces BUFF CLOTH, &c.
S. HOPKINS.

New-York, Nov. 30, 1782.

THOSE who have any demands against the late BENJAMIN BIRKETT, are desired to send in their accounts properly attested; and those who are indebted to him, or have transactions unsettled, are desired to close the same, and make immediate payment to

SAMUEL ELAM, Executor,
No. 211, Queen-Street.

FOR the speedy closing of his affairs, the effects of the deceased, consisting of plain and figured Sattins, Persians, Sarsenets, Modes, 4-4ths and 7 8ths Irish Linens, Moreens, Rattinets, Shalloons, Callimancoes, dark brown and striped Camblets, Dorsetteens, Damascus, Missinets, Lustres, Brilliants, Silverets, Cord Denims, Durants, Tammies, Crapes, Rupels, Silk Stockings, Hatts and Hatter's Trimmings, Coarse and fine Scotch Threads, &c.

A few Callicoes, and French Basket Buttons, with a small but well assorted parcel of black Lace, and rich striped and spotted Gauzes, Mens fine and military Shoes, Womens Callimancoe ditto, new Silk, Lungee, Romal, and Silk and Muslin Handkerchiefs, &c &c. will be sold by said ELAM on very reasonable terms for Cash only.

TO BE SOLD OR LET,

A GREAT number of LOTS OF GROUND, part of the estate of JAMES DELANCEY, Esq; now in England, lying between the Bowery Lane and the East River, and adjoining thereto, also four lots of ground, whereon is a double brick house, and one frame house, next to John Mott's in the Bowery; also four lots with a two story house, adjoining the lines, also another brick house with as many lots as will suit a purchaser, at present possessed by government as a magazine; also the MANSION HOUSE of the said James Delancey, and the out-houses thereto belonging, with either 32 or 64 lots, as will best suit the purchaser. For particulars enquire of James Rivington, or George Stanton, Attornies to the said James Delancey.

It is again earnestly requested that the tenants in arrear, pay their rents, or they must expect trouble.

One Guinea and a Half Reward.

RUN-AWAY, on the 15th ult. an INDENTED SERVANT-BOY, about 17 years of age, named *Samuel Wilkins*; he has fair hair; a little pitted with the small pox; is a smart active boy; had on when he went away, a blue jacket, round hat, and long trowsers, shoes and stockings, plated buckles. The above reward will be given to any person that will secure him or bring him on board of his former ship, *Generous Friends Transport*, one of the last fleet from England.

N. B. All Masters of vessels and others, are forwarned not to conceal or carry him off, as they shall answer for the same at their peril. [*3t.

New-York, Dec. 2, 1782.

JOSEPH STEVENS,
Livery Stable Keeper,

IS thankful to the Public for their past favours, and begs leave to acquaint them he has provided a neat Carriage, close and warm, with four able Horses, and a careful Driver, to go from this city to Fort Knyphausen, every Monday, Wednesday, and Friday, to set out from his house, No. 16, in the Broadway, near Fort George, at Eight o'Clock in the morning, and to return from Fort Knyphausen at Three o'clock in the afternoon, the same Days precisely.
Each passenger to pay One Dollar to and from thence.
Baggage and small parcels carried at a reasonable rate.
It set out for the first time last Monday being the 9th of this month.

A good Coach and Saddle Horses to be had on the shortest notice, and particular care taken of Horses at Livery.

By the Public's humble Servant,
JOSEPH STEVENS.

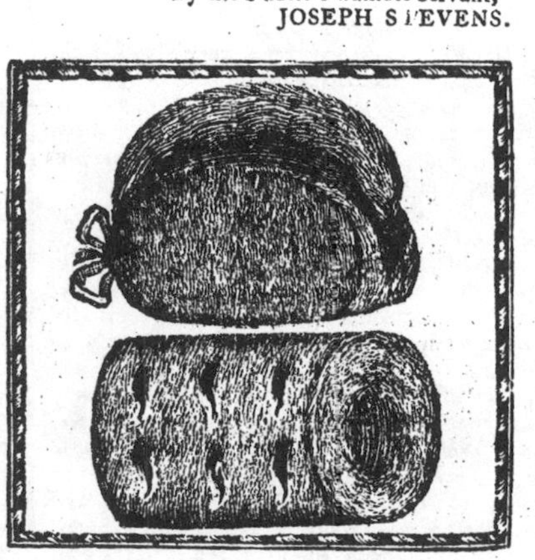

Daniel Hartung,
FURRIER from LONDON,
At the Sign of the CAP and MUFF,
No. 176, Queen-Street, near Peck's-Slip.
Has for Sale,

A General and complete assortment of Muffs and Tippets, the best of Martin and Martin Throat, Russia Squirrel, and ground Squirrel Lining for Cloaks, Trimmings for Ladies Riding Dresses, and likewise Gentlemens travelling Caps, Gloves lined with Fur, wholesale and retail.

N. B. The highest price given for all sorts of Fur.

Thomas Barrow,
No. 58, BROAD-STREET,
Has received by the IRIS,
From LONDON,
A very elegant Assortment of
PRINTS,
UNFRAMED,
Taken from the Paintings of the most celebrated Artists, many of them entirely new,

WATTS's Select Views of Gentlemen's Seats,
BUNBURY's Caricaturas, a great variety, and many of them new published,
Small Landscapes, in books for young Artists,
Boxes of prepared colours, with Pencils, &c. complete,
Colours in shells—fine dry Colours of all sorts,
Transparent Colours for maps and plans,
Best camel-hair Pencils, of all sizes,
Copal Oil Varnish and Whitehard, do.
Deep and Pale coloured Gold-Leaf,
Best London Crown-Glass, and framing do. for Pictures,
Oval Frames for Miniature and Profile.
Whiting, Chalk, and yellow Oaker, in Powder,
Red Lead, Lithurge, common Paints of all sorts,
Window Glass of every size.

By Samuel Birch, Esq;
Brigadier-General and Commandant of *New-York*, &c. &c.

A Proclamation.

WHEREAS the safety of the City, and the preservation of the Shipping require the Wharves to be kept as clear as possible, during the Winter.

It is therefore ordered, That after the 1st day of January next, no vessel be allowed to lay at, or near any wharf of this city, without having previously obtained Permits from the Superintendent of the Port, and coming within the following description:

Private Ships of War, and trading Vessels, to have Permits, not exceeding ten days, for repairing, fitting out, lading, and unloading.

Captured vessels to have Permits for the disposal of their cargoes, not exceeding 15 days, from the date of their condemnation.

All Owners, Merchants, and Masters of such Vessels (not employed in the service of Government) as intend wintering at New-York, are hereby ordered to remove their vessels to Newtown-Creek, by the said 1st day of January.

Any person offending against this Proclamation, will be subject to one month's imprisonment, in the Provost, and to the payment of such Fine as shall be adjudged by the Police, for the use of the city funds.

Given under my Hand in the City of New-York, this 14th day of December, in the year of our Lord 1782.

SAMUEL BIRCH.

By Order of the Commandant,
JOHN ST. CLAIR, *Secretary.*

CHOICE old Madeira Wine, London quality, neat as imported,
Irish low price Linens Sheetings, Tabbinets,
Printed Cottons, silk Crapes and Rigs,
Bed Ticken, Furniture, Check and Dimity,
Sail Cloth, No. 1, 2, 3, and 5,
And Bohea Tea, &c.

TO BE SOLD BY
WILLIAM BACKHOUSE, and Co.
WATER-STREET.
December 12, 1782. tf

To be Sold low for Cash,
By BRUCE and ADAMS,
At No. 3, Murray's Wharf, opposite the Cooperage,

OLD Cherry, Port and Lisbon Wines, per Cask or Dozen, old Jamaica Spirits and Rum, Coniac and Cherry Brandy; Gin and Lime-Juice, per Cask or Gallon; best London Bottled Porter; Hyson and common Teas, Gloucester, Cheshire and Country Cheese; Hams; Pearl and common Barley and Butter; Beef and Pork in Tierces and Barrels; Pickled and Dry'd Ox Tongues; Flour and fine Bisquet in Kegs; Codfish, Wax, Mould, and Dipped Candles, and Soap in Boxes; Sugars per Hogshead or Box: Also a quantity of English made Rivetts and Coopers Tools, and Chalk, reasonable, with many Articles in the Grocery line—

N. B. As Robert Bruce intends for Britain shortly for the benefit of his Health, wishes to intimate the same to his Friends and Customers, whose past Favous, he gratefully acknowledges, and wishes to close his Books as soon as possible.

A Negro Fellow, Wench, and three Children to be Sold together or separate, by R. B.

F O U N D,
By two Grenadiers, 37th Regiment,
A BLACK STRAP POCKET BOOK,

CONTAINING papers, protections, &c. with a name marked on it in gold letters.

The owner proving property and paying charges, may have it again. Enquire of the Printer.

Jamaica, Long-Island.
TO BE LET,
A well-accustomed Shop & Cellar,
The former is already shelved, and stands advantageously for Business.
Enquire of the PRINTER.

ALL Persons having any demands against the Estate of JAMES BURR, deceased, are requested to leave their accounts at his late Dwelling-House on Cow-Neck, or at Samuel Mabbets, in New-York. And all those that are indebted to said Estate, are desired to make immediate payment to

ISAAC BURR, ADMINISTRATOR.
December 13, 1782. *3t.

Further Advices by the Roebuck Packet.

CAMP of St. ROCH versus GIBRALTAR.

COPY of an INDICTMENT against GEN. ELLIOT, for destroying the Spanish Floating Batteries.

THE Marshals of France, in council of war assembled, after solemn deliberation, on behalf of their Most Christian and Catholic Majesties, the Kings of France and Spain, do present, That his Most Catholic Majesty, having combined with his Most Christian Majesty, and become a party in the war against his Britannic Majesty, for the sole purpose of re-annexing to the Imperial Crown of Spain that brightest and most central of its jewels, GIBRALTAR, which, to the infinite dishonour and mortification of the Spanish nation, had sparkled in and ornamented the British diadem for near threescore years past, their said combined Majesties did, on the 29th day of July, 1779, cause the said fortress of Gibraltar, then and still being under the government of Gen. George Augustus Elliot, a British subject, to be invested both by sea and land with their united and utmost forces, viz. 30,000 Spanish and 20,000 French troops, the flower of their respective armies, and 10,000 forcats, convicts, and galley slaves, for hazardous expeditions, and to save the blood Royal of France and Spain, and others of the noblesse, whose valour and thirst for honour led them to the said siege—And that the said fortress hath been closely besieged, and for a long space of time, to wit, three years and upwards, assailed with force and arms, to wit, with cannon and other great guns, mortars, and bombs, loaded with gunpowder, shells, and balls, and with divers and all other the most destructive engines and warlike instruments, heretofore invented, used or accustomed. YET (in despight thereof, and notwithstanding the town of Gibraltar, and every house there and within the said fortress, had been totally and effectually demolished by the incessant fire of red hot-balls and other laudable warlike instruments, and the inhabitants driven to reside in caves and hollows of the rock) he, the said Gen. Geo. Augustus Elliot, not regarding the Lives of his troops, nor the polite laws of modern war and the many BURGOYNARDS and other examples of his countrymen, which demanded, and would have justified, the surrender of the said fortress to the victorious arms of their said combined Majesties long since, to wit, several years ago; nor yet in any wise influenced by the horrible dissentions, party-rage, and destructive feuds, which have nearly destroyed the kingdom, whose welfare he pretends to have so much at heart; and notwithstanding he was appointed to his post by the late discarded administration; but being moved to such unexampled obstinacy by true British bravery and innate courage, (as he pretends) and by the fidelity due to his Sovereign and the honour of the British crown and arms, which he hath declared himself determined to defend to the last extremity, though with only a handful of men, viz. 5000 men or thereabouts; he, the said General, in pursuance of such obstinate determinations, had the audacity, after a three years siege, to set at naught his Excellency the Duc de Crillon, the Princes of the Blood, the forcats, convicts, and whole power of France and Spain, and to bid them all defiance:

[2d Count.] And the said Marshals of France, so in council assembled as aforesaid, do farther present, That their said Majesties of France and Spain, being so insulted and dishonoured by such the obstinacy of the said British Governor as aforesaid, did assemble, and cause to be assembled, all the able engineers, and other the greatest men of France and Spain, to invent new and the most diabolically-destructive engines that human wit could devise, who accordingly, pursuant to such Most Christian commands, did invent, and cause to be built, a great number, to wit, 20 huge floating batteries, whose roofs were bomb proof, and whose sides, like the solid rock of Gibraltar, were impervious to cannon balls; and the same INVINCIBLE ARMADA of floating batteries did man and fit out with an immense number of cannon, viz. 500 cannon of the largest bores, and 20,000 of the picked men and volunteers of the said combined army, headed by the Princes of the Blood, convicts and forcats aforesaid, and protected and supported by the whole naval power and combined fleet of France and Spain, to wit, 48 great ships of the line, and divers others of less force, under the bravest commanders, with an intent to take him the said obstinate Gen. Elliot, and the said impregnable rock of Gibraltar, utterly to demolish, and the said devoted garrison and troops to kill, destroy, and exterminate, to the immortal honor of their said Catholic and Most Christian Majesties and their arms, and the unbounded joy of the Spanish nation.

[3d Count.] And the said Marshals of France, so in Council assembled as aforesaid, do farther present, that the said Gen. G. A. Elliot, the polite and inoffensive rules of modern war not regarding, but craftily and subtily devising and intending the destruction of the said floating batteries, gun-boats and other the aforesaid unheard of, unusual, and deadly engines and inventions, so intended to be brought, levelled and directed against him, for the destruction of himself and his garrison, he, the said Gen. Elliot (for his own preservation, and that of his brave garrison, as he pretends, but, in fact and in truth, with intent to bring immortal and irretrievable disgrace, discredit, and dishonour upon the arms of their said combined

Monday, May 5, 1783. THE (No. 164)

NEW-YORK GAZETTE: AND THE WEEKLY MERCURY.

Containing the earliest Advices Foreign and Domestick.

☞ Printed by *HUGH GAINE*, at his BOOK-STORE and PRINTING-OFFICE, at the BIBLE and CROWN, in *Hanover-Square*.

HIGH-WATER, at *NEW-YORK*, this Week.

Monday,	34 Min. after 12	Friday,	2 Min. after 3
Tuesday,	26 Min. after 12	Saturday,	51 Min. after 3
Wednesday,	19 Min. after 1	Sunday,	38 Min. after 4
Thursday,	11 Min. after 2	First Quarter Friday.	

PHILADELPHIA, APRIL 24.

The Brig Minerva, Captain Hallet, of Boston, arrived here last Tuesday evening, in five weeks, from Bourdeaux. By her we are favoured with London papers to the 4th of March, from which we have selected the following intelligence.——

HOUSE of COMMONS.

FRIDAY, FEBRUARY 21.

MR. *Secretary Townshend* gave notice, that he would, on a future day, make a motion relative to the regulating the commercial intercourse between Great-Britain and North-America.

Lord John Cavendish informed the House, that at first it was his intention to wait till the Dutch articles were laid before them, in order that they might judge with the greater precision concerning the peace; but after the issue of the debate on Monday last, he was convinced that the farther consideration of these articles should immediately take place, without any interruption whatever. He did not argue in this manner from any pique or personal enmity against any man, but for the national good, which ought to be the first consideration of every Member of that House. It had been industriously spread abroad, that the part he took in Monday's debate, tended to militate against the peace, whereas he meant no such thing. His amendments tended to delay the consideration of the terms of the treaty, till such time as Parliament were fully informed of the different articles, and not to inform his Majesty that they had considered and approved of the treaty, when, in fact, they new very little about it. He did not at all mean no insinuate, that the treaty should not be looked upon as binding in every respect, and that it was ratified to all intents and purposes. He thought that the national honour and faith were pledged upon it, and he would by no means wish to have it believed without doors, that he entertained any the least idea of breaking this treaty although some very officious persons had industriously circulated such an opinion; but he assured the Hon. House, and he believed every gentleman upon the least reflection would agree with him, that the amendment on Monday last, which he had the honour to make had quite the contrary tendency. What motives such persons could have in circulating a report which carried along with it such notorious falsity, he could not pretend to determine; but he was sorry to think that it might be now fully propagated in the country, that those were his intentions. He then said, that although he thought that the national faith should be held as sacred and binding in every respect, and that the articles of pacification, which were now ratified, should be considered as finally entered into and agreed upon by the different powers, yet he begged leave to observe, that the peace was not so honourable to this country as might have been expected. He did not think that the framers of this treaty were entitled to such high compliments, or such distinguished praise, as their dependents had imagined. We were not in such a deplorable situation as they thought proper to represent. We had been victorious in many parts of the globe, and we should not have made such shameful and extravagant concessions as we had done. We had given up great and lucrative possessions, and gained nothing in return. We had lost our national importance, and diminished our grandeur.—We had tarnished our splendid victories, by yielding to our enemies such possessions as they could not with any degree of reason look for. He did not mean to criminate any of the gentlemen in Administration, but he thought, and he flattered himself every gentleman, who judged with candour and propriety, on a subject of so great importance, would coincide with him in opinion, by saying that there was fault somewhere, and ought to be enquired into. Perhaps it might appear that Government were not to blame in this treaty, but it should be so proved to the House. After some farther argument to the same purport, he made five motions to the following effect.

1. That the House will support his Majesty in the articles of peace already concluded between him and the different powers.

2. That they will assist his Majesty in dispensing the blessings of peace among his subjects.

3. That his Majesty, considering the circumstances of the times, acted right in granting independence to the Thirteen United States of America.

4. That it is the opinion of the House, that the cessions made on the part of Great-Britain, by his Majesty's Ministers, were too many, and too extravagant.

5. That it be recommended to government, to provide some way or other for the Loyalists, so as that they may be relieved from their present distressed situation.

Mr. St. John supported the noble mover. He thought our concessions were too many, especially when we considered the insignificance of what we had in return, and that the peace was a shameful one to Great-Britain.

Mr. Secretary Townshend did not attempt to defend the peace on any other than national principles. If gentlemen were resolved to make an enquiry into the treaty, let them do it in a fair and candid manner, and not be led away by party prejudices. Let them, if they pleased, make a motion for the immediate removal of the present Administration, if they thought they had not acted agreeably to the interests of the nation. If any man could lay any blame upon him, he would be ready to meet him whenever he thought proper; and he was certain that his colleagues, who acted in every respect with as much rectitude and probity, would be ready at any time for such an investigation. He said, he had no objection to the first, second, and third motions, but the fourth he would oppose, as he thought it uncandid and improper; that his Majesty's Ministers, if they had made any cessions, had certainly some compensation in return.—He likewise objected to the 5th, although he agreed that the Loyalists ought to be provided for.

Sir Cecil Wray declared, that he was an enemy to all parties, particularly those that were detrimental to the interests of the nation.

A desultory conversation then took place between Lord North, Sir Richard Sutton, Sir Horace Mann, Mr. Burrel, Secretray Townshend, General Conway, &c. concerning this point whether or not the different motion should be taken into consideration *in toto*, or debated upon one after another, when the latter was agreed to.

The first and second were then read, and passed *nemine contradicente*.

After which the third was read, when

Lord Newhaven and *Sir W. Dolben* wished to know what authority his Majesty had for dismembering the Empire? The bill that passed in Parliament, granting his Majesty power to make a Truce or Peace with America, did not grant him such authority. The framer of the bill certainly did not mean that his Majesty should have full power to grant America Independence. As the Honourable Gentleman was in the House, they would like to have his opinion upon it, and to know what his sentiments were when he brought the bill into Parliament?

Mr. Wallace said, that when the bill was brought into Parliament, it undoubtedly had that meaning, and that it granted his Majesty full power to give the Americans Independence, if that was the price of Peace.

A short conversation took place between the Attorney-General, Mr. Lee, and the Solicitor-General, relative to his Majesty's prerogative to grant Independence to America, in which they differed from one another, and promised at any time to meet each other on this point of law; but they deferred entering into the grounds of it then, as it would in all probability soon come before the House.

Sir Adam Ferguson, doubted much whether or not this was the original intention of the bill. But allowing that it was, surely, says he, his Majesty has no power to give away any principal part of Canada. The bill never went so far, and he denied the legality of such a procedure.

Lord North thought that we had given up too much, and wondered that we should have made such concessions; but he would not embarress Ministry by declaiming against their conduct, as he thought it an uncandid mode of proceeding. The motion was then agreed to.

The fourth was then read, when

Mr. Powys, in a speech of considerable length, inveighed against those who were dissatisfied with the peace, and was surprised that the noble Lord should have made such a motion. He respected him for his integrity and philanthrophy, and wondered how he could be guilty of so great an impropriety. He declaimed against party prejudices, and imputed a great part of our misfortunes to the noble Lord in the blue ribband.

Lord John Cavendish refuted the last Honourable Speaker in his attacks on him and his party; and said, he did not mean to impeach Administration, but he thought it necessary to enquire into the reasons of making such great concessions.

Sir Edward Astley despised all parties, and thought every one should unite in the cause of the nation. He would wish to see discord banished, and all sides of the House shake hands in an amicable manner, and exert themselves in the common cause. So far was his interest from Administration, that he assured the House he had not influence enough to make an officer of the Customs or Excise. He thought that the noble Lord in the blue ribband had plunged us in the ruinous and destructive war in which we had been engaged for many years. But the enormity of pensions had proceeded to such a height, that his Lordship had been rewarded with one, and his Secretary with another. With regard to this, his successors could not dare to blame him, as they had committed the like enormity. He was, therefore, amazed at the corruption of the times, and concluded with dissenting from the motion.

Mr. M'Donald opposed the motion.

Mr. Fox, in a long and very able speech, said, that we had made base and mean cessions to our enemies. The condition of our country was much more respectable than had been represented. France had decreased 13 in line of battle ships this last year, while those of Great-Britain had increased seventeen ships of the line. We had a great superiority in the West-Indies. Our fleet, he said was put upon the most respectable footing, by the great exertions of the first Lord of the Admiralty (Lord Keppel), a man who deserved well of his country, but who had been invidiously and maliciously calumniated. We had given away inestimable possessions, and we were wise *a fortiori*. What we had given to France was equal to a general restitution. He said he had taken notice of the *uti possidetis* on a former day, and he averred, that what he had done was as lucrative to France as a general restitution. This to him appeared *prima facie*; and at first blush he was convinced of our error. He lamented the untimely death of the Marquis of Rockingham, and paid many compliments to his memory. He said, he himself had withdrawn himself from the present administration, as soon as he found that the gentlemen with whom he confided in for many years, abandoned their principles. The present administration were formed from the ruins of the last, and he was sorry to see many gentlemen for whom he had the highest regard remain so long in administration. He blamed the Earl of Shelburne, and said, that he had never a great opinion of his Lordship. He was up three hours, and entered minutely into his political principles.

Mr. Chancellor Pitt made a long and elegant speech, in which he gave a narrative of the condition of our navy, and compared it with that of our enemies, by which he endeavoured to shew that Mr. Fox's statement was erroneous. He said, that if he and his colleagues should be forced from their situation, he would not erect, like Mr. Fox, a fortress for the invitation of a phalanx, but would leave to government the management of the state, unclogged by invidious opposition.

Sir Cecil Wray rose to explain, he was only the enemy of North's principles; but of all men in this country, he would select Mr. Fox to be Prime Minister.

Lord North made a long and most able speech, in which he confirmed what Mr. Fox had said. Their enmity had ceased with its cause. He had always found Mr. Fox a warm friend—a fair, but a formidable adversary.

Mr. T. Pitt arraigned the unnatural junction of men, the most adverse in principle, and told a story of a Barbarian, who meeting a friend as he was going to a feast, mangled and left him in a miserable condition; and afterwards, when he had found that they had bathed and bound up his wounds, he tore off the bandages and set them a-bleeding afresh.—This story he applied to Lord North.

Several other members spoke, and at length the House divided, ayes 207, noes 190 —— Majority against Ministry 17.

Lord John Cavendish then withdrew his fifth proposition respecting the Loyalists, and the House adjourned.

HOUSE OF COMMONS,

MONDAY, *March 3d.*

READ a first time the Bill for opening an intercourse with America.

The Secretary at War moved, that the House should go into a Committee, and vote one years supply for the army. He gave a particular account of the different estimates, and explained to the House the several extraordinaries that had been voted during the time that he had held his office in Administration.

Mr. David Hartley in a speech of considerable length said, that instead of one year's supply, he thought that six or nine months supply would be sufficient to answer all the purposes requisite. He did not, he said, speak to Administration, for were he to do so, it would be doing nothing, as there were at present no Administration in this country, therefore he hoped the House would take the matter into consideration, and insist that the troops should be immediately withdrawn from America.

The *Speaker* then put the question, when the House divided, and the numbers were,

Ayes - - -	183
Noes - - -	10

Majority against Mr. Hartley, 173

The House then went into a Committe of Supply, Mr. *Ord* in the Chair, when the sum of one million, that was mentioned on Friday last was granted.

The *Secretary at War* then resumed the former business relative to the estimates of the army, and entered fully into every particular. He then moved that the following sums be granted as a twelve months supply to the troops, and mentioned the various dates of the applications of these different sums.

TROOPS.	MONEY.		
Guards and those in garrison,	456 904l.	19s.	9½
Plantations, - -	310,623	16	6
Staff, - - -	15,096	17	2
East-Indies, - - -	15 074	10	0
Militia and Fencibles, -	165 418	10	0
From Ireland, - -	41,140	16	2
North-America, - -	25,126	3	1
Chelsea, - - -	96.719	7	11
Gibraltar, (Hanoverians)	28,017	11	0½
Hesse Corps, - -	367.203	9	10
Hanau Corps, - -	65,152	12	8¼
Brunswick Corps, -	36,747	0	0
Waldeckers, - - -	1,749	11	3
Brandenburgh Corps, -	51 501	19	3
Anhault Zerbst, - -	23,818	14	2¾

Mr. David Hartley used some arguments similar to what he had already advanced, and expressed his intention of moving for an Address to his Majesty, relative to the withdrawing the troops immediately from America.

Secretary Townshend observed, that it would take a considerable time to accomplish it, as it required an immensity of tonnage to convey the troops and the implements of war from that country: and was surprised that any gentleman could doubt the sincerity of this country to America, after what had passed.

Mr. Pulteney was equally astonished at the former Honourable Gentleman's sentiments with regard to our sincerity to America, and thought that administration should not be teized on the occasion, as he hoped that all cause of enmity between the two countries was now at an end.

Mr. H. W. Hartley warmly urged the Committee to take care in time, and not to vote a matter, the evil consequences of which were not seen at present, but he was persuaded would be greater than any of the Ministry, or any other person could possibly have expected. Mr. Hartley talked of the suspicions that had already been embraced respecting the sincerity of this country's conciliatory disposition towards America, and said, he was sorry such suspicions had been really entertained.

Mr. Sheridan rose immediately after Mr. W. Hartley sat down, and observed, tha[t] one man in that House holding a lang[uage]

m'lar to that the Committee had just heard, and hinting even at any suspicions of the sincerity of this country, with respect to her reconciliation with America, might create very serious jealousies, and do much mischief. Mr. Sheridan declared, that to say this country was not sincere in regard to the United States, Gentlemen must know and feel to be an assertion very ill founded indeed! This country was, this country could not but be sincere in what she had done; but it did not appear that it ought to follow, that New-York must be evacuated in any limited time.——If he understood the sixth article of the Provisional Treaty rightly, he meant that article which stipulated that there should be no further confiscations made, and that those persons in confinement at the time of the ratification of the treaty, should be immediately set at liberty. If he understood that article rightly, the words of the treaty referred to a future treaty, that remained to be made, and not the Provisional Treaty, should such be the fact Ministers undoubtedly would hold New-York till that treaty was concluded, otherwise the Loyalists would be completely abandoned, and stand but a poor chance of even reaping the little benefit held out to them by the 5th article. Mr. Sheridan dwelt for some little time on the difficulty that would be thrown in the way of the King's present servants, or of any Ministers that might succeed them, if the resolution was altered from the form to which it had been moved. The chief part of what he said, seemed to meet with the concurrence of the Chancellor of the Exchequer, as the Minister nodded his assent repeatedly, while Mr. Sheridan was speaking.

Sir *Cecil Wray* rose in some surprise, and said, what had fallen from the Hon. Gentlemen, had given him a much higher suspicion, and a much stronger doubt of the sincerity of this country towards America, than he had before entertained. Not evacuate New-York for Twelve Months! "God bless my soul (said SirCecil) what am I to conclude from such a declaration? Is it then intended to renew the American war, and to plunge this country still deeper into ruin?" He was pursuing this idea pretty strongly, while Mr. Sheridan was silently expressing his wonder, that what he had suggested should have generated so odd a construction, when

The *Chancellor of the Exchequer* rose and said, it was high time to put an end to a conversation, which if pursued farther, he saw clearly, might, in the present state of the country, do infinite mischief. He begged therefore that gentlemen would weigh their words before they ventured opinions that tended only to raise doubt, where there was no real foundation for it, and to excite jealousies that were wholly unmerited on the part of Great-Britain.

Mr. *Pitt* added some cogent reasons in support of the resolution in its present shape; and quoted the terms of the Provisional Treaty, which states, "that his Britannic Majesty shall, with all convenient speed, withdraw his armies, garrisons and fleets, from the said United States, and from every port, place and harbour within the same." After a word to or two more from Mr. Sheridan, the motions of supply were agreed to.

TRADE.

The Chancellor of the Exchequer brought in a bill relative to our exports to St. Vincents, Montserrat, Dominique, &c. which was read a first time.

He then moved for leave to bring in a bill to regulate our commerce between this country and America, which was agreed to, and the same to be taken into the consideration of the House to-morrow, and he deferred enlarging on it till the House was fuller. Adjourned.

LONDON, *February* 22.

Yesterday at five o'clock, immediately after the Levee was over, the Duke of Grafton went to St. James's, and after holding a private conference with his Majesty for upwards of half an hour, resigned the seals of his employment, as Lord Privy Seal.—This resignation is the prelude to several others that must necessarily take place in a few days. General Conway is expected to resign this day at the drawing room.

February 25. Yesterday at the levee the following Ministers of State intimated to the King their resolution of resigning their respective employments, namely—the Dukes of Richmond, Manchester, and Rutland, the Lord Chancellor, Lords Shelburne and Ashburton, General Conway and Mr. Pitt—*English Chron.*

Yesterday advice was received by Government from Mr. Fitzherbert, our resident at the Court of Versailles, that the French Cabinet were so much alarmed at our present embarkation of troops for the East-Indies, and seemed so little satisfied with the arguments he had urged in defence of the measure, that it would be prudent to be prepared for any hostile interruption which might be given to the passage of the said fleet. In consequence of the above advice orders are gone down to Portsmouth, for fifteen sail of the line to convoy it through the bay to a certain latitude.

Ireland is at this time pushing for a preference in the American market; not a single vessel has sailed as yet from England for any part of the now Independent States; but the ship Mary was to sail on Sunday from Dublin for Philadelphia; so that Ireland takes the lead of the three kingdoms in opening the trade to America.

We hear preliminaries with the Dutch were ally signed, and will be declared to the of Commons on Monday next.

March 4. We can assure our readers, that though the principal officers of the State are settled for the new arrangement, yet there is much to be done before the whole can be so compleated as to be given to the public, and we are afraid that some of the late administration, whose services promised great benefit to the nation, are to retire upon pensions.

The English Chronicle also gives the following as the arrangement of a new Ministry, confidently talked of yesterday at the West end of the town. The Duke of Portland, first Lord of the Treasury. Earl of Carlisle and Mr. Fox, Secretaries of State. Lord John Cavendish, Chancellor of the Exchequer. Earl Gower, President of the Council. Lord Beauchamp, Secretary at War. Colonel North, Paymaster of the Forces. Mr. Burke, Treasurer of the Navy. Lord Townshend, Master of the Ordnance. Earl Dartmouth, Lord Privy Seal. Lord Thurlow, to remain Lord Chancellor. Duke of Montague, Master of the Horse. Dukes of Manchester and Rutland, also to retain their places. The Duke of Devonshire, or Earl Fitzwilliam to go to Ireland. Lord Keppel, first Lord of the Admiralty, with Mr. Brett, Sir Robert Harland, Lord Mulgrave, Lord Lisburne, Lord Duncannon, and the Honourable Major Stanhope. Lords of the Treasury, Mr. Fitzpatrick, Mr. Frederick Montague, Mr. John Townshend, Lord Lewisham, and Lord Althorp. Mr. Richard Burke and Mr. Champion, Secretaries to the Treasury. Mr. Lee, Attorney General. Mr. Macdonald, Solicitor General. Mr. Wallace, to have the first vacancy in Westminster-Hall.

March 7. The Bill for the removal of all doubts relative to the Independency of the legislation and jurisdiction of the Parliament of Ireland, passed the British House of Commons without any particle of opposition, and was ordered to the Peers by the hands of Mr. Grenville.

CHATHAM, *April* 23.

HEAD-QUARTERS, April 18, 1783.

THE Commander in Chief orders the cessation of hostilities between the United States of America and the King of Great-Britain to be publicly proclaimed to-morrow at twelve o'clock, at the new building; and that the proclamation which will be communicated herewith be read to morrow evening at the head of every regiment and corps of the army; after which the chaplains, with the several brigades will render thanks to Almighty God for all his mercies, particularly for his over-ruling the wrath of man to his own glory, and causing the rage of war to cease among the nations.

Although the proclamation before alluded to extends only to the prohibition of hostilities, and not to the annunciation of a general peace, yet it must afford the most rational and sincere satisfaction to every benevolent mind, as it puts a period to a long and doubtful contest, stops the effusion of human blood, opens the prospect to a more splendid scene, and, like another morning star, promises the approach of a brighter day than hath hitherto illuminated the Western hemisphere.—On such a happy day, which is the harbinger of peace, a day which compleats the eighth year of the war, it would be ingratitude not to rejoice: it would be insensibility not to participate in the general felicity.

The Commander in Chief, far from endeavouring to stifle the feelings of joy in his own bosom, offers his most cordial congratulations on the occasion to all the officers of every denomination; to all the troops of the United States in general; and in particular to those gallant and persevering men who had resolved to defend the rights of their invaded country, so long as the war should continue.—For these are the men who ought to be considered as the pride and boast of the American army; and who, crowned with well earned laurels, may soon withdraw from the field of glory to the more tranquil walks of civil life. While the Commander in Chief recollects the almost infinite variety of scenes through which we have past, with a mixture of pleasure, astonishment and gratitude, while he contemplates the prospect before us with rapture, he cannot help wishing that all the brave men, of whatever condition they may be, who have shared the toils and dangers of effecting this glorious revolution; of rescuing millions from the band of oppression, and of laying the foundation of a great empire, might be impressed with a proper idea of the dignified part they have been called to act, under the smiles of Providence, on the stage of human affairs; for happy, thrice happy! shall they be pronounced hereafter who have contributed any thing; who have performed the meanest office in erecting this stupendous FABRIC OF FREEDOM AND EMPIRE on the broad basis of independency; who have assisted in protecting the rights of human nature; and establishing an asylum for the poor and oppressed of all nations and religions.——The glorious task for which we first fled to arms being accomplished—the liberties of our country being fully acknowledged and firmly secured by the smiles of heaven on the purity of our cause, and the honest exertions of a feeble people, determined to be free, against a powerful nation, disposed to oppress them; and the character of those who have persevered thro' every extremity of hardship, suffering, and danger, being immortalized by the illustrious appellation of the PATRIOT ARMY; nothing now remains but for the actors of this mighty scene to preserve a perfect unvaried consistency of character through the very last act, to close the drama with applause; and to retire from the military theatre with the same approbation of angels and men which have crowned all their former virtuous actions. For this purpose no disorder or licentiousness must be tolerated. Every considerate and well disposed soldier must remember it will be absolutely necessary to wait with patience until peace shall be declared, or Congress shall be enabled to take proper measures for the security of the public stores, &c. As soon as these arrangements shall be made, the General is confident there will be no delay in discharging, with every mark of distinction and honour, all the men inlisted for the war, who will then have faithfully performed their engagements with the public. The General has already interested himself in their behalf, and he thinks he need not repeat the assurance of his disposition to be useful to them on the present, and every other proper occasion. In the mean time he is determined that no military neglect or excesses shall go unpunished while he retains the command of the army.

The Adjutant-General will have such working parties detached, to assist in making the preparations for a general rejoicing, as the Chief Engineer with the army shall call for; and the Quarter-Master General will, without delay, procure such a number of discharges to be printed as will be sufficient for all the men inlisted for the war; he will please to apply to Head-Quarters for the form.—An extra ration of liquor to be issued to every man to-morrow to drink, "Perpetual Peace and Happiness to the United States of America."

[VOL. IV.] [NUMB. 161.

THE

NEW-YORK MORNING POST.

☞ *Printed by* MORTON *and* HORNER, *No.* 7, *Water-Street, between the Coffee-Houſe and Old-Slip.*

PUBLISHED EVERY TUESDAY AND FRIDAY.

FRIDAY, NOVEMBER 28, 1783.

New-York, Nov. 28.

Laſt Sunday Night arrived the Lord Hyde Packet, in 47 days from Falmouth.

The DEFINITIVE TREATY

between Great-Britain and the United States of America, ſigned at Paris, the 3d day of September 1783.

In the Name of the Moſt Holy and Undivided Trinity.

IT having pleaſed the Divine Providence to diſpoſe the hearts of his Moſt Serene and Moſt Potent Prince George the Third, by the Grace of God, King of Great-Britain, France and Ireland, Defender of the Faith, Duke of Brunſwick and Lunenburgh, Arch Treaſurer, and Prince Elector of the Holy Roman Empire, &c. and of the United States of America, to forget all paſt miſunderſtandings and differences that have unhappily interrupted the good correſpondence and friendſhip which they mutually wiſh to reſtore, and to eſtabliſh ſuch a beneficial and ſatisfactory intercourſe between the two countries, upon the ground of reciprocal advantages and mutual conveniencies, as may promote and ſecure to both perpetual peace and harmony, and having for this deſirable end already laid the foundation of peace and reconciliation, by the Proviſional articles ſigned at Paris on the 30th of November, 1782, by the Commiſſioners empowered on each part, which articles were agreed to be inſerted in, and to conſtitute the treaty of peace propoſed to be concluded between the crown of Great-Britain and the ſaid united ſtates, but which treaty was not to be concluded until terms of peace ſhould be concluded upon between Great-Britain and France, and his Britannic Majeſty ſhould be ready to conclude ſuch treaty accordingly; and the treaty between Great-Britain & France having ſince been concluded, his Britannic Majeſty and the united ſtates of America, in order to carry into full effect the proviſional articles above mentioned, according to the tenor thereof, have conſtituted and appointed, that is to ſay, his Britannic Majeſty on his part, David Hartley, Eſq; Member of the parliament of Great-Britain, and the ſaid united ſtates on their part, John Adams, Eſq; late a Commiſſioner of the United States of America at the Court of Verſailles, late Delegate in Congreſs from the State of Maſſachuſets and Chief Juſtice of the ſaid ſtate, and Miniſter Plenipotentiary of the ſaid United States to their High Mightineſſes the States General of the United Netherlands, Benjamin Franklin, Eſq; late Delegate in Congreſs from the ſtate of Pennſylvania, Preſident of the Convention of ſaid ſtate, and Miniſter Plenipotentiary from the United States of America at the Court of Verſailles and John Jay, Eſq; late Preſident of Congreſs, and Chief Juſtice of the ſtate of New York, and Miniſter Plenipotentiary from the ſaid United States at the Court of Madrid, to be the Plenipotentiaries for the concluding and ſigning the preſent Definitive Treaty, who, after having reciprocally communicated their reſpective full powers, have agreed upon and confirmed the following articles:

Art. I. His Britannic Majeſty acknowledges the ſaid united ſtates, viz. New-Hampſhire, Maſſachuſetts Bay, Rhode-Iſland and Providence Plantations, Connecticut, New-York, New-Jerſey, Pennſylvania, Delaware, Maryland, Virginia, N. Carolina, South-Carolina, and Georgia, to be Free, Sovereign, and Independent States; that he treats with them as ſuch, and for his heirs and ſucceſſors, relinquiſhes all claims to the government, property, and territorial rights of the ſame and every part thereof.

Art. II. And that all diſputes which might ariſe in future, on the ſubject of the boundaries of the ſaid united ſtates, may be prevented, it is hereby agreed and declared, that the following are and ſhall be their boundaries, viz. From the north weſt angle of Nova-Scotia, viz. that angle which is formed by a line drawn due north from the ſource of St. Croix River to the Highlands, along the ſaid Highlands, which divide thoſe rivers that empty themſelves into the river St. Lawrence, from thoſe which fall into the Atlantic Ocean. to the north-weſternmoſt head of Connecticut river; thence down along the middle of that river to the forty-fifth degree of north latitude; from thence by a line due weſt on ſaid latitude, until it ſtrikes the river Irriquois or Cataraqui; thence along the middle of the ſaid river into Lake Ontario; through the middle of the ſaid lake until it ſtrikes the communication by water between that lake, and Lake Erie, through the middle of ſaid Lake, until it arrives at the communication between that lake and Lake Huron, thence thro' the middle of ſaid lake to the water communication between that lake and Lake Superior; thence through Lake Superior, northward of the Iſles Royal and Phelipeaux, to the Long Lake; thence through the middle of ſaid Long Lake and the water communication between it and the Lake of the Woods, to the ſaid Lake of the Woods; thence through the ſaid lake to the moſt north-weſtern point thereof, and from thence on a due weſt courſe to the river Miſſiſſippi; thence by a line to be drawn along the middle of the ſaid river Miſſiſſippi until it ſhall interſect the northernmoſt part of the thirty-firſt degree of north latitude. South, by a line to be drawn due eaſt from the determination of the line laſt mentioned in the latitude of thirty-one degrees north of the equator to the middle of the river Apalachichola or Catahouche; thence along the middle thereof to its junction with the Flint river, thence ſtrait to the head of St. Mary's river; and thence down along the middle of ſaid river to the Atlantic Ocean, the river St, Croix from its mouth in the Bay of Fundy to its ſource, and from its ſource directly north to the aforeſaid Highlands which divide the rivers which fall into the Atlantic Ocean from thoſe which fall into the river St. Lawrence, comprehending all Iſlands within twenty leagues of any part of the ſhores of the united ſtates, and lying between lines to be drawn due eaſt from the points where the aforeſaid boundaries between Nova-Scotia on the one part, and Eaſt-Florida on the other, ſhall reſpectively touch the Bay of Fundy and the Atlantic Ocean, excepting ſuch Iſlands as now are or hereafter have been within the limits of the ſaid province of Nova-Scotia.

Art. III. It is agreed that the people of the United States ſhall continue to enjoy unmoleſted the right to take fiſh of every kind on the Grand Banks of Newfoundland, alſo in the Gulph of St. Laurence, and all other places in the ſea, where the inhabitants of countries uſed at any time heretofore to fiſh. And alſo that the inhabitants of the United States ſhall have liberty to take fiſh of every kind on ſuch part of the coaſt of Newfoundland as Britiſh fiſhermen ſhall uſe, (but not to dry or cure the ſame on that Iſland) and alſo on the coaſts, bays and creeks of all others of his Britannic Majeſty's dominions in America; and that the American fiſhermen ſhall have liberty to dry and cure fiſh in any of the unſettled bays, harbours and creeks of Nova Scotia, Magdalen Iſlands and Labrador, ſo long as the ſame ſhall remain unſettled; but ſo ſoon as the ſame or either of them ſhall be ſettled, it ſhall not be lawfull for the ſaid fiſhermen to dry or cure fiſh at ſuch ſettlement, without a previous agreement for that purpoſe with the inhabitants, proprietors or poſſeſſors of the ground.

Art. IV. It is agreed that the creditors on either ſide ſhall meet with no lawful impediment to the recovery of the full value, in ſterling money, of all *bona fide* debts heretofore contracted.

Art. V. It is agreed that Congreſs ſhall recommend it to the Legiſlature of the reſpective States. to provide for reſtitution of all eſtates, rights, and properties. which have been confiſcated, belonging to real Britiſh ſubjects; and alſo of the eſtates, rights, and properties of perſons reſident in diſtricts in the poſſeſſion of his Majeſty's arms, and who have not borne arms againſt the ſaid United ſtates; and that perſon of any other deſcriptions ſhall have free liberty to go to any part or parts of any of the Thirteen United States, and therein to remain twelve months unmoleſted in their endeavours to obtain the reſtitution of ſuch of their eſtates rights, and properties, as may have been confiſcated; and that Congreſs ſhall alſo earneſtly recommend to the ſeveral ſtates a reconſideration and reviſion of all acts or laws regarding the premiſes, ſo as to render the ſaid laws or acts perfectly conſiſtent not only with juſtice and equity, but with that ſpirit of conciliation, which, on the return of the bleſſings of peace, ſhould univerſally prevail: And that Congreſs ſhall alſo earneſtly recommend to the ſeveral ſtates, that the eſtates, rights and properties of ſuch laſt mentioned perſons ſhall be reſtored to them, they refunding to any perſon the *bona fide* price (where any has been given) which ſuch perſons may have paid on purchaſing any of the ſaid lands, rights, or properties ſince the confiſcation.

And it is agreed, that all perſons who have any intereſt in confiſcated lands, either by debts, marriage ſettlements, or otherwiſe ſhall meet with no lawful impediment in the proſecution of their juſt rights.

Art. VI. That there ſhall be no future confiſcations made, nor any proſecutions commenced againſt any perſon or perſons for, or by reaſon of the part which he or they may have taken in the preſent war, and that no perſon ſhall on that account, ſuffer any future loſs or damage, either in his perſon, liberty or property: and that thoſe who may be in confinement on ſuch charges, at the time of the ratification of the treaty in America, ſhall be immediately ſet at liberty, and the proſecutions ſo commenced be diſcontinued.

VII. There ſhall be a firm and perpetual peace between his Britannic Majeſty and the ſaid ſtates, and between the ſubjects of the one, and the citizens of the other; wherefore all hoſtilities both by ſea and land ſhall from henceforth ceaſe; all priſoners on both ſides ſhall be ſet at liberty, and his Britannic Majeſty ſhall, with all convenient ſpeed, and without cauſing any deſtruction, or carrying away any Negroes, or other property of the American inhabitants, withdraw all his armies, garriſons and fleets, from the ſaid united ſtates, and from every poſt, place and harbour, within the ſame, leaving in all fortifications the American artillery, that may be therein; and ſhall alſo order and cauſe all archives, records, deeds, and papers belonging to any of the ſaid ſtates, or other citizens, which in the courſe of the war may have fallen into the hands of his officers, to be forthwith reſtored, and delivered to the proper ſtate and perſons to whom they belong

Art. VIII. The navigation of the River Miſſiſſippi, from its ſource to the ocean ſhall forever remain free and open to the ſubjects of Great-Britain, and the citizens of the united ſtates.

Art. IX In caſe it ſhould ſo happen, that any place or territory belonging to G. Britain, or to the united ſtates, ſhould have been conquered by the arms of either from the other, before the arrival of the ſaid proviſional articles in America, it is agreed that the ſame ſhall be reſtored without difficulty, and without requiring any compenſation.

Art. X. The ſolemn ratifications of the preſent treaty, expedited in good and due form, ſhall be exchanged between the contracting parties in the ſpace of ſix months, or ſooner, if poſſible, to be computed from the day of the ſignature of the preſent treaty. In witneſs whereof, we the underſigned, their Miniſters Plenipotentiary, have in their name, and in virtue of our full powers, ſigned with our hands the preſent Definitive Treaty, and cauſed the ſeals of our arms to be affixed thereto.

Done at Paris, this 3d day of September, in the year of our Lord One Thouſand Seven Hundred and Eighty three.

(L. S.) JOHN ADAMS.
(L.S.) DAVID HARTLY.
(L. S.) B. FRANKLIN.
(L. S.) JOHN JAY.

GEORGE R.

George the Third, by the Grace of God, King of Great-Britain, France and Ireland, Defender of the Faith, Duke of Brunſwick and Lunenbourg, Arch-Treaſurer and Prince Elector of the Holy Roman Empire, &c. To all to whom theſe preſents ſhall come, Greeting:

WHEREAS, for the perfecting and eſtabliſhing the peace, friendſhip, and good underſtanding, ſo happily commenced by the Proviſional Articles, ſigned at Paris, the thirtieth day of November laſt, by the Commiſſioners of us and our good friends the United States of America, viz. New-Hampſhire, Maſſachuſetts-Bay, Rhode-Iſland, Connecticut. New-York, New-Jerſey, Pennſylvania, the three Lower Counties on Delaware, Maryland, Virginia, North-Carolina, South-Carolina and Georgia, in North-America, and for opening, promoting and rendering perpetual the mutual intercourſe of trade and commerce between our kingdoms and the dominions of the ſaid United States, we have thought proper to inveſt ſome fit perſon with full powers on our part, to meet and confer with the Miniſters of the ſaid United States, now reſiding at Paris, duly authorized for the accompliſhing of ſuch laudable and ſalutary purpoſes. Now know ye, that WE, repoſing ſpecial truſt and confidence in the wiſdom, loyalty, diligence, and circumſpection of our truſty and well-beloved David Hartley, Eſq; (on whom we have therefore conferred the rank of our Miniſter Plenipotentiary) have nominated, conſtituted, and appointed, and by theſe Preſents do nominate, conſtitute and appoint him our true, certain, and undoubted Commiſſioner, Proſecutor and Plenipotentiary, giving and granting to him all and all manner of faculty, power and authority, together with general as well as ſpecial order (ſo as the general do not derogate from the ſpecial, nor on the contrary) for us and in our name, to meet, confer, treat and conclude with the Miniſter or Miniſters furniſhed with ſufficient powers on the part of our ſaid good friends the United States of America, of and concerning all ſuch matters and things as may be requiſite and neceſſary for accompliſhing and completing the ſeveral ends and purpoſes herein before mentioned; and alſo for us, and in our name, to ſign ſuch Treaty or Treaties, Convention or Conventions, or other inſtruments whatſoever, as may be agreed upon in the premiſes; and mutually to deliver and receive the ſame in exchange, and to do and perform all ſuch other acts, matters, and things as may be any ways proper and conducive to the purpoſes above mentioned, in as full and ample form and manner, and with the like validity and effect, as we ourſelves, if we were preſent, could do and perform the ſame; engaging and promiſing, on our Royal word, that we will accept, ratify, and confirm, in the moſt effectual manner, all ſuch acts, matters, and things, as ſhall be ſo tranſacted and concluded by our aforeſaid Commiſſioner, Procurator, and Plenipotentiary; and that we will never ſuffer any perſon to violate the ſame in the whole or in part, or to act contrary thereto. In teſtimony and confirmation of all which, we have cauſed our Great Seal of Great Britain to be affixed to theſe preſents, ſigned with our Royal hand.

Given at our Palace at St. James's, the fourteenth day of May, in the year of our Lord one thouſand ſeven hundred and eighty-three, and in the twenty-third year of our reign.

I David Hartley, the Miniſter above named, certify the foregoing to be a true copy from my original Commiſſion, delivered to the American Miniſters this 19th day of May, 1783.

(Signed) DAVID HARTLEY.

The United States of America, in Congreſs aſſembled.

To all to whom theſe Preſents ſhall come, ſend Greeting.

WHEREAS theſe United States, from a ſincere deſire of putting an end to the hoſtilities between his Moſt Chriſtian Majeſty and theſe United States on the one part, and his Britannic Majeſty on the other, and of terminating the ſame by a peace founded on ſuch ſolid and equitable principles as reaſonably to promiſe a permanency of the bleſſings of tranquility, did heretofore appoint the honorable John Adams, late a Commiſſioner of the United States of America at the Court of Verſailles, late Delegate in Congreſs from the State of Maſſachuſetts, and Chief Juſtice of the ſaid State, their Miniſter Plenipotentiary, with full powers general and ſpecial to act in that quality, to confer, treat, agree, and conclude with the Ambaſſadors or Plenipotentiaries of his Moſt Chriſtian Majeſty, and of his Britannic Majeſty, and thoſe of any other Princes or States whom it might concern, relating to the re-eſtabliſhing of peace and friendſhip: And whereas the flames of war have ſince that time been extended, and other nations and States are involved therein; Now know ye, that we ſtill continuing earneſtly deſirous, as far as depends upon us, to put a ſtop to the effuſion of blood, and to convince the powers of Europe that we wiſh for nothing more ardently than to terminate the war, by a ſafe and honorable peace, have thought proper to renew the powers formerly given to the ſaid John Adams, and to join four other perſons in commiſſion with him; and having full confidence in the integrity, prudence, and abilities of the honorable Benjamin Franklin, our Miniſter Plenipotentiary at the Court of Verſailles, and the honorable John Jay, late Preſident of Congreſs, and Chief Juſtice of the State of New-York, and our Miniſter Plenipotentiary at the Court of Madrid, and the honorable Henry Laurens, formerly Preſident of Congreſs, and commiſſionated and ſent as our Agent to the United Provinces of the Low Countries, and the honorable Thomas Jefferſon, Governor of the Commonwealth of Virginia, have nominated conſtituted, and appointed, and by theſe preſents do nominate, conſtitute and appoint the ſaid Benjamin Franklin, John Jay, Henry Laurens and Thomas Jefferſon, in addition to the ſaid John Adams, Benjamin Franklin, John Jay, Henry Laurens, and Thomas Jefferſon, or the majority of them, or of ſuch of them as may aſſemble, or, in caſe of the death, abſence, indiſpoſition, or other impediment of the others, to any one of them, full power and authority general and ſpecial, conjunctly and ſeparately, and general and ſpecial command to repair to ſuch place as may be fixed upon for opening negociations for peace, and there for us, and in our Name, to confer, treat, agree, and conclude with the Ambaſſadors, Commiſſioners, Plenipotentiaries of the Princes and States whom it may concern, veſted with equal powers relating to the eſtabliſhment of peace; and whatſoever ſhall be agreed and concluded, for us and in our Name to ſign; and thereupon make a Treaty or Treaties, and to tranſact every thing that may be neceſſary for completing, ſecuring, and ſtrengthening the great work of pacification, in as ample form, and with the ſame effect, as if we were perſonally preſent and acted therein, hereby promiſing in good faith that we will aſſent, ratify, fulfil, and execute whatever ſhall be agreed, concluded, and ſigned by our ſaid Miniſters Plenipotentiary, or a majority of them or of ſuch of them as may aſſemble, or in caſe of the death, abſence, indiſpoſition, or other impediment of the others, by any one of them; and that we will never act nor ſuffer any perſon to act contrary to the ſame in whole or in part. In witneſs whereof we have cauſed theſe preſents to be ſigned by our Preſident, and ſealed with his Seal.

Done at Philadelphia, the fifteenth day of June, in the year of our Lord One Thouſand Seven Hundred and Eighty one. and in the fifth year of Our Independence, by the United States in Congreſs aſſembled.

(Signed) SAM. HUNTINGTON, Preſident.
CHA. THOMSON, Secretary.

WE certify the foregoing copies of the reſpective full powers to be authentic.---PARIS, SEPT. 3, 1783. (Signed)

GEORGE HAMMOND, Secretary to the Britiſh Commiſſion.

W. T. FRANKLIN, Secretary to the American Commiſſion.

NEW-YORK, November 28.

Laſt Tueſday morning the American Troops marched from Haerlem to the Bowery Lane. They remained there till about One o'Clock, when the Britiſh Troops left the poſts in the Bowery, and the American Troops marched into, and took poſſeſſion of the City in the following order, viz.

1. Corps of Dragoons.
2. Advanced Guard of Light Infantry.
3. A Corps of Artillery.
4. Battalion of Light Infantry.
5. Battalion of Maſſachuſetts Troops.
6. Rear Guard.

After the Troops had taken poſſeſſion of the city, their Excellencies the General and Governor made their public entry in the following manner:

1. Their Excellencies the General and Governor with their Suites, on Horſeback.
2. The Lieutenant Governor and the Members of the Council, for the temporary government of the ſouthern diſtrict, four a-breaſt.
3. Major General Knox, and the officers of the army, eight a-breaſt.
4. Citizens on Horſeback, eight a-breaſt.
5. The Speaker of the Aſſembly, and citizens on foot, eight a-breaſt.

Their Excellencies the Governor & Commander in Chief, were eſcorted by a body of Weſt-Cheſter Light Horſe, under the command of Captain Delavan.

The Proceſſion proceeded down Queen-Street, and thro' the Broadway, to Cape's Tavern

The Governor gave a public dinner at Fraunces's Tavern, at which the Commander in Chief and other General Officers were preſent.

After dinner the following toaſts were drank by the company.

1. The United States of America.
2. His Moſt Chriſtian Majeſty.
3. The United Netherlands.
4. The King of Sweden.
5. The American Army.
6. The fleet and armies of France, which have ſerved in America.
7. The memory of thoſe heroes who have fallen for our freedom.
8. May our country be grateful to her military children.
9. May juſtice ſupport what courage has gained.
10. The vindication of the rights of mankind in every quarter of the globe.
11. May America be an Aſylum to the perſecuted of the earth.
12. May a cloſe union of the States guard the Temple they have erected to Liberty.
13. May the remembrance of this Day be a Leſſon to Princes.

The arrangement and whole conduct of this march, with the tranquility which ſucceeded it, through the day and night, was admirable! and the grateful citizens will ever feel the moſt affectionate impreſſions, from that elegant and efficient diſpoſition which prevailed through the whole event.

Accounts from London by the Lord Hyde Packet aſſert, that there was on the firſt of October, no leſs than thirty one ſail of veſſels loading in the river Thames for the American States, viz. twelve for South Carolina, ſeven for Virginia and Maryland, ſeven for Philadelphia and North Carolina, and five for Salem and Boſton.

To His Excellency GEORGE CLINTON, Eſq; Governor of the State of New-York, Commander in Chief of the Militia, and Admiral of the navy of the ſame.:

The ADDRESS of the CITIZENS of NEW-YORK, who have returned from exile, in behalf of themſelves and their ſuffering brethren:

SIR,

WHEN we conſider your faithful labours at the head of the government of this ſtate, devoid as we conceive every free people ought to be of flattery, we think we ſhould not be wanting in gratitude to your vigilant and aſſiduous ſervices in the civil line.

The ſtate, Sir, is highly indebted to you in your military capacity.---A ſenſe of your real merit will ſecure to you that reputation, which a brave man, expoſing himſelf in defence of his country, will ever deſerve.

We moſt ſincerely congratulate you, on your happy arrival at the capital of the ſtate. Your Excellency hath borne a part with us in the general diſtreſs, and was ever ready to alleviate the calamities you could not effectually remove.--Your example taught us to ſuffer with dignity.

We beg leave to aſſure your Excellency, that as prudent citizens, and faithful ſubjects to the people of the ſtate of New-York, we will do every thing in our power to enable you to ſupport order and good government in the community, over which you have by the ſuffrages of a free and diſcerning people been elected to preſide.

Signed at the requeſt of the meeting,

THO. RANDALL,
DAN. PHOENIX,
SAM. BROOME,
THO. TUCKER.
HENRY KIPP,
PAT. DENNYS,
WILL, GILBERT, ſen.
WILL. GILBERT, jun.
FRANCIS VAN DYCK,
JEREMIAH WOOL,
GEO. JANEWAY,
ABRA. P. LOTT,
EPARAIM BRASHIER.

New-York, November 22, 1783.

His Excellency's ANSWER.

GENTLEMEN,

ACCEPT my moſt ſincere thanks for your very affectionate and reſpectful addreſs. Citizens, who like you, to vindicate the ſacred cauſe of freedom, quitted their native city, their fortunes and profeſſions, and ſuſtained with manly fortitude, the rigours of a long and painful exile, ſuperadded to the grievous calamities of a vengeful war, merit, in an eminent degree, the title of patriots, and the eſteem of mankind; and your confidence and approbation are honours, which cannot be received without the utmoſt ſenſibility, or contemplated without gratitude and ſatisfaction.

To your ſufferings, and to the invincible ſpirit with which they were ſurmounted, I have been witneſs; and while I ſympathized in your diſtreſſes, I have deeply lamented that I had not means to alleviate them equal to my inclination.

The aſſurances of your firm ſupport in the adminiſtration of government, give me ſingular pleaſure.---A reverence for the laws is peculiarly eſſential to public ſafety and proſperity, under our free conſtitution; and ſhould we ſuffer the authority of the magiſtrate to be violated for the ſake of private vengeance, we ſhould be unworthy of the numberleſs bleſſings which an indulgent Providence hath placed within our reach. I ſhall endeavour ſteadily to diſcharge my duty, and I flatter myſelf that this ſtate will become no leſs diſtinguiſhed for juſtice and public tranquility, in peace, than it has hitherto been marked, in war, for vigour, fortitude, and perſeverance.

Gentlemen,

Your kind congratulations on my arrival at this metropolis, after ſo long an abſence, are highly acceptable; and I moſt cordially felicitate with you on the joyful events which have reſtored us to the free and uncontroulable enjoyment of our rights.---- While we regard with inviolable gratitude and affection, all who have aided us by their council or their arms, let us not be unmindful of that Almighty Being, whoſe gracious providence has been manifeſtly interpoſed for our deliverence and protection; and let us ſhew by our virtues, that we deſerve to partake of the freedom, ſovereignty and independence, which are ſo happily eſtabliſhed throughout theſe united ſtates.

GEO. CLINTON.

New York, November 26, 1783.

To his Excellency GEORGE WASHINGTON, Eſquire, General and Commander in Chief of the Armies of the United States of America.

The Addreſs of the Citizens of New-York who have returned from Exile, in behalf of themſelves & their ſuffering Brethren.

SIR,

AT a moment when the arm of tyranny is yielding up its fondeſt uſurpations, we hope the ſalutations of long ſuffering exiles, but now happy freemen, will not be deemed an unworthy tribute.

In this place, and at this moment of exultation and triumph, while the enſigns of ſlavery ſtill linger in our ſight, we look up to you, our deliverer, with unuſual tranſports of gratitude and joy. Permit us to welcome you to this city, long torn from us by the hard hand of oppreſſion, but now by your wiſdom and energy, under the guidance of providence, once more the ſeat of peace and freedom. We forbear to ſpeak our gratitude or your praiſe---we ſhould but echo the voice of applauding millions; but the citizens of New-York are eminently indebted to your virtues, and we who have now the honour to addreſs your Excellency, have been often companions of your ſufferings, and witneſſes of your exertions---permit us, therefore, to approach your Excellency with the dignity and sincerity of freemen, and to assure you that we shall preserve with our latest breath, our gratitude for your services, and veneration for your character, and accept of our sincere and earnest wishes, that you may long enjoy that calm domestic felicity, which you have so generously sacrificed; that the cries of injured liberty may never more interrupt your repose; and that your happiness may be equal to your virtues.

Signed at the request of the meeting:

THO. RANDALL,
DAN. PHOENIX,
SAM. BROOME,
THO. TUCKER,
HENRY KIPP,
PAT. DENNIS,
WILL. GILBERT, sen.
WILL. GILBERT, jun.
FRANCIS VAN DYCK,
JEREMIAH WOOL,
GEO. JANEWAY,
ABRA. P. LOTT,
EPHRAIM BRASHER.

New-York, November 22, 1783.

His Excellency's Answer,
To the Citizens of New-York, who have returned from Exile.

Gentlemen,

I THANK you sincerely for your affectionate address, and entreat you to be persuaded, that nothing could be more agreeable to me than your polite congratulations: Permit me, in turn, to felicitate you on the happy restoration of your city.

Great as your joy must be on this pleasing occasion, it can scarcely exceed that, which I feel at seeing you, Gentlemen, who from the noblest motives, have suffered a voluntary exile of many years, return again in peace and triumph, to enjoy the fruits of your virtuous conduct.

The fortitude and perseverance which you and your suffering brethren have exhibited in the course of the war, have not only endeared you to your own countrymen, but will be remembered with admiration and applause, to the latest posterity.

May the tranquility of your city be perpetual. May the ruins soon be repaired, commerce flourish, science be fostered, and all the civil and social virtues be cherished, in the same illustrious manner, which formerly reflected so much credit on the inhabitants of New-York. In fine, may every species of felicity attend you, Gentlemen, and your worthy fellow-citizens.

GEO. WASHINGTON.

New-York, November 26, 1783.

O D E.

On the Arrival of their Excellencies General WASHINGTON and Governor CLINTON, in New-York, on the 25th November, 1783.

Tune—" *He comes! he comes!*"

THEY come! they come! the Heroes come!
With sounding fife, with thund'ring drum,
Their ranks advance in bright array.
The Heroes of AMERICA.

He comes! 'tis mighty WASHINGTON!
Words fail to tell all he has done;
Our Hero, Guardian, Father, Friend!
His fame can never, never end.

He comes! he comes! 'tis CLINTON comes!
Justice her ancient seat resumes.
From shore to shore let shouts resound,
For Justice comes with Freedom crown'd.

She comes! the white rob'd Virgin, Peace,
And bids grim War his horrors cease.
Oh! blooming Virgin, with us stay,
And bless, oh! bless AMERICA.

Now Freedom has our wishes crown'd,
Let flowing Goblet's pass around;
We'll drink to Freedom's fav'rite Son,
Health, Peace, and Joy to WASHINGTON.

CHARLES-TOWN, (South-Carolina) October 18.

Died at the Havanna after a few days illness Major Ichabod Burnet, Aid de Camp to the honourable Major General Greene.--He was buried with great solemnity in the sea; and a British frigate being in the harbour, the Captain manned his boat, and joined in the mournful procession. As the scholar, citizen and soldier, Major Burnet was equalled by few; his loss will be long and deeply impressed on the hearts of those who served with him in the field.

October 24 *The brigantine Delight, Captain Seater, belonging to Tortola, in going over the bar on Saturday last, had the misfortune to get amongst the breakers, and soon after went to pieces. Three of the crew perished, and the rest were taken up by some of the pilots. She was on her way to Beaufort for a cargo. It appears that it was not through any neglect of the pilot, or any person who was on board said vessel, that occasioned her loss, but may be attributed entirely to her not working as she ought in the heavy head sea.*

PHILADELPHIA, November 22.

The schooner Esther, Captain Towers, is arrived at Charlestown, after a passage of 22 days, having been dismasted in a gale of wind soon after leaving our Capes. The Betsey, Swinburn, from Virginia, is also arrived at Charlestown, having been 21 day at sea, and received considerable damages, having been thrown on her beam end, and obliged to cut away her masts.

Just arrived from Liverpool,

And now ready for Sale, on very low Terms for CASH only, on board the Ship ST. CUTHBERT, laying at Brownjohn's Wharf, the following Articles

V I Z.

LOAF SUGAR in hogsheads,
Mould and dipped Candles,
Best Turpentine Soap,
Bottled Beer and Porter,
Cheese in Casks and Hampers,
Earthen Ware in Crates well assorted,
Glass do. do.
Hard Ware, a few Casks assorted,
Brooms and Brushes,
An Assortment of Paints ground in Oil,
Mens low priced Hats,
Irish Linens,
Few Trunks Millenary, very fashionable,
And, a Quantity of COAL.

W A N T E D,
A Quantity of L U M B E R.

BURKE and DONNAN,

Beg leave to inform their friends, and the public, that they have commenced business at the Store of (formerly) Hull and Birks, late George Birks, at No 4, Beekman-slip where they have for sale on the lowest terms,

A General assortment of Groceries,	*Draught and bottled Porter,*
Wines,	*Butter,*
Spirits,	*Cheese,*
Rum,	*Ship Bread of the first quality,*
Gin,	*Mould Candles, &c.*
Bottled Ale	

All orders will be gratefully received and executed with the strictest punctuality.

November 28, 1783. 3m.

By A U T H O R I T Y.
Public Auction.
No. 244, Queen Street, opposite Mr. James Rivington's, opened by

P. Regnier, and Co.

IN which place they beg leave to acquaint the Public in general, and their friends in particular, that they purpose to carry on the business of Auctioneers in all its branches. they have Stores in the best parts of the town provided for the reception of all kinds of goods or merchandize, either from Europe or India or any kind of American produce, intended for public or private sale.

They will be highly obliged to all Merchants and Captains of Vessels, to favour them with a list of what they have for sale, they will endeavour to recommend themselves to their particular notice.

Landed Estates, Houses, Ships, and Money Securities, will be negociated or sold on the lowest commission.

The utmost attention will be paid to all kind of trust reposed in them, and the greatest deference paid to any commands.

They may be found in the above named Store from Six o'Clock every morning Sunday excepted, beginning Monday the first of December next, till two o'clock in the afternoon and from four o'clock till dark.

ONE Thousand Pounds of Depreciation Notes wanted immediately, for which cash will be given. Apply to Bingham and Marshall, No. 20, Hanover-Square.

WANTED immediately, a number of Wood Cutters. Good encouragement will be given by applying at No. 56, Queen-street, or to the Printers hereof.

For LONDON,
The Ship Friendship,
Samuel Milford, Master,

She sails remarkably fast, and can genteely accommodate a number of cabin passengers, has also commodious room in the steerage. She will sail on Saturday the 29th instant.-------For freight or passage apply to Joseph Wilks, No. 40, Hanover-Square, or to the Master on board at Brownejohn's Wharf.

WANMED, a Black Man that is a good Cook, and can be well recommended. Enquire at the Elizabeth-town ferry house, on the White-hall dock, or the Printers hereof.

Public Auction,
On Saturday Morning,
At the Office of John Delafield,
No. 5, Queen Street,

A small quantity of Furniture, neatly elegant, consisting of Mahogany Chairs, Window Curtains, Kitchen Utensils, &c.

At the same Time,
Two good Road Horses,
A quantity of Beef, and Hollands Gin, in double Cases.

P U B L I C A U C T I O N.
In a few Days,
For the benefit of the Under-Writers,

A large quantity of Cordage Canvas, Carpets, Rum, Madeira and Port Wine in bottles Porter and Glasgow Ale in bottles, Printed Books, Candles. Three Beef, Anchors, Boats, and a variety of other articles, saved out of the Brig New-York, Capt. Forter, from Glasgow.

The goods may be viewed till the morning of sale, at the office of John Delafield, No. 5, Queen-Street.

Catalogues will be ready to deliver in a day or two at the above office, and at the Coffee House.

Private Sale,

Malmsey, Madeira, very old & curious, Red Port Wine, in pipes and quarter casks, Porter in hogsheads, Saddlery Horn Combs, Watch Glasses, Hops in bags, Worsted Stockings, Fine Hyson Tea, Cocks, 30 Groce in a Bag English Canvas and Twine, Mess Beef and Pork &c. &c.

John Delafield No. 5, Queen-Street.

For Sale,
8000 *Acres of Land,*

A tract of land in Hardenburg's, or the Great Patent, containing about eight thousand acres. The title indisputable. If a purchaser offers for the whole quantity, a part of the money may remain on good security. For terms apply to

John Delafield, No. 5 Queen-Street.

For Sale, A valuable Farm,

Situate on the west side of Hudson's river a mile above Newburgh. containing about 135 acres, there is a good house on the estate, three rooms on the lower story, the bed chambers not yet finished, a good new kitchen and pantry, the cellar is also a good one, before the house is a spring, and a well of fine water. The orchard is large, well stored with apple trees in high perfection, which this year produced 65 hogsheads of cyder, besides an ample supply of fruit for the family. This estate has singular advantages, the farm extends 12 chains in width on the banks of the river, and is admirably well calculated for a ship builder. A good proportion of meadow and woodland, and a large lime kiln. Adjoining to the above estate is a tract of woodland of about 100 acres of excellent timber, that on moderate estimation will furnish 5000 cords of firewood. Further particulars may be known at the office of

John Delafield, No. 5, Queen-Street,

W A N T E D

Bills drawn by the Hon. Robert Morris, &c. &c. &c. on John Swanwick, Esq; also good Bills at a short date on Baltimore, apply to

John Delafield, No. 5, Queen Street.

W A N T E D

On the security of a House and Land in the Out-ward of this city, that lately let at 90 per annum, the sum of Forty Pound, apply at the office of

John Delafield, No. 5, Queen-Street.

State Securities.

Of several kinds ready for sale, Gentlemen inclined to purchase these truly lucrative Securities are very respectfully entreated to favour John Delafield with their address.

BROKER's OFFICE

No. 5, QUEEN-STREET,
JOHN DELAFIELD,

BEGS leave to acquaint his friends and the public, that he purposes carrying on the business of a BROKER, in all its various branches.

His house which is large, centrical, and in every respect well calculated for the business, is open for the reception of every species of dry goods; and warehouses are provided for rum, sugar, and other wet goods intended for public or private sale.

He will purchase on the shortest notice and on the best terms, all kinds of American and West India produce. In order to effect this business with certainty and dispatch, he will think himself obliged to all merchants and traders to favour him with a list of such goods as they have for sale. The utility of this plan, he trusts, will recommend it to the public, and be found beneficial to trade in general.

Landed estates, houses, &c. &c. bought and sold, and all kinds of money securities negociated on terms the most liberal to all parties.

Fidelity, honour, secrecy, and a strict attention to the interests of his employers, will be the basis on which he means to found his pretentions to public favour: those gentlemen who indulge him with their commands, may rely on every exertion in his power for their interest.

Supercargoes, Captains of ships, &c. &c. will find it their interest to apply immediately on their arrival, at this office.

New-York, Nov. 17, 1783.

SHEPPARD KOLLOCK,

(Late Printer of the New-Jersey Journal) Will publish, on WEDNESDAY next No. I, OF A PERIODICAL PAPER, INTITLED, THE

NEW-YORK GAZETTEER,
AND
COUNTRY JOURNAL.

Subscriptions, Advertisements, &c. are taken in at his House in Hanover Square. No. 22, and nearly opposite Mr. Hugh Gaine's.

T O B E L E T,

From now till May next, or a Lease for five years, and immediate possession given, That beautiful pleasant Seat of Mr. David Provost, deceased, called the

L O U V R E,

Situate upon York Island on the banks of the East River, opposite the five mile stone, containing about 100 acres of land, 10 of which are good fresh meadow, and more may easily be made, a good orchard, and plenty of the best fruit. the buildings consist of a commodious large house, four rooms well finished on the lower floor, a cellar under the whole, two large barns under one a fine dry cellar, on the brink of the river, three out houses, suitable for small families or convenient for servants, an exceeding good Cyder Mill, inclosed under a good frame building with a large loft over the same, one thousand rails with posts equivalent are housed upon the premises for the purpose of fencing it,

A L S O,

To lease for five years from May next, that snug agreeable seat of Mr. Provost, on Long-Island, within a quarter of a mile of Hell-Gate Ferry, containing about 35 acres of good upland, and 5 acres of salt meadow, on the premises are a neat house, barn and out-buildings, with a variety of choice fruit.

Two small houses now vacant, to let cheap in New-York, and immediate possession given, situate one in Gold Street, the other in Skinner Street. Enquire of the Printers.

New-York, Nov. 28, 1783.

WANTED, a Man Cook, that can dress victuals in a cleanly, plain way. Such a person, who may be desirous of going to England, may meet with good encouragement by applying at No. 206, Water-Street.

A WET NURSE is wanted in a gentleman's family; none need apply but those of good character. Enquire of the Printers.

A NURSE with a good Breast of Milk, is wanted in a genteel family; none need apply without good recommendations. Enquire of the Printers.

FOR VIRGINIA, the Ship OLIVE BRANCH, William Green, master, now laying at Cruger's wharf; will sail in a few days. For freight or passage apply to the master on board or to Robert Dunbar, No. 11, Queen-street.-----N. B. Forty barrels Ship Bread to be disposed of. Apply as above.

TO LET, a compleat front Store, well fitted for dry goods; a spacious dry Cellar, and a large back Warehouse.---Enquire at No. 202, Queen-street.

BEEF and Pork smoaked at the old Smoak House, at No. 126, formerly occupied by John Bennet, near the north end of the hay yard, fronting the N. river. By leaving directions a person will receive and deliver the beef and pork.----Three Lots of Ground to be let.

Josiah Shippey & Co.

No. 16, Little Dock Street,
Near Coenties-Slip,
Have to dispose of Wholesale and Retail,

HYSON, Bohea, And Congo } Teas.	Genuine Red Port Wine, in pipes, at 42 l.
Muscovado Sugar,	Hogsheads, 21l.
Coffee,	Quarter Casks, 11l.
Cinnamon,	Tin in boxes,
Jamaica Spirits,	White Lead in kegs,
West India Rum,	A variety of Hatters
French Brandy,	Trimmings, consisting of Linings, Loopings, Bowstrings, &c.
Holland Geneva, in hogsheads, casks and anchors,	
Claret in cases and by the dozen,	Seine Twine, &c. &c.

1000 Bushels of Indian Corn,
Which will be sold altogether reasonable.

CHRISTOPHER LEWIS LENTZ,
No. 32, Hanover Square,
Has for SALE, the following
GROCERIES,
And other ARTICLES,
Which he will sell cheap, for CASH only,
N. B. As he purchases but for ready Money, he therefore can give no trust.

LOndon particular Madeira,
Port,
Lisbon,
Claret,
Packoratte,
Rancio,
And Fontiniac
} WINES, by the pipe, and quarter cask, the oldest and best in this city,

French Brandy, Jamaica Spirits,
Holland Geneva, and many sorts of English and foreign Liqueurs,
London bottled Porter, and Dorchester Ale,
Foreign and English Wine, Garlic, Tarragon, and different Herb } Vinegars,
English and Foreign ready-made Mustard,
English and Foreign Flour of Mustard,
India Soy,
Mushroom Ketchup,

P I C K L E S.
Mushrooms, India Mangoes,
Wallnuts, Girkins,
Onions, French Beans,
Capers, Anchovies, and Olives.

P R E S E R V E S.
West-India Sweet-Meats, in Syrup,
Apricots, Peaches, Pears, Citron, Green Gages, &c. in Brandy Syrup,
Sugar Plumbs, Caraway Comfits, &c.
Syrup de Orgeat, Ditto Capilaire,
Ditto Rasberry, Ditto Lemon.
Orange Flour and Rose Water,
Double distilled Lavender Water,
Howe's Acid, Lemon and Lime Juice,
Lisbon Lemons,
Fine Hyson, single Hyson, Congo, Soushong, and Bohea Teas,
Chocolate and Coffee,
Double, single and Lump Sugar,
White and brown Sugar Candy,
Muscovado and Powder Sugar.

S P I C E R I E S.
Mace, Cloves, Nutmegs
Cinnamon, Alspice, Ginger,
Cayenne, white and black Pepper
Sago, Carraway Seed,
Pearl Barley, Rice,
Vermacelli, Macaroni,
Morells, Truffles,
Isinglass: Hartshorn Shavings,
Jordan and Shell Almonds,
Figs, Prunes, Currants,
Jar and Cask Raisins,
Salt Petre and Basket Salt.

Poland Starch, Hair Powder,
Wax, Spermaceti and Tallow Candles,
Castile and Turpentine Soap,
Fig and Powder Blue,
English and American cured Hams,
English and Irish pickled Tripe,
Spiced Salmon in kits,
Best London made Boots and Shoes,
Silk, Sattin, Morocco and Stuff Womens Shoes,
Childrens Shoes,
Hardware and Glass Ware,
Jewellery by the package,
Playing and Message Cards, with sundry Articles too tedious to mention.

Most of the above Articles being imported in the Iris, Captain Caldcleugh.

A few Casks of
Vermacilli and German Prunes,
To be sold at a very low price.

The CO-PARTNERSHIP
Of Jones and Ross,
OF this city, being nearly expired, they request all those who have any demands against them, may be pleased to bring in their accounts immediately, that they may be adjusted and paid; and it is expected that all those indebted to them, by bond, note, or book debt, will be speedy in the discharge of the same.

N. B. Malcolm Ross intends leaving this city in a few days.

New-York, November 3.

THOMAS MAULE.
No. 55, Queen-street,
Has received by the Vigilant,
And is now opening for SALE,
AN ASSORTMENT of European GOODS, which he will dispose of on the lowest terms for Cash, or good Bills of Exchange:—Moreens, black and coloured Calimancoes, Lastings, Tammies, Durants, Camblets, Shalloons, Rattinets, Modes, Sattins, Taffaties, Sarsnets, Amozeens, Lutestrings, Florentines, a good assortment of Ribbons, black and coloured sewing silks, scarf twist, black laces and edgings, Corduroys, Checks, Jeans and Pillow Fustians, Playing Cards, Ferrets, Galloons, Tapes and Bobbins, Pins, Whitechapel and other Needles, Writing Paper, Leather, Jean and silk Gloves and Mitts, Womens stuff shoes, Childrens Morrocco shoes, Womens superfine cotton hose, shirt buttons, hardware, plated buckles, &c.

I M P O R T E D,
In the last Vessels from ENGLAND,
And now opened for Sale at
RHINELANDER's STORE,
The Corner of Burling's Slip,
A large and general Assortment of
China, Glass, and Earthen Ware,
A L S O,
Ironmongery, and Cutlery,
WINDOW GLASS, from 6 by 8, to 22 by 16.
A Brig and Schooner for Sale,
About 160 hogsheads burthen each.

W I L L I A M S's,
No. 41, Smith-Street, between Pitt's Statue, and King-Street,
Have just received by the Ships VIGILANT and SKINNER, from LONDON,
A fresh Assortment of
IRONMONGERY *and* HARDWARE,
Which they are now selling on very low terms for Cash;---among a variety of others, are the the following Articles:
SHoemakers and Carpenters Tools, Curriers and Coopers ditto,
Locks and Hinges assorted,
Hand, Pit, and Cross cut Saw Files, Horse Rasps, &c.
Scale Beams and Steelyards,
Table Knives and Forks,
Scissors, Corkscrews, and Snuffers,
Cutteaux and Penknives,
Pocket and Memorandum Books,
Jewellery assorted,
Gilt, Plated, and Metal Buttons,
Japan Tea Trays, Tobacco Boxes, &c.
Brass and Iron And Irons
Brass and Wire Fenders,
Shovel and Tongs,
Brass Warming Pans, Mortars, Candlesticks, Weights, &c.
Copper Tea and Camp Kettles, Saucepans, Warming Pans, &c, Brass Cabinet work assorted,
Plated and Metal Buckles,
Plated and Steel Stirrups, Bitts Spurs, &c.
Plated Candlesticks, Waiters, &c,
Window Glass, Also Tin Ware in casks, Glass Ware in cases, fine and military Shoes and Boots, Womens Stuff Shoes, Perfumery, Millenery, and Stationary assorted in Trunks, Turnery assorted, and a few dozen patent silk Hose, to be sold very low.

ALL those who are indebted to the estate of Elias Ellis, deceased, by bond, note or otherwise, are requested immediately to discharge the same, and those who have any demands against the said estate, are desired to apply to the subscriber for payment.

Also to be sold at public vendue on the premises on the first day of December next or at private sale at any time before, one House or Lot of ground in Crown Street, near the Broad-Way, the house is one story and an half high, with a good kitchen back, and a good cellar under the whole, the lot is in breadth in front 24 feet and an half, and in the rear 20 feet 9 inches, & in length 87 feet, also one lot of ground in Temple Street, adjoining the rear of the before mentioned lot, being in breadth in front and rear 25 feet, and in length 50 feet and an half. Also one other lot of ground in Dey Street, being in breadth in front and rear 25 feet, and in length 85 feet. For further conditions apply to the subscriber, who will give an indisputable title for the same.

William Ellis, Executor.

M A R E Y,
LADIES HAIR DRESSER,
No. 7, Beekman Street,
BEGS *leave to inform the Ladies that he has newly removed to this city, with the intention of carrying on his business here, and will do himself the honour to wait on any Ladies who may choose to employ him.*

New-York, November 10, 1783.

THE Subscriber intends going in the first vessel to London and Germany. Any person that has any demands on me will call at my house to receive payment, and all those indebted to me will pay me immediately; the Tobacconist's business will be carried on by my wife, during my absence from this place

John Holtzman,
Chatham Street, No, 4.

For CORK, or any other Port in Ireland, or Bristol or Liverpool,
Should a full freight offer to either,
The Ship NANCY,
Captain WOODWARD,
A Remarkable fast sailing vessel, well found, has good accommodations for passengers, and will be ready to take in, in ten days. For freight or passage apply to the Captain on board, at Moore's wharf, or to

EDWARD GOOLD,
Hanover-Square,
Who has just imported in said Ship new mess beef in tierces, tallow in firkins. He has also for sale a bale of rugs, and a parcel of three years old Barbadoes Cane Spirit, just landed from the Brig Speedwell.

New-York Coffee House.
ALL Masters of vessels arriving in this Port are hereby informed, that the Subscriber who keeps the New-York Coffee House, has prepared a book in which he will insert the names of such as may please to call on him, the names of their vessels, the port from whence they came, and any other particular occurrences of their voyages, in order that the gentlemen of this city, or travellers may obtain the earliest intelligence thereof: particular care will be taken in the delivery of all such letters as may be entrusted to his care,

Cornelius Bradford.

New-York, 1st November, 1783.
THE Co-Partnership of ATTWOOD and FLLOYD, being this day final ly dissolved, all persons indebted to them are requested to make speedy payment to the subscriber; by whom also all demands on them (if such there are) will be immediately answered. The business in future will be carried on under the old firm of

A T T W O O D's
MEDICINAL STORE,
No. 207, Water-street,
Which is fresh supplied by the arrival of the Black Queen, and Skinner, ships, from London. The greatest care and attention ever has been paid in selecting the choicest articles, which a long connection with some of the first houses in England, has enabled the proprietor to obtain. The same assiduity will be continued to render this *general repository of Drugs and Medicines, Surgeons Instruments, &c. &c.* truly useful, and to merit the continuance of past favours conferred on

The Public's
Obliged and obedient
Humble servant,
THOs. BRIDGEN ATTWOOD.

N. B. Essence of Spruce,
Guava Jelly,
Tamarinds and
Castor Oil, } from Jamaica,
English Spanish, and American Honey.

Mount Hope Pig and Bar Iron.
Nail and Deck Nail Rods, Durham Tin Plate Steels, Close Steels and Franklins, Potash Kettles, Tea Kettles, Pye Pans, Griddles, and all cast Hollow Ware, Smoothing or Sad Irons, Andirons, &c. to be sold at No. 207, Water-street; where all orders are received, and executed, to the pattern given, at a short notice.

German Heart and Club Steel,
Window Glass of all sizes.

Cullimore and Sadlier,
No. 202, QUEEN-STREET,
Have just received per the NANCY, Captain WOODWARD, from CORK,
A few Tierces and Barrels best
M E S S B E E F.
Which they will sell very cheap for Cash.

November 4, 1783.

ARMSTRONG & MILLER,
No. 202, QUEEN-STREET,
Have on hand, and imported in the Black Queen, from London, which they will sell on the most reasonable terms for CASH,

BRitish Osnabrigs and sail Cloth,	Horn Combs and Spoons,
Yard wide Irish Linens,	Manchester Goods,
Printed Linens and Callicoes,	Superfine Broad Cloths,
Lawns,	A handsome assortment of Ribbons,
Men and Womens Thread and Cotton Stockings,	Glasgow plain Snuff,
Coloured Threads,	Jewellery,
Check and striped Hollands,	Gold and Silver Watches,
Sattinets,	Chains, Seals, &c.
Diaper Table Cloths	Solid Plate,
Worsted Binding,	Silver Buckles,
Tapes,	Plated Ware, &c.
Mens Leather Gloves,	STATIONARY and BOOKS,
Silk Gauze & Gauze Handkerchiefs,	Sadlery,
Queens Ware,	Ship Bolts, 3-4 and 7-8 inch. tf

Frederick Cockle,
No. 193, Queen-street, between Beekman and Burling-slips,
Has imported in the St. James and Albion, Just arrived from Bristol,
A general Assortment of
Ironmongery, Brasiery, Pewter, & Cutlery,
Amongst which are,
AWL Blades,
Table Knives and Forks,
Penknives and Cutteaux,
Spades and Shovels,
Shovels and Tongs,
Locks and Hinges assorted,
Scales, Beams, and Weights,
Steelyards, Bellows, Sad Irons,
Copper Tea Kettles, Saucepans and Coffee Pots,
Brass and Copper Warming Pans,
Brass, Iron, and Princes Metal Candlesticks,
Japanned and polished Steel spring Snuffers
Brass Pans, Mortars and Pestles,
Plated and Steel Bitts and Stirrups,
Gilt, plated, and Metal Shoe Buckles,
Paste Shoe, Knee, and Stock do.
Double gilt, plated, Metal, and Horn Buttons,
Paper Snuff Boxes and Ink Pots,
Wool Cards, &c. &c. &c.
A L S O,
A few Dozens of the best English tanned
SHEEP SKINS.
N. B. Old Copper, Brass, and Pewter taken in payment.

Nails, Anchors, Graplines,
Just arrived in the ABIGAIL and MARY, Captain TAYLOR,
And to be SOLD by
EDWARD GOOLD,
No. 34, *Hanover-Square,*
THE finest Hyson,
Bohea,
Soushong
and
Single } T E A S.
Rum, high proof Brandy,
Window Glass 7 by 9,
Gin in cases,
A few trunks of Womens best Callimanco Pumps, fashionable heels.
A few boxes of Citron,
And a very large Assortment of
D R Y G O O D S,
Suitable to the season. tf

HENRY NASH, and Co.
H A V E F O R S A L E,
At their Store on Cruger's Wharf,
The following Articles:
Which they will dispose of on the lowest terms, viz.
GENUINE Red and White Port Wine, by the Pipe, Hogshead, and Quarter-cask.
Ditto, Lisbon Wine, by the Pipe, Hogshead, and Quarter-cask.
Hyson Teas, by the Quarter-chest.
Sequin ditto, ditto.
Toulin ditto, ditto.
A few Packages of Flannels.

T O B E S O L D,
A Dwelling House and Lot of Land, situated in William Street, in a most excellent stand for business, for particulars apply to John Kelly, No. 33, Hanover-Square, New-York.

AS the Subscribers intend in the course of a few weeks, to leave this city, they inform their friends, and the Public in general, that they will transact such business in London, as may be committed to their management, with fidelity and dispatch.

ELIAS HARDY,
JOHN L. C, ROOME.

Mr. Hardy is already admitted in the Court of King's Bench and Chancery, and proposes resuming the practice of the Law in England.

New-York, October 14, 1783.

Mr. Hardy sailed for England by way of Nova Scotia, a few days past, and left in the hands of Mr. Roome, some bonds, notes, and other papers, to be delivered to his clients, who will be pleased to call for the same.

Deeds, Bonds, Notes, and other Papers, heretofore left with Mr. Roome, to be put in suit, will be returned to the proprietors on being called for.

A large and valuable LIBRARY, and some excellent Office Furniture, to be disposed of on terms advantageous to the purchasers.

Mr. Roome requests his friends, who have been obliged with the loan of books, or return them immediately, as he will fail for England in about a fortnight.

New-York, Queen Street, No. 225, October 27. 1783.

MRS. ANN TODD, living on Brownejohn's wharf; intending shortly to leave this city, requests all those to whom she is indebted to call and receive payment, and she hopes that all those who are any ways indebted to her, will be so good as to make speedy payment.

[VOL. III.] THE [NUMB. 114.]

SALEM GAZETTE.

THURSDAY, December 18, 1783.

PRINTED AND PUBLISHED BY SAMUEL HALL, NEAR THE COURT-HOUSE.

ANTIGUA.

HIS Excellency the Governor thinks fit hereby to notify to all Frenchmen and other foreigners, that they must forthwith leave the Island, and that such of them who may neglect to obey his Excellency's pleasure, will be apprehended, and put under confinement until a proper opportunity can be found of sending them off; and his Excellency requires of the Magistrates of this Island, and of the Constables, and other public officers, that they do apprehend, or cause to be apprehended, all persons under the above description, who may be found either in town or country, and to send them to the Deputy Provost Marshal, in whose charge they will remain until they quit the Island.

By his Excellency's command.

Clark's Hill, Oct. 24, 1783. THO. WARNER, Secr.

St. John's, October 24. On Monday last arrived here in seventeen days from Philadelphia, the ship Antigua Packet, Captain Carson. Her cargo consisting of various articles very much wanted, were not permitted to be landed, and she is gone to Leeward.

PHILADELPHIA, December 3.

On Saturday night last, about a quarter past ten o'clock, a smart shock of an earthquake was felt in and about this city; and about one o'clock on Sunday morning another, less violent, was felt by many people in the city and suburbs. Most of the houses were very sensibly shaken, so that in many the china and pewter, &c. were thrown off the shelves, and several persons were waked from their sleep.——We hope that the country has sustained no damage by this convulsion of nature, which brings fresh to our memory the late calamities of Sicily, &c. &c.

On Saturday the 15th ult. departed this life in Prince George County, Maryland, the honourable John Hanson, Esquire, late President of the United States in Congress assembled.

NEW-YORK, December 4.

The character of the British army exemplified, on their precipitate flight from this city, in cutting away the hailiards of, and greasing the flag-staff in the fort, lately called Fort George, strongly marks the character of those people, and demonstrates their meanness of spirit and indisposition to conciliate the affections of the Americans; men who have proved themselves their superiors in every virtue, and who may without arrogance be denominated their Conquerors.

It is too obvious to need any proof, says a customer, that nothing chagrins the Britons more than the Union Cockade which appears in the hats of the American officers, in honour to our worthy Allies.

DECEMBER 8.

At Frances's tavern, last Thursday at noon, there was a numerous meeting of officers of the first distinction in the American army, to take leave of their great Commander, General Washington; who on filling a glass of wine addressed his brave compatriots as follows:

"*With an heart full of love and gratitude, I now take leave of you: I most devoutly wish that your latter days may be as prosperous and happy, as your former ones have been glorious and honourable.*"

The respectable body convened on this important occasion, comprised the courageous soldier, the invaluable patriot, and sincere friend to the interests of society. Deeply impressed with a stedfast sensibility of his Excellency's amiable manners, and conspicuous virtues, an earnest anxiety to acknowledge them was minutely legible thro'out the whole meeting, and exercised the nicest feelings of human nature.

An affection so laudable and sincere on the part of the community, could not be enhanced by the highest finished eloquence; yet it must in strict justice be allowed, that they received his Excellency's concise and characteristic address with undescribable emotions of admiration and unfeigned esteem; and replied to it in animated terms, which reflect the highest honour on men vying with each other to express their veneration for so dignified a commonwealth, and its illustrious founders.—His Excellency the Governor, the attendant officers of state, and many citizens of repute, gave the most conspicuous proofs of their regard for the General's true merit, in a sincere and affectionate farewell.

The corps of light infantry was drawn up in a line; the Commander in Chief, about two o'clock, passed through them on his way to Whitehall, where he embarked in his barge for Powles-Hook. He is attended by General le Baron de Steuben; proposes to make a short stay at Philadelphia; will thence proceed to Annapolis, where he will resign his commission of General of the American Armies into the hands of the Continental Congress, from whom it was derived; immediately after which, his Excellency will set out for his seat, named Mount-Vernon, in Virginia; emulating the example of his model, the virtuous Roman General, who, victorious, left the tented field, covered with honour, and withdrew from public life, to enjoy *otium cum dignitate*.

We are informed that their Excellencies the Commanders in Chief of the British fleet and army, in America, with the last division of troops on board, have left Staten-Island, on their passage to England. General Sir Guy Carleton, Deane Poyntz, Esq. Paymaster-General, Brook Watson, Esq. Commissary-General, William Smith, Esq. and a number of Gentlemen, were passengers in the Ceres frigate, commanded by Captain Hawkins. In the Cyclops frigate, commanded by Captain Christian, were Hugh Wallace and James Jauncey, Esqrs. and many other Gentlemen. The Assurance man of War, Captain Swiney, with a great number of passengers, chiefly officers of the army, sailed for England some days before the above fleet. The ship Holderness, with the Commissariate Department, sailed likewise a few days before them for Halifax, in Nova-Scotia, where they are to act in the same line as they were accustomed to do in this city.

SALEM, December 18.

The Legislature of Connecticut, by their Resolutions passed at their Session in October last, did declare, that that State has the undoubted and exclusive right of jurisdiction and pre-emption to all the lands lying west of the State of *Pennsylvania*, and east of the river *Mississippi*, and extending throughout from the latitude 41d. to latitude 42d. 2m. north, by virtue of the charter granted by King *Charles* the IId. to the late Colony, now State of *Connecticut*, bearing date the 23d day of *April*, A. D. 1662: Which claim and right they are determined to assert and maintain. The Governor of the said State has accordingly issued a Proclamation, strictly forbidding all persons from entering upon or settling within the said territory, without special licence obtained of the General Assembly.

Last Thursday Capt. Baldwin arrived here in 15 days from St. Croix. By several late news-papers, printed at that island, we find, that the inhabitants of the British West-India islands are under alarming apprehensions of distress, occasioned by the Proclamation issued by their King on the 2d of July last, construed to exclude the citizens of these United States from trading in their ports. The sentiments of the people of Antigua are fully discovered in an address presented to General Shirley, their Governor, on the 10th of October, the substance of which address is as follows:

"Your Excellency must have beheld with pleasure, that upon the restoration of peace, this Colony came into the immediate possession of an unaccustomed plenty—a plenty they had long been strangers to, and had long wished for; and in the prospect of a long enjoyment of it, they had forgotten all the injuries, mischiefs and disappointments that were inseparably allied to the war.——In this momentary enjoyment, the publication of his Majesty's Royal Proclamation, dated at St. James's, the 2d day of July last, has taken place, which, by tolerating British vessels, navigated according to law, to trade with the United States of America, is construed to exclude, by implication, the United States of America from trading to our ports,——This interpretation of the Royal pleasure, arresting in so sudden a manner the commerce of America, at the very moment it was returning to our ports, has thrown the interest of the Planters into more confusion and distress than they ever felt at any stage or period of the war: because, by placing a false dependence upon a continuance of such supplies, the disappointment leaves them almost without remedy, and, from the best information, at a time when the provisions now at market will not answer the consumption of the Island for more than TWO MONTHS, and such provisions too, by the effect of the Proclamation, risen in their prices at nearly the rate of FIFTY PER CENT.——With the melancholy evidence of these facts before their eyes, and the more gloomy prospect of their future wants, the inhabitants at large have petitioned us, their Representatives, to lay their case before your Excellency, and to implore the aid of your Excellency in the adoption of such measures as may suggest themselves to your Excellency's wisdom, for their immediate relief.——We, knowing the just grounds of their fears and apprehensions, and not doubting but his Majesty, from his paternal care and affection for the remotest of his subjects, would approve and ratify your Excellency's conduct in exceeding his commands, when, from peculiar local and unthought-of circumstances, the strict execution of them would be ruinous to the smallest branch of his kingdom,—Do most humbly pray, your Excellency would be pleased to order and direct, that the produce of the United States of America may not only be imported into this Island in British ships and vessels, owned by British subjects, and navigated according to law, but that the same may be also imported in the ships and vessels of the subjects of the United States of America, and that the produce of this Island may also be exported in such last mentioned ships and vessels, upon payment of his Majesty's duties, until such time as his Majesty's pleasure shall be known, or until the Commercial Treaty, now negotiating between Great-Britain and the States of America, is definitively settled; and that your Excellency would signify such your pleasure to the Officers of his Majesty's Customs of this Island, or that your Excellency would take such other measures for our relief, as to your Excellency's wisdom shall seem meet."

The Governor's answer was in these words:——

"Gentlemen,

"I have carefully attended to the purport of your Address, and am very sorry to tell you, that it is totally out of my power to take any steps in this business, but those of strictly obeying his Majesty's Proclamation, which is backed likewise by an Act of Parliament, and doing my utmost to have it obeyed by all within my government.

"I flatter myself, Gentlemen, you do not doubt of my warmest wishes and inclination to serve this community, where it is compatible with my honour and duty."

Capt. Baldwin, on the 6th instant, in lat. 36. 27. long. 68. 40. spoke with Capt. Samuel Gill, in the schooner Commerce, from New-London, bound to Martinico; all well—though he had met with a very heavy gale of wind.

On the 27th ult. died at Beverly, in the 69th year of his age, Mr. JONATHAN PERKINS, a gentleman of a liberal education, who has been employed, for upwards of 50 years past, as a Schoolmaster, which trust he discharged with fidelity. He sustained the character of a worthy, honest man; and has left a sorrowful widow and a numerous acquaintance to lament their loss.

DIED—At Byfield, in Newbury, on Sunday evening last, the Reverend MOSES PARSONS, pastor of the church in that parish.—At Boston, Mrs. MARY CHAUNCY, in the 69th year of her age, consort of the Rev. Dr. Chauncy, of that town.

☞ *A meeting of the Fellows of the American Academy of Arts and Sciences will be holden, by adjournment, at the Hall of the Manufactory House in Boston, on the 31st instant.*

⁂ *Mr.* PIEMONT, *of Ipswich, since his loss by fire, as mentioned in our last, has provided himself with Stabling sufficient to accommodate his customers.*

NAVAL-OFFICE, Port of SALEM, December 17.

ENTERED.

Brig Harmony, L. Whitteridge,	from	St. Martins.
Schooner Industry, W. Baldwin,		St. Croix.
Brig Three Brothers, T. Rice,		Jamaica.

CLEARED.

Brig Recovery, W. Dennis,	for	West-Indies.
Brig Betsey, J. Burke,		West-Indies.
Schooner Cato, T. Dexter,		Nova-Scotia.

Brig Dispatch and Brig St. John, mentioned last week as cleared out, were inserted through mistake.

THURSDAY, SEPTEMBER 30, 1784. NUM. 424

THE

New-York Packet

AND THE

AMERICAN ADVERTISER.

PUBLISHED EVERY MONDAY AND THURSDAY.

PRINTED BY SAMUEL LOUDON, No. 5, WATER-STREET, between the COFFEE-HOUSE and the OLD SLIP.

CHIMNEY-OFFICE,

For the CITY of NEW-YORK,
No. 160, Water-ſtreet, the corner of Beekman's ſlip.

As the ſaid office wants a number of good ſweepers, great encouragement will be given, by applying immediately. 22

CHIMNEY OFFICE,

For the CITY of NEW-YORK.

WHEREAS, the ſubſcriber has made application to the Corporation for leave to open a Chimney Office in this city; and they have been pleaſed to recommend and encourage the undertaking, as promiſing advantages to the public: Therefore the ſubſcriber propoſes to procure a number of hands, ſufficient to clean all the chimnies of the ſubſcribers, to theſe propoſals in this city, as often as may be thought neceſſary.

He will keep an office where the name of every perſon who chooſes to favour this undertaking will be regiſtered, with the number of chimnies which are daily uſed, and the days, from time to time, on which they were laſt cleaned.

He will engage that every ſubſcriber, without the trouble of ſending or ſearching for a perſon, ſhall be waited on every ſix weeks, or month, if required, preciſely on the day, from the beginning of September until the latter end of April.

In the ſummer ſeaſon the kitchen chimnies to be ſwept every two months.

He will engage to pay the fine laid by law, if the chimney takes fire within five weeks after it has been cleaned by his people; unleſs the chimney be cracked, or the fire begin in ſome other part of the room.

That the perſons employed by the undertaker ſhall be diſtinguiſhed by caps, numbered, and having his name on them; that they ſhall be under the direction of a deputy, and attend to aſſiſt at all fires.

He promiſes to employ ſuch as have hitherto been engaged in this buſineſs, if they deſire it.

The payment for cleaning each chimney ſhall be no more than the cuſtomary price of one ſhilling and ſix pence, paid at the time to the deputy.

In conſideration of the great trouble and expence which muſt attend the eſtabliſhing ſo uſeful a regulation, the ſubſcriber entreats the ſubſcription of the inhabitants to an engagement not to engage any other than the perſons who may belong to the intended office, in cleaning their chimnies; ſo long as what is above propoſed, engaged and promiſed, ſhall be punctually obſerved by himſelf and ſervants.

A copy of theſe articles ſhall on the firſt day of entry on the buſineſs be delivered to each ſubſcriber, ſigned by the undertaker, to furniſh the means of forcing a compliance with what is engaged: It is alſo expected, that the ſubſcribers will pay for the number of chimnies (which will be only thoſe daily uſed) entered into the books, during the time above-mentioned, though they employ others than the office boys to do the buſineſs; unleſs it appears that they did not attend at the neceſſary time.

That the hours for cleaning the chimnies ſhall be from four to eight in the morning, and from two to ſun-ſet in the evening.

That each ſubſcriber, after each ſeaſon, ſhall be at entire liberty to withdraw his name from the office.

JOSEPH BECK.

We are become ſubſcribers to this plan,

JAMES DUANE, MAYOR,
RICHARD VARICK, RECORDER,
B. BLAGGE,
THO. RANDALL,
W. NEILSON,
W. W. GILBERT, } ALDERMEN.
AB. P. LOTT,
THO. IVERS,
J. BROOME,
ROB. BENSON, CLERK.

23

FRENCH LANGUAGE.

JAMES ROBINS, native of France and maſter of the French Language, will open his ſchool in Garden-ſtreet, oppoſite to the Dutch church, the firſt of next month, where gentlemen, who will honour him with their confidence, will be inſtructed with great care and cheerfulneſs. His ſchool will begin at 6 o'clock, in the evening and continue until 9. His price is Four Dollars per month, without entrance money. 23

FOR SALE,

At the Merchants Coffee Houſe, on Monday the 25th of October, at 12 o'clock,

Two Dwelling Houſes on the north ſide of Thames ſtreet, near the North-river, built on leaſe ground, about 16 years of which is unexpired.

Any perſon deſirous of purchaſing one or both of ſaid houſes at private ſale, or viewing the premiſes, may apply to Thomas Elliſon, in Broadway, or William Backhouſe, No. 163, Water-ſtreet.

Sept. 25. 23

TO BE SOLD,

A Likely Young NEGRO FELLOW, about 21 years of age, brought up to farming buſineſs, Enquire of the Printer. 15

Juſt Imported,

In the Reſolution, and other late veſſels from London,

And to be SOLD, by

James Beekman and Sons,

At their STORE, No. 241, Queen-Street,

An Aſſortment of

BROAD Cloths,
Caſſimers,
Wiltons,
German Serges,
Sagathies,
Shalloons,
Black Velverets,
Spotted do.
Black & blue Laſtings,
Sattinets,
Florentines, beſt qual.
Prunellos,
Princes Stuff,
Royal Rib,
Cotton Denim,
Black and brown Silk Crape,
Black Mode,
Buff printed Jane veſt Patterns,
Elegant tamboured & embroidered Silk do.
Black worſted breeches Patterns,
Black, blue & white worſted Hoſe,
Striped Hollands,
6 4, yd. wide, and 7-8 Cotton Checks,
Callicoes & Chintzes, a great variety,
Blue, red and purple copperplate furniture do.
Printed linen Handkerchiefs different colours,
White do. with blue, red and purple borders,
Barcelona,
Martinico,
Negligees, } Handkerchiefs
Romals,
Silk checks,
Beſt India Nankeens,
Flanders Bed Ticks,
Oznabrigs,
Ruſſia Huckaback,

Do. Sheeting, white & browns,
Princes Linen,
Ruſſia Drabs,
Bleached do.
Ruſſia Diaper,
Clouting do.
Dowlas,
Brown Sileſia,
Damaſk Table Cloths,
Modes and Sarſanets, black & white, pink and blue,
Black Taffity,
Perſian do.
Black Silk Mitts,
Sewing Silk of all colours,
Black,
Dutch, } LACE, a great varety,
&
Troly
Edging,
Scotch Thread,
Darning do.
Coſſe Muſlins,
Blue, red and purple copperplate do.
Cambricks,
Pocket do.
Clear Lawns,
Striped and ſpotted Scotch lawns,
Lawn Aprons,
Do. Handkerchiefs,
Striped and bordered Kenting, do,
Gauze,
Black & white Minionet,
Buckrams,
Quality Bindings,
Silk Ferrets,
Silk and worſted knee Garters,
Curtain Fringe, different colours,
Buttons, Tapes, &c.

23

JOHN HENRY,

No. 209, *QUEEN-STREET*,
Between BURLING'S SLIP & the FLY MARKET,
Has Imported in the Polly from Hull and other Ports,

A very general ASSORTMENT of

FALL GOODS,

Which, with thoſe he has on hand, will be ſold on the moſt reaſonable terms, either wholeſale or retail, as uſual.

SUPERFINE broad cloths,
Second do.
Third & middling do.
Rattinets and ſhalloons,
Twilled and plain Bath coatings,
Duffils,
Baizes,
Flannels,
Roſe blankets,
Striped do.
Corduroys & velverets,
Figured and plan fattin laſtings, &c.
Denims,
Forreſt and plain cloths,
Low priced Linſeys &c.

Callimancoes,
Durants,
Tammies, } all Colours.
Moreens,
Taboreens,
Yard wide, and 7/8 Iriſh linen,
Apron and yard wide cotton check,
And a variety of worſted hoſiery,
Ribbed, patent & plain ſilk and worſted do.
With every other article in the dry good line too tedious to enumerate.

23*

Corduroys and Cotton Velvets,

TO BE SOLD,

BY the piece, very low, as the importer, who is concerned in the manufactory, purpoſes embarking for England, in a few weeks. Enquire of William Morewood, No. 202, Queen-Street. 23

WANTED a ſingle man capable of managing a ſmall farm, and large garden in the Jerſeys. His character muſt bear a ſtrict enquiry. Apply to No. 4, Wall-Sreet. 236

BESLY and GOODWIN,

DRUGGISTS and APOTHECARIES,

No. 229, Queen-ſtreet, near the Fly-Market,

HAVE IMPORTED, in the Triumph, Captain Stout, and the Reſolution, Capt. Strannock, from London, a freſh aſſortment of all kinds of *GENUINE MEDICINES*, both of the Chymical and Galinical, which they will ſell wholeſale and retail, for Caſh, Public Securities or at ſhort credit.

As follows is part of their Aſſortment:

GENUINE red Peruvian Bark,
Antimony,
Æthiops mineral,
Aquar fortis,
Socororine aloes,
Spaniſh arnato, or otter,
Balſam of fir,
Borax, camphor,
Beſt powdered bark,
Caſtor, white wax,
Cochineal, vermillion,
Cream of tartar,
Engliſh ſaffron,
Conſerve of roſes,
Turner's cerate,
Lenitve Electuar
Powder of Jalap.y,
Powder of Ipecacuana,
Coriander ſeed,
Venice treacle,
Elixir of vitriol,
Do. proprietatis,
Eſſence of lemons,
Do. of Bergamot,
Goulard's extrct of lead
Liquorice juice,
Flowers of brimſtone,
Camomile flowers,
Gum arabic,
Gamboge,
Pearl barley,
Hiera picra,
Iſinglaſs,
Liquid laudanum,
Flakey manna,
Magneſia alba,
Oil of anniſeed,
Powder of rhubarb,
Tartar emetic,
Cardamom ſeed,
A quantity of juniper berries,
Oil of juniper,
Do. of lavender,

Oil of ſweet almonds,
Do. of vitriol,
Sirup of violets,
Pill cochiæ,
Carolina pink root,
Genetian root,
Valerian do.
Sago, ſalt-petre,
Sulphur viv.
Spermaceti,
Glauber's ſalt,
Sal armoniac,
Spirit of hartſhorn,
Compound ſpirit of lavender,
Sal. volatile,
Anniſeed,
Carraway ſeed,
Nut galls,
Anderſon's pills,
Britiſh oil,
Bateman's drops,
Hill's balſam of honey,
Court plaiſter,
Daffy's elixir,
Eſſence of peppermint
Godfrey's cordial,
Hooper's female pills,
Jame's fever powders,
Walker's jeſuits drops,
Lockyer's pills,
Lavender water,
Roſe water,
Green oil cloth,
Stoughton's bitters,
Turlington balſam,
Beſt Surgeon's inſtruments, in leather pouches,
Beſt lancets,
Do. common,
Ivory and pewter ſyringes,
Bell-metal, glaſs and marble mortars with peſtles, &c. &c. &c.

Thoſe gentlemen who chooſe to favour them with their cuſtom, may be aſſured of being ſerved on the moſt reaſonable terms, and their orders executed with punctuality and diſpatch, having been bred to the profeſſion, hope to make it their intereſt, and worth the attention of all who chooſe to favour them with their orders.—Medicine Cheſts with ſuitable directions will be made up on the loweſt terms and at the ſhorteſt notice.—Practitioners and country ſtore keepers may depend on being ſerved with care and attention. 223

JOHN IRELAND,

No. 68, Water-ſtreet, near Beekman's-ſlip,
Has juſt imported in the Reſolution, and other veſſels from Europe,

A large aſſortment of WOOLLENS,

Conſiſting of

LOW priced Coatings, red and green Baize, ſtriped and roſe Blankets, yarn and worſted Hoſe, feathered pluſh Waiſtcoats, fine Bath coating Great-Coats, full lined and velvet collars, with all ſorts of ready made Cloathing, fit for the approaching ſeaſon, which will be Sold on the loweſt terms for Caſh. 23

George and Samuel Douglas,

No. 233, Queen-Street,
Have Imported in the ſhip London, Captain Hopkins, juſt arrived from London,

A general Aſſortment of

DRY GOODS,

The principal part of which are adapted for the fall trade, and will be diſpoſed of on moderate terms, by the package or piece. Alſo, Leaf Sugar, Hyſon Teas, Shot, Soap, Candles, Saddlery, Tin Ware, and a few Hhds. beſt London Porter.

N. B. The above-mentioned ſhip will return to London with all convenient ſpeed. 22

For LONDON,

The SHIP

TRIUMPH,

JACOB STOUT Maſter.

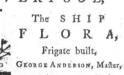

For freight or paſſage apply to Benjamin Stout, jun. No. 210 Queen-ſtreet, or to the Maſter on board, at the Commiſſary's wharf. 22

For LIVERPOOL,

The SHIP

FLORA,

Frigate built,

GEORGE ANDERSON, Maſter,

WILL ſail on the 8th of October. Any gentleman deſirous of a paſſage in this ſhip, will pleaſe to apply to Mr. Iſaac Moſes, merchant, or to the Captain on board, now lying at the Beekman's wharf. 22

TO BE SOLD,

THE double decked Polacre Ketch Boon, burthen about 150 tons, Spaniſh built, of red cedar and other durable wood, about ſix years old; can be ſent to ſea immediately with little expence being well found, and is the compleateſt veſſel in this port for carrying horſes or cattle, having a remarkable convenient deck for that purpoſe.

Now landing out of ſaid veſſel at Leffert's Wharf,

A Cargo of excellent Teneriffe Wine, of different qualities, ſuperior to any that has been imported into this place for theſe ten years paſt from that quarter.

Enquire at No. 28, King-ſtreet, for particulars. 2

TO BE SOLD,

The faſt ſailing SCHOONER

HENRIETTA,

Of about 120 tons burthen, Britiſh property.—Inventory to be ſeen on board ſaid veſſel at Brownejohn's wharf, or at No. 28, King-Street.

N. B. Now landing out of ſaid ſchooner, for ſale, a ſmall cargo of beſt Packing Salt, a few quarter-caſks of choice Old Wine, and 40 boxes of Lemons, in prime order, being only plucked thirty-five days from the tree 2

An ACADEMY,

Is now opened at No. 8, Frankfort-ſtreet,

WHERE youth are boarded and educated in every branch of uſeful and polite literature, and the minuteſt attention paid to their morals. As proper aſſiſtants (well verſed in the neceſſary requiſites for the inſtruction of young minds) are engaged, the ſubſcriber doubts not the countenance and protection of the generous public.

Evenings are appropriated to diſpenſe inſtructions in the French Language, in its grammatical purity, and in the lateſt and moſt approved method of Italian Book-Keeping, by The publics humble ſervant,

MICHAEL SHRIMPTON.

*** Conveyancing, ſuch as bonds, bills, releaſes, recognizances, articles of agreement, letters and warrants of attorney, awards, bills of ſale, gifts, grants, leaſes, aſſignments, mortgages, ſurrenders, jointures, covenants, co-partnerſhips, charter parties, letters of licence, compoſitions, conveyances, partitions, wills, ſailors wills, ſoldiers conveyances, &c. &c. And merchants books, correctly poſted with accuracy and diſpatch. 23

BROTHERS, COSTER, & Co.

No. 8, Duke-ſtreet,

Have juſt now opened, and for SALE,

A Large Aſſortment of

COARSE BROAD CLOTHS;

And a variety of GOODS, ſuitable to the ſeaſon, which they will diſpoſe of on very reaſonable terms. 23

UNITED WHALING COMPANY.

THE Members of the United Whaling Company, are deſired to attend their meeting, on the fourth day of October next, at ſix o'Clock in the Evening, at the Long Room of the Coffee-Houſe, it being the firſt Monday in the month.

By order of the Preſident,

JAMES GRIFFITHS, *Secretary.*

23

This Day is PUBLISHED,

And now selling by SAMUEL LOUDON,
Price two shillings and six-pence;

ARGUMENTS and JUDGMENT of the MAYOR's COURT of the City of NEW-YORK, in a cause betwen

ELIZABETH RUTGERS
AND
JOSHUA WADDINGTON.

N. B. The suit between *Elizabeth Rutgers* and *Joshua Waddington*, having from its peculiar circumstances been a subject of much public expectation, it has been judged, that a publication of the principles on which the late determination in the Mayor's Court was founded, might answer some beneficial purposes; and would at least serve to prevent misapprehension.

In compliance with the wishes and request of several citizens, the arguments and judgments of the Court are now given to the public.

E D U C A T I O N.

J. M E N N Y E,

At No. 32, Gold-street, fronting Beekman-street,

PROPOSES to open his EVENING SCHOOL, the 11th of next month; in which, and in the day school, he will teach the following branches of education:

THE ENGLISH LANGUAGE, agreeably to a system of grammar which he has compiled from the best authorities; by which, although in manuscripts, he has been able to bring youth faster on than he ever could by any yet in print. In confidence that this work will meet with a favourable reception from the public, he has put it to the press, depending entirely on its merits for a reimbursement of the expences attending the publication.

WRITING; and ARITHMETIC, in all or any of its parts, including the doctrine and application of vulgar and decimal fractions in all cases.

The fundamental branches of the MATHEMATICS, viz. EUCLID'S ELEMENTS, according to Stone, Cunn, Simpson, &c. PLANE and SPHERICAL TRIGONOMETRY; the CONIC SECTIONS; and ALGEBRA. On this foundation he teaches

MENSURATION, GEOGRAPHY,
GAUGING, ASTRONOMY,
SURVEYING, NAVIGATION,
DIALING, The USE of the GLOBES, &c.

Likewise the construction of the LOGARITHMETICAL TABLES, deduced either from the hyperbola, or the doctrine of fluxions, extended to any number of places which can be necessary, either in trigonometry, astronomy, or compound interest, even if the time should amount to thousands of years.

Also the construction of most of the MATHEMATICAL INSTRUMENTS in common use; that is, such as can be delineated on paper; among which are, the plane and Gunter's scales; the carpenters joint-rule; Everard's and Coggeshall's sliding-rules; the gauging rod; the sector and protractor; the divisions on the theodolite, plane-table, circumferentor, semi circle, &c. And the construction of the globes, maps of countries, plane and Mercator's charts: these last to any assigned radius or scale.

He teaches NAVIGATION to those who have but little time to spare by inspection only, and thereby commonly enables them to keep a journal in the course of a few weeks: but to such seamen, and others, as can give proper attendance, he communicates the whole, according to Hamilton Moore, and others; with this addition, that in all cases of finding the longitude by means of the nautical almanack, he instructs the seaman to enlarge his tables of logarithms to any number of places which the case may require. Upon the whole, he pledges himself to the public, that within the walls of a school, he will teach seamen every thing belonging to a ship's progress in the ocean, her lee-way, the variation of the compass, and her longitude in, according to the latest improvements published by the Commissioners of Longitude in England.

He likewise teaches BOOK-KEEPING, by double entry; instructing youths of a docile capacity, to transform any intelligible waste-book into a journal, and the journal into a ledger, having all its accounts balanced, from which they begin a new set.

He thought it necessary to be explicit on these two last branches, as he has frequently heard Captains of vessels affirm, that navigation could not be taught but at sea; and some merchants, that book-keeping could not be acquired but in their stores; yet he knows, from experience, that when these assertions have proved in appearance to be well-founded, either the scholar must have been a dunce, or the teacher an impostor.

He continues, at certain hours, to teach gentlemen privately, at his dwelling-house, No. 19, Ann-street, particularly such masters of vessels as think themselves deficient in any part of the theory of navigation.

In the day school he teaches Latin to a few: and youths who have had a regular education in the language, and who are sent to him, in order to study the mathematics, are exercised in translating from any of the classical authors, and in correcting the false syntax in Clarke's or Mair's introductions; on such a plan, however, as takes up but little of their time from mathematical pursuits.

KINGSTON ACADEMY, *September* 22, 1784.

THE annual Examination of the Students in this Seminary, will be held here, on Tuesday, the 12th of October next, precisely at ten o'clock in the forenoon. The young gentlemen will deliver essays and orations on various subjects; so that not only their knowledge in the classics will be enquired into, but their abilities in composition and reading of the moderns, will be discovered.

As the Rectorship of this academy will become vacant on the 18th of November first, by the resignation of Mr. Addison, any gentleman, whose abilities and moral character can be sufficiently attested, and who is willing to accept of the above office, will, by applying to the Trustees of the Freeholders, and Commonalty of the town of Kingston, be informed of the particular terms upon which they will supply the vacancy.

The Academy of Kingston has been of signal utility to the public. While the education of youth in many of the public schools of this state, has either in part or totally been interrupted during the war, this seminary has flourished; and a number of young gentlemen laid the foundation of their education here, who give the fairest prospects of being most useful members of the community. The Trustees think it almost unnecessary, to enumerate the many encouraging circumstances, to induce gentlemen to send their sons to Kingston, such as the healthy situation of the place, the cheapness of lodgings, and the few temptations to vice and immorality: Be it sufficient, that they assure the public, they are determined to watch over and promote the interests of their school, and that nothing shall be wanting on their part, which consistantly may be in their power, to render it extensive public advantage.

By order of the Trustees,
24 3w JOH. SNYDER, Speaker.

MARINE SOCIETY.

ON Monday the 11th Instant, at 6 o'Clock in the Evening, will be held at the Coffee-house, a quarterly meeting of the MARINE SOCIETY, of which the members are desired to take notice and give their attendance.

By order of the President,
ANTHONY GRIFFITHS, Secr'y.
New-York, Sept. 30, 1784. 24

P R I N T I N G
For Subscribers only,

A NEW SYSTEM of HUSBANDRY, suited to the climate and land of AMERICA, in 2 volumes octavo, in boards; price to subscribers Three Dollars, or Three and an half bound and lettered. No money required till the books are delivered.

By CHARLES VARLO, Esq.

This is a regular system of husbandry thro' all its branches, and treats of wheat, rye, barley, oats, naked oats, beans, peas; on Siberian wheat; on the white and grey vetch, tares, lentiles, &c. on hemp, flax and potatoes; on the management of all sorts of grass seeds, such as clover, lucerne, saintfoin, rye, grass and burnet; on rape, cole and mustard seed; on turneps, cabbage, and turnep-cabbage; on madder; on different sorts of turneps, with pickles to prevent black wheat, and the fly from destroying young turneps; also, on all sorts of manures, marles, clays and sands; on an artificial cheap compound manure; on rearing, breeding and feeding cattle; some chosen receipts for the cure of all sorts of cattle.

Also, a FEW HINTS humbly offered for the perusal of the different Legislatures of America, shewing some acts that might pass for the utility of the public, particularly, how to put a stop to runaway servants, and to reduce the price of labour to the standard of England, &c.

While the author or his Agents are on their travels, they will call on principal gentlemen that lie on their road, as all subscribers names will be printed in the work; and such as are missed of and wish to subscribe, are desired to forward their names and address to the Printer, before the work is out of press, which it is expected will be about the first of November next.

N. B. The Books will be printed on a large type. 24 3

A C A D E M Y.

MR. QUESNAY begs leave to inform the public, that his Academy, for the tuition of the

French Language, Drawing and Dancing,

is actually open at the Assembly-Room, in Broadway, and where it will be continued until the rooms in Broad-street, No. 32, shall be repaired.

Ladies and gentlemen who would wish to be farther informed, by applying in person, or by letter to MR. QUESNAY, at Mr. Stile's, corner of Broad and Princess-street, will be respectfully attended to. 24 3

Ten Dollars Reward.

RUN AWAY from the Subscriber, on the 24th inst. a NEGRO MAN named PETER, about 22 years of age, 5 feet 7 inches high, of a yellow complexion: Had on when he went away, a brown coloured coat, a blue and grey mixed coloured westcoat, a brown linen trowsers, and an English castor hat: He likewise took with him, a grey coat, leather breeches, and striped linen trowsers---it is supposed he will change his habit: --He talks English and Dutch, and if particular notice is taken of him in his walking his knees stand back more than common. Whoever takes up and secures said negro, so that his master may get him again, shall receive the above reward, and all reasonable charges, paid by EVERT W. SWART.

Fish Kill, Sept. 26. 24 3

TAKEN UP, by the Subscribers, about a fortnight since, a NEGRO MAN, of a dark yellow complexion, who calls himself JIM, about 5 feet, 6 or 7 inches high, supposed to be about 29 years of age: He has a remarkable scar of a burn on his buttock, and also several others on the lower part of his leg, and a ridge on his great toe. It is supposed that he belongs to some part of Virginia, and appears to answer a description given of a run-away, in a late advertisement, signed William Fitzhugh, of Boyd's Hole, King George county, Virginia. The owner of said Negro, can have him again, by applying at the New Gaol, of the city of New York, paying the offered reward and charges, to

JAMES CAMPBELL,
Mayor's Marshall.
NICH. COONRAD, Constable,
West Ward.

Wanted immediately to Hire,

A white Woman (or Negro Wench) who are single, and have no children, and who understand cooking, washing, and house-work, for a small family. They must be well recommended. Enquire of the Printer. 24

A NEGRO BOY,

Is wanted to be purchased,
Of about 17 or 19 years of age,
Who has been brought up to Family or House-Work.
Enquire of the Printer. 24 3

JAMES RENWICK,

No. 7, Great-Dock-street,

HAS IMPORTED,
In the last Vessels from EUROPE, *the following*
GOODS,
Which he will sell on the most reasonable terms,
VIZ.

PRINTED Cottons and Callicoes,
Fustians, Thicksets, Corduroys & Velverets,
Mens and boys coarse and fine Hats,
Mens, womens and boys cotton, thread and worsted Stockings,
Mens and womens Silk do.
Plain and figured Lawns,
Lawn bordered Handkerchiefs,
Printed Handkerchiefs and Scotch Thread,

Likewise a large Assortment of
Hardware, Cutlery and Ironmongery,

A few boxes long and short Pipes,
A few boxes well assorted Medicines,
Ladies elegant Stays, of the newest fashion. 24

HAYMAN LEVY,

No. 7, DUKE-STREET,
HAS FOR SALE,

The following GOODS, which he will sell on the most reasonable terms, for cash, short credit or country produce.

SHERRY WINE, in pipes & quarter casks,	Dutch lace,
Teneriffe do. in do. & half pipes,	Sewing silk,
Hyson, Souchong & Bohea } Teas,	Double sattin hair ribbons,
Striped & rose blankets,	Oznabrigs,
Green & spotted rugs,	Ticklenburgs,
Worsted, Cotten & Thread } Stockings,	Russia duck,
Chintzes, callicoes,	Do. sheeting,
Holland & Irish linen,	Ravens duck,
Callimancoes,	German dowlas,
Camblets, durants,	White chaple needles,
Corduroys, fustians,	Pins,
Cambricks, lawns,	Sattins and other silks,
	Queens ware assorted, by the crate, and a variety of other goods too tedious to enumerate.

24 8

Simon Van Antwerp, and Company,

At No. 45, Little Dock-street, a few doors to the eastward of the Exchange, near the Albany pier;

Have received by the last vessels from Holland, and the EDWARD, from LONDON, the following articles, which they will sell Cheap for CASH;

V I Z.

That antient and famous Medicine and Salve,
Known by the Name of
Haerlem Oil and Neurenberg Salve,

DUTCH mill saws,	Holland powder in quarter casks,
Coffee mills,	Choice Souchong Tea,
Dutch Cheese, (called) Cummina Kase,	Pearl Barley,
Slates and pencils,	Durham Mustard, in 1-2lb. bottles, 6doz. in a box,
Tea kettles,	White sugar Candy in small boxes,
White wash, Sweeping, Hearth, Shoe and Weavers } BRUSHES.	LONDON PAINTS. Viz.
Boenders,	White Lead, Spanish brown, And Yellow oaker, } Grond in OIL.
Scale beams,	London Glue,
Corn fans,	Blistered Steel,
Frying pans,	
Dutch Psalm books of the old version,	
Ivory combs,	09

A few London made SADDLES and BRIDLES.
And several Articles in the
GROCERY LINE.

ALSO, 165 dozen Shone's Best London PORTER, just arrived by the ship Resolution.

SURVEYOR-GENERAL's-OFFICE,

New-York, Sept. 30, 1784.

NOTICE is Hereby Given, to all persons claiming or interested in Lands legally purchased of the native Indians, prior to the fourteenth day of October, in the year one thousand seven hundred and seventy-five, and which do not lay westerly of a line beginning at the north-east corner of the state of Pennsylvania; thence running northerly along the west bank of the Mohawk or westerly branch of Delaware river, to opposite where Tianaderha falls into Susquehanna; thence to Tianaderha, and up the west side thereof, and the west side of its west branch to the head thereof; and thence to Canada creek where it empties into Wood creek; and which have not been patented, to produce and specify their respective claims, to the Governor, or person administering the government of this state for the time being, within one month after the expiration of six weeks from the date hereof; that such provision may be made therein, as justice shall require; agreeable to an act of the Legislature, entitled, "An act to encourage the settlement of the waste and unappropriated lands within this state," passed the 10th of May last.

24 12 *SIMEON DE WITT, Surveyor-General.*

ALL Persons having demands against the Estates of JOHN BOGART, Esq. and his Son HENRY BOGART, respectively deceased, are now for the last time requested to bring their accounts to CORNELIUS J. BOGART, Attorney at Law, No. 42, Beekman-street—as there is a necessity for making an immediate settlement of the said estates.——Sept. 29th, 1784.

FOR SALE,

A very handsome Saddle-horse, almost full blooded, and about five years old.—enquire as above. 24 6

A Woman capable of house-keeping, is willing to go into a genteel family in that character---She can get good recommendations. Apply to the Printer. 24

Joshua and Henry Waddington,

No. 30, Water-street,

Have Imported by the London and Resolution, just arrived from London,

A Capital collection of printed Cottons and Callicoes, admirably adapted for the approaching season,	$\frac{7}{8}$ and $\frac{4}{4}$ Irish Linens,
India Chints, Callicoes,	$\frac{5}{4}$ Irish Sheetings,
Rose Blankets of different sizes,	$\frac{7}{8}$ Irish Dowlas,
Superfine and second Broad-Cloths,	Printed linen Handkerchiefs,
Corduroys and Velverets,	Bandanoe and coloured silk ditto,
Pillow Fustians,	Rich Brocades and Tissues,
Plain and striped Camblets,	Gilt and plated Buttons,
Superfine blue and brown Brussels do.	Sewing Silk and Twist,
Black Sattinet Lastings,	Coloured and brown Thread,
Callimancoes,	White and brown Buckrams,
Moreens and mock Moreens,	Black and white Souffle and chain Gauzes,
Tammies and Durants,	White Minionet do.
Mens patent worsted Gloves,	Plain and spotted Lawns,
Mens knit worsted Hose,	Bordered lawn Handkerchiefs,
Mens patent ribbed ditto,	Superfine $\frac{5}{4}$ sprigged Muslins,
Mens, womens and boys white cotton Hose,	Womens patent black silk Mits,
	Table Knives and Forks,
	Pocket Knives,
	Buckles and Sleeve-Buttons.

A L S O,
A Box of Russia Rein Deer Tongues,
Hyson Tea of a superior quality. 24

LAWRENCE and MORRIS,

No. 16, Duke-street,

Have Imported in the last vessels from Europe, a handsome Assortment of GOODS, suitable to the season, which they will dispose of on very reasonable terms, for Cash, short Credit, Pennsylvania Bank Notes, Robert Morris's Notes, and divers kinds of country Produce, viz.

BROAD Cloths, of a variety of colours, & prices. Forest Cloths, do do.
Coatings, do. do.
Striped Duffils, Indian Blanketting,
Chintzes, Callicoes, and Cottons,
Yard wide and 3—8 Cotton and Linen Checks,
Yard wide and 7—8 Irish Linen,
Broad Laval, do.
Britannia, do.
Holland, do.
Check Handkercheifs,
Worstead, Cotton, Thread, and Silk Hose,
Silk of various kinds,
Womens and Mens cold and white Kid Gloves
Sewing Silks of all Colours,
Fine and coarse Threads,
Feathers and plumes,
Black and coloured Ribbons,
Cambricks and Lawns,
Embroidered Waistcoat Patterns,
Scotch check Handkerchiefs,
Cotton do. Red Ground,
Hats of various sizes &c. &c. &c.

They have also to dispose of a quantity of Brandy, in quarter Casks and Kegs. Several Casks of Bottled port Wine.

A good vessel of about 150 or 200 tons is wanted to charter or purchase. 24

FOUR GUINEAS REWARD,

RUN AWAY from the Subscriber, on the 18th day of September, a NEGRO MAN, named CÆSAR, about six feet high, well made, his skin yellow; has a fine set of teeth, and shews them much when he talks or laughs; walks with his toes much turned out: Had on when he went away, a blue cloth coat, and white swanskin jacket, and a good castor hat; and carried away with him a short keresy over jacket, and brown tow and striped Holland trowsers, one pair of mixed reddish breeches, mixed blue yarn and white cotton stockings, and two pair of shoes. Whoever will take up and secure him, in any gaol of the United States, so that the owner may have him again, shall have the above Reward and all reasonable charges.

24 4 *PHILETUS SMITH.*

F A S H I O N S.
F R A N C I S I' A N S,

at No. 51, BROAD STREET.

RESPECTFULLY informs his Customers and the Ladies in general, that he has received by the last arrivals from London, Patterns of the newest fashioned Hats, Caps, &c. that is worn there at present: And that Mrs. PANS has it now in her power to supply them with all kinds of MILLINERY, either in the *Gay London*, or in the *neat American Taste*.

In future, the Ladies will have an opportunity twice every Year, (at Spring and Fall,) of viewing both the *London* and *Paris* fashions.

He has for Sale on reasonable Terms, a fashionable assortment of Ribbons, Gauzes, Flowers, &c. and a few Ladies elegant Beaver Riding Hats, fit for the Season.

Sept. 26, 1784. 24 3m.

IMPORTED in the brig Lucy from Liverpool and other lateessels from London, Bristol and Glasgow, by

JOHN TAYLOR, & Co.

and now for Sale, by the package or piece, at their store, No. 225, Queen-Street, the following articles, viz.

MEN and boys coarse and fine hats,
Superfine and second broad cloths and shalloons,
Corduroys, velvets, sattinets and denims,

SATURDAY, July 1, 1786.] [VOL. II. No. 420.

The Daily Advertiser: Political, Historical, and Commercial.

"THE NOBLEST MOTIVE IS THE PUBLIC GOOD."

NEW-YORK: Printed by FRANCIS CHILDS, at the New Printing-Office, opposite the Coffee-House Bridge.

WILLIAM THOMAS,

No. 242, Queen-street, between Wall and King-street,

Has now for SALE the following articles of the first quality and latest importations, which he will sell cheap for cash, *viz.*

HYSON, souchong, & common teas,
Double and single refined, powder and Muscovado sugars,
Madeira, Port, Lisbon, Claret and Sherry wines,
Old Jamaica spirits,
Do. Coniac brandy,
Do. Holland gin, and Batavia arrack,
Genuine porter, bottled in London,
Bottled ale and beer,
Cheshire and double Gloucester cheese,
Irish butter,
Elegant spermaceti & wax candles,
Castile and turpentine soap,
Best blue Poland starch, per box, &c.
Fig and powder blue,
Coffee and Chocolate,
Barley, rice and oat meal
Sago, ground and razed ginger,
Mogul, Henry's and Andrew's playing cards,
Assorted Confectionaries,
Sugar Candy,
Preserved fruits in brandy, viz. apricots, pears, peaches and green gages,
Syrup of capillaire and Do. of lemon, orgeat,
Ditto of vinegar,

PICKLES,

Tamarinds,
French and Spanish olives,
Anchovies and capers,
Mushrooms,
India soy,
Ketchup, coratch and Quin's sauce.

SPICES.

Cinnamon, nutmegs, mace, cloves, alspice, cayenne and black pepper, per the quantity, &c.
Durham mustard,
Patent mustard, ready made in jugs,
Stoughton's bitters,
Soft and hard pomatum,
Jar and cask raisons, cheap per jar or cask,
Zants currants,
Preserved citron, per box, &c.
Soft shell'd almonds,
Madeira nuts,
Isinglass and corks,
Best Florence oil,
Spermaceti oil,
White wine vinegar,
Lemon and lime juice
Smith's acid of limes,
Tobacco pipes of all sorts,
Spanish segars, &c.

Every allowance will be made to those who buy by the quantity.

Two complete Iron Chests for Sale. *

Randall, Son & Stewarts

Have removed their UNIVERSAL STORE from No. 10, Hanover-Square, to No. 211, Water-street, and have just received by the brig Betsey, from London, ship Four Friends, from Liverpool, and Sloop Resolution, from Dublin,

A large and general assortment of East-India and European

GOODS,

Consisting of as follows, viz.

FUSTIANS, and jeans, Corduroys, & velverets,
Checks,
Irish linens,
Sheetings and Dowlas,
Flannels,
Printed linens,
Do handkerchiefs,
Pulicat, Romall, and Lunge silk handkerchiefs,
Barcelona ditto.
Silk bandanoes,
Cloths and cassimers,
Counterpanes,
Dimities,
Marseilles quilting,
Dippers,
Chintzes,
Cottons,
Callicoes,
Table cloths,
Calimancoes,
Durants, and tammies,
Shalloons, and rattinetts,
Camblets,
Princess stuffs,
Everlastings,
Sattinetts & bombazeens,
Moreens,
Humhum jaconet plain sprigged, striped, and crossbar muslins,
Laces and edgings,
Gauzes,
Thread leno gauze,
Teasty,
An assortment of ribbons
Cambricks and lawns,
Worked and plain border lawn aprons, and handkerchiefs,
India persians,
Sattins, modes, and taffities,
Sewing silk,
Ginghams,
Fans,
Women's silk and leather gloves and mits.
Mens thread gloves,
Mens patent brown and white thread hose,
White & colour'd threads
Buttons, twist,
Broad and narrow bunting,
Gartering, tapes, and bobbing.
Quality and shoe bindings
Sewing and seine twine,
Womens and girls calimanco and Morocco slippers and pumps,
Looking glasses,
Spy glasses,
Japaned ware,
Pott and common writing paper,
Pins and needles,
Spelling books,
Seamans daily assistants,
Mariners compass rectified,
Best London white lead ground in oil,
Yellow oaker in oil and dry,
Spanish brown do. do.
Red lead, do.
Prussian blue, do.
8 by 10 window glass,
4d. 6d. 8d. 10d. 12d. 20d. and 24d. nails in casks of 2 Cwt. each,
10d. 12d. and 20d. brads,
Shott,
Crowley's steel in whole and half faggots,
Tacks and clout nails,
Coopers rivetts,
2d. pump and shutter nails,
Best F and F F Holland powder,
Green and tonkay teas,
Glass ware in crates,
Doctors phials in crates,
Queens ware in crates,
Also, a very large assortment of ironmongery,
A quantity of beef and Pork,
Ship bread,
Bar iron, and
The best (white) Holland Geneva, in bu:s.

LIVERPOOL FINE SALT,

at one Shilling and Eight-pence per bushel. Enquire at No. 163, Water-street.

PUBLIC SECURITIES,

Of all kinds, particularly those of this state, BOUGHT and SOLD by *De La Mater & Hutton,* No. 36, Water-Street.

A quantity of FINAL SETTLEMENT certificates for SALE.

FOR SALE, BARBER's NOTES.

Enquire at No. 12, Little-Dock-street.

250 Ton of Square Oak Timber,

GOT for the European market, now ready to be delivered at the Port of HUDSON, to be SOLD or bartered for Goods, on very low terms. For further information apply to STEVENS and HUBBELL, No. 145, Water-street; who have a large supply of excellent LUMBER on hand for exportation or city use; a quantity of 2 and 3 inch oak plank, from 30 to 60 feet in length: 100 Barrels of PITCH in good order. June 16. tf.

Just Arrived from Bristol,

In the Peggy, Capt. Dekay, and to be SOLD cheap for CASH,

By Peter Mackie,

No. 34, Little-Dock-street.

4d. 6d. 8d. 10d. 12d. and 20d.

NAILS; where also may be had bar iron, Sweeds refined and bloomery, of all sizes, fit for chair, waggon and cart tire, country or ship work; share moulds of all sizes; hollow ware and castings of all kinds; blistered and other steel; pork and beef in barrels; butter in firkins, country cheese; chocolate; castile soap; choice indigo; G B wool cards; Scotch barley in kegs, rum, sugar, and molasses; and an assortment of HARDWARE and DRY GOODS. June 5.

FOR SALE,

At No. 12, Duke-Street, by JOHN DEWINT,

RUSSIA Duck, blue mark, at 4l. 16s per peice; Superfine broad cloth — 1l. 8s per yard; Second ... Bedtick, Russia drilling, white ... thread, German scythes, sugar candy in boxes, writing paper, brown sugar in hhds and barrels, St. Croix rum, and green coffee, RAW HIDES. May 9.

THE Subscriber has for Sale, at his House, No. 44, Broad-street, a neat assortment of DRY GOODS, Which he will dispose of low, for Public Securities. SIMON NATHAN.

ISAAC MOSES,

HAS for SALE at his STORE, *No. 37, GREAT-DOCK-STREET,* At reasonable prices,

HOLLAND GIN in cases, BOHEA, GREEN, SOUCHONG TEAS.

A very choice parcel of INDIGO, *well assorted,* TEA KETTLES, PAINTERS BRUSHES, TOYS in CHESTS,

A neat assortment of

DRY GOODS,

Consisting of superfine and common broad cloths, corduroys, brown holland, jeans, white Russia sheeting, 9-4ths and 10-4ths best Holland bed tick, ticklenburg, oznabrigs, and a small assortment of the most approved of BOLTING CLOTHS.

FOR SALE, BY

Simon Van Antwerp, & Co.

At No 45, Little-Dock-Street;

A Few kegs choice pickled sturgeon, cured in the Holland mode, for cash, or West-India produce. Also, at the same place, a few tons bar and pig Lead.

Also, a lot of ground in the corporation dock. Inquire of Simon Van Antwerp, near the premises.

A Genteel COACH

With HARNESS compleat, to be SOLD CHEAP. Enquire of the PRINTER.

TAKEN away from along side of the Schooner WILLING MAID, lying at Marston's wharf, on Wednesday night 22d inst. a Moses built BOAT, painted black and yellow on the gunwales, and daubed with red oaker and tar. She is branded on the inward part of the stern 'JONA. DICKENSON.' Whoever will bring said boat to William Eccles on said wharf or give intelligence to the Printer hereof so that she may be again returned, shall receive SIX DOLLARS reward, and no questions asked. June 23.

A small Quantity of EXCELLENT WAFERS To be SOLD CHEAP. Apply to the PRINTER.

Selling off Cheap!!!

At the Store of JOHN FERRERS, No. 20, Great-Dock-street, a variety of DRY GOODS and IRONMONGERY, which will be sold for CASH, at prices under what they can be imported.

Amongst them are the following articles,

MENS coarse and fine hats, mens and womens shoes, broad cloth, patterns of do. for coats, with trimmings compleat, an elegant assortment of silk waistcoat patterns, modes and sarsenet, Barcelona handkerchiefs, thread, sewing silks, India cotton, cotton for quilting, silk and other laces for stays, Files, hammers, locks, Shoe-makers tools, chissels and gouges, candlesticks, hand saws, drawing knives knives and forks, japan'd tea boards, grid irons, frying pans, and sad irons; with a variety of other articles not enumerated. June 26. 1m.

George Lewis & Co.

At their Printed Calico and Irish Linen Warehouse, No. 39, Queen-street, between Burling and Beekman's Slip,

HAve just imported by the latest ships from Europe a general assortment of the best fabrics of 7-8 and 4-4 Irish hollands, chintzes, printed calicoes and cottons, muslins, silk handkerchiefs, &c. &c. which from their well known connections in these articles, they are enabled to dispose of, by the trunk or piece on unusual low terms, for cash.

FANCY CLOTHS.

WILLIAM WILLEMENT,

No. 25, Broad Way, the corner of Crown-Street,

HAS just received by the Edward, Capt. Cooper, the Betsey, Capt. Watson, and other spring ships, a great variety of fashionable FANCY CLOTHS which are so much and so deservedly esteemed for their lightness, durability & neatness in fitting. Also superfine, second and inferior BROAD CLOTHS, of the newest and most approved colours, together with a general and handsome assortment of Crapes, Sattinetts, Bombazeens, Lastings, Prunellas, &c. &c.

Likewise some entirely new articles, suitable to the season.

Many of the above are admirably adapted for the West-Indies, and will be sold at the lowest possible prices. June 1.

George Barnewall,

Late partner in the house of Sarly and Barnewall has opened store No. 205 Water-street, near the Coffee-House, AND HAS FOR SALE, *A general assortment of* DRY GOODS.

Amongst which are the following articles, viz.

SUPERFINE and second broad cloths, shalloons, silk twist, tammies, durants, coatings, baizes, flannels, calimancoes, camblets, moreens, olive pillow fustians and jeans, printed jeans and jeanets India and French dimities, denims, sattinets Marseilles quiltings, moree gowns, Irish linens, chintzes, callicoes, mens womens and childrens white and black hats, gauzes, womens stuff shoes, mens and womens silk cotton and thread hose and gloves, men and womens worsted hose, thicksetts, printed beaverets, corduroys, velverets, pewter, white and common needles, No. 1 to 12, an assortment of hard ware, with many other articles too tedious to enumerate.

All which he will sell on the most reasonable terms for cash, short credit, and almost every species of country produce.

N. B. Any person wanting an excellent cellar or ore, near the water, may be supplied by applying as above.

Also, Just Arrived

From Dublin, A consignment of the following articles, viz.

A QUANTITY of yard wide and 7-8 Irish linen, a few packages of paper hangings, womens stuff and quilted petticoats, and a few dozen of leather breeches, low priced, all which will be sold cheap for cash. Apply as above

Sadler and *Bailie,*

Have removed from No. 9 to No. 31, in Hanover-Square, where they have FOR SALE.

IRISH linens 4-4 7-8 and 3-4 wide, well assorted,
Brown linens 3-4 wide,
Dowlass 7-8 do.
A large assortment of printed linens, of the newest patterns
A few pieces of linens pencilled, in elegant chintz patterns,
Silk and linen handkerchiefs,
Womens lasting and calimanco shoes and pumps,
Bunting for ships colours,
Manchester goods, consisting of corduroys, thicksetts, pillow fustians, southvellets, sattinets, dimity and jeans,
Irish coatings, frizes, ratteens, blankets and rugs,
Mens saddles and bridles,
Boots
Black silk lace,
Table and breakfast knives and forks, penknives, razors, scissars, buttons, locks and hinges, spurs, carpenters tools, with an assortment of Sheffield and Birmingham ware in small packages,
Glass ware in packages, consisting of decanters, tumblers, glasses, water bottles, &c.

Which they will dispose of by the piece or package for cash, or barter for pot and pearl ashes, May 4.

A few pipes CONIAC BRANDY, and some boxes Crown WINDOW GLASS, 7 by 9.

For Dublin,

The BRIGANTINE MARY, EPHRAIM TOWNSEND, Master.

WILL sail in ten days. For freight or passage apply to SAMUEL FRANKLIN, & Co. No. 183, Queen-street, or to the master on board at Franklin's wharf, near the New-slip.

For Philadelphia,

The SLOOP PATTY, RICLOFF ALBERTSON, Master. Lying at Hunter's Key, adjoining The Old Slip.

WILL sail in a few days. For freight or passage apply to the Master on board.

For Liverpool,

The SHIP BETSEY, WILLIAM HASELDEN, Master,

A BRITISH vessel, burthen about 250 Tons, with a Mediterranean Pass; will sail in 14 days. For freight or passage apply to WILLIAM KENYON, No. 189, Queen-street; who has for SALE as usual, a general assortment of

Earthen-Ware by the Crate.

On very low terms.

New-York, June 27, 1786.

For Charleston, (S. Carolina.)

The BRIG MERCURY, JAMES TINKER, Master, Now lying at Byvanck's wharf.

HAS excellent accommodations for passengers, will positively sail the 4th of July. For freight or passage apply to the master on board, or to ROBERT JAMES LIVINGSTON, No. 50, Smith-street.

For Newbern, (N. Carolina.)

To Sail by the First of July, The SLOOP Betsy and Polly WILLIAM STEVENSON, Master.

LYING at Beekman-slip. For freight or passage apply to GUION, CARTHY and Co. No. 164, Water-street.

TO BE SOLD,

The BRIGANTINE, JANE,

BURTHEN 100 tons, more or less, now lying at Beach's wharf, has had a thorough repair, and can be sent to sea at a small expence. Her inventory to be seen, and terms of sale known by applying at No. 4, Hanover-square. Where there is also for sale a few tons of Fustick, and a quantity of Mahogany. June 8.

For Norfolk, Richmond and Petersburgh,

The SCHOONER HAZARD, Patrick Elworth, Master,

WILL Sail on Saturday the 1st. July. For Freight or Passage Apply to the Master on board at Brownjohn's Wharf, or No. 40, Wall-street.

There is for SALE on board said Schooner, about 20 or 30 Chaldron of best VIRGINIA COALS. Apply to the Measurer on board.

David Longworth, Grocer,

At No. 57, Nassau-street; has for sale,

WInes, spirits, rum, geneva, brandy, cordials, molasses, white and brown sugars, coffee, hyson and green teas, fresh and best bohea tea, pepper, mustard, spices, ginger, raisins, currants, indigo, ag-blue in small boxes, &c. Poland and common starch, Scotch herrings in kegs, Block-Island cheese of the best quality, spermaceti oil for chamber lamps, Florence oil, vinegar for pickles at 1s6. per gallon, per 5 gallons; where may always be had, Gomez's best superfine warranted chocolate, wholesale and retail, at the lowest rate. Orders are received and punctually attended to, for chocolate, at the above place, he only having the sole vending of the same.

JOHN HIRNE,

LADIES HABIT-MAKER & TAYLOR, *No. 28, HANOVER-SQUARE;*

IS just arrived from EUROPE, and brought with him the *Newest and Genteelest* FASHIONS of PARIS and LONDON.---He hopes by Attention quick Dispatch and Cheapness, to merit the Countenance of the Citizens of New-York. 4w. June 19.

A large CELLAR to be Let.

THE BOSTON AND COUNTRY

Containing the lateſt Occurrences,

MONDAY,

[No. 1776.]

GAZETTE, THE JOURNAL.

Foreign and Domeſtic.

Auguſt 11, 1788.

Printed by BENJAMIN EDES and SON, No. 7, State-Street, BOSTON.

A FREE PRESS MAINTAINS THE MAJESTY OF THE PEOPLE.

Form of RATIFICATION *of the* FEDERAL CONSTITUTION *by the State of* New York.

In CONVENTION, July 26, 1788.

WE the Delegates of the People of the State of New-York, duly elected and met in Convention, having maturely conſidered the Conſtitution for the United States of America, agreed to on the 17 day of September, in the year 1787, by the Convention then aſſembled at Philadelphia, in the Commonwealth of Pennſylvania, *(a copy whereof precedes theſe preſents)* and having alſo ſeriouſly conſidered the preſent ſituation of the United States, DO declare and make known,

That all power is originally veſted in and conſequently derived from the people, and that government is inſtituted by them for their common intereſt, protection & ſecurity.

That the enjoyment of life, liberty, and the purſuit of happineſs, are eſſential rights, which every government ought to reſpect and preſerve.

That the powers of government may be reaſſumed by the people, whenſoever it ſhall become neceſſary to their happineſs: That every power, juriſdiction and right, which is not by the ſaid Conſtitution clearly delegated to the Congreſs of the United States, or the departments of the government thereof, remains to the people of the ſeveral States, or to their reſpective State governments, to whom they may have granted the ſame; and that thoſe clauſes in the ſaid Conſtitution, which declare that Congreſs ſhall not have or exerciſe certain powers, do not imply that Congreſs is entitled to any powers that are not given by the ſaid Conſtitution; but ſuch clauſes are to be conſtrued either as exceptions to certain ſpecified powers, or inſerted merely for greater caution.

That the people have an equal, natural and unalienable right, freely and peaceably to exerciſe their religion according to the dictates of conſcience, and that no religious ſect or ſociety ought to be favored or eſtabliſhed by law in preference of others.

That the people have a right to keep and bear arms: That a well regulated militia, including the body of the people *capable of bearing arms*, is the proper, natural and ſafe defence of a free State: That the militia ſhould not be ſubject to martial law, except in time of war, rebellion or inſurrection.

That ſtanding armies in time of peace are dangerous to liberty, and ought not to be kept up, except in caſes of neceſſity; and that at all times the military ſhould be under ſtrict ſubordination to the civil power.

That in time of peace no ſoldier ought to be quartered in any houſe without the conſent of the owner, and in time of war, only by the civil magiſtrate, in ſuch manner as the laws may direct.

That no perſon ought to be taken, impriſoned or diſſeized of his freehold, or be exiled or deprived of his privileges, franchiſes, life, liberty or property, but by due proceſs of law.

That no perſon ought to be put twice in jeopardy of life or limb for one and the ſame offence, nor unleſs in caſe of impeachment be puniſhed more than once for the ſame offence.

That every perſon reſtrained of his liberty is entitled to an enquiry into the lawfulneſs of ſuch reſtraint, and to a removal thereof, if unlawful; and that ſuch enquiry and removal ought not to be denied or delayed, except when on account of public danger the Congreſs ſhall ſuſpend the privilege of the writ of *habeas corpus*.

That exceſſive bail ought not to be required, nor exceſſive fines impoſed, nor cruel or unuſual puniſhments inflicted.

That (except in the government of the land and naval forces, and of the militia when in actual ſervice, and in caſes of impeachment) a preſentment or indictment by a Grand Jury ought to be obſerved as a neceſſary preliminary to the trial of all crimes *cognizable by the Judiciary of the United States*; and ſuch trial ſhould be ſpeedy, public, and by an impartial Jury of the county where the crime was committed; and that no perſon can be found guilty without the unanimous conſent of ſuch Jury. But in caſes of crimes not committed within any county of any of the United States, and in caſes of crimes committed within any county in which a general inſurrection may prevail, or which may be in the poſſeſſion of foreign enemy, the enquiry and trial may be in ſuch county as the Congreſs ſhall by law direct, which county, in the two caſes laſt mentioned, ſhould be as near as conveniently may be to that county in which the crime may be committed. And that in all criminal proſecutions the accuſed ought to be informed of the cauſe and nature of his accuſation, to be confronted with his accuſers and the witneſſes againſt him to have the means of producing his witneſſes, and the aſſiſtance of counſel for his defence, and ſhould not be compelled to give evidence againſt himſelf.

That the trial by Jury in the extent that it obtains by the common law of England, is one of the greateſt ſecurities to the rights of a free people, and ought to remain inviolate.

That every freeman has a right to be ſecure from all unreaſonable ſearches and ſeizures of his perſon, his papers, or his property; and therefore that all warrants to ſearch ſuſpected places, to ſeize any freeman, his papers or property, without information upon oath, or affirmation of ſufficient cauſe, are grievous and oppreſſive; and that all general warrants (or ſuch in which the place or perſon ſuſpected are not particularly deſignated) are dangerous and ought not to be granted.

That the people have a right peaceably to aſſemble together, to conſult for their common good, or to inſtruct their Repreſentatives; and that every perſon has a right to petition or apply to the Legiſlature for redreſs of grievances.

That the liberty of the preſs ought not to be violated or reſtrained.

That there ſhould be once in four years an election of the Preſident and Vice-Preſident; ſo that no officer who may be appointed by the Congreſs to act as preſident, in caſe of the removal, death, reſignation, or inability of the Preſident, and Vice Preſident, can in any caſe continue to act beyond the termination of the period for which the laſt Preſident and Vice Preſident were elected.

That nothing contained in the ſaid Conſtitution is to be conſtrued to prevent the Legiſlature of any ſtate from paſſing laws at its diſcretion from time to time to divide ſuch State into convenient diſtricts, and to apportion its repreſentatives to and amongſt ſuch diſtricts.

That the prohibition contained in the ſaid conſtitution, againſt *ex poſt facto laws*, extends only to laws concerning crimes.

That all appeals in cauſes determinable according to the courſe of the common law, ought to be by writ of error, and not otherwiſe.

That the judicial power of the United States, in caſes in which a State may be a party, does not extend to criminal proſecutions, or to authoriſe any ſuit by any perſon againſt a State.

That the judicial power of the United States, as to controverſies between citizens of the ſame State claiming lands under grants of different States, is not to be conſtrued to extend to any other controverſies between them, except thoſe which relate to ſuch lands ſo claimed under grants of different States.

That the juriſdiction of the Supreme Court of the United States, or of any other Court to be inſtituted by the Congreſs, is not in any caſe to be encreaſed, enlarged or extended by any fiction, colluſion, or mere ſuggeſtion, And,

That no treaty is to be conſtrued ſo to operate as to alter the Conſtitution of any State.

Under theſe impreſſions, and declaring that the rights aforeſaid cannot be abridged or violated, and that the explanations aforeſaid are conſiſtent with the ſaid Conſtitution; and in confidence that the amendments which ſhall have been propoſed to the ſaid Conſtitution will receive an early and mature conſideration; —WE the ſaid Delegates, in the name, and in the behalf of the State of New-York, DO, by theſe preſents, ASSENT TO and RATIFY the ſaid Conſtitution. *In full confidence nevertheleſs*, that until a convention ſhall be called and convened for propoſing amendments to the ſaid Conſtitution, the militia of this State will not be continued in ſervice out of this State for a longer term than ſix weeks, without the conſent of the Legiſlature thereof. That the Congreſs will not make or alter any regulation in this State reſpecting the times, places and manner of holding elections for Senators or Repreſentatives, unleſs the Legiſlature ſhall neglect or refuſe to make laws or regulations for the purpoſe, or from any circumſtance be incapable of making the ſame—and that in thoſe caſes, ſuch power will only be exerciſed until the Legiſlature make proviſion in the premiſes—that no exciſe will be impoſed on any article of the growth, production, or manufacture of the United States or any of them, within this State, ardent ſpirits excepted. And that Congreſs will not lay direct taxes within this State, but when the monies ariſing from the impoſt and exciſe ſhall be inſufficient for the public exigencies, nor then, until Congreſs ſhall firſt have made a requiſition upon this State, to aſſeſs, levy, and pay the amount of ſuch requiſition, made agreeably to the cenſus fixed in the ſaid Conſtitution, in ſuch way and manner as the legiſlature of this State ſhall judge beſt; but that in ſuch caſe, if the State ſhall neglect or refuſe to pay its proportion purſuant to ſuch requiſition, then the Congreſs may aſſeſs and levy this State's proportion, together with intereſt, at the rate of 6 per cent. per ann. from the time at which the ſame was required to be paid.

Done in Convention, at Poughkeepſie, in the County of Dutcheſs, in the State of New York, the 26th day of July in the year of our Lord one thouſand ſeven hundred and eighty eight.

By order of the Convention,

GEO. CLINTON, Preſident.

Atteſted,

JOHN M'KESSON, ABM. B. BANCKER, Secretaries.

Occurrences in Convention the ſame day, before the Conſtitution was ratified.

The queſtion being called, and the yeas and nays required, Mr. G. Livingſton roſe, and made the following addreſs:

Mr. Preſident,

I hope for indulgence from this honorable houſe, that I may ſhortly ſtate the reaſons which actuate me, for taking the part I do in the buſineſs before us. The great and final queſtion on the conſtitution is now to be taken. Permit me, ſir, again to ſay, that I have had a ſevere ſtruggle in my mind, between *duty* and *prejudice*.

I entered this houſe, as fully determined on previous amendments (I ſincerely believe) as any one member in it. Nothing, ſir, but a conviction that I am ſerving the moſt eſſential intereſts of my country, could ever induce me to take another ground, and differ from ſo many of my friends on this floor. I think, ſir, I am in this, purſuing the object I had at firſt in view; the real good of my country. With reſpect to the conſtitution itſelf, I have the ſame idea of it I ever had—that is, there is not ſafety under it, unleſs amended. Some time after we firſt met ſir, a majority of theſe in this houſe who oppoſe it, did determine not to reject it. Only one queſtion then remained—which was the moſt eligible mode, to enſure a general convention of the States, to reconſider it, to have the eſſential amendments ingrafted into it?

I do not here mean to go into the reaſons which have repeatedly been urged on this head—but only to ſay, that on the moſt mature and deliberate reflection on this momentous occaſion, the reſult of my judgment is—— that the adoption on the table, with the bill of rights and amendments contained in it, and the circular letter to the different States accompanying it, is, conſidering our PRESENT ſituation with reſpect to our ſiſter States, the wiſeſt and beſt meaſure, we can poſſibly purſue. I ſhall therefore vote for it.

As an American, I am proud of my country—as a Whig I love it, and *feel* the duty of guarding its rights and freedom, to the utmoſt of my power:—— And ſir, conſidering my ſituation in this houſe—as a repreſentative of a reſpectable county—I feel the weight of duty increaſing in a redoubled proportion.

Sir, I know I was elected a member of this convention, from a confidence the people had in my integrity.—And ſir, I truſt, I am at this inſtant, giving them an unqueſtionable evidence of it. The people of the county I have the honor to repreſent, are in general, thinking and ſenſible, —and I have not the leaſt doubt, but that they ſoon will, if they at preſent do not, ſee the propriety of the meaſure here purſued.

But ſir, I would beg leave to mention another conſideration, of a nature infinitely ſuperior to any thing, which poſſibly can be put in competition with it, as a motive of action——an approving *conſcience*, and an approving *God*. ——I muſt hereafter ſtand at a bar, where, if the moſt trifling conduct muſt be accounted for (and which I fully believe) ſurely this moſt *important* tranſaction of my life will be ſtrictly ſcrutinized:——To that awful being,—— who will there preſide——I would with due ſubmiſſion and humility, appeal for the rectitude of my intentions. I hope, ſir, the houſe will pardon me, for having been ſo powerful in this addreſs; I owe it, ſir, to them, as well as to myſelf: eſpecially to a part of one ſide of the houſe, who, I have no doubt, are actuated by the pureſt motives——and are equally conſcientious with myſelf, on this occaſion——and with whom, and every friend to his country, I will ſteadily perſevere, in every poſſible means to produre this deſirable object, a reviſion of the conſtitution.

For a conſiſtency in conduct to this *honorable houſe* to *my conſtituents*, ane to *my country*, on this occaſion, with the utmoſt chearfulneſs do I ſubmit myſelf.

Mr. Livingſton having concluded, Mr. Whiſner, from Orange, made a ſhort addreſs; after ſtating a few reaſons, having reconſidered the above ratification, ſaid he ſhould not give his aſſent to it.

The yeas and nays being then taken, it was carried, In the affirmative 30. In the negative 27.—— Majority 3

After ratifying, His Excellency the Preſident, according to notice given laſt Thurſday, addreſſed the Convention very politely: The purport of which was that until a convention was called to conſider the amendments now recommended by this convention, the probability was, that the body of the people who are oppoſed to the conſtitution, would not be ſatisfied—he would however, as far as his power and influence would extend, endeavour to keep up peace and good order among them: To which the members and ſpectators were very attentive —and more than a common pleaſantneſs appeared in their countenance.

A circular letter, addreſſed to the Executives of the other States, was then read, and agreed to, earneſtly requeſting them to co-operate with this ſtate in obtaining a conſideration of the amendments annexed to the ſaid ratification, by a convention to be called for the purpoſe. The ſaid letter was then ſigned by all the members preſent, and the Convention adjourned.

Anſwer to the QUESTION in our laſt.

ONE ſingle word, both ſexes comprehend,
In union dear; without confuſion, blend
Both heart and mind—the ſweeteſt joy of life!
In Hymen's chain—hail happy man and wife.
HE, HER, the HERO, and the HE,R,O,INE,
In one grand word, both ſex and honors join.
So let their joys abound in union ſweet:
The point obtain'd, my anſwer is compleat.

Gazette of the United States.

NUMBER I. | WEDNESDAY, APRIL 15, 1789. | PRICE SIX PENCE.

P L A N

OF THE

GAZETTE of the UNITED STATES.

A NATIONAL PAPER.

To be publiſhed at the SEAT *of the* FEDERAL GOVERNMENT, *and to compriſe, as fully as poſſible, the following Objects, viz.*

I. EARLY and authentick Accounts of the PROCEEDINGS of CONGRESS—its LAWS, ACTS, and RESOLUTIONS, communicated ſo as to form an *HISTORY of the TRANSACTIONS of the FEDERAL LEGISLATURE, under the NEW CONSTITUTION.*

II. IMPARTIAL SKETCHES of the DEBATES of CONGRESS.

III. ESSAYS upon the great ſubjects of Government in general, and the *Federal Legiſlature in particular*; alſo upon the *national* and *local* Rights of the AMERICAN CITIZENS, as founded upon the Federal or State Conſtitutions; alſo upon every other Subject, which may appear ſuitable for newſpaper diſcuſſion.

IV. A SERIES of PARAGRAPHS, calculated to catch the "LIVING MANNERS AS THEY RISE," and to point the publick attention to Objects that have an important reference to *domeſtick, ſocial,* and *publick happineſs.*

V. The Intereſts of the United States as connected with their literary Inſtitutions—religious and moral Objects—Improvements in Science, Arts, EDUCATION and HUMANITY—their foreign Treaties, Alliances, Connections, &c.

VI. Every *ſpecies* of INTELLICENCE, which may affect the *commercial, agricultural, manufacturing,* or *political* INTERESTS of the AMERICAN REPUBLICK.

VII. A CHAIN of DOMESTICK OCCURRENCES, collected through the Medium of an extenſive Correſpondence with the reſpective States.

VIII. A SERIES of FOREIGN ARTICLES of INTELLIGENCE, ſo connected, *as to form a general Idea of publick Affairs in the eaſtern Hemiſphere.*

IX. The STATE of the NATIONAL FUNDS; alſo of the INDIVIDUAL GOVERNMENTS—Courſes of Exchange—Prices Current, &c.

CONDITIONS.

I.

THE GAZETTE *of the* UNITED STATES *ſhall be printed with the ſame* Letter, *and on the ſame* Paper *as this publication.*

II.

It ſhall be publiſhed every WEDNESDAY *and* SATURDAY, *and delivered, as may be directed, to every Subſcriber in the city, on thoſe days.*

III.

The price to Subſcribers (excluſive of poſtage) *will be* THREE DOLLARS *pr. annum.*

IV.

The firſt ſemi-annual payment to be made in three months *from the appearance of the firſt number.*

SUBSCRIPTIONS

Will be received in all the capital towns upon the Continent; alſo at the City-Coffee-Houſe, *and at* No. 86, William-Street, *until the 1ſt of* May, *from which time at* No. 9, Maiden-Lane, *near the* Oſwego-Market, New-York.

N. B. By a new Arrangement made in the Stages, Subſcribers at a diſtance will be duly furniſhed with papers.

POSTSCRIPT.——*A large impreſſion of every number will be ſtruck off—ſo that Subſcribers may always be accommodated with complete Sets.*

To the PUBLICK.

AT this important Criſis, the ideas that fill the mind, are pregnant with Events of the greateſt magnitude—to ſtrengthen and complete the UNION of the States—to extend and protect their COMMERCE, under *equal* Treaties yet to be formed—to explore and arrange the NATIONAL FUNDS—to reſtore and eſtabliſh the PUBLICK CREDIT—and *ALL* under the auſpices of an untried Syſtem of Government, will require the ENERGIES of the Patriots and Sages of our Country—*Hence the propriety of encreaſing the Mediums of Knowledge and Information.*

AMERICA, from this period, begins a new Era in her national exiſtence—"THE WORLD IS ALL BEFORE HER"—The wiſdom and folly—the miſery and proſperity of the EMPIRES, STATES, and KINGDOMS, which have had their day upon the great Theatre of Time, and are now no more, ſuggeſt the moſt important Mementos—Theſe, with the rapid ſeries of Events, in which our own Country has been ſo deeply intereſted, have taught the enlightened Citizens of the United States, that FREEDOM and GOVERNMENT—LIBERTY and LAWS, are inſeparable.

This Conviction has led to the adoption of the New Conſtitution; for however VARIOUS the Sentiments, reſpecting the MERITS of this Syſtem, all GOOD MEN are agreed in the neceſſity that exiſts, of an EFFICIENT FEDERAL GOVERNMENT.

A paper, therefore, eſtabliſhed upon NATIONAL, INDEPENDENT, and IMPARTIAL PRINCIPLES—which ſhall take up the premiſed Articles, upon a COMPETENT PLAN, it is preſumed, will be highly intereſting, and meet with publick approbation and patronage.

The Editor of this Publication is determined to leave no avenue of Information unexplored:—He ſolicits the aſſiſtance of Perſons of leiſure and abilities—which, united with his own aſſiduity, he flatters himſelf will render the Gazette of the United States not unworthy general encouragement——and is, with due reſpect, the publick's humble ſervant,

JOHN FENNO.

New-York, April 15, 1789.

EPITOME OF THE PRESENT STATE OF THE UNION.

NEW-HAMPSHIRE,

WHICH is 180 miles in length, and 60 in breadth, contained, according to an enumeration in 1787, 102,000 inhabitants—is attached to the federal Government—engaged in organizing her militia, already the beſt diſciplined of any in the Union—encouraging the domeſtick arts—and looking forward to the benefits which will reſult from the operations of the New Conſtitution. New-Hampſhire, from her local adantages, and the hardihood of her ſons, may anticipate eſſential benefits from the operation of equal commercial regulations.

MASSACHUSETTS,

450 miles in length, and 160 in breadth, contained, according to an enumeration in 1787, 360,000 inhabitants—Since the tranquility of the State was reſtored by the ſuppreſſion of the late inſurrection, the whole body of the people appears ſolicitous for the bleſſings of peace and good government. If any concluſion can be drawn from elections for the Federal Legiſlature, this State has a decided majority in favour of the New Conſtitution. The great objects of Commerce, Agriculture, Manufactures, and the Fiſheries, appear greatly to engage the attention of Maſſachuſetts. Fabrications of Cotton, coarſe Woolens, Linens, DUCK, IRON, Wood, &c. are proſecuting with ſucceſs—and by diminiſhing her imports, and increaſing her exports, ſhe is advancing to that rank and importance in the Union which her extent of territory—her reſources—and the genius and enterpriſe of her citizens entitle her to—and although the colliſion of parties, at the moment of Election, ſtrikes out a few ſparks of animoſity, yet the deciſion once made, the *"Calumet of Peace"* is ſmoked in love and friendſhip—*"and like true Republicans they acquieſce in the choice of the Majority."*

CONNECTICUT,

81 miles in length, and 57 in breadth, contained, agreeably to a Cenſus in 1782, 209,150 inhabitants, enjoying a fertile ſoil, this truly republican State is purſuing her intereſt in the promotion of Manufactures, Commerce, Agriculture, and the Sciences—She appears to bid fair, from the peaceable, loyal, and federal Character of the great body of her citizens—from the Enterpriſe of her men of wealth, and other favourable circumſtances, to attain to a great degree of opulence, power, and reſpectability in the Union.

NEW-YORK,

350 miles in length, and 300 in breadth, contained, agreeably to a Cenſus in 1786, 238,897 inhabitants, This State appears to be convulſed by parties—but the CRISIS is at hand, when it is hoped, that the *"Hatchet"* will be buried. Exertions on one ſide are making for the re-election of Gov. CLINTON, and on the other for the introduction of the Hon. Judge YATES to the chair—both parties appear ſanguine as to their ſucceſs. It is ardently to be wiſhed, that *temper* and *moderation* may preſide at the Elections; and there can be no doubt of it, as that Freedom, for which we fought and triumphed, depends ſo eſſentially upon a FREE CHOICE.—It is greatly regretted, that this reſpectable and important member of the federal Republick, ſhould not be repreſented in the Moſt Honourable Senate of the United States. New-York, however, is riſing in her federal character, and in manufacturing, agricultural, and commercial conſequence: Evidenced in her federal elections—her plans for promoting Manufactures, and the increaſe of her Exports.

NEW-JERSEY,

160 miles in length, and 52 in breadth, contained, by a Cenſus in 1784, 149,435 inhabitants. This State is at preſent tranquil, although lately agitated by a very extraordinary conteſted election—which by a *timely* interference of the Executive, appears to be ſettled. The inhabitants of this State are warmly attached to the New Conſtitution—the bleſſings of peace, an equal trade, and good government, being properly prized by them. The Arts and Sciences are objects of importance in this State, and many of her ſons rank high in the Republick of Letters.

PENNSYLVANIA,

288 miles in length, and 156 in breadth—by a Cenſus in 1787, contained 360,000 inhabitants.—This extenſive and truly reſpectable State, is making great proficiency in her Manufactures, Agriculture, Arts and Commere. Her attachment to the New Conſtitution is unequivocal, and with a conſiſtency highly honourary to her *national* character, ſhe has lately made an effort, (which, though defeated for a time, will undoubtedly be ſucceſsful) to conform their State Conſtitution to that of the Union. The publick buildings in the city of Philadelphia, have been reſpectfully offered for the accommodation of Congreſs. Theatrical exhibitions are now permitted by law—and the city has been incorporated: Experience will determine the eligibility of the two latter tranſactions.

DELAWARE,

92 miles in length, and 16 in breadth, by a Cenſus in 1787, contained 37,000 inhabitants. This State, though circumſcribed in its limits, derives great importance from its rank in the Union—attached to the New Conſtitution, and having the honour to take the lead in its adoption, there is no doubt of its giving efficacy to its righteous adminiſtration.

MARYLAND,

134 miles in length, and 110 in breadth, by a Cenſus taken in 1782, contained 253,630 inhabitants. From its favourable ſituation in the Union, this State bids fair for proſperity, wealth, and eminence. Warmly attached to the New Conſtitution, and enjoying a central ſituation, the publications there have teemed with tempting inducements to Congreſs, to make Baltimore the Seat of the Federal Legiſlature.

VIRGINIA,

758 miles in length, and 224 in breath—by a cenſus taken in 1782, contains 567,614 inhabitants. From the natural ardour of her ſons in the cauſe of freedom, is frequently convulſed in her elections, and has been torn by factions.—Poſſeſſing an extenſive territory and a vaſt income, her funds are placed on a reſpectable footing; but as her repreſentation in the federal legiſlature is decidedly attached to the union and the new conſtitution—there is now no doubt but that ſhe will ſee her intereſt and glory finally connected with a few *temporary* ſacrifices upon the principles of mutual conceſſion.

SOUTH-CAROLINA,

200 miles in length, and 125 in breath—and contains, by a cenſus in 1787, 180,000 inhabitants, an important member of the union, has appeared lately to vibrate between oppoſing ſentiments—Her attachment to *national* meaſures we doubt not will evidentally diſcover itſelf when all *tender laws* and *pine barrens* ſhall be done away. The prohibition of the importation of ſlaves, and the proviſion lately made for the reduction of her foreign debt are federal traits—add to theſe that their electors have given an unanimous vote for his Excellency GENERAL WASHINGTON, as Preſident of the United States—by which the memorable circumſtance is authenticated, that the voice of the WHOLE CONTINENT has *once more* called our FABIUS MAXIMUS to reſcue our country from impending ruin.

GEORGIA,

600 miles in length, and 250 in breath,—by a Cenſus in 1787, contained 98,000 inhabitants. This ſtate is compleating her federal character by conforming her ſtate conſtitution to that of the union—and being the youngeſt branch of the family—and a frontier—ſhe will doubtleſs experience the ſupporting and protecting arm of the federal government.

FOREIGN STATES.

RHODE-ISLAND,

Is 68 miles in length, and 40 in breath, and by a Cenſus taken in 1783, contained 51,896 inhabitants. This ſtate has again refuſed to accede to a union with her ſiſter ſtates, and is now wholly eſtranged from them; and from appearances, will long continue ſo, unleſs the meaſure of the iniquity of her "KNOW YE" gentry ſhould be ſpeedily filled up—or the deluſion which has ſo long infatuated a majority of her citizens, ſhould be removed.—Anxious of enjoying the protection of the union, the inhabitants of Newport, Providence and other places, are determined to ſue for its protection, and to be annexed to Maſſachuſetts or Connecticut. This diſmemberment of the ſtate it is to be deſired, may be prevented by her being wholly graffed into that ſtock from whence through blindneſs ſhe has been broken off.

NORTH-CAROLINA.

Is 758 miles in length, and 110 in breadth, and by a cenſus taken in 1787, contained 270,000 inhabitants. A depreciated paper medium, and a deficiency of political knowledge, are conſidered as the cauſes of the anti-national ſpirit of this State. Her extenſive frontier, and being obliged to export the greater part of her productions through Virginia, it is expected will ere long evince the neceſſity of her acceding to the confederation. This indeed appears already to be the predominant idea of her citizens, by ſome recent tranſactions.

NOTE.

Some of the foregoing Obſervations are tranſcribed from the Maſſachuſetts Mag. an ingenious periodical publication of I. Thomas and Co. of Boſton, now in the fourth month of its progreſs as a Candidate for literary eminence, and publick patronage. The Enumeration of the Inhabitants of the ſeveral States, is taken from Morſe's AMERICAN GEOGRAPHY—a new work juſt publiſhed, which from its very uſeful and important contents, ſhould be introduced into every family of the United States.

CONGRESSIONAL AFFAIRS.

NEW-YORK, APRIL 15, 1789.

THE time appointed by the Congress, under the OLD CONFEDERATION, for the assembling of the SENATORS and REPRESENTATIVES chosen to administer the NEW CONSTITUTION, was the fourth day of March last; an unfavourable season of the year for journeying. Through unavoidable delays, a quorum of the members did not arrive in this city, till Monday the sixth inst. when being assembled, the Hon. JOHN LANGDON, Esq. was chosen President pro tempore. The votes of the Electors chosen by the several States were then opened and counted, and were as follows, viz.

GEORGE WASHINGTON,	69
JOHN ADAMS,	34
JOHN JAY,	9
R. H. HARRISON,	6
JOHN RUTLEDGE,	6
JOHN HANCOCK,	4
GEORGE CLINTON,	3
SAMUEL HUNTINGTON,	2
JAMES ARMSTRONG,	1
JOHN MILTON,	2
EDWARD TELFAIR,	1
BENJAMIN LINCOLN,	1

Upon which his Excellency GEORGE WASHINGTON, Esq. was announced PRESIDENT, and the Honourable JOHN ADAMS, Esq. VICE PRESIDENT of the United-States. This important business being compleated the Legislature of the United States, is thus arranged, viz.

GEORGE WASHINGTON, PRESIDENT,

JOHN ADAMS, VICE-PRESIDENT.

SENATORS.

New-Hampshire,	*John Langdon* and *Paine Wingate.*
Massachusetts,	*Caleb Strong* and *Tristram Dalton.*
Connecticut,	*William S. Johnson* and *Oliver Ellsworth.*
New-Jersy,	*William Patterson* and *John Elmer.*
Pennsylvania,	*Robert Morris* and *William Maclay.*
Delaware,	*George Read* and *Richard Basset.*
Maryland,	*Charles Carrol,* and *John Henry.*
Virginia,	*Richard Henry Lee* and *William Grayson.*
South-Carolina,	*Pierce Butler & Ralph Izard.*
Georgia,	*William Few* and —— *Gun.*

REPRESENTATIVES.

New-Hampshire,	*Benjamin West, Samuel Livermore* and *Nicholas Gilman,*
Massachusetts,	*Fisher Ames, George Partridge, George Thacher, George Leonard, Elbridge Gerry, Benjamin Goodhue, Jonathan Grout.*
Connecticut,	*Jonathan Sturges, Roger Sherman, Benjamin Huntington, Jonathan Trumbull, Jeremiah Wadsworth.*
New-York,	*John Lawrence, Egbert Benson, William Floyd, John Hathorn, Peter Sylvester, Jeremiah Van Renselaer.*
New-Jersey,	*Elias Boudinot, James Schureman, Thomas Sinnickson, Lambert Cadwallader.*
Pennsylvania,	*Frederick Augustus Muhlenberg, Henry Wynkoop, Thomas Hartley, George Clymer, Thomas Fitzsimons, Peter Muhlenberg, Daniel Heister, Thomas Scott.*
Delaware,	*John Vining.*
Maryland,	*Joshua Seney, Daniel Carrol, Benjamin Contee, George Gale, William Smith, Michael J. Stone.*
Virginia,	*James Maddison, Josiah Parker, Richard B. Lee, Theodoric Bland, Isaac Coles, Alexander White, John Page, Andrew Moore, Samuel Griffin.*
South-Carolina,	*General Sumpter, Edanus Burke, Tho. T. Tucker, D. Huger, William Smith.*
Georgia,	*Abraham Baldwin, James Jackson, George Matthews.*

The Hon. CHARLES THOMSON, Esq. was appointed to inform the PRESIDENT, and Mr. SYLVANUS BOURNE, the VICE PRESIDENT, of their respective elections. Those gentlemen sat out on their embassy the 7th inst.

PROCEEDINGS of CONGRESS.

In the HOUSE *of* REPRESENTATIVES *of the* UNITED STATES.

TUESDAY, APRIL 7, 1789.

RESOLVED—*That the RULES and ORDERS following, be established* STANDING RULES *and* ORDERS *of this House—to wit:*

FIRST.

TOUCHING THE DUTY OF THE SPEAKER.

HE shall take the chair every day at the hour to which the house shall have adjourned on the preceding day; shall immediately call the members to order, and, on the appearance of a quorum, shall cause the journal of the preceding day to be read.

He shall preserve decorum and order; may speak to points of order in preference to other members, arising from his seat for that purpose, and shall decide questions of order, subject to an appeal to the house by any two members.

He shall rise to put a question, but may state it sitting.

Questions shall be distinctly put in this form, viz. "As many as are of opinion that (as the question may be) say aye:" And, after the affirmative voice is expressed—"As many as are of a contrary opinion, say no."

If the speaker doubts, or a division be called for, the house shall divide, those in the affirmative going to the right, and those in the negative to the left of the chair: If the speaker still doubt, or a count be required, the speaker shall name two members, one from each side, to tell the numbers in the affirmative, which being reported, he shall then name two others, one from each side, to tell those in the negative; which being also reported, he shall rise and state the decision to the house.

The speaker shall appoint committees; unless it be determined by the house that the committee shall consist of more than three members, in which case the appointment shall be by ballot of the house.

In all cases of ballot by the house, the speaker shall vote; in other cases he shall not vote, unless the house be equally divided, or unless his vote, if given to the minority, will make the division be equal, and in case of such equal division, the question shall be lost.

When the house adjourns, the members shall keep their seats until the speaker go forth; and then the members shall follow.

SECONDLY.

OF DECORUM AND DEBATE.

When any member is about to speak in debate, or deliver any matter to the house, he shall rise from his seat and respectfully address himself to Mr. Speaker.

If any member, in speaking or otherwise transgress the rules of the house, the speaker shall, or any member may call to order; in which case the member called to order shall immediately sit down unless permitted to explain, and the house shall, if appealed to, decide on the case, but without debate: If there be no appeal, the decision of the chair shall be submitted to: If the decision be in favour of the member called to order, he shall be at liberty to proceed; if otherwise, and the case require it, he shall be liable to the censure of the house.

When two or more members happen to rise at once, the speaker shall name the member who is first to speak.

No member shall speak more than twice to the same question without leave of the house; nor more than once until every member choosing to speak, shall have spoken.

Whilst the speaker is putting any question, or addressing the house, none shall walk out of, or cross the house; nor either in such case, or when a member is speaking, shall entertain private discourse, or read any printed book or paper; nor whilst a member is speaking, shall pass between him and the chair.

No member shall vote on any question, in the event of which, he is immediately and particularly interested; or in any other case where he was not present when the question was put.

Every member who shall be in the house, when a question is put, shall vote on the one side or the other, unless the house, for special reasons, shall excuse him.

When a motion is made and seconded, it shall be stated by the speaker, or being in writing, it shall be handed to the chair, and read aloud by the clerk before debated.

Every motion shall be reduced to writing, if the speaker or any member desire it.

After a motion is stated by the speaker, or read by the clerk, it shall be deemed to be in possession of the house, but may be withdrawn at any time before decision or amendment.

When a question is under debate, no motion shall be received, unless to amend it, for the previous question, or to adjourn.

A motion to adjourn shall be always in order, and shall be decided without debate.

The previous question shall be in this form: "Shall the main question be now put." It shall only be admitted when demanded by five members; and until it is decided shall preclude all amendment and further debate of the main question.

On a previous question no member shall speak more than once without leave.

Any member may call for the division of a question, where the sense will admit of it.

A motion for commitment until it is decided, shall preclude all amendment of the main question.

Motions and reports may be committed at the pleasure of the house.

No new motion or proposition shall be admitted under colour of amendment, as a substitute for the motion or proposition under debate.

Committees consisting of more than three members, shall be ballotted for by the house; if upon such ballot the number required shall not be elected by a majority of the votes given, the house shall proceed to a second ballot, in which a plurality of votes shall prevail, and in case a greater number than are required to compose or complete the committee shall have an equal number of votes, the house shall proceed to further ballot or ballots.

In all other cases of ballot than for committees, a majority of the votes given shall be necessary to an election, and when there shall not be such majority on the first ballot, the ballot shall be repeated until a majority be obtained.

In all cases where others than members of the house may be eligible, there shall be a previous nomination.

If a question depending be lost by adjournment of the house and revived on the succeeding day, no member who has spoken twice on the day preceding shall be permitted again to speak without leave.

Every order, resolution or vote to which the concurrence of the senate shall be necessary, shall be read to the house, and laid on the table, on a day preceding that in which the same shall be moved, unless the house shall otherwise expresly allow.

Petitions, memorials, and other papers addressed to the house shall be presented through the speaker, or by a member in his place, and shall not be debated or decided on the day of their being first read, unless where the house shall direct otherwise; but shall lie on the table to be taken up in the order they were read.

Any fifteen members (including the speaker if there is one) shall be authorised to compel the attendance of absent members.

Upon calls of the house, or in taking the ayes and noes on any question, the names of the members shall be called alphabetically.

THIRDLY.

OF BILLS.

Every bill shall be introduced by motion for leave, or by an order of the house on the report of a committee, and in either case a committee to prepare the same shall be appointed. In cases of a general nature one days notice at least shall be given of the motion to bring in a bill; and every such motion may be committed.

Every bill shall receive three several readings in the house previous to its passage; and all bills shall be dispatched in order as they were introduced, unless where the house shall direct otherwise; but no bill shall be twice read on the same day without special order of the house.

The first reading of a bill shall be for information, and if opposition be made to it, the question shall be, "Shall the bill be rejected?" If no opposition be made, or the question to reject it be negatived, the bill shall go to its second reading without a question.

Upon the second reading of a bill, the speaker shall state it as ready for commitment or engrossment, and if committed, then a question shall be whether to a select committee, or to a committee of the whole house; if to a committee of the whole house, the house shall determine on what day. But if the bill be ordered to be engrossed, the house shall appoint the day when it shall be read the third time. After commitment, and a report thereof to the house, a bill may be re-committed, or at any time before its passage.

All bills ordered to be engrossed shall be executed in a fair round hand.

The enacting style of bills shall be, "Be it enacted by the Senators and Representatives of the United States in Congress assembled."

When a bill shall pass it shall be certified by the clerk, noting the day of its passing at the foot thereof.

No bill amended by the Senate shall be committed.

FOURTHLY.

OF COMMITTEES OF THE WHOLE HOUSE.

It shall be a standing Order of the day, throughout the session, for the house to resolve itself into a Committee of the whole house on the state of the Union.

In forming a Committee of the whole House, the Speaker shall leave his chair, and a chairman to preside in Committee shall be appointed.

Upon bills committed to a committee of the whole house, the bill shall be first read throughout by the clerk, and then again read and debated by clauses, leaving the preamble to be last consid[illegible]; the body of the bill shall not be defaced or interlined; but all amendments, noting the page and line, shall be duly entered by the clerk on a separate paper as the same shall be agreed to by the committee, and so reported to the house. After report the bill shall again be subject to be debated and amended by clauses before a question to engross it be taken.

All amendments made to an original motion in committee shall be incorporated with the motion and so reported.

All amendments made to a report committed to a committee of the whole shall be noted and reported as in the case of bills.

All questions, whether in committee or in the house, shall be propounded in the order they were moved, except that in filling up the blanks the largest sum and longest day shall be first put.

The rules of proceeding in the house shall be observed in committee so far as they may be applicable, except that limitting the times of speaking.

Extract from the Journal,

JOHN BECKLEY, *Clerk.*

WEDNESDAY, APRIL 8, 1789.

THIS day the Galleries of the Hon. House of Representatives were opened. The members being convened, the Hon. Chief Justice MORRIS, of the State of New-York, administered to the Speaker and Members of the House, the Oath required by the Constitution of the United States.

Upon motion of the Hon. Mr. PARKER, of Virginia, the House then resolved itself into a Committee of the whole, to take the state of the Union into consideration. This motion was agreed to, and the Hon. Mr. PAGE, of Virginia, took the chair.

Mr. MADDISON, of Virginia, after a few introductory observations on the great subjects of Finance, and the deficiencies of the federal Treasury, suggested the necessity of immediately adopting some measures upon the subject of National Revenue. With this object in view, he produced a Resolve, specifying certain articles upon which an Impost was proposed to be laid. The plan was similar to that recommended by Congress in 1783—and is as follows, viz.

[*RESOLVED, as the opinion of this committee, That the following Duties ought to be levied on goods, wares, and merchandize, imported into the United States, to wit.*

On Rum, pr. gallon, *of a dollar.*
On all other Spiritous Liquors.
On Molasses.
On Maderia Wine.
On all other Wines.
On common Bohea Teas, pr. lb.
On all other Teas.
On Pepper.
On Brown Sugars.
On Loaf Sugars.
On all other Sugars.
On Cocoa and Coffee.
On all other articles *per cent. on their value at the time and place of importation.*

That there ought, moreover, to be levied on all vessels in which goods, wares or merchandises shall be imported, the duties following, viz.

On all vessels built within the United States, and belonging wholly to citizens thereof, at the rate of *per ton*

On all vessels belonging wholly to the subjects of powers with whom the United States have formed treaties, or partly to the subjects of such powers, and partly to citizens of the said states at the rate of ,

On all vessels belonging wholly or in part to the subjects of other powers, at the rate of

Mr. BOUDINOT, of New Jersey, and Col. WHITE, of Virginia, spoke in favour of the Resolve, from the necessity of a temporary System's being immediately adopted; but as it was presumed, that gentlemen had not come prepared to discuss the subject, an adjournment was called for, when the Speaker, resuming the chair, the House adjourned till to morrow.

THURSDAY, APRIL 9, 1789.

The House having again resolved itself into a Committee. Mr. PAGE took the chair.

When Mr. SHERMAN, of Connecticut, proposed resuming the Resolve submitted to the Committee yesterday, by filling up the blanks.

Mr. GOODHUE suggested the propriety of again reading the Resolve—which being done,

Mr. LAWRENCE, of New-York, observed, that the immediate necessity of a publick Revenue, to answer the exigencies of the Union, was universally acknowledged, and the mode of raising it by Impost was generally supposed to be the best; but that as the resolve, at present proposed, was designed as a temporary measure; and it being requisite that some System should be speedily adopted, so as to embrace the advantages that would result from the Spring importations, it appeared to him the most eligible plan to adopt a general idea with respect to impost, and lay a pr. centum, *ad valorum,* on articles indiscriminately, in preference to specifying particulars at various rates.

Mr. FITZSIMONS, of Pennsylvania, in opposition to the Hon. Mr. LAWRENCE, replied, that a specification of certain articles, with various rates of Impost affixed to each, had been found to be more productive, easier collected, and a more certain revenue, than a pr. centum, assessed in a general way; that so far from wishing to abandon the original idea, he thought it of so much importance to be

Gazette of the United-States.

No. VI. From WEDNESDAY, April 29, to SATURDAY, May 2, 1789. PRICE SIX PENCE.

A SKETCH *of the* POLITICAL STATE *of* AMERICA.

NUMBER III.

AMONG the causes of a domestic nature, to which we can attribute our late unhappy situation, may be placed those ill-judged, impolitic commercial connections, and speculations in this country, consequent upon the peace, and none perhaps may be esteemed more pernicious to us, than our large importations of British luxuries, while we were prohibited to pay for them in any staples of our country; and little else than specie, which we most wanted at home, was suffered to be taken in return: For though the exportation of our Tobacco, in the first instance, promised a good freight, yet this, from a variety of causes, was soon found injurious, and in many instances, destructive to those who were largely concerned in it—to which the discouragement, arising from the high duties imposed by the British government, and the exorbitant commissions charged by their merchants, may be ascribed as efficient causes—while the narrow channel, through which it could be introduced into France, has never held out a sufficient inducement to the adventurer. Other evils which we have experienced may be said to have arose from too licentious notions of liberty, which the early policy of the day might have given rise to, as it would not have been prudent to inform the people they were contending only for a change of rulers—but absolute freedom, without restraint, was held out as the palm of victory: Thus the publick at large were led to confound the ideas of natural and political, or civil liberty—and by experience only, could be taught the essential difference. The same policy as above referred to, carried into the principles of taxation, may be viewed as another ground of our misfortunes, as government withholding for so long a time, in the early stage of the war, to raise any revenue by taxes, the community were led to suppose all future impositions of the kind as not arising from necessity, and to answer the exigencies of Government, but as the arbitrary mandates of their rulers, for their own power and aggrandizement—and even those who knew it to be the price of our liberty, were almost induced to relinquish an object so dear in its purchase.

The floods of unfunded paper money, issued as a substitute for taxation, gave every opportunity to the knavish and ill-minded part of the community, to cheat and defraud their neighbours, and all under the sanction of solemn acts of Legislative authority; and eventually a greater part of this ideal money sunk worthless in the hands of those who were best able to bear it—and without any prospect of redress: But during its currency, many people deferred calling for those dues which they knew no way of justly obtaining; but after the channels of justice were once more opened without any barrier, those of this class, some from motives of resentment, and others from real necessity, almost universally commenced their suits for those balances, which were by this time grown more burthensome by an accumulated interest; and perhaps the effects of those habits upon our future intercourse with each other, which were impressed by a long converse in large sums, may not be placed among the least injurious consequences from the use of paper money. I venture to rank them among the greatest, as fixed habits are not readily removed, and a certain association of ideas will frequently remain in the mind after the cause which produced them has ceased to exist.

AMERICANUS.

(To be continued.)

COMMERCE.

Further extracts from the " AMERICAN ESSAYS."

" Per varios casus, per tot discrimina rerum
" Tendimus."—— VIRG.

MULTIFARIOUS have been the speeches and publications upon the *now* visionary schemes of a rigid national economy, and *republican virtue*. Amusing pictures! But where are the originals! Painful retrospect! Blended—alas—with the diluvian wreck! And only serve to throw a melancholy gloom over all future prospects. The opinions, and habits of mankind, are perpetually changing, and therefore preclude all rational hopes of success, in the endeavors to apply the most approved practices and manners of ancient times to the present day.

It is true we are in our infant state, politically considered; but morally considered, we are by no means infants; we are beyond that period of flexible docility; we may be said to be at least initiated, if we are not adepts, in all the arts, refinements, habits, luxuries, extravagancies, follies, vices, and wants, of the oldest and most corrupt monarchies: Rome boasted her CINCINNATUS, and America can boast her CINCINNATI, a society, chiefly composed of military patriots, who may, with propiety, be said to be *followers*, tho' perhaps not all scrupulous *imitators* of their ILLUSTRIOUS PREDECESSOR.

Agriculture, arts, manufactures, and industry, are promising presages of future greatness; but if these are not attainable, without a rigid adherence to that simplicity of manners, which is said to have characterised those great and virtuous patriots of Greece and Rome, who have been so often held up as our great exemplers, I fear we may never expect to see them flourish in America.

When the great and important question of *national revenue* is agitating in the grand councils of the nation, it will be found necessary to recur to every probable source, and to contrive to give all possible encouragement and efficiency to each; this will naturally lead to the consideration of the importance of a *free, well regulated, and extensive commerce*, which upon the most accurate and profound investigation, of its various productive influence, and effects, *will discover*, what at this day, chiefly gives vigor, life, and energy to the husbandman, mechanic, manufacturer, and laborer; and from whence modern states principally derive the necessary resources for the support of government: In the solemn, national deliberations, upon this deep, this wide, this *immeasurable* subject, it will probably be found necessary, with our political, to unite the best commercial knowledge, and experience, that can be collected in America.

" Est laudatissimus, qui per se cuncta videbit;"
" Sed laudandus et Is, qui paret recta monenti."

The present exhausted state of our public and private finances, and the consequent want of means to supply the exigencies, and support the credit and dignity of government, are universally bruited, acknowledged, felt and deplored: The general decay of trade may doubtless be considered one of the principal causes, as also of the ruinous migration of our citizens from the sea ports into the remote interior country, and even *into the British, and other foreign dominions.*

The French merchants have made several attempts to carry on the whale fishery from Dunkirk, and although the King of France had furnished them with large sums of money upon the very advantageous terms of giving all the profits of that trade to the merchants, with the use of the money without interest, and sustaining all the loss of unsuccessful voyages, yet their fishery never succeeded, until Americans, principally from the State of Massachusetts, were induced by the very great encouragement offered by the merchants in Dunkirk, and the want of employ at home, to enter into their service, since which, the French government has prohibited the free importation of whale oil from foreign dominions. The English owe also their success in the whale fishery chiefly to Americans; for notwithstanding the immense bounties paid by the British government for its encouragement, they could never succeed until they employed Americans, who are also very well paid and greatly encouraged in their service.

The destructive influence of a declining commerce acts like a gangrene, which unless timely checked will soon spread over the whole body, and become incurable: Every lover of his country will therefore be solicitous to find out some speedy remedy for this alarming evil: *There are no possible adequate substitutes for the loss of commerce*: Our first grand object therefore is *its restoration*. I presume not to dictate or direct, it is a subject that will require the deepest deliberations and researches of the wisest and most experienced men in America fully to comprehend: It probably belongs to no one man existing, to possess *all* the qualifications requisite to trace the course of American commerce through all her numerous, intricate and yet untroden paths; and to point out those, and only those, that shall lead the United States to future glory and prosperity. I am sanguine in the belief of the possibility, that we may one day become a great, commercial, and flourishing nation; but if in pursuit of the means, we should unfortunately stumble again on *unfunded paper money*, or any similar species of *fraud*, we shall assuredly give a fatal stab to our national credit in its infancy, and blast the success of the best concerted plans: Palliatives at best are poor pitiful expedients, and never to be applied, but in the most desperate, or *incurable* causes. *Paper money* will invariably operate in the body politic, as spiritous liquors on the human body, which often produce a momentary relief, or giddy joy, *the effects of a delirium*; but while they intoxicate the brain, and lull the senses, they prey upon the vitals, *and ultimately destroy the constitution*: " But while a nation can preserve its credit at home, and abroad, there are " no difficulties to be deemed insurmountable." " Loaded with an enormous debt beyond the possibility of payment, and which would annihilate the credit of any other nation on the globe, and burthened with taxes which her *commerce* alone enables her to support; *Great Britain*, from her uniform sacred regard to all her pecuniary obligations, and transactions, foreign and domestic; and her constant punctual discharge of the interest of all loans; though just emerged from a long, expensive, unsuccessful war, now stands, commercially considered, the unrivalled mistress of the world: Her revenues are immense; her credit at home and abroad unbounded; her funds the great reservoir of the treasures of the globe; the bank of England full and runing over; ships openly, or disguisedly, but really owned by British subjects, swarming and evidently taking the lead in commerce of every other nation in all the parts of *Europe, Asia, Africa, and even in America*; openly monopolizing the trade in the few sea ports of *Austrian Flanders*, secretly possessing a large share in every lucrative branch of the *French* trade, particularly their African trade; draining *Portugal* and her *Colonies* in the east and west; leaving *Spain* but little to boast of all those precious *Mexican* and *Peruvian* harvests drawn from the bowels, or the bosom of her prolific earth; profiting greatly in her commercial intercourse with almost every other nation; and wisely jealous and tenacious of the exclusive possession of all the benefits arising from the trade with her own colonies.

Thus, *the little island of Britain*, maintains the right and glory of being considered, *and acknowledged* the *great Emporium of the world*. Yet such is the present state of corruption, dissipation, extravagance, and immense expence of that nation in every department, there are only wanted the united, well directed exertions of the *American States*, with industry, and their wonted activity and enteprize, soon to lop off many of the most valuable branches of their trade; it is well known that " the difference of three or four per cent. will carry the trade of the world." E. C.

NEW-YORK.

PROCEEDINGS of CONGRESS.

In the HOUSE *of* REPRESENTATIVES *of the* UNITED STATES.

TUESDAY, 28th APRIL, 1789.

DEBATE *upon the* IMPOST *on* MOLASSES *continued.*

Mr. MADISON, after an exordium, observed, This duty, it is said, will operate against a beneficial branch of commerce, carried on with our allies; but what was the state of facts previous to the revolution? This trade supported itself, notwithstanding the article of molasses was then subject to a duty, and foreign rum was imported duty free: Now, there is a heavy duty on rum, and yet this article, it is contended can not bear a tax—if the manufacture of rum was in a flourishing condition, when it had to combat a duty, and the influx of foreign spirits, it appears absurd to suppose, that the proposed duty, will annihilate the trade. There is a duty upon country rum, through the States, yet the trade is not destroyed; and if this duty is assessed on molasses, it is evident from these facts that the importation will not be diminished. It is considered by gentlemen as a necessary article of life—if this is granted, it must also be allowed, that a great proportion is consumed through the States—and where molasses is not used, it is more than balanced by Sugar—as that pays a higher duty.

It has been said, that this duty will be burthensome, as it will oblige the merchants to encrease their capitals—but this objection applies to other branches, and must be submitted to, or we must relinquish the idea of a revenue. The complaint respecting the fishermen appears ill founded, as no draw back is now allowed on the duty paid on rum consumed by them. The objection urged against the tax on account of smuggling (from the bulk and weight of this article), can not be considered as formidable. Mr. Madison was opposed to the substitute mentioned, an excise at the distill head, at present.

There was, he observed, an excise already upon rum in the States; but molasses, he believed, was free—and if a duty was now laid upon the latter, he had no doubt of an encrease in the sale of rum. Should this article be struck out of the report, it would be sacrificing the interest of three millions of people to support the interest of the distillers. This duty will not bear harder on the eastern than other exactions will on the southern States—he was therefore against a diminution of the six cents, or striking out the article.

Mr. AMES observed, that the Constitution under which this House was now deliberating was the result of commercial necessity—that from the opinion he had formed, and from the evidence he

[*Several other gentlemen ſpake upon both ſides of this queſtion; but our limits will not admit of inſerting their obſervations.*]

The queſtion being taken, the duty was continued at 6 cents.

Mr. SHERMAN moved, that card wire be added to the articles exempted from Impoſt—which was acceded to.

The Houſe having proceeded through the remainder of the report (except the duty on tonnage, which was poſtponed) appointed Mr. CLYMER, Mr. WHITE, and Mr. BALDWIN, a committee, to draft and report a bill.

A reſolution of the Senate was then read, purporting that they had appointed Mr. JOHNSTON, Mr. IZARD, and Mr. MACLAY a committee, to determine and report, reſpecting the papers in the late Secretary's office. The Houſe concurred, and appointed Mr. TRUMBULL, Mr. CADWALLADER, and Mr. JACKSON, to join the committee of the Senate.

WEDNESDAY, APRIL 29.

A letter from MATTHIAS OGDEN, Eſq. of New-Jerſey, addreſſed to the Speaker, incloſing a petition and remonſtrance of a number of citizens of New-Jerſey, alledging, that certain irregularities had prevailed at their late election, and that undue means has been uſed to bias the voters; alſo complaining of the return made by the Governor, was read, together with the petition, and committed to the committee of elections.

The Houſe took up the conſideration of the reſolution of the Senate for attending divine ſervice, in St. Paul's church, immediately after the oath is adminiſtered to the Preſident, and concurred therewith.

A committee was appointed to prepare an eſtimate of the probable amount of the revenue on impoſt, agreeably to the duties lately agreed to; and to procure an eſtimate of the public debt.

FRIDAY, MAY 1, 1789.

The Speech of the Preſident, to the two Houſes of Congreſs yeſterday, was read, and referred to a committee of the whole Houſe.

The Houſe then reſolved itſelf into a committee, and Mr. PAGE took the chair.

Mr. MADISON then introduced a reſolution to the following effect, viz.

Reſolved, as the opinion of this committee, that a ſelect committee of the Houſe be appointed, to prepare an addreſs to the Preſident, congratulating him on his appointment to the office of Preſident of theſe States by the unanimous voice of his countrymen—expreſſing the approbation of the Houſe of the liberal and patriotic ſentiments, contained in his ſpeech, and their concurrence in every plan which he has or may propoſe, to ſecure the liberties, promote the harmony, and advance the happineſs and proſperity of their country.—This reſolution being adopted, the committee was diſſolved, and the Speaker reſumed the chair—when the following gentlemen were elected a committee, agreeably to the reſolve—Mr. MADISON, Mr. CLYMER, Mr. SHERMAM, Mr. BENSON, Mr. GALE.

A propoſition for the appointment of a committee, to take into conſideration, what compenſation ſhall be made to the Preſident for his ſervices, was after ſome converſation referred to a committee of the whole upon the ſtate of the Union.

Upon motion of Mr. SHERMAN, to take up the order of the day—it was voted to come to the choie of a Chaplain—the ballots being collected—the Reverend Mr. LINN was choſen.

Adjourned until Monday.

NEW-YORK, MAY 2.

On Thurſday laſt, agreeably to the reſolution of both Houſes of Congreſs, the inauguration of THE PRESIDENT of the UNITED STATES was ſolemnized.

At nine o'clock, A. M. the people aſſembled in the ſeveral churches, with the Clergy of the reſpective denominations, to implore the bleſſing of Heaven upon the new govermemt, its favor and protection to the PRESIDENT, and ſucceſs and acceptance to his adminiſtration.

About twelve o'clock the proceſſion moved from the Houſe of the Preſident, in Cherry-Street—through Queen, Great Dock and Broad Sreets, to the Federal State Houſe, in the following order:

Col. LEWIS,
Attended by two Officers.
Capt. STAKES,
With the Troop of Horſe.
Artillery.
Major VAN HORNE.
Grenadiers, under Capt. HARSIN,
German Grenadiers, under Capt. SCRIBA.
Major BICKER.
The Infantry of the Brigade.
Major CHRYSTIE.
Sheriff.
Committee of the Senate.

Civil Officers.	Aſſiſtants.	PRESIDENT. His Suite.	Aſſiſtants.	Civil Officers.

Committee of the Repreſentatives.
Hon. Mr. JAY.
Gen. KNOX.
Chancellor LIVINGSTON,
Several gentlemen of diſtinction.

When within a proper diſtance of the State-Houſe, the troops formed a line on both ſides of the way, THE PRESIDENT paſſing through, was conducted into the Senate Chamber, and introduced to both Houſes of Congreſs.

Immediately after, accompanied by the two Houſes, he was conducted into the Gallery adjoining the Senate Chamber, and fronting Broad-Street, where, in the preſence of an immenſe concourſe of citizens, the Oath, preſcribed by the Conſtitution, was adminiſtered to him by the Hon. R. R. LIVINGSTON, Eſq. Chancellor of the State of New-York.

The Chancellor then proclaimed him THE PRESIDENT OF THE UNITED STATES, which was followed by the inſtant diſcharge of 13 cannon, and loud repeated ſhouts: THE PRESIDENT bowing to the people, the air again rang with their acclamations: He then retired with the two Houſes to the Senate Chamber, where he made the following SPEECH.

FELLOW-CITIZENS OF THE SENATE,
AND OF THE HOUSE OF REPRESENTATIVES,

AMONG the viciſſitudes incident to life, no event could have filled me with greater anxieties, than that of which the notification was tranſmitted by your order, and rceeived on the 14th day of the preſent month.—On the one hand, I was ſummoned by my country, whoſe voice I can never hear but with veneration and love, from a retreat which I had choſen with the fondeſt predilection, and in my flattering hopes, with an immutable deciſion, as the aſylum of my declining years; a retreat which was rendered every day more neceſſary as well as more dear to me, by the addition of habit to inclination, and of frequent interruptions in my health to the gradual waſte committed on it by time. On the other hand, the magnitude and difficulty of the truſt to which the voice of my country called me, being ſufficient to awaken in the wiſeſt and moſt experienced of her citizens, a diſtruſtful ſcrutiny into his qualifications, could not but overwhelm with deſpondence, one, who, inheriting inferior endowments from nature, and unpractiſed in the duties of civil adminiſtration, ought to be peculiarly conſcious of his own deficiencies. In this conflict of emotions, all I dare aver, is, that it has been my faithful ſtudy to collect my duty from a juſt appreciation of every circumſtance, by which it might be affected. All I dare hope, is, that, if in executing this taſk, I have been too much ſwayed by a grateful remembrance of former inſtances, or by an affectionate ſenſibility to this tranſcendant proof of the confidence of my fellow citizens; and have thence too little conſulted my incapacity as well as diſinclination, for the weighty and untried cares before me; my *error* will be palliated by the motives which miſled me, and its conſequences be judged by my country, with ſome ſhare of the partiality in which they originated.

Such being the impreſſions under which I have, in obedience to the public ſummons, repaired to the preſent ſtation; it would be peculiarly improper to omit in this firſt official act, my fervent ſupplications to that Almighty Being who rules over the univerſe; who preſides in the councils of nations, and whoſe providential aids can ſupply every human defect, that his benediction may conſecrate to the liberties and happineſs of the people of the United States, a government inſtituted by themſelves for theſe eſſential purpoſes; and may enable every inſtrument employed in its adminiſtration, to execute with ſucceſs, the functions allotted to his charge. In tendering this homage to the great author of every public and private good, I aſſure myſelf that it expreſſes your ſentiments not leſs than my own; nor thoſe of my fellow citizens at large, leſs than either. No people can be bound to acknowledge and adore the inviſible hand, which conducts the affairs of men more than the people of the United States. Every ſtep by which they have advanced to the character of an independent nation, ſeems to have been diſtinguiſhed by ſome token of providential agency. And in the important revolution juſt accompliſhed in the ſyſtem of their united government, the tranquil deliberations, and voluntary conſent of ſo many diſtinct communities, from which the event has reſulted, cannot be compared with the means by which moſt governments have been eſtabliſhed, without ſome return of pious gratitude along with an humble anticipation of the future bleſſings which the paſt ſeem to preſage. Theſe reflections ariſing out of the preſent criſis, have forced themſelves too ſtrongly on my mind to be ſuppreſſed. You will join with me, I truſt, in thinking, that there are none under the influence of which, the proceedings of a new and free government can more auſpiciouſly commence.

By the article eſtabliſhing the executive department, it is made the duty of the Preſident to "recommend to your conſideration, ſuch meaſures as he ſhall judge neceſſary and expedient." The circumſtances under which I now meet you, will acquit me from entering into that ſubject, farther than to refer to the great conſtitutional charter under which you are aſſembled, aud which, in defining your powers, deſignates the objects to which your attention is to be given. It will be more conſiſtent with thoſe circumſtances, and far more congenial with the feelings which actuate me, to ſubſtitute, in place of a recommendation of particular meaſures, the tribute that is due to the talents, the rectitude, and the patriotiſm which adorn the characters ſelected to deviſe and adopt them. In thoſe honorable qualifications, I behold the ſureſt pledges, that as on one ſide no local prejudices, or attachments—no ſeparate views, no party animoſities, will miſdirect the comprehenſive and equal eye which ought to watch over this great aſſemblage of communities and intereſts; ſo, on the other, that the foundations of our national policy will be laid in the pure and immutable principles of private morality; and the pre-eminence of free government, be exemplified by all the attributes which can win the affections of its citizens, and command the reſpect of the world—I dwell on this proſpect with every ſatisfaction which an ardent love of my country can inſpire. Since there is no truth more thoroughly eſtabliſhed, than that there exiſts in the œconomy and courſe of nature, an indiſſoluble union between virtue and happineſs; between duty and advantage, between genuine maxims of an honeſt and magnanimous policy, and the ſolid rewards of public proſperity and felicity. Since we ought to be no leſs perſuaded that the propitious ſmiles of heaven, can never be expected on a nation that diſregards the eternal rules of order and right, which heaven itſelf has ordained. And ſince the preſervation of the ſacred fire of liberty, and the deſtiny of the republican model of government, are juſtly conſidered as *deeply*, perhaps as *finally* ſtaked on the experiment entruſted to the hands of the American people.

Beſides the ordinary objects ſubmitted to your care, it will remain with your judgment to decide, how far an exerciſe of the occaſional power delegated by the fifth article of the conſtitution is rendered expedient at the preſent juncture by the nature of objections which have been urged againſt the ſyſtem, or by the degree of inquietude which has given birth to them.

Inſtead of undertaking particular recommendations on this ſubject, in which I could be guided by no lights derived from official opportunities, I ſhall again give way to my entire confidence in your diſcernment and purſuit of the public good.

For I aſſure myſelf that whilſt you carefully avoid every alteration which might endanger the benefits of an united and effective government, or which ought to await the future leſſon of experience; a reverence for the characteriſtic rights of freemen, and a regard for the public harmony, will ſufficiently influence your deliberations on the queſtion how far the former can be more impregnably fortified, or the latter be ſafely and advantageouſly promoted.

To the preceding obſervations I have one to add, which will be moſt properly addreſſed to the houſe of repreſentatives, it concerns myſelf, and will therefore be as brief as poſſible.

When I was firſt honoured with a call into the ſervice of my country, then on the eve of an arduous ſtruggle for its liberties, the light in which I contemplated my duty required that I ſhould renounce every pecuniary compenſation. From this reſolution I have in no inſtance departed. And being ſtill under the impreſſions which produced it, I muſt decline as inapplicable to myſelf, any ſhare in the perſonal emoluments, which may be indiſpenſably concluded in a permanent proviſion for the executive department; and muſt accordingly pray, that the pecuniary eſtimates for the ſtation in which I am placed, may, during my continuance in it, be limited to ſuch actual expenditures as the public good may be thought to require.

Having thus imparted to you my ſentiments, as they have been awakened by the occaſion which brings us together—I ſhall take my preſent leave; but not without reſorting once more to the benign parent of the human race, in humble ſupplication, that ſince he has been pleaſed to favour the American people with opportunities for deliberating in perfect tranquility, and diſpoſitions for deciding with unparalleled unanimity on a form of government, for the ſecurity of their union, and the advancement of their happineſs; ſo his divine bleſſing may be equally *conſpicuous* in the enlarged views, the temperate conſultations, and the wiſe meaſures on which the ſucceſs of this government muſt depend.

GEORGE WASHINGTON.

THE PRESIDENT, accompanied by His Excellency the Vice-Preſident, the Speaker of the Houſe of Repreſentatives, and both Houſs of Congreſs, then went to St. Paul's Chapel, where divine ſervice was performed, by the Right Rev. Dr. PROVOST, Biſhop of the Epiſcopal Church in this State, and Chaplain to the Senate.

The religious ſolemnity being ended, the Preſident was eſcorted to his reſidence.

Yeſterday morning THE PRESIDENT received the compliments of His Excellency the Vice Preſident, His Excellency the Governor of this State; the principal Officers of the different Departments; the foreign Miniſters; and a great number of other perſons of diſtinction.

We are informed, that THE PRESIDENT has aſſigned every Tueſday and Friday, between the hours of two and three, for receiving viſits; and that viſits of compliment on other days, and particularly on Sundays, will not be agreeable to him.

It ſeems to be a prevailing opinion, that ſo much of THE PRESIDENT's time will be engaged by the various and important buſineſs, impoſed upon him by the Conſtitution, that he will find himſelf conſtrained to omit returning viſits, or accepting invitations to Entertainments.

The tranſparent paintings exhibited in various parts of the city, on Thurſday evening, were equal at leaſt, to any thing of the kind ever before ſeen in America.

That diſplayed before the Fort at the bottom of Broad-way, did great honor to its inventors and executors, for the ingenuity of the deſign, and goodneſs of the workmanſhip; it was finely lighted and advantageouſly ſituated! The virtues, FORTITUDE,* JUSTICE,† and WISDOM‡ were judiciouſly applied; of the firſt, all America has had the fulleſt evidence; and with reſpect to the two others, who does not entertain the moſt pleaſing anticipations.

* THE PRESIDENT. † THE SENATE. ‡ THE REPRESENTATIVES of the United States.

His Excellency DON GARDOQUI's reſidence next caught the eye—and fixed it in pleaſing contemplation: The *Tout-en-ſemble* here, formed a moſt brilliant front; the figures well fancied, THE GRACES, ſuggeſted the beſt ideas; and the pleaſing variety of *emblems, flowers, ſhrubbery, arches*, &c. and above all the MOVING PICTURES, that figured in the windows, or as it were in the *back ground*, created by fixing the tranſparencies between the windows, afforded a new—an animated, and enchanting ſpectacle.

The reſidence of his Excellency, COUNT MOUSTIER, was illuminated in a ſtile of novel elegance; the ſplendid bordering of lamps ronnd the windows, doors, &c. with the fancy pieces in each window; and above all the large deſigns in front, the alluſions, of which we cannot at preſent particulaiy deſcribe, did great honor to the taſte and ſentiment of the inventor.

The above two inſtances of attention to honor this great and important occaſion, ſo highly intereſting to our "dear country," evince the friendſhip, the delicacy and politeneſs of our illuſtrious allies.

The portrait of "THE FATHER OF HIS COUNTRY" exhibited in Broad-Street, was extremely well executed, and had a fine effect.

There was an excellent Traſparency, alſo ſhewn at the Theatre, and at the corner, near the Fly-Market: In ſhort, emulation and ingenuity were alive; but perhaps were in no inſtance exhibited to greater advantage than in the diſplay of the Fire Works, which, from one novelty to another, continued for two hours, to ſurprize, by variety, taſte, and brilliancy.

The illumination of the Federal State Houſe, was among the moſt agreeable of the exhibitions of the evening; and the ſhip Carolina formed a beautiful pyramid of Stars:—The evening was fine—the company innumerable—every one appeared to enjoy the ſcene, and no accident caſts the ſmalleſt cloud upon the retroſpect.

ARRIVALS.

At the Port of New-York.

Wedneſday.	Brig Minerva,	Bell,	Cape de Verds,	39 days.
	Sloop Mary,	Daun,	St. John's.	
	Ann,	Lyburn,	Turks-Iſland,	15 days.
Friday.	Sloop Peggy,	Cahoone,	Rhode-Iſland,	1 day.
	Defiance,	Drew,	Baltimore.	
	Friendſhip,		Savanna.	

Gazette of the United States.

[No. XLIX.] WEDNESDAY, September 30, 1789. [Publiſhed on Wedneſday and Saturday.]

AYES. *Meſſrs.* Brown, Baldwin, Bland, Burke, Contee, Coles, Carroll, Gerry, Gale, Griffin, Jackſon, Lee, Madiſon, Mathews, Moore, Page, Parker, Smith, (M.) Sumpter, Seney, Smith (S. C.) Stone, Schureman, Tucker, White. 25.

Mr. AMES then moved to concur with the Senate in their amendment. Objections were made to this, and on motion the Houſe adjourned without coming to a deciſion.

MONDAY, SEPT. 28.

A meſſage was received from the Senate acquainting the Houſe, that they had appointed Mr. JOHNSON and Mr. IZARD a committee to join a committee of the Houſe to wait on the Preſident, and inform him that the Houſes had reſolved to adjourn the 29th inſt. to meet again on the firſt Monday in January. The Houſe accordingly appointed Mr. VINING, Mr. LEE and Mr. GILMAN, a committee for the purpoſe.

Read the report of the committee appointed to aſcertain the amount of the compenſations due to the members and officers of the Houſe.

The Houſe then proceeded to conſider the amendment of the Senate to the bill for fixing the ſeat of government.

Mr. MADISON moved a reſolution, as a proviſo to the bill, that nothing therein contained ſhould be conſtrued to affect the operation of the laws of Pennſylvania within the ſaid diſtrict of ten miles ſquare, until Congreſs ſhall otherwiſe provide by law. This was agreed to.

Mr. MADISON moved to ſtrike out of the amendment thoſe words which comprehend within the diſtrict ſuch parts of the northern liberties of Philadelphia as are not excepted in the Pennſylvania act of ceſſion. The queſtion on this motion was negatived.

Mr. GERRY then moved to refer the bill with the amendment of the Senate to the next ſeſſion, and that in the interim, commiſſioners ſhould be appointed to examine the river Delaware, and to report a proper ſite for the eſtabliſhment of the ſeat of government.

To this motion it was objected that it was not in order, ſince the queſtion for poſtponement had been decided in the negative on Saturday. Mr. GERRY defended the motion, as this was for a particular reference, the former for a general one, and therefore the queſtion was a new one.

The Speaker declared it not to be in order.

Mr. LEE moved to ſtrike out the clauſe providing that the temporary reſidence ſhould be in New-York. This was negatived.

Mr. BOUDINOT moved to amend the amendment of the Senate, by annexing to it a clauſe, providing that the ſeat of government might be any where on the Delaware within the State of New-Jerſey and Pennſylvania, or either of them, above Philadelphia, and below Howell's ferry. Negatived.

The main queſtion of concurrence was then put, and the yeas and nays were as follow:

AYES. *Meſſrs.* Ames, Benſon, Cadwallader, Clymer, Fitzſimons, Floyd, Foſter, Gerry, Gilman, Goodhue, Grout, Hartley, Hathorn, Heiſter, Huntington, Lawrance, Leonard, Livermore, P. Muhlenberg, Partridge, Van Ranſellaer, Schureman, Scott, Sherman, Sylveſter, Sinnickſon, Thatcher, Trumbull, Vining, Wadſworth, Wynkoop. 31.

NOES. *Meſſrs.* Baldwin, Bland, Boudinot, Brown, Burke, Carroll, Coles, Contee, Gale, Griffin, Jackſon, Lee, Madiſon, Matthews, Moore, Page, Parker, Seney, Smith, (M.) Smith, (S.C.) Stone, Sumpter, Tucker, White. 24.

A meſſage was received from the Senate with the appropriation bill in which they have concurred with amendments—Alſo, the bill to recognize and adapt to the conſtitution of the United States, the ordinances of the late Congreſs for the eſtabliſhment of troops on the frontiers, with ſundry amendments.

The amendments propoſed by the Senate to the appropriation bill were agreed to by the Houſe—Alſo, thoſe to the other bill, excepting the ſeventh, which occaſioned conſiderable debate. This amendment was to ſtrike out the two laſt ſections, which reſpects the number of militia to be called into ſervice, for the defence of the frontiers, from the States of Pennſylvania, Virginia, and Georgia—and to inſert in lieu thereof, a ſection to empower the Preſident of the United States to call out ſuch numbers as he may find neceſſary for the defence of the frontiers generally. On motion to concur with this amendment, the ayes and noes were called as follow, viz.

AYES. *Meſſrs.* Benſon, Carroll, Clymer, Foſter, Gilman, Lawrance, Lee, Madiſon, Partridge, Sherman, Silveſter, Smith, (M.) Stone, Thatcher, Trumbull, Wadſworth. 16.

NOES. *Meſſrs.* Baldwin, Bland, Boudinot, Burke, Cadwallader, Coles, Contee, Fitzſimons, Floyd, Gerry, Heiſter, Jackſon, Leonard, Livermore, Matthews, Moore, Muhlenberg, Van Ranſellaer, Schureman, Scott, Seney, Sinnickſon, Sumpter, Tucker, White. 25.

A report from the committee of conferrence on the diſagreement between the two Houſes, reſpecting the firſt amendment to the bill for regulating proceſſes in the courts of the United States, ſtating that they had come to no agreement, was received.

This bill was further amended by the Senate, and agreed to by the Houſe.

The committee to examine the enrolled bills, brought in a number which they had examined and found correct, to which the Speaker affixed his ſignature.

A meſſage was received from the Senate by their Secretary, informing the Houſe, that they had come to a reſolution, to defer the conſideration of the laſt amendment of the Houſe to the bill for eſtabliſhing the permanent ſeat of the Federal Government, to the next ſeſſion of Congreſs. *Adjourned.*

TUESDAY, SEPTEMBER 29.

A meſſage was received from the Preſident of the United States, by the Hon. Mr. JAY, with the following communications, viz.

UNITED STATES, SEPTEMBER 29, 1789.

Gentlemen of the Houſe of Repreſentatives.

His Moſt Chriſtian Majeſty, by a letter dated the 7th of June laſt, addreſſed to the Preſident and Members of the General Congreſs of the United States of North America, announces the much lamented death of his ſon the Dauphin. The generous conduct of the French Monarch and nation towards this country, renders every event that may affect his or their proſperity intereſting to us; and I ſhall take care to aſſure him of the ſenſibility with which the United States participate in the affliction which a loſs ſo much to be regretted, muſt have occaſioned both to him and to them. G. WASHINGTON.

United States, Sept. 29, 1789.

Gentlemen of the Houſe of Repreſentatives,

Having Yeſterday been informed by a joint committee of both Houſes of Congreſs, that they had agreed to a receſs to commence this day, and to continue until the firſt Monday in January next, I take the earlieſt opportunity of acquainting you, that conſidering how long and laborious this ſeſſion has been, and the reaſons which I preſume have produced this reſolution, it does not appear to me expedient to recommend any meaſures to their conſideration at preſent. G. WASHINGTON.

A meſſage was received from the Preſident of the United States, by Mr. Secretary LEAR, with four Acts of the Legiſlature, which have received the approbation and ſignature of the Preſident.

Mr. GERRY introduced a reſolution to the following purport, That it ſhall be the duty of the Clerk of the Houſe, and Secretary of the Senate, to tranſmit an atteſted copy of the Journals of each Houſe, to the Supreme Executive, and to each branch of the Legiſlature of the ſeveral States, reſpectively. This was adopted, and ſent to the Senate for their concurrence.

A meſſage was received from the Senate, informing, that they concur in the above reſolution.—Alſo, the bill to eſtabliſh troops, &c. for the defence of the frontiers, was ſent down by their Secretary—the Senate inſiſting on their ſeventh amendment to ſaid bill. Alſo the reſolution on the memorial of JOHN WHITE, concurred in, with amendments, which amendments were acceded to by the Houſe. The Senate alſo ſent down an act which they had paſſed in favor of the Baron de GLAUBECK.

The Houſe then took up the above ſeventh Amendment, and on motion to adhere to the original ſections, the queſtion being put was negatived.

The queſtion for concurring with the Senate was then carried in the affirmative, by a large majority.

The Houſe then paſſed the bill in form, for allowing the pay of a Captain for a certain time, to Baron de Glaubeck: which being enrolled, was ſigned by the Speaker. The buſineſs aſſigned for the preſent ſeſſion being finiſhed, the Speaker, purſuant to Reſolution, adjourned the Houſe to the firſt Monday in January next, then to meet at the city of New-York.

[The above, cloſes our account of the proceedings of the firſt Seſſion of Congreſs, under the New Conſtitution. We have aimed to be impartial and accurate—and as particular as our limits would admit. If the avidity with which the ſketches have been received and read, is not indicative of their intrinſic merit, it conveys theſe ideas very forcibly, that the Conſtitution is an object of prime conſequence, and that the tranſactions of the General Government are conſidered as highly intereſting to the good people of this confederated Republic. The original publication of theſe ſketches in the newſpapers of this city, has proved a fountain of information, to every part of the Union: The ſtreams conveyed through the medium of the innumerable channels of Intelligence, with which theſe riſing States are ſo highly favored, have ſerved to give the government a more realized exiſtence, by bringing it home to the door of every citizen. This method of laying open to the full view of the people the proceedings of their political Fathers, is productive of the happieſt effects: It prevents innumerable impoſitions ariſing from miſrepreſentation and falſehood; it unfolds principles, and exhibits characters in a juſt point of light; the people learn to know whom to truſt, and to give honor to whom honor is due. May the Freedom of the Preſs always be juſtly prized, and ſacredly preſerved by the free citizens of the United States.]

NEW-YORK, SEPTEMBER 30.

The PRESIDENT of the United States has been pleaſed to nominate, and by and with the advice and conſent of the Senate, to appoint,

JOHN JAY, of New-York, CHIEF JUSTICE.

JOHN RUTLEDGE, of South-Carolina,
JAMES WILSON, of Pennſylvania,
WILLIAM CUSHING, of Maſſachuſetts, } Aſſociate Judges.
RORERT, H. HARRISON, of Maryland,
JOHN BLAIR, of Virginia,

Diſtrict of MAINE.

David Sewall, *Judge*—William Lithgow, *Attorney*—Henry Dearbourn, *Marſhal.*

Diſtrict of NEW-HAMPSHIRE, John Sullivan, *Judge*—Samuel Sherburne, jun. *Attorney*—John Parker, *Marſhal.*

Diſtrict of MASSACHUSETTS, John Lowell, *Judge*—Chriſtopher Gore, *Attorney*—Jonathan Jackſon, *Marſhal.*

Diſtrict of CONNECTICUT, Richard Law, *Judge*—Pierpont Edwards, *Attorney*—Philip Bradley, *Marſhal.*

Diſtrict of PENNSYLVANIA, Francis Hopkinſon, *Judge*—William Lewis, *Attorney*—Clement Biddle, *Marſhal.*

Diſtrict of DELAWARE, Gunning Bedford, *Judge*—George Read, jun. *Attorney*—Allan M'Lean, *Marſhal.*

Diſtrict of MARYLAND, Thomas Johnſon, *Judge*—Joſeph Potts,* *Attorney*—Nathaniel Ramſey, *Marſhal.*

Diſtrict of VIRGINIA, Edmund Pendleton, *Judge*—John Marſhall, *Attorney*—Edward Carrington, *Marſhal.*

Diſtrict of SOUTH-CAROLINA, Thomas Pinckney, *Judge*—John Julius Pringle, *Attorney*—Iſaac Huger, *Marſhal.*

Diſtrict of GEORGIA, Nathaniel Pendleton, *Judge*—Matthew M'Alliſter, *Attorney*—Robert Forſyth, *Marſhal.*

Diſtrict of KENTUCKEY, Henry Inneſs *Judge*—George Nicholas, *Attorney*—Samuel M'Dowell, jun. *Marſhal.*

Diſtrict of NEW-YORK, James Duane, *Judge*—Richard Hariſon, *Attorney*—William S. Smith, *Marſhal.*

Diſtrict of NEW-JERSEY, David Brearly, *Judge*—Richard Stockton, *Attorney*—Thomas Lowry, *Marſhal.*

THOMAS JEFFERSON, SECRETARY OF STATE.

EDMUND RANDOLPH, ATTORNEY-GENERAL.

SAMUEL OSGOOD, POSTMASTER-GENERAL,

WILLIAM CARMICHAEL, Eſq. CHARGES DES AFFAIRES from the UNITED STATES to the COURT of SPAIN.

* *Mr.* Potts *was not acted upon, it having been ſuggeſted that there was a miſtake in the Chriſtian name.*

OFFICERS OF THE REGIMENT OF INFANTRY.

LIEUT. COL. COMMANDANT. Joſiah Harmar.

And a Brigadier General by brevet, he having been appointed ſuch by a Reſolve of Congreſs, of the 31ſt of July, 1787.

MAJORS. John Palſgrave Wyllys, John F. Hamtramck.

CAPTAINS. Jonathan Hart, David Zeigler, William McCurdy, John Mereer, David Strong, John Smith, Joſeph Aſhton, Erkuries Beatty.

LIEUTENANTS. John Armſtrong, John Pratt, Ebenezer Frothingham, William Kerſey, Thomas Doyle, William Peters, Jacob Kinſbury, Ebenezer Denny.

ENSIGNS. Francis Luſe, Cornelius Ryker Sedam, Nathan Mc Dowell, Abner Prior, Robert Thompſon, Aſa Hartſhorn, John Jeffers, Jacob Melcher.

SURGEON. Richard Alliſon.

MATES. John Elliot, John Scot, John Carmichael, Joſhua Sumner.

OFFICERS OF THE BATTALION OF ARTILLERY,

MAJOR COMMANDANT. John Doughty.

CAPTAINS. Henry Burbeck. William Ferguſon, Joſeph Savage, James Bradford.

LIEUTENANTS. John Pierce, Moſes Porter, William Moore, Dirck Schuyler, Mahlon Ford, Matthew Erneſt, Edward Spear, Ebenezer Smith Fowle.

SURGEON'S MATE. Nathaniel Heyward.

Extract of a letter from Paris, July 15.

"The Grenadier who ſcaled the outer barrier of the Baſtile yeſterday, has had a laurel crown decreed him: An old officer who was witneſs of his bravery and danger, tore from his own boſom the order of St. Lewis, and gave it to the grenadier in that moment, and ſaid, *take this,* THOU ART MORE DESERVING OF IT THAN I. Decorated with this, and the *Croſs* of the Governor of the garriſon, and the *cordon blue,* he has paſſed the ſtreets and the ſquare of Palais Royal twice—once ſupported by two grenadiers of his own corps (the Guards Francois,) and the next time mounted.—He is an old ſoldier, and bears applauſe like a man of good ſenſe and great fortitude."

By ſome late accounts it appears probable, that the rays of freedom will penetrate thoſe dark receſſes of ignorance and bigotry, the Monaſteries and Nunneries of France: Should this be the caſe, immenſe treaſures, that have for ages been ſhut out from the light of the Sun, will emerge into day.—Many a golden dove, that never moved, will find the uſe of its wings: Many a maſſy image, that has been confined for centuries, will find its legs and walk off—and being melted by the fire of Liberty, which reduces all bodies to a proper level, will diffuſe univerſal joy among the pockets of the people.

How many fair, but wretched victims to a blind zeal, will rejoice in thoſe glorious beams, which ſhall pervade the gloomy regions, where they thought themſelves immured for life! Their hearts will bound with rapture at the muſic of Freedom—and reſtored to Liberty, and the rights of humanity, life will aſſume a new aſpect, when it invites them to enjoy all that they were intended for by the beneficent author of exiſtence.

Extract of a letter from Boſton, dated Sept. 25, 1789.

"Yeſterday the Society of the Cincinnati in this town gave a moſt ſplendid entertainment at Concert-Hall to the Officers of His Moſt Chriſtian Majeſty's ſquadron. The tables formed a ſemi-circle. At the head of the Hall was placed a full length portrait of The Preſident, with the *real* eagle pendant from the *painted* button hole. On his right a diſplayed American Enſign. On his left a French ditto. Over his head was a Star, encircling three *Fleurs de Lis,* with the motto *eſto perpetua,* At the other end of the Hall, the eye was caught with a fine picture of His Moſt Chriſtian Majeſty, with the French Enſign on his right, and the American on his left: Over his head were the arms of France, the motto *Vive Louis XVI.* The Orcheſtra was covered with blue broad cloth, edged with white; the thirteen Stars, and Thirteen Fleurs de Lis formed on the ground a very beautiful Conſtellation: The bald Eagle ſoared from the centre: oppoſite the Eagle, on the other ſide of the room, was the arms of Maſſachuſetts, finely executed. The chandeliers and ſeveral parts of the room were ornamented with flowers, The whole forming as happy a *coup d'œil* as fancy can imagine. The choiceſt viands, the moſt delicate paſtery, and exhilerating wines crowned this feſtive board: happineſs ſat on each countenance, good humor and friendſhip reigned ſupreme: the toaſts were judicious, &c.

"The Active frigate ſailed yeſterday for New-York: She is gone to carry the reſpects of the Chef of the Diviſion, to The Preſident of the United States, the Ambaſſador of France, &c.

LONDON.

SORTIE OF GIBRALTER.——By Mr. *Trumbull.*

Of the merits of this picture there is a general concurrence of opinion. The ſubject is choſen with great judgement: And while the artiſt celebrates the glorious triumph of one nation, he has happily availed himſelf of the gallantry of an individual to palliate the defeat of the other. This is liberal; and the trophy due to courage receives new honors from its being conferred in a rival country.

As a work of art, whether we conſider the compoſition, the drawing, the expreſſion, the effect of light and ſhadow, or the coloring, we do not heſitate to pronounce, that we have ſeen only two productions on this ſcale of the Engliſh ſchool which we think equal to this: The death of Lord Chatham, and the pierſon of Copley, rank highly in our eſteem; but the *Wolfe,* tho in compoſition and deſign very beautiful, bears no proportionate claims to admiration with the picture before us.

Monday morning the Light Horſe, and the other Independent companies in this city, paraded in the Broad Way, under the immediate command of Col. BAUMAN—from whence they proceeded to the Race Ground, where they went thro a number of manœuvres in a manner that would do credit to regular troops; after which they exhibited a ſham fight, that afforded the higheſt entertainment to The Preſident, His Excellency the Governor, and a large concourſe of reſpectable characters.

We cannot but with regret mention one unhappy circumſtance which occured, Adjutant JOHN LOUDON, a moſt amiable and worthy character, in the prime of life, received a wound (as we are informed with a buck ſhot, through the careleſsneſs of one of the men in loading his piece) of which he expired on the field.—By this ſorrowful accident, has his family been deprived of a dutiful ſon, an affectionate brother, and ſociety of a worthy member.

Yeſterday the funeral ſolemnities of Mr. JOHN LOUDON were attended with every mark of public grief, which the truly affecting circumſtances of his death were calculated to inſpire. The Proceſſion was preceeded by two Companies of Light-Infantry, with arms reverſed, and the Holland Lodge of Free Maſons, of which he was a brother: On the pall were laid maſonic and military Inſignia: The diſtreſſed family; the reverend Clergy, and a numerous train of mourning friends followed: The military Band played a ſolemn Dirge, which according with the ſolemn ſenſations of a vaſt croud of citizens aſſembled on the occaſion, added greatly to the ſeriouſly impreſſive ſcene.

When a perſon dies in defence of a juſt cauſe, in the defence of his country or the protection of the rights of mankind, we may apply the expreſſion uſed by the author of CATO,

How beautiful is death when earn'd by virtue;

But when a perſon ſo truly and juſtly eſteemed falls a ſacrifice in a trifling way and on an unneceſſary occaſion, how ghaſtly! how ſhocking! how terrible is death!

ERRATUM.

In No. 47, we mentioned that the Ayes *and* Noes *on the bill for fixing the ſeat of the Government, were called for by Mr.* CARROL*—this is a miſtake—it was Mr.* BOUDINOT *who called for them. Thoſe who have copied the above error are requeſted to inſert this note.*

Gazette of the United-States.

[No. LI.] WEDNESDAY, October 7, 1789. [Publiſhed on Wedneſday and Saturday.]

By THE PRESIDENT
OF THE UNITED STATES OF AMERICA.
A PROCLAMATION.

WHEREAS it is the duty of all nations to acknowlege the Providence for Almighty God, to obey his will, to be grateful to his benefits, and humbly to implore his protection and favor: And whereas both Houſes of Congreſs have, by their joint committee, requeſted me "to recommend to the People of the United States, a Day of public Thankſgiving and Prayer, to be obſerved by acknowledging with grateful hearts the many and ſignal favors of Almighty God, eſpecially by affording them an opportunity peaceably to eſtabliſh a form of government for their ſafety and happineſs."

Now therefore, I do recommend and aſſign Thurſday the twenty-ſixth day of November next, to be devoted by the people of theſe States, to the ſervice of that great and glorious Being, who is the beneficent Author of all the good that was, that is, or that will be: That we may then all unite in rendering unto him our ſincere and humble thanks for his kind care and protection of the people of this country previous to their becoming a nation;—for the ſignal and manifold mercies, and the favorable interpoſitions of his providence in the courſe and concluſion of the late war;—for the great degree of tranquility, union and plenty, which we have ſince enjoyed; for the peaceable and rational manner in which we have been enabled to eſtabliſh Conſtitutions of Government for our ſafety and happineſs, and particularly the national one now lately inſtituted; for the civil and religious Liberty with which we are bleſſed, and the means we have of acquiring and diffuſing uſeful knowledge;—and in general, for all the great and various favors which he hath been pleaſed to confer upon us.

And also, That we may then unite in moſt humbly offering our prayers and ſupplications to the great Lord and Ruler of Nations, and beſeech him to pardon our national and other tranſgreſſions;—to enable us all, whether in public or private ſtations, to perform our ſeveral and relative duties properly and punctually;—to render our national government a bleſſing to all the people, by conſtantly being a government of wiſe, juſt and conſtitutional laws, diſcreetly and faithfully executed and obeyed;—to protect and guide all ſovereigns and nations, (eſpecially ſuch as have ſhewn kindneſs unto us) and to bleſs them with good government, peace and concord;—to promote the knowledge and practice of true religion and virtue, and the encreaſe of ſcience among them and us;—and generally, to grant unto all mankind ſuch a degree of temporal proſperity as he alone knows to be beſt.

GIVEN under my Hand, at the city of New-York, the third day of October, in the Year of our Lord one thouſand ſeven hundred and eighty-nine.

G. WASHINGTON.

By the PRESIDENT
OF THE UNITED STATES OF AMERICA.
A PROCLAMATION.

WHEREAS by virtue of powers given by the United States in Congreſs aſſembled, to Arthur St. Clair, Governor of the territory north-weſt of the Ohio, and Commiſſioner Plenipotentiary for treating with the Indian nations in the northern department, a Treaty was concluded at Fort-Harmar, on the ninth day of January laſt paſt, by the ſaid Arthur St. Clair, on the part of the United States, with the Sachems, Chiefs and Warriors of the Wyandot, Delaware, Ottawa, Chippawa, Pattiwatima and Sac Nations.

And whereas I have, by and with the advice and conſent of the Senate, in due form ratified the ſaid Treaty.—NOW Therefore, to the end that the ſame may be obſerved and performed with good faith on the part of the United States, I have ordered the ſaid Treaty to be herewith publiſhed; and I do hereby enjoin and require all Officers of the United States, civil and military, and all other citizens and inhabitants thereof, faithfully to obſerve and fulfil the ſame.

GIVEN under my Hand in the city of New-York, this twenty-ninth day of September, in the Year of our Lord one thouſand ſeven hundred and eighty-nine, and in the thirteenth year of the Sovereignty and Independence of the United States.

G. WASHINGTON.

By command of the Preſident of the United States of America,
H. KNOX,
Secretary for the Department of War.

GEORGE WASHINGTON, *Preſident of the United States of America.*

TO ALL TO WHOM THESE PRESENTS SHALL COME, GREETING:

WHEREAS a Treaty between the United States and the Wyandot, Delaware, Ottawa Chippewa, Pattawatima and Sac Nations of Indians, was in due form made and concluded at Fort-Harmar, on the ninth day of January laſt paſt, by Arthur St. Clair, Governor of the territory north-weſt of the Ohio; who was duly authorized thereto by the ſaid States on their part, and by the Sachems and Warriors of the ſaid Nations on their part: Which Treaty is in the form and words following, *viz.*

ARTICLES of a Treaty made at Fort-Harmar, between Arthur St. Clair, *Governor of the Territory of the Uuited States north-weſt of the river Ohio, and Commiſſioner Plenipotentiary of the United States of America; for removing all cauſes of controverſy, regulating trade, and ſettling boundaries, with the Indian nations in the northern department, of the one part; and the Sachems and Warriors of the Wyandot, Delaware, Ottawa, Chippewa, Pattawatima and Sac Nations, on the other part.*

Article I. WHEREAS the United States in Congreſs aſſembled, did by their Commiſſioners George Rogers Clark, Richard Butler, and Arthur Lee, Eſquires, duly appointed for that purpoſe; at a Treaty holden with the Wyandot, Delaware, Ottawa and Chippewa Nations, at Fort-M'Intoſh, on the twenty-firſt day of January, in the year of our Lord one thouſand ſeven hundred and eighty-five, conclude a peace with the Wyandots, Delawares, Ottawas and Chippewas, and take them into their friendſhip and protection: And whereas at the ſaid Treaty it was ſtipulated that all priſoners that had been made by their nations, or either of them, ſhould be delivered up to the United States: And whereas the ſaid Nations, have now agreed to and with the aforeſaid Arthur St. Clair, to renew and confirm all the engagements they had made with the United States of America, at the before mentioned treaty, except ſo far as are altered by theſe preſents. And there are now in the poſſeſſion of ſome individuals of theſe Nations, certain priſoners, who have been taken by others not in peace with the ſaid United States, or in violation of the treaties ſubſiſting between the United States and them; the ſaid nations agree to deliver up all the priſoners now in their hands (by what means ſoever they may have come into their poſſeſſion) to the ſaid Governor St. Clair, at Fort Harmar, or in his abſence to the officer commanding there, as ſoon as conveniently may be; and for the true performance of this agreement they do now agree to deliver into his hands two perſons of the Wyandot Nation, to be retained in the hands of the United States as hoſtages until the ſaid priſoners are reſtored; after which they ſhall be ſent back to their Nation.

Article II. And whereas at the before mentioned treaty it was agreed between the United States and ſaid Nations, that a boundary line ſhould be fixed between the lands of thoſe Nations and the territory of the United States; which boundary is as follows, *viz.*—Beginning at the mouth of Cayahoga river, and running thence up the ſaid river to the portage between that and the Tuſcarawa branch of Muſkingum, then down the ſaid branch to the forks at the croſſing-place above Fort-Lawrence, thence weſterly to the portage on that branch of the big Miama river which runs into the Ohio, (at the mouth of which branch the fort ſtood which was taken by the French in the year of our Lord one thouſand ſeven hundred and fifty-two,) then along the ſaid portage to the Great Miami or Omie river, and down the ſouth-eaſt ſide of the ſame to its mouth; thence along the ſouthern ſhore of Lake Erie to the mouth of Cayahoga, where it began. And the ſaid Wyandot, Delaware, Ottawa and Chippewa Nations, for and in conſideration of the peace then granted to them by the ſaid United States, and the preſents they then received, as well as of a quantity of goods to the value of ſix thouſand dollars, now delivered unto them by the ſaid Arthur St. Clair, (the receipt whereof they do hereby acknowledge) do by theſe preſents renew and confirm the ſaid boundary line; to the end that the ſame may remain as a diviſion line between the lands of the United States of America, and the lands of ſaid Nations, for ever. And the underſigned Indians do hereby in their own names, and the names of their reſpective Nations and Tribes, their heirs and deſcendants, for the conſideration above mentioned, releaſe, quit-claim, relinquiſh and cede to the ſaid United States, all the land eaſt, ſouth and weſt of the lines above deſcribed, ſo far as the ſaid Indians formerly claimed the ſame; for them the ſaid United States to have and to hold the ſame in true and abſolute propriety for ever.

Article III. The United States of America do by theſe preſents relinquiſh and quit claim to the ſaid Nations reſpectively, all the lands lying between the limits above deſcribed, for them the ſaid Indians to live and hunt upon, and otherwiſe to occupy as they ſhall ſee fit: But the ſaid Nations, or either of them, ſhall not be at liberty to ſell or diſpoſe of the ſame, or any part thereof, to any ſovereign power except the United States; nor to the ſubjects or citizens of any other ſovereign power, nor to the ſubjects or citizens of the United States.

Article IV. It is agreed between the ſaid United States and the ſaid Nations, that the individuals of the ſaid Nations ſhall be at liberty to hunt within the territory ceded to the United States, without hindrance or moleſtation, ſo long as they demean themſelves peaceably and offer no injury or annoyance to any of the ſubjects or citizens of the ſaid United States.

Article V. It is agreed that if any Indian or Indians of the Nations before mentioned, ſhall commit a murder or robbery on any of the citizens of the United States, the Nation or tribe to which the offender belongs, on complaint being made, ſhall deliver up the perſon or perſons complained of, at the neareſt poſt of the United States; to the end that he or they may be tried, and if found guilty, puniſhed according to the laws eſtabliſhed in the territory of the United States north-weſt of the river Ohio, for the puniſhment of ſuch offences, if the ſame ſhall have been committed within the ſaid territory; or according to the laws of the State where the offence may have been committed, if the ſame has happened in any of the United States. In like manner if any ſubject or citizen of the United States ſhall commit murder or robbery on any Indian or Indians of the ſaid Nations, upon complaint being made thereof, he or they ſhall be arreſted, tried and puniſhed agreeable to the laws of the State or of the territory wherein the offence was committed; that nothing may interrupt the peace and harmony now eſtabliſhed betwen the United States and ſaid Nations.

Article VI. And whereas the practice of ſtealing horſes has prevailed very much, to the great diſquiet of the citizens of the United States, and if perſiſted in can not fail to involve both the United States of America and the Indians in endleſs animoſity, it is agreed that it ſhall be put an entire ſtop to on both ſides; nevertheleſs, ſhould ſome individuals in defiance of this agreement, and of the laws provided againſt ſuch offences, continue to make depredations of that nature, the perſon convicted thereof ſhall be puniſhed with the utmoſt ſeverity the laws of the reſpective States, or territory of the United States north-weſt of the Ohio, where the offence may have been committed will admit of: And all horſes ſo ſtolen, either by the Indians from the citizens or ſubjects of the United States, or by the citizens or ſubjects of the United States from any of the Indian Nations, may be reclaimed, into whoſe poſſeſſion ſoever they may have paſſed, and upon due proof ſhall be reſtored; any ſales in Market Ouvert, notwithſtanding. And the civil magiſtrates in the United States reſpectively, and in the territory of the United States north-weſt of the Ohio, ſhall give all neceſſary aid and protection to Indians claiming ſuch ſtolen horſes.

Article VII. Trade ſhall be opened with the ſaid Nations, and they do hereby reſpectively engage to afford protection to the perſons and

Gazette of the United States.

[No. LXXVIII.] SATURDAY JANUARY 9, 1790. [Publiſhed on Wedneſday and Saturday.]

NEW-YORK, JANUARY 9, 1789.

CONGRESS.

JANUARY 6.

IN addition to the Members of Senate, mentioned in our laſt, Mr. Maclay, of Pennſylvania, being arrived, a quorum of the Senate was formed. A ſufficient number of the Members of the Houſe of Repreſentatives, were alſo in town; but through the indiſpoſition of one of the gentlemen, they did not proceed to buſineſs, and adjourned.

JANUARY 7.

Mr. Ellſworth, and Mr. Patterſon, of the Senate, arrived and took their ſeats.

HOUSE OF REPRESENTATIVES.

Mr. Wadſworth, Mr. Sturgis, Mr. Van Ranſellaer, Mr. Carrol, and Mr. Matthews, appeared and took their ſeats.

A meſſage was ſent to rhe Senate, informing them that a quorum of the Houſe was now aſſembled.

Mr. Boudinot, Mr. Sherman, and Mr. White, were appointed a committee to report the unfiniſhed buſineſs of the laſt ſeſſion.

A reſolution was received from the Senate, by which Mr. Strong and Mr. Izard is appointed a committee on their part, to wait on, and inform the Preſident of the United States, that the two Houſes of Congreſs are now formed, and requeſt to know of him, what time he will aſſign to meet them in the Senate Chamber, to lay before them the buſineſs he has to communicate. The Houſe concurred in this reſolution, and appointed Mr. Gilman, Mr. Ames, and Mr. Seney, a Committee on their part.

On motion, Reſolved, that two Chaplains of different denominations, be elected for the preſent ſeſſion—one by each Houſe, to interchange weekly.

Mr. Gilman of the committee appointed to wait on the Preſident informed the houſe that the Preſident had aſſigned To-Morrow, 11 o'clock to meet, and addreſs both Houſes of Congreſs, in the Senate Chamber. Adjourned to half after 10 o'clock, to-morrow morning.

JANUARY 8.

Mr. Wynkoop appeared this day, and took his ſeat.

The Houſe being aſſembled, adjourned to the Senate Chamber. At 11 o'clock, THE PRESIDENT of the United States, attended by his Aids, and Secretary, was received by the two Houſes of Congreſs in the Senate Chamber, when he was pleaſed to make the following SPEECH:

FELLOW-CITIZENS *of the* SENATE, *and* HOUSE *of* REPRESENTATIVES.

I EMBRACE with great ſatisfaction the opportunity, which now preſents itſelf, of congratulating you on the preſent favorable proſpects of our public affairs. The recent acceſſion of the important ſtate of North-Carolina to the Conſtitution of the United States (of which official information has been received)—the riſing credit and reſpectability of our country—the general and increaſing good-will towards the government of the union, and the concord, peace and plenty, with which we are bleſſed, are circumſtances, auſpicious, in an eminent degree to our national proſperity.

In reſuming your conſultations for the general good, you cannot but derive encouragement from the reflection, that the meaſures of the laſt ſeſſion have been as ſatisfactory to your conſtituents, as the novelty and difficulty of the work allowed you to hope.—Still further to realize their expectations, and to ſecure the bleſſings which a gracious Providence has placed within our reach, will in the courſe of the preſent important ſeſſion, call for the cool and deliberate exertion of your patriotiſm, firmneſs, and wiſdom.

Among the many intereſting objects, which will engage your attention, that of providing for the common defence will merit particular regard.—To be prepared for war is one of the moſt effectual means of preſerving peace.

A free people ought not only to be armed but diſciplined; to which end a uniform and well digeſted plan is requiſite: And their ſafety and intereſt require that they ſhould promote ſuch manufactories, as tend to render them independent on others, for eſſential, particularly for military ſupplies.

The proper eſtabliſhment of the troops which may be deemed indiſpenſable, will be entitled to mature conſideration. In the arrangements which may be made reſpecting it, it will be of importance to conciliate the comfortable ſupport of the officers and ſoldiers with a due regard to œconomy.

There was reaſon to hope, that the pacific meaſures adopted with regard to certain hoſtile tribes of Indians, would have relieved the inhabitants of our ſouthern and weſtern frontiers from their depredations. But you will perceive, from the information contained in the papers, which I ſhall direct to be laid before you, (comprehending a communication from the Commonwealth of Virginia) that we ought to be prepared to afford protection to thoſe parts of the Union; and, if neceſſary, to puniſh aggreſſors.

The intereſts of the United States require, that our intercourſe with other nations ſhould be facilitated by ſuch proviſions as will enable me to fulfil my duty in that reſpect, in the manner, which circumſtances may render moſt conducive to the public good: And to this end, that the compenſations to be made to the perſons, who may be employed, ſhould, according to the nature of their appointments, be defined by law; and a competent fund deſignated for defraying the expences incident to the conduct of our foreign affairs.

Various conſiderations alſo render it expedient, that the terms on which foreigners may be admitted to the rights of Citizens, ſhould be ſpeedily aſcertained by a uniform rule of naturaliza

Uniformity in the currency, weights and meaſures of the United States, is an object of great importance, and will, I am perſuaded, be duly attended to.

The advancement of agriculture, commerce, and manufactures, by all proper means, will not, I truſt, need recommendation. But I cannot forbear intimating to you the expediency of giving effectual encouragement as well to the introduction of new and uſeful inventions from abroad, as to the exertions of ſkill and genius in producing them at home; and of facilitating the intercourſe between the diſtant parts of our country by a due attention to the Poſt-Office and Poſt-Roads.

Nor am I leſs perſuaded, that you will agree with me in opinion, that there is nothing, which can better deſerve your patronage, than the promotion of Science and Literature. Knowledge is in every country the ſureſt baſis of public happineſs. In one, in which the meaſures of government receive their impreſſion ſo immediately from the ſenſe of the community, as in our's, it is proportionably eſſential. To the ſecurity of a free Conſtitution it contributes in various ways: By convincing thoſe, who are entruſted with the public adminiſtration, that every valuable end of government is beſt anſwered by the enlightened confidence of the people: And by teaching the people themſelves to know, and to value their own rights; to diſcern and provide againſt invaſions of them; to diſtinguiſh between oppreſſion and the neceſſary exerciſe of lawful authority; between burthens proceeding from a diſregard to their convenience, and thoſe reſulting from the inevitable exigencies of ſociety; to diſcriminate the ſpirit of liberty from that of licentiouſneſs, cheriſhing the firſt, avoiding the laſt, and uniting a ſpeedy, but temperate vigilance againſt encroachments, with an inviolable reſpect to the laws.

Whether this deſirable object will be beſt promoted by affording aids to ſeminaries of learning already eſtabliſhed, by the inſtitution of a national univerſity, or by any other expedients, will be well worthy of a place in the deliberations of the Legiſlature.

Gentlemen of the Houſe of Repreſentatives.

I SAW with peculiar pleaſure, at the cloſe of the laſt ſeſſion, the reſolution entered into by you, expreſſive of your opinion, that an adequate proviſion for the ſupport of the public credit, is a matter of high importance to the national honor and proſperity.—In this ſentiment, I entirely concur.—And to a perfect confidence in your beſt endeavors to deviſe ſuch a proviſion, as will be truly conſiſtent with the end, I add an equal reliance on the chearful co-operation of the other branch of the Legiſlature.—It would be ſuperfluous to ſpecify inducements to a meaſure in which the character and permanent intereſts of the United States are ſo obviouſly and ſo deeply concerned; and which has received ſo explicit a ſanction from your declaration.

Gentlemen of the Senate, and Houſe of Repreſentatives.

I HAVE directed the proper officers to lay before you reſpectively ſuch papers and eſtimates as regard the affairs particularly recommended to your conſideration, and neceſſary to convey to you that information of the ſtate of the union, which it is my duty to afford.

The welfare of our country is the great object to which our cares and efforts ought to be directed.—And I ſhall derive great ſatisfaction from a co-operation with you, in the pleaſing though arduous taſk of enſuring to our fellow citizens the bleſſings, which they have a right to expect, from a free, efficient and equal government.

G. WASHINGTON.

UNITED STATES, *January* 8, 1790.

The Preſident then retired—and the Houſe returned to their own room: When The Preſident's Speech being read by the Clerk, it was voted that the Houſe would to-morrow take the ſame into conſideration in a Committee of the whole on the ſtate of the Union.——On motion, it was voted to proceed to ballot for a Chaplain, when the votes being collected, it appeared, that the Rev. Dr. LYNN was re-elected.

Adjourned till to-morrow, 11 o'clock, A. M.

FROM THE POUGHKEEPSIE JOURNAL.

IN America we have very generally adopted the principle of a balanced legiſlature, and have thereby moſt probably reſcued free government from the violence, inſtability, and eventual tyranny, which have marked their progreſs in every part of the globe.—The report of the committee in the Pennſylvania convention which is now ſitting for the purpoſe of reforming their conſtitution (and which is the only one in the union that centers all legiſlative power in a ſingle houſe) contains a plan which appears to be an improvement even on our own models. Their legiſlature is to conſiſt of a governor, ſenate and aſſembly, with checks on each other, nearly ſimilar to the conſtitution of the United States. But the governor appoints all officers without any council of appointment. This is a real improvement on government in America. When appointments are confined to the executive department excluſively, and that executive is limited to a ſingle perſon, there is leſs room for cabal and intrigue, and much greater reſponſibility of character. The people then can be at no loſs for the perſon on whom to fix their cenſure or applauſe. On the plan of an executive council there may be very exceptionable appointments, and the public not diſcover the efficient cauſe of them. But the more the public eye is concentered on one perſon, the more he feels his reputation at ſtake, aud the greater neceſſity of acting with integrity and firmneſs.—It has been frequently remarked, that popular aſſemblies are apt to diſcover very little ſolicitude for public faith, and that this muſt have ariſen from the idea, that the diſgrace attending ſuch groſs violations of moral juſtice, was ſo weakened by being divided among a large number, as to act with ſcarcely a perceptible influence.

There is another article in the report of the Pennſylvania committee which is without example in the original compact of any people. It is ſaid of Charondas, one of the ancient lawgivers of Italy, in inſtituting laws for the government of Sybaris, that he ordered the ſons of every family to learn to read and write under maſters in the pay of the public: The Pennſylvania convention have imitated a conduct which has conſecrated to immortality the memory of this antient legiſlator: One of the articles which are reported in their plan, requires ſchools to be ſupported in each town at the cheapeſt rate by teachers at the public expence. It is an obvious truth, that a free people owe all their liberties to their information. The eſtabliſhment of public ſchools eſpecially among our eaſtern neighbours, have moſt eſſentially ſerved to diſſeminate among the people of this country a knowledge of their rights, and the means to defend them—and we derive all our governments and character from the ſeeds implanted by thoſe generous inſtitutions. Without very conſiderable information, and unleſs education becomes pretty general, a people cannot elect their rulers with diſcernment, nor will they indeed eaſily find men who are competent for the various duties of public life. I therefore conſider it proper to make the buſineſs of education a part of the ſocial compact. We find from daily experience that people will not do their duty voluntarily. Education, and by it here I mean the more ſimple and uſeful parts of inſtruction both in ſcience and in morals, is moſt unaccountably neglected by the people in general in this State. It is even conjectured that our legiſlature will never conſent to a law making it a duty of each town to ſupport a reſpectable ſchool for fear it would be unpopular, What a pity then it is we have no ſuch article in our conſtitution.

There are ſeveral other very valuable improvements in the plan reported in the Pennſylvania convention; and if it is finally adopted, as it moſt probably will be, their government, from being the moſt unſkilful, will become the moſt complete in the union.

EDENTON, December 20.

By accounts from Fayetteville we learn, that the General Aſſembly have elected the houorable ALEXANDER MARTIN, Eſq. Governor of this ſtate, in the room of his Excellency SAMUEL JOHNSON, Eſq. appointed a Senator to Congreſs of the United States: That Fayetteville was the place for the next ſeſſion of the General Aſſembly, and that the appointment of the other Senator had not been made, as there was not a majority of the Houſes in favor of any perſon.

NEW-YORK, JANUARY 9.

The Preſident of the United States, when he addreſſed the two Houſes of Congreſs yeſterday, was dreſſed in a crow colored ſuit of clothes, of American manufacture: The cloth appeared to be of the fineſt texture—the color of that beautiful changeable hue, remarked in ſhades not quite black. This elegant fabric was from the manufactory in Hartford.

The acceſſion of North-Carolina to the preſent confederation of the ſtates, is an event that gives ſincere pleaſure to the friends of our country; eſpecially as the majority is ſo large and reſpectable—and the joy excited on the occaſion, may be heightened, when the public are aſſured, as they are from the beſt authority, that the minority have diſcovered ſimilar ſentiments to thoſe which have done ſo much honor to the principles of patriotiſm, and good citizenſhip, diſcovered by the minorities in ſome of the other ſtates.

A noble ſpirit of emulation is diſcovering itſelf in the ſeveral ſtates—well endowed colleges, and other ſeminaries of learning are ſpringing up, upon liberal and enlightened plans—medical and other ſocieties are forming to extend the bleſſings of uſeful profeſſions, and extenuate the inevitable miſeries of human life—while the principles of benevolence are exciting the ſons of clemency, and compaſſion to deviſe the moſt feaſible methods to extinguiſh every veſtige of tyranny and ſlavery from off the face of the earth.—Our mechanics and artizans are forming into companies to enable them more effectually to promote their general intereſt.—Our merchants encouraged by the protection of the laws, and a uniform ſyſtem of revenue, are extending their enterprizes to all quarters of the globe—while their patriotic aſſociations ſtrengthen the hands of government, and prevent the honeſt and conſcientious traders from being ſacrificed by the arts of thoſe who would evade the laws.—To crown the whole, the great American Republic appears to realize its eligible ſituation, by giving the moſt indubitable evidence of its growing attachment to that Conſtitution, which with ſo much unanimity they have adopted—and which every day's experience proves was the great *deſideratum* in their late embarraſſed ſituation.

" United here, and realiz'd we ſee,
" LAWS, INDEPENDENCE, LIBERTY!
" The triple cord which binds all faſt,
" Like the golden chain of Jove,
" Combining all below, with all above,
" To make the ſacred Union laſt."

ARRIVALS.—NEW-YORK.

Wedneſday, Sloop Sea Flower, Whiting, Cape Francois, 30 days.
Thurſday, Brig Amelia, Lewis, Cape Francois, 9 days.

☞ *A few copies of The Preſident's SPEECH, on fine paper, may be had at the Office of the Editor.*

AMERICAN MINERVA,

AND THE

NEW-YORK (*Evening*) ADVERTISER.

NIHIL INVITA FACIENDUM MINERVA

Publiſhed (Daily) *by* GEO. BUNCE, & Co. *No.* 64, *Wall-ſtreet, nearly oppoſite the Tontine Coffee-houſe, at Six Dollars per annum.*

VOL. I.] FRIDAY, APRIL 25, 1794. [NUMB. 120.

THIS DAY will be LANDED *from on board the Sloop Polly and Phœbe at Hallett's Wharf, and for Sale by*
JOHN MARLEY, Front-ſtreet
20 hds. Sugar.
5 bls. do.
6 hds. Cocoa.
20 bgs. Cotton.
Who has alſo for Sale,
20 pipes Madeira.
90 quarter caſks Sherry.
10 pipes Liſbon.
20 quarter caſks Liſbon.
60 tierces Rice.
April 15, 1794. dtf.

CAROLINA INDIGO, of firſt quality, in large and ſmall caſks ſuitable for retailing.
16 hds. St. Croix Rum, old crop and high proof.
75 Tierces new Rice, for ſale by
LEFFINGWELL & PIERPONT.
March 29th, 1794. tf.

To be Sold,

AND entered upon the Firſt of May the noted Eſtate called *Johnſon Hall*, lying in the Mohawk Country in the State of New-York, formerly the Eſtate of Sir William Johnſon, containing about ſeven hundred Acres of land which is of the very beſt quality, together with the ſtock, and farming utenſels; the Buildings are large and convenient, and fit for a Gentleman's Seat. The payment will be made eaſy on good ſecurity.

For further particulars, enquire of George Metcalf Eſq. on the Premiſe, of Silas Talbot Eſq. at Philadelphia, of Samuel Ward and Brothers in New-York, or of the Subſcriber in Providence Rhode-Iſland.

JABEZ BOWEN.
March 14, 1794. d2m.

Juſt PUBLISHED,
And now ready for Sale, by
The Thouſand, Groce, Dozen or Single,
(Bound or in Sheets)
By GEORGE BUNCE, & Co.
No. 64, Wall-Street,
A New and Improved Edition of the Firſt Part of

Webſter's Inſtitute

(Printed under the Inſpection of the Author.)

Alſo FOR SALE, at the ſame place, A few ſmall ACCOUNT BOOKS, of 2 and 3 quires each.
New-York, March 25.

MUSEUM *and* WAX-WORK.
At the Exchange, New-York;

THIS beautiful place of public reſort is open every day [Sunday excepted] at 10 o'clock in the morning until one, and from 3 to 5 in the afternoon—And on Tueſday, Thurſday, and Fryday evenings in every week, at half paſt 6 o'clock, and continue open until 9.

Tickets for admiſſion, at two ſhillings for grown perſons and one for children.—Alſo annual tickets not transferable, at one dollar—to be had in the front room oppoſite the door of the Muſeum,

GARDNER BAKER,
Keeper of the Muſeum.

For HAMBURG.

The Brig REBECCA *Richard Brown* maſter, now lying at Schemmerhorn's Wharf, about 180 tons burthen, a ſtaunch faſt ſailing Veſſel, will Sail in a few days, having a great part of her cargo ready to go on board.
For freight or paſſage, apply to
ROBERT BOWNE, or
PETER SCHERMERHORN.
March 17th 1794. tf.

This Day will be Landed, at Jackſon's Wharf.
From the Schooner George, George Burr.
91 Hhds. high proof St. Croix Rum,
10 ditto Sugars. For ſale by
ISAAC RILEY,
Burling Slip.
April 22d, 1794.

For WILMINGTON, (N. C.)

The faſt ſailing Brig
CERES,
Will ſail the 25th inſt.
For Freight or Paſſage apply to DANIEL COTTON, on Crane Wharf, or to the Maſter on Board, at ſaid Wharf.
22d April, 1794.

Sales at Auction,

By A. L. BLEECKER & SONS.
On Thurſday the 15th May next, at the Tontine Coffee Houſe, at 12 o'clock.

THE following tracts of land, in Watkins and Flints purchaſe, in the county of Tioga, ſtate of New-York.

				Acres.
the ſouthweſt quar.	of townſhip no.	2	con.	9424
northweſt	do	do	4	5647
northeaſt	do	do	6	10525
ſouthweſt	do	do	7	9000
ſouthweſt	do	do	8	3950
northweſt	do	do	8	6230
ſoutheaſt	do	do	9	6250
ſoutheaſt	do	do	10	9000
northweſt	do	do	11	10475
				70,521

Theſe lands are rapidly encreaſing in value, large ſettlements are already made in ſeveral of the townſhips: the goodneſs of ſoil, and the advantages in point of ſituation, being ſo well known, renders any further deſcription unneceſſary. A map of the tracts and conditions of ſale may be ſeen at No. 10 Queen-ſtreet.

On Thurſday, the 15th day of May next, at the Tontine Coffee Houſe, preciſely at 1 o'clock, if not previouſly diſpoſed of at private ſale.

Three very beautiful ſituated houſe lots in this city, lying in front of the walk round the battery, and adjoining the new range of building, erected by Mr. Watſon and Mr. Penfield, and making the corner of State and White hall ſtreets, ſaid lots meaſures 27 feet each in front, and about 103 in depth.
April 2.

CARD MANUFACTORY.

ROGERS, CHOATE, & Co.
At their Card Manufactory oppoſite the Hoſpital, have for Sale.

A LARGE quantity of Wool, Cotton, Hatters and Clothiers Cards, which they warrant to be of the beſt quality and will ſell on reaſonable terms.

They alſo make Cards for Carding Machines, agreeable to any directions that may be given.

Orders left at the Manufactory or with Rogers & Woolſey, Queen-Street, will be regularly attended to.
April 1, 1794. d. 2w.

FOR SALE, BY
REUBEN SMITH, & Co.
The cargo of the
SLOOP FAVORITE,
Conſiſting of
Turks Iſl. Salt,
and Five Thouſand Weight
Caro. Indigo.
New-York, Feb. 17, 1794.

Circulating LIBRARY.

J. FELLOWS has lately added between five and ſix Hundred Volumes to his Library; conſiſting of French and Engliſh Novels, Romances and Miſcellaneous works; making in the whole, upwards of 1,000 volumes. Complete Catalogues of which containing the terms of Subſcription may be had gratis, at the Library in Water-Street, No. 131.

Cabinet Litteraire No. 131 Water-ſtreet, entre le Caffe, et King-Street, compoſe de livres Francois et Anglois. On deliverá gratis a ce Cabinet le Catalogue des livres qu'il contient, ainſi que les conditions de l'abonement.

To Country Merchants.

J. FELLOWS has for ſale by the quantity, Walkden's beſt black Ink powder, thick and thin Letter Paper---Walkingame's Tutors Aſſiſtant, being an improvement of the Schoolmaſter's Aſſiſtant---a ſmall abridgement of Cook's voyages---Cheſterfield's Advice to his Son---Leſſons adapted to the comprehenſion of Children, from three to ſix years of age, by the celebrated Mrs. Barbauld---Vicar of Wakefield, a Novel in very great eſteem---A few of the third part of Webſter's Inſtitute, and the laſt edition of his Spelling-Book.
Water-Street, No. 131. eod.

FOR SALE,
224 Tierces of New Rice,
50 Bolts of beſt Ruſſia Duck,
A few Tierces of good London Porter. *Apply to*
JOHN HALSEY,
No. 34, Princeſs Street.
April, 12.

For BALTIMORE,
The BRIG
ANN,
Will ſail the 20th inſtant, lying at Jackſon's Wharf.
For Freight or Paſſage, apply to
ISAAC RILEY,
April 17, 1794. Burling Slip.

FOR SALE,
By T. ALLEN, FRANCIS CHILDS, & Co. & J. FELLOWS, *at their reſpective Bookſtores,*

AN ESSAY ON SLAVERY:

DESIGNED to exhibit in a new point of view, its effects on *morals*, *induſtry*, and the *peace of ſociety*. Some facts and calculations are offered to prove the labor of *freemen* to be much more *productive* than that of *ſlaves*; that countries are rich, powerful and happy in proportion as the laboring people enjoy the fruits of their own labor; and hence the neceſſary concluſion, that ſlavery is *impolitic* as well as *unjuſt*.
PRICE 2s.

To be Sold,

A HOUSE and one acre of Land pleaſantly ſituate in the City of Perth-Amboy. Alſo a Farm conſiſting of Seventy-four acres of excellent Land, on which is an orchard of grafted Fruit-Trees within a mile of the ſame place, commanding a beautiful and extenſive proſpect.

For further particulars, enquire at No. 40 Broad-Street.
New-York, 13th March 1794.

NOTICE.
BOARDING & LODGING,
at BELVIDERE.

ONE Family only can be accommodated (at the delightful and healthy ſituation) with Convenient Rooms and a ſeparate Table, alſo Stabling for Horſes.---Apply at the Houſe to
JOHN AVERY.
New York, April 23, 1794.

Notice.

IN conſequence of the failure of the houſe of John Searle and Co. of this Iſland, the Subſcribers were appointed by the Miniſters of Her moſt faithful Majeſty, to receive and ſettle the debts of the ſaid Concern.---All Perſons therefore, who have any accounts with the ſaid houſe of J. Searle & Co, will pleaſe to forward them to John Abram's Eſq. Vice Conſul in New-York, who will tranſmit the ſame to us here---and ſuch as owe money will pleaſe to make payment thereof without delay.
(Signed) DANIEL HENRY SMITH.
PETER MONDONSA DRUMMOND.
Madeira, 29th Nov. 1793. d2m.

For CHARLESTON,

The Sloop
Harriot,
DAVID OSBORNE, Maſter.
WILL Sail in Six Days, for Freight or Paſſage apply to the Maſter on board, or to
R. SMITH, & Co.
April 23d. Crane Wharf.

Juſt publiſhed, and for ſale by J. Rivington, T. Allen, H Gaine, Berry, Rogers and Berry, F Childs & Co. J. Fellows, and the Printers hereof,

A PAMPHLET,
—CONTAINING—

R*EMARKS on the Revolution in France, the means by which it has been effected and its probable effects; with an application of the ſubject to the ſituation of America.* Price 25 cents.

Juſt Publiſhed, and for Sale,
By GEORGE BUNCE, & Co. No. 37, *Wall-ſtreet, nearly oppoſite the Tontine Coffee-houſe,*

The Prompter;

A COMMENTARY on COMMON SAYINGS and SUBJECTS, which are full of COMMON SENSE, the beſt ſenſe in the world.

THIS little book is written in a ſtile altogether novel, and is adapted to all capacities, as well as to all claſſes of people, merchants, mechanics and farmers. Such a reputation has this work acquired, that it has paſſed thro three impreſſions in the eaſtern ſtates, and many houſeholders deem it ſo uſeful as to purchaſe a copy for every adult in their families. —PRICE 2s.

BY order of the Hon. John Sloſs Hobart Eſq. one of the Juſtices of the ſupreme Court of Judicature of the State of New-York; Notice is hereby given to Joſeph Sacket of the State of Connecticut Mariner, that upon application by a Creditor of the ſaid Joſeph Sacket, and due proof made to the ſaid Juſtice purſuant to the Act, in ſuch caſe made and provided, he hath directed all the real and perſonal Eſtate of the ſaid Joſeph Sacket within the city and county of New-York, to be ſeized, and that unleſs the ſaid Joſeph Sacket ſhall diſcharge his Debts within one year from the publication of this notice, all his Eſtate real and perſonal will be ſold for the ſatisfaction of his debts.
Dated the 24th day of April, 1794.

PROPOSALS
For *Printing* by Subſcription,

A Poem,

ENTITLED

Greenfield-Hill.

BY TIMOTHY DWIGHT, D.D.

In *Seven Parts, viz.*

I. The Proſpect.
II. The Flouriſhing Village,
III. The Burning of Fairfield,
IV. The Deſtruction of the Pequods,
V. The Clergyman's Advice to the Villagers.
VI. The Farmer's Advice to the Villagers.
VII. The Viſion; or, Proſpect of the Future Happineſs of this Country.

IN the Pariſh of Greenfield is an eminence, called Greenfield-Hill; on which the writer of this Poem is ſuppoſed to ſtand. In this ſituation are ſucceſſively preſented to his eye a beautiful landſcape, the flouriſhing condition of the ſurrounding inhabitants, the town of Fairfield burned by the Britiſh not long before the Poem was begun, and the field in which the Pequod nation was finally deſtroyed.--These objects furniſhed the materials for the four firſt parts of the work.

As the writer is the Miniſter of Greenfield, and a well wiſher to its inhabitants, the ſubjects of the two ſucceeding parts very naturally aroſe in his mind; and to an American Poet thoſe of the laſt part would readily offer themſelves, on almoſt any occaſion.

A primary intention of the whole work is to engage the readers attention to ſeveral of the moſt important intereſts of mankind, and eſpecially to the ſtate of ſociety in this country.

CONDITIONS.

The work, comprized within 150 or 160 pages Octavo, will be printed on fine paper, and with a handſome type, and delivered to the ſubſcribers, ſewed in blue paper, for half a dollar; the uſual allowance being made to ſuch as ſubſcribe for a conſiderable number.

The writer of this poem is alſo employed in preparing for the preſs, a diſcourſe on the genuineneſs and authenticity of the New Teſtament; preached at New-Haven, September 11, 1793, by appointment of the General Aſſociation of Connecticut; which he offers to the public, with the following

CONDITIONS.

That it will be delivered to ſubſcribers, printed and ſewed as above, for one ſixth of a dollar, and will contain about 60 pages Octavo.

Subſcriptions received at this Office.

Webſters Inſtitute

2d & 3d PARTS,
For Sale by the Printers hereof.
15th April, 1794.

THE

MUSICAL MAGAZINE,

BY

ANDREW LAW.

Continued by Subſcription.

THE Muſical Magazine is to be a principal diviſion of a much larger work. It is to form the Third Part of the Author's Art of Singing; a work, part of which is already publiſhed, and the remainder in preparation for the preſs. The deſign, therefore, of the Magazine will beſt be underſtood by a ſummary deſcription of the whole work to which it belongs. The Art of Singing is to conſiſt of Three Parts: The Muſical Primmer; a Book, which contains a new reviſion of the Rules of Vocal Muſic, together with a number of Leſſons and Plain Tunes, deſigned expreſsly for the uſe of Learners. Secondly, The Chriſtian Harmony, in 2 vol.; this is to contain a ſelect variety of Pſalm and Hymn Tunnes, with a number of Airs and Anthems, calculated to ſupply Schools of Muſic, and Chriſtian Churches. And thirdly, The Muſical Magazine; which is the only part of the Work that is to be publiſhed by ſubſcription. The Magazine is to compriſe an additional publication of Favourite Pieces, Airs, and Anthems, and is deſigned for all ſuch as wiſh to furniſh themſelves with a variety of the moſt approved European and American compoſitions.

The Two Firſt Numbers are already compleated: with theſe, ſubſcribers may, therefore, be furniſhed immediately, by applying to the Bookſellers. In the courſe of the year, 1794, the Third Number will alſo be finiſhed; after which, the Numbers will follow each other, not oftener than twice in a year.

CONDITIONS.

THE Numbers will contain from 20 to 24 pages. Bookſellers, in various parts of the United States, to whom ſubſcription papers are returnable, will, from time to time, receive the numbers for delivery; and, each Number will be ſet, to ſubſcribers, at one ſixth of a Dollar. Thoſe who ſubſcribe for ſix Setts, will be entitled to a ſeventh gratis, and the common allowance will be made to Bookſellers, and other Gentlemen, who ſubſcribe for larger quantities. Subſcribers to receive their numbers at thoſe places, where the particular papers, to which they ſubſcribe, are returnable, unleſs they give ſpecial directions to the contrary.——N. B. Gentlemen, who take ſubſcription papers, are requeſted to return them by the firſt day of November, 1794; or ſooner, provided the probable ſubſcriptions be ſooner cloſed.

Subſcriptions taken in by the printers hereof, and by moſt of the Bookſellers and Printers in this City.

WHEREAS John Webbers of the city of New-York, Waterman, being indebted to John Somarindycke of the ſaid city, Grocer, deceaſed, by bond bearing date the tenth day of June, in the year one thouſand ſeven hundred and eighty-nine, in the penal ſum of five hundred and ſixteen pounds, conditioned for the payment of two hundred and forty-eight pounds, on or before the tenth day of June, then next enſuing the date thereof, the ſaid John Webbers with his wife Sarah, and on the ſaid tenth day of June, in the year one thouſand ſeven hundred and eighty-nine, for the purpoſe of ſecuring the payment thereof, mortgage to the ſaid John Somarindycke, all that certain lot, piece, or parcel of ground, ſituate in the outward of the city of New-York, on the eaſt ſide of Bloomingdale road, containing ſix acres, and one hundred and fifty-four rods, bounded as follows: Beginning at a ſtake and heap of ſtones, on the eaſt ſide of the ſaid road about half a rod, north of the fence made between the land of the late Arnout, deceaſed, and the land intended to be granted, and from thence running ſouth ſixty-two and half degrees, eaſt by the north bounds of the ſaid Arnout Webbers, land ſixty rods, to a ſtake and ſtones in the weſt bounds of the corporation lands ſo called, and from thence north thirty-four degrees, eaſt by the ſaid corporation lands fifteen rods, to a ſtake and heap of ſtones, thence north ſixty-one, eaſt ſixty-eight rods to a ſtake and heap of ſtones, on the eaſt ſide of the ſaid road, thence weſt twenty, ſouth eighteen rods to the place of beginning.—With a power in the ſaid mortgage contained, that if the ſaid money mentioned in the condition of the ſaid bond ſhould not be paid, when the ſame became due, that it ſhould be lawful for the ſaid John Somarindycke, his heirs, executors, adminiſtrators or aſſigns, to ſell the ſaid premiſes at public vendue, which ſale ſhould be an entire bar in law and equity againſt the ſaid John Webbers and Sarah his wife, their heirs, executors, adminiſtrators and aſſigns.

And whereas the ſaid ſum mentioned in the condition of the ſaid bond, with the intereſt is ſtill unpaid, Notice is therefore hereby given, that by virtue of the ſaid power in the ſaid mortgage, and purſuant to the act, entitled "an act, to prevent frauds by mortgages, and for ſecuring the purchaſers of mortgaged eſtates," paſſed the 26th of Feb. 1788: the ſaid premiſes will be ſold at the Tontine Coffee-Houſe in the city of New-York, on the firſt day of Auguſt next, at twelve o'clock in the forenoon of ſame day.

Dated this 20th day of January, 1794.

SARAH SOMARINDYCKE,
Adminiſtratrix of John Somarindycke dec.

January 20. 6m m.

Imported in the ſhip Draper, Mark Collins, maſter, from Dublin, by

BERRY, ROGERS & BERRY,

No. 35, Hanover-ſquare,

A LARGE AND VALUABLE

COLLECTION OF BOOKS,

Among which are,

The following eſteemed COPIES:

(All well bound, and of the beſt Editions—which will be ſold to the *Trade*, at the reduced price of 15 per cent. diſcount, from the Dublin retail price, and 10 per cent. diſcount to the public.) viz.

THE works of S. Johnſon, L.L.D. complete, in 6 vols. 8vo. with an eſſay on his life and genius, by Arthur Murphy, Eſq.

The hiſtory of Hindoſtan, by Alex. Dow, Eſq. 3 vols. 8vo. with plates.

Reynolds' hiſtory of the Eaſt-Indies and America, with maps and fine engravings.

Gibbons' hiſtory of the Roman Empire, 6 vols. 8vo. maps.

Hume's hiſtory of England, 8 vols. royal 8vo. beſt edition.

Late King of Pruſſia's hiſtorical works, 4 vols. 8vo.

Chambers' dictionary of arts and ſciences, 5 vols. folio, plates bound ſeparate.

Tales of the caſtle, by Mad. Genlis, 4 vols. 12mo.

Smith's wealth of nations, 2 v. 8vo.

Blair's lectures, on the Bells Le Nus, 2 vols. 8vo.

Cullen's Materia Medica, 2 vol. 8vo.

Bruce's Travels, 6 vols 8vo.

The right hon. Edmund Burke's works, 3 vols. 8vo. complete.

Wilſon's account of the Pelew Iſlands 17 engravings.

Reeves' hiſtory of the Engliſh law, 4 vols. 8vo

Comyns' digeſt of the law, a new edition, continued to the preſent time by Kyd, 6 vols. 8vo.

Bacon's abridgement of the law, 5 vols. royal 8vo. a new edition, with additions.

Wilſon's reports, 3 vols. royal 8vo.

Durnford & Eaſt's laſt reports, 4 vols. 8vo.

Burrow's reports, 5 vols. 8vo.

Croke's reports, royal 8vo.

Blackſtone's reports, 2 vols. 8vo.

Vattel's law of nations, 8vo.

Sheppard's touchſtone of common aſſurance.

BESIDES the above BOOKS, there is a number of other valuable copies expected every day, the whole of which would be worthy the attention of the Bookſellers of Philadelphia, Boſton, Baltimore, &c. December 20.

TO THE PUBLIC.

ONE ſtep is now made in improving this paper, an enlargement of the ſize. Various conſiderations concurred to render this ſtep neceſſary, and we preſume, our cuſtomers will be pleaſed with it. Further advances will be made, as ſoon as new letter arrives; and it depends on the encouragement given it by the public. to make the final improvement; which will be to print it on a *fine* paper.

Expected correſpondences wil ſoon enable us to make the Minerva more intereſting, either as a city or a country paper. In original matter, and candid diſcuſſion of public affairs, we truſt it has already an advantage over ſome papers. Empty declamation has rarely, if ever, found a place in it; and nothing will be admitted to offend a chaſte ear. It is our deſire that every thing inſerted in the Minerva may be *worth reading*.

In our Wedneſday's paper, there will be, as heretofore, a ſummary account of the moſt material occurrences, for country Subſcribers. But if any perſons chooſe to take more papers, than one, in a week, they may have what number they like.

As this paper circulates very extenſively, it will be found uſeful as an advertiſing paper; and as the ſize now affords room for more matter, a few more advertiſements will be acceptable.

The price of the daily paper is Six Dollars a year. Of the Wedneſday's paper 14ſ.

All Newſ-papers and other communications for the publiſhers, it is deſired, may be addreſſed to the firm of George Bunce & Co. All eſſays deſigned for inſertion, to the Editor, Noah Webſter Jun.

ADVERTISEMENT.

PUBLIC NOTICE is hereby given that on the thirteenth day of September next, at eleven o'clock in the forenoon at the Tontine Coffee-Houſe in the city of New York, will be ſold by the ſubſcriber at Public Auction, a tract of land ſituate in the town of Warwick, (formerly a part of the precinct of Goſhen) in the county of Orange and ſtate of New-York, which on the thirtieth day of May, one thouſand ſeven hundred and ſeventy-ſeven, was deſcribed as follows, to wit, All that tract of land ſituate in the ſaid Precinct of Goſhen, being part of a tract of land conveyed from the heirs of Lankaſter Syms to William Holly, beginning in the middle of the highway in the ſouth-eaſt line of the lands of Benjamin Davis, he purchaſed of ſaid William Holly, and the corner between ſaid Noah Holly and James Wright, and runs from thence along ſaid Daviſs' lands, ſouth fifty-ſix degrees weſt, two chains and twenty-ſeven links, and along the ſame ſouth forty-three degrees and thirty minutes weſt ten chains and five links, and along the ſame ſouth twenty-nine degrees weſt nine chains, ſouth fifty-ſeven degrees weſt ſeven chains and forty-ſix links, then ſouth forty-ſix degrees eaſt ſixteen chains and eighty-two links to the lands of Herman Rowley, a ſtake and ſtones; then along the ſame, north ſeventy-ſeven degrees and thirty minutes eaſt thirty-five chains, to two walnut ſaplings and ſtones, then along the lands of James Wright, north forty-ſix degrees weſt thirty-ſix chains and twenty-three links, to the place of beginning, containing ſeventy-five acres one quarter and thirty-eight rods. Being the tract of land which Noah Holly lately purchaſed of the ſaid William Holly.

The ſaid premiſes will be ſold agreeable to the law of the ſaid ſtate in ſuch caſe made and provided, by virtue of a power for that purpoſe contained in a mortgage executed by Noah Holly of the ſaid precinct, and Martha his wife on the thirtieth day of May, one thouſand ſeven hundred and ſeventy-ſeven, to William Wickham, to ſecure to the ſaid William Wickham the payment of one hundred and twenty-one pounds, with intereſt on a day long ſince paſſed, default having been made in the payment thereof.

WILLIAM WICKHAM.

Dated the 4th day of March, 1794. th6m

ADVERTISEMENT.

WHEREAS, WILLIAM CRUIKSHANK of the city of New-York Starch-maker, for ſecuring the payment of one hundred pounds, Current money of the ſtate of New-York, according to the condition of a certain bond or obligation, bearing date the 17th day of November 1792, and executed by the ſaid William Cruikſhank, unto George Hunter of the ſaid city of New-York, did, by Indenture bearing date the ſaid 17th day of Novembes 1792, mortgage to the ſaid George Hunter, for the term of years therein mentioned; all thoſe three certain lots of ground ſituated and being in the ſixth ward of the ſaid city of New-York, and diſtinguiſhed in a certain map made by Francis Marſchalk, late city ſurveyor, by lots No. 655 and 656 fronting Great George Street, and lot No. 659 fronting Heſter Street—which ſaid three lots were, by Indenture bearing date the 29th day of October 1791, leaſed by Nicholas Bayard, Eſq. to the ſaid William Cruikſhank, for the term of twenty-one years from thence next enſuing. And whereas in and by the ſaid Indenture it was covenanted and agreed, that if default ſhould happen to be made in the payment of the ſaid ſum of one hundred pounds, and Intereſt thereof, on the day therein mentioned, that it ſhould and might be lawful to and for the ſaid George Hunter, his Executors, Adminiſtrators, or Aſſigns, at any time after ſuch default made, to grant, bargain, ſell, aſſign and transfer the ſaid three lots of ground and premiſes, at public auction or vendue, agreeable to law, and to give a good conveyance therefor, during the term then unexpired in ſaid leaſe, to the purchaſer or purchaſers thereof, and to retain the ſaid ſum of one hundred pounds, and intereſt, out of the nett proceeds of ſuch ſale, and to return the overplus, if any, to the ſaid William Cruikſhank, his heirs, executors, adminiſtrators, or aſſigns.——And whereas the ſaid mortgage, and the bond therein referred to, have ſince, to wit, on the 16th day of January 1793, been aſſigned and ſet over, for a valuable and full conſideration, by the ſaid George Hunter unto Thomas B. Bridgen, of the ſaid city of New-York, whereby the right to ſue for, recover and receive the ſum of money, mentioned in the ſaid bond, and ſecured by the ſaid mortgage, and in caſe of default in payment thereof the right of ſelling the ſaid premiſes at Public Auction, hath devolved to to the ſaid Thomas B. Bridgen. And whereas the ſaid ſum of money, and the intereſt thereof, are yet unpaid, and are now as aforeſaid due and owing to the ſaid Thomas B. Bridgen.— THIS IS, THEREFORE, to give notice, to the ſaid William Cruikſhank, and all other perſons concerned, that unleſs the ſaid ſum of money, together with the intereſt due thereon as aforeſaid, are paid, diſcharged and ſatisfied on or before the firſt day of Oct. next, all the term of his demiſe herein before mentioned, then unexpired, of all and ſingular the ſaid mortgaged premiſes, will be ſold at Public Vendue, at the Tontine Coffee Houſe, in the city of New-York, on the ſaid firſt day of October next, at eleven o'clock in the forenoon, purſuant to the covenant and agreement in the ſaid Indenture of mortgage contained; and the directions of the Statute in ſuch caſe made and provided.

Dated this 20th day of March, 1794.

THOMAS B. BRIDGEN,
by his Attorney
fr. 6m. CHARLES BRIDGEN.

CAUTION.

THE Public are cautioned againſt purchaſing imperfect editions of *Webſter's Inſtitute; 1ſt Part.*

The genuine impreſſions of this work have, annexed at the end, "A Moral Catechiſm, or Leſſons for Saturday;" an improvement on former editions, and which can be publiſhed only by the true proprietors. The lateſt improved edition is publiſhed and to be ſold by GEORGE BUNCE, & Co. No. 64, Wall-Street, oppoſite the Tontine Coffee Houſe.

AT a Court of Chancery held at the Chancellor's Chambers, in the City of New-York the nineteenth day of March, in the year of our Lord one thouſand ſeven hundred and ninety four.

PRESENT.

The Hon. ROBERT R. LIVINGSTON Eſq. Chancellor.

Jeronimus Alſtyne Jun. and Marianna his wife John Young and Jonathan Pearſee Executrix, and Executors of the laſt will and Teſtament of George Campbell deceaſed. *vs.* WAL. LIVINGSTON.

FORASMUCH as it appears to this Court, that a Bill hath been filed in the above cauſe by Jeronimus Alſtyne Jun. and Marianna his wife, John Young, and Jonathan Pearſee Executrix and Executors of the laſt will and teſtament of George Campbell deceaſed, Complainants againſt Walter Livingſton defendant to obtain a Decree for the ſale of certain Premiſe, in the ſaid Bill mentioned to have been Mortgaged by the ſaid defendant, to the ſaid George Campbell deceaſed in his life time. WHEREUPON proceſs of ſubpœna to appear and anſwer hath been duly iſſued and returned, and the ſaid Defendant hath not entered his appearance in this ſuit, as the ſame ought to have been done according to the rules of this Court, in caſe the ſaid proceſs had been duly ſerved, and an Affidavit having been made to the ſatisfaction of this Court, that the Deponent therein named, had not upon due enquiry been able to find the ſaid Defendant, ſo as to ſerve him with a Subpœna, iſſuing out of, and under the ſeal of this Honourable Court, and that the ſaid Deponent had beeu informed, which information he verily believed to be true that the ſaid Defendant concealed himſelf within this ſtate in order to avoid being ſerved with the proceſs of any Court.

WHEREUPON it is ordered on motion of Mr. Roorbach, Solicitor for the Complainants that the ſaid Defendant appear to the ſaid Bill, on or before the expiration of eight weeks from the publication of this order, and in Default thereof, that the ſaid complainant's Bill be taken pro confeſſo to the end, that a decree may be made for the ſale of the ſaid premiſes, or ſuch part thereof, as to this Court ſhall appear juſt and right, and it is further ordered that a copy of this order within twenty days from the date hereof, be inſerted in at leaſt two of the public newſ-papers printed in the State of New-York, for the ſpace of eight weeks ſucceſſively.

Extract from the minutes.

PETER R. LIVINGSTON, Regr.

New-York, March 22, 1794. m8w.

FOR SALE,

By TH'S. ALLEN, J. FELLOWS, and the Printers hereof,

(PRICE TWELVE SHILINGS)

Webſter's Eſſays

On Moral, Hiſtorical, Political, and Literary ſubjects:

—CONTAINING—

REMARKS on the Education of Youth.

----On Principles of Government and Commerce.

----On Bills and Declarations of Rights.

----On Conſtitutions.

----On the Manners, Debts, &c. of America.

----On the Riſe, Progreſs and Conſequences of the late Revolution, with a hiſtory of the States from the cloſe of the war to the eſtabliſhment of our preſent Conſtitution.

----On the bad policy of Laws regulating the Intereſt of Money.

----On Allegiance, natural and local.

----On ſeveral ſubjects of Hiſtory and Antiquity.

----On diviſions of Property, Government, Education, Religion, Agriculture, Slavery, Commerce, Climate, and Diſeaſes in the United States----with other Miſcellaneous Eſſays.

BY order of the hon. John Sloſs Hobart, Eſquire, one of the juſtices of the ſupreme court of judicature of the ſtate of New-York, *Notice is hereby given*, to HENRY LORD, late of Bedford, in the county of Weſt-Cheſter, and ſtate of New-York, yeoman, but now reſiding in the city of St. John, in the province of New-Brunſwick, within the dominions of the king of Great-Britain, and all others whom it may concern, that upon application and due proof made to the ſaid Judge, purſuant to the act entitled, "An act for relief againſt abſconding and abſent debtors," paſſed the 4th day of April, 1786, he hath iſſued his warrant, directed to the ſheriff of the county of Weſtcheſter, commanding him, to attach, ſeize, take and ſafely keep, all the eſtate, real and perſonal, of the ſaid Henry Lord, an abſent debtor, of what kind or nature ſoever the ſame may be, and in whatever part of his bailiwic, the ſame may be found, with all evidences, books of account, vouchers and papers relating thereto; and that unleſs the ſaid Henry Lord, ſhall return and diſcharge his debts within one year after the publication of this notice, all the ſaid real and perſonal eſtate of him the ſaid Henry Lord, will be ſold, for the payment and ſatisfaction of his creditors. Dated this twenty-fourth day of December, 1793. 1ytu.

PUBLIC Notice is hereby given that on the thirteenth day of September next, at Eleven o'clock in forenoon at the Tontine Coffee Houſe in the city of New-York will be ſold by the Subſcriber at Public Auction; A tract of land ſituated in the Town of Warwick (formerly a part of the precint of Goſhen) in the County of Orange and ſtate of New-York, which on the thirteenth day of May one thouſand ſeven hundred and ſeventy ſeven was deſcribed as follows, to wit. All that tract of Land ſituated in the precinct of Goſhen, being part of a tract of land conveyed from the Heirs of Lankaſter Syms to William Holly, beginning at a ſtake and ſtones on the Weſt ſide of the high-way, and in the line of the Jerſey claim and the Eaſterly corner of a piece of land conveyed from ſaid Holly to Benjamin Davis, and runs from ſaid ſtake South forty-ſix degrees Eaſt forty chains and ſeventy-eight links to a black oak tree, then South ſeventy-two degrees Eaſt along the line that divides Banker's and Clowſes Tracts, five chains, and eighteen links to a ſtake in Buſhy-meadows, the North corner of Clows tract, then South ſeventy-ſeven degrees and thirty minutes, Weſt ſixteen chains and ſixteen links to two Walnut ſaplings and Stones, a corner between the lands of Robert Armſtrong deceaſed, and Henman Rowly, then North forty ſix degrees, Weſt thirty-ſix chains and twenty-three links to the middle of the high-way and the lands of Benjamin Davis, then along the ſame North fifty-ſix degree Eaſt four chains, and twenty-three links, and along the ſame North forty degrees, Eaſt ten chains and ſeventy-two links to the place of beginning, containing ſixty-two acres and forty rods: being the tract of land which James Wright lately purchaſed of the ſaid William Holly.

The ſaid Premiſes will be ſold agreeable to the law of the ſaid State, in ſuch caſe made and provided; By virtue of a power for that purpoſe contained in a mortgage executed by James Wright of the ſaid precinct, and Elizabeth his Wife on the thirtieth day of May one thouſand ſeven hundred and ſeventy ſeven, to William Wickham, to ſecure to the ſaid William Wickham the payment of Seventy-nine Pounds with intereſt on a day long ſince paſt, default having been made in the payment thereof.

Dated the 4th day of March 1794.

WILLIAM WICKHAM. th6m.

WE the ſubſcribers truſtees for the creditors of Jacob Leap an abſent debtor, do hereby requeſt that on the 26th day of May next at twelve o'clock in the forenoon of the ſame day, at the Tontine Coffee Houſe, in the city of New-York; a general meeting may be held of all ſuch creditors of the ſaid Jacob Leap, as ſhall chooſe to attend, to examine and ſee the debts due to each perſon aſcertained; and in order to a diſtribution, or diviſion amongſt the ſaid creditors (in proportion to their reſpective juſt demands) of all ſuch monies as ſhall have come the hands of the ſubſcribers as truſtees of ſuch eſtate or effects.

Dated this twenty firſt day of March, in the year of our Lord one thouſand ſeven hundred and ninety four.

NICH. COOKE,
LEBEUS LEOMIS,
W. LEFFINGWELL.

For ſale by the Printers hereof,

WEBSTER's DISSERTATIONS

ON THE

ENGLISH LANGUAGE.

(*Price Twelve Shillings.*)

New York, Feb. 1794.

THEATRE.

ON FRIDAY EVENING,
The 2d April, 1802, will be presented,
A Dramatic Romance, with Songs, Chorusses, &c.
(Eigth time) called,

BLUE BEARD,
OR, FEMALE CURIOSITY.

Music by Mr. Kelly.
Additional Music and Ochestra Accompaniments by Mr. PELISSIER.
With new Scenery, Machinery. Decorations, and Dresses, &c.

—MEN.—

Abomelique	Mr. TYLER.
Ibrahim	Mr. JEFFERSON.
Selim	Mr. HODGKINSON.
Shacabac	Mr. WILSON.
First Spahi	Mr. FOX.
Second Spahi	Mr. SHAPTER.
Third Spahi	Mr. HALLAM, jun.
Fourth Spahi.	Mr. HOGG.
Hassan	Mr. WILMOT.
First Slave	Mr. MACDONALD.

—WOMEN—

Fatima	Mrs. HODGKINSON.
Irene	Miss BRETT.
Beda	Miss E. A. WESTRAY.

Female Slaves, &c.
Slaves (Male and Female) Spahsi, &c. &c.

IN ACT I,
ABOMELIQUE ON HIS ELEPHANT,
And his Train of Guards, Slaves, Camels, &c. are seen descending.

IN ACT II,
THE ILLUMINATED GARDEN,
A Fountain playing in the middle, and other decorations.
PROCESSION OF SLAVES WITH DANCES.

TO WHICH WILL BE ADDED,
A celebrated Comedy, in two Acts, called,
THREE WEEKS AFTER MARRIAGE.
BOX, 1 Dollar—PIT, ¾—GALLERY, ½ Dollar

TONTINE CITY ASSEMBLY ROOM.

SATURDAY EVENING. 3d April, 1802, Mr. RANNIE will exhibit an entire new set of *Magical Delusions, Balanlances, Ventriloquism, &c.*—Amongst which, he will perform the most astonishing feat of carrying a table with a hundred wine glasses in one hand and a young man with the other, standing all the while upon a slack wire no thicker than the eighth part of an inch.

Admittance one dollar. Children half price.

☞ Doors open at 6, performance commences at 7.

Days of exhibiting, Tuesdays, Thursdays, and Saturdays.

April 2.

TAMMANIAL NOTICE.

THE Members of TAMMANY SOCIETY or COLUMBIAN ORDER, are requested to attend in their Great Wigwam on Monday the fifth day of April instant, one hour after the setting Sun; it being the stated annual meeting for the election of officers for the ensuing year. By order,

Season of Blossoms, year of discovery 310. } E. ROBERTS, Secretary.
April 2.

TO LET,

A FRONT ROOM and CELLAR within a few doors of the Tontine Coffee-house, in Water-street.—Enquire at No. 120 Water-street. April 2.

WANTED AT THIS OFFICE,

A CLERK, who can produce good recommendations for honesty and sobriety. An unmarried man will be preferred. April 2.

A JOURNEYMAN PRINTER,

WILL find employ, if application is made immediately at this office. April 2.

TO PRINTERS.

FOR SALE—A fount of English about 400 wt. also one of Pica about 300; each fount about one third worn, and will be sold low for cash—Apply to

H. C. SOUTHWICK,
April 2. At the Office of the American Citizen.

ARTIFICIAL TEETH.

I. GREENWOOD, DENTIST to the late PRESIDENT WASHINGTON, continues to make and fix Artificial Teeth in the neatest and most durable manner; he cleans and separates the teeth, and likewise performs every operation in the line of a Dentist. His abilities and candor are well known and approved by many of the first people in the United States, as well as foreigners.

N. B. I. GREENWOOD may be consulted at his house, No. 13 Chatham-row, near the play-house, as he does not attend abroad, except it is to relieve pain in difficult cases that comes within the line of his profession; and that he will do gratis, if required. His prices for replacing teeth, &c are moderate, that every person applying for his assistance may be benefited.

April 2. &w.

PORTER & PUNCH HOUSE.

CORs. RAWDON most respectfully informs his friends and the public, that he has taken the house No 63 Stone-street, (one door from the corner of William-street) lately occupied by John Wilkes, Esq. where he will open on the first of May, a PORTER and PUNCH HOUSE. As the apartments are neat and commodious, he can accommodate clubs and parties in a very handsome stile, as it will be his chief study to have always on hand a supply of the best wines, liquors, porter, &c. and with good attendance, he hopes it will be an inducement for gentlemen to resort to his house.

☞ Dinners and suppers for large or small parties—Also beef-steakes and oysters, &c. regularly furnished.

April 2. 2w.

SHERIFF's SALE

BY virtue of a writ of fieri facias to me directed and delivered, I will expose to sale at public auction, on Monday next, the 5th instant, at 10 o'clock, A. M. in Greenwich-street, between Vesey and Barclay-streets, a handsome and general assortment of household and kitchen furniture, in excellent order; consisting of a mahogany sideboard, mahogany bureaus, breakfast, card, and dining tables, mahogany bedsteads, chairs, and knife cases, sophas, fancy chairs, carpets, looking glasses, pictures, feather beds and bedding, bed and window curtains. An assortment of glass ware, china, also an elegant piano forte, Madeira wine, and cherry brandy in bottles, and a great variety of other articles.

JOHN STAGG Jun.
April 2. Sheriff.

SHERIFF's SALE.

BY virtue of several writs of fieri facias to me directed and delivered, will be sold at public auction on the premises, on Friday the seventh day of May next, at twelve o'clock of the same day, all the right, title and interest of William Turner, of, in, and to that certain messuage No. 76, and lot of ground, situate in Pine street, in the second ward of the city of New-York. And on the succeeding day, and at the same hour, will be sold, in like manner, on the premises, all the right, title, and interest of the said William Turner of, in and to that certain lot or piece of ground in the seventh ward of said city, in Crosby street, between William and Grand streets, together with the frame building, &c. thereon erected.

March 26 to May 8 JOHN STAGG, jun. Sheriff.

AT PUBLIC AUCTION,

ON MONDAY the 5th of April next, at No 54 Wall-street, will commence, (and continue from day to day until sold,) the sale of the whole stock in trade, of the late THOMAS GREENLEAF, deceased; consisting of a great variety of Books, Divinity, Law and Physic, History, Biography, Voyages and Travels, Politics and Government, Arts and Sciences, Philosophy, Novels, Poetry and Miscellany, School Books, Geography, Chap Books, Children's Books, Plays, Tragedies, a number of Maps, with a great variety of Pamphlets, &c. &c.

Also, a quantity of scaleboard, &c.

☞ Those persons, who have neglected settling their accounts altho' repeatedly requested, are informed, that this will be the last notice this way; as all accounts unsettled, will, on or before the 1st of May next, be put into the hands of an attorney.

March 30.

FOR SALE,

A NEAT and convenient Two-story House situate in Chapel-street, in the 5th ward of the city of New-York. The lot is in breadth, in front and rear 19 feet 8 inches, and in depth on each side, 75 feet. The house contains 4 fire places, beside a cellar kitchen, a bed room, and store room cieled in the garret; the whole finished in a neat and modern stile—For terms, apply to TUNIS WORTMAN, No. 18 Cortland-street.

N. B. If not previously sold, the above property will be exposed to sale at public auction on Friday the 9th day of April next, at the Tontine Coffee-house. March 30. dtf.

THE CITIZEN.

New-York, Friday, April 2.

We yesterday received the paper from Goshen, in the county of Orange. It contains a well written address to the electors of that county, and concludes with proposing James W. Wilkin, Esq. to fill the seat of that district in congress. The writer pays Mr. Wilkin a very handsome, and we believe, a very just compliment. He says "his character is certainly unblemished, his education liberal, his information extensive, his candour, probity, and republicanism undoubted." It is not for us to offer the most distant hint to the truly enlightened republican citizens of Orange; of persons who, *in our opinion*, ought to represent them in congress. They have the sole right, and they are undoubtedly competent to make their own choice. It is pleasing to see that they do not mean to go out of their county for a representative. We were however permitted to speak on this subject, we would say, in language the most unequivocal, that the citizens of Orange County ought to be represented in congress by a man *firmly attached to the present administration of our federal government*. We mean not to insinuate that a man ought to go hand in hand with the present administration whether right or wrong. We explode this *federal* doctrine. Every administration ought to accord with the constitution, which contains emphatically the expression of the public will. But we contend that even the *first* administration of the illustrious Washington was not *more*, *if as much* entitled to the confidence and support of the republicans as the present one. We behold the executive every day hazarding his own well earned popularity for the public good. We see him uncommonly solicitous to maintain in their purity and pristine vigor the freedom and independence of the Union; to reduce the enormous load of taxes which were wantonly and wickedly laid upon us by the last administration. We see him laudably recommending measures calculated to diminish almost to nothing thousands of useless officers and offices, created like so many satellites to add to the splendor and influence of former executives. Plain, unostentatious; with a vigorous intellect, and a mind stored with the richest gifts of nature; possessed of integrity immaculate; firm even to a proverb, and devoted to the promotion of the liberty and prosperity of our citizens, we have a chief like Epaminondas, ready to sacrifice his life on the altar of public good. Such a man, and such is our executive, is undoubtedly entitled to, and ought to receive the support of every real republican. Hence we repeat, that you, citizens of Orange county, ought to be *particularly careful* to send no man to represent you in congress who is not *honestly* and *warmly* attached to the *present administration*; to the present economical and republican system of things. There is a *peculiar necessity* at this moment for circumspection Your country calls upon you to be attentive to her interests. You are all with *perhaps a few exceptions* well affected to the present administration. You *may* have among you a *few men* more intent upon the promotion of self dishonorable views than the substantial interests of the nation. If you have such men among you avoid them. Let them sink into insignificance. Mr. Wilkin, Mr. M'Cord, and many other of your citizens are entitled to your confidence. They are frank, open, honest, candid Republicans.

We have taken the liberty to say thus much, not to dictate (were it in our power to do so) but to caution you against probable mischiefs.

The justly celebrated Counsellor Hay, of Richmond, Virginia, the author of the elegant and argumentative letters signed Hortensius, on the unconstitutionality of the sedition law, the same who left the Court in consequence of the tyranny of Chase in the trial of Callandar, is a candidate for a seat in the state legislature, for Richmond, in opposition to Mr. Rind, whose publication lately appeared in the federal prints. This is sufficient to shew that, although Mr. Rind may have disapproved of the administration of Mr. Adams, as stated by himself, he is not considered a *sound* republican. It evinces that his observation, respecting the repeal of the judiciary law are *ungrateful* to the republican citizens. Counsellor Hay is very popular, and his popularity has been very honorably acquired. We regret we have not room to publish his address. It is elegant without ostentation. It contains no avowal of his political creed; no promise to support particular measures. They were both unnecessary. His sentiments and talents are known and duly appreciated by his fellow-citizens.

It appears the federalists have nominated a person to represent the district comprehending Salem in the senate of Massachusetts, in opposition to the republican candidate, Capt. Crowninshield. A very admirable and no less cogent reason is brought forward to convince the people that the *federal* candidate ought to be elected. It is this. "That being a man of *great property* and willing to *give his time* to the public, he ought *gratefully* to be accepted." What a comfortable federal doctrine! What an insult offered to common sense! This candidate would no doubt *save the people* from their worst enemies, *from themselves*. In some of the English boroughs, the argument—immense wealth—would be omnipotent. But *here* it is both *mistimed* and *misplaced*. The reason assigned why he ought to be elected, is the most powerful one that can be adduced why *he ought not* to be elected.

We hear from a very respectable source that the republicans of Connecticut intend to support at the approaching election, Mr. Kirby, for Governor, and Mr. David Trumbull (brother to the present Governor) for Lieut. Governor of the state. The patriotism of Mr. David Trumbull, notwithstanding the federalism of his kindred, is above all suspicion. Although independent in fortune, he is is not less so in mind. Of Mr. Kirby nothing need be said His fidelity to republicanism has never been doubted. He is an ornament of the state, and valuable to the country. We congratulate the republicans on their choice. It is undoubtedly a very respectable one.

It has has been suggested to us, that the extract of a letter from New Orleans inserted in our paper of yesterday, is only intended to promote speculating views. Unless the person who communicated it comes forward to substantiate its authenticity, the extract will be considered as a fabrication.

We understand that a convention between the United States and Great Britain has been concluded, which terminates all the existing differences under the sixth article of the British treaty.

In this convention it is stipulated that all the claims of British subjects on the American government under the sixth article shall be commuted into an obligation of the United States to pay to the British government 600,000 pounds sterling, in three annual payments, the first instalment to be paid one year after the final ratification of the convention.

On the other hand, claims of American citizens for spoliated property are to be adjusted, as provided for under the British treaty, and payment to be made therefor by the British government at London at the above periods. *Nat. Intel.*

At the annual meeting of the Freeholders in Hopkinton, on the 1st of March, 1802, the Republicans, before prayers, brought forward a motion in the words following, viz.

"Inasmuch as calumny, reviling and abuse are spread in our land, against the administration of the general government, tending to weaken and destroy the union, and spread discord among brethren, in open violation of the new commandment which our saviour gave unto us, "*Ye shall love one another*:"—Therefore, we beg our Reverend Pastor to supplicate the throne of Grace for us—that he would save our land from such calamities—that he would in mercy bring those, who have so offended, to speedy repentance, and forgive them—that he would banish discord and restore and confirm tranquility and peace, and unite our hearts in the fear of God."

To the astonishment of all present, the Federal party came forward, and violently opposed the motion in the most abusive terms—at length the motion was put, and carried by the republicans, by a considerable majority in the affirmative. The federalists neverthelss still clamoured against such a prayer—the Republicans then proposed, for peace sake, to proceed as usual—Solemn prayer ensued, and the Revnd. ETHAN SMITH, in his prayer, seemed to notice the request, and prayed with the fervency of a true Republican. [*Concord paper.*]

ARTIFICIAL TEETH.

I. GREENWOOD, DENTIST to the late PRESIDENT WASHINGTON, continues to make and fix Artificial Teeth in the neatest and most durable manner; he cleans and separates the teeth, and likewise performs every operation in the line of a Dentist. His abilities and candor are well known and approved by many of the first people in the United States, as well as foreigners.

N. B. I. GREENWOOD may be consulted at his house, No. 13 Chatham-row, near the play-house, as he does not attend abroad, except it is to relieve pain in difficult cases that comes within the line of his profession; and that he will do gratis, if required. His prices for replacing teeth, &c are moderate, that every person applying for his assistance may be benefited.

April 2. &w.

CONGRESS of the UNITED STATES.

HOUSE OF REPRESENTATIVES.

Monday, March 15.

Mr. Randolph called for the order of the day, on the bill for repealing the internal taxes.

Mr. Griswold said, that he hoped the resolution which he had laid on the table for indemnifying for French spoliations would be first taken up. It was important before a decision was made on the repeal of the Internal taxes, that the extent of indemnities made by government would be known. He therefore moved a postponement of the bill on Internal taxes till to-morrow, that in the mean time his motion might be acted upon. He concluded by desiring the yeas and nays.

The motion of Mr. Griswold, on FRENCH SPOLIATIONS,

Is as follows.—"*Resolved*, That it is proper to make provision, by law, towards indemnifying the merchants of the United States, for the losses sustained by them from French spoliations, the claims for which losses have been renounced by the final ratification of the Convention with France, as published by proclamation of the President of the United States."

Mr. Lowndes observed that it was nearly two months since the committee was raised, to whom had been committed the petitions of Merchants, praying indemnities: notwithstanding this length of time, the committee had not yet met. He hoped this resolution would induce the committee to meet.

Mr. S. Smith said, that he had presented the first petition on the subject of French spoliations, and that it had been immediately referred to a select committee, who, though they had made progress in the business committed to them, had not considered it fair to decide until all the petitions expected on the subject had been received. One indeed had been presented only this morning. Gen. Smith asked if this mode was not perfectly just and fair. For himself on this subject he was precluded from voting, as he was deeply interested in the decision of the House He mentioned this circumstance that the reason might be understood why particular gentlemen from different parts of the Union did not vote on this question in its several stages.

Mr. Lowndes said he did not consider the right of deciding the principle delegated to the select committee. That must be decided in the House It was the duty of the committee barely to make arrangements to protect the House from imposition on the score of facts. If it shall be determined by the government that it is improper to make compensation—though he thought such a decision scarcely possible—the select committee may be discharged. If on the other hand it is thought proper to compensate, the committee may go into the investigation of details.

The order of the day is called for on repealing the Internal taxes. But ought not the House to understand the amount with which the government will stand charged on these indemnities, before these taxes are repealed? Mr. Lowndes said he was of opinion, the claims could not be rejected. They were too just to be disregarded. It was the duty of the government to protect its citizens from the depredations of an enemy. Government, for a certain national good, had thought proper to abandon the claims of its citizens on the French government. Surely no man would say, the government possessed the right to seize the property of a certain description of its citizens, and appropriate it to general purposes. He repeated, that their claims must be paid by the government. Was it not then proper to determine their extent before the internal taxes were taken off?

Mr. John C. Smith submitted it to the candor of the gentleman from Virginia, to wave his motion until that made by the gentleman from Connecticut respecting French spoliations, should be referred to a committee of the whole.

Mr. Mitchell felt it an obligation, that the case of those whom he had the honor to represent, and that of the other merchants in the United States, should be taken up and receive from this house the most deliberate and serious consideration. He had before submitted to the house his ideas on the proper course to be pursued, which it was not necessary for him to repeat. He would observe, that the resolution now made was so broad as entirely to defeat its object.—The first reference of this business was to a select committee instructed to examine all the papers and documents in relation to it, with an instruction to report their opinion to the house; on receiving which the house might be able to come to a decision. On the other hand, the present proposition goes to commit the house on the whole extent of the subject without any examination whatever.

Dr. Mitchell said, he would suggest a few reasons, which satisfied his mind that a decision should not be too rapidly pressed. The vessels taken by the French admitted of various classifications. One class consisted of those, that were captured before the dissolution of our treaty with France; another class of those which were captured after that event; another class of those that were captured by pickeroons without commissions; and another class where captures were ... goods. All these ...rations; and when ... house in a form so ...pitately to decide a ... government to make ...?

...doubt but that such ...ited States as came ...ated property, would ...ndemnity. He was ... such cases payment ...d the merchants as a ...nd that their interests ...e thought the more ...n of the bill on the ...nder the government ...dit.

... that the best way of ...merchants was not to ... other hand, he was ...f success would arise from an examination of the various classes of spoliations, from seperating them from each other, thereby enabling the house to act understandingly upon them. The resolution of the gentleman from Connecticut, was so vague as not to be susceptible of any distinct meaning. He hoped, therefore, the subject would be suffered to undergo a full and deliberate investigation in the select committee, which he, as a member of that committee, assured the house was progressing as fast as a sense of justice and a regard to our merchants required.

Mr. Dana. The object of the present motion is to take up the resolution of my colleague, and to make order upon it—not to decide definitively upon it. This being the true question, I hope the gentleman from New-York will not think it improper in me to say that many of his remarks do not apply to it. As the question is not whether we shall immediately decide the point; but only place it in a train for decision. It must be discussed either in a committee of whole, or in a select committee; and we ask the house now to decide which, that it may be progressing towards the final decision.

The resolution states a general principle. If it is the fixed determination of the majority, without an enquiry, not to grant any relief whatever, there is an end of the business. But if you agree to grant any relief, the resolution ought to be adopted. The principle is then established of indemnifying; after which you may discriminate.

The principle on which the resolution is founded is not that the government has declined to insist upon the claims of its citizens against the French; but that it has undertaken to abandon their claims, so that no citizen can now come forward with his claim either against the French government or any citizen of France. For this is the construction of the treaty as finally ratified by the government. It is a complete surrender and renunciation of all demands. Among the first claims of our citizens are some of private right, which, were it not for the treaty, could be recovered in the courts of France but which the treaty bars. This constitutes a class of claims which the government cannot refuse to indemnify. There are other descriptions of claims, which might require discrimination; in some of which the degree of compensation should be varied, and others, in which there should be no compensation whatever. I think, therefore, it is proper for the government to say the business shall be attended to; at some future time an enquiry may be made into the nature of the various claims. This is all we ask.

Mr. Griswold said that the great man from New-York had misapprehended the order of proceeding in that house. He supposes the present resolution so vaguely worded, as to be improper to be passed.—But if taken up, that very gentleman may offer any

NEW-YORK EVENING POST.

No. 826 — FRIDAY, JULY 13, 1804. — No. 40 Pine-Street

NOTICE...All persons indebted to the late Copartnership of George Ferguson & Co. are requested to make immediate payment to the subscribers, who have received an assignment of all the estate and effects of the said Copartnership for the benefit of all the creditors of the said George Ferguson & Co. And the creditors are also requested to present their respective demands, duly authenticated to Thomas Eddy, of the city of New-York, that they may receive such dividend as may hereafter be made of the estate and effects so assigned as aforesaid.

Richard Hartshorne,
Henry Shotwell,
James Byrd,
Thomas Eddy.

July 11. 3w

BY order of John B. Prevost, Esquire, Recorder of the city of New-York, Notice is hereby given to *Dat & Brocar*, absent debtors, and all others whom it may concern, that on application and due proof made to him, the said John B. Prevost, pursuant to the directions of the act of the Legislature of the state of New-York, entitled, "An act for relief against absconding and absent debtors," passed 21st of March, 1801, he hath directed all the estate, real and personal, within the city and county of New-York, belonging to the said Dat & Brocar, to be attached and safely kept—And that unless the said Dat & Brocar do discharge their debts within one year after the notice of such seizure, all their estate, real and personal, will be sold for the payment and satisfaction of their creditors.

May 28 3m — BOYD & DEY, Att's.

BY order of John B. Prevost, Esquire, Recorder of the city of New-York—Notice is hereby given to Benjamin Wayne, of Boston, in the Commonwealth of Massachusetts, ship-master, an absent debtor, and all others whom it may concern, That on application made to the said Recorder, by a creditor of the said Benjamin Wayne, pursuant to an act of the Legislature of the state of New-York, entitled "An act for relief against absconding and absent debtors," passed 21st March 1801, the said Recorder has directed all the estate, real and personal, of the said Benjamin Wayne to be seized, and that unless the said Benjamin Wayne shall discharge his debts within one year after the publication of this notice, all his estate, real and personal, will be sold for the payment and satisfaction of his creditors. New-York, 25th May, 1804.

JAMES SCOTT SMITH, Att'y. — May 28 3m

At a General Assembly of the State of Connecticut, holden at Hartford in said State, on the second Thursday in May, A. D. 1804.

UPON the Petition of Jesse S. Peck, of Wallingford, in New-Haven County, against his creditors, praying an act of Insolvency in his favor, shewing to this Assembly among other things that many of his creditors dwell out of this State and in places unknown to the petitioner, and praying that said petition may be continued to the next session of the General Assembly, to be holden at New-Haven on the second Thursday in October, 1804, for the purpose of notifying said creditors and all others concerned, of the pendency of said petition, by advertizing notice of the same in such newspapers and for such lengths of time as this Assembly may direct, as by petition on file. Dated April 10, 1804.

Resolved by this Assembly, That said petition be continued to the next session of the General Assembly, to be holden at New-Haven on the second Thursday in October, 1804, and that the petitioner give notice to said creditors and to all others concerned, of the pendency of said petition and that they appear at said last mentioned Session of Assembly, on the second day of said Session (if they see cause) then and there to shew reasons (if any they have) why the prayer of said petition should not be granted; by causing a copy of this Resolve to be published in the Evening Post, printed in the city of New York, and in the Connecticut Courant, printed at Hartford in this State, at least three weeks successively.

A true Copy of Record,
EXAMINED. By SAMUEL WYLLYS, *Sec'ry.*

June 29 3w*

IN CHANCERY.

Hester Gouverneur, and others, Executors, &c. of Nicholas Gouverneur, deceased, vs. Herman G. Rutgers, and others.

IN *pursuance of a decretal order made in the above cause by the Court of Chancery of the State of New-York, will be sold under the superintendance of the subscriber, at Public Auction, at the Tontine Coffee-House, in the City of New-York, on the twenty first day of August, 1804, at one of the clock in the afternoon, a certain lot of ground and dwelling house thereon, described in a mortgage thereof made by Herman G. Rutgers, and Sarah his wife, to Nicholas Gouverneur, as follows, to wit, "all that certain messuage or dwelling house and lot of ground, No. 3 situate in Cedar-street, late little Queen-street, in the City of New-York, butted, bounded and described as follows, to wit, on the north or rear by a lot of ground belonging to the devisees of Joseph Haynes, deceased, on the west by another house and lot of the said devisees, on the east by the house and lot of ground belonging to John Harris Cruger, on the south by the said Cedar-street, containing in breadth in front twenty-five feet and one inch, in the rear twenty-three feet and six inches, in length on the south east side one hundred and thirteen feet six inches, and in length on the north west side one hundred and twelve feet seven inches," together with all and singular, the appurtenances, &c. thereunto belonging. Dated the 15th day of June, 1804.*

THOMAS COOPER, *Master in Chancery.*

July 9

TO BE SOLD, a Country Retreat, situated in the pleasant village of Jamaica, on Long-Island, on the corner formed by the post-road, and the road leading to Black Stump, Flushing, &c. containing one acre of ground, or upwards, in a high state of cultivation, inclosed in a substantial fence, and abounding with a great variety of fruit and flowering trees, shrubs and plants. On the premises are a double two story dwelling house, a spacious barn, and other out-houses, a cistern and well of excellent water, with a pump in each. The improvements have been lately made, are replete with every convenience, and in excellent repair.—the house contains four rooms on each floor, besides three garret rooms, a milk room, kitchen, and two cellars, and has six fire places, two of them with marble and other suitable chimney ornaments.—The village contains three places of public worship, several seminaries of education, and affords the convenience of procuring supplies of all kinds.—Stages and market waggons are daily passing to and from New-York.

Possession may be had immediately if required, and terms made known by applying on the premises. — June 14 f tf

BUILDING LOTS...Three Lots on Broadway, and one acre of ground at Kips Bay, fronting on the Harlem road—For sale by JOHN HAGGERTY, 82 William-street.

July 3 2w

WANTED a Dry Nurse, none need apply without good recommendations—enquire at this office. — July 9

For HAMBURGH,
The ship Lydia, capt. Tredwell, lying at Pier No. 9, has more than one half of her freight engaged, for the remainder or for passage apply to GEORGE ERICH, 93 Front-street.
The Lydia will proceed to Lubeck, should the blockade of Hamburgh continue.

June 27 1m

For LIVERPOOL,
The staunch ship GEORGE & MARY, will positively sail in ten days, having three-fourths of her cargo ready to go on board Fifty tons heavy and Fifty tons light goods will be taken on very low freight. For terms apply to
June 18 — MINTURN & CHAMPLIN.

For NEW-ORLEANS,
The brig WILLIAM, P. W. Paillet, Master, has two thirds of her cargo engaged, and will be dispatched soon as possible—For freight of the residue or passage, apply to
JACOB & THOS. WALDEN, 66 South-street.
Who offer for sale landing from said vessel,
110 Hhds New-Orleans Sugar, strong grained and of superior quality,
34 bales Cotton,
IN STORE,
170 Qr. casks Sherry Wine of the most approved brands,
35 bbls Cider Brandy, strong proof & good flav.
4 pipes old L. P. Madeira Wine,
500 Red oak Hhds Shooks, best quality.
July 10 2w

ST. DOMINGO COFFEE in bags, barrels and Tierces, about 3000 wt. with Certificate—For sale by
MAXWELL HYSLOP, 18 Broadway.

Freight for Jamaica,
A good vessel bound to the port Kingston, may have a few barrels of Provisions and a quantity of Lumber by applying as above.
June 18.

Wanted to Purchase,
Two Schooners of about 100 tons each—Apply to
GRANT FORBES, & Co.
Who have in Store
Louisiana Sugars of the first quality for the sale, in parcels suitable to the retailers. Also, 82 hhds and 20 bbls Clayed Sugars. — June 23

For Sale, Freight or Charter,
The new brig WILLIAM TELL, burthen 120 tons by Carpenter's measurement, E. Glad, master, just arrived from Poughkeepsie, where she was built; she is a faithful built and handsome vessel, and will be fitted for sea with dispatch. If she should not be sold when completely fitted, a freight to Cadiz or Lisbon would be preferred. Apply to
CALDWELL & FOOTE, 74 South-street.
June 22

FOR SALE,
(A GREAT BARGAIN)
The brig HAMILTON, a prize vessel, purchased in the West-Indies, about 150 tons burthen, British built, and is coppered. She may be examined at the foot of James street—For terms apply to
May 15 — ROBERT LENOX.

EBENEZER STEVENS, 222 Front-street, has for sale,
350 lbs. first quality New-Orleans Indigo
60 pipes Barcelona Brandy,
4 do Cognac
80 do Sicily Madeira Wine
6 bales French Coffee Bags, best quality
3 do French Paper Hangings
2 do Umbrellas
2 cases Fowling pieces, single & double barrll'd
1 do common and embroidered Fans, Snuff Boxes and Pocket Books
2 do Ladies Straw and Crape Bonnets
2 do Fancy Articles, Chambray, Gauze, Plumes, Ornaments for Gowns, Wreaths and Garlands of Flowers, Diadems, &c. and
2 cases Ladies extra long Silk Gloves
ALSO,

The very fast sailing brig ENTERPRIZE, burthen 164 tons, pierced for 16 guns, and is in complete order. — July 7

FOR SALE,
The beautiful fast sailing Pilot Boat DASH, as she arrived from Port-au-Prince, burthen 51 tons, Inventory and conditions of sale to be known by application to
GILBERT ROBERTSON & Co.
July 10

For Sale Freight or Charter,
The schooner MARGARET, now lying at the subscribers Lumber Yard, burthen 99 1-2 tons, is a strong vessel and newly sheathed; will be ready to receive a cargo in 2 or 3 days—For terms apply to
BROADIE & DENNISTOWN, 146 Washington-street.
July 10

WANTED TO CHARTER,
(for a port in the Mediterranean)
A good vessel, burthen about 150 or 160 tons, immediate dispatch will be given. Apply to
JOHN MURRAY & SONS, No. 269 Pearl street.
July 2

SICILY MADEIRA WINE....50 pipes, of first quality, now landing from the brig Ann, from Marsala—For sale by
EBENEZER STEVENS, 222 Front-street.
Also,
7 hhds. Clayed Sugar,
5 do. Muscovado do.
7 barrels of Coffee.
From the brig Diamond, from Guadaloupe.
June 16

BEEF, PORK, ASHES, WINES, BRANDY, & ANCHORS....
40 bbls. prime }
76 do. cargo } Beef, Wilson's brand.
10 do. necks & shanks }
74 do. mess and prime Pork,
91 do. Pot }
39 do. Pearl } Ashes.
For sale by KANE & PLATT.
Also in Store,
Madeira, Sherry, Teneriffe, Port and Corsica } Wines, in pipes, hhds. and qr. casks,
15 pipes high 4th proof Barcelona Brandy,
A constant supply of Anchors. — May 16

RAISINS, SPERM CANDLES & GUNPOWDER TEA—
50 casks Raisins, 50 boxes Mucatel do
65 boxes Spermaceti Candles
10 chests Gunpowder Tea landing this day
For Sale by BRUCE & MORISON.
They have also in Store
140 hhds prime Godish
20 hhds Jamaica Spirits
20 pipes Cognac and Barcelona Brandy
12 do Hollands Gin
40 casks Hibberts Brown Stout
30 Qr casks Sherry Wine
7 pipes Madeira Wine
3 do Old Lisbon
First quality Claret in cases of 1 & 2 doz. each
15 chests Hyson
25 do Young Hyson } TEAS of latest importations.
30 do Souchong }
25 do Bohea }
Flotant and Spanish Indigo
Bullocks Cheese, 75 bags Race Ginger
Demi Johns and 12 bales soft shell'd Almons
Chocolate and Coffee
200 lb Nutmegs, 200 do Cloves
Cassai, Ginger, Pepper, Rice, Barley
Basket Salt, Citron, Mace, Mustard, &c. with a number of other articles which they will dispose of Wholesale and Retail. — June 22

GUN-POWDER & FOWLING PIECES. Just received, and for sale by the subscribers.
120 qr. casks single seal British Powder, a very approved quality,
20 do. double seal do.
20 do. cannister do.
500 do. tower proof do.
120 do. double do. do.
40 do. glazed do. do.
4 cases well assorted Fowling Pieces, and long deck Guns, and
2 do. twisted stub do. in cases, with implements.
ROBERT BACH & Co.
June 1 — 128 Pearl-street.

ONEIDA's CARGO.

A FEW boxes best chop Hyson Tea of this Cargo yet on hand—Also,
Hyson Chulan in small boxes for families
Imperial Tea, | Fans
Nankeens, | China Ware
Silks, | Rhubarb and
China Root, &c.—For sale by Wm Leffingwell, No. 50 Wall-street, or at
LEFFINGWELL & DUDLEYS, No 115 Front-street.
May 11

DUNSTABLE BONNETS, RUSSIA HEMP, &c....
2 boxes straw and chip Bonnets, of the first quality, with fancy chip Plumes,
11 tons St. Petersburg Hemp,
1 cask Felt Hats,
180 bbls. Mess, Prime and Cargo Beef,
30 do. Cargo Pork.
A few bbls. Prime Pork—For sale by
LEBBEUS LOOMIS, 45 William-street.
June 9

SUGAR & MOLASSES, of the first quality—Will commence landing this day, from on board the schooner Hampshire, from Trinidad, at Stevens'-wharf,
52 hhds. }
48 barrels, } Muscovado Sugar,
27 hhds. Molasses—For sale by
JOHN MURRAY & SONS, 269 Pearl-street.
May 21

TELESCOPES, MAPS, BUNTING, &c.—Imported in the ship Jupiter, Law, from London, 3 cases and 12 casks, containing an handsome assortment of—
Telescopes, Quadrants,
Maps of the coast of America, West Indies and Europe,
Buntings white and coloured,
Sail Needles, Paints in kegs and Paint Brushes, with a variety of other articles in the Ship Chandelery line, which are offered for sale on very moderate terms, by
JOHN MURRAY & SONS, 269 Pearl-street.
May 28

TO commence landing on Monday, the 18th June, the cargo of the brig Albatross, captain Woldes, from Leghorn.
6 boxes Marble Slabs,
300 Marble Tiles
116 pipes Corsica }
83 hhds. French } Wine,
250 boxes Soap, 6 boxes Manna,
12 bags Aniseeds, 189 boxes Olives,
17 boxes Straw Hats,
8 do. Silk do. 2 boxes Silks,
12 bags Juniper Berries,
2 boxes Black Crapes,
3 do. Chip Hats,
1 do. Straw Rims,
2 do. Writing Paper, of excellent quality,
2 do. Saffron,
527 do. Oil—For sale by
JOHN MURRAY & SONS, 269 Pearl-street.
June 16

OLIVER WOLCOTT & Co.
OFFER FOR SALE,
FIFTEEN bales Allahabad Cossas,
4 do. Jelapore Sawns,
4 do. blue Handkerchiefs,
10 do. Chintzes,
11 do. Twine,
307 bags Pepper,
120 do Ginger,
288 do Sugar, part of the cargo of the ship Allegany. — june 21

JOHN M'VICKAR & Co. have received per the ship Susan, John O'Connor, master, from Dublin, a further supply of—
7 8 and 4-4 Linens,
3-4 and 10-4 Diapers,
5-4 Sheetings,
Long Lawns and Table Cloths.
Also on hand,
100 cases Claret, two dozen each.
June 4

HEMP, IRON, LINEN, INK, WINE, &c....For Sale,
Russia Hemp, Iron, Diapers, and Sail Duck,
Irish Linens, Sheetings and Ticken, assorted,
Irish Whiskey, 4th proof, and Glassware,
A few kegs Printers Ink,
10 pipes superior quality Port Wine,
Old Madeira Wine, from $3 to 5 per gallon.
Apply to LOW & WALLACE, 24 Broadway
April 6 tf

BAR LEAD, SHOT, NAILS & CHEESE
896 kegs Patent Shot,
100 barrels }
50 kegs } BAR LEAD
20 casks Nails assorted
5 Hampers Cheese, received per ship Cotton-Planter, from Liverpool---For sale by
ROBERT GILLESPIE.
June 26

PORTER, COPPERAS, BARK, WINE, CORDAGE & HATS....
150 casks Hibberts best Brown Stout,
30 hhds. Copperas,
60 do. Quercitron Oak Bark,
104 coils Cordage,
3 pipes old London Particular Madeira Wine,
2 cases low priced Hats—For sale by
COIT & PHILLIPS, Corner of Carlisle and Washington streets.
May 12

LE ROY, BAYARD & M'EVERS, have for sale the following articles, which they will dispose of on reasonable terms, for approved notes.
Madras Handkerchiefs, in bales,
Mock Madras do. do.
Vantapaulum do. do.
Ginghams, do.
Sursackars, do.
Napkins, do.
Twilled Silk Hdkfs. in boxes }
50 cadies colored Sewing Silk, } from Canton.
50 do. black do. do. }
Also,
A few bales of Hessians. — April 24

STERLING PLATE & PLATED WARE.
THOMAS WARREN,
No. 61 MAIDEN-LANE,
HAS just opened and for sale an elegant assortment of the above articles, with a general assortment of—
Cutlery and Japan Ware,
Knife Cases and Tea Caddies,
Andirons, Shovels and Tongs,
Officers Swords, Sashes and Epaulets,
Prussia Binding, Vellum Lace, Cord, &c.
ALSO,
30 cases Pins, well assorted,
4 do. Metal, Plated and Gilt Buttons,
May 4

ROBERT LENOX,
HAS for sale, by the latest arrivals, the following Goods—
By the ships Grace, Peace and Plenty, and Nancy, from Calcutta,
A complete and well selected assortment of PIECE GOODS, Cotton, Lines and Twine, a large proportion of which is calculated for Sugar Bakers.
Ginger, Gunny Bags,
Gum Shillac, Gum Copal, and
Sugar, of a very superior quality.
By the ship Alleghany, from Madras,
A very handsome assortment of Pullicat, Ventapolam and Masulipatam Hdkfs. of the newest and most fashionable patterns.
By the ship Silenus, from Cape of Good Hope,
600 bags Brazil Sugar,
12 boxes Window Glass,
150 pieces Ebony Wood, and
5000 pounds Sapan Wood.
Also, by former arrivals,
A few boxes of Madras superfine Chintz,
100 pipes fine flavored Barcelona Brandy,
270 cases Bordeaux Claret,
A few tons Lignumvitæ,
A quantity of cases of 6 bottles, containing 4 gallons each, and
Old full-bodied MADEIRA WINE, fit for present use. — May 15

GUNS, SWORDS, EPAULETTS, &c....
3 cases first quality double barrel Guns,
1 do Hair trigger and pocket Pistols,
1 do Epaulets, Cords, Fancy Plumes, Wreaths, Fringes, Laces, &c.
1 do Military Feathers,
6 do Plated Ware, Castors, &c.
1 do Gigg Whips,
2 trunks Watch Glasses,
1 do Silk and Cotton Suspenders,
1 cask Cutlery,
1 do. Brittania Metal Tea Pots,
1 do Plating Mills 4 to 8 inches,
Received by the Martha, from London; Cotton-Planter, Oliver Ellsworth and Josiah Collins, from Liverpool, and for sale by
LEMUEL WELLS, & Co.
June 30 eod 1m

MADEIRA WINE....3 pipes and 14 hhds. choice picked London Particular Madeira Wine, 4 years old, now landing, for sale by LOW & WALLACE.
Also in store,
Russia Hemp, Sail Duck and Diapers,
Madrass Hdkfs. Ginghams, &c.
30 hhds. assorted Irish Glass,
12 kegs Printers Ink,
30 hhds. Draught Porter,
Old Madeira Wine, from three to five dollars per gallon, and
Superior Port and Claret Wines, in bottle & wood.
June 8 tf

EDWARD L. SCHIEFFELIN,
HAVING entered into co-partnership with Mr. JONATHAN SCHIEFFELIN, business will in future be conducted at the Store lately occupied by James Thomson, corner of Maiden lane and Pearl street, under the firm of
J. & E. SCHIEFFELIN,
Who have for sale a general assortment of *Drugs and Medicines*, which they will dispose of on the most reasonable terms, amongst which are, viz.

1000 lb Rhubarb,	50 doz large white skins
800 lb Yellow Bark,	3 cases Aq. Fortis,
1000 lb Sarsaparilla,	2 carboys Oil Vitriol
600 lb Camomile Flowers,	40 lb Oil of Mint.
	1000 lb Liquorice,
6 doz superior Castor Oil,	1000 lb Flor. Sulphur
	1000 lb Salts,
150 lb Nutmegs,	7 lb Pulv. Feb. Antim.
200 lb Cloves,	
200 lb Windsor Soap	COLOURS.
1000 doz Wash Balls,	200 lb Mineral Green, No. 1 & 4.
100 doz Roll Pomatum,	
200 lb Camphor,	200 lb Rose Pink,
200 lb Quicksilver,	Litharge, Blue Verditer,
1000 lb Pearl Barley,	Naples Yellow, Patent
200 lb Oil of Lavender	Yellow, &c.
1000 lb Rad. Gentian,	200 lb Cantharides.

MEDICINE CHESTS
From six dollars to twenty, and upwards, with new improved directions, and a general assortment of Patent Medicines, &c. — May 21

RICE, SUGAR, AND RUM....
180 tierces New Rice,
13 hogsheads Jamaica Rum,
5 hogsheads Sugar,
Now landing, and for sale by
EBENEZER STEVENS, 222 Front-street.
May 23

NEWEST FASHION.
CHIMNEY GLASSES....A few very elegant ones are now offered for sale by JOHN DIXEY, at his Looking Glass Store, 118 William-street,
As they are the first articles of this kind finished agreeably to the present prevailing fashion in Europe it is hoped they will merit the attention of persons of taste.
Also, an extensive assortment of Pier Glasses, Gerandoles, Widow Cornices, &c. in the newest and most approved stile. — March 28 eod

NOW Landing at Walton's-wharf from on board the ship Fame, from Bourdeaux, and for sale by the subscribers,
303 pipes best 4th proof Cognac Brandy,
700 boxes Claret Wine,
100 do. Capers, Olives and Anchovies,
100 baskets best Sweet Oil.
Also in Store,
300 bags Ginger,
200 casks Rice and 10 bags Cloves.
June 18 — MINTURN & CHAMPLIN.

BOURS, MAC GREGOR & Co. have received by the Telegraphe and Ontario, from Liverpool, and Brandywine Miller, from Greenock, the following Goods, which they offer for sale by the package or less quantity, on reasonable terms—
2 cases fancy and Bugs Trimmings, Gimp bindings, and other patterns,
3 do. black and white Silk Laces,
1 case black and white silk Bands and Tassels, white silk Epaulets, new patterns,
1 do. black Pattinet Laces and Lace Cloaks,
1 do. elegant 6-4 laced and soft twill muslins, and fashionable flush'd Shawls.
Also, by the late arrivals from Calcutta,
34 packages, consisting of—
Mow, Jallapore and Johanna } MAMOODIES,
Jugdea, Lckipore and Chittabully } BAFTAS,
Jallapore and Mow } SANNAS,
Beerboom Gurrahs,
Cossas and Company do.
Checks and Persians. — June 4

FOR SALE, 9 casks White Wine Vinegar, just received from Bordeaux—Apply to
LE ROY, BAYARD & M'EVERS, 66 Broadway.
June 13

INDIA GOODS, imported in the ship Alleghany, G G Coffin, master, from Calcutta, viz.
86 bales Piece Goods, assorted,
7 do. Twine,
619 bags }
20 chests } Sugar,
272 bags heavy Pepper,
67 do. Ginger—For sale by
BENJ. WOOLSEY ROGERS & Co. 235 Pearl-street.
April 26

SAMUEL MURGATROYD, No. 14 Stone street, has for sale,
277 cases of Claret,
36 cases sweet White Wine,
14 half casks White Wine,
9 tierces White Wine Vinegar,
Imported in the brig Rolla, from Bordeaux.
May 30 eod tf

BRANDY, OIL, BEANS, &c....
3 hhds and 58 bbls Cyder Brandy
11 bbls. Linseed Oil
200 bbls White Beans
10 hhds Yellow Corn Meal.—For sale by
GURDON & DANIEL BUCK, 84 South-street.
June 26

GREEN COFFEE.........Landing this day from on board the brig Dolly, Jacob Lewis, master, from Port-au-Prince—
1900 Bags }
8 Hhds. and } About 200,000 } First quality Green Coffee.
6 Tierces }
For Sale by
SAML. G. OGDEN, Gouverneurs-wharf.
June 27

NOTICE.....By order of John B. Prevost, Esq. Recorder of the city of New-York—Notice is hereby given to the persons constituting the co-partnership, or house of trade of Dat and Brocar of Cape Francois, merchants, absent debtors, and all others whom it may concern, that on application and due proof made to him the said Recorder, pursuant to the directions of the act of the Legislature of the state of New-York, entitled, "An act for relief against absconding and absent debtors," passed March 21, 1801, he hath directed all the estate of the said persons as constituting the said co-partnership or house of trade of Dat and Brocar, to be seized, and that unless they discharge their debts within one year after this public notice, all their estate will be sold for the payment of their debts. Dated, New-York 20th April, 1805.

April 20 — F 3m

ROBERT DUNLAP,
Merchant Taylor, 57 Chatham street,
RETURNS his sincere thanks to his customers and the public in general for their past favors, and hopes by strict attention to his business, to merit a continuance of their patronage.
N. B. Mens wearing apparel of every description made on the shortest notice—and should any garment made for a gentleman, not fit him, he is at liberty to return it free of expence. — June 6. tf

IN CHANCERY.
BUILDING LOTS AT BROOKLYN,
FOR SALE.

The President, Directors and Company of the Bank of New-York, vs. Comfort Sands, Henry Sands, & Isaac Kibbe.

A *DECRETAL order having been made in the above cause, by the court of Chancery of the state of New-York, whereby the mortgaged premises mentioned in the pleadings in the aforesaid cause, are directed to be sold at Public Auction, in the city of New-York, by one of the Masters of the said Court—The subscriber gives notice, that the sales of the said mortgaged premises will commence at Public Auction, at the Tontine Coffee House, in the city of New-York, on TUESDAY, the third day of July, 1804, at twelve of the clock, A. M. and will be continued by adjournment from time to time, until the same shall be completed.*

The said mortgaged premises are situate at Brooklyn, in the County of Kings, in this State, and consist of Building Lots of different dimensions, to the number of six hundred and upwards, as numbered on a certain map thereof, which may be seen at the office of the subscriber.

Some of the said Lots will be sold separately, and others of them in such parcels as to the subscriber shall appear likely to be most beneficial to the parties interested therein.

On some of the said lots there are dwelling houses, buildings, and other improvements. Dated June 11, 1804.

THOMAS COOPER, *Master in Chancery.*

June 11

P. S. The sales of the above property will be resumed and continued on Tuesday the 31st inst. at 12 of the clock, in the forenoon, at the Tontine Coffee-House in the city of New-York, to which time the said sales have been adjourned by the subscriber. Dated 10th July, 1804.

THOMAS COOPER, Master in Chancery.

July 11

FOR SALE OR TO LEASE, the House and Lot adjoining Mr Adams, on the east corner of the common, near the Episcopal Church, Newark. There is on the premises every convenience necessary for a family, a good garden, with a beautiful grass lot in the rear, and a new barn For terms apply to ELIAS VAN ARSDALE, Newark, or to JOHNSON TUTTLE, No. 31 Nassau-street, New-York.

April 14 f

United Insurance Company.

THE Stockholders in the United Insurance company in the city of New-York, are hereby notified that an Election will be held on Wednesday the 18th instant, at 10 o'clock in the forenoon, at their Office in Wall street, to fill up two vacancies in the Direction of the said company.

By order of the Directors,
JOSEPH STANSBURY, Sec'y.
July 6

THOMAS WHITE,

IN order to distinguish himself from other persons of the same name in New-York, has thought proper to add a letter to his; of which the public are requested to take notice—thus,
THOMAS T. WHITE,
July 9 1w Stanton-street.

WEST-CHESTER TURNPIKE.

NOTICE is hereby given to the Stockholders in this Company, that a dividend of Five Dollars on each share of the *Original Stock*, having been declared by a resolution of the President and Directors of said Company, the same will be paid at any time after the 16th of July inst: by PETER JAY MUNRO, Esq. Treasurer to said Company, at his office in Broadway, to the said Stockholders or to their agents, duly constituted and appointed.
By order of the Board,
JOHN P. DELANCEY, President.
New-Rochelle, July 11.

OFFICE OF THE NEW-YORK INSURANCE COMPANY.

THE Directors of this Company have this day declared a dividend of ten per cent. on the Capital Stock of the Company, payable to the Stockholders, or their legal representatives, at the Office of the Company on the 20th instant
HUGH ANDERSON, Sec'ry.
July 2.

POWLES-HOOK.

THE proprietors give notice that they have appointed William Halsey, Esq. of New-Ark, their agent to sell their lots at Powles-Hook and he will attend for that purpose at Powles-Hook on Thursday, Friday and Saturday in each week. In the intermediate time persons may apply to him at New-Ark; or to A. Dey, in Pine street, New-York. There are now building two wharves of considerable extent to accommodate shipping, and the proprietors offer to sell the lots fronting the water which are above *low water* mark and subject to any possible claim.
June 27.

LIFE OF WASHINGTON.

GENTLEMEN who are subscribers to the History of the Life of General Washington, in this city and its vicinity, are respectfully informed that the introductory volume is just received at E. SARGEANT & Co's. Book-store, 129 Water-street, near the Tontine Coffee-House. The second volume, which is now printing commences with the birth of Mr. WASHINGTON; gives an account of his early life; details his active military services in the Indian and French wars; and brings down the History of the American Revolution to the year 1776, including the battle of Princeton. This and the subsequent volumes, will be published as soon as possible.

Agreeably to the terms of subscription, the price of the second volume now becomes payable in advance. A few proof impressions of the Portrait of General Washington may be had if applied for immediately. July 11.

MAHOGANY, NICARAGUA WOOD, &c.

EIGHTY Logs prime large St. Domingo Mahogany, now landing from the sloop Eliza, at the back of the Circus, North-river.
20 tons large first quality Nicaragua Wood,
40 bales prime Upland Cotton,
2 hhds. Georgia Tobacco,
5 do. Carolina Pink Root.
4000 lbs. Gum Guaiacum. For sale by
THOMAS C. BUTLER,
July 7 1w 34 Frankfort-street.

MUSIC....J. WILLSON, Organist in Trinity Church, informs his pupils and others who may wish to be instructed in the modern style of playing the Piano Forte and singing, that he will devote two days in the week after the 6th of July to the attendance of those who leave town for the summer season and reside within about twenty minutes ride of the city.

New Music just published, composed by Mr. Willson.
I ask the esteem of but one (written by Clara,)
Let others wreaths of roses twine,
Javotte or the Maid of the Alps,
'Twas on a clear and cloudless night,
The Sky Lark,
O yes Sir, if you please,
And an easy Sonata for the Piano Forte, to be had of the Author 330 Greenwich-street near Harrison-street, and Messrs. Paff and Mr. Hewitt's, Maiden Lane. July 7 1w*

LINENS, &c....JOHN M'VICKAR, & Co. have received by the ships Diligence from Dublin, and Oliver Ellsworth from Liverpool, a complete assortment of—
7 8 and 4 4 Linens, 3-4 brown do.
9 8 and 5 4 Sheetings.
3-4 and 10 4 Diapers,
Long Lawns and Cambricks, which they will sell on moderate terms at their Store in Barclay street.
July 2.

REMOVAL.

WILLIAM CODMAN, has removed his Compting house from No. 30 William-street, to his new Store 28 South-street, between Old and Coenties-slips, where he will be happy to receive the commands of his friends in the line of general Commission business, and to store Goods of every description on the most reasonable terms.
He has on hand for sale,
4 tons English Gunpowder superior quality,
1 bale Dimity,
2 trunks and 1 case fashionable elegant Muslins,
1 do Cotton Hose handsomely assorted,
1 case ounce threads, Ginghams and Quiltings,
20 Qr. casks Lisbon Wine,
3 cases Nutmegs and Cloves,
150 pieces black Chinese Lustrings, 1st chop
60 colored Sinchews,
100 catties dark blue } Sewing Silk.
100 do assorted colours }
40 pieces Italian Lustrings,
8 bales blue Gilly Hdkfs and Sooty Romals.
July 5.

LINENS....JOHN M'VICKAR & Co. have received per the ship Juno, Stephen Merrihew, master, from Dublin, a few boxes 7-8 and 4 4 Linens, mostly low priced, which they will sell on reasonable terms. June 25

A FIRE PROOF STORE TO LET.

THE 4 story Fire proof Store No. 2 Gouverneurs-Alley, to Let—Apply to
RICHARD I. TUCKER,
June 27

FOUND in this city a Silver WATCH, the owner may have the same by proving property, paying charges and calling at 16 Anthony street.
July 9 1w*

WANTED TO LEASE for a term of years, a Farm within 25 miles of the city, containing from 150 to 300 acres of land, a good grazing farm, and one near a river would have the preference. Any person having such a one they would wish to hire on lease, may hear of a person wanting one by applying at the office of the New York Gazette and General Advertiser.
July 10 1w*

DOLLARS WANTED.......The highest premium will be given for Spanish Dollars, at No. 45 William street. May 24

MONEY WANTED....1000 or 1200 dollars wanted for one year, at legal interest, on unquestionable security. March 30 tf

THE highest price given for Specie Dollars, at No. 54 Wall-street. June 13 tf

DOLLARS WANTED....A premium is given for Dollars at No. 64 Pine-street. June 11

SUGAR....30 hhds superior quality Trinidad Sugar, just received and for sale by
GILBERT ROBERTSON & Co.
June 19.

SUGAR, COFFEE, COCOA, &c...59 hhds. first quality Muscovado Sugar
215 bags Cocoa
42 bags, 29 bbls and 11 half barrels Coffee, landing from the schr. Jack, from St. Lucia.
Also, 27 hhds and 1 tierce prime Sugar, landing from the brig Sukey and Polly, from Jamaica
IN STORE,
31 hhds Trinidad Sugar
6 pipes Bucellas Wine
12 do Old Madeira—For sale by
June 26 GILBERT ROBERTSON & Co.

HAVANNAH SUGARS.....200 boxes of White and Brown Havannah Sugars, just received per brig Romulus, and for sale by
LE ROY, BAYARD & M'EVERS.
June 27.

NANKEENS....20,000 pieces Yellow Nankeens, first chop, entitled to more debenture than any other parcel in this city, for sale by
WILLIAM LEFFINGWELL,
June 14 50 Wall-street.

SPANISH DOLLARS....The highest premium paid for SPANISH DOLLARS, at No. 44 William-street. July 3 tf

GIN....50 pipes of an excellent quality, just received from the distillery of Pierpont and Anderson, for sale by
LEFFINGWELL & DUDLEY,
July 2 116 Front-street.

AFLOAT...211 barrels Tar, 92 barrels of Spirits Turpentine, 29 barrels Rosin—For sale by R. LENOX.
June 19.

COFFEE....21,500 lbs. St. Domingo Coffee, in bags, for sale by
ELIAS KANE & Co.
June 6 182 Water-street.

COTTON AND RICE......75 square bales of Cotton of a very superior quality and 80 casks of excellent Rice, just received and for sale by
THOMAS BUCKLEY,
241 Front-street.
Who has in Store,
120 Hhds Kiln dryed Corn Meal,
300 dryed Hides.
July 3. 2w

RUM, MOLASSES, &c.....140 puncheons of Jamaica Rum landing from brig George, capt. Emmerson, from Jamaica,
61 Hhds.
6 tierces, } MOLASSES.
24 barrels,
2 Hhds. Honey.
50 Hides from on board the German Peggy, capt. Landers, from Havanna.
IN STORE,
100 Hhds prime Codfish,
450 barrels Turpentine, 10,000 feet Mahogany,
8 bales Sea Island Cotton,
50 pipes, Hhds. and Qr. casks Madeira Wine,
6 puncheons Windward Island Rum,
5 boxes Havanna Brown Sugar
7 cases Isle France Indigo
1 box Bengal Indigo, 1 Hhd. Honey
1 Hhd. Loaf Sugar—For sale by
E. BURRILL,
July 9 96 Murrays-wharf.

CLARET, NANKEENS, TOBACCO, &c

JOHN M'VICKAR & Co. No. 3 Barclay-street, have on hand the following consignments which they will dispose of on accommodating terms
23 hhds. Prime Richmond Tobacco,
840 pieces Blue Nankeens,
106 boxes Claret, each containing 2 dozen, and
A quantity of Lignum Vitæ. July 7

RICE....55 heavy tierces fresh Rice of an approved brand, just arrived in the brig Dean, capt. Edgar, from Savannah—which will be sold on reasonable terms, if taken from the wharf on landing
ALSO,
A few packages just landed of articles for the use of the *Military*, consisting of rich Epaulets and Counter Epaulets for Staff and other Officers; cocked and round Hats; full sized 18 inch Plumes of the last military stile in Europe. These will be shipped to one of the West India Islands if not sold previous to the 4th July. Apply to
GRANT FORBES & Co.
June 29 62 South-street.

HATS, received per the last arrivals, and for sale by
D. OAKEY & H. WATKINSON,
No. 51 William-street
8 cases mens fine London black HATS,
3 do do do drab,
4 do Children and Youths coloured Ruffs,
3 do and Girls Hawksbury Bonnets,
6 do Mens Plated Hats,
10 do Youth and Mens coarse do.
5 do do Plated Drab, Drab Green under and Black Green under.
9 do Leghorn and Straw Hats and Bonnets and Straw Flowers,
1 do Fashionable artificial Flowers.
July 10 1m

TO DRY GOOD MERCHANTS.

FOR SALE, the late STOCK in Trade of BEACH & WARD, No. 3 City-Hotel, Broadway, consisting of a general assortment of DRY-GOODS. The Goods will be sold low, and the terms of payment made easy, if they can be disposed of immediately. The stand can be rented by the purchaser. Apply to
S. GOULD, & Co.
July 10 Opposite the City-Hall.

DRY GOODS.

JUST received on consignment, 2 bales superfine London Broad Cloths,
2 bales superfine London Cassimeres,
1 case Cotton Hosiery,
4 cases Mens fine Hats,
1 case Norwich Shawls,
1 case Elastic plated Spurs—For sale by
MILLS & STEWART,
July 9 2w 193 Pearl-street.

ST. CROIX SUGAR....30 Hhds, & 24 bbls. of the first quality of Muscovado Sugar, imported in the brig Mountaineer, Rodgers, and 6 Hhds. and 43 bbls. of the first quality Muscovado Sugar, imported in the brig Phœnix, capt. Goodrich, both from St. Croix, will be landed tomorrow at the old slip and for sale by
CHARLES D. GOOLD.
July 9

A HORSE for sale, a chesnut bay, 15 1-2 hands high, 6 years old, warranted sound, good under the saddle and in every kind of harness—will be sold cheap. Enquire at the Washington Livery Stable, 278 Greenwich street.
July 10

NEW-YORK EVENING POST.

FRIDAY, JUNE 13.

With emotions that we have not the hand to inscribe, have we to announce the death of ALEXANDER HAMILTON. He was cut off in the 48th year of his age, in the full vigor of his faculties and in the midst of all his usefulness.

We have not the firmness to depict this melancholy, heart-rending event. Now—when death has extinguished all party animosity, the gloom that overspreads every countenance, the sympathy that pervades every bosom, bear irresistable testimony of the esteem and respect all maintained for him, of the love all bore him; and assure us that an impression has been made by his loss which no time can efface.

It becomes us not to enter into particulars; we have no doubt, that, in compliance with the universal anxiety of the inhabitants, a statement will soon be exhibited to them containing all the circumstances necessary to enable them to form a just opinion of this tragic scene. In the mean time we offer the following letter that we have received from the Reverend Bishop Moore. The testimony which this pious and venerable Clergyman bears to the virtues of the deceased, will we are sure not be lost on a discerning community.

As soon as our feelings will permit, we shall deem it a duty to present a sketch of the character of our ever-to-be-lamented patron and best friend.

Thursday Evening, July 12, 1804.

MR. COLEMAN,

The public mind being extremely agitated by the melancholy fate of that great man, ALEXANDER HAMILTON, I have thought it would be grateful to my fellow citizens, would provide against misrepresentation, and, perhaps, be conducive to the advancement of the cause of Religion, were I to give a narrative of some facts which have fallen under my own observation, during the time which elapsed between the fatal duel and his departure out of this world.

Yesterday morning, immediately after he was brought from Hoboken to the house of Mr. Bayard, at Greenwich, a message was sent informing me of the sad event, accompanied by a request from General Hamilton, that I would come to him for the purpose of administering the holy communion. I went; but being desirous to afford time for serious reflection, and conceiving that under existing circumstances, it would be right and proper to avoid every appearance of precipitancy in performing one of the most solemn offices of our religion, I did not then comply with his desire. At one o'clock I was again called on to visit him. Upon my entering the room and approaching his bed, with the utmost calmness and composure he said, "My dear Sir, you perceive my unfortunate situation, and no doubt have been made acquainted with the circumstances which led to it. It is my desire to receive the communion at your hands. I hope you will not conceive there is any impropriety in my request." He added, "It has for some time past been the wish of my heart, and it was my intention to take an early opportunity of uniting myself to the church, by the reception of that holy ordinance." I observed to him, that he must be very sensible of the delicate and trying situation in which I was then placed: that however desirous I might be to afford consolation to a fellow mortal in distress; still, it was my duty, as a minister of the gospel, to hold up the law of God as paramount to all other law: and that, therefore, under the influence of such sentiments, I must unequivocally condemn the practice which had brought him to his present unhappy condition. He acknowledged the propriety of these sentiments, and declared that he viewed the late transaction with sorrow and contrition. I then asked him, "Should it please God to restore you to health, Sir, will you never be again engaged in a similar transaction? and will you employ all your influence in society to discountenance this barbarous custom?" His answer was, "That, Sir, is my deliberate intention."

I proceeded to converse with him on the subject of his receiving the Communion; and told him that with respect to the qualifications of those who wished to become partakers of that holy ordinance, my enquiries could not be made in language more expressive than that which was used by our Church—"Do you sincerely repent of your sins past? Have you a lively faith in God's mercy through Christ, with a thankful remembrance of the death of Christ? And are you disposed to live in love and charity with all men?" He lifted up his hands and said, "With the utmost sincerity of heart I can answer those questions in the affirmative—I have no ill will against Col. Burr. I met him with a fixed resolution to do him no harm—I forgive all that happened." I then observed to him, that the terrors of the divine law were to be announced to the obdurate and impenitent; but that the consolations of the Gospel were to be offered to the humble and contrite heart; that I had no reason to doubt his sincerity, and would proceed immediately to gratify his wishes. The Communion was then administered, which he received with great devotion, and his heart afterwards appeared to be perfectly at rest. I saw him again this morning, when with his last faultering words he expressed a strong confidence in the mercy of God through the intercession of the Redeemer. I remained with him until 2 o'clock this afternoon, when death closed the awful scene—he expired without a struggle, and almost without a groan.

By reflecting on this melancholy event, let the humble believer be encouraged ever to hold fast that precious faith which is the only source of true consolation in the last extremity of nature. Let the Infidel be persuaded to abandon his opposition to that gospel which the strong, inquisitive, and comprehensive mind of a HAMILTON embraced, in his last moments, as the truth from heaven. Let those who are disposed to justify the practice of duelling, be induced, by this simple narrative, to view with abhorrence that custom which has occasioned an irreparable loss to a worthy and most afflicted family; which has deprived his friends of a beloved companion, his profession of one of its brightest ornaments, and his country of a great statesman and a real patriot.

With great respect, I remain
Your friend and ser't.
BENJAMIN MOORE.

At a numerous and respectable meeting of Merchants and other citizens of New-York, at the Tontine Coffee-House, last Evening, Mr. Wm. W. Woolsey was called to the chair, and Mr. Maturin Livingston appointed Secretary.

The Meeting having been informed of the melancholy event of GENERAL ALEXANDER HAMILTON'S decease, and being deeply sensible of the irreparable loss which the United States have sustained by the death of a man, whose public and private virtues have endeared him to his friends and acquaintances; whose patriotism, talents, integrity, and eminent services, have rendered him peculiarly valuable to his country; and being anxiously desirous to render to so great and distinguished a character the last tribute of respect in their power,

Resolved, That this meeting will unite with their fellow-citizens of all classes in every suitable demonstration of sorrow for the death of General Alexander Hamilton—And that, for this purpose they recommend to the citizens at large, to shut up their stores, and generally to suspend business on Saturday the 14th inst. and to assemble at the house of Mr. CHURCH, in Robinson-street, at ten o'clock in the forenoon, to form a procession to attend the remains of the deceased.

That it be recommended to the owners and masters of vessels to direct the Colours of all the vessels in the harbour to be hoisted half mast, during the whole of Saturday next—

That Mr. Henderson, Mr. M. Livingston, Mr. A. Jackson, Mr. J. Kane, and Mr. H. I. Wyckoff be a committee on the part of this meeting, to meet such persons as may be appointed by other bodies of their fellow-citizens, in order to make such further arrangements as the occasion may require.

WILLIAM W. WOOLSEY, Chairman.
MATURIN LIVINGSTON, Secretary.

The Committee of arrangement appointed at the meeting at the Tontine Coffee House on the 12th inst. in conformity with the sense of the meeting, expressed on that occasion, request their fellow-citizens in general to wear Crape on the left arm for thirty days, as a testimony of their respect for the Integrity, Virtues, Talents and Patriotism of Gen. ALEXANDER HAMILTON deceased.
July 13.

City of New-York, ss.

IN COMMON COUNCIL,

JULY 13, 1804.

Resolved unanimously, That the Common Council of the City of New-York entertain the most unfeigned sorrow and regret for the death of their fellow citizen, ALEXANDER HAMILTON, and with a view to pay a suitable respect to his past life and future memory, and to afford the most unequivocal testimony of the great loss which, in the opinion of the Common Council, not only this City but the state of New-York and the United States have sustained by the death of this great and good man, the Common Council do unanimously recommend that the usual business of the day be dispensed with by all classes of inhabitants.

And, *Resolved unanimously*, That the ordinance prohibiting the tolling of Bells at funerals be on this occasion suspended, and that it be recommended to those who have the charge of the Church Bells in this City to cause them to be muffled and tolled at proper intervals during the day of his interment.

And also, *Resolved unanimously*, That the members of the Common Council will in a body attend and join in the funeral procession of the deceased at the time and place appointed.

Likewise, *Resolved unanimously*, That a Committee of three be appointed to make such arrangements in behalf & at the expence of the Common Council of the City of New-York for performing the funeral obsequies of the deceased, as the said Committee shall judge necessary and expedient.

Extract from the Minutes,
T. WORTMAN, Clerk.

Agreeable to the notice in the Morning papers the gentlemen of the Bar met at Lovetts Hotel, to join in those expressions of sorrow so universally produced by the untimely death of General Hamilton. The meeting was very numerous, and all party distinction lost in the general sensiment of love and respect for the illustrious deceased. Mr. Harison in a few words with a faltering tongue and a feeling heart, adverted to the sad occasion most on which they were called together, & in the affectionate terms mentioned the private virtues, the splendid talents, and the useful services of this best and greatest of men. Amidst countenances which spoke no common grief the following resolutions were adopted.

At a general meeting of the Gentlemen of the Bar of the city of New-York, at Lovetts Hotel, on the 13th of July, 1804, Richard Harison, Esq. in the chair.

This meeting being deeply affected by the death of ALEXANDER HAMILTON, the brightest ornament of their profession, whom they have ever held in the most sincere esteem, and admiration; whose superior talents, distinguished patriotism, eminent services, and uniform integrity has procured him universal confidence and veneration, and whose loss they lament as a severe private affliction and deplore as a great public calamity:

Resolve, that they will unite with their fellow citizens to demonstrate in every suitable manner their sincere respect for the memory of General HAMILTON, and the deep sense of the loss which their country has sustained.

That they will wear crape as mourning for their deceased brother for the space of six weeks.

That Jacob Radcliff, Josiah O. Hoffman, Nathan Sanford, John Wells and Daniel D. Tompkins, be a committee to make any further arrangements that may be proper on this mournful occasion.

DANIEL D. TOMPKINS, Sec'y.

☞ The Committee request that the Gentlemen of the Bar will assemble precisely at ten o'clock tomorrow morning, at the house of the Sheriff in Murray street. July 13

New-York 12th July 1804.

BRIGADE ORDERS.

For the purpose of paying the last testimony military respect to Major General ALEXANDER HAMILTON, deceased, the Brigade Company of Artillery, the Sixth Regiment, and the Uniform Companies belonging to the other Regiments of the Brigade, will assemble on Saturday at 9 o'clock, A. M. with three rounds of blank cartriges in the Park, where they will be joined by the Regiment of Artillery—the whole will be under the command of Lieut. Col. Morton.

By order of Brig. Gen. Boyd,
NATHAN SANFORD,
Assistant Brigade-Major.

P. S. The officers not on duty are requested to attend at Mechanic-Hall in uniform, and with the usual mourning.

ARTILLERY.

REGIMENTAL ORDERS.

Agreeably to Brigade Orders of this date, the First Regiment of Artillery will parade in the Park, on Saturday morning at 9 o'clock. The first battalion with small arms, the second with field artillery, each man of the first battalion will provide himself with three rounds of blank cartridges, to perform the last military obsequies over the grave of the late General HAMILTON.

Captain M'Lean will take charge of firing the minute guns.

The officers will appear with crape on the left arm.

By order of Lieut. Col CURTENIUS,
ROBERT SWARTWOUT, Adj.
July 12

ARTILLERY.

Captain De Peyster's Company will assemble on the Company Parade, at half-past 8 o'clock on Saturday morning, in full uniform—Crape to be worn on the left arm.

By Order, &c.
J. D. KEESE,
July 13 Ordy. Sergt.

NEW YORK INDEPENDENT VOLUNTEERS

☞ IN pursuance of Regimental Orders of last night, you are ordered to parade on the Battery to-morrow morning, at 9 o'clock precisely, with three rounds of blank cartridges.

By order,
AND. SMITH, Sec'y.

☞ A meeting of the *Students at Law* of this City, is requested this evening at 7 o'clock, at the office of Jos. Ogden Hoffman, Esq. in order to consider in what manner they can best express their sincere regret for the death of the late Gen. HAMILTON.
July 13.

☞ The Students of Columbia College are requested to meet in the College Green, tomorrow morning at half after 9 o'clock precisely, with their gowns, for the purpose of joining in the funeral procession of the late General HAMILTON.

N. B. The Graduates of the College are also desired to attend.

TAMMANIAL NOTICE.

BROTHERS,

Your attendance is earnestly requested at an extra-meeting of the tribes in the great wigwam, precisely at the setting of the Sun, this evening, to make arrangements for joining our fellow-citizens and soldiers in a procession, in order to pay the last tribute of national respect, due to the manes of our departed fellow citizen and Soldier, General ALEXANDER HAMILTON.

By Order of the Grand Sachem,
JAMES D. BISSET, Sec'ry.
Season of Fruit, in the year of discovery 312 and of the institution 15th. July 13

☞ THOSE Members of the "General Society of Mechanics and Tradesmen of the City of New-York," desirous of paying the last tribute of respect to the remains of General HAMILTON, are requested to meet at their New Hall, on Saturday morning the 14th inst. precisely at 9 o'clock.

N. B. The editors of the morning papers are respectfully requested to insert the above tomorrow.

ST. ANDREWS SOCIETY.

☞ The Members of the St. Andrews Society are requested to meet at the Masonic Hall, tomorrow Morning, at half past 9 o'clock precisely, in order to join the Funeral Procession of their late much respected and sincerely beloved Brother, Alexander Hamilton, and to testify the grief and regret they feel, in common with their fellow citizens, at the irreparable loss this community has sustained by his untimely death.

A. GLASS, Sec'y.
July 13.

FUNERAL PROCESSION:

The Society of the Cincinnati being charged with the direction of the funeral ceremonies of its President General, the following is the order of procession which will take place tomorrow at Ten o'clock, as commemorative of an event of the deepest national regret.

ORDER OF PROCESSION.

1. The Military Corps commanded by Col. Morton
2. The Society of the Cincinnati.
3. Clergy of all denominations.
4. The Corpse.

5. The General's Horse.
6. Relations of the deceased.
7. Physicians
8. The Judges of the Supreme Court.
9. Mr. Gouverneur Morris in his carriage.
10. Gentlemen of the Bar and students at Law.
11. The Governor and Lieutenant Governor of the State.
12. The Mayor and Corporation of the City.
13. Members of Congress and Civil Officers of the United States.
14. The Ministers, Consuls and Residents of Foreign Powers.
15. The Officers of the Army and Navy of the United States.
16. Military and Naval Officers of Foreign Powers
17. Militia Officers of the State.
18. President, Directors and Officers of the respective Banks.
19. Chamber of Commerce and Merchants.
20. Marine Society, Wardens of the Port and Masters and Officers of all vessels in the Harbour.
21. The President, Professors and Students of Columbia College.
22. The different Societies in such order as their respective Presidents may arrange.
23. The Citizens in general.

The Military Corps commanded by Col. Morton being ordered to parade in the Park at 10 o'clock, accompanied with Six pieces of Artillery, two of the pieces will remain on the ground under the command of Capt. Maclean, and will fire minute guns from the movement of the Corps until it arrives at Trinity Church.

The Sixth Regiment with the Colours and Music of the several Corps will parade in Robinson street, on the south side fronting Mr. Church's house; Standards and Music in front of the centre—the Regiment in solemn attitude, resting on arms reversed. On waving the Standard of the Cincinati shrouded in Crape the Regiment will shoulder, and receive the Corpse proceeding from the House with presented arms, the colours and music saluting. On a signal Trumpet the Regiment will shoulder and the Troops in the Park will throw themselve in columns and occupy the Broadway with the rear of the column covering the head of Robinson-street, & halt. On a signal Trumpet the 6th Regiment in Robinson-street will wheel to the right, by Platoons, and occupy the street in front of the Corpse, in open Column, at half distances of Platoons, and with arms reversed wait the signal. On signal Trumpet the Column will move with Colours and Music in the centre of the Sixth Regiment, playing the Dead March, with muffled drums. Two companies detached from the military in the Park will cover the flanks of the Corpse, in single file, with trailed arms, from the rear of the Sixth Regiment down the line, and take their proper position as the Corpse enters Broadway. The Column advancing will wheel to the left round the Park, enter Beekman-street, and passing down Pearl will ascend Wall-street to Trinity Church; the leading wing will form close column to the right, on the Church walk, extending to the north corner of Wall-street dressing by the left and facing to the right, stand with ordered arms. The rear wing advancing, will form close Column to the left, and facing to the right, extending to the south corner of Wall-street, dressing by the right with ordered arms. Mr. Governeur Morris from the Portico of the Church, (the Corpse in front on a bier) will deliver an appropriate address at the conclusion of which the Corpse preceded by the Military and properly attended will proceed to the vault, where the military ceremonies will be performed, under the order of the Commandant, which will close the Solemnities of the day.

W. S. SMITH, *President.*
W. POPHAM, *Secretary.*

NOTE.—The gentlemen included in Nos. 2 and 3, will assemble, previous to the procession, at Mr. Church's house.—In Nos. 7 and 8, at College-Hall—In Nos. 10, 11, 12, 13 and 14, in the College Green.—In Nos. 15, 16 and 17, will parade in Church street, south of Robinson-street.—No. 19 in the Mechanic-Hall, and adjacent houses.—No 20 in the College—Nos. 22 and 23, in Church-street north of Robinson street.

*** No paper will issue from this office tomorrow.

MARRIED,

At Alexandria, (Ma.) on Saturday evening last, GEORGE WASHINGTON PARKE CUSTIS, Esq to Miss MOLLY FITZHUGH, daughter of William Fitzhugh, Esq. of that place.

DIED,

At Philadelphia, on the 7th inst. in the 34th year of his age, after a long and painful illness, capt. ROBERT CLAY.

EVENING POST MARINE LIST.

ARRIVED AT THIS PORT, — days

British Packet Lord Charles Spencer, Cotesworth, Falmouth via Halifax, 54
Brig Ranger, Hacker, Lisbon via Norfolk, 45
Schr Minerva, Nye, Richmond, 11

CLEARED,

Ships Four Sisters, Moores, Fecamp, Hicks, Jenkins and Co; Stephen, Burks, Liverpool, Fergnson and Day; brig Friends, Aderton, Jamaica, by Capt. Haff; schr Greyhound, Boyer, St. Jago de Cuba, by B. M. Mumford.

The British Packet Lord Charles Spencer, Cotesworth, from Falmouth via Halifax. She sailed in company with a fleet of 40 sail, bound to Quebec, Halifax and Newfoundland, under convoy of the the Eurydice, of 24 guns. July 7, in lat 40, spoke the ship Hampden, 70 days from Marseilles for Philadelphia.

The brig Ranger, Hacker, from Lisbon via Norfolk, has salt to John M'Pherson and Co. Spoke, in lat 37, 50, the brig Triton, Nichols, of Boston, 3 days from Norfolk for Copenhagen.

The schr Minerva, Nye, in 11 days from Richmond, has flour and cocoa, to W. & J. Radcliffe, Andrew Smith, and John Patrick. Passengers, Dr Leonard and Lady, Mrs Leonard, and Miss Leonard.

The arrival of the British ship London Packet from New-York at Guernsey, is mentioned in the London Star of the 16th May.

From the General Shipping and Commercial List, from May 1st to 15th.—For Philadelphia, from London, June 1, the Union, Thomas; for New-York the South-Carolina, Steel, June 6.—From Greenock, May 10, the Minerva, Carrick, for Wilmington; Spinster, M'Call, for Charleston, do.—Arrived at London, the Edward and Charles, from Charleston. At Gravesend, the Janus, Waterman, from Virginia. At Clyde, the Endymion, Miller from Virginia. At Falmouth, the Princess Augusta Packet, from New-York. At Amsterdam, the Patty, Hazard, from New-York; Harriet, Pierce, Baltimore; Aurora, Eden, Boston; and Mary, Crockatt, New-York. At Elsineur, the Pallas, Dalling, from New-York. At Deal, the Suffolk, Moore, from Virginia. At Liverpool, brig Mary, Harrow, from New-York. At Falmouth, the Amelia, M'Dermot, from Savannah; and President, from Baltimore. At the Texel, Anna Eliza, Olney from Providence. At Hoelvet, Victory, Becknell, from Boston; Faber, Fowles, Providence. At Dover, the Robert, Dunkin, from Baltimore. At Deal, the Ritson, Wakefield, from Virginia. At Embden, Anna, Koper; Andromeda, Tegeler; and Krone v. Bremen, Dannken, all from Baltimore. At Gravesend, the Virginia, Dixon, from Virginia. At Liverpool, Orange, Pelham, from North-Carolina. At Jahde, Speculation, Schilling, from Baltimore via Dartmouth. At Embden, the Levington, Sellens, from Baltimore; and the Fortuna, Morse from Philadelphia. At Falmouth, the Charlotte Murdoch, Walker, from Charleston. At Tonningen, the Ocean, Smith, for New-York.

Falmouth, May 4.—Brig Rover, Waite, for London, put in by contrary winds.

Plymouth, May 6.—Arrived, ship General Green, of and for Baltimore, from Amsterdam.

Deal, May 9.—Came down the river last night and sailed this morning, the Suffolk, Moon, for Virginia. Remaining in the Downs, the Ritson, Wakefield, for Virgina.

High Court of Admiralty, May 10.—Yesterday the Right Hon. Sir Wm. Scott, proceeded to the adjudication of the following cases:—Ship Aurora—ship and cargo restored, with ten weeks demurrage. The Harriet, Brasher, for a breach of blockade, ship and cargo restored, subject to the captor's expences. The Perseverance, Byrne—the ship was restored in this case with expences.

Halifax, June 28.—Monday sailed for Falmouth, the British Packet Leicester, Bell. Arrived, schr Charlotte Augusta, from New-York; brig Edward and Mary, Gibbons, from Liverpool, via Newfoundland.

Port of Philadelphia, July 12.

Arrived, schrs Amity, Trefethen, Portsmouth 13; Christopher Flower, Flower, North Carolina.

The ship Ganges, Callender, left Calcutta. Feb. 8, and was embargoed in the river until March 11. Left the Sand Heads, in co. with the ship John and James, ——, for Portland, and brig Lydia, Smith for Boston, and 30 British ships under convoy of the Crampus, Caroline, and Buffaloe ships of war under the command of Com. Page, bound to Madrass, &c. The Ganges, parted company the same night. Left at Calcutta, to sail about 15th March, ship ——, Town, of Salem, and ship St. Cuthbert, Brown, of New-York.—Two American ships went up the Ganges early in March, one the Portsmouth of New Haven.

In the bay of Bengal, the Ganges was boarded by the privateer brig Alfred, Capt. Trevio, and treated politely by the captain & officers, and informed they were 4 months out from the Isle of France, and had taken nothing.

The Ganges was off St. Helena the 1st of June—saw an American brig there from the Cape of Good Hope, and 3 British ships of war, waiting for the homeward bound fleets from China and Bengal.

WANTS a situation a Gardener from Dublin, who is a complete master of the business, as he has been employed by one of the first houses in Dublin. Apply at 17 Augusta-street.
July 13 2*

TOBACCO, RICE, &c....58 Hhds. Tobacco, best Georgia, will be sold on good terms for approved Bills on Liverpool or London.
10 tierces Rice.
18 bales best Upland Cotton—Apply to
BENJ. B. OSBORNE,
July 12 1w 67 South-street.

FOR ANTIGUA,

And will stop at Barbadoes or Dominique if freight offers, the brig ACTRESS, Edward Tinker, master. She is now graving and will sail in ten days. For freight or passage, (having excellent accommodations) apply to
A. KIRKPATRICK,
July 12 7 Fair-street.

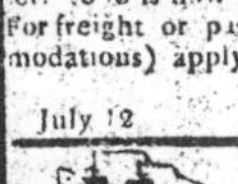

TRINIDAD.

Freight for 40 hhds. is wanted on board a good vessel bound to the Island of Trinidad. Apply to
JOHN MURRAY & SONS,
July 12 269 Pearl-street.

STOLEN on Tuesday Evening July 10th. from the subscriber, an ALARM SILVER WATCH, made by *Andrew Duchene.* Whoever will return the said Watch to the subscriber shall receive a reward of *Ten Dollars*, and no questions asked. Watch makers are requested to stop the Watch if offered for sale.
HUGH O. HARE, Baker.
July 11 3* 22 Bedlow-street.

THIS DAY IS PUBLISHED,
AND FOR SALE BY PETER A. MESIER,
107 PEARL-STREET,
A COMPANION FOR THE ALTAR,
Consisting of a short Explanation of the Lords Supper, and Meditations and Prayers, proper to be used before, and during the receiving of
THE HOLY COMMUNION,
According to the form prescribed by the Protestant Episcopal Church, in the United States of America.
BY JOHN HENRY HOBART, A. M.
AN ASSISTANT MINISTER OF TRINITY CHURCH, NEW-YORK.
Price 75 cents fine—62 cents common.

Contents—The usefulness of actual preparation before receiving the Lord's supper—The sacrament of the Lord's supper, and the necessary preparation for it stated and explained—The obligation of receiving the holy communion stated, and the various pretences for neglecting it considered and refuted—A prayer, &c.—Monday morning meditation: the christian directed in the examination of his spiritual character and state, &c. a confession of sins and prayer—Tuesday morning meditation: man in his natural state; the prayer—Tuesday evening meditation: man in his natural state; the subject of the morning meditation continued; the prayer—Wednesday morning meditation: repentance; the prayer—Wednesday evening meditation: resolutions of obedience; the invigorating and sanctifying agency of the holy spirit; the prayer—Thursday morning meditation: faith in Christ; the prayer—Thursday evening meditation: faith in Christ, as the son of God, and as a prophet, priest and king; the prayer—Friday morning meditation: thankful remembrance of Christ's death; the prayer—Friday evening meditation: thankful remembrance of the death of Christ; charity with all men; an act of thanksgiving for the sufferings and death of Christ; the prayer—Saturday morning meditation: the devout participation of the ordinances of the church; the appointed method of salvation, the prayer—Saturday evening meditation: the mode by which authority to administer the sacraments is to be derived from Christ, the divine head of the church; the prayer—Sunday morning meditation: the disposition with which the communicant should advance to the altar; the prayer—Devotions to be used at the administration of the Holy Communion; forms of daily devotion, &c. May 19 P&H tf

A YOUNG MAN, (PRINTER) capable of superintending a Printing Press, and willing to go to the southward, will hear of a good situation, by applying at this office. July 12.

A SERVANT....Wanted to purchase the time of a black Boy, 15 or 16 years of age. Enquire at this office. July 12

A REPORT prevailing that Mr. E. & A. SKETCHLEY intend removing their *Boarding School for Young Ladies* from Hærlem Lane, circulated no doubt with a view to their prejudice—they find it necessary to contradict it, and to inform the public the House is secured on lease, for two years from the first of May last.

Young Ladies confided to their care will be instructed in Reading, Writing, Cyphering, Grammar, Drawing, Geography, and the use of the Globes, Embroidery, and every other kind of Needle-Work, board and washing included for forty dollars per quarter.

Music, eight dollars per quarter.

Dancing, by Mr. L'Alliette, ten dollars per quarter, and five dollars entrance.

Each young lady finds her own bed and bedding, table spoon and tea do. which articles, when she leaves school, she takes away with her, and she must keep a quarter always paid in advance.

Parents and guardians are assured of the strictest attention being constantly paid to the morals, deportment, improvement and health of the scholars.
Hærlam Lane, July 12. d1w 2aw3w

TWENTY DOLLARS REWARD.

RUN-AWAY, from the subscriber, an apprentice Boy, named James Lockwood, about 20 years of age, by trade a Cooper. Had on when he left his master a blue and white broadcloth coat, white striped vest, black nankeen pantaloons, and a black hat; he is about 5 feet high pretty well set, short black hair, and dark eyes. he limps in walking owing to a stiffness in one of his knees, has a simple look, and is as simple as he looks. Any person who will take up said boy and deliver him to the subscriber at Oyster-Bay, or lodge him in any jail so that his master can have him again, shall be entitled to the above reward and all reasonable charges. All persons are forbid harboring said boy at their peril.
SAMUEL BANKS.
Oyster-Bay, July 5. P&H 1aw4w.

RUM....70 puncheons St. Croix and Windward Island Rum, will be landed this day at Old-slip. For sale by
July 11 KANE & PLATT.

INDIGO......19 tierces and 40 cases Isle of France Indigo, containing about 7000 lbs entitled to drawback—For sale by
MINTURN & CHAMPLIN.
July 6

A DROMEDARY,

TO be seen at Mr. Ros's Livery Stable, in Fair-street, the second door from Broadway. She is 4 years old, and suckles a young one three months old. She measures 9 feet 3 inches from head to tail, and 7 feet 2 inches round. They are the most docile animals in the known world—they kneel down, take on their load and rise at the pleasure of their keeper. She will stay here but a few days. Admittance 25 cents.
July 9 1w*

A Pleasant and Healthy Retreat.

FOR SALE, or to Lease for a term of years a small Farm and Dwelling House, &c. situated in Westchester county, lately the residence of Col. James Thompson, deceased. The house is situated on the main road leading from Peekskill landing to the Red Mills, 3 1-2 miles from the landing, and 1 1-2 from the post-road to Albany, pleasantly situated, and newly built in modern style. It contains a store ready shelved and a room for liquors, &c. on the first floor, 2 neat sitting rooms an entry and a kitchen on the next floor, and three bed rooms and a servants garret above. There is a newly built barn and stable, capable of containing horses, carriage, sleigh, &c. a new smoak-house and suitable out-houses, and a never failing well of excellent water. There is a large garden, well stocked with currant bushes, gooseberries, strawberries, asparagus bed, &c. next to which is a large young peach orchard, in full perfection, and of superior flavor; there are also 500 grafted apple trees now bearing fruit—the front of the land and house is ornamented with a row of lombardy poplars.—Most of the land has been newly laid down in clover. On the premises there is also a small tenement, fit for a servant or mechanic, and which may be generally rented.

The stand is excellent for a store, has been occupied as such for some time past, and always commanded a large share of country business. The situation of the house is uncommonly salubrious and healthy, and sufficiently near to command the conveniences of the village of Peekskill.

It would form a comfortable and cheap retreat for a family during the hot months, and would answer well for a retail city trader, disposed to continue his business there during a part of the summer. It has been lately put in complete repair.—The terms will be made quite easy.

For further particulars enquire of JOHN HANLON on the premises, or of the subscriber. Possession may be had immediately.
THEODORE F. TALBOT,
March 9 P&H tf 63 Pine-street.

ALL persons having claims against the estate of *Grant Bradley*, late of the city of New-York, merchant, deceased, are requested to send in their accounts duly authenticated, and those indebted to the estate are desired to make immediate payment to Edward M'Laughlan, No. 411, Broadway.
A. Bradley, Executrix.
John Eastmond, } Ex'rs.
Edw. M'Laughlan, }
July 9 eod2w

NOTICE....All persons indebted to the estate of Thomas Lawrence, of the city of New-York, Merchant, deceased, are requested to make payment to the subscribers, at No. 83 Cherry-street—And all persons who have any demands against said estate are requested to exhibit the same for payment.
ELEANOR LAWRENCE, Administratrix.
ARCHIBALD KERLY, Administrator.
July 10 2aw 3m

TO BOOKSELLERS.

FOR Sale (in sheets) 350 sets Shakespear's Dramatic works, printed complete, from Johnson & Steven's Text, in 8 vo. 12mo. containing Dr. Johnsons Notes and Preface, embellished with an engraved title page and vignette Head of the Author; printed at Boston, by Munroe and Francis. The terms which are liberal may be known by enquiring at this office.

TERMS.

For 25 sets	$3 75	For 75 sets	$3 30
50 do	3 50	100 do	3 10

To pay one third on delivery, the remainder in approved notes at three months.
July 3. oed 2w*

MORRIS TURNPIKE.

THE Proprietors of Stock in the Morris Turnpike Company, are hereby notified and required to pay to *Elias B. Dayton*, Treasurer of said Company, at his office in Elizabeth Town, in the county of Essex and state of New-Jersey, the sum of *Two Dollars* on each Share of stock by them respectively holden on the hooks of said company, on or before the sixteenth day of August next, and if not then paid, the same will be forfeited without further notice.
By order of the Directors of said Company,
GAB: H. FORD,
July 7, taw P&H 4w President.

Ordinance to prevent the firing of Guns Squibs, &c.

BE *it ordained by the Mayor, Aldermen and Commonalty of the City of New-York, in Common Council convened this tenth day of July* 1804, That if any person shall fire or discharge any Gun, Pistol, Rocket, Cracker or Squib, or other Fire-Work in any Street, Lane or Alley, Garden or other inclosure, or from any House, or in any other place where persons frequently walk to the south ward of Grand street, every such person, for every such offence, shall forfeit and pay the sum of Five Dollars, to be recovered with costs of suit, and if the person offending be a minor, servant or slave his or her parent, master or owner, as the case may be, shall be liable for the said penalty, and be sued in like manner, as though the said parent, master or owner, had been the party offending; and the Attorney of this Board, is hereby authorised to pay over one half of each penalty recovered, to any person who will give such information as to enable him to prosecute to effect, and recover the same.
A true Copy,
T. WORTMAN, *City Clerk.*

The printers employed by the Corporation are requested to insert the above three times in their respective papers. July 12.

WHEREAS default of payment has been made of the monies secured to be paid by a certain Bond and Mortgage, executed by Wilson Stout, of the town of Ulysses, in the county of Cayuga, in the state of New York, to the subscriber bearing date the ninth day of May, in the year one thousand eight hundred and three—NOTICE IS HEREBY GIVEN, that by virtue of a power contained in said mortgage, and in pursuance of the act in such case made and provided, will be sold at public vendue, at the Tontine Coffee-House, in the city of New-York, on Monday, the 8th day of October next, at ten o'clock in the forenoon of said day, all the right and title of the said Wilson Stout, to that certain lot of Land, lying in the town of Ulysses, county of Cayuga, aforesaid, being lot No. 15, with all the improvements thereon, containing six hundred acres, more or less. The title deeds, and every necessary documents from the clerks office to prove their indisputable title, will be produced on the day of sale.
JAMES BLANCHARD.
April 7 s. 6m

FOR SALE OR EXCHANGE,

FIVE Shares in two several tracts of land, situate in the county of Washington, in the Territory North-West of the Ohio—each share containing 1173 acres, and including a House lot in the town of Anannati. This land will be sold at a very moderate price, and a reasonable term of credit given upon good security, or it will be exchanged for improved real estate, at a proportional valuation, in either of the states of New-York, Connecticut or New-Jersey. The Agent of the proprietor represents it as a good allotment, and the title is unquestionable. Enquire of the printer.
June 22 2aw6wP&H.

NEW BOOKS.

JUST Received per the Juliana, from London, and for Sale by P. A. MESIER, No. 107 Pearl-street—
Travels from Hamburgh through Westphalia, Holland and the Netherlands, to Paris, by Thomas Holcroft, 2 vols. 4to.
Military Mentor, 2 vols 12mo—Do. Byography,
Public Characters, 1803 and 4,
Spirit of Public Journals, 1803.
The Decameron, or Ten Days Entertainment of Boccacio, 2 vols.
The British Drama, comprehending the best plays in the English language, 5 vols royal 8vo
Seward's Life of Darwin,
The Revolutionary Plutarch, exhibiting the most distinguished characters, Literary, Military and Political, in the recent annals of the French Revolution, 2 vols 12mo
The Anti-Gallican, or Standard of British Loyalty Religion and Liberty, including a collection of the principal papers, tracts, speeches, poems and Songs, that have been published on the threatened Invasion, 1 vol 8vo
Lady's Museum, 11 vols—Monthly Mirror, 16 do.
Monthly Visitor, new series, 7 vols
Potts' Law Dictionary,
Orlando Furioso, 5 vols royal 8vo
Naval Chronicle, 10 vols do.
Letters of Advice from a Mother to a Son,
Dalla's History of the Maroons, 2 vols 8vo.
History of Malta, 1 vol 12mo
The Works of Joseph Addison, collected by Mr. Tickle, 6 vols 8vo
Addisonia, 2 vols 12mo—Barr's Buffon, 15 vols
Berwick's edition of Ossian's Poems, elegant,
Johnson's Works, 12 vls 8vo—Do. Lives, 4 vls 18mo
Swift's Works, 19 vols 8vo—Swiftina, 2 vols 18mo
Sterne's Works, 4 vols 8vo—Do. do. 7 vols 18mo
Burke's Works, 8 vols 8vo—Gibbon's Rome, 12 do
Hume's England, with Smallet's continuation, 13 vols 8vo
Hume's, Smallet's, Cormick and Lloyd's England 26 vols. Cooke's edition—(Same book, fine paper, calf gilt)
Parson's edition of do. 21 vols.
Bensley's Milton, 2 vols 8vo, elegant,
Heptinstall's do. 1 vol royal 8vo do.
Lady Montague's Works, 5 vols do.
Pinkerton's Geography, 1 vol.
Lempriere's Classical Dictionary,
Bacon's Works, 10 vols 8vo
Reeve's Bible and Common Prayer, 10 vols, royal 8vo, morocco,
Porteus' Lectures on the Gospel of St. Matthew,
Galloway on the Prophecies,
Willson's Sacra Privata—Do. Parochalia,
Romaine's Discourses—Do. Life of Faith,
Do. Walk of Faith—Do. Triumph of Faith,
Do. Works complete, 10 vols 8vo
Stanhope's Epistles and Gospels, 4 vols, 8vo
Shepherd on the Common Prayer, 2 vols 8vo
Hooke's Ecclesiastical Polity, 3 vols 8vo
Knox's Christians Philosophy,
Whitaker on the Revelations,
Edwards on Free Will—Paley's Theology,
Letters to a Young Lady, on a course of English Poetry, by J. Aikin,
Gray's Poetical Works, elegant—Goldsmith's do.
Peasant's Fate—Collin's Poems—Roger's do.
Opie's do—Poetical Register,
Kisses, being an English translation, in Verse, of the Bassia of Johhanes Secundis Nicoliaus, elegt.
Murray's Materia Medica, 2 vols
Hooper's Medical Dictionary, 1 vol
Johnson's Animal Chemistry.

NEW NOVELS.

Adelphe and Blanche, or the Travellers in Switzerland, 5 vols
Vagabond, 2 vols
Mount Pausilyppo 5 vols
Two Marrilas, or the Mysterious Resemblance, 3 vols
Remorseless Assassin, 2 vols
Picture of the Passions, 4 vols
Union, 3 vols
Peep at the World, or the the Children of Providence, 5 vols
Frederick Montravas, 2 vols
Harry Clinton,
Spong Castle,
Mysterious Count, or Montrillo Castle, 2 vols
Watch Tower, 5 vols
Hell upon Earth 2 vols
Don Sancho, or the Monk of Hennares, 2 vols
Light and Shade, 4 vols
Depraved Husband, 2 vols
Pride of Ancestry or who is she, 4 vols
Citizen's Daughter or what might be, 1 vol
Henritta Belman or the New Family Picture, 2vols
Malvina, 4 vols.
Mothers and Daughters. May 22 eod

SCHOOL MONIES.

WHEREAS in persuance and by virtue of an act of the Legislature of the state of New York, entitled "An Act to direct certain monies to be applied to the use of Free Schools in the City of New York," passed 8th of April 1801. It is made the duty of the vestry, trustees and minister, elders and deacons of the several churches and religious congregations therein mentioned, to put out at interest at real security, the whole amount of the respective shares of money received by them respectively by virtue of the several acts of the Legislature, entitled "*An Act for the encouragement of Schools*"—and "*An Act to raise a sum of money for the use of the State by tax, and for the further support of government*," and annually to expend and apply the interest accruing thereon for the instruction of poor children in the most useful branches of common education.

AND WHEREAS it is further made the duty of the said vestries, trustees, ministers, elders, and deacons respectively, on the second Tuesday of July in every year, to make return to the Common Council of this City, stating in writing the amount and manner in which they have disposed of such shares of money, and how they have applied the income thereof, on pain of forfeiting such share or shares to the said Common Council to be applied by them in such manner, and for such purposes as is directed by the said act.

PUBLIC NOTICE therefore is hereby given that the Common Council will meet at their chamber in the city-hall of the city of New York on Tuesday next, being the second Tuesday in July instant at 4 o'clock in the afternoon, for the purpose of receiving the said returns agreeably to law.
TUNIS WORTMAN,
Clerk of the City and County of New-York.

The Printers employed by the Corporation are requested to insert this ordinance in their respective papers three times. July 3

JOHN HOGG, of the Theatre, begs permission to inform his friends and the public, that he has taken that noted PORTER-HOUSE, No. 11 Nassau-street, lately kept by Mr. Fryatt, where he will make it his duty to keep a choice assortment of all such Liquors and other refreshments and conveniences, as the public expect in a well kept house of this sort. June 28 tf

FOR SALE, that valuable FARM in Greenbush, County of Rensselaer, about two miles below the Ferry into Albany; containing 140 acres of Flats of the best quality, extending one mile and a quarter along Hudson's-river, with about 100 acres of Pasture and Wood-land. There is a good Dutch House, a large Barn, and excellent Granary, and a remarkable well-bearing Orchard of choice grafted Apple & Pear-trees, on the premises. This Farm will be sold cheap, or would be divided into nearly two equal parts. For particulars apply to the printer, or the subscriber, on the premises.
JOHN G. HILL.
Letters post paid, will be attended to.
Dec 6 m tf

HAS for sale, a variety of valuable Patent and Family Medicines, among which are, the *Sovereign Ointment for the Itch*, which is warranted an infallible remedy at one application, and may be used with the most perfect safety by pregnant women, or on infants a week old, not containing a particle of mercury or any dangerous ingredients whatever, and is not accompanied with that tormenting smart which attends the exhibition of other remedies.—*The genuine Persian Lotion*, so celebrated among the fashionable throughout Europe, as an invaluable cosmetic, perfectly innocent and safe, free from corrosive and repellent minerals, (the basis of other Lotions) and of unparalleled efficacy in preventing and removing blemishes in the face and skin of every kind, particularly freckles, pimples inflammatory redness, scurfs, tetters, ring-worms, sun-burns, prickly heat, &c. The Persian Lotion operates mildly, without impeding the natural insensible perspiration, which is essential to health, the skin delicately soft and permanent, rendering complexion, and restores and clear, improving the ver failing to render an ordinary bloom of youth; ne... tiful, and an handsome one more so.—*The Restorative Powder for the Teeth and Gums.* This excellent preparation comforts and strengthens the gums, preserves the enamel from decay, cleanses and whitens the teeth, by absorbing all that acrimonious slime and foulness, which suffered to accumulate, never fails to injure and finally ruin them.—*Tooth Ache Drops* the only remedy yet discovered, which gives immediate and lasting relief in the most severe instances.

Hamilton's Elixir, a sovereign remedy for Colds obstinate Coughs, Asthmas, Sore-Throats, and approaching Consumptions. To parents who have children afflicted with the Hooping Cough, this discovery is of the first magnitude, as it affords immediate relief, checks the progress, and in a short time entirely removes the most cruel disorders to which children are liable—the Elixir is so perfectly agreeable, and the dose so small, that no difficulty arises in taking it,

From Luther Martin, Esq. Attorney General of the state of Maryland.

GENTLEMEN,

I comply with your request in stating my opinion of Hamilton's Elixir—It has been used in my family for two or three years past with uniform success, whenever colds, coughs, or similar complaints have rendered medicine necessary—I have myself found it an excellent and agreeable remedy for a very painful and troublesome affection of the breast, accompanied with soreness, and with obstructed breathing.

On these accounts, I do not hesitate to recommend Hamilton's Elixir as a valuable medicine and deserving public attention.
LUTHER MARTIN.

Mr. Abijah Henly, Bridge-street, Baltimore, was cured by one bottle of Hamilton's Elixir, of a very complicated disorder, occasioned by a severe cold caught several months ago—He breathed with the greatest difficulty, and was often thrown into weakening sweats when he attempted to walk any distance, and his voice would frequently fail in such a degree that he could only attempt to whisper; he has been upwards of six weeks without a return of his complaints, and desires to give his public testimony in favour of this invaluable medicine.

Mrs. Elizabeth Jones, South Howard street, was greatly relieved of an asthmatic complaint of several years standing, by the first bottle of Hamilton's elixir, and by the use of 5 bottles she has acquired a degree of ease and strength to which she had been long a stranger. She had taken balsam of honey Church's cough drops, and other medicines, without any benefit, and sometimes to the evident injury of her breathing.

THE MEDICINES PREPARED BY RICHARD LEE have been in high estimation and general use throughout the United States for upwards of six years—many of them are sold for less than the drugs of which they are compounded could be purchased at a retail store.

It is no inconsiderable evidence of their utility that during the above period, numerous imitations of every article (the production of ignorance and inexperience, urged by envy and penury) have intruded on the public, seen a day and then perished—others now succeed them, which in like manner are fast descending to "the tomb of the Capulets," while our remedies become more generally used, and acquire a daily accession of well-earned celebrity.

To prevent the imposition of worthless or dangerous preparations, purchasers are requested to remember, that an engraved label, with the signature of Richard Lee, (to counterfeit which is felony) is affixed to each of his genuine medicines.

Druggists and country store-keepers will be treated with on liberal terms. December 28

R—— respectfully informs his friends and the public in general, that the large new house, called the ... in NEW-UTRECHT, near the Narrows, Long Island, is again opened for the reception of company. Parties wishing to dine there will please send to the subscriber, or BENJAMIN BIRDSALL, at Brooklyn, one day's previous notice thereof.

N. B. A STAGE will commence running on next Saturday, from Birdsall's, at Brooklyn, to Bath, and will start on every Tuesday, Thursday and Saturday from Brooklyn, at 11 A. M. and return to Brooklyn in the evening. Fare for each passenger *two shillings each way.*

Gentlemen may be accommodated with Horses and Carriages at Birdsall's, on any day in the week.

June 19 tf TIMOTHY TITUS.

FOR SALE, or to Let, an elegant Country Seat, situate on Long-Island, between Flushing and Jamaica. Said place contains 110 acres of Land, 20 of which are wood land. On the premises are an excellent two-story well finished house, with two large rooms, a pantry, and spacious hall on the first floor; two large rooms, two bed rooms, and a pantry on the second floor; two finished bed rooms in the garret; a kitchen and cellar under the whole house; a barn and other out-houses; a great variety of the best peach, apricot, and other fruit trees. The prospect is extensive, as you have a view of the country around for a number of miles, together with Flushing Bay and the Sound. Its healthy situation, its convenience to Flushing, where the boats are daily going to New-York, and the short distance to Brooklyn, render it a desirable situation for a merchant, a person wishing to retire from business, or a farmer. The same will be disposed of on reasonable terms. A considerable part of the purchase money may remain on mortgage for a number of years. Apply to

ISAAC LAWRENCE,
No. 205 Pearl-street, New-York.

June 15. tf

TO LET, a commodious House, in a healthy situation, fronting the North-River, in Hudson-street, containing eight fire-places—the rent moderate. Enquire on the premises, or at this office.

Also, for sale, an elegant Pedal Harp, one of the best in America. Enquire as above.

June 13 1m

IN CHANCERY.

John R. Livingston, vs. George Purvis. } *In pursuance of a decretal order of the Court of Chancery, of the state of New-York, made in the above cause, will be sold at Public Auction, by the subscriber, at the Tontine Coffee-House, in the city of New-York, on the 26th day of July, 1804, at one of the clock in the afternoon, all those certain three Lots or parcels of Land, situate in the Handenburgh Patent, in the county of Ulster, in the state of New-York, being distinguished by lots No. 90, 133, and 139, in the Great Lot No. 4—the said three lots together containing four hundred and eighty-six acres and one half, together with all and singular, the privileges and appurtenances thereunto belonging, &c.—Dated the 9th June, 1804.*

THOMAS COOPER,
Master in Chancery.

June 9

PIANO FORTE & MUSIC STORE,

JOHN & MICH. PAFF, No. 54, Maiden-Lane.—Respectfully inform their friends and the public in general, that they have removed from No. 85, to No. 54, Maiden-lane, and have received by the ship Martha, from London, a general assortment of MUSICAL INSTRUMENTS, and NEW MUSIC, viz. elegant and plain patent Piano Fortes; finger and barrel Organs; pedal Harps, Guittars, Drums, Fifes, Clarinets, Trumpets, French Horns, Oboes, patent and plain Flutes, Flagellets, Bassoon, Violins, Violin-Bows, Violincellos; the best (Roman) Violin, Harp, Piano Forte and Guitar Strings, New-Music, Songs, &c.

All which will be disposed of wholesale and retail on the most moderate terms.

ALSO,

TO LET, a very convenient large STORE, if application is made immediately. Apply as above.

June 28

LATELY PUBLISHED,
In Philadelphia ... 129 Water-tree.

E. SAVINGS from the most celebrated Books on HUSBANDRY and GARDENING and RURAL AFFAIRS, interspersed with remarks and observations, by a gentleman of Philadelphia, one vol. 8 vo. price 2 dollars.

The general opinion of this Compendium is displayed by the immediate sale of the first edition; its merit is stamped by the praise of the reviews (two of which are selected,) and the author's desire to render it more eminently useful, is conspicuous, by the introduction (in the second edition) of Gardening. This edition has also undergone general revision, and under many heads is given considerable increase of information.

Extract from the Monthly Review of February 1801.

"The compiler has extracted a great variety of information, which he has arranged in alphabetical order under distinct heads, from A to Z. We think that the publication will be very useful to Agriculturists. It may be considered as a concise Farmer's Dictionary."

Extract from the Review in the Gentleman's Magazine for June 1801

"This little work gives the *essence of the most recent publications* of many favorite authors on Agricultural and Rural Economy, together with the *surveys of the several counties* of England, Wales, and Scotland, drawn up at the desire of the Board of Agriculture. *Plants are described in their variety, quantity of seed necessary per acre,* according to the various modes of cultivation; *Method of Cultivating, Weeding, Cropping, and Seeding.*

"And lastly the several uses to which the produce, whether of *seed or haulm,* can be most *advantageously* applied. *Trees,* whether of the *fruit or forest* kinds, are also treated of as to their varieties, the nature of the soil they delight in, their quality and affections, as to their own growth, or to what may be in contact with them; and the various use of their blossoms, fruits, leaves; or their wood, are capable of. The *management of bees, the dairy* and *many other useful articles,* are likewise introduced; together with a Plate of some useful implements for Draining, Transplanting, &c.—the *manner by which Hay is saved in wet seasons* in the North of England, by a practice called *Tappling.* The whole is arranged with great conciseness and merit, and will prove a most desirable companion to such as have neither the means or leisure to peruse the bulky materials from which this cheap tract is judiciously selected."

A list of the Books out of which the author selected the principal part of the materials:

General views of agriculture of the different counties of England, Wales, and Scotland; drawn up at the request of the Board of Agriculture.
Transactions of the Society instituted in London for the encouragement of Arts, Manufactures, and Commerce.
Transactions of the Bath Agriculture Society.
Do. of the Highland Do.
Do. of the Dublin Do.
Statistical Survey of the County of Dublin.
General view of the Agriculture, &c. of the County of Wicklow.
Marshall's Rural Economy.
Youngs Tour.
Hunter's Georgical Essays.
Curtis's Practical Observations on the British Grapes.
New Farmer's Calendar, by Mr. Lawrence.
Domestic Encyclopedia, by Dr. Willich.
Darwin's Phytologia.
Withering's Botanical Arrangement of all the Vegetables naturally growing in Great Britain.
And Works of the following writers on Gardening, viz. Evelyn, Bradley, Miller, Abercrombie, Kennedy, Kyle, Preston, &c.

July 7

TO THE INHABITANTS OF NEW-YORK.

A NEW CHEMICAL COMPOSITION HAS FOR SOME TIME PAST BEEN DISCOVERED, & WAS DAILY USED BY MORE THAN FIVE HUNDRED PEOPLE LAST YEAR DURING THE PREVALENCE OF THE YELLOW FEVER IN THIS CITY, UNDER THE NAME OF

PATENT ANTISEPTIC GAS,

As a sure preventative against any infectious or contagious disorder, and as the most powerful agent to purify the air, to neutralize mephitic miasmata or putrid effluvia in the rooms of sick people as well as on board of vessels, in cellars & stores which may harbour principles of corruption, &c. &c. without removing any goods or furniture---and without the least inconvenience either to the assistants or to the persons themselves administering the said Gas.

Previous to the aforesaid epoch the Patentees were fully convinced by numerous experiments of the efficacy of their Gas, but, through delicacy, they would not pretend to set out their own facts to the public as a rule for its explicit confidence. And indeed they earnestly deprecate (even now) any idea of personal lucre, and above all that of being confounded with *Quacks:* therefore instead of bringing forth a long list of certificates on the efficacy of this *New Gas,* they will only beg leave to refer it to the opinion of every one who has made a proper use of it last season, and who had time and opportunity to ascertain its extraordinary virtue.

They are bold to say that the honor of their discovery is more flattering than any monied consideration; therefore, while they ardently wish with the rest of their fellow-citizens to see this flourishing town free from the return of such a dreadful calamity as the *Yellow Fever* or any other epidemic, they esteem it their duty to give more publicity this year to a *preventative* which cannot fail to subside many pernicious alarms, and is at the same time the best *agent** that can be employed during a warm season to purify the air, &c. as here above mentioned.

P. DELABIGARRE,
One of the Patentees.

N. B. The Antiseptic Gas is to be had with printed directions at No. 258, Greenwich-st.

** The Patentees do not condemn the common practice of using soap, lime, and strong lye to scour and cleanse houses, but every one knows that infection or contagion always exists in an aerial form, and that hidden focus often adhere to certain places, even to pieces of furniture to which neither soap, lime nor lye can be applied; is it not therefore obvious that a gaseous substance like the Antiseptic must be the only fit antagonist to penetrate every where, combat and destroy infection or any pestilential focus? The purification of four or five rooms with the Antiseptic Gas will cost less than the white washing of them.*

June 22. 2m

To the Admirers of the Feathered Creation.

H. J. HASSEY, 72, Wal-Street, begs leave to inform the public that he has been at a vast deal of trouble to procure the following collection of beautiful singing BIRDS, which cannot be equalled in this country.

Canari Birds of different notes and colours, English Gold finches, English Black-birds, Bullfinch, Mocking Birds, Red Birds, Robbins, Blue Jays, Indigo Birds, Boblinks, Yellow Birds, Hang Birds.

A large assortment of Cages with Globes in Gold Fish.

A few of the best Parrots for talking in this country.

HE HAS ON HAND,

A few Grey, Red and Flying Squirrels, Rabbits and Guinea Pigs. Birds and Cages bot' sold, and exchanged of every description.

N. B. Masters of vessels and others can be furnished with any other kind of Birds or Beasts that this country produces.

June 29. 1m

FOR SALE, 4 Lots of Ground, situated on the Bowery Road, opposite Rivington-street, about half a mile above the Bull's-Head, fronting the Bowery on the south-east, and Elizabeth-street on the north-west. There is on said Lots a dwelling house, stable, smoak-house, a well of good water, a number of excellent fruit trees, &c. For further particulars enquire of the subscriber, on the premises.

EDWARD PATTEN.

June 14 tf

NOTICE is hereby given, that the Commissioners in the case of *David Auchmoole,* a Bankrupt, and the subscriber, Assignee of the estate and effects of said Bankrupt, intend to meet, to make a dividend or distribution of the said estate and effects, on Wednesday, the 25th day of July, 1804, at the office of the commissioners, No. 32 William-street, in the city of New-York, at which time and place, any creditors who have not already proved their debts, will have an opportunity of proving the same.

The creditors of said estate are also requested to meet at the same time and place, for the further purpose of considering whether they will consent that the subscriber should compound & agree all matters in difference and dispute between the said estate and *James Deas,* and whether they will consent that any and what composition be accepted of said James Deas, for the debt he owes said estate.

SAMUEL M HOPKINS.

New-York, June 16 1m

FOR SALE, a second hand STAGE, in compleat order, having just undergone a thorough repair—will be sold or exchanged for one or two horses. For particulars enquire at the Washington Livery Stable, No. 278 Greenwich-street.

A large Room to Let, or will be Leased to companies, societies, or lodges, or would answer extremely well for an election room, it being in the centre of the fifth ward. Military companies may likewise be accommodated in it. Enquire as above

May 19 tf

SUMMER RETREAT....To Let for the Summer Season or a longer time, a neat and pleasant situated small House and coach house, on the Bloomingdale road, at the 5 mile stone. Enquire of Wm. A. HARDENBROOK.

June 26 tf

STRAY COW....A large Red Cow came in to the pasture of the subscriber at Lit le Bloomingdale, in the month of April last. The owner is requested to call pay expences and take her away. Wm. A. HARDENBROOK.

June 26. 1m

THOMAS FAIRCHILD,

RESPECTFULLY informs his friends and the public in general, that he has removed from No. 10 Fair-street, to No. 2 Cedar-street, where he now keeps a PORTER-HOUSE. He has a quantity of best Newark Mountain CYDER, bottled under his own inspection and warranted of a superior quality.—Also, London Brown Stout in bottles. His draft Beer for ordinary use, he ventures to say, is of a quality inferior to none in this city. Merchants, Masters of vessels and private Families, may be supplied on moderate terms. June 16 eod tf

TUTTLE'S HOTEL.

JOHNSON TUTTLE informs his friends and the public, that he has taken the Hotel in Nassau-street, lately occupied by Mr. Mathieu.—He begs leave to premise to such of his friends as do not reside in this city, that the house is large, airy, and pleasantly situated in the business part of the town, where they may be assured of accommodations superior to those of ordinary Hotels. He is happy to have it in his power to inform gentlemen travellers, that a part of his house *is detached from the public rooms,* which will afford them an agreeable seclusion at the same time it furnishes them with all the enjoyments and attention of a public house. The merchant and the man of business, be they of town or country, cannot fail of being accommodated agreeably to their wishes, as his house affords every variety, and the more particularly as it will be his study to fashion it to the taste and fancy of his guests. It is almost unnecessary to add, that public and private parties may be accommodated, on all occasions, at a very short notice.

May 10 tf P&H 1m

To the Ladies and Gentlemen.

W. S. TURNER, Surgeon Dentist, respectfully acquaints the Ladies and Gentlemen, that he practices in all the various branches of his profession. He fits Artificial Teeth with such nicety as to answer all the useful purposes of nature, and of so neat an appearance that it is impossible to discern them from real ones. His method of cleaning the Teeth is allowed to add every possible elegance to the finest set, without giving the least pain, or incurring the slightest injury to the enamel. In the most raging *Tooth-ache* his Tincture has rarely failed in removing the torture; but if the decay is beyond the power of remedy, his attention in extracting the tooth, and indeed of decayed teeth in general, (from considerable study and practice) is attended with infinite ease and safety.

Mr. Turner will wait on any Lady or Gentleman, at their respective houses, or he may be consulted at No. 12 Dey-street, where may be had, with directions, his Antiscorbutic Tooth Powder, a most innocent preparation of his own, from Chemical and Medical experience. It has been in great esteem the last ten years, and is considered as pleasant in its application, as it is excellent in its effect; it renders the teeth smooth and white, braces the gums, makes them healthful, red and firm, prevents decay, tooth-ache, that accumulation of tartar, (so destructive to the teeth and gums) and imparts to the breath a most delectable sweetness.

Sold by appointment of the proprietor, at G. and R. WAITE'S Patent Medicine Warehouse and Book-Store, No. 64 Maiden-lane. June 12

FOR SALE,

THE time of an excellent Wench, from the country, who understands all kinds of House work, particularly excels in washing and ironing, is very neat, honest and sober. Enquire at 89 Pearl-street. June 28

Establishment at Canton, in China.

THE subscribers give notice, that they have formed a commercial Establishment at *Canton, in China,* with Mr. *Ephraim Bumstead,* under the firm of EPHRAIM BUMSTEAD & Co. whose services in the purchase of China Goods, Sales of Merchandize, or the transaction of other business, they now tender to their friends and the public. The terms on which they execute business intrusted to them may be known on application to Messrs. *Grant Forbes & Co. in New-York, Messrs. John Stille, Jun. & Co. at Philadelphia,* or at their Counting-House, in Boton. JAMES & THOMAS H. PERKINS.

Boston, June 2. June 7 2m

NOTICE is hereby given to the creditors of Thomas Phoebus and Gilbert Golding, lately trading in the city of New-York, under the firm of Phoebus and Golding, that they present to the subscribers, Assignees of the said firm, on or before the first day of August next, their respective accounts, together with their vouchers for the same. The creditors are hereby informed that no payment will be made on accounts presented subsequent to that period.

ROBT. CHEESBOROUGH, PETER S. MERCER, } Assignees.

New-York July 3, 1804.

ALL persons indebted to the late firm of Phoebus and Golding, are hereby requested to make payment of the same to the subscriber, duly appointed Attorney to the Assignees of the creditors of the said firm, on or before the twentieth day of July inst. as after that period they will be put in suit. THOS. W. RATHBONE,

July 3. t&tAug.1 111 Water-street.

FOR SALE,

A TWO story dwelling house, brick front, pleasantly situated on the east side of Greenwich-street, late the property of Alexander Lamb, deceased, having 6 fire places, 4 dwelling rooms, 2 bed rooms, 2 cellar kitchens and two kitchen pantries—Also a cistern in the yard. The house is newly built and of the best materials. The lot on which the said building is erected is 26 feet by 100, on a lease of 60 years unexpired, at a ground rent of £14 per ann.—For further particulars enquire of the subscriber, corner of Greenwich and Brannon-street, or of Peter C. Schuyler, corner of Nassau-street and Maiden-lane.

ROBERT MURDON, Administrator of the estate of Alexander Lamb, deceased.

N. B. If the above premises be not sold at private sale before the 21st inst. they will then be sold at Public Auction, at the Tontine Coffee-House, at one o'clock in the afternoon of that day.

July 10—to 21.

FOR SALE AT GREENWICH,

EIGHT Lots of ground, delightfully situated, within one hundred yards of the Banks, running through from Hammond to Henry-streets, there is on the premises, a large and convenient Store, built last fall, forty feet in length and twenty in width, on Hammond-street, and in the rear on Henry-street, is a small Stable—upwards of sixty Lombardy Poplars are beautifully arranged around the premises.—The whole is inclosed in a new board fence. Terms of sale may be known by applying to

T. SALTER,
Corner of Courtlandt-street and Broadway.

July 10 2w

IMPROVED method of Cutting Hair by EDWARD FROST, at the Mirror of Fashion and original Manufactory for Ladies and Gentlemen's Artificial Heads of Hair, No. 121 William-street. Three different rooms are fitted up for the reception of Ladies and Gentlemen; those who please to honour him with their custom will be met with punctual attention by proper persons.

N. B. Every article in the Ornamental Hair Line made and sold to the trade on reasonable terms. Perfumery of the first quality.

July 9 1m

TO LET, a pleasant Summer Retreat, situate in the village of New-Utrecht, on Long Island, near the Bath, and about eight miles from Brooklyn Ferry. Enquire at No. 57 Stone-street. June 11 tf

LOTTERY NO. III.

FOR THE ENCOURAGEMENT OF LITERATURE.

SCHEME.

1	PRIZE OF	$25,000	IS	$25,000
1		5,000		5,000
1		2,000		2,000
1		1,000		1,000
18		500		9,000
60		200		12,000
120		100		12,000
200		50		10,000
500		20		10,000
9000		10		90,000
1	FIRST DRAWN NO. 1st DAY			500
1		5th		1,000
1		10th		1,000
1		15th		1,500
1		20th		1,500
1		25th		2,000
1		30th		10,000
1		35th		2,000
1		40th		1,000
1		45th		1,000
1		50th		500
9,913	PRIZES			$198,000
23,087	BLANKS.			

33,000 TICKETS AT 6 DOLLARS IS $198,000

Less than 2 1-2 Blanks to a Prize.

☞ Subject to a deduction of fifteen per cent.

The drawing of the above Lottery will certainly commence in the city of New-York, on the first Tuesday in December next, and will be continued, at the rate of six hundred tickets each day, until completed.

The managers having disposed of twenty thousand tickets, to a company of contractors in the city of New-York, the remainder will be sold for cash only, by the respective managers, until the first Tuesday in October next.—This is the third of five Lotteries, directed by an act of the Legislature, passed the 3d of April, 1801, entitled "an act for the encouragement of literature"—and "an act making further provision for improveing the navigation between the villages of Troy and Waterford, and for other purposes."

DAVID GELSTON,
THOMAS STORM,
DANIEL HALE, } Managers.
PHILIP TEN EYCK,
S. SOUTHWICK,

June 6, 1804.

NEW-YORK AND ALBANY *MAIL STAGE,*

LEAVES New-York every morning, at 6 o'clock, lodges at Peekskill and Rhinebeck, and arrives in Albany on the third day. Fare of each passenger through eight dollars, and 6d per mile for way passengers. For Seats apply to *William Vandervoort,* No. 48, corner of Courtland and Greenwich-streets, New-York, and of *T. Witmore,* Albany.

February 13—tf POTTER, HYATT & Co.

FOR SALE,

A HOUSE, part of the inside unfinished, and a lease of two lots of ground, 19 years unexpired, in a healthy and pleasant situation at the corner of Broadway and Greenwich road; there is a pump quite new, close to the door of an excellent spring of water, which will be found a valuable acquisition. The rapid improvements that are continually making and the increase of population will render it a valuable situation for a Grocery, Tavern or Tea garden, particularly in the summer season, being perfectly free from sickness. For particulars enquire at No. 63 Barclay-street.

May 22. tf

FOR SALE at Bloomingdale, six miles from the city, a valuable FARM, containing twenty acres, in the highest state of cultivation. On said premises is a new two story House, built in the modern style, consisting of 3 rooms, with a hall on each floor, and 3 finished bed chambers in the attic story, a convenient kitchen, pantry, and 2 cellars, a new barn, out house, &c. with a right of a good dock. The river affords a variety of scale and shell fish in their season, the land is ornamented with walks, and the best collection of fruit and forest trees, and for health and situation it is not exceeded by any on the Island. It is surrounded by a number of beautiful seats, inhabited by the most respectable characters, has a view of the Hudson for 20 or 30 miles, part of York bay to Staten Island, with an extensive view of the adjacent country. As it is the only farm for sale on the Hudson, and considering the rapid increase of population and property, with the various objects it embraces, it is worthy of immediate attention to those who wish to purchase so admirable a retreat. An indisputable title will be given, and half of the purchase money may remain on mortgage. For further particulars enquire at No. 124 Broadway.

N. B. As there are a number of building spots on said farm, the whole will be sold together, or in lots from half an acre to any larger quantity, for the accommodation of purchasers. Jan 9 tf

TO BOOKSELLERS,

FOR SALE 10 trunks of Books, containing the works of the most celebrated authors in the English language, all of the best *London Editions* in elegant bindings; among them are the following, viz.—The works of Hume, Smollet, Gibbon, Swift, Locke, Sterne, Pope, Baron, Smith, Buffon, Raynal, King of Prussia, Mavor, Encyclopedia Britannica, Henry's Great Britain, British Essayest's, Rollins, Junius, Josephus, Gillies, Edwards, Dibdin, Newton, Zimmerman, Thompson, Milton, Goldsmith, Robertson, Montague, Blair, Hawies, Doddridge, Knox, with a great variety of others, an invoice of which may be seen and terms known (which will be a very liberal credit for the greater part) on application to

GRANT FORBES, & Co. 62 South street.

Note—Should the above books not be disposed of by Thursday next, they will be sold at public auction. Catalogues published and notice given of the place of sale accordingly. June 18

TO PRINTERS.

THE following Printing Materials will be sold a great bargain, if immediate application is made, and a liberal credit given for approved endorsed notes, viz.—two Printing Presses, one new and very complete; one fount Brevier, never blacked; one fount Pica, new; Black Letter, of different kinds; one large marble Imposing Stone; Chases, of different kinds; Gallies; Composing Sticks; Frames, with racks and drawers, and many other articles. Apply at 245 Water-street.

June 1 tf

TO LEASE, several Lots of Land, containing from 4 to 6 acres, on each of which there is an excellent situation for a house. They are within 3 1-2 miles of the city, and lay on the *North-river* and Greenwich-road. For particulars enquire of

THOMAS B. CLARKE,
January 20 tf 16 Broad-street,

AN eligible situation for a Country Seat.— About Twenty Acres of improved Land, in Harlem Lane, at the 8 mile stone. There are several fruit trees on the place, and is in every respect well calculated for a gentleman's country residence. For further particulars apply to

May 17 JOHN MURRAY & SONS.

THE CIRCULATING LIBRARY, (*formerly H. Caritat's*) No. 1 City-Hotel, broadway, is offered for Sale. Proposals for its purchase will be received until the first of August. A priced catalogue will be exhibited, and the conditions of sale made known, to those who wish to treat for it, at the Library.

This collection, far more extensive than any of the kind which has been established in the United States, comprizes the most celebrated works in the English and French languages, in the several departments of polite literature, and generally two or more copies of each. It consists of more than ten thousand volumes, most of which are in a good condition, and none of those included in the catalogue unfit for circulation. The patronage which this establishment has hitherto received from the inhabitants of New-York and its neighbourhood, has been such as to indemnify the proprietor for the very considerable additions, which he has yearly made to it, and has afforded a very handsome profit after deducting the expences of managing it. This patronage may be secured, and still further increased, by any person who will devote himself to the business with assiduous attention, and who unites a suitable degree of industry to a tolerable knowledge of books. The catalogue will be found to contain not only every decent work yet imported into this country, belonging to the class of Novels and Romances, but a more general collection of books in the higher departments of literature; and of those which are generally classed under the head of Miscellanies, than can be found in any one bookstore in America. June 19 tf

GIBSON & DAVIS, Patent Piano Forte Manufacturers, from London, takes this opportunity to inform the Ladies and Gentlemen of the city of New-York, that they have removed from No. 53 Warren-street to No. 63 Barclay street near Greenwich-street, where all orders in the above business will be punctually attended to.

May 10

JOHN R. D. HUGGINS respectfully informs the Ladies and Gentlemen of New-York he has returned from Philadelphia, and will be happy to receive their commands. He has a great variety of New Fashions, which he intends immediately to put in practice.—Also, a large assortment of Tortoise-Shell Combs, on the most reasonable terms, at No. 92 Broad-way. June 18

ELECTUARY for the cure of the FEVER and AGUE and INTERMITTENT FEVER.

The subscriber having removed from the city of New-York to Newark, there to resume the practice of Medicine. In compliance with the wishes and advice of several friends, announces to them and the public, that this Electuary, which invariably removes the above diseases, in the course of a day or during an intermission, may, in future be had of Messrs. G. & R. Waite, 64 Maiden-lane, whom he has constituted his agents for the sale of said Medicine. To those who have used it no recommendation is necessary, and those who have not, may be fully informed of its qualities and effects by application to Mr. JOHN MURRAY, Pearl-street, who will attest that in more than 30 instances, to the best of his recollection, in which he has used it or recommended the use of it, during the last summer, it has never failed of success), or to Samuel Bayard, Esq. Cortland-street, Mr. Elias Haines, or Mr. Thomas Lovell, Broadway.

This Electuary (a small quantity of which removes the above diseases) may be taken easily in pills without any sensible operation and without any restriction as to diet, either in roasted apple, or if the patient can take the Medicines in a liquid state, then either in port or Madeira wines. With each box more particular directions are given.

ABRAHAM CLARK,
April 26. 6m eod late of Broadway.

FOR SALE, a COUNTRY SEAT, situate at Haverstraw, in the county of Rockland, 40 miles from the city of New-York, and a mile and a half from the landing, from whence vessels daily sail for the city. The House is two story high, well built, finished neatly in the modern stile, and commandsan extensive and elegant view of the Hudson. The Farm contains about 74 acres, mostly under cultivation, and in good fence, a large part of it stone wall. The house, barn and other buildings have all been built within 4 years. A more particular description of the premises may be had, and the terms of sale known, by applying to

SAMUEL SMITH,
341 Washington-street.

Also for sale the equal undivided moiety or half part of a tract of land, containing 3,200 acres situate in Township No. 2, in the first range of Towns in Steuben County (formerly Ontario). Apply as above. Jan. 19. tf

FOR SALE, a pair of Bay Horses, 15 1-2 hands high, 6 years old, free from any fault, broke to all kinds of harness, and will be sold cheap—they will answer a curricle extremely well, as they carry very lofty.

Also, a pair of bright Bay Horses, 14 1-2 hands high, 5 years old, suitable for a curricle, and broke to every kind of harness.

All the above Horses will be warranted sound, and free from any fault and defect. For particulars enquire at the Washington Livery Stable, No. 278 Greenwich-street.

N. B. The above horses have just came from the country, are excellent saddle horses, and remarkable good for the single harness. May 18

LIQUID BLACKING.

THE subscriber has imported this day, in the ship Halcyon, Rossiter, from London, a few groce bottles of Bunbury and Co. celebrated Royal Egyptian Liquid Blacking, prepared by that house only, and now universally used. Sold by WILLIAM HUTSON, (only) at his Perfumery and Fancy Store, No. 78 Broadway, at the Sign of the Rose and Eagle. March 1 tf

LIQUID BLACKING.

BLUNTS original Morocco Liquid Blacking, which is universally acknowledged superior to any other for preserving and giving a beautiful shining black gloss to Leather.

Several years experience has proved the excellence of this Blacking for the above purposes—during which period it has been made use of by numerous gentlemen of the first respectability, who affirm it to be superior to every other preparation of the kind for preserving and giving a beautiful gloss to Leather.

In addition to the above, it also possesses these peculiar advantages—It does not *cake* on the Leather—Boots or Shoes blacked with it will neither soil fingers in putting on, or the stockings in wearing—It need be applied but two or three times a week. Gentlemen using this Blacking and giving it a fair trial, and not approving it, their money shall be returned.

The original Morocco Liquid Blacking is prepared only and sold Wholesale and Retail by the proprietor, T. BLUNT, No. 81 Nassau-street, New-York, one door from Beekman-street, and by appointment at G. & R. WAITE's Patent Medicine and Book Store, No. 64 Maiden lane

*** Note. Each Bottle is sealed with a bill of directions, which unless signed in the hand writing of the proprietor, is spurious. Fifty per cent allowed to Storekeepers to sell again. ... 30.

NEW-YORK:
PRINTED AND PUBLISHED
BY
MICHAEL BURNHAM,
NO. 40 PINE-STREET.
PRICE, TEN DOLLARS PER ANN.

AMERICAN CITIZEN.

[No. 2301.] SATURDAY, AUGUST 22, 1807. [Vol. 8.]

FOR SALE,

The Sloop FAME, about 45 tons burthen, I. Denning, master, now lying in Burling Slip—or would be exchanged for a larger one. A bargain may be had in her by applying to

JUSTIN & ELIAS LYMAN, 80 South street

Also for sale—146 bbls Pot and Pearl Ashes. June 5

For Freight or Charter,

The superior built, fast sailing Ship PARNASSO, S. Allen, master, burthen 240 tons, one year old, and in complete order for the reception of a cargo. Apply to

POST & GRINNELL, corner South and Pine streets

Also, the brig PINDUS, Allen, master, burthen 215 tons, a substantial fast sailing vessel, six months old, and in good order for business. Apply as above.

Also, the Brig ROBERT BARCLAY, Brailey, master, burthen 220 tons, a well built, swift sailing vessel, 18 months old, and ready to receive a cargo. Apply as above.

For Sale, 150 bales prime Upland Cotton. june 24

FOR FRIEGHT OR CHARTER,

The good, fast sailing brig HARLEQUIN, Dickins, master, burthen about 178 tons. For terms apply to

JENKINS & HAVENS, South st. between Dover st. and Peck slip.

FOR SALE,

2000 bushels coarse and bright Isle of May Salt, discharging from on board the ship Thomas, and in Store,

Whale and sperm oil in small casks

30 boxes sperm candles

5000 goat skins, in prime order. july 17

FOR TONNINGEN OR HAMBURGH, (*If the Blockade of the Elbe be taken off*)

The Ship PASSENGER, Jas. G. Copinger, master, a fine staunch vessel, and a remarkably fast sailer, has half her cargo engaged and will be dispatched with all convenient speed—For freight or passage apply to the master on board at Pine street wharf, or

WM. ADAMSON, corner Pine and Front streets. april 30

For Freight or Charter,

The ship ISABELLA, 290 tons, 6 months old, daily expected to arrive in Virginia—The Ship *Charles*, 400 tons, 3 years old, sails very fast, and hourly expected at the Hook from Portland in ballast—The fine new ships *Clinton*, of 260 tons, and *York*, of 308 tons, lying at eastern ports, in readiness to be dispatched to such ports as freighters may wish—For cargoes apply to

JACOB BARKER, 34 Beekman-street. june 15

For Sale, Freight or Charter,

The brig CLINTON, burthen 190 tons, T. Allen, master, a substantial swift sailing vessel, one year old, and in complete order for the reception of a cargo. For further particulars apply to

POST & GRINNELL, Corner South and Pine streets

Also, for Freight or Charter.

The very fast sailing, staunch ship NIAGARA, capt Cross, 270 tons—has made only one voyage, and may be dispatched immediately—Apply as above. July 16.

FOR FREIGHT OR CHARTER,

The superior built, swift sailing ship HANNAH, E. Cottle, master, burthen 190 tons, one year old, and in complete order for the reception of a cargo. Apply to

POST & GRINNEL, Corner of Pine and South streets. July 8

FOR GREENOCK,

The fast sailing Brig ROVER, captain Towne, 197 tons, 6 months old, commences loading this day, and will have immediate dispatch. For freight of a few heavy goods or passage, having good accommodations apply to the master on board at Dover street wharf, or to

JACOB BARKER, 34 Beekman street. aug 4

FOR SALE,

The remarkable fast sailing Ship AMBITION, burthen about 333 tons, laying at Clason's wharf. For terms and inventory apply to

ISAAC CLASON, 61 Broadway. april 28

SLOOP EXPERIMENT,

For Passengers only.

ELIHU S. BUNKER informs his friends and the public, that he has commenced running a Sloop of about 110 tons burthen, between the cities of Hudson and New York, for the purpose of carrying passengers only. The owners of this vessel being desirous to render the passage as short, convenient and agreeable as possible, have not only taken care to furnish her with the best beds, bedding, liquors, provisions, &c. but they have been at very great expence and trouble in procuring materials and building her on the best construction for sailing and for the accommodation of ladies and gentlemen travelling on business or for pleasure.

The Experiment leaves Hudson every Sunday morning precisely at 8 o'clock, and New York every Wednesday evening at 6 o'clock, from Whitehall, in front of John B. Coles's flour store, throughout the season.

E. S Bunker having been several years engaged in the freighting business between New York and Hudson, has become well acquainted with every part of the river, and he hopes by attention and punctuality to merit the patronage of ladies and gentlemen who may have occasion to travel through this or the northern states.

Merchants and others residing in the northern, eastern and western countries, will find a great convenience in being able to calculate (at home) the precise time they can sail from Hudson and New York, without being under the necessity of taking their beds and bedding; and those in New York may so calculate their business as to be certain of comfortable accommodations up the river. Persons residing or coming to the different places on the river, south of Hudson, will be carefully taken on board or set on shore as the case may be. The very great improvements made within these few years on roads leading in most all directions from Hudson, will add to the convenience and facilitate the travelling in this way. aug 13

HIDES, OIL, &c.

2000 Spanish hides

20 barrels liver oil

500 calf skins suitable for the West India market

And a general assortment of leather as usual. For sale by

FERGUSON & SHIPLEY, corner Frankfort & Jacob st. march 27 tf

SUGAR, COTTON, INDIGO, &c.

69 hhds and 34 bbls Muscovado sugar

25 boxes white, and 39 boxes brown sugar

62 bales Carthagena cotton

28 seroons Indigo, 53 seroons bark

129 quintals fustic

301-2 do Brazilletto—landing this day at Courtland street wharf from on board the sch'r Betsey, Ripley, from Trinidad (Cuba) Apply to

ABM. KING, No 70 Courtlandt st

ALSO, if applied for immediately, the above vessel, 2 years old, 134 24 95 tons; sails fast, and can be sent to sea without any expence. Apply as above. july 26

DISSOLUTION OF PARTNERSHIP.

The co-partnership of *John Kane and Co.* is dissolved by mutual consent. The business will be continued by John Kane, who is duly authorised to settle the concerns of the company.

JOHN KANE.
OLIVER KANE.

JOHN KANE, No 277 Pearl street, has remaining on hand of late importations a general assortment of seasonable Goods, among which are—

Calicoes and Chintzes
Shawls and Pocket Hdkfs
Scotch, Madras and Malabar do.
Handsome printed Waistcoating
4-4, 9-8 and 6-4 Cambric and Book Muslins
Brown Linens, Cotton Shirtings
7-8, 4-4 and 5-4 linen and cotton Checks
Mens & womens white and col'd Cotton Hose
Cotton Cassimeres and Granderells
Hunters Cords and velveteens
Superfine and tabby Velvets
Undressed Bed Ticks
Linen and Cotton Stripes
5-4 and 6-4 Silk Shawls
Extra long silk and cotton Gloves
A large assortment of white thread Laces and Edgings, do. Cotton do. black patinet do.
An assortment of Ribbons, Velvet Bindings, white Threads, Tapes, Quality and Shoe Bindings, Sewing Silks and Twists, Rattinets, Shalloons, Calimancoes, Russelets, striped and plain Wildbores, black Bombazetts, &c. with a general assortment of Fancy Goods

He has also on hand, a good assortment of Calcutta and Madras Goods, consisting of, Beerboom Gurrahs, Baftas, Salempores, Emerties, Madras and blue Gilla Hkfs.

Also, a constant supply of Cut Nails of the very best quality, of the following size—4d, 6d, 8d, 10d, 12d, and 20d—all of which he will sell very low and at accommodating credits. june 27

SALT—Now landing from the ship Nancy, at Dye street wharf, a quantity of Liverpool grained and fine SALT—For sale by

JOHN DUFFIE & CO. or THOMAS FARMAR & CO. july 25

PRIME RICHMOND TOBACCO AND FEATHERS.

SIX hhds prime Tobacco, 12 small bales live Geese Feathers, landing from on board the sch'r Huldah and Anna, at Murray's wharf.

IN STORE,

10 hhds Muscovado Sugars
5 do prime Jamaica Coffee
9 pipes Corsica Wine, superior quality
Madeira, Port and Sherry do
10 pipes Amsterdam Gin
10 do Cogniac Brandy
6 do Barcelona do
10 hhds Jamaica Rum
8 do Country do
Old Cherry Brandy and Rum
15 boxes London Mustard, (fresh)
50 Demijohns, 30 Liquor Cases
4 bbls Hickory Nuts
Nutmegs, Cassia, Cloves, Pepper and Pimento
Claret in boxes, London Porter
Cheese in casks
Loaf and Lump Sugar
10 chests Souchong } TEAS
8 do Imperial and Gunpowder }
4 do Young Hyson }

With a general assortment of Groceries, for sale by

CLARK & OGILBY, 111 Front street

Ship Stores put up, and families supplied. march 23 tf

WILLIAM ADAMSON, No. 35, Pearl street, offers for sale, the cargo of the brig Triton, from Cette, now landing at Courtland-street wharf, viz.

100 pipes of brandy, 4th proof
20 whole and 20 half pipes red Cargo wine
20 casks do 100 do do
4 bales Silk goods, assorted
1 do Sattins 1 do Cambrics
1 do Kid Gloves
7 cases mens' Hats
3 hhds Cream Tartar
41 bundles Verdigrease
5 bales shelled Almonds
28 do Almonds in the shell
6 boxes Candles 1 box Soap
26 bags Corks

Also in store, a quantity of Claret Wine in hhds and boxes, and a few bales of Broad Cloths. july 1 tf

THE subscriber has received by the late arrivals from England, a complete assortment of Hardware and Cutlery Goods, which he offers for sale on liberal terms.

E. LYDE, JUN. 230 Pearl-st. near Burling slip. april 28

CLARET WINE.—Now landing from on board the ship Exchange, captain Weekes, from Bordeaux, 80 hhds Cargo Wine—For sale by

WM. ADAMSON.

A quantity of excellent Bordeaux Bottled Wine, Cette Brandy, and French Dry Goods in store. july 31

GOLD & SILVER WATCHES.

STEPHEN REED, No 70 Maiden-lane, has received per ship Clyde, from Amsterdam, a large, well chosen and elegant assortment of *SWISS WATCHES,* of various descriptions, and of the most tastey and approved patterns, which he will dispose of for cash or approved notes, wholesale and retail, on reasonable terms. july 10 tf

SLATE—200 boxes first quality Slate taken from a quarry lately discovered in Putny, Vermont, for sale by

JUSTIN & ELIAS LYMAN, No 80 South street. march 26

PORK, BUTTER, RYE FLOUR, &c.

90 bbls Mess Pork
8 do Prime do
110 firkins excellent Butter
100 bbls Rye Flour
300 sides Soal Leather
10 bbls Country Gin—For sale by

WM. HILLYER & CO. aug 17 1w

25 casks, 200 dozen CLARET WINE of excellent quality and fit for immediate use, for sale on moderate terms by

GEO. DE PEYSTER, No 11 Wall street

Fine Old Port and Madeira in casks and bottles. aug 4 1m

FOR SALE by *ABRAHAM REYNOLDS*, No 20 South street, near Coenties Slip,

200 puncheons of yellow Delaware and Jersey kiln dried Indian Meal, in quarter iron bound casks
1000 barrels do do do
400 do superfine Flour
400 do Rye Flour

Also just arrived by the Richmond Packet, captain Lefort, and for sale by A. Reynolds,

400 barrels of fresh Richmond S fine Flour
400 do do do fine do
50 do do do Middlings

The *Richmond Packet* lies at Coffee House Slip, and will sail in a few days. For freight or passage apply to the captain on board. aug 3 1m

ISAAC BLOOMFIELD, Merchant Taylor and Salesman, 256 Water street, having come to a determination to quit the business, offers the stand and stock in trade upon advantageous terms to any person who is desirous of entering into the above line. All persons indebted to the said Isaac Bloomfield are requested to make settlement before the 25th of July next, as all accounts undischarged at that time will be delivered to a committee of his creditors for collection. june 30 tf

OAKUM & BRUSHES—For sale at the *State Prison*, a quantity of Oakum of the first quality; also, Brushes of all kinds, and a quantity of Stockings. jan 16 tf

COTTON—140 bales superior Upland Cotton, now landing, for sale by

POST & RUSSELL, corner of Pine and South streets. july 31

SPANISH SEGARS—260 boxes 1st quality Spanish Segars, for sale by

IRVING & SMITH, 153 Pearl-st. aug 6

FLAXSEED WORKS FOR SALE.

A Complete set of Flaxseed Works in the fire proof store no 94 Front street, being one of the best and longest established stands in this city for the flaxseed business. The purchaser to become tenant of the store till the first of May next. Application to be made at no 6 Upper Read street. aug 17

HERMAN VOSBURGH,

MANUFACTURER OF PAINTS, VARNISHES, & No 53 *Chatham street New York*,

OFFERS for sale, a general assortment of Paints, Painter's articles, and Varnishes, of every description, wholesale, retail, and for exportation, at the lowest prices for cash, or the usual credit.

50 casks dry whitelead	500 wt mineral or blue
8 hhds whiting	black
8 do Paris white	3 casks black lead
2 do pumice stone	1 do powder blue
14 do lampblack	100 wt emery powder
10 casks ivory black	1000 wt blue vitriol
16 do powdered ochre	16 casks linseed oil
70 do Spanish brown	3000 wt putty in bladers
4 tons powdered Venetian red	250 kegs gr'd wh. lead
	300 do Spanish brown
6 casks blue verditer	150 do black paint
18 do mineral green	100 do Venetian red s
6 do olympian do	25 do gr'd verdigrise
4 do green verditer	100 do yellow ochre
6 do French green	130 doz paint brushe
10 do imperial patent verdigrise	assorted
	300 do sash tools do
700 wt Dutch pink	40 gross camels hair
600 do new yellow do	pencils
400 do patent yellow	24 doz pallet knives assorted
100 do sugar of lead	
1 hhd rotten stone	1600 books Dutch metal
16 do Italian ochre	Flake white
3 casks S. American gum copal	White chalk
	Red do
10 bags India do	Strewing smalts
1 cask gum asphaltum	Putty, window glass
1000 wt gum shellac	Powdered blue
100 do English umber	Flotant indigo
3 casks Prussian blue	Carolina do
2 bales Russia glue	&c &c

NB. The manufacturer begs leave to suggest that he grounds his pretensions to public patronage only on the knowledge of his business, and the quality of his articles, and in future his kegs shall be branded with his name, jugs of varnish sealed with his initials, pots and packages labelled with his name and place of abode, *and the contents warranted*. Feb 12

American Playing Cards.

FORTY-TWO boxes playing cards, just received from the factory, consisting of supergne and fine Eagles and Harry 8th and Merry Andrews—For sale on liberal terms by

N. JUDAH, 84 Maiden Lane. july 21

TEAS, &c.—120 qr chests hyson tea, 456 boxes Shulon do, 400 quarter chests hyson-skin do, 17 do Powchon do, 100 cr chests and 59 boxes Pecco, 1468 chests Congo tea, 1678 do compoi do, 1473 quarter chests, 798 eighths, 492 twelfths chests, and 105 boxes Souchong Tea; 2148 bundles cassia, 75 pecals Galinzall Root—the cargo of the ship General Hamilton now landing—*And in Store*, 874 chests souchong tea, per Aeolous—9 casks plated ware, containing castor and cruet frames, coffee and tea urns, epergnis, snuffers and trays, brackets, coffee and tea pots, oral dishes and covers, cream jugs, cake baskets, bottle stands, patent and plain candlesticks, sugar basons, cream ewers, fruit baskets, and a variety of cutlery and hardware, containing hand, pannel, sash, dove tail and tenant saws, scissors, razors and penknives on cards, knives and forks, penknives, razors, shoe knives, shaving boxes, &c. Also, several pipes Cogniac brandy—for sale by

Ingraham, Phenix & Nexsen. aug 11

WINE, TEA, SUGAR & RICE.

100 casks claret wine, on reasonable terms
100 hhds first quality brown clayed sugar
60 do 2-3d white and 1-3d brown
12 boxes fresh hyson tea, extraordinary fine, for family use
23 tierces rice—For sale by

ALEXANDER ZUNTZ, At his auction and commission store, 127 Water street. aug 15

JUST received and for sale by *Myers & Judah* No 150 Pearl street, 200 boxes first quality Segars, 50 ceroons royal Spanish Tobacco, 12 ons Camwood. aug 18

MONEY!

ACCOMMODATION OFFICE,

BY NUNES & GOMEZ, No. 74 MAIDEN-LANE, *Corner of William Street.*

FROM one dollar to any amount always ready to be advanced on the shortest notice, for a day, week, month, or longer if required, on deposits.

Bills, Notes, and other securities bought and sold on commission, and all money concerns transacted with the strictest punctuality and integrity. Eastern and Southern Bank Notes discounted.

NB. LOTTERY TICKETS for sale at the above office by B. GOMEZ. june 25 tf

BROKER'S OFFICE

AND COMMISSION STORE,

No. 145 FRONT STREET, THREE DOORS FROM THE MARKET.

The subscribers purporting to transact business as Brokers in general, inform the merchants of New York and masters of vessels that any charge left with them relative to business as above, will be prudently attended to; they will procure freights, charters, and also buy and sell vessels, merchandise of all descriptions, lands, &c. Transient persons not knowing the forms of our Custom House, may have their business dispatched expeditiously and upon easy terms. Conveyancing, &c; also money procured on notes, bonds, and mortgages. Seamen shipped, &c.

AARON KELLOGG & CO. aug 13 2w

SUGAR & COFFEE—43 tierces and 37 bags coffee, 35 hhds Havanna do. 114 boxes brown do do—For sale by

ALEX. ZUNTZ, at his auction and commission store, 127 Water st. aug 21

NOW LANDING,

100 boxes white Havannah sugar
110 brown do
300 boxes segars, first quality
21 ceroons indigo

IN STORE,

49 boxes brown Havannah sugar
121 white do
49 bales sarsaparilla
21 puncheons Grenada rum
33 pipes Cette brandy
9 ceroons flotant indigo
20 boxes chocolate
1 pipe Holland gin—For sale by

WM. F. PELL. aug 12

JACOB BARKER,

134 *Beekman street—Has for Sale,*

Who has for sale—6000 bushels coarse, 3000 do fine Liverpool salt, 100 crates crockery, 100 boxes spermaceti candles, 10 pipes, 20 half do and 15 qr casks LP Madeira wine, of an excellent quality, 200 dressed seal skins, 150 chests hyson, 30 do young hyson, and 30 do hyson skin teas, 100 hhds clayed and 50 do muscovado sugar, 4 bales yellow nankeens, 20 coils American cordage, 7 hhds molasses, 11 boxes Manilla indigo, 25 casks whale oil, 10 casks summer and 10 do winter oil, 12 bundles whalebone, 100 bls mackarel, 33 hhds codfish, 11 boxes saffron in oil, 30 boxes mould and 30 do dipped tallow candles. aug 4

IMPORTANT

To Owners & Masters of Vessels.

A PATENT has been obtained from the President of the United States, for the valuable purpose of extracting Fresh Water from Salt Water of the Ocean by evaporation and condensation, with a new constructed Camboose on a plan which is calculated to economise fuel in the course of cooking, when at the same time it will afford at the rate of from five to seven gallons of pure fresh water in an hour. This invention, properly considered, is no doubt one of the most important things to the commercial world which has ever been known, as it not only provides the ship's crew and passengers with pure and wholesome fresh water in the time of cooking, and without additional expence of fuel, but is a saving to the merchant of a great proportion of the room occupied by water casks in the hold of the vessel.

The machine has been put in actual practice, and by experiment in this city, under the most strict examination, it has satisfactorily proved to answer every purpose as above mentioned, as appears by certificates herewith published, signed by gentlemen of rank and commercial respectability:

The machine requires but a very small space and is easily secured; the importance of this discovery will therefore instantly present itself to all persons concerned in navigation, and will be particularly obvious to those whose misfortune it may be to be kept long at sea by distress of weather and suffering for water.

"We certify that the new invented machine for extracting fresh water from salt water, for which John Lamb has obtained a patent from the United States, on strict examination, appears to answer a valuable purpose, as it extracts pure fresh water from salt water, at the rate of from five to seven gallons an hour.

Samuel Osgood, Jacob Stout,
Wm. Denning, Corns. Brinckerhoff,
Acquilla Giles, Joseph Marshall,
Wm. I. Vredenburgh, Robert Cocks, jun'r
John Ten Eyck, Joshua Secos,
Wm. Pell, Isaac Brouson."
Peter Curtenius,

All persons are cautioned against making, using or vending any part or parts of the said machine unless legally authorised.

Apply to the subscriber at the Custom House, New York. JOHN KEARNEY.

The inventor and patentee are citizens of the state of New-York. Oct 13

WANTED, in a small family, a Woman Servant to do plain cooking, washing and ironing, and other house work. The family will reside about 3 miles out of town on this island during the summer months. Apply at this office. april 22 tf

WANTED, a White Woman who understands cooking. Enquire at No 85 Water street. aug 18

WANTED,

A Woman to do the work of a small family. Good wages will be given to one well recommended. Enquire at No. 120 Water street. august 11

WANTS A SITUATION,

A Young Man, aged 23 years, who has been a resident of the city for nearly 2 years, is willing to engage as a Clerk in a Counting House or out door business; speaks French, English, and Italian fluently, and will give satisfactory reference, by applying at No. 1 Burling slip, or 94 Chatham street.

NB. The reason of leaving his present employment is owing to the state of health. august 11

GEOGRAPHICAL COMPILATION

JUST received from Philadelphia, and for sale by *Brisban & Brannan*, No 1 City Hotel, Broadway, in 2 vols 12mo price in sheep, Geographical Compilation for the use of schools being an accurate description of all the empires, kingdoms, republics and states in the known world: with an account of their population, government, religion, manners, literature, universities, history, civil divisions, ecclesiastical hierarchy, principal cities, with an account of their importance, remarkable monuments, illustrious citizens, commerce and populations, &c. The whole arranged in a categorical form, compiled from the best American, English and French authors.

The subscribers to the above work in the city of New York are requested to send for their copies to No 1 City Hotel, Broadway. aug 17

ENGLISH STATIONARY.

JUST received and for sale by *Matthias Ward* No 149 Pearl street, a large supply of choice English Stationary—consisting of

Paper of every description
Parchment, quills, penknives
Pocket books, patent memorandum books
Mathematical instruments
India rubber
Ink stands of different sizes & distinctions
Letter racks, paper folders
Desk knives, sealing wax
Wafers, pounce, pounce boxes
Paints, crayons
Silver pencil cases,
Morocco purses, ink, ink powder, &c

which will be sold wholesale or retail upon very reasonable terms. may 11

THIS DAY is published by Samuel Stansbury, J. & T. Ronalds, J. Osborn, and G. F. Hopkins, and for sale at their respective stores, a neat and very accurate edition in 8vo of *Walker's Critical Pronouncing Dictionary*, and expositor of the English Language. Price in the best sheep binding, 3 dollars 50 cents.

In presenting to the public this edition of Walker's Dictionary, a work which more than any other has contributed to fix the varying pronunciation of the English language; the publishers hope that, in its typographical execution it will be found more correct than any other copy extant. Besides the claim to greater accuracy, they beg leave to state, that this edition possesses another advantage of no trifling importance, that of having the Appendix incorporated in the general vocabulary, an advantage of which the author regretted he could not avail himself in the last London copy; and which has been unaccountably overlooked in the former American edition.

Also just published and for sale as above, a neat octavo edition of the BIBLE, with Canne's Notes, price $3 and $3 50 cents. july 9

District of New York, ss.

BE it remembered, that on the tenth day of April, in the 31st year of the Independence of the United States of America, D. Smith and Forman, of the said district, hath deposited in this office the title of a book, the right whereof they claim as proprietors, in the words following, to wit: '*The Juvenile Spelling Book*; being an easy introduction to the English language, containing easy and familiar lessons in spelling, with appropriate reading lessons, calculated to advance the learners by easy gradations, and to teach the orthography of Johnson, and the pronunciation of Walker.'

In conformity to the act of the congress of the United States, entitled 'an act for the encouragement of learning, by securing the copies of maps, charts, and books to the authors and proprietors of such copies during the times therein mentioned.'

EDWARD DUNSCOMB, Clerk of the district of New York

The above book has lately been published by *Smith and Forman*, and may be had at their Bookstores no 70 Vesey street, and 213, corner of Greenwich and Barclay streets, by the dozen or single one, on more advantageous terms than any other speling book now extant.

Also may be had at the above stores, *Picket's Juvenile Expositor*, or Sequel to the common Spelling Book, which is generally allowed by teachers and others to be the best book for the instruction of youth ever introduced into schools. This appears evident from the rapid sale the 2d edition of this work has met with in the course of the last year. A *third* edition is now in the press, and will be published in the course of a few weeks. aug 5

PATENT BRIDGES

EITHER of TIMBER, STONE or CAST IRON, capable of being erected over rivers, lakes and swamps, of any space or dimensions, with a single arch of any altitude the local situation may require, so that shipping of the largest kind may sail under and the navigation in no wise be injured.—Timber Bridges of any extent may be erected over any lake, river or swamp, without the use of a centre or support of any kind while building, and be stronger on that account.

Also, patent arches of stone, &c. for buildings of any kind which may be built of any shape or extent of opening, whereby any weight of wall may be supported and secured from being thrown down by the fatal effects of fire, and also without depending on adjoining buildings for abutments—by the sole inventor, THOMAS POPE, Architect and Landscape Gardener, New York—

Who most respectfully begs leave to inform the public of the United States, and particularly those persons engaged in the erection of bridges about to be erected, that after a long persevering attention and assiduous study, combined with the experience of many years in the science of architecture, he has matured the aforesaid invention for bridges, &c. upon the most incontrovertable mathematical principles of self support, and to which no bounds of situation, locality of circumstance, strength, or space, can possibly be set, and which has been acknowledged by those who have already explored the same, to be superior in every sense of the word to any plan for bridges ever offered to the public, inasmuch as it removes all and every of those formidable objections that hitherto with so much propriety have been advanced. Would therefore most earnestly recommend to those about to erect structures of so much importance to the public to stay their hands and proceed no further till they have maturely examined the superior properties of this my invaluable invention for bridges.

NB. The aforesaid Thomas Pope, the patentee, may be consulted with on this or any other subject of his profession, by a line of notification to that effect, directed to no 30 Wall street, or 412 Greenwich street, New York.

Surveys of scites, plans, models and estimates for bridges furnished on the shortest notice.

Gentlemen's gardens, parks and pleasure grounds laid out in the most appropriate and picturesque style. may 18 c&wtf

AMERICAN CITIZEN.

NEW-YORK, AUGUST 22

His Majesty's Packet Prince Adolphus, New York, 21st Aug. 1807.

To the Editor of the American Citizen.

SIR,

In consequence of a publication in your paper of this day signed Washington Morton, I feel it a duty I owe the public and myself to make the following statement of facts as they occurred.

On Wednesday afternoon, steering for Sandy Hook within five or six miles of the Light House, saw a schooner, built and rigged exactly in the pilot boat style; the wind being light with a flood tide, my anxiety was of course great to have a pilot on board. A signal was hoisted and a gun fired, which not being noticed fired another gun some minutes after; being shotted I directed the master to be very careful to point the gun very wide of her, in a direction that would be impossible to do any mischief, as evidently appears from the ball falling four or five hundred yards astern of the said schooner.

The foregoing is corroborated by Mr. John Higinbothom's certificate, a citizen of the U. States, who was a passenger with me from Halifax. If doubts should still remain of the correctness of this account, Mr. John N. Macomb, who was on board the schooner, is referred to, and I am convinced he will acknowledge this statement candid and true.

I am, sir,

Your very obed't serv't.

JN: BOULDERSON.

New-York, 21st Aug. 1807.

I hereby certify that the statement hereon to annexed is correct and true, and that upon captain Boulderson's giving the master orders to fire the gun alluded to he replied, the shot will fall above a mile from her; the captain answered, better that than within twenty yards.

J. HIGINBOTHOM.

Sworn to this 21st day of August, before me,

J. ZUNTZ, N. Pub.

New York, Aug. 21, 1807.

SIR,

Hearing incidentally that the correctness of the facts stated in my note to you under date of the 20th instant, was intended to be impeached, I take the liberty of sending the enclosed affidavit.

Other testimony in corroboration shall be offered as occasion may require, though I hope that my own assertion of a fact would with all to whom I am known be abundantly sufficient.

I am, sir,

Your obedient serv't.

WASHINGTON MORTON.

AFFIDAVIT.

City and County of New-York, ss.

GEORGE REINS and JOHN HOPPER, both of the city of New-York, being duly sworn, say, that they were on board the schooner Pilot's Friend, off Sandy Hook, on Wednesday the 20th instant; that while lying to on the Banks, a ship, which proved to be the English Packet, came along about a mile to windward and fired a gun, at the same time heaving her main-top-sail to the mast; about 15 minutes after she fired a shot, which these deponents believe from the direction of it was fired at the schooner—And this deponent, John Hopper, remarked at the time, being on the end of the boom, that he could throw a stone to the spot where the shot struck, and is of opinion it struck about a hundred yards from the schooner, but never having seen a shot fired before, cannot be positive; and George Reins, for himself, says that the ship being rather a-head, the shot came over the bowsprit, nearly raking the schooner, and struck astern from *one* to 200 yards at farthest, as this deponent believes, he having seen many shot fired; that at the time the shot was fired these deponents were on the boom hauling the mainsail out, and immediately thereafter the schooner made sail and went along side the ship, and after some conversation between Mr. Morton and the captain, the ship squared away her main yard, and the schooner went into the Hook—And further say not. GEORGE REINS.

JOHN HOPPER

Sworn this 21st day of August, 1807, before me.

JOSHUA BARKER, *Special Justice.*

Want of room obliges us to postpone our comments on Capt. Boulderson's communication until Monday.

COURT MARTIAL OVER MAJ. SITCHER

"First Brigade of N. York State Artillery.

"BRIGADE ORDERS—July 7, 1807.

"The court martial appointed for the trial of major Andrew Sitcher, having found him guilty of the three first charges, and having sentenced him to be removed from office, and the major general, as appears by the annexed division order, having approved the sentence of the court, major Sitcher is therefore removed from command in the brigade. Major Snoden succeeds him in command until further orders. The court martial, in pursuance of division orders, is dissolved. By order of *Brigadier General MORTON,*

Brig. Maj. and Inspector.

(COPY.)

New-York State Artillery—Division Orders.

"New-York, July 6th, 1807.

"A general court martial, under the orders of the major general of the New-York State Artillery, was convened at the city hotel, in the city of New-York, on the second day of June last, and composed of the following officers:

"Brigadier General Morton, *President.*

"*Members*—Colonel Curtenius, Majors Loomis, Saltus, and Mumford; Captains Richards, Anth. Bleecker, Smith, Lovett, Alex. Bleeker, Swartwout, Hopkins, and Miller.

"Samuel Jones, jun. Judge Advocate.

"The court martial was ordered for the trial of major Andrew Sitcher, commanding a battalion in the first brigade of Artillery, on the following charges:

"*First*—For disobedience of orders in countermanding, without authority, the brigade order of the 10th April last.

"*Second*—For unofficer-like and improper conduct in countermanding the above mentioned order, with the view of mortifying some of the officers of his battalion, and of injuring the reputation and interest of said battalion.

"*Third*—For unofficer-like and improper conduct in countermanding the above mentioned order, and thus actually and seriously injuring the reputation, discipline and harmony of the said battalion.

"*Fourth*—For unofficer-like and ungentlemanly conduct in regard to Mr. M'Pherson, in omitting his name in the return made in February last, by major Andrew Sitcher, for appointments, contrary to his repeated and solemn assurances to captain Townsend, lieutenant Pinckney, and lieutenant M'Pherson, and to the known wishes of their company and themselves, and thus forfeiting all title to future confidence and respect.

"*Fifth*—For ungentlemanly and unofficer-like conduct to M. B. Seixas, in first voluntarily giving him a brevet appointment of quarter-master, and thus induce him to resign his situation as lieutenant, and go to great expence in equipment, and afterwards omitting his name entirely in his return for appointments, and when this perfidy was discovered and he taxed with it, in solemnly denying that there was any foundation for the accusation, and pledging his honor that Mr. Seixas' name was returned for quarter-master, all which was contrary to fact, thus degrading himself, and reflecting his disgrace on the whole corps.*

(Signed) CHARLES SNODEN,

"Major Battalion Artillery

"*Dated 19th April*, 1807.

"To the first, second and third of these charges the major plead not guilty, and excepted to the competency and relevancy of the fourth and fifth charges. The court martial, after having gone into a full and patient examination of the testimony produced, and heard the major on his defence, and after having maturely deliberated thereon, delivered the following sentence:

"The court having considered the first charge against major Andrew Sitcher, the evidence and his defence, are of opinion, that he is guilty of disobedience of orders, in countermanding, without authority, the brigade orders of the 10th of April last:

"The court having considered the second charge against major Andrew Sitcher, the evidence and his defence, are of opinion, that he is guilty of unofficer-like and improper conduct, in countermanding the brigade orders of the 1st April last, with the view of mortifying some of the officers of his battalion, and of injuring the reputation and interest of the said battalion:

"The court having considered the third charge against major Andrew Sitcher, the evidence and his defence, are of opinion, that he is guilty of unofficer-like and improper conduct, in countermanding the brigade orders of the 10th April last, and thus actually and seriously injuring the reputation, discipline and harmony of his battalion:

"The court being of opinion that the fourth and fifth charges against major Andrew Sitcher, and the matter therein contained, are not cognizable by the court, the same were, and hereby are dismissed:

"The court do sentence major Andrew Sitcher to be removed from office in the militia of the state of New-York.

"The major general is induced, by his high consideration for this important military tribunal, and by the respectability of the characters who compose it, as well by the expediency in relation to the discipline of the militia, to approve of the preceding sentence of the court martial. In approving the sentence of the court martial, the general cannot but observe, that taking into consideration that this being the first offence charged against major Sitcher, while an officer in the Artillery,† that the court might, with much propriety, have sentenced him to a much less severe punishment, and allowed him an opportunity to retrieve his military character.

"The court martial will consider itself dissolved at the reception of this order.—By order of *Major General Stevens.*

(Signed) "R. M. MALCOM, *A. D. C.*"

* These charges were laid before the council of appointment in April last, by the respectable President of the Court, but in defiance of the allegations, and before the issue of them was tried, Governor Lewis and his Council promoted Sitcher to the command of a regiment! A proceeding so scandalous requires no comment. It is understood that Lewis expected some *political* aid at the late election from the efforts of Sitcher.

† With due respect for General Stevens, I beg leave to say that his remark is not military. The general knew or he did not know that Sitcher had been *tried before*; if not, he should have enquired, but if he did, the observation, affecting discrimination, is disrespectful to the *Militia*, and unbecoming the *General.*

Sitcher has been several times tried for various offences; he is what at the Old Bailey would be termed an *old offender.*

The trial previous to the one in question in the service of the artillery, on which he was convicted and very properly cashiered, was upon the following charges: *I was a Member of the Court*, which sat three days.

Sitcher was commander of an uniform company of Infantry, of which Mr. Tiebout, I believe the printer, was in the ranks. Tiebout applied for permission to withdraw, which was refused by capt. Sitcher.

It happened, however, sometime after the application of Mr. Tiebout was refused, that Sitcher's brother, who it appeared in testimony was not very able to furnish himself with uniform, wished to join Sitcher's company. Sitcher, therefore, informed Tiebout that if he would give up the uniform to his brother, or part of it, I am not now certain which, he would suffer Tiebout to withdraw; Tiebout consented, *on condition*, that captain Sitcher would give him a certificate to exonerate him from doing duty in the beats, if called upon, with which condition Sitcher complied; that is to say, in plain language, capt. Sitcher was to give Tiebout a certificate that he was a member of his company, when in fact he was not!

Sitcher, having Tiebout's uniform for his brother, complied with the condition, and, as appeared in testimony, the certificate of Sitcher had excused Tiebout in the beats for non attendance.

But Sitcher, after some time, grew weary with renewing the fraudulent certificates, and at length refused to give them any longer—the uniform most probability being worn out!

Tiebout was now called upon to do duty in the Beats, but, not appearing, was fined.

In revenge, I suppose, against Sitcher, Tiebout, directly or indirectly, preferred the charges already in substance enumerated against him, and upon which, after an impartial and laborious investigation, Sitcher was found guilty by the court.

NEW YORK, *August* 20.

To the Editor of the American Citizen.

SIR,

I arrived this afternoon at 4 o'clock, in the steam boat, from Albany. As the success of my experiment gives me great hope that such boats may be rendered of much importance to my country, to prevent erroneous opinions, and give some satisfaction to the friends of useful improvements, you will have the goodness to publish the following statement of facts:

I left New-York on Monday at 1 o'clock, and arrived at Clermont, the seat of Chancellor Livingston, at 1 o'clock on Tuesday, time 24 hours, distance 110 miles; on Wednesday I departed from the Chancellor's at 9 in the morning, and arrived at Albany at 5 in the afternoon, distance 40 miles, time 8 hours; the sum of this is 150 miles in 32 hours, equal near 5 miles an hour.

On Thursday, at 9 o'clock in the morning, I left Albany, and arrived at the Chancellor's at 6 in the evening; I started from thence at 7, and arrived at New-York on Friday at 4 in the afternoon; time 30 hours, space run through 150 miles, equal 5 miles an hour. Throughout the whole way my going and returning the wind was ahead; no advantage could be drawn from my sails—the whole has, therefore, been performed by the power of the steam engine.

I am, Sir,

Your most obedient,

ROBERT FULTON.

We congratulate Mr. Fulton and the country on his success in the Steam Boat, which cannot fail of being very advantageous. We understand that not the smallest inconvenience is felt in the boat either from heat or smoke.

From the Richmond Enquirer.

TRIAL OF AARON BURR

(continued by adjournment and held at the Capitol in the Hall of the House of Delegates) for High Treason against the U. States.

FRIDAY, AUGUST 7th, 1807.

(Challenging of Jurymen concluded.)

8. Miles Selden declared, that it was impossible not to have entered into the frequent conversations which had occurred on this topic; and to have declared some opinion; that he had always said, that Col. B. was guilty of something, and that if he was guilty of treason against such a government, he would deserve to be hung; that he could not assert that he had always accompanied his opinions with this reservation; but that he was not afraid to trust himself in the rendering of a verdict.—Upon being interrogated, he said that he had frequently jested on this subject; and particularly recollected to have said in a sportive conversation with Col. Mayo, that this was a federal plot and that Burr had been set on by the federalists. Suspended.

9. Lewis Truehart had said, if the reports were correct, that Col. B. had been guilty of something inimical to the country, and that he always qualified his opinions in that manner. Col. Tinsley was then called in, who stated that from a conversation with Mr. Truehart he thought he had discovered that he had a general preposession against Col. B. Suspended.

10. William Yancey had expressed an opinion that Col. B. was guilty on newspaper testimony; but that he had no doubt, he should entertain a different sentiment, if other testimony were produced. Set aside.

11. Thomas Prosser had made numberless declarations about Col. B; that he had believed him to be guilty of a treasonable intention, but not of the overt act; on this point he had suspended his opinion, but he was rather inclined to believe that he had not committed it.

Mr. Martin. Can this gentleman be considered as an impartial juryman, when he thus comes with his mind made up on one half of the guilt? Suspended.

12. John Staples had been under the same impressions, which had been described by others; that he dared to say that he had said Col. B. was guilty of levying troops and making war upon the United States. Set aside.

13. Edward C. Stannard acknowledged that his prejudices against Col. B. had been deep-rooted; that he had no doubt of the criminality of his *motives*, but he had doubts of the commission of an overt act; he regretted that a man of his genius and energetic mind, should be lost to his country; upon being interrogated he observed, that he had doubts as to the overt act, because he believed him to be a man of such insidious intrigue as never to jeopardise his own life. Set aside.

14. Richard B. Goode stated, that from newspaper information and common report, he had formed an opinion unfavourable to Col. B. and that this opinion had been confirmed by what had fallen in this court from his own lips: but that without arrogating to himself more virtue than belongs to the human bosom, he was satisfied that he could render him strict and impartial justice. Some conversation here ensued respecting certain transactions which took place between him and captain Heath of the Manchester troop of horse. Mr. G. delivered a long narrative of these incidents, which he concluded by asserting that he had addressed a letter to capt. H. in which he had refused to act under a commander, who had sanctioned a man, that had been a traitor to his country. Set aside.

15. Nathanial Selden stated he had formed an opinion particularly from Gen. Eaton's deposition, that the intentions of the prisoner were hostile to the United States; but that he had also said, that he had seen no evidence to satisfy him, that he had been guilty of any overt act. Suspended.

16. Esme Smock declared that he had formed and expressed an opinion as to Col. B's treasonable designs; that he had formed that opinion from newspaper publications and common report; and that he had constantly conceived Col. B's intentions to be treasonable.

Mr. Wickham. Have you ever formed an opinion, that Col. B. was guilty of treason? I have in my own mind. Set aside.

17. Richard E. Parker had, like every other person, formed an opinion on this case, on newspaper statements; but he had heard very little of the evidence that may be adduced on this occasion. He had declared, that if these newspaper statements were true, Col. B. had been guilty; as to the doctrine of treason, he had not formed a conclusive opinion.

Mr. Burr. I have no objection to Mr. Parker. He is therefore elected.

A desultory argument here ensued about the propriety of swearing one juryman at a time. The counsel for the prosecution opposed; the counsel for the prisoner advocated the doctrine. The court decided that it would adhere to the practice of Virginia; and swear 4 jurymen at a time.

18. John W. Ellis had entertained and did not now entertain any doubts, that the prisoner had been guilty of a treasonable design. Suspended.

19. Thomas Starke, without any expectations of being summoned as a juryman, had stated his opinion to his neighbours, that Col. B. had been guilty of high treason. Set aside.

20. William White stated, that he had been in the western country in May last; and from Col. B's character and from the representations he had received of his conduct, he had been induced to say, that he was guilty of treason, and that hanging was too good for him. Set aside.

21. Wm. B. Chamberlayne stated, that he stood in a very peculiar situation; if as Mr. Wickham declared, any man was unfit to be a juryman who had asserted Col. B. to be worthy of death; he was ready to confess that he himself came under this restriction: He had so said; but he did not now believe that Col. B. had committed an overt act of treason, though he believed him to be guilty of the intention; he however believed that he could do him justice; and that he could conscientiously pass between him and his country. Set aside.

22. David Lambert wished to be excused on account of his indisposition: but the court rejected his plea. On being interrogated, he declared that he does not recollect to have formed an opinion for or against Col. B. Elected.

23. William Hoomes had no hesitation in saying, that he had often declared his opinion that Col. B. was guilty of treasonable intentions, and perhaps he might say, of treason itself. He had imbibed his impressions from every thing he had seen, heard or read. He had understood that Col. B's counsel had made preparations to prove that he had disqualified himself by his own declarations. He should thank them to develope their objections.

Mr. Burr. I assure you, Sir, no preparation has been made. Set aside.

24. Overton Anderson had often expressed an opinion that Col. B's views were inimical to the United States; these opinions he had principally formed upon newspaper statements; he did not recollect that he had ever asserted him to be guilty of treason; but he had sometimes given credit to the representations which he had heard, without particularly defining the degree of guilt in which they might involve the prisoner. Set aside.

25. Hugh Mercer upon being called, said, it was his duty to state, that an opinion which he had for some time past entertained of the character of Col. Burr, was unfriendly to a strictly impartial en-

L'ORACLE L'ECHO DU JOUR AND DAILY ADVERTISER.

{NEW-YORK, TUESDAY JANUARY 5, 1808.} PUBLISHED BY J. J. NEG[illegible]N, No. 133, WATER, CORNER OF PINE-STREET. [No. 3 — Vol. 1]

CONDITIONS.

L'Oracle & Daily Advertiser, se publiera tous les matins, à raison de 8 *Dollars* par an.

Les avis soit en Anglais ou en Français, seront insérés sur le même pied des autres journaux.

Nous prions les pesonnes qui envoyeront des annonces, d'être très-exact à spécifier la durée du tems qu'ils désireront que leurs avis paraissent, particulièrement ceux qui n'avertissent que rarement.

DESCRIPTION DE LA RELIGION DES QUAKRES.

Prise d'une vue de l'éducation, de la disciplines, des mœurs sociales, de l'économie civile et politique, des principes religieux, et du caractère de la société des Amis ;

Par THOMAS CLARKSON, auteur de différens essais sur le commerce des esclaves, &c.

Cet Ouvrage célèbre, qui a passé par deux éditions, à Londres, avec une vente sans égale, vient d'être publié dans cette Ville, par SAMUEL STANSBURY, No. 111, Water-St. deux portes au-dessous du Phoenix, *Coffee-House*.

The Annual Review de 1806, contient un détail descriptif de la Religion des Quakres, par Thomas Clarkson. Après avoir donné une variété d'extraits sur les différens chapitres sous lesquels Mr. Clarkson a divisé son Ouvrage, accompagné de remarques, conclut ainsi :

" Nous avons ainsi établi, autant que nos limites nous le permettaient, le contenu de ces précieux et curieux volumes. Ce livre a été généralement lu, une édition considérable a été vendue même avant d'avoir été annoncé ; il n'y a point de doute que ce livre n'occasionne beaucoup de controverse, et les *insectes* du jour qui ont mordu Mr. Lancastre n'épargneront pas Mr. Clarkson. Nous espérons que la partie théologique fera paraître des adversaires habiles. Ses idées sur l'Eucharistie méritent considération ;— nous n'avons jamais vu ce sujet si bien traité. Il ne faut pas considérer ce livre comme un ouvrage de controverse, mais comme une description exacte [illegible] le plus remarquable qui existe parmi nous : un peuple florissant au plus haut degré ; un peuple heureux par excellence, et parfaitement honnête ; et une explication frapante des principes qui le rendent tel. Cet Ouvrage formera une aussi grande époque dans l'histoire de la société, que celle de leur fameuse apologie ; il engagera tout le monde à bien penser d'eux, et peut-être entrainera-t-il, quoique sans intention, bien des personnes dans leur opinion ; car il y a encore des *chercheurs* dans le pays. Nous ne devons pas omettre d'observer que nous ne connaissons aucun livre moderne qui soit écrit d'un style si pur et si naturel ".

S. S. a aussi à vendre quantité de livres de littérature de différentes espèces, et des livres d'éducation, à l'usage des écoles, et aussi un assortiment complet de livres de comptes, de la papeterie anglaise et américaine, des procurations et des connaissemens en blanc, livres de marins, &c. en gros et en détail. jan. 4.

CONTES POPULAIRES,

Dernièrement reçus et se vendent chez Samuel Stansbury, No. 111 Water Street.

TO-MORROW AND THE CONTRAST.

Deux des Contes les plus estimés.

PAR MADEMOISELLE. EDGEWORTH,

Reliés en un volume de poche PRIX *75 cents.*

Ce n'est point à ceux qui connaissent les ouvrages de cette dame qu'on recommande celui-ci, il contient deux de ses plus intéressentes contes populaires, productions de genie qui ont reçues un tribut unanime et qui ne peuvent jamais cesser de plaire. Le premier est tiré de la nature même ; mais d'une touche si legere, mais pure, si libre et cependant si juste, qu'on peut à peine se persuader quil n'ait pas été écrit d'après des scênes naturelles, passées sous les yeux de l'auteur. Il a pour sujet *le Délai*, et il dépeint d'une manière si positive la naissance, les progrès et la fin de cette malheureuse habitude, que l'on ne peut douter que l'écrivain soit un stricte observateur du cœur humain et consommé dans l'art de le décrire. L'enjouement s'y mêle à la vérité, et quoiqu'on ne puisse s'empêcher de sourire aux désastres plaisans dans lesquels ce héros du conte est continuellement entrainé, on ne peut retenir des soupirs causés par la réflexion que rien n'est si ordinaire ni si vrai.

Le second est d'un genie différent. Il parait avoir pour but de montrer l'influence que l'éducation a sur le caractére et sur la destinée des hommes. On y voit deux familles, l'une vertueuse, l'autre dépravée, passer tout dès leur jeunesse et dans tout le cours de leur vie à travers une variété d'événements qui fournissent les moyens de connaitre les passions humaines et d'acquérir le talent de les décrire, qu'on observe dans le premier dexes contes, et qui caracterise si bien tous les ouvrages de cette Demoiselle —Enfin on a rarement donné au public un volume de cette taille, qui lui ait offert autant de plaisir, que peut lui en faire celui-ci.

Jan, 4.

CONDITIONS.

The Oracle and Daily Advertiser will be published every Morning at the Subscription of Eight Dollars per annum.

Advertisements either in the French or English language, will be inserted on the usual terms of other papers.

It is requested that our advertising friends will be particular in specifying the period and duration of time in which they wish their notices to appear, especially those *who only* insert occasional advertisements.

A PORTRAITURE OF QUAKERISM

Taken from a view of the Education and Discipline, Social Manners, Civil and Political Economy, Religious Principles and Character of the Society of

FRIENDS,

BY THOMAS CLARKSON, A. M.

Author of several Essays on the Slave Trade, &c.

This celebrated Work which has passed thro two heavy editions in London, with unprecedented rapidity, has lately been published in this City

By SAMUEL STANSBURY,

NO. 111 WATER-STREET, TWO DOORS BELOW THE PHOENIX COFFEE-HOUSE.

The Annual Review for 1806, contains an account of the Portraiture of Quakerism, by Thomas Clarkson ; after giving a variety of Extracts from the different heads, under which Mr. Clarkson has divided his work, accompanied by remarks, it concludes as follows :

"We have thus, as far as our limits would permit, stated what are the contents of these highly curious volumes. The book has been very extensively read, a large edition having been sold, even before it was advertised. It will doubtless provoke much controversy, and the Buggs of the present day, who have been biting Mr. Lancaster, will not spare Mr. Clarkson. The theological part will, it is to be hoped, call out abler opponents. His opinions upon the Lord's Supper, deserve consideration, we have never seen the subject so ably treated. The book, is not to be considered as a controversial work, but as a faithful Portraiture from the life of the most remarkable people existing among us, a people eminently flourishing, eminently happy, and eminently moral, and as an able elucidation of the principles which make them so. Its publication will form as great an era in the History of the Society, as that of their famous Apology ; it will induce all persons to think [illegible], and perhaps, though it [illegible] written with no such intention, it may lead others to join [illegible], for there are still *seekers* in the land. We must not omit to mention, that we know of no modern book which is written in so pure and natural a style."

S. S. Has also for sale, a variety of Books in Miscellaneous Literature, and most School Books.

Also, a complete and extensive assortment of Merchants Account Books, English and American Stationary. Mercantile and Notarial Blanks, Seamens Books, &c wholesale and retail dec 11

POPULAR TALES.

JUST RECEIVED, AND FOR SALE, BY

SAMUEL STANSBURY,

No. 111, *Water-street*,

Two of the most highly esteemed TALES, by Miss EDGEWORTH,

TO-MORROW, AND *TH CONTRAST*,

Bound in a neat pocket volume—*Price 75 Cents.*

TO those who are acquainted with the writings of this lady, the present work needs no recommendation. It contains two of the most interesting of her "Popular Tales"—productions of genius, which have received the tribute of universal applause, and which can never cease to charm. The former of these is drawn from life with a pencil so glowing, yet so chaste, so free and yet so correct, that one can scarcely be persuaded it has not been written from scenes actually before the author's eyes. Its subject is *procrastination*—and it depicts the rise, progress confirmation and effects of that mischievous habit in a manner which proves the writer to have been both a scrutinizing observer of the manners of men, and an adept in describing them. Humour is here blended with truth—and while we cannot forbear a smile at the ludicrous disasters into which the hero of the tale is perpetually betrayed, we cannot repress a sigh at the reflection that they are so common and so true.

The latter is of a different cast. It appears intended to exhibit the effects of education in the formation of character, and in shaping the destinies of men. A virtuous and a vicious family are traced from childhood through a variety of fortunes to a settlement in life, and while the [illegible] of the narrative affords ample opportunity for [illegible] knowledge of human nature and talent at description, which is noticed in the former tale, and which so eminently characterise all this lady's writings. Upon the whole, a volume of this size has been rarely presented to the public, for the perusal of which they will be better rewarded.

oct 14

BLOOMINGDALE TAVERN.

JOHN S. TAYLOR.

RESPECTFULLY informs his friends and the public, that he has relinquished the GROCERY BUSINESS at No. 19 Bedlow street, and that he has taken the house recently occupied by Mr. Rogers, as a Tavern at Blooming-Dale, where his friends and the public in general may depend on meeting with that attention which ought ever to characterize the keeper of a public house.

His friends and acquaintances are particularly invited to give him a call on Tuesday evening next, the 25th inst. when he hopes to convince them that his endeavors to please will give general satisfaction.

N B. All orders relating to his present or former business, will be attended to, if left at No [illegible] Wall street. Nov. 22. tf

HUNTER'S SACRED BIOGRAPHY.

COLLINS & PERKINS, No. 189 Pearl-street have received for sale, a handsome edition of the above valuable work, in Four Volumes—at—Eight Dollars bound. Dec I.

For New-Orleans,

TO sail positively on Sunday next —the new pilot boat built schr MARIA, burthen about 70 tons, will take 200 bbls on moderate terms, if application is immediately made—she has also excellent accommodations for passengers. For particulars, apply to CHARLES M'CARTHY, Ship and Merchandize Broker, No. 134, Front-street, or to Capt Batee, at Moore's wharf, near Beekman's Slip. Dec. 29—5t

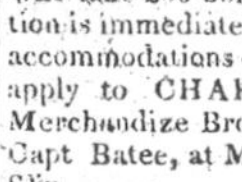

SHIP MINERVA

The Ship MINERVA, J. Burdick master, will sail for Charleston on Wednesday next. For freight or passage apply on board at Murray's wharf, or to E. BURRILL,

Who has for sale on board the Wm. and Mary, 670 bushels of good Barley.

IN STORE,

100 sides of Carolina Soal Leather.

Dec 28

For Freight or Charter,

TO any Port in the West Indies or the United States, the Schooner Belvidere, John Henley, master, burthen 800 barrels, for terms apply to the master on board at Old Slip or to

DIVIE BETHUNE &C

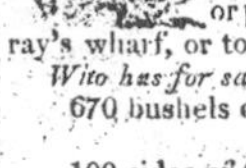

For Sale, Freight or Charter,

The staunch fast sailing ship INDEPENDENCE, 246 tons burthen, 3 years old, in good order, and may be sent to sea with small expence. Apply to

N. L. & G. GRISWOLD, 86 South street.

FOR NORFOLK & RICHMOND,

The well-known fast-sailing schr. RICHMOND, Isaac Seaman master, a regular trader, will sail on the 22d inst—For freight or passage (having elegant accommodations) apply to captain Seaman on board, in the coffee-house slip, or to DIVIE, BETHUNE & CO.

Dec. 16.—10t.

For Sale, Freight or Charter.

The staunch fast sailing brig SUSSEX, 116 tons burthen, in complete order to receive a cargo.

Apply to

N L & G GRISWOLD,

Dec 17 86 South-street.

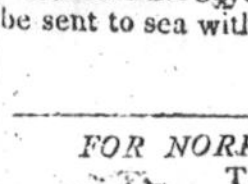

The staunch fast sailing brig Three Friends, 166 tons burthen, is one year old, and may be sent to sea with small expence. Apply to

N. L. & G. GRISWOLD,

Dec 4 86 South street

Coffee, Pimento, Rum, Logwood, &c.

170000 lb. green coffee in bags and barrels
100 bags pimento
50 puncheons Jamaica rum
90 tons campeachy logwood
30 pipes cogniac brandy
50 tons clean hemp
12 do. English cordage

Glass and earthen ware asorted—For sale by

ROBINSON & HARTSHORNE,

nov 21 Greenwich-street

COTTON, GIN, OIL, &c. &c.

57 bales prime upland cotton
60 pipes best Amsterdam gin
400 gin cases
80 pieces low-priced ravens duck
100 large demijohns
2 boxes Dutch brushe
50 jugs linseed oil
40 boxes Pattegrass cheese
7 do. round do.
100 bbls. herrings
15 casks rice
25 pieces English patent canvas
7 puncheons West India rum
100 chests souchong tea
2 tierces Isle of France indigo
25 elephants' teeth
10 bales liquorice root
50 lbs. hay saffron
125 pieces Russia canvas in cannisters
60 do. ravens do.—for sale by

E. BURRILL,

oct 17 96, Wall-street

Cotton Bagging, Canvas, &c.

Hemp Cotton Bagging, different qualities,
Do. Coffee do.
Heavy twilled Sacking,
Brown and bleached tow Oznaburgs,
British Canvas No 1 to 7,
Brown Hollands in boxes,

just received per brig Betsy from Dundee, & and for sale by

DIVIE BETHUNE & Co.

ALSO IN STORE,

250 pieces Canvas, No. 1 to 7,
4 boxes bleached Sheetings, 4-4 & 9-8,
2 bales do. 7-8 Shirtings,
15 do. flax and tow Oznaburgs,
1 case white stiching thread.

dec 7

MINTURN & CHAMPLIN,

At Franklin's Wharf, Have for sale,

HYSON, hyson skin, souchong and bohea Teas, of the first quality, assorted chests,
50 chests superior souchong Tea, in papers,
4th proof cogniac Brandy,
Heavy Pepper, Catalonia Wine,
300 boxes Capers, Olives, Anchovies, and Cornichons,
100 boxes very superior Claret, vintage 1802, 12 bottles each,
400 boxes Claret, 12 bottles each,
10 boxes do of 72 bottles each, put up for the Calcutta market,
China Ware, consisting of cups & saucers, [plates, &c.
70 boxes Camphor,
500 bundles Cassia,
20 packages green Windsor Chairs,
100 do plain and figur'd straw Carpeting
24, 26, 28 and 30 oz. sheathing Copper,
10 bales brown Sheetings, and
7 bales Brabants Linens. Oct 9

OLIVER WOLCOTT offers for sale, the cargo of the ship Trident from Canton, consisting of

Imperial, Hyson, Young Hyson, Souchong, Bohea and Hyson skin Teas in whole, half and quarter chests.
Long and short pieces white nankeens
Short yellow nankeens,
24 boxes, containing

Sinchews,	Lutestrings,
Green Umbrella Silks,	Striped Vest patterns,
Handkerchiefs,	Black Sattins,
Sarcenets,	Mock Damask, and

assorred Buglepo es
5 Boxes Camphor of the best quality.
a few boxes pearl-handle pocket-combs

April 8 tf

BAGGING, OZNABURGS & SUGAR

JUST received per ship YOUNG FACTOR, from London,

20 bales bread bagging
4 do flax and tow oznaburgs
1 do twilled sacking

Per brig THETIS, from New-Orleans, 25 boxes brown Havanna sugar, entitled to debenture. For sale by DIVIE BETHUNE & CO

Dec. 2

HERMAN VOSBURGH,

Manufacturer of Paints, Varnishes, &c.

No. 53 Chatham-street, New-York,

OFFERS for sale, a general assortment of Paints, Painter's articles, and Varnishes of every description, wholesale, retail and for exportation, at the lowest prices for cash, or the usual credit

30 casks dry white lead	50 wt mineral or blue black
60 hhds. whiting	3 casks black lead
8 do. Paris white	1 do powder blue
13 do pumice stone	100 wt emery powder
14 do lampblack	1000 wt blue vitrol
20 casks ivory black	16 casks linseed oil
16 do powdered ochre	3000 wt putty in bladders
70 do Spanish brown	250 kegs grd. wh. lead
4 tons powder'd Venetian red	300 do Spanish brown
6 casks blue verditer	150 do black paint
18 do mineral green	100 do Venetian red
6 do olympian do	25 do gr'd verdigrise
4 do green verditer	100 do yellow ochre
6 do French green	130 doz. paint brushes assorted
10 do imperial patent verdigrise	300 do sash tools do
700 wt Dutch pink	40 gross camel's hair pencils
600 do new yellow do	[illegible] knives assorted
400 do sugar of lead	1600 books Dutch meta
1 hhd rotten stone	Flake white
1 do Italian ochre	Red do
14 casks South American gum copal	Strewing smalts
10 bags India do	Putty. Window galss
1 cask gum asphaltum	Powdered lue
1000 wt gum shellac	Flotant indigo
300 do English umber	Carolina do. &c. &c.
3 casks Prussian blue	
2 bales Russia glue	

N. B. The manufacturer begs leave to suggest, that he grounds his pretentions to public patronage only on the knowledge of his business, and the quality of his articles, and in future his kegs shall be branded with his name, jugs of varnish sealed with his initials, pots and packages labeled with his name and place of abode. *and the contents warranted.* Feb 7. tf

NEW-YORK CARD MANUFACTORY

SAMUEL WHITTEMORE & CO

No. 100, WALL-STREET,

KEEPS constantly for sale, as usual, a general assortment of Cotton and Wool Cards, Nos 4, 6, 7, 8, 9 and 10, cotton, and 3, 4, 5 and 6 wool. Also, cards for carding machines of every description, and clothiers' and hatters' jacks ; all of the first quality, and on the most accommodating terms. Also, a general supply of English comb plates for carding machines.

*** All orders executed with dispatch.

sept. 4.

MRS. L. GRIFFITHS,

Late of Beaver Street, Silk, Cotton and Woolen Dyer and Calico Glazier—No 40, Pearl Street,

CLEANS, dyes, and dresses all kinds of silks, satins, crapes, gauze, fringes, muslins, &c. to any shade or color.

Also, camel hair shawls, silk stockings, and all kind of damaged goods, cleaned or dyed.

Gentlemen's clothes, carpets, bed-furniture, and blankets scoured and cleaned, umbrellas cleaned, dyed and repaired, and all kinds of chip hats dyed and blocked to any shape.

N B. Hair and Feathers dyed scarlet, or to any other shade, for military companies, tipt, cleaned, &c. tf sept 22

GLASS-WARE, IRON-WARE, PAINTS, &c.

TO-MORROW will commence landing, the cargo of the ship William, Rawson, from Newcastle, consisting of

40 casks Nails, 70 chaldrons Coals,
20 ditto Patent Shot, 20 do. dry white Lead,
130 kegs Ground ditto
50 crates Sheet Glass,
75 boxes Window Glass
30 hhds assorted Glassware,
33 ditto green Copperas,
20 bundles sheet Iron,
8 tons Nail Rods,
1412 Iron Pots, 1½ to 10 gallons,
70 boxes Tin Plates,

Adn from the ship Maine, Dowdall, from Bristol,

200 casks dry Spanish Brown,
200 kegs White Lead, ground in oil, for sale by D. BETHUNE & CO.

Dec 15

RICHMOND TOBACCO. 56 hhds. prime Richmond Tobacco, partly of the new crop, landing this day at Murray's wharf, from the schr Weymouth, For sale by

Dec. 19. DIVIE BETHUNE, & CO.

LISBON LEMONS—170 boxes fresh Lemons just received per schooner American, Capt Hunter, and for sale by

SAML. WHITTEMORE & Co

Dec. 3. 100 Murray's Wharf

REGISTER OFFICE

FOR HOUSES AND STORES,

No. 101 WATER STREET.

THE owners of Houses and Stores, in the city, and also in the country, are hereby informed that a Book is opened at the above place for Registering all Houses, Stores, &c. for sale or to let.

The uncertainty of Landlords, depending upon the usual mode of putting up bills, which are generally destroyed, and their relying on a friendly reception of enquiring Tenants, at the house or premises, and who are often refused admittance, induces a belief, that every person having Tenements to sell or let will see the propriety and advantage of having them recorded at this Office, as all those who wish to buy or rent can have free access to every information concerning the same, *gratis*.

The small expence to Landlords, only one Dollar each, and the great convenience to Tenants, must be a sufficient inducement for their encouragement of the undertaking.

N. B. All commands by letter, post paid, will be strictly attended to.

Dec 18 eodtf

NEW-YORK INSURANCE COMPANY

THE Stockholders are hereby notified, that the Annual Election for Twenty-one Directors, will be held at the Office of the Company on Monday, the 11th day of January. The poll will open at 10 o'clock in the forenoon, and close at 2 o'clk

HUGH ANDERSON, Sec'ry.

Dec 23 tJan11

THIS DAY IS PUBLISHED,

BY E. SARGEANT,

39 WALL-STREET,

The Fourth American Edition of the

WILD IRISH GIRL.

A National Tale—By Miss Owenson.

Dec 16

JUST PUBLISHED,

AND FOR SALE BY E. SARGEANT,

NO. 39 WALL-STREET,

THE WILD IRISH GIRL.

A National Tale,

By Miss Owenson.

The third American Edition—Price $1 25 cents

Also, just published and for sale as above,

THE NOVICE OF SAINT DOMINICK.

By Miss Owenson.

2 vols. 12mo—Price $2 50 cents.

E. S. [illegible] ready for publication, a New Novel by Mrs. Roach, author of the Children of the Abbey, entitled,

THE DISCARDED [illegible]

ALL persons are forbid trusting any of the Crew of the British Ship THORNTON, without an order, as I will pay no debts of their contracting JOHN JUBB.

dec 24

TO BOOKBINDERS.

SIX tons Binders' Boards of the first quality, and red, blue and black Roans and Skivers, For sale by SAMUEL STANSBURY,

oct 10 No. 111, Water-street.

MRS. OPIE'S TALES.

JUST published and for sale by E. SARGEANT, No. 39, Wall-street—[illegible] Tales, [illegible] Opie, in two volumes, first American, from the second London edition. Dec 16

LANDS FOR SALE.

EIGHT building Lots, situate in Stuyvesant-st. near St. Marks-church, commanding a fine view of the East-river—*Also to let for a term of years*, several acres of land, worthy the attention of Gardners &c. For particulars, apply to

NICHOLAS WM. STUYVESANT,

Dec. 22 1m Stuyvesant-street

FORSALE,

Or exchanged for real estate in New-York.

A LOT of Land containing 170 acres, situated in the town of Hadley, in the county of Saratoga, being part of the patent granted to John Glen and 44 others, distinguished on a general map of the same by lot No. 120. For particulars, enquire of Ezra Sargeant, bookseller, Wall-street, New-York, or Edmund M. Blunt, Newburyport, Massachusetts. Nov 2

A FARM FOR SALE.

A FARM for sale on Throgs Neck, Westchester, distant from New-York fourteen miles, containing thirty acres, more or less, on which is erected a large dwelling house two-stories high, a new barn, two wells of water, well fruited, such as a young orchard with Newtown pippen trees ; also, peaches, plumbs, pears and cheries.—The buildings are in good repair, and the farm is devided into convenient lots and walled with a stone fence, produces fresh hay, about five or six acres of woodland, salt meadow, &c. all lying about one mile from two main landings, very convenient for fishing, fowling, and a variety of shell fish. For further particulars, apply at the office of the Daily Advertiser, No. 71, Pine-street, or on the premises of

Nov. 24—dtf FREDERICK REGER.

TUITION OF THE

MODERN LANGUAGES

A H. PALMER respectfully informs his friends and the public that he continues teaching the French, Italian, Spanish, and German languages, and the English language to foreigners by the most approved methods.

He gives private lessons in those languages, and teaches the French, and Italian to females at their houses

A. H. P. intends commencing a course of instruction to a select class in the Spanish Language three evenings in the week, during the ensuing winter. Terms, evenings of tuition, &c. will be made know by applying at the School Room, No. 270 Pearl-street,

N. B.—Translations from the above, and the Portuguese and Dutch Languages.

Oct 27 3m

THE WAR.

"LET THE RALLYING WORD, THROUGH ALL THE DAY, BE "*LIBERTY OR DEATH*."

VOL. I. NEW-YORK.....SATURDAY, JULY 11, 1812. No. 3

THE WAR,

WILL BE PUBLISHED EVERY SATURDAY,

(FOR THE EDITOR)

At $2 per annum, payable quarterly in advance.

At No. 473 Pearl-street, New-York.

CONGRESS.

[SECRET JOURNAL.]

HOUSE OF REPRESENTATIVES.

Monday, June 1, 1812.

A confidential message in writing was received from the president of the United States, by Mr. Coles, his Secretary, which he delivered in at the Speaker's table.

The House was then cleared of all persons except the members, clerk, sergeant-at-arms and door-keeper, and the doors were closed, and the said message was read.

[Here follows the message of the president as already published in the war.]

A motion was then made by Mr. Randolph that the same message be referred to the committee of the whole house on the state of the Union.

And the question thereon being taken it was determined in the negative, yeas 37, nays 82.

On Motion of Mr. D. R. Williams,

Ordered, that the said message be referred to the committee on that part of the president's message which relates to our foreign relations.

And then the house adjourned until to-morrow morning 11 o'clock.

Tuesday, June 2.

The house met, and

On motion of Mr. Harper,

Adjourned until to-morrow morning 11 o'clock.

Wednesday, June 3.

Mr. Calhoun, from the committee on foreign relations, to whom was referred the message of the president of the United States, of the 1st inst. made a report, stating at large the causes and reasons of a war with Great Britain; which being read,

Mr. Quincy moved that the doors be now opened, that the injunction of secrecy on the said message be removed, that the same be promulgated, and that the subsequent proceedings thereupon be had with open doors.

And the question thereupon being taken,

It was determined in the negative—

YEAS. Messrs. Baker, Bleecker, Boyd, Breckenridge, Brigham, Champion, Chittenden, Cook, Davenport, Ely, Emott, Fitch, Gold, Goldsborough, Hawes, Hufty, Jackson, Key, Law, Lewis, Macon, M'Bryde, Milnor, Mosely, Newbold Pearson, Pitkin, Potter, Quincy, Randolph, Reed, Richardson, Ridgely, Rodman, Stanford, Stewart, Sturges, Sullivan, Taggart, Talmage, Tracy, Van Cortlandt, Wheaton, White, Williams, Wilson—46

NAYS. Messrs. Alston, Anderson, Archer, Bard, Bartlett, Basset, Bibb Blackledge, Brown, Burwell, Butler Calhoun, Cheves, Cochran, Clopton, Condit, Crawford, Davis, Dawson, Desha, Dinsmoor, Earle, Findley, Fisk, Gholson, Goodwyn, Green, Grundy, B. Hall, O Hall, Harper Hyneman, Johnson, Kent, King, Lacock, Lefevre, Little, Lowndes, Lyle, Maxwell, Moore, M'Koy, M'Kee, M'Kim, Metcalf, Mitchill, Morgan, Morrow, Nelson, New, Newton, Ormsby, Pickens, Piper, Pleasants, Pond, Ringgold, Rhea, Roane, Roberts, Sage, Sammons, Seaver, Sevier, Seybert, Shaw, G. Smith. J. Smith, Strong, Taliaferro, Troup, Turner, Whitehill, Winn, Wright—76.

A motion was then made by Mr. *Randolph*, that the proceedings upon the said message of the President be had and conducted with open doors.

And the question being taken,

It was determined in the negative—

YEAS. Messrs. Baker, Bartlett, Bleecker, Boyd, Breckenridge, Brigham, Champion, Chittenden, Cooke, Davenport, Ely, Emott, Fitch, Gold, Goldsborough, Hawes, Jackson, Key, Law, Lewis, Macon, M'Bryde, Milnor, Mosely, Pearson, Pitkin, Potter, Quincy, Randolph, Reed, Richardson, Ridgely, Rodman, Stanford, Stewart, Sturges, Sullivan, Taggart, Talmage, Tracy, Van Cortlandt, Wheaton, White, Williams, Wilson, 45.

NAYS. Messrs. Alston, Anderson, Archer, Bard, Bassett, Bibb, Blackledge, Brown, Burwell, Butler, Calhoun, Cheves, Cochran, Clopton, Condit, Crawford, Davis, Dawson, Desha, Dinsmoor, Earle, Findley, Fisk, Cholson, Goodwyn, Green, Grundy, B Hall. O Hall, Harper, Hufty, Hyneman, Johnson, Kent, King, Lacock, Lefever, Little, Lowndes, Lyle, Maxwell, Moore, M'Koy, M'Kee, M'Kim, Metcalf, Mitchill, Morgan, Morrow, Nelson, New, Newbold, Newton, Ormsby, Pickens, Piper, Pleasants Pond, Ringgold, Rhea, Roane Roberts, Sage, Sammons, Seaver, Sevier, Seybert, Shaw, G. Smith, J. Smith, Strong, Taliaferro, Troup, Turner, Whitehill, Winn, Wright—77.

The said report was then, on motion of Mr. *Calhoun*, ordered to lie upon the table.

Mr. Calhoun, from the same committee, on leave given, presented a bill, declaring war between Great Britain and her dependencies and the United States and their territories, which was read the first time.

And opposition being made thereto by Mr. *Randolph*,

The question was taken in the form prescribed by the rules and orders of the House, to wit "shall the bill be rejected?"

And determined in the negative,

YEAS. Messrs. Baker, Bartlett, Bleecker, Boyd, Breckenridge, Brigham, Champion, Chittenden, Cooke, Davenport, Ely, Emott, Fitch, Gold, Goldsborough, Hufty, Jackson, Key, Law, Lewis, M'Bryde, Metcalf, Milnor, Mitchill, Mosely, Newbold, Pearson, Pitkin, Potter, Quincy, Randolph, Reed, Ridgely, Rodman, Stanford, Stewart, Sturges, Sullivan, Taggart, Talmage, Tracy, Van Cortlandt, Wheaton, White, Wilson—45.

NAYS. Messrs. Alston, Anderson, Archer, Bard, Bassett, Bibb, Blackledge, Brown, Burwell, Butler, Calhoun, Cheves, Cochran, Clopton, Condit, Crawford, Davis, Dawson, Desha, Dinsmoor, Earle, Findley, Fisk, Gholson, Goodwyn, Green, Grundy, B. Hall, O. Hall, Harper, Hawes, Hyneman, Johnson, Kent, King, Lacock, Lefever, Little, Lowndes, Lyle, Macon, Maxwell, Moore, M'Koy, M'Kee, M'Kim, Morgan, Morrow, Nelson, New, Newton, Ormsby. Pickens, Piper, Pleasants, Pond, Richardson, Ringgold, Rhea, Roane, Roberts, Sage, Sammons, Seaver, Sevier, Seybert, Shaw, G. Smith, J. Smith, Strong, Taliaferro, Troup, Turner, Whitehill, Williams, Wright—76.

The said bill was then read the second time and committed to a committee of the whole House to-day.

The House resolved itself into a committee of the whole House on the said bill; and after some time spent therein, Mr. Speaker resumed the chair and Mr. Bassett reported, that the committee had according to order the said bill under consideration, and made some progress therein, and had directed him to ask leave to sit again.

Ordered, That the committee of the whole house have leave to sit again on the said bill.

And then the House adjourned, until to-morrow morning 11 o'clock.

Thursday, June 4, 1812.

A motion was made by *Mr. Milnor* that the doors be now opened.

And the question being taken,

It was determined in the negative.

The House then resolved itself into a committee of the whole House on the bill declaring war between Great Britain and her dependencies and the United States and their territories; and after some time spent therein, Mr. Speaker resumed the chair and Mr. *Bassett* reported that the committee had according to order had the said bill under consideration and made no amendment thereto.

A motion was then made by Mr. *Quincy*, to amend the said bill by adding thereto a new section, as follows:

" Sec. *And be it further enacted*, That from and after the passage of this act, the act entitled " An act concerning the commercial intercourse between the United States and Great Britain and France and their dependencies and for other purposes," passed the 1st day of May 1810, and also the act entitled " An act supplementary to the act entitled " An act concerning the commercial intercourse between the United States and Great Britain and France and their dependencies and for other purposes," passed the second day of March, 1811. And also, the act entitled " An act laying an embargo on all ships and vessels in the ports and harbors of the United States for a limited time," passed the 4th day of April, 1812, be, and the same hereby are repealed."

A motion was thereupon made by Mr. Nelson, that the bill and the proposed amendment be recommitted to a committee of the whole house.

And the question being taken thereon,

It passed in the negative.

(To be continued in our next.)

REPORT.

The committee, to whom was referred so much of the President's message as relates to Indian affairs,

REPORT:

That the attention of the committee has been directed to the following inquiries:

1st. Whether any, and what agency the subjects of the British government may have had in exciting the Indians on the western frontier, to hostilities against the United States.

2d. The evidence of such hostility, on the part of the Indian tribes, prior to the late campaign on the Wabash.

3d. The orders by which the campaign was authorised and carried on.

The committee have obtained all the evidence within their power relative to these

THE WAR.

NEW-YORK:

SATURDAY MORNING, JULY 11, 1812.

☞ Our city patrons are respectfully solicited for their indulgence with regard to such omissions of our carriers as may occasionally occur; for it cannot be expected that their new task has already become so familiar to them as to prevent a few such inaccuracies.

The Fourth day of July was celebrated in this city with a zeal, a splendour, and an unanimity of sentiment unprecedented. The military and different societies formed in processions agreeable to previous arrangements. Two orations were delivered, one before the Tammany and other republican societies; the other, before the Washington and Hamilton societies. The acerbity of party formed no feature in either oration; the orators did themselves honor, and spoke the sense of their constituents. One principle seemed to animate all, a determination to support their government, to resist the common enemy, and, on the altar of liberty, to swear eternal fealty to the principles of the revolution. Such were the sentiments that marked the day, and concluded the evening; no riot, no disturbance, all harmony, good will, and concord. Toasts in our next.

From all quarters, we learn that the news of war was received with joy and enthusiasm, and has been followed by a general display of loyalty—hundreds and thousands of volunteers every where offered their services to government. The newspapers are filled with particulars of patriotic meetings and resolutions and instances of individual enthusiasm, editors of all political complexions are loud in their appeals for a suspension of party animosities, and a general concurrence in supporting our government. It is impossible for us to give place at present to the many instances of patriotism which came to our knowledge even within the short space of one week. We can only give in this number a few, drawn indiscriminately from the pile. The news of war was unexpected in Canada, and will, we predict, cause equal astonishment in England, where it undoubtedly will be unpopular. In all the seaports we perceive there is a general preparation for sending out privateers, many have already sailed, and as many more are preparing to depart as will, we believe, destroy British commerce, their 1200 vessels of war to the contrary, notwithstanding. The British ministers have withdrawn their services, and left the Prince Regent to be advised by other men, and wise indeed must they be if they will quickly heal the wounds inflicted by their predecessors.

TO CORRESPONDENTS.

Avast, gentlemen!—Seventy-six, two Washingtons, Common Sense, and Junius—We cannot give you all room this day, you will be introduced in turn

Seventy-six was too long for our present number, we were obliged to curtail it, the spirit is however retained.

Columbus is a bad politician and a doubtful patriot, he is laid aside.

We cannot understand An Artillerist, and we suspect he would be equally unintelligible to our readers—an interview would be desirable.

LATE NEWS.

A pilot boat, laden with a large quantity of English goods, has been seized by the collector of Eastport.

Recapture. The brig Pickering, Davis, from Gibraltar, was taken by the frigate Belvidera and ordered to Halifax; she was retaken when within six miles of Halifax light, by the crew, *assisted by four of the prize crew*,* and carried into Gloucester.

Several waggons, with arms and ammunition, and military stores, together with five pieces of cannon, were sent on to the frontiers at Fort Niagara—several detachments of troops have marched for the same destination.

The British have taken a vessel on lake Ontario, laden with produce, owned by Mr. Abraham Dox, of Geneva. They also captured another vessel on lake Erie, belonging principally to Mr. Peter H. Colt, who was on board. Lieut. Gansevoort, of Fort Niagara, with a sergeant, who happened to be over the river, at the time the news of war was received, were detained by the British.

A prize. The Ontario, a fine new schooner of 87 tons, was taken by captain Tarrar, deputy collector, and brought into the port of St. Vincent, last week.

On Thursday evening the British brig of war Colibri, captain Thompson, arrived off Sandy Hook, in eight days from Halifax, with dispatches.

Captain Thompson came up in a pilot boat, and informed us that the Belvidera frigate, captain Byron, had arrived at Halifax; that on the evening of the 23d of June, the Belvidera had a running fight with the United States frigate President, commodore Rodgers, from 6 to 9 o'clock, P. M.—that the Belvidera had two men killed, and twenty-two wounded, four badly, and the ship considerably injured.

All citizens of the United States, residing in Quebec, have been ordered to quit that city by twelve o'clock on the first July, and the district of Quebec by twelve o'clock on the third July. An indulgence of ten or twelve days is granted to persons having business to settle, on their finding approved security.

FOREIGN.

IRISHMEN THE CHAMPIONS OF LIBERTY.

In an event of a war between the United States and England, the British troops will have new enemies to encounter, in the presence of the IRISH residing in America, who may, at the smallest computation, furnish an army of 20,000 men, and with such facility, that it will not be necessary to seduce them into the ranks by the offer of bounties. Their attachment to their new country and the abhorence of the men who drove them from the land of their fathers, contribute to make them the most formidable enemies the British will have to contend with in the new world.

Irish Magazine.

"We have been favoured with a copy of the embargo act lately passed by the American congress. We contemplate the evils of which such a measure may be productive with the greatest anxiety; we do not wish to be the prophets of calamity, but the situation both of our armies and our allies in the peninsula will call for all our commiseration if we should see them reduced to depend entirely on this country for supplies of grain. Cadiz* and Lisbon are, as we rejoice to hear, in no immediate want, but their present stores, though considerable, can be only of short duration where armed bodies are to be maintained in a ravaged and exhausted country."

Liverpool Mercury.

* This circumstance is a happy presage of what may be expected from the unfortunate impressed sailors of Britain, when unwillingly opposed to Americans. Of 9 men put on board the Pickering, by the commander of the British frigate, four proved friends to America. If this bears a just proportion to the number of our friends in the entire British navy, we may soon expect peace on our own terms. *Editor.*

(COPY.)

GENERAL ORDERS.

HEAD-QUARTERS, NEW-YORK, *July* 6, 1812.

The General announces to the troops in the city and harbor of New-York, the death of Brigadier General GANSEVOORT, at Albany, on the 2d instant. In testimony of respect to the defender of Fort Schuyler in 1777, of an officer of intelligence, bravery and distinguished military merit during the revolutionary war, the colors will be hoisted half staff high for the day; and the officers wear the usual badge of mourning for one month. By order.

R. H. MACPHERSON, Aid-de-Camp.

July 7.

For the War.

PATRIOTISM AND LOVE.

My country calls—must I away?
 While *honor* urges to the field,
Love holds me here with equal sway:
 Shall I to *love* or *honor* yield?

O, Myra! shall I leave thy charms,
 Thy cheering smiles and converse sweet,
For the rude camp, the din of arms,
 Where death and devastation meet?

But duty calls me to the field,
 My country's wrongs demand redress;
Shall softer ties to valor yield,—
 Will honor prove my love the less?

"No! Henry, let not this pretence
 Cause thee thy duty to forego;
If patriot valor urges hence,
 Then, Henry, love shall urge thee, too.

"I would—but *will not* keep thee here,
 For thou thy country's friend must prove:
The soul that shrinks when foes are near,
 It *must*— it *will* be false in love.

"Go, Henry, go—thy Myra's pray'rs
 Attend thee on thy valiant way,
Though absent, she'll partake thy cares,
 Till thou return'st—yet, Henry stay."

O, could two patriot lovers part,
 Without one pledge their loves to tell!
How *fearless!* yet the trembling heart,
 Dares not to *speak* the last farewel!

One chaste embrace—one gentle kiss;
 A hopefel smile—an anxious sigh;
Who would not *merit* such a bliss,
 Nor fear for such a bliss to die?

"Now, Myra, Heaven must be thy guard;
 The signal waves—adieu! adieu!
While *honor* calls me thitherward,
 I'll be inspir'd by love and you!

"No fear shall this proud arm restrain,
 Till the vindictive foe shall cease;
Then I'll return to thee again,
 To live and love in lasting peace!"

July—1812. ZEPHRI.

☞ Distant subscribers are requested, when sending orders for our paper, to mention if they wish it forwarded from the first number.

THE LONG ISLAND FARMER.

AGRICULTURE—THE HANDMAID OF COMMERCE.

Number 80.] JAMAICA, Queens County, THRSDAY, JULY 11, 1822. [Volume II.

PRINTED AND PUBLISHED BY
H. C. SLEIGHT,
EVERY THURSDAY,
IN THE WEST END OF THE OLD ACADEMY, MAIN-STREET, NEXT DOOR TO LAMBERSONS' STORE.

TERMS.

$2 50 cents, payable half yearly, or $2 in advance.

To companies of 10, or more, who send for their papers, a discount will be made.

*** Interest charged on all delinquents.

††† No paper discontinued until all arrearages are paid.

☞ Postage must be paid on all Communications, or they will not receive attention.

ADVERTISEMENTS

Official advertisements at the rate established by law.

Other advertisements on the usual terms.

One square per week, $12 per annum. Two squares, $20.

THE WREATH.

FROM THE STATESMAN.

God said, "LET THERE BE LIGHT."

"LET there be Light," Jehovah said,
And nature sprang to birth;
Darkness before his presence fled,
And beauty crowned the earth.

Man, by his word, from dust he form'd,
And woman from his side;
Their souls with fire ethereal warm'd,
To heaven's dread King allied.

But soon the gloom of sin o'erspread
The lustre of the mind;
No light the lamp of Reason shed,
And man again was blind.

His walk was darkness; and despair
Upon his spirit prey'd;
Weary and worn with racking care,
Along life's waste he stray'd.

Th' ETERNAL saw: "Let there be light,"
Again in heaven was heard;
And lo! man's weak bewilder'd sight
The STAR OF BETHLEHEM cheer'd.

The Sun of Righteousness, his beams
Upon the spirit shed;
The sleep of sin, and error's dream,
Were o'er, when Jesus bled!

BOSTON BARD.

FROM THE CONNECTICUT MIRROR.

The Rev. LEVI PARSONS, who was associated with the Rev. Pliny Fisk, in the Palestine Mission, died at Alexandria, February 10th, 1822.

GREEN as Machpelah's honour'd field
Where Jacob, and where Leah lie,
Where Sharon's shrubs their roses yield,
And Carmel's branches wave on high;
So honour'd, so adorn'd, so green,
Young Martyr! shall thy grave be seen.

O how unlike the bloody bed
Where pride and passion seek to lie:
Where Faith is not! where Hope can shed
No tear of holy sympathy!
There withering thoughts shall drop around
In dampness, on the lonely mound.

* * * * * *

On Jordan's weeping willow trees
Another holy harp is hung;
It murmurs in as soft a breeze
As e'er from Gilead's balm was flung,
When Judah's tears in Babel's stream
Dropp'd—and when "Zion was their theme."

So may the harp of Gabriel sound,
In the high heavens to welcome thee,
When rising from the holy ground
Of Nazareth and Galilee—
The saints of God shall take their flight
In rapture to the realms of light.

MISCELLANY.

FROM THE EMPORIUM.

THE MONEY COINER.

"Look into those they call unfortunate,
"And, closer view'd, you'll find they are unwise."—*Young.*

There is not a word in the whole vocabulary of the English language, more frequently misapplied, than the word "*unfortunate.*" Mr. A. a respectable merchant of my early acquaintance, neglected, one cold winter's night, to take care of his store fire, and, before morning, the building, with half his fortune in it, was reduced to ashes. Nothing would suit my old friend Timothy Tandem, when he came out to see me last January, but he must drive across the ice on the Shippany creek; he was warned that it was a hazard, but on he dashed, and his fine horse and gig, worth 800 or so, went to the bottom, and his pocket-book, containing a round 1200 dollars, was missing, when he came out. And my next neighbour, who has all the celebrated harangue of Poor Richard at the vendue by heart, and retails more proverbs than he sells bushels of corn, forgot the other evening to put up a pair of bars that led into an eight acre grain field, and next morning he found six or eight of his cattle had made a repast upon it that proved fatal to half of them. My poor friends are pitied for their misfortunes, and these *mysterious* dispensations of providence have each occasioned their nine days of wonderment; while Jack Hoyt, the robber, who was sent to the state prison a month ago, on a ten years apprenticeship, did not hear a sympathetic sigh from the concourse who listened to his sentence, all agreeing the punishment was scarcely equal to the crime for which it was inflicted.

This Providence, about which so much is said, I believe is, after all, a fair dealer; and I made up my mind in this respect long before I came across the little sentence I have placed at the head of my narrative today. When we meet with losses, and are suffering under the effects of our own errors and carelessness, we cry out, "unfortunate! unfortunate!" ascribe the disasters that overtake us, to the hand of an over-ruling power, and are ready to question the justice of our punishment; while these losses and disasters are the natural consequences of our own doings, and could not in fact be prevented from falling upon us but by the direct and particular interposition of a miraculous power. This will be illustrated as I proceed to introduce to my readers an honest-hearted soul as ever lived—Charles Clemens of Alesbury, alias "The Money Coiner," a hand-and-glove acquaintance of Bob Hawthorn of Holburn Hill, and whose hammer is at this moment sounding in my ear.

Charles came down to Alesbury from among the mountains, just before I left the village to reside in Philadelphia. He was a raw country lad, and so awkward in his manners and appearance that the boys of the village used to crack many a merry joke upon his broad brimmed hat and clownish address. For lack of a better place, he was apprenticed to Giles Overshoot, the whitesmith. It was a poor business, in a country where pewter dishes and wooden spoons were served up at the dinner-table of the 'squire; but it afforded Giles the means of supporting a lazy family, and of keeping his credit tolerably well at the alehouse. With him Charles learned the business, and came out with credit, slim as, from a variety of circumstances, his chance appeared at first.

By this time the silver-smithing business had become better than it was. The girls had taken it into their heads that their city friends looked better in silks and lockets than they did with their homespun frocks and their rosy cheeks—and these becoming fashionable for an evening walk, they soon brought the furniture of the table into corresponding style. Charles set up a shop, not in opposition to his old master, for opposition means to oppose, to injure, but with the view of benefiting himself, the business, and the public, by bringing the trade to more perfection than it had been brought there, and in the honest emulation to which he aspired he was successful. His hammer never ceased from that time till now. He married, and children grew up around him, but he set them to work as soon as they left the school; he had not an idler about his premises; he not only set an example of constant and unremitting industry, but in his frugal habits, in his moral and religious deportment, in his regular and religious duties, he was a pattern to all who knew him. Charles Clemens never neglected his shop—never broke his promise—never slighted his work—never cheated a customer; and Chas. Clemens soon had a purse full of dollars, a cellar full of beef and cider, a house of his own, and two or three handsome lots around it.

Giles, on the other hand, found his business declining; his old customers one after another dropped off; and, as may be supposed, he saw them calling upon his fellow tradesman with not much of complacency. Still, however, upon reviewing, he was well assured that in the aggregate since Charles had set up for himself, the greatest part of the business had come to the old shop, tho' now indeed the balance seemed inclining fast to the new one. How could it be that he, with a smaller and older family than Charles, should be [illegible] rich? It was a mystery he could not unravel; and he resolved to watch him closely. Night after night, as he returned from the tavern, he saw a light over the way, and heard the hammer that was charming his customers from him, busy; and again its clink was heard at the first blush of day. He reflected, and observed, and reflected; and at last, apparently big with some new idea or discovery, he posted down to the magistrate's, craved an audience, and informed that he had ascertained, beyond all controversy or doubt, that Clemens was in the habit of coining spurious metal into dollars. This discovery was, indeed, an unraveller, and he proved it by an argument drawn from the circumstance that his rival worked at unseasonable hours, in secrecy, alone, and that he had accumulated more than was possible to be accumulated honestly, from the business he did.

His honour smiled very good naturedly, but sent for the offender, and promised that justice should be done him, if the charge was made out. Charles soon appeared in his leather apron and check shirt. "If," said he, in answer to the argument of his accuser, "I have made a living and laid up money, I owe it to other means than those alleged; while I have worked hard, as my hands attest, I have spent but little, as all know: my boys assist me in the shop, my girls spin, and my apprentice, because I am always with him, earns me a round sum every year: the necessaries of life are few, and we want no more. Thus I live; and if you, Giles Overshoot, would cease to spend your yearly hundred at the alehouse, and would earn your three hundred at the hammer; if you would put out your children, or make them earn their living at home; if you would do as much work as you can, with as little expense as possible, and then live frugally and sparingly, you would deserve the appellation of Money Coiner as much as I do." The audience laughed heartily; Giles hung down his head; and the rival tradesmen shook hands before they parted.

FROM THE DEMOCRATIC PRESS.

Fables.—The following anecdote of Dr. Franklin was recently told by the ex-president, John Adams. The aversion of Mr. Adams to Dr. Franklin is so well known, that we may be certain the anecdote is at least as creditable as it is reported to the intellect and patriotism of the Doctor. It is a well conceived, well expressed, and most appropriate fable.

The Doctor was in company with some of his literary friends in London, when the subject of *fables* was the topic of conversation. It seemed to be the general sentiment that the subject was exhausted. The Doctor was appealed to for his opinion, who said that he thought quite otherwise, and that there was still a rich fund, on which future Æsops might delight and instruct mankind. Lord Spencer asked him to give them a specimen of his powers in that scene. The dispute between G. Britain and her colonies had been under discussion; when, in allusion to that subject, he fabricated the following fable, which may be considered *prophetic* as to the result of that controversy:

"An eagle, scaling round a farmer's barn, spied in the yard a *hare*, and darting down upon him, seized him in his claws, and mounted with him high in the air. But he soon found that the animal had clasped his body with her fore paws, to the great interruption of his wings; and had grasped his legs with her hind paws, so that he could with difficulty preserve his balance in the air; and, what was worse, she had seized his throat with her jaws; and above all, he found to his sorrow that he had mistaken a *cat* for a *hare!* The eagle says to the cat, 'Let go your hold and I will release you.' 'Oh no!' said the cat, 'you brought me up here against my will, and I have no notion of falling from this height, to dash myself to pieces. You must stoop and set me down.'

Yankee Clown.—In one of the courts of judicature in Massachusetts, some 18 or 20 years ago, an uncouth young fellow of the age of 18 was introduced into court, as a witness for the plaintiff; upon which the defendant arose, and objected to his being admitted as a witness, "for (said he) he does not know enough to understand the nature of an oath; therefore he ought not to be allowed his evidence in this court. And to convince you, gentlemen, that this is the case, I will ask him a few questions." He then turned to the young fellow, and said, "Who made *you?*" To which he awkwardly replied, "I don't know—*I spose 'twas Moses.*" His answer, gentlemen, I think, is sufficient to convince you, that what I have said respecting him is true, without any further evidence;" and sat down again. The young fellow by this time began to scratch his head, and feel somewhat chagrined that he should be thus taken off, and begged leave of the court to ask the gentleman, who had just interrogated him, a few questions. "Who made *you, sir?*" To carry the joke still farther upon the awkward lad, he replies, "I don't know—*spose 'twas Aaron.*" "Well, (says the fellow,) we read in the good Book, that Aaron made a *Calf;* but I *dident know the darn'd fool had got here.*"

Mr. *Heron*, a minister in New-England, when dying and leaving a family of small children, his poor wife fell a-weeping, and said, alas! what will become of all these children? He pleasantly replied, "never fear—He that feeds the young ravens will not starve the young *Herons;*" and it came to pass accordingly.

Two genuine sons of Hibernia having just landed at New-York, stepped into a small grocery, in order to take a cooling draught. While the storekeeper was engaged in drawing the exhilarating beverage, one of them espied a steam boat coming down the river. Not knowing what it was, he hastily stepped to the door and says to his companion, 'Jammy, Jammy, just for once be after looking this waw." "Och" says the other, "Dont be exposing yourself now; it is nothing but a *Grist-mill afloat.*"

Religious Department.

FOR THE LONG-ISLAND FARMER.

CHRISTIAN UNION.

To all in whose hearts the *love of Christ* prevails over the miserable considerations which have too long divided and almost distracted the *body of Christ;* to all who lose sight of the distinctions which *names* have produced, in their love for *Christians*, any indication of increasing harmony among professors of the Lord Jesus, of different denominations, will be matter of joy and rejoicing.—To me, it has long been a subject of grief and mourning, that those who "see eye to eye" so perfectly upon the great fundamental doctrines of the Gospel as do the Baptists and Congregationalists, or Presbyterians—whose communion with the Father and with his Son Jesus Christ is the same—that *they* should have so little communion and fellowship one with another. I am persuaded that, to produce a commingling of hearts, it is only necessary that they should become more acquainted with each other, and know the sentiments and feelings common to both. Let us break down the middle wall of partition. Let us avail ourselves of the privilege of uniting, heart and hand, with all who bear the image and do the works of our Master; and thus constrain those who make our apparent differences an objection to our [illegible] Behold, how these Christians love one another." Christ said, not to one sect nor to another, but to his followers, to *Christians*, "By this shall all men know that ye are my disciples, if ye love one another."

I have been led to these observations by reading the following communication in the Christian Watchman, a very valuable Baptist paper, printed in Boston. The communication is from a committee appointed at the Union Prayer Meeting, held in the Baptist Meeting-house in Worcester, Mass. Feb. 27, 1822, to consider how far the two denominations, Congregationalists & Baptists, were agreed, and how far they might consistently and properly be united.

A PRESBYTERIAN.

"We are agreed in the first place, in our views of the *fundamental doctrines* of Christianity. The total depravity of the natural heart; the necessity of regeneration by the influence of the Divine Spirit; the Deity and atonement of Christ; justification by faith; the necessity and certainty of the saints' perseverance in [illegible] the everlasting happiness of the righteous; and the endless punishment of the wicked in the future world, are doctrines which we unitedly receive and inculcate as pillars in our system of religious truth.

2. We are agreed in *Christian experience.* So far as we have evidence that we are followers of Christ, we believe we have experienced the same great change, and are now the subjects of religious views, feelings, and affections, which are in kind the same.

3. We are agreed in respect to the grand object of our pursuit. The glory of God in the advancement of Christ's kingdom, and the salvation of souls we unitedly regard as an object of supreme importance—an object compared with which all others lose their value, and appear as trifles.

4. We are agreed respecting the *means* by which this great object is to be promoted. The word of God, a preached Gospel, meetings for religious conference, the Christian Sacraments, Baptism and the Lord's Supper, the singing of praises, prayer, in public and private, together with contributions for religious charitable objects, we number amongst the most prominent means, which we are authorized to use in attempting the enlargement of our Redeemer's kingdom.

5. We are agreed in considering the churches we respectively represent as *churches of Christ*, churches which he has owned and blessed; nor do we discover any material difference of opinion in regard to the rights, powers, and discipline of these churches.

6. We are agreed in acknowledging each other as *regularly ordained ministers* of Christ, and thus *qualified officially* for the performance of all ministerial acts.

Indeed, the differences by which we are specifically separated are few. In regard to the *nature* or *mode*, and the *subjects of Christian Baptism*, and the *exterior qualifications for communion at the Lord's Table*, we have not the happiness at present to harmonize. The Scriptures we mutually receive as our rule of faith; but particular passages relating to these subjects, which we agree in considering subjects of importance, we have not yet been enabled to interpret in the same way.

The points above noticed in which the denominations composing this meeting are agreed, appear to us to lay the foundation for the following conclusions:

1. Ministers and Christians of these denominations may, with great propriety, unite, as occasion shall offer, in *meetings for public prayer,*—meetings similar to those which have already been attended, and from which this paper has originated.—Interspersed with the devotions of these meetings, brief remarks may be made, and religious intelligence communicated. It is recommended that each meeting be concluded with a discourse to be delivered ordinarily by one of a different denomination from him who has invited the meeting. In every thing pertaining to these meetings, there should be an entire reciprocity; and nothing should be said or done, which can have a tendency the most remote to disturb the feelings of any brother.

2. To members of churches in regular standing, who request *certificates of dismission* and *good standing*, from the churches of one denomination to those of the other, such certificates *may*, and *ought*, without unreasonable delay, to be given; and, by the church to which they are addressed, they ought to be received in evidence of Christian character, as though they had come from a church of its own denomination.

3. It is proper and right, that between the ministers of our respective congregations there should be an occasional interchange of public labours; leaving it to every minister (as in all cases it should be) to regulate his own exchanges.

4. It should be the constant endeavour, both of ministers and Christians of the two denominations, to treat each other, so far as they may [illegible] *brotherly manner;* ever remembering the direction of our Saviour, "Whatsoever ye would that men should do to *you*, do ye even so to *them.*"

Finally—As we are hoping and expecting, through infinite grace, to be united for ever in the kingdom of our God above, we will unite in the desire and prayer, that our present differences of opinion may soon cease; that existing impediments to perfect union and communion may be speedily done away; and that the promised period may be hastened when the "Watchmen shall see eye to eye, and the Lord shall bring again Zion."

All which is respectfully submitted.

JOSEPH GOFFE,
NICHOLAS BRANCH,
JONATHAN GOING,
ENOCH POND,
} *Committee.*

The committee of Publication would only add, that the above report was considered, and accepted, in two successive Prayer meetings, and that several clergymen in the region, of both denominations, who have been consulted respecting it, have signified their full approbation."

part of her dress. He was too polite not to yield to her request. In a moment she disappeared in the crowd, and could not afterwards be found. The young gentleman was left with a sleeping infant in his arms, surrounded by his jeering companions, and was perhaps the only person present who could not raise a smile at witnessing his early and unwelcome paternity.—*N. Y. Amer.*

THE FARMER.

JAMAICA:

THURSDAY, JULY 11, 1822.

Accident.—We understand that a young man, named Frost Carpenter, was killed, and several others wounded, in the evening of the 4th instant, at Musqueto Cove, by the bursting of a cannon. It is said that, *in the night*, they got possession of the cannon, charged it heavily, forced a stone into its mouth, and fired it in that situation.

Extract from a letter of an officer attached to the U. S. ship Franklin, received by a friend in Philadelphia.

"We have on board a Mr. Kennedy, who formerly belonged to the U. S. Marine Corps. He resigned and came out to this country with the unfortunate General Carrera, who was well known in the United States.

"In a battle fought some months since, General Carrera was taken prisoner, shot, and quartered. Mr. K. was taken at the same time, and would have suffered the fate of his general, had he not received in the action a musket ball, which entered his left and passed out of his right eye. He had the rank of captain in the service of Carrera. He arrived here totally destitute of every thing—and all that he has received for his services is the loss of both eyes.—He will return to the U. States in the frigate Constellation.—*Freeman's Journal.*

SUMMARY

Conspiracy of the Negroes.—The following persons of colour were convicted at Charleston, of an attempt to raise an insurrection in Carolina, and sentenced to be executed on the 2d instant, viz: Denmark Vesey, a free black man; Rolla, Batteau, Ned, slaves of his Excellency Thomas Bennett; Peter, the slave of James Poyas, Esq.; Jesse, the slave of Thomas Blackwood, Esq.

A new Post-Office has been established at Baptist-Town, N. Jersey, and Wm. Bray, esq. appointed postmaster.

Female Courage.—An attempt of the convicts in the Baltimore Penitentiary to escape, was lately frustrated by a female, who, discovering their designs, immediately ran towards the alarm bell to give notice of it; and, though repeatedly threatened by the prisoners with instant death, she had courage and presence of mind sufficient to accomplish her purpose, without receiving any injury.

Swindler.—A person, answering the description of the swindler, who lately imposed on the inhabitants of Worcester, has been committed to the workhouse at New-Haven, till his identity is ascertained.

Lightning.—The ship Newburyport, of Newburyport, which sailed on Monday, last week, from Baltimore for Limerick, was struck by lightning the following day at the mouth of the river, by which her foretopmast was split, and four men hurt, two badly, from the electric fluid that descended to the cabin.

Accident.—A sailor was killed on Friday last in Water-street, N. York, by the falling of an anchor, weighing about 900, which he inadvertently laid hold of while passing it.

Fire.—Two wooden buildings, in which were eleven looms, and a quantity of unfinished cloth, attached to the Woollen Factory at Steubenville, Ohio, were destroyed by fire on the 21st ult. The loss is estimated at $3000.

Murder.—A coroner's jury at Boston, has returned a verdict of Murder, on examining the body of Thomas Branagan, a native of Ireland, and a labourer, found dead in a house near the dock. A warrant had been issued against Owen Sherry, charged with the crime, but he had decamped. A woman named Mary Reed had been committed as an accomplice in the murder.

Canal.—The Cleveland Herald says, that the project of a Canal, on the courses of Cuyahoga and Muskingum rivers, is feasible beyond the most sanguine expectations entertained of this route. The Portage Lake, covering about 500 acres, is so situated as with no great labor to be made to discharge itself either way. To this lake the main branch of the Muskingum approaches within about two miles, and may be conducted, with small expense, into it, and thence by its outlet into lake Erie.

Advices from St. Louis of the 3d June, state that the boat sent up by General Ashley, containing the provisions, ammunition, guns, troops, &c. for the expedition to the mountains, was sunk in the Missouri river, about 20 miles below Fort Osage.—Preparations were making to repair the injury, and every exertion used to prevent delay in the progress of the company to their destination.

Ancient City.—The ruins of an extensive city, said, in the Savannah Georgian, to have been discovered a few years since in Guatimala, Mexico, have been surveyed by a learned Spaniard, & drawings made of its curiosities, which have been sent to London, and will soon be presented to the world. The city had been covered for ages with verbage and underwood.

Hail Storm.—The county of Dutchess was visited, on the 1st inst. with a most violent hail storm. It lasted about an hour and a half.—The hail extended between one and two miles in width. It came from the northeast, passed by the back of Fishkill and over Beckmantown. In the latter place it prostrated all the crops, rooted up a great number of trees, both forest and fruit, killed some young cattle, and broke most all the panes of glass in the meeting house, and a great number in the village. It was succeeded by a torrent of rain, which almost surpasses description.

A mad dog was killed on the 8th inst. in Broadway, New-York, opposite Washington Hall.

The Post says that a number of human bones were discovered by workmen who were digging for the foundation of a house, at the corner of Fulton and Gold-street, New-York.

MARRIED,

On Saturday last, by the Rev. Mr. Martindale, Mr. *Samuel L. Smith*, to Miss *Amelia Hewlett*, both of Long-Island.

FORUM.

THE LONG-ISLAND FORUM

WILL be opened again at Mr. Eldert's Hotel, in this village, THIS EVENING, at *half past seven* o'clock, when the following question will be discussed, viz.

"*Which is the stronger passion, Ambition or Love?*"

The debates will continue for the season on every other Thursday, and not on Saturday, as it had been intended.

The proceeds arising from the sale of tickets (after deducting the expenses incurred by the society) will be devoted to charitable purposes.

Tickets 25 cents. Each ticket will admit two ladies and a gentleman—to be had at the bar of the Hotel.

A LIST OF LETTERS

Remaining in the Post Office at Jamaica, July 1, 1822.

SMITH Hicks, 4, John W. Seaman, Aury Remsen, John Down, Henry Davis, Alexander Sharp, Jesse Leverich, Christopher Howard, Zebulon Valentine, Rev. Solomon G. Ward, William Spragg, Rachel Tredwell.

ELIPHALET WICKES,
Post Master.

LIST OF LETTERS

Remaining in the Post Office at the Alley, July 1, 1822.

SAMUEL Brainard, Leonard I. Frost, Lewis Bixby, John Roe, I. F. Lawrence, Esq. Miss Jane D. Lowerree, Mrs. Charlotte Jointer, *Flushing.*

S. B. BARNUM,
Post Master.

SURROGATE'S SALE.

BY order of John W. Seaman, Esq. Surrogate in and for the county of Queens, notice is hereby given, that the undersigned Administrator on the estate of Jacobus Losey, late of the town of Jamaica, in said county, deceased, will sell, at Public Vendue, on the premises, on Saturday the 24th day of August next, between the hour of one o'clock in the afternoon and the setting of the sun of that day, all the right, title and interest of the said Jacobus Losey, deceased, of, in and to all that certain piece or parcel of land, with the buildings thereon, situate, lying and being at a place called Springfield, in the township of Jamaica, and bounded as follows: Easterly by the land of Isaac and John Vannausdol, until it comes to main Springfield road, and thence bounded westerly by said road, and northerly partly by the land of Samuel Mills and partly by the land of Samuel Higbie; it being one equal seventh part of the farm of John Losey, deceased.

STEPHEN WOOD.

Dated July 11, 1822. 80 6w

NEW-YORK PRICE CURRENT.

Wholesale Prices—Corrected Wednesday.

ARTICLES.	per	From	To
DOMESTIC GOODS.			
White Shirting	yd.	14	18
Brown do.	—	11	14
¾ Checks	—	16	18
⅞ Checks	—	19	21
4-4 Check	—	20	28
Stripes	—	15	17
Plaids	—	14	21
Bedticks	—	30	35
Chambrays	—	16	17
FEATHERS, live for	lb.	13	50
American	—	37	45
FISH, dry Cod	cwt.	3 00	2 25
Scale	—	1 75	2
pickled Codfish	bbl.	4 50	5
Salmon	—		
Fall Mackerel	—		
No. 1	—	8 50	9
No. 2	—	6	6 50
No. 3	—	3 25	3 50
Con. Mess Shad	—	11 50	11 75
Herrings	—	2 75	3 00
do. Nova Scotia	box	1 50	
N. England		65	
FLAX	lb.	8	9
FLOUR & GRAIN			
N. York spf.	bbl.	6 25	
Philadelphia	—	7	
Baltimore	—	7	
Alexandria	—		6 50
Fredericksburg	—	6 37	
Rich'nd city mills	—	6 62	
country do.	—	6 37	6 50
Petersburg	—	6	
Middlings, fine	—	4 75	5
Rye Flour	—	4 00	4 12
Indian Meal	—	4	4 12
in hogsheads	hhd.	18	19
WHEAT, N. River	bush	1 31	1 34
Virginia	—		
N. Carolina	—		
Rye	—	73	75
Corn, yel. North	—	78	80
Southern	—	75	
Barley	—		
Oats	—	47	
MOLASSES, Antig'a	gal.	31	33
Surrinam	—	31	33
Mart. Guad.	—	31	33
Trinidad	—	31	32
Havana	—	29	30
N. Orleans	—	38	40
SUGAR, Mus. prime	cwt	11 00	12
2d & 3d qual.	—	8	10
N. Orleans prime	—	10	11
2d & 3d qual.	—	9	10
Havana White	—	14	14 50
2d & 3d qual.	—	13	14
Havana Brown	—	9	9 50
2d & 3d qual.	—	8 50	9
Brazil Brown	—	9	
Calcutta White	—	10	
Brown	—	9 50	
Lump	lb.	14	16
Loaf	—	16	18
GLASS, Am. 7 by 9	100f	7	
8 by 10	—	8	
10 by 12	—	9	
GLUE, Irish best	lb.	22	28
American	—	16	20
GUNPOWDER, Am.	25lb.	4	6
English	—	6	7 50
HAMS, Virginia	lb.		10
North River	—	8	9
HEMP, Russia clean	ton	230	240
Out shot	—	220	230
Amer. dew rot	—	200	
HOGS' LARD	lb.	8	
HONEY, American	—	8½	9
Havana	gal.	53	
HOPS, 1st&2d sort	lb.	10	12
LUMBER, b'ds oak	M ft.	18	
N Riv. Pine (Yard Prices)	—	16	17
Yel. Pine (Yard Prices)	—	18	20
Al. pine bds. (Yard Prices)	pce	15	
Scant'g pine (Yard Prices)	M ft.	14	15
Oak (Yard Prices)	—	25	
Oak timber (Yard Prices)	sq.ft.	20	
Shingles Cy- [prus (Yard Prices)	M	3	
Pine (Yard Prices)	bund	1 75	
Staves W O pipe (Yard Prices)	M	58	
hhd (Yard Prices)	—	36	
b'l. (Yard Prices)	—	25	
R O Hhd. (Yard Prices)	—	20	
hhd beading (Yard Prices)	—	41	
Hoops (Yard Prices)	—	24	
NAVAL SORES, Tar	bbl.	1 62	
Pitch	—	2	2 12
Rosin	—	2	
Turpentine, soft	—	2 50	
Spirit of	gal.	40	
OILS, Lins'd Am.	—	73	75
Whale	—	30	
Sea Elephant	—	35	
Sperm. summer	—	68	70
winter	—	87	90
Liver	bbl.	15	
PEAS, white, dry	7 bu.	6	7
PORK, cargo	bbl.	7 25	
prime	—	9 25	
mess	—	14	14 25
SEED, Flax, clean	cask		
rough	—		
Clover	lb.		
WINE, Madeira	gal.	2 25	2 50
L. P.	—	2 75	3 50
Sherry	—	1 37	1 50
Colmenar	—	65	
Teneriffe L. P.	—	1 25	1 37
Cargo	—	1	
Lisbon	—	1 12	1 25
Malaga	—	62	
Port	—	1 87	2 50
WOOL, me'no wshd	lb.	60	70
unwash'd	—	35	45
½ breed wash'd	—	40	50
¾ breed wash'd	—	50	55
unwash'd	—	30	
Amer. Hatters	—		
BEEF, Mess	bbl.	8 50	
Prime	—	4 75	5
Cargo	—	4	
Boston No. 1	—	none	
Boston Mess	—	none	
BUTTER, 1st qual.	lb.		
for exportation	—	9	12
COFFEE, W. I. best [green	—	28	
Borbon	—	28	
Java	—	28½	

BY order of the Honorable Effingham Lawrence, first Judge of the Court of Common Pleas, for Queens county, notice is hereby given for the Creditors of *Walter F. Townsend*, of said county, an Insolvent debtor, to appear before the said Judge, at his dwelling house in Flushing, on the thirty-first day of August next, at ten o'clock in the forenoon of that day, to show cause, if any they have, why an assignment of the said Insolvent's estate should not be made, for the benefit of all his Creditors, and that the person of the said Insolvent may be for ever thereafter exempted from all arrest or imprisonment for or by reason of any debt or debts due at the time of making such assignment, or contracted for before that time, though payable afterwards, and also, if in prison, from his imprisonment, agreeably to an Act of the Legislature of the State of New-York, entitled, "An Act to abolish imprisonment for debt in certain cases. Dated the 6th day of July, 1822.

TO BE SOLD

At Private Sale,

The property of the late TUNUS COVERT,

PLEASANTLY situate on the Babylon turnpike, about two miles from the village of Hempstead and near Ram Point, containing ten acres of land, with convenient buildings thereon, viz. a good HOUSE with three rooms on the first floor, and an entry running quite through, a Kitchen adjoining with a cellar under the same and a well of excellent water near the door; also, a good Barn, Waggon-House, Carpenter's shop and other requisite buildings, all of which being nearly new are in good repair.

If the above property be not sold before SATURDAY, the THIRD of AUGUST, it will on that day be exposed at PUBLIC VENDUE, on the premises at 2 o'clock, P. M.

ALSO—at Private Sale, the *HOUSE* and *LOT* of the Subscriber, which he now occupies, situate in the village of Hempstead, on the Main street, west from the Episcopal Church; the house has three rooms and an entry on the first floor, with a large Workshop adjoining, and a Kitchen in the rear with a Pump by the door; a good Barn, Waggon House, Chair House, and other requisite buildings; the lot contains half an acre. For further particulars, inquire of HENRY COVERT.

Hempstead, 27th May, 1822. 74tds

SAM'L S. CARMAN,
Clock and Watch Maker,
and Jeweller,

INFORMS his friends, and the public in general, that he has commenced the above business, in all its various branches, in the house opposite the Hon, Rufus King's residence, where, by care and attention, he hopes to merit and receive a liberal encouragement from his numerous and respectable friends.

N. B. Clocks and Mantle Time Pieces repared at the houses of those who desire it, and warranted to keep good time. All kinds of Jewellery made and repaired in the neatest manner.

CASH given for old Gold and Silver.

Jamaica, May 23, 1822. 73 ft

WILL BE SOLD, at Public Auction, on Wednesday the 1st day of January, 1823, at one o'clock in the afternoon, on the premises, ALL and singular the premises herein after described, situate, lying and being in the town of Hempstead, county of Queens, and state of New-York, viz. all that certain piece or parcel of land and tenement, situate, lying and being in the town aforesaid, and bounded as follows, viz. southerly by land of Jonah Skidmore, easterly by the road that leads from the plains to Samuel Wright's, northerly by the road that leads along by said premises to Foster's meadow, and westerly by the mill-brook,—containing, by estimation, five acres, be the same more or less, reserving & excepting the privilege of ponding in said swamp. Also, one other piece or parcel of land situate near the same place, and bounded as follows, viz. easterly by the road leading from the plains to Samuel Wright's, southerly by the road leading to Foster's meadow, westerly by the mill ... land, being the place whereon Samuel Pearsall then lived—containing, by estimation, eight acres, be the same more or less, together with all and singular the buildings, fences, trees, privileges and appurtenances thereunto belonging or any way appertaining. The above described property will be sold by John Rider and Luke Covert, as executors of the last will and testament of John Covert, deceased, by virtue of a power contained in a mortgage executed by Samuel Pearsall to the said John Covert, deceased, on the 12th day of April, in the year of our Lord 1821, to secure the payment of the sum of two hundred and fifty dollars, with lawful interest, on or before the 1st day of May then next ensuing, default having been made in said payment. Dated the 27th day of June, 1822. 78

Six Cents Reward.

RAN away from the Subscriber, on the 9th inst. a Black Woman, about 23 years of age, named BET. All persons are forbid harboring, trusting, or employing her, under penalty of the law. Whoever will return her to the subscriber, shall receive the above reward, but no charges paid.

JAMES HENDRICKSON.

Six Cents Reward.

RAN away from the subscriber, on the 31st of May, a black boy named DAVID APPLEBY, five feet 3 inches high, very black, and very large white teeth. All persons are warned against harboring or employing said boy, at the peril of the law. Whoever will secure said boy and return him to his master, or lodge him in any public prison, shall receive the above reward, but no charges paid.

HEWLETT TOWNSEND, Sen.

Agricultural Notice.

THE Board of Managers of the QUEENS COUNTY AGRICULTURE SOCIETY, at a Meeting held on the 4th day of June, 1822, offer the following Premiums, on *Agriculture, Domestic Manufactures*, and *Animals*. All premiums under $6 will be paid in money—all premiums of $6 and upwards, will be paid in a piece of *Plate*, of corresponding value.

AGRICULTURE.

For the best piece of Indian corn
not less than two acres, $12
the second best do. 6
the best acre of Potatoes, 8
the best half acre of Ruta Baga, 8
the best ...
the second best do. 6
the best two acres of Rye, 10
the second best do. 6
the best acre of Flax, 8
the best 2 acres spring Barley, 8

FAMILY DOMESTIC MANUFACTURES.

For the greatest number of yards of Cloth manufactured in any one family, $10
the best piece of Woollen Cloth, fifteen yards in length, and not less than ¾ in width, spun in the family, 10
the second best do. 6
the best piece of Flannel, 20 yards in length, and ¾ wide, 6
the second best do. 3
the best piece of Linen Diaper, 20 yards in length, and ¾ wide, 3
the second best do. 8
the best piece of linen Shirting or Sheeting, 20 yards in length, and one yard wide, 8
the best pair of Woollen Stockings, (knit,) 2
the second best do. 1 50
the best pair of linen thread Stockings, (knit,) 2
the second best do. 1 50
the best pair of cotton Stockings, (knit,) 2
the second best do. 1 50
the best piece of woollen Carpeting, not less than 25 yards in length, and one width, homemade, 10
the second best do. 6
the best pair of woollen Mittens, (knit,) 2

ANIMALS.

For the best Bull raised or owned in the county, not under 18 months old, $10
the best Cow for milk and form, 10
the best pair of working Oxen, not less than 4 years old, owned for one year in the county, 10
the best Bullock, fatted in the county, 10
the best merino Ram, raised or owned in the county, 8
the best 4 merino Ewes, do. do. 8
the best Ram, other than merino, do. do. 8
the best 4 Ewes, do do do do. 8
the best Boar, not less than one year old, raised or owned in the county, 8
the best Sow do. do. 8
the best two shoats or Pigs, not over ten months old, 3
the best Stud Horse, owned in the county, not less than three years old, 15
the best breeding Mare, of like description 12
the best yearling Colt, raised and owned in the county, 10
the best Calf, not exceeding ten months old, 6

Committee on Agriculture.

Singleton Mitchell, Thos. Tredwell.
Lewis S. Hewlett,

On Manufactures.

Benj. Platt, Benj. Tredwell,
John H. Jones, Thomas Phillips.
Benj. Wright,

On Horses and Cattle.

Wm. Jones, John Tredwell,
Daniel Bedell, Benj. Platt.
John A. King,

On Sheep and Hogs.

James Lent, John J. Schenck,
Nicholas Wyckoff, Richard Cornell.
E. Lawrence.

Candidates for Premiums offered by the society shall, prior to the day of exhibition, give to some member of the committee ten days notice, in writing, of their intention, together with a description of the article or animal to be exhibited.

The annual exhibition of Domestic Manufactures, of Animals, and of Products of Agriculture, will take place at the Court House, on Thursday the 17th day of October next.

By order,
JOSEPH S. DODGE,
Recording Secretary.

TO THE PUBLIC.

WHEREAS I, *SILAS SMITH*, have reported that Benjamin S. Birdsall, and James Pinkney, did, on or about, the first of November last, assert that the abovenamed parties did, in the night time, kill other persons' Sheep on the Great Plains, and that I caught them at it, which is a great slander upon the characters of the said Birdsall and Pinkney, Now, therefore, I, the said Silas Smith, do hereby acknowledge that I have asserted a falsehood, and confess *myself* to be a *LIAR* in that assertion, and am willing this should be published by the said Birdsall and Pinkney.

I, Silas Smith, do further say, and agree with the above persons, that if I, the said Silas Smith, do ever assert any thing of the kind again, I am willing to be subject to a prosecution, and this writing shall be brought against me as evidence of my guilt of slander. Signed by me, in the presence of the subscribing witnesses, this fifth day of June, in the year 1822.

SILAS SMITH.

Witnesses.
Timothy C Youngs,
Samuel Mott, Sheriff,
Charles Coles,
Richard Valentine,
Wright Nichols,
George W. Layton,
James ...
Smith Thorn. 76

JAMAICA & BROOKLYN
POST COACH.

THE subscriber returns thanks to the public, for the very liberal encouragement which he has heretofore received, and having become the proprietor of this line of stages, (which he has taken under his personal charge) hopes by his strict attention to merit a continuance of Public Patronage. The route (12 miles) will be performed in the short space of *NINETY MINUTES, or LESS.*

The Stage will start every morning, (Sundays excepted) at seven o'clock, from *Smith Hicks'* Hotel, Jamaica; and from *Townsend Cock's*, (formerly *John Bedell's*,) at Brooklyn, (west side of the Ferry) every afternoon, at 5 o'clock.

Seats can be taken at *Simmons' & Mott's*, No. 4, Fulton slip, New-York, at *Townsend Cock's*, Brooklyn, or at the *Stage House*, Jamaica, at either of which places baggage and small parcels will be received, and strict attention paid to their delivery.

Passengers will be called for and set down in any part of either village.—*Fare 50 Cents.*

Conveyances will be provided for passengers wishing to go beyond the village of Jamaica.

JOHN SUTPHIN, *Proprietor.*

Jamaica, June 13, 1822.

TO BE SOLD, at Public Auction on the thirteenth day of December next, at two o'clock, P. M. at the house of David Kelly, Innkeeper, Hempstead Harbor, by the subscribers, heirs of the late Richard Valentine, dec'd. That certain messuage, or tenements, and lot of Land, situate in the town of North Hempstead, Queens county, and state of New-York, beginning at a road, southeast corner of land lately belonging to Wilson Williams and Jane Smith; southerly, to a marked butternut tree; south easterly to a marked chesnut saplin; thence continuing south easterly to a marked saplin; easterly to an apple tree by road side; northerly, by the west side of the road to the place of beginning, containing three quarters of an acre, more or less—except a gate-way or road one rood wide, as it is now running from the main road westerly through the above mentioned premises. The said land and tenements will be sold by virtue of a power contained in a mortgage executed by John H. Williams, and Rebecca his wife, to the late Richard Valentine, deceased, to secure the payment of two bonds, one made by John H. Williams and Wilson Williams, for two hundred and fifty dollars, payable, with interest, on the 1st day of May, 1804; the other by John H. Williams for two ... interest, on the 1st of May, 1812, default having been made in said payments. Dated June 13, 1822.

SIDNEY SEAMAN.
PHEBE W. VALENTINE.
ANN S. VALENTINE.

BY order of the honorable Effingham Lawrence, first Judge of the Court of Common Pleas, for Queens County, Notice is hereby given for the creditors of *William L. Van Zandt*, an Insolvent Debtor, to appear before the said Judge at his dwelling house, on the 20th day of August next, at ten o'clock in the forenoon of that day, to show cause, if any they have, why an assignment of the said insolvent's estate should not be made, for the benefit of all his creditors, and that the person of the said Insolvent may be forever thereafter exempted from all arrest or imprisonment for or by reason of any debt or debts due at the time of making such assignment, or contracted for before that time, though payable afterwards, and also, if in prison, from his imprisonment, agreeably to an act of the Legislature of the State of New-York, entitled, "An Act to abolish imprisonment for debt in certain cases." Dated the 28th day of May, 1822.

THE
CHRISTIAN HERALD,
AND
SEAMAN'S MAGAZINE,

Is published under the patronage of the "Society for Promoting the Gospel among Seamen in the Port of New-York."

Instituted in 1818—Incorporated by the legislature of N.York in April, 1819.

EDITED BY A MEMBER OF THE BOARD OF DIRECTORS.

TERMS.

I. A Number, consisting of 32 pages octavo, on fine paper, and a new type, and stitched in a coloured cover, will be issued on the first and on the third Saturday of every month.

II. An Appendix, of from 24 to 32 pages, containing a titlepage, preface, a copious index, and such other articles as properly belong to the volume, will be added, making in the whole one volume of 25 numbers (about 800 pages) in a year.

III. The price is three dollars a year to those who pay in advance, and four dollars to those who pay at the end of the year. Notwithstanding the addition of an Appendix, the price will not be increased.

[illegible] before the last number of any volume is published. will be considered as pledged to take the succeeding volume.

V. Agents in the country are entitled to ten per cent. for collecting and remitting, besides a copy gratis.

VI. This work is devoted to the common cause of Christianity, and will not advocate the *peculiar* tenets of any sect or party.

The price of this work is as low as any of the kind published in the United States, and much lower than most of them: this fact renders a large subscription list necessary for its support; and it is to be hoped that those who approve of its plan and execution will not only give it their own patronage, but recommend it to their friends and neighbours.

This work gives an account of the formation and proceedings of those institutions which tend directly to improve the religious and moarl condition of mankind. A few pages of each number are devoted to such original essays and reviews as are designed to animate its readers, of every denomination, to take their part in the benevolent labours of the present day. A "*retrospect*" of those political events which affect the interest of morality and religion, will be found in the first number in each month.—Holding a correspondence with all those societies which are established to promote true religion among seamen, we shall be able to give our readers the earliest and most important intelligence suited to that department of our work. The following testimonials will show the character of the work:

I have been a reader of the Christian Herald from its first appearance, and I have no hesitation in expressing my approbation of its excellence and utility, as a source of very extensive intelligence respecting the transactions of the religious world, as well as a means of instruction on a variety of interesting subjects connected with the faith and practice of Christians. This recommendation is not to be understood as an acquiescence in every sentiment and statement of a work to whose pages so many contribute; but in its general character, and especially since the union with the original design, of the interesting department relating to the spiritual interests of seamen, I consider this miscellany as one of the most valuable in our country, and sincerely wish it may have a circulation proportioned to its merits.
JAMES MILNOR,
Rector of St. George's Church.

We heartily concur in the above recommendation of Dr. Milnor.

J. M. MATHEWS,
Pastor of the R. D. Church in Garden-st.
WILLIAM GRAY,
Stated Preacher in Bancker-st. Mission House.
ARCHIBALD MACLAY,
Pastor of the Baptist Ch. Mulberry-st.
JOSEPH S. C. F. FREY,
Pastor of the Presbyterian Church in Vandewater st.
JOHN WILLIAMS,
Pastor of the Baptist Ch. in Oliver st.
[illegible] of the Church of United Brethren, city of N. York.
May 1st, 1822.

Having been for some time a patron and reader of the Christian Herald and Seaman's Magazine, and being personally acquainted with the editor, I am gratified with the opportunity of saying, that I highly and peculiarly value this publication. Its plan is singularly adapted to be extensively useful, and especially to the Christian community in the vicinity of this metropolis. I cordially wish it the patronage of men, and the benediction of God. SAMUEL H. COX,
Pastor of the Spring st. Presbyterian Ch.
New York, 1st May.

Having been for some time constant readers of the Christian Herald and Seaman's Magazine, we most cheerfully recommend the work, as being evangelical in its doctrine, catholic in its spirit, and well calculated to foster the active piety which distinguishes this day of benevolent enterprise.

ELIHU W. BALDWIN,
Pastor of the Seventh Presbyterian Church, Sheriff st.
WARD STAFFORD,
Pastor of the Bowery Presb. Church.
New-York, April 27th, 1822.

I most heartily concur in the above recommendation of the Christian Herald and Seaman's Magazine; I also add, that I cannot but believe that it will be come still more and more interesting, from the intelligence it will contain in regard to the progress of the gospel among seamen. God is beginning to raise up a seed among them—they are to be missionaries to tell of the Christian's God and Saviour to the heathen by their lives. Every Christian will love to hear the earliest intelligence in regard to them. This will be no inconsiderable advantage of the present work I heartily wish it success, and wish that it might be in the hands of many Christians.
JOHN TRUAIR,
Minister of the Mariner's Church.

I have taken the Christian Herald from its commencement. It has always been an interesting work, but is now becoming every month more and more so. I know of no periodical paper which is more useful or interesting to the Christian reader. ASA HILLYER,
Pastor of the Presb. Ch. in Orange, N. J.
Orange, N. J. May 1.

Having been in the habit, for a considerable time, of perusing "The Christian Herald and Seaman's Magazine," I consider it [illegible]lical and catholic in its principles and spirit, and can with confidence recommend it to [illegible] denominations, as a strictly impartial and highly useful miscellany. CAVE JONES,
Residing in New-York, and officiating in the Episcopal congregation in Jersey City.
April 29th, 1822.

The Latter Day Luminary, of March, 1822, published at Washington City, by a Committee of the Board of Managers of the General Convention of the Baptist Denomination in the U. States, in noticing the Christian Herald and Seaman's Magazine, says—

"It gives us pleasure to notice, publicly, the evangelical piety and catholic spirit that glow in the pages of this valuable work. We feel persuaded that the cause of religion will be extended by its wide circulation, and therefore recommend it to the patronage of christians generally. The moderate terms on which it is offered renders an unusual subscription necessary to its support. We hope that friends enough will be found to establish it on a firm and lasting basis."

** Communications relating to this work must be addressed to the "Editor of the Christian Herald and Seaman's Magazine," No. 128 Broadway, New-York, at the Bookstore of E. Bliss & E. White.

SUBSCRIPTIONS received by Dr. BLATCHFORD, of this village.

HOUSE
OF
REFRESHMENT.

STEPHEN HOLT

HAS removed his well known Establishment to the new four-story brick building, directly opposite the corner of Water and Fulton streets, where he will be happy in accommodating his friends, and the Public, in

Boarding, Lodging, Breakfasts, Dinners, & Suppers,

either separately or in parties, and he flatters himself in giving perfect satisfaction.

PASSENGERS arriving in the city, can at all times be accommodated, and no situation in New-York is more favorable or convenient for Masters of Vessels.

Likewise, MARKETMEN, and LONG-ISLAND PEOPLE, will find it to their advantage to call, as they will be furnished with sufficient store room for their Produce, GRATIS, at Nos. 22 and 23 Fulton Slip.

56—tf New-York, Jan. 1, 1822.

TO LET,
The Dwelling-House and Office

LATELY occupied by the Editor of the LONG-ISLAND FARMER. The house is pleasantly situate on the Main-street, has a good garden, &c.—is an excellent stand for any kind of Mechanical business, or for a small Store. Inquire of Messrs. [illegible]

Jamaica, May 1, 1822. 70tf

TO be sold at public auction, on the 9th day of November next, at 2 o'clock in the afternoon, on the premises hereafter described, all that farm situate in the town of Hempstead, Queens county, about one mile west of the presbyterian church, and adjoining the turnpike, on the south, that leads to Jamaica; on the west, land of Daniel Stillwell; on the north, land belonging to the estate of David Gildersleeve; on the east, land of Daniel Remsen—containing twenty acres, be the same more or less. The above premises will be sold by the subscriber by virtue of a power contained in a mortgage executed by James Deryea and Phebe his wife, to the subscriber, on the 15th day of February 1820, to secure the payment of the sum of seven hundred dollars, on the first day of May ensuing, with interest at six per cent. default having been made. Dated the 9th day of May, 1822.

71 LININGTON DURLON,

MAGISTRATE'S
BLANKS
FOR SALE AT THIS OFFICE.

BROOKLYN
CIRCULATING LIBRARY,
At the Office of the Long-Island Star, Fulton-street, Brooklyn.

THIS Library is improved by the accession of numerous modern publications, and now comprises as follows:

	VOLS.
History, Biography, Voyages, Travels, &c.	490
Novels, Tales and Romances,	915
Periodical Works, old and new,	92
Poetry,	140
Plays, (143 plays included)	36
Pamphlets, including 300 different tracts, being literary, scientific and political, orations, sermons, &c.	80

Terms of Subscription, payable in advance.

For a year,	$4 00
six months,	2 50
three months,	1 50
one month,	0 75

Any person not a subscriber may take books by paying for an octavo volume *twelve cents* per week, and for a duodecimo volume (which is the common size of novels) *six cents* per week.

Most of the new publications are added to the library [illegible] as they are out of the press.

A new catalogue is just printed, which is given to subscribers.

Brooklyn, March 14, 1822.

JAMAICA STAGES

THE subscribers respectfully inform their friends and the public that one or both, of their Stages start every morning (Sundays excepted) at seven o'clock, from *Hewlett Creed's* Inn, at Jamaica, and from *Coe S Downing's* at Brooklyn, east side of the Ferry, every afternoon, at FIVE o'cloc, for Jamaica.

Seats may be taken at *Mott & Williams'*, or at *G. & E. W. Nichol*, Fulton Slip, where baggage and small parcels will be received, and delivered according to the directions.

The proprietors of this line of Stages, will provide conveyances for those passengers who wish to go beyond the village of Jamaica.

JOHN VAN NOSTRAND } Pro'rs
JOHN SUTPHIN
Jamaica, Jan. 10, 1821.

TO BE SOLD on the twenty-fifth day of October next, a ten o'clock, A. M. on the premises herein after described, ALL that tract of land situate in the township of Oysterbay, in Bethpague, purchases and bounded as follows:—beginning at a stone at the north east corner of said tract of land, running southwardly along the highway that leads from Bethpague to south, till it comes to the land of Jonas Loses, then westwardly along Loses' land then southwardly by Loses' and Benjamin Saxton's land, then westwardly by Saxton's land to Henry Whitson's land, then northwardly by Whitson's land to a tone at the north west corner of the tract of land, then eastwardly by Elishua Post's and to the place of beginning, containing sixty acres more or less. The above premises will be sold by virtue of a power contained in a mortgage, executed by Peter Nostrand and Susan his wife to the subscriber, on the eighth day of December, one thousand eight hundred and eighteen, to secure to him the payment of six hundred dollars, with interest, at six per cent, on the first day of May, 1819—default having been made in said payment. Dated the twenty-fifth day of April, 1822.

69 JACOB WHITSON.

TO be sold, at Public Auction, on the twenty-eighth day of September next, at 1 o'clock in the afternoon, on the premises, hereafter described, to wit: ALL that lot of Land in the town of Hempstead, Queens county, butted and bounded as follows: beginning by the highway that leads from the Brook to Lawrence Seaman's, and running northerly adjoining said highway till it comes to land of William Thurston, then running easterly adjoining [illegible] brook, then running southerly adjoining the brook to the highway that leads from William Weeks' to David Beadell's, then running westerly adjoining the highway to the place of beginning; the second piece of land, opposite the first described piece, bounded on the north by the highway that leads from David Beadell's to William Weeks', on the east by the brook, on the south by the brook, and on the west by the highway that leads from the brook to Lawrence Seaman's, the two pieces containing two acres, be the same more or less. The said premises will be sold by virtue of a power contained in a mortgage, executed by Thomas Cooper, to the subscriber, on the 15th day of May, in the year of our Lord one thousand eight hundred and twenty, to secure to him the payment of two hundred and fifty dollars, on the first day of May then next, with legal interest, default having been made in said payment. Dated the 28th day of March, in the year of our Lord 1822.

BENJAMIN SAMMIS.

BLANK
MORTGAGES
For sale at this Office.

TO BE SOLD
At Private Sale,
A FARM.

SITUATE in the township of Jamaica, Queens county, about 6 miles from the village of Jamaica, and two from a good landing. Said farm is well watered, contains about 200 acres of land, with a sufficient quantity of Woodland, and a good lot of fresh and salt meadow which will cut nearly 100 loads of fresh and salt hay annually. There is on said farm a good dwelling house, barn, and other out houses, a good apple orchard, a number of pear trees, and a good well of water near the door. The situation is very pleasant, being open to the South Bay, which abounds with fish and fowl. Any person wishing to purchase a part or the whole of said farm may know the terms by applying to the Subscriber on the premises, who will give a good title for the same.

SAMUEL CORNELL.
Jamaica, Feb. 8, 1822. 58—tf

TO THE PUBLIC.

NOW PUBLISHING, IN
NUMBERS,
BY DANIEL FANSHAW,
No. 20 Sloat-Lane,
NEW-YORK.
THE HIGHLY ESTEEMED WORKS OF THE
REV. JOHN NEWTON.

The above Work is printing on fine paper, with new type, and is furnished to Subscribers at *two thirds* of the Bookstore price, as the publisher conceives that such as are furnishing the means for conveniently accomplishing an object should be more favored than they usually are.

The whole Work will make 5,888 pages, or 81 numbers; and to be comprised in six large Octavo Volumes.

It will be delivered to Subscribers at 12½ cents per Number.

Each Number will contain 48 pages.

One number will be delivered each week, until the Work is finished.

The Likeness of the Author will accompany the first Number.

Any person obtaining 10 Subscribers, and becoming responsible for them, shall be entitled to one copy.

The Works of the Rev. JOHN NEWTON are so well known, and so highly appreciated by those who have perused them, that, to such any thing by way of recommendation is needless. It is deemed advisable, however, to inform such as have not had an opportunity of reading them, that they are truly Spiritual Works, and afford an excellent fund of [illegible] instruction to Christians of every denomination.—As the writings of Mr. Newton are not of a sectarian Character, but speak to the heart and experience of every follower of the Redeemer, the Christian will find in them much useful information, suited to every trial which may be fall him in his pilgrimage through this world.

Among the wealthy part of the Christian Community they are well known and highly valued; but the poor of the Redeemer's fold, to whose capacities and trials they are most peculiarly adapted, have not heretofore had an opportunity of obtaining them, as this is the FIRST EDITION ever published in NUMBERS in this country.

Persons wishing to possess themselves of a copy by obtaining Subscribers for the work, can be supplied with proposals at the above mentioned place. The proposals contain the recommendations of upwards of 50 Clergymen, of various denominations, of the cities of N. York and Philadelphia; several of whom express themselves much gratified with the easy manner in which the poorer part of their flocks can now get possession of such a Spiritual Companion.

** The Editor of the Farmer having been appointed Agent to the above Work. for Long-Island, respectfully solicits subscriptions for it.

January, 1822. 55

TO be sold at Public Auction, on the 25th day of August next, at two o'clock, P M. on the premises hereafter described, ALL that certain messuage or tenement and lot of land, situate in the township of Newtown, in the county of Queens, and state of New-York, bounded as follows, viz:—southerly, on the highway; westerly and northerly, on land of Abraham Culver; and easterly, on land of Francis Titus—containing half an acre of land. The above premises will be sold by virtue of a power contained in a mortgage, executed by William McLaughlin and Temperance his wife, late Temperance Duryea, which said Temperance is the administratrix of the goods, chattels, and credits, which were of Abraham Duryea, late of the city of New York, deceased, to the subscribers, as executors of the last will and testament of James Leverich, late of Newtown, in Queens county, deceased, on the seventh day of July, in the year of our Lord, one thousand eight hundred and eighteen, to secure to them the payment of one thousand dollars, with lawful interest, on or before the seventh day of July then next—default having been made in said payment.—Dated the twenty-first day of February, 1822.

WILLIAM LEVERICH.
JAMES LENT.

PROPOSALS
For Publishing by Subscription,
A COMPANION
FOR THE
LORD'S DAY;
BEING THE MEDITATIONS
OF THE
Humble and the Experienced Christian
On each of the sections of the
HEIDELBURGH CATECHISM,
BY THE CELEBRATED AND PIOUS FRANCISCUS RIDDERUS, OF ROTTERDAM.

First published in that city in the year 1670.

TRANSLATED
BY JOHN BASSETT, D.D.
Minister of the Gospel,
Bushwick, L. I.

TO WHICH WILL BE ADDED, AN APPENDIX TO EACH SECTION, CONTAINING

The Sentiments and the Christian Experience of the Fathers, from the days of the Apostles to the end of the sixth century;

With a view to demonstrate, that their sentiments and Christian experiences perfectly comport with those taught in our excellent system of Divine Truth.

CONDITIONS.

I. The work will be delivered to subscribers in numbers. Those who reside in the cities of New-York, Albany, and New Brunswick, will receive them on the last Saturday in every month.

II. It will be printed on paper of an excellent quality. Each number will contain 56 pages, stitched, and covered, at 25 cents.

III. The whole work will contain, probably, from twelve to sixteen numbers.

IV. Those who subscribe for ten copies of the whole work, and become responsible for the payment of the same on delivery, shall receive one copy gratis. The usual allowance to booksellers.

V. The work will be put to press as soon as five hundred subscribers shall have been obtained.

☞ Subscriptions for the above work, received at this office.

LAY'S
Map of N. York.
A NEW EDITION

OF LAY'S MAP OF NEW YORK, the size is 4 feet 4 inches square, comprising the principal part of the states of Pennsylvania and New-Jersey, with part of the states of Connecticut, Massachusetts, Vermont, and also part of Upper Canada,

Recommended by the very respectable gentlemen, as follows:

We have examined a Map of the State of New-York, including the upper part of the State of Pennsylvania, published by Amos Lay, and it appears to us to be accurate, and to contain all the counties up to this time correctly designated, and to be well worthy public patronage.

Dewitt Clinton, *Governor;* James Kent, *Chancellor;* John Tayler, *Lieut. Governor;* Elisha Jenkins, *Mayor of Albany;* M. Van Buren, *Attorney General;* S. Van Rensselear, *late Lieutenant Governor;* Robert Troup, *Agent of Pultney Estate;* Daniel D. Tompkins, *Vice President;* John W. Van Ness, Jonas Platt, *Judges Sup Court;* Nathan Ford, *First Judge of St. Lawrence County;* Gideon Granger, *late P. M. General;* Abraham Van Vechten, *late Attorney General;* Joseph Ellicott, *Resident Agent of the Holland Land Copany;* Andrew Ellicott, *Professor of Mathematics, West Point.*

I have examined the above map, and think it a desideratum; its execution, so far as Mr. Lay is concerned, is, in myopinion, correct, and well; and I recommend it to those who wish to acquire a knowledge of the country it embraces, as equal and even superior to any extant.
A. SPENCER,
Chief Justice of the State of N. Y.

The Map is for sale by the author, at his Map Establishment, No. 649, South Market-Street, Albany.

Map in the Sheet,	$ 6.
Portable in Book,	10.
Mounted and Varnished	10.

The above Maps are for sale at the Office of the Long-Island Farmer.
Jamaica, Aug. 23, 1821.

BY order of the Honorable Effingham Lawrence, first Judge of the Court of Common Pleas, for Queens county, notice is hereby given for the Creditors of *James Duryea*, of said county, an Insolvent debtor, to appear before the said Judge, at his dwelling house in Flushing, on the thirteenth day of July next, at ten o'clock in the forenoon of that day, to show cause, if any they have, why an assignment of the said Insolvent's estate should not be made, for the benefit of all his Creditors, and that the person of the said Insolvent may be for ever thereafter exempted from all arrest or imprisonment for or by reason of any debt or debts due at the time of making such assignment, or contracted for before that time, though payable afterwards, and also, if in prison, from his imprisonment, agreeably to an Act of the Legislature of the State of New-York, entitled, "An Act to abolish imprisonment for debt in certain cases. Dated the 25th day of May 1822.

BLANK DEEDS
For Sale at this Office.

CLERK WANTED

A LAD, about 15 years of age, of good moral and industrious habits, to serve in a Country Store.—Enquire of
WRIGHT & HERRIMAN.
Jamaica, June 6, 1822.

Jamaica Bakery
AND
FLOUR STORE.

THE subscriber, grateful for the favors which he has received from his friends and the public, begs leave to inform them that he has on hand, and for sale a constant supply of

BREAD,

Made of the best superfine flour. Together with all articles in his line, such as *Biscuit, Crackers, Rusk, &c.* warranted to be of the best quality.

His Bake-Waggon will go every Tuesday and Saturday to Flushing and Whitestone; every Thursday from Jamaica to the plains, thence to Success; thence by the way of Great Neck and Cow Neck to Hempstead-Harbor; thence returning through Foster's Meadow, by the head of Springfield to Jamaica; to Far-Rockaway every Wednesday, and return through Springfield.

He trusts by a continuance of attention to his business, to merit general approbation and support.

SILAS ROE.
Jamaica, April, 1822. 69-6m

TO BE SOLD, at public auction, on the sixth day of December next, at one o'clock in the afternoon, on the premises, ALL AND SINGULAR the premises hereafter described, situate, lying and being in the town of North Hempstead, in the county of Queens, and state of New York, viz: one tract of land at the head of Hempstead Harbour, on the westerly side thereof, and bounded as follows: northerly by a line beginning at a marked locust tree, standing by the highway; westerly from the house formerly occupied by Abraham Coles, and running westerly from the said tree a straight course until it strikes a marked butternut tree standing at the east end of a certain stone fence; thence westerly a straight course until it strikes a marked cherry tree; thence westerly a straight course to a marked sassafras tree standing by the highway; westerly by the said highway as the fence now stands; southerly by the land late of John M. Smith, Rem Kesshow, and John H. Williams, as the fence now stands; easterly by the highway, as the fence now stands, to the place of beginning—containing thirty four acres, be the same more or less, (excepting a lot of land on the south corner, joining on the west side of the road, which Caleb Valentine sold to James W. Smith, as the same is now enclosed in fence, containing two acres, be the same more or less.) ALSO that certain other tract of land and swamp, and land covered with water, divided from the above by the highway leading up the west side of Hempstead Harbour, and bounded as follows, viz: beginning at the northeast of a corner of an old bakehouse, running thence southwesterly to the northwest corner of Daniel Hoogland's garden fence; thence southerly along the fence, as it now stands, by the highway, to a marked locust tree; thence a due east course until it strikes the grist mill pond; thence a circular course round the southern and easterly sides of said pond, by the edge thereof, until it strikes the grist mill dam; thence westerly along the said dam to the place of beginning—containing fourteen acres, be the same more or less. ALSO, another small pond or piece of land covered with water, and situate at the west end of the said grist mill dam, together with a dam around the same, and a privilege of passing on the westerly side thereof, between it and the fence, with waggons or carts—one quarter of an acre, be the same more or less; together with the grist mill dam and grist mill erected on the northerly side thereof, streams of water and water courses, buildings, rights, members, hereditaments and appurtenances belonging or appertaining; always excepting and reserving so much of the first mentioned tract of land as can be included in a circle of sixty feet diameter around a certain spring or well of water, situate and made in the large sand bank nearly west of William H. Valentine's paper mill, and adjoining the road, the centre of said circle being the centre of the said circle; and also excepting the privilege reserved to William Onderdonk and Benjamin Onderdonk, their heirs and assigns, of carting earth or sand out of said bank. The above described premises will be sold, by virtue of a power contained in a mortgage executed by Caleb Valentine and Eupheme his wife, to Thomas Tredwell, Benjamin Allen and Daniel Bogert, on the thirtieth day of December, 1820, to secure to them the payment of the following sums: to Thomas Tredwell, six hundred and five dollars; to Benjamin Allen, two thousand four hundred and twenty dollars; and to Daniel Bogert, one thousand seven hundred and forty six dollars, on or before the first day of May then next, with interest, default having been made in the payment of the said sums. Dated the sixth day of June, 1822.

THOMAS TREDWELL,
BENJAMIN ALLEN,
DANIEL BOGERT.

American Eagle.

V[illegible] No. 43—TWO DOLLARS per annum. HUNTINGTON, (L. I.) THURSDAY, AUGUST 4, 1825 Payable half yearly.

THE AMERICAN EAGLE,

Is published every Thursday morning

BY HIRAM HERSKELL,

AT THE MODERATE PRICE OF TWO DOLLARS PER ANNUM.

(Payable half yearly.)

POETRY.

From Blackwood's Magazine.

THE MAGIC LAY OF THE ONE-HORSE CHAY.

Air—Eveleen's Bower.

Mr. Bubb was a Whig orator, also a soap Laborator,
For every thing's new christened in the present day;
He was followed and adored by the Common Council Board,
And lived quite genteel with a one horse chay.

Mrs. Bubb was gay and free, fair, fat, and fortythree,
And bloomy, as a peony in buxom May;
The toast she long had been of Farringdon Within,
And filled the better half of the one-horse chay.

Mrs. Bubb said to her lord, "You can well, Bubb, afford
Whate'er a Common Councilman in prudence may;
We've no brats to plague our lives, and the soap concern it thrives,
So let's have a trip to Brighton in the one-horse chay.

"We'll view the pier and shipping, and enjoy many a [dipping,
And walk for a stomach in our best array;
I long, more nor I can utter for shrimps and bread and butter,
And an airing on the Steyne in the one-horse chay.

"We've a right to spare for nought that for money can be bought,
So get matters ready, Bubb, do you trudge away;
To my dear Lord Mayor I'll walk, just to get a bit of [talk,
And an imitation shawl for the one-horse chay."

Mr. Bubb said to his wife, "Now I think upon't, my [life,
'Tis three weeks at least to next boiling day;
The dog days are set in, and London growing thin,
So I'll order out old Nobbs, and the one horse chay."

Now Nobbs, it must be told, was rather fat and old,
His colour it was white, and it had been gray:
He was round as a pot, and when sound whipt would [trot
Full five miles an hour in a one-horse chay.

When at Brighton they were housed, and had stuft and caroused
O'er a bowl of rack punch, Mr. Bubb did say,
"I've ascertained, my dear, the mode of dipping here
From the ostler, who is cleaning up my one horse chay.

"You're shut up in a box, ill convenient as the stocks
And eighteen pence a time are obliged for to pay;
Court corruption here, say I, makes every thing so high
And I wish I had come without my one-horse chay."

"As I hope," says she, "to thrive, 'tis flaying folks alive,
The king and them extortioners are leagued I say:
'Tis encouraging of such to go and pay so much,
So we'll set them at defiance with our one-horse chay.

"Old Nobbs, I am sartin, may be trusted gig or cart in,
He takes every matter in an easy way;
He'll stand like a post, while we dabble on the coast,
And return back to dress in our one-horse chay."

So out they drove, all drest, so gaily in their best,
And finding in their rambles a snug little bay,
They uncased at their leisure, paddled out to take their pleasure,
And left every thing behind in the one-horse chay.

But while so snugly sure that all things were secure,
They flounced about like porpoises or whales at play,
Some young unlucky imps, who prowled about for [shrimps,
Stole up to reconnoitre the one-horse chay.

Old Nobbs, in quiet mood, was sleeping as he stood;
(He might possibly be dreaming of his corn or hay)
Not a foot did he wag as they whipt out every rag,
And gutted the contents of the one-horse chay.

When our pair had soused enough, and returned to their buff,
Oh, there was the vengeance and Old Nick to pay!
Madam shrieked in consternation, Mr. Bubb he swore damnation
To find the empty state of the one-horse chay.

"If I live," says she, "I swear, I'll consult my dear Lord Mayor,
And a fine on this vagabond town he shall lay!
But the gallows thieves, so tricky, hasn't left me e'en a dicky,
And I shall catch my death in the one-horse chay."

'Come, bundle in with me, we must squeeze for once,' says he,
"And manage this here business the best we may;
We've no other step to choose, nor a moment must we lose,
Or the tide will float us off in our one-horse ceay."

So noses, sides, and knees, altogether did they squeeze
And packed in little compass, they trotted it away,
As dismal as two dummies, heads and hands stuck out, like mummies,
From beneath the little apron of the one-horse chay.

The Steyne was in a throng as they jogged it along,
Madam hadn't been so put to it for many a day;
He pleasure it was damped, and her person somewhat cramped,
Doubled beneath the apron of the one-horse chay.

'Oh would that I were laid,' Mr. Bubb in sorrow said,
'In a broad-wheeled wagon, well covered with hay!
I'm sick of sporting smart, and would take a tilted cart
In exchange for this bauble of a one-horse chay.

'I'd give half my riches for my worst pair of breeches,
Or the apron that I wore last boiling day;
They would wrap my arms and shoulders, from those impudent beholders,
And allow me to whip on in my one-horse chay.

Mr. Bubb ge-hupped in vain, and strove to jirk the rein,
Nobbs felt he had his option to work or play, (a race,
So he wouldn't mend his pace, tho' they'd fain have run
To escape the merry gazers at the one-horse chay.

Now, good people, laugh your fill, and fancy, if you will,
(For I'm fairly out of breath, and have said my say)
The trouble and the rout to wrap and get them out,
When they drove to their lodgings in the one horse chay.

The day was swelt'ring warm, so they took no cold or harm,
And o'er a smoking lunch soon forgot their dismay;
But, fearing Brighton mobs, started off at night with Nobbs,
To a snugger watering place, in their one-horse chay.

MISCELLANY.

CONJUGAL AFFECTION.

Among the many striking examples of female tenderness, affection, and constancy, which modern times have furnished, the following is worthy of record:—Mr. Weiss, who was town surgeon of Neumarkt, prompted by that ardent patriotism which inflamed the bosoms of the Prussians of all ranks at the commencement of the conflict in 1812, exchanged that situation for the post of surgeon to the Neumarkt Landwehr. The corps formed part of the force employed in the siege of Glogau. In the execution of the duties of his office, he caught the epidemic fever. No sooner did his wife receive the account of his situation, than she immediately hastened to him from Newmarkt. She found her husband in the height of a typhus and insensible, in a cottage at Nosswitz, near Glogau. Scarcely had she undertaken the office of nurse, when a sortie (made 10th Nov. 1813) by the garrison of Glogau threw the whole neighbourhood, and that village in particular, into the utmost consternation. All its inhabitants besook themselves to flight. She alone was left, with her apparently expiring husband, in the cottage, against which the hottest fire of the enemy's artillery was directed, probably because it was distinguished from the other houses by a tiled roof—several grenades breaking through the roof, set the floor on fire. Having carefully covered up her patient, and, as it were, buried him in the bed clothes, she ran out for a pail of water, extinguished the fire, and again directed her attention to the beloved object of her anxiety. She found him, to her great joy, in a profuse perspiration; but the incessant shower of balls rendered her abode more and more dangerous. A twelve pounder fell close to the bed of her husband, but without doing him the slightest injury.—Resolved to die with him, she lay down by his side, and thus awaited their common fate.—Noon arrived, and this time the Prussians had driven back the enemy into the fortress. She was earnestly entreated to provide for her safety, as it was impossible to tell whether the enemy might not attempt a fresh sortie. She, however, scorned every idea of removing to a place of security herself, unless she could save her husband also; and, though the removal of the patient was deemed impracticable, she nevertheless determined on this hazardous and only way of ensuring safety.

Having tied his hands and legs, to prevent him from moving and taking cold, she laid him, closely wrapped up with bed and bedding, in a cart covered with boards, in which she took her stand, and looking at him every minute. She slowly pursued her course towards Schmarsau, but scarcely had she left Nosswitz, when the besieged began to fire from the fortress, in that direction. The balls flew thickly about the cart, and the affrighted lad who drove took shelter, sometimes under it, and sometimes under the horses. She was fortunate enough to escape it without injury, and arrived with her patient at Schmarsau, which was already thronged with wounded, and applied for a lodging at the cottage. The mistress of the house, whose husband had died of a nervous fever, fell on her like a fury, turned the horses' heads, and protested, with many bitter execrations, that she should not cross her threshold. In this desperate situation, our heroine had recourse to a decisive expedient. Almost beside herself, she drew her husband's sword, and, pointing it to the woman's breast, declared that she would run it through her heart, unless she immediately admitted her husband. Terrified at this unexpected menace, the other complied, and the patient was carried into the house, which previously contained fifteen wounded. His wife, however, perceived with horror that her beloved charge manifested not the least sign of life. The bystanders advised her to give herself no farther trouble about him, and offered to lay him out for dead. To this she positively refused to agree; and, laying him in the bed, she incessantly rubbed his stiffened body, and with a teaspoon administered some wine, the only medicine within her reach. With the following morning, the expiring spark began to revive, and her joy was unbounded. She continued her attentions, and in a few days had the inexpressible satisfaction to see him out of danger. She now obtained a distinct apartment of her landlady, who began to behave to her with more kindness than at first. When her husband was sufficiently convalescent, she returned with him, to Neumarkt, to complete his recovery. Unfortunately, during her absence, one of their two children, a fine boy, was taken ill, and him her maternal care was unable to save. In the beginning of Feb. her husband again returned to resume his perilous duty with his battalion before Glogau.

PIRACY, AS IT REALLY IS.

We have read a pamphlet of about fifty pages, entitled "A Narrative of the shipwreck of the Brig Betsey, of Wiscasset, and murder of five of the crew, by pirates, on the coast of Cuba, Dec. 1824"; which discloses scenes of horror and suffering that are almost incredible. The author is Daniel Collins, one of the only two survivors of the crew; and we are assured, by persons of respectability, that his relation is entitled to belief. It is well written; and, as it is published for the benefit of an unfortunate seaman, we hope it will meet with a liberal sale. We annex a short extract, giving an account of the murder of the writer's companions.—*Wash. Gaz.*

"The seven pirates and four fishermen, as before, now proceeded with us towards the beach, until the water was about three feet deep, when they all got out; the two fishermen to each canoe, hauling us along, and the pirates walking by the side of us, one to each of our crew, torturing us all the way by drawing their knives across our throats, grasping the same, and pushing us back under the water which had been taken in by rocking the canoes.—While some of us were in the most humiliating manner beseeching of them to spare our lives, and others, with uplifted eyes, were again supplicating that Divine mercy which preserved them from the fury of the elements, *they* were singing and laughing, and occasionally telling us, in broken English, that 'Americans were very good beef for their knives.' Thus they proceeded with us nearly a mile from the vessel, which we were now losing sight of by doubling a point at the entrance of the cove before described; and when within a few rods of its head, *where we had before seen the human bones,* the canoes were hauled abreast of each other, from 12 to 20 feet apart, preparatory to our execution.

The stillness of death was now around us—for the very flood-gates of feeling had been burst asunder, and exhausted grief as its fountain. It was a beautiful morning—not a cloud to obscure the rays of the sun—and the clear blue sky presented a scene too pure for the deeds of darkness. But the lonely sheet of water, on which, side by side, we lay, presented that hopeless propect which is more ably described by another.

———'No friend, no refuge near:
All, all is false and treacherous around:
All that they touch, or taste, or breathe,
is Death.'

We had scarcely passed the last passing look at each other, when the work of death commenced.

They seized Captain Hilton by the hair—bent his head and shoulders over the gunwale, and I could distinctly hear them chopping the bone of the neck. They then wrung his neck, separated the head from the body by a slight draw of the sword, and let it drop into the water. There was a dying shriek—a convulsive struggle—and all I could discern was the arm dangling over the side of the canoe, and ragged stump pouring out the blood like a torrent.

There was an imploring look in the innocent and youthful face of Mr. Merry that would have appealed to the heart of any one but a pirate. As he arose on his knees, in the posture of a penitent, supplicating for mercy, even on the verge of eternity—he was prostrated with a blow of the cutlass, his bowels gushing out of the wound. They then pierced him through the breast in several places with a long knife, and cut his throat from ear to ear.

The captain's dog, repulsed in his repeated attempts to rescue his master, sat whining beside his lifeless body, looking up to these blood hounds in human shape, as if to tell them, that even brutal cruelty would be glutted with the blood of two unoffending victims.

Bridge and the cook, they pierced through the breast, as they had Merry, in several places with their knives, and then split their heads open with their cutlasses. Their dying groans had scarcely ceased, and I was improving the moment of life that yet remained, when I heard the blow behind me—the blood and brains that flew all over my head and shoulders, warned me that poor Russell had shared the fate of the others; and as I turned my head to catch the eye of my executioner, I saw the head of Russell severed in two nearly its whole length, with a single blow of the cutlass, and even without the decency of removing his cap. At the sound of the blow, Manuel, who sat before me, leaped overboard, and 4 of the pirates were in full chase after him. In what manner he loosed his hands, I am unable to say—his escape, I shall hereafter explain. My eyes were fixed on my supposed executioner, watching the signal of my death—he was on my right and partly behind me—my head, which was covered with a firm tarpaulin hat, was turned in a direction that brought my shoulders fore and aft the canoe—the blow came—it divided the top of my hat, struck my head so severely as to stun me, and glanced off my left shoulder, taking the skin and some flesh in its way, and divided my pinion cord on the arm. I was so severely stunned that I did not leap from the canoe, but pitched over the left side, and was just arising from the water, not my length from her, as a pirate threw his knife, which struck me, but did not retard my flight an instant; and I leaped forward through the water, expecting a blow from behind at every step.

The shrieks of the dying had ceased—the scene of horrid butchery in the canoe was now over—Manuel and I were in the water about knee deep—2 of the pirates after me, and all the rest with the fishermen, except one pirate, after Manuel. We ran in different directions.

WARM WEATHER.

From the Boston Gazette, July 14.

The weather since 6 o'clock Sunday morning, has been uncommonly hot and oppressive—in fact we have never experienced any think like it.—The Daily Advertiser of yesterday contains the following observations of the temperature of the three previous days, made from a thermometor in a shady position, and protected as far as possible from radient heat. Observations made in other positions, vary a few degrees from those here mentioned.

Sunday–Sunrise,		63
"	3 " P. M.	95
"	Lowest in the night,	77
Monday–Sunrise,		77
"	3 " P. M.	100
"	Lowest in the night,	78
Tuesday–Sunrise,		80
"	2 " P. M.	100
"	4 " P. M.	98

This excessively warm weather, as may be readily imagined, has been the cause of much inconvenience and uneasiness to our citizens, and its effects upon the laboring classes have been particularly destructive. The deaths from exposure to the heat and imprudent drinking of cold water, we think may be estimated at *twenty five or thirty*—and a majority of these are unfortunate sons of Erin.

Yesterday our streets wore a solemn appearance—the funeral hearse was seen moving in every direction. The following persons were buried in the course of the fornoon:—[Here follow the names of twenty persons.]

One of our physicians informed us yesterday morning, that he was called on the previous day to visit *thirteen* persons who had been suddenly attacked, from an imprudent use of cold water—three of these cases proved fatal, and some of the others were doubtful; the city contains between sixty and seventy physicians. We have also conversed with a friend residing in the vicinity of Broad-street, who saw three Irishmen draw their last breath between the hours of 1 and 2 o'clock on Tuesday.

We have heard of the destructive effects of the weather to the brute creation. The owners of the Providence line of stages, it is mentioned, have lost several fine animals, and deaths have occurred on other brutes.

Most of the workmen employed in building stores and houses, or in other exposed situations have been compelled to quit their work, and seek safety in the shade. The Patriot states, that some slaters, on the roof of a building, became paralised by the influence of the sun, and were so weak as to require assistance to get down. Several privates of a company, ordered to attend a funeral on Monday morning, became so faint as to be obliged to leave the ranks; one of them died on Tuesday.

We understand, that, at the request of his honor the Mayor, the master builders have agreed to abstain from labour, during the continuance of the warm weather, from 12 o'clock, M to 5 P. M. This arrangement, if the weather should continue, as it has been since Sunday morning, may be the means, under Heaven, of preserving the lives of a number of human beings.

"*Salem, July* 13.—Terrible weather; some of our glasses in the shade are as high as 104. Several gentlemen who have been in Mocha, when for many days the thermometer stood from 102 to 108, say they never felt the heat more oppressive there."

Providence July 13.—On Sunday the thermometer kept at the Branch Bank, in the shade, ranged at 90, on Monday at 91, and yesterday at 92. Other thermometers stated it at 99 1-2, on Monday, which we are inclined to think more correct. The excessive heat of Sunday and Monday last, was fatal to the fish in Brush Pond, near Mashapaugh Pond, in Cranston. This pond is about three acres, and the water between 2 and 3 feet in depth—yet so intense was the heat that all the fish therein were suffocated. Several hundred perch, pickerel, &c. some weighing a pound and a half, were found floating on the surface of the water, and large quantities were taken from the bottom, without any signs of life.

State of the thermometer at the Academy, Albany:

	7 a m	2 p m	9 p m
July 14.	67	85	75
15,	60	0	81
16,	71	91	82
17,	74	93	

State of the thermometer at the Pine Orchard on the Catskill Mountain, in the shade:

TO be sold by the subscribers, at the inn of William Griffin, at Riverhead, on the third Monday of July next, at three o'clock afternoon, at public auction by virtue of a power contained in a mortgage bearing date the fifth day of March, 18[illegible] and executed by Joshua Horton, and Joshua H. Horton, of Southold in Suffolk county, for securing the payment of two hundred and eight dollars and fifty cents, on demand, with interest, to Persis Booth, then a widow, but now the wife of Enoch Jagger—"ALL that certain tract or parcel of woodland, lying at a place called Hog Neck, in the town of Southold, aforesaid, and bounded southerly, easterly and northerly by a highway, and westerly by the land of Joel Overton, and Eleazer Overton deceased, containing by estimation twenty five acres, be the same more or less." Dated January 5, 1825.

ENOCH JAGGER.
PERSIS JAGGER

WHEREAS John Conkling and Rhoda his wife, of the town of Southold, county of Suffolk, and state of New-York, did, on the tenth day of March, in the year one thousand eight hundred and twenty-one, to secure the payment of three hundred dollars, with the interest to become due thereon, mortgage unto Phineas King, of the town of Shelter-Island, County and State aforesaid, all that certain tract or parcel of land, situate in the town of Southold, in the village called Hashmomick, in the County and State aforesaid, containing, by estimation, twenty four acres be the same more or less, and bounded easterly by the land of Jeremiah Moore, southerly by the land of Jared Hand, westerly by the land of Joseph C. Albertson, and northerly by the land of Thomas Conkling. And whereas default has been made in the payment of the said sum of money—notice is hereby given, that, by virtue of a power contained in the said mortgage, the said land will be sold at public auction, at the house of John Conkling in Southold, aforesaid, on the twenty third day of June next, at one o'clock in the afternoon. Dated this 8th day of December, 1824.

PHINEAS KING.

BY virtue of a power contained in a mortgage, dated December 7th 1819, and given by Philetus Hart and Mary his wife, of Smithtown, Suffolk County, to Phebe Platt of the same place; will be sold at public auction at the dwelling house of the said Phebe Platt in Smithtown aforesaid, on the first day of September next at two o'clock in the afternoon; two several tracts of land situate in Smithtown aforesaid one lying at Bread and cheese-hollow, bounded easterly by land of Selah Gildersleeve, southerly by the highway, westerly partly by land of Zephaniah Ketcham and partly by land now or late of John Gildersleeve, northerly by land now or late of John Gildersleeve, containing five acres and an half more or less; the other consisting of upland and meadow, lying in Sunkmeadow, bounded easterly by land of Matthew Gardiner, southerly by the highway westerly by land of Isaac Buffet, northerly by the main creek, containing three acres more or less, with the appurtenances.

PHEBE PLATT.

Dated March 1st 1825. Wm P. Buffett, Att'y.

NOTICE.

BY virtue of a power contained in a mortgage executed by Phinehas F. Corey, of Sag Harbor county of Suffolk, and state of New-York, to Hannah Stratton, of Greenfield, county of Saratoga, dated the twenty sixth day of August, eighteen hundred and twenty two, for securing the payment of nine hundred and ninety nine dollars and twelve cents, with the lawful interest, will be sold at public auction, at the house of Robert Fordham, inn keeper in Sag Harbor, on the fifth day of July next, at three o'clock, P M.—ALL that certain lot of land, with the buildings thereon situate, lying and being at Sag Harbor, in the township of Southampton, county of Suffolk, bounded on the south by the street or highway, forty feet in front; on the east by the land of the heirs of Benjamin Price; north by the land of the heirs of Benjamin Price, forty feet, and on the west by the land of Joseph Crowell, jr. containing by estimation one eighth of an acre, be the same more or less—Default having been made in the payment of the said sum of money and interest.

Dated the thirteenth day of December, 1824.

HANNAH STRATTON.

H. Halsey, att'y.

Suffolk County. }
Surrogate's Office, } ss.

NOTICE is hereby given to all persons having demands against the estate of John Hendrickson, late of Huntington, in the county aforesaid, deceased, to exhibit the same, duly attested, to the Surrogate of said county, at his office in Southold, on the nineteenth day of July next, at one o'clock in the afternoon, when and where a final distribution of the said estate will be made.

EBEN. W. CASE, Surrogate.

Dated at Southold, April 8, 1825.

BY virtue of a power contained in a mortgage, dated the seventh day of December, A. D. one thousand eight hundred and ten, and given by Oliver Youngs and Sarah his wife, of Huntington, Suffolk county, to Treadwell Scudder, Moses Rolph, and Anning Moubray, Executors of Jarvis Rogers deceased,—will be sold at public auction on the premises, on Thursday the twenty seventh day of October next, at two o'clock in the afternoon, that certain tract or parcel of land, described in said mortgage as "situate in the township of Huntington, on the neck of land called Sumpawams, and bounded as follows:—on the west by the road that leads up the said neck; on the north by the lands of Penn Weeks, Jun'r.; on the east by the swamp or pond, and on the south by the land belonging to the heirs of David Davis, deceased, containing, by estimation, twenty one acres, more or less," with the appurtenances. Dated April 21st, 1825.

TREADWELL SCUDDER, }
MOSES ROLPH, } Executors.
ANNING MOUBRAY, }
W. P. Buffett, att'y.

SALE OF LANDS FOR TAXES.

STATE OF NEW-YORK, }
COMPTROLLER'S OFFICE. }
ALBANY, May 16, 1825.

NOTICE IS HEREBY GIVEN, That lists of lands liable to be sold for arrears of taxes have been forwarded to each of the County Treasurers, and the several Town Clerks in this state; and that so much of the said lands will, ON THE SEVENTEENTH DAY OF JANUARY, 1826, and the immediately succeeding days, be sold at public auction, at the Capitol, in the city of Albany, as will be necessary to pay all taxes, interest and charges due, assessed or to be assessed thereon, at the time of such sale.

W. L. MARCY, *Comptroller.*

June 9.

NEW-YORK

WHOLESALE PRICES CURRENT.

ARTICLES.	PER	PRICES. dol. ct.	dol.
ASHES, Pot,	ton	107 50	
Pearl,		115	
BEANS,	7 bu.		11
BEEF, Mess,	bbl.	8 75	9 2[illegible]
Prime	--	5 75	6 2[illegible]
Cargo	--	4 25	
BREAD, Pilot	cwt.	4 25	
Navy	--	2 50	
Crackers	--	5 75	6 75
BUTTER, for exportation	lb.	8	10
Goshen	—	16	20
CANDLES, Mould		11	
Dipped	—		1[illegible]
Sperm	—	34	30
Wax	—	60	
CHEESE,	—	7	9
COAL, Liverpool	chal.	10 50	11
Lehigh	—		
Virginia	—	8	10
COFFEE, W. India, 1st qual.	lb.	19	2[illegible]
CORDAGE, Foreign	cwt.	11	11 50
American		11	
Patent	—	11	
COTTON, Sea-Island	lb.	24	28
Georgia Upland	—	22	27
New Orleans	—	27	30
DOMESTIC GOODS.			
SHIRTINGS, Brown 3-4	yard	10	14
Bleached	--	11	16
SHEETING, brown 4 4	—	13	16
do 5-4	—	19	22
bleach'd 4-4	—	16	24
do 5-4	—	22	25
Waltham Cottons.			
No. 1 brown	—	17	
do bleach'd	—	18 1-2	
No. 2, brown	—	21	
do bleach'd	—	22 1-2	
No. 3, brown	—	28	
do bleach'd	—	30	
No. 4, do	—	23	
Fine do	—	26	
AIDS,	—	13	16
RIPES, fast colors	—	13	16
INETS	—	45	25
Checks	—	12	16
Checks	—	15	17
on Yarn, No.5 a 10 lb.		24	24
11	—	24	28
12	—	25	25
13	—	26	25
tinets Warps	—	40	42
SH, Dry Cod	cwt.	2 50	3
ll Mackerel	bbl.	5 75	
nnecticut Mess Shad		9	9 5
AX,	lb.	8	0
FLOUR AND GRAIN.			
ew York superfine	bbl.	5 37	
Western		5 87	6 0
hiladelphia		5 25	5 37
ltimore		5 50	
e Flour		2 62	2 75
lian meal		2 75	2 87
HEAT, North River,	bushel	1	1 06
YE,		50	51
ORN, yellow. North		47	51
white		50	50
ATS,		29	38
EATHERS American	lb.	30	75
Gunpowder, American,	25 lb.	3 50	5 10
HAMS, Virginia,	lb.	8	9
North River,		8	
Hog's Lard,		8	9
Honey, American		8	10
Hops, 1st and 2d sort,		15	17
IRON, Country, bar,	ton	80 00	90 00
LEATHER, sole	lb.	24	25
Dressed upper	side	2 25	3
LUMBER, N Riv Pine Boards	M ft.	15	
Albany Boards	piece	18	
Shingles, cyprus,	M.	3 25	3 50
Pine,	bundle	2 75	3 55

PROPOSALS

For publishing a pereodical work, entitled

THE

Long Island

JOURNAL OF PHILOSOPHY,

To be printed at Huntington, L. I. and conducted by SAMUEL FLEET.

THE sphere of this work will be very extended, occasionally containing selections from the transactions of learned societies, both of our own and of foreign countries—Reviews—Extracts from publications on Natural Philosophy—Mechanics—Chemistry—Natural History—Anatomy—Geology and Mineralogy—Geography, Agriculture, and the fine and useful Arts.

Although the work will be principally confined to the above subjects, yet when nothing very interesting or useful can be written or extracted on them, the Editor will not hesitate to assume great latitude in the introduction of subjects which he shall judge compatible with the work, and which he shall find by experience agreeable and profitable to his subscribers. Such subjects as relate to Long Island will be early noticed. When any important changes occur in the government or policy of nations, in the religion and morals of a people, they will receive due attention.

A great objection against a general dissemination to most of our scientific and literary Journals, is, that a plan is adopted and continued in, even when there is not information of much moment: Such a course is well adapted for improvements in the sciences, and is suitable for scholars, but not for the generality of readers. The object, therefore, of this work is to render accessible to the Long Island public the various information found in large publications and periodical Journals. The great and valuable discoveries in Philosophy and the Arts, of the present century are to be found in scientific Journals published in various parts of this and of other countries The Editor will have access to many of these, and he hopes by great exertion and application to give satisfaction to his friends and the public.

A number of literary gentlemen from the counties of Suffolk and Queens have generously offered to contribute to its support. And from the fact that there is no publication of the kind on the island, the proprietor entertains a hope that it will meet with a favorable reception.

SAMUEL FLEET.

Huntington, Jan 8, 1825.

CONDITIONS

This work will be published on the first Wednesday of every month, on good paper, with a fair type, and will contain forty eight pages, (octavo) with a printed cover. The price will be three dollars and fifty cents per annum, payable on the delivery of the sixth number. The first number will be issued in May.

☞ The following gentlemen have given their names to recommend the work, and they will use their influence to give it a general circulation:—Hon. Silas Wood, Hon. Nathaniel Potter, Rev. Mr. Brown, Rev. Mr. Fowler, Col. Isaac Conklin, Dr. D. W. Kissam, Dr. Benjamin Bowers, Moses Rolph, Esq. Mr. Christopher Ming, Geo S. Phillips, P M Smithtown; Selah B. Strong, Esq. Drown Meadow.

New-York American.

(FOR THE COUNTRY.)

VOL. VII....No. 631] NEW-YORK, FRIDAY, APRIL 7, 1826. [OFFICE 3 NASSAU-STREET.

A Description of the Hetton Rail Road in England, by William Strickland, Esq. Civil Engineer.

The Hetton Rail-Road extends from the town of Sunderland, on the River Wier, to the Hetton Collieries. Its length from the pit to the staith, is seven miles five furlongs; it has an *ascent* of two hundred and 66 feet; and a series of *descents*, equal to five hundred and forty-six feet; making in the whole, 812 feet of elevation and depression, overcome by a series of *levels* and *inclined planes*. The first portion of the road, from the pit to the foot of the ascending plane, is one mile seven and a half furlongs in length; and its general descent is one ninth of an inch to the yard, with a portion of it (five-sixteenths) which is equally favorable for loaded and light carriages. A single loco-motive engine, with twenty-four waggons in train, has drawn six hundred tons per day, going nine *gauts* equal to thirty-five miles forwards, and returning.

On another portion of the way, in length two and a half miles and sixty yards, with a descent, for the greatest part, between four and five sixteenths of an inch to the yard, on which the loaden waggons tend to move of themselves, and consequently produce less stress on the light train, two loco-motive engines, in use at the same time, have conveyed the quantity above-mentioned.

Stationary *reciprocating engines* are placed at the summits of the inclined planes. These engines draw loaden and light waggons, alternately each way; and each successive station performs its operation in the same time; the relative speed of the waggons being according to the distances between the engines, so that their respective journies may be completed in similar times, and maintain a uniform succession of carriages each way, by means of ropes, alternately winding and unwinding upon drum wheels, eight feet in diameter.

On one of the inclined planes, the ropes are upwards of two miles in length, being supported by light cast-iron concave rollers, fixed at a distance of forty or fifty feet apart, in the centre of the way, between the rails; and as the ropes are *wound on* and *off* the drum, the small rollers revolve and keep them from coming in contact with the soil of the road.

Where the road-way deviates from a straight line, *in plan*, or where the *plane* winds to the *right or left*, the axes of the rollers are placed in nearly a vertical direction; in order to keep the line of draught mid-way between the rails.

It will be perceived by the engraved view, that this road is formed over an undulating or hilly country; and that the transportation of all the articles from the Collieries and its neighborhood, is made to surmount a series of very considerable ascents, by means of fixed engines, placed on their summits; and the motion given by these machines to the waggons reciprocally, is equal to nine miles an hour.

The rails are made of cast iron, four feet in length; and are known generally by the denomination of the edge or round top rail, of Losh & Stephenson.

The loco-motive engines are made of thick sheet iron, and are obviously of the high-pressure kind; they are only made upon *level lines of road*; for the engine itself, in any material ascent, consumes a great portion of its power in the movement of its own weight and that of its fuel; and any sudden rise would annihilate its object and use.

TOWN OF SUNDERLAND. GENERAL VIEW OF THE HETTON RAIL-WAY, LEADING FROM THE COAL MINES TO THE TOWN OF SUNDERLAND.

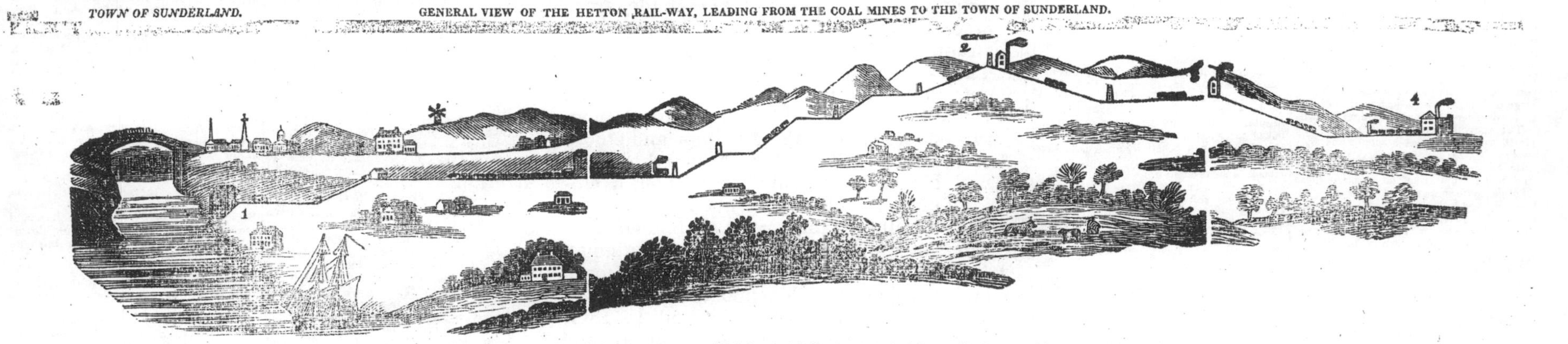

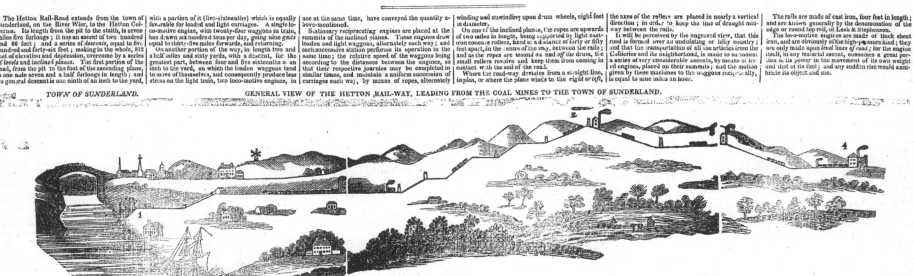

1. Staith.—2. *Fixed Engine.*—3. *Fixed Engine.*—4. *Pit.*—*Whole length of the Road, 7 miles and 5 furlongs. The elevation and depression overcome, 812 feet.*

From the "fixed engines" at the summit of each elevation, extend ropes each way, which on one side *draw up* the train of waggons, on the other *lower* them to a level, upon which they are conveyed by the *locomotive* engine, until they reach an ascent or descent, when the ropes from another reciprocating engine are attached.

The figure below is admirably illustrative of the appearance of the loaded train while upon the level.

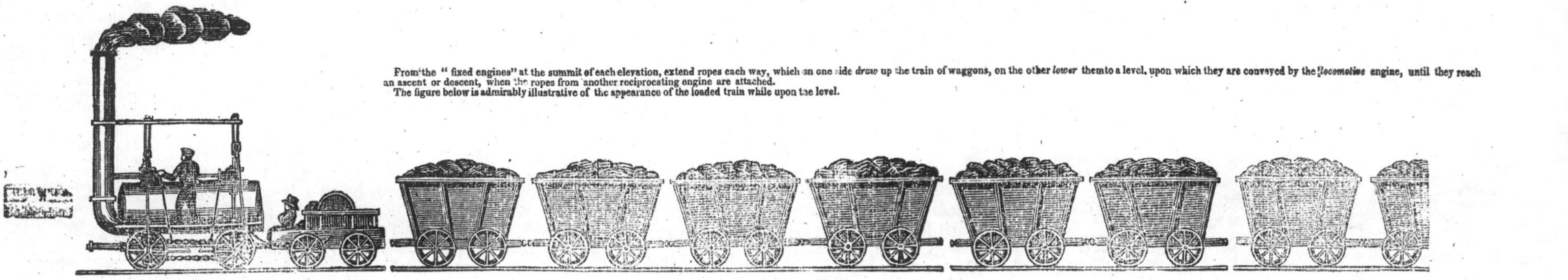

Locomotive Engine, 12 horse power; wt. 5 tons—Cost in England £600. | Tender with coals and water. | The train consists of 24 Chalder waggons, containing 90 tons.

NEW-YORK AMERICAN.

TUESDAY EVENING, APRIL 4, 1826.

We ask attention to the report of the Committee of Foreign Relations in the House of Representatives. It is conclusive.

Bellum Medicum.—The report in the House of Assembly respecting the Medical College in this city, and in answer to the report on the same subject in the Senate, will be found in our columns to-day. *Non nobis tantas componere lites.* We meddle not—though one thing appears to us pretty certain, that between the professors and the trustees, the legislature and the regents, the College will be destroyed, and this city will lose the honor and the profit, at least for a time, of a great medical school.

Extract from a letter dated Washington, Saturday evening.

"The debate on the constitutional amendment was brought to a close to-day. After Mr. Trimble, Mr. Vance, and others, had spoken, Mr. Webster moved that the Committee rise, with a professed intention of moving, when in the House, to discharge the Committee, and take a vote on the resolutions. The Committee accordingly rose, and the House discharged it from further considering the subject, and proceeded to the vote in the house. There was a very large majority for the first resolution, which expresses the abstract proposition *that it would be desirable that the President would be chosen without the necessity of a resort to Congress.* This was considered as the language, in effect, of the existing constitution; and against the abstract proposition, therefore, members thought it invidious to vote, although they might not believe that any provision could be substituted, on the whole, preferable, for the case of a failure on the part of the people to make a choice. The resolution was ordered to be referred to a committee of twenty-four, to see what amendment could be proposed. This is probably the last that will be heard of it for the present, there being very little or no probability that the Committee will suggest any thing, in which even a majority of the House will concur.—The other resolution, viz., that for providing a general district system, was lost by a majority, I think, of twelve votes. No other business was transacted in the House, and the Senate did not sit.

"It is said the joint committee on the subject of the day of adjournment met, but were not able at present to come to any conclusion."

The Vulcan Iron Works between Rivington and Arundel-streets, has become known to us, as probably to many others, by the opposition which, according to advertisements in the newspapers, is stirred up against an application making by the proprietors of those works, for an act of incorporation. Presuming that an establishment which could excite the apprehensions of many considerable master workmen, must at least be worth a visit, we have devoted a half hour or so, to an hasty examination of its vast and well-arranged workshops, and must frankly say that in our judgment, no reansonable request which the proprietors of so fine, effective, and valuable establishment can make, ought to be refused. It is perhaps the only one in the city where every article of iron work, from the smallest tack, to the chain cable of a line of battle ship is manufactured. It is however too vast a concern for individual enterprize, and a charter is asked for, in order that a joint stock company may be formed to carry on its operations. Is there any reasonable objection to this request? yes, say the master mechanics, it is a monopoly—it enables men who are not mechanics, to earn the profits of mechanical labour. But surely the application of additional capital to any branch of industry, cannot justly be called monopoly; and yet such is the only result aimed at, in seeking for a charter. The law allowing limited partnerships is so badly drawn, and so limited in the amount which it provides for, as to prevent the present applicants from associating under it. The principle however is the same, & in asking, therefore, to be associated, these gentlemen are not asking for any thing new or unknown to our laws, but merely that in the spirit of existing laws, they may be permitted to associate and create a joint stock for manufacturing purposes. The objection that the establishment is not under the control of mechanics, may be very important to those master workmen whose profits it interferes with, but cannot be so to the public, whose interest it is to buy what is best at the cheapest rates. If the Vulcan Company cannot work as well and as cheaply as individuals, they will certainly not succeed; but if they work as well, or better, and as cheaply, or more so, they will, and ought to be sustained. It is for the interest and credit of the city, and for the advantage of some 300 or 400 workmen who are employed in this establishment, that it should not be overthrown by interested, (we do not mean to use the word in an offensive sense) opposition. We hope the Legislature may pass the general act, authorizing, under proper restrictions, associations for manufacturing and other purposes, and then this Company can come in under its sanction, without further difficulties. If not, we trust that they will obtain a charter.

By the York our regular files of London papers are continued to the 24th Feb. inclusive.

In the Courier of the 24th, is a speech of Mr. Huskisson, in justification of the principles of free trade, as pursued by the government, which produced very great effect—as well from its sound and admirable views, as from the references to the sentiments of the merchants of London, expressed in their petition in 1820, and of Mr. Baring on the floor of the house.—The object in view was on the petition of the Spitalfields and Coventry silk weavers, to induce ministers to go back to the old system of prohibitory duties—which alone, it was contended, could relieve the existing distress. This last position is most conclusively overthrown by Mr. Huskisson, who as well as Mr. Canning, declared that the course pursued by government, had been deliberately adopted and would not be departed from. Mr. Canning said it was a policy which "he should have no hesitation in allowing to stand or fall by."

The Courier of 23d Feb. acknowledges the receipt of New-York papers of the 5th February, making only 18 days from the time they were published here till extracts were made from them in London.

The Stephania, from Havre brings us our Paris papers to the 24th Feb. inclusive. We do not find in them any thing that had not been anticipated by the previous Liverpool arrivals.

The editor of the Journal du Commerce had, on a complaint made by M. de Salaberry, a member of the Chamber of Deputies, been ordered to appear at the bar of that house on 7th March, to answer for certain articles published by him in December last when the Chamber was not in session.

It is curious enough, that in making his accusation to the Chamber, against what he calls the license of the Journal du Commerce, M. de Salaberry quotes Hamilton's famous definition on Harry Croswell's trial, of the liberty of the press, with great eulogium on its justness and on the character of its author.

A report was circulating in the Paris Exchange on the 23d Feb. of the death of the Emperor of Austria, but it does not appear to have obtained credit.

French Funds.—5 per cents, 98 70; 3 per cents 65 40.

The prompt and clear answer of the Secretary of State to the call of the House, to know how far the government had authorized any pledge to the American nations, that in case of foreign European aggression upon them, the United States would interfere in their defence, has disappointed many expectations. It was thought by the malcontents, that they had caught the Secretary tripping; but he comes out clear and uncommitted.

THE U. STATES & SOUTHERN REPUBLICS.

The following message was received from the President of the United States, and read at the Clerk's table:

To the House of Representatives of the U. States.

WASHINGTON, 30th March, 1826.

In compliance with a resolution of the House of the 27th inst. requesting a copy of such parts of the answer of the Secretary of State to Mr. Poinsett's letter to Mr. Clay, dated Mexico, 28th September, 1825, No. 22, as relates to the pledges of the United States therein mentioned: And also requesting me to inform the House whether the United States have, in any manner, made any pledge to the Governments of Mexico and South America, that the United States would not permit the interference of any foreign Power with the independence or form of government of these Nations; and if so, when, in what manner, and to what effect: And also to communicate to the House a copy of the communication from our Minister at Mexico, in which he informed the Government of the United States that the Mexican Government called upon this Government to fulfil the memorable pledge of the President of the United States, in his message to Congress, of December, 1823: I transmit to the House a report from the Secretary of State, with the documents containing the information desired by the Resolution.

JOHN QUINCY ADAMS.

DEPARTMENT OF STATE,
Washington, 29th March, 1826.

The Secretary of State, to whom has been referred by the President, the resolution of the House of Representatives of the 27th March, 1826, requesting him to transmit to that House certain parts of the correspondence between the Department of State and the Minister of the United States at Mexico, and to communicate certain information therein mentioned, has the honor to report—

That no answer was transmitted from this Department to the letter of Mr. Poinsett, No. 22, under date at Mexico, on the 28th September, 1825. That No. 18, from Mr. Poinsett, under date the 13th of the same month, and No. 22, relate to the same subject; the first stating the obstacle which had occurred to the conclusion of the commercial treaty, in the pretension brought forward by Mexico to grant to the American Nations of Spanish origin, special privileges which were not to be enjoyed by other Nations; and the second narrating the arguments which were urged for and against it, in the conferences between Mr. Poinsett and the Mexican Ministers: that No. 22 was received on the 9th of December last, and the answer of the 9th of November, 1825, from this Department to No. 18, having been prepared and transmitted, superseded the necessity, as was believed, of any more particular reply to No. 22.

That extracts from the general instructions to Mr. Poinsett, under date the 25th March, 1825, are herewith reported, marked A: that the United States have contracted no engagement, nor made any pledge to the Governments of Mexico and South America, or to either of them, that the United States would not permit the interference of any foreign Power with the independence or form of government of those nations; nor have any instructions been issued, authorizing any such engagement or pledge. It will be seen that the message of the late President of the United States of the 2d December, 1823, is adverted to in the extracts now furnished from the instructions to Mr. Poinsett, and that he is directed to impress its principles upon the Government of the United Mexican States. All apprehensions of the danger to which Mr. Monroes alludes, of an interference, by the Allied Powers of Europe, to introduce their political systems into this Hemisphere, have ceased. If, indeed, an attempt by force had been made by Allied Europe to subvert the liberties of the Southern Nations on this Continent, and to erect, upon the ruins of their free institutions, monarchical systems, the People of the United States would have stood pledged, in the opinion of their Executive, not to any foreign State, but to themselves and to their posterity, by their dearest interests and highest duties, to resist to the utmost such attempt; and it is to a pledge of that character that Mr. Poinsett alone refers.

That extracts from a despatch of Mr. Poinsett, under date the 21st August, 1825, marked B. are also herewith reported, relating to the movements of the French fleet in the West India seas, during the last summer. That his previous letter, to which he refers, on the same subject, with the accompanying papers, is accidentally mislaid, and cannot therefore now be communicated: which is less regretted, because the information contained in that now reported, it is presumed, will be entirely satisfactory.

All which is respectfully submitted.

H. CLAY.

The message was ordered to lie on the table, and, with the accompanying documents, was ordered to be printed.

A.

Extracts from the general instructions of Mr. Clay, Secretary of State, to Mr. Poinsett, appointed Envoy Extraordinary and Minister Plenipotentiary to Mexico, dated

Department of State, Washington, 25th March, 1825.

The mission on which the President wishes you with all practicable despatch to depart would at any time be highly important, but possesses at this moment a peculiar interest. Every where on this continent, but on the side of the United Mexican States, the United States are touched by the colonial territories of some sovereign authority fixed in Europe. You are the first Minister actually leaving the United States, to reside near a sovereign power established and exerted on this continent, whose territories are conterminous with our own. You will probably be the first Minister received by that power from any sovereign state, except from those which have recently sprung out of Spanish America. The United Mexican States, whether we regard their present posture, or recal to our recollection their ancient history and former times, are entitled to high consideration. In point of population, position, and resources, they must be allowed to rank among the first powers of America. In contemplating the progress in them towards civilization, which the aborigines had made at the epoch of the Spanish invasion, and the incidents connected with the Spanish conquest which ensued, an irresistible interest is excited, which is not surpassed, if it be equalled, by that which is awakened in perusing the early history of any other part of America. But what gives, with the President, to your mission peculiar importance at this time, is, that it has for its principal object, to lay for the first time the foundation of an intercourse of amity, commerce, navigation, and neighborhood, which may exert a powerful influence for a long period upon the prosperity of both States.

In more particularly inviting your attention to the objects which should engage it on your mission, I will in the first place refer you to the general instructions which were given by my predecessor, on the 27th May 1823, to Mr. Anderson, the Minister of the U. States at Colombia, of which a copy is annexed, and which are to be considered as incorporated in them. So far as they are applicable alike to the condition of Colombia and Mexico, and shall not be varied in this or subsequent letters, you will view them as forming a guide for your conduct.

In that letter of the 27th May the principles which have regulated the course of this government in respect to the contest between Spanish America and Spain, from its origin, are clearly stated, explained, and vindicated, and the bases of those upon which it is desirable to place the future intercourse between the United States and the several governments which have been established in Spanish America, are laid down. So that although that letter was intended to furnish instructions for the American Minister deputed to one of those governments only, it should be contemplated as unfolding a system of relations which it is expedient to establish with all of them. From that letter, as well as from notorious public facts, it clearly appears that the people and the Government of the United States have alike, throughout all stages of the struggle between Spain and her former colonies, cherished the warmest feelings and the strongest sympathies towards the latter. That the establishment of their independence and freedom has been anxiously desired; that the recognition of that independence was made as early as it was possible, consistently with those just considerations of policy and duty which this government felt itself bound to entertain towards both parties: and that, in point of fact, with the exception of the act of the Portuguese Brazilian government, to which it was prompted by self-interest, and which preceded that of the United States only a few months, this government has been the first to assume the responsibility and encounter the hazard of recognizing the governments which have been formed out of Spanish America. If there ever were any ground for imputing tardiness to the United States in making that recognition, as it respects other parts of what was formerly Spanish America, there is not the slightest pretext for such a suggestion in relation to Mexico. For within a little more than a year after its independence was proclaimed, the United States hastened to acknowledge it. They have never claimed, and do not now claim, any peculiar favour or concession to their commerce and navigation, as the consideration of the liberal policy which they have shown towards those governments. But the President does confidently expect, that a priority of movement, on our part, which has disconcerted plans which the European Allies were contemplating against the independent governments, and which has no doubt tended to accelerate similar acts of recognition by the European powers, and especially that of Great Britain, will form a powerful motive with our southern neighbours, and particularly with Mexico, for denying to the commerce and navigation of those European States, any favours or privileges which shall not be equally extended to us.

"You will bring to the notice of the Mexican Government the message of the late President of the United States to their Congress on the 2d December, 1823, asserting certain important principles of international law, in the relations of Europe and America. The first principle asserted in that message is, that the American continents are not henceforth to be considered as subjects for future colonization by any European powers. In the maintenance of that principle, all the independent governments of America have an interest, but that of the United States has probably the least. Whatever foundation may have existed three centuries ago, or even at a later period, when all this continent was under European subjection, for the establishment of a rule formed on priority of discovery and occupation, for apportioning among the powers of Europe parts of this continent, none can be now admitted as applicable to its present condition. There is no disposition to disturb the colonial possessions, as they may now exist, of any of the European powers, but it is against the establishment of new European colonies upon this continent that the principle is directed. The countries in which any such new establishments might be attempted are now open to the enterprise and commerce of all Americans, and the justice and propriety cannot be recognised of arbitrarily limiting and circumscribing that enterprise and commerce by the act of voluntarily planting a new colony without the consent of America, under the auspices of foreign powers belonging to another and a distant continent. Europe would be indignant at any American attempt to plant a colony on any part of her shores; and her justice must perceive in the rule contended for, only perfect reciprocity.

The other principle asserted in the message is, that whilst we do not desire to interfere in Europe with the political system of the Allied powers, and should regard as dangerous to our peace and safety any attempt on their part to extend their system to any portion of this hemisphere. The political systems of the two continents are essentially different. Each has an exclusive right to judge for itself what is best suited to its own condition and most likely to promote its happiness—but neither has a right to enforce upon the other the establishment of its peculiar system.

This principle was declared in the face of the world at a moment when there was reason to apprehend that the allied powers were entertaining designs inimical to the freedom, if not the independence of the new Governments. There is ground for believing that the declaration of it had considerable effect in preventing the maturity, if not in producing the abandonment of all such designs. Both principles were laid down, after much and anxious deliberation on the part of the late administration. The President, who then formed a part of it, continues entirely to coincide in both. And you will urge upon the Government of Mexico the utility and expediency of asserting the same principle on all proper occasions.

B.

Extracts of a letter from Mr. Poinsett to Mr. Clay, dated

MEXICO, Aug. 21, 1825.

The correspondence respecting the reported movements of the French fleet in the West India seas, which accompanied my last letter, was attended with circumstances which I had not then time to communicate.

The intelligence was received on the 15th instant, by the Secretary of State. On the morning of the 16th, he called upon the Charge des Affaires of his Britannic Majesty, and showed him the letters from the agent of this government at Jamaica. Mr. Ward came immediately to me, to consult what was to be done, and expressed a wish that we should act in concert. As I had not seen the Secretary, nor the letters to which he alluded, I could only reply that I was perfectly willing to do so, provided this government in their communications with us placed both our governments on precisely the same footing. He immediately went to the palace, and saw the Secretary of State, to whom he explained his desire that the notes to be addressed to us should be *verbatim et literatim* the same. Late in the afternoon the Secretary called on me, and exhibited the letters he had received from Jamaica, and which induced him to believe that France entertained hostile intentions against this country. In this conversation I assured him of the friendly disposition of the United States; and that they would not view with indifference the occupation of the Island of Cuba by France, especially if it were the result of any hostile views towards Mexico; but at the same time, hinted that the imprudent conduct of some of their commanders might have induced Spain to cede the Island to the French, rather than have it wrested from her, in the manner proposed by Santa Ana, of which they were fully aware.

When Mr. Ward was informed that the Secretary had said nothing to me of his interview with him, nor of his intention to make the notes to be addressed to us on this subject, similar, he waited on the President, and reiterated his request. The President, after assuring him that this should be done, declared that he himself was ignorant of the arrival of this important intelligence, until he saw it published in the Sol.

On the ensuing day, notes concluded in exactly the same words, were received both by Mr. Ward and myself. I objected to the language, and waited on Mr. Alaman to state my objections. The original notes, after stating that we had declared, in the most solemn manner, that we would never consent that any third powers should interpose in the question between Spain and her former colonies, and that the conduct of France, on this occasion, is certainly an interposition, which, however cloaked, is not the less inexcusable, goes on to say, "The President, therefore, instructed me to inform your Excellency of these important occurrences, so that by bringing them to the notice of your government, it may demand of His most Catholic Majesty such explanations as the same requires."

I told the Secretary that the declaration of the President, and the known friendly disposition of the Government and of the people of the United States towards those countries, did not confer upon this government the privilege of demanding our interference as a right. He expressed his readiness to alter the phraseology of the note, and it was done. The note to his Britannic Majesty's Charge des Affaires was afterwards altered in the same terms, and the substance of our answers corresponded.

A motion was made by Mr. Herrick, of Maine, that 3000 extra copies be printed—ayes 59, noes, 41.—There being no quorum,

On motion of Mr. Vance, of Ohio, the House adjourned.

[From the Albany Argus and Daily City Gazette.]

LEGISLATURE OF NEW-YORK.

IN SENATE,

Monday morning, April 3.

Bill read a third time and passed:

To amend the charter of the La Fayette insurance company in New-York.

The committee of the whole then took up the consideration of the bill for the apportionment of the members of assembly, and for the arrangement of the senate district. The report was agreed to, ayes 16, noes 12, and the bill was ordered to a third reading.

The bill in relation to the canals was then taken up in committee of the whole, Mr. Nelson in the chair.

Mr. Wright's motion to strike out the first six sections, (which establish a canal board of six commissioners, one commissioner at a salary, and the remaining five at per diam allowance) was first in order. Messrs. Ogden and Spencer opposed the motion, and supported the bill; and the latter admitted, that whilst he did not belive that the change would be a matter of economy, he believed that political considerations, or a more equal division of the members of the board amongst the two parties, required an increase of the number. Mr. Colden replied, and contended that the effect of the bill was to legislate the present commissioners out of office, that the object was political, that he was not prepared to pursue a course towards these commissioners which must imply a censure of their conduct or an admission that they are incompetent, that the injustice of such a course had been seen in a previous well-known instance, and that he was especially not prepared to convey this censure, immediately after an investigation, which, whilst it had exhibited the worst of feeling and intention towards the commissioners, had resulted in their most perfect and honoroble exoneration from all the charges. He was also opposed to the proposed addition to the canal board, as unnecessary and more expensive.

The result was, that the question was taken upon each section separately, and each was stricken out by a vote of about 18 to 9; the 7th section was so amended as to make the superintendents of repairs to be appointed by the canal commissioners; and the several remaining sections, 25 in number, were variously though not materially amended, and adopted; when two additional sections having been offered by Mr. Wright, the committee rose and reported, and the senate adjourned.

Court for the Correction of Errors.

Monday, April 3.—Mr. Livingston offered a motion, to rescind the order taken at the previous sitting, to hold an extra session of the court at the capitol in the city of Albany; and that such session be held in the city of New-York. The motion prevailed by the following vote.

Ayes.—Mr. Chancellor, and Messrs. Allen, Burrows, Burt, Colden, Haight, Hart, Jordan, Keyes, Lake, Livingston, McIntyre, Nelson, Ogden, Smith, Spencer, Stebbins, Viele, Wilkeson.—19.

Noes.—Mr. Chief Justice Savage, Mr. Justice Woodworth, and Messrs. Bowman, Brayton, Earll, Elsworth, Hager, Mallory, McCall, McMichael, Wooster, Wright—12.

And the court adjourned until the first Monday in September, in the city of New-York.

The Senate yesterday confirmed the appointment of George Hay, Esq. to be district Judge for the Eastern District of Vircinia.

We are much gratified, and our readers will be equally so, to understand that a supplemental article to the treaty with the Creek Indians, was yesterday sent to the Senate for confirmation, which it is expected, will entirely remove the objections which existed to the treaty in its original form. The arrange-

From the Boston Courier.

NATURAL HISTORY.

A curious circumstance in Natural History is related in the last number of the American Quarterly Review. The large winged grasshopper, which flutters with so much vivacity through our meadows during the autumn, feeds upon vegetable matter, and deposits its eggs upon vegetables for the purpose of being supported till matured. Before the grasshopper takes wing, another insect, the ichneumon, alights upon its body, and thrusts under its skin a number of its eggs, by means of a tubular, awl-shaped oviduct. These eggs slowly acquire perfection, become living worms, and feed upon the body of the hapless grasshopper, until themselves are ready to take wing. So admirably do they perform their office, that they do not injure the vital organs of the insect they are internally devouring, until they are just ready to change their state; and at the proper season, hundreds of grasshoppers, in this condition, have just strength enough remaining to flutter to a tree or fence, and with a dying effort fix their hooked feet so firmly as to retain their position long after death. Examine their bodies at this season, and you find an empty shell, or one filled with large and active worms, just ready to burst their coverings and become winged insects.

The recently published number of the North American Review supplies us with another description of a natural object, but little known to common readers, though said to be familiar to the sight of those who navigate between the tropics,—the beautiful and enigmatical insect, commonly named the Portuguese man-of-war. It is from a memoir by Dr. Tilesius, who accompanied M. de Krusenstern in his voyage round the world.

"This singular animal had several times been delineated, described, and endowed with names, yet not only its denominations were various, but also the nature and characteristics ascribed to it. According to some it was a Polypus, according to others a Zoophyte, and others ranged it among Mollusca. Naturalists who followed in the steps of Linne, have called it the *Physalis*. Wonderful as are all the works of Providence, admirably fitted as are the several parts of each created being for their several functions, complex in their composition as they sometimes at first seem, while yet they are always found to be really so simple and suitable in their action, on a nearer investigation, we may, nevertheless, venture to rank this little animated creature among the most curious phenomena of nature. A worm between 6 and 8 inches in length, which is found but in certain latitudes, has seemingly the skill and knowledge of an experienced navigator, and is in itself a little ship. Its evolutions are according to the winds; it rises and lowers its sail, which is a membrane provided with elevating and depressing organs. When filled with air it is so light, that it swims on the surface of alcohol, and is at the same time provided with a structure, which furnishes it with the necessary ballast.

When high winds would endanger its existence it descends into the deep, and is never seen on the surface of the water. From the under side of the body proceed fibres, which extend twenty feet in length, and are so elastic and delicate, that they wind in a spiral form like a screw, serving at once as anchors, defensive and offensive weapons, pneumatic tubes and feelers. The insect has the colors of the rainbow; its crest, which performs the office of a sail, is intersected with pink and blue veins, trimmed with a rosy border, and swells with the wind, or at the animal's pleasure. The fibres contain a viscous matter, which has the property of stinging like nettles, and produces pustule. It acts so strongly, that vessels in which they have been kept for a time must be repeatedly washed before they can be used. These fibres may be cut off without depriving them or the rest of the insect of the principle of life; and the separation takes place spontaneously, whenever the glutinous matter comes in contact with a hard surface, like the sides of a glass globe. The insect has, however, dangerous enemies in small dolphins, and medusæ, against which neither its nautical skill nor its poison can defend it. To the natural philosopher, this little animal is a curious exemplification of the principles of hydrostatics and of hygrometry, as its bladder is perhaps among the best substances that can be used for the delicate instruments of the latter science. To the physiologist it has the same importance as the rest of that class of beings, of which every part is endowed with an uncommonly strong principle of vitality, and which have therefore not improperly been called *biota* by Dr. Hill. To a contemplative mind the wonderful organization of the Physalis must be a new proof that hardly any great effort of human ingenuity, perseverance, courage, and skill, is without a duplicate of more astonishing workmanship, simplicity, and sagacity, in beings coming from the hand of the Author of creation. If navigation is justly deemed the most daring enterprise of man, it may be considered as a remedy against pride to know that there exists a worm, which an all powerful Providence has at once made a navigator and a ship, a hydrostatic and pneumatic engine, a being destitute of mind, and yet one that watches the winds, and rides on the waves."

Rum Anecdote of the Olden Time. To show in what estimation the primitive settlers of New-England held the necessity and use of ardent spirits, the history of the first barrel of rum ever brought into Norwalk, (Conn.) is here subjoined. A packet master had returned from Boston, and it was noised abroad, that he had brought a barrel of rum. The civil authority, the selectmen, and principal inhabitants of the town, came together and inquired if the thing was so. He assented. They declared with one voice, "You shall never land it on our shores! What, a whole *Barrel* of Rum! It will corrupt our morals and be our undoing!"

National Philanthropist.

A good plan. A friend complained to his neighbor of the heavy amount of his bill for meat; "but," added he, "I am determined to have no more butcher's meat in my house this year at any rate." "Not this year!" said his neighbor, "why the year is but just begun." "True," rejoined the other, "but I mean to pay ready money for it in future, and then it will be *my* meat, and not the *butcher's*."

Religious.

From the Boston Recorder and Telegraph.

GENERAL ASSOCIATION OF MASSACHUSETTS.

This body assembled at Worcester, in the First Church, on Tuesday, the 26th ult., at 5 o'clock, P. M., and was organized by choosing Rev. Samuel Osgood, of Springfield, Moderator, Rev. Enoch Pond, of Ward, Scribe, and Rev. Josiah Bent, of Weymouth, Assistant Scribe. All the Associations previously connected with the body were represented, and two additional Associations recently formed, viz. the Middlesex Union Association, and the Association of Taunton and vicinity, were received into the connexion in the manner prescribed by the rules of the General Association. Delegates were also present from most of the foreign bodies connected with this Association.

Among the articles of business transacted by the Association, the following are worthy of particular notice:—

A request was complied with from the General Conference of Maine to become connected with this Association on the same terms as other foreign bodies. The question, "Has the Committee appointed by the General Association to certify the regular standing of Ministers travelling out of the State, a right to recommend one who has been deposed by an Association connected with this body," was, unanimously answered in the *negative*. In reference to the subject of the ordination of Evangelists referred to this meeting by the last General Association, the following vote was passed:—"That an Association of Congregational Ministers, acting in their associated capacity, are authorized to ordain Evangelists." To a request from the General Assembly of the Presbyterian Church to consent to such an alteration in the terms of Union between that body and this Association, that the Delegates from each to the other respectively shall not hereafter, as has been the case heretofore, have the right to vote, it was answered, that "the principles of the compact between that body and the General Association of Massachusetts have been, in their operation, productive of much good, and that there is nothing in them inconsistent with the general design of this body—therefore, resolved that this body cordially invite a continuance of the friendly intercourse hitherto sustained on the principles already established." In relation to a proposal from the General Association of Connecticut, to this and other general ecclesiastical bodies in New-England, to appoint a joint Committee to "prepare a common summary of Christian doctrine, to be reported to each of those bodies for their adoption," it was voted, "that although there may seem to be some advantages attending the experiment, the difficulties which would attend it are such as render it inexpedient for this body to unite in the appointment of such a Committee." Resolutions were passed approving the recent measures adopted at Philadelphia preparatory to the organization of a national institution to promote the formation and prosperity of Bible Classes, also "the object and operations of the American Sunday School Union, and, as its treasury is much embarrassed, earnestly recommending to the churches to make their Ministers members for life by the payment of thirty dollars, and otherwise to aid the funds of the Society and recommending our schools to connect themselves with that Soaiety, either directly, or through the medium of its Auxiliary Unions." On the subject of Temperance the following resolutions were passed:—

"1. That we cordially approve the object, and operations of the American Society for the Promotion of Temperance, and we earnestly hope that the practice of entire abstinence from the use of distilled liquors will become universal.

2. That we will abstain from the use of distilled liquors ourselves: that we will not have them used, except as a medicine in case of bodily infirmity, in our families; that we will not provide them as articles of entertainment for our friends; and that we will, in all suitable ways, discountenance the use of them in the community."

The religious excercises during the meeting of the Association were the following, all of them well attended:—

On Wednesday and Thursday mornings, there were prayer meetings at 5 o'clock, and on Tuesday, Wednesday and Thursday evenings, sermons preached by the Rev Mr. Armstrong one of the Delegates from the General Assembly, the Rev. Mr. Edwards, of Andover, and the Rev. President Humphrey. On Wednesday afternoon, at 3 o'clock, the Associational sermon was preached by the Rev. Samuel Sewall of the Andover Association. Immediately after this service the narratives of the state of religion in the several Associations were given in presence of the congregation. These narratives were unusually interesting. In two of the Associations, the Berkshire and the Suffolk, nearly every church was reported to be now enjoying the blessing of a revival. In most of the other Associations revivals now exist, and in all there are appearances which promise the speedy enjoyment of yet greater blessings. Never since 1740, perhaps since the settlement of the country, have there been so many revivals at one time in the State of Massachusetts. The reports from the foreign bodies represented at the Association were also unusually interesting. On Thursday morning, the annual report of the Executive Committee of the Domestic Missionary Society was read—a most interesting and animating document; and the Society, by a unanimous vote, united with the Massachusetts Missionary Society, which is now connected with the American Home Missionary Society. In the afternoon, at 3 o'clock, the annual sermon before the Domestic Missionary Society of Massachusetts, was preached by the Rev. Elias Cornelius, Secretary of the American Education Society, and a collection taken to aid feeble churches in this Commonwealth. After this service, the sacrament of the Lord's Supper was celebrated by the Ministers present, and a large number of private Christians from Worcester and the neighboring towns.

Jews' Synagogue. This building has lately been erected in New York, by the German and Polish Jews, and was recently dedicated. The editor of the New York Enquirer, who is a Jew, gives the follow-

New York, July 6. The blacks of this city and the vicinity had yesterday, in pursuance of a previous arrangement, a celebration of the day of their emancipation from slavery throughout this State. It is supposed that fifteen hundred joined the procession, which was conducted with a degree of sobriety and decorum highly honorable to this class of people.

An incident took place in the course of the procession, which is not only diverting, but will serve to show the admirable subordination of this band of new-made freemen. While passing through Greenwich street, a violent shower overtook them.—The heavens seemed for a moment to pour out their wrath on the procession: the whole band dispersed, and sought temporary shelter under the awnings and stoops of the shops. The Marshal found himself, with his aids, suddenly left without a single follower. He faced about, unmindful of the pelting storm, and exclaimed in a voice of thunder, "For shame, gentlemen—for shame! you behave like boys! form, and move on!" This appeal had the desired effect: the men returned to their posts; the banners were again raised, and the procession moved forward under increasing showers of rain.

In relating this incident, we by no means wish to throw ridicule on the ceremony.—Too many of our more favored race, are disposed to condemn the degraded African, and his claim to be raised to a higher state of existence. Such is not our disposition.

A numerous body of men, joining in a tribute of joy and gratitude for liberty so long denied them—a long oppressed race added to the ranks of freemen, is, to the eye of philanthropy, a sublime and grateful sight. With such feelings we looked upon the celebration of yesterday, and the difference of color was forgotten.—*Amer.*

to the European Philhellenists, to whose active exertions the melioration of affairs is ascribed. Eight months before the date of the manifesto, Eastern and Western Greece, it is said, were under the Turkish yoke, and now, "not an enemy is found from the environs of Athens to the point of Macrynoros, and the gates of Missolonghi." Karaiskaki, encamped not far from Athens, was constantly engaged in sharp skirmishes with the enemy. Other troops had arrived for the defence of the city, under Colocotroni. The nation is congratulated on the arrival of Lord Cochrane.

Odessa, May 8. Letters from Constantinople, of the 2d instant, assert, that the Grand Sultan had dismissed the Seraskier, Redschid Pacha, (Commander in Chief,) and had appointed the Aga Pasha in his place; and that the latter had been succeeded in the command of the troops on the Bosphorus by Chossor Pasha. The dismissal of the Seraskier is said to have been in consequence of his inefficiency in conducting the siege of Athens, and the determination of the Sultan to have no *drones* in his service by land or sea; and to promote none but active officers.

New York, July 10.

Mexico. We have received by the brig Sea-Nymph, from Tampico, a copy of the message of Guadalupe Victoria, President of Mexico, to the Congress, at the closing of the session, on the 21st of May last.—We learn from it generally, that their relations with foreign powers were on a friendly footing—that their internal affairs were in a prosperous situation, and that the internal dissentions in some of the provinces had been quelled.

In alluding to the ratification of a treaty of amity, commerce and navigation with Great Britain, the message states that she has, on its return to Mexico, "promised us a Ministry Plenipotentiary—and at the same time, one named by this government, will enjoy that honorable rank in the capital of the nation, which exercises so great an influence over the destinies of Europe."

Of the United States, the message merely says that the treaty which had been concluded between the two countries had been ratified, with some modifications and alterations by the Senate of the Union—which alterations would require a renewal of the negotiations, &c.; that the best harmony existed between the two countries, and both were anxious to arrange a treaty of limits and boundaries, "so essential to the preservation of the good understanding of two neighboring and friendly nations."

Gardner, (Me.) June 22.

Brick-making. Mr. David Flagg, jr. of this town, has constructed a machine for making bricks, which promises to be of great utility in the manufacture of that article. The machine now in operation, is moved by one horse, and it makes or strikes the bricks as fast as three or four persons can take them away and place them on the yard. It requires two persons to supply it with mortar, one to wash moulds, and another to place the empty moulds upon the machine. With this number of hands, from 18 to 20,000 bricks may be made in a day. While observing the operation of the machine a few days since, we had the curiosity to count the number it turned off in five minutes, which was 144. The bricks made in the machine, are more handsome and much more compact than those manufactured in the ordinary manner by hand.

the twentieth toast had just been read, and the men appointed for the purpose, were preparing to accompany it with the discharge of a twelve pounder, when the gun went off, while they were in the act of ramming down the cartridge. By this accident, Terenbe Bady and William Hyatt, two very worthy young men, were severely wounded. Mr. Bady's head, face, neck and arms, are very much injured—his wounds are dangerous, and but little hope is entertained of his recovery. The family to which Mr. Bady belongs, appears to have been particularly unfortunate in their sufferings from powder, as two of his brothers were killed by an explosion at Mr. Dupont's mills. Mr. Hyatt's injuries, though not so extensive as Bady's, are very distressing, and they are irreparable, for he has lost an arm.—*Wilmington Watchman.*

Singular Notice. Appended to a notice of the intended celebration of the 4th of July, at a spring near the town of Milton, N. C. we find the following expressive nota bena:—We have been requested to state, that the services of Jacob Thomas and wagon have been engaged to carry home all who may become *intoxicated* on the occasion. We hope their services will not be called for.—*Fayetteville, N. C. pa.*

The Providence American says:—"The above, nevertheless, shows a decent respect for good order, and we think Mr. Jacob Thomas and his wagon entitled to honorable mention for their services. If men could be carted home on these occasions as soon as they become intoxicated, much of the noise, riot, and obscenity of which they are guilty when they become a little *more* than intoxicated, would be avoided. Besides, sufficient disgrace might be attached to this mode of conveyance to make people loth to become candidates for so public an exhibition of their drunken imbecility."

Resuscitation of the Drowned. As this is the season when persons frequently lose their lives by drowning, it may not be amiss to publish the best method for resuscitating them when taken from the water, instead of the old usage of holding them up by the heels, rolling the body upon a barrel, &c. which of itself is enough to kill one. This prescription has been often before published, but will bear repetition.

When a person is taken out of the water supposed to be drowned, the first and chief object is to make the body warm and restore respiration, breathing. To effect these, dry the body as speedily as possible, and place it in blankets in bed. Continue to rub the body with the dry cloths. Apply bladders or bottles of hot water or heated bricks to the soles of the feet. Let the patient have plenty of air according to the season, and give him every opportunity to breathe. If breathing does not soon occur, inflate the lungs by closing one nostril and blowing up the other with a pair of bellows or the mouth. Continue these operations until the arrival of a physician, who ought to be sent for with all possible speed. If no physician can be procured, the warm bath and bleeding may be added. The above modes of recovery should be continued for three hours, if animation be not sooner restored; and the operators should not be discouraged from the circumstance of the patient having been under water even more than half an hour.

Albany Daily Advertiser.

From the Kentucky Reporter.

Isaac B. Desha. We understand that Governor Desha has pardoned his son Isaac. The power to grant pardons before conviction, though questionable, has been repeatedly asserted and exercised by former Governors of Kentucky, and perhaps other states. The whole of the late term of Harrison Circuit Court, was devoted to this case. Nine Jurors only, were obtained on the last day, the prisoner having exercised to the extent of the law, the privilege of peremtory challenge. The Judge refused to renew the recognizances of his sureties, or again liberate the prisoner on bail, in consequence, we presume, of the state of his health not now requiring such indulgence. The Governor being present when the Judge remanded his son Isaac to jail, addressed the people in a speech of considerable length, and concluded by reversing the order of the Court and setting his son at liberty. We are not informed of any form observed by his Excellency, except the speech, in which it is said, he treated the court with great indignity.

[A Kentucky paper, speaking of Desha, says he looks as well as he did before he cut his throat, though not quite so fleshy. He breathes through a silver tube inserted in his throat, which has to be frequently changed or cleansed. When it is removed he strangles, and were it not replaced, would soon suffocate. Whether guilty or innocent, he has suffered worse than the pains of death, and will carry with him to the grave a mark which nothing can efface.]

From the Schoharie Republican.

A few days since, a farmer in the town of Jefferson, (N. Y.) heard loud talking and angry words bandied about among his dung-hill fowls, and being a man of a pacific disposition, no ways inclined to countenance family quarrels, and withal being curious to know the cause of the disturbance, and who was in the right, and who in the wrong, with divers other causes him thereunto moving, he leisurely bent his course toward the scene of cackeling and confusion aforesaid, which, as is recorded in the cause of Bullum, *vs.* Boatum, was "very natural for a *man* so to do." Arrived in the vicinity of the disturbances above particularly referred to, he observed his dung-hill cock, who is a great pugelist, and in the enjoyment of all his physical strength, engaged in a mortal combat with a striped snake of about 18 or 20 inches in length, the cock to all appearance, having the decided advantage, over his more wiley though less nervous adversary, dealing his blows in quick succession, employing alternately his bill and spurs with true pugelistic skill and science. But the cunning serpent, well aware that victory must declare against him by fair combat, brought into requisition a portion of the innate cunning, for which that reptile has been celebrated from the beginning of the world to this present time; and seizing his antagonist by the thigh, in the rear, he completely secured himself from any further danger from him. Thus situated, the cock very naturally thought his only "safety was in flight," he accordingly "cleaved the air majestically with his wings," the snake keeping fast his hold, and dangling like a tag-lock, underneath, until the cock, overcome with fatigue, alighted on a neighboring apple tree. The snake immediately coiled his tale round a branch of the tree—the cock again attempted flight, but he could scarcely clear the limb, from which he hung with his head downwards, making every effort to escape, but all in vain, until the farmer came to his assistance—killed the snake, and set him at liberty.

From the Essex County, (N. Y.) Republican.

Bear Fight. Mr. Andrew C. Bigelow, and Mr. Harvey Bliss, of Ticonderoga, while engaged in fishing in a small canoe, a few weeks since, on Long Pond, discovered a huge bear playing in the water near them. Being armed only with a fowling-piece loaded with shot, they discharged it into his face, which so enraged the monster, that he swam towards them with full speed, apparently determined on revenge for being thus insulted while quietly bathing for his own amusement. The bear made repeated attempts to overturn the canoe, but the men, not having time to reload their pieces, as often applied their paddles opon his pate, until they succeeded in conquering him. He was dragged ashore, and found to weigh five hundred pounds.

Virginia *vs.* Pennsylvania. Niles's Register states, that Virginia, by adhering to her *doctrines*, has advanced the number of her people 160,000 in 30 years, from 1790 to 1820; and that Pennsylvania, by adhering to her *practices*, has *increased* her people 625,000 in the same time, or more than all Virginia contains; and the wealth of Pennsylvania, has proportionably advanced. Thus—

	1790	1820	1830
	People.	*People.*	*Calculated.*
Virginia,	442,117	602,974	690,000
Pennsylvania,	429,099	1,094,398	1,340,000

The first period shows a difference in favor of Virginia, of 13,000—the second in favor of Pennsylvania, of 447,000; and the next census will increase this balance to 650,000, or more, and the people of the United States, located in Pennsylvania, will be more than twice as numerous as those who shall be located in Virginia, yet the latter has fifty per cent. more territory, and a much larger quantity of good land than the former, and is, in every respect, as well fitted by Providence, for the comfortable subsistence of a dense population of industrious and enlightened citizens.

We stated last winter that a large majority of the Louisiana Legislature were decidedly friends of the Administration. It excited a doubt among some of our readers. We have now before us the Argus of New Orleans, dated June 6, which contains a letter to the editor from a member of the Legislature. In referring to the fact that Gen. Jackson had accepted an invitation tendered to him by that body to join in a celebration on the 8th of January, 1828, the writer says:—"The resolution was supported by the warm friends of the Administration, and could not have been adopted without their support, there being only twenty-five Jacksonites, in both houses, out of sixty-seven members."

We refer again to this fact with no intention of making any calculations upon the future Presidential vote, but as a confirmation of our former statement.

U. S. Gazette.

Thames Tunnel. After copying the account of the bursting in of the tunnel under the river Thames, at London, the editor of the Greenfield Gazette adds the following information.

This stupendous undertaking is not likely to fail in consequence of the late disaster.

The final success of it was at first doubted. One former attempt has, we believe, been made to construct a tunnel under the Thames, and abandoned. The present work has been in progress some few years, and was completed nearly two-thirds of the distance across the bed of the river, when the water burst in. It has been regarded by some in this country, as rather an affair of curiosity and wonder, considering the magnitude and boldness of the undertaking, than a work of public utility. But it is of great importance to the city of London, and the population of the south of England.

There are six bridges across the Thames in London, viz:—London Bridge, which was begun in 1176, and finished in 1209, Westminster Bridge, begun in 1739, and completed in 1750, Blackfriars, commenced in 1760, and finished 1768. Waterloo, Vauxhall and Southark bridges, were all built within the last sixteen years. The three last are toll bridges, the others free. None of them have draws to admit the passage of vessels. London Bridge is situated lowest on the river; and as no sea vessels can come past it, all the navigation of the river is crowded into a narrow space below the bridge. A vast deal of business is done on each side of the river, below, as well as above this point. The erection of another bridge below the London Bridge is out of the question. It would crowd the navigation still further down, and in fact remove it from the business part of the city.

The tunnel will be about a mile below London Bridge, and is to answer all the purposes of a bridge, without interruption to the navigation.

It is intended to accommodate a large proportion of the travel that is now drawn to London Bridge. And some conception can be formed of its importance, from the fact, that from 60,000 to 90,000 footmen, and about 5000 carriages, of all descriptions, pass the bridge daily. And when the tunnel shall be completed, it will present a spectacle of no ordinary interest and grandeur. The commercial wealth and naval power, of the British empire, riding 50 feet above a ceaseless current of her population, passing from one section of the metropolis to the other!

New Haven, July 10. Mr. Joseph Lancaster, who lately arrived in this city from South America, says the New York American, has proceeded to Philadelphia, where he intends to publish a history of his expedition to Colombia, which will also contain a view of the present situation of that republic. It is said Mr. L. never received the $20,000 for the draft given him by Bolivar, it remaining at present unpaid in London. The opinions which he entertains of South America, are not the most favorable, and are very freely expressed.—*Herald.*

Manufacturing Establishments in New York. In the county of Oneida, says the Buffalo Journal, the original amount of capital invested, is estimated at $482,000—present value, $393,000—depreciation, $89,000. They have all sprung into existence since 1810, and pincipally between '12 and '16. These factories, keep in operation, in the aggregate, 14,945 spindles, 378 power looms, and employ 745 men, boys, and girls. Several of the cotton establishments are rapidly extending their business, and improving their buildings and machinery.—*Williamstown Advo.*

Mixing Salt with Hay. An English agriculturist gives the following information in answer to inquiries made of him respecting his mixing salt with hay when getting it into stack, and giving it to his horses and stock:—"I have used salt to hay in unfavorable seasons upward of thirty years, which hay has been regularly consumed by all my horses, and likewise by my cows, bullocks and sheep; and every description of stock has done well with it. I now do and shall continue using salt with my hay, whether the season prove foul or fair. My rule is to mix about a peck to a load, keeping a boy sprinkling whilst unloading.—Last year I spread ten bushels of salt per acre on some land sown with barley, and the part salted was two shades lighter color than the unsalted, and produced an increase of four bushels per acre; and it should be remembered, that the beneficial effects from salt do not cease with the first crop."

Appointments by the Governor and Council.

Hon. Nahum Mitchell, of East Bridge water, and Samuel M'Kay, Esq. of Pittsfield to be commissioners, and J. F. Baldwia, Esq. of Boston, Engineer, to survey a Route for a Railway from the city of Boston, westward, to the Hudson river.

Hon. John Mills, of Southwick, Willard Phillips, Esq. of Boston, and James Hayward, Esq. of Cambridge, to be Commissioners of the Board of Internal Improvements; and James Hayward, one of the Commissioners, to be also Engineer of the Board.—*Boston Patriot.*

In celebrating the National Independence at Bath, N. Y. a dreadful accident took place. In firing a six pounder, a young man by the name of Morgan, a private in Capt. Bell's artillery company, rushed forward before the gun to ram down more wadding at the moment the match was applied to the priming. His arms were both shot off, and his body mangled in a shocking manner. He is yet alive, but his physicians think it impossible to save him. This was the dreadful effects of intoxication, as Morgan was at the time intoxicated, as was his general habit on all public occasions. This ought to be a warning to others.—*Albany Gaz.*

On the 4th inst. at the celebration of that day at Glen's Falls, three men were injured for life by the premature discharge of a field piece. The gun had been fired, when an attempt was made to re-charge it without properly swabbing it out; the cartridge took fire after being about half rammed down, and in the explosion carried away both arms, and otherwise injured one of the men employed in loading the piece, and one of the arms of another was shot off, and the man tending the vent had all the fingers of his hand torn off. The man who lost both arms is since dead.—*Ibid.*

The Farmington Canal is in a state of great forwardness; $342,017 have been expended on it, and the fund unexpended is $107,343.—30 miles are finished; 14 nearly so; and the remaining 13 half excavated.

NEW-YORK SPECTATOR:

VOL. XXXIV. | FRIDAY, JULY 8, 1831. | NO. 46 PINE-STREET.

PUBLISHED BY FRANCIS HALL & CO.
EVERY TUESDAY AND FRIDAY,
AT THE
CORNER OF PINE & WILLIAM STREETS,
Opposite the Bank Coffee-House.

—:o:—

SATURDAY EVENING, JULY 2.

GREAT FIRE.—About 2 o'clock this morning, a fire broke out in the centre of the block bounded by Amity, Greene, Mercer and Fourth streets. So rapid was the progress, that all the buildings on the block except one (it was only partly built on) were either totally destroyed or greatly injured. We have just returned from the spot, and give below as correct an account of the disaster as we could collect.

From the best information, we believe the fire was the act of an incendiary, and commenced under the stairway of the carpenter's shop, owned and occupied by Mr. Nathan H. Topping, which contained a large quantity of lumber and stock, valued at from four to five thousand dollars, all of which is entirely consumed. The tools belonging to some dozen journeymen, were in the shop, and all are gone, which is a severe loss to the respective owners.

On Greene-street, there were only two dwelling houses, which were elegant two story brick, with a basement—both were owned by Mr. Topping—one was occupied by Mr. Topping and Mr. John Conner—the other by Mr. Timothy Wood and Dr. De Wolf. These buildings are totally destroyed. They were valued at 8,000, on which Mr. Topping had an insurance of $5,000. Mr. T. had also an insurance of $1,000 on his lumber; he estimates his loss, exclusive of the insurance, at $7,000.

On Amity street.—The only house not injured, is the large one on the corner of Mercer, occupied by Warren De Lancy, Esq. The next is the marble factory belonging to Mr. William Frazee: this is much injured. Adjoining were two three story brick dwelling houses owned by Mr. Frazee, both occupied by him, one as a dwelling, the other a shop or show room: both greatly injured—next to these was a two story brick dwelling, owned by Richard I. Wells, Esq. and occupied by Mr. Mark Spencer, considerably injured. Mr. Frazie was insured for $4000, which will more than cover the loss sustained. Mr. Wells' property was insured for $3000.

On Fourth-street.—Two two-story brick front dwelling houses, owned by David S. Jones, Esq.—No. 125 occupied by Mr. Birbeck, and Mr. M'Guire, and No. 127 by Mr. Fisher and Mr. Drayton—both so much injured as to be useless and will probably be pulled down: insured for $2500.

On Mercer-street, the only building, in front, was a two-story frame building, owned and occupied by Mr. James Williams, who kept a Dairy; this dwelling was but slightly injured, but Mr. W. sustained a severe loss in the destruction of his extensive stables which were in the rear of his dwelling—fortunately he got out all his cows and horses: he estimates his loss at upwards of $2,000.

The whole amount of property destroyed is estimated at $20,000, about one-half of which was insured.

We are happy to learn that a good supply of water was obtained from the new hydraulic works in the neighborhood of the Bowery Hill.

CABINET LIBRARY.—Carey & Lea, have commenced the publication of a series of valuable works, under the above title. The first No. being a very handsome and compact duodecimo, of 300 pages, has reached us. It is a narative of the War in Germany and France, in 1813, and 1814, by Lieut Gen. Charles William Vane, Marquess of Londonderry.—The leading English periodicals have spoken of this work in terms of high praise. The noble author had previously acquired much reputation for his Memoirs of the Peninsular Campaigns; and we have read enough of this present work, to warrant the favor with which it has been received by the press abroad. The substance of this volume was originally written in a series of letters, to the relation of the noble author, (the late Lord Castlereagh, as we infer) embracing an account of all those important military operations which came under the author's immediate notice, during the campaigns mentioned in the title. These letters have now been thrown into the form of an unbroken narrative, with little alteration, other than such as was necessary to the change of manner. The sketches of the numerous military events of those important campaigns, being thus fresh as it were from the field, are greatly enhanced both in value and interest.—No. II. of this series of works, is to consist of the "Journal of a Naturalist"—a delightful book—to be succeeded by Military Memoirs of the Duke of Wellington, &c. It is to be published monthly.

THE PERSIAN ADVENTURER.—Carey & Lea.—This is a continuation, in two volumes, by the same author of the popular novel called the Kuzzilbash, published a few years ago; which, as most readers will remember, was after the pattern of Anastasius and Hadji Baba. An oriental Gil Blas is conducted through various scenes, both among the roving Turcomans and the more refined inhabitants of the eastern capitals; and the manners, customs, character, diplomacy, &c. of the people are pleasingly illustrated. The writer, who has been in the East, and is conversant with the entertaining peculiarities which he describes, makes a most attractive use of his materials. He says he has been induced to vary the title of his work, in the continuation, because a bookseller told him he had been asked whether the "Kuzzilbash," (which means Red Head,) was a *cookery book*. We anticipate much pleasure from the perusal of this second part.

FIRST LESSONS; *or, Elements of Thought and Language, expressed by pictures and words; classed according to Walkers' Pronounciation. By Elizabeth Oram.*—We know of no manual better calculated than this for the purpose of teaching children the alphabet, and the different sounds of the vowels. The objects selected to fix the attention are well chosen, and the typographical execution is remarkably neat and perspicuous. By the association of images, giving ideas to the infant mind, with the sounds of the words which represent them, the task of instruction has always been made lighter; and philosophy dictates this method as the best, the sneers of the "Dutchman's Fire Side" to the contrary notwithstanding. The lady who has prepared this little work is well known as one of the best instructresses in the country.

RHODE ISLAND.—The National Convention at Newport, have nominated Hon. Messrs. Tristam Burges, of Providence, and Dutee J. Pearce, of Newport, as candidates for re-election as Representatives to Congress. The friends of the administration have likewise held a convention; but their ranks in Rhode Island are so thin, that they dared not venture upon a nomination, and therefore adjourned without doing any thing, and without day.

PROVIDENCE AND BOSTON STEAM-BOATS.—We are gratified to perceive that the Directors of the Providence and Boston Steam-boat Company, have changed the time of departure of the Franklin, from Providence, so that hereafter that boat will not leave on the Christian Sabbath.

The Eagle Fire Insurance Company have declared a dividend of four per cent. for the last six months, payable on the 15th inst.

The Howard Insurance Company have also declared a dividend of four per cent. for the last six months, payable on the 11th inst.

A laborer was seriously injured this morning at the new building adjoining this office: those repeated accidents are from the want of ordinary care.

ERRATUM.—In the leading article of last evening's paper, towards the close, speaking of a certain political party, or rather a combination of the fragments of all parties, we denominated it "the most wicked and "*dangerous*," &c. The compositor, however, preferred some other dialect—the *Carraboo*, we believe—to our Norman or Scottish English, and therefore, instead of "*dangerous*," printed a word which it would be truly dangerous to undertake to pronounce, or even to spell again.

PROCEEDINGS OF THE NEW-YORK HORTICULTURAL SOCIETY, June 27.—Mr. Hyslop, gardener to N. Prime, Esq., presented two bunches of white Muscadine Grapes, in full maturity, of excellent flavor, weighing 11 and 12 ounces.

Mr. Smith, Seedsman, 372 Broadway, a plate of red Morello, from a tree imported from France; 1 do. of Bleeding Heart; 1 do. Harrison's Heart; 1 do. of Yellow Swiss.

Mr. Morrow, 2 heads Lettuce, weighing 1¼lbs., and 2 do., 1 lb., 14 oz.

Mr. Still, 2 long Prickly Cucumbers, 11 and 12 inches in length; 2 cluster do. 7¼ inches each.

Mr. Floy, a Lonicera flexuosa, L. Fraseri, L. caprifolium italicum, Champney's cluster, Grenville and Royal Roses, Clematis viorna, Magnolia glauca.

Messrs. Prince & Sons, from their garden at Flushing, Andromeda speciosa, a beautiful plant with white flowers, a native of Carolina; a Pæonia fragrans, and from two to six specimens of upwards of *one hundred* varieties of Roses, making a very splendid display of some of the most fragrant, beautiful, singular and delicate of this favorite and charming flower.

June 21—Mr. Neal presented a beautiful Scabiosa, Double Lychnis, Fox Glove, Geraneum Nosegay, do. deep scarlet, Provence Rose, 2 kinds of Coreopsis, white Lily, 20 seedling double Carnations, and blue bulbous Iris.

Mr. Floy, Magnolia glauca, Hoya carnosa, Passiflora alata, Petunia nyctaginiflora, monthly sweet Honey Suckle, Clematis viorna, Wellington's Geraneum, Nereum splendens.

Mr. Shaw, 12 Gooseberries, weighing 3 ounces 11 pwt.

Mr. Morrow, six Turnip Beets, weighing 1 lb. 13¼ ounces.

Mr. Hogg, 20 uncommonly fine Holly Hocks, 12 Carnations, a first rate Amaryllis purpurea in pot, Geraneum triste, Coreopsis lanceolata, C. tinctoria, scarlet Lychnis, orange Lily, Lythrum salicaria, Spirea ulmaria, flore pleno, S. lobata, Lysimachia verticillata, Œnothera, Chenolea barbata, Delphinium grandiflorum, D. Chinensis, Betonica grandiflora, Lonicera Fraseri, seedling Chinese Rose, Valeriana officinalis, a seedling Phlox.

Mr. Wilson, 8 varieties, and 12 seedling Carnations, among which were the Pride of the Isles, Pan's playmate, and Royal Crown.

Mr. Oakley, a beautiful Bouquet of Pinks, scarlet Lychnis, Chinese and Moss Roses, Gnaphalium, Veronica spicata, Malva officinalis, Coreopsis grandiflora, French Honey Suckle, French Marygold, Lythrum, and others.

Mr. Cooke, six large Gooseberries.

June 28—Alderman Wells presented 12 Gooseberries, 3 ozs. 4 pwt. 4 gr. Delphinium grandiflorum, handsome double Holly Hock, and, from the garden of Rev. Mr. Ives, the very beautiful and singular Rosa microphylla.

Mr. Wilson, 4 quarts of Antwerp Raspberries remarkably fine and large, 46 varieties of double China Pinks, 30 of single do., Lychnis fulgens, Campanula speculum, and several other choice flowers.

Mr. Oakley, 12 different sorts of Carnations.

Mr. Warner, a plate of very fine Black Heart Cherries.

Mr. Neal, 10, do. do.

Mr. Knox, 12 Gooseberries, 4½ oz.

Mr. T. Bridgeman, a bushel of superior Vicia faba, English Broad Bean, accompanied by a letter to the Editor of the New-York Farmer.

Bowery Road, June 28, 1831.

Sir,—Being desirous that the Vicia faba, or English Beans, be fairly tasted, and more generally introduced into this community, I have sent one bushel, to be distributed amongst those of the members of the Horticultural Society, who may be desirous of tasting them.

They [illegible] boiled in England, with bacon, pork, or fat [illegible] should boil about half an hour. If boiled without [illegible] require a few minutes longer, and [illegible] be [illegible], &c., the same as Lima Beans. [illegible] mixture of varieties; viz: Early [illegible] Windsor, Green Nonpareil and [illegible] well.

[illegible] very respectfully,

T. BRIDGEMAN.

PROGRESSIVE INCREASE OF DUTY.—On and after the first instant, the Tariff provides that the duties on the subjoined articles are to be increased as follows:—

Flax, from 45 to 50 dollars per ton.
Hemp, from 55 to 60 dollars per ton.
Indigo, from 30 to 40 cents per pound.
Sail Duck, (of all kinds) from 10 to 10½ cents per square yard.

The accounts from the Russian capital to the 5th May, mention that the little success which had attended the operations of the army in Poland under Gen. Diebitsch was a source of much dissatisfaction. The Emperor of Russia, it is mentioned, had expressed himself strongly upon the subject. A confident expectation was, however, indulged that, before the summer, Diebitsch would be in the capital of Poland, and that the Poles would be compelled to submit to any terms that may be offered. The Emperor appeared not to want for money to carry on the war, which will prove a much more expensive one than was at first imagined. Fears were beginning to be entertained of the spreading of the cholera morbus more extensively throughout the Russian dominions than last year. It had already recommenced its ravages in Birsk.

The King of Denmark, to prevent unnecessary litigation, has established a Court of Equity, or Arbitration, the members of which are paid entirely by government, and no expense is incurred by the parties appealing to its decision.—No suit can be instituted in any court without a certificate to state that the parties have ineffectually attempted to have it settled by arbitration.

FROM LAGUAYRA.—Extract of a letter from a gentleman who has been several years in Laguayra, to his friends in Washington, dated, June 11, 1831.

"Venezuela is still in revolution to the windward, but I think will be speedily concluded, and I hope without bloodshed. The Congress is still in session. We have just received intelligence from Bogota that General Flores from the Southward, has acknowledged the Constitutional Government, under the authority of the duly elected Vice President Caicido—Mosquera the President being in the United States. Not a word is said of what has become of Urdaneta, who has been governing these militants for some months, and who put out Mosquera and Caicido. Commissioners are about to be sent from Venezuela to Bogota to endeavor an arrangement. I do not think Venezuela will go further than to confederate, and be herself a free state—not again to consolidate the power over this part of Colombia, (Venezuela proper,) at Bogota. I think it probable some attempt will endeavor to be made after the form of the government of the United States. This country is much depressed and extremely poor, and agriculture (the foundation of *all prosperity here*) is reduced to a bare cultivation for subsistence—nothing but years of peace, a good government and strong, with a change of the laws on the subject of property, can restore the present miserable state of Venezuela."

Brazil.—Capt. Weld, of the schr. Horatio, who left Para on the 2d ult. states that the country was in a very unsettled state. There were 3000 troops at Para, who have not received any pay for the last 14 months, in consequence of which, together with the unpopularity of the President, fears were entertained that they would break out in open rebellion, in which case, foreign property would be unsafe. The President had in some measure allayed the ferment, by issuing a proclamation promising to pay them. The British Consul was endeavoring to charter the American schr. Washington's Barge, for the purpose of proceeding to Bermuda, to order a British vessel of war to sail immediately for Para, to protect British property.

FIRES.—About two o'clock on the morning of the 27th ult. a fire broke out in the cooper shop owned by R. Beach, and occupied by Mr. P. Darrow, on the south side of the Acqueduct, at Rochester, which with a new building erected for a store house, and B. Campbell's floating mill, and the stone building adjoining, occupied as a saw mill and store house, also owned by Mr. Campbell, were entirely destroyed, with most of their contents. It was with great difficulty that Beach and Kempshall's large mill was saved, as it took fire in several places. The Acqueduct House was partly destroyed. Loss estimated at $22,000. Insurance $10,000.

The steamboat Ousatonic, which plies to Nahant, while lying at Tileston's wharf, Boston, took fire on Wednesday morning about 3 o'clock, near the boiler, and was considerably injured before the fire could be got under. Eight men and boys were sleeping on board, and narrowly escaped being burnt to death. two of them were scorched and one jumped overboard, but was saved. Their clothing was destroyed. This boat was much injured by fire, night of April 24, 1830, and rebuilt.

On Wednesday evening, about 10 o'clock, the [illegible] victualling cellar of Antoine Malfeit, Merchants' Row, under the hardware store of Messrs Proctor and Palmer, was found to be on fire; although the doors were kept tight by the Fire Department until the water was ready to follow, it was upwards of an hour before the fire was extinguished. The damage was confined to the cellar.

Case of Barker.—In our last, we briefly alluded to the singular circumstances connected with the murder of this unfortunate man, and to the fact that matters were in a train to ferret out the murderers. We have since made further inquiry into the affair, and are enabled to subjoin a more correct statement.

A man named Barker, who followed the business of a Drover, was for many years in the habit of visiting this city, disposing of his stock, and making purchases for the west.—In his habits he was exceedingly eccentric—in his dress still more singular and unique. He usually wore a leathern belt round his middle, in which was secured his money; a kind of moccasons for shoes; and for a covering, occasionally, a large cloth drab coat, which he has been seen to have on him in the hottest days of July.

The last visit this Barker made this city, was in the summer of 1825. He brought as usual, a large drove of horses, and by their sale came in possession of a considerable sum of money. He started away from his lodging place, one evening, leaving word that he intended going to the cellar of one Smith Crowell, residing in Shippen-street, and that he should return before bed time. He, however, did not return that night, nor in the morning, and some of his acquaintances feeling uneasy in regard to his safety, as they knew he had money with him, went in search. They found him in Shippen-street, lying on the pavement, a few rods from the celler above alluded to, and in the agonies of death! He was immediately conveyed to the hospital, and promptly received medical aid, but he died in a few hours after.

The circumstances, as many of our readers will remember, created considerable excitement at the time. The parties supposed to be implicated in the murder—for that he was murdered was beyond question—were arrested and examined before Mayor Watson, but discharged for want of evidence.

Barker's family resided in Canada. His wife did not receive the news of his death for a considerable time after, and since then she has been anxious to come on, and use every exertion to bring the culprits to merited punishment. She heard of her husband's death by letter, but that he was murdered was, she says, revealed to her in a dream, and her present visit to this city was more immediately undertaken at the instance of certain impressions which laid strongly on her mind, that her husband had been foully dealt with.

On last Saturday week, she communicated these and other particulars to Mayor Richards, and solicited his aid in the affair. She desired the arrest of Crowell, and also that he would send for two other individuals supposed to be concerned, who were some time ago committed to prison in New York, for robbery; that another examination might take place, in the hope of eliciting something bearing on the point. Crowell was brought up and examined, but there did not appear to be any *positive* proof against him, although many implicating circumstances were adduced. He was, however, committed to prison, where he now remains, bail being refused by Judge King, when brought before him a few days after his committal by the Mayor on a writ of *habeas Corpus*.

It is thought by those best acquainted with this affair, that Barker was poisoned with laudanum.—*Saturday Evening Post.*

The result of the experiment on the Rail-road, on Tuesday afternoon, with the York locomotive engine, was highly satisfactory. A speed of twenty miles an hour was, we, learn, easily attained and preserved, although there was attached to the engine a carriage containing a number of passengers. The private trials of the locomotives are expected to be repeated daily, and will doubtless continue to attract spectators to the scene of operations.

Yesterday afternoon the locomotive started form the depot on Pratt street with a train of five cars, four of which were laden with stone and the fifth with passengers. The entire weight of the train, exclusive of engine, was about fifteen tons; and with this load the locomotive travelled at the rate of ten or fifteen miles an hour. A large concourse of spectators witnessed the experiment with high gratification. The New York locomotive was also on the road during the afternoon, and travelled with considerable velocity.—*Balt. Am.*

NEWARK, July 1.—*Davis's Trial.*—On Tuesday morning last the Special Court of Oyer and Terminer was opened; but owing to the non-appearance of several witnesses on the part of Davis, the court took a recess until the afternoon, when at the re-opening, Davis was brought in. On entering the bar he threw a hasty glance towards the bench and deliberately took his seat in the rear of his counsel. The Jury were then called. A pannel being completed, the cause was opened by Amzi Dodd, Esq. the Prosecuting Attorney in behalf of the State, and five witnesses examined. Court adjourned about 9 o'clock in the evening until 7 next morning. On Wednesday, nineteen witnesses were examined. An argument of considerable length took place in the afternoon on the admissibility of a certain examination of the prisoner, taken by two magistrates, several days after he had been in jail, which examination was declared by the Court inadmissable as testimony against the prisoner.—*Newark Eagle.*

MELANCHOLY ACCIDENT.—On Thursday evening a decent colored man named Jacob Miller, fell from on board the sloop Samuel, near Fort Diamond, and was drowned.

OPTHALMIA.—We are glad to be informed that the children afflicted by opthalmia, who were removed from the Alms House are recovering from the effects of the disease, in their now location on Blackwell's Island.

CORONER'S OFFICE, 145 Greenwich-street.—The Coroner was called to view the body of an unknown man, found floating at the dock foot of 13th street. He had on a blue frock coat, striped woollen vest, light blue satinet pantaloons, white shirt, and boots. He appeared to be about 25 years of age, and to have been recently drowned.

ALSO, to view the body of an unknown man, found at the foot of 19th-street. He had on a black cloth coat, yellow striped valencia vest, brown drilling pantaloons and white shirt. He appeared to be about 30 years of age, and to have been drowned a short time. It is supposed that his name is William Horrocks from letters found in his possession.

A daring robbery was committed on Wednesday evening upon the person of Benjamin Knower, Esq. President of the Farmers' and Mechanics' Bank of Albany, while on his passage in the steamboat Ohio to this city. After the arrival of the boat, Mr. Knower discovered that his pocket-book had been taken from him while he was asleep, and a draft for $800 drawn by the Rochester bank on one of the Hartford Banks abstracted, together with about twenty dollars in small bills. A large amount of drafts upon the United States Branch Bank in this city remained in his pocketbook untouched. The villian is supposed to have left the city in the steamboat Superior, for Hartford.—*Journal of Com.*

The Boston Transcript states that on Thursday morning a man by the name of Bronson, who said that he belonged to the State of New York, and has boarded at the Rail Road Hotel, Pond-street, for the last fortnight, was heard by the family, just before the alarm of fire, coming down Stairs.—He passed through the kitchen cellar, next through the bar-room cellar, and then into the bar-room, took eleven dollars in cash from the bar, and suited himself to a pair of boots belonging to one of the boarders. He then left the Hotel and crossed Warren bridge, and was seen returning again to the city with the crowd that was crossing to the fire, from Charles town. He has been traced no further.

MERITORIOUS ACTION.—In a heavy squall in this harbor on Wednesday afternoon, a small sail boat capsized, at some distance from the shore, in which were Mr. and Mrs. Turner of this city, who had started to visit Deer Island. Mr. Jotham Monroe, a respectable waterman, who was alone in his sail boat about a mile distant, saw the disaster, crowded all sail at the risk of his life, and succeeded by very great exertion, first catching Mrs. Turner from the water as he passed, and then Mr. T. both being on the point of sinking.—The case has been represented to the Humane Society.—*Bos. Pat.*

In Londongrove, Chester county, on the 20th instant, a very serious accident occurred.—Ann Brown, ascended a a cherry tree, fell therefrom, and broke her neck. She has left a husband and two children to mourn her untimely death. Ann was many years a resident of West Chester.

A fourth unsuccessful attempt has been made, in Bristol district, (Mass.) to elect a representative for Congress.

It is stated by one of the Washington letter writers that the Secretary of the Senate and Clerk of the House of Representatives, with all their deputies, are engaged in preparing for the press the legislative and executive documents authorised last session to be printed by Gales & Seaton. Many important documents have deen found, relating to the early legislation of the United States, which were never printed.—Among them is a volume of correspondence between General Washington and Mr. Jay, in relation to the treaty made by the latter with Great Britain. Also, a very able report of General Hamilton; and a great many communications relating to the campaigns of Harmar, St. Clair, and Wayne, against the Indians north-west of the Ohio.

THE CROPS.—The Richmond Compiler says:—"The harvest for early wheat is nearly completed in Virginia.—The purple straw is almost all cut—and the harvest of the latler wheat is in many places commencing. We have various accounts of the productiveness of the crop. In the low grounds it is generally good—the upper lands have been much infested by the fly, and the crop will be cut short. In general, the quality is said to be very good."

The Lynchburg Virginian says, that "the wheat harvest in this neighborhood has just commenced here, fifteen to twenty days later than last year. On the 15th of June, 1830, new wheat was delivered in our mills. The crop of wheat in this section of country has been improved some by the late rains, but it must be a very little one, though the quality is said to be excellent"

SHIP BUILDING IN MAINE.—In addition to the ship Constellation, of 400 tons, recently launched from the shipyard of Peter Grant & Sons, in Hallowell, it is stated in the Advocate that there are now two fine ships on the stocks, one of 300 tons owned by Robinson & Page, and the other of 450 tons by Rufus K. Page. They are under the superintendence of E. G. Pierce, and the workmen make use of coffee and beer instead of ardent spirits. The Constellation was built, launched, and has gone to sea *without ardent spirits*. There are also two schooners of 100 tons each building in Hallowell, by Isaac Smith and S. C. Grant.

Extract of a letter received in Charleston, dated, Point Petre, May 16, 1831.

"As I expected, the Governor of this Island has just issued an ordinance to open the ports, for four thousand barrels of Flour, and for the exportation in foreign vessels, of five thousand hhds. of Sugar. The introduction of foreign Flour will begin on the 1st of June, and continue until the 1st of September, as well for the exportation of Sugar. Prices—Flour, 75 to 80 francs per brl. free of duty, but one per cent; Rice, 25 to 27f; Tobacco, 38f.; Corn, white, 20 to 25 francs per barrel of 3½ bushels; Staves, $5 per M.

PASSENGERS.

The packet ship Canada, sailed yesterday for Liverpool, with the following passengers:—Mrs. Hays, son and daughter, of N. York: Mr. J. Battersby and lady, of South Carolina; the Hon. J. Poinsett, of do; Mr. J. Watson, of do; Mr. William Hewitt, daughter and servant, of Havana: Messrs. James, Ball, of Mexico. Joseph Hall, of Mobile; P. E. Livaudais, and William, Alderson, of New-Orleans; John Mackie, of Scotland; Joseph Stamps, of England; and John Avery, of Belfield, Virginia.

In the ship Hannibal, sailed for London—Mrs. McCombs, of London; Mr. Hervieu, of France; Mrs. Trollope and 2 daughters of England; Mrs. Hebard, of New York; Miss Spence, of Brooklyn; Mr. Gappen, lady and daughter, of Quebec; Mr. Gallot, of London; Mr. G. A. Stobz and 2 sons, of Vera Cruz; Mr. Johnston, of Montreal; Mr. Adams, of New York.

In the ship Henri IV., sailed for Havre:—Mr. and Mrs. Verdier, of Charleston; Mr. D. Conick, of Philadelphia; Mr. Sandon, Mr. Espada, General Bazagan, and Mr. S. Idalgo, of Mexico; Mr. Pichon and servant, of France; Dr. Mosely, U. S. N.; Philip Matton, of Paris.

In the brig Roanoke, from Gottenburg:—Madame Christian Bomanand daughter, of Carlscroon; and Jonas Auguste Lunberg, of Stockholm.

SALES THIS DAY AT THE STOCK EXCHANGE.

$1000		United States Fives, 1835	106½
100	shares	United States Bank,	130¼
120	do	Bank of America,	101
30	do	Delaware and Hudson Canal Comp'y,	67
70	do	do do do do do	67½
140	do	do do do do do	67½
50	do	Dry Dock Bank,	106½
50	do	Butchers & Drovers' Bank,	104½
50	do	Mechanics' and Traders' Bank,	105½
50	do	National Bank,	106
60	do	Merchants' Exchange Bank,	105
150	do	Louisiana Bank,	121
20	do	N. Y. Life Insurance and Trust Co.	119½
20	do	Phœnix Fire Insurance Company,	92½
10	do	Paterson Rail Road Company,	120½
50	do	do do do do	120
10	do	do do do do do	121
25	do	Ithica and Owego Rail Road Company,	104½
60	do	Harlem Rail Road Co.,	115

The Case of the Cherokee Nation against the State of Georgia; argued and determined in the Supreme Court of the United States, January Term, 1831.

OPINION OF THE MINORITY.

Mr Justice THOMPSON—Entertaining different views of the questions now before us in this case, and having arrived at a conclusion different from that of a majority of the court, and considering the importance of the case and the constitutional principle involved in it, I shall proceed, with all due respect for the opinion of others, to assign the reasons upon which my own has been formed.

In the opinion pronounced by the court, the merits of the controversy between the state of Georgia and the Cherokee Indians have not been taken into consideration. The denial of the application for an injunction has been placed solely on the ground of want of jurisdiction in this court to grant the relief prayed for. It became, therefore, unnecessary to inquire into the merits of the case. But thinking as I do that the court has jurisdiction of the case, and may grant relief, at least in part, it may become necessary for me, in the course of my opinion, to glance at the merits of the controversy, which I shall, however, do very briefly, as it is important so far as relates to the present application.

Before entering upon the examination of the particular points which have been made and argued, and for the purpose of guarding against any erroneous conclusions, it is proper that I should state, that I do not claim for this court, the exercise of jurisdiction upon any matter properly falling under the denomination of political power. Relief to the full extent prayed by the bill may be beyond the reach of this court. Much of the matter therein contained, by way of complaint, would seem to depend for relief upon the exercise of political power; and as such appropriately devolving upon the executive, and not the judicial department of the government. This court can grant relief so far only as the rights of person or property are drawn in question, and have been infringed.

It would very ill become the judicial station which I hold, to indulge in any remarks upon the hardships of the case, or the great injustice that would seem to have been done to the complainants, according to the statement in the bill, and which for the purpose of the present motion I must assume to be true. If they are entitled to other than judicial relief, it cannot be admitted that in a government like ours, redress is not to be had in some of its departments; and the responsibility for its denial must rest upon those who have the power to grant it. But believing as I do, that relief to some extent falls properly under judicial cognizance, I shall proceed to the examination of the case under the following heads.

1. Is the Cherokee Nation of Indians a competent party to sue in this court?

2. Is a sufficient case made out in the bill, to warrant this court in granting any relief?

3. Is an injunction the fit and appropriate relief?

1. By the constitution of the United States it is declared (Art. 3, § 2), that the judicial power shall extend to all cases in law and equity, arising under this constitution, the laws of the United States, and treaties made or which shall be made under their authority, &c. and between a state or the citizens thereof, and foreign states, citizens or subjects.

The controversy in the present case is alleged to be between a foreign state, and one of the states of the union; and does not therefore, come within the eleventh amendment of the constitution, which declares that the judicial power of the United States, shall not be construed to extend to any suit in law or equity commenced or prosecuted against one of the United States by citizens of another state; or by citizens or subjects of any foreign state. This amendment does not, therefore, extend to suits prosecuted against one of the United States, by a foreign state. The constitution further provides, that in all cases where a state shall be a party, the supreme court shall have original jurisdiction.—Under these provisions in the constitution, the complainants have filed their bill in this court, in the character of a foreign state, against the state of Georgia;—praying an injunction to restrain that state from committing various alleged violations of the property of the nation, claimed under the laws of the United States, & treaties made with the Cherokee nation.

That a state of this union may be sued by a foreign state, when a proper case exists and is presented, is too plainly and expressly declared in the constitution to admit of doubt; and the first inquiry is, whether the Cherokee nation is a foreign state within the same sense and meaning of the constitution.

The terms state and nation are used in the law of nations, as well as in common parlance, as importing the same thing; and imply a body of men, united together, to procure their mutual safety and advantage by means of their union. Such a society has its affairs and interests to manage; it deliberates and takes resolutions in common, and thus becomes a moral person, having an understanding and a will peculiar to itself, and is susceptible of obligations and laws. Vattel, 1. Nations being composed of men naturally free and independent and who, before the establishment of civil societies, live together in a state of nature, nations or sovereign states, are to be considered as so many free persons, living together in a state of nature. Vattel 2, § 4. Every nation that governs itself, under what form soever, without any dependence on a foreign power, is a sovereign state. Its rights are naturally the same as those of any other state. Such are moral persons who live together in a natural society, under the law of nations. It is sufficient if it be really sovereign and independent: that is, it must govern itself by its own authority & laws. We ought, therefore, to reckon in the number of sovereigns those states that have bound themselves to another more powerful, although by an unequal alliance. The condition of these unequal alliances may be infinitely varied; but whatever they are, provided the inferior ally reserves to itself the sovereignty or the right to govern its own body, it ought to be considered an independent state. Consequently, a weak state, that, in order to provide for its safety, places itself under the protection of a more powerful one, without stripping itself of the right of government and sovereignty, does not cease on this account to be placed among the sovereigns who acknowledge no other power. Tributary and feudatory states do not thereby cease to be sovereign and independent states, so long as self government, and sovereign and independent authority is left in the administration of the state. Vattel, c 1, pp. 16, 17.

Testing the character and condition of the Cherokee Indians by these rules, it is not perceived how it is possible to escape the conclusion, that they form a sovereign state. They have always been dealt with as such by the government of the United States; both before & since the adoption of the constitution. They have been admitted and treated as a people governed solely and exclusively by their own laws, usages, and customs within their own territory; claiming and exercising exclusive dominion over the same; yielding up by treaty, from time to time, portions of their land, but still claiming absolute sovereignty and self government over what remained unsold. And this has been the light in which they have, until recently, been considered from the earliest settlement of the country by the white people.—And, indeed I do not understand it is denied by a majority of the court, that the Cherokee Indians form a sovereign state according to the doctrine of the law of nations; but that, although a sovereign state, they are not considered a foreign state, within the meaning of the Constitution.

Whether the Cherokee Indians are to be considered a foreign state or not, is a point on which we cannot expect to discover much light from the law of nations. We must derive this knowledge chiefly from the practice of our own government, and the light in which the nation has been viewed and treated by it.

That numerous tribes of Indians, and among others, the Cherokee nation occupied many parts of this country long before the discovery by Europeans, is abundantly established by history; and it is not denied but that the Cherokee nation occupied the territory now claimed by them long before that period. It does not fall within the scope and object of the present inquiry, to go into a critical examination of the nature and extent of the rights growing out of such occupancy, or the justice and humanity with which the Indians have been treated, or their rights respected.

That they are entitled to such occupancy, so long as they choose quietly and peaceably to remain upon the land, cannot be questioned. The circumstance of their original occupancy is here referred to, merely for the purpose of showing, that if these Indian communities were then, as they certainly were, nations, they must have been foreign nations to all the world; not having any connexion, or alliance of any description, with any other power on earth. And if the Cherokees were then a foreign nation, when or how have they lost that character, and ceased to be a distinct people, and become incorporated with any other community?

They have never been, by conquest, reduced to the situation of subjects to any conqueror, and thereby lost their separate national existence, and the rights of self-government, and become subject to the laws of the conqueror. Whenever wars have taken place, they have been followed by regular treaties of peace, containing stipulations on each side according to existing circumstances; the Indian nation always preserving its distinct and separate national character. And notwithstanding we do not recognize the right of the Indians to transfer the absolute title of their lands to any other than ourselves, the right of occupancy is still admitted to remain in them, accompanied with the right of self-government, according to their own usages and customs; and with the competency to act in a national capacity, although placed under the protection of the whites, and owing a qualified subjection so far as is requisite for public safety. But the principle is universally admitted, that this occupancy belongs to them as a matter of right, and not by mere indulgence. They cannot be disturbed in the enjoyment of it, or deprived of it without their free consent; or unless a just and necessary war should sanction their dispossession.

In this view of their situation, there is as full and complete recognition of their sovereignty, as if they were absolute owners of the soil. The progress made in civilization by the Cherokee Indians cannot surely be considered as in any measure destroying their national and foreign character, so long as they are permitted to maintain a separate and distinct government; it is their political position that constitutes their *foreign* character, and in that sense must the term *foreign* be understood as used in the constitution. It can have no relation to local, geographical, or territorial position. It cannot mean a country beyond sea. Mexico and Canada is certainly to be considered a foreign country, in reference to the United States. It is the political relation in which one government or country stands to another which constitutes it foreign to the other. The Cherokee territory being within the chartered limits of Georgia, does not affect the question. When Georgia is spoken of as a state, reference is had to its political character and not to boundary; and it is not perceived that any absurdity or inconsistency grows out of the circumstance, that the jurisdiction and territory of the state of Georgia surround or extend on every side of the Cherokee territory. It may be inconvenient to the state, and very desirable, that the Cherokees should be removed; but it does not at all affect the political relation between Georgia and those Indians. Suppose the Cherokee territory had been occupied by Spaniards or any other civilized people, instead of Indians, and they had from time to time ceded to the United States portions of their lands precisely in the same manner as the Indians have done, and in like manner retained and occupied the part now held by the Cherokees, and having a regular government established there; would it not only be considered a separate and distinct nation or state, but a foreign nation, with reference to the state of Georgia and the United States. If we look to lexicographers, as well as approved writers, for the use of the term *foreign*, it may be applied with the strictest propriety to the Cherokee nation.

In a general sense it is applied to any person or thing belonging to another nation or country. We call an alien a foreigner, because he is not of the country in which we reside. In a political sense we call every country foreign, which is not in the jurisdiction of the same government. In this sense, Scotland before the union was foreign to England; and Canada and Mexico foreign to the United States. In the United States all transatlantic countries are foreign to us. But this is not the only sense in which it is used.

It is applied with equal propriety to an adjacent territory, as to one more remote. Canada and Mexico is as much foreign to us as England or Spain. And it may be laid down as a general rule, that when used in relation to countries in a political sense, it refers to the jurisdiction or government of the country. In a commercial sense, we call all goods coming from any country not within our own jurisdiction, foreign goods.

In the diplomatic use of the term we call every minister a foreign minister who comes from another jurisdiction or government. And this is the sense in which it is judicially used by this court, even as between the different states of this union. In the case of Buckner vs. Finlay, 2 Peters, 590, it was held that a bill of exchange drawn in one state of the union, on a person living in another state, was a foreign bill, and to be treated as such in the courts of the U. States. The court says, that in applying the definition of a foreign bill, to the political character of the several states of this union, in relation to each other, we are all clearly of opinion, that bills drawn in one of these states upon persons living in another of them, partake of the character of foreign bills, and ought to be so treated. That for all national purposes embraced by the federal constitution, the states and the citizens therefore are one; united under the same sovereign authority, and governed by the same laws. In all other respects, the states are necessarily foreign to, and independent of each other; their constitutions and forms of government being, although republican, altogether different, as are their laws and institutions. So in the case of Warder vs. Arrell, decided in the court of Appeals of Virginia, 2 Wash. 298. The court in speaking of foreign contracts, and saying that the laws of the foreign country where the contract was made must govern, add—the same principle applies, though with no greater force, to the different states of America; for though they form a confederated government, yet the several states retain their individual sovereignties; and, with respect to their municipal regulations, are to each other foreign.

It is manifest from these cases, that a foreign state, judicially considered, consists in its being under a different jurisdiction or government, without any reference to its territorial position. This is the marked distinction, particularly in the case of Buckner vs. Finley. So far as these states are subject to the laws of the union, they are not foreign to each other. But so far as they are subject to their own respective state laws and government, they are foreign to each other. And if, as here decided, a separate and distinct jurisdiction or government is the test by which to decide whether a nation be foreign or not, I am unable to perceive any sound and substantial reason why the Cherokee nation should not be so considered. It is governed by its own laws, usages and customs; it has no connexion with any other government or jurisdiction, except by way of treaties entered into with like form and ceremony as with other foreign nations. And this seems to be the view taken of them by Mr. Justice Johnson in the case of Fletcher vs. Peck, 6 Cranch, 146; 2 Peters's Condens. Rep. 308.

In speaking of the state and condition of the different Indian nations, he observes, "that some have totally extinguished their national fire, and submitted themselves to the laws of the states; others have by treaty acknowledged that they hold their national existence at the will of the state, within which they reside; others retain a limited sovereignty, and the absolute proprietorship of their soil. The latter is the case of the tribes to the west of Georgia, among which are the Cherokees. We legislate upon the conduct of strangers or citizens within their limits, but innumerable treaties formed with them acknowledge them to be an independent people: and the uniform practice of acknowledging their right of soil by purchasing from them, and restraining all persons from encroaching upon their territory, makes it unnecessary to insist upon their rights of soil."

Although there are many cases in which one of these United States has been used by another, I am not aware of any instance in which one of the United States has been used by a foreign state. But no doubt can be entertained that such an action might be sustained upon a proper case being presented. It is expressly provided for in the constitution; and this provision is certainly not to be rejected as entirely nugatory.

Suppose a state, with the consent of congress, should enter into an agreement with a foreign power (as might undoubtedly be done, Constitution, Art. 1, § 10) for a loan of money; would not an action be sustained in this court to enforce payment thereof? Or suppose the state of Georgia, with the consent of congress, should purchase the right of the Cherokee Indians to this territory, and enter into a contract for the payment of the purchase money; could there be a doubt that an action could be sustained upon such a contract? No objection would certainly be made for want of competency in that nation to make a valid contract. The numerous treaties entered into with the nation would be a conclusive answer to any such objection. And if an action could be sustained in such case, it must be under that provision in the constitution which gives jurisdiction to this court in controversies between a state and a foreign state. For the Cherokee nation is certainly not one of the United States.

And what possible objection can lie to the right of the complainants to sustain an action? The treaties made with this nation purport to secure to it certain rights. These are not gratuitous obligations assumed on the part of the United States. They are obligations founded upon a consideration paid by the Indians by cession of part of their territory. And if they, as a nation, are competent to make a treaty or contract, it would seem to me to be a strange inconsistency to deny to them the right and the power to enforce such a contract. And where the right secured by such treaty forms a proper subject for judicial cognizance, I can perceive no reason why this court has not jurisdiction of the case. The constitution expressly gives to the court jurisdiction in all cases of law and equity arising under treaties made with the United States. No suit will lie against the United States upon such treaty, because no possible case can exist where the United States can be sued. But not so with respect to a state; and if any right secured by treaty has been violated by a state, in a case proper for judicial inquiry, no good reason is perceived why an action may not be sustained for violation of a right secured by treaty, as well as by contract under any other form. The judiciary is certainly not the department of the government authorised to enforce all rights that may be recognized and secured by treaty. In many instances, these are mere political rights with which the judiciary cannot deal. But when the question relates to a mere right of property, and a proper case can be made between competent parties, it forms a proper subject for judicial inquiry.

It is a rule which has been repeatedly sanctioned by this court, that the judicial department is to consider as sovereign and independent states or nations those powers, that are recognized as such by the executive and legislative departments of the government; they being more particularly entrusted with our foreign relations. 4 Cranch, 241, 2 Peter's Cond. Rep. 98; 3 Wheat. 634; 4 Wheat. 64.

If we look to the whole course of treatment by this country of the Indians, from the year 1775, to the present day, when dealing with them in their aggregate capacity as nations or tribes, and regarding the mode and manner in which all negotiations have been carried on and concluded with them, the conclusions appear to be irresistible, that they have been regarded, by the executive and legislative branches of the government, not only as sovereign and independent, but as foreign nations or tribes, not within the jurisdiction nor under the government of the states within which they are located. This remark is to be understood, of course, as referring only to such as live together as a distinct community, under their own laws, usages and customs; and not to the mere remnant of tribes which are to be found in many parts of our country, who have become mixed with the general population, of the country; their national character extinguished; and their usages and customs in great measure abandoned; self-government surrendered; and who have voluntarily or by force of circumstances which surrounded them, gradually become subject to the laws of the states within which they are situated.

Such, however, is not the case with the Cherokee nation. It retains its usages and customs and self-government, greatly improved by the civilization which it has been the policy of the United States to encourage and foster among them. All negotiations carried on with the Cherokees and other Indian nations have been by way of treaty with all the formality attending the making of treaties with any foreign power. The journals of Congress, from the year 1775 down to the adoption of the present constitution, abundantly establish this fact. And since that period, such negotiations have been carried on by the treaty-making power, and uniformly under the denomination of treaties.

What is a treaty, as understood in the law of nations? It is an agreement or contract between two or more nations or sovereigns, entered into by agents appointed for that purpose, and duly sanctioned by the supreme power of the respective parties. And where is the authority, either in the constitution or in the practice of the government for making any distinction between treaties made with the Indian nations and any other foreign power? They relate to peace and war; the surrender of prisoners; the cession of territory; and the various subjects which are usually embraced in such contracts between sovereign nations.

A recurrence to the various treaties made with the Indian nations and tribes in different parts of the country, will fully illustrate this view of the relation in which our government has considered the Indians as standing. It will be sufficient, however to notice a few of the many treaties made with the Cherokee nation.

By the treaty of Hopewell of the 28th November 1785, 1 Laws U S. 322, mutual stipulations are entered into, to restore all prisoners taken by either party, and the Cherokees stipulate to restore all negroes, and all other property taken from the citizens of the United States; and a boundary line is settled between the Cherokees and the citizens of the United States, and this embraced territory within the chartered limits of Georgia. And by the sixth article it is provided, that if any Indian, or person residing among them, or who shall take refuge in their nation, shall commit a robbery, or murder, or any other capital crime on any citizen of the United States, or persons under their protection, the nation or tribe to which such offender may belong shall deliver him up to be punished according to the ordinances of the United States. What more explicit recognition of the sovereignty and independance of this nation could have been made? It was a direct acknowledgment, that this territory was under a foreign jurisdiction. If it had been understood that the jurisdiction of the state of Georgia extended over this territory, no such stipulation would have been necessary. The process of the Courts of Georgia, would have run into this as well as into any other part of the state. It is a stipulation analogous to that contained in the treaty of 1794 with England, 1 Laws U. S. 220, by the 27th article of which, it is mutually agreed, that each party will deliver up to justice, all persons who, being charged with murder or forgery committed within the jurisdiction of either, shall seek an asylum within any of the countries of the other. Upon what ground can any distinction be made, as to the reason and necessity of such stipulation in the respective treaties. The necessity for the stipulation in both cases must be, because the process of one government and jurisdiction will not run into that of another; and separate and distinct jurisdiction, as has been shown, is what makes governments and nations foreign to each other in their political relations.

The same stipulation, as to delivering up criminals who shall take refuge in the Cherokee nation, is contained in the treaty of Holston of the 2d of July 1791, 1 Laws U. S 327. And the eleventh article fully recognizes the jurisdiction of the Cherokee nation over the territory occupied by them. It provides, that if any citizen of the United States shall go into the territory belonging to the Cherokees, and commit any crime upon, or trespass against the person, or property of any friendly Indian, which, if committed within the jurisdiction of any state, would be punishable by the laws of such state, shall be subject to the same puishment, and proceeded against in the same manner, as if the offence had been committed within the jurisdiction of the state. Here is an explicit admission that the Cherokee territory is not within the jurisdiction of any state. If it had been considered within the jurisdiction of Georgia, such a provision would not only be unnecessary but absurd. It is a provision looking to the punishment of a citizen of the United States for some act done in a foreign country. If exercising exclusive jurisdiction over a country is sufficient to constitute the state or power so exercising it a foreign state, the Cherokee nation may assuredly with the greatest propriety be so considered.

The phraseology of the clause in the Constitution, giving to Congress the power to regulate commerce, is supposed to afford an argument against considering the Cherokees a foreign nation. The clause reads thus, "to regulate commerce with foreign nations, and among the several States, and the Indian tribes." Constitution, Art 1, § 8. The argument is, that if the Indian tribes are foreign nations, they would have been included, without being specially named, and being so named imports something different from the previous term of "foreign nations."

This appears to me to partake too much of a mere verbal criticism, to draw after it the important conclusion, that Indians are not foreign nations. But the clause affords, irresistibly, the conclusion, that the Indian tribes are not there understood as included within the description of the "several States;" or there could have been no fitness in immediately thereafter particularizing "the Indian tribes."

It is generally understood that every separate body of Indians is divided into bands or tribes, and form a little community within the nation to which it belongs; and as the nation has some particular symbol by which it is distinguished from others, so each tribe has a badge from which it is denominated, and each tribe may have rights applicable to itself.

Cases may arise where the trade with a particular tribe may require to be regulated, and which might not have been embraced under the general description of the term *nation*, or it might at least have left the case somewhat doubtful; as the clause was intended to vest in Congress the power to regulate all commercial intercourse, this phraseology was probably adopted to meet all possible cases; and the provision would have been imperfect, if the term "Indian tribes" had been omitted.

Congress would not then have regulated the trade with any particular tribe that did not extend to the whole nation. Or, it may be, that the term *tribe* is here used as importing the same thing as that of the term *nation*, and adopted merely to avoid the repetition of the word nation: and the Indians are specially named, because there was a provision somewhat analagous in the confederation; and entirely omitting to name the Indian tribes, might have afforded some plausible grounds for concluding that this branch of commercial intercourse was not subject to the power of Congress.

On examining the journals of the old Congress, which contain numerous proceedings and resolutions respecting the Indians, the terms "nation," and "tribe," are frequently used indiscriminately, and as importing the same thing; and treaties were sometimes entered into with the Indians, under the description or denomination of tribes, without naming the nation. See Journals 30th June and 12th July, 1775; 7th March, 1776; 20th October, 1777, and numerous other instances.

But whether any of these suggestions will satisfactorily account for the phraseology here used or not, it appears to me to be of too doubtful import to outweigh the consideration to which I have referred to show that the Cherokees are a foreign nation. The difference between the provision in the constitution and that in the confederation on this subject appears to me to show very satisfactorily, that so far as related to trade and commerce with the Indians wherever found in tribes, whether within or without the limits of a state, was subject to the regulation of congress.

The provision in the confederation, Art. 9, 1 Laws United States, 17, is, that congress shall have the power of regulating the trade and management of all affairs with the Indians not members of any of the states, provided that the legislative right of any state within its own limits be not infringed or violated. The true import of this provision is certainly not very obvious; see Federalist, No. 42. What were the Legislative rights intended to be embraced within the proviso is left in great uncertainty. But whatever difficulty on that subject might have arisen under the confederation, it is entirely removed by the omission of the proviso in the present Constitution; thereby leaving this power entirely with congress, without regard to any state right on the subject; and showing that the Indian tribes were considered as distinct communities although within the limits of a state.

(*Concluded on fourth Page.*)

den, all of this city.

On the 28th ult. by the Rev. Mr. Cuyler, at Poughkeepsie, Mr. Charles S. Phelps, merchant, of Staten Island, to Miss Harriet Butler, daughter of Charles Butler, Esq. of Poughkeepsie; and at the same time and place, Lieut. John C. Carter, of the U. S. Navy, to Miss Elizabeth S. Phelps, daughter of B. B. Phelps, Esq. of New-York, and sister of Charles S. Phelps.

At Blauveltville, Rockland county, on the 28th ult. by the Rev. Mr. Thompson, John Nichol, of the firm of Trowbridge & Nichol, of this city, to Juliana, daughter of the Rev. Andrew Thompson, of the former place.

DIED.

Yesterday, William Knowlton, formerly of Hartford, Vt., aged 27 years.

Last evening, Stewart C. son of S. C. March, aged 14 months.

At Brooklyn, L. I., on the morning of the 29th ult. John, only child of Capt. George Hughes, of the scarlet fever, aged 2 years and 6 months, after an illness of six days.

At Brooklyn Heights on Friday the 1st inst. Teunis Joralemon, Jun. son of Judge Joralmon.

The relatives and friends of his father, are requested to attend his funeral this afternoon at 5 o'clock, from the house of his father, upper end of Hicks-street.

At the residence of Col. James Brown, in Maury county, Tenn., on the 3d of June, Jane Brown, born the 22d of June 1740—died in the 91st year of her age. Her husband James Brown, was murdered, in her presence, by the Cherokee Indians, on the 9th of May, 1788, and herself and five children made prisoners. Her husband, in company with Colonels John and Daniel Gillespie, (her brothers,) were leading men and valiant soldiers at the battle of Guilford court house in the war of the Revolution. She lived through the struggles of those times, and was again with her family amidst the troubles and Indian cruelties, that marked the early history of Tennessee. She remained a prisoner among the Indians, with a daughter seven months old, for seventeen months, and amidst the troubles, trials, and privations, of Indian bondage, clung to her children with an intrepidity of affection, that brought her and them off together—except her son George, who remained five years a prisoner, and with a piety and patriotism unusual in later days, instilled into the youth of her children such a love of country, and hatred of tyranny, as made them dutiful sons, pious parents, valiant and patriotic soldiers. Her son, Colonel Joseph Brown, one, of the children made prisoners, still lives among us. He settled with his mother near Nashville, in the year 1792; his virtues as a son, neighbor, parent, and patriot soldier are known to all.—*West Mer.*

At Middletown, Conn., on the 25th inst. M. A. Raynaud, a native of Malta. This gentleman was formerly a Surgeon in the French Navy—he afterwards resided as a practitioner in the West Indies, (Trinidad) and visited the United States in the hope of having his health improved by change of climate.

SHIPPING INTELLIGENCE.

ARRIVED,

Ship James Cropper, Garey, from Bristol, mdze.
Brig Martha, Edwards, from Amsterdam, with gin, &c.
Brig Martha, Edwards, 47 days from Amsterdam, with gin.
NEW-BEDFORD, June 29.—Arr. brig Thos. Winslow, Cornell, from Bahamas, with 119 bbls. oil.
Cl'd, brig Parthian, Hammond, South Atlantic.

TUESDAY EVENING, JULY 5.

DEATH OF JAMES MONROE.

Yesterday, about half past 3, P. M., the venerable Ex-President, James Monroe, expired at the residence of his son-in-law, Samuel Gouverneur, Esq., in this city. The event has been for some time past expected, and, for the last few days, momentarily looked for. His spirit was permitted to linger in th body until his country's birth-day came, and departed while a grateful nation, for whose independence he had fought and bled,—which venerated him while living and hallows his memory now, as in the front rank of its benefactors,—was holding its universal Jubilee.

Thus of the six former Presidents, by a coincidence for which it would be difficult to find a parallel in history, three have been called away in a good old age, on the same proud anniversary. Their fellow-citizens knew not in the midst of their rejoicings, while arms were glittering, salutes resoundind and bells ringing gladsome peals, that death was dealing with the fathers of their country. Else had "the day been darkened and the pomp o'ercast." While we write, minute guns are firing, and the bells tolling; and the sad solemnities due to the honored remains of one of the very few "last of the Romans" will soon succeed the festivities of yesterday. The moral illustration this affords is too striking to need being pointed out.

Mr. Monroe's biography is written in the annals of his country; and the events of his life are connected with those prominent in the pages of her history, from the time when, while yet a youth, he bled in her service at Trenton,* until recently he sat in the Convention which amended the constitution of his native State. During his administration of the government, the nation flourished in unexampled prosperity; developing its unlimited resources with vast rapidity, and maintaining with dignity its peaceful relations with all the world. To him may with truth and peculiar aptness be applied the eloquent apostrophe of Tacitus to Agricola,—'*Tu vero felix, non tantum clantate vitæ, sed etiam opportnnitate mortis.*' Happy is it for his country, that the reproach of total ingratitude cannot in his instance be cast upon her. The long withheld debt was paid, just in time to save her honor, and to gild the evening of his days, which had else, after all the obligations she owed him, closed in sorrow and penury.

Mr. Monroe was born in September 1758, in the County of Westmoreland, Virginia, and died in his 73d year. In September last he lost his wife, long the cherished companion of his prosperity as well as of his adversity. Embarrassments and afflictions no doubt contributed to hasten his decease. His desire of returning to Virginia, and there closing his days, was often and earnestly expressed.—We learn that he retained all his mental faculties to the last, and was perfectly composed and calm.

When the noise of firing began at midnight, he opened his eyes inquiringly; and when the cause was communicated to him, a look of intelligence indicated that he understood what the occasion was. There can be little doubt that the simultaneous departure of his two predecessors on the same day was present to his mind.

We understand that the funeral will take place from the house of S. Gouverneur, Esq. on Thursday next, at 4 o'clock, P. M. We presume it will be recommended from the proper quarter, to the citizens generally, to close their stores and shops during the movement of the procession.

* We have been been favored with the following memorandum in relation to his military services. He entered the army at 18 years of age, and marched under Washington as a Lieutenant, in the retreat through Jersey. He volunteered to attack the Hessians at Trenton, and assumed the command of his company when Captain Washington fell. He was severely wounded in the neck, and carried from the field. He stood by La Fayette, when the latter was wounded at Brandywine; and was subsequently selected by Congress to command a regiment, which was to be raised by Virginia.

LATEST FROM ENGLAND.

By the arrival on Saturday of the ship James Cropper from Bristol, London papers of the 18th were received, and Bristol papers of the 31st, containing London dates of the 30th. No news of specific importance was contained in them, except an account of a gallant expedition into Volhynia by General Chrzanowski, the particulars of which will be found among our extracts.

ENGLAND.

All is quiet in this country and the greatest confidence entertained by the people in the success of the Reform Bill.

The King has conferred the order of the Garter upon Earl Grey.

The distress in Ireland continues to increase.

The report of O'Gorman Mahon's having been killed in a duel, is without foundation.

It is said that the patent creating the Lord Mayor of the city of London a baronet, is in progress, and will be announced in Friday's Gazette.

Money Market and City Intelligence, Friday Evening, May 27.—The Stock Exchange transactions are still, more or less, under the influence of the settlement of the account. In fact there has not been for many years an occasion of the kind which has produced so much inconvenience and mischief among the members of the Stock Exchange. Not only the immediate connexions of the parties who have become defaulters, but a majority of the whole body, have suffered perhaps directly or indirectly by the failures. Several small failures have occurred to-day, but fewer than might have been anticipated, and none at all approaching in magnitude to the two first announced. The scarcity of stock, as regards Consols, has a good deal diminished since yesterday, and on the other government securities, of which not being at all the subject of speculative transactions, there has been all along an abundance, money could have been obtained to-day on more favorable terms. The prices are well maintained, and unusually free from fluctuation. Consols for the opening in July left off at 83⅝ to ¾, and for money at 83¾ to ⅞. Exchequer Bills are at 7s. to 8s. premium.

The Foreign Stock Market presents no new feature. The prices are there also well maintained. No speculation of the least moment is at present going on in any of the foreign funds.

Additional failures had taken place among the London stockjobbers, which made a momentary sensation, from the effect they produced on private interests.

"An amnesty is expected in favour of the exiled Piedmontese. It is said that Austria has already turned her attention to the affair."—*Times.*

The Princess Butera, so celebrated for her beauty, wit, wealth, and her misfortunes, died recently at Naples. She married for her second husband a Hanoverian Lieut. named George Wilding, who is now at Vienna.

... of foreign wines upon which duty has been paid for home consumption imperial measure), for the year ending January 5, 1831, is 6,628,490, and the net amount of duty received, 1,524,177l. 18s. 3d.

Spirits.—The quantity of spirits (imperial measure) exported from Ireland to England, during the year ending January 5, 1831, is 426,322 gallons. The quantity of spirits exported from Scotland to England, during the year ending January 5, 1831, is 2,724,221 gallons; to Ireland, 1,006,493 gallons.

Salt.—The quantity of foreign salt imported into Great Britain and Ireland in the year 1830, amounts to 373,128 bushels.

Tobacco and Snuff.—The quantities of leaf Tobacco, manufactured Tobacco, and Segars, and Snuff, entered for home consumption in the United Kingdom, for the year ending the 5th January, 1831. amount to 29,406,402 lbs.—The amount of duty received thereon is 2,938,050l. 10s. 10d.

Half Pay.—The half-pay and retired allowances, civil and military, paid in the year 1830, is as follows:

	l.	s	d.
Army : :	2,939,606	9	6
Navy : :	1,531,646	17	11¾
Ordnance : :	357,090	0	0
Civil Department :	485,370	18	7
Total	5,313,714	6	0¾

FRANCE.

London, May 29.—We have just received by express the French papers of Thursday, which contain nothing to countenance the report of the sudden return of the King of the French to Paris, as reported in the following letter of our Dover correspondent, who, we have reason to believe, has in all respects been grossly misinformed. These papers contain nothing worthy the delay of extracting:—

"Dover, May 27.—A report has reached us this afternoon, by the arrivals from France, that an Austrian army of 100,000 men is marching to invade France. The King of the French has certainly been suddenly recalled from his tour, to Paris; whether in reference to the above affair or not we must leave for time to determine. Mr. Crotch, one of the Government messengers, arrived this afternoon from Rome."—*Correspondent of the Globe.*

A great number of Frenchmen are proceeding to Algiers by Toulon, in order to settle in that country, where they can easily procure land at a rent of 2 francs 50 cents per acre.

Cholera Morbus.—A letter received from St. Omer states that symptoms of that dreadful disease the Cholera Morbus, have appeared among some English families in that town. We trust our Ministers will take every precaution to keep the horrid disorder on the other side of the channel.—*News.*

The Courier Francais gives the following as rumors of the day:—"The diplomatic circles have been occupied within the last month on the subject of an interchange of notes, to which great importance is attached. M. Casimir Perrier has sent to both Vienna & Berlin, requiring either an entire or partial reduction of the present exorbitant military establishments, which, by exciting alarm, paralyze commerce. The Cabinet of Vienna replied, that Austria required nothing better than to place her army on the footing of peace, but that this could not be done till certain important questions, connected with the present state of Poland and Italy, were decided. France rejoined that these questions had been settled by the Congress of Vienna, and that nothing prevented the Powers from coming to an understanding as to the events that have taken place since the revolution of July, and modifying the stipulations of the Congress of Vienna; that with regard to Italy, Austria had even exceeded her rights in exercising an interference in the police of the Italian states, and that these states could no longer form a pretext for new armaments. In what related to Poland, the overtures of the Emperor Nicholas having been rejected, it had been represented to him, that as the present state of Poland might disturb the peace of Europe, France and England conceived it essential to call the attention of his Imperial Majesty to the Conventions of Vienna, which secured the constitutional independence of Poland. It is this last note that gave rise to the rumors of war that have been current lately."

French Funds.—*Paris, May* 25.—Five per Cents., 91f. 40c. 25c. 10c. 91f. 90f. 80c. 90c. 80c. 75c. 90f. 70c. 40c. 50c. 60c. 80c. 91f. 91f. 40c. 50c.; New Loan of 1831, 91f. 5c. 91f. 90c.; Four per Cents., 75f. 50c.

On the 17th inst. the students of the college of Braincon proceeded in a body to the Hotel de Ville, where they destroyed the busts of Louis XVIII and Charles X. and then demanded that an old white flag, that had been preserved as an historical memento, should be burnt the next day, which was promised them.

Paris, May 25th.—At one o'clock on Monday the King viewed the National Guards of Eu and the environs, amounting to 2,200 men, who were commanded by the Duke de Nemours, their colonel.

Several medals were then delivered. Afterwards the king visited Trepol, a small sea port a short distance from Eu, and went on board of some vessels in the roads.

At 5 o'clock the royal party returned to the Chateau.—His Majesty left Eu on Tuesday for Amiens, where he is to remain till to-morrow morning, when he will proceed to Beauvais, and in the evening arrive at Saint Cloud.

For some time a gastric fever has prevailed at Berlin, and at the present time no less than 30,000 persons are affected by it. The complaint is epidemic, but is not dangerous.

From the Times of the 28th.

BELGIUM.

By the Brussels mail, which arrived yesterday, we received the Belgic papers to the 25th. At Namur a conflict took place on the 22d between a company of Lancers and a corps of Volunteers, in consequence of which General Mellinet, who commanded the latter, was put under arrest. The unsettled state of the Government renders such instances of military insubordination by no means surprising. The proceedings of the Congress on the 23d are important, though the 22d Protocol, which appeared in our paper of yesterday, had not been communicated to the Belgian Legislature. It will, doubtless, give a still more interesting color to the discussions of that assembly. We are, indeed, informed that the communication of that document has actually been made to the Belgian Minister for Foreign Affairs, accompanied by a note, requiring the assent of his Government to the award of the Five Powers on or before Wednesday next.

The Dutch Government, it is said, has refused to acknowledge the receipt of the overture for a negotiation between Belgium and Holland, made by M. Lebeau, the Belgian Secretary for Foreign Affairs.

[The Protocol above referred to, is excluded for want of room.]

London, May 30th.—Although the discussions concerning the election of Prince Leopold to the throne of Belgium have not yet commenced, it is evident, from the preliminary proceedings and the express declaration of the deputies, that his Royal Highness will have a great majority of the Congress in his favor. Out of 122 of the members present, 96 declared themselves his supporters, and only two pronounced themselves against him, the rest reserving their votes.—*Times.*

POLAND.

LONDON, May 30.—The latest news from Berlin is to the 21st, and from Warsaw to the evening of the 17th inst. at which time no news had arrived of the then hourly expected collision between Diebitsh and Syrzynecki. Both armies are manoeuvring—the Russians to operate against Warsaw on the opposite side of the Vistula from the previous line of action, and the Poles to defeat this fresh assault on their capital. The country upon the line of march was desolate, and the cholera morbus, according to our pri... letters, frightfully extending its ravages; it had spread into Austrian Gallicia. In Lithuania the Russian are pursuing a savage extermination. They are hanging and shooting even their wounded prisoners, and the peasants and scattered Polish partizan corps are executing on the spot in their turn; a terrible retaliation.

The French papers of Friday, contain a long report (copied from a Warsaw paper) of the proceedings of the Lithuanian insurgents, presented to the National Government of Poland by an Envoy from Lithuania. The insurrection is said to have extended to Grodno and Minsk, and the Government of Wilna alone is said to have 60,000 insurgents under arms. They have established provisional governments, and have begun founderies of gunpowder.—The peasants fight with the greatest bravery against their Russian oppressors, and "if Lithuania falls," says the report, "she will carry to her grave the consoling idea that she preferred to sacrifice every thing rather than supply arms and means to subjugate the Poles and their common country."

The Russians have sent back to Warsaw two doctors made prisoners at Minsk. The Russians at Lublin have become a great prey to the fever; in the hospital at Opoli they have 6,000 sick.

Commercial letters from St. Petersburg state that the Russian officers of the Court, and other nobles of the land, are clothing, arming, equipping, at their own expense, an army of 100,000 men to march against the Poles.

From the London Times of the 27th.

We publish with unfeigned satisfaction, letters from Warsaw, bringing intelligence from the Polish armies so late as to the 16th—only 11 days old. Those communicate a gallant and important exploit of the Patriot General Chrzanowski, who was despatched by the Commander-in-Chief with a corps of 8,000 men to disturb the left flank and rear of the Russian army, an expedition into Volhynia, which was conducted with marvellous intrepidity and success, that brave officer bursting through successive lines of Russian posts, beating the enemy in several engagements, and though in the midst of 24,000 Russians, under Generals Kreutz and Witt, capturing 800 prisoners, with which he entered the fortress of Zamosc in triumph. The main object of this well-conceived and brilliant enterprise was to substitute a new force in Volhynia for that which, since the misfortunes of General Dwernecki, has been withdrawn from the patriot cause, by the more than dubious unfriendliness of Austria towards the Polish liberties. The new chieftain has thus proved himself at the outset a worthy successor to the brave and skilful Dwernecki; though we trust he is not destined to experience the same vicissitude of war, or the same treachery from pretended neutrals.

The Prussian Government, it grieves though it does not surprise us to see, has begun the game of "cordons sanitaires" against the emancipation of Poland. If the English and French Cabinet once put themselves in motion, the old comrades of Russia in the crimes of the 18th century had better behave with more circumspection in what belongs to the laws of neutrals.

The Allgemeine Zeitung states that it is at length determined that the soldiers of Dwernecki's corps shall be sent in several detachments to Transylvania and Moravia and that Laybach is assigned to General Dwernecki and the majority of his officers as their abode.

TO THE NATIONAL GOVERNMENT.

I have the honor to announce to the National Government, that the Gen. Chrzanowski occupies Kock, where he fell in with the rear guard of the Russian General Thiemen, composed of Cossacks, and of the cavalry regiments of Czarnomorski and Attamanski, which are considered as the *elite* of the Russian light cavalry. This rear guard also consisted of many detachments, making part of the third corps of the cavalry of reserve.

Without the loss of a single soldier, General Chrzanowski made 158 prisoners in Kock, among whom are four officers. ... baggage wagons, loaded with various military effects, and another carrying portable camp chapels; a magazine containing a considerable quantity of cloth also fell into his possession. An aid-de-camp of General Kreutz, named Kindrakoff, is among the prisoners; lastly, he took 393 Polish florins in silver, which has been forwarded to the general military chest. The regiments Czarnemorski and Attamanski saved themselves by swimming across the river Wieprx, near Lysobiki. SKRZYNECKI.

Jedrzejow, May 11, 1831.

TURKEY.

Letters from Constantinople of the 25th, and from Smyrna of the 19th ult. have been received. The Sulton was using great exertions to put down the insurgents in Albania and elsewhere. An army of 30,000 men, with a large train of artillery, had assembled near Adrianople, and was preparing to march against the rebels; and a squadron, composed of a frigate and several sloops, had sailed for the coast of Albania to blockade its ports. If his men remained faithful, little doubt was entertained that the Sultan would triumph at last over the rebels. But there seems to be a good deal of apprehension on that point, as a great number of desertions had lately taken place among the troops under the order of the Grand Vizier; and the cause of the rebels appears to be more generally popular than that of the Sultan. The fact is, that three-fourths of the male population of the Ottoman empire were members of the corps of Janissaries, and if the Sultan had succeeded for a time ... discontent, for having forcibly disbanded that corps, he has not been equally fortunate in securing popularity to the system by which it has been suspended. If discontent at the measures of the Sultan had not been generally prevalent, he would not have been so wholly forsaken by his subjects as was the case in his last war with Russia.

It is deplorable to see the obstinacy with which the partizans of perpetual barbarism and national degradation oppose all views and measures tending to their amelioration; but had Mahmoud adopted less sanguinary means than those to which he has had recourse for the execution of his praiseworthy designs, it is probable that he would have secured the support of a much greater number of his subjects than has been the case. It is by a system of terror alone that he has ever sought to enforce obedience to his will, and this has proved by no means the surest mode of conciliating the numerous portion of those who are inimical to his views. Among the difficulties by which he is at present surrounded, the want of money does not appear to be the least. He had extorted loans from most of the wealthy Jews in the capital, which the lenders well knew he would never repay. Most of the Armenians, who had formerly possessed wealth, had been already stripped by him of all they possessed, and therefore could no longer supply his wants. His Greek subjects have long ceased to have much to give, and his Mahometan ones are not disposed to allow his innovations to extend to taxation over themselves. Under these circumstances, the Sultan's affairs were in such a precarious state, that the loss of a single battle with the rebels would it was feared by those who wished him well, lead to his dethronement, and possibly to the loss of his life. There were still many in the capital who were ready to rise against him the moment that a good opportunity occurred.

At Smyrna English trade was very brisk. A great number of ships were loading for England. The exchange there was 78½, and at Constantinople 79½.

Constantinople, April 25.—Daud Pacha, the rebellious governor of Bagdad, has submitted to the Porte.

The Turkey mail arrived this morning, with accounts from Smyrna of the 19th, and from Constantinople to the 26th ult. They are generally silent as to the insurrections mentioned in French papers; there is, however, no doubt a great movement, as 500 persons were put to death in one night, and a great number of bodies had been seen in the Bosphorus; but the details we are unable yet to give.—*Times.*

Belgrade, May 7.—We learn from Nissa, under the date of the 28th of April, that the vanguard of the insurgents, commanded by the Pacha of Wrana and Persorein, attacked on the twenty-first of April, the Grand Vizier's troops near Pielepo, but was completely beaten and put to flight with the loss of 1000 men. Mustapha Pacha, on hearing this news, immediately advanced to repair the disaster, and met with the Grand Vizier's troops on the 23d. A terrible battle began, and the cannonade was heard the whole day, but the result is not known. The mail from Constantinople has arrived here by way of Sophia as usual.

We learn with satisfaction, through the German papers, that the troops of the Sultan have gained advantages over the Pachas who had rebelled against the civil and military institutions of this reforming Prince.

Letters from Semlin contradict, in the most positive manner, the intelligence of the defeat of Reschid Pacha, and his decapitation. They heard at Belgrade, that the Grand Vizier had attacked and beaten the insurgents. A price has been set on the head of the Pacha of Scutari. Proclamation to that effect has been made in all the mosques of Constantinople.—*Augsburg Gaz.*

ITALY.

The following is an extract from the Dauphinois:—Savoy is tranquil, and, like Piedmont, waits for the effect of the good dispositions acquired from the new King.—Like Piedmont, it is ready to use every exertion to crush the Austrian influence, and to unite itself to France sooner than recognise as a sovereign a slave of Metternich.

"The Piedmontese troops, being aware of the approach of the numerous corps of Austrians, are continually on their guard. The tendency of feeling, which under Charles Felix was concealed, but is really in Favor of the French, scruples less to show itself since the acession of the Prince of Carignan to the throne. The soldiers in general burn with the desire of coming to open hostilities with the oppressors of Italy.

SPAIN.

The *Ami de la Charte* gives an account of the capture of Beranger, one of the most notorious chiefs of the bands in the district round Vitre, who, with several of his associates, was taken on the 17th.

The Breton gives an account of the arrest of another Chouan chief, named Duclos, who belonged to the ex-royal Guards. On the 15th, 4,000 men arrived at Vitre, and took up their quarters in the town and neighbourhood. It appears, by a letter from St. Brieux of the 14th, that a rather serious engagement had taken place between a brigade of gendarmes, stationed in Plumiex, near Lachese, in the Cotes du Nord, and a party of Chouans, in which the gendarmes, from inferiority of numbers, were forced to retire, and being again suddenly attacked by surprise in their quarters, they were disarmed by the rebels. One of the gendarmes is missing; but it is reported that he was killed.

"Private letters from Madrid of the 10th instant announce that some persons are daily hanging there, but that they are merely robbers. As for persons accused of political transgressions, the military commission is in no haste to try them, but rather endeavours to make them forgotten, and to save them, because they belong to families whose powerful interest has succeeded in softening the judges."

These letters give also vague and uncertain rumours of the rising of the peasantry, brigands, and others. They seem entitled to so little credit that we do not publish them.

A case of some importance was recently decided in the Courts of Lower Canada. In 1794, Jean Doriegani, an alien, came to the province with three sons and a daughter, all *aliens*, and acquired real estate. By his will in 1800, he constituted his sons his universal legatees, bequeathing a pecuniary legacy to the daughter. He left the province afterwards, and died in his native country. The daughter married, and the plaintiffs in the suit, issue of the marriage, brought their action to recover the land from their uncles. They contended, and it was so decided by the Court, "that by the law of France, an *alien* might acquire and hold real estate, of which he might dispose, by sale deed, or gift, donation, or other mode of conveyance, to take effect during his natural life; but that he could not devise except in favor of his natural born children, neither could he be inherited to by his natural descendants, *alien born*; so much so, that the natural born grandson could exclude his alien father from the succession."

The country possessing its own local jurisdiction, it was adjudicated that recourse must be had to the laws of France; and judgment was given for the plaintiffs.

Peter B. Davis, who was acquitted on the charge of murder, at the Special Court held in Newark last week, was yesterday morning arraigned on three indictments for forgery, pleaded guilty to them all, and was sentenced to twenty-four years imprisonment in the State Prison. As he is considerably above fifty years of age, it is scarcely probable that he will outlive the term of his confinement; and it is probable that the Jury, knowing he could never go at large, gave on this account more weight to the doubts in his favor, on the trial for murder.

Counterfeit.—We were shown this morning a counterfeit five dollar bill on the Morris Canal Bank. Its general appearance is good, and would be taken by those not very conversant with the signature of the Cashier, which is not a good imitation. The paper, also, is of a lighter texture than the genuine bills. It is dated January 1, 1831, payable to Jno. Hone, Jun., C. D. Colden, President; Robert Gilchrist, Cashier.

Charles Carroll.—Intelligence was received on Saturday that the venerable survivor of the signers of the Declaration of Independence, was dangerously ill, and not expected to recover.

A student of the Virginia University, lately made a calculation, founded on data derived from the most accurate tables of mortality, that the chances were more than 1721 millions to one, that Jefferson and Adams would not both die on the day upon which they actually expired.

Dividends.—The Neptune Insurance Company have declared a dividend of six per cent. for the last six months, payable on demand.

The New York Insurance Company have declared a dividend of five per cent. for the last six months, payable the 11th inst.

Yesterday morning at 9 o'clock, a child was bitten by a mad dog, in Walnut-street. The animal was pursued and shot, after having bitten another dog.

Col. Trumbull's Gallery.—We learn with pleasure that the exhibition was visited yesterday by the Mayor and both boards of the Common Council, by the members of the Cincinnati, and by great crowds of citizens. This is as it should be.

☞ A communication, relative to the Grand Lodge, will receive attention on the return of the Editor, to whom it is addressed.

PORTUGAL ... Miguel ... an advertising friend, and we have always treated him and his works very tenderly, on that account, as all our readers know. Our correspondent, who asks for the insertion of the subjoined well written communication, ought, regularly, to have forwarded it to the Editors of the National Intelligencer; as the communication to which it is a reply originally appeared in that paper, and the almost proverbial urbanity of those gentlemen would have insured for it a courteous reception. We have consented, however, at his instance, and because it contains facts, belonging, in a manner, to history, to give it an insertion; looking for our pay to Queen Maria da Gloria, when she gets her rights. If there be any personal allusions of an offensive kind, we do not understand them.

To the Editors of the Commercial Advertiser.

Gentlemen—A writer who signs himself *aisdamonaj*, (some Scandinavian deity no doubt) but whom we shall style *d'Asam-ja*, for abbreviation's sake, only using a few of the many letters he is pleased to assume for a cognomen, has found the editors of the Washington *National Intelligencer* kind enough to insert in their paper of the 13th inst. a long communication on the subject of an article in that same paper of the 28th May, headed *France and Portugal*. It is not the first time that the columns of that journal have been open to articles from the same pen, under different signatures, all tending to vindicate the conduct of the aptly called *Monster*, Miguel, unfortunately, of Portugal; and forsooth why should *he*, this same *d'asam-ja* not write and endeavor to vindicate him with all his might? "It is money makes the bear to dance." We hope the editors of that paper will show their impartiality and goodness by inserting the present article.

This writer would make us believe that what has been said on the subject of the cruelty, tyranny, and despotic sway of Miguel, is a tissue of falsehoods, with the only object of disturbing the *happiness* enjoyed by the Portuguese nation under the *mild* and *pexemlary* government of the *King our Lord by the Grace of a Faction*.

He denies that "Bonhomme" was flogged in the streets of Lisbon. He would also deny, no doubt, that "Claude Souvenet" was sentenced to ten years' transportation to the infected climes of Massangano, Africa, and for why? because———but here are the very words from a document before us, published at Lisbon, by order of the existing government—"that in his porter house No. 78, in the street of the Arco do Bandeira, some agents of the aforesaid revolution met; that the soldiers who were bribed over would go there, to whom was freely and gratuitously offered Porter and Biscuits; that from the said porter house they would go to a fourth story of a building opposite, where the meetings of the Revolutionists took place, and where porter and biscuit would be sent from the porter house. The defendant denies that his bar-keeper had his authority for so acting; and furthersays, he was wholly ignorant of their proceedings, because he resided at a great distance, in Valde Pereiro: but this denial and plea of ignorance, do not exculpate him, for he is answerable for what is done in the porter house, being owner thereof; and also that he acknowledges in the interrogatories put to him, that he was advised by his clerk to make his escape, which proves a connivance between the defendant and his clerk. He is besides affected to liberal ideas and republican principles, "(aye, here's the rub!)" as is proven by sundry newspapers found in his possession, but amongst which, however, no paper was found that can criminate him as to the premeditated revolution." Now here we have word by word the court's argument, upon which this man was convicted; and mark, it is drawn up and published by the government itself. We would appeal to this country of Jurors, and ask if any impartial twelve of them would, upon this evidence, have brought in a verdict of guilty against this man, for promoting the pretended revolution, which might have been discussed and agreed to in his very porter-house, and he still innocent; and in fact the very body of the document, above translated, acknowledges there was no proof against him, as an agent or abettor of this dreamed of revolution—*but he dared to hold liberal ideas and profess republican principles*: these were more than sufficient to condemn him. We only marvel at the mildness of the sentence—ten years imprisonment and hard labor—poh! the gallows would hardly atone for such impudence and mighty crimes.

And as we are quoting from this very *equitable* and *justifiable* document, we will endeavor to give one other example of the reigning mercy,—Maximo Joaquim Lopes and Joao dos Santos e Oliveira, the first condemned to be transported for *life*, and the second for *ten* years, to Mocambique, Africa, upon the following evidence: "Against these defendants it is proved that they had a knowledge of the projected Revolution, and did not give information thereof; for so it is sworn to by the witness Marques at folio 106; who declares he was spoken to on the subject of the revolution. The defendants absolutely deny they had any knowledge of it, and set forth the bad character and reputation of the said witness, adding that although they had made signs to him near the public promenade, still those signs were not for a revolution, but to give him to understand they were going to the theatre of the Rua dos Condes after the first act;" and upon similar grounds, with little more or less variation, were twelve human beings disposed of at the same time, seven of whom were sentenced to be strangled, the heads separated from the bodies and all consumed by fire, and the ashes scattered to the winds; others transported for life, and a few for ten years, to the African colonies, a sure and lingering death. The gallows for these last would have been more merciful.

That there are laws in Portugal we will grant to Mr. "d'Asam-ja," and that there are judges also; and would to God the first were sacredly discharged by the latter; but they are venal hirelings for the execution of their masters' blood-thirsty propensities. As a further illustration of our saying, this appears the proper opportunity to mention the fact that Col. Perestrello, one of the victims judicially murdered in March 1829, was arraigned, tried, convicted, and executed, under the assumed name of Lieut. Vellez! The witnesses for the prosecution swore that the said Perestrelio was Vellez, under whose orders they had served in the same regiment!! It was only after this unfortunate nobleman's head was severed from his body, and stuck on an iron pike, that the baseness of the evidence was ascertained by the public, and his features and real name recognised!!

These examples will prove the evidences *clearer than noon-day*, which Mr. "d'Asam-ja" asserts (in suspicious Latin) are required by D. Miguel's Courts of Justice, in order to inflict punishments—and such as these are the *full convictions of guilt* that demand judgment at their hands. This same "d'Asam-ja" will please bring to his recollection the condemnation, and execution of Mr. Brito of Oporto, for the *crime* of having given a dinner to some constitutionalists, then lately arrived there from England; he *ought* to recollect this glaring outrage, and Nero-like tyranny; for Mr. B. was, if we mistake not, a *near relative* to this same correspondent now at Washington, or thereabouts. Such as these are the feelings of the partisans of Don Miguel—let America appreciate the estimation such a party deserves, who endeavor to exculpate the murderers of their fellow-citizens—ay, of their very relatives, and who dig the grave of their common country!

This correspondent would make us believe that the *generous* and *gallant* French nation, as he hypocritically calls it, (for as a Miguelite he must hate her,) will not demand reparation for misdemeanors of Miguel's government towards her subjects: "for," says he, "we must believe the courts of Portugal, acting in conformity with their laws, have not done any thing for which they deserve to be blamed." Our Washington *friend* little dreamed, while penning his last communication, that Miguel himself would have given him the lie so soon; for among the dismissals for glaring outrages, demanded by the British nation, we find that (and in the *Lisbon* Gazette, too, of which only the idea was so indigestible to Mr. d'Asam-ja,) of the judge, Silva Belforte—and mark—one of the Bench who condemned the Frenchman, Souvenat, and the others already alluded to, and who had a hand, no doubt, not only in the outrage committed against the Englishman, Roberts, but also in the arrest of Mr. O'Neil—by the bye, another relative of Mr. d'Asam-ja, if we err not.

The display of Decrees in the Lisbon Gazette of the 4th May, in acquiescence to the demands of England, must have horror stricken this vindicator of Miguel's rights to the throne, and defender of his *lenient* government; they were as unexpected to him as they are degrading to that cowardly and dastard Prince, who finds no credit in London since the bankruptcy of the firm of Wellington, Aberdeen & Co.

Mr. d'Asam-ja appears to question that remonstrances have been made by France, and if made, "why should they," says he, "be less respectful of Portugal? (D. Miguel.) Why more neglectful of the usual forms among civilized nations, than in those which France has employed in negociating with other countries?" &c. He argues as if D. Miguel were an acknowledged sovereign among the European nations—as if he governed in conformity with the laws of the country he tyrannises over. D. Miguel is an outlaw among the crowned heads of Europe; he cannot, therefore, be treated as on a par, and from his conduct, must be intimidated and forced to act towards foreigners with due justice and equity. Would to God he could be compelled to act so likewise towards the Portuguese; but it is to be hoped the time is at hand, when they may arouse from the panic which his atrocities have created, and hurl this *Leech* from the throne he has usurped and disgraced.

Such eulogiums of D. Miguel & the *present* justice of the Courts of Portugal, under his control, as the writer of the communication alluded to has been in the habit of lavishing, since his residence in this country, might very well pass unanswered and unmasked among the oppressed Portuguese nation, in the Octavo Official, and only "Gazette of Lisbon" wherein his idol has been likened to the Archangel Michael! Not so in these United States, where, thanks to her liberal and unequaled political institutions, the press is free to all and every one.

We are now anxious to see the arguments this same Mr. "d'sam-ja" or "Aisdamonaj," (who appears to have them at his fingers ends, to suit every purpose, and every color) will use to justify the contents of the Lisbon Gazette of 4th May, with the unalterable equity of Miguel's Courts of Justice.

CASTRO.

New-York, 17 June, 1831.

* Mr. d'Asam ja was editor, if we are not in error, of this Gazette—it was *then* a government *constitutional* paper.—*Dict. des Girouettes.*

Aligatorical Eloquence.—The following extract is said in the Illinois Gazette to be a fair sample of the demi-civilised oratory of Jackson dimagogues in that quarter.—We doubt it not. It smacks of being genuine; and we will be bound that the Boanerges who executed it, was half-horse, half-alligator, and a touch of the earth-quake.

Gentlemen—I'm for Jackson! though I say it myself—yet I say it any how, Jackson is all horse, and I'm his friend through fire and thunder. You see gentlemen Indians I dont go in for a man's holding an office too long, and old Hickory says he wishes he may be shot if he's going in for Presidential chair longer than the next time of the 'lection.—Now dont yot see how consideration he is—see he wants to let Clay *take a fork* at Washington. And more nor that, he's opposed to appointing members of Congress, he gave them their walking papers quicker,—I mean Van Buren, Ingham, Branch, Eaton, &c. And he has now got a set that never were in Congress, and he says if they ever wish to be he's done with them. Now you see gentlemen Indians, I take the right look at these matters, and though I say it myself, Jackson is the best man in America—there aint no man that is the *first beginning of a man*—no not a *priming* compared to the old General and he's a *republicau* too, *at that*. Now I'll give you a history of Henry Clay, from the *first jump* of him. No. I'll be d———d if I do neither, for he aint *no account*. Come Gentlemen let's liquor and than I'll *explaterate* more. Now, Gentlemen, I seem to have more spirit than I had afore and I'll just *whale* it *into* that Van Buren—don't you see how old Jackson *flung* him the minute he began his d———d John Quincy Adam's ways of writting long letters—don't you take the idea—by gosh did he think Old Hictory was such a blasted fool, as he looked. Now just think of a fellow living in the same town and to set down and write a letter to another chap! caze he was too d———d lazy to walk a mile or so! why did'nt Van just go and *tell* the old man he wanted to *break for high timber*? He thought Jackson could'nt write *no more than a shot gun*, and I'll tell you more—folks says that Van was rascal enough to write old Hickory's answer, and that's worse than counterfeiting—blast him! Come let's liquor again—come here to Jackson and blast all his *satellites*! Spawn I mean.

From Smyrna.—By the brig Palestine, arrived at Boston from Smyrna, we have received a letter from a correspondent at that place, with the Courier of April 3d.

The monopoly of opium had been transferred from Smryna to Constantinople; but on a petition from the Frank merchants it was to be restored, and hopes were even entertained that it would be destroyed. The Courrier strongly edvocates the heroic Poles.

At the Central School at Ægina, in Greece, there have been unfortunate disturbances among the pupils.

From the Baltimore American of Saturday.

Various and very exaggerated reports have been in circulation during the last two days, in relation to the disorderly conduct of the workmen employed on the third division of the Baltimore and Ohio Rail Road, in consequence of the failure of one of the contractors to pay them their wages.—The particulars of this affair, as far as they had transpired up to Thursday night, are thus detailed in the Gazette of yesterday afternoon:—

"The misconduct of one of the contractors to lay rails on the third division of the Baltimore and Ohio Rail Road, in omitting to apply the funds he had received from the company, to pay the workmen hired by him, the wages due for their labor, had excited among a portion of them much discontent, which having come to the knowledge of the directors, an agent was deputed to inquire into the circumstances, who, during last week, had several interviews with the discontented workmen, which resulted in an arrangement that appeared generally satisfactory to them. Under that arrangement, the agent on the part of the Company, and with the consent of the contractor, had agreed to apportion among the workmen the whole balance of money which the contractor would be entitled to receive for the work done.

On Wednesday last, the agent having proceeded to the appointed place, met the workmen, prepared to comply with the arrangement as agreed on; but a portion of the workmen then declared themselves dissatisfied, because the amount proposed to be paid was much less than what was due to them from the contractor, and threatened to destroy the rails and other works of the company unless the whole demand was paid. With this demand the agent informed them he was neither prepared nor authorised to comply.—Some of the workmen evinced a disposition to accept of the payment pursuant to the terms agreed on; but this was prevented by the disaffected, who, in proof of their determination to put their threats in execution, commenced the work of destruction in presence of the agent. He immediately returned to this city, and communicated the information to the directors.

On application to Judge Hanson, a warrant was issued to the Sheriff of Baltimore county, requiring him to arrest the persons engaged in the riotous proceeding, and the Sheriff proceeded the same night to the house of a gentleman in the neighborhood of the rioters, intending to summon a sufficient number of the nearest inhabitants to enable him to execute the warrant.

Yesterday (Thursday) information was received from the Sheriff, that sufficient force could not be obtained in the immediate neighborhood to sustain the civil authority, and enable him to arrest the rioters, who had chosen a leader and declared their determination to proceed in injuring the road, and destroying the property of the Company. A requisition was then made of the Officers of the Militia of the city, by whom a force was promptly furnished, which we have no doubt has proved adequate to effect the object. They departed from the city on Thursday night after nine o'clock on this unpleasant expedition."

The detachment marched to the Pratt-street Depot about nine o'clock on Thursday night, in a soaking rain, and, when they left the paved streets, through mud frequently more than ankle deep. A number of deputy sheriffs and bailiffs accompanied them. They were conveyed on the Rail-road to Ellicott's Mills, and after a short detention, the carriages proceeded on the Second Division until within about two miles of its termination, where their further progress was arrested by the working cars left on the Road.—The detachment alighted, and having formed the order of march, proceeded along the line to the commencement of the Third Division, which they reached about day-light. As they advanced along the line, they made prisoners of a number of the rioters, a portion of whom were found asleep in their cabins. Many were evidently taken by surprise, being entirely unaware of the approach of a military body to aid the civil authority, and a few made attempts to escape. The detachment marched about seven miles on the Third Division, assisting and supporting the Sheriff in the discharge of his arduous and fearlessly executed duty. Among the persons arrested are those who are known to have been the promoters and ringleaders of the outrageous proceedings directed against the work of the Rail-road. In many places the stone rails have been defaced on the upper side, and the iron rails torn off, and at the quarries a large quantity of prepared granite rails has been broken or otherwise injured.—The wooden rails were either mutilated or burnt. No material injury was sustained by the bridges or culverts. The amount of damage done is variously estimated, and although no precise judgment can be at present formed of its true extent, it is believed that it will not exceed, directly, five thousand dollars. The rioters, to the number of forty, were brought into town yesterday evening, in charge of the detachment, and were safely lodged in jail to await the judgment of the law.

The Sheriff has remained on the line of the road, for the purpose of making further arrests, and to prevent further violations. He is supported by an armed body which volunteered for the duty out of the main detachment. The officers who accompanied the detachment were Generals G. H. Steuart and S. C. Leakin, Cols. B. C. Howard, S. Barry, and B. U. Campbell; Major E. L. Finley; Captains Deems, Hickman, Cook, Hodgkinson, and Pindell; and Majors W. H. Van Wyck and Geo. Brice, aids to Generals Steuart.

The following letter from the General commanding was received yesterday afternoon:—

To the Honorable Nicholas Brice,
Chief Justice of Baltimore City Court.

Sykes's Mill,
8 o'clock, A. M. 1st. July, 1831.

Sir—Our detachment from the Light Brigade, with the aid of the Rail-road cars, advanced rapidly to this place, distant about thirty-two miles from Baltimore, on the route of the Rail-road.

We left the cars about day-light below the Forks of Patapsco, and on the march from that place we surprised and arrested a number of person suspected, and several well known to be concerned in the recent riotous proceeding on *this* division of the road.

The combination has been a formidable one, and much injury has been done from the forks of the River for ten miles upwards. The second Division has not sustained any injury. Fortunately the beautiful bridge across the Patapsco, twenty six miles from town, *is safe*. I believe, however, it was the intention of the rioters to blow up this bridge in the course of this day. In a few minutes we shall take up the line of march homeward, leaving a detachment here, and you may expect us early this evening.

Very respectfully,
Your obedient servant,
G. H. STEUART.

The name of the defaulting contractors is Truxton Lyon, of Pennsylvania.

BRIGADE ORDERS.

First Light Brigade, M. V. 1st July, 1831.

It must be satisfactory to the public to know that the duty assigned by the civil authority to the light Brigade, has been promptly, successfully, and humanely executed. The small force hastily collected at a late hour yesterday evening, proceeded during the night to the scene of depredation on the third division of the rail-road, where they arrived at day light, (distant about twenty-six miles from the city,) and this afternoon at half past 4 o'clock, the troops returned with about 40 prisoners; most of them are believed to have been active, and some of them are *known* to have been the principal transgressors in the recent riotous proceedings.

Great injury has been done on the third division of the road commencing at the 26th mile from Baltimore, but the intended blowing up of the fine granite bridge over the Patapsco at the 28th mile, fixed upon for this day, was happily prevented by the seasonable appearance of the troops.—Every attention was paid to the comfort of the corps on duty by the officers and agents of the Rail-road Company, and it is due to the Messrs. Sykes, and also to Mr. Whitter, at Sykes' Mill, to acknowledge the great hospitality and kindness which they manifested on the occasion.

Brigadier General Leakin of the Artillery brigade volunteered to accompany the expedition, and his active exertions and those of the officers in the United States service and others who accompanied the expedition, are duly appreciated. Much is due to Captain Ripley of Fort McHenry for his obliging assistance, without which there would have been delay in the departure of the troops, for want of ball cartridges. It must not be concealed from the generous citizens of Baltimore that there is a great suffering and distress among the families, especially the wives and children of the deluded workmen on the third division of the rail-road, who engaged in the recent riots, and of course prompt assistance will be afforded to *those* unhappy sufferers—at the same time it may be looked for that the *offenders themselves* will be dealt with as justice may require, according to the evidence in each case.

It is a pleasing reflection to the commanding officer that no violence was resorted to, none being found necessary; and that a sufficient force was left at Syke's mill to preserve order and assist the Sheriff in arresting more of the rioters.

By order,
WILLIAM H. VANWYCK,
Brig. Maj. and Ins.

From the Patriot of Saturday evening.

This forenoon the military detachment which remained on the ground came into the city bringing with them eighteen more prisoners, who have been lodged in prison.

We understand that such was the confidence of the workmen in the integrity of the Contractor, that many of them, as well as others deposited their little funds in his hands for *safe keeping*. In this unpleasant business there are many innocent sufferers, particularly among women and children, for whom liberal supplies of provisions and clothing have been sent out; and many persons who have visited the place have contributed to their relief. Now that order is restored a new Agent will be immediately upon the ground and recommence the works.

From the Quebec Gazette.

The numerous friends of the Earl of Dalhousie in these Provinces, will participate in the satisfaction with which we publish the following news from India of, at least, a month later date, than the accounts copied in the London papers, of the serious difference existing between the Governor General and the Earl, as Commander in Chief on that station. The reports have evidently been much exaggerated, had so serious a step as His Lordship having been placed in arrest occurred, it is obvious that he could not have resumed his duties until his conduct had been investigated by higher powers, and that could only be done in England. But it will be seen that his Lordship was on the 4th January exercising the functions of his command and on a tour of military inspection.

Extract of a Letter from an Officer of the Staff of the Commander in Chief in India dated Benares—In Camp—4th January, 1831.—received at Quebec via Boston, 27th June, 1831.

"Lord Dalhousie's health is improved most amazingly, and His Lordship yesterday morning inspected a Brigade of three regiments of Infantry and a regiment of Cavalry—had a Levee of nearly 300 people in the afternoon—a large party at dinner, and in the evening attended a Ball given by the Officers of Cantonments, and did not feel in the least fatigued:—Lady D. is also in perfect health. We break ground to-morrow for the first time in the marching way and will inspect at every station as we pass along."

Storm.—On Friday last considerable damage was done to the crops in the southern section of this county by hail of a large size and a violent wind. In Charles Carr's neighborhood, the forest trees were blown down, and some injury done to the buildings. The hemp, young corn, and small grain were prostrated.—*Lexington Reporter.*

ANOTHER GREAT FIRE.

A most destructive fire occurred last night in the upper part of the city, which nearly destroyed an entire block of buildings, bounded on the north by Charlton, on the south by Vandam, on the east by Varick, and on the west by Hudson street, the value of which, with furniture, &c. is estimated at upwards of ONE HUNDRED THOUSAND DOLLARS. The fire spread with such rapidity, that many families barely escaped with their night clothing, and in one instance, a person was dragged from his bed, after the bedstead was on fire. In addition to the property destroyed, we regret to add that several persons are missing, whom it is feared have perished in the flames. Two children, who were left locked up in a room by their parents, who had gone to the Theatre, have not been found. Several firemen, we understand, are seriously injured.

The fire broke out in the carpenter's shop of Wm. J. Burke, in the rear of 66 and 68 Charlton-street. Mr. B. had a large quantity of lumber on hand, which was all on fire before the engines could reach the scene of conflagration; and unfortunately the distance from a supply of water was so great that a dozen buildings were in flames before a drop could be thrown on them. The chief supply was from the Hudson River, and when the fire broke out the water was so low that the suction rooted in the mud, and soon gravelled the boxes. From appearances this morning we have no doubt that many families are in great distress. It is computed that not less than *one hundred and twenty-five* families are rendered houseless by this disaster, several of whom, who resided in the rear, are reduced to beggary. One family we saw, a widow with several children, who had saved nothing but the few rags on them when they retired to rest.

The following is the result of our investigation, and we believe is correct so far as collected:—

On Vandam-street.—No. 67, a double two story frame building, owned by John L. Anderson, and occupied by Abraham Chatterton and Mr. Isaacs, partially destroyed.

No. 65, two story brick house, occupied by Capt. Beebee, and one other family, burnt down; not a vestige left.

No. 63, two story brick front building, together with large stables in the rear, owned and occupied by Mr. Martine, burnt down.

No. 61, two story brick house, owned and occupied by Mr. James Throop, and one other family, entirely destroyed.

No. 59, two story brick house, owned and occupied by Garret Hopper, destroyed.

No. 57. Two story brick house, owned and occupied by widow Green, and two or three other families, destroyed.

Next to the above was the Baptist Church, called the North Beriah. This was entirely destroyed—a frame building, and insured for $3,500, about one half of its value.

No. 53. Two story brick, occupied by Mr. Scott and Mr. Ingersoll, destroyed.

No. 51. Two story brick, occupied by Andrew Boden, and others, destroyed.

No. 49. Two story brick, owned by Jno. Demarest, occupied by Jasper Brockway, and Mr. Van Volkenburgh, destroyed.

No. 47. Two story brick house, occupied by Peter Bogart, and Mr. Townley, destroyed. A building in the rear of this, occupied by several families, was totally destroyed.

No. 45. Two story brick, occupied by James Jones, and two other families, destroyed—insured for $1,200.

No. 43. Corner of Varick, two story, brick front, owned and occupied by Anthony Compton, grocer, destroyed—insured for $1,500.

On Varick street.—Only two buildings are saved. One the store of Mr. Delano, on the corner of Charlton, the other a large livery stable, occupied by Mr. Sparks: the latter was considered fire proof—all the frame work of the windows was burnt.

No. 163. Two story building, owned and occupied by Mrs Lucinda Summerville, and a junk shop, destroyed.

No. 161. Two story brick, owned by Mr. Delano, occupied by Mr. Thorp, and Mr. Green, destroyed. This house had been insured until within a few hours of its destruction: the policy having expired.

On the corner of Charlton and Varick.—Mr. Delano—house slightly injured.

On Charlton-street.—No. 66 and 68, Mr. Burke's dwelling house and Carpenter's shop—destroyed.

No. 70, two story brick building—entirely destoyed—occupant not known.

No. 72, two story brick building, owned by Owen Haley, occupied by Patrick Hairu, Benjamin Oliver, and one other family—destroyed. A frame building in the rear of this, occupied by four colored families, destroyed.

No. 74, two story brick front, occupied by Thomas Thomas, John Lee, John Kittler, and Samuel Brown, destroyed.

Also, a two story frame building in the rear, occupied by Robert Small, Henry Smith, Robert Anderson and Mrs. Hulsey, destroyed.

No. 76, two story brick front, occupied by Messrs. Cole, Jones, Brower, and Berdon, destroyed.

In the rear of the last, two 2-story frame buildings, occupied by Joseph Griffeths, Mr. Culbertson, Mrs. C. Woolsey, Mr. M'Donough and John O'Donnell, destroyed.

No. 78, two-story brick front, occupied by Wm. Lewis, John Ackerman and Samuel Wallace, destroyed.

In the rear of the above, a two-story frame building, occupied by Mr. Anderson, Mr. Hopper, Edw. Shannon, and another family, destroyed.

No. 80, two-story brick front, occupied by John Green, Mr. Grey, Oliver Bloodgood and three others, destroyed.

No. 82, two-story frame building, owned by John Charters, occupied by Thos. Kinster, Mr. Scott, Geo. Smith, Mrs. Murphy and Samuel Young, much injured.

In addition to the foregoing, several back-buildings were destroyed.

The houses on the opposite side of Charlton-street were several times on fire, but, by the exertions of the firemen, were soon extinguished.

So far as we have been able to ascertain, about one half of the property destroyed was insured.

Yesterday afternoon about 4 o'clock, the roof of the drug-store, on the corner of Fulton and William-streets, was discovered to be in flames, but by the extraordinary exertions of an engine company, whose house is nearly opposite, the fire was soon subdued. This fire, and it is believed the extensive one of last night, were caused by the violation of the corporation law, in throwing squibs and crackers about the streets and into houses and yards. Besides the great loss of property, lives have thus been sacrificed.

We have just learned that a little son of Mr. Grinnell, the painter, aged about eight years, in attempting to take hold of the drag-rope of engine No. 24, was thrown down and trampled to death, by the company, who were not able to stop the machine in season.

PASSENGERS.

In the schr. Tallahasse, from Magnolia:—Mrs. Haskins and daughter, W. G. Burgess and lady, Mr. Chaus, Mr. Wilson, Mr. Stephens, Mr. Fuller, L. Goldsborough, N. L. N. and M. Lyon.

SALES THIS DAY AT THE STOCK EXCHANGE.

$10000	Ohio Sixes, 1850,	119
$10000	do do do do do do	119⅛
$800	Corporation Fives,	112
400 shares	United States Bank,	127⅛
20	do Delaware and Hudson Canal Company,	67¼
167	do do do do do do	67
200	do Mechanics and Traders Bank,	106
30	do Louisiana Exchange Bank,	121
210	do N. Y. Life Insurance and Trust Co.	119¼
20	do N. Y. State Marine Insurance Co.	102
50	do do do do do do	101⅛
10	do Globe Fire Insurance Company,	120
40	do Ætna Fire Insurance Company,	103
100	do Paterson Rail Road Company,	120
50	do do do do do do	119⅞
60	do Harlem Rail Road Company,	115⅞

MARRIED.

On Sunday evening, by the Rev. Mr. Baldwin, Mr. Silas Wood, to Miss Sarah Ann Cooper, all of this city.

DIED.

On the 2d inst. Mrs. Elizabeth Gale, in the 78th year of her age.

Yesterday afternoon, after a lingering, illness, Thomas Briscoe, in the 32d year of his age.

On the morning, of the 4th inst. Frances Evelina, only daughter of John T. Mayo, Esq. aged 15 months. She was laid in the same grave with the former companion of her father.

Suddenly yesterday morning, Capt. George Taylor, aged 77 years. His remains were taken to Catskill his former residence for interment.

SHIPPING INTELLIGENCE.

ARRIVED,

Ship James Cropper, Garey, Bristol, 31st May, to G. Gallagher & Co—92 steerage passengers. Left no Americans. Spoke, 3d ult, lat 30, long 10 30, brig Superior, (Br.) from Honduras for Jersey. Same time, brig James of Salem and brig Lucilla, both from Matanzas, latter for Bremen. 13th, lat 43 30, long 35 30, passed brig Thetis of Sunderland. 18th, lat 40, long 43, schr Lexington, of Rochester, whaling. 19th, lat 41, long 49, exchanged signals with Br. brig Sir William Wallace, bound East. 25th, at midnight, blowing fresh from N. N. E. was run foul of by a large ship standing east—the main yards became wrecked, and the lee braces giving way we cleared each other. We lost all the head yards, the main royal yard, the main sail, fore top sail, and main top gallant sail, were all much torn—the other vessels truck fell on our deck—having cleared each other very soon, owing to the tumult, we were unable to learn her name or destination.

NEW-BEDFORD, July 1.—Arr. brig Marcella, Swift, from Cagliara, and 50 days from Gibraltar.

Sailed, ship Emerald, Norton, South Atlantic.

2d, arr. sloop Rodman, Wood, from NYork.

3d, sailed, ships Condor, Luce, Brazil Banks; Minerva, Leonard, South Atlantic.

QUEBEC, June 26.—Arr; brigs Braganza, Gelling, fm Bristol; Hope, Colgin, Belfast; Minerva, Somerville, Yarmouth; schr Gleaner, Bascombe. Antigua.

THE MAN.

NO. 38.—VOL. I. NEW YORK, APRIL 4, 1834. PRICE ONE CENT.

GREAT MEETING OF MECHANICS AND WORKING MEN OF THE CITY OF NEW YORK.

" The greatest public meeting probably ever held in this city, was drawn together last [Wednesday] evening, at Tammany Hall, by the call of the mechan ics, Artisans, and other Working Men. Not merely was the great room of that edifice crowded, but the stair cases, halls, passages, and committee rooms, were all densely filled, and a multitude, consisting of several thousands, unable to obtain an entrance, took possession of the Park, there organized themselves, and adopted proceedings in perfect consonance with those of the meeting within the walls of Tammany Hall. Of the proceedings of that meeting it would be difficult to speak in terms of too extravagant approbation. There never was a more numerous, a more enthusiastic, or a more decorous public meeting, at any time, or on any occasion, in this city. The whole vast throng seemed actuated by one mind and one heart. The sentiments of the multitude were expressed in shouts so unanimous and accordant, that they seemed like the uplifting of one mighty voice. That voice, reaching the ears of those who were engaged in corresponding proceedings in the Park, was ever and anon answered by them with hearty cheers, which floating back to those who crowded the great room of Tammany Hall, seemed like the reverberated echo of their own loud acclamations."

We have thus far used the language of the Evening Post in relation to the meeting on Wednesday evening, because we could not make use of language more suitable for the occasion. The meeting was addressed, with eloquence that we never heard surpassed, by Messrs. E. J. Webb, Moore, Walton, Marsh, Bowie, and Carr ; and resolutions of the most patriotic character were passed with a unanimity and enthusiasm that left not a doubt on our mind as to the issue of the coming contest.

In listening to the patriotic remarks of the various speakers on this occasion, the conviction was forced upon us that *such* men were the founders of our constitution, and that had *such* men been continued in our legislative halls, the *rich* would not now be arrayed against the *poor* at our elections, for legalized monopolies and a spurious currency would not have made the many dependent upon the few for the means of existence, and there would have been but one class, a class neither rich nor poor, but the class of citizens enjoying in equality and abundance the fruits of their industry, and nothing more.

We would have given a year of our existence to have had present on this occasion, face to face with the assembled thousands, the national legislators who misrepresent the people by advocating the perpetuity of a chartered monopoly, a manufactory of spurious currency, the head of a system of spurious currency manufactories, which are preying upon the very vitals of the body politic. Had these men been present at the meeting, they would have heard clearly explained the cause of the evils which now oppress the useful classes, and they would, those, at least, of them who have a spark of honesty and patriotism in their composition, have returned to Washington determined to aid the honest efforts of the President to restore the Constitutional Currency.

The following is the official account of the proceedings of the meeting.

☞ **At a meeting of Mechanics and Working Men, held at Tammany Hall, on Wednesday evening, April 2d, James Connor was chosen Chairman, Joel Curtis and Robert Beatty, Assistant Chairmen; John Windt and William Dymock, Secretaries.** The call of the meeting having been read, it was moved that a committee of five retire to report resolutions expressive of the sentiments of the meeting; and the following gentlemen were appointed: Messrs. Bowle, Commerford, Darling, Fenwick, and Hill. During the retirement of the Committee, a unanimous call of the meeting elicited an eloquent and impressive address from Mr. Edward J. Webb, at the close of which he read several resolutions, that were heartily responded to, asserting the fact, that the prevailing money distress owed its origin not to the removal of the deposites, &c., but to a former error of Congress in chartering the Bank, thus giving some citizens exclusive privileges, contrary to the Constitution, &c. [The mover subsequently withdrew them, as they were connected with other matters not immediately relating to the objects of the meeting.]

Mr. Ely Moore having arrived at the meeting, an ardent call for him was continued, until he rose and was welcomed with the most enthusiastic cheering by the dense throng. After this expression of feeling had subsided, Mr. Moore delivered a patriotic address in favor of the objects of the meeting, distinguished alike for strength of argument, appropriate application, and beauty of diction; the breathless silence of the vast multitude, now and then broken by an outburst of feeling, is the best evidence of its commanding eloquence; while the truth of the reasoning was testified in the spontaneous and animated affirmatives of the assemblage. Mr. Moore sat down amid the most flattering testimonials of approbation. The following preamble and resolutions were then read and unanimously adopted.

PREAMBLE.

We, the Mechanics, Artizans, and other Working Men of the city of New York, feel it a duty we owe to ourselves and our country, to come forward at the present crisis, and give a decided expression of opinion on the great question that now agitates the nation.

We want but little more to convince us that the cause of the Bank is aristocratic and unjust, than the simple fact that we find the same men arrayed in its favor who have always been opposed to our best interests ; who endeavored to deprive us of the right of suffrage ; who opposed the last war, and almost every other democratic measure that has ever been brought forward in our State or General Governments. The presses that are now sounding the tocsin of alarm, and abusing our worthy, respected, and truly patriotic President, because he would not bow his neck to the Bank, and sell the Liberties of his Country for paltry Gold, are the same vehicles through which our would-be-aristocrats have heaped on us, the actual producers of that very wealth on which they found their respectability, every vile, filthy, and opprobrious epithet that their diseased imaginations could invent. When we find these men and their hirelings all at once pretending to have a wonderful sympathy for our interests, we conclude that their object is to cajole, wheedle, and deceive ; and when we are aware that they have threatened and are now threatening to discharge from employment those who can see through the cheat, and are independent enough neither to be bullied nor bought by them, we consider ourselves called upon to declare once for all ; that we know our own interest too well to be deceived ; we would not be worthy to have a vote did we allow any man to dictate how it should be given ; and we have nothing to barter but the labor of our hands. We are opposed to the United States Bank from *principle* and from deep conviction of its enmity to the best interests of every man who would wish to enjoy the fruits of his own industry.

It is an overgrown monopoly, with a power that no trading institution should possess. It boasts the power to crush nearly all our local Banks, to break half of our merchants and traders ; and in fact, judging from the language of the Bank presses, it has the power to regulate and control nearly all the commercial operations of the country. Now, although we are not willing to allow that it has all this power, yet we are well aware that it has more than it ever *ought* to have had, and that we must endure considerable privation and suffering before things find their true levil again after the Bank has received its death blow and ceased to exist. Still we believe the gloom will be only transitory ; and that the industry of our country, relieved from such an incubus, will spring up with fresh energy, and the sun of our prosperity shine with greater splendor than before.

Can we give way under a little temporary privation, when we recollect what the heroes of the Revolution suffered before their objects were achieved? Perish the thought! We will never allow the domineering and purse proud spirit of aristocracy to ride triumphant over that liberty and those institutions purchased by the blood of heroes. Nay, rather than see our Republic—the Polar Star of every lover of freedom throughout the earth—overthrown by a corrupt and powerful monopoly, not under the control of the People, we will endure every evil that flesh is heir to. Therefore be it

Resolved, That we view the approaching election as a contest exclusively of principle, in which the dearest interests of freemen are involved; one of moral and natural right against aristocratic usurpation; of honest industry against the corrupting influence of a monied monopoly; and embracing in its results, whether or not the sacred Charter of our Liberties shall be trampled upon by a proud, insolent, and overwhelming Faction.

Resolved, That an institution like the United States Bank, under the most favorable circumstances, would be dangerous to the liberty and happiness of the Republic; but on reviewing the past conduct of the present Bank, the high handed measure adopted to retain its power, to coerce the People and the Government, by preventing and entirely prohibiting the Government Directors from a participation in the management of its affairs, by speculating on the national credit, bribing and [illegible]ting the press, causing unnecessary distress [illegible]strious classes for an honest expression of [illegible]se reasons combined would carry conviction [illegible] every candid man, that its recharter would [illegible] subvert the Liberties of our Country.

Resolved, That the course pursued by our patriotic Chief Magistrate, in relation to the Bank of the United States, and the subsequent removal of the Government Deposites, deserves and will receive our hearty and undivided support.

Resolved, That the President and Members of Congress, who have determined to use their best exertions to restore the constitutional currency, merit the grateful acknowledgements of every working man and friend of the Constitution.

Resolved, That the present attempt of the hireling presses of the Bank to communicate and vilify our venerable and worthy Chief Magistrate, deserves utter contempt and detestation; his whole life has been devoted to the service of his country, the measures of his administration are truly patriotic, and his Veto on the Land Bill alone entitles him to our everlasting gratitude.

Resolved, That we are of opinion that the existing distress has been most rationally accounted for in the Report of the Committee of which Preserved Fish was Chairman, and James J. Roosevelt, jr. was Secretary; and the present efforts of a reckless set of politicians, and would be office holders, to increase and aggravate that distress, merit the condemnation of every good citizen.

Resolved, That we deprecate the conduct of certain employers of this city who have attempted to interfere with the right which every freeman ought to possess undisturbed—that of voting according to the dictates of his own mind on all public measures; and we pledge ourselves to resist every such attempt to coerce us.

Resolved, That CORNELIUS W. LAWRENCE is deserving of our unanimous support, being no new convert to the principles for which we contend. He was a candidate for Alderman of the 6th ward some years ago, and avowed himself at that time, when our principles were not so popular as they are now, in favor of all our leading measures. We call upon every man who values the existence of our liberties, and who wishes to see honor, principle, and consistency triumph, to come forward and give Cornelius W. Lawrence his decided support.

Resolved, That we will lay aside all minor considerations at the present contest, and support in our different wards those candidates, and those only, who are decidedly opposed to the Bank.

Resolved, That we recommend to the Mechanics and Working Men in the various wards to come out in their strength, and render every assistance in their power to the good cause in this struggle.

Resolved, That we view with distrust the course pursued by our opponents in calling on trades and occupations separately to express opinions on political subjects, as tending to create schisms and contentions among us as mechanics, and calculated eventually to overturn the great safeguard of our rights, a UNION OF TRADES.

A resolution was then offered by Mr. Commerford, and carried, disclaiming the idea of our State Legislature being in favor of continuing the prison monopoly, and in proof a notice of Mr. Humphrey's report on the subject to the legislature was read.

A number of speakers then addressed the meeting in a spirited and eloquent manner, among whom were Messrs. Bowie, Walton, Walsh, and Carr.

It was then unanimously Resolved, That a copy of the proceedings be transmitted to the President, and also to each member of Congress.

Resolved, That the proceedings of this meeting be signed by the Chairman and Secretaries, and published in all the democratic papers in this city. Adjourned.

JAMES CONNOR, Chairman.
JOEL CURTIS, } Assistant
ROBERT BEATTY, } Chairmen.

JOHN WINDT, } Secretaries.
WILLIAM DYMOCK, }

N. B. Several volunteer resolutions were passed, which it was deemed unnecessary to publish at length, their substance being embodied in those reported by the committee.

LETTER OF MR. LAWRENCE,

ON THE MEASURES OF THE WORKING MEN,

In answer to a Committee of the Working Men of the Sixth Ward, when a candidate for Alderman of that ward in 1831.

NEW YORK, March 26, 1831.

Mr. Henry Durell, Corresponding Secretary, &c.

SIR,—In reply to your communication, bearing date 17th inst. received by me last evening, I have no hesitation in avowing the sentiments I entertain on the subjects referred to by you, so far as I have been enabled to form opinions understandingly in relation to them. Perhaps under the existing circumstances in which I find myself unexpectedly placed by my fellow citizens, I ought to deprecate a course which might seem to court publicity to the opinions of a private individual; but, as the sentiments I shall avow are in strict accordance with former expressions, I do not perceive that I can withhold them without a violation of that courtesy which is due to the respectful terms in which the enquiries are couched.

Upon a review of the topics embraced in the code of measures to which you have referred, they appear to me to be principally such as cannot be affected by legitimate proceedings of any municipal bodies. Yet as the whole force of public opinion and public policy consequent thereon, receive an impulse from individual sentiment, I shall state freely the views I entertain, and by which my public conduct would be influenced should the kind intentions of my fellow citizens be realized, who have, in a manner and under circumstances which forbade a refusal on my part, placed me in the attitude of a candidate for public office.

In reference to the first subject—"Equal Universal Education"—I am a decided advocate of the universal diffusion of the lights of knowledge. I think that the advantages of education should be thrown open to all classes—that the spread of information, and the cultivation of intellect, should be coextensive with the increase of our population. On this subject I cannot be misunderstood—no man more ardently desires to see established, throughout our country, a school system on a firm and liberal basis, where the advantages of learning should be accessible to all who seek them. I am satisfied that the elevation of our national character depends more upon this, than upon any other separate measure of public policy.

On the subject of "Abolishment of Imprisonment for Debt"—I am decidedly of opinion that the measure is a just one, so far as the honest debtor is concerned. The debtor who surrenders his property for the benefit of his creditors can never be a proper subject for incarceration in a prison; but where different circumstances exist, and a debtor refuses to account with his creditors, or to surrender property known to be in his possession, I certainly think there should be some process of compulsion.

With regard to the "Present Militia System"—I am decidedly favorable to a revision—its operation now is essentially oppressive.

In reference to the "Abolition of all licensed Monopolies"—I am not fully aware that I understand the scope of the question. It is often more easy to find objections to existing errors than to apply a remedy. On the broad ground, I admit the justice of the general proposition, that it is objectionable to give any man or set of men, privileges which interfere with the just rights and liberties of others.

"A less expensive Law System," is a subject on which I am so little experienced that I do not consider myself competent to give a decided opinion in relation to it. Redress of injuries, and protection of rights and property, are guarantied

Report of the Post Master General.—This able document presents us with results, which are not only creditable to Mr. Kendall but are gratifying to his immediate friends and will prove satisfactory to the public at large.

It appears from the Report oft hePostmaster General, that after his accession to the office, on the 1st of May, such measures were taken, that, on the 1st July, the balance of the debts over the means of the Department, (excluding certain claims which the Postmaster General did not think himself authorized to allow,) was reduced to $23,700 59. Including these claims, the balance, then, against the Department, will stand $180,709 59. Such was the then improved condition of the Department, upon a summary of its debts and credits, supposing these last all collected in. As this could not be done, and as a large portion of the means of the Department taken into the above estimate, consisted of these balances due to it, not immediately available, the Report states the measures adopted, as calculated most speedily and satisfactorily to discharge the debts of the Department. The principle chiefly and properly acted upon, was to give preference to payments for services performed in the last quarter, throughout the Union, and apply the surplus to the extinction of the old debt.

Having pursued strictly the system adopted, the Postmaster General reports these results:

The payment of all the contractors throughout the Union, for services in the quarter in which he come into office, except some suspensions.

The payment of all such claims for the next quarter, as have been made ready for a justment.

The discharge of $187,086 of the old debt out of the postages since July 1st, of which $67,304 36 was to the banks.

Cash on hand $73,737.

Claims for arrearages are now paid as fast as they are presented, and can be adjusted.

Only about $205,000 now remain due to the banks. Of this one-half will be paid in January, and the balance in April.

After the extinction of the debt, and before the close of the present session of Congress, the Department will be in the receipt of an annual surplus of about $400,000, applicable to the extension of the mail routes.

Various improvements have been introduced into the financial operations of the Department.—The chief of these is the system of prompt collections from about 9,000 offices quarterly. No one can fail to perceive the benefit to result from this plan. It keeps the public money from lying idle in the hands of the receivers, subject to the accidents of death, insolvency, &c., and applies it at once to the payment of demands against the Department, without the agency of third persons, or the instrumentality of drafts, laboriously prepared in the office.

During the past fiscal year, the government post-routes covered upwards of one hundred and twelve thousand miles, and the mail were carried thereon nearly twenty-six millions of miles! The number of post offices on the 30th June, was ten thousand seven hundred and seventy.

Mr. Kendall complains of the monopolizing disposition evinced by several rail road companies, with whom he has not yet been able to effect any arrangement for the transportation of the mails.

In reference to the circulation of incendiary publications, he says:

"A new question has arisen in the administration of this department. A number of individuals have established an association in the Northern and Eastern States, and raised a large sum of money, for the purpose of effecting the immediate abolition of Slavery in the Southern States. One of the means resorted to has been the printing of a large mass of newspapers, pamphlets tracts and almanacs, containing exaggerated, and in some instances, false accounts of the treatment of slaves illustrated with cuts calculated to operate on the passions of colored men, and produce discontent, assassination, and servile war. These they attempt to disseminate throughout the slave holding states, by the agency of the public mails.

As soon as it was ascertained that the mails contained these productions, great excitement arose, particulaaly in Charleston, S. C, and to ensure the safety of the mail in its progress Southward, the postmaster at that place agreed to retain them in his office until he could obtain instructions from the Postmaster General. In reply to this appeal he was informed, that it was a subject upon which the Postmaster General had no legal authority to instruct him. The question again came up from the Postmaster at New York, who had refused to send the papers by the Steamboat mail to Charleston, S. C. He was also answered that the Postmaster General possessed no legal authority to give instructions on the subject; but as the undersigned had no doubt that the circumstances of the case justified the detention of the papers, he did not hesitate to say so. Important principles are involved in this question, and it merits the grave consideration of all departments of the Government.

It is universally conceded, that our States are united only for certain purposes. There are interests, in relation to which they are believed to be as independent of each other as they were before the constitution was formed. The interest which the people of some of the States have in slaves, is one of them. No State obtained by the union have any right whatsoever over slavery in any other state, nor did any state lose any of its power over it, within its own borders. On this subject, therefore, if this view be correct, the states are still independent, and may fence round and protect their interests in slaves, by such laws and regulations as in their Sovereign will they may deem expedient.

Nor have the people of one State any more right to interfere with this subject in another State than they have to interfere with the internal regulation, rights of property, or domestic police, of a foreign nation. If they were to combine and send papers among the laboring population of another nation calculated to produce discontent and rebellion, their conduct would be good ground of complaint on the part of that nation; and in case it were not repressed by the United States, might be, if perseveringly persisted in, just cause of war. The mutual obligations of our several states to suppress attacks by their citizens on each others' reserved rights and interests, would seem to be greater, because, by entering into the Union, they have lost the right of redress which belongs to nations wholly independent. What claims may be set up or maintained, to a right of free discussion within their own bordors, of the institutions and laws of other communities, over which they have no rightful control, few will maintain that they have a right, unless it be obtained by compact or treaty, to carry on such discussions within those communities, either orally, or by the distribution of printed papers, particularly if it be in violation of their peculiar laws and at the hazard of their peace and existence. The constitution of the United States provides, that "the citizens of each state shall be entitled to all privileges and immunities of citizens in the several States;" but this clause cannot confer on the citizens of one state, higher privileges and immnities in another, than the citizens of the latter themselves possess. It is not easy, therefore, to perceive how the citizens of the Northern States can possess or claim the privilege of carrying on discussions within the Southern States by the distribution of printed papers, which the citizens of the latter are forbidden to circulate by their own laws.

Neither does it appear that the United States acquired, by the constitution, any power whatsoever, over this subject, except a right to prohibit the importation of slaves after a certain date. On the contrary, that instrument contains evidences, that one object of the Southern States, in adopting it, was to secure to themselves a more perfect control over this interest, and cause it to be respected by the sister States. In the exercise of their reserved rights, and for the purpose of protecting this interest, and ensuring the safety of their people, some of the States have passed laws, prohibiting under heavy penalties, the printing or circulation of papers like those in question, within their respective territories. It has never been alleged that these laws are incompatible with the constitution and laws of the United States. Nor does it seem possible that they can be so, because they relate to a subject over which the U. States cannot rightfully assume any control under that constitution either by law or otherwise. If these principles be sound, it will follow that the State laws, on this subject, are, within the scope of their jurisdiction, the supreme laws of the land, obligatory alike on all persons, whether private citizens, officers of the State, or functionaries of the General Government.

The constitution makes it the duty of the United States, 'to protect each of the States against invasion; and, on application of the Legislature, or of the Executive, (when the Legislature cannot be convened,) against domestic violence.'—There is no quarter whence domestic violence is so much to be apprehended, in some of the States, as from the servile population, operated upon by mistake or designing men. It is to obviate danger from this quarter, that many of the State laws, in relation to the circulation of incendiary papers, have been enacted. Without claiming for the General Government the power to pass laws prohibiting discussions of any sort, as a means of protecting States from domestic violence, it may safely be assumed, that the United States have no right thro' their officers or departments, knowingly to be instrumental in producing within the several States, the very mischief which the constitution commands them to repress. It would be an extraordinary construction of the powers of the General Government, to maintain that they are bound to afford the agency of their mails and post offices, to counteract the laws of the States, in the circulation of papers calculated to produce domestic violence, when it would at the same time, be one of their most important constitutional duties to protect the States against the natural, if not necessary consequences produced by that very agency.

The position assumed by this Department, is believed to have produced the effect of withholding its agency, generally, in giving circulation to the obnoxious papers in the Southorn States. Whether it be necessary more effectually to prevent, by legislative enactments, the use of the mails, as the means of evading or violating the constitutional laws of the States in reference to this portion of their reserved rights, is a question which, it appears to the undersigned, may be submitted to Congress, upon a statement of the facts, and their own knowledge of the public necessities.

The postmaster general proposes reorganization of the department in several particulars; and his suggestions appear to be judicious. The most important is that relating to a new construction of the financial branch, so as to place it on the same footing with those of the other departments, and secure a more exact and responsible system of payments, by the appointment of an auditor. Mr. Kendall's views upon this subject are interesting, well expressed, and worthy of attention.

He suggests the expediency of altering the rates of postage, so as to make them conform to the national currency, in graduations of 5, 10, 15, 20, 25 and 30 cents, and so arrange the distances to which the rates are applicable, as to make them double at each increase of rate from the lowest to the highest. The effect of this arrangement would be a great increase of simplicity, and decrease of labor in keeping and examining accounts.

He pays a compliment to the various subordinate officers employed by the department, which we have no doubt is merited, and suggests the propriety of increasing their compensation; a suggestion in which we are disposed to coincide.

He pays a deserved compliment to his predecessor, and thus concludes:

The undersigned cannot close this communication, without paying a humble tribute to the worth of a patriot and friend—the late Postmaster General. It may be said of him, as the head of this department, that the reason he had not a better fortune was, he was too good a man. In other positions, and under other circumstances, he would have been one of the greatest and most useful as he was one of the best and most highly endowed of our public men. Having for more than twenty years been acquainted with Mr. Barry, and been honored with his friendship; knowing his private worth, his love of country, and his disinterestedness, and having always had an abiding confidence in his integrity and honor, it would be to the undersigned a source of lasting regret, if any thing said or done by him, in the administration of this department, should be understood as intended or calculated to depreciate his virtues or cast a stain upon his memory.

TWO DAYS LATER FROM LONDON.

The Packet ship Ontario, Capt. Huttleson, arrived off this port last evening from London, via Portsmouth. Capt. H. sailed from the latter port on the 2d November. By this arrival we have the London Courier of the evening of October 31.

The accounts from Spain continue to be highly favorable to the administration of M. Mendizabal. The directive Junta of Cadiz have made a report to the queen regent, in which, after expressing their entire satisfaction with the measures adopted and promised by the government, they offer their frank, decided and unanimous co operation in its efforts to restore peace and establish the throne of queen Isabella. The whole of the juntas have now submitted.

The government has issued a decree appointing a commission to restore harmony between the kingdom of Spain and the South American States which were formerly integral parts of the Spanish empire.

Various other measure of a highly popular character have been adopted.

Forces were concentrating upon the north, from all parts of the kingdom, and it was believed that within a short time the royalist troops opposed to Don Carlos, would amount to one hundred thousand men. The report of Gen. Iturrdale having joined the queen's party, with sixteen of his friends, is repeated and believed.

Advices from Egypt still announce a speedy resumption of hostilities against the Pacha by Sutlan Mahmoud.

The King of Prussia has pardoned 1380 out of 1400 inhabitants of the Dutchy of Posen, condemned to loose their property for assisting the Poles against the Russians. The fines imposed on the remainder have been reduced.

The papers still speak of a large reduction of the standing armies, by the five great powers of Europe.

The cholera appears to have disappeared from Genoa, and Leghorn, and to have much abated throughout the Roman and Neapolitan states generally.

A slight difficulty of etiquett has risen between lord Durham and the Russian commandant of Odessa, the latter having neglected to salute the British admiralty flag, displayed on board the transport ship in which his lordship had arrived at that port. The Russian excused himself on the plea that he did not know the flag, it having never before been seen in the Black Sea. The excuse is said not to have been satisfactory.

The marquis of Wateford arrived at Waterford from New York, on board his yatcht Gem, on the 27th of October.

DESTRUCTIVE FIRES.

About eleven o'clock last nigt, a fire broke out in the hardware store of Fullerton & Pickering, 173 Water street, which was entirely consumed with its contents. About three o'clook it again broke out and communicated to five or six adjoining houses which were completely distroyed. Messrs. Fullerton & Pickering were insured for $10,000, which it is believed will cover their loss. No. 171 was occupied by Joseph Barron, furrier, and by Mr. Hill as a boarding house. No. 169 by H. Huges & Co., dealer in saddlery. No. 167 was Mrs. Yeo's leather tore. The roof of 175, occupied by Wm. H. White, was broken in by the fall of a chimney.—We have not been able to ascertain the amount of loss, but we think it will not fall short of fifty thousand dollars, about one third, or one half, insured.

About three o'clock, another destructive fire broke out in Chrystie st. between Delancy and Rivington strs, which consumed seven two story brick buildings.

The firemen enacted wonders. The weather was, and is now, most bitterly cold.

The value of property destroyed at the Christie st. fire is estimated at $20,000. We do not know what portion was insured.—*N. Y. papers of Wednesday.*

The New Haven Herald states that Judge John M. Niles of Hartford, has been appointed by Gov. Edwards, to fill the vacancy in the U. S. Senate, occasioned by the death of the Hon. Nathan Smith.

Letters from Richmond, Va., say that the Whig members of the Legislature had held a meeting, and nominated Hugh L. White, as their candidate for the Presidency.

Ohio.—The Legislature of the State of Ohio met at Columbus on Monday the 7th inst. Elijah Vance was elected Speaker of the Senate, and William Sawyer Speaker of the House of Representatives. Both are Van Buren men. Vance received 19 votes against 16 for others, and Sawyer 45 votes against 23 for others.

Chicago—By a recent census, the population is ascertained to be 3,295. Cook Co. in which Chicago is siuated, has a population of 9,773.

The Rochester Daily Advertiser states that a correct account of the quantity of flour embargoed by the ice in the canal, has been taken, and that it is less than 40,000 barrels.

The waiter alone, in a first rate London Hotel, requires at least ten dollars a week from each person for his own private fees. Besides this there are other servants to pay, the bill exclusive. Two guineas are often charged for a room one evening, with a pair of wax candles. Stage-drivers at the end of a day's journey expect two shillings English (four shillings our money) extra from each passenger. Payment to ordinary servants in New York money, is as follows: for bed one night, two shillings to the maid—the porter two shillings—waiter two shillings—boots one shilling—all exclusive of the bill.—*N. Y. Mirror.*

MAP OF THE FIRE.

Believing that our readers will be anxious to understand the exact locality and extent of the fire, we have caused a plate to be engraved.—The black places indicate the premises swept by the conflagration; the small white squares and oblongs show the buildings saved. The spot where the fire began is shown by the letter X.

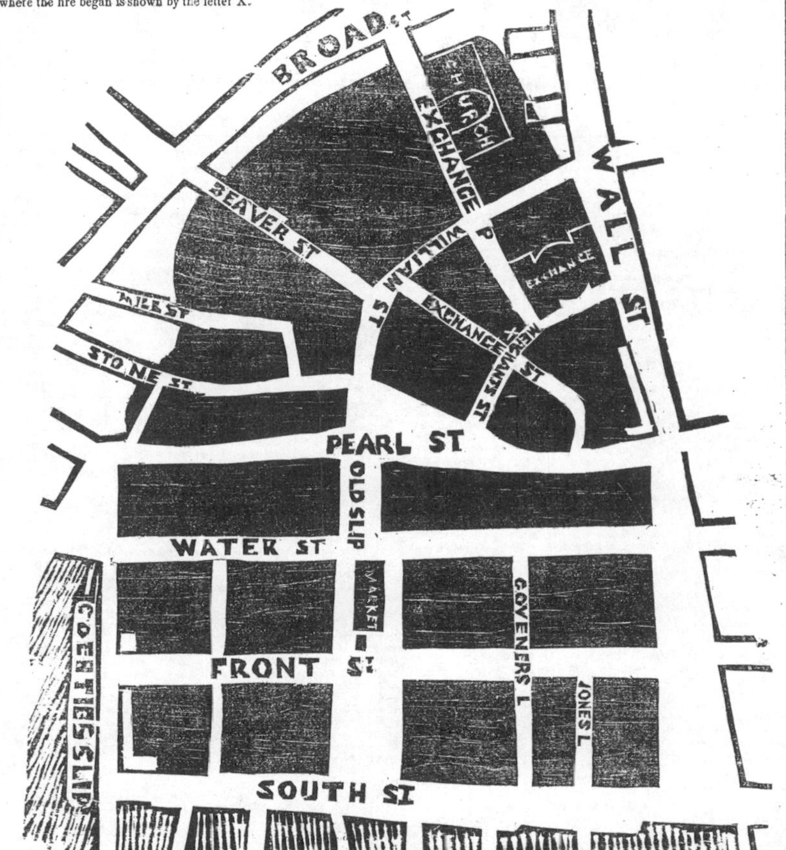

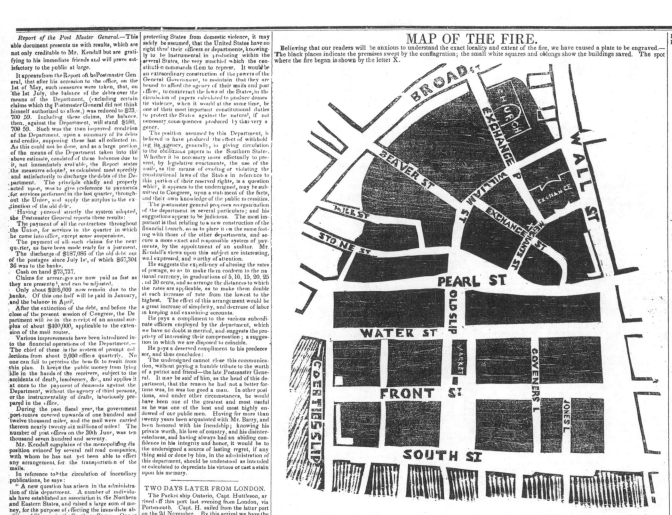

Destructive Conflagration !

Millions of Property Destroyed !!

New York has been SIXTEEN HOURS IN FLAMES. Since the conflagration of Moscow, no calamity, by fire, so extensive, and so dreadful, has befallen any city in the world.

The fire broke out in Merchant street, in the triangular block, formed by Wall, William and Pearl streets at about 9 o'clock Wednesday evening, Dec. 16. The weather was so cold the engines could not be worked. Powder was obtained from the Navy Yard and whole blocks of buildings were blown up in advance of the fire in order to stay the progress of the flames.

Excepting three or four buildings between Merchant and Pearl sts. the whole south side of Wall street from William street to the river was destroyed.

Also from William to Broad, greatly injured in the rear.

Exchange street both sides, from Broad street crossing William to Merchant street with Garden street Church.

Merchant street, both sides, from Wall street to Hanover Square.

William street, both sides, to Hanover Square.

Pearl street, both sides to Coenties Slip including the whole sweep of Hanover Square.

Stone street, from Hanover Square to the lane leading to Coenties Slip.

Exchange street and part of Beaver street from Pearl to Broad.

Water street, both sides from Coffee House to Coenties Slip.

Front street both sides, from Coffee House Slip to Coenties.

South street from Coffee House Slip to Coenties do.

South side of Coffee House Slip from Pearl st to East River.

Both sides of Old Slip, (including Franklin Market) from Pearl street to East River. North side Coenties Slip from Pearl to river. Jones' Lane, Governeur Lane, Cuyler's Alley and part of Mill street.

But little danger was done to the shipping.

The loss is estimated at $15,000,000. Amount of insurance on the property destroyed is about $10,000,000. Several of the Insurance Offices are ruined.

The Post Office, from which every thing was saved, has been removed to the Custom House.

The following is the number of buildings destroyed in different streets:

26 on Water street,	38 on Old slip,
79 on Pearl street,	16 on Coenties slip,
3 on South street,	60 on stone Street,
76 on Water street,	3 on Hanovers quare,
80 on Front street,	23 on Beaver street,
16 on Hanover street,	20 on Governeur's lane,
62 on Exchange place,	10 on Jones' lane
61 on Exchange street,	20 on Cuyler's alley,
44 on William street,	38 on Mill street,

Total 674

most of which were 4, 5 and 6 stories high.

PEARL STREET.

Nos.	*Occupants,*	*Business.*
73	Wm Van Antwerp & Co	hardware
74	Deniston & Disbrow	do
75	Veighte & Lippincott	crockery
	Samuel Aymar & Co	
	This store was blown up.	
76	Harris & Chauncey	china & earth'ware
	Towsend Harris	
77	John V Greenfield	
78	Suydam, Jackson & Co	merchants
79	Benjamin Stephens	
	J W & H P Corlies	Crock'ry
	N W Easton	
80	John Stewart & Co	dry goods
11	Ehl, Brailey & Co	
	Harris & Chauncey	
	Towsend Harris	
82	A & D Henry	
	Michael T Bergen	dry goods
	Jeanrenaud & Beguin	French import.
	Boynton & Brooks	dry goods
	Jackson, Deuel & Co	do
83	Underhil & Seymour	crockery
84	Gould & Conklin	dry goods
85	Tweedy, Mozier & Co	do
	John L H M'Cracken	importer
86	Kortright, Anderson & Co	dry goods
87	Weed & Little	
88	Flint & Bacon, Pearl St House & Ohio Hotel	
89	Gideon Frost & Co	dry goods
	Martin Mantin	French imp.
90	Doughty, Dibblee & Co	dry goods
91	Deraismes & Brother	French fancy
92	Marsh & Compton	dry doods
	William Bloodgood & Co	do
93	Freeland & Hoffman	do
94	Crocker & Williams	do
	Edward Noltenius	French imp
96	Legoox & Plunket	French imp
	Besley & Fitch	dry goods
97	Halstead, Haines & Co	do
	Jas Bottomley Jr	importer
98	Vietor & Duckwitz	French imp
99	Elliott, Huntington & Co	hardware
	C Palmer	do
100	Henry H Leeds	dry goods
	Andrews, Myer & Co	do
101	Sword, Halstead & Cornigg	
102	J U Muller	French imp
103	Andrews & Hunt	dry goods
	N J Becar & Co	French imp
104	F A Benjamin	merchant
	Ira Smith & Co	dry goods
105	Unoccupied	
106	Rebuilding, not occupied	
107	J B Glentworth & Co	shoe dealers
108	Bell, Ogilvie & Co	
109	Greenway & Henry	dry goods
	Riggs, Taylor & Co	do
109 1-2	Jas M'Call	
110	Crosby, Candee & Scribner	dry goods
	Philip & Eytinge	do
111	Post, Gibson & Post	do
	T F Brett & Doremus	do
112	Langdon & Andrews	do
	A Chardon	Fr dry goods
112	Ceeler, M'Neil & Co	dry goods
	B Lupin & Co	Fr imp
114	Wm Kobbe	importer
	Pomeroy, Wilson & Butler	dry goods
115	Bostwick & Taylor	do
	John Gravillon & Co.	do
116	Brown and Hone	do
	John Durand & Co	Fr imp
117	Hillyer & Bush	dry goods
	Baker, Johnson & Co	
	A S Parrot	merchant
118	Grant & Barton	dry goods
	Jas D Ruosch	importer
	S Boiceau & Co	Fr imp
	Miller, Ripley & Co	
119	Mesier, Coates & Co	dry goods
120	Seaman, Lee & Ward	do
	C Calemard & Co	Fr imp
121	Rhoades, Weed & Co	dry goods
	F B Rhoades & Co	do
122	Arthur Tappan & Co	do
123	Davenport, Wyckoff & Co	do
124	Seaman, Van Wyck & Norton	do
	J M Jacquelin	Fr imp
	L Allien	Fr goods
125	Baily, Keeler & Remsen	imp
	H F Bowen	dry goods
126	W A Beecher	do
	Lawrence & Beardsley	do
	Chevrolat, Freres & Co	Fr imp
127	Farnham & Bolton	dry goods
	Caulkins & Darrow	umbrella store
128	Clark, Smith & Hyde	dry goods
	Suydams & York	
	Babcock & Suydam	Fr imp
129	Wanzer & Harrison	clothing manuf
	J & D Clark & Hunt	dry goods
130	Edward Hardy	imp of hoisery
	Warren Carter	merchant
	John Loyd	dry goods
	B Lupin & Co	Fr imp
131	Cormstock & Andrews	dry goods
	Henry Babad & Co	Fr imp
132	Sherman & Gillilan	imp dry goods
	Little, Shaw & Co	do
133	Samuel Cochran	dry goods
	M Vedder	clothing
	Warriner, Birch & Whittemore	
134	Baker, Johnson & Co	clothing mer
	Downer & Co	dry goods
135	Robertson & Eaton	do
136	West & Oliver	do
137	Martin & West	do
	Joseph Dupre	Fr imp
138	Hyde, Hickok & Greenman	hardware
	F J Conant	clothing manuf
139	Henschen & Unkhard	importers
	E Kellogg & Co	dry goods
140	Frost, Dickinson & Co	do
	Jesse Miller	importer
141 & 143	R H Osgood & Co	dry goods
	Levi Cook & Co	fancy goods
	Churchill, Southmayd & Co	dry goods
142	J & W Kelly & Co	do
	James Lee	importer
144	Daniel Smith & Co	clothiers
	Wm Kain & Co	dry goods
145	Nelson, Caulton and Co	do
146	Foster & Easton	do
147	Skidmore & Wilkins	do
	L F Varet	Fr imp
148	Robbins & Painter	dry goods
149	Conklin, Herring & Co	do
150	G W Tyson & Co	hardware
151	Not burnt	
152	Miller & Hicks	auctioneers

WATER STREET.

43	John Wright jr & Co	earthenware
44	Brown & Betts	
46	Evans & Carman	merchants
47	Joseph Gaillard	
48	Lt Atkinson, R M agent for Canada Co	
	Tallmadge & Van Pelt	grocers
49	H & D Cotheal	merchants
50	J & J Raymond	glass-cutters
	W W Pratt	ship merchant
52	Hartman & Birdsall	produce brokers
	Thomas Betts & Co	confectioners
	Geo A Gannett & Co	
54	Silas Constant	oil merchant
55	Wm A F Pentz & Co	merchants
	Dudley & Stuyvesant,	merchants
56 & 58	Pearl-street and Ohio House, extended from Water to Pearl streets	
56	Doughty Diblee & Co	
	Jonathan H Ransom	shoes
57	Nichs Berthoud	merchant
59	J H Devoe & Co	groceries
60	Billings & Matthews	merchants
	Chas Cartlidge	earthenware
61	John Noble	wine merchant
	Lansing & Munroe	do
	Kudolph Braem	merchant
62	P W Hinton	
	Bergh & Arcularius,	gravers
63	Pomeroy & Bull	merchants
64	Wilson & Cobble	do
	Wm McLeod	do
65	F M Babcock	
67	J P Phœnix & Co	merchants
68	E & J B Delano	grocers
	Alexander J Cotheal	
71	Jno W Taylor	groceries
73	cor Old slip, Gay & Gallaway	iron store
77	cor Old slip, Dane Lord	druggists
78	Thos F Field	crockeryware
79	Geo Churchwood	com merchant
	Chas A Jackson	provision broker
180	H Rodermond	hair dresser
81	Mrs C Gardner	dwelling house
82	Wm E Dunscomb	
	M Connonly	shoe store
84	Seaman, Lee & Ward	dry goods
	Holmes & Myers	crockeryware
85	Hendricks & Brothers	copper store
87	R C Wetmore	crockery
88	T J Barrow & Co	do
89	Thos D Moore	glass agent
	J Field	crockery
90	T B Coddington	copper store
	Samuel Coddington	com merchant
91	Ebenezer Cauldwell	china dealers
	John Alexander	merchants
	John Gray	do
92	T C Seixas	do
93	R V W Thorne & Co	cotton and hay presses
94	through to Pearl, Suydam & York,	dry goods
	John A Moore	copper dealer
95	C Hixon & Co	
97	J Delano	dwelling and store
98	thro' to Pearl, Little Shaw & Co	dry goods
	Sherman and Gillelan	
99	T T Kissam	crockery store
100	thro' to Pearl Downer and Co	dry goods
101	E Cook and Co	china store
102	thro' to Pearl, West and Oliver	dry goods
103	Chas J Gayler	iron-safe maker
104	Hyde, Hickock and Greenman	hardware
	F J Conant	clothing store
105	H W Cauldwell	
	Seaman and Brothers	druggist
106	John A Moore	iron store
107	John C Jackson	crockery store
	J Cheesman	do
108	J S Bryant & Co	
	Corn's Oakley	tobacconist
109	Wm Churchill & Co	ea & gl ware
	Daniel Colt	crockery ware
110	Mrs Miller & Co	tobacco & snuff warehouse
111	R Vandewater	crockery store
112	U H Levy	druggist
113	Wm J Burritt	do
115	Wm Norris	tinman
116	Wm Minns	bookseller

FRONT STREET.

41	Thomas Woodward	oil store
43	Henry Suydam	merchant
44	J W Kellam	merchant
45	C & R Wardell	grocers
46	Gilbert, Walker & co	grocers
48	Woodgate & Davis	grocers
49	J & R Millbank	grocers
	C I W Wood	merchants
50	Peck & Walton	merchants
51	Robert Smith	merchant
52	Robb & Hasbrouck	merchants
53	Jonathan Leech & co	oil manufacturers
	R Burdick	merchant
54	Hinman & Nash	merchants
55	Mr Spencer	
	Mr Denton	merchant
56	Holmes, Bailey & co	merchants
57	Conover & Labagh	grocers
	A S Marvin	merchant
58	Allen & Phelps	merchants
59	Brigham & Fay	merchants
	Means & Sprague	merchants
60	Warren & Brintnall	
	Drake & Fryatt Commission	merchants
61	Herring & Green	merchants
62	McDonald & Arnold	merchants
63	Henry Marvin	merchant
64	P H & A W Titus	merchants
65	J W Halstead	merchant
66	F & T Denham	coopers
67	Mr Lathan and several families,	
68&70	Wisner, Gale & co	merchants
69	Lewis Denney	cooper
71	Whitney & Storm	merchants
72	Edward Doran	cooperage
73	Whitney & Storm	merchants
74	Jesse Reed & co	merchants
75	William Aymar	merchant
	Nichol & Aymar	ship chandlers
78	J Applegate	grocer
79	W W Todd	merchant
80	David Johnson & H Snyder	merchants
81	S Storm	flour merchant
82	McCoun & Sherman	merchants
	Waddell & Macoomb	merchants
83	Strong, Ballagh & co	grocers
84	L N Dillicker	grocer
85	John H Smith	oil merchant
87	Smith & Rudd	merchants
88	Hawkins & Logan	tobacco merchants
	Briton L Wooley & co	merchants
89	J C Cooper	importer of liquor
	Abraham Dally	inspector of spirits
90	Wood, Grant & co	
91	Condit & Scott	merchants
92	J E Harper & Son	merchants
93	A V Winans	
96	R Maitland & Sons	
98	T Irvin & co	hardware merchant
99	Benedict & Wetmore	
100	Parker, Howard & co	merchants
	Putnam & Slocum	merchants
101	J Batmet	merchant
	Chamberlain, Phelps & co	merchants
	J E Barrill	merchant
	Williams & Roberts	merchants
102	William Banks	merchant
	McIntosh & Rhynd	merchants
103	Houghton & Boardman	merchants
104	John Wilson, jr & co com'n	merchants
105	George Douglass & co	merchants
	G W Brinckerhoff	merchant
106	Naar & Brothers	merchants
108	John P Garcia	
109	Nathaniel Ely	
	J E Bettney	merchant
110	Nicholas Cruger	merchant
	W W Russell	merchant
	J S Bryar	merchant
11	J Cram	merchant
112	W C Wilcox	merchant
117	Baldwin & Henriques	com'n merchant

SOUTH STREET

23	E & J B Herrick	comm'n merchants
24	J S Schermerhorn & Son	merchants
25	A G & A W Benson	com merchants
	John T Balch	merchant
26	Howes, Godfrey & Robinson	merchants
27	Milon Bostwick	grocery
	Wm Churchill & co	imp of crockery
	Martin W Brett	merchant
	Frederick A Burrall	merchant
	James Munson	block and pomp maker
28	Richardson & McCobb,	merchants
29	James H Braine	merchant
	P I Farnham & co	merchants
	Charles N S Rowland	merchant
30	Jacob Badger	comm'n merchant
	Middletons & co	comm'n merchants
31	Chastelain & Ponvert	merchants
32	Saltus & co	merchants
33	John S Bagley & co	ship chandlers
	John W Westervelt	counting room
	E W Baker	counting room
	George Eichell	sail maker
34	John Q Aymar	merchant
	Benjamin Aymar & co	comm'n merchants
35	Peter Donnally	grocery
	Nesmith & Leeds	comm'n merchants
	Upper part, (two families)	dwelling
36	Manuel Depuger	merchants
	Lewis A Berte	city weigher
	Palmer & Hamilton	merchants
37	E & NO Ward	ship chandlers and gro's
38	Fowler, Gordon & co	merchants
	J A Gordon	Tuscan Consul
	Henry B McCobb	merchant
39	J M Reed	grocery
40	Action Avrill	grocery and ship store
	Hy & Wm Delafield	com'n merchants
41	Perkins & McLellan	com'n merchants
	Ebenezer Bartlett	com'n merchant
42	Campbell P White	merchant
43	Eleazer E Bradshaw	merchant
	Peter Edes	merchant
	Wm Sterling	merchant
44	Thomas Marean	merchant
	Moses Taylor	merchant
45	Henry Coit & co	merchant
46	Osborn & Youngs	com'n merchants
	Wm Whitlock Jr	shipping merchant
	Hy & Wm Delafield	store house
47	Augustin Averill	com'n merchant
	Wm Bainewell & co	merchants
48	Hellam Chesebrough	grocery
49	J Bulkley	ship chandler
50	Joseph W Alsop Jr & co	merchants
	Smith & Town	merchants
51	Richards & Richardson	merchants
	F G Thurston	com'n merchants
52	Moller & Oppenheimer	merchants
53	Edward Banker	ship chandler
	Schermerhorn, Willis & co	merchants
54&55	Howland & Aspinwall	merchants
57	Boorman, Johnson & co	merchants
59	William Taggard & co	merchants
	James Hunter	grocer

WALL STBEET.

13	Benedict & Benedict	watchmakers
	R L Nevins & co	brokers
33	Fulton Fire Ins. co	
	W Fitch	broker
	G R Barker	broker
	Wm Cairns jr	broker
	F & Isaac Bronson	
35	New York American	
	Rail Road Journal	
	American Farmer	
	James Cayler	book binder
	P Chubb & co	brokers
	T & C Wood	stationers

MERCHANTS' EXCHANGE.

	Merchants' Exchange co	
	Franklin Insurance Company	
	Neptune Insurance Company	
	Ocean Insurance Co	
	Union Insurance Co	
	N Y State Marine Insurance Co	
	Daily Advertiser Office	
	Journal of Commerce	
	James Bleecker & Sons	
	Franklin & Jenkins	
	Board of Brokers	
	Chamber of Commerce	
	Israel Foote	
	W B Doughty	city surveyor
	Joseph A Adams	wood engraver
	Samuel S Doughty	city surveyor
	Wm S Bernard	engraver
	Arthur Stewart	chronometer maker
	Nicholas Campbell	grain broker
	Joseph H Colton & Co	map makers
	Kerr & King	coffee rooms
	Post Office	
	Alexander J Davis	architect
	A A Leggett	telegraph
	Gilpin's Reading Room	
	R M Penoyer	auctioneer
	Jersey city Ferry Co	
	Boston and Providence Rail Co	
	Rawdon, Wright & Co	engravers
47	J L & S Joseph	brokers
	S & M Allen	do
	A Lemoine	
	Wm O'Brien	
	G Griffin	
	Atlantic Insurance Co	
	Chas G Havens	
49	John J Boyd	broker
65 1 2	Sturtevant & Jones	auctioneers.
67	A S Glass & Gerards	auctioneers.
71	F J Bearnes	auctionesr.

PHENIX BUILDINGS.

	George Barrell	broker
	Wm Caboone	do
	Bowne & co	stationers
	Andrew Bache	weigher
	Wm B Knight	broker
73	J Matthews	broker
	Wm Plimpton	
	R Elwell	
75	P Embury & co	importers champaigne
	Deen, Grenzeback & co	tobacconists
77	Bayard & Deloynes	liquor merchants
79	N W Easton	
81	Dill & Clark	notaries and shipping agents
	D Murphy	printing office
83	John Reese	
87	A Ballermaun	
89	J W Purdy	grocer
91	Wm P Morris	
	Berry Flanders	sail maker
	Doane, Sturges & co	
93	James M Christie	
	Aaron H Palmer	
	Noah Talcott	broker
	Clarkson & co	
	Seamen's Savings Bank	
	Jackson Insurance Co	
	S N Judah	
	L Lorut	
	Marius Panon	
	All intermediate not burnt	

EXCHANGE PLACE.

1	D & E L Perkins	
	Edwin F Woodward	
3	John R St Felix & co	
4	Lane & Lamson	imp. dry goods
	Clark, Rockwell & Gilbert	
6	Ch H Sand	importer
7	Henry Payson	dry goods
	Rapelye, Wetherspoon & co	cotton brokers
8	Enon & Phelps	merchants
	D Crassous	broker
	F Crassous	
9	J U Neiderer	importer
11	Cooke, Angell & co	dry goods
12	Wetzler, Diederick & co	importers
	Staples, Wooly & Clark	
13	Leary & co	
15	Leopold Bierwith	
	Leroy & Perry	brokers
	S V S Wilder	merchant
	Partridge	
	Blackstock, Merle & co	
	Wm W Talcott	broker
	John Reinicke	
	John A Morton, jr	merchant
	Merian & Bernard	do
	J W Partridge,	
16	T & E Townsend	
	C G Fehr	importer
17	Decasse & Meige	importers
	Weeks & co	stock brokers
	Cammann & Whitehouse	do
	Shipping and Com. List	
	G & E Curtis	
	P & J B Staples	
	J Neilson jr	broker
	Hallowell Granite Company	
18	Wemple & Christe	
	Robert B Atterbury	
	Henry W Christie	
	Booth & Atterbury	brokers
19	Lucius Pearl & M Anstice	do
	Archibald Rogers	
20	J W & T Nesmith	
	Elisha Lewis & co	
21	Callemard & Kleffier	importers
22	Hicks, Lawrence & co	auctioneers
	J Taylor	importer
23	Thomas, Son & Adams	merchants
26	Burrill & Tilden	do
27	M Caffe	
	Thomas, Fuller & Son	
	E Tremaine	
28	Voison & Tardy	importers
	Silas Bronson	merchant
20	Crumbie & Draper	importers
	Andrew Broome	dry goods
	C O Halsted & co	
30	Austen, Wilmerding & co	auctioneers
31	North, Hoyt & co	dry goods
32	Satterlee & Masters	
	James Bronder	broker
	Wm Tuzell	do
	Lee, Savage & co	
34	H Hennequin & co	importer
	McCarty & Bartow	auctioneers
	Robert S Bartow	
36	Hone, Coster and co	
	Rogers and co	
40	Lewis Stasser	importer
	F Gillet and co	merchant
	Charles Antoine	do
	Armsby and Gillet	do
42	N Castelais	importer
	Nelson J Elliott and co	
44	E Fountaine and co	
	John Butterworth	merchant
46	A Lentilhon and co	importers
	Thomas Lord	
48	Stone, Swan and Mason	importers
48 1-2	Hubbard and Carey	hardware
50	D N Lord	importer
	Robert Sedgwick	attorney
52	Edwin Lord and co	
	A Le Barbier and co	importers
	Francis Bacon	merchant
56	Tucker and Lauries	merchant
58	W A Depeyster	importer
	P O'Neill	porter house

WILLIAM STREET.

1	Shanan, Cutter and Bulkley	
	Holbrook and Ferne	hardware
2	Doremus and Smith	merchant tailors
	Joseph Attinelle	Custom House Broker
	Sailors and Masters'	chronometer makers
	J Avreosane	
	Wm Dobbie	broker
	F Bishop	dry goods
	Williamson	book binder
	J M Elliott	printer
3	P Freeman and co	
	Barbey and Cottenet	merchant
4	Raymond and Dexter	dry good
	Harvier and Smith	French importers
5	Thiron and Maillard	merchants
	Lewis Gayot	do
	Gillian, Rosart and co	commission merchants
6	Loth and Ferry	basket store
7	Timothy Callahan	
8	Osborn and Buckingham	printers
10	Jno Jamieson	saddler
11	Henry Smith	
13	Snowden and Bogardus	merchants
	Abm Vannest	
15	F T Laqueer	hardware merchant
	Thompson, Austen and co	French importers
17	Henry Bates	dry goods
	Hugh Auchincloss and Son	merchants
	J L Moore	fancy dry goods
18	N M Brown	porter vault
	Edw Langdon	hardware
	Lemit and Blancan	Fr. importers
19	Blenkard and Hutton	do
	Henry Wells	dry goods
20	Piedanna and Mauroy	Fr. importers
	Edw. Ferguson and co	merchants
22	Struther and Haff	do
23 & 25	Delmonico and Brothers	hotel, &c.
33	W M Hicks and co	auctioneers
	Chuard and Boell	Fr. importers
35	D Baker	
	Corlies, Haydock and co	auctioneer
37	Adee, Timpson and co	do
38	Perkins, Hopkins and White	
	Leggett, Wooster and Frame	
36	S Agley, Sparks and Allen	dry goods merch's
40	R and H Cheesebrough	
	T S Shepherd	
41	Burns, Halliburton and co	dry goods
42	Law and Todd	do
43	J W and A Otis	do
45	R Curtis	broker
	L J Belloni	
	Luckee and Crape	lawyers

MERCHANT STREET.

1	Brett and Vincent	
	F A Loshe	
2	J Wichelhausen	
3	Van Schaick, Noyes and co	1st floor, jobbers
	James Denison	
	William Binns	importer
5	J and A Brown and co	importers
7	Wm Redmond	
20	Farr and Farnham lower part	
	E Bubet	
	Henry Davrernville	
22	S V Bouland	French importer
	Bostwick and Booth	
23	J Harrison	
24	Palmer, King and Gonverse	
25	Comstock and Andrews	
26	L Ferraton	
27	Ricketts and Rantlett	
28	S Soher	
	F Le Clerc	French Importer
	Bradley and Taylor	4th story
	Leonard Bradley	dry good
30	Clark and Welton	Commission merch'ts

BEAVER STREET.

51	E C Ketchum	family of 5
59	Mary Wellington	dwelling, 3 story
	William Cullen	cooper

COENTIE'S SLIP.

2	George A Riell	tobacconist 3d story
	Day and Riley	stationers
4	Chaldwick	victualling house
6	O Cobb	
8	Scott	hardware store
10	P O'Brien	grocer
12	Edgar J Oliver	
	W Hayden jr	

GOUVENEUR LANE.

4	Thaddeus Phelps and Co	
	Delano and Sons	
	S W Pentz	cooper
	S Broom	
	Kliff and Murray	
9	R C McClellan	carpenter shop

HANOVER SQUARE.

1	Billett, Lander and son	French Importers
2	John Lang and Co	Gazette Office
	W L Bradbury	printer
	Wright, Winston and Co	merchants
	Joseph N Balestier	attorney

STONE STREET.

56	Deraismes and Brother	
58	Francis S and Alexander G Cochran	
59	John Cole	sail maker
59 1 2	Charles Bicknell	
60	James Bottomley jr	importer
	James Conolly	dwelling
	Jacob H Corlies	dwelling
	Joseph Collet	

JONES' LANE.

Moller and Oppenheimer
Schermerhorn and Marsh
Benedict and Wetmore
J Hunter Graham
L Lincoln

OLD SLIP

1	New building not finished	
	Widow Mary Sutton	
	Jeremiah Briggs	ship master
3	New building not finished	
5	New store not finished	
6	J W Towt	saddlery and hardware
	J Staeble	German importer
7	New store not finished	
8	R and E Patterson	druggists
	R E Alcock	china manufac.
9	Wakeman and Smith	dry goods
	Burr Wakeman	carpet store
10	Graham, Mabee and Co	druggists
	Isaac F Smyth	com'n merchant
	Edward Lammer	
11	J D Kleugden	merchant
	W McFarlane	merchant
12	John Reid	hardware
	Wm P Furniss	commiss. merch.
	James McComb	commiss. merch.
	Geo N Crawford	
14	Dr Lord	druggist
22	A Pentz	cooper
23	Daniel Coglan	rope and paper
	Dean and Masston	merchants
25	Nicoll and Aymar	ship chandlers
	H Durbrow	sail maker
	Bridget Conolly	
27	Kemp and Farnham	grocery
	George O Van Amrin	
29	J Alkins and Co	
31	Whittlesey and McCrea	
32	W T Frost	painter
	Allen McDongal	grocer
33	Mary Hingston	block and pump maker
	Bromeley and Wilson	sail makers
	J M Reed	grocery
	J Ludlow	rigger
34	William Boyd	merchant

The conflagration of Wednesday night was distinctly seen at New Haven, a distance of 84 miles.

Plundering at the Fire.—The Police Officers were all day on Friday engaged in recovering property which was stolen at the fire, and bro't to the Police Office upwards of $20,000 worth, chiefly in dry goods. The Police Office was crowded all day with persons in search of their property, and several found articles there belonging to them.

THE EMANCIPATOR.

Proclaim liberty throughout all the land, unto all the inhabitants thereof.—Lev. 25 : 10.

Vol. II.—No. 46.——Whole No. 98. NEW-YORK, THURSDAY, MARCH 15, 1838. Joshua Leavitt, Editor.

PUBLISHED WEEKLY,
BY THE AMERICAN ANTI-SLAVERY SOCIETY.
GEORGE RUSSELL,
PUBLISHING AGENT,
NO. 143 NASSAU STREET.

Terms—$2 per annum, always in advance.

Five dollars in advance, will pay for one copy three years.

Those who will forward the money for five copies *in advance*, shall be entitled to one copy gratis.

Thirty dollars will be received in payment of 20 copies provided they are all ordered at one time, and directed to one post office.

All authorized agents for the publications of the American Anti-Slavery Society, are requested to act as agents for this paper.

☞ All communications must be POST PAID. On all letters enclosing money, double postage should be paid. Otherwise, the addition (as is right) is made at this Post Office, and must be paid out of the money enclosed.

Piercy & Reed, Printers, No. 7 Theatre Alley.

THE EMANCIPATOR.

The West Indies.

We have for some time had in contemplation to devote a considerable space to selections from our files of West India papers, as affording our readers a sort of familiar insight into the condition of society, and the aspects which those interesting communities are assuming in their transition state, from the depths of hopeless slavery, through the absurd and pernicious apprenticeship system, to the elevation of entire personal freedom and equality of civil rights, irrespective entirely of caste or color, which will certainly take place on the 1st of August, 1840. To the philosophical philanthropist, it cannot but be an exceedingly interesting study, to trace the developments of human improvement under the very curious combinations in which those islands are now placed. A white population accustomed to absolute and irresponsible control, and this power suddenly taken from them, and their recent slaves placed under the exclusive power of law, and soon to be on a civil equality with their former masters; the demoralizing influences of slavery, the low state of religion, the ignorance of the peasantry, the revengeful feelings of the petty aristocracy, the distinctions of color, and the prejudices of caste, with numerous other peculiarities, conspire to make the experiment now in progress one of the most intricate and instructive that has ever been performed. If liberty, education and Christianity can mould a happy and well organized community out of these commingled sorts, the problem of improveableness may be considered as settled for the whole human race.

I. SUGGESTIONS FOR IMPROVEMENT.

The papers before us are an index of the topics with which the public mind is occupied. Suggestions of improvement constitute now a very large proportion of the matters discussed in these journals.

A writer in the Jamaica Royal Gazette discovers that the cruel and disgusting modes of punishment which slavery has introduced, are not adapted to the present state of society.—He therefore proposes to have the American system of prison discipline introduced, of confinement combined with labor on public works, and that men acquainted with the management of the system shall be hired to come from the United States to superintend it. We commend this to the attention of the United States Congress, in the preparation of their code of laws for the District of Columbia. Let them adopt the same rule both in regard to crimes and punishments both for black and white citizens, and one of the objects of government then will have been obtained.

Another improvement urged is the construction of steam instead of cattle mills, for the grinding of the sugar cane, and also the improvement in the construction of the mills, by substituting horizontal instead of perpendicular rollers. A saving of labor will thus be effected in feeding the mill, together with a less liability to accidents in feeding.

A new impulse is also given to scientific pursuits, as is indicated by the establishment of a periodical, called "The Jamaica Journal of Arts, Sciences and Literature," edited by W. Arnold, M. D. The editor of the Gazette speaks highly of the work, and says, "Such a publication is much wanted in Jamaica, and we hope it will meet the support it so richly deserves, not only on account of the enlightened and scientific editor, but also on that of the spirited publishers who have at much expense and risk determined if possible to redeem the character of the Jamaica public, from that disgrace which must inevitably fall upon them, in the want of support to any work of more than ordinary capability."

II. LEGISLATION.

The subjects of legislation afford an indication of an altered state of society. It must be new times in a slave country, to find the legislators inquiring and legislating *for the benefit* of those who were lately slaves and lived for the use and advantage solely of their owners. In the records of the Jamaica House of Assembly we now find such proceedings as the following:

Mr. Thompson moved that a committee be appointed to enquire into the state of the children of apprentices declared free by the Abolition Act, and those born since, and to ascertain the means of providing for their future welfare, including a general and agricultural education.—The committee was accordingly appointed, consisting of Messrs. Thompson, John Brown, Barclay, Hamilton, and Guy.

Mr. Barclay presented a Bill to declare children legitimate by the subsequent marriage of their parents—Read the first time, and the second reading fixed for the 21st inst.

Mr. Mitchell presented a petition from the Clergymen and other inhabitants of Kingston, in favor of the National School. Ordered to lie on the table.

Dr. Whittaker, pursuant to notice, moved that no grants should be given for the erection of sectarian chapels, unless available for educational purposes. After some debate, the motion was withdrawn.

On motion of Mr. Grossett the correspondence between Lord Sligo and Lord Glenelg, relating to the working of the 9 hours system, was ordered to be printed for the use of members.

Mr. Sanguinetti moved that the Provost Marshal General do make a return of all apprentices convicted in the Grand Courts of Assize and Quarter Sessions, the nature of their offences, &c., from the 1st August, 1834 to 1837, and the manner in which the convicts have been disposed. Agreed.

On motion of the same honorable gentleman, a message was agreed to be sent to his Excellency the Governor, requesting the Special Magistrates' return of all the apprentices who had purchased their remaining term of apprenticeship, and the sums paid by them for the same, &c.

Mr. Jordon, from the committee to bring in a bill for the amalgamation of the Maroons, presented the same, which was read the first time.

Mr. Allwood presented a petition from the parish of Hanover, praying for aid towards finishing their chapel at Green Island. Lie on the table.

Mr. Barclay presented a petition from St. Thomas in the East, praying for aid in extending the means of religious instruction. Lie on the table.

Mr. Barnet presented a similar petition from the parish of St. Ann's. Lie on the table.

Mr. Osborn presented a petition from several Rectors, praying the means of diffusing Religion in the eastern district of St. Andrews and Parish of Port Royal. Ordered to lie on the table.

Mr. Good presented a petition from the Roman Catholics of the county of Middlesex, praying the aid of the house in the erection of a place of worship. The same.

Some of the debates, that arose in connection with these proposals, afford still greater insight into the machinery of society in its present transition state. On the marriage bill, declaring children legitimate on the subsequent marriage of their parents:

Mr. Barclay said, that in moving the second reading of this bill, he should not detain the house at any length, as he could not anticipate much opposition to it. The measure was first introduced into the house in 1832, and carried by a large majority. He then gave it his best support, and had seen no reason since to alter his opinion; on the contrary, every successive year, and the changes they had brought with them, had more and more strengthened his conviction of the advantages which our community would derive from such a law. Policy, justice, humanity—every consideration was in favor of it. He could understand why laws should prevent man from committing a wrong, but he could not understand, nor admit the wisdom of their standing as a bar to a man remedying a wrong, and doing that which, in the sight of God and of man, was clearly and acknowledgedly right.—Was it consistent with reason, with justice, or with Christian precepts, that a man, conscious of having done a wrong and seeking to remedy it, should be prevented from doing so? If such a principle would be abhorrent in the most ordinary concerns of life, how much more so was it when applied to the case of innocent children?—To judge of the benefits of this measure, it was necessary to revert to the rapid changes which our society had been undergoing, and to the state in which many females at present stood. A few years ago marriages between the white and colored classes were altogether unknown; but connections were formed between white men of the highest respectability and colored females of the most unsullied character. Those connections, although not sanctioned by a marriage solemnity, had been nevertheless most faithfully maintained by the parties; their children had been brought up with the utmost care and affection; many of them had been sent to England to be educated; and the question was, whether the law should continue to deny the father the power of giving them the rights of legitimate children, if he himself wished to do so by intermarriage with the mother?—He (Mr. B.) thought not. On the contrary, it was his decided opinion that such a course ought to be encouraged and promoted to the utmost extent. It would promote domestic happiness—it would unite society, and raise the moral character of the community, by giving those young persons such a stand in society as would place them on the same rank with their fathers, and thereby give them a strong inducement to pursue an honorable and useful course of life. Objections had indeed been made to the measure as having an immoral tendency; but where, he would ask, was the proof? The same law ruled in Scotland, and had done so for ages. Had this effect been to make that an immoral country? No such thing. In that country a father had the power (and a merciful power it was) of legitimatizing his children born out of wedlock if he thought proper, and no injury to society had resulted from it. There could be no objection to agree to the principle of the bill, which was to unite in closer ties the parent to the child, and the child to the parent.

Second reading agreed to.—*Chronicle.*

The following is the exact form of a resolution adopted by the Assembly, by a vote of 19 to 9, with reference to the abolition of the apprenticeship:

"Resolved, That this house, having reference to the Address presented this day to his Excellency the Governor, wherein they declare their anxiety to adopt all measures calculated to secure a successful transition from the apprenticeship to freedom, deem it highly inexpedient to entertain any measure having for its object the abbreviation of the apprenticeship as fixed by the Abolition Act."

Mr. Jordon, the member for Kingston, moved as an amendment, that the Assembly are ready to adopt measures for giving equal freedom to all the apprentices on receiving from the Parent Government compensation to those who are entitled to their services for the remaining period.

The honorable gentleman alluded to the discontent that might prevail in August, 1838, when prædial apprentices saw their relations and friends relieved from the apprenticeship whilst they were obliged to continue in it for two years longer. He thought it therefore better for the interests of the country to adopt the means of abolishing the system, rather than to shut the door against all discussion on the subject. Jamaica would never be in the situation she ought to be, as long as the system was continued, but the peace and security of the country depended upon doing away with it. The prosperity of the country depended upon every man standing in the same situation, and being governed by the same laws; not until then would the trade of Jamaica be increased, and its wealth be developed. No man was more desirous than he was, that this his native country, should enjoy peace and prosperity. He thought it would be the greatest blessing for Jamaica to put an end to that state of things. The apprenticeship system had been productive of collision from the very first; and the different classes of society have in consequence been opposed to each other. He asked what state of things was it, when the peasantry were in arms against their masters, and the proprietory against the peasantry? Had any one party been satisfied? No! Not alone had mutual confidence been destroyed, but disputes had arisen not only between the master and the magistrates, but between the magistrate and the executive; by which means the executive have been bothered with things with which he had nothing to do. It had produced a difference of opinion between the planters of the country and the inhabitants of Great Britain. The planters had been accused of injustice, cruelty, and withholding the indulgences from the negroes which they were accustomed to; on the other hand, the people of Britain were accused of lies, and wilful misrepresentations. Capital and wealth were withheld from the country, for no man would invest his capital in the soil of the land during such conflicting state of society.

Mr Anderson said, many think that this apprenticeship term operates as a suspension of the prosperity of the island. I think so. I am satisfied that it does, and that I am suffering in fortune, and that we are all suffering on account of it. Instead of shutting out inquiry, we should court it. I will not go over the important and impressive statements of my respected and honorable friend Mr. Jordon. But I hope they will be pondered by us all in our private retirements. Surely, with such a basis for enquiry as he has had, it would be most unwise to shut out the possibility of enquiry. It is strange how some gentlemen dread the day of freedom, as if it were to be the beginning of days of darkness and adversity. Why are they afraid to trust themselves to the principles of our common nature? It is absurd to suppose, as some do, that the negro will only work for meat and drink. Why, meat and drink are the very little of all *our* objects of expenditure. The negroes, like us, would desire to be well clothed—to *have* their wives and children well clothed—to get education, and to rise, if possible, to some little eminence in their station. I have had some little experience of the negro character, and I have found him actuated by motives similar to my own. As face answers to face in a glass, so have I found the mind and heart of the negro to answer to the mind and heart of the white man! It would really, sir, become us more to sit in solemn inquiry upon this *topic*, than to pass a resolution to shut out enquiry. I mean enquiry by a committee that will *take evidence* and report. I should like to see a few *negroes* brought up to give evidence before the committees of this house. Theirs is a description of evidence that has seldom appeared here.

Mr. Milner was opposed to any agitation of the subject. They were now entering upon a new state of society, and it was of far greater importance that they should occupy their time in preparing such laws to meet the coming change. For some time after the passing of the abolition act, it was difficult to get the various classes of society to understand the real state in which they stood in relation to each other; and it was but too true that the greater difficulty existed among the prominent classes of the community, than among the laboring classes; all classes, however, now better understood their position and prospects, and discarding the mean idea of compensation, and entertaining a higher motive, he must again express the honest and unbiassed conviction of his heart, that it would be impolitic and inexpedient to disturb the present system, more especially at a moment when the minds of the people had become sobered down to a proper understanding of their situation.

Mr. Grosset thought the apprenticeship necessary to teach the negroes habits of industry; but he was happy to observe that even in the short period of three years, the apprentices had improved in their ideas of freedom, which they always used to contemplate as freedom from labor; whereas they begun to perceive that rational liberty included the necessity of labor, and therefore he apprehended no danger, unless a system of agitation and misrule was pursued.

III. MORALS OF SLAVERY.

The following remarks, by a writer in the Royal Gazette, of course wholly in the planters' interest, will show to our northern readers, a new evidence of one of the revolting features of slavery.

If the moral character of the island, as well as its pecuniary means, is susceptible of improvement and should be improved, we ask why is concubinage on estates longer tolerated or marriage interdicted? True it is that the apprentices are allowed in this respect to please themselves—then, we ask, why should marriage be a disqualification in an overseer? It is a notorious fact that the present race of overseers and bookkeepers are far superior to those of a quarter of a century ago—they are now generally men of good education, and of respectable connections in Britain. Would it not therefore best agree with their inclination to enjoy the comforts of a matrimonial state, and seeing rising around them a respectable family, than either having to put up with the miseries of celibacy or indulging in the criminalities of concubinage and perpetuating illegitimacy on their offspring? The future welfare of the island demands, therefore, the immediate extinction of so unjust, so degrading an interdiction. Had matrimony been encouraged in by gone days at this moment we should have a numerous and hardy legitimate race of creoles. The reverse is the case—but the day has begun to dawn upon Jamaica when the mispolicies of the past will be corrected.

IV. HORRORS OF THE APPRENTICESHIP.

The following letter from the Rev. J. Clark, Baptist missionary, dated from Brown's Town, in the parish of St. Ann's, has appeared in the Falmouth Post.

"*Sir*,—There are in this island, as you well know, numbers of men who wantonly trample on the rights of humanity, and unblushingly violate the laws of God: they place themselves beyond the reach of the influences of religion; the course of justice is too much obstructed to bring upon them the punishments which they richly deserve—since the only way to arrest them in their career of wickedness is to hold them up to the contempt and execration of mankind.

"I have heard of but few men better deserving so dishonorable a distinction than a Mr. Daniel Waldon, overseer of Hyde Park pen in this district.

"A woman named Betsey Edwards came to me last week with the following tale of sorrow:—About six or seven months since she gave birth to a child. On recovering from the effects of her confinement, she was obliged [according to the custom generally prevailing in this neighborhood] to take her child with her into the field when she went to her daily labor; the child was ill; she had no one to nurse it, but was compelled to carry it on her back or to lay it on the ground while she finished her work. Exposure at so tender an age to the cold, damp, and heat, brought on fever, on which the mother went to Mr. Waldon and requested to be taken into the hospital, with her infant, that she might pay it the attention it demanded during the continuance of the fever: such an indulgence he would not allow her; she begged for medicine to administer to it—but this favor was also refused!

"The child lingered, suffering from fever, for two months, and it was not until the afternoon on which it died, when too late to afford effectual relief, that Mr. Waldon would allow the poor mother relaxation from field labor to attend to the wants or to mitigate the sufferings of her dying infant!

"On the same day, George Williams, a member of my congregation and a worthy man, came to me evidently much distressed in mind. He is an apprentice and field constable on the same property, and has a daughter of 16 or 17 years of age, also an apprentice there. Respecting this girl he had felt much solicitude, and had a pleasing confidence that she was walking in the path of virtue. Preparations had been making for her marriage, which it was arranged should take place at Christmas. But the father's peace of mind has been destroyed—the daughter disgraced, her prospects of happiness blighted, and her heart almost broken by the iniquitous conduct of the overseer, the same Daniel Waldon. He had for some time endeavored to seduce the girl, but she resisted his repeated overtures, and as she had friends around her and her father to whom she could fly for protection, he was not able to accomplish his iniquitous design. Thus baffled, he sent the girl to Dover, (a property 12 or 14 miles distant from Hyde Park,) to pick pimento, and there aided by a bribed panderer to his lusts, he at length succeeded in accomplishing her ruin.

"She returned to her home, depressed in spirit and ashamed to make known her disgrace. Her mother enquired into the cause of her sorrow, and obtained from her an account of the circumstances. The father grieved at his daughter's dishonor, went to the author of her shame, who, in terms too gross to repeat, added insult to the injury he had inflicted.

"This Daniel Waldon is the same individual who caused Jane Simms to be stripped at the door of his house, and her person exposed to his brutal gaze. (See evidence taken before the Commissioners at Brown's Town.)

"What, sir, are stripes and dungeons when compared with cases such as these? The lacerated back of the poor slave may heal—the long incarcerated victim of oppression may, when he again breathes the free air of heaven, recover his elasticity of spirit—but, 'can the mother forget her sucking child?' Can the wounded feelings—the bleeding heart of the father ever be healed? can the poor girl's disgrace ever be wiped away, or her virtue, (the only treasure a female slave is likely to possess) ever be restored!"

V. SLAVERY IN THE UNITED STATES.

V. SLAVERY IN THE UNITED STATES.

So twenty-five members of the states which encourage or rather depend on slave labor, marched out of the House of Representatives, at Washington, on the 20th ult., with a view to cut short the debate on the petitions for the abolition of slavery in the District of Columbia! What an inconsistent animal is that cooking animal, the *homo sapiens!* Jonathan will help the Canadians to assert and vindicate their entire and absolute liberty, but he will not allow his own brother buckras to talk of giving liberty to Quashie or Cudjoe. This is another matter likely to breed mischief to the world. There are no slaves in Spanish Columbia, and it will be difficult to keep any peaceably in the United States of Columbia; yet, without them we know not what is to become of the planters of Georgia, Louisiana, South Carolina, &c. It will be impossible to uphold slavery in the midst of civilized people, who have disdained it, and the attempt to persist may very likely lead to a separation of the states. What will Brazil do? The southern states of America must unite with Cuba and Porto Rico, and then—what comes next? The southern states of America may form one vast republic.—*Despatch.*

Of all the advocates for the universal abolition of slavery, none have so much cause to be strenuous as the British West Indian colonists and planters. The state of slavery was confessed to be milder and the condition of the slave to be more favorable in these colonies, than in those of any other nation. Our countrymen have been the only people who have not forgotten the man in the master; yet have they been the first to consent to the abolition of slavery, readily sacrificing their individual interests to the common cause of humanity

The Governor has transmitted a message to the Assembly on the allowances to the apprentices. He complains that on many estates the utmost rigor has been exercised, in depriving the laborers of every allowance, that no cooks are allowed to the field hands to prepare their food, and no carriers to bring them water, no attendants or medicine for the sick, and no forbearance towards pregnant women and mothers. On this subject, one of the island papers remarks:

In this message his Excellency makes two grave and important admissions; he says "that *prudent* and *humane* planters have already adopted what is recommended," and the consequence is that "*their* properties present the good working of this system in peace and industry without their resorting to the authority of the Special Magistrates." And again, that "there are *other* properties where neither the law of apprenticeship, nor the usages of slavery have been found sufficient to guard the *rights* of the apprentices." With this admission, we ask how it can possibly be expected that the peasantry can sit down with any satisfaction, or labor with any degree of pleasure while such fertile sources of evil continue? They must be remedied and right early! We feel certain that some of our legislators will exclaim, "What! give the apprentices cooks, water carriers, hospital attendants, food, time, fish and other allowances! Why, the Government may as well rob us of their services by declaring them free at once." Such we say is *likely* to be the petulant tone of the old school party, and we hope that we may be agreeably disappointed; that the influence of wise heads and more liberal hearts will have some weight upon the minds of honorable members, and that they will be induced to give way to the *pressure of necessity* and to the loud calls of humanity.—*Falmouth Post.*

VII. MISSIONS.

The Baptist Missionary Society held its anniversary at Spanishtown, Jan. 15. The building was brilliantly illuminated, and it was estimated that not less than 3000 people assembled within and around the place.

The following gentlemen addressed the assembly: The Rev. J. Tinson, the Rev. B. B. Dexter, the Rev. J. Clark, Brown's Town, the Rev. H. C. Taylor, the Rev. J. M. Phillippo, the Rev. J. Clark, Jericho, the Rev. Wm. Knibb, the Rev. J. Reid, the Rev. T. F. Abbott, the Rev. W. Whitehorn, the Rev. J. Hutchins, the Rev. J. Kingdom, Charles Harvey, Esq., and John King, Esq.

The spirit and interest of the meeting were nobly sustained throughout, and would have done credit to the Platform of the Metropolis in England. The collection it appears, amounted to upwards of 70*l.*, and hopes are entertained that this sum will be speedily increased to 100*l.* sterling. The business being gone through, the whole assembly rose, and sung with great animation and effect, "Praise God from whom all blessings flow," and the meeting separated.

The opening of the chapel and school-house at Shortwood, was celebrated Dec. 26, with sermons by Rev. J. Tinson and J. Wooldridge.

We are happy to learn that the attendance at public worship on Sabbath days is good, and that the school has commenced, under the administration of the Rev. D. S. Ingraham, with a good attendance of children from the neighboring estates and pens. It is intended also, as soon as the crop season is over, to commence an evening school for adults, of which the negroes seem anxious to avail themselves.

To the hon. Joseph Gordon, the Custos, the hon. John Mais, A. Aikman, Esq., John Fowles, Esq., Edward Jordon, Esq., Robert Osborn, Esq., Alex. Forbes, Esq., and other magistrates and proprietors, or residents of the parish of St. Andrew's, thanks are due for the liberal encouragement they have afforded to the object; and we are happy that their liberality is so likely to be rewarded, not only by the addition made to the beauty of their rural scenery, but by the wholesome influence of sound scriptural instruction diffused among their laboring peasantry.

[Mr. Ingraham, the teacher, is a young American, who went with his wife from Oberlin, last fall, to see what openings for usefulness he could find among the freedmen of the West Indies.—Ed. Eman.]

Liberty should be *immediate, unconditional* and *universal.*

Christianity in contrast with Colonization.

It is a favorite hobby with some very worthy people among us, to attempt the education of pagan Africa, by Colonization—i. e. by a course of measures directly the reverse of those which they propose to employ in every other portion of the pagan world. We are aware how difficult it is to induce hobby-riders generally to look candidly at facts which bear against their favorites. Yet we cannot but think it is our duty still to keep reiterating the facts, as they come to our hand, with the hope that some at least will thereby be induced to abandon their dreams about "missions made easy" and "short cuts to civilization," and be content to follow in the old beaten track of apostolic precedent—preaching the gospel to every creature. We are gratified in reading the following article in the valuable periodical, entitled "The Spirit of Missions," published by the Board of Missions of the Protestant Episcopal Church in the United States.

Christianity the means of civilization.—In the Christian Observer for November, are copious extracts from a Report of a Select Committee of the British House of Commons, (appointed in 1813, and renewed in 1835,) to consider what measures ought to be adopted "to promote the spread of civilization" among the aborigines of the British settlements, &c., "and to lead them to the peaceful and voluntary reception of the Christian religion."

This valuable parliamentary paper contains much important and authentic evidence. We give some extracts bearing on the interesting question of civilization as attempted with or without Christianity.

1. From the evidence of D. Coates, Esq., one of the Secretaries of the Church Missionary Society.

"I find the perceptive part of Christianity tends to make men peaceable, honest, sober, industrious and orderly. These, in my opinion, are the very elements of civilization in the moral sense of it.

"I find in the christian scheme, the doctrines of man's fallen state through sin—redemption by Christ—renovation by the power of the Holy Ghost, and the great and awful sanction of an eternal judgment. Now it is clear to my mind, that the impression of these great principles on the heart of man, tends directly to make him humble, self-denying, philanthropic, beneficient, apart from the consideration of those effects of the doctrines, which may be considered more strictly of a religious or theological kind. These principles, I apprehend, cannot exist in force in any community, without the moral and social well being of that community being greatly promoted.

"I look again at the christian scheme, and observe the very emphatic description of the gospel; it is declared to be 'the power of God.' I think that the phrase must be understood to imply in any reasonable interpretation of the words,

of the gospel.
ess by which
iore powerful
ined.
I find it to be
as the Bible
l beneficence,
en I think the
bring the rev-
eir temporal,

e history of
nost civilized
spel operates
most civilized
ospel in Bri-
labors of the
ealand.
retary of the
are that our
mpt to civil-
reception of
of that kind
iissions. He
troducing civ-
A number
, was engaged
Mr. Wilber-
reat expecta-
However, it
ion, that the
into execu-
hem to perse-
l men willing
to teach them
eave their na-
a, and settle
the gospel.—
about two or
mission is of
en to the gos-
of a change
xperienced its

ization follow-
sumption that
iting it; but I
something be-
ner does the
n, than it leads
een to be in-
ther in a state
lic worship of
oon made to

feel, under the teaching of the missionaries, that a more decent exterior is necessary, and thus the first step is taken in civilization, and clothing is introduced. As the next step, the gospel induces a settled course of life, and tends to promote industry. The people having become desirous to hear the gospel preached, find it necessary to renounce their wandering life, and to have a settled abode, in order that they may enjoy the regular ordinances of religion. That follows as a kind of necessary consequence. They cannot attend the ministry of the gospel, the influence of which they are beginning to feel, and the ministry of which they are desirous to enjoy, without changing their mode of life. Having changed their mode of life, so far as to take up a settled abode, industry becomes necessary for them to maintain themselves; they are no longer dependent upon the chase, and industrious habits are consequently formed. Education, which is another step in the process of civilization, seems naturally to follow. The missionary, in preaching to the heathen, does not deliver his own opinions; he does not speak on his own independent authority; but he tells the people whom he addresses, that the doctrines he delivers are all found in a book which he holds in his hand, and which he calls the word of God, and which he tells them it is important that they should be able to consult. This creates in their minds a desire for school instruction, and many are found in the character of pupils, anxiously endeavoring to learn to read the word of that God who has been so lately made known to them. Then follows another stage of the civilized process; the gospel originates the moral virtues, truth, honesty, fidelity, chastity; and denouncing polygamy, a fruitful source of evil among savage people, it maintains the sanctity of the marriage vow; and thus does it produce, as its direct and proper effect, the virtues which constitute to so great an extent the bond of civilized life. In intimate connection with the moral virtues, the gospel brings in the humanity of life. While it enforces that the husband be faithful to his one wife, it enjoins also that he shall love her as his "own flesh," and thus it raises woman from that state to which heathenism invariably depresses her. The gospel teaches parents to love their offspring, and to regard them as immortal spirits confided to their care, and which they are under obligation to train for eternity; and the mind of the heathen being brought under the influence of this teaching, at once infanticide is abolished. The gospel imposes on children a corresponding obligation to love and reverence their parents, and no sooner is this obligation felt by the heathen than they are seen comforting and supporting their aged parents, instead of leaving them to perish in the jungle, or be devoured by wild beasts. Then again the gospel enjoins on all to be merciful and forgiving one to another, as they hope to be forgiven of God, and this is no sooner admitted than an end is put to violence and deeds of blood. It is in this way I see the connection between Christianity and civilization, and perceive how the former originates the latter."

From the evidence of Elisha Bates, a member of the Society of Friends.—"The Society of Friends have been engaged for many years past in efforts for the civilization and improvement of several tribes of Indians in the United States. The yearly meeting of Ohio, to which I belong, has had, for a number of years, perhaps thirty or forty, the remnant of the Shawnee tribe under their care. I am myself a member of the committee that has had charge of that concern, and have been since the year 1817.

"I think that the Society of Friends, and the Indians of different tribes in the United States, have been in some sort of connection since the year 1681. The plan which the Society of Friends adopted, in their early intercourse with the Indians, was to attempt civilization *first*. Within the last few years we have had occasion to review the whole course of proceedings, and we have come to the conclusion, from a deliberate view of the past, that we erred, sorrowfully erred, in the plan which was originally adopted, in making civilization the first object; for we cannot count on a single individual, that we have brought to the full adoption of Christianity."

The Rev. Mr. Williams says: "I think the South Sea Islands are assuming a very great importance in connection with our nation generally. A few years ago they knew nothing of European manufactures, and now there are hundreds and thousands of them wearing European clothing, and using European articles, such as tools, &c. Wherever Christianity is introduced, of course European clothing and habits are introduced. There is not a single person, in any of our congregations, but is dressed very respectably. I suppose there were 100 tons of sugar made in the Island of Tahiti last year; we have taught them that art. I have not sent out a single native missionary from my station, that I had not taught my self the art of turning, rope-making, soap-boiling, salt-making, sugar-making, carpentering, &c. We put them under a course of instruction in the useful arts before we send them away. Instead of their contemptible huts along the sea beach, there will be a neat settlement, with a large chapel in the centre, capable of containing 1,000 or 2,000 people. A school-house on one side, and the chiefs' or the missionaries' house on the other, and a range of white cottages a mile or two miles long, peeping at you, as it were, under the splendid banana or bread-fruit groves, so that their comfort, as well as their happiness is increased, and altogether their character is elevated."

From a Speech of the Bishop of Winchester, at the Annual Meeting of the Church Missionary Society.—The true Missionary Spirit.—"I cannot but remind you that, to the blessing of God in answer to the prayers of Christians, the success of our missions is owing; and if we look for more converts from among the millions yet unconverted, it must be by the outpouring of prayer by us at home. It is thus we shall be daily with our missionaries in the spirit, and thus shall we be enabled to dwell in closer union with the Head. That is the secret of success—union with Christ.

"One of our missionaries speaks of 'preaching straight forward' the gospel of Christ. That must be the spirit of their teaching. That is the means of cementing their union in Christ; and thus we must build up all our missions; all—all—all in Christ! We must preach the gospel straight-forward—first to our own hearts, and then to the people."

ANOTHER TESTIMONY.

In the same publication we find the following additional testimony, taken from the journal of the Rev. Dr. Savage, Episcopal Missionary at Cape Palmas. It shows conclusively that what the natives desire is light, not colonies; that the only thing which has induced them to admit or tolerate the colonies has been the hope of receiving through these the benefits of education; that this hope has entirely failed, and recourse must now be had to the *appropriate* means, preaching, teaching, and that so far as the enlightenment of Africa is concerned, the twenty years of previous time, and the hundreds of thousands of dollars expended in colonization, have been worse than wasted.

Desire of the natives.—To test the sincerity of their desire for schools, I put a number of interrogations to their king and head men, somewhat as follows: "Why do you desire schools for your children?" "That they may sabby (or know) book," was the reply. "And what do you mean by sabbying book—what book?" "God's book," was promptly answered. But, as I have before remarked, they have not a very definite idea of their wants in this respect. This desire does not arise from a sense of sin. The necessity of pardon, and a mediation or atonement, enters not into their religious rites nor conceptions. The system of sacrifices, as among almost all their known heathen nations, is absent.—Occasionally something is found among some tribes approaching to it in shade only, but no real identity can be made out. Their whole aim seems to be to keep off, or to conciliate the *devil*. The religion of Africa, along its western coasts, has no reference whatever to an *offended God*. A supreme being, other than an evil one, does not fall within their recognition, except so far as they have been taught in their intercourse with christianized people, and alas! all that many of them know of God, is to take his name in vain, and in the profanest manner, which too they have learned from the same source. Their desire for schools, therefore, cannot arise from a *hungering* and *thirsting* after righteousness, or a longing for the truth as it is revealed in the gospel, upon which Christ has pronounced a blessing. But, as I have also before remarked, from a wish to be like the Americans,—and to be like the Americans is they know not what; all they know about it is, (in their own vague dialect,) to be "*fine*"—"*fine*." "White man pass black man" is the universal confession of the African negroes, and for one black man to be in some degree like him, is to pass, (or surpass,) another. To reduce this desire to a healthful, practical influence, and to convert it into an *open* door for the entrance of light and true religion, remains within the power of the patient, judicious, and devoted missionary. And it seems to me, that the present moment is one of the highest importance in regard to the speedy success of the religious teacher. The waves of commerce from other nations are rapidly rolling in upon this vast continent. The eye of cupidity is opening upon it. It is beginning to enlarge too, beneath the vision of natural science. Curiosity and speculation are awake to its mighty, though unknown resources, of geographical knowledge and wealth. Its inhabitants too begin to feel that they also, with other nations, form a part of this lower world. They see that, on the one hand, their country, so long neglected, possesses attractions in the eyes of the commercial world, and that they themselves are becoming objects of interest to the benevolent and the Christian. They feel that a change of the same kind awaits them, and their minds are open to that kind of influence to which they may be first subjected. Any one, who has made the African character his study, must know how easily can be engrafted upon it the vices and degrading habits of that class of civilized society, who visit them *from any other than* from motives of Christian benevolence. It is all important, therefore, that upon the same stream that bears onward the slaver, the merchant and the man of science and research, should likewise carry forward the messenger of grace—the missionary of the cross. It is only by the self-denying efforts of the latter that they are convinced that the object of the white man is to do them good. But why wait for the tide in the affairs of commerce and of scientific exploration? Why should not the Christian teacher, if his object be holy—if the Africans be indeed so ignorant, so degraded, so lost to virtue;—why should not *he*, professing to love his neighbor as himself, precede all others in the great work to be done among this people? He should be first to find out their moral condition, and to make known their moral wants. But where is he? His footsteps mark only the whitened *beach*, and there they are but "few and far between." The burning deserts—the gloomy and almost impenetrable forests, the lakes and the rivers of the interior, have all been visited and revisited by the white man—the profanely curious. But where is the Christian, the man of God, who, before them, should have planted *his* feet, shod with the preparation of peace? The desert and the forest—the mysterious waters—the sunken native of the interior, still, and alas! will long send back the echo, *where is he?* How long, oh Lord! how long?

Another question put to the king of Rabookah was, "What will you do to aid us in opening a school among your people?" His reply was, "I will furnish all the timber, my people shall do all the labor, if you will find the nails for a house, and I will furnish food, all the same as my people eat, for the teacher." I was urged to make a solemn promise that I would open a school at once. They literally pleaded with outstretched arms for this privilege so easily granted by the people of America!

These facts speak for themselves. I leave them with the committee. I leave them with the church; and imploringly ask, "Will you not send us more helpers—more teachers?—Shall these poor starving people plead in vain? Shall they be turned off by the church of Christ to grope their way down to endless despair?

> Shall *we*, whose souls are lighted
> With wisdom from on high
> Shall we, to men benighted,
> The lamp of life deny?"

Loyalty of Colored Citizens.

The recent insurrection in Canada placed the people of color on both sides of the line in a delicate situation, for reasons which will be obvious, when it is known that there are in Canada probably not less than 5000 fugitives from republicanism, "as we understand it." The following proceedings in Toronto and in Buffalo, will show that good sense and honest integrity have carried them through, straight and safe.

From the Toronto, U. C. Christian Guardian.

The more we become conversant with the people of color, and have opportunity to observe their character and conduct in this city, the more confirmed are our convictions of the extreme wickedness or ignorance of those who would rank them as an inferior order of beings to the whites, and would treat them accordingly.

The resolutions which we have published by request in another column, will be read with interest. They prove that those who passed them are capable of discriminating between right and wrong, and of sympathising with the afflicted, even of another color. The reference to the murder of the abolitionist Lovejoy, is peculiarly creditable to them. Mr. Augustus, the Secretary, is a man who, though born and brought up in slavery, has, since his escape, made such improvement of his advantages, that we have often listened to his extemporaneous addresses at meetings of the Anti-Slavery Society with astonishment and pleasure.

THE MEETING.

At a meeting of the colored inhabitants of the city of Toronto, convened by themselves, at the residence of Mr. Wm. Osborne, on Saturday, January 13th, 1838, Mr. Stephen Dutton was called to the chair, and Mr. Wm. Augustus was appointed Secretary,—

The following resolutions were unanimously adopted:

Moved by Mr. M. B. Truss, seconded by Mr. H. Coles,—

1. That we have learned with the most painful and indignant feelings, the continued determined opposition which is arrayed against the friends of our colored brethren in the United States, in their efforts to secure the inalienable right of personal freedom to two millions and a half of human beings, who are held by tyrants in a state of abject slavery, and especially manifested in a resolution of the American Congress, as published in a recent number of the *Emancipator*, the effect of which is to stifle the voice of complaint and remonstrance, however respectfully presented in the petitions of the free in behalf of the oppressed.

Moved by Mr. John L. Randolph, seconded by Mr. Wm. Hickman,—

2. That the recent outbursting of the true spirit of slavery in a nominally free state, in the murder of that pious and talented advocate of human rights, the Rev. E. P. Lovejoy, has excited in our breasts feelings of the warmest condemnation of the perpetrators of that unparalleled outrage, mingled with the deepest and most affectionate commiseration for his bereaved widow and children; and has called forth our earnest prayers to Almighty God—prayers which we doubt not will be heard and answered—that this tragical affair may be overruled for the more speedy extinction of a system—the whole history of which presents an unbroken chain of deeds of cruelty, darkness, tyranny, and blood.

Moved by Mr. Samuel Thompson, seconded by Mr. Geo. Brown,—

3. That it is due, not only to ourselves and to the government under which we have the happiness to live, but especially to our colored brethren in the United States—as well the free as those who are yet groaning in slavery—and to that portion of the white population who are striving for universal emancipation, that they should be made acquainted with the true state of the colored population of Canada, and with the happy situation in which we are placed as compared with our former condition.

Moved by Mr. Richard Burke, seconded by Mr. George Williams.—

4. That we express the universal feeling of our colored brethren throughout this Province, when we state our perfect contentment with our political condition—living, as we do, under the influence of free and equal laws, which recognize no distinction of color in the protection which they afford and the privileges which they confer; and that we distinctly contradict all statements to the contrary which have been industriously circulated in the states, by slaveholders and others of a kindred spirit, for the purpose of creating a belief that colored people are unprepared for freedom, and that our emigration to this country has effected no real improvement in our circumstances.

Moved by Mr. Wm. Augustus, seconded by Mr. George Wilkinson,—

5. That we wish it to be known that the unfortunate occurrence which took place at Niagara in the month of September last, in the case of Moseby, the self-emancipated slave, and which has excited much painful feeling and some prejudice among our brethren in the neighboring states, is in reality mainly attributable to the unprincipled conduct of the slave master, who, in order to effect his design to re-enslave Moseby, alleged against him the commission of an offence—for which, whatever might be its character in the eye of Canadian law, he was not amenable to the laws of slave states; and that we have every reason to believe that similar pretences in future will receive that degree of scrutiny from the authorities of this Province, which will afford ample protection to the injured.

Moved by Mr. William Hickman, seconded by Mr. James C. Brown,—

6. That the philanthropy which induced the British nation to strike the fetters from the limbs of our brethren in the West Indian colonies, at an expense of nearly a hundred millions of dollars, and which is now prompting the British public to demand the completion of their emancipation by the abolition of the apprenticeship system, has laid the whole family of colored men under obligations of gratitude; and that we earnestly hope and pray that the time is not far distant when America shall manifest similar magnanimity, and remove at once the stain which blots her banner, and the intolerable burden which oppresses two and a half millions of the natives of her soil.

It was then ordered that the proceedings of this meeting be sent to the Christian Guardian and Toronto Patriot for publication; and that other papers friendly to the cause of human rights, especially the anti-slavery journals in the United States and in England, be respectfully requested to copy them.

William Augustus,
Secretary.

From the Utica, N. Y. Friend of Man.

The following reaches us in a hand bill form. Of the circumstances which occasioned it, we know nothing except what the reader will gather from the perusal. We have italicised a few words of it, which seem to give a clue to the circumstances of the writers.—Ed. F. of M.

AN APPEAL TO THE CITIZENS OF BUFFALO.

Fellow Citizens:—Although incompetent to do this appeal justice, still, the present crisis demands that something should be done. *The approbrious epithets continually poured out against the colored citizens*, and the contemptuous manner in which we are treated by the aged and the young, is enough to debase our minds and paralize all our efforts. We would ask where can be found, under heaven, a class of men thus treated, that have been more subservient to the laws, made a more rapid progress, and less expense to the city, than we, the colored citizens of Buffalo? And we would also ask if this has not always been the case with the respectable part of the colored community; and why are we thus treated; why is it that on almost every subject brought up that leads to excitement, no matter where it originated, that the heaviest threats and greatest prejudices rest upon the colored people? Are we deserving of such treatment? Is it right that the whole colored community should be implicated for the opinions or misconduct of some of their people? Is it that we have proved untrue to our country? Surely not. Does not Botta's History, page 113, of your own country, prove to the contrary? You will there find among the first American blood shed in defence of her rights, that of a colored man; and in the last war they were efficient auxiliaries in the navy, and received the thanks of the commander-in-chief for their services after the victory of New-Orleans. Yes, sirs, and the one who penned this appeal, my father endangered his life and boldly stood up to defend the institutions of the country, and there are others in this city whose fathers were slain in battle to achieve that glorious victory and obtain those inalienable rights which have been so cruelly wrested from us; *and as far as we can ascertain respecting the present excitement against us, it originated from the fact that a number of colored people were engaged with the government forces in Canada*; is it justice to implicate us on their account? *Our interests are not identified with theirs*; they are under a separate government and are amenable to the laws under which they live, and we do assure you our interests are as much at stake, our feelings as strongly attached to this government, and as fully prepared to act in its defence, if necessary, as any other citizens amongst you, and we hope and trust such feelings will no longer be harbored against us. It must be expected that there will be some thoughtless and malicious persons in the community; but the undersigned, and numbers whose names are not here, are willing to aid in protecting the city against any aggressors.

Abner H. Francis, John L. Watson, Payten Harris, James Linchcomb, Rev. Geo. Weir, John H. Morrel, Anthony Curtus, Thomas Harris, Randall Cezar, Henry Jackson, F. Jinkins, David Smith, G. Dover, John Williams, Daniel Moten, A. Washington, Richard Jones, Robert Banks, Robert Brister, Nimrod Linchcomb, James Garret, Lewis White, A. P. Brokenborough, Henry Moxley, John Cary, Limus Miller, F. Washington, W. E. Low, Richard Scott, James Clarkston, Carr Johnston, Samuel Charles, Henry Hawkins, Joseph Adams, Joseph Whitfield, Henry Fields, Nath. Steward, A. E. Crosby, Dennis Marshal, George B. Conway, Joseph C. Gilman, George S. Whitfield, D. Lewis, Robert Moore, Wm. Qualls, John Dandridge.

Buffalo, Jan. 4th, 1838.

Since the above was prepared for the press, we find in the Friend of Man, for Feb. 28, a letter from Mr. Abner H. Francis, a colored citizen of Buffalo, dated Feb. 21, giving the following explanation of the handbill. The manliness of our friends, in thus appealing to the reason and humanity of their fellow-citizens, is worthy of all praise, and must gain for them a general respect and confidence. Mr. F. says,

"At the time of the great excitement in this city, occasioned by the interference of some of the citizens with Canadian affairs, a rumor went the rounds that the colored citizens of this city had held public meetings and passed resolutions expressive of our determination to aid and abet the government of Canada, which was strictly false, but produced quite a desperate feeling against us. Shortly after it was ascertained that among the Canadian forces were a number of colored people, and as usual (as if we had an interest at stake with them) the rabble became furious towards us, and it was almost impossible for us to walk the streets without molestation. One colored man was taken up upon charge of attempting to fire the city, which upon trial proved unfounded, and if we had not circulated the said hand bills as soon as we did, some of us, no doubt, would have shared the fate of our esteemed and much lamented friend, Lovejoy—murdered by the hands of an infuriated and lawless mob. But thank God, the excitement ceased, and we were once more permitted to pursue our daily avocations in peace."

Interesting Correspondence.

Communicated for the Philanthropist.

LANE THEOLOGICAL SEMINARY.

Walnut Hills, near Cincinnati, Ohio, January 3, 1838.

Hon. Wm. Slade:

Sir—The undersigned, being candidates for the sacred ministry, and soon to enter on that holy office, feel no disposition to employ their thoughts upon the reigning topics of political controversy; yet we cannot forbear this expression of personal gratitude for the signal service which you have recently rendered to humanity and truth, in moving to instruct a committee to bring in a bill for the abolition of slavery in the Ditrict of Columbia.

Governed by the wholesome restraints of a religious profession yourself, yet compelled to act in a body, some of whose members seem to know no restraint except what one violent passion imposes on another, your situation must be trying beyond ordinary conception; and the merit of your recent services is enhanced by the consideration that your duty must be discharged at the risk of your life.

Aware of these facts and circumstances, we beg leave respectfully to assure you, that the interest we feel in your efforts, as well as those of our venerable ex-president, is of

THE SUN

COUNTRY EDITION. SATURDAY MORNING, AUGUST 3, 1839. WEEKLY----NO. 142.

ARRIVAL OF THE STEAM SHIP BRITISH QUEEN.

MONDAY MORNING, JULY 29, 1839.

ARRIVAL OF THE BRITISH QUEEN. SIX DAYS LATER FROM LONDON. HIGHLY IMPORTANT NEWS.

[illegible] longest under the water [illegible] been looked for during [illegible] of the [illegible] much anxiety, arrived at Sandy Hook ab[illegible] o'clock on Sunday, morning, and at 10 o'clock was in her berth at Clinton Slip.

She sailed from Liverpool on the 11th inst., and Portsmouth on the 12th, bringing London and Liverpool papers to the former date—six days later than those received by the Great Western.

THE BRITISH QUEEN.

This magnificent vessel, which to-day makes her first appearance in American waters, was built, as our readers are probably already aware, expressly for a regular packet between this port and Liverpool. She is the largest and finest ship ever built in Great Britain, her length exceeding by thirty-five feet that of any vessel in the British navy. She is commanded by Lieut. Richard Roberts, R. N, the favorite and accomplished late commander of the Sirius. She is registered at 1862 tons, and her engine is of 500 horse power. Her extreme length, from figure head to taffrail, is 275 feet; length of upper deck, 245 feet; length of keel, 223 feet. Her breadth within the paddle boxes is 40 feet 7 inches; including the boxes, 64 feet; and her depth is 27 feet. The diameter of her paddle wheels is 31 feet 6 inches; length of stroke, 7 feet. The estimated weight of her engines, boilers and water, is 500 tons; estimated weight of coals for 20 days, 600 tons; weight of cargo, 500 tons; and her draught of water with the above weight and all stores, 16 feet. The frame work of her engines is in a massy gothic style, while the working parts, for strength, beauty, and excellence of fitting, are admirable. Each engine stands upon a single plate of metal, weighing 35 cwt.; four pieces of the frame work weigh each 16 tons; the cylinders weigh each 12 tons; the diameter of the [illegible] diameter of the boilers, any number of [illegible] else [illegible]. She has in all four [illegible] without the other [illegible] which can be used at one [illegible] to find out [illegible] of the others. The float boards, [illegible] feet 6 inches long, are arranged in 3 distinct parts, presents a resistance of 3 feet in breadth. According to her depth in the water the revolutions in her paddle wheels will vary from 15 to 18 in a minute. She is supplied with Hall's Patent Condensers, and thus the same water with which she fills her boilers in the Clyde, will, with a little addition, serve until her arrival in New York. She has iron tanks between the timbers in the hold, capable of holding 200 tons of water, all of which is accessible to the pumps, and can be thereby drawn out and conveyed by pipes to the different berths. But over and above this, she has a patent still with her, and convert can salt water into fresh for her boilers, and for the use of her passengers, as may be required.

The extent and splendor of her finish and furniture, and of her accommodations for passengers, are in keeping with the unparalleled stupendousness of her structure and machinery. We have received from her agents here a beautiful lithographic view of the interior of this superb steam ship, in which are represented her fore saloon, ladies' saloon, and main saloon, with a plan of the cabins. Judging from this view, there is not a hotel in Broadway, and there are but few parlors up-town or down-town, which quite come up to this palace of the seas. But, though thus prepared, on going on board of her we found that the *picture* was but an indifferent representation of the reality.

She carries 32 hands immediately connected with the superintendence and management of the engines, and her crew in whole, including officers and seamen, engineers, cooks, stewards, etc, amounts to 85. In respect of stores and general fitting out, she is admirably found, and every thing is on the most improved construction. Her chain cables are 1 7-8 iron, and are of the same kind as is used for a 74 gun ship. Her small bower, best bower, and sheet anchor, weigh respectively 32 cwt. 2 qrs. 18 [illegible]; and 47 cwt. 1 qr. 2 1 lbs. No pains, no time, expense, have been spared in obtaining perfection; and taking her all in all, we may safely say she is unequalled by any vessel afloat. Amongst other conveniences for passengers, we had almost forgotten one. On the deck there is a neat erection, in which cold, warm, or shower baths, may be obtained by the passengers.

The deck is what is called a flush deck, perfectly continuous from one end to the other, instead of having higher and lower portions, forming poops, half poops, &c, as most common in vessels of her size. The deck is a long promenade, and the distance from stem to stern is a good rifle shot; her breadth on deck being some sixty feet. Descending to her engine rooms, the engine does not strike the spectator as being extraordinarily large; but when once at the bottom of it, looking up, you perceive the men who guide the whole machinery, and regulate and direct the combined strength and simultaneous energy of 500 horses, with greater success than the tyrant Philopater his galley of 3000 slave power, and feel that you are in the presence of one of the noblest of human creatures, the impersonation of the adage, that "knowledge is power"—power applied to the benefit and improvement of humanity. The engine is some thirty feet high, occupying a length of 84 feet.

[illegible] he is steered by a double wheel, similar to those [illegible] by London East Indiamen, or line of battle [illegible]. The rigging of the vessel is low and snug, rather than taunt; but her yards are prettty square, and as she has studding sail booms fitted on them, she is able, when necessary, to display a good breadth of canvass to the breeze.

She is coppered up to 17 feet, and is expected, when loaded, to draw 18 feet aft, and 17 1 2 forward. Notwithstanding the great capacity of this magnificent vessel, she does not look so large as many would expect; probably the beauty of her mould tends to detract a little from the apparent bulk. When down to the depth aforementioned, we do not think she much exceeds in appearance a first class frigate.

The external appearance of the ship, seen from the shore, is imposing and beautiful. The figure-head is a graceful representation of the youthful monarch of Britain, so well proportioned as to seem not more than usual height, although twelve feet in stature; and it is only when the sturdy fellows who form her crew approach the sovereign, that her Patigonian size is determined by their Lilliputian dimensions. The appendages of the figure head and cut-water are beautifully outlined, moulded, and covered with gold, and the effect of the vessel at the bow on the whole is very majestic. Passing round to her stern, the vessel is still very fine; the carving of the stern is in perfect keeping with the rest of her ornamental work, and the stern galleries are elegant and well placed. The rigging is also well proportioned; her masts are beautiful, and her yards are of great stretch and excellent proportion. There she rides majestically, Queen of the Seas, the noblest steam ship the world has ever seen.

At the expense of heavy cost and some trouble, we have procured a stereotyped copy of a London lithograph of the British Queen, cut on wood with great accurracy, by which we are enabled to present our readers with a minutely correct view of the exterior of this noble vessel.

THE STEAMBOAT JOHN FITCH.

In direct contrast with it we have placed a model of the first application of steam to propelling of boats, made by John Fitch, at Philadelphia, and exhibited by him on the Delaware in the year 1786. At the time of making the exhibition, he remarked to the few scientific gentlemen who would condescend to witness it: "This, gentlemen, will be the mode of crossing the Atlantic in time; and although I may not live to see it, you may, when steam will be preferred to all other modes of conveyance;—and they will be particularly useful in crossing the Mississippi. He then retired, when a person present observed in a tone of deep sympathy, "Poor fellow, what a pity he is crazy!" To an understanding of the cut, it may be well to state that the six paddles on each side of the boat were scooped out in the form of a spoon, and by the machinery the six fore and six aft paddles were alternately raised from and immersed in the water.

THE NEWS.

There is nothing in the news from England to change very materially the aspect of affairs in the money market. A severe pressure continues to be felt, but it has been perhaps in some measure alleviated by the determination of the Bank of England not to increase the rate of interest to 6 per cent., a step which was seriously apprehended, and also by the opening of the budget in the House of Commons, by which it appeared that there was an increase in the revenue, on the quarter, of £308,175 and on the year of £2,076,659; the principal increase being in the customs and excise.

The prices in the stock market had rallied slightly, but showed a good deal of fluctuation. The state of foreign exchanges was considered unsatisfactory.

The cotton market continues dull, and the demand very limited.

The Times says, the speculators in cotton and other articles, complain most loudly of the conduct of the Bank of England, as it has afforded a complete check to their operations; that it is fully expected that at the conclusion of the present year there will be a surplus stock of American cotton of from 250,000 to 300,000 bales, and that too at a period when there is every probability of most abundant crops in the United States, in India and Egypt. The prospect for cotton speculators is, upon the whole, gloomy enough.

The following was the state of the money market on the 10th inst.

CITY, Wednesday evening, July 10.—The permanent securities have advanced a fraction on yesterday's quotations. Consols left off at 92 1-2 to 1-4 for money, and 93 5-8 to 3-4 for account. The same party who were selling so largely of Exchequer Bills on Monday, attempted to-day to place a further amount of those interests, but the market was so sensitive, that they made very little progress. A decline in the premium to 20s. has put a stop to their operations for the present. They left off at 20s. to 22s. premium, and bank stock at 191 1-2 to 2.

In the Foreign Market Two-and-a-half Per Cent. Dutch Stock was quoted 54½ to ¾, Brazilian 77 5-8 to 7-8, Chilian 37½ to 8½, Columbian 33 to ¼, Five Per Cent. Portuguese 33 3-4 to 4, and Active Spanish, with the overdue coupons, 18 3 4 to 19.

A case of default occurred at the Stock Exchange to-day, and we are sorry to say it was that of an old and respected member of the house.

Nothing of importance was done in any description of shares.

In the House of Lords on the evening of the 5th inst., the Archbishop of Canterbury brought forward his resolutions upon the subject of national education. The Sun says, "a long and spirited discussion ensued, which lasted till nearly 3 o'clock, and ended in a division. The numbers were—contents present 171, proxies 58; non-contents present 80, proxies 38, total 229 and 118—majority for the Priestcraft, and against education, 111."

In the House of Commons, on the evening of the 10th inst. the Metropolitan Police Bill, that had caused considerable sensation, was re-committed, after a curious conversation relating to the Metropolitan Police at Birmingham. In committee, also, all the material clauses of the bill were agreed to, except that to prevent women of bad character assembling in public houses, which, on motion of Mr. Hume, was omitted, and that relating to the suppression of gambling in the streets and highways, was also struck out, after a division, on motion of Mr. Clay.

Arrests of the persons engaged in the bloody riots in Manchester were still being made, and the city continued in a very unsettled state. On the 9th there were serious demonstrations of a renewal of violence and bloodshed, but by a prompt rally of the military, the use of fire-arms was prevented, though the mob pelted the military with stones. Several arrests were made on the occasion. A riot which took place on the 5th, wore for a time a very serious aspect, and led to the arrest of numerous prominent persons, among whom was the celebrated Doctor Taylor, who has been fully committed for trial for the part he is alleged to have taken in the Digbeth affair.

A great riot broke out at Ramsgate on the 8th inst. in consequence of the conviction of several fishermen for hawking fish about the streets. While the commitments of the prisoners were being made out large numbers, principally of Torbay fishermen and women, assembled until the rioters increased to 5000. On the arrival of a fish van to convey the prisoners to Sandwich jail a tremendous rush was made at the vehicle to arrest its progress.—The prisoners called out to the mob to rescue them, and the carriage was carried some distance by the mob. The Police, in their efforts to disperse the mob, were attacked with showers of stones, &c. and compelled to retreat. The mob then broke the windows, forced the door, and, in the midst of the melee, the prisoners and three others were rescued and escaped amid the cheers of the mob. Ellis, and another policeman, were dreadfully beaten, kicked and dragged along the ground. One prisoner has since been arrested, and the police were in pursuit of the others.

The remains of the Lady Flora Hastings were on the 10th, early in the morning, removed from Buckingham Palace on board the Royal William steamship, lying at the St. Katharine Docks, for the purpose of being conveyed to the last resting place of her Ladyship's maternal ancestors in Scotland. So numerous were the applications for permission to form part in the sad procession that it was found absolutely necessary to restrict it to those were related to the noble family or who were on terms of the closest intimacy with them. At the request of her father a *post mortem* examination of her body was made, the result of which put forever at rest all doubts as to her innocence of the scandal which had been attached to her.

There appeared to be much distress in some parts of Ireland. Col. Percival said in the House of Commons that there were many families living on one meal a day, and that of potatoes of the worst description. Mr. O'Connell said of the western coast of Ireland, that the misery was becoming so oppressive that it was absolutely necessary some steps should be taken without the least delay. Mr. Sergeant Jackson said he had received similar accounts from the south-western parts of Ireland, where the distress was most appalling. At Rantry 2000 were in a state bordering on starvation out of a population of 7000. Notwithstanding this the Chancellor of the Exchequer said that he thought that the less discussion there was on this subject the better—and he thought the better plan would be to lay the letters relating to the affair before the government. No action appears to have been had upon it.

The London Morning Herald says:—"So characteristic are the Americans in all they do, that part of a public procession, on the anniversary of the evacuation of New York, is described to have consisted of a party of butchers, drawn in a sort of rustic arbor or shambles, "tastefully festooned with *sausages*."

The Provincial Bank of Ireland has raised the rate of interest on bills to six per cent.

The Junior Fellows of Trinity College, Dublin, have drawn up a petition to the Queen, praying that her Majesty would be graciously pleased to repeal the statute of celibacy which prevents them from marrying. The petition will be presented to her Majesty by Dr. Lefroy, one of the members of the University.

At a late assizes at Lancaster, a very old man, an Irishman was sentenced to fourteen years' transportation. He bowed profoundly to the court, and thanked his lordship, "For, indeed," said he, "I did not think I had so long to live, till your lordship told me."

THE EGYPTIAN WAR.

CONSTANTINOPLE, June 19.

[From the Correspondent of the Morning Post.]

The Trebizond steamer, which arrived here on Sunday, brought a Tartar with despatches from Hafiz Pacha, containing an account of an engagement which took place between the advanced guard of the Turkish army and the Egyptian cavalry, and in which the latter were repulsed with great loss. But though this intelligence has been in some measure confirmed by advices received from Alexandria and Beiroult up to the 31st ult., the affair will, in all probability, turn out to have been nothing more than a skirmish. The Sultan, on receiving the news, gave a liberal *bakshish* to the bearer of it; and with the noisy festivity in which he delights, set the guns of all the batteries thundering. His health, however, has within the last few days been very indifferent, and yesterday the report of his medical attendants was extremely unfavorable, and even alarming; but this morning he is reported to be doing well again.

Mehemet Ali Bey, the bearer of the firman of investiture and the Sultan's instructions to Hafiz Pacha, proceeded in the Stamboul steamer to Samson on the 13th inst. On his reaching head-quarters Hafiz Pacha, it is said, will assume the offensive.—His operations have hitherto been confined to a march in the direction of Aintab, which was made to favor the revolt of several villages which had risen against Ibrahim at the instigation of their Sheiks. It was in executing this movement that his troops fell in with the Egyptian cavalry, and defeated them. I have heard it asserted at the Porte that they have also taken Aintab by storm; but the report, as far as I can ascertain, is unfounded. It is by no means probable that a decisive action will take place for a month to come. Hafiz Pacha, as I wrote to you last week, has only just been appointed to the command of all the Sultan's forces, and it will take him some time to concentrate the various divisions now at Kataya, Angora, and Bagdad.

FRANCE.

The trial of the insurgents of the 12th and 13th of May was still progressing on the 8th inst.—which was the 12th day of the trials.

The French papers contain nothing to call for particular notice.

"On the 9th the Peers met to deliberate on the verdict. Sixty questions, upon each of which a ballot will take place, were submitted to them, and the fate of Barbes, Mialon, and Martin Bernard gave rise to animated discussions the result of which would not, it is expected, be known before the 11th. In the event of any prisoners being condemned to death, they will be executed 24 hours after the sentence, and Louis Phillippe alone can save them—an event of extreme improbability, as every public office in Paris was put in a state of defence for the day of execution. Additional troops had been summoned to the French capital, which gave rise to the supposition that mercy would not be extended.

"It is presumed, from the number of insurgents of May yet to be tried, that the affair will not be concluded before the end of the year. In less than 48 hours an army of 100,000 men can be collected in Paris, where there are 16 regiments, besides 28 others cantoned at Vendome, Meulon, Versailles, Beauvais, St. Germain, Fontainbleau, Compeigne, Rambouillet, Orleans, Chartres, Amiens, Rouens, &c.

"PARIS, Tuesday, July 9.—The Five Per Cents left off at 111f. 90c. for the account, and 111f. 80c. for cash, as yesterday. The Threes closed at 79f. 50c. for cash, a rise of 15c.; and 79f 70c for the account, 10c. higher The Four-and-a-half per Cents 106f.; the Fours 103f. Bank of France Shares 2,705f, 5f. lower; Lafitte, nothing quoted.

"The Railroad Shares occupied the Money Market very strongly this day. The decision of the Chamber of Deputies in favor of the Government loan of five millions to the Versailles Left Bank Company produced the extraordinary rise of 122f. 50c. from yesterday's quotations, which were 175f., and are now 297f. 50c. Jobbing of the Court in favor of this company was openly hinted at, and some severe remarks were passed upon the honesty and wisdom of Deputies who could reject a work of public utility like the Havre and Paris Railroad to encourage two railroads to an uncommercial place like Versailles.

SPAIN.

Ximenes has been appointed Minister of Finance, and Alaix Minister of War. The first act of the new ministers was to change several of the provincial intendants. This measure had given universal satisfaction, and would exercise an influence at the next elections in favor of the Queen.

Narvaez has been appointed to command the army of the centre. The Carlists at Carrete had escaped, and by a rapid flight evaded the army of Narvaez. In the Carlist ranks great dissension prevailed, and one of Cabrera's aids had been shot by order of a court martial.

The Count d'Espange was preparing a large expedition at Berga, destination unknown.

THE HAGUE, July 6.—The marriage of the Hereditary Prince of Orange with the Princess Sophia of Wirtemburg is now null, according to the laws of the country. The new civil code of the Netherlands, like that of France, requires that a marriage should be preceded by two publications at the respective domiciles of the future husband and wife. The wise nogotiator at the Hague is supposed to have thought that this formality could be dispensed with. The publication did not take place at the Hague, although the marriage was celebrated at Stutgard. Were the husband to die now, leaving his wife *enciente*, the child would be illegitimate. The King is furious at this unexampled omission. Measures are being taken to repair the error, but the affair has made a great sensation.

We learn that the King, in his quality of Grand Duke of Luxemburg, is negotiating with the Pope for the exercise of the Catholic religion in his duchy; it was formerly in the see of Liege, but a separate bishop is talked of now.

There is a great deal of talking at Rotterdam about building a suspension bridge to unite the Isle of Fymon, celebrated for its iron works, to the town This has been tried before, but failed.

PASSENGERS BY THE BRITISH QUEEN ARRIVED THIS MORNING.

J L Little, R Martuscilli, C Abrahamson, Major Chase, C Fay, P Millhiroff, W B Huggins, D E Fermex, U Kraff, J W Coolidge, Fred'k Stobrar, Sam'l Cunard, S Breiter, W Munron, F Breisley, Ab. Wagman, H Von Voss, H Harmony, W H Thompson, G Hammond, Wm Dickinson, C A Auffin, Vrot T Palmer, E Pleasants, D B Green, C H Cope, T C Grattan, Mrs Green, Edmund Grattan, Thomas Harrison, O Mauron, Captain Leslie, J S Bates, William H Hart, Jonas Phillips, Mr Hemmerling, T Dickman, Fred Bunchler, Mrs. Grattan, D T Vail, Mrs Chase, Miss Grattan, Mrs Vail, Miss Wetherill, Maria Timeno, Dr McNought, Miss Mills, Miss Weir, A E L Weiderholdt, Miss Chambers, Mrs Thompson, A M Feltus, Aug C Cowman, A Gonim, A H Palmer, E Bedard, L Massue, C C Mills, S T Harrison, Dr S Hasley, J L Schrage, Montant C Gayarre, Col J W Webb, Mr Archibald, Mrs Starr, Master Webb, Mrs Archibald, Mrs Starr & servant, C F Baxter, Lewis Rogers, two masters Starr, H W Root, Amie Maosue, John Chambers, Cap Cumberland, jr, H Wier, jr, H Bentley, Mrs Cumberland, Cap Spaulding, L W Heath, A Sutton, H Sancard, Wm Maunder, G F Stoor, James Adgers, J De Bruggen, J W Staugley, F W Geiffer, Jacob Cootes, Thomas Green, H Johnson, A Allen, Eli Smith, H F Jaques, F Wright, O E Carmichael, C Demotte Destount, Courtenay Taggart, C F Baxter, Capt Irwin, W H Hackett, G D Wetherell, Francis Smith, Jno Smith, Mrs Baxter, Col Mudge, R H Eddy, B. Gordon, Thos Patterson, Col. Vernon, H L. Coppel, Morgan Hamilton, K. L. Smith, W. Rich, S. J. Patterson, Robert Hornden, G. H Featherstonhaugh, McCorquadale, Wm McGregor, John McQueen—5 servants.

LOG OF THE STEAM SHIP BRITISH QUEEN.

July 12—Sailed from Spithead at 1 o'clock P. M.—Wind WSW.

July 13th—Lat 49 32, lon. 5 45—St. Agnes Lighthouse NE ½ E. 9 leagues. Distance run, 245 miles.

14th—Wind WNW to S lat. 49 34, lon. 11.22—moderate and cloudy. Distance 218 miles.

15th—Wind WNW. lat. 49 23, lon. 15.50—strong breezes. Distance 181 miles.

16th—Wind SW by W & W. lat. 49.20, lon. 21.18—fresh gales and squally—head sea. Distance 210 miles.

17th—Wind N & NNW lat. 48.6, lon. 25.46—strong breezes, with head sea. Distance 198 miles.

18th—Wind N by W. lat. 46 56, lon. 30.10—strong breezes, with head sea. Distance 193 miles.

19th Wind N by W. & NW by W lat. 46.13, lon. 34.47—moderate breezes, with swell. Distance 198 miles.

20th—Wind WNW. lat 45.30, lon. 39 1—strong breezes and fresh gales, head sea—ship very easy. Distance 182 miles.

21st—Wind WNW. lat 45 4, lon. 42.1—fresh gales, with increasing sea. Distance 138 miles.

22d—Wind WNW. lat. 44.33, lon. 46 27—moderate breeze. Distance 190 miles.

23d—Wind WSW. lat. 43.42, lon. 51.2—light and fresh breezes. Distance 214 miles.

24th—Wind W by N. lat. 43.17, lon. 55.40—fresh breezes and squally. Distance 207 miles.

25th—Wind NW. lat. 42.23, lon. 60.30—light breezes and cloudy. Distance 221 miles.

26th—Wind W & WSW lat. 41.24, lon. 65 34—moderate breezes and fine. Distance 240 miles.

27th—Wind N. and variable, lat. 40.19, lon. 70.35—moderate and fine. Distance 240 miles.

EVENING PALLADIUM.

VOLUME I.—NUMBER 4.] NEW HAVEN, CONN., WEDNESDAY EVENING, OCTOBER 9, 1839. [SINGLE PAPER 2 CENTS

THE EVENING PALLADIUM

IS PUBLISHED ON MONDAYS, WEDNESDAYS, AND FRIDAYS—AT $2,50 PER ANNUM—AT 131 CHAPEL-STREET.

J. F. BABCOCK, EDITOR AND PROPRIETOR.

THE NEW HAVEN PALLADIUM

Is published every Saturday morning, on a sheet more than double the size of the Evening Palladium, at $2 per annum in advance. A discount made to those who receive their papers in bundles.

WEEKLY ALMANAC.

D. M.	OCT. 1839.	SUN RISES.	SUN SETS.	HIGH WATER.	MOON. R. & S.
7	Monday,	6 20	5 40	10 49	SETS.
8	Tuesday,	6 22	5 38	11 29	5 44
9	Wednesday,	6 23	5 37	A 12	6 8
10	Thursday,	6 24	5 36	0 58	6 37
11	Friday,	6 25	5 35	1 45	7 12
12	Saturday,	6 26	5 34	2 35	7 53
13	Sunday,	6 27	5 33	3 27	8 43

THE AMISTAD.

The following NARRATIVE is translated for the New York Express, from the Spanish paper "*Noticioso de Ambos Mundos.*

To-day, at last, we publish the sad narrative of the voyage of Messieurs Ruiz and Montez on board of the schooner Amistad; it is very concise and unadorned. It will undoubtedly be found wanting in style, and many details have been omitted, as the minds of the narrators have not yet regained the necessary composure, nor their memory the strength requisite for the undertaking, after such dreadful sufferings, the relation of which would according to their own statement take up a large volume. Perhaps with time they will recollect other important details which may hereafter be published; we notice however that at present they do not explain the manner in which the two white sailors escaped, and no mention is made of them having been compelled to drink salt water for several days and to bathe themselves in the sea to quench their thirst.

VOYAGE OF THE SCHOONER "AMISTAD."

On the 28th day of June, 1839, at 4 o'clock in the afternoon, there sailed from the port of Havana, the Spanish schooner Amistad, Capt. Ramon Ferrer, of about 45 tons burthen, bound to the port of Guanaja, which is 14 leagues distant from the city of Puerto Principe and 110 leagues from the city of Havana. The crew of said vessel consisted of two sailors whose names were Jacinto Verdaque and Manuel Padilla, the first a native of Catalonia, and the second of Santa Domingo, the cook named Celestino, who was a mulatto, the slave of the Captain, and a black boy about 16 years of age, who was also a slave of the Captain. There were also on board of the said schooner two passengers whose names were Don Jose Ruiz, a native of Rodezno, in Old Castille, of about 24 years of age, and Don Pedro Montes, a native of the city of Tortosa, a province of Catalonia, aged 58 years, and both residents of Puerto Principe, in Cuba. There were also on board 53 negro slaves, of whom 49 belonged to Senor Ruiz, and 3 little negro girls and a little negro boy were the property of Don Pedro Montes. These gentlemen were taking their slaves to the city of Puerto Principe for their service. The said vessel having passed the Moro at 5 o'clock in the afternoon, of the 28th of the said month of June, on her voyage aforesaid. On the night immediately after her departure, one of the sailors observed that the slaves were coming up from the hold to the forecastle, and that they made some noise, on which account the sailor reprimanded them and told them to be quiet and go down into the hold. On the third day after their departure, as the moon rose, say about 11 o'clock at night, being one league distant from the Cape called Bahia de Cadiz, there arose from the land a storm, and it became necessary to lower the sails; the storm, which lasted an hour and a half or two hours, passed over, and all on board, with the exception of the helmsman, went to sleep. The slaves were some in the hold, and some on deck. When all were sunk in sleep, they heard and were awakened by a great uproar, and Don Pedro Montes and the Captain got up, and the former observed that the slaves were killing the cook. Senor Montes and the two sailors ran to his assistance, Senor Montes having a knife in his hand, and one of the sailors a stick, and they made them retire behind the foresail; Senor Ruiz stood before the Caboose and halloed to the slaves to be quiet and to go down into the hold; one of the sailors who had no arm of defence told Don Pedro Montes, that if the cook (who was already dead) had a knife about him he should take it and give it to him. In this emergency, he hallooed to Don Pedro Montes to kill some of the slaves, but the latter from compassion, only wounded a few of them to frighten them. The Captain observing what was going on and with a view to appease the negroes, told his slave boy Antonio to bring a basket of sea biscuit, and to throw some to the negroes over the hatches; then some of the negroes advanced from under the foresail to gather the biscuit, but they were all now armed with cane-knives, which they had taken out of a box that was in the hold. The Captain then hallooed to the little black, his slave, to bring him his dagger.—Montes again attacked them with his knife, and they retired behind the foresail, the negroes striking blows at Montes with their sticks and cane-knives, which he parried with a pump handle which he held in his left hand, and he attacked them, at the same time, with the knife in his right. During this struggle Don Pedro observed that the negroes were going to strike him with an oar—he then retired under the foresail and seized the oar by the flat part of it, and endeavored to draw toward himself the negro who held the oar; then two other blacks seized the oar, and some other negroes with another oar struck Senor Montes about the legs and other parts, until one of the sailors halloed to him to let go the oar or they would kill him; at this time the knife dropped from the hand of Montes, in consequence of a blow which he received on the arm, and while stooping and looking for it about the floor, they gave him a powerful blow on the head with a cane knife, and he fell senseless on the deck. Before this occurrence the same sailor had halloed to Montes not to be stooping looking for the knife, because they would kill him. Montes tried to rise, but his strength failing him he staggered to the cabin, and fell headlong below, and when in the cabin he had sufficient presence of mind to creep behind some barrels of sea biscuit upon which he found an old sail, which he threw upon himself. As soon as it was day-light a black (who caused himself to be acknowledged the chief or ringleader of the mutineers) came down with a cane knife in his hand, accompanied by another black, and hearing the hard breathing of Montes came furiously upon him and struck at him two or three blows with the cane knife, when the other black who accompanied the ringleader seized the latter by the arm as he heard Montes begging for his life; then both seized Montes by the arms and took him up, and the first object which Montes saw was Don Jose Ruiz seated upon the hen-coop with both hands tied. The two negroes then untied Ruiz, and tied one arm of Ruiz to another of Montes, and threatened to kill them, making at the same time horrible gestures, while Ruiz and Montes begged for their lives. At last they again loosened them; they stripped Montes of his clothes, which were covered with blood from his wounds; they took from him the key of his trunk and brought him clean clothes, which they made him put on. After finishing this operation they ordered Montes to take the rudder and govern the vessel. Montes now being placed at the rudder cast a look over the whole deck to see if he could recognise any of his companions; he saw the deck covered with blood and that the negroes were washing it; and as Montez saw only Ruiz and the cabin boy Antonio, (who spoke Spanish well,) he supposed that they had murdered the captain, the two sailors, and the cook; the black boy Antonio told him afterwards that they had killed only the captain; Montes knew already that they had murdered the cook, whose body covered with wounds was at the stern in the boat, where the cook used to sleep. After placing Montes at the rudder the negroes ordered him to steer toward the rising of the sun, which Montes obeyed, but he always kept the sails flapping in the wind, and the vessel made very little headway. In this manner passed the whole of that day until the moon rose at midnight, when there blew a violent squall from the land, and it became necessary to lower the sails and to keep only the foretopsail. At this time the negroes were so frightened that they kept saying that they were going to die, that they would be drowned. Montes then tacked to the west, and when the squall ceased he bore away before the wind. In the morning, about two hours before daybreak, the vessel got in soundidgs, and Montes tacked to sea; as soon as it was day he tacked again to the soundings. The vessel was now in soundings and the day was quite clear, when the negroes observing that Montes had made the vessel turn around during the squall, imagined that he wished to take them to Havana; they held a consultation among themselves below in the cabin, and then came up with the intention of killing Ruizzand Montes—Jose Senqui, the ringleader, holding a dagger in his hand; Montes perceiving that Senqui was advancing as if to kill him, fell upon his knees and begged him to spare his life, telling him he had a family and children. They steered towards soundings, and about mid-day they saw the keys or shoals (Los Roques,) and as the negroes always kept one of their number at the mast-head, as soon as he saw the Roques, he exclaimed that he saw houses, and that it was Havana; the others then became enraged, and made Montes change the course of the vessel, but Montes told them they were not houses but rocks, and that if they proved to be houses they might cut his throat. Upon this they allowed Montes to steer toward the keys, being satisfied with his assurances. They thus passed two days, making very little headway, and cast ancher at night, as there was very little wind. This was done by Montes with the view of suffering the vessel to be taken by some man of war cruizing in those seas, as there are usually many English and other national vessels cruizing thereabout, but unfortunately they only saw a merchantman which appeared to be an American, and althouhh she came very near she paid no attention to the Amistad, though Montes endeavored by all possible means to make them understand that there was nobody on board who could govern the vessel, as he repeatedly steered to the windward and immediately after to the leeward. On the following day the wind blew from the south though not strong, and they steered toward the east, coasting along the keys, in the direction of Anguilla, Montes all the time expecting to be taken by some vessel. Near Anguilla they saw a hermaphrodite brig sailing westward; perceiving that it took no notice of them, Montes asked the negroes if they wished to go to a free country where there were no slaves; his object was to escape to shore with Ruiz and the boy Antonio, who served them well and faithfully. They answered they were willing to go, upon which Montes steered N. E. in the direction of the island San Andres, anchoring for two nights successively on the shoals. After three days they arrived at the island, the weather having been calm; they arrived at three o'clock, P. M., and anchored as near shore as possible. They immediately lowered the boat, and the ringleader Jose, with four blacks, got into it to go ashore, leaving Montes and Ruiv on board, when suddenly observing a great smoke ashore, they returned, got aboard, and set sail; but as they were very scant of water and on allowance, the negroes asked Montes if he knew any place where they could get water; he answered he did, and as his object was always to escape ashore, to suffer himself to be taken by some other vessel, or to escape in the boat, he steered toward the little Keys near San Andros; and passing among them he went to Green Key, about 18 leagues distant from New Providence, where he knew there was water. In five days they arrived at Green Key, having kept but little sail set, and made slow progress. Upon their arrival the negroes performed some superstitious ceremonies, each one casting into the water the clothes he wore and putting on new. Having anchored, they lowered the boat, and Montes wishing to get into it, under the pretext of showing where there was water, but in reality with the intention of escaping, they did not allow him, but made him stay aboard, and only four negroes, with the boy Antonio, went ashore, taking two demijohns for water and a loaded pistol to make a signal if they found it.

Before going they inquired of Montes where they might find water. They reached land, run the boat aground, and went in search of water according to the directions given them by Montes; they found it at last, filled their demijohns, came to the beach near the vessel, and discharged the pistol. At the moment those aboard heard the sound they kneeled and prostrated themselves before Montes, returning him thanks, touching his hands, and telling him that he was a very excellent man, so much were they in want of water.—The boat arrived from shore, the negroes rushed upon the water, and the two demijohns were immediately emptied. The negroes that had been ashore manifested the delight with which they had drunk, and they were all exceedingly rejoiced, together with Ruiz and Montes, who partook of the water. They weighed anchor and went to the north part of the Island, approaching nearer to the spot where the water had been found; —another reason for anchoring there was, that it looked stormy towards the South, and if the wind blew from that quarter the vessel might run aground. The negroes went again for water with five or six demijohns, pots and bottles, and though they brought them full it was again soon drunk up.

After having been taking in water for two days, on the morning of the third day the wind having blown fresh, their cable parted before they had a full supply and they were obliged to set sail, and thus the plans of Ruiz and Montes to escape in the boat were frustrated, which plans they would have otherwise undoubtedly accomplished, In the morning Montes asked them if they wished to anchor again with another anchor and chain which were left, in order to get a full supply of water and wood, as the latter was also scarce. They answered no, and then Montes steered towards New Providence, and as they arrived near this Island about ten o'clock in the day, they saw two fishing smacks. One of them was about approaching the vessel when the negroes obliged Montes to bear away to the East, to escape it: at night they anchored in soundings near the shore of New Providence. On the following day, they again set sail, and as the current is very strong there at the rising and ebbing of the tides, Montes always kept the vessel making very little way, and the sails flapping in the wind as if they were lying-to, and they again anchored in the same place. When at anchor they saw a fishing smack, and supposing that the schooner wanted a pilot to steer her into port, it came within hailing distance, when the negroes were alarmed and seized their cane knives, and the people on board the smack perceiving this, were afraid and put off. Montes supposing that the smack would give information in the port, full of hopes kept sailing about in that part for seven days without the negroes perceiving it. At last they observed what was going on and they compelled Montes to steer towards the rising sun, which he did and went towards the Exuma Keys. As soon as the negroes saw so many keys, they made Montes steer towards the West without being aware of what they were doing; but at sun-set observing that the vessel was going towards the West, they became exceedingly enraged at Montes because he was taking them towards Havana. He then explained to them that they themselves had so ordered it and they answered that Montes ought to have apprised them of it; he replied that they were very noisy and would not let him do what was best. Then they allowed him to steer towards the East and they came to anchor near a key and as the tide ebbed at midnight the vessel began to touch bottom; alarmed at this, the negroes awoke Montes, who was resting overcome with fatigue, and they made him set sail, steering again towards the Exuma Keys; as soon as they approached them they were afraid of touching bottom again, and as one of them was at the mast head they saw an open sea with no land visible. They ordered Montes to steer towards it, and he answered that they could not pass that way; but they, without paying any attention to what Montes said began to direct the vessel, which made it every moment strike upon the rocks and and it was next to a miracle that it was not wrecked. Having made some progress in this manner the negroes were convinced they could not pass that way and left the command of the vessel to Montes, who took them to the same key where they had been the day before and they again anchored near it, and Don Pedro Montes told them that it was their fault they had not yet left the place. They were persuaded it was so, and much pleased with Don Pedro, they shook hands with him and told him he was a fine man, and in future to do as he pleased without minding their talk. At daybreak of the following day they again steered towards the Exuma Keys; at five o'clock in the afternoun they anchored near a key, where there was a small English vessel at anchor, the people on board of which, observing the schooner, were afraid, and took their vessel through a narrow channel into the island. That night the negroes slept with their knives under their heads, and at daybreak the same small vessel passed them astern; upon this the negroes got up and seized their weapons; but the small vessel went on, passed through the keys and went out to sea. They soon set sail again, and went after the small vessel towards Long Island, at the request of the blacks. In the morning they arrived at the windward of Long Island, and again saw the same small vessel going into that Island. Montes then asked the blacks if they wanted to follow the small craft, as the water was almost gone. They answered in the affirmative, and after running aground once, they went in after the said craft; but as they had gone in so far that it was too shallow, and the negroes saw three dwellings on the shore, they put out again, and as the current was very strong against them, and there was very little breeze, and it was late, they were compelled to anchor. At this time the negroes lowered the boat, and went ashore towards a dwelling for the purpose of getting water and buying rum with the money they had purloined. Montes having previously told them, that there were only negroes in that part and no slaves; but upon their meeting two white men, as the negroes belonging to the dwelling were out engaged in the fields, they were afraid, returned to the vessel, and set sail, and went to a point of the Island where there was another house. Here they anchored—the negroes went ashore and returned at about 8 o'clock in the evening, saying that the people of the house had run away from them, and that they had seen many chickens, goats and sheep. Shortly after, there came astern a boat with two white men, —the negroes seized their knives,—the two men of the boat asked what vessel or schooner it was, and the blacks without answering, asked in turn where the boat was going; and the two men replied in English, "We are going home, of course." The negroes asked if they had fish; they answered they had, and went ashore.

On the following day they set sail, and they fired a gun from the house as a signal to call them ashore, and the negroes fired a pistol. Montes then saw with the glass that six or seven men, black and white, were coming from the house to the shore, and as soon as they came to the beach, they again fired twice. As there was but little breeze, they saw them for a long time on the shore,—the negroes understood that they were invited to land, but fear prevented them. At last they got out and put to sea. On the next day they again tacked towards the Island; and as the negroes every day searched the hold, they found seven demijohns of red wine in the locker. They began drinking the wine, which lasted only two days, and some got drunk, particularly one of the ringleaders. In the afternoon they arrived at Long Island on the sea side, where they saw seven or eight houses, and the negroes made preparations to go ashore; and as they were drunk and quite merry, perceiving some negroes ashore, they began to deck their persons with the clothes of the passengers, of the dead captain, and with India silk handkerchiefs as belts, which they got out from the cargo, saying they were going ashore to drink rum and make love. They accordingly lowered the boat, and as they were going into it fully armed, Montes perceiving that they were much excited by drink, and fearing that they might commit some crime ashore for which he and Ruiz would have to suffer, advised and persuaded them to return aboard, which they did. They put off as before to the SSW. and in the morning they came to the same place whence they had sailed;—they put out in the afternoon, discovered a large brig, and although she must have observed that the schooner had only the mainsail, the jib and the foretopsail set, when she might have all sail set—the brig paid no attention to them.

They again steered towards the Exuma Keys with the view of getting water, and again the same smack which they met at Long Island followed them, no doubt intending to plunder them if they were wrecked on those shoals. Two days after they ran aground, having mistaken the Key, as they had lost all reckoning. When aground the negroes began to perform superstitious ceremonies; they threw their shirts overboard, the pots and other utensils, and they brought to Don Pedro a piece of plate, a pistol and other articles that he might throw them overboard. It appears that the object of these ceremonies was to break the charm in which they supposed they were; they said the plate, which was white, was to please God, and that the dirty and black articles were to appease the Devil. At this place the vessel lost the kelson and false key upon the rocks, and the rudder got off and thereupon one of the negroes was going to cut Montes' throat, when another seized him by the arm at the very moment of striking the blow. Soon after the schooner anchored in three fathoms and a half of water; and here Montes began to repair the sails, which were torn, and to caulk the boat to go in search of water. While thus engaged, there came three boats from one of the keys, with 18 or 20 blacks. Before the boats approached, the negroesin the schooner made Ruiz and Montes go down into the cabin, as they always did when a vessel or boat approached.—The blacks in the boats seeing those in the schooner, were afraid and returned ashore. Next day they weighed anchor and they went for the purpose of getting water towards the Key whence they supposed the three boats had come, but shortly after weighing anchor the bow of the schooner struck on a reef, which made the schooner labor much and made her recede a considerable distance. They went to the Key thinking they were in soundings, but soon found that they were getting out to sea; they approached the Key as much as possible, and the negroes seeing rocks at the bottom and being afraid, refused to anchor, and they steered to sea.

After being two days out of soundings, they found that they were quite out at sea, at which Montes be-

[*Continued on* LAST *page.*]

[*Concluded from* LAST *page.*]

a small barrel of water and some apples and biscuit. As the other two pilots approached, the negroes armed themselves and the pilots went away, and when they were a great distance off, the blacks made Montes come on deck after having had a consultation together, and made him kneel down, telling him that they were going to kill him, because they believed he had brought them to that place to take them again to Havana. Many came up to him saying they were going to cut his throat, and the ring-leader, Jose Senqui, seized a dagger and a sword. Upon this all commenced to sing and dance, preparing themselves thus to kill Montes; as soon as the song was ended Jose Senqui came upon Montes, held the dagger and sword to kill him, and making the most horrible contortions with his eyes, and as he was going to give the blow, two other negroes took hold of his arm. After this horrible scene, they again placed Montes at the helm, made Ruiz come up and made him sit down upon the quarter deck, saying they would not kill him. On the next day they made Montes repair the sail, and as there was but little wind, they made very little headway; in the afternoon another pilot with about ten men approached and they made Ruiz and Montes go below. This pilot asked the same questions as the former, and the negroes told them that they did not want any thing; the pilot got angry and had some high words with the blacks, who, seeing that the former wanted to get possession of the vessel, armed themselves, and began to sing in the same manner as when they prepared to kill Montes. The blacks then compelled Montes to steer Eastward. They then saw a ship which appeared to be English, and as she approached the negroes made Ruiz and Montes go below.—This ship passed so near that the negroes said they had seen two dogs aboard. That same day they saw many vessels. At night they began to steer to the North, passing many large and small vessels. Shortly after this Montes gave the helm to Ruiz, requesting him to be very particular to steer to the North; and as the wind blew fresh, he luffed up, and the boom struck the ring-leader, Jose, and almost killed him, which alarmed all the other blacks. Montes again took the helm, and steered towards the NW., and all fell asleep soundly, and Montes being alone at the helm, in the morning he perceived what appeared to be a star, and which after a while he recognized as a light house; he then let the vessel go towards land, intending to run her aground, but it occurred to him that they might kill him as they had attempted it before, and as they were so near the land and all were asleep, he woke one of the blacks up and told him that he thought he saw land, and that they slept too much; the negro replied that it was land, and that the light was from some house on the coast of Africa, and told Montes to steer towards it; he did so, and as the wind was not strong in the morning, they were a short distance from the light house. The negroes perceived many vessels towards the opposite coast, made Montes steer towards the light, and they anchored about one mile from the shore. They then lowered the boat, and four or five blacks went ashore with two demijohns and found plenty of water; they filled the demijohns, and came aboard for others, and they began to take in a supply of water, leaving the foretopsail set. They were engaged all that day bringing water, and one of the blacks ran away and went to a neighboring house, where he slept all night. Some of the negroes remained on shore to observe if Montes jumped into the water. In the morning of the following day they again went for water, and as the negro who had run away did not appear, they said ironically to Montes and Ruiz that the people of that country must be very free indeed, when they had bound their comrade. Though Montes told them this could not be the case, they persisted in their assertion, and said that they had found a piece of the rope with which they had bound their companion, and the traces on the ground over which they had led him. At ten o'clock a person from the house brought the negro to the beach, and his companions were much rejoiced at seeing him. Then the ring-leader, Jose, another black, and the boy Antonio, determined to go ashore to the house, Montes and Ruiz urging them to do so. In about an hour or an hour and a half they returned, with a bottle of gin and some sweet potatoes. At about two o'clock in the afternoon three or four men appeared on the beach on horseback and in a gig, and made a great noise, two or three of the blacks then came aboard and carried two muskets ashore. About four o'clock the white men went away and the ringleaders and some other blacks came on board of the schooner, saying that on the following day the white men would come on board.

Shortly after the white men returned and began to cry out to the negroes to look out because a man-of-war was coming. This was true, as there was at a distance an American brig which proved to be the U. S. brig Washington, commanded by Lieut. Gedney. The brig lowered her boat and the negroes perceiving her to be a man-of-war, two of the ring-leaders and two others went below, took out two trunks and a portmanteau, and got into the boat, which was a very fortunate occurrence for Ruiz and Montes, for if they had been on board when the brig's boat arrived they would have killed them, as they had told them they would do in such an event. At last the deliverers from the brig arrived on board, being about six in number, and learning from Don Jose Ruiz, who came up when the boat approached, all that had happened, Lieut. Meade and officer Porter, who had come in the boat, made all the negroes go below into the hold. When they were all below, Mr. Porter went ashore in the boat with four sailors in pursuit of the negroes who had remained on the beach, among whom was the leader, Jose Senqui; but Mr. Porter met the boat coming towards the Amistad. The negroes in the boat perceiving the brig's boat coming in pursuit of them, turned again for the shore, and Mr. Porter then fired a pistol over their heads, which made them afraid, and they allowed themselves to be taken on board of the Amistad. As soon as Senqui came on board he went down into the hold, but bouncing up again he jumped into the water. Then Mr. Porter got into the boat with some sailors and pursued him, but Senqui swam away, and when the boat approached him he dove and again came up some distance from the boat, until Mr. Porter pulled out a pistol and threatened to shoot him if he did not surrender. Then Senqui approached and they hooked him by his clothes with the boat hook, took him in and brought him on board of the Amistad. Messrs. Ruiz and Montes gave many and repeated thanks to their deliverers for the service they had rendered them, and for the kind manner in which they offered them clothes and every kind of comfort when they went on board the brig. The negroes being secured on board of the Amistad, and Ruiz and Montez with the negro Senqui being on board of the brig Washington, the schooner was towed by the brig and taken into the port of New London, in the State of Connecticut, where they arrived on the 26th day of August, 1939, after having been 60 days at sea.

EVENING PALLADIUM

NEW HAVEN, OCTOBER 9, 1839.

THE NEXT CONGRESS.—The New York Express, republishes the list of the members of the new Congress. Mississippi is to choose on the 15th of November, and as fifteen days are allowed to furnish returns to the Governor, there is no probability that the members from that State, will be in Washington, in season to vote for the Speaker. The Express says—"The members chosen and the four members in South Carolina and Massachusetts,—will decide the result. No member we are told, can be returned from Mr. Harrison's district in Missouri by December. By the last dates from St. Louis, we learn that the Governor had not then issued a proclamation for an election, and as the sheriffs are required to give thirty days notice of the days of election, it will be impossible for an election to be held, and the result ascertained, in time for the members elect to reach Washington by the opening of the next Congress.—Who will be the Speaker of the next house, remains a matter of doubt. If the State Rights men are true to themselves, and the majority who elected them, the choice will fall upon a Whig,—probably upon Mr. Bell of Tennessee."

☞ Assessors and Board of Relief only were chosen at our town meeting last Monday. The locos made a rush and expected to catch the Whigs sleeping; but they found themselves mistaken, and were beaten more than two to one. The gentlemen chosen Assessors, are Messrs. Frederick Lines, Elihu Atwater, Wyllis Peck, Amos Bradley, and Isaac Foot. Board of Relief—Messrs. Stephen Bishop, John Durrie, Eli B. Austin, Isaac Dickerman, Alfred Daggett. The proposed amendment to the Constitution received 126 votes—against it *one.*

THANKSGIVING.—The Governor has appointed Thursday, the 28th of next month, to be observed as a day of Thanksgiving in this State.

The Fair of the American Institute opened in New York on Monday, and will probably continue open for some days.

Elections took place in Ohio, Pennsylvania, and New Jersey, yesterday. The results will be interesting, although no members of Congress have been chosen. We shall have the news in a few days—perhaps a little from New Jersey to-day.

MARYLAND.—The election news from Maryland is confirmed. The members of Congress last year stood four to four—now they stand five locos to three Whigs—a Whig loss of one. The Whigs have been more scared than hurt in regard to Maryland. The turning of the scale was in Baltimore city, where a small majority secured two members. Luck, mere luck, as well as the government patronage, is almost invariably with the locos. The names of the members chosen are John Dennis, (district No. 1); Wm. Cost Johnson, (No. 5); Daniel Jennifer, (No. 7)—*Whigs.* P. F. Thomas, (No. 2); J. T. H. Carroll, (4th); S. Hillen, Jr. (do.); Francis Thomas, (6th)—Loco Focos. In the House of Delegates, there are 31 Whigs and 47 Loco Focos. In Calvert county, there is a tie, 2 and 2.

The Bank of Middlebury, Vt., has declared its intention to wind up its business, as has the Willoughby Bank at Brooklyn.

The Halifax gale of Sept. 13th, was severely felt also on land. At Antigonish, vessels were driven ashore, and a new one, which was building, was scattered to pieces. Trees, barns, &c. were blown down in every direction.

Mr. Ambler, of Fauquer county, Va. recently sold, it is said, mulberry trees to the amount of $10,000, the produce of half an acre!

"I would myself banish all paper money.—*Tom Benton's Letter.*

Save enough to stiffen your cravat.—*Baltimore News.*

DEGENERACY.—A grandson of the patriot and statesman, Gov. Hancock, was brought before the Boston police court on Thursday of last week as a common drunkard.

THE VOYAGE OF THE AMISTAD.—We publish today the narrative of the voyage of Messrs. Ruiz and Montez, on board the schooner Amistad. It is their side of the story, and is quite interesting, as it is a more connected detail of events than any thing we have seen. Remembering what we have heard of this affair, we are surprised that the Spaniards have not told a worse tale; for although it is bad enough at best, it yet does not represent the negroes to have been half as ferocious and blood-thirsty, as did the reports at the time of their capture. In fact, this account, in several particulars, acknowledges a manifestation of confidence and gratitude decidedly creditable to any set of men, and especially to the poor wretches referred to. Their whole object and aim appeared to be *home,* as was so frequently expressed in the earnest inquiry, "where is Africa?" If home was all, they certainly are not the bucaniers they were at first supposed to be.

Mr. Pickens, of South Carolina, is spoken of as the Administration candidate for Speaker of the House of Representatives.

The New Orleans Advertiser of the 24th Sept. says, the epidemic is rapidly abating.

The tops of the mountains in the neighborhood of Rutland, Vt., were covered with snow on Saturday last.

THE CURRENCY.—At the North little is said about a National Bank. The merchants and manufacturers sweat and groan under the present state of things, and think hardly any change in regard to the currency can be for the worse—any change but the sub-treasury, and this they know to be too "disorganizing and revolutionary" to be tolerated under any circumstances. At the South, however, where sub-treasuryism has been in better odor, and where opposition to a national bank has been very general, they seem to be out of all patience with the operations of the 'experiment,' and clamor loudly for a National Regulator of the Exchanges. The locos occupy a consistent ground now. They are for hard money, no credit, and the sub-treasury. These three jingle well together. Enlightened business men go for the credit system under a proper regulation—not as it was in 1836, when it resembled a locomotive dashing furiously off without an engineer to direct it—but as it was when it had a National Regulator for its guide. Then it moved off steadily, drawing a full train of merchandize, the products of prosperous commercial and manufacturing industry. The question of a National Bank will one day, and not long hence, become a party question again. The locos will as usual fall in with the popular current, admit the proposition to be democratic, declare they were always in in favor of one, and opposed only to Biddle's Bank, and will perhaps triumph on this very issue. They have come into several whig measures in this precise manner—but this will be better than persisting in error. Nevertheless, it should be a serious question with the voters, whether such reckless managers ought to be much longer entrusted with political power. We are sure they would not be if some men were not '*too busy*' with their private affairs to attend to their public duties; and others too easily humbugged by false issues, to appreciate the demands which our business and political institutions have upon them.

☞ We are greatly pained to hear of the death of Judge BUEL, the famous Agriculturalist, and a most worthy man. On his way to this city to deliver an Address to the Agricultural and Horticultural Societies, he was taken ill at Danbury, at which place he died on Sunday.

TOWN MEETINGS.—The Town Meetings, generally held on Monday, as far as heard from, afford no encouragement to the loco focos. In Derby, after counting the ballots three or four times, a majority of one was declared for the loco focos, at the moment three or four whigs appeared to vote, who had arrived *too late.* Waterbury has gone for the locos by 40, which is a gain to them. North Branford has given a whig majority of 19; a whig gain. Guilford, East Haven, Orange, Milford, Woodbridge and Madison, whig. Hamden, Branford, Bethany, Wallingford, and North Haven, loco as usual. In North Haven the loco majority was reduced to 14.

Wolcott, loco, as usual. Prospect, tie—good grit, voted till midnight.

On the whole the elections in our county are a little better than we expected.

GOOD.—New Milford, whig—Perry Smith to the contrary notwithstanding.

The number of deaths in N. York, from the 28th day of September to the 5th day of October, 1839, is 39 men; 35 women; 41 boys; 39 girls.—Total 154.

Be contented and thankful; a cheerful spirit makes labor light, sleep sweet, and all around happy—all of which is much better than being only *rich.*

THE FIRE IN NEW YORK.—The names of most of the sufferers by the great fire in New York, as published in the city papers, are as follow—on Water street, S. D. Halsey & Co. Jessup & Gilbert, Simeon Dunn & Co. H. E. Shackerly, J. W. Brodie, J. Hunt & Co. Z. B. Goodwin, James A. Kissam, Stephen King, A. Megary, J. & L. Brewster, Eli White, R. & H. Haight, W. & A. White, John Hunt, Alfred Seton, E. C. Boughton, Vaeder, Little & Merrick.

On Burling Slip—Gen. Storms, Stephen W. West, David Keys, Jewett & Son, George C. Fowler, C. Ballou & Co. R. M. Demill, Mitchell & Co. W. E. & J. Craft, B. Z. Waite, Pollen & Colgate, J. C. Ashley, Hope Mills, C. Fulton.

On Fulton street—Mr. Thompson, N. & L. Bradford.

On Fletcher street—Mr. Hawkes, Ross, Duffy & Son.

MR. EDITOR:—Judge Darling made himself very busy, before the meeting on Monday last for the choice of Assessors and Board of Relief, in calling on such Whigs as were known to be opposed to the canal, and urging them to be present and support an "*Anti-Canal Ticket,*" which he had made up. When the time arrived, we were surprised to find among the strongest supporters of this "*Anti-Canal Ticket,*" Wm. Mix, Esq. and Silas Mix, Esq., two gentlemen who have labored and *talked* more in behalf of saddling the city with that concern, than almost any other individuals. This is enough of itself, to show the motives of the Locos who would introduce this subject into our political contests. They care nothing for it themselves, but hope to divide the Whig ranks. They will find their labor lost. *Anti-Canal and Anti-Loco Foco.*

From the Hartford Courant we learn that one of the hands on board the steamboat Cleopatra, was drowned while assisting to land a passenger at Wethersfield. The passenger was saved by clinging to his trunk.

The N. York Express says, the two slavers brought to New York, by the British brig Buzzard, are to sail in a few days for Jamaica, the government of the U. S. having declined to exercise any jurisdiction over them.

SNOW STORM.—We learn from the Buffalo Journal that there was a severe snow storm in that place and vicinity, on the night of the 27th ult. It was followed, not by frost, but a perfect congelation. On the highlands, at a distance from the lake, the snow fell to the depth of six or eight inches!

CHARGE OF FORGERY.—Two charges were made on Monday at New York, against Albert L. Merriam, of the firm of Kellogg & Merriam, for forging the names of Miller & Bancker, as endorsers on notes which he passed to Foulke & Son, in payment of coffee. One of the notes was for $965 85, and the other for $637 45. He was fully committed.

KIDNAPPING.—The Massachusetts Spy, says of Shearer, the scoundrel who was recently detected in kidnapping a colored boy, that since his arrest he has confessed that he has followed the business of kidnapping six years past, and that he is connected with a gang of kidnappers whose organization extends from New England to Virginia.

Mr. Wood, the Philadelphia murderer, it would seem, according to an article in the Pennsylvanian, put his daughter to death because her marrying Mr. Peak led to the disappointment of some ambitious schemes which he had formed. He was an Englishman by birth, and his intention was to return to his native country, as soon as he had acquired a fortune, and marry his daughter to some person of high rank. So fixed was his intention to accomplish this end, that he was averse to his daughter mingling with society, fearing that some one would obtain her affections. He was, nevertheless, a very indulgent parent, and appears to have absolutely adored her whom he so ruthlessly murdered.

TOWN MEETINGS.—In many of the towns in the State, elections were held yesterday for the choice of Selectmen, &c. In Suffield, the Whigs chose the first selectman by one majority; the Locos succeeded in carrying the remaining two, each by a majority of one. From Berlin, we learn that the Whigs carried the town clerk by a small majority, but our informant came away too soon to give us any further information.—*Hartford Courant.*

LATE FROM CHINA.—Advices from Canton to the 22d May were received at New York on Saturday, by the ship Canada, which brought a cargo of teas and silks. The correspondent of the Journal of Commerce, in a postscript to his letter, says: "The trade is about being stopped again." The Government has issued an edict, decreeing death and the confiscation of goods to all found engaged in the importation of opium.

A MOST DISTRESSING SHIPWRECK.—We learn from the Baltimore Patriot that Captain Little, of the ship Glasgow, at that port from Liverpool, reports on the 18th Sept. in lat 39 40, long. 61 20, wind light from the westward and baffling, he discovered at a distance the appearance of a raft with something on it, bore up and sent his boat and took from it three human beings, with scarcely any life in them—took them on board, and learnt that they were the only survivors of a crew of 19 men, belonging to the ship Arab, Capt. Robertson, of and for Hull, from Balize, Honduras, with a cargo of mahogany. During the gale of the 13th September, she was dismasted, and finally went entirely to pieces. Those saved were on the side of the poop, being four planks twenty feet long.—They had been on this raft five days without any thing except two coca nuts, which they found, and were in a most wretched and starving condition when taken off, and would not have survived another day. There were originally nine upon the raft, including the mate, but they had previously died, or becoming deranged for want of food had jumped into the sea.

[*Continued from first page.*]

came much disheartened, seeing that they had only one cask of water, no sails, no instrument of navigation, and that it was the bad season of the month of August; and as the negroes compelled him to steer E. and E. S. E. he supposed that they would find no land and perish from want, without meeting any vessel to give them aid. Montes finding himself in this difficulty, addressed Ruiz, telling him he would venture to go to the United States; Ruiz answered that he thought it was well to propose it to the blacks, but Montes was so disheartened that he replied it was of no use, that he had made up his mind to die. Ruiz however insisted and proposed the matter to the negroes, who asked how many days it would take to get there. Montes answered, in 8 or 10 days, if the weather was good.

It is proper to observe here, that during the days that the schooner had been among the Keys, the negroes had consumed the best of the provisions,—had opened and destroyed several cases of clothing, and every instant threatened Don Pedro with death, and even attempted to kill him and Ruiz while sleeping, for which reason they always asked one of the leaders, who promised to befriend them to sleep near them. The negroes finally consented to go to the United States, having been informed first that it was a country where there were no slaves. They steered N. N. E. Don Pedro then being quite fatigued asked Ruiz if he would undertake to steer the vessel, and he answered that he would, provided Don Pedro would direct him. On the second day after changing the course to the United States, at day break they saw a ship which passed very near without paying any attention to them. On the fourth or fifth day they saw a schooner astern, which they observed was steering North and they followed her course. At night they steered N. N. W. Two days after that they saw a ship and a brig steering N. E.; they then made the same course all that day and all night, being now in the soundings of the U. States. On the following days, as they saw no more sails, and Montes intended to go to the Southern part of the U. States because it was the nearest, they steered N. W. The wind blew fresh from the N. E. and it began to rain. Two days after this they saw a ship and afterwards a schooner at sunset; as the latter approached she steered E. S. E. and they followed after her because a storm was coming. After sunset there blew a gale and the sky became clouded, which made them strike all sails and put the foretopsail on deck and lay to with only the foresail, and the other schooner did the same.

At day-break the weather became calm and having split the foresail, and being obliged to strike it they remained without any sail, because the jib and mainsail were also torn; and yet it became necessary to set up the piece of the mainsail which was left. In about half an hour afterwards there blew a violent gale from the N. W. and they had to remain under bare poles. Montes then told Ruiz that they could not escape from that danger, that they would certainly perish, as they had no sail and the sea was very strong. The negroes were so frightened that for the first and only time they allowed the Spanish flag to be hoisted as a signal of distress to two ships which were in sight under bare poles; but it was to no purpose, for either they did not see the signal or they paid no attention to it. Finally it became calm and they again set the piece of the mainsail and the jib and steered N. E. After two days they saw an English man-of-war, which passed them within half the distance of cannon shot and hoisted her flag: but the schooner did not return the signal and she passed on without taking notice of it, to the great mortification of Ruix and Montes. On the following day in the afternoon they saw two schooners, and so much were they now in want of water, that the negroes at the request of Ruiz and Montes to make a signal of distress, hoisted up a piece of plate at the mainmast, but would not allow the flag to be hoisted.

Then the nearest schooner came within hailing distance and the negroes as usual made Montes and Ruiz go below; they then asked those on board of the schooner if they were very far from Africa, and if they would sell them water, rice and rum. The people on board of the schooner at first were afraid, but finally determined to come alongside of the vessel, and they sold the negroes a quarter cask of water, some segars, sweet potatoes, and sea biscuit, for which they paid a doubloon and a few shillings, the blacks having gone on board of the schooner and some of the people from the schooner having come on board of the Amistad. Finally they fastened a rope to the Amistad and began to tow her, saying to the negroes that they would give them next day plenty of rice, water, &c. if they had plenty of money. Ruiz and Montes, being tired of staying below, asked the negroes to let them come up; they did so, and then Ruiz and Montes perceived that the schooner was towing them to the West; Ruiz perceived that the schooner had on her stern the word *Kingston*, which undoubtedly was the name of the place where she was built; he also saw another inscription, but could not read it. At dusk the blacks set a jib, and the men on board of the schooner having told them to take it down, they refused to do so, and then the men on board of the schooner cut the rope, at which the blacks became exceedingly angry. Montes then steered towards the N. E., and in the morning the same schooner hailed the negroes, who again made Ruiz and Montes go below, and after having a talk with the men from the schooner, the latter went away, and the negroes made Ruiz and Montes come up. In the afternoon a pilot boat hailed the pilot, and asked the blacks if they wanted a pilot, and whence they came; the blacks made no answer, but asked the pilot if he knew where Africa was, and he, not understanding them, answered "from New York." Next morning they saw three pilot boats and many other vessels; one of the pilots came near and asked the same questions as the first; and he replied in answer to the negroes, that "they were 25 miles distant from New York," and asked them if they were from Havana or San Domingo.—They were a long time talking together without understanding each other well, and the pilot gave them

[*Concluded on second page.*]

NEW HAVEN STEAMBOATS.

THE Steamboats will alternately continue to leave New Haven daily, at 8 o'clock, A. M. Returning leave New York daily, at 7 o'clock, A. M. Freight taken as heretofore, excepting such Goods as are of foreign growth or manufacture.

CHAS. W. HINMAN, Agent,
For 'the Successors of the New Haven
Oct. 1.—50 Steamboat Co'.

FARE REDUCED.

Hartford and New-Haven Railroad.

U. S. Mail Route—Summer Arrangement.

STEAM BOAT, RAIL ROAD & POST COACH LINE,

Between NEW YORK and HARTFORD.

THE Cars will leave the Steamboat Wharf in New Haven daily, on the arrival of the Boats from New York, at about 1 P. M., and passengers for Hartford, Middletown and the intermediate towns, will proceed immediately by Railroad to Meriden, from thence in Post Coaches to Hartford, arriving about 4 P. M.

Post Coaches leave Hartford daily at 4 in the morning, and reach the depot in Meriden at a 1-4 before 7 The cars proceed immediately, and arrive at the Steamboat Wharf at 8 o'clock; and at about 2 o'clock P. M. the same day, passengers taking this line are landed in the city of New York.

Passengers from New York, taking this line, are requested to procure tickets on board the Boat, for Hartford, Middletown and the places intermediate; and passengers from Hartford to N. York are requested to provide tickets through, at the Stage Office kept at the United States Hotel in Hartford.

Fare between New York and Hartford,	.	$3 00
" " "	Middletown,	2 75
" " "	Berlin, . .	2 50
" " "	Meriden,	2 25
" " "	Wallingford,	2 00

RAILROAD & POST COACH ACCOMMODATION LINE.
Between New Haven and Hartford.

The cars will leave the depot at the Railroad Office in New Haven, at 5 o'clock, A. M., daily, (Sundays excepted) for Meriden and the intermediate towns, and passengers will reach Hartford by Post Coaches, about 9 o'clock, A. M. Returning, the Coaches will leave Hartford at 2 o'clock, P. M., and the cars arrive in New Haven at half past 5 o'clock.

Tickets to be had at the Railroad and Stage Offices in New Haven, and the Stage office in Hartford.

Fare between New Haven and Hartford,	.	$1 75
" " "	Berlin, . .	1 25
" " "	Middletown,	1 50
" " "	Meriden,	75
" " "	Wallingford,	50
" " "	North Haven,	25

MERCHANDIZE

Will be promptly forwarded between New Haven and Meriden, also between Meriden and New York, in connexion with Steamboats and Packets running between New Haven and New York.

JOHN T. CLARK, General Agent
of the H. and N. H. Railroad Co.
April 20, 1839. 26tf

COAL.

THE subscriber would respectfully inform the public that he is now receiving his supply of Lehigh, Beaver Meadow, Lackawana, Peach Orchard and Tuscarora, Schuylkill COAL, of the best quality, which is offered for sale in lots to suit purchasers at the lowest market prices.

Orders left with Lucius Gilbert, P. Saunders, A. & F. Lines, Noble Towner, Nicholson & Clark, Smith & Austin, or the subscriber, will be promptly attended to

TRUMAN BENEDICT.
Corner of Water and Brewery streets.
July 20. 1y39.

COAL.

THE subscriber is receiving his regular supply of Lehigh, Beaver, Meadow, Lackawanna, Peach Orchard, and Tuscarora Schuylkill COAL of the best quality, which is offered at the lowest market price.—He would respectfully invite his friends and the public generally to hand in their orders early, as the summer season is the most favorable time for laying in coal.

Orders left with Messrs. Eli B. Austin, Young & Uhlhorn, Samuel Wadsworth, E. S. Rowland & Co., N. C. Hall, C. K. Brown, or the subscriber, will receive prompt attention.

ISAAC T. HOTCHKISS.
July 13—38tf.] Long Wharf.

Crockery, Stone Ware, and Fire Brick.

CALL on E. E. HUGGINS, 135 Chapel st. for the above articles, in large or small lots. They are all for sale cheap for cash. Oct. 2. 50

AT a Court of Probate, held at New Haven, Oct. 4th, 1839, on the estate of

MERWIN ANDREW,

late of Orange, deceased. Ordered, that the Executors exhibit their Administration account to this Court for adjustment, at the Probate Office in New Haven on the 14th day of October, 1839, at 9 o'clock, forenoon; and that all persons interested in said Estate, may be notified thereof, the Executor will cause this order to be published in a newspaper printed in New Haven, and post a copy thereof on the sign post in said Orange. Attest, JOHN BEACH, Clerk.

English 3 Ply Carpeting, &c. &c.

JUST received and for sale on the most reasonable terms, at the *Broadcloth and Carpet Store,*

No. 2 Central Row,

English 3 ply, superfine, fine & common Carpetings, Cotton Ingrained and striped do.
4-4, 3-4, 5 8, 1-2 Venetian Carpeting, the best assortment ever offered in this city,
Druggett, Floor Baize, Canton Matting,
Brussels and Wilton Hearth Rugs,
Manilla and India Matts, Floor and Table Oil Cloth, Blk., and green worsted Fringe, green Cord, &c. &c.
Sept. 21.—48] HENRY HUGGINS.

FURS ! FURS ! FURS !

THE subscriber has just received from New York, a large and splendid assortment of Furs of all descriptions, among which may be found, Buffalo Robes, Gentlemen's No. 1, Sea Otter, and Shetland Seal Caps, Mens and Boys Nutria, Muskrat Sealette and Hair Caps; Seal, Nutria, Genet, Coney, and blk. Astrachan Skins and Collars, Fur Gloves, Swan's Down Neck Furs, &c. &c. all of which together with a general assortment of Hats, Cloth Caps &c. will be sold low. The public is respectfully invited to call and examine. WM. E. VIBBERT.

N. B. Ladies Muffs made to order.
Sep. 28.—3w 49

School Book Repository.

To Teachers of Music, Country Choirs, and Amateurs generally.

MUSIC BOOKS.—SACRED.

MASON'S Sacred Harp; do. Choir, or Union Coll.
do. Boston Academy's Collection.
do. Handel and Hayden Society's do.
do. Musical Exercises used in teaching, as a substitute for the Black Board.
The Manhattan Collection, by Thos. Hastings.
The Sacred Choir, by George Kingsley, author of "Sacred Choir."
The Musical Cabinet, by Alling Brown.
Spiritual Songs; The Christian Lyre.

SECULAR.

The Odeon, by Mason and Webb.
The Boston Glee Book, by do.; The Lyrist, by do.
The Social Choir, by Geo. Kingsley, vols. 1 and 2.
The Juvenile Singing Book, by Mason.
Burrows' Thorough Base Primer.
" Piano Forte Primer.
Mason's Musical Manual.
The American Elementary Singing Book, by E. Ives, Jr.
Preceptors for the Flute, Violin, Fife and Clarionett, all the different editions lately published.
Also, most of the Hymn and Psalm Books in use, blank Music Paper, &c. &c. for sale by
Oct. 2.—1 DURRIE & PECK.

NOTICE

IS hereby given to the residents and non-residents of the town of Waterbury, liable to pay taxes on the list of 1833, that the subscriber has received warrants to collect a Town tax of ten cents on the dollar, and a State tax of one cent on the dollar, on said list—and that he will be at the Mansion House of Edward Chitenden, on Thursday, the 24th of October—and at the inn of Baldwin Beecher, on Saturday, the 26th of October, 1839, for the purpose of receiving said Taxes, at from 1 until 5 o'clock, P. M.

MOSES S. COOK, *Collector.*

N. B. Those who neglect to pay their Taxes on or before that time, may expect to pay such fees as the law allows.

Waterbury, Sept. 30, 1839. *50

THE Court of Probate for the District of Waterbury, hath limited and allowed six months from the date hereof, for the Creditors to the Estate of

MICHAEL BOWERS

late of Middlebury, deceased, to exhibit their claims for settlement. Those who neglect to present their claims properly attested, within said time, will be debarred a recovery. All persons indebted to said Estate, are requested to make immediate payment to

HORACE MANVILL, } Adm'rs.
ADAM LUM, }
Middlebury, Oct. 2. *50

AMERICAN PRINTS.

2 CASES of a good style—dark and fast colors at 12½ cents per yard—also 1 case at sixpence—just received by S. B. CHITTENDEN.
Oct. 2. 50

PAPER HANGINGS AND BORDERS for sale cheap by S. B. CHITTENDEN.
Oct. 2. 50

ENGLISH HORSE NAILS.—The subscriber has received a lot of English Horse Nails, of superior quality, for sale by the bag of 100 lbs. or at retail.
Oct. 2.—50 BENJ M. SHERMAN.

NOTICE.

R. HOTCHKISS & SON having taken into partnership Mr. Henry Hotchkiss, the business will hereafter be conducted under the name and firm of R. HOTCHKISS, & SONS.
Oct. 2.—3t. *50.

TO BOOK AGENTS.

A few responsible persons, who would be disposed to circulate a new and salable work in the middle, southern, or western States, can have employment by calling at the office of the subscriber in York st.
Oct. 2.—50 HORACE MANSFIELD.

RODGER'S FINE CUTLERY.—An extensive assortment constantly for sale by
Oct. 2.—50 DURRIE & PECK.

CHAIRS.

ROSE WOOD, Mahogany, Fancy with cane and flagg seats, together with a large assortment of Winsor Chairs.—Also a great variety of Rocking Chairs at BOWDITCH'S warerooms.
Sept. 2. [Orange st.] 50

STATIONARY.—A new lot of Quills, Sealing Wax, Black Sand, Fine Letter and Note Paper; Pocket Books, &c. &c. DURRIE & PECK.

THE subscriber has received a large assortment of Britannia Metal Lamps, Japanned Lamps of superior quality, suitable for workshops; brass and iron Candlesticks, Snuffer Trays, &c.
BENJ. M. SHERMAN, Chapel-st.
Oct. 2. 50.

BEDSTEDS, BEDS AND MATRESSES.—A large assortment on hand and for sale at BOWDITCH'S Warerooms.
Oct. 2. [Orange st.] 50

SOFAS AND SOFA BEDS.—A large assortment of the latest fashion, some splendid patterns at BOWDITCH'S Warerooms.

WELCH FLANNELS.—A good assortment—and the genuine article, for sale by
Oct. 2.—50 S. B. CHITTENDEN.

BROADCLOTHS CASSIMERES.—Gentlemen are invited to examine the assortment in the Cloth Room of S. B CHITTENDEN.
Oct. 2. 50

FRENCH SHOES.—The latest fashions constantly on hand and for sale by WM. A. LAW.
Oct. 2. [84 Chapel st.] 50

NEW BOOKS.—Opinions of Lord Brougham on Politics, Theology, Law, Science, Education, Literature, &c. &c., as exhibited in his Parliamentary and Legal Speeches and Miscellaneous writings.
Hamilton King, or the Smuggler and the Dwarf. For sale by YOUNG & UHLHORN,
Oct. 2.—50 No. 1 Exchange Place.

PLOUGHS.—A new pattern, highly approved, made and sold by KILBORN & SMITH.
Also, Harrows, Ox Shovels, &c.
Oct. 2—50 East side the Hillhouse Basin.

KNIVES & FORKS.—A fine assortment of Knives and Forks, Carvers and Steels, Bread and Butcher Knives, for sale by NATHAN SMITH,
Oct. 2—50 at the old stand of Coley and Smith.

WOOLEN GOODS.

JUST received at No. 1. Central Row—BROADCLOTHS, PILOT CLOTHS and BEAVER CLOTHS, of various shades and qualities:—Also a full assortment of Cassimeres and Sattinets all of which are for sale on accommodating terms.
Oct. 2.—50 SANFORD & BLISS.

GUILFORD TURNING SHOP.

RICHARD CHITTENDEN & JOHN F. KIMBERLY, will execute all orders in the Turning line at their shop near the Town Mill in Guilford. Waggon Hubbs, Swivle Trees, Bedstead Post, pillars for Porticos, &c. &c. made to order with neatness and despatch. All kinds of Cabinet work will be done and every exertion made to please customers in that line of business. Also a share of public patronage is respectfully solicited.
Guilford, Oct. 2. 50

PICTORIAL edition of the Book of Common Prayer, together with the form and manner of making, ordaining and consecrating of Bishops, Priests and Deacons; illustrated with *seven hundred* wood cuts, to which are added original notes, and an Introductory History of the Liturgy, by the Rev. Henry Stebbing, M. A. For sale by YOUNG & UHLHORN,
Oct. 2—50 No. 1 Exchange Place.

W. G. MUNSON,

DENTIST.

RESPECTFULLY informs his friends and the public that he still continues his office at his residence in Wall street, 3d door west from College-st.

Refer to Doct. T. P. BEERS, }
" N. B. IVES, } *New Haven.*
Dea. ISAAC THOMPSON, }
June 16. 34tf.

NEW GOODS.

(*At the Centre Store, Phoenix Building, Chapel street.*)

SMITH MERWIN, MERCHANT TAILOR, has returned from New York with a first rate selection of Fall and Winter Goods for gentlemen's apparel to which he would respectfully invite the attention of his customers, and the public. Among them are BROADCLOTHS of superior quality viz: Wool Dy'd Blk and Blue Blk. Blue, Invisible Green, Olive and Brown, Superior Beavers, Blk. and Blue Blk. Green and Pilot Cloth CASSIMERES of Blk. and Blue Wool, Dy'd, British Queen, London check, Partridge breast, Doe Skins, and fancy Cassimeres of all kinds.

The VESTINGS are rich fig'd silk velvets and Satins, plain do. Brocade, Cashmere, Persian Shawl and Superfine Valentias, Fig'd Silks and quiltings for Surtout and Coat Facings. Satin and heavy Silk Cords and Agraffes for Cloaks, Merino and Kid Gloves Rich Fig'd Silk and plain Gum Elastic Suspenders; Elegant Fig'd Satin Cravats; Silk and Linen Hdkfs. Stocks of various patterns; Collars and Bosoms, Linen and Cotton; fine Skirts, Woolen and Cotton knit Skirts and Drawers, &c. &c All of which were bought for cash, and will be sold on such terms, as cannot fail to suit the purchaser.
Oct. 2.—2w. 50

Notice to Silk Culturalists.

THE subscriber will contract to deliver one hundred thousand of the MORUS MULTICAULIS, in the fall of 1840, either by the foot or tree, at quite reduced prices from this fall sales, warranted as good as they will average throughout the State. He has likewise 10 good Cows, and 8 last Spring Calves; 300 bushels of Oats; 100 do of Rye, and 2000 weight of Cheese, on which the premium was awarded at the Agricultural Fair, in New Haven. CLAUDIUS ALLEN.
Cheshire, N. H. Co. Oct. 2. 50

PRINDLE'S ALMANAC.

For the year of our Lord

1840:

For sale by the gross, dozen, or single, at the Book and Stationary store of A. H. MALTBY.
Oct. 2. 50

RICH Fig'd Satin Cap Ribbons, entire new style; cheap Chantilly Veils this day rec'd. and for sale by Oct. 2.—50 WM. A. LAW.

WALTON HOUSE,

NO. 328

PEARL-STREET—FRANKLIN SQUARE,

NEW YORK,

BY ARCH'D A. PETERSON.

From the similarity of the names, many persons suppose the "WALTON HOUSE" to be connected with the "Walton Mansion House." A. A. P. therefore deems it necessary to state that no connection whatever exists between them. October, 1839. tf50

CHARLES ROBINSON,

ATTORNEY & COUNSELLOR AT LAW, and Solicitor in Chancery: Notary Public: Commissioner for the State of Maine: also Agent for the N. American & Hudson Insurance Companies of New York. Oct. 2—50

NOTICE.

THE electors of the Town of New Haven are hereby warned to meet at the City Hall, in said town of New Haven, on the first Monday of October, 1839, at 9 o'clock in the forenoon, then and there to signify by their vote their approbation or disapprobation of the proposed amendment of the Constitution of this State, passed at the session of the General Assembly of said State holden at Hartford on the first Wednesday of May, A. D. 1839, relating to the admission of Electors.

SCOVIL HINMAN, }
CHARLES W. CURTISS, }
JESSE KNEVALS, }
DAVID H. CARR, } *Constables.*
GEORGE W. JONES, }
GARDNER MORSE, }
CHAUNCEY BARNES, }
New Haven, Oct. 2, 1839. 50.

NOTICE

IS hereby given to the legal voters of the town of New Haven, that a Town Meeting will be held at the City Hall, in the city and town of New Haven, on the first Monday of October next, at 2 o'clock in the afternoon, for the choice of Assessors and Board of Relief.

BENJAMIN BEECHER, }
LEVI GILBERT, }
NAHUM HAYWARD, }
ISAAC JUDSON, } *Selectmen.*
MARCUS MERRIMAN, }
PHILIP S. GALPIN, }
RICHARD M. CLARK, }
New Haven, Oct. 2, 1839. 50.

THIS WEEK

THE subscriber will receive this week a most valuable assortment of goods. It is very generally known that Dry Goods are sold this season at a great sacrifice from last year's prices, and that within the last few weeks some styles of goods have fallen from 5 to 10 per cent. It will be the object of the undersigned to take advantage of this depreciation in buying,—and sell accordingly.

☞ Rich and beautiful styles of Goods on Saturday.
Oct. 2 : 50] GEORGE RICE.

MERINO TRIMMINGS and FRINGES, for Shawls in Red and Blk. a fresh supply for sale by Oct! 7.—51 WM. A. LAW.

THE EXTRA SUN

Drawn by W.K. Hewitt. N. Currier Lith. & Pub. 2 Spruce St. N.Y.

Awful Conflagration of the Steam Boat **LEXINGTON** *In Long Island Sound on Monday Eveg. Jany. 13th 1840. by which melancholy occurrence; over* 100 PERSONS PERISHED.

PUB. AT SUN OFFICE

THE LEXINGTON

Left New York for Stonington, at 3 o'clock on Monday afternoon, Jan. 13, 1840. About half past 7 o'clock, when off Eaton's neck, L. I., the wood-work, casings, &c., about the flues, were discovered to be on fire. An alarm was immediately given, and all efforts to subdue the flames proving unabailing, the pilot headed the boat directly for Long Island shore. When she had got within about two miles of the shore her engine suddenly stopped. In the mean time the life-boat and small boats had been got out, but the former was broken to pieces by being struck by one of the wheels, and the latter were swamped by mismanagement in lowering them into the water crowded with passengers. No relief was therefore obtained from either of the boats. All hopes of escape to those on board, except by clinging to such articles of freight as would sustain them, were now cut off. The freight of the Lexington consisted principally of cotton, on which some of the passengers tried to save themselves, but none succeeded except Capt. Hilliard, Mr. Manchester, the pilot, Charles Smith, one of the firemen, and a passenger who had been picked up and taken to River Head, and who was so far gone as to be unable to disclose his name.

It was believed, however, that he would survive. Capt. H. continued upon his bale of cotton until 11 o'clock A. M., Tuesday, when he was taken off by a sloop which went out from Southport, having been thus exposed about 15 hours. The same sloop rescued the other two, who were clinging to a fragment of the boat. The bodies of two others, one a colored woman, were likewise taken from a part of the wreck, on which they had perished with cold. The steamer Statesman on Thursday also picked up one body and thirteen trunks. The bodies of Hempsteed, the chief engineer, and Sands, the head waiter, have also been recovered.

The number of passengers on board is not known with any degree of certainty. It is most probable, however, they numbered about EIGHTY—of whom but two were rescued alive. The boat's company numbered THIRTY, of whom also but two were saved.

We regret to have to add, that among the passengers were the wife and two interesting children o Russell Jarvis, Esq., formerly of Boston, more latterly editor of the Philadelphia World, and at present editor of the Evening Tattler in this city. Capt. Hilliard, whose attention had been attracted to this interesting and unfortunate family at the table, saw Mrs. Jarvis floating with one of her children in her arms, on a bale of cotton. The other child had leaped overboard, as had also a great many other passengers—some twenty of whom had life preservers on. When observed by Capt. H., Mrs. Jarvis was franticly calling upon the persons in the water to preserve her child and bring it to her on the bale. Mother, children, passengers and all, however, sunk to a common grave.

The steamboat Statesman on Friday repaired to the scene of the disaster, and returned on Saturday, bringing five bodies, one of which was that of Mr. Stephen Waterbury, of this city, and another that of Mr. Paulo Upson, of South Egremont, Massachusetts, two others those of Benjamin Leddeu and Silas Thorburn, hands on board the steamer, and the fifth that of a boy 4 or 5 years of age. The arms and the face of the child are much scorched; its face is frightfully distorted with the agonies of its dreadful death. Its dress is a dark red merino frock and pantalettes, and mottled cotton socks—no shoes. It has, too, a green veil round the upper part of the body, partly burnt.—The faces of both seamen are also shockingly scorched, particularly that of one man, whose left eye seems to have been burnt out; the eyebrows are literally charred. All the bodies are frozen stiff, and partially covered with ice.

On Friday night, Capt. Comstock despatched a letter to this city, in which he says that "Captain WILLIAM TERRILL, master of the sloop Improvement, was, with his vessel, within four or five miles of the Lexington at the time she commenced burning, and thinks if he had immediately repaired to her assistance, he would have saved a great number of lives. The reason he gives for not doing so is, *that he would have lost his tide over the bar*, at the port to which he was bound, and accordingly he pursued his inhuman course, leaving upwards of 100 persons to die the worst of deaths. The circumstances of this unparalleled cruelty will hereafter be more clearly exposed, and I trust he will receive its merited deserts."

This conduct of Capt. Terrill has elicited an universal burst of indignation against him in this city; and for his safety's sake, we advise him not to venture too much in public here.

We understand that a great number of trunks, &c., which have floated ashore have been broken open and rifled; and that the trunk of the Rev. Dr. Follen was found in the woods, some distance from the shore, rifled of every thing but papers.

To the names of the sufferers already published, we regret to have to add those of Mr. John Marshall, glass worker, of this city, and of Mr. Baum, son of the clerk of the Washington market.

We learn also, that the body of Cortland Hempstead, first engineer of the Lexington, has been picked up at Southport. Jos. Robinson, the head cook of the Lexington, whose name is reported among the lost, was not on board at the time of the calamity, having been detained at home by sickness. His place was supplied by the second cook, Howell; and Isaac Putnam, (colored,) supplied the place of Howell.

Capt. Manchester, the pilot, is now at Southport, and is slowly recovering. He states that he remained at the wheel until he was actually burnt out. He descended, and got to the aft deck, where was Mr. Harnden of the express Line, Mr. Hoyt, baggage master, and two or three others. He succeeded in getting out the life boat; he lowered it into the water, and threw his pea jacket into it. Unfortunately at this time the painter gave way, and the life boat was sucked under the wheel, thus depriving those who looked for safety in this boat of all hope. The flames now advanced rapidly to the aft part, and to prevent its progress, the pilot and others broke open some specie boxes, and emptying them of the worthless dross, used the boxes as buckets to keep off the flames and prevent their progress. Finding this in vain, Capt. Manchester, taking his clasp knife from his pocket, jumped overboard to a cotton bale he saw near the vessel. In endeavoring to get on it, he found another man already sustaining himself by it. In his attempt to get on both fell into the water. Captain Manchester rose, and supported the man until he could get on. Then using his knife, he cut holes in the bale, by which he supported himself. Captain Manchester's companion died in the course of the night. The pilot was picked up on the bale, as has been stated.

David Crowley, the 2d mate of the Lexington, floated ashore near River Head on Wednesday evening, having been afloat on a bale of cotton 48 hours. His extremities were frozen as stiff as marble. The preservation of his life, during so protracted a siege of suffering, is indeed wonderful. Charles Smith, the deck hand, who was picked up by the sloop, says that he jumped overboard at 8 o'clock, and swam to a bale of cotton: after floating on which five hours and a half, he got back to the wreck, and warmed himself by the fire, and then got on the part of the wreck from which he was taken off.

We are informed, in a letter received yesterday, that Mr. T. M. H. Lyon, of Boston, was on board the Lexington at the time of the disaster, and doubtless shared the sad fate of the rest. It is also feared that Mr. Wyman Osborn was on board, as there was found a letter with an envelope requesting him to deliver it. Mr. Jonathan G. Davenport, of Middletown, N. J., was also on board, and was lost.

The Boston Transcript gives the names of four deck hands and of eleven colored waiters who were on board the Lexington, as follows:

Deck hands—Charles Williams, Ben. Laddle, C. Hunber, Joel Lawrence.

Colored waiters—Mr. Sands, Danl. Aldridge, Mr. Gilbert, Oliver Howell, King Cade, Jos. Costin, John B. Tab, E. Parkson, John Masson, Solomon Askons, Isaac Putnam.

It is reported that the Collector received instructions yesterday from the Comptroller of the Treasury to make a thorough investigation into the cause of the destruction of the steamer Lexington, to the end that it may be reported to the department, whether the act of Congress in relation to the navigation of steamboats has been complied with.

A letter received yesterday from Stony Brook, written yesterday morning, says:—"There is a report here this morning that two more men have come ashore alive from the wreck of the Lexington, opposite Greenport. If this be true, it will make six that have been saved."

The Lexington—more bodies recovered.—The bodies of Mr. H. Craig and of Mr. Charles Brackett, of this city, of Mr. A. Green, of Providence, and of Mr. David Green, of Philadelphia, on Tuesday floated ashore at Stoney Brook, in one of the Lexington's small boats. They were secured by a very poor man residing near the spot, and were yesterday brought by him to this city. The rewards offered for the recovery of the bodies of those unfortunate gentlemen, amounted to over $1000.

A gentleman who came yesterday from Eaton's Neck, informs us that the sum of $15,000 in bank notes was found upon the person of Mr. A. Green, entirely uninjured. He had on board in specie and bank notes $60,000. The sum recovered was promptly transmitted to this city, and speaks well for the integrity of those into whose hands fate threw so tempting a sum.

The following letter, which we received last evening, we insert with the hope that, authentic as is the source from which the information arises, there may be some mistake about it. We trust the individual implicated will be able to clear his skirts of the damning accusation; and we shall be infinitely more ready to afford him the means of doing so through our columns, than we have been to give currency to the charge.

JANUARY 22d, 1840.

To the Editors of the Sun:

Gentlemen—I am informed by a letter received this afternoon from New London, Conn., in which implicit reliance may be placed, that Captain James Kenny, of packet sloop James Lanpheer, plying between here and New London, saw the ill-fated Lexington when she took fire and was within an hour's sail of her at the time; furthermore Captain Kenny says he knew, or had reason to suppose it was the Lexington, but still contined on his course without deigning to offer the least assistance. If true, such inhuman conduct will, I trust, receive the eternal execration of his outraged fellow beings. If untrue, I trust he or his friends will come forward and rescussitate his name from a coalition with Terrell, and thereby save him from eternal infamy.

Yours Respectfully,
THOMAS MONSON, 392 Broome street.

The following are all the names of the many passengers who have perished by this dreadful calamity, as far as we were able to gather them.

Passengers.

Mrs. Russell Jarvis, and two children,	New York
Mr. Fowler,	do
Stephen Waterbury, (firm of Mead & Waterbury, 25 Cedar street)	do
Rev. Doct. Follen and wife, formerly of the Unitarian Church, Chambers street,	Boston
Thomas James, Tailor, Fulton street,	New York
John Winslow, (firm of D. L. & J. Winslow)	Providence
Mrs. Alice Winslow, widow of Henry A. Winslow, who was accompanying the corpse of her husband to Boston for interment,	do
John L. Winslow, father of the above,	New York
Charles Bosworth, 97 Frankfort street,	do
H. C. Craig, firm of Maitland, Kennedy & Co.,	do
Robert Schultz,	do
Chas. Brackett, (clerk with N. Brackett,)	do
Richard W. Dow, firm of Dow & Co.	Brooklyn
Charles S. Noyes, clerk with C. B. Babcock,	New York
Albert E. Harding, firm of Harding & Co.,	do
E. B. Patten, 183 Walker street,	do
Mr. McKinney,	do
Hezekiah Lawrence, firm of Kelly & Lawrence,	do
Mr. Bullard,	do
Thomas J. Taylor, firm of James & Taylor,	do

Adolphus S. Harnden, of the Boston and New York Express Package Car Office, having with him about $18,000 in specie, and 70 or $80,000 for brokers in Eastern money.

Capt. Eben S. Kimball, (just from Valparaiso)	Salem
" John D. Carver, barque Brontes,	Plymouth
" Pierce, mate of do.	Portland
" John J. Low, agent Boston Insurance Company,	Boston
" Theophilus Smith,	Dartmouth
Capt. Benjamin Foster,	Providence
" Smith,	Dedham
" Chester Hilliard, (saved)	Norwich

These Captains had recently returned after several years absence, and were on their way to visit their families at the East.

David Green,	Philadelphia.
Samuel Henry,	Boston
Charles H. Phelps,	Stonington
C. W. Woolsey, sugar refiner,	East Boston
John Brown, do	do
John Hoyt, (Mail Contractor)	Boston
Mr. Everett, returning from the burial of a brother who died here last week,	do
Henry J. Finn, Comedian,	do
Charles Eberle, of the Theatre,	do
Royal T. Church,	Baltimore
Richard Pickett, (clerk with Marquand & Co.)	Newburyport
John W. Karle,	Baltimore
Mr. Walker,	do
Mr. Weston (firm of Weston & Perdexter,) lady and child,	do
John G. Brown, firm of Shall & Brown,	N. Orleans
Master Woodward, son of Charles,	Philadelphia
J. A Leach, firm of Leach & Lovejoy	Boston
N. F. Dyer, (formerly of Braintree)	Pittsburg
William Ray, late of the barque Bohemia,	Kennebunk, Me.
Nathaniel Hobart,	Boston
H. C. Bradford, (from Kingston, Jam.)	do
John G. Stone,	do
John Lemist, Treas. Boston Leather Co.,	Roxbury
Jonathan Linfield,	Stoughton, Mass
Philip Upton,	Egremont, do
P. Van Cott,	Stonington
Mr. Stuyvesant,	Boston
Capt. Mattison,	
Robert Williams,	Cold Spring, N. Y.
Samuel Henry, firm of S. & A. Henry	Manchester, Eng.
Wyman Osborn,	
T. M. H. Lyon,	Boston
John B. Marshall,	New York
Mr. Baum,	do
J. G. Davenport,	Middletown, N. J.
Wm. A. Green, agent of Minot Shoe Co.	Maine
Thomas White, firm of Sands & White,	Boston
A Green, firm of Allen & Green,	Providence
J. Porter Felt, jun.,	Salem
W. A. Mason,	Gloucester, Mass.
Robert Blake,	Wrentham, do
A. Green, firm of Green & Allen,	Providence
Isaac Davis,	Boston
Mr. Peck,	Southington, Ct.
Abraham Howard, firm of Howard & Mersey,	do
P. O. Swain,	
Isaac Davis,	Boston
William Nichols, steward of S. B. Massachusetts,	
Robert Blake, Pres't Wrentham Bnak,	Wrentham, Mass.
Mr. Bosworth,	Royalton, Vt.
Jesse Comstock,	Providence
Mr. Brooks, comb store,	Boston
Erastus Coleman, of the Pavilion,	do
John Corey,	Foxbury, Mass.
Charles [illegible], son of the late Gen. Samuel Lee, of Barre, Mass.	Barre, Mass.
Mr. Martin, and Son,	Manchester, Eng.
William H. Wilson, formerly of Worcester,	Williamsburg
Thomas Blecker, carpenter,	Dedham, Mass.
John Brown, colored, 26 Varick st,	New York
William Nichols and Joshua Johnson, both colored men,	Providence
Daniel McFarlan, mate of brig Clarissa.	
James Walker, seaman,	Cambridgeport
John Gordon, do	do
Patrick McKenna, 7 Monroe st,	New York

Officers, &c. of the Lexington.

George Childs, captain.
Edward Thurber, 1st mate.
David Crowley, 2d do
Cortland Hempstead, chief engineer.
Wm. Quimby [illegible] do
S. Manchester, pilot, (saved.)
Martin Johnson, wheelsman.
H. P. Newman, steward.
R. B. Shultz, fireman.
Benj. Cox, do
Charles Smith, do (saved.)
One other, do
Eight deck hands.
Two wood passers.
One boy, deck hand.
Joseph Robinson, cook, (colored.)
Oliver Howell, 2d do do
Robert Peters, do do
Susan C. Hulcomb, colored, chambermaid.
Jacob Sands, do head waiter.
Seven others, do waiters

Investigation into the affair of the Lexington Steamer.—In consequence of the urgent solicitations of many of our most respectable citizens, and out of regard to the dictates of an imperious sense of duty, the Coroner yestereay summoned an intelligent jury, not only to view and pronounce upon the cause of death of the dead of the Lexington, that were rescued from the water and brought to this city, but also to examine, critically, testimony relative to the manner of building that boat—her former and late condition—the cause, if possible, of the dreadful catastrophe that befel her, and every other fact and circumstance of any interest to the public, or calculated to soothe the anxious solicitude of the surviving friends of the immolated victims of this horrible disaster.

The first witness examined was Mr. Joseph Bishop, who with his partner, Mr. Simonson, was employed to build the boat by Mr. C. Vanderbilt, and who accordingly built her in the latter part of 1834 and beginning of 1835, of the best possible materials, and bolted and fastened her together, and secured her in the strongest and best possible manner, without regard to cost or expense. She was 205 feet long on deck from stem to stern post, breadth 22 feet, and 40 feet across the wheel houses from side to side. She was launched in April, 1835, and her first trip was in June of that year. Her timbers were part of oak and part of chesnut—plank, oak as far as the waist, then of pine—futlocks part of oak and part of chesnut—floor timbers 16 inches in depth and 5 in thickness, about 6 inches apart amidships, and from that to 16 inches apart towards the ends. The deck floor was of white pine, 2¼ inches thick; her keel and kelsons were four feet deep, of three pieces of oak, besides a bilge kelson. Round the chimneys all precaution was used that ever was used in any other boat. She was repaired about two months since on the railway of the dry dock, and part new copper and part new plank put on, and put in as good repair as possible. He considered her perfectly safe, sound and seaworthy.

CAPTAIN HILLIARD'S TESTIMONY.

Capt. Chester Hilliard sworn.—I was born in Norwich, Connecticut—am 24 years old. I have latterly followed the sea—been a sailor for upwards of six years. Left Norwich about 8 years ago, and removed to Port Ann, N. Y., about ten miles this side of Whitehall, on the Northern Canal, for two years, and learned the woolleen manufacturing business. Went to sea then with Capt. Hunt in the ship McClellan, now belonging to New Orleans.—The ship then belonged to Messrs. Howland & Aspinwall. Have been only in Mr. Howland's and Collins' employ ever since I went to sea. First went before the mast as a raw hand—went 5 voyages as a foremast man, occupying about 3 years. Then went as 3d mate of the ship Sheridan, Capt. Russell, one voyage—then 2d mate of ship Mississippi, Capt. H. Davis, to New Orleans, then to Liverpool—then as 1st officer in same ship to New Orleans, Beebee, master, who died, and I took the ship home. I then made another voyage in her to New Orleans, as captain, and arrived here four weeks ago next Saturday. I went on board the Lexington as a passenger on Monday, the 13th inst., about three o'clock, to go to Stonington. I was bound to Norwich—have no family—had 3 own brothers and 2 sisters, and 2 half brothers and 1 half sister. My father was a seaman. Did not know the number of passengers on board—judged from what I saw at the table that there were 150—that statement is since, I believe, too large. Did not pay very particular attention to the stowage of the cargo. I should think the greatest share of the cargo consisted of cotton, stowed under the promenade deck—did not notice other parts of the cargo. There was plenty of room left for a person to pass between the wheelhouse and engine room—there was a tier of cotton bales stowed there, I think against the wheel house. There were three baggage cars and a gangway plank on the forecastle, which was pretty nearly all that was there. The life boat was on the promenade deck, starboard side, forward of the wheel house. I took no notice of her except that she was covered over with canvass, until that was torn away for her to be launched. I saw the two quarter boats hang on the davits, and saw them afterwards lowered away. Supper was served near [illegible] o'clock—there were three tables set more than half the length of cabin, all of which were full, and some waited for the second table. Nothing observed wrong before supper.

We were proceeding at the rate of from 12 to 14 knots an hour. The tables were cleared away about an hour before the alarm of fire was heard; I was at the point of turning into my berth, in the after cabin, No. 49, starboard side, when I heard the alarm, and had my coat and boots off. At the time I did not apprehend any thing serious, but slipped my coat, boots and hat on, and went up on deck; took my overcoat in my arms. When I got on deck I discovered the casing around the smoke pipe on fire, and I think part of the promenade deck. The after part of the casing was on fire above the main deck when I first came up. I thought the fire might be extinguished with proper exertions. Did not see any fire below the main deck. Cannot say whether that casing was around the steam chimney or not. Did not see the captain; from what I could judge from the crew, they were at work at the fire engine, trying to rig it. I should think they had not used buckets at that time. I did not see any used; I saw a good many fire buckets on board; can't tell how many; did not get the fire engine to work. I left soon after this and went on the promenade deck. When I first came on deck my attention was turned to the rush of the passengers towards the quarter boats. My attention was drawn that way on account of the stupid determination manifested by the passengers to destroy themselves and their only means of safety. I repaired to the starboard boat, which was lowered away until it touched the water pretty evenly, when some one I think cut the forward tackle fall, as it was disengaged and the boat swung immediately round; she was entirely filled with water, there being about twenty persons in it at the time. That boat passed immediately astern, entirely clear.— They then cleared away the other boat pretty much the same way. She was also full of passengers, and swung around much in the same way as the former, and passed to the stern—the passengers were thrown out. By that time the fire had increased so rapidly that I thought the best thing that could be done was to run the boat on shore. For that purpose I went up to the wheel house, supposing Captain Childs would be there. He was there, and I told him the best thing would be to run the boat ashore. He said the boat was already heading for the land. The fire at this time began to come up through the promenade deck on the sides, and the wheel house was so filled with smoke that we could not see. There were some two or three on the promenade deck, near the wheel house, whose attention was turned to the life boat.

I told them if any thing was done it must be very quick or the boat would burn up. The boat was cleared away—I helped to tear the tarpaulin off her. I had made up my mind however not to go in her, as I supposed as a matter of course that as they passed her down they would get in and fill her and she would be lost. They got hold of her and got her overboard—what became of her I dont know.—The fire at that time began to burst up through the promenade deck in different places, and I went aft and went down on the main deck. They were then at work with the hose—saw them screw the hose on the force pump—did not know before they had a force pump. It was so thick with smoke that I could hardly see what they were about, and they were soon all compelled to leave the pump and hose. The communication at that time was cut off between the fore and after part of the vessel. This was 20 minutes after the first alarm was given. The engine stopped in about 15 minutes after the first alarm. I then recommended to the deck hands and passengers to throw the cotton overboard, because if they did any thing it must be done quickly. We all joined and threw over the ten or twelve bales that were not on fire on the larboard side of the boat. I then took a piece of rope 4 or 5 fathoms or less, and spanned a square bale of cotton with it (the last I think that was not on fire near me) the bale about 4 or 5 feet long and three feet across, left an end of rope about 4 fathoms, took a round turn of the rope around the rail, and aided by a boat hand slipped the bale off below the guard, having a part of the rope in my hand, and we both got on the bale before it was in the water. This was abaft the wheel house. The boat then lay broadside to the wind. This was on the larboard side of the boat, under the lee. When we got into the water with the bale it was one-third out of the water with both of us on it. The wind was pretty fresh, and the boat drifting at the rate of about a knot and a half an hour, and we found the bale rather difficult to navigate. We coiled the rope away on the bale of cotton. My companion [illegible] the idea of leaving the boat at once, but wished to hang on to the boat under the guards, but I determined to get out of the way before I got burned to death, as I knew if I staid much longer we should have hot quarters. We accordingly shoved the boat along under the stern. We immediately drifted to the windward of the boat or the boat from us. This was exactly eight o'clock, as I looked at my watch. We both sat astride of the bale, face to face, keeping the bale end to the sea with a piece of board we had picked up.

When I came aft on the bale when we left, saw a lady and a few passengers, and the ladies' cabin all on fire. The most of the passengers had before left. The reason that I noticed the lady was that her child was overboard, having been thrown or fallen overboard. We passed by it so near that I could put my hands on it as it lay on its back—the [illegible] as we passed it sung out for us to save the child—it appeared to be a female child, and was perfectly dead. There were some persons only on the forecastle at the time. It was pretty rough, and I had as much as I could do to take care of the bale of cotton. My feet and legs were in the water, which would splash over the bale, and I was wet up to my middle. I was in sight of the boat until she went down—[illegible] then perhaps a mile from her. It was cloudy [illegible] we left the wreck, but it cleared off and we had a fine night. I looked at my watch every half hour, and think the boat went down at 3 o'clock. It was so cold that it was necessary to make efforts to keep myself warm by whipping my hands and arms. About 4 o'clock the bale capsized with us owing to a heavy sea—I went over [illegible]—we managed to get on the bale which was the other side up, and then losing the piece of board—the bale became ungovernable after that, and we had to let it go as it could. My companion complained much of the cold on first setting out, and did not seem to have that spirit about him that he ought to have, and fretted himself about things that he had no business to, and that could do no good. He said his name was Cox, and that his wife lived at No. 71 Cherry street.

Before we capsized he seemed to have given up all hope, and appeared to me as if he thought he could not be saved. Shortly after leaving the steamboat, I gave him my waistcoat, as he had only a flannel shirt, pantaloons, drawers, boots and cap on. He was one of the firemen. After the bale upset, he remained with me for two hours or two and a half, until near daylight. The last half hour he became perfectly stupid, had lost the use of his hands, and could not help himself. I beat his hands and rubbed and pounded him to try to keep the blood in circulation as he did nothing for himself. It was very rough at that time, and I had to hold on to the rope around the bale. The bale got nearly broadside to the sea, gave a lurch, and my companion slipped off, and went down without a struggle. I had as much as I could do to keep on the bale. The man fell off about half past 6 o'clock.

I then got more on the middle of the bale some time to make it ride as it should, and kept in that situation until about an hour before I was taken up by the sloop, when I sat down on the bale; as the wind had died away, and the water became smooth, I waved my hat to the sloop, and made what motion I could to those on board, as the sloop came out on purpose to see what she could find. It was the sloop Merchant, Capt. Meeker, of Southport, and he did all in his power, and deserves great credit; he tried to get out the night before, to the aid of those on board the steamer, but got the sloop aground on the bar, and could not get out; they however unloaded her in part, taking out a portion of her cargo, and one of her anchors, to get her over the bar; she had to beat out to where I was, as the wind was ahead, and they were on to me almost before I saw them; they picked me up at about 11 o'clock; they had been in and spoken the light-boat, on the Long Island shore, to find out where the fire was, before they found and picked me up; they took me on board the sloop and paid every attention to my wants; I was not frozen any. The captain took me down into the cabin, and then went to cruise about, and picked up two other live persons, and also two dead bodies. The live persons were Capt. Manchester, the pilot of the Lexington, and the other Charles Smith. Capt. Manchester was on a portion of the wheel-house, and Smith found on and taken from off a bale of cotton; Capt. Manchester was picked up first; I was below when both were picked up, which was within half an hour. Capt. Manchester was pretty much exhausted when found, which was about 20 minutes after I was. Smith was a fireman, and belongs to Norwalk, Ct., and was not so much exhausted as Capt. Manchester. They were both put to bed. The sloop still continued to cruise for three hours longer—picked up two dead bodies from a piece of the wheel house. The sloop then returned to Southport. The steamer Nimrod overtook us when we were half way to Southport, came along side, and I went on board of her. She was bound to Bridgport, where I arrived in about three quarters of an hour, went on shore, and went to Captain Davis, an old friend of mine, with whom I formerly sailed. I staid there that night, went on board the steamer Nimrod the next morning at eight o'clock, and came on to this city. Capt. Child, when he went to the wheel house, appeared to be very much confused.—He said nothing that I heard, except that they were running for the land. He then went into the wheel house, and I am inclined to believe, staid in there and was suffocated. I do not know this, but am inclined to believe so from the fact that he was not seen afterwards. I was under the impression that the tiller ropes had burnt off, but don't know the fact; I only supposed so. I did not say, as was published, that the tiller ropes were actually burnt off. I think there was a communication from the forward to the after part of the boat, on the promenade deck, at the time they launched the life boat. I did not observe that the tiller was or was not unshipped at the time. I had a talk with Capt. Vanderbilt, and might have said to him that when I first saw the fire two or three buckets of water would have put it out. I think there would have been no trouble in putting it out when I first saw it, had they gone the right way to work. I will not say that two or three buckets full would have completely put it out.

Had I had command of the Lexington I think I should have stopped the engines, manned the buckets, and put the fire out, which might at first have been done. I should have tried also to save the boats. A man, however, under such circumstances, has many things to attend to, and it is hard to know what to do first. The captain had the fire to attend to, also the boats and other things, and I think it would have been a very difficult matter to have preserved the boats, on account of the rush of the passengers into them. The quarter boats might have carried fifteen persons each to the shore in safety.

—

The inquest then adjourned to Thursday.

NEW-YORK RAIL-ROADS.

1. New-York and Erie Rail-road.—This road commences at Tappan, (now called Piermont,) in Rockland county, on the Hudson river, 25 miles from the city-hall in New York, and running first a north-westerly, and then in a westerly direction, passes through every county on the southern border of the State, and by the towns of Goshen, Deposit, Binghamton, Owego, Elmira, Corning, Hornellsville, and Olean to Dunkirk, on lake Erie, a distance of 457 miles. If a road should be made, as is contemplated, on the east side of the Hudson, from a point opposite Piermont, to connect with the Harlem rail-road, and through that road with the city of New York, the whole distance, by this route, from the city of New York to lake Erie would be 484 miles.

The distance, from the city of New-York to Dunkirk, by the route first surveyed, was 508 miles, and the grades, in some places, were very unfavorable. By surveys recently made by E. F. Johnson, Esq. and others, the distance has been reduced to 484 miles, and the grades to 60 feet to the mile. Recent surveys have also enabled the directors to dispense with inclined planes, and to make other valuable improvements, particularly in the grades in Sullivan, Broome and Alleghany counties. It is believed too, that the whole line from Dunkirk to New-York may be reduced to 475 miles.

The importance of this rail-road will be apparent when it is considered that it will connect the city of New York with a very extensive and fertile agricultural and grazing country; with the Chenango canal, at Binghamton; with the fertile country on Cayuga lake, by the rail-road from Owego to Ithaca; with the country on Seneca lake, by the Chemung canal, at Elmira; with the iron and coal regions of Pennsylvania, by the rail-road from Blossburg, at Corning; and with the extensive vallies of the Genesee and Alleghany rivers, by the Genesee canal at Olean point. The road will be one unbroken line from the Hudson to lake Erie, and it has a great advantage over any other road from New York to lake Erie in being under only *one charter*.

The cost of the road for a single track, owing to the cheapness of lumber and other favorable circumstances, is estimated at only $6,000,000. By a law passed in 1838, the state agreed to furnish $3,000,000 towards the construction of the road, on condition that the company expended an equal sum from their own resources, the company being authorised to receive this amount in sums of $100,000, as often as $100,000 was expended. Under this law they have received $400,000. At the last session of the legislature a law passed to grant the company in the proportion of $2 for every one dollar they shall expend, the company pledging the road to the State as security for the interest and principal of the loan.

In connection with the New York and Erie rail-road, we must mention two branches, viz: First, the *Ithaca* and *Owego* rail-road, 29 miles long, which is completed and in successful operation, opening a communication with Cayuga lake, and through that lake with the Erie canal; and Second, the *Corning and Blossburg* railroad, 40 miles long, by which the coal and iron of Pennsylvania are brought to the Chemung canal, and through that canal and Seneca lake conveyed to the people in the interior of New York, who in return send their salt and plaster, through the same channels, into Pennsylvania.

2. New-York, Albany and Buffalo Rail-road.—This rail-road, or rather series of rail-roads, commences opposite the City Hall in New York, and has been completed to Harlem, 7 miles and three quarters, by the *New York and Harlem Rail-road* company, at an expense of $1,100,000.

From Harlem, the *New York and Albany rail-road* company are to continue it through Westchester, Putnam, Dutchess, Columbia and Rensselaer counties to Albany, a distance of 140.7 miles, in the whole of which there are but two summits, one of 305 feet, near the centre of Westchester county, and the other of 769 ft., near the N. E. corner of Dutchess county; and the grades will in no case exceed 30 feet to the mile. Proposals have been made to build this road, and furnish the requisite number of engines and carriages for putting it in operation, in thirty months, for $2,640,000; or, if an entire iron rail is adopted, of suitable size and weight, $3,120,000. For a particular account of this road see our paper of September 5th.

The next link in the chain is the *Mohawk and Hudson* rail-road, extending from *Albany to Schenectady*, 15 miles and seven-eighths. This road was one of the first that was completed in the United States, and cost $1,100,000, or more than $70,000 per mile. It has two inclined planes which can be dispensed with, as the line of the road can be altered so that there shall be no grades of more than 60 feet to the mile.

From *Schenectady to Utica*, a distance of 78 miles, the road, being located by law on the north side of the Hudson, cost $1,540,000 for a single track, with 20 miles turnout in the centre. The company are prohibited by law from carrying freight, although they have offered to pay the same tolls into the State treasury, as are charged on the Erie canal; and yet the income, derived exclusively from the transportation of passengers and the U. S. mail, permits the company to divide 11 per cent. per annum!

The *Utica and Syracuse* rail-road, the next link in the chain, is 54 miles long, with a single track, and is built partly upon piles. It was completed on the 3d of July, 1839, at a cost of $900,000, and between that date and the 1st of January, 1840, (less than six months,) there were received from passengers and for the transportation of the U. States mail $117,614, yielding, after deducting expenses, a nett revenue of ten per cent. in less than half a year!

From *Syracuse to Auburn*, a distance of 26 miles, an excellent road has been completed at an expense of $460,000. It is considered one of the best roads on the line, and yields a fair income.

The *Auburn and Rochester* rail-road passes some distance south of the Erie Canal, through the flourishing villages of Geneva and Canandaigua, a distance by this route of 77 miles and a half. The part of the road between Rochester, and Canandaigua, 35 miles, is finished and in operation. The whole road, it is estimated, will cost $1,250,000, and with the aid of the state may be completed at the close of the year 1841. A road from Auburn to Rochester through Lyons, and along the banks of the Erie canal, it is said, would be 24 miles shorter than this road through Geneva and Canandaigua, equally practicable, and even more favorable in the grades.

The *Tonawanda* or (*Rochester and Buffalo*) rail-road has been finished to Batavia, 32 miles, at an expense of $400,000. From Batavia to Buffalo, by the direct route, the distance is 34 miles, making the whole distance from Rochester to Buffalo by the direct route only 66 miles, and so near a straight line, that the road would diverge only three-quarters of a mile to pass by Batavia. The road is represented on our map as passing in this direct line. If, however, it should diverge still farther, to pass by Attica, as is contemplated, the whole distance from Rochester to Buffalo would be increased to more than 70 miles. The road from Rochester to Buffalo, it is expected, will be finished in 1841.

From this view it will be seen that a line of rail-roads can be located on this route from the City Hall in New-York to Buffalo on Lake Erie, through a remarkably level country, and only 440 miles in length. The distance as given on our profile is 470 miles; but 30 miles, it is supposed, may be saved by adopting the short routes from Syracuse to Rochester, and Rochester to Buffalo.

In connection with this line of rail-roads we must mention the roads which cross it, join it, or approach it at different points, in their order.

The *Hudson and Berkshire* rail-road proceeds from the city of Hudson across the route of the New-York and Albany rail-road, 31 miles, to the west line of the State of Massachusetts, at West Stockbridge, whence it is continued for two miles, till it unites with the great Western rail-road of that state, and will thus supply, when the New-York and Albany rail-road is finished, the only link necessary to complete an *unbroken* rail-road line from New-York to Boston. This road has been in operation more than two years. In addition to passengers and merchandize, a considerable business is done in the transportation of large blocks of marble from the quarries at West Stockbridge to the city of Hudson.

The *Schenectady and Saratoga* rail-road, 23 miles long, cost $277,237 for a single track. At Ballston this road is connected with Troy, by a road which cost $450,000. Both these roads have been in successful operation for several years, and an extension of the line is contemplated by a road from Saratoga to Whitehall, 43 miles. When completed, *Troy and Lake Champlain* will be connected by a line of rail-roads 73 miles in length.

The *Catskill and Canajoharie* rail-road, 78 miles long, it is expected, will be completed with the aid of the state, and connected with the Hudson and Berkshire rail-road, at a cost of $1,200,000 in the year 1842. The first 22 miles from Catskill were graded, and the rails laid, several months since. This road will have the advantages of saving about 30 miles of the distance between New-York and Utica, and of striking the Hudson below the Overslaugh; but from the height of the summit to be overcome, (1180 feet, as given in our profile,) we presume the grades must be very steep, and unfavorable to the transportation of heavy produce.

A rail-road is contemplated which shall leave the Catskill and Canajoharie rail-road, at a point a few miles north of Schoharie, and proceed in a westerly direction for 16 miles up the valley of Cobleskill, (a branch of Schoharie creek) to its source, and thence in a south-westerly direction, down the valley of Schnewas creek, (a branch of the Susquehannah,) and down the valley of the Susquehannah till it meets the New York and Erie rail-road a little west of Deposit. We have given a profile of this road, but have not inserted the route on our map. Its whole length would be 53 miles.

A charter has been granted for a rail-road to leave the great line of rail-roads at *Rome*, and proceed west to *Oswego* on lake Ontario, about 60 miles; and for another, to leave the same line at *Syracuse*, and proceed to *Oswego* down the valley of Oswego river, 35 miles.

A rail-road is contemplated which shall connect *Auburn with Ithaca*; the route to proceed from Auburn along the east side of the Owasco lake to its southern extremity, and thence south till it joins the Owego and Ithaca rail-road at its summit, eight miles south-east of Ithaca. We have given profiles of the Auburn and Ithaca, and of the Ithaca and Owego rail-roads, showing them in their proposed connection.

From *Buffalo*, a rail-road has been built to *Niagara Falls*, 23 miles, at an expense of $110,000 for a single track on wood; and from Niagara Falls another has been built to *Lockport*, 20 miles.

3. The *St. Lawrence and Champlain* rail-road, from Ogdensburgh by Malone to Plattsburg, has been surveyed, under orders from the legislature, by Edwin F. Johnson, Esq., who found the distance 120 miles, and estimated the cost at $1,451,805. This route crosses the Chateaugay river, a few miles east of Malone, and is called the Chateaugay route. Mr. J. also surveyed another route, which commences at Port Kent, on lake Champlain, at the mouth of the Au Sable river, and proceeds up the valley of that river, on the north side, nearly to its source; thence, across the highlands, to the valley of Racket river, down which it descends till it meets the Chateaugay or northern route, 2 or 3 miles west of Potsdam. Profiles of both these roads are appended to our map.

We conclude this notice with a brief statement of the comparative advantages of the great cities on the Atlantic coast for communication with the great valley of the West by rail-road.

The distance of the *city of New York* from lake Erie, by the *New York and Erie rail-road* is only 484 miles, with grades in no case exceeding 60 feet to the mile, the highest summit to be overcome being 1,770 feet, and the road is *in one unbroken line*, and *under one charter*, and can be built for $6,000,000.

2. The distance of *New-York* from lake Erie by the *New-York, Albany and Buffalo* rail-road is 470 miles; and this distance may be reduced to 440 by improvements in the western part of the route. The highest summit to be overcome is only 912 feet, and the grades throughout are almost, if not quite, as favorable as if the country were a dead level, the descents being gentle, and with the course of the heavy transportation. In no part, except for about 5 miles between Albany and Schenectady, do the grades exceed 30 feet to the mile. This line of rail-roads will cost when completed more than $10,000,000; and it will labor under the disadvantage of being under the control of nine or ten distinct companies.

3. From *Boston* to Lake Erie, by the *Massachusetts Western rail-road* to the western line of this state, and thence via Albany, and the rail-road line just referred to, is 525 miles; or 55 miles farther than from the city of New-York to the same lake. The highest summit to be overcome in Massachusetts is 1440 feet, and the grades in crossing the Green Mountains run up to 80 feet in the mile. From Boston to the Hudson river this line of rail-road will cost $6,500,000.

4. The communication of *Philadelphia* with the ocean by the Delaware river and bay, is obstructed by ice in the winter; and her connection with the valley of the Ohio is by a mixed line of rail-roads and canals, the Allegany mountains being passed by a rail-road with ten inclined planes at an altitude of 2,397 feet above tide-water.

5. The rail-road from *Baltimore* thro' Maryland to Wheeling, on the Ohio, has to surmount an elevation of about 2500 ft.

6. From *Albany* to Rome, by rail-roads already finished, is 109 miles, and from Rome to Oswego, by the contemplated rail-road, is 60 miles, making the whole distance from Albany to Oswego, by rail-road, 169 miles. This is the shortest route from the tide waters of the Atlantic to the great lakes; and when the contemplated rail-road from Hamilton in Upper Canada to Detroit is completed, it will probably be, in summer, the quickest and pleasantest route to the far West from New York and the Eastern states.

NEW-YORK RAIL-ROADS.

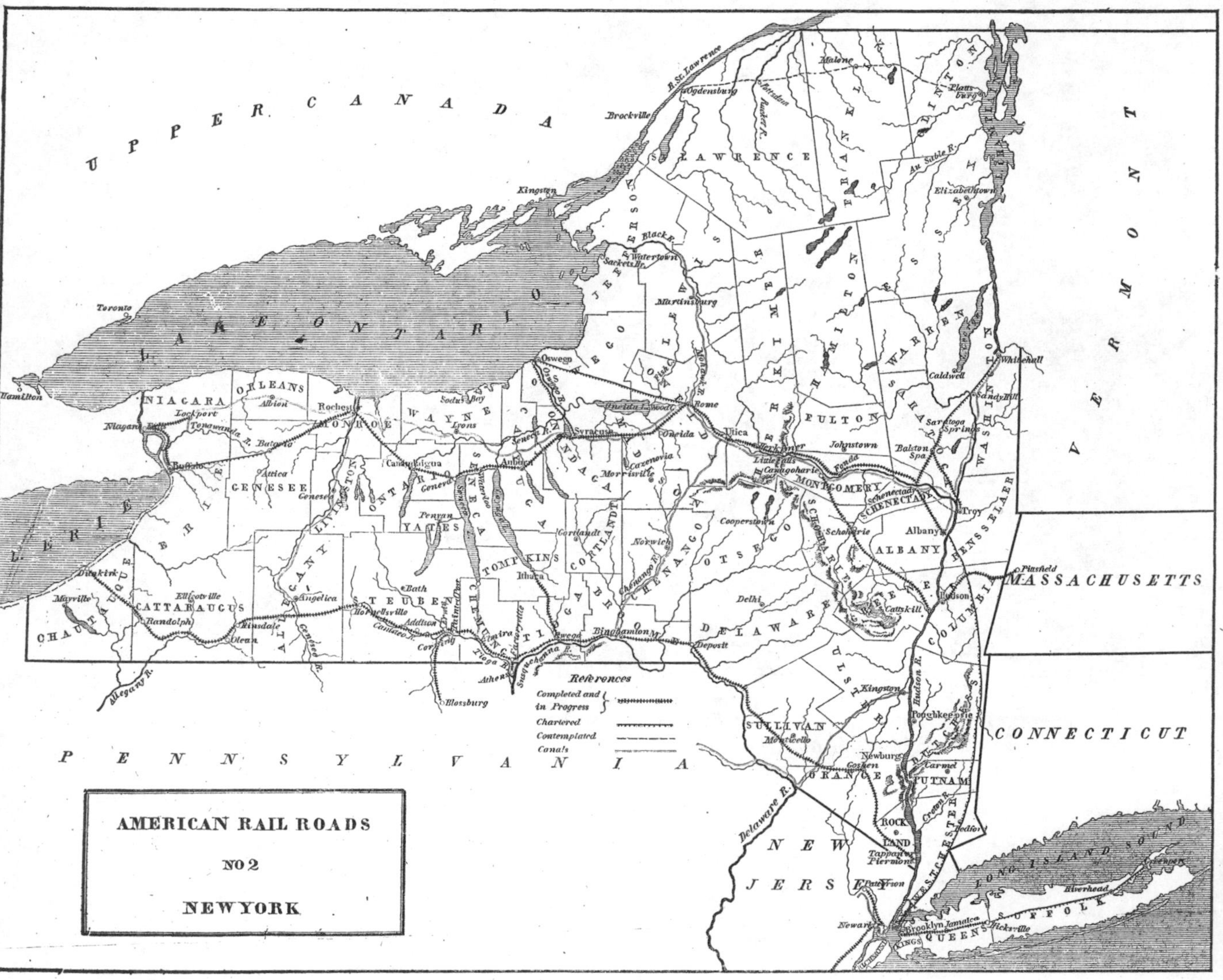

PROFILES OF THE PRINCIPAL RAIL-ROAD ROUTES IN THE STATE OF NEW-YORK.

Vertical scale 1,000 feet to 1 inch. Horizontal scale 40 miles to 1 inch.—Portions shaded, complete and in operation.

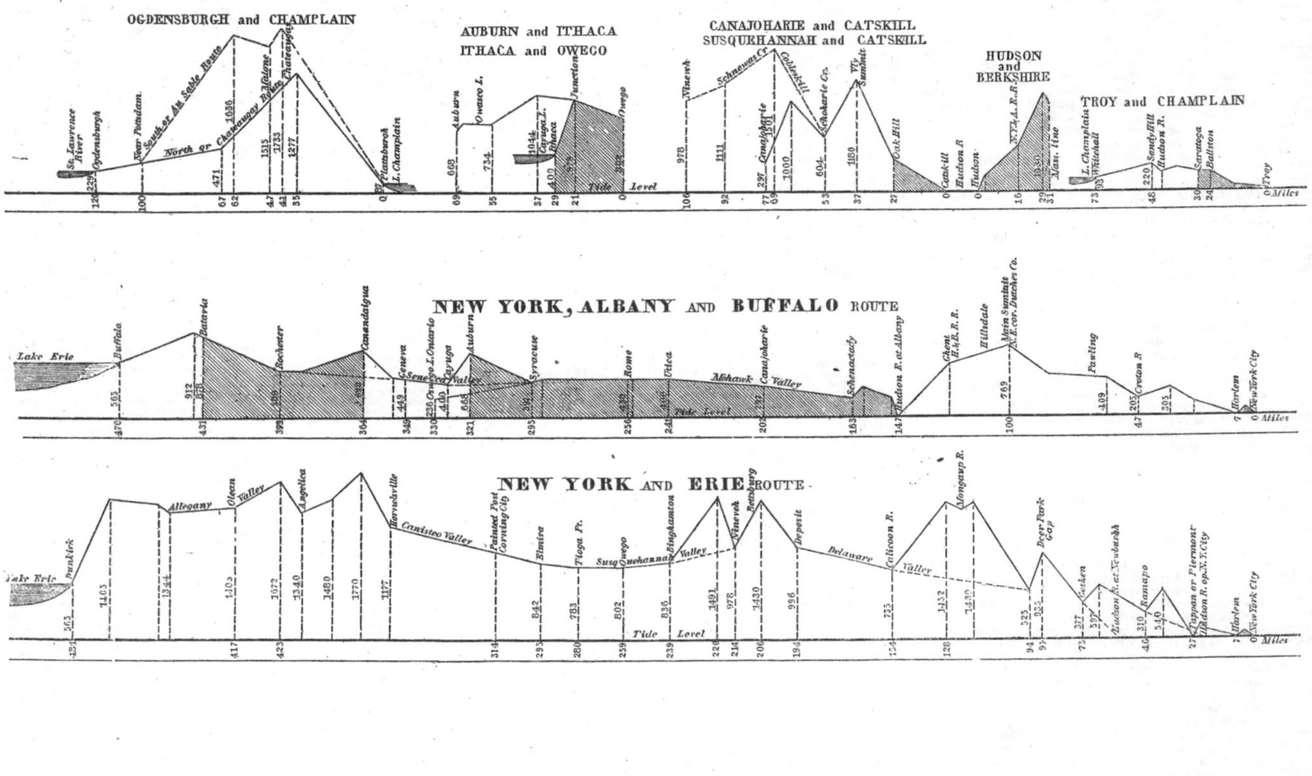

LIST OF RAIL-ROADS IN OPERATION IN THE STATE OF NEW-YORK, OCTOBER, 1840.

Names.	*Miles.*	*Name.*	*Miles.*	*Name.*	*Miles.*
Long Island,	27	Mohawk and Hudson,	16	Lockport and Niagara Falls,	20
Harlem,	7	Utica and Schenectady,	78	Buffalo and Niagara Falls,	22
Hudson and Berkshire,	31	Syracuse and Utica,	54	Ithaca and Owego,	29
Troy and Ballston,	24	Auburn and Syracuse,	26	Blossburg and Corning city,	14
Saratoga and Schenectady	22	Auburn and Rochester,	35		85
Catskill and Canajoharie	26	Rochester to Batavia,	32		241
	137		241		137

Total Rail-Roads in operation, 463

LADIES' MAN.

AND

EVERY BODY'S BEAU.

DEVOTED TO NEWS, POLITICS, THE DRAMA, THE WOMEN, AND ALL KINDS OF WIT, FUN AND FLASH IN THEIR PROPER SPHERES.

VOL. I.—NO. 1. NEW YORK, SATURDAY, AUGUST 18, 1844. PRICE TWO CENTS.

LADIES' MAN.

SUSPICION, AND A PAIR OF BREECHES--A VERY FARCICAL SCENE!

A good thing occurred in those amorous "diggins" out south the other day; much too good to keep, even though it smacks a little of crim. con. but here it is, fresh from 'Raccoon Holler.'

A lady there had for some time suspected her lord of dividing his attentions between herself and a fairer fair one, the wife of a neighbour; and divers and various were the expedients resorted to by the jealous one to overcome that "tedious difficulty" of which Iago speaks when bringing about the "strong proof" which was yet only shadowed forth in "imputation and strong circumstances." At length the moment arrived when the awful secret was to be revealed. The suspected husband had mysteriously absented himself, and this was "confirmation strong as holy writ" that he was domiciliating at the whereabouts of his charmer. Thither did the neglected wife repair, and softly did she steal beneath an open casement to catch whatever sounds might emanate from the chamber within, and soon she believed her worst suspicions were confirmed, and revenge became her only meditation. What punishment would she not have inflicted on him had her power been equal to her will; but she contented herself, in order to have an evidence of his guilt, with seizing hold of his cast-off breeches, and instantly decamped in silent rage.

When arrived at her own lodgings, she turned the key upon the naughty world and threw herself upon a sleepless couch. In half an hour her naughty husband arrived, whistling as usual to his bed chamber. 'Wretch!' thought the wife, 'how can he thus endure his situation in half nakedness, sans pants, sans coat, sans almost every thing!' He however raised the latch with as much confidence as if he had never given cause for a key to be turned against him, when lo! to his utter astonishment, the 'open sesame' was not responded to. 'What can this mean?' thought he, 'sure I think my wife honest, but damn me if I like appearances.' Rap, rap, rap, was only answered by a mysterious fumbling within, and an occasional deep sigh. A sturdy kick however, soon introduced the visiter to his wife's sanctum, which though wrapt in the 'blackness of darkness" was soon illuminated by a certain appendage of modern democracy, a loco foco match. 'Hallo, here!' said he, as soon enabled him to discover the breeches, 'what in the name of chastity does this mean? So, madam, I have caught you at last!' and he looked into every hole and corner of the bed room, until he came to a partly raised window, when his passion suddenly raised to its grand climacteric, and the tragic scenes of Othello seemed about to be realized. But the wife by this time had ventured to peep from between the bed curtains, when she discovered to her consternation that her lord was full dressed, and in his own praper clothing, and that the awfully suspicious breeches which he held in his hand, were those of the husband of her supposed rival.

It may well be imagined that many difficulties stood in the way of a satisfactory adjustment of all the troubles of the evening, and it was not until the suspicious breeches had been restored to to their proper owner, and the avowal of the lady of the wearer had been made, that he had not on that evening been making sans culotte exhibitions abroad, that entire domestic tranquility was restored, and the green eyed monster entirely rooted out of the hearts of either party.

WOMAN.

As the dew lies longest and produces most fertility in the shades so women in the shade of domestic retirement, sheds around her path richer and more permanent blessings than man, who is more exposed to the glare and observation of public life. Oh, WOMING, pure, genuine 'clar grit' virginity, we owe thee much.

A WIFE WANTED.

The editor of a paper in Pennsylvania, says he wants a wife; and he thus enumerates the necessary qualifications:

"She must be a girl whose eyes beam with love tenderness and pity; twinkle with fun, frolic and mischief, and heighten up the flash with the immortal part of its frail tenement; whose countenance is illuminated by virgin innocence and purity; chastened by humility, and happy from the practice of every homely virtue; and a heart to feel, and a hand to relieve, and a bosom to sympathize with misfortune; one who can mend breeches, make shirts, scrub floors, peal taters and cook dinners.' Now, girls, put in your claims, if you will have him on these terms.

Woman is
In infancy a tender flower,
Cultivate her;
A floating bark in girlhood's hour,
Softly freight her.
A fruitful vine when grown a lass,
Prune and please her;
Old, she is a heavy charge, alas!
Support and ease her.

We observed on Wednesday evening, when taking a stroll along West Broadway, a scene which did us much surprise, and cause modesty to recede with blushes. It was no more nor less than a gal sitting on her feller's knee, billing and cooing at the front window, to the astonishment and disgust of the passers by. Oh, decency for heaving's sake.

As we were sitting in the garden of Otto Cottage at Hoboken, on Saturday afternoon, we observed a certain married man, a broker, walking about the place, with a little French bonnet maker of the Bowery. Come, my covy, that won't answer.

We observed Jimmy D. of Spring street, on the Battery, on Sunday afternoon, with Sal G——s. Oh!

LADIES' MAN

NEW YORK, AUGUST 18, 1844.

PUBLISHED EVERY
SATURDAY MORNING, BY
JOHN DALRYMPLE.

Sold at the FRANKLIN NEWS DEPOT, No. 321 Broadway, (next the Hospital)

All communications addressed to the Ladies' Man, directed as above, will receive attention. Letters through the Post office must be post paid.

Rumors, Wants to Know, Wonders, and Advertisements, not exceeding 6 lines, 12 1-2 cents, or two cents per line. Communications, from the Ladies especially, solicited.

Here I am, The Ladies' Man, (and Every Body's Beau. Ain't I first rate, and no mistake. There, I see by that smile on your pretty face that you think so. Indeed I was always a favorite with the feminine women ever since that good old lady first found me 'in the woods,' and held me up blushing and rosy as a full-blown holly-hock to the delighted gaze of my blessed mammy, one fine frosty morning, afore day. Yes, the ladies love me, and I love them. Oh how nice it is to hug their heads, and smack their strawberry lips, all in an innocent friendly way, of course. It was always a fashion I had this sparking, and gallivanting the little heavenly feminine angels. Somehow I never could help it. It was bred in the bone and never could be got out. I am little its true, but I have a mighty soul. I espouse the cause of women with all my heart, soul and breeches, and will defend them, bustles and and all, against all assault upon their beauty and purity, even if we have to get on two bricks to do it. So look out, you nasty good for nothing hemales, and don't 'try for to come it' over the innocent and unsuspecting, or we shall down upon you like a rush of soap-suds into a sink.

TEMPERANCE, CORSETS, KISSES! &C. &C.

The Ladies, who go in for temperance so 'good and strong,' that they kiss the gentleman's lips to find out whether they had been drinking JULIPS, brandy smashers, &c. are mighty ticklish about the claims of the gentlemen to feel of their waists to see if they wear corsets or not. Now who's to decide in so ticklish a matter? We don't like the job, for we are partial to the ladies and might be tickled into the advocacy of corsets, albeit we really think they are worse for their tender bodies than julips or smashers. We are for temperance in all things, so the ladies will know where to find us, at all times; but we have a thought that may settle the question, without much FEELING in the premises. This is to enter into a compact with the gentlemen that if they shave off their filthy buffalo whiskers and their imperial upper lip soap locks, or nasty-cat-tail swabs, you will cut the corset strings, instanter. That now is a fair offer, ladies, and if the gents won't go it, stick to your corsets and you'll be as fair as ever.

There are some other little preliminaries that ought to be settled in the premises, and while our pen is in the business we may as well allude to them, however ticklish. The ladies complain that the gentlemen talk so much about their bustles behind their backs and rarely, if ever, come out plumply as the ladies do in that matter, or, as with rouge before the face. They sneakingly assail our dress, taste and standing, say they, without as much as saying a word to us, pro or con. As well might they speculate upon our stockings, or petticoats—which we dare them to do—as to trouble their heals with our bustles; or corsets. In this we say boldly, they are right, for though we dare not trouble our heads about these things, especially after such a threat; yet they are as near and dear to us as the others. Out, then, gentlemen, with your critical acumen upon matters know nothing about, whatever you may care for them. And, what is more, the girls say you never shall know any thing about them if you don't let their dresses elone and mind your own business. There, now, that is right spunky; it is right into them tooth and nail. Now ladies, following in the footsteps of our 'illustrious predecessor,' Mr. Van Buren, out west—may'nt we have a kiss all round for that. We shan't mind if there's but one who refuses, as with the worthy ex-president, there will be enough for the present, as he thought.

That the Old Maid's Garret and Tattle Club met as usual on Saturday last, at the Old Maids' Hall, in Broom street.

After the minutes of the last meeting were read.

Miss Tell-tale stated that Miss All-love kept a house in Leonard street, for the accommodation of single gentlemen and their wives.

Miss Watch-them said that some queer sights might be seen in the yard of said house, from the neighbors' windows.

Miss Say-nothing stated that she did not like to talk about her neighbours, and she would say nothing about Miss Easy going to be married to Mr. Nurse-it, because 'tis an act of necessity.

Miss Crab-apple Dignity, strted a Mr. Minststick, of Centre street, member of the Squirt Club, wears corsets, and no suspenders to his——[Here she was interrupted by Miss Modesty exclaiming: 'Don't mention the nasty things."

On motion of Miss Scratchem, a committee of three was appointed to make Mr. Mintstick some ch—no, that is—shirts without sleeves!

Miss Knowall, stated that Miss Willing had received a present from a married man that his wife did'dt know anything about.

Miss Suspicion thought that Miss Willing would receive another kind of present before long. Miss Fearful said they had better say nothing about it, as such things would tell for themselves.

Miss Manhater stated that Mr. LAST has quit going to see Miss Late-hour; cause vy? her daddy gave him the STRAP because he would not MEND a bed cord he broke. So here's an END to AWL his courtship poor SOLE.

Miss Tell-tale stated that the pretty Miss Black-eyes of Grand street, has a red headed beau. Here the committee from Marth Sly, the fish girl, entered add reported that Marth. would soon have to trade for a very important piece of furniture, in the matter of house-keeping. At this moment, the trap door on which I was sitting (not being admitted into the room) gave way; down I came in the midst of the ladies of advanced age, vulgarly called old maids. Picture to yourself, gentle reader, (for I cannot describe) the excitement of the moment. Suffice it to say, that I was handed out of the window in no gentle manner; but thanks to a tub of water that was sitting in the yard, I escaped with only a good ducking. I hastened home, said amen, and put myself to bed, where I lay all night dreaming of old maids, wildcats, and a thousand other horrible things. SPY.

That the Ladies' Man, and Every Body's Beau, having arrived in New York intends bringing out his dear little weekly paper every Saturday, at the request of a large portion of the up-town population, and the sweet feminines in particular. That's true, we intend to go it while we're young, and refuse the ladies nothing.

BOWERY THEATRE.

A splendid spectacle called Putnam or the Iron Son of 76, written by the gifted Banister has had a tremendous rush at this establishment for a week past. The horse is the best ACTOR of the whole lot however, always excepting the pretty women and they can't be beat, no how you can fix it.

CHATHAM.

Our friend Deverna has also gotten up the horse spectacle of Putnam. It is a thrilling thing, enough to curl a fellow hair into knots, so as to require the use of a curry comb to get it smooth again.

NIBLO'S.

The entertainments at this popular establishment are under the sole direction of Mr. Mitchell, who appeared on Monday in his original character of Broomy Swash, in the laughable farce of Aldgate Pump. The Spirit of the Rhine, a new operetta, was also produced for the first time, in which Mr. Nickinson sustained the character of Ignatius Stuffilecrafts to good advantage.

PARK.

Simpson is in Europe. The cobwebs in dusty magnificence, hang in this temple, and spiders are left alone in their glory!

The Annual Pictorial Herald.

NEW YORK, JANUARY 1, 1845.

The Dying Coon's Advice to Posterity.

Great Pedestrian Feat.

Field Sports of the West.

The Lost Wager.

Things as they were to have been.

General Jackson's March.

The "Young Hickory of the West."

The Mill-Boy of the Slashes.

FAME!

Silas Wright visited By General Macombs.

The Polk-a!

A Leap for Life.

Celebrated Character in the Beggar's Opera.

Scene from The "Coon," a tragedy in one Act.

A Settler.

Two Gentlemen of Verona.

Old Kentucky.

The Town Pump.

That Trunk.

St. Patrick's Cathedral, Prince Street.

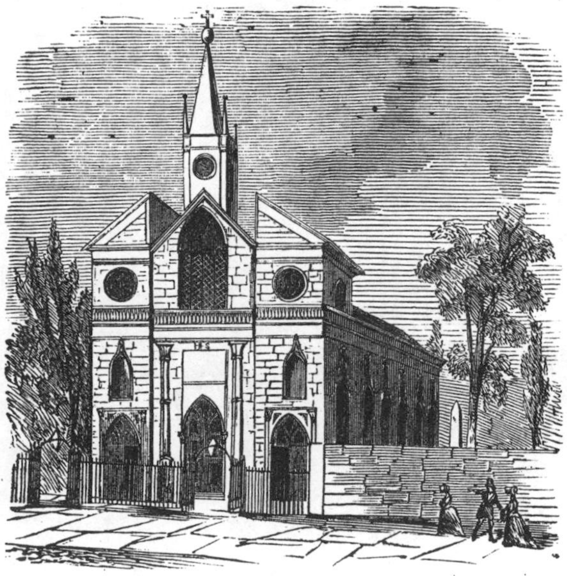

St. Peter's Church, Barclay street, New York.

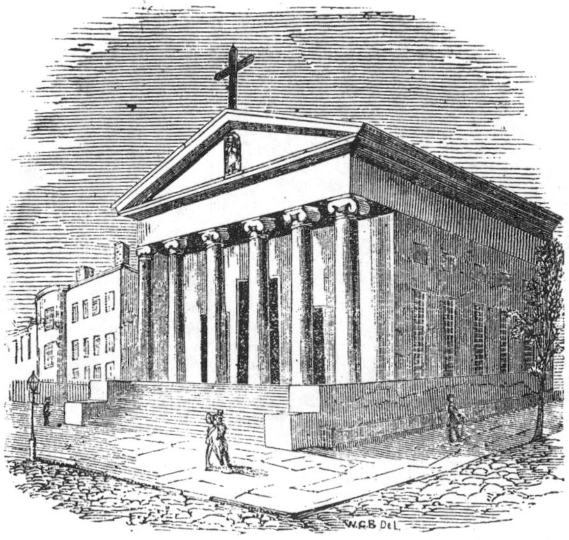

Dr. Potts' New Church.

Interior of St. Patrick's Catheral.

University, New York.

St. Thomas' Church.

Trinity Church.

Interior of St. Peter's.

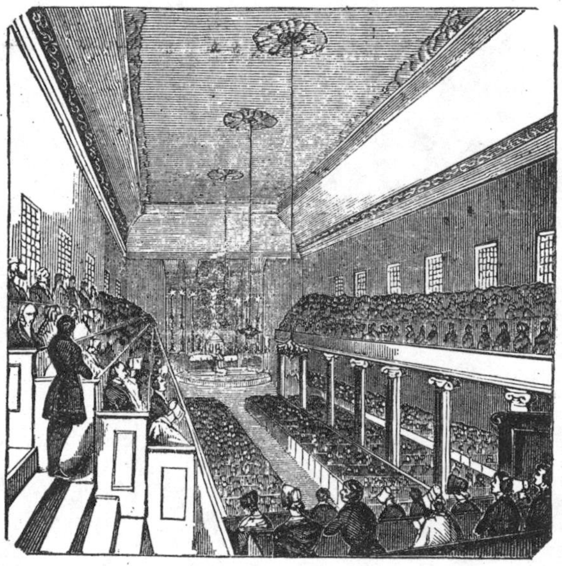

St. Paul's Church, Broadway.

Interior of the Brick Church.

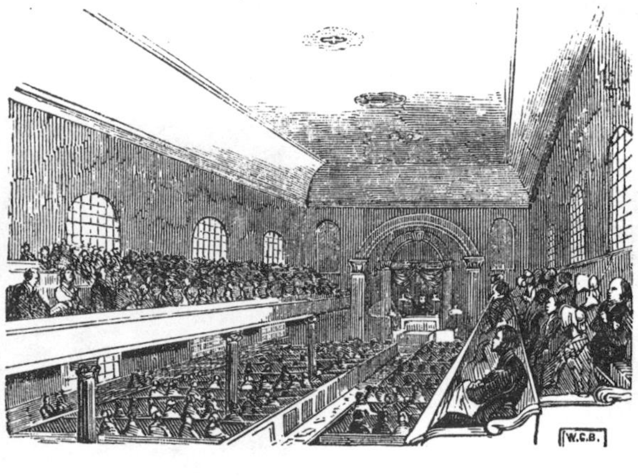

Exterior View Of the New Post Office.

Interior of the Post Office.

One of the Corps de Ballet.

Parlor Scene in a Fashionable Boarding School.

A Chevalier.

The Opera House, New York.

The Board of Brokers, Wall Street.

Fanny Ellsler.

The Milliner.

New York Gallery of the Fine Arts, Broadway.

Interior of the Church of the Messiah.

Chasseur d' Afrique.

The Polka, as taught by Mons. Korponay.

M. Heinrick, the Composer.

Betty, the handsome Chambermaid at the Astor.

NEW YORK PATH-FINDER.

Devoted to Steamers, Railroads, Omnibusses, Stages, Expresses, Hotels, Packets, Advertisements, News, &c. &c.

VOL. 1.---NO. 39. NEW YORK, THURSDAY, JUNE 8, 1848. CORRECTED SEMI-WEEKLY

PUBLISHED EVERY
MONDAY AND THURSDAY,
—BY—
HOLBROOK & BARTLETT,
NO. 123 FULTON STREET,
2d Door from Nassau St. (Up Stairs.)

Terms of Subscription,

$1,50 per year in advance, or $2 at the end of the year. Single Copi[illegible] Cents.

Terms of Advertising,

For 1 square, (18 lines Agate) 4 weeks..........$4,00
½ " 9 " " 4 " 2,00
¼ " 4 " " 4 " 1,25
Monthly payments in advance.
For 1 square, (18 lines Agate) 1 year..........$40,00
½ " 9 " " 1 " 20,00
¼ " 4 " " 1 " 12,00
Quarterly payments in advance.

DAILY CIRCULATION!

☞ **1,000 Copies per Day** given to **Travellers** *coming* to the city by the different *Railroads and steamboats*, making at least **30,000 different Persons** who Read the **Path-Finder** *every month.* Our Agents are at **White Plains, Albany, Piermont, Paterson, Newark, New Brunswick, Perth Amboy, Jamaica, Fall River, Stonington, Norwich, New Haven and Bridgeport.**

Railroad Directory.

NEW JERSEY RAILROAD AND TRANSPORTATION COMPANY.

SPRING ARRANGEMENT.

On and after April 17, 1848, passengers will leave the foot of Courtlandt street as follows:—

NEW YORK AND NEWARK.

Leave New York—At 8 AM, Newark Accom; 9 AM, Phil & Elizabethtown; 10.15, N. B. Accommodation; 11, Newark freight; 12 M, Newark Accommodation; 2 PM, Elizabethtown Accommodation; 3, New Brunswick freight; 3.30, Newark freight; 4, Newark Accommodation; 4.30, Trenton Accommodation; 5, New Brunswick Accommodation; 6, Rahway Accommodation; 7, Newark Accommodation; 11.30, Wednesday nights.

Leave Newark—At 7 AM, Newark Accom: 7½ N. B. Freight; 8 AM, Rahway; 8¼ N. B. Accom.; 8¼ Newark Freight; 9 Newark Accom.; 9¾* Trenton Accommodation; 11*, Elizabethtown Accom.; 1 PM, Newark Freight; 2, Newark Accom.; 4, Elizabethtown Accommodation; 5, New Brunswick Accom.; 6, Newark Accommodation; 8¼* Philadelphia line;* 10.40 Wednesday nights.

On Sunday—Leave New York at 9 AM, and 4½ PM. Newark at 1¼ PM* and 8¼* PM.

NEW YORK AND ELIZABETHTOWN.

Leave New York at 9 AM, Philadelphia and Elizabethtown; 10¼ New Brunswick Accommodation; 2 PM, Elizabethtown Accom.; 3, New Brunswick freight; 4½, Philadelphia and Trenton Accom.; 5, N. Brunswick Accom.; 6, Rahway; 11½, Wednesday nights.

Leave Elizabethtown—At 6¾ AM, New Brunswick freight; 7½, Rahway; 8.10, New Brunswick Accom; 9¾, Trenton Accommodation*; 10½*, Somerville; 12¾, PM., Philabelphia; 3½, Elizabethtown Accom'n; 4½, New Brunswick Accommodation; 8, Phila.;* 10.20, Wednesday nights.

On Sundays—Leave New York at 9 AM, and 4½ PM; Elizabethtown at 12¾ and 8 PM.

NEW YORK AND RAHWAY.

Leave New York—At 9 AM, Philadelphia; 10¼, N. Brunswick Accom.; 3 PM, N. Brunswick freight; 4½, Trenton Accommodation; 5, N. Brunswick Accom; 6, Rahway; 11½, Wednesday night.

Leave Rahway—At 6½ AM, N. Brunswick freight; 7½, Rahway Accom.; 7.50, New Brunswick Accom; 9,* Trenton Accom.; 12½ PM, Philadelphia; 4½, New Brunswick Accommodation; 7¾,* Philadelphia; and 10 Wednesday nights.

On Sundays—Leave New York at 9 AM, and 4½ PM; Rahway at 12½* and 7¾ PM.

NEW YORK AND NEW BRUNSWICK.

Leave New York—At at 9 AM, Philadelphia; 10¼, Accommodation; 3 PM, freight; 4½, Trenton Accom; 5, New Brunswick Accommodation.

Leave New Brunswick—At 6 AM, freight; 7½, New Brunswick Accommodation; 8½,* Trenton Accom.; 12 M,* Philadelphia; 3½ PM, Accommodation; 7¼*, Philadelphia.

☞ Those marked thus [*] leave upon the arrival of the train from Philadelphia and Trenton—whether sooner or later.

FARE—To or from Newark, 25 cents; Elizabethtown and Rahway, 31¼ cents; New Brunswick, 50c; except in the Philadelphia and Trenton Accommodation.

Passengers purchasing tickets at the office, receive a ferry ticket gratis, except in Wednesday night extra train, 8¼ PM. Philadelphia from Newark.

TABLE OF DISTANCES AND FARES.

From New York to	Miles.	Total.	Fares. Way.	Total
Jersey City	1	1	4	4
Newark	8½	9½	25	25
Elizabethtown	5¼	14¾	12	31
Rahway	5¼	19¾	12	37
Metuchin	7	26¾	12	38
Flemington	2¼	28¾		
Freeman's	1	29¾		
Campbell's	2	31¾		
New Brunswick†	1½	33	25	50
Dean's Pond	8	41		
Kingston	4	45		
Princeton	4½	49½		2.00
Trenton	10	59½		2.50
Tullytown	6	65½		
Bristol	4	69½		3.50
Philadelphia	20½	90		4.00

* Sundays, fare 50 cents. † Sundays fare 75 cents.

PATTERSON RAILROAD.

SUMMER ARRANGEMENT.

On and after Monday, May 1, 1848, the trains will leave as follows:—

Leave New York at 9 AM, and 12.30 and 5 PM.
Leave Patterson at 8 and 11.30 AM, and 4 PM.
On Sundays—Leave New York at 9 AM, and 5 PM.
Leave Patterson at 8 AM, and 4 PM

Passengers are advised to be at the Ferry a few minutes before the hour of starting.

Stages for Little Falls twice per day. On Mon. Wed and Fri on arrival of 1st train from New York for Hamburg via Pompton, Newfoundland, and Deckertown.

TABLE OF DISTANCES AND FARES.

From N. Y. by Ferry to	Miles.	Total.	Fares. Way.	Total
Jersey City	1	1	4	4
Bergen Junction	1½	2½	18	18
Seacaucus	2½	5	12	25
Boiling Spring	4	9		
Passaic Bridge	2	11	12	38
Aquackanonk	¾	11¾	12	50
Ackermans	1	12¾		
Patterson	3¾	16½	18¾	60

MORRIS AND ESSEX RAILROAD.

SUMMER ARRANGEMENT.

On and after Monday, May 1, 1848, passenger trains leave as follows:—

Leave New York at 8 AM, and 4 PM.
Leave Newark at 8.45 AM and 4.45 PM.
Leave Morristown at 7 AM and 2 PM.

On arrival of 1st train from New York, stages leave Morristown for Schooley's Mountain, Washington, Belvidere, and Easton; for Owego, Milford, Newton, Stanhope and Succasuny Mon. Wed. and Fr.; for Rockaway, Dover, Sparta, and Newton, Tu. Th. and Sat.; for Basking Ridge every evening.

Passengers go through to and from Jersey City without changing cars. On leaving the city, pessengers will deposit their baggage in the car at the foot of Cortlandt st, where an agent will be in attendance to receive it.

All packages or bundles must be entered on the way bill, or the company will not hold themselves responsible.

Freight will be forwarded immediately to Morristown from Albany Basin by Stephens & Condit's Daily Transportation Line to Newark, or from the Transportation Office of the N. J. R. R. Transportation Company, foot of Liberty street.

IRA DODD, Superintendent.

TABLE OF DISTANCES AND FARES.

From N. Y. by ferry to	Miles.	Total.	Fares. Way.	Total
Jersey City	1	1		
Newark	8½	9½	25	25
Orange	4	13½	12	37
Millville	6	19½	19	56
Summit	3	22½	13	69
Chatham	3	25½	12	75
Madison	2½	28	12	87
Morristown	4½	32½	13	1,00

ELIZABETHTOWN AND SOMERVILLE RAILROAD.

WINTER ARRANGEMENT.

Leave by New Jersey Railroad, foot of Cortlandt st, at 9 AM, 2 and 5 PM.

Leave by steamboat from pier No. 1 North River, to connect with the same train at 9 AM, 1 PM, (freight train) and 5 PM.

Stage Lines leave Somerville for Easton, Pa, on arrival of 1st train from New York, fare $2,75, returns at 8 AM. in time for 3d train for New York; for Flemington, N. J., on arrival of 1st train from New York; for Rahway on arrival of 1st and 3d trains, returns in time for steamer from Elizabethport at 7.30 AM. and 3.30 PM, for New York.

For seats apply to A. D. HOPE, Merchants' Hotel, 41 Cortlandt st.

TABLE OF DISTANCES AND FARES.

From N. Y. by steamer to	Miles.	Total.	Fares. Way.	Total
Elizabethport	15	15	18	18
Elizabethtown	1½	16½	6	18
Westfield	5	23½	18¾	50
Scotch Plains	3	26½		62
Plainfield	2	28½		62
New Market	3	31½		62
Bound Brook	4	35½	25	75
Somerville	5	40½	12	87½

NEW YORK & HARLEM R. ROAD.

SUMMER ARRANGEMENT.

On and after Monday, April 24, 1848, the cars will leave the City Hall, New York, as follows, until further notice:—

Harlem, Morrisania and intermediate places, at 5.30, 7.10, 8, 9, 10 and 11 AM, 12 M, and 2, 3, 4, 5, 5.30 and 6.30 PM.

Fordham and Williams' Bridge, at 5.30, 7 and 9 AM, 12 M, and 3, 4.30 and 5.30 PM.

White Plains and Tuckahoe, at 7 and 9 AM, and 3 4.30 and 5.30 PM

Pleasantville, Mount Kisko, Mechanicsvills and Croton Falls at 7 and 9 AM, 4.30 PM.

Returning will leave

Harlem and Morrisiana, 7.08, 8, 9 and 11 AM, 12 M, and 1.40, 3, 4, 5, 6 and 7.30 PM.

Fordham and William's Bridge at 6.45, 8 and 9.10 AM, and 1.15, 3.40, 5.30 and 6.35 PM.

Tuckahoe and White Plains at 7.15 and 8.35 AM, and 3, 4.45 and 6 PM.

Croton Falls at 7.30 AM, and 1.45 and 5 PM.

All the Morrisania trains leaving City Hall at 5.30, 7.10, 8, 9, 10 and 11 AM, 12 M, and 2, 3, 4, 5, 5.30 and 6.30 PM, and returning at 7.08, 8, 9 and 11 AM, 12 M, and 1.40, 3, 4, 5, 5.45 6 and 7.30 PM. will stop at 42d, 51st, 61st, 79th, 86th, 109th, 115th, 125th and 132d streets.

The accommodation train for Croton Falls at 9 AM and returning at 1.15 PM and also the accommodation trains for White Plains at 3 PM and returning at 4.45 PM, will stop at all places beyond Morrisania to land and receive passengers; and will stop to receive passengers going up, and to land them coming down, at all the streets above named.

The Croton Falls trains (except the accommodation trains) will not stop below Fordham, except at Broome street and at 32d street, unless to receive passengers at Harlem going beyond White Plains or to land them on coming down at Harlem.

The Morning Train of Cars from Croton Falls at 7.30 and the afternoon train at 4.30, will not stop between White Plains and New York except at Tuckahoe, Williams' Bridge and Fordham.

The morning train from White Plains will not stop below Fordham, except to land passengers at Harlem

A car will precede each train ten minutes to take up passengers in the city. The last car will not stop except at Broome street and 32d street.

On arrival of trains stages leave Harlem for Macomb's Dam, High Bridge, Carmanville, Kingsbridge, and Manhattanville; Bedford for Bedford Village and Poundridge, fare 25c; Williamsbridge for E. Chester, W. Farms, W. Chester, Pelham, New Rochelle, and Mamaroneck, 25c; Mechanicsville for Cross River, fare 37c, South Salem 50c, and Ridgefield 62c; Croton Falls daily, Sundays excepted, on arrival of 8 AM and 2.30 PM for Danbury, fare 50c, Sodom 25c, Bethel 50c, Mill Plain 37c, Mill Town 37c, Lake Mahopac 25, Somerstown 19c, and Tu,Th&Sat for Patterson 62c, and Paulings 87c; Williamsbridge for Yonkers, 25c; Hart Purdy's for Ridgebury, 87c, North Salem 25c, Salem Centre 25c. Transient Stages at White Plains for Portchester and Rye; Croton Falls for Dover Plains TuTh&Sat; return MW&F.

TABLE OF DISTANCES AND FARES.

From City Hall to	Miles.	Total.	Fares. Way.	Total
27th street	2½	2½	6	6
32d Street	½	3	6	12
Fordham	10	13	10	20
Williams's Bridge	1½	14½	5	25
Hunt's Bridge	3¼	17¾	6	31
Underhill's	2	19¾	12	37
Tuckahoe	1	20¾	12	37
Harts	4	24¾	12	50
White Plains	1¼	26	12	50
Davis's Brook	2	28	12	62
Pleasantville	3	31	12	62
Chapeqaa	2	33	12	75
Mount Hisko	6	39	12	75
Bedford	3	42	12	88
Mechanicsville	6	48	12	88
Purdy's	3	51	12	1,00
Croton Falls	2	53	12	1,00

LONG ISLAND RAILROAD.

SUMMER ARRANGEMENT.

On and after Thursday June 1st, 1848, trains will run daily, Sundays excepted, as follows:

PASSENGER TRAINS,

Leave Brooklyn for Greenport, at 9 30 AM.
Leave Brooklyn for Farmingdale, at 9.30 AM, & 4 PM.
Leave Brooklyn for Jamaica at 9.30 AM, 4 & 6.30 PM.
Leave Greenport for Brooklyn at 9.30 AM.
Leave Farmingdale for Brooklyn, at 7 AM, & 12.40 PM.
Leave Jamaica for Brooklyn at 8 AM, 1.45 & 5.30 PM.

FREIGHT TRAINS.

Leave Brooklyn for Greenport and intermediate places at 8 AM.
Leave Greenport for Brooklyn and intermediate Places at 8 AM.

From this date the fare will be increased to 2½ cents per mile—the fare not to exceed $2 for any place on the road.

DAVID S. IVES, Sup't.

On and after Monday, May 1, and until further notice, the 4 PM. train from Brooklyn will run to Farmingdale, daily, Sundays excepted—Sat. to Yaphank

Stages from Jamaica for Rockaway, fare 50c; Branch for Roslyn, 37c; Hicksville for Cold Spring, Huntington, and Oyster Bay, (north and south) from 25 to 50c; Deer Park for Coram and Babylon; Thompson for Islip, and Mechanicsville; Medford station for Patchogue, and Port Jefferson; Yaphank for Millville and Carman; St George's Manor for Moriches; Riverhead for Quog, and the Hamptons.

TABLE OF DISTANCES AND FARES.

From Brooklyn to	Miles.	Total.	Fares. Way.	Total
Bedford	2½	2½	5	5
East New York	3	5½	10	15
Union Course	2½	8	10	20
Woodville	½	8½	5	20
Jamaica	2½	11	10	30
Brushville	3	14	10	35
Hyde Park	3	17	10	40
Branch	3	20	10	50
Hempstead	1	21	5	55
Carle Place	1	22	10	55
Westbury	1	23	5	55
Hicksville	3	26	10	65
Farmingdale	5	32	15	75
Deer Park	6	38	15	90
Thompson	4	41	20	1.10
Suffolk Station	2½	43½	5	1,15
Lake Road	5½	49	15	1,20
Medford Station	6	55	15	1,35
Yaphank	5	60	15	1,50
St. George's Manor	6	66	15	1,65
River Head	8	74	20	1,85
Jamesport	5	79	10	1,95
Mattituck	4	83	10	2.00
Cutchogue	3	86	10	2,00
Hermitage	4	90	10	2,00
Southold	1	91	5	2,00
Greenport	4	95	10	2.00

PITTSBURG AND WHEELING.

To Pittsburg and Wheeling, Cincinnati, by Morning and Evening trains from New York Philadelphia, Baltimore and Cumberland, without delay. Passengers having a choice of a day or night travel over the Mountains, by the Great U. States Mail and Passenger Route. Through in 48 hours from New York to Pittsburg, Wheeling, thence to Cincinnati, St. Louis, New Orleans, and the South and West.—passengers going directly through by the U. S. Mail trains.

Leave New York, foot of Liberty st, daily, at 9 AM, and 4.30 PM, for Philadelphia, and connect with lines for Baltimore.

Leave Philadelphia by 10 PM train for Baltimore, and arrive in time to connect with 7,15 AM train for Pittsburg and Wheeling, going directly through without delay.

Leave Philadelphia, by Railroad from the corner of Eleventh and Market street, daily at 8.30 AM for Baltimore and arrive in time to connect with 4 PM. train for Pittsburg and Wheeling, and going directly through without delay.

Leaves Philadelphia, Sundays excepted, at 2.45 PM, by steamboat from Dock st wharf for Baltimore.

The only line on Sunday from Philadelphia for Baltimore is by Railroad, at 10 PM.

Leaves Baltimore daily at 7.15, and 4 PM, by the Baltimore and Ohio Railroad.

Leave Cumberland at 6 AM. and 6 PM, by twenty daily lines of the National Road and Good Intent Stage Lines, and arrive in Pittsburg or Wheeling, next evening and the following morning.

Passengers for Pittsburg take the splendid new and modern built steamboats at Brownsville, and thereby have only 74 miles of staging on the whole route.

For through-tickets by this route, apply in Philadelphia at the Railroad Office, corner of Market and Eleventh sts; at 45 South Third st; or on board steamboat, Dock st wharf.

Fare through from Philadelphia to Pittsburg, $12; to Wheeling $13, with the privilege of stopping at Baltimore, and resuming seats at pleasure.

☞ Passengers are cautioned against purchasing tickets in New York for Baltimore, Pittsburgh or Wheeling, purporting to go by the above mentioned Lines, as no one is authorized to sell tickets in New York for these lines.

For farther information apply to

J. L. SLEMMER, Agent.

At Adams & Co's Express Office, 16 Wall st, at 11 AM, or 29 Broadway, cor. Morris st. je5

CAMDEN AND AMBOY RAILROAD.

This Line for Philadelphia and intermediate places will leave Pier No. 2. N. R. foot of Battery Place, by steamboat JOHN POTTER, or South Amboy, Sundays excepted, at 6 AM, and 1 PM.

Passenger will take the cars from South Amboy o Camden and arrive in Philadelphia, about 11.30 PM., and 6.30 PM.

Fare to Philadelphia $3; for forward deck passengers to Philadelphia, $2,50; Emigrant and Transportation Line every day, by steamer Transport, at 3.30 PM, fare $2,25; Freehold and Monmouth via stages rom Hightstown and Wests Turnout; from New York to Freehold by West's Turnout 87½; from New York to Freehold by Hightstown, $1,50; to Spotswood and Wests, 75c; South Amboy, 25c; Perth Amboy, 12½c.

Fifty pounds of baggage will be allowed to each passenger in this line, and passengers are expressly prohibited from taking anything as baggage but their wearing apparel, which will be at the risk of its owner.

I. BLISS, Agent.

TABLE OF DISTANCES AND FARES.

From N. Y. by steamer to	Miles.	Total.	Fares. Way.	Total
South Amboy	27	27	25	25
South River	5	32	37½	
Spotsford	6	38	12½	75
West's	4	42	20	75
Prospect Plains	3	45	12½	
Hightstown	4	49	20	1,50
Centreville	4	53	15	1,75
Hungry Hill	3	56	15	
Sand Hills	2	58	15	2,00
Bordentown	5	63	20	2,50
Kincora	4	67	12½	
Burlington	4	71	25	
Rancocas	6	77	12½	2,87
Brick S. House	7	84	12½	
Philadelphia	6	90	12½	3,00

NEW YORK & ERIE RAILROAD.

SUMMER ARRANGEMENT.

From Monday, May 1, 1848, until further notice.

For Passengers—Leave NEW YORK from the foot of Duane st, at 7 AM, and 4 PM, for Piermont, Blouveltville, Clarkstown, Spring Valley, Monsey, Ramapo, Monroe Works, Turners, Monroe, Oxford, Chester, Goshen, New Hampton, Middletown, Howells, Otisville and Port Jervis.

For New York and intermediate places, leave PORT JERVIS at 6 AM and 3 PM; Otisville at 6.35 AM and 3.35 PM; Middletown at 7 AM and 4 PM; Goshen at 7.20 AM and 4.20 PM; Chester at 7.30 AM and 4.30 PM.

☞ All Baggage at the risk of the owner, unless put in charge of the Baggage Masters. Fifty lbs. of personal baggage allowed to each passenger. No Freight taken by the passenger trains.

For Freight—Leave New York at 5 o'clock PM, per barges Samuel Marsh, Henry Suydam, Jr., and Dunkirk. Leave Port Jervis at 9 AM; Otisville at 10 AM; Middletown at 11 AM; Goshen at 12 M, and Chester at 12.30 PM.

MILK will be taken morning and evening by trains running expressly for that purpose.

H. C. SEYMOUR, Superintendent.

TABLE OF DISTANCES AND FARES.

From N. Y. by steamer to	Miles.	Total.	Fares. Way.	Total
Piermont	25	25	25	25
Blauveltville	4	29	10	25
Clarkstown	5	34	10	30
Spring Valley	3	37	6¼	37½
Monsey	1	38	5	40
Sufferus	5	43	12½	60
Ramapo Works	2	45	6	70
Sloatsburg	1	46	5	75
Monroe Works	7	53	15	87½
Turner's	5	58	12½	94
Monroeville	3	61	6¼	1,00
Oxford	2	63	5	1,00
Chester	3	66	6¼	1,05
Goshen	5	71	10	1,12
New Hampton	4	75	10	1,18¾
Middletown	3	78	6¼	1,25
Howell's	2	80	12½	1,37½
Otisville	5	85	12½	1,50
Port Jervis	13	98	25	1,75

HOUSATONIC RAILROAD.

The steamer NIAGARA, Capt. J. Brooks, Jr, will leave N. York, from the pier foot of Market st., East river, daily, Sundays excepted, at 6 AM, for Bridgeport where, passengers take the elegant and commodious cars of the Housatonic Railroad, arriving at State Line at 3.30, and Albany at 4.30 PM.

A Baggage Master will go through from city to city.

Stages run in connection with the cars for Lee, Lenox, Old Stockbridge, Curtisville, Winstead and Norfolk. Also to Litchfield, Woodbury, Danbury and Bethel.

☞ No Agent of this Company is authorized to take charge of specie, Bank Notes, or valuable papers, or to receive them for transportation on any condition.

Freight received at the depot foot of Market street, from 7 AM. to 5.06 PM—positively not after that hour.

G. M. PERRY, Agent, Office on the Pier.

TABLE OF DISTANCES AND FARES.

From N. Y. by steamer to	Miles.	Total.	Fares. Way.	Total
Bridgeport	60	60		
Stepney	10	70		
Botsford	5	75		
Newtown	4	79		
Hawleysville	4	83		
Danbury				
Brookfield	6	88		
New Milford	6	95		
Gaylord's Bridge	7	102		
Kent	6	108		
Cornwall Bridge	9	117		
West Cornwall	4	121		
Falls Village	6	127		
Canaan	6	133		
Sheffield	6	139		
Great Barrington	6	145		
Van Dusenville	2	147		
West Stockbridge	8	155		
State Line	3	158		
Albany				

EXPRESS MAIL LINE TO BOSTON.

VIA STONINGTON AND PROVIDENCE.

The steamers C. VANDERBILT, Capt. Stone, and MASSACHUSETTS, Capt. Potter, will run throughout the season, in connection with the Stonington and Providence and Boston and Providence Railroads, leaving New York daily, Sundays excepted, from pier No. 1, North River, at 5 PM, and Stonington at 9 PM, or upon the arrival of the mail train from Boston.

The steamers are unsurpassed in speed, splendor and comfort, having each of them 60 large commodious private state rooms, and berths for 500 persons, besides large private rooms for families and parties.

The steamers are officered by the most experienced men, and will shorten the passage between New York and Boston from 1½ to 2 hours, thereby arriving in ample time for all the lines running from New York, North, South and West, and all the lines from Boston, North and East.

The C. VANDERBILT, will leave New York on Tuesdays, Thursdays and Saturdays.

Leave Stonington Mondays, Wednesdays, and Fri.

The MASSACHUSETTS will leave New York on Mondays, Wednesdays and Fridays.

Leave Stonington Tuesdays, Thursdays and Sat'ys.

N. B.—Passengers, on the arrival of the steamers at Stonington, proceed immediately, in the splendid railroad cars, to Providence and Boston, without any delay, or remain on board the steamer, and leave in the Accommodation train at 6.30 AM, which connects at Providence with the 9.30 AM. train for Boston; and a baggage master accompanies each train through to Boston, to take charge of the baggage.

For passage or freight, inquire on board the boats, at pier No. 1, North River, or 10 Battery place.

TABLE OF DISTANCES AND FARES.

From N. Y. by steamer to	Miles.	Total.	Fares. Way.	Total
Stonington	126	126	2,00	2,00
Kingston	23	149	75	2,75
Providence	25	174	75	3,00
Mansfield	17	191	50	3,50
Boston	25	216	75	4,00

NEW LINE FOR BOSTON.

VIA NEWPORT AND FALL RIVER.

The superior first class steamers BAY STATE, and GOVERNOR, of great strength and speed, particularly adapted to the navigation of Long Island Sound, running in connection with the Fall River and Old Colony Railroads a distance of 53 miles to Boston only.

Leave pier No. 3 North River, near the battery daily.

The BAY STATE, William Brown, master, will leave New York on Tu. Th. and Sat., at 5 PM.

The GOVERNOR, T. G. Jewett, master, will leave New York on Mon. Wed. and Fri, at 5 PM.

These steamers are fitted with commodious state rooms, and every arrangement for the security and comfort of passengers, who are afforded by this route a night's rest on board, and on arrival at Fall River proceed per railroad, reaching Boston early the following morning; or can remain on board (getting their breakfast if wished for) until the starting of the accommodation train at 6½ AM, which reaches Boston at about 9½ AM. A baggage master is attached to each steamer, who receives and tickets the baggage and accompanies the same to its destination.

The rates for passage and price of state rooms (one dollar) the same as the other lines.

A steamer runs in connection with this line to and from Providence, daily, except Sundays.

Freight to Boston is taken at the same rates as by the other regular lines, and forwarded with greater expedition.

For freight or passage, apply on board, and either to TISDALE & BORDEN, 70 West st, or at the office of the Line, at the corner of Washington st, and Battery Place.

TABLE OF DISTANCES AND FARES.

From N. Y. by steamer to	Miles.	Total.	Fares. Way.	Total
Newport	152	152	3,00	3,00
Fall River	17½	169½	50	3,00
Myrick's Corner	12½	182	37	3,35
South Braintree	29½	211½		4,00
Boston	21½	223		4,00

REGULAR MAIL LINE TO BOSTON.

VIA NORWICH AND WORCESTER.

Without change of cars or baggage or without crossing any Ferry.

Passengers taking their seats at Norwich are ensured their seats through to Boston; this being the only inland route that communicates through by steamboat and railroad. Passengers by this line are accompanied through by the conductor of the train, who will have particular charge of their baggage, and who will otherwise give his attention to their ease and comfort.

This line leaves south side pier No. 1, North River, foot of Battery place, daily (Sundays excepted) at 5 PM. and arriving in Boston in time to take the Eastern trains.

The steamer KNICKERBOCKER, Capt. Van Pelt, will leave every Monday, Wednesday and Friday, at 5 PM, from pier No. 1, N. R. foot of Battery place.

The steamer WORCESTER, Capt. J. W. Williams, will leave every Tuesday, Thursday, and Saturday, 5 PM.

For furthur information inquire of I. H. VANDERBILT, No. 8 Battery place. N R.

TABLE OF DISTANCES AND FARES.

From N. Y. by steamer to	Miles.	Total.	Fares. Way.	Total
New London	116	116	2,00	2,00
Allyn's Point	8	124	25	2,00
Norwich	7	131	25	2,00
Danielsville	25	156	65	2,65
Worcester	34	190	85	3,00
Framingham	23	213	70	4,00
Boston	21	234	50	4,00

U. S. M. DAY LINE TO BOSTON,

VIA HARTFORD & NEW HAVEN.

From Peck Slip E. R.

NEW ARRANGEMENT—From May 3d, 1848.

The new and splendid steamer COMMODORE, Capt. Lefever, will leave every morning, (Sundays excepted,) at 7 o'clock.

An Express Train will leave New Haven on the arrival of the Commodore, conveying passengers to Hartford, Worcester and Boston, and arriving at the latter place at about 7 PM. Fare through to Boston, $5, paid on board the boat. Fare Worcester, $4.

Evening Line to New Haven—The steamer NEW YORK, Capt. R. Peck, will leave every Tu. and Th, at 4 PM, and Sat. at 3 PM.

FOR HARTFORD DIRECT.

The steamers NEW CHAMPION, Capt. Tinklepaugh, or HERO, Capt. Roath, will leave every afternoon, Sundays excepted, at 4 PM.

Freight by all the above boats received until within one half hour of starting.

For further information, inquire of Jno. Saxton, 112 South st; G. W. Corlies, 283 Pearl street.

N. B.—All persons are forbid trusting any one on account of the above boats or owners.

TABLE OF DISTANCES AND FARES.

From N. Y. by steamer to	Miles.	Total.	Fares. Way.	Total
New Haven	78	78	1,50	1,50
Hartford	36	114	1,00	2,50
Springfield	26	140		3,25
West Brookfield	29	169		
Worcester	25	194		4,00
Framingham	23	217		
Boston	21	238		5,00

OCEAN STEAM NAVIGATION CO.

U. S. MAIL LINE TO SOUTHAMPTON AND BREMEN. From the beginning of the year 1848, the steamers of this Company will sail regularly once a month, as follows:—

FROM NEW YORK.

HERMANN......Capt. Crabtree....June 20, 1848.
WASHINGTON...Capt. J. Johnston..July 20, 1848.

FROM BREMEN.

HERMANN..........July 15, 1848.
WASHINGTON..........August 15, 1848.

FROM SOUTHAMPTON.

HERMANN..........July 20, 1848.
WASHINGTON..........August 20, 1848.

Passage from New York to Southampton or Bremen, $120.

From Bremen or Southampton to New York $150.

For passage or freight apply at the office of the Ocean Steam Navigation Company,

60 Broadway, New York.

BRITISH AND NORTH AMERICAN ROYAL MAIL STEAMSHIPS.

Appointed by the Admiralty to sail between Liverpool and Boston, and between Liverpool and New York, calling at Halifax to land and receive passengers and Her Majesty's mails.

AMERICA.........Capt. C. H. E. Judkins.
EUROPA.........." E. G. Lott
NIAGARA........." Alexander Ryrie
CANADA.........." W. Douglass.
CAMBRIA........." William Harrison.
HIBERNIA........" A. Shannon.
BRITANNIA......." W. J. C. Lang.
CALEDONIA......." J. Leitch.
ACADIA.........." J. Stone.

From Boston.		*From New York.*	
NIAGARA	June 14.	HIBERNIA	June 7.
AMERICA	" 28.	ACADIA	" 21.
CAMBRIA	July 12.	BRITANNIA	July 5.

Price of Passage to Liverpool..........$120
Price of Passage to Halifax..........$20

These ships carry experienced Surgeons. No berth will be secured until paid for.

No Freight received on days of sailing.

NOTE.—All letters and newspapers must pass through the Post Office. Merchandise and Specie (except for personal expenses,) shipped under the name of luggage, will be charged as freight and liable to Custom House regulations.

Apply to EDW. CUNARD, Jr.,
my29 38 Broadway, New York.

CHARLESTON LINE OF STEAMSHIPS

NORTHERNER & SOUTHERNER, leave every alternately Saturday, at 4 PM, from pier foot of Clinton st, opposite the Tobacco Inspection, East River.

No berths secured until paid for.

All bills of Lading signed by the Clerk on board.

Specie will be received until 12 M. on the day of departure.

Passengers by this vessel are requested to send their baggage on board previous to 12 o'clock on the day of departure.

Consignees are requested particularly to attend to the receipt of their goods on the arrival of the steamer.

For freight or passage, apply to

SPOFFORD, TILESTON & CO.,
dec14 48 South street.

NEW YORK, ALBANY AND TROY

LINE for ALBANY & TROY direct from Pier at the foot of Cortland st. Persons taking this boat will arrive in Troy in time to take the earliest morning trains west for Buffalo; and north to Saratoga, Lake George and Champlain.

The steamboat TROY, Capt. Wm. H. Frazee, Monday, Wednesday and Friday at 6 PM.

The low pressure steamboat EMPIRE, Capt. W. W. Tupper, Tuesday, Thursday & Saturday, at 6 PM.

For passage &c, apply on board, or to S. S. CHAMBERLIN, at the office on the wharf. Freight must be put in charge of the Freight Agent, or the company will not be responsible for loss. Ap10

PEOPLE'S LINE, ALBANY, DAY & NIGHT.

DAY STEAMER.

HENDRICK HUDSON......Capt. A. GORHAM,

Tuesdays, Thursdays and Saturdays at 7 o'clock A.M., from the foot of Barclay street, making the usual landings, returning on the opposite days.

SIX O'CLOCK THROUGH STEAMERS.

ISAAC NEWTON..........Capt. W. H. PECK,
OREGON..........Capt. A. P. ST. JOHN,

Daily (Sundays excepted) at 6 P.M., from Pier between Cortland and Liberty streets.

U. S. MAIL LINE STEAMERS.

NORTH AMERICA.........Capt. T. N. HULSE,
SANTA CLAUS.........Capt. ELMENDORF,

Daily at 5 o'clock, P.M., from the Pier North side of Barclay street.

All the above boats connect regularly with the R. Road cars bound West, East & North from Albany.

Freight taken at moderate rates, and when required forwarded by Railroad from Albany without delay.

For Freight, apply at People's Line Office, 144 Greenwich street; to P. C. SCHULTZ, Pier between Liberty and Cortlandt streets; or to Wm. Lane, wharf between Barclay and Robinson sts. my25

NEW ROCHELLE, GLEN COVE, &c.

SPRING ARRANGEMENT.

For New Rochelle, Glen Cove, Oyster Bay and Cold Spring, commencing Monday, April 17th 1848—The steamboat CROTON, Captain Charles Peck, will leave New York from Fulton slip every day at 2 PM.

Returning, will leave Cold Spring every day at 6 AM; Oyster Bay 6.15 AM; Glen Cove 7.15 AM, and New Rochelle 7.45 AM, touching at Whitestone each way.

Stages will be in readiness at the respective landings to convey passengers, as usual.

Fare to New Rochelle 25 cents; Glen Cove 37½ cts; Oyster Bay and Cold Spring 50 cents.

ELIZABETHPORT & N. Y. FERRY.

NEW ARRANGEMENT.

Through without landing. The steamboat WATER WITCH, will, on and after Monday, April. 3d, 1848, ply daily, from Elizabethport to New York (Sundays excepted) as follows:—

Leave New York at 9 AM, and 1 and 5 PM.

Leave Elizabethport at 7.30 and 10.45 AM, 3.30 PM.

Touching at Port Richmond from Elizabethport at the 10.45 o'clock trip; also from New York at 1 trip.

N. B.—Passengers for Westfield, Scotch Plains, Plainfield, Bound Brook, Somerville, by the Elizabethtown and Somerville Railroad cars, will leave New York, in the 9 o'clock boat in the morning, and in the 1 and 5 boat in the afternoon.

The HorseCar will leave the front of the Union Hotel, quarter of an hour previous to each boat.

All baggage at the risk of its owner.

The Baskridge stage leave by the 9 boat.

STATEN ISLAND FERRY.

On and after Saturday, May 20th, 1848, the steamboats SYLPH and STATEN ISLANDER will make the following trips, until further notice:—

Leave New York at 7, 9, 10 and 11 AM, 1, 2, 3.10, 4, 5, 6 and 7 PM.

Leave Quarantine (Staten Island) at 6, 8, 9, 10 and 11 AM. 1, 2, 3, 4, 5, 6 and 7 PM.

FLUSHING AND ASTORIA.

SPRING ARRANGEMENT.

For Flushing, Astoria and Ravenswood.—On and after Wednesday, April 12, 1848, the steamboat WASHINGTON IRVING, Capt. S. Leonard, will run as follows, daily, (Sundays excepted.)

Leave Flushing at 7 AM, and 2.30 PM, and Astoria at 7.30 AM, and 3 PM.

Returning—Leave New York, from Fulton Market Slip, at 9.15 AM, and 5 PM.

Fare to Flushing, 25 cents; to Astoria, 12½ cents.

NORWICH, WORCESTER & BOSTON—PROPELLER LINE.

The steamers QUINABAUG, Capt. Williams, SHETUCKET, Captain Gert, and DECATUR, Capt. Havens, will hereafter leave pier No. 3, N. R, instead of Old Slip, every TUESDAY, THURSDAY & SATURDAY, at 4 PM.

For freight, which will be taken at low rates, or passage, having excellent accommodations, apply to the captain on board, or to

I. & N. BRIGGS, 40 South st.

PERTH AMBOY & N. BRUNSWICK

The Steamer ANTELOPE, Capt. S. Van Wickle will leave pier foot Robinson st, daily at 2 PM, landing at Rossville, Woodbridge, Totten, Perth Amboy and Frenchis.

Bank Note Table.

Corrected Weekly for the N. Y. Path-Finder.
By C. & E. W. THWING, 37 WALL STREET.

NEW YORK.	
Atlas Bank, Clymer (Stock)	5 dis
Atlas Bank, do (Real Estate)	30 dis
Bank of Brockport, Brockport	25 dis
Bank of Buffalo, Buffalo	50 dis
Clinton County Bank	10 dis
Clinton Bank, New York City	50 dis
Commercial Bank, New York City	10 dis
Commercial Bank of Bufialo	10 dis
Commercial Bank of Oswego	5 dis
Farmers' Bank at Malone (closing)	2 dis
Farmers' Bank, Cattarsugus	fraud
Farmers' Bank, Warwick (closed)	2 dis
Farmers and Drovers' Bank, Buffalo	2 dis
Hamilton Bank, Madison County	10 dis
Manufacturers, Bank, Ulster (closed)	1 dis
Oswego Bank, Oswego (closed)	10 dis
State Bank of New York, Buffalo	75 dis
Staten Island Bank, Port Richmond	50 dis
St. Lawrence Bank, Ogdensburg	60 dis
Watervleit Bank, West Troy	10 dis
MAINE.	
Bangor Commercial Bank, Bangor	closed
Bank of Old Town, Orono	broken
Bank of Portland, Portland	closed
Bank of Westbrook, Westbrook	3 dis
Calais Bank, Calais	10 dis
Citizen's Bank, Augusta	fraud
Frankfort Bank, Frankfort	fraud
Georgia Lumber Co, Portland	broken
Globe Bank, Bangor	fraud
Lafayette Bank, Bangor	closed
Maine Bank, Portland	closed
Mercantile Bank, Bangor	4 to 5 dis
Neguemkeag Bank	closed
Oxford Bank, Fryeburg	fraud
People's Bank, Bangor	closed
Sagadahock Bank	closed
NEW HAMPSHIRE.	
Exeter Bank, Exeter	closed
Union Bank, Portsmouth	closed
Wolfborough Bank	broken
VERMONT.	
Agricultural Bank	broken
Bank of Bennington, Bennington	broken
Bank of Windsor, Windsor	broken
Commercial Bank, Poultney	broken
Essex Bank, Guildhall	broken
MASSACHUSETTS.	
American Bank, Boston	broken
Amherst Bank, Amherst	broken
Chelsea Bank, Chelsea	broken
Cohannet Bank, Taunton	broken
Commercial Bank, Boston	broken
Commonwealth Bank, Boston	broken
Franklin Bank, Boston	broken
Fulton Bank, Boston	broken
Lafayette Bank, Boston	broken
Manufacturers and Mechanics', Nantucket	45a50 dis
Middlesex Bank, Cambridge	broken
Newburyport Bank, Newburyport	broken
Norfolk Bank, Roxbury	broken
Phœnix Bank, Charlestown	broken
RHODE ISLAND.	
Pascoag Bank, Pascoag Village	broken
Providence County Bank, Smithfield	broken
R. I. Agricultural Bank, Johnston	broken
NEW JERSEY.	
Delaware Bridge Co	80 dis
Farmers & Mechanics' B'k, N. Brunswick	broken
Manufacturers' Bank, Belleville	broken
Monmouth Bank, Freehold	fraud
Morris Canal & Bkg Co, Jersey City	no sale
Plainfield Bank, Plainfield	60 dis
PENNSYLVANIA.	
United States Bank, Philadelphia	25 dis
Berks County Bank, Reading	broken
Lehigh Coal & Nav. Co's Scrip	40 dis
Lumberman's Bank, Warren	broken
Northampton Bank	broken
Pittsburg City Scrip, Pittsburg	10 dis
Susquehanna Co. Bank, Montross	3 dis
Towanda Bank, Towanda	fraud
West Branch Bank, Williamsport	2½a3 dis
MARYLAND.	
Baltimore and Ohio Railroad Co, Baltimore	10 dis
Bank of Salisbury, Salisbury	broken
Commercial Bank, Millington	broken
Farmers and Millers' Bank, Hagerstown	broken
GEORGIA.	
Bank of Ruckersville	broken
Central Bank, Milledgeville	broken
Commercial Bank, Macon	broken
ALABAMA.	
Planters and Merchants' Bank, Mobile	25 dis
MISSISSIPPI AND FLORIDA.	
☞ All the Banks in these States are broken.	
ARKANSAS.	
Bank of the State, Little Rock	75 dis
Real Estate Bank, Little Rock	75 dis
TENNESSEE.	
Bank of Tennessee and Branches	6 dis
Farmers and Merchants's Bank, Memphis	failed
Planters' Bank and Branches	5 dis
Union Bank and Branches	5 dis
ILLINOIS.	
Bank of Illinois, Shawneetown	75 dis
State Bank of Illinois, Springfield	50 dis
OHIO.	
Bank of Xenia	10 dis
Bank of Mount Pleasant	10 dis
Belmont Bank of St. Clairsville	10 dis
Bank of Hamilton	25 dis
Bank of Marietta, Marietta	25 dis
Commercial Bank of Sciota	10 dis
Farmers' Bank of Canton, Canton	broken
Granville Alex. Soc	62 dis
Lancaster Ohio Bank, Lancaster	25 dis
Urbana Banking Company	62 dis
State Bank and Branches	1½ dis
MICHIGAN.	
Bank of St. Clair, St. Clair	75 dis
IOWA TERRITORY.	
Miners' Bank, Dubuque	50 dis
NEW BRUNSWICK.	
All Banks in this Province	7 dis
NOVA SCOTIA.	
All Banks in this Province	10 dis
N. Y. State	½ dis
Boston	½ dis
Philadelphia, Albany, &c	½ dis

MISCELLANEOUS.

A Western Court Scene.

BY JENY NOBS.

Judge B—— of Missouri, was in many respects, a remarkable man. He stood six feet two in his boots, and was as fond of a frolic as the most rattling lad in the county. He could drink more liquor, "lift" a heavier "bag o'meal," and play a better game of "poker," than any man in his circuit. These admirable qualifications, of course, rendered him the most popular judge on the bench of his State. Yet he never lost his dignity while on the bench. *There*, he was stern, haughty and dignified. The least approach to familiarity, while he was sitting in court, was always resented by a fine, and sometimes by imprisonment.

Well, it happened one day, while he was "holding court," that Mr. Dewzenbury, a rough-looking, but independent customer came into the court room with his hat on his head. This the judge considered an indignity offered to the court, and forthwith ordered Mr. D. to take off his hat.

To this Mr. Dewzenbury paid no attention, which being observed by "his honor," he ordered the sheriff to "take that man's hat off."

"Take your hat off," cried the sheriff.

Mr. Dewzenbury remained motionless, while the judge proceeded to business. At last, raising his eyes, "his honor" again discovered the incorrigible standing with his hat on his head.

"Sheriff!" cried the court, "take that man's hat off."

The sheriff approached and repeated the command of the court.

"I'm bald," said Mr. D., "and can't comply."

"You can't," exclaimed the judge, waxing angry, "then I fine you five dollars for contempt of court."

"What's that you say, judge?" replied Mr. D., as he walked deliberately up to the judge's stand.

"I fine you five dollars, sir, for contempt of court."

"Very well," said Mr. D. as he carefully put his hand into his pocket and pulled out a fifty cent piece. "Very well, here's the money," handing the judge the half dollar; "this squares us judge. *You owed me four dollars and a half when we quit playing poker last night, and this half makes us even.*"

The bar roared, the crowd smiled, and the judge pocketed his "change" without uttering a word.

A capital story is told of the law-and-order people of Boston. The city marshal, it is said, a very precise and particular man, who knows what duty is, discovered, some days since, an omnibus standing in a street where it had no right to stand, and without a driver. The driver had, in all probability, gone to take a glass of lemonade—nothing stronger is drank in Boston. The marshal mounted the box, and proceeded to drive the buss to the stand. The horses being rather spirited, defied the efforts of the marshal to keep them at a pace regulated by the ordinances, and when he arrived at the stand, he proceeded to enter a complaint against himself, for furious driving, and was fined four dollars and costs!—*Sunday Times.*

It is seldom we fall upon so many truths in brief, as are contained in the following lines from a philosophic correspondent. They are a short sermon, which we commend to all who are o'ervaulting in their ambition.

Our *ingress* in life is naked and bare,
Our *progress* through life is trouble and care,
Our *egress* out of it we know not where,
But doing well *here*, we shall do well *there*,
I could not tell *more* by preaching a year.

BORN TO LOVE PIGS.—Willis says, in his home Journal, "I have a peculiar fondness for domestic animals, not excepting *pigs and chickens. I was born to love them.*" He appears to be an extraordinary linguist, too, for he adds—"they all talk to me in a language I understand."

ELIHU BURRITT has published in London a volume entitled "A Voice from the Forge." A leaf from the only one more left of the Razor Strops will soon be put to press; also, a Groan from an old paving stone by Smooth Pavements Russ, Esq. This last work will no doubt be a bricky affair.

There appears to be considerable excitement to know where Santa Anna has *vamosed* this last time. When he embarked from Mexico, by consent of our government, it was said that he was going to Jamaica. Advices have been received from that Island, but there is no mention made of Santa Anna's arrival, although full time has elapsed for the completion of the voyage. Perhaps he has gone back to Mexico.

DECIDEDLY ORIGINAL.—An editor out West wishing to give some faint idea of a contemporary's meanness, says, that his soul is so small that it might dance a hornpipe in a mosquito's watch-fob!

RATHER PROLIFIC.—The females in California think nothing of having twenty, twenty-five, or even thirty children—they begin to have them, says a writer from that country, when they themselves are quite children, and continue to have them until they are obliged to put on spectacles to see them!

Custom House Rates of Gold.

Rates allowed in the Custom House for Gold coins, as per act of Congress in 1834 fixing the value thereof:

U. S. Eagle, (old emission)	$10 66
U. S. Eagle, (new emission)	10 00
English Guinea	5 07
English Sovereign	4 84
English 7 shilling Piece	1 69
French Double Louis, (before 1786)	9 69
French Louis "	4 84
French Double Louis, (since 1786)	9 15
French Louis "	4 57
French Double Napoleon	7 70
French Napoleon	3 85
Frankfort-on-the-Main Ducat	2 27
Hamburg Ducat	2 27

NEW YORK PATH-FINDER.

HOLBROOK & BARTLETT,
PUBLISHERS AND PROPRIETORS.

THURSDAY, JUNE 8, 1848.

☞ For terms of Subscription, Advertising, &c. see first page.

☞ The Boston Agency for this paper is at the **Path-Finder office**, 5 Washington street Boston. Advertisements and Subscriptions for the **Boston Path-Finder** received at this office, **123** Fulton street.

V. B. PALMER, Tribune Building, is an authorized Agent for this paper.

To Business Men.

For the purpose of inviting custom rom the Country, the PATH-FINDER is one of the best papers to advertise in that has ever been offered o the public. The publishers, at their own expense, give it a gratuitous

DAILY CIRCULATION

n the Steamboats, and Railroad Cars oming to this City, where it is read by housands of people on their way to New York city expressly to make purchases. Merchants, Mechanics, Artisans, and others who have, or desire to have, business transactions with people living out of the City, will find their interests promoted by Advertising in the PATH-FINDER.

REMOVAL.

The PATH-FINDER Office has been Removed to No. 123 FULTON Street, 2d Door from Nassau St, (Up Stairs.)

Steamboat Landings.

The unusual number of steamboats that arrive daily in our city cause large crowds of vagabonds to gather about them, insulting and imposing in many different ways on the passengers, which to a looker on, although very disgusting, is sometimes quite amusing. The greatest imposition is practised by the hackmen, and although there have been hundreds of complaints, the city authorities as yet have taken no step to remedy the evil. A few days since, standing on one of the piers we could but notice the situation of a poor country fellow who arrived. Two hackmen seized him, with "have a hack sir," and notwithstanding his repeated answer of no, they paid no attention to it whatever. One had him by the arm, dragging him up the pier, the second by the skirt of the coat, which would not bear too much pulling, soon gave way, splitting it open up to the shoulders. As soon as this happened a general laugh burst forth, whilst another man rushed in and giving the countryman a knock on the head, crushed his beaver down over his eyes, at the same time subjecting him to a kick rom one of the crowd. The poor fellow was glad enough to get out of the way. This affair happened on a pier where there was an M. P. stationed, who took no more notice of it than as if it had not happened. We do not say that hackmen alone were engaged in this, for a crowd of apparent loafers were standing round, some soliciting baggage, others looking as if they were watching an opportunity to relieve some stranger of his pocket book. There is no subject that calls for more immediate action than this, and stringent laws should be passed for the protection of the travelling community, and suppression of these gangs, who, if they cannot get a job are sure to insult strangers on their arrival. Strangers should take warning and look out for these fellows, for they infest every landing, and impose in every manner that can be conceived of, without open violation of law, especially on the unsophisticated stranger.

General Taylor.

The old General has been summoned to attend the Court Martial now being held at Fredericktown, and we understand a committee has already been appointed to invite him to visit this city, which there is no doubt he will accept. Many of his personal friends confidently expect he will receive the nomination of the Whig party for President, and if so, there will be but little doubt of his going in. This being nomination week, we shall soon know who is to be the candidate, and although the friends of Clay anxiously expect *him* to be the man, there seems to be hardly a possibility of a chance. Should he receive the nomination however, there will be still less chance of his election, as in this case there will be a third party. The party called the Barnburners in this city, have already expressed their determination of making Gen. Taylor their candidate, and by a late meeting in Philadelphia, we see it announced that the Taylor men were quite sure of his getting the nomination on the first ballot. In a day or two we shall know who is to be the man, and shots will begin to pour in from all quarters. Gens. Cass and Butler as yet have received much praise throughout the country, but when the campaign fully sets in, we presume they will share the same fate as many others, and conflicting stories be told from every part of the Union.

THE PARK FOUNTAIN.—This would be beautiful fountain that is so seldom seen playing, would lead people to suppose that Croton water was very scarce. It generally "spouts" about one hour each day, and then at the convenience of those who have charge of it. Several enquiries have been made through the papers, why there is not some regulation as regards the time of playing, as there are but very few who now enjoy the sparkling scene. If the water is so scarce that the authorities cannot afford us but one hour a day to admire this beautiful fount, certainly that hour should be fixed so that the thousands who would like, can enjoy it.

A CRUEL ROBBERY was committed in Albany on Thursday night, on board the steamboat Admiral. The parties robbed were Mrs. Igglesworth, of $410 in gold; Mrs. Little, 17 sovereigns; and Wm. Burgess of 8 sovereigns and one Queen Anne shilling. These persons were all poor immigrants on their way est, and are left nearly destitute.

Railroad Matters.

The road which is to run between Worcester and Nashua is rapidly progressing, and will be completed so as to convey passengers between the two places by the 1st of January next. Part of the road will be open for travel during the next month.

The Eastern Railroad Company have voted unanimously to accept the act of the Legislature, authorizing them to extend their road into the city of Boston, over the bridge of the Boston and Maine Railroad Company.

The Maine papers say that the railroad connecting the city of Bath with Brunswick will be completed the ensuing fall. In a few months the cars of the Atlantic and St. Lawrence road will be running to North Yarmouth. The road from Portland to Montreal, and one to Waterville, through Lewiston, as also one by way of Brunswick to Augusta, which are now under way, must effect great changes in the western part of Maine, and greatly improve the price of lands.

A writer in the Rochester Advertiser, who has recently visited Ogdensburg, gives some interesting particulars of the progress of the Boston and Ogdensburg Railroad, which is to connect this city with St. Lawrence. There are now employed by the company about fifteen hundred men, with horses, carts, &c., and it is intended to increase the number to several thousand as the work progresses. Of the number now engaged, about two hundred are operating in the vicinity of Ogdensburg, in digging, drawing and floating lumber, building wharves, carting stone and gravel, &c. This railroad runs from Ogdensburg east, between 80 and 90 miles without curve or grade, being the longest piece of road in the Union so favorably situated. To this port it is expected that a large proportion of the commerce of the great western lakes will wend its way, and that as the population of the Western States and Canada increases, the agricultural and manufacturing interest, and consequently the commercial interest of that portion of the country will also increase, and centre at Ogdensburg; that vessels and Railroads will freight from the western country, and instead of unloading their cargoes at Buffalo, to be towed the length of the State of New York by *horse power*, they will rush forward by the power of steam to meet the Boston and Ogdensburg railroad cars, waiting to convey their freight to the waters of the Atlantic. Another feature presents itself strongly for Ogdensburg. The river St. Lawrence, every foot of which is a good harbor for trade and commerce to enter, will also become a resort of vessels and sailors for winter quarters. The abundance of timber for ship building which the surrounding country contains, the facilities to obtain ship stores, &c., from the east, all seem to secure new and real advantages to *the projected city of New Boston*. The Bostonians have already purchased large quantities of land in the vicinity of the village, which, together with the railroad, has caused the real estate in and near the village to advance more than *two hundred per cent.*

The Directors of the Hartford and Providence Railroad Corporation advertise in the Hartford Courant for proposals, and are prepared to put the road under contract to Williamantic, 29 miles. The Courant says that, by the report of the Engineer, made to the Directors last week, the route was shown to be much more feasible than had been anticipated.

The Albany and Schenectady Railroad Company (formerly Mohawk) have declared a dividend of 3 1-2 per cent. payable to the New York stockholders on the 15th inst. at the Mechanics' Bank. The receipts of this Road in May were an increase of 16 per cent. on the receipts of May 1847.

PICKPOCKETS.—These professional gentlemen are quite plenty at this time, probably on the watch for Southerners, who are daily arriving in this city, and generally carry large sums of money with them. Hardly a day passes but that we hear of one or more cases of this kind, and as the police are on the watch, and know many concerned in this business, we understand many have taken to going to church, and there sit during services with sanctified air, but always on the alert for *game* when the congregation disperses. One of these worthies was arrested last Sunday, in the act of abstracting a pocket book from a gentleman's coat pocket, and carried to the Tombs, where undoubtedly the remainder of the day was spent in private devotion. A Sunday paper, in speaking of these characters, says—"if a few policemen should go to church occasionally, it might subserve the ends of justice, and drive out all rogues from the sanctuary, unless there was danger of the preacher being left without a congregation."

INTERESTING TO WINE DRINKERS.—In the year 1821, there was visiting at Brighton, (Eng.,) a gentleman 92 years of age, who had never before been ten miles from London, and who, it was said, had frequented an Inn in Bishopgate street, daily, for upwards of fifty years; at which it was further reported, he allowed himself five bottles of wine per diem; and that upon calculation and proof, it appeared he had actually drank, at the above named house no less a quantity than 35,600 bottles, or 57 pipes of that generous and genial juice.
[*Boyle's Chronology of 18th & 19th Centuries.*

Now Professor Brande, in his paper on fermentep liquors,—in the philosophical transactions,—says that "Port wine and Raisin wine, and some others, appear to contain about half their bulk of pure brandy; and that a man who drinks two bottles of strong bodied Port, swallows exactly one bottle of the strongest brandy."

PORTERS' SOCIETY.—We understand a number of waiters and porters have formed a Society, the object of which is to ensure compensation for their services, and form a fund for the assistance of sick members and their families. Such a Society would undoubtedly be very useful, as it is very much needed, and all belonging to such Society should be regularly licensed by the Mayor and Aldermen. Should this be carried through, and regular stations adopted, it would be found very beneficial to the public and profitable to the Society.

Amusements.

THE BROADWAY THEATRE was well filled on Tuesday night, it being for the benefit of Messrs. Kipp & Brown, who met with a great loss. The managers are deserving of much credit for their liberality, and the public will be sure to reward them by a succession of crowded houses. On Saturday evening the proceeds are to be devoted to the family of the late Samuel Pray, who lost his life a few weeks since, when the house was on fire. The cause is a deserving one, and we hope a full house will be in attendance.

THE BOWERY THEATRE is doing a fair business at the reduced prices. The beautiful drama of Ehrnestine having been played for several night, on Wednesday night Mr. Marshall, a deserving actor, took a benefit, and acted the part of Richard III, with good effect. The company is one of the best selections in the country, and everything is produced in first rate style.

NIBLO'S ASTOR PLACE, since opening has been crowded every night with the elite of the city, to witness the performances of the Viennoise children. A first rate company is attached to the house, and under excellent management, which will make it one of the most popular places of amusement in the city.

THE CHATHAM THEATRE is but a continuation of crowded houses, and as "Mose" cannot be seen only through this week, every body must improve the opportunity, or lose the sight of the greatest piece of fun ever produced.

CASTLE GARDEN.—M'lle Auguste appeared on Monday night, to a very good house, and as she has thousands of admirers, cannot but prove a good card. This is one of the finest and coolest places in the city, and no stranger should leave the city without paying a visit here.

BANVARD'S PANORAMA.—Strangers visiting the city should not fail to witness this beautiful painting of the Mississippi, which is now on exhibition at Panorama Hall, No. 598 Broadway. We understand it is soon to be removed, and those who do not see it now will loose the opportunity of seeing the most magnificent work ever produced. The country is shown for 1200 miles, and Southern and Western life fully described. We hope no one will fail of seeing it, for its merits are well deserving the public patronage.

STRAWBERRIES.—We are now in the midst of these berries, for they are as plenty and a good deal more plenty than blackberries. They are hawked about the streets by hundreds of women, and sold at from three to five cents per basket. Others have made quite a business of it, and many cart them round in wagons. We were amused this morning at seeing one man, who was in a wagon well loaded with this fruit, carrying with him a horn or trumpet, where at the corner of the streets he would stop and play some lively tune, which would have done credit to a professor. A crowd would soon gather round him, and he would do a great business in disposing of them at from three to four cents per basket. These luxuries are so plenty that all can indulge, and to look through our markets one cannot resist the temptation.

NEW MUSIC.—Jaques & Brother, music publishers, 358 Broadway, have just added to their extensive stock a large addition of new music, among which we notice the Christys' favorite melodies, arranged for the Piano Forte, containing five different airs, which they sell for the low price of 25 cents. Also Christys' Polka, Jenny Lind Waltz, and several others no less favorites. We cannot mention the large number we saw added to their assortment; suffice it to say, that all and everything that is new can be found at their Bazaar; as also many beautiful Quicksteps, dedicated to different companies, and arranged for the Piano Forte. One great feature in this establishment they sell at remarkably low prices, which ensures them a good share of trade, and enables them to furnish a much larger assortment than many other houses. Give them a call and get suited with all kinds of music.

J. H. GREENE, the reformed gambler, is lecturing on lotteries, exposing the schemes practiced. This is a new kind of expose and although many have but little faith in the drawing, from the thought of their being practised in the manner, Greene is now showing them. He says that the drawers so plan them as only to draw a prize when they think proper, and that in every lottery, not one thousand dollars in twenty ever goes out of the proprietor's hands. This should prove a warning to those who are in the habit of purchasing tickets, as it shows how little chance they stand of getting any thing more than their money back.

ARTIFICIAL LEG.—The late war with Mexico has been the cause of not only dis*arming* many who were engaged in it, but also caused many to return minus that useful limb called the *leg*. To those who have been so unfortunate as to lose the *right* or the *left*, either in war or accidentally, we would advise them to call on Mr. Selphos, No. 24 Spring street, who manufactures an article so perfectly life like as to answer all purposes of the real one. Mr. Selpho has been a number of years in the business, and has many credentials from those who have seen them in use, among which is one from Dr. Mott, Professor of Surgery. He also manufactures artificial hands in an exact manner, and all who have been unfortunate in losing either of the above limbs should call here, where plenty of high testimonials can be seen.

STEELE'S PATENT FEATHER DUSTERS, are the articles to keep counters and cases clean during the warm and dusty season. They are an article manufactured altogether different from the original styles, and far superior, being put together so as to hold the feathers without their breaking. They are universally used in our Broadway stores and genteel houses, and strangers who would purchase an elegant brush made from the most beautiful of Peacock feathers, should call at 305 Pearl stieet.

The Hon. Lewis Cass the present nominee of the Democratic party for the Presidency will arrive in this city to day. He will undoubtedly meet with a warm reception, although but little notice has been given of his arrival. He is to be accompanied by several "lions" and no doubt a handsome turn out will receive them. The man whom a great party selects for its chief magistrate and though charged with many foibles, he has passed through a long public career, and should be treated with respect from all parties to which he is entitled too.

MEETING IN THE PARK.—The Democrats held a great meeting in the Park, Tuesday afternoon, when a large crowd was addressed by several eminent speakers, among whom was John Van Buren. This party is called the "Barn-burners" and were opposed to the nomination of Cass and Butler. A great deal was said about the Hunkers and Barn burners,—the two titles for the Democratic parties, but the meeting passed off very quietly considering the occasion, with loud hisses and cheers.

THE DOG LAW.—Dog killers are scarce, and notwithstanding a law was passed, ordering all dogs to be killed seen running at large unmuzzled, as yet no one seems to have taken up the business. A few days since seventy-three unmuzzled dogs were counted in passing from the lower part of Spring street to the corner of Broadway and Leonard street; and there are now thousands running in the streets without home or master. It is time a proper regard was had for the safety of the city from hydrophobia.

JAMES C. MULL, the young man who was shot and stabbed in Albany, on Sunday week, by the madman Kelley, died on Thursday morning of his wounds.

The Steamer to-day will take about $300,000 in coin, and the United States on Saturday as much more. The remittances going for France are sent by the United States as more direct.

☞ The reader's attention is requested to the advertisement of Dr. S. S. FITCH, on the prevention and cure of Consumption.

Home Produce Market.
REPORTED FOR THE N. Y. PATH-FINDER.

PROVISIONS.			
Butter, lump, lb	18a25	Hams, Western	7a 9½
Butter, tub	15a18	Lard, Western keg	6a 8
Eggs, doz	11a	Veal	8a12
Beef, fresh lb	6a12	Calves, alive	4a 5
Beef, salted	6a 9	Mutton	4a 9
Beef, smoked	10a12	Chickens, pair	a75
Hogs, whole	7a10	Turkeys, each	100a150
Pork, fresh	8a10	Duck, pair	a75
Pork, salt	6a10	Wild Pigeons, doz	a75
Hams, Boston	9a12		
FISH.			
Tongues & Sounds	6a 7	Eels	6a 6
Bass, lb	8a10	Tautog	a 8
Codfish	4a 6	Perch, lb	8a 12
Frost Fish, bch	none		
VEGETABLES.			
Potatoes, bbl	300a	Turnips, white	a50
Potatoes, swt, bkt	a500	Cranberries	a12
Turnips, Russia	none	Beets	200a
FRUIT.			
Apples, dried, lb	4a 5	Oranges, doz	12½a31
Apples, bushel	a300	Lemons	16a18
Walnuts, lb	6a 7	Figs, lb	6a12

TATHEM BROTHERS, } Action for the infringe-
THOS. OTIS LEROY & } ment of a re-issued Pa-
DAVID SMITH. } tent for making Lead Pipes; defence, want of novelty, and that the re-issue was improper. Damages laid at $20,000—trial commenced May 4th—verdict rendered for defendants May 9th, 1848.
For plaintiff, Messrs. Staples, Goddard & Cutting.
For defendants, Wm. Curtis Noyes and J. W. Girard, Esqs. 4w-myl5

POETRY.

[From the Yankee Blade.]

The Fisher Boy.

TRANSLATED FROM THE GERMAN.

The waves glide smoothly, with gentle swell,
Lulling the sense with a dreaming spell.
A tiny boat is floating by;
Little dreams he who holds the helm,
That danger and death are hovering nigh;
That some silvery ripplets will him o'erwhelm.
He said and sighed, "It were most sweet
To have 'neath the tide a cool retreat."
E'en as he spoke, before his sight
A Water-Spirit fair and bright,
Uprose herself from out the sea,
Upbraiding him with cruelty.
She sang a lay so sweet and sad,
She won the heart of the fisher lad;—
"Why, with cruel art, O, mortal,
Lure my children to their doom;
Why entice o'er death's dark portal
From thy quiet and happy home?
Would'st not thou, then, be happy, too?
Forsake the busy haunts of men,
Enter the region of eternal dew,
Where want and sorrow come never in."
His bounding pulses quicker beat,
No mortal maiden doth entreat;
All, all to happy would he be,
With such a bride, his home the sea,
With eager eye and heart elate,
The Fisher-boy doth rush on fate.
One step, the frail boat's edge is crost—
They dive adown, and he is lost.

New York, May, 1848. TOTOTOT.

I. O. of O. F. Directory.

IN THE CITY OF NEW YORK.

SUBORDINATE LODGES.

CLINTON HALL, cor. Beekman and Nassau sts.

National, No. 30....Mon	Templar, 235......Thurs
Commercial, 67....Tues	Excelsior, 126........Fri
Merchants, 150.....Wed	Orion, 278...........Sat

71 Division street.

Mutual, 57..........Mon	Continental, 117....Wed
Empire, 64..........Mon	Knickerbocker, 22..Thurs
Mercantile, 47.......Tues	Marion, 34........Thurs
United Brothers, 52.Tues	Mt. Vernon, 73.......Fri
Howard, 60.........Wed	

NATIONAL HALL, Canal street.

Teutonic, 14........Mon	Perseverance, 17...Wed
City, 151...........Mon	Metropolitan, 33...Thurs
Gettys, 11..........Tues	Oriental, 68........Thurs
Washington, 12....Tues	Fidelity, 87.........Thurs
New York, 10.......Wed	Germania, 13........Fri

38 Canal street.

Mariners, 23........Mon	Cohota, 137.........Wed
Concorde, 43........Tues	Hospitaller, 295......Fri
Hancock, 49 ......Thurs	

411 Broadway.

Hinman, 107........Mon	Crystal, 315.......Thurs
Eureka, 177........Tues	Sincerite, 233 ....Fri
Olive Branch, 31....Wed	

132 Bowery.

Oregon, 178.........Mon	Columbia, 1.......Thurs
Hermitage, 165.....Tues	Beacon, 228...........Fri
Independence, 158..Wed	

187 Bowery.

Diamond, 140.......Mon	Croton, 78..........Wed
German Oak, 82....Tues	Covenant, 35.......Thurs

MILITARY HALL, Bowery.

Strangers Refuge, 4..Mon	Fountain City, 15...Wed
Island City, 331.....Tues	Alleghania, 183....Thurs

Hester street, corner Bowery.

Pilgrim, 243.........Mon	Globe, 337...........Wed
Tradesmen's, 314...Tues	Ocean, 321.........Thurs

Forsyth street, corner Broome.

Schiller, 129........Tues	Warren, 253.......Thurs

Clinton street, corner Grand.

Manhattan, 20......Mon	Ark, 28.............Wed
Enterprise, 36......Tues	Harmony, 44......Thurs

Hudson street, corner Grove.

Greenwich, 40......Mon	Meridian, 42........Wed
Tompkins, 9........Tues	Grove, 56..........Thurs

327 Bowery.

Jefferson, 46........Tues	Acorn, 237..........Wed

71 West Seventeenth street.

Siloam, 210........Tues	Chelsea, 84 ....Wed

Avenue C, corner Third street.

Mechanics, 113......Mon	Eckford, 234........Wed

Eighth avenue, corner Twenty-ninth street.

Blooming Grove, 182..Th	Fitzroy, 326.........Wed

DEGREE LODGES.

Manhattan, No. 2..	Avenue C, cor. 3d street..	Thurs
New York, 1......	National Hall...............	Fri
United Brothers, 5..	Broome street, cor. Forsyth..	Fri
Hudson, 4.........	Hudson street, cor. Grove...	Sat
Clinton, 6.........	71 Division street...........	Sa

SUBORDINATE ENCAMPMENTS.

Mount Horeb, No. 12.	National Hall..	2d & 4th Thurs
Mount Hebron, 2....	National Hall..........	2 4 Fri
Mount Sinai, 3.......	National Hall..........	1 3 Fri
Mosaic, 6...........	Grand st, cor. Clinton...	1 3 Fri
Mount Olivet, 10....	Avenue C, cor. 3d st....	2 4 Fri
Jerusalem, 28.......	Hudson st, cor. Grove...	1 3 Fri
Mount Zion, 31......	71 West Seventeenth st..	1 3 Fri
Egyptian, 35........	71 Division street.......	1 3 Fri
Marine, 37..........	Broome st, cor. Forsyth.	1 3 W
Manitou, 45.........	193 Bowery.............	2 4 Fri
Samaria, 41	411 Broadway..........	2 4 Fri
Palestine, 9.........	411 Broadway..........	2 4 Sat
Damascus, 18.......	71 Division street.......	2 4 Sat
Lebanon, 19........	71 Division street.......	1 3 Sat

Map of Hudson River.

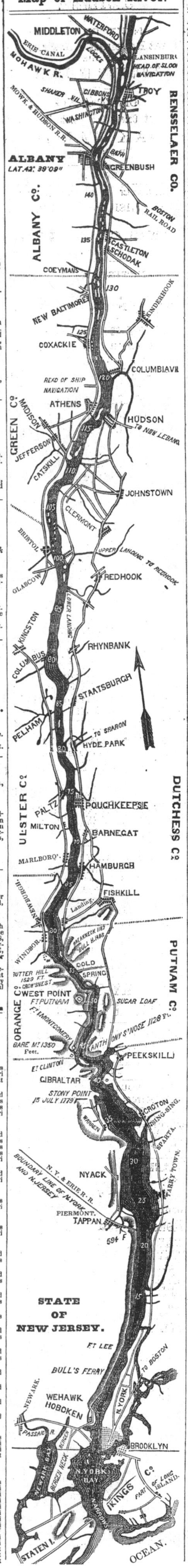

Directory to Expresses.

Albany, Wells & Co, 10 Wall, 4½ PM.
Amherst, Adams & Co, 16 Wall, 4.30 PM.
Amsterdam, Wells & Co, 10 Wall, 4.30 PM.
Auburn, Wells & Co, 10 Wall, 4.30 PM.
Augusta, Me, Gay & Co, 1 Wall, 4.30 PM.
Baltimore, Adams & Co, 16 Wall, 3 and 4 PM.
Baltimore, Livingston & Co, 6 Wall, 3 and 4 PM.
Ballston, Wells & Co, 10 Wall, 4.30 PM.
Bangor, Gay & Co, 1 Wall, 4.30 PM.
Batavia, Wells & Co, 10 Wall, 4.30 PM.
Boston, Adams & Co, 16 Wall, 4.30 PM.
Boston, Harnden & Co, 6 Wall, 4.30 PM.
Boston, Gay & Co, 1 Wall, 4.30 PM.
Bound Brook, Hope, 41 Cortlandt, 8.30 AM, and 4 PM.
Brattleboro', Adams & Co, 16 Wall, 4.30 PM.
Brooklyn, Pierson, 17 Wall st
Brownsville, Adams & Co, 16 Wall, 4 PM.
Buffalo, Wells & Co, 10 Wall, 4½ PM.
Canandaigua, Wells & Co, 10 Wall, 4.30 PM.
Charleston, Adams & Co, 16 Wall, 4 PM.
Cincinnati, Adams & Co, 16 Wall, 4 PM.
Cincinnati, Livingston & Co, 6 Wall, 3 and 4 PM.
Cincinnati, Wells & Co, 10 Wall, 4.30 PM.
City, Boyd's, Principal Office 45 William.
Cumberland, Livingston & Co, 6 Wall, 3 and 4 PM.
East Brooklyn, Callow, 45 Fulton.
Easton, A. D. Hope, 41 Cortlandt, 8.30 AM. and 4 PM
Elizabethtown, Hope, 41 Cortlandt, 8.30 AM 4PM.
Elizabethtown, Gilmore, 6 Wall, 4½ PM.
Fall River, Gay & Co, 1 Wall, 4.30 PM.
Fonda, Wells & Co, 10 Wall, 4.30 PM.
Farmington, Adams & Co, 16 Wall, 4.30 PM.
Fredericksburg, Adams & Co, 16 Wall, 4 PM.
Fredericksburg, Livingston & Co, 6 Wall, 3 & 4 PM.
Genoa, Wells & Co, 10 Wall, 4.30 PM.
Georgetown, D. C., Adams & Co, 16 Wall, 4 PM.
Greenfield, Adams & Co, 16 Wall, 4.30 PM.
Harrisburg, Adams & Co, 16 Wall, 4 PM.
Harrisburg, Livingston & Co, 6 Wall, 3 and 4 PM.
Hartford, Adams & Co, 16 Wall, 5½ AM.
Herkimer, Wells & Co, 10 Wall, 4.30 PM.
Lancaster, Adams & Co, 16 Wall, 4 PM.
Little Falls, Wells & Co, 10 Wall, 4.30 PM.
Louisville, Adams & Co, 16 Wall, 4 PM.
Louisville, Wells & Co, 10 Wall, 4.30 PM.
Louisville, Livingston & Co, 6 Wall, 3 and 4 PM.
Meriden, Ct, Adams & Co, 16 Wall, 4 PM.
Montreal, Virgil & Rice, 10 Wall, Mon. 4½ PM.
Nantucket, Godfrey & Munro, 6 Wall, 4 PM.
Newark, C. Adams, 222 Broadway, 12 M, and 6 PM.
Newark, Baldwin, 6 Wall, 11 AM, & 5 PM.
Newark, Lewis, 16 Wall.
New Bedford, Godfrey & Munro, 6 Wall, 4 PM.
New Brunswick, Gilmore, 6 Wall, 4 PM.
Newburgh, Vixen, 10 Wall, 3½ PM.
New Haven, Adams & Co, 15 Wall, 6 AM.
New London, Adams & Co, 16 Wall, 4.30 PM.
New Market, Hope, 41 Cortlandt, 8.30 AM, and 4 PM.
Newport, Gay & Co, 1 Wall, 4.30 PM.
Norfolk, Adams & Co, 16 Wall, 4 PM.
Northampton, Adams & Co, 16 Wall, 4 PM.
Norwich, Adams & Co, 16 Wall, 4.30 PM.
Oneida, Wells & Co, 10 Wall, 4.30 PM.
Oswego, Wells & Co, 10 Wall, 4.30 PM.
Paterson, Van Gieson, 6 Wall, MW&F, 3½ PM.
Petersburg, Adams & Co, 16 Wall, 4 PM.
Philadelphia, Adams & Co, 16 Wall, 3 & 4 PM.
Philadelphia, Harnden & Co, 6 Wall, 3 & 4 PM.
Philadelphia, Livingston & Co, 6 Wall, 3 and 4 PM.
Phœnixville, Livingston & Co, 6 Wall, 3 and 4 PM.
Pittsburg, Livingston & Co, 6 Wall, 3 & 4 PM.
Port Clinton, Livingston & Co, 6 Wall, 3 and 4 PM.
Portland, Gay & Co, 1 Wall, 4½ PM.
Pottstown, Livingston & Co, 6 Wall, 3 and 4 PM.
Pottsville, Pa., Livingston & Co, 6 Wall, 3 and 4 PM.
Plainfield, Hope, 41 Cortlandt, 8.30 AM, and 4 PM.
Princeton, Gilmore, 6 Wall, 4 PM.
Providence, Harnden & Co, 6 Wall, 4.30 PM.
Providence, Ewins & Co, 16 Wall, 4.30 PM.
Quebec, Virgil & Rice, 10 Wall, Mon. 4½ PM.
Rahway, Gilmore, 6 Wall, 4 PM.
Reading, Pa., Livingston & Co, 6 Wall, 3 and 4 PM.
Richmond, Adams & Co, 16 Wall, 4 PM.
Rochester, Wells & Co, 10 Wall, 4½ PM.
Rome, Wells & Co, 10 Wall, 4.30 PM.
Saratoga, Wells & Co, 10 Wall, 4.30 PM
Savannah, Adams & Co, 16 Wall, 3 and 4 PM.
Schenectady, Wells & Co, 10 Wall, 4.30 PM.
Scotch Plains, Hope, 41 Cortlandt, 8.30 AM, and 4 PM.
Somerville, Hope, 41 Cortlandt, 8.30 AM, and 4 PM.
Springfield, Adams & Co, 16 Wall, 5.30 AM.
St. Louis, Adams & Co, 16 Wall, 4 PM.
St. Louis, Wells & Co, 10 Wall, 4.30 PM.
St. Louis, Livingston & Co, 6 Wall, 3 and 4 PM.
Stonington, Harnden & Co, 6 Wall, 4.30 PM.
Stonington, Ewins & Co, 16 Wall, 4.29 PM.
Syracuse, Wells & Co, 10 Wall, 4.30 PM.
Taunton, Godfrey & Munro, 6 Wall, 4 PM.
Thompsonville, Ct, Adams & Co, 16 Wall, 4 PM.
Trenton, Gilmore, 6 Wall, 4 PM.
Troy, Pullen & Co, 10 Wall, 4½ PM.
Unionville, Adams & Co, 16 Wall, 4 PM.
Utica, Wells & Co, 10 Wall, 4½ PM.
Washington, Adams & Co, 16 Wall, 3 & 4 PM.
Washington, Livingston & Co, 6 Wall, 3 and 4 PM.
Waterloo, Wells & Co, 10 Wall, 4.30 PM.
Watertown, Wells & Co, 10 Wall, 4.30 PM.
Waterville, Wells & Co, 10 Wall, 4.30 PM.
Westfield, Hope, 41 Cortlandt, 8.30 AM, and 4 PM.
Wheeling, Adams & Co, 16 Wall, 3 & 4 PM.
Wheeling, Livingston & Co, 6 Wall, 3 and 4 PM.
Williamsburg, Hewins, 17 Wall, 11.30 AM, 3.30 PM.
Wilmington, Adams & Co, 16 Wall, 4 PM.
Windsor, Ct, Adams & Co, 16 Wall, 4.30 PM.
Worcester, Adams & Co, 16 Wall, 4.30 PM.

Legal Interest Table,

Exhibiting the legal rates of interest allowed in the different States and Territories within the United States, with the punishment inflicted for usury in eah State.

MAINE—Six per cent; forfeit of the claim for usury.
NEW HAMPSHIRE—Six per cent; forfeit of thrice the amount unlawfully taken.
VERMONT—Six per cent; recovery in an action, with costs.
MASSACHUSETTS—Six per cent; forfeit of thrice the usury.
RHODE ISLAND—Six per cent; forfeit of the usury and interest on the debt.
CONNECTICUT—Six per cent; forfeit of the whole debt.
NEW YORK—Seven per cent; usurious contracts void.
NEW JERSEY—Seven per cent; forfeit of the whole debt.
PENNSYLVANIA—Six per cent; forfeit of the whole debt.
DELAWARE—Six per cent; forfeit of the whole debt.
MARYLAND—Six, and on tobacco contracts eight per cent; usurious contracts void.
VIRGINIA—Six per cent; forfeit double the usury taken.
NORTH CAROLINA—Six per cent; contracts for usury void, and forfeit double the usury.
SOUTH CAROLINA—Seven per cent; forfeit of interest and premium taken, with costs to debtors.
GEORGIA—Eight per cent; forfeit thrice the usury and contracts void.
ALABAMA—Eight per cent; forfeit of interest and usury.
MISSISSIPPI—Six per cent. on contracts made since 1840; eight on loaned.
LOUISIANA—Five per cent; bank interest 6; and conventional as high as 18; beyond that, contract void.
TENNESSEE—Six per cent; usurious contracts void.
KENTUCKY—Six per cent; usury recoverable with costs.
OHIO—Six per cent; on written agreements may go as high as 10.
INDIANA—Six per cent; a fine of double the excess.

Packet Directory.

Alexandria, weekly, 110 Wall.
Apalachicola, 84 South.
Every 10 days, 38 South.
Baltimore, New Line, Wed. and Sat., 106 Wall.
Regular Line, Wed. and Sat, 120 Wall.
Union Line, every Saturday, 40 South.
Boston, New England Line, semi-weekly, 25 South.
Commercial Line, semi-weekly, foot Maiden Lane.
Tremont Line, semi-weekly, 38 South.
Lewis Line, semi-weekly, 26 South.
Charleston, Steamship, every Sat, 48 South.
Commercial Line, every Wednesday, 67 South
Union Line, weekly, 88 South.
Derby, Steam Propeller Line, semi-weekly, 40 South.
Galveston, Texas Line, 91 Front.
Georgetown, weekly, 110 Wall.
Glasgow, 1st and 15th, 87 South.
Havre, French Transatlantic Steamships, 9th and 24th, 14 Broadway.
Union Line, 8th, 16th and 24th, 22 Broad.
1st and 15th, 88 Wall.
Hartford, Trans. Line, Tu. and Fri. 40 South.
Key West, 84 South.
Liverpool, Cunard Line, (steamers) D. Brigham, Jr, Agent, 6 Wall 1st and 16th each month.
New York and Liverpool, 6th, 78 South.
Old Line Liverpool, 1st and 16th, 38 Burling slip.
The New Line Liverpool, 21st, 87 South.
New Line Liverpool, 26th, 56 South.
Black Star, weekly, 275 Pearl.
London, 1st, 8th, 15th and 24th, 70 South.
1st, 8th and 24th, 70 South.
Mobile, City Line, every 10 days, 110 Wall.
New Orleans, Holmes Line, every Mon., 85 South.
Merchants' Line, weekly, 67 South.
Stanton Line, every 10 days, 61 South.
New Line, weekly, 120 Wall.
New York Line, weekly, 115 Wall.
Norfolk, Bedell's Line, every Saturday, 100 Wall.
Norwich, Propeller Line, tri-weekly, 40 South.
Petersburg, Old Line, every Mon., 153 Maiden Lane.
Philadelphia, Old Line, every 3 days, 42 Front.
Swift-sure Line, every day, 40 South.
Providence, Union Line, semi-weekly, foot Maiden Lane.
Richmond, Old Line, 134 Front.
Savannah, weekly, 186 Front.
Old Line, weekly, 67 South.
New Line, weekly, 96 Wall.
Brig Line, every Monday, 110 Wall.
Wilmington, N. C., New Line, weekly, 159 Front.
Regular Line, 72 Wall.
Worcester, Propeller Line, tri-weekly, 40 South

Markets.

Catharine, Catharine slip, Cherry to South.
Centre, Centre, Grand to Broome.
Chelsea, Avenue 9th near 18th.
Clinton, Washington and West, bet. Spring & Canal.
Essex, Grand, Essex to Ludlow.
Fulton, South, bet. Fulton & Beekman, East River.
Franklin, Old slip.
Gouverneur, Gouverneur c. Water.
Greenwich, Weehawken c. Christopher and West.
Jefferson, Avenue 6th c. Greenwich lane.
Monroe, Corlears, between Monroe and Grand.
Manhattan, Houston c. First.
Tompkins, Avenue 3d bet. Sixth and Seventh.
Union, Second c. Houston.
Washington, Washington c. Vesey & Fulton, N. R.

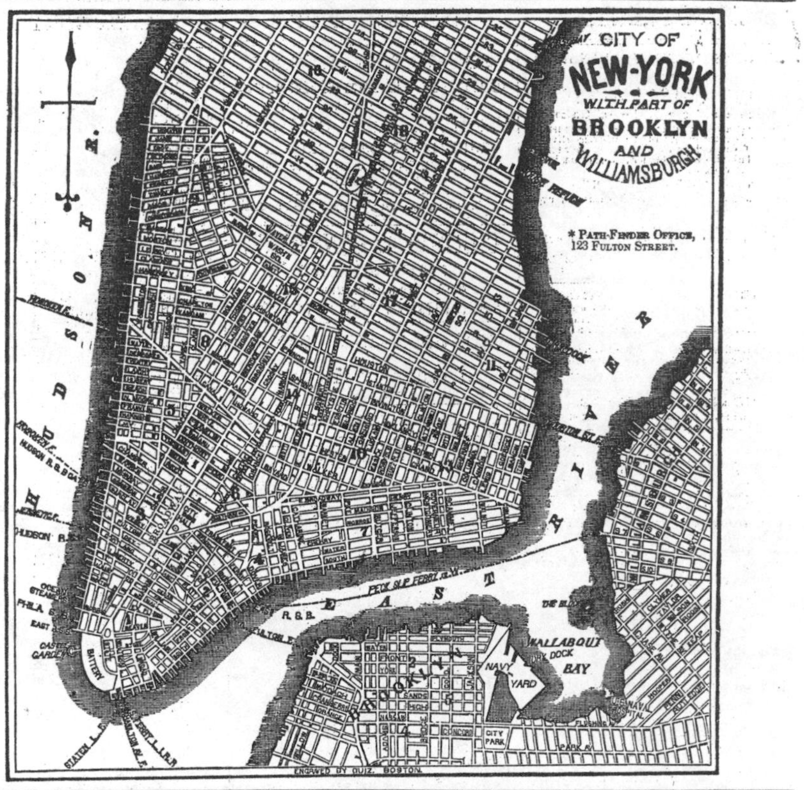

Directory to Hotels.

Astor House....231 Broadway...	Colman & Stetson.	
Atlantic Hotel..3&5 Broadway..	Wm. C. Anderson.	
Barclay st House....John Patten....	foot Barclay st.	
Bond street House....665 B'dway....	Charles Plinta.	
Carlton House..350 & 352 Broadway..	P. H. Hodges	
City Hotel.......119 Broadway......	F. Blanchard.	
Clinton Hotel.......3 Beekman......	Simeon Leland.	
Croton Hotel.....144 Broadway.....	John L. Moore.	
Delmonico's....25 Broadway...	P.A.&L.Delmonico.	
Dunlap's Hotel......135 Fulton.....	W. G. Dunlap.	
Dunning's Hotel....66 Cortlandt...	Smith Dunning.	
Eastern Pearl st. House..309 Pearl...	George Seeley.	
Exchange Hotel...133 Fulton..........	Case & Co.	
Franklin House...197 B'dway...	Hayes & Treadwell.	
Globe Hotel.........66 B'dway....	James H. Page.	
Hotel de Paris.....290 B'dway......	Antoine Vignes.	
Howards' Hotel....176 B'dway...	Thomas & White.	
Hudson R. House..73 Robinson..	E.&J.Chamberlain.	
Judson Hotel.......61 B'dway.......	Curtis Judson.	
Lovejoy's Hotel....34 Park row...	Lovejoy & Libby.	
Mansion House....39 Broadway....	Wm. J. Bunker.	
Merchants' Hotel...41 Cortlandt....	Wm. Muirheid.	
National Hotel......5 Cortlandt.......	J. B. Curtis.	
New York Hotel...721 B'dway...	Joseph B. Monnot.	
Park place House...1 Park place..	James G. Elliott.	
Pearl st. House.....88 Pearl.....	Bishop & Leonard.	
Rathbun's Hotel.....163 B'dway....	Benj. Rathbun.	
Rochester Hotel...31 Courtlandt st...—		
Shakspeare Hotel. Wm. c.Duane.	Bergen&Galabrun.	
Tammany Hall...166 Nassau...	Joseph W. Howard.	
Taylor's Hotel....28 Courtlandt st....	Eldad Taylor.	
Tremont Temp....110 B'dway....	H. Waterman, Jr.	
United States Hotel.... 200 Water.....	H. Johnson.	
Western Hotel....9 Cortlandt....	Dwier & Barber.	

Places of Amusement.

Astor Place Opera House, between Broadway and Bowery.
American Art Union, Collection of Paintings, Broadway, between Broome and Spring street.
American Museum, corner of Broadway and Ann st.
Banvard's Panorama, Broadway, adjoining Niblo's Garden.
Bowery Theatre, Bowery, between Bayard and Walker.
Broadway Theatre, Broadway, between Pearl and Anthony st.
Castle Garden, Off the Battery.
Chatham Theatre, Chatham st, between Pearl and Roosevelt st.
Circus, Bowery Amphitheatre, Bowery, between Bayard and Walker sts.
Elysian Fields, Hoboken Ferries, foot of Barclay, Canal and Christopher sts.
Grant Thorburn's Flower store and Picture Gallery, 15 John st.
Mitchell's Olympic Theatre, Broadway, between Howard and Grand sts.
National Academy of Design, cor. Broadway and Leonard sts.
New York Gallery of fine Arts, in the Rotunda, in the Park, cor. Centre and Chambers sts.
Niblo's Garden, corner Broadway and Prince sts.
Palmo's Opera House, 41 Chambers st.
Park Theatre, on Park Row, opposite the Park.

Banks in New York.

Name.	*Location.*	*Ds. of Dis.*
American Exchange*....	50 Wall..........	W&S.
Bank of America.......	46 Wall..........	Tu&F.
" Commerce*......	32 Wall..........	Tu&F.
" New York......	Wall c William...	Tu&Th.
" the State of N.Y.	30 Wall..........	Tu&F.
Butcher's & Drover's....	Bowery c. Grand..	W&S.
Chemical*.............	216 Broadway....	Daily.
Citizens...............		
City..................	52 Wall..........	M&Th.
Dry Dock Banking Co...	Avenue D. c. 10th.	Tu&F.
Fulton*...............	Pearl c Fulton....	W&S.
Greenwich.............	402 Hudson.......	Tu&F.
Knickerbocker..........		
Leather Manufacturers..	45 Williams......	Tu&F.
Manhattan.............	40 Wall..........	M&Th.
Mechanics'............	33 Wall..........	W&S.
Mechanics' Banking Ass..	38 Wall..........	Tu&F.
Mechanics' and Traders'.	370 Grand........	M&Th.
Merchants'............	42 Wall..........	W&F.
Merchants' Exchange...	Greenwich c. Dey.	W&S.
National..............	36 Wall..........	Tu&F.
North River...........	Greenwich c. Dey.	Tu&F.
Phœnix................	45 Wall..........	W&S.
Seventh Ward..........	Pearl c. John.....	Tu&F.
Tradesmen's...........	177 Chatham.....	Tu&F.
Union.................	34 Wall..........	M&Th.

Bank of U. S. at Philadelphia..Agent at 1 Hanover st.
Commercial, (in hands of receivers). No 1 Hanover st.
N. A. Trust and Banking Co....Receiver 38 Wall st.
*Free Banking Associations.

Banks for Savings.

Bank for Savings in the City of N. Y.	107 Chamber.	Daily, 4 to 6 PM.
Bowery Savings....	128 Bowery..	M, Th&S 5 to 7 PM.
Greenwich Savings..	11 Sixth Av..	M, W&F 5 to 7 PM.
Seamen's Savings...	82 Wall......	Daily, 11 AM, 2 PM.

Post Office Regulations.

Under the Laws of March 1, 2 and 3, 1847.

Postage on all Letters under 300 miles........	5 cts.
" " " over 300 "	10 "
On all Newspapers (from the office of publication,) within the State..................	1 "
If out of the State, and more than 100 miles...	1½ "
All transient Newspapers, each............	3 "
Circulars and Handbills..................	3 "

Every letter or parcel not exceeding half an ounce in weight, shall be deemed a single letter; and every additional weight of half an ounce or less, shall be charged with an additional single postage.

Advertised letters to be charged with the cost of advertising the same, in addition to the regular postage.

Transient Newspapers, Circulars and Handbills, must in all cases be pre-paid.

Letters to different persons cannot be enclosed in the same envelope under a penalty of *ten dollars*.

Letters, Newspapers and Packages, not exceeding one ounce, addressed to officers, musicians and privates of the United States Army in Mexico, *free*. The address must state 'belonging to the army.'

Members of Congress to have the Franking privilege as fully as before the passage of the Act of 1845.

Travellers Route to Chicago.

New York to Albany............................	miles 151
Albany to Buffalo	325
Buffalo to Cleveland..............................	192
" to Detroit......................................	312
" to Milwaukie.................................	639
" to Racine	914
" to Southport..................................	949
" to Chicago....................................	1004

Specie Table.

Gold Coin—Victoria Sov's..................	$4,87 to 4,90
Light do	$4,83 to 4,85
Guineas, (full weight)......................	5,00 to 5,16
Twenty franc pieces.......................	3,80 to 3,80
Spanish Doubloons........................	16,00 to 16,25
Silver Coin—Am. dol's, halves and qurs..	par
Mexican dollars...........................	to 1 prem
Mexican quarters and small pieces.......	2 to 3 dis
Spanish dollars............................	1 to 3 prem
English crowns............................	1,06 to 1,09
English shillings...........................	22 cents
Five franc pieces..........................	94½ to 95

Directory to Omnibusses.

Astoria & Yorkville, Chatham and Bowery to Yorkville and Hell Gate Ferry, hourly, from 7 AM, to 7 PM.
Bloomingdale & Manhattanville, over Tryon Road, hourly, from 7 AM to 6 PM.
Bull's Head, 24th st and 2d Av. through Bowery and Broadway to foot Whitehall, every 5 minutes, from 6 AM to 10 PM.
Chelsea, 9th Av. cor. 23d st, to Bowling Green, every 10 minutes, from 6 AM to 10 PM.
Dry Dock, Whitehall, through Grand and Columbia sts to Dry Dock, every 2 minutes, from 6 AM to 10 PM.
Empire, 6th Av. cor. 23d st, to foot Whitehall, every 5 minutes, from 6 AM to 10 PM.
Fulton Ferry, 7th Av. cor. 19th st, through Broadway to Fulton Ferry, every 5 minutes, from 6 AM to 10 PM.
Greenwich, 9th av. cor. 27th st, through Broadway to Bowling Green, every 5 minutes, from 6 AM to 11 PM.
Harlem, Tryon Road to Harlem Bridge, every 15 minutes, from 5½ AM to 9 PM. Also at 11½ PM.
Knickerbocker, 8th Av. cor. 23d st, to foot Whitehall st, every 4 minutes, from 6 AM to 10 PM.
Connects at 8th Av. with Bloomingdale stages.
Madison, 4th Av. cor. 23d st, to South Ferry, hourly, from 6 AM to 10 PM
Manhattan, Whitehall, through Bowery, Houston & Av. C to 10th st, every 5 minutes, from 6 AM 10 PM.
Murphy & Co's, 3d Av. cor. 28th st, through Bowery and Brodway to foot Whitehall st, hourly, from 5½ AM to 11 PM.
Murphy & Co's, Tompkins Square, through Bowery and Broadway to foot Whitehall st, hourly, from 5½ AM to 11 PM.
Telegraph, Williamsburgh Ferries to Jersey City Ferries, every 15 minutes, from 6½ AM to 9½ PM.
Waverly, 6th Av. cor. 23d st, through 6th Av. to 8th st, down Broadway to foot Whitehall st, every 4 minutes, from 6½ AM to 10 PM.

Directory to Ferries.

Brooklyn, foot Whitehall, every 8 minutes, from 4½ AM, to 12½ PM.
Brooklyn, foot of Fulton st, running all the time.
Brooklyn, Catharine slip, running all the time.
Brooklyn, foot Walnut st every 15 minutes, from 6 AM, to 10 PM.
Bulls, foot Canal st, 10 AM. and 3 PM; Tu&Sat 7 PM.
Fort Lee, foot Canal, 10 AM. and 3 PM; Tu&Sat 7 PM.
Hell Gate, 86th st, every 15 min, from 6 AM to 7 PM.
Hamilton Av., foot Whitehall every half hour, 5½ AM. to 8½ PM.
Hoboken, foot Barclay, every 15 minutes, from 5½ AM. to 6½ PM.
Hoboken, foot Canal, every 15 minutes, from 6½ AM to 12 PM.
Hoboken foot Christopher, every half hour, from 6 AM. to 8 PM.
Jersey, foot Cortland, every 15 minutes from 6 AM
Elizabethport St Bt & Summerville Railroad, Battery place 9 AM, 1 and 5 PM.
New Brighton & Pt Richmond, Battery place 9½ AM, 1 and 4 PM.
Staten Island, foot Whitehall, 9 and 11 AM, 1, 3½ and 6 PM.
Williamsburg, Peck slip, every 15 minutes, from 3 AM to 10 PM.
Williamsburg, foot Grand st, from 3 AM to 12 PM.
Williamsburg, foot Houston, from 3 AM to 11 PM.
Greenwood Cemetery, East side Battery, 10½ AM, and 2, 4 and 5½ PM.

Mail Arrangement.

New York Post Office.

Nassau street, between Liberty and Cedar streets.

CORRECTED WEEKLY.

Office Hours—From 8 AM. to 6.30 PM.
Sundays, from 9 to 10 AM, from 12½ to 1½ PM.

Time of Closing Mails.

North—Albany, closes daily, 3½ PM. Sundays, 1½ PM.
Erie Railroad via Piermont and S. Middleton, 2 PM.
Peekskill via Yonkers, &c, 6 AM.
East—L. I. Railroad via Jamaica to Greenport, for all offices on the Island east of Jamaica, 6 AM.
Mails by this Line for Hempstead, Jamaica, &c, 6 AM.
Brooklyn mails at 6½ and 9½ AM, and 3½ PM.
Williamsburgh, Newton, Flushing, &c, 2 PM.
Tompkinsville, North Shore and Richmond, 9 AM.
Richmond Valley and Rossville, Tu. and Fri. 9½ AM.
Great Eastern Mail via Stonington & Norwich, 3½ PM.
New Haven Mail to Hartford, except Sundays, 5 AM.
Bridgeport and offices on line Housatonic R'road 5 AM.
White Plains, 6 AM.
Land Mail to New Haven, &c, 6 AM., except Sun.
South—Southern Mail, via Washington City to New Orleans, 7½ AM, and 3 PM; Sundays 1½ PM.
Jersey City, Newark, &c, by this route, 3 PM.
Southern Way Mail, including all offices on Railroad to Philadelphia, 7 AM.
Monmouth Co, N. J, via Trenton, Tu. and Fr. 1 PM; via New Brunswick, Mon. and Th. 12 PM
Hackensack, via Hoboken, Tu., Th. and Sat. 2 PM.
Freehold, by Steamboat, daily, 12½ M.

When Due.

The Southern Mails, 11 AM. and 10 PM.
The Northern Mails, 6 AM.
The Eastern Mails, 7 AM.
The Long Island Mails, 3 PM.
The Jersey Mails, 10 AM and 3 PM.

City of New York.

Fare for Hack and Cab Hire, &c.

For conveying a passenger any distance not exceeding one mile, 25c; two passengers, 50c, or 25c each; every additional passenger, 25c.

For a passenger any distance exceeding a mile, and within two miles, 50c; every additional passenger, 25 cents.

For one passenger to the the New Alms House, 50c; returning, 50c; for two passengers 75c for the two, and 25c going, and 25c returning, for every additional passenger.

For the use of a Hackney Coach, Carriage or Cab, by the day, with one more passengers, $5.

For the use of a Hackney Coach, Carriage or Cab, by the hour, with one or more passengers, with the privilege of going from place to place, and of stopping as often as may be required, as follows, viz:—first hour $1; second hour 75c; every succeeding hour 50c.

For children between 2 and 14 years of age, half price only; for children under two years of age, no charge.

Every driver or owner of a Hackney Coach, &c., shall carry, in and upon his Coach, Carriage, or Cab, in addition to the person or persons therein, one trunk, valise, saddle bag, carpet bag, portmanteau, or box, if he be requested so to do, for each passenger, without charge; but for every trunk or other such articles above named, more than one for each passenger, he shall be entitled to the sum of six cents.

In case of disagreement as to distance or price, to be determined by the Mayor, or Superintendent of Hackney Coaches.

The owner or driver of any Hackney Coach, Carriage, or Cab, shall not be entitled to recover any pay from any person from whom he shall have demanded any greater price of rates than authorized to receive.

No owner or driver of any Hackney Coach, Carriage, or Cab, in the City of New York, shall ask, demand, or receive, any larger sum than he or they may be entitled to receive as aforesaid, under the penalty of ten dollars for such offence, to be sued for and recovered from the owner or owners or drivers of any such Hackney Coach, &c, &c.

Complaints of any violation of this Law, can be made at the Mayor's Office, City Hall, or at the Office of the Chief of Police, in the *New* City Hall, (rear of the *City Hall*,) under the Marine Cour

Table of Distances.

Battery.	*Exchange.*	*City Hall.*	*to*
¼ of a mile			Rector street.
½	¼		Fulton.
¾	½		Warren.
1	¾	¼	Leonard.
1¼	1	½	Canal.
1½	1¼	¾	Spring.
1¾	1½	1	Houston.
2	1¾	1¼	Fourth.
2¼	2	1½	Ninth.
2½	2¼	1¾	Fourteenth.
2¾	2½	2	Seventeenth.
3	2¾	2¼	24th.
3¼	3	2½	29th.
3½	3¼	2¾	34th.
3¾	3½	3	38th.
4	3¾	3¼	44th.
4¼	4	3½	49th.
4½	4¼	3¾	54th.
4¾	4½	4	58th.
5	4¾	4¼	63d.
5¼	5	4½	68th.
5½	5¼	4¾	73d.
5¾	5½	5	78th.
6	5¾	5¼	83d.
6¼	6	5½	88th.
6½	6¼	5¾	93d.
6¾	6½	6	97th.
7	6¾	6¼	102d.
7¼	7	6½	107th.
7½	7¼	6¾	112th.
7¾	7½	7	117th.
8	7¾	7¼	121st.
8¼	8	7½	126th.
8½	8¼	7¾	131st.
8¾	8½	8	136th.
9	8¾	8¼	140th.
9¼	9	8½	145th.
9½	9¼	8¾	150th.
9¾	9½	9	155th.

Table of Distances.

FROM NEW YORK CITY TO

	Miles.		*Miles*
Acquackanock	13	Kinsgbridge	13
Astoria, L. I.	6	Lakeville	19
Bath, L. I.	9	Long Branch	30
Bedlow's Island	2	Manchester	18
Blackwell's Island	4	Manhassett	20
Bellville, N.J.	9	Manhattenville	8
Bergen, N.J.	3	Middletown, N.J.	26
Bloomfield, N.J.	13	Middletownpoint	24
Bloomingdale	5	Morristown	28
Brooklyn	½	Morrisiana	9
Bulls Ferry	6	Newark	9
Chatham, N.J.	20	New Brighton	6
Chelsea	16	New Brunswick	30
Clifton	8	New Rochelle	20
Cold Spring, L.I.	30	Newton, L.I.	8
Communipaw	3	New Utrecht, L.I.	9
Coney Island	13	Nyack	27
Dobbs Ferry	22	Orange, N.J.	13
East Chester	16	Oyster Bay, L.I.	30
East New York	6	Paterson, N.J.	17
Elizabethport, N.J.	12	Perth Amboy	24
Elizabethtown, N.J.	14	Piermont	24
Factoryville	9	Plainfield, N.J.	26
Flatbush	4	Port Chester	30
Flatlands	8	Port Richmond	9
Flushing	11	Rahway, N.J.	19
Fort Hamilton	9	Ravenswood, L.I.	5
Fort Lee	10	Red Bank, N.J.	26
Fort Washington	10	Richmond	13
Glen Gove	28	Rockaway, L.I.	20
Governor's Island	1	Rossville	18
Gowanus	3	Rye	28
Gravesend	11	Singsing	34
Greenburgh	22	Shrewsbury, N.J.	28
Green Wood Cemetery	3	South Amboy, N.J.	26
Hackensack	13	Springfield, N.J.	18
Harlem	7½	Stapleton	7
Harsimus	2	Tappan	27
Hastings	20	Tarrytown	27
Hemstead	22	Tomkinsville	
Hicksville	27	Weehawken, N.J.	
Hoboken	2	Westchester	14
Irving	26	West Farms	13
Jamaica	12	White Plains	26
Jericho	28	Williamsburg, L.I.	1
Jerusalem	28	Yonkers	17
Jersey City	1	Yorkville	5

Table of Distances,

BETWEEN NEW YORK AND ALBANY.

East Side River. From New York to..	*Mls*	*West Side River.* From New York to..	*Mls*
King's Bridge	13	Piermont	24
Yonkers	17	Ramapo	44
Dobb's Ferry	22	Munroe Works	52
Tarrytown	28	Turners' Depot	57
Sing Sing	34	Newburg	74
Croton River	36	Marlborough	82
Peekskill	46	Milton	86
Phillipsburgh	55	New Paltz	90
Fishkill	65	Esopus	99
Poughkeepsie	78	Rondout	107
Hyde Park	84	Kingston	109
Rhinebeck	94	Glasco	118
Redhook, Lower	100	Saugerties	121
Redhook, Upper	103	Malden	124
Clermon	108	Catskill	133
Blue Store	110	Atheus	139
Hudson	121	Coxsackie	147
Sturveysant Falls	129	N. Baltimore	153
Kinderhook	134	Coeymans	155
Schodack Centre	144	Albany	167
Greenbush	153		
Albany	154		

Parks and Squares.

Abingdon Square, Hudson st, between Bank & Troy.
Battery, foot Broadway, between Pier No. 1 N. River and Pier No. 1 E. River, contains 11 acres.
Bloomingdale Square, between 8th and 9th avenues, and 53d and 57th streets.
Bowling Green, foot Broadway, near the Battery.
Chatham Square, junction Chatham and Bowery st, and East Broadway.
Gramercy Park, between 3d and 4th av, and 20th and 21st streets, 2 miles from City Hall.
Hamilton Square, between 3d and 4th avenues, and 65th and 69th streets.
Hudson Square or *St. Johns Park*, between Hudson, Beach, Laight and Varick streets.
Madison Square, 5th av, cor 23d st.
Manhattan Square, between 8th and 9th avenues, and 77th and 81st streets.
Murray Hill Square, 4th avenue, between 31st and 34th streets.
Observatory Place, on Prospect Hill, between 4th and 5th avenues, and 89th and 94th streets.
Park, between Broadway, Chamber, Park and Centre streets, contains 10¾ acres
Reservoir, Distributing, between 5th and 6th avenues, and 40th and 42d streets.
Reservoir, Receiving, between 6th and 7th avenues, and 79th and 86th streets.
Stuyvesant Square, 2d av, between 15th and 17th sts.
Tompkins Square, between 7th and 10th streets, and avenues A and B.
Union Place, at the termination of Broadway and Bowery sts and University place, contains 10 acres, and is 1¾ miles from City Hall.
Washington Square, between 4th st, Waverly place, University place and McDougal street, contains 9¾ acres, and is 1½ miles north of City Hall.

New York Day Book

New-York, Saturday Evening, August 18.

PRINCIPLE WITH INTEREST.

THE SEASON.—The movement of commercial visitors to the city continues, and it is very striking in contrast with the dullness of the previous two months. At RATHBUN'S Hotel yesterday at dinner the whole of the large dining-room was occupied with guests, so that it was difficult, for those who came a little behind time, to find a place in the crowd.

The Astor-House, Irving-House, and all the principal Hotels show the same throngs of guests.

The streets occupied by the jobbers give similar evidence that a very active business season has already fully commenced,—all the more active for recent temporary obstructions.

THE RAILROAD MONOPOLY.—A SIGN OF CHANGE.—After several years of painful and oppressive silence, the *Tribune* of this morning unlocks its rigid jaws, and utters an echo of the Day Book's condemnation of this infamous and murderous monopoly. Why ? Why, at *this* time ? Why not sooner ? If the *Tribune* had not been bribed into silence years ago, this monopoly would have been crushed ere this.

As the *Tribune* finds it for its advantage to follow the lead of the Day-Book in this matter, it may do so to greater advantage in other particulars.

The Bursting of the Trouble.

For the past two days, the papers have been burdened with heavy reports of the two Loco-Foco Conventions at Rome, in this State, assembled professedly for the purpose of re-uniting the two rascally factions.

The Day-Book has not troubled its readers with the dirty details of these plotters' work. It now gives the following as a compendium and "conclusion of the whole matter."

No Union.

THE FINAL—5 P. M.

The Convention came to order, and at half-past four received a message from the Free Soilers stating that they had no farther communication to make, Mr. Cutting moved some resolutions, which were carried, after which speeches were made by Messrs. Cutting, Bowne, Chatfield, and Peckham, when it was moved and carried unanimously that the Convention adjourn *sine die*. Six cheers were here given for Marcy and three for the democratic party. The greatest enthusiasm and unanimity of feeling characterized the closing scenes of the Convention.

CHRISTY closes his entertainments here during the next week. The Hall is to be cleaned, repaired, improved, and decorated ; and he avails himself of the interval to refresh his company of "Minstrels" in the air of the sea-shore. On Monday evening, they will perform at Fort Hamilton. They leave very full houses here. During the whole of this week, they have had constantly increasing audiences, as the city has filled with strangers ; and their return on "Monday week" will be impatiently awaited by a host of their "inveterate" auditors as well as by curious strangers attracted by their fame.

THE GRAND OPERA AND BALLET at the Broadway Theatre are perfectly successful. 'ERNANI' was never so well performed in New York, nor to so large an ordiance as to the Broadway this week.—The queenly and brilliant Tedesco is alone a sufficient attraction to a spectator, even if he were deprived of the sense of hearing. It is difficult to imagine a higher musical excellence, than her performance of *Elvira*. Signor VITA is majestic and faultless in Charles V. He gives the part its just dignity and prominence, and far surpasses Taffanelli's performance of the same. CORRELLI performed *Ernani* with good taste and action, but with a damaged voice ; and, last evening, Signor Vietti was substituted for him with manifest advantage, though the latter lacks the force necessary to do full justice to the character. NORELLI in Silva maintained his well-known excellence.—Altogether, the corps is remarkable for the excellence of its prominent members.

The Monplaisir company have made the *ballet* a very brilliant and popular affair, and have held crowds of applauding spectators in attendance through the week.

California Correspondence.

COLLOMA, UPPER CALIFORNIA, June 9, 1849.

Dear Doctor :

A friend of mine having determined on returning home, I embrace this opportunity of sending this epistle. It is the first chance I have had since I have been at the mines, for I am cut off from the low country, no way of sending a letter at all. I suppose you have been expecting to hear from me for some time. Yes, Doctor, here I am at last, where I had so much desired to be, in the Gold Regions of California; but I am greatly disappointed in every thing. There is plenty of gold here, that is certain ; but it is scattered so thinly over a vast extent of country and is so difficult, or rather it is so laborious to obtain it, that few can stick to the digging long enough to make any thing handsome. Old laborers say it is the hardest work they ever underwent. You have to work under a broiling sun, and pick among the hard rocks, and almost break your back stooping and lifting large stones ; a person has no conception of the labor. A great many who came out with me are about returning, or have already returned. A person by working hard, may average an ounce per day in the good places, sometimes they make more and sometimes less. I should advise no one to come out unless he be a carpenter or blacksmith, or a gunsmith. The medical profession is already well represented here, there are too many of them to make much. There was a better chance when I first came. Dr. B—— is established here, I saw him sell an ounce of quinine for $20 worth of dust a few days after our arrival, but things are greatly changed already.—Everything nearly, is as cheap as the States, except some luxuries. Ale is $4 per bottle—brandy $3,56—champaigne $12—flour is 50 cts. per lb.—salt pork 74 cts.—sugar 50 cts.—coffee 40 cts.—fresh beef cannot be had at present ; some sold the other day for $1 per lb., a poor old ox at that. I am greatly disappointed in the climate; the days are sometimes as hot as I have felt in Mexico, and the nights are bitter cold and chilly always. The country up here is black and barren, and nothing I think can ever be cultivated to advanteger Grass cannot grow. I went digging a little when I first came up here. We went to a place called Weaous Creek, and came near being caught by the Indians with whom we are at war, and lost ourselves and suffered much with hunger. We were out five days. I afterwards opened a shop and am doing tolerable well. I paid $50 a month for a log hut. I have now built a house of my own which cost me near $400. Our party has split up. H. and B. have gone up the Sacramento, and R. has opened a groggery. I am undergoing a most miserable existance here, nothing to do but go to bed as soon as night comes, unless I choose to associate with gamblers and cut-throats or drunkards. I am really sorry I left New York; however, I shall be able to make something in a FEW YEARS. Believe me, all India Rubber Goods are a humbug, not worth a copper. I send you a specimen of the root of evil. I send each of the youngsters a piece, which they must take care of and keep it to remember me.

Yours, truly, B. F.

Report of the Board of Health.

MAYOR'S OFFICE,
New York, August 18, 1849.

The Sanitary Committee of the Board of Health report 67 new cases, and 24 deaths of Cholera as having occurred during the last 24 hours.

	Cases.	Deaths.	Disch'd
In Centre Street Hospital,	–	–	–
In William Street "	11	3	4
In Stanton-street "	6	3	2
In 13th Street "	2	2	2
In 35th-street Hospital	3	1	2
In Penitentiary "	—	—	—
Bellevue Hospital	—	—	—
Lunatic Asylum	—	—	—
In Ward's Island "	—	—	—
In Col'd Home	—	—	—
Randall's Island	—	—	—
In Private Practice,	45	45	—
Total,	67	24	10

BROOKLYN.

OFFICE OF BOARD OF HEALTH,
August 18, 1849.

Since yesterday 15 deaths by Cholera were reported to this office. The number of cases will not be furnished in future.

CHAS. S. J. GOODRICH.
Physician of Board.

Progress of the Cholera.

BUFFALO, Friday, Aug. 17, 2 P. M.—There have been 22 cases of Cholera and 13 deaths during the 24 hours ending noon this day.

There were, from 30th May, to August 11, (ten weeks) 1802 cases, and 594 deaths of Cholera at Buffalo.

ALBANY, Friday, Aug. 17, 6 P. M.—Seven cases of Cholera and 6 deaths are reported to-day. No cases or deaths at Rochester.

TROY, Aug. 15, 12 M.—Four fatal cases of Cholera have been reported to the Board of Health the last 48 hours.

August 16, 12 M.—Five fatal cases of Cholera have been reported to the Board of Health this day.

WEST TROY, August 16.—Only two cases of Cholera have been reported to the Board of Health during the last two weeks, one of which proved fatal.

FISHKILL, Thursday, Aug. 16.—We are happy to hear that the sickness still so prevalent in our midst is becoming mild and manageable, and that those who have long been lying low are rapidly advancing to convalesence. These are principally dysentery and diarrhœa, with some few cases of fever. The Cholera appears to have subsided, though diseases appear to become of that type, in some cases.—*Standard.*

BOSTON, Friday, Aug. 17, P. M.—There have been reported since yesterday, 9 deaths from Cholera, 5 of which were Americans and 4 foreigners. There are now remaining in the Hospital 19 cases. The deaths have fallen off one-half.

PROVIDENCE, Friday, Aug. 17.—Five deaths from Cholera occurred in this city yesterday.

HARTFORD, Friday, Aug. 17.—Mr. Alvin Perkins, potter, residing in Morgan street, was attacked with Cholera yesterday, and died about 4 P. M. He was in a collapsed state when medical attendance was called. We understand he ate freely of clams in the morning.

Last evening an Irish woman residing in Asylum street was in the last stages of the same disease.

PHILADELPHIA, Friday, Aug. 17, P. M.—The report of the Board to-day is but 5 cases and 1 death—the death being in the County Prison.

FATAL RESULT OF DELAY IN A CASE OF CHOLERA.—On Friday evening last, David T. Thompson, of Salem, driver of an express wagon at East Boston, though having a slight diarrhœa, was well enough to be about his usual avocation. He took nothing of consequence to check his diarrhœa, and at 3 o'clock the next morning, was seized with cramps and soon with purging. Still he did not send for a Doctor, until after 5 o'clock, when nothing could be done to save him, and he died at 2 P. M. on Saturday. It is the opinion of the physician that if he had been sent for an hour or two earlier, he might have saved Thompson's life.—*Daily Republican.*

NEWARK, Aug. 16.—Five new Cholera cases are reported since yesterday, Mrs. Bridge, 11 Maiden Lane, taken last night, died this morning ; a colored man, near Nine Row died yesterday. Three others reported are likely to recover. The man in Quarry-st. in collapse yesterday, died last night

Aug. 17.—Eight new cases of Cholera and 5 deaths have occurred, among which we noticed the death of Mr. James Turnbull, for many years at the head of one of the large carriage-making establishments.

THE CHOLERA still continues among us, and several fatal cases have occurred during the past week. The dysentery and diarrhœa are also very prevalent, and quite a number of persons are down with one or the other of these diseases. The former is of very malignant type, and several deaths have occurred from it during the last week or two. We learn also that the dysentery is very prevalent at Lfrtle Falls, in this county, and that a number of persons had fallen victims to it within the lasr week.—*Patterson Int.*

An instance of unprecedented and afflicting mortality in one family circle in Paterson is mentioned by the Jersey City Sentinel. The grandmother, the father and mother, an uncle, an aunt, and a nephew of Mr. Henry Demarest, (of the firm of Demarest and Brown of Jersey City,) having fallen victims to the Cholera at Paterson within ten days.

A similar case of family affliction occurred during the last week in Mannington, Salem County—Mr. James Brooks, jr., having lost his father, mother, wife, and a sister-in-law. The last named, Ann Kendall, of Phila., bein on a visit to Mr. B's. family—having had the premonitory symptoms when she arrived—died within 48 hours. Mrs. Brooks was taken after the funeral on Monday and died nevt morning. On Tuesday the father, who had come from Cumberland County with his wife on a visit, also died, and on Friday afternoon his wife was taken ill, and died of the same disease. A sister of Mrs. Kendall (who was with her,) James Brooks, Jr., and several children, had slight attacks, but throught the prompt administration of remedies are convalesceent.

A number of persons in the vicinity are said to have been more or less affected, but it is believed that the cases cannot justly be pronounced more than bad attacks of cholera morbus. The Salem Ssandard of yesterday says :

"The ravages of the disease in this family are believed to have been occasioned by local causes, and we hear it variously attributed to an impure cellar and well, the close proximity of a buried hogshead, the resceptable of impure substances, and the clearing of what is known as 'Heron Swamp.'"

PITTSBURGH, Friday, Aug. 17.—Birmingham is almost deserted, business suspended, and charcoal burning in the streets all day. The disease is confined to where it first broke out, and where 21 died within the past 24 hours.

CINCINNATI.—Eighteen interments to 16th inst. in two days.

CHOLERA EXPENSES AT CINCINNATI.—The *Gazette* estimates the expenses to the city and township at $19,000.

HARRODSBURG, (Ky.)—The Harrodsburg Ploughboy of Aug. 9, says :

Since our last issue the Cholera has been somewhat on the increase at this place, 21 deaths haning occurred in addition to the number before recorded.

The Maysville Herald of Aug. 8, says :

To-day we hear of no deaths or new cases of Cholera.

In Millersburg there were two deaths on yesterday, and some five or six cases.

In Paris, up to 5 o'clock yesterday, there were only three new cases.

QUEBEC.—The number of deaths to the 11th inst. is 857.

MONTREAL, Friday, Aug. 17.—There were 3 interments from Cholera to-day.

SAUT ST. MARIE.—A number of deaths have occurred at the Sault. Among them we notice Capt. Hicks, the newly-appointed Receiver at that place. Capt. H. was from Adrian, Mich., and commanded one of the companies of Michigan Volunteers during the Mexican war. Mr. Edward Clark of Woreester, Mass., Superintendent of the Marquette Iron Co., died on Tuesday, the 7th inst. ; Maj. Martell died on the same day. Three Indians died the same day.

Capt. Benjamin of the Franklin, which arrived at Cleveland, informs us that nine deaths in all had occurred from Cholera. The visitors had all left for the lower regions, and the Indians living on the point had scattered fer parts unknown.

TAUNTON, Friday, Aug. 17.—There were reported yesterday 4 deaths from Cholera. All the cases in this place, so far, have proved fatal.

CHOLERA ABOUT THE LAKES.—With the exception of Sandusky City, the Lake towns and cities, so far, have not been severely scourged by the epidemic, and it is generally abating. The reports from Milwaukie, Chicago, Detroit, Toledo, Sandusky and Buffalo are favorable, and show a decline in number of cases and fatality. Very few cases are reported at Detroit or Toledo.

Occasional cases are reported an the steamboats and other Lake shipping, but in no instance has the cholera made such havoc among emigrants and others on boat or vessel, as frequently occurred on the western rivers when the disease was at its height.—*Cleveland Herald.*

A WEDDING SUIT AND A WINDING SHEET.—The Rev. Mr. Cooper, Bethel Chaplain at Sandusky, left the city during the prevalence of the cholera, for one of the adjoining towns, to be married. It having been reported that he left through fear of the Cholera, it is now stated, upon authority, that he left to fulfil a long-standing engagement to be married, and died the very morning appointed for the marriage.

The Milwaukie Sentinel says : "We understand, by a gentleman from Racine county, that the Cholera has raged with considerable severity in the Norwegian settlements in that county ; some 40 deaths having occurred from that disease in the town of Norway, withtn the past few days."

IMPORTANT DISCOVERY IN IRELAND.—If there be faith in chemistry and the O'Gorman Mahon, a discovery has been made in Ireland which is likely to be more important to this country than the discovery of gold in California, will be to the United States of America. According to the statement of the gentleman in question, the peat or "turf" of the Irish bog is capable of being converted by a cheap and simple process, into a variety of matters of the utmost value. One-fourth of Ireland is bog ; therefore, one-fourth of Ireland is composed, on the showing of chemistry and The O'Gormon Mahon, of carbonate of ammonia, [soda, vinegar, naphtha, candles, camphine oil, common oil, gas, and ashes. Only think of fifty square miles of candles lying under the feet for the picking up, the ocean of oil of that dimension, or the volume of gas—to say nothing of the vinegar. "A new light" in every sense of the word, was east upon the House of Commons, by The O'Gormon Mahon in discussing the subject. Where Edmund Burke introduced a rusty dagger, his fellow-countryman introduced a piece of candle, made from the bogs of his native land, and well it burned, according to the newspapers.

The interest of this discussion was derived from the fact that Lord Ashley bore testimony to the integrity of the patentee—a Mr. Owen ; but it is singular, to say the least of it, that the patentee and the discoverer should be both Welshmen—Mr. Owen and Mr. Rhys. It is, however, a discovery which, if it be truly represented, must open in the United Kingdom, mines of wealth worth a thousand Californias, mines of wealth, having these extraordinary properties, that all the cost of exploring them will be clear gain to the people, while the place from which the treasure is to be withdrawn, will be enriched by its removal.

Lord Ashley's statement of the amount of valuable materials, into which 100 tons of peat was convertible. 100 tons of peat, which cost £8, and the labor of converting it about £8 more, contained—

Carbonate of ammonia,......	2602 lbs,	value	£32 10 2
Soda,......	2128 lbs,	"	8 16 6
Vinegar,......	600 lbs,	"	7 10 0
Naphtha,......	30 gls,	"	7 10 0
Candles,......	400 lbs,	"	17 10 0
Camphine oil,......	600 lbs,	"	5 0 0
Common oil,......	800 lbs,	"	3 6 8
Gas,......	— –	"	8 0 0
Ashes,......	— –	"	1 13 4
Total,......			£91 16 8

Mr. Owen, he said, had tried this experiment not merely on 100 tons, but on thousands of tons of peat, during the whole of the last twelve months. He had expended his captal on it, and received his remuneration, and was willing to stake his character and fortune on the issue. He (Lord Ashley) wished to add, that after the peat was cleared away the soil was found fruitful beyond all description, because it was absolutely saturated with ammonia ; and consequently, not only would the country be enriched by the conversion of the peat into valuable materials, but the soil itself would afterwards be found in a far more cultivatible condition.

The introduction of steam navigation, railroads, agricultural chemistry, the application of the electrical fluid (itself unknown 200 years ago,) to uses unimagined 20 years ago, and many other new applications of physical powers, afford pregnant proof of the inexhaustible resources of *material nature.*

TELEGRAPHIC STOCK.—The following statement of the receipts of three of the O'Rielly lines of Telegraphs, says the *Buffalo Commercial* shows that the business of telegraphing must be very profitable. Although in its infancy, the amount paid for telegraphing is not far from three quarters of a million of dollars! We were not aware of the extensive business done by these lines. Within a few days, the *Detroit Free Press* says: We have received a private report of three of them, from which we gather the following receipts :

Philadelphia and Pittsburg,......	$110,811
Pittsburg, Cincinnati and Louisville,......	98,736
Louisville and St. Louis,......	63,312

THE COURTS.

AT CHAMBERS—Before Judge Ulshoffer—In re Diedorich Schulenburg, who appeared for his discharge on writ of Hebees Corpus from arriving as one of the crew of the Danish Ship "Westphalio." In this case the man had signed shipping arrticles, binding himself not to leave the vessel in a foreign port nor to sue for his wages ; on discharge went before a Consul of his own nation ; yet, the judge held that the stipulation was not binding on him in a matter which concerned the personal liberty of the seamen. The applicant was discharged.

Riot in the First Ward.—Several of the Police of the 1st Ward, while in the act of arresting two men named Tracy and Brenan, on a charge of disorderly conduct last evening, were attacked by a large number of the friends of the accused, who seemed determined to rescue them. The mob threw stones and other missels at the officers, but did not succeed in rescuing either of the prisoners from their custody. Tracy in his desperate endeavors to get away divested himself of all his clothing, and when taken before Capt. Wiley at the station house, presented the appearance of an amateur "model artist." Justice McGrath this morning discharged Brennan from custody, the officer not appearing against him. Tracy was committed to answer.

Stealing Gloves.—Two women named Ann Nolan and Julia Ann Watson, were taken into custody for stealing 12 pair of gloves from Otto Sahrader. The prisoners were discharged by Alderman Kelly of the 6th Ward, notwithstanding the property was found in the possession of Ann Nolan, who accounted for one pair of the gloves by depositing 50 cents with the remaining 11 pair of gloves. She was discharged by Alderman Kelly on presumption that the complainant did not come honestly by the property. The Alderman gave orders to have the property returned.

Assault with a Pitcher.—At an early hour this morning Lydia Ann Mins was arrested for striking Harriet Jane Grayten with a pitcher, inflicting a severe wound. She was locked up.

Conspiracy.—A man named John R. Manchester, was arrested late last evening by officer Crout, on a warrant in which he stands charged on complaint of J. M. Bennett, with the above crime. He was detained.

Charge of Grand Larceny.—Last evening, Caroline Goldsmith, was taken into custody for grand larceny, in stealing from J. A. Schatz. Committed by Justice Mountford.

Assault and attempt at Robbery.—Officer Drago last evening arrested a chap named John Hall, residing at No. 8 Carlisle-street, on a charge of assault and battery. and attempt at highway robbery on John Lewis. Committed.

A runaway girl.—Officer Wiley yesterday arrested a young woman named Sarah Jane Coyle, who was arrested as having run away from her parents residing in Wilmington, Del. She was sent back.

Foundling.—A female child about three weeks old, was found last night on the stoop of house No. 119 Bedford st., and was provided for, preparatory to being sent to the Alms-house.

Stage driver Arrested.—Henry Hasson driver of stage No. 18, Bulls Head Line, was arrested last evening for racing in Broadway and running against another omnibus. He was discharged to appear this morning at court.

Deserter.—James Cody was arrested last evening a deserter from the U. S. A. He was sent back.

Charge of Rape.—A young man named Isaac Perkins was arrested on a warrant charged with the above offence upon Eliza Carter, of No. 8 Goerick street. He was held to answer.

From the Syracuse Daily Star.

The Tragedy in Yorkville, Mich.

We have now been allowed the use of a private letter to a gentleman of this city, and the sad murder of young Kellogg is fully confirmed. It appears that the elder son has for some time suspected the mental aberation of his father and thought he might commit suicide. Mr. Kellogg seems to have entertained the idea that there would be a famine and that he would not live long. He said he did not think his sons capable of supporting themselves without his assistance and counsel, and he was determined to take both with him.

In order to kill William he detained him at the store until all the rest had left. He then wrote two or three letters, and requested William to copy them. While he was copying, he went to the Tavern, procured an axe, returned and put it down behind his son, who observed him, but had no idea a father's hand would be raised against him. But while engaged on the second letter, the insane man raised the axe, struck him with the blunt end on the back of his head, breaking his skull most horribly. William fell from the chair, and was repeatedly struck, the blows terribly mangling his head. Mr. Kellogg then shut the door and locked it, and with the axe, went to the house of his elder son, with the full intent to kill him. He had gone to bed leaving the candle burning. The Father came to his bed-room door, waited a few moments and then went out and came to the window, watching until the light was extinguished. But his son hearing a noise arose and re-lit the candle, which served to turn him off. He went down to the bridge, and was making preparations for a plunge and strike against the timbers, the sooner to end his life; but some one saw him and asked him if he He replied "Yes I feel very bad." He then started for the house. One of the girls waked young Mr. Kellogg and said his father acted very strangely. He at once arose and went in pursuit of him. He saw no light in the store ; called William, but he made no reply. He then awoke a man by the name of Ide, and while in the act, saw him walking along the bank of the millpond. The son ran around and headed him off; and he then ran into the bushes. Several men were now at hand; but he evaded them and finally plunged in against a beam for the purpose of making himself senseless. A Mr. Eldred jumped in after him, and found him twenty feet from the store, in fifteen feet of water striving to keep his head under. It was with great difficulty he was rescued as he was bent on drowning himself. He was constantly repeating, "I have killed William" and that he was the murderer. They went back to the store, broke it open, and found the poor boy lying in his gore, a most horrible spectacle. He did not die as soon as was expected, but lived on in the most excruciating pain, until the 9th when he departed. The father felt dreadfully and thought he should be hung. A jury of physicians have pronounced him insane. An inquest and legal investigation have taken place and a verdict returned in accordance with the above facts. Young Mr. Kellogg, will place his suffering parent in some insane asylum. Thus has this very dreadful affair been fully confirmed by the surviving son. We had strongly hoped it was untrue, but alas, we have no more room for doubt. William is dead, and the father a mad man.

ST. LOUIS, Friday, Aug. 17.

INCENDIARISM.—New attempts at incendiarism continue almost daily, and in some instances the villians escape, although the police are actively on the look out.

The health of the city is improving.

The weather is still exceedingly warm, the thermometer reaching 94 in the shade.

Captain Dan Drake Henrie whose hair-breadth escapes from the Mexicans, when taken prisoner with C. M. Clay and others, and who was the theme of admiration. died at the Hospital of the Sisters of Charity.

True bills have been found by the Grand Jury against Joseph Wilkinson and George Moore for the late murder of negro John.

BOSTON, Friday, Aug. 17—P. M.

FIRE AT LAWRENCE, MASS.—The repair-shops and car-houses attached to the Boston and Maine Railroad at Lawrence were destroyed by fire last night. The loss is estimated at $25,000, on which there was no insurance.

From the European Times.

The English Dry-Goods Market.

MANCHESTER MONTHLY REPORTS.—In our last circular we had the satisfaction of describing the transactions of the month of June as having been of a very extensive character ; and to-day as regards those of the closing month we have no hesitation in pronouncing them as of immense magnitude, as will be collected from the following report :

9-8 and 6-4 Grey Tangibs, 20 yards, which, in all qualities, have been in great demand during the month, are from 1 1-2d to 3d per piece higher. All descriptions are very scarce.

6-4 Grey Gold-End Jacconets, 20 yards, [have again experienced a very extensive demand, and are as regards qualities adapted for India, fully 1 1-2 d to 3d per piece higher. Such descriptions are now higher than they have been at any period during the present year, and the rates now demanded could easily be realised for immediate delivery. All the manufacturers, however, being under contract for some weeks to come, buyers manifest no disposition to enter into fresh contracts at the present prices for completion at an extended period. Of such there are necessarily no stocks; and with regard to the medium and best qualities, which are realizing a similar advance, a considerable business has been done in them also. Stocks of these are moderate. A fair demand has existed for all qualities in 12 yards, which may be considered fully 1 1-2d per piece higher. Of them stocks are light.

6-4 Gold-End Cambrics, 12 yards, have improved in value to the extent of fully 1 1-2d per piece. No very great amount of business has been done in them, and stocks may be considered comparatively plentiful. The demand for tape checks, fancy muslins, &c., has been good, and though an advance of about 1 1-2d per piece is demanded, all descriptions, or nearly so, may be purchased at or about last month's quotations. Stocks light.

36-inch Power-loom Shirtings, 66 and 72 reeds, 37 1-2 yards, which are from 7 1-2d to 9d per piece higher than they were at the end of June, have experienced a demand much in excess of the supply. There are consequently no stocks, and orders for immediate delivery in either reed could not be executed, as all the manufacturers are producing to order, and under engagements in many instances for some weeks hence. The same may be reported of all the lower reeded cloths, if we except that they have realized an advance equal to 9d per piece. For instance, some descriptions which we purchased at the end of June for 6-9 could not be had to-day under 7-6. We may notice that all descriptions of 36-inch shirtings have become very much dearer and scarcer, owing to so many of the manufacturers who had suitable looms having turned their attention to the manufacture of wider widths, such as 40 inches.

40-inch Gold-End Shirtings, 66 and 72 reeds, 37 1-2 yards, notwithstanding the immense increase of production, are still very scarce ; the supply so far having been very inadequate. An advance has been established during the month of 4-12d to 6d per piece. All descriptions of the lower reeded cloths—6s's for instance and under—have likewise experienced a very extensive demand, and are now realizing, though more is asked, 3d to 6d per piece more than could have been obtained for them a month ago. Generally they are very scarce with many manufacturers under contract for some time. In some instaeces, however, orders are approaching early completion, and here and there a few may be met with. Considerable quantities of 72's, 66's, 64's, and 60's continue to be taken for printing purposes : a fact which has necessarily diminished the consumption of 7-8ths printing cloths, and tended to make 40 inch shirtings more scarce. Wider widths, say 45, 50, and 54-inch shirtings, have also been in very good demand throughout the month, and are scarce. Upon them the advance will amount to about 3d per piece in all reeds.

27-inch Printers, 66 and 72 reeds, 28 yards, have also been in very great demand, including 26-inch in the former reed, throughout the month, and are as regards 66's about 3d per piece higher. 72's may be said to have advanced fully 4 1-2d per piece All qualities in each reed are very scarce. The demand for the lower reeded cloths has been very considerable, and the advance upon them will vary from 1 1-2d to 3d per piece. Of such there are no stocks. 27-inch twills are scarce, and about 1 1-2d to 3d per piece higher. Good 28-inch 66's and 72's are likewise scarce, with the former 3d to 4 1-2d per piece dearer, and the latter 1 1-2d to 3d. As frequently noticed previously, this width in each reed is but of iimited production. All descriptions of 9-8ths in 66's and 72's have been in very great demand, and are fully 4 1-2d to 6d per piece higher than they were at the end of June. There are no stocks, and orders for immediate delivery could not be executed, as all (or nearly) the manufacturers are under contracts. The same may be said of all the lower reeded cloths in 9-8ths.

T CLOTHS.—The low qualities are quoted 1 1-2d per piece higher and the best 3d, and a fair business has been done in each. Both descriptions are plentiful. With respect to the medium fabrics, of which stocks are heavy, very little has been done in them, and though an advance of 1 1-2 to 3d per piece is asked, extensive purchases might be effected at the rates ruling a month ago.

9-8 GREY MADDAPOLAMS, 24 yards, in all qualities, have experienced a very extensive demand throughout the month, and, as has been stated with respect to certain other descriptions of goods, orders for immediate delivery could not be executed, as all the manufacturers are under contract for some time to come. The low qualities may be considered 1 1-2d and 3d per piece higher, and the medium and best 6d.

9-8 and 6-4 LONG CLOTHS, 36 yards, exhibit an apparent improvement in value varying from 1 1-2d to 4d per piece, according to quality. These, however, form but a very inconclusive data, as many descriptions must be considered nominal in price in the absence of any general or active demand. All descriptions are plentiful in stock, and the demand during the month has been chiefly confined to the low qualities. The absence of active operations [on Greek account tells seriously against such goods and T cloths.

DOMESTICS, in the low and narrow descriptions, have been in very good demand, and are scarce. Upon such an advance varying from 1-16th to 1-8th per yard has been established. As regards some of the medium qualities the same may be reported, but generally no improvement has taken place. Stocks are moderate, and with respect to the best and heavy makes, little or no alteration can be noted. Of such stocks continue heavy, and for quantities the manufacturers would hardly be able to realize any advance. Still, generally, the position of this description of cloth is better.

Velveteens and Moleskins are, as regards the latter, about 5 per cent higher, with much lighter stocks, a very good demand having prevailed throughout the early part of the month. One-half ells and five-eighth velveteens, which have likewise advanced about 5 per cent, have been in very good demand, and are very scarce. As regards price velvets, they are very scarce, the demand for them fully equal to the supply.

Prints, with which the market is still very barely supplied, continue to be in very good demand, and particularly so as regards 5-4th's for the country trade. All the printers are very busy, and various new dark styles have since our last report, made their appearance.

Some of the calico printers are well supplied with cloth, bought at comparatively lower prices than are ruling at present, which enables them to sell prints at proportionably cheap rates, and less interruption is therefore experienced in the execution of orders in these and other fancy goods. The accounts which we have recently received from America, Mexico, and some other important markets for prints do not, however, give much encouragement for purchases even at the old prices, and printers therefore have little inducement to pay the advance upon grey cloth.

The prospects for the harvest remain good, notwithstanding the late rain by which which wheat has been laid in some localities.

We perceive the same disinclination to purchase at present, on the large home-trade houses, as exists among the foreign houses. We do not attribute this to the late railway exposes as some are inclined to do, nor take any change in the general aspects of affairs, but solely to a caution generally exercised by the home-trade houses when the purchases on foreign accounts are partially suspended. The consumption of cotton is equal to about 32,000 bags per week, and can be maintained only when all markets inland and foreign remain in a satisfactory state.

NORFOLK, Friday, Aug. 17.

SAILING OF THE STEAMER LEGARE, &c.—The U. S. Steamer Legare sailed from this port yesterday. The steamer Sea Gull has arrived.

Commercial and Money Matters.

FRIDAY, August 17.

SALES AT THE SECOND BOARD.

$5,000 U S 6s '56.... 107		50 Erie RR........ 59⅞
100 shs Read RR.... 34		36 do.......... 59¾

SATURDAY, August 16.

SALES AT THE STOCK EXCHANGE.

$5,000 U S 6s '67...s3.114½	20 shs Manh Bk.....103
4,000 do.......114⅝	1 Bank of NY.....128
10,000 do '68.....114¾	30 Brook & Jam RR. 84
5,000 do.....s3 114¾	150 Canton......... 38⅜
8,000 do coup....114¼	10 Harlem......... 53
4,000 Treas 6s.....113⅞	150 do.......s10 52¾
600 do.......114	150 do......b30 53
5,000 NY Cor bds '75 102	50 de.......... 52⅞
1,000 Penn 5s...... 87¼	350 do.......... 52¾
10,000 do....... 87⅛	25 Long Island...s3 19¾
5,000 do.....s3 87⅛	50 Erie RR.....b90 60
5,000 Int Imp stk.s90 43	100 do......b60 60
1,000 Read Bds..... 57¼	36 do.......... 59⅞
100 shs Far Trust... 38⅛	5 do.......... 59¾
100 do........b3 38	50 do......b90 60¼

Commercially the European news by the steamer does not amount to much, and the heaviness of government stocks abroad has originated a corresponding depression here.

The coming crops are represented as being in fine condition, and the yield promises to be abundant.

Under such auspices, it is not to be wondered, at the anxiety of speculators to realize, and we consequently find the shipments continually as active as ever; amounting last week to 32,047 bbls. of flour, and 86,207 in corn ; and that too in the face of an over stocked market.

This unusual movement can be attributed to nothing else then to the unexpected increase of the past year's crop ; amounting in fact to over 136,684 bbls. since the opening of river navigation.

The new crop is now upon us, and a few days will find the fresh stock rapidly arriving, when present prices must give way.

There is no change to notice in the money market as yet, but with the rapid accumulation of specie in the coffers of the customs, in payment of importations, together with the renewed activity of the Fall trade, an increase in the value of mouey may be daily expected.

New-York Markets.

Reported for the Evening Day-Book.

SATURDAY Morning, Aug. 18.

ASHES.—The market is steady, with sales of 40 bbls at $6 00 for Pot and Pearl.

COTTON.—There is but little doing in this stable, the market is in favor of the buyer, with sales of 800 bbls.

FLOUR, &c.—Our market for Western and State Flour for the new and medium grades is again 6¼ better, induced by the limited receipts, and a good speculative demand for Western account. Considerable parcels have been withdrawn from the market. There is less doing for the East aud city trade. The sales of the day reach 5,800 bbls a4 00a4 62½ for some ; 4 25a4 7 for Fine ; 4 25a4 87½ for Uninspected ; 5 44a5 50 for common State and mixed Western ; 5 50 a5 56½ for straight State and good Michigan : 5 56a5 68¾ for fine Genesee and favorite Indianna ; 5 75a 5 81 for good staaight Ohio ; 5 87½a6 12½ for Fancy State and Ohio ; 5 87½a6 12½ for Extra Ohio ; and 6 12½a6 62½ for Extta Genesee, (old.) and 6 75a7 00 for new. Southern Flour is in firm demand, with sales of 10,000 bbls a5 37½ a5 44 for Alexandria, and old Brandywine, and 5 50 for new Brandywine. Rye Flour is better, with sales of 680 bbls a3 25a3 37½. Corn Meal is scarce, better, with sales of 600 bbls Jersey, part to arrive a3 31 a3 37½.

GRAIN.—Our market is firm for Wheat, but the supply of prime is limited ; the sales include 8,000 bush inferior Upper Lake on terms not made public—and 1,400 bush Ohio in store at about $1 15. Rye is again better with sales of 4,000 bush at 62a62½c delivered. Corn is rather better with a fair demand, and sales of 23,000 bush at 60 for heated ; 62a63½ for Western yellow ; 63a 63½ for Jersey and Northern yellow ; and 53½a64 for flat yellow. Oats are down and quiet at 39a40½ for Northern . 34a35 for Jersey.

WOOL—There is but little activity in this staple, the receipts continue large, reaching 1,000 bales within foar days, the tendency is still upward, the sales reach 30,000 lb the past two days at 27a28 for common ; 33 for ¾ blood; 35 for marine, and 39 for Saxony. There is a steady demand for Lambs pulled at 27a29 ; manufacturers buy sparingly.

PROVISIONS.—The market is very dull for Pork, some 400 bbls sold in lots to the trade, at 10 75 for mess; 10 25 for thin mess; and 9 00 for prime. Lord is firm, there is some demand for superior lots for the French market. The sales are 950 bbls at 5a6c for common to white grease; and 7c for very extra leaf lard. Beef is firm but quiet, at 13 50a$14 for mess. Cut meats are steady, with sales 26 bbls good hams, at 7c. Butter is less active but firm, at 10a14½c for Western; and 7a11½c for Ohio. Cheese is more plenty, and saleable at 2a7c.

LIME—We notice sales of 1,000 bbls Thomastone at 85c, cash.

HAY—There is no change in the market, sales of 1000 bales, at 45a50c.

IRON—A firmer market, with sales of 60 tons American on private terms, and 200 tons Scotch pig, at $22, six months.

GINSING—We notice a sale 1,200 lbs, good white, at 30c, cash.

NAVAL STORES—The market if better for Spirits, with sales of 50 bbls at 34½, cash; and 900 bbls Tar, at 1 87½, cash.

FREIGHTS—Are entirely nominal, and but listle offering

New-York Markets.

Reported for the Evening Day-Book.

SATURDAY, Aug. 18—12 o'clock M.

ASHES—The market is steady at $6 00 for Pot and Pearl.

COTTON—Private advices are more favorable than the published accounts by the steamer, and the market is firm.

FLOUR, &c.—There is but little change to notice in our market, the storm in the morning restricted the sales. They reach 2,000 bbls, at 4 00a4 62½ for some; 4 25a475 for Fine; 5 00 for common State and mixed Western.

GRAIN—There is but little prime Wheat here, and we have no sales of any kind to export; the demand is good for milling. Rye is better, with small sales, at 62a62½ cts. Oats are dull and down: sales at 38a40 for Northern, and 34a34 for Jersep. Corn is dull but firm; sales 3000 bushels at 52a63½ for Western mixed; 63a63½ for round yellow, and 64 for flat yellow.

WHISKEY—The market if bare; to arrive 26c is offered for Ohio and Prisen; Drudge is held at 26c, time.

PROVISIONS—There is nothing doing in Pork, holders are firm at $10 75 for mess, and 9 for Prime. Beef is in steady demand at 13 50a14 for mess. Cut meats are quiet at 7 for Ham and 5 for shoulders. Butter and checco are quiet, prices steady. Lard is in fair demand at 6½a7 for good, to extra there is some inquiry for the French market for extra quality.

DAY-BOOK MARINE JOURNAL.

PORT OF NEW-YORK, AUGUST 18, 1849.

ARRIVED THIS MORNING.

U S M Steamship Tennessee, Captain Cole, 63 hours from Savannah, to S S Mitchell. Saturday morning, 7 o'clock, 17 miles N of Barnegat, passed Bark Missouri, bound in.

Passengers—W F Bryant. Mrs Bryant & Son, Mrs Cowles Mrs Chandler, Mr J H Whitttlesay, Mrs Whittlesay, John R Wilder, G S Harping, S P Griffin, USN, J S Fay, John Treanor, H P Hastings, John F Christian, E A Glass C Petty, M J Gayton, Charles Millard E W Pervine, Wm Oliver, Sohn Willard, A Girrard, P McGreedy Wm Belden, J E Clarke, J M Muldon R G Hobbs, B A J L Robinson, G R Barker, J L Cornish, D A McRae, A Huntington, A Allen, J W Saunbers, Mr Roberts, W Davis, L Davis, Mr Moore, J R Crozier, G H Bestwick, and two in the steerage

Sch Exchange, Sweet, fm Suffolk, Va.
Sch Mary Ann & Susan, Browne, fm N Carolina.
Sch May Crabtre, fm N Carolina
Sch Belle, Brittingham fm Virginia.
BELOW—Bark Missouri, fm Malaga, to Chamberlain & Phelps. Also 1 Ship and 1 Brig unknown.
Wind—S E.

New-York Daily Times.

THE NEW-YORK DAILY TIMES IS PUBLISHED EVERY MORNING (*Sunday excepted*,) at the office, No. 113 NASSAU-STREET, between Beekman and Ann, just behind the Old Park Theater, and delivered to subscribers in the city, Brooklyn, Williamsburgh and Jersey City for six cents a week; or, when they prefer, they can pay in advance at the Desk for six months or a year at the same rate. Single copies, ONE CENT. Mail subscribers, FOUR DOLLARS a year.

THE NEW-YORK EVENING TIMES IS PUBLISHED EVERY EVENING, (*Sundays excepted*,) on the same terms as the Morning Edition.

THE NEW-YORK WEEKLY TIMES, A VERY LARGE NEWSPAPER FOR THE COUNTRY, is published every *Saturday Morning*, at the low price of $2 per annum. Ten copies for $15, or twenty copies for $20, will be sent to one address, and the paper in no case continued beyond the time for which payment is made.

Payment in all cases must be paid in advance.

RAYMOND, JONES & CO., Publishers.

New-York Daily Times.

VOL. I.....NO. 1. NEW-YORK, THURSDAY, SEPTEMBER 18, 1851. PRICE ONE CENT.

New-York Daily Times.

THE NEWS FROM EUROPE.

ARRIVAL OF THE EUROPA'S MAILS.

AFFAIRS IN ENGLAND.

The Election in France---Arrests, &c.

APPREHENDED DISTURBANCE IN AUSTRIA.

SOUTHERN EUROPE.

The Royal Mail Steamer *Europa* arrived at Boston yesterday morning, at about 6 o'clock. Her mails were sent on by the New Haven Railroad train, which left at 8 o'clock, and reached this city at an early hour last evening.

By this arrival we have received our regular English and French files, with correspondence, circulars, &c., to Saturday, September 6th—the *Europa's* day of sailing.

The news by this arrival has considerable interest, though it is not of startling importance.

In ENGLAND, political affairs are quiet. The *Humboldt* arrived at Southampton on Thursday, the 4th, with the news of the execution at Havana of the fifty men under Col. Crittenden's command. The details of the news are given at length in the London papers.

In FRANCE attention is chiefly absorbed with speculations on the approaching Presidential election. The Prince de Joinville is clearly to be a candidate, and will doubtless be a more formidable opponent of Louis Napoleon than any other that could be selected.

Another "Conspiracy" has been discovered in Paris; forty-seven arrests have been made by the Police.

In AUSTRIA hostility to the government still smoulders under the surface with occasional outbreaks. An affray took place near Gross-Waradin, between a rustic wedding party and several *Gendarmes*, of the most brutal character.

In PORTUGAL attention is absolved by an accusation of a Cabinet Minister of bribery. He has resigned and come before the courts of law.

The news of KOSSUTH's release is confirmed, but the time is now said to have been the 13th of September. It is said that he proposes to go first to England and provide there for the education of his children and then proceed to the United States.

The money market presents no feature of marked interest.

GREAT BRITAIN.

The Queen was absent on her visit to Scotland where she had been very enthusiastically received. The Exhibition continues to attract numerous visiters. The attendance and receipts were:

Tuesday, ...	49,866 persons—	£2,407,15s.
Wednesday, ...	41,917 persons—	2,080,12s.
Thursday, ...	44,209 persons—	2,137,18s.

The necessity of reducing prices is strongly urged.

In Dublin it is stated that the Government intend to send four additional regiments of infantry from England, to enforce obedience to the law. The correspondent of *The Times* denounces this as simply preposterous.

The Freeman's Journal announces the death of one of the celebrities of the memorable year 1843, namely, the Rev. Thomas Tierney, one of the two clergymen included in the monster indictment of the then Attorney General, Mr. A. B. C. Smith. Up to 1843 he was one of the most active supporters of the Repeal movement headed by O'Connell.

DUBLIN, Sept. 4.—The weather has been extremely fine during the present week, and the agricultural reports from all parts of the country are proportionably favorable. In the south, harvest operations are nearly completed, and the yield is said to be good, both as regards quantity and quality. Of the potato the reports continue conflicting, but, making every due allowance for the loss by the fatal epidemic, there appears to be no rational doubt that enough will be saved to supply the wants of a greatly diminished population. In the meanwhile the tide of emigration still rolls on.

A new feature in connexion with emigration has just manifested itself, in the departure, by the emigrant ship Celeste, for Quebec, of a number of comfortable families, of the farming class, from the neighborhood of Park, near this city. So fertile and remunerating were the lands of Park considered for the last 30 years, that they were designated "the golden gardens of the city," yielding as they did successive rotation crops (chiefly vegetables and prime feeding for milch cows) throughout the year. The scene is changed, and the result now is, that the greater portion of the people of Park, a most industrious and expert class of agriculturalists, are determined to endure no longer the hardships to which they were of late years subjected to meet solely the demands of "tax gatherers, poor rate collectors, and landlords," without being able to provide ordinary comfort for their families.

The performances of the American yacht continue to attract attention. Several writers in *The Times* and other papers are drawing attention to the peculiarities of her construction and recommending the imitation of her to English builders.

The American and English Yachts.

To the Editor of The Times:

SIR—It is always regarded in history as peculiar to the most distinguished generals, that they have best known how to turn disasters to profitable use, and have frequently converted the ruins of defeat into foundations of victory. We are now in circumstances which give full scope to the display of such qualities, if we possess them. We have been beaten—signally defeated—on our own element. Our yacht squadron, so long masters of the Solent, hitherto victorious in all sea fights, are completely routed—I had almost said, put to flight. For a long time, not one of the Solent Sea Kings could be found to face the enemy or accept his challenge, and the American would have returned without his gage being taken up, had not the little Titania, of only half the tonnage, and therefore no adequate match, been courageous enough to hazard a defeat. Even the Alarm, which had been so long the champion of the English waters, declined battle. The victory of the America is complete.

[The writer then goes on at considerable length to specify the peculiarities of the *America* and concludes thus:]

I have entered thus minutely into all these points, because I conceive it to be of great importance that we should wisely and in time prepare ourselves for the probable contest of next year. We are more likely to fail next year by a blundering imitation of the unessentials of our victor than by any other course. It is most undesirable that we should be driven by a sudden defeat to abandon any of the excellent points which our own long experience may have taught us to be unquestionably excellent. The roominess, the comfort, the excellent sea-going qualities, the ease of motion in bad weather, are points in our own yacht-building which we must on no account abandon. It is our duty, therefore, to see what we must do to win next year.

1. We must build yachts of the newest construction, of as large a size as may be likely to come against us—*i. e.* somewhat larger than the America; and not allow ourselves to be caught, as this year, with a vessel of half the tonnage only fit even to accept the challenge.

2. We must adopt the best scientific principles of construction for the build of our new yachts, instead of allowing old maxims of routine to govern us. The Americans have boldly adopted the wave system, and applied it to the America in an unmitigated form; we must as boldly adopt it, and give speed to our vessels by offering to the water that form which shall produce the least disturbance in it, and receive from it the least resistance.

3. We must not abandon such forms of midship section as have been found to give easy motion and good sea qualities to our own yachts.

4. We must thoroughly revise our system of rigging and cutting sails. The true theory of sails is that they are flat boards. All mechanical means must be adopted to give them that form, and make them keep it. The superior cut of American sails has long been matter of notoriety to seamen. Sail-cutters have long resisted the abandonment of cherished prejudices on this head. They must now at once adopt the true sail-theory of plane surfaces, and carry it out—whether with the use of booms or a new cut, or both, they must well consider.

5. As to rigging, the simpler the rigging, the fewer the ropes, the better. The Americans have long been distinguished in this respect for simplicity and efficiency. Multiplicity of ropes and blocks is an old-fashioned error, out of which we are rapidly escaping, and the America merely gives us a fresh impulse in this direction.

In conclusion, I have only to express a hope—one which has prompted this letter—that we shall not degenerate into vulgar imitation of our victor, a course in which we shall always be behind him; but rouse ourselves to apply more independently than hitherto the resources of our science and skill to the attainment of that superiority in yacht building, which we have hitherto fancied we possessed. I have the honor to be your obedient servant, A MEMBER OF SEVERAL YACHT CLUBS.

From The London Spectator, Aug. 30.

Off one of our great naval ports, the shipbuilding of England has been challenged by an alien vessel, and defeated totally. It is a remarkable incident, and not satisfactory to the national pride.

We may find solace in the fact that it is due to "accident." Strange as it must appear, it has only been in comparatively recent times that attempts have been made to reduce the water-cleaving power of the ship to scientific rule; and hitherto science has not been happy in its efforts. The victory of the America, if we are not mistaken, practically refutes the newest hypothesis in the search for the philosopher's stone in the science of shipbuilding. The principle of Mr. Scott Russell's plan, we believe, was based on the fact that water displaced by a body which is removed fills the vacuity, not so much by falling in at the sides as by rising from below; hence it was calculated that if a vessel was built sharp and deep toward the bows, broad and shallow toward the stern, the very act of the water in rising to supply the displacement would aid the impetus on the body of the vessel; and experiment tended to justify that expectation. The make of the America, we understand, is quite the reverse of that just described: the bows are sharp, and the breadth of beam, which is considerable, is greatest about parallel to the mainmast; so far coinciding with the other model. But the draught of water at the bows is trifling—about three feet; and it deepens to three times as much toward the stern.

The make is not conducive to great freightage capacity; yet its origin is commercial. American shippers have inclined lately to prefer speed to large capacity; as they find that rapidity, by facilitating certainty of movement and a multiplicity of voyages within a given time, returns a larger profit than slower and more uncertain voyaging with greater bulk. The model of the America is the result.

The *good luck* of the discovery has first fallen to the United States; but there is no room either for chagrin or dismay. Ship-building in this country is not stagnant; a considerable number of ships are made annually, and there can be no doubt that any well-tested model will soon find its way to our docks. We shall not therefore, be much behind in the practical progress of ship-building. Nor is it to be assumed, that because empiricism has beaten science, that the latter is to yield in despair. On the contrary, empiricism has always been the jackal to theoretic science, and every discovery by the working shipwright only brings us nearer to the desideratum—a scientific rule. We have heard an American express the hope that England, by beating America, would give the impulse for a new effort, which should again give his country a new triumph. Such friendly emulation is not rivalry: it is but the pride of him, who for the moment gets foremost in the search for the common good. A more invidious feeling would have kept the America at a distance from our waters: as it is, our friends hasten over, with a natural pride, to make us a party in the new idea.

From the London Examiner, Aug. 30.

The American challenge stipulating for at least a six-knot breeze, proves that the America must be a wholesome as well as a fast craft. A six-knot breeze with a dead beat in a head sea would be too much for many of our crack yachts, which, if they are brought to reducing sail, are overwhelmed by the excess of their masts and spars in a sea way.

The truth is, they are built for the inside of the Isle of Wight, and for owners who take to yachting for fashion's sake, knowing nothing about the matter, having no real taste for the sea, subject to sickness, and confining their trips to Hurst Castle to the west, Ryde and Portsmouth to the east, and preferring to them the Southampton water if a weather-tide raises a popple on the gentle Solent. The great pleasure of these gentlemen is to swagger about in sea-toggery, and to have boats'-crews in smart equipment dangling after them. Many a yacht hardly stirs from its moorings at Cowes in a whole season; but to make up for that inaction, there is plenty of boat-work, rowing backwards and forwards, hailing and signalling. There are exceptions; there are some score of the two hundred members of the Royal Squadron Club who are good seamen, ay, and competent navigators to boot; but the great majority are unskilled. The other Clubs contain a much larger proportion of seamen among their members, because with them it is not a matter of fashion so much as it is with the aristocratic Squadron. Some years ago a member of the Thames Club undertook to man his yacht (between 60 and 70 tuns) with gentlemen, members of the Club, exclusively, not employing a single working-man, and to sail her against any vessel of the Squadron, manned in like manner; but the challenge fell to the ground. And well it might, for though there are some few members of the Royal Yacht Squadron who know whether a gaff-topsail is properly set or not, we have our doubts whether there is one who could go aloft and lace it to the topmast. But no matter how shallow the taste is, or how much is mere fashion, the fashion is a good one, and has excellent consequences susceptible of further improvement, which we trust the present lesson of the America will stimulate.

The veteran yachter, the Marquis of Anglesea, upon seeing the America, is reported to have remarked, "If she is right, we are all wrong."

It is to be borne in mind, however, that something besides speed is to be considered in the yacht. A yacht must have stowage and accommodation, and both these points are in the America sacrificed to speed. Still we have no doubt that something may be learnt from a craft which requires a six-not breeze, and beats our clippers; and it is her model, not her canvass, that must be looked to for the lesson.

Kossuth and Austria.

From The London Daily News, Sept. 2.

This is the day on which the Sultan promised to liberate Kossuth, Perczel, Bathyani, and the illustrious prisoners of Kutahia. Since the fact was first announced, as it was by us some weeks back, a regular fire of menace has been kept up by all the organs, or would-be organs of the great military governments. They would break with the Porte, the ambassadors should be withdrawn, retaliation taken by reëxciting the Bosnian insurrection; and the whole East was to be convulsed because Kossuth was allowed to receive visits at Bayswater instead of planting cabbages and defending himself against assassins at Kutahia.

The question is, in truth, one of mere sentiment and humanity; for no one hopes or thinks to work harm to the Empires of Austria and Russia, or to disturb their peace by liberating Kossuth. Admiration for the past, not intrigue for the future, is the sole motive with our Hungarian sympathizers. But the solemn politicians of St. Petersburg and Vienna cannot understand that the most practical of earthly races, the Anglo-Saxon, should simultaneously, in England and in America, have been taken with such enthusiastic sympathy for the Hungarian cause, and for its chiefs, unless some deep policy lay at the bottom of it. We need not say to English readers that neither Britons nor Americans have the least admixture of policy in their love of Hungary and Kossuth. It is from sentiment, the unmingled homage paid to brave men struggling in a righteous cause.

The future fate of Hungary and its definitive connexion with Austria, are things, we believe, very much in Austria's own power. After the complete conquest it has effected, great wisdom, moderation, and liberality on her part might, we have no doubt, secure Hungary to the HAPSBURGS and to the Austrian power too firmly for KOSSUTH and all his influence to shake. But there is no wisdom, moderation, or liberality in the conduct of Austria.

Not only is barefaced tyranny the adopted principle of government, but it is the avowed one. Until now the Austrian ministers were supposed to be responsible to the nation, or to some imaginary States. Hopes of a constitutional system, at least for the future, were not at an end. The fiction of ministerial responsibility did not the least detract from the absolute power of the government. But the young Emperor would not tolerate the decorous fiction. And he has published a solemn decree, declaring that his ministers are only responsible to himself. Every one well knew such to be the fact. Why then declare it? In order to promulgate divine right in theory as well as practice, and to seek to establish it as a philosophic truth, what was already established in the only way it could be established, by force.

Such *doctrinaires* of despotism, such puerile politicians, monarchs whose sovereignty is unbounded by the horizon of their staff, and statesmen who have taken a personal pique to constitutions—such men as these cannot found an empire, re-attach defective provinces, or give that confidence and freedom, without which industry cannot breathe, nor prosperity be developed. The hope of consolidating such an empire as that of Germany, by denying in royal and imperial edicts, the *grundrecht* or national rights, voted by national assemblies, and promulgating instead the law of ministers, being only responsible to sovereigns, and sovereigns to GOD; this is the current mistake of seeking to pacify the nineteenth century by reducing it to the ignorantism and servility of the fifteenth.

The big children, who assert that political wisdom is the gift of Heaven, and who prove themselves possessed of it by governing in this way, may well dread Kossuth, as they must dread every independent man that wields a sword or a pen. Well may they tremble at every shadow. And yet they are wrong to dread individuals, and mean to move Heaven and earth to fetter down one political Prometheus like Kossuth. For their system of government soon converts a whole people into a tacit band of conspirators, biding their time to be insurgents, and only biding that opportunity from the certainty, that a fatuitous goverment cannot fail to afford it.

However, we may foresee all this in the inevitable course of things, we have no wish to interfere, to foment conspiracies, or keep alive a war of jealousy with a great European power, whatever the folly of its misgovernment. Such abuses always cure themselves without foreign intervention; and if we should hail with pure welcome and delight the coming of Kossuth to our shores it is with no desire to prompt or aid him to a renewal of that contest, which for the present epoch has been decided in the field.

FRANCE.

PARIS, Wednesday Evening, Sept. 3.

The announcement of the Prince de Joinville as candidate for the Presidency of the Republic has created a great sensation here, and affords the Paris papers ample food for comment. It would appear that a considerable portion of the Orleanists are dissatisfied with the appearance of the Prince de Joinville as a candidate. Some of them fear that he will be beaten, and that the defeat will have an injurious effect on the consideration of the Orleans family with the country. Others look on the candidateship with coldness, because it was started by *The Ordre*, the organ of M. Thiers. An article appears in *The Assemblée Nationale* of to-day, which has excited great surprise. That paper, which is the organ of M. Guizot and of the Fusionists, declares that if the Prince de Joinville should be so ill-advised as really to throw himself into the revolutionary conflict of 1852, "it would not hesitate to combat with all its force a candidateship which would be a serious injury to the Monarchical principle, and would throw the country into an ocean of difficulties and dangers." Upon the whole, the impression created among the Orleanists, by the announcement, appears to be that the policy of allowing a Prince of the House of Orleans to appear as a candidate for the Presidency of the Republic, is extremely doubtful in itself, and that, at all events, the announcement is premature. As regards the Legitimists, they declare their determined hostility to the "adventure," and treat the whole affair with ridicule. *The Univers*, the organ of M. de Montalembert and the clergy, also opposes the Prince de Joinville, and foretells that the result must be "the abasement, and probably the ruin, of the Orleans family, which has so long, so terribly, and so perseveringly erred."

It must be admitted that the Prince de Joinville is decidedly the most formidable opponent that Louis Napoleon has yet had to contend with. The friends of the President are fully alive to the danger, and are using every effort to meet it. None of Louis Napoleon's friends seem to think that the Prince de Joinville will have a majority of votes at the election, but they know that all the votes given to the Prince de Joinville will be taken from Louis Napoleon, so that the final choice of a President will probably be left to the Assembly, which is not by any means well-disposed towards the present President.

The number of councils-general, which up to the present time have recorded resolutions in favor of the revision of the Constitution amounts to about sixty. Out of this number about fifteen have declared themselves in favor of the prolongation of the Powers of the President.

The council of war of Marseilles has just pronounced judgment on five men belonging to the 11th regiment of dragoons, who were tried for having excited their comrades to insubordination and revolt, in June last, at Orange. Four of them have been condemned to death, and the fifth acquitted.

P. S. 6½ *o'clock.*—For several days vague rumors of a plot, discovered in Paris, have prevailed. Last night a number of arrests were made, in relation to which I have just heard the following account. It has for some time been known to the police that Ledru Rollin and Mazzini's Central European Committee were in correspondence, through the Central German Committee of London, with a German committee sitting in Paris. A man named Meir was the delegate employed to transmit instructions to the Paris committee from the two committees in London. Besides this, an advocate, named Maillard, formerly secretary to Ledru Rollin, was instructed by the latter to organize an insurrectional committee in Paris, ready to take arms at a signal to be given by the Central European Committee of London. Such was the activity of Maillard that he had formed the neucleus of a society that had put itself in communication with the departments, and had made such progress as to be able to send to London within the last few days to take Ledru Rollin's final instructions.

It was on the return to Paris of the emissary sent on this occasion that the Prefect of Police informed the authorities that the time had come for putting a stop to all these proceedings. Warrants were issued simultaneously to arrest persons designated at St. Amand. Forty-seven arrests have been made. All the prisoners have been sent to the prison of Mazas, and this explains the reason why the Prefect of Police has within these few days sent away several prisoners who were there, in order to have vacant cells at his disposition.

The most prominent among the persons arrested are M. Dalicau, the director of *The Voix du Proscrit*, and M. Maillard, the advocate. The rest are obscure individuals, principally journeymen, tradesmen, and mechanics. One of them named J. J. Cherval, a lithographer, is described as an "Irish subject." Last night, at about 9 o'clock, 60 "Sergens de Ville" marched to the Café de la Haute-Saône, Rue Grenelle St. Honoré, where they arrested a dozen persons. Several brigades of police were sent in the night to different quarters of Paris, wich instructions to execute warrants of arrest. As many as 80 prisoners have already been sent to the Mazas prison.

It is said at the Palais de Justice that most important papers, emanating from the London Committees, have been seized.

Paris is absolutely quiet, and no alarm or even excitement has been produced in the public mind.

AUSTRIA.

VIENNA, Aug. 27.—The decrees of the Emperor on the responsibility of the ministers, and on the revision of the constitution, *octroyée* in March, 1849, amount to a complete retrogression to absolutism.

In Italy, Radetski fears an outbreak, and the army is said to be reinforced for the third time—ten thousand men are to march to the Piedmontese frontier. There is a report that the dissensions between the Croat and Hungarian soldiers are daily increasing, and that they led to a bloody conflict in the neighborhood of Verona. The papers remain silent on such events, but the letters from Italy mention it as a fact. In Hungary the gendarmerie had had several conflicts with the peasants, and a tragedy which in the month of June happened at Szent Maria, near Gross-Waradin, is soul-stirring, like an episode of a French novel. I relate it as I had it from an Hungarian gentleman of the Bihar county, who happened to be at Vienna.

At a peasant's wedding, when the procession of the betrothed was moving toward the church, the gendarme approached the bride and summoned her immediately to divest herself of the red, white and green ribbons which she had in her tresses, according to the custom of the country girls, saying that these colors were revolutionary. The bridegroom objected, saying that after the ceremony the bride would comply with the desire of the gendarme, but that now they could not keep the priest waiting at the altar. The gendarme retired, the procession proceeded to the church, but at the moment the bride was kneeling at the steps of the altar to receive the benediction, the gendarme rushed forward and cut her tresses and ribbons with scissors from her head. In Hungary it is considered a great insult to a female to cut her hair; it conveys the notion of infamy. Naturally an affray took place; the gendarme was assailed by the bridegroom, other gendarmes arrived in aid of their fellow-official, the people, though without arms, rushed upon them, and the result was the slaughter of seven men, three gendarmes and four peasants, amongst them the bridegroom and the brutal assailant of the bride.

The Preussische Zeitung says, that Austria has just obtained by negotiation a military right of way through Bavaria for the passage of troops to the federal fortress of Mayence.

A telegraphic dispatch from Ischl, received in Vienna on the 31st, announces that the Emperor of Austria will prolong his stay in that watering place until the 6th inst. Nothing has transpired relative to the interview between him and the King of Prussia.

SPAIN.

MADRID, Aug. 29.—The principal topic of the provincial journals is still the serious effects produced by the long drought and extraordinary heat. At Madrid we have now been four months without rain. The country is burnt up, and fires, extending in some cases over many leagues, are no doubt the result of this state of things. Great scarcity of water was felt at Saragossa, and throughout Aragon, and the most rigorous measures had been decreed by the authorities to preserve a supply for the most indispensable purposes.

A Gijon letter of the 25th says that five leagues of the railway there would shortly be open to public traffic, and speaks of the great natural difficulties overcome in constructing it.

TURKEY.

CONSTANTINOPLE, Aug. 16.—The liberation of Kossuth is now decided upon by the Sublime Porte.—In spite of all the threats of Russia and Austria, the porte stood her ground, and when reminded by the English government of its promise, the Divan replied, "We keep it." Kossuth is, therefore to be released on the 13th September. His intention, as far as I could ascertain, is to proceed first to England, to leave there his children, and to provide for their education, and after a stay of a fortnight, to sail to the United States, there to express his thanks to the Congress and the President.—But the Captain of the steam frigate Mississippi, which has waited for Kossuth since the month of June, objects to this arrangement; he wishes to carry Kossuth without delay to New-York. I do not know, therefore, whether you will have the pleasure of seeing the mighty man—who, even when in prison in Asia Minor, frightens the Czar and the Kaiser—before December.

The dismissal of the seraskier, Mehemet Ali Pasha, made here, for a moment a painful impression, for everybody knew that he, the brother-in-law to the Sultan, was the greatest enemy to Russia in the cabinet. But it soon became obvious that this step had no political importance whatever.

PORTUGAL.

LISBON, Aug. 29.—Public attention is chiefly directed towards the accusation of bribery preferred against Senhor Ferrao, which compelled him to retire from the Ministry. The accusation is of so serious and grave a nature that the Ministry had a meeting upon the subject (Senhor Ferrao not having been present at it), when, it is said, it was determined that he should be invited to resign and carry the accusation before the tribunals, he being accused of having received from the contract of tobacco 2,093,600 reis. This Senhor Ferrao has done.

The heat and the drought this year is without example. Accounts from the country say the small rivers are drying up.

The ports of Ceara in the Brazils are declared infected with the yellow fever, and those of Moroco with cholera.

The Government has advertised for proposals to complete the roads and form new ones in the Minho. The former contractors, conceiving it an infringement of their rights, protest against it, and say they shall have recourse to the tribunals. There is to be a new road from Oporto to Braga, and another from Oporto to Guimaraens.

It appears that several officers of the 14th, at Vizeu, endeavored to make their escape, but were prevented and placed in arrest. A general officer is implicated in the attempted insurrection.

Another serious conspiracy, that was to have broken out at Vizeu, and had extensive ramifications, has been rendered abortive.

The elections of the electoral Commissioners are in the gross in favor of Government and Septembristas.

BREMEN.

The treasurer of the head corporation school of Bremen, who held large sums of money in trust for that establishment, as well as for other institutions, has been arrested, charged with embezzling upwards of 120,000 thalers. The arrest of this man, whose name is Haase, who was an alderman of the city, and a most esteemed member of the corporation, created quite a sensation.

BAVARIA.

AUG. 29.—The sale of cavalry and artillery horses has suddenly been stopped, and new purchases are to be made by order of the Minister of War. We are told that the late movement of troops was in consequence of some possible eventuality in France. But the Munich correspondent of a Brussels paper, who is apparantly well informed, says the military movements are nothing more than the ordinary garrison changes, consequent upon the manœuvres which take place in the autumn of every year.

FRANKFORT.

The Frankfort Diet has taken its first resolution, says *The Augsburgh Gazette*, in commercial affairs. It has adopted as the basis of deliberation in these matters, the resolutions of the Dresden Conferences. *The Augsburg Gazette* says that the Diet has again called special men together, to give it special information on the subject.

The same journal affirms that the Diet have come to the formal resolution, that it has authority to establish a common principle on which to act in regulating the constitutions of the divers states.

PRUSSIA.

The provincial diets are beginning to meet. That of Brandenburg and Lusatia met on the 31st ult., sixty members being present, under the presidency of M. Von Flottwell, who made a speech in his capacity of royal commissioner. Count Arnim Boitzenberg, Marshal of the Diet, and chief of the party of the extreme right in the second chamber of Prussia, replied to M. Von Flottwell.

A letter from Berlin of the 29th ult., states that the minister of state, Von Thill, is dangerously ill. The Diet of the province of Prussia will meet on the 14th inst.

ITALY.

The Genoa Gazette announces from Cagliari that the levy of recruits in the island of Sardinia has been effected without the slightest resistance, but that a serious affair occurred in the north of the island. It appears from this account that Major de Sant Elia, one of the recruiting commissaries, while on his way to Nulvi, with an escort of twelve dragoons, was attacked by a party of bandits, who fired four shots at him; his horse was wounded, and the flap of his coat pierced with a ball. Three of his escort were also wounded. The bandits have not been arrested.

The King of Naples, says *The Brussels Independent*, has just appointed a commission for the reform of the prisons in his kingdom. His Majesty, in order that the truth may be known, has requested several members of the *corps diplomatique* to follow the labors of this commission, and to visit, with its members, the different prisons in the city of Naples.

The Pope is about to erect the city of Hamburg into a bishopric.

The Opinione of Turin announces military evolutions on a large scale, representing the battle of Montenotte, which, in 1796, opened Italy to the invasion of the French. General La Marmora is entrusted with the general direction of the evolutions.

LOMBARDY.

The Milan Gazette of the 28th ult. announces that the brigadier of carabineers, who, in 1849, arrested Ugo Bassi, (the priest who acted as chaplain to Garibaldi's troops, and was shot by the Austrians,) has been assassinated at Commachio.

TUSCANY.

The Tuscan Monitore publishes a series of regulations issued by the minister of worship at Florence on the 28th ult., concerning the right of censorship reserved to the bishops by the new concordat. By these regulations every bishop has the right of censorship over ecclesiastical works to be published within his diocese; a work rejected by one bishop cannot be approved by another, and there is no appeal from the decision of a bishop in such matters.

THE PAPAL STATES.

A dissolution of the Ministry has taken place, we learn, at Naples, and another Cabinet been formed. The names of the members of the new Administration had not been made public at the date of the last advices. [*Galignani.*

SWITZERLAND.

According to letters from Berne of the 29th ult., the damages caused in the canton by recent inundations are valued at 2,400,000 fr., or about £96,000. Subscriptions are open all over Switzerland to cover the losses of the inundation. The city of Berne has already subscribed 12,000fr.

ICELAND.

The Diet of Iceland was opened on the 5th July at Reikiavik. Amongst the bills presented was one enacting that from the 15th June, 1852, foreign vessels shall be allowed to enter the port of Reikiavik without passports of the authorities of the island, and shall be treated as Danish vessels.

Fugitive Slave Riot in Lancaster Co., Pa.

Our readers will be already advised of the occurrence of a lamentable riot and loss of life at Christiana, Lancaster Co., Pa., on the 9th inst.,—growing out of the attempted capture of two fugitive slaves by their owner.

In order to give the conclusion of this affair in an intelligible shape, a brief summary of the circumstances of the case may be necessary.

A party composed of Edward Gorsuch, of Baltimore county, Md., his two sons, Dickerson Gorsuch and Joshua Gorsuch, Dr. Thomas Pierce, Henry C. Kline, a Deputy Marshal, and two police officers from Philadelphia, started from Philadelphia, with a warrant issued by Edward D. Ingraham, United States Commissioner, to arrest two fugitive slaves belonging to Edward Gorsuch, who were supposed to be in the neighborhood of Christiana, in Lancaster county. After spending a day in Chester county, they arrived at break of the next day, at the place in which it was supposed the fugitives were harbored. This was a two-story stone building, on the farm of Levi Pownall, about three miles from Christiana. As the party approached the house, one of the fugitive slaves was identified, but took shelter in the house, and was followed by Mr. Gorsuch and his party. While in the house, an axe was thrown at the Deputy Marshal, and he fired. The negroes returned the fire, and the whites retreated outside of the house, where they were again fired upon.—Neither party being yet injured, a parley ensued, and the Deputy Marshal read aloud his warrant for the apprehension of the negroes.

In the midst of this parly, a horn was blown by some one in the house, when sixty or eighty armed blacks rushed upon the party from the adjacent woods and cornfields, and after a few words discharged a volley. At this fire, the elder MR. GORSUCH fell dead, and his son DICKINSON was shot in the breast and lungs. DR. PIERCE was also shot in several places, but succeeded in making his escape, together with the Marshal.

The matter rested, from some oversight, till Friday morning, when information of the unhappy event was given to the authorities of Lancaster County, and legal steps were taken for the arrest of the blacks. Nine of them were at once arrested. On Saturday morning, the United States Commissioner and the United States District Attorney proceeded to Lancaster County for the purpose of investigating the affair. Twenty-five arrests were made in the course of the day, and a large amount of arms was captured. Thirteen witnesses were examined, who testified that the firing was principally from the blacks. On Sunday, the party of U. S. authorities returned to Philadelphia, and ten prisoners, found guilty of participation in the riot, were confined in Moyamensing prison. Their names are as follows: Joseph Scarlet, (white) Wm. Brown, Ezekiel Thompson, Isaiah Clarkson, Daniel Caulsberry, Benjamin Pendergrass, Elijah Clark, George W. H. Scott, Miller Thompson, and Samuel Hanson, all colored. The three last-named, were placed in the debtors' department, and the others in the criminal department of the prison, to await their trial on the charge of treason and levying war against the United States.

The examination was resumed before United States Commissioner Ingraham, at Philadelphia, on Monday last. A number of additional arrests were made, and Henry Green, William Williams, John Halliday, Wm. Brown, Geo. Read, John Jackson, Thos. Butter, and Benjamin Johnson, were fully committed.

Hopes are entertained of the recovery of young Gorsuch.

On Monday, a proclamation was issued by Gov. Johnston, offering a reward of $1000, for the arrest of the guilty parties. The proclamation is strongly expressive of the energetic character of the Executive.

GOV. JOHNSTON has replied, in the following excellent letter, to a memorial addressed to him by a number of citizens of Pennsylvania, requesting him, as the Chief Executive, to "vindicate the laws and uphold the dignity" of the Commonwealth. The common-sense view of the subject which characterizes this production will commend it to the candid reader:

Letter from Gov. Johnston.

PHILADELPHIA, Sept. 14, 1851.

To Messrs. John Cadwallader, A. J. Roumfort, Jas. Page, and others:

GENTLEMEN: Your letter, without date, was this afternoon put into my hands by one of the servants of the hotel. The anxiety which you manifest to maintain the laws of the land and the public peace, is fully appreciated, and I have great pleasure in informing you that more than twenty-four hours before the receipt of your letter the parties implicated had been, through the vigilance and decision of the local authorities, arrested, and are now in prison, awaiting an inquiry into their imputed guilt. Tee District Attorney and Sheriff of Lancaster County, acting in concert with the Attorney General of the State, deserve especial thanks for their prompt and energetic conduct. This was all done early on Saturday morning, and duly reported to me by the local officers.

The testimony taken by the United States Commissioner, who arrived at a later period on the ground, a printed copy of which has accidentally reached me this afternoon, confirms me in the belief that the State authorities had vindicated the law, and to a large extent arrested the perpetrators of the crimes.

The cruel murder of a citizen of a neighboring State, accompanied by a gross outrage on the laws of the United States, in the resistance of its process, has been committed; and you may be assured that so soon as the guilty agents are ascertained, they will be punished in its severest penalty by the law of Pennsylvania. I am very proud that the first steps to detect and arrest these offenders have been taken by Pennsylvania officers.

Permit me, gentlemen, having thus removed all just cause of anxiety from your minds, respectfully to suggest that the idea of rebellion or "insurrectionary movement" in the county of Lancaster, or anywhere else in this commonwealth, has no real foundation, and is an offensive imputation on a large body of our fellow citizens. There is no insurrectionary movement in Lancaster county, and there would be no occasion to march a military force there, as you seem to desire, and inflame the public mind by any such strange exaggeration. I do not wish our brethren of the Union to think that, in any part of this State, resistance to the law goes undetected or unpunished, or that there exists such a sentiment as treason to the Union and the constitution.

The alleged murderers of Mr. GORSUCH, whose crime is deep enough without exaggerating it, have been arrested and will be tried; and they and their abettors will be made to answer for what they have done in contravention of the law. But in the meantime, let me invite your coöperation, as citizens of Pennsylvania, not only to see that the law is enforced, but to add to the confidence which we all feel in the judicial tribunals of the land, by abstaining from undue violence of language, and letting the law take its course. Depend upon it, gentlemen, there is in Lancaster county a sense of duty to the laws of the land, manifested in the easy and prompt arrest of these offenders, which will on all occasions show itself in practical obedience.

The people of that county are men of peace and good order, and not easily led aside from the path of duty which the constitution prescribes. They and every Pennsylvanian love the constitution and the Union. They will detect, as they have done in this case, and arrest and punish all who violate the laws of the land. There is no warrant, depend on it, for representing the men of Lancaster county as traitors and participants in an "insurrectionary movement." You do them, unintentionally, I have no doubt, great injustice.

I am deeply indebted to you for affording me the opportunity of expressing my views. But for your communication it might not have been able to do so. You and my fellow citizens at large, may be assured of my firm determination at all hazards and under all circumstances, to maintain the supremacy of the constitution, and enforce obedience to the law, alike of the United States and of this commonwealth.

In order that I may be sure that my answer may reach its destination (your letter having but accidentally come to my hands,) I have requested Mr. White to put it in the hands of Mr. John Cadwallader, whose signature, I observe, is first. I am, with great respect,

your obedient servant,

WM. F. JOHNSTON.

The Baltimore Sun of yesterday, learns from a private source, that the Executive of Maryland, Gov. LOWE, will take immediate action upon the official information which he has received relative to the riot. A special messenger has already been despatched to the President with a communication on the subject.

A mulatto man, supposed to be the slave Pinkney, owned by Mr. Garsuoh, was seen yesterday on the hills near Lancaster, and several citizens had gone in pursuit of him.

NEW-YORK CITY.

☞ The weather was the theme upon which we hinged an item for our morning edition, but we have been forced to forgo the infliction of it upon the public, by the proceedings of the Boston Jubilee, which our special correspondent has forwarded us. Never mind, the President cannot always be lionising through the country, and as soon as he returns home, we shall endeavor to do this important subject full justice.

DEATH OF A BAPTIST MISSIONARY. We regret to announce the death of REV. WM. T. BIDDLE, of this city, who departed this life yesterday morning, at the house of Rev. John Dowling, D. D., where he was making a temporary home, in anticipation of his early departure for his field of labor in Burmah, at or near the station lately occupied by Rev. Dr Judson. The intelligence of Mr. Biddle's death will be received with deep regret by a wide circle of friends, who were looking to his future career with large hopes, warranted by the honor with which he acquitted himself at Hamilton University, where he has just graduated. He was married but a few weeks since, and in a few days was to have sailed for his future home in India. The funeral exercises were held at the Berean Baptist Church, cor. of Bedford and Downing streets, and were attended by a large and deeply affected audience. The body is to be taken, this morning, to Brookfield, Conn., the residence of his father, Rev. M. Biddle, where closing exercises will be held previous to interment.

EXECUTION OF THE TWO CONDEMNED MURDERERS.—Between the hours of 10 and 11 o'clock to-morrow morning, *Aaron Stookey* and *Henry Carnal*, the Frenchman, are to undergo the penalty of death, for the murder of two fellow beings. Yesterday afternoon, each culprit seemed greatly troubled in mind, and they appeared to dread the awful fate that awaits them. The gallows will be erected in the City Prison yard, this afternoon, by direction of Sheriff Carnley, who, we understand, will hang the culprits simultaneously. The evidence of guilt was clearly proved against these murderers at the time of their trials, and, if any, very brief confessions will be made respecting their perpetrating the horrible deeds for which they are to suffer the extreme penalty of the law.

☞ The Board of Supervisors met yesterday, Mr. DELAMATER, of the XVIth Ward, in the Chair.—Eleven members were present, but neither the Mayor nor the Recorder. The minutes of the last meeting were read and approved. Several petitions for the correction of taxes were referred, but no other business transacted. The Board adjourned to Wednesday next.

FIRE IN HUDSON-STREET.—At an early hour on Tuesday evening, a fire was discovered in the upper part of a dwelling house at No. 159 Hudson-st., occupied by Stuart F. Randolph, Esq., which originated from the soot in the chimney taking fire, and before it could be put out, the chimney burst, and set fire to the wood work of the attic rooms. Hose Company No. 24 and other companies of the fire department, were promptly on the ground, but before they could arrest the progress of the flames, the building was inundated with water, which damaged the furniture about $500.

FIRE IN SPRING-STREET.—At half-past 12 o'clock yesterday afternoon, a fire was discovered in the Cabinet shop of Mr. George Boyd, at No. 151 Spring-street, which originated from a quantity of sparks that were blown from an adjoining blacksmith's shop. The firemen were promptly on the ground and the fire was speedily extinguished, before any material damage was sustained.

RUN OVER BY AN ICE CART.—Yesterday afternoon, about 3 o'clock, a young man by the name of George Fuller was thrown from an ice cart, in Spring-st., the wheels of which passed over his body and severely injured him. Capt. Turnbull, of the 8th patrol district, had the injured man conveyed to the N. Y. Hospital, where he received medical aid.

DISTURBANCE BETWEEN RIVAL BLACKSMITHS.—For some weeks past, a feeling of jealousy has existed between a number of workmen employed in the smith shop of Messrs. Marshall & Townsend, Stage Proprietors and others in the employ of the 6th-avenue Omnibus line, whom the former parties charged with waylaying them in the night time for no good purpose. On Tuesday night several of these rival mechanics met at the corner of 7th-av. and 22d-st., and angry words passed, which, no doubt would have resulted in a desperate and fearful conflict, had not a posse of the 16th ward Police reached the scene of disturbance, in a few minutes after the gangs had assembled. Three of the workmen (employed by Messrs. M. & T.) named John Green, Bernard Daly, and John Davie, made complaints against seven of their opponents, by the names of Bernard Matthews, Henry Malloy, Martin Kehoe, Patrick McCourt, John Mathews, Hugh Matthews, and Dennis Broderick, all of whom were immediately arrested, conveyed before Justice Blakely, and committed to prison upon charges of assaults with intent to kill. The latter prisoner was armed with two large knives, and a deadly weapon, known as a "slung shot," and he was accordingly committed for "felony."

STEAMERS.—The *Marion*, Capt. BERRY, arrived from Charleston, yesterday morning. She has experienced heavy northeasterly gales during the passage, and consumed all her fuel when thirteen days from the Delaware Breakwater, at which place she was obliged to put in for a supply. The *Marion* brings $30,000 in specie.

The *Alabama*, Capt. LUDLOW, from Savannah, arrived on Tuesday evening.

The *Winfield Scott*, Capt. COUILLARD, sailed for New Orleans at 3 o'clock yesterday afternoon.

"THEY COME."—Six vessels arrived at this port on Tuesday bringing an addition of 1,300 to our population.

Ship Rajah, from Liverpool	27
Ship Duchesse d'Orleans, from Havre	379
Ship Philadelphia, from Liverpool	598
Bark Jason, from Bremen	184
Bark Scotland, from Newport, Wales	11
Brig Lulea from Gottenburg	83
Total	1,282

☞ The packet-ship *American Congress*, sailed from this port, for London, yesterday. She took out $160,000 in specie.

☞ The Board of Assistant Aldermen closed their session for September, last evening. Our sketch of the proceedings is driven out by the Foreign News, but we are consoled by the reflection that our readers will find a full record of their doings in *The Evening Times*, which will be published at 1 o'clock this afternoon.

☞ The Fountain in Washington Square gets on towards completion with moderate speed. It is to be a very large circular basin, with a central jet and several side jets. The excavation is made, the wall around the border of the basin is nearly done, and the workmen were yesterday laying a bottom of hard plaster. The fountain will be a very fine one, and will increase greatly the attraction of this beautiful park.

NEW STEAMBOAT LINE.—The staunch little steamer, the C. Durant, has been placed on the East River, to run between this city and Flushing, touching at Astoria and Strattonport, by Mr. Flammer, the enterprising proprietor of the latter village. The fare has been reduced to one shilling, and the boat is to make two trips each way a day, and is to be a permanent arrangement. We hail with pleasure every new enterprise that will bind the Metropolis and the quiet and beautiful rural districts in its closer contact.

DEATH IN A CELL.—At a late hour on Tuesday night, policeman Coulter, of the Fourth Patrol District, found an unknown female, aged 35 years, lying in Madison-st., laboring under the effects of delerium tremens, and apparently lifeless. A dray was procured, and the poor woman was conveyed to the Station-house, where she seemed to somewhat revive, but was yet under the influence of strong drink, and was accordingly placed in a cell in the female department, where she was found a corpse in about two hours after. Yesterday morning the Coroner held an inquest on the remains, and the jury rendered a verdict of "Death by an apoplectic fit."

DEATH FROM CONVULSIONS.—The Coroner held an inquest yesterday, at the Bellevue Hospital, upon the body of a young woman named Sarah Carr, born in New-York, and aged 21 years, who, it appears, was admitted into the above institution on the 15th inst., in a fit of convulsions, and after lingering a few hours, died from the effects of the same. A verdict was rendered in accordance with the foregoing facts.

☞ A Bloomer Costume made its appearance in Sixth-avenue day before yesterday. A crowd of "Conservatives" manifested their hostility to this progressive movement by derision. "New ideas" are compelled to wage fierce battle in this world before they obtain recognition and favor. Two Bloomers appeared in Broadway and two in Washington square yesterday.

☞ It has been stated that Senator Douglass was too ill to fulfil his engagement, to deliver the oration at the State Fair. We understand that he has so far recovered from his indisposition, that he left for Rochester last evening.

FALSE ALARM.—The Hall bell rang an alarm at 9 o'clock last evening for the Sixth District, but our item gatherer failed to discover the first spark of a fire.

ANOTHER.—About 2 o'clock there was an alarm in the Second District—but the fire was not visible.

WOMAN POISONED.—Coroner Geer was called yesterday to hold an inquest on the body of a married woman by the name of Mrs. Eliza Knecht, lying dead at her late residence, No. 204 Seventh-street. A jury was was empanneled, and the first witness sworn was Mr. Leonard Smith, a resident of the same house, who deposed that deceased had been married about nine months, and that the husband only lived with her the first four weeks after they were united, since which time he had been absent until Sunday afternoon last, at 4 o'clock, when he called upon his wife and remained with her during the night; he then states that she was seized with violent pains and cramps at 11 o'clock that (Sunday) night, and in great distress; her husband remained with her till Tuesday morning and then left, at which time she was apparently beyond all hopes of recovery, and continued to labor under severe convulsions. Dr. Ruppenrecht, residing at No. 21 Avenue B., was next called, and deposed, in substance, as follows: I was called, on Tuesday morning, to visit deceased, and was informed that she was on the eve of confinement; but upon examination, found that no symptoms of that nature exhibited themselves, but discovered that she was laboring under severe and repeated convulsions, and all efforts to save her life proved of no avail, and she died at 5½ o'clock on Tuesday evening. I then made a *post-mortem* examination and found the stomach in a high state of inflammation, and all her internal organs exhibiting signs of poison. The medical gentleman then closed his testimony, by saying, that it was his opinion, that deceased came to her death by taking some corrosive poison in a fluid state, and there being no further evidence adduced, the jury rendered a verdict, "That the deceased came to her death by the administration of some corrosive poison given to her by some person, to this jury unknown." The deceased was a native of Germany, twenty-nine years of age, and had she lived a month longer, she would have undoubtedly been the mother of an offspring. As the case now stands, a strong suspicion rests upon the husband of deceased, and we trust our worthy coroner will cause a diligent search to be made for him or any other person who may be suspected of being in any way connected with the horrible affair.

ACCIDENT TO AN OMNIBUS-DRIVER.—Yesterday morning the driver of a Broadway omnibus, named John Ashbury, was severely injured by falling from the top of his vehicle and striking his head upon a curbstone, causing a dangerous fracture of the skull and other serious injuries to his limbs. He was conveyed to the N. Y. Hospital, by a citizen, and placed under the care of a skillful surgeon.

A SAD AND FATAL ACCIDENT.—About 8 o'clock yesterday morning, a brick layer named Patrick Halligan, residing at No. 27 West 17th-st., met with a sad and fatal accident, while at work upon the fourth story of a new brick building, in the course of erection in 14th-st, near the 6th-av. It appears that the unfortunate man was engaged in placing a row of bricks on the outside wall, and in consequence of missing his footing, he was precipitated to the ground and instantly killed.—His body was removed to the residence of his family to await a coroner's inquest.

ARREST OF AN ESCAPED PRISONER.—On the 29th of July last, a man by the name of William Clark made his escape from a cell in the City Prison, where he was confined upon a charge of Grand Larceny, in stealing a gold watch and several chains from a jewelry store at No. 4 Maiden-lane, for which he was subsequently indicted. Nothing was heard of the accused until yesterday, when a telegraphic dispatch was received from the Chief of Police at New-Orleans, La., by Mr. William Edmonds, the efficient Keeper of the Prison in Center-st., which conveyed the intelligence of Clark's arrest in that City. Mr. Edmonds immediately telegraphed to the authorities of New-Orleans, requesting them to detain Clark in custody, until such time as a requsition could be obtained from Governor Hunt and forwarded to them by one of our Police officers, who will bring him back to this City.

COURT CALENDAR.—*Thursday.*—U. S. CIRCUIT COURT—Nos. 2, 18 to 36. CIRCUIT COURT—Nos. 577, 578, 583 to 586, 588 to 591, 350, 403, 296, 592. COMMON PLEAS—Nos. 281, 540, 563, 575, 582, 586, 594, 599, 601, 603, 605, 611, 639, 640.

BROOKLYN.

BRIGADE INSPECTION AND REVIEW.—The annual parade and review of the Fifth Brigade, Gen. H. B. Duryea, comprising the thirteenth regiment, Col. Abel Smith, and fourteenth regiment, Col. Philip S. Crook, located in Kings County, will take place at Brooklyn on Monday, the 29th inst. The artillery and cavalry will parade on the east side of Henry-st, right on Pineapple-st.; the infantry of the 13th regiment on Orange-st., right on Hicks-st.; the infantry of the 14th regiment on Cranberry-st., right on Hicks-st. The regiments will be formed at 8½ o'clock, A. M., precisely; and punctuality will be strictly required, so that the march may be taken up at the hour of 9 o'clock, A. M., precisely. Major General Aaron Ward and staff will be present at this Parade. The light artillery companies of Captains Olney, (Brooklyn City Guard,) Graham, (Ringgold Horse Guard,) and Taft, (Williamsburg Artillery,) will parade with their Batteries, Capt. Neely's Dragoons (Washington Horse Guard) will act as an escort to the Brigadier General. The companies of Capt. John Willss and Henry Willss will do duty as *Light* Infantry and foot Rifles. In addition to the companies above named, there are attached to this brigade the Pierson Light Guard, Capt. R. B. Clark; Putnam Continentals, Capt. J. H. Morgan; Washington Life Guard, Capt. Sharpe; 1st Continentals, Capt. B. F. Hoagland; 1st Sarsfield Guard, Capt. ——; 2d Sarsfield Guard, Capt. ——; Union Blues, Capt. Burnett; National Guard, Capt. Sprague; Franklin Guard, Capt. Baldwin; Steuben Guard, Capt. Schaffer; Emmet Guard, Capt. Dodge; Shields Guard, Capt. Smith; Kings County Troop, Capt. Suydam; and some three or four companies from Williamsburgh. It is anticipated that this will be the finest parade ever witnessed in Brooklyn, and preparations are making to give much *eclat* to the occasion. This ought to be the best disciplined brigade in the State.

PREPARING FOR MUSTER—OFFICERS' DRILLS.—Our gallant militia men are brushing up right smartly for training. We see that orders have been issued to the officers and non-commissioned officers of the 5th Brigade to assemble in Fatigue dress, white trowsers, armed and equipped for Battalion drill and practice, at the City Armory, in Henry-street, on yesterday, the 17th inst., and Wednesday, the 24th inst., at 9 o'clock, A. M., on foot. Gen. Duryea, the worthy District Attorney of Kings county, is the commander of this Brigade.

LONG ISLAND VEGETABLES.—The State of Long Island is some on tomatoes. We were shown the other day, a tomato raised by Mr. Frederick Rowland of Hempstead, one of those vegetables which measured 22½ inches around it, and weighed 2 pounds 3½ ounces. Who can beat it!

New-York Daily Times.

NEW-YORK, THURSDAY, SEPT. 18, 1851.

☞ The first number of the NEW-YORK WEEKLY TIMES will be issued on Saturday of next week, September 27. It will be a very large paper, printed upon a quarto sheet, just twice as large as that of the Daily Edition, and will contain an immense amount of reading matter of all kinds, including that published in the daily paper during the week. Individual subscribers and clubs in the country would do well to send in their orders as soon as convenient. The price to Clubs of twenty is but *one dollar* a year. Postmasters are authorized to act as agents.

☞ If any of our subscribers, in this city or in Brooklyn, fail to receive their papers *before seven o'clock* they will confer a favor by leaving word to that effect at the office.

☞ We have received a great number of letters from gentlemen in various parts of the country, seeking employment upon *The Times*. In all cases where it has been possible, we have replied by letter; but some sixty or seventy still remain unanswered. We beg the writers to believe that nothing but incessant occupation has prevented us from paying attention to their requests. Our establishment is now *full*, in every department.

A Word about Ourselves.

We publish to-day the first number of the NEW YORK DAILY TIMES, and we intend to issue it every morning, (Sundays excepted) for an indefinite number of years to come.

We have not entered upon the task of establishing a new daily paper in this city, without due consideration of its difficulties as well as its encouragements. We understand perfectly, that great capital, great industry, great patience are indispensable to its success, and that even with all these, failure is not impossible. But we know also, that within the last five years the reading population of this city has nearly doubled, while the number of daily newspapers is no greater now than it was then;—that many of those now published are really *class* journals, made up for particular classes of readers;—that others are objectionable upon grounds of morality;—and that no newspaper, which was really *fit* to live, ever yet expired for lack of readers.

As a *Newspaper*, presenting all the news of the day from all parts of the world, we intend to make THE TIMES as good as the best of those now issued in the City of New-York;—and in all the higher utilities of the Press—as a public instructor in all departments of action and of thought, we hope to make it decidedly superior to existing journals of the same class. Of course, all this cannot be done at once; some little time is necessary to get the machinery in easy working order—to arrange for correspondence, to receive exchanges from various quarters of the world, and to enable assistants to find just the places in which they can work most efficiently. We hope, however, at the very outset, to show that we are *disposed*, and in course of time that we are *able*, to make as good a newspaper in all respects, and in many a much better one, than those hitherto offered to the New-York public.

We have fixed the price of THE TIMES at *one cent* each copy, or six and a quarter cents a week, delivered to subscribers. Carriers, of course, make their profit upon this; so that the amount which we receive barely covers the cost of the paper upon which it is printed, the deficiency being made up by advertisements. We have chosen this price, however, deliberately, and for the sake of obtaining for the paper a large circulation and corresponding influence. That influence shall always be upon the side of Morality, of Industry, of Education and Religion. We shall seek, in all our discussions and inculcations, to promote the best interests of the society in which we live—to aid the advancement of all beneficent undertakings, and to promote, in every way, and to the utmost of our ability, the welfare of our fellow-men.

During the past summer, the public press throughout the country has speculated and predicted, to a very considerable extent, and in all possible ways, upon the character and purposes of this journal. It has been praised and denounced in advance, for principles to which it was supposed to be devoted and for purposes which it was said to entertain. Some have said it was to be an *abolitionist* paper—a *free-soil* paper—devoted to the work of anti-slavery agitation—radical in everything, reckless of constitutions, laws and the public good. Others have ascribed its establishment to a design to push individual interests or party schemes: one announces that it is to sustain Mr. WEBSTER, another General SCOTT, and another Mr. CLAY for the Presidency. In fact, almost every possible variety of sentiment and of purpose has been ascribed to it in one quarter or another.

We have not the least fault to find with all this. Some of it proceeded from a malicious desire to prejudice the public mind against it, while much of it sprung doubtless from that propensity to *gossip* which governs tea-tables and newspapers, and which readers of all classes are suspected of not disliking overmuch. None of it is likely in the long run to prove injurious; on the contrary, it has contributed greatly towards making our project known, and has stimulated public curiosity concerning it, to a degree which our own exertions might have striven for much longer in vain. We are, therefore, rather thankful for it than otherwise;—while to those numerous journals throughout the country, whose love of fair play as well as personal kindness, has led them to interpose on our behalf, any expression we might make would fall far short of the gratitude we feel.

Upon all topics,—Political, Social, Moral and Religious,—we intend that the paper shall speak for itself;—and we only ask that it may be judged accordingly. We shall be *Conservative*, in all cases where we think Conservatism essential to the public good;—and we shall be *Radical* in everything which may seem to us to require radical treatment and radical reform. We do not believe that *everything* in Society is either exactly right, or exactly wrong;—what is good we desire to preserve and improve;—what is evil, to exterminate, or reform.

We shall endeavor so to conduct all our discussions of public affairs, as to leave no one in doubt as to the principles we espouse or the measures we advocate. And while we design to be decided and explicit in all our positions, we shall at the same time seek to be temperate and measured in all our language. We do not mean to write as if we were in a passion,—unless that shall really be the case; and we shall make it a point to get into a passion as rarely as possible. There are very few things in this world which it is worth while to get angry about; and they are just the things that anger will not improve. In controversies with other journals, with individuals, or with parties, we shall engage only when, in our opinion, some important public interest can be promoted thereby:—and even then, we shall endeavor to rely more upon fair argument than upon misrepresentation or abusive language.

We hope to make the DAILY TIMES acceptable to the great mass of our people, and shall spare no effort to do so. We have an abundance of means,—plenty of able and experienced assistance, and every facility for making at once, the *best* and the *cheapest* newspaper in the United States. We know how much easier it is to say this, than it is to do it: but we hope to show, in due course of time, that we have not failed in our promise, or disappointed any just expectation.

We shall seldom trouble our readers with our personal affairs; but these few words, at the outset, seemed to be required.

New-York Politics.

Both the great political parties are in the field for the November Contest. The two Conventions assembled at Syracuse last week, and their proceedings in detail have already been spread before the public. The Democratic Convention assembled first and adjourned last. The ill-feeling which has been growing up between the two sections of that party, during the past few years, was still so strong as to make the task of "harmonizing" one of no little difficulty. The members of the Convention, however, went at it with a good degree of courage, and followed it up with tenacious perseverance. Their efforts were crowned with a good degree of success.

The proceedings at the outset rather staggered the Hunkers. Having counted upon a very decided majority in Convention, and being determined to use their power with remorseless severity, they were dumbfounded to find it suddenly smitten from their hands. A goodly portion of their number fraternized with the Radicals, and gave them the organization of the Convention. The Hunkers struggled against the current, fighting every inch of ground, making sharp speeches and fulminating very intelligible threats. The Radicals talked less, and were anxious to harmonize, but were bent on doing it in their own way. Their Committee reported a series of resolutions, re-affirming those of the State Convention of 1848—of which the following is the only one pertinent to the chief topic of division:

Resolved, That, devoted to the principles and forms of our confederation, ever mindful of the blessings it has secured to ourselves and to mankind, and regarding the citizens of all sections of our country as members of a common brotherhood, we cherish the union of the States as the ark of our political covenant, and that we deprecate all sectional agitations at the North or South calculated to impair its sacred obligations, or to threaten its perpetuity.

Another resolution declaring,

"That the Democratic party in the State of New-York will faithfully adhere to the recent settlement by Congress of the questions which have unhappily divided the people of these States, and will neither countenance nor sanction any sectional agitation or legislation on the subjects embraced in that settlement,"

was laid upon the table by a decisive vote, and one adopted in its stead, simply "congratulating the country upon the recent settlement by Congress of the questions which have unhappily divided the people of these States."

In the Ticket nominated, the Radicals have decidedly the preponderance.

The Whig Convention was entirely harmonious. The Albany platform was re-affirmed, and a full ticket nominated, each section of the party being fairly represented; the following are the nominations of each party:

WHIG.	DEMOCRATIC.
For Judge of the Court of Appeals.	
SAMUEL A. FOOTE.	A. S JOHNSON.
For Secretary of State.	
JAMES C. FORSYTH.	HENRY S. RANDALL.
For Comptroller.	
GEORGE W. PATTERSON.	JOHN C. WRIGHT.
For Treasurer.	
JAMES M. COOK.	BENJAMIN WELCH, Jr.
For Attorney General.	
DANIEL ULLMAN, Jr.	LEVI S. CHATFIELD.
For State Engineer and Surveyor.	
HEZEKIAH C. SEYMOUR.	WM. J. McALPINE.
For Canal Commissioner.	
HENRY FITZHUGH.	HORACE WHEATON.
For State Prison Inspector.	
ALEXANDER H. WELLS.	HENRY STORMS.

We think that the Whig ticket will receive the full support of the Whig party in the State. Both sections of the party are represented upon it, and both are apparently satisfied with it. The election this fall is important, not only from its effect on State interests, but from its relation to the Presidential contest of 1852. In that contest both sections of the Whig party have, and will feel, an equal interest; and they will therefore, naturally put forth equally strong exertions to show to the Whigs throughout the Union, that the vote of New-York will in 1852 be cast for the Whig Presidential Candidate. This consideration will not be without weight, although the State interests involved might well be relied on to induce a full Whig vote for the Whig ticket.

In the Democratic party, although no formal division has taken place, we doubt if the ticket will receive a unanimous support. Its nominees—those of them who will be, if elected, members of the Canal Board, with two exceptions—belong to the radical section of the party. If they succeed, they will arrest the progress of the Erie Canal Enlargement as provided for by the law of last session. Their determination on this subject is too well known to be concealed; their success will postpone the completion of that great work for many years. We do not believe that the entire Democratic vote can be cast for a ticket, from the election of which such a result is to be apprehended. The Erie Canal has passed the point at which it can be made the foot-ball of political parties. Its vital importance to the State has been too clearly demonstrated, and is too generally felt to allow its interests to be neglected. Another stop law, like that of 1842, would not be voted by the Democratic party at the present day.

At present, therefore, we are inclined to think, the Whig party enter upon the canvass with prospects of success

HON. JOHN G. PALFREY, editor of the *Boston Commonwealth*, is offered up by his friends as a candidate for the Governorship of the good Commonwealth of Massachusetts. The particular cue we presume, upon which the hopes of his election are based, is of Mr. HORACE MANN's dictation, to wit, animosity more personal than political, more virulent than wise, to Mr. WEBSTER, and a good hearty contempt for any sentiments short of the craziness of Garrison, or the smartnesses of Wendall Phillips. As the majority of his supporters will doubtless come from men of that ilk, it is pleasing to find them at last so far in the attitude of friends of the Union and the Constitution as is indicated by their resolutions. This fact will console us for anything short of Mr. Palfrey's defeat: perhaps, for even that.

☞ REVOLUTIONS IN GERMANY are to be effected, says *The Tribune*, by means of "communications and suggestions, forwarded to Dr. Karl Tausenau, Holborn, London." The extraordinary facility thus tendered our "Vaterland heros" will naturally be embraced as decidedly preferable to any disbursement of funds or resort to arms, so long regarded as obsolete ideas in that connection; and if the cheapness and safety of the scheme fail to recommend it, a desire to encourage the international postage system may be taken into account. A "war of posts" we thought was a style of tactics disused in these latter days.

☞ Another Mexican Foray is currently talked of at New-Orleans, and rumor is so far explicit as to indicate Tamaulipas, Leon and Coahuila, as the Provinces to be dismembered; and that forces for the expedition are rallying in that city and at several points in Texas. There is nothing intrinsically improbable in the story. It is only one more of those chronic diseases bequeathed us by the Mexican affair; and portions of our population will be carried off by it every once in a while. A little more of the sharp practice of a Cuban Captain-General will be required before such unpleasant recurrences are effectually stayed.

TOO LATE BY HALF.—*The London Times*, by way of a flyer, promises that ere August next, every English Yacht will be built and rigged à la America. If so, they will infallibly be beaten again, for American progression is after the geometrical order, and we shall double our speed in a year.

Cuba.

Our readers have undoubtedly made themselves familiar, through the public journals, with the history and result of the late invasion of Cuba. We shall not, therefore, repeat them.

The issue of this attempt will probably prevent any new one, for some years to come. Nothing can be clearer than the fact, that, for the present at least, the inhabitants of Cuba do not desire their freedom. This has been made so evident by the fearful hostility which LOPEZ encountered from the inhabitants of the island, from the hour when he first landed upon their coast, that any new invader will require conclusive evidence of their favorable disposition, before he will trust himself among them.

There has been a good deal of sympathy throughout the United States with the project of revolutionizing Cuba. The island is large, rich, and of undeveloped resources.—Americans naturally think that it is not well taken care of now; and they crave the task of cultivating its soil, governing its people and pocketing its rich returns. The opinion, moreover, has very widely prevailed, that the Cubans were grievously oppressed by their Spanish rulers, and that the severity of their oppression alone prevented them from making some effort to throw it off. The presence of an armed force in their midst, however small, ready to start the battle against their tyrants, it was supposed, would summon them by thousands to the standard of revolt, and convert the colony into a free republic. These statements have been made upon high authority, and repeated and believed for years past. Men high in office, men who had lived in Cuba and were supposed to be familiar with the sentiments of its people, have uniformly represented that they were ripe for revolt, and desired only the presence of a small military band to serve as a nucleus for their force.

Whether it be right or wrong,—whether it be in accordance with, or against, the principles of international law,—whether it be any of their business or not,—the Americans will always sympathize with any people struggling, or supposed to be struggling, against oppression. There may be some among us who can look coolly upon such contests, and regulate their sentiments concerning them by their intellectual notions of law and national duty:—but the great mass of the people of the United States, acting solely from the impulses of free hearts and quick sympathies, will always sympathize with, and stand ready to aid, so far as they can, every nation, or colony, which may desire and endeavor to throw off hurtful and unjust restraint and to secure for themselves the same proud position and the same independence of political action, which we enjoy. It would be strange indeed, if it were otherwise. Prizing freedom, as we do,—and believing as we profess to believe that freedom is the natural right of every people,—brought into national existence, as we were, under the influence of this belief, and through the aid of sympathizing allies, it would be strange indeed, if we could look with cold indifference upon the efforts of others to throw off unjust oppression, and to regulate their political conduct by laws of their own enactment.

Certain it is, that no struggle for liberty will ever go on in any part of the earth without enlisting the sympathy, the good will and, if it be possible consistently with other duties, the aid of the American people. It is not strange, therefore, that Americans should have sympathized with what was supposed to be the desire of the Cubans for liberty.

We do not suppose that any considerable number of those who invaded Cuba enlisted under the influence of such feelings. They were induced to enlist, in most cases, by promises of large rewards. Cuban scrip had been isssued and widely scattered, and the most lavish promises were made to induce them to join the expedition. Believing that the Cuban population would aid them, American adventurers, never too scrupulous as to the nature of the enterprises which attract their minds, enlisted and were ruined. They found no aid. Not a Cuban joined them. They were treated as pirates and robbers, from the first moment of their landing until their destruction was accomplished. Nor could they, nor did they, expect any other treatment in case of failure. Even if a revolution had been in progress there, they would have been rebels and would have been treated as such. They ceased to be American citizens the moment they set out, as invaders, for the shores of Cuba. They became amenable to Spanish law, and they expected to meet its vengeance if they failed to overthrow it. As there was no revolution there—as the people of Cuba did not wish their aid and joined the government against them—they were invaders, waging war, on their own responsibility, upon the Spanish authorities. Their own government was at peace with Spain; and their conduct was, therefore, criminal at home as well as in Cuba. They violated American law, as well as the laws of Cuba.

The conduct of the Spanish government seems to have varied with its sense of danger. When Col. Crittenden's command was captured, LOPEZ and his force were in arms. The government undoubtedly was alarmed, and the impulse of vengeance, the desire to strike terror into their enemies, drove cool judgment from its seat. Crittenden and his fifty companions were, therefore, shot. Nothing could be better calculated to arouse the fiercest spirit of hatred and hostility among the American people than such an act as this; and if thousands had afterwards joined the invaders, (as they probably would have done but for the capture of Lopez,) this act would have done much to incite them to it. After LOPEZ was executed and his force in captivity, the government seems to have resumed, in some degree, its dignity and judgment. Passion did not prevent it from being considerate. And the release of VAN VECHTEN, KERR and others will do more to prevent future invasions of Cuba from the United States, than the slaughter of thousands in the field or upon the scaffold.

UNION IN PHILADELPHIA.—The people of Philadelphia are once more moving in the matter of a union of the various districts that enter into that composite city. A meeting for the consideration of the subject has already been called. The great difficulty has hitherto been the equalization of the debts and politics of the different sections, in case of consolidation. Whether the result has been cyphered up, and in favor of which of the great parties the doubts have terminated, we are not informed; but the indications seem to be that the next session of the Legislature will see the business accomplished.

"Judging from the tenor of the latest news from the French republic, there is as strong a disposition to *revolve* as ever, and the worst of these revolutions is, that the wheel that makes them has an *irregular motion*."
[*Commercial, last Eve.*

☞ What if the *Commercial*, like another Leverrier, undertake to account for these perturbations of France in her orbit, by ascertaining some obscure object outside to produce them. Nicholas and Nesselrode control the disturbing forces, perchance.

☞ We are indebted to COZENS BROTHERS, News-Agents, for Philadelphia papers in advance of the mail.

Snap-Shots at Books, Talk and Town.

Old sporting-men know very well what snap-shooting is; they know that there is very little method in it, and that, at the first sound of the "whirr," they must be ready to crack away. It is as unlike as possible to your "lying low" with a heavy ducking gun, and blazing mercilessly into a flock of canvas-backs; there is all the difference, in short, between the two, that lies between your long-barrelled editorial, leveled at some group of political canvassers, and those *quick shots* with which we mean to bring down the swift-winged, and yet the most plump, items of Books, Talk, and Town.

—Miss HAYS, for the moment, is the lion of the town; and Captain NYE, of the *Pacific*, will perhaps have made himself as pretty, and as undying a fame, for his courtesies to the "Swan of Erin," as has crowned the *Atlantic*, WEST, since he conducted the Swedish Nightingale to our shores.

There are reasons which will make Miss HAYS a favorite, independent of her musical attainment; nor do these reasons spring out of an extraordinary record of charities, or any anticipated liberality; they belong rather to her nationality.

When poor Ireland,—distressed, uncertain, travailing through doubt, and misery, and vain surges of action, toward relief, throws off to the world—like a phosphoric spark upon the waves—an emanation of genius, whether of poesy or of song, the world—and the American world above all, stands ready to welcome it, and to herald it with a hearty huzza.

The Sunday lookers-on have represented her as beautiful and winning; and they tell long stories of her triumphant progress to the Astor House, and of her cordial reception by the hosts. The last we can well believe; and the first, we are willing to take on trust. But we would entreat Miss Hays not to render herself the victim of any set of *claqueurs*; and can assure her, moreover, that merit in her realm of song, added to the chivalrous welcome which must belong to a graceful daughter of misery-striken Ireland, cannot fail to win her fair applause, without any of the aid of purchased adulation.

—Next to Miss HAYS, the weather has rounded the periods of gossip; and a change of 30° Fahrenheit, even in our ever changeable climate, is not a thing to be hurried from the after-dinner talk, with a mere shrug. It has changed indeed—this somerset of the air—the whole look of Broadway; and grass-cloth jackets, and white hats, have given way—like the fading substances in the Scotch wizards fingers—to black coats and winter beavers.

Sunday saw, we fancy, the last shiver of the summer muslings, and the work-day week has opened with lady fingers, clad in padded *visites*. And it is an odd Sunday, that lies in the metropolis between the summer and the winter. The show churches are indeed full—but full of strangers; and the old-fashioned worshipping-places, which have only their religion to commend them, show a beggarly account of empty pews. And we have even fancied,—though may Heaven grant that our fancy is wrong!—that the clergymen, too, have felt the poverty of listeners, as a shield of excuse, for a poverty of doctrine.

But the summer is on the heel; the in-coming cars and boats are showing their burden of nurses and children; and the door-plates of the up-town avenues are shining with the preparatory burnishing of the summer servants. You may even see lights at evening in parlor windows, and the market men at the area doors, with a stout joint in the basket, that a week ago could boast only—a steak.

The street, too, our saucy, and noisy Broadway, is whipping its aspect into a winter dress; and the unmistakeable southern guests, with their jaunty and careless air, are giving place to the hurried, and care-worn looks of the Town.

— Sporting-men, just rounding the Pot-rock, from a summer's gala in the Sound-waters, are toasting the two-masted Yacht, which has just now astonished the Englishers. Even the slowly-satisfied "*Times*" sets down the triumph of Commodore Stevens as the triumph of the year, and the whole sea-coast population of an Island, that has made its prowess by its sea-going craft, is on a sudden startled by the stranger that has won their birthright.

The papers tell us that all the Yachts of Southampton waters, are taken into the dock to be Americanised, and that even the first vessels of the squadron are trimming their sails after our *barbarian* fashion. This is indeed a loud cause of triumph; and we only hope that those concerned will wear their honors modestly; and that America will learn to take off the wiry-edge of its success by an abandonment of that old system of boasting which has so long been the plague-spot of the nation. Whatever England may do, it is to be hoped, that one day we may become conscious of the fact, that a really strong man has no need to tell of his strength; and that *honor unclaimed, is honor made double*.

— The book-men are just now bidding upon the summer's surfeit of literature, and some time, it may be worth our while to take our readers into the rooms of this traffic; and to show what manner of auctioneering disposes of the blood, brains, and worry of luckless authors.

We shall sometimes, too—true to our subject-heading,—take note of the books of the day;—unravel their narative into a newspaper column and give the public, whom we have taken in hand to serve,—a running synopsis of their story. And if we give, now and then, a critical shot at their manner, method or morals, we shall do it with all the modesty, and perhaps the occasional misses, which belong to our swift shooting.

As for the amusements, we shall bring them in our range very much as inclination may prompt, and shall render them over in epitome, or in critique, to those who have a liking for our off-hand opinions. We have only now to set down as a part of the news of the day, the arrival of Miss ADDISON, well spoken of as an actress, and the return of that successful comedian, Mr. Hackett.

☞ The Negro Riot at Lancaster will prove, after all, to be a *negro* riot, involving neither the prompting nor participation of the Whites. Of course, there are peace-loving prints quite willing to make the latter share all the criminality of the tragedy, probably in order to soothe the apprehensions of Union-loving people everywhere; but there is a sad lack of evidence to go upon. The affair occurred in the midst of a Quaker population, and it will be remembered that the obligations of that Society to peace and submission are rather more inveterate than their aversion to Slavery. The activity of the neighborhood in assisting the ends of justice; the unanimity of the local indignation against the perpetrators of the crime, go far to refute the first random rumors so prejudicial to the good fame of the vicinage; and we will wager a trifle that no future developments will damage it in the least.

There is neither charity nor fairness, nor any motion toward either, in this attempt to inculpate a quiet and harmless community, without diminishing the *prestige* against the actual offenders. The virulence of party feeling may dictate, and indeed that alone will dictate the use of any portion of the transaction for partisan objects. Whether *The Pennsylvanian* will persist, as it threatens, for lack of other ammunition, in pressing the matter into a service where it has no place and can effect nothing but harm, we shall see. If it does so persist, it is more than probable that Mr. Buchanan and not the Whig party will be the sufferers by a blunder so decidedly and obviously worse than a crime.

☞ The hour of departure for the Southern mail, in consequence of the destruction of the Hackensack bridge, has been altered to 2½ P. M. instead of 3½, as heretofore. It is to be hoped the wealthy corporations who control the right of transit over that stream will take care to erect a fire proof structure next time. Why not construct a stone arched bridge at once?

FIRE AT LOUISVILLE.—The telegraph last evening brought word of an extensive fire at Louisville, at its hight, at the moment of despatch. The Galt House and the adjoining ware-house of B. O. Davis were in a fair way to be consumed.

Recent Deaths.

The public papers have already announced the deaths of several distinguished gentlemen in various parts of the country. Of Hon. LEVI WOODBURY and the Rev. STEPHEN OLIN, D. D., extended notices have already been published. One or two others, however, have also died, of whom adequate obituaries have not yet been given.

Among these was the Rev. THOMAS H. GALLAUDET, LL. D., well known as the pioneer of Deaf-Mute Instruction in this country, who died at his residence in Hartford, on Wednesday, the 10th inst., at the age of 64. At an early period of his life, Mr. Gallaudet became interested in the cause of the Deaf and Dumb, and an accidental circumstance decided his future career. In the autumn of the year 1807, a child of Dr. Mason F. Cogswell, then residing in the city of Hartford, became, through the effects of a malignant fever, first deaf and then dumb. Mr. Gallaudet, a young man of talents, education and benevolence, interested himself in the case of this unfortunate child, and, with a strong desire to alleviate her condition, attempted to converse with and instruct her. His efforts were rewarded with partial success; and through the exertions of Dr. Cogswell, Mr. Gallaudet was commissioned to visit Europe for the purpose of qualifying himself to become a teacher of the Deaf and Dumb in this country. Seven gentlemen of Hartford subscribed a sufficient amount of funds to defray his expenses, and on the 25th of May, 1815, Mr. Gallaudet sailed for Europe.

Meanwhile, the friends of the project employed the interval of time in procuring an act of incorporation from the Legislature of Connecticut, which was accomplished in May, 1816. In May, 1819, the name of "the American Asylum at Hartford for the Education and Instruction of the Deaf and Dumb," was bestowed by the Legislature on the first Institution for the Deaf-Mutes established in the United States.

After spending several months in the assiduous prosecution of his studies, under the Abbé Sicard and others, Mr. GALLAUDET returned to this country in August, 1816. He was accompanied by Mr. Laurent Clerc, a deaf and dumb Professor in the Institution of Paris, and well known in Europe as a most intelligent pupil of the Abbé. Mr. Clerc is now living in a vigorous old age, and is still a teacher in the American Asylum at Hartford. The Asylum was opened on the 15th April, 1817, and during the first week of its existence numbered seven pupils; it now averages 220 annually. Mr. Gallaudet became the Principal of the Institution at its commencement, and held the office until April, 1830, when he resigned, and has since officiated as Chaplain of the Retreat for the Insane at Hartford. His interest in the cause of Deaf Mute Education has always continued unabated, and his memory will be warmly cherished by that unfortunate class of our fellow beings as well as by a large circle of devoted friends. The tree which was planted under his supervision and was tended by his care, has borne good fruit.

JAMES FENNIMORE COOPER, known throughout the world as the first of American Novelists, died at his residence, at Cooperstown, on the 14th inst., at the age of 62. Born in 1789, at Burlington, N. J., and graduated at Yale College in 1805, he entered the Navy as Midshipman the next year, but after six years left the service. In 1811, he was married to Miss Delancey, sister of the Episcopal Bishop of Western New-York, and soon after published his first novel—*Precaution*, a tale of English Society. It was, however, a failure; but, *The Spy*, which followed it, gave him rank at once, as one of the most brilliant Novelists of the day. The public is familiar with his subsequent literary history. After having given to the world a series of truly American novels,—American in scenery, character and tone, and exalted American Literature to a rank in European estimation which it had never before approached, he incurred the enmity of the American public, by censures of American manners. He had spent some years in Europe and returning to the United States, published two or three books in succession, in which he held up, for censure and reform, those faults of his own countrymen, to which residence abroad had called his attention. The lesson, however well meant, was not well received. His books were savagely reviewed, and he, personally, was unsparingly denounced. He carried the contest from print to courts of law, and waged active war with the whole newspaper press. The result, of course, without regard to verdicts, was injurious to him, and for the last few years he has not been a favorite in the United States.

In Europe, and especially on the Continent, no American name stands higher than that of COOPER. The attendant at the Castle of Chillon, on the northern shore of Lake Geneva, points to his name, cut by his own hand, in stone, upon one of the pillars of Bonnivard's dungeon, before any of the rest, except BYRON's, and in every part of the Continent, his name is known and honored. In England, his reputation as a writer is second only to that of IRVING. He was not only a Novelist, but a man of strong intellect, clear and quick in his apprehensions, fearless in conduct and gifted with a force of will, which would have made its mark conspicuous in any calling upon which he might have entered. His genius is one of which America should be proud.

Hon. SETH E. SILL, of Buffalo, of the Supreme Court of this State, elected in the VIIIth District, died on Monday afternoon, after a brief and painful illness. Judge SILL was a native of Saratoga Co., but became a resident of Buffalo early in life, and commenced his professional career in that city, in 1836. Possessing remarkable aptitude for legal study and investigation, and habituated to severe and constant professional industry, he always commanded the respect of the profession and the confidence of the community. He achieved the success due to eminent capacity and unstained integrity.—Judge SILL had already acquired a distinguished reputation on the bench, and his loss at this early period of his judicial life will justly be esteemed a public calamity. His term would have expired on the 31st December, 1853.

Rev. SYLVESTER GRAHAM, the founder and untiring advocate of the Vegetarian System of dietetics, died at Northampton, Mass., on Thursday, 11th inst. Dr. Graham was chiefly known for his strict adherence to the system which, for some time, bore his name. His writings on the subject were numerous and popular, and his labors, as a lecturer, were incessant. The most important of his works are, *Lectures on the Science of Human Life*, first published in Boston in 1839; and *Lectures to Young Men on Chastity*. The "Science of Human Life," is a work in two large volumes, containing a systematic, and in some degree, a scientific exposition of the author's peculiar views, and has had a rapid sale.—It passed through several editions in this country, and has lately been re-printed in England, where its sale is quite extensive. Dr. Graham was a native of Suffield, Ct., and at the time of his death was aged about 55. His character evinced energy and decision, and his influence on the public mind was rather beneficial than deleterious. Of his theories, each will form his own judgment; the projector, at least, was undoubtedly honest and sincere in sustaining them.

Prof. BEVERLY TUCKER, of William and Mary College, Virginia, died at Winchester on the 25th ult. Mr. Tucker was one of the Federal Judges of the Territory of Missouri before its admission as a State; and was subsequently State Judge in Virginia for a number of years, when he resigned, and accepted the chair of Professor of Law at William and Mary College. He was a member of the last Nashville Convention, and is known as the author of a work published fifteen years ago, entitled *The Partisan Leader*. Mr. Tucker's age was about 67.

Hon. FRANKLIN WITT, one of the earliest settlers of Illinois, and at the time of his death a State Senator, died at Whitehall, Ill., on the 27th August.

☞ We see it stated that the first train of cars passed over the railroad from Elmira to Canandaigua on the evening of the 15th. This road has a broad gauge, and is only an extension of the New-York and Erie Road to Canandaigua. Active measures are in progress to continue it directly to Niagara Falls.

Britain's Verdict.

The crowning triumph of American genius may perhaps be found in the amended temper of the English press, since they have been forced to admit our supremacy in mechanical skill, whether tried on land, in the lists of Hyde Park, or on water with the Baltic and the America.—Their admissions, unquestionably, flow with the viscidity of the "Thames 'neath London Bridge;" they have all the punch-like raciness of mingled sugar and lemon; all the courtesy—nationally characteristic—of a beaten gamester, entirely and hopelessly cleaned out. But for all that, they are quite acceptable, and much to be thankful for.—If we fail to appreciate them duly, it argues a sad deficiency of taste to offset super-abundance of invention.

We are nationally vain. Young people are apt to be; and though the head may be old, the shoulders beneath it are still youthful. Approbativeness, as in all pursuit-of-knowledge-under-difficulty-folks, swells like an iceberg on that same national cranium. "Some steeds," says Savage Landor, "go best in silence, with no other impulse than the spur and gad; others require the shouting and hand-clapping of the Roman Corso." We are of the latter sort; and if our juvenile energies, aiming as they steadily do, to the mastery of the true and the attainment of the beautiful, are stimulated by the applauding cry of spectators, in Heaven's name let the welkin ring! Praise, even if it exceed due appreciation, is never objectionable: let them lavish it as they may, but let us pass on.

And one word more, not the less important because uttered curtly. Reflecting men will not fail to note the gigantic proportions of American productions, when set down beside the last efforts of British mechanism. Boasting less of the results than of the means displayed to achieve yet greater works, we are satisfied with pointing to what the "*Times*" once sneeringly designated as "mere machinery." Our implements are made to act where wider elbow-room and less labor are afforded; our steamships and pleasure yachts tell of longer stretches to be spanned; and perhaps the old fling at the magnificent distances of the American capital embodies the form-type of American character. For the magnitude of our enterprizes John Bull has more wonder than sympathy. Our pieces are adapted to a larger theatre. American agricultural machinery would presently turn half their farm labor adrift. The American steam navy is a prophecy of the disuse of many a long-lived Indiaman or slow-paced South Sea trader; and to our clipper fleet all the British sea-craft will have to give way. To Americanize British land and sea machinery would half revolutionize Britain; and our patterns, after all, would be like the vicar's picture, too large for the house. At least so says Yankee vanity; what if its crest does swell a trifle at our blushing honors?

☞ On Saturday last, three of the Christiana offenders were brought up upon *habeas corpus* before Judge Lewis, in the District Court, at Lancaster, and an endeavor was made to procure their discharge. The Judge very promptly refused to entertain the application, on the ground that the parties were actually awaiting a postponed hearing, before Ald. Reigart. The Court was then adjourned, and the hearing proceeded with. This judicious course adds one to the many instances which have secured for Judge Lewis so enviable a position among American jurists. Several of his decisions, and among them, those in relation to the rights of married women and the legal obligation of the Sabbath observance, have been generally hailed as the dawn of brighter ideas on the bench; the admixture of a trifle more common sense with common law, and of reason with the solemn stupidities of precedent. Whatever may be thought of Ellis Lewis's politics, his fine juridical abilities call for but one opinion.

The Nicaragua Route.—England and America.

From the London Examiner, Aug. 30.

In February, 1849, *The Times* directed public attention to the desirableness of a transit route from the Atlantic to the Pacific, by way of Lake Nicaragua. At that time we Englishmen possessed every advantage for undertaking it. The enterprise, however, according to some, was not sufficiently exclusive, and would merely result in the loss of our capital for the benefit of the Americans, who were "too shrewd to undertake it themselves." A few months afterwards the announcement came that the Americans, aroused to the value of the route, had lost no time in opening negotiations in Nicaragua, and had actually succeeded in concluding a contract. The cry was then raised that they were seeking to grasp Central America; that they would construct the canal and exclude our vessels from entering it upon equal terms, and that we must forthwith prevent their proceedings by contesting, in the name of the King of Mosquito the right of Nicaragua to concede the route. The answer to this was the arrival of two commissioners from the canal company to offer to English capitalists, upon little more than nominal terms, a clear half of all the privileges which they had acquired by their promptitude, and which were now held under a joint guarantee of protection from the governments of the United States and Great Britain. The desire for participation, however, was again cooled as soon as it was found that it could be gratified. The prudence of Englishmen in 1850 was enough to compensate for the entire history of 1846, and where £800,000,000 had once been considered a moderate outlay to be incurred during two or three years for local traffic, the possible expenditure by England and the United States combined of £300,000 per annum for twelve years to revolutionise the traffic of the globe was something almost too much even for a congress of capitalists to contemplate. A direct purchase, therefore, was out of the question, and it was apparently only from a sense of patriotism and of the shame that would be incurred if the power of accepting the offer should be wholly lost to us, that at the eleventh hour an agreement was entered into with the view of securing its renewal at a fair price if the company should ultimately succeed in demonstrating the feasibility of their undertaking. All kinds of evil foreboding followed. A more remarkable history of discouragements was perhaps never recorded, and was certainly never terminated in a more concise or interesting way than by one of the simple paragraphs in the American news of Monday morning: "The passengers by the Pacific steamer arrived at San Juan del Sur (Nicaragua) with the California mails on the 29th of July, crossed the isthmus in thirty-two hours, and arrived at New-York after a passage from San Francisco of about twenty-nine days." Thus, within thirty months of the time when the question of Nicaragua first became generally discussed, the American company have entered into and secured a contract with that State, have gained the advantage of a protective treaty between Great Britain and the United States, have established a line of the fastest steamers both on the Atlantic and Pacific, have completed a survey which shows that the difficulties which for 300 years have frightened the world from attempting a junction of the oceans were absolutely fabulous, have carried 200 passengers in a few hours down a river which was represented as almost impracticable from shoals and rapids even for Indian canoes, have removed all the uncertainties and terrors that rendered the Isthmus the great stumbling-block of a safe and cheap passage to Australia, have brought California a week or ten days nearer to New-York, and have secured for themselves the monopoly of a traffic which is the most marvellous that has ever been known, and the disposal of fertile lands and trading stations and natural docks, that promise ultimately to receive the commerce of the world.

// TAYLOR'S BULLETIN.

JOHN TAYLOR, Proprietor. "Ich Dien." **JOHN F. WHITNEY, Publisher.**

VOL. 1. MONDAY, FEBRUARY 23, 1852. NO. 4.

RAILROADS.

N. York & Philadelphia R. R. via C. and Amboy R. R.

PIER NO. 1 NORTH RIVER.

Leave N. York for Philadelphia at 10 AM. and 4 PM.

N. York for Philadelphia via N. Jersey R. R.

PIER, FOOT OF COURTLAND & LIBERTY STS.

Leave N. York for Philadelphia 6, 9 AM, and 5 PM.

Morris & Essex R. R.

PIER, FOOT OF COURTLAND ST.

Leave N. York for Dover 8.30 AM and 4 PM.

N. J. Central R. R.

PIER, FOOT OF COURTLAND ST.

Leave N. York 9 AM and 4.30 PM.

Ramapo & Patterson R. R.

PIER, FOOT OF COURTLAND ST.

Leave N. York for Sufferns 8 AM, 2.30 and 4 PM.
" " " Patterson 8 and 9.15 AM, 12.30, 2.30, 4 and 4.45 PM.

Erie R. R.

PIER, FOOT OF DUANE ST.

Leave N. York for Dunkirk 8 AM, 5 PM.
" " " Elmira 8 AM, 12M and 5PM.

Hudson River R. R.

OFFICE IN HUDSON ST., NEAR CHAMBERS.

Leave N. York for Albany and Troy 8 AM, 1.15 and 5 PM.

Leave for Peekskill 7, 8 AM and 1.15, 1.30, 4.05 and 5 PM.

Long Island R. R.

FOOT OF ATLANTIC ST., BROOKLYN.

Leave Brooklyn for Greenport 7, 9 AM and 3 PM.
" " " Jamaica 11 AM.
" " " Farmingdale 9 AM and 3 PM.

Harlem R. R.

DEPOT AT CITY HALL.

Leave N. York for Harlem and Mott Haven 7, 8.30, 10 and 11.30 AM, 1.30, 3.30, 4, 4.30, 5.30, 6.30, 8 and 11 PM.

Leave for Fordham 7, 7.30, 8.30, 10 and 11 AM, 1.30, 2.30. 3. 4, 4.30, 5.30, 6.30, and 11 PM.

Leave for White Plains 7.30 and 10 AM, 2.30, 3.30 and 4.30 PM.

N. Y. & New Haven R. R.

DEPOT AT 29 CANAL ST.

Leave N. York for New Haven 7, 8, 11 AM, and 3, 4 and 4. 55 PM.

Housatonic R. R.

DEPOT AT 29 CANAL ST.

Leave N. York 8 AM.

FERRIES.

Brooklyn—foot Whitehall, Fulton, Catherine sts., and Gouveneur Slip.
Bull's Ferry—foot Spring st.
Calvary Cemetery—foot E. 23d st.
Fort Lee—foot Spring st.
Hell Gate—foot do.
Hamilton and Gowanus—foot Whitehall st.
Hoboken—foot Barclay, Canal and Christopher sts.
Jackson—foot Gouverneur st.
Jersey City—foot of Courtland st.
New Brighton & Elizabethport—Battery Place.
Port Richmond do do.
Snug Harbor do do.
Staten Island—foot Whitehall and Cedar sts.
Williamsburgh—foot Grand and Houston sts., Peck Slip.

STEAMBOATS.

Albany, People's Line—pier between Courtland and Liberty sts.
Albany—foot of Courtland, Robinson and Chambers sts.
Albany & Troy—foot Courtland and Barclay sts. (morning and evening.)
Amboy—pier 1 N. R.
Astoria—Peck Slip.
do & Ravenswood—Fulton Market Slip.
Bridgeport—foot of Catherine Slip and foot of Market st.
Caldwell's Landing, West Point and Cold Spring—foot Warren st.
Castleton—foot Battery Place.
Catskill—Albany Basin, foot Cedar st., N. R.
Dobbs' Ferry—pier, foot Chambers st.
Elizabeth Point—foot Battery Place.
Fall River via Newport—pier 3 N. R.
Fishkill—foot Robinson st.
Flushing, Astoria & Ravenswood—Fulton Slip, E. R.
Fort Lee & Bull's Ferry—foot Hoboken Slip.
Glen Cove, Oyster Bay, &c—Fulton Market Slip.
Grassy Point—pier, foot Murray st.
Hartford—Peck Slip.
Haverstraw—foot Chambers st.
Hudson—foot Cedar st., N. R.
Kingston—foot Chambers st.
Kingston & Rondout—Delaware & Hudson Canal line, foot Jay st.
Long Branch & Shrewsbury—pier 24 E. R.
Morristown—foot Dey st.
Newark—foot Barclay st.
New Brunswick—piers, foot of Robinson and Barclay sts.
Newburg—foot Murray st.
New Brighton—foot Battery Place.
New Hamburgh & Malborough—foot Murray st.
New Haven— Peck Slip.
New London—foot of Courtland st.
New Rochelle—Fulton Market Slip.
Newport, Fall River & Boston—pier 3 N. R.
Norwalk (Conn.)—Catherine Slip.
Norwich do. pier 18 N. R.
Oyster Bay, Glen Cove, &c—Fulton Market Slip.
Peekskill— pier, foot Chambers st.
Philadelphia, Cape May—pier 12 N. R.
Philadelphia, Camden & Amboy—pier 1 N. R.
do Emigrant and Transportation Line—pier 1 N. R.
Port Richmond—foot Battery Place.
Poughkeepsie—pier, foot Murray.
Providence and Boston, via Stonington—pier 2 N. R.
Quarantine—foot of Whitehall st.
Rhinebeck—foot Robinson st.
Saugerties—foot Chambers st.
Sing Sing—pier, foot Chambers st.
South Amboy and French's Dock—foot Barclay st.
Staten Island—foot Battery Place, Whitehall and Cedar sts.
Tarrytown—pier, foot Chambers st.
Yonkers—pier, foot Murray.

Places of Public Amusement.

BROADWAY THEATRE—Between Pearl and Anthony.
BROUGHAM'S LYCEUM.—Broadway, near Broome.
NATIONAL THEATRE.—Chatham, between James and Roosevelt streets.
BOWERY THEATRE.—Bowery, between Bayard and Walker streets.
BURTON'S THEATRE.—Chambers street.
NIBLO'S GARDEN.—Broadway, corner of Prince st.
AMERICAN MUSEUM.—Broadway, corner of Ann st.
OPERA HOUSE.—Astor Place.
TRIPLER HALL.—677 Broadway.
CASTLE GARDEN.—Battery.
MECHANIC'S HALL.—472 Broadway, above Grand st.
FELLOW'S MUSICAL HALL.—444 Broadway.
CIRCUS.—Opposite the Bowery Theatre.

EXHIBITIONS OF PAINTINGS.

AMERICAN ART UNION.—497 Broadway.
DUSSELDORF GALLERY.—548 Broadway.
NATIONAL ACADEMY OF DESIGN.—663 Broadway.
GALLERY OF THE FINE ARTS.— " "

OBJECTS OF INTEREST.

Croton Water Works.	High Bridge, Harlem.
Trinity Church.	Merchant's Exchange.
Custom House	Institution for the blind
Insti'n for the deaf and dumb	City Hall and Park
Navy Yard and Dry Dock	Bellevue Hospital
Bloomingdale Lunatic Asy'm	Greenwood Cemetery

EXPRESSES.

Adams & Co—16 Wall st., Boston, Philadelphia, Baltimore, Washington, Wheeling, Richmond, Norfolk, St. Louis, California and Foreign.
American Express Co., Wells. Butterfield & Co—66 Courtland st., and 10 Wall st., Buffalo, Erie, Cleveland, Louisville, Cincinnati, St. Louis, &c.
Archer & Bostwick—1 Hudson st., Westpoint, Newburg, Kingston, Rondout, Saugerties, Poughkeepsie, Hudson and Catskill.
Baldwin's—6 Wall st., Newark.
Berford's—2 Vesey st., California.
Boggs'—69 Maiden Lane, Albany.
Carpenter's—21-2 Courtland st., City.
Coffin's—69 Maiden Lane, City.
Cooper's—71 do do
Davenport & Mason—6 Wall st., Taunton, New Bedford and Nantucket.
Day's—16 Wall st., Newark, N. J.
Einstadter's—44 Beaver st., City.
Gregory's California Package and Parcel, Thompson & Hitchcock—139 Pearl st., cor. of Wall.
Harnden's—6 Wall st., Boston, Providence, Philadelphia, New Haven, Hartford, Springfield and Foreign.
Henry's—58 William st., Newark.
Kennedy's— do City.
Kinsley & Co.'s—1 Wall st., Boston, Fall River, Newport, Philadelphia, Lancaster, Harrisburgh, Wilmington, Norfolk, Richmond, Pittsburgh, Cincinnati, Lexington, Louisville, St. Louis, New Orleans.
Livingston & Co.'s—6 Wall st., Philadelphia, Baltimore, Washington, Pittsburgh, South and Foreign.
Livingston & Fargo—10 Wall st., Cincinnati, Louisville, St. Louis, Detroit, Chicago, Cleveland, Milwaukee and to all the Western States.
Lucas'—38 Cedar st., Brooklyn, Long Island, Williamsburgh, Newark & Bloomfield, N. J.
Ludlow & Co.'s—6 Wall st., City.
Macdonald's City Package—33 Liberty.
Mather's—71 Maiden Lane, Brooklyn.
Norton & Co.'s—South Ferry, Greenport.
Price's—18 Liberty st., Brooklyn.
Miles & Co.'s—6 Wall st., Patterson, N. J.
Pullen, Virgil & Co.'s—10 Wall st., Troy and North, Montreal and Quebec.
Stanley's—58 Williams st., Brooklyn.
Hale & Co.'s—70 Wall st., Trans-Atlantic.
Wells Butterfield & Co.'s—10 Wall and 64 Courtland sts., Utica, Syracuse, Albany, Oswego, Rochester, Buffalo and intermediate places, and on the N. Y. & Erie R. R.

RATES OF FARE FOR HACKNEY COACHES, CARRIAGES, OR CABS.

1. For conveying a passenger any distance not exceeding one mile, 37 1-2 cents; and for every additional passenger, 25 cents.
2. For conveying a passenger any distance exceeding a mile, and within two miles, 50 cents; and for every additional passenger, 25 cents.
3. For conveying a passenger to the New Alms House, and returning, 75 cents; and for every additional passenger, 37 1-2 cents.
4. For conveying a passenger to 40th street, and remaining half an hour and returning, $1; and for every additional passenger, 25 cents.
5. For conveying one passenger to 61st street, and remaining 3-4 of an hour, and returning, $1,50; and for every additional passenger, 25 cents.
7. For conveying one or more passengers to Harlem, and returning, with the privilege of remaining three hours, $4.
8. For conveying one or more passengers to King's Bridge, and returning, with the privilege of keeping the Carriage, or Cab all day, $5.
9. For the use of a Hackney Coach, Carriage or Cab, by the day, with one or more passengers, $5.
10. For the use of a Hackney Coach, &c., by the hour, with one or more passengers, with the privilege of going from place to place, and of stopping as often as may be required, as follows, viz: for the first hour, $1—for the second hour, 75 cents; and for every succeeding hour, 50 cents.
11. In all cases where the hiring of a Hackney Coach, &c., is not at the time thereof specified to be by the day or hour, it shall be deemed to be by the mile.
12. For children between two and fourteen years of age, half price is only to be charged; and for children under two years of age no charge is to be made.
13. Whenever a Hackney Coach, &c., shall be detained, excepting as aforesaid, the owner or driver shall be allowed after the rate of 75 cents for an hour; 37 1-2 cents for every subsequent hour, and so on in proportion for any part of the first and subsequent hour which the same may be so detained.

TAYLOR'S SALOON.

337 BROADWAY.

BILL OF FARE.

ICE CREAMS.

Lemon	1s
Vanilla	1s
Strawberry	1s
Pine Apple	1s

FRUIT ICES.

Orange	1s
Pine Apple	1s
Raspberry	1s
Strawberry	1s
Roman Punch	1s
Meringues a la Creme	1s
Pyramid Meringues	6d
Charlotte Russe	1s
Calves-foot Jelly	1s
Brandy Fruits	1s
Preserved do	1s
Orgeat	6d

SOUPS.

Green Turtle	3s
Mock do	2s
Terrapin	2s
Oyster	1s 6d
Beef	1s
Vermicelli	1s
Maccaroni	1s
Pea	1s
Mutton Broth	1s
Soup Julien	1s

FISH.

Smelts	2s
Lobster	1s 6d
Salmon	3s
Salt Salmon	1s 6d
Shad	2s
Mackerel	2s
Salt Mackerel	1s 6d
Trout	

MADE DISHES.

Mutton Chops	2s
Lamb do	2s
Pork do	2s
Beef Steaks	3s
Venison do	4s
Boned Turkey	2s 6d
Chicken, (Oyster Sauce)	3s 6d
Fricasse of Chicken	3s 6d
Broiled do	3s
Cold Roast Chicken	3s
Chicken Salad	4s
Lobster Salad	3s
Veal Scollops	2s 6d
" Cutlets, (Sauce Piquant)	2s 6d
" " (Bread Crum'd)	2s 6d
Sweetbread larded	3s 6d
" plain	3s
Maccaroni au gratin	2s
" a l'Italien	2s
Calves' Head a la Tortue	2s 6d
" (Egg Sauce)	2s 6d
Broiled Kidney	2s
Kidney (Champagne Sauce)	2s 6d
Squabs	3s
Stewed Terrapins	4s
Frogs	2s 6d
Soft Crabs	3s
Lambsfries	3s
Turtle Steaks	2s 6d

JOINTS.

Roast Beef	2s
Roast Lamb	2s
Roast Veal	2s

GAME.

Partridge	
Woodcock	
Quails	
Snipe	
Squab Owl	

VEGETABLES.

Beets, Celery and Spinach	6d
Potatoes, fried and mashed	6d
" Maitre d' Hotel	1s
Tomatoes	6d
Mushrooms	2s
Cucumber	6d
Peas	1s
Salad	6d
Radishes	6d
Asparagus	1s 6d

OYSTERS.

Raw	1s
Roasted	2s
Fried	2s 6d
Stewed	1s
Broiled	2s 6d
Pickled	1s
On Chafing Dish	4s per doz

HAM.

Fried	2s
Broiled	2s
Cold Broiled	1s 6d
Ham and Eggs	2s 6d

OMELETTES.

With Ham	2s
" Herbs	2s
Sweet Omelettes	2s
Sweet, with Currant Jelly	3s
Plain Omelettes	1s 6d
Welsh Rarebits	1s
Tea, Coffee and Chocolate	6d
" " with Cream	1s
Rolls and Butter	6d
Tongue	2s
Pickled Tongues	1s 6d
Sandwiches	6d
Sardines	1s 6d

TOAST.

Buttered	6d
Milk	1s
Dry	6d
Toasted Rusk	6d
Muffins	6d
Apple Fritters	1s 6d
Pancakes	1s 6d

EGGS.

Poached	1s 6d
Boiled	1s 6d
Fried	1s 6d

PIES.

Strawberry	6d
Cherry	6d
Almond	6d
Pumpkin	6d
Peach	6d
Apple	6d
Plum	6d
Mince	6d
Custard	6d
Cocoa Nut	6d
Gooseberry	6d
Rhubarb	6d
Greengage	6d
Huckleberry	6d
Cranberry	6d
Rice Pudding	6d
Tarts, Cream Cakes	6d
Boston Cream Cakes	6d
Cocoa Nut Tarts	6d
Oyster Pies	6d
Cheese Cakes	6d
Bath Buns	6d

CAKES.

Sponge Cake	6d
Pound "	6d
Lafayette "	6d
Ladies' Fingers	6d
Cocoa Nut Drops	6d
Macaroons, &c	6d

FRUIT.

Grapes	
Peaches	
Apricots	
Plums	
Nectarines	
Almonds and Raisins	
Cherries	
Figs	
Apples and Oranges	
Bananas	
Stewed Prunes	

WINES, ON DRAUGHT.

Madeira	6d	Glass.
Port	6d	"
Sherry	6d	"
Claret	6d	"
Cider	6d	"
Claret Punch	1s	"

BOTTLED.

Maderia	12s	quart.
Port	12s	"
Sherry	12s	"
Claret	6s and 8s	"
Claret	3s and 4s	pint
Hockheimer	8s and 12s	quart
Neirsteiner	8s	"
Cabinet Steinberger	20s	"

CHAMPAGNE.

Heidsick	16s	quart.
"	8s	pint.
Virzeney	16s	quart.
"	8s	pint.

CORDIALS.

Cinnamon	1s
Rosolio	1s
Annisette	1s
Noyeau	1s
Curacoa	1s
Maraschino	1s
Kirsch Wasser	6d
Extrait d'Absinthe	6d
Cherry Bounce	6d
parfait Amour	1s

NEWSPAPERS.

AMERICAN.—Courier and Enquirer, Tribune, Evening Post, N. Y. Pathfinder, Herald, Courier des etats Unis.

ENGLISH.—London Punch, London Times, Illustrated News.

FRENCH.—Charavari and La Presse.

GERMAN.—Deutche Schnell Post and Illustrite Zeitung.

SPANISH.—La Cronica.

J. TAYLOR begs to announce that he has lately increased his arrangements for supplying parties, and is now prepared to furnish them in a style that has never been surpassed in this country. He has engaged the best workmen in both the Confectionary and Cooking departments, and has imported an entirely new set of Moulds from Paris. He has also purchased a very splendid set of Table Ornaments for loaning to parties, of the latest fashion and most costly description, and feels confident of giving satisfaction to those who may favor him with their orders.

ARTICLES FURNISHED FOR PARTIES.

Ornaments and Pyramids of Nongat, Grapes, Oranges, Spun Sugar, Ratafias, Kisses, Cocoa Cakes, Macaroons, &c.
Ice Cream and Fruit Ices, in plain and fancy moulds.
Roman Punch.
Small fancy forms of Ice Cream and Ice.
Biscuit Glaces.
Bombes Glaces.
Mille Fruits Ice.
Plum Pudding Glace.
Charlotte Russe, ornamented.
" " plain.
" " imperial.
Jelly in Moulds—Wine, Orange and Rum.
" " Macedon.
" " Mosaic.
Oranges a la Surprise.
Chantilly Cakes.
Gateaux a la Polonaise.
Grand Meringues.
Meringues a la Creme.
Brandy Fruits.
Crystalized do.
do Bonbons.
Grapes, Pears, Apples, Lady Apples, Lemons, Oranges, &c.
Small Ornamental Cakes.
Loaves of Wedding Cake, ornamented.
Boxes " do
French and Flower Mottoes, very handsome.
Fancy and Plain do
Boned Turkeys.
" Capons.
" Game.
Dishes of Cold Game.
Game Pattes.
Ornamented Hams and Tongues.
Chicken and Lobster Salads.
Pattes de foie Gras.

Silver Forks, Spoons, Ladles, Trays, and Cake Baskets.
Brackets and Candelabras.
All kinds of Glass and China Ware.

GOOD WAITERS AND MUSICIANS FURNISHED.

Extra Bill of Fare.

Fresh Pickerel	2s
Smoked Salmon	1s 6d
" Herring	1s 6d
" Mackerel	1s 6d
Venison Scollop	4s
Croquettes de riz	1s
Chicken a l'Italien	3s 6d
Fillet de Bœuf, with Olives	4s
" " Madeira Sauce	4s
Beef Steaks (Anchovy Sauce)	3s 6d
Calves' Head a la Matelottes	3s
Fried Sausages	1s 6d
Minced Beef, with Poached Eggs	2s
Hashed Meat	1s 6d
Bologna Sausages	1s 6d
Stewed Kidney, with Onions	2s
" " a la Maitre d'Hotel	2s
Anchovy and Sardine Salad	4s
Herring and Oyster do	3s
Omelette, with Apricots	2s 6d
Asparagus	2s
Ham and Eggs	2s 6d
Broiled Ham	2s
Grilled "	2s
Roast Partridge (Bread Sauce)	8s
Broiled do Salmee	7s
Anchovy Toast	1s
Tongue Sandwiches	1s
Anchovy do	1s
Boned Turkey do	1s
Beef do	6d
Bread and Butter, with Anchovy	1s
Bread and Milk	6d
Vol au Vent a la Francaise	1s

ILLUSTRATED NEWS.

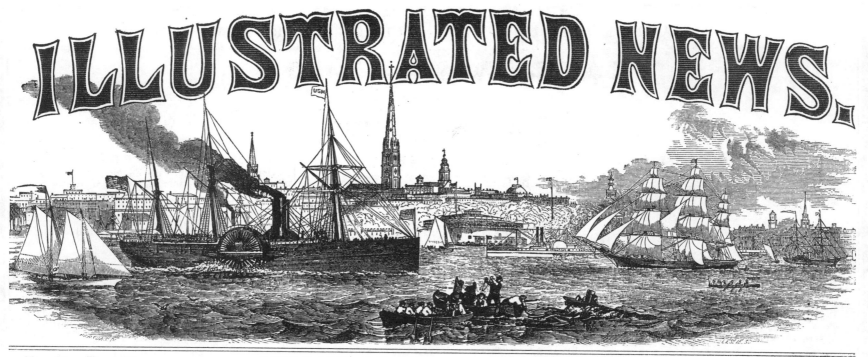

No. 46. Vol. II. NEW YORK, SATURDAY, NOVEMBER 12, 1853. Six Cents.

PUBLISHER'S NOTICE.

The Great Presentation Plate will be published in connection with the regular issue of this paper on Saturday, November 26th, 1853, being about the period of our annual thanksgiving, and forming an appropriate Thanksgiving Gift.

Great delay has been occasioned in its issue by breakages of the wood blocks on which it is engraved, and difficulties of electrotyping the large plate on which it is printed. Being the largest wood engraving ever issued in America, the Publishers have been subjected to many accidents in its preparation not encountered in smaller engravings.

FIREMEN'S ANNUAL PARADE—FIRE-PROOF BUILDINGS.

Our sketch represents a portion of the procession in Broadway, passing some of the very fine buildings recently erected there, conspicuous among which is observed that of Thompson's, and that occupied by the extensive daguerrean establishment of Mr. Brady, an interior view of whose saloon we have heretofore given in our paper. The festival was very generally observed among the firemen, and excited considerable interest, drawing together a very large number of spectators along the line of march. It is estimated that about thirteen thousand persons joined in the procession. The display was brilliant, and the music from the numerous bands contributed greatly to the gratification of the spectators. Altogether, it may rank as one of the most noted displays yet made by our gallant firemen.

It is fortunate for our citizens that we are provided with such an excellent fire department, picked out of the flower of our population, who are willing and anxious to devote their services, at all times, and all seasons, without fee and without reward, to the preservation of property. In no other city in the world does such an extensive and able organisation exist, and no other city, unfortunately, requires such an organisation more. Were it not for the abundant supply of Croton water, now at our command, we believe New York would almost be entirely re-built every thirty years. The aggregate number of fires in our metropolis almost staggers belief. There are thousands of petty cases, where a well directed bucket extinguishes fire at the outset, and the occurrence never is known by the public. The number of fires in our city since the introduction of Croton water, does not appear diminished, but, on the contrary, has increased more than proportionately with its growth. But the destruction of property is not so great—and but one general conflagration has since swept over our city—that of 1845—made general, after being once subdued, by the explosion which scattered burning fragments over a very large area of surface.

But however effective our fire departments may be, and whatever activity is extinguishment of fires may be exhibited, it is desirable that our citizens should turn their attention to the erection of buildings not so easily swept away by the devouring element. In London, Paris, and other European cities, conflagrations are of rare occurrence. It is attributable to a variety of causes, but among the principal may be named the different construction of dwellings, tiled floors, and greater care in construction of flues. In our country the abundance of wood, the higher price of labor, and the comfort in using the material, effectually prevents the general use of tiled floors. But floors, and other portions of the wood-work of buildings, can be made nearly fire-proof, in our present styles of building, at comparatively light cost.

Experiments have been made, as far back as 1772, in checking the progress of fire through wooden floors. It was then shown that a board of fir-wood, half an inch in thickness, covered with earth one inch in depth, resisted the steady action of an intense fire, next the earthen side, for the space of four hours. A building then constructed on this principle, was fired as an experiment, wooden casings being protected, as far as possible, with plaster, and the building remained enveloped in smoke for four days, at the expiration of which time some portions of it were charred through, but other portions had wholly resisted the fires built, and these had become extinguished.

In 1776 a Mr. Hartley introduced a system of casing with thin iron plates, leaving a vacuum between the iron and the wood, the same in its general principles as the plan above referred to. He estimated that the same could be applied to buildings at a cost of five per cent.

By extra lathing and plastering, repeating the coats three or four times over, experience has shown that ceilings of buildings can be made fire proof. This protects the under side of floor joists. A floor of earth or mortar, from one to three inches in depth, can be laid over the tops of the floor joists, upon which the wooden floor of the room may be laid, and burned away, in case of fire, without communicating to the floor joists, provided all openings be entirely closed in the ceiling next below, and the earthen floor next above. These should be impervious. It is evident that some such simple precautions may be made at slight expense—it is evident that in the course of competition among monetary corporations a difference of rates of insurance will eventually be established upon buildings of this nature—it is evident that, in the course of time, rents must decline, and with this decline will be sought every mode to lessen risks of fire. We would be glad to see the good work commence.

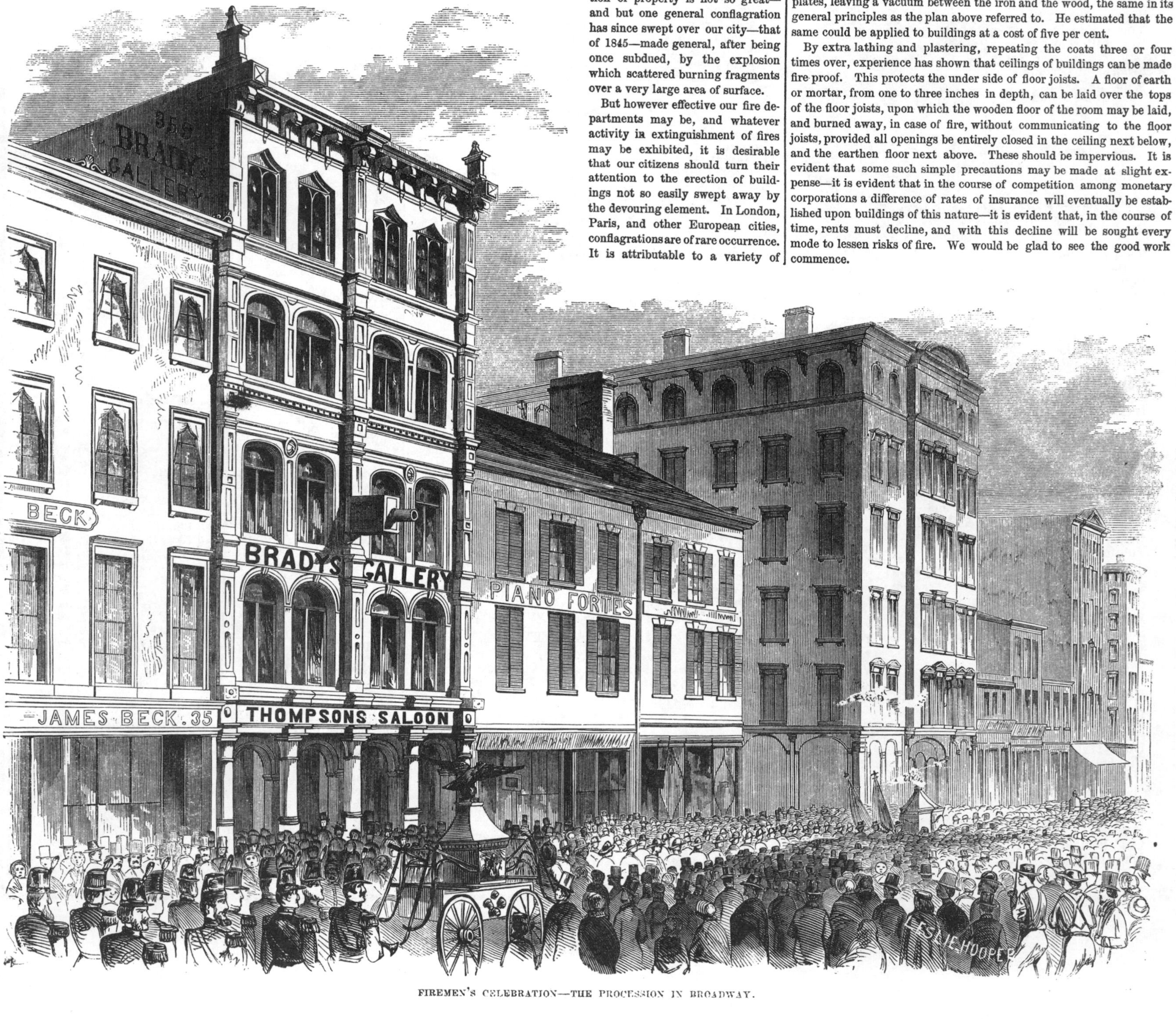

FIREMEN'S CELEBRATION—THE PROCESSION IN BROADWAY.

CAPTAIN. CAP-COVER FOR RAIN. CHIEF. RESERVE CORPS. LIEUTENANT. PRIVATE.

NEW REGULATION UNIFORM OF THE NEW YORK POLICE.

NEW YORK POLICE.

We give herewith a view of the new regulation uniform of the police of New York, which has just been adopted, and, as we think, very properly. The police of every large city, in our opinion, should be uniformed; this is also the opinion of many good judges in such matters, and we observe that the plan is to be adopted in Philadelphia, and also in Cincinnati. Let not Boston be behindhand in adopting a measure that would undoubtedly add to the efficacy of this arm of the municipal authority.—For the Chief of Police, the emblem of office is a gold star, with a gold ribbon underneath holding a gold shield. The dress is a double-breasted frock coat of navy blue cloth, the skirt extending two thirds of the distance from the top of the hip to the bend of the knee. There are two rows of buttons on the breast, ten in each row, the distance between each row being five and one half inches at the top, and three and one half inches at the bottom. The collar is of black silk velvet, rolling, and buttons close up at the throat; the cuffs are two and a half inches deep, and go round the sleeves parallel with the lower edge, and buttons with three small buttons at the under seam; the pockets are in the folds of the skirt, with one button at the hip and one at the end of each pocket, making four buttons on the back and skirt of the coat—the hip button ranging with the lower button on the breast. For the Captains of Police, the emblem is a silver star, with a silver disc about a quarter of an inch wide, having engraved upon it the name of the captain, and the district to which he is attached. The dress is the same as the chief, with seven buttons on the breast, double rows. For Lieutenants of Police, the emblem of office is a silver star, surrounded with a small silver wire; and the dress is the same as the captains, with eight buttons on the breast, double rows. For the Sergeants of Police the emblem of office is a plain copper star; and the dress is a frock coat of navy blue cloth, single-breasted, nine buttons on the breast, and buttons close up at the throat, with a rolling collar of black velvet. The skirt extends two thirds of the distance from the top of the hip-bone to the bend of the knee; the cuffs are two and a half inches deep, go round the sleeves parallel with the lower edge, and button with two small buttons at the under seam; the pockets are in the folds of the skirt, with one button at the hip and one at the end of each pocket, making four buttons on the back and skirt of the coat—the hip button to range with the lower button on the breast. For Policemen, the emblem of office is a plain brass star, with the number of his warrant stamped thereon; the dress is the same as the sergeants. In addition to the above, each officer and policeman is furnished with a navy blue cloth cap, made in the style of the officers of the highest grade in the Navy, on the front of which is the word "Police," in raised letters, the number of the warrant of each policeman, and the letter of the section to which he belongs. During night patrol duty, the policemen wear a leather cap in the form of a helmet, with a rim around it resembling the cap worn by the New York firemen, with the word "Police," in large, white, metal letters, a star and the number of the district to which they belong on the front of the cap. Thus this important arm of the law for the great metropolis of America may be said to be in a state of thorough organization, and complete in all its departments. There can be no doubt but that all persons, legally endowed with authority, should be so uniformed, as to carry with them, even to a casual passer-by, the sign of their authority, and then none will pretend to dispute it. A year's experience in the matter will show other cities of the Union the great excellence and importance of such a measure; and, as we have intimated above, we hope to see it generally adopted.

THE TURKS.

Below we have presented four characteristic pictures of Turkish peculiarities, which are truthful and expressive. Any item relating to this peculiar people, is, at the present time, vastly interesting, as exhibiting facts concerning a race so different from our own, or any with which we are closely brought in contact, and as representing a nation now struggling in war for the preservation of their nationality. The sympathy of the whole civilized world is with them; and their oppressor, the haughty emperor of Russia, is as bitterly denounced and detested by honest people as the Turks, in the present conflict, are honored and upheld. Travellers tell us that we are mistaken with regard to the efficiency and courage of the Turkish troops. Once let them have their religious zeal awakened—let their devotional feelings be connected with the idea of revenging their wrongs, and they are nearly invincible. The troops of Russia, on the contrary, have to march thousands of miles from the land of their birth to seek the Turks, and then have to fight them in a climate, where, while the Mussulmen are perfectly at home and acclimated, the Russians die off like sheep with fever and disease. There are many reasons why we think that Nicholas, with all his boasted strength and power, is weak here. He has many circumstances to contend with besides the bravery of the Turks. His own army dislike his service. They are impressed men, who fight because they are compelled to do so; and already, in one instance, has a whole regiment of Poles revolted and gone over to the Turks. Might does not always make right. On the other hand, the army of the Sultan is constantly being augmented by the joining of some of the best German, Hungarian and French officers in Europe; and his people are all loyal, united and determined. The Russians are wholly the aggressors, are away from home, the Turks are fighting for their families and their firesides. There can be no comparison between troops actuated by such contrary motives—one army fights with heart and soul, the other because its officers order it to do so! Thinks any one that there will not be a plenty of Russian bullets shot at random? Thinks any one that the Turks will throw away their fire? No, no; Nicholas is too hasty this time. And, though we do not pretend to be any prophet, yet we think his future career can never equal his former power and splendor.

TURKISH LADY AT HOME. TURKISH POLICEMAN. TURKISH SOLDIER. TURKISH FRUIT-VENDER.

ASTOR HOUSE. BARCLAY STREET.

A PANORAMIC VIEW OF BROADWAY, NEW

WARREN STREET.

A PANORAMIC VIEW OF BROADWAY, NEW

LA FARGE BUILDINGS. DUANE STREET.

A PANORAMIC VIEW OF BROADWAY, NEW Y

ADWAY BANK. PARK PLACE MURRAY STREET.

CITY, COMMENCING AT THE ASTOR HOUSE.

CHEMICAL BANK. CHAMBER STREET IRVING HOUSE.

CITY, COMMENCING AT THE ASTOR HOUSE

HOSPITAL.

CITY, COMMENCING AT THE ASTOR HOUSE.

[For description, see page 173.]

SLEIGHING IN BROADWAY.

HARPER'S WEEKLY.
A JOURNAL OF CIVILIZATION.
VOL. II.—No. 87.] NEW YORK, SATURDAY, AUGUST 28, 1858. [PRICE FIVE CENTS.

THE BURNING OF THE CITY HALL, NEW YORK, AUGUST 18, 1858.

SUPPLEMENT.

NEW YORK EVENING EXPRESS.

"One Country--One Constitution--One Destiny."

THURSDAY EVENING, SEPTEMBER 2, 1858.

THE GREAT JUBILEE.

ATLANTIC TELEGRAPH CELEBRATION.

IMPOSING SPECTACLE!

Half a Million of People in the Streets!

A FULL ACCOUNT OF EVERYTHING THAT WAS DONE.

SOLEMN SERVICES AT TRINITY CHURCH.

THE TE DEUM, ETC.

BISHOP DOANE'S ADDRESS.

Grand Military and Civic Procession.

The Montreal Artillery Men.

THE MARCH TO THE CRYSTAL PALACE.

Interesting Ceremonies There.

Immense Crowd.

SPEECHES AND MUSIC.

NIGHT SCENES.

THE FIREMEN'S TORCHLIGHT PROCESSION.

THE ILLUMINATIONS.

Brilliant Display of Fireworks

ETC., ETC., ETC.

HAIL COLUMBIA!

YANKEE DOODLE!

GOD SAVE THE QUEEN!

Wednesday, September the 1st,—was the day appointed for the opening of the Atlantic Telegraph cable to the public, and also the day appointed for the great celebration of the greatest achievement of the age.

People began to celebrate it on the eve. For long hours after dark on Tuesday night, hundreds were engaged in putting up decorations, and arranging banners for the great festival.

At early dawn the city was astir. Already drums and trumpets were heard in the streets,—although the hour for forming the grand parade was not until 1 o'clock.

At sunrise flags of every nation on the globe were flying to the breeze. The morning was beautiful, mild, clear, with very light air from the West. Flags on masts would hardly fly; but on almost every house the bunting was thrust out of windows or depended from poles fastened on the roof, so as to hang down and display every fold of the colors. Never has so general a color-setting been seen in New York. With the least breath of air, the city, from a house top, looked like a fluttering kaleidoscope. As far as the eye could reach, on the bay, all the rivers, over the rivers, in the country,—every one who could raise a piece of colored stuff hoisted it for a flag. The shipping at our piers were gorgeous. The Express Office displayed a superb new National Standard, from a mast fifty feet high. From the City Hall French's, Old Tammany, the Astor House, Custom House, Exchange, and all the public buildings, banners were displayed. From some houses banners were hung at every window.

Business was suspended by general consent.—The Custom House was open for one hour only for the clearance and entry of vessels—from 6 to 10 A.M. The Post Office kept Sunday hours. The people created a new universal Holiday and kept it as such. Every one gave himself up to one sole object, "to celebrate the cable," and every one did it with all his might. Never was there such a celebration since New York was New York. Never such display; such lavish outlay, such unanimous enthusiasm.

Broadway was in a blaze of glory. Swept perfectly clean, but not sprinkled, it was a beautiful parade ground, and was full of paraders all day. The celebration ceremonies commenced formally with the grand Religious Services at Old Trinity, and we give the occurrences there, therefore, the place of honor in our columns.

Vol. VI.—No. 25. NEW YORK, SATURDAY, OCTOBER 9 1858. Four Cents.

BENICIA BOY'S SPARRING EXHIBITION AT MOZART HALL.—THL "BOY" AND JONES IN THE WIND-UP.

LATEST SPORTS ABROAD.

From Bell's Life in London, September 13.

THE RING.

FIGHTS TO COME.

SEPT. 21.—Brettle an1 Brown's Novice—£100 a side, London.
21.—Hannagan and Harrison—£15 a side, Liverpool.
21.—Tyson and Hall—£25 a side, London.
21.—Davis and Harper—£25 a side, Birmingham.
OCT. 5.—Brookes and Thomas—£25 a side, London.
NOV. 9.—Finighty and Norton—£25 a side, London.

BAILEY AND HOWE.—These men met last Monday to fight, but were prevented by the Blues. On Wednesday they again came together, and fought 23 rounds without any definite result, and were for the second time interrupted. The referee appointed a third time and place; but before Howe had reached the spot the police once more appeared on the ground. The referee must therefore name another time and place.

BRETTLE AND BROWN'S NOVICE.—The final deposit of £25 a side for this match is to be staked at Alec Keene's, Three Tuns, Moor-street, Soho, on Tuesday. At this deposit, final arrangements are to be made as to the mill. Both men are reported to be in fine form, and that there will be a fight is not doubted for a moment.

NORTON AND FINIGHTY.—Another deposit of £2 10s. a side for this match was made at Mr. Skinner's, Stone Stairs, Ratcliff, on Wednesday.

HARPER AND DAVIS.—These midland district men have made the whole of their money good for their fight which comes off on the 21st instant, and it has been mutually agreed to fight within 40 miles of Oldbury.

YOUNG HANNAGAN and Young Harrison are matched to fight for £15 a side on September 21. The first deposit of £5 a side is down. The lads fight in the Liverpool ring at catch weight.

JERRY NOON IN THE FIELD AGAIN.—Having heard that several of the great guns have asserted that they can win easily, Jerry Noon will fight either blacks or whites at 9st. 2lb. or 9st. 4lb. in three months from the time of drawing articles, for £100 a side; he thinks, never having been stopped by outsiders, he has yet a chance to checkmate them.

BENJAMIN LEECK, lately arrived from America, [who is he?] will fight George King of Liverpool, for £50 a side. Money ready at John Chown's, Green Man, Jane-street, Commercial road.

PEDESTRIANISM.

PUDNEY AND ROWAN.—MATCH FOR £50.—The four miles race between the noted pedestrians, James Pudney of the Commercial-road East, and John Rowan of Gateshead, for £25 a side, came off on Monday last, on Mr. Baum's enclosed running-grounds, White Lion, Hackney Wick. The match, from the celebrity of the parties, and their well-known "antecedents," had excited the most lively interest in all persons who patronize this species of athletic sport, and there were no less than 1,300 spectators assembled to witness the result. The contending parties in the match had competed on a former occasion, at Newcastle, in a match of six miles, but then Rowan received a start of 100 yards, and proved rather an easy winner. The distance on Monday was but four miles (26 laps round the course and 180 yards,) and Rowan got a start of only 50 yards. The course had been repeatedly and carefully rolled by a heavy roller in the early part of the day, and was in admirable condition; indeed, all the arrangements made br Mr. Baum and the well-known Bill Price seemed to give universal satisfaction. At about six o'clock both men appeared on the ground, apparently in first-rate "fettle." Pudney, who was the favorite at 5 and 6 to 4, stands some two or three inches taller than his opponent, and is also his senior by some years. Rowan is, nevertheless, a compact, well-made little fellow. He had trained for the match at Jack Levitt's Racecourse, Newcastle, while Pudney had undergone his probationary movements at Garratt-lane, under the watchful supervision of G. Clarke of Yarmouth. On the signal for starting being given, both men bounded away from their respective marks and "pursued the even tenor of their way" as follows: During the first mile Pudney gained considerably on his opponent, and at the end of the second had considerably reduced the gap between them; in the seventh lap Pudney had got within eight yards of his man, and at the conclusion of the eighth not more than two yards separated them; it was now evident that he could win the race when he pleased. In the eleventh he fell off a little, but resumed his position in the twelfth; in the run home of the thirteenth he had breasted him, but again fell off slightly in the fourteenth, a disadvantage which he fully recovered in the fifteenth; in the sixteenth the men alternately had the lead, and at the end of the eighteenth, Rowan, seeing it was all up with him, gave in (complaining of a bad foot,) to the great delight of the Metropolitans, and the signal dismay of the gentlemen "frae the North," who had backed their pet to a considerable amount. Of course Pudney finished the distance by himself, doing his four miles, at his ease, in twenty-one minutes ten seconds.

GREAT PEDESTRIAN MATCH IN KENT.—The announcement that "thirty gentlemen of Whitstable" would contend against a similiar number selected from various parts of the Isle of Thanet drew together. on Monday last, at Birchington, about four miles from Margate, a vast number of spectators to that romantic and delightful part of Kent. We imagine that, to the great majority present, the system adopted in this kind of competition was a novelty, being so unlike the old style of pedestrianism in any other part of the country. We will attempt to describe the manner in which the match was carried out. As before observed, there were thirty runners on each side, the Whitstable party being attired in pink guernseys with white drawers, and their opponents in both habiliments of white. Bounds were marked out, the Pink having the right hand side and the Isle of Thanet men the left, the umpires being stationed at the extreme end between the two lines of demarcation. Each party had to run out inside and return outside their respective boundary. They then gradually neared each other, tempting an opponent to follow, and once out of bounds an exciting chase ensued, a touch only being considered a chalk or stroke. In such a case great judgment is necessary, for to follow or not entirely depends on what sort of a man an attempt is made to capture. The usual plan, we believe, is for a rather indifferent runner to become as it were a decoy, with a man of swifter powers to back him up as his second, the others being on the look out all the time. The decoy ought to be a good jockey, to lead one of the opposite side out of his bounds, so that the second may chase him. They are not compelled to keep within the field, and while this mode of running is going on as many men on each side as think proper may follow in succession, but care must be taken to avoid those behind, as the last runner out is at liberty to take, or at least to touch any man before him. If managed properly the competition frequently becomes most exciting. A good general in each camp is essentially necessary one, in fact, who knows the qualities of each runner, and starts his men with judgment, in order to conteract the tactics of the opposing side. It is easy to imagine that some splendid running is displayed when once in the field which extended over fifteen acres. The games consisted of seven strokes, and when one was made all returned to their tents and started afresh. The weather was extremely propitious, and the majority of the company of a *distingue* character, many ladies honoring the competitors with their presence. Booths and tents were erected on the ground, and there was no want of refreshments, at a moderate scale of charges.

The Whitstable party were the favorites, for independent of its being well known that they frequently practise together, they were, as a body, a finer set of men than their opponents; many of whom, however, displayed much muscular power, and were excellent runners. Most of the competitors ran bare footed, and others in stockings, but not one wore shoes. The peculiar style and swiftness of the running, especially by the Whitstable men, elicited frequent bursts of applause. The contest was kept up with great spirit for upwards of two hours, but thh Isle of Thanet men were defeated in every instance, although there was no lack of energy on their part. This may be accounted for from the fact of the men being gathered together from various parts of the island, and not having any, or perhaps very little, practice as a "body corporate."

DESTRUCTION OF THE NEW YORK CRYSTAL PALACE BY FIRE, OCTOBER 5, 1858.

HARPER'S WEEKLY.
A JOURNAL OF CIVILIZATION.

VOL. II.—No. 98.] NEW YORK, SATURDAY, NOVEMBER 13, 1858. [PRICE FIVE CENTS.

CONTENTS.

THE NEW BRICK CHURCH IN FIFTH AVENUE.

WE herewith present an engraving of the New Brick Church in Fifth Avenue, which was dedicated to the service of Almighty God on 31st October. The venerable pastor, Rev. Dr. Spring, officiated on the occasion with his usual solemnity and earnestness. His text was in Leviticus, xix., 30: "Ye shall reverence my sanctuary." After a few words of joyful gratitude on the auspicious occasion, he proceeded to set forth the reasons why men should reverence the sanctuary—1. Because it is the house of God; 2. For its moral and religious power; 3. For its conservative influence; and, lastly, for its social influence in the community. These considerations were urged with remarkable force, and with a beauty of illustration in some measure peculiar to Dr. Spring, but at this time with more than his usual felicity. Perhaps the best passage in the sermon was his exhibition of the conservative influence of the sanctuary. Having completed the discussion of the theme, the pastor called upon the people to stand up, and the whole assembly rose and stood, while, in measured and majestic words, he devoted the house to the worship of the Triune God!

It will be remembered by the subscriber to *Harper's Weekly* that in No. 19 we gave a portrait of Dr. Spring and a view of the "Old Brick Church" in Beekman Street. That venerable building, which had been used as a church for ninety years, was pulled down last year to make way for a row of massive stores; and the congregation and the pastor moved "up town." They selected a site on the corner of Thirty-seventh Street and Fifth Avenue, on the top of Murray Hill, in the most aristocratic quarter of the city, and there they have built their new house—of which the engraving on this page will give the reader a very fair idea.

Dr. Spring, the venerable clergyman, whose name will ever be identified with this handsome building, is now in the seventy-fourth year of his age. He came here thirty-eight years ago, and ever since, in the eloquent language of the New York *Observer*, "has stood like a pillar in the midst of this great city, a tower of strength in the times that tried men's faith, and patience, and principle; the patron and friend of Christian benevolence; the wise and prudent counselor of the young and old; the example of holy living and patient continuance in well doing, while change and decay have been going on around him. He has buried more than one generation. He has preached more than seven thousand sermons! He has made full proof of his *ministry!* About three years ago he was threatened with blindness. For many long and weary months he was in darkness. A skillful operation removed the *cataract*, and he now reads and writes with ease, and bids fair to continue long the pastor of the flock that he came to in his youth—his first, his only, his beloved charge."

The new church is a massive building. The ground measurement is 75 by 145 feet; main auditory, 50 feet in height. With the galleries, from 1500 to 2000 people can be accommodated. The spire is 250 feet high, the cap-stone weighing 2500 pounds.

The interior of the church is admirably arranged. The organ is behind the pulpit, and a recess, or organ-loft, at its side, is designed for the leader of the congregational music. There are three aisles, leaving four blocks of pews, 146 in all, on the ground floor, which will seat 1200 persons. The galleries have 18 pews on each side, 36 in all, seating 200 more. Scagliola columns behind the pulpit support a ceiling; and the old tablet, "Holiness to the Lord," known to all frequenters of the Old Brick Church, is renovated and placed here. The pulpit is in a semicircular recess, and the general effect of this end of the church is very grand. The vestibules of the church are laid with marble; the gallery stairs are of oak. Rooms for the pastor, the trustees, and church purposes are provided; and there is a fine lecture-room in the rear, on Thirty-seventh Street. The old bell is in the new spire, to call, in its old tones, the children to worship as it has called their fathers. The church is lighted by one large chandelier of 100 burners, with an arrangement for lighting and extinguishing them all at one instant. The spire is to receive a fine clock, and this is the only apparent indication that the erection is not complete.

The Building Committee, of which Paul Spofford, Esq., is chairman, have given the church their time and labor, and to their admirable taste, care, and foresight alone, we believe, is to be ascribed the magnificence and appropriateness combined which make the New Brick Church one of the great architectural ornaments of New York city.

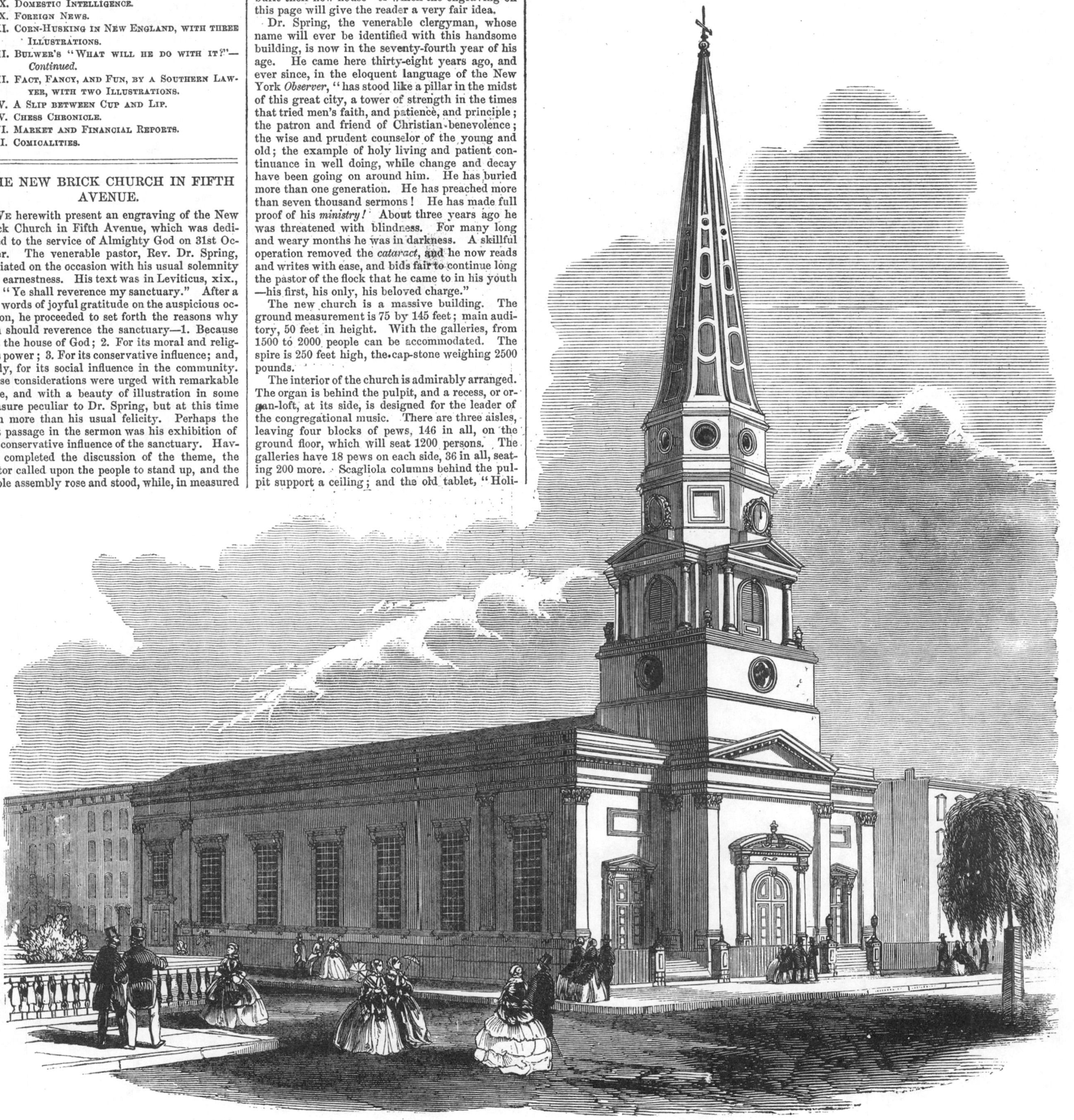

THE NEW BRICK CHURCH IN FIFTH AVENUE, NEW YORK.

FRANK LESLIE'S ILLUSTRATED NEWSPAPER

Entered according to Act of Congress in the year 1859, by FRANK LESLIE, in the Clerk's Office of the District Court for the Southern District of New York.

No. 193.—VOL. VIII.] NEW YORK, SATURDAY, AUGUST 13, 1859. PRICE 6 CENTS.

THE GREAT WAR
ON THE
NEW YORK PIGGERIES.

THE piggeries and offal boiling establishments in Hog town and its vicinity, having become such a nuisance to the neighborhood, that to endure it any longer was impossible, steps were taken by the police to remove them, and hostilities were commenced on Tuesday, the 26th of July.

At half-past eight on this eventful morning, a party of police from Twenty-second Precinct, under the command of "General" Downing, assembled in front of Mr. Wattemeyer's, corner of Fifty-fourth street and Fifth avenue, and organized their forces for another attack on the offending piggeries.

The fortress first attacked was that belonging to Mr. McCormick, on Fifty-ninth street, between Sixth and Seventh avenues. Notwithstanding the apparently impregnable position of General McCormick, the rock was scaled, and its owner forced to treat for peace. He obtained a suspension of hostilities for two hours, which, by order from Inspector Delavan, was afterwards increased to two days, in consequence of the difficulty of disposing at once of so many hogs.

From Fifth-ninth street the army marched to the piggery of Godfrey Brumme, in Fifty-seventh street, between Seventh and Eighth avenues. The hogs here were summarily expelled, their quarters were razed to the ground, and a plentiful supply of lime was sprinkled on the refuse of the pen.

Terence Cahill, Patrick Bohen and Laurence Lyons were also favored with a visit from the army, and their piggeries shared the fate of General McCormick's.

These gentlemen having been duly disposed of, the grand movement of the day was made to the "famous quadrilateral," bounded on the north by Fifty-second street, on the south by Fiftieth street, and flanked by Sixth and Seventh avenues. This spot is the grand centre of the operations; the steam from the bone boiling kettles is sometimes so intensely penetrating that the passengers in the Sixth avenue cars are obliged to stop their breath with their handkerchiefs while passing the block, and for several minutes afterwards. Nearly all the pigs had been previously removed from the quadrilateral, but the ominous cauldrons were there still, the majority of them still containing the abhorrent mess composed of swill of all kinds and all kinds of offal. Strange to say, but few of these cooking utensils were removed by the party of exterminators. After visiting one or two unimportant establishments, the army ceased from its labors, and adjourned for refreshment to Mr. Wattemeyer's, and their absence was taken advantage of by the enemy, who immediately set about repairing the broken defences, and driving back the pigs to their old quarters, the temporary pound which was erected on Fiftieth street being most unceremoniously broken down.

On the following day operations were resumed, the forces parading at the same place.

They proceeded at once, in two ranks, to the scene of action. In the forenoon they visited all the localities in the neighborhood of Fifty-ninth street, on both sides of Seventh avenue. All those persons who had not yet re-

THE PORCINE WAR—MRS. MC'ELROY EXPRESSES TO OUR ARTIST HER VIEWS ON THE UNITED STATES IN GENERAL.

A SCENE AT THE BATTLE OF HOGTOWN.

VOL. I., NO. 43. F. GLEASON, PUBLISHER. BOSTON, SATURDAY, OCTOBER 22, 1859

[Written for Gleason's Pictorial Battle Ship.]

STRENGTH OF WOMAN'S LOVE.

(STANZAS FOR MUSIC.)

BY J. ALFORD.

Why do I thus behold thee
O'erwhelmed with sighs and tears?—
How oft have I implored thee
To banish hence thy fears?
Doubt not the vows I've plighted;
For thou shall mourn me dead,
My hopes of heaven be blighted,
Ere I another wed.

What though the world may chide me,
And look on thee with scorn;
Sincere affection guides me,
Then look not thus forlorn.
Doubt not the vows, etc.

What more can I assure thee,
Thy confidence to gain?
O, cease, then, I conjure thee,
Nor plunge me deep in pain.
Doubt not the vows, etc.

JUDGE HALIBURTON.

The return of the author of the celebrated "*Sam Slick*" papers to England, and his recent election to Parliament, render our publication of his portrait this week, both seasonable and appropriate.

Mr. Haliburton originally prepared those papers anonymously for a journal in Nova Scotia. He resided, at the time, and for many years afterward, in Halifax. The delineation of Yankee character in these writings was by no means remarkable for verisimilitude, but it was certainly an improvement upon that outrageous caricature, the stage Yankee, and had the additional advantage of being the medium of a great many common sense views of life, exquisitely spiced with delicate touches of sarcasm and humor. Sam Slick commented freely upon every phase and condition of society, as well as the follies of individuals, and scarcely any subject deserving of satire escaped perforation from his salient pen; yet he was never bitter, never ill-natured, and consequently his shots never failed to tell.

The editor of the journal in which they appeared afterwards collated them, and gave them to the world in the shape of a duodecimo volume, with Judge Haliburton's name appended, and it had an extensive sale, being recognized at once as being peculiarly original and meritorious.

Its popularity in America soon reached England, and a London publisher made overtures to Judge H., and finally purchased the copyright. Its success in Great Britain was equal to its sale in this country, and Sam Slick's droll but shrewd sayings were quoted in all classes of society, and even in Parliament.

In 1842, Judge Haliburton became an *attache* of the American legation in London, and in the following year published his observations upon what he saw there, in a volume entitled "Sam Slick in England." In it he seems to have taken the most flattering views of English customs and personal peculiarities, his predilections all tending that way; still, the satirical touches, and the same sly humor as marked the Clock-Maker were not lacking in it, and Jonathan, in his turn, was afforded some fun at the expense of the cockneys.

Later still, the Judge published an historical work on the settlement of New England. It is, we believe, not more than two or three years since Mr. Haliburton took up his residence in England, and in May last he was elected a member of the House of Commons. The London press in commenting upon the personal appearance of the new member, said there was nothing to indicate that he was the famous humorist "Sam Slick," or anything more than a round, ruddy, good-natured gentleman from the rural districts. His "maiden speech" was not regarded as a success, and no one expects that he will win any laurels in Parliament. Still, we have no doubt he will be a very useful member.

JUDGE HALIBURTON (SAM SLICK.)

FULTON FERRY, BROOKLYN.

On this page, we give a large and accurate illustration of that great floating thoroughfare, the Fulton Ferry, and its buildings on the Brooklyn side.

We have spoken so fully of the ferry accommodations of New York in connection with our recently-published engravings of the famous South Ferry and the ferry boats, that to describe minutely the very similar appointments of the Fulton, would be a work of supererogation.

In the present picture, the water, all alive with various craft, is the East River. On the left is the steamer Metropolis, of the Fall River route from New York to Boston, coming in with all her flags flying. Almost simultaneously, the boats of the Norwich and Worcester line, and the Stonington, laden with passengers from Boston, pass majestically by Brooklyn and round the Battery to their respective piers on the North River side. The three boats arrive usually between six and seven A. M., unless detained by fogs or head winds on Long Island Sound, which is frequently the case.

The vessel numbered 10 is a fore-and-aft schooner, belonging to a regular line. Of all the ferries which connect Long Island with New York, the Fulton makes the most rapid trips and is most frequented. Merchants, mechanics, pleasure-drivers, fancy men with fast horses and faster women, funeral processions bound to Greenwood Cemetery, military companies, milkmen, market-men, butcher and grocer wagons, organ-grinders, ladies and children—an innumerable and heterogeneous crowd, bipedal and quadrupedal—may be seen at most any hour, but especially in the early and latter periods of the day, on board a Fulton ferry boat.

Such facilities, and the rapid growth of New York, have built up Brooklyn almost magically since 1830. At that time there were few houses and no business done there; now it is a great and populous city, which has lately absorbed to itself in one municipality the towns of Williamsburg and Bushwick. Its City Hall will compare favorably with any in the United States, being built of white marble, in elegant architectural style, and covering an area of 162 by 102 feet, with a dome and cupola reaching to 150 feet from the ground.

THE GREAT MYSTERY.

The body is to die; so much is certain. What lies beyond? No one who passes the charmed boundary comes back to tell. The imagination visits the realm of shadows—sent out from some window of the soul over life's restless waters—but wings its way wearily back with no olive leaf in its beak as a token of emerging life beyond the closely bending horizon. The great sun comes and goes in heaven, yet breathes no secret of the ethereal wilderness. The crescent moon cleaves her nightly passage across the upper deep, but tosses overboard no message and displays no signals. The sentinel stars challenge each other as they walk their nightly rounds; but we catch no syllable of their countersign which gives passage to the heavenly camp. Shut in! Shut in! Between this and the other life there is a great gulf fixed, across which neither eye nor foot can travel. The gentle friend whose orbs we closed in their last sleep long years ago, died with rapture in her wonder-stricken eyes, a smile of ineffable joy upon her lips, and hands folded over a triumphant heart; but her lips were past speech, and intimated nothing of the vision that enthralled her."—*Dr. Holland.*

VIEW OF THE FULTON FERRY BUILDINGS, BROOKLYN, LONG ISLAND, N. Y.

THE NEW YORK YACHT CLUB SAILING IN TWO SQUADRONS, AS THEY APPEARED APPROACHING NEW BEDFORD HARBOR.—From a Sketch by our Own Artist.

THE NEW YORK YACHT SQUADRON OFF NEW BEDFORD HARBOR.

The New York Yacht Squadron made an excursion to New Bedford Harbor, on Tuesday last, and presented a magnificent spectacle. The Commodore issued orders, whilst at Newport, for the fleet to lay to, as the yachts arrived off the Dumplings, and go into New Bedford in two lines, the Commodore to lead the starboard and the Vice-Commodore the port division, the second and third classes to start at 8, and the first class at 9 A. M.

The wind was leading from the Light-ship, a fresh full-sail breeze. The gun from the Maria reverberated over Newport, and away flew the second and third classes, except the Mallory and Manersing—each waiting for the other to start—the Manersing leaving at 8:15, and the Mallory a short time after. The first classes were off at the signal-gun at 9. The Irene, Ray, America and Narragansett took the lead, the Manersing overhauling them fast. The America and Ray held their speed well, but the fleet Manersing at length passed them and led the squadron, rounding to at the Dumplings, and firing the gun of victory.

The yachts passed the lighthouse and rounded to in the following order: Manersing, America, Ray, Bonita, Narragansett, Irene, Alpha, Gypsy, Madgie, Rebecca, Maria, Julia, Bessie, Mallory, Widgeon, Haze, Norma, Favorita, Zinga, Una, Juliet, Scud, Restless, Charlotte, and Rowena. The fleet then formed in two lines, headed by the Maria and Favorita, and went into the harbor of New Bedford, (the whole town turning out to behold the beautiful sight), amid the the roar of cannon, every mast in port decorated with bunting, and the docks thronged with spectators. Mr. Rutherford's yacht, the Ray, fouled the Madgie, in coming to anchor, and carried away her own top-mast and the Madgie's gib boom, and also rent her own mainsail.

Our engraving represents the general appearance of the Squadron off New Bedford Harbor.

OUR MARBLE PALACES.

THE MARBLE PALACE OF MESSRS. LORD & TAYLOR, 461 TO 467 BROADWAY, N.Y.

We beg to call the attention of our readers this week, to our illustration of the splendid store of Messrs. Lord & Taylor, Nos. 461 to 467 Broadway, corner of Grand street. This beautiful building, which is entirely new, having been finished only in August last, consists of five stories and basement; it is constructed of white marble from the Chester quarries, and is of the modern Italian school, from the designs of that eminent architect, Griffith Thomas, Esq. The length of the principal front in Broadway is eighty-eight feet by one hundred feet deep on Grand street. A noble arch of richly gilded and ornamented metal work, extending upward to the second story, forms the entrance on Broadway, while on either side are immense windows, each formed of a single sheet of highly polished plate glass. The upper stories are ornamented with finely chiseled balustrades and richly-cut scroll brackets, the whole being surmounted by a colossal marble cornice and pediment. The interior is fitted up in a most elaborate manner, combining elegance and utility; and leaving nothing to be desired in order to facilitate the proper working of so large an establishment. The first floor is lighted behind by semi-cupola windows, in strong metal frame work. This, with the basement and second floor, are devoted to retail trade, while the three upper stories are exclusively for the wholesale or jobbing department, and for offices. Goods are received and dispatched by the Grand street entrance, being raised or lowered by a steam elevator, the steam from the boiler of which, also warms the building.

This well-known firm, which has been established now thirty years, have two other places of business; the principle one being 255 to 261 Grand street, its dimensions being 100 feet by 200 feet deep, and is solely devoted to the retail trade; their third store being 47 and 49 Catharine street. The total number of their employes amount to six hundred. Strangers visiting New York will find this magnificent building well worthy of their inspection.

The firm of Lord & Taylor is one of the most important in the United States—their wholesale business in the interior and in the West, is immense, and puts them in the first rank of our merchant princes. Their retail trade in the city is very extensive, and as they keep none but the best goods and employ no one in their establishment who is not a gentleman both in education and in manners, the popularity of this house for fair prices and courteous attention to customers, is second to none in the city.

THE CITY OF MONTREAL.

The city of Montreal, interesting always on its own account, for the histories and traditions which belong to it, assumes just now an unwonted importance in consequence of the proposed visit to it of the Prince of Wales.

As a commercial city, Montreal has won a high position. It is beyond all question the first city in British North America. The people seem to have an energy which reminds one of the United States. Happily situate, at the head of ocean navigation, and at the mouth of the Ottawa and Upper St. Lawrence, it has naturally become a general depot for Canadian produce. The Grand Trunk Railway will doubtless increase its importance, and assist in developing its fine surrounding country. It boasts nearly 75,000 inhabitants, the largest cathedral in North America, a splendid market-house, and other public buildings, and, above all, that monument of engineering skill, the Victoria Bridge. Montreal will give the Prince a favorable idea of British North America.

"Why does father call mother honey?" asked a boy of his elder brother—"Can't think, except it's 'cause she wears a large comb in her head."

OUR MARBLE PALACES—THE NEW STORE OF MESSRS. LORD & TAYLOR, NOS 461 TO 467 BROADWAY, NEW YORK.—(See page 261.)

FRANK LESLIE'S ILLUSTRATED NEWSPAPER

Entered according to the Act of Congress, in the year 1860, by FRANK LESLIE, in the Clerk's Office of the District Court for the Southern District of New York.

No. 275.—VOL. XI.] NEW YORK, MARCH 2, 1861. [PRICE 6 CENTS.

THE PRESIDENT ELECT ON HIS WAY TO WASHINGTON.

From Cincinnati to Columbus—Arrival at Columbus—Escorted to the Governor's Room—The President at Cleveland—The President meets Ex-President Fillmore at Buffalo—Arrival of the President at Albany—At Troy—Arrival at New York—The President at the City Hall, &c.

From Cincinnati to Columbus.

IN our last number we left Mr. Lincoln at Cincinnati, which city he left on the 13th. His departure was attended with little ceremony. At nine o'clock the President elect with his family drove to the depot, where a large crowd had gathered. An eye-witness says that his appearance was careworn, and his face crowded with wrinkles. It must be confessed that, although he travels only in the daytime, yet the labor is great, since the stoppages are very numerous, and he is obliged or expected to make a speech at all of them. On his way from Cincinnati to Columbus he made nearly half a dozen. The principal ones were at Morrow, Xenia and London, at all of which places there were great concourses of people. At Xenia they acted more like crazy people than American citizens. Here rather an amusing episode occurred. We quote from our friend Howard of the *Times*, and knowing his appreciation of the good things of this world, we cordially re-echo his sorrows:

"It was about one o'clock when we reached that point, and as we had breakfasted quite early in the morning, the anticipated and promised lunch was regarded most favorably by the several eyes of faith, and the various unemployed digesting apparatuses that floated and uncomfortably moved from car to car most restlessly. Imagine the feelings of the President elect, of all the corporals, of the high and mighties, of the four reporters and the untitled hangers-on, when it was announced by the chairman of the gastronomic department that a lunch, varied and extensive in its dainties, had been prepared, had been left on the table in the depot, and had been devoured by the voracious and Democratic crowd, who now, with well-filled paunches, with bread and buttery hands, and with the most comfortable abdominal sensations, were clamoring for a third speech from their dear old Rail-Splitter."

The philosopher of the party seems to be the Prince of Rails, or the President Lincoln's eldest son, for the historian relates that he took out his meerschaum and puffed vigorously.

We have not space to dilate upon the little passage of arms between Miss Mary Jane Stuart and Old Abe, although it involved a nosegay and a kiss, nor will we say anything of the young damsel who begged the President to let his whiskers grow. The gravity of the occasion compels us to skip these episodes.

The Arrival at Columbus.

The State House of Columbus is a fine imposing building, and the reception was worthy the occasion and the *locale*. Great credit is due to the various State and local officials who managed it, prominent amongst whom was Adjutant-General Carrington, of this State, on whom devolved the entire charge of the party during their trip through Ohio. Drawn up before the depot was a very fine array of military; at one end of the line was a cannon, which momentarily thundered out a hearty how-are-you; carriages for the guests, one and all, little and big, were provided at the other end of the line, while far off, as far as the eye could reach, and in numbers so great that no mortal man could easily number them, stretched thousands and thousands of cheering, hurrahing, welcoming citizens. A fine band of music preceded the procession, and while the multitude rolled after, like the waves of the ocean, and their voices roared afar off like the sound of many waters, the President elect was drawn in hospitable triumph to the State Capitol.

He is escorted to the Governor's Room

Through lines of unarmed men, in which elegantly furnished cham-

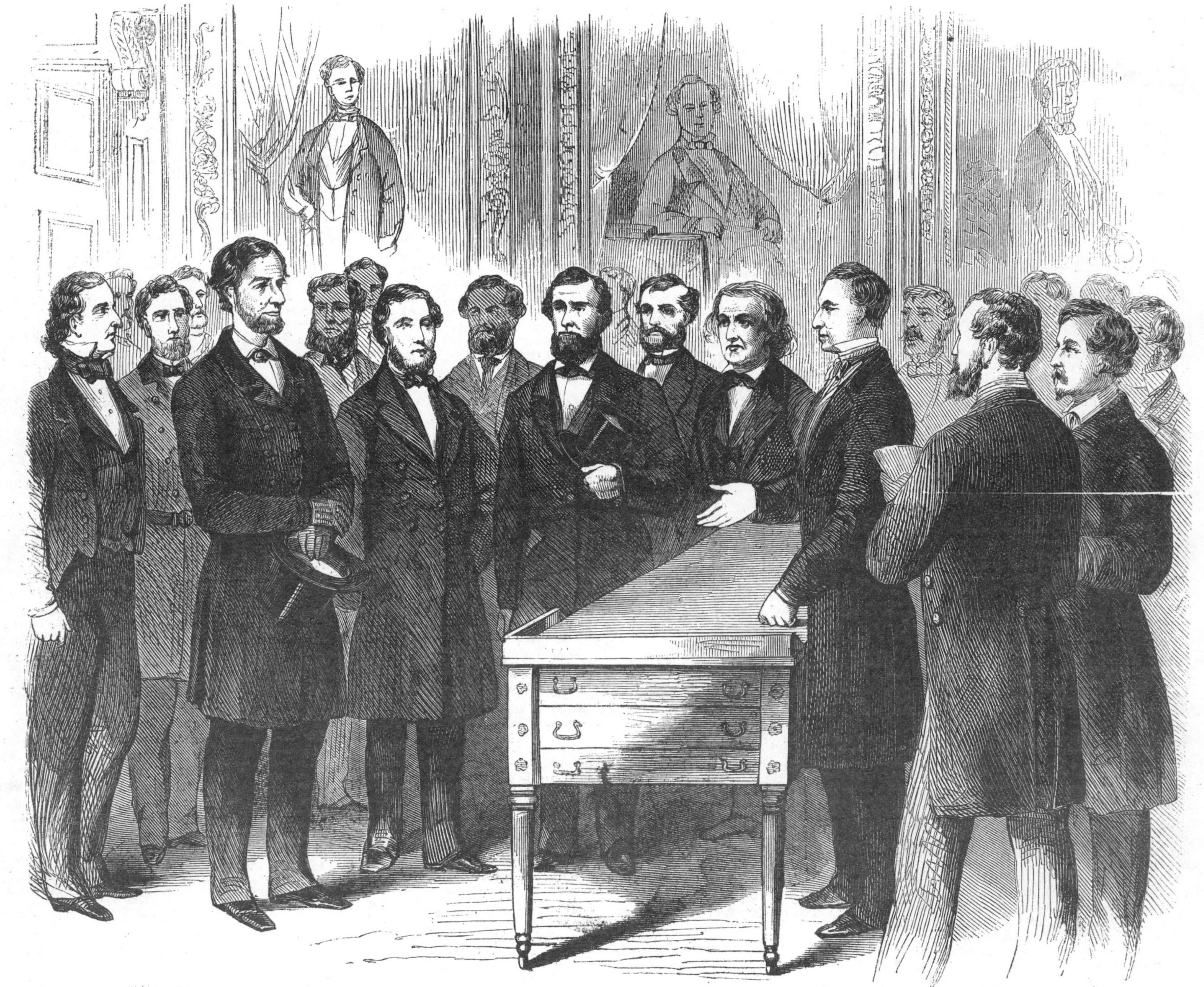

THE PRESIDENTIAL JOURNEY—RECEPTION OF PRESIDENT LINCOLN BY FERNANDO WOOD, MAYOR OF NEW YORK, AT THE CITY HALL, ON WEDNESDAY, FEB. 20TH, 1861.—FROM A SKETCH BY OUR RESIDENT ARTIST.

New-York Semi-Weekly Tribune.

VOL. XVII. NO. 1,670. NEW-YORK, TUESDAY, MAY 28, 1861. THREE DOLLARS A YEAR.

THE MURDER OF COL. ELLSWORTH.

TEARING DOWN THE REBEL FLAG.

PUNISHMENT OF THE MURDERER.

MINUTE AND ACCURATE ACCOUNT.

From Our Special Correspondent.

WASHINGTON, Friday, May 24, 1861.

I have already given by telegraph a brief account of the successful movement of to-day, and of our sorrowful calamity, and I hasten to send such details as my own observation enables me to supply. The part of the expedition with which I moved was that under command of the late Col. Ellsworth. His Regiment of Zouaves was certainly the most actively employed, and was the earliest upon the hostile ground; and with him were associated the most startling events of the day. Of the general forces which are now assembled in Alexandria, others can speak better than I, for their operations were wholly distinct, until the time of the junction, when they were combined under one command. The exact nature of the inroad, as well as the means by which it was to be effected, were of course withheld from the public up to the latest hour, and the only sure method of gaining accurate knowledge of the result was by joining what seemed likely to be the leading body in the movement.

It was generally understood in Washington, on Thursday evening, that an advance of some sort was contemplated, though the rumors fixed no exact time or point of assault. But as the night advanced, the slight fever of excitement which the half-authorized intelligence created, wore away, and the city fell into its usual tranquillity. The contrast between its extreme quiet and the bustle which pervaded some of the expectant camps, was very remarkable. I crossed the Potomac, from Seventh street, in a little boat, and before I had half reached the Zouave camp, unusual indications of busy preparation came echoing over the water. The night was peculiarly still and clear, and the moon so full and lustrous, that the camp was almost visible from the opposite shore. Above the slight murmur caused by the rustle of arms and the marching, a song would occasionally be heard, and once the whole regiment burst out into "Columbia, the Gem of the Ocean," with all the fervor they could bring to it. It was not early when I reached the camp, but the exercise was still progressing under the vigilance of the Colonel, who threw in now and then clear and energetic counsels for the guidance of his men in the morning's work. Before midnight everything needful had been done, and the troops were scattered to their tents for two hours of rest. The Colonel did not sleep until much later. He sat at his table completing the official arrangements which remained to him, and setting carefully before his subordinates the precise character of the duties they were to be charged with. After this he was alone, and I thought, as I entered his tent a little before he turned to his straw and blankets, that his pen was fulfilling a tenderer task than the rough planning of a dangerous exploit. He was so much a stranger to fear, this brave little Colonel, that his friends sometimes wondered at him; but it seemed, then, that he was not insensible to the awful hazards of his station. I hope that those who were nearest to him will find a touch of consolation in the assurance that the last moments he passed alone were given to them.

For more than an hour the encampment was silent. Then it began to stir again, and presently was all alive with action. At 2 o'clock, steamboats appeared off the shore, from one of which Capt. Dahlgren, the commander of the Navy-Yard, came to announce that all was ready for the transportation. The men marched forward in line, and were drawn up by companies to the beach. At this time, the scene was animated in the highest degree. The vivid costumes of the men—some being wrapped from head to foot in their great red blankets, but most of them clad in their gray jackets and trowers and embroidered caps; the peaks of the tents, regularly distributed, all glowing like huge lanterns from the fires within them; the glittering rows of rifles and sabers; the woods and hills, and the placid river, which here meet in exquisite proportion, enfolding all—and all these suffused with the broad moonlight, were blended in such novel picturesqueness that no man among the throng could fail to be moved by it. The embarkation was rapidly conducted, and, although the spot chosen was not apparently the most advantageous, was completed in less than two hours. The entire regiment, excepting the small guard necessarily left behind, nearly one thousand men, were safely bestowed and on their way down the river by 4 o'clock, just as the dawn began to shine over the hills and through the trees.

The night had passed without any noteworthy incident. It had been thought possible that the rebels, who could by some means undoubtedly have gained premonition of the movement, might fire the bridge by which other regiments were to advance upon them, and thus diminish the attacking force for a time. Nothing of this kind, however, had been attempted, and as we steamed down the river (very slowly, for the boats were heavily laden), there was no sign that we were expected, or that any inroad was provided against. This seemed at first suspicious, especially as on nearing Alexandria we found it sharing the same appearance of repose. It could hardly be credited that at least a rumor of warning should not have reached them. But if it had, it would appear that their enormous self-confidence was not to be even thus disturbed, for it afterward was found that no preparations either for resistance or for evacuation had been made until early in the morning, when, if I am rightly informed, the sloop-of-war Pawnee had sent ashore a summons to surrender the town, which I believe the garrison were considering, or had partially assented to, when we arrived. It was not until our boats were about to draw up to the wharf that our approach was noticed in any way; but at the latest minute a few sentinels, whom we had long before discerned, fired their muskets in the air as a warning, and, running rapidly into the town, disappeared. Two or three of the Zouaves, fancying that the shots were directed toward them (which they certainly were not), discharged their rifles after the retreating forms, but no injury to anybody followed. The town was thus put on its guard, but yet so early was the hour, and so apparently unlooked for our arrival, that when we landed, about half-past 5 o'clock, the streets were as deserted as if it had been midnight.

Before our troops disembarked, a boat, filled with armed marines, and carrying a flag of truce, put off from the Pawnee, and landed ahead of us. From the officer in charge we learned that the Pawnee had already proposed terms of submission to the town, and that the Rebels had consented to vacate within a specified time. This seemed to settle the question of a contest in the negative; but in the confusion of mustering and forming the men, the intelligence was not well understood, and received but little attention. Indeed, I am quite sure that the Pawnee's officer did not seek Col. Ellsworth, to communicate with him, and that the Colonel only obtained a meager share of information by seeking it directly from the bearer of the flag of truce himself. No doubt this omission arose from the confused condition in which affairs then stood. But it would have caused no difference in the Colonel's military plans. No attack was meditated, except in case of a forcible resistance to his progress. On the other hand, the idea of the place being under a truce seemed to banish every suspicion of a resistance either from multitudes or individuals. It was just possibly this consideration that led Col. Ellsworth to forego the requisite personal precautions, which, if taken, would have prevented his unhappy death. But I am sure none of us at that time estimated the probability of the danger which afterward menaced us. Perhaps the thought of actual bloodshed and death in war was too foreign to our experiences to be rightly weighed. But it certainly did not enter our minds then, as poor Ellsworth's fate has since taught us it should have done, that a town half waked, half terrified, and under truce, could harbor any peril for us. So the Colonel gave some rapid directions for the interruption of the railway course, by displacing a few rails near the depot, and then turned toward the center of the town, to destroy the means of communication southward by the telegraph; a measure which he appeared to regard as very seriously important. He was accompanied by Mr. H. J. Winser, Military Secretary to the Regiment, the Chaplain, the Rev. E. W. Dodge, and myself. At first he summoned no guard to follow him, but he afterward turned and called forward a single squad, with a Sergeant from the first company. We passed quickly through the streets, meeting a few bewildered travelers issuing from the principal hotel, which seemed to be slowly coming to its daily senses, and were about to turn toward the telegraph office, when the Colonel, first of all, caught sight of the Secession flag, which has so long swung insolently in full view of the President's House. He immediately sent back the Sergeant, with an order for the advance of the entire first company, and, leaving the matter of the telegraph office for a while, pushed on to the hotel, which proved to be the Marshall House, a second-class inn. On entering the open door, the Colonel met a man in his shirt and trowsers, of whom he demanded what sort of flag it was that hung above the roof. The stranger, who seemed greatly alarmed, declared he knew nothing of it, and that he was only a boarder there. Without questioning him further the Colonel sprang up stairs, and we all followed to the topmost story, whence, by means of a ladder, he clambered to the roof, cut down the flag with Winser's knife, and brought it from its staff. There were two men in bed in the garret whom we had not observed at all when we entered, their position being somewhat concealed, but who now rose in great apparent amazement, although I observed that they were more than half dressed. We at once turned to descend, Private Brownell leading the way, and Colonel Ellsworth immediately following him with the flag. As Brownell reached the first landing-place, or entry, after a descent of some dozen steps, a man jumped from a dark passage, and hardly noticing the private, leveled a double-barreled gun square at the Colonel's breast. Brownell made a quick pass to turn the weapon aside, but the fellow's hand was firm, and he discharged one barrel straight to its aim, the slugs or buckshot with which it was loaded entering the Colonel's heart, and killing him at the instant. I think my arm was resting on poor Ellsworth's shoulder at the moment. At any rate, he seemed to fall almost from my own grasp. He was on the second or third step from the landing, and he dropped forward with that heavy, horrible, headlong weight which always comes of sudden death inflicted in this manner. His assailant had turned like a flash to give the contents of the other barrel to Brownell, but either he could not command his aim or the Zouave was too quick with him, for the slugs went over his head, and passed through the panels and wainscot of a door which sheltered some sleeping lodegrs. Simultaneously with this second shot, and sounding like the echo of the first, Brownell's rifle was heard, and the assassin staggered backward. He was hit exactly in the middle of the face, and the wound, as I afterward saw it, was the most frightful I ever witnessed. Of course Brownell did not know how fatal his shot had been, and so before the man dropped, he thrust his saber bayonet through and through the body, the force of the blow sending the dead man violently down the upper section of the second flight of stairs, at the foot of which he lay with his face to the floor. Winser ran from above crying, "Who is hit?" but as he glanced downward by our feet, he needed no answer.

Bewildered for an instant by the suddenness of this attack, and not knowing what more might be in store, we forbore to proceed, and gathered together defensively. There were but seven of us altogether, and one was without a weapon of any kind. Brownell instantly reloaded, and while doing so perceived the door through which the assailant's shot had passed, beginning to open. He brought his rifle to the shoulder, and menaced the occupants, two travelers, with immediate death, if they stirred. The three other privates guarded the passages, of which there were quite a number converging to the point where we stood, while the Chaplain and Winser looked to the stair-case by which we had descended, and the adjoining chambers. I ran down stairs to see if anything was threatened from the story below, but it soon appeared there was no danger from that quarter. However, we were not at all disposed to move from our position. From the opening doors, and through the passages, we discerned a sufficient number of forms to assure us that we were dreadfully in the minority. I think now that there was no danger, and that the single assailant acted without concert with anybody; but it is impossible to know accurately, and it was certainly a doubtful question then. The first thing to be done was to look to our dead friend and leader. He had fallen on his face, and the streams of blood that flowed from his wound had literally flooded the way. The Chaplain turned him gently over, and I stooped and called his name aloud, at which I thought then he murmured inarticulately. I presume I was mistaken, and I am not sure that he spoke a word after being struck, although in my dispatch I repeated a single exclamation which I had believed he uttered. It might have been Brownell, or the Chaplain, who was close behind me. Winser and I lifted the body with all the care we could apply, and laid it upon a bed in a room near by. The rebel flag, stained with his blood, and purified by this contact from the baseness of its former meaning, we laid about his feet. It was at first difficult to discover the precise locality of his wound, for all parts of his coat were equally saturated with blood. By cautiously loosening his belt and unbuttoning his coat, we found where the shot had penetrated. None of us had any medical knowledge, but we saw that all hope must be resigned. Nevertheless, it seemed proper to summon the surgeon as speedily as possible. This could not easily be done, for, secluded as we were in that part of the town, and uncertain whether an ambush might not be awaiting us also, no man could volunteer to venture forth alone, and to go together, and leave the Colonel's body behind, was out of the question. We wondered at the long delay of the first company, for the advance of which the Colonel had sent back before approaching the hotel, but we subsequently learned that they had mistaken a street, and gone a little out of their way. Before they arrived we had removed some of the unsightly stains from the Colonel's features, and composed his limbs. His expression in death was beautifully natural. The Colonel was a singularly handsome man, and, excepting the pallor, there was nothing different in his countenance now from what all his friends had so lately been accustomed to gladly recognize. The detachment was heard approaching at last, a reënforcement was easily called up, and the surgeon was sent for. His arrival, not long after, of course sealed our own unhappy belief. A sufficient guard was presently distrib[illegible] over the house, but meanwhile I had rem[illegible]ed the Colonel's earnestness about the tele[illegible] seizure, and obtained permission to guid[illegible] [illegible]d of Zouaves to the office, which was found to be entirely open, with all the doors ajar, yet apparently deserted. It looked a little like another chance of a surprise. The men remained in charge. I presume it was not wholly in order for me, a civilian, to start upon this mission, but I was the only person who knew the whereabouts of the office, and the Colonel had been very positive about the matter. When I returned to the hotel, there was a terrible scene enacting. A woman had run from a lower room to the stairway where the body of the defender of the Secession flag lay, and recognizing it, cried aloud with an agony so heart-rending that no person could witness it without emotion. She flung her arms in the air, struck her brow madly, and seemed in every way utterly abandoned to desolation and frenzy. She offered no reproaches—appeared indeed almost regardless of our presence, and yielded only to her own frantic despair. It was her husband that had been shot. He was the proprietor of the hotel. His name was James T. Jackson. Winser was confident it was the same man who met us at the door when we entered, and told us he was a boarder. His wife, as I said, was wild almost to insanity. Yet she listened when spoken to, and although no consolation could be offered her by us for what she had lost, she seemed sensible to the assurance that the safety of her children, for whom she expressed fears, could not possibly be endangered.

It is not from any wish to fasten obloquy upon the slayer of Col. Ellsworth, but simply because it struck me as a frightful fact, that I say the face of the dead man wore the most revolting expression of rage and hatred that I ever saw. Perhaps the nature of his wound added to this effect, and the wound was something so apalling that I shall not attempt to describe it, as it impressed me. It is probable that such a result from a bullet-wound could not ensue once in a thousand times. Either of Brownell's onslaughts would have been instantaneously fatal. The saber-wound was not less effective than that of the ball. The gun which Jackson had fired lay beneath him, clasped in his arms, and as we did not at first all know that both barrels had been discharged, it was thought necessary to remove it, lest it should be suddenly seized and made use of from below. In doing this, his countenance was revealed.

As the morning advanced, the townspeople began to gather in the vicinity, and a guard was fixed, preventing ingress and egress. This was done to keep all parties from knowing what had occurred, for the Zouaves were so devoted to their Colonel that it was feared if they all were made acquainted with the real fact, they would sack the house. On the other hand, it was not thought wise to let the Alexandrians know thus early the fate of their townsman. The Zouaves were the only regiment that had arrived, and their head and soul was gone. Besides, the duties which the Colonel had hurriedly assigned before leaving them had scattered some companies in various quarters of the town. Several persons sought admission to the Marshall House, among them a sister of the dead man, who had heard the rumor, but who was not allowed to know the true state of the case. It was painful to hear her remark, as she went away, that "of course they wouldn't shoot a man dead in in his own house about a bit of old bunting." Many of the lodgers were anxious to go forth, but they were detained until after I had left. All sorts of arguments and persuasions were employed, but the Zouave guards were inexorable.

At about 7 o'clock, a mounted officer rode up, and informed us that the Michigan 1st had arrived, and had captured a troop of rebels, who had at first demanded time for reflection, but who afterward concluded to yield at discretion. Not long after this, the surgeon made arrangements for the conveyance of Col. Ellsworth's body to Washington. It was properly vailed from sight, and, with great tenderness, taken by a detachment of the Zouaves and the 71st New-York Regiment (a small number of whom, I neglected to state, embarked in the morning at the Navy-Yard, and came down with us), to the steamboat, by which it was brought to the Navy-Yard. It now remains in the care of Capt. Dahlgren.

Washington is greatly excited over the strange news, and there seems to be much doubt among the citizens as to what has really been accomplished. I am as yet ignorant of the movements of other troops sent to occupy the place, but there can be no question but that an ample force, for all the purposes we need to carry out, is now there. I only attempt to furnish a record of that part of the expedition which I witnessed, and to supply the particulars, which would surely be sought after, of the bereavement which has caused our grievous sorrow. I am sure that no young officer in our Northern land could be more sincerely and universally mourned than Col. Ellsworth will be. Perhaps none so much so, for his name was a familiar token for all that was brave, and loyal, and true. There is not a town that did not know him, and could not speak of him to his honor. His friends, while lamenting his early fall, may assure themselves that he perished in performing a daring and courageous action—in resenting a shameful and long undredressed insult to his Government and the Chief Magistrate of his country. It may be said that his deed was rash, but I should not like to hear this reproach too hardly urged against him. He was young, and ardent, and full of ambition, and perhaps knew not that sense of caution which a colder nature would possess. But it would be well for many of us if we were as free from faults, and as rich in manly virtues, as was this gallant, noble and devoted soldier.

I find that I have been free in speaking of my own very slight connection with the events of this morning. It certainly was not from any anxiety on my part to do so; but because I could not, in making a rapid and yet particular narration of a matter in which so few persons acted, avoid alluding to each incident precisely as it occurred, without pausing to consider, at this time, the question of personality.

COLONEL ELMER E. ELLSWORTH,

ASSASSINATED AT ALEXANDRIA, MAY 24, 1861.

[A Biography of Col. Ellsworth was printed in THE TRIBUNE of Saturday.]

The following is the card of the proprietor of the Marshall House, whose death is recorded in the above letter:

MARSHALL HOUSE,
JAMES W. JACKSON, Proprietor,
Corner of Pitt and King streets,
ALEXANDRIA, Virginia.

Virginia is determined, and will conquer under the command of JEFF. DAVIS.

The subjoined plan shows the position in which the late gallant Colonel Ellsworth fell. Only a section of the Marshall House is represented. There are wings on either side, and at the back, a number of passages converging at the point "C." It was from one wing through the door K that Jackson's wife appeared, to seek her husband:

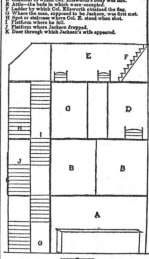

A Office of Marshall House.
B B Lodging-rooms.
C Passage in which Jackson was concealed.
D Chamber in which Col. Ellsworth's body was laid.
E Attic—the beds in which were occupied.
F Ladder by which Col. Ellsworth obtained the flag.
G Where the man, supposed to be Jackson, was first met.
H Spot or staircase where Col. E. stood when shot.
I Platform where he fell.
J Platform where Jackson dropped.
K Door through which Jackson's wife appeared.

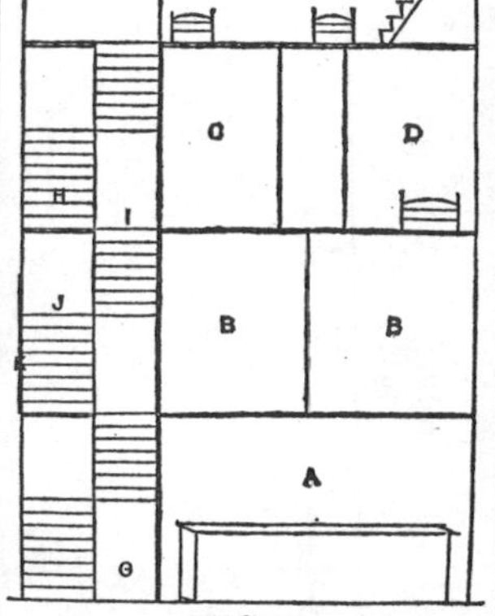

HOW THE NEWS WAS RECEIVED.

The news of Col. Ellsworth's murder was received everywhere with a thrill of horror and sorrow and indignation. The flags were at once put at half-mast, and in almost every city and town resolutions appropriate to the event were passed. On Saturday morning the remains of Col. Ellsworth were conveyed to the east room of the President's house, where for several hours they lay in state. The coffin was draped with the American flag, and adorned with choice flowers. The face was exposed to the public. Many persons, principally soldiers, visited the White House to take a farewell look at him.

Owing to the immense throng of anxious gazers on the remains of the deceased, the funeral cortege delayed moving from the Executive mansion till near 1 o'clock. All along the line of Pennsylvania avenue flags were displayed at half-mast and draped in mourning.

Every available point, including the windows, balconies, and house-tops, were thronged with anxious and sorrowful spectators. Various testimonials of respect were paid. All the bells of the city were tolled, and the heads of the soldiers and troops uncovered.

Several companies of the City corps, followed by the New-York 71st Regiment, Marines, and the local cavalry corps formed the military escort, with their arms reversed and colors shrouded.

The hearse was followed by a detachment of Zouaves, one of whom, the avenger of Col. Ellsworth, carried the identical Secession flag torn down by the deceased.

Then followed the President, accompanied by Secretaries Seward and Smith, and the rear of the procession was composed of carriages containing the captains of the Zouave Regiment.

The special train bearing the body arrived at New-York on Sunday morning, and the remains were at once attended to the Astor House. At 9 o'clock priaate services were there held, after which the coffin was taken to the Governor's Room in the City Hall. The building, within and without, was draped in mourning. For three hours the multitude poured into the Hall, anxious to look upon the face of the dead. The coffin was literally buried beneath the floral offerings which had been laid on it. A large and splendid military escort, the firemen in a body, distinguished military and civic officials, and a large concourse of citizens formed the procession which attended Ellsworth's remains to the steamer waiting to take them to his home, in Mechanicsville. The occasion was one of the most oppressive solemnity, and the sorrow of all was unfeigned and poignant.

The following is a copy of the last letter written by Col. Ellsworth, except one to his affianced bride, written at the same time, just before moving on Alexandria:

HEADQUARTERS 1ST ZOUAVES, CAMP LINCOLN,
WASHINGTON, D. C., May 23, 1861.

My Dear FATHER and MOTHER: The regiment is ordered to move across the river to-night. We have no means of knowing what reception we are to meet with. I am inclined to the opinion that our entrance to the City of Alexandria will be hotly contested, as I am just informed a large force have arrived there to-day. Should this happen, my dear parents, it may be my lot to be injured in some manner. Whatever may happen, cherish the consolation that I was engaged in the performance of a sacred duty; and to-night, thinking over the probabilities of the morrow and the occurrences of the past, I am perfectly content to accept whatever my fortune may be, confident that He who noteth even the fall of a sparrow will have some purpose, even in the fate of one like me.

My darling and ever-loved parents, good bye; God bless, protect, and care for you. ELMER.

SKETCH OF COL. ELLSWORTH'S LIFE.

The announcement on Friday of the assassination of Col. Ellsworth by one of the retreating enemy, who lingered on the spot after the capture of Alexandria, was the signal for profound and intense excitement throughout the city. His name had been familiar to all classes of our population, since the military visit which called forth such universal enthusiasm; and his recent energy, boldness, and determination in organizing a regiment for the defense of the country has been the theme of applause and admiration from every tongue. He fell in the exercise of a characteristic trait, which has often been the subject of remark. Not content with assuming the direction of the soldiers under his command, he was always foremost in action—attending with his own eye to the execution of details which are usually left to subordinates, and as far as possible performing with his own hands the services which he had a right to demand from his subalterns. Fired with this impetuous zeal, he rushed forward on gaining the soil of the rebels, to tear down in person the waving emblem of Secession, but before he could return to his comrades he was slain by a dastardly shot from a Virginian, who met with summary retribution at the hands of an incensed soldier of the deceased, before he could slink away to boast of his ignoble deed. The death of Ellsworth, like that of Warren on Bunker Hill, will send a thrill of indignant rage throughout the land. His blood will cement the covenant to which our armed hosts have sworn, to count their lives as nothing in support of their cause. Henceforth his name will be a watchword in the camp, a war cry on the battle field, and as a flame of fire in the hearts of his brave Zouaves who burn to avenge his death.

Col. Elmer E. Ellsworth was a native of Malta, Saratoga County, N. Y., where his bereaved parents are now living, and although he had attained so prominent a position in our military service, was yet in early youth at the time of his death, having scarcely completed the twenty-fourth year of his age.

For the last few years he had been a resident of Chicago, where he was engaged in the practice of law, but was distinguished for his love of military affairs and his remarkable zeal and efficiency as an officer and disciplinarian. Previous to his entering the service of the United States, with his regiment of New-York Zouaves, he held the office of Quartermaster of the Northern Division of Illinois and Paymaster-General of the militia of that State. His first company of Zouaves was formed in Chicago in the Spring of 1859, and soon became famous for their admirable drill and wonderful feats of activity. In the course of a year, their peculiar tactics had excited so much attention that a strong desire was expressed that they should visit the East, and accordingly, in July, 1860, they left Chicago for a military tour to New-York and other cities of the seaboard. Their reception in this city formed a new era in the history of the militia. The enthusiasm which was excited by their strange and picturesque costume, the astonishing precision of their drill, and their reckless exhibition of strength and skill, pervaded the whole country, and received a fresh impulse on the recent call to arms for the suppression of rebellion. Col. Ellsworth himself was prompt in his answer to the summons of the Government. He lost no time in the offer of his services, and in less than three days after his proposal to form a Zouave Regiment from the Fire Department of New-York, over a thousand brave fellows had enlisted under his command. Since they were mustered into actual service, there has been but one opinion of their value and effectiveness. Amply have they redeemed their brilliant promise, by the noble performance of their late duty. Devoted to their gallant commander, whose personal qualities were as winning as his military genius was remarkable, his death has been the occasion to them of overwhelming grief, that can only be appeased by their share in the triumph which his cowardly assassination did not permit him to witness.

Col. Ellsworth was a man of exemplary moral habits, and a model of temperance and integrity. It is said that he never tasted a drop of liquor, nor smoked a cigar in his life. At the time of his martyr's death, he was engaged to be married to Miss Spofford, an estimable young lady of Rockford, Illinois. The personal sorrow for his untimely loss can hardly be more poignant than the indignant national grief, which is pledged both to honor the memory and avenge the murder of the departed.

ELLSWORTH.

We mourn, alas! thy hapless fate!
And yet 't was glorious thus to die;
Thine eye with victory's gleam elate,
And Freedom's banner floating high.

Thy hand the rebel flag had torn
From off its pinnacle of pride;
And we, alas! can only mourn
That one so young, so brave, has died!

For now thy noble hopes are crushed,
Thy glowing dream of conquest o'er;
The pulses of thy being hushed
Amid the coming battle's roar.

Yet we will still remember thee,
And round thy pallid brow still spread
Sweet garlands, to thy memory,
Thou first among our glorious dead!

Troy, N. Y., May 24. J. L. Y.

THE NEW YORK SUN,

Published daily, Sundays excepted, at the Sun Buildings, cor. of Fulton and Nassau sts, and delivered to Subscribers in New York City and vicinity at SIX AND A QUARTER CENTS PER WEEK.

☞ When sent by Mail, four dollars per year.

THE WEEKLY SUN is published at 75 cts. a year; sixteen months, $1; single copies, 2 cts.

Address "The Sun" Establishment, New York.

THE SUN.

IT SHINES FOR ALL

NUMBER 9161 — NEW YORK, TUESDAY, NOVEMBER 19 1861. — PRICE ONE CENT

THE NEW YORK SUN

TUESDAY MORNING, NOV. 19, 1861.

The Rebel Commissioners Slidell and Mason. Further Particulars of their Mission to Europe.

The arrest of the rebel envoys continued to be the theme of much discussion yesterday. The following further particulars are given from a variety of sources.

If the Charleston rebels should dare to carry out their threat to hang Col. Corcoran, there is no man upon whom the retribution, which is sure to follow, can be so fitly visited as John Slidell, the rebel commissioner, whose arrest we announced yesterday. No man is more directly responsible for the great southern conspiracy, of which he sought to be the European representative, and for his treason, there is not even that poor excuse which might be urged in behalf of Mason and others, on the score of their southern birth. Slidell is a native of this state—the son of one of those "greasy merchants" of whom the cotton chivalry have so much to say. His father was an honest tallow chandler, doing business in the neighborhood of what is now Broome or Grand street, and old residents of the city can remember his factory, which in their day stood upon the outskirts of the town, near the Slidell mansion, a pretty cottage surrounded by a garden, where John and his brothers had their playground when children. Even in those days the family were accustomed to receive much southern company, and it is probable that the associations into which young Slidell was then brought may explain his removal to the South, and his subsequent career growing out of that. It is only just to his relatives, some of whom are still residents in this city, to say that his secession sentiments find no sympathy with them.

INTERVIEW WITH LIEUT. FAIRFAX.

When Lieut. Fairfax, of the San Jacinto, reached the deck of the Trent, he met the Captain and inquired if he had Mason and Slidell on board. He hesitated in answering, when Mr. Fairfax discovered Mason at a distance seated. Observing this, the Captain stated that they were on board, and Mr. Fairfax approached the rebel envoy, and inquired if he was not Mr. Mason. Mason arose and stated that he was, when Mr. Fairfax announced that he had orders for his arrest. Mason turned to the captain and asked if he intended to allow this outrage to be committed upon his flag. The captain made some response, which was inaudible to my informant. Mr. Slidell at that moment came up from the cabin, and he also was informed by Mr. Fairfax that he had orders for his arrest.

The ladies of the suite coming up at the moment, a conversation in an under tone was commenced, which was followed by a very affecting scene, as it became apparent that they were to be separated. They expressed themselves confidently that they would never see Mr. Slidell or Mr. Mason again, and when the offer was made to his family to accompany him, Mr. Slidell objected, and asked that they continue the voyage.

In private conversation, it is supposed that they gave to Eustis and McFarland instructions what to do when they reached Europe, and were much astonished to learn that they were also to be transferred. Their baggage was brought up and examined, and various papers, which were supposed to be of service to the Government, were taken possession of. A considerable amount of money was found. Their wearing apparel was transferred to the boats, and soon the prisoners were on board the *San Jacinto*. Mason was very haughty in his manner for a time after reaching the vessel, but Slidell was pleasant and easy in his manner.

HOW THEY REACHED CUBA.

We take, as the most reliable account from the rebel source, the following from the Charleston *Mercury* of Nov. 2, relative to the movements of the rebel Commissioners:

For some time past the papers of the interior have been indulging in sly hints as to the whereabouts of Messrs. Mason and Slidell. We have hitherto made no allusion to their movements; but, the causes which induced our reticence being removed, we may now, without indiscretion, narrate the facts of their embarkation. The Commissioners having resolved to make the venture of running the blockade of Charleston, after mature deliberation, selected for the experiment the staunch and swift little steamer Theodora, which was therefore got ready for sea with all dispatch. The preparations having been completed, they embarked a little before midnight on Friday, October 11. The party of passengers who were starting on this very unusual and somewhat hazardous trip, consisted of the following persons:

Hon. J. M. Mason, of Virginia.
Mr. Macfarland, Secretary to Mr. Mason.
Hon. John Slidell, of Louisiana.
Mrs. Slidell.
Miss Mathilde Slidell.
Miss Rosine Slidell.
Mr. Eustis, Secretary to Mr. Slidell.
Mrs. Eustis, who is a daughter of Mr. Corcoran, the Washington banker, now in Fort Lafayette.
Colonel Le Mat, of Louisiana, the inventor of the grape-shot revolver.

And two or three other gentlemen, whom it will be best for the present not to name. The night was pitch dark, and about midnight a light rain began falling, which rendered the chances of being detected by the blockaders exceedingly slim. At one o'clock on Saturday morning, the hasty "good bys" and "God speed yous" having been said, the cables of the Theodora were loosened, and she glided down the harbor on her important mission. As the steamer passed Fort Sumter every light on board was extinguished, and away she went, right through the fingers of the blockaders, far out to sea. On the evening of the 11th she reached Nassau in safety, where, had the opportunity been a favorable one, the Commissioners would have disembarked; but on inquiring, they ascertained that the English steamer connecting with that point touched at New York. However gratifying a sight of New York might have been under other circumstances, the Commissioners determined in this instance to forego the pleasure. So the Theodora left Nassau and steamed away towards Cuba. On the 16th inst. she arrived at Cardenas, where the Commissioners landed. The news that a southern steamer had arrived, with Messrs. Mason and Slidell on board, which was telegraphed from Cardenas to Havana, was scarcely credited at the latter place. But when, on the 17th inst., the Theodora came up the harbor of Havana, displaying the Confederate flag, the quays were immediately thronged with thousands of wondering spectators, and a most cordial and enthusiastic reception was given to the adventurous little craft. The Yankees in Havana were as a matter of course, much disgusted at the welcome given to the Theodora. But, on the other hand, the ladies of Havana prepared a splendid Confederate flag for the steamer, which was presented to the captain with appropriate ceremonies. The ladies of Matanzas also took advantage of the chance to send hither a splendid flag for the Hampton Legion. The steamship Columbia, formerly a Charleston vessel, but now in the armed service of the Yankees, was, at the time, in the harbor of Havana. Luckily, however, she was not ready to put to sea. Her consort, the Keystone State, had gone to New York with a southern steamer, loaded with a valuable freight of arms and munitions, and which, unfortunately, had been captured while endeavoring to make the run to Tampa, Fla. So the Theodora left the friendly port of Havana unmolested, and, with a freight of coffee, sugar, saltpetre, sulphur, acids, lead, iron, shot, block tin, &c., ran quietly in—we won't say where—bringing a number of Charlestonians, who had reached Havana from Southampton about the time the Theodora made her appearance. It is ascertained that the Yankees keep a fast yacht constantly plying between Key West and Havana, simply for the purpose of gaining intelligence of our naval movements. The Theodora is a private vessel, and is unarmed.

THE COTTON can't be removed from the plantations of Louisiana for the want of rope and bagging. We'll give the rebels a little more rope, and then do the bagging ourselves

War Intelligence.

THE ENGAGEMENT AT THE MOUTH OF THE MISSISSIPPI.

The Boston *Journal* publishes the following extracts from private letters dated on board the Preble, at the Mouth of the Mississippi, Nov. 9:

"At half past two o'clock on the morning of the 13th, an iron machine rounded the point above us and floated down the river with the current, made in direction of the Richmond. We ran up a red lamp, the signal of danger. The men always sleep on their guns, so that we were well prepared for this infernal machine, as it turned out to be. As it floated by us we could have given it a broadside, but having no signal from the Post-Captain's ship, were not allowed to. This machine, for we have no other name for it, is long and low, in shape like a cigar. It has no deck, but is apparently cased in railroad iron. It has probably been severely tested, else it would never have ventured on the batteries of three ships as it did. Soon as it was seen by us, it steamed up and went off for the Richmond. There was a schooner alongside of her that she had coaled from the day before. This machine or battering ram aimed at her port bow, but the schooner being in the way, she was obliged to turn, and that diminished the force of the blow somewhat. She struck the vessel on the starboard side, under her third port, about four feet below the water, making a hole a foot square. The water rushed in in a torrent. A rubber stopper was slid down the side of the ship, and by working the steam-pumps she was kept free. After this 'black ram,' as the tars called it, had left the Richmond, it went on toward the Vincennes, approaching within forty yards of it. The Vincennes turned short round, and came over to us. The Richmond's guns on the port side had been run in the day before, to allow the schooner to get alongside. She at this moment got them to bear, and poured shot and shell into the black ram, though most of the missiles went beyond their mark. As he ranged alongside of us we gave him three broadsides. Most of the shots struck him, though but one took effect. Shot 'one' was a shell from the sixty-eight pounder. It struck him plump on the smoke-stack, knocking said stack out of sight. As he passed our bow he fired a rocket over our forecastle, which was a signal for his chummies up the river. Lights sprung up all over the river above us, and fire-ships chained together came toward us from every direction. So rapidly they approached that all four of the vessels were obliged to slip anchor. We could see five steamboats and a bark behind the fire-ships, and it were madness to think of fighting fire. We retreated in good order down the Southwest Pass. The order from Capt. Pope was for all of us to go over the bar. The Preble obeyed in good shape. The pilot of the Vincennes, not thoroughly acquainted with the channel, got her aground. The Richmond, now essaying to aid the Vincennes, got aground also. The Preble stood off the bar for an anchorage. We found a suitable place and dropped the kellock. Very soon the flag-boat of the secessionists, named the Ivy, appeared in the Pass three miles up, and commenced firing her rifled cannon at the Richmond. The Post-Captain signaled for us to beat up to him, but having a very heavy head wind and current, we could make no headway, and were obliged to witness the fight without the enjoyment of participation. The Vincennes aground, stern up the river, could get none of her broadside guns to bear on the enemy. But Capt. Handy had his cabin stove to pieces to enable him to work two sixty-eights out of the cabin ports astern. The Ivy seeing the helplessness of the Vincennes, steamed down toward her, probably with the intention of boarding her. The little Water Witch, with her four guns, now ran in between them, and by a well directed broadside, knocked the whole upper part of the Ivy's stern off. The steam bark now came down toward the Richmond, who was aground, broadside up the Pass. The Richmond drove her off by a few well thrown shot and shell. The other steamers being banged up badly, the fleet concluded to leave. They went up the Southwest Pass, and then down "Pass a l'Outre." Their intention was to run the blockade so as to get the steam bark to sea as a privateer. This bark, according to secession papers that we found at Ship Island, had been lying in New Orleans for some time, and the Secessionists had conceived the idea of getting her to sea in this manner. However, it was "no go" with her, for at Pass a l'Outre the Colorado was on guard, in company with the new gunboat from Boston. The Northeast Pass is guarded by the Niagara, assisted by one or two small gunboats. The Chivalry had no other alternative but to return to New Orleans and make their brags.

During the engagement the Vincennes was deserted by order of Capt. Pope. Capt. Handy spiked his guns, and wrapping the American flag around him, set fire to a fuse connected with the magazine and left his ship. As soon as the secessionists were driven off an officer returned to the Vincennes and put out the fuse. The Water Witch then proceeded to Pass a l'Outre and came back with the South Carolina. Both together could not get the Vincennes off. The Huntsville came in next day, and by throwing overboard all the guns except the four 8-inch ones and two 12-pound howitzers, the three steamers towed her off. She will be obliged to go to Key West for an armament. Capt. Handy lived in the ward room, his cabin being utterly destroyed. The Water Witch was not damaged at all, though she was in the thickest of the fight. The Richmond's post quarter-boat was stove, and a shell went through her side on her gun deck. None of our men were killed, though the enemy, from the number of shell that exploded on their decks, must have had not a few killed and wounded. The Nightingale is here with only six feet of water under her. She cannot be got off by all the steamers here.

The Guyandotte Affair.

The Cincinnati *Commercial* has the following later news from Guyandotte, Virginia:

"The officers of the steamer Anglo Saxon inform us that only some fifteen or sixteen houses were burned at Guyandotte—that the majority of the buildings in the town were not burned. The burned district, however, comprises the most valuable business houses and dwellings. The excitement is intense along both shores of the Ohio, above and below Guyandotte. Many, fearing an attack from the rebels at Catlettsburg and Ceredo, had removed their families and household goods to the wharf-boats and across the river to the Ohio shore. The carcasses of fourteen dead rebel cavalry horses were found in Guyandotte and vicinity. When they were attacked a number of the unarmed Union soldiers of the Fifth Virginia effected an escape by swimming the Ohio river to the opposite shore. One poor soldier, when about one-third of the way across, and finding he could not reach the Ohio shore in safety, returned to the Virginia side, landing below Guyandotte. He surrendered to the heathen mob of rebels and begged for quarter, when they replied, "We do not take prisoners," and thirsting for blood, cut his throat from ear to ear."

Decisions Under the Tariff.

Secretary Chase has made the following decisions in cases of appeal from duties imposed by the collectors of various ports:

Articles styled by the importer "engravings or plates," and entry claimed thereof at ten per cent. *ad valorem*, are decided to be lithographic show bills or hand bills designed as advertising posters, and are liable to a duty of fifteen per cent. as "printed matter" under section 18 of Act of March 2, 1861—the work being executed by the press alone.

Woolen jackets not made on frames, but hand knit, open in front, with buttons and sewed button holes and pockets, must be entered at the rate of 12 cents per pound, and in addition twenty-five per centum on the value.

On cigars of all kinds, whatever their invoice price, a duty of ten per cent. is fixed in addition to a specific rate per pound according to their value.

The Maryland Election.

The returns from Maryland show the following vote:

Bradford, (Union)............57,502
Howard, (Peace)..............26,070

Bradford's majority....31,432

The Legislature stands as follows:

Senate..Union........13 Secession..........8
House..Union.........68 Secession..........6

Seven of the eight secessionists in the Senate hold over from a former election—only one having been chosen at the recent canvass.

DID THE only white man found at Beaufort, S. C., being drunk, represent the *spirit* of the Southern Confederacy?

MICHAEL CORCORAN, COLONEL OF THE SIXTY-NINTH REGIMENT, N. Y. S. M.

Sketch of the Life of Colonel Corcoran, and late interesting letters from him at Castle Pinckney, S. C.

We present our readers above, with an accurate portrait of Colonel MICHAEL CORCORAN, of the 69th Regiment, New York State Militia, who is now a prisoner of war at Castle Pinckney S. C. It is probable, however, that he has been removed to some other place, since his selection by lot to be hung, as elsewhere referred to. A painful interest attaches to the name of the Colonel, who is one of the bravest and best officers within the lines of our whole army, it having become known that he has been selected by the Rebel government to be hung, in case the pirates of the Rebel privateers are condemned to death by the people of the North. And such is the rashness and infatuation of the Confederates, that no deed may be deemed too reckless or unprincipled for their perpetration. Further intelligence may be expected upon this head, it being only necessary to allude to the fact to explain the intensity of devotion to this gallant officer, which is exhibited by all classes of his countrymen in this city and elsewhere. We append a brief sketch of his career, which will be read with great interest:

Colonel Corcoran was born on the 21st day of September, 1827, in Carrowkeel, county Sligo, Ireland. His father, Thos. Corcoran, was a retired half pay officer who had served in the West Indies for several years, and married Mary McDougald, the mother of *our* Colonel, after he retired to private life. Both families were of honorable and patriotic stock.

After receiving the benefits of an English education, at the age of 19 Michael entered the Irish Constabulary establishment, and remained in it three years, during which period he was stationed at Creeslough, in the county Donegal. In this capacity he was distinguished for his energy, activity, honesty and fidelity, and commanded the esteem and confidence of his superiors. He resigned his place in 1849, and turned his face toward "the land of the free and the home of the brave" in America. Soon after his arrival in New York, he entered the employment of Mr. John Heeney, of "Hibernian Hall." At length he succeeded his employer in the proprietorship of the establishment, and remained in the business until the early part of the present year.

He early became a member of the 69th Regiment, enlisting as a private under Capt. John Judge, of Company I, (since changed to Company A. He was soon elected Orderly Sergeant, and his energy, military spirit, and popularity advanced him step by step to 1st Lieutenant and Captain of his company, receiving also from time to time numerous testimonials of the respect and esteem of his companions.

Capt. Corcoran was a faithful servant of the state in what is known as the "Quarantine War," being then senior captain of the 69th; and the Inspector General's return pays a distinguished tribute to his military character. In this official recognition of true and modest merit the Inspector said: "What I might say of Capt. Corcoran, commanding 'A' Company, as to his military knowledge, would not add to his already well-known reputation as the best, if not the very best officer of his rank in the First Division." This was high praise, and occurrences since, and recently, show that it reflects not less credit on the officer who conferred than on him who received it.

On the 25th day of August, 1859, he was elected Colonel of the 69th, and his name and that of the regiment have, since that time, been almost synonimous in the public mind. On the occasion of the visit of the Prince of Wales to this city, Colonel Corcoran refused to parade his men in honor of the representative of the crown and government under which his countrymen have suffered so much, and by which many of the best of them have suffered banishment. Whatever may have been thought of the act as a matter of taste or judgment, no one ever questioned the honesty of the motives which governed him on that occasion. The breaking out of the rebellion found him, however, under charges before court martial, and many of the officers of the regiment doubted the propriety of going to the defense of the capital without their Colonel, especially as they fully approved of his act. Immediately, however, the gallant Colonel addressed them a letter imploring them to think only of their adopted country, and to stand by the Flag of the Union, without regard to him. That letter had the desired effect, and the brave Irishmen of the 69th were not backward in responding to the call of the President.

On the 20th day of April last, "a special order" was "promulgated" stating that "the Eighth regiment, Col. Lyon, and the 69th regiment, Lieut. Col. Nugent, are hereby detailed for immediate service at the National capital." On the same day, "special orders No. 9," announcing that "in pursuance of special orders No. 58, from general headquarters, the court martial detailed for the trial of Colonel Corcoran, of the 69th regiment, is dissolved and the charges dismissed; and Colonel Corcoran is directed, forthwith, to resume the command of his regiment."

Our citizens have not forgotten the memorable 23d of April, when the 69th, with their popular colonel, so proudly welcomed again to his command, after an almost triumphal march through Broadway, took their departure in the steamer James Adger, for Anapolis. It was a day of excitement and alarm for the safety of the city of Washington, but it was a day of pride to the citizens of New York, when two such regiments as the 8th and 69th so promptly responded to the call of their country.

We need not follow Colonel CORCORAN and his regiment to Anapolis, during their service in protecting the railroad to Washington, or the time they were quartered at the Catholic College on Georgetown Heights; nor into Virginia, and at length to Bull Run. All the facts connected with these movements are familiar as matters of history to all our readers. Everywhere Colonel CORCORAN and his command received the applause of the public for their soldierly appearance and conduct. At the battle of Bull Run, he was taken prisoner, and the most that we know of him since has been gathered from letters received from Richmond, brought under flags of truce to our lines, and then forwarded by mail. A portion of these letters we publish today, and from them our readers will gather a more accurate account of the brave action of the 69th Regiment at the battle of Bull Run, than from any other source, while the Colonel's description of the circumstances in which he is now placed will be of high interest to his friends.

LETTER TO MRS. CORCORAN.

RICHMOND, Va., July 29, 1861.

My Dear Wife—I wrote a letter to Captain Kirker a few days since, acquainting him of my being in close confinement here, also Captain McIvor and Lieut. Connolly, with about 37 other officers and 603 non-commissioned officers and privates from various regiments. Among them are Sergeants Murphy and Donohue, and 35 privates of my own regiment. We are all in good health. I was very ill for the first two days after my arrest, but feel quite well at present. I am deeply afflicted at the loss of Acting Lieut. Col. Haggerty, who was among the first that fell on the battle-field, and several of my brave soldiers. It is, however, consoling that they attended to their religious duties for that day. I have had many narrow, hair-breadth escapes, but God, in his infinite mercy, has been pleased to preserve me. I am uneasy to know the fate of many officers and men whom I had not seen in line immediately after the battle, among whom are Captains Thos. Francis Meagher and Kavanagh, and Acting Adjt. (late Captain) John A. Nugent. My regiment came off the field in admirable order, and was on the road to Centreville, when I halted to rest and await orders for future action, knowing that our artillery would need protection in returning. Two regiments that had not been in line, and were retreating in disorder, being on my flank, and when the cavalry were seen advancing towards us, these regiments broke precipitately through my lines, throwing us into disorder—causing a general flight, I dismounted and crossed a rail fence, over which they had gone, and got the color bearer to halt, calling on the men to rally around the flag. Just at this moment a discharge of carbines from the pursuing cavalry and from our artillery drowned my voice, and destroyed all my efforts to muster the men. I had only nine men who heard me and halted, and these, with the two officers and myself, were immediately surrounded and taken to Manassas. We left there on the following morning and arrived here on Tuesday night. Lieutenants Bagley and Gannon, with two Colonels, one Lieutenant-Colonel, and other officers and privates, arrived here this morning. Some of our wounded have also been brought here, but I have not yet learned their names. Give my love to your aunt and William, Captain Kirker and friends.

Your affectionate husband.

MICHAEL CORCORAN.

Col. Corcoran's Letters Last Received.

The following letters are just received, and possess a more than usual interest from the fact that the prisoner is now surrounded by a most excited state of feeling against the North, the bitterness of which breaks forth on every occasion:—

CASTLE PINCKNEY, S. C., *October 21st*, 1861.

Captain James B. Kirker:

MY VERY DEAR FRIEND:—Your letter bearing date 16th August last, has just come to hand, and the delay seems to have been on your side of the line, as it leaves the post-mark, "Norfolk, October 14th." However, its receipt, even at this time, has afforded me the most infinite pleasure. I have written you a letter dated on the 14th instant, which I hope you may receive, and which I intended as my last effort, but the officer in charge here has been kind enough to give me hope that my answers to yours will be forwarded.

In my last, I mentioned that the people of Charleston had treated us with considerable courtesy on the occasion of our arrival in and departure from that city, but neglected to state another favorable change in our treatment here. The officers have the liberty of the island on which the Castle is situated, from reveille to retreat, and are allowed on the ramparts until tatoo. The rank and file are allowed the liberty of the interior yard during the aforesaid hours. This is quite a change from Virginia hospitality, where we had not been permitted one moment for air or exercise during the fifty days of our detention in the ever memorable Tobacco Factory, and without bedding of any kind.

The Bishop of this place visited me and spoke in that mild gentlemanly and Christian spirit for which all our clergy everywhere, and under all circumstances, have been so truly characterized. He handed me all the funds in his possession, and of which I stood in the greatest need, and appointed to come here on last Thursday to celebrate mass and attend to the religious necessities of the prisoners, but the day proved so wet and stormy that it was impossible, without imminent danger, to cross over from the city, but we expect him at his earliest convenience. This is the first time that any apparent interest has been taken in our spiritual welfare

The good sisters of our faith residing in Richmond, (who, thank God, can rise above all national or sectional strife, and contention of this world, with their usual self sacrificing and Christian disposition to render aid and comfort to the afflicted,) attended to such of our wounded as were at the general hospital, and our officers and men who were there, and who represent all classes of religion, are unanimous in their praise of the care and attention bestowed in dressing and cleaning the wounded, and many attribute their recovery to their untiring exertions.

The health of the officers at present is generally good. Lieut. Underhill, of the Eleventh New York Volunteers, has had a very severe attack of typhoid fever, but is now perfectly recovered. Some four or five of the rank and file, mostly from the Michigan regiment, are in hospital. The general health of all is as good as might be expected under ordinary circumstances, but all are sadly in want of new clothing and bed covering; straw beds have been furnished.

You may give yourself no uneasiness about me for money, as I understand that one hundred dollars have been forwarded by you to my credit, which I hope to receive in a few days. This will suffice for Lieutenants Connelly, Dempsey & Co. The latter belongs to the Second N. Y. We are a well united body, and what one has becomes general property. I understand a similar amount has been forwarded to Lieutenant Bagley, whom I believe to be still at Richmond, with Captain McIvor and Lieutenant Gannon, but I am under the impression that the rank and file of our regiment have been sent to New Orleans. Money goes pretty fast, as most articles are sold at a high price. I might have had enough for my own immediate wants, were it not that I found it necessary to purchase shirts, handkerchiefs, &c., for those of our wounded who were in the hospital, next to the building I was in. I also advanced $20 to the privates of our regiment, who were confined in the building with myself. To most of our wounded, who were in the general hospital, I found it impossible, even after a written request and numerous verbal applications, to have any assistance rendered.

The loss of property from my trunks I am charitably disposed to attribute to a great desire that probably existed to be possessed of something to remember me by. They will probably return them, when they learn of my existence.

Many friends must excuse me for not writing to them, with whom I would desire to correspond, under any other circumstances than those which exist at present. I shall endeavor to write to Major Bagley and Mr. Wm. J. Kane about the 1st of next month. I am much pleased to learn that Richard O'Gorman, Esq., has returned in safety to New York, particularly so at this juncture. I believe him to be possessed of all these excellent qualities which make man noble. Please present him with my warmest regards.

Remember me kindly to those legions of *true friends* you have mentioned, as I do not wish to name any, where there are so many equally deserving. I have written a letter to Father Mooney, and one in answer to Lieut. Giles.

Lieut. Connolly joins in kindest remembrance to you. When you chance to see Lieut. Connolly's brothers, tell them he is in excellent health, and has written home a few days ago; he is most anxious to receive a letter from home. Kind love to Mrs. Corcoran, Mrs. Heaney and Mrs. Kane. Believe me,

Your ever faithful friend,

MICHAEL CORCORAN,
Col. 69th Reg't, N. Y. S. M.

CASTLE PINCKNEY, S. C., Oct. 14, 161.

Capt. JAMES B. KIRKER—

My Very Dear Friend—I have had the most infinite pleasure of receiving your long and anxiously expected letter on the 1st ult., and another from Mr. Kane some short time afterwards, both of which, with others from Captain Clark, and various inquiries after friends who were members of the regiment, have remained unanswered solely in consequence of the announcement previous to their receipt that the means of transportation had been stopped. I had a very lengthy communication ready for mailing to you at that time, but I have now concluded to hand it to you whenever I may have the happiness of meeting you.

The receipt on yesterday of quite a number of letters by my fellow-prisoners from New York and other sections of the country, which came by way of Fortress Monroe to Norfolk, inspires me with the hope that a few lines may possibly reach you. The prisoners here who left Richmond on the 13th ult., consist of 34 officers and 120 non-commissioned officers and privates; amongst the former are 3 colonels, a lieut.-col., and a major. Lieut. Connolly and a private named John Owens are all of the 69th that are here, although all were most anxious to be together, and my officers endeavored to effect an exchange with some of the others, but their efforts were in vain, as all were too anxious to get away from the *hospitality of Virginia*. I believe most of the 69th were sent to New Orleans.

This place is already well known, therefore needs no description. The casements are occupied as quarters. As no visitors are allowed here, we are not so subjected to the idle and offensive curiosity of spectators, as was the case at Richmond, where crowds were permitted to assemble in front of our prison, to stare at us all day whenever we went to catch a breath of air at the windows, while the more favored individuals obtained passes to enter, and in many cases took occasion to ask all kinds of questions. Indeed, the people of Charleston presented a striking contrast of gentlemanly behavior towards us, on our arrival and departure, although large numbers were present on both occasions, not a single offensive word was spoken or act committed.

We are all here in great need of clothing, and in many cases without a single cent to procure any of the different things essentially necessary. I received some funds from a relative in Richmond, which have been expended, and Lieut. Connolly and myself are amongst the bankrupts for some days past. I am well satisfied there are several in Charleston who would divide their last dollar with me, but I cannot accept it as there appears to be no possible way of repaying, perhaps for years. Indeed some gentlemen were so kind as to make inquiry if I needed anything, to which I replied in the negative, and while at Richmond I received a communication from a gentleman from Montgomery, Ala., who is said to be one of the wealthiest gentlemen in that city, stating that he was most desirous of supplying me with anything I required.

I am quite satisfied to remain here as long as it may be considered necessary to serve the purposes of my Government, or our people; but I am exceedingly anxious that the rank and file of the different regiments should be seen to as soon as possible. The poor fellows are all most earnestly devoted to the best interests of their country, and are suffering much from want of proper clothing or any changes of under-garments. Many are without shoes, coats, or bed-covering, which is a cheerless prospect, with the near approach of cold weather; and, above all things, their poor families, in many cases, must certainly suffer from want of the assistance they could render if at liberty—and many are of the three months volunteers, who made no provision for absence beyond that time, and whose future welfare depends upon their return at the very earliest period.

I regret I cannot give the desired information of the missing to their friends. My facility for obtaining intelligence or visiting our wounded was of the most limited character.

The officers from the city of New York, in addition to the two already named, are Captains Griffin, Downey and Farrish; Lieuts. Fay, Underhill, Hamblin and Worcester; Doctor Griswold and Chaplain Dodge. I have not seen any of them since that day, but one man named Collins, who has been permitted to return to New York.

I have been informed that Capt. O'Neil of Co. D, was wounded in the right arm, and was last seen in one of the hospitals in company with Sergt. Major Tracy. That day my whole attention was drawn to the command, as I was without a single member of my field or regular staff officers during the entire day. Captain Meagher and Nugent, who were acting as staff officers, I had not seen after the last time we were engaged, as they did not keep up with the regiment. I believed them, with other officers, to be among the killed and wounded. Those officers rendered me good service in the early part of the day and last engagement, as also several other officers, whom I hope to mention when I may have an opportunity of making my report. I have been surprised to hear that a report has been put in circulation derogatory of Capt. McIvor. My space [illegible] me only to say that a braver or more attentive officer than he, was not present on the battle field.

I rejoice you have got the flag. I have heretofore refrained from mentioning anything about it, but ask Capt. Wildey if he did not find it in a small house about 200 yards to the left of the road leading to Centreville, where we left it safe, and which cost those their liberty who remained to shield it.

The color bearer was not shot down, nor the colors temporarily lost.

"Absence makes the heart grow fonder." Yes, I love my friends, whom I know to be honest and true, with (if possible) tenfold devotion; to all such please remember me. Friends will please pardon me for not writing to them individually. This is intended as my last effort while so much uncertainty of my letters ever reaching their intended destination continues to exist. I hope Mr. Kane's services and the assistance which he renders, you, will be duly appreciated by those in whose behalf and for whose benefit you are laboring. I shall at all events feel ever grateful.

Lieut. Dempsey, for whom you inquired, is quite well and here with us. Mrs. D. may feel quite at ease about him. Lieut. Connolly writes to his family this day, being also in hopes it may find its way. Give my love to Mrs. Corcoran, and believe me,

Your sincere friend,

MICHAEL CORCORAN,
Col. 69th Regt. N. Y. S. M.

Organization of the Irish Brigade

In connection with the above interesting sketch and correspondence, the organization of the above brigade, composed of many of the officers and men forming the 69th Regiment, of which Col. Corcoran was commander, will prove of interest:—

After the expiration of their three months' service and return of the 69th Regiment, State Militia, Lieut.-Col. Nugent, in company with Capt. T. F. Meagher and other officers of the regiment, planned and commenced the organization of this Brigade, to be composed of 5 regiments, and commanded by Brig.-Gen. Shields, of the U. S. Army, a distinguished officer of Irish birth. Three of five regiments were to be raised in this city, one in Boston and one in Philadelphia. They were to be commanded as follows:—1st Regt, Col. Nugent; 2nd, Col. Patterson; 3d, Col. Murphy; 4th, Col. Baker; 5th, Col. Meagher. The first of these, Col. Nugent's, was composed in great part of members of the gallant 69th, and at the solicitation of its officers, Gov. Morgan assigned to it the number in the volunteer roll, borne by them in their former organization, the 69th. We append a sketch of the departure of the 69th (volunteers,) and also of the presentation of stands of colors to the other New York regiments of the brigade.

Color Presentation to the Irish Brigade, and Departure of the 69th Regiment.

The departure of the 69th Regiment, N. Y. S. V., or First Regiment of the Irish Brigade, yesterday, for the seat of war, was made the occasion of one of the most impressive military displays which our citizens have witnessed since the opening of the present campaign. Magnificent stands of colors had been prepared for each of the New York regiments of the Brigade, and were to have been presented to them at an earlier day, but in consequence of some necessary delays in the arrangements, the ceremonies were postponed until yesterday. Public notice having been given in all the morning papers of yesterday, of the intended ceremonies at the residence of Archbishop Hughes, in Madison Avenue, near Thirty-sixth street, an immense crowd was gathered at an early hour in all the streets in that vicinity, to await the arrival of the gallant 69th and their comrades in the Brigade. The crowd, composed of both sexes and of all ages, classes and nationalities, extended from Madison avenue to the East River, on both Thirty-fourth and Thirty-fifth streets, it not being positively known at the foot of which street the troops would land—but, through the exertions of the police, an open space was kept for the approach of the troops to the place for the presentation. The presence of such vast numbers, on a morning as unpleasant as that of yesterday, and their patient waiting

THE NEW YEAR'S ADDRESS

OF THE

NEWSMEN

OF THE

NEW YORK HERALD,

To its Subscribers and Readers, January 1, 1862.

ONCE, again, in her course
Round the centre and source
Of her life, light and beauty, our planet has run
Her circle of seasons. Again 'tis begun;
Unfailing and true, as through thousands of years,
In that concord sublime of the heavenly spheres.
When human affairs are thus govern'd—ah! then
The millenium will shine on the children of men.
But, hold! 'tis no part of the Newsman's economy
To leave Mother Earth for the realms of astronomy.

THE UNION—live the Union!
With the New Year's dawn we bring
Our tribute to the Union, and
Rejoicing while we sing
Of its unconquerable power,
That it has passed its darkest hour.

THE UNION, 'twas the Union
Which closed our last refrain;
With the Union—*vive la* Union,
We begin our present strain—
As, like a bird upon the wing,
The past year's grand events we sing.

THE UNION—from our Union
What blessings have been given,
Descending upon all alike,
As the gentle dews of Heaven.
Sacred this war, though saints deplore,
Which aims these blessings to restore,
North, South, East, West, forevermore.

How glorious and grand
Our country did stand;
How happy and prosperous our Heaven-favored land,
As it were but yesterday amply possessing
All resources and forces of power, every blessing
Which earth can bestow—with a government proved
The best since our globe out of chaos was moved—
So strong, foreign threats we dismissed in contempt;
So benign, we imagined our Union exempt
From traitors and treason for ages to come—
When the whole land was roused by the roll of the drum
Of a fierce insurrection, the silliest and worst
With which any people have ever been cursed;
A war continental, and, sad the confession,
Inflamed by this will-'o-the-wisp of Secession.
The fruits of a long agitation of slavery,
The work of fanatics, and treason, and knavery—
Secession, rebellion, sword, fire and slaughter,
On mountain and plain, on the land and the water,
Are wasting our country. These things be our theme,
Though strange, wild and dark as the fantastical changes of
some horrible dream.

Ere the first morning sun
Of the year Sixty-One,
This insane rebellion had fairly begun.
Crazy South Carolina had bolted, and raised
Such a fuss, such a muss, that it crackled and blazed
Like a fire o'er the South, while "Old Buck" stood amazed—
Still pouting and doubting,
Or waking to quaking and shaking,
And whining, and pining, and dining, and wining;
While sappers and miners were sapping and mining,
And smoking, and joking, and croaking,
And pledging and hedging;
In promises spacous and gracious,
In performances often fallacious;
Still grumbling, and mumbling, and fumbling,
While the country to ruin was tumbling;
To conspirators wincing and mincing,
Their ways were so very convincing.
Decoyed, still among them he cuddled,
Bamboozled, befogg'd and bemuddled;
Still moaning and groaning,
Beseeching and preaching,
And moping, and groping, and hoping,
Gallivanting, and canting, and soaping,
Till his Cabinet revealings
Of treason and stealings,
Reduced the old man to a poor trembling mouse,
Afraid of his shadow even in the White House;
But, deserted, beleaguered, and weak from old age,
The HERALD stuck by him till drawn from the stage.

As it was, had it not
Been for Old Winfield Scott,
And his vigilant eye on the fire-eaters' plot,
"Old Buck" and "Old Abe" would have fallen a prize
To a Jacobin mob under Skyrocket Wise;
And our National Capital, in their possession,
Would have been the headquarters of rampant secession.

But Scott saved "Old Buck,"
And "Old Abe" had the luck
To be warned in good time, by a whisper from Puck,
Of cutthroats in Baltimore, lying in wait—
So casting aside his official estate,
And rigg'd as a Scotchman, and travelling all night,
By a roundabout road, with the morning's gray light,
"Honest Abe" safe in Washington, caused some surprise,
And some fun at his run and his Highland disguise.

Yet still there were dangers;
But Scott had his rangers
Maintained on the watch, till the crisis was past
Of the inauguration,
Which brought to the nation
The hope that the clouds were dispersing at last.
'Twas a foolish and almost a fatal delusion,
For the rebels were widening their plots of confusion.
Seven States had gone out—
With the Palmetto shout
Of mock independence they went up the spout—
Had set up Jeff. Davis—were hotly employed,
With the cannon and muskets provided by Floyd,
In arming for war, while imploring for peace,
Only asking a full and a final release,
Only calling to us, in an innocent tone,
"We are sinking the Old Ship, pray let us alone."

To "Honest Abe Lincoln,"
A queer fact to think on,
They sent up this olive branch, all the time arming;
But he, not quite ready, was patient and steady,
And his answer delayed, till the case was alarming.
For, under this fooling, secession was cooling—
"They must strike or it dies," so their fiat went forth,
And then Sumter's story, of Anderson's glory,
Aroused like a trumpet the Sons of the North.

With the flames and the smoke,
And the thunders which broke
From the walls of Fort Sumter, our people awoke,
Our proud Empire City still leading the way
To the nation's high cause in her battle array.
By thousands and millions, from Kansas to Maine,
Our people came out, this high cause to maintain;
Lifting high the old flag from the East to the West,
And resolved that its wrongs should be amply redressed.

And the South! Why, God bless ye,
All over Secessia,
Its Jacobin clubs all opposers expelling,
Carousing, and threatening, and arming, and yelling,
Soon reduced every State in revolt to their sway,
And dragg'd in four more to their rebel array—
North Carolina, Virginia, Arkansas, Tennessee—
And how, from an outrageous case, you shall see:—
A club of conspirators, summoned by Wise,
Came down upon Richmond, and took by surprise
A loyal Convention, as robbers sometimes
Take a traveller's watch, and his jewels and dimes.
Like brigands, they forced that Convention to sign,
In secret, their bill of Secession. 'Twas fine
Thus to make of Virginia, with all her old pride,
A mule, yea, a jackass, for Davis to ride.

Thus the people down there in the "Ancient Dominion"
To the Jacobins yielded their right of opinion;
For her traitors declared that you cannot refuse,
With four hundred thousand fat niggers to lose.
Unless you fall in, and before its too late,
We'll take them, and drive you, disgraced, from the State;
Fit only to dwell in that Yankee communion
Which seeks to beguile us with songs of "the Union."
Thus the poor "Old Dominion" succumb'd, it is true,
And thus situated, what else could she do?
But Western Virginia (where the almighty nigger
Is accounted a humbug, and cuts a small figure)
Stood fast by the Union, and still standing fast,
Defies all Secessia, and will to the last.

Old Virginia was cold,
And before we were told
That she had been captured, and shackled, and sold,
In pursuing the plans of Floyd, Letcher and Wise,
Harper's Ferry and Norfolk were seized by surprise—
The one to secure a great arsenal of rifles,
And muskets, and pistols, and other such trifles;
The other to capture a squadron which lay
Asleep in the trap of Elizabeth Bay,
And the Navy Yard there, with its millions of stores
Of warlike materials, and cannon by scores.
But when traitors contrive, and resolve, and conspire,
In plots such as these, they should look out for fire.
Harper's Ferry they seized; but too late at the scene,
A fire had despoiled them of that magazine.
Wise was not half so smart as the madman John Brown,
When with twenty-five followers he captured the town;
And Letcher fell short of his grand speculation
At Norfolk—'twas spoil'd in a grand conflagration.
Best of all, the conspirators had to forego
All their plots for the seizure of Fortress Monroe,
So that still we retained that strong lock and its key,
Which shuts up the State, like a wall, from the sea.
And over the Bay, we have lately brought back
The counties Northampton and old Accomac,
Rendered famous by Wise, and its bountiful dishes
Of ducks, oysters, crabs, and all sorts of choice fishes.

And Maryland next,
By conspirators vex'd,
And caught in their toils, was extremely perplex'd
What to do, where to go, till our soldiers dispers'd
Those Baltimore roughs—of all ruffians the worst—
And her bridge-burning night birds, a dastardly crew,
And warned them to find something better to do.
And thankful that city may be, and with reason,
In losing her bold legislators of treason;
And thankful, in view of her late pranks so dashing,
That she has escaped a most terrible thrashing.
And thanks for the now full and cordial communion
Between the Old State and the North and the Union.

Big Bethel—a blunder;
Vienna—no wonder;
Rich Mountain—a sharp peal of good Union thunder.
'Twas there in his victories McClellan displayed
That genius and skill in war's terrible trade
Which have placed on his shoulders the mantle of Scott,
"*Sans peur, sans reproche*" without blemish or spot.

Bull Run! 'twas "On to Richmond,"
Cried Greeley and his crew—
"Onward," their hue and cry; so march'd
Our army raw and new.
It went rejoicing in its strength,
And in its grand display;
Bleeding and broken, it return'd
From that disastrous day.
That Sabbath morning brightly dawn'd
Along our glittering lines,
For miles o'er fields of grass and grain,
And groves of oaks and pines;
In the pomp and pride of battle
As on a gay parade,
But ah! how different was the scene
Beneath that evening's shade!
The conflict opened gloriously
Along our fiery track,
And full three miles we still advanced
And drove the rebels back;
From bridge, copse, trench and battery,
Our flag still rising higher,
And through a storm of shot and shell,
Through dust, and smoke, and fire;
Until we thought the day was ours—
When wearied from the fight,
By thousands we sat down to rest—
But 'twas a brief respite:
For the rebel Johnston's squadrons
Had come, and with them, too,
Our fancied day of Austerlitz
Was changed to Waterloo.
Our Grouchy was Old Patterson,
Some sixty miles away,
With five and twenty thousand men,
And thus we lost the day.
And yet while brave men are esteemed
For deeds of glory done,
New York will boast her heroes,
At the battle of Bull run.

With this change in the tide,
Kentucky was tried
By secession, but loyal Kentucky allied
To three strong Union States, looming up at her side,
And cherishing still the wise teachings of Clay,
Found secession a game which she never could play.
Although she betrayed quite a weak partiality
For that wretched secession device of neutrality,
Which means, if you give all we ask, and disown
The Union and fight it, we'll let you alone.
But this sort of luck was too mean for Kentuck,
And driven to close quarters, she fights like a buck,
And the secession crew may regard themselves lucky,
If with a whole skin they escape from Kentucky.

Unhappy Missouri!
Its most savage fury
This fierce war has brought upon loyal Missouri.
Over her fair fields its march may be traced,
By broad belts of country despoiled and made waste;
Their people like wandering gypsies are found,
Their homes laid in ashes or torn to the ground;
Their women and children, exhausted and falling
In death on the highway—still piteously calling
Upon their protectors, cut down by the fury
Of savage marauders. Unhappy Missouri!
Yet Boonville, and Springfield, and Carthage will stand,
And Lexington, high with the names of our land
Of heroes immortal; and Belmont, in story
And song, will live long in the annals of glory.
But will glory repay the poor mothers and daughters
Made widows and orphans by such dreadful slaughters?
Our country, we answer—whatever the cost,
We must rescue our country, or all will be lost.

And East Tennessee,
Stronghold of the free—
That it should be rescued all good men agree,
And promptly, we hope, Parson Brownlow will hear
The sounds of its coming deliverance near.
And that from those mountains we'll open the gates
To reunion in all the "Confederate States."

Well done! We can boast
On our Southern seacoast—
Our Soldiers and Sailors. Come join in the toast.
Captain Wilkes, 'tis conceded, has done pretty well,
For those lost children, Mason and Johnny Slidell,
Head chiefs of secession, and of it crammed full,
And nabb'd from that kidnapper known as John Bull.
He has heard all about it; and pitching, and rearing,
He calls it an "insult outrageous and daring."
A most diabolical act of aggression,
Which must be atoned for. "Huzzah!" cries Secession.
A shout which informs that now our true plan
Is to keep England quiet as long as we can.
And to give her no cause for a league with Jeff. Davis,
With her much needed stores, and her armies and navies.
The *Times*, call'd the Thunderer, has not deigned to flatter us
And pooh-pooh's that little affair at Cape Hatteras—
That neat operation which broke up some juggling
And a brisk little trade in the business of smuggling.
And at Chicamacomico—mark well the spelling—
Those land crabs for once, got a good Union shelling.

But in South Carolina!
Oh! Cesar! and Dinah!
Where secession is worshipp'd as something divine-ah!
There we brought down their boastings in terror and sorrow.
For as once, it rained fire and brimstone from Heaven—
For sins which could not, by the Lord, be forgiven—
On the vile city Sodom and wicked Gomorrah;
So the sun was obscured by the smoky eclipse,
From that tempest of fire from our circle of ships,
As they moved like a shoal of sea monsters at play,
In that beautiful water of Port Royal Bay.
"It seemed," said a darkie, "You done us so brown,
Dat de earth was gwine up, and de heavens comin' down."

Hark! Louder and higher
Comes that wild cry of "Fire."
From Charleston—wide raging—dome, tower and spire
Are flaming and crackling; and in the wild glow,
The woodlands above and the waters below,
Fort Sumter the bay, and its isles, and the ocean,
Are illumined as by some volcanic commotion.
A city laid waste, in this dread visitation
To treason, secession and nullification.

Billy Wilson's game chickens,
Down there at Fort Pickens,
Were really beginning to spoil for a fight,
When the rebels surprised them,
And nearly capsized them,
Stealing down on their camp, under cover of night;
But our fellows soon rallied, and then from their slaughter
The rebels, like ducks, scampered off to the water.
Since which, General Brown, these attentions rewarding,
Has quieted Bragg with a wholesome bombarding.

Captain Hollins, the hero
Of Greytown, the Nero,
Has fallen in glory somewhat below zero.
Since that brilliant achievement, in which he essayed
To open our tight Mississippi blockade,
His "Turtle" did wonders; but, as the fact shows,
His "Turtle" did nothing but break his own nose.
"We peppered them well, the Hessian crew, darn 'em."
Oh! Hollins, you humbug, don't tell that to Barnum.
But our chaps? Well, so far as we are enlightened,
Our chaps, though not hurt, were most shamefully frightened.

But, in this rattling fashion,
For days we might dash on,
Yet one moment longer we ask your compassion.
We have a grand army, and what is its score?
Six hundred and sixty-five thousand, and more.
And the line around which this immense army hovers?
Two thousand miles long is the line which it covers,
With our Navy—no longer contemptibly small—
Two hundred and fifty odd vessels in all.
And the men? Some twenty-five thousand. The cost?
Including what's stolen, and squandered, and lost,
And contractors' big swindles, and oysters and toddy,
Bad beef, and bad pork, and bad blankets and shoddy,
Our Army and Navy's expenses and pay
Are not quite two millions of dollars a day.
Mon Dieu!—and no battle—this really is funny.
Is this war, then, reduced to the bluff game of money?
Perhaps; yet why should this excite any wonder?
'Tis the pause in the storm ere it breaks forth in thunder.
Has the Sumter been caught? Yes—that is, she's been found
A half dozen times, though still bobbing around.
And when will they hang those condemned privateers?
Wait a bit—think of brave Col. Corcoran, my dears.
But an exchange of prisoners?—our soldiers demand it.
Very true; but you know, well, we can't understand it.

Good morning! time passes:
Touch lightly your glasses.
Peace, peace to the brave fellows slain at Manassas,
And all o'er the land, in this deadly contention
Of brothers with brothers. And yet we must mention
A thing or two more; for you know that at parting
With friends it requires a good deal of starting.
The Potomac blockade: can't tell what the matter is;
Perhaps we're afraid of those secession batteries;
Or, perhaps, we may think them entitled to no regard
Till McClellan has settled with Toutant de Beauregard.
Whatever the mystery, it seemeth outrageous
That the rebels in that noble river should cage us,
And that we are contented at long range to shell them,
With forces on hand quite enough to expel them.
The Potomac! fair stream of America's pride,
Of Washington's birth—where he grew up and died;
Where the chief and the shrine of Mount Vernon forever
Will brighten the face of the beautiful river—
The Potomac, alas! that its shores should now be,
From its rise in the mountains far down to the sea,
The scene of red slaughter, of scouts, guerrillas,
Camps, armies and batteries, and forts and flotillas.
Shade of Washington! rise, interpose and restore
Our land to thy faith in the Union once more!
And what of Fremont? Why, his case simply teaches
That a man, now and then, gets too big for his breeches.
And our secession peace men—that rascally set?
Inquire at Fort Warren or Fort Lafayette.
And our hot abolition disturbers and screechers—
The Garrisons, Greeleys, and Cheevers and Beechers?
Still scattering their firebrands of discord, and brewing
In Congress their schemes for the nation's undoing.
If they had their deserts they would now be held faster
Than any ass of the class of the Abbe McMaster.
But let "Honest Abe" still maintain his position,
Resisting this rank anti-slavery sedition,
And soon we shall silence its base coalition.

Bon jour! We are sure
That you cannot endure
This long rigmarole. Yet a word in your ear:
With the day's liberalities,
Not to say prodigalities,
The Newsman, you know, has his "Happy New Year."
Shall we summon the shadow of Douglas, who died
Holding up for the Union, and fast by its side?
Or need we recall such as Baker and Lyon,
And Ellsworth and Ward? In the sweet peace of Zion
May they rest. So, good morning! but yet, by the way,
Good luck to George Opdyke, our Mayor to-day.
With "great expectations" he's this day anointed,
And they are not likely to be disappointed,
If we may rely on his friends, who assure us
That if we are sick he's the doctor to cure us.
But we very much fear he will never cry "Land, ho!"
If hampered and worried like Mayor Fernando.
We hope for the best; and we hope very soon
That the *World*, and the *Times*, and the howling *Tribune*
Will find abolition sedition a sell,
And "cease to do evil and learn to do well."
We hope this rebellion will shortly be ended—
That the States in revolt will be soon again blended
With the States still in loyalty true to the Union,
And blended for ages in cordial communion.
In this hope that our skies will again soon be clear,
Dear ladies, to you, and all friends, far and near—
To "Honest Old Abe," and (he's right, never fear),
To our Army and Navy a "A HAPPY NEW YEAR."

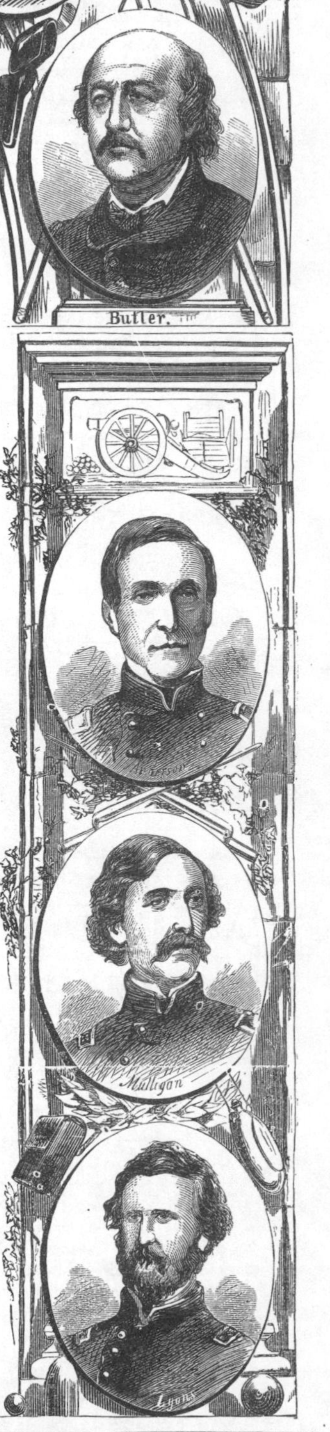

NEW YORK DAILY NEWS.

VOL. VII......NO. 182. NEW YORK, THURSDAY, JULY 16, 1863. PRICE TWO CENTS.

THE RIOT!!

Terrible Scenes in Nineteenth Street.

THE MILITARY AND THE MOB.

CHARGES AND COUNTER CHARGES

Colonel Jardine Mortally Wounded.

One Captain, Two Lieutenants and Fifteen Privates Killed.

HOWITZERS OPEN ON THE MOB

The Street Strewn with the Bodies of Men, Women, and Children.

SCENES IN THE ELEVENTH AVENUE.

THE MILITARY FIRE ON THE MOB.

THIRTY MEN AND WOMEN KILLED.

LIST OF THE SLAIN.

A Woman Shot Through the Heart.

DEATH OF COLONEL O'BRIEN.

RAID UPON THE BLACKS.

SEVERAL NEGROES HUNG.

ONE NEGRO DROWNED

BLOCKS OF NEGRO DWELLINGS BURNED

LETTER FROM GOV. SEYMOUR

Firemen and Citizens Organizing for Defense.

RIOT ON STATEN ISLAND.

Railroad Depot Burned—Lyceum Sacked, and a Negro Hung.

GREAT FIRE IN BROOKLYN

CONFLAGRATION IN NEWARK.

ARRIVAL OF TROOPS.

Gen. Dix to be Assigned to the Department of New York.

INCIDENTS, ACCIDENTS, &C.

[*For reports of riotous proceedings during the early part of the day, see second page.*]

Notwithstanding all that was done on Tuesday to satisfy the turbulent populace; and the confident hope of all good citizens that the riot would cease with Tuesday night's excesses, the riot raged yesterday more fiercely than on any previous day, although the personnel was greatly changed. There were but few, comparatively speaking, of those who rose for the purpose of opposing the draft in the ranks of the rioters yesterday. The mob seemed composed mainly of the vagabonds of the town—pickpockets, thieves, and the multitude of "prowlers about the streets." Many of the workingmen and firemen who had strenuously opposed the enforcement of the draft, as soon as its suspension was announced, joined the ward organizations for the protection of unoffending persons and property. The terrible scenes which occurred in Nineteenth street, in the Eleventh avenue, and elsewhere, exceed any which have occurred since the riot began. Arrangements have been made for the arrival of large re-enforcements of military to-day, and General Dix is to be assigned to the command of the Department of New York.

Yesterday's Proceedings.

The authorities in the City Hall fondly hoped on Tuesday night that the mob was crushed, that all apprehensions of further violence were groundless, and that peace absolute and serene would reign throughout the municipal borders and there would be naught to molest nor make afraid.

How near the truth came the prophecyings of these high officials, let the teeming columns of THE NEWS of to-day, filled as they are with the record of bloodshed and mischief, explain.

During the earlier hours of the morning, that is from one o'clock to six, that part of the city which is bounded by Wall street, the East and North Rivers, and the Battery, was comparatively quiet, although the authorities had every reason to believe that an attack upon certain public buildings in Wall street would be made at that time.

AT THE CUSTOM HOUSE.

One hundred of the clerks and a large number of other employees, fully armed, were kept on watch all night, expecting a visit from the fearful "mob." There are but two places into which the visitors could by any possibility have gone, and these were so guarded by well armed and determined men, that any attempt to break in would have resulted in an absolute failure, and in loss of life to whomsoever might make the foolish trial.

THE BANKS

are all safe and it is far more than likely that the fears of the officials at those necessary institutions are but the creations of their own lively imaginings; for to the best of our knowledge and belief, there has been no intimation nor thought of an attack upon them. The removal of the specie from several of them seems so absurd, that were we not familiar with the fact, we should regard the report as ridiculous in the extreme. No mob on earth, unprovided with artillery, could effect an entrance to the banks or their vaults, and it seems to us, that the less said about that, the better.

IN GREENWICH AND WASHINGTON STREETS,

however, affairs wore a far less peaceful look than in Wall street and Broadway. At about 2 o'clock in the morning a gang of men and boys, numbering perhaps sixty or seventy, went howling through the streets from the Battery up, rumaging even lager bier saloons, routing out the proprietors and other inmates, and playing grand havoc generally with everybody and everything. A German named Breussing, who keeps a small-sized restaurant near Morris street, had been in bed with his wife and children just long enough to reach the cheerful land of noddom, when he was awakened by a terrific pounding at his door and a stentorian voice thereat, intimating to him the propriety of an immediate opening. He went cautiously to the door and said he had closed for the night and did not propose to re-open. The order to "open and be d—d" was reiterated by half a dozen voices, and with trembling hands he obeyed the first part of the direction leaving the other portion to the decision of a more righteous tribunal. Instantly the scoundrel crew sprang in, seized the frightened Teuton by the throat and demanded a treat. This so soon as he was released he liberally gave, and his night-gowned frow came out to assist in doing the honors. The men, seemingly ashamed of their actions, the woman having quietly remonstrated with them, quietly retired, having done no damage save the upsetting of all the decanters, barrels and demijohns they could find, kicking the proprietor into his back room and saluting each for himself the indignant lady. Had they confined themselves to such pilferings as this, there would not have been so much cause for complaint, although that was bad enough, but we regret to say that

ARSON, in its worst form, was attempted and almost accomplished by the same set of ruffians, who made this section of the city hideous with their outrages for the space of three or four hours. Near the corner of Washington and Rector streets there is a large tenement and boarding house, occupied mainly by the poorest of the poor, against whom the rioters could by no possibility have even a pretended cause for hostility. On the lower floor, however, is a groggery, and in that commenced the row, which came near terminating in a most fearful calamity.

Having effected an entrance to the bar room the rioters made free with everything within reach, and then began to upset the liquor upon the floor. This the man in charge endeavored to prevent, but he was hustled into the street in short order, and the cry was raised, "Fire it! Fire it!" As is well known, but a spark is needed to set such tinder as these mobs are composed of into the most furious flames, and acting upon the suggestion they began to suit the action to the word.

Luckily, the main body of the gang had gone off into Greenwich street, "blackberrying," as they facetiously term their negro hunts, and but ten or a dozen of the fellows were left. These, however, proceeded to kindle a fire upon the bar room floor, when suddenly, and to their entire surprise, the barkeeper, accompanied by some half a dozen friends and neighbors, rushed in upon them and clubbed them most unmercifully. One of the rioters was so injured about the head and neck that he was unable to skedaddle with his friends, and was left upon the bar room floor, surrounded by broken bottles, puddles of rotgut and charred chips, until toward daybreak, when the liberal doucings of water he received and the fearful amount of brandy he was made to swallow, started up his faculties, and he was permitted to go in peace.

During the progress of the row the families in the upper part of the house became terribly alarmed and excited. They threw many of their effects from the windows and prepared to evacuate in full force. Had the fire been kept alive but a few moments longer, the house and all in it, and the tinder block which adjoins it, must have gone the way of destruction.

In the meantime the larger portion of the gang went from shop to shop "helling around" for no particular purpose, but just having a good time generally.

There was no one to stop them in their course, all the police being needed elsewhere, and they managed to scare all the women, batter a great many inoffending citizens, destroy any quantities of lager and other "beverages," and stir up the locality in a way which was new, startling and slightly disagreeable.

During the remainder of the day this portion of the city was very quiet, several gangs of men marched from the docks up toward the Park, and on further up town, but molested no one down town, nor did they create disturbance of any kind.

Toward eight o'clock this morning, a

NEGRO WAS CHASED

by a mob of half-grown men, every one of whom looked like a jail bird, from Burling Slip through South street, by the Fulton Ferry, and to the corner of Peck Slip. At this point, the man stumbled and his pursuers pounced on him with fiendish yells of triumph. In a struggle which ensued, the poor fellow got away again, and ran several yards, when the crowd again caught him, and beat him most unmercifully.

It seemed for a time as though the man's life was good for but a brief season, but fortunately for him a number of sailors belonging to vessels in the vicinity hearing the disturbance and the cries of the negro, rushed out from the eating house and charged the cowardly assailants pell mell and in true sailor style. As is always the case with miscreants, who war upon single individuals, the rioters were arrant cowards and ran from the stalwart thrashings of the men of the seas as if they had been whipped dogs. The negro was taken into the eating house, a glass of brandy was given him and he was sent home under a convoy of two of the noblest hearted men we have heard of in many a day.

In the house where this colored man lives there are five colored families, and of the seven men over nineteen years of age, five have been overhauled by mobs and cruelly beaten. The normal fruits of this savage treatment has not yet appeared. We have not seen a single negro who counseled opposition or spoke of revenge.

ONE OF THE MOST TERRIFIC FEATURES

of this riot was the double murder, which was committed yesterday morning, in Thirty-second street, near Sixth avenue. The facts, as gathered from a reliable reporter, are these, and as there are many exaggerations of the affair in circulation, which will, if believed, certainly cause trouble and bloodshed, we have taken great pains to get at the exact truth:

At half after six yesterday morning a middle-aged negro, named Potter or Porter, was passing quietly down Thirty-second street, near the avenue, when he was met by a fireman, an ex-Zouave, named Manney, who hailed him, asking where he was going. The negro, not understanding, apparently, what was said, made no reply, and Manney, with the most kind intentions, told him that the excitement was still very great, that the mobs would certainly be around to-day, and would doubtless kill him or severely beat him, if they should catch him. Still, apparently misapprehending Manney's intentions, and probably misunderstanding his language, the negro drew a revolver and discharged it with fatal effect. He shot twice certainly, each ball striking Manney full in the forehead, and entering his brain. He then started to run, but was soon overtaken by a crowd of excited and infuriated people, and by several of the firemen residing near by, who chased him a short distance, and soon overtook him.

The heart sickens at the recollection of the fearful and

DREADFUL SCENE

which followed. The negro was pounded, battered, kicked, pummeled, stoned, thrown down, trampled upon, and fairly bruised into jelly. A bloody pulp was all that was left of the mistaken murderer in a very few moments; but even this was considered slight revenge, and the mutilated mass of blood and bones and quivering flesh was carried brutally to a tree, to a limb of which it was hung, amid the cheers and jeers of the indignant crowd.

Poor Manney had the best of medical attendance, but probably for naught. Dr. Brooks, who was called to dress his wounds, declared that the case was a hopeless one, and that he would not probably live an hour. He was taken to Bellevue Hospital, and is probably gone to his last account long since.

In the tenement house where Manney lived, and in which some say the negro also lived, resided several Irish and negro families. Until now there has been but little trouble between them; in fact the house has been one of the most quiet tenement houses of the neighborhood. Since the present "uprising of the people," however, there has been considerable ill feeling, and during the day before yesterday the white families were moving out. Regardless of any fact, however, save the one all-convincing one that negroes were in the house, the crowd, which by this time had assumed the proportions of a mob, surrounded the building, and having saluted it with yells of unequalled fury and rage, set fire to it, and then moved on to other scenes of violence. Fortunately the fire was extinguished before it had got fairly under way, and the additional horror was thus spared.

In the afternoon about 3 o'clock, a large mob, among whom are many of the men who "assisted" at the foregoing outrage, gathered in the rear of the premises No. 147 East Twenty-eighth street, and inaugurated a renewal of

NEGRO OUTRAGES

which, for barbarity and recklessness of life and property, exceed anything before attempted. In the alley-way which leads from that point, reside a small colony of negroes, numbering in all about twenty-five families. To drive these people out and destroy their local habitation, was the least brutal of the intentions of the mob, which, with shoutings and profanity which do dishonor to the infernal regions, rushed unannounced into the very presence of their victims. Very many of the negroes had run off, but enough remained to invite the outrageous indecencies of the mob. For some minutes their search for the colored people was in vain, but they soon found one whom they

MURDERED WITH A CROWBAR

in the following manner: Van Clef (the negro) was found crouching behind a bedstead by two young men, one of whom had a large crowbar in his hand. The negro was at once hauled into the middle of the room, when he was pulled about by the hair, kicked and beaten over the head and finally punched and pounded with the crowbar until he was apparently lifeless. The crowd played with him for a little while, and then, as other victims were found, threw the mutilated and dying man into the alley, while they turned their attention to the other candidates for public notice. No other absolute murder was committed here, but many poor creatures were mercilessly beaten and thoroughly used up, so that when the crowd left them there was but little choice between life and death in their appearance or sensations.

From this place the mob went into Broadway alley, into a house kept by a black man named Dudley. They threw the furniture into the street and beat Dudley so badly about the head and chest, that he was not expected to survive. The women were frightened, as well they might be, out of their senses, and ran to and fro, crying for help and begging for protection, while their husbands and sons were beaten and murdered, their homes destroyed and their dwellings set on fire. Their attempts to save some of their goods were set at naught by the mob, and after suffering much from the brutal treatment of the rioters, they started with their little ones for the Central Office to seek a lodging and a protection from further violence.

TERRIBLE SCENES IN NINETEENTH STREET.

Over One Hundred Killed and Wounded.

At about 8 o'clock, as about one hundred citizens and returned soldiers, all armed, under the command of Col. Cleveland Winslow, late of the Duryee Zouaves, were passing through Nineteenth street, near Second avenue, they were attacked by a large number of rioters. Brickbats and other missiles were hurled upon them from the housetops. One man who had followed Col. Winslow's force, and had repeatedly fired into the ranks, was shot by one of the volunteer soldiers, who stepped from the ranks, leveled his musket and fired. The man dropped, and was left lying in the street. Two howitzers were then loaded and fired into the crowd, making great havoc and causing them to retire down First avenue. Col. Jardine, late of Hawkins' Zouaves, was severely wounded by a shot in the leg, and was taken to a house in 19th street, which the crowd afterward threatened to attack and take possession of the wounded officer. By a charge made upon Col. Winslow's force, one captain, one lieutenant and fifteen privates of his command were killed. Col. Winslow charged five distinct times upon the crowd. The effect of these charges were most terrific, the street was strewn with bodies, at least twenty or thirty dead and fifty wounded. As soon as the crowd dispersed, Col. Winslow came to the Central Office and reported the result of the engagement, which was the most desperate which has taken place since the commencement of the riots in the city. Capt. Ukell and Lieut. Brown were killed; Lieut. Upton and Col. Jardine were shot in the groin. Col. Winslow, as soon the crowd was driven off, marched his men down the Second avenue to Fourteenth street, thence to Third avenue, and thence to the Seventh Regiment Armory, to await further orders. He first reported to Gov. Seymour, at the St. Nicholas, and was ordered by the Governor to report to Gen. Brown, at Headquarters.

General Brown, as soon as the particulars of the fight were related to him, ordered a company of regulars, 200 men, commanded by Captains Putnam, Shelley and Rowolle, and a large body of policemen, to the scene of the slaughter, with instructions to use every effort to procure the body of Colonel Jardine and take it to a place of safety. The military carried two field pieces.

The Regulars arrived upon the ground about 10 o'clock. An immense crowd was found waiting to give them a warm reception. The house into which Col Jardine was taken, after he had received his wound, was surrounded by the rioters, who refused to disperse until they had contested the position with the soldiers. Capt. Putnam then ordered his men to turn the howitzers upon the crowd. The pieces, two in number, were loaded with canister and orders were at once given to fire. The artillerists then poured their death-dealing volley upon the crowd, which dispersed rapidly, bearing off their killed and wounded. The soldiers now marched to the house in the cellar of which Col. Jardine was lying, and removed the wounded man to a carriage in which he was taken to headquarters and afterward to the St. Nicholas, where he was attended by several physicians, who pronounced his situation extremely critical. Both of his legs were broken and he was severely wounded by a musket ball in the body. The other wounded officers were also taken to the St. Nicholas.

Frightful Scenes in 11th Avenue.

The following account, taken from the lips of an eye-witness, of a mission undertaken and successfully carried through by Judge McCunn on yesterday afternoon, presents the most astounding revelation of affairs in our city which has yet been presented to our readers:

It seems that Governor Seymour, who is doing all that he can to restore the quiet and peace of our city, sent for Judge McCunn yesterday afternoon, and after consultation with him upon the state of affairs in the upper districts of the city requested him to make a grand tour through the disaffected districts, that the true state of the internal sentiment of the people might be ascertained, and that so far as was possible, he (Judge McCunn) might allay the apprehensions of the citizens, and induce them to return to their ordinary avocations, and keep the peace of the city and county.

This mission, dangerous as it would seem to be, the Judge cheerfully undertook, and having ordered a carriage, drove first to the scene of the morning's conflict, concerning which, the most astounding accounts were circulating, all of which were calculated to do great damage to the cause of "law and order."

He first went to the corner of

SEVENTH AVENUE AND TWENTY-NINTH STREET.

where quite a large crowd had assembled, evidently intending to do further damage to the body of a negro who was crouching piteously at the foot of a large tree. A body of military under charge of a Lieutenant, whose name he did not gather, was stationed there, and the preparatory movements toward firing upon the crowd had been made when the Judge called out in an authoritative manner, "Lieutenant, don't fire!"

Col. Myers, under whose superior command the force was, demanded the name of the interrupter and wanted to know by what authority he presumed to interfere with the operations of the soldiers.

The Judge replied that he was the City Judge of New York and had come as a special messenger from Gov. Seymour; that he believed the crowd would be more easily dispersed by a word from him than by a volley from the soldiers, and that, if the Colonel had no objections, he would try the experiment and save the shedding of innocent blood.

The Colonel, of course, agreed to this course, and Judge McCunn, stepping forward, spoke as follows:

SPEECH OF JUDGE M'CUNN.

MY FRIENDS: You should not remain here longer. You are here for no lawful purpose, and I counsel you as your friend, to go to your quiet homes. You know who I am, and you know full well that to the extent of my power I will, as I always have, protect you. [Cheers.] Gov. Seymour [Cheers for Seymour] is in the city; he has already appealed to the President to retrace his steps in regard to the draft and has secured its suspension. The Courts yesterday afternoon decided that the draft was unlawful, [Applause] and if it is your pleasure, I will read you that decision. ["Go on, old boy."] (The Judge here read the decision rendered by him at Chambers, on Tuesday, which was received with cheers and applause.) Now, my friends, I have a message from the Governor.

The Governor, who is the people's friend, now as ever, has instructed me as his messenger, to say to you, that he will sustain the decision of the Courts of the State to his very utmost power; that the rights of no citizen shall be trampled upon, that if you are true and good men you will respect his advice, his counsel, and request that you go at once to your homes, and participate no further in these lawless proceedings. [Applause.]

At the conclusion of the Judge's speech the crowd slowly dispersed, giving cheers now and then for him and for the Governor.

For some unaccountable reason two of the soldiers discharged their muskets before the crowd had fully obeyed the direction of Judge McCunn, and immediately thereafter screams were heard from a large tenement house in the vicinity, and it was reported and believed that a man was killed. The Colonel promptly disarmed the soldiers and put them under arrest.

In the Eleventh avenue the Judge found a most terribly excited population. In many houses families were lamenting the death of husbands, sons and fathers from the effect of

THE MORNING'S FIGHT.

So near as the facts could be ascertained, the truth would seem to be that early in the day all along that portion of the avenue groups of men, women and children, gathered for the various purposes of discussion and observation. About noon, two companies of artillery passed along, making no disturbance, and causing no excitement. At 3 o'clock, or in that neighborhood, a force of soldiery marched up, under command (it was said) of Lieut. Ryer, whose presence attracted a still greater crowd, and called forth some hostile demonstrations.

Whatever may have been the immediate cause (and concerning this there are so many conflicting stories that we prefer to give none), the fact is that the troops

FIRED UPON THE CROWD

with fatal effect, instantly

KILLING SOME THIRTY

people, men, women and children. The effect was immediate, and the frightened people took to their houses and other shelter without waiting a second encounter.

The following is as correct a

LIST OF KILLED

as can be procured, and is long enough and fearful enough to enforce the advice and request of the Governor, as well as of all right-minded men, that the people would much better disperse and go quietly to their homes, than by riotous demonstration draw upon themselves and their families such fearful punishment as this.

Michael Ryan, Eleventh avenue, killed.
Daniel Kiernan, Eleventh avenue, killed.
Patrick Garvey, Eleventh avenue, killed.
John Grey, Forty-second street, killed.
John Kearney, Eleventh avenue, killed.
Patrick Quinn, Eleventh avenue, killed.
James Garrett, Eleventh avenue, killed.
Mrs. Thornton, Eleventh avenue, shot through the heart.
Child of Mrs. Thornton, Eleventh avenue, shot through both legs.
Patrick Casey, Eleventh avenue, killed.
Mrs. Lawrence, Eleventh avenue, killed.
Two Germans, names unknown, Forty-second street, killed.
Two Germans, names unknown, Forty-third street, killed.
Mrs. Lawrence and child, Eleventh avenue, killed
Mrs. Kirtland, Eleventh avenue, killed.
Richard Stafford, Eleventh avenue, killed.
C. Larkin, Eleventh avenue, killed.
Woman, name unknown, killed.
Lawrence Ryan, Eleventh avenue, killed.
Mr. Ackley, Eleventh avenue, killed.

The above twenty-three names are all that could be obtained up to the hour of going to press, but it is known that several others were mortally wounded. The greatest consternation prevails in the neighborhood, the women and children filling the air with their cries and lamentations, while the men who were happily spared from the dreadful fate of their friends and companions sat mournful and sullen.

The people, with what degree of fairness we know not, charge that the firing was reckless and wholly unjustifiable, but what the truth of the matter is, nothing but a legal investigation can determine.

At the request of Major General Sandford, Judge McCunn went over to the arsenal, whose adjacent precincts are picketted, sentinelled, and guarded with all the paraphernalia of war and strife.

While they were talking, firing was heard, and the General suggested that the mob was firing upon the pickets. Judge McCunn volunteered to go out and ascertain. He went to the corner of Thirty-first street and Seventh avenue (at 8 o'clock in the evening) in company with the Captain, and found that the pickets had been firing without orders. They were at once disarmed, placed under arrest and sent to the arsenal.

While the Captain and Judge McCunn were talking, a man named Henry Schultz, who said that he was a member of the Seventh regiment, came up to them and joined in the conversation. At this time, a woman started to cross the street; she was ordered back by Schultz; she continued her course, when Schultz levelled his gun, fired at her, and

SHOT HER DEAD.

in her tracks. The most intense excitement prevailed at once, and great trouble was anticipated, and would undoubtedly have ensued had not the murderer been instantly disarmed and sent to the Arsenal under arrest. The woman, whose name was Mrs. Thornton, was taken into an adjoining house, while a very natural gloom settled upon one and all.

A representation of these facts having been made to Gen. Sandford, he called in all the pickets and replaced them by others who were cautioned and counseled as to their duties and responsibilities by the General before they were sent out.

On the corner of Twenty-eighth street and Seventh avenue Judge McCunn, who was accompanied by Mr. Dunn, saw a large crowd gathered about a tree on which

HUNG THE BODY OF A NEGRO.

With his own knife Judge McCunn cut the rope which held the yet animate sufferer by the neck, and directed some men whom he recognized in the assemblage to take him into a house and care for him. This was done, and the Judge addressed the crowd in terms very similar to those in which he spoke before and accomplished the same results.

The above report was made to Governor Seymour by Judge McCunn in person. The Governor congratulated him on the good service he had done, and indorsed all that he had promised in his behalf.

A more extraordinary night's work has probably not been recorded in the annals of this most extraordinary outbreak of the people.

The Thirteenth Ward.

A mob gathered yesterday afternoon in Grand street, at the head of Mangin street, for the purpose of repeating some of the scenes of the previous night. Word was immediately brought to the Thirteenth Precinct Station House, when the police, under the command of Capt. Steers, proceeded to the scene of disturbance. When they arrived they were hooted by the mob, and some stones were thrown at them, when they immediately charged upon the mob, whom they succeeded in dispersing and arresting two of the ringleaders, named John Maher, who had a loaded pistol in his possession, and Francis Lamb. The arrests were made by Officer Johnson and Roundsman Holden, of the Thirteenth Precinct.

The police of the Thirteenth Precinct, under Capt. Steers, are patroling the Ward, and bringing all those who have had the misfortune to be born black to a place of safety, until the excitement shall have passed over.

A military vigilance committee, composed of citizens under command of Captain Huston, formerly of the Twelfth regiment N. Y. S. N. G., is forming in the Thirteenth Ward. Their headquarters are at the Thirteenth Precinct Station House. Already 400 names are enrolled. The following are the officers: William. H. Huston, Captain: John J. Tooker, Lieutenent; Bernard Rody, formerly of Wilson's Zouaves, Lieutenant; Frank Snyder, Lieutenant; Joseph T. Ellery, Lieutenant. They are to do duty under Captain Steers, of the Thirteenth Precinct Police, about 100 of whom, armed with muskets, patrol the ward.

In the Seventh Ward there is also another large armed patrol of citizens patrolling the ward.

Scenes at Harlem Bridge.

In Harlem and Yorkville all was quiet up to 12 o'clock. It was rumored that an attempt would be made to burn the bridge over the Harlem River, but the report was not verified up to the hour at which our reporter left Harlem. All the streets approaching the bridge were strongly guarded at favorable points, and long lines of policemen extended from the bridge to the different points where an attack was expected.

A large number of special officers were on duty, and strong detachments of these, intermingled with the regular police, were stationed at short intervals on all the avenues of approach. Near One Hundred and Twenty-sixth street, about one hundred men of the Twelfth Regular Infantry were stationed, ready to fall in at a moment's notice. The utmost vigilance was exercised to prevent any persons, not properly authorized, from approaching the bridge. Every carriage passing was closely examined, and any passer-by, who was unable to give an account of himself, was summarily arrested. Up to a late hour no disturbance was apprehended in this locality.

Firemen's Organization in the First Ward.

All is quiet here at 11 o'clock, P. M. Alder-

CONTINUED ON EIGHTH PAGE.

Published by the Brooklyn and Long Island Fair, for the Benefit of the U. S. Sanitary Commission.

R. S. STORRS, Jr., D.D., Editor. BROOKLYN, THURSDAY, FEB. 25, 1864. Price, 5 Cents. No. IV.

A LADY'S GREETING.

Beat, noble Drum! beat loud and strong—
Roll the deep bass of Liberty!
Thrill thro' the pulses of this throng—
Till every chord responds to thee!

Tell them, thine are but echoing notes
Of Drums that beat in camp and field,
Where'er our starry banner floats,—
Or Victory with Blood is sealed!

Feb. 24, 1864.

THE FAIR.

Another day of delightful weather has favored the Sanitary Fair, and many thousands of our citizens and strangers took advantage of it to visit the Exhibition. The increased charges for admission seemed to make little or no difference in the numbers present, and the Academy and adjacent buildings were yesterday as crowded as on the previous days. The eating arrangements had been improved, and in every respect the machinery of the great Fair moved smoother than before.

The total receipts for entrance tickets sold up to last evening were eighteen thousand eight hundred and three dollars. The sales have amounted to nineteen thousand two hundred and fifty dollars; and Cash contributions amount to nineteen thousand six hundred and fourteen dollars.

The previous receipts in the Treasurer's hands from all sources amounted to fifty-nine thousand five hundred and seventy-eight dollars. Total cash in hands of Treasurer last night $117,236.

The Executive Committee, in view of the great rush to the Fair—necessitating last night the closing of the doors as early as eight P. M.,——advise visitors from New York and elsewhere to come as early in the day as possible. The Fair buildings are open to the public at eleven A. M.

LONG ISLAND.

The impression which most people have of Long Island, is that it extends for a hundred miles, more or less, due east from the Ridgewood Reservoir; is fifteen or twenty miles in width; is as flat as a floor, with a soil several degrees dryer than brick dust; is nearly as picturesque, in its natural features as the bare top of a carpenter's bench, and about as generally and generously fertile as a graveled roof after the winds have powdered it with dust. That such a piece of country should have had any pleasant and inspiriting history, should now have any rich resources, or show any hardy and intelligent life happily developed among the people who inhabit it—this is to such a thing incredible. Their idea of the Island resembles it, more than anything else, to an enormous strip of dirty brown flannel; intended originally to swathe the chafed shores of Connecticut and New York, but dropped unluckily twenty miles out at sea, and, though useless there, too big to be picked up and applied to the parts it was meant to cover, by anything less than the fingers of an earthquake! Brooklyn Heights they acknowledge to be delightful; but the intervening country, from there to the Lighthouse on Montauk Point, they suppose to be made up of sand-plains, pine woods, and scrub-oak barriers.

It is one and a great incidental good effect of the present Fair that it will make Brooklyn itself better acquainted with the Island on which it stands, and will show to those who visit us from abroad how industrious, prosperous, patriotic and humane are the farmers, manufacturers, mechanics and fishermen who have their homes to the eastward of us, and who have sent to the Fair their generous contributions.

Long Island is, in fact, remarkable on its northern shores for an undulating, picturesque and diversified surface; sometimes rising into abrupt and high hills; often pierced by short and deep inlets from the sea; with brooks as noisy, and villages as bright, as any found among the Green Mountains; with farms as easily and naturally divided as are those of Vermont into lowlands and uplands, for tillage and for pasturage. On the southern and eastern shores the land is flatter and more level. But the soil even there is often rich and rewarding; the lands are well watered—neither parched in a drought, nor soaked and drowned after continuous rain; the orchards are fruitful; the roads are excellent; and the delicious sea air, fresh from the ocean—which is all that separates the bar beyond the South Bay from Cuba—with the birds and fish which are the constant spoils of the Bay, make this part of the Island even more delightful, especially in summer, to tourists and visitors make it a much-loved home, for all the year round, to those who dwell on it.

Long Island has had too a history to be proud of. After the City of New York, it was the first part of the State to be settled, by both the Dutch and English colonists. Hudson and his men landed on Coney Island in 1609. Southold was settled in 1640. The Hamptons are towns two centuries old. Flushing was settled in 1645, and Newtown and Jamaica not long afterwards. Previous to the Revolution, the Island was far the most important part of the whole colony. A century ago, its population was larger than that of the City of New York; and was more than one-third of that of the entire province. The great patents of Suffolk County—one of them covering 30,000 acres, another covering a hundred square miles—furnished residences for families of almost baronial possessions and dignity. The first Academy in the State was established at East Hampton, in 1785. "Erasmus Hall," at Flatbush, was its immediate successor. One of the earliest papers, the Suffolk *Herald*, was published in 1791. The first paper mill in the State was built at Roslyn. A race-course was established on Hempstead plains two hundred years ago; and Sag Harbor, in the palmier days of the whale fishing, was one of the most important stations of that adventurous and profitable enterprise.

Some of the most eminent men of the State, too, and even of the Nation, were either born upon the Island, or, having had the misfortune to be born elsewhere, did what they could to amend their condition by choosing it for their residence. Egbert Benson, Rufus King, Melancthon Smith, Cadwallader D. Colden, the two Samuel Joneses, Judge Radcliffe, William Floyd and Daniel Lewis, signers of the Declaration, Chancellor Sandford, Judge Reeve, De Witt Clinton. Dr. Mitchell was born here, famous for his immense learning, and his equal eccentricities; Dr. Valentine Mott; Dr. John Jones, the physician of Franklin, and the surgeon of Washington, So were Commodore Truxton, Col. Talmadge, Gen. Woodhull, and many others, distinguished in the military or naval service of the country. Mount, the unequalled delineator of the comic in American life, is a native Long Islander; and Bryant, the chief in age and place among our living American poets, has made for himself a delightful home on the Northern Shore.

It is altogether time that the city of Brooklyn knew more of the Island upon whose western extremity it is planted, and that the bonds of alliance and intercourse between it and the counties lying eastward of it were more vital and numerous than they hitherto have been. We trust they will be so hereafter; and that the present grand patriotic enterprise, to which all have contributed, will shine in the history of both the City and the Island, as the glorious clasp—purer than pearl, and more brilliant than diamond—closing and perpetuating the alliance between them.

MY EXPERIENCE OF THE FAIR.

II.

The plot thickened as the days went on. Mrs. Watts herself became a member of the Committee on Eternal Arrangements, and made a practice of leaving the house immediately after breakfast, to return only at supper-time. I remarked that this was not beneficial to the baby, and I soon began to see with pain its effect upon my wife. In addition to cares and labors incessant, the committee seemed to borrow trouble from discord. The ladies were evidently not a unit. They differed from each other on many and important points. I am afraid they sometimes let their angry passions rise. One day Mrs. W. came home in some agitation, with flushed cheeks, and a red halo around each sparkling eye. I was putting the finishing touch to the last of my Star-Spangled Banner letters, and from wise motives I took no notice of her mood. She resented my calmness by slamming the doors and scolding the servants, and finally, to cap the climax of her unreason, she was about to apply corporal punishment to our innocent baby as a remedy for stomach ache. It was time for me to interfere.

To open the subject, I said, mildly, "My love, what is the matter?" My love suddenly laid down the baby, and burst into tears, sobbing out the familiar, but not intelligible phrase:

"That's what's the matter!"

Now the appearance of tears convinced me that I had read the case aright, and I applied at once the proper remedy. I took the dear little tempestuous woman on my knee, and questioned her in my most soothing conjugal tones: "Poor Susan! have they abused you and insulted you, and are you indignant, and can't you bear the chairman? and has Mrs. Sawfiler an intolerable temper? and are you so sick of it? and do you wish it was over? and have you resigned your place because you wouldn't be put down?" To all these questions she vehemently nodded assent. She was not surprised that I knew all about it. I know all about most things—in which I am not unlike the late Baron Humboldt. I continued: "Now, my love, shall I set it all right, and put everything *couleur de rose*, as before?" Ah, that wasn't possible. "Nonsense, now listen. You haven't been snubbed, nor slighted, nor insulted, nor have the ladies you liked a week ago all turned to fiends incarnate; but you are a poor, overworked, weary, hysterical little goose. Now, drink some warm tea, soak your feet in hot water, and go to bed at 9 o'clock. In the morning you will be willing to do your share, without a murmur, towards the relief of those brave men who have suffered without complaining, for you!"

Susan was struck with the eloquent termination of my remark. She thoughtfully took her head out of my vest, and said, "The Fair is for those dear Soldiers, so it is! I do believe we had forgotten that!" Whereupon she followed my directions, and medicined herself with the mystic mandragora of sleep. In the morning she was

CENTR
PEDESTRIANS.
MUS
THE LAKE.
THE LAKE NEAR

L PARK
EQUESTRIANS.
HE MALL.
Th. Nast.
THE TERRACE.
MER.
THE BOW BRIDGE.

OUR VOLUNTEER FIRE DEPARTMENT—A SERIES OF ILLUSTRATIONS REPRESENTING THE

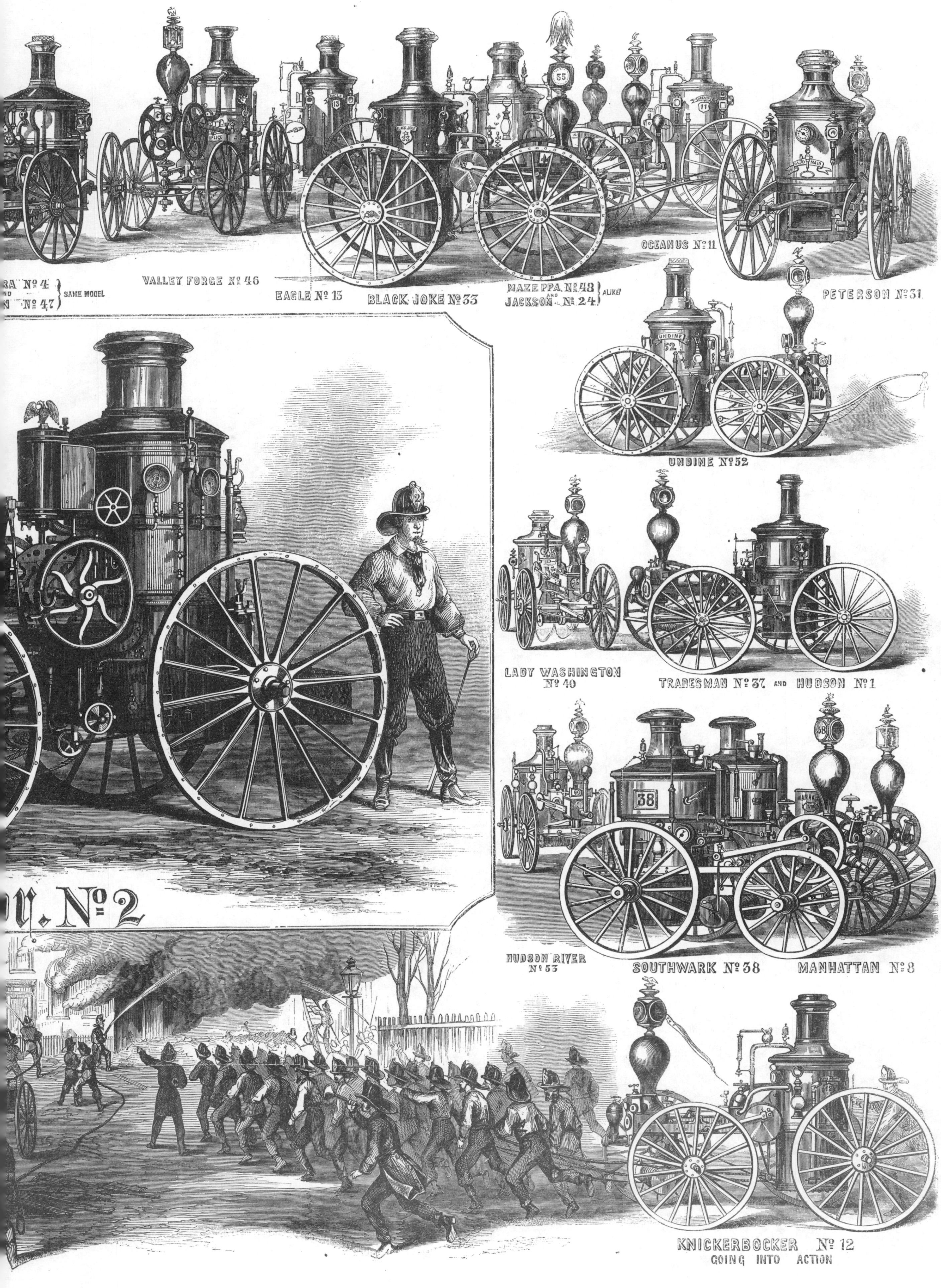

US STEAM FIRE-ENGINES NOW USED IN NEW YORK.—Sketched by A. Berghaus.

NORTH, SOUTH EAST & WEST,
MOURN.
END OF SUFFRING HUMANITY IS GONE
OUR CHIEF HAS FALLEN

FUNERAL HONORS TO PRESIDENT LINCOLN.—THE CATAFALQUE PASSING UP BROADWAY, NEW YORK, APRIL 25, 1865,

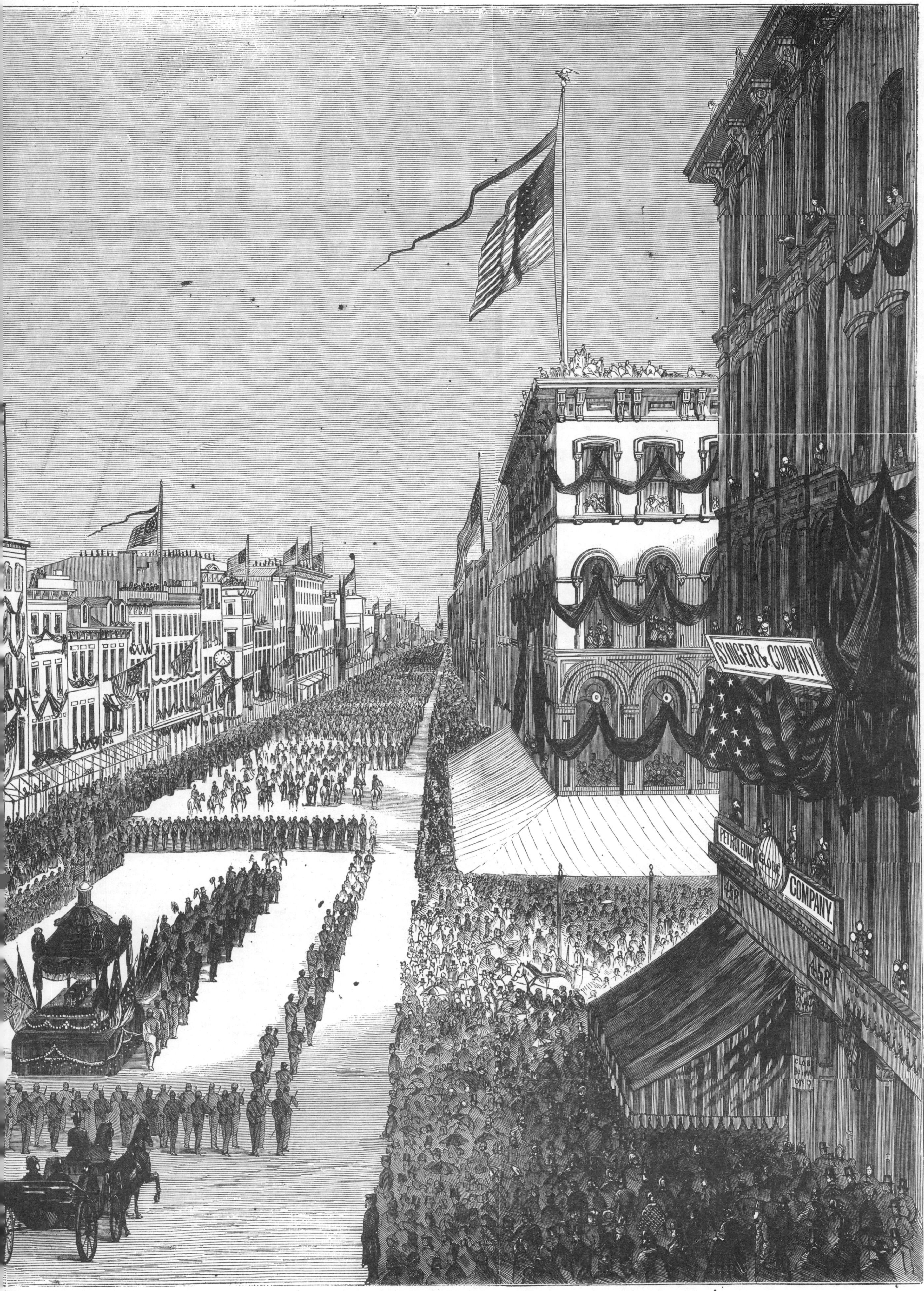

HE PRESENCE OF NEARLY A MILLION SPECTATORS.—From a number of Sketches taken at different points by our Special Artists.

The World

VOL. IV.—NO. 1209. NEW-YORK: MONDAY, MAY 2, 1864. PRICE THREE CENTS.

THE PROPOSED BRIDGE OVER THE EAST RIVER.

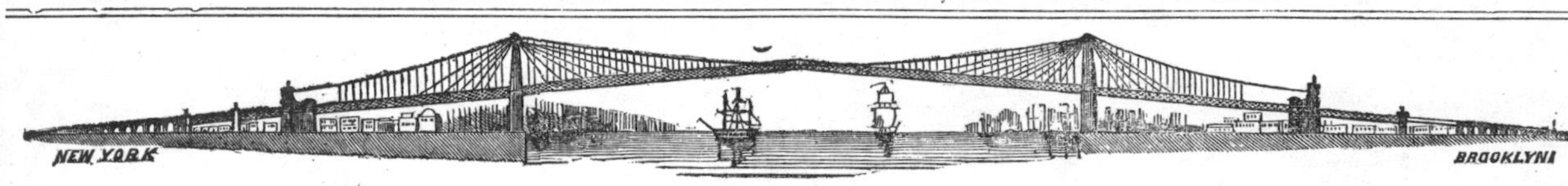

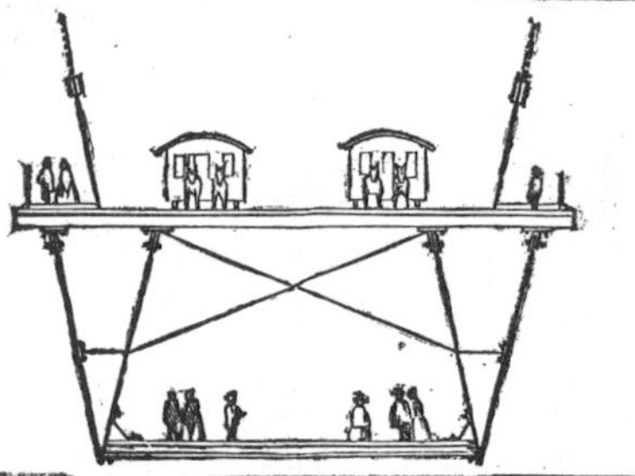

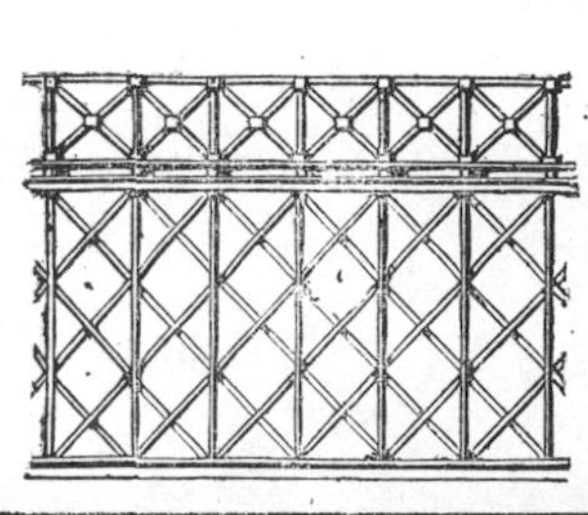

NEW-YORK AND BROOKLYN UNITED.

Project for a Grand Suspension Bridge Over the East River.

PLAN OF THE STRUCTURE.

Full Description of the Working Plan of the Designer.

HOW THE SISTER CITIES WILL BE JOINED.

Railroads, Carriage Roads, and Foot Walks all Provided for Traveling Among the Clouds.

Estimated Cost Three Millions of Dollars.

Magnificent undertakings—undertakings which, in their first inception, seem from their very magnitude to be impossible, are the special wonders which mechanical engineering every now and then contributes to the sensationalism of the age. Projects are started which the general public look upon with awe and astonishment, marveling at the power and energy with which inventive genius puts some grand idea into tangible shape, and treats as playthings, what, to the uninitiated mind, seem insurmountable obstacles to its accomplishment.

A great many people regarded Brunel as little more than a lunatic when he conceived the scheme of boring a tunnel under the bed of the Thames river, and by that means connect portions of London which the necessities of navigation prevented from being bridged. Yet he managed to infuse his own enthusiasm into a sufficient number of persons to secure the money he required for his purpose, and from that moment the thing was practically done. True, he was foiled again and again. More than once the water broke through, and put him farther back than his original starting point; but it is the peculiarity of mechanics that when certain calculations, made in conformity to certain laws, have produced a definite theoretical result, nothing but faintness of heart or lack of money can prevent its actual achievement.

Within a short lifetime the world has been filled with stupendous monuments of engineering skill and perseverance—works, indeed, that seem simple enough when they are done, but which it almost looks like human presumption even to have imagined. There are Stephenson's tubular bridges, in the construction of which he has set at defiance and conquered every known difficulty that mathematics and mechanics could encounter. There is the tunnel through the Pyrenees piercing a range of mountains that had hitherto been—comparatively speaking—an impassable barrier between France and Spain; and the Suez canal—delayed for years by English hostility—which will yet unite European waters with the Indian ocean.

The splendid schemes by which the chief cities of the United States are supplied, as are no other cities in the world, with one of the paramount requirements of health and cleanliness, are not by any means the least important or signal engineering triumphs. The works which bring the waters of the Croton river to New-York are the admiration of the world. And it is in devising a vast plan at an enormous initial expense to supply some common want that modern engineering particularly distinguishes itself. The theory of those who have the courage to conceive these grand designs is, that anything that anybody can be brought to use and, in time, look upon as a necessity, must, as a matter of course, be ultimately profitable in one way or another to the whole community. The underground railroad lately opened in London is a case in point. When the project was started, it looked like madness. Populous streets had to be tunneled under, property of enormous value to be purchased or guaranteed against damage, sections of the line to be so built as absolutely to sustain all the superincumbent weight beneath which they passed; all for—what? Just to add to a line of travel already carried along and intersected by innumerable thoroughfares, a new road which should have other merits than those of being a little more rapid and direct. The liabilities to be incurred were tremendous enough to appal the soul of the stoutest speculator; yet means were found to organize a company, sanguine people took shares and the matter progressed. The difficulties met with were greater even than had been anticipated, and the outlay proportionally larger; but the thing was persistently put through, and it is now stated that its profits exceed all preliminary calculation. There can be little doubt that the underground railroad suggested as a relief for Broadway would become equally popular and successful.

Another project, still more comprehensive in its scope and aims, has just been brought to public notice—a project which at first seems almost too colossal and fraught with too many impediments to be seriously entertained. Yet science declares that is feasible, and science seldom makes mistakes in such matters. The idea is not wholly new. It was first developed at the time the Suspension Bridge was successfully constructed at Niagara, and it has been revived once or twice in some form or another since then. But it has never been put in its present shape before. The idea is that of bridging the watery chasm which divides this city from Brooklyn. Messrs. Adams and Craven (engineers of the Croton water works) are authors of the plan, and the details of the proposition that they offer may be thus described. It may be mentioned, by the way, that a model of the contemplated structure was exhibited at the Metropolitan Fair, where it attracted general attention and no small share of admiring curiosity.

This bridge is designed to connect the system of city railroads of New-York with that of Long Island, without impediment to the navigation of the East river; to which end the connection is made from the centers of travel as now existing at Chatham square in New-York, and Fulton street square in Brooklyn. The width of the East river on this line, between the commissioners' line for pier-heads in New-York and the same line for bulkheads in Brooklyn, is but little over one thousand three hundred feet in length.

Erecting masonry suspension piers at these points two hundred and twenty-five feet high above high water, enables a suspension bridge to be thrown over the river, which in the center will clear the highest ships' masts, and give a grade of bridge less abrupt than many of the city railroads as now traveled. The length of the suspension is but a fraction greater than that of suspension bridges already built and in use in this country and in Europe, so that its feasibility in this respect is established. There only remains to determine the means by which acknowledged strength and stability may be given to it, to meet the requirements of such a structure in this locality.

The great improvements in the manufacture of steel, brought about by the increasing demands for this material, in almost every branch of art, from the enormous amount consumed in light fabrics to the ponderous bars and masses required in railroad tracks and and machinery and in heavy artillery and armor plating, points to this material as now within reach and as affording a high degree of strength, with comparative lightness, thus peculiarly fitting it for the purpose in view.

Extensive experiments on the tension of cast-steel show an ultimate strength as high as one hundred and seventy-three thousand pounds to the square inch in bars, whilst iron under the same circumstances cannot be depended upon for over sixty thousand pounds. Iron wire may be estimated as high as ninety thousand pounds, but the drawing of steel into wire will give its strength more than double the best iron wire.

The steel for the proposed cables will be drawn into ribbons, four inches wide by one-eighth inch in thickness, and can be manufactured with certainty, with an ultimate strength of one hundred and fifty thousand pounds to the square inch. The standard of strength announced, however, is, that its breaking-strain will be one hundred and thirty thousand pounds to the square inch, and the posts of the bridge would be so proportioned that the strain at no point would be more than twenty-six thousand pounds to the square inch, or *one-fifth* of the estimated breaking-strain.

The cables, of which there are two, each consist of three hundred and eighty-four ribbon of steel, four by one-eighth inch, arranged in four rows of ninety-six in each row, and secured by wrought-iron gripes at each five feet in the length of the cable, to which the suspenders of wire rope are fastened. These cables pass over cast-iron saddles at the top of the suspension and anchorage towers, which rest on cast-steel rollers six inches in diameter, bearing on bed-plates of cast-iron secured to the heads of the towers. The land cables have the same weight, angle and action over the saddles of the towers as those of the main chain.

At the anchorage towers the chains pass down over a saddle with friction rollers and are secured below the masonry to a system of screw piles, and also to a heavy bed plate embracing the bond of the tower masonry with a suspension posed weight greatly exceeding the tension of the anchor chain. The result of the tension of the anchor chains at the anchorage saddle is taken by a discharging arch which springs from the foundation ninety feet in advance of the anchorage-well. The whole of this masonry is built with hoop iron bands between the corners. The main towers having a base of forty-four by eighty-six feet, will be built of heavy masonry, dowelled at each corner, and with a well hole by which the saddles may be examined at any time. Wrought iron beams three feet deep will be built in the arches connecting the towers, the weight of which is distributed on the foundations equally. The upper floor beams are wrought iron girders sixteen inches deep at intervals of five feet. The lower floor-beams are nine inches deep at the same interval. Both floors are braced diagonally by iron rods. Both foot ways of the upper platform have wrought iron tube truss hand rails five feet deep, two to each footway, the suspender rods being fastened to the posts of the inner-hand rail, thus adding materially to the vertical stiffness of the bridge floor. The over-floor stays are fastened to the cast-iron saddles at the top of the towers, thus relieving the cables of a portion of the weight of the bridge, and adding to the stiffness of the flooring.

the whole bridge is of iron and steel, with the single exception of the flooring planks, which are of oak and pine, in two thicknesses of 1⅛ inch each, fastened to the floor-beams diagonally across the bridge. The cables are to be galvanized and painted, and further protected from the weather by a projectng sheet of copper. The iron-work will all be galvanized and painted white.

It is proposed to make the upper floor which is thirty-six wide, a tall brigde for foot-passengers, horses and carriages, and two or three railroad tracks, connecting the railroad system of Long-Island with that of New-York city, and will be entered at the extreme ends. The lower floor twenty-three feet wide, and eighteen feet below the upper, connected to it by four steel-plate lattice trusses diagonally braeed, will be a free-bridge for foot-passengers solely, and is entered by inclosed stair-ways at the anchorage towers.

I will be seen that the bridge is made up of a central suspension bridge of one thousand three hundred and fifty feet span, a land suspension on each side of six hundred and five feet, three wrought iron truss bridges on piers, a girder bridge of three spans, and the remaining distance will be sustained on arches of masonry. The bridge is suspended above the piers and wharves on each side, so as not to interfere with their proper use, and enters Catharine street on one side and Fulton street on the other, without interfering with their traffic.

SUMMARY OF DIMENSIONS.

Length of Suspension bridge	2,560	feet.
Length of truss bridges	610	feet.
Length of iron girder bridge	260	feet.
Length of arches	400	feet.
Total length of bridge	4,250	feet.
Weight of iron and steel	3,535	tons.
Masonry in towers, piers and arches	88,800	cubic yds.
Between suspension towers	1,350	feet.
Center of bridge above high water in East river	125	feet.
Bridge at the towers above high water	93	feet.
Deflexion of center cables	99	feet.
Weight on center cables when the bridge is loaded with troops on the upper, and foot passages on the lower floors	2,500	tons.
Strain on the cables at points of support when loaded as above	4,500	tons.
Section of steel cables	400	square in.
Grade of bridge five feet per hundred feet.		
Deflexion at the center caused by a change of temperature of hundred degrees	3	feet.

ESTIMATED COST OF BRIDGE, THREE MILLION DOLLARS.

A good deal could be said in favor of the construction of such a bridge, and the advantage it would be to the growing mutual interests of the sister cities, which now only communicate at the pleasure of the Union Ferry Company. Its projectors claim for it great superiority over any plan for tunneling, even though the first cost of the latter might be less. They also believe that the two cities will, within a very few years, see the accomplishment of the idea, and marvel that they did without such an obvious need so long. The subject is unquestionable one of extensive public interest. It would be a fine thing to be able to ride or walk over to Brooklyn, especially in the winter time, when passengers by the ferries have been known to remain ice-bound in the river for hours. Sensible, practical men, put the project forward, and no harm at least can be done by taking it into serious consideration.

ARMY OF THE POTOMAC.

Continued Reinforcement of the Rebel Army in Virginia.

ALL QUIET AT THE FRONT.

[SPECIAL DISPATCH TO THE WORLD]

WASHINGTON, May 1.

Advices from your correspondents with the Army of the Potomac are as late as 1 o'clock this afternoon. There is nothing of special interest going on. The weather continues clear and cool, and the roads are in magnificent condition.

Reinforcement of General Lee's Army.

[SPECIAL DISPATCH TO THE WORLD.]

There are unmistakable signs that Lee is receiving large reinforcements. Refugees declare that trains from Richmond and Lynchburg are laden only with troops. New intrenchments along the Rapidan are seen from our signal-station on Pony mobntain, while the important fact appeared that Lee's left wing, stretching toward Madison Court House, has lately been drawn back

Soldiers Ordered to their Regiments.

WASHINGTON, April 30.

A special order, issued by the War Department this morning, requires all enlisted men now in this city on detailed duty, to report forthwith to their regiments in the field, unless they can produce from proper medical authority certificates of physical inability, and are unable to perform the duties of the field.

General Sigel's Command.

General Sigel is at Martinsburgh, on the Baltimore and Ohio Railroad. He reports that there are no rebel forces in the Shenandoah valley.

Raid by Moseby's Guerrillas.

Moseby's guerrillas came within fourteen miles of the city last night, and captured eighteen members of a New-York regiment.

From Fortress Monroe.

FORTRESS MONROE, April 29.—Private Jacob Morgan, of the Eighth Connecticut regiment, was shot for desertion in Norfolk yesterday afternoon.

The French vessels which went to City Point recently to bring away tobacco from Richmond, have all returned, light, to Hampton Roads.

The steamer New-York, with sick rebel prisoners, has sailed for City Point in charge of Major Mulford.

The Quota of Missouri Full.

ST. LOUIS, April 30.—Congressman Hall, from Washington, says that the credits of enrolled militia, re-enlisted veterans and colored troops, reduce the quota of Missouri to 530. The negroes enlisted since the 1st of April more than cover this, freeing Missouri from the draft.

The New Jersey Normal School.

NEWARK, N. J., April 30.—Professor Phelps having resigned as principal of the New Jersey Normal School, John S Hart, LLD., who was principal of the Model School, has been made sole head of both schools, the two offices having been combined.

Sale of Prize-Steamers.

BOSTON, April 30.—The prize-steamers Scotia and Mary Ann were sold at auction to-day. The former brought $24,250, and the latter $31,000.

JERSEY CITY.

FUNERAL OF THE LATE CHIEF OF POLICE REILY.

The funeral of the late Edward D. Reily, chief of police of Jersey City, took place yesterday afternoon. The body was borne from the late residence of the deceased to the church of the Immaculata, preceded by the mayor, mayor elect, the Common Cuncil, and city officers in carriages, the police department, and Liberty Engine Company No. 1, and followed by the relatives and a large body of citizens. The services in the church were conducted by Rev. Father Senez. At the conclusion the remains were conveyed to St. Peter's Cemetery, Hudson City, where they were interred. The fire-bell was tolled during the passage of the procession, and thousands of people crowded the streets through which it passed.

GOVERNOR PARKER TO LECTURE IN JERSEY CITY.

Governor Parker has signified his intention to deliver a lecture in Jersey City, at the Congregational Tabernacle, on Thursday evening next, May 5, for the benefit of the Soldiers' Relief Society. The subject of the lecture will be "The Early History of New Jersey."

CHOKED TO DEATH.

A boy named Alexander Corbett, whose parents reside in Jersey City, was choked to death on Friday last by a piece of meat lodging in his throat. Coroner Farrel viewed the body, and gave a permit for burial.

NO DRAFT IN JERSEY CITY.

The draft that has been ordered to take place in New Jersey on the 3d instant, will not affect Jersy City in the least, the quota of that city under all the calls of President for troops being full.

AUCTION AT THE FAIR BUILDINGS.—The temporary buildings connected with the Metropolitan Fair will be sold at auction at 10 o'clock this morning, at the Fourteenth street buildings.

NEWS FROM WASHINGTON

WASHINGTON, May 1.

Messrs. Gooch and Wade, who were deputed by the Committee on the Conduct of the War to visit Fort Pillow, and inquire into the facts regarding the treatment of the colored troops after the surrender of that place, returned to-day. From the evidence adduced, and depositions taken, the statements made in regard to the barbarities and cruelties were fully corroborated. The committee visited quite a number of the poor creatures, and saw with their own eyes the outrages which had been perpetrated. The report will be completed and laid before Congress at once. The committee called upon the President this evening, and gave him a full account of the affair. This is a new source of embarrassment to Mr. Lincoln, and he is greatly troubled to know how to treat it. He has announced that retaliatory measures will be adopted.

THE BRAZILIAN MINISTER.

His Excellency M. M. Lisboa, the Brazlian minister, took leave of Secretary Seward and the members of the diplomatic corps to-day, and left on the afternoon train for New-York en route for home. Before leaving he procured estimates of Messrs. Kennard & Co. for their American fire-alarm and police telegraph for the city of Rio Janeiro.

ORDERED TO THE FIELD.

Enlisted men who have been detailed here as clerks for some time have been ordered to rejoin their regiments. The fact causes much excitement among a large class in the departments.

THE MONROE DOCTRINE.

The joint resolution which unanimously passed the House of Representatives about a month ago, protesting against the Frencu occupation of Mexico and the establishment of monarchical institutions on this continent, still sleeps in the Senate's Committee on Foreign Relations, which it is permitted to do for reasons of state policy.

MEDICAL STORES.

The army appropriation bill appropriates $2,715,000 for medicines, instruments and dressings.

WASHINGTON, April 30.

THE SIXTY-DAY TARIFF.

The President has approved of the joint resolution temporarily increasing the duty on imports fifty per centum. It is, therefore, a law.

PAY OF NEGRO TROOPS.

While the Senate's amendments to the Army Appropriation bill were under consideration in the House to-day, Representative Schenck, chairman of the Military Committee, proposed to substitute for the sections relating to negro soldiers the Senate bill equalizing the pay of all soldiers of the army, which had been passed upon by that committee with some modifications, and also increasing the pay, etc. The Senate having become impatient at the delay of the House not acting upon their bill, incorporated its provisions in the Army Appropriation bill, which provision, with the amendments by the Committee on Ways and Means and those of the Military Committee, formed the basis of the House proceedings of to-day, and the result is as stated in the congressional summary.

ABANDONED PROPERTY.

The Secretary of the Treasury has communicated to Mr. Washburne, of Illinois, chairman of the Committee on Commerce, the draft of a bill relative to abandoned property, with various suggestions concerning the necessary legislation upon the subject.

The first section sanctions sales of live stock, planting implements, and machinery, at the points where collected, instead of sending them to some place in the loyal states, as required by the present law.

The second section connects the care of abandoned plantations with the general care of the freedmen, whose support must be derived from the cultivation of these lands, unless they are to become a burden on the treasury. This provision involves little expense or delay.

The third section provides that fees shall be charged for permits, graduated according to the magnitude of the transaction, and that they be paid into the treasury, after deducting the attendant expenses; also the moneys arising from the leases of abandoned lands.

The fourth section meets the cases of persons residing within the lines in insurrectionary tates, who claim to conduct trade and transport supplies therein, without being subject to the prohibitions and penalties applying to persons from other states.

The fifth section is intended to sanction restrictions upon trade and transportation, in the loyal states even, for the purpose of preventing supplies to the rebels.

The sixth section repeals the existing distribution of one half the proceeds from abandoned property to informers and customs officers, and leaves the whole matter with the court decreeing the forfeitures.

THE PACIFIC RAILROAD.

The Pacific Railroad bill, as reported by Mr. Stevens from the House Select Committee, provides that the grant of lands shall not impair any pre-emption homesteads, swamp-land, or other lawful claim or government reservation. It proposes to repeal the provision for the reservation by government of a portion of the construction bonds. The Central Pacific Railroad Company of California is authorized to issue first mortgage bonds, not exceeding the amount of the government bonds, to which the lien of United States bonds shall be subordinated. Any other road of the line may issue one-half the amount of United States bonds and have the same precedence. It fixes the number of directors to be elected by the stockholders at twenty, and the number to be appointed by the President at ten.

PRIZE-LAW.

The secretary suggests the necessity of revising the law governing maritime prizes, now construed to cover captures in inland waters, and even property taken from shores.

THE BANKRUPT BILL.

There is now a probability that this important measure will become law before the close of the session. It is generally felt that some relief must be given to those who must eventually succumb to the enormous pressure of taxation, and the derangement of the currency. The measure, in its details, is generally approved.

THE BANKING BILL.

The Senate failed to pass the Banking bill to-day. It will probably not get through before Tuesday or Wednesday next.

BAD STORIES ABOUT THE TREASURY CLERKS.

Washington is full of stories of startling developments, certain to be made before the Special Committee authorized to-day on Treasury Department. Affidavits and witnesses are ready to testify that, in addition to gross frauds, a regular system of prostitution is carried on in the female bureau of the Treasury, with the connivance of its band of officials, and that a code of morals exist, degrading to women as it is repugnant to decency, and calling for the brand of infamy on those at the bottom of it. Many of the female clerks have been secured as witnesses.

DIPLOMATIC CHANGES.

A letter from the Secretary of State calls the attention of the House Committee on Commerce to several ammendments to the Diplomatic and Consular Appropriation Bill recommended by the Finance Committee at the suggestion of the Secretary, and designed to secure the more efficient working of the consular system and execution of the law of last Congress, requiring all invoices of goods imported into the United States to be authenticated by our consuls by which the consular fees will be increased during the presnt year more chan one hundred thousand dallars sad also protect our revenve from the operations of smuuglers in Canada. It now asked to transfer salaries of fiften hundred dollars from tho now unimportant ports of Otranto, Taranto, Ancona, Napoleon Vndee, to Conculates at Brisdince, Gibraltar, St. Helena, and Boulogne. Authority is requested to appoint two Consuls in Canada, at Clifton, Conticook, Erie, Goderich, Kingston, Fort Sarnia, Preston, St. Lambert Lougueil, Tsrant, and Windsor a salaries of fiftaeu hundred dollars each.

INTENDED SMUGGLING OF IMPORTED GOODS.

The Secretary says that he has reliable information from Canada, France, Switzerland, and even China, that arrangements are in progress for shipping large quantities of teas, silks, velvets and other rich goods to Canada, with the intention of attempting to smuggle them into the United States under the prospective high tariff. An increase of the consulate salary at Nassau is also recommended. In consequence of the fraudulent under-valuation of silks and velvets, requiring the employment of an expert, and the necessity of triplicate invoices at Lyons, France, $500 addition salary is recommended for that consulate.

THE TAX ON STATE BANKS.

The Senate this afternoon adopted the amendment to the currency bill, taxing state banks half yearly one-half per cent. on their circulation, one-fourth per cent. on deposits, and one-fourth per cent. on capital other than United States bonds.

SUBSCRIPTIONS TO TEN-FORTY LOAN.

The amount of the subscriptions to the Ten-Forty Loan reported at the Treasury Department reaches $854,000.

FRAUDS IN COTTON.

Most of the cotton purchased has, by fraudulent practises, gone into individual hands, and very little money has been realized to the government from the cotton owned by the southern Confederate States. The secretary favors the abrogation of the whole system, and the purchase and transportation of the cotton exclusively by he government.

SENTENCE AHPROVED.

The President to day approved of Butler's sentence in the case of nine officers who resigned the service in his department just on the eve of this campaign. They are reduced to rank as privates, to serve until the end of the war.

ADMIRAL DAHLGREN RETURNED TO CHARLESTON.

Admiral Dahlgren has returned to Charleston to remain in command of the iron-clad fleet for the present at least. He will also be at the head of the South Atlantic Blocading Squadron.

THE WORLD.

The DAILY WORLD, published every morning and evening (Sundays excepted), price THREE CENTS; mailed at EIGHT DOLLARS a year; served by carrier, EIGHTEEN CENTS per week

The SEMI-WEEKLY WORLD, published Tuesdays and Fridays, THREE DOLLARS a year; two copies to one address for FIVE DOLLARS.

THE WEEKLY WORLD, TWO DOLLARS a year; three copies FIVE DOLLARS; five copies EIGHT DOLLARS; ten copies FIFTEEN DOLLARS; twenty copies to one address TWENTY-FIVE DOLLARS. The Semi-Weekly and Weekly sent to Clergymen at the lowest club rates. Specimen numbers forwarded on application.

TERMS—Cash, invariably in advance.

All letters should be addressed to THE WORLD, 35 PARK ROW, New-York City.

FROM THE SOUTHWEST.

General Steele's Army Reported to be at Camden, Ark.

A BATTLE AT ELKIN'S FERRY.

The Enemy Driven from their Intrenchments and Pursued to Washington.

ST. LOUIS, April 30.

Advices from Camden, Arkansas, say that General Steele's army is there. General Thayer joined General Steele at Elkin's ferry, on the Little Missouri river, where the rebels were driven from a line of breastworks commanding the river bottom.

The enemy next stood at Prairie d'Anna, which was fortified with a line of rifle pits, and epaulments for guns *en barbette*, a mile and a half long. General Steele flanked their position, and General Price skedaddled, after a brisk fight, toward Washington. Other skirmishes occurred during the march, but our total loss was less than two hundred.

Price supposed General Steele was going to Shreveport via Washington, and moved his command from Camden to Washington after the fight at Prairie de Anna.

General Steele pursued the rebels toward Washington, and then suddenly turned and pushed for Camden. Price discovered his mistake, and started for Camden also. A desperate race ensued, and although heavy skirmishing occured all the way, Marmaduke being in front and Dockery in the rear with cavalry and artillery. Steele came out victor, and entered the enemy' fortifications unopposed.

Camden is strongly fortified with nine forts, all its approaches are well guarded, and it can be held against a largely superior force.

A large rebel transport was captured thirty miles below Camden.

It is understood that reinforcements and supplies are going overland from Little Rock to General Steele, he not being able now to draw either from General Banks.

General Steele's force is fully twenty thousand strong, and can whip Kirby Smith should he attack him. No fears need be entertained of his safety.

Camden,

the scene of General Steele's success, is the capital of Washita county, Arkansas, on the right bank of the Washita river, and one hundred and ten miles from Little Rock. It was a very handsome town. It is the head of navigation for large steamers, and is connected with Fulton, on the Red river, by a plank road recently constructed. If, as is represented, General Steele has twenty thousand men, he has enough to accomplish his object. Washington is in Hempstead county in a northwest direction from Camden.

FROM NEWBERN.

NEWBURN, N. C., April 24—4 P. M.

The capture of Plymouth, including General Wessels and his command, by the rebels, is confirmed. Nothing is known of the movements of the rebels here. It is reported they have gone to Virginia. Should the rebels attack Little Washington or Newbern their punishment will be fearful.

The proceedings of the rebels at Plymouth will not compensate them for the severe loss they sustained. From all accounts General Wessels and his little band of fifteen hundred veterans fought like heroes for four days and nights, leaving the rebels dead in heaps in every street, which they admit will number seventeen hundred.

We hear at this point all kinds of reports in regard to the rebel ram on the Neuse river above this city.

FIGHTING IN KENTUCKY.

Fifty-one Prisoners and Twenty-four Horses Captured.

CINCINNATI, April 30.—A detachment of the Forty-fifth Kentucky, of Hobson's division, under Captain Adams, attacked the rebels in Brent Hill county, Kentucky, killed four, and captured sixteen men and twenty-four horses.

Adams then pushed forward and defeated Everett's command, killing two of his officers and capturing thirty-five men.

The First of May.

HOUSEHOLD MOVING ALREADY NEARLY FINISHED.

To-day is, in a legal sense, the 1st of May, and the law allows tenants to keep possession of their rented houses until 12 o'clock, noon. Probably the greater part of the annual moving was done during the latter part of the previous week, as it was observed that thousands of carmen were at that business. Of late years, also, people are getting in the habit of anticipating May-day by forty-eight hours or so to avoid the general rush and wreck that result in crowding the furniture and household goods of half the population of the city into the streets at the same time. This has somewhat toned down the tumultuous performances that of earlier years occurred on this memorable anniversary, so that to-day's moving will only be the remnant of the May-day home-finding. The carmen have been busy enough for a week, and will be for some days to come. Of course there is the usual amount of extortion. The prices fixed by law are quite moderate, being sixty-two cents per load for the carrying of household furniture a half mile in distance, and sixty-two cents additional for the loading, unloading and housing. If these rates are exceeded to imposition, any policeman can take the culprit before Mr. Morton, the city marshal, for the rectification of such things. The legal prices for cartage on May-day are the same as on other days.

New choirs, or partially new appeared in some of the churches yesterday. M. Heller, the magician officiated as organist at the Twenty-eight street Catholic church.

SPORTING INTELLIGENCE.

THE PRIZE RING.

For the next day or two the pugilistic and fistic fraternity of this city will be in a high state of ferment as to the result of the long-pending match between the two celebrated English boxers Patsey Marley and Dooney Harris. For two months past these men have been in active training, the former in the vicinity of the Fashion Course; Harris has taken his "breathings" at McGuire's, Harlem Lane.

The fight will come off, in all probability, on Tuesday noon, the time and place to be made known to the favored few at the well-known sporting houses of Harry Hill and others in the secret. The match will be for $1,000 a side, and at present Harris has the odds in his favor, although unknown this side the water, from the fact that he is allowed to fight at catch weight, is the tallest in stature, has the longest reach, and is considered the ablest boxer and wrestler of the two. Marley proved himself a tough customer in his engagement with Con Orem, which resulted in a draw from interference after a two hours'

Diphtheria is prevailing to an some portions of Maine.

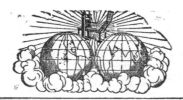

THE NEW YORK HERALD.

WHOLE NO. 10,546. NEW YORK, FRIDAY, JULY 14, 1865. PRICE FOUR CENTS.

CONFLAGRATIONS.

Destruction of Barnum's Museum.

SUPPOSED ORIGIN OF THE FIRE.

Gratuitous Distribution of Curiosities.

A BOA CONSTRICTOR LOOSE.

THE LEARNED SEAL SAVED.

Eighteen Buildings in a Blaze.

Jeff. Davis Loses His Head and Has His Wardrobe Confiscated.

RUMORED LOSS OF LIFE.

The Herald Establishment in Imminent Danger.

Saved by the Firemen and the Home Department Apparatus.

SCENES IN THE STREETS.

The Noble Firemen of New York Assisted by the Noble Firemen from Brooklyn and Hoboken.

SAVING THE FLAG.

ARREST OF PICKPOCKETS.

LOSSES AND INSURANCES.

Condition of the Burnt District Last Night.

Extensive Conflagration in West Forty-fourth Street.

Nine Buildings Burned and Seventy-five Families Turned Out of House and Home,

&c., &c., &c.

About half-past twelve o'clock yesterday an alarm of fire was given, which was discovered to have been caused by flames originating in the lower portion of Barnum's Museum, corner of Park row and Ann street. There was immediately a grand rush for the burning district.

The scene on Broadway, fronting old St. Paul's, in the early stages of the fire, was an interesting and impressive one, and one which will not soon be forgotten by those who, being caught by the crowd, were compelled—some of them unwillingly—to witness it. The engines had not yet arrived upon the ground. The firemen, some with coats on, but more trying vainly to find the sleeves of those they would put on—men coming upon the run, knocking down old women, boys, and even men, like mere chessmen, as they ran. And the crowd thickened with the usual accumulation of interested and disinterested spectators; some coming to see what was to be seen, but a larger number to encumber the sidewalks and thoroughfares with their persons, ostensibly to get out of the way, but really to get in the way of the steam fire apparatus, when it should arrive on the ground. And it was not long before it came. And of course there were some severe accidents to those same individuals, who were so thickly planted as to be unable to move from their places. Yet, strange to say, none were in this way killed outright, that we have heard of. Down Broadway, up Broadway, from Fulton street, from Chatham street and Park row, from Vesey street, from Barclay street, and from innumerable alleys and by-streets, came still more people to add to the already vast and excited assemblage, all to witness one of the most wonderful spectacles ever exhibited to an awe-stricken multitude, even in the centre of sights and shows, pageants and parades, the city of New York.

THE FIRE BREAKS OUT.

It was perhaps some fifteen minutes from the time when the first alarm was given before there were visible outward indications of the fierceness with which the conflagration was burning within the Museum building. These indications were evinced by an individual who went about the second story balustrade of the structure with a club in his hand, breaking the panes of glass in the windows. Smoke poured out in dense volumes, showing that, wherever the fire had first taken, it had already reached the second floor. And the smoke was quickly followed by the flames, darting out in sheets and in tongues, licking up the combustible awnings and transparencies and large paintings with which the walls were nearly covered, and communicating thence to the woodwork about the casements and doors. A similar scene was being enacted at the Ann street front of the Museum Up to this time but little had been done toward saving property or putting out flames, those near at hand having spent some fifteen minutes of valuable time in trying to save a case of stuffed animals.

In the front ladders were placed, and men were passing from the balcony into Knox's, and down the ladder, bearing such curiosities as they could lay hands on. They continued at this work till the flames wrapped about the topmost rounds of the ladder. The police then appeared and cleared the street immediately in front of the burning edifice.

At one o'clock forked tongues of flames were darting through every window, wreathing the painted medallions outside with chaplets of fire, and sweeping away at a single touch the veracious canvass representations of the whales, giantesses and alligators within. At this time the flames shot up into the air to a marvellous height, and to spectators standing in the City Hall Park seemed to extend in an oblique direction as far as Powers' Hotel, five buildings the other side of Ann street. The heat reflected by the conflagration was intense. On the steps of the City Hall it could be distinctly felt.

THE ASTOR HOUSE.

Opposite the Museum, on Broadway, St. Paul's church stood an isolated object. Had that front offered more obstruction, or had it been a solid block of buildings, the danger of the fire spreading on the other side of Broadway would have been imminent, as the wind impelled the flame and cinders at one time strongly in that direction. The Astor House, on the adjoining block, opposed its armor of granite, while its roof swarmed with the little army who constituted the employes of the establishment. This systematic organization kept the roof and every point of danger well defended, and, although the inmates were all more or less excited, the special police or watchmen kept the doors guarded, and the vast crowd in the street expended their ingenuity in vain in endeavoring to circumvent the special police and effect an entrance for so splendid an opportunity of seeing "Barnum's" in its last scenic glories.

Messrs. Stetson and J. E. Devlin had just returned from down East to take timely charge of their establishment on this occasion.

General Hooker and staff, with numerous other dignitaries now stopping at the Astor House, witnessed the conflagration from the windows.

A SCARE AMONG THE CROWD.

As the flames stealthily crept from window to window of the Museum, and the crowd stood in awed silence waiting further developments, a pregnant suggestion passed from mouth to mouth, "Was there anything explosive in the building?" Mobile, Chattanooga and Gallatin presented themselves to recollection, and tacitly the dense throng began to move backwards. At this instant one of the engines in front of the Astor House suddenly let off steam, and the loud and powerful blast breaking in upon the previous stillness of the crowd, and following upon their whispered speculations, sent a panic through their midst. The retreat became a stampede; those who sought to stand up against the pressure of the crowd were knocked down and trampled under foot, and some were injured. It was but a momentary panic; in a few seconds more the causelessness of the alarm was apparent, and order was restored.

SEEING THE CURIOSITIES.

The majority of the crowd seemed delighted at the chance of seeing the curiosities gratis. One of the employes of the Museum, who passed through the crowd with a bunch of coral in one hand and a stuffed raccoon in the other, was loudly cheered. But the excitement rose to its height when the giantess, the fat lady and the white woolly-headed Albino passed down Fulton street, followed by a number of the ladies of the *corps de ballet*, who, poor things, had lost all of their theatrical wardrobe. The pantomime of the Green Monster was to have been performed at the Museum in the afternoon; but the Monster was consumed with the whales, the Happy Family and the snakes. The fat lady, the giantess and the ballet girls found a temporary refuge in a newspaper office, where they rehearsed their losses to a small but select audience, and the Albino was spirited away to a more private location, where she could not be seen without paying for the privilege. About one hundred persons must have been thrown out of employment at the Museum, and many of the pantomimists, dancers and keepers will find it difficult to obtain employment at this dull season for amusements. The crowd did not think of this, however. They were incessant in their cries of "boiled whale," "fried snakes," "broiled monkey," and "roast elephant," thus displaying a sort of *gamin* wit and a perfect familiarity with the contents of the Museum. "Throw me out one of the canoes," or "Pitch me the bow-constructor, I wants it for a tippet," or "How are you, learned seal?" provoked continual laughter. We suggest, however, that the fire has rather a serious side to it, and that the members of the theatrical profession in this city ought to organize a mammoth benefit at the Academy of Music, the proceeds to be divided among those whom this conflagration has deprived of their engagements for the summer. Let this suggestion be adopted without delay.

HOW THE ANIMALS FARED.

When the fire first broke out and the smoke commenced to penetrate the galleries there arose the most peculiar Babel of sounds which it was ever allotted to mortal to hear. The Happy Family quite belied their cognomen—the monkeys jabbered, the dogs barked, the cats mewed, parrots screamed, bears growled, kangaroos kangarooed, paroquets screamed "otter, otter," and the poor otter, not caring for the smoke, buried himself in his native element. The birds fluttered against the bars of their cages and sang most doleful melodies. To save those poor animals was one of the first things thought of, and the first who presented himself to our notice was poor "bruin" himself, making the descent of the ladder in a very peculiar manner. He seemed quite savage and not at all inclined for fun. Accustomed to be looked at through iron bars, he seemed at a loss to understand his present situation. Several times, as his feet slipped through the rounds of the ladder, the tightening of the rope by which he was held caused him to pale visibly, and certainly show his canines, or, more properly, *bearines*. After some considerable time he reached not the top of the ladder, but the foot, and once on *terra firma* he looked as contented as a bear could look under the circumstances.

Louder grew the jabberings of the monkey tribe, who leaped frantically about, the boa constrictor writhed in agony as the heat became stronger, and a dismal series of wails from the whales, who had not been used to tropical seas, mingled with the rhapsodies of the astrologer, the pantings of the fat woman and the groanings of the giantess. The two latter were half frantic, and the maniac penman made the most artistic flourishes with his quill. Poor Ned, the educated seal, who was wont to astonish spectators with his sagacity, who used to turn the handle of a barrel organ, and do everything but speak, was seized upon by a couple of men, one evidently a Hibernian:—"Bad luck to ye, he's bitin' me, Mick;" and so he was. "Fetch me a basket" was the cry, and still Ned wriggled about in the most fishy manner, the crowd making way on every side. At length his rescuers succeeded in bringing Ned to a place of safety, and we may at some future time see him perform as of yore.

With these exceptions, we fear all the extensive and interesting collection of animals fell a prey to the fiery element, with the exception perhaps of a few birds, which may have succeeded in flying away. The crowd outside were most anxious about "dumb crathurs who niver done no one any harm, barrin' the bite the sale giv me," as our friend the Hibernian called them, and anxious inquiries were made as to whether the water in the aquasia wouldn't prevent their finny inhabitants from being burned.

It may be some time before we can have so fine a collection of tropical fish as was in the Museum. The aquaria were made on the most approved plan, and arranged so that the water was kept fresh by the passage of air through them. The collection of birds, too, was most extensive. The animals were numerous and well trained, so that they all lived together without any squabbling—making one think that even by training the millennial characteristic of "the lion lying down with the lamb" not so strange after all. The collection comprised a large variety of the monkey tribe, kangaroo, cat, dog and other species, and afforded much amusement to the children of our city, to whom a visit to Barnum's was always a great treat. Country cousins, too, who viewed the white cat that had no tail, and therefore could not "a tale unfold," will have no place where to study the beauties of natural history, and many now will feel sorry for having given the monkey blind nuts, now that he is no more. Many will think of Jocko who used to submit to their persecutions "without a word of anger or reproach." Poor Jocko! Unfortunate pussy! you are now where even the great showman himself cannot find you. We drop a tear for your memories, and though you sometimes attempted to bite our fingers when we approached too near your prison house, still we will faithfully adhere to the injunction, "*Nil mortuis nisi bonum.*"

When the flames communicated to Knox's hat store, a person who shall be nameless for his heartlessness in joking upon a very serious subject, shouted at the top of a good pair of lungs:—"Be jabers, now the fire will be *felt*." In a moment more that identical jocular individual had his head beaten lustily with a fireman's trumpet. He evidently felt the blow, and will blow no more on that score.

ESCAPING FROM THE BUILDING,

on the part of the employes, firemen, and those who had been aiding in making confusion worse confounded within the walls of the Museum, began to become a matter to be thought about. In fact many had already thought on the subject and evacuated the premises.

A JEFF. DAVIS AUGURY.

But before looking out for their own bacon, one or two persons thought they had better do something more towards saving what it were useless to pursue. One took the stuffed effigy of Tom Thumb and gave it a toss out of the window. Of course the General went to general smash upon the pavement below, to the imminent risk of the crowns of the people standing there as spectators. Another seized the wax figure of General Grant, rushed to the balcony, had almost succeeded in handing him intact to a person below, when a stream of water struck him amidships, and he had to drop Grant to save himself from falling. The General was, undoubtedly, consumed. And still another man, in the excitement consequent upon such an imminent danger to himself, took a third stuffed figure, rushed frantically to the front window, leaped with it to the portico, cried out for some one to help him, and then, lo and behold! he found out that he had saved the effigy of Jeff. Davis. He thought it too late to back out, had not time to consider exactly what was best to do, but was brought to a decision by a shower of hisses and groans from the multitude, who had recognized the arch traitor. The man, determined to save something for Mr. Barnum, persevered in his endeavors, handed Jefferson D. down to a person on the sidewalk, and as he did so the head of the ex-President of the defunct confederacy became detached from its spinal connections and fell upon the ground, to the no small satisfaction of those witnessing the scene. It was subsequently found hanging to a lamp post by St. Paul's, in Fulton street. Some were superstitious enough to augur from this incident that Jeff. Davis' neck was in a slightly dangerous predicament even at that moment. The fall of the conspirator's head produced no end of remark, and more cheers, groans and hisses.

And then the building was cleared of human beings. All saw the necessity for leaving at once, and left.

THE FLAMES SPREAD.

It was a quarter-past one o'clock when the Ann street wall of the Museum fell outwardly, disclosing to full view the fiery furnace raging within. Happily no one was fatally injured by the *debris*, for the intense heat had driven everyone back yards from the flaming mass. A sort of framework was dimly discerned in the second floor, and was popularly believed to be the cage of the once "Happy Family."

At a quarter to two the Broadway end of the building came down with a sound like the roar of distant artillery. For some seconds the very sun itself was obscured by the black cloud of smoke and dust that rose from the floating cinders and dust and ashes.

At two o'clock the Ann street gable, rounded and perforated by the flames, still stood out gaunt and grim in the lurid light, looking not unlike a stray fragment of the ruins of the Coliseum at Rome. At twenty minutes past two fresh engines still came up and got into play. Eight broad jets of flame are issuing from the orifices in the side of Knox's store—the roof gives way and the fire at the front increases in volume and intensity.

THE LAST OF THE MUSEUM.

At half-past two P. M. the last remaining gable of Barnum's and some of the side brickwork of Knox's building fell heavily upon the burning ruins—Pelion heaped upon Ossa.

A smouldering heap, scarcely more than ten feet high, is all that is now left of the great American Curiosity Shop.

BARNUM AND BARNUM'S MUSEUM.

It is appropriate in this connection to give a few words regarding the man who is so great a loser and the building and its contents. Mr. Barnum began his career as a showman in 1835, by exhibiting Joyce Heth, a colored woman, who was the reputed nurse of General Washington. He advertised widely, and people flocked from all quarters to see the old woman. Mr. Barnum made enough out of this speculation to organize a travelling show. In 1841 he bought Scudder's Museum, paid for it in a year, and, adding to it the contents of Peale's Museum, formed what has since been known as Barnum's American Museum. Here he has since remained, and has realized from the undertaking two colossal fortunes, one of which he lost in his unlucky clock speculations. Here he has exhibited all the remarkable curiosities which money and enterprise could procure. A model of Niagara Falls, the Fejee Mermaid, the diorama of the removal of the remains of Napoleon I. from St. Helena to Paris, the Happy Family, the What is It, the Lightning Calculator, the hippopotamus, whales, alligators, prize babies, big dogs, prize poultry, Tom Thumb and wife, the Belgian giant, Commodore Nutt, Minnie Warren, Calvin Edson, the living skeleton; Julia Pastrana, the bearded woman; the (so called) Madagascar Albinoes and quite a regiment of giants, dwarfs, fat boys and fat girls have at various times been the attractions of this unique place of amusement. There was also a large collection of minerals, shells and stuffed birds and animals, which were of real value and cannot be easily replaced. A series of portraits of men eminent in the early annals of our history have been destroyed. Though valueless as works of art, they were not without historical value. A number of revolutionary and other relics are also consumed. Indeed, the accumulations of over twenty years have been utterly destroyed. Of late, however, the establishment has not been adequate to the wants of its patrons, and not equal to the position of a metropolitan museum. The wax figures and other recent additions are no great losses; but the conchological, mineralogical, ichthyological, zoological and ornithological specimens were of genuine merit, though of late visitors had neglected them for the more showy attractions of the "lecture room" and the platform of living curiosities.

Mr. Barnum was absent at the time the fire broke out, in Connecticut. He was telegraphed for at once and left for town in a special train.

FEARS AND RUMORS.

"Was there any one remaining in the building?"

"For God's sake tell me if they all got out."

"Two of my children were there."

"Six men burned in the ruins."

"Several firemen killed by the falling walls."

—And all this as the resistless flames devoured their way with hideous unrelenting maw. These and kindred exclamations passed about among the crowd, and every moment new horrors were added. It was late in the evening before the apprehensions thus excited of human life sacrificed began to be allayed. Several were badly scorched but none are known to have been killed.

SUPPOSED LOSS OF LIFE.

A returned soldier informs us that during the fire he was forced to jump from one of the third story windows of Barnum's Museum, and that he was in company with James Burns, of Lancaster, Pa., a member of Company A, Sixty-ninth regiment N. Y. V., who he has every reason to believe perished in the flames.

STILL MORE BUILDINGS

were destined to fall victims to the insatiate element.

More engines. More water. More smoke. More stifling heat. More cries of frightened women and shrieks of steam whistles. The conflagration seems to go forward—forward; and more houses are swallowed up. More property gone to naught. More hearts wrung. More fortunes turned to dross.

IT IS A FIERY CARNIVAL.

While the fire raged fearfully the scene at the HERALD corner was one of considerable excitement. The opposite side of the street was lined to the curbstone with men who stood to gaze at the fiery spectacle—the flames then towering at their highest. On these blazing fragments fairly rained down, some of these "sparks" being large pieces of wood a foot square, and though the crowd stood, it didn't stand still, as there was a great deal of dodging to do. Wherever the fragments touched combustible material they lighted up new fires, and every awning was ablaze. Up and down the street excited men ran, making violent gesticulations to call every one's attention to the fact that his awning was on fire, and still more excited men busied themselves with efforts to duck their old duck or to tear it down. Around the corner the brass "steamers" worked away, awfully busy, with their short, rapid puffs lost now and then in a shrill, spiteful scream. There was a steady current of men down the street, as if in procession, with spoils. One had an eagle without wings; another, an indescribable monster of the reptile race; several had bright plumaged birds and rare curiosities. There was an unheard of antiquarian taste made manifest, and men bore away the burden of Barnum's glories with delight. Some had been to Knox's, and had more hats than they had heads for. And every now and then the movement of this procession was accelerated tremendously by a grand rush down the street of every one in it, as some one shouted that a wall was coming down, or as some little remnant of panic was communicated from Broadway. Then the street was clear for a few minutes, and the crowd would sway back and fill it up once more with the gazing, curious throng.

Hundreds of prophets came into the HERALD counting-room to make the assurance that the HERALD buildings would certainly go, and to express in advance their regret for such a public calamity. Indeed, there was a very general expression on the part of the people of hope that the HERALD would come out of this fiery ordeal as triumphantly as it had come out of so many others And, thanks to

THE HERALD FIRE APPARATUS,

it did come out safely. While the flames were yet confined to the Museum building the houses at the east end of the block were endangered by the numerous burning cinders which were blown about by the very high wind.

THE ROOFS OF VARIOUS BUILDINGS.

The firemen, working with great and commendable energy on the burning buildings on Broadway, were unable to pay due attention to the roofs of the Belmont Hotel, Ellis' store, &c., and here the HERALD fire apparatus came into good play, and, with all due deference to the Fire Department, saved the threatened buildings mentioned from destruction. Had the several roofs upon which the huge burning cinders were falling in a profusion which looked frightful during a few minutes' delay in the supply of water, caused by the bursting of a section of our hose, became once fired, all after efforts of the firemen would have been unavailing. The HERALD apparatus kept the roofs of all the buildings from the rear of the Museum flooded with water, and undoubtedly saved them from the flames.

As soon as it was discovered that the fire was in the vicinity of the HERALD office the engineer of the office, Mr. John Clark, was ordered to get steam up. He replied that he always had enough steam on to run the two Whitworth Number Four Double Acting Force Pumps with which the office is supplied, and which only require about thirty pounds pressure of steam to run them. Mr. Wm. F. Smythe, superintendent of the HERALD office, as well as of the HERALD Fire Department (which is complete, embracing the entire force of pressmen, compositors, stereotypers, &c.), soon had the members at work, and the hose belonging to the establishment was stretched from the basement to the roof in an incredibly short space of time. The stream was turned on, but the force of the pump was too great for one section of the hose, which burst. Mr. Clark was standing near the pump at the time, and the hose striking him, knocked him a distance of twenty feet or more, throwing him violently to the floor and under the boilers. John Robertson, a young man attached to the establishment of the Continental Bank Note Company, was standing by and was also considerably injured. Although his breath was knocked out of him, he retained his presence of mind and immediately rushed to his employer's establishment, and in a few moments returned with several sections of hose. As the "Continental" has the good sense to use Whitworth's pump, their hose exactly fitted that in use in the HERALD establishment, and served to fill up the deficiency in our length of apparatus, caused by the bursting of the section in the basement.

Our hose was over three hundred and fifty feet in length, extending through seven stories, to the roof of the HERALD office. Through this length of four-inch hose the admirable, though little, pump of which we are possessed forced a stream which, escaping at the pipe, was thrown nearly one hundred and fifty feet further. We were able with it not only to flood the roof of the HERALD office, but, by extending our hose to the buildings more immediately threatened, to throw a heavy stream on Knox's building and the burning Museum. This was a service we had not anticipated being able to extend to our neighbors; but, by the energy of the HERALD firemen, and the particularly noticeable daring of Wm. Bennett, ex-foreman of Engine 22, and Wm. G. Cowles, both HERALD compositors, who ventured on to the roof nearest the Museum, and who, though the heat was intense enough to drive away less experienced firemen, remained constantly at their post, and fairly rivalled the exertions of the Paid Fire Department, we were enabled to do so. If the old Fire Department ever wishes an occasion, in the spirit of generous rivalry, to "break a lance" or "try a stream" with the new department, we advise them to choose for the exponents of their ability the HERALD Fire Company, with Bennett and Cowles at the "butt," and such as George Clark, James Ennis, George Foos, and the others who are too numerous to mention, "on the brakes."

The HERALD apparatus had five streams of water upon the fire at one time.

The Fire Department worked nobly as soon as it had its apparatus arranged, and but for its exertions and the blessing of Croton water the entire block must have been destroyed, and perhaps others with it; for, in a number of instances, the flames were communicated to the roofs and canvass awnings of buildings a block distant from the one on fire. Though unceasing in their exertions the firemen seemed to look upon the conflagration solely from a professional point; and one of the most active of the body remarked, looking at Knox's store, "By Heavens, that alone would have made a pretty fire at night." Apparently he considered it a waste of good material to use up so many buildings at once.

FROM THE ROOF OF THE HERALD BUILDING.

After the fire had burned for more than an hour the mass of flame which was concentrated in the houses between the Museum and the HERALD building was terrific. It reached from Fulton to Ann streets in a solid body, and seemed for a long time to refuse submission to the floods of water so assiduously poured upon it by the firemen from above and below. The spectacle at this time, as seen from the roof of the HERALD office, was very grand, although a position on the roof was almost untenable from the intense heat, and showers of burning embers, which were falling like rain. Our fire staff had their hose at full work here, keeping the roofs thoroughly wet. The sparks from the burning buildings set fire to some awnings on the west side of Fulton street, and for a time created some alarm in that direction, but they were torn down before the fire communicated to the signs and window frames. The roofs of the houses for several blocks around, at all sides, were crowded with spectators watching with anxious interest the fate of the HERALD buildings, which were at that time, and for some time previous, in imminent peril.

THE HERALD OFFICE

was in imminent danger until after three o'clock in the afternoon, but happily escaped with but slight damage. At one time the cinders fell so fast down the chimneys that papers in the grates of several of the apartments were fired But there was little confusion in the establishment. The files were placed in a convenient position for removal should it become necessary, and other preparations quietly entered into which, in the event of catching fire, would insure the safety of the most valuable portion of the library and the manuscripts in the offices. The editors became for the nonce impromptu firemen, the reporters sharpened their pencils and started out upon their usual duties, and the cashier remained at his post and actually contracted for the insertion of some advertisements in this morning's issue of the newspaper while the fire was the hottest and the excitement about the building the most intense. There was no bravado, but all felt that everything was being done that could be done for saving the building and its contents by the brave firemen and the employes of the establishment, and that gave confidence and firmness to each individual to calmly await the culmination of events.

INCIDENTS.

It would be useless to attempt to give all the sad, serious, laughable and other incidents connected with this conflagration. The following are only a few of the large number related:—

A PANIC.

At about half-past one, while the fire in Barnum's was burning furiously, a horrible shriek was heard to emanate from the ruins; an unearthly sound, which so startled the crowd standing in front of St. Paul's church, that a general rush was made up and down Broadway and the utmost confusion prevailed. Several people were knocked down and crushed. The impression on the minds of many was that an explosion had taken place, others cried out that it was only the fearful shrieks of the whales which were being consumed in the debris. The most likely cause was the bursting of the apparatus which supplied the aquaria in which the beautiful fish from all quarters of the earth were accustomed to swim, but will swim no more. The panic for the time was complete, and as the crowd gathered again many were the comments upon the loss which the students of natural and unnatural history, especially from the country parts, would sustain by the destruction of the multifarious curiosities. One man with an artistic air remarked that the only things he regretted were the old coins and fine specimens of ancient armor. Another wondered if the monkeys were saved, while the deepest solicitude was expressed by others as to the fate of the fat women, whose small powers of locomotion it was feared would retard their escape. "The HERALD office is in a bad fix," said an anxious-looking old gentleman; "I hope the fire has not reached it." "Let it go, and be damned," said a rough, groggy fellow, evidently a bummer of some engine house; "it goes in for the paid fire department, and the firemen are down on it." "It is very strange then," replied another, "that the firemen are working so bravely to save it." "That's so," cried out a number of voices simultaneously. "Oh, we'll take care of the HERALD," sung out a lusty fireman, who was lugging his hose through the crowd. A cheer greeted this remark, and again the mass of people were scattered by the crash of a falling roof, and policemen flew here and there to clear the space, now rendered dangerous by the constant tumbling of fragments of stone from the front of the Museum, which was rapidly crumbling to pieces.

A LUCKY ESCAPE.

Among the works of art which fortunately escaped destruction in Barnum's Museum were twenty-four gigantic pictures, illustrating the battles of Washington during the Revolutionary war, painted by Mr. John McNevin, which were to have been exhibited at the Museum as a panorama in a few days, but had not reached their destination, and were lying in a building close by. The studies for these pictures had been carefully examined by the late Washington Irving, and were in fact revised by Mr. McNevin in many of the details at the suggestion of that distinguished author. They were thus preserved by the lucky accident of delay in delivering them.

STATEMENT OF THE AQUARIAN.

Mr. Oscar Kohn, the aquarian of the Museum, makes the following statement containing additional particulars of the conflagration:—I came back from my dinner at about a quarter-past noon, when I observed a rush down the stairs; proceeding at once to the engine room in the basement I saw the fire directly over the boiler, and then went to the ground floor and saw the flames burst from the ladies' private room; the giantess, Anna Swan, stood at the head of the stairs as if swooning from the effects of the smoke, which then came down in columns; I took her to the Belmont House; coming back I found it impossible to enter the upper stories; Miss Swan lost everything except the clothes she wore; she had in her trunk about one hundred and twenty dollars in gold, some greenbacks and all her clothing.

THE BROOKLYN DEPARTMENT

turned out in pretty full force to help put out the fire, a number of machines coming across, including steamers Nos. 7, 9, 14 and 17, and Hose Companies Nos. 4, 6, 8, 9 and 14. To the members of these companies, as well as to those of our own department, the thanks of the city should be returned that the loss is not very much larger than it is.

THE TELEGRAPH WIRES

upon Broadway, in front of the Museum, were heated to such a degree as to melt, and their gutta percha covering dropped upon the clothing and in the faces of the people standing beneath.

ST. PAUL'S STEEPLE

was at one time on fire—the wooden portion—and there were well grounded apprehensions entertained that it might also be consumed. But timely exertions and the putting out of wet blankets saved it as well as the Astor House.

THE GREEK SLAVE.

An officer of the Broadway squad succeeded in saving the Greek slave. He carried it into an Ann street store.

REMOVING THE FLAGS.

The removal of the flags from the Museum roof, by John H. Carman, caused great cheering, as the populace expected their destruction. This brave fellow chose to risk his life, to save the dozen "Star Spangled Banners" which "in triumph" were waving above the heat and roar of the flames, and in the midst of dense volumes of smoke, which often obscured them from sight.

THE COMPANIES AND THE STREAMS.

The following is deemed an accurate enumeration of the engine and other companies having water upon the fire yesterday, with their foremen's names, their streams of water and other particulars connected with the department:—

NEW YORK COMPANIES.

Engine Company No. 8, one stream, through 490 feet of hose, G. Patterson, foreman.

Engine Company No. 53, two streams, through 500 feet of hose, T. Duffey, foreman.

Engine Company No. 11, two streams, through 550 feet of hose, C. Johnson, foreman.

Engine Company No. 40, one stream, through 450 feet of hose, H. Bonner, foreman.

Engine Company No. 31, two streams, through 450 feet of hose, F. Mahody, foreman.

Engine Company No. 30, one stream, through 300 feet of hose, C. Loughran, foreman.

Engine Company No. 14, one stream, through 450 feet of hose, J. Massey, foreman.

Engine Company No. 7, two streams, through 1,000 feet of hose, T. Eustis, foreman.

Engine Company No. 13, two streams, through 250 feet of hose, T. Cornan, foreman.

Exempt Engine Company, two streams, through 900 feet of hose, John Gorman, foreman.

Engine Company No. 20, one stream, through 250 feet of hose, J. Kanfect, foreman.

Engine Company No. 42, two streams, through 600 feet of hose, Wm. Corgan, foreman.

Engine Company No. 5, one stream, through 600 feet of hose, Thos. McCauley, foreman.

Engine Company No. 38, two streams, through 400 feet of hose, A. H. Mitchell, foreman.

Engine Company No. 21, two streams, through 650 feet of hose, P. Galligan, foreman.

Engine Company No. 16, and Engine Company No. 24. These companies retired from the fire before we could ascertain the names of their foremen.

Alert Hose Company No. 41, Mr. Shields, foreman.

Warren Hose Company No. 33, Charles Bacon, foreman.

Niagara Hose Company No. 2, J. Castell, foreman.

Ed. Forrest Hose Company No. 5, M. Miller, foreman.

Lady Washington Hose Company No. 49, H. A. Seeley, foreman.

Phœnix Hose Company No. 22, Geo. Anderson, foreman.

M. T. Brennan Hose Company No. 60, M. J. Keeser, foreman.

Atlantic Hose Company No. 15, J. Toobe, foreman.

Nassau Hose Company No. 56, J. Sullivan, foreman.

Humane Hose Company No. 20, Robert McGinn, foreman.

Hose Company No. 3, R. H. Woodruff, foreman.

Eagle Hose Company No. 1 Louis Hoppz, foreman.

Hose Company No. 50, J. Garvey, foreman.

City Hose Company No. 8, T. P. Curtiss, foreman.

H. Howard Hook and Ladder Company No. 11, J. Morrell, foreman.

Mutual Hook and Ladder Company No. 1, ——

McClellan Hook and Ladder Company No. 4, M. Loftus, foreman. The wall fell on one of the members belonging to this company, who was taken to the City Hospital.

Lafayette Hook and Ladder Company No. 6, F. W. Melville, foreman.

Baxter Hook and Ladder Company No. 15, L. W. Parkes, foreman.

BROOKLYN COMPANIES.

Engine Company No. 9, one stream, through 750 feet of hose, P. Cornell, foreman.

Engine Company No. 19, one stream, through 600 feet of hose, J. Connor, foreman.

Engine Company No. 5, one stream, through 600 feet of hose, D. McNamara, foreman.

Atlantic Hose Company No. 1, R. J. Luckey, foreman.

Washington Hose Company No. 6, Wm. Gardner, foreman.

Crystal Hose Company No. 4, Thos. Fowler, foreman.

Waterwitch Hose Company No. 8, T. D. Plumb, foreman.

Americus Hose Company No. 7, P. Boyle, foreman.

Frontier Hose Company No. 5, Chas. B. Farley, foreman.

Mechanic Hose Company No. 2, R. Williams, foreman.

HOBOKEN COMPANIES.

Charles Chamberlain, Chief Engineer.

Engine Company No. 1, with hose tender, L. Osdenrof, foreman.

Engine Company No. 2, with hose tender, John Kennedy, foreman.

Ocean Hose Company No. 1, P. Law, foreman.

These companies brought with them 2,200 feet of hose.

THANKS

should be returned to Mr. John Brosnan, of No. 143 Fulton street, for the kind proffer of refreshments to the firemen, which were very acceptable under the pressure of arduous labor and the scorching heat to be endured. And the HERALD office is especially indebted to Exempt Engine Company, to No. 5 Engine Company, and to Nos. 20 and 56 Hose for their promptitude and herculean exertions in aiding to preserve the establishment from the threatening flames. They will never be forgotten. In fact, the entire department will ever be remembered with feelings of liveliest gratitude for favors rendered us, as well as to neighboring citizens.

WASHINGTON'S BILLIARD TABLE,

which was in a billiard hall in Fulton street—Bassford's—was completely destroyed, with the other contents of the place. This valuable and interesting relic was the property of the family of the late Recorder Lee, of Philadelphia. It was thought highly of, having been played upon by General George Washington.

MR. KNOX'S BUSINESS

will be carried on at 533 Broadway hereafter, he having been compelled "by the force of circumstances," and a very hot fire, to remove from his old location, 212 Broadway.

PICKPOCKETS AT THE FIRE.

During the progress of the fire in Broadway yesterday afternoon a fine opportunity was afforded the light-fingered operators to ply their profession, and it is needless to say that they improved it. Henry Jackson, George Douglass, James Smith, Godfrey Mish, Henry Mursken, James Clancy and James Lemord were arrested by officers McGloin, McGuire and Dwyer, of the Third precinct, and officer Dowdell, of the Tombs Police Court, charged with picking pockets of men at the fire, stealing from stores, &c. Lemord had secured quite a load of plunder, and when taken was marching off under the weight of a piece of cloth, several hats, reticule, two valises, two pieces of flannel, &c., &c. All the above named prisoners were detained in the Third precinct station house to await an examination before Justice Hogan this morning.

Robert and James H. Walsh, brothers, were arrested by officer Kinney, of the Twenty-sixth precinct, charged with relieving John W. Sharman, residing at 196 Fulton avenue, Brooklyn, of a gold watch, as he was looking at the blazing Museum. The watch was recovered, and Captain Brackett detained the prisoners for a hearing.

The Second precinct police arrested John Fox, Henry Suhoff, James McDonald and Andrew S. Gilso, charged with stealing boots from No. 6 Ann street. Frank Fover was conveying away a cask of wine, when taken in charge and lodged in the station house. James Cameron, Thomas Newton, Geo. Thompson, James McCord and John Ulfosser were arrested, charged with stealing boots which were found in their possession. James Kirby, John Spencer, John Sullivan and James Welsh, known to the police as pickpockets, were taken out of harm's way and sent to the station house.

Mr. Daniel Stewart, of Johnstown, Fulton county, this State, lost a two hundred dollar gold watch and chain, while standing in the crowd opposite the Museum. The accused parties will be examined before Justice Hogan at the Tombs.

BURNED OUT.

Yesterday evening, huddled together by the side of Lovejoy's Hotel, were a number of frightened women, sitting upon hastily packed bundles and trunks, and hugging, with forlorn looks the fragments of crushed bonnet boxes. These were Barnum's lady assistants, burned out of house and home. They are to be pitied.

Losses and Insurances.

There seems to be but little doubt that the fire originated in a room used for storage in the vicinity of the boiler, in the cellar, and is supposed at present to have been caused by the heat of the boiler on the first floor, and under the stairs made at the rear part of the Museum for egress. The flames spread up the stairs, and in a few minutes communicated from floor to floor. In half an hour from the first discovery of the fire the entire building was in flames, and shortly afterward the walls fell in. Owing to there being a communication from the Museum to No. 10 Ann street, and from there to 151 Fulton street, the flames took that direction, and in a very short time the flames were bursting forth from the windows of the Fulton street building. The Museum numbered Nos. 218 and 220 Broadway, and extended over Nos. 214 and 216, the theatre occupying the upper floors. The fire extended down Broadway to the corner of Fulton street, totally destroying the buildings and their contents.

The buildings destroyed are as follows:—

Barnum's Museum, Nos. 218 and 220. Loss on stock estimated at about $300,000; insured for $60,000. The building is owned by the Olmstead estate. Loss $40,000; insured for $80,000.

ON BROADWAY.

No. 216—Occupied on first floor by G. W. White, hatter. Loss $10,000. Part of the goods were taken out. Insured for $15,000. The upper part occupied as part of the Museum.

No. 214—First floor occupied by P. L. Rogers' Sons, clothiers. Stock removed. Loss $15,000; insured for $34,500, as follows:—Bowery, $2,500; Phenix, $2,500; Atlantic, $2,500; New Amsterdam, $2,500; Harmony, $3,000; Lenox, $3,000; Montauk, $1,500; Yonkers, $2,000; Morris, $2,000; Manhattan, $5,000; New England, $3,000; Indemnity, $2,500; Home, of New Haven, $2,500.

Second floor—Billiard room of J. T. Reeves. Loss $10,000. Insured.

Basement—"Captain's Live and Let Live" restaurant. Loss $5,000; insured.

Wm. Van Name occupied the basement of No. 216 as a restaurant. Loss $8,000; insured.

Building No. 214 is totally destroyed. Loss $15,000; insured. It belonged to the Morris estate.

No. 212—First and top floors occupied by Charles Knox, hatter. Loss estimated at $80,000; insured for $30,000.

Second floor—B. H. Horn, optician; also patent agency of Coombs & Brown.

Third floor—J. Briggs, corn doctor, and Mr. Barringer, broker.

The basement was occupied by William Branch as a restaurant.

The whole building was destroyed, together with its contents. Loss on building $15,000; insured for $20,000. It was owned by the Lorillard estate.

FULTON STREET.

No. 155—Gentlemen's furnishing goods store, owned by Willetts & Skidmore. Loss $3,000; insured.

No. 153—Porter house, owned by Mr. Wortendike. Loss $1,000.

No. 151—Hat store of Sherwood & Metzinger. Loss $3,000; insured.

No. 149—Liquor store, owned by John Duane. Loss $3,000. Upper part by A. Bassford, Jr., as a billiard saloon. Loss $8,000; insured.

Buildings Nos. 149 and 151 are totally destroyed.

No. 147—First floor, stationery store of Stearns & Beale. Damage by water about $2,000; insured for $12,000 in the Phenix, Croton and Hanover Insurance Companies. Second floor, tailor's store of Hamilton & Thompson. Damage slight; insured. Third floor, Slater & Riley, printers. Loss $200; insured. Fourth floor, Harvey & Ford, ivory turners. Loss $50; insured for $3,500, in the Tradesmen's Insurance Company. Fifth floor, Austin & McGill, blank book binders. Loss $300; insured for $3,000, in the Mechanics' Insurance Company.

No. 145—First floor, Savery's dining saloon. Damage $200; insured for $4,000, in Park Insurance Company. Basement, wine store of F. C. Hansen. Loss $100. Third floor, S. Bradford, printer. Damage $150; insured for $3,000, in the Mechanics' and Traders' Insurance Company.

The buildings Nos. 145 and 147 are owned by Josiah Macy. They are damaged to the extent of $500; insured.

ANN STREET, UNDER THE MUSEUM.

J. E. Nolan's sample room. Insured for $4,000, in the Fulton Insurance Company; total loss.

Boot and shoe store owned by Mr. Irwin. Loss $2,000.

Truss store of J. J. Glover. Loss $1,500.

Truss store of Wm. Marsh. Loss $1,500.

New York Optical Instrument Company. Owned by Charles F. Lemke. Loss about $8,000. Insured for $2,000 in Goodhue Insurance Company.

J. R. Surbrug, cigars. Insured for $4,800 in Manhattan Insurance Company. Loss $1,500.

Mr. Higginson, barber shop, in the basement. Loss $500.

No. 8 Ann street, restaurant kept by Mr. F. V. Groot. Loss $2,500. No insurance.

Nos. 10 and 12—First floor, boot and shoe store of Jones & Kenwood. Loss $5,000. Upper floors, W. N. Clapp, printer. Loss $2,000; W. S. Wilder, paper ruler. Loss $1,000. T. E. Bartow, printer. Loss $1,000. The building is owned by the Chandler estate. It is damaged to the extent of $6,000; insured.

Nos. 14 and 16—Occupied by J. J. Byrn, tailor; C. Bellman, wood engraver; J. Ross, porter house and J. J.

CONTINUED ON FIFTH PAGE.

GREAT BASE BALL MATCH BETWEEN THE ATLANTIC AND ECKFORD CLUBS OF BROOKLYN, AT THE UNION BASE BALL GROUNDS, B

N, E. D., OCT. 13, WITH PORTRAITS OF THE LEADING PLAYERS OF THE PRINCIPAL CLUBS OF NEW YORK, BROOKYN AND NEWARK.

SCENE AT POLICE HEADQUARTERS—CAPT. JAMES LEONARD INSTRUCTING NEWLY-APPOINTED POLICEMEN.

revent an immediate breach of the peace, or to quell a disturbance actually commenced.

C.—"What is your duty towards a prisoner?"

S.—(Sec. 32.)—"Any officer, roundsman, or policeman, who shall wilfully maltreat, or use unnecessary violence towards a prisoner or citizen, shall, on complaint being made, and the fact established by competent testimony, be immediately dismissed from office."

And so on through 173 sections does Capt. Leonard teach and examine his pupil, renewing the schooling from day to day, until, at the end of 30 days, Smith is supposed to be fit for final examination, and is brought up for that purpose and put through his paces. If he answers even in the spirit of the Manual, he goes upon duty, but if not, he is turned back to the school for farther instruction.

While this is going on, the recruit every day is passing through the hands of Mr. W. H. Simonds, who is supposed to be the physical instructor, as Capt. Leonard is the mental teacher.

Mr. Simonds puts in the hands of the recruit the baton, and in doing so, teaches him how to use it. In this part of his schooling, Smith is put through all the movements of self-defence and attack, the same as a recruit will be taught the use of the musket, bayonet, or sword, if he enters the army. It was this tuition that made the police force so valuable during the riots of 1863, and will always make them equal to twenty times their number in a street battle.

To the public all that we have been telling should be especially interesting, not only from the elements within itself, but from the fact that it exerts an influence over their daily life, and teaches them that they can sleep with safety in their beds, and walk with safety in the streets.

HON. ELIJAH F. PURDY.

WE regret to announce the death of Hon. Elijah F. Purdy, which occurred at his residence in Ludlow street, at 12 o'clock, on the night of the 8th of January. His disease was pneumonia, with which he has been confined to his house for some time, though it is only within the last two or three days that serious fears have been entertained in regard to his recovery.

Mr. Purdy was born in Westchester county, N. Y., about 70 years ago. He came to New York in the year 1819, and commenced business as a cartman, but shortly quit that business for the grocery trade, in which also he was successful. He took an active part in politics, and first became conspicuous in the support of Andrew Jackson for the Presidency. Shortly after this election he was elected Alderman from the Ward of his residence, and has been very frequently elected to office since, having held, among other important public trusts those of Supervisor, Surveyor of the Port of New York, and Commissioner of Emigration.

From the beginning of his political career he has been a member of the National Democratic party, and in city politics he has been one of the chief pillars of Tammany Hall. During the late war his services in filling the quota of the city were given heartily, and without the expectation of adequate reward, and were of very great value to the city and to the general Government. He held throughout the war, and up to the time of his death, the office of Supervisor.

In private life Mr. Purdy was a most amiable and genial man. His personal and official integrity has never been questioned. His death will be regretted deeply by his numerous personal friends, and will be felt as a loss by the Democracy of the State, and particularly of the city, to whose success he had so often and so greatly contributed. He was married early in life, and leaves surviving him a widow and six children—three sons and three daughters.

A RAINY NIGHT IN FRONT OF THE THEATRES.

NEW YORK in a rain storm or a snow storm changes its entire character. In the first case, the entire people fall into the blues; in the second, they rise almost to frantic hilarity. The city, on a rainy day, almost suspends business, but on a rainy night it does not suspend its amusement. We remember the time when a rainy night killed a benefit at the theatre, but the temper of the people has changed within a few years; and now, unless it rains emphatically cats and dogs, the inside of the dramatic temple shows little difference. This may be attributed to various causes. Perhaps, to the belief of some people, that upon such a night they will have more room; perhaps to their insatiate appetite, which will let nothing stand in the way of their pleasures; and perhaps that omnibus and car communication to every part of the city is so easy that it is about as dry travelling as staying at home. Sufficient to say that if the audience is not as brilliantly dressed upon a rainy night, it is as numerous.

Our illustration is at the front of the house after the performance. Then and there comes the crash of war, or something worse. The din of clashing omnibusses and the eager cry of the drivers: "Broadway—up—Twenty-third street—Madison square—Here you are!—South Ferry—Ninth avenue—Hurry up!" And through this confusion the artillery of the policeman, slamming the bus doors with a loud "Move on!" and "This way, madam!" gives, for about five minutes the nearest approach to Pandemonium that we know of. Umbrellas are at a premium, and the smartest man is he who is active, and, by having eyes all over him, and popping about like a pea on a hot shovel, gets his ladies snugly omnibussed in the least time, and gives them the smallest amount of fluidity on their precious persons.

In connection with this matter we have often thought that it would be a brilliant idea for our theatres to have an awning reaching well over the sidewalk, which could be put up when wanted, and act as a protection to the fairer part of the audience from the front of the house to the curb. A few such attentions to their patrons, *after* they have left the theatre, would be more telling than all they could offer before they entered it.

SCENE AT POLICE HEADQUARTERS—MR. W. H. SIMONDS INSTRUCTING POLICEMEN IN THE BATON EXERCISE.

The Ball Players' CHRONICLE.

A Weekly Journal Devoted to the Interests of the American Game of Base Ball and Kindred Sports of the Field.

VOL. 1. | THOMPSON & PEARSON, Publishers. | NEW YORK, OCTOBER 17, 1867. | HENRY CHADWICK, Editor. | No. 20.

Base Ball.

THE GAME IN NEW YORK.

THE ATLANTIC AND UNION MATCH.

The Championship Pennant Leaves Brooklyn for the First Time.

Great Excitement in Morrisania.

On Thursday, October 9th, 1867, an event occurred which will be noteworthy as a prominent chapter in the annals of the game in this section of the country, for on that day the laurels of the championship of the United States were wrested for the first time from the Atlantic Club by a club not located in Brooklyn. For ten years past the championship has been held by Brooklyn clubs, the Atlantics being the first champion club of the United States, and the last, up to the 9th of October, 1867. For an interval of two years, however, the title was held by another Brooklyn club—the Eckford Club of the Eastern District, who were champions during 1862 and 1863; but with this exception, the Atlantics have flown the whip pennant, and bravely held their own against all comers for the past ten years.

On the day in question the Union Club became the champion club of the United States, by virtue of the winning of two games in succession of a home-and-home series with the Atlantic Club of Brooklyn, their first game being won at Morrisania, July 31st, by a score of 32 to 19, and the second, Oct. 9th, by a score of 14 to 13—an aggregate of 46 to 32. Before proceeding to give the details of this last game, we propose briefly to review the season's play of the Union Club.

The Unions began play for the season in a regular match game, on the 18th of May, their adversaries being the Atlanta Club of Tremont. This they won by a score of 48 to 10. On the 25th of May they played the Athletes of Washington Heights, and then made the highest score known in the history of the club, the Unions winning by the totals of 101 to 13 in a game of six innings only. On the 4th of June they entered the championship arena, encountering the noted Irvingtons for the first time, and this time met with defeat by a score of 26 to 17. On the 12th of June victory perched upon their banner in a contest with the Eureka Club at Newark, the score being 26 to 12; and on the 15th of June they captured a trophy from the Eclectics by a score of 45 to 10 in a game of seven innings. The return match was played on June 29th, the Unions again winning, but only by a score of 36 to 32. On the 2d of July their return game with the Irvington Club was hastily played, and another defeat was the result, the Irvingtons winning by a score of 26 to 22. They now realized the fact that they were not properly prepared for the championship contest, and they wisely resolved upon a week's tour through the western part of the State for practice; and accordingly they left town, July 7th, and on the 8th played the National Club of Albany, winning easily by a score of 47 to 16. On the 9th they met the noted Unions—ye "Haymakers"—at Lansingburg, and this time they had foemen worthy of their steel, and for the first time the Unions had to yield to a "country club"—the score standing at 51 to 23 against them. This repulse only spurred them to extra exertions, and on the 10th they defeated the Utica Club by a score of 49 to 26, and on the 11th the Excelsiors of Rochester, by a score of 34 to 15—closing their week's play with a victory over the noted Niagaras of Buffalo by a score of 25 to 19. On the 13th they returned home—tired, of course, but greatly improved by the practice, as their play in the next two games fully proved.

On the 31st of July we find them again entering the championship arena, and this time they face the champions themselves, and it being a contest between a nine well practiced in home positions, against a nine entirely out of practice, the result was the signal success of the trained nine of the Unions by a score of 32 to 19. This victory offset the Irvington defeats, and after a practice game with the Atlantas, of Tremont, Aug. 6th, which they won by a score of 31 to 16, they encountered the Mutuals on the 14th of August, at Brooklyn, and it not only proved to be a brilliant victory, but the finest fielding game the two clubs had ever played before, the result being the success of the Unions by a score of 9 to 8. Union stock was now at a high premium, and when their fine nine entered the field, Aug. 19th, to meet the Athletics, and finish their home-and-home game with them, every one anticipated another signal triumph for the gallant Unions. But Dame Fortune, with her usual fickleness, deserted them on this occasion, the result of the contest being their signal defeat by the Philadelphians by a score of 23 to 10, the only consolation being that the Athletics also defeated the Mutuals the next day. The Unions did not again play until Aug. 25th, when they visited Newark and played the Active Club, winning by a score of 22 to 12, and on the 27th they had a close game with the Eckfords, but came off the victors by a score of 25 to 23. On the 31st of Aug. they took another little country trip to get their hands in again, and visiting Norwich played two games there, first with the Pequot Club, winning by the score of 33 to 8, and then with the Riverside Club, score 66 to 17. On Sept. 10th, they defeated the Eurekas again by a score of 33 to 14, and on the 12th polished off the Excelsiors, of Rochester—then visiting New York—by a score of 29 to 21, and on the 17th won another trophy from the Actives, of Newark, by a score of 22 to 11. On the 19th of Sept. they met the Orientals, with four of their nine absent, and this carelessness cost them the game by a score of 42 to 19 against them. Two days after, Sept. 21st, they visited Philadelphia, and again being short-handed, sustained defeat at the hands of the Athletics, but only by a score of 36 to 32. On Sept. 23d, they were defeated by the Mutuals by a score of 20 to 24, thus losing two games out of the series of three between them, and the next day they played their return game with the Unions, of Lansingburgh, at Brooklyn, and were beaten by a score of 26 to 21. On the 28th of September they met the Actives, and after a closely contested game, came off the victors by a score of 15 to 11. This was the last game prior to their meeting with the Atlantics, their total scores in the above matches being 872 against 543. They play one more game before they close the season, and that is their return game with the Athletic Club. Early in the season they notified clubs that their season would close Oct. 16th.

We now come to the contest of Oct. 9th, on which occasion they played their return match with the Atlantic Club, at Brooklyn, in the presence of about three thousand people, the attendance not being as numerous as it would have been had such a fine game and a close contest been anticipated; but in view of the recent defeat of the Mutuals by the Atlantics, and of the Unions by the Haymakers, it was pretty generally expected that the Atlantic Club would have but little trouble in winning a ball, even from the crack club of Morrisania. The uncertainty of ball matches in general and of the result of contests in which the Union Club take part in particular, should have taught the habitues of our leading contests better; but it did not have that effect, and the result was a comparatively slim attendance. The Unions had out the strongest nine on this occasion they ever presented in a match, while the Atlantics were not only minus the services of Charley Smith, but had a nine out which was not as happy a family as it is requisite to have to fully develop the strength of a nine.

The game began at 2.50 P. M. with the Atlantics at the bat, Pearce leading off with a safe hit to centre field, on which he easily secured his base, Start following suit with a safe bounder to right field, both being helped round by passed balls. Galvin then came to the bat, and, banging away at the first ball within reach, sent it high to left field, and it fell very prettily into Smith's hands, Start getting home by the operation, Pearce having preceded him. Crane also sent a high ball to right field, directly into Beals' hands; and as Mills also popped one up for Shelley to take, the innings closed for the two runs scored by Pearce and Start. Smith led off on the Union side, and hit a "corker" to centre field; but Galvin judged the ball finely, and bottled Smith's corker in style. Martin then sent a hot bounder to Crane, which Fred passed to Start, but scarcely in time, the ball certainly not being handled before the striker reached the base; but the umpire thought it had, and Martin had to retire; whereupon up went a regular old Morrisania growl from the Union backers and hisses from the betting men of the crowd who had invested on the Unions. In view of the fact that the two clubs had experienced difficulty in getting any one to act as umpire, and that the secretary of the National Association—as fair and square a ball player as there is—had undertaken the disagreeable task, common courtesy for the favor done should have led the partisans of the clubs to have held their peace at least, if they could not approve. But betting men do not know the meaning of the word when they have money at stake, and club partisans are no better; and hence both are always down upon the umpire the moment he commits an error of judgment, except when it favors their side. Those who desire to escape insults and abuse would do well to refuse to act as umpire in any match on which the betting crowd have money invested. Let these growlers be taught a lesson, for it is about time they were.

Pabor followed Martin, and he gave Start a chance to field him out, but Joe failed to hold the ball in time, and Pabor made his base, and by passed balls got round to his third; and as Ferguson gave Austin a life on a muffed ball, Pabor scored his run, Akin being third out, by the good fielding of Zettlein to Start. This left the totals of the first innings at 2 to 1 in favor of the Atlantics.

In the second innings Ferguson led off with a high ball to right field, which Beals caught in brilliant style. McDonald then sent a ball to Akin, which was thrown poorly to Goldie, who failed to hold it, and McDonald reached his base. Zettlein was next, and by a bounding ball out of Akin's reach secured his base. Kenney, too, sent one of the same kind to Akin; but the latter stopped it beautifully, and, sending it straight to Goldie, caused Kenney's retirement, McDonald getting home at the same time. Goldie, seeing Zettlein running to third, hastily threw the ball to Shelley, but out of reach, and the "charmer" got in—and just in time, too, for Pearce afterwards retired on a foul fly well taken by Birdsall. This left the Atlantics' total at 4, and the Unions went in to get square. Birdsall led off well with a good bounder to Kenney, on which he secured his first, but, as Kenney let the ball go by him, David ran to his third; and after Shelley had tipped out, David came in on Beals's hit, Tommy being well put out by Zettlein and Start, and Goldie closed the innings by retiring from a ball prettily caught by Crane—the totals standing at 4 to 2 in favor of the Atlantics, the ratio of the first innings' lead being kept up.

Start opened play in the third innings by giving Goldie a chance to field him out, Joe taking a back seat in consequence. Galvin was next, and he hit a beauty to left field, easily making his base, and, Crane following suit well, things began to look favorable for a good score; but Mills failed to come to time, and, giving an easy chance to Martin, became the second hand out. Ferguson, however, came to the rescue with a beautiful grounder to right field, easily getting his base, and sending Galvin in; and as Beals, seeing Crane running home, threw the ball in to Birdsall, Ferguson ran to second, Crane getting home, from the ball being thrown in too high. Although Beals was playing finely in the field, and had played the point correctly, the wind alone taking the ball out of reach, he did not escape the growlers, the find-fault style of thing prevailing too much in the Union Club for their own welfare. Ferguson was on his second, with two runs in, when McDonald gave Austin a chance for a good fly catch, which was well attended to, and the innings was finished, with the Atlantic score at 6—a very poor score from the beginning for Atlantic batting. Smith led off on the Union side, and, hitting what he thought a safe one to right field, took his base; but Kenney ran a long way in for the ball, and took it on the fly in splendid style, it being the best catch on the Atlantic side. Martin tried the same kind of ball, and this time it was a success, and Martin made his base; and Zettlein throwing a ball poorly to Start, Martin got round to his third. Pabor then hit a ball to Start, who fielded it in time to first; but this time the umpire erred on the other side, and, thinking Pabor had reached his base as soon as Start, gave Charley it. The Atlantics looked surprised, but said not a word, and the Union growlers kept quiet, the umpire doing right always when he errs on the side we bet on. This squared things in regard to the errors of judgment complained of, as Martin got in and Pabor had a life given him. Afterwards a muff by Crane helped Pabor round, and Austin's good hit sent him home. Austin, in running to second, was caught napping by Crane, who received the ball from Mills in time to touch Austin, but he failed to reach him, although it must have looked to the umpire as a plain out, for Austin was ten feet off his base when Crane had the ball; but the growlers said it was "rough," and again pitched into the umpire, they complaining of two decisions against them thus far in the game to one in their favor. Two hands were out and two runs were scored when Akin hit a high ball to right field, which was a far less difficult one to catch than the one Kenney had previously held; but this time Kenney dropped it, and Akin made his base, and, Birdsall following with a good hit, two men were on the bases when Shelley gave Kenney another chance for a catch; but it was scarcely within reach, and as it was neither caught nor stopped Shelley made his third base, and Akin and Birdsall got home; and as Beals sent a "corker" to left field and Goldie followed suit, Shelley and Beals got home, four runs being added after Kenney's first mis-catch, Goldie being on the second base when Smith was well put out by

THE HORSE MARKET, BULL'S HEAD, NEW YORK CITY.—SKETCHED BY A. R. WAUD.—[SEE PAGE 109.]

The Revolution.

PRINCIPLE, NOT POLICY JUSTICE, NOT FAVORS.—MEN, THEIR RIGHTS AND NOTHING MORE: WOMEN, THEIR RIGHTS AND NOTHING LESS.

VOL. IV.—NO. 7. NEW YORK, THURSDAY, AUGUST 19, 1869. WHOLE NO. 85.

The Revolution.

PUBLISHED WEEKLY, $3 A YEAR.
NEW YORK CITY SUBSCRIPTIONS, $3.20.

ELIZABETH CADY STANTON, Editor.
SUSAN B. ANTHONY, Proprietor.

OFFICE, 49 EAST TWENTY-THIRD ST.

WOMAN SUFFRAGE CONVENTION AT NEWPORT, R. I.

A WOMAN SUFFRAGE Convention, under the auspices of the National Association, will be held in the Academy of Music at Newport, Rhode Island, on Wednesday and Thursday, the 25th and 26th inst.

The success attending the recent gathering at Saratoga, warrants the most sanguine hopes and expectations from this also. The intense interest now everywhere felt on the great question, renders all appeal for a full attendance unnecessary.

Among the speakers will be Mrs. Elizabeth Cady Stanton, Mrs. Paulina Wright Davis, Mrs. Celia Burleigh, Rev. Phebe A. Hannaford, Mrs. Charlotte B. Wilbour, Miss Susan B. Anthony, Theodore Tilton and Hon. James M. Scovel.

Names of other speakers will be announced hereafter.

In behalf of the National Woman's Suffrage Association,

ELIZABETH CADY STANTON, Pres.

PAULINA W. DAVIS, { Advisory Counsel for the State of Rhode Island.

AT the regular weekly meeting of the National Woman's Suffrage Association, on Tuesday, August 10, there was a full attendance. The President, Mrs. Stanton, presided. Mrs. Blake was elected Secretary *pro tem.*

Mrs. Stanton made a few remarks on the tone of the press in regard to the Association.

Mrs. Lozier spoke of the improving effect of these weekly meetings on the women themselves.

Mrs. Blake delivered a short address on the evils of woman's education.

Mrs. Wilbour read an essay on the elevating influence the ballot would have for woman.

Mrs. Stanton called attention to the dreadful condition of our city prisons. A Committee consisting of Mrs. Lewis, Barlow, Lozier and Bronson, was appointed to visit them, and after a short debate on the style of the reports of these proceedings in the daily papers, the meeting adjourned.

JOHN STUART MILL.

BY HON. S. S. COX.

MR. COX, whom some persons and papers designate, for some reason, "Sun Set Cox," is travelling in Europe and reporting his progress quite extensively, and often to excellent purpose, in the New York *World.* The following account of his visit to John Stuart Mill will be acceptable and entertaining to readers of THE REVOLUTION:

What makes Avignon to me so dear to-day? Not the machiolated battlements, perfect as gems upon its unflawed walls; nor anything within these walls; nor the voiceful Rhone and its panorama of magnificence. None of these. Turn to the East; overlook the cathedral towers; the gray roofs of the stony city, on the hither side of the mountains, and amidst the green and gold meadows. Fix your eye upon a spot very dark with cypress; a grove of trees in symmetry, here and there specked with marble monument. This is the Cemetery of Avignon. Within it lies the body of Harriet Mill, and near by lives her ever-mourning husband, John Stuart Mill. He lives here because she is here buried.

This fact makes Avignon as full of interest as the Rhone is of beautiful islets. It is, indeed, an unwritten elegy, too sweet for the lyre, lute, or voice. Why the best thinker with the best heart upon this star lingers (not in exile), but lingers nearer home, within a few steps of his wife's grave? why, yielding his intellect to the labors incident to his progressive and thoughtful mind, he yet weeps "a grief forever fresh," here in this lovely land so full of tender and graceful associations? why that mind so ardent in all good words and works, so logically trained, so quickly responsive, so grandly attuned to the higher harmonies, should here day by day come to lay his heart against the white marble of the mute tomb? These are questions that have their answer, and their answer is in the still small voice of the bereaved and devoted heart.

It is the fashion now, even in England, and much more in America, to applaud the acumen and goodness of this philosophic statesman. Sneered at, at times, as a chimerical theorist, with many erratic orbits in his starry progress, he is nevertheless to-day the most potential mind living. I am no worshipper of heroes, but I owe much to Stuart Mill, and my admiration is not of recent date. Long before he attained his splendid fame, as a student I read after him. If I needed any apology for my admiration of the man, I am pardoned when I say that at college, and, as early as 1847, I wrote criticisms for the American Reviews on his writings. The old *Knickerbocker* has a "chapter of fallacies," which were suggested by his logic, and a Western quarterly, published by Louis Hine, a thinker of the advanced class, was, I fear, made heavy with some flounderings of mine in the positive philosophy, Compte's Social Science," and "Mill's Ethology." Will this be excuse enough to the reader for neglecting romantic ruins and faded frescoes in old churches and palaces—to renew with me my earlier devotion at the shrine of a master now acknowledged by all? I had corresponded with Mr. Mill on matters of common interest, in connection with the enfranchisement of industry; and called to see him in England and found him gone! Hardly expecting, yet a little hoping to find him at his home here, I drove to his house. At least, if the human presence was not there, it would have been interesting to see where he had been.

A fine road follows the walls of the city and bank of the Rhone, and leaves the latter—still to follow the walls—a continuous line of shaded boulevards, which leads you to the eastern side of the city. Near the gate which leads you to the Valley of the Vaucluse you turn to the East. Under the shade of Lombardy poplars and plane trees, growing luxuriantly under the irrigation from the Canal of the Durance, long avenues of grateful shade over a white and dusty road, we drive toward our "Mecca of the mind," the home of John Stuart Mill. Our driver knows the way. When I asked him, he said: "*Oui! Oui! Monsieur Meele, Anglais. Oh! Oui!*" He stops, after a half hour's drive, in front of a gate covered over with green vines. The stone globes on the posts of the gate are almost hid with the growth. We alight with some trepidation; we ring. A servant or workman appears: "Is Mr. Mill at home?" *He is.* "Will you take this card to him?" *He does;* and while *we* wait—for I am not alone—I take a memorable inventory of the place and its embellishments. Opposite are wheat fields. The grain is just cut. The sheaves are lying about in rich disorder. Willows are bending over the gullies by the dusty way; within the enclosure are cypress-hedges, and laurel in plenty to make a shaded alley from the gate to the house. The house was not large; hardly to be called a country seat, but quite secluded, cool, and comfortable. Sauntering down the avenue, waiting for the servant, Mr. Mill himself appeared. I recognized him at once from the photograph he sent me last year. He gave us a cordial greeting, and welcomed us to the little reception room of his house. He has fair, light hair, half bald, with a slight hesitation in speech and voice, indicating feebleness of vocal apparatus, if not of body. He seems to be suffering from a nervousness of the muscles of the face. He is not, by any means, feeble in body, though he walks lame. Our driver says he is the greatest walker in or around Avignon. He starts off and never stops till he runs into the mountains, many miles off. His little room was decorated with engravings of the Virgin, etc. In the hall, in a vase, were some *herbs de plume*, a smoky, plumy curiosity of vegetation. What kind things he said, especially of America, it would be very pleasant to record. The temptation to write conversations with eminent men is very dangerous, and I refrain. He spoke of the latest book

Will News Agents please hang this up so that everybody can see BUFFALO BILL.

STREET AND SMITH'S

NEW YORK WEEKLY

A JOURNAL OF USEFUL KNOWLEDGE ROMANCE AMUSEMENT &c.

Vol. XXV | *FRANCIS S. STREET, FRANCIS S. SMITH,* } *Proprietors.* | NEW YORK, DECEMBER 23, 1869. | TERMS { *Three Dollars Per Year. Single Copy, Six Cents* | No. 6.

MENTAL PHOTOGRAPHS.

BY NED BUNTLINE.

I watch faces in the street-cars,
Ever when a ride I take,
And with still and quiet glances
Oft an earnest study make.
Here some miser mean and crusty,
There a spendthrift full of pride,
Here a widow, low whose means are,
There a matron well supplied.

Here a lawyer keen, devising
Some new quibble for the court;
There a merchant, looking over
Lists of ships just come to port—
Here "a green 'un" from the country,
Hands in pockets holding tight,
While his eyes distend in wonder
At each new, surprising sight.

Here a work-girl, neat tho' humble.
There another better dressed—
One whose eyes are calm uplifted,
One whose eyes are ne'er at rest—
Telling, oh, how plain and sadly,
Whence the silks and feathers came,
And that beauty but a curse is
When the tempter leads to shame.

Forms I see by Nature perfect—
Others padded out by art,
Faces where the rising blush shows
When the warm blood leaves the heart:
Other's red with Gouraud's liquid,
Others still, by use of wine—
Only here and there I see one
Look to me "a face divine."

Look as if its thoughts were holy,
Look as if 'twas fit to die,
Leaving earth. so full of grossness,
For a home beyond the sky.
Such a face I love to study,
In its pure and holy mien,
Only sad when realizing
They are "few and far between."

Ned Buntline's Great Story!!

Buffalo Bill.*

THE KING OF BORDER MEN!

The Wildest and Truest Story I Ever Wrote.

BY NED BUNTLINE,

(E. Z. C. JUDSON.)

CHAPTER I.

An oasis of green wood on a Kansas prairie—a bright stream shining like liquid silver in the moonlight—a log house built under the limbs of great trees—within this humble home a happy group. This is my first picture.

Look well on the leading figure in that group. You will see him but this once, yet on his sad fate hinges all the wild and fearful realities which are to follow, drawn to a very great extent, not from imagination, but from life itself.

A noble looking, white-haired man sits by a rough table, reading the Bible aloud. On stools by his feet sit two beautiful little girls, his twin daughters, not more than ten years of age, while a noble boy twelve or thirteen, stands by the back of the chair where sits the handsome, yet matronly-looking mother.

It is the hour for family prayer before retiring for the night, and Mr. Cody, the Christian as well as patriot, always remembers it in the heart of his dear home.

He closes the holy book and is about to kneel and ask Heaven to bless and protect him and his dear ones.

Hark! The sound of horses galloping with mad speed toward his house falls upon his ear.

"Is it possible there is another Indian alarm?" he says, inquiringly.

Alas, worse than the red savages are riding in hot haste toward that door.

"Hallo—the house!" is shouted loudly, as a large cavalcade of horsemen halt before the door.

"What is wanted, and who are ye?" asked the good man, as he threw wide open the door and stood upon its threshold.

"You are wanted, you black-hearted nigger-worshiper, and *I*—Colonel M'Kandlas—have come to fetch you! And there's the warrant!"

As the ruffian leader of the band shouted these words, the pistol already in his hands was raised, leveled, fired, and the father, husband and Christian, fell dead before his horror-stricken family.

"If them gals was a little older—but never mind, boys, this will be a lesson for the sneaks that come upon the Border—let's be off, for there's plenty more work to do before daylight!" continued the wretch, turning the head of his horse to ride away.

"Stop!"

It was but a single word—spoken, too, by a boy whose blue eyes shone wildly in a face as white as new-fallen snow and full as cold—spoken as he stood erect over the body of his dead father, weaponless and alone.

Yet that ruffian, aye, and all of his mad, reckless crew, stopped as if a mighty spell was laid upon them.

"*You*, Jake M'Kandlas, have murdered my father! You, base cowards, who saw him do this dark deed, spoke no word to restrain him. I am only Little Bill, his son, but as God in Heaven hears me now, I will kill every father's son of you before the beard grows on my face!"

"Hear the little rooster crow. He'll fight when his spurs grow, if we don't cut his comb now," cried the leader, with a mocking laugh, and he raised his pistol once more.

"Monster, you have robbed me of a husband; you shall not kill my boy," shrieked the mother, as she sprang forward and drew her son up to her own bosom.

"Colonel, there's a big gang of men comin' over the prairie. We'd better git," cried a scout, riding in at this moment.

"Aye! For I don't want to kill a woman, if I can help it. Column to the right, boys, and follow me."

In a minute, at full speed, the party dashed away after their leader, and the wretched family were left alone with the dead.

Frozen with terror and awe, the beautiful twins, Lillie and Lottie, crept out to the doorway, where their mother and brother knelt over the stiffening form of him who had been so good and kind—their dear father.

Oh, what a picture! Grief was still. Nor sob, nor tear, not even a moan arose. They were dumb with agony—paralyzed with a sense of utter bereavement.

They scarcely raised their heads as a noble-looking officer, in the United States uniform, rode up, followed by a body of cavalry.

"Who has done this foul murder?" he cried, as, springing from his horse, he advanced to the mournful group.

"Jake M'Kandlas, and may God, in His just vengeance, spare him for *my* hand!" said that pale boy, in a tone so low, so deep, and with a look so wildly stern, that the officer looked at him in wonder.

"Heavens, how savage!" muttered the officer, as he marked the look of ferocity which accompanied the words.

"Tell me, madam, if you please, how this occurred, and which way the murderer or murderers went. My name is Sumner, and I serve a government which will avenge, if it cannot always prevent outrage," continued the officer, addressing the poor widow.

Tears and sobs now came to her relief, and amid them the sad tale was told.

The officer detailed a small party to assist her in the last sad offices for the dead; but himself, heading the rest, dashed away over the prairie, in the hope to catch and punish the murderers. Vain hope!

Mounted on the best stock in the land—the most of it stolen—M'Kandlas and his party were already miles away, speeding to coverts known to but few, and those few of their own kind.

All this occurred in those dark days when the struggles on the border were the theme of conversation and dispute all over our land, and it was but one of a thousand, or even more, such cases—*real*, terrible, and unnatural as it may seem.

"Mother, don't cry any more," said Little Bill, when, with his two young sisters, he stood beside the new-made grave. "Tears will not bring him to life. You have these to look out for at home. You need all your strength now."

"You are not going away, William?"

"Not far, mother—not far. But there were thirty of them beside old M'Kandlas, and it may take me some time to kill them *all*."

So quietly, almost gently, did the boy speak, that one would hardly think his young mind capable of studying out, his small hand of doing such deeds as he contemplated.

Ah! little do the thoughtless know how character is formed, how destiny shapes our course, how circumstance forces us, as it were, upon a tide from which we may not turn.

In years a boy, in mind, in a preparation for a wild, desperate, eventful life, already a *man*.

Such was the hero of our story then, and now our prefatory chapter ended, we must leap over a lapse of years and spring into the full interest of our story.

BUFFALO BILL.

CHAPTER II.

ANOTHER PICTURE.

It is now 1861. The old log house has disappeared, but in the same noble grove a pretty white cottage is seen. Around it trellised bowers of vines and climbing roses, a lovely flower garden, and in the foreground not far away, are fine grain fields, broad acres, well stocked with sheep cattle and horses. Barns and haystacks all tell a story of good farming and profitable results.

On the embowered porch of this cottage sits the widow, still in her mourning garb, worn for him whose death we pictured in the first chapter, and near her stand two lovely girls—the twin sisters, Lillie and Lottie, now in the early bloom of beautiful womanhood.

They look alike, are dressed alike and are exceedingly beautiful.

I will not waste time in description—just imagine hazel eyes, dark brown hair, slightly brunette complexion, and figure of perfect symmetry, and you have them before you.

Lillie held a letter in her hand which the mounted mail carrier had left as he swept by, adding in hurried words:

"The war is begun—the rebels are fortifying posts all over the south and threaten Washington from Manassas.

Lillie's loving eyes sparkled as she read the letter, and she cried out:

"Oh, mamma, mamma! brother is coming home! He says he will be here before the sun sets on the twenty-fifth! The letter is from Fort Kearney, and has been long in coming."

"Is not to-day the twenty-fifth?" asked Lottie.

"To be sure it is, and he will be here. Our William is wild, but he never tells a falsehood. He is too proud for that! Heaven bless him!" said the mother, in a low, earnest tone.

"He is not coming alone," said Lillie. "One whom he calls "Wild Bill;" I wonder if he has become tame himself—he speaks of as a very dear friend, one who has three times saved his life. The other one he calls Dave Tutt, says he is handsome and brave, but I know he doesn't like him, for he doesn't speak of him as being good at heart and true as steel, as he does of the other.

"It lacks scarce a half hour of sunset," said the mother. Tell our good Kitty Muldoon to put on the tea-kettle and hasten preparations for supper. Tell her how many will be here and to let nothing be lacking. Thanks to my good son and that Providence, which has smiled on his efforts, our home is ready to welcome him to comfort when he comes!"

Lottie called out in her clear, ringing voice:

"Kitty Muldoon!"

"Here, miss, here fresh as a daisy and three times as natural," cried a plump, cherry-cheeked young girl, with just enough of the brogue on her tongue to tell that most likely sweet Erin's Isle was her birth place. Dressed as well as the sisters, she looked more like a companion than a servant.

"And what is it, me darling Miss Lottie, that Kitty can be after doing to plase you?"

"Mamma wants you to hurry and get supper, good Kitty, for her brother and two of his friends are coming here to-night."

"The young master and two of his friends?"

"Yes, Kitty—so make haste!"

"Are they young men, Miss Lottie."

"Yes, to be sure they are."

"And are they half as handsome as the young master and as tinder of heart as he is."

"Oh! botheration, I expect so. What is it to you, Kitty."

"Sure, miss, to me 'tis nothing. But to you and swate Miss Lillie, it may be something, since it's a beau apiece for yez, if they're but worth the looking at and spaking wid."

"Oh you good-for-nothing——"

Kitty did not wait to hear the rest of the not angry expletive, but ran laughing away to carry out the wishes of her mistress.

At the same instant Lillie, who had been glancing through an avenue which led westward in the grove, cried out:

"They are coming! They are coming!"

And three minutes later, their horses frothy and hot, three riders at full speed dashed up to the gate fronting the cottage.

"Oh brother! brother!" cried the two sisters, joyously, and all heedless of the stranger eyes now looking on them, they rushed out to embrace and kiss him.

Buffalo Bill, for this was he, had learned to hide all his feelings, but with a gentle tenderness he shook himself out of their embraces, and presenting his two friends by name, hurried on to meet the dear mother, who, with glistening eyes, waited to greet her idol and her pride.

"My good mother!" was all he said, as he pressed his manly lips to her white forehead.

"My dear son!" was all she said, but pages would not describe the reverence in his tone, or the undying love in her look.

Bill now presented his friends in more form to his mother than he had deemed it necessary in the case of his sisters.

"This, mother," said he, presenting a young man who, in form and appearance, resembled himself very closely, though he was an inch taller and hardly so muscular, "this is my mate—this is Bill Hitchcock, the best friend I ever had, or ever will have, outside of our own family. Three times has he saved me from being wiped out. Once by the Ogallalas, once when I was taken with the cramps in the ice-cold Platte, last winter—and once when old Jake M'Kandlas and his gang had a sure set on me. He and I will sink or swim in the same river, and that's a safe bet. Bill, that's my mother, and a better never trod the footstool!"

Wild Bill, with a natural grace, bent his proud head and took the hand of the lady, saying, in a tremulous tone:

"I'm glad to see you, ma'am, for I've got a good old mother that I haven't seen this many a day, and this rayther brings her up afore me!"

"And this other," continued Bill, "is Dave Tutt. He is good on a hunt, death on the reds, and as smart as bordermen are made now-a-days. Now, boys, you're all acquainted, make yourselves at home. The darkey out there has got the horses, and he'll see them all right. I know that mother will soon have a good old supper for us."

"Yes—Kitty is getting it ready as fast as she can, and I'll go and help her," said Lillie, who did not like the wild, passionate gaze which Dave Tutt seemed to fix upon her.

I don't like to use time or space for description, but as the three men now before us are *real*, not fictitious characters, I think it due to them and the reader to paint pen-portraits of the trio.

Three more perfect men in point of personal beauty never trod the earth.

Wild Bill, six feet and one inch in hight, straight as an ash, broad in shoulder, round and full in chest, slender in the waist, swelling out in muscular proportions at hips and thighs, with tapering limbs, small hands and feet, his form was a "study." His face, open and clean, had regular features, the nose slightly aquiline. His large bright eyes, now soft and tender in expression, were a bluish gray in color, shaded by lashes which often drooped over his bronzed cheek as he looked down, somewhat confused in female society, to which he was unused. His long brown hair fell in wavy masses over his shoulders, but it was fine, soft and glossy as silk.

The same picture will do for Buffalo Bill, only this difference noted. The eyes of the latter were nearer a blue in color, his hight one inch less, and his hair a little more wavy and a shade lighter.

Dave Tutt, nearly of the same hight, was equally well formed, but there the resemblance ceased.

His eyes were black as jet and deeply set, though his features were perfect, and, when he chose, his expression soft and winning. His hair, curling slightly, was black and glossy. But with all his beauty, there was a sensual expression about his mouth, so utterly different from that in the other two, and a fierce, passionate longing in his eyes, which made the two girls, instinctive in their purity, shrink from him.

Lillie, toward whom his glances seemed from the first to be directed, especially felt, and scarcely could conceal an aversion.

Now this most unpleasant picturing duty is over and I can heave ahead on my story.

Pretty Kitty Muldoon was busy setting the table in the dining-room when Buffalo Bill, unobserved, came slyly in and, bending his tall form over her shoulder, suddenly touched his lips to hers.

Bounding aside, quick as a fawn with a bullet in its heart, she wheeled and brought the palm of her fat, chubby hand into contact with his cheek with a force that made him see stars and brought unbidden tears into his laughing eyes.

"Bad 'cess to yez, Master Bill, and it's at yer ould thricks ye are!" cried Kitty, laughing at the woful look he put on. "Sure haven't ye sisters as swate as honey purtier than the wild roses to be kissin' wid, instead of slobberin' over a bit of a wild Irish girl like meself!"

"Why, Kitty, I hadn't seen you for so long, I couldn't help it. Thunder and whip-stalks, but you hit hard! My cheek tingles yet!"

"Faith then it'll make your memory better sir, but may be I did hit a bit harder than I had razon for sir, for you're a good son and brother, and I know you'd cut your right hand off before you'd harm a poor girl like me, or see harm come to her."

"That is so, Kitty, that is so, and now here's something to wear I brought from the traders. It's a new dress, and if it isn't just like those I brought for mother and sisters it is just as good and cost as much."

"Thank ye, Master Bill, thank ye for your kind thought of the poor girl that has no one to think after her but you and yours. Sure the angels sent me here when I came, and I hope they'll kape me here till I die, for it's like heaven to work for them that's so good to me! But call your friends, Master Bill, for the supper is all ready, and it's nice enough for a king and a king's people, sure!"

CHAPTER III.

There was no piano in that Kansas cottage, but two sweeter voices, alto and soprano, never thrilled a human ear than filled the sitting-room with melody as Lillie and Lottie sang song after song to please their brother and his guests after night set in.

The good mother with her knitting and Kitty already engaged in sewing on her new dress, listened while they worked. The young men smoked, for in the Far West the pipe seems *apropos* everywhere, and from time to time expressed themselves warmly in praise of the treat they were receiving.

The night was lovely. A gentle breeze rustled through the leafy trees, the moon shone out brightly, though passing clouds at times obscured it for a minute or two, the air was soft and balmy. In through the open window came the delicious perfume of rose and honeysuckle, taking away at least a part of the tobacco-taint in the atmosphere.

That sweetest of all songs, more dear to the writer than any song ever sung, "Thy bright smile haunts me still," had just been sung by the twins, when Mrs. Cody, whose face was toward the window screamed out in sudden terror, and rose to her feet with a face so deathly pale that it seemed as if she was death-stricken.

"What is it, mother?" cried Bill, springing to her side.

"The window—*he* was there!" she gasped, and then she swooned away.

"*He?* Girls look out for mother! I'll see what *he* was at the window!" cried Bill, and he sprung to the open casement.

As he did so, a bullet whistled past his ear and struck the opposite wall, while a hundred wild yells proclaimed that Indians had surrounded the house.

Wild Bill, cool and collected, instantly blew out both the lights, exclaiming:

"Darkness here and moonlight out thar! We'll be all right in a shake. Jump for your tools boys, mine's handy! Gals, lay low out o' range, we'll soon let the reds know old hands are here."

The three young men, reinforced by three negroes and one white man, the farm hands, were ready for work in less than a minute, and as the Indians did not seem disposed to make a rush for the inside of the house, crept quickly to points where from the doors and windows they

* This is the *nom de chasse* of Wm. F. Cody, the greatest hunter, guide and scout in the far West, now employed in that capacity in General Augur's Department, and a great favorite with Generals Custer and Sheridan. A man who has killed sixty-nine buffaloes in one day's hunt, has earned the name, I think.

The Jewish Times.

VOL. II. NEW YORK, FRIDAY, APRIL 1, 1870. No. 5.

CONTENTS.

☞ "DURCH KAMPF ZUM FRIEDEN!" ☜

By special agreement with the publishers of the *N. Y. Belletristisches Journal*, we will in a short time commence to publish an English translation of the Prize-novel "Durch Kampf zum Frieden," by *Ewald August König*. This novel received, among a great number of others presented by the best novelists of Germany, the price of one thousand dollars, which the publishers of the *N. Y. Belletristisches Journal* had publicly offered, and it undoubtedly is one of the best literary productions of modern novelistic works.

THE SEDER.

A VILLAGE TALE. BY DR. L. STEIN.

(From the *Freitag Abend*).

I.

THE DAY OF PREPARATION.

The house is cleaned and all leaven removed—*Pesach* may enter—his home is ready for him!

Moses Cohn, a rich man, was about kneading, in company of his son Benjamin, a pretty little boy about ten years old, the sweetest of loams, which was ever made by a loam-maker, that sort of loam, which is so well-known by Jewish children "*Charosess*." It is a *mixtum compositum* of nuts, almonds, pieces of apples, raisins, cinnamon, and other aromatic ingredients, which kneaded and well mixed with wine, form a brown mass, which symbollically represents the material, of which Pharaoh's slaves built the pyramids—a bold comparison to which only an imagination may rise, that accepts anything as plausible that tastes well.

The little Benjamin, therefore, with his little knife, which his mother had just bought for him, for the *Pesach* festival—it was very nice, and had a white bony handle with red stripes—and which he examined with great satisfaction, cut bravely into the almonds and nut kernels, and handed the pieces to his father to be used in the mixture, without taking anything therefrom, because the object for which it was used had impressed him with a sort of religious awe. Who looked at the conscientious boy could not surmise that the same boy was destined by pious custom and holy simplicity, to steal this evening of his father the "*Mazzah*," and to be rewarded and praised for it, as it was done by our old relatives—the Spartans!

However, this *Mazzah*-theft was perpetrated quite openly and honestly, and as little Benjamin asked his father, while preparing the *Charrosoth*:

"What will I get, papa, if I carry out the *Mazzah* affair this evening quite deftly?" he was answered.

"What you will get? No small affair! A quarter of a pound of almonds and raisins, and a quarter of a hundred Welsh nuts, of such size that the nuts of all the children in the village will not come up with yours in the game to-morrow, as little as once the little folks did with the sons of Anak!"

Little Benjamin saw that his father was in good humor, and with good business tact he made use of the opportunity.

"But what, my dear father, will I get, if I will translate this evening the 'Hagadah' (the ritual in use on Passover night) with Dikduk (grammatically)?"

Properly, the father was to be surprised with that, and in so far little Benjamin would have done better to keep silent about it. But the little merchant wanted to enjoy his profits it advance, and make all that could be got out of the good humor, his father was in. The news made, indeed, the desired impression on his father; he closed his left eye—what he always did when in good humor—twinkled with his right eye, and pinching the young scholar in the cheek, he said:

"You, Benjamin, my darling! you—if you can do that, I shall have you a new suit made for the second holidays, a full new suit, my boy!"

"Father, I can do it. You will see that I can."

"You!" exclaimed the man, increduously. "I will bet, your own Rebbe (teacher) can't do it, and you pretend to know it?"

"Father, I can do it."

"And of whom have you learned it?"

And little Benjamin also closed the left eye, and twinkled equally as masterly with his right one, and said, roguishly, laying his little finger on his cherry-red lips:

"Father, that stands in private *schmone-esre* (prayer composed of eighteen benedictions) that dare not be said loud!"

"Well, whisper it then."

"Not at all, father, not at all."

"I command you, however, to do it?"

"I dare not, father; I dare not."

"What! how?" exclaimed the old man; "not to obey me; not to follow my command? Tell it to me this instant; I want to know it! I want to send before night to the man, who really has taught you the *Hagadah* with *Dikduk*, a couple of bottles of the best wine I have got, so that he may also drink the 'four cups' with *Dikduk!*"

"My dear father," roguishly answered the little traitor, "he that has taught me, does need no wine to be sent to him. That he is such a learned man, you could hardly believe! He drinks wine with you, ignorant and still learned!"

"By my life!" exclaimed the father, in assumed anger; "the good-for-nothing boy wants to fool me!"

"Wait, I will show you!"

And little Benjamin, as the father, made believe that he would run after him, would have got into a bad dilemma by his partial treason, if at that moment, like a helper in need, the barber would not have made his appearance, in order to get Mr. Cohn's whiskers ready for the festival, and which had to last him for a whole week.*

Reb Koppel, that was the name of the barber, was at the same time a *Schaddchan*. "What sort of a creature is that?" Oh, a most important one in human, and, especially, in Jewish society. A *Shaddchen* makes *Shidduchim*, a Shidduch means no more nor less than, if successful, the uniting of man and woman into happy wedlock.

A *Shaddchan*, therefore, is a parcel of fate; *Reb Koppel*—whose name auspiciously sounded like *cupola*—was more; he was a sort of providence for the marriageable people for twenty miles around. He kept conscientiously a book of all the male and female candidates for marriage, and "Dr," and "Cr," played an important *rôle* in this interesting ledger. Of course, occasionally did mistakes creep in. It was namely the habit of the "*Shaddchan*" to rubricate the candidates according to their circumstances.

* Jews according to strict orthodoxy dare not use the razor, but scissors only, to cut off their whiskers.

The Jewish Times.

Five Dollars per Annum. Ten Cents per Copy.

☞ All communications to the JEWISH TIMES should be addressed to M. ELLINGER, Publisher, No. 7 Murray Street, Room No. 5, New York.

NEW YORK, FRIDAY, APRIL 1, 1870.

MOUNT SINAI HOSPITAL.

We called attention in last week's issue to a meeting, called for Sunday morning next, at half past ten o'clock, A.M., of all the Presidents of the various Jewish congregations, to consider the best means to interest the Jewish population in the successful erection of the new Hospital buildings.

The invitations extended to the various Presidents to attend a meeting which was to have been held a fortnight ago, were responded to by but four of them, let us hope at the next meeting every congregation will be represented. The Mount Sinai Hospital is, and ought to be, the property of all the Israelites in this city, and all of them should acquire this right and title by proportionate contributions; the mite of the poor weighs as heavy in the scales of charity as the pound of the rich, and there are but few Jews, who not only, will not refuse to contribute when applied to, but will cheerfully embrace the opportunity to lay their *Shekel* on the altar of charity.

It becomes, however, more especially the duty of those congregation, who have as yet done nothing toward subscribing to the Hospital fund, to make an earnest effort and put their shoulder to the wheel, as their character of honesty and sincerty is at stake. Yes! We say it boldly, the establishment and maintenance of a Jewish hospital is a concession to the piety and reverence yet entertained by a number of our co-religionists for the antiquated dietary regulations; is a sacrifice offered at the shrine of toleration and is a tribute of respect to the conscientious scruples of Israelites, who look upon the Mosaic sanitary precepts as religious ordinances. The congregations who thus far have born the heaviest burden in the support of our public charitable institutions, have for themselves discarded the observance of these laws as a religious obligation, but they have nevertheless, and most cheerfully supported a Jewish hospital, so as to provide for the sick poor in a manner agreeable to his religious conviction.

The Mount Sinai Hospital had thus far its staunchest friends and supporters in the members of the Reform congregations, and it is certainly a very moderate demand, if they ask the other congregations to come to their assistance in the establishment of an institution which is maintained in the interest of conservative Judaism. Few are so poor that they cannot contribute something to this proud monument of Jewish liberality, charity and philanthropy, and few so callous as to refuse their co-operation, if the matter is presented in the proper light; and who will forego the satisfaction of having a share, be it ever so small, in this grand temple of brotherly love?

Let those then, whose bounden duty it is to guard the moral and material interest of their congregations be on hand, to take an active part in the momentous question at issue, and there is no doubt, that with powers united, the great work must succeed to the glory of Israel and humanity!

NO PUBLIC MONEYS FOR SECTARIAN EDUCATION.

At a mass meeting of prominent, intelligent and influential citizens, held at Cooper Institute, on Wednesday evening last, the following resolutions, protesting against the appropriation of public moneys for the purposes of sectarian education, were unanimously adopted:

WHEREAS, It is a fundamental principle of our whole polity to keep Church and State entirely separate—a principal incorporated into our National Constitution, and also into every one of our State Constitutions; and

WHEREAS, It is our profound convicton that the sacred interests of religion, of conscience and of domestic peace require this separation to be strict and perpetual; and

WHEREAS, This sound principle has been violated in this State and City, and more than half a million dollars annually of the public money of this City is abstracted from the City Treasury and given to certain churches and sectarian schools; thus uniting Church and State, and making the State support the Church; and

WHEREAS, The union of Church and State, in all ages and in all countries, has led to oppression and bloodshed; and

WHEREAS, Education is essential to the intelligent exercise in a free country of the rights of citizenship, and to the preservation of our free and tolerant Government, hence the American doctrine that the State owes an education to all its children as an obligation, and not a charity, and each child has a right to demand from the State a generous and unsectarian secular education, such as shall fit him to be a citizen of a free and tolerant Republic; and

WHEREAS, In every country where the State assumes this obligation, intelligence and prosperity increase, while, on the other hand, in every country where secular education has been left to the Church, ignorance, bigotry and oppression, political and religious, continue; therefore,

Resolved, That we enter our emphatic protest against the appropriation of public money of property by City, State or National authorities for the establishment or support of sectarian schools and institutions.

Resolved, That every such appropriation is a violation of the sacred principles of religious liberty and equality before the civil law of all denominations, principles which have been the glory of our institutions in the past, and have been illustrated in the complete separation and independence of Church and State.

Resolved, That any and every religious sect which attempts to support its churches, sectarian schools or church charities by the public money raised by general taxation is, by that act, uniting Church and State, introducing sectarian bitterness into politics, and deserves the condemnation of all good citizens.

Resolved, That every such appropriation of public money is an attack upon the free non-sectarian public schools of this State, which schools now—with a liberality worthy a great Republic—offer, free of cost, to every child in the State a generous and tolerant education.

Resolved, That section 10, chapter 876 of the law of 1869, relating to the City of New York, which in fact, though not in name, appropriates nearly a quarter of a million of dollars anually to a few sectarian schools in this City, is unnecessary, was not called for by the people, is a violation of the American doctrine of equal toleration to all religious sects and public support to none, and unless

The World

VOL. XI. NO. 3319. NEW YORK: SUNDAY, SEPTEMBER 18, 1870. PRICE FIVE CENTS.

MURDER MAP OF NEW YORK.

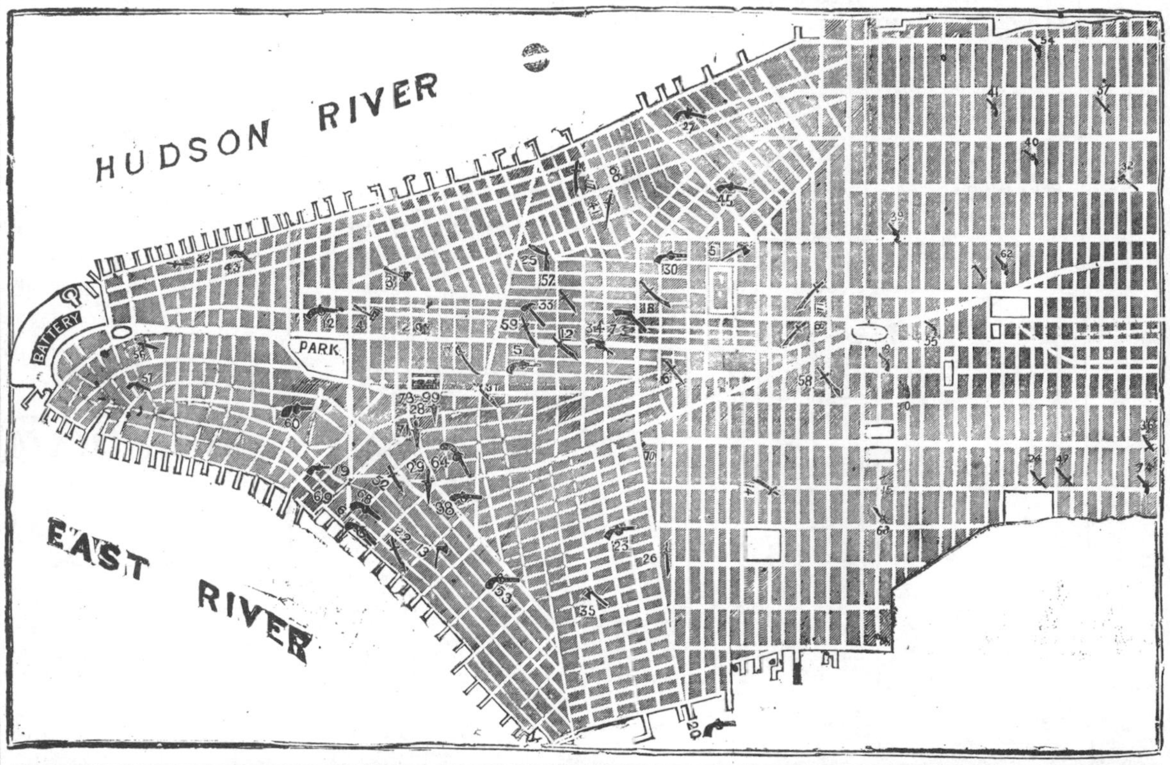

THE MURDER MAP.

The Ways and Means of Murder in the Metropolis.

A BLOOD-RED RECORD.

The Crimes of Two Generations in a Great City.

PISTOL, CLUB, AND DIRK.

Romance and Mystery, Reality and Horror.

CRIMES OF PASSION AND AVARICE,

&c. &c., &c.

If every murder ever perpetrated in New York were denoted upon a map of the size presented to-day by a mark not larger than a grain of wheat it is not too much to say that the bloody *indicia* would blot out the topography of the city. To describe those murders, further, even in the most cursory manner would fill every column in THE WORLD, and for these reasons we merely map and describe, to-day, first, those mysterious butcheries which may be called the historic murders of New York, and, second, the chief homocidal crimes which have polluted the city within the past ten years. Even within these narrow limits, it will be seen that the map is marked in seventy-eight (78) places, with the indications of death, and to this monstrous list, for the work has gone on while this article was writing, are to be added two more occurring in the past week. Seventy odd murders occurring in a single decade, for the murders prior to 1860 we note are but half dozen in number, is a fearful exhibit and the record darkens when we remember that it is only the known and premeditated butcheries we note. The "found drowned," the "disappeared," the men and women slain in what appears sudden recontres would, if the truth could be but known, dot the city much more thickly than we have already marked it, but, declining to go into conjecture, we have set down only those well ascertained cases in which name, date, locality, and circumstance can be given, the figures on the map denoting the locality and instrument.

1. THE NATHAN MURDER.

First in the list of those crimes which appal, not less by the mystery attending them than by the intrinsic awfulness, comes the murder of Mr. Benjamin Nathan at his residence, No. 12 West Twenty-third street, on the 29th of July, 1870. Mr. Nathan was by birth and family a genuine "old New Yorker," born in the city himself, as was his father, and, if we mistake not, his father before him, and had lived in the city all his life. He was in religion an Israelite, and by avocation a broker. In this calling he had amassed a very handsome fortune, said to have been one of the largest in the city, and in the enjoyment of this affluence, the practice of the charities for which his name was eminent, and in the care and society of his family, bade fair, at the opening of the summer just passed, to live prosperous and respected for many years. With the approach of warm weather he had, like most of our well to do citizens, moved out into the country with his family and only occasionally visited the city upon business. On one of these trips the tragedy connected with his name and localized on the map by the figure 1 occurred. Visiting the city on the 28th of July, 1870, on some business matters which do not appear to have ever been very satisfactorily explained, Mr. Nathan repaired at the close of the day to the residence of a relative and there spent the evening in a social way. On leaving he was desired to stay all night, the argument being that he would be more comfortable than at his own house, which was then in some disorder owing to the absence of the family and the fact that workmen were engaged in repairs, but, declining these friendly solicitations with the remark that his own house was "safe," he departed. Why he should have made this remark about the safety of his mansion does not well appear, since the subject of danger was not mentioned, and it is a curious coincidence that afterwards in the testimony on the inquest it should appear that he had referred some years before to this same topic of safety. Perhaps the theme may have been brought up in the course of conversation, but for all that is known in the evidence the remarks appear isolated, and suggest by that isolation the query whether some vague premonition may not at odd times in his life have crossed the murdered man's brain. Be that as it may, however, Mr. Nathan went to his own house and there retired to rest in a second-story front room, upon which opened a small cabinet, or library, containing an iron safe. Some time after midnight one of his sons, Mr. Washington Nathan, returned home, fastened the front door with all the usual precautions, and repaired to his own room on the third floor, pausing a moment at the door of his father's apartment, which stood open, to see if the old gentleman was awake. Stretched upon his couch the father lay asleep, and turning from the door the young man went to his own room and retired. At 1 o'clock that morning the policeman upon that beat tried the door of No. 12 West Twenty-third street, and found it fast; at some time between 2 and 3 a physician residing on the corner of Twenty-third street and Fifth avenue was aroused by his wife, who had been awakened by a sound apparently from Mr. Nathan's mansion, which just adjoined. Husband and wife then listening, heard several sounds seemingly in that mansion, which resembled the somewhat violent slamming of a door. The sounds ceasing, the couple watched for a few minutes to see if any person issued from the dwelling, and then, dismissing the subject as probably after all but trivial, repaired to rest. Between 4 and 5 the policeman, pacing his beat over again, a second time tried the door of the Nathan mansion and again found it fast At about 5:30 a newsboy saw a man ascend the "stoop," pick up a piece of paper therefrom, apparently a bank check, and walk away. At 5:45 General Frank Blair, the Democratic candidate for the Vice-Presidency in 1868, rising to close the blinds in his room on the Twenty-third street side of the Fifth Avenue Hotel in order to shut out the light which had disturbed his slumbers, saw a young man, afterwards shown to be Mr. Frederick Nathan, son of the deceased, sitting at a third-story window of Mr. Nathan's mansion, and apparently enjoying the freshness of the early morning air. Leaving the window after a moment or so, the young man was seen moving about in the room, apparently about to dress himself, and with this General Blair, closing his window blinds, saw no more. At 6 the cry of "murder" rang through the street. General Blair, the policeman, and others saw two young men in their night-clothes standing on Mr. Nathan's "stoop," blood on the socks and shirt of one of them, and both uttering that awful cry. On entering the house, outsiders found an iron bar of the shape indicated at 1 upon the map, just inside the door, clotted with blood and hair, and on ascending to the second-story front room discovered the body of Mr. Benjamin Nathan stiff and cold upon the floor, the corpse in the attitude of having fallen in a struggle, the rich carpet soaked for a yard or so in every direction about it with blood, the safe in the cabinet open, papers scattered about the floor, and the dead man's watch and diamond studs gone. When this is said, all is said of the Nathan murder that is now known. Who did the deed, why, how, when, in what manner he or they entered or how left, is a mystery deeper than broods over any murder ever known in the annals of New York. Motive, manner, and murderer are alike buried in obscurity, and all that is known is that in his own house, which he thought so safe, the rich man fell by a bloody, a horrid, a cruel death. The strange character of the instrument used in his murder, the publicity of that neighborhood in which the deed was done, and the utter powerlessness of wealth, which we are all accustomed to think so all-powerful, to prevent or detect the monstrous violence, are salient points in this Twenty-third street tragedy which have wonderfully impressed the public mind. The utmost ingenuity of the whole administration of justice, the extremest power of money, the old adage that murder will out, are all so utterly set at defiance by this deed, that it stands forth so undeniably the first in atrocity and mystery as to justify the bad pre-eminence of 1 upon the map.

2. MARY ROGERS.

By looking to the place denoted by 2 upon the map the reader will see where Mary Rogers, the Beautiful Cigar Girl of New York, whose tragic murder has been woven into fancy by Edgar A. Poe in his murder of Marie Roget, not to speak of lesser *litterateurs*, once resided. Her cigar store, and a store attended by a beautiful girl was a novelty years ago, was on the lot next above the hospital ground, going up Broadway, and now that a street has been cut through that ground the site of the store is occupied by the second large modern store from Thomas street as you face it on Broadway. Taken to Hoboken, on some promised excursion of pleasure, Mary Rogers was brutally murdered, how, or exactly in what manner, was never ascertained; but, if the reader has ever perused Poe's "Marie Roget," he might like in some account of the historical murders of New York to know just where the beautiful cigar-girl crossed the threshhold of her home the last time.

3. HELEN JEWETT.

If the reader will take the trouble to go to the spot represented on the map by the figure 3, he will find before him a fine, new, iron-front store, painted a pure white, and in strong contrast by its clean and stately appearance to the dilapidated rookery next door and the shabby, old-fashioned dwelling, swarming with negroes, which rots just opposite. This store, No. 41 Thomas street, stands on the spot where, up to a brief time since, mouldered the house in which the beautiful Helen Jewett, the very Lais of New York courtesanship, was murdered thirty-four years ago. Look on No. 42, the dwelling opposite, where the inmates sprawl about the door and dozé in the sunshine, and in the relics of old-time elegance which peer out of all its dirt and dinginess you will see that the houses of this neighborhood were even fashionable a generation since. Number 41 was in certain circles, in 1836, extremely so. It was the finest establishment of its kind in America, and Helen Jewett, its chief attraction, so amazingly lovely that it is recorded visitors to the city in those days, from all parts of the country, would repair to the house simply to gaze upon the magnificence of that beauty which had extended its reputation over the United States. Robed in the costliest of fabrics and glittering with gems, she whose life was destined to have so terrible an ending in the scene of her triumphs, would sweep through the parlors like a Paphian queen; and there are yet living old New Yorkers who recall from the memories of their "hot youth" the tribute of admiration her appearance on these occasions would produce. Just 23, of a form that was voluptuousness itself, with a skin of silver whiteness, and an eye like melting fire, Helen Jewett might at this time have realized the antique idea of Venus, and in her history could well approve herself from her youth up a veritable devotee of desire. Her real name was Dorcas Dyon, born at Augusta, Maine, in June, 1813, of Welsh parents who had but recently emigrated to the United States. At *eleven* years of age she became too intimate with a lad named Sumner, and soon fell. Sumner was at once sent to sea, and, the secret of his disappearance being unknown, Helen was sent to school and elegantly educated by a wealthy old gentleman of the neighborhood who marked the sprightliness of the poor little Welsh girl. Thus educated and befriended for a respectable life, it seemed as if years of usefulness were opening before little Dorcas, when one day in walking by a grove a stalwart form in sailor's garb stepped out. It was Sumner, and that meeting sealed the girl's fate. Her parents were dead, her patron cast her forth as lost, and her lover having been summoned away by his calling, Helen, as she is henceforth to be known, was forced to face the world. For such beauty it has few frowns, and it was not long before a very wealthy "protector" in Portland became so infatuated with his purchase that he proposed marriage. At this moment a notice of the arrival of Sumner's ship fell under Helen's eye. She wrote to him, they met, the meeting was discovered by her would-be husband, and once more the girl was on the world. It complicated her misfortune that just here Sumner died. His sea life had given him consumption, and, after lingering awhile, he expired in Helen's arms. To the last she never forgot him, and a strange tenderness is recorded in her accent and demeanor whenever an allusion to her early life brought up the memory of the Maine sailor boy. Portland, on her lover's death, becoming insupportable, Helen fled to Boston, and must have arrived there in a state bordering on insanity. She was found fainting in the street by some negroes, who carried her to their hovel and robbed her of her money, jewelry, and clothes. That night a descent was made upon the den for some prior thefts of its inmates, and Helen along with the blacks was brought into the police court. Here a "protector" stood ready immediately on her discharge, and once more the girl entered on a life of shame which bade fair to end as it had in Portland—in honorable marriage. All was arranged between herself and a wealthy broker, when an anonymous note to the prospective husband revealed the past career of his intended wife. Helen then bent her course toward New York, and arrived here when about nineteen. The "town" was taken by storm. The equipment of a queen was put at this modern Nell Gwynn's service, and clad in magnificent raiment, and carrying a letter in her hand—always carrying a letter—the beautiful Helen anticipated on every fine day a generation since the modern song of "Walking down Broadway." One day in these rambles Sumner's successor came. Richard P. Robinson, a youth of but some nineteen, and, though born in the land of steady habits, with the fire of a dozen tropics in his veins, met the "Queen of the Pave," as the old-fashioned slang of the day had it; and, being as handsome for a man as Helen was for a woman, or perhaps (who knows?) resembling Sumner, caught the royal eye. Helen, whose Welsh blood was not the only point in which she resembled Nell Gwynn, instantly conceived for the dashing stripling that affection which a life of simulated passion does not always destroy in a woman of her class. Nell Gwynn is reported to have remained true to her royal lover, the second Charles, to the last, an affection remembered by him on his death-bed in almost his last petition—"Don't let poor Nelly starve;" and certainly Helen Jewett seems to have truly loved "Frank Rivers," as Robinson in her society was known. Out of the very intensity of this feeling it is commonly supposed there arose that tragedy which marks an instrument of death at figure 3 upon our map to-day. Luxuriant as were the charms proffered his acceptance, "Frank" tired of his impetuous beauty. There came a day when virtue asserted its right supremacy over him, as at some time it does over even the most dissolute; when he thought it better to have one chaste woman for his own than all the harlots of Paphos. He desired to marry a virtuous lady, and, as the first step, began that process of "breaking off" which has avenged so many illicit connections on those who have lewdly formed them. Lost in everything else, Helen could not endure to be bankrupt in her love too. Crimination and recrimination followed, and there is a dim intimation of a threat on Helen's part that if Robinson withdrew from her society she would avenge the slight by exposing his acquaintance with her to the young lady he sought to marry. The only date assigned to anything of this kind, however, was November, 1835, and it was not until the 10th of April, 1836, that Helen Jewett was murdered. On Saturday night, the 9th of April, 1836, Helen said she expected "Frank Rivers," there being two persons of that name who visited the house; between 9 and 9:30 there came a man to the door with his face muffled in one of the Spanish cloaks then much worn, and this man the keeper of the bagnio swore was Robinson; Helen accosted him as "Frank," and, still without removing his cloak, the man ascended with her to her room. At eleven the landlady was summoned to bring wine, and through the half-opened door, as she handed the salver in, discerned a man, whose face she could not see, lying on the bed. Helen came to receive the wine, and that was the last ever seen of her alive. At two, Maria Stevens, whose apartment was near Helen's, and who, as the record states, "was kept wakeful by disturbances which to her were not uncommon," heard in Helen's room a deep, sullen blow, which seemed to shudder along the floor. Prompted by that indefinable instinct which so often develops itself in cases of murder, Maria left her room, and stepping across the corridor, listened at Helen's door. Two or three broken sobs, "which," to quote from the record again, "her strange experience told her might proceed from a very ordinary cause," was all she heard, and thinking nothing further of the matter she retired to her own room. Presently the sound of Helen's door gently opening and then softly closing again claimed her attention, and, running to her own door, she saw, as she opened it, a man wrapped in a loose cloak gently making his way down stairs. In one hand, hidden under his cloak, he appeared to have some object, and in the other, which was free, carried the glass lamp ordinarily used in Helen's room. Seeing this much, Maria started to see more, but as she was about to follow the man, the person who was occupying her room that night reached forth his hand and plucked her in, with the order to cease her folly and close the door. This careless demeanor—for the visitor with her had heard the blow, and thus had as much occasion for suspicion as herself—allayed her anxiety, and she soon fell asleep. The man she had seen was, of course, the murderer of Helen Jewett, but Maria had not seen his face, and, while she always avowed that she knew the murderer, is not known to have ever declared it to have been Robinson. Her death before the trial left her testimony unavailable, and for the further circumstances of the case we must rely upon the evidence of others who were asleep at the time the deed was done. About 3 o'clock the keeper of the house was roused to let "her man" in, and after opening the front door, was surprised to find Helen Jewett's lamp burning on the parlor table, and the back door of the house open. Supposing some one in the yard, she called out, but receiving no answer, ascended with the lamp to Helen's room. The door at once opened, and at that moment a stifling volume of smoke rushed forth in the woman's face. Rushing over to Maria Stevens's room, she beat wildly on the door, and aroused the house with her screams. Maria instantly rushed forth, and in conjunction with the landlady, attempted to enter Helen's room. Again and again the dense, black, pungent smoke drove them away, but as the draught fanned the fire into brightness they were enabled finally to reach the bed. Helen lay dead upon it, a clean, deadly cut in the centre of her forehead from the part in the hair straight down between the eyes, her body bathed in blood, and the bedding smoking and smouldering beneath her, too thoroughly saturated in gore to blaze. Search was at once given, and in the back yard, jutting on Hudson street, was found a stool close to the fence, as if one had raised himself up on it to surmount the barrier. Not far off was found a cloak, and close to that again a hatchet. This cloak was sworn to as belonging to Robinson, and the hatchet was identified by the porter of the store in which Robinson was employed as belonging there, and one which he had missed the day before the murder. Further than this was the evidence of the women in the house that Robinson was certainly the man who was admitted at nine or half-past, and had retired to Helen's room; and with so much the case against Robinson virtually stands. For him, are the facts that when the police entered the house an unknown man who afterwards escaped was found near the door of Helen's room; that the hatchet was covered with dew, as if it had lain where it was found for hours, and that it had no blood upon it; that the cloak was sworn to by the women of the house; that ill-feeling, produced by rivalry and jealousy, existed toward Helen on the part of those women; and finally that the keeper of a grocery store in Liberty street swore most positively that Robinson was in his store smoking from nine till after ten on the night of the murder, the hours between which he was declared by the women of the bagnio to have entered that house. The result of the trial was a verdict of not guilty; and on his release Robinson, who was looked on with grave suspicion in the community, went to Texas, where he married, became the father of a large family, and some years since died. With some not inconsiderable reason to believe him guilty, the case yet remains a mystery, and if the Nathan tragedy be the most awful, the Helen Jewett murder is the most romantic in the history of New York crime. Novels have been written upon it, one in particular by George W. Matsell, formerly Chief of Police in this city; and on the death, but a few days since, of the venerable Joseph Hoxie, Robinson's old employer, the number of reminiscences evoked of the scene in which a generation since he played a part, amply testify to that strong hold which the murder at No. 41 Thomas street has maintained on the public imagination for thirty-four years. Impure as she was, the strong affections of the unfortunate Helen, her amiable disposition, her surpassing beauty, her accomplishments, her youth, and her terrible ending seem to have made an impression upon her day which has extended down to this a commiseration and allowance that pardon in her fate the faults of the poor Welsh orphan girl.

4. THE COLT MURDER.

Few who have ever entered the up-stairs saloon of Delmonico's restaurant at the corner of Broadway and Chambers street, and seated themselves at the table next the third window from Broadway, on the Chambers street side, would care to be told that they had washed down the *entrees* with claret on the very spot where, at 3:15 in the afternoon of Friday, September the 17th, 1841, murder poured out a redder fluid than any wine. Then and there Samuel Adams was murdered by John C. Colt with such circumstances attending the deed as make it most memorable in that sanguinary book, a few pages of which this article unfolds. John C. Colt, who was born in Hartford, Conn., in 1809, occupied a room on the second floor of the granite building still standing on the northwest corner of Chambers street and Broadway as a teacher of book-keeping, and to this room Samuel Adams, a printer, came on the day above named to urge payment of a bill for publishing a manual of book-keeping some time prior printed by him for Colt. What occurred will be first told from outside. Next to Colt's room, the floor, now thrown into one saloon, then being subdivided into separate apartments, was the writing academy of A. H. Wheeler, a pair of folding doors, ordinarily kept locked, being between the two rooms. At 3:15 on the 17th of September, 1841, Mr. Wheeler and one of his pupils, then busy in the academy, heard from Colt's room a sharp, clashing sound, resembling the striking of foils, which lasted but a moment, and was succeeded by a violent fall. "What's that!" was the exclamation, the old instinct which seems ever to betray murder in its sounds at once awaking. Mr. Wheeler went to Colt's door and listened. All was still. He then tried to look through the keyhole, but the key was out and the slide down. Running his pen through he pushed this to one side, and, in about the centre of the room, saw a man in his shirt sleeves bending down over something and slowly moving his arms as one does in sawing. For ten minutes this continued, the arms sawing, sawing the air, and then the former rose, placed something, what exactly could not be seen, on the table, and returned to the bending posture and the sawing motion. Returning to his own room, the professor found his pupil had listened intently at the folding doors, but heard nothing save one soft sound like a footstep gently slide over the floor. The police were sent for, but in some way failed to appear, and after a while the professor and his pupil went home, leaving in the academy a young man who was temporarily out of a room, having hired Colt's apartment, to have been delivered up that day by Colt, but withheld on the plea of his not being quite ready to move. This young man heard some one come out of the room at dark, lock the door and go away, shortly after returning, unlocking the door and then locking it again. Then came a sound of scrubbing close to the folding door, interspersed with a sound of rinsing a cloth in water. Shortly after the young man fell asleep and slept until 6 the next morning, when he was waked by the sound of nailing up a box in Colt's room. On going to breakfast he perceived a box at the head of the stairs, and on returning the box was gone. Samuel Adams was shortly after missed. Colt, among others, was asked if he had seen him, but said that he had not, expressed surprise at his disappearance, and even called one day at his place of business to ascertain if he had been heard from. Finally suspicion became so strong that an advertisement was issued for any cartman to come forward who might have carried a box from the corner of Chambers street and Broadway on the morning of the 18th of September, 1841. Early in the day a cartman waited on the authorities to say Mr. Colt had engaged him at that time, and that he had carried a box for him to the ship Kalamazoo. The cargo of the vessel was at once discharged, a vile stench before the unlading was half completed warning the officers of the certainty of their search, and almost at the bottom of the cargo the box described by the cartman was found. In it was a decomposing human body, clad only in a shirt, and tied up into small compass by a rope fastened around the neck and thence down about the legs, forcing the knees up upon the trunk and the head down on the chest. The face could not be recognized, but a ring upon the hand was sworn to as belonging to Samuel Adams, and from the testimony of Adams's shoemaker, who measured his foot, and that of his father-in-law, who testified to some private marks on the body, it was sufficiently established that the missing man was found. The forehead and right side of the head were beaten in, and a small hole was found above and behind the left ear. The box was identified as one that had long stood in Colt's room. Colt was at once arrested, and, after some delay, a most exciting trial began, the accused displaying the utmost resolution, except at one awful moment when he fairly broke down. Unknown to him the head was introduced into court, wrapped in a cloth, which one of the testifying physicians held in his lap. It having been decided it was evidence the physician rose from the table where he had been sitting near the prisoner, threw off the cloth, and taking a bloody hatchet which had been found in Colt's sleeping apartment, laid the weapon as close as a bullet in its mould in every gash and orifice the gaping skull contained. Colt hid his face in his hands. The verdict was guilty, and the 18th of November fixed as the day of execution. At 12 o'clock noon, the execution being fixed for 4 P. M., Colt was married to Caroline Henshaw, his mistress, whose testimony on the trial, as she described how he came home to her on the night of the murder, was listened to with absorbing interest, and, as the two were left together for a short time after the ceremony, it became a general impression she supplied the doomed man with a small clasp-knife that had been hidden in her luxuriant hair. However that may be, after she had gone Colt was left to himself to await the fatal hour, and when, shortly before the time, the officers went to lead him forth, he was found dead, the knife sticking in his heart. He had cut a small round hole in his clothes just over the heart, placed the point of the weapon upon it with one hand and with the other driven the steel in with such force that the handle of the knife was broken, though the blade went true. Just as the suicide was discovered, the Tombs was found to be on fire, and out of the confusion of the two occurrences grew a vulgar tradition that John C. Colt was spirited away and some dead body left for appearance sake in his cell. Of the suicide, however, there is as little doubt as the murder; and in a plea to the jury Colt confessed that he had killed Adams, claiming it done in the heat of blood, and that the concealment was an afterthought. Of Adams, the story is told that the night previous to his murder his wife dreamed that she saw him killed as it afterwards happened, and begged him not go to out that day; and, as a further reminiscence, it is reported in the journals of the time that a strange portent, in the shape of a bright star in the firmament at noonday, was visible on the day of the suicide.

5. THE LUTENER MURDER.

About ten o'clock on the morning of Tuesday, the 10th of January, 1854, one of those pushing, driving, "live" business men who give New York its energy was scudding along down town on the east side of Broadway, and had just stepped up from the cross-walk upon the curb on Grand street, when a sound which he took for a pistol shot rang in his ears. For an instant he stopped, the instinct of murder, so to speak, asserting itself, and looked eagerly around, but on every side the street was as it always is, and only remembering that he had an engagement at bank, that day, that business men must be prompt, and that he would be behind time if he delayed at what, after all, was probably nothing, he struck into that shuffling gallop of a walk only to be seen in its perfection when the business men of New York come down town in the morning, and would perhaps never have remembered the shot, and the pause it caused him, had it not been brought to his attention by the announcement that a murder had been committed that morning at No. 458 Broadway. Now 458 Broadway conveyed no very distinct impression, but when it appeared that that number was at the corner of Grand, and that just there he had heard the sound, as he hurried by at 10, the fact rose into importance and was made known. So far as has ever appeared no living soul ever heard that shot save the belated business man, the murderess, and the murdered, if, indeed, it be the case that any man hears that shot which instantly deprives him of life. On the second floor of No. 458, Doctor William R. T. Lutener had his office, and on this Tuesday morning, in the winter of 1854, came down from his residence as usual, entered his office at night, and after a pleasant word to the woman who kept the rooms in order, drew up his chair facing the window, so as to have his back to the door, and in that attitude opened the morning paper and began to read. Having occasion to leave the building the charwoman who had retired from the room when the doctor entered, started on her visit at 9:30 and remained absent for about an hour. At 10, as stated above, the business man heard a shot in passing just under the windows of the office, and at 10:30, when the old woman dropped in the room to see if her employer wanted anything, a terrific scream rang through the building. Before her affrighted eyes was the doctor dead upon the floor, prone upon his face, his hand tenaciously clutching the paper he had been reading, and a bullet hole in the back of his head. He had been shot from behind as he sat reading the paper within thirty minutes of the time the old woman left the building, and he dropped forward dead upon the floor. Shot by whom? The only answer is that this is one of the mysterious murders of New York. Several persons passing up and down the stairs, the building being full of offices, remembered seeing a woman thickly veiled pass into that particular door and out again almost instantly, but beyond this nothing was ever known. Differences having been shown to have existed between Dr. Lutener and a Mr. and Mrs. Hays, living near his residence, suspicion fell on Mrs. Hays, but the murder was, beyond all doubt, shown to have been committed between 9 and 10, and just as fully beyond doubt did Mrs. Hays show by reputable witnesses, that during that time she was transacting some business in Wall street. With this proof, the only thing that seemed a clue, vanished, and the mystery of the murder still remains.

6. THE BURDELL MURDER.

One morning in the winter of 1856-7 a little boy employed by Dr. Harvey Burdell, of No. 31 Bond street, to wait upon him went to the Doctor's door and attempted to enter. Something lay against the door on the inside and prevented his pushing it open at first, and upon a second effort, pushing it more forcibly, the lad saw blood. He gave the alarm instantly, and Dr. Harvey Burdell's body was found lifeless in the room, stabbed with several deep, mortal thrusts, and pricked, one can hardly use an an apter term, by over a score of little digs or dabs from a knife or poniard point. There was blood all about the room, in one place a tremendous splash upon the wall, as the knife had evidently struck an artery; blood upon the door and along the sides of the room, as the doctor, bleeding profusely, had been forced up against them; blood upon the stairs outside, and gory finger marks as ensanguined hands had groped down as far as the basement of the dwelling. A chair by a secretary was overturned, and papers strewn about the desk—a counterpart so far of the Nathan murder—and all the internal evidence was that the doctor had been first struck from behind as he sat at his desk; had then risen and fought all around the room until he fell. Being a powerful man, it was argued at the time that his adversary who had grappled with and stabbed him again and again must have been a man of great strength, even conceding that the first blow partly disabled his victim, and yet the many little spiteful stabs, evidently inflicted by a weak, uncertain hand, came in to complicate the question of who did the deed. In the house, which belonged to Dr. Burdell, lived a widow named Cunningham with two daughters, and a young man named Snodgrass and an older man, Eckel, who boarded with Mrs. Cunningham. From certain developments brought out on the inquest an extreme intimacy between Eckel and Mrs. Cunningham was evidenced, and upon this and the further fact that there were some troubles, pecuniary and other, between Mrs. Cunningham and Dr. Burdell, public opinion soon settled down to the conviction that Eckel did the fatal stabbing, and Mrs. Cunningham, either during the struggle or after its termination, had vented her animosity by venomous—even if futile—"pokes" with a poniard. As a further circumstance, a cobbler swore that on the night of the murder he stopped on the "stoop" of Dr. Burdell's house to tie his shoe, and that a man, whom he identified as Eckel, came to the front door and, partly opening it, roughly ordered him away. But it all came to nothing. The man was dead—murdered—and that was the end of it. What else is to be said of this butchery being more in the nature of circumstance than bearing directly on the main points, who? why? whither? Bloody and awful as the case was, it had yet its titillating side, morsels of the inner life of the house, salacious, dramatic, and humorous, which for days were eagerly devoured by the public. With Eckel as the heavy villain and Mrs. Cunningham as a managing mamma of a Borgia type, the young man Snodgrass was the light comedian, and the fair Augusta Cunningham the walking lady. While the elders, as the public believed, plotted the deed even down to drugging some punch for the rest of the household, that they might sleep soundly. Snodgrass was pictured forth as now playing "Villikins and his Dinah" upon his banjo, and now reading Byron to the languishing beauty, nothing loth. When the law gave up "beat," Snodgrass and his banjo went to California, Eckel drifted out into business somewhere in the city, and Augusta and Mrs. Cunningham for a time disappeared. But a few months, however, and the whole tragedy was brought into view again. Claiming to have been married to Doctor Burdell, and indeed that she was married at the time claimed to *some* man was sufficiently proven, Mrs. Cunningham announced herself as the mother of a child by the murdered man, and laid claim to his property. The child, however, was proven surreptitious, and then Mrs. C. again disappeared, though up to within a recent date occasionally noticed in the papers as turning up at such and such a place. Eckels figured within a year or so in a prosecution for defrauding the revenue in the matter of a distillery in which he was interested, and not long since died, passing away, it is said, after he had declared that there was something on his mind which he wished and was just about to reveal.

7. THE BURKE MURDER.

On the southeast corner of Broadway and White street stands a store, No. 378, on the second floor of which, some two years and a half after the murder of Dr. Lutener on the second floor of another large building likewise on a southeast corner—Broadway and Grand street—occurred the murder of Bartholomew Burke. This man was the porter of a tailoring establishment carried on some fourteen years since at 378 Broadway, and of such good habits that when on the morning of the 18th of July, 1856, a clerk in the establishment arrived at his place of business, he was surprised to find the store still closed. While wondering at this circumstance as something that had never occurred before in several years, the clerk's eye fell

Continued on Eighth Page.

THE MURDER MAP.

Continued from First Page.

on a blood spot on the door knob, and with that instinct which tells of murder in everything was at once struck with such consternation that he rushed out in the street for the police. The door was broken open and Burke was found dead upon the floor, run through and through the body by a short, sharp-edged sword which lay beside him, where the murderer had dropped it when it had done its work. Also, beside the body, lay a huge pair of shears with which Burke had evidently fought though vainly for his life. Over the guard of the clumsy weapon the keen sword had passed, and been thrust up to the very hilt in the unfortunate porter's body. Where it came from and who had used it were never discovered. No noise had been heard either by the family living above the room in which the murder occurred, or any person passing in the street below. All that was made clear was that Burke had been in a saloon in the basement of the building that night, and there drank with an unknown man whom he brought in and with whom he passed out, first buying a pot of beer to carry with him; that two men were seen afterwards at one of the windows of the room with two beer-mugs on the sill before them; and that within a hundred feet of the door of the building a citizen hurrying by late that night met a man whose face he did not notice, and of whom he only remarked, first, that he was whistling a popular air, and, second, that he had a bandaged hand. As blood was found on the outer knob of the door, and some drops upon the stairs to about half way down, it was surmised that this whistler with the bandaged hand was the murderer; that he had been cut in the hand by Burke, in his defence, with the shears, and, remembering, when half way down the stairs his hand was dripping witnesses put a bandage upon it and passed out. Inside the room, which, as mentioned, was a tailor's store, nothing belonging to the proprietor was missing, and, though the murdered man's trunk had evidently been searched, there was nothing going to show that anything had been removed. A wash-basin in one corner was found full of bloodied water where the murderer had washed his hands, and this was all. Burke had a few hundred dollars in the bank, as was afterwards discovered, but no attempt was made after the murder to draw it out. From the murdered man's quiet habits, and the fact that his past life was neither mentioned by himself nor made known by others, the case was left even without the chance of finding a clue from antecedents, and as it was found a mystery, so remains.

8. THE ROGERS MURDER.

Early on the morning of December 31, 1868, Charles M. Rogers, an elderly gentleman, living at No. 42 East Twelfth street, stepped out upon the sidewalk in front of his residence to remove the snow. Two ruffianly looking fellows were just then passing, and taking off his overcoat and handing it to his companion, the shorter of the two advanced toward Mr. Rogers, the taller running across the street and calling out from that sidewalk, "Jim, don't do it." Disregarding this advice, the desperado snatched Mr. Rogers's watch and pocket-book, dropped them in his coat pocket, and started to run. The old gentleman seizing upon him, tore from him in the struggle that side of the sack coat containing the pocket with his property, and in that instant the ruffian plunged a huge knife into his bowels. The old man fell upon the instant, the ruffians at once fled, and that is all that is certainly known of that. In the pocket torn away from the murderer, was an empty envelope with this writing, "James Logan, N. Y. Cythy—this will be handed ye by Tom," and at first this was thought a clue. James Logan No. 1 and James Logan No. 2, with divers Toms and Jims, supposed to be the tall fellow, were arrested and much talked about, but the whole thing came to naught. It was a mystery when Mr. Rogers was found bleeding on the snow and so remains.

9. 10. WALTON AND MATTHEWS.

Coming to the murders in this city from 1860 to 1870, the first that merit special attention are two by the same hands within a few minutes of one another, on the night of Saturday, the 30th of June, 1860. John Walton and Thomas Pascal, his nephew, were walking along Eighteenth street, near Irving place, and without the least indication of such a purpose, a passer by shot Mr. Walton through the head and ran. Mr. Pascal, assisted by a gentleman named John W. Matthews, immediately pursued the murderer into Irving place, and opposite No. 47 in that street he turned upon them—being hard pressed—and shot Mr. Matthews dead. After two years delay Charles Jeffrards was convicted, and while under sentence of death in the penitentiary, was himself murdered by a fellow-convict.

11. MRS. SHANCKS.

A little after 8 A. M. on Friday morning, December 7, 1860, Mrs. Sarah Shancks, residing at No. 22 East Twelfth street, sent her servant out for breakfast, and shortly after the girl's return her mistress was found dead upon the floor, her head smashed in, apparently with various instrumentalities, a broken chair and vase, and several broken bottles lying about, and her throat cut with the knife brought in with her breakfast. The crime was supposed to have been committed by a worthless fellow who had been disappointed in marrying her, no doubt with intent she should support him out of her little thread and needle store.

12. CROGEN.

Thomas F. Crogen, porter at the St. Nicholas, was stabbed in front of that hotel on Monday morning, November 11, 1861. No execution of murderer.

13. MARY ANN WEBER.

On the next day, November 12, 1861, Mary Ann Weber was murdered at No. 40 Hamilton street with an axe by her husband.

14. HOFFMAN.

Samuel Hoffman was murdered before his wife's eyes at No. 141 First avenue, on the 14th of November, 1861, by Dr. Moses Lowenberg, who stabbed him with a knife, and was sentenced, in 1862, to be hanged, but never executed.

15. M'GILL.

On Sunday, December 8, 1861, Thomas Alexander McGill, living at No. 292 First avenue, murdered his mother by throwing her out of the window, whereby she was dashed to pieces, *apparently* by accident, on the stones below. The atrocious nature of this deed suggesting insanity, that amiable plea prevailed, and the matricide was sent to the Insane Asylum, to be in due time cured and kill some more.

16. LEVY.

Bernard Levy was found murdered—his throat cut from ear to ear—on Saturday morning, December 14, 1861, at 146 Canal street, in his store, in which he slept, with a large case knife close to the body and covered with blood. Supposed to have been done by some bravo at the instance of a loose woman, Louisa Briedsback, whom Levy had discarded for her incessant drain upon his purse, but nothing certainly known, save the gaping throat.

17. MORTON.

Thomas Morton was stabbed to death on Christmas night, 1861, at the corner of Greenwich and King streets; supposed to have been by a particular friend. No execution.

18. FOWLER.

Andrew J. Fowler was murdered at 80 West Houston street, on Wednesday, January 2, 1862, some unknown signalizing the good resolutions of the new year by cutting a man's jugular vein.

19. RYAN.

Thomas Ryan was murdered on New Year's night, 1862, at 81 James street, by Frederick Lowe.

20. LEWIS.

Bernard Lewis, a scene painter at Laura Keene's, drew some $700 savings from the bank, went upon a spree, beginning May 20, 1862, and was missing from that time till June 4, when he was found in the water at the foot of Houston street with a bullet hole between the eyes.

21. REAL.

John C. Real—not the John Real who was hanged August 5, 1870, and then canonized—was called on at 3 P. M. on the 13th of June, 1862, at his place of business, the third floor of No. 256 Broadway, by Mary Stewart, who, claiming to be his wife, called him out upon the landing and shot him with a pistol she had bought that morning for the purpose. It is a delicate refinement in this case that the ball was not so large as a pea, and yet went so near through him that the doctors chipped it out of the opposite side to its entrance with almost a lancet scratch.

22. WAGNER.

John Wagner was murdered on Monday, the 4th of August, 1862, on the corner of Catharine and Cherry streets, by being stabbed in the stomach by a knife in the hands of Joseph Barrow.

23. JOSEPHINE WEILER.

Ernestine Josephine Weiler was shot through the heart with a revolver ball at No. 154 Essex street on the 26th of August, 1862, by her husband, Jacob Weiler, who was sentenced to the penitentiary for life, is now there, and will remain there till the next soft-hearted Governor pardons the "poor fellow" out.

24. GALLAGHER.

Martin Gallagher was murdered on the 31st of August, 1862, in First avenue, near Twenty-sixth street, by William McFaden, who thrust a long, narrow, keen butcher knife with such tremendous force that it took the strength of two men to draw it out.

25. THOMPSON.

Amanda Thompson cut her husband's throat with his own razor as he slept, severing carotid and jugular, and rejoiced in the deed. Done at 41 Sullivan street, on the 29th of September, 1862.

26. DONNELY.

John Donnely was murdered by an unknown negro, who cut his lungs to pieces with a dirk at 1 A. M., on the 5th of August, 1862, at the corner of Avenue B and Houston street.

27. WILLIAMS.

Henry L. Williams, police officer, was murdered by a revolver shot in the groin, given by Edward McCormick, in front of 142 Charles street, on the 13th of October, 1862.

28. KANE.

John Kane was on Saturday, December 12, 1862, murdered by a negro named Harkless Little, at 164 Leonard street, by being stabbed in so scientific a manner that the physicians reported three quarts of clotted blood in the cavity of the thorax.

29. UNKNOWN.

On Friday night, January 1, 1864, one unknown man stabbed another to the heart with a dagger in Chatham square, and then made his escape. The body was never identified.

30. MARY ANN SHIPLEY

was murdered January 25, 1864, at 217 Sullivan street, with a revolver, by a negro named Eli Brown.

31. FITZPATRICK.

Michael Fitzpatrick was murdered at the corner of White and Elm streets, on the 2d of February, 1864, by Richard Fairbanks. Both mere lads; the motive, revenge; the weapon, a sharp shoe-knife.

32. HUNTER.

On the 19th of February, 1864, at 339 Seventh avenue, Edward Hunter murdered his wife with a hatchet, his little son George witnessing the deed and saying afterwards his father waked him at 10 that night by beating his mother "with a shoe." When convicted, Hunter confessed and justified the deed. Sentenced for life—*i. e.*, till the next "good" Governor.

33. JAMES.

Mary Ann James was hammered to death on the 20th of February, 1864, at 61 Grand street, by one unknown, but supposed to have been her paramour, Krell.

34. MULDOON.

John Muldoon was murdered at No. 83½ Mercer street, on Sunday, the 12th of June, 1864; pistolled by one unknown.

35. MARY WAGNER.

Mary Wagner was murdered on the 21st of July, 1865, at No. 156 Broome street, by her husband, George Wagner, who drove the hatchet so utterly into her head that even the back part of the weapon became imbedded in her skull.

36. SMITH.

James Smith, throat cut, July 25, 1865, in East Thirty-second street, near Second avenue.

37. VAN DEREN.

Joseph Van Deren was murdered on the 29th of July, 1865, at No. 40 Beaver street, by a shot in the heart, administered by James F. Oram.

38. TRISTAM.

"Did anyone ever hear or know," says Mr. Walter Shandy, "of anyone of the name of Tristram doing any good?" On the 8th of August, 1865, at No. 34 East Broadway, Richard Tristram murdered his brother Thomas by shooting him through the lungs into the spinal column.

39. WALKER.

On Tuesday, the 15th of August, 1865, Thomas Walker, police officer, was murdered at 130 West Seventeenth street by John Ward, who pistolled him as he came up at a decoy cry of distress. Ward sentenced for life, *ut supra*.

40. NEWLET.

Officer John Newlet, in the same squad with above, was murdered in West Twenty-fifth street on the 7th of November, 1864, by one unknown, who blew his brains out and walked off into mystery.

41. RAMMING.

On the 15th of October John Ramming was murdered at No. 372 Hudson street by one unknown, who jammed a dirk knife into his eye and thence upward into the brain.

42. DUNLAP.

Patrick Dunlap by Edward Johnson, January 12, 1866, at 150 Washington street, with a pocket-knife.

43. CARLL.

William Carll was murdered by a gang at 66 Cortlandt street, on Wednesday, February 7, 1866, by shooting.

44. POLLOCK.

On Saturday, May 26, 1866, Richard Pollock was murdered with the knife at 166 East Fourth street by William McCormick.

45. FITZMEYER.

Frederick Fitzmeyer, just arrived from Europe, stepped out to breathe the strange air at No. 51 Frankfort street, between 1 and 2 A. M. on Tuesday, September 11, 1866, and was murdered by a ball behind the left ear, why or by whom unknown.

46. FURNARI.

Petro Furnari was murdered by a shot through the body at 145 Elm street on the 22d of September, 1866, by Alessandro A. Urania, who put a pistol to his head as the officer reached out his hand to arrest him, and blew out his own brains.

47. WESTCOTT.

On the night of the 3d of November, 1866, Walter Westcott was murdered at 443 First avenue, by one unknown, who slashed him across the stomach until his bowels fell out.

48. MILLER.

Charles Miller, by Charles Jones, negro, at No. 46 Thompson street, December 28, 1866, with a knife thrust in the heart.

49. VANDERMARK.

Sophia Vandermark was murdered on the 5th of January, 1867, at No. 140 Ninth avenue, by Thomas M. Burke, who shot her dead and then blew out his own brains.

50. KLEMAN.

Regina Kleman murdered her brother, Louis Kleman, by splitting his head open with a hatchet, at No. 52 Sixth avenue, on the 29th of January, 1867.

51. HEINRICH.

Jacob Heinrich by William Snobell, with a knife, on Monday, February 18, 1867, at No. 225 West Twenty-eighth street.

52. WEIBEL.

Tuesday, April 16, 1867, at No. 33 James street, Charles Godfrey Weibel murdered his wife, Ann, by cutting her throat from ear to ear.

53. LIVINGSTON.

John R. Livingston was murdered by Vincent Cody, who shot him above the left eye, on Thursday, April, 18, 1867, at No. 17 Jefferson street, for which Cody was sentenced to imprisonment "for life."

54. M'CAFFERTY.

Ann McCafferty was murdered by her husband, James, who shot her in the neck, on Tuesday night, May 15, 1867, at No. 250 Tenth street, and "was sound asleep" when the officers entered.

55. KING.

On Monday night, June 10, 1867, at No. 30 East Nineteenth street, Alfred M. King murdered his wife, Mattie C., and then with the same pistol shot himself.

56. COBAY.

Catharine Cobay was murdered by one unknown, who cut her throat with a broken tumbler while asleep at No. 137 Mott street, on the night of Friday, the 21st of June, 1867.

57. BOSTWICK.

Christian Bostwick, negro, by John Higgins, Sunday, July 21, 1867, at No. 531 Broome street. Beaten to death.

58. CADENA.

Matilda Cadena, negress, murdered by her husband Cripino, a Cuban negro, on the 4th of September, 1867, at No. 15 East Eleventh street, the work being begun with a flat-iron, and finished with a dagger. Cadena sentenced to imprisonment for life.

59. M'CHESNEY.

Robert McChesney, police officer, was murdered on the corner of Canal and Mercer streets, on the night of the 19th of October, 1867, by Margaret Welsh, alias Fanny Wright, a harlot, who sprang upon him as he rapped for assistance to carry the tigress to the station-house, and slashed his carotid artery clear through.

60. FREEL.

Daniel Freel by Jeremiah Handigan, corner of Pearl and Franklin streets, Tuesday, November 5, 1867. Pistol.

61. SCOTT.

David Scott, by James Griffin, Wednesday, December 11, 1867, in Cherry street, near James. Pistol.

62. SHARPLEY.

Thomas Sharpley, by Edwin Kelly, December 11, 1867; Fifth Avenue Theatre. Pistol.

63. JACOBS.

Charles Jacobs, by —— Kelly, January 4, 1868, at No. 262 First avenue. Knife.

64. CONNELL.

William Connell, by Richard Casey, January 4, 1868, corner of Bowery and Bayard street. Pistol.

65. MULLEN.

Lawrence Mullen, by Wm. O'Brien, Monday, January 27, 1868, corner of Broad and Beaver streets. Knife.

66. PENDAR.

Margaret Pendar, murdered by her husband John, at No. 591 Greenwich street, February 29, 1868. Choked, bitten, hammered to death.

67. GARDNER.

Louis Gardner was murdered on the 6th of April, 1868, at No. 100 Mott street, by one unknown, a lad of 15, who stabbed him to the heart and escaped.

68. SHERMAN.

Mary Sherman, by her husband John, at No. 67 James street, on Friday, 8th of May, 1868. Beaten to death.

69. NICHOLSON.

Teresa Nicholson, waylaid by husband Patrick, and shot June 20, 1868, at No. 329 Water street.

70. M'BRIDE.

Ellen McBride, hammered to death by unknown at No. 127 East Houston street, on the 29th of June, 1868.

71. RILANDS.

On the 4th of July, 1868, John Rilands was murdered in Baxter street, near Park, by Donati Magaldo, a gigantic Italian, who stabbed him with a carving-knife, ground edge and point, Magaldo sentenced to imprisonment for life.

72. BAUMANN.

On Sunday, the 2d of January, 1870, George Baumann murdered his mistress Annie McNamara, at the bagnio No. 65 Elizabeth street, and then shot himself.

73. LOGAN.

On Wednesday, the 5th of January, 1870, James Logan, commonly known as Logan No. 2, and supposed to have murdered Mr. Rogers in East Twelfth street on the 31st of December, 1868, was murdered at No. 25 West Houston street by Jerry Dunn, who escaped. Pistol.

74. SMEDICK.

On the 5th of August, 1870, John Real was hanged for the murder of Jno. Smedick, police officer, whom he murdered by shooting from behind a box in First avenue, between Thirty-second and Thirty-third streets, on 23d of July, 1868.

75, 76, 77. KENNEDY, M'DONNALD, GEORGE.

On the 1st of December, 1864, at about 4 A. M., the warden on duty near "Bummer's Hall," or the place of confinement for small offenders, drunkards, and so on, in the Tombs, was astonished to hear tremendous cries of "Help," "Murder," "Police," issue from that place. Rushing to the grated door he beheld a drunkard named Donovan, who had been incarcerated as a lunatic from liquor, dashing furiously with the iron poker belonging to the room among his companions, who were fleeing from him and screaming for help. Wardens and police from outside rushed in as soon as possible, but not until two men, McDonnald and Kennedy lay dead upon the floor, their brains scattered about the room, and a third, named George, was in the agonies of death with a broken skull. Donovan utterly refused to cease his violence, despite the shots fired at him, and it was not until the whole force rushed en masse upon him that he could be overpowered. Besides this tragedy under the very shadow of the gibbet, those who have been hanged in the Tombs from 1849, an average of one a year, make up the sum total of the figures which appear under the gallows on the map.

RELIGIOUS NOTICES.

A MEETING OF THE COMMONWEALTH OF HUMANITY for devotional exercises (without regard to sect or party), will be held to-morrow at 10:30 A. M., 3, and 7:30 P. M., in Metropolitan Hall, 93 and 95 Sixth avenue, opposite Eighth street. Contribution taken up. And for social improvement, Wednesday evening, 767 Sixth avenue, near Forty-fourth street, second floor.

A REGULAR QUARTERLY MEETING OF THE Protestant Episcopal Sunday-school Association will be held in the Sunday-school room of St. Ann's Church, Eighteenth street, near Fifth avenue, on Monday, September 19, at 7:30 P.M. Rev. Wm. Tatlock, of Stamford, Ct., will deliver an essay on "The Aim of the Sunday-school Teacher, and how best it may be attained." Subject for discussion: "How can the Catechism best be taught in our Sunday-schools?" All are invited to attend.

CHURCH OF THE HOLY LIGHT, SEVENTH avenue, next to Thirty-fourth street.—Divine service at 10:30 A. M. The Rev. Eastburn Benjamin will preach.

EVANGELICAL LUTHERAN CHURCH OF THE Holy Trinity, Twenty-first street, between Fifth and Sixth avenues, Rev. G. F. Krotel, D. D., Pastor. Services resumed Sunday, 18th inst., at 10:30 A. M., and 7:30 P. M. Sunday School at 2:15 P. M.

FORTY-SECOND STREET PRESBYTERIAN Church, near Eighth avenue.—Preaching to-morrow morning and evening, by the Rev. H. L. Singleton, of Wilmington, N. C.

GRACE CHURCH, BROADWAY AND TENTH street. The afternoon service will be resumed in this church to-morrow at 4 o'clock. Morning service at 11 A.M.

SAINT PAUL'S REFORMED DUTCH CHURCH, Reservoir Square, Fortieth street, between Fifth and Sixth avenues, Rev. Alexander Thompson, D.D., Pastor—Please God, Divine service on Sunday, 18th inst., at 10:30 o'clock A.M., and 7:30 o'clock P.M. Sunday-school and children's service at 9 o'clock A.M.

SAINT THOMAS PARISH.—THE NEW CHURCH, Fifth avenue and Fifty-third street, will (by Divine permission) be opened with appropriate services Thursday, October 6, at 11 A. M. Rev. Dr. Morgan will officiate in the Church of the Resurrection, Madison avenue, corner of Forty-seventh street, on Sunday next. Service commences at 10:30 A. M.

THE ANTHON MEMORIAL CHURCH, FORTY-eighth street, west of Sixth avenue, will be reopened on Sunday, September 11. Services at 10.30 A. M. and 5 P. M.

THE TOWERS MUST FALL—THE MUCH-ABUSED Messenger of Christ will preach the Word of Prophecy, on Sunday at 3 P. M., in the University, Washington square. Seats free. Subject: "The Approaching Doom of the Nations."

THERE WILL BE A MEETING AT THE "NEW Jerusalem Church," Thirty-fifth street, between Park and Lexington avenues, Sunday evening, at 8 o'clock, for reading the works of Emmanuel Swedenborg and for instruction in the doctrines of the "New Church." The public are cordially invited. Rev. Chauncey Giles will preach in the morning at 11 o'clock.

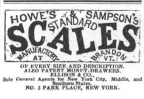

The New-York Times.

VOL. XX.......NO. 6189. | NEW-YORK, SATURDAY, JULY 22, 1871. | PRICE FOUR CENTS.

THE SECRET ACCOUNTS.

Proofs of Undoubted Frauds Brought to Light.

Warrants Signed by Hall and Connolly Under False Pretenses.

THE ACCOUNT OF INGERSOLL & CO.

The following accounts, copied with scrupulous fidelity from Controller CONNOLLY'S books, require little explanation. They purport to show the amount paid during 1869 and 1870, for repairs and furniture for the New Court-house. It will be seen that the warrants are drawn in different names, but they were all indorsed to "INGERSOLL & Co."—otherwise, J. H. INGERSOLL, the agent of the Ring. Each warrant was signed by Controller CONNOLLY and Mayor HALL. What amount of money was actually paid to the persons in whose favor the warrants were *nominally* drawn, we have no means of knowing. On the face of these accounts, however, it is clear that the bulk of the money somehow or other got back to the Ring, or each warrant would not have been indorsed over to its agent.

We undertake to prove whenever we are afforded the opportunity, that the following account is copied literally from the Controller's books, and forms a part of the documents to which the public is entitled to have access.

The dates given for the work done are obviously fraudulent. For example: On July 2, 1869, a warrant was drawn for furniture supplied for County Courts and offices, from Oct. 18 to Nov. 23, 1868, for $42,560 64. On July 16—fourteen days afterward—another warrant was drawn for $94,038 13 for furniture supplied to the same offices from Nov. 7 to Dec. 31. That is to say, the bill was fully paid by the *first* of these two warrants down to Nov. 23. And yet a fortnight afterward another warrant was drawn paying the bill over again from Nov. 7. It is obvious that the fictitious dates were not remembered by the City authorities when these warrants were drawn. Many similar cases will be observed in the figures given below.

It will be seen that on one day furniture is supposed to have been supplied to the amount of $129,469 48—at least a warrant for that sum was signed by HALL and CONNOLLY in favor of C. D. BOLLAR & Co., and indorsed by INGERSOLL & Co.

1869. INGERSOLL & CO. 1869.

Date of Warrant.	*Character of Work. Date on Which Work was Supposed to be Done.*	*Amount Drawn.*
July 2.	—Paid for Furniture in County Courts and Offices from Oct. 18 to Nov. 23, 1868	$42,550 64
July 16.	—Paid for Furniture in County Offices from Nov. 7 to Dec. 31, 1868	94,038 13
Aug. 4.	—Paid for Furniture in County Offices July 19, 1868	53,206 75
Sept. 7.	—Paid for Furniture in County Offices Aug. 30, 1868	60,334 71
Sept. 8.	—Paid for Furniture in County Courts and Offices Sept. 23, 1868	42,901 47
Oct. 22.	—Paid for Iron Railing, Cases, Stairs, &c., Check in name of M. W. Davis, indorsed by Ingersoll & Co., July 29, '68	63,201 16
Oct. 23.	—Paid for Carpets, &c., in Co. Courts and Offices, Check in name of J. A. Smith, indorsed by Ingersoll & Co., Aug. 10, '68	27,154 55
Oct. 28.	—Paid for Furniture in County Courts and Offices Dec. 28, 1868	28,032 11
Nov. 5.	—Paid for Carpets, &c., in Co. Courts and Offices, Check in name of J. A. Smith, indorsed by Ingersoll & Co., April 6, '68.	36,422 10
Nov. 17.	—Paid for Carpets, &c., in Co. Courts and Offices, Check in name of J. A. Smith, indorsed by Ingersoll & Co., Jan. 26, '68.	32,617 13
Nov. 16.	—Paid for Carpets, &c., in Co. Courts and Offices, Check in name of J. A. Smith, indorsed by Ingersoll & Co., July 29, '68.	32,185 20
Nov. 19.	—Paid for Furniture, &c., in County Courts and Offices, Oct. 18, 1868	10,494 61
Nov. 24.	—Paid for Furniture, &c., in Co. Courts and Offices, Check in name of C. D. Bollar & Co., in'd. by Ingersoll & Co., Aug. 17, '68.	32,826 81
Dec. 3.	—Paid for Furniture, &c., in Co. Courts and Offices, Check in name of C. D. Bollar & Co., in'd. by Ingersoll & Co., Nov. 9, '68.	32,682 38
June 8.	—Paid for Furniture, &c., in Co. Courts and Offices, Check in name of C. D. Bollar & Co., in'd. by Ingersoll & Co., May 8, '69.	129,469 48
June 15.	—Paid for Carpets, &c., in New Court-House, Check in name of J. A. Smith, indorsed by Ingersoll & Co., April 16, 1869	72,605 97
June 8.	—Paid for Furniture, &c., in New Court-House to April 8, 1869	90,923 40
Dec. 16.	—Paid for Furniture, &c., in County Court-rooms and Offices, April 26, 1868	54,243 57
Jan. 11.	—Paid for Furniture in Armories and Drill-rooms, Nov. 12, 1868	38,906 71
Jan. 19.	—Paid for Furniture in same, Dec. 3 and 22, 1868	31,801 95
Feb. 27.	—Paid for Furniture in same from Jan. 13, 1869, to Feb. 9, 1869	55,791 56
April 26.	—Paid for Furniture in same, March 11, 9186	39,844 68
June 5.	—Paid for Furniture in same, Nov. 17, 1868	26,325 26
Sept. 20.	—Paid for Furniture in same, May 26, 1869	[illegible]
Feb. 18.	—Paid for Shades, &c., Check in name of J. A. Smith, indorsed by Ingersoll & Co., Dec. 21, 1868	15,786 40
May 12.	—Paid for Shades, Curtains, Cornices, &c., Check in name of J. A. Smith, indorsed by Ingersoll & Co., April 6, 1869	19,163 65
June 7.	—Paid for Repairs, &c., Check in name of J. A. Smith, indorsed by Ingersoll & Co., March 13, 1869	22,496 33
May 12.	—Paid for Repairs, &c., Check in name of C. D. Bollar & Co., indorsed by Ingersoll & Co., April 9, 1869	21,969 13
June 5.	—Paid for Repairs, &c., Check in name of C. D. Bollar & Co., indorsed by Ingersoll & Co., to Feb. 3, 1869	38,907 43
Sept. 30.	—Paid for Fitting up Armories, Check in name of C. D. Bollar & Co., indorsed by Ingersoll & Co., Sept. 1, 1868	44,737 45
Sept. 20.	—Paid for Fitting up Armories, Check in name of C. D. Bollar & Co., indorsed by Ingersoll & Co., July 1, 1869	32,112 78

GEORGE S. MILLER, 1869—*All the Checks Indorsed by Ingersoll & Co.*

July 2.	—Paid for Repairs to Court of Common Pleas to Oct. 17, 1867	$905 51
July 2.	—Paid for Repairs to Courts and Offices from Aug. 1 to Oct. 20, 1868	6,089 24
July 28.	—Paid for Repairs to County Offices, Dec. 23, 1868	10,647 56
July 28.	—Paid for Repairs to County Offices and Courts, Nov. 20, 1868	11,849 54
Sept. 8.	—Paid for Carpenter-work, County Offices and Courts, from Nov. 12, 1868, to Dec. 12, 1868	48,833 23
Dec. 3.	—Paid for Repairs to County Offices and Buildings from Oct. 21 to Oct. 31, 1868	28,038 74
Dec. 29.	—Paid for Repairs and Alterations, County Offices and Buildings, July 21, 1868	27,885 04
Jan. 11.	—Paid for Repairs in Armories and Drill-rooms from Nov. 27 to Dec. 19, 1868	15,415 14
Jan. 19.	—Paid for Repairs in Armories and Drill-rooms from Oct. 23 to Dec. 4, 1868	14,691 78
Feb. 27.	—Paid for Repairs in Armories and Drill-rooms from Jan. 14 to Jan. 30, 1869	27,937 51
May 12.	—Paid for Carpenter-work in Various Armories from Jan. 30 to March 23, 1869	27,651 40
June 7.	—Paid for Carpenter-work in Various Armories from April 23 to May 18, 1869	38,676 50
June 7.	—Paid for Carpenter-work in Various Armories from March 30 to April 16, 1869	13,864 07
Sept. 20.	—Paid for Carpenter-work in Various Armories from May 25 to June 9, 1869	14,130 36
Oct. 11.	—Paid for Carpenter-work in Various Armories from May 25 to June 29, 1869	49,753 80

A. G. MILLER, 1869—*Checks Indorsed by Ingersoll & Co.*

Dec. 20.	—Paid for Repairs to County Offices and Buildings, March 8, 1868	$34,785 03
Dec. 20.	—Paid for Repairs to County Offices and Buildings, July 7, 1868	18,222 47
Sept. 28.	—Paid for Repairs to County Offices and Buildings, July 2, 1869	48,798 63

1870. INGERSOLL & CO. 1870.

Jan. 17.	—Paid for Furniture Furnished County Court-rooms and Offices, July 17, 1868	$20,655 72
Jan. 24.	—Paid for Furniture Furnished County Court-rooms and Offices, May 13, 1868	33,538 36
Feb. 7.	—Paid for Furniture Furnished County Court-rooms and Offices	11,186 92
Feb. 16.	—Paid for Furniture Furnished County Court-rooms and Offices, Aug. 21, 1869	29,404 48
Feb. 23.	—Paid for Furniture Furnished County Court-rooms and Offices, Sept. 23, 1869	51,813 77
Feb. 26.	—Paid for Furniture Furnished County Court-rooms and Offices, Oct. 6, 1869	26,981 90
Feb. 26.	—Paid for Furniture Furnished County Court-rooms and Offices, Sept. 3, 1869	33,037 15
May 6.	—Paid for Furniture Furnished County Court-house, Dec. 10, 1869	64,954 87
May 21.	—Paid for Cabinet-work County Court-house, July 23, 1869	70,117 59
May 21.	—Paid for Cabinet-work County Court-house, Oct. 17, 1869	64,984 82
May 28.	—Paid for Furniture County Court-house, Oct. 21, 1869	40,314 09
May 28.	—Paid for Furniture County Court-house, Nov. 3, 1869	39,844 19
May 30.	—Paid for Furniture County Court-house, Dec. 27, 1869	68,218 82
June 3.	—Paid for Furniture Furnished in County Buildings and Offices, Feb. 5, 1870	54,030 26
June 10.	—Paid for Furniture, Clocks, &c., Furnished in County Buildings and Offices, March 23, 1870	69,719 10
June 13.	—Paid for Furniture and Cabinet-work in County Court-house, April 18, 1870	98,259 07
June 20.	—Paid for Cabinet-work in County Court-house, Feb. 3, 1870	66,292 33
June 27.	—Paid for Cabinet-work and Furniture in Armories and Drill-rooms, Feb. 27, 1869	58,330 93
June 30.	—Paid for Cabinet-work and Furniture in Armories and Drill-rooms, Feb. 6, 1870	54,053 33
June 30.	—Paid for Cabinet-work and Furniture in Armories and Drill-rooms, March 26, 1870	29,129 99
Aug. 1.	—Paid for Furniture in Court-rooms and Offices, March 28, 1870	91,325 50
Mar. 14.	—Paid for Furniture in Armories and Drill-rooms, Nov. 3, 1869	58,987 60
April 16.	—Paid for Furniture in Armories and Drill-rooms, Sept. 11, 1869	28,608 68
Aug. 31.	—Paid for Fitting up District-Attorney's Office, Aug. 22, 1870	30,000 00
Aug. 30.	—Paid for Fitting up Commissioners of Taxes' and Receiver of Taxes' Offices, June 30, 1870	40,000 00
Aug. 30.	—Paid for Fitting up Register's Office, Aug. 3, 1870	10,000 00
Oct. 26.	—Paid for Fitting up Surrogate's Office, Sept. 3, 1870	12,000 00

C. D. BOLLAR & CO.—*Checks Indorsed by Ingersoll & Co.*

May 7.	—Paid for Furniture, &c., Furnished in County Court-house, Sept. 16, 1869	$39,260 17
May 7.	—Paid for Furniture, &c., Furnished in County Court-house, Oct. 18, 1869	35,114 08
May 13.	—Paid for Cabinet-work Furnished in County Court-house, July 18, 1869	89,379 00
May 21.	—Paid for Fitting up in County Court-house, March 6, 1870	39,950 18
May 21.	—Paid for Fitting up in County Court-house, Jan. 20, 1870	39,614 59
May 27.	—Paid for Cabinet-work Furnished in County Court-house, Aug. 23, 1869	125,830 56
June 10.	—Paid for Cabinet-work Furnished in County Court-house, April 16, 1870	67,487 21
June 30.	—Paid for Fitting up Armories and Drill-rooms, Jan. 7, 1870	49,208 14
June 30.	—Paid for Fitting up Armories and Drill-rooms, March 13, 1870	37,072 16
Aug. 1.	—Paid for Cabinet-work, &c., done in County Buildings and Offices, March 12, 1870	60,503 43

J. A. SMITH—*Checks Indorsed by Ingersoll & Co.*

May 6.	—Paid for Carpets Furnished in New Court-house, June 22, 1869	$34,082 25
May 7.	—Paid for Curtains and Shades Furnished in New Court-house, Sept. 23, 1869	36,083 80
May 21.	—Paid for Carpets and Shades Furnished in County Buildings and Offices, Feb. 21, 1870	34,515 73
May 28.	—Paid for Carpets and Shades Furnished in County Buildings and Offices, Feb. 21, 1870	73,602 46
June 3.	—Paid for Carpets and Shades Furnished in County Buildings and Offices, Dec. 27, 1869	63,175 51
June 6.	—Paid for Carpets &c., Furnished in County Court-house, Aug. 3, 1869	42,291 45
June 6.	—Paid for Carpets, &c., Furnished in County Buildings and Offices, June 21, 1869	44,259 23
June 6.	—Paid for Shades Furnished in County Buildings and Offices, Sept. 16, 1869	36,987 25
June 24.	—Paid for Carpets Furnished in Armories and Drill-rooms, Dec. 22, 1869	36,441 42
June 30.	—Paid for Carpets Furnished in Armories and Drill-rooms, March 16, 1870	37,426 87
July 26.	—Paid for Carpets Furnished in County Court-house, April 17, 1870	72,819 81

GEORGE S. MILLER—*Checks Indorsed by Ingersoll & Co.*

Jan. 17.	—Paid for Carpenter-work in Court-rooms and Offices, Aug. 19, 1868, to Sept. 11, 1868	$20,291 44
Jan. 17.	—Paid for Repairs and Alterations in County Buildings, June 7, 1868	23,005 83
Jan. 24.	—Paid for Repairs and Alterations in County Offices, Aug. 5, 1868	26,952 99
Jan. 28.	—Paid for Repairs and Alterations in County Offices, Sept. 23, 1868	25,366 49
Mar. 21.	—Paid for Repairs and Alterations in County Offices, May 13, 1869	20,255 00
April 8.	—Paid for Repairs and Alterations in County Offices, Aug. 7, 1869	18,955 69
April 8.	—Paid for Repairs and Alterations in County Offices, July 23, 1869	22,494 74
April 8.	—Paid for Repairs and Alterations in County Offices, June 10, 1869	21,418 99
May 7.	—Paid for Carpenter-work in Court-house, May 13, 1869	42,128 47
May 13.	—Paid for Carpenter-work in Court-house, Sept. 29, 1869	38,902 22
May 21.	—Paid for Carpenter-work in Court-house, Dec. 15, 1869	34,990 66
May 28.	—Paid for Repairs in County Buildings and Offices, Aug. 31, 1869	39,361 21
June 3.	—Paid for Repairs in County Buildings and Offices, Sept. 22, 1869	37,326 02
June 6.	—Paid for Repairs in County Buildings and Offices, Dec. 18, 1869	32,381 73
June 6.	—Paid for Repairs in County Buildings and Offices, Oct. 25, 1869	35,663 82
June 10.	—Paid for Fitting up New Court-house, Jan. 12, 1870	44,474 30
June 17.	—Paid for Repairs in County Buildings and Offices, Jan. 25, 1870	48,768 21
June 20.	—Paid for Carpenter-work in Court-house, Feb. 9, 1870	40,965 41
June 27.	—Paid for Repairs in County Buildings and Offices, March 29, 1870	44,874 59
June 30.	—Paid for Repairs in Armories and Drill-rooms, Aug. 3, 1869	40,549 24
June 30.	—Paid for Repairs in Armories and Drill-rooms, Sept. 8, 1869	35,748 79
July 8.	—Paid for Repairs in Armories and Drill-rooms, Feb. 10, 1870	29,317 59
July 8.	—Paid for Repairs in Armories and Drill-rooms, March 2, 1870	46,947 32
July 26.	—Paid for Repairs in Armories and Drill-rooms, March 31, 1870	49,251 31
Aug. 9.	—Paid for Repairs in County Buildings, April 12, 1870	40,607 49
Aug. 12.	—Paid for Repairs in Armories and Drill-rooms, April 2, 1870	48,639 49
Aug. 12.	—Paid for Repairs in Carpenter-work in Court-house, March 23, 1870	46,343 45
Mar. 14.	—Paid for Repairs in Armories and Drill-rooms to Nov. 13, 1869	38,084 28
Mar. 31.	—Paid for Repairs and Carpenter-work in Armories and Drill-rooms, July 6 to July 31, 1869	45,266 04
April 16.	—Paid for Repairs and Alterations in Armories and Drill-rooms, Aug. 3 to Aug. 13, 1869	25,948 38
April 16.	—Paid for Repairs and Alterations in Armories and Drill-rooms	8,147 88

A. G. MILLER—*Checks Indorsed by Ingersoll & Co.*

June 24.	—Paid for Cabinet-work in Court-house, Jan. 9, 1870	$49,082 30
June 27.	—Paid for Cabinet-work in County Buildings and Offices, March 29, 1870	85,163 22
June 30.	—Paid for Cabinet-work in County Court-house, April 2, 1870	59,932 01
Aug. 1.	—Paid for Cabinet-work in County Court-house, Oct. 8, 1869	69,537 68
Aug. 9.	—Paid for Cabinet-work in Armories and Drill-rooms, April 16, 1870	77,949 58
Mar. 28.	—Paid for Repairs in Armories and Drill-rooms, Aug. 28, 1869	49,742 45
Mar. 31.	—Paid for Repairs in Armories and Drill-rooms, Oct. 20, 1869	38,818 84
April 16.	—Paid for Fitting up Armories and Drill-rooms, Oct. 2, 1869	22,612 10
	Grand Total	**$5,663,646 83**

WASHINGTON.

Clearing up a Muddle in the Revenue Department—Lively Work in the Pension Bureau—Imports of Australia—Immigration at New-York—Kuklux Investigation—National Bank Circulation.

Special Dispatch to the New-York Times.

WASHINGTON, July 21.—It will be remembered that over a year ago Congress tried to give an expression of its will concerning the reduction of a part of the income tax, but failed to find language to convey its purpose successfully in regard to the payment of certain income taxes for the last five months of 1870. Judge DOUGLAS, the acting Commissioner, had the question of how the law should be construed before him, and gave the Government the benefit of the doubt. Commissioner PLEASONTON reversed the decision, and the corporations paid their semi-annual interest without withholding the amount of the [illegible] have done. The Attorney-General in turn reversed PLEASONTON'S decision, putting the case back where Judge DOUGLAS placed it, and now the corporations resist collection, on the ground that they acted on the instructions of an agent of the Government in neglecting to retain the amount of the tax, and that they are not liable to sustain loss because of the reversal of the decision on which they acted. Solicitor BANFIELD has been considering their plea, and today handed the Secretary of the Treasury his opinion as to the legality of action for the collection of these taxes. The opinion will be made public to-morrow, together with the Secretary's decision based upon it. This is another case which must make Commissioner PLEASONTON aware that he is one of the Secretary's subordinates, and that he is so regarded by the President.

BRISK WORK IN THE PENSION OFFICE.

A statement was not long ago published which showed that there were about 106,000 pension claims unexamined on the files of the Pension Office. Those who are anxiously looking for action upon applications will be glad to hear that the daily average work of the Pension Office under the new Commissioner, Gen. BAKER, has been already about doubled. Yesterday 188 certificates for pensions were issued, the largest number ever issued from the office in one day. The first week in June, which was the first week after Gen. BAKER came into the office, 423 certificates were issued. Since then there has been a general constant increase and last week 915 were issued. This week the number is expected to reach 1,100, and during July 4,000 are expected to be signed. At this rate the office will be gaining on its work instead of falling further behind, and an effort will be made to bring the work up to time as soon as possible with the limited force which can be employed.

SECRETARY DELANO.

Secretary DELANO has written that his return will be delayed till Tuesday next.

Dispatch to the Associated Press.

AUSTRALIA'S IMPORTATIONS.

A statement has been compiled at the Treasury Department from the latest statistics, showing the imports into Australia and New-Zealand, as follows: From Great Britain, £17,924,420; from the United States, £1,354,38[illegible]; all other countries, £3,812,478. Stated by per centage, they are as follows: From Great Britain, 77 6-10; from the United States, 5 5-10; all other countries, 16 6-10. The Parliament of New-South Wales has recently voted a subsidy of $75,000 to a monthly line of American steamers between San Francisco and Sydney. The imports of Australia and New-Zealand being largely manufactured goods, it is believed that a very large and profitable commerce will spring up with our Western Coast.

IMMIGRATION AT NEW-YORK.

The official returns received at the Bureau of Statistics show that during the quarter ending June 30, 1871, the total number of passengers arrived at the port of New-York from foreign countries was 107,114, of whom 64,213 were males and 42,901 females. Of the total number arrived, 101,015 were actual immigrants—males, 60,082; females, 40,933. Ages—Under fifteen, 19,812; fifteen and under forty, 71,056; forty and upward, 10,147. The deaths on the voyage were 92, of whom 54 were males and 38 females. The principal nationalities of the immigrants were as follows: England, 17,845; Scotland, 4,613; Wales, 399; Ireland, 26,149; Great Britain, locality unknown, 5,672; Germany, 30,814; Austria, 1,983; Sweden, 5,727; Norway, 1,286; Denmark, 1,143; France, 849; Switzerland, 1,305; Spain, 104; Italy, 8,671; Holland, 409; Belgium, 78; Russia, 295; Poland, 183; Cuba, 43; Bermudas, 77.

THE KUKLUX INVESTIGATION.

The Kuklux Committee, today, examined a witness named McBRIDE, who testified that while a teacher of a colored school in Chickasaw County, Mississippi, a band of disguised men seized and whipped him, and insisted he should leave the country. Other colored schools were broken up in that section. Three witnesses from North Carolina are in attendance, and will testify relative to the existence of Kuklux organizations in that State. A telegram was read in the Committee from a citizen of Macon, that he telegraphed on the 11th of July he was ready to report, but received the next day a telegram from the Sergeant-at-Arms of the Senate, telling him he need not come, as the Committee had not time for more witnesses. The Sergeant-at-Arms being out of town could not explain, but at the instance of the Democratic members this Georgian and six or more others were resummoned by telegraph to appear before the Committee.

NATIONAL BANK CIRCULATION.

The total circulation issued to the national banks to date is $318,686,999. The act of July 12, 1870, authorized the issue of $54,000,000 additional circulation, and the establishment of gold national banks, to which circulation can be issued upon the deposit of United States bonds, at the rate of eighty per cent. upon the par value thereof. Since the passage of the act, circulation has been issued to the following States: Virginia, $744,000; Illinois, $3,066; West Virginia, $950,000; Michigan, $1,[illegible]; Kentucky, [illegible]; Indiana, $1,174,000; Wisconsin, $534,000; Ohio, $760,000; Tennessee, $1,300,000; Iowa, $1,076,000; Louisiana, $1,300,000; Minnesota, $380,000; Georgia, $561,000; Kansas, $176,100; North Carolina, $609,000; Missouri, $1,290,000; South Carolina, $258,000; Nebraska, $212,000; Texas, $145,000; Colorado, $61,000; New-Mexico, $155,000; Oregon, $137,000; Alabama, $260,000; California, $3,205. The law requires that one-half of the increased circulation shall be apportioned among the States not having an excess already, according to population, and one-half according to the existing banking capital resources and business of such State and Territory. The census returns of the valuation of property and banking capital have not yet been received, and the proportion of circulation for the States of Ohio, Indiana and Illinois cannot probably be ascertained with any accuracy until about the 1st of October. It is probable, however, that there will be sufficient circulation for all of the Southern and Western States when the full census returns are received. No additional circulation can be issued to the Eastern and Middle States.

THE ABUSED CAR-HORSES.

Inspection of Stables by Henry Bergh—Sickening Sights—Comparative Views.

Yesterday, Mr. BERGH and Mr. A. H. CAMPBELL, the President and Superintendent of the Society for the Prevention of Cruelty to Animals, accompanied by Dr. LIANTARD, of the New-York Veterinary College, and a TIMES reporter, made a tour of inspection of the principle car companies' stables to examine the horses, the condition of the stables, the quality of feed, and the general order of the homes of the best servants of mankind. The first stables inspected were those of the Fourth-avenue line. The Superintendent, Mr. MESSEROE, received his visitors very politely, and showed them over the premises. This line had lost eighteen out of ninety-four cases with the new disease. Ninety out of the ninety-four affected were mares, and the eighteen that died of the disease were mares. The hospital yesterday had sixty disabled horses in it. Only a very small portion, however, were down with the malady, the others being sick with sore feet, quittors, sore backs, and otherwise disabled. Some of the poor creatures had fearful wounds on the fetlocks, caused by their injuring themselves in the numerous switches on the line. This is reckoned the hardest road for horses of any in the City. The feed given the horses of this line is half oats and half corn. The condition of the stables is tolerable. The open windows of the stable in which the sick horses were, looked into a yard belonging to the proprietors of the Fourth-avenue stage line, and the filth and mud in this place was knee-deep. The stench must be anything but conducive to the recovery of the sick horses. The feed was examined and found of medium quality.

The stables of Messrs. WILKINS & MARSHALL, the proprietors of the Fourth-avenue stage line, were next visited. The stables were three tiers deep, and the atmosphere of the lowest was very bad. The refuse besides ran through from the top to the lower stable, rendering it altogether quite unfit for the purpose, in addition to which it is quite underground, and excepting just at the entrances quite dark. In a dirty yard were fifteen horses turned out for exercise in course of recovery from the disease. The stock consisted of 330 horses. Eighty had been attacked, out of which number eleven mares had died. One of the proprietors drew Mr. BERGH'S particular attention to one horse which had been kept from work two weeks simply because he had a sore back. Mr. WILKINS, one of the proprietors, said he felt certain that the disease was easily curable if attended to quickly. He said the first symptoms were swelling of the hind legs and running at the eyes, but Dr. LIANTARD did not at all agree with this view. The horses were fed on half corn and half oats.

The stables of the East Belt line, at Thirty-seventh-street and First-avenue, were next inspected. Here were found 400 horses, a great proportion of which were in appearance very unfit for the every day toil required of them. There were about seventy cripples in a deplorable condition, and many more with large sores and ulcers on the fetlocks. Superintendent TERRY was asked if the latter were worked, and replied that he was compelled to work such stock or he must stop the line; and besides, he thought such horses better working than standing idle. Mr. BERGH did not agree with him, and cautioned him not to use many of the suffering beasts which were noticed in the stalls. The horses go over eighteen miles every day, and the daily feed of each consisted of twelve pounds of meal and four and a half pounds of ground oats. The line had lost forty animals, principally mares, with the new disease. There were only six cases now under treatment.

The stables of the Second-avenue line were next overhauled. Mr. SHAW reported that they were now quite free of the disease, not having had a case for two weeks. They had lost eleven horses out of 135 stricken down with the malady. The stables were in pretty good condition, but there were no signs of bedding, and apparently the poor beasts, after toiling over sixteen miles every day, had nothing but the hard and damp boards to lie on at night. The stock consisted of 750 horses. Daily feed, ten pounds—half oats and half corn. The hospital had some twenty patients in, under the homeopathy treatment.

The stables of the Third-avenue line were visited. In them were 1,600 horses. In an extra stable were a number of "green horses," which the hard work of the road had crippled. In the hospital were several bad cases, the poor creatures being covered with blisters, and scars arising therefrom. Two or three appeared in a dying state. There were no signs of bedding in a large portion of the stables. The feed taken from some of the mangers was sour, and as poor as any that had been inspected. The stablemen stated that the animals did not like it, and no wonder.

The stables of the Sixth-avenue line were found in admirable order, or as Mr. BERGH said, they were "perfect models." Everything was in first-rate order—perfect system reigning throughout the establishment. The best of feed [illegible] seventeen pounds each horse. [illegible] were all good, sound animals. They were lying in their stalls on clean bedding. Mr. BIDGOOD only reported four cases of the disease, all of which were slowly recovering. He said that the Company had decided not to use in future any kiln-dried corn. After being dried it was found to have lost its virtue, and when sown it would not grow. The horses of this line had seventeen pounds of feed per day supplied to each.

The stables of the Forty-second-street, or Cross-town line, which has of late given Mr. BERGH and his officers so much trouble, were next visited. The clerk was very civil, and called the stable-keeper, A. CHALMERS, to escort Mr. BERGH and his party over the premises, but CHALMERS recognized the visitors, kept out of the way, and was found only after great trouble. He said he had received strict orders from JOHN GREEN, the President, not to show any one over the stables, and especially Mr. BERGH nor any of his officers. The reason of this refusal was quite apparent, for a more filthy, dilapidated and unwholesome-looking place, even from the outside, is difficult to conceive of. The office is dirty, and a coke dealer would hardly deign to use it. The waiting-room is an inch deep in dirt, and the seats covered. Some half-dozen dirty-looking ruffians were squatting inside the shed, who were pointed out to our reporter as drivers and conductors of the "line." Mr. BERGH told CHALMERS he knew perfectly well the reason he was refused admittance, for he had gone over the cellars, called stables, a year ago, and had found them in an awful condition. CHALMERS denied that the stables were in a bad condition. It is strange that Mr. BERGH and his party should be so cordially received and treated so well at every other stable that was visited, and invited to call at any time and point out such horses as he might feel justified in ordering to be relieved of work, and yet be refused even admission to the "sheds" of the Green line. Mr. BERGH begged that CHALMERS would request Mr. GREEN to go over the Sixth-avenue stables, and then "go and do likewise."

DESTRUCTIVE FIRE.

Several Buildings in West Forty-Seventh and Forty-Sixth Streets Destroyed or Damaged.

Another destructive conflagration occurred last evening, which was discovered at about 9 o'clock, in the two-story saw and planing mill of KINNEY & CLARK, Nos. 628 and 630 West Forty-seventh-street, and which, being first seen in the boiler-room, probably originated from the furnace. The flames spread with extraordinary rapidity, and almost before the engines arrived the entire building was enveloped, and the fire communicated to adjacent property. The mill was entirely destroyed with all its contents and the loss will probably reach $15,000. Next west was the lumber yard of JOHN W. STEVENS & BRO., where stock to the amount of about $5,000 was destroyed. Next east was a five story building, Nos. 622, 624 and 626 West Forty-seventh-street, occupied as a morocco factory, by C. P. Buckin, the top floor of which was reached by the flames and the loss will probably exceed $5,000. The fire even reached across the street to the two story dwelling of THOS. ING, whose loss is $500; also to the building No. 627, owned by JOHN DARRAGH, and the lower floor of which was occupied as a stable and the upper portion as a tenement. The Twenty-second Precinct Police got out a great portion of the furniture of the tenants and the thirty horses in the stable, so that the loss was chiefly confined to the building, which will require $1,500 for repairs. No. 629 was occupied as a stable by HENRY BENKIN, whose loss is $500, and the slaughter-house of RICHARD DONOVAN, in the rear, was also slightly damaged. The fire also extended from the rear of the houses on the south side of the street to the raw-hide establishment of WM. CARR, Nos. 641 and 643 West Forty-sixth-street, whose loss is chiefly confined to the building, which is damaged $1,500. The fire at one time threatened to destroy the entire block, and that result would have undoubtedly followed, but for the great exertions of the firemen, ably directed by Chief Engineer PERLEY and the district engineers.

Meeting of the Riot Relief Fund Association.

A meeting of the Twelfth of July Relief Fund Association was held last evening at No. 295 Third-avenue, Dr. J. C. HANNAN presiding. The General Committee already appointed was authorized to begin the collection of subscriptions, and was authorized to name a subcommittee to investigate cases of distress arising out of the late riot. The election of a treasurer was deferred to the next meeting, each member of the Committee being ordered to report to the Secretary all collections made in the meantime. The name of JAS. H. GOODMAN, attorney-at-law, was added to the General Committee, which will meet at No. 204 East Twenty-first street next Friday evening. Our reporter was informed that the subscriptions already promised amount to $700.

AFFAIRS IN EUROPE.

Mr. Gladstone's Sensational Flank Movement Against the Lords.

The Constitution Declared to be Violently Wrenched.

Parliament Brought into Contempt Before the People.

German Troops Ordered to be Withdrawn from Amiens and Rouen.

Formation of a Spanish Cabinet by Marshal Serrano.

Tumultuous Scene on the Adjournment of the Cortes.

GREAT BRITAIN.

The London Journals on the Recent Act of the Government—The Queen's Warrant Laid on the Table of the House of Commons—The New Castle Strikers.

LONDON, July 21.—The *Times* says the act of the Ministers abolishing the system of purchase of army commissions by royal warrant is a violent wrench of the Constitution, and a wanton setting aside of the will of the House of Lords. The *Times* regrets that this grave issue has been raised, but expresses the hope that the Lords will in their future action think of the effect upon the officers of the army rather than the indignity to their own privileges. The *Daily News* approves the conduct of the Government in making themselves the exponents of the popular will, and recommends that the Lords pass the bill abolishing the purchase of Army commissions. The *Telegraph* is exultant over the action of the Ministry, and says that Mr. GLADSTONE will be the more popular for vindicating the dignity of the House of Commons, in securing the harvest of its laborious session, and for reorganizing the defenses of the country and guarding the interests of the Army. The *Post* says the course of the Government has been somewhat unconstitutional, bringing, it believes, Parliament into contempt before the people. The *Standard* asserts that Mr. GLADSTONE has grossly violated the privileges of Parliament, wasting its time, and precipitating a constitutional crisis. In the House of Commons, this afternoon, Mr. CARDWELL, Secretary of State for War, laid on the table the Queen's warrant abolishing the system of purchase of army commissions.

[illegible] held a meeting today, and resolved to make no compromise with their employers.

FRANCE.

The Paris Elections To-Morrow—Rumored Resignation of the Orleans Princes—German Evacuation of the Northern Departments Ordered.

PARIS, July 21.—The Radicals are actively canvassing for the municipal elections to be held next Sunday. The contest grows more and more exciting. In the Assembly, today, Minister LAMBRECHT explained that the state of siege was still maintained in Paris, because the reorganization of the Police had not yet been completed. Notwithstanding the adverse report of the Committee of the Assembly, M. THIERS intends to defend his policy of protection before the Assembly. It is rumored that the Duke D'AUMALE and the Prince DE JOINVILLE have resigned their seats in the Assembly. President THIERS will shortly leave Paris for one of the watering-places. *Le Monde*, the ultra Catholic organ, demands that the Government support the Pope in the exercise of his temporal rights. Criminal proceedings have been commenced against the *Avenir Nationale* for calumniating the Government. The Prussian troops have received orders from Berlin to evacuate the Cities of Amiens and Rouen, and the Departments of the Somme, Lower Seine and Euse. Rouen will be evacuated to-morrow.

GENERAL EUROPEAN NEWS.

Serrano Forms a New Ministry in Spain—Adjournment of the Cortes—Alsace and Lorraine—A Fleet Preparing to Convey the Grand Duke Alexis to America.

MADRID, July 20.—Marshal SERRANO has been intrusted by King AMADEUS with the formation of a new Ministry, and has already designated the following members: Minister of Justice, Señor GOMEZ; Minister of Foreign Affairs, Señor CAUDAN; Minister of Marine, Admiral MALCAMPO; Minister of Finance, Señor CAMADIO. The Cortes has adjourned tumultuously amid the protests of the minority.

VIENNA, July 21.—Count AGENOR GOLUCHOWSKI has been appointed Governor of Galicia.

BERLIN, July 21.—Several decrees are published today, organizing Courts of law in Alsace and Lorraine.

LONDON, July 21.—The Grand Duke CONSTANTINE, of Russia, has arrived in England. A naval squadron is fitting out at Cronstadt to accompany the Grand Duke ALEXIS to America.

The "Reformed" Hackmen—Opposition to the Proposed New Regulations.

The Hackmen's Association met last evening in Apollo Hall, in Prince-street, with a very large attendance. JOHN MARRION, the President, occupied the chair, and J. PHILLIPS was Secretary. A dozen new members were elected, and $149 50 was received for dues and fees.

A resolution was passed to expel any member of the association who should take passengers with the Transfer Companies' tickets. The initiation fee was changed to $5 for owners, and $2 for drivers.

The Treasurer reported that the expenses for the past week had been $217, and the cash in hand, previous to the meeting, was $215.

The new regulations proposed by Mayor HALL did not meet the views of the hackmen. Several members spoke in opposition to them. They considered them as unjust and unconstitutional; they would drive the men out of their business, and the men who had new carriages would get all the business, while those who had second rate or middling carriages would have to go to the wall. They deemed the clause which prevents the hackmen from soliciting passengers as illegal, and they would contest it in Court if necessary. It was a job got up to benefit a few politicians who are engaged in the business, who wish to monopolize it and drive the poorer men out of it altogether. A committee was appointed to visit the Mayor and explain the views of the hackmen, and request him to modify it.

A HAPPY HOME FOR ORPHANS.—A REVEREND PRECEPTOR'S PUNISHMENT FOR LITTLE CHILDREN.

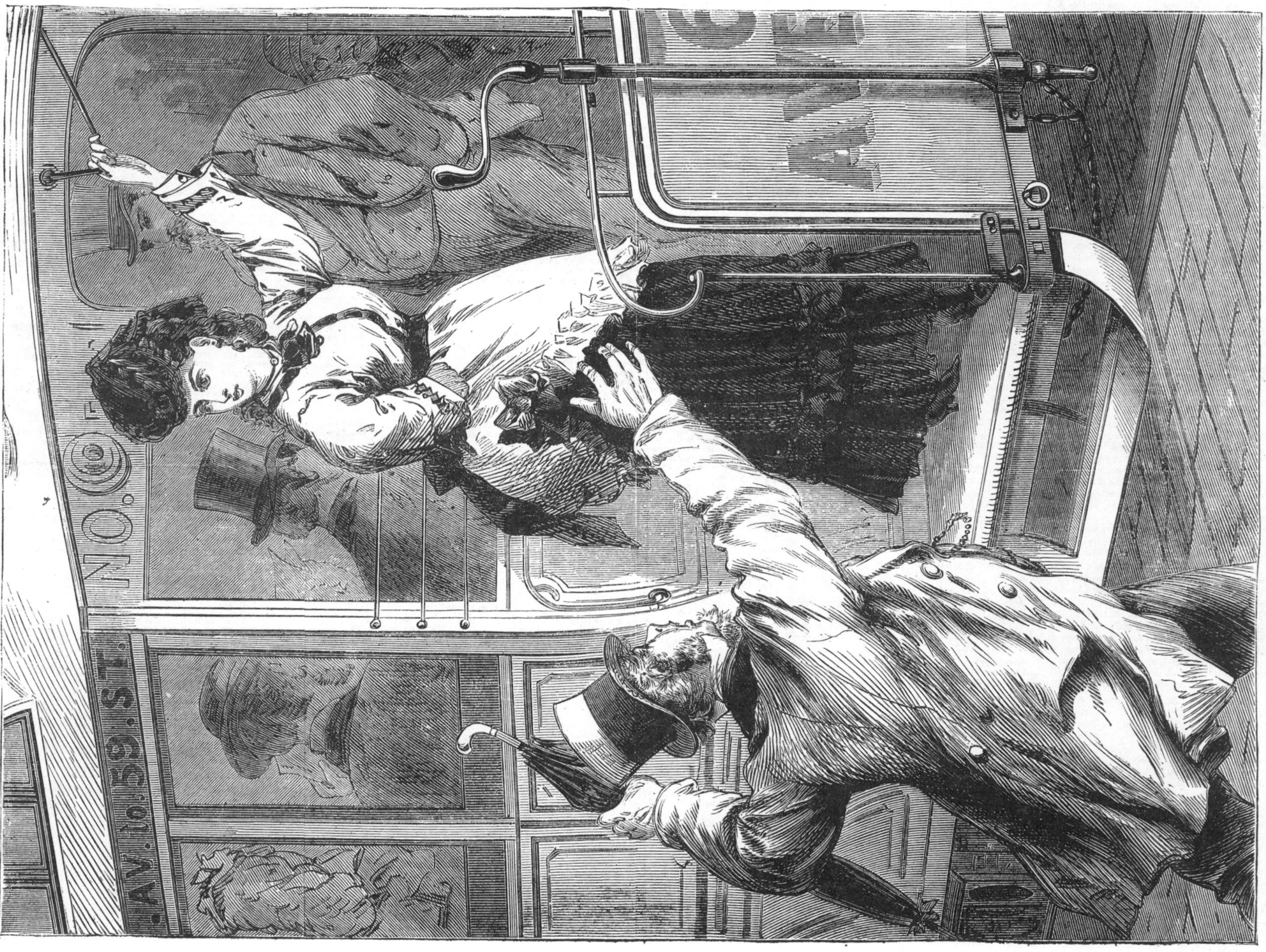

WHAT WE ARE COMING TO!—FEMALE TRAMWAY-CAR CONDUCTORS.

FOREST FIRES IN THE WEST.

SIMULTANEOUSLY with the news of the burning of Chicago came the intelligence of vast conflagrations in the forests and prairies in the States of Michigan, Wisconsin, and Minnesota. These terrible fires have probably destroyed many times the number of those who fell victims of the burning of Chicago, though the damage to property is much less in actual value.

The worst calamity occurred in the State of Wisconsin, where, in the woods between Green Bay and Fox River, a conflagration raged many days, laying waste a strip of country thirty miles wide in Shawana and Oconto counties. The towns of Marinette, Peshtigo, and Little Sturgeon Bay were destroyed. At Peshtigo 320 lives were lost, seventy-five at Little Sturgeon, and hundreds more in other places, while many families were driven out of house and home. Farm buildings, fences, and bridges all over the country were swept away. Thousands of square miles of valuable pine forests were destroyed. Bears and other wild beasts were driven in dismay from the woods, and were flying about in every direction. All supplies of food for man and beast have been destroyed, and starvation during the coming winter stares them in the face. The double-page illustration in this number of the *Weekly* gives a graphic idea of the terrors of this unexampled conflagration.

It has been estimated that in the State of Wisconsin the fire extended over an area of 150 square miles, through a region of pine and hardwood timber, which was thickly settled. The drought in August had dried up springs, streams, and vegetation, and parched the ground to such a depth below the surface that the soil itself burned, and living trees were falling from the action of the fires which undermined them. All outstanding property was swept away, there being no water available to stop the fires. Barns and their contents, hay-stacks, corn, wood, and other property, with hundreds of miles of fences, were burned. The hardest fights against the flames were made at the saw-mills located among the pine forests of Green Bay region, but many of them have been burned.

THE HON. JOEL PARKER, GOVERNOR ELECT OF NEW JERSEY.
[PHOTOGRAPHED BY C. D. FREDRICKS & COMPANY.]

WOMEN AT THE POLLS.

FIVE adventurous women of this city marched boldly to the polls on last election day, and demanded to be allowed to vote. Among them was Mrs. VICTORIA WOODHULL, who, fresh from an interview on the house-top with the roving spirit of DEMOSTHENES, drove up early to the polls in a fine carriage. This lady was more determined and more demonstrative than her sister reformers. She was not to be bluffed off without an argument. Her lawyer was at hand, but she required no prompting. When her right to vote was denied, she planted herself on the Constitution of the United States, and insisted that the inspector should read the clause on which she founds her claim. The objection that no copy of that document was at hand was immediately met by the production of a pocket edition with which the fair claimant had come provided. The Republican inspector was inclined to receive her vote, but his Democratic colleague was immovable. He would not even look at the Constitution, and finally put an end to the scene by telling the persistent lady that she "obstructed the polls, and must get out." Miss TENNIE C. CLAFFLIN met with the same rebuff; and then, seeing that their efforts were fruitless, the ladies departed. Our artist has delineated this serio-humorous rencontre in the sketch on this page.

The only one of the five who succeeded in voting was a Mrs. MILLER, who afterward openly boasted that she had cast a ballot for TWEED. The *World* suggests that if this is a fair sample of the use which women will make of the ballot, the opposition to their demand will be stronger than ever, and humorously expresses the fear that Mrs. MILLER may have "chosen some untrustworthy Greek—ALCIBIADES, perhaps, or possibly PISISTRATUS—as her guide and counselor." DEMOSTHENES is wholly occupied by his prior engagement with Mrs. WOODHULL, but the *World* suggests the names of several other distinguished Grecian spirits who might be glad to undertake the task of directing Mrs. MILLER's political conscience.

THE HON. JOEL PARKER.

WE give on this page a portrait of this gentleman, who has just been chosen for the second time to fill the gubernatorial chair of New Jersey. Mr. PARKER owes his election more to the personal esteem in which he is held by his fellow-citizens than to the strength of the Democratic party, the Republicans having a numerical majority in the State. He was first elected Governor in 1862, and proved himself to be an honest and able administrator of affairs, and so truly patriotic that in several of the strongly "Copperhead" counties of New Jersey he was burned in effigy by members of his own party.

HUMAN MISERY IN LONDON.

M. TAINE, in his notes upon England, gives an equally terrible account of the two extremes of human life as they appear in the most neglected and poorest districts of London. Speaking of Shadwell, he describes "small streets, dusty courts, infected by a smell of rotten rags, and tapestried with poor clothing and linen hung out to dry. The children swarm. At one moment," says M. Taine, "I had fourteen or fifteen round me, dirty, barefooted, the little sister carrying the baby in her arms, the nursling of a year old, with its bald white head. Nothing can be more distressing to see than these white bodies, these flaxen tangles, these pasty cheeks plastered with dirt of long standing. They come running up, showing the gentleman to each other with curious and greedy gestures. The motionless mothers look out from the door-ways with lack-lustre eyes. The narrow dwelling may be seen within, often one single room in which all is heaped together in the foul air. The houses often consist but of one story; they are low and narrow hovels in which to sleep and die. What an abode in winter, when the window remains shut through continuous weeks of rain and fog! And that this brood may not die of hunger, the father must not drink, must never be without work, must never be ill. Here and there is a heap of street sweepings. Women were working among the rubbish. One of them, who is old and faded, had a short pipe in her mouth. They raised themselves from their work to look at me, showing brutalized, disquieting faces, like female Yahoos: perhaps that pipe, with a glass of gin, is the last idea which comes uppermost in their idiotic brain. Could any thing be found therein above the instincts and appetites of a savage or a beast of burden? A miserable black cat, lank, lame, and bewildered, watched them out of the corners of its terrified eyes, and stealthily searched about a dust-heap; the old woman followed it with looks as wild as its own, mumbling as she did so, and evidently calculating that it represented two pounds or so of meat!" M. Taine thinks the street boys of this part of London more wretched-looking and more repulsive than the Parisian "voyou," and attributes this to the "climate being worse, and the gin more murderous." But the same story is true of most large cities. Our own New York could supply M. Taine with pictures quite as terrible in their repulsive misery as those which he has drawn of the London slums.

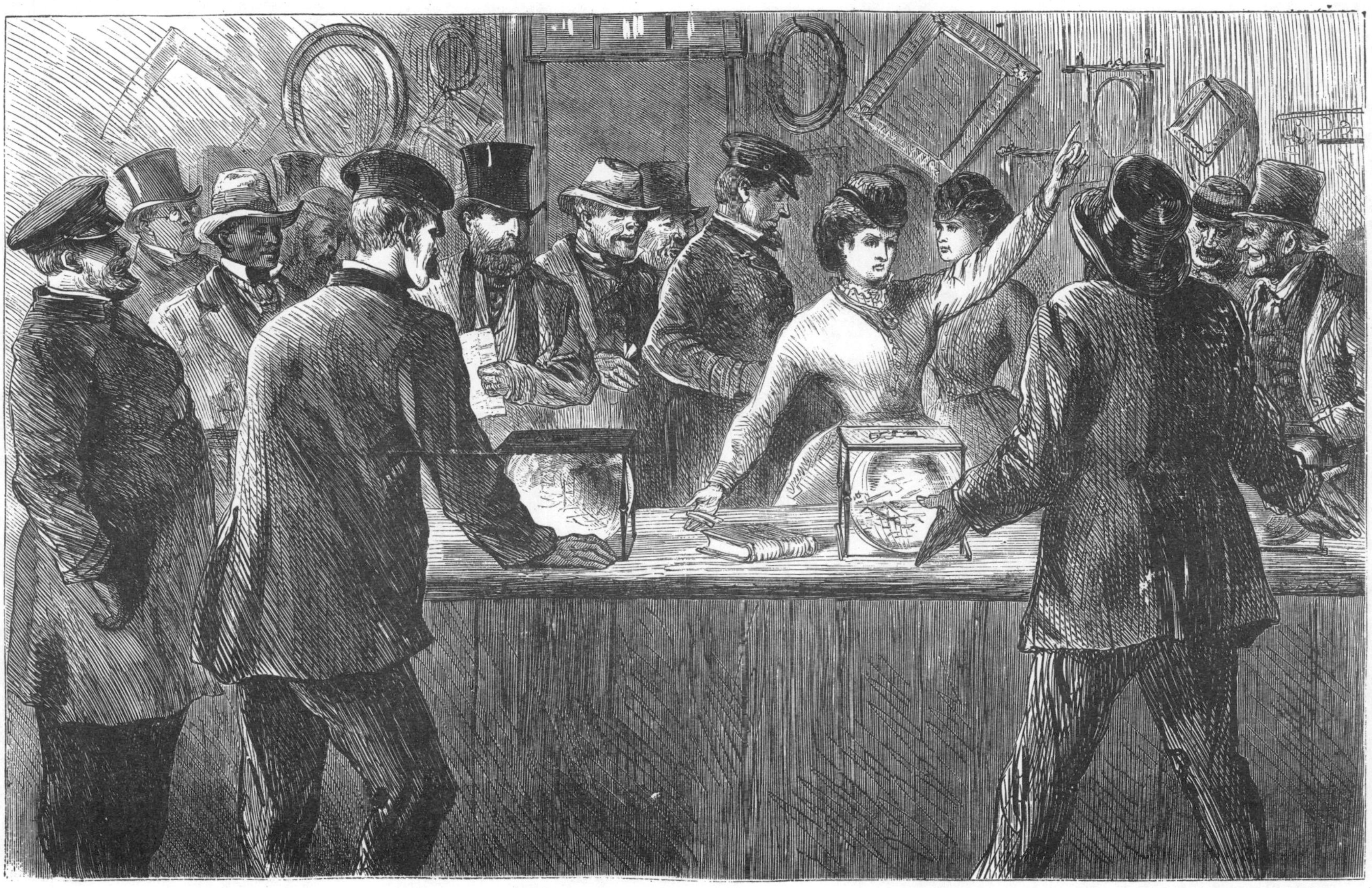

MRS. WOODHULL ASSERTING HER RIGHT TO VOTE.—[FROM A SKETCH BY H. BALLING.]

The Life and Death of James Fisk Jr.

FOR SALE BY ALL NEWS DEALERS.] NEW YORK. [PRICE 10 CENTS.

THE LIFE AND DEATH OF JAMES FISK, Jr.

THE ASSASSINATION.

A Twelfth Night Tragedy.

JAMES FISK, JR., is now but a memory.

The career of this eccentric personage has been as brilliant as a rocket—it has terminated in the darkness of death, and, like a rocket, has left but a flash behind, to mark where and what it had been.

It is for us here and now to discuss, by pen and pencil, the details of the shooting of James Fisk, Jr., by Edward S. Stokes.

The tragedy was but the sequel to a farce; the murder was but the culmination—the finale of the tediously disgusting Stokes-Fisk-Mansfield litigation, involving certain correspondence of Fisk with Mansfield; certain pecuniary transactions between them, complicated with the monetary affairs

STOKES ENCOURAGES JOSIE IN COURT.

of Stokes, and indirectly connected, so it has been presumed, with the gigantic operations known formerly as the Erie and the Tammany Rings.

On Saturday, January 6th, 1872, James Fisk, Jr., had, to all appearance, won the suit, and was master of the situation; Judge Brady had given a decision in his favor; he had succeeded in obtaining, so it's said, an indictment against Miss Mansfield and Mr. Stokes on his charge of black-mail; he had, through the lawyers, worried Stokes on the examination, and even moved his former mistress to tears; he was flushed with triumph, and, in the plenitude of his victory, drove, on Saturday afternoon, January 6th, to the Grand Central Hotel, and alighted thereat, for the purpose of visiting some of his lady friends—Mrs. Morse and her daughters.

But at the very moment of might, in the very zenith of glory, in the full flush of life and vigor, the end came.

His former friend, his discomfited enemy, Edward S. Stokes, met him as he was ascending the ladies' entrance to the hotel, and then and there shot him.

HELEN JOSEPHINE MANSFIELD-LAWLOR.

THE SHOOTING.

While Mr. Fisk was mounting the staircase of the ladies' entrance, before he had reached the third step, his deadly foe, Edward S. Stokes, suddenly made his appearance from his place of concealment, and a shot rang out which struck Fisk in the abdomen, two inches to the right of the naval, and three inches above it, passing downward, backward, and to the left, inflicting a terrible wound. Fisk fell, shouting "Oh!" and immediately scrambled to his feet again, when Stokes again levelled his revolver and fired another shot, the ball passing through and out of Fisk's left arm, without touching the bone. Fisk turned to run, but fell a second time and slid down to the bottom of the stairs, where he was picked up by the crowd, among whom were several of his acquaintances, who had gathered on hearing the report of the pistol, and carried upstairs to rooms 214 and 215, where he was laid upon the bed, and the house physician summoned.

THE ARREST.

Then the alarm was given and the police notified. Stokes did not attemp to leave the hotel. Officer McCadden and Captain Byrne, of the Fifteenth Precinct, came in and arrested him. He said nothing. Captain Byrne said, "Your name is Stokes?" and Stokes bowed, and said, "Yes." The captain said, "Where is the pistol?" and Stokes told the captain where it was.

A crowd had gathered around, and Stokes was taken up-stairs. The

THE LUNCH BEFORE THE MURDER.

mob of men who had rushed from all parts of the hotel, especially from the barber-shop hard-by, in all stages of apron and lather, attempted to follow, but were kept back by two waiters who had been placed at the foot of the main stairs. Another waiter stood guard in the private entrance to the hotel and refused admission to all comers. The crowd in the main hall gave a murmur of disappointment as they saw Stokes being taken away. Men were there in their shirt-sleeves fresh from the billiard-room with cues in their hands; loungers from the street, actors from the theatres, guests of the hotel, thieves from the Eighth Ward, and a swarm of detectives from Police Headquarters were there also.

THE IDENTIFICATION.

Immediately subsequent to his arrest, Captain Byrne, on taking Stokes up-stairs, brought him to the room in which Fisk lay on a lounge, and

STOKES LYING IN WAIT FOR HIS VICTIM.

EDWARD S. STOKES.

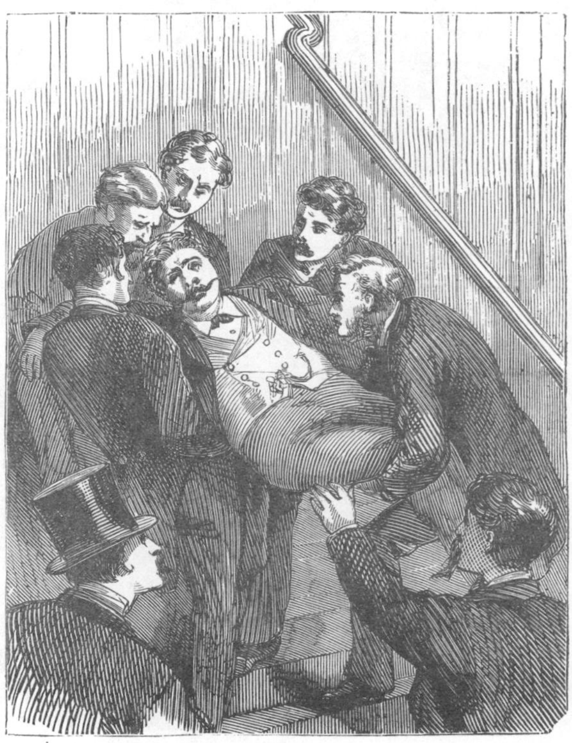

CARRYING FISK FROM THE STAIRCASE TO HIS ROOM.

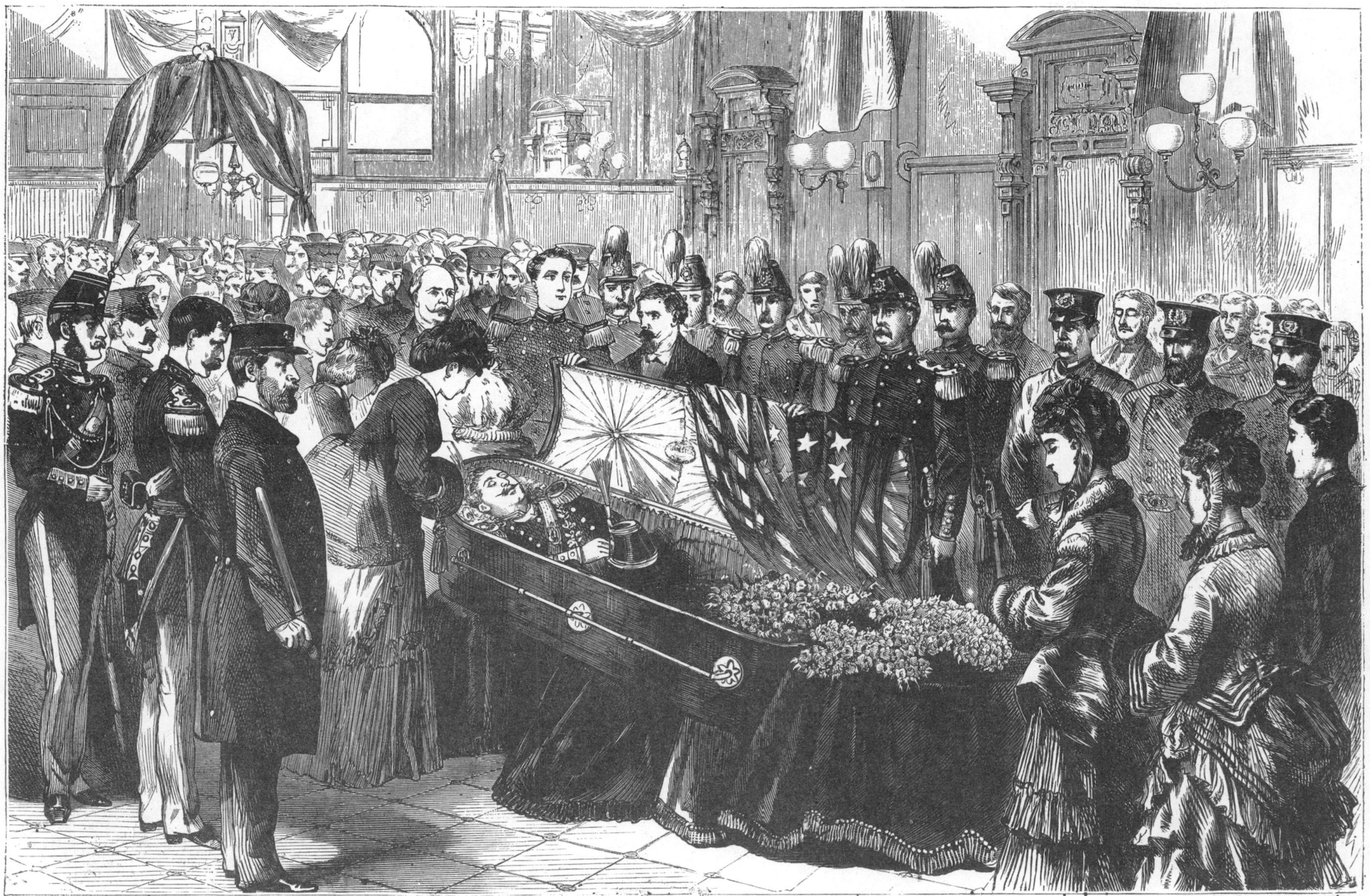

OBSEQUIES OF THE LATE COLONEL JAMES FISK, Jr.—THE REMAINS LYING IN STATE IN THE CORRIDOR OF THE ERIE RAILWAY OFFICES IN THE GRAND OPERA HOUSE.

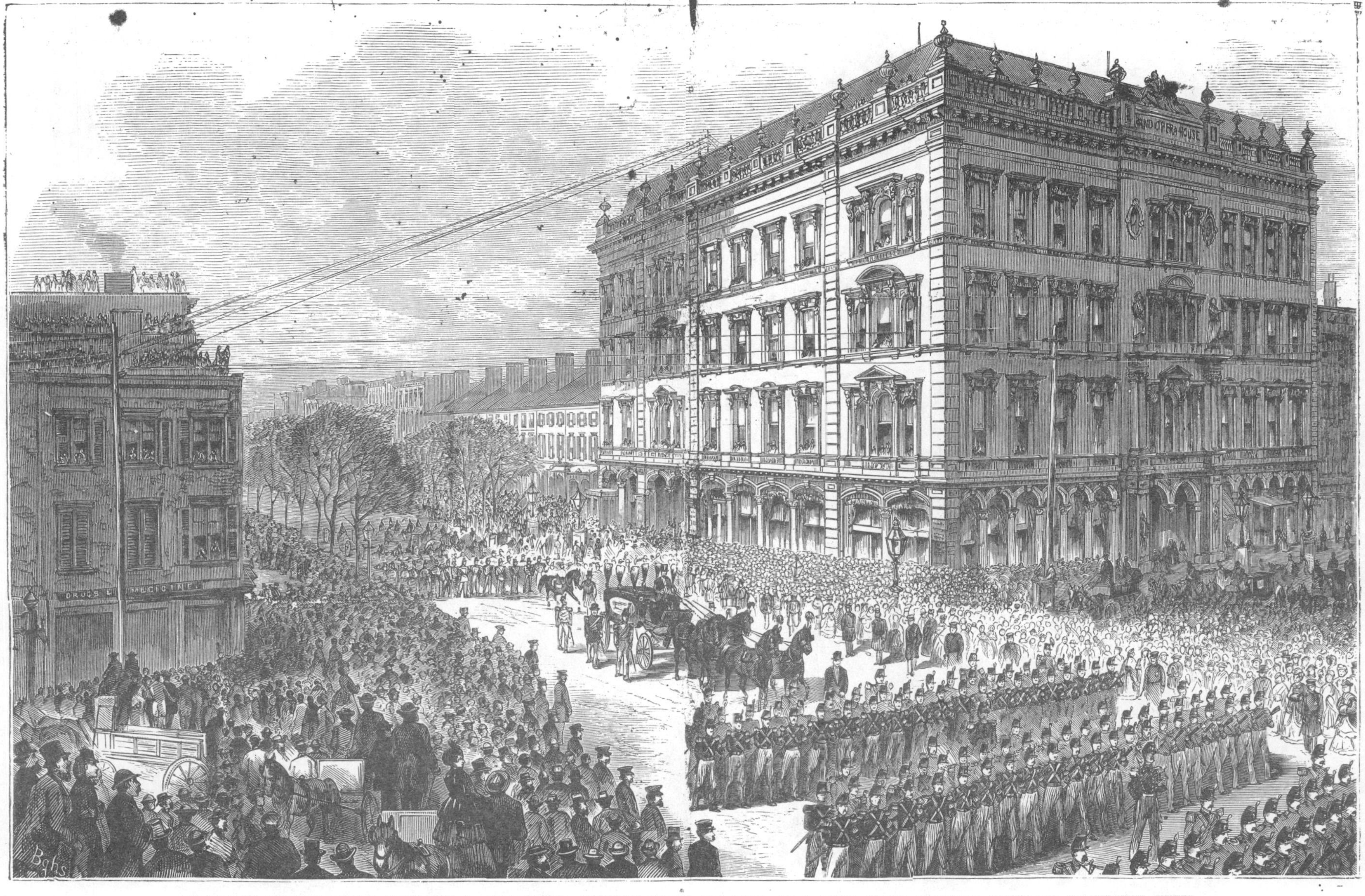

OBSEQUIES OF THE LATE COLONEL JAMES FISK, Jr.—THE FUNERAL PROCESSION LEAVING THE GRAND OPERA HOUSE, CORNER OF EIGHTH AVENUE AND TWENTY-THIRD STREET.

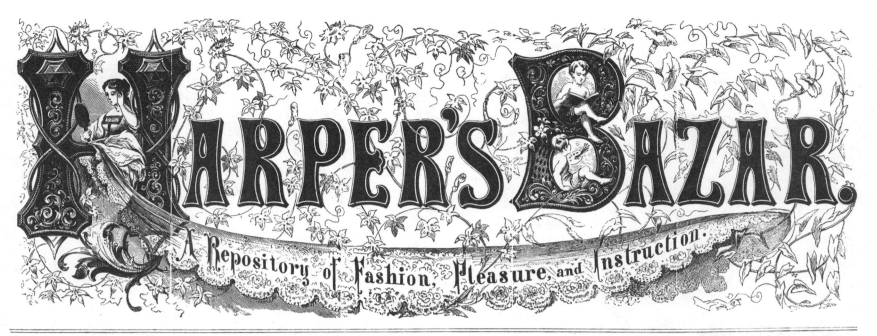

HARPER'S BAZAR.

A Repository of Fashion, Pleasure, and Instruction.

Vol. V.—No. 2.] NEW YORK, SATURDAY, JANUARY 13, 1872. [SINGLE COPIES TEN CENTS. $4.00 PER YEAR IN ADVANCE.

LADIES' AND CHILDREN'S DRESSES.—[See Page 18.]

Fig. 1.—Suit for Girl from 5 to 15 Years old (with Cut Paper Pattern). Fig. 2.—Dinner Dress. Fig. 3.—Evening Dress.

[Cut Paper Patterns of Suit for Girl from 5 to 15 Years old, with Double-breasted Sacque, Postilion Basque, Apron-front Over-Skirt, and Under-Skirt, in eleven Sizes, from 22 to 32 Inches, Bust Measure, sent, Prepaid, by Mail, on Receipt of Twenty-five Cents.]

THE

GREELEY CAMPAIGN

BUDGET.

No. 1. ORNUM & COMPANY, PUBLISHERS, NEW YORK. PRICE FIVE CENTS.

FOR PRESIDENT,
HORACE GREELEY,

FOR VICE-PRESIDENT,
B. GRATZ BROWN.

HORACE GREELEY'S THE MAN.

BY MAJOR JACK STRATMAN.

AIR: *"Moon behind the hill."*

The time has come for all of us,
There's no use now to wait;
And understand what we're about,
Before it is is too late.
To bring about the good old times,
We've got to change the plan,
And to fight it out on this 'ere line,
O! Greeley is the man!
(Repeat the last four lines for Chorus.)
To re-construct this mighty land,
And do the thing that's right;
We don't want any nonsense now,
Or else there'll be a fight.
We've had enough she-nan-i gan,
Since Congress last began,
And to make peace and prosperity,
O! Greeley is the man!

Chorus

O! now's the time for all of us
To act and have a voice,
And what I sing of Greeley to you,
Is now the people's choice.
We want a man that's staunch and true,
To act as well as plan,
Who's got the nerve to back it up;
And Greeley is the man!

Chorus.

So rally boys! get up and get!
There's no use now to wait,
But take this matter right in hand,
Before it is too late.
And give this Greeley to Uncle Sam—
You'll not regret the plan—
To fill the White House Chair, you bet,
O! Greeley is the man.

HURRAH FOR THE OLD TREE CHOPPER.

Hurrah for Horace Greeley,
The Tree Chopper, honest and true!
Hurrah for him with a will and a vim,
With your votes and your victory, too.
For when he springs into the combat
With his battle axe heavy and broad,
He will level the tree of rank and robbery
And chop off the head of Fraud.

Hurrah for Horace Greeley!
Woe, woe, to the men who frown,
When the People's Man in the crushing van
Cuts the place-brought hireling down!
For his weapon is made of Vengeance,
And its handle is made of Right,
And his arm is strong against the wrong,
That would throttle the people's might.

Hurrah for Horace Greeley!
Stand fast by the People's Man,
The old Tree Chopper of Chappaqua,
Who bravely leads the van!
Go sharpen your battle-axes!
Prepare for the combat red,
And strike with the Just till low in the dust,
The Wrong and its tools lie dead.

OUR FUTURE PRESIDENT.

Horace Greeley, nominated at Cincinnati for the Presidency, was born on the 3d February, 1811, in Amherst N. H. Greeley's youth seemed to have been passed amidst considerable though not unusual hardships. At ten years of age his parents removed to Vermont. After assisting his father in the farming operations for three or four years, he was apprenticed to a printer in East Pulteney, in that State. After working in Erie, Pa., for a few months as journeyman printer, he went to New York City, and entered upon journalism as a profession. As a whig he entered into politics and published a number of campaign papers, all of which failed. In 1836, he married Miss Cheney of North Carolina.

In 1841, the New York *Tribune* was started by Horace Greeley, and it is with that paper, now in existence, with which his name is considerably known. In 1848, Greeley was elected to the House of Representatives to fill an unexpired term. In 1850, he published "Hints Towards Reforms," partly lectures and partly essays. In 1851, he visited Europe, and was chosen chairman of one of the juries at the World's Fair. In 1844, he strongly supported Clay for the Presidency; in 1852, Scott, and in 1856, Fremont. In 1860, he supported Lincoln, and published his notable letter dissolving the firm of Seward, Weed and Greeley. In 1867, Greeley became part bail for Jefferson Davis, of Mississippi, arraigned before the United States Circuit Court for levying war against the United States. Greeley opposed Johnson's administration throughout. He supported, on the impeachment project, and sustained Secretary Stanton in his refusal to resign his portfolio at the request of the President. In 1868, Greeley and the *Tribune* supported General Grant for the Presidency. Greeley is in his 62d year, and has been prominent in the politics of the country for more than thirty years.

AFTER ELECTION IS OVER.

AIR: *"After the Opera is Over."*

After election is over,
Old Horace will take the big chair,
Ulysses and his carpet-baggers,
To clear out will quickly prepare.
The people are speaking their verdict,
Ulysses has taken alarm,
The racers, gift-trotters, and bull-pups
Are shipped to the St. Louis farm.
After election is over,
And counting the ballot is done,
The followers of Honest old Horace,
Will cheer for the vic'try they've won.

After election is over,
Grant's porter his luggage must pack;
Catell must go home to Camden,
And Robeson take the back track,
Farewell then to all the bribe-takers.
No plunder, the people insist,
Grant's host of relations they'll banish,
From old Jesse down through the list.

After election is over,
Fair Cuba, we swear, shall be free,
Let Grant go to Santa Domingo,
His mahogany crony to see.
Prince Fred and the fair Princess Nellie,
No longer shall ape royal airs;
No flunkeys shall tarnish our banner,
When Horace shall manage affairs.

DOCTOR GREELEY.

A CAMPAIGN SONG.

AIR: *"The Umbarella."*

The Great Republic is awake,
It surely is surprising,
Through East and West and North and South,
The people are uprising.
They're tired of war and party hate,
And patriot hands grasp freely,
The Union through love to bind
With Honest Horace Greeley.

For Horace is a man of peace,
Who knows the war is over,
And with the garb of charity
His country's wounds would cover.
A friend of liberty to all—
The doctor who can heal ye,
The sickened body politic,
Is good old Doctor Greeley.

With universal amnesty,
And with impartial suffrage,
A single term will do to cure
The evils of this tough age.
His vermifuge, Reform, will purge
The State of rascals scaly,
And blood-suckers will run away,
From fearless Doctor Greeley.

The Tribune of the people, he
Has never failed to tell them
The honest truth, and hunted down
The villains who would sell them.
Oh, Horace is a man of peace,
A friend of freedom really—
We'll have him for our President—
Hurrah for Doctor Greeley!

WOODHULL & CLAFLIN'S WEEKLY.

PROGRESS! FREE THOUGHT! UNTRAMMELED LIVES!

BREAKING THE WAY FOR FUTURE GENERATIONS.

Vol. V.—No. 11.—Whole No. 115. NEW YORK, FEBRUARY 15, 1873. PRICE TEN CENTS.

THE

LOANER'S BANK

OF THE CITY OF NEW YORK,

(ORGANIZED UNDER STATE CHARTER,)

Continental Life Builing,

22 NASSAU STREET, NEW YORK.

CAPITAL.................................. $500,000
Subject to increase to..................... 1,000,000

This Bank negotiates LOANS, makes COLLECTIONS, advances on SECURITIES and receives DEPOSITS.

Accounts of Bankers, Manufacturers and Merchants will receive special attention.

☞ FIVE PER CENT. INTEREST paid on CURRENT BALANCES and liberal facilities offered to our CUSTOMERS.

DORR RUSSELL, President.
A. F. WILMARTH, Vice-President.

JOHN J. CISCO & SON,

Bankers,

No. 59 Wall St., New York.

Gold and Currency received on deposit subject to check at sight.

Interest allowed on Currency Accounts at the rate of Four per Cent. per annum, credited at the end of each month.

ALL CHECKS DRAWN ON US PASS THROUGH THE CLEARING-HOUSE, AND ARE RECEIVED ON DEPOSIT BY ALL THE CITY BANKS.

Certificates of Deposit issued, payable on demand, bearing Four per Cent interest.

Loans negotiated.

Orders promptly executed for the Purchase and Sale of Governments, Gold, Stocks and Bonds on commission.

Collections made on all parts of the United States and Canadas.

HARVEY FISK. A. S. HATCH.

OFFICE OF

FISK & HATCH,

BANKERS AND DEALERS IN GOVERNMENT SECURITIES,

No. 5 Nassau st., N. Y.

☞ *Opposite U. S. Sub-Treasury.*

We receive the accounts of Banks, Bankers, Corporations and others, subject to check at sight, and allow interest on balances.

We make special arrangements for interest on deposits of specific sums for fixed periods.

We make collections on all points in the United States and Canada, and issue Certificates of Deposit available in all parts of the Union.

We buy and sell at current rates, all classes of Government Securities, and the Bonds of the Central Pacific Railroad Company; also, Gold and Silver Coin and Gold Coupons.

We buy and sell, at the Stock Exchange, miscellaneous Stocks and Bonds, on commission, for cash.

Communications and inquiries by mail or telegraph, will receive careful attention.

FISK & HATCH.

A FIRST-CLASS

New York Security

AT A LOW PRICE.

The undersigned offer for sale the First Mortgage Seven Per Cent. Gold Bonds of the Syracuse and Chenango Valley Railroad, at 95 and accrued interest.

This road runs from the City of Syracuse to Smith's Valley, where it unites with the New York Midland Railroad, thus connecting that city by a direct line of road with the metropolis.

Its length is 42 miles, its cost about $42,000 per mile, and it is mortgaged for less than $12,000 per mile; the balance of the funds required for its construction having been raised by subscription to the capital stock.

The road approaches completion. It traverses a populous and fertile district of the State, which insures it a paying business, and it is under the control of gentlemen of high character and ability. Its bonds possess all the requisites of an inviting investment. They are amply secured by a mortgage for less than one-third the value of the property. They pay seven per cent. gold interest, and are offered five per cent. below par. The undersigned confidently recommend them to all class of investors.

GEORGE OPDYKE & CO.,
No. 25 Nassau Street.

TO INVESTORS.

To those who wish to REINVEST COUPONS OR DIVIDENDS, and those who wish to INCREASE THEIR INCOME from means already invested in less profitable securities, we recommend the Seven-Thirty Gold Bonds of the Northern Pacific Railroad Company as well secured and unusually productive.

The bonds are always convertible at Ten per cent. premium (*1.10*) into the Company's Lands, at Market Prices. The rate of interest (seven and three-tenths per cent. gold) is equal now to about *8 1-4* currency—yielding an income more than one-third greater than U. S. *5-20s*. Gold Checks for the semi-annual interest on the Registered Bonds are mailed to the post-office address of the owner. All marketable stocks and bonds are received in exchange for Northern Pacifics ON MOST FAVORABLE TERMS.

JAY COOKE & CO.

BANKING HOUSE OF

HENRY CLEWS & CO.,

32 Wall Street, N. Y.

Circular Notes and Letters of Credit for travelers; also Commercial Credits issued available throughout the world.

Bills of Exchange on the Imperial Bank of London, National Bank of Scotland, Provincial Bank of Ireland and all their branches.

Telegraphic Transfers of money on Europe, San Francisco and the West Indies.

Deposit accounts received in either Currency or Coin, subject to Check at sight, which pass through the Clearing House as if drawn upon any city bank; interest allowed on all daily balances; Certificates of Deposit issued bearing interest at current rate; Notes and Drafts collected.

State, City and Railroad Loans negotiated.

CLEWS, HABICHT & CO.,
11 Old Broad St., London.

BANKING & FINANCIAL.

THE ST. JOSEPH AND DENVER CITY RAILROAD COMPANY'S

FIRST MORTGAGE BONDS

Are being absorbed by an increasing demand for them.

Secured as they are by a first mortgage on the Road, Land Grant, Franchise and Equipments, combined in one mortgage, they command at once a ready market.

A Liberal Sinking Fund provided in the Mortgage Deed must advance the price upon the closing of the loan. Principal and interest payable in GOLD. Interest at eight (8) per cent. per annum. Payable semi-annually, free of tax. Principal in thirty years. Denominations, $1,000, $500 and $100 Coupons, or Registered.

Price 97½ and accrued interest, in currency, from February 15, 1872.

Maps, Circulars, Documents and information furnished.

Trustees, Farmers' Loan and Trust Company of New York.

Can now be had through the principal Banks and Bankers throughout the country, and from the undersigned who unhesitatingly recommend them.

TANNER & CO., Bankers,
No. 11 Wall Street, New York.

AUGUST BELMONT & CO.,

Bankers,

50 WALL STREET,

Issue Letters of Credit to Travelers, available in all parts of the world through the

MESSRS. DE ROTHSCHILD AND THEIR CORRESPONDENTS.

Also, make telegraphic transfers of money on California, Europe and Havana.

TOLEDO, PEORIA

AND

WARSAW RAILWAY,

SECOND MORTGAGE CONVERTIBLE 7 PER CENT. CURRENCY BONDS.

INTEREST WARRANTS PAYABLE

OCTOBER AND APRIL,

PRINCIPAL 1886.

We offer for sale $100,000 of the above bonds in block. By act of reorganization of the Company these bonds are convertible into the First Preferred Shares of the Company, which amounts to only 17,000 shares, and into the Consolidated Bonds (recently negotiated at Amsterdam) of six millions of dollars, which cover the entire line of 230 miles of completed road, together with all the rolling stock and real property, to the value of more than ten millions of dollars. The road crosses the entire State of Illinois and connect with the mammoth iron bridges spanning the Mississippi at Keokuk and Burlington. The income of the road for the year will net sufficient to pay interest on all the bonded indebtedness and dividend on the preferred shares.

For terms apply to

CLARK, DODGE & CO.,

Corner Wall and William Streets.

MAXWELL & CO.,

Bankers and Brokers,

No. 11 BROAD STREET,

NEW YORK.

WOODHULL AND HER OFFENSES.

A LEGAL FRAUD EXPOSED—THE RIGHTS OF THE PRESS DEFENDED—A CRITICISM BY EDWARD H. G. CLARK, OF TROY, N. Y.

[*From the Troy Daily Press, January* 25, 1873.

Mrs. Woodhull is undoubtedly the most obnoxious person to-day in the United States. But has she reduced forty millions of people to cowards—afraid not to defend her (which no one might wish to do), but all equally afraid to say one honest word, even in explanation and criticism of her offenses. This word I purpose to speak. Truth awaits it. Violated law demands it. A careless and confused nation needs it.

On Saturday the 2d of last November, Victoria Woodhull and Tennie C. Claflin were arrested under charge of publishing obscene literature. The charge rests on two articles which appeared in WOODHULL & CLAFLIN'S WEEKLY of November 2, 1872—one entitled "The Beecher-Tilton Scandal Case," and the other, "The Philosophy of Modern Hypocrisy—Mr. L. C. Challis the Illustration." Both of these articles are simply horrible in their statements, and, if slanders, should consign their authors to prison without stay or mercy. But neither article contains one word that is not current in every dictionary, and perfectly familiar throughout English literature. There are no immodest cartoons, as the dispatches of the Associated Press have untruthfully reported; nor does either article convey any description of wickedness different from other and customary accounts of crime.

I will not repeat the Challis story. But suppose that any journalist publishes an aggravated case of seduction, and brands the guilty parties as "scoundrels," throwing no charms about the deed, but making it cruel, ghastly, damnable. Say, for instance, that he tells of three young girls, scarcely more than children, brought from Philadelphia into the "best society" of New York, ruined by two middle-aged *roues*, and then cast out into a life of shame and despair. Let him add that the seducers gloated over their crime—one of them in so brutal a manner that he claimed to carry with him the evidence that his victims had been innocent until he reduced them to guilt and misery. A journalist publishing such a tale as this would take a grave responsibility. If true, I think it ought to be told, as a warning to society. If false, the publisher should be punished with the utmost severity of the law. But will any reader of a daily newspaper dare assert that the supposititious story here given is obscene? It is in every way as fairly liable to the charge of obscenity as the Challis story in WOODHULL & CLAFLIN'S WEEKLY. But is it obscene? If so, let Mr. A. J. Comstock instigate one more arrest as soon as desirable. 'Tis not exactly a religious question here involved; but 'tis a question, at least, of the right to speak and print in a great republic. For even such a right, Mr. Comstock, alias Mr. "Beardsley," may yet find—when his position is once understood—some very stubborn challengers.

It is of course wholly unnecessary in the present article to ask, for any purpose, whether Mrs. Woodhull's Challis story is true. "How this may have appeared to the jury," says a legal critic of the case, "we do not know;" but it "did appear from the published court reports that the matter contained in this libel was true." Suppose we deny it? But every man of the world knows that precisely the same kind of sin takes place in New York every day. Shall no person, no journal ever dare to expose and denounce the sin again, because one Anthony J. Comstock stands ready to snatch his body with the cry of "Obscene print?" If so, Mr. Comstock is much more dangerous than Mrs. Woodhull; and the Young Men's Christian Association, which seems to covet the honor of being his special backer, is only a Yankee "Inquisition," as odious and stupid as was ever that of Spain.

But the motive of the Woodhull scandals! Blackmail.

Perhaps it was so. Mrs. Woodhull has been charged with this offense "in the house of her friends." A "Professor Denton" has brought her among the Spiritualists, and Susan B. Anthony among the advocates of Woman's rights. On the other hand, Theodore Tilton acquits her of it, even now, as "something not in keeping with her character." The testimony in the Challis case is worthless. What, then, is the result? The public may suspect Mrs. Woodhull of blackmailing; but they have no evidence of it. It may be worth a moment of patience, therefore, to inquire into the motive of the Woodhull and "slanders," as given by the authors themselves.

It is everywhere understood that these women hold and advocate the doctrine called free love. I suppose it is possible to explain what they mean by free love, without being held responsible for the thing itself. I suppose it is possible to make this explanation, without agreeing with Woodhull and Claflin in their sentiments. At any rate, the explanation is necessary.

The theory of free love, then, maintains the right of the individual—any man or woman—to love and be loved with no restraint except individual taste and conscience. It does not mean polygamy; it does not mean prostitution. It may mean the mutual love of one man and one woman for life, like that of marriage. But it insists that without love individuals shall not be bound by legal forms. In the extreme view, held by some exponents, it would revolutionize our present social system, and result in a sort of universal Oneida Community, with bed and nursery common to a nation—its sons and daughters bred according to the "science of stirpiculture."

Certainly there is no danger of the world's taking such a dubious leap as this, with any great haste. The very thought of it strains, and sickens, and terrifies us. But Mrs. Woodhull, as Theodore Tilton long ago explained, having been an exceptional sufferer in marriage—neglected, abandoned, frozen—crushed by abuse into bearing an idiotic child—has come to curse the whole institution of marriage, and to accept the extreme position of free love. She and her sister Tennie C. Claflin avow and preach it.

But for the advocacy of such a complete heresy, they have naturally become social outcasts. They tell the story themselves in their suppressed WEEKLY. Obliged, from loss of money, to give up a house which they owned in New York, they were refused the rental of other houses, refused board, refused accommodation at the New York hotels, and Mrs. Woodhull says that she and her child were finally obliged to sleep on the floor of her business office in Broad street. "Good enough for her!" says the conventional respectability of the whole world. But before Mrs. Woodhull was actually turned into the streets, she obtained board for a while at the Gilsey House. She was presently requested to leave, on the ground, not of improper acts, but that she "published a paper in which free love was advocated and the people would not tolerate any such thing." Yet at this Gilsey House Mr. L. C. Challis was a welcome guest, with the whole dandy crew of New York rottenness in broadcloth.

Woodhull and Claflin contend that such a state of affairs brought home to them, in the liveliest manner, the social inequality of men and women. The most consummate rake might board at the Gilsey House, or the Fifth avenue, for no other purpose than to "seek whom he might devour;" while they must be kicked out, not for immoral practices, but for entertaining a certain theory—false, I think, and wicked, but which, if so, cannot be very dangerous.

"After carefully considering all these things," exclaims Mrs. Woodhull, "can any one wonder that we have been compelled to turn upon our accusers? Can any one wonder if we take the roofs off the hotels and expose the lechery that exists there; if we strip the masks from the faces of our maligners, and show them to be the rotten masses they would have it thought we are? We make the formal declaration that, whenever a person, whom we know to be a hypocrite, stands up and denounces us because of our doctrines, and not because of our immoral practices, we shall unmask him."

Now the indignation, the sense of injustice here expressed, would seem to account for the publication of the Challis story about as well as any supposition of blackmail. As both motives are impartially presented, the "gentle reader" may take his choice between the two.

But the suppressed WEEKLY, again, contains an article by Miss Claflin, in which *her* reasons are also given for the hateful method of personal exposure. She insists that society throughout is a chronic injustice to women, as the most thoughtful men of the world, up to John Stuart Mill, have long admitted. She demands "absolute equality everywhere." If the loss of virtue is a disgrace to unmarried women, then the same should be held of men. If the mother of a child out of legal wedlock is ostracised, then the father should share the same fate. If a life of female prostitution is wrong, a life of male prostitution is equally wrong. If the male debauchee is allowed to circulate in respectable society, and marry women with unsoiled robes, then the female debauchee should be allowed the same privileges, and be treated in the same manner. "This," says Miss Claflin, "is justice—not mercy, not charity!" She says that she wishes people to be virtuous; and as strange as it may appear to the public, she claims to be virtuous herself. But, whether virtuous or not, she would level up the virtue of men to just as high a plane as men demand for women. Has Mr. A. J. Comstock a special work to perform in preventing the equal chastity of the sexes? And is such, too, the present call of the Young Men's Christian Association? And now

"THE BEECHER-TILTON SCANDAL CASE."

The American press has been wonderfully patient in bearing the peculiar muzzle that this tale of horrors has put over its mouth. Mrs. Woodhull declares in her article itself, that for two years before its publication, "the press, by a tacit, and in the main, honorable, *consensus* to ignore all such rumor until they enter the courts, or become otherwise matters of irrepressible notoriety, abstained from any direct mention of the subject." Nearly three months have now passed since the publication, and the press has maintained the same silence, perhaps with an equally honorable motive. But, taking this course, what has the press been obliged to do? Not merely to keep the American people in the dark regarding a libel, but to see them hoodwinked, blinded—deliberately ensnared and deceived by a gigantic farce of moral and legal false pretense. The charge against Woodhull and Claflin of publishing obscene literature in either the Challis or the Beecher-Tilton case, can never be sustained unless courts are packed on purpose to do it.

The New York courts themselves are doubtless aware of this fact. The whole charge is a fraud. Possibly George Francis Train, who has culled all the most lamentable passages of the Old Testament into his *Train Ligue* and printed them under the most sensational and disgusting heads, can be punished in some way for such sorry work. The spirit of his publication seems partly obscene; and the letter is gross beyond measure. Yet as the letter is the letter of the Bible—simply intensified and horrified by separation and coarse exhibition—it will doubtless require a very long and a very dirty trial before a thing so technical as the law can convict even him of a misdemeanor. But the offense of Woodhull and Claflin, if a legal offense at all, is libel. It is a monstrous libel, but it is nothing else; and in procuring the arrest of these women for "publishing obscene literature," Mr. A. J. Comstock has taken a coward's advantage of an exasperated public sentiment—has used the laws of his country to blind the eyes of her citizens, and has buried a true issue under a false one. In doing so, he is perhaps only a zealot without discrimination; he is perhaps the conscientious dupe of stronger minds who need bad services; he is possibly their mere pander. But in any event he has struck a dastard's blow at liberty and law in the United States.

I should be strongly tempted to reproduce the substance of the Beecher-Tilton scandal case if the friends of Mr. Tilton had not lately promised the public that he would soon give the "true version" of the story. There are no legal obstacles to this repetition that I should heed for an instant. It is solely a matter of conscience and honor. The position taken by both Mr. Beecher and Mr. Tilton invites publicity. Both decline to proceed against Mrs. Woodhull for libel; both refuse to deny anything she has said. This position might be wisely taken by Mr. Beecher, if innocent; more wisely still, if guilty. But to Mr. Tilton it was at once the grave of hope. He had vindicated Mrs. Woodhull, in advance, as "the sincerest of souls"—"a woman speaking the truth, punctiliously, whether in great things or small." This "sincerest of souls," who "speaks the truth punctiliously," had received Mr. Tilton's indorsement when she published a statement blasting the character of his wife, clouding the prospects of his children, and leaving some rather doubtful spots on his own reputation. Could Mr. Tilton afford to sit ten weeks in silence under this publication? He has seen fit to do so; and at the end of that time he has broken silence—and for what? To doubt the *technical correctness* of Mrs. Woodhull's account; to acknowledge that a "true story" underlies the false one, and to say that "when the truth is a sword, God's mercy sometimes commands it sheathed." Here is a negative confession. At the same time, a rapturous friend and admirer of Mr. Tilton uses the Chicago *Times* as a sort of official organ, to declare Mr. Tilton's opinion, to-day, that Mrs. Woodhull "is innocent of the attempt at black-mailing." "She is thoroughly in earnest," says Mr. Tilton's friend. "She believes what she says, and thinks she is doing Mr. Tilton a service by repeating it." The "service," of course, is not an immediate one. It is the "emancipation," as Woodhull would call it, of all chafing natures in New York, Brooklyn and the world, from the "enslavement" and "general corruption" of the "system of marriage." No wonder such a "service" is reluctantly accepted in public by all parties concerned.

But if Mr. Tilton is really about to unfold "the true story" of the Beecher-Tilton scandal, it should not be anticipated by any reproduction of the "false story." And perhaps enough has been said in this article to set before its readers the true case of Woodhull and her offenses. The American people should understand it—not at all on account of the woman, but on their own account. I, for one, certainly, have no personal interest in Mrs. Woodhull. I have never seen her but once, and then I conversed with her perhaps ten minutes in a public hall. Miss Claflin I have never seen at all. But in talking with Mrs. Woodhull (it was a year or two ago), I instantly perceived her to be just what Theodore Tilton says the is now—"a woman thoroughly in earnest," who "believes what she says;" "a strange combination of good and evil;" "destructive in her tendencies;" "faithful only to her own ideas,"—a fanatic of fanatics, able, out of balance, and with a will as unyielding as the clutch of death. This fierce, reckless, tireless enthusiast, is burning alive with the belief that the world is rotten, and that she can better it. She has taken the most desperate means of personal assault to aid her purpose. If she has fabricated a slander of such magnitude as the Beecher-Tilton scandal case, she has pretty well earned a hanging at the first lamp-post.

She has not been attacked by the rabble of the streets; but Mr. A. J. Comstock, with his false pretense of "obscene literature," has proceeded against her in a more suspicious way. He has violated both law and common sense; he has headed public opinion in a *virtual* mob, but a mob too craven to strike in the light; he has cheated justice, and deceived a nation. I think his course is one to debauch the courts, to rot the church, to destroy criticism, to garrote liberty. This is my reason (I make no *excuse*) for writing the present article. It is a duty that *some one* owes to his country.

EDWARD H. G. CLARK.

COMMENTS BY "THE PRESS."

We publish on our first page to-day a calm and dispassionate, but very outspoken and fearless, review of the charges against Woodhull and Claflin. The article is not intended as a defense of these people, but a defense of the great principles of liberty and justice to which all are entitled. That there is urgent need for just such a fair and just consideration of the case, must be recognized by all, but only a man whose life is pure and character spotless, can do it with safety. Such an one has written the article we publish today. This article, from the subject, will command attention, and from the well-known purity of the writer's life, must carry great weight with it among those who think.

WOODHULL'S DEFIANCE.

[*From the New York Herald, Nov.* 17, 1872.]

LUDLOW-STREET JAIL,
NEW YORK, Nov. 16, 1872.

To the Editor of the Herald:

No one can be more conscious then I am that prudent forethought should precede any appeal made to the public by one circumstanced as I am; and I think I have not ignored that consciousness in asking the attention of the public through your columns.

Ever since it became generally known by the press that I am constitutionally, theoretically and practically a social revolutionist, the disscussion of the principles upon which my theories are based have been excluded from their columns, while I have been subjected to all sorts of personal abuse To those who do not know me personally I am this or that, which renders me an object of fear or hate—either a "ghoul," a "vampire" or a "devil."

I have been systematically written down as the most immoral of women, but no act of mine has been advanced in support of the charge. My theories have been first misstated or misrepresented, and then denounced as "revolting." Thus have I been gratuitously misinterpreted by the press to the public, whose interests it professes to watch over and protect. But has it ever occurred to this great public, which now holds up its hands in horror of me, that, even in its estimation, manufactured by the press as it has been, I am no worse than, thirty years ago, were the prime movers in the anti-slavery movement in the estimation of the public of that time? Is it remembered how they were abused by the press, imprisoned by the authorities, and stoned and almost hanged by the people? And yet, strange as it is, on the great broad earth, there are none more esteemed and respected to-day than are the veritable persons who so recently were generally condemned. And what is still more strange, some who were thus condemned, forgetting the lesson of their own exper iences, earnestly join the present persecution. Verily, history does repeat itself, even within the remembrance of a single generation.

Who, in their own time and among their own people, have been the bad people of the past? Were there ever any more loudly decried and persistently persecuted than Christ and His apostles and disciples, than Galileo, Luther, Calvin, Fox, Harvey, Ann Lee and Murray, and Douglass, Garrison and Philips! In some form each and all of these were the advocates of new ideas of freedom, as I am now the advocate of freedom in its full sense, and they were persecuted by the public of their times, as I am by the public of to-day, because they advocated ideas which were not fully comprehended. The public of their time i[illegible]reted the freedom they advocated to mean anarchy, a[illegible] public now interpret the freedom I advocate to mean anarchy. But nobody now pretends to condemn them; but everybody [illegible]ites in commending them for the courage which gave [illegible]e strength to do right in spite of the public preju[illegible]d yet eveybody fails to learn the lesson taught by the[illegible]nces.

But what is the great danger which [illegible]c pretends to fear from me? The plain statement of what I desire to accomplish, and it is this at which the public howls, is this: I desire that woman shall be emancipated from the sexual slavery maintained over her by man.

It is by reason of her sex only that woman, whether as wife or mistress, now supports herself; and man is determined not to give up this domination. This is all wrong, and against it I long since declared war—relentless and unceasing war. I desire that wo[illegible] shall, so far as her support is concerned, be made indepen[illegible]f man, so that all her sexual relations shall result fro[illegible]r reasons than for maintenance; in a word, shall be w[illegible]nly for love.

Is there anything so dreadful, [illegible]e public has conjured up in its mind that there is, in this? Ask those about to enter marriage "for a home," those who have already done so and the so-called prostitutes, if they think this is a dangerous and terrible proposition? And yet it is the sum and substance, the intent and effect, of my "revolting theories." These theories ought to appear dangerous to such men only as now purchase women by money, who, under other circumstances, would be unable to command them by love. They ought to appear dangerous to such women only as now prefer to sell themselves to men they loathe for money, support or "a home," rather than to rely for them upon the power of love from these they love, lacking money. I can think of no other classes who should be frightened of me.

"But," say the press, "we are threatened by a great public danger if this be permitted to go on. Let me see if it be possible to find what that danger is. "But these bad women, of bold and unabashed front, have flaunted their degradation and lived upon it," and "have hurled defiance at decency and virtue." A heinous crime; truly a most heinous crime! I have been bold and unabashed enough to make a plain statement of facts which I found existing in and detrimental to the community, and, according to the immaculate press, have thus defied decency and virtue.

Now, let me ask this condemning public to stop right here, [illegible] Does the defiance to decency and virtue emanate from [illegible] or from those who commit the acts which I expose; is it in the facts themselves or in their exposure; is it in their existence or in making their existence known? Answer this upon your honor, great public, and then condemn me if you can.

Again: "Among the most dangerous forces is so-called free thought, that would make immorality free from all restraint, and that, under the name of liberty of the press, would make the journal the vehicle not only for the vilest slanders, but for the filthiest expression of debauched thought." And again I ask: Does the immorality consist of the facts that exist in the community; or is it in making them known to the unsuspecting, to the great honest and moral masses? And is the act of thus making them known "the filthiest expression of thought," or giving expression to filthy facts? Answer this also, and then condemn me if you will.

The persecution to which I am subjected seems to me to be the effort of the magnates of society to hide from the great public, over which they assume to preside, the pitfalls into which, rather than that I should point out the danger and its location, they would have the public walk blindfolded to its destruction. A danger, to be dangerous, must remain unsuspected, since from the very moment it is exposed, the danger ceases, and nobody knows that fact better than the very persons who, in the name of the public, are now pursuing me. I have had the courage to warn the public of a subtle poison that is being stealthily but steadily distributed in society, undermining the very foundation of morality in the human heart and erecting in its stead the most consummate but degrading hypocrisy. Where the moral conse[illegible]tors would have the public think virtue exists if the assumed masks be stripped off, the foulest slime will be discovered.

The great public danger, then, is not in my exposure of the immoralities that are constantly being committed, but in the fear that their enactors will be shown up to the public they have so long deceived. The public is in no danger from me; but those who are distilling poisons and dig[illegible] pitfalls for it are in danger, and will remain in danger so long as I live; and, since this is known, their danger must be abated, at whatever cost of public justice or private right. To the public I would say, in conclusion, they may succeed in crushing me out, even to the loss of my life; but let me warn them and you, that from the ashes of my body a thousand Victorias will spring to avenge my death by seizing the work laid down by me and carrying it forward to victory. Very respectfully,

VICTORIA C. WOODHULL.

"THE WORKER."—This is the name of a new paper issued in the interests of the workingmen, and especially in those of the Internationalists. The appearance and character of the first number give promise of usefulness, and evidence that it ought to meet with a cordial support from the laboring classes. We shall give more extended remarks of this sheet next week.

REV. STEWART ROBINSON RECEIVES A LESSON.

LOVELAND, O., Dec. 1, 1872.

EDITOR COURIER-JOURNAL, KY.:

Permit me to ask, through the columns of your paper, what is the matter with Stewart Robinson? What is he mad about? Don't he know how to submit gracefully to the defeat of his split-pea batteries in the ranks of the invincible progressionists of the age? It seems not. His lecture, delivered in Baltimore, entitled "The New Sociology," and reproduced in the *Courier Journal*, has made me ask, "what is the matter with Stewart Robinson."

He is called Rev. Stewart Robinson. "What's in a name?" Certainly I shall not accord to him the title even of Christian Gentleman, much less Rev. Christian Gentleman, till he learn to express himself with more decency toward a large class of high-souled, earnest-minded, womanly women, whom he stigmatizes as "peripatetic Jezabels," "strong-minded hags" and the like elegant adjective phrases.

I had almost said the man had broadly written himself an ass in that learned (?) lecture, as he assuredly did when he helped increase Mrs. Stanton's large audience in Louisville by his ill-advised protest against that lady's right to lecture in said city. Since Stewart Robinson chooses so maliciously to term many noble members of my sex "perepatetic Jezables" and "strong-minded hags," I see no reason why I should falter over beating the devil with his own base weapons and calling him, in the person of Stewart Robinson, a most egregious ass. Certainly no well-sexed man would be guilty of standing up before an intelligent audience in these days, and using such coarse terms toward even abandoned women, much less an intelligent class of free thinking, nobly working women, no matter how widely he might deem them in error.

Will Stewart Robinson look about him to where our representative women stand in glorious phalanx, with their feet upon the burning plow-share of public opinion, and steady gaze fixed straight upon the "mark of their high calling," awed at no defeats, rising constantly to renewed endeavors, proving themselves hourly more and more worthy the steel of their opponents? Then let him dare in his pusilanimity to call them "peripatetic Jezabels" and "strong-minded hags." Strong minded they are, aye, and strong-souled, too, attributes which Stewart Robinson must yet demonstrate he possesses. When will the prejudiced fanatic learn that abuse is no argument, and calling vile names no proof of power? Is Stewart Robinson a married man? If so, then has his wife no softening influence to refine his innate brutality? But I forget: "the woman is subordinate to the man." God have mercy upon the souls of all women subordinate to a foul-mouthed coarse-grained, man!

The man's dastardliness in classing Mrs. Stanton with Josephine Mansfield and Laura Fair, when he knows how low those women are, in his esteem, at least, is almost too much for human nature, when he must know there is not a higher and finer type of womanhood, gracefully passing away in a comely old age, than Elizabeth Cady Stanton presents to the world to-day. "But she is a womans rights woman, forsooth, and goes upon the rostrum to lecture!" when Stewart Robinson makes it a point not to be "dar." Oh pitiful chip under the wheels of Juggernaut! What a sadness must have pervaded Mrs. Stanton's assembly in Louisville, all because he wasn't "dar!"

As regards the Rev. (?) gentleman's tirade against that *true* gentleman, scholar, philosopher and statesman, John Stewart Mill, let it pass for the flea in the lion's mane: John Stewart Mill, will probably never know it's "dar."

Concerning S. Robinson's views upon the "Social Question," we must inform him, for he seems ignorant upon the point, there are greater minds than his that see a wide-spread devastation and desolation in the present state of social life to-day, and possibly S. Robinson himself could contribute his own skeleton to the social catacombs. S. Robinson must meet those "greater minds" more fairly and squarely if he would cope with them, for they are worthy of truer steel than the *refined* and *gentlemanly* and *scholarly clergyman* has yet flourished in the sunlight.

Stewart Robinson may be content with t[illegible] puritanic *regime*, when witches were burned, when "[illegible]etic Jezabels" did not go about opening ministerial c[illegible], and revealing skeletons in their reverences' closets[illegible] there are good souls and true, who earnestly long for a ne[illegible]tmosphere, and who have agitated the social evil till it is now before the people—*the grand question of the hour!* Let Stewart Robinson stand from under when his own structure comes tumbling down.

In conclusion, let me tell him there *are* women fitted to teach as lecturers, there *are* women fitted to teach in the pulpit, though Othello lose his occupation; there *are* women well qualified to hold official positions. *Established facts must be respected*, though the Bible burn in a fire! When established facts preside, who cares a farthing whether Stewart Robinson is "dar" or not? Let him return like the hog to his vomit, and be compelled to eat those nasty words he used concerning women.

HELEN NASH.

RESOLUTIONS.

At a meeting held in St. Louis, Sunday, January 19, 1873, in Avenue Hall, in which were gathered many liberals and free-thinkers, the following resolutions were read and adopted:

Having carefully read the article styled by some the "Beecher Scandal," in WOODHULL & CLAFLIN'S WEEKLY, and for publishing which, Mrs. Woodhull and Miss Claflin have been incarcerated in prison, and held there by a demand for exorbitant bonds for their release—we can truthfully assert that said article does not contain any language that is obscene, or in any way calculated to corrupt good morals, but rather tending to awaken sober thought and elevating to the tone of society. Therefore be it

Resolved, That the action of the Grand Jury of New York in filing a bill of indictment against the defendants at so short a notice, and before giving them an opportunity for a hearing in their defense, bears abundant evidence of a tyrannical usurpation of power, and a disposition to trample under foot, with impunity, the most sacred of human rights—*a free press, free speech*, and *bodily freedom*.

Resolved, That the conduct of the New York officials and their abettors in this matter is an unpardonable insult to civil liberty.

Resolved, That we extend our fullest sympathy to Mrs. Woodhull and Miss Claflin, in their martyrdom for the right, and express our determination to thoroughly ventilate their case before the public until ample justice is meted to them. And be it further

Resolved, That a copy of these resolutions be tendered to the leading liberal journals of this country and Europe, for publication.

COMMISSIONER DAVENPORT'S DECISION.

After a three-week's consideration, Commissioner Davenport rendered the following extraordinary decision, upon which we shall reserve comment until our next issue, merely remarking that, practically, it is a discharge, since he says it does not come within the "purview" of the statute:

"I have carefully examined the various grounds of defence urged on behalf of the prisoners, together with all the authorities cited on both sides, and but for the ruling in a recent English case (Regina agt. Shore,) not cited, should have considerable doubt as to the Challis articles being, as is claimed by the prosecution, obscene in law.

"The case of Shore is so nearly parallel, however, to that of these defendants, and the grounds of defense and arguments of counsel so much the same as to compel me to adopt the ruling therein and hold the article in question to be obscene.

"Upon the further question as to the intention of Congress in the framing and passage of the statute under which these proceedings were instituted, I am quite clear that a case of this character was never contemplated, and under ordinary circumstances I should at once release the accused.

"In view, however, to the importance as well as to the subtlety of the questions involved, the anxiety of the prisoners, as well as the community for definite settlement of the whole matter, I am disposed to and shall hold the prisoners to await the action of the Grand Jury, to the end that a judicial determination by the Circuit Court of the United States may be had, and the rights both of the prisoners and the public be finally ascertained.

In connection with this decision, the *Brooklyn Eagle*, of the 4th inst., says:

DAVENPORT DONE.

What there is of Commissioner Davenport is remarkable enough. He was never of more that microscopic magnitude, mental and physical, and there isn't so much of him as there used to be, since Lawyer Choate took hold of him before the Assembly Committee on Cities at Albany the other day. The remains of Davenport, however, got off a wonderful opinion yesterday, which the *Eagle* published in its four o'clock edition. He decided that "the law of Congress" under which the women, Woodhull & Claflin, were arrested "never contemplated any such case, and that, under ordinary circumstances he would not hesitate to release the accused." What the extraordinary circumstances are under which he holds the accused, by a law to which he decides they are not obnoxious, are left to the imagination, but can easily be supplied. He also admits that all American practice, rulings and decisions are against him; but he has found a recent English case which he declares leaves him to do that which he himself brands as illegal. This case he neither reproduces nor names. There is every reason to believe that the Commissioner never perused the case. He is quite capable of such an omission, and of misunderstanding it, even if he did peruse it. His further fallacy for holding the accused is the assumption that the matter is "subtle," and that the people and defendants are both very curious and anxious to have it decided judicially. This assumption is only justified by the other assumption, that under no circumstances will a decision by Davenport be accepted as judicial in any respect. The "opinion" thoroughly exculpates the accused from having violated any American law, and then holds them amenable to it. Davenport did not display so much ingenuity in "this opinion" as he used to display in mutilating war correspondents' letters at Bermuda Hundred—even after he had rifled the Government mails to get at them. *Dogberry* was a Chief Justice Marshal 'long side of Davenport. There is no doubt these notorious women are more helped by the asininity of those who on one side do proceed, and who on the other fail to proceed against them, than by any other cause or means. It has been reserved for the hardy canonical Challis to initiate the sole proper proceeding against them—a suit for libel, and even he seems to prefer persecution to prosecution of them.

The editor of one of the most influential papers west of the Alleghanies says:

MRS. WOODHULL & MISS CAFLIN—Having an hour, I called. I much regret my call was *too late* to see you. This, however, you may *as well understand*. Opinion *is forming*, and you shall not fight the case *alone*. If the women have not the *power*, or the courage, to stand by the truth, there [illegible] a few men who *will* to the *last* extremity.

TERMS OF SUBSCRIPTION.

PAYABLE IN ADVANCE.

One copy for one year,	$3 00
One copy for six months,	1 50
Single copies,	10

FOREIGN SUBSCRIPTION

CAN BE MADE TO THE AGENCY OF THE AMERICAN NEWS COMPANY, LONDON, ENGLAND.

One copy for one year,	$4 00
One copy for six months,	2 00

RATES OF ADVERTISING.

Per line (according to location), From $1 00 to $2 50

Time, column and page advertisements by special contract.

Special place in advertising columns cannot be permanently given.

Advertiser's bills will be collected from the office of the paper, and must in all cases, bear the signature of WOODHULL & CLAFLIN.

Specimen copies sent free.

Newsdealers supplied by the American News Company, No. 121 Nassau treet, New York.

All communications, business or editorial, must be addressed

Woodhull & Claflin's Weekly,

48 Broad Street, New York City.

WOODHULL & CLAFLIN'S WEEKLY.

NEW YORK, SATURDAY, FEBRUARY 15, 1873.

TO THE PRESS.

The course the Government has pursued to suppress the WEEKLY, and thereby to establish a precedent which, followed, may extend to any recalcitrant journal, having been most disastrous to us financially, we ask both friends and foes to extend us the journalistic courtesy to insert the following in the several papers under their control:

WOODHULL & CLAFLIN'S WEEKLY, an Independent Journal open to the absolutely free discussion of all subjects in which human welfare is involved, and which is especially the organ of social reform, is published by Victoria C. Woodhull and Tennie C. Claflin (Woodhull & Claflin), at No. 48 Broad street, New York, upon the following terms:

One copy one year,	$3 00
Five copies one year,	12 00
Ten copies one year,	22 00
Twenty copies one year,	40 00

Six month, half these rates.

The WEEKLY occupies a somewhat remarkable, certainly a most exceptional, position in regard to its contemporaries, the reformatory, religious and secular press. Outside of some half-a-dozen journals, there is little contained in the public press which is of use to the editors either as news or otherwise. But we know that the entire press, while for the present mainly silent upon the great question that is now agitating public thought, is deeply interested in the main feature of the WEEKLY. Formerly when we were in better pecuniary circumstances than we now are, we sent the WEEKLY regularly to about one-third of the press of the country, and we are more than repaid by the modifications of public opinion upon reformatory questions which have indirectly resulted therefrom.

There are about six thousand newspapers and journals of all sorts in the United States. We want to send the WEEKLY to each of them; but this would be at an expense to us, for printing and paper only, of over ten thousand dollars, which we cannot afford. But we will furnish it to all papers that want it at $2 per annum—our lowest rates for large clubs. This course suggests itself to us because we have already received numerous applications from editors for the best terms upon which we will furnish the WEEKLY to them. This is a small matter for individual papers, while the press, as a whole, would be a very mighty one for us to exchange with—one which its representatives cannot expect us to bear. If the WEEKLY were a political or religious or a literary journal merely, we should not presume to thus address the press, to which, in many instances, we are under great obligations; but it is exceptional, being the only advocate of social freedom in the world. And this, coupled with the fact, that momentous issues will be discussed in its columns during the entire year, is an excuse for this presentation.

INSTRUCTIONS TO SUBSCRIBERS.

In writing to us persons should sign their names carefully, so that their need be no mistaking them; many come to us so carelessly written that one cannot decipher them.

Again, many persons neglect to include their State in the date; and if, as often is the case, the postmaster's stamp on the outside of the envelope is a mere daub, we are utterly in the dark about the location of the writer; unless, perchance, the town be an uncommon one, when we can guess in what State it may be.

The letter should also state whether the inclosed remittance is for a renewal or for a new subscription. Failing in this we are compelled to spend a large amount of time to determine it. In case any one receives two papers from this neglect, they should inform us at once, so that one may be discontinued.

CLUB! CLUB!! CLUB!!!

We return special thanks to our friends who have so readily gone earnestly to work to extend our subscription list. We are daily in receipt of numbers of letters containing remittances for clubs. This is the way to show love for, and zeal in, any cause advocated by a special journal.

To all our friends, everywhere, we say, go and do likewise! The friends in every town and city should see to it that a club of five for every thousand people be immediately formed. We have said that we have wrought alone as long as we can. We now, want the joint efforts of all who believe in freedom in its full sense.

A REQUEST TO OUR FRIENDS.

Since the newsmen in the country cannot obtain the WEEKLY through the accustomed channel—The American News Co.—many of them suppose the WEEKLY to be dead. Now we are aware there is a demand through this medium for a hundred thousand copies per week, which is suppressed by the refusal of the above mentioned company to furnish them. We ask our friends in all towns where there is a news depot, and especially the cities, to interest themselves sufficiently to call repeatedly upon the newsmen and urge them to order a supply directly from us. We are sending them regularly through the mail in packages to suit all customers; and where the newsmen are subsidized against the WEEKLY, we ask our friends to order weekly supplies to fill this demand. Hundreds of people would buy the WEEKLY from news agents and ultimately become interested in it, who, at first, would not subscribe. Perhaps there is no way our friends could do us so great service as in this way, and we hope they will press their news agents everywhere to order the WEEKLY direct from us, until the Great Monopoly—the American News Company—will consent to furnish it.

THE WEEKLY.

Having now re-entered upon the regular issue of the WEEKLY, we trust our friends, who heretofore have waited for this event, will now come at once to our support. We have no cause to complain of the responses that have been made to our several appeals for assistance, but, on the contrary, every reason to return thanks for their heartiness; and those friends whose names are already enrolled on our lists, as having given a willing ear to our appeals for the sustainment of the WEEKLY, will ever occupy a fresh remembrance in our hearts.

But there is a still larger class than is represented by these who, not so deeply interested as they are, have waited to see if we should be able to publish the WEEKLY. They have realized the fearful odds in numbers and wealth, against which we have struggled and have doubted our strength, courage, or ability to withstand them. Hundreds of letters, full of encouraging words and expressions of esteem, say, "There are many persons in this vicinity who are desirous of reading the WEEKLY, and who will subscribe as soon as it is positively ascertained that you will be permitted to publish it.

To the writers of these letters, and to those for whom they speak, we would now prefer a special request, asking that they at once send forward their names. If everybody should wait to see if everybody else moves first, nobody would move at all, and we should be left without support. Every person who has any love for the cause that we advocate, or who believes that in our persons the freedom of the press and free speech have been attacked, should not hesitate a single day to give us all the aid in their power.

It must not be forgotten that our resources are now confined to the income from the WEEKLY, and that to it we are compelled to look for all the means required to publish it, and therefore that the delay of even a single week in remitting dues or sending on remittances for new clubs and subscriptions, may endanger our ability to send out the strong aliment of the new social dispensation.

Then let every friend begin earnestly to labor. Let him or her join hands with us and make common cause for the paper at which the whole force of the Government and the Young Men's Christian Association has been directed to prevent its publication. Let him or her find out every progressive spirit within their sphere and bring them within the range of the WEEKLY'S advocacy. Let the club lists be poured in upon us in double numbers. They have already come in most satisfactory and promising numbers; but we want a perfect deluge. The intense interest everywhere present regarding the new social dispensation is rousing everybody to inquiry. No other paper in the world contains any light whatever upon this all-important subject. Every other journal is afraid to discuss it either pro or con, and thus a double labor is left for us to perform. But this we can easily do if our friends, upon whom we must rely, do their part. If, by their efforts, we are relieved from anxiety as to the future of the WEEKLY, we can give double force and increased effect to its already well-freighted columns.

Therefore, thanking our friends for the very generous aid already extended, we urge them to renewed and wider efforts to add to the number of our readers, and to thus work at the circumference of the movement, while we delve at the centre.

ARE COURTS MERE MACHINES MOVED BY MONEY?

We have always had a great reverence for our system of administrating civil and criminal law. We have always supposed that the results of its administration in civil cases was justice after a sort; but if the highest legal lights are to be believed, the efforts of their profession are mainly directed to influences other than those of securing their clients' rights by lawful means. These things we have heard talked of so freely that we come to believe there was really little justice to be obtained by invoking the [illegible]sts of law.

We had, however, no idea th[illegible] a still more outrageous practice had crept into criminal cases. It was a reproach upon our institutions [illegible]we could not accept, to think that the system of crimi[illegible]sprudence was or could be reduced to a mere engine [illegible]ce and revenge. It was a thought too horrible to [illegible]ined that a person could be falsely accused of a crime and "railroaded" to a penitentiary with no hope of escape. No one blames any person, or any lawyer for making use of every possible means to secure a verdict of "not guilty;" but when Judges and Prosecuting Attorneys so far exceed the legal limits of law and established practice as to make before trial public declarations of the guilt of persons to be tried or prosecuted therein, it becomes a matter worthy of the deepest and most serious alarm, since in no ancient despotism did a[illegible]ore arbitrary practice than this obtain.

Under this method [illegible]ure any person who from any reason whatever may [illegible] himself in opposition to the great weight of public opinion may be set upon by the representatives of this public opinion charged with any crime and be convicted and sentenced without even having conceived a criminal intention. It is useless to say this is not true, since within three months we have heard no less than four prominent lawyers say, "that we have, in this city, a way of railroading people to Sing Sing." Now each of these four lawyers could not possibly have asserted the self-same thing unless there were some foundation in fact for the assertion, while to admit that there is a foundation in fact for it is to open wide the door to the practices to which we have called attention.

During these three months just past we have had a pretty thorough introduction to all the various preliminary processes, and by it have become somewhat familiar with many things of which previously we had no other than hearsay knowledge. We have been brought face to face with prejudice in all its forms; we have been made to feel keenly that the officers—the servants of the people; indeed, our servants—in no single instance have administered these functions without respect to persons. At every point we have been confronted by the effects of personal feeling obtaining the control over what should [illegible] action.

We say, and we desire any person to controvert it, that no person acting as a public servant has any right to permit his personal prejudice to enter in and modify his action in administering the functions of his office; and further, we most emphatically declare and again challenge contradiction, that any officer who permits his action to be biased by his personal feelings is unfit to be an officer and earns, if he do not receive, impeachment.

And least of all, should a person occupying the high position of judge so degrade himself and the office he fills as to attempt to decide upon any law whatever before the evidence in such case is all before him; but we have the sad spectacle in our own case of a person who may try one of our cases, saying "he will give us the full extent of the law." How is that person fitted to administer justice to us? Can he, indeed, with any self-respect, even attempt to try our case? And can we, with any hope for justice, submit to be tried before him? We leave these questions for the calm deliberation of our readers and pass to state more terrible considerations.

Last week, in an article entitled "Our anonymous correspondents," we stated certain things with which we are threatened, among which was this—that any amount of money necessary to accomplish it was already provided to secure our conviction. Had not these anonymous threats been a reflection of what was openly stated, we should never have given any of them a second thought; but as they were really the same as came to us from other than unknown sources, we believe them to be the evidence that the things at which they point have a tangible existence, and that they are to be used against us.

But with even all this staring us in the face, we should coolly, calmly and confidently stand before the courts and know that justice would be done—that truth and right would triumph; but when to all these is added the apparently authoritative declaration that our cases are already decided, it becomes our duty to ask, and to ask seriously, what do these things mean? And thus, seriously, we do ask those lawyers who have said that our cases are already decided, who it is that has decided them, and how do they know that the decisions have been made? If it were one or two who say these things it might still be questioned if there were any foundations for them; but when several, and they among the prominent criminal lawyers, in different places and at different times, and under different circumstances, and to different persons, make the same declarations, it seems impossible not to come to the conclusion that there must be somewhere some general understanding about the cases, from which understanding these several persons have obtained the same information.

THE NEW SENSATION

A LIVELY, ROMANTIC PAPER FOR THE PERIOD

Vol. I. No. 2. NEW YORK, JUNE 28, 1878. Price Ten Cents.

THE FASTEST GIRL IN NEW YORK.

A SENSATIONAL STORY OF NEW YORK CITY LIFE BY COLONEL CABOT.

THE DAILY GRAPHIC

AN ILLUSTRATED EVENING NEWSPAPER.

39 & 41 PARK PLACE.

VOL. III.---NO. 225. NEW YORK, FRIDAY, NOVEMBER 21, 1873. FIVE CENTS.

AT LAST.

THIRD EDITION.

THE WAR CLOUD.

THE RECALL OF SICKLES EXPECTED—PRESIDENT FIGUERAS SENT TO ENGLAND ON A DIPLOMATIC MISSION.

MADRID, November 21.—United States Minister Sickles still remains in this city. His recall by the Government at Washington would not come unexpected here, following the rupture in the diplomatic relations between the United States and Spain.

LONDON, November 21.—It is officially announced that Senor Figueras, President of the Spanish Cortes, is coming to London, having been intrusted by his Government with an important diplomatic mission in relation to the Virginius affair.

GENERAL SHERMAN INSPECTING THE FORTIFICATIONS—REPORTED ATTEMPT TO ASSASSINATE GENERAL SICKLES—EXCITEMENT IN WASHINGTON.

WASHINGTON, November 21.—The press despatches from Madrid announcing the insult to our Minister created considerable feeling in official and other circles this morning, and intensified if possible the war feeling pervading all classes here.

Secretary Fish has advices from General Sickles relative to the demonstration against him, which the Secretary says show that the press despatches, while not wholly groundless, are somewhat exaggerated.

The Secretary has just laid before the President the latest intelligence from General Sickles.

The Cabinet will meet at noon with all the members present, Secretary Robeson having returned to Washington this morning.

It is reported here that General Sherman left here ast night on a tour of inspection of the fortifications of the Atlantic and Gulf coasts.

Later.

Further despatches from Madrid received here this morning report that a second attempt has been made to assassinate General Sickles, and that he was wounded. The report is not credited in official circles, though outside of official circles it is generally credited.

Further despatches are momentarily expected from General Sickles, and are looked for with great anxiety.

FRANCE.

MACMAHON CONGRATULATED BY FOREIGN REPRESENTATIVES—THE RECONSTRUCTION OF THE CABINET.

PARIS, November 21.—Under instructions from their respective Governments, a number of the ministers attached to the foreigns embassies in Paris have called upon President MacMahon and tendered to him the congratulations of their Governments upon the prolongation of his term of office.

The Duke de Broglie, who was charged with the reconstruction of the French Ministry, has decided to make but few changes in the complexion of his Cabinet.

It is announced this morning that he retires from office as Minister of Foreign Affairs, and will assume the Vice-Presidency of the Ministry, without a portfolio.

M. Decazes has been appointed to succeed the Duke de Broglie as Minister of Foreign Affairs.

THE WAR IN AFRICA.

THE ASHANTEES AGAIN DEFEATED BY THE ENGLISH FORCE.

LONDON, November 21.—Despatches to the Government from the Ashantee expedition in Africa state that Sir Garnet Wolesley's forces met and defeated the Ashantees at Dunquah on the 27th of October. The loss on either side was slight.

GENERAL NEWS.

ANNUAL REPORT OF THE INTERNAL REVENUE COMMISSIONER.

WASHINGTON, November 21.—The Commissioner of Internal Revenue states in his annual report that the aggregate receipts from all sources, exclusive of the direct tax upon lands and the duty upon capital, circulation, and deposits of national banks, for the fiscal year ending June 30, 1873, were $114,075,456. There were refunded during the last fiscal year for taxes illegally assessed and collected $61,866,777. The increase in the receipts from the gallon tax on distilled liquors being $1,003,276, and from the spirit tax of rectifiers and dealers in liquor $1,094,264, there is a total increase of over $11,000,000 from these sources. The total receipts from tobacco for the fiscal year ending June 30, 1873, were $34,386,303.02; showing an increase over last year of $650,132.57. The Commissioner urges that Congress should fix by law the exact compensation of collectors, and speaks in the highest terms of the new system known as the Act of December 24, 1872, which abolishes the offices of assessor and assistant assessor, and shows that under its operation $1,600,000 have been saved to the Government.

FUNERAL OF THE LATE EX-GOVERNOR VROOM.

TRENTON, N. J., November 21.—The funeral services of ex-Governor Vroom took place this morning from his residence on State street at nine o'clock. It was attended by Governor Parker, ex-Governor Olden, and all the State officials, the Chancellor, and several members of the bar; also by a large number of prominent citizens from all parts of the State. Flags were hung at half-mast on the Capitol building and the State offices, and many places of business were closed out of respect to the deceased.

After the funeral services the remains were taken on a special train to Somerville, N. J., where the body was interred in the family vault. Nearly all the residents of the town of Somerville were present to witness the interment. The pall-bearers were Chancellor Green, ex-Governor Olden, Chief-Justice Beasley, Governor Parker, Attorney-General Gilchrist, Abraham Browning, Courtland Parker, and Judge Scudder.

WEATHER REPORT.

WASHINGTON, November 21—11:30 A. M.—For the Middle States, southeasterly and southwesterly winds, temporarily rising temperature, increasing cloudiness, and possibly occasional rain to-night. For New England, northwesterly winds, shifting to southeasterly, cold and partly cloudy weather.

INGERSOLL REARRESTED.

THE INDICTMENT FOR FORGERY TO BE PRESSED FOR TRIAL ON MONDAY.

Last night James H. Ingersoll was rearrested on the suspicion that he proposed to escape, and is now in charge of the Sheriff while endeavoring to arrange for the continuance of his freedom on bail.

To-day in the Chambers of the Supreme Court, before Judge Barrett, a petit jury was drawn for his trial on Monday.

The charge on which he is to be tried is forgery in the third degree. He and John D. Farrington, Jr., are jointly indicted for forging an endorsement on warrant No. 6295—a county warrant drawn in favor of Heath & Smith on the Broadway Bank for $15,138.40 for mason-work, &c., on the new County Court House from October 14, 1869, to December, 1870.

TWEED'S ROMANTIC LIFE.

A CAREER OF UNEXAMPLED CHANGE OF FORTUNE—FROM THE PAVEMENTS OF CHERRY STREET HIGH UPON THE LADDER OF FAME.

The history of the life of William M. Tweed presents a curious record of vicissitudes and alternations of good and bad fortune. His career has had many curious and contradictory phases, from that of the bungling apprentice in a chair shop to that of the political autocrat of a great city, the maker of Mayors and Governors, and the dispenser of millions of dollars' worth of patronage. An intermediate picture of his life would represent him as a red-shirted fireman in the days when the "Mose" of the Bowery stage was the type of the New York volunteer fireman—a member and foreman of "Big Six" in the days of its rivalry with the famous "Black Joke," when such rough warfare as dumping a hostile engine over a dock was freely indulged in. In this as in all the other positions he has filled in life he developed the exact traits to fit him for the leadership of the daring and reckless men by whom he has been constantly surrounded and looked up to. He was always bold, prompt, reckless, and unscrupulous. His friendships have always been warm and devoted, and towards his friends he has proved generous, open-hearted, and open-handed; and, on the other hand, his enmity, when it is aroused, is implacable and endless. In the face of his success in

CLIMBING FROM OBSCURE POVERTY

to a position of enormous wealth and almost boundless power, there is no denying his possession of practical ability in no ordinary degree; but the principal characteristics of the man which contributed to this success appear to have been his indomitable will, his ever-present ambition, and a sort of personal magnetism which, without any ability either as a conversationalist or orator, made him immensely popular both with the b'hoys of Big Six in the days of the old Fire Department and with the magnates of Tammany in its zenith of prosperity and power.

William Marcy Tweed was born, as the political biographists would say, of poor but honest parents, on the 3d of April, 1823. His paternal grandfather was a Scotchman; his father, Richard Tweed, was born in New York City and his mother on Long Island. Their residence at that time was a two-story brick house at No. 24 Cherry street, which has since been supplanted by a lofty tenement-house. Before the Revolutionary war there was an Indian massacre at Corlear's Hook, whereupon the inhabitants of the city enacted a law prohibiting the approach of the Indians nearer the settlement than the Minnahanock, now Blackwell's Island. A fort was soon afterwards built on Cherry street for the protection of the whites, and the house in which Boss Tweed was born occupied a part of the site of that fort. He was the youngest of three children, having a brother, Richard Tweed, Jr., and one sister. His father was a chair-maker, and, being of limited means, both Richard and William were kept hard at work in the shop from an early age, and consequently had scarcely any opportunities for schooling. It soon became evident, however, that William's genius did not lie in the direction of chair-making. He had no mechanical skill whatever, and could not handle edged tools without spoiling his work and cutting his fingers, and he proved to be much more fond of skylarking than labor. His father used to exclaim that

THE DEVIL WAS IN THE LAD

for mischief, and was wont to base all manner of lugubrious predictions upon his partiality for play, although it is not reported that he ever prophesied that his son would become a Congressman. The old gentleman appears to have finally despaired of ever making a respectable mechanic of his young hopeful, and he obtained for him a situation as a clerk in the saddlery and hardware store of Isaac Fryer, at No. 277 Pearl street. Here he remained for about one year, and obtained some knowledge of business and book-keeping. At the end of the year, his father's business affairs having become more prosperous, he was sent for a year's schooling to the Rev. John T. Halsey, of Elizabethtown, N. J. Here he is credited with having done his best to improve his opportunities, and he became at least a fair penman and a ready cipherer. On his return from school he became a clerk in the tobacco store of J. & G. C. Alexander, No. 107 Front street, and remained there about two years at the munificent salary of one dollar per week. In the meantime his father had become a partner of the firm of D. Berrien & Co., brushmakers, at No. 357 Pearl street, and William became a clerk in their store, and two years later was made a junior partner in the firm. Here he remained for a few years, and in 1851, having accumulated a small capital, he embarked in the chair business with his brother Richard Tweed, Jr., at their father's old stand, No. 5 Cherry street. A few years before this the famous Americus Engine Company No. 6 had been organized, and its double-decked machine had been such a wonder of size in comparison with the primitive apparatus of the other companies that it had been christened Big Six.

FOREMAN OF "BIG SIX."

Young Tweed had been an active member of the company from its organization, and, proving popular among his fellow-bunkers, he was in 1850 unanimously elected foreman. This office he held for about eighteen months, and nine years afterwards, while William B. Dunley was foreman, he again acted in that capacity during a trip made by the company to Canada and the Niagara Falls. In those days the engine companies supplied in a great measure the place of the political clubs of the present time, and the members, especially of so large and powerful a company as the Americus, wielded a large share of political influence. The membership of Big Six included Tweed, Edward J. Shandley, Michael J. Shandley, John J. Blair, John J. Reilly, and a dozen others whose names have since become known in politics, and Tweed had not been a member of the company for many months before he began to make a figure in the politics of the Seventh Ward. He soon became known as a shrewd manipulator of primaries and efficient worker on election days, and a practical exponent of the good old plan of voting early and voting often for the straight Democratic ticket. Such bright and shining abilities as these were not destined to be unrewarded, and in 1853 he was elected to his first office—that of Alderman from the Seventh Ward. At about the same time his brother withdrew from the chair business, and he continued alone, and made some money. He soon, however, became impregnated with a speculative mania, and began to dabble in Erie and other particularly lively railroad shares, and the result was that he managed to lose all the little capital that he had scraped together by honest industry and chair-making. From the year 1853 he appears to have devoted himself entirely to politics.

A CONGRESSMAN.

After serving one year as an Alderman he ran for Congress against Joe Hoxie, was elected by a good majority, and served until 1856. In 1856 he was made School Commissioner for the Seventh Ward, and held this office two years. In 1858 he was elected to the Board of County Supervisors, and remained in the Board until legislated out of it, with the rest of the Tammany members, by a new city charter. He was Deputy Street Commissioner and the real head of the Department from 1861 to 1870. He was elected to the State Senate from the Fourth District, comprising the First, Second, Third, Fourth, Fifth, Sixth, Seventh, Thirteenth, and Fourteenth Wards of this city, in 1867, and re-elected in 1871. He was Chairman of the Tammany Hall General Committee for ten years, beginning in 1861, a sachem of Tammany for the same length of time, and the Grand Sachem of the Order during the last three years of the old *regime*, being the successor in that position of John T. Hoffman. In 1870 he reached the summit of his power, being made Commissioner of Public Works—an office created especially for him by the Tammany Ring charter of that year, and one in which he exercised the power of an absolute autocrat. This was then the only department of the City Government whose chief was not under the control of a board, and it was the most important and powerful department of the whole municipal machinery. It combined the functions of both the Street Department and the Croton Water Department, and had practically unlimited power in the construction, maintenance, and repairs of the entire system of public works. The patronage of the Department, all of which was in the personal gift of the Commissioner, amounted to millions upon millions of dollars per annum, and the immense power thus placed in the hands of Tweed fully justified his popular cognomen of

THE "BOSS."

Had he been termed the "Dictator" or the "Emperor" the titles would have been hardly less appropriate; and his power and position during his lease of this office were the nearest approach to Cæsarism that has been seen in this country either before or since. His headquarters were at the corner of Park place and Broadway, and his magnificent apartments presented every day the appearance of a President's levee, with the halls and anterooms crowded from nine A. M. to four P. M., and with a throng of obsequious ushers and retainers carefully guarding all approaches to the great man of the hour. Nor were his other surroundings on a less magnificent scale than those of his official headquarters. In addition to a handsome house at No. 197 Henry street, by means of which he claimed a residence in the Seventh Ward, he owned and occupied a palatial mansion at the corner of Fifth avenue and Forty-third street, and a splendid villa at Greenwich, Ct. He was also the president and principal patron of the Americus Club, the famous political coterie which had taken the place of the old-time engine company, and was often found enjoying himself at their magnificent club-house at Indian Harbor, on the shore of Long Island Sound. He was a director and large stockholder in the Erie Railroad, under the Fisk-Gould *regime*, and a director of a dozen other corporations. He was, in short, at the zenith of his power, and it was at about this time that the Tweed Testimonial Association was formed for the purpose of erecting a marble statue of the great Boss in the Central Park. This organization had a list of officers including judges, editors, bank presidents, and all the highest dignitaries of the city, and had its headquarters at the Oriental Club on East Broadway. Elaborately engraved circulars and certificates of subscription were issued, and money was flowing into the treasury from Tweed's office-holding friends, until the opportune exposure by the press of the gigantic frauds of the Tweed Ring put a sudden stop to this additional project for the glorification of the potent Boss, and culminated in his precipitate downfall and humiliation in a manner which is familiar to all our readers.

HIS SOCIAL LIFE.

Mr. Tweed was married early in life to Miss Scaden, and has eight children, of whom only one—General William M. Tweed, Jr.—has appeared prominently before the public. General Tweed obtained his epaulettes in the volunteer militia and his admission to the bar on the same day. His principal military achievement has been to command the "Shandley Legion," an impromptu quasi-military organization which made a street parade on Thanksgiving Day, 1870, in honor of Judge Edward J. Shandley. As a lawyer, he is a member of the firm of Tweed & Edelstein, and is said to have been particularly fortunate in the matter of profitable references. He was also a member of Governor Hoffman's staff.

Mr. Tweed's social reputation is that of a blunt, hearty, genial companion. He possesses the power of making friends easily, and he has an equal faculty of making his enemies comprehend his sentiments. He is temperate in his habits and has an iron constitution. In his younger days he had the reputation of being almost invariably successful with the fair sex; and there are many stories circulated confidentially among his acquaintances which would seem to show that he had sometimes carried his penchants far beyond the bounds of prudence. In recent years a report, which may be groundless scandal, has connected his name with that of a mysterious lady whose residence is in a fashionable street among the forties, and not far from Fifth avenue, and at the grand annual balls which used to be given by the Americus Club, when the Academy of Music and Irving Hall were thrown into one, the beaming face and blazing diamonds of the gallant Boss were a sure guide to the locality of the handsomest women on the floor.

THE SEARCH FOR SHARKEY.

HUNDREDS OF DETECTIVES SCOURING THE CITY—MAGGIE JORDAN, MRS. ALLEN, AND THE PRISON KEEPER PLEAD "NOT GUILTY."

Sharkey is still at large. This is not for want of clues however. Captain Irving and his force have struck any number of warm trails, and Pinkerton's detectives are following up at least as many more.

Maggie Jordan, Sarah Allen, and Keeper Lawrence Phillips were brought from their cells this morning and taken before Justice Bixby in his private room. William H. Howe was counsel for all three. Warden Johnston was present but took no part in the proceedings. The people were not represented except in the person of the Justice.

Maggie Jordan was dressed in black, as usual. She wore a smiling face, and was evidently elated at the success of her scheme. She told Mr. Howe that she would be willing to go to prison for five years so long as she knew that Sharkey was safe. She was born in New York, and was twenty-one years old. She pleaded not guilty, waived an examination in a careless tone, and was committed in default of $10,000 bail to await the action of the Grand Jury.

Mrs. "Wes" Allen is a woman of the medium height, and was dressed neatly and in sober colors. Her hair is brown, but her eyes appear to be of a very light blue. Her face, though not as interesting as Maggie Jordan's, might by many be accounted more beautiful. It was flushed during the examination and her eyes were wet with tears. She answered questions in a low voice, and when asked to sign her name to her plea declared that she was too nervous to write. She was therefore told to make her mark, which she did. It is a cross consisting of two scraggy, uncertain lines. She broke into tears several times, saying she felt "so bad." "Just think of it," she said. "The idea that he (her husband) should be in one prison and I in another. When he hears of this it will almost make him cry, too."

She gave her age as twenty-five years, and said she lived at No. 66 Sixth avenue. She pleaded not guilty, and her further examination was set down till two o'clock to-morrow afternoon.

Keeper Lawrence Phillips pleaded not guilty. He is twenty-nine years old, and lives at No. 221 East Twenty-ninth street. His examination also was set down for to-morrow at two P. M.

Judge Barrett has granted writs of habeas corpus for Maggie Jordan and Mrs. Allen, returnable to-morrow.

CASTELAR AND BRADLAUGH.

It is well known that when Charles Bradlaugh was in Spain last spring he had several interviews with leading Republicans, Castelar among the rest. In a recent lecture at Bridgeport, Ct., Mr. Bradlaugh is reported as saying that "about the 3d of May last I was conversing with a number of Spanish gentlemen in Spain on the situation in Cuba, when one, a leading statesman, said: 'I am in favor of seeing the Cubans gain their independence; I am in favor of their establishing a republic; I sympathize with them in their struggles, and am with them in everything but one thing, and that is when they say, "Death to Spain," for I am a Spaniard.' That statesman's name is Emilio Castelar." In a private conversation with a gentleman whose name is well known to lecture-goers, Mr. Bradlaugh said that Castelar remarked to him in substance, "There are two revolutions in Cuba—that of the Casino Club, and that of the insurrectionists. I am in favor of the insurrectionists, who contend for free Cuba and the emancipation of slaves." These reports, probably of two conversations, show plainly enough what are the feelings of Emilio Castelar, and indicate the direction which his action will take, however it may be thwarted by elements beyond his control.

FOURTH EDITION.

THE WAR PROSPECT.

GENERAL SICKLES SURROUNDED BY A MOB IN MADRID—A RUMOR THAT HE HAS ASKED FOR HIS PASSPORTS—INCREASED ACTIVITY IN THE WAR AND NAVY DEPARTMENTS.

WASHINGTON, November 21.—A despatch was received to-day by Secretary Fish from Minister Sickles, stating that he was threatened by a mob who assembled in front of his residence on the night of the 19th instant, but that they were dispersed by the Spanish military authorities before he was subjected to indignity. The Spanish Government is considered strong enough to maintain order in Madrid. A large number of officers on detached service were ordered to the various available vessels of the navy to-day. Most of the assignments are to take effect on the 1st of December.

A large number of army officers were also assigned to duty.

SECOND DESPATCH.

WASHINGTON, November 21.—A long cable despatch in cipher was received at the Department of State from General Sickles, shortly after twelve o'clock to-day, and was at once translated and disclosed to Secretary Fish at the Cabinet meeting.

It is supposed that the despatch relates to the further outrages reported to have been committed on the American Legation in Madrid. Intense anxiety prevails here to ascertain from official sources the exact state of affairs at Madrid, as well as the official details of the reported insults offered to this Government on the person of our Minister.

A complete statement of the financial resources of the Government and the unexpended balances standing to the credit of the various Departments, made by order of the Secretary of the Treasury, has just been delivered to Mr. Richardson at the Cabinet meeting.

THIRD DESPATCH.

BOSTON, November 21.—There is a rumor here to the effect that General Sickles, our Minister at Madrid, has demanded his passports. The rumor created a sensation in Boston, and the public are on the *qui vive* for further news in regard to the Spanish situation.

GREAT FIRE IN OTTAWA.

THE ESTIMATED LOSS $250,000.

OTTAWA, Ont., November 21.—A fire broke out on Sussex street this morning, destroying seven large brick stores, and a number of fine dwellings were also consumed. The loss is estimated at $250,000. The amount of the insurance is unknown.

The Ottawa River is completely blockaded with ice and snow. A number of vessels are frozen in with their cargoes. There is excellent sleighing in this vicinity.

LATEST GENERAL NEWS.

DISASTERS TO CANADIAN SHIPPING.

MONTREAL, Can., November 21.—The steamship Pro Tem, bound for Plymouth, England, with a cargo of phosphate, went ashore at St. Denis Point, and is a total wreck.

There are several schooners and barges ashore up the river, and assistance is impossible on account of heavy ice.

IMPROVEMENT OF TRADE IN NEW ENGLAND.

FALL RIVER, Mass., November 21.—The Fall River mills will run on full time beginning January.

PAWTUCKET, R. I., November 21.—The Stater Cotton Company, at this place, will resume on full time on Monday next.

DEDHAM, Mass., November 21.—The Merchants' Woollen Company, at this place, employing seven hundred hands, is running extra hours to fill orders.

THE FARMERS IN THE ILLINOIS ELECTION.

CHICAGO, November 21.—The returns of the election show that the whole vote (one hundred and two counties) is a little more than 336,000. The whole vote in the sixty-six counties in which the farmers made battle was 176,263, viz.: Farmers, 94,188; all others, 82,075. The same ratio of votes extended through the whole State would have yielded the farmers about 22,000 majority over all.

THE SPRAGUES' FAILURE.

PROVIDENCE, R. I., November 21.—The Cranston Savings Bank of this city and one of the Spragues institutions will be placed in the hands of a receiver.

HENRY WILSON ON THE CUBAN QUESTION.

BOSTON, November 21.—Henry Wilson has given his views on the Cuban question. He said that such a succession of cruelties as had been practised on Cuba of late years should be ended by some nation in the interests of common civilization. He expressed his fear that the form of government was not sufficiently established in Spain to stand the test of a war with this country, and that the effect of such a war would be to recreate a monarchy. He believed no hasty or ill-advised action would be taken by the Government. He expressed his regret at the foolish talk published about taking Cuba and settling with Spain afterwards. He spoke strongly against the sensational utterances of newspapers on the subject.

DESTRUCTIVE FIRE IN NEVADA.

SAN FRANCISCO, November 21.—On Thursday morning a fire began in a Chinese wash-house, in the town of Eureka, Nevada. The flames spread rapidly, and destroyed the whole block. The establishment of the Eureka *Sentinel* was completely destroyed, the loss being $12,000. Several other losses make the total about $40,000.

THE WISCONSIN ELECTION.

MADISON, Wis., November 21.—Complete returns from the State election give Taylor (Opposition), for Governor, 15,400 majority over Washburne, who is the lowest on the Republican ticket. Frisby, for Attorney-General, is 3,000 ahead, chiefly in his own and adjoining counties.

THE UNEMPLOYED POOR.

CONFERENCE OF SENATORS AND ASSEMBLYMEN-ELECT WITH THE COMPTROLLER—MR. GREEN'S VIEWS.

A committee of the New York delegation to the Legislature, consisting of Charles S. Spencer (Chairman), Peter Woods, J. Coughlin, Senators Fox and Ledwith, Mr. Biglin, and Mr. Waehner (Secretary), this morning waited upon Comptroller Green for the purpose of ascertaining what means that officer could devise for raising money for the various departments in order that the laboring classes might be supplied with opportunities for work during the present dull season.

After a few preliminary statements by Mr. Spencer in relation to the distress now prevalent, the Comptroller said:

"Your object, as I understand it, is to get sound and reliable information as to what is practicable to be done for those men who have been thrown out of employment. How is that to be accomplished? The taxes for the ensuing year are already 3½ per cent.—that is to say, where a tax-payer paid $250 last year he will pay $350 next year. Would it be desirable to still further increase that taxation? My own opinion is that it is quite heavy enough; and when I say this I don't refer to tax-payers who have millions, but to the poorer classes of persons who own property, and who are illy able to bear these burdens. Besides, any addition that you make to taxation could not come into effect till after the 1st of January, so that your object would be defeated because you want immediate relief. What provision, then, can be made for this purpose? I have had a careful estimate made as to the amount of bonds the Finance Department is authorized to issue for public works, and I find that for the public parks there is authorized $700,000; for the Croton water mains, $1,000,000; of dock bonds, $1,000,000; for the New York Bridge Company, $150,000. There are also bonds for street improvements, and, indeed, sufficient to carry on work abundantly. Now, how is the money to be obtained on these bonds? We must keep within the limits of the law. Capitalists are very careful how they invest their money. But I have been down in Wall street this week, and I may say that I have found every disposition on the part of the capitalists to aid us in this emergency. I have advertised in this morning's papers for loans on bonds amounting to $2,717,000, and I have every reason to hope that they will be promptly taken; and I shall not hesitate to make demands on the capitalists to meet the emergency you have suggested."

Mr. Spencer said in reply: "We understand that work could be done more advantageously by day work direct from the Department than by contracts, and that the Board of Aldermen can, by a two-thirds vote, rescind that part of the charter making it obligatory on the departments to take contracts for all jobs over $1,000."

Mr. Green—Yes, that is so; but I have nothing to do with that.

Mr. Spencer—You think there is a probability of this money being raised?

Mr. Green—I think the capitalists are disposed to come forward and assist us.

At this point of the preceedings Mr. Wales, President of the Park Commission, entered the room, and was questioned as to his ability to employ men.

Mr. Peter Woods said the situation of affairs in regard to working-men was most serious; and he hoped that all the departments would do their best in regard to employing men. There ought to be employment furnished for fifteen thousand.

Senator Ledwith—How many men do you think you could take on between this and New Year's.

Mr. Wales thought he could take on about a thousand.

Senator Ledwith—Then you don't think you could spend this $700,000 that is to be raised for you during the next six weeks.

Mr. Wales—No; I do not—especially if snowy or wet weather was to come on.

Mr. Spencer—The men ought to be employed shovelling snow off, and then shovelling it on again.

Mr. Delafield Smith, corporation Counsel, said no one felt more heartily than himself for our laboring fellow-citizens, and, so far as possible, all technicalities which stood in the way or impeded the action of the departments would be disregarded. The laws would in all cases be construed in a broad and liberal sense for their benefit.

Mr. Spencer—The state of affairs is simply dreadful. Hundreds of applications are daily made to me and to the other representatives, from men out of employment. Men cannot stand it to see their wives and children starving. Something must be done immediately.

After some further discussion the Committee took their leave of the Comptroller and proceeded to the Department of Public Works, where they were introduced to Commissioner Van Nort, and the case stated to him by Mr. Spencer.

In reply Mr. Van Nort said that if the funds were placed at his disposal he could take on ten thousand men within the next six weeks. There was plenty of work to be done. He was now taking on men every day. No case of real distress was sent away, but all men in want who applied were furnished with a ticket for work.

The Committee then called on the Mayor and received his assurances that he would do all that lay in his power to further their object, in providing work for men in idleness.

TWEED AS A PRISONER.

WHAT JUDGE DAVIS SAYS REGARDING THE PRIVILEGES ACCORDED BY THE SHERIFF.

The action of Sheriff Brennan in allowing Mr. Tweed to transact business and arrange his affairs about town after his delivery into the Sheriff's custody has been questioned by many persons whose opinions on legal matters are of weight.

Judge Davis was visited by the writer and asked whether such liberty could be granted to a criminal after a verdict of "guilty" had been rendered.

"I would rather not express an opinion," said the Judge. "The question may arise, and then I shall render a decision upon the bench."

"But is not such action unprecedented? Is not a criminal supposed to be in confinement while he awaits sentence?"

"I can only say this: When Mr. Tweed was found guilty he was placed in the custody of the Sheriff. Papers were made out commanding the Sheriff to take entire charge of him. From that moment the Sheriff became responsible for the criminal. If I am called upon to do so, I shall give a very decided opinion upon the subject."

Last night Mr. Tweed slept at the Metropolitan Hotel, and after breakfasting sumptuously this morning he was driven to his office at No. 85 Duane street, in company with Deputy Sheriff Shields and his assistant, Cahill. The ex-Boss reached his office a little before noon, and remained there during the whole afternoon with the doors locked, and admittance refused except to a few of his most intimate friends. To-morrow morning at ten o'clock he is to be taken to the Court of Oyer and Terminer to receive his sentence, and there appears to be no doubt on the part of his counsel that its severity will only be limited by the longest term of imprisonment allowed by law. An appeal will then be taken, but, pending the appeal, there will then be no method of preventing his being placed in actual confinement in either the City Prison, the County Jail, or the Penitentiary.

INGERSOLL TO BE LOCKED UP.

NO BAIL ACCEPTABLE TO THE DISTRICT ATTORNEY.

[Continued from Third Edition.]

Assistant District-Attorney Allen said this afternoon that no bail would be accepted in the case of James H. Ingersoll, who was surrendered by his bondsmen and is to be tried on Monday. Late this afternoon Ingersoll was consulting with his lawyer at the latter's office in Pine street, and had not yet been taken to the Tombs.

MORE MEN EMPLOYED AT THE NAVY YARD.

Fifty additional men were given work at the Brooklyn Navy Yard to-day. They were given to the foremen on the Swatara, Roanoke, Florida, and Colorado. It is said the Spaniards on board the Arapiles do not like the appearance of the Roanoke, as she looks rather formidable. They have made many inquiries about the effect of her shots and the effect of shells or shot on her turrets. They are exceedingly anxious to get away, having received orders to sail for Cuba as soon as possible.

THE REV. HENRY MORGAN AT COOPER INSTITUTE.

The Rev. Henry Morgan is to give his last lecture at Cooper Institute on Sunday evening, choosing "Fast Young Men" for his subject. It is one of his most successful efforts.

CITY NOTES.

Mrs. Maria Jourdan Westmoreland, at the request of a large number of literary admirers, will deliver her lecture, "Shot at Social Myths," at the Union Square Theatre to-morrow evening.

Gilmore's Twenty-second Regiment band gives the first of a series of grand promenade concerts at the armory of the regiment, on Fourteenth street near Sixth avenue, to-morrow evening.

At a meeting of the Police Board to-day, Detectives Radford, McCord, Dickson, Eustace, Kelso, Simington, Tully, and Moore were transferred to patrol duty; and Ward Officers J. J. Dunn, R. Fields, R. King, P. Leahy, J. H. Woolsey, J. Von Gerichten, and Z. H. Mullen were ordered to fill their places. The above transfers cause a good deal of comment at headquarters.

AWFUL CALAMITY.

The Wild Animals Broken Loose from Central Park.

TERRIBLE SCENES OF MUTILATION

A Shocking Sabbath Carnival of Death.

SAVAGE BRUTES AT LARGE

Awful Combats Between the Beasts and the Citizens.

THE KILLED AND WOUNDED

General Duryee's Magnificent Police Tactics.

BRAVERY AND PANIC

How the Catastrophe Was Brought About---Affrighting Incidents.

PROCLAMATION BY THE MAYOR

Governor Dix Shoots the Bengal Tiger in the Street.

CONSTERNATION IN THE CITY

Another Sunday of horror has been added to those already memorable in our city annals. The sad and appalling catastrophe of yesterday is a further illustration of the unforeseen perils to which large communities are exposed. Writing even at a late hour, without full details of the terrors of the evening and night, and with a necessarily incomplete list of the killed and mutilated, we may pause for a moment in the widespread sorrow of the hour to cast a hasty glance over what will be felt as a great calamity for many years. Few of the millions who have visited Central Park, and who, passing in through the entrance at East Sixty-fourth street, have stopped to examine the collection of birds and animals grouped around the old Arsenal building, could by any possibility have foreseen the source of such terrible danger to a whole city in the caged beasts around him, as the trivial incident of yesterday afternoon developed. The unfortunate man to whose fatal imprudence all accounts attribute the outbreak of the wild animals of the menagerie has answered with his life for his temerity, but we have a list of calamities traceable from his act which one life seems inadequate to expiate. We have a list of forty-nine killed, of which only twenty-seven bodies have been identified, and it is much to be feared that this large total of fatalities will be much increased with the return of daylight. The list of mutilated, trampled and injured in various ways must reach nearly 200 persons of all ages, of which, so far as known, about sixty are very serious, and of these latter three can hardly outlast the night. Many of the slightly injured were taken to their homes, so that for at least another day the full extent of the calamity cannot be measured. We have only to hope that no further fatalities will occur. Twelve of the wild, carnivorous beasts are still at large, their lurking places not being known for a certainty, but the citizens may rest assured that if they will only exercise ordinary prudence and leave the task of hunting down the animals to the authorities, who have, somewhat tardily, taken the matter in hand, there will be no further casualties to register as the outcome of the unfortunate act of a reckless keeper in Central Park. It was an apparently small cause for a huge and horrible result, but the overturning of a kerosene lamp in a dingy cowshed in Chicago laid the Queen City of the West in ashes, and the spark from a hod carrier's pipe was parent to the flames that destroyed in a night the great granite buildings of Boston as if the solid stones were fuel. It is not long since a herd of Texan cattle threw New York's million of human beings into consternation, defied the police force and injured so many. It was at least to be hoped that the somewhat similar, although more fearful calamity of the breaking loose of the wild beasts at Central Park would have found Superintendent Walling with some plan to meet the emergency. In all such cases promptitude is invaluable, and although General Duryee deserves credit for his plan, formed, we are assured, on the instant, and carried out so far with effect, we must regret that he was not earlier informed of the terrible event. A telegram from police headquarters to the General's residence did not reach him, and thus a valuable hour was lost, as he was first informed of the catastrophe by seeing the mutilated body of the unfortunate sewing girl, Annie Thomas, borne on an improvised stretcher to the Thirty-first precinct station house, near West Eighty-sixth street. He was visiting at the house of a friend, and the passing crowd with the mournful burden on the shoulders of the police, attracted the attention of a young daughter of his friends. Her screams brought the entire party to the windows. In an instant the General was in the street. Learning from a hundred tongues the horrible truth in the few words, "the wild animals at the Park have broken loose," he ran like a deer to the station house, and seating himself by the telegraph instrument directed from that point the operations which first resulted in staying the panic. Had he lost the time which it would have taken to reach Police Headquarters, it is impossible to say where the panic and affright and their consequent fatalities would have ended. Commissioners Matsell and Disbecker were heard from at various points throughout the evening, but their efforts were not of a nature to produce any good result. Orders and counter orders were issued by them in confusing succession. Happily the steps taken by General Duryee made them practically subordinates and diminished their inefficiency—to give their stampeded zeal no harsher term. Commissioner Voorhis could not be found during the entire evening. To General Shaler, also, the thanks of the community are due. His promptitude in calling out the Seventh, Eighth, Ninth and Sixty-ninth regiments, a call manfully responded to, and placing them at the service of General Duryee deserves unqualified praise. It is to be hoped, too, that the proclamation issued by Mayor Havemeyer, after consultation with General Shaler and Commissioner Duryee, will meet with the obedience which its gravity merits. Discipline is the only means of meeting and conquering such an untoward chain of circumstances, and we here point out that the obedience which is given by the militia to General Shaler, by the police to General Duryee, the hero of the hour, should be cheerfully rendered by the citizens at large to the proclamation of his Honor the Mayor. The deaths and mutilations are already too numerous to risk their increase, and the authorities will only serve the common cause by enforcing the law against those whose curiosity leads them to defy the mandates of the civil power.

The following is the Mayor's proclamation:—

A Proclamation.

MAYOR'S OFFICE, SUNDAY NIGHT, Nov. 1, 1874.

All citizens, except members of the National Guard, are enjoined to keep within their houses or residences until the wild animals now at large are captured or killed. Notice of the release from this order will be spread by the firing of cannon in City Hall Park, Tompkins square, Madison square, The Round and at Macomb's Dam Bridge. Obedience to this order will secure a speedy end to the state of siege occasioned by the calamity of this evening.

An account will be opened at the City Hall of the city of New York for contributions to the sufferers.

THE CATASTROPHE.

The location of the zoological collection in the Park is well known to most New Yorkers; but it appears that changes were made recently in the disposition of the various animals, and to realize the exact nature of the catastrophe it becomes necessary to indicate where the various animals were situated yesterday when the frightful event occurred that spread such terror throughout the city. If you enter the menagerie from Fifth avenue you will find on either hand, running parallel to the street, the houses where the herbivorous beasts were domiciled. In former times several bears from the northern regions occupied the right hand corner, where a few beautiful zebras lately gladdened the eye. To the extreme left were the cages of the several foreign birds formerly devoted to a large collection of monkeys. To the extreme right were the vultures and eagles, and the visitor, by making a short circuit of the large building, known in times gone by as the Arsenal, found himself in front of a handsome wooden structure, one story high, where the principal wild animals resided. Of course the residence of the sea lion was known to everybody. On the inside of the garden the stately giraffe occupied a somewhat large enclosure, and adjacent were a number of pelicans, intermingled with several specimens of the ostrich tribe. The bears were in isolated cages on the green sward, near the common pedestrian route from the Fifth avenue entrance.

THE PROMINENT ANIMALS

in the quadrangle nearest to Fifth avenue were the bison, the nylghau, the zebu, the sacred bull, cow and calf, the zebras, the young elephant, the capybara, the guanaco, the fat tailed Syrian var, the aoudad and the fallow deer. In the valuable monkey collection was the sooty mangabey, the bonnet macaque, the Toque monkey, the pigtailed monkey, the Arabian baboon, the black handed spider monkey, the brown capuchin, the Teetee and the black eared marmoset. Such was the scene before

THE TERRIBLE EVENTS

of yesterday—the bursting forth of the most ferocious of the beasts within the menagerie of the Park, the awful slaughter that ensued, the exciting conflicts between the infuriated animals, the frightful deaths that followed, the destruction of property and the fearful and general excitement, making an era in the history of New York not soon to be forgotten. How singular that Sunday, of all days in the week, should make the occasion of such great panics as mark the record of the past four years. It was a Sabbath morning that witnessed the destruction of Chicago and Boston, and a Sabbath afternoon beheld the streets of New York given up to the fury of a drove of Texan cattle. It was on a Sabbath that the Westfield exploded her boiler. But yesterday capped the climax of unthought possibilities, and it was the Sabbath, too, that deepened the significance of the great disaster.

As everybody knows, the Central Park on Sunday is the popular resort of all classes. The rich and fashionable in their carriages and the poor and humble on foot, alike sally forth to enjoy its beauties. It is safe to say that at least 20,000 people filled the various walks, drives and avenues yesterday. To nine-tenths of the pedestrian visitors the Menagerie is a chief source of attraction. That it contained the elements of sanguinary disaster to a multitude of human beings hardly entered into the philosophy of anybody. It would be vain of the writer to presume himself capable of picturing the harrowing scenes of which he was a distressed and involuntary spectator. To give, for instance, an adequate conception of the frightful incident where Lincoln, the Numidian lion, urged to indescribable fury by the bullets that pierced his flanks and shoulders jumped into a landaulet occupied by a nursemaid and her four young charges, mangling the delicate little things past all sign of recognition, would be a difficult task. But let me endeavor to describe the fearful scenes with some attempt at order. My head is so confused and my nerves so unstrung with the fearful scenes through which I have passed that I confess I am hardly equal to picturing them.

FIRST OMINOUS SYMPTOMS.

The writer stood within a hundred yards of the menagerie when the first ominous symptoms of the approaching catastrophe were heard. The doors of the main structure, wherein the principal wild animals were confined, were closed at five o'clock. Hundreds of people, men, women and children, were still lingering in the vicinity. Five or six of the Park police were stationed in the neighborhood. One stood at the entrance on Fifth avenue and Sixty-fourth street, making a record of the number of visitors passing in. Another was stationed for a similar purpose on the roadway approaching from the southeastern entrance, at the corner of Fifty-ninth street. Within the arsenal there appears to have been a number of the Park police. The Captain was off duty and did not appear until late at night. Mr. Conklin, the director of the menagerie, was at his post, like a good soldier. It was

A CALM, PEACEFUL AND PLEASING SCENE

in the early hours of the afternoon. Children ran about from cage to cage in the perfect fulness of delight. A stream of people released from the cares and labors of the week wandered through the grounds, pausing here to admire the beautiful zebras and stopping there to laugh over the amusing antics of the monkeys. The idea of danger could only be suggested to create laughter and derision. Certainly nobody seriously contemplated the possibility of peril where seemingly massive cages restrained the wild and savage instincts of the various beasts of prey. The rhinoceros appeared the

PICTURE OF STUPID AMIABILITY;

the Numidian lion wore a look of the grossest indolence, the Bengal tiger seemed as harmless as a prostrate forest tree, the bears invited a caressing acquaintance, the boa constrictor might have been petted with the hand, the elephant eating biscuits from the fingers of a little child suggested an extreme condition of tameness and docility. In all the rest, saving the restless and savage-eyed hyena, the spirit of the day appeared to dwell.

THE ORIGIN OF THE AWFUL CALAMITY.

In a very few moments the whole aspect was destined to be changed. It is now well authenticated that Chris. Anderson the keeper, one of whose charges was Pete, the rhinoceros, in walking around after the public was excluded, stopped in front of the den of the huge animal above mentioned. He was seen to poke his cane through the bars at the great beast, and was warned by Keeper Miller to desist. The latter was leaving the building at the moment he remonstrated with Anderson, and to this circumstance, doubtless, owes his life. He says that Keeper Hyland also called out to Anderson. The latter had a fashion, it appears, of teasing the animals, although he was often known to eject persons from the building for similar practices. Anderson paid no attention to the warnings of his fellow keepers, and, it is thought, a heedless thrust must have entered the eye of the rhinoceros. A number of boys who were peering in through the windows on the north side of the building attracted the attention of the writer by their cries,

"LOOK, HE'S BREAKING OUT!"

There was a crashing heard within and the boys were seen to flee precipitately. I rushed to the window, drawn by a curiosity which was irresistible. My example was soon followed by others, many women struggling for a place. It was some moments before I could make out what was transpiring within. A keeper was standing in the middle of the open space apparently spellbound. Another was standing further down, grasping a crowbar, his gaze directed toward the pen of the rhinoceros. The short, angry, squeaking cry of the rhinoceros, like sudden blasts on a fishhorn, were heard amid the sound of snapping bars and crashing planks. It at once struck me that the huge animal was breaking down the walls of his pen in the endeavor doubtless to reach his tormentor. Not aware of any cause for this sudden exhibition of rage, none of the fascinated crowd at the window measured the danger of their position or the object of the infuriated beast. The keeper (afterward found to be Anderson) now rushed forward and struck at the animal. We could not see whether his blows reached the rhinoceros or not, but their effect was soon told. A crash which shook the building followed and the front of the pen fell outward and the horrid, misshapen mass of Pete, the rhinoceros, rushed out, his double-horned head close to the ground. Anderson made a spring sideways to evade the monster's onslaught and might have succeeded in gaining at least temporary safety by this means but he was too close to the animal, for the latter, swinging his unwieldy body toward him, knocked him down with a touch of his shoulder, and an instant after had trampled him out of recognition. Backing down from the mangled body with a swiftness almost incredible from his bulk, the rhinoceros plunged his horrid horn into the dead keeper, dashing the last possible spark of life out against the walls of one of the pens, which likewise gave way. All this tragedy transpired in an instant. Horror stricken, I tried to push my way from the window, but the crowd was now dense behind me, and I could not stir. I cried:—

"For God's sake, let some one run to the police station for help!"

I struggled to get out, putting my hands against the window and my feet below it, and pushing with all my might. An accursed curiosity in the crowd, who were only vaguely conscious of what was transpiring, made my efforts useless. When I looked in through the window again the destruction at the further end had increased, the rhinoceros breaking open the dens of the animals on the left hand side.

THE KEEPER, HYLAND,

whom I had first seen standing spellbound, was advancing, pale as marble, and a navy revolver in his hand, toward the enraged rhinoceros. The animal saw him, turned and made for him in an instant. He sprang aside and fired. The ball hit the rhinoceros on the left shoulder, for he swerved over for an instant; but it can scarcely have more than hurt him a little, as he turned with a whiff, whiff, whiff snort, his head down toward the keeper. The latter, with cat-like agility, retreated toward the lions' and tigers' cages, evidently making for the space between them; but too late. The horrid horn impaled him against the corner cage, killing him instantly, tearing the cage to pieces and releasing the panther, who landed in the middle of the open space with a spring. The cries of all the animals were now joined in horrid chorus by the loud and long-sustained roar of the lion and lioness, the tigers and all the wild beasts, that doubtless had their carnivorous instincts whetted by the smell of human blood and the sound and sight of the bloody struggles outside their bars.

"THE WILD ANIMALS ARE LOOSE,"

I yelled, and the savage chorus within bore out my words. At last curiosity seemed to give way. The crowd fled in all directions, women falling as they ran, and no one staying to help them out of the way of the coming danger, which was then shaping itself so swiftly. I ran to the police station in the Arsenal Building, and found that the sergeant on duty was dozing quietly. I shook him up, told him in a few words what was the matter, and ran round to the space in front of the Arsenal. There I found Keeper Miller talking to the policeman, who was just coming off duty. Miller laughed at my story.

"Come around," I said earnestly.

"Too thin, young fellow," said the policeman.

"Don't you hear?" I said, as the roaring of the animals sounded ominously in our ears. The sergeant now came running out in search of the policeman.

"Anderson and Hyland are killed," said he to Miller. "Why don't you stir yourself."

Miller is a tall, stalwart man of about thirty-three, and it is but just to say that from the moment the sergeant spoke he sprang into action. He rushed into the keeper's room and grasped a sixteen shooter rifle, which is kept loaded for such emergencies, and ran out through the central door in the rear of the Arsenal to the window the crowd had just deserted. What he saw evidently appalled him, as he let the butt of his rifle fall to the ground and continued gazing in through the window like one in a dream. From his own lips I have learned what he saw. He said:—

"An attentive glance through the window revealed the fact that

THE HUGE RHINOCEROS HAD BROKEN LOOSE.

He had apparently made no more of the massive barrier that enclosed him than of a sheet of pasteboard. I saw the dead bodies of Hyland and Anderson, the former nearer to me than the other. The panther was crouched over Hyland's body, knawing horribly at his head. I recognized his body by the striped shirt which I could just see hanging tattered from the arm. It was growing dark, and this made everything look twice as fearful. I saw the rhinoceros plunge blindly forward against the double tier of cages where the black and spotted leopards, the striped hyena, the prairie wolf, the puma and the jaguar were lying. Judging from the condition of the cages the onset of the powerful and infuriated rhinoceros must have been tremendous. In some cases the bars were only bent to an elbow, but, as a rule, they snapped asunder like kindling wood before the smashing weight brought against them

THE RELEASE OF THE ANIMALS

mentioned angered still more the lions and tigers and all the rest within the building. The rhinoceros in the meantime was busy in the work of destruction. In a few moments more he had broken down the pens of the wild swine, the manatee, the American tapir, the two-toed sloth and the pair of kangaroos. Just then, too, Lincoln, the Numidian lion escaped from his cage, through some unfortunate oversight committed at feeding time. The bolt of his prison door was insecure, and when the raging rhinoceros butted his head against the bottom it flew wide open. Hardly had Lincoln the lion bounded into the centre aisle of the building when the three cages containing the black and spotted leopards, the tiger and tigeresses, the black wolf and the striped and spotted hyenas were sprung open by an overpowering charge from the now desperate rhinoceros. The noise of this crash might have been heard several blocks away. It was followed by a series of fights between the liberated beasts. Close by a window on the western side of the building the black wolf sprung upon the flanks of the Bengal tiger. The lion stood a little distance away pawing the floor, awaiting rather than offering an attack. Between the wolf and tiger the conflict was brief. The latter, shaking off the feeble hold of the other, turned quick as lightning on his hind legs, and falling, with open, gleaming jaws, upon his less muscular foe, rolled him over in the dust. The great fight ensued

OVER THE BODY

of poor, brave Hyland. There was evidently a fight over the body of Anderson; but I could see nothing more than a mingling, gleaming mass, whence arose the most awful cries. Nearer to me, where Hyland lay, the lioness, the panther, the puma, and presently the Bengal tiger, were rolling over and over, striking at each other with their mighty paws. The lioness tore the skin off the puma's flank with one blow. The coming of the tiger was something terrible. I never shall forget the awful, splendid look of him as he landed with a spring in the thick of them. I could not move. It was too awful for anything. Oddly enough, while the fight was going on, now one furious beast tugging and crunching at the arms or legs of the corpse, now letting go with his teeth to plant his paws upon the bleeding remains and snap with his dripping jaws at another beast, writhing and awful as they were, I could not help looking at Lincoln, the lion, who was standing behind them, pawing the ground, roaring and lashing his sides with his tail, every muscle in uneasy tension. All of a sudden I had a flash.

"BY GOD, HE'S LOOKING AT ME."

I said to myself. It seems to me I felt him looking at me. I saw him crouch. I turned and ran. My God, I had no idea there was anybody near me.

Miller had not been a minute and a half at the window when I saw him run towards me, shouting, at the top of his lungs,

"THEY'RE COMING; THEY'RE ALL LOOSE."

It is here necessary to explain Miller's statement. "My God? I had no idea there was anybody near me." Those who ran from the window in the first instance had not run far before they looked back. There was, of course no pursuit, and a great many lingered by, but at a safe distance. The coming of the keeper, however; his standing listless looking before the window for over a minute, had had the effect of inspiring a return of confidence in the more curious, and when Anderson, frightened by the eye of the lion, ran precipitately toward the Arsenal there were perhaps a dozen persons near the window. He had only sped a few paces when, with a terrific roar

LINCOLN, THE LION, CAME CRASHING THROUGH THE GLASS.

I saw a young man fall from a blow of the awful paw, and another crushed to earth beneath the beast's weight. The crowd fled in all directions, but the lion did not pursue. Planting his paws upon one of the bodies he filled the air with the fearful rumble of his roar. I started to run, but Miller called on me to stop. I turned and saw him kneel down deliberately and take aim. There was a good chance for a shot, as the lion stood almost facing him, but with the right shoulder more toward him. I have no reason to doubt the steadiness of Miller or his reputation as a shot, but I waited with inpent breath as he took aim. He had hit him. I could not see where, but the wound was far from fatal. The bellowings were renewed, his mane erect, his tail switching his sides, while he pawed the earth and swung his huge head from side to side. Drawn by the report of the rifle and the roaring of the beasts, crowds of people were entering the enclosure from the Sixty-fourth street entrance. I saw that already a number of Park

POLICE, ARMED WITH REVOLVERS,

and citizens with rifles, were on the ground. I had no weapon and so ran down the incline by the refreshment stand, toward Fifth avenue; and almost on my heels, as it were, came the Numidian lion, with a series of bounds. So sudden, fierce and powerful was the leap he made into the midst of the storming party that he paralyzed the coolest calculations and scattered half a hundred armed and unarmed men like chaff before the wind. Springing in the air over the stooped form of Policeman Murray, who ducked in time to save himself from possible death, Lincoln landed in a fast widening

CIRCLE OF FEAR-STRICKEN PEOPLE,

of fainting women, screaming children and terrified men. Lincoln paused for perhaps a second, lashing himself with his tail and glaring horribly around him. On the ground before him were two young men, who had tripped and fallen in the precipitate retreat from before the building. They were struggling fast to rise, and had nearly succeeded, when Lincoln, with another awful roar that echoed over the Park, pounced upon the nearest, and, with one stroke of his fore paw, tore clothes and flesh to pieces. A shout of horror went up from the distant witnesses of the deed; but they were given little time to meditate upon it. I was just in the angle between the two aviaries, which contained yesterday the doves and the eagles respectively, when the last mentioned deed of blood was enacted. I was about to escape by rushing past the house where the wild animals were caged, and had just reached the path near the sea lion's tank, when what I had feared most came to pass. The rhinoceros, in his infuriated career, had at last found the gate and crashed through it. Had he done so at first there would have been less lost lives to count. A storming party, which had been formed by Colonel Conklin, of keepers, citizens and police, near the Fifty-ninth street entrance, and which was powerfully aided by the arrival of a platoon from the Nineteenth precinct, under Captain Gunner and Mr. Hunt of Ninety-third street, was within a hundred yards of the building when the rhinoceros emerged, giving his short, vicious cry. His appearance was the signal for a misdirected volley, which, of course, did little or no execution on his thick, tough hide and double-horn-protected proboscis. It confused him momentarily, however, for he turned and re-entered the building on a sort of ambling trot. Misled by this retreat a cheer went up from the firing party, and they rushed forward, Colonel Conklin leading to secure the door. Had the great brute deliberately planned an ambuscade it could not have better succeeded. When the party were within a dozen feet of the door the puma sprung through the shattered portal into their midst, overthrowing several, doubtless injuring some. Almost on the heels of the puma came the black and spotted leopard, followed by the jaguar, the African lioness and tiger. The latter came forth with a slow and stealthy tread. Archambeau, one of the keepers, had the temerity to try and lasso the beast, knowing that there was none more dangerous and bloodthirsty in the whole collection.

THE TIGER SAW THE OBJECT

of the keeper, and without a moment's warning sprung fifteen feet into the air and caught Archambeau by the right shoulder. The two went down together, the tiger on top. Instant preparations were made to save the poor fellow, when unfortunately the rhinoceros came lumbering at a half trot out of the entrance and drove the rescuing party from their purpose. He also drove the tiger before him, but at the same time planted one of his enormous feet on the prostrate Archambeau and squeezed the breath from his body. The storming party was for the moment completely disorganized. The animals were running in various directions, and the attacking forces and the curious spectators were fleeing in every direction, scaling rocks, climbing trees, falling in their flight, and a case is reported of a citizen stabbed at this moment by an Italian over a quarrel as to which should first ascend a tree. The wounded man, Calvin Morley, of Flatbush, L. I., is at Bellevue Hospital, but cannot give the police any description of

THE MAN WHO STABBED HIM.

I mention this terrible incident from a host of others to show how overwhelming was the fright and how blinding the stampede. The lion had escaped the bullets of the firing party in the front inclosure, or rather being maddened to further desperation by them careered wildly through the Fifth avenue entrance, and was followed shortly after by the Bengal tiger, a number of demoralized Park policemen, who still had a sentiment of duty, pursuing them with halloes, as if they were sheep, not sheep devourers.

CONFUSION AND DESTRUCTION.

From this point it has been found extremely difficult to gather anything like a coherent or complete story of the depredations of the uncaged beasts. From a number of statements made to our reporters by eye-witnesses, many of these statements abounding in patent impossibilities, but all of them given with an apparent conviction of truthfulness, the following continuation of the story is given. The writer of the preceding on the pell-mell breaking forth of the animals ran to the Seventy-fourth street entrance and hurried down to the Windsor Hotel, whence he telegraphed to the HERALD office for assistance.

THE CONTINUATION OF DESTRUCTION.

The rhinoceros, after trampling down the keeper, Archambeau, made directly for the cage of the brown bear, which stood on the grass recently. The ease with which he overturned the structure well illustrated the vast muscular power of the brute. The brown bear escaped with some bruises. The grizzly bear, on being knocked out of his house, advanced to give fight, but was bowled over on the grass three times in succession.

THE LEOPARD

after killing a little child and mutilating several women who strove to run before him, made his way into the inclosure containing the pelicans, the pea fowl and ostrich and killed all before him. The terror among the storming party lasted long enough to give ample time to the escaped animals to spread havoc all through the park and city besides.

THE JAGUAR

had been forgotten at meal time, and, made desperate by hunger jumped over the fence surrounding the tall and gentle giraffes, and in less time than it takes to tell it had slaughtered one of the noble but helpless animals.

OVER ONE HUNDRED SHOTS

were fired at the rhinoceros in vain. His sides appeared to be covered with slabs of wrought iron. "Shoot him in the eye" was the general cry, but no one was lucky enough, as all were nervous with fright, to strike that particular organ. A long reaching crowbar, however, struck him in a sensitive spot under the jaw, not with the effect of checking his headlong career, but only to drive him onward to

WORSE DEEDS THAN EVER.

In the same half trot with which he issued from his quarters and swaying like a ship at sea, he struck over to the cages near Fifth avenue, where the herbivorous animals were stationed. The havoc made in this direction was frightful. All the cages tumbled to pieces, and, to add to the destruction and confusion, the liberated elephant joined forces with the rhinoceros, and the joint attack of the weaker animals, such as the camel, the zebras, the sacred bull, the guanaco and the llama was simply irresistible. The sacred bull was killed instantly, and one of the mild-eyed zebras was crushed without pity. The other escaped into the Park and ran toward Eighth avenue. He is reported to have badly bitten and kicked a number of daring boys who endeavored to effect his capture. He is still at large.

THE BIRDS.

The destruction of the bird cages was marked by terrific screaming. The eagles fought gallantly for their eyries, but nothing could withstand the united charge of the elephant and rhinoceros. It was late in the evening before the organized force of the menagerie subdued the former of these two powerful animals, and not before both had destroyed several lives and ruined a vast deal of property. The rhinoceros, the parent of all the destruction, made away toward the Mall when

THE ELEPHANT HAD BEEN LASSOED

by the hind leg, a huge log being tied to the end of the stout rope with which the leg was lariated so as to impede his progress, while other parties with ropes similarly hampered the other legs, until they were able to throw him on his side and effectually "hobble" him so that he could not rise. They were then about to shoot him at point-blank range, when the strange sight was presented of the elephant's keeper, with streaming eyes and outstretched arms, planting himself between the pointed and cocked lines of the angry crowd, who had seen the deaths and mutilations and the prostrate beast, whose trumpetings of defiance were still ringing on the ear. The keeper would not move, and, with many curses, the great brute's life was saved.

THE RHINOCEROS

escaped, as we have said, toward the Mall. Here he attacked a party of young girls, killing the sewing girl, Annie Thomas, and frightening the others terribly. One of them, subject to heart disease, Ellen Schubert, has received such a nervous shock that her death may be looked for at any moment. The beast left the Park at one of the upper Eighth avenue entrances, and gored a horse at Ninetieth street, overthrowing the heavy wagon to which he was harnessed, and dislocating the shoulder of Isaac Parker, milkman, who was driving. In this neighborhood he overthrew a shanty on the rocks, which fell before him like a house of cards. The wretched inmates were at supper, and the falling planks took fire. All the family escaped except a child in the cradle, which was burned to a crisp. Continuing on his career until he reached Eleventh avenue, he was followed by a crowd of men and boys, who were evidently unaware of his ferocious nature. He must, too, have been nearly spent with his terrible efforts but continued on toward the North River. A fortunate accident put an end to his career. It was now very dark, and he was seen to fall into a sewer excavation on the Boulevard, fifteen feet deep. Had it been a week day, and at an earlier hour, he would, no doubt, have ended his life in killing, by falling on some of the men at work. As it was, he fell inglorously.

The Park from end to end is marked with injury, and in its artificial forests the wild beasts lurk, to pounce at any moment on the unwary pedestrian.

THE LEOPARDS AND WOLVES

made short work of the deer, and all the blood for which they are responsible is not even yet fully computed. The subsequent fight between

THE LION AND TIGER,

when they met on the open space at Fifty-ninth street, outside the Park wall, in the presence of a thousand terrified spectators, was the great combat of the day. The lion tore away at one bite half the tiger's flanks, while the latter, with characteristic ferocity, buried his teeth in the lion's neck until the king of beasts howled with the keenest anguish. Now it was the lion underneath and the tiger on top. The next moment positions were reversed.

BLOOD COVERED THE AVENUE,

and off in the distance the awestruck spectators looked on in breathless fear. Finally the two sanguinary brutes rushed from each other as a bullet from the rifle of General Wingate, who came promptly on the ground, whistled between their ears. Lester Wallack took aim at the same moment from behind the unfinished iron building on the east side, and perforated the tiger to some slight degree. Many other gentlemen came rushing to the scene in the meantime, among them ex-Mayor Hall, Erastus Brooks, of the *Express*; Manton Marble and Mr. Bangs, of the *World*, who had been visiting Governor-elect Tilden, and were on their way uptown in a carriage; Judge Daly, Judge J. R. Brady, General Arthur, Hugh Hastings and Prosper Wetmore. But they were all a trifle nervous from running, and the beasts escaped on their raid down town, where, as everybody knows by this, they had a bloody and fearful carnival.

TRAGIC DEATH OF THE BROWN SEA LION.

When the ponderous rhinoceros plunged through the sea lion's cage the latter was in an apparently profound sleep. Awakened by the startling noise around him, and struck with terror at the appearance of his visitor, the poor seal uttered one long, piercing howl, partly resembling the shriek of a locomotive, and the next moment tumbled into his tank and disappeared. The rhinoceros, breaking down the whole structure, was soon floundering in the tank also. Then it was the sea lion, driven to bay, showed fight; but the contest was as unequal as a ferryboat in conflict with an iron-clad man-of-war. For a time the seal seemed to stand a chance for his life. Being lithe and slippery, he easily avoided the unwieldy attacks of his visitor. Indeed, he had every hope of safety but for an unfortunate slip made by the rhinoceros, who, keeling suddenly over, fell with all his immense weight on his prostrate foe and killed him. During the fight the roars of the sea lion were incessant and painful to hear. It was unlike any other cry of bird, or beast, or fish. It was something strange and weird, and had a half human sound that struck the ear with a singular impression. The little seal escaped by hiding under the water.

DEATH OF THE ANACONDA.

In the destruction of the various cages the anaconda was roused from his torpor, and pivoting himself upon his tail made a spring at the neck of the tall and beautiful giraffe that occupied the adjacent cage. Only a few boards separated the two. The long slender neck of the giraffe bending over the partition proved a tempting mark for the anaconda. The graceful neck was quickly bowed to the ground in the coils of the powerful constrictor. The giraffe made but a feeble struggle and death speedily ended his sufferings. Then it was the awful spectacle was seen of the anaconda seeking to swallow the body of his victim. He had but commenced this disgusting task when he was observed by Dr. F. A. Thomas, of Eighty-third street, who attacked the reptile, armed with a sabre, who at one blow severed the great snake's body and then retreated in haste.

IN THE MONKEY HOUSE.

When the elephant smashed the cages with his trunk and drove the monkeys into every hole and corner the scene of disorder and noise was perfectly indescribable. The monkeys screamed and laughed and laughed and screamed. Two green monkeys perched themselves on the elephant's back, but for a very short time. Over twenty monkeys escaped from the house and made off in various directions. Two of them climbed into a carriage standing outside the Park on Fifth avenue. One was killed by the laughing hyena, several were wounded by the black wolves; but, considering the risks they ran and the familiarity they made with many of the liberated beasts of prey, they escaped very well.

THE NEWS OF THE PROCEEDINGS

in the Park, and the terror excited throughout the city at the prospect of having a visit from the wild animals at the domestic fireside, drew an immense number of sporting men and Yorkville fast boys and rowdies in the direction of the menagerie. There was dangerous sport enough for everybody as far as hunting down the fugitives went. They penetrated everywhere. The African lioness, after saturating herself in the blood of eighteen victims—men, women and children—was finally killed at Castle Garden by a party of emigrants. She lay down under one of the great trees in the Battery Park, having leaped the rails. Although followed at a safe distance by a large crowd, she was allowed to remain in this position.

A PARTY OF SWEDISH HUNTERS,

who had arrived in the Thuringia, on their way to farms in Nebraska, undertook to kill the beast, although bears were the only large animals they had practised on. Ten in number, and armed with rifles, they scattered themselves in a semicircle in pairs, and advanced, crawling on their bellies, until within a few paces of the recumbent lioness. Her head was turned toward Broadway, but, suddenly suspecting danger, she arose and shook the heart of the onlookers with her sounding roar. It was at this moment that Jansen Bjornsen, the leader of the hunters, blew his shrill whistle, and five rifle balls were buried in the body of the lioness. She fell with a dull thud evidently dead, but the five hunters whose guns were still charged rushed up and emptied their pieces into the prostrate carcass. This was the signal for a deafening cheer. The hunters were carried round on the shoulders of the First warders, and the proprietor of the Stevens House and Nicholas Muller headed a subscription list with $50 each as a testimonial to these brave children of the Norseland for their maiden service to the great Republic. It is announced that Superintendent Webster, of Castle Garden, will receive subscriptions. It is said that nearly $500 is already down on the lists. Commissioner Lynch has put his name down for $10, Whitelaw Reid subscribes $50, C. A Dana adds $50 also.

THE BENGAL TIGER

having counted up a score of victims, surrendered his life to the trusty rifle of our aged Governor, John A. Dix, who shot him as he rounded Madison avenue and Thirty-fourth street. This was an extremely fortunate occurrence. The Governor, a splendid shot, was in town in the nick of time. This gallant act will be remembered by the citizens of New York, although it is now too late to mark that esteem at the ballot box. It may be mentioned as a fortunate circumstance that a minute after the death of the tiger Archbishop McCloskey's carriage drove up. A fright or injury to the horses by the ferocious beast might have ended the career of the aged prelate. Hearty congratulations were exchanged between the Governor and Archbishop.

FRIGHT ON FIFTH AVENUE.

The crowded condition of the Fifth avenue sidewalks on Sunday afternoon is well known to all, and the effect upon the host of elegantly dressed promenaders when the breaking loose of the beasts was made known was curious. When the beasts made their escape from the building mainly devoted to the great *carnivoræ* a number of excited people rushed down Fifth avenue, shouting as they ran. It caused a general stampede of the fashionables, who ran in various directions down side streets and into the churches, which thus received full congregations long before the hour of service. The Hon. Richard Schell, who was standing near the Brick Church on Murray Hill, and who at first believed the report of the breaking loose to be a cruel hoax, told one of our reporters that the rapidity with which the avenue was cleared beggars description. The excited, shouting party

SEEMED TO SWEEP THE AVENUE

before them. In ten minutes there was not a soul visible in either direction from the Park to the Fifth Avenue Hotel. It was puzzling to think where they had gone. Mr. Schell proceeded to state that be turned and walked up the avenue, but met no one for three-quarters of a mile. He felt then fully convinced it was a hoax. As he neared the Park, however, he heard a number of shots fired. He, in turn, became excited, and commenced running toward the Arsenal. On his way he was met by a party

BEARING A DEAD BODY,

that of a youth, fearfully disfigured about the head and face. A terrifying roar was heard behind them, when the party let the body fall and ran precipitately. Mr. Schell ran too, and jumped in among some shrubs off the main road. The incline leading to the Arsenal is unfinished, and up this road he saw some animal of the tiger species come with a light, swift movement. The beast was evidently following the blood trail, for he went straight up to the abandoned corpse, and after striking one paw upon the breast and touching it with his head, as if smelling, he gave forth a series of horrible howls. "I felt my blood run cold," said Mr. Schell, "but kept perfectly still, lest the brute should be attracted to me from

THE HORRID MEAL

he was evidently about to commence. I soon heard a number of shouts and saw a party of citizens and police running toward the animal, but unconscious of the fact. They were running away from danger in their rear. I shouted to them. They suddenly halted and looked back. Two of the party fired revolvers at the animal, which, to their relief and mine, uttered a howl of anguish and ran, pursued by men who themselves were running away (from the lion they said). I ran until I gained the entrance to the Park and made down Fifty-ninth street, as the animal was proceeding at a limping trot down Fifth avenue. I had not proceeded far when I saw a large object careering madly toward me. I recognized it as a buffalo bull. I turned to run back toward the Park, when to my horror I observed an animal ambling toward Fourth avenue. I saw it was a brown or black bear. I rushed up the stoop of one of the houses and tugged at the bell. I saw as I turned that the buffalo and the bear had met, and that a fight was in progress. I cannot tell which got the better. The fight was short, and I heard that the bear was seen to limp away. I got into the house, but was almost summarily ejected, although I made an urgent appeal to be allowed to remain." The animal first referred to by Mr. Schell is, doubtless, the one that

ENTERED THE CHURCH OF ST. THOMAS,

of which Dr. Morgan is pastor, at the corner of West Fifty-third street, causing such a deplorable panic, with injuries to many. A party carrying one of the wounded down Fifth avenue to St. Luke's Hospital, at Fifty-fourth street, was tracked by him. Just as the bearers neared the corner a deep bass growl was heard behind them, and losing their presence of mind, they ran down the avenue and past the hospital. Descrying the church a little ahead they hurried toward it and entered the edifice, with fright on every countenance. The sight of the wounded man caused the greatest consternation. Shrieks were heard on all sides. The women grasped their protectors and the utmost confusion succeeded. The church door must have been left open, for a minute after the animal (cougar, some say, panther others) came stealthily, with his head down to the blood trail and growling gutturally. His presence once discovered, a frightful scene ensued. Men and women rushed in all directions away from the beast, who sprang upon the shoulders of an aged lady,

BURYING HIS FANGS IN HER NECK

and carrying her to the ground. In the haste to get away over the seats many injuries were sustained, Mrs. Catherine Ransom, of West Forty-fifth street, breaking her leg by falling between two pews. Some one ran to the Windsor Hotel for assistance, and one of the guests ran with a loaded rifle to the church. The beast was in the middle aisle, sitting crouched above the form of his victim, when a tall, fair man, with a rifle in his hands, entered. Without a moment's hesitation he brought the weapon to his shoulder and fired. The beast tumbled over and the rifleman ran up and struck him over the head, driving the hammer through the brute's skull. When the aged victim was examined life was found to be extinct, although the flesh wound in the neck was in itself not of a very dangerous nature. Up to this hour the remains have not been identified. An inquiry at the hotel as to the name of the rifleman elicited the single word,

"RIGBY!"

In several parts of the city the greatest danger resulted from people firing rifles and pistols from windows. There is no instance reported of any of the animals having been hit, while it is believed many citizens were struck by the missiles. One policeman, Officer Lannigan, of the Seventh precinct, was wounded in the foot near Grand street by

A SHOT FROM A WINDOW,

during the chase after the striped hyena, which was mistaken by the crowd for a panther. This cowardly brute was finally killed by a bartender, armed only with a club. He was treated as a second Sampson by the entire neighborhood, and is undoubtedly a young man of courage. His name is Dan Brenan, and he is a native of the Nineteenth ward. Counsellor Spellissey distinguished himself by stopping a causeless stampede in the Fourteenth ward.

THE FERRYBOAT CARNAGE.

Perhaps the most deplorable of all the incidents of the terrible evening was that which took place on the ferryboat of the Twenty-third street line, North River. Several of the animals made their way down Fifth avenue. Among them was one of large size (almost the only description now obtainable). It is thought to have been one of the tigers, but its passage along West Twenty-third street appears to have been unnoticed in the general amazement. At any rate, just as the gatekeeper at the Twenty-third street ferry was closing the gates he saw a fierce animal bound past him and rush on to the ferryboat. The boat was well loaded. Some horses attached to light wagons were seen to rear and show every sign of terror, and then rush forward

INTO THE RIVER,

carrying their human loads with them. Several people were mangled by the ferocious brute in a very few minutes. The boat had just begun moving as the beast leaped on board. When the pilot saw the horses and wagons going overboard, the boat was not quite clear of the dock. He immediately

RUNG TO REVERSE THE ENGINES

and put back. To this providential circumstance must be attributed the saving of so many lives. Numbers were seen to plunge overboard to escape the beast, which at last sprung into the water after a young man. The wonderful escape of Larry Jerome is an incident of breathless interest. Overborne by the crowd, he was forced into the river, and although a heavily built man, is a splendid swimmer. He was seized around the neck by a desperate man, whom he shook off with the greatest difficulty. Striking out for shore, he touched against a female who appeared to have given herself up to death. He piloted her to the spiles near the dock, and both were rescued by the fast gathering crowd. The tide was running swift ebb, and it is feared most of the bodies have been carried out to sea. This is one of the cases in which days must elapse before the full list of fatalities is known.

THE HOSPITAL HORRORS.

In Bellevue Hospital many touching sights were seen. The doctors were kept busy dressing the fearful wounds, and the cries of the unfortunates in the accident ward were most painful to hear. It was necessary to perform a number of amputations instantly. One young girl is said to have died under the knife. Few of the wounded were visited by their families last night, but the ministers of the Gospel of all denominations took their places by the bedsides of the unfortunates. The handsome face of Rev. George H. Hepworth was seen bending over a moaning street Arab. Bishop Potter, Rev. Mr. Morgan Dix, Rev. Mr. Armitage, of the Fifth avenue Baptist church, and Fathers Farrelly and McGlynn were seen moving among the sufferers, ministering to the souls of the suffering and the dying.

The following is a partial list of the casualties:—

LIST OF KILLED.

James Radley.	—— Hyland.
Owen O'Reilly.	John Judge.
Peter Ryan.	William Meredith.
Michael Murphy.	Jacob Kuhne.
Peter Kerr.	Benjamin P. Steiner.
Thomas B. Styles.	Thomas Fagan.
James Hewson.	George Cross.
Ellen Lalor and three children.	John F. Coleman.
	Abel Garrett.
Stephen Long.	F. D. Comstock.
Mary Brady.	Fred. C. Gamble.
Fred McDonnell.	George Hanley.
Alex. H. Henderson.	Stephen Bruce.
Pedro Velasquez.	William Mapes.
Christopher Andersoa.	Annie Thomas.

LIST OF WOUNDED.

John Morrissey, very slightly.	John Connors.
	Mark Haselstein.
General Butler.	Jacob Wort.
Alexander O'Leary.	Julia Denison.
James Haydon.	Anne Cushman.
Michael Rafferty.	Sarah White.
George D. Bancroft.	Mary Ann Gough.
Silas Hammersmith.	Pat Byrnes.
Julien D. Brown.	George Seaver.
Amos Hardy.	

Of the number actually killed it will be impossible to tell for some days. Of those wounded no full list can be ascertained. The charge of the savage beasts was the most unexampled in the history of cities. They tore through the leading thoroughfares with all the freedom they might have enjoyed in their native wilds.

LIST OF THE SLAUGHTERED ANIMALS.

1 rhinoceros.	1 American tapir.
1 zebra.	1 anaconda.
6 American deer.	1 woodchuck.
2 giraffes.	4 Syrian sheep.
1 American bison.	1 American eagles.
1 [illegible] porcupine.	1 two-toed sloth.
1 prairie dog.	1 great kangaroo.
1 sea lion.	1 alligator.
2 leopards.	2 water turkeys.
1 grizzly bear.	4 pink-footed geese.
1 brown bear.	2 pelicans.
1 striped hyena.	1 trumpeter swan.
1 ocelot.	1 clapper rail.
2 brown Capuchin monkeys.	1 red-breasted merganser.
1 bengal tiger.	1 pied-bill grebe.
1 Chacma baboon.	1 pine snake.
2 camels.	1 Derbian wallaby.
1 Sambur deer.	1 Dorcas gazelle.
1 African lion.	1 nylghau.
1 African lioness.	1 guanaco.

ANIMALS AT LARGE.

The following animals are at large in various parts of the Central Park and city, and, of course, are extremely dangerous:—The cheetah, the manatee, the Cape buffalo, the panther (a most ferocious beast, supposed to have killed the two policemen near the Belvidere tower and eaten the goats whose skeletons were found on the Ramble), the opossum (not dangerous), the wild swine, the paisano (a vicious beast, supposed to be on the west side of town, in the neighborhood of Manhattan Market, and credited with killing the young lady found near Sir Walter Scott's statue), the mangabey, the puma lion (a very savage animal) destroyed most of the deer in the northern enclosure and bit a large piece out of the shoulder of Henderson the policeman; supposed also to have killed the nursery girl discovered in the Carrousel. Three snakes escaped and are believed to be hid away in the grass and shrubbery near the Casino. More than a dozen monkeys are playing truant through the Park and are not to be depended on when they become hungry. The black leopard, whose fight in the building with the Bengal tiger disabled him considerably, is limping about the upper end of the Park. The Polar bear that killed the two keepers, Ryan & Murphy, is said to have been shot by Recorder Hackett near the upper reservoir. There is a sharp look out for the black wolf. He escaped into the city, but looks so much like a Dutchman's dog he may evade detection until he has committed some lamentable tragedy. The musanga paradoxure and many other beasts of prey whose names are not immediately available are scattered over the island. Five or six bald-headed eagles escaped and many valuable tropical birds. The prairie wolf is not to be found, the suricate is also missing and no tidings have been received of the brown coatimundi.

GENERAL DURYEE,

by the excellent disposition he made of the police force, saved hundreds of children in the vicinity of Tompkins square from being devoured. Had the same precautions been taken on the west side of town the American buffalo and the brown bear would never have accomplished so much fearful havoc.

NATIONAL GUARD PRECAUTIONS.

General Shaler deserves credit also for having orders promptly issued to turn out the National Guard, as the danger from the wild and savage animals at large in all the thoroughfares proved too much for the police. The scene at the Fifth Avenue Hotel when the Malayan tapir that killed the two policemen burst in among the mob of gentlemen standing in the portico can never be forgotten. John Morrissey escaped with a flesh wound. General Butler, who had come on in the morning, was in conversation with General Gilmore, and received a bite in the calf of the leg. Major Bundy, of the *Mail*, and Mr. Stone, of the *Journal of Commerce*, assisted to calm J. Jones, the button manufacturer, who was thrown into a paroxysm by the appearance of the animals. Secretary Robeson and Alderman Vance were thrown violently against a pile of baggage. Leonard Jerome pursued the animal two blocks after it disappeared from the hotel, and made some excellent practice with a revolver but failed to bring the brute down. The Buffalo overturned Earl Roseberry's carriage in front of the Brevoort, and subsequently ran into another carriage, containing Moses Hanz, of Forty-first street, but without doing any serious damage.

It would be impossible at this late hour to describe the numberless scenes of dismay and disaster. The hospitals are full of wounded. There are fifteen bodies at the Morgue and several in the various precincts. A sentiment of horror pervades the community.

THE GALLANT POLICE.

It is now time to say that the police deserve the greatest credit for their courage, if not for the success in dealing with this unheard of danger. Everywhere they are at the front, and among the slain and mutilated they count heavily. General Duryea's order to clear the streets was a master stroke of policy. It gave the rapidly gathered off platoons work they could undertake without further direction, while it gave the squads of officers he despatched to the angles of the leading thoroughfares a chance to deal efficiently with the animals running a muck and without further danger to citizen life. There was only a case reported of a citizen shot by a police bullet, and, as the unfortunate victim had been warned to leave the streets, the officer cannot be blamed.

THE MORAL OF THE WHOLE.

Of course the entire story given above is a pure fabrication. Not one word of it is true. Not a single act or incident described has taken place. It is a huge hoax, a wild romance, or whatever other epithet of utter untrustworthiness our readers may choose to apply to it. It is simply a fancy picture which crowded upon the mind of the writer a few days ago while he was gazing through the iron bars of the cages of the wild animals in the menagerie at Central Park. Yet as each of its horrid but perfectly natural sequences impressed themselves upon his mind, the question presented itself How is New York prepared to meet such a catastrophe? How easily could it occur any day of the week? How much, let the citizens ponder, depends upon the indiscretion of even one of the keepers? A little oversight, a trifling imprudence might lead to the actual happening of all, and even worse than has been pictured. From causes quite as insignificant the greatest calamities of history have sprung. Horror, devastation and widespread slaughter of human beings have had small mishaps for parent time and again.

HAVANA LOTTERY.

DRAWING OF NOVEMBER 23, 1874.

CLASS 936.

No.	Prize.	No.	Prize.	No.	Prize.	No.	Prize.	No.	Prize.
58	$300	6255	$300	12283	$300	18972	$300	25685	$300
68	300	6275	300	12420	300	18994	300	25739	500
151	300	6288	300	12425	300	19008	1000	25805	300
240	300	6325	300	12567	300	19018	300	25828	300
256	300	6361	300	12696	300	19071	300	25868	500
260	300	6390	300	12700	300	19158	300	25880	300
277	300	6465	300	12701	300	19161	300	25888	300
309	300	6597	300	12777	300	19241	300	25959	300
315	300	6687	300	12791	300	19275	300	25968	300
365	300	6641	300	12831	300	19320	300	25987	300
373	300	6717	300	12883	300	19387	300	26046	300
390	500	6727	300	12917	300	19411	300	26081	300
490	300	6770	300	12971	300	19431	300	26094	300
539	300	6807	300	13029	300	19443	300	26114	300
565	300	6808	300	13130	300	19474	300	26129	300
591	300	6906	300	13133	300	19565	300	26158	300
592	300	6908	300	131[illegible]9	300	19607	300	26193	500
634	300	6957	300	13218	300	19826	300	26208	500
645	500	7057	300	13307	300	19865	300	26225	500
744	300	7086	300	13315	300	19916	300	26256	300
715	300	7164	300	13374	300	19940	300	26352	300
800	300	7178	300	13391	300	20095	500	26379	10000
871	300	7250	300	13628	300	20174	300	26436	300
885	300	7253	300	13658	300	20190	300	26499	300
901	300	7254	300	13719	300	20208	300	26543	500
919	300	7262	300	13796	300	20218	300	26643	300
945	300	7275	300	13839	300	20222	500	26710	500
948	300	7315	300	13843	300	20257	300	26734	500
974	300	7353	500	13906	300	20261	500	26736	300
1002	300	7362	300	13978	300	20269	300	26781	300
1005	300	7372	300	14078	300	20336	300	26802	300
1091	300	7375	300	14102	300	20342	300	26810	300
1231	300	7409	500	14116	300	20381	300	26857	300
1239	300	7465	300	14132	300	20408	300	26947	300
1263	300	7471	300	41140	300	20470	300	26961	500
1289	300	7473	300	14183	300	20492	500	26966	300
1315	300	7496	300	14230	300	20560	500	26984	300
1353	300	7544	300	14259	500	20731	300	26993	300
1425	300	7601	300	14380	300	20737	300	27031	300
1442	300	7683	300	14394	300	20875	300	27046	300
1443	300	7686	300	14399	300	20908	300	27050	300
1451	300	7723	300	14433	300	20933	500	27061	300
1464	500	7876	300	14458	300	20974	500	27073	300
1500	300	7914	300	14498	300	21015	300	27143	300
1607	300	7941	500	14522	300	21100	300	27199	500
1661	300	7960	300	14535	300	21125	300	27266	500
1692	300	7974	300	14579	300	12187	300	27247	300
1820	300	8000	300	14600	300	21201	300	27377	500
1853	300	8082	300	14674	300	21262	500	27384	300
1867	300	8083	300	14695	500	21355	300	27385	300
1880	300	8148	300	14745	300	21391	300	27424	300
1899	300	8250	300	14836	300	21447	300	27489	300
1914	300	8340	300	14841	300	21466	300	27556	500
1972	300	8341	300	14858	500	21511	300	27632	500
1975	500	8346	300	14932	300	21530	300	27674	300
1988	300	8365	300	14956	300	21540	500	27695	500
2055	300	8426	300	14995	500	21548	300	27748	300
2106	300	8460	300	15084	300	21560	300	27779	500
2107	300	8491	300	15059	300	21596	300	27788	300
2170	500	8554	300	15062	300	21669	300	27885	300
2178	500	8672	300	15068	300	21715	300	27893	300
2193	300	8716	300	15082	300	21722	300	27895	300
2195	500	8754	300	15085	300	21842	300	27899	300
2250	300	8778	300	15159	300	21858	500	27924	1000
2258	300	8798	300	15274	300	21911	300	27940	300
2310	300	8814	300	15331	300	21981	300	28005	500
2350	500	8827	300	15342	300	21947	300	28030	300
2359	500	8918	500	15349	300	21997	500	28087	300
2409	300	8925	300	15402	300	22020	500	28133	300
2459	1000	8938	300	15411	300	22022	300	28168	300
2502	300	8959	300	15527	300	22041	300	28227	300
2507	300	8994	300	15536	300	22061	300	28242	500
2544	300	9041	300	15635	300	22075	300	28288	300
2632	300	9084	300	15643	300	22116	300	28321	300
2642	300	9159	300	15654	300	22131	300	28359	300
2729	300	9251	500	15697	300	22160	300	28431	300
2808	300	9336	1000	15804	300	22181	300	28458	300
2873	500	9355	300	15806	300	22237	300	28517	300
2876	300	9367	300	15827	500	22246	300	28554	300
3018	300	9485	300	15832	1000	22345	300	28556	300
3030	300	9527	300	15846	300	22365	300	28610	300
3048	300	9529	300	15873	300	22375	300	28621	300
3076	300	9537	500	16055	300	22521	300	28657	300
3133	1000	9549	300	16064	300	22534	500	28718	300
3198	500	9562	300	16116	300	22536	300	28752	500
3226	300	9610	300	16200	300	22537	300	28856	300
3319	300	9658	300	16202	300	22571	300	28858	300
3363	300	9740	300	16214	300	22574	300	28891	300
3409	300	9798	300	16247	300	22675	300	28903	300
3419	300	9837	300	16268	300	22708	300	28906	300
3422	300	9900	300	16280	300	22724	300	28912	300
3428	300	9994	300	16281	300	22837	300	28932	300
3456	500	10019	300	16289	500	22863	300	28955	300
3457	300	10020	500	16362	300	22901	300	28976	300
3459	300	10036	300	16431	300	22936	300	29049	300
3522	300	10082	300	16488	500	22945	500	29176	300
3569	300	10108	300	16549	300	22966	300	29210	300
3627	300	10110	300	16579	500	23005	300	29236	300
3664	500	10120	300	16604	300	23036	300	29306	300
3711	300	10150	300	16620	300	23059	300	29312	300
3843	300	10174	300	16710	500	23086	300	29391	300
3860	300	10216	500	16794	1000	23088	300	29429	300
3886	300	10226	300	16812	300	23130	300	29483	300
3903	300	10288	300	16816	300	23164	300	29583	300
3913	300	10291	500	16872	500	23187	300	29587	300
3959	1000	10292	500	16879	300	23199	300	29601	300
4192	300	10297	500	17025	300	23213	500	29677	300
4207	300	10323	300	17027	300	23223	500	29706	300
4217	300	10324	500	17045	300	23248	300	29752	300
4219	300	10329	300	17117	300	23254	300	29769	500
4248	300	10333	300	17120	300	23259	300	29775	300
4265	500	10395	300	17135	300	23432	300	19788	300
4272	300	10453	300	17138	300	23445	300	29815	300
4283	300	10532	300	17142	300	23471	300	29844	300
4289	300	10567	300	17162	300	23495	300	29859	300
4378	300	10622	300	17188	500	23589	300	29921	300
4456	300	10625	300	17209	300	23745	300	29923	300
4479	300	10705	300	17220	300	23777	500	29977	300
4481	300	10720	300	17223	300	23784	500	[illegible]	[illegible]
4517	300	10811	300	17237	300	23838	300	30060	[illegible]
4553	300	10812	300	17268	1000	23970	300	30101	300
4628	300	10827	300	17277	500	24030	300	30216	300
4749	300	10845	300	17284	300	24142	300	30342	300
4772	300	10877	300	17285	300	25186	300	30429	300
4804	300	10911	300	17351	300	24210	300	30441	300
4811	300	10924	300	17380	300	24238	300	30459	300
4828	500	10926	300	47387	1000	24277	300	30503	300
4849	300	11046	300	17403	300	24297	300	30541	300
4900	300	11058	300	17491	300	24310	300	30612	300
4955	300	11082	500	17585	300	24376	500	30720	300
4995	300	11107	300	17638	300	24426	300	30780	300
5076	300	11109	300	17695	300	24450	300	30932	300
5139	300	11129	300	17737	300	24474	300	30944	300
5148	300	11146	300	17748	300	24494	300	30992	300
5164	300	11153	300	17889	300	24541	300	31008	300
5229	10000	11194	300	17895	500	24606	300	31027	300
5275	300	11256	300	17987	300	24611	300	31048	300
5281	300	11273	300	18014	500	24623	300	31090	500
5352	300	11287	300	18018	300	24624	300	31095	500
5366	500	11316	300	18053	500	24661	300	31124	500
5392	300	11342	500	18084	300	24755	300	31133	300
5421	300	11425	300	18146	300	24759	500	31246	300
5426	300	11491	300	18150	300	24835	300	31350	300
5475	300	11541	500	18285	300	25849	300	31408	300
5511	300	11543	300	18312	300	24900	500	31434	300
5589	300	11609	300	18320	300	25034	300	31438	300
5612	500	11616	300	18350	300	25053	300	31455	500
5620	300	11617	300	18514	300	25056	300	31511	500
5655	300	11645	300	19518	300	25083	300	31532	300
5663	300	11658	300	18530	300	25092	300	31560	300
5689	300	11677	300	18536	300	25102	300	31563	300
5697	300	11732	300	18541	300	25115	300	31615	300
5736	300	11762	500	18586	300	25139	300	31632	300
5824	500	11794	300	18621	300	25210	300	31660	300
5846	300	11795	300	18632	300	25258	300	31727	300
5852	300	11990	300	18659	300	25264	300	31740	300
5913	300	12008	500	18682	500	25266	300	31755	300
5920	500	12072	100000	18737	300	25344	300	31778	300
6014	300	12115	300	18756	500	25501	300	31786	500
6033	300	12160	300	18764	300	25519	300	31787	300
6114	300	12183	300	18844	300	25598	500	31912	300
6136	25000	12204	300	18885	300	25616	300	31922	300
6165	500	12225	300	18936	300	25619	300	31966	300
6201	500	12240	300	18970	300	25636	300	31967	300
6227	300	12273	300						

APPROXIMATION PRIZES.

$100,000. No.	Prize.	$50,000. No.	Prize.	$25,000. No.	Prize.	$10,000. No.	Prize.	$5,000. No.	Prize.
12071	$500	20932	$500	6135	$300	5228	$300	26960	$300
12073	500	20934	500	6137	300	5230	300	26962	300
12074	500					26378	300		
12075	500					26380	300		
12076	500								
12077	500								
12078	500								
12079	500								
12080	500								

(Signed) ADOLFO GASSET, Central Administrator

VICTOR DE PAGES, El Contador.

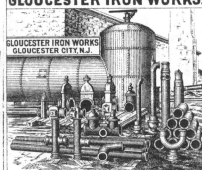

15 Cents.

Pictorial History

OF THE

Beecher-Tilton Scandal.

Its Origin, Progress and Trial, Illustrated with Fifty Engravings from Accurate Sketches.

REV. HENRY WARD BEECHER, THE DEFENDANT IN THE SCANDAL SUIT.

MRS. ELIZABETH R. TILTON.

FRANCIS D. MOULTON, THE MUTUAL FRIEND AND CHAMPION-WITNESS OF AMERICA.

THEODORE TILTON, PLAINTIFF IN THE GREAT SCANDAL SUIT.

THE PRINCIPALS IN THE ACTION.

THE
Humors OF THE Brooklyn Scandal

OR THE

FUNNY SIDE OF A SERIOUS SUBJECT.

NEW YORK, 1875. PRICE 10 CENTS.

THE LOGIC OF THE HOUR.

BUTCHER BROWN.—"I SAY, PARSON JONES, I DON'T OBJECT, YOU KNOW, TO HAVING A PEW AT THE CHURCH, AND HEARING YOU PREACH; BUT DON'T COME AROUND HERE VISITING MY FAMILY UNLESS I'M HOME."

THE DAILY GRAPHIC

AN ILLUSTRATED EVENING NEWSPAPER

39 & 41 PARK PLACE

VOL. VIII. | All the News. Four Editions Daily | NEW YORK, THURSDAY, JULY 15, 1875. | $12 Per Year in Advance. Single Copies, Five Cents. | NO. 732.

BLOWING BUBBLES OF FINANCIAL FROTH.

Master Jay Gould (to Miss Commodore)—"SAY, SISSY, IF I BLOW AND BLOW AND YOU BLOW AND BLOW, WHICH OF OUR BUBBLES 'LL GO OUT FIRST? THEY'RE NEARLY THE SAME SIZE NOW."

Miss Commodore—"YOURS, BUBBY. YOU SEE, I HAVE BLOWN THEM EVER SO LONG, AND THE BUBBLES KNOW ME. THIS ONE 'LL LAST AS LONG AS I LIVE; I'M USED TO WATER AND—AFTER ME THE DELUGE."

NEW YORK CITY.—SCENE FROM THE SECOND ACT OF THE NEW PLAY, "THE CRUCIBLE," NOW PERFORMING AT THE PARK THEATRE, ON BROADWAY.—SEE PAGE 271.

NEW YORK CITY.—HOLIDAY EXHIBITION OF DOLLS IN A WINDOW AT MACY'S, FOURTEENTH STREET AND SIXTH AVENUE, FOR THE BENEFIT OF INFANT ASYLUMS.—SEE PAGE 271.

FIFTH YEAR. NEW YORK, FEBRUARY, 1876. VOL. 5, No. 5.

Published by FRED. J. MILLER, Builder of Fire Apparatus and Manufacturer of Fire Department Supplies of every description, 65 Liberty Street, New York.

CHAMPION STATIONARY CHEMICAL FIRE TANK.

It is admitted by practical and scientific men that the day is not far distant when the mode of extinguishing fires will be entirely changed, and instead of using simple water in large quantities, as at present, fire destroying chemicals will be added to water, and used in much less quantity, requiring less powerful apparatus. The simplest and most practical apparatus for producing and applying carbonic acid gas in solution with water for extinguishing fires is that made by the Champion Fire Extinguisher Co., of Louisville, Ky. The wheeled engines made by this company and in use in the principal fire departments of the country, are giving the greatest satisfaction, peforming wonders by the large amount of fires that are extinguished by them.

As an evidence of the great value of the engines made by this company, we give the record of the Champion Engine in use in the Buffalo Fire Department, as reported by the Chief Engineer to the Common Council of that city for the year 1875:

"Mar. 12, 1875. Arrival of "CHAMPION" Chemical Engine.
15, Fire in Scovill's Car Wheel Works, Louisiana street, extinguished by CHAMPION alone.
23, Frame houses, 154 and 156, Tennessee street—good service.
25, Frame house, 47 Chestnut street—good service.
29, Frame house, 220 Jersey street—good service.
April 3, Coit Block, Swan street—good service.
3, Comstock's Hat Store, Pearl street, extinguished by CHAMPION alone.
4, Old fire in Coit Block, extinguished by CHAMPION alone.
15, Barn, Carey street—good service.
23, Dwelling, 155 Seneca street—good service.
25, Dwelling, corner Court and Pearl, extinguished by CHAMPION alone.
29, Frame building, Water street—good service.
May 16, Freight car, B. & J. R. R., extinguished by CHAMPION alone.
20, Fire in County Jail, extinguishe by CHAMPION alone.
27, Fire in Dudley's Oil Refinery, extinguished by CHAMPION alone.
June 14, House, 32 Miami street, extinguished by CHAMPION alone.
26, Soap Factory, 39 Lloyd street, extinguished by CHAMPION alone.
July 23, Slattery Bro.'s Ice House, Louisiana street, (on call from American District Telegraph,) extinguished by CHAMPION before arrival of Steam Fire Department.
Aug. 8, Hat and Cap Store, 184 Main street, extinguished by CHAMPION alone.
Sep. 13, Residence, 110 Swan street, extinguished by CHAMPION alone.
13, Ganson Block—good service.
Oct. 2, Hotel, Swan street, extinguished by CHAMPION alone.
20, Tug Bryant, Buffalo river—good service.
31, Brick and Frame, corner Canal and Lloyd streets—good service.
31, Frame dwelling, corner Scott street and Burwell Place, extinguished by CHAMPION alone,
Nov. 16, Stores, 360 and 362 Main street—good service.
17, Propeller Mohawk, Erie Basin—good service.
19, Hazard and Excelsior Elevators, and Commercial Block—extra good service.
Dec. 10, Residence, 104 Carolina street—extra good service.
19, Express Printing Co., Swan street—extra good service.

At the burning of the elevators, November 19, the Commercial Block situated on the corner of Main and Ohio streets, took fire several times, and once on the dome, and the velocity of the wind was so great that water thrown from the steamers was blown away and could not strike the fire. The "Chemical," which was being used to good advantage on the dock, was called into requisition, and played through 300 feet of hose, which being light was easily taken up through the building to the roof, extinguishing the fire and saving the block, valued at $35,000.

At the fire, May 27, Box 23, Dudley's Oil Refinery, the department had been at work over one half an hour before the Superintendent of the Fire Department telegraphed for the "Champion Chemical," which arrived promptly, extinguishing the fire in about fifteen minutes. This Engine has been worked for five consecutive hours at the fire November 19."

"During the early part of last Summer, E. E. Raht, sup rvising architect of *The Tribune* building, made a thorough investigation of fire-protective apparatus with the design of procuring for *The Tribune* building the most effective arrangement of the kind which has been invented. After testing the machines of several companies, he gave a contract to the Champion Fire Extinguisher Company of Louisville, Ky., for one of its "self-acting, stationary, chemical fire engines," which has just been set up in *The Tribune* Building. A number of gentlemen assembled in *The Tribune* composing rooms yesterday afternoon to witness the first trial of it. The engine is is only necessary to pull the wire rope on any floor, open the stop-cock, and direct the stream on the fire, the whole occupying about 20 seconds.

In the first trial made yesterday afternoon, the "trip" was pulled from the composing room, eleven stories above the engine, and 20 seconds afterward, a stream of water charged with carbonic acid gas was pouring from the nozzle. With an elevation of 176 feet, and a length of pipe and hose amounting to 251 feet, a stream of water was thrown horizontally 75 feet from the nozzle against a stiff wind. It was estimated by those present that the stream of water could be kept up about half an hour. Several interruptions were made, as the stream was directed from different windows. After the force of the engine was exhausted the spectators went to the basement, and witnessed the "tripping" of the tank. All the gentlemen present expressed satisfaction with the working of the apparatus.

The main point in which this apparatus is believed to be superior to all others is the quickness with which the stream can be directed on the fire after it is discovered. A single person in any story, on discovering the flames, can immediately do the work which with other engines requires the aid of additional persons, and usually a journey to another room and back again. In an ordinary building several stories in height, before a person could descend from the top to the basement, or warn the engineer of the danger, the fire might gain such a headway that no power could extinguish it. The apparatus is moreover simple in construction, and so made that it will not fail to act at a moment's notice, though allowed to stand for ten years without a change of chemicals. Another important advantage is that the action of the chemicals, which come up mingled with the water, is such as to aid materially in stopping the fire. They do not seem to extinguish so much as instantly to smother it, and so render the charred wood incombustible."—*N. Y Tribune, Feb. 11th.*

NEW TRIBUNE BUILDING, NEW YORK, SHOWING CHAMPION CHEMICAL TANK IN SUB-CELLAR AND CONNECTED WITH TWELVE FLOORS.

The Self-Acting Chemical Tank for use in Warehouses, Factories and large buildings, now being supplied by the Champion Co., is so constructed that a powerful stream of Carbonic Acid Gas and water is instantly available upon any floor of a building where placed, and it can be operated by one person, being free from the complicated parts to be found in all other chemical engines.

Among the number of these Tanks lately put in use, are those in the new *Tribune* Building in this city, a cut of which we give in connection with this article, and in the building occupied by Jordan, Marsh & Co., Boston, the following extracts being the accounts published at the time the said Tanks were tested: placed in the sub-cellar of the building, and consists of a cylindrical tank, holding 180 gallons of water, and hung on pivots in such a way as to be inverted on the lifting of a latch rod. 60 pounds of Bi-carbonate of soda are mixed with the water, and in the top of the tank is a jar containing 28 pounds of sulphuric acid. When the tank is inverted the chemicals are mingled together and produce carbonic acid gas, by the expansive force of which the water is driven out with a pressure of 150 pounds. From the tank to the top of the building runs a stand-pipe, to which is attached a stop cock and hose in each story, A wire rope, connecting with the "trip," also runs through the building. In case of fire, it

Messrs. Jordan, Marsh & Co., have just placed in the basement of their retail store a machine for the extinguishment of fires that, in the simplicity of its construction, and completeness, seems to be exactly the thing long sought after. The apparatus consists of a stationary chemical engine, built by the Champion Fire Extinguisher Co., of Louisville, Ky. Connected with the engine is a stand-pipe, with hose attached on each floor, and a trip or latch rod passing up beside the stand-pipe, a simple upward pull of which puts the machine in operation and sends the carbonated water flying to the top of the pipe. An ordinary stop-cock is then opened and the liquid applied by means of the hose to any point at which a fire may occur. Heretofore powerful extinguishing apparatus has required the exertions of several experienced men to put it to work, or at least a man has to go to where the engine is located, set it in motion and then pass back to the vicinity of the fire, thereby consuming valuable time, which, as evidenced nearly every day in the newspaper accounts, results in a disastrous conflagration. In brief, where apparatus cannot be brought to bear on a fire within a few seconds it is comparatively worthless. Jordan, Marsh & Co., having experienced the disaster of delay, have provided themselves with an engine that may be relied on at any and all times to apply a powerful extinguisher to any point of their store within fifteen seconds of the discovery of a fire. This seems incredible, but an actual test made last Friday from the fifth floor, sent a stream through the pipe at the end of the hose in ten seconds. An exhibition of the working of the engine was made yesterday in the presence of the Fire Commissioners, a number of prominent insurance men and other interested gentlemen, and the apparatus received their unqualified approval.—*Boston Post.*

Any communications sent direct to company's office, at Louisville, Ky., or to the General Agent, 57 Liberty street, this city, will receive prompt attention.

CHAMPION FIRE EXTINGUISHER CO., LOUISVILLE, KY.

Champion Three-wheeled Engine,

Price $850.

Hand Extinguisher,

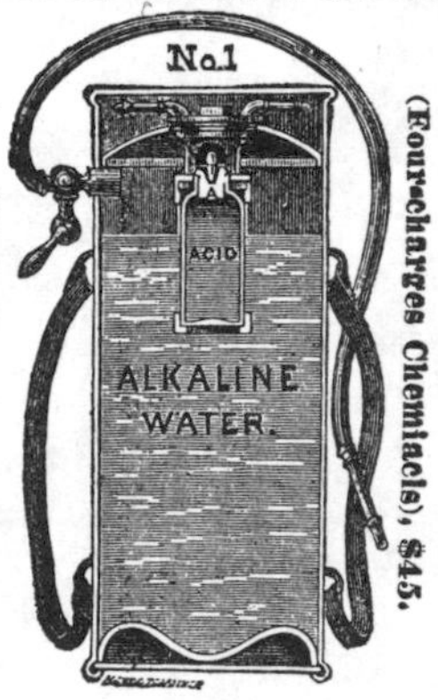

(Four charges Chemicals), $45.

Champion Two-wheeled Engine,

Price $750

Champion Chemical Engine.
No. 1, capacity, 250 gallons, fully equipped, - $3,000 to $3,500
No. 2, capacity, 200 gallons, fully equipped, - $2,500 to $3,000
No. 3, capacity, 160 gallons, fully equipped, - $2,000 to $2,500

Champion Hook & Ladder Truck.

Price, fully equipped, $1500.

The Champion Chemical Engines and Fire Extinguishers are in use in a large number of the Fire Departments of the Country. Among the places using them are the following: Boston, Cincinnati, Buffalo, Jersey City, Atlanta, Ga., Topeka, Kans, Milwaukie, Peoria, Greencastle, Ind. U. S. Government, Pennsylvania R. R. Co. and Baltimore and Ohio R. R. Co. The Company have in actual service 140 Wheeled Engines and about 10,000 Hand Extinguishers.

Clapp & Jones Manufacturing Co., Hudson, N.Y.

BUILDERS OF THE CELEBRATED PISTON STEAM FIRE ENGINE

Hose Carriages, TENDERS, &c.

IMPROVED WATER WORKS FOR Cities & Towns.

STEAM PUMPS.

And all kinds of Fire Apparatus,
Manufacturers' Agents for Vulcanized Rubber "TEST" Hose.

A New Steam Fire Engine For Sale.

A Second-Class Steam Fire Engine, new and in perfect order, with tongue for hand power and pole for horses; Single Pump, 4x10; Steam Cylinder, 8x10; Boiler 5 feet high, 32 inches diameter; 100 1½-inch tubes; Boiler covered with Russia Iron; the Running Gear is neat and light; Engine handsomely painted, weight, about 3,600 pounds; will sell this Engine very low.

Further particulars can be had of **FRED. J. MILLER, 65 Liberty Street, New York.**

Robert Jones,

BUILDER OF EVERY DESCRIPTION OF

Fire Apparatus.

Pine's Improved Hook & Ladder Truck, Ladders on Rollers, arranged to be drawn by horse or hand.—Weighs 1200 lbs. less than any other Truck, with ladders on rollers now in use.

Latest Improved Extension Ladder, Hose Elevator and Fire Escape.

Office and Manufactory:

133 & 135 Nassau St., Brooklyn, L. I.

Between Jay and Bridge Sts.

JOSEPH PINE, Supt.,

Formerly of the firm of Pine & Hartshorn, and late Superintendent for E. B. Leverich.

SHALER'S Patent

Flash Torch.

Just the thing for Torch-Light Processions—gives three times the light of old style torch. A flame can be thrown three feet into the air by blowing through the tube in handle.

Price $7.50 a dozen;
or, in large quantities $50 a hundred

Sample will be sent to any address on receipt of 75 cents.

MANUFACTURED BY
G. H. BABCOCK & CO., 34 New St., N. Y.
Also for sale by
FRED. J. MILLER, 65 Liberty St., N.Y.

Silver-Plated Parade Trumpets.

Ready for immediate delivery.

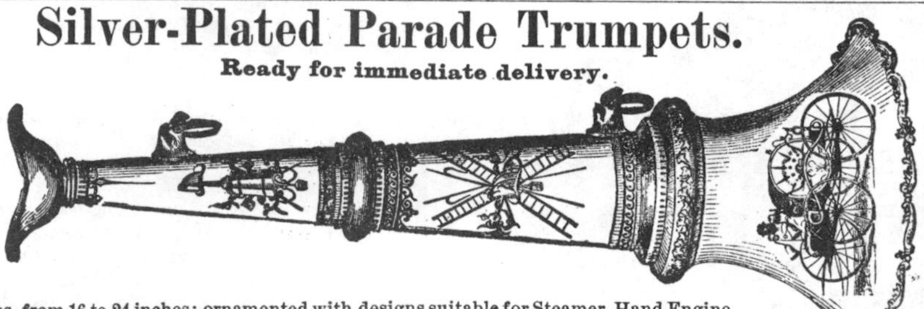

All sizes, from 16 to 24 inches; ornamented with designs suitable for Steamer, Hand Engine, Hose or H.& L. Cos. Orders by telegraph shipped same day received. For prices see page 7.
Made by FRED. J. MILLER, 65 Liberty Street, N. Y.

BUTTON ENGINE WORKS.

WATERFORD, N. Y.

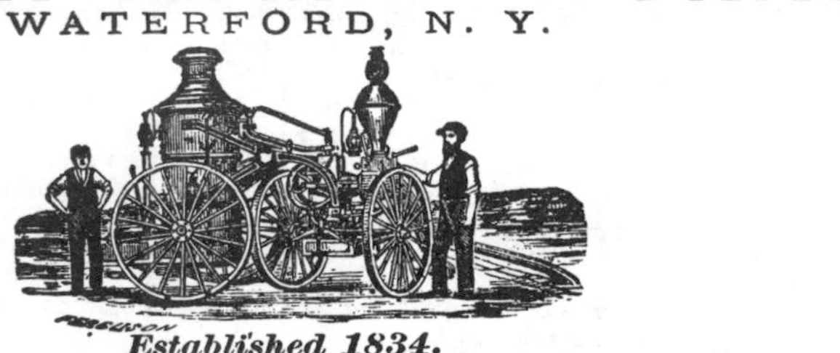

Established 1834.

Steam & Hand Fire Engines, Steam Pumps, Hose Carriages,
Hook and Ladder Trucks, and all kinds of Fire Apparatus.

L. BUTTON.
THEO. E. BUTTON.

☞ SEND FOR ILLUSTRATED CIRCULAR.

COLE'S EXCELSIOR HOSE OIL STUFFING.

This preparation has now been in use nearly ten years, and experience has proved it to be very far in advance of anything that has ever been devised for use upon Leather Hose. I claim for this Stuffing that it is **by all odds the best Leather Preservative in the world;** that, after the animal or fish oils are forced out (which can only be accomplished by oiling from the inside) that the hose can be rolled up compactly, and put away for months through the heated term without risk of heat or mould; that they will remain soft and pliable twice as long as with any other treatment; that it is more easy of application; that it is nearly a water-proof; and that its properties are such as to greatly increase the elasticity of the leather, and thereby enable it to resist a much greater strain; that it can be kept for years in the original package without injury or brushed off the rivets leaving them nearly as clean as when first made, and if thoroughly filled will not again corrode change. After the hose have been oiled a short time, they can be cleaned with a stiff brush, and the verdigris thereby removing the principal objection to the use of Leather Hose, whilst its cheapness must commend it to popular use. Price, $1.25 per gallon—no charge for package when sold by the barrel; in less quantities packages charged extra.

This Stuffing can be used with any of the Patent Oilers or Pumps in use by the fire departments.

TESTIMONIALS:

We have used the Cole's Hose Oil Stuffing, have carefully noted its effect upon the hose, and are well satisfied with the results.
JOHN W. REAGAN, Assistant Engineer, Boston Fire Department.
GEORGE HOBSON, Chief Engineer, Lowell, (Mass.), Fire Department.

I must say, honestly, that Cole's Oil is the best that we have ever used in this department; it preserves the leather, making the hose soft and pliable without leaving that coat of grease so common to other oils, and so disagreeable to handle; it also prevents mildew and rust. AMBROSE BEATTY, Chief Engineer, New Britain, (Conn.), Fire Dept.

We have used Cole's Oil Stuffing. We find in our experience that it *stops the corrosion of the rivets and prevents mildew;* is remarkably softening to the leather, whilst the hose are free from the *nasty gurry* which follows the use of other oils when the hose are used. I believe it to be by all odds the best thing out for the purpose for which it is designed.
S. E. COMBS, Chief Engineer, Worcester Fire Department.

Think the Cole's Hose Oil Stuffing to be the best for hose we have ever seen.
J. H. DADMUN, Chief Engineer, Ashland, (Mass.), Fire Department.

Sole Manufacturer W. D. COLE, Ashland, Mass.,
Also for sale by **FRED. J. MILLER, New York City.**

ROUND THREAD COUPLING CO.

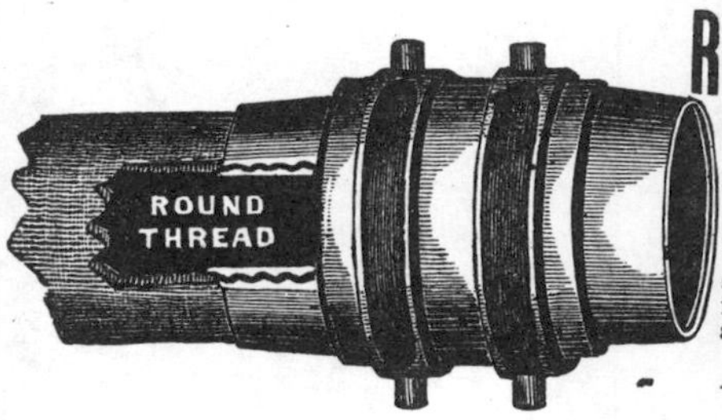

33 Beverly Street, Providence, R. I.

All sizes of Hose Couplings and Fittings on hand and made to order; also the best **Controlling Nozzle** in use. All kinds of Fire Department Supplies at short notice. Sole maker of the Patent **Round Thread Coupling**—which will commend itself to all who want a good one. Can refer with pride to any in use. Perfect satisfaction guaranteed when properly applied to the hose.

E. M. WALDRON.
A. McQUEEN Salesman.
Can be obtained of Fred. J. Miller, NewYork.

FRED. J. MILLER,

65 Liberty street, N. Y.,

MANUFACTURER OF

POLICE EQIPMENTS,

Of Every Description.

Hats, Caps, Belts, Clubs, Hand Cuffs, Nippers, Leg Irons, Badges, Dark Lanterns, Jail Locks, etc.

SEND FOR CATALOGUE.

THE "GOULD" STEAM FIRE ENGINE.

The Champion of the World.

The "FAME," of Wilmington, Del., a First-class, having thrown 354 feet 4 inches, from an 1½ inch nozzle.

MANUFACTURED BY
B. S. NICHOLS & CO., Engineers & Machinists, *Burlington, Vermont.*

Steam Fire Engine Heaters, and Fire Apparatus.

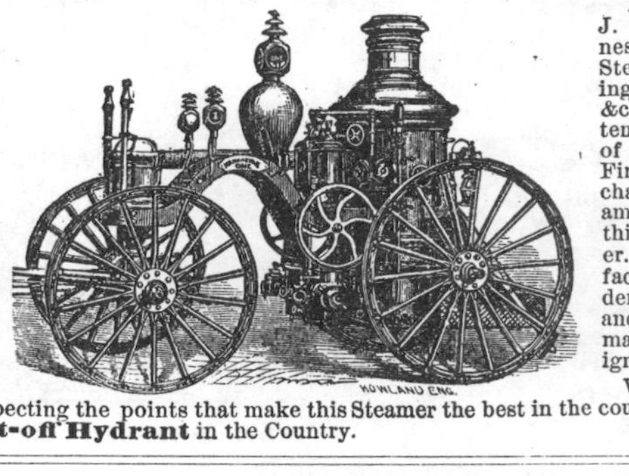

Having bought of Mr. R. J. Gould, his entire business in the manufacture of Steam Fire Engines, including Patterns, License, Tools, &c., we wish to call the attention of Chief Engineers of Fire Departments and Firemen generally, to the change, and to solicit an examination into the merits of this justly celebrated Steamer. We have the most ample facilities for supplying any demand for these Steamers, and the mechanical skill to make them perfect in design, finish, and efficiency. We shall always be glad to give any information respecting the points that make this Steamer the best in the country. We also make the best **Independent Shut-off Hydrant** in the Country.

Caswell's Improved Coupling Co.,

CHICAGO, ILLS.,

DEALS IN AND MANUFACTURES ALL KINDS OF FIRE DEPARTMENT SUPPLIES.

The Caswell Improved Coupling is *entirely free* from *complicated* parts. It can be attached or detached to hose *easier* than any other coupling made. It was the *favorite* at the Convention of Chief Engineers

Caswell's Coupling. (*Devices for Attaching and Detaching Free of Cost,*) - - - **$5.50 per Set.**
Caswell's Improved Hose Suspender, - - - - - - - - - - - **6.00 per Doz.**
Caswell's Impr'd Coupling and Hydrant Wrench Combined, - - - **6.00 per Doz.**

LIGHT, DURABLE, AND CHEAP.

Nozzles Tips and **Pipes** made to order at low prices.
Buildings equipped with the best **Hose** and **Fire Extinguishers,** at short notice.
Hose Carriages, Hook and Ladder Trucks of the best manufacture furnished on application.
Steam Fire Engines of all classes furnished.
We deal in only the *best class* of **Steam Fire Engine Hose,** which we invite Fire Committees and others about to purchase to examine.

Head Office, 138 Lake Street, Factory, 353 Canal Street.

Send for Circular and full Price List.

THE ILLUSTRATED WEEKLY

PURE, INSTRUCTIVE, AMUSING.

VOL. II—NO. 34. NEW YORK, SATURDAY, AUGUST 19, 1876. $3.00 A YEAR.

CORNELIUS VANDERBILT.

[DRAWN FOR THE ILLUSTRATED WEEKLY FROM A PHOTOGRAPH BY GURNEY.]

CORNELIUS VANDERBILT.

SKETCH OF THE CAREER OF NEW YORK'S RAILROAD KING AND MILLIONAIRE.

Cornelius Vanderbilt, the eldest son of Cornelius and Phœbe Vanderbilt, was born in 1794 on Staten Island. His parents were well-to-do people. His father seems to have been an ordinary person, but his mother is described as a woman of great energy, with sparkling eyes and a commanding will. Her son attributes much of his success in life to her implanted vigor and virtue in his nature. The elder Vanderbilt died in 1832, and his widow survived him about thirty-five years. Seven children were born to them—five sons and two daughters. Jacob, twelve years the junior of Cornelius, lives on Staten Island. He bears a strong resemblance to the millionaire. His estate is worth about $250,000.

Cornelius began life at sixteen, when he was known as a "dare-devil" youth, as captain of a sailboat running from the beach at Whitehall to Staten Island, and carrying passengers at 18 cents each. At that time the population of New York was only 80,000; and Staten Island was inhabited by farmers, gardeners and fishermen. Five years later, he and his br other-in-law, Captain De Forrest, launched the Charlotte, in which Cornelius was accustomed to make trips south, bringing home on these occasions large and remunerative freights. About two years later he began his "steamboating" career, his first engagement, given him by Thomas Gibbons, being as captain of a steamer plying between New York and New Brunswick. He continued in this service twelve years, during which period he married his first wife, Sophia Johnson, who kept a hotel both at New Brunswick and on the dock at Staten Island. The match contributed to Vanderbilt's financial scccess; for under his wife's management the hotel at New Brunswick, which they occupied rent free on account of its not having paid under former occupants, became a success, it being well patronized by the steamer passengers. By the year 1829, when Vanderbilt was thirty-five, he found himself worth $30,000, and determined to go into business on his own account. This was a bold venture, as the steamboat owners at that time were men of much ampler means than his; but his energy overcame all opposition. By the year 1851 he had accumulated a vast fortune and controlled the steamboat interest, having vanquished, without pecuniary aid from any source, all his opponents, including the powerful firm of the Messrs. Stevens, of Hoboken. It was during this period of his life that he acquired the title of "Commodore," by which he has been known ever since.

His subsequent business achievements gave him a world-wide reputation. In 1857 he established a line of steamers from the port of New York to San Francisco, via Nicaragua. In 1862 he presented to the United States government a new steamer of 5,000 tons burden, which cost him $800,000, and at the time was earning him $2,000 a day. For this public service Congress passed a resolution of thanks to him. His cruise in the steam-yacht North Star and his visit to Russia were his last conspicuous acts as a steamboat owner.

About this time began his brilliant career as speculator in railroad stock. His first venture was in Harlem railroad stock, then for sale at a nominal figure. By 1858 he was master of this road, and enjoying thereby a large augmentation of his fortune. He now attempted to gain control of the Hudson River railroad, which runs parallel with the other.

His success in this enterprise was first indicated in the uniformity of rates on the two roads and the issuing of through tickets available on both. These arrangements were in remarkable contrast to the frequent misunderstandings which had characterized their previous management. The name of John N. Tobin, who had assisted the "Commodore" in his ferry business, and had afterwards been transferred to the Hudson River office, was announced as president of the road, but in a few years Vanderbilt's name took its place, and the great speculator was the acknowledged head of both roads.

At this time Corning was president of the New York Central. In 1864 Vanderbilt gave him his influence to the extent of half a million of stock to enable him to maintain his position against the at-

HAYES
CAMPAIGN
COMIC PICTORIAL.

TILDEN'S WELCOME TO TWEED.

What might be expected if Tilden should be elected. "Should auld acquaintance be forgot!" "Oh, Willie(am M. Tweed) we have missed you, welcome, welcome home."

The Sun.

VOL. XLIV.—NO. 69. NEW YORK, WEDNESDAY, NOVEMBER 8, 1876. PRICE TWO CENTS.

THE PRESIDENT ELECT

Samuel J. Tilden Elected President of the United States.

THE EMPIRE STATE FOR TILDEN.

New York City Gives Him Over 53,000 Majority.

Connecticut, New Jersey and Indiana Safe.

The Pacific Coast Joins the Victorious Phalanx.

THE NATION REDEEMED.

The South Solid for Honest Government and Reform.

The latest returns seem to leave no doubt of the election of Tilden and Hendricks. The probabilities are that they have received about 205 Electoral votes. This would leave to Hayes and Wheeler 164, and give Tilden and Hendricks 41 majority. In this estimate we concede Ohio, Michigan, Nevada, and Wisconsin to the Republicans. We are not sure that they have carried them all. We concede New Jersey and California to the Democrats. We are at this moment not quite certain about either of them. However, we hav no doubt of Tilden's election.

THE STATES.

FOR TILDEN AND HENDRICKS.

[illegible]	10	Missouri	15
[illegible]	6	New Jersey	9
[illegible]	6	New York	35
[illegible]	6	North Carolina	10
[illegible]	3	Oregon	3
Florida	4	Tennessee	12
Georgia	11	Texas	8
Indiana	15	Virginia	11
Kentucky	12	West Virginia	5
Louisiana	8		
Maryland	8	Total	205
Mississippi	8		

FOR HAYES AND WHEELER.

Colorado	3	New Hampshire	5
Illinois	21	Ohio	22
Iowa	11	Pennsylvania	29
Kansas	5	Rhode Island	4
Maine	7	South Carolina	7
Massachusetts	13	Vermont	5
Michigan	11	Wisconsin	10
Minnesota	5		
Nebraska	3	Total	164
Nevada	3		

NEW YORK.

The returns from the interior of the State of New York at 1 o'clock, when this edition went to press, were very meagre, but sufficient to indicate that the State has gone for Tilden by a handsome majority, and that the entire Democratic State ticket is elected. The Republicans claim the defeat of Congressman Ward in the Eighth District. The Assembly is very close, with a probability that the Democrats will have a small majority.

Estimated Majorities by Counties Compared with the Official Majorities in 1872.

Counties.	1872. Grant. Maj.	1872. Greeley. Maj.	1876. Tilden. Maj.	1876. Hayes. Maj.
Albany	621	—	1500	—
Allegany	3169	—	—	2500
Broome	1397	—	—	800
Cattaraugus	2008	—	—	1000
Cayuga	3212	—	—	2000
Chautauqua	3251	—	—	3000
Chemung	622	—	600	—
Chenango	1296	—	—	600
Clinton	480	—	—	700
Columbia	—	585	1300	—
Cortlandt	1229	—	—	900
Delaware	1017	—	—	400
Dutchess	—	401	—	500
Erie	5364	—	—	3500
Essex	1789	—	—	700
Franklin	1295	—	—	1000
Fulton	624	—	200	—
Genesee	1454	—	—	800
Greene	—	263	1000	—
Hamilton	—	139	—	—
Herkimer	1450	—	—	700
Jefferson	2712	—	—	1500
Kings	—	4740	18000	—
Lewis	369	—	400	—
Livingston	1403	—	—	1000
Madison	2198	—	—	1800
Monroe	3772	—	—	500
Montgomery	371	—	850	—
New York	—	23139	53550	—
Niagara	1008	—	—	700
Oneida	3305	—	—	200
Onondaga	2961	—	—	3650
Ontario	1531	—	—	500
Orange	763	—	1000	—
Orleans	1466	—	—	800
Oswego	3115	—	—	2800
Otsego	160	—	450	—
Putnam	309	—	250	—
Queens	423	—	2000	—
Rensselaer	3265	—	1000	—
Richmond	171	—	1500	—
Rockland	—	210	1000	—
Saratoga	2222	—	—	1500
Schenectady	567	—	400	—
Schoharie	—	913	1800	—
Schuyler	492	—	—	300
Seneca	36	—	600	—
Steuben	1611	—	800	—
St. Lawrence	6936	—	—	6000
Suffolk	1678	—	500	—
Sullivan	198	—	1000	—
Tioga	854	—	—	400
Tompkins	949	—	—	800
Ulster	90	—	2000	—
Warren	1093	—	200	—
Washington	2770	—	—	2200
Wayne	2385	—	—	1200
Westchester	—	879	2500	—
Wyoming	1608	—	—	1200
Yates	938	—	—	400

Grant's majority over Greeley in 1872, 53,480

THE VOTE IN SOME OF THE PRINCIPAL CITIES.

Auburn gives Hayes 665 majority, a Democratic gain of 199.

Syracuse gives Hayes 332 majority, a Republican gain of 405.

Elmira gives Tilden 166 majority, a Democratic gain of 327.

Palmyra gives Hayes 138 majority, a Democratic gain of 8.

Schenectady gives Tilden 267 majority, a Democratic gain of 399.

Ithaca gives Hayes 139 majority, a Republican gain of 121.

Binghamton gives Hayes 89 majority, a Democratic gain of 14.

Newburgh gives Hayes 220 majority, a Republican gain of 80.

Kingston gives Tilden 524 majority, a Democratic gain of 251.

Oswego gives Tilden 220 majority, a Democratic gain of 293.

Whitehall gives Tilden 129 majority, a Democratic gain of 84.

Oswegatchie gives Hayes 336 majority, a Democratic gain of 93.

Jamaica gives Tilden 339 majority.

Dunkirk gives Tilden 227 majority, a Democratic gain of 39.

Allegany gives Tilden 145 majority, a Democratic gain of 109.

Rome gives Tilden 440 majority, a Democratic gain of 358.

Utica gives Tilden 94 majority, a Democratic gain of 319.

Saugerties gives Tilden 181 majority, a Democratic gain of 355.

Lockport gives Tilden 94 majority, a Democratic gain of 200.

Albany county elects two Democratic Assemblymen and defeats Hamilton Harris, Republican candidate for Congress.

Troy gives Tilden 1,267 majority, a Democratic gain of 1,702.

Kingston gives Tilden 564 majority, a Democratic gain of 291.

State Officers Elected.

Governor—Lucius Robinson.
Lieutenant-Governor—William Dorsheimer.
Canal Commissioner—Darius A. Ogden.
Inspector of State Prisons—Robert H. Anderson.
Judge of the Court of Appeals—Robert Earl.

Congressmen Probably Elected.

Dist.		Dist.	
1	James W. Covert (D).	18	Andrew Williams (R).
2	William D. Veeder (D).	19	A. B. James (R).
3	T. A. Dakin (D).	20	John H. Starin (R).
4	A. M. Bliss (D).	21	T. H. Matteson (D).
5	N. Muller (D).	22	George A. Bagley (R).
6	S. S. Cox (D).	23	Scott Lord (D).
7	A. Eickhoff (D).	24	William A. Baker (R).
8	E. Ward (D).	25	Frank Hiscock (R).
9	Fernando Wood (D).	26	John H. Camp (R).
10	Abram S. Hewitt (D).	27	Elbridge G. Lapham (R)
11	B. A. Willis (D).	28	Jere. W. Dwight (R).
12	C. N. Potter (D).	29	J. N. Hungerford (R).
13	John H. Ketcham (R).	30	E. Kirke Hart (D).
14	George M. Beebe (D).	31	Charles B. Benedict (D)
15	Stephen L. Mayhan (D).	32	D. N. Lockwood (D).
16	Terrence J. Quinn (D).	33	Geo. W. Patterson (D).
17	Martin I. Townsend (R)		

Judges of the Supreme Court Probably Elected.

Seventh District—George W. Rawson (R).
Eighth District—Albert Haight (R.)

State Senators Elected to Fill Vacancies.

Fifth District—Frederick W. Seward (R).
Thirty-first District—E. C. Sprague (R).

Assemblymen Probably Elected.

*Reëlected. †Democratic gain. ‡Republican gain. Democrats, 65; Republicans, 63. In the last Assembly there were 72 Republicans and 56 Democrats.

ALBANY COUNTY.
1—James Fisher, (R.)
2—J. R. Herrick, (D.)
3—*Wm. J. Maher, (D.)
4—†E. Curran, (D.)

ALLEGANY.
*S. Baldwin, (R.)

BROOME.
E. C. Moody, (R.)

CATTARAUGUS.
1—T. J. King, (R.)
2—E. Shannon, (R.)

CAYUGA.
1—*G. I. Post, (R.)
2—J. S. Brown, (R.)

CHAUTAUQUA.
1—*Wm. H. Whitney, (D.)
2—*T. A. Case, (R.)

CHEMUNG.
H. H. Rockwell, (D.)

CHENANGO.
C. C. Dalrymple, (R.)

CLINTON.
S. P. Bowen, (R.)

COLUMBIA.
1—S. W. Ham, (R.)
2—*J. T. Hogeboom, (R.)

CORTLAND.
‡Delos McGraw, (R.)

DELAWARE.
1—W. J. Welch, (R.)
2—*J. H. Maynard, (D.)

DUTCHESS.
1—*T. Hammond, (R.)
2—*DeWitt Webb, (R.)

ERIE.
1—J. L. Crowley, (D.)
2—†J. G. Langner, (D.)
3—*E. Gallagher, (R.)
4—*Charles F. Tabor, (D.)
5—*B. Cluffee, (D.)

ESSEX.
Benjamin D. Clapp, (R.)

FRANKLIN.
*John I. Gilbert, (R.)

FULTON AND HAMILTON.
Cyrus Stewart, (D.)

GENESEE.
E. Taylor, (R.)

GREENE.
O. T. Humphreys, (D.)

HERKIMER.
*M. A. McKee, (R.)

JEFFERSON.
1—Chas. R. Skinner, (R.)
2—*L. Becker, (D.)

KINGS.
1—J. M. Clancy, (D.)
2—†R. Marvin, (D.)
3—John Shanley, (D.)
4—J. G. Tighe, (D.)
5—†W. C. B. Thornton, (D.)
6—*Jacob Worth, (R.)
7—*C. L. Lyon, (D.)
8—†Thomas Cames, (D.)
9—John McGroarty, (D.)

LEWIS.
Wm. W. Rice, (D.)

LIVINGSTON.
A. L. Angle, (D.)

MADISON.
1—A. N. Sheldon, (R.)
2—M. Billington, (R.)

MONROE.
1—*W. Hodges, (R.)
2—*J. S Graham, (R.)
3—*H. Glass, (R.)

MONTGOMERY.
E. Wemple, (D.)

NEW YORK.
1—James Healey, (D.)
2—T. F. Grady, (D.)
3—W. H. Rooney, (D.)
4—*John Galvin, (D.)
5—†Peter Mitchell, (D.)
6—P. J. McAleer, (D.)
7—*I. I. Hayes, (R.)
8—Martin Wachtmann, (D.)
9—W. H. Corsa, (R.)
10—*J. Hoffman, Jr., (R.)
11—E. C. Cowdin, (R.)
12—M. E. Hourahan, (D.)
13—*R. H. Strahan, (R.)
14—L. F. Cozans, (D.)
15—J. G. Dimond, (D.)
16—F. Spinola, (D.)
17—J. E. Coulter, (D.)
18—*S. J. O'Hare, (D.)
19—T. E. Ecclesine, (D.)
20—†J. L. Sline, (D.)
21—*J. P. Fallon, (D.)

NIAGARA.
1—*A. A. Bissell, (D.)
2—*J. W. Brown, (R.)

ONEIDA.
1—G. W. Bagg, (D.)
2—E. Case, (R.)
3—B. D. Stone, (D.)
4—*Walter Ballou, (D.)

ONONDAGA.
1—T. G. Alvord, (R.)
2—*C. E. Smith, (R.)
3—*C. F. Herbst, (R.)

ONTARIO.
1—H. C. Harmon, (D.)
2—‡A. T. Winch, (R.)

ORANGE.
1—J. G. Graham, (R.)
2—S. T. Durland, (D.)

ORLEANS.
*J. D. Billings, (R.)

OSWEGO.
1—*G. B. Sloan, (R.)
2—George M. Case, (R.)
3—DeWitt C. Peck, (R.)

OTSEGO.
1—*J. S. Davenport, (D.)
2—‡S. R. Barnes, (R.)

PUTNAM.
*Hamilton Fish, Jr., (R.)

QUEENS.
1—E. F. Jones, (D.)
2—George E. Bulmer, (D.)

RENSSELAER.
1—John H. Burns, (D.)
2—John J. Filkins, (R.)
3—R. A. Derrick, (R.)

RICHMOND.
†S. R. Brick, (D.)

ROCKLAND.
*Geo. W. Weiant, (D.)

ST. LAWRENCE.
1—*David McFalls, (R.)
2—*A. P. Hepburn, (R.)
3—*L. C. Lang, (R.)

SARATOGA.
1—†Geo. W. Neilson, (D.)
2—*Isaac Noyes, Jr., (R.)

SCHENECTADY.
Charles Hastings, (R.)

SCHOHARIE.
J. M. Brown, (D.)

SCHUYLER.
*William Gulick, (R.)

SENECA.
A. L. Childs, (D.)

STEUBEN.
1—*Wm. B. Ruggles, (D.)
2—*J. E. B. Santee, (R.)

SUFFOLK.
Francis M. Brill, (D.)

SULLIVAN.
T. A. Niven, (D.)

TIOGA.
*E. B. Gere, (R.)

TOMPKINS.
‡S. R. Wickes, (R.)

ULSTER.
1—*Thomas Hamilton, (D.)
2—N. Lefevre, (D.)
3—I. W. Longyear, (D.)

WARREN.
*Robert Waddle, (R.)

WASHINGTON.
1—*T. J. Potter, (R.)
2—I. V. Baker, Jr., (R.)

WAYNE.
1—*E. W. Gurnee, (D.)
2—J. Thistlewaite, (R.)

WESTCHESTER.
1—James R. Angel, (R.)
2—Wm. F. Moller, (D.)
3—†Geo. E. Craft

WYOMING.
*Arthur Clark, (R.)

YATES.
*John Sutherland, (D.)

THE CITY.

The Vote for President by Assembly Districts.

Assembly District.	Tilden, Dem.	Hayes, Rep.	Cooper, Ind.
First	4939	1569	7
Second	4272	926	16
Third	4093	917	13
Fourth	6193	1299	15
Fifth	4595	2702	18
Sixth	4081	1228	5
Seventh	3149	3292	12
Eighth	7000	3110	20
Ninth	4443	4175	4
Tenth	4972	2321	25
Eleventh	3665	4265	14
Twelfth	4681	1898	10
Thirteenth	3841	3563	12
Fourteenth	3888	1552	19
Fifteenth	5045	3000	11
Sixteenth	5814	2610	10
Seventeenth	7334	4536	7
Eighteenth	5060	2735	14
Nineteenth	3364	1349	3
Twentieth	8962	4583	8
Twenty-first	8184	4777	18
Twenty-third Ward	2459	1424	0
Twenty-fourth Ward	1277	762	7
Total	112,208	58,658	252

Tilden's majority over Hayes.....53,550

At the time of going to press the returns from the city are too incomplete to admit of exact figures being given, except as to the Presidential candidates. The indications are that Mr. Robinson's majority for Governor and Mr. Ely's for Mayor will each be nearly as large as Mr. Tilden's. Of course the entire Tammany ticket shares in the great Democratic victory.

The Vote in Kings County.

Wards.	President— Tilden.	Hayes.	Governor— Robinson.	Morgan.
1	1623	1907	—	—
2	1379	467	1369	851
3	1654	1441	—	—
4	1433	1136	4383	1193
5	2759	763	—	—
6	3384	1575	—	—
7	2925	2650	—	—
8	1828	996	1768	1048
9	1965	766	—	—
10	3208	1455	—	—
11	2275	1974	—	—
12	3157	458	2474	2016
13	1341	2093	1849	2178
14	3535	819	—	—
15	1977	1955	—	—
16	3198	2283	3078	2384
17	2711	1714	2612	1824
18	1855	1439	1855	1439
19	1978	2143	—	—
20	1747	2568	—	—
21	2552	1925	—	—
22	1877	1698	—	—
23	951	1318	606	1340
24	600	482	655	499
25	1319	1283	—	—
Flatbush	766	359	—	—
Flatlands	—	—	—	—
Gravesend	—	—	—	—
New Lots	1413	759	—	—
New Utrecht	—	—	—	—
Total	—	—	—	—

Gov Tilden's majority in Kings county is 17,100, and including the three county towns so far heard from is 18,202. In the town of Flatlands, which has for thirty years gone Republican, Tilden gets 24 majority.

WESTCHESTER COUNTY.

WHITE PLAINS, Nov. 7.—Gov. Tilden will have 2,500 majority, and Robinson 2,600 majority. Clarkson N. Potter is elected to Congress by 2,500 majority. The entire county ticket is elected by 1,800 majority. James R. Angel, Republican, will probably be elected to the Assembly in the First District, and W. F. Moller, Dem., in the Second District. It is rumored that Gen. James W. Husted will be defeated in the Third District by George E. Craft.

MAINE.

PORTLAND, Nov. 7.—The following is a statement of the vote cast in the principal cities of this State:

	Hayes.	Tilden.		Hayes.	Tilden.
Portland	3405	2749	Bath	1136	666
Lewiston	1385	1152	Saco	881	471
Rockland	917	654	Brunswick	502	385
Auburn	1086	630	Gardiner	559	303
Biddeford	933	950			

Fifty towns give Hayes 17,298; Tilden, 12,242, and Cooper, 74; Hayes's majority, 5,056; against the same towns in September, Republican, 19,067; Democrat, 13,926; Republican majority, 5,141; showing a Republican loss of 85 votes.

The results from one hundred towns give Hayes 32,336; Tilden, 23,542; and Cooper, 74. Hayes's majority is 8,794; his plurality, 8,720. In September the same towns gave the Republicans 35,537, and the Democrats 27,396, a Republican majority of 8,141. The Republican vote is 9 per cent. smaller; the Democratic vote 14 per cent. smaller. The aggregate vote is 55,952 in these towns, against 62,933 in September, a decrease of 11 per cent. If the remainder of the State gives the same ratio, the aggregate vote will be about 121,000, of which the Republicans will have 69,000, the Democrats 52,000, a majority for Hayes of 17,000.

In 1872 Grant had 61,426, and Greeley 29,097, making Grant's majority 32,328.

NEW HAMPSHIRE.

CONCORD, Nov. 7.—Seventy towns and cities give Hayes 12,254; Tilden, 11,371; scattering, 26.

In 1872 the same places gave Grant 10,975; Greeley, 9,684; scattering, 66; a Republican net loss in these places of 368.

The incoming returns continue very favorable for the Republicans. The excitement is intense. Ex-Gov. Harrimon, from reports received up to half-past 7 o'clock, predicts that Hayes and Wheeler will carry New Hampshire by a majority of 2,500.

One hundred and five towns and cities give Hayes 19,625, Tilden 17,386, scattering 54. In 1872 the same places gave Grant 17,366, Greeley 14,675, scattering 150. Republican net loss in these places, 356.

CONCORD, Nov. 7.—Think New Hampshire has gone Republican by about two thousand—a Democratic gain of one thousand to twelve hundred.

ISAAC N. BLODGETT,
Chairman Democratic State Committee.

One hundred and forty towns and cities give Hayes 30,368; Tilden, 26,785; scattering 59. In 1872 the same places gave Grant, 26,951; Greeley, 21,863; scattering 222. Republican net loss in these places, 1,352.

VERMONT.

CASTLETON, Nov. 7.—Castleton, Rutland county, Vermont, gives a Republican majority of 121.

WHITE RIVER JUNCTION, Nov. 7.—Eighty-nine towns in Vermont give [illegible] ,256; Tilden 12,379. The same towns g[illegible] 3,536; Greeley 6,810. Republican g[illegible] Democratic gain of 5,569.

Returns from 89 town[illegible] 5,256, Tilden 12,379, scattering 1[illegible] ns gave, in 1872, Grant 23,536, Greel[illegible] O'Conor 216; Hayes's majority over T[illegible] ,863; Hayes's gain over Grant, 1,720; Ti[illegible] majority over Greeley and O'Conor, 5,353.

One hundred and fifty-two towns to be heard from gave Grant 17,945; Grant's majority over Greeley and O'Conor was about 30,000 in 1872.

MASSACHUSETTS.

BOSTON, Nov. 7.—Boston gives a majority for Tilden and Adams. Morse (Dem.) is elected in the Fourth Congressional District over Frost. Dean (Dem.) probably in the Third District—a gain. The Eighth District is very close. A very large vote was polled, and the returns are coming in slowly.

EDWARD AVERY.

BOSTON, Nov. 7.—Twenty-four towns give Hayes 6,718; Tilden, 3,836; Rice, 6,308; Adams, 3,816; Baker, 435. Nine wards in Boston give Hayes 6,893; Tilden, 7,419. Rice has a majority of 52 in these wards.

BOSTON, Nov. 7.—One hundred and twenty-three towns give Hayes 51,494, Tilden 31,601, Rice 47,308, Adams 30,379, and Baker 4,573. Butler in the Seventh District, Banks in the fifth, Claflin in the Eighth, Crapo in the First, Robinson in the Eleventh, Rice in the Ninth, and Norcoss in the Tenth are elected to Congress as Republicans. Harris in the Second District and Loring in the Sixth, both Republicans, are probably elected. Dean in the Third and Morse in the Fourth Districts, Democrats, are probably elected.

The present Congressional delegation stands, Republicans 5, Democrats 6, a Republican gain of 4 Congressmen; and if the vote continues in the same ratio, it will carry the State for Hayes by a plurality of 50,000.

The vote of cities:

	Hayes.	Tilden.	Rice.	Adams.	Baker.
Somerville	1846	1262	1734	1177	136
Chelsea	2184	1207	1948	1282	—
New Bedford	2649	1488	2013	1445	647
Newburyport	1269	937	1125	897	104
Cambridge	3654	3527	3427	3463	—
Lynn	2757	2322	—	—	—
Newton	1026	531	1007	510	31
Quincy	867	852	811	871	31
Taunton	2060	1060	1674	1054	388
Brocton	1373	613	1147	608	249
Plymouth	820	363	762	353	54
Springfield	2919	2098	2740	2234	103
Lowell	4003	3089	3831	1919	226
Salem	2485	1572	2288	1486	252
Fitchburg	1177	943	1283	902	196
Marblehead	676	832	605	761	147

One hundred and sixty-three towns and cities give Hayes 65,893; Tilden, 43,436; Rice, 61,534; Adams, 41,961; Baker, 5,831.

The following is the vote of Boston all but one ward: Hayes, 19,138; Tilden, 22,296; Rice, 18,073; Adams, 21,575; Baker, 1,135.

One hundred and ninety-seven towns give Hayes 95,578; Tilden, 70,644; Rice, 88,804; Adams, 70,905; Baker, 8,085.

Four counties complete give sixty-one Republican and ten Democratic members of the Legislature. All but three towns in the Fifth District give Banks 9,741; Frothingham, 9,155. Other towns will increase Banks's majority about 200. The Third District elects Dean (Dem.) for Congress by 43 plurality. Morse (Dem.) is also elected in the Fourth District. Butler, in the Seventh District, has about 3,000 plurality over Tarbox and Hoar.

RHODE ISLAND.

PROVIDENCE, Nov. 7.—Partial returns from all parts of the State show that Hayes will have from 5,000 to 6,000 majority. Eames and Ballou, Republican Congressmen, are both reëlected by a large vote. There have been no disturbances. All three of the State constitutional amendments are rejected.

CONNECTICUT.

NEW HAVEN, Nov. 7.—Returns from 79 towns show a loss of 1,000 over the spring election of 1876, when Gov. Ingersoll carried the State by 7,600. The State is for Tilden by about 5,000. Landers (Dem.) in the First Congressional District, and Phelps (Dem.) in the Second, are elected, the latter by about 1,200 majority.

HARTFORD, Nov. 7.—Indications all point to the success of the Democratic National and State ticket by about 5,000 majority. Hawley is probably defeated for Congress by over 500. Hartford gives Tilden 983 majority.

Hartford gives Hayes 4,033; Tilden, 5,019; Cooper, 79; Smith, 8; Robinson, 4,128; Hubbard, 4,940; Atwater, Greenback, 68; Cummings, 12. In 1872 Greeley's vote over Grant was 469; in 1876, Ingersoll (Dem.) over Robinson, 676. Democratic gain over 1872 of 517, and 310 over 1876.

For Congress—Hawley, 4,234; Landers, 4,837; Landers's plurality, 603. In 1875 Landers's plurality 469. Democratic gain on Congress of 134.

Bridgeport gives Hayes 2,389; Tilden, 3,134; Robinson, 2,388; Hubbard, 3,124. Democratic gain, 198.

Norwalk gives Hayes 1,358; Tilden, 1,245; Robinson, 1,341; Hubbard, 1,234. Republican gain, 55.

New Britain—Hayes, 1,183; Tilden, 1,352; Robinson, 1,176; Hubbard, 1,357. Republican gain, 120.

Norwich gives Hayes 1,995; Tilden, 1,747; Robinson, 1,972; Hubbard, 1,766; Democratic gain, 53.

Ninety-four towns give Hayes 32,322; Tilden, 33,145; Robinson, 32,266; Hubbard, 33,267. These towns last spring gave Robinson 24,435; Ingersoll, 28,398; Democratic majority so far 1,001, against 3,963 last spring.

HARTFORD, Nov. 7.—New Haven reports 1,800 plurality for Tilden, which, with returns from 120 other towns, gives Tilden about 2,500 plurality. It is probable that the election of Governor may go to the Legislature, which the Republicans claim, and they probably have the Senate without doubt. The Hartford *Times* thinks Hawley is elected by a small plurality.

Midnight—Hawley is defeated for Congress in the First District by about 150.

The Senate in all probability is Republican, the Republicans carrying the following of the twenty-one districts: Second, Sixth (probably), Eighth, Ninth, Twelfth (probably), Thirteenth, Fourteenth, Fifteenth, Nineteenth, Twentieth and Twenty-first. Returns from seventy-eight towns show a net Republican gain in the lower House of thirty. There seems no doubt that the Legislature is Republican in both branches.

NEW JERSEY.

Large Democratic Gains Reported from Every Part of the State.

The triumph in Jersey City is overwhelming, and Democrats thronged the streets last night despite the rain, and rejoiced with each other in congratulations and handshaking. At the *Argus* office the returns from the different States were mirrored on a broad sheet of bunting by means of a stereopticon, and thousands gathered and cheered to the echo the glorious intelligence of Tilden's triumph. In the editorial rooms were seated Sheriff Laverty, Senator Abbett, ex-Senator McPherson, who is on the electoral ticket; Assemblyman Hannon, ex-Assemblyman Stevens, the Hon. Martin M. Drohan, and all the influential Democrats of the city. A private wire was in operation, from which the news was flashed of the complete rout of the Republicans.

The Pavonia Club, the leading Republican organization of the city, received the returns at the Catholic Institute, John E. Jennie, Colonel of the Boys in Blue, and ex-Mayor Gopsill, with a number of officeholders and the Custom House and Port Officer, sat on the platform as if they were officiating at the burial of some friend. The returns were read for a few hours and then deafened and discomforted by by the applause and cheers of the Democrats who filled the lower part of the hall, the gas was extinguished, and the crowd made their way to the Police Central Office where the Republican Police Commissioners were receiving the receiving the returns from the city. An immense throng had gathered in the lobby, and it was with extreme difficulty that the police could preserve order. In consequence of the election of a United States Senator by the next legislature there was great anxiety to ascertain the vote in the Assembly Districts.

Early in the evening the returns flowed in from the districts, and as they indicated a triumph over the Ring Commissioners that have so long misgoverned the city, the throngs shouted themselves hoarse.

The greatest triumph is the defeat of William J. Gregory, Robeson's candidate in the Sixth District. This is a Democratic gain which has formed a rout. T. C. Brown, the present Assemblyman, a respectable merchant of Jersey City, was refused a renomination, and Robeson's tool received the prize. Mr. James Stevens, the Democratic candidate, who wins by at least 300 majority, says that Gregory placed $10,000 in the district. He organized a Robeson Battery, and equipped it at a cost of $1,500. Efforts were made at colonization, but Mr. Stevens watched the scheme so closely that it was defeated. There was great rejoicing in Jersey City last night over the result.

The first District, which was represented in the last Legislature by William A. Lewis, the Republican Corporation Counsel is regained to the Democracy, Martin M. Drohan, Democrat, being elected by 325 majority. This is a Democratic gain of 375.

The Second District elects Thos. J. Hannon, Democrat, by 2,100 majority. The Republican candidate, Wm. Gerdts, ran slightly ahead of his ticket.

In the Third, which is the banner Republican district of the county, the Republican majority has been reduced twenty-five per cent. Marmaduke Tilden, the Republican [illegible] Republican loss of 400.

The contest in the Assembly Districts has been fierce and bitter. At this hour the count shows the election of Robt. M. Jarvis, Democrat, in the Third District, over Marmaduke Tilden, Republican, by 18 majority. The delegation from the county will stand 6 Democrats to 2 Republicans, a gain of 4 Assemblymen.

In the Fourth District, local differences and the presence of two Democratic candidates in the field reëlect Henry Brautigam, Republican. His majority over Major Alex. W. Harris, the regular Democratic candidate, will be about 150, a slight Democratic gain.

The Fifth District, which comprises old Hudson City, is strongly Republican, elects Lewis A. Brigham, Republican, by less than one hundred majority.

The Seventh District, which comprises the city of Hoboken, gives a sweeping majority for Rudolph F. Rabe, Democrat. He claims 2,100 on a vote of 3,700 over his opponent William Barnett, Republican.

The Eighth District comprises the outlying townships of the county, and includes Weehawken, Union Hill, West Hoboken, and Harrison. The returns at headquarters last night showed Paxton (Dem.) elected by 300 majority over Jacobus.

The result in the Congressional district shows that Hardenbergh (Dem.) is elected by 2,500 majority over Stastny, Republican.

Hudson county will give Tilden about 3,500 majority, a Democratic gain over the vote of 1872.

LATER—Returns show Tilden's majority in Hudson county about 4,800. The city is wild with delight.

ELIZABETH, Nov. 7.—An unusually heavy vote was polled in Elizabeth and Union county, and thus far the indications are that the Democratic plurality in both will reach 1,000. Democrats have made gains in the major portion of the towns. In Elizabeth, the Hon. John Egan has been reëlected to the Assembly from the First District by a majority estimated at 600, an increase of 285 over last year. From returns received from Crawford, Westfield, and Scotch Plains, of the Second Assembly District, it is thought that Chas L. Abry will defeat Moses F. Cory, whose majority of last year has been reduced by at least 300, a gain of 351.

Cornelius A. Runkle, Democrat, has gained 216 in Rahway, and his election over Benjamin A. Vail is considered almost certain.

The Hon. Miles Ross's majority in the county will reach between 800 and 900, a heavy gain over last year.

Mercer county gives Tilden 300 majority, a gain of 700 over the vote of 1872. Democrats claim the election of the three Assemblymen.

In Passaic county the vote on electoral ticket is very close. G. A. Hobart (Rep.) is elected to the State Senate, with Stevenson and Sanderson (Dems.), and Cunningham (Rep.) to the Assembly, a Democratic gain of one Assemblyman.

New Brunswick City and six towns give Tilden 145 majority. Ludlow (Dem.) is probably elected State Senator by about 200 majority—a Democratic gain of a Senator. Three Democratic Assemblymen probably elected—a gain of one.

The city of New Brunswick gives Tilden a gain of 881 votes. Democrats claim the county by a small majority.

Indications are that Tilden has carried the State by 5,000 majority.

The Legislature will doubtless be Democratic.

PENNSYLVANIA.

PHILADELPHIA, Nov. 7.—Philadelphia gives Hayes and Wheeler 16,000 to 17,000 majority. Pennsylvania is undoubtedly for Hayes by from 10,000 to 15,000 majority.

Returns from nearly every precinct of this city indicate a Republican majority on the Presidential ticket of 15,200. The city gave a Republican majority of 17,200 last year.

Returns from 24 towns and townships outside of the city, principally in Chester, Berks, and Delaware counties, show a net Republican gain of 84 on the vote for Governor in 1875.

MARYLAND.

BALTIMORE, Nov. 7.—Tilden's majority in this city is 9,600; in the State not less than 14,000. Five Democrats elected to Congress. The Sixth District doubtful.

Official returns from all the wards in this city give a Democratic majority of 10,099. In this Congressional district, comprising the First to the Ninth Wards, inclusive, Kimmell's (Dem.) majority is 5,827; Fourth, Swann's (Dem.) majority over 2,500. Returns from every portion of the State show Democratic gains.

VIRGINIA.

NORFOLK, Nov. 7.—The election was quiet. This city gives Tilden a majority of 958; Goode, Democratic, for Congress one of 965, and a Democratic gain of 574.

Elizabeth City county gives a Republican majority of 830 and a Republican gain of 200.

RICHMOND, Nov. 7.—Tilden's majority in Richmond will be 1,500. Returns from the surrounding counties show Democratic gains over the vote of 1874. The only close contests for Congress are in the Second and Fourth Districts. The remaining seven districts will elect Democratic Congressmen. The returns from the Second District show that Goode Dem. is gaining over the vote of 1874. The Democratic majority in Alexandria is 270, and about the same majority for the State Constitutional amendment. Gen. W. H. F. Lee is elected to the State Senate. There is no doubt of Hunter's reëlection to Congress by a majority of several thousand.

NORFOLK, Nov. 7.—The majority for Goode (Dem.) for Congress in Portsmouth is 1,118, a Democratic gain of 965.

WEST VIRGINIA.

WHEELING, Nov. 7.—The Democrats gain in every precinct heard from. Wilson's majority in the first Congressional District will be 20,000. The majorities for Martin and Kenna in the second and third are very large. Tilden's majority will reach 20,000.

NORTH CAROLINA.

WILMINGTON, Nov. 7.—The election closed without the slightest disturbance. Lilesville, Anson county, gives a net Republican gain of 8. The Third Ward of this city gives Hayes 311, Tilden 304. Democratic gain 13.

The Second Ward of this city gives a Democratic gain of 103, and the Fifth Ward a Republican gain of six. Lilesville gives a corrected Democratic gain of 15, and Lawrinburg, Richmond county, a Democratic gain of 34.

RALEIGH, Nov. 7.—Raleigh city and township give a Democratic gain of 100. All points in the State heard from give Democratic gains. Mecklenburg county, the home of Vance, gives a Democratic gain of 300.

WILMINGTON, Nov. 7.—The returns thus far received show an almost universal Democratic gain. Wilson county gives a Democratic gain of 400, and the indications all favor a decided Democratic majority in the State.

Later.—The returns continue favorable to the Democrats. The Republicans claim the State by a small majority, but admit that it will be very close. The Democrats claim the State by 5,000 to 10,000 majority. The *Star* estimates the Democratic majority at 4,500 to 6,000.

The Democrats have made gains in the following counties: Lenver, 125; Cleveland, 700; Mecklenburg, 350; Wake, 500; Rockingham, 200; Guilford, 250; Wayne, 300; Rowan, 400.

SOUTH CAROLINA.

CHARLESTON, Nov. 7.—Unofficial returns from various sections of the State show large Democratic gains everywhere, as compared with the vote of two years ago. No Republican gain is reported anywhere. The Democratic Committee are jubilant. The Republicans are unwilling to grant that Chamberlain's majority of 1874 is overcome.

The returns come in slowly. The Democrats claim the State by 4,000 majority. Barnwell, Aiken, Edgefield and Abbeville counties, heretofore Republican, are claimed by the Democrats.

CHARLESTON, Nov. 7.—Unofficial but trustworthy returns from about half of the State show a Democratic gain of over 12,000, as compared with the vote of 1874, when Chamberlain had 10,000 majority over Green (Fusion). The Republicans claim that Charleston county will give a heavy Republican gain to offset the Democratic gains. The result hangs upon coast counties not accessible by wire.

COLUMBIA, Nov. 7.—Returns coming in very slowly. Heavy Democratic gains everywhere. In nine counties heard from, Hampton receives 7,600 majority, a Democratic gain of 1,000 over the vote of 1870, when the Republican majority was 34,000. Indications point to a close vote.

The Democrats most probably gain two Congressmen—Aiken in the Third and Evins in the Fourth. No disturbance occurred anywhere. In the morning many Democratic negroes were intimidated, but as the day progressed the Democrats rallied and voted a large number of them. The vote was the largest ever polled, as the negroes repeated heavily.

GEORGIA.

COLUMBUS, Nov. 7.—Muscogee county gives Tilden 1,400 majority, as also a like number to Harris (Dem.) for Congress. This district goes Democratic by a heavy majority.

AUGUSTA, Nov. 7.—The returns seem to indicate the election of an unbroken Democratic [illegible] to Congress. There has been a large vote polled in the State. Every county in the Eighth District has gone Democratic. Richmond County gives over 3,000 Democratic majority.

SAVANNAH, Nov. 7.—Chatham County gives Hartridge for Congress over 600 majority; Tilden's majority 800. Seven hundred negroes voted the straight Democratic ticket. Everything passed off quietly, although there was a crowd of negroes in the town all day.

ATLANTA, Nov. 7.—The State gives a majority of from fifty to sixty thousand for Tilden. The Congressional ticket is reëlected throughout the State.

ALABAMA.

MONTGOMERY, Nov. 7.—The election was quiet throughout the State as far as heard from. Hayes's majority in this city will be 1,600. The few boxes heard from indicate a large Democratic majority in the State. It is safe to say that seven Democratic Congressmen have been elected.

MOBILE, Ala., Nov. 7.—The indications are that Bromberg (Dem.) has carried the county by 3,500 majority. Tilden and Hendricks's majority will equal, if it does not exceed, Bromberg's. Everything is quiet.

MONTGOMERY, Nov. 7.—On largely increased vote indications from all points are that Alabama has gone Democratic by 30,000 majority. Bromberg, Independent candidate for Congress in the First District, carries Mobile county by 3,500 majority. The Democrats gain largely in the Fourth District. Probable election of the entire Democratic delegation to Congress. Election entirely peaceful as far as heard from.

M. D. GRAHAM,
Chairman Democratic State Ex. Committee.

MONTGOMERY, Nov. 7.—Returns show Democratic majorities from all directions indicating at least 25,000 majority in the State. Seven Democratic Congressmen are certainly elected. In the Fourth District Harrison, the present colored member, is opposed by Rapier, colored ex-member, who is supported by Senator Spencer and all the Federal officials. Shelby (Dem.) is making gains, but not enough is known to warrant an estimate.

LOUISIANA.

NEW ORLEANS, Nov. 7.—One of our most prominent physicians, who has lived in the same house since 1861, and whose name was erased on the sewing machine circulars, being refused the privilege of voting, was required to go to the supervisor of election, Pat Creigh, to get his permission to vote. The office was in the third story of a dram shop. On each story at the doors were stationed armed policemen, through which the Doctor had to pass to reach this dirty creature, who, on finding himself confronted, gave a note to the commissioner of election, saying, "Allow Dr. Brickel to vote." This is one instance in many. Everything is progressing quietly in the city and country. A large vote is being polled. There is no doubt of our success.

J. W. PATTON,
Chairman Dem. State Committee.

NEW ORLEANS, Nov. 7.—The Democratic State Central Committee have received despatches claiming 1,500 majority in Claiborne parish, and 1,000 majority in Lincoln parish, a net gain of over 1,300 in the two parishes.

NEW ORLEANS, Nov. 7.—The election has ended very quietly here and throughout the State. As far as heard from heavy Democratic gains, owing to the colored people voting that ticket, are reported in the parishes of Claiborne, Morehouse and Ouachita. In East Feliciana, one of the disturbed parishes, the colored vote has been almost solid for the Democratic ticket. A majority of 6,400 is reported in the parishes named. They have heretofore been strongly Republican. This city is Democratic by a large majority.

W. H. ROBERTS, New Orleans *Times*.

NEW ORLEANS, Nov. 7.—Louisiana certainly Democratic by from twelve to fifteen thousand. Large Democratic gains from every parish heard from. Perfect quietness all day. City largely Democratic.

J. W. PATTON.

NEW ORLEANS, 10 P. M.—We have carried our city and State by large majorities in spite of fraud and intimidation. We have elected five Congressmen certainly, probably six.

I. W. PATTON.

ARKANSAS.

LITTLE ROCK, Nov. 7.—The returns from five wards and one township are as follows: Democratic, 992; Republican, 954. For Congress, Stuart, Dem., 672; Cravens, Dem., 301; McClure, Rep., 905; Rice, Greenback, 78, Dell, Rep., none; Ward, Rep., yet to hear from. Election quiet, and orderly.

MISSISSIPPI.

JACKSON, Nov. 7.—We have advices from all parts of the State. Democratic gains everywhere. Our majority will be at least 30,000. Five Democratic Congressmen elected, and good prospects for the sixth. Election quiet and peaceable.

J. Z. GEORGE.

LOUISVILLE, Ky., Nov. 7.—Private news from all over Mississippi from superintendents to Mr. Van Horne, Division Superintendent of the Western Union Telegraph Company, reports the election of five and perhaps more Democratic Congressmen, and says that the State is Democratic by over 30,000.

MISSOURI.

ST. LOUIS, Nov. 7.—The election passed off very quietly. An unusually heavy vote was polled. The appointment of several hundred United States Deputy Marshals caused great dissatisfaction among all good citizens of both parties, and resulted in an increase of several thousand votes for the straight Democratic ticket. Very little scratching done. Returns coming in slowly, but thus far show heavy Democratic gains.

FLORIDA.

LAKE CITY, Nov. 7.—Returns come in slowly. The southern and western counties show large Democratic gains. The Republicans have small gains in the eastern counties. The State looks Democratic. Definite returns are expected about midnight. The Democrats claim the State.

TENNESSEE.

MEMPHIS, Nov. 7.—The election here today was unusually quiet. A very heavy vote was polled, that of the city being over 10,000, or 1,000 over any former vote. It is believed that Thomas, the Independent Democratic candidate for Governor, has carried the county by over 1,500, and that the Republicans have elected their legislative ticket. The Democrats generally concede the election of Randolph (Republican) for Congress over Young (Democrat), the present incumbent. The official vote will not be known until a late hour.

KENTUCKY.

LEXINGTON, Nov. 7.—Official vote of the city gives—Tilden, 1,579; Hayes, 2,172; a Democratic gain of 454 on the vote of 1872. Blackburn (Dem.), for Congress, 1,594; Shackelford (Rep.), 1,895.

LOUISVILLE, Nov. 7.—Tilden's majority in Kentucky is estimated at over 60,000.

LOUISVILLE, Nov. 7.—Majority in city, 7,005; in State, 60,000 to 70,000. We have carried every Congressional district.

T. L. BURNETT,
Chairman Dem. Central Committee.

LOUISVILLE, Nov. 7.—The total vote of the city of Louisville was 17,321, of which Hayes has 5,158 and Tilden 12,163, a Democratic majority of 7,005, and a Democratic gain of 3,509. The State probably goes Democratic by over 60,000. The Democrats elect Congressmen in every district, they being as follows:

First, Andrew Boone; Second, James McKenzie; Third, John W. Caldwell; Fourth, J. Proctor Knott; Fifth, Albert S. Willis; Sixth, John G. Carlisle; Seventh, J. C. S. Blackburn; Eighth, W. J. Durham; Ninth, Thomas Turner; Tenth, John B. Clarke.

IOWA.

CHICAGO, Nov. 7.—Returns have been received from fifteen townships in Iowa, showing heavy Republican majorities.

Partial returns from 17 counties in Iowa show a Republican gain of 714; a Democratic gain of 52, net Republican gain 662.

MICHIGAN.

DETROIT, Nov. 7.—Returns from thirty-two townships give Hayes a net Republican majority of 831, a Democratic gain of 1,590 as compared with the vote of 1872. The same towns give Crosswell (Republican) for Governor a net majority of 463.

Twenty-eight towns and three cities give a net Democratic gain of 126 over 1874.

Sixteen precincts of Detroit give a Democratic majority of 1,116, a gain of 300.

Eighteen out of twenty-three precincts in Detroit show a Democratic majority of 1917, a gain of 1,600. [illegible] majority of 2,154, a net Democratic gain of 2,612 as compared with 1872. The same towns give Crosswell (Republican) for Governor a net majority of 348.

Returns from 78 townships and precincts give Hayes a net Republican majority of 2,669, a Democratic gain of 3,652 as compared with the vote of 1872. The same towns gave Cresswell (Republican) for Governor a net majority of 809.

WISCONSIN.

MILWAUKEE, Nov. 7.—Madison gives a net Democratic gain of 380, which proportion indicates that Tilden has carried the State.

Returns from fifty towns and wards in Wisconsin give Hayes a majority of 1,300, a Republican gain of 947.

Ninety-eight towns and wards give Tilden 12 majority; a Democratic gain of 994. This does not include any returns from the city of Milwaukee, where there are indications of a large Republican gain.

11:20 P. M.—Twelve of the thirteen wards of Milwaukee and one town give Tilden 1,206 majority. The Democratic majority in the county will not exceed 2,500. One hundred and fifty-four towns and wards, not including the above, give Hayes 1,050 majority—a Democratic gain of 910.

NEBRASKA.

OMAHA, Nov. 7.—The election passed off quietly. A heavy vote was polled in this city. No returns are yet in from the State. Both parties claim Douglass county. Local factions have caused much scratching. The straight ticket so far counted in this city shows a Democratic plurality.

OMAHA, Nov. 7.—Partial returns from Colfax county show 58 Republican majority; the same from Buffalo county, 144 Republican majority; Dodge county, 110 Republican majority; Memaha county is claimed by the Democrats; Saline county Republican by about 400; Democrats claim Platte county by 150 majority. No official returns have been received.

MINNESOTA.

ST. PAUL, Nov. 7.—Returns received to 9 o'clock indicate a full vote and a heavy Republican majority on the general ticket. Dunnell (Rep.) in the First Congressional District will be elected; Stewart (Rep.) in the Third and probably Strait (Rep.) in the Second.

ILLINOIS.

CHICAGO, Nov. 7.—Returns from twenty townships in Illinois show general Republican majorities. The vote for Cooper in some of the interior counties is nearly equal to that for Tilden.

CHICAGO, Nov. 7.—At 9 o'clock it is evident that Aldrich (Rep.) is elected from the First Congressional District, Harrison (Dem.) in the Second, and Lemoyne (Dem.) in the Third. The Germans cut Brentano heavily. Chicago will doubtless go 3,000 for Tilden.

Cairo, 56 majority for Tilden; a Democratic gain of 230.

Returns from 20 towns in Illinois give Hayes 4,339; Tilden, 3,484; Cooper, 84; Republican gain over the vote for 1872 of 1,234; Democratic gain 1,328, being net Democratic gain of 94.

CHICAGO, Nov. 7.—Eleven precincts in this city and 39 towns in the interior of the State give Hayes 13,290, Tilden 10,397, a small Democratic gain over the vote for Governor in 1872, when the State went Republican by over 50,000. There is no doubt of a large Republican majority in the State.

Returns from 82 towns in Illinois give Hayes 23,081; Tilden, 18,501; Cooper, 321; net Democratic gain, 397.

INDIANA.

INDIANAPOLIS, Nov. 7.—The election has been remarkably quiet in this city. Up to noon the Democrats had a decided advantage. The Republicans were slow and spiritless in coming out, but toward afternoon they became alarmed and drummed up their forces, and regained some of their lost ground before the polls were closed. From present indications the vote has not fallen more than several hundred short of October in this county, but Democratic gains are conceded so generally by the Republicans that the Republican majority will be reduced. The precise figures cannot be furnished much before midnight. The prospects in the State at large for an overwhelming victory are settled at this early hour. Twenty townships, mostly from the north, now reported, show a Democratic gain of 131. The tables of returns are thus reversed at the outset compared with October. Reliable private information gives gains in counties of Porter, Scott, Vanderburgh, Vigo, Greene, and many precincts in all localities. In the counties of Fountain and Hamilton the Independents have voted almost solid for Tilden.

At 8.10 P. M. the returns from forty townships give Tilden 5,806, and Hayes 5,801. The same places in October gave Williams 6,789, and Harrison 5,898.

Reports are in from sixty townships, and show Democratic gains of 239 over October. This ratio of increase will give Tilden the State by 10,000.

Returns from eighty townships give Tilden 13,376, Hayes 13,433. The same places in October gave Williams 13,325 and Harrison 13,702. The indications are that Tilden's majority in the State will be from 7,000 to 10,000.

10 *P. M.*—The Democratic increase still continues at the same figure as last reported.

One hundred townships give a gain over October of 245. The Republicans concede the State. Pools are offered and refused on 8,000 for Tilden. Radical demoralization is general.

Returns from 100 townships in 54 counties give a net Democratic gain of 245.

Returns from 180 townships give Tilden 35,948, Hayes 35,324. The same places in October gave Williams 35,141, Harrison 35,193, a net Democratic gain of 667.

INDIANAPOLIS, Nov. 7—Midnight.—Everything indicates that Indiana will go for Tilden and Hendricks by a majority approaching ten thousand. This estimate is based on returns from 200 townships, which show a Democratic gain of 716, and on the further fact that the precincts from which the reports are still to come are heavily Democratic. Taking the State as a whole, the vote has not fallen much short of October, and there are the same mysterious variations in the vote. In some strong Democratic counties there have been slight Republican gains, owing in large measure to Republican Independents having returned to their first love, while again there are Democratic gains in Republican counties of the North where issues have been free from the independent vote. Returns from counties where Democrats were largely represented in the greenback movement indicate that they have come back almost solid.

The Greenback vote in the State will hardly exceed five thousand, if it reaches that figure, which now seems doubtful. Holloway has telegraphed Morton that the State is lost beyond doubt, and nothing but depression rules in the radical headquarters.

The most intense interest and excitement are manifested in the streets. All eyes are turned on New York, and the Republicans are assuming a tone of confidence over the small gains reported from the interior of New York.

The betting at the pool rooms is even on 20,000 Democratic majority in New York, while on the general result Tilden is the favorite by large odds.

The Democrats are crowding headquarters in immense numbers and cheering themselves hoarse, while the Republican rooms are comparatively deserted. The vote in the city is not yet in. Both parties claim an increase, but it will be slight and of no consequence on the general result in the State.

OHIO.

CINCINNATI, Nov. 7.—The Democratic and Republican gains are nearly even, with the figures slightly in favor of the Republicans. Hayes will probably carry the State by ten thousand.

Reports from 308 wards, townships, and precincts in about sixty counties, including about half of Cleveland and one-third of Cincinnati, show Hayes gain of 4,407, Democratic 4,566; net Democratic gain as compared with Gubernatorial election in 1875, 159.

11 *P. M.*—Reports from 168 voting places show a net Democratic gain of 108. It is now pretty certain that Hayes's majority in the State will be about the same as the Republican majority at the last election.

Midnight.—The Democrats have made considerable gains in the northern part of the State, which more than counterbalance the Republican gain in Southern Ohio. Hayes's majority in the State must be light, if he carries it, and the Democrats are now hopeful of giving it to Tilden.

COLUMBUS, Nov. 7.—Returns from 448 townships and voting precincts in Ohio, covering sixty-five counties, show a net Democratic gain of 266, as compared with the Gubernatorial vote of 1875.

THE PRESIDENT-ELECT AT HOME.

How he Received the News of his Election to the Chief Magistracy.

Gov. Tilden sat very quietly in his house at Gramercy Park all last evening, and received the news through a private wire and from minute messengers from the Democratic [illegible] were with him early to hear the returns, and to their number were added the Governor's political friends, who poured in later in the evening to tender their congratulations. At About ten o'clock Messrs. Algernod S. Sullivan and Augustus Schnell arrived at the head of the delegation from Tammany Hall to request the Governor to go down to the Wigwam and receive the congratulations of the Sachems. But the Governor thought it would hardly do so to take time by the forelock, and said it was better to wait until the result was placed beyond a possible doubt. An hour later the Hon. John Kelly, ruddy and joyous, appeared and had an interview of considerable length with the President elect. The Governor was calm and composed under his budding honors. From the start he had worn a quiet, assured air that was so assured that it could hardly become more confident, and he became even quieter as time wore on. His first congratulatory despatch, which was from Summit, N. J., was received with manifest satisfaction. Nor were his guests noisily excited over the news of his elevation to the Chief Magistracy. The despatches were read with composure and the Governor received all congratulations very quietly.

Disasters at Sea.

HALIFAX, Nov. 7.—An American brig, lumber laden, is reported ashore at Porter's Passage, east of Halifax. The schooner Morning Light, from Boston, is ashore at Cape Negro. Late reports from Newfoundland say there have been as many as thirty shipwrecks on that coast since the 1st of October. Several lives were lost. The schooner Minnie Cronon of Halifax, which left Bay of Islands on the 15th of October for Pictou, has been fallen in with dismantled and sinking. The crew and three or four passengers are supposed to have been lost. The schooner Lizzie of Tregmouth, from St. Johns for Glace bay, went ashore at Port Nova on Friday night last, and is a total wreck. The crew were saved.

Miss Marshall Ahead.

Misses Von Hillern and Marshall reëntered the track in the Central Park Garden at about 5 o'clock yesterday morning, and at 11:30 Miss Von Hillern had walked seventy-five miles, after a rest of four hours. Miss Marshall completed her 100th mile at 3 o'clock P. M. Miss Marshall walked thirty miles during the day, and Miss Von Hillern twenty-one.

Valuable Land Patents Granted.

WASHINGTON, Nov. 7.—The Commissioner of the General Land Office, to-day, issued a patent for the Rancho Jamul, embracing two square leagues in San Diego county, California., Henry H. Burton, Maria Burton, and Nellie Burton, confirmees; and also a patent for the Rancho Piedra Blanca, comprising 48,806 acres in San Luis Obispo county, José de Jesus Pico, counrmee.

The Guests of G. W. Childs. A. M.

WASHINGTON, Nov. 7.—The President and Mrs. Grant, with Secretary Fish, will leave Washington for Philadelphia to-morrow, and be the guests of G. W. Childs during their stay in the city—until the close of the Centennial Exhibition.

The Eastern Question.

LONDON, Nov. 8.—The *Standard* announces in an official form that the Marquis of Salisbury will be appointed special Ambassador to act with Sir Henry Elliott as English plenipotentiary at the contemplated conference.

Death from Lockjaw.

Larry Holten, ex-policeman, died in Newark, on Monday, from lockjaw, caused from a bite on the thumb received in a drunken quarrel with Patrick McManus, three weeks ago.

Weather Office Prediction.

Falling, possibly followed by rising barometer, northwest to southwest winds, and occasional rain, with stationary or lower temperature.

SPARKS FROM THE TELEGRAPH.

A special to the London *Standard* from Belgrade reports that Gen. Tchernayeff arrived there on Tuesday, accompanied by 200 Russian officers.

JOTTINGS ABOUT TOWN.

Patrick Dinsen dropped dead on the sidewalk at 1,405 Second avenue last evening.

Henry L. Collins, captain of a Providence schooner that is lying at Hoboken, was enticed into a Washington street den, and drugged and robbed, early yesterday morning.

The Hon. Thomas K. Downing of Port Chester was thrown from his carriage yesterday, and had four of his ribs fractured, besides other severe and possibly fatal injuries.

HORSE NOTES.

Goldsmith Maid will winter in California.

Charles Robinson of Fishkill has purchased Aboemarle for $4,000.

Add was sold at the Pimlico meeting to A. D. Brown of Baltimore for $3,000.

Murrain continues to rage in and near Cairo, Egypt. Nearly 3,000 horses have died in that city alone.

C. McArdell of Middletown, N. Y., has sold Midnight to Charles Reed, Mayor of Erie, Pa., for $11,000.

Flora Temple is in her thirty-second year. She is kept in a comfortable box on her owner's farm at Chestnut Hill, Philadelphia.

The once-renowned race horse Wild Irishman, the last surviving son of imported Glencoe, died on the Hon. A. B. Conger's farm in Rockland county on the 11th ult.

THIRTY-TWO PAGES

SPIRIT OF THE TIMES

"THE SPIRIT OF THE TIMES SHALL TEACH ME SPEED" King John Act IV.

A Chronicle of the Turf, Field Sports, Aquatics, Agriculture, and the Stage.

VOL. 93—No. 9. NUMBER 3 PARK ROW. | NEW YORK, SATURDAY, APRIL 7, 1877. | SUBSCRIPTION: FIVE DOLLARS A YEAR.

DELMONICO'S CAFE (Broadway and Twenty-sixth Street).

For a picture of social life among the upper classes of New York society, our artist has happily chosen, for this week, an interior view of the new and palatial up-town Delmonico restaurant, extending from Broadway to Fifth Avenue, on Twenty-sixth Street, with entrances on both the former thoroughfares. The name of Delmonico has become the synonym for high living, and for all that is super-excellent in the culinary art throughout the country, and before it the glories of all other restaurateurs pale their ineffectual fires. Rivals in this, and in other cities, have their specialties, and enjoy the fruits of their comparatively petty successes, but Delmonico, by universal consent, holds the proud place of high priest of gastronomy in America. The family have been engaged in the business of caterers to the *bon vivants* of the metropolis

HOW THE STREETS OF NEW YORK ARE CLEANED.—DRAWN BY W. P. SNYDER.—[SEE PAGE 927.]

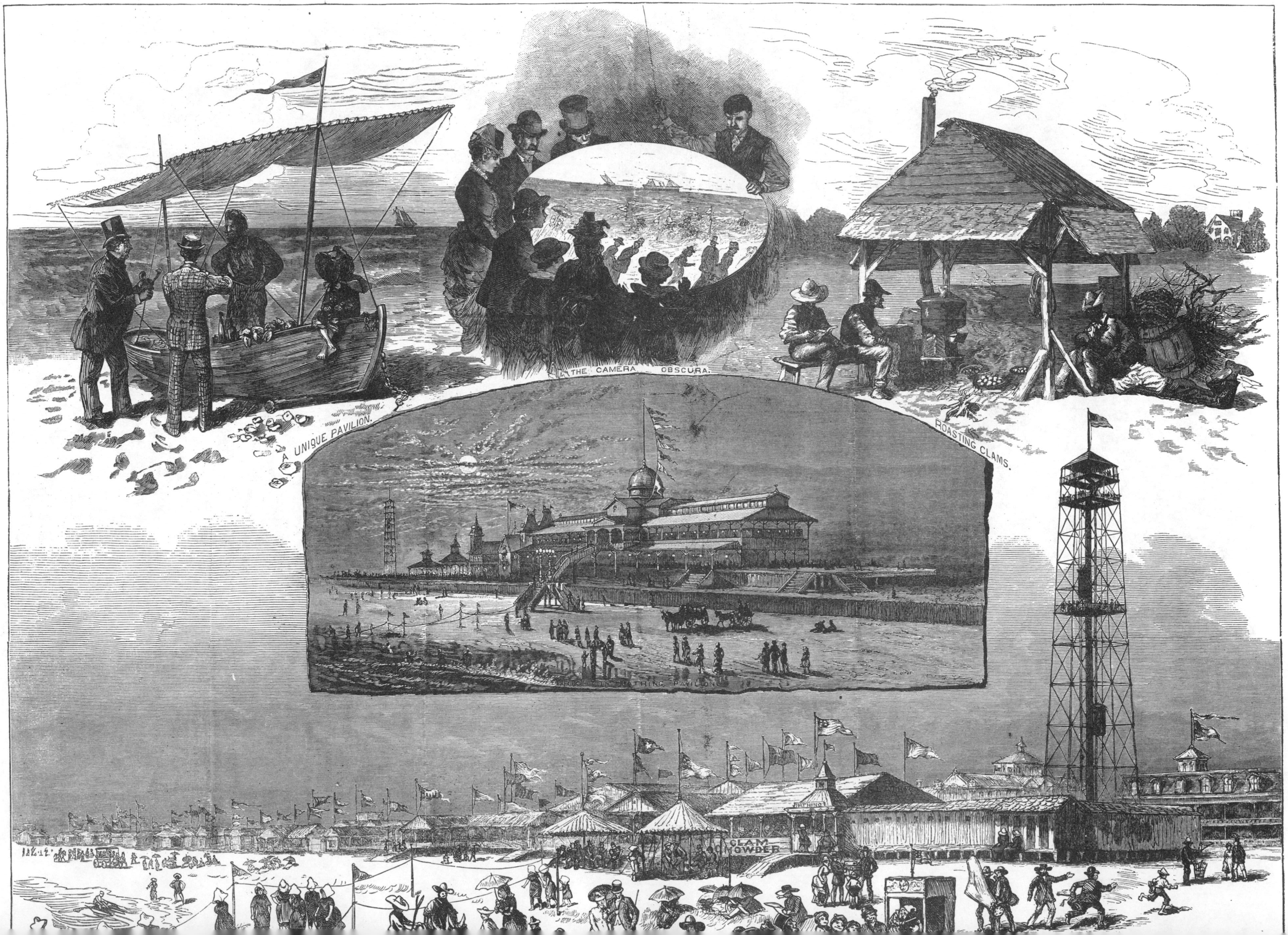
A UNIQUE PAVILION.
THE CAMERA OBSCURA.
ROASTING CLAMS.
CLAM CHOWDER

SCENES AND INCIDENTS ON CONEY ISLAND.—DRAWN BY W. A. ROGERS.—[SEE PAGE 630.]

THE ILLUSTRATED POLICE NEWS
LAW-COURTS AND WEEKLY RECORD

Entered according to Act of Congress in the Year 1880, by the ILLUSTRATED POLICE NEWS PUBLISHING COMPANY, in the Office of the Librarian of Congress at Washington.

VOL. 27—NO. 695 FOR THE WEEK ENDING SATURDAY, FEBRUARY 21, 1880. PRICE TEN CENTS.

1970-1033

HOW INIQUITY PROFITS BY THE TRIUMPHS OF INVENTION—HOUSES OF QUESTIONABLE RESORT PROVIDED WITH TELEPHONE FACILITIES—HOW GIRLS ARE SUMMONED FROM A DISTANCE TO MEET GENTLEMEN CALLERS—A DETECTIVE'S DISCOVERY IN NEW YORK.

THE NEW YORK STOCK EXCHANGE.—Drawn by Graham and Thulstrup.—[See Page 614.]

NEW YORK STOCK EXCHANGE.

WHEN in 1865 the New York Stock Exchange erected its building on Broad and New streets, just out of Wall, the members thought that they had made ample provisions for the future. They had a five-story building, with a frontage on Broad Street of forty-five feet and a depth of eighty-eight feet, with a T on New Street eighty by sixty-eight feet. This building was divided into suitable rooms, the most important being the Board Room, which was fifty-three feet wide and seventy-four feet long. This seemed a large enough room. There were in the Exchange then 400 members, and although the price of a seat in the Exchange was but $3000, it was not expected that in sixteen years the membership would be nearly three times as great. But to-day there are 1100 members of the Stock Exchange, and the price of a seat has risen steadily, until $34,000 has been recently paid. This increase in membership, and consequent increase in resources, led the members to think of increasing their facilities for doing business. The old building was daily proving inadequate. Not only was it not large enough to accommodate the members, but it was not large enough to accommodate the hundreds of telephones, telegraph instruments, and "tickers" that have so multiplied within the last ten years.

It was decided to enlarge their quarters. A building committee, composed of DONALD MACKAY, President of the Stock Exchange, A. M. FERRIS, Vice-President of the Stock Exchange Building Company, HOWARD LAPSLEY, and FRANK STURGIS, took the matter in hand. The committee bought on Broad Street, adjoining the Stock Exchange Building, a lot twenty-four feet wide and eighty-six feet deep, and on New Street they bought a lot sixty-eight by seventy-two. This increased the frontage on Broad Street one-third, and doubled the New Street frontage. Then began the work of adding to the old building, and making of both new and old one symmetrical and convenient whole. It was a work requiring considerable more architectural skill than to build a new building. JAMES RENWICK was the architect to whom the work was given. An inspection of the building as it stands to-day shows just how successful he has been. The old Broad Street front was taken down, the interior changed in many particulars, and now the Exchange has a building that is apparently very complete. Work was begun in June, 1880. To-day the painters are putting the finishing touches on the walls and wood-work of the interior. The Broad Street front is sixty-nine feet in width, and from the sidewalk to the top of the cornice of the fifth story the distance is 101 feet, and to the top of the French roof 120 feet. The front is of marble, elaborately carved in the French Renaissance style. The portico of the first story has eight polished and carved red granite columns flanking the three windows and two doors. The key-stones to the windows and doors are richly carved, with the heads of Fortuna and Plutus in bass-relief, surrounded by foliage, flowers, and fruits. The portico projects four feet from the front, and bears in large letters the words "New York Stock Exchange," cut in the frieze. The central pediment has a very richly carved tympanum. The four stories above the first have each five windows, and in the central tympanum of the fifth story is a carved shield, with the monogram of the Exchange cut upon it. The work on the building has now cost $275,000, and will reach nearer $300,000 when everything is completed.

Entering by the right-hand door, one passes into the Long Room—a department devoted to telegraph desks, messengers' desks, and seats for subscribers. There has been no change made in the Long Room, which is forty feet wide by sixty-nine feet long. Parallel with this, and entered both from the street by the left-hand door and from the Long Room, is a large apartment, thirty-two feet wide and sixty-six feet long, elegantly finished in black walnut, elaborately frescoed, and which will be very carefully furnished, for it is to be the smoking and lounging room of the members of the board, and none but a member will be admitted to its pleasant precincts. The attractions of this room are two huge fire-places of yellow Echaillon marble, carved in the most approved Renaissance style. From flourishing foliage drop coins, and over the head of Fortuna a bear and a bull rampant contend in battle.

Back of these two rooms runs at right angles a long passage to Wall Street. It is twenty-four feet wide here, and gives ample room for scores of telephones that hang in rows along the walls. From this passage many swinging doors open into the great Board Room, the room of the building. There is not such another in this city certainly. It is 140 feet long, fifty-four feet wide, and from the floor to the lofty panel of the iron ceiling is fifty-five feet. Two tiers of windows open upon New Street, and give abundant light. Under these windows run railings, behind which messengers wait in business hours. At each end of the room is another railing, behind which subscribers can congregate, and communicate with the brokers upon the floor. On each side of the huge room rise ten great red granite pilasters, with marble bases and bronze capitals. These pillars are thirty-five feet high, and from the cornice over them the ceiling is groined for twenty feet, as far as the centre panel. The effect is good, for there is the appearance of strength and gracefulness combined. At each end of the room is a gallery, from which visitors can look down upon the conflicts between bulls and bears in the arena below. The President's desk is on the east side of the room. The board prefers to retain the old one, which is massive, and dark with age. The walls and ceiling are painted in the richest and most elaborate style of Renaissance decoration. Blue and gold are the predominating colors, but by no means the only colors; for in painting the arabesques of flowers and foliage, and the fabulous beasts of the Renaissance, all the colors of the rainbow are used, and some not in the ordinary every-day rainbow.

Having paid his $34,000 for a "seat" in the Exchange, the member finds that he has no seat. The floor of the Board Room is destitute of seats, save a few here and there around the walls. There is nothing to impede the course of the members in their struggle with fortune, save a row in the centre of six small iron posts seven feet in height, each bearing the name of some stock which is dealt in. For instance, one post bears on one side the name, "Western Union"; on the other, "Wabash Common." Then at different points on the walls are cards with the names of other stocks upon them. These are guides for the members. If one wishes to deal in Western Union, he sees on entering the room the card, and near he finds the men who are dealing. He hurries up to the group, which may be idly talking at that moment, and shouts the figure that he will give for 100 shares. Instantly there is a commotion. Half a dozen men yell at him the figure that they will take; others join in bids. They shake their fists at each other; they reach after each other's hands; they crowd and push, and yell and vociferate. Such a scene in such a group the artist has depicted in the illustration upon page 613. He gives the action well, but he can not reproduce the noise. But multiply this group by ten, fifteen, or twenty, and then imagine the noise that goes up among the blue and gold and fruits and flowers of that gorgeous ceiling on a "lively day in the street." Visitors lean over from the galleries and wonder at the tumult below. They can not catch a word that is said, nor can they see a reason for the tumult. They see two men who are gesticulating in a throng grasp each other's outstretched fingers, then suddenly subside, step back, mark upon a small pad, tuck the memoranda in their pockets, and then perhaps rush over to another group, and go through similar operations. That simply means that Mr. Bull has sold, say, 200 shares of Wabash Common to Mr. Bear for 48⅜, or whatever the price may be, and that each has made a memorandum of the transaction. At such a time the floor of that big room presents a remarkable sight. Crowded with struggling men, some with blanched faces as they see their fortunes slipping from them, a hoarse tumult of discordant cries goes up with a cloud of dust raised by the shuffling feet. The floor is white with bits of paper—torn memoranda or notes of reference or instruction. Messenger boys, gray-coated and white-capped, dart hither and thither through the throng. Anxious messengers and subscribers hang over the railings endeavoring to catch the eyes of struggling brokers. There is nothing elsewhere like the scene.

Formerly there was another element added to the confusion. A broker being wanted by a subscriber, a messenger walked through the room, calling his name in a tremendous voice. The effect was curious, this monotonous, steadily repeated cry arising amidst the tumult of the brokers. Now this is done away with. In front of each visitors' gallery are series of disks of iron, painted black. They are on hinges, and when they fall on their hinges they disclose under them numbers in white that may be read the length of the room. To each broker is assigned a number; this number corresponds to his name. The disks are worked by electricity, by an operator outside of the room. Say that President MACKAY's number is 10. A messenger wishes to communicate with him. He goes to the operator of the disks and makes known his wishes. The operator touches a button, and in the Board Room a falling disk reveals a big white 10 on a black ground. President MACKAY sees it, and knows that he is wanted at the railing. This simple arrangement will do away with much of the noise of the room.

There is nothing above the Board Room but the roof. It occupies all of the New Street frontage. The remaining stories of the building are in the Broad Street building proper. On the second floor is the Government Room, a fine large apartment, forty by seventy feet, hung with crimson cloth, amphitheatrical in arrangement, furnished with massive leather-cushioned chairs, where government bonds are sold. Besides this, there are the President's and Secretary's rooms. The three other stories are divided each into six committee rooms. The halls and rooms are finished in ash, frescoed finely, and well lighted. In the basement are safe-deposit vaults, rooms for messenger boys, and complete steam and ventilating apparatus.

[Begun in HARPER'S WEEKLY No. 1251, Vol. XXIV.]

CHRISTOWELL.

A Dartmoor Tale.

BY R. D. BLACKMORE,

AUTHOR OF "MARY ANERLEY," "LORNA DOONE," "CRIPPS, THE CARRIER," ETC.

CHAPTER XXXI.—(*Continued.*)

THE SILVER KEY.

ACCORDINGLY, when this faithful person, punctual to her hour on Sunday, had made a pre-eminent dinner, and admired the view of a crowd in the Park (who might be taken thus far off for London trees walking off their woes), and then had refused more Frontignac—a wine that has gone the way of all fashion—because she was determined to consider slowly what Mr. Snacks had said about investment, when she happened to confess that she had put by, in spite of hard times, just a little bit of money; and when she had been persuaded, as a favor to everybody present and especially her host, to relent from that refusal, and touch flower-bells with Mr. Snacks (who was an exceedingly pleasant man), really such a desire to please those who had pleased her so much became established in her kind heart that Mrs. Giblets and Mrs. Snacks, and even Mary—although she was ordered to run away three times, and so lost three half-minutes before she ventured back again—one with another, putting things together, could enter into all the affairs of that interesting house almost as clearly as if they had the privilege of living there.

To put into a few words a story which cost many, the present Earl Delapole, although by nature of haughty and imperious vein, in his later years had fallen deeply under the influence of a man who had made his way upward from post to post. From the position of farm bailiff and rent-collector's deputy upon a small part of the Earl's estates he had risen to be the general agent, steward, manager, and master. There still were times when the rightful lord, who was of a very suspicious mind, would rebel, break out most violently, and order his enemy to quit his sight and his premises forever. At such times Mr. Gaston used to fling out of the house and bang the door; but the next day he was back again, having made himself indispensable: all that violence only tightened the noose, as with a well-set wire. Mrs. Tubbs could not say whether she considered him a rogue or not; perhaps, if he had not been so boisterous and so domineering, she would have thought him deficient in principle; but she had never known a rogue with a voice so loud and a face so red.

The Earl, who was now in his eightieth year, was falling more and more completely into the power of this tyrant. No one ever came to brighten his dullness or divert his mind toward any kind of charity, although he must have a mint of money, in land and houses and leather bags. Mr. Gaston would take good care of that. Only his doctor, Sir John Tickell, who always went about with a trumpet—which perhaps was make-believe, because he hated questions—and his lawyer, Mr. Latimer, though even he seemed to be shut out now, and his shaver (who could not be shut out), these were all that were let in now with any sort of grace about it. If any old gentleman who had carried on highly in the fine old times with his lordship desired to shake him by the hand once more, and to lighten it up for him to hold on, and to say things witty, as they used to be, there was no other message, when his card came in, but that his lordship was in great pain to-day. And so the very best of them dropped off—gentlemen who must have been the foremost of their day in carrying on high wickedness. Mrs. Tubbs liked them, because they were gentlemen, not such soft-mouths as you see now. But although she liked them, and they liked her (as their compliments on her appearance proved), she durst not authorize man or maid to show them up to his lordship's room. And this had grown sadly upon the Earl, quite according to Mr. Gaston's wishes, ever since the grandson died, following that poor lord his father, who had never been much to speak of. However, it was known among the older ones that there was another son somewhere, or at any rate there used to be; but the Earl had refused to have him mentioned, because of some trouble that he had been through. And although he might forgive him now, for the sake of the land and the title, Mrs. Tubbs was sure that Mr. Gaston would give him no chance of repentance.

"That is how things always goes with our great families," said Mr. Snacks, a liberal of the largest order, who liked the world to go up and down—"men who think that nothing less than a coach and four of their own driving is fit to come through their property. Their time is pretty well up on this earth. But the son, if there is one, should be looked up, to make a good title to the company."

Through the caution of the timber merchant, none of those present knew as yet that the missing son could be found on Dartmoor, though some of them began to suspect it.

"But if these troubles go on much longer, what am I to do?" asked the good housekeeper, who felt that she might have unburdened her mind so as to bring worse burden afterward. "I can throw up my situation of course, and goodness knows it is a gloomy one."

"No, ma'am, no," exclaimed Mr. Snacks; "you must not contemplate such a step. For the good of the family, you must not do that. You are so placed that an immensity depends upon your discretion and forbearance. To-morrow is Monday. I will feel my way toward getting you those shares we spoke of. If I succeed, as I fully hope to do, your money will be doubled by Friday morning. My investments are never speculative, but sound as the Bank of England. I will not say a syllable to disturb your mind. Cast off every thought about it. I shall act for you with even more discretion than I should employ about my own affairs. And I think I can promise you another thing. From my intimate acquaintance with the Docks, I shall have the pleasure of telling you next Sunday, if you most kindly renew your visit, the latitude and longitude of Captain Tubbs, and perhaps the very day when he must come home, after making all allowances for wind and weather."

This brought a very nice smile into the eyes of the housekeeping lady, who was not so very old; and if Mr. Gaston could have seen how warmly and gratefully she wished her new friends good-night, perhaps it would have made him grind his teeth, and hesitate about his next proceeding.

CHAPTER XXXII.

UNDER THE ASH-TREE.

THE evening of a ripe summer day was slanting down the western heights, and spreading waves of peace and rest (too soft to be called shadows yet) along the fertile lowland and the villages, where people talk. The striped proceedings of the harvest, and the winding tree-girt woods, and meadows coned with hay uncarted still (because of summer floods), patches also streaked according to the coat they had put on (whether of beans, or rape, or turnips, or the hungry and hungrifying potato, or brown vetches spent in pods), and the green leisure of soft pasture filled with alders by the brook—these and a thousand other beauties, spreading wide content to gaze at, lay in the mellow summer eve below the rampart of rough moor.

Returning from Christowell in time to get her father's supper ready, Rose, with one hand full of woodbine, blue-cap, and dark beads of worts, espied a lovely place to rest in and enjoy the varied view. A bend of the wandering lane lay open where a gate had once kept guard; for time had dispersed the gate, and man and his cattle had done very well without it. Over the moss-browed granite posts, whose heads were antlered like a stag's, a grand old ash-tree, hung with tassels, spread a cool awning; to improve the sight, ferns and foxgloves and puce heath flowers fringed the descent of the steep foreground, while the lowland distance was beginning to acknowledge the cast of these great hills.

Here she sat to think a little of the beauties earth presents, and perhaps (although she was so young) of the many troubles it inflicts. She was capable, as she thought, of putting two and two together; but this capability had not brought the comfort of so rare a gift. Nothing came of meditations, and perhaps the wisest plan would be to stop them altogether.

The sweetness of the hovering light and calm of summer fragrance were enough to

A GAME OF LAWN TENNIS, STATEN ISLAND CLUB GROUNDS.—Drawn by J. W. Alexander.—[See Page 653.]

AMERICAN OPIUM-SMOKERS—INTERIOR OF A NEW YORK OPIUM DEN.—Drawn by J. W. Alexander.—[See Page 682.]

HARPER'S WEEKLY.
JOURNAL OF CIVILIZATION.

Vol. XXV.—No. 1300. FOR THE WEEK ENDING NOVEMBER 19, 1881. TEN CENTS A COPY. $4.00 PER YEAR, IN ADVANCE.

THE GRAND STREET TENEMENT-HOUSE DISASTER.—Drawn by Graham and Thulstrup.—[See Page 775.]

her nose up, for she hated that man, if possible, more than she feared him; and then, with feminine insolence, she took his best umbrella from the stand, and quitted the premises by the little door where poor Mrs. Snacks had been so unwell.

There was no rain yet; but flips of reflected lightning, here, there, and everywhere, shone upon the roadway, or flickered at the corner, or flitted behind some big tree or black house. Mrs. Tubbs went on bravely; of all the works of the Lord she feared man only, finding him to be the only bad one. She said this to herself, to make the best of things—because there were no men about, but plenty of the higher works of Providence—as she hastened toward "Amalgamation Villa," the hospitable abode of Mr. Snacks.

That gentleman was up, and wide-awake, carefully conning share lists—for the weather was never too hot for that—and as soon as he had heard the tale he went for his hat, a writing-case, and a double-barrelled pistol, which he loaded and pocketed without the knowledge of the ladies. "Now, we'll checkmate the red-faced man," he said to Mrs. Tubbs as they set forth together. "No lawyer in the land can draw a better will than I can. Ha! here comes the rain, and in earnest too! Take my arm, madam; I will keep you dry."

The old house was shaken to its deep foundations by the din of rolling thunder, and the long windows glared with the fire of the skies; but the old earl was sitting with the leaded lattice open, cherishing the last breath of above-ground air. The butler of the house, a very timid old dependent, had been sent up by the housekeeper before she hurried forth. He was standing by the curtain now, overcome with want of courage, flinching from the lightning and the tempest roar outside; flinching even worse from that which he must soon look straight at—the growth of death before him—and still, from habit, peering toward the staircase door in fleshly dread of his bugbear, Mr. Gaston.

"Here I am, my lord," said Mr. Snacks, advancing boldly, "grieved to hear how much your lordship has suffered from the recent heat. At last the change has come, and I hope it will benefit your lordship."

"That is no concern of yours. You are here to draw my will. To what firm do you belong?"

"The long-established firm, your lordship, of Snacks, Giblets, Tucker, & Co. I am the senior partner, William Snacks, entirely at your service."

"If you were not respectable," said the earl, with his old keen look revived—for he did not like the style of man—"Tubbs would not have called you in. And if you can draw a valid will, it does not matter who you are. Now put into legal form what I tell you. 'I, Earl Delapole'—describing me aright—'leave all that I have to dispose of to my only surviving son, Lewis Arthur, now Viscount Pole, for his absolute use, and I appoint him my sole executor, if he be surviving. But if he be dead, I leave all the above to his children, if any; and if none, to the right heirs of my lands and titles, appointing in that case as my executor Mr. Thomas Latimer, of the firm of Latimer & Emblin, who have long been my solicitors. For legacies, I leave £1000 to Mrs. Tubbs, my housekeeper; to each of my domestic servants, £50; and to my agent, George Gaston, the pair of felt slippers which he stole from me to come skulking about my door at night.' Be sure you put that in. Tell me when you are ready."

Entering into the spirit of the man—hot and imperious to the last—Snacks, with his writing materials ready, called for a large supply of candles; for the play of lightning round the house and across the open windows dimmed, and sometimes seemed to quench, the pale and feeble light inside. Then, with a good many amplifications and fine sweep of verbiage, in the manner of the most accomplished lawyer—who after slaying his slain three times drags him nine times round the walls—Mr. Snacks discharged his meaning, and comparatively that of the testator also. "There is no time to waste in words; put it anyhow," said the earl, who knew much more of law than his new lawyer. "I have little to dispose of. The land is all secured. The chief thing is about executor. Gaston was that; but he won't be now. I feel better. It has done me good to discharge this bit of business. Snacks, you shall have fifty guineas—though you are no lawyer, any more than I am, and I remember something about you now—when you bring me a receipt for this concern from Latimer & Emblin. They are to keep it dark, you know—not to write to me about it—only to see that it is valid, and give you a private receipt for it. Now let us have the witnesses. Tubbs is no good; Tubbs is a fat legatee—no allusion to your figure, loyal Tubbs. I am not going to die yet; don't you think it. I love the lightning; it has set me free. Be off, all of you, as soon as this is done with. I shall go to sleep exactly as I am. Give the devil legal notice that I don't intend to die."

His lordship was right. After duly executing this last will and testament, he turned over in his chair, and his mind was so relieved that he enjoyed a bowl of ox-tail soup next morning.

[TO BE CONTINUED.]

THE TRANSPLANTATION OF BONE.

The engrafting of flesh is a surgical feat which has been frequently accomplished with success; but the first-known instance of transplanting a piece of bone from one living person to another was announced at a recent meeting of the Royal Society of England. In 1878, a young child was admitted into the Glasgow Infirmary with necrosis, or mortification of the right humerus, or bone of the upper arm. The mortified part was removed from the bone, but even after fifteen months no fresh bone had grown to fill up the gap. This extended to two-thirds of the entire shaft, and it became necessary to try and transplant a piece of alien bone into the place. On three several occasions portions of living bone were transplanted into the child's arm, the pieces being obtained from osseous wedges which had to be excised from the healthy bones of other patients. The pieces were divided into many small fragments before being applied, and in course of time they united together into a solid rod, thereby converting a helpless arm into a useful one. The operation is of great importance as demonstrating that a piece of transplanted bone is capable of living and growing on another system, to the benefit of the latter.

THE TENEMENT-HOUSE CALAMITY.

The sudden collapse of two old tenement-houses in this city a few days ago is a shocking illustration of the ignorance of builders, the inhumanity of some landlords, and the utter imbecility of the department whose business it is to protect the community against the possibility of such calamities.

To most people it would seem that the best thing to have done with a building half a century old, or more, resting on crumbling foundations laid in wet "made ground," and carried up on rotten walls, was to pull it down, and substitute for it a structure that was not likely to tumble into the street one day and bury its living inmates beneath its ruins. But the owners thought differently. Two years ago, instead of levelling it to the ground, or strengthening it as it then stood, they set about to "fix it up." The blundering stupidity with which this was done is almost incredible. The rickety concern could hardly stand as it was. It already staggered, so to speak, under the load it bore, and they undertook to "fix" it by giving it still more to carry. The corner building at the time referred to had a peaked roof, and was three stories high. The builder changed it into a four-story flat-roofed house. It is said that in making the alterations serious mistakes were made. The party-wall between the houses, which was twelve inches thick at the basement and eight inches thick on the upper floor, was strained and overweighted by the insertion of beams and the building of an additional floor, while a partition was taken away to make the bar-room larger, so that the beams of the second floor no longer rested on it, and oscillated whenever an elevated railroad train passed, thus weakening their hold in the walls. These risks were not warranted by the materials used in erecting the house fifty years ago. The wood-work was not first-class, and the bricks were laid in mortar which was as friable as brown sugar. Additional risk was incurred when, in re-arranging the saloon, heavy iron girders were put over the windows in Grand Street and South Fifth Avenue. An eight-inch iron column was placed in front of the entrance to the liquor store, which ran diagonally across the northwest corner of the store. On this column, for several days immediately prior to the accident, the whole weight of the building is said to have rested.

Strange to say, the Building Department, after a careful (?) inspection of the premises, gave the necessary permission to do the blundering work, the inspector declaring in his report that the building was "in a good and safe condition to be altered and enlarged in the manner proposed."

Two months ago the occupants of the house remarked that something was wrong. When trains passed on the elevated railroad, or heavy wagons went along Grand Street or South Fifth Avenue, it vibrated to an extraordinary degree. Furniture got out of place, articles left on tables fell from them, window-casings bulged, and doors could not be closed or opened. Six weeks ago, at night, several persons in the houses were startled by a crack and a jar, and discovered a yawning rent in the party-wall. One of the tenants spoke to his landlord, and insisted that a complaint be made to the proper authorities, and that the buildings should be repaired. The landlord says he complained to the Building Department, but that nothing was done. A second complaint brought an inspector, who examined the buildings, and reported them both unsafe. Why the owners or the authorities did not at once order the tenants out, nobody can tell. But the coroner's jury, if it does its duty, is very likely to ask the question, and to insist upon an answer.

WAIFS AND STRAYS.

The question whether eggs should be sold by number or by weight has been under discussion in Paris. All of the usual arguments in favor of either method have been put forth. Men of mathematical and statistical proclivities have been at work on the problem, and have learned that eggs laid by the more generous fowls, such as Black Spanish, Houdans, and Creve-Cœurs, average seven to a pound, while Hamburgs and some other varieties lay eggs so small that nine or ten are required to tip the pound weight. It has not occurred to any ingenious Frenchman that, in view of the varying thickness of the shells, a more equitable method than either of those under discussion would be to open the eggs, and sell them at so much a quart for solid meats, as oysters are sold.

Henry Johnson, a colored man in Sumter County, South Carolina, procured from a conjurer a charmed bullet, and shot John Davis, with whose wife he was in love. He thought that he was thus protected from punishment, but to his surprise and that of the negro spectators in the court-room, he was found guilty of murder, and sentenced to be hanged. He still expects to escape the gallows, however, and his belief is strengthened by the fact that while his trial was going on two of the jurors were suddenly taken sick, and had to be replaced by others, and that within three hours after he was sentenced, the sheriff, a robust man in the prime of life, dropped dead.

The pen with which President Garfield wrote his last letter to his aged mother is in the possession of White House Steward Crump, who was a faithful attendant at the President's bedside until he was prostrated with malaria.

A man entered the dining-room of a hotel in Deming, New Mexico, rapped a guest over the head with the butt of his revolver to secure attention, and announced that he was "looking for somebody on the shoot." He found a person who answered to that description, and the ruffian was carried out with a bullet in his head.

A "boy preacher" has been tried before a Western Conference on several grave charges, among them swearing, drunkenness, lying, smoking, and "claiming to be a Republican when he was a Democrat." The last-named offense shows that he was not wholly callous as to what others might think of him.

A colored gallant who eloped from Richmond, Virginia, with the daughter of William Brown, will be surprised, perhaps, when he reads the description of his bride by one who should know. In an advertisement offering five dollars for her arrest her father describes the young woman as being "of a dark gingerbread-color, with a bushy head of hair and full eyebrows." Love may be blind, but the injured parent has no doubts as to the accuracy of his vision.

The Baron Haymerle, the Austro-Hungarian Premier, whose death occurred not long ago, died literally of a broken heart. The autopsy disclosed a rent more than an inch long in that organ. European physicians regard the case as one of extraordinary interest.

A wax figure of Guiteau has been placed in Madame Tussaud's "chamber of horrors." This is a fate that even the most vengeful of the writers of postal cards to the assassin had not invoked upon him.

An English newspaper has exclusive information to the effect that an agent has been sent from Ireland to gather potato-bugs in Colorado, to be let loose in the fields of England.

In order to stop a panic in his church, a clergyman in Bradford, Pennsylvania, led off in a hymn at the top of his voice. His singing was so unmusical that the congregation believed that he had become terrified beyond control, and the panic increased in violence.

Mr. Harlan, the mulatto who ran for the Ohio Legislature in a Republican district, and was defeated, visited President Arthur after the election. In the course of his call he remarked that he was "a half-breed, but not in politics."

The French soldiers in Tunis were presented with little plates of metal on which their names were engraved, to be fastened to strings worn around their necks. The soldiers were told that these tags would enable the survivors to identify the bodies of those who should fall in battle. It is not difficult to think of an occasion more cheerful than these presentations must have been.

The will of Gerhart Bechtel, who died some time ago in Berks County, Pennsylvania, contains this provision: "And I further disinherit and prohibit from participation in the distribution of my estate such of my male descendants as persist in wearing mustaches."

It is told of a veteran horse-trader that when he went to sell the carcass of one of his unfortunate purchases to a soap-fat man, he not only felt compelled to speak at length concerning the kind disposition of the animal, but knowingly stated the age of the horse to be some five or six years less than it actually was.

Early in October a prominent newspaper advertising agent whose head-quarters are in Connecticut received a cable dispatch from his correspondent in London asking him to procure a copy of an advertisement that had been sent to a New York paper, to secure its publication as "reading matter" in all the papers of standing published south of Philadelphia, and to charge the expense to his account. The advertisement was an ingeniously worded attempt to "bull" Confederate bonds. The instructions were carried out, and the costs of correspondence by cable and of advertising were not a small item. The gentleman who attended to the advertising in this country knows nothing further about the London scheme; but it is evident that the persons for whom his correspondent was acting must have spent some time collecting Confederate bonds, in order to have held enough of them to warrant the outlay in running the price up to the point at which they could profitably "unload."

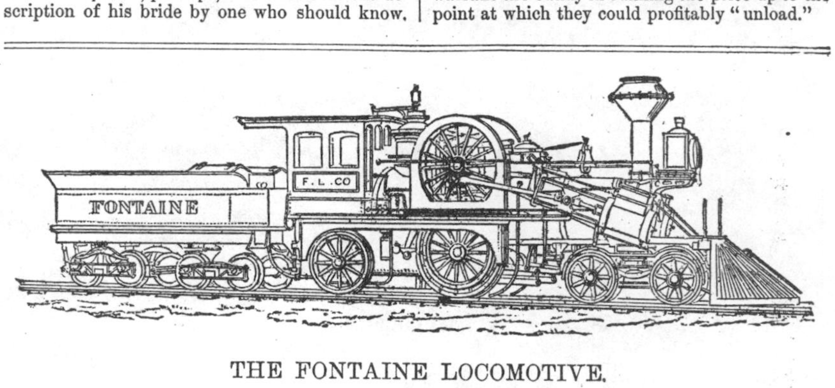

THE FONTAINE LOCOMOTIVE.

This locomotive, a companion to which has been in use for some time on the Canadian Southern Railway, presents some novel features of construction. It has two sets of driving-wheels, one resting upon the other as shown in our illustration. The larger driving-wheels are secured to an elevated axle above the boiler, running in boxes supported by a strongly braced frame. These wheels do not touch the rails, but have a firm frictional contact with the under set. The motion communicated to the upper wheels is transmitted to the lower ones by means of friction only. The lower wheels are constructed with two treads, the periphery resting upon the rails. The other and smaller tread supports the upper wheels, which are of somewhat greater diameter.

The inventors of this locomotive, which was constructed at the Grant Locomotive-Works, at Paterson, New Jersey, claim that it is capable of attaining a speed of ninety miles an hour; but, after trial on the Pennsylvania Railroad, experts declare that the damage to the tracks is greater than the economy in time, and that while upon a perfectly straight road the locomotive might make a splendid performance, it is not adapted to contending with the difficulties presented by heavy grades and sharp curves. An officer of the Pennsylvania road says of it: "Now, for instance, we take an engine of the kind known as 'long-legged loco. No. 10,' hitch on ten cars, and start her off. Away she goes, swinging around curves and climbing mountain-sides, and giving the speed that the builder calculated in his model. I doubt if the Fontaine engine could make any kind of time up a mountain-side with one car, and I should feel considerably alarmed in a swing around a curve behind the new machine. You can rest assured that such a style of engine will never be adopted on this road, and I do not think it will be wanted in the West, for it could not run against the heavy winds they have on roads out there."

THE ELECTRIC LIGHT IN HOUSES—LAYING THE TUBES FOR WIRES IN THE STREETS OF NEW YORK.—DRAWN BY W. P. SNYDER.—[SEE PAGE 394.]

THE BROOKLYN DAILY EAGLE.

VOL. 44.—NO. 143. BROOKLYN, THURSDAY, MAY 24, 1883. THREE CENTS.

UNITED!

Brooklyn and New York by the Great Bridge.

THE MIGHTY STRUCTURE COMPLETED

The Story of its Origin and Erection.

EARLY DISCUSSIONS ABOUT BRIDGING THE RIVER.

The History of the Ferries—Primitive Means of Crossing the Stream—The First Steamboat—Mode of Transit Before the Bridge was Built.

THE WORK OF CONSTRUCTION INAUGURATED.

Preliminary Legislation—The Formation of the New York Bridge Company—How the Money was Raised—Political and Mechanical Obstacles Overcome. The Enterprise Under Control of the Municipal Authorities.

THE BUILDING OF THE BRIDGE.

The Labors of the Engineers—Working on the Foundations Below the River Bed—Fires and Blow Outs—The Towers and Anchorages—How the Cables were Spun—A Detailed Description of the Bridge.

THE PIONEERS OF THE WORK.

The Roeblings and What They Did—Engineer—John A. Roebling's Early Plans for Spanning the River—A Martyr to Duty—Colonel Washington A. Roebling as Chief Engineer—His Services for Fifteen Years—The Assistant Engineers and the Tasks They Accomplished.

THE TRUSTEES AND DIRECTORS.

Citizens and Officials who Took Charge of the Business of the Bridge—The Career of William C. Kingsley—His Relations to the Project—Picturesque Incidents in the Life of Bridge Magician Stranahan—Biographies of the Men Conspicuously Identified with the Management.

THE COST OF THE BRIDGE.

Fifteen Millions Expended Upon It. The Amounts Furnished by the Two Cities—Bridge Bonds. The Rates of Toll.

MEN WHO DIED IN THE HARNESS.

The Long Mortality List—A Score of Lives Lost on the Work—The Breaking of the Strand and the Caisson Disease.

THE RAILWAY SYSTEM.

How the Cars are to be Operated by the Endless Wire Rope.

SUSPENSION BRIDGES OF THE PAST.

A Talk with Colonel Adams—The Celebrated River Spans of Europe and America.

THE FINISHING WORK ON THE BRIDGE.

A Detailed Account of the Greatest Engineering Feat of the Century.

Proudly uprearing its mighty towers, secure in the integrity of its massive cables, spanning with the graceful arch of its splendid superstructure the perilous rush of the swiftly flowing river, the great bridge, which is in the future to weld together the two cities, stands to-day a completed monument to human ingenuity, mechanical genius and engineering skill. Sentinel like it watches at the eastern gateway of the continent, formidable in its gigantic proportions, picturesque in the sweep of its symmetrical trusses, significant in the purpose of its design and erection, the greatest work wrought by the hand of man within the limit of the quickly vanishing century. With its completion are realized the hopes of millions of people, the fruition of fourteen years of faithful and persistent toil, and the fulfillment of the audacious and ingenious plans of its projectors. Its opening to public use marks an enormous stride in the march of American progress, adequately supplies the most pressing wants of the Metropolis and its sister city, and unfolds a prospect for the future dazzling in its brilliant possibilities. An enduring reminder of past endeavor, a finished avenue of popular convenience in the present and a majestic bow of promise for the advancing years, the structure may well be contemplated with pride and satisfaction by the people of New York and Brooklyn. The solution by its success of the suspension bridge problem in its entirety is a companion star in the galaxy of our national achievements to the wonderful utilization of steam and the phenomenal development of electricity. It will forever rank with such stupendous works as the Mount Cenis Tunnel, the Atlantic Cable and the Union Pacific Railway, and taken altogether will surpass anything in the nature of bridge construction likely to be witnessed by men now living.

At this time, when resplendent decorations, stately processions, the booming of cannon, the strains of martial music, the eloquence of fervid oratory and the swelling acclamations of assembled thousands betoken the long anticipated hour of its completion the EAGLE deems it fitting, with the extension of its congratulations, to review the story of this historic undertaking, to tell what the bridge is and how it was built, and to describe the men who conceived and carried out the project. From the date of the earliest discussion of the possibilities of bridging the river down to this time, the advance of the work in its various stages has been carefully and accurately noted in these columns; and it is needless to add that the EAGLE has believed in the project throughout and championed it in the face of assaults of almost every description. A collation of the facts bearing upon the subject could not fail to be of absorbing interest to-day and will prove of value in after years. Such a narrative must entertain all who find pleasure in reverting to the past history of the city. And yet, in following the details of the story it hardly appears surprising when the extraordinary expansion of Brooklyn is remembered. It seems but yesterday that the only mode of crossing the river was by the primitive skiffs, and that woodland and uncultivated meadow stretched closely to the water's edge. Even a Brooklynite of the last century would open his eyes in blank astonishment at the advances made within a score of years, for many citizens still well preserved readily recall the time when the site of the City Hall was environed with corn fields, and the tinkle of the cow bell was heard where now flourish the crowded marts of local trade; when ancient stages rumbled in tedious movement to the scattered Long Island settlements; when the horse car, now trembling before the advent of rapid transit, was an unknown luxury; when hardly a single shanty relieved the bleak desolation of Coney Island beach, and the suggestion of a bridge in mid air across the East River would have been regarded as an impossibility. With the urban circle compactly occupied by enduring structures, and stately edifices lifting their lofty facades on every thoroughfare; with the tide of increasing population overrunning the wonderful figure of 600,000; with rapid transit almost upon us and the suburbs springing into renewed life; with Prospect Park blooming in its sylvan loveliness, and Ridgewood water pouring in crystal abundance into every household; with the Island beaches blossoming in the opening of the Summer's prosperity and the magnificent boulevards and numerous railway lines wooing excursionists to the ocean side the transformation from the early days suggests the employment of the magician's wand and to the oldest inhabitant a revival upon an exaggerated scale of Rip Van Winkle's amazement. Undoubtedly the river span will at once be utilized to a vast extent, but the uses to which it may be put in years to come and the influences which it will exert upon the development of Brooklyn and Long Island, upon the railway and steamship traffic of the country and upon the future of the great Metropolis are hardly recognized in the excitement of the moment. In more ways than have yet been thought of the bridge will prove a boon to the metropolitan population. The seasons of discomfort and peril from ice and Winter storm on the ferries are relegated to the field of unpleasant memory; the dangers of collison are removed; the vexations and delays caused by fog and wind are overcome, and the people are as safe in crossing the turbid waters of the river as they are upon any city street. Beside all this there is the opportunity opened up to the overcrowded population of the Metropolis to secure within easy reach of their places of business occupation the comfortable homes, the educational advantages and the many benefits which Brooklyn offers to all dwellers within its boundaries. In the narrative herewith presented are given an exhaustive sketch of the early days on the East River, and the foundation and conduct of our ferry system from the establishment of the first ferry; a summary of the discussion and agitation which led up to the inauguration of the bridge enterprise, together with the story of the New York Bridge Company and the record of the Board of Trustees; a complete history of the method of con-

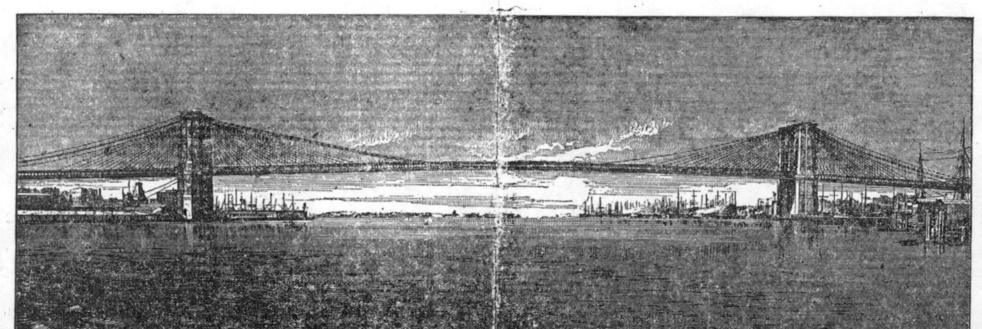

A River View of the Bridge, Looking Towards the Bay.

First Ferry to Long Island, 1686.

Brooklyn Ferry House, 1746.

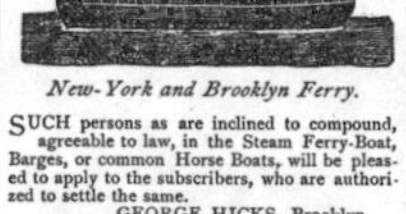

New-York and Brooklyn Ferry.

SUCH persons as are inclined to compound, agreeable to law, in the Steam Ferry-Boat, Barges, or common Horse Boats, will be pleased to apply to the subscribers, who are authorized to settle the same.

GEORGE HICKS, Brooklyn,
JOHN PINTARD, 52 Wall st.

Commutation for a single person not transferable, for 12 months,	$10 00
Do. do. 8 months,	6 67

May 3, 1814 6m.

Steamboat Nassau, 1814.

RECENT EVENTS.

The recent history of the East River ferries is almost too well known to require extended mention here. The inauguration of the bridge project led the management to recognize that the days of the river boats were numbered so far as a monopoly of the traffic was concerned, and they fully appreciate the effect that the great highway will have upon their fortunes. Persons familiar with the ferries of the world freely admit that the service of the Union Ferry Company, the accommodations for passengers and the moderate rates of fare place these ferries upon a plane superior to any similar lines of travel. When one considers the difficulties of navigation on the East River, the dangers arising from fog, ice and the swiftly passing craft that traverse the streams it can easily be realized that the company has been endowed both with singular good fortune and excellent management. Of course, a corporation of such vast importance and ample resources was compelled to encounter persistent and forcible opposition, legislative and otherwise, but the shrewdness of its management and the fact that its conductors are so thoroughly familiar with public questions and so completely identified with the fortunes of the city has enabled them to triumph over antagonism that would prove fatal to a less skillfully conducted enterprise.

The reader cannot fail to notice with interest the pictures herewith presented in these columns, showing the first steamboat operated on the Fulton Ferry and the Fulton, the most recently constructed of the Union Ferry Company's fleet. The representation of the craft

Steamboat Fulton Now Running.

The Bridge as Seen From the Brooklyn Side, Including the Fulton Ferry House.

Continued on Fourth Page.

THE NATIONAL POLICE GAZETTE

THE LEADING ILLUSTRATED SPORTING JOURNAL IN AMERICA.

RICHARD K. FOX, Editor and Proprietor. | Three Months, $1.00 | NEW YORK, SATURDAY, JANUARY 3, 1885. | One Year, $4.00. | VOLUME XLV.—No 380. Price Ten Cents.

JOYS OF TRAVEL ON THE ELEVATED.

HOW PASSENGERS GET MIXED UP, AMID SHRIEKS AND LAUGHTER, TO THE CONSTERNATION OF THE FAIR SEX AND THE ENJOYMENT OF THE MEN.

FRANK LESLIE'S ILLUSTRATED NEWSPAPER

Entered according to Act of Congress, in the year 1885, by Mrs. Frank Leslie, in the Office of the Librarian of Congress at Washington.—Entered at the Post Office, New York, N.Y., as Second-class Matter.

No. 1,551.—Vol. LX.] NEW YORK—FOR THE WEEK ENDING JUNE 13, 1885. [Price, 10 Cents. $4.00 Yearly. 13 Weeks, $1.00.

1. OFFICIAL PRESENTATION OF THE STATUE OF "LIBERTY ENLIGHTENING THE WORLD," PARIS, JULY 4TH, 1884. 2. M. FRÉDÉRIC-AUGUSTE BARTHOLDI. 3. SECTIONAL VIEW OF STATUE, SHOWING IRON CORE AND BRACES.— SEE PAGE 271.

FRANCE-AMERICA.—THE GIFT OF THE FRENCH REPUBLIC TO THE UNITED STATES.

LET THE ADVERTISING AGENTS TAKE CHARGE OF THE BARTHOLDI BUSINESS,
AND THE MONEY WILL BE RAISED WITHOUT DELAY.

The World.

THE WORLD'S
GREAT LIBERTY EDITION
Containing the Names of 20,000 Participants in Yesterday's Celebration.
A Complete History of the Day and Its Events.

VOL. XXVII., NO. 9,201. 16 PAGES. NEW YORK, FRIDAY, OCTOBER 29, 1886. 16 PAGES. PRICE TWO CENTS.

TO LIBERTY!

The Colossal Statue Dedicated With Splendid Ceremonial.

It was a Fitting Tribute to the Sister Republic's Magnificent Gift.

An Army in the March—A Great Fleet on the Water.

Our President Greets the Representatives of France.

And a Million of Our People Gather for the Notable Event.

The Rain Fell, but Patriotism and Ardor Glowed Fervidly.

A Detailed Record of the Day and Its Ceremonies.

Bartholdi Witnesses the Crowning Glory of a Great Career.

"The World's" Share in the Great Work Gracefully Acknowledged.

More than Twenty Thousand Men Take Part in the Parade and About Three Hundred Vessels of All Descriptions Form in Line in the Pageant on the Water—The Scenes on the March to the Battery—Under "The World's" Triumphal Arch—On the Battery—Exercises on Liberty Island—Speeches by M. de Lesseps, W. M. Evarts, Chauncey M. Depew, M. Lefevre and Others—Throngs of Enthusiastic People on the Street—The President's Part in the Ceremonies—What the People Have to Say—Artists on the Statue—Other Incidents of the Day.

Baptized with rain-drops the Bartholdi Statue of "Liberty Enlightening the World" was yesterday dedicated in the presence of a million of people with fitting ceremonies, and all resounding hosannas suitable to an occasion in itself significant from an artistic standpoint, but made doubly interesting by reason of its close combining of two great republics by one common band of union, upon which is blazoned:

Vive
L'Entente Fraternelle
des
Deux Republiques.

The story of the day—how majestic in its simplicity, how comprehensive in its significance. Belting the globe, from point to point the current ran, telling to all the nations of the earth the consummation of a long anticipated incident in the marvellous progress of a new land to her place in the community of nations, wherein, so long as time shall endure she will shine radiant and beneficent in all that is good and strong and lovely. Interesting as the occasion was, it was not so alone by reason of the personal presence of the great artist who designed and completed the statue, Bartholdi, attended as he was by men whose names are known in every civilized land as types of the intellect, the enterprise, the pushing zeal which, combined, create empires and bind them together by political as well as commercial ties; not alone by reason of the personal presence of the Chief Magistrate of the nation, surrounded by officers of the army and the navy high in rank, famed for their deeds—nor by reason alone of the extraordinary assemblage of favored sons, Cabinet Ministers, Senators, Governors, Mayors and dignitaries of varied names—all this was interesting, but by no means the chief feature of the day. That, by common consent, must be conceded to be the wondrous outturning—the unprecedented outpouring of the men, women and children of the metropolis, of the vicinage, of the State, of the nation itself, aggregating so multitudinous an army that no eye could number them, no xpert comprehend them, as massed here, marching there, gathering like a majestic cloud of witnesses, they hung upon the proceedings of the day with unfeigned solicitude and genuine cordial participation.

The arrangements were perfect.

Too great praise cannot be awarded to Gen. Stone and those associated with him for the preparation of a programme so comprehensive, dealing as it did with the moving of a navy on the waters and the marching of an army through the streets. But the sun—had the sun shone with accustomed brilliancy, had New York enjoyed the balmy breath so usual on October days—a miracle would have been enacted, for the lily would have been painted and the gold refined. Dampened as were the streets, chilly as was the air, drizzling as the rain, what more imposing could be imagined, in spite of petty drawbacks, than the colossal gathering which rested its main body on and in the vicinity of Madison Square, extending the entire length of the island to the Battery, cheering, shouting, huzzaing, patiently waiting and enthusiastically enjoying the coming of the parade!

Early in the forenoon, how bright, how grand, the picture at the reviewing stand. Radiating from the President-centre were hundreds of men known in all distinguished lines of occupation. Far as the eye could reach, north, south, east and west stood enthused, excited throngs. The city was one vast cheer. Gayly the bunting defied the rain. The colors of the two republics blended into every conceivable shape, shared each with the other the salute, the recognition, the fraternity of the multitude. The magnificent arch in front of the amply decorated buildings of THE WORLD newspaper was fit exponent of the decorations which garlanded every heart, which danced in every eye, which waved in every hand. The City Hall, the Post-Office, hotels in every section of the city, private residences and clubs vied with each other in an endeavor to give to the physical aspect of the metropolis something analogous to the bright spirit of rejoicing that stirred in every human breast.

There were no accidents.

There was some delay, but when the magnitude of the programme is taken into consideration and the multiplicity of its details is recalled the wonder is that with such clearness, exactness, promptitude and success everything moved from the salutional gun at sunrise to the ceremony of unveiling.

THE ARMY AND THE NAVY.

The two parades!

Which was the finer, which the better, which the more attractive? Who can answer? Resting on the gentle bosom of the Hudson, passing down to the unequalled water approaches of our great city, saluting with sonorous boom, moved an aggregation of shipping in little and in big which the most exalted naval chief might well feel pride in directing. Tiny boats, little sail craft, superb private yachts, huge-tonnaged merchantmen, magnificent steamers and thundering ironclads lay side by side with pleasure craft of every name, and little screaming tugs sent forth their shrill signals, adding their clarion notes to the magnificent diapasons which rolled from the cannons rife around our fort-beleaguered shores. The flags, the dressing of the ships, which encountered every glance of every eye, how bright and beautiful and gay and enlivening they made the scene!

Everything passed along with quiet ease as though the helm itself was in the hand of some sturdy mariner upon whose autocratic will depended every motion of every participant in that greatest of all naval exhibits. And as it was with this unparalleled development upon the bosom of the waters so was it with a characteristic processional development upon the shore. Our foreign guests looked on with unfeigned amazement. Citizen soldiery by the thousands, citizen firemen by the thousands, veterans by the thousands, bands of music in sweet harmony made the spaces echo with melodious and patriotic strains. Gayly caparisoned steeds bore gallant men in attractive uniform. Our crack regiments marched with customary precision, and the free and easy bearing of our firemen, paid or volunteer, attracted the attention it so richly deserved. Well might the President feel proud of his position at the head of a nation, part and parcel of which is this great metropolis, and why should not the Governor smile time and again as the saluting masses passed along, correct in equipment, admirable in bearing, perfect in universal picture?

UP AND DOWN THE CITY.

But again it was not that our distinguished guests from abroad were pleased, not that the Chief Magistrate of the nation nodded approval, not that the Governor's face was wreathed in smiles, that success was assured, but because as this uniformed portion of the city, of the State and of the nation marched proudly by, the smile which illumined the countenances of those upon the reviewing stand acted as a signal which flitted quickly from point to point, starting cheers and shouts and bravos through all the air. With quick intuitions the multitudes, eager to repeat their enjoyable participation in the scene, as if by common impulse ran from place to place. All travel by surface cars and private conveyance was stopped. But the hurrahing crowds cared for no perfunctory service. Pedestrianism was the order of the day, and as the head of the column touched first Madison Square, then the City Hall Park, then THE WORLD Building, and last the Battery, a hundred thousand people massed themselves at the several places, while a continuous and processional panorama of restless and accompanying humanity kept step to the music of the bands and marched the entire distance from start to finish.

How beautiful our bay!

Under sun or cloud its beauty never fades. With capricious mood to-day it glints the sunshine from its rippling waters; to-morrow it reflects the heavy, lowering clouds down in its deeper depths; but it is always commanding, spacious, imposing, safe. It never fails to challenge the admiration of the artist, to stir the heartfelt gratitude of sturdy seamen. Yesterday, however, it bore most favorable comparison with its choicest appearance during any of our recent festal days; then its disclosures were narrowed to two classes of marine endeavor—yachts and pleasure craft; but yesterday, while from neighboring forts, placed here and there, boomed many a time and oft a thundering recognition of the occasion, while there flew in the stiff breeze from every available point the tricolor and the flag of the Union, while pleasure boats and yachts and all manner of minor craft moved, restless, here and there, seeking vantage ground for observation of the central figure of the day, there was added also a grand, suggestive naval architectural display, in which the nations clasped, as it were, hands in a common endeavor to be glad and joyful over a supreme success. Radiating from the island, on which rest the feet of her towards whose fire-illumined crown, in many decades yet to come, will turn the eyes of wistful sailors, were long lines of vessels, biding each its opportunity or taking each its place as a participant in the ceremonies that were to crown the formal installation of the statue.

The Parade Passing Under "The World's" Arch.

THE SCENE ON THE ISLAND.

It was an imposing group that sat or stood on Liberty Island yesterday.

Their names are names of men known not alone in metropolitan circles, in cosmopolitan clubs, but throughout the varied channels of the world's outworking. Their voices are recognized in the halls of legislation. Their presence is familiar in the forum, in the Senate chamber, in courts of law, in the sanctum and in the pulpit. Their opinions are quoted as arguments by other men. The graceful limning of the artist, the ponderous declaiming of the orator, the forceful writing of the journalist, the grave assertions of the preacher, the sagacious predictions of the statesmen emanate at various times, and in sundry places, from the men who sat or stood during the dedicatory services on Liberty Island. And what was the interesting feature there? Surely not the music, nor the signal gun attracting the attention of the universe to what would soon be done, nor the earnest prayer, nor the charming compliments of De Lesseps, nor the eloquent presentation address by Mr. Evarts, nor the unveiling of the statue itself, nor the salvo salute from all the guns in the harbor, nor the short, curt acceptance by the President, nor the charming phrases of Levaivre, nor the versatile talent displayed by Mr. Depew in his commemorative address, but rather in the homely doxology played by the band, sung by the assembly, echoed by the people and carried by the press through all the land, indicative of the universal sentiment expressed 10,000 times 10,000 by more than one million of people in this city yesterday, and by more than fifty millions of people through the borders of this great land, "well done good and faithful servants;" a universal recognition on the part of the people that the design and completion and presentation of this magnificent gift of Bartholdi and his fellow-countrymen, and its solid location by the people of the country, stirred to patriotic endeavor by the example and arguments of THE WORLD newspaper, had found a universal benediction summed up in words taken from sacred writ, "well done good and faithful servants." Sentiment suggested the gift. Sagacity selected the site. Practical generosity erected the statue. And yesterday the people's gratitude accepted the one and indorsed the others.

ASSEMBLING FOR THE PARADE.

A Brilliant Scene on Fifth Avenue when the Great Parade Began.

The busiest scene of the busy day was that presented during the early morning hours, when the great marching column was gathering itself into a concrete whole. There were over 20,000 individual units each to find his particular place in the long line, and when each member of this or that organization had donned his uniform and had set out to his appointed rendezvous, he found the streets already crowded with sightseers tramping to secure points of observation. The whole town was up before the sun, and that did not require any extra activity either, for Mr. Sol was an unaccountable sluggard and sulked behind a veil of clouds throughout the all-important day. By daybreak, or the hour when the day should have broken, the streets had a midday look so far as crowds were concerned, and at a dozen score armories and meeting-places men were reporting for the pleasant duty of doing honor to the occasion. Many eyes were pointed skyward, but the general opinion was that it was not to be a drenching day, and the majority were in the right, even while they carried umbrellas, ready to defy the downpour when it should come.

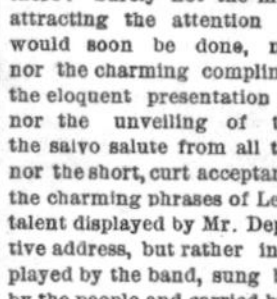

GEN. SCHOFIELD.

The people at large made a descent on Fifth avenue and captured that thoroughfare in most complete fashion. Residents of the fashionable street were perforce obliged to remain indoors, since each stoop and areaway was blocked by a jam of folks who had come to testify their regard for the day and the gift while they gratified their love for the military and band music at the same time. The crowd was a good-natured one. Each was willing to assist a fellow-spectator to a good spot, after he had himself been satisfied, and the police had little difficulty in keeping the long lane open for the passage of the paraders. It was nearly five miles from the starting point to the finishing post in the historic pageant, and every inch of space on either side from whence even the most sidelong glimpse of the moving panorama could be had, had its occupant.

ARRANGING THE PARADE.

To get everybody to his or her place, to fill the front of the house, or the part reserved for spectators and then arrange the *dramatis personæ*, or those who were to take more formal part in making up the show, was the work of the morning hours. The police ushered the populace to its place, the Grand Marshal and his aids saw to it that the parading column was set a-going in proper fashion. The town went band mad, for every organization made it a cardinal point in arranging its programme for the day to secure a band, and so from such superb moving masses of harmony as Gilmore's or Cappa's down to the modest little band set a-going for the day, the listeners along the route had their ears set jingling with all manner of music. The result was at times discordant, but the intention was good, and the general effect of the grandest holiday sort.

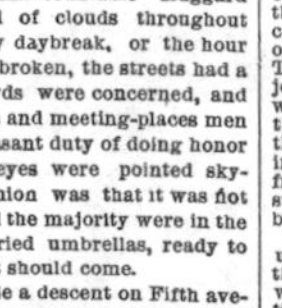

ADMIRAL LUCE.

Each band began its blare of brass and its rub-a-dub of parchment as soon as its uniform was put on, and each marched to its place in the line with its freshest effort in the way of noise. Each had a cohort of followers, and it looked as though the whole city was crowding up against the rampart of police on either side of the Fifth avenue roadway.

The effect during these early hours of the forenoon was somewhat confusing. This way and that way went bodies of marching men seemingly without any order or method, yet out of this chaos was coming the beautiful entity which a short time after came down the avenue in one of the finest street displays which this city of many processions and a long series of historic shows of the sort has ever seen.

At 8.30 nearly a hundred first sergeants were busy in nearly a score of armories rattling over the names of the National Guardsmen and getting in response a rattling shower of "Here" repeated nearly five thousand times. The absentees in the Guard were few and far between. Every man knew that his absence would be noted, that away from the ranks he would not attain an historic importance by having his name appear in THE WORLD'S list of participants. The Seventh and Twenty-second each knew that thrice ten thousand critics would be in waiting to make the old-time comparisons between them, and each command turned out in full strength. Overcoats covered up the pretty uniforms and the men seemed out for more serious duty than that of taking part in a sort of pedal *feu de joie*. The men were out to take the weather as it came, and through rain or shine they were ready to go over the line of march. Not a few of them fell into place after the rendezvous had been reached. The Eleventh Regiment, for instance, had a way peculiarly its own of going to the place assigned it. Each man, starting from home with his wife and neighbors and having safely lodged them in a good position for seeing, sought out his own place for marching. Far up about the Fifth avenue entrance to Central Park Gen. Fitzgerald and his well-mounted staff gathered about them the several commands of the First Brigade. Further up the avenue were the naval and regular army sections of the line. They came without extra flourish, were ready on time and when the signal came from the Grand Marshal for the start there were none more prompt in moving forward than the regulars. About the Windsor Hotel carriages by the hundred were grouped, and the impatient pawing and neighing of nearly a thousand horses made a sort of pandemonium. The drivers held an informal meeting and a very large majority of the members of the Cabbies' Union were present to talk over their affairs. The carriages were for the use of distinguished guests who could not lower their dignity nor soil their shoes by slipping along over the mud-plastered pavement.

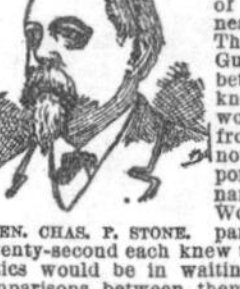

GEN. CHAS. P. STONE.

PHILADELPHIA PEACE-PRESERVERS.

Queer-looking policemen as to uniform, but fine fellows as to physique, crowded West Forty-eighth street. They were the police force of Philadelphia or a section of it, brought on to show the metropolis that the "Finest" is a generic term.

Brooklyn, too, had something to be justly proud of in the way of peace guardians and sent on a sample lot well worthy of marching beside the Philadelphians. West Forty-eighth street shook as with a fair-sized earthquake when the order came to fall in and the big men in helmets started on their long tramp.

The Grand Army men had several streets to dispose themselves in and took them up in small measure with the vets proper, and in large measure with the boy bands, now a part of each post. The little Zouave fifers and drummers were in high feather and rattled through their marching airs in fine style when not watching the acrobatic performances of their drum-major. The boys were thoroughly alive to the spirit of the day and the fact that a special holiday had set them free from school duties made them the merrier still. Their efforts in furnishing marching music were very successful and not a few grandpapas kept step to the fife notes of their grandsons. Here and there in the ranks was a bit of a girl in Zouave uniform and pretty enough to set everybody applauding.

THE STUDENTS' DIVISION.

The educational division was a capital one so long as it was kept in motion. The collage lads looked upon the whole affair as a sort of gigantic cane-rush. They came to the place assigned them with a roar of hurrahs. They shouted their college cry at every street corner. A balcony full of ladies set them off again in shouts of greeting. They saluted everybody and everything and enjoyed the largest sort of a day. Mortar-board hats were worn by many and canes by all. Once started they marched in broad company fronts and won the best word of the Grand Marshal by obeying his injunction to walk in close order fourteen files front. From curb to curb was the delight of the student-soldiers and each carried his cane in a new bit of tactic-fashion.

There were war veterans—those who had been under fire—and other veterans who had come from the National Guard. The latter were close weather-watchers and twinging gout and flashes of rheumatism, coming with the mist, kept the ranks low. Col. Winchester established his headquarters on East Forty-second street, and, wrapping his big martial cloak about him, defied the elements. His Seventh Regiment Veterans mustered in good force but the other uniformed battalions were conspicuously absent.

BRAVE OLD FIREMEN.

The firemen's section of the parade was one of its most successful features. The old Volunteers seemed rather pleased than otherwise that there was something to fight, and tackled the weather which the clerk had sent with an old-time vigor. The hauling and hustling of the machines was no small task, but there were many hands to make light work, and then everybody constituted himself a committee of one to find out why the start was not made on time.

East and west in the several side streets, with the heads of their respective divisions resting on Fifth avenue, the several marshals waited. More than a mile long was the portion of the avenue set apart for the wheeling into line of the various sections of the main column. There was not confusion enough to be worth the mentioning. There were too many old campaigners in every organization to allow anything in the shape of a muddle. When the platoon of mounted police started, everybody was ready to fall in behind the carriages which conveyed the President and members of his Cabinet from the residence of Secretary Whitney down the avenue to the reviewing stand. Banners and bands were the common features which ran from end to end of the enormous line.

The start was capitally made, no more behind time than a reasonable calculation would have allowed for, while the interest in the event and its significance was evidenced in such a column of volunteers on such a day of mud beneath and mist above. Down the avenue the column marched, between two walls of living beings who cheered and applauded every step.

The line of march was down Fifth avenue from Fifty-seventh street to Waverley place, through Waverley place to Broadway, down Broadway to Mail street, through Mail street to Park Row, through Park Row to Broadway, down Broadway to Bowling Green, where the several corps not previously detached were dismissed.

The procession was led by the Seventh Regiment and followed by the Sixty-ninth Regiment, the Eighth Regiment, the Eleventh Regiment, and the Twenty-second Regiment, with Gilmore's band ahead, brought up the rear of the military procession.

The civic parade was led by the Grenadier Rochambeau and was followed by the Societie Israelite, the Garde Lafayette, the Societies of Red Men, the Italian companies, the distinguished visitors in carriages, the visiting policemen, the volunteer fire brigades, accompanied by their drum corps.

A more detailed account of the order of march will be found on another page, with the names of most of the men taking part in the parade by companies and societies.

PAST THE REVIEWING STAND.

President Cleveland, M. Bartholdi and the French Guests Greet the Throng.

There had congregated in Madison Square an immense crowd. Everybody seemed seized with the desire to get as near as possible to the west stand, erected just below the Worth Monument, where the procession was to be reviewed by President Cleveland, the members of his Cabinet, the French guests, Gov. Hill and staff, and the Diplomatic Corps. Directly opposite the reviewing stand was the grand stand, which was literally packed with people, a majority of whom were ladies. The cordon of police was none too strong to restrain the crowd from forcing its way on to the stands, and ladies ineffectually pleaded to be passed on them. There was the usual jostling for place and those who had the pick in position held their advantage despite mist and rain. They patiently waited until 10.30 o'clock, when the Presidential party arrived in carriages. The latter were preceded by the Old Guard, that acted as escort, headed by the United States Marine Band. There was considerable cheering as the carriages halted and the party alighted. The Old Guard formed in two lines opposite the stand and presented arms. The martial form of Gen. M. T. McMahon, the United States Marshal, ushered the party up the short flight of steps leading to the stand. President Cleveland promptly took his position in the little box built out in front that had been reserved for him, after bowing his acknowledgment of the enthusiastic reception he received. William C. Whitney, Secretary of the Navy; Thomas F. Bayard, Secretary of State; L. Q. C. Lamar, Secretary of the Interior; Postmaster-General Vilas and Col. Daniel A. Lamont, the President's private secretary, accompanied him.

M. SPULLER.

NOTABLES WHO ATTENDED.

Grouped around him were Lieut.-Gen. Phil Sheridan and Col. M. V. Sheridan, Col. S. C. Kellogg and Col. Blunt, his aides; Major-Gen. Schofield, commander of the Department of the Atlantic, and staff; Admiral Luce, U. S. N., commanding the North Atlantic squadron, and staff; Gen. Hazen, chief of the United States Signal Service; Gen. Rufus F. Ingalls, Quartermaster-General, U. S. A.; A. A. Adee, Second Assistant Secretary of State; Col. Roger Jones, Assistant Inspector, U. S. A.; Wm. K. Knox, Alexander Lumley, C. Minzesheimer, Gen. Duryee, Lieut. Waring, Second Infantry, U. S. A.; Alfred Bijot, Justices Brown and Benedict, of the United States Supreme Court, Capt. Haskell, U. S. A.; Lieut. Pitcher, U. S. A.; Lieut. Jones, U. S. A.; ex-Mayor Wickham and Senator Amasa J. Parker, of Albany. Gen. Daniel E. Sickles, in the full uniform of a major-general of volunteers and resplendent in gold lace, with his breast covered with decorations, made an imposing appearance and was one of the most striking figures of all the notables. Senator William M. Evarts, President of the American Committee of the Statue, and his confrères, were on hand. Aside from them there were few other prominent New Yorkers, and most of them belong to the French colony.

All of the distinguished French guests occupied the northern end of the stand. There was Count Ferdinand de Lesseps, perhaps the most *distingué* man of the group; M. Bartholdi, Admiral Jaures, M. Spuller, M. Deschamps, Col. Bureaux de Pusy, M. Villegente, M. Hielard, M. Napoleon Ney, M. Cottu, M. Hector de Castro, Baron Salvador, M. Albert Thomegueux, M. Halphen, M. Albert Lefaivre, Gen. Pelissier, M. Desmons, M. Leon Robert, Col. Laussedat, M. Giroud, M. Charles Bigot, M. Leon Meunier, M. Auguste Caubert, M. Georges A. Glaenzer, M. Godchaux, M. d'Orgeval, M. Clapot and M. Rajon. They were accompanied by Charles Colne, Secretary of the Panama Canal Company, and an escort of army officers consisting of Lieuts. Chase, Tassett, Newcombe and Parker.

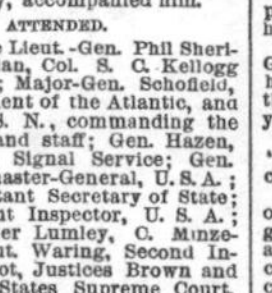

M. DESMONS.

GOV. HILL'S PARTY.

It was noticeable that Gov. Hill's party kept well in the background. Besides the Governor there was Lieut.-Gov. Jones, Secretary of State Frederick Cook, and Gen. Wiley, Gen. Schaeffer, and Col. Judson, of the Governor's staff.

A representation of the Society of the Cincinnati were present by special invitation. They were Judge-Advocate Asa Bird Gardiner, LL. D., Secretary-General; John Schuyler, Treasurer-General; Herman Burgin, Assistant General; Rear-Admiral James W. A. Nicholson, U. S. N., of Massachusetts; Clifford S. Sims, of New Jersey; William Wayne, of Pennsylvania; James M. Varnum, of Rhode Island, and Col. Oswald Tilghman, of Maryland. The latter wore the eagle that Washington sent to Paris in 1783, when the society was organized, and from which one was made for Col. Tenon Tilghman. The Diplomatic Corps was under the escort of Sevellon Brown, Chief Clerk of the State Department at Washington. There were twenty-five or thirty gentlemen in the party. While all the South and Central American States were represented by diplomats of highest rank from the several States accredited to the United States, none of the Ambassadors from European countries were present.

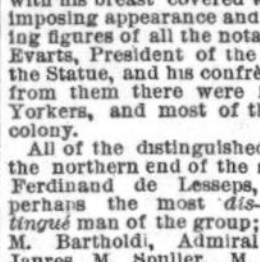

ADMIRAL JAURES.

LEON MEUNIER.

Some of the legations were represented by secretaries or Chargés d'Affaires, but Germany and England had no representatives whatever. The Belgian and Swedish Ministers to the United States sent their regrets to Gen. Stone that they could not participate. Both of the Ministers are in the city, but have just returned to this country from home, and their health is such that they were not permitted by their physicians to brave exposure. Count Sala, the Italian Chargé d'Affaires, and M. Greger, Secretary of the Russian Legation, represented their governments. The other notable members of the Diplomatic Corps were in the order of their rank: Ministers Stephen Preston, of Hayti; Don Matias Romero, of Mexico; H. A. P. Carter, of the Sandwich Islands; Domingo Gana, of Chili; Don Toriellos, of Guatemala; Don Quesada, of the Argentine Republic; Don Miguel Velasco y Velasco, of San Salvador; A. M. Soteldo, of Venezuela; Sig. Flores, of Ecuador, and the Ambassadors of Bolivia and the United States of Colombia. Quite a number of the Ministers were accompanied by their Secretaries of Legation.

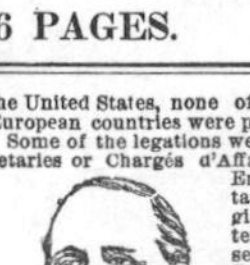

GEN. PELISSIER.

PRESENTED TO THE PRESIDENT.

After all the distinguished party had taken their positions, an informal reception was held, the French visitors being presented to the President, Cabinet officers and members of the army and navy. Gen. McMahon took his stand by the side of the President, and during the progress of the procession he explained the interesting points in the history of different organizations and the special significance of their presence in line. Gen. Stone and several aides to the Grand Marshal remained at the stand to see that the general orders were carried out, and to give others should they become necessary. In nearly every instance the bands played the "Marseillaise" as they came up to the stand, and, after passing, many of them played "Hail, Columbia," or "Columbia, the Gem of the Ocean." The military organizations gave the regulation salute, while the civic societies saluted by dipping their colors.

A color guard of the Old Guard stood on either side of the President's box to respond to these salutes. The precision with which this was done was something extraordinary. Many of the salutes, however, were personally acknowledged by President Cleveland by lifting his hat. Whenever a tattered ensign or battle flag passed he invariably stood with uncovered head.

One of the most interesting incidents was the presentation of flowers to him by three little girls. When the Fred Hecker Post, No. 408, G. A. R., came up, three little girls dressed as daughters of the regiment tripped out from the ranks where they were marching and courtesied to the President. Each bore in her hand a basket of flowers, artistically arranged, which they held upward so that Gen. McMahon could reach them.

"FOR M. BARTHOLDI."

"Thank you," said the President so cordially that the little ones looked inexpressibly happy. But they lingered yet longer, while one little tot, Mamie Fest, an orderly sergeant of the Post, shook out the folds of a handsome silken banner on an ornamental staff. On one side was the Stars and Stripes and on the other the French tri-color. When Gen. McMahon took the staff the little one apparently thought that he mistrusted that all their gifts were for the President, which made her nervously cry out: "That's for M. Bartholdi." So it turned out to be, for the name of him for whom it was intended was artistically embroidered on the French national colors. The inscription read this way:

To M. BARTHOLDI.
In Memory of Liberty-Loving France.
New York, 1886.
Presented by May Fest.

Count De Lesseps gallantly raised his hat to the little donor, and looking as happy as though he had been thus remembered, hastened to M. Bartholdi's side and graciously handed him the very appropriate souvenir of the day, making a pretty little speech as he did so. On the occasion of the Grant obsequies, in August, 1885, these three little girls—Annie Gerber, Lizzie Hafner and May Fest—presented baskets of flowers to the President. He seemed to remember them yesterday, for when one of the Cabinet officers stooped down to examine the floral gifts, the President said:

"The little girls don't forget me. I am very fortunate to be thus remembered with flowers."

MR. EVARTS HAPPY.

Senator Evarts appeared to be in a very happy frame of mind. The fine physique and excellent marching of the Philadelphia policemen evoked great applause and cheers as they came down the avenue.

"You would hardly expect so many policemen from such a quiet city, would you?" queried the Senator of his neighbor, who had lauded the Quaker City contingent.

"Well, they can be spared from their city, I suppose, because all their enterprising citizens are here to-day."

Private Secretary Lamont tried to be funny with Gen. Hazen. While the rain was coming down the hardest the former asked: "What do you think of the prospects of the weather, anyway? Couldn't you do better than this?"

"Now, look here," responded Gen. Hazen, "I've heard that a thousand times, and if I had a chestnut bell I would ring it on you."

It is said that there has never been such a turnout of firemen in years, and the laddies came in for a good share of the cheers. Harry Howard received a perfect ovation as he hobbled along as best he could, with his paralyzed limbs, at the head of his column. Ladies fluttered their handkerchiefs and men cheered at the faithful veteran fireman who made such sacrifices to do his duty and help make the parade worthy the grand object.

THEY WERE NOT INTRODUCED.

Naturally there were some ludicrous incidents, but none more so than the exhibition which two women made of themselves trying to be presented to the President. They got on to the reviewing stand in some manner and elbowed their way through the crowd to the President's box while the procession was passing. Senators and Cabinet officers were pushed aside, but when the persistent females got up to the object of their curiosity their courage failed them. They successively asked Secretaries Bayard and Whitney to introduce them to the Chief Magistrate, but were very properly disappointed. The faithful Lamont eyed them suspiciously, which led several gentlemen, who mistook him for Detective Price of Capt. Williams's force, whom he much resembles, to imagine that something other than curiosity impelled the females to obtrude themselves in the manner they did. But Lamont merely eyed them and looked disgusted, and everybody refrained from reminding them of the havoc they were working and the distress they were causing by letting their umbrellas drip and their feet to roam over other people's bunions.

Secretary Whitney chuckled when he overheard the remark of a reporter that the campaign of 1888 had already opened, apropos to the deferential salutes of the President to colored and Italian organizations. But the President certainly stood up to his task like a man and went through the form of raising his hat and bowing no matter how hard the rain fell. When Gen. Stone informed him that an approaching division was composed of French military and civic organizations the President took off his hat and remained uncovered during most of the time it was passing and for a longer period than on any other occasion of the day. He met his reward in the peculiarly gracious French manner of saluting, by kissing the sword hand.

There was an exciting episode when a steam fire-engine dashed past the stands with clanging bells, followed by a hose company, and later by a water tower. They forced their way through the crowd and raced up Fifth avenue in an opposite direction to the parade. A great contrast was shown by this exhibition to the old methods of protecting the city as the volunteer firemen were then passing, and one company was trundling an old-time machine. In their eager haste to get through the crowd an engine toppled over a truck packed with people. Fortunately no one was seriously hurt, although Mrs. E. Burke, of Cottage street, Jersey City, was badly cut about the head. She was taken into the Hotel Bartholdi, at the corner of Twenty-third street and Broadway, and cared for. There was some alarm when an ambulance followed not far in the wake of the fire-engines, as it was feared that some injuries had resulted from the fire. But this proved to be the transfer of a patient from one hospital to another. There was not much occasion for concern about the fire, although people mistrusted there must have been some large blaze where there was so much smoke, for it rolled up in columns and settled over the square. The man who tends the furnace in the basement of the New York Club, at Twenty-fifth street and Fifth avenue, started up his fire with wet wood, causing a tremendous cloud of smoke to roll up.

GILMORE TO THE FORE.

Pat Gilmore's big band headed the second division of the parade. Just before it reached the reviewing stand it struck up the "Marseillaise," and it was played so admirably that everybody who lives anywhere near New York knew who was giving such a rendition of the patriotic fervor of the national French hymn. The guests from across the sea were very noticeable and they applauded heartily. "Yankee Doodle" was blended with the "Marseillaise" with equally fine effect. But as the band came abreast the President they saluted him with "Hail to the Chief," and Gilmore was rewarded by a personal recognition by the President, who also bowed profoundly and lifted his hat. Quickly the change was made to the "Marseillaise" again after the stand was passed, and the sea of people in front of the Fifth Avenue Hotel re-echoed the cheers of the throng further up the avenue.

When the Seventh Regiment passed, the President saluted them gracefully and audibly expressed his admiration of their fine appearance and marching. He appeared in a very amiable frame of mind, but paid so strict attention to the moving column that one might have mistrusted that he was either trying to pick out somebody in particular or was counting the passing thousands. His hearty welcome of Count de Lesseps and M. Bartholdi was by no means the least interesting feature of the occasion. He invited them, with their associates, to visit Washington, and they assured him that it would give them pleasure to do so. They will go to the National Capital on Monday and pay their respects to the President in person at the White House.

The head of the procession passed the reviewing stand at 10.40 o'clock and it was 1.15 o'clock when the last organization came up. Several times during that two hours and thirty-five minutes the suggestion was made to the President that perhaps he might wish to lunch or go to a neighboring hotel to rest. But he merely shook his head and maintained his position. The entire party remained until the review was over. Then Gen. Schofield stepped up to the front of the platform, and saluting Gen. Stone, who was on horseback, said:

GEN. STONE COMPLIMENTED.

"Gen. Stone, permit me to congratulate you. This is one of the best managed parades I have ever seen. You ought to be proud of the day."

The President started to say something, when he was interrupted, but he nodded his head as if in approval of the compliments of Gen. Schofield.

The Presidential party quickly entered carriages and were driven to the foot of West Twenty-third street, where they went on board the United States steamer Despatch. The French guests were taken on board the United States revenue cutter Grant.

Before the head of the procession reached the square all the street cars were stopped in Broadway, and they formed a continuous string for blocks on each side. The tops of buildings were taken as points of observation by scores of people and the roof of the Hoffman House was a regular gallery. Venturesome youths climbed telegraph poles in the vicinity of the stand, and from their perilous position it looked as though this crop of fruit would ripen too quick and fall to the ground to the imminent danger of any one who stood in the way. And down Broadway the scenes on Fifth avenue were repeated.

UNDER "THE WORLD'S" ARCH.

Cheering the Paper which Aided the Two Nations in their Work.

It was about 12.30 when the head of the column was seen marching across the plaza in front of City Hall, and when it turned into Park row a marked down towards THE WORLD'S triumph arch a cheer went up from the thousands of people congregated about THE WORLD Building. All of the way down from Canal street they had been cheered and the people lined the sidewalk.

The side of the Federal building fronting on Park row had but little decoration, the main display, under the direction of custodians Fryer and Conley, having been made on the side fronting on Mail street; but the scarcity of bunting was made up by human decoration. Every point of vantage was occupied by men, women and children, friends and relatives of the Government officials. On window sills and ledges ladies bravely watched the parade. Looking from THE WORLD'S arch in the direction of the City Hall Park one could see but a mass of humanity extending from the doors and windows of the buildings far out over the curb where the blue-coated policemen stood to mark the line. It was an orderly crowd and stood in the cold wind and rain of an October day waiting with remarkable patience the advent of the monster parade which was given in honor of the emblem of this Government.

This was the same up Park row as far as the eye could see. From the bridge entrance down to where the plaza begins, was but a repetition of the crowd about the arch. It was a good-natured crowd, too, for it waited and made glad the waiting by songs, cheers and play.

Turning round and looking south, toward old St. Paul's, the scene was the same, yet changed. Instead of innumerable black hats and bonnets, with an occasional umbrella, were thousands of faces turned towards the arch waiting for the promised procession and whiling away the time with loud cheers for THE WORLD, Bartholdi and Liberty.

The Astor House, its sombre gray front only relieved by the tri-color which floated from the flag-staff, was like the Federal building as regards crowds. Each window and balcony was filled with men and women.

THE CENTRE OF ATTRACTION.

It did seem as though everybody downtown wanted to get in front of THE WORLD office, appreciating the prominent part that paper had taken in placing the statue on its pedestal. The arch itself was a most imposing structure. It is the largest ever erected in this city, and, as told in THE WORLD of yesterday, spanned the street and was over sixty feet high. It was entirely covered with evergreens and on the summit were placed two globes and a statue, the familiar heading of THE WORLD, on either of which were the words:

"La Belle France" and "The United States."

Underneath and running entirely across the arch, was the following:

"Vive l'Entente Fraternelle des deux Republiques."

On each end waved the tri-colors and the stars and stripes—the red, white and blue, the emblems of the great republics of which it was said a hundred years ago, "it is but an experiment." The front of THE WORLD building was literally covered with flags and bunting, almost hiding the windows, while the counting-room was also decorated with appropriate designs.

In short, every building had its thousands of occupants, every window was crowded, every roof was filled with people desirous of seeing the great parade.

THEIR PATIENCE REWARDED.

First the distant sound of the drum was heard, and the people held their breath; then the faint strains of music, and they grew restless; at last the gay uniforms of Cappa's band were seen turning into Park row, followed by the Seventh Regiment marching in twenty-four file front. Then the crowd could not, would not keep quiet and it broke out into one long, continuous cheer. Hats were waved, and the best efforts of the musicians were drowned in the hearty welcome accorded. Down they come toward the arch, the band playing and the regiment marching in close ranks until the arch was reached, when above the din of the music and the shouts of the enthusiastic crowd was heard the order "Halt!" and they stopped as though they were one man.

"Present arms!" and the thousand guns came from the shoulder like one.

"Carry arms!" "Forward; march!" and without losing a step they were off again, down towards the Battery. All along the lines of spectators handkerchiefs and hats were waved by tireless arms, but the troops moved on regardless outwardly of the honor paid them. Their only salute was given to THE WORLD.

THE GALLANT SIXTY-NINTH.

The approach of the Sixty-ninth Regiment headed by Bayne's Band playing a pot-pourri of Moore's melodies was also greeted with loud cheers. The men were clad in the State regulation uniform, with knapsacks and blankets. They marched well, presenting a solid front as they came under the arch. Notwithstanding the iron-clad rule of the National Guard to keep "eyes front," it was noticed that they could not resist their curiosity of looking up with admiring eyes on the beautiful structure above them. As they passed under and executed the order to carry arms, some one in the crowd called out "Rah! for THE WORLD," and it was taken up all along the line and was generously responded to by all.

Next in order came the Ninth Regiment, Col. Seward, marching to the music of the "Marseillaise" given by Conterno's Band, and they were followed by the Twelfth Regiment, with Dodworth's Band at its head. Then came Eben's Fife and Drum Corps, leading the Seventy-first Regiment, down under the arch.

The scene of the panorama below in the direction of the City Hall was something to be remembered. Across the Park with its mass of packed humanity over to Broadway could be seen rows of glistening bayonets marching down tow[illegible]

THE CAMP OF BUFFALO BILL'S WILD WEST, STATEN ISLAND.

COHEN'S SATURDAY BUDGET

and N Y. WEEKLY PRESS.

VOL. II, NO 10. NEW YORK & BROOKLYN, SATURDAY, MARCH 19, 1887. 3 CENTS

THE GREAT PREACHER.

LIFE AND DEATH OF REV. HENRY WARD BEECHER.

His Early Struggles—Development of His Liberal Views on Religious Matters. The Brooklyn Scandal—General Review of a Most Eventful Career.

Henry Ward Beecher, whose death and funeral services have lately drawn the attention of the country, inherited from his parents, Lyman and Roxana Foote Beecher, the two greatest blessings of an earthly nature—a perfectly sound body and a cheerful disposition. It was remarked from the start that in body, mind and disposition he was almost a perfect blending of both parents, while his nine brothers and sisters—for it was truly a patriarchal

MR. AND MRS. BEECHER.

family—partook more of the father's or the mother's nature. The family was thoroughly American. In 1638 a yeoman named Andrew Ward and a widow, Hannah Beecher, came to New Haven in the same vessel from England; from the latter Roxana Foote, from the former Lyman Beecher, descended, and these two united in marriage Sept. 19, 1799, locating first at East Hampton, L. I., and afterward crossing to Litchfield, Conn. Henry Ward was their eighth child.

The family was not only thoroughly American, but also thoroughly Calvinistic—thoroughly New England in blood, faith and manners. It was a family of talent, too. If Henry Ward had died in infancy, the name of Beecher would still have been enrolled forever in American history; if he had been a lawyer or a doctor, his father would have held a still higher rank as the great preacher than he now does as Dr. Lyman Beecher. Noted as he was in his time, he is now known to most young Americans chiefly as the father of the great Brooklyn divine. And eminent as other members of the family are in their separate walks, their eminence is made comparative obscurity, and they are often referred to merely as the brothers or sisters of Henry Ward. To this general statement there is one brilliant exception—the name of Harriet Beecher Stowe will shine among the great ones of earth and she will be honored and loved as long as the English language is read and human hearts beat in sympathy with the oppressed. For it was her pen that roused the heart and conscience of the common people against slavery.

The children of Dr. Beecher were reared in a rather strict, old fashioned way. Festivals for children, fancy toys and story books were unknown in the Connecticut of that day; but they had a severe moral training, and with it much freedom in the open air, in the woods and the fields. Of this experience Mr. Beecher said: "I think I was well brought up, because I was let alone. Except here and there, I hardly came under the parental hand; but I knew where the sweetflag was, where the

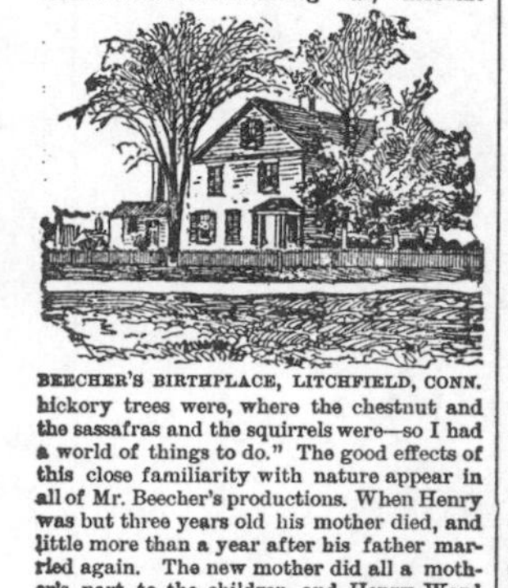

BEECHER'S BIRTHPLACE, LITCHFIELD, CONN.

hickory trees were, where the chestnut and the sassafras and the squirrels were—so I had a world of things to do." The good effects of this close familiarity with nature appear in all of Mr. Beecher's productions. When Henry was but three years old his mother died, and little more than a year after his father married again. The new mother did all a mother's part to the children, and Henry Ward always spoke of her with the utmost reverence; but he confesses that she was a woman to be venerated rather than warmly and tenderly loved, and that her religion was of a strangely severe and solemn kind. He confessed that he could not open his heart to her, and often felt his emotions chilled. The family discipline was somewhat less severe than was usual at that day in New England, but there was strictness enough. Especially were the children trained to habits of truthfulness; duplicity in any form was the one unpardonable offense in a true New England household.

It was while he was attending a mathematical school, which his father had persuaded him would be necessary if he went to sea, as he at one time wished to do, that Henry Ward Beecher professed religion and united with his father's church in Boston. All his thoughts now turned toward the ministry, and as soon as he could prepare therefor he entered Amherst college.

His classmates were not impressed with his scholarship, but in the debating club he soon took high rank. He also became an enthusiast on the subject of phrenology, and was very early distinguished as an ardent speaker against slavery. Here, too, his religious views underwent a peculiar change. Dr. Lyman Beecher was then the great orthodox divine of New England, and Henry Ward has rec-

BEECHER'S FIRST CHURCH, BATAVIA, O.

orded the terrible struggles his own mind went through in revising and finally rejecting some of the harsh features of the old creed. After his graduation in 1834 he followed his father's family to Cincinnati, where Dr. Beecher had become a professor in Lane seminary. He entered at once upon the study of theology in that institution, but as the divergence of views between him and his father became more marked, he fell into another state of deep depression. His older brother had just withdrawn from the ministry on the ground of unbelief in the standards set up, and for a season Henry Ward suffered great darkness and confusion of mind. From this he emerged with an enthusiastic conviction of the truth of the more liberal views he had previously held only tentatively.

The congregation at Lawrenceburg, Ind., of which he was first made pastor, was poor; the lower part of the town was subject to overflows, and there was sickness and want of energy. But Mr. Beecher acted as his own sexton, and by enthusiastic devotion to duty was building up a church when he received a call to Indianapolis. In that city, he says, he dropped the study of theology and began the study of mankind; the effect on his preaching was so marked as to attract wide attention. He became a magnetic and popular preacher. He had married just before leaving Cincinnati, and in Indianapolis he and his wife led very active lives for a little over seven years, when he received his call and made his last change to the Plymouth Congregational church of Brooklyn, with which his name and fame have been identified for nearly forty years. On Sunday, Oct. 10, 1847, he preached his first sermon in Brooklyn, then a city of 60,000 people, with but two Congregational churches and thirty-nine of all other denominations.

His first sermon at Plymouth created a sensation. In it he declared with extreme plainness his position on all the leading national questions—slavery, the Mexican war, temperance and other issues; but as to theology, contented himself with saying that he should strive to make his preaching "a ministry of Christ." He was publicly installed as pastor Nov. 11, 1847, and in the next ten years Plymouth church grew rapidly, grew to be not only one of the great churches of the land, but a great center of liberality. In 1849 Mr. Beecher suffered his first severe illness, which left him enfeebled for a long time, and in 1850 the society sent him to Europe, where he remained three months. His next visit there was in 1863, when he did that great work in England which made him so dear to all Union loving Americans. This is no place to relate that wonderful story. Suffice it to say that American statesmen credit him with having "converted the

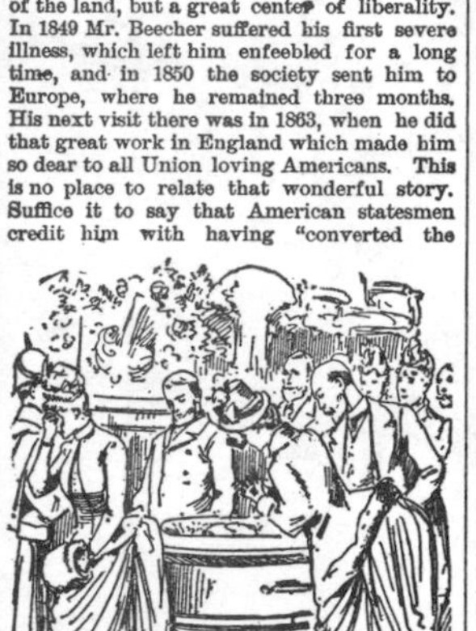

THE BODY LYING IN STATE.

British people to a just view of the American Civil War." Mr. Beecher himself always looked upon this as the most trying experience of his life, though he had been very active and prominent in the anti-slavery agitation preceding the war, and had fought for freedom of speech in the darkest hours. Of one of the gatherings he addressed in England he said: "The uproar would come on and drown my voice—then I would wait and get in five minutes or so. The reporters would get that down. Occasionally I would see things that amused me and laugh outright; the crowd would stop to see what I was laughing at and I would sail in with a sentence or two."

Mr. Beecher returned home to be welcomed as no returning American had ever been, and to remain for nine years the great representative American, the honored patriot, the influential politician and the one pulpit orator whose life was an almost constant ovation.

Then came the great cloud upon his fame, which had lifted, indeed, but was not entirely cleared away even at his death. In this space it can only be touched upon—a large volume would be needed to give the details of the "Great Brooklyn Scandal" of 1872–75. It was emphatically a Brooklyn scandal, not exclusively a Beecher scandal; for its destructive fury made havoc in many circles, sundered lifetime friendships, destroyed the peace of families, bankrupted business men, poisoned schools and churches and wrought a moral desolation which even now we cannot estimate. Take any view we can of it, some people have been cruelly wronged; place the guilt where we may, many people have perpetrated the vilest treachery and some the most unblushing perjury. In fact, the saddening conclusions which logically follow any verdict are so depressing that many good men shrink from them and refuse to make up their minds at all. But in spite of this blot Henry Ward Beecher will live in American history as one of the really great men of his age. We do well to honor him as a patriot, orator and friend of the oppressed, ignoring any personal weakness; his monument is in the hearts of millions, and his career will long remain as a bright chapter in the history of Brooklyn.

FLORAL DECORATIONS.

The steadfast devotion of Mrs. Beecher to her husband and family is well known. She was a teacher before marriage, and was noted for conscientious devotion to duty. It is not too much to say that the funeral of the dead pastor was unique. In accordance with his wish, flowers were everywhere—the very pall was covered with flowers, and no near friend wore mourning. There was a private service at the house Thursday, and on Friday a public service at Plymouth church, where the floral decorations were the most profuse. The body lay in state part of Thursday, all of Friday and part of Saturday. Nearly 100,000 people viewed it.

CHARLES W. FOSTER.

The Versatile Humorist of The Omaha World.

Charles W. Foster, the humorist of The Omaha World, is very generally regarded as a new writer, his paragraphs and dialogues in that paper having sprung into popularity at the moment of their first appearance, but the fact is that he was trained for the work by years of arduous and responsible service in the most trying departments of journalism, his writings showing in every line the broad scope of an "all around newspaper man." He served for fifteen years on Philadelphia papers, beginning as a reporter and ultimately becoming successively the managing editor of three daily publications, The Press, News and Call of that city; and during this long term as a general worker had no opportunity or desire to give his humorous faculties full play. In The News and The Call he conducted "funny columns" which were widely quoted, but managerial responsibilities prevented him from doing himself justice. On The Omaha World he is not thus handicapped, and hence the marked difference in results. He is a devoted student of human nature. Mankind is his hobby. Given a character and an occasion it is easy for him to guess what it would be natural for that character to do. Mr. Foster's humor is thus full of revelations, his little surprises seeming inexhaustible. Born and reared in the anthracite coal and canal regions of Pennsylvania, spending many of his early years in mining towns, he had the double advantage of association with people of the highest refinement and personal acquaintance with characters such as could only be found there. For months he was one of the denizens of a mining district, one-half of whose inhabitants were arrayed against the other, the law abiding portion being drilled and uniformed in regular military organizations and many places being practically under martial law. Following his natural bent, he did his best to probe the cause of dissaffection to the bottom, often taking long tramps through the gang infested forests at night in hopes of adding to his stock of information, the points publicly presented being apparently of little moment. Men were being shadowed, beaten and shot seemingly without motive and a reign of terror had begun, which continued with little interruption for years. From such scenes he was suddenly transferred to an academy in a large city. After a few years he returned to his mountain home at Mauch Chunk, Pa., revisited the mining towns and was then sent to Dio Lewis' gymnastic school near Boston, where outside of the hours of exercise he had nothing to do but study the universal Yankee as he exists in New England. After preparing for college, entering and remaining a few terms he abandoned the classics and spent several years in business pursuits, which took him into adjoining states and threw him among people of every imaginable sort. His journalistic experience in Philadelphia embraced every duty which a newspaper worker can be called on to perform, and led him into all grades of society, from the frequenters of the lowest dives and denizens of the most revolting slums to the visiting wearers of coronets and their cultured American hosts. His reportorial duties fortunately happened to extend over the Centennial year, and, being at the Exposition daily, he acquired a familiarity with national traits and customs only possible to the carefully observing traveler. It will be seen, therefore, that The Omaha World man has not achieved popularity at a bound. He has labored as only journalists can or will labor at his chosen profession, and his bright sallies are but the glintings of sunshiny drollery along the rough but diversified hedges of wide experience.

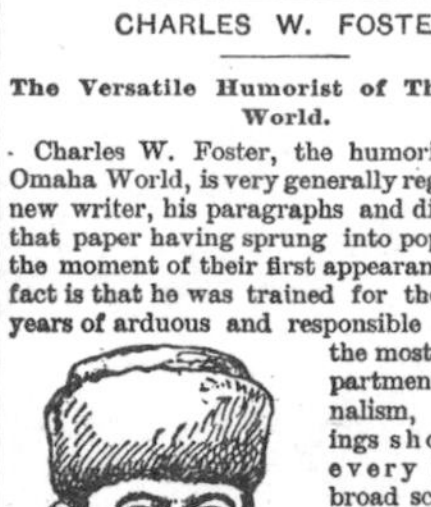

CHARLES W. FOSTER.

"Pet" Names in London.

The use of "pet" names is said to be the cause of much trouble in London. Several ladies of position have been married recently under sobriquets that do not bear the slightest resemblance to their baptismal names. And, more curiously, people attempt to ignore or vary the designations of their ancestors who bore Christian names that are not considered fashionable now.—Chicago Times.

CAPT. J. B. EADS.

A GREAT ENGINEER GONE TO HIS REWARD.

His Passionate Love for Machinery When But a Lad—His Struggles and Successes—Anecdote Showing His Own Personal Bravery and Regard for His Men.

Capt. James B. Eads, whose death at Nassau has been announced, was a great figure in the mechanical and engineering world, and has left many monuments behind him which go to prove it.

He was born in Lawrenceburg, Ind., on May 20, 1820. His love of machinery developed at an extraordinarily early age and when he was 9 years old his attention was attracted to the steam engine. His father's family moved to Louisville, Ky., at that time and the young lad was much interested in the workings of the engine of the boat on which they were, with their household goods, transported thither. James asked a great many questions of the engineer and so thoroughly familiarized himself with the principle of the engine that he believed he could make an engine all by himself. A little more than two years later he had succeeded in finishing a small model which worked by steam very satisfactorily. His father was so well pleased by the lad's success that a small workshop was fitted up for him, and there the future engineer constructed miniature saw mills, fire engines, steamboats and electrical machines. He used to spend much time with the family clock, greatly to the dismay of his mother, no doubt, and when he was 12 he could pull a patent lever watch in pieces, clean and repair it, with all the skill of an experienced jeweler.

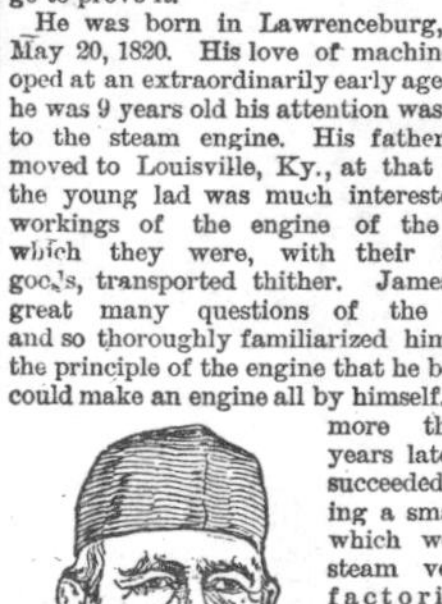

CAPT. EADS.

When he was 13 years of age his father met with financial reverses and the boy was forced to leave school and prepare to win his bread and his way in life by his unaided efforts. That same year (1833) the family went to St. Louis. The steamer in which they traveled burned in the night during the trip, and young Eads landed in St. Louis without coat or shoes on the very spot now covered by the abutments of the great steel bridge which he many years afterward designed and put up.

Selling apples on the streets was the way he took to make a living, for no other occupation presented itself for a long time, and in this way he not only supported himself but contributed considerably to the maintenance of his mother and sisters. After a while he built a diving bell boat for the purpose of recovering the cargoes of sunken steamers, and later a company was formed and soon its business extended over the entire river, from Balize to Galena, and branched out into some of its tributaries.

The following very characteristic anecdote of Capt. Eads is taken from an admirable sketch of his life published about a year ago in The Popular Science Monthly:

"His first undertakings in the peculiar and instructive study of hydraulics occurred while he was constructing the first diving bell boat, not then completed. A barge loaded with about a hundred tons of pig lead was sunk upon the rapids of the Mississippi river, near Keokuk, in fifteen feet of water. A contract was made for the recovery of this lead. He had had no experience whatever with the submarine armor or diving apparatus of any kind; but, engaging a diver from the lakes who was familiar with it, with an armor, an air pump and a sailor skillful in the use of rigging, he started—at that time only 22 years of age—to the scene of the wreck. Obtaining a barge, this was promptly anchored over it and preparations made for the diver to go to work; but the current was found so exceedingly rapid that it was impossible to use the armor with any safety. A belt around the diver's waist was attached by a cord to the bow of the boat to hold him against the current, and a ladder procured on which the diver undertook to descend, but it was impossible for him to control his body in the current. Determined not to be baffled, Mr. Eads immediately visited the town of Keokuk and purchased a forty gallon whisky barrel with which to improvise a diving bell. With several pigs of lead secured around one end of the barrel by a network of ropes, and with that head taken out, a block and tackle attached to the network at the other end and a temporary derrick erected, he was soon prepared to commence the recovery of the cargo. But the diver demurred and would not descend in this dangerous looking apparatus. Mr. Eads then set an example which he has followed throughout all his varied experience as an engineer, which was never to ask a man in his employ to go where he was unwilling to trust his own life. The bell thus suspended was held against the current by a rope which led up to the bow of the barge, and a strap across the lower end of the barrel was used as the seat for the diver in it. He at once got into the diving bell and ordered his men to lower him down. He had a trace chain attached to a lead line, the lower end of the trace chain having a ring in it, and with this he was readily enabled to form a loop, which was placed over one of the pigs of lead, and at a given signal it was hoisted up. A small cord sufficed to draw it back to him while he was still in the bell; and in this manner a number of pigs weighing seventy pounds each were recovered before he started to come up—the air pump all the time supplying him with air. But in the mean time, having cleared the space beneath the bell, the guy line moved it farther and farther up stream in compliance with his signals, and instead of the line being slacked out again when his men commenced raising the bell, it was held so far forward that the derrick capsized, having no guy to hold it in the opposite direction. His assistants seized the block and tackle and pulled the whisky barrel up to the surface of the water by hand. But it was so weighted with the lead around it that they could not raise it higher. Not knowing what was the matter, he waited patiently, the air pump running with redoubled velocity, supplying him with plenty of air. He soon saw the fingers of a man under the chime of the barrel, and, recognizing this as an invitation, he seized the man's hand and got out from under the barrel, much to the delight of all on board. The derrick was then secured against any possible catastrophe occurring again, and, after a number of successful trips to the bottom, the diver was content to do the remainder of the work."

Of his Mississippi river improvements, his achievements building gunboats on short notice during the war, the building of the great bridge over the Father of Waters at St. Louis, and his ship railway scheme, which is still undeveloped, besides other great engineering feats, the reading world is already well informed. It is now thought that the ship railway scheme will fall through. He leaves a wife and daughter.

THE CALHOUN MONUMENT.

It Will Be Unveiled at Charleston on the 26th of April.

The 26th of April next will be a day of importance in Charleston, S. C., for on that date will there be unveiled the monument to John C. Calhoun that has been made by Mr. Albert E. Harmisch.

Calhoun was a great figure in the history of South Carolina, and, indeed, his name is written in large characters upon the pages of the annals of the nation. The movement to erect the monument was set on foot in 1854, when eleven ladies met, formed an association for the purpose of raising funds and set to work. By the end of the year $8,000 had been raised, and canvassers were sent out to augment this sum. By 1860 it had been increased to $20,000, and the money came from rich and poor alike. Then came the war, and of course there was a cessation of efforts in behalf of the fund. But it was not lost in the general wreck of fortunes which accompanied the struggle, and this happy re-

THE CALHOUN STATUE.

sult was due to the intelligent zeal of Mrs. M. A. Snowden, treasurer of the association, and in 1880 the market value of the securities in which the money had been invested was $54,194.77. Four years before this time the actual work of building the monument was resolved upon. Thirteen gentlemen of Charleston were made a commiteee, with Maj. Henry E. Young chairman, and the contract was made with Mr. Harnisch to execute the statue and design the pedestal for $44,000. The contract called for a bronze statue of Calhoun, to be placed on a pedestal of Carolina granite, and four allegorical figures of Truth, Justice, Constitution and History. The figure of Calhoun is fourteen feet high, and represents him addressing the senate. Hon. L. Q. C. Lamar will make the dedicatory address. The monument is placed in Marion square, opposite the South Carolina military academy, on Calhoun street.

MR. ALFRED SULLY.

Sketch of a Railroad Man Who Has Suddenly Become Prominent.

Mr. Alfred Sully has not been especially prominent before the American public until lately. But his reported deal with Mr. Robert Garrett for a controlling interest in the Baltimore and Ohio railroad—that magnificent heritage of the Garrett family—has brought him into the people's view, and his every action and his every characteristic is likely to be scrutinized with the closest attention for some time to come. Alfred Sully was born in Ottawa, Canada, May 2, 1841. It was not until he was 30 years of age that he went into railway service. He was educated for the law and was duly admitted. In 1871 he became counsel for the Davenport and St. Paul Railroad company, but occupied this post but one year. From 1877 to 1880 he was counsel for the New York and Manhattan Beach Railroad company, and held a position on the directorate of this road from 1877 to 1883. From 1879 to 1888 he was secretary and member of the executive committee of the Indiana, Bloomington and Western Railroad company, and was later made vice president of the same company. He has also at various times been connected with the financial and executive departments of the Long Island City and Flushing Railroad company, the Ohio and Southern Railroad company, the Central Iowa, the New York, Susquehanna and Western, and other lines. Mr. Sully has a keen, shrewd, strongly marked face and keen eyes.

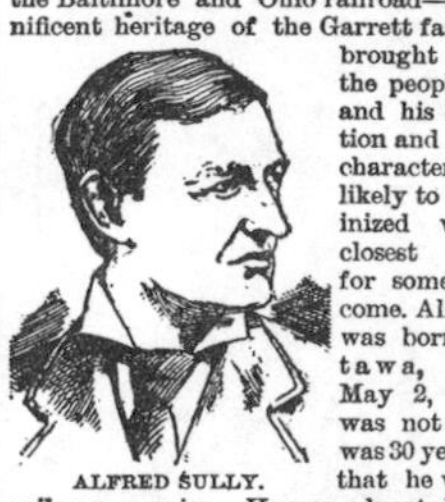

ALFRED SULLY.

Cable dispatches from Vienna announce a most decided success of "Bellman," the latest comic opera by Suppe, the brilliant composer of "Boccaccio" and "Fatinitza," which was performed for the first time at the Theater an der Wien on Saturday last. Mr. Conried has acquired the right of production for this country, and will add it to his repertory of comic operas, which he will produce during the coming summer and next season.

THE METROPOLITAN MUSEUM.

How the Sunday Opening Plan is Progressing.

When the question of opening the New York museums to the public on Sundays was first proposed it had many less adherents than it has now. At that time—several years ago—even those citizens inclined to liberalism felt very delicate about handling the Sunday question. It was an untried and seemingly dangerous experiment, a complete change from old customs, opposed to old laws and old sentiments. Since then, however, the public has either grown a long way toward the Sunday opening or it has grown nearer to them. Perhaps its progress was helped along by the success which met the introduction of music into Central park on Sundays. This is now an established Sunday amusement, and a decorous one withal. "Sunday," say those who favor Sunday opening, "is the laboring man's day. Art and music are educators; not only educators, but apostles and makers of proselytes. There is no way during the week when these two, man and art, can reach one another. Yet they should and must come together." On the other hand it is held that the proposed innovation will tend to greatly increase the desecration of the Sabbath, which the opponents of the plan hold is already too general in New York.

The Metropolitan Museum is almost free—that is, an admission fee of twenty-five cents is charged on Mondays and Tuesdays, while the four following days no charge is made. It is situated in one of the most beautiful parts of Central park, almost directly opposite the Obelisk, that Egyptian monolith that cost one of the Vanderbilts $100,000 to bring to this country. The Museum building is of red brick, with white marble trimmings. It does not present at all a handsome appearance, the style of architecture being unimpressive, and the marble trimmings are stained with the lapse of years. The building, however, is not yet finished, as a new wing is to be added on the side shown in the picture. The basement floor contains a collection of laces, tapestries, etc., calculated to attract and hold the admiring eyes of lady visitors. There is also on this floor a most interesting exhibition of Mexican and Indian art. On the first floor the statuary finds room. Handsome cases, containing collections of rare old glass and silver ware, are ranged around the room, and at one end are a number of Indian tombs and idols. The actors' monument to Edgar Allan Poe is at the main entrance to the floor.

METROPOLITAN MUSEUM OF ART.

Above are the galleries of paintings, the east devoted to the old masters and the west to the modern school. Between these two are long cases of rare pipes, snuff boxes, cutlery, porcelain ware, etc.

And the people who go there are as varied as the objects to be found therein.

There is the bright, bustling school girl, striving to crowd a whole day's work into half an hour. The open eyed, smudge faced street gamin, with his ever ready criticism. The young person whose education has been neglected and who finds this an awful bore. The cultured young lady, who has been there time and again, who always gushes over the same "Madonna and Child." The professional artist, with his quiet appreciation or condemnatory expression of countenance. The old connoisseur, the park policeman, the nursemaid, the baby, the unemployed young man and the retired old one, all flock here on the free days. For be it known, the pay days are favored by my lady in her carriage, who disburses twenty-five cents on Mondays and Tuesdays for what she could view gratis on other days. Some things are rushed by, some are dwelt before for an hour. In some is found a reminiscence of the country lane, or the stretch of sea shore of childhood's days. Here, in a pictured face, may be the counterfeit presentment of living countenance, there the perfect expression of something we have dreamt or thought. The old Bibles, too, with their gaudily colored and impossibly formed prophets and good men, are often and curiously viewed.

The museum has increased greatly in size and interest since it found its present abiding place in Central park. Formerly it occupied quarters in a musty old brown stone building on Fourteenth street, now the home of a furniture store and a lager beer saloon. Probably the saloon has more customers in a day than the museum had visitors in a week. But private philanthropy took the struggling infant to its arms. Foreign consuls, world travelers, æsthetically inclined merchants and dilettante bankers, who fonnd recreation and pride in scouring the earth for artistic treasures, generously dumped these treasures into the vacant cases and corners of the Metropolitan. Some of the collections are merely loaned, while others have been gifts and bequests outright. All is not good that is contained within its walls. From grave to gay, from grand to mediocre, its contents range.

Many of the directors of the museum are averse to opening it on Sundays, while the board of aldermen has issued a resolution in its favor. No matter how the question is decided the institution, while not equaling the Corcoran Art gallery and one or two other collections in some particular department, is without doubt the best in our part of the world.

Sharing the Profits.

The plan of sharing profits among the employes of productive establishments is receiving more and more attention from employers of labor, and the announcements of the intention to carry on business upon this basis are constantly increasing in number. If the system grows in popularity at its present rate of increase in two or three years more it will perhaps be found to have supplied a solution to some of the most vexatious of labor problems.—Boston Herald.

FRANK LESLIE'S ILLUSTRATED NEWSPAPER

·BLIZZARD·

Entered according to Act of Congress, in the year 1888, by Mrs. Frank Leslie, in the Office of the Librarian of Congress at Washington.—Entered at the Post Office, New York, N. Y., as Second-class Matter.

No. 1,697.—Vol. LXVI.] NEW YORK—FOR THE WEEK ENDING MARCH 24, 1888. [Price, 10 Cents. $4.00 Yearly. 13 Weeks, $1.00.

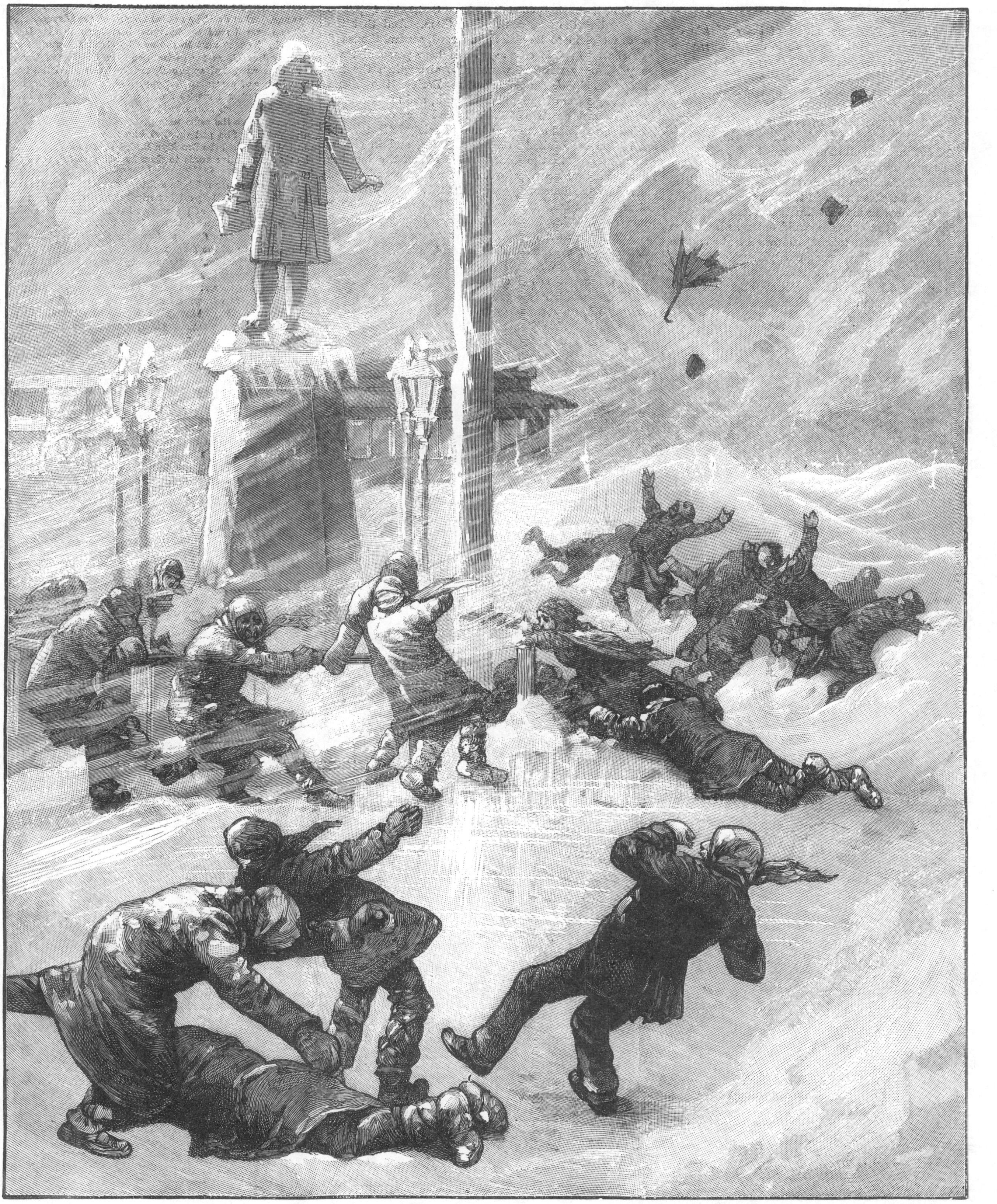

THE GREAT STORM OF MARCH 12th-13th.—SCENE IN PRINTING-HOUSE SQUARE, NEW YORK CITY, SHOWING THE TERRIBLE FORCE OF THE BLIZZARD.

From a Sketch by a Staff Artist.—See Page 85.

BROADWAY, AT THE HEIGHT OF THE BLIZZARD—IMPROVISED HEADDRESSES OF PEDESTRIANS.

CROSSING EAST RIVER ON THE ICE.—DANGERS OF THE BREAK-UP.

THE COAL FAMINE—HAULING COAL IN BROOKLYN BY MEANS OF BOATS.

FINDING THE BODY OF GEORGE D. BAREMORE IN A SNOWDRIFT ON SEVENTH AVENUE.

BROKEN TELEGRAPH-POLES IN WEST ELEVENTH STREET.

MELTING SNOW.

CRAWLING OVER THE HARLEM BRIDGE.

THE SOLE SURVIVOR OF THE SCHOONER-WRECK, OFF BRANFORD BEACON.

SUBURBAN TRAINS SNOWBOUND.

SCENE IN A FERRY-HOUSE.

SCENES AND INCIDENTS OF THE GREAT STORM OF MARCH 12TH–13TH IN AND AROUND NEW YORK CITY.

FROM SKETCHES BY STAFF ARTISTS.— SEE PAGE 85.

The Sun.

VOL. LV.—NO. 195. NEW YORK, TUESDAY, MARCH 13, 1888. PRICE TWO CENTS.

BLIZZARD WAS KING

The Metropolis Helpless Under Snow.

HARDLY A WHEEL TURNS

Business Knocked Flat as if by a Panic.

PLAYS, TRIALS, FUNERALS, ALL POSTPONED.

Fifty Train Loads of Passengers Stuck on the Main Lines.

WHERE THEY ARE, HEAVEN KNOWS.

A Wonderful Change in Our Ways of Living and Moving Sprung on Us in a Night.

ELECTRIC LIGHTS OUT.

MIGHTY LITTLE NEWS GOT INTO TOWN OR GOT OUT OF IT.

GOING TO LET UP NOW

The Elevated Roads After a Day's Paralysis Get a Half Hold Again on Travel.

It was as if New York had been a burning candle upon which nature had clapped a snuffer, leaving nothing of the city's activity but a struggling ember.

At little after 12 o'clock on Sunday night, or Monday morning, the severe rain that had been pelting down since the moment of the opening of the church doors suddenly changed to a sleet storm that plated the sidewalks with ice. Then began the great storm that is to become for years a household word, a symbol of the worst of weathers and the limit of nature's possibilities under normal conditions.

At a quarter past 6 o'clock, when the extremely modified sunlight forced its way to earth, the scene in the two great cities that the bridge unites was remarkable beyond any winter sight remembered by the people. The streets were blocked with snowdrifts. The car tracks were hid, horse cars were not in the range of possibilities, a wind of wild velocity howled between the rows of houses, the air was burdened with soft, wet, clinging snow, only here and there was a wagon to be seen, only here and there a feebly moving man.

The wind howled, whistled, banged, roared, and moaned as it rushed along. It fell upon the house sides in fearful gusts, it strained great plate glass windows, rocked the frame houses, pressed against doors so that it was almost dangerous to open them. It was a visible, substantial wind, so freighted was it with snow. It came in whirls, it descended in layers, it shot along in great blocks, it rose and fell and corkscrewed and zigzagged and played merry havoc with everything it could swing or batter or bang or carry away.

It was Monday morning, when a day of rest from shopping had depleted the larders in every house, and yet there were no milk carts, no butcher wagons, no basket-laden grocer boys, no bakers' carriers. In great districts no attempt was made to deliver the morning papers. The cities were paralyzed.

Few of the women who work for their living could get to their work places. Never, perhaps, in the history of petticoats was the imbecility of their designer better illustrated. "To get here I had to take my skirts up and clamber through the snowdrifts," said a washwoman who came to the house of the reporter who writes this. She was the only messenger from the world at large that reached that house up to half past 10 o'clock. "With my dress down I could not move half a block." It was so with thousands of women; the thousand few who did not turn back when they had started out. Thus women were seen to cross in front of THE SUN office and at many of the busiest corners up town. But all the women in the streets assembled together would have made a small showing. They are said to be much averse to staying in, but they stayed in as a rule yesterday.

At half past 10 o'clock not a dozen stores on Fulton street, in this city, had opened for business. Men were making wild efforts to clean the walks, only to see each shovelful of snow blown back upon them and piled against the doors again.

"Have the girls come?" an employer asked of his porter.

"Girls!" said the porter. "I have not seen a woman blow through Fulton street since I've been here."

The street was dead. Here and there a truck moved laboriously, but more trucks were stuck in drifts and the horses were being led away from them. The elevated roads were running trains semi-occasionally at this early hour, and mainly over only certain parts of their routes. Only one East River ferry, the Fulton, was making its trips. The Brooklyn elevated was chock-a-block with an engine broken down and a solid line of trains from the ferry to Greene avenue. The big bridge was next to useless. A dense mass of men were packed in the Brooklyn depot, and a shuttle train, run by a dummy, was pecking dainty mouthfuls out of the great multitude, running now and then. The cable whirred along, but it never would have done to hitch cars to it. That would simply have been to have the grips torn out of the car bottoms. The attendants would not allow any man to attempt to walk over the aerial footway.

The Fulton ferryboats picked their way across the turbulent river as blind men grope without their sticks. The water was black and boisterous, the air above it white and roaring. When a boat would hold not another passenger it crawled out into the storm. The Staten Island boats ran in a desperate effort to mind their time table. Nothing was ever known to make any difference to a Staten Island boat except when the Westfield burst her boiler in 1871. The Jersey ferries, at least those that wharf down town, ran as best they could, and they brought unofficial rumors that not a railroad wheel was turning in New Jersey.

You could not see New Jersey from New York; you could not see Brooklyn or even Governor's Island. But the storm was plain to see, to hear, to feel, and to fight.

What a storm! What a day! What a crippling of industry! Policemen who did not hide in doorways plodded along the middle of the streets. In Brooklyn a chimney took fire somewhere up at the head of Broadway, and a hose carriage was seen going to it with four horses at the rate of two miles an hour. At Broadway the firemen must have thought all the horse cars in town were huddled there in a heap, for they were blockaded there.

Nassau street from the *Tribune* building to the southern end of the Vanderbilt building and the Kelly building opposite had become a funnel, a wind-condensing cañon. The gale there swept the flagging clear and took men off their feet so irresistibly that they were seen falling and lying down everywhere, and therewhile the air seemed littered with flying hats and pierced with the yells of the merry idlers who blocked the doorways and looked on at the fun.

Cabmen at the Astor House were demanding five to eight dollars to carry passengers up Broadway below Central Park. Cab horses were breaking down and tiring out, and their drivers were resting them wherever one went. Whoever faced the wind had his breath driven down his throat, his eyes blinded, his ears frozen, and his hands numbed. Whoever went with the gale achieved the velocity of a cutter. As is usual when there is snow in the air, the laboring men and the small boys yelled at the top of their voices. Never was there heard in New York such a chorus of shouts, curses, appeals, idle screams, and peals of laughter.

"How on earth did you get here?" was what each man asked every other man who appeared in the down-town streets.

Every man had a moving tale of hair-breadth escapes, of blockades and breakdowns, of pugilistic set-tos with the gale, of mirings in fabulous drifts, of queer sights, of hampered business and snow-choked plans gone in the storm.

The Stock Exchange could not provide the means for gambling, the banks were without hands to do their work, the Stewart will case in the Surrogate's Court developed nothing but an abandoned court room. THE SUN found its never-hindered energy confronted with a situation wherein reporters could not make their way about, messages by wire would not go or come, and for a time all the news seemed to be of wires down, business suspended, public places gaping tenantless, and only a 'phone wire to Philadelphia and another to Boston in shape for work.

THE EVENING SUN was on deck precisely as if the elements were at rest and a summer calm hallowed the atmosphere. It brought out what it happily called a "Blizzard edition," to find its way to the eager hand of every man on the streets who could read, to be welcomed with exclamations of delight in the clubs and hotels, better yet, to do what no other evening newspaper succeeded in doing—to present fully and compactly, and in its own inimitable style, a complete view of the atmospheric disaster that had befallen every inch of the country that could be heard from. Its account of the fate of the great metropolis left nothing to be desired or provided.

As the hours went on and noon drew nigh the storm lost none of its severity. Dusk came and then darkness, and the wonderful visitation was still in progress. Still the streets were banked high with rifts of snow, still the wind roared and howled and bellowed and flung itself against the city's walls, still the horse cars were cut off from their tracks and the pillared roads were idle, still the wagons were few, the women were obliterated from the outdoor scenes, the pelting snow and sleet blinded men's eyes, the cold wind numbed man and beast, the uproar of wild voices continued.

The streets were littered with blown-down signs, tops of fancy lamps, and all the wreck and débris of projections, ornaments, and movables. Everywhere horse cars were lying on their sides, intrenched in deep snow, lying across the tracks, jammed together and in every conceivable position. The city's surface was like a wreck-strewn battle field.

Locomotion was especially difficult on account of human helplessness. Men were constantly thrown against one another and were continually falling on the sidewalks. A woman attempting to cross Nassau street was obliged to call for help. She said she had lost her strength, and her clothing was so entangled with her limbs that she could not move. Two men helped her to the sidewalk. Up town, well-dressed women begged the drivers of private carriages to let them into the vehicles. Their manifest helplessness often got them the opportunities to ride.

So fierce was the wind that sparrows could not fly against it. They rested in the windows of THE SUN building, and started out against the air to stand still with wings fluttering vainly. If they attempted to fly with the gale they were hustled along like stones thrown with fearful force.

So amazing, so unprecedented was the situation that at 3 o'clock in the afternoon the only vehicles in Printing House square were two abandoned horse cars covered with sleet stuck horseless in the snow. The only human beings to be seen were a fat policeman knee deep in a drift and three boys on the sidewalk.

Clothing, the like of which is seldom seen in town, was brought out. Men appeared in quaint caps, in enormous thigh boots (some looking like theatrical properties), in vast coats of cloth, rubber, canvass, fur, oilskin, sou'westers, Indian moccasins, trousers legs tied at the bottom with twine—everything, anything that could keep out the weather was to be found on the people in the street.

The busiest streets were lifeless, the wires were down at last—not subwayed, but hanging in tatters. The houses were coated with sleet, the general tone of every scene was white, the general motion was whirling, the general sound was roaring.

When dusk came there was no abatement of the fury of the blizzard. It howled more and more loudly, accentuated by the darkness and absence of all distracting sounds. New York had at last experienced at least one day with a Western blizzard. At last weather had been felt the like of which no old inhabitant ventured to say he had ever seen in this neighborhood. The city went into its gas-lighted rooms and its heated houses, and its parlors and beds tired, wet, helpless, and full of amazement.

'Tis an ill blizzard that blows no one good, says the proverb, and in this case the good came to the liverymen. Here is how it worked: A gentleman living near Central Park went to the Fifty-ninth street station of the Third avenue elevated. It was packed, and the people said they had been there two hours. He went home, was thawed and dried, and made ready for another venture. He plodded, between ankle-deep and knee-deep, to the Sixth avenue road. The same conditions there. He turned back and went to a stable. There they would take him to the Post Office for $10. He would not pay so much, for he did not know that at that time there were no carriages in most stables, and men were paying $8 to go down town from Twenty-third street. While this traveller waited he learned that a carriage was to be sent down to the Produce Exchange to bring a broker back. Could he not go in that for $5? No; but he could for $10. He would not pay $10. Would he pay $7? No; not a cent more than $5. Well, he could go for that. He was a lucky man. Others walked or stayed at home.

Men walked to business from the other side of Brooklyn, from Harlem, from Jersey City Heights. Those who chose the main avenues made their way with reasonable ease, but nearly every one had more or less of side street experiences, and these they will narrate for twenty years, or as long as they may live.

AN UNHEARD-OF DAY IN TOWN.

Ways Without End in Which that Storm Flabbergasted Us.

The morning rush down Broadway was a very little one considered as a rush. It was to be called that only because it was the time when there usually is a rush. A thin stream of plodding pedestrians strung along the drift-heaped sidewalks struggled down town, snow covered, ice fringed, breathless, and perspiring under the close wraps that were necessary to shut the fine snow out from necks and wrists. They were mostly young men and boys, who were continuing the journey interrupted by blocked elevated trains or stalled street cars. A few elderly men struggled with them in the restless, eager mood that comes of the fact that promissory notes and little matters of that sort stop not for blizzards.

A few women and girls also faced the storm. They were the weakest and least prepared of any for the contest. Yet many of them laughed gayly as they plunged and slipped along. Others proceeded slowly and painfully, and despite additional pairs of coarse stockings drawn over their shoes and the most careful use of their meagre wraps they were evidently suffering. They attracted attention and excited pity, no doubt, but no one could spare the time and strength to turn this sentiment into practical assistance. So they helped themselves as best they could, and floundered through drifts and across streets knee-deep with floury snow; or with equal effort tried to brace themselves against the wind when they struck a clear spot. The contest was bitter, and they were often driven to doorways to gain breath and strength.

In the roadway the yellow cars were few and far between. The reporter saw but three between Tenth street and the City Hall. None of them was making any progress, though in one case six horses were tugging in vain at the traces. One with four horses was in much the same fix, and the third, with a single team, stood motionless, no effort or strength being left in horses or driver.

The vehicles that were getting along were very few. Cabs, coupés, and carriages were the liveliest, while the big double wagons of the express companies seemed to be making pretty good weather of it. Trucks were far from plenty, but their drivers were, as usual, in good spirits and good tongue. One of them advised the three drivers of the six-horse car team to "swim out when you are over your head." As he disappeared in the snow-clouded air a burst of profanity followed him that ought to have melted the snow which clogged the wheels of the car.

BROADWAY STORES SHUT AND SNOWED UNDER.

The persistency with which these men and women struggled toward the usual scene of their daily labors was usually but poorly rewarded. The business done anywhere was inconsiderable, and in many cases the doors were closed altogether and half hidden in drifted snow. As late as 10 o'clock in the down-town streets and avenues clerks and shop girls stood shivering in doorways and hallways, sheltering themselves as well as they could, and anxiously waiting for the arrival of the holder of the keys. Only about half, as a rule, of the force in all the business houses, banks, and offices was on hand by noon, and this number was not added to during the slow-moving hours of the afternoon up to the time that an early closing was generally determined on to give everybody a chance to try and get home.

In the Equitable Insurance office 93 out of 205 clerks made their appearance, and no officer of higher rank than the assistant cashier was on hand. The offices throughout this and the other big buildings were only half of them opened, and these but half tenanted. Business was practically at a standstill, and one or two elevators were enough in the biggest buildings to take care of all the traffic. Those who had persevered in their efforts to get to business despite the elevated, surface, bridge, and ferry blockades had done so in the hope that things would be cleared up during the day, and the home trip would be easy. As the day wore on and this hope faded away they began to regret their success of the morning, and to wish that they had not left home. The scenes of the morning were the suggestion of yet more trouble to come.

Men who had paid $5 or $10 for a short carriage ride on the way down, or anything from 25 cents to $1 for the privilege of using a ladder to climb down from an elevated train stalled between stations, were quite naturally prone to wonder how much it was going to cost them to get home, as the conditions had grown worse instead of better. The only way they could withdraw their minds from these dreary forebodings was to discuss the peculiar experiences of the city's blizzard day. When snugly ensconced for the time being, it added to their feeling of comfort to relate the incidents they had observed of the details of the hard lot of others. The policemen, the letter carriers, the newsmen, and the milkmen were the principal objects of this kind of attention

WOES OF MILKMEN, NEWSMEN, LETTER CARRIERS.

The milkmen had all succeeded in getting their supplies from the railroad depots before the storm had developed to its full intensity. But in the work of distribution they were caught badly. In many cases it was nearly noon before, with their horses jaded and themselves half frozen, they stopped the service, with most of their customers supplied. With the newsdealers it was much the same. They got their usual stores of papers in due season, but when it came to serving routes the conditions were such that few attempted it. Customers who came after their papers were very welcome to them, but the job of leaving them from door to door was too much for the dealers. They preferred to be "stuck" with whatever unsold papers their luck might determine. The letter carriers made a great struggle to get out the two early deliveries of Sunday stuff, but so many business places were closed, and the work was so difficult, that not much headway was made.

The policemen were scarcely to be seen. The snow was so thick and their storm-coated uniforms looked so much like everybody else's clothes that it took sharp eyes to tell where they were. But they were on hand when anything happened, and that was all the time, for events crowded each other's heels all day long. Falling awnings, signs, and telegraph wires were constantly endangering lives, and not a few narrow escapes were recorded. At 32 Vesey street a section of the iron awning in front of the Metropolitan Hardware Company's store fell under its weight of snow. A postman had just passed under it, and just missed being caught in the wreck. In Courtlandt street, Capt. Slevin stopped a lady who was rushing blindly along. A falling sign that the Captain's quick eye had espied fell just in front of her. It smashed a big plate-glass window.

Spruce and Nassau streets was one of the breeziest corners down town. Park row and Beekman street was an equally exposed place. Men and women alike were unable to retain their feet there. They were blown with wildly fluttering garments and most undignified haste across the street and landed in the opposite gutter every which way. The Western Union corner was in some mysterious manner made equally difficult to travel upon. The wind had swept it clear of snow and on its glare ice surface at times no progress could be made except on all fours. Many a man rounded it in this fashion careless of the fate of the hat or umbrella that had gone in the first gust.

MARKETS IDLE—SCHOOLS CLOSED.

Washington Market's early birds of business men were on hand and ready for customers before the storm had entirely blocked things. But the blockade was around ahead of the buyers, and they were so few that there was really no use for the stand keepers to have opened at all. It is positively stated by some of the marketmen that there was not an average of two customers to each stand in all the people that had visited the place up to noon. By that time nearly every one had given up the expectation of doing any business, and closed up.

The public schools were all opened on time, the resident janitors making this a certainty; but the teachers and scholars reported in such meagre numbers that scarcely one of them remained open for an entire session. The slim attendance and the general disorganization of the day made the exercises necessarily brief and unimportant. Some of the children narrowly escaped getting lost on their way home. No schools were open in the afternoon at all.

"WHAT WAS THE DAY MADE FOR?"

A messenger boy, whose errand set his reluctant face against the full fury of the storm, said sadly to a companion, "I wonder what a day like this is made for, any how." He had just floundered through a drift three feet high on the sidewalk in front of St. Paul's Church. It was one of the most peculiar snow formations in the city. Between it and the iron railing of the church yard a space two feet wide was left comparatively free from snow. There is no better way of showing how completely business and traffic were at a standstill than to say that this space was ample here, where a twenty-foot sidewalk is ordinarily all too narrow. Other big and dangerous drifts were on the Park row side of the Post Office. Two men were actually pulled out of it unable to help themselves. One of them, who is supposed to be Herman Oelke of 1 Cannon street, was so thoroughly overcome by exposure that Hudnut's brandy did not revive him, and he was taken to the Chambers Street Hospital in a comatose condition. On West street the drifts were very deep and the wind that swept over the river was piercing and strong. Women here had frequently to call upon utter strangers for assistance to get along.

BLIZZARD RIGS.

The blizzard rigs of the down-towners were diversified and curious. Oilers in full suits, from sou' westers to rubber boots were seen, and all sorts of moccasins and waterproof foot gear were common. Edward S. Innett, one of the Governors of the New York Athletic Club, was one of the best fixed men about. With perfect protection he had provided for a fair degree of activity in getting about. Over a stout pair of walking shoes he had drawn a pair of bicycle stockings that reached outside his trousers above his knees. Over the stockings were ordinary light rubbers. His overcoat was short and he wore a light silk handkerchief about his neck to keep the snow out. A thin skull cap under a soft felt hat completed his costume and made his comfort secure. Some English tourists were his only rivals as to completeness of preparation for the arctic weather, but the homely, though excellent, device of heavy woollen sock overshoes and trousers bottoms was frequently seen. Porters and others who believed in this, but who were frugal-minded, tied bandages or bagging around their feet. The practice of tying the trousers about the ankles to prevent the fine snow from getting over the tops of gaiters and low shoes was very general. A large proportion of New Yorkers never wear any heavier foot gear than a calfskin shoe or gaiter. These people were in a fine fix yesterday, despite the strings thus brought to their aid. They started out blithely in the morning in the same spirit that the scoffers felt when they told Old Noah that it wasn't going to be much of a shower. They got back, if they got back at all, with frosted toes, wet feet, and a stock of the seeds of pneumonia, rheumatism, and other ills sufficient for an army. The people unprepared for such an experience as yesterday, and yet sufficiently unwise to venture out and toy with the blizzard, were legion, and the doctors and the undertakers will be the beneficiaries. P. C. Benjamin of the Merchants' National Bank of Wall street, who walked down from the Ninth ward and arrived on time, without any elaborate preparations for the experience, is not one of these. He declared to congratulating friends that his feet were not even wet.

MAILS AT A STANDSTILL.

The mail service of the city succumbed to the storm early in the day. The employees came to their posts pretty promptly, but the carriers went out almost empty handed, as the railway mail service was about paralyzed. Superintendent Jackson of the railway mail service said that all his means of obtaining information were cut off. What little mail was brought in by the collectors and from the sub-stations during the morning was despatched from the general office.

At 1 o'clock he telegraphed to all the railway termini for advice as to the possibility of getting the afternoon mails out.

Postmaster Pearson said that the service was about demoralized and that business was nearly at a standstill.

There were forty out-of-town mails due between 4 o'clock yesterday morning and noon. Of these only four arrived—the Washington, Baltimore, and Philadelphia mail over the Pennsylvania Road at 4:05 A. M., came in the office at 6:30. The Boston mail due at 4:10 A. M. over the New York and New England Road was received at 6:30 o'clock. The Chicago mail, due over the New York Central Road at 6:45, reached the office at five minutes before 1 o'clock. The Boston and Springfield express due at 7:05, arrived at 12:40. At the close of the day's business no other mails had been received, and the exact locations of the trains unknown.

YOU COULD TELEGRAPH HARDLY ANYWHERE.

"There is not a single wire working between New York and the South," said Wire Chief Baldwin of the Western Union Telegraph Company in the afternoon. "As early as 9:30 last night we received news to the effect that sixty poles, bearing some of our most important wires, had fallen in Washington. Shortly after that information we lost Baltimore, then we lost Washington, and then Philadelphia. We have but ten wires to Buffalo, and should have fifty, while to Albany we have not quite ten, and they are working very badly. Our only way to reach Chicago is around by the Lake Shore and Western, through Buffalo. Even those wires may be down before Monday.

As far as Harlem and a little beyond where our lines run in aerial cables we are all right, but past the point where the wires separate we have no connection. Never before in the history of telegraphy has New York been cut off from communication with the rest of the world. The European cables, while all right in themselves, are useless on account of the destruction of the shore lines. Why, we have no connection with Newark, and New Jersey is further away than ever. The damage I cannot even approximate. The sleet storm of '81 was the most destructive ever known before this, the damage running into the thousands. We have hundreds of men ready to send out for repairs, but cannot send them now, as they could do no work. As soon as the storm ceases we shall at once begin repairing our lines. The Hudson River lines came out better than all, and we have connection with Poughkeepsie yet. The lines in and around New York will be fixed as soon as possible, the vicinity of the damage making the work of repairing easier. Should the storm abate to-night, we will probably be all right by the end of the week."

TELEPHONE WIRES IN AN AWFUL TANGLE.

The telephone wires, though in short circuits and short stretches, did not escape damage. Even if they had held their own weight of snow and resisted the strength of the wind, the wreck of the other wires would have brought them to grief. There were a great many subscribers who could ring up the central offices, yet it seldom happened that any two of these wanted each other. So the operators spent the day in varying the "Hello! hello!" of every day with an equally monotonous cry of "We can't get them!"

Superintendent Hibbard of the Metropolitan Telephone Company was far from being a cheerful man yesterday. "We are in a bad fix," said he, "but we cannot tell how badly off we are. We cannot tell how much of our trouble is due to our own wires being down, and how much of it is due to other wires being down on ours. In West Eleventh street there are several blocks of poles down. They carried hundred of wires, and many of them are ours. Some of the poles crashed through the house windows, and the wreck was a lively one. At Fulton and Washington streets, Brooklyn, there is another bad mess, and in Mott Haven the breaks and tangles are frightful. We have a strong force of linemen at work. They cannot climb poles or make repairs in such a storm as this, but they can untangle the wires, straighten them out, and roll them up. That will get them out of the way of travel and avoid a great deal or danger."

THE PROBLEM OF GETTING HOME.

By 3 o'clock the generally hopeless character of the outlook had entirely depressed those who had ventured out to do business, but who had been rewarded with very indifferent results. Anxious inquiries as to whether any cars were running on the surface or anywhere had been made all day whenever two persons met, and the answer was uniformly discouraging. So the thoughts of home became stronger with every moment, and the wonder of how it was to be reached became greater. By 4 o'clock all considerations of business had been outweighed by these, and nothing was left open except the saloons, which had been pretty well filled all day, in the absence of any business stir. The absence of the usual crowd down town was a matter of congratulation when the tide set homeward. With not a wheel turning on any of the regular lines of travel, it was well that scarcely five per cent. of the usual crowds were down town. The majority, under the impulse of stern necessity, set themselves sturdily to the task of footing it. Broadway was the most popular track (although the Bowery was better), and a black procession of pedestrians soon marched along its more sheltered western sidewalk. It was laborious work, the wind being dead ahead and laden with cold, fine snow, as well as keener and harder particles blown off the roofs. But many of the bravest walkers of the morning faltered at the thought of the return. It was not alone the difference between a fair wind and a head wind. The lameness and fatigue resulting from the unaccustomed and vigorous work of the down trip was the chief trouble. And so it happened that hundreds of men who are in a position to look lightly on five or twenty dollars when compared to comfort and ease, determined that there should be no more walking in theirs.

FANCY PRICES FOR CABS.

It was then a question between getting hotel accommodations or getting a conveyance. And it was speedily developed that there was not enough of either sort of relief to go round. The hackmen were the first to be found in inadequate supply. Such of them as had braved the storm, and there were many who would not on their own account and on account of their horses, were all too few to take the anxious up towners home. The work was too slow and hard for many trips to be made. The Astor House was the best place to see the demand. All below that were exhausted by 4 o'clock, or engaged at a price that put them beyond temptation, and the improvident men who had rested in the belief that the railroads would be all right by that time, and had not ordered carriages from uptown set their faces toward the Astor House to get cabs there. The down towners had all got $20 for a trip up town. A coupe or a coach either got this price. In one case it was $10 apiece, and in the other it was $5, as four could be carried. A gentleman with a lady at the corner of Courtlandt street and Broadway paid $20 to be taken to Fiftieth street. Detective Phil Reilly waited three hours for a chance to pay $5 to be driven to his home in Bank street. He had walked down, and figured that it would be more economical to ride than to take the risk of walking back. The struggle for carriages was very exciting. The starter and the colored boss porter in the corridor were subjected to all sorts of blandishments by the applicants. It finally got to be necessary for a man to canvass the crowd until he found three others who lived near him. Then, by a compact job, with the customary $5 a head, the Jehu could be tempted. This price was frequently raised to $10 apiece for four by impatient ones who were afraid of getting left. It looked like big money, but it was killing work, and the livery men said they did not feel as though they could afford to work their horses even at these prices.

DOWN-TOWN HOTELS SWAMPED.

The men who determined to stay down town, and thus provide for both the getting home and getting back to business in the morning, were soon in as bad a fix as those who sought transportation. The Astor House was the first point of attack naturally. It began very early to turn away applicants for rooms. At 5 o'clock Manager Keefe said that he had refused 400 who wanted to register. Later on he booked some more as a special favor, and gave them cots and shake downs in the corners of the halls. The Eastern Hotel, the Stevens House, the United States Hotel, Sweeny's, and Everett's were soon swamped. At 6 o'clock not a room could be got in any of them. Extra cots and all sorts of makeshifts were brought into play, and as many as four men in an ordinary single room was a frequent occurrence. The opportunities for racketing and unlimited poker were not to be neglected. The stock of playing cards at the stands in the hotel corridors was soon exhausted in every case, and the absence of sleeping accommodations did not bother many of those who got shelter and a deck.

MACY'S GIRLS SLEEP IN THE STORE.

The saleswomen in Macy's store who live too far from the store to walk home and depended on the cars were invited to stay all night by the proprietors. It was a regalar picnic. The men were all obliged to shift for themselves, and walk or not, as they liked. When they were gotten rid of, mattresses were produced, and everything necessary to make the girls comfortable was provided by the firm. The girls thought it great fun to camp out in that fashion at first, but before morning doubtless many of them wished they were at home.

BUSINESS KNOCKED OUT FLAT.

First Time the Weather Ever Floored the Stock Exchange—Brokers in Carts.

It was startling to see how effectually Wall street and the Exchanges, the Clearing House, the banks, the Sub-Treasury, the Custom House, and the business that centres about them were knocked out. All the great Exchanges were practically closed at noon. The slim attendance on the Stock Exchange made the great Board mournful. Vice-Chairman Henriques was around on time to bang the big ivory hammer that opens the session in the morning, but before him were but twenty-one brokers. There are usually 500. The Wormser brothers, Mr. G. B. Schley, Charley Johnes, and Mr. John Kirkner were in the little band, and Secretary George W. Ely was up stairs in his office thawing out. He and others on the Exchange had ploughed through the snow drifts from their homes up town, some felt flush enough to pay from $15 to $35 for cabs to bring them down, but most of them were carried a block or two by elevated trains and were shot along by the blizzard the rest of the way. Mr. Ely said he knew of two brokers who were brought down half the way in a butcher cart, but at the Morton House the butcher boy driver and his horse gave out, and his passengers did the best they could after that.

Commodore Bateman started out from his home at the Windsor Hotel in a butcher cart, but that butcher boy dropped the doughty Commodore after a block or two, and his passenger struggled back to the Windsor and stayed there. An elevated train which started from Harlem with Brother Jones of Dow, Jones & Co., and a contingent of brokers, was practically abandoned at Twenty-third street, after taking nearly four hours to get there. The brokers flocked to neighboring restaurants and hotels, and the billiard rooms and barrooms were thronged from that time out.

While there were but twenty-one brokers on the floor at the opening of the Exchange, there was even a smaller number of customers distributed through the offices of the 600 and odd active members of the Exchange. The thousands of private wires leading to Chicago, Boston, Philadelphia, Washington, and other speculative centres had been snapped like cotton twine, and while the London cables were working, Wall street and all financial and commercial folks were absolutely cut off from their out-of-town constituents. The streets were strewn with broken telegraph wires. Stout cables hanging from swaying telegraph poles parted, and many a struggling pedestrian, in addition to all his misery, was tripped by them.

Shortly before noon, when the attendance on the Stock Exchange had increased to a little over a hundred, it was announced that one wire was working to Chicago. This was a small ray to the benighted, but the blizzard-struck brokers were too indifferent to brighten much. They swapped their experiences with their neighbors on the floor, and finally decided to give it up and shut up shop for the day. Vice-Chairman Henriques got out his ivory hammer again and called them around him. This resolution was then adopted:

That it is the sense of the members present that all dealings, so far as possible, be suspended, and deliveries go over until to-morrow, March 13.

Furthermore, all loans were extended until to-day. This is the first time in its history that the weather has knocked the Stock Exchange out. It was closed for a few days during the Black Friday panic, and since then only once on a business day. That was when Vice-President Hill died suddenly on the floor of the Exchange.

After the little throng had decided to quit, it was figured up that the transactions for the session had been 15,200 shares.

There were two cabs in front of Delmonico's when the brokers abandoned the Exchange. One driver got $35 and the other $40 to go to the Fifth Avenue Hotel. The other brokers got home the best way they could. Many of them went to the offices of the elevated roads, at 71 Broadway, to inquire about the chances of getting up town. They were greeted with a big placard stating that the road was blocked, and they were informed that not a single executive official of the elevated roads had turned up at the offices.

Judge McCue, the new Assistant Treasurer, managed to get to the Sub-Treasury, but half of his clerks were away, and at the Clearing House business was clogged until nearly dusk by the absence of the clerks. All the banks managed to make their clearances, but in several of them certifications were refused because of the absence of Presidents, cashiers, and tellers.

Collector Magone, Surveyor Beattie, Deputy Collectors Dunn, Guthrie, Nicoll, and McGee, Democrats, were at their posts in the Custom House. Of the force of 1,500 in the Custom House and the Barge Office, 500 were kept away by the blizzard. The duties of those on hand, however, were light, as business along the docks was practically abandoned. A good many of the female inspectors were on hand.

The Produce Exchange was closed at 2 o'clock. When the doors were opened seven stanch men were on hand. At one time there were ninety-five brokers on the great floor, but all efforts to do business were abandoned long before 2 o'clock struck. Some of the valiant ones were Alex. Meakim, Samuel L. Finlay, James Christie, Latin Scholar White, and Michael Hennessy. The flour men didn't show up at all. The freight men were without any occupation and sensibly stayed home, and at no time were there over a score piping around the grain pit, where hundreds usually cluster and howl. The average daily attendance on this Exchange is 1,700.

The Consolidated Stock and Petroleum Exchange, the Cotton, the Maritime, and the Coffee Exchanges assembled from 20 to 120 persons, where 300 to 1,200 are usually seen. The doors of the Real Estate Exchange were not opened.

A peculiar and interesting feature of the brokers who braved the blizzard was their demand for fresh linen when they got down town. The few haberdashery stores in the neighborhood of the Exchanges were positively thronged with them calling for fresh collars and shirts that had been soaked and wilted by the shooting and penetrating snow. Mufflers were of no account. The icy particles scorned them. All the hat stores down town sold cases of Scotch caps with peaks in front and rear; but of all the blizzard barons down town the cabmen were the mightiest.

HARLEM TO CITY HALL—TIME, 2H. 11M.

The Horse was Game, but the Man Thinks he Won't Go Back Until May.

A gentleman who lives at 128th street and Sixth avenue and who does business near the City Hall, made the distance in two hours and eleven minutes yesterday morning, probably the fastest time on record for the day. This is the account as he gave it to a SUN reporter:

"I left my house on 128th street at 9½ A. M. and at once discovered that it was snowing. I opened my umbrella, and a howling wind swept around the corner from Sixth avenue and took that umbrella out of my hand and lifted it over the roof of a neighboring flat house. Next my Derby hat flew off my head and went skimming over the snow drifts at the rate of about sixty miles an hour. I let it go, returned to my house, put on an old hunting cap, tied up my ears in a woollen muffler, and started out again to go to my business. I met a friend who yelled to me that the Sixth avenue trains were not running, so I steered for Third avenue. Arriving there I found that the trains were not running there either. On Second avenue there were no trains either. The cable road in 125th street had stopped, and business men by scores were walking from one L road to another in the effort to go south.

"I had to get down town, and I went to a livery stable to get a conveyance. There was one cutter, one horse, and one driver left. I hired all three for $15 and started out. That was at 10:20 o'clock. The driver told me that the horse was liable to run away if he got excited, but he didn't get excited. Well, we started down Third avenue on a fast trot, and then the fun began. The air was so full of little fine needles of snow and the wind tore by us at such a rate that that horse staggered about like a drunken man. But he was game. He put his head down and trotted ahead in the teeth of the blast. His mane and tail were masses of ice, and his hide was thickly veneered with it. You know I wear eyeglasses. Well, my eyeglasses were covered with ice so thick that I had to lick it off every five minutes. I couldn't get them clear any other way.

"We passed Third avenue surface cars all the way down. They were all deserted and most of them were off the track. The horses had all been taken back to the stables. The brewers' wagons were out, though, out in force, and each one had from four to ten great Normandy horses. Even the great strength of these huge draught animals was not enough to pull the wagons through some of the snow drifts, and the drivers were lashing the poor beasts with their whips and cursing them with great vigor. The sidewalks were almost deserted as well as I could see through my ice-covered glasses. As we kept moving southward at the great speed of four miles an hour, the sleet striking my face made me feel as if it was raining carpet tacks. My moustache froze solid, my eyebrows did likewise, and little icicles formed on my eyelashes and got into my eyes. They hurt like hot cinders.

"At Eighty-fourth street I got out, went into a dry goods store, and bought two toboggan caps for the driver and myself. We pulled them down over our ears and tied mufflers over our faces, leaving only the eyes exposed. Then things were more pleasant. The driver was 61 years old, but he didn't grumble a bit.

"'I'm an old New York tough,' he said, 'I've lived here, man and boy, all my life, but I'll be — if ever I seen the likes o' this ride, an' I doan' wanter.'

"And still that good horse went staggering ahead. We tilted nearly over several times and twice we ran into pillars of the elevated road, for we couldn't see where we were going half the time. As we passed Seventy-sixth street I saw a great crowd of people gazing up at the scene of the accident on the elevated. They were all standing with their backs to the wind. Deserted wagons stood at the curb all the way from Harlem to the City Hall, and we met any quantity of men who had unhitched their horses and were taking them to shelter. At Ninth street the fury of the wind redoubled, and when we got to Park row the horse was forced to stagger a little more slowly.

"I arrived opposite THE SUN office at 12:31 o'clock, having made the trip in a little more than two hours, and I don't believe anybody beat it yesterday. One of the driver's fingers was frozen, and the horse was completely exhausted. No, I am not going home to-night. I have telegraphed to expect me in May."

THE BRIDGE DID NOBLY.

Beaten by the Storm at First—Mr. Barnes Foots it and Just Misses Perishing.

With the exception of an hour from 9 to 10 A. M. yesterday cars ran on the Brooklyn Bridge at intervals. The bridge was enduring a severe test, but President Howell said that not the slightest vibration was discovered in the solid piers. A northwest storm does not strike the bridge so fair as a southeast or southwest storm. Delay was caused by snow and ice. Regular trains ran yesterday morning to 5:10, when the cable was started. For two hours the cable did satisfactory work, but before 8 o'clock snow and ice accumulated on the tracks, and the momentum of the cars was not sufficient to take them to the platforms. Engines had to pull the trains into the stations. The intervals between the trains grew longer, and the crowd which every morning rides over the bridge to New York was jammed up at the entrance of the bridge on Sands street.

The string of people became so dense and so vociferous that the police feared trouble, and wooden bars were put up at the gate in front of the ticket choppers after a crowd had assembled on the upper landing. The barriers were broken down, and with a yell the crowd burst through. They did not gain anything by it except to get under cover. The situation was made more vexatious by an accident on the New York side. A train of three cars was pulled by a motor from the north track a short distance west, when the last car slipped off from the icy rails, and it had to be raised with jackscrews. This caused a delay of considerably over half an hour. Meanwhile the Brooklyn crowd of passengers waited.

The bridge promenade was closed at 6 o'clock A. M. by order of Sergeant Phillips of the bridge police. When the crowd was biggest in front of the boxes a young man who said that he was Mr. Barnes, and was Secretary of the American Exchange, limited, at 162 Broadway, and that he had walked from Greenpoint, begged Sergeant Phillips to let him walk across the bridge, because he feared he would lose his place if he was late. Sergeant Phillips consented, and the young man walked or rather staggered across the bridge until he became benumbed by cold and sore from being knocked against the iron railings by the wind. The policemen in their two snug houses under the towers had been warned by Sergeant Phillips by telephone to look out for Barnes. When Barnes arrived over the land span in New York he staggered and fell. Policemen followed him, and as he did not rise they yanked him to his feet and marched him to the bridge entrance. Alone, he would have perished.

Some passengers secured cabs to ride across and others climbed upon trucks.

Superintendent Martin arrived in the middle of the forenoon in a cab and ordered the cable to be stopped, because the grips failed to hold. Trains of two cars and two engines were put on, and afterward three cars and two engines, with a headway of from five to ten minutes. In the afternoon the Brooklynites returning caused a big and perpetual jam on the bridge approaches in New York. Men, in their haste to get into the cars, smashed car windows and crushed each other's hats.

Superintendent Martin hired a gang of Italian laborers to keep the tracks clear, but most of them deserted before night.

The bridge, on the whole, justified its creation yesterday.

TRAVEL BY RAIL KILLED.

MORE THAN 50 TRAINS STALLED HELPLESS BETWEEN STATIONS.

No Telling Where They Are or What's Become of the Passengers—Only One Train Gets Into the Grand Central—None Goes Out—Every Railroad Into New York Beaten, and Abandoning the Field for the Day—The Fourth Avenue Tunnel Choked With Snow—Serious Delays.

Not a train had moved out of the Grand Central Depot all day, and only one had come in. President Chauncey M. Depew of the New York Central was one of a dozen men in the executive offices who reported for duty. Fifty were missing.

"Well, how did you get here?" was the abrupt question with which he greeted the SUN reporter late in the afternoon.

"I have just received a telegram from Buffalo," he added, "which states that the sun is shining brightly there, and that what little ice remains in the city is melting rapidly and running off in water through the gutters. That's cheering news, isn't it?"

The pleasant frame of mind that characterized Mr. Depew was not shared by his subordinates. Every attempt to communicate with station agents after 8 A. M. had proved unsuccessful. The waiting rooms were crowded with travellers anxious to depart, and persons waiting to hear from friends who were en route to this city. To neither could the officials give the slightest satisfaction.

HAULING IN THE BOSTON EXPRESS.

Nor was the condition of affairs on the New Haven any better. The one train that succeeded in getting through was a train that had started long before the storm began. The express that leaves Boston at 10:30 P. M., and which is due in New York at 6:20 A. M., got as far as Hartford before any part of the storm was encountered. That was 2:41 A. M. The train had started under a comparatively clear sky. Clouds were encountered at Hartford, but the air was mild, and there was no reason to expect anything more than a light rain storm. At New Haven, at 3:58 A. M., snow was coming down lightly but regularly. The further the trains travelled from that city the denser the storm became. At Stamford the first signs of the blizzard that was prevailing in New York showed themselves. From thereon the storm was similar to the one that prevailed in New York. The wind drove against the train and around it so that the engineer didn't know which way it was coming. The storm increased in intensity. Snow drifts had covered the tracks in all places where these run through depressed cuts. The wind decreased the heat in the cars and the passengers began to don their wraps. Those that had sleepers piled their overcoats on to their blankets and swore at the porter. Sleep was impossible after leaving Stamford because of the frequent stops and the jerks as the trains started.

The train reached the Harlem bridge three hours late. From there its progress was much impeded, until it finally stopped altogether at Fifty-ninth street. All attempts to move it from there proved futile. A bank of snow fully five feet deep had formed across the track. It was now after 11 A. M., and all the passengers were fully awake and aware of the situation. They got out and discussed the difficulty among themselves. Some were prepared to leave the train, but the announcement that a messenger had been despatched to the Grand Central Depot for assistance deterred them. In a short time an engine came puffing along slowly, and assisted after the drift had been cleared away in pulling the train through. When the passengers arrived in the depot they were still further disgusted upon learning that no cars or elevated trains were running. Cabs were finally secured by such as could pay $5 a mile, and the others had to walk. The train was five hours late.

THE STAMFORD LOCAL STUCK AT 110TH STREET.

That was the last and only train to reach the depot. The only other that came anywhere near it was the Stamford local, on the same road. That left Stamford at 5 A. M. It had reached 110th street at 10½ A. M. This train was crowded with brokers and business men. The Boston express had passed the same spot with difficulty a half hour previous, and the wind and snow had put in effective work since then. The drifts were piled so high that it was impossible to pass them. After a number of vain attempts a brakeman was sent on foot to the depot. He had hard work getting there, but his errand was fruitless. The officials had been endeavoring for some time to get an engine through the Fourth avenue tunnel, but had found it now absolutely impossible.

The passengers were furious when the messenger returned with his answer, but there was no help for it. One courageous passenger who was on important business refused to be comforted, and started off on foot. He succeeded in pushing his way through the drifts, and reached the Grand Central Depot by way of the tracks an hour and a half later. He was completely exhaused, and paid $20 for a cab to take him down town. He refused to tell his name. The remaining passengers stayed in the cars, and took such comfort as they could out of the provisions supplied by a neighboring restaurant at the order of the railroad company.

NO NEWS OF THE MISSING TRAINS.

The leading officials of the railroad had become convinced of the danger that lay in the attempt to run trains early in the day. None had been allowed to leave the depot, and frantic attempts were made to reach the agents along the route. It was impossible to communicate with any of them after 8 A. M. No word had been received from the agent at New Haven after midnight on Sunday, and even Mount Vernon could not be reached after 8 o'clock. The last word received by wire from any official connected with the road stated that telegraph wires were down everywhere, and that the poles lay across the tracks in many places. The long-distance telephone owned by the New Haven Company could not be worked either. The tunnel from Fifty-ninth street to Ninety-sixth street was blocked.

TRYING TO FEED THE BESIEGED.

The train despatcher said that eight local trains on the Harlem division of the road were stalled between stations. As far as possible word had been conveyed to the conductors to supply the passengers with provisions and such other comforts as could be obtained These messages were sent by wire and fast messengers, but their efficacy was admittedly doubtful where the trains were far from caterers and retaurants, and had to depend on the propinquity of farm houses. Superintendent Turner said that he had done all he could to relieve passengers, but, in the uncertainty prevailing, could venture no opinion as to their condition. None of these local trains, of course, are fitted with any sleeping accommodations, and the result last night cannot have been pleasant. Not the slightest tidings had been received as to the condition of the trains on the main line, but the superintendent thought that these had all been stopped in time. Where trains were delayed in towns over night the company will pay hotel bills. In the depot a group of conductors of the road were gathered. They said that three and four engines had been put on single trains that were stalled along the route, but without any appreciable effect. They said that the tunnel in the city was not only blocked at the entrances, but that the air holes along the street had admitted the snow in large quantities, and that under these holes the snow was seven feet deep. Where the tracks ran in cuts with banks on each side, the snow had filled up the depressions even to the tops of the banks. They declared that four trains were stalled along the main road be-

THE CENTENNIAL CELEBRATION.—SCENE AT THE REVIEWING-STAND ON MADISON SQUARE—THE PRESIDENT SALUTING THE PROCESSION.
FROM A PHOTO.—[SEE PAGE 230.]

A BEAUTIFUL INCIDENT OF THE CENTENNIAL CELEBRATION.—GIRLS FROM THE NORMAL COLLEGE STREWING FLOWERS IN THE PATH OF PRESIDENT HARRISON AT THE ENTRANCE OF CITY HALL.—Drawn by Miss G. A. Davis.—[See Page 230.]

THE NEW BASE BALL PAVILION.

IT WILL BE THE LARGEST AND FINEST IN THE WORLD WHEN COMPLETED.

The monstrous and handsome pavilion on Gotham's new base ball park, which this afternoon will contain a select and enthusiastic crowd of admirers and supporters of the Giants, is a marvel in at least one respect: It is just two weeks ago since Architect John J. Deery drew his first line on it, and to-day it will accommodate in comfort 8,000 people.

Readers of THE GRAPHIC who will not have the pleasure of being present at the grand opening to day can form an accurate idea of the magnificent monument to Architect Deery's skill and the animated scenes on and in front of it by scanning the accompanying pictures made by THE GRAPHIC artist.

The pavilion—grand stand is obsolete now—is the largest of any of the bare ball pavilions in the country and, although designed and built in such a wonderfully short time, it is also the most complete in detail. It is not entirely finished yet. Only the first tier or deck will be occupied to-day, but work will be pushed until it is complete, the artisans stopping only for games. The dimensions and plan of the pavilion are interesting. It is 320 feet long on the field side, with the narrow depth at the ends of fifty feet and the wider depth in the centre, sixty feet. Its total length on the street or rear side is 410 feet. In shape it is the central part of a large segment of ninety feet radius, meeting slanting lines, each ending at eighty feet beyond first and third bases It is ninety feet from the home plate to the centre of the stand.

The first three rows of seats are entirely without obstruction In the fourth row is a line of supports, twenty-two in number, which is not great for the distance of 320 feet

The stand is supplied with tilting seats, with plenty of foot room in front. There are ten aisles 3 feet 6 inches wide There are two staircases 8 feet wide from the rear to the second tier, each having a projection terminating in a round tower, supporting flagstaffs. There are also spaces used for ladies' retiring rooms and dressing rooms for the players

The restaurant will be easy of access from both the pavilion and the open seats. At the corner of Eighth avenue and 155th street is a concourse thirty-two feet square where the people will assemble from the elevated railway platform as well as from the street. In the centre is a large ticket office with turn-stiles on either side to pass eight lines of people through simultaneously. They next go into another concourse, 30x32, from which a staircase eighteen feet wide leads down to the free seats. A small octagon ticket office is located there, where tickets to the pavilion are sold, and aisles lead to both the lower and upper tiers. There are stairways on both sides, so arranged as to distribute the crowds going in or coming out.

Between the pavilion and the free seats is a passage ten feet wide for carriages The free seats extend on each side of the pavilion at an angle of eight degrees in three courses of sixty feet each, making a continuous railing fronting the field of 690 feet.

The field is twenty feet wider than the Boston field and forty wider than the Chicago field. The centre field is not as long as that at Boston, but is just about the same as the Philadelphia centre field. Longer right field hits can be made on the Philadelphia, Boston or Chicago grounds than here

The grounds have been perfectly drained and the infield and centre field are in perfect condition to-day, but the left and right are a little soft, as the drains were only connected with a sewer on Saturday afternoon

The pavilion is portable The common idea is that this location is permanent, but it is not The managers expect to remain there only two or three seasons. They have better and larger grounds in view which cannot be obtained now, but will be eventually. Therefore the pavilion has been so constructed that it can be taken down, moved and rebuilt readily. It will be completed during the month

INSURING HAPPY DAYS.

[From To-day.]

Giggs—By the way, old man, I see your mother-in-law is cutting a great swell down in Narragansett. Has she got any means?

Figgs—Well, I should hope so! I pay her $10 a day, cash in advance, to keep away from the house.

THE GRAND STAND.

ENTRANCE AND REAR OF GRAND STAND.

[FROM DESIGNS BY J. J. DEERY, ARCHITECT.]

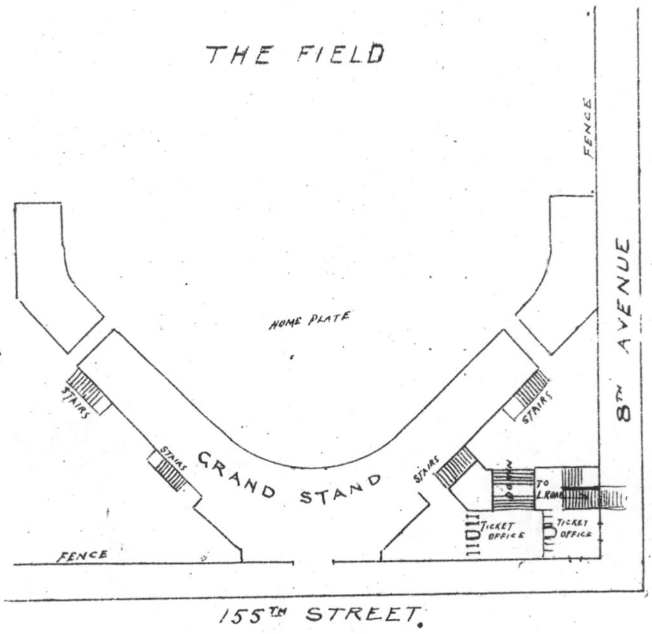

PLAN OF THE GROUNDS.

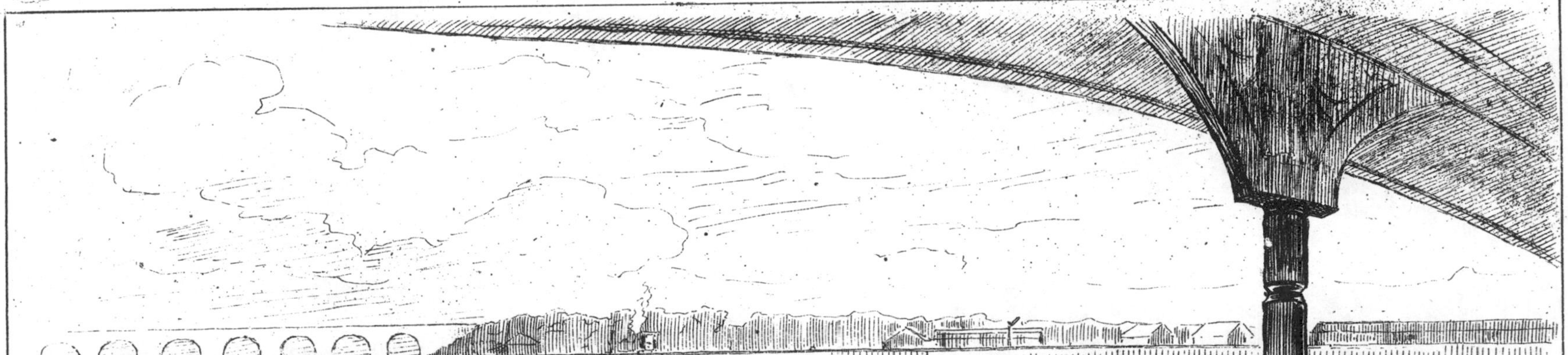

THE VIEW FROM THE GRAND STAND.

THE NEW POLO GROUNDS AT ONE HUNDRED AND FIFTY-FIFTH STREET AND EIGHTH AVENUE.

Photos. of the Sullivan-Kilrain Battle.

NEW YORK ILLUSTRATED NEWS.

JOHN L. SULLIVAN SPORTING EDITOR.

Entered as Second Class Matter at the New York, N. Y., Post Office, for 1889
Copyrighted for 1889, by the Proprietor, 252 Broadway, N. Y.

Vol. II. No. 78. New York, Saturday, July 27, 1889. Price 10 Cts.

THE CHAMPION'S COLORS GIVEN AWAY WITH NEXT WEEK'S ISSUE.

HE HAS DOWNED THEM ALL.

John Lawrence Sullivan Knocks Out all Fakes and Remains the Undefeated Champion of Champions.

"NELLIE · BLY."

G. P. HALL & SON, PHOTOGRAPHERS. COPYRIGHTED BY PRESS PUBLISHING CO. PHOTO ENG. CO. 67 PARK PL. N. Y.

The New York WORLD'S Correspondent,
who Placed a Girdle Round the Earth in 72 Days, 6 Hours, and 11 Minutes.

Nov. 14th, 1889—Jan. 25th, 1890.

SUPPLEMENT—THE WORLD, N. Y., FEB. 2, 1890, VOL. 30, NO. 10,393.

BASEBALL STARS.

Biographical Sketches of Those Who Will Play To-day.

LEAGUERS AND PLAYERS.

How They Look and What Experts Think They Can Do.

With the umpire's cry of "Play ball!" this afternoon the greatest season in the history of the American national game will be begun. The conflict between the two principal Leagues will be exceedingly bitter and will form an interesting topic of public comment until the season closes.

With that THE EVENING SUN has nothing to do. Its only interest will be to publish the same full and correct accounts of baseball games that it has in other seasons. Of the merits of the teams the public will undoubtedly be able to decide to its entire satisfaction.

Upon one point, however, everybody in this great city is agreed, and that is that every club that bears the name "New York" on the shirt fronts of its players is expected to carry it to the front and hold it there until the championship is won.

It will be neither League nor Brotherhood that will hold popular favor, but "Champions."

The metropolis has two great clubs, from both of whom great things are expected. Both have the material to head the list in their respective races.

That they are a fine-looking body of men the subjoined cuts clearly indicate, and THE EVENING SUN publishes the ages, weights and heights of the two teams:

NEW YORK NATIONAL LEAGUE CLUB.

	Age.	Weight.	Height. Ft.	Height. In.
P. J. Murphy	29	170	5	10
R. D. Buckley	29	187	5	10½
J. A. Sommers	23	186	6	
T. O'Rourke	28	180	5	—
M. Welch	31	155	5	7
H. Boyle	29	190	5	11
A. Rusie	19	190	5	11
J. C. Burkett	21	155	5	8
R. Murphy	23	176	6	1
J. Sharrott	20	163	5	8½
S. Crane	30	190	6	—
M. Scanlon	25	190	6	1½
C. E. Bassett	26	170	5	10½
J. Denny	29	190	6	—
J. Glasscock	30	170	5	9
J. Hornung	32	158	5	8¾
M. Tiernan	23	160	5	8¾
A. F. Clarke	24	155	5	7½
C. L. Dooley	24	178	6	—
F. Siefke	20	165	5	11

NEW YORK PLAYERS' LEAGUE CLUB.

	Age.	Weight.	Height. Ft.	Height. In.
W. Ewing	30	180	5	10½
W. Brown	27	190	6	1
H. Vaughn	26	180	5	11
T. J. Keefe	31	185	5	10½
E. N. Crane	26	210	5	9
H. M. O'Day	27	190	5	11¾
J. Ewing	26	168	6	1
R. Connor	32	205	6	2
D. Richardson	27	165	5	8
A. W. Whitney	31	160	5	7
G. Hatfield	35	169	5	9½
J. O'Rourke	38	185	5	8
G. F. Gore	32	185	5	10½
M. J. Slattery	24	190	6	—

The average of the twenty League players is 26 years, 173¾ pounds, 5 feet 10¼ inches.

That of the fourteen Brotherhood players is 29 years, 183 pounds, 5 feet 10¼ inches.

This places them very nearly on a par. The only decided differences are in the ages and weights, and the suppleness and enthusiasm of the younger players may fairly be considered an offset to the greater muscle and heaviness of the older ones.

THE PLAYERS' LEAGUE.

Sketches of Buck Ewing and the Members of the Brotherhood Club.

William Ewing, the manager and captain of the New York Players' League club, was born in Pendleton, O., thirty years ago. He stands 5 feet 10½ inches high and weighs 180 pounds. Buck's first experience as a baseball captain and manager occurred when he was about 14 years old, when he had charge of all the business affairs of a club in his native town, whose playing stock consisted of a ball and bat and a capital of 75 cents.

He first played professionally with the Mohawk Browns in Cincinnati in 1878 and 1879. He there attracted the attention of Manager Horace Phillips, who signed him with the Rochesters in 1880. After a short experience there he joined the Troy club. In company with Welch, Connor and other old Giants, he left the Laundry City club in 1883 and signed with the New York League club, with which club he remained until the recent baseball disruption.

Ewing is generally considered to be the best general baseball player in the country. As a backstop he stands in a class by himself. He is a pitcher of unusual excellence, and would doubtless rank with Welch and Keefe if he devoted his entire time to that kind of play. He excels also as an outfielder and on the bases. He is one of the safest hitters in the country, and possesses remarkably clever judgment in running bases.

Ewing drove a distillery wagon for a living when he first began to play ball, and is not ashamed of it now that he is a magnate as well as player and enjoys an enormous salary. Frequently on Western trips when the train was passing Cincinnati he would call attention to the little distillery, a couple of miles from the city, where he first began to earn his living.

William Brown, the big, good-natured Californian who so acceptably fills the place of backstop when Ewing does not play, is one of the best players in that position. There is no limit to his grit, and he is also a good, hard hitter. Bill's only drawback is a disposition to get rattled at exciting moments. With Ewing's coolness he would have no superior in the country.

Brown is a native of the Golden State, and is about 27 years old. He is 6 feet 1 inch in height, and weighs 190 pounds. His professional career has been brief. He had been playing but a year or two in California when he was signed by the New Yorks three years ago.

Harry Vaughn, the new catcher of the Players' club, is a native of Rural, O. He is 26 years old, is 26 years old, is 5 feet 11 inches tall and weighs 180 pounds. He rather a good-looking fellow and deserves an apology for the injustice of the cut. He has only played professionally since 1887 and has always been associated with long John Ewing as a battery. Their transfers from one club to another have always been made together. Vaughn's first professional experience was with the New Orleans club. In 1888 he played in Memphis, and last season he was with the lamented "Colonels" of Louisville. He is a very earnest player and has made a good impression here in his practise work.

Timothy J. Keefe, the star twirler of the local Brotherhood, is such a familiar figure to New Yorkers that any extended reference to his career is unnecessary. He is regarded by many baseball enthusiasts as the most skilful pitcher in the country. Two years ago he was admittedly so, but last year he fell off somewhat in his work and now his admirers are content to rank him with Clarkson at the head of the list. "Sir Timothy" has been a ball player since 1875, when he played at Lewiston, Me. In 1876 he played with "our boys" of Boston. For the next two years he was with the Westons. In '79 he joined the Uticas; in '80 he twirled in Albany and Troy. He became conspicuous in the baseball world in 1884 and 1885 with the Metropolitans. He signed with the New Yorks in 1885.

Keefe was one of the leaders in the Brotherhood movement, and won golden opinions by his manliness in expressing his judgment against the contract jumpers on both sides. Keefe is a fine looking man, with a coolness of judgment that no situation, however exciting, seems to disturb. He is 5 feet 10½ inches high, and weighs 185 pounds.

Edward N. Crane, the famous speedy pitcher, was born in South Boston 26 years ago. He is 5 feet 9 inches in height and weighs 210 pounds. Crane is not only a first-class twirler, but has had considerable experience as an outfielder. He was one of Spalding's round-the-world baseball tourists, and his massive physique attracted attention everywhere. In Italy and Paris he was termed "The Hercules." Crane is probably the best long-distance baseball thrower in the world. His exhibitions in Australia and England were regarded as little short of marvellous. Crane began his professional career with the Boston Unions in 1884. Since then he has played with the Providence, Buffalo, Washington and Toronto clubs. He joined the New Yorks two years ago. He is one of the heaviest batters among the well-known pitchers.

Henry M. O'Day made a great reputation for himself in the world's championship series between the New York and Brooklyn clubs. His fine work was largely instrumental in bringing the pennant to the metropolis. O'Day has played professionally since 1883, when he played with the Toledos. In 1885 and 1886 he was with the Pittsburgs and Detroits. Toward the close of the latter year he joined the Washingtons, and remained there until last August. President Day then purchased his release and gave him his first opportunity to distinguish himself. He was born in Chicago in 1863, stands 5 feet 11¾ inches high and weighs 190 pounds.

John Ewing, the new addition to the Players' club's pitching talent, is a brother of the celebrated Buck, but does not resemble him in any way. He is extremely tall and comparatively thin. His height is 6 feet 1 inch, and he weighs 168 pounds. He has been pitching to Vaughn since they first played professionally with the New Orleans club in 1887.

Long John, as he is termed, has good speed and command of the ball, and has shown good work in the exhibition games. If it is in him he is certain to develop into a great twirler under the instruction of his little brother Bill. He is 26 years old.

Roger Connor is one of the biggest and best first basemen in the country. He was born in Waterbury, Conn., in 1859. He was a sturdy youth, and grew to large proportions so rapidly, in fact, that when quite a young man he was called the Giant. He is over 6 feet 2 inches tall and weighs 205 pounds. His first professional baseball appearance was in 1888, when he joined the New Bedford team. He remained there two years, and in 1880 joined the Troys. His work on that team, mostly at third base, was of such a phenomenal character that in 1883 Jim Mutrie secured him for the New York team. Of his connection with the Giants it is almost unnecessary to speak. Everyone who ever visited the old Polo grounds or the new one at 155th street knows how admirably he has guarded first bag. Many a pitcher has come to dread him. The longest hit on the old Polo grounds was made by Rogers. It was over the right field fence in a game with the Bostons three years ago, and was a drive that aroused the wildest enthusiasm among the spectators. He afterwards duplicated the hit. He was also the first player to lift a ball over the centre field fence of the new Polo grounds.

Daniel Richardson, the great second baseman, has probably the shortest professional history of any prominent ball player in the country. Previous to joining the New Yorks in 1884 he had only played with the Elmira *Telegram* team of his native city. Danny is a great general player and is a twirler of no mean ability. He was originally taken on trial by the New Yorks. They were on the point of releasing him because there was no room for him when an accident to a fielder gave him a chance to show his skill. By the time the players had recovered another accident gave him an opportunity to display his ability in some other position. His merit was so positive that he was made a regular player. Danny is proud of the fact that he is a fellow townsmen of Gov. Hill. He is 27 years old, 5 feet 8 inches tall, and weighs 165 pounds.

Arthur W. Whitney, familiarly known as Artie, Whit, and the Count, has had a long baseball experience. He was born in Brockton, Mass., 31 years ago, is 5 feet 7 inches tall, and weighs 160 pounds. He first played professionally with the Fall River Club in 1877, in company with Gore and Mutrie. In 1878 and '79 he played with the Lowells, in 1880 with the Worcesters, '81 and '82 with the Detroits, '83 with the East Saginaws, and 84-87 with the Pittsburgs. In the latter year his release was purchased by the New York. Whitney is not only a great favorite on account of his skill as a ball player, but has won admiration by his modest, gentlemanly qualities, and the excellent care he takes to keep himself in condition.

There is no more earnest player in the profession than Gil Hatfield. He is a Hoboken boy, 35 years old, 5 feet 9½ inches tall, and weighs 169 pounds. He first learned the rudiments of the national game on the turf of the Elysian fields, but it was not until 1882 that he figured professionally. He was then a member of Jim Mutrie's Metropolitan reserves.

In 1883 he played in Hartford, Conn., '84 and '85 in Newark, '86 and '87 in Portland, Me., and in 1888 was signed by Mutrie to play with the Giants. His position is short stop, but heretofore he has not had much opportunity to distinguish himself. This year, however, as a member of the Brotherhood team, he will play that position regularly, and will probably give a good account of himself. It is the opportunity of his life, and if he will only remain cool at critical moments he is sure to succeed.

James O'Rourke is one of the oldest ball players. He and old Deacon White have ambled on the green diamond for so many years that they have become as sensitive about their ages as an old maid. O'Rourke is about 38 or 40 years old. He is 5 feet 8 inches tall, and weighs 185 pounds. He was at one time one of the best outfielders and general ball players in the country, but his present excellence is mainly as a batter. In this respect he has always held a very high position though it is marred somewhat by his inability to bat out a sacrifice when it is wanted.

George F. Gore was at one time considered the best centre fielder in the country, but, like his comrade O'Rourke, he has deteriorated in this respect, and is now more conspicuous for his safe, heavy batting qualities than his ability as a fielder. Gore began his professional career with the Fall River club in 1877, of which Jim Mutrie was manager. Mutrie had seen him play with the Resolutes at Portland, Me., the year previous, and took him on trial. Gore did not show up well at first, but Mutrie knew he was a ball player and took him along when he became manager of the New Bedfords in 1878. In that year Gore joined the Chicagos and remained with "old Anse" eight years. It was during this period that Gore shone as one of the star fielders of the country. Gore was born in Hartland, Me. He is 32 years old, stands 5 feet 10½ inches high, and weighs 185 pounds.

Michael J. Slattery is a South Boston boy, 24 years old. His native place has turned out more ball players than any other locality, and it is due to his early training that he occupies such a high place in the baseball world to-day. When 18 years old his playing attracted the attention of the organizers of the Boston Union Club, and he played with them through that memorable season. In '85 he played in Biddeford, Me., '86 with the Haverhills, '87 with the Torontos, and in '88 he made his debut before a New York crowd. He is a splendid fielder, a first-class base runner, hard hitter, and in general an A 1 ball player. He is 6 feet in height and weighs 190 pounds.

MUTRIE AND HIS MEN.

The Giants of To-day and What They Have Done.

James Mutrie, the handsome hustling manager of the New York National League club, is a native of Chelsea, Mass., and was ushered into the world of baseball strifes and struggles in 1870. "Smiling Jeemes" is a hard worker and enjoys the distinction of having managed more penant-winning clubs than any other man in the country. He numbers his championship flags at twelve and feels confident that fourteen will be the number when this season is over.

Mutrie began his baseball career as the catcher and shortstop of the Lewiston club of Maine. In 1876 he became captain and manager of the Fall River club. He afterward acted in the same capacity for the New Bedfords and Brocktons and piloted both to the New England championship. In 1880 he came to New York and helped to organize the famous Mets, and won several championships with them.

In 1885 he became manager of the New York National League club. His career with that famous organization is too well known to need more than a reference. Mutrie is one of the best judges of a baseball player in the country. Hanlon, Whitney, Gore and Latham were under him as youngsters. Jim is an exceedingly kind manager and nothing is too good for his "boys" if they will only play winning ball. He never gives up a fight, and his encouraging cry of "Have sand, have stomach!" is familiar all over the country.

Capt. John Glasscock, the short stop, also enjoys the Sullivan-Ewing distinction; he is considered in a class by himself. His name and that of Third Baseman Denny's has become almost inseparably linked in the baseball world. They are generally acknowledged to be pre-eminently the two best fielders in their positions in their country. Their exhibition, apart from the rest of their associates, is usually considered an art by itself.

Glasscock is a native of Wheeling, W. Va., and is 30 years old. He began his career as a ball player in 1876, as third baseman of the Standards of his native city. He first became well known when he joined the Buffalo club in the fall of 1877. In 1878 he played with the Alleghanys of Pittsburg, and, after it disbanded, joined the Cleveland club, with which he remained until 1882. He played at short in 1879, and soon came into prominence by the reason of his excellence. He afterward played with the St. Louis Unions, afterward changed to the St. Louis Maroons, and remained there until the club was transferred to Indianapolis, three years ago.

He is one of the heaviest and safest batters in the country, and is a first-class base runner. He stands 5 feet 9 inches high and weighs 190 pounds.

Jeremiah Denny is a New York boy, but his family removed to California when he was very young. He is a strapping specimen of a man. He is six feet tall and weighs 190 pounds. He is the third baseman par excellence of the country, and has no equal as a fielder in his position. He is a veritable stonewall at third, and leading pitchers have frequently said of him that he stops apparently easy balls that with other third basemen would be counted safe hits.

For several years past the New York club has been anxious to get him. Now that he is here he has already given evidence that the cranks will enjoy an exhibition of fielding for a whole season such as has never before been witnessed in this city.

Denny first became prominently known as a ball player in California in 1881. In 1882 he joined the famous old Providence team, and remained there until the club disbanded. He then joined the St. Louis League team, and was transferred from there with Glasscock, Boyle and others to the Indianapolis club in 1887.

Patrick J. Murphy, who will be one of the League club's principal backstops this year, was born at Auburn, Mass., 29 years ago. His professional career has been comparatively brief. He first played in the semi-professional team of Worcester, Mass. He joined the Newarks in 1885, but late in the season played with the Jersey City team. In the fall of 1887 he was signed by the New Yorks.

Murphy is a first-class catcher, an enthusiastic ball player, and a great coacher. He is as agile as a cat on his feet and stops the wildest of pitched balls. He works to win from start to finish, and without regular work this season he will show that he holds a place among the leading backstops of the country. He is 5 feet 10 inches tall and weighs 170 pounds.

Richard D. Buckley, the clever Hoosier catcher, was born in Troy in 1860. His professional career began in 1884 with the East Ends of Pittsburg. In 1885 he played with the Binghamtons; in 1886 and 1887 with the Syracuse club, and after that with the Indianapolis club until he came to New York. He is a quiet, hard-working player, and puts up a fine game at third. He is a hard hitter and is not afraid to sacrifice at the proper time. He is a heavily-built man, 5 feet 10½ inches high, and weighs 187 pounds.

J. A. Sommers is already quite well known in this vicinity as a backstop, having played with the Metropolitans at Staten Island in 1887. He has improved materially since then, and will give a good account of himself this season. He was born in Cleveland, O., 23 years ago. He is 6 feet tall, and weighs 186 pounds. His professional career began with the Cleveland Reserves in 1884. Since then he has played with the Geneva club, the Hamiltons of Ontario, Metropolitan, Boston and Chicago clubs.

Tom O'Rourke is a New York boy by birth.

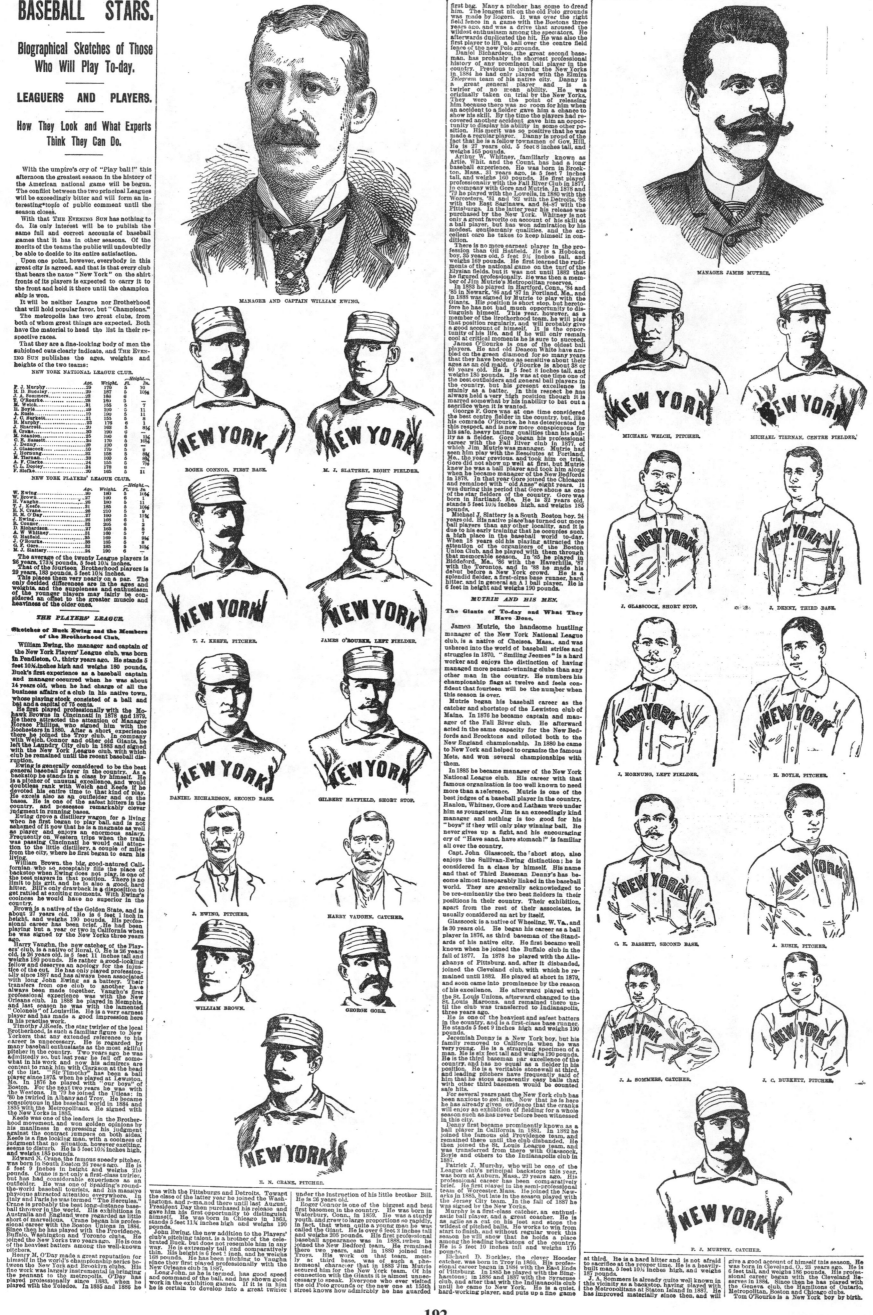

MANAGER AND CAPTAIN WILLIAM EWING.

ROGER CONNOR, FIRST BASE.

M. J. SLATTERY, RIGHT FIELDER.

T. J. KEEFE, PITCHER.

JAMES O'ROURKE, LEFT FIELDER.

DANIEL RICHARDSON, SECOND BASE.

GILBERT HATFIELD, SHORT STOP.

J. EWING, PITCHER.

HARRY VAUGHN, CATCHER.

WILLIAM BROWN.

GEORGE GORE.

E. N. CRANE, PITCHER.

MANAGER JAMES MUTRIE.

MICHAEL WELCH, PITCHER.

MICHAEL TIERNAN, CENTRE FIELDER.

J. GLASSCOCK, SHORT STOP.

J. DENNY, THIRD BASE.

J. HORNUNG, LEFT FIELDER.

H. BOYLE, PITCHER.

C. E. BASSETT, SECOND BASE.

A. RUSIE, PITCHER.

J. A. SOMMERS, CATCHER.

J. C. BURKETT, PITCHER.

P. J. MURPHY, CATCHER.

THE TWO NEW HOTELS AS THEY WILL STAND AT FIFTH AVENUE AND FIFTY-NINTH STREET, NEW YORK.
Drawn by Hughson Hawley.

THE NEW HOTELS ON THE PLAZA, NEW YORK.

Advantage of position, that is the architect's battle with his art. Unlike an Alexander, he cannot manœuvre for it. There is a fixed factor, and he is owner of the lot, and master of the situation. "Put up my building here. These are my limits, and I want my structure lofty, imposing." He is indifferent as to the narrowness of the street, and so, following his behest, up goes the towering edifice. Would you see the pinnacle of it, take it all in, as it stands? Then your position would be such as to dislocate your neck.

Advantage of position is an architect's bit of good luck, and nowhere else in New York has it been better afforded than at that locality on Fifth Avenue and Fifty-ninth Street where spreads out the Central Park Plaza.

Where Fifty-ninth Street enters Fifth Avenue, to the right and left of it, there have been for many a year two lots, not exactly without structures on them, but the buildings were of a sorry kind. These were beer-houses, serving to quench the thirst of those going and coming to and from Central Park. A number of years ago the master thief of city corporations had devised some grand plan of a caravansary of mammoth proportions, which was to cover the whole block between Fifty-eighth and Fifty-ninth streets, and a commencement had been made. Adjacent to the superb entrance to Central Park such structures were eyesores. Everybody knew, however, that they were but temporary blemishes on the face of this fine plaza. Now they are no more, for two superb hotels are in process of erection, as shown by the illustrations.

The building to the left of Fifty-ninth Street, with its frontage on Fifth Avenue, is the hotel to be known as the New Netherland, to be built by Mr. William Waldorf Astor. To-day steam-drills are pecking away at the rock, and within ten days the foundations will be put in place. The building will have a frontage of 100 feet on Fifth Avenue, with a depth of 125 feet on Fifty-ninth Street. The hotel is to be of seventeen stories, and below the street level there will be cellar and sub-cellar.

The mechanism of the modern hotel is complex. It bears a certain semblance to a factory. Catering to the many requirements of those who are to live in the 370 guest-chambers of the New Netherland, it is a nice calculation to find out what is the exact numerical force of those whose business it is to care for the paying occupants. In this hotel, cellar, basement, first, second, and the seventeenth stories are what are designated as "the working stories" of the house. The nicety of appreciation on the part of an architect who makes the interior plans of the hotel of to-day must be apparent. Many diverse problems must be solved. It may be house-keeping on a grandiose scale, subjected to the same rules, only it is the expansion of them all which increases the difficulties. Ventilation! Why, the fussiest people, not the less sensible as far as pure air is concerned, are those who, taking rooms in a hotel, notwithstanding the elegance of the table, pack up their baggage and quit in high dudgeon on the suspicion that a room or a hall has a fluffy or musty odor. To give privacy, with hundreds of people in a house, seems paradoxical. Everything must be accessible. A single dark room breeds vermin, and all hotels have the Croton bugs they deserve. In the economic and social conditions, if an architect has *carte blanche* to do as he will, as is supposable in the case of the New Netherland, nothing less than perfection is aimed at.

The building follows the Romanesque. The first four stories are of Belleville brownstone. From the fifth to the twelfth story the superstructure will be of buff brick. The next story, to the balcony, will be stone-faced, and the four uppermost ones will follow the slant of the roof. What the architect—Mr. William H. Hume—has tried to do, the height of his edifice being so much in excess of the base, is to break the great upstretch of the building by accentuating the horizontal details; and where the skill comes in is to accomplish this without shock. Mr. Hume has the advantage of knowing fairly well what will be the effectiveness of his building, because with the width of the plaza before him, he is not at work in the dark. The Roman arches are on the Fifth Avenue façade. A word might be said about Roman arches. Modern necessity skimps the Roman arch of the grandiose. The Roman built neither hotels nor newspaper offices, and was, fortunately, indifferent to rentals. We cramp all entrances because they do not "pay," and portals of noble construction are only to be found in structures intended for pompous or glorious services.

As to the interior decoration, there will be a fine staircase, with marbles and bronzes. The ground for the New Netherland was broken at the close of last year, and some time in the fall of 1892 the hotel will be opened for guests.

On the other side of Fifty-ninth Street a hotel is being built by Judge P. Henry Dugro and Mr. F. Wagner. The first story now shows above the sidewalk. The hotel stands on a 75-feet frontage on Fifth Avenue, and has a depth of 150 feet on Fifty-ninth Street. The architect, Mr. Ralph S. Townsend, is constructing an edifice in the Italian Renaissance style. It is to be built of brick, with an entire facing of Indiana limestone, which is a material of a light gray with a faint warmth of buff. On the Fifth Avenue front there will be a handsome portico, with a width of 45 feet, supported by eight columns of polished granite. The structure will be of twelve stories, with basement and sub-basement, and will contain 325 rooms. This hotel was commenced in the spring of 1890, and will be finished some time in 1892. The interior of the house will be of marble, with mural decorations in white and gold. In both houses the skeleton structure is of rolled iron and steel. Perhaps $4,000,000 would about cover the cost of building these two hotels.

HOTEL WALDORF.—Drawn by Hughson Hawley after the Architect's Designs.

first President. He resigned after the first meeting. He was President of the Coney Island Jockey Club at the time of his death.

Mr. Jerome was at one time an enthusiastic yachtsman. He owned the *Undine*, and later the *Restless*. He was joint owner with Mr. James Gordon Bennett of the *Dauntless*. His steam-yacht *Clarita* was not a success, and he gave up the sport.

In early life he married Miss Clarissa Hall, the sister of Mrs. Lawrence Jerome. They had three daughters, all of whom married Englishmen. The eldest married Mr. Moreton Frewen; the second, Lord Randolph Churchill; and the third, Captain Leslie, of the Guards, the oldest son of Sir John Leslie, Baronet.

The residence which Mr. Jerome built for himself and family in Madison Square was at the time the most sumptuous in New York. It is now the property of Lady Randolph Churchill, and is occupied by the University Club. It was previously occupied by the Union League and the Turf clubs.

THE WALDORF.

In the abstract the critical faculty when applied to architectural composition might be indifferent to the utilitarian idea, and yet the one of fitness, appropriateness, cannot be overlooked. It is obvious that you may not design a prison like a theatre, nor a minster like a mart, simply because the usage of each building is fitted for its peculiar requirements. An edifice, then, is endowed with a certain individuality.

In the hotel construction of to-day a better taste, though it has no liking for what is unattractive, discredits the gorgeous. Where in a vast city there is put under a single roof, as in a hotel, about the population of a village, a building suggestive of a barrack would repel guests. An attractiveness, a certain cheerfulness, and at the same time a dignity not too oppressive of its kind, are the qualities which Mr. H. J. Hardenbergh, the architect of the Waldorf, has impressed on his structure.

This hotel, the name of which, the Waldorf, is now made public through Harper's Weekly for the first time, is being built by Mr. William Waldorf Astor. The ground was broken early this year, and by the fall of 1892 it will be finished. It stands on the northwest corner of Thirty-third Street and Fifth Avenue, and on the site of the old Astor mansion. In order to secure ample room, several of the houses on Thirty-third Street have been pulled down. The façade on Thirty-third street will be 250 feet, and on Fifth Avenue 100 feet, or half of the block. The architect has had, then, the good fortune to command ample room for his structure, and with such a base is chary of building up to the clouds.

The style of the hotel is German Renaissance, in keeping with its name. Not quite as florid as is the Italian, under certain wise modifications German Renaissance acquired greater robustness. Details are more impressive, because not so overwrought. Mr. Hardenbergh has introduced on the Thirty-third Street side a charming loggia, with an open story above it; and on the Fifth Avenue side has repeated the loggia, giving to this particular one a much greater height. The conception is excellent, since it breaks lines and takes away any appearance of conventionality.

The building will have twelve stories. The first two stories are to be of Maynard stone, which is of a warm reddish hue, and the rest will be made up of Baltimore brick, which will continue the predominant tone color of the stone. The embellishments and decorations will be of terra-cotta, and the whole surmounted with a roof covered with red tiles. At the corner the usual hard up and down line will be done away with, for here there will be a rounded termination, coming out from the sides above the second story and continued to the top, and capped with a conical roof. That difficult thing, a fine sky-line, the architect has succeeded in obtaining. With a fair width on Fifth Avenue, as the building has a height of 180 feet, it will be tall enough to be visible at a good distance.

Of all things in the world, it must be the conception of the architect which is of slowest birth. It comes haltingly, piecemeal, subjected to endless refinings before it can be welded into one homogeneous whole. The comely outside can be reached only by adaptations of the inside requirements, and so looks and utility have to go hand in hand. Five hundred guest-rooms, with offices, restaurants, ballrooms, court-yards, mean something more than the mere spaces they occupy. Modern requirements are infinite. A man not given to devising plans fitted to hygienic necessities would give it all up with an addled brain were he told that every bathroom in the Waldorf must be so arranged that it shall be ventilated not by means of shafts, but by actual access to the open air. Mr. Hardenberg, by a series of open courts, not wells, has so planned it that what seemed impossible has been attainable. When a property owner holds in his possession the title-deeds of all the adjacent ground, such a thing is feasible, as in the case of the Waldorf.

All the work of the hotel, everything that comes into the house, all unsightly objects, for there is nothing elegant in a traveller's luggage, finds its entrance through a driveway ending in an internal court on the Thirty-third Street side. Below, in the basement, are the electrical and the ice machines, and that expanse of laboratory where cooks pervade. And the wine cellar? That alone is a distinguishing feature.

What of the elegances? The climate of New York city is eccentric. In the Waldorf there is to be a famous court of 40 by 50 feet. In winter this will be roofed by glass and thoroughly warmed, so as to be habitable. In summer away will go the roof, and above, a hundred feet higher up, will be the sky and the fresh air. It is by means of many similar courts, not all parade ones like the one described, that perfect ventilation is attained. Should there be festivities, here are many dining-rooms, where future company will meet, and contiguous to these banqueting places a whole series of rooms arranged so as to open *en suite;* and so can be had all the requirements of a private house.

We have flattered ourselves that, so far, the hotels of the United States were fairly comfortable. As imitation is the sincerest flattery, London and Paris have followed in our wake. In the last number of Harper's Weekly illustrations of the New Netherland and a second hotel opposite to it on Fifty-ninth Street and Fifth Avenue were presented. The Waldorf, the subject of this article, makes, then, the third house. All of them will add to the comfort of that world which visits New York for business or pleasure.

FURNISHED ROOMS TO LET.

A NICE FURNISHED ROOM in private family; $1.25 per week. 725 East 163d st., first floor.

548 EAST 142D ST.—A large, comfortably furnished front room to let, with gas and bath; $3 per week. Ring Ahrens' bell.

FURNISHED ROOM for married couple or two gents, also single rooms. Address Mr. Lohr, 974 East 163d st., near Union ave.

FURNISHED PARLOR FLOOR—Furnished parlor floor to let; heated and bath; three rooms; $6.00 a week; 974 East 163d st., near Union ave., or E. Kronemeyer, grocer, 3545 Third ave.

FURNISHED ROOM—A private family will rent large, handsomely furnished room; also back parlor. 720 East 138th st.

A PRIVATE FAMILY will rent large handsomely furnished second-story room; also back parlor; fine location for physician. 720 East 138th st.

FURNISHED ROOM—Nicely furnished front room in private house. 522 East 143d st., near Third ave

FURNISHED ROOM—Nicely furnished front room; three windows, with ante-room; basin hot and cold water; bath; furnace heat; private house, 209 Alexander ave.; rent reasonable.

NICELY FURNISHED ROOMS on second floor, front or rear; convenient to electric and elevated roads; private family. Call at 3002 Third ave.

PROFESSIONAL.

NURSE—A nurse for ladies during confinement; doctors' reference; terms, $1.00 per day. 2987 Third ave., between 153d and 154th st. Call or address

CLAIRVOYANTS.

CLAIRVOYANT—The wonderful Gypsy, Nino, can be consulted daily on all matters of libel. 220 East 128th st.

DRESSMAKING.

DRESSES made at from $5 00 up. Late styles. S. T. Taylor's system of cutting. 1030 East 138th st.

DRESSMAKER—Competent dressmaker would like private customers by the day or week; understands children's clothing. 1001 Jackson ave., near 165th st.

HELP WANTED—FEMALE.

HOUSEWORK—Girl for general housework; no washing; go home nights; reference as to character. 314 Alexander ave.

LADIES, you can have the best help of all nations at Mrs Samsels' Employment Office, 2627 Third ave., near 143d st.

WANTED—A good girl for general housework; good wages. 948 Fleetwood av., bet. 163d and 164th sts.

GERMAN GIRL, for general housework; no washing. 876 Forest ave., near 161st st.

HELP WANTED—MALE.

WANTED—25 boys and girls to learn trade. Apply B. L. Young, 427 East 144th st.

WANTED—Five good, reliable boys who are willing to work from 5.30 a. m. to 11 a. m.; small salary at the beginning. Call Monday morning, from 8 to 9, at the Advocate office, 175th st. and Third ave.

SITUATIONS WANTED—MALE.

DRIVER AND STABLEMAN wishes situation; honest and sober. 551 East 152d st., rear house

BOY, 19, wants situation; anything; can give the best of references. J. McVeady, 1976 Main st., West Farms.

SITUATIONS WANTED—FEMALE.

DAY'S WORK WASHING AND IRONING. Mrs. Harper, 92 162d st. and Brook ave.

YOUNG WOMAN would like to do plain sewing of any kind, or take home washing. Mrs Boosmann, 579 East 149th st., first floor.

WASHING, ironing neatly done home; will go out by day. Mrs. Balzer, Camp's flats, Webster ave., bet. 176th and 177th sts.

WASHING—A woman wants to take in washing. 1624 Vanderbilt ave.

HOUSEWORK—A respectable colored woman, middle aged, wants housework in a small family; give reference. 113 West 159th st.

ROOMS AND BOARD.

TO LET—Furnished room, with or without board. J. Freund, 2343 Ryer ave., cor. Kirk pl

PRIVATE FAMILY of two adults will accommodate table boarders. Apply 2581 Third ave.

FURNISHED ROOM to let, with or without board; private house. 686 East 134th st.

ROOMS AND BOARD—366 Willis av.; private house.

FURNISHED ROOMS, with or without board; private family. 1262 Vanderbilt ave.

BOARDERS WANTED—1698 Bathgate ave.; terms reasonable.

FURNISHED ROOM—Private family will rent large, handsomely furnished room; board if desired. 720 East 138th st.

HOUSES TO LET.

WHOLE HOUSE of seven rooms for $15 on 164th st., next door east of Brook ave.; will be put in good repair. Enquire Morris, Third ave and 163d st.

HOUSE TO LET—$18 per month; improvements. J. Hoffman, 614 East 155th st

TO LET OR FOR SALE—House of nine rooms; hot and cold water; bath; heater; on 167th st.; rent low for winter; price, $4,750. Apply 1062 Forest ave.

175TH ST., 747 EAST—In whole or part; 14 rooms; inquire S. A. Thompson, 84th st. and Third ave

HOUSE TO LET CHEAP—1187 Railroad ave., near 167th st; large rooms; all improvements; would let for business purposes. Hendrickson, 877 Cauldwell ave., near 161st st.

COTTAGE TO LET—Pelham ave. and Lorillard st.; all improvements; seven rooms; rent $25 00 per month. Apply at Coffin's Real Estate Office, Fordham Depot.

EIGHT ROOM HOUSE—Croton water, Avenue St. John, Fordham; rent $16 per month; also 4 rooms, croton water; rent $8 per month. Wm. G. Mulligan, northwest cor. Third and Tremont ave.

FLOORS TO LET.

TO LET—A floor of three light rooms and pantry. 7?9 East 163d st., bet. Third and Washington aves.

$13—DESIRABLE SECOND FLOOR, five rooms, large; all improvements. 1638 Bathgate ave., 172d st.

A FINE all-light warm floor in three-story brick house; high stoop; all improvements. Dining room separate, $14. 666 145th st., near Willis ave.

FURNISHED ROOMS—Second floor to let, furnished or unfurnished; six rooms; bath; cheap rent. 2324 Bathgate ave.

FLOOR in private house; all modern improvements, including heat; rent $15. 713 East 141st st.

TO LET—Upper part of house; six rooms; bath; all improvements. 725 East 163d st., near Brook ave

APARTMENTS TO LET.

FOUR ROOMS in private house. Trolley cars pass the door. Rent, $11. 1030 East 138th st.

FLATS TO LET.

2615 THIRD AVE., NEAR 140TH ST.—All improvements, including bath and private hall.

4 rooms, 2 flights up	$14.00
3 rooms, ground floor	12.00
2617 Third Ave.:	
4 rooms, 3 flights up	$11 00
3 rooms, 2 flights up	9.50

Apply to OTTO ZIMMERMAN, 2615 Third ave.

SINGLE FLAT, all improvements and furnished Rooms. 725 East 163d st.

LOST AND FOUND.

LOST—Two weeks ago a neck nat. scarf, between Mt. Hope and Tremont. Suitable reward. Mrs. Dryer, Gray and Topping sts., Mt. Hope.

FOR SALE.

CHATTEL MORTGAGE SALE—Fixtures and furniture of barber shop. Sale to day, 10 a. m., at 597 East 167th st. By order of Rob't Hill Attorney for Mortgagee.

$40.00. FOR SALE—Old house on Franklin ave.; Park Department. F. Boss, 177th st and Third ave.

TWO SHOW CASES, fishing tackle, toys and candies. 952 East 149th st.

FOR SALE—3 horses, 2 platform spring wagons, 1 phaeton, 1 double set of harness, 1 brass beam scale. L. Ford, 698 East 165th st.

FURNITURE FOR SALE—$150 buys new furniture, 4-room flat; one flight; rent, $16. Drew, 364 West 118th st.

DELICATESSEN STORE—For sale at reasonable price; in good German vicinity, on account of other business. F. Scheele, 790 Forest ave., saloon.

FULL LOT, corner 166th st. and Union ave. $3,500; plot with house, corner 166th st and Tinton ave., $11,000; 664 East 162d st., 7-room house, lot 17x100, $3,200. Hendrickson, 877 Cauldwell ave., near 161st st.

FOR SALE—One Baltimore fireplace heater; one steam pump; one small horizontal engine; one 6-arc light dynamo. S. A. Thomas, 468 Mott ave.

MILK ROUTE—100 quarts daily; seven cows and two heifers; also horse and wagon if desired; the whole to be sold very cheap. Apply to Owen Toher, 184th st. and Third ave.

MEDICAL.

MRS HEIDECKER, skilful midwife; confinement with board for nine days, $12; infants adopted. 725 Third ave., near 45th st.

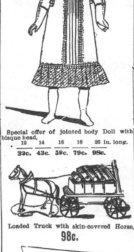

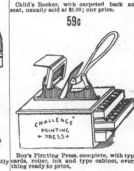

Bloomingdales
3rd Ave. Corner 59th St.

Thousands of people are selecting their presents now. We are doing what we can to help other thousands to do likewise. Goods selected now stored at our expense. Sure deliveries on any day you may designate. Holiday Catalogue free to any address.

Bloomingdales
3rd Ave. Corner 59th St.

Great Holiday Sale of Fine Laces.

Holiday Sale of made-up Lace articles at greatly reduced prices.

Irish Point and Cluny Lace Tidies, 16x18 inches square, reduced from $1.50 to

.98

Table Runners, Bureau Scarfs and Chiffonier Tidies of Renaissance Lace, each

8.00

Small Companion Tidies, each

.75

Fancy Persian Tidies, 98c. to

1.75

Toilet Sets of four pieces, made of China Silk and Val. Lace; sizes to order, per set

3.75

Cluny Scarfs, Chiffonier and Sideboards, sizes to order, $2.98, $3.50 and

3.98

Antique Tidies, each 6c. to

1.75

Renaissance Lace for window and table decorations; insertions to match, 49c., 59c., 75c. and

.98

—:o:—

Mufflers and Handkerchiefs.

Holiday Sale of Ladies' and Gentlemen's Silk and Linen Handkerchiefs, Silk and Cashmere Mufflers, Children's Fancy Box Handkerchiefs, and Handkerchiefs of all kinds in fancy boxes, especially suitable for Holiday Presents. There will be no advance in our prices, no matter how great the rush.

Children's Fancy Handkerchiefs, 3 in a box, 15c. per box; 6 in box at per box,

.27

Children's Initial, 3 in a box, at per box,

.28

Ladies' Initial Hemstitched, each............ .5
Ladies' Initial Hemstitched............ .15
Gentlemen's Initial Hemstitched............ .15

Ladies' all-linen Initial, former price was 35c.

.21

Gentlemen's fine all-linen Initials at

.30, .49 and .75

Gentlemen's White Hemstitched, all-linen,

.25 to 1.00

Ladies' White Hemstitched, all-linen,

.20 to .75

Special sale of Chiffon Hand Embroidered Handkerchiefs—very great bargains

At .15............sold for .25
At .25............sold for .50
At .48............sold for 1.00
At .75............sold for 1.98

Mufflers, Cashmere............ .23
Cashmere and Silk............ .45
All Silk............ .65
All Silk............ .75
All Silk............ .98

—:o:—

Great Holiday Picture Sale.

A fine assortment of the latest French fac-similes in white and gold Bow Knot Frames, worth 2.00, at

1.25

Same in fleur de lis frames, worth 2.50, at

1.49

Genuine Free Hand Pastels in white and gold frames, reduced from 4.50 to

2.98

Artist Proof Etchings, in handsome oak and steel frames, reduced to

.98

A large assortment of Engravings in handsome oak frames, reduced from $2.50 to

1.69

An Immense Stock of Framed Oil Paintings, Pastels, Etchings, etc.

The Finest Assortment of Fancy pictures in Oval, Bow Knot and Fancy Frames.

The Latest Patterns of genuine imported gold Florentine Frames for cabinet, and larger sizes at very low prices.

Frames to Order a Specialty.

Holiday Book Sale.

NOTE.---In quoting the publishers' list prices we do not wish to convey the impression that other dealers ask these prices. Every progressive Retailer sells books at less than the publishers' list prices. We are certain, however, that no other house sells Books at anything like our special prices. Mail orders should be sent in at the earliest possible moment. General Holiday catalogue FREE to any address.

Here Are Special Prices:

"OUR LEADER SERIES."

Handsome cloth bound books: Arabian Nights, Child's History of England, Deerslayer, East Lynne, Grimm's Fairy Tales, Handy Andy, Ivanhoe, Jane Eyre, John Halifax, Last Days of Pompeii, Lorna Doone, Oliver Twist, Pathfinder, Pioneers, The Prarie, Robinson Crusoe, Romola, Rory O'More, Irving's Sketch Book, Tom Brown, Twenty Thousand Leagues, Willy Reilly, etc., published at 1.00 and 1.25; our sale price,

.15

10,000 SETS.

Dickens, 6 vols., English cloth, published at 6.00,

1.98.

Dickens, 15 vols., published at 15.00,

3.49.

Thackeray, 10 vols., published at 10.00,

2.47

Lyall, 6 vols., published at 7.35

1.39

Lamb, 2 vols., published at 2.50,

.47

Cooper's Leather Stocking Tales, published at 6.25,

.98

Eliot, 6 vols., published at 9 00,

1.37

Emerson, 2 vols., published at 2.50,

.47

Hugh, 2 vols., published at 2.50,

.47

Sue, 2 vols., published at 2.50,

.47

Macaulay's England, 5 vols., published at 6.25,

.98

Shakespeare, 3 vols., published at 6.00,

1.29

Irving, 6 vols., published at 12.00,

3.48

Longfellow, 2 vols., published at 2.50,

.79

Dumas, 8 vols., published at 12.50,

1.79

Gibbon's Rome, 6 vols., published at 9.00,

1.98

Scott's Waverley Novels, 12 vols., published at 18.00,

3.69

Shakespeare, 4 vols., published at 6.00,

1.15

Webster's 5.00 Original Dictionary,

.69

Shakespeare, 1 vol, English cloth, large print, fine paper, fully illustrated, published 3.50, at

.69

Chambers' Encyclopedia, 12 vols., cloth, published at 25.00, at

4.89

Chambers' African Explorers and Adventures, 2 vols., published at 3.00,

.98

Prescott's Ferdinand and Isabella, 2 vols., published at 3 50,

.98

Scott's Waverly Novels, 12 vols., half Russia, published at 24.00,

6.98

These popular sets, English cloth, library binding, large print, extra fine paper—

Eminent Americans, by Lossing, in two volumes, published at 2.50,

.98

Set Fielding's Works in two volumes, published at 2.00,

.79

Byron, Spectator, Boswell and Disraeli's Works, three volumes, cloth and gold, published at 6.00,

2.88

New and Interesting

—

BOOKS
for Young Folks.
Beautifully Illustrated.

Young Folks at Home, Children's Delight, Our Boys and Girls, Wide Awake Pleasure Book, Sunshine for Babyland, published at 1.25 and 1.50,

.24

29c. and 35c.

—

"Special Popular Books,"
By Mark Twain.

Huckleberry Finn, Tom Sawyer, Prince and Pauper, bound in cloth,

.59

Little Lord Fauntleroy.

1.12

Elsie Books,

.49

Wide Awake, published at 1.00,

.25

Wood's History of the United States, Arctic Travelers, Life of Napoleon, Stanley's Travels, Out-door Sports, Old and New Testament, published at 1.25,

.35

—

Instructive, Interesting and Amusing.

THE ROUND ABOUT BOOKS.

The Fall of Sebastopol, by G. A. Hentz. Fighting the Saracens, by G. A. Hentz. A Voyage in the Sunbeam, by Lady Brassey. Young Americans in Tokio, by Edward Greey. Our boys in India, by Harry W. French. Young Americans in Tezo, by Edward Greey. Drifting Around the World, by Captain C. W. Hall. Our Boys in China, by Harry W. French. Young Americans in Japan, by Edward Greey.

The above are beautifully illustrated, handsomely bound, large print and extra fine paper. We sell them in:

Picture Covers, published at $1.25,

.69

Cloth and Silver Covers, published at 1.75,

.89

The Universal Cook Book, oilcloth binding, by Mrs. D. A. Lincoln, Miss M. Parloa, Marion Harland, and others, published at $1.25,

.59

Miss Parloa's Cook Book, oilcloth cover, published at 2.00 and sold by us for years at 1.19, at

.59

Captain Mayne Reid's Works, published at 1.25,

.47

Popular Boys' Books, handsomely bound in cloth and gold, published at 1.25 and 1.50, by such popular authors as Alger, Ellis, Chipman, Fitts, Prentice, Otis, Converse, Castlemon, Hill and Calhoun,

.59

Alice's Adventures in Wonderland, published at 1.25, sold at

.35

St. Nicholas, per volume

1.34.

Harper's Young People,

1.79

Ballantyne's Works, published at 1.25,

.59

The Sunbeams and Our Little Ones. The most popular Calendar for 1893, published at 50c.; our sale price

.15

50,000 Children's New, Amusing and Instructive Books, suitable for boys and girls of all ages, with handsomely illuminated covers and fully illustrated, more than 500 kinds, published at from 35c. to 1.00,

5c., 8c., 10c., 12c., 15c.

The Young American Annual. A great book for young folks. 480 pages of instructive, amusing and pleasing histories, adventures, stories, anecdotes and incidents, mainly American characters. Edited by the Rev. Samuel Fallows, M. D. Fully illustrated. Printed in large type, on fine paper, beautifully bound in English cloth and gold. Published at 3.75.

.98

Wide Awake, Sparkles for Bright Eyes, Merry Christmas, etc. Published at 1.25, at

.21

Homespun Yarns, Grandma's Stories, Our Girls, Our Boys, etc. Published at 1 50, at

.29

Girl's Annual. Published at 1.50, at

.29

Children's Life of Jesus, Grandma's Old, Old Stories, etc. Published at 1.50, at

.29

Chatterbox,

.36

The Sunday. Published at 2.00, at

.59

Giovanni and the Other, a new book by Mrs. Burnett, author of Little Lord Fauntleroy, etc. Published at 2.00, at

.89

Frank Leslie's Christmas Book of Fairy Tales for 1893, handsomely illustrated and elegantly bound. Published at 1.25, at

.35

Elegant assortment of Gift Books, illustrated with fine Steel Engravings and Colored Plates.

Every book published can be found in our book department. Largest and most complete in the city. Goods can be selected now and delivered on any day you may designate. Special terms to Dealers, Committees, etc.

5.00 Atlases at 1.59

The C. A. Gaskell's Complete Family and Business Atlas of the World, of 1893, handsomely bound in library cloth. Published and sold at 5.00; our price

1.59

Silk Dress Patterns for Holiday Gifts.

150 Dress Patterns, good quality black gros grain silk, sufficient for full costume; a great bargain,

8.25

175 Dress Patterns, excellent quality black gros grain silk, rich finish, sufficient for a full dress; a great bargain,

11.75

125 Dress Patterns, elegant quality black Faille Francaise, sufficient for a full costume; a great bargain,

8.75

75 Dress Patterns, a superior quality and excellent wearing article, sufficient to make a full dress pattern; a great bargain,

11.98

Look at this elegant Christmas Present: A handsome Colored Bengaline Serge in stripes and figures, all evening shades and street colors, a full dress pattern; a great bargain,

6.35

—:o:—

Dress Robes.

Elegantly Embroidered Dress Robes for holiday gifts, in cashmere at

3.50

Silk Embroidered Dress Robes for holiday gifts, in all-wool cashmere serges and cloth, for

5.98

One lot of 250 Dress Robes for holiday gifts, made of cloth, cashmere and brocades—trimmed with fine chenille lining and edged with fur—actually worth 12.00 for

6.98

A finer grade, reduced from 18.00 and 25.00, for

10.98 and 14.98

To-morrow morning we begin a great sale of 10,000 Dress Patterns put up expressly for holiday gifts.

2,000 Dress Patterns for holiday gifts, in cheviot or cashmere, fully worth double; each

1.79

1,250 Dress Patterns for holiday gifts, in English jacquard and crocodile, in a large variety of designs, each fully worth double; each

2.25

750 Dress Patterns for holiday gifts, in English body cashmere and all-wool cheviots, fully worth double; each

2.79

1,000 Dress Patterns, for holiday gifts, in all-wool serges, henriettas and black brilliantines; fully worth double,

3 69

800 Dress Patterns, for holiday gifts, in a superior quality, all-wool bedford cord, crocodile and goods sold at 1.00 yard; fully worth double,

4.25

1,000 Dress Patterns, for holiday gifts, in all-wool camels' hair brocades in all the newest and fashionable colors; fully worth double; our price, each

4.98

5,000 Dress Patterns, in gingham, cambric, cordurette, recoles, etc., each 75, 85, 1.00, 1.25 and

1.50

2,000 All-Wool Homespun Skirts, especially adapted for holiday gifts, each 75, 1.25 and

1.50

Lot of Embroidered Flannels, per yard, 63, 69, 75, 85, and

1.00

Solid Gold Jewelry.

Solid Gold Rings, .39, .49, .69, .98, 1.39.
Solid Gold Lockets, 1.69, 2 98, 3.98.
Solid Gold Earrings, .69, .98, 1.25 per pair.
Solid Gold Scarf Pins, .47, .69, .98, 1.19, 1.69.
Solid Gold Sleeve Buttons, 1.69, 2.49, 2.98, 3.98.
Solid Gold Necklaces, 2.19, 2 69, 2.98, 3.98.
Solid Gold Lace Pins, 2 98, 3 98, 4 98.
Solid Gold Cuff Pins, .85, 1.19, 1.49, 1.69.

BLOOMINGDALE BROS. THIRD AVE., COR. 59TH ST. BLOOMINGDALE BROS.

Colored Supplement.

The World.

"Circulation Books Open to All."

Colored Supplement.

NEW YORK, SUNDAY, MAY 21, 1893.

BROADWAY CABLE CAR POSSIBILITIES.

ARGYLL ON WEALTH.

His Grace Defines It in His Book "The Unseen Foundations of Society."

THE DISTINGUISHED AUTHOR FALLS FOUL OF HENRY GEORGE AND ADAM SMITH.

Political and Social Economy from an Ethical Standpoint—Does America's Prosperity Rest Upon Law and the Security of Possession?—Views on Productive and Unproductive Labor—A Tribute to Democratic America from an English Aristocrat—Everything Here Is on a Gigantic Scale.

At a time when there has grown up a strong scientific protest against the older schools of political economy, and men very far removed from philosophy and metaphysics are discussing with practical sense and a vigorous conviction the relation of all three elements which go to make up the modern social solidarity, the calm utterances of a conservative scholar like the Duke of Argyll cannot fail to be of service and of deep interest.

His book of nearly six hundred pages, which he calls "The Unseen Foundations of Society," specifically claims to be an examination of the fallacies and failures of economic science, due to neglected elements. It is something more. Analysis no doubt is its chief merit, but the historic method employed and the synthetic grouping of facts point very clearly to the formulation of a doctrine, and making all allowance for "the personal equation" of a writer who is avowedly a free-trader of the orthodox Cobden school, the views and the conclusions are sufficiently broad and accurate to commend this book to all who are interested in the study of social science.

Perhaps there is no subject of human thought and no motive of human action which at this time are so operative and so urgent as the relation of wealth and the owners of wealth to the community, and any dispassionate and scholarly attempt to arrive, through the fogs and figments of abstruse doctrinaires, at the abiding elements in human character and the possible human basis of social prosperity and permanence, will be welcomed whenever there is an honest desire to form and to diffuse clear views.

The author, in his preparatory work of clearing the ground of the abstract rubbish that Adam Smith and Ricardo have left behind them, points out that the continual and abounding source of error in the philosophies of social science lies in "neglected elements;" that is to say, not only in facts which may be unknown, but quite as often in the omission of facts which may be so well known and familiar that they are not treated as worthy of notice, and this great and fruitful source of fallacy is never so baneful as in the sciences which deal with facts and phenomena that are purely mental. It is for this reason that the author rejects the mathematical process of Jevons, and declares that the application of mathematical methods to economic science is essentially delusive because it tends, more than any other, to multiply the number of neglected elements.

He is equally intolerant of the definitions of the older writers, mentioning, as a curious fact, that Adam Smith, in his "Wealth of Nations," did not even attempt to define "wealth," but carelessly uses the phrase "the necessaries, conveniences and amusements of life" as comprising all there is to wealth. Cliffe Leslie's compact definition that "wealth comprises all things which are objects of desire, limited in supply and valuable in exchange," the author is inclined to think could be improved, or at least simplified, by such a mere description as this: "Wealth is the possession, in comparative abundance, of valuable things."

But even this is inadequate for the author's purpose, and he sets about to give a definition of wealth which shall embody in it all the heads of his thesis. He even puts it in syllogistic order, and he declares that wealth is—

1. The possession
2. in comparative abundance
3. of things
4. which are the objects of human desire
5. not obtainable without some exertion
6. and which are accessible to men able as well as anxious to obtain them.

His apology for this formal and ample statement is that its propositions will be at once recognized as the language of common sense and universal experience. He proceeds, however, to deliver an essay on each proposition.

It is only necessary to refer to those points which have of late been most in dispute, or have been most successfully sophisticated by popular writers and speakers.

Thus, the things which constitute wealth depend for their value upon the desires, tastes and powers of other men, and nothing is so difficult, says the author, as to fix in the ordinary man's mind that no labor, whether of hand or of brain or of both combined, can by itself put the stamp of wealth upon things if other men do not desire them.

In the fifth proposition care has been taken to meet the popular fallacy that the common elements of air and water in a sense represent wealth.

But the author well says they could be thus exemplified in the eyes of those who forget the fundamental element of possession. In so far as air, earth or water, or any other natural agency, needs to be possessed before it can be turned to use, in so far it can never be got for nothing.

Finally in this scheme we see in the sixth proposition a proposition to recognize the relativity and interdependence of wealth, and the writer claims that this view places at once on the firm basis of an almost self-evident fact, the conclusion of which is too often regarded as a mere sentimental theory, that the true and ultimate interest of every individual man is bound up inseparably with the interests of human society as a whole. The very possibility of wealth for all depends on the wealth of all around us. We cannot get wealth except by serving them directly or indirectly, and conversely we cannot serve them without at least promoting the means on which our own wealth depends. It is thus not a theory or a mere sentiment, but a scientific fact, that society is an organism every part of which acts and reacts upon each other and on the whole.

So far the definition and the elucidation of wealth falls within the province of economics. But the author appears to have felt as he went along that it should extend into ethics. He points out to the reader, it is true, but as if to himself, that there are some things which, as a matter of fact, are objects of human desire, but which do not constitute wealth. The scalps and the skulls of enemies are the most coveted objects of desire to not a few savage races, yet he thinks they are not a possession which can constitute wealth. We fail to see the force of this observation, for they may be regarded as wealth in a degree corresponding to the savage's condition and relations to his fellows. But that aside, the author believes the skulls and scalps to represent desires which must always be fatal to the possibility of wealth being attained. He therefore exultingly goes back and corrects the fourth proposition so that it reads: "Which are the objects of legitimate desire."

This is a discovery, he maintains, which teaches us a great lesson. There is no science which does not touch other sciences at more than one point of contact; no definition, if it be a true one, can be independent of qualifications due to the interference of adjacent truths in a different yet cognate sphere of thought. He declares that his first definition would be perfect if the sphere of economics could be cut off completely from the sphere of ethics.

As to the sources of wealth, this author is very severe upon those writers who have cut the idea down to the materialistic elements in the conception. He calls Henry George's difinition of wealth the crudest and rudest ever presented in the name of science. Wealth, according to that writer, is "matter of the universe worked up into desirable form." In like manner our author finds that the definition of the source of wealth has been affected by the badness of the preconceptions as to that in which wealth consists. Nowhere, he declares, in the history of a "shattered science" is anything more astonishing than the wide acceptance which has been given to the formula, "Land, labor and capital." Land, he says, cannot mean, as it usually does, the mere soil, or some particular area. Labor cannot mean, as it usually does, mere handiwork. Capital cannot mean, as it usually means, mere storage of wealth; for the simple reason that the soil without many adjuncts and many agencies external to itself is inert and valueless, and labor must be taken as meaning the whole mental as well as the whole bodily activities of men. Capital, we are told, is essentially a consequence, and not a cause. It is nothing but the product of the other two great sources of wealth—namely, the energies of a man and the working of these on the materials of external nature. It is characteristically a product of mind. To save and to store is essentially the work of purpose and intention. Capital is not a mere source of wealth; it is simply another word for wealth itself when put to a particular kind of use.

The soundness of these views will be questioned. Indeed, it is not difficult to see that the fervor of His Grace's attack upon certain phases of the social question has led him to take the technical and doctrinaire view which he deprecates so vehemently in the older writers. Nothing, he declares, can be worse in its practical effects than the common distinction or antithesis which we see every day in newspaper headings between labor and capital.

But it is doubtful if the newspapers use the words with any implication of elemental antithesis. They merely serve to express two economic conditions of energy which are patent factors in life around us.

With another distinction that has been made of late between productive and unproductive labor he has no patience at all, and declares that "it has played havoc with economic science." On no question of economics has the thinking of the orthodox school been more slovenly than on this, or on any other has their teaching been more fallacious. It has flattered, he says, particular classes to think that they are the only producers and to envy and hate other classes whose effective share in production may be much larger and more potent than their own.

It is at this point, we think, that the personal equation comes more distinctly into view in the book than at any other. He speaks of the root of this fallacy being deeply imbedded in Adam Smith's mind, and declares that he relegated to the unproductive class, in one indiscriminate jumble, all sovereigns, officers of justice, the whole army and navy, lawyers of all kinds, along with players, buffoons and opera dancers. "What are we to think," exclaimed the Duke of Argyle, "of the undiscerning thought which classifies soldiers, sailors, magistrates, police and lawyers as all belonging to one category of unproductive laborers? What can be more certain or obvious than that all the conditions of society which afford external peace and internal security are the most fundamental of all conditions on which the enjoyment and increase of wealth depend?"

It is doubtful if this philosophic statement will quite hold its own in the face of the fact that there are at this moment in Europe nearly six million soldiers who sow not, neither do they reap, but who are affording an internal security that would be almost absolutely guaranteed if they were turned into producers.

Very interesting are the historical studies in which the sources of the first possessions of wealth are traced, the causes of comparative abundance pointed out and the conditions which confer value on things determined. The author does not try to avoid the blunt avowals of early Jewish history—that possession was the result of bloody conquest—but he points out with a sure apprehension of the facts that the total destruction of the sources of wealth in those vast tracts of Asia which once fed the world was owing to the insecurity of possession. The absolute insecurity of all property was the universal experience of the people, and the stupendous phenomenon of populous cities sinking into the sand and scarcely leaving a trace of their opulence and vice is shown to be the result of uncertain and destructive forces which have continued down to our day.

The unseen causes here are religious mainly, but affecting government polity and social usage. It is in bringing into view these much neglected causes that in the author's view make up the badness that was destructive of individual liberty and secure possession that the book assumed an ethical import wholly unique in the treatment of social science. We perceive here and there, it is true, the influence of a distinct theological tendency of thought; but while insisting that religion has played a much larger share in the history of economics than it is given credit for by economists, the author does not neglect what he conceives to be the other historic factors.

Thus, he gives great weight to the Roman establishment of jurisprudence.

When she fell she transmitted those principles to Europe, and she thus planted deep in the western nations the root conception of law, upon which all wealth depends.

The Duke of Argyll makes no mention of the social phenomena which Guizot saw so clearly and placed so complacently at the foundation of European progress, which was that for the first time three diverse elements came together at the fall of Rome and produced that live diversity in unity which is everywhere seen in Nature herself. The three unlike elements were the municipal system of Rome, the Christian Socialism, and the austere independence of the invaders.

In considering some of the social problems of the day, the Duke falls foul of Henry George, with the asperity that we might expect from a writer so far removed from Mr. George's point of view. He thinks that the American writer's wonderful confirmation of Malthusian views and his vehement denunciation of Malthusian law, is one of the curiosities of literature; he attributes Mr. George's contradictions to his inability to trace causes to the constitution of man, and his inexcusable determination to find them in the systems under which man lives. He calls him a pessimist, and exhibits a grim humor in quoting his account of the corruption of the American Government, and placing against it his panacea of extending the control of that corrupt Government over the entire soil of the country.

Everything in America, says the Englishman, is on a gigantic scale, even its villainy, and the villainy advocated by Mr. George is as striking as the Mammoth Cave or the Tammany Ring, and naturally enough he comes with facile bitterness to the ethical weakness of Mr. George's scheme of repudiation.

He asks: "If the doctrine he established, that no faith is to be kept with the owners of land, will not the same principle apply to tenancy, as well as ownership? If one generation cannot bind the next to recognize a purchase, can one generation bind another to recognize a lease?" All national debts in Mr. George's view are as unjust as property in land, and are to be treated with the sponge. Whenever, says the Duke, "the people see any large handful in the hands of any one, they have a right to take it, in order to save themselves from the necessity of submitting to taxation."

It is interesting to quote the author here in his remarks on our civil war, which he makes a pungent example of Mr. George's methods.

"We all know," he says, "that not many years ago the United States was engaged in a civil war of long duration, and, at one time, of doubtful issue, and on which the national existence hung. I was one of those, not too many in this country, who held from the beginning of that terrible contest that the North was right in fighting it. Lord Russell, on a celebrated occasion, said they were fighting for dominion. Yes, and for what else have nations ever fought, and by what else than dominion have great nations ever come to be? But behind and above the existence of the Union as a nation there was the further question involved, whether, in this nineteenth century of the Christian era, there was to be established a great dominion of civilized men, which was to have negro slavery as its fundamental doctrine and the cherished basis of its Constitution.

"On both of these great questions the people of the Northern States had before them as noble a cause as any which has ever called men to arms. It is a cause which will be forever associated in the memory of mankind with one great figure—the figure of Abraham Lincoln, the best and highest representative of the American people in that tremendous crisis. In nothing has the bearing of that people been more admirable than in the patient and willing submission of the masses, as of one man, not only to the desolating sacrifice of life which it entailed but to the heavy burden of taxation which was inseparable from it. It is deplorable—nothing I have ever read in all literature has struck me as so deplorable—that at this time of day, when by patient continuance in well doing the burden has become comparatively light and there is a near prospect of its final disappearance, one single American citizen should be found who appreciates so little the glory of his country as to express his regret that it did not begin this great contest by an act of stealing. Yet this is the case with Mr. Henry George, who, in strict pursuance of his dishonest doctrines of repudiation respecting public debts, and knowing that the war could not have been prosecuted without funds, speaks with absolute bitterness of the folly which led the Government to shrink from at once seizing the whole of all but a fraction of the property of the few individual citizens who had the reputation of being exceptionally rich."

And here we have to take leave of the moralizing economist for the present, with regret, for, however much we may differ with him in the point of view and however often we may feel that from his position and his experience, he is much closer in touch with abstract principles than with social facts, evolved out of the collision of antagonistic elements, we, nevertheless, acknowledge the excellence of his rigid moral standard, the purity of his motives, and the dispassionate and lofty scholarship which has brought to a hitherto arid science some of interest, of human sympathy and all of the graces of a pure literary style.

NYM CRINKLE.

Suicides from the Eiffel Tower.

[*From the London Daily News.*]

Two persons, our Paris correspondent says, committed suicide on Sunday on the Eiffel Tower. One was M. Delarue, a secretary and clerk at the Colonial Ministry. He threw himself over the parapet of the third platform and fell to the second, where he was taken up dead. He was forty-two, a bachelor and had just been jilted. The other was a clerk in the stores, or "Magasins Generaux," of the Rue de Flandre, and a mere lad. He was seventeen, and had also, according to a letter found in his pocket, not only been slighted by a girl with whom he was in love, but owed £15, which he found he could not pay at once. The creditor being impatient he determined to settle the matter by the cowardly and in his case the dishonest resource of suicide. Before ending his life he spent the last 5 francs that remained to him on a Sunday dejeuner at the first platform restaurant, and at the coffee and liqueur stage blew his brains out.

HARPER'S WEEKLY
A JOURNAL OF CIVILIZATION

VOL. XXXVIII.—No. 1937.

NEW YORK, SATURDAY, FEBRUARY 3, 1894.

TEN CENTS A COPY.
FOUR DOLLARS A YEAR.

AT THE OPERA.

A PERFORMANCE OF "CARMEN" IN THE REMODELLED METROPOLITAN OPERA-HOUSE, NEW YORK.—DRAWN BY E. V. NADHERNY.—[SEE PAGE 111.]

GOLF—THE GREAT SOCIETY SPORT AS PLAYED IN HOGAN'S ALLEY.

Disappointed.

hey strayed into a garden where
hrysanthemums were rich and fair.
e said: "This garden is like you."
"e means 'tis sweet," she thought, but
he
ntinued, low and mournfully,
ecause it, dear, has bloomers, too."

NO CONFIDENCE.

Shopkeeper—Shall I send your parcel by mail?

New Woman—Male? Shame on you; send it by express.

PROVIDED FOR.

Mrs. Dix—What will Dick do with himself while you are gone to Europe?

Mrs. Hicks—His father is going to buy him a sixteen-bladed knife.

Answered.

The bloomer girl sat on the fence
To take a well-earned rest,
For she had biked from early morn
With unrelenting zest.
"My bloomin' lass, what ails the wheel?"
A passing swain inquired.
And with a saucy smile, she said:
"Why—don't you see?—it's tired!"

SOMETHING TO BRAG ABOUT.

Plymouth Roche—My great-grandfather came over in the Mayflower.

Tommy Traddles—Bah! Me brudder plays on de feetball team.

EASIER.

Banks—Old Soak is in trouble, and they want you to bail him out.

Tanks—Why don't they use a stomach pump?

Immodest Nature.

The winter now is near at hand,
The days are short and cold,
The trees no longer can command
Their foliage of gold.
The bleak winds bend each supple bough,
And Boston girls declare
They're too immodest anyhow,
Because their limbs are bare.

WOMAN, EVER SUPERSTITIOUS

He—Things have been at sixes and sevens with me to-day.

She—That's unlucky; six and seven make thirteen.

ADVICE, BUT NO CASH.

Dusty Rhodes—Give me a dime, boss? I'm out of work.

William Ann—Go to the Devil! He finds work for idle hands to do.

THE EARLY BIRD CATCHES THE WORM.—NIT.

Her Quick Perception.

"You are concealing something from me!"

His words were bitter, his accents sharp. So sharp that the maiden whom he addressed started, as though frightened, and blushed deeply.

"It is no use denying it," he repeated, with more sadness than bitterness now; "you are concealing something from me."

The girl hung her head in silence, and made no attempt at denial.

Shortly after, he left her without the usual good-night.

Stung to the quick with his reproaches and realizing the truth of his accusation, she received him the next evening, when he called, in her most decollete evening gown.

SHOCKING.

Elder Berry—Joblots nearly threw his wife into a fit at church to-day.

Mrs. Berry—How?

Elder Berry—Whispered to the usher to put him down for a call at 12.30.

INDEFINITE.

Bell Boy—Col. Juniper sends this card for you to register him by.

Clerk—It's a wine card; ask him if "Kentucky" is where he lives or what he wants.

1898 on the Farm.

The shades of night were slowly descending, the dew was also arriving, and the usual "indefinable feeling of impending danger" was on time. Mary Jane had almost finished her milking, when suddenly, with a final switch of her tastefully decorated tail, the usually peaceful bovine raised her left Trilby and, with a fierce kick of protest, upset the brimming pail. As Mary Jane quickly arose from her cobbler leather-seated rocker she might have been heard to sorrowfully murmur, "Another pair of my best bloomers completely ruined."

COULDN'T STAND IT.

Wool—Hanks and Scroggs hadn't spoken for twenty years until last week.

Van Pelt—How did it come about?

Wool—Hanks started to paint his house and Scroggs wanted to dictate the color.

WAKED 'EM UP.

Wool—I was on a Fifth avenue stage to-day and the team came near running away.

Van Pelt—What was the matter?

Wool—A farmer was ahead with a load of oats.

Bottomless.

as near the dawn of morning, the
was dark and still,
Claus was trying hard his
fil.
his y.

MR. SPATTS'S MISTAKE.

"I have kissed you nine times this evening, darling," said young Mr. Spatts, who was trying to take his leave of his sweetheart.

She fired up, and in an imperious manner exclaimed:

"Go, Mr. Spatts, never to return! I cannot trust my happiness with a man so coldly calculating as to count his kisses!"

AN O[illegible]D ONE.

?" asked the In-
y. "I'm a little
try to vote but

eanliness is

uble rates
af of the

On the Bridge of Sighs.

"Gee!"

A howl of anguish arose from the man with the pale pink whiskers.

"I've an awful stitch in my side!"

The Brooklynite beside him held fast to the handrail.

"That comes from"—

(He helped the sufferer through the surging throng as he spoke.)

—"getting hemmed in a crowd."

The other said nothing, and in silence they threaded their way through the devious mazes of the new bridge terminal.

ONE OF MANY.

Wool—Fields tells me he has put in the last year or two in foreign travel for the health of his family.

Van Pelt—That's right; he's a Jersey commuter.

THE WORM TURNS.

Election Inspector—Any visible marks on your face?

Van Pelt—Two ears, two eyes, one mouth.

Election Inspector—Such marks as that wouldn't distinguish you from me.

Van Pelt—I said one mouth—not mouth enough for two.

GOING AT A BARGAIN.

Miss Gotrox—I've got a bargain in a title.

Miss Neighbob—Who is he?

Miss Gotrox—That's telling; but he's a real duke, and I can get him for $999,999.99.

MOST LIKELY.

Saidso—Wonder what makes a lobster so red?

Herdso—Guess it must be what he sees at the seashore.

FIGURES IN THE THEATRE.

AN EXHIBITION OF THOMAS A. EDISON'S VITASCOPE.

Mistakes of "Thoroughbred" that Do Not Lessen Its Fun—The Tickers that Do Not Work Together in "Speculation"—John Hare's Reappearance Delayed.

Vaudeville took in a brand-new item last evening, the fact being made clear by the first public showing at Koster & Bial's of Thomas A. Edison's "vitascope." Its sub-title in the programme was the "projecting kinetoscope," and it was in effect a development of the kinetoscope that produced the pictures in life size. The producing apparatus was located in the second balcony, where the spaces back of two of the semicircular sections of the balcony front were built up in turret form to a height of six feet. In the front of each turret were two holes a few inches in diameter, through which the light was cast upon a drop curtain. In the centre of this curtain there was a painting of a huge picture frame that enclosed a white cloth. When the music hall was darkened and all was ready to begin, a whirring noise was audible from one of the up-stairs turrets, and simultaneously the two holes in it were brightly lighted. In a few seconds there appeared on the white space of the curtain a picture of two short-skirted dancers, who held a big umbrella in front of them. They kept up nimble dancing, changing the position of the umbrella from time to time, so that one second their faces were in sight and the next all that could be seen of them was their twinkling feet. The steps could be followed just as closely as if the dancers were in view in flesh and blood, and colors were in evidence in the costumes. Even more surprising than this was the second showing, which was a view of waves tumbling in upon a beach. At one side a stone pier ran out into the water, and along this the surf rolled, each wave hugging the stones and seeming to gather force till it broke in spray at the front of the pictures. By the time the foam-topped water receded another big roller would come sidling along the pier and dash into white fragments as had its fellow. The succession of waves included billows of different sizes, and when a big one would come rolling in its top would become higher and steeper, a little ripple would come at the crest, and then the whole bank would fall forward, and the irregular masses of foam would go tumbling on up the sands in the manner that sends beach promenaders scattering for dry spots. It was the next thing to seeing the real damp article and a closer copy than would have seemed possible.

It was so realistic that the only safe successor for it was a comic picture, and the selection was a burlesque bout of boxing between a very tall man and a short one. The contest included frequent knock-downs and many comical antics on the part of both sluggers. It simply threw upon the curtain a familiar form of exercise by knock-about variety pairs, and their punishing practices were copied exactly, from the long, swinging side blows to the kicks that were the fallen man's portion. Next came a picture that included a score of persons. There was a gayly dressed brass band, a group of women in the scanty attire of stage spectacles, and others in ornate costumes. The band marched in from the centre, dividing in two columns, one turning to each side. Then the others formed in line in an orderly manner, and a vocalist stepped out before them. Just after she bowed the screen was blank for a fraction of a second, and the band's march began again. The final item was a serpentine dance, which was shown quite as naturally as the other matters had been. The waving of the skirts was continuous, various colors were shown in them, and the legion of dancers tripped about over the space of canvas after the Loie Fuller manner.

The whole display was thoroughly novel, and it was greeted in a way to satisfy those persons that complain of the manner in which home talent is received in comparison to the greetings of entertainers from over seas. It seemed to be only a beginning, and one that opened up almost unlimited possibilities, while it at the same time presented several pictures, the waves particularly, that were very fine.

and that the rise or fall of an eighth, or anything else that is happening, must be of great interest in all the brokers' offices in the city. The tickers are made so prominent in this scene that the audience cannot help seeing them and noticing them all the time, whether they are immediately concerned with the dramatis personæ or not. If we have realism on the stage, there is no harm in having it fairly real. Mr. Seabrooke comes out pretty strongly later in this act as a serious actor, and the final impression is that he has played one of *John Fullerton's* most difficult scenes with unexpected success. But the tickers don't know their business.

John Hare's illness still delays his reappearance at Abbey's, but it is confidently expected that he will be able to act in "A Pair of Spectacles" and "Old Cronies" on Saturday night. The time and place of the single all-star performance of "The Rivals" in this city will be the afternoon of May 7 and the American Theatre. The cast names William H. Crane as *Sir Anthony*, Robert Taber as *Captain Absolute*, Joseph Jefferson as *Bob Acres*, Joseph Holland as *Falkland*, J. N. C. Goodwin as *Sir Lucius*, E. M. Holland as *Fag*, Francis Wilson as *David*, Mrs. Drew as *Malaprop*, Julia Marlowe Taber as *Lydia*, and Fanny Rice as *Lucy*. A company

Rudyard Kipling, the Rev. Dr. Rainsford, Theodore Roosevelt, Cardinal Gibbons, and Chauncey M. Depew. She said that the object of widening the road was that it might be used by prosaic trolley lines and elevated railroads.

Thomas B. Connery, Mrs. Sophie M. A. Hensley, Mrs. Alexander Newcomb, and several others asked the Mayor to reject the bill. Park Commissioner McMillan spoke in favor of it and advocated the removal of the cottage to a point where it will be safe. Mr. McMillan said that if the cottage remains where it is, in less than eighteen months it will be torn down by the Bureau of Encumbrances.

At the conclusion of the hearing Mayor Strong said that he thought he would have to accept the bill. He was sorry that he couldn't please everybody, but he hoped that the Poe cottage would be saved.

Is This Turtle 125 Years Old?

NEW LONDON, Conn., April 23.—A turtle was found on the Eugene F. Stillman farm yesterday. On the top of the shell were the initials "P. M." (Paul Maxson), with the date 1797. On the lower side of the shell were also "A. S., 1808" and "J. F. S., 1855." The last initials stand for the names of Adm. Stillman, grandfather of Eugene Stillman, and J. F. Stillman, father of Eugene F. Stillman. This turtle is thought to be 125 years old.

MRS. DRIFTER'S BANK BOOK.

A WOMAN WHO WANTED TO SHARE DUTIES AND INCOME.

She Tries Her Hand at a Separate Bank Account with Some Mishaps—Now She No Longer Yearns to Demonstrate the Superior Business Abilities of Woman.

Drifter and his wife have been chums, in the truest sense of the word, ever since their marriage. If he felt a yearning for an afternoon's revelry at the baseball park, Mrs. Drifter was eager to go along and share his hopes and disappointments. To him all Mrs. Drifter's hats, wraps, and furbelows, when exhibited for criticism, were "dreams, my dear, simply great. No other woman could have done so well on so little money."

She joined a bowling club and pretended to enjoy the weekly sessions; drank steins of beer with Drifter and his friends, and he smothered his dislike for "those young cubs and chattering girls" and whirled for a season with his comrade-wife in a junior cotillon society.

Mrs. D., in her girlhood, lived in California. She came East and married without having crossed the portals of a woman's club, without having any longing for suffrage, and was content to be taken care of, petted, and humored; while in turn she smoothed all the wrinkles out of Drifter's life by a chummy interest in everything he did, said, or liked.

So far so good. But when the Drifters got the suburban fever and settled upon their home in a cottage at Gravesendhurst there came an interruption to the comradeship. As Drifter says:

"The little girl was never one of your know-it-all, self-reliant, head-of-the-firm women. Not much. She always said that figures bothered her, and that when she wanted more money than I gave her or she could find in my pockets she'd ask for it. Some kind friend, while on a shopping expedition with my wife, threw a brand into the Drifter circle. That night I got this piece of information:

"'Drifter, every wife should take her share of the responsibilities of the household. Woman should not be afraid to handle business affairs. Experience teaches us that woman is a better manager of the home finances, and——'

"'What the dickens are you driving at, little one?' I asked.

"'A woman loses her independence, sacrifices her individuality, and becomes merely an ornament, a plaything, a——'

"'Hold on! hold on!' I gasped. 'Have you joined the Female Society to Prevent Husbands from Caring for Wives, or is this a notice of proceedings for separation, Madam?'

"'Drifter,' came the measured reply. 'I have leaned upon you too much. I must not only be a sharer in your pleasures, but in your trials and—and—I—I—m-u-s-t have a separate bank account. There!'

"The cat was out of the bag. A separate bank account. The dream of the new woman. The terror of the bank officials. I didn't rave around nor refuse my wife's request. I politely intimated that my own account frequently got me into hot water, said a few words on the subject of protested drafts, and brought tears from the feminine partner of the house of Drifter when I wound up by remarking:

"'I did think my slender account and all you could gather out of my pockets had satisfied you, Mrs. Drifter.'

"Conversation flagged that evening. The next morning I learned that Mrs. Drifter intended to purchase the new furniture for our Gravesendhurst cottage, to buy groceries in quantities, and run the affair entirely on her own plans.

"'It will give me something to do,' she said. 'The storekeepers will have more respect for me, too, and you won't have any bother at all about fitting up the house or running it.'

"That day I devoted largely to starting my wife out on her adventures, those of a young woman with her first bank account. I handed her a check on a New York trust company for a few hundred dollars, took her over to a Brooklyn bank, and got the cashier to enroll her as a depositor. The usual formalities were complied with, and then trouble commenced. With bank book and pocket check book in hand Mrs. Drifter felt her new independence. She decided to raid the bank at once.

"'I will draw some money out now,' she said, sweetly.

"I let her proceed. She didn't get far. The old cashier kindly insinuated that in the banking business it was customary to realize upon checks or drafts deposited on a new account before honoring demands. He told her that her husband would 'have no difficulty in getting a small check cashed for your shopping needs.'

"That nearly upset the little woman. We went out. I took her to lunch.

"'I don't think much of that bank,' she said. 'Why, they've got the use of my money, drawing interest and all that, and then to tell me to wait a day or so. Perhaps you will lend me some money until that funny old cashier finds out who I am.'

"I gave her a few pointers as to the checking out of funds; showed her the importance of simple subtraction as applied to bank balances, and dwelt at some length on the necessity of entering on each stub the name of payee and for what purpose each check was drawn. I also advised her to call on me from time to time to look over her accounts. Then woman's new sphere of activity dawned upon me. Said my wife!

"'Now, Drifter, dear, once for all, do stop joking. You look over my accounts and keep 'em straight? Not much. I'll trouble you simply to give me some more checks to put in that funny little window there at the bank, and I will do the bookkeeping.'

"'Go it,' I remarked, and she did. Three days later I was called to the telephone. Mrs. Drifter had started in to furnish the dining room and kitchen of our cottage by the sea, and was cutting holes in her separate bank account. In her search for bargains she got rattled and lost her shopping bag. It contained purse and check book. The message over the telephone urged me to meet Mrs. Drifter at once at one of the big Brooklyn stores. I went. My wife tried to appear unconcerned. I didn't see much cause for worriment until she confided thus:

"'There wasn't much money in the purse, and probably some honest man will find it and return it, or some poor woman who needs the money may get it, but that nice new check book and my deposit book! And think how business-like I have been. I had signed my name to five or six checks and they were all ready to fill out.'

"'Great Scott! wait here,' was all I could yell, and I bolted for the bank, feeling that my wife's separate bank account was a peach for any sharper who found those checks signed in blank. I explained matters at the bank, got a pitying stare from the teller, and after a two hours' tramp found the missing bag and contents intact. I didn't growl. What's the use? She'd started out on her career of individuality, divided responsibility, and all the other dreams of latter-day women, and I knew I must stand by, ready to lend a hand.

"Well, the thing went along. I didn't monkey any with the books of my former chum. When at home together I saw that there was a tired look about her eyes, an expression which seemed to say, 'I wish the darned bank account was in a hotter place than Gravesendhurst,' but I let her new venture severely alone. When necessary I handed over checks for her to deposit. That was all. She got the furniture, fitted up the house, meanwhile getting thinner each day and less companionable. Finally a crash came. This time the telephone rang with emphasis.

"'Mrs. Drifter is very sick, sir. Keeps calling for you and saying, "Come home, I give up, I'll never do it again." I've been trying to find you for an hour, sir. I'm so scared for the poor dear lady.'

"This from the new girl. Of course I got home as quickly as the trolley cars could carry me. Then the secret came out. Between sobs and moans I learned that some grocer of whom Mrs. Drifter had ordered a bill of goods had grossly insulted her.

"'He insulted me, me, your wife,' she sobbed. 'The woman who has no one to protect her if you fail her. Why, why should a weak, frail woman have to stand the insults of rude, rough men when she has a husband who ought to attend to all the business matters?'

"This was rich, indeed, but I didn't load my six-shooter and sail out after the offending tradesman. I soothed the little woman, assured her that I was a brute to have allowed her to wrestle with the worldly problems of trade, barter and bills, and begged forgiveness for having, as she said, imposed upon her the whole work of furnishing the house and worrying her poor, tired brain with prices and figures and horrid old bank books.

"I found that the grocer's insult consisted in returning a dishonored check, drawn by Mrs. Drifter on her own and only bank account, for \$53.16, and marked plainly in red ink at the bank 'N. G.' That was all, except that the grocer had written: 'I return your check. Evidently some mistake. Shall I send a bill to Mr. Drifter?'

"'What does he mean by disfiguring my check with horrid slang? Tell me. How dare he put "N. G." on one of my checks? What can be done to him? Isn't it the same as forgery?' asked my wife. I looked over her books, found that her additions and subtractions were sadly mixed, and that two other checks were due to come back also disfigured with those horrid words 'N. G.,' for she had overdrawn her account to the tune of \$208. And those stubs! Bless her heart! she took me literally. She tried to keep track of her expenditures so as to give me a surprise in bookkeeping. She succeeded. To give you an idea: Instead of filling out the stub thus:

Apr. 1. ...... \$53.
M. Macaroni,
For groceries,

Mrs. Drifter had actually endeavored in every case to put down each separate item on each bill paid by check. The one given in payment of an order of groceries was a dream. The order embraced everything from spaghetti to roach powder, and the poor woman, with a new and separate bank account, endeavored to transfer all the items to the stub. She religiously filled that stub in her fine handwriting, then started in and covered two sheets of note paper and pinned those to the suffering stub.

"She doesn't run a bank account now," concluded Drifter. "And she's gained ten pounds since becoming again my chum and 'an ornament' to the cottage at Gravesendhurst."

SOME GOSSIP OF THE HOUR.

A pretty Southern girl who is attending a fashionable school in the city has been entertaining an older sister for a week or two.

"How long will your sister remain?" asked a friend the other day.

"Well, Miss ——, I really don't know."

"Hasn't she decided yet?"

"No—o! she hasn't made up her mind whether to stay two weeks longer with me or buy a hat!"

A few days after this conversation the friend met the Southern girl again.

"Is your sister still here?" she asked.

"No; she bought the hat!"

Apropos of the South, a Louisiana man called the other evening on a young woman who has a flying squirrel for a pet. According to him, the parrot and the flying squirrel are the most popular pets down in his State. It is no uncommon thing to see a woman on a street car carrying a little squirrel attached by a fine gold chain, but the queerest phase of their popularity is the fondness which the commercial traveller has for them. The Louisiana man said that he himself knew at least half a dozen travelling men who always took their squirrels with them. They carry them in their pockets and become very much attached to them.

This bit of information reminded a lady who was present of her little niece, who has an absorbing affection for all animals in general, and horses in particular. Not long ago the child's father was driving across a railroad crossing when his carriage was struck by an engine, he himself injured, and the horse so badly hurt that it was found necessary to kill him. The child seemed considerably more impressed by the fact that the horse was injured than she was by her father's condition, and when she heard that Colonel, as the horse was called, must be killed she wept unceasingly. Finally she came to her mother and said:

"Mamma, will Colonel go to heaven?"

"I don't know, dear," was the evasive reply; "some people think there is a heaven for horses and for all animals."

"But, mamma, do you think Colonel will go to heaven?" persisted the child.

"Well, if there is a heaven for horses, Colonel will surely go there," said her mother, reassuringly. "At any rate, dear, the Bible says that whatever is necessary for your happiness you will find in heaven."

That settled the question. Colonel was necessary for her happiness, so the child felt that she was sure to find him waiting for her. A day or two later she came to her mother again.

"Mamma," she said, "I'll tell you what I'm going to do. Colonel has gone to heaven, and when I grow up I'm going to get a gray horse just like Colonel; then, when he dies, he'll go to heaven, too, and when I die and go to heaven I'll have a team!"

This reminded some one else of the small Chicago girl who had been playing with her older sister and appeared before her mother in great distress of mind.

"Why, what is the matter, dear?" said her mother, taking the child up to soothe her.

"Oh—ma—ma!" with convulsive sobs. "Gladys 'sicked' a worm on me!"

The truth of that old saying about the ruling passion strong in death was exemplified the other night when a manufacturer of a certain well-known patent medicine accidentally fell out of the window of a large apartment house near Central Park. The man was picked up in an unconscious condition, and the doctors worked with him some time before he revived. As he opened his eyes and realized that a physician was bending over him, he said, feebly:

"Doctor, have you—ever—used our—pills?"

He was something like an American man who was in Venice a year or two ago, and strolled into Florian's café in the Piazza San Marco, unaccompanied by any of his travelling companions. Two young Englishmen came in a moment later and sat down near the American. The latter began a wild attempt to call the waiter in Italian, and then gave that up for an equally ludicrous attempt in French.

"Confound it!" he said to himself, "I don't know what to call the heathens!"

"Just say waiter," suggested one of the Englishmen, taking pity on him. "Most of them understand a little of our language."

"Oh, do you speak English?" exclaimed the American rapturously. "Thank heaven, I've found some one I can talk to!" and he insisted on shaking hands.

"Come and have something with us!" he urged.

The Englishmen demurred, but the American was so delighted to find an opportunity of speaking his native tongue that he insisted. Finally the two Englishmen named a drink and the waiter went off with the order.

"By George!" said the American, beaming at his new acquaintances, "I certainly am glad to see you! Let me give you my card!" and diving into his pocket he brought up a handful of long, narrow, thin packages, wrapped in pink paper and bearing the inscription: "Choochew Pepsin Chewing Gum."

"Choochew;" said the American, pointing to the name on the package. "That's me! Ever use my gum?"

Mr. Jones of Iowa was in town last week. He had a good deal to say about the weather—in which he was not alone.

"Well," he remarked, as he mopped his forehead, "I'd like to know what sort of weather they're having up in the northern part of the State. I used to go there a good deal along about this time of year and there were always great heaps of snow out in the yard of the little old hotel. You know these left-over snowdrifts! All muddy and dirty and honeycombed, but still hanging on!

"I noticed these drifts, and I said that I thought the season must be more backward than it is out in Iowa, where we really begin to have spring early in April. There was one old fellow sitting there with his feet up on the stove and his hands in his pockets.

"'Wall,' he said with a Yankee drawl, 'you see we're sitooated most peculiar. We git sech a powerful lot o' snow durin' the winter that it can't git warm till that there' snow melts, an' the snow can't melt till it doos git warm, so there we be!'"

Never was a matter more literally brought home to the minds of the people than the Raines bill was last Sunday morning. The housewives of the town hadn't thought much about it; hadn't supposed it particularly concerned them, except by way of their husbands, and they were quite willing to have the saloons closed to the men of the family. But when the maid was sent out for the fresh vegetables, which the housewife has been in the habit of getting Sunday morning from the grocer, and came back empty handed, why, that was a different thing altogether! It is astonishing how much depends on the point of view!

When one reflects on a few such tales as this one ceases to be hurt that the English have queer opinions of us. The writer was travelling in England last year and was going from Lichfield to Coventry, when two Americans, a man and his wife, entered the compartment. They had taken the wrong train a number of hours earlier, owing, as they insisted, to the guard's fault, and had lost a good deal of time and money thereby. As a consequence they were not in a particularly good humor, and things English were with great unanimity hateful to them. Particularly did they condemn and upbraid the railway system. They paid their compliments in succession to the station arrangements, the baggage system—or lack of it—and then the passenger coaches of different classes. They did not recognize their fellow passengers as Americans, so carefully explained the difference in systems.

"Why, said the man, the idea o' havin' first class an' second class an' third class! You bet we don't have nothin' o' that sort in America!"

"No, sir!" echoed his wife.

"We wouldn't put up with anything like that! Why, when I go anywhere on the train I can sit in any seat I want to, and the President o' the United States, maybe, 'll be sittin' right alongside o' me!"

There was a vivid picture in the minds of his hearers of the President hobnobbing with the irate fellow passenger, swapping stories and cigars in the smoker, sharing his lunch basket or taking coffee and sandwiches in his company at the lunch counter. Had they been English they would have had a most peculiar idea of American customs.

The writer was telling this story to an American friend he ran across in London not long afterward, and was marvelling much that he should have been mistaken for an Englishman, when the friend smiled.

"That reminds me," said he, "of a young fellow I ran across down on the Isle of Wight. We were together a whole day very nearly, and I supposed he was English, for he had all the earmarks, clothes, figure, accent, and everything. Finally the conversation drifted to politics, and I gave him an elaborate explanation of our entire political system, to which he listened politely and, as I thought, with interest.

"'Now,' I said finally, 'I am a Republican, but under the circumstances I describe I should vote the Democratic ticket.'

"'Yes,' he said quietly, 'I have always voted the Democratic ticket myself.'

"I stared at him.

"'Why—where are you from?' I demanded.

"'Philadelphia,' he said.

"I didn't know whether to kick him or kick myself!"

CALVE HELPS MT. HOLYOKE.

SHE ASSISTS MISS ELY'S SCHOOL AT A PUBLIC RECEPTION.

Shakes Hands with Eighteen Hundred Persons, Who Gave a Dollar Apiece for the Privilege, and Endears Herself Forever to the Hearts of All the Schoolgirls.

A white cloud of schoolgirls and Emma Calvé smiling and radiant in the midst thereof! It was a sight for gods and men, although there were few of either species there to see it. Nevertheless, there was a crowd. Miss Ely's big yellow school on the Riverside Drive got almost purple in the face, it was so full to overflowing with women, all in their best spring clothes.

Why did they go to the big yellow school? and why did they wear their best spring clothes? and why, above all, did they pay a dollar apiece to go in at the iron gates?

Simply and solely for the purpose of seeing and shaking hands with Calvé. Oh, to be sure, there was something about a seminary, Mt. Holyoke Seminary, which wanted ever so many thousand dollars and to which all the profits of the afternoon were to be turned over. But not half a dozen people out of the eighteen hundred who swarmed into the building ever thought of the seminary.

Calvé did not remind them of it. She probably had the vaguest ideas on the subject anyway. And as for associating Calvé with a seminary where the girls assist with the housework and are taught the good, old-fashioned domestic arts—why, no two things could be wider apart. She had consented, at the urgent solicitation of a friend who happened to be interested in the seminary, to lend her presence in its aid, and so she appeared at 4 o'clock in a ravishing toilet and an equally ravishing smile.

Ah, that was a moment never to be forgotten in the lives of the cloud of schoolgirls who hovered in the broad doorways. And it was followed by 120 other unforgettable moments, every one more thrilling than the one before. The postman who takes up the mail from that neighborhood will be heavy laden for the next few days as he gathers up the fat epistles which those girls will write describing "how we entertained Calvé."

Without a doubt, they did entertain her. Calvé has had glimpses of many phases of American life, but yesterday afternoon, for the first time, she came into close contact with the American boarding schoolgirl on her scholastic heath. And there were so many of them, and they were so rapturous!

But there was one of them in particular who, by virtue of her familiarity with French, became, as it were, the guide, philosopher, and friend of the distinguished guest. She never quitted Calve's side for an instant, and, between introductions, she chatted with the singer in a way which turned the other girls green with envy.

The manner of those introductions was most imposing. In the first place there were two men at the gate to take the tickets of the multitude, and there were several policemen scattered about to see that the house was not swept from its foundations. At each corner of the long veranda was a large printed sign:

BICYCLES CHECKED.

When one looked at the assemblage of irreproachably clad men and of women in silks and satins and laces, those printed signs seemed to shout out a most amusing misconception. Bicycles seemed as far from the nature of that crowd as Calvé is from the Mt. Holyoke Seminary.

When the arriving hosts had given up their tickets or their dollars at the gate, they found themselves on a short walk leading up to the steps. At these steps a problem confronted them in the shape of a rail put up so as to make a passageway to the front doorway, while by taking the other side of the rail one could reach the veranda with its gay crowds. It was the front doorway, however, which led to the drawing room, where two men quickly put the arriving guests into line and ascertained their names. One of the men announced each name with tremendous lung power and a distinctness which was all thrown away on Calvé, who didn't know one name from another.

You would never have suspected her of indifference, however. When the name had been announced the woman (forty-nine out of fifty were women) found herself face to face with a radiant vision, which smiled with a warmth and grace that was charming. And then, before the woman knew it, she had shaken hands with Calvé and was moving out into the hall beyond. The vision wore a black and white silk skirt, a waist of creamy accordion-plaited chiffon, with rows of black insertion, and a white hat trimmed with black lace and pale green poppies. She carried a bunch of red roses. This much the women gathered en route.

Later in the afternoon Calvé eternally endeared herself to those hovering schoolgirls by dividing up her bouquet among them, and it is safe to say that three dozen red roses are now reposing between the covers of three dozen different school books.

"I tell you what," said one of the girls after Calvé had gone, "we did pretty well with those roses. Miss Ely gave 'em to her, but we girls got 'em all back again!"

After Calvé had stood in the drawing room about an hour receiving the interminable handshakes of the crowd, some one took her out on the veranda to show her the view. The cloud of white-robed girls clung to her all the way. Then, as by inspiration, some one suggested that she have a bit of refreshment. Instantly a detachment of the cloud broke off, and in two minutes one girl came back with a glass of iced tea, followed by a girl with a cup of hot chocolate, followed by another girl with a plate of sandwiches, and another with a plate of cakes, and another with a paper napkin.

Having reposed poor Calvé a trifle, she was led back to her post, with the cloud still following, of course, bearing first a chair, then a half empty glass, then the chocolate, and so on. Whenever Calvé moved she was followed by a surge in the multitude. They stood about her in serried ranks and watched her every move.

"I wish I could see her!" said one little woman plaintively. She had taken the wrong side of the rail and had come in from the veranda by means of a window, so that she was quite on the outskirts of the crowd which hemmed Calvé in.

"Just push right through!" said her friend, and showed her how to do it.

It was a proud day for the girls. They stood about, those of them who were not in the cloud at the time, and told their visiting acquaintances all about Calvé.

"You never saw anything like the way some of the people act," said one of them. "Why, Calvé had hardly got inside of the house when a man rushed up to her, pulled a picture out of his pocket and asked her to sign it. Calvé turned to her secretary, Mme. d'Hardelot, and said, '*Assez mauvais goût!*' Pretty bad taste, you know, that means."

In the crowd which hung densely about the group of palms where Calvé stood were half a dozen young girls in short dresses and with long hair down their backs. They were trembling with excitement. Most of them had been presented; but there was one little girl, with her hair in two long braids, who hadn't "been up," and who longed yet dreaded unspeakably to do it.

"Oh, go on, Mildred!" pleaded the others.

"I'm afraid to!" said Mildred, clasping and unclasping her hands in great excitement. "I don't know what to do."

"Why, you don't need to do anything! She'll just shake hands like this," illustrating, "and then you go on."

"But I think I ought to say something."

"She can't understand a word of English."

"But I might say it in French."

"Well, why don't you?"

"I don't know what to say."

"Tell her you're charmed to meet her. That's the proper thing."

But Mildred hung back, and trembled between fear and desire for a full hour before she finally screwed her courage to the sticking point, and fell into line. Her little friends stood on their tiptoes to watch her, and when Mildred paused and made her little speech to the great singer they almost broke into applause. As for Calvé, she held the child's hand and looked down so kindly and answered so sweetly that little Mildred came back fairly hysterical with joy.

And it was pleasant, too, to see the great artist when an elderly woman was presented to her. For most of those who passed she had only a gracious smile, but when a white-haired old lady would come up to her, Calvé bent low over the proffered hand with at least the appearance of great respect.

When Calvé went to the dining room for a cup of chocolate just before 6, the crowd still followed. They stood about her and hemmed her in, and when she sipped her chocolate they drew a deep breath, and when she took a bite out of a sandwich they whispered it to each other. After that, she bade the girls good-by and took her leave. The verandas were packed; the steps swarmed; and about the door of the carriage hung that white cloud of girls, with here and there a vivid blot of scarlet—one of Calvé's roses.

Among those present were: Mrs. J. W. Pinchot, Mrs. Stuyvesant Fish, Mrs. Abram S. Hewitt, Mrs. Reginald De Koven, Mrs. H. D. V. Post, Mrs. Benjamin Knowles, Miss Florence, Mr. and Mrs. William M. Ivins, Consul-General Brawaert, Gen. and Mrs. Viele, Mrs. Andrew Carnegie, Mr. and Mrs. H. E. Krehbiel, Mr. Ben Davis, Mr. F. K. Bristol, Mr. St. Clair McKelway, Mrs. Alfred Harrison, Mrs. Berwind, Mrs. Sheldon, Mrs. Fahnestock, Mrs. J. E. Parsons, Mrs. Edey, Mrs. Henry Ward Beecher, and Mr. and Mrs. C. R. Miller.

A RIDE WITH A MADMAN.

Constable Cray's Experience with the "King of Hell."

SOMERVILLE, April 23.—A horse covered with foam and attached to a light road wagon, in which was seated a big, wild-eyed man, by the side of a little man who struggled to control the animal, dashed up Bridge street last night. The rig brought up with a short turn at the County Hotel. The big man made a leap to the sidewalk and the little man was in hot pursuit. He placed a restraining hand on the big fellow's arm and said: "Now, Hanky, let's go for a beer."

The little man was George Cray, a constable from Montgomery township, and the big man was "Hank" Lake, the self-proclaimed "King of Hell," who has recently been terrorizing the farmers near Kingston. Lake, who weighs 260 pounds and is known throughout Montgomery township as "Big Hank," was discharged recently from the Trenton Insane Asylum. Last week he turned up at his old home and proclaimed himself "King of Hell." He proceeded to create a domain by setting fire to several acres of woodland. After his fuel had been exhausted he amused himself by knocking out the windows of the houses in the neighborhood with a gun loaded with bird shot.

When he was remonstrated with he peppered away at the inmates, but injured no one seriously. He was finally subdued by a demijohn of Jersey lightning passed to him at long range by a courageous neighbor. He dozed for two days, and then the rum gave out and he started on another rampage with renewed vigor. He defied the authorities and said he had been appointed to bring about the destruction of the world.

Constable Cray started on Hank's track at 3 o'clock yesterday morning. He came up with him unexpectedly on a by-road near Rocky Hill. The little constable could get no assistance and was obliged to resort to strategy. With honied words and a promise of a keg of beer he induced the madman to climb in his wagon, and then started on a fifteen-mile drive to the county jail at this place.

On the road Lake became imbued with a delusion that the horse had wings and could fly, and then Constable Cray had the most thrilling experience of his life. The horse was forced along at a terrific pace down steep inclines and over rough country roads. At times the madman would give way to a series of yells, which terrified both man and beast. The drive of fifteen miles was made in one hour and ten minutes. Considering the mountainous country travelled, this is one of the most remarkable feats on record out here.

After arriving here Cray conducted the lunatic to a private room in the hotel and gave him a drink of beer, after which he persuaded him to follow him to the county Court House, where he was handed over to the Sheriff. Lake will be returned to the insane asylum at Trenton.

BOOTH-TUCKER'S BOOMERANG.

His Statement Causes Four More Officers to Leave the Salvation Army.

As a result of the recent publication of the correspondence between Commander Ballington Booth and the International Headquarters of the Salvation Army, three staff officers and one field officer left the Army yesterday and joined the Volunteers. The correspondence was given to the press in the hope that it would stop the resignations from the Army. All the officers who resigned yesterday gave that correspondence as the reason why they could no longer serve under Gen. Booth. The staff officers who resigned are Staff Captain D. D. Walton, Capt. David Arthur Johns, and Capt. Lucy Kirk. The field officer is Capt. John Denton, who for some time has been stationed at Olean. After handing in their resignations all the officers applied to Commander Booth for permission to join the Volunteers. They were accepted. Capt. Johns has been the private secretary of Commander Booth-Tucker.

Staff Captain Walton, in his letter of resignation, said:

"The words of Commander and Mrs. Ballington Booth on Feb. 24, in their explanation to the staff, sunk deep into my soul. I have been unsettled ever since, and explanations, so called, and contradictions, and the publication of the correspondence have only confirmed my conviction that they have not been treated with justice. I have been in the Salvation Army thirteen and a half years, an officer eleven years, and a staff officer over eight years. I feel a regret in asking you to accept my resignation. This is no hasty or ill-considered step, and costs me something. My respect for the deposed Commander is such that I shall ask him if he has a corner for me."

TRIED BRIDGE JUMPING.

Mrs. Conover, Who Has Acted Queerly, Attempts Suicide.

BELLEVILLE, April 23.—At 4:30 this afternoon Mrs. Nettie Conover, 32 years old, attempted suicide by diving from the Belleville Bridge into the Passaic River. She has been acting queerly for ten days. She left her husband and went out to work as a domestic servant. Then she gave up her situation.

On Tuesday night she went to the residence of Mrs. Garrison, at William and Quinton streets, climbed through a window, went to one of the sleeping rooms, undressed, and got into bed. The family discovered her at 2 o'clock in the morning and notified the authorities. When two constables arrived at the house she told them that they would have to take her through the streets naked if they wanted to arrest her. It was decided that she should remain in the house until morning. Then, when the constables called, they found that she had disappeared.

To-day she was seen climbing over the bridge railing, and Comer Vogt and his son Nicholas, who were putting up electric wires across the bridge, tried to prevent her from plunging into the river, but she plunged head foremost into the water, twenty feet below the bridge. Vogt and his son procured a rowboat and went to her rescue. The big sleeves of her waist kept her afloat until the men in the boat got to her. Then they pulled her into the boat and she was taken to the Belleville township lockup. She will be arraigned before Justice Sandford to-morrow.

MOUNTING A HUGE MASTODON.

The Largest Specimen in This Country Being Prepared at Rochester.

ROCHESTER, April 23.—The largest mastodon in this country is now undergoing mounting at Ward's natural science establishment. This monster was found in New Jersey.

"This specimen," said Mr. Ward, "is being mounted for Rutgers College. It is supposed the huge beast wandered through the forests of New Jersey thousands of years ago, and while wallowing in the mud sank so deeply that he was unable to extricate himself and perished. Fortunate was it for science that the death of the animal came about in this manner, for had he perished on the solid soil his bones would have been destroyed. The muck that covered his bones kept them in a good condition through the centuries which intervened from the time of his death to the finding by a farmer a few years ago. Its height is from twelve to thirteen feet, and with tusks its length is twenty-four feet."

MR. VANDERBILT'S CALLER

Pronounced Temporarily Deranged and to Be Put in an Asylum.

Estella Burmeister, who was arrested on Wednesday for trying to have an interview with William K. Vanderbilt and sent to the insane pavilion of Bellevue, was examined yesterday by the hospital physicians. They say that she is at least temporarily deranged. Yesterday morning her sister, Mrs. M. A. Horton of Berlin, Pa., went to Bellevue Hospital and told Dr. Russell that Miss Burmeister had acted queerly for some time, and that her trouble was probably the result of overwork.

After satisfying the hospital authorities that she was Miss Burmeister's sister, Mrs. Horton took the woman away, and they started for Philadelphia. Miss Burmeister will be sent to a private asylum.

CIGARS IN A STATE HOSPITAL.

Were They Made in Violation of the Revenue Laws?

James M. Platfoot, superintendent of the Long Island State Hospital, was before United States Commissioner Morle in Brooklyn, charged with a violation of the revenue laws by allowing cigars to be made and sold in the institution. Superintendent Platfoot admitted that one of the insane patients had been in the habit of making the cigars for his own use and that of some of the officials, but denied that they had been sold outside. He was placed under \$500 bonds pending examination. The revenue officials who visited the hospital found 500 cigars and a quantity of tobacco in one of the cottages.

Killed Her for Ruining His Life.

CHICAGO, April 23.—James K. Culbertson of this city, formerly of Chambersburg, Pa., shot and killed a woman named Lily McCormick at 69 Church street last night and then shot himself. He cannot live. Culbertson has made an ante-mortem statement in which he says that the McCormick woman had been the ruin of his life and he decided to kill her. After committing the murder the idea of suicide occurred to him. When arrested he had two revolvers in his possession, and fired two shots at Detective Sergeant Driver, who subdued him after a struggle.

MARINE INTELLIGENCE.

MINIATURE ALMANAC—THIS DAY.

Sun rises.... 5 08 | Sun sets.... 6 49 | Moon sets.. 8 17

HIGH WATER—THIS DAY.

Sandy Hook. 4 26 | Gov. Island. 4 43 | Hell Gate.. 6 36

Arrived—THURSDAY, April 23.

Ss Anchoria, Young, Glasgow.
Ss American, Butz, Rotterdam.
Ss Scottish Hero, Singer, Hamburg.
Ss Idaho, Marshall, Glasgow.
Ss Trave, Thalenhorst, Southampton.
Ss Pro Iamo, Jackson, Baltimore.
Ss El Dorado, Baker, New Orleans.
Ss Mark Lane, Bate, Palermo.
Ss Yumuri, Mathiesen, Santa Martha.
Ss Algoma, Cumming, Philadelphia.
Ss Guyandotte, Walker, Norfolk.
Ss Gen. Whitney, Bearse, Boston.
Ss City of Fitchburg, Webber, Fall River.
Bark Olive Thurlow, Gooding, Port Spain.

[For later arrivals see First Page.]

ARRIVED OUT.

Ss Lahn, from New York, at Bremerhaven.
Ss Kaiser Wilhelm II., from New York, at Naples.
Ss Spaarndam, from New York, at Rotterdam.
Ss Massilia, from New York, at Marseilles.
Ss Dresden, from New York, at Bremerhaven.
Ss Mississippi, from New York, at London.
Ss Wells City, from New York, at Bristol.
Ss Italia, from New York, at Naples.
Ss Flaxman, from New York, at Santos.
Ss Standard, from New York, at Swinemunde.
Ss Iroquois, from New York, at Charleston.

SIGHTED.

Ss Hekla, from Copenhagen for New York, passed Dunnet Head.
Ss La Campine, from New York for Antwerp, passed Prawle Point.
Ss Werkendam, from Rotterdam for New York, off Isle of Wight.

SAILED FROM FOREIGN PORTS.

Ss Manitoba, from London for New York.
Ss Castle Eden, from Batoum for New York.

SAILED FROM DOMESTIC PORTS.

Ss Hudson, from New Orleans for New York.
Ss El Norte, from Port Eads for New York.
Ss El Monte, from Port Eads for New York.

OUTGOING STEAMSHIPS.

Sail To-day.

	Mails Close.	Vessel Sails.
Portia, Newfoundland	11:00 A. M.	1:00 P. M.
New York, St. Domingo	1:00 P. M.	3:00 P. M.
Algonquin, Charleston	....	3:00 P. M.
Colorado, Brunswick	....	3:00 P. M.
Sail To-morrow.		
La Gascogne, Havre	6:00 A. M.	9:00 A. M.
Campania, Liverpool	11:00 A. M.	2:00 P. M.
Anchoria, Glasgow	10:00 A. M.	12:00 M.
Veendam, Rotterdam	7:00 A. M.	9:00 A. M.
Fulda, Genoa	8:00 A. M.	10:00 A. M.
Thingvalla, Christiansand	11:00 A. M.	1:00 P. M.
Persia, Hamburg	....	3:00 P. M.
Mobile, London	....	1:00 P. M.
Fontabelle, Barbadoes	9:30 A. M.	12:00 M.
Philadelphia, La Guayra	11:00 A. M.	1:00 P. M.
Vigilancia, Havana	10:30 A. M.	1:00 P. M.
Tjomo, Martinique	10:00 A. M.	12:00 M.
Andes, Jamaica	10:00 A. M.	12:00 M.
Silvia, Jamaica	11:00 A. M.	12:00 M.
Carib Prince, Pernambuco	1:00 P. M.	3:00 P. M.
Seminole, Jacksonville	....	3:00 P. M.
Knickerb'ker, New Orleans	....	3:00 P. M.
Leona, Galveston	....	3:00 P. M.
El Sud, New Orleans	....	3:00 P. M.
Sail Tuesday, April 28.		
Trave, Bremen	7:00 A. M.	10:00 A. M.
Curacoa, Maracaibo	11:00 A. M.	1:00 P. M.
Comanche, Charleston	....	3:00 P. M.

INCOMING STEAMSHIPS.

Due To-day.		
Llandaff City	Swansea	April [illegible]
Victoria	Gibraltar	April [illegible]
Seminole	Charleston	April 21
St. Paul	Southampton	April 18
Britannic	Liverpool	April 15
Palatia	Hamburg	April 12
Zaandam	Amsterdam	April 11
Mozart	St. Lucia	April 17
Prins Willem III	Port-au-Prince	April 18
Aachen	Bremen	April 11
Nacoochee	Savannah	April 21
Panama	Havana	April 20
Due Saturday, April 25.		
Umbria	Liverpool	April 18
Idaho	Greenock	April 11
El Norte	New Orleans	April 21
Kansas City	Savannah	April 22
Due Sunday, April 26.		
La Bretagne	Havre	April 18
Panama	Cherbourg	April 18
Caribbee	St. Thomas	April 20
Orinoco	Bermuda	April 23
Due Monday, April 27.		
Ethiopia	Glasgow	April 16
Nomadic	Liverpool	April 17
Maasdam	Rotterdam	April 15
Nuestria	Gibraltar	April 13
Yumuri	Havana	April 23
Due Tuesday, April 28.		
Aller	Bremen	April 18
Southwark	Antwerp	April 18
Massachusetts	London	April 16
Belgravia	Gibraltar	April 14
Vasco	London	April 13
Caracas	La Guayra	April 22
Pascal	St. Lucia	April 21

DIED.

BISHOP.—Entered into paradise, Estelle, wife of the Rev. Hutchus C. Bishop, Wednesday, April 22, 1896.

Funeral service at St. Philip's Church, Saturday afternoon, at 3 o'clock. Interment at Kensico.

GRAUX.—At the residence of his parents, Manhattan av., on Thursday, April 23, Gaston H. G. Graux, only son of Jules L. and Lillie Graux, in the 12th year of his age.

Funeral services at St. Vincent de Paul's Church, 23d st., near 6th av., on Saturday morning at 11 o'clock. Please omit flowers.

McEVOY.—On April 21, Hannah, widow of John McEvoy.

Funeral from her late residence, 153 East 53d st., Friday, April 24, at 10 A. M. Religious services in St. Patrick's Cathedral. Friends and relatives are invited.

MAY.—On Wednesday, April 22, 1896, Mary E., beloved wife of George W. May.

Funeral services Friday evening, April 24, at 8 o'clock, at her late residence, 235 Rodney st., Brooklyn, N. Y.

McEWEN.—Entered into rest at Saratoga on Tuesday, April 21, in the 21st year of her age, Ellen Dudley McEwen, only child of Sarah Watrous and the late Robert Charles McEwen, M. D.

Funeral services at the house, Franklin square, Saratoga Springs, on Friday morning at 11:30. Interment private.

McLAUGHLIN.—On Wednesday, April 22, James McLaughlin of 52 Jane st.

Relatives and friends are invited to attend the funeral from the residence of John F. O'Hara, 811 Washington st., Hoboken, N. J., Saturday morning, April 25, 1896. Burial at Calvary Cemetery.

RANKEN.—At Jersey City, on Wednesday, April 22, 1896, William B. Ranken.

Funeral services will be held at the residence of his son-in-law, R. W. R. Koester, 63 Madison av., Jersey City, on Friday evening, April 24, at 8 o'clock. Interment at convenience of the family. Philadelphia and Washington papers please copy.

Pages 17 to 32. NEW YORK JOURNAL Pages 17 to 32.

SUNDAY, OCTOBER 11, 1896.

HAS PUBLIC TASTE SUNK TO THIS DEGRADING LEVEL?

If the New York Theatre-Goers Unblushingly Flock to See a Vulgar Young Woman Undress Herself on the Stage, What May We Expect Next?

"SHOULD BE SUPPRESSED," SAYS DR. PARKHURST.

Rev. Dr. Charles H. Parkhurst: "Concerning the particular performers of whom you speak I can, of course, say nothing, for I have not seen them; but if, as you say, they were expelled from Germany by the Government, there must be something more or less objectionable about them—something which will not, I am sure, add to their popularity among the really respectable people of New York. For the same reason that I am not qualified to speak more definitely of these performers, I am also unqualified to talk with accuracy concerning the general moral influence of the present day of New York theatres and music halls. For a long time I have been too busy to visit them. That I do not, in the abstract, disapprove of the theatre will be plainly shown when I say that I believe an evening each week devoted to laughing at a good comedy would benefit me very greatly. Hearty laughter at clean fun is recreation of a healthful sort; but I am convinced that a large part of the fun on the stages of our theatres is not clean. Laughter at dirty fun means demoralization of the worst kind. Therefore, in my belief, there is much in the theatres which should be suppressed. The public conscience has, perhaps, been dulled by long contemplation of questionable stage doings, but it will awaken. It always does. Until it does awaken, and thoroughly, the thoughtful people, who see the danger with which this phase of our recreation menaces our minds and morals, cannot expect the managers to cease to bring forth their filth, the Legislature to pass preventing laws, the police to not interfere in extreme cases.

"LEWD AND INDECENT." SAYS CHARLOTTE SMITH.

Mrs. Charlotte Smith: "I witnessed the performance of the Barrison sisters and never saw an exhibition in any theatre more suggestive, lewd and indecent. It was disgraceful. The whole aim of these women seemed to be to excite the base emotions of the audience. Their dresses had been constructed with this one object in view, and all their motions were simply vicious and libidinous. Before the curtain went up the ten legs of these Barrisons could be seen by the audience under the edge of the curtain, indecently twisting and wriggling, as they sat upon the floor. This was designed to whet the appetite of the spectators. Then they came out and turned their backs to the audience, lifting up their dresses in a vulgar and indecent manner. Their underclothes had been specially made to excite the spectators, with many arts plain to the feminine eye. None of these women could either sing or dance well, and the audience did not appear to expect them to. They have nothing to recommend them beyond notoriety and the indecency of their exhibition. The elder Barrison undressed on the stage and gave an exhibition on horseback that was even more disgraceful than that of her sisters, while the song that she sang would not have been permitted for a moment if translated into English. The Barrisons exert an immoral influence. A law ought to be passed putting a stop to such exhibitions, and I will make a recommendation of this kind to the Legislature this Winter."

ALAN DALE SAYS---

"THEY ARE THE LIMIT."

The Shocking Performance of Miss Lona Barrison at a New York Theatre.
1
2
3
4
5
6
7

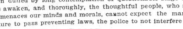

Fat, boozy youths, with convex shirt fronts and water-on-the-brain foreheads, accompanied by lydies of apparently decollete habits, occupied the boxes at Koster & Bial's dark blue establishment in Thirty-fourth street last Thursday night. They were trying frightfully hard to be saucy and abandoned and up-to-date and Parisian. They had read in books on "How to Be Devilish, Though Sixteen," that the thing to do was to appear in an ennui of dazed imbecility, to loll, to pose, to publicly caress their companions, and to applaud nothing. The men were probably clerks in Wall Street offices $10 a week and a day off); the women were emancipated typewriters, kitchen maids gone wrong, Sarah Janes and Susan Annes, out for a night's naughtiness.

New York, when it gets devilish, is hilariously funny. To see it striving to cast off the proper fetters of a brand-new civilization, and trying to imitate the innate evil of London and the pictorial, tinsel wickedness of Paris, is, for the student, a delightful find for mirthful entertainment. I watched some of these youths as they bestowed an occasional gratuity of a nickel upon an obsequious waiter, and ordered "beers" with the lordly hauteur of My Lord Tomnoddy, and I knew that the following day all New York would be agog with such reports as "John Jones went out last night and spent $2.25" and "George Smith did Koster & Bial's like a prince to the tune of $4.30."

To feed imbeciles with imbecility is a pretty good maxim. It is the axiom at Koster & Bial's this week, and it will be the axiom for eight weeks to come, unless we have an earthquake or a tornado, or some equally revolutionary bouleversement. Mr. Bial is not catering to the intellectual naughtiness that causes us to accept Yvette Guilbert and Anna Held—genuine artists who are neither vulgar nor shocking—or to the cerebral spiciness that makes problem plays and problem novels timely and apropos. He is apparently pandering to the cheap boys and cheaper girls who want to give the evil in them an inexpensive outing. There [illegible] thousands of them, of course, and if they are willing to give [illegible]heir hard-earned and meagre coin, why—says the manager—[illegible] do it. It's current coin. It is just as good as the money [illegible] to the Empire and Garrick theatres.

[illegible]keleton dudes, and Big Elizas, and dual-headed Jo-Jos—as [illegible]l as the Lady with the Pig-Face and the Gentleman with the quadrup'[illegible] Skin, are of no account at present. Huber's Museum is surely not "in it" with Koster & Bial's these weeks.

Consider for a moment the managerial tactics that have given us the poor little Barrison sisters—faint, sketchy little ladies who look as though they couldn't say "Boo!" to a goose. A few years ago they sang "Daddy Wouldn't Buy Me a Bow-Wow" for the benefit of the ladies in the shopping district of Twenty-third street who had a few minutes to spend at the Eden Musee. They were cunning little things, all fluffy gold hair and flat Dutch-doll faces. The trouble with them was, though, that they couldn't do anything. They had voices like ravens, and you forgot their dainty appearance because they were so hopelessly clumsy and awkward. They were failures, because they had nothing to offer but a mere quintuple prettiness, and it is possible to get that sort of thing in combination with talent. They skirmished about and got "jobs" at roof gardens and other resorts. They trotted about Broadway, all dressed alike, in tow of their astute manager, but New York wouldn't be captured. The Barrison girls went away.

And now they are back again. Nobody has seen them since the days of their drab, dark failure, but the fat, boozy boys with the water-on-the-brain foreheads, and the lydies of decollete habits are clamoring for admission to Koster & Bial's. Something has happened, between the date of the Barrisons' departure and the Barrisons' return, to give them a fictitious value. Mr. Bial doesn't pretend that they can act any better, or sing any better, or dance any better. They have grown no younger. Only leading ladies grow younger as the years roll by. Why, then, do we see the names of the Barrisons in large letters on our fences to-day? What have they done?

As poor Bessie Bellwood would have said: "That's where the larf comes in." No reports have reached us of any improvement in the work done by these girls. In fact, it is reported that they went to the Alhambra, in London, for an engagement of eight weeks, and stayed there seven days. Stories, however, were cabled over about suicides committed on their account by addlepated Germans. We were told that their fatal beauty had wrought such havoc among the jeunesse doree of Berlin that they had been banished from the German country. New York had seen them. New York had refused them, but—Mr. Bial knew this gallant metropolis. He reasoned that the "advertising" they had received gave them intrinsic value, just as the head of Guiteau, worthless carrion under ordinary circumstances, becomes worthy of alcoholic preservation when haloed with notoriety.

Mr. Bial dreamed of our latent naughty streaks. He saw the callow boys trooping forth to see damsels whose notoriety far exceeded any native talent: he beheld visions of box-office prosperity that Cissy Fitzgerald, with her moribund wink, and Eugene Stratton, without a suicide to his account, could never achieve. He engaged the Barrisons, and back they came.

"Send all your interviewers and your artists," telegraphed Mr. McConnell to the newspapers, and when I saw him before their opening at Koster & Bial's he said to me: "Mark my words, old chap. Monday night will be Barrison night in New York. You can have your Georgia Cayvans and your "Secret Services" and your legitimate. The town will go crazy over these girls. It is in the air. Mark my words. They are the limit."

And they are.

They are the limit of crass stupidity, of incredible clumsiness, and of the very cheapest sort of a vulgarity that can appeal to nothing but mere slumminess. I went to the music hall after having read the comments of my colleagues setting forth the disappointing tameness and the irretrievable propriety of the Barrisons. I went because I don't always believe what I read, and I thought that possibly the Barrisons were going to be downed by a concerted effort to rob them of their advertised German evil. I have already described the condition of the house, with its teeming boxes, clogged lobbies, a plethora of pale youths and silly women. A sensation of pleasurable excitement titillated my veins. I felt that I was going to be electrified. I began to consider what kind of suicide I should prefer if I found that life without the Barrisons proved insupportable.

There were reporters around, and in a sheer spirit of charity I said to myself: "If I find that suicide is inevitable, I'll plunge from the top of the house into the orchestra, crying 'Lona!' and give my friends something to write about." I could see it all in the papers on the following day: "Alan Dale dies for the Barrisons!" "A critic succumbs to five pale girls!" and so on. I also felt that Mr. Bial—charitable Mr. Bial—might, for the sake of the ad., settle a trifle on the loved ones at home, and that perchance Fleron, with the truculent hat, might be induced to "do something" for my "widows and orphans."

You see, I was quite prepared to be inflamed. In fact, I courted inflammation. And as Miss Lona Barrison appeared I began to sniff around for a little evil. (Evil is generally sniffable, don't you think?) Where was her beauty? That was the first question I asked myself. A complexion like boiled veal, hair like the "bleached blondes" of Rice's chorus, and a figure that had neither symmetry nor grace of any sort, sent me into the region of perplexity. She wore a dude costume and sang a song in the most execrable French in a voice that would have disturbed the tranquillity of the Seven Sleepers. Then she took off her coat, waistcoat and trousers, stood before us in a pretty suit of lace and satin, and ambled off the stage.

"It's a fraud," I cried. "There must be something more. I cannot kill myself for Lona. It would be too silly. Such a story wouldn't be worth more than three-quarters of a column, at $8 a column, to any paper."

There was something more. Lona waited outside a few minutes for applause that didn't come. The fat, boozy youths and the decollete ladies were sober enough to look as though they felt they were being buncoed. Silence prevailed for a few minutes, and Lona reappeared on a large white horse, and astride it. The horse was lovely, glossy and milk white. It danced, and it pranced, and a few hands beat a faint applause, which Lona greedily took unto herself, away from its equine proprietor. Then she sang a song in French, the refrain of which was "Ca fait mal." The audience didn't understand her in the least, so I may as well tell you that she meant to convey the impression that it is uncomfortable for a lady to ride a horse manwise. Poor Lona tried so hard to look saucy and self-conscious that I felt sorry for her. In reality she was as spicy as a tapioca pudding and as vivacious as mucilage. The horse—poor dumb beast—had genuine terpsichorean skill. He was worthy of Barnum's circus. Lona could learn more by looking at that horse than she acquired during her alleged triumphant occupancy of Berlin.

When she had left the stage, without any attempt on the part of the defrauded audience to cheer her by applause, some trained dogs came ou to remove the gloom that had settled upon the house. Clever little dogs! Faithful, cunning canine actors, relying on sheer ingenuity for their bread and bones! The dogs stayed but a short time, and gave way to the five Barrison sisters. They showed us their legs first, for they sat with them poked out under the curtain. I like a leg or two occasionally, but it must be a leg in the true sense of the word. The spindleshanks that the Barrisons betrayed were so screamingly funny and so bewilderingly emaciated that I had hard work to keep in my seat. In fact, I don't mind saying that the only things immoral about the Barrisons are their legs. They are an affront to symmetry. They should be sewn up in masses of petticoats and kept from an unfortunate public. Amputation would be justifiable. There are wooden legs to be had far more shapely than the limbs of these five silly exaggerated girls.

"What a fake!" cried a boozy youth beside me.

And his companion, a girl wearing all the colors of the rainbow, exclaimed: "Oh, mamma!"

And then the poor little Barrisons began to do what they had been taught to do for the delectation of imbeciles. They sat on the stage looking hopelessly ill at ease, and ridiculously cheap, and sang a vulgar but stupid song, dealing with the physiology of generation. There was no tune to it, no metre to it, no rhythm to it, nothing latent, nothing chic, nothing clever. It was thrust at the boozy, callow boys and the ladies of decollete virtue—and it made not the least appeal to them. The young folks who had come out to be devilish, looked wearied and disgusted.

After this first song they shrid mh wm

They had two more songs, though they were not encouraged to sing them. The applause, like the letter, never came. They returned with a ditty about "The Johnny You All Know," and they went through it as though it were a suet dumpling. Not a gleam of intelligence gleamed in their eyes. Not a wicked look was cast in any direction. Five little frumps tugging away at a cheap concert hall chanson was all we saw. It was really too bad. Such utter inanity made you feel that you might as well have left your brains at home.

And then, "Linger Longer, Lucy!" Ye gods and little fishes! After Yvette Guilbert, these dummies dared to tackle it. I assure you that Ventriloquist Noble's lay figures were actresses compared with these dreary sisters. That German Count was no fool when he killed himself. The Barrison sisters would drive any well regulated audience to death, not for love, but for disgust. What think you of the impudence of a troupe that will foist such ditties upon a public who has always respected and upheld talent. It is all very well for a manager to cater to the streak of naughtiness in our natures by engaging women on the strength of their notoriety; but, when he has netted them, let him see to it that they have something to offer. We can't live at a place of amusement on old stories, which may after all be untrue. For I believe that they are untrue. I don't believe that the Barrisons ever created any excitement in any civilized community. I discredit it. If there was a suicide on account of these five pallid, little nothings, I want to see the corpse.

There is not very much harm in notoriety, if there be anything to back it up. It is hard to get a public hearing sometimes. Managers wont take risks, because this public is a faddy one. The legitimate frequently dies from inanition. Clever people with talent to emit are forced to the wall because there is no booming process to launch them forth. Notoriety has its uses and its abuses. The Barrison sisters have abused it. They had the finest chance in the world to make a big hit in New York. The metropolis had given them more attention than Irving or Bernhardt or Duse could secure. Mr. Bial believed that his appeal to callow youths would be but temporary, and that the Barrisons would be something that would set the town talking.

They have fallen as flat as a pancake, and their fate will teach New York a needed lesson. In no other metropolis in the world could such a farce as this Barrison affair have been perpetrated, and Mr. Bial must redeem himself speedily in the eyes of a public that considers his house the best of its kind in town. I'm one of that public. I'm very fond of Koster & Bial's. Whenever I feel blue or depressed I go there, and before the evening is over I am better. But I vow that the engagement of the Barrisons has shaken my faith in Mr. Bial's judgment. It looks very much as though he took us all for "jays," or for the boozy boys and decollete women I saw in his house last Thursday night. We all like Mr. Bial, but we like ourselves much better. We are not going to shelve our self respect or doff our complacency.

In other words, we are not going to be buncoed. If naughtiness is advertised, we want naughtiness and not vulgarity. We like our fare seasoned with a spice of deviltry occasionally. We are not at all squeamish. But Albert—dear Albert Bial—don't sell us wool for silk, or delft for Dresden china. Furnish us with the brand you advertise, and we'll buy it. After all, it's a simple business proposition, and there's no getting away from it.

ALAN DALE.

The Sun.
NEW YORK, SEPTEMBER 21, 1897

There has been, as it appears, no difference of opinion as to what constitutes and what falls short of the requirements of a good moral character in Connecticut, but the provision which relates to the ability to read "any article of the Constitution or any section of the statutes of the State" has been thought to be ambiguous. Some of the election officers declare that such reading should be, and by law must be, in English, while others have, with equal vigor, contended that the ability to read in any language the Constitution or statutes was all the law required.

By the Federal census of 1890 the foreign-born population of Connecticut was 183,000, and the number of foreign-born male persons over the age of 21 was 78,415. At that time 65 per cent. of the male voters in Connecticut were native born and 35 per cent. were foreign born. The ambiguity of the Constitutional provision has led to the acceptance in some counties of the votes of citizens having no intimate knowledge of English, and to the rejection in other counties of similar applicants. In order to bring about uniformity in the matter there was submitted to the Legislature in 1895 a proposed amendment, which was ratified by both houses; and this year this amendment is to be voted on by the people of the State. It is as follows:

"Every person shall be able to read *in the English language* any article of the Constitution or any section of the statutes of the State before being admitted as an elector."

In other words, it will no longer be sufficient for an applicant for the rights of citizenship in Connecticut, if the proposed amendment is adopted, to demonstrate his educational proficiency by reading the Constitution in the language with which he is familiar; he must be able to read it in English. The voters of the State are asked to give their sanction to this change, the practical effect of which will be to render uniform henceforth the conditions of suffrage in Connecticut. The rejection of the amendment would do away with the requirement that English shall be spoken and understood.

There is now a large Canadian French population in Connecticut. It is increasing at a lively rate, and perhaps it is on account of this that the proposed amendment has found favor; perhaps it is prompted by the desire of Connecticut electors generally to restrict the suffrage by excluding from it other newcomers. However that may be, the question will be voted upon next month and determined, so that in the future this Constitutional provision may be no longer indefinite or ambiguous.

In New York State there is no Constitutional requirement that English should be understood, either by citizens or Sheriffs.

By Rail to Hudson Bay.

The project of building a railroad from Winnipeg to Hudson Bay, with a view to connecting the road with a line of steamers, the whole forming a new grain route to Europe by way of Hudson's Straits, has long been familiar. But while that scheme is still under consideration, a rival enterprise has lately appeared in the proposed extension of the Quebec and Lake St. John Railway from its present terminus to James Bay, which forms the southernmost part of Hudson Bay.

This project, of course, has no new grain route in view, but a plea of special interest just now is made for it as a possible route from eastern Canada to the Yukon gold fields. For this purpose there would be water travel by Chesterfield Inlet and English River as well as by Hudson Bay. In addition, it is hoped that the fisheries, the timber, and the minerals of the Hudson Bay region may furnish support for the proposed new road.

The existing railway, it appears, is 190 miles long, extending to Roberval, on Lake St. John, while the distance thence to James Bay would be nearly twice as great, a considerable part of it through a hilly region, but the beginning and nearly or quite all of the [illegible] half lying in comparatively level territory. To the cost of con-

or several pounds heavier than this year's chain variety.

It is intimated that the new chainless wheels will be sold for considerably more than $100, perhaps $125. It will be necessary for the public to give the machines a good test before being able to say what they are worth, but it must be admitted that the day of high-priced bicycles has gone by, and wheelmen are firm in their demand for lower prices.

Is There a Santa Claus?

We take pleasure in answering at once and thus prominently the communication below, expressing at the same time our great gratification that its faithful author is numbered among the friends of THE SUN:

"DEAR EDITOR: I am 8 years old.

"Some of my little friends say there is no Santa Claus.

"Papa says 'If you see it in THE SUN it's so.'

"Please tell me the truth; is there a Santa Claus?

"VIRGINIA O'HANLON.

"115 WEST NINETY-FIFTH STREET."

VIRGINIA, your little friends are wrong. They have been affected by the skepticism of a skeptical age. They do not believe except they see. They think that nothing can be which is not comprehensible by their little minds. All minds, VIRGINIA, whether they be men's or children's, are little. In this great universe of ours man is a mere insect, an ant, in his intellect, as compared with the boundless world about him, as measured by the intelligence capable of grasping the whole of truth and knowledge.

Yes, VIRGINIA, there is a Santa Claus. He exists as certainly as love and generosity and devotion exist, and you know that they abound and give to your life its highest beauty and joy. Alas! how dreary would be the world if there were no Santa Claus. It would be as dreary as if there were no VIRGINIAS. There would be no childlike faith then, no poetry, no romance to make tolerable this existence. We should have no enjoyment, except in sense and sight. The eternal light with which childhood fills the world would be extinguished.

Not believe in Santa Claus! You might as well not believe in fairies! You might get your papa to hire men to watch in all the chimneys on Christmas Eve to catch Santa Claus, but even if they did not see Santa Claus coming down, what would that prove? Nobody sees Santa Claus, but that is no sign that there is no Santa Claus. The most real things in the world are those that neither children nor men can see. Did you ever see fairies dancing on the lawn? Of course not, but that's no proof that they are not there. Nobody can conceive or imagine all the wonders there are unseen and unseeable in the world.

You may tear apart the baby's rattle and see what makes the noise inside, but there is a veil covering the unseen world which not the strongest man, nor even the united strength of all the strongest men that ever lived, could tear apart. Only faith, fancy, poetry, love, romance, can push aside that curtain and view and picture the supernal beauty and glory beyond. Is it all real? Ah, VIRGINIA, in all this world there is nothing else real and abiding.

No Santa Claus! Thank GOD! he lives, and he lives forever. A thousand years from now, VIRGINIA, nay, ten times ten thousand years from now, he will continue to make glad the heart of childhood.

The talk of the Low adulators about his running "compelling Tammany to nominate the best man it can get" amuses everybody who really understands the political situation. Low's persistence in his independent candidacy, as all politicians know, would be the signal to Tammany to make a square and out-and-out organization ticket. Tammany has no fear of Low. It regards him as a friend.

The initiative and referendum can be heard clattering over the Chicago pavements. Cook county has an association of philosophers of great name, the Sovereign Citizens. The Sovereign Citizens are not so called in honor of the Hon. JAMES RODOMONT SOVEREIGN, but because, like him, they are full of sovereignty and

What double-extra Gothic ignorance is this? The South wish to put out one of the brightest lights of its literature, a very candle and cresset of the literature of the world? The South seek to suppress the playful historian of France? Why, if TOM WATSON'S poll should set itself on fire there's not a hand in Georgia but would turn a hose or douse a bucket at that bronze temple of intellect and historical humor.

The Hon. FRED E. WHITE, the Democratic candidate for Governor of Iowa, was frank enough at the beginning of his campaign to admit that the silver dollar might come to be worth ten cents, and his frankness has won for him a certain sympathy, which he needs as his canvass goes on. He was nominated three months ago, and the platform of the convention which nominated him asserts that the Iowa farmers are marketing their products "at less prices than ever before." The Iowa farmers are the best judges of the truth and value of that assertion. The Iowa Democrats bet on calamity and they have lost. They are not likely to indulge in an early convention again.

The Hon. JAMES K. JONES of Arkansas is a well-meaning soul enough, and as a political manager he is exceeded in skill by only a few babes in arms, but he needs judicious editing. Somebody should try to reconcile JONES with JONES and not permit the Fall JONES to contradict the JONES of Spring. If JONES tried to have the Arkansas Democracy do what he advised the New York Democracy to do, the Arkansas Democracy would drive JONES into the woods or a recantation. But JONES is not to be blamed too much for his little contradictions. JONES has been mightily muddled as to his intellectuals ever since the election, and he was fairly well muddled during the campaign. The people insisted upon electing MCKINLEY, whereas JONES had elected BRYAN, and ever since JONES has been figuring and assailing the Money Power. Yet, in advising the New York Democrats to forget the Chicago platform, what was JONES doing but advising them to truckle to the Money Power? JONES is inexplicable, or else it is not worth while to explain him.

Here is a picture from real life in Pratt county, Kan., a personal from a local paper: Mr. GREEN last Saturday lost a $800 diamond in his wheat field.—*Kansas City Journal.*

Another instance of the wicked work of Prosperity. If wheat had not been bribed by the money kings to stop going hand in hand with her sister silver, Mr. GREEN would have been in no hurry to visit his wheat field. He could have gone to a Populist convention and enjoyed the resolutions. The price of wheat is boosted by the plutocrats and straightway Mr. GREEN is working hard in his wheat field and is punished for his weak yielding to Prosperity by losing one of his diamonds. The indirect results of the ravages of Prosperity must be awful to number and look at. Many a Kansas farmer must have lost valuable diamonds which he might have kept if the country could have been blest with continuing bad times.

Lord Salisbury's Kind Heart Gives Way.

From the Spectator.

It is no use to conceal the fact that the struggle over the peace negotiations has ended in a victory for German diplomacy. At first it was said that this had been agreed to, but Friday's telegrams show that the negotiations are still dragging, and it is alleged that the rest of the powers now argue that a beginning must be made with the payment of the war indemnity before the Turks move. Of course, if this is insisted on, the delays may be endless, for evacuation becomes dependent upon the power of Greece to get a loan. But the necessity for getting the money quickly will probably oblige her to make worse terms than she need. Though, as we have said above, Germany has triumphed, we admit that Lord Salisbury had no choice but to give way. The prolongation of the negotiations meant the prolongation of the Turkish occupation. But since Germany had no objection to that occupation and Lord Salisbury had, Lord Salisbury was at the mercy of the German negotiators. They could play the waiting game. He could not without bringing even more miseries on Thessaly.

Knew More Than His Examiners.

From the Alexandria Gazette.

WASHINGTON, Sept. 18.—A young deaf-mute named Merrill, a student of the college of deaf-mutes out at Kendall Green, some time ago took a civil service examination for a position in the Weather Bureau. When it came to solving an example in spheritrigonometry, he astonished the examiner by asking for a table of logarithms. The examiner finally wrote that the rules forbade the bringing of any papers or books into the room, and could hardly be convinced that the solution of examples of this kind was impossible without what the mute young man called for. After a confab the examiner went around the room and struck off the question from the papers, noting that a great many had attempted a solution

TO THE EDITOR OF THE SUN—*Sir:* Are you willing to print the letter of a Low-minded man? Pardon the pun. Our candidate's name never did inspire anything but puns in my mind; puns and a vague sense of disagreeable duty. I am going to vote for him for the same reasons that will influence hundreds of others. These reasons may interest you. Possibly you can answer them. If so you will relieve me of a great burden, the burden that conscience sometimes imposes on our intellectual tastes.

Low is the perfect type of the virtuous commonplace. He is as innocent of wrong as a little paper man cut out of a Sunday school leaflet. He is the most average person I have ever known. He is a copybook aphorism stereotyped on ruled lines. He is the apotheosis of the humdrum. Virtue safeguarded by stupidity, sanctity well ballasted with phlegm. These are his qualities.

And what better would you ask for a public servant? Think of the safety of such a man. Think of his moral example. His success would be the triumph of sheer moral spotlessness, unaided by intellect. Dulness may hope for anything if he succeeds. Only be good and let who will be clever. Can you find a better lesson for the masses?

Has he done anything? Not much; but think how he has baffled Satan! Political wisdom? God forbid. It is the knowledge of evil. His attitude is that of the monk, *scienter nesciens, sapienter indoctus.* A city is a business concern, and the Mayor should have the qualities of a bank cashier, no more. Low has no more. We admire him for the qualities he lacks and respect him for what he isn't. He is so negative that we find nothing in him to oppose; so tasteless that he must be nutritious, like gruel.

Thence comes it that I shall vote for him. This bread and butter statesman, how I—but I shall feel better afterward, I know. Sneer at this if you will, but there are 124,999 other signers who feel this way.

Pardon me if for a moment I burst into song:

Were he less stupid, he might be less moral;
Were he less prosy, he'd be less benign;
For in the lack of intellectual brilliance
It is presumed his virtues brighter shine.

So, with a sense of all his moral beauty,
I shall endeavor righteously to pump
Vigor enough to vote, as is my duty,
Feeling the while I'm voting for a chump.

NEW YORK, Sept. 20. CIT.

Hospitals for Family Use.

TO THE EDITOR OF THE SUN—*Sir:* In Sunday's SUN in an article on life in hospitals, I saw a statement to the effect that the prejudice among people against going to hospitals was slowly but surely disappearing and I write this to ask why something shouldn't be systematically done to remove the prejudice completely and quickly? I have been sick seriously five times in my life (I am now 60), and the first three times my wife and family would not listen to my going to the hospital. Really the way they talked about it you would have thought that a hospital was some kind of a dangerous and disreputable place. In each of these illnesses the expense in money was between $250 and $300, not to mention the upsetting of all our domestic arrangements and the wear and tear on wife and daughters, my wife being sick in bed for three weeks after I got well. The fourth illness necessitated an operation which had to be performed at the hospital, and when I had once fixed myself there I got the doctors to say that it would be dangerous to move me. The result was that an illness of six weeks was passed in the hospital at a cost of $150, no upsetting of the home life, careful attention, the right kind of food served at the right time, callers only when I should see them, and, generally speaking, such an improvement over the old way that made an entire change in the opinion of my family. Last year I had a four weeks' attack, and the very first day my wife carried me away to the hospital, and after four weeks I was out again in fine shape, and I believe at least two weeks earlier than if I had tried to turn my home into a hospital, where all the family had to be more or less sufferers because I was. That's why I am so anxious to see sick people go to the hospitals, where they are expected to go and every provision is made for them. L. Z. G.

John Brown's Pistol.

TO THE EDITOR OF THE SUN—*Sir:* At the risk of offending the guileless Third avenue curiosity shop keeper who thinks he owns "the pistol which John Brown used at Harpers Ferry," the story of which is so interestingly told in THE SUN of to-day, I should like to say that shells were not used in revolving pistols in John Brown's time. Cartridges were then made of a thick and greasy paper capped with a bullet, which was rammed home with a rammer and lever, which formed a part of the mechanism of the weapon. So you see that if the pistol be genuine the cartridges are bogus, as also is the exploded shell from which it is alleged John Brown fired his last shot. By all means the curiosity shop keeper should satisfy himself that he has not been deceived.

The late Gov. Henry A. Wise of Virginia received from admirers more than two dozen dragoon pistols and Colt's revolvers, said to have been taken from John Brown in the engine house, while there are few homes in West Virginia that do not contain a rifle, pistol, and dagger taken from the man whose "body is mouldering in the ground, while his soul goes marching on." There is a dealer in this city who has built a block of houses with money made by selling pistols and pikes taken from Brown, and his supply is still ample for the demand. G. WILFRED PEARCE.

WASHINGTON, Sept. 19.

The True Place for Low.

TO THE EDITOR OF THE SUN—*Sir:* As Mr. Low, from his own writings and declarations, is not a Republican, having resigned from the party because he did not believe in protection to American industries, why does he call for Republican support? He should go to Tammany, and as their natural friend ask them for its support. Of course, by simply staying in the field he would help Tammany, but it would be squarer for him to go over to it openly.

BROOKLYN, Se[illegible] ALWAYS A REPUBLICAN.

Weather Indications: FAIR; COLD.

863,956
WORLDS CIRCULATED YESTERDAY

The World.

"Circulation Books Open to All."

Weather Indications: FAIR; COLD.

863,956
WORLDS CIRCULATED YESTERDAY

"Circulation Books Open to All."

VOL. XXXVIII. NO. 13,330. {Copyright, 1898, by the Press Publishing Company, New York World.} NEW YORK, THURSDAY, FEBRUARY 17, 1898. PRICE {ONE CENT in Greater New York and Jersey City. TWO CENTS outside of Greater New York and Jersey City and on trains.

MAINE EXPLOSION CAUSED BY BOMB OR TORPEDO?

Capt. Sigsbee and Consul-General Lee Are in Doubt---The World Has Sent a Special Tug, With Submarine Divers, to Havana to Find Out---Lee Asks for an Immediate Court of Inquiry---260 Men Dead.

IN A SUPPRESSED DESPATCH TO THE STATE DEPARTMENT, THE CAPTAIN SAYS THE ACCIDENT WAS MADE POSSIBLE BY AN ENEMY.

Dr. E. C. Pendleton, Just Arrived from Havana, Says He Overheard Talk There of a Plot to Blow Up the Ship---Capt Zalinski, the Dynamite Expert, and Other Experts Report to The World that the Wreck Was Not Accidental---Washington Officials Ready for Vigorous Action if Spanish Responsibility Can Be Shown---Divers to Be Sent Down to Make Careful Examinations.

DRAWN FROM A DESCRIPTION BY EYE-WITNESSES ON THE STEAMSHIP CITY OF WASHINGTON WHO SAW THE EXPLOSION, FOLLOWED BY "A VOLCANO OF FIRE AND SHOWERS OF BOATS, BODIES, IRON AND GUNS," CABLED TO THE WORLD BY ITS OWN CORRESPONDENT IN HAVANA, SYLVESTER SCOVEL.

THE WHOLE STORY OF THE DISASTER TOLD IN A FEW WORDS.

Growing Belief that It Was Not Accidental—Visitor from Havana Reports that He Overheard a Plot—Sigsbee and Lee Suspicious.

In an official cable to the State Department Lee makes the significant request that a court of inquiry be held to ascertain the cause of the explosion.

Capt. Sigsbee officially cabled Secretary Long his conclusion, after a hasty examination, that the disaster was not caused by an accident.

He expressed a belief that whether the explosion originated without or within, it was made possible by an enemy.

Dr. C. E. Pendleton, who has just arrived from Havana, says that he overheard there a conversation in which it was declared that there would shortly come a great sensation; that there were wires all around the Maine and that she could be blown to pieces at a moment's notice.

Capt. Zalinski, perhaps the foremost living expert upon explosions in warfare, declares that he is almost sure that the Maine was destroyed by a dynamite torpedo or bomb.

A despatch from Washington says that Secretary Long and Assistant Secretary Roosevelt called all the chiefs in the Navy Department in consultation yesterday morning to secure expert opinion as to the cause of the Maine's loss and its effect on the navy.

Consul-General Lee cables officially that the number of victims is 260. Lieuts. Merritt and Jenkins are still missing.

Another Washington despatch says that the United States Government will maintain a firm and determined attitude. If it appears that the Spanish are responsible for the Maine's destruction the most vigorous action will be taken.

It is presumed that their orders are to steam directly to Havana or to join Admiral Sicard's fleet off the Dry Tortugas.

The Spanish cruiser Vizcaya has not arrived in this port. Capt. Paul Boyton told a World reporter last night that he would like

VIEW OF DOWN TOWN, NEW YORK,

VIEW OF DOWN TOWN, NEW YORK

VIEW OF DOWN TOWN, NEW YORK, TA

AKEN FROM NORTH RIVER—1897.

TAKEN FROM NORTH RIVER—1891.

FROM A SOUTH STREET ROOF—1897.

Great Is Greater New York.

STARTLING FACTS AND FIGURES.

GREATER NEW YORK is now a fact in law. When its first tax budget, amounting to about sixty-five millions of dollars, is collected the tax-payers will realize that it is a fact in figures also. Look at it in any way we may, the imperial city is the most complex and tremendous fact on the earth. New problems, some of them presented by new conditions, some by the weaving together of old and new, are to be worked out in this metropolis.

Not to speak at present of the other parts of the territory involved, there have never before been united two cities such as New York and Brooklyn. There are no adjoining communities more unlike. Brooklyn has been a community, the city of neighborhoods; an aggregation of people who retained in a measure village customs. The New York of Manhattan Island was and is cosmopolitan. The Brooklyn man may be a New-Yorker in business hours and a Brooklynite at night and on holidays. New-Yorkers, in this respect, do not lead double lives.

One of the problems which the greater New York must first solve is to make the people of these two dissimilar boroughs realize and magnify their common citizenship. There must be a welding of interests. This will take time. But until it is accomplished Greater New York will continue to be a fact in law and finance only. The public has been inundated with statistics about the greater city. The people have learned that all history might be searched in vain to find another metropolis with such an extensive water front, consisting of river, bay, kill, sound, and ocean, adapted to all sorts of commerce, domestic and foreign. They need not be told that the city, with sagacity on the part of its rulers, cannot help becoming, during the next half-century, a commercial emporium for which a comparison cannot be found in the world's history.

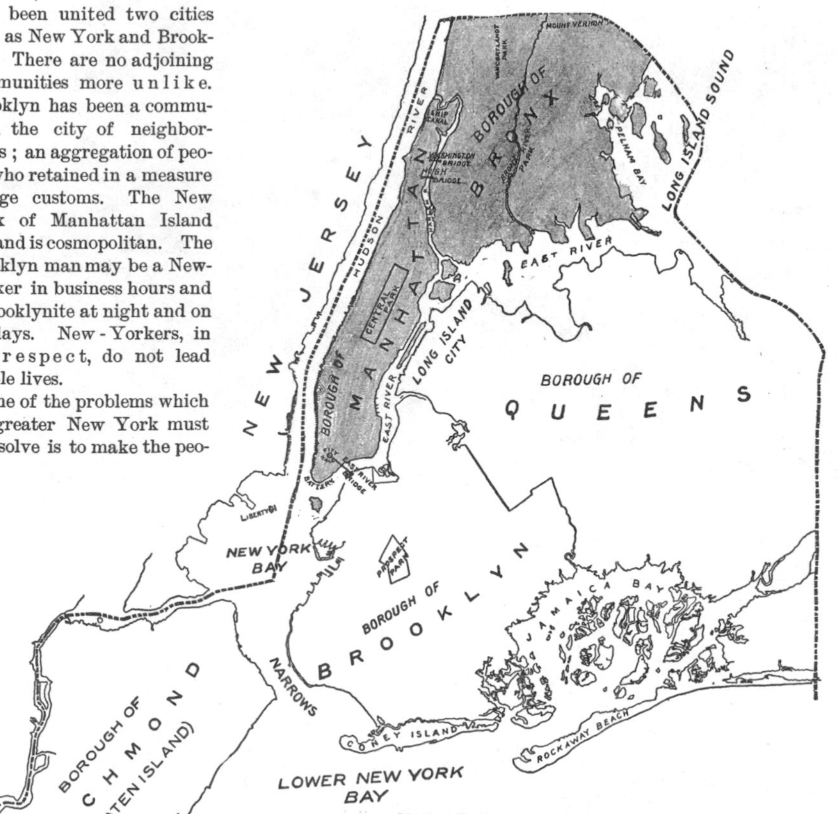

MAP OF GREATER NEW YORK.
The shaded part indicates the former area of New York City.

The statistician has convinced us also that in manufacturing pursuits the city on Manhattan Island has long been the greatest in the United States. The greater New York, the same authority tells us, is to be by far the most important manufacturing city in the world. It is possible that at present the metropolis has not as much ready money in its vaults as London has. We may, however, safely assume that it is a matter of a few years only before New York will be surpassingly pre-eminent as a financial centre.

While the enthusiastic manipulator of figures has been dilating on the commercial, manufacturing, and financial prominence of Greater New York he has forgotten the singular fact that it is the greatest agricultural city under one government on the globe. The larger part of its territory is under cultivation to-day. Richmond and Queens counties are almost wholly farm lands, with more acreage than all the other boroughs put together. The agricultural and garden products of the city reach a total value as great as that of some granger States. During the next few years politicians at least will realize the importance of the agricultural element of the greater New York. The limits of the new city embrace one hundred and ninety-six thousand eight hundred acres. Territorially it is the largest of cities, and it is as large as some of the States in the Union. Of the commonwealths, only New York, Pennsylvania, Illinois, and Ohio exceed it in population. London is the only other metropolis with more inhabitants. Our friend, the statistician, says that in 1945 the two cities—London and New York—will have an equal number of residents. New York has more miles of paved streets, sewers, and street-railways than any other city. Its debt exceeds that of all the States in the Union.

New York is to be a city of bridges and tunnels. The various boroughs must be connected in order that the convenience of the people may be served and that the communal feeling may be developed. One new bridge over the East River is being constructed; two others are projected. A magnificent bridge over the Harlem River is nearly finished, and contracts have been made for the erection of two others. Staten Island may be connected, by a tunnel under the Kill von Kull, and thus, by railway and ferries or by a tunnel under the Hudson, with Manhattan Island.

The Public Library in Bryant Park, the zoological and botanical gardens, the additions to the museums of art and history, and the public baths which are under way, are merely the beginning of colossal undertakings in this and other directions for the comfort, convenience, and instruction of its citizens. Parks and recreation piers are to be increased in number, and magnificent drives are planned. The ocean beach of the new city will afford opportunity for the laying out of water-front parks which in accessibility, healthfulness, and popularity will not be equaled in the wide world.

Including the underground rapid-transit road as planned, and not taking into account the cost of its probable extensions, the expenditure for the great public improvements along the lines indicated will be nearly two hundred millions of dollars. This sum does not include the cost of the ordinary city's work, such as street extension, paving, and the like.

Every nine minutes an infant is born in Greater New York, and every ten and a half minutes some soul quits its body. There are eighteen thousand families whose average income is less than seventy-five cents per day, and three hundred persons who possess a fortune of two million or more dollars each. The assessed value of the real estate is $2,367,659,607, and the value of the personal property is $404,201,063. Think of these figures!

This article might continue to repeat figures, dazzling and depressing, munificent and miserable, striking and stupendous. There are heights and depths in statistics as in everything else. Poverty, as well as property, can be computed. Suffering and joy can be averaged. Perhaps sufficient figures have been cited for one time. New York is vast in population as well as in mathematics. The consolidation brings into it a large element of American-born citizens, and hereafter, for a generation at least, the probability is that a majority of the residents of the city will be natives of the United States. Heretofore foreigners have been numerically in the majority. From every section of the country the reproach came that New York was a foreign city. The consolidation, however, does not eliminate the foreigner from the East Side, where he has made that section un-American in population, language, and customs. The assimilation of this element and the amelioration of its condition, through association, education, increase of intelligence, and improvement of its habitations, constitute one of the most puzzling of the problems that confront the new metropolis. HENRY McMILLEN.

Sunset on the Brooklyn Bridge.

A STRIKING WORD PICTURE.

MEN called it the sun for want of a better name. All day it had been lavishing its kindly rays upon the great city, cheering the hearts of women and little children. And now it was setting behind the Statue of Liberty, its feeble imitator. The western sky was filled with sombre clouds. There were pearl-gray tints, deep violets, and purples in profusion. It seemed as if the sky was draping itself in mourning because the sun was resting his ruddy chin on the edge of New Jersey, and taking a last look for the day at the magnificence and squalor of the great city.

Slowly he sank from view, tingeing the edge of a white cloud with fire. Then, as if smitten with remorse at his enforced desertion, he shot up a prodigal wealth of color upon the heavens. The aerial mountain ranges took on crimson hues, as if some supernal Titan blacksmith was blowing his furnace to Vesuvius heat, and the deep cloud-valleys blushed with a roseate glow. It was such a fine, exquisite warmth of color as is seen in a crematory furnace before incineration begins. The sky was blushing for the follies of Wall Street and Fifth Avenue.

Farther up toward the zenith were splashes of crimson on a vagrant cloud. The sun was making an ineffectual effort to fight the shadows of his adversary, night. A massive, vapory cliff was daubed for an instant with terra-cottas and yellows such as no palette ever held. Then came Twilight with her misty pigments. She toned down the glaring tints with neutral touches. With cruel insistence she threw a veil of sombreness over the heavens until there was left only a thin, irregular line of molten gold touching the remoter hills with ineffable glory.

This, too, was soon wiped out by the sponge of Twilight, and night had come. And with it came the moon, full-orbed, beneficent, with her benediction of silver. She touched the trembling waters rushing to the sea, and each tossing wave-crest smiled. She silvered the clouds and quenched all the stars except those in the remote depths of infinity, which peeped out slyly as if afraid of being scolded by the queen of the heavens. Then there blossomed out upon the night the magical beauty of lights forged in the brain of a pallid workman—white lights flashing with the insistence of harnessed lightning.

The bridge had put on its necklace. Red lights hung from the rear of swiftly-moving trains—unwinking bull's-eyes looking into the night. Long processions of yellow lights in the perspective radiated like the spokes of a wheel. Armies with torches. Green and red waving lights perched at the ends of jutting piers. Window-lights in ferry-boats. Bouquets of lights in city squares. Colored magic-lanterns in the fairy palaces of Williamsburg. A faint glow on the far horizon, like the fading glory of a prairie on fire. Below, the black, swirling river, reflecting on its ebon surface shifting chunks of amethyst and crimson light. ERNEST JARROLD.

An Up-to-date Philanthropist.

THE scene depicted by Mr. de Lipman on the front page of this number of LESLIE'S WEEKLY has attracted the attention of thousands of New-Yorkers who have chanced, on Sunday evenings lately, to be passing the Worth monument, at the intersection of Broadway, Fifth Avenue, and Twenty-fifth Street, in the heart of the metropolis. Those who have had the curiosity to stop and look into the crowd have been rewarded by seeing in action a philanthropist whose breezy and bustling method of work constitutes an interesting variation upon the ways of the average street evangelist or missionary of the slums.

Frederick Rotzler, city missioner, is a bluff, hearty sort of person who looks as though he would rather work, or even fight, than preach. Evidently his appearance does not belie his character. He has started in to hold up the well-dressed throngs of Broadway and Fifth Avenue, and beg from them the price of a decent bed (fifteen cents) for each of the fifty or sixty homeless vagrants that he always has lined up and waiting there. And his scheme has met with more than a little practical success. There are usually more tramps than the passing contributors can be induced to pay for; but sometimes as many as a hundred men (the most needy and apparently deserving have first chance) are provided with a decent night's lodging. If they had attempted to beg it on their own hook they might have failed, or perhaps landed in the police-station. Mr. Rotzler says to the passers-by, in effect: "Here are these poor chaps without a place to lay their heads, this cold night. Can't you help us out? A quarter will fix two of 'em—for a number have a nickel or a dime of their own. Who'll give us a helping hand?" This is a strong, direct appeal to the average man or woman. Contributions come in rather briskly; and when they have ceased, the missionary marches his men off to a cheap but good lodging-house in East Twenty-third Street, and pays for their beds himself.

Just how far this sort of thing may go, or how much permanent good it may accomplish, it would be idle to speculate. Presumably, Mr. Frederick Rotzler does not worry his head about that—and there is no reason why he should. The regular charity organizations have salaried officers who do all the thinking that is required, and oftentimes their deliberations fail to keep pace with the necessities of the poor outcasts who are supposed to be among the beneficiaries of the charitable funds. Then the direct methods come into play. There is no red tape about the city missioner. He is like Jim Bludso, who—

"Seen his duty, a dead sure thing,
And did it—thar and then."

Intercollegiate Chess.

THE photograph here reproduced shows the outward aspect of affairs at an interesting moment during the third round of the intercollegiate chess tournament in New York City. The contest has engaged the crack players of Harvard, Yale, Princeton, and Columbia, the arena of their struggle being the Columbia Grammar School. In the picture we see Southard, the Harvard champion, on the right, pitted against Seward, of Columbia, on the left. The principals are wrapt in a Yogi-like intensity of thought; the score-keeper holds an attitude of pleased expectancy; while the privileged spectators stand about with facial expressions suggestive of the inscrutability that reigns at a high-limit game of poker.

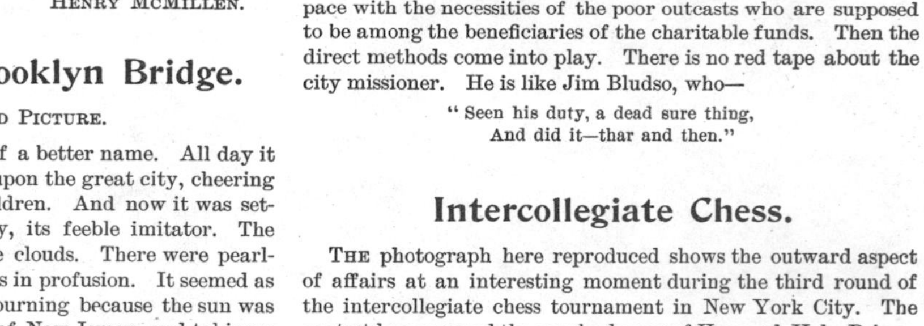

Photograph by Hare.
INTERCOLLEGIATE CHESS MATCH.

MADISON SQUARE, INTERSECTION OF FIFTH AVENUE AND BROADWAY—GENERAL WORTH'S MONUMENT IN CENTRE.
Copyrighted by J. S. Johnston, New York.

WALL STREET—TRINITY CHURCH IN BACKGROUND.
Copyrighted by J. S. Johnston, New York.

THE CITY HALL, BROOKLYN.

THE BROOKLYN BRIDGE, UNITING THE BOROUGHS OF NEW YORK AND BROOKLYN.

THE GREATER NEW YORK.—BORN, JANUARY 1st, 1898.

[SEE ARTICLE ON PAGE 26.]

Bright, Newsy, Truthful. Order from Newsdealers.

The North Side News.

Clean, Local, Vigorous. Subscribe Now $1 per year.

Published Weekly in the Interests of the Great North Side.

Vol. II. No. 18. NEW YORK, SATURDAY, APRIL 30, 1898. Price, 3 Cents.

BUSINESS MEN PROTEST.

A DELEGATION FROM THE NORTH SIDE BOARD OF TRADE CALL ON THE MAYOR AND COMPTROLLER.

Pleasantly Received by the Mayor, Who Assures Them of His Sympathy—The Comptroller Not in—A Way Out Promised by His Deputy.

The North Side Board of Trade met on Wednesday evening pursuant to a call for a special meeting signed by the following members: Henry Schrader, Albert E. Lickman, Adam P. Dienst, M. S. Leahy, Frank P. Mott, Charles S. Adams, J. S. Carvalho, O. G. Angle, A. Weiner, Martin Lipps and John M. Tierney.

The call for the special meeting asked for the appointment of a committee to call upon the Mayor and Comptroller in relation to the stopping of public works, owing to the non-payment of contract money. After considerable discussion it was decided, on motion of Mr. S. S. Oliver, that the above-named gentlemen, together with the gentlemen present and all those who could be notified, should call upon the Mayor on Thursday and attend the meeting of the Board of Estimate and Aportionment at 3 o'clock.

There seemed to be considerable difference of opinion among the members as to the selection of a spokesman. All the gentlemen seemed able to present formidable arguments and reasons why public works in this borough should not be stopped, but each man seemed a bit wary of presenting these cogent reasons to the ogre of the City Hall. Finally they achieved a brilliant coup. They selected a man who was absent, and therefore couldn't decline. On motion of Mr. C. W. Stoughton, Mr. De Witt C. Overbaugh, was selected as spokesman, Mr. Overbaugh having previously signified to Mr. Wells his intention of joining the committee. The board then adjourned, to meet at 2.30 on Thursday at the City Hall.

Despite the rain, quite a number of gentlemen gathered in the rotunda of the City Hall. Among them were James L. Wells, D. C. Overbaugh, Martin Lipps, A. P. Dienst, O. G. Angle, C. W. Stoughton, A. E. Lickman, M. J. Leahy, M. Redmond, P. J. Collins and others.

Mr. Overbaugh, who had had honors thrust upon him by being selected to speak for the committee, was rather inclined to decline, but finally consented. While the members were deliberating they learned that the Board of Estimate and Apportionment had met and adjourned. It was then decided to call and interview the Mayor.

That functionary received them most graciously, and politely asked how he could serve them. Mr. Wells announced that the gentlemen were a delegation from the North Side Board of Trade, and then introduced Mr. Overbaugh. Mr. Overbaugh began by stating the objects of the gathering. The non-payment of money to the contractors, he said, was causing great delay and distress. He alluded to many public works in detail, and particularly to the hardship which was being caused to the mechanics and the tradesmen. Many public works would have been stopped long ago but for the dealers in materials, who had been most lenient with the contractors. Mr. Overbaugh asked the Mayor to use his best endeavors to have this serious condition of things remedied, and predicted that if something were not done not only would the public be much inconvenienced and hardship be caused, but the public health would be menaced in many swampy localities, where sewers had been opened and owing to a lack of funds must remain incompleted. Other gentlemen spoke in the same vein. During the various remarks the Mayor stood with his hands in his pockets, listening attentively. When they had finished he assured them that he was in hearty sympathy with them and their aims, and realized perfectly the gravity of the situation. He, however, had no jurisdiction in the matter, he assured them, because all such questions should be referred to the Comptroller. It was evident that the Mayor had his usual chip on his shoulder and yearned for battle, for he could not refrain from making various disparaging remarks concerning the last administration. As the burden of the Mayor's song seemed to be, "See the Comptroller," the delegation withdrew, taking with it the assurances of the Mayor's most distinguished consideration.

Once out in the corridors, the members held a conference and decided to take the Mayor's advice, so, in line of battle, they charged through the rain over to the Comptroller's office, only to find that he had left for the day. Deputy Comptroller Michael T. Daly received the delegation, however, and had a conference with Messrs. Wells, Overbaugh and Dienst. From Mr. Daly they learned that a plan was under consideration by which the contractors could be satisfied. The manner in which this was to be done was not divulged, but the members of the Board of Trade received assurances that a way out of the present difficulty would be found. So the committee came away in high spirits.

It is not out of place to say here that if the citizens of other sections of the city would take the trouble to look after these things, and stick to them with as much pertinacity and energy as the North Side Board of Trade, the Taxpayers' Alliance and other like organizations handle such affairs, they would secure more benefits. Great are the men of the Borough.

DROWNED IN PELHAM BAY.

The body of an unknown man awaits identification at the Fordham Morgue. It was taken from Pelham Bay Tuesday by the Bronx Park police, and the body seemed to have been in water several days. The man appeared to have been about 40 years old, five feet and five inches tall and with dark hair and eyes. He wore a black pea jacket and vest and black trousers, with laced shoes that had recently been bought, and a red necktie.

He had a long scar on the left cheek. A card was found in the man's pockets bearing the memorandum "Mrs. Fitzpatrick, Nov. 10, 1897."

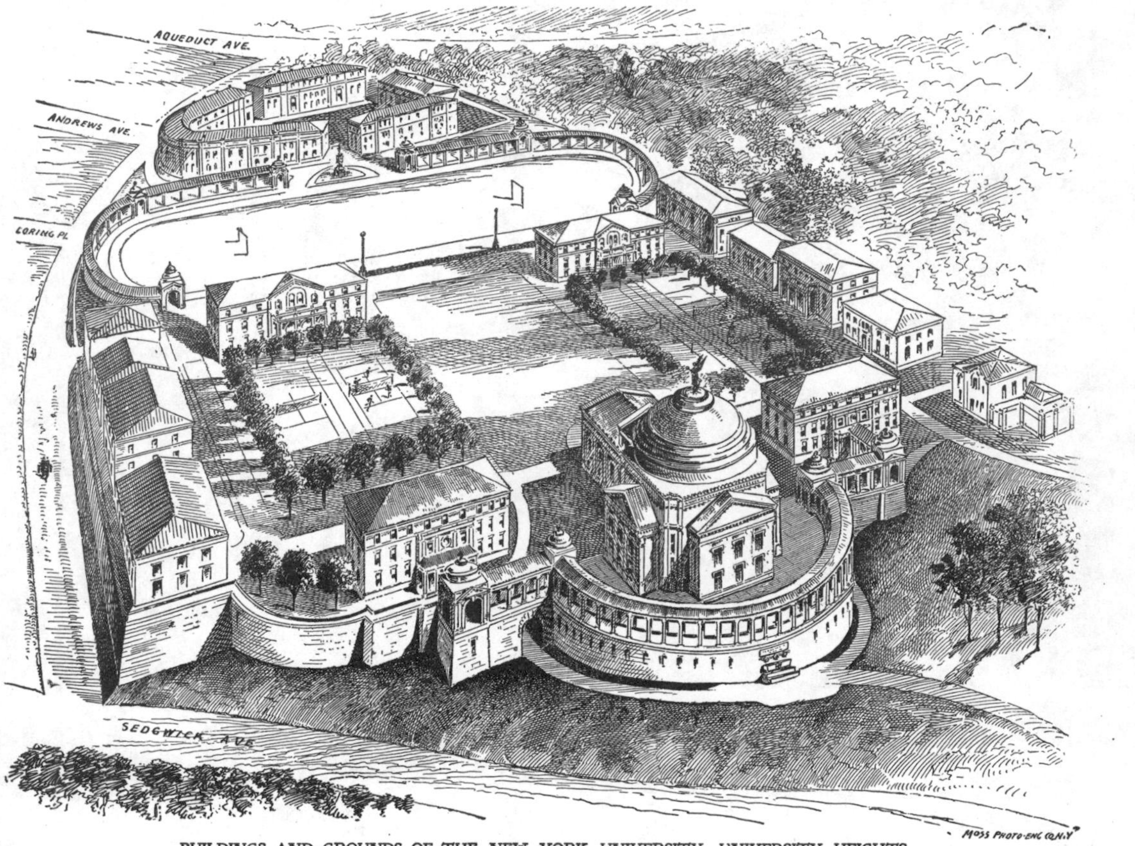

BUILDINGS AND GROUNDS OF THE NEW YORK UNIVERSITY, UNIVERSITY HEIGHTS.

THE LOCAL BOARD.

Petitions for Various Public Improvements Approved—The Sampson Street Matter Finally Laid Over.

The local board held its regular meeting in the president's office at 2 p. m., on Thursday. Councilmen Hottenroth and Murray and Aldermen Geiger and McGrath were present.

A petition was presented for the regulating and grading of 230th street, from Daily avenue to Spuyten Devil road. On motion of Councilman Murray the board passed on the petition favorably. A petition was presented for a sewer from Jerome avenue to the concourse, and in the concourse from 179th street to Tremont avenue, and in Walton avenue from 179th street to Burnside avenue in Morris avenue to Tremont avenue, from Burnside avenue to Creston avenue, and from 178th street to Burnside avenue. On motion of Alderman Geiger the matter was recommended.

A petition was received from the principal and teachers of Public School No. 61 to asphalt Third avenue in front of the school, they complaining that the noise of the passing wagons interfered greatly with their work.

On motion of Councilman Hottenroth the matter was referred to the Commissioner of Highways, as the local board. had no power to take action in the matter, as the city would have to pay for entire cost of the work.

A petition was presented for the paving with asphalt of Jackson avenue from 164th street to 166th street. On motion it was laid over.

The old matter of the paving of Simpson street from 167th street to Freeman street was brought up. Mr. Gallagher, who last week questioned Mr. John De Hart's ownership of any property on this street, was present with fifteen residents to protest against pavement of any kind. Mr. John De Hart had only one follower, but as Mr. De Hart is a host in himself, he did not need many backers. He had with him, moreover, his deeds to prove his ownership to property fronting on the street in question and he proceeded to present many weighty arguments why the street should be improved.

After much discussion Councilman Hottenroth moved that the matter be laid over indefinitely, and it was so ordered.

A petition was presented for the paving with granite blocks of Westchester avenue from Rogers Place to Prospect avenue, and on motion of Alderman Geiger it was recommended.

Commissioner Kearny, of the Department of Public Building, Lighting and Supplies, asked that two rooms be set aside in the annex to the Municipal Building for his department. The board then went into executive session to try and map out a plan to divide up the rooms as fairly as possible among the various departments.

TROLLEY LINE BLOCKED.

One of the cars of the Union trolley line burned out its armatures while going over Harlem Bridge late Sunday afternoon, and another car started to push it up to the shops at West Farms.

The conductor of the disabled car forgot to fasten his trolley pole and, as the two whizzed along under the elevated railway structure at Third avenue and 145th street, the pole struck the wooden trolley support and tore away about a hundred feet of it.

The pole became tangled in the "L" structure, and in the effort to get loose short connections were made between the wire and the ground that sent out flashes and roars that frightened the passengers. The line was blocked for a long time.

THE NEW YORK UNIVERSITY.

THE REMOVAL TO BRONX BOROUGH FROM WASHINGTON SQUARE A GREAT STEP FORWARD.

Great Increase in Undergraduate Students—Athletic Sports Receiving More Attention, and the Development of a College Spirit Among the Many Advantages that Will Accrue.

For many years the New York University occupied the dingy old gray building in Washington square, and while its graduate departments were known and valued for their contributions to the knowledge of the world, the situation was not a good one for the undergraduate departments. In fact, the university work far exceeded the college work in importance, and under such conditions the developing of a college spirit was out of the question.

The schools of law, medicine and engineering which had grown up around the college had always been independent of the council in the management of their moneys, and practically of their entire work, and so they remained until 1885,

Even the finances of the college itself had for some years been resigned by the council into the hands of a few professors who consented to serve for whatever dividend they could make to themselves out of the income, after paying the fixed charges. The responsibility for the college however, was resumed by the corporation at the date named above—1885.

By successive steps the council has now assumed the direct control and financial responsibility of all the schools, having accepted that of the medical college last year. Thus at last a true university organism has been completed, and to-day this corporation is in reality what it has been for two-thirds of a century in name—the New York University.

In 1885 the Undergraduate College and the School of Enginering were conducted by twelve professors and instructors. Of these, seven had each a room assigned him for his work—the professors of chemistry and geology a private room in addition. The remaining five taught in the chapel, law room, library or council room, as was found convenient. The entire college work was thus carried on in thirteen rooms—two upon the ground floor, nine upon the main floor, two upon the upper floor of the building at Washington square.

There were no accommodations for professors or students outside these thirteen rooms, the passageways and the janitor's office, excepting the literary rooms of the two societies, and the observatory room in the southwest tower.

The election of studies for students was confined to a choice between the classical and scientific courses. These differed in that the latter substituted science for language to some extent, and offered modern languages instead of ancient throughout. The instruction was all given in three continuous hours; much good work, however, was done. The sound rule for undergraduate instruction was observed, that it must introduce the student into each of the three great fields of thought—namely, language and literature; philosophy and history; the exact and descriptive sciences. Also the old traditions of rhetorical training for all students, required attendance at prayers, and instruction in morals and religion were carefully maintained.

The advancement of the university since 1885 has been steady and wholesome. The number of undergraduates increased about 25 per cent. Still the environment was anything but ideal, and it was felt that if the college was to go on to increased usefulness some site better adapted to the needs of the undergraduate department must be secured. With rare wisdom the university authorities finally decided, after carefully examining many sites offered, to accept the Mali homestead, extending from Macomb's Dam road to the Harlem River. The tract purchased extends from Sedgwick avenue to Aqueduct avenue, and contains twenty-two acres, a boat house site on the Harlem River extending from the bulkhead back to the railway. There are also purchased two plots for the purpose of establishing a university community and opening streets and passageways to the railways and the river. These plots comprised about twen-

(Continued on Page 2.)

NEW YORK UNIVERSITY ATHLETIC TEAM.

THE MAINE.

Remember the Maine—
Her boys live again!
Risen are they from the dark Spanish flood.
Hark! O'er our broad land
The heroic band
Aloud from the deep calls for vengeance in blood.
Their stern battle cry,
'Tis "Conquer or Die!"
List! How it echoes from near and afar,
From hilltop and vale,
And on every gale
Sound thundering notes of grim visaged war!
The battleship, too,
Still manned by her crew,
In majesty floats fiercely facing the foe.
No longer a wreck,
Her turret and deck
For action are cleared to strike the first blow.
Brave spirits! By ye
Shall Cubans be free,
And Liberty's hosts in triumph be led;
With martyrs of old
Thy names be enrolled,
A glory resplendent for ever to shed!

—Roger H. Lyon.

OLD GLORY WAVES AT LAST.

The Municipal Building Has Secured a New Flag and the Clerks Are at Last Satisfied.

It's all right now. The municipal building finally has its flag flying. Ever since December, when the old flag blew down, the building has had no banner, and the employes have been unhappy. Since the war excitement began, this lack has been particularly noticeable. Recently the two hundred odd clerks began to be uneasy and irritated, and to wonder who was to blame. So vigorously did they express themselves that the Deputy Commissioner of Public Buildings, Lighting and Supplies, Mr. Best, managed to have a good deal of business elsewhere, while his messenger, Mr. Daniel Schwegler, went about with a hunted, worried look. Finally, it was reported that a flag would be sent up, to arrive on Tuesday. Disgust changed to joy, and the employes immediately set about planning a suitable demonstration. It was finally arranged that when the time came for raising the flag, all the clerks should mount to the roof, and there, led by the quartet of the Washington Club, were to sing: "The Star Spangled Banner," "America," and other patriotic songs, while President Haffen was to pull the halyards and raise the flag.

Tuesday arrived, and so did the flag, a handsome banner, twelve feet by twenty-four. Just before the time for the exercises to begin, it was discovered that the halyards had been blown away and that some one would have to climb the flag pole and affix new halyards. Meanwhile, the exercises were postponed temporarily. But, alas! when the employes went to work on Wednesday morning, they discovered that the flag was already up and had been flying since 7.30. The celebration had to be abandoned. But the patriotism is still there and so is the flag.

STRUCK BY LIGHTNING.

During the thunder storm on Sunday afternoon lightning struck the residence of Mrs. Clio Butterkofer at 1103 Woodruff street. The house is a two story frame building, situated in the middle of a large plot of ground. One wing of the house is semi-detached, with windows on three sides. The lightning came through the west window, tore down some plaster, set the place on fire and knocked Mrs. Butterkofer senseless. She was speedily restored by her family, and the fire was extinguished by the Fire Department. The damage was $200.

BETTER POLICE PROTECTION.

THE REDISTRICTING OF THIS BOROUGH WILL CONSERVE TO THAT END.

Details of the Plan Explained—The Boundaries of the Renumbered Precincts—An Inspector to Be in Charge at Crotona Park.

Chief of Police McCullagh has made many radical changes in the police force lately and the most noteworthy is the redistricting of the precincts, a step which was made necessary by the addition of Brooklyn, Staten Island, etc., under the Greater New York charter. This step is of particular interest to the Borough of the Bronx, where the rapid growth of population had not been matched by an increase in police and fire protection. Lately the Fire Department has begun to remedy this defect, and now the Police Department has taken a like step.

Perhaps the most radical change in the new arrangement is the creation of a new precinct composed of Bronx Park and portions of the Thirty-fourth, Thirty-fifth and Thirty-eighth precincts. This is a matter which has long needed attention. The Thirty-fourth Precinct has had enough territory within its borders to make a good sized Western city, and to properly patrol it, with but comparatively few men, has been a difficult matter and has puzzled Capt. Schmittberger sorely.

The following schedule will show the old and new precinct numbers and the location of the station houses:

Old No.	New No.
34th,	31st, Highbridge.
35th,	37th, Alexander avenue.
36th,	33d, 160th street.
37th,	34th, Tremont.
38th,	38th, West Chester.
39th,	38th, Sub., Wakefield.
40th,	35th, Kingsbridge.
41st,	Bronx Park.
42d,	36th, Steamer "Patrol."

The new precincts and their boundaries have been defined by Chief McCullagh as follows:

The Thirty-fourth Precinct will be what is now known as the Thirty-first Precinct (Highbridge). Boundaries: Beginning at Cromwell's Creek and the Harlem River, thence along the centre line of said creek to the centre line of Jerome avenue, to centre line of Kingsbridge Road, to Harlem River, along the shores of the Harlem River to place of beginning, including all streets and avenues within said boundaries. Station house, Highbridge.

The addition of a portion of the territory of this precinct to the present Thirty-fifth Precinct will make its boundaries as follows: Beginning at Cromwell's Creek and the Harlem River, thence along the shores of the Harlem River to the centre line of Fordham Landing Road, to Jerome avenue, to Cromwell's Creek, to the place of beginning, including all streets and avenues within said boundaries. Station house will be at Highbridge street. Contains no parks.

The Thirty-fifth Precinct will be what is now known as the Thirty-seventh Precinct (Alexander avenue). Boundaries: Beginning at the centre line of 49th street and Long Island Sound; thence along the centre line of 149th street to the New York Central and Hudson River Railway, to the centre line of Cromwell's Creek, to the Harlem River, along the shores of the Harlem River, Bronx Kills and Long Island Sound, to the place of beginning, including all streets, avenues and roads within said boundaries. Station house, Alexander avenue and 138th street. It contains St. Mary's Park (acreage 28.70, now patrolled by three park policemen), and will be made one additional day and night post. Its addition will not change the boundaries of the precinct.

The Thirty-sixth Precinct will be what is now known as the Thirty-third Precinct (161st street). Boundaries: Beginning at the centre line of 149th street and Long Island Sound; thence along the centre line of 149th street to the New York Central and Hudson River Railway, to Cromwell's Creek, to the centre line of Jerome avenue, to centre line of East 170th street, to centre line of Franklin avenue, to centre line of Jefferson avenue, to centre line of Boston road, to centre line of Home street, to centre line of Bronx River, along centre line of Bronx River to Long Island Sound, along the shores of Long Island Sound to centre line of 149th street, place of beginning, including all streets and avenues within said boundaries. It contains Cedar Park (acreage 17.470, now patrolled by three park policemen). Two posts are to be made of present Post 52, one taking in Cedar Park and all that portion of Post 52 south of 161st street, and the other new post taking in the remainder of present Post 52. The addition of this park will not change the boundaries of this precinct.

The Thirty-seventh Precinct will be what is now known as the Thirty-fourth Precinct (Tremont). Boundaries: Beginning at the intersection of the centre lines of 170th street and Jerome avenue; thence along Jerome avenue to the centre line of Van Courtlandt avenue, to Reservoir Oval East, both sides, to centre line of Gun Hill road, to centre line of Olin avenue, to centre line of the bridge across the Bronx River at Williamsbridge, to northern boundary of Bronx Park, thence to east side of Harlem Railroad, to centre line of Pelham avenue, to centre line of Southern Boulevard, to centre line of Kingsbridge road, to centre line of the Bronx River, to centre line of bridge over Bronx River at Westchester avenue, to centre line of Home street, to centre line of Boston road, to centre line of Jefferson street, to centre line of Franklin avenue, to centre line of 170th street, to place of beginning, including all streets and avenues within said boundaries. Stationhouse, Tremont. It contains Claremont and Crotona Parks. Claremont Park (acreage, 38, is now patrolled by three park policemen) will be made an additional day and night post.

(Continued on Page 3.)

Pages 25 to 32. NEW YORK JOURNAL AND ADVERTISER. Pages 25 to 32.

SUNDAY, MAY 29, 1898.—Copyright, 1898, by W. R. Hearst.

Two Monster Events for Decoration Day in Aid of Maine Fund.

MOST GORGEOUS SPECTACLE EVER SEEN.
JIMMY MICHAEL'S WILD RIDE FOR GLORY.

NEW YORK LETTER CARRIERS' BAND.

FRANK E. HOUTS, Bandmaster.

WILLIAM J. FOWLER, Assistnat Bandmaster and Librarian.

Cornets—Al. Littau, James Greer, Fred A. Hoelzer, John J. Collier, John Blake, William H. Jacobs, P. F. Keller, Thomas H. Cordery, J. Rosenthal. Altos—M. J. Sullivan, H. A. Field, Charles Kraft, George W. Belasco, Gus Trautfeld, Peter J. Lambe. Baritones—Thomas Merchant, W. H. Barker. Basses—George Schlabach, Thomas F. Whalen, Fitzsimmons. Drums—George R. Greer, James Cavanaugh, M. Barnard, A. J. Plummer. Clarinets—Henry V. Clayton, P. T. Maloney, Alex J. Hogg, William P. J. Curtiss, John Cross, James F. Graham, T. G. Macpeak, W. J. Corbett, H. B. Lubkert, Charles Holbert, Joseph Cermack, E. Brusson, Benjamin F. Noah, William Eaton, J. Winner, J. J. Brady. Flute and Piccolo—John F. Mahoney, John A. Lawrence, George F. Gallot. Trombones—Jere F. Donovan, Louis E. Land, J. M. Zumkley, J. D. Lawlor, Charles D. Flesche, A. Jacobs.

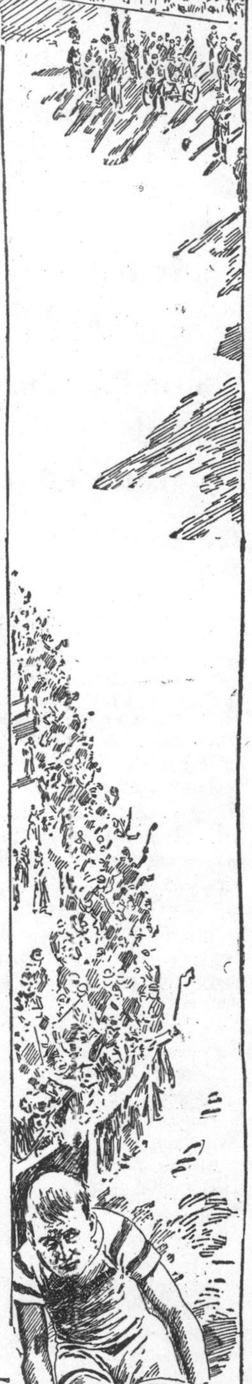

MONSTER FIREWORKS AT MANHATTAN BEACH

Pain's Realistic Description of Dewey's Storming of Manila To-morrow Night Will Be the Event of the Day.

PAIN'S greatest fireworks exhibition, depicting Dewey's storming of Manila, and the sinking of the Spanish squadron, which will be given at Manhattan Beach Monday evening, will be by far the greatest pyrotechnical display ever seen in this country.

This exhibition is given in aid of the Journal's Maine Monument Fund. Every effort has been made to make "Maine Night" at the noted Summer resort famous in the annals of the beach. The list of attractions surpass anything ever before offered. The New York Letter Carriers' Band, sixty strong, has volunteered its services for the evening.

"We do this," said President Fitzgerald, "to show our interest in the movement to erect a monument to the Maine dead. It is a noble work, and anything we can do to advance it will be gladly done."

The twenty war ships that took part in the battle will appear brilliantly lighted. Dewey, on the flagship, will begin the manoeuvring, and, coming closer and closer to the enemy, the firing will begin. Then come shots from the land forces. As the balls one after another splash in the water at the sides of the American vessels sparks colored like foam rise up, and the shots, hot from the cannon's mouth, sink with a hissing noise into the sea.

Then comes the defeat of the Spanish vessels. Some are on fire; others have turned tail and are scuttled by their own seamen; the others are seen as the American guns pour their heavy fire into their sides.

The reproduction of the great battle will be on a stage more than three hundred feet in width. This will allow room for the war ships to move exactly as they moved in Manila Bay, and the effects of the light will make the distances appear as they appeared on the day of the fight. At the first signs of victory will come the hurrah of the American sailors; the American flag will be seen as it is raised for the first time on the island, and amid changing lights will appear the Stars and Stripes.

JIMMY MICHAEL IN THE RACE OF HIS LIFE.

Paced by Electric Tandem at Ambrose Park, He Will Try to Make a New World's Ten-Mile Record.

THE Journal's Decoration Day meet at Ambrose Park, in which the famous Jimmy Michael will race for a new ten-mile world's record, paced by the electric tandem, will be the cycling event of the day.

Everything is in readiness for Michael's noteworthy dash against electricity. Then, too, this may be the fleet bicyclist's last public appearance for some time. He has sent a letter to President McKinley, volunteering his services in organizing a cycle corps of couriers, and he thinks his offer will be accepted. This, then, should bring a big crowd to Ambrose Park to witness the midget in his marvellous attempt at record breaking against the electric tandem, which has attracted so much attention in the cycling world.

All the other contestants are in fine fettle to make a great showing. The race of Boulay and Goodman will be most exciting. The men are in the pink of condition. Each is anxious to win, and the friends of both are equally confident. Goodman, however, says he will make the race of his life.

All the other prominent professionals who will take part in the meet are in condition to make an excellent showing. The lists of amateurs comprise the best in the country. They number among them the following:

A. H. Kraskey, of Hoboken, N. J.; W. E. Siebert, of Hoboken, N. J.; Peter G. Van Cott, of New York; S. J. Adelman, of Brooklyn; Harry Sherman, of Brooklyn; Chester A. Neill, of Brooklyn; Harry Heyde, of New York; Fred Gohde, Riverside Wheelmen; John M. Derby, Jr., of New York; A. E. Vulchneir, of Brooklyn; Paul S. Young, of Brooklyn; G. H. Alpers, of Brooklyn; H. E. Boardman, of Hoboken, N. J.; A. R. Jacobson, of New York; A. O. Huselton, of Brooklyn; E. W. Conradson, of Brooklyn; W. W. Staylor, of New York; W. P. Kurchen, Andrae Wheelmen; Jack Fleiger, of New York; Harry Rowland, Jr., of Corona, L. I.; George Taylor, Nameless Wheelmen; William Spree, of Brooklyn; Ralph Ottavis, Wolff-American Wheelmen.

TWO unparalleled events will take place Decoration Day in aid of the Maine Monument Fund.

One will be Jimmy Michael's furious ride against the electric tandem, which is one of the features of the great meet at Ambrose Park under the auspices of the Journal.

The other event is the reproduction by Pain of the stirring scenes in the harbor of Manila when brave Dewey stormed the forts of Cavite and annihilated the Spanish squadron. This is scheduled for the evening at Pain's Amphitheatre, Manhattan Beach.

No such elaborate exhibition of fireworks has ever been prepared as the portrayal of Dewey's remarkable achievement in the Philippines. Every incident will be accurately given with a fiery realism never before equalled.

At this mammoth pyrotechnical display the famous Letter Carriers' Band will give a series of patriotic selections suitable for the occasion. Other spectacular attractions will be provided, and the night bids fair to be a most memorable one.

The cycle meet at Ambrose Park is the chief bicycle event scheduled for the day. In addition to Jimmy Michael a long list of other professionals will take part, including Goodman, and Boulay, the French rider. The contest between these two crack cyclists will be close and exciting.

The list of amateurs includes every noted one in this vicinity. Valuable cash and souvenir prizes are provided for each event.

A MILLION AND A QUARTER A DAY. 1,250,000. A MILLION AND A QUARTER A DAY

LARGEST ON EARTH!

An Instructive Table of Comparative Daily Circulation of the Leading Newspapers of the World.

New York Journal	1,213,751
Paris Petit Journal	1,000,000
London Daily Mail	525,000
London Daily Telegraph	250,000
London Standard	250.000
London Chronicle	200,000
London Daily News	200,000
London Times	40,000

NEW YORK JOURNAL

AND ADVERTISER.

WEATHER.

The local Weather Bureau's prediction for New York City and vicinity is as follows: Warmer; southerly winds.

For New York, New Jersey, Eastern Pennsylvania and Connecticut: Fair; warmer; southwesterly winds.

The highest temperature yesterday was 83 degrees at 4 p. m.

The lowest temperature yesterday was 59 degrees at 6 a. m.

NO. 5,700. Copyright, 1898, by W. R. Hearst.—NEW YORK, SATURDAY, JUNE 25, 1898.—12 PAGES. PRICE ONE CENT In Greater New York and Jersey City. Elsewhere, TWO CENTS.

TROOP OF ROUGH RIDERS AMBUSHED, SHOT DOWN AND KILLED BY SPANIARDS.

Young Hamilton Fish One of the First to Meet a Soldier's Fate.

Many of New York's Society Youths Among the Killed and Wounded.

Journal's Correspondent, Edward Marshall, Seriously Wounded in Front Rank.

Ten Men Killed and Thirty-six Wounded, Including Many of the Officers.

Special Cable to The Journal.

PLAYA DEL ESTE, June 24, by Journal Dispatch Boat Simpson.—There was hot, bloody fighting this morning between Colonel Wood's Rough Riders and the Spanish in ambush. After a forced march the troopers dismounted.

They heard the enemy felling trees three miles inland from here. Eight miles from Santiago occurred a fierce charge through the grass and chaparral.

They were met by a withering volley.

The dead are:

Captain Allyn Capron.

Hamilton Fish.

Captain Luna.

Privates James Crews, Edward Culver and Dawson, of Troop L.

Harry Heffner, of Troop G, and three others.

Wounded — First Regular Cavalry:

Major Bell.

Captain Knox.

Captain McCormick.

Lieutenant Byran.

First Volunteer Cavalry:

Major Brodie.

Captain McClintock.

Lieutenant Thomas.

Privates Darnett T. Isabel and Keene S. Whitney, Troop L.

Sergeant Cavanagh.

Corporal Stewart.

Private M. Coyle.

Troop G—G. W. Arinto.

Troop F—A. Rebrutisch.

A. F. Hartle.

Fred Beal.

And twenty-one others.

The rough riders had begged to be sent to the front at once. They marched over the foothills from Daiquiri last night.

Colonel Leonard Wood, who was reported killed, is all right.

He and Roosevelt led the charge with great bravery, scorning to lie in the grass or underbrush, as the Spaniards did. The enemy was driven back toward Santiago with heavy losses.

Our base had been changed from Daiquiri to Siboney.

Roosevelt was supported by the Second Massachusetts and First regular cavalry.

The army is to advance on Santiago to-morrow.

Forty Cubans were killed in to-day's fighting.

The Montgomery, Suwanee, Scorpion, and Wampatuck shelled the woods hotly this morning at Siboney, covering the landing of supplies and horses.

Edward Marshall, the Journal correspondent, was seriously wounded at the front with Roosevelt. Journal Correspondent Laine is with him. Journal Correspondent Menichol and G. A. Coffin, the Journal artist, have gone with food and water and a surgeon to bring Mr. Marshall to the coast.

General Castillo with two thousand Cubans reports engaging the Spaniards at Guasima, capturing two railroad trains laden with food and a hundred tons of coal. He killed many of the enemy. Our own losses were fewer than fifty.

The Spaniards, reinforced from Santiago with ten field pieces, are fortifying the hill at Sevilla.

In the battle to-day Roosevelt's men utterly routed the Spaniards in splendid style.

Transports are on the way to Cerradero to get Garcia with his forces.

THE KILLED.

Captain Allyn Capron.
Captain Luna.
Hamilton Fish.
James Crews, private.
Edward Culver, private.
—— Dawson, private of Troep L.
Harry Heffner, private of Troop G.
Three others.

THE WOUNDED.

Major Bell, First Regular Cavalry.
Captain Knox, First Regular Cavalry.
Captain McCormick, First Regular Cavalry.
Lieut. Byran, First Regular Cavalry.
Major Brodie, First Volunteer Cavalry.
Captain McCormick, First Volunteer Cavalry.
Lieut. Thomas, First Volunteer Cavalry.
Damett T. Isabel, Private.
Keene S. Whitney, private, Troop L.
Sergeant Cavanagh.
Corporal Stewart.
M. Coyle, private, Troop G.
G. W. Arinto, Troop F.
A. Rebrutisch, Troop F.
A. F. Hartle, Troop F.
Fred Beal, and twenty othe.s.

(From His Latest Photograph.)

HAMILTON FISH, JR.

Killed in Ambush with the Rough Riders on the Way to Santiago.

OFFICERS OF ROOSEVELT'S ROUGH RIDERS, WITH THEIR MACHINE GUNS.

BRILLIANT DEEDS OF DARING BY NEW YORK'S BRAVE BOYS.

SERGEANT HAMILTON FISH, WHO FELL AT LA QUASINA.

LANDING OF THE FIRST BOATLOAD OF AMERICAN SOLDIERS AT BAIQUIRI.

KNOBLAUCH AND JUDSON, WHO DIVED IN SHARK-INFESTED CUBAN WATERS FOR LOST AMERICAN GUNS.

DRAMATIC SCENES IN THE TERRIFIC CHARGE OF THE ROUGH RIDERS at La Quasina; the First Landing at Baiquiri, and the Historic Attack of the Americans on Santiago.

COL. "TEDDY" ROOSEVELT LEADING THE CHARGE OF THE ROUGH RIDERS.
(From press description.)

HOW HAMILTON FISH DIED—FROM THE DESCRIPTION BY THE WORLD CORRESPONDENT WHO WITNESSED HIS DEATH.

NEW YORK HEROES AT THE FRONT.

AMERICA'S "kind-hearted policy" in the conduct of the present war has not prevented the making of American heroes. In the few brief months since the war began important additions have been made to the list of famous fighters who will live in the history of the world.

Not all the glory has been won during the crash of battle and the roar of guns. Old fighters tell us it is comparatively easy to be brave there with one's comrades fighting round one, with the enemy before one, and with honor to be gained by doing one's duty. The fighting instinct is strong in the normal man. Whatever his ordinary environment or condition may be, line him up before the Spaniards with a musket in his hands and let him understand that he is fighting for his life, as well as for his country, and he will fight while there is life in him, or cheer on his comrades when his own fight has been ended by the enemy's bullet.

He doesn't think, for he hasn't time to think; there is too much to be done. If at the end he realizes that he is leaving this little earth his mind is still on the battle that is going on around him. He watches it to the last—as Capt. Capron did—or perhaps, just at the end, he recalls the One Woman and sends her the message on which she will draw for comfort through the weary years to come. It is all fine, and the story of it is read with a thrill by the men and women who stay at home—but it is not the highest kind of courage after all. That shows when the man goes to his duty and his death alone, without the sweep and charge of the army to bear him along; without the inspiration of the presence and approval of his officers and comrades. There has been much of this quiet heroism shown during the Spanish-American war. It should not be obscured by the more brilliant exploits that have come to the attention of the public.

Many of the stories of heroism told in the newspapers and around camp fires in Cuba have to do with New Yorkers. The most reckless and dare-devil exploits on Cuban soil have been the work of men from Manhattan Island. The fight of the Rough Riders will go down in history as one of the most daring of modern times. Men and women of the coming generation will thrill over it as those of to-day were thrilled when they read of it. It is said truly that no other regiment of volunteers ever made so brave a showing. But it is not alone "Teddy" Roosevelt, yelling at the head of a terrific charge, that holds the attention. The New York trooper who gave to a wounded comrade his shelter behind a tree and stepped out into the hailstorm of bullets to be himself brought down by them the next minute; the New York surgeon, Dr. Church, who calmly dressed wounds on the battlefield while the Mauser rifles of the enemy barked around him; the New York correspondent, Edward Marshall, who, thought to be fatally wounded on the field, dictated for his newspaper the story of the battle—all these are fine exploits to read and think about in this eminently practical age.

Before that memorable battle the New York Rough Riders had distinguished themselves in various ways. Alfred M. Judson and Charles E. Knoblauch, both of this city, won honors by diving into the shark-infested waters at Baiquiri for necessary guns and bugles that had been lost from the landing boats. Judson was a member of Squadron A, of the New York Volunteer Cavalry. One hundred and two men were chosen by lot to go South. Mr. Judson was not among them, so he promptly joined the Rough Riders and sallied forth for glory. His friends felt he would miss no chance to win it and they were right. Mr. Knoblauch is a well-known oarsman, athlete and polo player.

During this same landing of the American troops at Baiquiri the first two men to touch Cuban soil were also Rough Riders—Lieut. Simmons and Private McFarland, both of New York. They might have been picked off by the bullets of the alert enemy, but they were not. Two more New Yorkers—Major Henry La Motte and Sergt. Dennis J. Kick—hoisted the American flag on the blockhouse at the top of the hill near which the landing was made. The Spaniards, who might have been expected to interfere with this performance, lay low and regarded it with warm interest.

The quiet heroism of "Jack Berlin," who fell in the fight at Sevilla, must not be overlooked. "Berlin" was Jacob Wilinski, a New York boy of sixteen, who ran away from home and enlisted under an assumed name in Company K, First Cavalry. His height and athletic build—he was over six feet tall—counteracted the youthfulness of his smooth cheeks and boyish eyes. He said he was twenty-one, and went to the front with that patriotic falsehood still on his lips. No one fought more bravely or died more "gamely" than this waif from New York's tenement district.

The daring of H. Alsopp Borrowe, who has volunteered to operate the famous gelatine gun, has already been fully described in the Sunday World. The tendency of this terrible instrument to blow to pieces its operator as well as the enemy is recognized with awe by fighting men. It is a significant fact that whereas 2,000 men volunteered to go with Hobson on his expedition with the Merrimac, only Borrowe responded to the call for volunteers to operate the dynamite gun. He will have all the glory of the achievement, and his enthusiastic friends hope he will live to enjoy it.

The first boatload of soldiers for Shafter's invading army was landed in Cuba by Naval Cadet John Halligan, of the flagship Brooklyn. The Cubans who were at the landing enjoying this inspiring sight presented to Mr. Halligan a large silk Cuban flag as a memento of the occasion.

RISKS OF THE AMERICAN SOLDIERS.

IN order to arrive at an intelligent view of a soldier's risks it is necessary to get at some common basis with regard to his length of service. The chances of a man who enlists for three months must, generally speaking, be better than those of a man who enters the army for three years. Mr. Fox, having spent years in the study of the Government statistics, has completed a calculation by which the total enrolment on the Northern side has been reduced to a basis of three years' service. Taking this as a standard, he finds that the percentage of killed is 5.1.

Death in battle is by no means the only casualty. A man may be wounded and yet not die or be totally incapacitated. There is a satisfactory way of arriving at the probable number who suffered wounds that were not mortal. The records of many battles in the civil war are complete, not only with respect to the killed, but wounded. Taking the records of thirty-eight such battles (and among them are some of the bloodiest in the entire war), it is found that 34,542 were killed outright and 186,777 were wounded. In this the ratio of wounded to killed is 4.8. This ratio, it is believed, is a perfectly safe one. By reference to the Franco-Prussian war there is found a justification of this ratio, for in that conflict the proportion of wounded was a trifle more than five times the number of killed. On the basis of 100 men, therefore, it is probable that while 5 would be killed 24 would be wounded.

There is a greater danger than death in battle which soldiers must face—disease. This is shown in a startling way by the grand total of deaths in the Northern army during the civil war. As stated above, the killed in battle numbered 110,070; those who died of disease numbered 199,720, and this immense figure does not include deaths in Confederate prisons, death from accident, suicide and murder.

Mr. Fox has found that upon a basis of three years' service the percentage of deaths from causes other than battle is near 12, and there is no reason to suppose that in the present war the deaths from disease will be less than they were thirty-five years ago. The great advance in knowledge of sanitation will be more than counterbalanced by the greater difference in climate.

From the Franco-Prussian records it appears that less than 2 per cent. died during the campaign from causes other than injuries received in battle. Both German and French soldiers fought in a familiar climate, and their campaign was not so extended as to carry them to the trying weather of either a severe winter or a hot summer. In fact, it was over in seven or eight months.

No statistics are available to show the percentage of promotions during the civil war. It is an interesting fact that the percentage of deaths in battle is greater among the officers than among the privates.

The percentage of line officers killed in battle is 8, and the percentage of staff officers a little greater.

Generally speaking, an officer who is severely wounded will either give way to somebody from an inferior position, or will be himself promoted for bravery, and thus cause a vacancy. So it seems fair to assume, on the basis of 100 men, about 19 of whom will be officers, that 8 per cent. of the latter will be killed and five times as many wounded. A calculation on this basis will show that not less than six officers out of every company of 100 will either be removed by death or other casualty, and thus make room for promotion.

This does not take into account the possibilities of vacancies occurring among the officers by reason of death by disease.

In a company of 100 soldiers engaged in a three years' service there will be not less than six promotions. The more one considers it the more this seems to be a very conservative estimate, for promotions by brevet on account of distinguished bravery often occur and carry with them the higher title to which the soldier aspires.

The chances thus far estimated concern only men enlisted for land service, including all the branches, artillery, cavalry and infantry. It appears from the official figures of the civil war that the chance of coming out alive is very much greater in the navy than in the army. The percentage of killed and mortally wounded in the Northern army during the civil war was .0136. In other words, less than two out of every 100 were killed in battle, and the percentage of wounded is only a trifle greater. Putting both together, it appears that only three men out of every 100 enlisted in the navy were injured in any way. It further appears that in the navy deaths from disease and accident are no greater than in civil life.

It must be borne in mind that this computation of chances for death, wounds and promotion is based upon three years' service, and an assumption that fighting will be severe. No one expects the war to last so long. If it lasts but one year the percentages should be but one-third of those stated.

Bright, Newsy, Truthful.
Order from Newsdealers.

The North Side News.

Published Weekly in the Interests of the Great North Side.

Clean, Local, Vigorous
Subscribe Now $1 per year.

Vol. II. No. 33. NEW YORK, SATURDAY, AUGUST 13, 1898. Price, 3 Cents.

THE BICYCLE PARADE

THE ENTIRE POPULACE OF THE NORTH SIDE TURNS OUT TO VIEW THE MOST BEAUTIFUL SPECTACLE EVER SEEN IN BRONX BOROUGH.

NO PUBLIC EVENT HAS EVER BEFORE EXCITED SUCH GENERAL INTEREST AND AROUSED SO MUCH ENTHUSIASM.

The Hearty Applause with Which the Wheelmen Were Greeted Proved the Genuine Appreciation Felt by All Classes—Special Features Noted and Accorded—Extra Demonstrations.

Shortly before 2.30 on last Saturday afternoon a woman, accompanied by several small children, were journeying uptown in an open trolley car. As the conveyance reached 149th street the larger of the little ones clutched her mother's arm and cried excitedly, "Look, mamma look!" Instantly the eyes of all the passengers were turned in the direction indicated by the eager child's outstretched finger, and surprise was followed by amusement as they beheld the form of a person arrayed in a costume most unusual riding a wheel with all permissible speed, headed southward.

Explanations were demanded of the conductor for the presence of the strange figure, and that accommodating official promptly informed them that the great bicycle parade was to occur that day and that the object that had excited so much wonder and amusement was simply one of the many grotesque riders hurrying to the place of rendezvous at Alexander avenue and 139th street.

When this information had been secured the majority of the travelers who were destined for a day's outing in the parks, decided to stop and witness the parade, and in a trice the car was emptied and the passengers, following the direction taken by the wheelman who had first aroused their interest, walked down to the place from which the parade was to start.

As they drew nearer and nearer to the place of rendezvous the number of wheelmen on the streets increased momentarily, and their exclamations of wonder became more and more pronounced as wheelman after wheelman, some with beautiful decorations, others in the plain uniform of their club, passed them. Finally arriving at Alexander avenue their amazement was without bounds as they beheld the rows and rows of clubs, grotesque and fancy riders that lined that broad thoroughfare from end to end, and saw that still others were arriving and taking positions in the side streets.

As quickly as possible they pushed their way through the crowds and took their positions as near the curb line as possible that they might see the entire procession start on its way through the streets of the borough.

Meanwhile the residents of the borough who, through the medium of the "North Side News" had been informed of the route of the parade were hurrying to the nearest vantage point, determined not to miss a single feature of what they knew would be a most interesting and pleasing spectacle, and long before the time for the parade to start had arrived every inch of curb space of the entire route had been pre-empted and latecomers were forced to stand in the rear of their more progressive fellows and crane their necks to see what they could of the greatest bicycle parade ever held on the north side.

The parade had been scheduled to start at 3 o'clock sharp, but owing to the tardy arrival of several of the clubs, it was almost 3.30 when Grand Marshal Otho G. Angle gave the word and the official bugler, Albert Knowles, in turn gave the signal that started the parade on its triumphal journey over the principal streets of the borough.

Then as file after file of wheelmen rode along, the crowds greeted them with cheer on cheer. Probably never before in the history of the Twenty-third and Twenty-fourth wards has so much enthusiasm been manifested by the people. At last something had happened to take them away from the consideration of their own personal affairs and give them a common interest in a demonstration that they felt belonged to them.

Enthusiasm has been raised in times past by a political parade, but in that only the followers of the party under whose auspices it was given could wax enthusiastic. In the "North Side News" bicycle parade, however, all parties, all factions, all citizens, irrespective of age, sex or nationality, could feel a personal interest and pleasure in it and that they did was evidenced again and again by the hearty and spontaneous applause that greeted the wheelmen from the beginning to the end of their long ride.

In not a single instance was any one known to do aught but praise the beautiful appearance of the clubs, the handsome decorations, laugh at the appearance of the grotesque riders or marvel at the agility of the trick riders. On the contrary, all who witnessed the parade were enthusiastic, and words of commendation and approval were heard on every hand. Evidently the carping critic that is ever ready to cry down local efforts was afraid to make his presence known, or he had betaken himself to a more fruitful field.

The second "North Side News" Bicycle Parade has come and gone. In spite of the fact that this was a poor year for bicycle parades, so poor that the "North Side News" was the only paper that had courage enough to try to hold a parade, the second parade was by far a greater success than the first.

Long before the time set for the parade to start Willis and Alexander avenues, and the streets through which it was to pass, were lined with people. Many stood in the hot sun a long time,

(Continued on Page 2.)

1. Hempstead Wheelmen.
2. Modern Sweat Shop.
3. Lanigiro.
4. "North Side News" Girl, Miss Jessie Manheimer.
5. Miss Florence Mergenthaler, Best Decorated Girl Rider.
6. Trick Rider.
7. August Buscher, Best Decorated Gentleman's Wheel.
   Mrs. E. L. Fox, "Dawn of Peace."
8. Lady Cyclones.
9. Mr. and Mrs. Fisher, Best Decorated Tandem.
10. District 11 Street Cleaning Department.
11. Miss Florence Mergenthaler, Miss Ada Goodbody and Miss Hattie Steurer, Decorated Wheels.
12. Melrose Turn Verein Wheelmen.
13. Goddess of Liberty.
14. White Duck Wheelmen.
15. Westchester County Wheelmen.
16. Prospect Wheelmen.
17. Chief Marshal Otho G. Angle, Albert W. Knowles, Bugler, and Marshal's Aides.

PARADE IN DETAIL.

DESCRIPTION OF THE VARIOUS ORGANIZATIONS AS THEY WHEELED THROUGH THE STREETS TO THE ADMIRATION OF THE CITIZENS.

DEMONSTRATIONS OF APPROVAL METED OUT WITH GREAT PRODIGALITY AND IMPARTIALITY TO ALL THE CLUBS.

The Visitors Within Our Gates Greeted as Warmly as the Home Boys—Fancy Dress Riders Excite Admiration—Grotesque Riders Furnish Amusement—Trick Riders Arouse Wonder.

The vast throngs on Alexander avenue were just beginning to become impatient. A man took out his watch and looked at it. "Time is up," he said," addressing nobody in particular. At that moment the clear notes of a bugle rang out three times, and simultaneously a small boy, who had secured a point of vantage in the branches of a tree, yelled: "Here dey come!" And, sure enough, they were coming, and the crowd immediately gave evidence of its appreciation by a mighty shout.

Then the first division of the bicycle parade came in sight, led by Roundsman Schuessler, followed by two files of four police. Immediately after them came the first band wagon, followed by Chief Marshal Otho G. Angle and Assistant Marshals Charles D. Steurer and Richard F. Junker and their staff of couriers, led by Chief Courier David A. Best.

Then, following, in files of four, came the representatives of non-competitive visiting clubs, Company A, Harlem Military Cadets, Gilso Camp, 133, S. O. V., and the Department of Street Cleaning representatives, unattached riders, including the decorated wheels and the grotesque and trick riders.

Then, following the second band wagon, the second division, led by the Lanigiro Wheelmen, who were followed in order by the Bowling Green, Hempstead, Wolff American, Emanon, Westchester County, Union League and Calumet Wheelmen—all of whom made a handsome appearance, and were greeted with much appreciation.

Then, following the third band wagon, came the representatives of the clubs of the borough in the following order: Royal Cycle, Melrose Turn Verein, White Duck, Prospect, Cyclone, Lady Cyclones, Y. M. C. U., Williamsbridge, Police.

At first the crowds on the sidewalk seemed to be impressed with the scene as a whole, then, as the entire line got into motion, the work of the clubs and the individual riders began to appeal to them.

The bicycle police, of course, rode with the ease and precision of the veterans they are, and won much applause all along the route. The next club to attract attention was Company A, Harlem Military Cadets, who made a soldierly appearance. Following close behind the Military Cadets came the representatives of Gilso Camp, 133, S. O. V., with thirteen in line. That this number was not unlucky was proven when the judges decided that their appearance entitled them to the Kiesling cup, the prize offered for the best appearing division of the military.

The next club to win the plaudits of the crowd were the representatives of the Street Cleaning Department, headed by their captain, James Conlin.

Dressed in their regulation uniform they made a fine appearance, and won the prize for the best-appearing division of city employees. The Ebling Trophy will henceforth grace the office of Stable I—. Then came the fancy dress, decorated wheels, grotesque and trick riders. There were so many of these and all were so excellent that any extended mention in a general article is out of the question. Mention, however, should be made of a few that showed they had taken special pains to add to the attractiveness of the display.

Easily first among the decorated gentlemen's wheels was that of Mr. August Buscher, who on every hand was greeted with hearty applause by the men and the admiring glances of the ladies. He was awarded the afternoon tea, the prize offered for the best decorated gentleman's wheel.

The prize for the best decorated ladies' wheel was won by Mrs. S. L. Fox of 949 Home street. Her conception, "The Dawn of Peace," was most beautifully gotten up, and the decision of the judges meets with the approval of all who witnessed the parade.

There were so many handsome appearing girl riders under 15 that it was a difficult matter for the judges to decide which of them made the best appearance. Finally they decided that Miss Florence Mergenthaler of 147 Willis avenue was entitled to that honor, while Miss Ethel Turner, Miss Alice Grady, Miss Helen Brombacher, Miss Frances Edell, Miss Hattie Steurer and Miss Ada Goodbody were all thought worthy of special mention.

The best appearing boy rider under 15 was decided to be Master George Fisher. Eugene S. Alfeld was given special mention for being the smallest boy in the parade.

The grotesque riders were more than usually well gotten up, many of the costumes showing much thoughtful care in their preparation. Among those that won the approval of the crowd and the commendation of the judges were "The Modern Sweat Shop," represented by Messrs. Hitorff and Smith; "Trilby and Svengali," represented by Mr. and Miss Kierst; T. Venator, a Coney Island belle; George Holghauer, a colored girl; John Pabst, clown: Wm. Bernhardt clown; Mr. Turner as "Uncle Sam;" Mr. Green, clown; Edmund Collins, as a sweet girl of sixteen; Mr. Vordermeir, a broken-down sport; John Naughton, a rough

Bright, Newsy, Truthful. Order from Newsdealers.

The North Side News.

Clean, Local, Vigorous. Subscribe Now $1 per year.

Published Weekly in the Interests of the Great North Side.

Vol. II. No. 37. NEW YORK, SATURDAY, SEPTEMBER 10, 1898. Price, 3 Cents.

TROLLEY ROAD EXTENSION.

IMPORTANT CHANGES THAT WILL BE OF ADVANTAGE TO THE DISTRICT.

Double Tracks on West Farms Road—New Line to Kingsbridge—New Line from Unionport to Westchester Avenue—More Cars and Better Service Promised—A Ride from Harlem to Yonkers Line for Five Cents, or to Any Part of Yonkers for Ten Cents—Other Advantages.

The recent developments in the Union Trolley Company will prove of much interest to residents of the Borough of the Bronx. In the first place, there is now being built at West Farms a new car house. The building is 300 feet long, 100 feet wide, and one story high, and will accommodate 125 cars. As soon as this is completed new cars which are now contracted for will be placed upon the lines, thus giving better service. Better than this even, the necessary arrangements have now been completed whereby the Union Railway Company will be enabled to lay a double track from West Farms out along the West Farms road to Morris Park avenue, and up Morris Park avenue past the race track to Bronxdale. This will prove of immense advantage to travelers over the lines out of West Farms, for, as every one knows, the present single track system causes considerable confusion at West Farms, and beyond at the intersection of the West Farms road with Morris Park avenue. This double track will alleviate this difficulty, and will enable the cars destined for Westchester and Unionport to proceed on their way without waiting the arrival of a car from Williamsbridge, or will not delay the Williamsbridge cars as they are now delayed at that point. The work will be pushed immediately. This track is to be laid to the north of the present track, and will not in any wise interfere with the fine macadam roadway.

In addition to this it is the intention as soon as possible, which will be as soon as the bridge over the West Farms Creek can be completed on Westchester avenue, the line will be built connecting the present terminus of the Unionport line, in front of the Swan Inn, with the Westchester avenue and Boulevard lines, and on this road cars will be run on the loop system, that is, they will go over the present line through Westchester to Unionport, and down over the new line to Harlem Bridge. It is also the intention to have at the terminus of these two lines at West Farms and at Unionport a car which will be used entirely for local transit, running back and forth over the line and turning out at the switches for the through cars, giving them the right of way.

On the west side the line up Broadway from Kingsbridge to Yonkers is now in operation, and as soon as possible a line will be built connecting the present Highbridge line with the Kingsbridge line, and the fare from the Yonkers line to Harlem Bridge will be five cents. The consents of the property owners for the building of this road have been all secured and the work will be started as soon as arrangements can be made.

The advantages to the west side residents, and the effect on the building operations in Highbridge and Kingsbridge and vicinity can hardly be calculated. Unquestionably a boon will be the result of this development and the railway facilities.

The Union Trolley Company has also secured the Yonkers lines, and at present they give transfers over the Mount Vernon lines to Yonkers. The fare from any part of Yonkers over the Union trolley system to Harlem Bridge will in a short time be but ten cents, and from the New York City line to Harlem Bridge five cents.

As soon as the road now being constructed between Mount Vernon, Pelham and New Rochelle can be completed and a right of way secured over the tracks of the New York and Harlem Railroad in West Mount Vernon through cars will be run between Yonkers and New Rochelle for a five cent fare.

These extensions of the trolley system will do much to make both the citizen on the east in the new territory recently annexed to New York and the citizens of the west side of the borough happy. The increased track facilities on the Mount Vernon line alone will do much to develop Bronxdale, Williamsbridge, Wakefield and South Mount Vernon, for with the additional tracks and turn outs the cars will be run on a greatly reduced headway, and delays now so frequent will not occur.

On the Westchester and Unionport line the extension to Westchester and the Southern Boulevard lines will work almost a revolution. Property values in the Unionport section should fairly jump when this really delightful section is made accessible by this new improvement, which will give the residents quick and cheap access to the city, while the extension of the Highbridge line to Kingsbridge and the city limits will develop a great deal of property now lying idle.

IN AID OF THE SOLDIERS.

A very pleasant entertainment was given by ten children Friday evening, Sept. 2, at the residence of Mr. W. Brawley, 783 East 187th street, for the benefit of the sick and injured soldiers in the war with Spain.

The programme was as follows: A charade, in which Martha Brawley, Lottie Maines, Agnes L. Babcock, May Creeden, Gertrude McGerry and Willie Blawvelt took part. Edith F. Babcock sang. Francis Glew, Gertie McGerry and Martha Brawley recited. Magic lantern exhibition by James Maloney and George P. Babcock acted as ushers. The evening was very much enjoyed by a large and appreciative audience. The success of the entertainment was entirely due to the efforts of the children. They realized $5. The parlors were very tastefully decorated with the national colors.

WHERE IS PETRONE?

He Went on an Excursion Monday and Has Not Since Been Seen.

Renovald Capabiango, a stone mason, who lives at 583 East 149th street, obtained a summons on Thursday for Pasquelo Branopano, a blacksmith, who lives at 529 East 149th street. Capabiango told Magistrate Wentworth that Branopano had gone on an excursion on Labor Day with Nichol Petrone, a nephew of Capabiango, whose home is at 528 East 149th street. They left the foot of East 117th street about 9 o'clock in the morning to go to Boynton Beach, and returned about 11 p. m., and landed at Market street. While Branopano and his sweetheart, Josephine Bettini, 20 years old, of 520 Morris avenue, returned safely to their home, his nephew, Petrone, failed to put in an appearance, and has not yet been heard from. He secured the summons to try to ascertain the whereabouts of his nephew, and also to get an explanation of Branopano as to how he came into possession of certain articles of his nephew's, which are enumerated as follows: A coat, a gold ring and a revolver. Both Branopano and Josephine Bettini, when interviewed, said that they went on an Italian excursion with Petrone. He drank quite a little, but was not drunk, but he got into a quarrel with some strange Italians whom they did not know, but afterward they saw them shaking hands, acting as if they had made up their little difference. At one time they say they heard him say he would shoot the man with whom he was quarreling. Hearing this Branopano went up to him and remonstrated with him and persuaded him to give up the revolver. This Petrone did. Afterward, he removed his coat, and while removing it pulled off his ring from his finger. These two articles they took care of for him, and that is how they came into their possession. They sailed to Boynton Beach without any trouble, and only remained there a half hour, and then returned. They saw Petrone get on the boat on the return trip. While coming up the river they heard rumors that somebody had fallen overboard, but they were warm and very much interested in each other, and took no notice of the rumor. When they reached Brooklyn Bridge and found that the boat was about to land they missed Petrone, and went to look for him. They searched the boat high and low, but could not find him. Then they remembered the rumors that somebody had fallen overboard, and they began to fear that Petrone was the man, and that he was thrown overboard by the Italians with whom he had quarreled. When the boat landed at Market street Branopano and Josephine Bettini scanned the faces of every one of the passengers as they came off, but no Petrone appeared. They returned to their homes finally, much worried over the loss of their friend, and Branopano has done everything possible to find him. He searched the Morgue, went to the hospitals and has done his best. He tried to convince Petrone's uncle that he was in no way responsible for his nephew's disappearance, but without success. He has tried in every way to find the missing man, but without avail. The general belief is that Branopano had nothing to do with Petrone's disappearance, as the two men were on the best of terms. In the Morrisania Police Court on Friday the case against Branopano was dismissed.

MAPES ESTATE ASSOCIATION.

At the regular meeting of the Mapes Estate Property Owners' Association, held on Sept. 6 at Kronemeyer's Hall, the president, W. H. Parker, called the meeting to order, and the following business was transacted:

The question of laying a private sewer was discussed and no decision reached.

The following committees were appointed: Committee to visit Postmaster Van Cott in reference to beter postal facilities and a new mail box, to be placed at the corner of Commonwealth avenue and West Farms road—Mr. F. S. Leland, W. H. Parker, J. Riesnacker, A. Kroneneyer and Charles Knauf.

Committee to secure an all night car on West Farms, road from Third avenue, 177th street and Unionport: Mr. M. C. Whittick, P. A. Hartnett and F. S. Leland.

Committee to secure a polling booth on or near the Mapes estate in place of the Unionport booth. The growth of this district will run the number above the limit for the Unionport booth and the association feels there should be a redivision of the district, thereby saving the journey of two miles to register and to vote: F. S. Leland, P. A. Hartnett and Chas. Corbett.

The secretary was requested to write the Fire Department in regard to the inspection of fire plugs, as it is understood they have not been tested for several months, and the quick service in case of fire is endangered.

The secretary was also requested to send notification of its meetings to the "North Side News," and it was the wish of the members that this paper be represented at their meetings.

A CAMP SITE OFFERED TO THE GOVERNMENT.

The following is a copy of a telegram addressed to Secretary Alger, which explains itself:

Gen. Russell A. Alger, Secretary of War, Washington, D. C.:

We hereby tender to the Government the free and unlimited use of 160 acres of land at Grey Oaks, Westchester County, N. Y., with abundant pure water supply, for camp purposes. All honor to our brave soldiers!

CHARLES M. KAEPPEL & CO.
161st st. & 3d ave., New York.

Grey Oaks is a small village in Westchester county, on the New York and Northern Railroad, two miles north of Yonkers and distant 15 miles from the City Hall. The Hudson River and the Palisades are only one mile away. It is the most healthful locality, situated as it is on a high ridge, 600 feet above the sea level. The station is on the property and has ample facilities for transportation. The land is wooded. The air is salubrious and bracing and pure water can be obtained in abundance from the Saw Mill River which runs through the property. Altogether, it is a most favorable locality for a Government camp.

BRONX BOROUGH'S FIRST SYNAGOGUE.

THE HANDSOME NEW EDIFICE OF THE CONGREGATION HAND IN HAND FORMALLY DEDICATED ON SUNDAY.

Impressive but Simple Ceremonies—Excellent Sermons by Rabbi Dr. J. Silverman of Temple Emanu-El and Dr. J. Blum, Rabbi in Charge of the New Temple—Excellent Music by the Choir.

The torrid heat of last Sunday afternoon had no apparent effect on the size of the congregation which gathered to participate in the dedication of the Temple Hand-in-Hand, on 145th street, between Willis and Brook avenues. At half past three o'clock, a procession headed by Wm. Daub, the president, flanked by Albert E. Davis, the architect, and Philipp Freudenmacher, the builder, and followed by the officers of the congregation, emerged from the basement entrance and passed out in front of the building and up the entrance steps to the front door, where it stopped, while the builder handed over the keys to President Daub. Mr. Daub accepted them on behalf of the congregation and thanked the builder and the architect for the conscientious performance of their duties. The doors were then thrown up and the procession passed through the vestibule and up the aisle of the Synagogue to the music of the excellent organ which is located in the choir loft, immediately over the vestibule.

As soon as the congregation was seated the choir sung S'en Sh'orim; then the President lighted the Ner Tamid and immediately all the electric lights were turned on, the choir singing: "Let There be Light," which was very impressive. The entire programme was as follows:

Presentation of the key of the temple to the president, William Daub, by the builder, Mr. F. Freudenmacher.
Prelude by organist.
Procession marching into the synagogue.
S'eu, Sh'orim.................Chorus
Lighting of Ner Tamid.
Song, "Let There Be Light"..............Choir
Song, Ono, "Procession with Thora"........Choir
Opening prayer................Rev. Dr. Vidaver
Ma Tovu..............Choir
Sermon..............Rev. Dr. J. Silverman
Duet, "The Lord, Our Guide," Tillie Siegel and Milton Daub.
Sermon..............Rev. Dr. A. Blum
Solo, "Dedication Hymn"....Miss Harriett Loeb
Solo, "Trust in the Lord"........Miss T. Siegel
Remarks by some visiting clergymen.
Yigdal..............Choir
Benediction.

INTERIOR OF THE NEW TEMPLE "HAND IN HAND."

The sermon by the Rev. D. J. Silverman of Temple Emanu-El, on "Ideals of Modern Judaism," was one of great excellence. He spoke of the ideals that have moved the world since the beginning of time and showed how that each ideal achieved and opened the way for a still greater one. The ideal of modern Judaism was justice, liberty and truth. The entire discourse was most thoughtful and interesting and held the close attention of the vast congregation.

The duet by Miss Siegel and Milton Daul was excellently rendered.

Following the able and eloquent sermon of Dr. Blum, Miss Harriet Loeb sang the Dedication Hymn with much sweetness.

The Rev. Spencer L. Hillier, pastor of the First Presbyterian Church of Morrisania, spoke briefly, praising the energy of the congregation and congratulating the people on their success.

The Congregation Hand-in-Hand was organized July 22, 1891, its meeting place being North Side Republican Club Hall, Third avenue and 142d street. Until the election of the Rev. Dr. Abraham Blum as Rabbi, Mr. Nathan Lipman acted as officiating minister, generously refusing to accept compensation for his services, in recognition of which he has recently been voted a life interest in a pew in the new Synagogue. The Rev. Dr. Blum was formerly superintendent of Lebanon Hospital.

Mr. Isaac Piser, vice-president of the Congregation Hand-in-Hand, and who took a prominent part in its organization, was also one of the organizers of the present Temple Israel, in Harlem.

The Ladies' Henrietta Benevolent Society, composed of the leading ladies of the congregation, is a valuable auxiliary in its work.

The accompanying exterior and interior views will give an idea of the appearance of the Synagogue. It was erected from the plans and under the supervision of Albert E. Davis, architect, by Ph. Freudenmacher, mason, and Edward Stichler, carpenter. The plumbing was executed by Robert F. Seiffert, the iron work by Ph. Dietz, the metal ceiling by the Berger Mfg. Co., decorated by A. Pinkovitz, the electric work by Edwards & Co., the ark and pulpit by C. Rieger's Sons, decorated by Moeller & Potts, the gas and electric fixtures by R. Louis Steiner, the stained glass work by Richard N. Spiers, the mill work by John Lanzer, the general painting and varnishing by F. Pusemann, the tiling by Edmund O'Connell and the bluestone by Low & Flogans.

In furnishing the names of those who did the work mentioned, to the representative of the North Side News, Mr. Davis said: "The public seldom stops to inquire who the different ones are whose work is represented in a building, yet if each did not do his work properly the architect's labor would be in vain. It is

THE NEW TEMPLE.

a pleasure to testify to the faithful work of the corps of mechanics, artisans and laborers employed on this building. There was no attempt to shirk or evade any work, but each performed his assigned duty cheerfully and conscientiously and all seemed imbued with a sincere desire for the success of the completed work."

The officers of the congregation are as follows:

Wm. Daub, president; Isaac Piser, vice-president; Selig Hecht, treasurer; Jacob Siegel, recording secretary; Jacques Newgass, financial secretary. Trustees: S. Feust, H. H. Weil, M. Pollack, E. Fleishl, N. Lipman, Sol. Kohn, J. Weil, M. Katz, Ch. Richter. Rev. Dr. A. Blum, Rabbi; Rev. N. Lipman, Cantor. Building Committee: Sigmund Feist, J. Weil, H. H. Weil, D. Ottenberg, W. Daub, N. Lipman, M. Pollack, S. Kohn, I. Piser, J. D. Siegel, J. Loewy, Ch. Kaye, D. Hoexter. J. Davis, architect; F. Freudenmacher, builder. Sunday School Directors: A. Briegger, H. H. Weil, J. Weil, W. Daub, superintendent.

FORDHAM HOSPITAL MOVES FURTHER AWAY.

The New Building Will Doubtless Be Better Suited for Its Purpose.

Those who complain that Fordham Hospital is too far removed from the centre of population have had their argument strengthened by the fact that Fordham Hospital has been moved still further away. On Wednesday, Aug. 31, the transfer was made from the old headquarters in Valentine avenue to the new home on St. James street and Macomb's Dam road. Fourteen patients were transferred at that time in ambulances.

The new building, like the old, is the property of Dr. Eden. The old building, which was once Dr. Eden's residence, is used for administrative purposes, while the hospital proper is in a long two-story frame building that runs directly back. There are accommodations for forty patients in the four wards, the latter being divided into the male medical, the female medical, the male surgical and the female surgical wards.

The hospital staff includes a visiting board of eight physicians, a house corps of four as follows: House Surgeon James D. Murphy, M. D., Senior Surgeon James Brennan, Junior Surgeon A. B. Brown, M. D., and Ambulance Surgeon Henry Belt, M. D. The doctors are assisted by seven nurses from the training school for nurses on Blackwell's Island. The clerk of the hospital is Mr. J. F. Wood, who has won the good opinion of all the newspaper men whose business takes them there by his friendly and courteous treatment of them.

Persons going to the hospital should take the Jerome avenue trolley and get off at St. James street. The hospital is but two or three blocks to the west.

A RELIEF ASSOCIATION.

THE PATRIOIC CITIZENS OF KINGSBRIDGE HOLD A MAMMOTH LAWN FETE.

Brilliant Illuminations Make the Sealey Property Like Fairyland—Col. Roosevelt Was Expected but Did Not Appear—A Large Delegation from Tremont Present.

One of the largest events in the borough occurred on Thursday night at Kingsbridge.

The Kingsbridge Soldiers and Sailors' Relief Association held a mammoth lawn fete on the grounds known as the "Sealey Property." The grounds were like fairyland. Long lines of Japanese lanterns stretched in every direction. Brilliant rockets and Roman candles vied with the still more brilliant electric lights. The Kingsbridge Brass Band discoursed sweet music. There were gypsies and soldiers in profusion like a masquerade ball. In a dimly illumined marque on the lawn an oracle was ensconced, and revealed the future to the inquisitive. The Sealey house itself was ablaze with lights.

A large delegation from the Seventy-first Regiment Aid Society was present from Tremont. There were five wagonloads of people, and the noise of their singing and cheering could be heard for a long distance.

Shortly after nine Capt. H. H. Brown of Kingsbridge stepped upon the piazza and extended a hearty welcome to the visitors. He reviewed the work of the association, and in closing called upon Miss Grace Dodge. Miss Dodge paid a warm tribute to Col. Roosevelt in all his various fields of service. He was very well acquainted with Kingsbridge and Riverdale, Miss Dodge said, and was known favorably to them before he achieved a world-wide reputation. Col. Roosevelt had been expected to attend and make an address, but in both he disappointed them. Miss Dodge was followed by Col. Joseph A. Goulden. Col. Goulden has the knack of making an excellent patriotic speech without any more hackneyed phrases and allusions than are absolutely necessary, and he did not belie his reputation. He paid a glowing tribute to the soldiers who had so admirably prosecuted the war, and said that he was almost tempted to wish that the war was not over, in order that more than one New York regiment might have an opportunity to distinguish itself in the field. "But, nevertheless," he said in closing, "I thank God the war is over."

After the speeches were concluded there was an apparently unlimited supply of fireworks that had been donated by Pain of Manhattan Beach.

The committee in charge was composed of Mrs. F. M. Todd, chairman; Mrs. R. Alexander, Mrs. R. Rhatigan and Miss Edna Brown.

THE ROOSEVELT BOOM IN BRONX BOROUGH.

A Campaign Club Organized in Tremont Last Tuesday Night.

Col. Theodore Roosevelt's boom for Governor has struck the Borough of the Bronx. A meeting was held at 721 Tremont avenue on Tuesday evening, and the Roosevelt Campaign Club was organized with the following officers: President, Rufus R. Randall; Secretary. William A. Cameron; Treasurer, Mr. Thomas P. Lewis. The remaining officers are to be elected at a subsequent meeting. The following committees were appointed: Resolutions, Lewis, McDade, Babcock; Constitution and By-Laws, Cameron, Eckley, Lewis; Press Committee, McDade, Hardy, Tait, Stephens, Regan; Committee to Nominate General Committeemen, Schmid, Graham, Babcock, Thomas, Eckley.

At this meeting the following preamble and resolutions were unanimously adopted:

Whereas, Col. Theodore Roosevelt has been suggested as a candidate for Governor of the State of New York, and,

Whereas, The time to nominate such a candidate has almost arrived, and,

Whereas, Col. Roosevelt has fully demonstrated to the people of this State (as well as of the United States) his ability, integrity and unimpeachable honesty, as shown by his record:

First—As Member of Assembly of the State of New York;

Second—As United States Civil Service Commissioner;

Third—As President of the Board of Police Commissioners of the city of New York;

Fourth—As Assistant Secretary of the United States Navy;

Fifth—His well-known record for bravery and humane treatment of all under him in the Santiago campaign while colonel of the Rough Riders; and,

Whereas, We believe the sentiment of the voters of Bronx Borough, irrespective of party, is that he be nominated for Governor; therefore be it

Resolved, That our organization, composed of members of different political parties, pledge to Col. Theodore Roosevelt our support to secure his nomination and election as Governor of the State of New York; and be it further

Resolved, That the secretary be instructed to send a copy of these resolutions to Col. Roosevelt, to the several delegates from Bronx Borough, to the several conventions and to the public press.

ST. MARTIN'S LYCEUM EXCURSION.

On Labor Day, Sept. 5, the members of St. Martin's Lyceum, of Belmont, gave an excursion to Grand View Grove, Long Island Sound. The largest barge afloat, the Starina, was used, and a delightful time was had. The boat was crowded to its utmost capacity; and, indeed, if the boys have another excursion, which is earnestly to be hoped they will, there will be a demand for more barges. Much credit is due to all the members. The committees were composed of:

Officers—President, G. F. Heggins; Vice-President, Luke Murphy; Treasurer, H. T. Arnold; Secretary, J. Naughton; Sergeant-at-Arms, M. H. Kennedy.

Arrangements Committee—R. E. Arnold, chairman; G. Williams, F. Sheppard, P. McAvoy.

Floor Committee—J. Slavin, floor manager; Chas. Briggs, J. Leddy, assistant floor managers; F. Erhart, L. Kennedy, J. McShane, J. F. Flannigan, C. P. Cotter, F. Golman.

Reception Committee — Chr. Tighe, chairman; Wm. Fox, T. Wellstead, H. Mott, G. Briggs, M. Naughton, H. Hudson, L. Bossard.

THE SEVENTY-FIRST REGIMENT AID SOCIETY.

An Interesting Meeting Held Last Monday Night—Plans for the Banquet Perfected—Other Matters of Interest Discussed.

Suburban Hall was well filled on Monday night at the regular meeting of the Seventy-first Regiment Aid Society.

Although the necessity for the work of this society has in some measure disappeared there is no decrease in the interest and enthusiasm.

Further details were given by Colonel Goulden of the reception to be given the returned soldiers at Morrisania Hall, 170th street and Third avenue, on Thursday, Sept. 29th. The address of welcome will be made by the Hon. Louis F. Haffen, President of the Borough, and will probably be replied to by Captain E. F. Austin of Company L, Seventy-first Regiment. Music will be provided by an orchestra of six pieces. The menu will probably be as follows:

Consomme.
Roast Beef with Mushrooms.
Chicken.
Potatoes. Lettuce Salad.
Coffee.
Ice Cream.

An entertainment will also be furnished, consisting in part of vaudeville by the A. M. Palmer Dramatic Society and the remainder by volunteer talent. A dance will bring the reception to a close. A communication was received from the Tremont Fife and Drum Corps offering its services. The matter was referred to the reception committee with power.

The secretary read letters from the railroads in answer to his asking for reduced rates for soldiers who wished to go into the country. The Erie, the New York Central and the Pennsylvania agreed to carry soldiers at half rates to any point on their systems.

The society extended a vote of thanks to those who had aided it at its recent lawn party. Among them were the Union Railway Company for the use of a car for transporting the Protectory Band free, to the New York Catholic Protectory for free services of its band, to the North River Electric Light Company for free use of arc lights for the lawn party, and many others.

Mr. F. E. Saward was called upon and spoke interestingly, comparing the soldiers of the present war with those of the Civil War, and contrasting Gettysburg with Santiago.

The society had quite a number of boxes and barrels of material which the return of the soldiers had left on its hands. There was some discussion as to the final disposition of these goods until a member of the Seventy-first, who was present, suggested that the material be sent to the Sixth Infantry now at Montauk Point. This will be done and the goods will be sent with the compliments of the Seventy-first Regiment Aid Society.

The next meeting of the society to be held on Monday, Sept. 12, promises to be most interesting. Major Keck and Captain Rafferty, both of whom distinguished themselves in the battle of Santiago, will be present and speak.

WITH MILITARY HONORS.

Private McKeever Is Laid to Rest in Woodlawn Cemetery.

Private E. Percy McKeever of Company K, Seventy-first Regiment, who died in Mount Sinai Hospital of typhoid on Wednesday, was buried at noon on Friday of last week from his late residence, 2526 Marion avenue, Fordham.

Some two score of his comrades of the Seventy-first, among whom was a firing squad of eight men from the armory, under command of Corporal William MacAdam, met at Fordham Station and marched in column of two up to the McKeever residence, where they stacked arms on the lawn. The Episcopal service was read by the Rev. Herbert McElroy of St. James' Church. There was no music. The casket was of oak, with silver trimmings, and was covered by an American flag. Aside from the friends of the family, a delegation from the Seventy-first Regiment Aid Society of the Borough of the Bronx, headed by its president, J. Thomas Stearns, was present. The floral offerings were numerous and costly. The pall bearers were members of Company K—McKeever's own company.

On arriving at Woodlawn the pallbearers walked on either side of the hearse, while the remainder of the soldiers marched behind as a guard of honor.

After the casket had been lowered into the grave the firing squad fired the usual "three rounds blank," and as the echoes died away there rose on the air the strains of the sweetest and saddest of all the bugle calls—"Taps"—the soldier's good night, in this case, typical of the last sleep of the soldier.

E. Percy McKeever, before the war broke out, was a clerk in the bond department of the American Surety Company, and was but twenty-one years old. He served throughout the Cuban campaign, but was taken sick with typhoid fever on the transport St. Louis. On his arrival at Montauk Point he was taken to the Detention Hospital. His father, who is a lawyer, with an office at 121 Broadway, secured a furlough for him and took him to Mount Sinai Hospital, where he died on Wednesday.

WAS ONLY ENJOYING HIMSELF.

Dennis Burke, of 646 East 148th street, was arrested at one o'clock by officer Burke of the 35th precinct, on the complaint of David Allan, of 2607 Third avenue, for having taken a horse and wagon from his barn. Burke was employed by Allan, who keeps a cigar store, until last Saturday. When he left on Saturday, he took the keys of the stable with him, and since then has been going there, and taking the horse out, and treating his friends to a ride. On Thursday, Allan went to the barn to get his horse, but found it gone and sent out an alarm. He was looking for the horse when Burke drove up with it, and Allan had him arrested. Burke said in court that he had only done it for fun, and as there was no harm done to the horse, Allan did not press the complaint, and the magistrate discharged him.

THE EISENHUTH MOTOR VEHICLES.

Among the entries for the *Cosmopolitan* race, May, 1896, was John W. Eisenhuth, formerly of San Francisco, Cal., but now of New York. Mr. Eisenhuth is an old student of the gas engine, and an indefatigable inventor. He claims to have been the first to build a gasolene engine, and the first to adopt the electric ignition to the gasolene engine. He was unable to complete his vehicle in season for the race, on account of the shortness of the time for preparation, but finished it later and made a number of trial runs on the road. The weight of the rig is about 900 pounds, a reduction of about 100 pounds having been made by omitting two of the four cylinders of the original motor. When it is said that the four-cylinder motor developed over 25 HP. it will be seen that Mr. Eisenhuth intended to win the race if abundance of power would do it. The two cylinders alone give 14 HP., which Mr. Eisenhuth states was sufficient to carry the wagon through 22 inches of snow, and up the steep incline at Eagle Rock, near Orange, N. J.

The speed of the motor can be varied from 180 to 900 revolutions per minute, and nearly all the speeds of the vehicle are obtained in this way. A single low gear is provided for very heavy grades.

The cable transmission, which is employed only on this wagon, the inventor states he has found to be efficient, developing less friction than other forms. This cable is also employed for a brake.

One lever steers, controls speed and applies the brake.

Mr. Eisenhuth is about to bring out a light tricycle, a motor cab weighing only 750 pounds ready for a 200-mile run, a parcel delivery and a brougham, on large quantities of any one of which he is prepared to estimate. His office is at 40 Wall street, New York.

THE ALTHAM MOTOR CARRIAGE.

The Altham motor carriage, the first illustration of which appears in this issue, is the invention of George J. Altham, of Fall River, Mass., and is being manufactured for the market by the Altham International Motor Co., 27 State street, Boston, Mass. It is the result of several years' research by a mechanic of first-rate abilities, and possesses a number of distinctly original features, especially the method of cooling the cylinders by an air blast instead of by water, the transmission of power without the use of belts, gears frictions or chains, and the ease of the control of speed.

MOTOR CARRIAGE OF JOHN W. EISENHUTH, NEW YORK CITY.

Bright, Newsy, Truthful. Order from Newsdealers.

The North Side News.

Published Weekly in the Interests of the Great North Side or Bronx Borough.

Clean, Local, Vigorous. Subscribe Now $1 per year.

Vol. II. No. 45. NEW YORK, SATURDAY, NOVEMBER 5, 1898. Price, 3 Cents.

ROOSEVELT AROUSES REPUBLICANS!

TREMENDOUS OVATION RECEIVED BY THE ROUGH RIDER AND OTHER DISTINGUISHED AND ELOQUENT SPEAKERS AT TUESDAY NIGHTS GREAT MASS MEETING.

SUCH GENUINE HEARTY AND CONTINUOUS ENTHUSIASM WAS NEVER BEFORE MANIFESTED AT A POLITICAL MEETING HELD IN BRONX BOROUGH.

Cheer Follows Cheer as Col. Roosevelt, Chauncey M. Depew, Col. Abe Gruber, John Proctor Clarke and Others, Point out the Weakness of the Democratic Position—Morrisania Hall Packed as never Before in all its History and Thousands Turned Away from the Doors — An Immence Torch-Light Procession Parades the Streets — Fire-Works and Bands of Music cut no small Figure in the Demonstration.

The amount of interest in a political gathering cannot be gauged by the attendance when, as was the case at Zeltner's Morrisania Hall Tuesday night, not half the people who come can be accomodated.

Before 7 o'clock the hall began to fill, and the stream of people entering was composed so largely of ladies that when the meeting was opened fully one-tenth of those present were of the sex which does not vote, although it undoubtedly exercises a great influence over the result of an election.

At an early hour the hall was filled. Soon after it was crowded. And before very long it was packed. Had there been room for all who were turned away, and for all who would have come had there been any reasonable prospect of obtaining admission, the audience would have been at least four times as great as it was.

Cheers and applause are never lacking at a Republican meeting on the North Side, but ordinary cheers and applause are but as the summer breeze to the tornadoes which swept through the hall repeatedly during the meeting held to greet and to honor the Republican candidate for Governor.

Mr. William H. Ten Eyck called the meeting to order, and introduced as the president of the meeting Hon. Ernest Hall.

ADDRESS BY THE PRESIDENT.

Judge Hall said that he was proud at being called to preside over such a magnificent gathering, the greatest meeting ever held in the Borough of the Bronx. "This hall," said he, "now contains more people than within my recollection formed the entire population of the Twenty-third and the Twenty-fourth wards combined. As there are many ladies present I ask the gentlemen to remove their hats and to refrain from smoking. We shall have to-night to address us, in addition to the candidates for Congressman, Senator and for Assemblyman, Abraham Gruber, Chauncey M. Depew, Theodore Roosevelt and last, but not least, John Proctor Clark. Each of these is better than any other. I particularly request that all remain to hear the last speaker, and I assure all that if they do not they will experience a loss they will regret. I have said little in this campaign, but the little I have said and the little I wish personally to say concerns the judiciary. The Tammany tiger has laid its foul paw on the ermine of justice, and, unless the people of the city of New York now arise and stamp out the foul blot, we must pass through years of trouble and tribulation before it is eradicated. It was once said, if a man served long and well, 'Well done, thou good and faithful servant.' Tammany Hall has reversed that rule this year and says, 'Good and faithful servant, we'll see that you are well done.' New York has good reason to be proud of her judiciary. No purer set of judges ever sat on the supreme bench in this State than sits there to-day. Judge Daly, however, because he refused to obey the dictates of Tammany Hall, is denied by that power a renomination. No purer, no more upright man than Judge Daly ever graced the bench of any court. Tammany Hall wants only judges that will do something for Tammany Hall. If we have judges who are subservient to the wishes of the boss of Tammany Hall, what chance would a man not belonging to that organization have? I don't believe that the people of this city will submit to any such state of affairs. I believe that on the eighth day of November they will arise in their might and say, 'Thus far shalt thou go, and no farther.' I call your attention to the danger with which you are menaced by the hydra-headed monster which is not content with control of all the other offices, but wants to drag the judicial ermine in the mire."

Several campaign songs were sung by the Diamond Quartette to popular airs, including "There'll Be a Hot Time," &c. One verse sung to that air was:

There were men of every station in that gallant regiment;
There were sons of millionaires; there were men without a cent.
There were men of fame in letters; there were men who couldn't write;
But just ask the Spanish soldiers if those riders couldn't fight.

HON. J. IRVING BURNS.

Judge Hall then introduced Hon. J. Irving Burns as a man who had served faithfully and ably in the Senate of the State of New York and as one who could be relied on to serve with equal faithfulness and ability if elected as a Congressman.

"This campaign," said Senator Burns, "is really more of a business campaign than a political campaign. You know what occurred two years ago at Chicago. The Democratic party adopted a platform which embodied its ideas on free silver. At St. Louis the Republican party adopted a platform which declared for a money standard and used the word 'gold.' Those two platforms are before

COLONEL THEODORE ROOSEVELT.

the people to-day as much as they ever were. The Republican party still calls for the gold standard. The issue of two years ago confronts you to-day. If you say that the silver issue is dead you say what is not true. Every candidate on the Democratic ticket in the State to-day voted for free silver; but in Syracuse they and the men who named them for office were afraid to go on record. Every man is interested when the welfare of his family and the condition of his pocket are concerned, and never were they more affected by the possibilities of the result of a political campaign than they are now. Most men have families. If they haven't, they should have them. (Laughter.) The hearthstones and firesides are threatened as they were two years ago. If you do not give heed to this issue, but let the situation go by default, you'll go into the slough of despond and everlastingly rue your action. Wherever you go you'll find Democrats of high character and standing favoring the election of Roosevelt. You'll find ex-Governor Waller of Connecticut occupying this position and ex-Mayor Hewitt and ex-Mayor Grace urging the same thing. You'll find on the platform to-night Mr. Purroy, who says he can't stand it, and he's with the Republican party. You can't pick up a paper without reading of men who have been Democrats, but who will vote with the Republicans this year, and on the eighth day of November thousands of Democrats will stand by the Republican party.

"I feel sure that you'll elect your candidates for Senator and Assemblyman. Nothing is more important than that, because they'll vote for a sound money Senator. I have served in the Legislature with Mr. Mathewson, and I know just what he is. He was always present, active and efficient, and studying the interests of his constituents. You want him there again. You must have him there. I know him from the crown of his head to the soles of his feet, and I commend him to you as deserving your earnest and energetic and positive support. It is also important that you send Mr. Cronin to the Assembly. He has made the effort before. The tide was running the other way then, but, thanks be to God, it is running our way now, and he will be carried by it to his seat in Albany. As for myself I haven't much to say. As a Congressman I shall be in a sense your servant. I know all about the Harlem Kills, about the Bronx, about the harbor facilities needed and about rapid transit. I have done all I can to help you along in the past, and I shall do so in the future. If I succeed it will be both my duty and pleasure to do all I can in lines that will help you. In Westchester I am your near neighbor now. Already our relations are close, and many of our interests are mutual, but my election as Congressman will make our relations more close, and I shall be positively one of you."

HON. DOUGLAS MATHEWSON.

Hon. Douglas Mathewson was introduced by Judge Hall, who said of him: "Elected by the Republican party, he served the interests of the people in every way. He is a gentleman of honesty and ability, an upright lawyer and an enterprising citizen. I introduce to you the man whom I hope will be your next Senator."

Mr. Mathewson said he was glad to see so many Democrats present, for "the issue this year really is not between Republicans and Democrats, but between Tammany Hall on one, and the American citizens of the State of New York on the other side. I ask my Democratic friends whether they are proud of their party to-day? Do they believe that Richard Croker is a fit successor to such men as Jefferson, Jackson and Samuel J. Tilden? Do they think that any voter who aids the boss of Tammany Hall in his efforts to control the judiciary is showing himself true to the best principles of the Democratic party? Do they think that any good Democrat should vote for an administration under which the man who knows the judge has a better chance of securing a judgment in his favor than has the man who has right on his side?"

DR. DEPEW ARRIVES.

Mr. Mathewson had spoken less than five minutes when there arose at the entrance of the hall a slight commotion, and a voice shouted, "What's the matter with Depew?" "He's all right," was the reply, and then there arose a perfect din of yells and cheers and a storm of applause, which occasionally subsided but only to gain in force. Mr. Depew shook hands with several of the gentlemen on the stage and bowed to the audience before taking his seat.

Mr. Mathewson resumed his speech when quiet had been restored. He had been allowed ten minutes, he said, but he knew that the audience was more desirous of hearing others present than of hearing him, and he would occupy even less than the time assigned him. "But," said he, "I will take time to make one earnest request: I ask that when on the morning of Election Day you go to the polls, leaving behind you the enthusiasm which has been aroused in you by the words of orators, by patriotic music, by displays of the national emblem, by the shouts and cheers of your fellow citizens, you allow yourself to be influenced only by what you believe

(Continued on Page 2.)

FRANK K. BOWERS,

Republican Candidate for Assembly Thirty-fourth District.

Frank K. Bowers was born in Easton, Pa., on March 12, 1867. He secured an education in the public schools of Easton, and on graduation entered the Easton Business College. In 1888 Mr. Bowers came to New York city, where he soon

became interested in local politics, and took an active interest in it. He soon acquired a reputation as a skillful organizer of political forces, and the Loyal Republican Club of Harlem, of which he was a member, elected him to its presidency. In his new post Mr. Bowers showed marked ability, and his work was made evident in many campaigns. Mr. Bowers was one of the leaders in the agitation for a new primary law.

CHARLES H. CRONIN, REPUBLICAN CANDIDATE FOR ASSEMBLY IN THE THIRTY-FIFTH DISTRICT.

Charles H. Cronin was born in Fordham in 1865 and has resided there ever since. After receiving an excellent education in grammar school No. 64 he engaged in business with James L. Wells, 59 Liberty street. Mr. Cronin is an active member of the North Side Board of Trade, taking part in the discussions there and earnestly advocating the de-

velopment of his section. He also belongs to the Taxpayers' Alliance and is president of the Fordham and Belmont Property Owners' Association. As the presiding officer of the last-named organization Mr. Cronin has done much to further the aims and purposes it has in view. His Republicanism is of the stanchest kind and his treatment of public questions has always been of a practical character.

HON. J. IRVING BURNS.

Republican Candidate for Congress Sixteenth District.

JAMES IRVING BURNS, CANDIDATE FOR CONGRESS, IS FOR SOUND MONEY AND BUSINESS PROSPERITY. EVERYBODY SHOULD VOTE FOR HIM, IRRESPECTIVE OF PARTY.

THREE YOUNG THIEVES CAUGHT.

Walter Brinkworth of 173 Cottage place, David Webb of Woodruff street, and Edward Alliger of 1633 Bathgate avenue, were arrested by the police of the Tremont station for breaking into the dwelling house of Dr. Walters of Crotona Park, north of Franklin avenue, on Sunday afternoon. It appears that about 5 o'clock on that day, when Joseph Walters and his brother Roy came home, they noticed that some one was moving the blind in the house. So they went around to the rear in time to see Brinkworth jump out of the window. Webb was in the back yard and they discovered on his person some souvenir spoons. The two boys who were captured told Detectives Kane and Delaney that Edward Alliger had got into the house and stolen the spoons, and Alliger was thereupon arrested, too. When they were brought to court they denied that Alliger had anything to do with it, and Alliger was discharged. Brinkworth and Webb were held in $1,000 for Special Sessions.

PERTINENT QUESTIONS ANSWERED.

THE "NORTH SIDE NEWS" RECEIVES REPLIES FROM CANDIDATES ON MATTERS OF INTEREST TO THE PEOPLE.

All Are in Favor of Doing Their Best to Support This Borough's Local Interests—Democrats Dodge the Silver Issue—Republicans Meet It Squarely.

Believing that on the eve of this most important election the residents of this borough would be interested in knowing the position of the candidates who seek their suffrage on certain important matters, the "North Side News" sent out early in the week the following letter, addressed to the candidates for Senator and Assemblymen:

New York, Nov. 1, 1898.

Dear Sir—As you are a candidate for office in this borough to represent the people of the north side, we would like to have you answer the following queries, if possible on Wednesday of this week:

First—If elected to the office to which you aspire, would you further such bills as would benefit the north side interests? Especially do we desire that you express yourself on the question of rapid transit facilities and lower rates of fare within the borough limits.

Second—Would you favor such measures as would put residents of this borough on all commissions, such as acquiring title in the street opening proceedings, etc., when the improvement affects our borough?

Third—Would you favor and use your influence to secure for the north side a fair representation in the various city departments, such as the Board of Education?

Fourth—Would you favor a bill to restore to the north side the Department of Street Improvements, thus doing away with the present clumsy, expensive and inadequate system as provided for by the charter?

Fifth—Will you pledge yourself to vote for a United States gold Senator?

By answering these queries you will greatly oblige the public, whose suffrage you seek.

Yours respectfully,
NORTH SIDE NEWS.

To this letter the following replies have been received:

New York, Nov. 2, 1898.

North Side News, 2829-2833 Third Ave., The Bronx, City.

Gentlemen—In response to your categorical letter of inquiry dated and received by me yesterday, I answer as follows:

First—In response to your first inquiry as to whether, if elected to the honorable office for which I have been nominated, I would further the passage of such bills as would benefit the north side interests, I answer without qualification, YES; and as I think a man's record is a far stronger expression of his views than any statement he may make, I want to reinforce my affirmative answer by referring you to my record as member of Assembly in the Legislature of 1897, a record which will show that I introduced and succeeded in passing bills which became laws that brought over a million and a half dollars of the city money into our district for the benefit of north side interests, and also assisted in the Assembly in passing bills of Senator Guy's of equal benefit to the now Borough of the Bronx. On the question of rapid transit and lower rates of fare within the borough limits, I am in favor of compelling the extension of the elevated roads and also of the passage of laws which will permit the present Rapid Transit Commission to proceed to complete its work and to take from the Mayor of this city the power which he now has and which he has used during the present year to prevent that commission from making any progress whatsoever. I believe that there should be a uniform fare of five cents upon all roads within the city limits, and in and out of public office I have used my best efforts for the passage of such a law.

Second—In response to your second inquiry as to whether I would favor such measures as would put residents of this borough on all commissions having in charge matters affecting our borough, I answer YES. I believe that the neighborhood affected by the proceedings of any commission should have representation upon that commission and that the commission should not consist, as is often the case at present, of gentlemen from all parts of the country except the Borough of the Bronx. I might also add that I believe the present street opening and condemnation laws should also be amended so that the city could not as at present take a man's land and his house and not pay him for the same until a year or more after they have done so; in other words, that property must be paid for before it is taken away.

Third—In response to your third inquiry, concerning the representation of our borough upon city boards, I would say that I believe that the Bronx is and is to be one of the great boroughs of our city, and as such should secure its proper representation upon every city board and in every city department.

Fourth—I am in favor of an amendment to the city charter which would restore to the north side its former Department of Street Improvements, or an equivalent to it, and upon this subject I would again call your attention to my record in the Legislature, when I presented and worked for such an amendment, and then voted against the adoption of the charter for the reason, among others, that provision for such a department was not incorporated in the charter in place of what I then contended was, and which has since proven itself to be, an illy arranged, expensive and entirely unsatisfactory scheme for doing the work that that department had done prior to our being merged in Greater New York.

(Continued on Page 2.)

MR. MATHEWSON'S RECORD.

As Compared with that of His Opponent for Senatorial Honors.

Comparison between the records of Mr. Mathewson, who represented the Thirty-fifth Assembly District in the Legislature of 1897, and that of Mr. Mitchell, who in 1898 succeeded him, certainly makes a showing more than creditable

to the former, and one in which Mr. Mitchell and his friends have little reason to take pride. Not all of the bills introduced and successfully championed by Mr. Mathewson are included in the following statement, but the principal ones are given:

Mr. Mathewson's Record.		Mr. Mitchel's Record.
Bills introduced, carried and now laws:		Only one bill, which became a law, introduced, and that: "An act to amend the fisheries, game and forest law and the acts amendatory thereof, relating to the use of nets."
For Jerome ave., paving.	$150,000	
Making one-half expense of public places at Tremont and Burnside aves. a city charge, and saving same from assessment on property owners, saving about. ..	70,000	
Bridge over Bronx between Williamsbridge and Wood lawn.	150,000	
Same at W. Farms.	77,000	
For improvement of Spuyten Duyvil Parkway . .	150,000	
Placing one-half of expense of widening Washington ave. on city, estimated to save adjacent property owners about.	400,000	
For bridges over railroad at Gerard, Walton and River aves., and at Fort Independence st.	150,000	
For public place at Melrose station, about.	75,000	
For Garden in Van Cortlandt Park..	50,000	

Mr. Mathewson voted for dollar gas, and he worked and voted for the maintenance of the Department of Street Improvements. He assuredly proved himself worthy of the trust reposed in him, and no voter who realizes how essential it is that a worker and an enthusiast should represent the Borough of the Bronx in the Senate can hesitate long before deciding for which one of these two candidates his vote should be given.

OPEN AIR MEETING IN THE THIRTY-FOURTH DISTRICT.

Eight new transparencies, elaborately lettered and decorated in red and black, were carried in the parade which preceded the meeting held Wednesday evening in the store at the corner of Brook avenue and 139th street, under the auspices of the North Side Republican Club. A drum and fife corps furnished the music for the parade. When the meeting opened all the seats were filled, and soon nearly all the standing room was occupied. Headley M. Green presided and made a short address before introducing Hon. J. Irving Burns. Senator Burns' address was practical and to the point, and ex-Alderman School, who followed him, spoke highly of the record and abilities of the candidate for Congress. Mr. Nierney, one of the County Committee speakers, was next introduced, and made a good impression on all who heard him.

REPUBLICAN MEETINGS.

Three meetings which showed the energy of the Republican leaders and the loyalty of the Republican voters were held Thursday evening, one at Melrose Turner Hall, where John Kirst presided; another at 212 Willis avenue, under the direction of Headley M. Greene, and the third at Little Coney Island, West Farms. In every instance the attendance was limited only by the capacity of the place of gathering. The speakers included Hon. J. Irving Burns, Hon. Douglas Mathewson, Jacob Kemple, Howard E. White, Charles Hoeherstadt, Jr., Hon Ernest Hall, Patrick Brown and Charles H. Cronin. Owing to severe illness in his family, Frank K. Bowers, candidate for Assemblyman, who had been expected to address the Willis avenue meeting, was unable to be present.

Roosevelt Arouses Republicans.

(Continued from Page 1)

your duty to be. Are you going to vote the ticket headed by a typical American and bearing the names of men who will stand up for local interests which Tammany Hall has sought to strangle? or will you vote the ticket headed by the man agreed on by Richard Croker and Hugh McLaughlin and bearing the name of a candidate for Congressman who refuses to tell you how he stands on silver and free trade? If Sagasta were here and had a vote, would he vote for Theodore Roosevelt or for Van Wyck?"

"THE KING OF ALL."

As Mr. Mathewson took his seat amid applause, Judge Hall arose to introduce Dr. Depew, saying: "In this country, in England, and wherever the English language is spoken or understood, there stands as one above all others, a magnificent specimen of American manhood and the king of all orators in the English language, Chauncey M. Depew, whom I now have the honor to introduce."

For several minutes Dr. Depew did not attempt to speak, for the greeting he received was so vociferous that had he undertaken to utter a word he could not have been heard ten feet away. After a time the audience became tired and subsided, and then he said:

"It is a great pleasure to meet you here to-night—that is, what is left of me. The enthusiasm shown here to-night is shown by all of us young fellows under fifty all over the State. Last week I had an opportunity to test the question of the probable result of the election. In four days I traveled over one thousand miles and made sixty-four speeches. I had the inspiration of a good cause, the magnetic influence of a magnificent leader who accompanied me and the vigor of youth. (Laughter.) Wherever I went, and I covered nearly the whole State, the question was 'What are you going to do down in New York?' In New York city the question asked of men who come from up the State is, 'What are you going to do?' I dislike to assume the role of a prophet, but there always are certain indications which tell a veteran campaigner what the result will be. I believe I may justly call myself a veteran campaigner. I canvassed this State two weeks after I graduated from Yale College, and I have been at it ever since. And that was ten or fifteen years ago. (Laughter.) When a man has gone through this State almost every year and met men who have a natural and acquired faculty for knowing the political tendencies of their neighbors, he can tell very nearly what the result of an election will be. I am now ready to make a prophesy, in fact, two prophesies. One is that the next Governor of this State will be Theodore Roosevelt and the second is that the next Legislature will be Republican in both branches."

CHEERS FOR ROOSEVELT.

Dr. Depew was here interrupted just as Mr. Mathewson had been. There was a fresh commotion at the entrance of the hall, and cheers for Roosevelt. He turned toward the door and then toward the audience, saying, "No. Roosevelt will not be here for an hour yet;" but just then Roosevelt appeared struggling through the crowd to the platform, and the cries and shouts and yells which filled the house even exceeded the demonstrations with which Depew had been received. As the gubernatorial candidate reached the platform a floral horseshoe about five feet in height and composed of chrysanthemums and roses, among which appeared two American flags and two yellow silk pennons on which were embroidered in letters of gold the words, "Governor Roosevelt," was lifted to a position on the platform amid renewed cheers and shouts.

What greater test of enthusiasm for the head of the Republican ticket could there be than that which resulted in forcing such a noted orator as Chauncey M. Depew to remain silent? Mr. Depew probably never waited so long in his life for an opportunity to be heard. Not that the audience intended to be discourteous, but the presence of the hero of San Juan so aroused everyone present that the only way of restoring order was to allow the demonstration to continue until every throat was hoarse and every hand was smarting.

At last Dr. Depew was able to say, as he retired to his seat, "The Rough Rider has ridden faster than all the calculations made for him. He is here, and I'm sure you want to hear him."

The audience evidently had found its second wind, for, as Roosevelt took his position at the front of the platform, there burst forth such a storm of applause that it seemed as if a fresh force had taken possession of the hall. Shots from even Mauser rifles never came with the frequency and vigor with which the cheers came from those present. Roosevelt looked weary and worn, but when he was allowed to speak there was nothing in matter or manner which indicated that he was suffering from any fatigue other than physical.

"I am," said he, "glad to have a chance to say a few words to you. I wish it might be my good fortune to meet all the voters of this State in this campaign, to meet them face to face and go over the issues with them. Our opponents have not met us on half the issues involved. They are afraid to meet us on all. There are none that we are afraid of. Remember that you are not only New Yorkers, but that you are Americans, vitally interested in not only the welfare of the State, but in the welfare of the nation, which is greater than even the greatest State. You cannot divorce your State and national interests. Up here you have special interests which I shall carefully consider. You are interested in the matter of rapid transit. If I am elected that is one of the matters to which I shall give most patient and thorough attention. I recognize the importance of the question, and I shall bend every energy I have toward working out its solution. You also are interested in having an honest government and a pure judiciary. The man who presumes to say that you have as New Yorkers interests isolated and apart from national interests is a fraud. You cannot cast your ballots only as New Yorkers. You must vote not only as New Yorkers, but as Americans, too. I am more than glad that our opponents dwell on State issues. I hope you'll think on them deeply, for the more you think on them the more you'll distrust those who dare to tell you that they will be honest at Albany when here in New York they drag the ermine of the judiciary in the mire of the lowest politics. You don't need in your public office great talent or great brilliancy as much as you need common sense, common honesty and courage. Our opponents have talked about the canals. I shall go into that matter most carefully if I become the Governor of this State. If there is trouble with the system there shall be a change in the system. If any man has been dishonest or inefficient, that man shall be punished to the full extent of my power, no matter what his party or personal influence may be.

"I can get along all right with a free silver man. I think he is mistaken, but I respect him for having the courage of his convictions. The man whom I cannot get on with is the man who hasn't any convictions concerning gold or silver that outweigh his desire to get votes. Such a man hasn't the courage requisite in any man who desires to probe dishonesty. The one public officer in whom every citizen has a constant and abiding interest is the judge, the man to whom is given power over the liberty and property of every man. It is of incalculable moment that the judge shall be influenced in his decisions only by considerations of fealty to his oath of office and what the public interests demand. Woe to the people of the city and State of New York if the men who exercise such a power over their very lives and all they hold most dear and precious is compelled to yield timid obedience to a political dictator.

"I appeal not only to Republicans, but to every Democrat who puts the welfare of the nation and the honor of the commonwealth above mere partisan consideration. We stand for keeping untarnished the judiciary of the State. We flinch from no issue. We call for honest finance. We entreat you not to let the great State of New York turn her back on what she did two years ago. You remember how, two years ago, thousands were out of work, trade was depressed, mills and factories were idle and distress reigned. We have improved on this condition, not as much as I could wish, but to some extent. In the Spring of 1897 twenty-five out of every one hundred members of labor organizations were out of work. In the Spring of 1898 only six of each one hundred were unemployed. I am sorry we haven't jobs for the six, but I am glad for the nineteen. If you sag back, dire will be the results. I appeal to you to stand with us for the sake of the honor and the glory of the old flag."

DEPEW AGAIN.

Cheers for "The Rough Rider" were called for by Judge Hall, and the audience responded in a manner which must have been gratifying to the gallant soldier, no matter how accustomed he may have become to demonstrations of that nature. The cheering gave Dr. Depew the cue for resuming his interrupted speech. "I have," said he, "found this year no halls large enough for the people who want to see Col. Roosevelt and assure him of the heartiness of their support. All outdoors is hardly big enough to hold them. A man who is touring the State in a political campaign can almost invariably tell the feeling of the people by the atmosphere which surrounds him. He can always feel a chill when the current of popular feeling is against the cause which he represents; but when the people's views and preferences are in harmony with his, he feels in the air an electricity which means that his ticket will be elected. And that is the experience I have had all over the State.

"Some Democratic friends of mine, and I have many of them, said to me early in this campaign: 'Chauncey, if you have any ambition for yourself, don't say a word in public about this so-called Imperial question. We're not fitted to take care of distant possessions!' But, my friends, we've got 'em. What are we going to do with 'em. Andrew Carnegie advises us to scuttle and run. Did we scuttle and run at Bunker Hill? (Applause.) Did we scuttle and run when we fought Great Britain in 1812? Did the next generation scuttle and run when the question of the great Northwest Territory arose? At the end of 100 days, by the grace of God and the valor of Dewey and Schley and Sampson, we had driven Spain off the Western hemisphere. At the beginning of 100 days there were four great powers—Great Britain, Germany, Russia and France. At the end of 100 days there were five great powers, and the greatest of all was the last. (Applause.) I reckon we're equal to any job we may have in hand. I once knew a boy in Peekskill who inherited a little money and opened a little store. Every Saturday night, when he closed up, he thanked God that the Sheriff hadn't done it for him. Other boys went out into the world. Some became distinguished and others became only ordinary railroad presidents. (Laughter.) I often go up to Peekskill to see the old boys, and particularly the old girls—I look after their daughters now (laughter)—and on one of my visits I was told that Jim Ten Eyck had inherited a hundred thousand dollars. I ran over to his little store to congratulate him, but he was depressed instead of elated, and said, 'Oh, Chauncey, just think of the responsibility!' We don't want any such timid, unenergetic, emasculated men to decide what our foreign policy shall be. We don't want men who are afraid of responsibility. We want to uphold William McKinley in every way, and we want with one voice, one effort and one energy to send to Albany the young man to whom you have given so rousing a reception here to-night. The microscope of slander and venom can find not a stain on Roosevelt anywhere.

"When I was in Washington early in the Summer I was told by several ladies that it was a shame that Theodore Roosevelt should be allowed to enlist. He was, they said, needed at Washington, and he could serve his country there fully as well as he could in the field. They spoke of the fact that he had not much money, and said that he ought not to be allowed to leave his wife and six children, the oldest only fourteen years of age and the youngest but a few months. He ought not to tear himself away from his little ones for whom he had such great love in his heart. There were plenty of men without families who were anxious to enlist. Why should he go. 'We told him all this,' said one of the ladies, 'and his reply was: "I believed the war had to come. I believed the war had to come now. I have done as much as any man to bring it about, and, having done so, I must be as near the front as anybody."'"

Cheer after cheer greeted this narration, and the cheering was renewed when Dr. Depew concluded his address by saying: "One of the greatest glories possible for this State will be in having Theodore Roosevelt for Governor."

ABRAHAM GRUBER.

Introduced as "The Little Giant of the Republican Party," Abraham Gruber was loudly applauded. "The issue," said he, "is not between Republicanism and Democracy. It is between patriotism and Crokerism.

Let the Croker croak till sore with pain,
Let the tiger claw with all its powers;
On Election Day we'll remember the Maine,
And Santiago's hero will be ours.

"We should remember two Maines. One is the gallant battleship so shamefully destroyed, and the other is 'the raging main' which Croker crosses twice a year when he comes to visit this country. (Laughter.) The first time he comes to get what our Hebrew friends call 'mazuma,' and the second time to nominate candidates to govern the American people. When last he came, the New York Sun, which has a habit of interviewing distinguished foreigners (laughter) published an interview with him in which he remarked, after receiving a negative reply to a question whether Roosevelt had been wounded, that a war record did a man no good unless he had been wounded."

"I want to say right here," continued the speaker, "that if, instead of being confronted by Spaniards with Mauser rifles, he had been confronted by the adherents of Tammany Hall who have pistol records, he undoubtedly would have been wounded if not killed. Look at these two men—Roosevelt and Croker. While one was baring his breast to Spanish bullets, the other was racing horses on English soil; and Croker returns to insult Roosevelt as not even the Spaniards would insult him! What is the spectacle that Croker presents to the people of the city of New York? A man who for twenty-four years has been too strong to work! A man who in all that time, although he has held no office of emolument and has been engaged in no recognizedly legitimate business, has amassed a fortune, and is the owner of race horses of immense value and a town house in New York and one in England, and who is the reputed owner of the New York Baseball Club. He parades up and down the town, and says that the organization he represents is the friend of the poor. Yes, very much as Dick Turpin and Blueskin were! I ask my Irish friends—and I am justified in calling Irishmen my friends, for I once came very near being an Irishman, when I proposed to an Irish girl and she wouldn't have me—I ask my Irish friends what they would do to a countryman of theirs who spent in England all the time he didn't need to control affairs at home? They would lie behind the hedges and fill him with buckshot! And that's what we have got to do with Van Wyck this year! Mr. Croker is the most pronounced type of the absentee landlord the United States has ever known. Mr. Croker is not only playing the horse races, but he is trying to play the German and Hebrew races. He thinks the Germans vote with their stomachs and not with their heads. Van Wyck will have some Germans with him, but there are Germans who are patriots and to whom the old flag is dearer than beer during prohibited hours. Talk about beer! If there is any man here who can't get all he wants on Sunday, let him rise. Two years ago the trouble was in getting the price. (Laughter.) The only trouble now is the trouble that comes afterward because of the beer you didn't want. The Democrats have no issue, and they cannot succeed when they turn their backs on the most vital questions affecting every man in New York, be he rich or poor, be he great or be he lowly."

The speaker was interrupted by a disturbance created by a man in the audience, but a policeman soon removed the objectionable individual and Mr. Gruber went on. Speaking of the election inspection system he said that it had been made necessary by the high handed treatment of McCullagh and the substitution of Devery. "Some people are offended," said he. "Every bum and tramp is offended, the proprietor of the Dewey Theatre is offended, every panhandler below Fourteenth street is offended; but no honest man has been deprived of his vote and none will be. The Democrats are throwing scandal and slander and mud. How they can throw it! How they revel in it! I like a three-bagger myself, but you never saw such enthusiasm at a ball game as you can see among the Tammany heelers when some Democratic orator is trying to besmirch some fair American name.

"If charges are made against the Mayor, his judge will be the Governor. The town is now wide open. The time is not far off when the Republicans and honest Democrats will arise and demand that the chief executive of the city be called to account. What would happen then, with Gussie the Governor and Bob the Mayor? 'Ting-a-ling' would go the telephone bell. 'Give me umpty-steen Fourteenth street.' 'Is that you, Dick?' 'Yes, Bob; what's the matter?' 'What'ell! Here's a lot of guys making charges against me.' 'All right, I'll fix that.' And then a conversation occurs between Fourteenth street and Albany, and the man at the Albany end says: 'What! Charges again Bob? Send 'em up here, and I won't do a ting to 'em.' (Laughter.)

"But this is not going to occur. I want to say that the Republican leaders in the State of New York and the Democratic leaders have simply no conception of the amount of sympathy that exists among the plain people of the State of New York for Theodore Roosevelt. They have no idea of the ground swell that will break for Teddy on election day. Teddy's square, Teddy's got courage and Teddy loves the people. A vote for Teddy will be a tribute to patriotism and a tribute to heroism, and the votes that will be given him will show that the fires of patriotism burn as brightly in 1898 as they did in 1776 and in 1861."

HON. JOHN PROCTOR CLARKE.

Hon. John Proctor Clark was the last speaker. With a justifiable sneer he said: "Think of a party which doesn't allow its speakers to wave Old Glory for George Dewey!" Mr. Clark eulogized Roosevelt, and in a very dramatic manner compared the career of the Republican nominee with the careers of the men who are seeking to defeat him. "If the people of New York put Van Wyck in the Governor's chair," said he, "every bronze soldier and sailor in the State will turn his back on the people and blush with shame. I shall vote for Theodore Roosevelt because in twenty years of public service, with his character as easily read as an open book, and under the fierce light of publicity, he has worn the white flower of a blameless life and has lived up to the noblest thought and noblest aspirations of the great party to which he is proud to belong, and which will make Theodore Roosevelt the next Governor of the State of New York."

VICE-PRESIDENTS AND SECRETARIES.

The gentlemen who had been selected as vice-presidents and secretaries, most of whom occupied seats on the platform, were:

Vice-Presidents.

John J. Amory.	Rev. R. F. Humphries.
Blakeslee Baines.	I. R. Johnston.
Dr. Irving S. Balcom.	Isaac G. Johnston.
J. I. Ball.	Dr. I. C. Jones.
Edward Barker.	Israel C. Jones.
John E. Barstow.	Rev. H. Kastendieck.
Rev. Jonathan Barstow.	Charles Knapp.
Richard H. Du Barry.	Francis V. Keil.
Rev. J. T. Bates.	William Kirst.
Edward Becker.	M. J. King.
C. A. Becker.	Joseph Lowey.
Abraham Bennett.	Phil Link.
Chas. Berrian.	Dr. D. Lewis.
Samuel L. Berrian.	Phil Luther.
William Birchall.	Geo. Mariamson.
Samuel M. Bixby.	Edgar S. Marsden.
James A. Blakely.	Angelo Maunello.
E. G. Blauvelt.	Dr. H. M. McCracken.
Edw. J. Blauvelt.	I. H. McCracken.
James B. Blossom.	Hon. Samuel McMillan.
Wm. H. Boak.	Rev. H. V. R. Meyers.
John W. Bolton.	Dr. L. A. Mesereau.
W. A. Bolton.	Rev. C. W. Millard.
Charles F. Bradbury.	Rev. G. H. Miller.
Prof. Geo. F. Bristow.	Col. John Miller.
W. I. Brown.	John W. Miller.
John S. Bush.	Louis Mitchell.
Peter Call.	Wm. R. Montgomery.
Wm. A. Cameron.	Richard H. Moran.
Frederick E. Camp.	G. P. Morosini.
George F. Campbell.	Frank P. Mott.
James T. Campbell.	A. A. Nevins.
William Campbell.	Hon. W. W. Niles, Jr.
Elijah D. Clark.	Rev. George Nixon.
Wm. N. Clark.	Hon. Jacob M. Patterson.
Jacob Cole.	
Chas. V. Cowenhoven.	Hon. Henry D. Purroy.
D. S. Crawford.	Charles Radginsky.
Dr. J. A. Cutter.	R. R. Randall.
Charles Deitweiler.	Sidwell S. Randall.
Leonard F. Dietsch.	Owen Roberts.
J. S. Dingwall.	Max Rosenweig.
Cleveland H. Dodge.	Alfred P. Roth.
A. S. Dominick.	George Rudolph.
Chas. A. Dubois.	Henry Schappert.
Hugh Duffy.	C. W. Schmidtke.
John E. Eustis.	John Schulz.
William Ebling.	Geo. W. Stephans.
Louis Erickworth.	Wm. Stonebridge.
Dr. James Ferguson.	Rev. J. Sumner Stone.
Peter Friess.	Henry L. Stoddard.
Moses Fridiger.	W. L. Sands.
Ludwig Frederick.	Charles D. Steurer.
Otis L. Fowler.	Anthony Stumpf.
Rev. Franklin Gaylord.	J. Thomas Stearns.
Alfred Graven.	Geo. Stroninger.
John H. Gratacap.	Robt. N. Shepherd.
Wm. H. Gur.	W. Stebbins Smith.
Wm. H. Haebeck.	Robert Sheppard.
Harry Haight.	Otto T. Schmidt.
H. B. Hall.	Rev. Wayland Spaulding.
Sumpter L. Happy.	
James S. Healy.	Hiram Tarbox.
John T. Heath.	H. B. Thayer.
George Hey.	Fred Von Beesten.
Thomas Higgs.	N. L. Vogt.
William Hodgson.	Enoch Vreeland.
Garrett Hopper.	Samuel Walker.
David S. Hotaling.	David L. Woodall.
George W. Holding.	A. Wuensch.
Rev. Spencer L. Hillier.	Frank D. Wilsey.

Secretaries.

David B. Hart.	P. G. Woodstrom.
B. U. Keyser.	David Adamson.
John W. Valentine.	Wm. H. Yale.
Louis Horstman.	O. Longacre.
J. B. Lord.	Isidor Hildebrandt.
Wm. E. Sickles.	Chas. Rathfelder.
Theo. M. Milspaugh.	Wm. H. Henry.
Thos. G. Holland.	Jas. G. Henry.
Chas. H. Kirk.	J. Van Brunt.
Edward Foley.	H. C. Calkins.
E. L. Bianchi.	Chas. Iker.
Peter Celi.	Louis Doernberg.
John J. Weeks.	Chas. R. Jung.
Constantine Frederick.	Chas. W. Roxbury.
Henry Fischer.	Geo. Dennerlein.
Chas. Duda.	John Quigley.
Sebastian Fischer.	W. S. Beckley.
Geo. H. Taylor, Jr.	W. G. Rule.
John J. Adams.	R. N. Cotter.
J. S. Dale.	Geo. P. Esch.
F. V. R. Dodge	B. Joost.
Fred Hautau, Jr.	Emil Haas.
Al. Fox.	J. H. Elliott.
Albert Crouter.	Ed. Ruehl.
M. D. Sanger.	John Yule.
Jas. E. Randolph.	Geo. Holding.
Fred J. Kirchner.	W. N. Newroth.
Chas. E. Voigt.	Harry Williams.
Lewis Wirth.	Walter Chisholm.
Chas. E. Messler.	John Biggart.
Stephen F. Hill.	F. E. Camp.
Frank E. Purdy.	John McK. Camp.
John Yule.	Theo. L. Dusinbarre.
Chas. Dannewitz.	John W. Botton.
Adrian McLeod.	Andrew Devoe.
Wm. Hennessey.	Daniel Mapes.
Geo. Clampit.	Geo. Clampit.
D. R. Bolster.	Dr. John E. Comfort.
Jos. J. Schmidt.	Christ. F. Leonard.
J. C. Brolles.	Wm. G. Ball, Jr.

While Morrisania Hall was crowded to suffocation, a crowd numbering well up in the thousands was outside clamoring in vain for admission. The faithful party rulers were gathering at the different headquarters to participate in the parade that was to have escorted Col. Roosevelt to the meeting. Unfortunately for them the colonel was so much ahead of time that they were deprived of that pleasant duty. The parade was nevertheless a great success, and was participatd in by fully two thousand steadfast believers in good government and sound money; and if manifestation of enthusiasm is any indication of the feeling of the people the demonstrations all along the line of march would indicate that this district will be overwhelmingly for Roosevelt on next Tuesday. The clubs that participated in the parade were the North Side Republican Club, the Union Republican Club, the Morris Heights Republican Club, and the Theodore Roosevelt Campaign Club. The entire route of the parade was enlivened by magnificent displays of fireworks, and although the paraders arrived too late at the hall to get anywhere near enough to hear the speakers, they were well satisfied with what they had accomplished towards arousing enthusiasm for the ticket.

INCIDENTS OF THE MEETING.

One election district captain was heard to remark: "I have made a thorough personal canvass of my district, and I find it in better shape for the Republicans this year than ever before. This is not conjecture, mind you, but the result of my personal observation."

The first applause of the evening was elicited by the appearance upon the platform of the Hon. Douglas Mathewson, candidate for Senator. The crowd recognized him instantly and gave him an ovation which was repeated when he arose to speak.

One of the features of the evening was the unusual number of ladies who were present. It seems to be a peculiarity of the Republican meetings that there are many ladies present. One young lady was heard to remark that she thought political meetings were "lovely," and now that she had attended a Republican meeting she would like to attend one of the Democratic. Her escort told her that she had better confine her attendance to Republican meetings, as there seldom were any ladies at the Tammany demonstrations.

Somewhere in the northwest corner of the platform there was a gentleman who had with him a wild yell, that has seldom been equaled in this borough. The clarion note which he gave forth at intervals had in it all the timbre of a fog siren, and the tone color of a steam calliope. Ex-Tax Commissioner James L. Wells sat almost in front of the gentleman who gave forth the hideous yell, and not only was Mr. Wells startled each time, but as some of the people in the hall looked at Mr. Wells as if he had been guilty of the top note, he looked correspondingly embarrassed. Mr. Wells finally heaved a sigh of relief when the operatic enthusiast subsided.

Chauncey M. Depew certainly had a hard time endeavoring to deliver his speech. While he was in the first part of it, those near the door heard cheering in the street. Presently there was a commotion in the doorway, with more cheering, and every one turned around to look. "That's all right, gentlemen," said Mr. Depew, "Col. Roosevelt won't be here for an hour yet." The words were hardly out of his mouth before Col. Roosevelt pushed through the door, and, with difficulty, made his way to the crowded platform. Mr. Depew, of course, gave way to him, and when Col. Roosevelt had spoken and left, he continued his speech. He had spoken but a few moments, however, when a brass band at the head of a marching procession outside drowned out the Doctor's voice. He stopped and said, plaintively: "I can talk against a locomotive, but I cannot beat a brass band." Presently the band moved on, and Mr. Depew resumed his remarks; then another band came by, and later in the evening still another. Mr. Depew was very good natured, but a less experienced speaker would probably have had a hard time.

A WORD TO THE LABORING CLASSES OF THE 34TH ASSEMBLY DISTRICT.

Attention is directed to the claims that are being made and widely circulated about the so-called friend of labor, Mr. Lyman W. Redington, who asks for the support of the voters of this district and a re-election to the Assembly. This is a conspicuous case of false pretense; and voters must not be misled thereby.

During the term of Mr. Redington's service (?) at Albany, he failed to introduce or pass a single measure, interesting or benefiting the voters of the district he was supposed to represent.

He did introduce a bill purporting to be for the welfare of the laboring man; but was it?

This bill provided for a minimum rate of wages, as follows: "Unskilled laborers employed in the construction of public works by the State, or by sub-contractors, contracting for the construction of any part of such public works, shall not be less than at the rate of fifteen cents per hour.

This was substantially a legal proposition to reduce rather than advance wages. The prevailing rate was above that figure. No sane man will believe that contractors will pay more than the legalized minimum sum; and the bill introduced was therefore a premium on injustice to the laborer.

Eight hours being a legal day's work, the wages of the working man at fifteen cents per hour would aggregate $1.20 per day. None but American citizens can be employed on public works.

How do our citizens regard the proposition to place them on an equal footing with the under-paid labor of foreign lands?

The Republican Legislature would not sanction such a proceeding, and the measure failed to become a law. The records at Albany fail to show any act or proposed act credited to Mr. Redington, intended for the interest of his district. Workingmen and all interested in labor, vote for Frank K. Bowers for Assembly. He has been brought up and trained in the workshop. He has always been the friend of the laboring man, and a strong advocate for the interest of labor.

He is not a theorist, but a practical man of work. He has in addition thereto, parliamentary and legislative ability. He is a man of the people and will work for the people. Vote for him.

TAMMANY AND THE SCHOOLS.

Differences in the Republican and Democratic Methods of Handling the Bulwark of American Institutions.

A cursory review of the work accomplished for public instruction in our city since 1895 may be profitable at this time. Although the Board of Education is non-partisan in its composition it will not take a prophet to see what has been done under a Republican administration.

The impetus given public schools by the $5,000,000 authorized school-house bond issue by the Republican Legislature of 1895 came at a time when, by reason of the neglect, indifference and gross intent of Tammany's mal-administration covering a period of twenty years, fifty thousand children were turned into the streets, deprived of that sacred God-given right of having public instruction furnished them.

Every dollar of this handsome sum of $5,000,000 was applied by a Board of Education selected by a Republican city administration for the purchase of school sites, and several most commodious and well appointed school buildings were at once constructed in the most densely populated districts of the city. This amount of money was found insufficient to provide for all the children in all the districts, which for twenty years of Tammanyized city domination had been left without school accommodations; therefore the Legislature of the State was again appealed to, and with promptness the Republican Assemblymen and Senators rallied to the support of a bill prepared by the New York City Board of Education, asking for $9,000,000 for school purposes.

In 1897 the School Board, still finding that many children were yet out of school and many children who desired to acquire a higher education were deprived from so doing, the State was again appealed to by the Board of Education and the sum of $12,500,000 was asked for and granted by a Republican Legislature —$10,000,000 for the acquisition of sites and the erection thereon of school houses, and $2,500,000 for the erection and equipment of three high school buildings, which the Board of Education had determined to launch.

Three high schools were at once organized and set to work in old school buildings temporarily fitted up for the purpose—one in East 12th street, and another in East 13th street, and the third in the Borough of the Bronx at East 158th street. In addition to the high schools, a thoroughly equipped training school was provided and equipped to augment the supply of efficient teachers provided by the Normal College. Then the Tammany tiger again secured control of the City Hall, and being always willing to obstruct and never to advance public instruction, raised its brazen paw and placed it upon the Board of Apportionment, and for a subterfuge cried, "Debt limit exceeded! No more bonds can be issued for the erection of school houses!"

The children unprovided for can stay in the streets. Why? Is the debt limit provided by law reached? Tammany has said yes, but now, upon careful search, he says, "No; I was mistaken about the debt limit, but the schools will have to wait my pleasure. I have no time to consider the necessity of the children or the wants of the people."

This authorized school-house bond issue is the people's money, and he who holds it up is guilty of a crime against the children and the city and against the people. Will they hold him responsible? Let their voices be heard through the ballot and the tiger will tremble and cower, for he ever fears the light.

ATTEMPTED TO JUMP OFF HARLEM BRIDGE.

Policeman Dennerlein of the 138th street station, while patrolling the north end of the Third Avenue Bridge on Thursday afternoon, discovered a man attempting to climb over the parapet. He was caught just in time to prevent him from jumping over into the Harlem River. He announced to the policeman that he had committed a great crime, and for years had prayed to God to forgive him, but without avail. Finally, he said, God told him to jump into the Harlem and go straight to hell.

Dennerlein took his prisoner to the station house, where he gave his name as John White, no home, no friends. In court he told the same story and asked Magistrate Mott to send him to hell. The Magistrate told him the law gave him no power to commit to that place, but would send him to Bellevue. The man gave the Magistrate to understand that he considered that much the same thing.

FLORENCE LODGE SOCIAL.

The Florence Lodge Social Club held their monthly reception at the Arion Liedertafel Hall on Tuesday evening. The grand march was led by George Pearlbrook and wife. A handsome fan was drawn for by the ladies, and Miss A. Murphy was the holder of the lucky number. Among those present were Mr. and Mrs. Terrell, Mrs. Wurms, Mr. John Doyle, Miss Brady, Mr. John McCarthy and wife, Mr. H. Breuster, Mr. M. Davis, Charles Schuberger and Miss M. Winter, Mrs. Wagner, Mr. Otto Brown and Miss Wagner, Mr. Pearlbrook and wife, Mr. F. Saiers and Miss Siemers, Mr. F. W. Fleischmann and Miss A. Murphy, Miss M. Rowan, John L. Sullivan and ladies, Mr. P. J. Gillespie and wife, the Hon. John McCarthy, and Hon. James E. Brown.

Henry D. Purroy addressed the Republicans of Tremont Thursday evening and said that although he was nothing but a rebel Democrat, he intended, in the interests of good government, to vote the entire Republican ticket. Samuel McMillan, ex-Park Commissioner, and Hon. Ernest Hall also spoke. The meeting was largely attended, and the greeting given to the speakers and to their addresses indicated that the spirit of the Republican party is more active and widespread in Tremont than ever before.

A grand rally of the James G. Blaine Campaign Club, of the Thirty-fourth Assembly District, will be held on Saturday evening, Nov. 5, 1898, at 8 o'clock, at the North Side Republican Club Hall, 2661 and 2663 Third avenue. The following eminent speakers will address the meeting: W. A. Ullman, Chas. E. Whitman, Gilbert R. Hawes, James Irving Burns, candidate for Congress; Douglas Mathewson, candidate for Senate; Frank K. Bowers, candidate for Assembly. J. Stewart Wilson will preside. There will be music and fireworks. Singing by the Diamond Quartet.

CHIEF-OF-POLICE DEVERY GIVING ORDERS TO THE BICYCLE SQUAD.

WEARIED POLICEMEN RESTING IN THE CARS, NEW YORK.

HOOTING A NON-UNION MAN.

AT THE SECOND-AVENUE CAR-HOUSE.

CLEARING THE TRACK.

CLINTON L. ROSSITER,
President Brooklyn Rapid Transit Company.
Photograph by Gardner & Co.

WOMEN DISCUSSING THE STRIKE.

HERBERT H. VREELAND,
President Metropolitan Traction Company.

JAMES PINES,
Master Workman, D. A. 75, K. of L.

STRIKERS WATCHING FOR A CAR.

JOHN N. PARSONS,
General Master Workman, K. of L.

THE STRIKE OF THE TROLLEY EMPLOYÉS IN NEW YORK CITY.—[SEE PAGE 753.]

THE NEWEST COUNTY.

NASSAU TO COME INTO EXISTENCE ON LONG ISLAND NEXT YEAR.

TOWNS CONTAINED IN THE NEW COUNTY, AND ATTRACTIONS OF THE REGION.

By act of the Legislature of 1898 the State of New-York will have an additional county after January 1, 1899, to be known as Nassau. It will be the smallest of the island counties, but as its population will be nearly fifty thousand it will outrank many of the sixty-one counties of the State.

The new county is made up of the towns of North Hempstead and Oyster Bay and that part of the town of Hempstead that is outside of the Borough of Queens, and will include great stretches of farming land, miles of perfect roads, homes which were built in the early days of the Republic and buildings of the most modern style of architecture. Within its boundaries are the homes of some of the most important clubs of the country, and its citizens are well known in the business, political and social circles of the State. Nassau County begins its political career by furnishing to the State a Governor, an honor which many of its older sisters have never enjoyed.

STATISTICS OF THE NEW COUNTY.

The new county is twenty-two miles across from the Atlantic Ocean to Long Island Sound and about sixteen miles long from the eastern boundary line of the Borough of Queens to the western boundary line of Suffolk County. The most important places in the county are Hempstead, Glen Cove, Rockville Centre, Freeport, Oyster Bay, Hicksville, Port Washington, Roslyn, Sea Cliff, Farmingdale, Lynbrook, Garden City and Manhasset, and there are a number of smaller places, among which are Syosset, Locust Valley, Glen Head, East Williston, Massapequa, Mineola, East Norwich, Westbury, Jericho, Jerusalem, Merrick, Great Neck and a number of other "necks." The assessed valuation of the real estate of the county is estimated at $25,000,000. Aside from a large manufacturing plant at Glen Cove there is little manufacturing in Nassau County, and in some of the districts titles can be secured only on condition that the land shall not be used for business purposes. But that does not preclude commerce in its villages, many of which are making rapid strides in the direction of maintaining large and well-assorted stocks of goods by means of which the home trade is retained.

The schools of the county are among the features which the residents take pride in showing to the public. Besides the two large educational institutions at Garden City there are about seventy schoolhouses in the county, and a trip through Nassau will reveal the fact that in each locality the people point to their school as "the best in the county." In the matter of churches Garden City is also in first place, with the beautiful Cathedral of the Incarnation, but there are, besides this house of worship, ninety-one churches within the county.

Hunting, golf, shooting and yacht clubs attract people from the surrounding country, but the villages have an eye to the higher education of the public also, which is evinced by the maintenance of public libraries at Sea Cliff, Hempstead, Roslyn, Oyster Bay, Rockville Centre, Massapequa and Great Neck.

THE COUNTY SEAT.

The question, Where shall the county seat be? was submitted to the vote of the people, and decided in favor of Mineola, where for many years the Long Island fairs have taken place. A plot of four acres of land was donated for county buildings by the Garden City Company, and plans for a courthouse are now being made.

The voters showed their preference for Mineola, and also gave Colonel Roosevelt, of Oyster Bay, a majority of about one thousand two hundred. The following will be the first county officers: Robert Seabury, County Judge and Surrogate; James P. Nieman, District-Attorney; Thomas Patterson, County Clerk; William H. Wood, Sheriff; H. M. W. Eastman, County Treasurer; George D. Smith, Superintendent of the Poor. The salary of the County Judge and Surrogate will be $3,000 a year; the District-Attorney, County Treasurer and Sheriff will receive "a salary not to exceed $2,500 each, the County Clerk $3,000 and the Superintendent of the Poor $1,500."

THE SHOW PLACE OF THE COUNTY.

On account of the fairs which have been held there at regular intervals Mineola is one of the best-known places in the county, but a mile from the site of the new courthouse is the real show place of the new county—Garden City—which is reached by a perfect road on which one may see in the season many beautiful specimens of blooded stock and numbers of handsome vehicles of all kinds. The graceful spire of the Cathedral of the Incarnation and the smaller towers of St. Paul's and St. Mary's school may be seen from the spot where the courthouse will stand, but one must go to it and drive or walk through its broad, winding and well-kept shaded streets to realize what a beautiful place it is.

Toward the south, about two and a half miles from Mineola, is the pretty town of Hempstead, with its quaint, old-fashioned houses and streets perfectly macadamized, its electric lights and modern water system, as well as a reminder of the days of long ago in the shape of a hotel where Washington was a guest and old St. George's Church, with its communion service given to it by Queen Anne. Near this pretty village are the headquarters of the Meadow

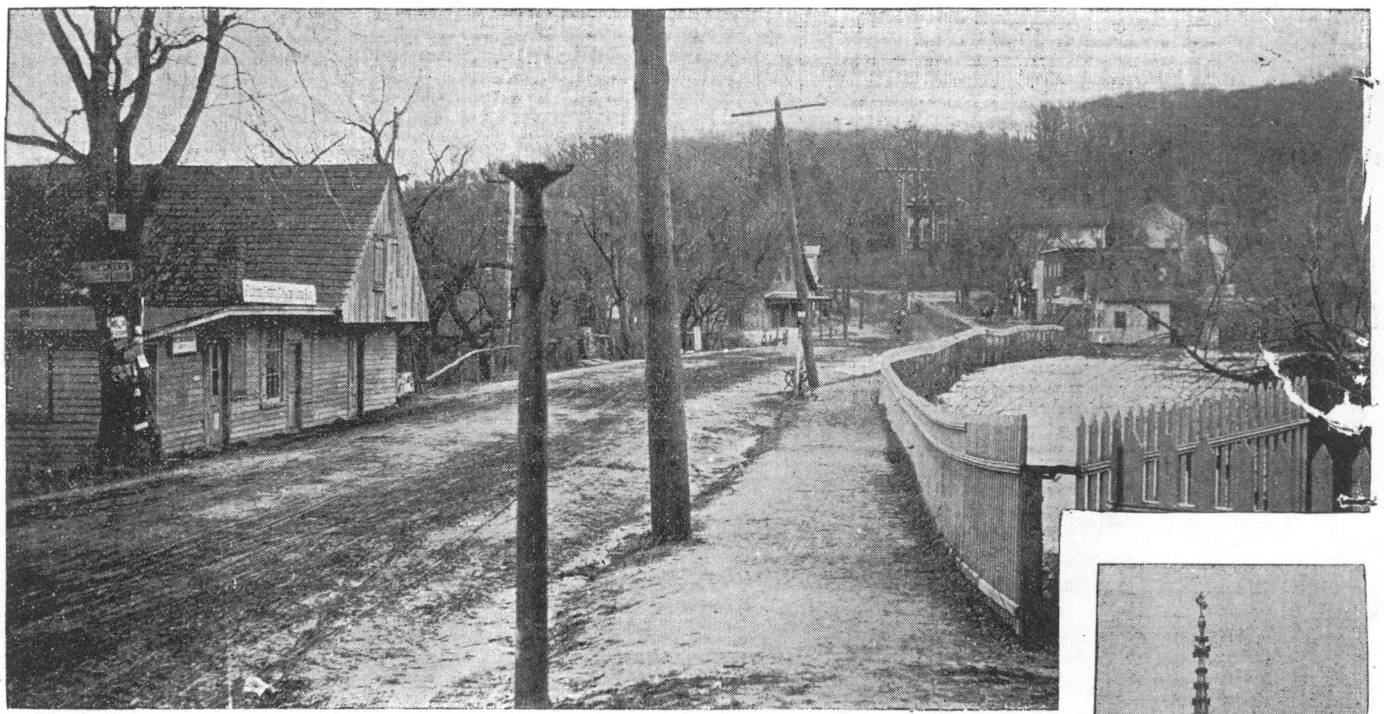

A STREET IN ROSLYN.

WILLIAM CULLEN BRYANT'S GRAVE AT ROSLYN.

THE CATHEDRAL OF THE INCARNATION, GARDEN CITY.

PLACE'S POND, NEAR HEMPSTEAD.

SEAWANHAKA-CORINTHIAN YACHT

SCENES IN THE NEW

SIDNEY DILLON RIPLEY'S HOME, HEMPSTEAD.

SCENE AT MINEOLA FAIR.

THE INGRAHAM HOUSE, HEMPSTEAD.

THE WARD MEMORIAL, ROSLYN.

CLUB HOUSE, AT OYSTER BAY.

ST. GEORGE'S PROTESTANT EPISCOPAL CHURCH, HEMPSTEAD.

COUNTY OF NASSAU.

Brook and the Farm Kennell clubs, and all around are the houses of men who are well known in the commercial and social circles of New-York. There are five churches in the place, two schools, two newspapers and a number of good hotels.

SOME LEADING HOUSEHOLDERS.

Among those who have fine homes near the place are August Belmont, O. H. P. Belmont, Sidney Dillon Ripley, O. W. Bird, Rutherford Winthrop, H. Van R. Kennedy, J. S. Smith-Hadden, and a short distance away, at Hempstead Gardens, is the beautiful estate of Austin Corbin. Mrs. Adolph Ladenburg, R. N. Ellis, Dudley Winthrop, William C. Whitney, J. F. D. Lanier, Perry Tiffany, Charles H. Mackay, Foxhall Keene, E. D. Morgan, Stanley Mortimer, Thomas Hitchcock, jr., and Sidney J. Smith are also among those who have fine homes in Hempstead and North Hempstead.

One of the Hempstead churches, Christ's First Presbyterian Church, is said to be the oldest in the county.

Roslyn, according to the views of the Long Island historian, "gives one a foretaste of the hills which abound along the north shore, and which are a never-ending source of delight to the lovers of the picturesque." The village is in the valley, has about eight hundred inhabitants and is one of the favorite Long Island summer resorts. Here William Cullen Bryant lived and wrote and received the visits of Whittier, Emerson and Beecher, and here a modest monument marks his grave.

OYSTER BAY, COLONEL ROOSEVELT'S HOME.

Probably no place in the county has received so much attention recently as Oyster Bay, the home of Theodore Roosevelt. It is situated at the terminus of one of the branches of the Long Island Railroad, and because of its charming situation has long been a favorite vacation place for people from New-York. At the entrance to the bay the Seawanhaka Yacht Club has erected its clubhouse, an imposing structure, from the verandas of which there is a fine view, across well-kept lawns and flower beds, on the water, and there in the yachting season may be found the representative yachtsmen and yachtswomen of New-York. The village of Oyster Bay was founded by the Quakers, and it still bears the imprint of the Friends who dominated it for a century and a half.

Among the well-known residents of Oyster Bay are, besides the Governor-elect, William J. Youngs, T. S. Young, jr., F. H. Benedict, Gerald Beekman, J. William Beekman, Edward H. Swan, F. T. Underhill, E. M. Townsend, E. M. Townsend, jr., James K. Gracie, J. Reeve Merritt, James A. Weeks, Austin Weeks, Frank Work, jr., W. F. Trotter and W. H. Burgess. On Centre Island, besides the Seawanhaka Yacht Club, are the places of Colgate Hoyt, D. Leroy Dresser and Charles W. Wetmore, and at Cold Spring are the homes of Robert De Forest and Walter Jennings.

Glen Cove, about nine miles from the county seat, with a population of about two thousand five hundred, has made remarkable progress in the last few years, and its beauties are being appreciated by the residents of New-York. Much of the land on the Sound shore is controlled by two syndicates, one called the North Country Club and the other the Red Spring Syndicate. Good roads lead to the thriving village, and the starch company which has been operating there for many years gives employment to many of the residents.

THE PRATT ESTATE.

One of the largest places in the village is the Pratt estate, which covers about one thousand acres, with a large frontage on Long Island Sound. On the estate is the tomb of Charles Pratt, whose public spirit and charity endeared him to his contemporaries and cause the present generation to honor his memory. He planned a model school building for the place, which was erected after his death by his sons. In connection with the school is an agricultural department, which is operated upon a part of the estate, where young men receive practical instruction in agriculture.

The fine roads, the beautiful scenery and the model homes have less interest for some of the people of Glen Cove than the Queens County Golf Club, which will soon begin the erection of a $25,000 clubhouse on a piece of property recently acquired. The purchase was effected by Harvey Murdock, president of the club, and the members now look forward to having one of the best courses in the country. When the clubhouse and the six thousand yards' course have been completed the name of the club will probably be changed to the Nassau County Golf Club.

Among those who have fine homes in this part of the new county are Percy Chubb, J. Rogers Maxwell, Leonard J. Busby, Leonard Jacob, Edward Ladew and Jacob Ladew.

Dana Island is also one of the attractive features of Glen Cove. At Great Neck is Graceland, the summer home of ex-Mayor William R. Grace, and one may find in nearly every village in the new county palatial homes and artistic grounds belonging to people who are well known in New-York.

Sea Cliff is beautifully situated on a commanding point overlooking the sheltered bay.

The new county reckons among its advantages the fact that all its important points are accessible by the Long Island Railroad, and that good service brings the inhabitants within easy reach of New-York. A spirit of pride has been awakened by the establishment of the new county, and Nassau, which is already one of the finest sections of Long Island, will doubtless become more so under the new order of things.

New-York Tribune.

Vol. LIX....No. 19,312. NEW-YORK, SATURDAY, SEPTEMBER 30, 1899.—EIGHTEEN PAGES. PRICE THREE CENTS.

GLORIES OF THE NIGHT.

BEAUTEOUS FORMS OUTLINED IN GLORIOUS FIRE.

THE HUDSON LIGHTED UP BY MYRIADS OF BOMBS AND ROCKETS—WARSHIPS AND YACHTS LAVISHLY ILLUMINATED — MANY THOUSANDS VIEW THE DISPLAY.

The night has a thousand eyes, the day but one, and so it was natural that the beauties of last night's Dewey ceremonies should exceed those of the day a thousandfold. No more gorgeous spectacle could be imagined than the warships lying on the black surface of the river, with every line and spar picked out with electric lights. On either side of these stretched the fleet of yachts, with thousands of lamps also in glow. The heavens shone with the glare of fireworks, and even the prosaic ferryboat took on new grace when touched by the fairy wand of the electricians.

The fireworks show last evening was a fitting climax to the day's celebration. It began opposite the Olympia's anchorage, just below Grant's tomb, where a series of scows were anchored. They were manned by a large force of Mr. Pain's faithful salamanders, who live in fire and are as little scathed by it as was the burning bush in Moses's vision, and who seem to breathe the choking vapors of the fireworks' aftermath with supreme pleasure.

These humble mud scows were loaded to the gunwales with serried rows of rockets, whole picket fences formed of Roman candles, an endless array of mortars, bombs and all those sorts of fiendish inventions in which Mr. Pain most delights himself. When seven bells rang from the Olympia's deck, the aerial artillery was let loose. From that time on it was one continuous glare of many colored fires, and a continuous roll of rattling explosions, till the fiery trail of the serpent wound its way down around the Battery, enfolding Governor's Island and Bedloe's Island in its coils, and expired at 10:30 o'clock in a final burst of glory.

It was Manhattan Beach multiplied a hundred times, and amplified in a hundred ways. One moment whole flights of rockets would stud the sky with strings of floating lanterns, and the next a myriad constellation of floating stars would take their places. All manner of hissing, sizzling, bursting things tore hither and thither through the startled air and died the many hued deaths of a thousand chameleons.

The old mud scows were transformed each into a floating section of Hades, wherein a score of devils in old felt hats and shirt sleeves hopped cheerfully about, each stirring up his particular style of an inferno wherever he went.

All the beautiful effects with which the visitor to Manhattan Beach is familiar were produced, but on a much grander scale. Many new features were added. Among these were the electric bombs, which certainly electrified every one within five miles by their earsplitting detonation. Another new device was a species of bomb that burst into an enormous starfish of fire. Sporadic arms of fire radiated from the explosive centre, producing a vivid effect.

While the fireworks popped, the jackies on the Olympia cheered and the steamboat whistles screeched. Then the Olympia's crew, not to be outdone, put their excellent brass band into commission, and the strains of "There'll Be a Hot Time in the Old Town To-night" joined with the bursting of bombs and the screaming of a thousand tormented fire spirits whose seeming agony ceased only when they fell back hissing into the waters of the Hudson.

After half an hour of this sort of thing the cargoes of these scows were exhausted. Then three tugs hitched on to another string of similarly laden scows anchored out in the stream, and started with them down the river with the "continuous performance" Hades still going on. A pushing crowd of excursion boats had gathered in a black circle about the fireworks scows, almost hiding them from the Olympia even. The sailors got a good view of the picture of Dewey, however, and cheered it loud and long.

Slowly the procession wended its way down the river, the three puffing tugs in advance, the volcanic scows straining at the hawsers behind them vomiting up red, white, blue and green shapes of every possible design, and the great black fleet of excursion craft hanging in the rear like a threatening storm cloud.

On the way other fireworks could be seen popping up from the Jersey shore, and twinkling behind Manhattan Island. The piers and buildings along the New-York shores were a blaze of light. The warships and the yachts shone like ships of stars, and the matchless beauty of the American flag floating from the gaff of each in the stiff southerly breeze glorified and etherealized by the pure white rays of the searchlight focussed on it, was enough to make a patriot of an Atkinson.

When the warships were left behind, and the flotilla approached the Battery, the plot thickened. The crush of steamboats became something to make even an international yacht race veteran pale. All sorts of craft, from the giant steamer Plymouth, of the Fall River Line, to the smallest naphtha launch, were gathered to view the display on Governor's Island. From the top of old Castle William, and from the sea wall to the east of it, there went up another rush of rockets and bombs, which wrought aerial effect of every conceivable design. Liberty looked over from Bedloe's Island with a glare of red fire to rouge up her rusty old charms, and companion displays shone against the Brooklyn skies in many places.

The fireworks scows coming down the river circled about with their batteries still belching up every imaginable variety of combustible and

Continued on fourth page.

ADMIRAL DEWEY ON THE BRIDGE OF THE OLYMPIA REVIEWING THE PARADE.

THE OLYMPIA ENTERING THE HUDSON RIVER SURROUNDED BY TUGS.

Photograph taken from roof of the Bowling Green Building.

PROGRAMME OF THE DEWEY CELEBRATION FOR TO-DAY.

7:00 a. m.—Sub-committee of the Reception Committee will board the police boat Patrol at West Fortieth-st. to take Admiral Dewey off the Olympia.

7:30 a. m.—Admiral Dewey will board the Patrol.

8:00 a. m.—Admiral Dewey will be landed at the Battery and be driven up Broadway escorted by Squadron A.

8:30 a. m.—Dewey and his escort will reach the City Hall, where he will be met by the Mayor and the city's guests.

9:00 a. m.—A loving cup will be presented to Dewey by the Mayor on behalf of the city, and hundreds of school children will sing patriotic songs.

10:00 a. m.—Dewey and the city's guests will be driven to the Warren-st. pier, where they will board the Sandy Hook, which will land them at West One-hundred-and-twenty-ninth-st. Breakfast will be served on the boat.

11:00 a. m.—Dewey will take his place near the head of the parade line, which will start from One-hundred-and-twenty-second-st. and Riverside Drive, marching south.

2:00 p. m.—Parade is expected to reach Madison Square, where Dewey will review the column.

6:00 p. m.—Last of the line is expected to pass the reviewing stand.

7:00 p. m.—Dewey will dine with his relatives on shore.

8:00 p. m.—Performance of "The White Squadron" at the Metropolitan Opera House, for the benefit of the Dewey Home Fund.

8:30 p. m.—Smoker for the sailors of the Olympia at the Waldorf-Astoria.

ROUTE OF THE PARADE.

From One-hundred-and-twenty-second-st. and Riverside Drive, down the Drive to Seventy-second-st., east along Seventy-second-st. to Central Park West, down Central Park West to Fifty-ninth-st., east along Fifty-ninth-st. to Fifth-ave., down Fifth-ave. to Washington Square. Dewey will leave the line at Madison Square and review the parade, just before it passes under the triumphal arch.

A PAGEANT FOR DEWEY.

THE OLYMPIA LEADS A HOST TO HONOR THE ADMIRAL.

WARSHIPS, YACHTS AND ALL MANNER OF CRAFT FORM A LINE THAT EXTENDS FOR MILES—MAJESTIC COURSE FROM TOMPKINSVILLE TO GRANT'S TOMB.

Lo, the leader in these glorious wars,
. . . .
He on whom from both her open hands
Lavish Honor showered all her stars,
And affluent Fortune emptied all her horn!
Yea, let all good things await
Him who cares not to be great,
But as he saves, or serve, the State.

There is a new law for those Americans who have won great fights for their country abroad. When such a great warrior comes home he must go, with due attendance, to the north of the Island of Manhattan, and he must salute the great warrior who sleeps there. The great warrior who sleeps does not see him who has watched and waited and fought and kept the country safe, as he once watched and waited and fought and kept it; he does not hear his salute; he does not know that he is passing by. At least, the part of him that lies there does not see and hear and know. He does not answer the salute. But cannon voices answer for him. From the floating forts of iron upon the river and from the pile of granite upon the hill the deep throats of war shout the greetings of peace. When this is done the new conqueror may pass on his way and go where he will.

A year ago came two rear admirals—Sampson and Schley—from the battle where they had destroyed a hostile fleet, to salute the resting place of General Grant. An admiral came yesterday to do the same observance. He had come half way round the world, from where he had fought such a fight as never was fought before, and where he had upheld the dignity of the flag of the United States as it seldom was upheld before in a foreign land. He came endeared to his countrymen as no other man of the last quarter of a century has been. They have seen in him more than in any other the type of all that they should wish to see in themselves and in one another, the type of all that is fine and deep and true and brave in the American character.

And so the people of the United States waited for his homecoming with eagerness, that they might make him see how they valued his services in their behalf, and, far more, his strong and true and gallant and gracious character as their representative, before themselves and before the world. If the celebration of yesterday and to-day does not mean that, it is a mere gigantic picnic, and all the money that is spent on it is wasted.

LAST YEAR'S PAGEANT AND THIS YEAR'S.

Those who saw the water pageant of last year and the one of yesterday could scarcely fail to be impressed with one of the manifest differences between them. Last year seven warships—all the armored craft of the United States Navy—filed up the Bay and up the river before the multitudes gathered to greet them, and under all the rejoicing and through all the cheers there ran a feeling of deep awe, and there was a sense of the nearness of war, of destruction and of death that gave a solemnity to all the triumph. The ships looked like fierce dealers of justice and death, where justice should demand death. They were gray and dark. They had the scars of battle upon them. Their flags were battle flags. Where the water lapped away from their hulls the green weeds of the tropic seas were seen clinging; they had had no time to be spruce and dapper. They were working ships, fresh from rough work. All about them spoke of guardianship for their people and of destruction to their foes. And so when the people saw them they thought, even while they cheered, of the few dead of their own and of the many dead of the enemy.

But the ships of yesterday! Every one of them was gleaming white. In neatness, in beauty—as far as a warship can be beautiful, and that is sometimes pretty far—they were like rich men's yachts. There were the yachts of many rich men in the parade, but not one of them was better kept, better groomed, neater, trimmer, finer than the ships of the Navy, which were built not for pleasure but for giving and taking hard blows.

THE BIRTH OF THE NEW NAVY.

It is strange that foreigners should ever have sneered at the United States Navy. It is stranger that Americans should ever have distrusted it. Yet both these things happened. Many a man who threw up his cap yesterday in genuine enthusiasm for the Admiral dared only half believe, when he heard that he had sailed from Hong Kong, that he could overcome the Spanish ships at Manila. For years there was no American Navy, as far as ships were concerned. Then the Government awoke and saw that there should be one. The people knew that there were no modern warships, and so they thought that there was no Navy. They did not realize that a navy is made more of men than of ships, and that the men of the Navy, through all those piping times of peace, were as fine and true and thorough seamen and fighters (though they never fought) as ever stepped on a deck—or off one.

Then came the new ships; and what did an absurd Government do but paint them white. That ended their reputation before it ever began. "These warships?" cried the knowing ones. "They are yachts! They are pleasure craft for their officers, and the taxpayers have to support them." Thus will men with deep inner consciousness read the future by the shallowness of the present, instead of by the depth of the past. These poor, garrulous ones had never read history enough to know that in every American sea fight the Americans had made a gallant showing, and in almost every one they had con-

The 20th Century Newspaper

"An American paper for the American people." PHILIPPINES · HAWAII · PORTO RICO · CUBA

NEW YORK JOURNAL AND ADVERTISER

"WANT" TO FILL ALL WANTS IN TO-DAY'S JOURNAL. ADVTS.

NO. 6,338. SUNDAY—Cloudy. Copyright, 1900, By New York Journal and Advertiser.—NEW YORK, MARCH 25, 1900. SUNDAY—Cloudy. PRICE FIVE CENTS.

THE MAIN SHEET OF TO-DAY'S EDITION OF THE JOURNAL CONSISTS OF 24 PAGES.

MULTITUDE CHEERS AS THE MAYOR DIGS FIRST EARTH FOR TUNNEL. AN EPOCH OF CIVIC PROGRESS BEGINS--15 MINUTES TO HARLEM.

Speakers Declare That the Event Marks an Era of Municipal Ownership and the End of Letting Public Franchises Without Compensation to the City, and Pronounce for the Extension of the Subterranean System.

Bird's-eye View of the City Hall Park Just Before the Mayor and His Party Broke the Ground.

A HANDFUL of men stood yesterday in a little clear space surrounded by many tens of thousands of New Yorkers, and carried out a quiet little ceremony over what looked like the beginning of a grave.

The likeness to some quaint funeral was heightened when a man in a tall hat, the Mayor of New York, seized a spade and began to delve in the earth. In fact, it was a burial, but a joyous one, as the banners and the bands attested.

They were beginning the Rapid Transit Tunnel, called, contemptuously by the few who once opposed it, the "hole in the ground." In that hole were interred resistance to progress and the policy of gift franchises.

FOR THE BENEFIT OF THE PEOPLE.

If the city was committed to anything by the incident, it was committed to the doctrine that hereafter all profitable enterprise of a public nature shall be the city's undertaking for the benefit of its citizens. The speakers commented upon that as the leading thought in the orations that none of the thousands heard.

Silas B. Dutcher, the president of the Ramapo Water Company, who was one of the framers of the charter of the greater city, was within hearing when President Orr, of the Rapid Transit Board, said incisively and as deliberately as if he intended that man alone to hear it:

"Let us contrast for a moment the outcome of the tunnel contract with an estimated outcome of the lately proposed contract to provide New York with in increased water supply. New York (by the latter contract) would have paid during forty years to a private corporation that does not appear to own much more than a name, about two hundred million dollars and have nothing to show for it.

CITY WILL OWN THE PROPERTY.

"At the expiration of fifty years the city will own this tunnel railroad that will have cost $36,500,000, WITHOUT THE EXPENDITURE OF A SINGLE DOLLAR."

Ideas of this kind, vistas of real homes far from the crowded streets, brought within easy reach of the business quarter; pride in the fine city this is, and in the finer city that it is growing to be; a certain civic exulting hard to make words of, but defined in the thrill that familiar patriotic airs played by the bands produced, in the joyousness of the banners reflected in men's faces—these things held a great multitude of folk tightly against barriers of policemen through several hours of comfortless waiting and stretching of necks, able to see little and to hear nothing at all.

WILL BE READY IN FIVE YEARS.

The work on the tunnel itself will begin to-morrow. Within a few weeks it will be under way at a score of places along the well-known route. Within five years, it is expected, people will be using the tunnel.

The ceremony of yesterday was appropriately enough taken from an idea furnished by a Journal reader in response to the Journal's offer of a fifty dollar prize. Appropriately, because the

LONDON'S LORD MAYOR CONGRATULATES NEW YORK.

Copyrighted, 1900, by the New York Journal and Advertiser.

LONDON, March 24.—To the Editor of the New York Journal:

On behalf of the corporation of the imperial city of London I congratulate New York City on commencing the important work of an underground city railroad.

This system has proved of incalculable value to London, where important extensions are now being carried out.

ALFRED NEWTON,
Lord Mayor.

STATISTICS OF THE GREAT TUNNEL.

Length of all sections, feet	109,570	Local stations	43
Total excavation of earth, cubic yards.	1,700,228	Express stations	5
Earth to be filled back, cubic yards	773,093	Station elevators	10
Rock excavated, cubic yards	921,128	Track, total linear feet	305,380
Rock tunnelled, cubic yards	368,606	Track, underground, linear feet	245,514
Steel used in structure, tons	65,044	Track, elevated, linear feet	59,766
Cast iron used, tons	7,901	Contract cost	$35,000,000
Concrete, cubic yards	489,122	Number of men to be employed (estimated)	10,000
Brick, cubic yards	18.519	Time allowed for completion	3 years
Waterproofing, square yards	775,795	Duration of McDonald's contract	50 years
Vault lights, square yards	6,640		

TIME TABLE OF THE TUNNEL DAY CELEBRATION.

Mayor arrived at City Hall	10:45 a. m.
Workmen took up slab in pavement	11:45 a. m.
Procession formed in City Hall rotunda	1:05 p. m.
Procession moved down City Hall steps	1:18 p. m.
Mayor began his speech	1:21 p. m.
Commissioner Orr began speaking	1:32 p. m.
August Belmont handed silver spade to Mayor	1:45 p. m.
Ground was actually broken by Mayor	**1:48 p. m.**
Comptroller Coler began speaking	1:55 p. m.
Tablet was placed in position	2:15 p. m.
Mayor and party returned to City Hall	2:20 p. m.

ACTUAL WORK ON THE GREAT TRANSIT ROAD BEGINS TO-MORROW.
CEREMONY CARRIED OUT ACCORDING TO A JOURNAL PRIZE PLAN.

The Mayor Declares for More Tunnels.

In his address, before piercing the earth, he announced that the Rapid Transit system must be extended to unite all the boroughs, and declared that he engaged in the first rapid transit movement many years ago. The Mayor said that he was then very skeptical as to an ultimate realization of the plan.

First Spadeful Goes Into the Mayor's Hat.

Mr. Van Wyck took i' away for a souvenir in the only receptacle that was handy, even if it spoiled his brand new "tile." A man tried to grab a handful of the precious earth, but the Executive guarded it with jealous care. The other distinguished city officers present also followed Van Wyck's example. Later there was a crush on the part of the public to get some of the precious earth.

Orr Compares the Tunnel and Ramapo.

The President of the Rapid Tra nsit Board congratulated the citizens on an undertaking that will give them the railroad to Harlem without costing a dollar, whereas the defeated Ramapo grab would have cost $200,000,000 and given them nothing. Silas B. Dutcher, president of the Ramapo Company, was one of the throng that listened to him.

Contractor Pilkington Will Start Lowering the Bleecker Street Sewer at Once to Clear the Way for the Shaft.

fight for the rapid transit tunnel owned by the city for the citizens has been the Journal's fight for the people.

THOUSANDS SEE THE EARTH DUG UP.

A BROAD-SHOULDERED, overall-garbed man with a pick smote the concrete pavement of City Hall Park yesterday morning, and the work of digging the rapid transit tunnel that is to bring Harlem as near to Park place as Fourteenth street is now was begun.

There was no noise, music or speeches, except the remark of the foreman of the gang of laborers, who said after he had smitten:

"Here, now, get in there lively!"

The laborers fell to, and in a few minutes a quadrangle of cement had been raised from the pavement and the earth beneath had been loosened so as to be ready for the silver spade that was to do the official turning of the first earth.

"Your name, sir?" asked one who wished to preserve the identity of him who had started the greatest municipal work ever undertaken.

"Aw, gwan," said the foreman.

Construction of the great tunnel was begun officially with splendid pomp and exciting circumstance. In the presence of a throng as great as the total population of many cities which are considered metropoli Mayor Van Wyck plunged his gleaming spade deep into the soft earth and raised on high the first shovelful of soil of the thousands of tons that must be moved before New Yorkers are whirled underground from business to home.

Thirty Thousand Cheered.

A thin rain of earth ran over the shoulders of the argentine spade and trickled back to earth, while the bands flared forth "The Star-Spangled Banner" and thirty thousand men roared themselves hoarse as they cheered the ceremony that means so much to New York in particular and the whole civilized world in general, for the rapid transit tunnel is the city's own enterprise.

Around the Mayor were grouped the most prominent men of the city. Beyond them, and kept from overwhelming the official party with a tidal wave of enthusiasm, was a sea of people.

The Day Was Very Fine.

There never was a more beautiful day for an out-of-doors ceremony than yesterday. There was only a trace of Winter's cold left in the air and the sun stared down on flag-donned City Hall Park until it was as if roofed with rainbows. High above the fluttering frivolities of signal flags and bunting that had no meaning beyond brightness and color, the Stars and Stripes stood out in the sky immobile as steel.

Kites held these national flags up against the wind. The national flag, the State flag and the city flag floated from the three staffs of the City Hall, which was otherwise bedecked from dome to foundation with bannerets, standards and streamers.

Repeatedly the police cleared the thousands out of the park hours in advance of the ceremony, but when the time drew near the people were allowed to encroach until only the space immediately before the steps of the City Hall was clear for the active participants in the event.

Eight thousand invitations had been issued that gave admission to the park and none was wasted. Beyond the confines of the square there were unnumbered other thousands that packed the surrounding streets. Every window in the tall buildings that look down upon the square framed as many heads as could crowd into it.

City Hall Was Crowded.

Meanwhile inside the City Hall were crowded the Councilmen and Aldermen and other city officials, the dignitaries invited to take part and the wives and sisters of many of them. There were so many people that even inside the building lines of policemen were extended through the corridors to keep them open for the procession that was to issue from the Mayor's office. In his room the Mayor sat alone at his desk going on with his routine duties. Gradually a movement began to his office. Men passed by and shook his hand and congratulated him in regular order, and so began a remarkable reception, the more extraordinary as it was entirely impromptu.

MAYOR VAN WYCK AT HEAD OF PROCESSION.

AT last the procession started from the Mayor's office. The Chief Magistrate went ahead, attended by his messenger carrying the Mayor's official flag. Close behind him marched President Orr, of the Rapid Transit Commission, followed by John B. McDonald, the contractor, and August Belmont, president of the Subway Construction Company. Then came the presidents of the Council and the Board of Aldermen. The members of the Municipal Assembly fell in behind these, and the rest followed as they could. Proudest among the marchers was Councilman Wise, who carried the silver spade with which, in accordance with the happy suggestion of a Journal reader, the first earth was to be turned.

As the head of the procession passed out the door the band burst into the national anthem. The first sight of the Mayor started the huge crowd to cheering, and the sea of men and women swayed and weaved under the stress of the excitement. As the Mayor stepped out a phalanx of photographers started up and turned their batteries upon him. From various points came the rolling fire of cinematographs and biographs. The great ceremony is certainly adequately preserved in picture shape.

Quickly the official party grouped about the hole in the cement. Mr. Wise in a few words, which nobody a yard from him could hear in the turmoil of cheers, introduced the Mayor and presented to him the silver spade. The blade was bright as the sunlight it flashed back, and the handle was of precious wood, polished until its gleaming rivalled the blade, but it was a spade in size and shape; just such a spade as multiplied by thousands will cut the long tunnel below the city's streets.

The Mayor Speaks of Progress.

Then followed the Mayor's speech, breathing the spirit of the day and the deed. New York's chief magistrate is a reserved citizen on ordinary occasions, but there are some things that can rouse him, and this was one.

He was followed as a speaker by President Orr, who read a historical address detailing the story of the trials of the Rapid Transit Commission down to this, the successful culmination of its efforts.

After President Orr had spoken the Mayor raised the beautiful spade on high, where all could see it. The cheering began anew.

Reminiscence of the Mayor.

"About fifteen years ago," said the Mayor, "I was secretary of a Rapid Transit Railroad Committee, having for its object an underground railroad of which Dwight L. Olmstead was chairman. We held several meetings at the Murray Hill Hotel and invited contractors and capitalists to come before us and give their views on this very important subject. We met with great discouragement, and I was among those who felt that the project could not be carried out.

"I said to my old friend Senator Francis M. Bixby, who was a member of the committee, that I feared that there never would be an underground rapid transit railroad in New York.

"He said, 'yes, there would be;' that I would live to see its completion. If I had thought of this incident before I came out here I would certainly have had ex-Senator Bixby here at my side to-day. So you see it is possible for a loyal friend sometimes even temporarily to forget a friend on an occasion like this.

"I little thought in those days that I would be standing here to-day engaged in this interesting ceremony, and you have no idea of the great pleasure this event gives to the members of the Rapid Transit Railroad Commission and to myself. To the toiling masses of this city this day is of great import and meaning. It means to them very much indeed, and I now will begin the work by turning the first shovelful of soil, and then the construction of the underground rapid transit railroad tunnel will be under way."

First Spadeful Is Raised.

With that the Mayor stepped into the depression. The bright silver spade kissed the yellow dirt. The Mayor's foot pressed it home. He raised it—a good shovelful and the dull yellow of it set the crowd wild. Bombs and rockets burst from the roofs of the tall buildings and a tremendous cheer went up.

Men looked at their watches to note the moment. It was, to be exact, 1:48.

The Mayor let half the shovelful trickle back to earth; then he looked for a receptacle for the rest. Nothing had been provided, so the Mayor of Greater New York set his high hat on the pavement and, as carefully as if the shovel held gold dust instead of common earth, he poured the soil into it, and then gathered up his hat and held it to his side.

President Orr took the next trick at the spade. He did double duty and passed it on to Contractor McDonald. There was nothing finicky about the shovelful McDonald gouged from the earth. August Belmont spaded up a spoonful, and then the Rapid Transit Commissioners, the Aldermen and Councilmen all had a turn.

Much Applause for Coler.

Comptroller Coler's speech closed the ceremonies. He made himself heard further than the others, and the people cheered the official in proportion to the regard in which he is held.

The Mayor and his party started back into the building, and then came the most characteristic episode of the day—the scramble for a few grains of the earth for reliquary purposes.

Hawkers appeared everywhere through the crowd offering small packages of earth for 10 cents a package, but the people wanted no false earth. The police had hard work preventing a disaster, so great was the pressure of those who wanted a crumb of ground.

Reception Ends the Occasion.

An informal reception closed the official day—a day of graver meaning, greater promise, deeper import, than even the cheering crowd that made City Hall Park a solid mass of humanity fully realized.

MAYOR POINTS PROUDLY TO IT.

MAYOR VAN WYCK began the speech-making, referring with pride to the city's greatness and with enthusiasm to the magnitude of the work begun and its far-reaching effect. He said in part:

"No Roman citizen ever entertained a keener pride in the glory of that imperial city than does the New Yorker in the fame of his home city. The foundation of her structure is too solid to be shaken by the unjust attacks of the misinformed stranger or the misguided son. The people can ever be relied upon to resist both.

"The Erie Canal made our city the commercial and financial metropolis of the world, with a population of three and a half millions of people, for whose accommodation and comfort this rapid transit underground road is necessary. The contrast exhibited between the two periods is striking and instructive. De Witt Clinton saluted in 1825 a city of one hundred and sixty thousand souls. We speak to a population of three and a half millions. Then the slow stage coach was the only means of passenger transportation, now superseded by steam and electricity.

"The people of Greater New York are to be congratulated that, with all of her former heavy expenditures, and, at times, somewhat reckless issuance of bonds, she is now, for the first time, able to undertake such an expensive enterprise which will furnish the first real test of the experiment of municipal ownership of public utilities on such a scale as will be decisive of that principle."

ORR'S IDEAL OF RAPID TRANSIT.

PRESIDENT ALEXANDER E. ORR, of the Board of Rapid Transit Railroad Commissioners, reviewed the work culminating in the ceremony of the hour. He stated a definite ideal of rapid transit, of which the tunnel is the beginning:

"A system of economical passenger transportation from all sections of the city that will continuously meet the requirements of our continually increasing needs."

Mr. Orr also contrasted effectively the contract framed by the Board for this work with the Ramapo water contract. He said:

"The removal of the spadeful of earth by our respected Mayor, which, according to the programme, we are soon to witness, will be the inauguration of a system of municipal transit which, if courageously carried out, will continue to stimulate our marvellous development and knit together all the sections of this great city in fact, as they have been lately united in name.

What Rapid Transit Is.

"Rapid transit for New York, briefly stated, is this: A system of economical passenger transportation from all sections of the city that will continuously meet the requirements of our continually increasing needs; and this, we claim, will be assured by an intelligent development of the tunnel system inaugurated here to-day."

Mr. Orr reviewed the progress of city transportation from "Shank's mare" to omnibus, horse car and elevated railroad, and to the realization of the approaching need of better facilities, which led to the Rapid Transit act of 1891, which named the first Commission.

Dwelling briefly upon the failure of private capital to adopt the first plans, Mr. Orr told of the next move, the popular vote in 1894, authorizing municipal construction at public expense, and outlined the law under which the road is to be built.

The Benefits Are Obvious.

"The benefits of this Rapid Transit law to both the city and the lessee are obvious. They are just and protective to the former, and at the same time generous and economical to the latter, and very creditable to all who were concerned in their enactment.

"But to illustrate more fully the advantages to the city, let us contrast for a moment the outcome of this tunnel contract with an estimated outcome of the lately proposed contract to provide New York with an increased water supply. In the latter case, if the proposition had been accepted (and it is likely it would have been had not the watchful and intelligent supervision of the financial office of the city exposed its disadvantages), New York would have paid during the sixty years of contract duration to a private corporation which at the present times does not appear to own much more than its name an estimated rent of two hundred millions of dollars and have nothing whatever on hand to show as an asset for that enormous expenditure.

"In the former case, at the expiration of a shorter period (fifty years), the city will own this tunnel railroad that will have cost $36,500,000, and which is the key to the rapid transit situation, without the expenditure of a single dollar for construction or interest, it having simply used its credit under carefully guarded guarantees for the time being in the advanatge of the lessee, who meanwhile pays the interest as it falls due and provides for the liquidation of the bonds at the expiration of his lease.

Her Rights Must Increase.

"And there is a lesson to be learned from this which we will do well to contemplate. If New York is to possess in the future the magnificent proportions her past history warrants us to expect, her municipal rights and franchise privileges must also increase in value in like degree. It is our bounden duty, therefore, to guard with jealous care those that yet remain to us and hold them in such control that they will never pass from us in perpetuity, as has been too often the case heretofore, but only farmed out for fixed periods of tenure, so that from time to time the city may enjoy a fair proportion of the increased values which it lrealy creates."

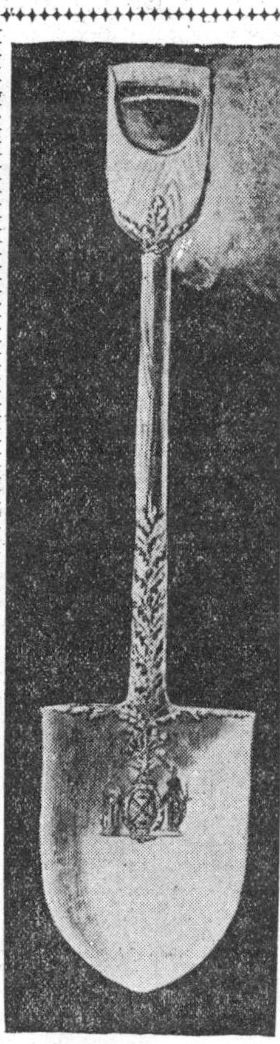

This Is the Spade That Did It.

The handle is made of wood from one of Alexander Hamilton's trees and from Commodore Perry's flagship. The blade, of silver, bears an inscription and the arms of the city and State.

Winner of the Journal's $50 Prize.

S. J. Flanagan suggested the plan of ceremonies followed by the Municipal Assembly's committee which arranged it.

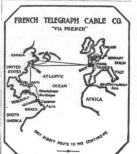

COLER SEES A NEW ERA.

Comptrolle rColer spoke with serious emphasis of the policy of holding municipal ownership of profitable public enterprises for the benefit of the city. He said:

"We celebrate to-day something more than the mere incident of breaking ground for a great public improvement. We celebrate by this ceremony the inauguration of a new and important policy in city government—the policy of municipal ownership and control of great public franchises and utilities. I earnestly hope the memorial tablet to be here placed commemorates not only the commencement of a great and beneficent public enterprise, but marks as surely the end of reckless extravagance in giving valuable privileges to private corporations, instead of making them permanent sources of income to the municipality, as this Rapid Transit road will surely prove.

Beginning of a Vast City.

"We are paying now almost $15,000,000 a year for legislative consolidation, or, in other words, for the sentiment that demanded a city great in wealth, in area and population. The building of this railroad will be the beginning of a vast system of rapid transit that in a few years will extend to every borough and every section, thereby creating a Greater New York in fact as well as in name.

"The practical solution of this rapid transit problem is an object lesson to that fast growing number who are interested in the great question of municipal ownership, and will go far to strengthen their faith in its ultimate triumph."

FIRST WORK ON A SEWER.

THE first real work to be done is the lowering of the Bleecker street sewer from Greene to Elm street to get it out of the way of the tunnel. James Pilkington, the only sub-contractor named as yet by Contractor McDonald, will start in on this job bright and early to-morrow morning.

He will dig the first hole at Greene street. The sewer west of Elm to Greene flows into the East River. He will make it flow westward. There are 900 lineal feet of sewer, the grade of which will be altered. It will cost about $15 a foot to do this, or $14,000 in all.

Mr. Pilkington expects to do a large share of the vast business of moving existing subterranean pipes and conduits out of the railroad's right of way.

Chief Engineer Parsons said yesterday that a large number of contractors were at work on estimates to be furnished Mr. McDonald, but that the latter had not closed with any of them yet. Forty-second street will be opened among the first, according to the chief engineer.

HERE IS REAL SPEED AT LAST.

HERE is the time table for express trains that has been figured out for the tunnel:

Stations.	Minutes.
City Hall	—
Fourteenth street	4
Forty-second street	6
Seventy-second street	9
Ninety-sixth street	12
One Hundred and Sixteenth st.	15

List of the Stations.

The list of stations on the underground road is to be as follows:

Barclay st. and Broadway.	137th st. and Boulevard.
Chambers and Centre sts.	145th st. and Boulevard.
Worth and Elm sts.	153d st. and Boulevard.
Canal and Elm sts.	157th st. and Boulevard.
Spring and Elm sts.	169th st. and Boulevard.
Bleecker and Elm sts.	181st st. and Boulevard.
Astor place.	Dyckman st.
14th st. and 4th ave.	215th st and Boulevard.
18th st and 4th ave.	Canal.
23d st. and 4th ave.	Bailey ave.
28th st. and 4th ave.	110th st. and Lenox ave.
33d st. and Park ave.	116th st. and Lenox ave.
42d st. and Madison ave.	125th st. and Lenox ave.
42d st. and Broadway.	135th st. and Lenox ave.
50th st. and Broadway.	141st st. and Lenox ave.
59th st. and Boulevard.	Mott ave.
66th st. and Boulevard.	Melrose and N. 3d aves.
71st st. and Boulevard.	Jackson and Westchester aves.
79th st. and Boulevard.	Prospect and Westchester aves.
86th st. and Boulevard.	Southern Boulevard and Westchester ave.
91st st. and Boulevard.	Jennings place.
96th st. and Boulevard.	177th st. and Boston road
103d st. and Boulevard.	Bronx Park.
110th st. and Boulevard.	
116th st. and Boulevard.	
Manhattan st. & Boulevard	

PRAISE FOR THE JOURNAL.

THE breaking of ground for the tunnel signalized a notable victory in the Journal's fight for municipal ownership of public franchises. It was recalled by many of those who took a prominent part in yesterday's ceremonies that the Journal was the original advocate of the construction of the underground rapid transit road by the city.

On April 19, 1899, the Journal offered to head a popular bond subscription to build the underground road with the sum of $5,000,000. The Journal's plan as set forth at that time was as follows:

"The Journal demands that the city lay aside $10,000,000 a year out of its revenues to build the rapid transit system, or else issue bonds sufficient to build the system. In the latter case the Journal will itself subscribe to $5,000,000 of the bonds and guarantee to float the remainder by popular subscription. In any case, the rapid transit system must be built and owned by the city."

Orr, Coler, McDonald, August Belmont and Many Public Officials Wielded the Spade for Glory's Sake After the Mayor.

Victory for the Public.

Yesterday's celebration was, in its most significant feature, the victory of municipal ownership and control of public franchises, which cause the Journal has championed from the beginning.

"The Journal deserves the thanks of all citizens for its efforts," said Corporation Counsel John Whalen. "I have always believed that the city should control its public utilities, and with the construction of the rapid transit tunnel we are taking a big step in that direction. By utilizing the tunnel for a telegraph, telephone and electric lighting system of its own we will have the beginnings of municipal ownership of a lighting plant."

"The press, and especially the Journal, has taken the right stand on the municipal ownership question," said Comptroller Coler, "and certainly deserves its share of the credit for the victory that we celebrate to-day."

Alderman Muh, chairman of the Tunnel Celebration Committee, said: "I believe in the Journal. I have been with it right along in its fight for municipal ownership, and the paper ought to get credit for its share in the victory now."

Commendation by Mr. Orr.

"I think the press of the city, and the Journal in particular, deserves the appreciative commendation of all true citizens for the stand taken in the fight for rapid transit," said Alexander E. Orr, president of the Rapid Transit Commission. "I hope that with this example before us we will hereafter reserve to ourselves the control of what is left of our valuable municipal franchises."

"The Journal's public spirit is deserving of sincere commendation," said Councilman Wise, chairman of the Committee on Celebration.

$50 BROUGHT OUT THE IDEA.

The Journal offers a prize of $50 for the best suggestion of a programme of ceremonies to mark the beginning of the construction of the underground system of rapid transit. The competition is open to all, and the suggestions will be submitted to the officials in charge for decision. . . . What programme for the ceremony is best suited to mark the beginning of the greatest public work ever undertaken for a municipality? Send in your suggestion.—From the Journal of January 19, 1900.

It was the suggestion of a Journal reader that was used at the ceremonies of breaking ground for the tunnel yesterday.

The winner of the Journal prize was Stephen J. Flanagan, of No. 1237 Broadway. His suggestion was contained in the following letter:

New York, Jan. 18, 1900.

W. R. Hearst, Esq.:

Dear Sir—In regard to rapid transit, I suggest that the Mayor take out the first shovelful of earth and that the shovel be made of silver, the shovel to be kept in City Hall afterward. That Mr. Coler make the principal address. That there should be present all who are connected with its building, as near as possible. That the Council and Aldermen be present. Yours, with gratitude,

STEPHEN J. FLANAGAN,
1237 Broadway, New York.

HUMORS OF THE TUNNEL DAY.

Such flags were never seen before. The genius who designed them surely had nights of fitful dreams.

"I have seen mornings when I would not care to look at some of them," one man remarked. A discussion followed in a little group near the fountain. Nobody could find the flag of a single nation. One man saw a cross of white on a black background, and said: "There is the Jolly Roger, sure enough. Maybe it was sent by the gamblers as a compliment to the Police Department."

Another saw the five of clubs on a white background. "Yes," he said, "there is the coat-of-arms from the Tenderloin. I wonder if it is marked."

It was a proud day for Captain Chapman. There were policemen galore, indeed, at one time there were more policemen than spectators, but in it and everywhere was Chapman. From the unknown wilds of Mercer street he had come forth to enjoy his former glory for the moment. His whiskers wafted high in the breeze, the white silk cord of his club dangled gracefully at his side. The cry "There's Chapman, the ex-czar of the Tenderloin," was always followed by a pleasant smile amid the parting of the whiskers.

"There's the fellow that raided the couchee-couchee dinner," said one of a crowd, and all eyes were turned in his direction.

"They all seem to know me," the captain remarked.

The small boy from the East Side is a condensed encyclopedia on names of police officers. In fact the ceremonies of a great public occasion are of much less interest to him than the appearance of the finest. He stands with his friends and points first to one and then the other, calling the names and enjoying the wonder and admiration of his friends.

"Deres Chapman, deres Delaney, deres Thomas, deres Cortright, an' deres Ayers, an'"—a boy was calling to a group of youngsters.

"Who's Ayers," another boy asked.

"Why, he's de cop on Cherry street."

"An' do yer know dat's Ayers?"

"Sure. Aint he de cop dat pinched me brudder John for trowin a ball in de street las' spring?" returned the first boy with a glow of pride.

It was an eventful day for "Weary Watkins." His place on a park bench became a reserved seat for once. He was fairly an object of selfish interest. While others were craning their necks for a view of the show, the author of a monograph on "dimes, and how to get them," had an eye to business. Every seat held a bloated tramp when the crowd poured into the park.

"A reserved seat for a dime," cried Weary Watkins."

Ten customers ran for the seat, and the first cousin of Weary Watkins stood on his seat and cried:

"A good reserved seat for a quarter."

"It's a poor tunnel that don't carry a good draught," said the first cousin as he walked away with the price of a night's lodging.

A woman, once determined, is a problem for the police. It isn't quite gallant to swing a club over her back, and it isn't altogether pleasant to be the object of interest in a hair pulling match. This woman was certain that she had rights, and she meant to assert them. Three times she broke through the police lines and each time was dragged back with a little more force. Finally the officer said impatiently:

"Now if you come through this line again I will lock you up."

The woman's voice fairly drowned the band. "You will lock me up, will you. You lay a hand on me, you nasty, blue coated wretch, and I'll bite your nose off."

Then two policemen came and escorted the angry woman away from the crowd and told her to depart in peace.

The venders of souvenirs were not overlooking stray wagers. They were on hand to supply our cousins from Connecticut and New Jersey.

"An exact imitation of the spade used by Mayor Van Wyck, made out of solid silver, and all for five cents," was the cry."

"For land's sake, how can ye do it," an old woman stopped to inquire.

"Why, madam," said the affable salesman. "The adoption of the gold standard a few weeks ago by Congress was followed by a great drop in silver. With my large resources I was enabled to take advantage of the market. Take one as a double souvenir of this occasion and the adoption of the gold standard law."

Vol. XLIV. No. 2272

HARPER'S WEEKLY

July 7 1900

CONTENTS

THE HARLEM RIVER SPEEDWAY, NEW YORK CITY

A GAME OF "DROP DEAD" IN THE JEWISH QUARTER.

THE LEMONADE VENDER AND HIS CUSTOMERS.

NINETY-THREE IN THE SHADE IN CHERRY-ST.

CHUMS.

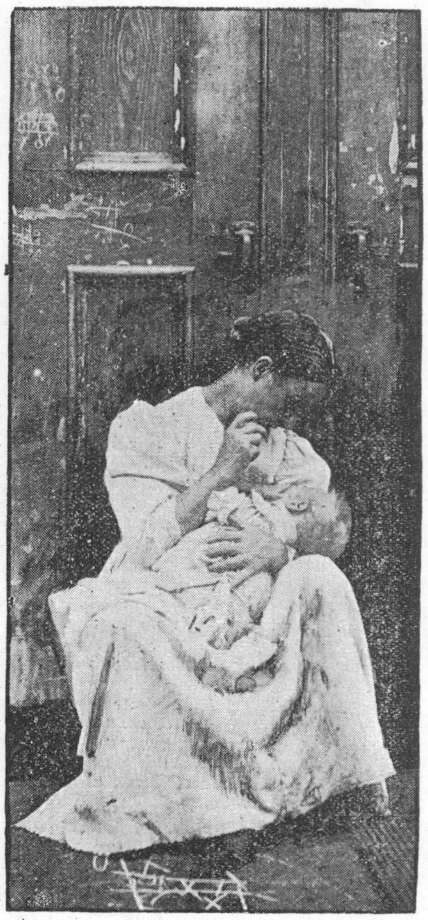

THE SICK CHILD.

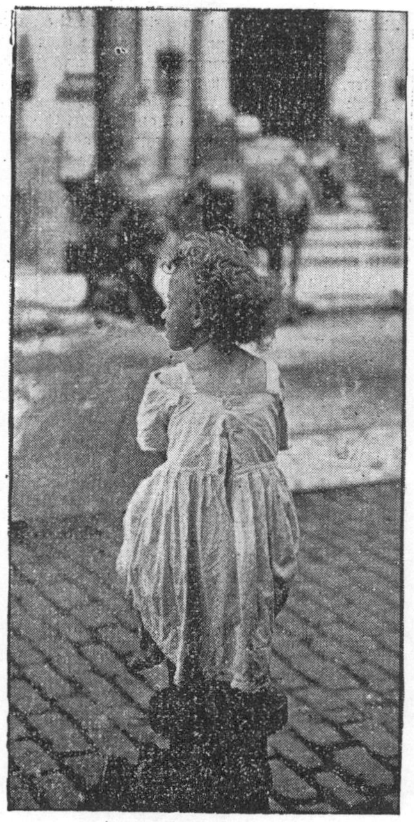

WAITING FOR A BREEZE.

LITTLE MOTHERS IN ISRAEL.

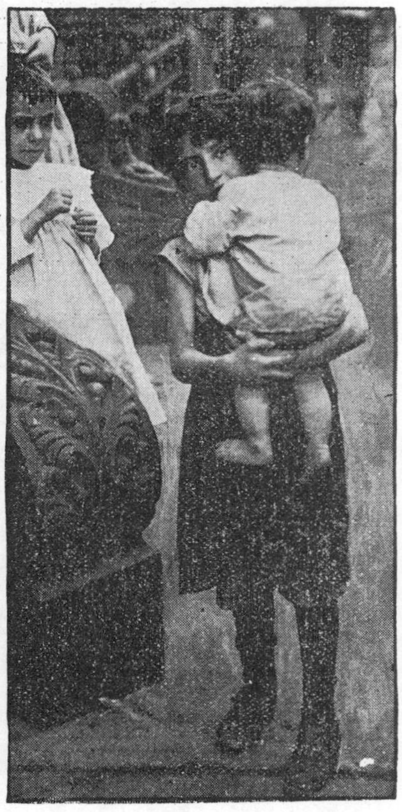

BABY AND HIS NURSE.

THE TENEMENT CHILD IN THE CITY.

THE STREET MERCHANTS.

SOME OF THEM ARE WELL TO DO, THOUGH THEY DRESS SHABBILY FOR EFFECT.

A day with the street merchants of New-York, sometimes inappropriately designated as fakirs, is interesting. Some of these merchants of the highways are rich, some are clever, a few are honest and many are neither conscientious nor cleanly. Among the thousands there are a few odd characters who are so well known as a result of having long frequented the same public places that they are pointed out as interesting figures in the daily grind of business. A few are proud of the success they have achieved, but the great majority appear to be just sufficiently ashamed of their calling to shrink from unnecessary publicity. Some of the wealthier appear to lead double lives. Their families are comfortably housed, and they affiliate socially with people who would hesitate to address them on the corners where they push their business enterprises. Others simply eke out a miserable existence by their vocations, and have few friends even in the poor sections of the city where they live. But few, if any, are American born, and Greeks, Polish Jews and Italians constitute the majority. There are some Irishmen, but the proportion of that nationality is small.

AT HIS FATHER'S STAND.

Maurice Kaufman sells men's garters, sleeve elastics, cuff retainers and necktie fasteners, from the areaway of the Park National Bank, near Fulton-st. His father had been there over twenty-five years when he died last February, and had amassed a comfortable fortune during that time. Maurice, who is twenty-five years old, dresses well, is at the old stand by the bank entrance early and late, and has a thriving trade. His father was the owner of tho patents for the garter he always sold, and had by his own genius greatly improved the invention.

A dealer in periodicals, whose trade is extensive and who has been at his present stand many years, and a seller of badges conduct their business between the Kaufman stand and the entrance to the St. Paul Building. The badge seller prepared for a big day's business last October, during the Sound Money parade. When it began to rain, about 8 o'clock in the morning, he hoisted an umbrella and called attention to the fact that his McKinley and Roosevelt buttons were waterproof. He sold out before the parade started.

One door below the garter man is a man of perhaps sixty, neatly dressed and apparently prosperous, who sells nothing but small metal chicks with a bulb and hose attachment, by which the diminutive creature, intended as a lapel ornament, is made to chirp lustily. His cheerful smile is a powerful magnet to attract attention to his wares, and he sells them at the rate of a hundred or so a day.

"MOTHER" IS BLIND.

The blind pencil merchant of the Equitable Building is an interesting woman. She is neatly but plainly clad, and sits in her place against the wall day after day waiting for customers. She never speaks to anybody unless addressed, and greatly dislikes to have a crowd collect about her. She is known to other street merchants near by merely as "Mother," and likes to be so addressed.

There is a vender of mechanical toys who frequents lower Broadway who is something more than interesting. He is unique. He may be fifty and he may be twenty years older.

"My wife and children," said he in fair English the other day, "are dressed as well as anybody's and are looked up to. I am, too, when I'm at home, but it wouldn't pay to dress well for my business. When my friends happen along where I'm selling toys, I don't know them, and they don't know me. I'm an American, if I was born in Europe, and I've made enough in thirty years to live like an American, but in business I'm still a Jew."

The Greek flower merchant is young and his style of beauty is Grecian, if not classic. He dresses well, and his stand at No. 34 East Fourteenth-st. is a model of neatness. His name is Christos Keama, and he is a diplomat. He drives a thriving trade with the women who throng the thoroughfare, and rarely fails of a sale to anybody who stops to admire his flowers.

"DIRTY SHOESTRINGS."

There is in Sixth-ave. a swarthy, not too clean fellow who sells shoelaces, and who is known to the frequenters of the locality only as "Dirty Shoestrings." An angry man the other day accosted him with: "Those shoestrings are rotten! They're not worth taking home! You ought to be arrested for fraud!"

"Buy my shoestring—no rot," said the pedler, placidly.

"I bought yours. That's what I'm talking about!" cried the irate man.

"Me no sell rot shoestring," said "Dirty" calmly. "Buy my shoestring—no rot." The argument continued about three minutes, but "Dirty's" position was the same at its end, when his former customer rushed off to escape an apoplectic fit.

What induces Karl, the pretzel pedler, to frequent the shopping district in Fourteenth-st. is apparently an unfathomable mystery. Nobody has ever seen him sell anything, as far as can be learned, and of all the people in New-York none seems less likely to buy pretzels than the shoppers in that street. The Park Row newsboys have a great fondness for pretzels, and business is good in the upper end of Frankfort-st., but Fourteenth-st. is different; yet Karl, who is a Greek, is to be found there always. Both he and his outfit are ill adapted to make one feel hungry.

The two-foot rule man and the needle threading thimble man, formerly of the sidewalk near the Western Union Telegraph Building, are there no more. The rule man is further down the street and on the opposite side. He seemed gloomy the other day. He simply held up a handful of rules to invite trade. He formerly loquaciously guaranteed every foot of rule he sold to contain twelve good and lawful inches and offered a large reward for every inch of shortage. He said the business had played out and that people didn't seem to care how long anything was any more. "They've quit measuring, apparently, for I don't sell one rule where I used to sell twenty," said he. "I don't believe people care for rules any more—not even the Golden Rule!"

HE DIED FROM NATURAL CAUSES.

REPORT IN THE CASE OF WERKERLE, WHO WAS TAKEN FROM BELLEVUE WITH BRUISES.

Coroner's Physician Williams yesterday made a report from an autopsy he had made on the body of Adolph Werkerle, of No. 29 [illegible]-st. On June 30 Werkerle was sent from Bellevue insane pavilion to the Manhattan State Hospital. It was found that there were bruises on Werkerle's body. The Manhattan State Hospital authorities got a signed statement from the Bellevue Hospital authorities acknowledging the presence of bruises.

On July 1 Werkerle died. Just previously he had developed a high temperature, complained of abdominal pain and vomited blood. The body was taken to the morgue. No certificate as to the cause of death was given by the Manhattan State Hospital authorities. They said, however, that the man had suffered from acute mania and exhaustion.

Dr. Williams said this afternoon that the autopsy showed conclusively that Werkerle died from natural causes.

SEVEN HORSES SUFFOCATED.

ANOTHER WILL PROBABLY DIE AS THE RESULT OF A BASEMENT FIRE.

Seven horses were suffocated early yesterday morning in a fire which burned out the first floor of the three story brick building No. 66 Clinton-st. Bloomburg & Hottzman occupied the first and second stories and the basement. Eleven horses belonging to East Side pedlers were in the basement. Joseph Pollak, the night watchman, was asleep in a wagon on the first floor at 1:30 o'clock when he was awakened by the kicking of the horses. The building was full of smoke. The firemen had great difficulty in getting at the fire.

When they were able to enter the building they found four of the eleven horses alive and led them to the street. One of the horses was badly burned about the head and will probably have to be shot.

INFRINGEMENT OF PATENT ALLEGED.

A bill of complaint was filed in the United States Circuit Court yesterday by Gifford & Bell, attorneys, of No. 141 Broadway, in behalf of the Westinghouse Electric and Manufacturing Company, against the Lorain Steel Company and H. C. Evans, its agent in this city. The court is asked to issue an injunction restraining the defendants from continuing to manufacture dynamo electric machines invented by Norman W. Storer in 1892, the patents for which, it is declared, were assigned to the Westinghouse Company in 1896. It is also asked that an accounting be had to compel the defendants to pay to the Westinghouse company the amount of loss sustained by them through the sale of the machines.

TO VISIT BUFFALO.

Companies B and I, of the 7th Regiment, have decided to visit the Pan-American Exposition. They will leave the city on Saturday, August 31, and return on the morning of September 3. An election has been ordered in Company H for a second lieutenant, vice Joscelyn, promoted to the first lieutenancy. The only candidate, it is expected, will be First Sergeant William B. Miles.

TYPES OF STREET MERCHANTS.

KARL, THE PRETZEL PEDLER.

KEAMA, A GREEK FLOWER SELLER.

VENDER OF MECHANICAL TOYS.

"DIRTY SHOESTRINGS."

THE SURRENDER OF ISIDRA TORRES.

AN INSURGENT LEADER WHO HAD DONE MUCH DAMAGE GIVES UP WHEN FUNSTON GETS ON HIS TRACK.

Washington, July 6 (Special).—As soon as General Funston had delivered Aguinaldo at Manila and was refreshed with a week's rest he went up into the north a little way, in Bulacan Province, and by his infectious enthusiasm stirred up his subordinates, with the result of securing the surrender of Isidra Torres.

Bulacan is one of the smallest but richest provinces in the archipelago, with extensive plantations of sugar, cacao, rice, and indigo; many mills and manufactories, iron mines, stone and alabaster quarries, gold washings and other varied industries, but for nearly two years Torres had kept its "pacificos" in constant terror and paralyzed its highly productive resources, besides furnishing no end of excitement and chagrin for the American troops of occupation. General Grant had repeatedly endeavored to apprehend him, and last September had succeeded in effecting the surrender of most of his force at San José, after a memorable and relentless "hike," but Torres easily eluded the trap. When Funston came on the scene, two months ago, Torres was as defiant as ever, but, on account of the lack of men, was not inflicting as much damage as he did earlier. Nor was he finding resistance to the Americans quite as profitable as it had been. Perhaps the fame of Funston's exploit of the month before impressed him with the probable futility of hoping to dodge the Kansas leader indefinitely, for at the end of April General MacArthur received this telegram from General Wheaton, commanding the Department of Northern Luzon:

Following from General Funston to-day: "The insurgent Isidra Torres presented himself to Captain McRae at Norzagaray, with six men and one rifle. This is the result of Captain McRae's activity and the thrashing administered to a part of Torres's outfit yesterday. Torres will be held a prisoner until instructions to release him are received from your headquarters. In view of the fact that he did not give himself up until he was afraid of being caught or killed, I recommend that he be held until an investigation of some of the atrocities supposed to have been committed by his orders can be made. The wife and brother of the insurgent lieutenant who guided Captain McRae on his expedition have been kidnapped, and Torres admits that he knew about it. Torres states that Morales, with all that is left of his force, will surrender at Malabon in a few days. Much credit is due to McRae for his activity and good judgment in the recent operations. FUNSTON."

ISIDRA TORRES.
Filipino general who surrendered when Funston got after him.

Captain James H. McRae, 3d Infantry, is a Georgian who was graduated from West Point in 1882 and who has been in most of the hard campaigning since the spring of 1898 without a volunteer commission. The War Department has not been informed as to the disposition made of Torres.

THE WONDERFUL MADGE.

A SCOTTISH BUILT YACHT THAT WON MANY VICTORIES NOW GOING TO PIECES ON ONTARIO'S SHORE.

Rochester, N. Y., July 6.—Twenty years ago a Scottish built yacht lit up the racing heavens of two hemispheres like a comet. Victory after victory followed in her wake, until no one could be persuaded to compete against her. One of the most famous yacht builders who ever lived admitted that he had designed six yachts to beat her, and the sixth crossed the line as far astern as the first. Racing men will nod their heads knowingly when they hear her name. It was the Madge.

To-day she lies rotting on the banks of the Genesee River at Charlotte. Her story reads like a romance and possesses an interest that is almost human in its pathos.

The Madge was a forty-six foot cutter. Watson designed her and has since said that her equal he expects never again to see. It is doubtful, of course, that she could stand much of a show against the modern racing machines whose masts buckle in heavy weather, but in her day, and judged from the point of view of those times, she was probably no less than her designer asserted her to be.

Watson built the Madge for Coats, the English thread maker. She was delivered in 1878 and at once began her career of victory. She was 46 feet 1 inch over all, 7 feet 10 inches in the beam and drew in salt water 8 feet. She was of the pure keel cutter type. Watson put into her the best that he had, for to-day her frame timbers are as firm and solid as the hour she slipped into the water.

For two years the Madge cut a wide swath in English and Continental waters. At last, like Alexander, she could have wept for others to conquer. Her owner thereupon sent her across to Auchincloss Brothers, his agents in New-York. She arrived in 1880. That summer she began a cisatlantic career around New-York which kept the world talking. The older yachtsmen will remember her. For two years she won race after race. Once only was she beaten. The Shadow, a Boston yacht, did the trick. The Madge lost her spreader and topmast, and even thus disabled trailed in only twenty minutes behind her rival.

The Madge's New-York owners decided to buy the America's Cup defender, the Mischief, in 1882, and therefore had no further use for the faithful Madge. The Madge was not in that class, but some think she could have taught the big raters a trick or two at their own game.

The fresh water career of the Madge began when the Mischief was built. Captain George P. Goulding, of Charlotte, purchased her. She never felt the ocean again. With her Captain Goulding in two years won thirteen prizes and beat every boat which raced with her.

In 1884 Fife designed the Yama for an Oswego man. He came to America to see that his craft behaved herself properly. It was then he confessed that he had built six boats for the express purpose of beating the Madge, and failed to achieve his object.

The same fate that pursued the Madge in England followed her here. Captain Goulding could find no one to race with. He offered to sell the famous yacht to Rochester yachtsmen for one-third of what he paid for her. They declined, and the captain ran her on the river bank, where she has been lying for eleven years, a useless hulk. A painter is now sketching her hull just as she lies. The picture will be sent to England, where her fame is yet green.

Her mast stands on the lawn of Æmilius Jarvis, of Toronto, Canada. Her spars are in use on his yacht, the Merrythought. Jarvis purchased them for $25 when he brought the Minota over to race against the Genesee for the Fisher Cup last fall. He said they were precious mementoes of the most remarkable yacht for her inches that was ever built.

A HAPPY OMEN.

ALLIANCE BETWEEN CHURCH AND STAGE MAKING PROGRESS.

The alliance between the Church and the Stage is, obviously, making progress, Mrs. Cora Urquhart Potter having become so far mollified toward the ecclesiastical establishment that she actually stood up, in the church, at Gorleston, Suffolk, England, on June 29, and recited "Vital Spark of Heavenly Flame"! Not very long ago the Heavenly Flame of this remarkable performer was, it will be remembered, directed against the venerable Bishop of New-York, whom she designated, in print, as "all fuss and feathers." Her present gravitation toward a more Christian frame of mind relieves the tension, and is, at least, auspicious. It is not every day that the Church is favored to this extent and in this manner. The effect was prodigious,—"the congregation listening reverently"; the Vicar ("whose idea was to enhance the attractions of the service"), being so profoundly moved that he rushed home to write a play for Mrs. Potter's use, and the Bishop of the diocese making haste to "forbid a repetition of the incident"—in order, probably, to head off Mrs. Langtry, Mrs. Patrick Campbell, Miss Olga Nethersole, and Miss Sadie Martinot, and thus to spare the public heart from too great a strain of religious ecstasy. The poem that Sister Potter recited, on this holy occasion, is Pope's well-known and justly celebrated imitation of the Emperor Hadrian's apostrophe to his parting soul,—the mellifluous "Animula, blandula, vagula,"—and edifying indeed must have been the spectacle that this new style of pulpit performer presented when reciting it:

I.

Vital spark of heavenly flame
Quit, oh quit this mortal frame!
Trembling, hoping, ling'ring, flying,
Oh, the pain, the bliss of dying!
Cease, fond Nature, cease thy strife,
And let me languish into life!

II.

Hark! they whisper; angels say,
Sister spirit, come away!
What is this absorbs me quite,
Steals my senses, shuts my sight,
Drowns my spirit, draws my breath?
Tell me, my soul, can this be Death?

III.

The world recedes; it disappears;
Heav'n opens on my eyes; my ears
With sounds seraphic ring.
Lend, lend your wings! I mount! I fly!
O Grave, where is thy victory?
O Death, where is thy sting?

NOTES OF THE STAGE.

Francis Wilson in "The Strollers" at the Knickerbocker Theatre is drawing good audiences despite the hot weather. Into the last act have been introduced new spectacular effects.

"Florodora" enters on the thirty-fourth week of its run at the Casino to-morrow night. In the excessive heat which prevailed throughout last week the audiences continued good.

"Lend Me Your Wife" is the chief production this week at Proctor's Fifth Avenue Theatre. The programme also includes a one act drama entitled "Sunset." Vaudeville turns are given between the acts. Among these features are dances by the Christoffersons in a specialty typical of the Norwegian peasantry. The kalatechnoscope will give new views of Sir Thomas Lipton's America's Cup challenger, Shamrock II. Others on the programme are Sydney A. Harris, singer; Ritchie and Frances, buck and wing dancers; Miss Belle Williams, a singer of "coon" melodies, and William Voxie, card and coin manipulator. Those who take part in "Lend Me Your Wife," in which Roland Reed once starred, include his daughter, Miss Florence Reed, and Julian Reed, who was his stage manager. Charles S. Abbe will take the part played by the late comedian, and Miss Beatrice Morgan has the leading woman's part.

Robert Hilliard heads the programme at Keith's this week in his one act play, "The Littlest Girl." Second on the bill are McIntyre and Heath, in "On Guard." Others on the bill are Louise Gunning in Scotch songs; Pascatel, "the aerial marvel"; Hedrix and Prescott, dancing specialties; Manning and Davis, in "The Irish Pawnbroker"; the Three Keatons, Raymond and Caverly, Young and Brooks, "Chalk" Saunders, Moore and Lessing and the biograph and stereopticon.

"The King's Carnival" ended its run last night at the New-York Theatre, and the lower part of the house will remain dark until the fall. The show at the Cherry Blossom Grove, on the roof, will continue, according to present plans, the rest of the summer. Among the features of the programme is Carl Marwig's ballet, "The N[illegible] Star," representing a winter carnival at Mor[illegible] The Three Brooklyns will be retai[illegible]ned fro[illegible] and others are Harry Bulge[illegible] "The [illegible]ders," the four Luken Brot[illegible] ners, Re[illegible]ards and Hills and Silviar[illegible]y. A c[illegible] given to-night.

Additions have been made to t[illegible] "People Talked About" at the F[illegible] moving pictures have [illegible] be shown hourly. The daily concerts will be continued.

Charmion still heads the programme at Koster & Bial's roof garden. Others are Post and Clinton, Rena Aubrey, the Four Madcaps, novelty dancers and acrobats; Reta Curtis, Belle Gordon and the Glenroy brothers. A concert will be given to-night.

Additions have been made to the programme at Hammerstein's Paradise Gardens this week, among which are Trovolo, with his automatic walking figures; Hale and Francis, O'Meers sisters, Prince Satsuma and others. Concerts are given every Sunday night.

Rose Coghlan begins a midsummer engagement of four weeks in Denver on July 21. Her last week there will be devoted to a production of "Fortune's Bridge," a melodrama, written for Miss Coghlan by her brother, the late Charles Coghlan.

Flora Zabello, who sang the leading part in "San Toy" at Daly's Theatre last season, has been engaged for the production of "The Messenger Boy." The singing of the "Maisie" song falls to her.

In "Tom Moore," in which Andrew Mack will appear next season at the Herald Square Theatre, August 31, the first act is on Irish soil, while the scenes of three other acts are laid in London. Of the thirty characters but four are Irish. The story, which to a great extent follows actual incidents in the life of Tom Moore, treats its principal character with considerable dramatic license, but there is no intricate plot and no intensely wrought up dramatic situations. The cast of principals is as follows:

Tom Moore	Andrew Mack
Prince of Wales	Myron Calice
Sir Percival Lovelace	George F. Nash
Lord Moira	Theodore Babcock
Robin Dyke	George Deyo
Sheridan	Giles Shine
Beau Brummel	H. P. Stone
Terrence Farrell	Frank Mayne
Buster	Eddie Heron
McDermott	R. J. Dillon
Dabble	Thomas Jackson
Bessie Dyke	Josephine Lovett
Winnie Farrell	Susie Wilkinson
Lady Fitz Herbert	Jane Payton
Mrs. Malone	Margaret Fielding

The following programme is presented at Pastor's this week: George Evans, "the Original Honey Boy," in monologue, Fox and Foxie, the clown and his dog; the Three Westons—Sam, Carrie and Florence—in "Let 'Er Go"; Casey and Leclair, "The Irish Tenants"; Miss Leah Russell, mezzo-soprano, in an imitation of a Hebrew soubrette; Hosmer and Ross, in "At Swords' Points"; the Lawrence sisters, in singing specialties; Milt and Maud Wood, acrobats and dancers; Lola Vougere Trio, with their Mexican dogs; Miss Olla Hood, "lady barytone"; Saunders and Burdell, in "Under the Gas Light"; Arlington and Delmore, "The Occident and Orient," incidents of travel, art and science, and the American Vitagraph.

At Terrace Garden this week will be produced Auber's "Fra Diavolo." Hubert Wilke will play the leading part, and Frederick Knights the Lorenzo; Beppo and Giacomo will be in the hands of Frank Deshon and George W. Callahan; Harry Carter will be Lord Allcash and Mme. Mathilde Cottrelly Lady Allcash; John Wheeler will essay the role of Matteo, Miss Morgia Lytton that of Roberts, and Miss Bonnie May that of Francesco. Miss Villa Knox will be Zerlina.

Among the features at the Madison Square Garden Roof Garden for this week are Lottie Gilson, James Thornton, Louis Granat, Tsudo, the Revere Sisters, Neva Aymar, Boyce and Wilson, Edwina, Swift and Huber, the Alsacian Four, Adele Purvis Onri and others. A concert will be given to-night.

FUNERAL OF DR. MAYNARD.

The funeral of the Rev. Dr. Newland Maynard at the Church of the Ascension, Tenth-st. and Fifth-ave., yesterday morning was in charge of the rector, the Rev. Dr. Percy Stickney Grant, and two assistant ministers of the parish, the Rev. R. T. Quinnell and the Rev. Lester Bradner, jr. The music was in charge of Charles Heinroth, organist. Miss Fannie Rice, soprano, and Henry W. Roe, barytone, sang the following hymns: "Now the Laborer's Task Is Over," "Asleep in Jesus, Blessed Sleep," and "Nearer, My God, to Thee." At the end of the regular Episcopal services the Rev. Dr. Grant made a brief address touching on some reminiscences of Dr. Maynard's life and characteristics. The body was buried yesterday in St. Michael's Cemetery, in a plot owned by the Church of the Ascension.

ELECTION IN THE TWELFTH.

Company I of the 12th Regiment will hold an election for a first lieutenant to-morrow night, and the candidate is Second Lieutenant George W. Preece, [illegible]ho was taken away from the company some [illegible] ago at his own request because he did not [illegible]rve under Captain Raborg. This was in [illegible] troubles which culminated in the res[illegible]aptain. There is an attempt being [illegible]er of the company, who is a [illegible]aborg, to get up opposition

TOPICS IN CALIFORNIA.

EPWORTH LEAGUE CONVENTION—THE MINT LOSS—PROFESSOR WENDELL'S CRITICISMS.

[BY TELEGRAPH TO THE TRIBUNE.]

San Francisco, July 6.—Great preparations are being made for the Epworth League convention, which meets here on July 18, and continues for a week. It is estimated by the railroad managers that fifty thousand persons will come here during the week. An unusual number of applications has been received by the league managers in all parts of the country, because of the attractiveness of this excursion trip across the continent and the liberality given in the choice of railroad routes coming and going. Every effort will be made to give the visitors a generous welcome. At Sacramento, Stockton, Los Angeles, Fresno, San José and other places which the league will pass through fruit and flowers will be distributed free to all the members. The ferry building and the City Hall will be illuminated every night with electric lights, and the Mechanics' Pavilion, where the exercises will be held, will be handsomely decorated. The main streets will also be decorated with the red and white colors of the league.

The theft of $30,000 from the San Francisco Mint, which was discovered this week, will probably lead to more care in handling and guarding coin both here and at the other mints. Experts declare that the main cause of the theft was the crowding of $25,000,000 into a vault intended to contain only $5,000,000. The result was terrible confusion and a mass of coin which it was physically impossible to count every day, as the law provides. The theory of the experts is that some officials of the mint saw the opportunity for stealing which the confusion offered, and took six bags, each containing $5,000. This loss will probably result in better arrangements for guarding the coin, and new checks to such an offence.

William A. Brandes, of Oakland, who beat his young stepdaughter to death and then hanged her to a bedpost to give the impression of suicide, was convicted this week of manslaughter and sentenced to ten years in the Folsom Prison. The judge scored the jury in the severest terms for their failure to bring in a proper verdict. Under the evidence a life term would have been light punishment for the crime.

The Pacific Union Club this week gave a farewell dinner to J. C. Stubbs, who has departed for Chicago to take charge of the traffic management of the Southern and Union Pacific companies, the Oregon Short Line and the Oregon Railway and Navigation Company. Fifty friends of the popular railroad man were present.

The Southern Pacific Company has given notice that after August 1 no liquors will be sold on any of its ferryboats that ply between here and Oakland and Alameda, as well as on the big saloon and Vallejo boats. The bar privileges on these boats brought in $150 a day. This action is only the natural consequence of the abolition two years ago of bars and saloons from all the stations, except at the eating stations for the benefit of travellers. One result of the closing of the bars on the ferryboats will be to reduce intoxication and disorder on the return of the Sunday picnic crowds, and the action of the railroad company is warmly commended by those who have the cause of temperance at heart.

Dr. Herbert M. Hopkins, instructor in Latin at the University of California, has been called to the chair of Latin at Trinity College. Dr. Hopkins is a graduate of Columbia, of the class of '93, and received his master's degree from Harvard in 1896. His election to a full professorship at Trinity is regarded as a high honor at his age.

Professor Barrett Wendell, of Harvard, created a mild sensation at the summer school of the University of California by a sharp criticism of the papers handed in by his class in English literature. He asked the members to state in writing the benefits and objects which they expected to gain in the course. Many took occasion to fill the papers with laudatory references to the professor. One woman said: "She had long worshipped him from afar off, and now came to sit at his feet and gather inspiration from his gifted lips." He declared he had never known of a woman making such a fool of herself on a single page before, and he called most of the papers "disgusting slop."

The Cypress Lawn Cemetery Association has let a contract for a seven story and basement apartment house in Turk-st., near Market-st. It will be of brick and terra cotta, and will have 232 rooms.

Harry Morosco this week sold his lease of the Grand Opera House to Charles L. Ackerman and Morris Meyerfield, jr. The lease has three years to run. Morosco tried melodrama and comic opera, but in neither of these two things could he make this big house south of Market-st. pay. It is understood that there will be no change made in the character of the house by the new management. The Frawley company is now playing there, with E. J. Morgan as the leading man. The opera house is owned by John W. Mackay and James L. Flood, but it has never paid the interest on the investment because of its location. Blanche Bates has done a big business in her second week of "Under Two Flags," and the play is billed for two weeks more, and, with fine scenery, a large company and Blanche Bates's personal popularity and splendid acting, it will probably draw well till the end of the season; but it is risky to attempt to run anything for a month in San Francisco.

Edna Wallace Hopper will go back to New-York nearly $500,000 richer than she came West. Her mother left to her practically all the fortune that she inherited from Dunsmuir, the coal millionaire. Edna's brother, who is a Denver barkeeper, gets only $100 a month.

SUICIDE OF AN OLD MAN IN THE PARK.

A park policeman found an old man unconscious in the Ramble, near the Bow Bridge, in Central Park, early yesterday morning. He had taken carbolic acid. The man was taken to the Presbyterian Hospital, where he died at 7 o'clock. He was Frederick See, a tailor, of No. 241 West Twenty-sixth-st. William See, a son, who is a painter, of No. 387 Eighth-ave., identified the body.

See was a retired tailor, seventy-five years old. He had been melancholy since the death of his wife six years ago.

HE COULD NOT MAKE AN AUTOPSY.

It had been intended to have an autopsy on the body of James Burke, who was discovered dead in his room on the top floor of No. 127 Chrystie-st. on Friday morning, but Coroner's Physician Williams, who viewed the body yesterday afternoon, found that it was in such an advanced state of decomposition that it was impossible to perform the autopsy. There was no fracture of the skull.

out possessing what is now called the "double escapement."

Through the kindness of Mr. Henry Ziegler, of the firm of Steinway & Sons, who made measurements of the different parts of the instrument for The Tribune, some comparisons are possible which serve to illustrate the wonderful progress that has been made in pianoforte construction since Cristofori came forward with his invention. The Steinway concert grand pianoforte is eight feet and ten inches long and five feet wide. It has a compass of seven and a quarter octaves, eighty-eight notes from subcontra A, sixth ledger space below the bass staff, to C on the ninth ledger line above the treble staff. Its longest string is six feet seven and one-half inches in length, its shortest only two inches; but the longest string has a steel core two millimetres thick, and with the wire which is wound around the core the string is five millimetres thick. The thickest string on the Cristofori pianoforte is not so thick as the thinnest string on the Steinway. The string on the Steinway which produces the same tone as the lowest note of the Cristofori is trebled and wound, and each string is two millimetres thick; the top note of the Cristofori register is five and a half inches long in the Steinway instrument and exerts a pull on the frame of 170 pounds for each of the three unison strings. A few of such strains would crush the wooden frame of the Cristofori pianoforte, but the Steinway concert grand is called on to endure a strain of about 43,000 pounds. H. E. K.

BEAUMARCHAIS'S WATERWORKS.

A RELIC OF THE PAST IN PARIS TO BE DESTROYED.

Paris correspondence of the Pall Mall Gazette.

The municipality has decided to do away with a relic of the past of which the history is interesting, but of which it must be admitted the continued preservation could serve no purpose. It is the Chaillot waterworks that are thus doomed to disappear. Some very illustrious men were mixed up in the earlier stages of their history. The "Chaillot steam pump," as the enterprise was originally designated by the public, was long regarded as one of the engineering marvels of the capital. It was the first attempt to supply Parisians with water brought to their doors, or, at any rate, into their district, by mechanical means. Two brothers of the name of Perier conceived the notion of the undertaking toward 1780, and were successful in interesting in their scheme that incorrigible speculator and incomparable dramatist Beaumarchais. The author of "Le Barbier de Séville" having obtained the necessary licenses from the authorities, two steam pumps, which it should be mentioned were imported from England, were set up in the Chaillot district, and were used to pump the water of the Seine into reservoirs constructed on the neighboring high ground, not far from where the Trocadéro now stands. A system of pipes carried the water to four fountains established in convenient centres. Payment of about £2 a year entitled the customer to a muid or some sixty gallons of water each twenty-four hours.

The ration was regarded as lavish, microbes were still an undiscovered terror, and Paris was lost in admiration of the new departure. Its promoters, of course, made money rapidly, and equally of course they were the butt of rival financiers. A violent campaign, led by no less a personage than Mirabeau, was started with a view to causing a fall in the shares of the company, which in two or three years had risen to over five times their original value. Beaumarchais replied to the onslaught with his accustomed verve, and by his famous pamphlet, the "Mirabelles," seemed for the moment to have pulverized Mirabeau, whose reputation hung in the balance until he turned the tables on his assailant by a scathing attack which brought about the ruin of the original company. The enterprise was not, however, allowed to collapse, but after a brief interregnum was bought by the city of Paris, in whose possession it has been ever since—existing, it need not be said, in a modified form.

CONEY ISLAND FUN.

HOW CENTRIFUGAL FORCE CAME INTO VOGUE WITH "LOOP THE LOOP," "FLIP FLAP" AND THE "BARREL OF LOVE."

Coney Island has added a phrase to its complicated vocabulary of pointed slang and mixed up English as the "barkers" howl it. Strange to say, for once the new words are not in the least slangy, but highly technical and secure of their place in all dictionaries.

"Centrifugal force" is the phrase which Coney Islanders have recently become acquainted with. They have their own ways of pronouncing it and give it a variety of meanings, some of which are at great variance with Webster. But with "Loop the Loops" and "Flip Flaps" and other amusement contrivances in which centrifugal force plays a part, it will not be long until every one at the island knows what it means and how it works.

THE "BARREL OF LOVE AT CONEY ISLAND.

"What is this centrifugal force business?" asked a Coney Island pony driver of the man who sells popcorn in the streetcar terminal.

"It's what sticks a fly to the ceiling," was the ready answer. "If you got enough of it you could stand upside down."

Just across the street a "barker" cried in deep and strenuous tones:

"Here it is! Here it is! The great and only 'Loop the Loop'! Everybody tries it, everybody likes it! Here's where we turn you upside down for the small and insignificant sum of one dime—ten cents!"

"Have you got the Santiago loop?" demanded some one in the crowd.

The crowd went in and for a time was content to watch others "looping the loop." The cars, filled with four people, tore down the incline and up and around the spiral arrangement that makes the loop. It looks dangerous to see the car with its human load whirl round the circle, but in a moment they are out of the loop and gliding slowly up the second incline.

"I wouldn't try that for $50,000!" exclaimed one woman, who had said the same thing about riding the donkey further up the street, which she afterward rode.

"Ah, come on and loop," insisted her escort.

"It wouldn't hurt a baby," said the ticket agent. "We've carried more than three hundred thousand people, and never had an accident."

At last she was persuaded to make the trip. She didn't know just exactly what happened, and while the sensations were not unpleasant, she hardly cared to try it again. In that she differed from two young men, who looped seventy times without leaving the car a few days before. They got a reduced rate after the twentieth round, and were none the worse for their extended trial.

The greater part of the "Loop the Loop" attraction is like the ordinary roller coaster. The difference lies in the bewildering, twisting loop. The cars are pulled to the top of an incline by a cable, and are started down one which is more steep by an automatic brake. At the bottom of the incline is a circular affair of steel resembling two sections of a spiral stairway. The car describes the circle with great speed, and the headway gained sends it up another incline, whence there is an easy switchback descent to the starting point. Only one car is allowed on the loop section of the track at a time. In case a car should break in the loop, it would simply seesaw for a few moments without harming anything. There might be trouble if two cars were allowed on the loop at the same time, but it is impossible under the block system used.

One has sensations in looping the loop, but, like everything else that comes in a hurry, there is trouble in remembering them. A Tribune reporter looped five or six times before he could remember much about it. The most feeling came with the rapid fall down the incline. It was something like the sensation one has in a falling elevator. The loop part was over almost before one knew it. The blood did not have time to rush to one's head. A few stars twinkled in the sunlight—where stars should not be—as the car went up the second incline, but they were all gone by the time the car reached the ground.

The loop is constructed under patents issued to Edwin E. Prescott, of Arlington, Mass. The steel loop is thirty-five feet high, and the distance around is a little more than seventy feet. The car is upside down for about one second. Similar loops are running at Atlantic City and at Boston. The only accidents so far have resulted from people putting their hands outside the car, which caused them to receive slight flesh wounds. William B. Van Duzen, the manager, is confident that the courts will permit him to continue operations.

The "Flip Flap" is one of the attractions at Captain Paul Boynton's chutes. It is called a centrifugal railway, and the cars do a turn around a wooden loop. The road is built on the mono-rail system, invented by Captain Lina Beecher. The track is in the centre of the trestle work, and the cars run on two wheels placed bicycle fashion. As a precaution, there are guide wheels at each side which run on tracks on the lower side of the trestle. The cars are virtually clamped to the track. Every precaution for the safety of "flip-flappers" is taken, and so far there have been no accidents.

"You can send a bucket of water around the loop in one of our cars, and not a drop will be spilled," said Captain Boynton yesterday. "Centrifugal force never fails to do the work, and a person could not fall out of a car if he tried. The same system which we use on the 'Flip Flap' road will one day bring Chicago within five hours of New-York. Such a road is a possibility, and a company is being formed to build it."

The "Barrel of Love" has been rolling at Coney Island for several seasons, but only this year has centrifugal force figured in the crier's descriptions. Before he told of the safety of the strap which went across one's waist. The barrel of this attraction is fifteen feet in diameter, and it rolls in a curved track. It turns one over several times for a single fare, and as the speed is not great, the riders know very well that they are upside down. Once in a long while the barrel will stop with its passengers in the air, and the attendants have a busy time getting them down. Just where the love part of this attraction comes in no one seems to know, not even the people who run the show.

In applying the principle of centrifugal force to their amusements Coney Islanders cannot say that they have a decided novelty. As much as a half century ago centrifugal railways amused the youth of Great Britain who visited the Liverpool Zoo and other amusement centres in England. The cars in those days carried only one person, but they turned upside down just as completely as do those at Coney. Of course, the English were not so undignified as to speak of "looping the loop" or "flipping the flap." To that extent Coney Island is original.

THE BATH OF THE ORANGE.

From The Los Angeles Herald.

Fresh from the tree an orange is still very much alive, with the oil cells expanded and the mystery of growth not yet suspended. Cut off from the sap supply, a change takes place. The skin draws closer to the pulp and gives off moisture that would cause sweating if the fruit were packed at once. But first these dust stained travellers must have a bath.

By the bushel—if only this were the land of the good old bushel basket—the newcomers are dumped into a long, narrow tank of water, at one end of which is a big wheel with a tire of soft bristles. The wheel revolves so that the lower edge works in connection with another set of brushes in a smaller tank below, and the oranges, after bobbing about in the big tank, pass between the wet brushes and come out bright and clean.

This washer is a neat machine and does away with the more primitive yet picturesque method of hand washing.

At some of the smaller packing houses may still be seen groups of women, sometimes white, sometimes brown skinned, each with a tub of water and brush, scrubbing busily away at the yellow piles that never seem to grow less till the last hour of the day.

After their bath the oranges are spread out in the sun to dry on long, slanting racks. At the lower end they roll off into boxes, to be carried away to the warehouse for their rest.

An orange needs a deal of grooming, it would seem, before it is ready for market. The washing was not enough. There must be a brushing, too. And after the days of curing, the oranges are fed into a hopper which drops them single file onto a belt that runs between revolving cylindrical brushes. This for a smooth, shiny look.

ARCTIC VEGETATION.

LIGHT COMPENSATES FOR INADEQUATE WARMTH.

From The British Geographical Journal.

Professor J. Wiesner, of Vienna University, who for some years has been engaged in researches on the requirements of plants in the matter of light, has come to the following conclusions with regard to the plants of the arctic regions. The demonstration previously put forward by him with regard to low and middle latitudes, that with the increase of latitude the light requirement of plants also rises, has been shown, by observations made in Norway and at Advent Bay, Spitzenbergen, 78:12 north latitude, to apply equally to sub-arctic and arctic regions. The reasons for this marked need of light are the low temperatures which prevail at the vegetative period, the want of heat being made up for by excess of light, the amount of which must therefore increase with the decrease of temperature. It thus comes about that a limit is set to the migration toward the Pole of bush and tree vegetation less by the cold of winter than by the constantly increasing need of light, which can, of course, be less and less satisfied. As a rule, the plants of the Far North can stand but a small diminution of their quantum of light, such as is caused by the interception of the sun's rays through the configuration of the country.

Dr. Peucker's researches on mountain shadow have shown how the amount of light required can be laid down with precision in each particular case. The intensity of the direct sunlight to which arctic plants are exposed is very slight, for it only becomes perceptible when the sun reaches an altitude of 15 degrees above the horizon, whereas in the most favorable case, on June 21, the sun only attains, at Advent Bay, an altitude of 30 to 35 degrees. Direct sunlight here at best reaches the strength of the light radiated from the whole expanse of the sky, the so-called "diffused light," so that the whole illumination available for polar plants is at most double the amount of the diffused light. The high Alpine plants of mean latitudes, on the contrary, enjoy an amount of illumination which may be estimated at a maximum of at least four times that due to the diffused light, the sun reaching a midday altitude in summer of 66 to 69 degrees. These differences result, as Bonnier has shown, in considerable variations in the organs of plants of like species, which occur both in high Alpine and high Arctic regions. In middle latitudes the effect of aspect on vegetation is very striking, the northern slopes of mountains being often bare of plants. But in view of the much nearer approach to a complete circuit round the horizon made by the sun in arctic latitudes it is easily seen that this influence is less felt there than anywhere.

Of much interest, lastly, is the demonstration of the influence exercised by differential lighting on the form of trees, the low angle at which light is received especially favoring the pyramidal shape in arctic latitudes, though this is by no means detrimental under the more nearly vertical lighting of low latitudes. The cypresses of the South are, in fact, protected by their form from the injurious effects of a vertical sun, while the same form enables the firs, pines and white poplars of Norway and Sweden to make the most of the horizontal rays of the Northern sun.

The New York Press

LARGEST REPUBLICAN CIRCULATION BY MANY THOUSANDS OF COPIES A DAY.

VOL. XIV.—WHOLE NO. 5,024. NEW YORK, MONDAY MORNING, SEPTEMBER 2, 1901. BC 2 PRICE ONE CENT in Greater New York, Newark and Jersey City; TWO CENTS everywhere else.

GREAT RAIN DELUGES CLEVELAND, IMPERILING MANY LIVES AND DOING $1,000,000 DAMAGE

Residents, Particularly the Wealthy, Spend a Night of Terror.

HOMES ARE DESTROYED AND RAILROADS TIED UP

Life Saving Crew and Boat Are Taken Seven Miles Through City to Rescue Families.

Special to The Press.

CLEVELAND, Sept. 1.—After a night of terror, in which the heaviest rain storm ever known in this city poured down for hours, imperiling many lives and damaging hundreds of thousands in property, the city at dawn to-day presented a scene of unparalleled devastation and destruction. Despite the danger of the night, so far as known not a life was lost.

The surging waters spread over an area in the East End nearly eight miles long and a mile and a half wide.

This extended from Woodland Hills avenue to East Cleveland and back to East Madison avenue.

MILLION IN DAMAGE.

The losses already reported are estimated at more than half a million, and besides these $100,000 damage has been done to the city parks. Thousands of smaller losses to homes and grounds probably will swell the total to a million.

Phenomenally heavy rains began falling at midnight. The downpour was unaccompanied by lightning or thunder and there was not enough wind to add to the damage. The deluge did it all unassisted. The sewers and gutters of the city streets were unequal to the occasion and the water swept through miles of streets, doing damage over a wide section of the best part of the city. It was nearly 10 o'clock before the rain completely ceased.

Great volumes of water poured over from [illegible] and Giddings brooks, down [illegible] street, swamped Vienna street, rushed over Cedar avenue, back over in East Prospect street, rushed like a millrace down Lincoln avenue to Euclid avenue, and then on to Glen Park place, where houses were undermined as though built of straw and almost incredible damage done to streets and property.

RICH IN DANGER.

Over a large share of the exclusive residence territory the water rushed with terrific force, varying in depth from one to six feet. Culverts, trestles and bridges were torn down, and for hours nothing seemed capable of stemming the tide.

Hundreds of residents who were imprisoned in their beautiful homes like stranded islanders were almost panic-stricken, expecting to be called upon to wade out into the swirling waters at almost every minute. Danger signals were flashed about the city as speedily as the disabled telephone system would allow and the work of rescue began. Rowboats plied back and forth, assisting whole families from perilous positions, but these proved pitifully inadequate and it was soon found necessary to go to the extraordinary precaution of calling on the United States life-saving crew from the river, a distance of seven miles.

LIFE CREW IN SERVICE.

The lifeboats were quickly loaded on wagons and hurried to the scene of destruction.

The torrent surged with awful force for hours in Deering street, from Fairmount to the Boulevard, and more than a dozen families were penned in with water five and six feet deep surrounding their homes. At this point the life-saving crew worked valiantly, and, assisted by squads of firemen and policemen, finally succeeded in landing the terror-stricken people in places of safety.

The fear was greatly enhanced by the momentary expectation that the great Shaker Heights dam would break loose and entail added destruction.

RAILROADS TIED UP.

Both the Lake Shore and the Nickel Plate railroads were tied up by washouts east of Cleveland. No Lake Shore train came into Cleveland from the East between 7 o'clock this morning and 5 this afternoon. Then the Lake Shore trains were only able to reach the city by way of the lines of the Nickel Plate. The latter system was tied up for about the same length of time.

Every street car line in the city was tied up for a part of the day at least, and some lines cannot be run for several days. In places the tracks are buried under several feet of earth washed over them. At other places the ground has been washed from under the tracks, leaving the rails and ties suspended in midair.

Euclid Heights, with its millionaire colony, is cut off from the city by destruction of the Cedar Gleen driveway, through which the Heights line of street cars run. The carriage way is destroyed and it was impossible for the residents of the Heights to get to church except by wading through a foot of water, and after dark even that was dangerous, because there were great holes edged with treacherous, caving earth, where the footways and streets had been.

BOULEVARD RUINED.

The magnificent Lower Boulevard, running through Wade, Gordon and Rockefeller parkway parks to Lake Erie, one of the finest drives in the world, practically is ruined, covered with mud from overflowed Doan Brook and washed out at many points.

Two cemeteries were torn up by the floods that swept through them. Coffins were disinterred and floated about on the muddy water with their silent occupants. Boys on rafts and boats towed them about without thinking what they were. A lake a mile long and covering parts of half a dozen streets formed in an almost inconceivable short space of time in the vicinity of Forrest street, Wilson avenue and the Nickle Plate Railroad, where a culvert choked. The bridge was once washed out by a similar accident, and a large part of the streets were saved by the work of the public works gangs.

CARRIE NATION SWEEPS THROUGH CITY AND IS ARRESTED, BUT SOON RELEASED

Visits Many Barrooms, Denounces the Owners and Is Made a Prisoner Near Devery's Four Corners—In Lecture at Night She Denounces Corsets.

LIKE a storm from her own Western country Carrie Nation swept across New York city yesterday. Swayed by her impetuosity, she attacked Richard Croker's club, entered saloons, investigated music halls and faced street mobs. Even when the police, assiduous for the preservation of law and order, sallied forth from Devery's corner to arrest her, she faced them serenely and marched blithely away with them toward the martyrdom that threatened her.

Mrs. Nation was due in the city at 7.30 a. m. from Danville, Ill., where she had smashed the Elks' beer display and delivered a lecture, but the train was almost three hours late.

"That train," said Mrs. Nation, "was nothing but a saloon on wheels. They were all the time passing drinks around. Soft drinks? Nothing of the kind. I smelt 'em and I read the names on the meenoos.

"Now, I want to get ready for church. I don't care what kind, so it's a church. I'd kind of like to go to a Free Methodist church, if I knew where there was one; but there's good in all churches."

"How about Christian Science?"

"Don't take me there. I'd call the preacher a liar and raise a row."

Mrs. Nation's "getting ready" consisted in exchanging the linen duster which she had worn in traveling for a white linen garment of the same general style. With this she wore a small black bonnet. She attended services in St. Patrick's Cathedral, lamenting that she was too late for the opening music.

"I used to be a singer myself," she said, "but when I was in jail the tobacco smoke there clogged my bronchi and hurt my voice.

INTERESTED IN MARTYRS.

"That was a good sermon," she said when she came out, "and I enjoyed the service, but I do wonder what they were roasting that martyr on the gridiron for."

This referred to one of the stained-glass windows which had seemed to fascinate Mrs. Nation, who has a personal interest in martyrs and roasting.

Mrs. Nation was mildly interested in Fifth avenue, but grew enthusiastic when the Democratic Club was pointed out to her.

"Croker's club? I'm going in there," and up the steps she started. At the door she was stopped by a porter and a Tammany politician.

"Ladies not admitted on Sunday? But the Good Book says it is not good for man to be alone. Now, what's you reason for not letting women in?"

"Rules of the club," said the superintendent, coming to the door. "No, I won't tell you why." Like Commissioner Murphy, the superintendent refused to enter into a discussion.

WANTED TO HOLD SUNDAY SCHOOL.

Stepping over the threshold she said, "Well, now I've been inside the door you might as well let me all the way in."

But the superintendent was obdurate.

"I know why you don't want women; it's because you drink in there from Saturday until Monday. Do you have a Bible?"

"Yes."

"Well, if you'll let me come in I'll hold Sunday school."

"That is not the purpose of this club."

"No, I guess not," laughed Mrs. Nation. "Well, I'll come some other day."

At Seventh avenue and Fiftieth street, seeing the open side door of a saloon, she walked in, followed by a crowd.

REMARKS ABOUT "POISON."

"Well, well, this is too bad," said she, looking at the men drinking beer. "Here you poor workingmen are spending your money for this poison."

"It's all the pleasure we have," objected one of the men.

"It's poison," she repeated, "and you ought to be saving your money for your families."

"Ain't got none."

"Give me a bottle," said she, "and I'll show you what I do in Kansas."

"I'm tending to my business, and I wish you'd tend to yours," the bartender protested, placing himself defensively between the bottles and the smasher. "Don't you do it!" as she threatened to make an attack.

"Why, you told me to attend to my business, and that's smashing hell holes and keeping men from destroying themselves. I wish I had my hatchet. Any one got a hatchet?" she inquired, cheerfully.

Then she shook hands with the bartender and left the saloon amid great cheering.

OBJECTED TO DIANA.

On her return to the hotel Mrs. Nation asked for the proprietor.

The clerk said he was not in.

"Well, there is a woman without any apparel on out there in the lobby, and I want him to put some clothes on her. Would you want your wife exposed to such indecency?"

The clerk stared blankly at his visitor.

"The statue of Diana," some one suggested, "is what Mrs. Nation objects to."

"I'll speak to the proprietor about it," the clerk promised.

"Well, I'll put something on her if he doesn't."

In the afternoon Mrs. Nation started out to do the "hell holes," of which she had heard New York was full. She was disappointed to learn that they could not be seen in full running until late at night. She was bent upon discovering what evil was awake at that hour, however, and started for a tour through the Tenderloin. She found the door of the first place she tried, in Twenty-ninth street, locked. "That's good," she said, but she looked disappointed. At the northeast corner of Twenty-ninth street and Sixth avenue she entered a saloon by the side door.

KNEW THE TASTE OF IT.

"Oh, you poor boys," she cried, as she rushed upon a group of sailors with beer mugs in their hands.

"We sell only soft drinks here," shouted the bartender.

"Is that so? Let me taste," she said to one of the sailors, and taking his glass from him she lifted it to her lips. "That's no soft drink. I know beer when I taste it."

"Have you a hatchet?" she asked the bartender.

"No, but I've got a hammer," he retorted.

"I suppose you would call it breaking the law if I smashed your place, where you break the law by selling liquor on Sunday. Don't you ever close up your drunkard factory? You are too good looking to be a malicious pauper. That's what a saloon-keeper is."

"Don't throw bouquets so fast. This ain't a church meeting. You'd better take a walk."

"Well, I'm not ready to go. If you have this place open for business I can stay."

PLEASED AT THE HONOR.

When she got ready to go Mrs. Nation shook hands with the bartender, who said he had been "pleased to have the honor."

A policeman seeing the crowd had come to within a few yards of the place, but hearing what was going on inside, had turned his attention to business in another direction.

Saloons in the neighborhood began to lock their side doors.

Crossing from Broadway in Thirty-fourth street Mrs. Nation and her party walked down Eighth avenue to the Abbey, between Twenty-seventh and Twenty-eighth streets. Mrs. Nation started in at the side door, but a man there said, "Nothing doing on Sunday."

"Now, that's real good," said Mrs. Nation "I want to shake hands with a man who respects the law like that." The man gave his hand, but looked embarassed by the tribute to his goodness.

"Let's rush Carrie!" cried a boy, and a party of hooting youths nearly carried her off her feet. By this time she was the centre of a mob.

"This is too close to Devery's corner. Something will happen, some one cried. Just then Patrolman No. 3769 seized Mrs. Nation by the arm, two other policemen following him.

ARRESTED FOR RAISING A CROWD.

"What have you been doing?" he demanded.

"Nothing," she replied, calmly. "I haven't hurt anybody or used any bad language."

"Well, you're under arrest."

"What for?"

"Raising a crowd and causing disorder."

"Bless me, I didn't tell them to come. I've just been looking into saloons and places that are open to the public."

Upon her promising to go to her hotel they released her and put her on a car.

In the evening Mrs. Nation lectured in Carnegie Hall.

"Less than a month ago," she began, "I was in a cage and I had hardly enough to feed me. Now, I am seeing places that I never expected to see."

She told young girls to save young men—not to be silly and say they liked the smell of a good cigar. "The men wouldn't walk with you, girls, if you had those things in the corners of your mouths."

Moses, she said, was a good smasher. He smashed the golden calf.

She blamed women partly for the evil conditions that prevail in New York. "Woman is not one of those soft things that can sit down and squeeze their waists with corsets. How I hate corsets! Such creatures make their heart and liver into one solid lump. A young man should write to a girl that he couldn't marry her if he found that she wore corsets."

GREAT CRUSH IN THE CAR.

Almost as many persons waited in West Fifty-sixth street during the lecture as were inside. At 9.30 o'clock Mrs. Nation came out of the entrance in that street and went to Broadway, where she boarded a car. It looked for a moment as if some one would be hurt in the rush to ride on that car. Mrs. Nation and her manager sat in the first seat. The car held probably the biggest load it ever had known. Mrs. Nation, as she said in her lecture, believes that women should not wear corsets. Perhaps that will explain in a measure why nine people sat on the seat opposite her and only seven with her. The seats ordinarily hold five. She saw a big policeman on the step.

"What are you doing here?" queried Mrs. Nation.

"I was sent here to take care of you," he replied.

The policeman and Mrs. Nation rode free.

"I don't pay any fare," she said to the conductor. "I guess I'm a deadhead. We've got trolley cars in Kansas, but they ain't as big as these."

One man in the seat opposite her was of small stature, but she told him that a certain bread would do him "a whole lot of good," adding, to his discomfiture, "You'd get a little bit of flesh on your bones if you'd eat some of that."

"Do you speak again in New York?" she was asked.

"I don't know. But if I could get all you men thoroughly aroused New York wouldn't be so wicked."

The crowd noticed her looking at the Delavan sign. A youth told her the place was owned by Tom O'Rourke.

"Is it a nice place?" she asked. When told it was a saloon she said "Oh!"

That the vice of the Tenderloin should be so alluring amazed her. "This is a wicked town," she continued, with emphasis on the "is."

"Goodby, Carrie. I must leave you," sang the crowd as she got off the car at the Victoria. She said something about a night visit to the Tenderloin, but was told that the great white lights were not burning, the owners of resorts having closed in fear of her.

"Then I'd better stay right here," she said, "if that's the effect of my presence."

Then she took the elevator for her room, saying:

"I've had a perfectly splendid time to-day."

She will go to Steeplechase Park, Coney Island, to-day and will speak there at temperance meetings every afternoon and evening this week, except on Wednesday, when she is to talk in Boonville, near Utica.

CROWN PRINCE IN BLENHEIM.

Frederick William Guest of Duke and Duchess of Marlborough.

LONDON, Sept. 1.—Crown Prince Frederick William of Germany arrived last night at Blenheim Palace on a visit to the Duke and Duchess of Marlborough.

The Duchess of Marlborough formerly was Miss Vanderbilt of New York.

DRUNKEN DRIVER A POLICEMAN

Leaves Post, Steals Cab and Tears Through Tenderloin.

COLLISIONS NARROWLY AVERTED

Lashes Maddened Horse for Many Blocks, Assaults Boy and Disappears with the Rig.

In full uniform, Louis Lurs, attached to the West Thirtieth street police station, when intoxicated on post last night, jumped into a cab that was standing in front of the Parker House, at Thirty-ninth street and Broadway, and, seizing the reins, started the horse on a mad gallop that almost ended disastrously. A charge of larceny will be made against him this morning.

Dashing up Broadway, with the cab swaying from side to side like a locomotive scaling the mountains, the policeman caused persons to flee in all directions. Lashing the horse with a long whip, the cab sped to Forty-second street, where a collision with a crosstown car was narrowly averted.

Charles Morris of No. 427 West Fiftieth street, who has the privilege of the cab stand in front of the Parker House, had placed his nephew, Louis Marguet, 16 years old, in charge of the cab after the driver had returned from a call from a Sixth avenue restaurant.

FELLOW TOOK POSSESSION.

The driver had gone to his supper, and the lad was patting the horse's head. Lurs, the policeman who was on post at that corner, came up, and before anybody could lay a hand on him jumped into the cab. Marguet saw that the policeman was grossly intoxicated and divined his intentions, but before he could get in the cab after the policeman the horse had started up Broadway.

Not to be daunted, the young lad swung on to the seat on the top of the cab behind and seized the reins, pulling with might and main to bring the horse to a halt. But the policeman, who had grabbed the lines also, proved too strong for the boy, and snatched them from his hands. Then the mad gallop began. In front of the Vendome Hotel, at Fortieth street and Broadway, the horse came to a sudden stop, and the policeman jumped from the cab and ordered Marguet from the box. The boy refused, whereupon the policeman took hold of him, and, drawing his night stick, struck him on the hip.

RUNS WILD ONCE MORE.

Dragging Marguet by the back of the neck, he threw him against the curb and mounted the box himself, and lashing the horse furiously, started on a mad gallop again. Looking over his shoulder, he shouted back to the boy, "You can go to ——." There was a large crowd of men standing in front of the Vendome and they called to the policeman to stop, but he cursed them all roundly and kept at his breakneck pace.

As the cab, swaying to and fro, dashed past Forty-second street, almost striking a crowded car, a man who was standing on the corner shouted, "Are you engaged?"

"It's none of your damned business," was the policeman's choice Tammany phrase.

The cab continued up Broadway to Forty-fourth street, when the policeman turned the horse to the left and it went racing down to Seventh avenue. Turning into that avenue several persons were almost knocked down, but the policeman heeded nothing and raced down the avenue.

At Forty-second street a crosstown car was taking on some passengers. It did not start up soon enough for the policeman, who, lashing the whip across the horse's head, called to the motorman: "Get a move on!"

ESCAPED BY A HAIR.

A collision was imminent, but the motorman fortunately turned on the lever and the car shot ahead, not a moment too soon, for the wheel of the cab just grazed the rear dashboard of the car.

Between Forty-first and Forty-second streets the cab was turned around again and the policeman drove back to Forty-second street and thence down that crowded thoroughfare to Eighth avenue. With a whoop he then went like mad down Eighth avenue, shouting at the top of his voice. Persons fled in terror as the cab dashed by and warning shouts to the drunken policeman had no effect. Motormen stopped their cars to let the cab pass by and on every block it seemed that an accident would occur.

At Thirtieth street and Eighth avenue the cab was lost to view and persons on that thoroughfare breathed a sigh of relief.

CAB WAS A WRECK.

George Gibbs of No. 577 Grand street discovered the cab standing at Thirty-eighth street and Seventh avenue with nobody in it. He drove the horse to the West Thirtieth street police station. It was found that both forefeet of the horse were injured and that it was so exhausted that it was ready to drop. The cushion of the box seat and the rest were broken and a valuable robe was missing.

Both lamps on the side of the cab were broken and panes of glass in the back were smashed to pieces.

Captain Flood was surprised last night when Roundsman Bauer reported to him that the policeman who was on post in Broadway, between Thirty-seventh and Thirty-ninth streets, was missing.

When the captain heard of the cab escapade he immediately ordered an investigation. He sent for the Marguet boy and got him to give a description of the policeman who had stolen the cab. Captain Flood was indignant, and told the lad to be in the police station to-day to look over every policeman in the precinct. The description the lad gave of the policeman answered that of Lurs, who was supposed to have been on post in Broadway at the corner where the cab was taken from.

DROWNED IN SAILING ACCIDENT

Morris Sutphen, a Johns Hopkins Professor, the Victim

Special to The Press.

LONG BRANCH, N. J., Sep 1.—Morris Sutphen of Morristown, N. J., a professor in Johns Hopkins University, was drowned last night by the upsetting of a catboat. Three other occupants of the boat held on and were rescued by Edward Peterson.

The party left the Oceanic for a sail, and at Highland Beach their boat ran into a drawbridge and was upset. Sutphen tried to reach the shore, but became exhausted and sank. His body has not been recovered.

MYSTERIOUS DOUBLE MURDER; STEWARDS HACKED TO DEATH IN SIWANOY GOLF CLUB

WOMAN OF 101 YEARS PLAYING IN STREET

Her Mind Shattered, She Imagined She Was a Child Again.

DID NOT KNOW WHERE SHE LIVED

Pathetic Scene in Court, When Arraigned as Vagrant, White-Haired Son Came and Led Her Away.

Many persons who happened to be near Ninth avenue and Twenty-fifth street on Saturday night found it worth their while to stop and watch with interest a curious group on a doorstep there. The central figure was an old, old woman, poorly dressed—miserably in fact—but evidently a jolly companion for half a dozen children.

Patrolman Willimese, noticing the crowd and hearing the laughter of the children, stopped to see what it all meant. He caught sight of the old woman's face and saw that it wore the smile of an infant. Her mind evidently was gone, and imagining that she was a child again she was playing merrily all the cunning little games that had come back to her from a memory that failed her in all else.

WAS A CHILD AGAIN.

The policeman asked the woman her name and where she lived. The smile faded away and with a frightened look she said that she was doing no harm and only wanted to play with the children again. When he took her to the police station she only could say again, in German, that she did not know who she was or where she lived. She had been wandering about for a long time in the rain, as her clothes were soaked through, her gray hair bedraggled and her shoes filled with water.

The sergeant asked if she were hungry and she said no, though she was tottering with weakness. He sent out for a hearty meal, which she simply devoured. Then he gave her what dry clothing he could find and stretched a blanket for the poor creature on the floor. She then went to sleep as quickly as a child, after mumbling a few words in German that might have been thanks or a baby prayer come back to her shattered mind.

MOTHER AND SON MEET.

Yesterday morning she was taken to the Jefferson Market Court, and, noticing her great age, Magistrate Mayo said he was most unwilling to commit her as a vagrant, but there was nothing else to do. The papers were being made out when a white-haired old man limped into the courtroom. He said he was Michael Beyerlen, an employe in the Street Cleaning Department, and the woman was his mother, Barbara, who lived in No. 339 East Forty-first street. She paid no attention to her son, and he explained that her mind was a blank most of the time and that her only enjoyment was in playing with children.

"How old is she?" asked the Magistrate.

"One hundred and one," said the son. "I am more than 60, but I am able to care for her yet. Let her come with me and I will watch her carefully. See, she is beginning to recognize me again."

The woman who had passed the century mark had put her hand in his, and thus they left the courtroom.

ANOTHER ANDREE RUMOR.

Indians Again Reported to Have Found Bodies in North.

KANKAKEE, Ill., Sept. 1.—Walter W. Cobb and G. W. Shields, young men of Kankakee who have just returned from a forty-five days' trip through the Hudson Bay region, bring back a story told by Indians of the far North that may relate to the missing explorer Andree and one of his two companions.

In Moose Factory, a Hudson Bay trading post at the mouth of Moose River, the men there reported that a party of Indians who came down from the north last spring told of the finding of the bodies of two white men at a point 900 miles north of Moose Factory. The story of the Indians was that the bodies were found in a broken basket, their description of which seemed to indicate a balloon basket, and that the bodies had been buried by Indians. The Indians brought nothing in support of their story, but the men in Moose Factory were inclined to believe the tale.

KELLER LETTER TO COME BACK

Barker Defense Association Probably Will Get It To-day.

Special to The Press.

NEWARK, N. J., Sept. 1.—It is likely the open letter of the Thomas G. Barker Defense Association to the Rev. John Keller, urging him to bring action for slander against Mrs. Barker, will be returned to the senders to-morrow. The letter was registered, and the thirty-day limit under which it may be retained in the Arlington Post Office expired last night.

During the month a carrier has taken the letter three times to the boarding house in which Mr. Keller lives, but each time nobody at the house would take it and sign the receipt. The letter was mailed on August 1 in New York.

IOWA PASTOR CALLED HERE.

Metropolitan Temple Wants the Rev. Robert Bagnell.

SIOUX CITY, Ia., Sept. 1.—The Rev. Robert Bagnell, pastor of the First Methodist Church of Sioux City, has been called to the chief pastorate of the Metropolitan Temple in New York.

Mr. Bagnell has not yet accepted the call. He is one of the best known of the younger M. E. ministers in the West.

DROPS DOWN DEAD AS SHERIFF APPEARS

Victim Was Charged with Illegally Transferring Big Estate.

$100,000 INVOLVED IN THE SUIT

Remarkable Will Contest Delayed by the Death of the Principal Defendant.

WESTBROOK, Conn., Sept. 1.—When told that he had been accused of inducing Mrs. Juliette A. Stannard to transfer her estate of $100,000 to him illegally, and told that he must appear in court and make a legal fight to retain the property, George D. E. Post of this place to-day dropped dead in the presence of the Sheriff, who served the papers on him.

The death of Post will compel the postponement of the suit for the possession of Mrs. Stannard's estate, which was scheduled to begin on next Tuesday.

Post and his wife were the defendants in what has indications of proving one of the most remarkable will contests ever recorded in this State. The suit is instituted by Carroll E. Kingsley of Westbrook, who is the administrator of the estate of Mrs. Stannard. Kingsley is acting on behalf of the heirs of Mrs. Stannard.

He asserts he has evidence that Mrs. Stannard was persuaded by Post and his wife to deed all her property to them without receiving any recompense in return. Undue influence to obtain possession of the estate is alleged. The property was transferred to the Posts about a year ago. Mrs. Stannard died on January 16. Her relatives, who expected to divide her estate, found themselves in possession of nothing except her personal property.

The Posts are distant relatives of Mrs. Stannard and she had lived with them for several years. Post was about 60 years old and was a prominent business man. Mrs. Stannard was one of the largest real estate owners in town. It is said that the question of Mrs. Stannard's mental soundness when she transferred the estate will be raised. Post, who fell a victim to the excitement attendant on the beginning of the suit over the property, was subject to attacks of heart failure.

HYDROPHOBIA KILLS YOUNG GIRL

Had Taken Pasteur Treatment for Bites Inflicted in June.

Hydrophobia, caused by the bite of a mongrel dog on June 13 last, resulted yesterday in the death of the daughter, 7 years old, of John Kohlmeier, a hardware dealer of No. 252 East Sixty-second street. The little girl was attacked by the dog and bitten on the right eyelid, right cheek and right lip. The wounds were cauterized immediately by Dr. Mund of No. 308 East Sixty-second street. The girl then was taken to the Pasteur Institute, where she underwent a full course of its treatment, lasting forty-eight days.

Early in July the child went to her father's summer home at Port Richmond, S. I., and until last week apparently was in the best of health. On Friday she began to show symptoms of hydrophobia and on Saturday, being worse, she was brought to the city. Mr. Kohlmeier says that on Saturday he communicated with the Pasteur Institute, informing them of the condition of his daughter, and was told that if hydrophobia had developed after having taken their full course of treatment nothing could be done, and the child must die. She suffered terrible agony in her last hours.

MINISTER WU TING FANG GOING

Popular Chinese Diplomat Will Be Transferred to England.

LONDON, Sept. 2.—"Li Ching Fang, the adopted son of Li Hung Chang, having declined the St. Petersburg Legation," says a dispatch to the Times from Pekin, "China has appointed Sir Chih-Chen Lo Feng-Luh (Chinese Minister in London) to St. Petersburg, transferring Wu Ting Fang from Washington to London."

Wu Ting Fang has been the most popular minister China ever sent to the United States. Since his arrival here three years ago he has made a reputation as an after-dinner speaker and wit, and has done much to assist in maintaining the American position in his country. His departure will be regretted by diplomats and his many friends.

39 GO DOWN WITH STEAMER.

TREBIZONDE, Asiatic Turkey, Sept. 1.—The Belgian steamship Noranmore, bound from Batoum for Bombay, sank near Athina. With the exception of one man the entire crew of forty were drowned.

The Noranmore was a turret deck steamer, the largest of that type afloat. She registered 5,640 tons gross and had a length of 420 feet and a beam of 50 feet.

The vessel practically was new, having been built in 1899. She formerly plied in the service of the Johnson line and visited the ports of Boston and Baltimore. The Belgian Maritime Trading Company of Antwerp were the owners of the Noranmore.

VENEZUELA NOW EXPECTS WAR

CARACAS, Sept. 1.—The Venezuelan Government has published a memorandum remitted to all foreign nations in explanation of the attitude it has adopted in the Venezuelan-Colombian controversy.

In diplomatic circles here the question is considered serious.

PARIS, Sept. 2.—A dispatch from Caracas asserts that the memorandum issued by the Venezuelan Government to foreign Powers in explanation of its course in the Venezuelan-Colombian difficulty says that hostilities between the two States are imminent.

Another Employe Who Discovered the Bodies Placed Under Arrest.

CRIME THOUGHT TO BE WORK OF BURGLARS

Organization a Fashionable One, Formed to Rival Westchester Country Club.

IN THE exclusive Siwanoy Country Club near Chester Hill, in Mount Vernon, David Scott, the club steward, and Captain John Stevens, his assistant, were found murdered yesterday morning. Both men are negroes and slept in the same room on the third floor of the club house. Warner Sims, the club cook, also a negro, and whose room was not ten feet away from that occupied by the murdered men, was arrested on suspicion and later in the day Frank Dennington, a waiter, was locked up by orders of Chief Foley of the Mount Vernon police.

There is great mystery as to how the two men met their death. There are three theories, one that Sims, the arrested man, committed the crime to obtain a tin box containing $175 of the club's money which the steward had in his room. This box and its contents are missing. The second theory, and one which has many facts to warrant its entertainment, is that burglars gained admission to the house by the rear entrance in the early morning and that the double murder was incidental to their purpose of robbery. The third is that the two men, the steward and his assistant, quarreled and fought to the death after having gone to their room shortly after midnight.

WORK ON THE MYSTERY.

Mount Vernon people, club waiters and others were about equally divided among the three theories last night. Chief of Police Foley said he had formed no opinion as yet, and that he wanted a day or two longer to work on the mystery before he committed himself.

Mayor E. W. Fiske was at Police Headquarters for several hours yesterday, and took part in the examination which Sims, the cook, underwent at the hands of Chief Foley. The Mayor made many suggestions, and when Sims was stripped and carefully examined for marks of blood Mayor Fiske personally assisted in the inspection. Blood was found on the heel of the arrested man, but as he had been the first to discover and report the crime and as the room in which the dead man lay was covered with blood, his explanation that he had stepped in a bloody pool on the carpet was plausible.

The rear doors of the club house were found broken and their glass shattered when the police first arrived at the scene, and this made it appear to have been the work of burglars. Those who think that the evidence is strongly against Sims, however, said that he could have easily arranged this appearance of burglary after having slaughtered his fellow servants.

TO RIVAL WESTCHESTER CLUB.

The Siwanoy Country Club was opened on July 4 last with a reception, which was a social feature in Mount Vernon. A committee of patronesses, which included many of the social leaders of the city, received guests, and the new club started in with a boom, as far as social prestige is concerned. The Lucas brothers, who come from one of the oldest families in Westchester County, inspired the organization of the club, which has fine golf links as well as all the other accessories of a first-class country club. The odd name, Siwanoy, is that of the tribe of Indians which formerly occupied the land now laid out as a golf course.

The club house is an old manor house, formerly the Glover residence, and stands at Sageman's Corners, about ten minutes' ride by trolley from the New Haven station. There are about thirty-five acres of ground about it. The old manor was remodeled inside and out, and fitted with all the modern appointments of a club, and the golf enthusiasts of Mount Vernon, many of them New York business men, congratulated themselves that they had established at their own doors an institution that some day was bound to rival the famed Westchester Country Club.

WAS BUTLER FOR ROBERT GARRETT.

Dr. A. M. Campbell was elected president and the other officers are: Frank W. Mack, vice president; W. N. G. Clark, secretary; Arthur D. Stone, treasurer, and Alfred E. Taylor, captain. The Board of Governors

THE WEATHER REPORT.

INDICATIONS FOR TO-DAY.

For Eastern New York, Eastern Pennsylvania and New Jersey—Generally fair Monday and Tuesday; light to fresh east to north winds.

For Western New York—Generally fair Monday and Tuesday; light north to east winds.

For New England—Generally fair Monday and Tuesday, preceded by showers Monday in Maine; light to fresh winds, mostly easterly.

Temperature here yesterday, according to Perry's thermometer:

	1900.	1901.		1900.	1901.
3.00 a. m.	73	70	3.30 p. m.	83	74
6.00 a. m.	72	68	6.00 p. m.	78	72
9.00 a. m.	75	71	9.00 p. m.	76	70
12.00 m.	77	78	12.00 mid.	74	6[illegible]

Average temperature yesterday, 71½; average temperature for corresponding date last year, 76¾.

Weather Bureau's local observations:

	8 A. M.	8 P. M.
State of weather	Lt. rain.	Clear
Wind, direction	N. E.	N. E.
Wind, velocity	10	7
Temperature	68	71
Humidity	88	84
Precipitation	0.57	T.

Maximum temperature, 74, at 4 p. m.; minimum, 68, at 6 a. m.

New-York Tribune.
ILLUSTRATED SUPPLEMENT.
SUNDAY, MARCH 23, 1902.

NEW OFFICIALS, A RAILWAY FIREMAN AT THEIR HEAD, WILL SOON BE IN CONTROL OF THE "GATEWAY TO AMERICA."

Loose practices discovered at Ellis Island and the Barge Office, in this city, in connection with the admission of immigrants, have caused President Roosevelt to consider a change desirable.

UNWASHED BUT STURDY STOCK FROM THE SOUTH OF EUROPE.
Photographed upon arrival at Ellis Island.

IMMIGRANTS LEAVING THE BARGE OFFICE.
For their first ride up Broadway.

FRANK P. SARGENT.
He is Grand Master of the Brotherhood of Locomotive Firemen, and is slated for Commissioner General of Immigration.

BAGGAGE OF IMMIGRANTS.
Each one frequently seems to carry enough for a Saratoga belle.

TERENCE V. POWDERLY,
The Commissioner General of Immigration, whose term soon expires.

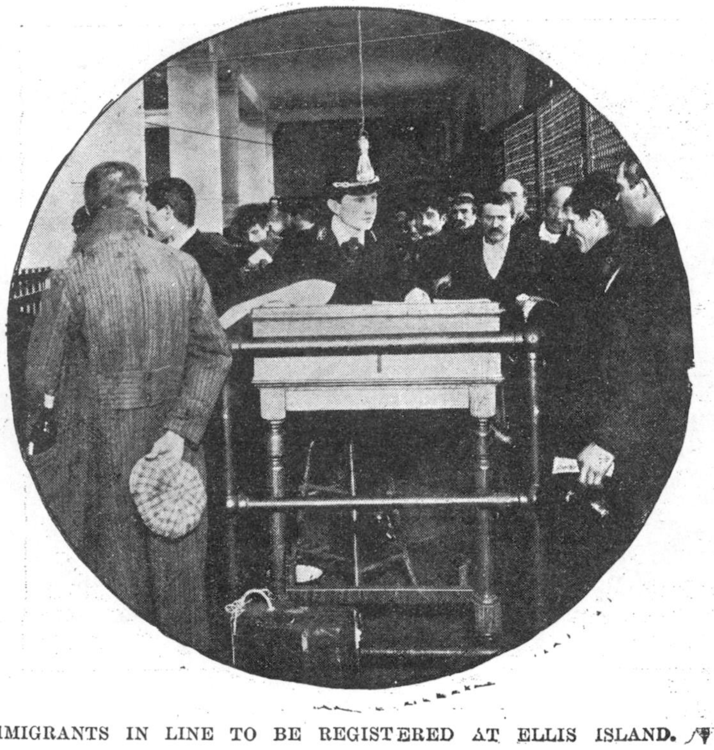

IMMIGRANTS IN LINE TO BE REGISTERED AT ELLIS ISLAND.

IN THE PEN AT ELLIS ISLAND FOR "DEFERRED" AND EXCLUDED IMMIGRANTS.

NEW-YORK HAS MANY IMPRESSIVE SKYSCRAPERS — BUT NONE MORE REMARKABLE THAN THE FLATIRON.

ship was out of the bay. They were tremendously happy over it, and more or less excited, as it was their first ocean voyage. The woman was afraid of being seasick, and asked every one she met for a "sure cure." The new husband was brazen in his scorn of the sea.

"I will not be seasick," he said, "and I won't bother with any of your old cures."

The bride kept up her hunt for a "cure," and at last succeeded. An old traveller told her to put a piece of brown paper over her chest and keep moving about on deck as much as possible. She had faith in the cure, but could not persuade her husband to paper his chest. He called it foolishness.

The steamer ran into a blow just outside of the Hook, and for twenty-four hours few passengers were in sight. It was exceedingly rough, but the bride did not seem to mind. She was one of the three women who dared come to meals, and she had to come alone, which looked bad for the bridegroom.

The third day out she got him on deck, a pallid wreck of a happy, boasting bridegroom. He lay in a steamer chair in the lee of a lifeboat and tried to forget. She danced up and down the deck, always in sight of his chair. After an hour she had the stewards help him below. She remained on deck to read and please the other passengers with her smile.

"You have been reversing the usual order," said one. "On honeymoon voyages it is usually the bride who gets seasick."

"I am not so sorry for John," she said. "He laughed at my brown paper cure, and it serves him right. If I had been sick I naver would have heard the last of it. I just had to stay well."

A WONDERFUL BUILDING.

THE FLATIRON, WITH SHARP EDGE, COULD ACCOMMODATE AN ORDINARY VILLAGE POPULATION.

The Flatiron Building, at the intersection of Broadway, Fifth-ave. and Twenty-third-st., New-York, is a marvel of tall building construction. It takes its name from the ground plan, which roughly resembles the form of a sadiron. Its greatest length is 190 feet in Broadway. It is 173 feet long in Fifth-ave., and 86 feet 8 inches in Twenty-second-st. Since the removal last week of the scaffolding, which partly concealed the outlines, there is scarcely an hour when a staring wayfarer doesn't by his example collect a big crowd of other staring people. Sometimes a hundred or more, with heads bent backward until a general breakage of necks seems imminent, collect along the walk on the Fifth-ave. side of Madison Square and stay there until "one of the finest" orders them to move on.

No wonder people stare! A building 307 feet high, presenting an edge almost as sharp as the bow of a ship to one of the most frequented openings along Broadway, is well worth looking at. The mere statement of the height in feet conveys only an imperfect idea of the towering structure. It is more impressive to say that if it fell over to the eastward it would almost reach Madison-ave. It would more than reach from Twenty-second-st. to Twenty-first-st. if it should fall along Fifth-ave.

The Flatiron is not the tallest building in New-York, but it is the slenderest—as a bright girl expresses it, "the most aquiline." "It's the sharpest thing any architect ever perpetrated," according to another authority.

It looks tall enough above ground, but there are 35 feet of it buried, the bottom of the boiler-room being that far below the street grade.

If all its floors should be divided into offices there would be seventeen on each floor, and if there were an average of five persons to the office the population of the building would be 1,700, or more than that of a respectable suburban village, for the Flatiron is twenty stories high.

The architects responsible for this unique structure are D. H. Burnham & Co., of Chicago, and the corporation which is investing $1,500,000 in it is the Fifth Avenue Building Company. It is to be ready for occupancy early in the fall.

DR. PATTON'S DUAL CITIZENSHIP.

A LOYAL AMERICAN, BUT LEGALLY A SUBJECT OF THE KING.

Princeton, June 28.—Dr. Francis L. Patton, of Princeton University, who recently resigned the presidency of that institution, enjoys the distinction of a dual citizenship, in all probability a distinction held by no other college president in the United States, and perhaps by no other in the world. He is both a citizen of the United States and at the same time a subject of Great Britain, and this is the explanation: In the early years of the last century his grandfather lived in New-York and was engaged in the coastwise trade between New-York and the West Indies. He was a native born American. On account of the annoyance and losses due to the impressment of seamen and other outrages which led to the war of 1812, he removed to Bermuda in order to save his business. He and his family lived there during the rest of his life, and one of his sons, the father of Dr. Patton, who was born in New-York, married while in Bermuda, and it was there that Dr. Patton was born.

According to the law of Great Britain, which holds that any one born on British land is a subject of Great Britain, Dr. Patton is a subject of the King. President Patton's father, who was a citizen of the United States, never took the oath of allegiance to Great Britain, and according to the American law, which provides that the children of any citizen of the United States born in any land, whether under the Stars and Stripes or some other flag, are citizens of the United States, Dr. Patton is an American citizen.

President Patton scouts the idea that he is a British subject and not a citizen of the United States, as has been generally rumored. He is a citizen of both countries, and this because he has never declared his citizenship. He could enjoy the right to vote to-morrow if he should declare his citizenship, but the reason he has not done so is that an ancestral estate was left to him in Bermuda, and if he declared himself a citizen of the United States this estate would escheat to the crown. That this estate might be passed on to his children is the reason he has refrained from declaring his citizenship. Notwithstanding, he is a true and loyal American, and in full sympathy with the progressive movements of the American people and the country in which he has lived since he was eighteen years old.

THE FLATIRON.
The remarkable new skyscraper at Twenty-third-st., Fifth-ave. and Broadway; D. H. Burnham & Co., architects.

SAXONY'S NEW KING.

NINE OTHER REIGNING SOVEREIGNS BEAR, LIKE HIM, THE TITLE OF DUKE OF SAXONY.

Although the kingdom of Saxony is considered abroad as one of those petty States of Central Europe that have become merged into what is now known as the German Empire—States that are bound by the march of events gradually to lose both their independence and their identity, their rulers sinking more and more into the position of mere vassals of the German Kaiser—yet the royal House of Saxony is undoubtedly the most important of the Old World in these modern times. For its members occupy no less than ten of the thrones of Europe, namely, those of Great Britain, Prussia, Portugal, Belgium, Bulgaria, Saxony, Saxe-Weimar, Saxe-Altenburg, Saxe-Meiningen and Saxe-Coburg and Gotha.

All these rulers bear, in addition to their other titles, that of Duke of Saxony. Bound together as they are by ties of kinsmanship and of dynastic policy, it will be readily seen that in this manner the royal House of Saxony possesses a prominence in the so-called concert of nations that is quite out of proportion to the relatively insignificant kingdom of Saxony, where a new monarch now reigns in the place of kindly, unaffected and sensible old Albert, whose two most intimate friends and cronies were Emperor Francis Joseph of Austria and the late Emperor Frederick of Germany. Foes in the war of 1866, comrades and fellow-commanders in the war of 1870, there was no one whom Frederick trusted more implicitly than King Albert of Saxony, and, full of apprehension for the future, he besought the latter a short time before his so tragic death to befriend his eldest boy and to stand by his side as a mentor with all the indulgence of a father.

Albert may be said to have responded nobly to this dying request of "Unser Fritz," and no one is more ready than Emperor William himself to acknowledge how much he owes to the paternal counsels, to the sagacious advice and to the ever kindly interest and sympathy of the good old King who has now gone to his rest. How completely the Kaiser deferred to the judgment of his father's best friend is shown by the manner in which he withdrew from the position which he had assumed in connection with the controversy about the regency of the principality of Lippe on his Saxon majesty pronouncing himself in favor of the claims of Count Lippe Biesterfield, as opposed to those of Prince Adolphus of Schaumburg-Lippe. It was a bitter pill for Emperor William to swallow. Yet he took his medicine without a murmur, and, far from allowing it to impair in any degree his affection for King Albert, treated him, on the contrary, thereafter with even still more filial devotion and regard than before.

King George, who has now succeeded to the throne of his childless brother, was, like the latter, one of the most successful and brilliant commanders of the war of 1870, holding the rank of field marshal general of the German army. While it cannot be said that there are any such relations between him and the Kaiser as prevailed between the latter and King Albert—namely, like those of father and son—yet there is no doubt but that the new ruler of Saxony is to a greater extent in political and military sympathy with Emperor William than his predecessor on the throne.

Thus, he shares his views with regard to the Poles, and provoked a scene during the grand manœuvres of the German army in Posen some two or three years ago by insisting upon the removal of the national flag of Poland, which had been hoisted by the Polish noble owning the chateau in which he and several other German royal princes had been quartered during the mimic warfare. He declared that he would not remain in the chateau unless either the flag of the German Empire or that of Saxony were raised in its stead, calling attention to the fact that he was there not as a guest, but by virtue of that law which compels German citizens of a district where military operations are in progress to lodge and board a certain number of officers or men. It was this action on the part of King George of Saxony which served to call public attention throughout Germany to the aggressive nationalism on the part of the Poles, and which precipitated the disappearance from the court of Berlin of certain brilliant representatives of the Polish aristocracy, who were charged with misusing the imperial favor which they enjoyed for the purpose of promoting their political intrigues.

King George, who is above everything else a soldier, alike by taste and training, has been a widower for sixteen years, his consort having been a sister of the late King of Portugal. Passionately fond of music and a devout Catholic, in spite of his being the granduncle of the King of Italy, he has three sons and two daughters still living. His eldest boy, Frederick Augustus, now heir apparent to his throne, is married to the Archduchess Louise of Austria, daughter of the Grand Duke of Tuscany, and one of his daughters, Marie Josepha, is the wife of Archduke Otho, who, in view of the morganatic marriage of his elder brother, Archduke Francis Ferdinand, is bound in due course to succeed to the throne of Austria-Hungary.

Yet another son of King George is a priest.

New-York Tribune.

ILLUSTRATED SUPPLEMENT.

SUNDAY, JULY 12, 1903.

SOME OF THE NINE NEW THEATRES THAT WILL GREET MANHATTAN PLEASURE SEEKERS NEXT SEASON

LYRIC THEATRE.
third-st., near Broadway.

THE NEW LYCEUM.
In Forty-fifth-st., near Broadway.

HUDSON THEATRE.
In Forty-fourth-st., near Broadway.

DRURY LANE THEATRE.
In Thirty-fourth-st., near Eighth-ave.

THE COMEDY THEATRE.
Forty-ninth-st. and Seventh-ave.

STEAM SHOVEL PLOUGHING UP THE FOUNDATIONS OF HOUSES ON THE SITE OF THE NEW GRAND CENTRAL RAILWAY TERMINAL IN THIS CITY.

(W. D. Inslee, Photographer.)

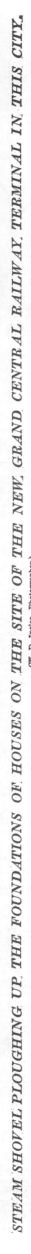

New-York Tribune.

[Copyright; 1903: By The Tribune Association.]

V^OL. LXIII....N^O. 20,853. To-day, rain or snow and warmer. To-morrow, fair and cooler. NEW-YORK, SUNDAY, DECEMBER 20, 1903.—FORTY-FOUR PAGES. PRICE FIVE CENTS.

SCENES AT THE OPENING OF THE NEW WILLIAMSBURG BRIDGE.

GUSTAV LINDENTHAL. JACOB A. CANTOR. MAYOR LOW. (Copyright, 1901, by Pach Brothers.) J. E. SWANSTROM.

CITY AND MANHATTAN OFFICIALS GOING TO MEET BROOKLYN OFFICIALS.

MAYOR LOW DELIVERING HIS ADDRESS.

BROOKLYN AND MANHATTAN OFFICIALS APPROACHING THE BROOKLYN END.

SENATOR HOAR ANSWERED

MORE LIGHT ON PANAMA.

Further Correspondence Justifying the President's Policy.

[FROM THE TRIBUNE BUREAU.]

Washington, Dec. 19.—The President to-day transmitted to the Senate the correspondence which passed between the State Department and Minister Beaupré at Bogota. The receipt of these communications was a source of gratification to the Republicans and a source of embarrassment to the Democrats, because the untenability of the Democratic position is still further emphasized. This correspondence is held to be a complete answer to Senator Hoar's inquiry as to what led this government to anticipate a revolution on the isthmus. It is shown that as far back as September 10 Minister Beaupré cabled the State Department that the appointment of Obaldia as Governor of Panama was regarded as the "forerunner of separation," and that a resolution which amounted to censure of the government had been passed by an almost unanimous vote, the only Senator de-[illegible] the action being the son of President [illegible]n. From experience, according to leading [illegible]can Senators, this government would have been most culpable had it not made preparations to protect the traffic across the isthmus, and would have incurred just condemnation had it been so remiss.

Attention is further called to the fact that on October 28 the news of a probable revolution on the isthmus "leaked out" in Bogota. The Republicans have no fear that they can not demonstrate to every unprejudiced person the entire propriety with which the administration acted in the premises, but they admit they are at a loss for some method by which to bring the Democrats to a realization of the responsibility they are incurring in permitting their efforts to annoy the administration to cre[illegible] a false impression in Colombia and afford encouragement to General Reyes, the Colombian commissioner now in this country.

WHAT THE PAPERS SHOW.

The papers transmitted by the President comprise correspondence between the State Department and Minister Beaupré, at Bogota, relative to the Hay-Herran treaty, consisting of 120 letters and telegrams sent between March 18 and November 18, 1903.

On April 7 Secretary Hay instructed Mr. Beaupré to inform Colombia that the requests of Colombia to canal and railroad companies for appointment of agents to negotiate cancellation of the present concessions were covered by the treaty, "and any change would be in violation of the Spooner law and not permissible."

On April 15 Mr. Beaupré again reviewed at length the feeling in Colombia toward the treaty. On its negotiation he says: "I am convinced the public had never expected better terms."

In a letter on the subject of public opinion adverse to the treaty Mr. Beaupré says:

It is utterly impossible to convince these people that the Nicaragua route was ever seriously considered by the United States, that the negotiation concerning it had any other motive than the squeezing of an advantageous bargain out of Colombia, nor that any other than the Panama route ever will be selected.

WANTED MORE MONEY.

The public discussion, he says, was largely along the line of the loss of national honor by the surrender of sovereignty, while private discussion was to the effect that the price was inadequate.

Mr. Hay, on May 30, asked whether there was any opposition from European sources. He called the situation "seemingly grave."

On June 9 Mr. Hay sent this dispatch to Mr. Beaupré:

The Colombian government apparently does not appreciate the gravity of the situation. The canal negotiations were instituted by Colombia, and were energetically pressed upon this government for several years. The propositions presented by Colombia, with slight modifications, were finally accepted by us. In virtue of this agreement our Congress reversed its previous judgment, and decided upon the Panama route. If Colombia should now reject the treaty, or unduly delay its ratification, the friendly understanding between the two countries would be so seriously compromised that action might be taken by the Congress next winter which every friend of Colombia would regret.

PRICE SET ON RATIFICATION.

On June 10 Mr. Beaupré wrote that a decided effort was being made to change public opinion into a more favorable consideration of the treaty. Mr. Beaupré said he had been informed by Mr. Mancini, agent at Bogota, of the Panama Canal Company, that he had been told ratification could be secured by the pay-

Continued on third page.

NO ANSWER FROM JAPAN.

Reply to Russia May Be Delayed for a Few Days.

Tokio, Dec. 19.—Japan's answer to Russia has not yet been sent. Owing to the indisposition of the Russian Minister, Baron de Rosen, it will probably be delayed for a day or two.

AN ULTIMATUM DENIED.

Rumor of Japanese Action in Dispatch from Tientsin.

London, Dec. 19.—A special dispatch from Tientsin says it is reported that Japan has sent an ultimatum to Russia. Baron Hayashi, the Japanese Minister to Great Britain, positively denied that an ultimatum had been sent, and the report has not been confirmed from any source. It is regarded as impossible that such important news should come first from Tientsin.

NO LOANS IN SIGHT.

Bankers Here and in England Not Likely to Give Aid.

London, Dec. 19.—The Rothschilds have heard nothing of any suggestions that Russia will attempt to raise a loan of $125,000,000, or any other amount, in Great Britain, and they declare that the report is palpably unfounded. Russia, they say, could not raise a loan here, and, judging from their latest advices from Paris, it would probably be equally difficult for Russia to raise more money in France.

It is stated in other quarters that, even were a Russian loan issued elsewhere, there is little likelihood of any portion of it being underwritten in London.

The report in circulation to the effect that Russia was about to open negotiations with a view to securing a loan in New-York is not credited in financial circles here. The Russian government, it is learned, made similar overtures unsuccessfully about six months ago.

A few days ago representatives of the Japanese government conferred with New-York bankers respecting the feasibility of a projected effort by Japan to float a large loan here, making no secret of the fact that the money, if secured, might be used for war purposes. These negotiations also were unsuccessful.

International bankers here are substantially unanimous in the opinion that, all other considerations being eliminated, domestic financial needs make any sort of a foreign loan impracticable at this time.

In February, 1902, it was reported that the Japanese government was negotiating for a loan here, but nothing ever came of the movement. Early in 1900 a syndicate of New-York banks, trust companies and life insurance companies purchased an issue of $25,000,000 4 per cent bonds of a Russian railway, which were guaranteed as to both principal and interest by the Russian government.

CHINESE OFFICIAL DEGRADED.

Tien-Tsin, Dec. 19.—Chang Yi, Director of the Northern Railways, has been degraded and stripped of all rank.

USE CARS FOR FUNERALS.

Feared That Drivers' Strike Will Cause Epidemic in Chicago.

Chicago, Dec. 19.—Undertakers' wagons and streetcars were used to convey the dead to the cemeteries to-day. In nearly every instance the funerals were watched by union pickets to see that no livery carriages formed part of the funeral procession. The most prominent funeral of the day was that of Judge Jonas Hutchinson, for fifteen years on the bench of the Superior Court. The body of Judge Hutchinson was taken to Oakwoods Cemetery in an undertaker's wagon, while the private carriages of his personal friends were used for the pallbearers and immediate friends of the family.

Police protection against strikers for funeral processions on their way to the cemeteries was demanded of Police Chief O'Neill this evening by a committee from the joint livery association, and was promptly promised by the chief. He ordered the police inspectors to afford every protection in their power, but refused to allow the officers to be seated on or drive the vehicles bearing the bodies.

"This interference with the burial of the dead is the meanest bit of business the police have had to cope with, to my knowledge," the chief said. "I do not know how the thing could be carried any further."

No attack has yet been made on ambulances bearing the sick, but the undertakers express fears that such will soon take place. Chairman Perrigo said that teamsters had threatened to drive the poles of their trucks through ambulances, but so far they have not done so. Particularly in cases of death from diphtheria and scarlet fever, in which burial must occur within twenty-four hours or before dark of the day following death, the strike is expected to have grave results. Interference with burials of such bodies might result in the spreading of epidemics.

GAGGED AND TIED SELF.

GILBERT CONFESSES.

Did It to Break Off Engagement—The "Drug" Was Whiskey.

The mystery surrounding the case of Otto Gilbert, who was found in a buggy at Irvington Friday evening, bound hand foot, and apparenly under the ifluence of a drug, was cleared away yesterday when the young man confessed that he had planned the whole affair with the object of breaking off his engagement with the young woman who he was to marry to-day. His plot was successful so far as the engagement was concerned, for the wedding was declared off, although his fiance, Miss Nellie Curry, of South E-st., Irvington, had already received many gifts, and all preparations for the ceremony had been made.

Gilbert was found with his hands and feet bound together with a piece of rope, and in his mouth was a gag of his own handkerchief. His watch was missing and the chain dangling. He was taken to the police station in the Town Hall. He remained semi-conscious for several hours. According to his confession a too free indulgence in whiskey was the sole cause of his stupor.

Yesterday morning he told Judge Irving H. Taylor a remarkable story about meeting three men in Yonkers, drinking with them, and being taken by them in a closed carriage, with a handkerchief saturated with drug over his face. It had made him unconscious. When he awake he found himself in a dark room. The three men, all of whom were armed, were with him, and from that time until he left the room there was always one man on guard over him. He said they tried to induce him to give them a check for $1,500 that he had on deposit in the Dry Dock Savings Bank in this city, but he refused, though he did give them on order for $25 on a Harlem man.

Then, Gilbert said, they took him to Tarrytown and made him hire the horse and buggy, threatening him with death if he told anybody what happened. Then there was another trip to Yonkers and further efforts to induce him to give them the check. Then, accompanied by one of them, he declared, he started for Irvington, but after passing Hastings he didn't remember anything that occurred until he was restored to consciousness in the police station at Irvington.

The story was told so plausibly that the police officials decided to take him to Yonkers. Before starting, however, Judge Taylor examined him rigidly, with the result that he broke down and confessed that the whole story was a "fake." He found that he could not support a wife, and thought if he made up the kidnapping story he would be released from his engagement to Miss Curry.

After he had made his confession Gilbert was arraigned in court and fined $15 for "drunkenness in the street." He could not pay and was locked in a cell. If it is not paid by to-morrow morning Gilbert will be taken to the White Plains jail to serve one day for every dollar.

In his confession Gilbert declared that he came to this city Tuesday and pawned his watch, and with this money went to New-Hampshire, where he had wealthy relatives, expecting to borrow enough money to pay for his wedding trip. When he arrived there his courage failed him, and he returned to Irvington without asking for a loan. On Thursday he wrote Miss Curry that his body would be found on the aqueduct.

On Friday he went to Tarrytown, hired the horse, drove to Yonkers and bought a bottle of whiskey. He then started back for Irvington, frequently sipping the whiskey from the bottle. When he neared the town of Greensburg he slowed the horse up, stuffed the rag into his mouth, then took his handkerchief and, folding it into a bandage, tied it over his mouth, the knots being back of his head. He then took a rope, tied his legs together, and made a slip noose on each end of the rope. Through this noose he put his hands, and, doubling up his feet, drew the noose taut on each wrist, cutting into the flesh, and thus causing the bleeding. Finally he became drowsy from the liquor. Miss Curry's mother is said to have been strongly opposed to the match. Yesterday she declared that when Miss Curry showed Gilbert a $10 gold piece which had been sent by her uncle as a wedding present, Gilbert remarked that he didn't think his landlady had ever seen a $10 gold piece and he would like to show her one. According to Mrs. Curry, he took the coin, and that was the last the Curry family has seen of it. It is also declared that a few months ago he gave Miss Curry an engagement ring. The last time he saw her he asked to look at it, and as she took it off her finger it dropped, and he accidentally stepped on it, crushing it. He took it, saying he would have it repaired.

Last Sunday night, in company with Miss Curry, Gilbert went to see Father Early to sign the anti-nuptial papers, for which he had to pay a fee. He did not have the money and the papers were not signed. Father Early is the pastor of the Church of the Immaculate Conception at Irvington, who was in controversy with Miss Helen Gould.

IRELAND FOR CARDINAL.

Philippine Settlement Betters Archbishop's Chances.

(Special to The New-York Tribune by French Cable.)
(Copyright; 1903: By The Tribune Association.)

Rome, Dec. 19.—The agreement reached between Governor Taft and Archbishop Guidi in regard to the purchase of the lands of the friars in the Philippines has increased the probabilities that Archbishop Ireland will be made a cardinal. His friends here wish to remind the Pope that Leo promised to reward Archbishop Ireland with the red hat after a settlement of the Philippine question. The cardinals belonging to the religious orders, however, besides the Spanish cardinals, are not satisfied with the agreement, and are more than ever determined to oppose the nomination of Archbishop Ireland, whom they consider to be chiefly responsible for what appears to them their defeat. It is reported that Cardinals Martinelli and Vives y Tuto will be charged by the others to speak on the subject to the Pope.

OHIO WILL BE IN LINE.

Colonel Herrick Expects Roosevelt's Nomination and Election.

Governor-elect Myron T. Herrick, of Ohio, says there is practically no doubt of President Roosevelt's nomination and election next year. Mr. Herrick came on from Washington yesterday with Mrs. Herrick and will spend to-day in town, starting for his home in Cleveland early this week. He was at the Cabinet dinner in Washington on Thursday night.

"There is practically no doubt that President Roosevelt will be nominated by the Republican National Convention next June and that he will be elected," he said last night to a Tribune reporter. "The many rumors afloat about Ohio hostility to him are largely without foundation. Senator Hanna has said more than once that he was not and is not hostile to him. Ohio will give the Republican ticket its enthusiastic support. Ohio Republicans are not plotting and scheming for Presidential honors, as some of our Democratic friends seem to think. The nomination of McKinley came naturally. The country wanted him, and he justified our faith. Generally speaking, I think Republicanism is in a wholesome and militant condition. It certainly is in Ohio.

"Shall you go to the national convention?"

"It is customary for the Governor of our State to go. I expect to be there," said Mr. Herrick.

When Colonel Herrick's Vice-Presidential boom was referred to he smiled and said nothing. He will be sworn in on January 11.

THE KAISER SPEAKS AT HANOVER.

A Stirring Address to Officers—His Voice Strong and Clear.

Hanover, Dec. 19.—At a dinner given in honor of the centennial of the formation of the Hanoverian regiments to-night Emperor William, replying to a toast and speaking loudly and distinctly, said:

With hearty thanks I raise my glass and I hope all will follow the example. To the health of the German legion, in memory of its incomparable deeds, which, in conjunction with Blücher and the Prussians, rescued the English army from destruction at Waterloo. To the past of 1866, when, brave and undaunted, the untarnished shield of Hanoverian honor was held high and bright. To the past of 1870, to the hero of Beaune la Rolande, who, alas, is no longer among us. To the present, which is here assembled and which I here greet, and to the future, which I hope may be as brilliant, pure and beautiful as the past. The German legions and its traditions: Hoch! Hoch!

As his majesty left the hall there was a remarkable outburst of cheering, which was long continued.

This morning the Kaiser reviewed the regiments and several thousand veterans of the Hanoverian army. He ordered a commemorative medal to be struck.

SAND MAY SOON COVER THE MOCCASIN

The Submarine Torpedo Boat Rapidly Settling Where She Grounded.

[BY TELEGRAPH TO THE TRIBUNE.]

Norfolk, Va., Dec. 19.—The United States submarine torpedo boat Moccasin, which broke loose from the naval tug Peoria in a recent gale and was blown ashore at Little Island, on the Virginia coast, is buried in six feet of sand, and the outlook for floating her in the near future is not bright. The wreckers expected a very high tide so that they could float the vessel, but the Moccasin has been steadily settling in the sand, and at the rate that she is sinking will soon be entirely buried. Besides the tugs of the Merritt Wrecking Company, the government has two tugs at the scene.

BRIDGE OPENED AMID CHEERS.

MAYOR HEADS CEREMONY ON NEW WILLIAMSBURG STRUCTURE—FIREWORKS LIGHT UP NIGHT.

Parade Through Brooklyn, Decked Out in Gala Attire, and Reception for City Officials—Housetops and Roofs Crowded with Sightseers.

Mayor Low, accompanied by city officials of all the boroughs of the greater city, formally opened the new Williamsburg Bridge in the afternoon while thousands cheered from surrounding house and building tops.

Brooklyn was decked in gala attire for a procession in honor of the bridge opening. A luncheon and reception was given at the Hanover Club for Mayor Low and other officials.

A marine parade and fireworks at night ended the opening ceremonies.

ROCKETS BLAZE IN SKY.

Vessels Parade Under Bridge While Spectators Line Shore.

No one had a better view of the superb fireworks which ended the opening of the new Williamsburg Bridge than those on the huge fleet of towboats in the naval parade. Nothing marred the display, there was not a single accident, and everything went with the smoothness of clockwork from the time the first rocket marked its fiery path in the sky until a blazing "Good night" signified its close.

Soon after dark the bridge was outlined by thousands of incandescent lights. At either end of the bridge, surmounting the towers, were the national colors. At the base of the short poles were burned great flares of red fire. At a little distance the star spangled banner seemed to be a blazing bit of color.

At 8 o'clock a rocket sent high into the air signalled the beginning of the display. A moment later at equal distances twenty aerial bombs were sent aloft, bursting with cannon-like reports two hundred feet above the bridge. Then, with no warning, the bridge was suddenly transformed into a sheet of flame. From tower to tower the flames turned and writhed and flared high in the air, illuminating the waterfront for blocks.

Then came a kaleidoscopic medley of colors, red, green, purple, orange, velvet—more colors than a French ribbon dealer could enumerate—from huge rockets that sailed two hundred feet above the bridge. Some of them broke in huge showers of glinting balls of fire; others burst into long connected streams of parti-colored flames, while others displayed long, thin, hair-like streams of glowing red.

Every time that an unusually beautiful piece was discharged it was greeted by a salvo of cheers from the hundreds that thronged the waterfront, and by ear splitting shrieks from the whistles of the great fleet of towboats that lay just below and above the bridge. One of the finest things shown was the aerial girandole. Over two hundred and fifty 6 and 8 pound rockets were sent aloft at once. All were so timed and aimed that they met in a point high above the centre of the bridge. Then they exploded almost simultaneously. The long, scintillating streams of blazing stars in thirty different colors shot outward in every direction. For a moment they hung almost stationary in the sky, and then slowly and gracefully sunk, disappearing one by one. Right after this a volley of twenty meteor-like blazing balls were sent upward. When they burst great fiery dragons zig-zagged in every direction. Ten enormous shells were then discharged. When they burst an iridescent sheet of gold hung fully a minute in the sky before the shimmering particles faded slowly away.

PORTRAITS IN FIREWORKS.

Later the boats kept their whistles shrieking until steam was exhausted, over a string of flaming fountains that were displayed at short intervals the entire length of the bridge. A full hundred feet upward were thrown a thousand gleaming bith of fire, that blazed and glowed like diamonds in the air. The gleaming violet and purple of the stars blazed forth like the discharge from a steel retort.

Two things stood apart from the others in the applause that they evoked. Portraits of the late Andrew H. Green, Mayor Low, Mayor-elect McClellan, Senator McCarren and Senator Timothy J. Sullivan were shown in fireworks. The pictures were colossal in size, being 50 by 50 feet. The first to be shown was that of Mr. Green. When in appeared, limned in fire, in the centre of the vast arc, there was a roar from the river that could have been heard for miles. The whistle cord of every boat was tied down,

Continued on second page.

THE FORMAL OPENING.

Cannon Boom, Whistles Shriek and Thousands Cheer the Ceremonies.

Amid the boom of cannon, the blare of steam whistles from hundreds of river craft and the cheers of thousands of sightseers on the roofs of the surrounding buildings, Mayor Low yesterday traversed the new Williamsburg Bridge, and a few minutes later declared it formally open, thereby repeating his action in dedicating the Brooklyn Bridge almost twenty years ago. The ceremonies attending the opening of the great structure included military, civic, naval and religious exercises, and ended in the evening with a grand display of fireworks and a naval parade which was brilliant and impressive, for while the exercises of the day were important as formalities, those of the evening far outrivalled them from a scenic standpoint.

It was nearly 1 o'clock when the procession attending the progress of the Mayor to the bridge formed at City Hall. Round the square the yellow colors of Squadron A had added an effective bit of color for nearly an hour, and the busy policemen, shuffling their dark blue coats amid the lighter hues of the National Guardsmen, had with difficulty restrained the thousands of sightseers who surrounded City Hall. Greeted by the flashing of sabres, the Mayor, accompanied by the heads of departments and the Manhattan members of the Board of Aldermen, entered carriages and drove slowly up Broadway, amid the cheers of crowds along the street. The real enthusiasm began when the procession turned into Broome-st. and began to traverse the Italian quarter. Here the cheering grew louder at once, amid a display of brilliant festoons of bunting.

When the carriages crossed the Bowery and passed into the East Side, the demonstration became still more animated. From the crowded tenement houses, all boasting at least a flag, and in many cases a profusion of bunting, the greeting to the Mayor was cordial in the extreme. The crowd was so dense that only the extreme precautions taken by the police prevented accident. As the line of carriages passed along Broome-st. to Clinton they moved through companies of the 71st Regiment, drawn up in company front and presenting arms in salute. It was nearly 2 o'clock when the twenty-seven carriages carrying the Mayor's party reached the Manhattan end of the bridge and the party entered the plaza.

THE PROCESSION ON THE BRIDGE.

The decorations at this end of the bridge were striking. Around the iron girders and the structure intended for the elevated tracks great festoons of Christmas greens had been hung, while aloft hundreds of gay colored flags and strips of bunting waved in the keen, crisp breeze. As the Mayor left his carriage the roofs along the line of the approach to the bridge echoed with the cheers of the thousands who had crowded to the tops of the tenement houses to view the spectacle, and after he had reached the bridge there arose from the streets below the dull, hoarse sounds of the shouting multitude in the vacant squares where Poverty Hollow was situated before the razing of buildings for the new bridge.

At the Manhattan end of the bridge the procession formed, headed by Mayor Low, whose flag, borne by one of the City Hall attendants, led the line. James B. Reynolds and William J. Moran, the Mayor's secretaries, walked with him, and Health Commissioner Lederle, Lieutenant Colonel Spiers, aid to Major General Corbin, and Commander E. B. Barry, aid to Rear Admiral Rodgers, followed. Behind these were various city officials, including Police Commissioner Greene, Corporation Counsel Rives, Dock Commissioner McDougall Hawkes, Park Com-

EXTRA. The Evening Sun. EXTRA.

TEMPERATURE. Min., 58. Max., 64.

Cloudy and warmer to-night; to-morrow fair. Fresh S. to S. W. winds.

VOL. XVIII. NO. 78. NEW YORK, WEDNESDAY, JUNE 15, 1904.—*Copyright, 1904, by The Sun Printing and Publishing Association* PRICE ONE CENT.

THE GEN. SLOCUM BURNED IN EAST RIVER

Hundreds Killed on a Sunday School Excursion.

WOMEN AND CHILDREN LEAP OVERBOARD

FINDING BODIES

Captain and Most of the Crew Saved.

BOAT IS BEACHED

Terrible Scenes on North Brother Island.

CALLS FOR ASSISTANCE

All the Hospitals in the City Are Summoned to Help.

From 300 to 500 persons, according to the best estimate that can be made most of them women and children, lost their lives by burning or drowning this morning between 10 and 11 o'clock when the steamboat Gen. Slocum caught fire off East 138th St., beached on North Brother Island and burned to the water's edge. The extent of the catastrophe can hardly be accurately estimated, but it is believed to be of more awful proportions in its loss of life and heart rending character than the Hoboken fire or any other harbor horror in the last generation. The victims in to-day's tragedy were excursionists under the auspices of St. Mark's Lutheran Church, on Sixth street and had started upstream for Locust Grove, L. I., hardly an hour before the fire broke out in the kitchen in the steamboat's bows. There had been about half as many childrena as adults on the excursion, the total number of whom was put at from 1,500 to 2,000.

WILD PANIC STARTED AT ONCE.

Terrible scenes were enacted when the fire broke out. The passengers went into wild panic on the instant of the discovery of the fire. The blaze started in the steamboat's bows when she was off Hell Gate and was fanned aft by the progress of the boat upstream. Instead of beaching on the sunken meadows, as might have been done, the boat was headed for North Brother Island.

By the time the island was reached the steamboat was enveloped in flames, and hundreds of the passengers had jumped overboard.

By 11 o'clock almost 200 bodies had been stretched out on the plaza on the island. There were then from twenty-five to thirty rowboats and launches in the river picking up bodies and rescuing such as were still alive. The police then put the loss of life at 500, at least.

The captain of the steamboat and most of the crew were saved. How any escaped from the blazing furnace except such as could swim was one of the marvels of the day.

BOAT CROWDED.

The General Slocum was licensed to carry 2,500 passengers. Persons who saw the Lutheran excursionists go aboard from 7:30 o'clock in the morning until the boat sailed from Third street said that they had no doubt that it carried the full limit o passengers. The excursionists were bound for Locust Grove, L. I., and the promise of a fair day on the water and ashore brought out a teeming crowd.

CONDITIONS RIPE FOR PANIC.

Perfect conditions for panic were offered. Upon these merrymakers, revelling in the prospect of a happy outing, hardly an hour after the steamboat got under way broke the cry of "Fire!" There was a clatter of hurrying feet, a surge of the throng away from the bows, where smoke curled up, and then panic at its worst was let loose.

CHOICE OF DEATHS OFFERED.

Women went literally insane at once. Some had allowed their little charges to be separated from them, and in that frantic mob there was no chance for reunion. Men, maddened by fear, trampled down women and children to get to the sides and leap overboard. To most of the terrorized multitude it was but a choice of deaths that offered.

To stay on board meant the awful certainty of being burned alive. To take to the water meant for all but a few the certainty of death by drowning.

CHILDREN THROWN OVERBOARD.

All the way for the half mile that the General Slocum steamed to the North Brother Island beach shore observers were rendered frantic by the pitiable sight which that blazing mass presented. Men and women were seen clinging to the sides like flies and dropping by twos and threes as strength gave out or hope died. They jumped by tens and dozens. Those of them who could swim preferred the desperate possibility of keeping afloat. Most heartrending sight of all it was to see the children thrown overboard by those who had them in care.

Like lightning the news of the disaster spread along both shores of the river and long before the steamboat hit the North Brother Island beach rowboats, launches, sailing craft and tugs were making all the speed they could to help.

Many survivors owe their lives to the fact that the watermen rose to the emergency so quickly.

Just as the steamboat grounded the hurricane deck fell in. A great burst of flame, smoke and sparks went up and the whole vessel was in a second afire from stem to stern, from water's edge to pilot house. In the seething pit which her hull had become were entombed no one knew how many of the unfortunates who had set out so little a while before in search of innocent pleasure and found a terrible death.

RUSH OF RESCUE AND RELIEF.

It was not until about 10:15 o'clock that the Fire and Police departments had any news of the fire. The first intimation came in an alarm from the box at 138th street and the Southern boulevard. Two minutes later a man of the name of Thompson called up the Police Department from a Melrose Exchange telephone and said:

"A big steamboat is on fire in the East River off 138th street. I think it's the General Slocum. She is heading upstream and people are jumping overboard."

Ten minutes later the same man reported again:

"The General Slocum has gone ashore on North Brother Island. Her decks have collapsed and she will burn to the water's edge."

A catastrophe of horrifying proportions was indicated by this information, and every agency of relief and rescue at the city's command was set in operation forthwith.

ALL FIREBOATS OUT—ALL AMBULANCES.

With the same speed with which the firemen on shore answer any call all the fireboats in the city's service were despatched to the scene. Every hospital in the city sent ambulances to the foot of 138th street, where a receiving station was established to which the men in boats could bring up the bodies of the dead and living picked up. Ambulances carried the injured and the dying to the hospitals, while police surgeons and Board of Health physicians worked side by side with the ambulance doctors in applying emergency measures to save life and relieve suffering before the injured were sent away. A huge guard of police reserves promptly commandeered from Headquarters threw a cordon around several piers along the river front, so that there should be no interference with the surgeons.

ISLAND FACILITIES OVERWHELMED.

Before noon this appeal came from North Brother Island to Police Headquarters:

"Send all the help you possibly can."

There was fire fighting force enough about the island then. The fire apparatus on the island had been turned on the blazing steamboat early, and tugs had joined the fireboats in throwing water on the flames. The fire had done its work, though.

The dead aboard the steamboat were many. The firemen, volunteer and regulars, at work on the hull knew that the best that they could do would be to recover some blackened cinders that had so shortly before been the bodies of men, women and children instinct with life and ho

They worked on at their task unheeded. What was paramount on the island was the task of saving from death the half drowned, half burned alive unfortunates who had been brought ashore. Fully half the maimed and suffering survivors were brought to the island or reached there by their own efforts, and by far the greatest proportion of the dead. The island's medical staff and hospital facilities were simply overwhelmed, and even when the appeal to Police Headquarters had been made many physicians and nurses had gone over from this side.

WORK OF RESCUE.

Tugs and Rowboats Swarm to Pick Up the Bodies.

Capt. Burgi, superintendent of the gas house at 13gth street, as soon as he saw the panic stricken passengers jumping into the water, set out in his 40-foot steam launch, the Elsa, and picked up a number of drowning women and children, finally saving and taking to shore about fifty persons.

"Most of the crew were good swimmers, and when the frantic passengers became unmangaeable they jumped overboard and swam to shore. The captain was saved in this way, but Michael McGrath, the steward, and a fireman named Birch, perished in the attempt to reach the shore.

The Gen. Slocum is lying off North Brother Island, with tugs and rowboats alongside of her. Seven streams of water were playing into the steaming ruin of her decks, beneath which, it is thought, lie the bodies of many women and children.

Many spectators who saw the fire from its start until the wreck was beached on the shore of North Brother Island say that the first seen of the flames was when the steamboat was approaching 120th street, at which time smoke was seen pouring from her hold, but the passengers were apparently kept quiet for some time.

These spectators say that before the boat was beached, and when there were still many on her decks who would not jump into the water, the superstructure collapsed and carried down with it the roof of the main cabin, burying beneath this mass of wreckage a number which cannot be guessed.

There were at least 2,000 human beings on the boat, it is estimated, when the flames broke forth, and of these by far the greater part were women and children.

Twenty-five rowboats put out from shore as soon as the passengers began to jump, and these succeeded in picking up many persons; but a large part of those who jumped into the water did not come to the urface again.

MINISTER'S STORY.

The Rev. Mr. Haas Tells of the Big Disaster.

The Rev. George C. F. Haas, the pastor of the church, was saved, but his wife Gertrude and his daughter Anna are among the dead. The Rev. Mr. Haas told this story of the disaster:

"The fire started in the kitchen in the forward part, when we were off 84th street. I understand that some fat that boiled over started the blaze and that the men in the kitchen, instead of fighting it, ran for their lives.

"At that time most of the women and childred were jammed in the rear of the boat, where the band was playing.

"Why the captain did not point the boat for the meadows I do not understand. He kept on and the fresh wind from the Sound drove the fire back through the different decks with lightning rapidity.

"In three minutes from the time the fire started all the decks were ablaze.

"Such scenes as followed I don't think were ever witnessed before I was in the rear of the boat with my wife and daughter. Women were shrieking and clasping their children in their arms. Some mothers had as many as three or four with them. Our case seemed hopeless. Death from fire was to be escaped only to die in the water.

"When the fire shot up to the top deck and drove the crowd back the panic was terrible to witness. The crush from the forward part of the boat swept those in the rear along. The women and children clung to the railings and stanchions, but could not keep their holds. I with my wife and daughter were swept along with the rest.

"I believe that the first that fell into the water were crushed over. When they went there seemed to be a general inclination to jump. The women and children went over the railings like flies. They preferred to take a chance in the water rather than wait sure death in fire.

"In the great crush many women fainted and fell to the deck, to be trampled upon. Little children were knocked down. Mothers with their little boys and girls in their arms would give wild screams and then leap into the water. We could see boats pulling out from the shore by this time, and a faint ray of hope came to us.

"With my wife and daughter I had been swept over to the rail. The fire then looked as if it would devour us the next instant. I got my wife and daughter out on the rail and then we went overboard. I was in such an excited state that I don't remember whether we were pushed over or jumped.

"When I struck the water I sank and when I rose there were scores about me fighting to keep afloat. One by one I saw them sink around me. But I was powerless to do anything. I looked around for my wife and daughter, but could not see their faces anywhere. They probably sank as soon as they struck the water.

"With a great effort I managed to keep afloat, but my strength was about gone when a man on one of the tugs picked me up."

THE DEPARTURE.

The excursionists, about 1,500 strong started from the church in Sixth street before 8 o'clock, and with a band at the head marched to the foot of Third street, where the Gen. Slocum was waiting. The little children were decked out in their gayest attire and carried flags. Their mothers were well supplied with lunch baskets. The Rev. George C. F. Haas, the pastor of the church, was at the head of the procession with his committee, working hard to make the outing of his flock a great success.

Into the big steamboat the excursionists poured, and soon all the decks were packed. A squad of men from the Union Market and Fifth street police stations had been stationed at the pier to keep order, and several policemen from the harbor squad had been detailed to see that things ran smoothly on the boat.

All were on board by 8:30 o'clock, and with flags flying from many poles, the band playing a lively air and the crowd on board cheering and waving handkerchiefs to those left behind, the big steamboat pulled out for her fateful trip up the Sound.

CALLING AID.

Chief Inspector of Police Moses Cortright sent the following message to Commissioner Lantry:

"The steamboat General Slocum is on fire in midstream off 138th street. Send all aid you can."

Superintendent Brennan, of the Police Telephone Bureau, notified all the hospitals in Manhattan to send all their available ambulances to the foot of East 138th street.

The Board of Health was notified to send its available doctors to the scene.

The Board of Education was ordered to send its corps of 100 physicians.

Over 500 policemen are on hand, either at the foot of 138th street or on North Brother Island.

Inspector McClusky sent fifty detectives.

St. Vincent's Hospital sent four doctors and eight nurses.

Roosevelt Hospital sent two ambulances, twelve doctors and ten nurses.

An appeal was sent from Riverside Hospital on North Brother Island to Police Headquarters at noon.

"Send all the aid possible. We need all the help we can get," it read.

Mayor McClellan, as soon as he heard of the disaster, ordered all boats of the various city departments to go to the scene at once and render whatever assistance they could. The fire and police boats and the boats of the departments of Charities and Corrections were sent to the scene.

PARISH STRICKEN.

As soon as the news of the great disaster spread through the lower East Side, St. Mark's Church, in Sixth street, was besieged with an anxious and grief stricken throng that wanted to know the details. Nearly all in the crowd had relatives on board the Gen. Slocum.

As the first stories of the fire came in, the emotions of the crowd were intensified until nearly all were weeping and wringing their hands. The full extent of the horror became known when a report came in from Police Headquarters that there were at least 500 dead.

Anxious inquiries were made for the pastor, the Rev. George C. F. Haas, but there was nothing definite known about his fate.

Before noon the word was spread around to the different places where the husbands and fathers of those on the Slocum worked and after the noon hour a large crowd of men visited the parish house. Most of them waited only for a word to find out the full extent of the distaster, and then rushed for the trains to take them to Harlem.

FINDING BODIES.

At 11:25 o'clock the following message was received at Police Headquarters from the Alexander avenue police station:

"Forty or fifty bodies are lying on the beach on the north end of North Brother Island.

'Five bodies are in this station house including one of an unidentified woman.

"Eighteen bodies are on board of the fire boat Zephar Mills.

"CAPT. GEOGHEGAN."

DEAD ON RIKER'S ISLAND

The bodies of seven women and two children are on Riker's Island, having been picked up in the river by a rowboat.

A woman and two small boys were picked up alive by the same boat and taken to Riker's Island.

RESCUES FIFTY.

The steamboat Massasoit came into the dock at 138th street with fifty survivors on board, whom she had picked up in the river.

PICKED UP BURNING.

Another steamboat succeeded in picking up about thirty persons, all women or children, many of whom had been seriously burned and were in great agony. Others the boat had picked up by means of life lines and buoys out of the river. The crowd which had collected about the dock stretched along for blocks and became so excited that it was found necessary to call out the reserves from all over that part of the city to preserve a vestige of order.

THE GEN. SLOCUM.

The General Slocum was built by Devine Burtis, South Brooklyn, in 1891, and has had Capt. Van Schaick as her chief officer during the greater part of her history.

The licensed capacity of the General Slocum is 2,500. Her dimensions are: Length, 263.3 feet; breadth, 38.6 feet over moulding; 65 feet over all; depth, 12.14 feet. Her normal horse power is 15,000.

Last spring the big excursion boat was thoroughly overhauled, and was never in better condition than on the day she was put in commission for this season. Her first trip this year was made on May 22, and every day since she has been out.

At the offices of the Knickerbocker Steamboat Company, it was said that the General Slocum carried her full complement of officers, deckhands and engineers this morning, and that the boat was equipped with a fire engine, the use of which the crew had learned by constant drill.

SAVED MANY.

Policemen James Collins and Herbert Farrell, of the Alexander avenue station, were at the 134th street ferry when they saw the fire shoot up from the General Slocum. The policemen turned in an alarm and then took a boat from a lumber schooner and put out to the burning steamboat.

"At that time the people were jumping from the boat," said Farrell in telling his story. "The Slocum was still going on and seemed to leave a trail of human beings in her wake. Collins and I dragged out twenty-two in all. Two of them died before they were taken ashore."

A SURVIVOR'S STORY

Annie Nordorf, 20 years old, of 93 Second street, who was one of those saved, says that she went to the picnic with her 5-year-old cousin, Annie Burhardi.

"The first intimation I had of the fire," she said, "was when I saw smoke pouring from the decks in the direction of the bow. Fortunately I was at about the middle of the boat, for straightway there was a rush for the stern, and in less time than it takes to tell it, the whole forward deck seemed to be on fire and those who were in the bow were caught in a trap of flame and had no choice but to jump. As I remember it there were a whole lot of people caught this way in the bow. I think that there were fully 1,500 persons on the boat. Our pastor, Mr. Haas, was saved, I know, for I saw him taken off by a tug. Annie Mack, of 401 Fifth street, I am sure was burned to death.

"The excitement on the deck got worse every minute and there was no managing the passengers. They rushed this way and that, screaming and shouting and pushing one another out of the way. After what seemed to me to be ages I saw a tug push a big flat barge up to the steamboat, and I with a lot of others jumped onto this and was saved. I got separated from my little cousin, and I don't know what has become of her."

Herbert S. Nulson, an employe of the De La Vergne Refrigerator Company, said that he was working in a tower in the company's factory at the foot of East 138th street when a fellow employe called:

"Here comes a big boat up the river, and I believe she's on fire."

"I looked down the river," said Wilson, "and saw this steamboat, which I was sure then was the Gen. Slocum. The flames were just beginning to make headway when I first saw her, and by the time she came opposite us, I could see that her decks were crowded with women and children, who began to jump into the water. I was certain then that the captain would come to land at the foot of East 138th street, as it seemed the only logical thing for him to do. It was a straight short course. But no, for some reason he kept out in the river and headed for North Brother Island.

LOST WIFE AND FIVE CHILDREN.

A man told Policeman Peck, who is in charge of the police telephone at the foot of 138th street that his wife and five children had been killed. He went away dazed without giving his name.

CAPTAIN ARRESTED.

William Van Schaick was the captain of the Slocum.

He was saved, as were nearly all of the crew.

The captain was arrested.

SAW THE SLOCUM GO BY, BAND PLAYING.

Many persons along the Astoria shore saw the Slocum pass up the river on her ill-fated trip. Among these persons was John E. Ronan, who is employed in the Dock Department at the foot of Broadway.

Mr. Ronan said he was in his office and from a window had a good view of the river. He said the General Slocum came steaming by at about 10 o'clock. The three decks of the boat were crowded with gay excursionists, most of them women and children. The steamboat was gay with flags and bunting and the strains of the band on board could be plainly heard from the shore.

As the Slocum passed through Hell Gate the excursionists cheered and waved handkerchiefs, hats and umbrellas to those on shore.

Mr. Ronan said there was nothing unusual in the passage of the Slocum; at least he noticed nothing to lead him to believe that there was any unusual excitement on board.

Mr. Ronan did not see any indication that the boat was on fire at this time. He remarked to a companion in his office how fine the Slocum looked as she passed and what a jolly crowd she had on board.

Ronan said that he watched the General Slocum until she got beyond Hell Gate and headed up the East River toward Ward's Island. When he last saw her there were no signs that the vessel was on fire.

Other persons who saw the Slocum at about this time tell similar stories.

MOB HANGS WOMAN.

Rope Breaks and She Is Riddled with Bullets—Still Alive.

LOUISVILLE, Ky., June 15.—A mob took Maria Thompson, a negro woman, from jail at Lebanon Junction, near here, at 2 o'clock this morning and hanged her to a tree. The rope broke and the mob searched the neighbordood for another rope, but none could be found. The woman was then riddled with bullets.

The Coroner arrived four hours afterward, expecting to hold an inquest, but the woman is still alive. She is now reported to be dying.

The Thompson woman last night attacked John Irvin, a wealthy farmer, with a razor for some reason which is not known. She almost severed his head from his body and he died within ten minutes. The woman tried to escape, but was caught and taken to jail.

WEATHER REPORT.

Local Indications.

For the thirty-six hours ending at 8 P. M. Thursday: Partly cloudy and warmer to-night; to-morrow fair. Light to fresh south to southwest winds.

Temperature of Air.

8 A. M.	58	2 P. M.	—
10 A. M.	62	3 P. M.	—
11 A. M.	64	4 P. M.	—

Official Barometer.

8 A. M.	30.14	2 P. M.	—
10 A. M.	30.15	3 P. M.	—
11 A. M.	30.12	4 P. M.	—

Official Humidity.

8 A. M.	80	2 P. M.	—
10 A. M.	78	3 P. M.	—
11 A. M.	72	4 P. M.	—

Miniature Almanac.

From noon June 15.

A.M.	P.M.	P.M.
Sun rises ...4:27	Moon sets.. 9:03	Sun sets 7:33

High Water.

Sandy Hook. 8:37 P. M.	Gov. Island. 9:16 P. M.	Hell Gate. 11:05 P. M.

New-York Tribune.
ILLUSTRATED SUPPLEMENT.
SUNDAY, JULY 17, 1904.

PLAN OF THE PENNSYLVANIA RAILROAD'S NEW STATION ON MANHATTAN ISLAND.

Photographed from the model now on exhibition at St. Louis.

THE THIRTY-FIRST-ST. FRONT OF THE GREAT STATION, SHOWING CAR TRACKS UNDER THE STREET LEVEL.

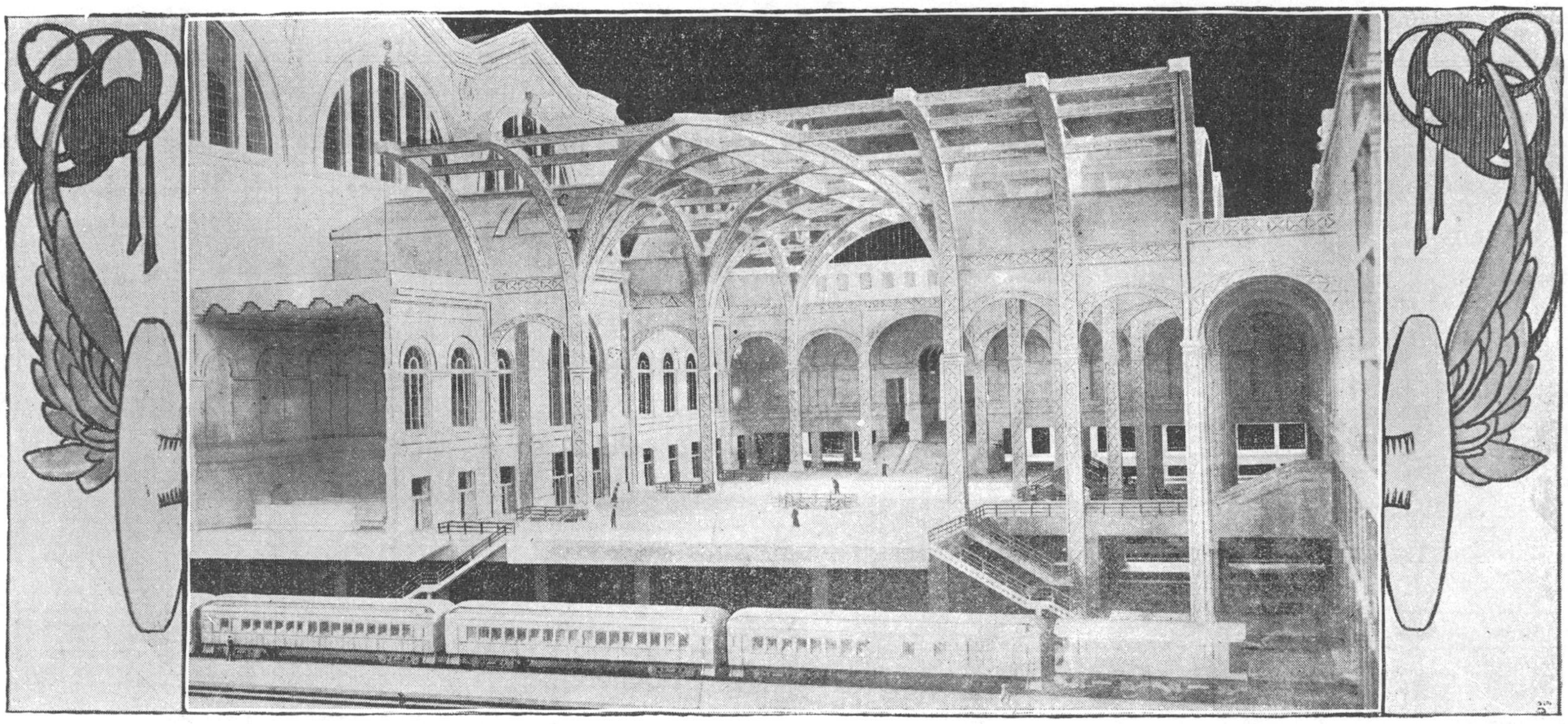

AN INTERIOR VIEW OF THE GREAT STATION, SHOWING CARS UNDER THE PASSENGERS' WAITING ROOM.

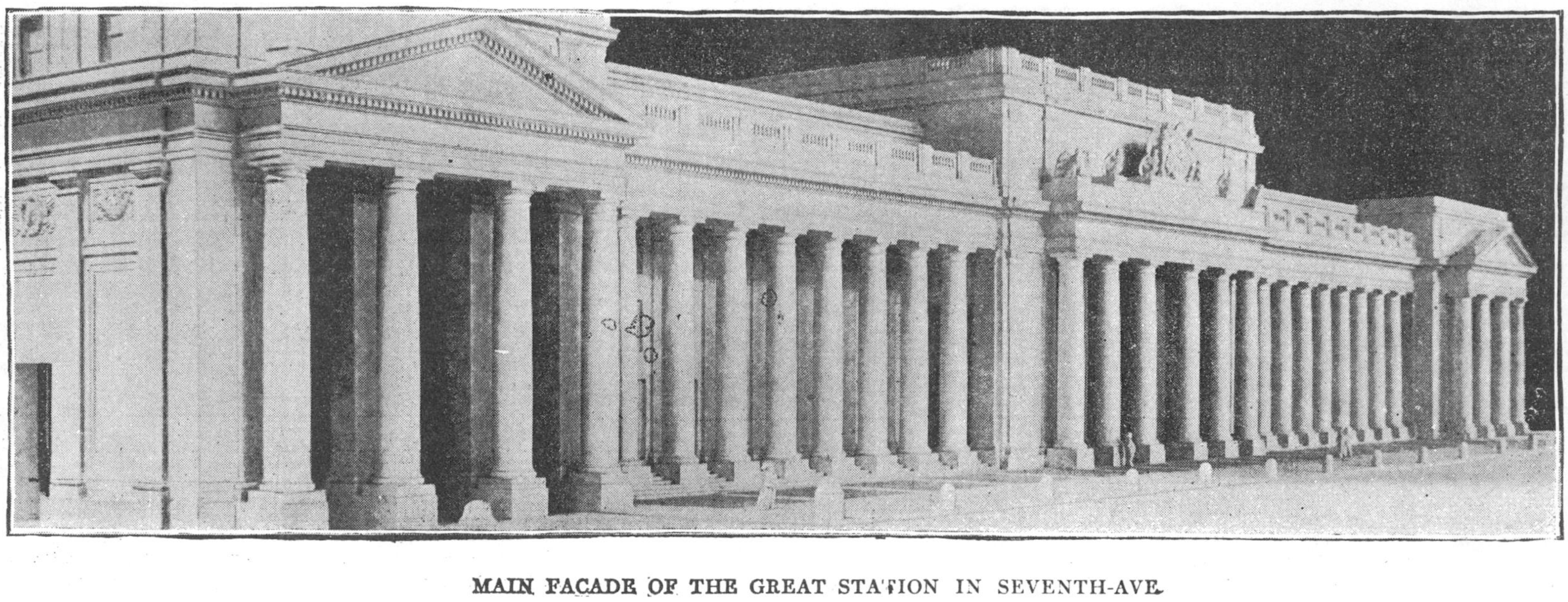

MAIN FACADE OF THE GREAT STATION IN SEVENTH-AVE.

MAGAZINE SECTION

The New York Press

SUNDAY, JULY 24, 1904.

When the Multitudes Flee the City

They Are Proud of Their Cities and "Scared of" Them, Too

"STEP lively!"

It is the summer song of the big ones—the American cities that spread over all that they can seize of creation.

They're all proud of them—the citizens who have helped build them and are pushing them along; proud of them and scared by them when the heat sweeps down. You can't crowd stone and iron together by the hundreds of tons, cover acres of ground with them, pile them up till they hide the sky, without paying for it.

Sea breeze, lake breeze, mountain breeze all wither when they strike mile-long streets, beset with steam engines on each side, meshed with arteries and veins carrying live steam below the surface and exhaling fiery air from thousand of stacks.

When the heat sweeps down the little kings of the cities are the men who stand at every vent-gate leading to car or boat, singing the song that never ceases, from the Atlantic to the Pacific—"Step lively!"

No command in the United States, from Section 1, Article 1, of the Constitution down, is obeyed so implicitly. Perspiring, wilted, ready to drop, the crowds awaken to one last burst of energy when they hear it, as foot-sore troops make a last dash when the bugle calls. With a rush and a crush they pile into the vehicles that are to bear them to places that they hope are cool.

Heat has become such a terror to the cities that a wave of suffering sweeps from New York across the continent, gripping Pittsburg and Cleveland and Chicago and Detroit and all the rest long before the weather observers suspect that it is time to issue the annual bulletins about the hottest day ever on the record for humidity.

The day the first straw hat appears the rush to escape town begins, and if the sufferer has to wear his winter overcoat on the way, he still thanks his stars that he has escaped the heat of his beloved town, of which he is so extremely afraid.

Later, when it becomes really warm, every other citizen is highly inflamed of countenance and may be seen dragging family festoons after him, all equally inflamed, and all bound to escape into a cool some place or another at whatever cost of time or anguish.

The heat of the towns often is largely imaginary, but there is nothing imaginary about the heat which the escaping multitude creates for itself in its wild rush to "escape."

There is no more noble example of human suffering borne patiently in a good cause than is that of an American crowd undergoing summer pains cheerfully for hours in order to get away from their beloved cities.

From every town railroad tracks run out, planned strategically to keep open the lines of summer retreat. Luckily, as the cities grew and increased their demands for avenues of flight, the electric roads came into being and opened hundreds of miles of country all around the house-masses. The marine engineer, too, has thrived vastly in catering to the annual flight; and if he has not made the American excursion boat a miracle of safety, he has at least made it a wonder for carrying the biggest possible live cargo the greatest possible distance in the shortest possible time.

But, though they link mile on mile of track, pile wheel on wheel on the iron road, add knot on knot to speed on the water, and each year press sea and lake and river down with still more floating monsters, the fugitives beat their capacity. And every day the crowds of most of the big cities have to fight anew, not for seats, not even for standing room, but for mere hanging room.

Every American city is proud of something that it owns which is the biggest in the world; and so almost every one of them is convinced, half with disgust and half with pride, that its crowds are the biggest, its conveyances the most inadequate and its general rush for trolley cars, steam trains and steamboats the fiercest.

As a matter of fact, when a cityfull begins to move out in a hurry—a barrelful trying to pour out of a few bungholes—there is bound to be a helter-skelter time at the bungs. And the differences between the scenes at the various city bungs are only differences in the temperaments of the people.

"Little old New York," being the first halting place of the foreign crowds, has the worst—not so much in temper as in sheer inability to do anything except to push.

Possibly if a given New York crowd of, say, 15,000, could be segregated, kept intact and driven half a dozen times over a given route, it would learn to be quite an intelligent crowd, able to take measurable care of the comfort of all.

But New York's crowds are ever new. Each hour there are new atoms in each that have it all to learn.

This makes the daily New York flight a rout that reproduces all the misery of the flight from a stricken field. The crowd prepares for a rush for the cars, not when they come in sight, but when the gongs are heard blocks away. A stranger, suddenly transported to the entrance to the big suspension bridge, or to the landings of the steamboats, might well laugh in the face of the man who strove to convince him that the fighting, shouting, red-faced, crazy crowds were going for pleasure. He would refuse to believe that anything except the terror of sudden and terrible death could induce human beings to battle so.

When a car approaches, a mob many times as big as could possibly be accommodated by it rushes up the track to meet it, swarms over it fore and aft, climbs with bland ferocity over the passengers who are trying to get out, and glares with a united glare at the slower mob that charges behind.

Man, the hero, the strong and undaunted, seizes woman, the weak, the gentle and timid, and hews his way over young and old to reach a spot where he can seize some part of the car with a death grip. And having succeeded at last, ten to one he finds that his gentle protege has climbed in ahead of him, while other gentle ones, defeated, divide their time between glaring balefully at her and repairing damages.

New York, of course, imagines that it has the only experiences of the kind. New York raises its three million pairs of hands each day over each new happening and calls on high heaven to witness that such a happening never happened to any city before.

But, as a matter of fact, if the crowds of other cities do not all incline as New York's crowds do, to purvey sudden death to each other every time they go out for a day's chaste pleasures, there are few cities, big and little, that "let their children go" without squeezing them good and hard at the gate.

The trolley car with its cheap fares has done it. When steam railroads provided the only means of exit, the fares were high and the crowds remained neatly and unobtrusively separated into units in their houses and streets. The trolley car, a modern magician, raised the multitude over night with its spell of a five-cent fare; and alas! like most magicians, it is helpless to cope with the monster it has made.

It is a monster like all monsters from the time of fairy tales to the present day—fearful in size but lamentably clumsy and helpless in other ways. Like the dear old dragons, it spits fire and smoke in its battle for seats, and having fought the fight, it pants, buttonless, breathless, disheveled, clings to straps with finger-tips, and is ready to have its head scratched by the princess and be deceived into doing it all over again next day.

But it isn't an entirely easy-going monster. One of its peculiarities is that it is easily pleased with some things and excessively particular about others. It is a hard monster to figure on.

One thing with which it isn't easily pleased is the place to which it goes

It's the American Habit---Run Away to Some Other Place

through such travail and labor. The old bare inclosure, with its dry, brown earth packed into hopeless solidity, which was unblushingly named a "grove" a few years ago, has had to hide itself. My Lord the Monster has a dainty appetite nowadays. He is even being educated beyond Ferris wheels and toboggan slides. He demands architecture, splendor and miracles for his summer amusement.

So New York has raised a city of vision on the ruins of old nasty Coney Island for him. Philadelphia sends trolley cars through glorious scenery into great parks—trolley parks, such as Willow Grove, that are more beautiful than any one thought of making even the biggeest municipal parks a few years ago. Steamboats carry her throngs down the Delaware to the Capes, a day's trip now that once was a voyage. On the river lies Washington Park-on-the-Delaware, to which more steamers carry more crowds every day.

Pittsburg's monster piles itself into trolley cars that speed for miles into the open country until they, too, reach great trolley parks, laid out with everything to please My Lord. River steamers wait at every pier to bear masses along the Ohio, Monongahela and Alleghany rivers, where resorts are scattered for miles along the shores.

Cleveland has its Manhattan and Euclid Beaches, where an inland Coney Island waits. Great lake boats leave it daily every hour in the day crowded from rail to rail with excursionists bound for a score of places, big and little, far and near, along the beautiful lake.

Detroit sends her crowds out by trolley to her Saratoga of Mount Clemens, and by boat to her famous Flats, where yacht villages and fishing villages and house-boat villages have been reared by the fugitives from the city.

Boat and car whirl out of every portal in Chicago and Boston and St. Louis—yes, and out of the smaller towns, too, that are set in trees themselves and have gardens around each house. Even there you will find a crush in the cars or the boats.

It is the American habit. When it gets hot, run away to some other place.

AUTO DERBY HERE

19 Cars to Start for Vanderbilt Cup

FAST TIME EXPECTED

Winner Likely to Do Better Than Mile a Minute.

FOREIGNERS FAVORITES

Thousands of Spectators Will Witness 283-Mile Race for Championship.

Over a twenty-eight and a fraction mile course that resembles, roughly, a butcher's cleaver, and is situated in the heart of Long Island, nineteen daredevil auto drivers, representing America, Germany, France and Italy, will to-morrow contest in the second international auto race for the Vanderbilt cup, emblematic of the American road-racing championship. With higher power machines and a course extremely fast, comparatively level and with few bad turns, new world's records are almost certain to be established in the struggle to complete the ten laps that constitute the race, in the least possible time. This, the third great auto road race held in this country and the second of international importance, promises to surpass in interest, speed and personality both its predecessors.

The world's most prominent and daring drivers in the latest racing game are represented in the entry list and have been preparing and tuning up their machines, that range from 90 to 130 horse-power, for the past two weeks, and in practise have repeatedly covered laps at speeds that averaged much better than a mile a minute. That the winner's time will be greater than sixty miles an hour for the 283 miles that is included in the ten laps of the 28.3 mile course appears certain. Both the Americans and foreigners that handle the steering wheels in the cars entered for the cup race have time and time again traveled around the circuit in better than twenty-five minutes, which is approximating sixty-eight miles an hour. Allowing elapsed time for tire changes and tank replenishing, it is considered by the experts that have followed the practise of the drivers that the winner's time will be well inside five hours unless a heavy rainfall just previous to the race makes such high speed out of the question.

That the sport-loving public of the country and of the metropolis, in particular, appreciate the opportunity that eighteen or more giant racing machines dashing along the country roads will give for spine-racking thrills is fully demonstrated by the demand for accommodations about the course. Every available room in hotel and farmhouse for miles about the circuit has been engaged for several weeks. Cots and chairs in hostelry halls and dining rooms are bringing $3 to $5 to their owners, and automobile parking places along the grand stand stretch near Mineola range in price from $10 to $50, according to their proximity to the official starting and finishing point. Grand stand and parking concessions for the day brought the farmers who are fortunate enough to own roadside property along the course near Mineola prices for which the property could have been bought six months ago.

Prospective lodgers who visited the hotels and farmers' houses along the twenty-eight mile circuit yesterday in search of lodging to-night heard their pleas for accommodations refused at place after place. Much as the proprietors hated to see the golden flood turned backward from their doors, the fact that every available foot of sleeping space had been engaged for several days left them helpless to garner in any more of the harvest of currency that sweeps by. The same conditions prevail in the grand stands. Every seat in the main stands was sold weeks ago. From time to time additions have been put up, to be snapped up before the last board was nailed in place. To meet the demand for seats at points of vantage private parties have erected stands to accommodate the overflow, and success was assured in every case before their completion.

The thousands of spectators who will go down in the early morning hours, both by automobiles and railroad, will have plenty of places from which to witness the race. Seats there will be none, but for miles along the course the roadbanks, fields and fences offer fairly comfortable quarters from which to watch the speeding, leaping combinations of machinery and humanity that form the entry in the contest where a false turn means disaster and death for car and driver. Starting from New Hyde Park, the point of the course nearest to New York, the Jericho turnpike stretches away eastward for nine miles to Jericho. Here a sharp turn to the north carries the racers to East Norwich, where another turn to the left sends them tearing along westward to Bull's Head Corner, where again the drivers steer their cars around a sharp right-angle corner and travel directly south in the Isaac U. Willetts road, where the course winds in and out eastward to Lakeville. Here the turn is again a left-handed one to the south, and the fastest speeding stretch of the course carries them to New Hyde Park, where the one-and-a-half mile straightaway brings the racers back to the grand stands and the starting point. All around this twenty-eight miles of roadway each corner and stretch will have its group of sightseers to-morrow, ranging from a few hundreds to thousands, according to the accessibility of the point.

All Long Island roads don't lead to Mineola, although visitors in carriage and car will find no great trouble in reaching the starting point of the race. From New York city the best route for autoists is from Thirty-fourth street by ferry to Long Island City. From the ferry house turn left under the viaduct to Jackson avenue. Follow car tracks on asphalt to Hoffman boulevard, a macadam street with asphalt cycle path. Cross the railroad tracks and bridge at Hoffman boulevard and Hillside avenue and turn left past Disbrow's garage and follow Hillside avenue to its end. Then turn right, past a high hedge on a narrow road and into Jericho turnpike. Turn to left and under railroad bridge to grand stand at Mineola.

The Williamsburg Bridge route is a sharp turn right and under elevated track, to right again one block; then left two blocks, right one block and left into Bedford avenue to Eastern Parkway. A left turn connects with the Brooklyn Bridge route.

The Brooklyn Bridge route is across the plaza to Liberty street, which leads to junction of Fulton and Clinton streets; through Clinton street to Schermerhorn, then left to Nevins street; turn right into Nevins street and continue to Dean street; turn left into Dean to Flatbush avenue and continue to the plaza. Bear to left and into Eastern Parkway. This is the juncture of Williamsburg Bridge and Brooklyn Bridge routes.

From this junction continue on Parkway until it joins Bushwick avenue and turn right. Follow Bushwick avenue by cemetery on left, and at foot of a hill turn into Jamaica turnpike, with its brick pavement and double trolley tracks. Follow tracks three miles to Richmond Hill. In the village turn left between a market and opposite drug store and continue on a curve to right, crossing a trolley and railroad track near the station on right and reach Hillside avenue. Go straight to a railroad viaduct and follow straight road closely. Don't use two streets crossing acutely, branching off at right. Continue to Hoffman boulevard and use the latter part of the Long Island City route.

The Long Island Railroad has made all arrangements for a series of special trains to Mineola, which will run as follows: Trains will leave New York, East Thirty-fourth street, for Mineola, 3:35, 4.00, stopping at Garden City one hour, 5.00, 5:40, 7:00, 7:50, 8:30, 8:50, 9:00, 10:20, 10:50, 11:00 A. M. Frequent trains returning from Mineola and special trains immediately after finish.

Thirty-fourth street ferryboats will be run at frequent intervals from 3:30 A. M. for accomodation of automobolists. Trains leave Flatbush avenue terminal, Brooklyn, for Mineola, at 5:38, 7:03, 7:55 and 8:30 A. M. and for New Hyde Park at 5:38, 7:03 and 7:55 A. M. Returning, trains leave Mineola 11:53 A. M. and 12:53, 1:40, 2:59 and 3:34 P. M., and New Hyde Park 11:58 A. M. and 1:45 and 3:04 P. M.

Unless there are one or more eleventh-hour withdrawals, eighteen, and possibly nineteen, cars will start in the mad dash around the ten-lap circuit in an attempt to bring an automobile championship and trophy to their country. As the teams stand at present America, France and Italy are represented by complete teams of five cars. Germany has four cars entered and one is a doubtful starter. To offset this handicap the German team drew No. 1 in the starting poll, and as a result Jenatzy will be first away in his 120 horse-power car on the stroke of 6 o'clock to-morrow morning. A minute later Duray will be second away, the first of the five French cars. America, having third place, starts Dengley at 6:03, and Italy follows fourth, with Lancia as their first starter.

The second relay of starters finds Foxhall P. Keene as No. 5 and second starter for the German team. Following him a minute later will go Wagner, of the French team; while Tracy, in his Locomobile, is seventh. Nazzari in his Fiat completes the second relay for the Italians. At 6:08 Warden is scheduled to start for the German team, but owing to his accident of two days ago it is doubtful if he starts. Following in tenth place is Szisz, of the French team, a growing favorite for winning honors. Eleventh place will find Walter Christie on the mark for the American team, to be followed a minute later by Cedrino for Italy. The thirteenth starter although his car bears the letter X in place of the fateful number, will be Campbell, for the German team.

At 6:13 o'clock Heath, fourth starter for the French and winner of last year's race, will get under way, to be followed by Lytle, of the American team. Chevrolet will be next at the line for Italy. There will be no car bearing the No. 17, for while this place was assigned to Basil for the German team the car in which he was to ace was declared ineligible by the committee and withdrawn. No. 18 will be Hemerey, the last starter for France, while America will be represented by White as No. 19, and Italy by Sartori, No. 20 and last starter.

Of these drivers, the leading auto racers of the four countries competing, three are decided favorites over the others. Lancia, in his 120 horse-power Fiat, has ruled a leading choice for first place since his arrival at the course. A reckless, dare-devil driver, ready to take advantage of every opportunity or slip of his opponents, yet careful of his car and tires, he has done magnificent work both here and abroad. Less was known of Szisz, who starts No. 10 in a 90 horse-power Renault, but his wonderful driving since his appearance on the course, and the way in which he handles his car on the bad corners, lead many to think that he will be first at the finish, at better than a mile a minute for the whole 283 miles. Hemery, who will drive off No. 18 in an 80 horse-power Darracq, is still another driver who has a large following. As winner of a number of European road races he has both the experience and the nerve to drive his car round and round the course at a speed that will keep him up with the leaders if not in first place himself.

Janetz, who starts first in the race and who will have a clear course for at least a round or two, is picked by some to win, and his work in practise has shown that he can hold his own with the fastest of the other foreigners for the limited number of laps tha the early morning hours of practise permit. Of the Americans Tracy, in the Locomobile, and Dingley and Lytle, in Pope Toledos, are selected as likely to make the best showing for the Americans, but that any of the trio will win is considered out of the question. Accidents and tire troubles are likely to figure prominently in the race, and for this reason a dark horse may speed away with the $2,000 trophy donated by William K. Vanderbilt, Jr.

The crowd that will pack the grand stand at the starting tape will see the race only as a roaring procession of flying cars, each moving at a seeming uniform speed, flash past the spectators. The real race will be run, for the spectators, on the scoring board, where the silent, watchful timekeepers will tally the time of each car as it whirls about the course. Men, expert in watching the sweep of the split second hand of a stop watch, have been watching, regulating and planning for weeks in preparation for the catching of each car's official time.

When the race begins, at 6 o'clock by watches held by four timers at the start, there will be equally trained men at all the intermediate stations around the course Each man will sit all during the race, his eyes on his watch and a telephone at his side. As a car passes his tape its time is flashed back to the grand stand and is chalked on the board. If the message comes "Car No. 10 passed at 6:07:03" the grand stand can see in fancy just where car No. 10 is and when it is likely to come booming down the track from Hyde Park to the stand. After it has passed the starting tape its time is fixed by four split-second hands on four timers' watches. It may vary a trifle, each timer catching the car differently, perhaps. The middle fraction is taken and a rapid calculation is made of the elapsed time from the start by means of the official time clock, which runs steadily on. The time for the entire lap is then scheduled on the board.

Society in general, and particularly that portion of the fashionable world which is intensely interested in the auto, will view the start and finish of the big contest from an extensive box grand stand. Among the boxholders who will view the race from this point of vantage are: Alfred Gwynne Vanderbilt, Alex. C. Young, Benjamin Stern, W. J. P. Moore, E. R. Thomas, Leon Rubay, Mrs. Clarence Mackay, J. L. Breeze, Arthur G. Hoffman, W. K. Vanderbilt, Jr., Robert Lee Morrell, Charles J. Glidden, Robert Graves, W. C. Temple, H. Van Rensselaer Kennedy, R. Lincoln Lippitt, O. H. P. Belmont, W. Gould Brokaw, Foxhall Keene, Albert C. Bostwick, Clarence Grey Dinsmore, E. R. Hollander, John C. King, H. A. Lozier, Col. E. H. R. Green, Garret A. Hobart, W. G. McAdoo, Col. John Jacob Astor, J. Horace Harding, John T. Pratt, H. L. Bowden, H. B. Hollins, E. N. Dickerson D. J. Post, F. G. Stewart, H. B. Joy, R. A Alger, H. W. Bull, H. R. Worthington J. K. Christie, Harry Payne Whitney, H. J Moulton, A. W. Brand, H. H. Hunnewell E. de Clifford Chisholm, Major C. J. S. Miller and F. E. Kessinger.

DRIVERS AND STATISTICS OF CARS ENTERED IN VANDERBILT CUP RACE.

No.	Car.	Driver.	Entrant.	Nationality.	H. P.	No. Cyl's.	Type.	Drive.	Make of Tires.	Speeds.
1	Mercedes	Jenatzy	Robert Graves	German	120	4	Gasoline	Chain	Continental	Four speeds and reverse
2	De Dietrich	Duray	M. De Dietrich	French	130	4	Gasoline	Chain	Michelin	Four speeds and reverse
3	Pope-Toledo	Dingley	A. L. Pope	American	60	4	Gasoline	Chain	Diamond	Two speeds and reverse
4	Fiat	Lancia	Hollander & Tangemann	Italian	120	4	Gasoline	Chain	Michelin	Four speeds and reverse
5	Mercedes	Keene	F. P. Keene	German	120	4	Gasoline	Chain	Continental	Four speeds and reverse
6	Darracq	Wagner	Darracq & Co.	French	80	4	Gasoline	Shaft	Michelin	Four speeds and reverse
7	Locomobile	Tracy	Dr. H. E. Thomas	American	90	4	Gasoline	Chain	Diamond	Three speeds and reverse
8	Fiat	Nazzari	Hollander & Tangemann	Italian	120	4	Gasoline	Chain	Michelin	Four speeds and reverse
*9	Mercedes	Warden	J. B. Warden	German	120	4	Gasoline	Chain	Continental	Four speeds and reverse
10	Renault	Szisz	Renault Brothers	French	90	4	Gasoline	Shaft	Michelin	Three speeds and reverse
11	Christie	Christie	J. L. Breese	American	60	4	Gasoline	Shaft	Goodrich	Two speeds and reverse
12	Fiat	Cedrino	Hollander & Tangemann	Italian	90	4	Gasoline	Chain	Michelin	Four speeds and reverse
X	Mercedes	Campbell	S. B. Stevens	German	120	4	Gasoline	Chain	Continental	Four speeds and reverse
14	Panhard	Heath	Panhard & Levassor	French	120	4	Gasoline	Shaft	Michelin	Three speeds and reverse
15	Pope-Toledo	Lytle	A. A. Pope	American	90	6	Gasoline	Chain	Diamond	Three speeds and reverse
16	Fiat	Chevrolet	Hollander & Tangemann	Italian	90	4	Gasoline	Chain	Michelin	Four speeds and reverse
18	Darracq	Hemery	Darracq & Co.	French	80	4	Gasoline	Shaft	Michelin	Four speeds and reverse
19	White	White	R. H. White	American	40	2	Steam	Shaft	Diamond	Two speeds and reverse
20	Fiat	Sartori	A. G. Vanderbilt	Italian	90	4	Gasoline	Chain	Michelin	Four speeds and reverse

*No. 9, Warden, doubtful starter. No. 17, Basil, non-starter.

AUTO DRIVERS OF INTERNATIONAL REPUTATION WHO WILL COMPETE IN VANDERBILT CUP RACE ON LONG ISLAND TO-MORROW.

SZISZ. LANCIA. HEMERY. JANETZY.

INTERESTING FACTS REGARDING TO-MORROW'S GREAT AUTO RACE.

Title	Vanderbilt Cup Race.
Distance	283 miles.
Trophy	Vanderbilt Cup, value $[illegible],000.
Course	Ten times round 23.3 mile circuit.
Number of entries	Nineteen.
Doubtful starters	One.
Starting time	6 A. M.
Starting point	Mineola, Long Island.
Corners on course	Six.
Weight of cars	Maximum 2,204 pounds.
Horse-power of cars	From 40 to 130.
Speed expected	Sixty-two to sixty-six miles an hour.
[illegible]	Eighteen gasoline, one steam.
[illegible]	Lancia, Hemery, Szisz, Jenatzy.

TEMPERATURE MAXIMUM MINIMUM

WEATHER FORECAST
Partly cloudy.

The Globe
AND Commercial Advertiser. EST'D 1797.
NEW YORK'S OLDEST NEWSPAPER.

6 O'CLOCK NIGHT EDITION

109TH YEAR. NUMBER 330. VOLUME 109. NEW YORK, TUESDAY, JUNE 26, 1906. ONE CENT.

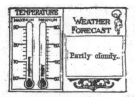

WOODBURY FAVORED BY COMMITTEE

Ivins Report Recommending His Removal From Office Rejected.

TWO MINORITY REPORTS MADE

Street Cleaning Department is Scathingly Arraigned by Attorney of Inquisitors.

SAYS HE IS INCOMPETENT

Also Accuses Him of Inefficiency, Waste, Neglect of Duty and Extravagance.

William M. Ivins, counsel for the aldermanic street cleaning investigating committee, submitted his report and findings, including a recommendation for the dismissal of Commissioner Woodbury, to the committee this morning. After a stormy consultation his recommendations were rejected by the majority of the committee, and Mr. Ivins left the committee room in disgust.

The recommendations made by Mr. Ivins were supported by two members of the committee, Chairman Max S. Grifenhagen of the Twenty-fifth Aldermanic District, and Alderman D. W. B. Brown of the Twenty-ninth Aldermanic District. Alderman Robert L. Downing of the Forty-fifth Aldermanic District, Brooklyn, expressed himself as favoring all the recommendations of Mr. Ivins except that in regard to the removal of the street cleaning commissioner, Major Woodbury, and he told the committee that he would prepare a separate report.

Alderman Frank L. Dowling of the Ninth Aldermanic District, the only Tammany member of the committee, submitted a minority report, signed by himself and Thomas J. Mulligan of the Bronx, an M. O. L. man.

The reports of Mr. Ivins and Alderman Dowling were submitted to the Board of Aldermen at its meeting to-day. Alderman Meyers, the Republican leader of the Board of Aldermen, said he favored the Ivins report and saw no reason why it should not be adopted. He intimated that he would do his best to have the Ivins report adopted at the next meeting of the board, but no action would be taken upon it this afternoon.

The reports were all submitted to the Board of Aldermen this afternoon and ordered printed. The question then went over to next Tuesday's meeting.

Recommends Dismissal.

The Ivins report contains twenty-two specific recommendations, as follows:

"That, in the interest of the good government and the welfare of the city, Commissioner John McGaw Woodbury be removed from office for incompetency; inefficiency, favoritism, and neglect of duty, waste and extravagance, and violation of the provisions of the city charter.

"That the department be completely reorganized by a new and competent commissioner, and that there be a deputy commissioner for the borough of Brooklyn.

"That the mayor require the commissioner of street cleaning to adopt a new and proper system of accounting, as may be prescribed by the commissioners of accounts and the Department of Finance.

"That the system of trial of subordinates for offenses against the rules of the department be so changed that fines shall be imposed only after trial, and an opportunity on the part of the accused to produce evidence in his own behalf.

"That the commissioner be required by the mayor to comply with the provisions of sections 419 and 541 of the city charter with regard to purchase of supplies or hiring of material in excess of $1,000.

"That the present system of snow removal, which showed a loss to the city of over one million dollars in a single season, be abandoned, and that contracts be let upon the basis of payment for snow actually removed, and not otherwise.

Refuse Would Make Land.

"That immediate steps be taken to put the city in a position where it shall not be dependent upon the Brooklyn Rapid Transit after the present contract for final disposition in Brooklyn.

"That all refuse in the future be used for the purpose of making public lands for the city, which will amount to at least $1,000,000 a year in the next twenty years.

"That the contract with the New York Sanitary Utilization Company be terminated at the earliest possible date and the city remove and render its own product of garbage.

"That no picking or culling of rubbage be permitted at the docks in Manhattan and the Bronx, or at the receiving stations in Brooklyn.

"That the contract with the American Railway Traffic Company be enforced without delay as to the erection of proper receiving structures; the picking of

(Continued on Fourth Page.)

J. OGDEN ARMOUR BACK.

Among the passengers on the steamer Kronprinz Wilhelm, which arrived from Southampton to-day, were Mr. and Mrs. J. Ogden Armour, Lieut. U. S. Grant, U. S. A., and Prof. J. T. Hatfield of Northwestern University.

MILLIONAIRE MURDERER AND WOMAN WHO WAS THE CAUSE OF HIS CRIME

ROGUES' GALLERY PHOTOGRAPH OF H. K. THAW.

EVELYN FLORENCE NESBIT, FORMER MODEL AND ACTRESS.

INQUEST ON TO-MORROW

The Informal Inquiry in the Kinnan Murder Case Is Ended.

The formal inquest into the murder of Mrs. Alice Kinnan, who was killed on the front piazza of her home in Washington avenue in the Bronx on the evening of June 8, will be begun to-morrow morning at the office of Coroner McDonald. A majority of the witnesses who appeared during the informal inquiry by Coroner McDonald and Assistant District Attorney Cardozo have been subpenaed to appear.

Several relatives of Mrs. Stenton, mother of the murdered woman—among them being a nephew who is a clergyman—were busy to-day looking for a competent attorney to care for Mrs. Stenton's interests during the formal inquest, and later to represent her in case a trial is evolved.

Mr. Cardoza was too ill to-day to give personal attention to the case, but Acting Capt. Price, head of the Bronx Detective Bureau, and Coroner McDonald were busy working up what details they have at hand in preparation for the inquest.

Acting Capt. Price and Coroner McDonald would not discuss the case, and if they have found the alleged evidence which they have declared would lead to an arrest by Friday they are reserving the surprise for the inquest.

Mrs. Stenton has issued a defiance to the police, the coroners of the Bronx, and the office of the district attorney.

As she sat on the porch of the Miller home, at Sixth avenue and 200th street, to-day she said.

"I will go out of here dead before I will be subjected to such treatment again."

She declares that at the hearing on Saturday she was browbeaten and bulldozed in an outrageous manner.

"I am feeling comfortable and not the least worried," she said, "but I am not going down again to that inquiry. They got me down there the other day by deceiving me, because I had believed in Capt. Price when he told me it would be merely to ask a few questions in private.

"They browbeat and bullied me and showed no respect for my gray hairs. Just imagine four strong young men trying to force a confession out of an old woman without a friend near her.

"I am not a murderer, and I am not going to be treated in this way again. I'll go out dead before I will be subjected to that thing again. They showed no pity for an old woman who had lost her daughter, but instead seemed to want me to confess that I had killed Alice. But I have some rights and I will be protected."

Mrs. Miller, at whose home Mrs. Stenton has been staying for ten days, objects strongly to the continuance of the police surveillance upon her house. She says the detectives who are kept there night and day are a nuisance, and have no right there. She says she wants the police to arrest Mrs. Stenton and take her away, or else to take the detectives away. If they are not going to arrest Mrs. Stenton, Mrs. Miller says the police should not keep such a watch upon her and the family in the house. Mrs. Miller says it is extremely annoying to have the detectives watching every move she makes and trying to hear every word she says, and trying to hear every word she says, and she wants the situation changed.

MURPHY FAVORS McCABE.

It was announced at Tammany Hall this afternoon that Charles F. Murphy was in favor of calling a meeting of the Democratic state committee for some date between July 8 and 15, and that he was in favor of McCabe of Albany for state chairman.

YALE VS. HARVARD.

SCORE BY INNINGS:

Yale........	0	0	0
Harvard.....	0	0	

RYE RACED FAST MILE

Ridden by Miller, Greenan Horse Goes Distance in 1.39 1-5—Prince Hamburg Wins.

THE WINNERS.

First Race—Prince Hamburg, 9 to 10, first; Sir Lynnewood, 6 to 1 for place, second; Cinna, 8 to 5 to show, third. Time, 1.18 2-5.

Second Race—Rye, 2 to 5, first; Water Tank, 3 to 1 for place, second; Klingsor, 8 to 5 to show, third. Time, 1.39 1-5.

Third Race—Red River, 4 to 1, first; Sewell, 2 to 1 for place, second; Bat Masterson, even to show, third. Time, 1.06 4-5.

(Special to The Globe.)

SHEEPSHEAD BAY RACE TRACK, N. Y., June 26.—Bright, sunshiny weather and an excellent card combined to keep the attendance up, here this afternoon. Probably about 8,000 people were scattered in the field and in the stand when proceedings began. Hardly a breeze was blowing, and those that made the journey from the city in the hope of escaping the heat did not find any relief.

Both the Zephyr Stakes, for two year olds, and the Swift Stakes, for three year olds, brought out excellent fields, and the races were interesting. The track was fast.

Martin Won for Favorite.

Jack Martin brought Prince Hamburg home a winner in the first race of the day, but it was by the very short margin of a head. He was the choice in the betting, had the speed to go to the front at the start and stay there all the way. In the strech he apparenly was winning easily when the long shot, Sir Lynnewood, closed with a tremendous rush after coming wide. Martin saw him coming and rode the finish he is capable of. He won by a nose, while Sir Lynnewood was two lengths in front of Cinna. Bohemia got away badly, and was pinched in on the rail all the way. It was a dash of six and one-half furlongs on the main course, and the time, 1.18 2-5, equalled the track record held by Mineola and Martinmas.

Rye Romped In in Second.

Christie Sullivan's game little plater Rye romped off with the second race. It was a selling event at a mile, and with Miller in the saddle he was made a prohibitive choice. The colt went to the front at the start and set a fast pace, and at the end was three lengths in front of Water Tank. Klingsor was third, four lengths back.

LENIENT WITH CAPT. WYNNE

President Permits Convicted Naval Officer to Resign.

(Special to The Globe.)

WASHINGTON, June 26.—President Roosevelt has approved the recommendation of the Navy Department that Capt. Robert F. Wynne, who was tried for insubordination, be permitted to resign.

Secretary Bonaparte laid the matter before the President to-day after E. S. Theall, counsel for Captain Wynne, had called at the Navy Department and submitted a brief, in the nature of a protest, against the proceedings of the court-martial end of the reviewing authority, Rear Admiral Evans, which is now before the department for final action.

The court-martial made no recommendation for clemency. The Navy Department has recommended to the President approval of the sentence, but in view of Capt. Wynne's service and the provocation under which he acted in the most serious offense charged, the department has advised that execution of the sentence be delayed until Capt. Wynne can be given opportunity to resign. This recommendation of the department is now before the President.

NEW HITCH ON THE RATE BILL

The Senate Sends It Back for Further Conference After Killing Report.

(Special to The Globe.)

WASHINGTON, June 26.—The Senate to-day disagreed to the conference report on the rate bill, returned the bill to conference, with the Senate insisting on its amendment, and selected Elkins, Cullom, and Tillman again to represent it on the conference committee.

All this came in the session that followed an all night conference on the question of adjournment at Speaker Cannon's home. They decided that no adjournment resolution should pass the House until the pure food immigration, naturalization, rate, and meat inspection bills had been agreed on in conference.

The disagreement was on the pipe line and commodity amendments and on the anti-pass amendment. The conferees so modified the amendment prohibiting carriers from transporting their own commodities as to prevent its application to any carriers but railroads, thus exempting the pipe lines from the prohibitions of the commodity amendment.

To this Senator Tillman vigorously objected yesterday, saying every senator who voted for it would go forth "branded on his forehead with the letters 'S. O.'" The debate was continued to-day, Senator Long of Kansas urging that pipe lines ought not be prohibited carrying their own product.

Senator Clapp of Minnesota had a letter read from a southwestern oil man, a friend of his, who declared the Standard Oil was stirring up the agitation against the pipe line features of the rate bill and had asked him to send dispatches to such senators and representatives as he knew.

It is expected the action of the Senate to-day will compel agreement on a stronger anti-pass provision and will force a rigid provision as to pipe lines.

The conference on the agriculture appropriation bill developed that the differences between the House and Senate in regard to the meat inspection amendment probably will be sent back to the two houses for further action or for instructions to the conferees. The Senate representatives refused absolutely to consider the provisions making an appropriation for the government to pay the cost of inspection and insisted upon the retention of the provision in the Beveridge bill requiring that the date of inspection be placed upon cans of meat.

Another meeting will be held at four P. M., when the conference will decide, finally, whether there is a possibility of agreement concerning the meat inspection amendment.

The Omnibus Public Building bill was passed by the House, one hour having been consumed in its reading and consideration.

The "pork barrel," as the so-called omnibus public building bill is generally called, was rolled into the House to-day by Mr. Dalzell (Pa.), who reported a broad and comprehensive rule for its consideration. The rule provides that while the consideration of the bill shall be the same as under suspension of the rules, its passage shall rest on a vote of the majority instead of by a two-thirds vote.

To be consistent, Mr. Williams (Miss.), the leader of the minority, called for a division, and by the overwhelming vote of 193 to 21 the previous question was ordered.

KAISER ON CRUISE.

On Board Meteor on Trip From Kiel to Eckernfoerde.

KIEL, Germany, June 26.—The yachts Meteor, Hamburg, Iduna, Clara, Susanne, Orion, Navahoe, Comet, and all the other large yachts cruised from Kiel to Eckernfoerde over a fifty-two-mile course today, followed by the steam yachts.

Emperor William was on board the Meteor, but the steamer Hamburg went to Eckernfoerde and his majesty and his party will pass the night on board that vessel. The yachts will cruise back to Kiel to-morrow.

SUMMING UP LOVETT CASE

The Divorce Contest Is Likely to Go to the Jury This Afternoon.

William E. Dennis, the hand writing expert, called yesterday by the defense in the suit of George E. Lovett against his wife, Grace, for an absolute divorce, resumed the stand to-day in Part III. of the Supreme Court, in Brooklyn.

The calling of this witness was avowedly for the purpose of proving that Mrs. Inez Courtenay, the former dear friend of the defendant, and now a witness for the husband, had written the alleged "threatening letters" to herself. They have been credited to Mrs. Lovett.

Mr Dennis proceeded to give crayon demonstration to show that the same "features" existed in the words "you testify" in the samples written by Mrs. Courtenay in court as in the original letter. A number of other words and letters were descanted upon to show a similarity in general characteristics.

Witness became somewhat confused in handling the various exhibits, and persisted in an endeavor to show a similarity of the writing in exhibit E (Mrs. Lovett's handwriting) to that of the specimens written by Mrs. Courtenay—until Mr. Ketcham, counsel for the defense, with considerable show of annoyance, requested him to dismiss exhibit E from his mind for the present. Counsel for the plaintiff appeared to be much amused at the blunder of the witness.

After the exhibits had been finally arranged so as to permit of no further bad breaks, Mr. Dennis proceeded with equal facility to point out dissimilarities between the handwriting of Mrs. Courtenay and that of the specimens written by Mrs. Lovett in court.

Mrs. Lovett was recalled to the stand and declared that she did not write or print the letters threatening Mrs. Courtenay's life or the envelopes enclosing them. She also denied that she ever had seen them before.

William J. Kinsley, the handwriting expert, recalled for plaintiff, stated that after a careful examination of exhibits he was prepared to give it as his professional opinion and conviction that the specimens written by Mrs. Courtenay in court and the threatening letters and envelopes enclosing them were not written by the same hand.

This closed the testimony on both sides, and court adjourned for recess.

Counsel on each side announced that they would require two hours for summing up, thus making it probable that the case would go to the jury this evening.

PULAJANES SURRENDER.

Last of Rebel Leaders on Island of Cebu Now Prisoners.

MANILA, June 26.—The Pulajane leaders Quentin and Adva have surrendered to Governor Osmena and the constabulary. They were the last of the men arrayed against the Americans on the Island of Cebu who remained at liberty.

The rifles and ammunition of the members of their band were also surrendered.

LITTLE WINS MATCH.

Kreigh Collins Loses Tennis Tournament at Wimbledon.

WIMBLEDON, England, June 26.—In the second round of the lawn tennis championship games here to-day Raymond D. Little (American) beat P. T. G. Pipon by 3—0. The scores were 6—1, 6—4, 7—5.

In the third round (singles) K. Powell beat Kreigh Collins (American) by 3—2 after a hard fought tussle. The scores were 6—4, 3—6, 6—4, 4—6, 6—2.

In the first round of the doubles Kreigh Collins and Raymond D. Little (Americans) were given a walkover.

Little was also given a walkover in the third round of the singles.

THAW THREATENED TO KILL WHITE, SHE SAYS, TWO YEARS AGO

Woman Friend Tells of Hearing Remark In Restaurant.—Mazie Follette, Evelyn Nesbit's Chum, Denies the Charge Against White.

PRISONER'S WIFE FOUND; SAYS: "I DIDN'T THINK HE'D DO IT"

Thaw Examined by Alienists in His Cell in the Tombs—Plea Will Be Insanity—Treated Like a Common Criminal—Handcuffed and Photographed.

Mrs. Evelyn Nesbit Thaw, for whom the police have been searching since midnight, was found this afternoon by a Globe reporter, to whom she made this significant statement regarding the shooting of Stanford White by her husband:

"Harry must have been mad. I didn't think he would do it."

Mrs. Thaw was found at the Cambridge Court Hotel.

Thaw is a prisoner in the Tombs. It has been learned that two years ago he threatened to kill White.

The prisoner was taken from the Tenderloin station at 9 o'clock this morning, handcuffed to Detective Brown. He was first taken to police headquarters and afterward to Jefferson Market Court, where he was remanded to the custody of the coroner without bail.

Dr. Carlos F. MacDonald, Dr. Austin G. Flint, and Dr. Mabon, noted alienists, examined him this afternoon. The defense will be insanity.

The inquest has been set for Thursday. Mr. White's funeral will be held on the same day.

Thaw was taken from the coroner's court across the "Bridge of Sighs" leading to the Tombs at 11 o'clock to-day. As he was led from the office of Coroner Dooley, into whose custody he has been remanded by Magistrate Barlow, Thaw spoke no word, nor did he give the slightest sign of failing nerve. Throughout the conference which preceded his commitment to the Tombs he remained quiet—almost indifferent. His eyes gazed straight ahead of him. He responded to questions with a start as if his thoughts were far away.

A startling statement was made this afternoon by Masie Follette, former stage chum and intimate friend of Evelyn Nesbit. Miss Follette said:

"Say for me that there is absolutely no truth in Harry Thaw's accusation that Stanford White ruined Evelyn Nesbit. I have known all three of them for many years, and I know the charge is false.

"Mr. White was a man who was always glad to assist young actresses. He did so out of the goodness of his heart, and no one can say a word against him."

Tells of Threat.

A close woman friend of the late Mr. White and Mr. and Mrs. Thaw, who is identified with the theatrical profession, made the following statement concerning the relations of the murdered man and the Thaws:

"Two years ago Harry Thaw while in a restaurant declared: 'I will kill him,' meaning Mr. White. We thought nothing of it at the time, but soon found out that he had a mania on the subject. He had been threatening to kill Mr. White ever since.

"I believe Mrs. Thaw put him up to it. I have heard her repeatedly accuse Mr. White of accomplishing her ruin. I have heard her say so in Thaw's presence plenty of times. Even when strange men would be with her in such a public place as a restaurant she has declared the same thing. It was very disgusting to us who knew better.

"I have been her friend for many years, but I am very bitter against her now. I believe she told Thaw of that charge against Mr. White in order to justify herself.

"Mr. White came to see me about a month after the marriage of Evelyn Nesbit and Mr. Thaw and told me that the night before he had passed the couple in the restaurant of the Hotel St. Regis. Mrs. Thaw averted her head and refused to notice him. Mr. White felt badly about the snub and said so."

Where His Wife Is.

The mystery of the disappearance of Thaw's wife was solved this afternoon, when a Globe reporter found her at the Cambridge Court Hotel, in Forty-ninth street, where she was registered under the name of "Miss Wilkins."

Mrs. Thaw arrived at the Cambridge Court very early this morning under the escort of George C. Carnegie, Harry Thaw's friend, to whom he sent word shortly after the shooting. Mrs. Thaw was no stranger to Cambridge Court, for she made her home there for a number of years prior to her marriage with Thaw.

Mrs. Thaw refused to make any statement at the hotel, but early this afternoon, in response to a telephone summons, went to the office of Lewis Delafield, at 1 Nassau street.

Mrs. Thaw on her way to the lawyer's office was accompanied by her chum, Miss May McKenzie, an actress. They spent half an hour with Lewis Delafield. When they left they were accompanied by Mrs. Thaw's brother and W. P. Delafield and went to the latter's office at 66 Wall street.

While she was there a subpœna server attached to District Attorney Jerome's office served Mrs. Thaw with a subpœna to appear before the grand Jury Thursday morning.

W. P. Delafield, talking to a reporter for The Globe, said:

"Mrs. Thaw will appear before the coroner at the proper time. She is not a fugitive from justice, but will appear when wanted. Meanwhile she will not discuss the case."

"It is too terrible to think of," said Mrs. Thaw, when approached by a Globe reporer. "I cannot say anything now. Harry must have been mad. I didn't think he would do it."

Mrs. Thaw was gowned entirely in brown and wore a brown veil that almost concealed her features. Miss McKenzie wore a black gown and black veil.

A large crowd quickly learned who the two women weer and they were followed by hundreds as they passed from 1 Nassau street to 60 Wall street.

Fled to Get Her Letters.

It has been learned that immediately after the shooting last night Mrs. Thaw fled to the apartments of Miss McKenzie, at 148 West Forty-ninth street. Then, accompanied by Miss McKenzie, she went to her apartments in the Lorraine and gathered up large quantities of letters and other things. The two young women then went to the Cambridge Court Hotel, where they spent the night.

Among the bundle of letters Mrs. Thaw secured at the Lorraine were a number written to her by Mr. White. There are now in the possession of W. P. Delafield.

After Mr. Delafield secured the letters he immediately sent for George Coleman Carnegie and William Thaw to confer over the bearing these letters may have in the trial of the slayer of Mr. White.

Wants Champagne for Dinner.

Thaw is registered at the Tombs as Harry Thaw, born United States; thirty-three years of age and a student. His cell is 8x9 by 12 feet high.

For the present Thaw will not have the full privileges accorded to other prisoners. He will exercise with a keeper. He has already had two meals in the prison, eating his luncheon while his counsel was conferring with him. When his dinner was ready at 1 o'clock, he asked for a bottle of champagne, but upon being told that no liquors could be served, he ordered the biggest bottle of mineral water that could be procured. This was supplied.

When the caterer inquired as to whether Thaw would pay for his meals as he was served, he replied:

"I guess I'll take them on credit for awhile and pay by check, if you are satisfied."

The caterer was satisfied, of course.

Just before dinner was served the alienists, including Dr. McGuire, spent ten minutes with the murderer.

Drs. Macdonald and Flint refused to say anything, but Dr. McGuire, while refusing to say anything officially, was frank enough to admit he believed he discovered symptoms of emotional insanity and that he thought he had discovered indications of incipient paresis. Just what these in-

New-York Tribune.

PART II. SUNDAY, JANUARY 12, 1908. EIGHT PAGES.

THE NEW PUBLIC LIBRARY BUILDING FOR THE CITY OF NEW YORK.

This great architectural monument, designed by Messrs. Carrère & Hastings, has now reached a stage toward completion at which its beauties can be fully realized for the first time. In these pages, with picture and text, The Tribune places before its readers a survey of it more comprehensive than hitherto has been possible.

FIFTH AVENUE FRONT OF THE NEW BUILDING AND 42D STREET SIDE.
The front extends from 42d street to 40th street and is 390 feet long. The depth is 270 feet. The cost will exceed $7,000,000.

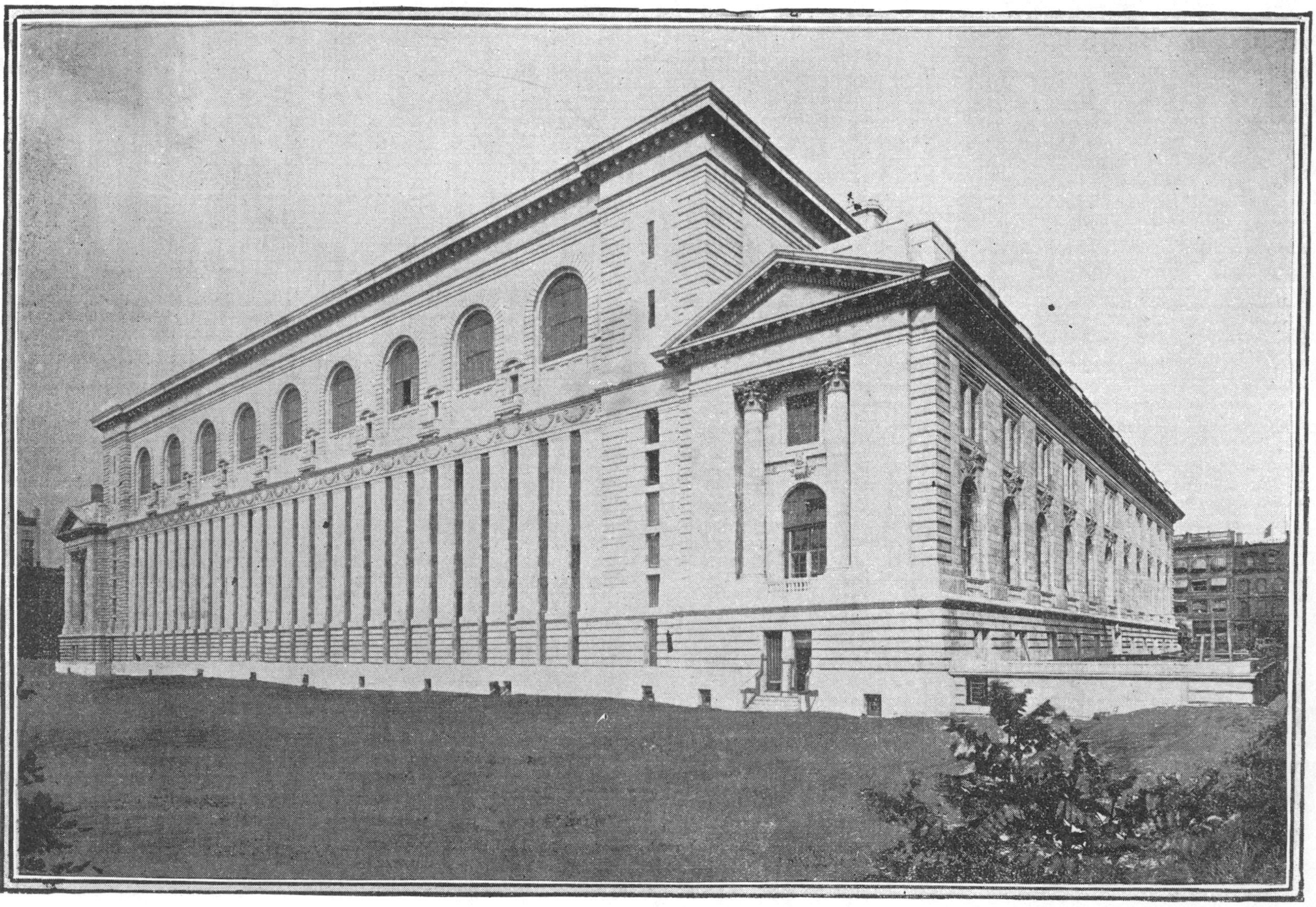

BACK OF THE NEW BUILDING AND 40TH STREET SIDE AS SEEN FROM BRYANT PARK, ON THE EASTERLY EDGE OF WHICH THE LIBRARY STANDS.
Showing the long, narrow windows lighting the big stack room, which is stratified into seven floors. Showing also the arched windows of the main reading room.

New-York Tribune.

PART II. SUNDAY, FEBRUARY 2, 1908. EIGHT PAGES.

AN INDISPENSABLE COMMODITY OF WHICH THE TYPICAL NEW YORKER GETS TOO LITTLE.

Yet sleep is free to all, is as cheap as air, has been called "the balance that sets the king and the shepherd, the fool and the wise man even," and may be just as sweet upon a rock as in an emperor's bed.

(All from stereographs, copyright by Underwood & Underwood, New York.)

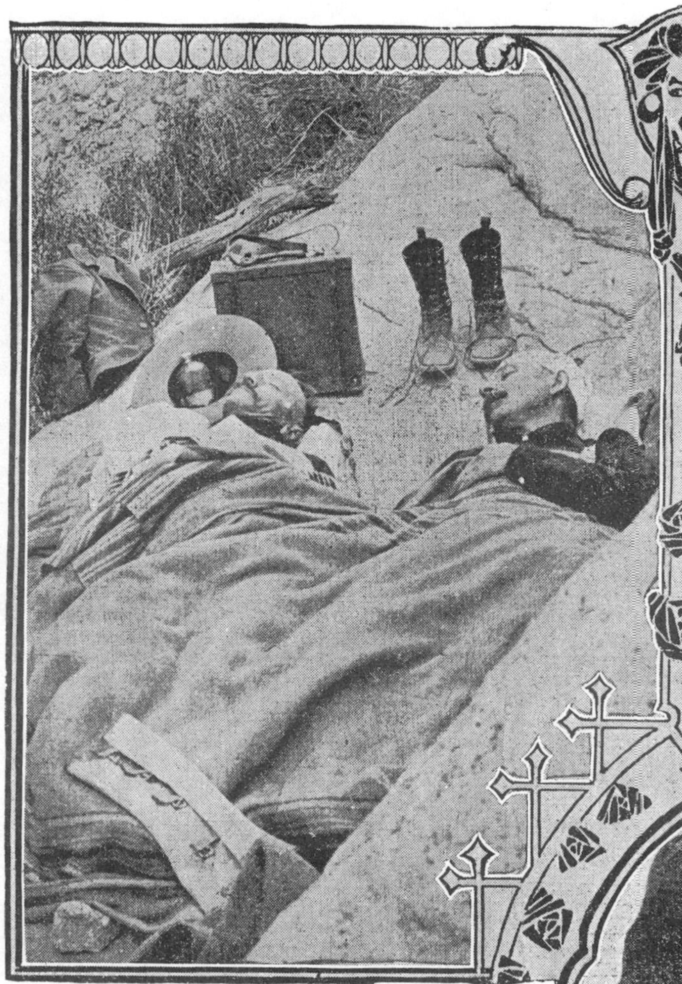

SLEEPING ON "BED-ROCK."
Miners camping on soft side of a ledge.

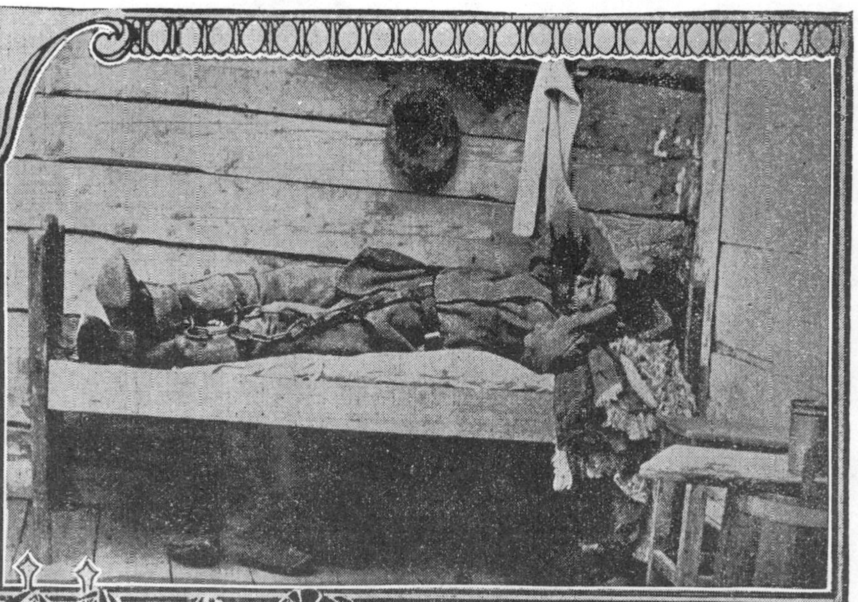

SLEEPING IN FETTERS.
Russian convict in a Siberian prison.

SLEEPING ON MOTHER'S SHOULDER.
Greek farmhand's baby slung in hammock.

SLEEPING IN LUXURY.
One of the most celebrated beds in the world—the gilded couch of Louis XIV preserved at Versailles.

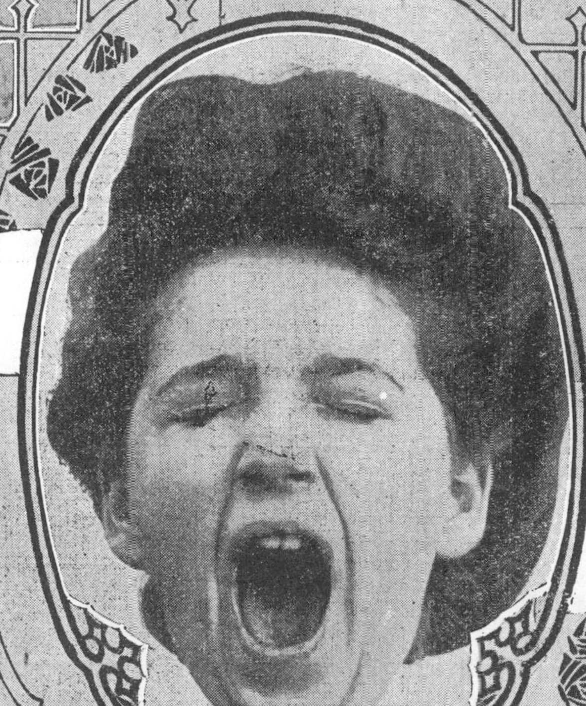

SLEEP'S HERALD—A YAWN.
One of the most infectious symptoms on earth.

SLEEPING ON A QUEER PILLOW.
The Japanese use a low rail of wood, with a thin cotton pad over it.

SLEEPING IN A SMOTHER.
Old-fashioned box bed, piled high with feather beds and inclosed by curtains.

PART V. New-York Tribune. PART V.

NEW-YORK, SUNDAY, MARCH 21, 1909.

1909 SPRING FASHIONS 1909

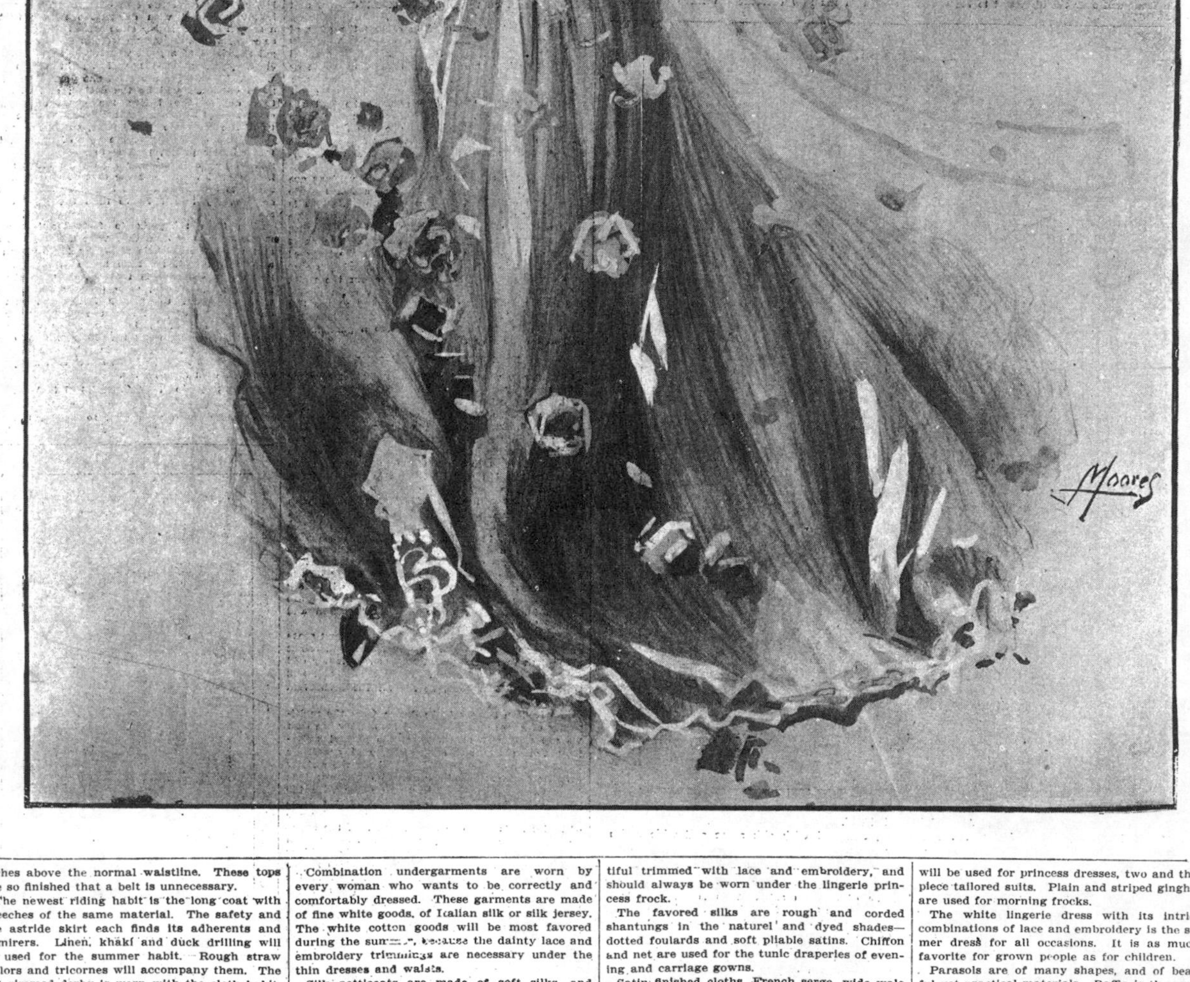

THE STYLE SUMMARY

FEATURES OF SPRING AND SUMMER MODES.

Changes Are Many, and Varied Fashions Will Show Woman at Her Best.

A season of beautiful colors is before us. All the new shades are soft, rich and dull with the exception of cherry, and it is by no means the garish tone of old, but has submitted to the general softening. No one color will be more fashionable than another.

A decided change has come in the mode of hair dressing. The fashionable coiffure is low in front, extended at the sides, and arranged in puffs just above the nape of the neck. It may be parted or worn as the wearer desires.

Hair ornaments are quite different, and are made to accord with the new styles of hair dressing. Ball and loop pins, wide barettes, the Psyche pin, and flat as well as upstanding bandeaux are the latest shapes. Tortoise-shell, jet, pearl and rhinestone are most favored in the new hair ornaments.

The new hats require the new hair dressing in order that they may be correctly placed upon the head. Millinery is more entrancing than ever. The mushrooms and pokes give a delightfully piquant air to the face and general contour. They are most comfortable, too, for they come well down over the head. The large hats are of the Louis XVI period, with beautifully curved brims and high crowns. Rough straw vies for favor with smooth straw in both medium and large hats. Millinery trimmings include flowers, fruits, velvet and satin ribbons, wings, aigrettes and ostrich plumes.

Hat pins with large jet or colored stone heads are novel. The jet pin may be worn with a hat of any color, but the colored stone must match the hat with which it is worn.

Mesh veils in large and small woven dots are new. The octagon mesh both with and without the dot is the latest arrival. Colored veils will be worn to match the hat. Becoming veils show a combination of black with a color. The chiffon veil with satin striped border is the newest motor veil.

Motor coats are mostly dust and waterproof, whether they be made of the light ballou silk or the heavier cloths. Many clever and serviceable ideas are shown in the new motor coats, which are all full length, with long protecting sleeves.

The lingerie waist is to be the waist of the summer season. It is more dainty than ever, and fashionable ones are all shown with the long sleeve similar to that in the latest French costumes. Colored embroidery is shown on some of these new waists, but by far the greater number are entirely white. There are several new waist materials.

Skirts for the two piece tailored suit, with which the lingerie waist will be worn, are made in princess style with the top coming a few inches above the normal waistline. These tops are so finished that a belt is unnecessary.

The newest riding habit is the long coat with breeches of the same material. The safety and the astride skirt each finds its adherents and admirers. Linen, khaki and duck drilling will be used for the summer habit. Rough straw sailors and tricornes will accompany them. The flat rimmed derby is worn with the cloth habit.

The white short glove is fashionable for street use, and the long one for evening wear. White and yellow chamois will be fashionable for day time during the warm weather. Heavy tan gloves are most used for riding, driving and motoring.

Combination undergarments are worn by every woman who wants to be correctly and comfortably dressed. These garments are made of fine white goods, of Italian silk or silk jersey. The white cotton goods will be most favored during the summer, because the dainty lace and embroidery trimmings are necessary under the thin dresses and waists.

Silk petticoats are made of soft silks, and with jersey silk tops and messaline flounces. The princess silk petticoat comes in white and colors. Silk knicker and sheath bockers are worn with evening gowns, and by some women all the time.

The white nainsook princess petticoat is beautiful trimmed with lace and embroidery, and should always be worn under the lingerie princess frock.

The favored silks are rough and corded shantungs in the naturel and dyed shades—dotted foulards and soft pliable satins. Chiffon and net are used for the tunic draperies of evening and carriage gowns.

Satin finished cloths, French serge, wide wale diagonals and mannish mixtures in unobtrusive colorings are used for the tailored suits. Black and white sheperd's checks are fashionable for tailored suits and dresses.

Linens in white and beautiful colors are to be the acme of smartness for the summer. These will be used for princess dresses, two and three-piece tailored suits. Plain and striped ginghams are used for morning frocks.

The white lingerie dress with its intricate combinations of lace and embroidery is the summer dress for all occasions. It is as much a favorite for grown people as for children.

Parasols are of many shapes, and of beautiful yet practical materials. Raffia is the newest fabric for the parasol. Handles are of long and medium length, made necessary by the high crowns of the new hats.

The Dutch collar promises to be the fad of the season. Yet it will not oust the high unlined lace stock collar from the favor of many women. There is a time and place for each. Irish lace is a great favorite for all forms of white neckwear. Hand embroidery also merits consideration. The stiff linen collar still holds sway for general use.

The newest shoulder scarf is made of soft silk or satin ornamented with five narrow rows of marabou, between which the silk, often of a contrasting color, shows to advantage. The embroidered net scarf is another new arrival, and is shown in both silk and tinset nets.

Skirts incline to greater fullness. For the street they are instep length with a few plaits sometimes set in about the bottom. For the evening costume they are much fuller than the extremely narrow models of the winter, but these still cling about the figure owing to the soft fabrics employed. Trained skirts are correct for costumes intended for formal afternoon occasions.

Tunic draperies of various lengths are seen on many of the imported costumes intended for carriage and evening wear. They are made of the material itself or of chiffon, net or marquisette.

Coats for the tailored suit are of knee length, and built on long lines that give the slender hipless figure. Coats for general utility purposes are full length. Lace and net coats intended for evening wear are of many lengths. Lingerie coats of openwork embroidery stop a trifle above the knees.

The princess gown is to be the dress of the season. It is made on the modified Empire and Directoire lines, as well as on those of classical princess cut and the latest moyen age type. The princess gown is shown in materials and trimmings suitable for every occasion.

High ribbon and feather ruches that fasten tight about the throat are smart for street wear. They are either in the color of the suit or in a contrasting color that matches the hat. The long feather stole continues a great favorite.

The bronze shoe is among the newest and smartest footwear for spring. Buck and suède ties and pumps in tan, gray and black, tan Russian leather, black patent leather and gunmetal are other new styles. The white shoe will be the popular summer shoe.

The new purses are made of colored and black morocco and pigskin. They are generally square. There are many new and useful articles in leather for the traveller and motorist.

Corsets are long, and continue to accent the slender lines that produce the hipless figure. Hose supporters are now used in the back as well as in front and at the sides of the corset. The brassiere is a necessary addition to the corset for the full figure.

SOME OF THE CHANGES.

High crowned and close brimmed mushrooms.

Large hats with broad brims.

The princess gown and knee length hipless coat.

Long sleeved gowns and coats.

Reviews of the Financial Week.

LA SEMAINE A LA BOURSE DE PARIS

Malgré la Proximité des Vacances de Pâques, la Hausse a Eté Générale.

LA RENTE FAIT EXCEPTION.

Elle n'a pu conserver l'Avance prise à la Fin de la Semaine dernière.

Depuis que la question orientale a été enfin réglée, non pas sans doute à l'entière satisfaction de tous, mais du moins de façon à assurer pour un temps un "modus vivendi" acceptable, la Bourse, libérée de tout souci immédiat, a pu donner libre cours au désir d'affaires et d'activité dont elle avait déjà fait montre au début de l'automne et que les événements des Balkans étaient venus si malencontreusement arrêter. Le marché n'avait d'ailleurs pas à se préoccuper des conditions dans lesquelles ce règlement était intervenu, ni à prendre parti pour personne. Il n'a donc envisagé que le résultat en lui-même qui, pour lui, signifie la disparition d'un élément dont l'influence dissolvante ne s'est que trop et trop longtemps fait sentir sur les transactions.

Aussi le mouvement de hausse, qui avait accueilli, dès qu'elle fut connue, la nouvelle de l'entente austro-serbe, n'a-t-il fait que s'accentuer, malgré la proximité des congés de Pâques. L'abondance monétaire constatée en liquidation de fin mars et affirmée également par la décision de la Banque d'Angleterre de ramener à 2½ pour cent son escompte officiel, n'a pas non plus été étrangère à ce mouvement. Les capitalistes, gros et petits, ont fait largement emploi de leurs disponibilités, ce qui a donné au comptant une toute autre allure. Le paiement des coupons et des loyers d'avril va d'ailleurs ramener de l'argent frais sur le marché.

Excepté la Rente.

La Rente seule a fait exception au milieu de la hausse générale. Elle n'a pu conserver l'avance qu'elle avait prise à la fin de la semaine dernière, après la nomination de la commission sénatoriale chargée de l'étude du projet d'impôt sur le revenu. Le comptant surtout a été lourd. On s'est fort ému, en effet, dans le monde des petits rentiers, de la réunion au cours de laquelle 10,000 ouvriers environ de l'industrie privée ou fonctionnaires de l'Etat ont acclamé des discours révolutionnaires et des exhortations à la grève générale et au chambardement.

Il est évident maintenant que l'idée de la grève générale fait des progrès énormes dans les milieux ouvriers, entraînés par quelques agitateurs professionnels, et se rendant mal compte des conséquences qu'une pareille démonstration aurait pour le pays. C'est même l'énormité de ces conséquences qui fait que la grève générale ne pourra jamais être qu'une démonstration, violente à vrai dire, de la puissance syndicale, mais qui ne sera que de courte durée. Jeudi la Rente s'est un peu relevée à l'annonce d'une mystification dont ce pince-sans-rire de Pataud aurait à son tour été victime.

La lourdeur du 3 pour cent Français a profité aux fonds d'Etats étrangers, qui ont été particulièrement bien tenus, notamment l'Extérieure espagnole, qui en tenant compte du coupon qui vient d'être détaché a franchi le pair, et les diverses catégories de Rentes russes, toutes en avances sensibles.

Le compartiment des Sociétés de Crédit a fait preuve également d'activité et de fermeté. Le marché va devoir s'occuper dès la rentrée de l'augmentation de capital de trois établissements: la Société Générale, le Comptoir d'Escompte et le Crédit Mobilier. C'est là un excellent élément d'activité pour notre place en attendant les émissions nouvelles en préparation. Le Rio Tinto clôture très ferme à 1,784 malgré une certaine lourdeur du cuivre métal à Londres. La Central Mining progresse vivement à 368 en sympathie avec l'excellente tenue du compartiment des mines d'or.

Marché en Banque.

En dehors de quelques rachats, qui se sont produits sur les valeurs industrielles russes, l'activité continue à se porter sur les valeurs sud-africaines. Celles-ci se présentent en plus-value presque générale et l'ampleur des négociations démontre qu'une appréciation nettement optimiste prévaut dans les milieux jusqu'ici réfractaires à tout ce qui concernait les entreprises sud-africaines. Les efforts qui ont été faits pour établir ces dernières sur une base industrielle inattaquable portent leurs fruits, et le public s'intéresse plus largement de jour en jour à celles d'entre elles dont les résultats régulièrement en progrès se traduisent par des dividendes nettement supérieurs aux nombreuses valeurs métallurgiques ou métallifères dont la cotation actuelle ne fournit qu'un taux de capitalisation souvent trop insuffisant.

La Rand Mines est celle dont l'avance a été la plus sensible; elle clôture à 217fr. Il est hors de doute que les exercices qui vont suivre seront de plus en plus productifs, car toutes les filiales de ce grand trust sont maintenant en marche. Mais ce n'est guère que d'ici deux ans que l'on pourra se rendre compte du surplus énorme de profits qui en résultera. Il est en tous cas certain que les bénéfices actuels sont plus importants que ceux de l'an dernier et que le portefeuille a acquis une sensible plus-value.

L'East Rand et la Goldfields progressent respectivement à 129fr. et 134fr. Sur la première de ces valeurs de gros achats de portefeuille ont été effectués. La Robinson Gold reste fermement tenue à 260fr. Sa production du mois de mars est des plus satisfaisantes. Elle présente une augmentation de profits de près de £5,000 sur le mois précédent. A signaler également les excellents rendements obtenus par la Rose Deep et la Durban Deep, dont les progrès constants depuis plusieurs mois méritent d'attirer l'attention. Elles s'avancent respectivement à 117fr. et 65fr.

La Simmer and Jack est fermement tenue à 51.75. La Robinson Deep a été également recherchée à 131fr. et jeudi de gros achats se sont produits sur la Village Main Reef, qui clôture à 103fr. La Transvaal Land progresse à 66.50.

NOTABLE ADVANCES IN WALL STREET.

Business Is Active During Week, Improving Trade Conditions Causing Generally Good Feeling.

WHEAT AND COTTON GO HIGH.

Stocks of Mackay Companies Also Soar, and Chesapeake and Ohio Shares Upward Tendency.

[BY COMMERCIAL CABLE TO THE HERALD.]

NEW YORK, Sunday.—"Uncle Daniel" Drew's advice, "When the saps are runnin' up the trees, sonny, buy securities," was pretty generally followed last week. As a result there was activity during the four business days and a notable advance in prices. Improving trade conditions, particularly in the West, were a strong cause of good feeling, and the passage of the tariff bill by the House was another.

The speculative spirit extended to the markets for commodities and was attended with a notable rise in cotton and a sensational advance in wheat. The latter was attributed mainly to the manipulation of the pool controlled by "Big Jim" Patten, of Chicago, with auxiliary operations on the New York Produce Exchange. Wheat for export in this city at $1.36 is 14 cents a bushel higher than a week ago, which means a 50-cent advance in the quantity required to make a barrel of flour. The advance in flour itself in this market is only 30 cents, the discrepancy being suggestive of the speculative nature of the rise in wheat.

An advance in wheat, due to scarcity, usually has a sympathetic effect on the prices of other grains upon which the poorer consumers must fall back. Oddly enough, corn is at precisely the same price as a week ago, and oats are lower. A curious thing is the arrival at this port of cargoes of oats from Argentina. That country has only recently taken to planting oats, and it certainly is surprising that it can send them here, a distance of 8,000 miles, and pay 15 cents a bushel duty, the market price here being 56½ cents a bushel.

The rise in cotton for the week was 35 points in staple, on spot, to 10¼ cents, say $1.70 a bale. The demand from foreign spinners since the clearing of the Balkan situation and the improvement in home trade are possible reasons, although speculators have laid most stress on the dry weather in Texas and are predicting the failure of a crop not half of which has yet been planted.

Turning again to Wall Street, the most notable advances were in stocks of the Mackay companies and their auxiliary, the American Telephone and Telegraph, which is up more than six points. Similarly there was a sharp rise in Chesapeake and Ohio, which, on Thursday, sold at 76¼ on reports as to the amount to which the dividend is to be increased this spring, and Wall Street interprets the high price as meaning that the dividend will be larger than had heretofore been expected.

The detailed report of the New York Central for the last calendar year, now issued, shows that a decrease of $9,500,000 in the gross receipts was met with a reduction of $10,250,000 in the operating expenses, and that the company had a good surplus over the dividends.

AMERICA'S LUMBER SUPPLY GROWS SMALLER RAPIDLY.

Mr. C. A. Robertson Says That Failure to Protect Timber Areas Will Cause Distress.

[FROM THE HERALD'S CORRESPONDENT.]

BERLIN, Friday.—"Twenty years from now the problem of how and where to obtain a sufficient supply of lumber will bother the people of the United States," says Mr. O. A. Robertson, of St. Paul, Minn., one of the leading lumber dealers of the North-West.

Mr. Robertson, who is stopping at the Hotel Bristol, was talking to-day with the HERALD correspondent on the subject of the lumber supply, which gives every evidence of failing to meet the demand sooner or later. In this connection, I ventured the remark: "I presume you are interested in a maintenance of the customs duty on lumber imported into the United States."

"Not exactly," he replied, with a smile. "Our properties are located in Canada, and we ship to the United States; therefore in considering tariff legislation the shoe may pinch us on the other foot. We want to see the tariff reduced."

Great Areas Destroyed.

Continuing on the topic of the future scarcity of lumber in the United States, Mr. Robertson said: "The great fault of the present, which will cause the distress of the future, is the failure to protect the timber areas. Contracting companies cut away the heavy timber and leave the undergrowth exposed to the dangers of fire, or the undergrowth is destroyed to make either waste land or farm land. Thus the young growths perish, and nothing remains to replace them. This situation constitutes a positive danger to the welfare of the country. Many admirable resolutions are made, officially and privately, but little is done in the line of practical reform.

"The great lumber states of the North, including Michigan, Wisconsin and Minnesota, are already swept clean of lumber, and most of that which remains in the North is found in the States of Oregon and Washington, but the supply in these districts will last only a certain number of years. There remains the Canadian supply, on which the United States is drawing rather heavily at present, and on which it will be obliged to draw more and more.

"A few figures will illustrate the diminishing importance of Minnesota as the lumber-distributing point of the North-West. The mills of Minneapolis sawed 500,000,000 feet of lumber in 1900 and 170,000,000 feet in 1908. The amount for this year will be still less."

Mr. Robertson's lumber interests are those of the Union Lumber Company, of Winnipeg, which does a big business throughout Canada and the United States. The company has seven mills, which saw, on an average, 200,000,000 feet of lumber a year.

Mr. and Mrs. Robertson and two children have just arrived in Berlin from Paris. Mr. Robertson will return to St. Paul soon, embarking on the Deutschland at Hamburg next Thursday, but he will come to Europe again in July to rejoin his family.

THE NEW QUEENSBORO BRIDGE

New Queensboro Bridge Costs New York City $20,000,000

Informal Opening of Second Largest Cantilever Structure in World Is Enthusiastically Celebrated.

(From the NEW YORK HERALD of March 31.)

New York and her sister borough Queens were brought into closer union yesterday, when the Queensboro Bridge, the first overhead link between the crowded island of Manhattan and the roomy, rapidly growing borough across the East River, was thrown open to the public.

Twenty thousand persons swarmed across the north footpath within two hours after Mayor McClellan declared the new avenue of traffic opened. At the same time a stream of automobiles, trucks, moving vans, old fashioned buggies and spring wagons, "Harrigan" hacks and vehicles of every possible variety were passing over the broad, well paved roadway which stretches for a mile and a half from East Fifty-ninth street to Jackson and Jane streets across the river.

Of the twenty thousand pedestrians who fought their way through the crowds and stampeded across the bridge from either side like a herd of animals, each one seemingly was determined to be the first to make the trip. There were foot races of Marathon merit. There were matches between women which were picturesque if not record breaking. And while all this was going on upon the north footpath, there were races below between automobilists and between drivers of all kinds of vehicles from beer wagons to buckboards.

It had been understood that there should be no speechmaking and no ceremonies of any kind, but the enthusiasm of the Queens citizens—all of whom expect the new bridge to send real estate values in Queens away up at once—overcame them, and when the Mayor and his little official party, occupying four automobiles, got to the centre of the structure at precisely half-past two o'clock they were held up by a delegation of citizens from Queens. There were twenty-two automobiles, a marching club of about one hundred members and a martial band. The Mayor was cheered with real enthusiasm. The automobiles fell in behind the Mayor's official party and followed him over and back.

While the bridge was actually opened to the public yesterday, the formal opening will not take place until June 12.

Work on the bridge, which is the second largest cantilever structure in the world, was begun in 1904. The first contract was let in November, 1903, and others followed rapidly. Although not beautiful when compared with the Brooklyn bridge the structure is one of the best specimens of bridge building in the world and will provide accommodation for enormous traffic. It was expected when work was begun that the total cost would not be more than $10,000,000, but strikes, changes in specifications and other things increased the cost. It is estimated to have cost the city approximately $20,000,000.

There is but one roadway on the new bridge and that is in the middle of the structure. It is as wide as the two roadways on either the Brooklyn or the Williamsburg bridge. There are two footpaths, one for pedestrians bound for Queens and one for Manhattan bound pedestrians. Up to the present time no arrangements have been made to establish a transit system in connection with existing lines either in Manhattan or Queens.

Strength and Confidence Shown by London Markets

With End of the Balkan Trouble and Cheap Money, Professionals Begin to Lay in Stock.

LONDON.—There are really only four working days to deal with this week, for the Stock Exchange decided to quit business from Thursday afternoon till next Tuesday morning, but though the time was short, it was not altogether without incident, and the tone of the market has been stronger and more confident than for a long time. The clearing up of the Balkan trouble coincided with cheapening money at the end of the quarter, and professionals immediately began to lay in stock in the hope of a public demand springing up later on.

The rise is no doubt partly due, according to "The Statist," to buying back by "bears," who were encouraged by the long drawn-out Near Eastern crisis to speculate for the fall. For a considerable time they operated profitably. "Now, of course," it says, "they are buying back actively; and it is clear from the magnitude and suddenness of the rise that the account open for the fall must have been very large. No doubt, also, dealers have protected themselves by putting up quotations. During the long crisis they did not care to lay in more stocks than was absolutely necessary, and as soon as confidence revived and buying on a considerable scale set in they naturally put up quotations."

It is further pointed out in "The Economist" that "the distribution of dividends has brought a lot of funds back into the money market and loan rates are really nominal. A certain amount of this money is finding its way into the Stock Exchange, and there is a good investment demand from the public; but it must never be forgotten that sharp rises of this sort are partly artificial, and if the public does not come up to expectations there must follow a proportionate decline.

"The advance in British Government securities has been led this week by British funds. In ten days Consols have advanced by about 1½ points, and other Government stocks have gained in proportion. In fact, the whole tone of the Consol market is different, and neither the prospect of fresh taxation nor the danger of a new expensive naval programme has prevented prices from rising.

As soon as the Easter holidays are over the "Statist" considers that it is reasonable to anticipate that the public will begin to buy more freely, mainly because decisive proof has been manifested that all the Governments of the world are sincerely desirous of maintaining peace.

"The section for foreign Government securities has not been so buoyant as it was on the first announcement of the Balkan settlement, but the changes made have all been in an upward direction. This week prices have been supported by buying orders from the Continent. Russian Fives have almost touched par, and the Fours are higher at 86½. Japanese, Chinese and Chilian securities are all higher.

"The appearance of the genuine investor in the market for British rails at last has been shown during the week by the demand for safe, non-speculative stocks and in particular by the amount of attention devoted to home railways. The general advance last week has been followed by still greater advances in the last three days under the stimulus of cheap money and the distribution of quarterly dividends during the last two weeks."

THE NEW YORK HERALD.

PRICE: PARIS and FRANCE, 15 Centimes. ABROAD, 25 Centimes.

EUROPEAN EDITION—PARIS. WEDNESDAY. MAY 12. 1909.—EIGHT PAGES.

NO. 26.560.

FEATURES ON INSIDE PAGES.

PARIS PRESS CRITICISES DEBATE IN PARLIAMENT

Adjournment of Chamber Till Thursday Is Adversely Viewed by Many Editorial Writers.

Scores Neglectful Deputies.

The adjournment of the debate on the post office agitation is severely criticized by various newspapers. The "Radical," a Governmental organ, says: "The Chamber yesterday committed the most egregious blunder in postponing the debate. The public is feverishly awaiting a solution of this strike menace, and those who read the full report of yesterday's proceedings may ask with perfect reason why the discussion was not carried through. Six o'clock is an early hour, and even an all-night sitting is not too much to devote to a question of such urgency. Meantime discontent keeps growing and hot heads grow more restless. From this slackness—this semi-indifference—the gravest complications may arise. In the most insignificant business house, when difficulties have to be met, no time is wasted, and it is sad to see our Deputies so neglectful of elementary principles."

Will Not Face the Issue.

On the same subject, the "République Française" (Moderate-Progressist) remarks: "The discussion has barely commenced, as it would appear that no one in the Chamber wants to see it commence in earnest—at least in the present legislature, but what the public demands to know is if the nation is to remain in authority over its administrative services or if the State servants are to rule the nation. The latter must not remain the victims of injustice or of favoritism, but it is not for them to cooperate to enforce their views. It is for the nation to exercise in their favor its right of control and authority. These are the principles, but they seem too crude to be faced by Parliament."

Blames Institutions, Not Individuals.

The "Soleil," Royalist in tone, comments: "M. Deschanel put the matter in a nutshell yesterday when he said: 'It is the public authorities who have given the example of anarchy,' and, seeking the guilty parties, he continued: 'It is not the individuals who should be accused—it is the institutions. Our body politic is ill—not from faults and errors of particular persons, but from the corrupt leaven and noisome drugs which have been administered to it for fifty years.' It is an illusion to suppose that changing men will change this state of things. The roots must be got at—the institutions must be suppressed."

Public Demands More Energy.

In similar strain, the "Eclair" (Nationalist) observes: "The adjournment of the debate on the Post Office crisis has not delayed the strike, which would appear to be voted. The lack of enthusiasm in Parliament has been taken for an easy-going attitude—practically a defiance—which suits the book of the violent spirits. The public is nervous and has a right to demand that its interests be considered, and that it shall not suffer by a conflict for which it is in no wise to blame. Some definite statute is urgently required which shall guarantee service under the State, but which in return will impose implicit obedience upon State servants."

An Armistice for the Government.

Still on the same lines, the "Rappel" (Socialist-Anti-Ministerial) says: "'Whom the gods wish to destroy they first render mad' wrote the ancient poet. It would seem that our statesmen are seeking to precipitate a social collision, prelude to the cataclysm, whose gravity all must admit. What cannot be pardoned in M. Barthou's (Minister of Public Works) speech yesterday is that it strikes a warlike note instead of evincing a statesmanlike circumspection. At a time when conciliation is required, to approve the recent punishments and threaten their speedy repetition is to perpetuate the conflict, accelerate the arrival of further trouble and invite a supreme upheaval. The Chamber felt that it could not approve such untimely declarations and adjourned the debate, giving, as one might say, a twenty-four hours' armistice to the Government."

News Notes.

Fire broke out yesterday morning at the Pavillon de Flore. Firemen promptly reached the Louvre and extinguished the fire.—Eclair.

The premises of M. Magne, clothes dealer, 173 rue Marcadet, were destroyed by a violent conflagration yesterday afternoon. M. Lépine, who hastened to the scene of the fire in an automobile, ran down a man. The latter received nothing more than a few bruises.—Petit Journal.

Charles Meyer and Marcelle Hureaux, suspected of having thrown a young girl into the Seine on March 31, have been released, no serious charge having been found against them.—Eclair.

A violent scuffle took place yesterday at the military camp at La Braconne (Charente) between some territorials of the 33rd regiment and gendarmes, who tried to prevent them escaping from camp. The gendarmes were pelted with stones and officers had to restore order. —Eclair.

Tired of life, Elisabeth Berton, an octogenarian, 60 rue de la Convention, threw herself into the Seine yesterday from the Auteuil viaduct. Immediately rescued, she is now at the Boucicaut Hospital.—Eclair.

While digging a trench yesterday in the avenue de Versailles, navvies came upon a live shell, dating from the German war. It was removed by the military authorities.—Echo de Paris.

STRIKE IS AGAIN DECLARED BY FRENCH POST-OFFICE EMPLOYÉS

Decision Is Come to Suddenly on Unexpected Attitude of Chamber in Adjourning Vote Until To-Morrow — At Great Meeting at the Hippodrome, 6,000 Persons Acclaim the Resolution.

For the second time within a couple of months the French postal and telegraph employés have declared a strike.

The order for the cessation of work was issued by the Federal Committee last evening, a few minutes after it became known that the Chamber of Deputies had decided to adjourn the further discussion of the situation until Thursday, and it was to a certain extent given immediate effect.

There is a trite saying that it is the unexpected which always happens, and this is assuredly true of the events which led up to the strike declaration last evening. For days past the Federal Committee had been drawing up its plan of campaign. It had decided upon the course of action which should be taken if the debate in the Chamber ended in the defeat of the Government. In that eventuality everyone was to remain at work. A similar decision was come to in view of the Government undertaking to reinstate those officials who had been dismissed because of the speeches they had made. Again the committee had deliberated and decided that in the event of the Chamber recording a vote which it regarded as adverse to its interests, they would proclaim the strike at the great mass meeting which was held at the Hippodrome last night. But there was one phase which they had not taken into consideration, and it was just this condition which the committee had suddenly to face when the Chamber, whether by accident or intention, decided to hang matters up until Thursday.

AT HIPPODROME MEETING STRIKE IS ACCLAIMED.

But Many Employés May Await Chamber's Vote.

The vote of the Chamber and the order to strike naturally added increased interest to the meeting which had been called at the Hippodrome last night. Long before half-past eight there was great animation in its vicinity, and by the time business commenced the immense building was filled from floor to ceiling, many of those present being postmen or telegraphists in uniform, while there was also a large number of women post-office employées present.

M. Marmonnier presided, and in a few short words recapitulated the history of the recent strike and the reasons for the present movement. He then at once posed the question, "Strike or continuation of work?" The answer was not doubtful. When he asked, "Those in favor of the strike raise their hands," a forest of arms rose. "Those against the strike?" he asked. Not a hand moved. "The strike is declared!" he said.

This declaration was received with great enthusiasm. Half the immense audience was on its feet, cheering and clapping its hands.

After this declaration, however, the enthusiasm fell off somewhat. The reason was probably that succeeding speakers for the most part confined themselves to statements of what had happened when the strike was declared and which are recorded elsewhere.

It required the intervention of M. Chastenet, one of the postal staff who was dismissed on Saturday, to revive the enthusiasm. His attack on the Prime Minister and the Parliament was greeted with applause which lasted for some minutes.

It was then proposed that the committee of the federation should resign and be succeeded by a committee of which the names should be kept secret. This was accepted with enthusiasm. The list of all the points at which the strike committee had organized centres was read out, and others were added.

Finally the following resolution was adopted:—

"The clerks, under-clerks and laborers of the Post and Telegraph Department, assembled on May 11 to the number of 10,000 at the Hippodrome, united in a common sentiment of revolt and indignation at the disloyalty of a Government, forgetful of its word of honor in persecuting employés for having freely expressed their way of thinking; resolve to cease work; to continue the struggle to the bitter end and until complete satisfaction shall have been obtained, and boldly demand the right of forming a trades union, cost what it may."

The impression of a HERALD correspondent present at the meeting was that, though the strike has been decreed, many post-office officials will await the result of the adjourned sitting of the Chamber before joining the movement. Many seemed to be in doubt as to future action. At the same time if only the 6,000 employés present in the Hippodrome join the strike movement the disturbance in the post and telegraph service will be considerable.

CONFIDENT OF M. SIMYAN DEFINES THE SITUATION.

Government Is Ready for All Eventualities.

As soon as M. Simyan heard of the decision and the result of the Hippodrome meeting, he returned, says the "Petit Parisien," to the rue de Grenelle, where he had a conference with the heads of the staff, and then proceeded to the Ministry of the Interior, where M. Clemenceau and M. Barthou were waiting to discuss the situation with him.

A person who is in M. Simyan's confidence made the following declaration to the "Petit Parisien": "The Government is determined to act. Moreover, the situation is such that it is impossible to withdraw. It is ready for all eventualities, though of course the morning can only show the extent of the strike. Perhaps the numbers of those who at once stopped work on the declaration of the struggle will not have increased. Would that it might be so!

"It is therefore only in several hours that the Government will put into force the measures it has taken. The army will take charge of several of the services. If the Central Post Office is deserted, the telegraphic operators of the engineer corps, who can now work the various instruments, and the telegraphists from the Saumur School and sailors from the fleet will replace the strikers. If the travelling sorters abandon their work, the troops will replace them, and what the Government cannot do private enterprise will complete, for as you know the Paris Chamber of Commerce and other bodies have arranged to start temporary post-offices. Then wireless telegraphy, posts for which have been established at quite a number of places, will be brought into play and will relieve the general work.

"Up to the present no acts of damage have been reported. The great switchboard of the Central Post Office will be guarded by soldiers. There is nothing to fear there. All precautions have been taken, and I can only repeat that the postal employés have nothing to gain, for the Government will act unflinchingly."

AT THE RAILWAY STATIONS.

Travelling Sorters Abandon the Mail Vans.

The strike especially made itself felt last night at the railway stations where quite a number of travelling sorters did not start with the mail vans. The mail train which leaves the Lyons terminus for Besançon had a staff of twenty-seven only instead of fifty-three. At the Gare du Nord eighteen sorters out of a total of sixty declined to leave on their usual journeys. From the Eastern station about 100 sorters usually leave each night. Nine only were absent last night. On the Orleans line the number who stopped work was seventeen out of sixty-five. When the strike order reached the Saint-Lazare station a train was leaving for Cherbourg with twenty sorters at work. Thirteen at once left the train and declined to go on the journey.

As soon as the Chamber's action became known, the greatest excitement prevailed at the Central Post-Office, the Bourse and the other big centres. The order to strike followed almost immediately, and the reports to hand would seem to indicate that it was given effect with great rapidity. By eight o'clock it was known that the employés of some of the post-offices, and notably at the rue d'Amsterdam and the rue de Provence, had ceased work. A number of postmen declined to undertake the last delivery of letters and preferred to march off to the Hippodrome meeting, while the sorters of the night mails declined to leave Paris in the post-office vans.

MAGNITUDE OF STRIKE CANNOT YET BE JUDGED.

Much Depends on Attitude Assumed by Other Corporations.

It is impossible at the present juncture to give any idea as to the magnitude the strike may assume. At the beginning of the week it was rumored that the railway servants, and, indeed, many other labor corporations, would act with the post-office and telegraphic employés and so bring about a general stoppage of business. Whether M. Pataud's dreams of a general strike are to be realized, to-day may show, but it is certain that the post-office employés have the sympathy of the various other labor corporations, which, if they do not join in the struggle, will at all events assist largely financially.

The "Herald's" Special Wire.

Throughout the night the HERALD's special wire with London worked normally until 2 a.m., when a disorganization took place, and notwithstanding all efforts no further decipherable messages could be received. It may be that this condition arose through an accident, but under the circumstances the more logical conclusion seemed to be that at some point several wires had been tied together, thus rendering all messages sent over them unintelligible. This method of rendering the telegraph wires useless, it will be remembered, was adopted by the strikers in March.

BROTHERS WRIGHT GET ROUSING RECEPTION FROM NEW YORKERS

Tugboats, with Groups of Friends and Committees of Welcome, Surround the Kronprinzessin Cecilie as She Moves up to Quarantine with Aviators on Board.

[BY COMMERCIAL CABLE TO THE HERALD.]

NEW YORK, Tuesday.—Greeted by hundreds of harbor whistles and nearly overwhelmed by the congratulations of their friends, Messrs. Wilbur and Orville Wright, accompanied by their sister, Miss Katherine Wright, arrived on the Kronprinzessin Cecilie this morning.

Before the vessel reached Quarantine she was surrounded by tugboats and other small craft, each bearing groups of friends or reception committees. The Aero Club of America, the Aeronautic Society, the Automobile Club and the Lawyers' Club each sent representatives, all cheering spiritedly. As the small boats hovered about the liner the Wrights

MR. WILBUR WRIGHT.

stood by the rail, calmly appreciative. The brothers occasionally lifted their hats and Miss Wright now and then smiled and waved her handkerchief in acknowledgment.

When the committees and friends went aboard the Wrights were almost carried

MR. ORVILLE WRIGHT

off their feet by the demonstration. They were requested to pose for their photographs, but resolutely declined. Miss Wright slipped away with a friend to escape attention, and finally the brothers, followed by a crowd that choked the promenade deck, withdrew to a quiet corner and told the reporters to open fire.

Mr. Wilbur Wright looked bronzed and hard, and his brother Orville was much stronger than when he left here last January. He announced that he will be able to continue his work and will finish his Government trials. The Wrights spoke in high terms of the treatment they had received in Europe, especially in France.

Miss Wright Defends Europeans.

But Miss Wright also permitted herself to be interviewed. When asked jokingly about the attentions she and her brothers had received from Royalties, she replied: "I am sorry so much flippant stuff has been printed about the notable persons who have shown their interest in what my brothers are doing. I love America, but the American people don't always understand the Europeans. They are an appreciative people and think about things more seriously than we do. Naturally it gratified my brothers and myself to realize that Europeans, from the highest to the lowest, were interested in what Wilbur and Orville were doing, and were willing to recognize their achievements. I won't listen to anyone saying unkind things about the European people without protest."

Mr. Wilbur Wright said, concerning their plans: "Aside from the Government trials, which will probably take place in June, it is not our intention to make any flights in this country during the summer. We shall go directly to our home in Ohio and will probably manufacture the seven aeroplanes which have been sold in this country.

"After these contracts are out of the way other business matters will be attended to. One, or both of us, will return to Europe, probably in August. We shall go directly to Berlin, where flights will be made. After that our European programme is not ready to be announced."

Asks for News of Lieut. Calderara.

Asked if they contemplated the manufacture of machines on a large scale in Ohio, Mr. Wilbur Wright replied that he could not say until certain business matters had been settled. He asked eagerly for news of his pupil, Lieutenant Calderara, who was recently injured in Rome. He spoke highly of the skill of his French and Italian pupils, and said that the ordinary man could become a good aviator in eight or nine days.

Upon the arrival of the liner at the pier at Hoboken a large crowd gave the Wrights another noisy welcome. The Wrights were entertained to luncheon at the Waldorf-Astoria Hotel by the Aero Club. To-morrow they will be the guests of the Aero and Automobile Clubs at a luncheon in the Lawyers' Club, when speeches are expected from them. Miss Wright will be entertained by the Women's Colonial Club. They plan to leave for Dayton to-morrow afternoon.

DAYTON PREPARES TO FETE AERONAUTS' RETURN HOME.

Round of Festivities to Last Two Days Is Planned.

[BY COMMERCIAL CABLE TO THE HERALD.]

DAYTON, O., Tuesday.—The general committee which is organizing the festivities in honor of the brothers Wright has planned a two days' celebration on June 17 and 18, including the firing of cannon, ringing of bells, blowing of whistles and an aeroplane flight by one or both the Messrs. Wright.

The presentation of national, State and city medals will be made at the fair grounds in the presence of two regiments of the Ohio National Guard.

On the second day there will be an automobile parade.

Welcomed in "Herald" Cartoon.

[BY COMMERCIAL CABLE TO THE HERALD.]

NEW YORK, Tuesday.—Mr. W. A. Rogers' cartoon in the HERALD to-day is entitled "Welcome Home." It exhibits Uncle Sam, with wings, flying over the skyscrapers and welcoming Messrs. Wilbur and Orville Wright, who are coming up the bay in their aeroplane, having left the steamship Kronprinzessin Cecilie.

Lieutenant Calderara Recovering.

(BY TELEPHONE TO THE HERALD.)

ROME, Tuesday.—Lieutenant Calderara, who was injured by a fall from his Wright aeroplane on the Centocelle manœuvre ground a few days ago, is now improving rapidly and probably will have quite recovered in a few days. He is now able to get out of bed without feeling any pain.

The aeroplane is being repaired somewhat slowly, as certain exchange parts which it is impossible to make in Rome and which have been ordered from Paris are lacking. It will take about twenty days to complete these repairs instead of the eight or ten which had been at first stated, so that if no complication arises the aeroplane will be once more ready for use about the end of the month.

AMERICAN EDITORIAL OPINION

Many New Yorkers Fail to Appreciate the Opportunities for Real Estate Investments in Their City.

The NEW YORK HERALD says: "That the average New Yorker does not appreciate the great opportunities for real estate investment in his own city, was the assertion made in an interview with Mr. Dean Alvord, published in the real estate section of the HERALD. Out of town investors, he continued, seem better able to see things in their true proportions.

"Judging, however, from the strong tone of realty throughout the New York district, and the lively interest manifest everywhere in the growth of sections in population and wealth, this will not much longer remain true. Certainly to a resident of New York there should be nothing more deserving of consideration for investment than real property judiciously selected."

The Income Tax.

An income tax is regarded as a discrimination against the honest in favor of the dishonest.

Makes Perjurers.

San Francisco "Chronicle": "Any income tax is objectionable for these reasons: It makes perjurers of the majority of those subject to its provisions; consequently it is grievous discrimination against the honest and in favor of the dishonest. Nothing approaching a reasonable enforcement of an income tax is possible without drastic and costly methods of collection most exasperating to the public. It takes, in the aggregate and to a degree not approached by any other form of tax, great sums which in due course would be reinvested and provide employment and dissipates them."

Would Work Hardship.

New Orleans "Picayune": "A tax on small incomes would work great hardship, but unless the tax is uniform—that is, it falls on every person having an income—it would be plainly unconstitutional."

Tax All or None.

New Haven "Journal-Courier": "A fair income tax would be to tax all incomes, whatever their size. There would then be no discrimination, and the people would contribute in proportion to their ability to pay. The moment the law regards men in a different light a principle has been introduced into the life of the Republic which is clearly repugnant to its free institutions."

Tax on Labor.

Washington "Post": "The income tax will be levied on a bank. With what result? The bank will advance its rate of discount, and instead of recouping the thing once it will collect it off its customers many times. The same is true of the railroad, and in the end it is a tax on labor."

Double Taxation.

Philadelphia "Record": "If an income tax could be thoroughly collected there would be much to recommend it as a substitute for existing taxes. But it is always urged as an additional tax. It is a form of double taxation; it is more easily evaded than any other tax, and its collection involves an inquisition which Englishmen and Germans chafe under. Frenchmen have stoutly resisted thus far and Americans have submitted to only in a great emergency, and then the yield of the tax was disappointing."

For What Purpose?

Boston "Herald": "If the income-tax must come, let its purpose be definitely stated and understood. Is it to be a revenue measure scheme for the shrinkage of 'swollen fortunes?' The point of view and the purpose may be important in determining its standing before the people, as well as before the courts."

Would Enlarge Ananias Club.

Philadelphia "Inquirer": "An income-tax would make the Ananias Club the largest institution of the kind in the world."

CONSIDERABLE PROGRESS MADE WITH TARIFF BILL.

Public Sentiment Appears to Have Excited an Influence on Republican Insurgents.

[BY COMMERCIAL CABLE TO THE HERALD.]

WASHINGTON, Tuesday.—Public sentiment appeared to have exerted its influence to-day on the Senate Republican insurgents who are engaged in obstructing the Tariff Bill. Considerable progress was made with the bill.

There were two test votes in the glass schedule. Senator Augustus O. Bacon, a Democrat, offered two amendments reducing the duty on cheap china. The first was defeated by 50 votes to 27, and the second by 54 to 25.

Senator Robert M. La Follette stood in the breach in both votes. On one amendment all other insurgents deserted him; on the other, Senator Joseph L. Bristow, of Kansas, and Senator Coe I. Crawford, of South Dakota, voted with him.

The refusal of the insurgents to assist the Democrats in any way is making bad feeling, the country realizing that delay in the tariff is due only to the filibustering part played by the Republicans, who can obtain no changes. Considerable criticism has been indulged in over such a narrow policy.

GERMAN LEGATION CRIME

[BY COMMERCIAL CABLE TO THE HERALD.]

VALPARAISO (viâ New York), Tuesday. —The Public Prosecutor asks the death penalty for Beckert, formerly treasurer of the German Legation, who is charged with murdering the janitor of the Legation and then burning the body.

SPORTING NEWS.

FRENCH POSTAL STRIKE INTERESTS LONDON PRESS

Situation It Creates in France Occupies Attention of Leader Writers This Morning.

[BY THE HERALD'S SPECIAL WIRE.]

LONDON, Wednesday.—The French postal strike and the situation in Persia are the questions to the fore in this morning's editorials. The "Morning Post" points out that with the reassembly of the French Chamber of Deputies yesterday began a period which may hold much in store for the Clemenceau administration. "Much," it proceeds, "will depend on the manner in which the difficulty with the State functionaries is finally regulated. If the Government eventually shows a firm hand and shows its worthiness of the continued confidence of the country by a statesmanlike manner of dealing with the question, a second Clemenceau administration is not unlikely. At present, however, the current seems to be running steadily against the Radical party."

Enthusiasm Cooling Off.

The "Standard" says: "The enthusiasm of the employés for the militant policy of their committee has cooled off a great deal during the past few days. The last manifesto of the federation was rather less aggressive than its predecessors. Instead of exhorting its members to prepare for immediate social war, it devotes itself to praising their haughty calmness and elevated tranquillity under the provocation they have received. The Government, it declares, is seeking to force the oppressed 'postiers' into an immediate strike; but these high-minded officers are not to be induced to abandon an attitude of dignified patience. All this looks very much as if the leaders of the agitation were a little uncertain of their ground."

DIPLOMATISTS ARE AMONG PASSENGERS FOR EUROPE.

The Kronprinz Wilhelm Also Carries Several Prominent Opera Singers and Other Well-Known Persons.

[BY COMMERCIAL CABLE TO THE HERALD.]

NEW YORK, Tuesday.—On the Kronprinz Wilhelm to-day departed several members of the Diplomatic Corps in Washington. These were Baron Mayor des Planches, the Italian Ambassador, with Baronessa des Planches; General Morteza Khan, the Persian Minister, and Prince de Windisch-Grätz, attaché of the Austro-Hungarian Embassy.

The Kronprinz Wilhelm also took a galaxy of opera stars, including Miss Geraldine Farrar, who is accompanied by her father, Mr. Sidney D. Farrar; Mme. Maria Gay, Signor Antonio Scotti and Signor Giovanni Zenatello. Other passengers were: Mr. and Mrs. T. J. Blakeslee, Mr. and Mrs. Hugo Blumenthal, Mr. and Mrs. John F. Campion, Mr. R. M. Haan, Mr. and Mrs. H. R. Ickleheimer, Mr. William H. Moore, Mr. Amos Pinchot, Mrs. J. W. Pinchot, Mr. and Mrs. C. E. Reed, Mr. and Mrs. Harlow F. Robinson and Mr. and Mrs. H. M. Wright.

Among those leaving by the Hamburg for the Mediterranean were: Mr. and Mrs. Walter Allen, Mr. and Mrs. J. M. Allen, Mr. and Mrs. Charles W. Boyden, Mr. Kyrle Bellew, the actor; Dr. and Mrs. P. F. Chambers, Mr. and Mrs. J. G. Coolidge, Mr. and Mrs. Herbert S. Houston, Mr. and Mrs. E. B. Hayden, Mr. William R. Laidlaw, Mr. and Mrs. Nahum Stetson, Mr. and Mrs. Edwin P. Shattuck, Mr. Walter R. Willets, the Misses Gertrude, Edna and Elsie Willets, Mr. and Mrs. Charles A. Williams, the Misses Williams, and Mr. and Mrs. T. H. Wilkinson.

On the Potsdam for Rotterdam departed: Mrs. Frances Andrews, Mr. and Mrs. Guy E. Beardsley, Mr. and Mrs. Andrew F. Derr, the Misses Derr, Miss Louise Gilmore and Mrs. W. C. Peet.

SENOR CASTRO TO PAY FOR USE OF MIRAFLORES PALACE

Venezuelan Courts Order Retribution for Arbitrary Occupation of Senora Crespo's Property.

[BY COMMERCIAL CABLE TO THE HERALD.]

CARACAS (viâ New York), Tuesday.—The deposed President Castro has been condemned by the Courts to pay six years' rental and heavy damages for the arbitrary occupation of the Miraflores Palace, which property belongs to the widow of the late President Crespo.

RESULTS OF BASEBALL GAMES.

[BY COMMERCIAL CABLE TO THE HERALD.]

NEW YORK, Tuesday.—Baseball games played by major league clubs to-day resulted as follows:—

NATIONAL LEAGUE.—New York 3, Chicago 4; Brooklyn 2, St. Louis 1; Boston 8, Cincinnati 10; Philadelphia 1, Pittsburg 7.

AMERICAN LEAGUE.—Detroit 16, New York 5; Cleveland 1, Boston 5; Chicago 5, Washington 3; St. Louis 3, Philadelphia 0.

Standing of the Clubs.

Following is the standing of the clubs, including the games played yesterday:—

NATIONAL LEAGUE.

	W.	L.	P.C.		W.	L.	P.C.
Pittsburg	14	7	.667	Brooklyn	9	10	.474
Chicago	13	10	.565	Cincinnati	11	13	.458
Philadelphia	11	9	.550	St. Louis	9	14	.391
Boston	10	9	.526	New York	7	11	.389

AMERICAN LEAGUE.

	W.	L.	P.C.		W.	L.	P.C.
Detroit	14	5	.737	Philadelphia	9	9	.500
Boston	11	8	.579	Cleveland	8	11	.421
Chicago	11	8	.579	St. Louis	6	11	.353
New York	11	8	.579	Washington	5	13	.278

FETE AT COMPIEGNE.

The town of Compiègne is, in its turn, about to celebrate Jeanne d'Arc. A historic cavalcade and a reconstitution of a tournament of the epoch will form two of the principal features.—Petit Parisien.

New-York Tribune.

PART II. SUNDAY, NOVEMBER 27, 1910. EIGHT PAGES.

WHERE CAN WE DOCK THIS MARINE MONSTER WHEN SHE REACHES THE PORT OF NEW YORK?

Cross section of the White Star Steamship Titanic, now almost ready to be launched. A $12,000 model of her has been put on exhibition in this city. She is 882 feet 6 inches long and Manhattan's longest pier is 57½ feet shorter. If her vast hull were empty, thirty-six full sized replicas of Hudson's famous Half Moon could be laid crosswise in her, under full sail, and still leave 270 feet of unoccupied tapering space at bow and stern; or twenty-eight full-sized replicas of Fulton's Clermont could be piled up like cord-wood inside her, without utilizing 282 feet and 6 inches of tapering space fore and aft, where several more could be stowed away. An ordinary railroad locomotive with tender, and drawing eight Pullman sleepers, could be laid upon her deck abaft the spot near the captain's bridge, where our artist has cut her in two. From keel to funnel top she is nearly as tall as the Postal Telegraph Building, fronting on City Hall Park.

New-York Tribune.

[Copyright, 1911, by The Tribune Association.]

Vol. LXX....No. 23,506. | To-day, fair and warmer. To-morrow, rain; south winds. | NEW-YORK, SUNDAY, MARCH 26, 1911.—FIVE PARTS—SIXTY PAGES. | PRICE FIVE CENTS.

MORE THAN 150 DIE AS FLAMES SWEEP THROUGH THREE STORIES OF FACTORY BUILDING IN WASHINGTON PLACE

DIAGRAMMATIC SKETCH OF THE SURROUNDINGS OF YESTERDAY'S FIRE HORROR.

Bodies of some of the unfortunates who jumped from the windows, lying where they struck the pavement.

Scores of Girls Leap to Death in Streets Ten Stories Below Them.

HAD NO CHANCE FOR LIFE

Unable to Reach Elevators or Stairways, Employes Rush to Windows.

CROKER BLAMES ESCAPES

None on Outside of Building, Says Fire Chief, Saying That Is Reason for Fearful Loss of Lives in Disaster.

ELEVATORS SAVE HUNDREDS

Frightful Panic as Trapped Workers Fight Like Furies for Places in Cars, Almost the Only Means of Escape, as Flames Sweep Through the Workrooms.

A hundred and fifty or more lives were lost in a fire that swept through the three upper stories of a ten story factory loft building at the northwest corner of Washington Place and Greene street at 5 o'clock yesterday afternoon.

Fire Chief Croker said:

"This calamity is just what I have been predicting. There were no outside fire escapes on this building. I have been advocating and agitating that fire escapes be put on buildings just such as this. This large loss of life is due to this neglect."

Fire Commissioner Waldo backed up the Chief. Buildings Superintendent Miller was out of town.

Scenes of almost indescribable horror attended the catastrophe. Scores of girls leaped from windows eight, nine and ten stories above the street to their death. In one place so many bodies fell that the glass and iron deadlights in the pavement were broken.

A fire escape in a light shaft proved a veritable death trap. More than fifty girls were found dead at the bottom of the shaft.

Heroic elevator operators saved hundreds of lives. When one man abandoned his car one of the horrorstricken crowd in the street broke through the police lines, reached the elevator and ran the car for ten more trips, saving nearly five hundred more lives.

It was just 4:40 p. m. when the alarm of fire was first raised in the big ten story loft building. That was five minutes before closing time, and many of the girls employed in the building were putting on their hats and coats. It is not known who first discovered the fire, or what caused the outbreak, but within thirty seconds after the cry of "Fire!" had been raised the girls nearly all of them Italians, began a mad rush for the two passenger and two freight elevators.

When they found that they could not all escape by way of the elevators the panicstricken women turned and dashed for the windows on the Washington Place side of the building. The windows were raised or broken open with frenzied blows and the women climbed out on the narrow ledges in front of each window. That happened before any firemen had reached the scene, and although scores in the street cried to the maddened girls not to jump their warnings were not heeded.

Within three minutes, more than fifty women leaped from the ninth floor, only to have their lives crushed out on the sidewalk below. The sight of so many human beings being dashed to pieces sickened the crowd, and the shrieks of the victims and of hysterical onlookers made the scene one of indescribable horror.

No accurate estimate of the loss of life could be had as late as midnight, the number of dead being variously placed at from 150 to 250, but it is probable that the first estimate is more nearly correct, although the firemen and police said that many bodies were at the foot of the light shaft in the rear of the building. A hundred bodies were in the Morgue at 10 o'clock.

The building, according to every official at the conflagration, was fearfully deficient as to means of exit in case of fire. While it was supposed to be fireproof and had one fire escape on a light shaft, the only way of escape that seemed to be available to the unfortunate hundreds who worked on the three upper floors, where the fire was confined, was by the elevators. For some reason the stairway was not used. It is safe to say that all those who survived the holocaust have the elevators and the elevator operators to thank for their lives. The lone fire escape, instead of being a way to safety, proved just the reverse. In that one spot alone more than fifty women lost their lives, being caught as though in a trap.

Slack Season Reduced Workers.

The building, which, the police say, is owned by John C. Asch, of South Norwalk, Conn., fronts a hundred feet on Washington Place and the same on Greene street. The three upper floors are occupied by the Triangle Waist Company and the Meyers, Crown & Wallach Company, manufacturers of clothing. These two firms employed probably between eight hundred and nine hundred women. There were 1,500 machines in the Triangle Waist Company's plant, but because it is a slack season only about half the machines were in use when the fire broke out.

East of the factory building, and with its walls adjoining, is the New York University building, also ten stories in height. On its top floor is the New York University Law School, students of which saved many lives. When some of the Triangle company's employes, with clearer heads than their unfortunate fellow workers, gained the roof of the burning building they managed to make their way to the roof of the American Book Company's building and thus escape in safety to the street.

No living person has so far been found who was in the cutting room of the Triangle Waist Company, on the eighth floor, to tell of the terror of those first few seconds after the alarm of fire was sounded. The terror of the hundreds of helpless girls on that floor can only be imagined. It is certain that many of the unfortunate creatures were killed not by fire, but in the mad trampling of many hundreds of feet.

Some of the elevator men told tales which seem beyond belief in their grewsome details. They told of how young Italian girls, their eyes starting from their heads in terror, fought with insane strength and savagery to gain the elevators. Women threw themselves against the iron barriers surrounding the elevator shaft and screamed for help. The scenes when each elevator rose to the eighth floor again, after carrying down a previous load of human freight, were frightful.

Women would cling to the wire netting with hands and even by their teeth, determined not to give way for those behind. Their clothing was torn from their bodies, yet they would not give up their positions until forced t[illegible] weight of numbers behind [illegible] eral dead and mutilated [illegible] stretched about the entran[illegible] vator shafts, not killed by [illegible] to pieces, almost, by fre[illegible] hands. It was a mad fight [illegible] some of those who did man[illegible] their way to the elevators ne[illegible] reach the first floor.

Fearful Crush in Elevators.

The four elevators had an outside capacity, probably, of fifteen or twenty persons apiece. Yet on every trip they made—and they must have made a dozen—women and young girls to the number of fifty were jammed in helpless masses in the small cars. In many cases the screaming women made flying leaps at the car entrance, landing on the heads of those already inside.

The passenger elevators were run by Joseph Zitto and Joseph Gasper. They continued to make their trips until it was impossible to run against the wall of fire which burst through the elevator shaft. Gasper continued until the cables of his car threatened to give way under the intense heat.

Zitto, it is said, after making half a dozen trips, left his car on the first floor and made his way to the street. He has not been seen since. His car was idle only a few minutes, however. A man named Gregory—no one knows more about him than that—was in the crowd watching the women leaping from the windows. When he heard that the elevator had been deserted, he pushed his way through the crowds and made his way into the foot of the elevator shaft. Firemen tried to stop the man, but he cried out that he knew how to run the car, and was allowed to pass.

Gregory then took charge and made at least ten trips to the tenth floor, each time carrying down at least thirty girls. He stopped only when the mechanism of the car failed as it reached the third floor on one of its downward trips. Gregory tried with frantic strength to send

FIRE CHIEF CROKER.

GIRLS FIGHT ON LADDERS

Many Pushed Off in Crowding to Cross an Airshaft.

STUDENTS AID IN RESCUES

Rooms in New York University Burned in the Rescue of 50 Women from Fiery Death.

About fifty girls who were foremost in the rush for the rear windows, looking on the small court formed by an airshaft in the rear of the burning building, were taken to safety by ladders placed across the shaft from the windows of the School of Law and Commerce of the New York University, in Washington Square. A few students who were in the University Building at the time, studying in the libraries, were attracted to the windows by the screams of the imprisoned women. They immediately rushed to the street and called the attention of the firemen to the possibility of rescuing them from the windows.

Ladders were carried up to the floors opposite the eighth, ninth and tenth floors of the burning building and pushed across the court. Lines of hose were also brought up through the building and played on the windows to keep the flames back, while a number of firemen went part way across and guided the panicstricken girls over the narrow means of escape furnished by the ladders.

The ladders were soon crowded as the girls fought for a chance to climb out on to them. Many were pushed off by others behind them, falling to their death in the pivement of the court a hundred feet below. As fast as they were within reach the students and gremen dragged them into through the windows of the University Building.

It was impossible to control them. All that those engaged in the work of rescue at this point could do was to throw all their weight on the end of the ladders and attempt to steady them in this way, keeping the frantic efforts of those still in the building from pushing the ends of the ladders off of the window sills, and hurling those already on them into the court below.

Fighting for place, some were pushed off of the edges, to hang by their hands until they finally weakened and had to let go. Many with safety all but within their grasp were sacrificed in this way, and the bottom of the airshaft become piled high with their bodies.

The work at this point soon had to be abandoned, for the flames quickly swept through the windows, burning those still left behind, and driving back those who were trying to rescue them from the windows of the University, and setting fire to some of the rooms in the university, where much damage was done.

SAYS MANY FACTORIES HAVE NO FIRE ESCAPES

Former State Labor Official Declares Conditions Here Are Disgraceful.

BLAMES CITY DEPARTMENTS

William W. Walling Points Out Warning in Report Against Just Such Disaster as Last Night's.

"This calamity is just what I have been predicting. There were no outside fire escapes on this building. I have been advocating and agitating that fire escapes be put on buildings just such as this. This large loss of life is due to this neglect."

This statement, made by Fire Chief Croker last night, on the absence of fire escapes from the burned building in Washington Square, was warmly supported by William W. Walling, who resigned his office as First Deputy Commissioner of the State Department of Labor about a month ago. Mr. Walling declared that the conditions existing in the factories and mercantile establishments in this city in this respect were disgraceful and even criminal.

He said that the inadequacy of fire escapes on many of these buildings had been known a long time to the department with which he was connected, but explained that the Department of Labor no longer had jurisdiction over the placing of fire escapes, this work being within the authority of the Fire Department and the Department of Buildings, and Mr. Walling unhesitatingly held these two city departments responsible for the condition of affairs that every day threatened just such catastrophes as occurred last night.

Mr. Walling talked on a subject with which he was intimately acquainted when he said that if the authority to enforce the law with regard to fire escapes had remained with the state officials it would have been more stringently observed than has been the case since it became the function of the city departments. "There is a large number of buildings in this city to-day," said Mr. Walling, "that are not properly equipped with fire escapes, and many more that are not equipped at all. If a fire started on the first floor of one of these inadequately equipped buildings no human being could possibly escape injury, and more than likely would be killed.

Work Transferred to the City.

"The Department of Labor had jurisdiction over the placing of fire escapes up to about six or seven years ago, and I want to say that the work was performed better then than since the power was transferred to the Fire Department and the Building Department. That part of the work of the factory inspectors of our department was taken out of their hands by a decision of the court, the Court of Appeals upholding, under the New York City charter, the jurisdiction of the two city departments that I have mentioned. Before that time we would make reports to them of the inadequacy of the provisions for escape from fire in factories, and frequently the answer would be that in their opinion the build-

Continued on second page.

CORRIGAN CHALLENGES MAYOR TO OUST HIM

"In the Fight to Go the Limit," Magistrate Says of His Attack on Police Methods.

ARRESTS DROP 29 PER CENT

Bureau Gives Figures—E. A. Philbin Says Corrigan's Statement of Conditions Is Entirely Correct.

"I challenge Mayor Gaynor to try to remove me from office," said Magistrate Corrigan yesterday. "The Mayor has no power of removal over me. The Appellate Division is the only body with the power of removal over city magistrates."

Magistrate Corrigan had been all the afternoon in consultation with his friends over police conditions in this city when he issued his challenge to the Mayor.

"I am in this fight to go the limit," he continued. "It was only after deliberate consideration that I sent my letter to the newspapers. I have been a close observer of police conditions in New York for many years and the places I have held in the District Attorney's office and on the bench qualify me to speak as an expert. My letter expressed my deliberate opinion.

"For several months I have had it in my mind to write this letter. I intended to write it last summer, but I learned that the Mayor was about to go to Europe, and I held off then until his return. It would do no good to write the letter while he was away, and I did not want to be put in the position of making an attack on him behind his back, though this is in no way to be considered a personal attack.

Waited for Mayor to Get Well.

"After the Mayor was shot I waited again until he should recover from his wounds. Now I feel that it is impossible to wait longer. The conditions are such that they cry for action, and something must be done to make life and property safe in this city and to end the open and constantly increasing violations of the law.

"I have started this fight and I am in it to stay the limit."

Magistrate Corrigan would not talk about the evidence he had to present to the grand jury, if one should be called to investigate the conditions he has recited in his letter, but it was known among his friends that he hoped for and urged a grand jury inquiry. He has a large amount of detailed evidence to present before that body, and he is prepared to suggest many lines for investigation, but he does not want to inform beforehand those whom he considers responsible for the conditions, so that they may build up their defences.

The Bureau of Municipal Research issued yesterday a table comparing the number of arrests for various crimes in the last six months of 1909 and 1910. The table showed a total of arrests in 1909 of 102,774, and a total in 1910 of 73,014, a decrease in 1910 of 29,760, or 29 per cent. The arrests for homicide in the last six months of 1909 numbered 397, while in 1910 the number was 227, a decrease of 42.8 per cent.

"Force Is Demoralized"—Philbin.

Eugene A. Philbin, who was appointed District Attorney by Governor Roosevelt to succeed Asa Bird Gardiner, upheld yesterday the position taken by Magistrate Corrigan.

"The force, as a force, is demoralized," he said, speaking of the police. "Never in my time has it been in such a state, and I believe that whether his statement was judicious and well timed or not, Magistrate Corrigan was entirely correct in his description of the conditions. Men are afraid of their commanding officers, not in the old sense of knowing that they must obey them, but in the sense of having no confidence in them. They are afraid to make an arrest, almost to call their souls their own. Of course, such a condition is intolerable."

When Patrolmen Rafferty and De Milto went to the Harlem police court yesterday for warrants for the arrest of the managers of a boxing bout at the New Polo Athletic Club on Friday night Magistrate Butts added his opinion to the many already expressed in condemnation of the administration of the Police Department.

"It is a confession through you policemen of the general inefficiency of the Police Department," said the magistrate, "and reflects no credit upon police affairs of the city of New York for you to ask for a summons or a subpœna when you make no sworn statement of a crime being committed. Now understand, I don't blame you two policemen, or your lieutenants or your captain, but it certainly shows the inexperience, if not the stupidity, in the police administration of New York. The court is powerless to put in motion its usual process in this case, and your application for a warrant is denied."

NEW FEAT IN WIRELESS

Message Sent 2,500 Miles from Ship at Sea to England.

Halifax, N. S., March 25.—What is said to be an entirely new feat in direct wireless communication, the sending of a message over the Atlantic a distance of 2,500 miles from a ship at sea to England, was reported by the White Star Dominion liner Megantic, which arrived to-day from Liverpool.

While off the coast last night the purser of the Megantic, Mr. Pomeroy, sent a wireless dispatch to Liverpool via Poldhu, Cornwall. The message was received, and to-day when the ship docked a reply by cable was handed to the purser.

Hitherto messages from ships in this part of the Atlantic have gone by way of Cape Race or Glace Bay, and a range of six hundred miles has been considered as practically the limit.

FINDS $1,250,000 IN RUINS

Guineas Coined in Reign of George III Discovered in Jersey.

London, March 25.—Treasure trove to the value of $1,250,000 is reported from Jersey, where it was uncovered by Athelstan Riley, while he was pulling down the ruins of an old manor house built in the thirteenth century with the object of using the stone to enlarge his present manor.

The discovery includes ancient urns filled with spade guineas, coined during the reign of King George III and bearing the British arms on a spade-shaped shield. One urn bears the monogram of Vespasian, the Roman Emperor.

JAPAN'S EMPEROR REPLIES

President Taft's Expression of Good Will Appreciated.

Washington, March 25.—President Taft was deeply gratified to-day to receive from the Emperor of Japan a message warmly reciprocating the President's expressions of good will and friendship toward Japan, made to the Japanese Ambassador, Baron Uchida, several days ago. Baron Uchida called at the White House this afternoon and delivered in person the Emperor's message, which is as follows:

To the President of the United States of America.

I was greatly pleased to receive your very kind message conveyed to me through my ambassador in Washington, and I thank you for it. I was already well convinced that you had given no credence to the false and wicked reports regarding Japan, but it was especially a source of profound satisfaction to me to receive from you the assurance that the relations of amity and good understanding between our two countries were never better or more cordial than at this time. I am most happy to be able entirely to reciprocate that assurance.
MUTSUHITO.

President Taft has been extremely anxious to set at rest the various reports of differences between this country and Japan, especially with reference to the mobilization of troops in Texas. He declared the other day that he was at a loss to understand the motive behind such "malicious and baseless stories." He sent for Baron Uchida to express this sentiment to him, and to ask that he convey the message to the Emperor.

KNOCKS OUT HEAD WAITER

Waldorf Attendant Lands on Jaw of Man Above Him.

The usual decorum of the main dining room in the Waldorf was eclipsed for a few moments early last evening while Paul Pinedaud, one of the waiters, was engaged in knocking Louie Knutti, the head waiter, flat on the floor. It is said the trouble began when Pinedaud refused to gratify the wishes of one of the diners, who asked for a menu card. The diner complained and the head waiter demanded explanations from Pinedaud. The latter grew offensive and Knutti discharged him.

Pinedaud, instead of raising his voice, raised both fists and landed three blows in quick succession on Knutti's jaw. The head waiter went down like an ox. Pinedaud lit out for the laundry room, where a locker contained his street clothes. J. B. Smith and A. F. Costigan, two house detectives, went after him. With his back up against his locker, Pinedaud kept both detectives at bay and landed a blow on Smith's jaw.

Patrolman Moore was called in and with the aid of the detectives placed Pinedaud under arrest.

VOTE SELLING IN KENTUCKY

New Batch of 210 Indictments Returned in Floyd County.

Prestonburg, Ky., March 25.—The grand jury of Floyd County, which has been investigating vote selling, has returned 210 indictments. Many more true bills will be found against voters before the inquiry is concluded. This is an increase of about one hundred indictments over the last report.

Similar conditions are said to exist in [illegible] and Magoffin counties, and their grand juries will begin an investigation soon.

BOY'S THRILLING ESCAPE

Slides Down Elevator Cables from Tenth Story.

One of the most dramatic incidents of the fire was the experience of Hyman Mechler, a young Jewish boy, of No. 332 East 15th street. Mechler was caught on the tenth floor. He slid down the elevator cables to the cellar, where he remained wedged beneath the car for five hours. He was found by a man belonging to the fire patrol in water up to his neck. He had escaped drowning by hanging at arm's length to the cable. The boy was chopped out and taken to St. Vincent's Hospital.

"There must have been 250 girls on the floor with me," Mechler said. "I was working at a cutting machine, and ran for the staircase with two girls, but it was afire. Then I slid down the elevator rope. I thought I would be drowned before I was found."

FREE CHICKEN LUNCHES

Lead to Discovery of Ancient Cold Storage Fowl.

[By Telegraph to The Tribune.]

Cincinnati, March 25.—What amounted to practically a raid on cold storage poultry was completed to-day by Dr. Blume, the city meat inspector. Within the month he and his assistants have condemned twenty thousand pounds of cold storage poultry. Dr. Blume says he found meat that had been in cold storage for five years, some venison actually being stamped 1905.

Dr. Blume said that what first attracted his attention and suggested the investigation was the fact that cheap restaurants were selling a chicken dinner for 15 cents and that some saloons were supplying chicken in their free lunches. "I conjectured," Dr. Blume said, "that something must be the matter with poultry that could be sold at that figure."

SUUN DECORATES DENTIST

Chinese Prince Was Relieved of Toothache in Philadelphia.

[By Telegraph to The Tribune.]

Philadelphia, March 25.—Prince Tsai Suun, uncle of the Chinese Emperor, got the toothache while he was here last September, and went to Dr. E. Druitt Crawford, wo stopped the imperial pain. Dr. Crawford has now received word, through the Chinese consulate in San Francisco, that Tsai Suun has conferred a decoration on him.

Dr. Crawford was surprised to hear of the decoration. The Emperor's uncle had paid his fees like any other solvent patient, and the dentist thought the incident closed. The decoration is a silver disk, on the obverse side of which is an anchor, three stars and Chinese characters. The other side shows a laurel wreath, in the centre of which are more Chinese characters.

MRS. WARD MUST PRESS SUIT.

Supreme Court Justice Guy decided yesterday that Mrs. Rachel M. O. Ward, widow and executrix of the estate of John Q. A. Ward, the sculptor, who died some time ago, must prosecute the suit begun while the sculptor was alive against the Society of the Army of the Cumberland or the suit will abate.

Weather Forecast: FAIR. "Circulation Books Open to All." **The World.** "Circulation Books Open to All." Weather Forecast: FAIR.

VOL. LII. NO. 18,332. Copyright, 1911, by The Press Publishing Co. (The New York World). NEW YORK, MONDAY, OCTOBER 30, 1911. PRICE { ONE CENT in Greater New York and Jersey City. TWO CENTS outside of Greater New York, Jersey City and on trains.

JOSEPH PULITZER FROM A PAINTING by JOHN S. SARGENT.

JOSEPH PULITZER DEAD

The Director and Proprietor of The World Expires Suddenly on His Yacht at Charleston, S. C., on Way to Jekyl Island —His Wife, Summoned by Wire, Finds Him Unconscious —His Death Peaceful, His Last Words, "Softly, Quite Softly."

HIS BODY TO BE BROUGHT HERE ON SPECIAL TRAIN.

It Will Leave Charleston This Afternoon—Burial Probably Will Be on Wednesday in Woodlawn—His Career as Soldier, Lawyer, Legislator and Journalist—Tributes to His Memory.

(Special to The World.)

CHARLESTON, S. C., Oct. 29.—Joseph Pulitzer died to-day. His end came at 1.40 o'clock in the afternoon in his room on his yacht Liberty, lying in the harbor of Charleston. The cause of Mr. Pulitzer's death was heart failure. He had been ill less than two days.

The first indication of his serious illness was apparent to his aids and attendants on Saturday morning. A telegram was sent to Mrs. Pulitzer advising her of the sudden illness of her husband, although the telegram stated that Mr. Pulitzer's condition was not considered serious. She left New York at 3 o'clock on Saturday afternoon and reached Charleston at 1.20 o'clock this afternoon. When Mrs. Pulitzer boarded the Liberty Mr. Pulitzer was unconscious. He did not regain his faculties before the end came, twenty minutes later.

With him at the time of his death were Mrs. Pulitzer and their youngest son, Herbert, who had accompanied his father when the latter left New York on Oct. 20.

Was Going to Jekyl Island.

Mr. Pulitzer was in fairly good health when he left New York and had projected to journey to Jekyl Island, off the coast of Georgia, for a short stay. Yesterday morning while the Liberty was approaching Charleston Mr. Pulitzer became suddenly ill and the yacht put in for Charleston to secure the services of a physician and to summon Mrs. Pulitzer.

Last night Mr. Pulitzer seemed to be in a slightly improved condition, though he did not sleep very well. This morning he seemed to be better and telegrams were sent to the other members of his family at New York advising them of the fact.

Just before noon Mr. Pulitzer seemed to be sinking. It was not until this time that his companions on the yacht realized the gravity of his condition.

Shortly before 1 o'clock Mr. Pulitzer awoke after having been asleep for three hours. He complained of a pain in his heart. Soon after he became unconscious and remained in that condition until the end.

Telegrams were immediately sent advising the other members of the family of his death. Ralph Pulitzer, his eldest son, was in New York; Joseph Pulitzer jr., his second son, in St. Louis; Miss Edith, one of his daughters, in France, and Miss Constance, another daughter, in Colorado.

His Last Words.

The death of Mr. Pulitzer was peaceful. His last words, before he lost consciousness, were: "Leise, ganz leise" (softly, quite softly). They were occasioned by the reading by a German secretary who had been entertaining Mr. Pulitzer, just half an hour before his death, with an account of the reign of Louis XII. of France. Toward the end of the chaptered from which the secretary was reading, Mr. Pulitzer spoke these last words.

Mr. Pulitzer was attended during his brief illness by Dr. Robert Wilson of Charleston and by Dr. Guthman, the yacht's physician.

The body of Mr. Pulitzer will be taken to New York on a special train of Pullman cars, which will leave Charleston at 4.30 o'clock to-morrow afternoon.

The funeral of Mr. Pulitzer will be held at Woodlawn cemetery in New York, probably on Wednesday of this week.

THE PUBLIC CAREER OF MR. PULITZER.

Soldier, Lawyer, Editor, Legislator and the Founder of Two Newspapers.

Joseph Pulitzer, proprietor of the New York World since 1883; born in Budapest, Hungary, April 10, [illegible] educated by private tutor; came to the United States in 1864; served until the end of the civil war in a cavalry regiment; went to St. Louis; became a reporter on the Westliche Post (a German newspaper) in 1868; later became its managing editor and part proprietor; in 1878 bought the St. Louis Dispatch and united it with the Evening Post as the Post-Dispatch, which he still owns; was elected member of the Missouri Legislature in 1869, and was a member of the Constitutional Convention in 1874; was a delegate from Missouri to the Democratic National Convention in 1880, and served on the Committee on Platform; was elected to the Forty-ninth Congress in New York for the term 1885-1887, but resigned after a few months' service; was a delegate to the Cincinnati Liberal Republican Convention which nominated Horace Greeley for President; after that a Democrat; advocated the National (Gold Standard) Democratic ticket in 1896; in 1893 endowed with $1,000,000 the Columbia College of Journalism, with an agreement to give an additional $1,000,000 when the school should be in successful operation; in 1887 his health was broken by overwork and he has since been an invalid, totally blind.

—From "Who's Who in America," 1911.

His Hand Always on the Helm.

Condensed in these lines are briefly set the boundary marks of the public life of Joseph Pulitzer. It ended in 1887 with a nervous breakdown, followed by a steady loss of eyesight relentlessly creeping on until the darkness of total blindness shut in upon his ardent spirit. He was then an eager, restless, resistless, tireless man of forty, in the prime of his days. For twenty-four years he has dwelt in the shadow; his public appearances have been few. He conserved his health with the greatest care, spending his summers at his home in Bar Harbor and his winters at Jekyl Island, Ga., or on the Riviera—always where he could live the most in the open air and get such exercise as he could take. For three years he has spent most of his time on his yacht Liberty, built for his comfort, where he could largely find his way about unaided, where he could dine on deck and where he could walk a free deck for hours in the salt sea breeze.

Yet in all the years his guiding hand and dominant mind controlled the policy of The World. To it always and to the very last he gave his thought, his love, his energy, his hope, and all the attention that his health and circumstances would permit. The World was Joseph Pulitzer's creation. It will be his monument.

America His Opportunity.

The Republic spelled opportunity to the youth passionately devoted to freedom and liberty. America embodied that to him in his boyhood in Hungary. When seventeen found him a well grown lad over six feet tall, broad shouldered and rugged, he persuaded his mother to let him answer the call he heard across the seas. Arriving at Hamburg he was robbed; but that did not even halt him. He worked his way across the Atlantic, and on his arrival at once enlisted in the war for the Union, joining on Sept. 30, 1864, the Lincoln Cavalry (the First New York Cavalry). He served under Sheridan's command in the Shenandoah Valley until mustered out at the end of the war, after riding in the ranks at the famous review in Washington.

Opportunity that had loomed so large seemed a vanished thing when the young soldier with his discharge papers found himself but one of the hundreds of thousands seeking it, searching for any kind of work.

New York was crowded with them, and a night on City Hall Park benches set his face to the West—the real heart of the country. "I spoke little but German then," he has said, "and I realized that I was not likely to learn much English among the Germans I knew. So I started for a real American city in the interior, one away from the sea. I chose St. Louis because I had heard most about it, and was amazed when I got there to find it even more German than I had found New York."

His First Work.

A want advertisement in a newspaper called for men, former cavalrymen preferred, to care for mules and horses at the Jefferson Barracks. "It was a long walk," he reminiscently said. "I made the trip four times, for I had to go back for my discharge papers. But I got the job. The food was vile. As soon as I could get my wages I quit and went back to the city. Then I got a room and paid my board in advance as far as my money would go and hunted a better job. This plan I kept up."

Oddly enough his one accomplishment then, that had practically saved his life in camp, again brought him friends who were to prove most valuable. He played a very good game of chess (a very welcome thing in winter quarters), and drifted one day into the back room of a German saloon and restaurant that was the club for the local chess players. In his eagerness he protested at a move of one of the masters. "Perhaps you can do better" was the retort. He sat down and did better and earned a welcome and many friends.

Joseph Pulitzer first sought his opportunity in the law. As he worked here and there for his daily bread, he sought out a library and spent his nights studying law. Keenly interested in public affairs, attracted by politics, and having a readiness at oratory, he soon made a reputation in St. Louis. He was admitted to the bar in 1867 and looked forward to a career there. Fate disposed otherwise. The great German paper of the Middle West was the Westlicher Post, owned by Dr. Emil Praetorius and edited by Carl Schurz.

It needed a reporter, and the managing editor, who played a good game of chess also, thought of his old antagonist, Joseph Pulitzer. He knew his ability, was familiar with his energy, enthusiasm and zeal, and offered him the job.

Joins Our Staff.

"Why, I can't write!" was the answer of the young man, amazed and laughing.

The editor said he knew better and persisted. Joseph Pulitzer gave up his budding law practice and in 1868 joined the staff of the Westliche Post. He was then twenty-one years old.

Old newspaper men in St. Louis still tell stories of the new reporter's zeal, energy and success in his work. He would dash out on a fire alarm regardless of coat or hat; he worked all hours, pushed everywhere. Soon he was made city editor and the work went on with greater force. The new executive drove every one, himself most of all. Politics attracted him more than ever. He was elected a member of the Missouri State Legislature in 1869, and was a member of the State Constitutional Convention in 1874. He became of more value to the Westliche Post, was made its managing editor and later part proprietor.

He Becomes a Democrat.

The post-bellum corruption of the Republican party made Mr. Pulitzer a hearty supporter of the Liberal Republican movement that culminated in the Cincinnati Convention in 1872, which nominated Horace Greeley for President. He went there as a delegate from Missouri and was made one of the secretaries. In the campaign that followed he was in great demand throughout Ohio and the Middle West to follow and answer Carl Schurz, and nightly addressed large audiences of Germans in fiery speeches on the issue of the campaign. The second administration of Grant put him squarely in the Democratic party. He fought with all his might for the election of Tilden in 1876 and taxed his physical resources in speechmaking and campaigning.

He had withdrawn from the Westliche Post. Much as that work had been to his liking, he had steadily looked forward to the time when he could have his own paper, make it according to his own rapidly crystallizing ideas of what the public wanted and should have as news, and where he could think as he pleased, say what he thought and fight the battles of the people with whom he had lived, labored and endured. He had intended to spend a year or more in travel and study in Europe. But in the trying times following the election of 1876 he went to Washington at the personal solicitation of Charles A Dana and wrote signed political letters of the exciting times during and following the Electoral Commission that attracted wide interest.

This but delayed his trip. On his return to St. Louis fortune was awaiting him in a guise which none but a strong self-confident man would have penetrated. The St. Louis Dispatch had fallen into evil days, its circulation had dwindled to nothing, its plant little better than junk, and the Sheriff was in charge. But it had one thing of value—an Associated Press franchise, all important to an evening paper.

Mr. Pulitzer Bought It.

At the Sheriff's sale he bought the paper for $2,500. His plans were immediately made known. The other evening paper, the Evening Post, seeing that it had killed off one rival but to find a newer and stronger one rising Phoenix-like from its ashes, capitulated rather than fight. It had a good plant, and in two days the two papers were consolidated as the Post-Dispatch to begin its long career of public usefulness and prosperity. Mr. Pulitzer soon bought out the interests of his partners and became sole owner and editor.

The work that Mr. Pulitzer did with the Post-Dispatch in St. Louis in the way of public service did not satisfy his ambition. He looked for a New York opening, for a national field. He was prepared to venture all he had of health, ability, energy, knowledge and money, confident of success. Once he thought he could buy the New York Star, but that paper was tied too tightly to John Kelly, who valued its services to his political machine too much to let it go into the possession of a fighter so independent as Mr. Pulitzer. The entire control or not a share was Mr. Pulitzer's ultimatum.

He Buys The World.

The New York World under the editorship of William H. Hurbert, with a circulation of 20,000, had then a place in the community fixed by the fact that it was owned by Jay Gould. Everything that it printed was under suspicion of having been colored or influenced by the arch manipulator of Wall street. It was not prosperous; it was for sale. Mr. Pulitzer, in May, 1883, bought it of Jay Gould personally. One block of twenty-five shares was held elsewhere.

"You do not object, of course, Mr. Pulitzer, to So-and-So's keeping those twenty-five shares; he's a good fellow," said Jay Gould.

"Certainly not," retorted Mr. Pulitzer, "if you do not object to my carrying on the editorial page every day: 'Notwithstanding the fact that Jay Gould still owns twenty-five shares, he does not control or influence one line in this paper.'"

Mr. Gould sold the entire paper and Mr. Pulitzer became the sole owner of The New York World. He issued the first number on May 10, 1883. No one could ignore the change of ownership, of policy, of methods, of character, of all that goes to make the paper that for over twenty-eight years has under his absolute control and active direction served the cause of the people. News filled the front page from which it had been crowded off by advertisements; foreign news gave place to the vital doings of the day at home, and a new note of striking virility rang from the editorial page. There appeared his salutatory, his confident appeal to New York. We print it elsewhere. Never in these years has a word of it been recalled or changed. It has been iterated and reiterated on every occasion.

His First Platform.

In those columns also Mr. Pulitzer laid down the planks of his first platform, to be fought for with tireless endeavor and unending devotion and with a true instinct and adept skill new to Park Row and the city.

Here are some of the planks in that platform:

- The taxation of luxuries.
- The taxation of inheritances.
- The taxation of monopolies.
- The taxation of large incomes.
- The taxation of the privileges of corporations.
- A tariff for revenue.
- Reform of the Civil Service.
- Punishment of corrupt office holders.
- Punishment of vote buying.
- Punishment of employers who coerce their employees in elections.

The World has kept these pledges of adherence to vital Democratic principles, though often furiously assailed by politicians and by great Democratic party organs.

Three days after he took control, Mr. Pulitzer began to raise funds through the columns of his paper to build the pedestal on which Bartholdi's Statue of Liberty Enlightening the World now proudly greets the incoming immigrants and returning citizens. The American committee had failed to arouse the people to the necessity of supplying a fitting pedestal for the gift. The press sneered. The World's early efforts failed, but with a larger clientele of readers, undaunted it took up the work again on March 15, 1885. The rich were unmoved, but in small sums the people gave $100,000 through the columns of The World, and the work was achieved. The President and his Cabinet, with a notable company, participated in the elaborate ceremonies of the inauguration on Oct. 22, 1886.

The hardest kind of hard work, incessant oversight, new methods, brought readers at once. Circulation increased. The far-seeing proprietor ordered a new press. Before it was completed he ordered a second. The cautious Hoe said: "Are you sure you need it?" and demanded a mortgage on the entire plant. For once Mr. Pulitzer was obliged to violate his cardinal principle of life—never to give his note or other obligation to any man—and assented. Mr. Hoe ceased to insist and refused to accept the mortgage. He has been building bigger and bigger presses for The World ever since.

The Folger Campaign.

The campaign was hot that fall. The breach between the Stalwarts and Half Breeds had wrecked the Republican party, and President Arthur's Secretary of the Treasury, Folger, was running for Governor, opposed by Grover Cleveland, the reform Mayor of Buffalo, as little known to New York as the new proprietor of The World. Mr. Pulitzer threw himself and his paper heart and soul into the campaign and rejoiced in the landslide that followed. He upheld the administration in Albany and worked sturdily for Cleveland's nomination and election to the Presidency in 1884. His work was the more valuable and made a wider impression because the defection of the New York Sun (Mr. Dana seeing fit to support Gen. Butler) left The World the only great Democratic newspaper in the city.

Grover Cleveland, who observed The World from the standpoint of a candidate for the Presidency, has borne eloquent testimony to Mr. Pulitzer's work, writing of it thus with the calm consideration of later life:

> I never can lose the vividness of my recollection of the conditions and incidents attending the Presidential campaign of 1884—how thoroughly Republicanism was intrenched—how brilliantly it was led—how arrogant it was—and how confidently it encouraged and aided a contingent of deserters from the Democratic ranks.
>
> And I recall not less vividly how brilliantly and sturdily The World then fought for Democracy; and in this, the first of its great party fights under present proprietorship, it here, there and everywhere in the field, showered deadly blows upon the enemy. It was steadfast in zeal and untiring in effort until the battle was won, and it was won against such odds and by so slight a margin as to reasonably lead to the belief that no contributing aid could have been safely spared. At any rate, the contest was so close it may be said without reservation that if it had lacked the forceful and potent advocacy of Democratic principles at that time by the New York World the result might have been reversed.
>
> In the Presidential canvass of 1892 I was again a witness of the World's Democratic zeal and its efficient party work. In that struggle it left nothing undone that any newspaper could do to aid the cause, and it certainly accomplished much.
>
> I have spoken specifically of the two campaigns with which I was personally most familiar, and in which I had the opportunity to share campaign activities, though I do not intend to speak of them as exceptional instances of The World's achievements.

The World grew rapidly under Mr. Pulitzer's hand; the quarters on Park Row opposite the Post-Office were extended and enlarged only to be hopelessly outgrown. Mr. Pulitzer on April 10, 1888, bought the historic French Hotel property at the corner of Park Row and Frankfort street, and the following year began to erect the Pulitzer Building, where The World is now published. Here again he was a pioneer, for he was the first to use the steel skeleton construction in a large business building. His four-year-old son, Joseph Pulitzer jr., laid the corner stone on Oct. 10, 1889, as part of imposing ceremonies, but the founder and proprietor was absent. From a sick bed at Wiesbaden he had cabled his message to his beloved paper and the people. It is printed elsewhere.

Mr. Pulitzer had broken down in harness. To the severe work of editing the morning edition of The World, and supervising his St. Louis Post-Dispatch by wire and mail from New York, he had in the fall of 1887 added the Sunday edition of the Post-Dispatch, and had started the evening edition of The World. With all this he was working with increasingly inadequate mechanical equipment and planning new presses and a new building.

He had in 1885 been elected to the Forty-ninth Congress from a New York City district, but had found it impossible to fulfill the duties of a Congressman at Washington to his own satisfaction and had resigned.

The strain was too much. There was a limit even to the endurance of his iron constitution and his highly sensitive nerves. He had never given a thought as to whether or not he should do a thing, but had done it. He had given his health no thought. Was it not good? And little to the care of his eyes. They had always been shortsighted, but had been abused by strain and ceaseless work under naked gas jets and in improper light.

Notable Things Done Under Direction of Mr. Pulitzer

The World First Advocated Election of Cleveland, Attacked His Bond Policy, Exposed Insurance Evils, Fought Free Silver and Opposed "Jingo" Policy in Venezuela Dispute.

These are some of the achievements of The World under the direction of Mr. Pulitzer:

Three days after assuming control of The World Mr. Pulitzer undertook to daise by popular subscription the funds necessary to build a pedestal for the Bartholdi statue of "Liberty Lighting the World." More than $100,000 was raised by this method and the statue was dedicated on Oct. 22, 1886.

Mr. Pulitzed began his fight for a Federal income tax five days after taking control of The World.

In 1884 Mr. Pulitzer, through The World, advocated the nomination of Grover Cleveland for President by the Democratic National Convention in the face of the opposition of Tammany Hall. Mr. Cleveland was nominated and elected.

The World led the fight against the election to the Court of Appeals of Judge Maynard and advocated the taking of the judiciary out of politics. Judge Maynard was defeated by more than 100,000 votes.

The World opposed the adoption of the Free Silver idea in the Democratic platform which nominated Mr Bryan in 1896 and repudiated both Mr. Bryan and his platform. It foretold exactly the States that would give the majority vote in the Electoral College to McKinley.

The World predicted the renomination of Theodore Roosevelt to succeed himself in 1904, and urged the nomination by the Democrats of Grover Cleveland.

The World opposed the intervention proposed by the "jingo" policy of President Cleveland in the dispute between Venezuela and Great Britain. It despatched 500 cablegrams and telegrams to the leading men of England and the United States urging them to oppose the policy of the Cleveland Administration. The replies upholding the attitude of The World influenced the abandonment of the policy by Mr. Cleveland. Both King Edward, then the Prince of Wales, and Gladstone sent messages advising "common sense" and the peaceful settlement of the controversy. This was accomplished as the direct result of the agitation by The World. The World's service was recognized by the peace and arbitration societies of Great Britain.

Opposed Plans for Bond Issue.

The opposition of The World to the deal between the Cleveland administration and the syndicate headed by J. Pierpont Morgan, by which the syndicate was to have secured the entire issue of $63,300,000 Government bonds under private arrangement "at about the same price," which would have netted the syndicate an enormous profit. The World sent out 10,370 telegrams to bankers throughout the country, urging them to protest against the deal and subscribe for the bonds. Replies were received from 7,130 bankers and published. The World headed the subscription list with $1,000,000 and the aggregate of other subscriptions was more than $300,000,0000 at "the market price." The bonds were then offered at public sale.

The World assumed the initiative in the effort to put a stop to the Boer war. It appealed to both the Boers and the British governments to settle their dispute by arbitration. Many eminent men including President Kruger of the Boer Government, President Steyn of the Orange Free State, Cardinal Logue, the Archbishop of Canterbury, Archbishop Ireland and thousands of prominent men of all nations joined with The World in urging the arbitration of the controversy between the two countries.

The World first called attention to the deplorable condition of the people in Cuba as a result of the cruelties practiced there by the Spanish Government for more than a century. It was this service in revealing the actual conditions that led the United States Government to demand justiec for the Cubans, and failing to secure considerations of its demands to declare war, which resulted in the freedom of the people of Cuba and the establishment of a republic. The World published the first authentic description of the battle of Manila Bay. The World published the first news of the blowing up of the Maine, and the first information of the taking of Santiago by Gen. Shafter.

The World first published the news of the fatal illness of Queen Victoria.

The World published the first list of the securities left by the dead millionaire, Cornelius Vanderbilt.

The first news of the sinking of the

MAGAZINE. JUNIOR EAGLE.

THE BROOKLYN DAILY EAGLE

MAGAZINE. JUNIOR EAGLE.

*** NEW YORK CITY, SUNDAY, JANUARY 26, 1913. THREE CENTS.

John D. Rockefeller's $100,000,000 Foundation

Scope of the Great Philanthropic Project That Provides for Future Generations of the World

By Frederick Boyd Stevenson

To create a fund of $100,000,000 for the Rockefeller Foundation, the object of which is promote the well being and to advance the civilization of the people of the United States in the acquisition and dissemination of knowledge, in the prevention and relief of suffering and in the promotion of eleemosynary and philanthropic means of any and all of the elements of human progress, the National House of Representatives last week passed the Peters bill, and the indications are that the measure, which is now before the Senate, will be passed by that body and become a law before the adjournment of the present Congress.

This stupendous charitable enterprise providing for the relief of mankind and the advance of human knowledge and betterment far into the future—an enterprise, the magnitude of which and the scope of which has no parallel in history—cannot be grasped or understood by a mere announcement of the figures representing the vast sum to be placed at the disposition of the incorporators and their advisers.

John D. Rockefeller has been picturesquely presented as the richest man in the world. His wealth has been variously estimated from half a billion to a billion dollars and more. He has been described as the world's greatest almoner and the newspapers and the periodicals have published long lists of his supposed donations for charitable and philanthropic purposes. But thus far no authorized compilation of these donations has been made. Mr. Rockefeller has been a large giver. Many of his large gifts have been made public, but no one outside of himself and those who aid him in his charitable distributions know the full extent of his philanthropy. The association of his name, therefore, in connection with a project of such great proportions as the proposed Rockefeller Foundation, carries with it an idea of "bigness."

But to most of us the term "one hundred million dollars" is only a term. We have become familiar with rows of nine and ten figures in the dollar lines in connection with gigantic private corporations, but they convey to us only a faint realization of the actual value and the power of a concentrated fund of wealth, for they bring to our minds simply visions of stocks, bonds, inflated securities and overestimated productions.

In the Rockefeller Foundation we have presented to us an actual accumulation of tangible wealth to be maintained as a permanent fund, until dissolved by act of the Congress, the principal of which shall remain intact, and the earnings of which shall be entirely devoted to the purposes for which it is formed. Here, then, at a low estimate—exclusive of increments—will be an annual income of $5,000,000 for philanthropic and charitable work.

THE ROCKEFELLER SYSTEM OF GIVING AWAY MILLIONS TO PHILANTHROPIC WORK.

When Mr. Rockefeller began, many years ago, to work out plans of systematic philanthropy he formed these plans on the same general basis on which he had constructed his vast private corporations—that is: on business principles. He held that mere reckless giving was a detriment, rather than a cure, for poverty and human distress. And he, therefore gathered around him a corps of "expert givers" whose sole duties have been to personally supervise the Rockefeller benefactions.

The rules which govern John D. Rockefeller's philanthropic work are as rigid and exacting as those which governed the numerous business interests of which he has been absolutely the master. He perfected a machine that is a marvel in the mercantile world. He has also perfected a machine that is a marvel to the great almoners of the philanthropic world. This machine is organized and equipped for the sole purpose of giving away money. But every dollar that is given away by it must be as strictly accounted for as every dollar must be accounted for by that other wonderful machine that has ground out the millions. The organization of this great philanthropic machine is as perfect as human forethought and ingenuity can make anything perfect. The one idea in its establishment has been to guard against waste and useless charity, one of Mr. Rockefeller's predominating beliefs being that money given away without thought, and with no especial aim in view except to temporarily relieve, does more harm than good. He, therefore, established this bureau of charity which has a definite system of philanthropic work.

In the telephone directory, under the call "Standard Oil Company, 26 Broadway," appears the caption, "J. D. Rockefeller, Cashier's Department." This is the surest and the quickest means of communication with the Rockefeller bureau for the dispensation of millions. While no legitimate appeal for aid coming within the scope of Mr. Rockefeller's charities goes unanswered, every precaution is taken to guard against trivial requests for assistance and the bestowal of benefactions to persons or institutions regarded as unworthy.

At the head of the charity bureau is Starr J. Murphy, an attorney. Mr. Murphy has charge of a large corps of assistants, investigators and clerks, whose sole business is to carry out his directions as the administrator of the philanthropic output. In every case submitted to him Mr. Murphy makes a thorough investigation. The first question asked is: Is it a worthy charity? The second is: Will assistance result in permanent good? Mr. Rockefeller's greatest fear was that there might be a waste of money due to lack of system. But the admirable system adopted by Mr. Murphy has almost wholly dispelled this fear, and his report on any given case is accepted as final.

Of late years Mr. Rockefeller has made this business of giving away great sums of money his personal affair. He now takes no active part in the business of the remarkable corporations which he established. Practically his whole attention is absorbed in the general superintendence of his larger gifts, and every one of his great donations can be authoritatively traced. One noticeable trait of his policy has been to conceal all benefactions. This, of course, has been impossible with donations like the General Education Board, the University of Chicago and other colleges and the Sanitary Commission for the Eradication of Hookworm disease, but in his private charities Mr. Rockefeller has given millions of dollars of which the public knows nothing.

JOHN D. ROCKEFELLER.

WHY ROCKEFELLER BEGAN TO STUDY THE GREAT SCIENCE OF GIVING.

Up to 1892 Mr. Rockefeller had probably given away $7,000,000, exclusive of his gifts to the University of Chicago. He afterward is said to have declared that at that time not more than 5 per cent. of this $7,000,000 had accomplished any really good results. If so, here was $6,650,000 gone astray—perhaps doing more harm than good. This was not in accord with that chief article in the Rockefeller creed that every dollar invested in anything—whether business or philanthropy—must show a satisfactory return. And so he began to study philanthropy as he studied business. In trying to solve the problem of giving away money wisely he effected a tentative organization by placing a man in charge of a charity bureau. This man was Frederick T. Gates, a former minister of the gospel. It became Mr. Gates' duty to record all applications for aid and make an investigation into each case, separating the worthy from the unworthy, reporting all the details to Mr. Rockefeller.

This was a great improvement on the method, or rather, the lack of method in the past, but it was still too limited in its scope to solve the problem of judicious charity. To Mr. Rockefeller the amount to be given was a secondary matter. He was willing to give away vast sums if he could be satisfied that these sums would produce the desired results. Making millions he regards as child's play compared to successfully giving away millions. Then he evolved a new plan for the formation of a philanthropic bureau, and he placed Mr. Murphy at the head of the new system, still retaining Mr. Gates in his field of usefulness.

Mr. Murphy and Mr. Gates have charge of the benefactions of Mr. Rockefeller, subject to his general superintendence. Those cases which are purely religious in their character are usually placed under charge of Mr. Gates, and those which involve great amounts of money for gifts that partake more of a business nature are looked into personally by Mr. Murphy, who directs certain experts in certain cases to investigate the details. If all the reports are favorable, the gift is finally disposed of in such manner that every penny of it does the work expected of it. In certain cases Mr. Murphy and Mr. Gates unite their forces. For instance, the incorporators of the Rockefeller Foundation, now before the United States Senate, are John D. Rockefeller, John D. Rockefeller, jr., Frederick T. Gates, Starr J. Murphy, Harry Pratt Judson, Simon Flexner, Edwin A. Alderman, Wickliffe Rose and Charles O. Heydt. Jerome Davis Greene, who is general manager of the Rockefeller Institute for Medical Research, has been active in forming the details of the Foundation.

Mr. Rockefeller's main idea is to carry out his belief that the best and most effective philanthropic work can be accomplished by concentration. With this thought in view his policy, therefore, to have his gifts equaled, if not more than equaled, by other gifts for the same purpose, is a rational idea, and leads up to the general principle of self-support and individual effort. In this connection he believes that education is the prime factor in producing the best men and the best women, and this belief accounts for the large donations he has made to educational and research institutions.

PROVISIONS OF THE BILL NOW BEFORE THE SENATE OF THE UNITED STATES.

The plan of the Rockefeller Foundation is the climax to the extensive system organized by him to give away millions of dollars. It is the beginning of a great forward movement for the advance of civilization, based on the principles of humanity. It includes in its scope not only the United States and its territories and possessions, but also foreign lands. It is provided in the bill that Congress may at any time impose such limitations upon the objects of the corporation as it may deem the public interest demands, and all property received must be accepted and held subject to this proviso. The powers of the corporation are to establish, maintain, and endow institutions and other agencies for carrying on the objects of the work in hand, to purchase, hold, sell and convey real estate necessary or convenient for such objects, to erect buildings, employ teachers and agents, to make donations for similar objects, to collect statistics and information and to publish and distribute books. The total amount of property held at any one time, whether absolutely or in trust, must not exceed $100,000,000, exclusive of increases in values subsequent to its receipt. The income of the property must not be accumulated or added to the principal, but to be currently applied to the objects of the corporation. The corporation is empowered to distribute the principal of any property fifty years after its receipt and is required to make such distribution after one hundred years, if so directed by Congress.

The number of members is to be not less than nine nor more than twenty-five. If the number falls below nine no gifts can be made until the vacancies are filled. Members are to be divided into three classes, the term of service for three years, one-third of the members to be eltced each year. Members are to be elected by the members of the corporation subject to disapproval by a majority of the following persons: The President of the United States, the Chief Justice of the Supreme Court, the President of the Senate, the Speaker of the House of Representatives, and the presidents of Harvard University, Yale University, Columbia University, Johns Hopkins University and the University of Chicago. The principal office of the corporation is to be in the District of Columbia.

All personal property used for the purpose of the corporation is to be exempt from taxation by the United States or any territory or district of the United States, but this provision does not affect the taxation of either real or personal property under the laws of the State in which it may be situated. No officer, trustee, member, or employe is to receive any pecuniary benefit except reasonable compensation for services affecting the purposes of the corporation. An annual report is to be filed

Continued on Page 2.

THE BROOKLYN DAILY EAGLE
PICTURE AND SPORTING SECTION NEW YORK CITY, WEDNESDAY, APRIL 9, 1913. PICTURE AND SPORTING SECTION

BROOKLYN TEAM STARTS 1913 PENNANT RACE

Today is the day of days in Brooklyn baseball. By special dispensation of the high Moguls of the National League the season opens in Brooklyn a day ahead of the regular opening on the big circuit. This privilege was accorded to provide an unrivald opening for our new Ebbets Filed, one of the finest baseball parks in the country.

So here we are, all ready for the big show—an opening game against the Philadelphias that's bound to prove a real thriller.

President Charles Ebbets and his side partner, Edward J. McKeever, take pleasure in presenting for your consideration the aggregation of Brooklyn balltossers who have aspirations of taking a climb up the ladder of fame this year.

If you don't know the young men in the picture, here's the architect's plans and specifications to help you out:

Back row, left to right: Wheat, Stengel, Kirkpatrick, Curtis, Cutshaw, Wagner, Smith, Yingling, Rucker, Ragan. Middle row: Hummel, Daubert, Hall, Callahan, Dahlen, Miller, Meyer, Moran, Phelps. Front row: Fisher, Erwin, Mascot, Allen, Fischer.

If you're not on deck when Borough President Steers throws the ball out for the opening of festivities this afternoon you're missing one grand big, glorious occasion.

View of Ebbets Field During Its Baseball Baptism

Brooklyns Show Great Finishing Powers By Beating Yankees in the Ninth

First Game on the New Grounds Ends in a Victory for the Local Team by 3 to 2—Thrilling Battle Ushers in the Local Season. Home Runs by Stengel and Daubert Are Features.

BY "RICE."

MANY a baseball game famed in song and story and carefully cherished in the history of the sport has been played on Brooklyn diamonds, but no more dramatic contest ever took place within the confines of Long Island than that yesterday, in which the Brooklyn National League team beat the New York American Leaguers by 3 to 2 in the first game ever played on Ebbets Field, the $750,000 park that was completed this week.

No writer of the most thrilling "thrillers" could have conceived a greater series of consecutive thrills than those endured by the crowd of 25,000 which filled every seat in the huge plant. It was an unparalleled performance of unlimited variety and under circumstances that may never be repeated in this generation of fans.

Brooklyn first won the game by home runs by Stengel in the fifth and Daubert in the sixth innings, the while Nap Rucker for five innings held the Yankees safe. The Yankees waited until the ninth inning, when a wild heave by Frank Allen on a hopeless prospect of catching Ed Sweeney at first, with two already on bases, let in Midkiff, who was running for Chase, and Manager Frank L. Chance.

Brilliant stuff prevented Sweeney from scoring from second, and Brooklyn opened its half of the ninth with the score a tie, thousands of home rooters, faint-hearted, not to say dismayed, at the sudden turn of affairs, and the contingent of thousands of shrieking Manhattanites wildly jubilant and confident.

Little cared they for the heart ache it would have caused President Ebbets, the McKeever brothers, Manager Dahlen and all the rest if the Superbas had been beaten in their first game in their new park. They were just as anxious to see Chance come out on top in his first game as manager of the New York Americans, and they did not give a hoot for the tender sensibilities of upright Brooklynites.

Wheat Scored the Winning Run.

Zachary Wheat, our Indian left fielder, took a long chance as first man up in the ninth and laid down a charming little bunt, to the huge surprise of big Ed Sweeney, who had been catching at a championship rate. Ed retrieved the ball but scarcely in time to have caught Wheat at first, and the Indian was credited with a hit. Sweeney should have let well enough alone, but he became as badly rattled as Allen had been in precisely the same circumstances five minutes before, and slammed the ball away to the right of Chance. Wheat had overrun first and was deep in right before he realized the throw had gone wild. He turned as shortly as he could on the slippery ground and hastened straightway for second, getting there by a close shave.

If Sweeney was surprised by the measley hit of Zachary Wheat he was astounded when Jake Daubert, whom he esteemed the most dangerous batter on the Brooklyn list, dumped a sacrifice, advancing Wheat to third. It had been a great day for the Dutch, with Stengel and Daubert in the home-run division and Daubert the hero of a wonderful line catch and of the said sacrifice. It was up to regular people to show that they could do things, and J. Carlisle Smith with the fine sentiment of a true Southern gentleman, suh, and a Cavalier of ancient lineage, offered himself as the burden carrier of a great responsibility.

Letting a couple go by because they did not comply with his ideas of what a good ball should be, "Red" fell upon the third with prodigious force. Far from the maddening crowd it whizzed, past the outstretched fin of Ray Fisher, and thence into the hinterland between second and short. It may be going yet for all we know. The last we saw of it, it was on its way. Zachary Wheat just naturally strolled home and the game was won.

Some Game, All Right.

Was it a good game, as games go? the gentle reader asks. It was. Errors were made—and they were costly errors—but the general play was astonishingly good, and the adherents of each team had every right to congratulate themselves upon the prospects for the coming major league campaigns. The big honors went to the catchers and the two short stops. Otto Miller fully justified the claims of his friends that he be ranked as high as any catcher in the National League. His work was not only perfect, but it was done in two or three instances on badly pitched balls hard to handle.

Otto was ably abetted by Bob Fisher, who was letter perfect in the knack of grabbing miscellaneous heaves out of the atmosphere and putting the ball on the runner. It was obvious that the sprightly actions of Miller and Fisher had completely upset the plans of Chance, who was anxious to play the game on a peppery basis and run on the slightest occasion.

Big Ed Sweeney was as keen and as accurate in his nipping of runners as was Miller, while Derrick followed closely in the footsteps of Fisher in helping his catcher. No one play by the nippers of base thieves stood out so conspicuously as the catch by Daubert off Sweeney in the fifth inning, but for steady efficiency they took the prize.

That catch by Daubert in the fifth was one of the thrillers we have mentioned, and shall have a whole paragraph to itself. Sweeney, first up, cut loose at a shoot that exactly suited his fancy, and sent a screaming line drive to Daubert's right. It was labelled a three-bagger and had passed the official test prescribed for such. Not one of the thousands of fans and fannettes present thought Daubert was doing more than making the usual spectacular and futile stab at that kind of a wollop, but Jake had his own view of the case to present, and went after it in earnest. He took a tremendous leap upward and to his right, got the ball in his gloved hand and came back to earth, turned around by the impact of the blow. You should have heard 'em yell! It must have given Hal Chase an inkling of the reason why Brooklynites regard Daubert as the best first baseman in either league.

Superbas Had the Edge on the Yanks

Comparing the two teams, we should say that Brooklyn had something of an edge on the Yankees. Both were working on the principle of running out hits and running bases to the full extent of their ability of venturing a lot to gain a little. Brooklyn was more successful than the Yankees.

One instance of new life Dahlen seems to have put into his men was furnished by "Red" Smith in the second inning. With one out he singled clearly to center. The drive was a prosaic journeyman hit, with no distinguishing features. In fact, it was so commonplace that Wolter eased up in chasing the leather. Noticing that lapse on the part of Wolter, and that the ball was rolling slowly in the soft ground, Smith continued right on to second, reaching there less than an inch to spare and thereby stretching his single into a double.

Benny Meyer and Zach Wheat worked the hit and run to perfection in the fourth inning, Wheat shooting the ball through shortstop as accurately as if he had used a rifle. It was not a hard drive, and it was a desperate chance to take in going to third, but Meyer went the route and reached the goal in safety. It was the kind of spirit Brooklyn has long needed, and Dahlen was warmly congratulated after the game upon the new life he has injected into his hirelings.

Benny Meyer a Welcome Addition.

Benny Meyer was the only brand new face in the Brooklyn lineup, and Benny bore the earmarks of a welcome addition to our happy family. He is a sizeable chap, thoroughly impregnated with pepper and ginger; got a clean hit off Caldwell in the first inning, and worked him for a pass in the fourth. He grounded to third in the sixth inning, and fanned in the eighth. In the field he did not have a chance of any kind.

Another athlete with limited chances was Hal Chase. The fans were eager to see how he would shape up as a second baseman, but will have to keep their curiosity unsatisfied until another day. The only offering sent him was a fly from Otto Miller in the fourth inning and of a kind that had nothing to do with second baseing more than with first baseing.

Nap Rucker pitched to win and pitched well in the five innings he worked. The Yankees reached him for four hits, two of which came in the second inning and caused much uneasiness among the elect, but Nat had the read mid-season stuff with which to tighten up and had little difficulty in pulling himself out of the hole.

Allen was inclined to be wild, but his pitching was decidedly impressive, and in the ninth inning, when he had been personally responsible for the tieing of the score, he demonstrated his nerve by the manner in which he suddenly checked the Yankees, who had a man on second and one out.

Two home runs were made off Caldwell, but do not for a moment think he did not pitch six swell innings. Four base swats are more or less lucky incidents when made off a good pitcher, as the New York fans will assure you when they discuss the savage assault of Frank Baker upon the diversified deliveries of Messrs. Marquard and Mathewson in the lamentable strife of 1911 with the Athletics. Caldwell had speed, curves and breaks galore and could tighten up like a drum. Ray Fisher, who succeeded him, was not so impressive, but looked good at that.

How They Scored.

How Brooklyn made the winning run has been related succinctly and truthfully, wherefore we now proceed backward, as it were, and take up the yarn of the other two counters.

It came to pass in the fifth inning that after Miller had flied to Chase, Nap Rucker withdrew and Moran batted for him. Caldwell had apparently heard of Moran's weakness in getting caught off his base, and after Herbert had drawn a pass, the New York pitcher played entirely for the runner. His dope was right, for he did snag Moran after numerous attempts, although the decision caused argument. That brought Stengel up with two out. Stengel swung viciously on a fast shoot and knocked it skyward toward left centre, and then a freak of baseball was injected into the proceedings to furnish fodder for the Stove League.

Wolter was running fenceward at full speed as the ball fell in front of his face. It bounded so that it came into contact with Wolter's uprising right foot and was kicked straight and true toward the left centre wall, which it reached in due time and about ten feet ahead of the hurrying Wolter. Stengel never slacked tack or hauled sheet, but kept on agoin' and got home with time to spare. It was not a real "boot" or error on Wolter's part, but just one of those curiosities of coincidence that go to make baseball what it is.

Daubert's Untarnished Homer.

Daubert's homer in the sixth was untarnished. Meyer had rolled out to Hartzell, and Wheat had been caught stealing after a walk. Jake landed on a fast shoot with every ounce of his strength and drove the ball past Wolter and onto the furthermost recesses of center field. It was a clean home run inside the grounds, a feat which some of the fans who had been fooled by the color effects into believing the park was smaller than it is had thought impossible.

New York's two runs in the ninth came with startling suddenness. Chase opened by walking and took second on Chance's single to center. Sweeney bunted toward Allen, who got the ball too late to catch Sweeney at first, but threw anyhow, and with all his might. It was a delirious chuck and went deep into right field. Midkiff, who had run for Chase, and Chance, scored with ease, but Sweeney was held at second. Derrick essayed a sacrifice, but Miller grabbed the bunt and threw to Smith at third, catching Sweeney between second and third, where he was exterminated. Fisher struck out and Derrick was caught stealing second.

GIANTS TRIM ORIOLES; TESREAU IN GREAT FORM.

Baltimore, Md., April 5—The New York Giants easily defeated the Baltimore Internationals today by a score of 12 to 3. In the five innings Tesreau pitched, he struck out seven men and did not allow a run. Roth also struck out seven men in five innings. Score by innings:

	1	2	3	4	5	6	7	8	9	R.	H.	E.
New York	0	1	2	2	3	0	1	3	0	12	15	1
Baltimore	0	0	0	0	0	1	2	0	0	3	5	3

Tesreau, Wiltse, Mathewson and Meyers; Shawkey, Roth and Bergen.

THE SCORE.

NEW YORK AMERICANS.

Name.	AB.	R.	1B.	TB.	SH.	SB.	SO.	BB.	PO.	A.	E.
Daniels,rf.	4	0	1	1	0	0	0	0	3	0	0
Wolter,cf.	3	0	1	1	0	0	0	1	1	0	0
Hartzell,3b.	3	0	1	1	0	0	0	1	2	2	0
Cree,lf.	4	0	0	0	0	0	1	0	1	0	0
Chase,2b.	3	0	1	1	0	0	0	1	1	0	0
Stump,2b.	0	0	0	0	0	0	0	0	0	0	0
Chance,1b.	4	1	2	2	0	0	0	0	7	0	0
Sweeney,c.	4	0	1	1	1	0	0	0	6	4	1
Derrick,ss.	4	0	0	0	0	0	0	0	4	1	0
Caldwell,p.	2	0	1	1	0	0	1	0	0	2	0
Fisher,p.	2	0	0	0	0	0	2	0	0	1	0
*Midkiff	0	1	0	0	0	0	0	0	0	0	0
Total	33	2	8	8	1	0	4	3	‡25	10	1

BROOKLYN.

Name.	AB.	R.	1B.	TB.	SH.	SB.	SO.	BB.	PO.	A.	E.
Stengel,cf.	3	1	1	4	0	0	1	1	4	0	0
Cutshaw,2b	4	0	1	1	0	0	0	0	1	3	2
Meyer,rf.	3	0	1	1	0	0	1	1	0	0	0
Wheat,lf.	3	1	2	2	0	0	0	1	1	0	0
Daubert,1b.	3	1	1	4	1	0	1	0	11	0	0
Smith,3b.	4	0	2	3	0	0	0	0	1	2	0
Fisher,ss.	3	0	0	0	0	0	0	0	5	1	0
Miller,c.	3	0	0	0	0	0	1	0	4	5	0
Rucker,p.	1	0	0	0	0	0	0	0	0	3	0
Allen,p.	1	0	0	0	0	0	1	0	0	1	1
†Moran	0	0	0	0	0	0	0	1	0	0	0
Total	28	3	8	15	1	0	5	4	27	15	3

*Ran for Chase in ninth inning.
†Batted for Rucker in fifth inning.
‡One out when winning run scored.

Score by Innings.

	1	2	3	4	5	6	7	8	9	
New York	0	0	0	0	0	0	0	0	2	2
Brooklyn	0	0	0	0	1	1	0	0	1	3

Basehits by Innings.

	1	2	3	4	5	6	7	8	9	
New York	0	2	0	1	1	0	0	2	2	8
Brooklyn	2	1	0	1	1	1	0	0	2	8

Two-base hit—Smith. Home runs—Stengel, Daubert. Balk—Allen. First base on errors—New York, 2. Left on bases—New York, 7; Brooklyn, 5. Time of game—2 hours and 1 minute. Umpires—Emslie and Hurst.

Pitchers' Summary.

Name.	Igs.	AB.	R.	H.	BB.	SO.	HP.	WP
Rucker	5	18	0	4	1	1	0	0
Allen	4	13	2	4	2	3	0	0
Caldwell	6	21	2	6	3	3	0	0
Fisher	2 1-3	7	1	2	1	2	0	0

YANKEE TRACK TEAM TO INVADE AUSTRALIA

San Francisco, April 5—Announcement was made today by James E. Sullivan, secretary-treasurer of the Amateur Athletic Union, that an all-American track and field team would visit Australia and New Zealand this year. The team will leave for Australia in December and return in April.

William Unmack, a writer on amateur sports on the Pacific Coast and a native of Australia, will manage the team.

NATIONALS WIN THIS TIME.

Washington, April 5—Washington took the second and last game from the Boston Nationals in their exhibition series here today, 8 to 7. The game was slow and uninteresting. The score:

	1	2	3	4	5	6	7	8	9	R.	H.	E.
Washington	0	0	0	0	4	1	0	1	2	8	11	1
Boston	1	0	1	0	1	0	0	4	0	7	8	2

Cashion, Groom and Ainsmith and Williams; Perdue and Devoght and Rariden.

PIRATES HAD EASY TIME.

Kansas City, April 5—Batting two Kansas City pitchers hard and taking advantage of two errors, the Pittsburg National League Baseball Club today administered a 14-to-1 defeat to the locals. Score:

										R.	H.	E.
Pittsburg	0	0	0	5	2	2	0	0	5	14	19	0
Kansas City	0	0	0	0	1	0	0	0	0	1	5	2

Adams and Kelly; Schlitzer, Reagon and Murphy, Kritchell.

JOE WALL'S TIMELY HOMER.

"Joe" Wall's All-Leaguers traveled to Irvington, N. J., yesterday and won a close eleven-inning game from the All-Stars of that place by a score of 2 to 1. Wall won the game for his team by a home run drive in the final inning.

BROOKLYN SEA DOGS TAKE RELAY RACE

Second Naval Battalion of Brooklyn Leads Home Runners in Seventh Regiment Games.

HALF MILE GOES TO GRANT.

New Armory Record Made by C. N. King in the Obstacle Race.

The sixty-third annual games of the Seventh Regiment were held last night at the armory. A large crowd turned out and was treated to some fine sport. The feature event was the one-mile military relay race, handicap, in which nine teams representing regiments in the Metropolitan District, started.

The Second Naval Battalion team from Brooklyn captured this event in the good time of 3:29 3-5. Although the handicaps were in their favor, the naval boys ran a very gritty race, and captured it only after a very hard run from the Seventy-first Regiment.

Tom Paton, the Columbia track man, ran last for the Seventy-first, and all but caught Reynolds of the sailors, at the tape. Paton ran a great race and picked up ten yards, but was just beaten out of the victory.

E. G. Grant, representing Company M, carried off first place in the half-mile handicap, beating a large field. Grant came up from the rear with a great burst of speed and just managed to nose out J. V. Converse. "Tony "Tink, the old Columbia star finished a good third.

A new armory record was made when C. N. King of Company F won the obstacle race in the time of 52 seconds flat. The old record, made last year, was held by R. Vallbracht, Company H, who finished second. G. G. Moore, the Company G veteran, was a very close third.

The summary:

880 yards handicap—Won by E. G. Grant, Company M. (30 yards); J. V. Converse, Company F (8 yards), second; A. Zink, H. D., third. Time, 2:4 4-5.

Tent-raising contest—Won by Company F, time 1:53 4-5; Company B, second, time 2:27 4-5.

Half-mile roller skating, novice—Won by W. A. Seibert, Company B; G. A. Carson, Company B, second; W. W. Friend, Company B, third. Time, 1:53 1-5.

Shot-put, 16 pounds, handicap—Won by P. Harnishfager, Company C (12 feet); J. J. Elliott, scratch, second; R. Sherman, Company L (11 feet), third. Winning put, 30 feet 4½ inches.

Obstacle race, 220 yards, scratch—Won by C. N. King, Company F; R. Vollbracht, Company H, second; G. G. Moore, Company G, third. Time, 52 seconds (new armory record).

93 yards, novice—Won by T. R. Smith, Company F; L. Carrean, Company G, second; R. L. Baldwin, Company H, third. Time, .08 3-5 seconds.

93 yards, handicap—Won by J. S. Richmond, Company F (7 feet); L. C. Perkins, Company C (7 feet), second; W. J. Ebbets, Company D (12 feet), third. Time, 9 4-5 seconds.

One-mile roller skating, handicap—Won by H. Deane, Company E (60 yards); G. G. Grenz, Company E (70 yards), second; A. E. Helmrich, Company A (70 yards), third. Time, 3:25 2-5.

Hospital and litter race, handicap—Won by Company E, second team (5 yards), (Knox, Crawford and Seguin); Company E (5 yards), (Schwab, Meeker and Woodward) second; Company F, first team (scratch), (Reilly, Quinn and King), third. Time, 20 seconds.

CRESCENTS BEAT YALE IN CLOSE SOCKER GAME.

New Haven, Conn., April 5—The Crescent Athletic Club of Brooklyn, N. Y., defeated Yale at socker this afternoon 4 to 3.

PHILLIES AND MACKMEN PLAY EIGHTEEN-INNING TIE GAME

Longest Battle on Record Between National and American League Clubs.

Philadelphia, April 5—The Philadelphia Americans and the Philadelphia Nationals today played the longest interleague baseball game in the history of the two major organizations, the contest being called at the end of the eighteenth inning on account of darkness with the score standing 2 to 2.

Brown, the Athletic's young righthander, pitched the entire game and was hit safely only thirteen times, while the Phillies used Alexander for five innings, Chalmers two and Brennan eleven. They allowed the former world's champions a total of only ten hits.

The Americans got the jump on their local rivals by scoring their only two runs in the first inning. E. Murphy singled and went to second on Oldring's sacrifice. Collins and Baker walked and Murphy and Collins scored on a single by McInnes. In the succeeding seventeen innings the Americans had chances to score, but sharp fielding kept them from the plate.

The Phillies made their two tallies in the ninth. After Knabe had been thrown out, Centerfielder Capron singled. Lobert hit to Baker, who threw wild to Collins, and Capron went to third. Rightfielder Miller singled, scoring Capron. Lobert came home on Luderus' sacrifice fly to centerfield.

Counting today's contest, the teams have played five games, the Americans winning the first four. Manager Dooin left the game at the end of the seventh inning, having been notified that his brother had died today at Muncie, Ind. The score:

Americans. 2 0 0 0 0 0 0 0 0 0 0 0 0 0 0 0 0 0—2 10 1
Nationals.. 0 0 0 0 0 0 0 0 2 0 0 0 0 0 0 0 0 0—2 13 2

Batteries—Brown and Egan; Alexander, Chalmers, Brennan and Dooin and Killifer. Umpires—Klem and Connolly.

WHILE WE TRIMMED THE YANKEES

President Ebbets and his associates are warmly to be congratulated upon their refusal to sell standing room at Ebbets Field, yesterday. They not only had a new park, but in the lobby an entirely new method of selling tickets and almost an entirely new crew of ticket sellers and turnstile men. Had an effort been made to keep on selling tickets after the normal seating capacity was disposed of, there would inevitably have been confusion and trouble.

* * *

The amount of interest in Frank Chance and his team must have surprised even President Frank Farrell and Chance himself. There was a tremendous outpouring of rabid Manhattan cranks, who began wildly dashing for tickets a couple of days before the game and could not get enough to satisfy them. They were for Chance hook, line and sinker. Playing as they will at the Polo Grounds this year, the Yankees, with any kind of luck, will draw as many people in the season of 1913 as they have drawn in the four previous seasons put together.

* * *

Heavy rain in the early morning hours of yesterday very largely upset the dope about the condition of the grounds. They were rather slippery and the men were not sure of their footing, which made the high-class performance so early in the season all the more remarkable.

* * *

Zach Wheat, in batting practice before the game, won the distinction of being the first man to put a ball over the fence at the new park. He lifted a high fly over the right field wall, which was just about equivalent to doing the same stunt at old Washington Park, where the fence was two or three feet further out, but was not so high.

* * *

Stengel's homer was freakish because of the kick Wolter administered to the ball, but it was a furious clout at that. On good, hard-dried ground it would probably have gone for a homer anyhow.

* * *

Manager Dahlen showed mid-season conversation when he argued with Tim Hurst over the calling out of Stengel at second in the eighth and with Emslie because of the balk he called on Allen in the sixth. Bill was tremendously interested in winning that first game in the new park and by no means regarded it as a mere exhibition for practice. The play on Stengel was peculiar. He drew a pass and Cutshaw attempted to sacrifice. Sweeney grabbed the bunt and took a long sporting chance by firing to Derrick at second to head off Stengel. From the press stand it looked like Derrick did not get near the bag to make a force and also completely failed in his obvious stab on the runner. It was taken for granted that Stengel was safe and the crowd was amazed when in a moment or two he started for the bench with a loud outcry against the veteran Timothy Hurst. But, Tim insisted Stengel was out, and out he remained.

* * *

Great opportunities were afforded the humorists when Roy Hartzell dashed madly through the band in the first inning after Wheat's foul fly to left. He scattered musicians and instruments in every direction, but became so tangled up he failed to make the catch. Unregenerate space writers immediately filed long yarns to the effect that the ball had cracked the big bassoon and that Hartzell had gone kerplunk through the bass drum.

* * *

Benny Meyer almost made a startling catch, and likewise almost made an error on Frank Chance's short fly to him in the second inning. Benny got near enough to the ball to hold it, but the bad footing made him wobble, and he dropped the offering. He was lucky to get there at all, and unlucky to miss the opportunity to figure in a sensation. At last reports he was consulting a fortune-teller to find out whether he was a hero or a dub. The scorers gave Chance a hit, which let Benny out, and he should not worry.

* * *

Daubert's catch of Cree's foul in the eighth when two were on bases, retiring the side, drew a round of applause. Jake had to run backward and sidewise over an extremely uncertain ground, and it was more than an even money bet that he would take a tumble instead of getting the ball, but he got it, all right.

* * *

Wheat's hit that started the winning streak in the ninth was an illustration of the perversities of baseball fate. Wheat tried to make a home run but sliced the ball, driving it into the ground toward third, exactly where an ideal bunt would be laid. Sweeney was rattled by the proceeding and made the wild throw that enabled Wheat to advance all the way to second on that misshapen swat.

* * *

Not the least pleasing feature of the big game to the fan who was at the Borough Hall at 2:30 o'clock was that he walked leisurely up the "L" stairs, waited just a minute for a "special train to the ball grounds," and then dropped into his seat in the grandstand at ten minutes of three.

BROOKLYNITE SECRETARY.

Dr. C. C. Taylor Among New Officers of Cosmopolitan Cricket League.

New officers for the approaching season were elected yesterday at the annual meeting of the Cosmopolitan Cricket League held at the headquarters of the league, 2150 5th avenue, Manhattan. Delegates were present from the Veteran Cricket Club, Spartan Cricket Club, Orient Cricket Club, West Indian Cricket Club and the Newark West Indian Cricket Club. Those elected to office were the following:

George McDermon, Veteran C. C., president; Forster Phillips, Spartan C. C. vice president; Dr. Charles C. Taylor, Orient C. C., 518 Classon avenue, Brooklyn, secretary; Percy Barrow, Orient C. C., treasurer; A. Jones, Veteran C. C., D. Mercer, Spartain C. C., and J. Augustus, Newark West Indian C. C., trustees.

Last season, a cup placed in competition by President McDermon was won by the eleven representing the Orient Cricket Club. A schedule for the coming season will be made up shortly.

OTHER BASEBALL RESULTS.

At Chicago—Chicago, 5; Indianapolis, 2.
At Washington—Washington (A. L.), 8; Boston (N. L.), 7.
At Baltimore—New York (N. L.), 12; Baltimore, 3.
At Kansas City—Pittsburg, 14; Kansas City, 1.
At Greensboro—Buffalo, 6; Greensboro, 4.
At Richmond—Washington Yannigans, 9; Richmond, 1.
At Norfolk—Philadelphia (A. L.) Yannigans, 5; Norfolk, 1.
At Newport News—Providence, 15; Newport News, 7.

FLORAL TRIBUTES TO BROOKLYN CLUB OWNERS

25,000 Fans Welcome Superbas to New Home

CHAMPION TRAVERS AGAIN NAMED AS THE ONLY SCRATCH GOLFER

Metropolitan Golf Association Handicap List Shows a Great Slaughter Among Players in the Ratings for Season of 1913.

The handicap list of the Metropolitan Golf Association for 1913 was announced yesterday by the handicap committee, which consists of A. H. Pogsan, Fox Hills, chairman; Wyatt W. Taylor, Ardsley; George H. Barnes, Apawamis; Oswald Kirkby, Englewood, and A. M. Reid of St. Andrews.

There has been a very severe going over the list, compared with the handicaps of 1912, as may be seen from the following table. There were 540 names in the 1912 list, but there are only 536 in this year's. The changes are shown by this table:

	1913.	1912.
Scratch	1	5
Handicap 1	3	0
Handicap 2	0	2
Handicap 3	3	9
Handicap 4	15	23
Handicap 5	37	61
Handicap 6	91	77
Handicap 7	100	103
Handicap 8	131	91
Handicap 9	155	168
	536	540

In this association, as in the U. S. G. A., only one player is placed on scratch—Jerome D. Travers of Upper Montclair, the present national and metropolitan champion. Last year there were five on scratch—Travers, Frederick Herreshoff, Walter J. Travis, Oswald Kirkby and Albert Seckel. Seckel drops out of the Metropolitan list, as he is now entirely affiliated with the Riverside (Ill.) Golf Club. The following is the list of handcaps up to and including the handicap five men:

Scratch—J. D. Travers.

Handicap 1—Walter J. Travis, Oswald Kirkby and Frederick Herreshoff.

Handicap 2—None.

Handicap 3—E. M. Byers, F. S. Douglas and W. K. Whigham.

Handicap 4—E. M. Barnes, Max Behr, T. V. Bermingham, S. D. Bowers, A. F. Kammer, H. K. Kerr, A. M. Reid, G. P. Tiffany, H. J. Topping, W. R. Tuckerman, John M. Ward, Robert C. Watson, Roy Webb, Gardiner White and E. M. Wild.

Handicap 5—B. T. Allen, Chisholm Beach, B. S. Bottome, W. B. Brenner, George T. Brokaw, C. A. Dunning, D. B. Fuller, jr., Archie Graham, S. J. Graham, W. L. Hicks, H. B. Hollins, jr., McKim Hollins, James R. Hyde, P. W. Kendall, Devereux Lord, M. G. Macdonald, M. R. Marsden, Donald McKellar, W. F. Morgan, jr., John Naething, W. D. Batterson, John Reid, jr., James M. Rhett, Charles H. Seeley, H. V. Seggerman, J. F. Shanley, Wallace Sinclair, J. Harold Slater, J. N. Stearns, jr., C. J. Sullivan, W. W. Taylor, C. E. Van Vleck, jr., C. Gilbert Waldo, jr., and Marshall Whitlatch.

E. M. Byers, though generally known as a member of the Oakmont (Pa.) Golf Club, gets into the list by virtue of his membership in the National Links at Shinnecock Hills. Byers won the national championship at Englewood in 1905. The rating of Devereux Lord, The Eagle trophy winner in 1911 and 1912, is the same this year as last.

Max Behr, the former New Jersey champion, has fallen from three to four, and E. M. Barnes, who distinguished himself last fall at the National Links tournament by defeating Harold Hilton of England, goes up a point from five to four. Gilman P. Tiffany falls from three to four, although he regained the title of Hudson River champion last year.

Of the sixty-eight clubs, members of the M. G. A., sixty-four reported this year. The four delinquents are the Fairview Country Club, the Golf Club of Glen Ridge, the Rockaway Hunting Club and the South Shore Field Club.

FRESHMEN WIN TROPHY AT ST. JOHN'S MEET

Athletes of the college and preparatory departments of St. John's College held their annual field day at St. John's field, Lewis and Willoughby avenues, yesterday. The freshmen proved the strongest point winners among the collegians by romping away with the trophy, with a total of 46 points. Their nearest competitors were the seniors, who earned 9 points. The juniors scored 7 points and the sophomores failed to get a place in any of the events.

The best race in the collegiate competition was the 440-yard run, which was captured by Phil McCaffrey, in 56 seconds. McCaffrey beat out Quinn and Rogan at the tape, after a hard race.

The representatives of the fourth year of the high school department pulled down the honors in their division, with a total of 34 points, as against 21 for the third year students.

Summaries:

100 yard dash—Won by Rogan; Quinn, second; O'Hara, third. Time, 11 seconds.

440 yard dash—Won by McCaffrey; Quinn, second; Rogan, third. Time, 56 seconds.

One mile run—Won by O'Hara; Weber, second; Quinn, third. Time, 4:57.

High jump—Won by Walsh; White, second; Rogan, third. Height, 5 ft. 7 in.

Running broad jump—Won by McCaffrey; Rogan, second; Walsh, third. Distance, 18 ft. 5 in.

Discus throw—Won by White; Walsh, second; Quinn, third.

Point score—Freshmen, 46 points; seniors, 9 points; juniors, 7 points; sophomores, 0.

PREP EVENTS.

100-yard dash—Won by Brady; Bowman, second; Dilla, third. Time, 11 seconds.

440-yard dash—Won by Brady; Howard, second; McBride, third. Time, 58 seconds.

1 mile run—Won by McBride; Graham, second; Bogely, third. Time, 5 minutes 32 seconds.

High jump—Won by Blake; Williams, second; Enkovitz. Height 5 feet 3 inches.

12-pound shot—Won by Kiernan; Williams, second; Brady, third. Distance 33 feet 2 inches.

Running broad jump—Won by Villa; McCrail, second; Graham, third. Distance 17 feet 3 inches.

Pole vault—Won by White; Howard, second; Walker, third. Height 9 fet 9 inches.

100-pound class relay—Won by third year (Flannigan, Matthews, Geller, Mulligan); commercial department (Stoth, Collins, Col'ett, Hughes), second; second year (Torney, Cragin, Shanion, Bradwick), third. Time, 1:02.

Point summary—Fourth year, 34 points; third year, 21 points. Commercial Department, 16 points; second year, 14 points; first year, 3 points.

GARRISON OFFERS CUP FOR HORSE SHOW EVENT.

Washington, April 5—In order to show his great personal interest in the enlisted personnel of the Army, Secretary Garrison has decided to donate a silver cup as a prize for the enlisted men to be competed for at the third annual military horse show to be held at Fort Myer, Va., April 28, 29 and 30. Special preparations are being made for the coming show, and the best cavalry horses in this section of the United States, including thoroughbreds presented by leading sportsmen, will take part in the various events. The President and other high officials of the Government at Washington are expected to attend the exhibition.

LEHIGH BEATS MIDDIES.

Annapolis, Md., April 5—In a close lacrosse game that required two extra periods before the tie was broken, Lehigh today defeated Navy by a score of 4 to 3.

BAY RIDGE SHUT OUT WITHOUT SINGLE HIT

In a game in which Brahe, the winning pitcher, refused to allow his opponents a single hit, the St. John's Prep baseball team defeated the Bay Ridge High School nine at St. John's Field yesterday by 5 to 0. Brahe had the Ridgeites at his mercy and was the individual star of the game, though he received excellent support from his teammates.

The Lewis avenue lads began to circle the bags in the second chapter. A row of clean hits, together with some fine base running and good headwork enabled the home players to score two runs. They did not score again until the sixth, when two more counters augmented their lead. In the seventh they earned another, and this was their last.

The Bay Ridge boys worked hard to connect with the delivery of Brahe, but to no avail. The St. John's twirler also did fine work in the field and at the bat. He had two put-outs, five assists and scored a run and a hit.

The score:

Bay Ridge. Name.	r.	1b.	po.	a.	e.
Doyle,1b..	0	0	5	0	0
Bright,3b..	0	0	3	2	3
Mat'aze,cf	0	0	1	0	0
Michael,ss	0	0	2	4	0
Corwin,c..	0	0	9	0	1
Carlsons,p	0	0	0	0	0
Cadell,rf..	0	0	1	1	0
Reardon,lf	0	0	2	0	0
W'sbar,2b	0	0	0	0	0
Collyer,lf.	0	0	1	0	0
Total	0	0	24	7	4

St. John's Prep. Name.	r.	1b.	po.	a.	e.
A.Ch'b'x,ss	0	0	1	1	0
M'Kenna,3b	1	0	1	1	0
J.M'rphy,1b	0	0	70		0
Brahe,p. ..	1	1	2	5	0
Walker,cf.	2	1	0	0	0
C.C'b'x,c,rf	0	1	6	0	0
Carey,lf...	1	0	0	0	0
McG'gal,2b	0	0	3	0	0
Morrissey,c	0	0	6	1	1
Nicklas,ss.	0	0	1	0	0
W.Murphy	0	0	0	0	0
Total	5	3	27	8	1

Score by Innings.

	1	2	3	4	5	6	7	8	9	
Bay Ridge	0	0	0	0	0	0	0	0	0	0—0
St. John's Prep.	0	2	0	0	0	2	1	0	..	—5

Left on bases—Bay Ridge, 6; St. John's Prep., 6. First base on errors—St. John's Prep., 3; Bay Ridge, 1. Stolen bases—Carey, Brahe, McKenna, Doyle, Reardon. Double play—Brahe and J. Murphy. Bases on balls—Off Brahe, 5; off Karlsons, 4; off Cadell, 3. Struck out—By Brahe, 12; by Karlsons, 4; by Cadell, 2. Hit by pitcher—By Brahe (Reardon). Passed ball—Corwin. Umpire—Mr. Albert, Fordham.

TOPPING WINS ON EXTRA HOLE

Defeats H. K. Kerr for the Chief Pinehurst Match in Brilliant Uphill Game.

Pinehurst, N. C., April 5—Harold J. Topping of Greenwich, Conn., won the championship trophy in the thirteenth annual United North and South Amateur Golf tournament, today, by defeating Hamilton K. Kerr one up on the thirty-seventh green. The contest was one of the most brilliant ever played here.

At the end of the morning round Topping was two down. In the afternoon the first five holes were halved, Kerr gaining a lead of three up on the twenty-fourth and halving the twenty-fifth. By spectacular play Topping evened the match on the thirty-third hole, halved the thirty-fourth, won the thirty-fifth, adn lost the thirty-sixth for a tie, and took the extra hole and the match.

In the championship consolation Harold Weber of Inverness, Ohio, defeated Chisholm Beach of Fox Hills, 8 up and 6 to play. Other division winners in the order given, were: J. P. Garner of Midlothian, Ill.; G. E. Wincher, Wheeling, W. Va.; the Rev. T. A. Cheatham, Salisbury, N. C.; M. W. Pinckney of Homewood, Chicago, and R. A. Sigert of Bethlehem, N. H. The closing tournament of the schedule is set for April 10, 11 and 12.

LACROSSE SEASON OPENS AT BAY RIDGE

Crescents, with New Players in Line, Defeat Stevens Institute 8 to 3.

The Crescent Athletic Club opened its lacrosse season at Bay Ridge yesterday by defeating the twelve from Stevens Institute by a score of 8 to 3. Both teams put up a fine contest, considering it was their first appearance, and there was plenty of excitement for the few hundred spectators who journeyed to the grounds.

The New Moon players jumped into the lead soon after the start, when Walbridge caged the ball on a long, pretty short. The same player added another immediately after the face-off. The home team scored four more goals before the Hoboken aggregation tallied. A few minutes before the whistle blew Van Siclen sent the ball past Dufresne, the Crescent goaltender. The first half ended with the score: Crescents, 6; Stevens, 1.

The visitors braced in the closing period and played the Crescents to a stand-still. Birkenstock, the Stevens captain, and Lawrence scored for the Jerseyites, while Waldridge and Park added two to the home team's total, making the final score: Crescents, 8; Stevens, 3.

Walbridge and Oates starred for the winners, while Van Siclen did the best work for Stevens.

Several new faces appeared in the line-up of the local club men, among them being Keep, Allen, Park and Hallock, the interscholastic hockey star. Manager Lionel Moses has arranged a hard schedule for the Crescent twelve.

The line-up:

Crescent A. C. (8)	Position.	Stevens (3)
Dufresne	Goal	Humphries
Dobby	Point	Parsons
McIntyre	Cover point	Campbell
Andrews	First defense	Bassett
Keep	Second defense	Barnard
Oates	Third defense	Birkenstock
Allen	Center	Lawrence
Taylor	Third attack	Van Siclen
Hallock	Second attack	Karst
Kennedy	First attack	Henry
Park	Outside home	Collins
Walbridge	Inside home	Moss

Referee—L. Moses, Crescent A. C. Goal umpires—Maddern and O'Dougherty. Goals—Walbridge, 4; Oates, 2; Kennedy and Park for Crescent A. C., and Birkenstock, Van Siclen and Lawrence for Stevens. Substitutes—Wardell for Kennedy. Time of halves—20 minutes.

TIGERS HAVE CLOSE CALL.

Louisville, Ky., April 5—Hard hitting by both teams featured the exhibition game here today between the Detroit Americans and the local team of the American Association. There were ten hits for extra bases. Crawford, of Detroit, led with a triple and a double. Timely errors of the visitors aided the locals to win, 8 to 6. Score:

	1	2	3	4	5	6	7	8	9	R.	H.	E.
Louisville	0	0	0	1	4	1	1	1	.	—8	7	1
Detroit	0	0	0	0	1	2	2	0	1	—6	9	4

Batteries—Salmon, Richter and Roth, Clemmons; Boehler, Hall and Stanage, Gibson.

ATLANTAS DOWN TORONTOS.

Atlanta, Ga., April 5—In a closely contested game here today Atlanta took the third straight game of the exhibition series with the Toronto Internationals, winning by a score of 9 to 8. The locals pounded Rudolph and Lush for a total of 11 hits.

PIRATE SECONDS BEAT WICHITA

Wichita, Kan., April 5—The Pittsburg National League second team defeated the Wichita Western League Club today 9 to 5.

LAWSON FINISHES FIRST IN TWELVE MILE RUN

Hoboken had a great day when the first twelve-mile road race, conducted by the Hudson Dispatch, was held, under the direction of Johnny Hayes, the Olympian Marathon winner in 1908.

Over 10,000 persons stood along the course, which trailed through Union Hill, Hoboken, West Hoboken and Jersey City. One hundred and twelve runners toed the mark.

Hannes Kohlemainen, the flying Finn, caused great disappointment when he did not start. Dies of the Knights of St. Anthony, led for a little over nine miles, when he weakened.

The race was won by T. Lawson, Irish-American A. C. Fred Heller, the hill-and-dale king of the Knights of St. Anthony, was the only Brooklyn runner that figured in the prizes. Harry Smith, the national ten-mile champion, finished third, and also captured the fast time prize. He covered the distance in 1 hour 2 minutes 35 seconds.

The course was mostly cobble stone, and many of the runners were foot-sore when they finished.

The Irish-American A. C. won the team prize after a hard battle.

Order of finish:

Name and club.	Hdcp.	Actual Time.
1. T. Lawson, Irish-American....	9:30	1:09:31
2. L. H. Roche, unattached......	1:00	1:11:03
3. H. Smith, unattached.........	2:30	1:02:35
4. H. Frick, Bronx Church House	9:30	1:10:36
5. H. McCloskey, Yonkers Y. M. C. A.	9:30	1:10:22
6. H. Nye, Mohawk A. C.........	8:30	1:09:45
7. A. Baldes, Jersey Harries......	1:00	1:12:22
8. C. L. Gilmore, St. Augustus C. C.	1:00	1:11:23
9. J. J. McNamara, I. A. A. C.	4:00	1:05:26
10. F. M. Heller, St. Anthony....	5:30	1:07:26
11. R. Springsteen, Yonkers Y. M. C. A.	5:00	1:06:43
12. B.J.Casseles, Jersey Harriers.	9:00	1:12:01
13. M. Brand, St. Ansleun.........	0:00	1:12:12
14. M. Maier, Morningside A. C..	5:30	1:07:53
15. W. Galvin, I. A. A. C.........	4:30	1:06:54
16. J. Guerin, unattached	7:30	1:10:14
17. C. Porles, Sheridan A. C......	9:00	1:11:51
18. H. Skellet, Pennant A. C....	9:00	1:11:51
19. R. Nickelson, Yonkers Y. M. C. A.	0:10	1:13:01
20. H. Lucas, Morningside A. C.	6:30	1:09:16
21. J. Hopkins, St. Bartholomew A. C.	9:00	1:12:22
22. J. Gaddy, St. Bartholomew's A. C.	0:00	1:13:37
23. A. Larson, Yonkers Y. M. C. A.	1:00	1:14:38
24. H. Jenson, unattached	4:30	1:08:30

TEAM SCORE.

Irish-American	1	9	15	41	43—109
Jersey Harries	7	12	21	48	65—153
St. Ansleum	13	27	23	45	52—173
St. Barthlomew	21	22	29	36	58—156
Pennat A. C.	18	56	59	61	68—252
Holy Family	25	47	60	67	70—259
Bronx Church House.........	4	39	42	57	69—212

MEADOWBROOK HUNTERS FOLLOW THE HOUNDS.

(Special to The Eagle.)

Westbury, L. I., April 5—A fine, clear day, and the prospect of one of the best runs that have been held by the Meadowbrook hounds this spring, brought a large number of riders to the old Quaker Meeting House here this afternoon to take part in the regular Saturday run of those hounds.

The meet was near the Jericho Turnpike and the sight of the hounds and scarlet coats and velvet caps of the riders attracted the attention of the large number of motor parties, so that by the time the acting master was ready to put the hounds in, over fifty automobiles were lined up along the road.

A number of novices, well mounted, however, were at the meeting place, but the sight of five and six feet rail fences soon had their nerve, and they pulled out long before the check was held.

Those who managed to stick to the end were Acting M. F. H. James Park, Alfred Davis, Henry F. Godfrey, W. Russell Grace, H. E. Drier, Henry W. Bull, Leo Martin, Douglas Campbell, James W. Appleton, A. Schwartz, J. Watson Webb, A. Boyer, James Coogan, W. F. Carson and Whip Cummings.

SHOOTING TITLE FOR VANDERVEER

Captures 1913 Championship of the Crescent Athletic Club with Good Score.

J. H. Vanderveer won the 1913 shooting championship of the Crescent Athletic Club at the Bay Ridge traps yesterday. The event was the feature of the final shoot of the New Moon season, and attracted a field of twelve gunners. Conditions were ideal for the sport, and some exceptionally good scores were made.

The championship was decided at 200 targets, in strings of 100. Vanderveer was in exceptionally good form, and finished the first string with a score of 87, three better than that made by J. F. James and F. B. Stephenson.

Vanderveer shot a total of 91 on his second string. This is one of the best performances of the year, and gave the new champion a total of 178. J. F. James was second, with 172, while F. B. Stephenson captured third prize with a score of 171. C. Blake, the 1912 champion of the club, finished in fifth place, with 167.

The 1912 championship was decided in January of this year, and it is an unusual thing to run off two championships in three months, but the shooting committee explained that the club is generally a year behind with its target event, and since it is doubtful whether there will be shooting at Bay Ridge next year, it was thought better to hold the 1913 championship at this early date.

Besides the title event, there was also a shoot for a Take Home Trophy, at 100 targets. John H. Hendrickson was the high gun, with 95 from the scratch mark, but since he is not a member of the club, first prize went to J. H. Vanderveer, who broke 94, with the aid of a handicap of 8. David T. Leahy was second, with a score of 90 and a handicap of 8.

J. F. James and G. G. Stephenson, jr., tied for the annual Remsen Cup, with three legs apiece, and after three shoot-offs the prize went to Mr. James.

The scores:

TAKE HOME TROPHY—100 TARGETS—HANDICAP.

Name	H'c'p.	String of 25.				T'l.
*J. H. Hendrickson.......	0	24	22	25	24	95
J. H. Vanderveer.........	8	25	25	24	20	94
D. T. Leahy..............	8	25	22	24	19	90
A. Corlies................	4	20	23	25	19	87
J. F. James...............	0	21	22	21	20	84
F. B. Stephenson.........	0	24	22	19	19	84
R. C. Williams...........	16	21	20	25	17	83
C. R. James...............	0	20	22	23	18	83
C. Blake..................	0	21	21	22	19	83
G. G. Stephenson.........	8	18	17	20	24	79
F. S. Hyatt...............	8	17	19	21	21	78
J. Bingham...............	16	21	18	21	18	78
A. Blake..................	16	18	16	19	19	72
F. Crampton..............	16	19	19	16	18	72
M. Stiner.................	0	18	18	15	19	70

CLUB CHAMPIONSHIP, 1913—200 TARGETS.

Name	String of 100.		T'l.
J. H. Vanderveer..........	87	91	178
J. F. James...............	84	88	172
F. B. Stephenson.........	84	87	171
D. T. Leahy..............	82	88	170
C. Blake..................	83	84	167
A. Corlies................	83	83	166
C. R. James..............	82	83	165
M. Stiner.................	70	86	156
F. S. Hyatt...............	72	72	144
R. C. Williams...........	68	67	135
A. Blake..................	56	67	123
F. Crampton..............	56	56	102

REMSEN TROPHY—25 TARGETS—HANDICAP—SHOOT OFF.

Name	H'p.	T'l.	Name.	H'p.	T'l.
J. F. James........	0	20	G. G. Stephenson.	1	20

THIRD SHOOT OFF—SAME CONDITIONS.

Name	H'p.	T'l.	Name.	H'p.	T'l.
J. F. James........	0	22	G. G. Stephenson.	1	21

THIRD SHOOT OFF—SAME CONDITIONS.

Name	H'p.	T'l.	Name.	H'p.	T'l.
J. F. James........	0	19	G. G. Stephenson.	1	15

*Guest.

SPECIAL STAND FOR THE "SUN GODS"

THE laugh was on Charley Ebbets when the fans in the great steel and concrete stand at Ebbets Field yesterday gazed across the Montgomery wall and saw a densely crowded wooden stand perched on the heights, which were facetiously dubbed McKeever's Bluff. A property owner with a disregard for the feelings of the Brooklyn Club owners, but a genius for business, had built a wooden stand for the bleacherites who did not care to cough up half a dollar to see the game. It did not take long to fill the stand to overflowing at a quarter a throw, and there was a waiting list of several thousand who could not be accommodated. It is probable, however, that the property owner will have to make hay while the sun shines, as President Ebbets intimated that there will be some obstruction to the view of the patrons of the stand before many games have been played.

BIG DEMONSTRATION PLANNED BY DIRECTORS OF THE P. S. A. L.

Thousands of Schoolboys to Take Part in Field Day at Central Park, June 6—Many Prominent Citizens on Committee.

The greatest demonstration of schoolboy athletics and physical training, and at the same time the largest field day ever held in the world will be staged in Central Park on the afternoon of Friday, June 6, by the Public Schools Athletic League.

On a huge field containing 360,000 square feet of the green, or 600 feet square, 10,000 grammar grade boys from the public schools of all boroughs will be assembled, and simultaneously perform various drills and compete in a programme of athletic events. The entire 10,000 boys, or the full quota of twenty regiments, in unison will bend, breathe, stretch and go through the other features of the new two-minute drill, and the exercises of the new public school course of study.

A single pistol shot will start from 100 to 200 relay teams of fifty boys each in a contest for school supremacy. The other events, such as the jump, hurdle and discus drill, will be on a similar wholesale plan, with from 5,000 to 10,000 boys all in action at one time.

This monster demonstration of the work of the public schools and the Athletic League, in numbers exceeds all athletic gatherings except the adult turnfest at Prague, in 1912. It will distance anything heretofore attempted with boys. The field day will be in charge of the following committee of the P. S. A. L.: Chairman, Gustavus T. Kirby, president of the A. A. U., director of the P. S. A. L.; General George W. Wingate, president of the P. S. A. L.; S. R. Guggenheim, treasurer, P. S. A. L.; C. Ward Crampton, M. D., director of physical training, New York Public Schools, secretary P. S. A. L.; Vincent Astor, director, P. S. A. L.; Luther Halsey Gulick, M. D., director, P. S. A. L.; Dr. Edward W. Stitt, District Superintendent of Schools, and director of the P. S. A. L.

Park Commissioner Stover Interested.

Park Commissioner C. B. Stover, while not a member of the working committee, has offered to co-operate in every way possible. Through Mr. Stover, the P. S. A. L. committee obtained the use of the huge field in Central Park needed to handle the 10,000 boys and provide the necessary stands for special guests. Similarly, Thomas W. Churchill, president of the Board of Education, and City Superintendent William H. Maxwell have assured the committee of the co-operation of the public schools.

While the detailed programme of events is not yet completed, Dr. Crampton, who will have charge of handling the boys and of school arrangements, states that the big problem of mobilizing and transporting the boys to and from the field has been settled. Through the active interest of superintendents, principals and teachers, he says, it will be possible to handle and drill this large number without any confusion. The P. S. A. L. will provide the large number of starters, clerks of course and judges necessary to start the boys and judge fairly the winners. While the actual schools which will send from one to five teams of fifty boys have not yet been finally determined, the work of drilling the boys for the events and to act as a chorus for patriotic singing was begun during the past week. One of the chief features of the day will be the salute to the American Flag and the singing of "The Star Spangled Banner" by the entire 10,000 junior athletes.

An invitation to see these 10,000 future citizens in action will be extended by the committee, to the President of the United States, ex-Presidents Taft and Roosevelt, the Governors of New York and neighboring States, the Mayors of New York, Boston, Philadelphia and other large cities, the Aldermen and heads of city departments, Borough Presidents and many others prominent in civic and educational affairs. Surrounding the actual field, the committee hopes to have from 20,000 to 40,000 interested spectators.

Gustavus Kirby Is Enthusiastic.

The direct purposes which the committee hopes the demonstration will accomplish are: (1) To show the value of general athletics under the P. S. A. L. system of having all boys take part in games and contests, and so to secure additional opportunities for New York boys to enjoy normal sports. (2) To demonstrate the new course of study in physical training and induce parents to cooperate in the proper physical development of children: (3) To show the discipline, patriotism, personal and civic pride and high character fostered among boys by sane athletics.

In discussing the demonstration, Mr. Kirby, chairman of the committee, said: "We want to make this field day one of the greatest object lessons in health and citizenship any country has ever been privileged to witness. I can imagine no more inspiring or impressive sight than will be afforded by these 10,000 healthy, happy, well-disciplined boys when they all are in action at the same time."

General Wingate, president of the league, said: "For one thing, our determination to hold this meet on such a gigantic scale shows our everlasting confidence in the New York boy as we of the P. S. A. L. have come to know him. This also is a compliment to the superintendents, principals and teachers who make it possible to handle boys in such numbers. It will open the eyes of many New Yorkers when they see the manliness, fine bearing, health, keen mindedness and absolute self-respect and obedience of these 10,000 boys taken at random from public schools located on easy ways of transportation to the Park."

ST. JOHN'S COLLEGE TIES FORDHAM NINE

The St. John's College team gave the Bronxonians a great surprise by holding them to a tie score at Fordham Field, yesterday. Carey, the clever southpaw of the Brooklynites, held the home team safe at all times, and but for ragged fielding on the part of his teammates during the latter part of the fray, would have gained an easy victory. Kehoe, the veteran twirler of Fordham, proved to be easy picking for the Saints, and was supplanted by "Runt" Walsh in the fifth, who retired the side by the strike-out route in the fifth and sixth and fanned two in the eighth. Score:

Fordham. Name.	r.	1b.	po.	a.	e.
Kane, cf..	0	0	0	0	1
Fl'ag'n,1b.	0	0	7	0	0
Shark'y,2b	0	0	0	2	0
Kehoe, lf.	0	0	0	1	0
Carrol, ss	0	0	3	0	0
Virlano,3b	0	0	2	2	0
M'Eri'n,ss	0	0	0	0	0
Elliffe, c.	1	2	14	2	0
Dooling,rf	2	2	1	1	0
Walsh,p...	0	0	0	0	0
Flanagan*	1	0	0	0	0
Totals.....	4	4	27	8	1

St. John's. Name.	r.	1b.	po.	a.	e.
Dorl, 2b...	0	2	3	2	1
M'Don'll,rf	0	1	0	0	0
Burchel,1b	0	0	10	0	1
Tracey,, cf	1	1	2	0	0
Crenny, 3b	0	0	1	1	0
Carey, p...	1	3	0	6	0
Damico,lf	1	2	1	1	0
Costello,ss.	1	0	2	3	1
Mahoney,c	0	1	7	1	0
Totals.....	4	10	26	13	4

*Batted for Elliffe in ninth.

Score by Innings.

	1	2	3	4	5	6	7	8	9	
St. John's	0	0	1	2	0	0	0	0	1	—4
Fordham	0	0	0	0	0	0	2	0	2	—4

Left on bases—St. John's, 5; Fordham, 7. Two-base hits—Tracey, Damico, Dooling (2). Three-base hits—Carey. Sacrifice hits—Kehoe. Stolen bases—Sharkey, Kane, Dooling. Double plays—Mahoney to Crenny. Bases on balls—Off Carey, 4; off Kehoe, 1. Struck out—By Kehoe, 8; by Carey, 4; by Walsh, 11. Wild pitches—Carey (2), Kehoe. Passed balls—Mahoney. Umpire—O'Connell. Time of game—2 hours and 10 minutes. Attendance—500.

HARVARD WINS RIFLE EVENT.

Washington, April 5—Harvard University, without a defeat, won the Eastern League Intercollegiate, rifle-shooting championship. Massachusetts Agricultural College was second, with one defeat, and Princeton University, third, with two defeats. In the Western League the series resulted in a tie, which must be shot off between the West Virginia University and Iowa State University, both having won twelve matches and lost one. The team winning the shootoff will meet Harvard to determine the United States intercollegiate championship.

CHESS CHAMPION BACK AFTER LONG ABSENCE

Although he had an engagement to play in Columbus, Ohio, which, notwithstanding the recent misfortune which befel that section of the country, had not been canceled, Frank J. Marshall, the United States chess champion and winner of the recent masters tournament at Havana, the home of Capablanca, came right through from Chicago, arriving home yesterday. Marshall had returned by way of New Orleans, where he played for a week at the New Orleans Chess, Checkers and Whist Club. He visited Lafayette, La., Dallas, Nashville, Memphis, St. Louis and Chicago, but decided to limit his tour in order to get back to New York as soon as possible. Mrs. Marshall, who was with the champion in Cuba, accompanied him, and both were glad to get home, after an absence of two months.

While in Chicago, Marshall gave one performance at the rooms of the Kenwood Chess Club, where he met twenty-one players at as many boards. He won all of the games without permitting any-one so much as a draw. Within a week Marshall expects to leave again for Montreal, where he will spend several days. Upon his return to the States he will visit Pittsburg, where a master exhibition is being arranged for him. No steps, the champion said, had been taken toward bringing about another match between him and Jose R. Capablanca, who is still in Havana.

NEW SUBWAYS MEAN PROSPERITY FOR BROOKLYN

CONTRACTS making effective the dual subway system were signed March 19, 1913. This is a big date in the history of New York City and a bigger one in the history of the Borough of Brooklyn. It marks the realization of a practical plan for alleviating the transportation problem in the entire city, but it brought Brooklyn into the five-cent zone and tied it up with the heart of the busiest and wealthiest city in the world.

The city, the New York Municipal Railway Corporation, representing the B. R. T. and the Interborough Rapid Transit Company, are the partners in this giant traction enterprise which joins to the old subway and elevated lines, valued at $270,000,000, new lines to cost $330,000,000.

The city's rapid transit lines will be increased in mileage from 308 track miles to 609 track miles; the increase of the New York Municipal Railway Corporation being from 105 to 258 miles, and of the Interborough Rapid Transit Company, from 203 track miles to 351.

Dual Subway System Gives Transit Relief to All Boroughs.

The dual system grew out of offers made by the two big traction companies after the Public Service Commission had laid down an independent system to be known as the Tri-Borough, since it ran from the Bronx to Brooklyn through Manhattan. The Tri-Borough omitted Queens and Richmond, whereas the dual system makes adequate provision for Queens and has laid down a plan for the future development of Richmond.

The agitation for the Tri-Borough began in August, 1907. On November 24, 1909, ground was broken for the Fourth avenue subway, the first link in it. On October 27 the Public Service Commission received bids for the construction of the remainder of the city-built line.

On November 1, 1910, William G. McAdoo, now Secretary of the Treasury, but then president of the Hudson and Manhattan Railroad, proposed to put up $50,000,000 to equip the new subway and to become its operator. This move spurred the Interborough Rapid Transit Company to activity, and on December 5, 1910, it put in an offer to the city to extend the present subway system, of which it is the operator, on terms that were considered more favorable than those proposed by Mr. McAdoo. On December 12 the Hudson and Manhattan Company withdrew from the subway field.

B. R. T. Enters Field and Proposes to Operate Subways.

On December 20, the Public Service Commission reported in favor of the Interborough's plan and forwarded it to the Board of Estimate. The Board withheld action and so made possible the dual system, for on March 2, the Brooklyn Rapid Transit Company, suddenly entering the field, proposed to operate all of the Tri-Borough lines in Brooklyn with the exception of the Broadway-Lafayette loop and to tie up their elevated lines with a subway in Broadway, Manhattan.

A special committee on pending transit proposals had been appointed (January 19, 1911), by the Board of Estimate, consisting of George McAneny, borough president of Manhattan; Cyrus Miller, borough president of the Bronx, and George Cromwell, borough president of Richmond. On June 13, 1911, this committee and the Public Service Commission reported in favor of accepting the proposals of both companies with such slight changes as were necessary to weld them together. The two proposals covered the entire city.

On June 21, 1911, the Board of Estimate and Apportionment accepted this report. On June 27, 1911, the B. R. T. accepted the city's plan for joint operation. On the same day the Interborough Rapid Transit Company refused to accept the terms and conditions and, in one act, withdrew from the field.

Negotiations with the Interborough Company were resumed, and on July 19, 1911, the company made another offer. The following day the McAneny Committee reported in favor of the Interborough's new plan, but the Board rejected the proposal of the company. On February 27, 1912, the Interborough came forward with another plan. This was accepted May 22, 1912.

Act of Legislature Made City Partnership Possible.

During the final negotiations the Public Service Commission took to the Legislature and had passed an enabling act permitting the city to go into partnership with a private corporation. The question of whether or not the city violated the Constitution and pledged its credit in allowing the traction companies to take the first money out of the joint earnings, giving their investment a preference over the city's money, was carried to the Court of Appeals and there decided. The Court held that the city did not pledge its credit and paved the way for the dual system.

On March 4, 1913, the contracts were approved by the Public Service Commission. On March 18 they were approved by the Board of Estimate. On March 19 they were signed, sealed and delivered.

Practically all of the $314,858,200 to be put into subways is expended by the city, the traction companies having no direct supervision over the most of the funds. The Interborough Company is to third track and extend its elevated system with its own money, and it is the boss of this job. The B. R. T. is to third track and extend its elevated lines and it controls this expenditure. Everything else is done by the city, the companies merely turning over the sums agreed upon. The Interborough's expenditure for elevated roads is $25,000,000 and the B. R. T.'s $15,000,000. The Interborough is to put $21,000,000 into new equipment and the B. R. T. $26,000,000.

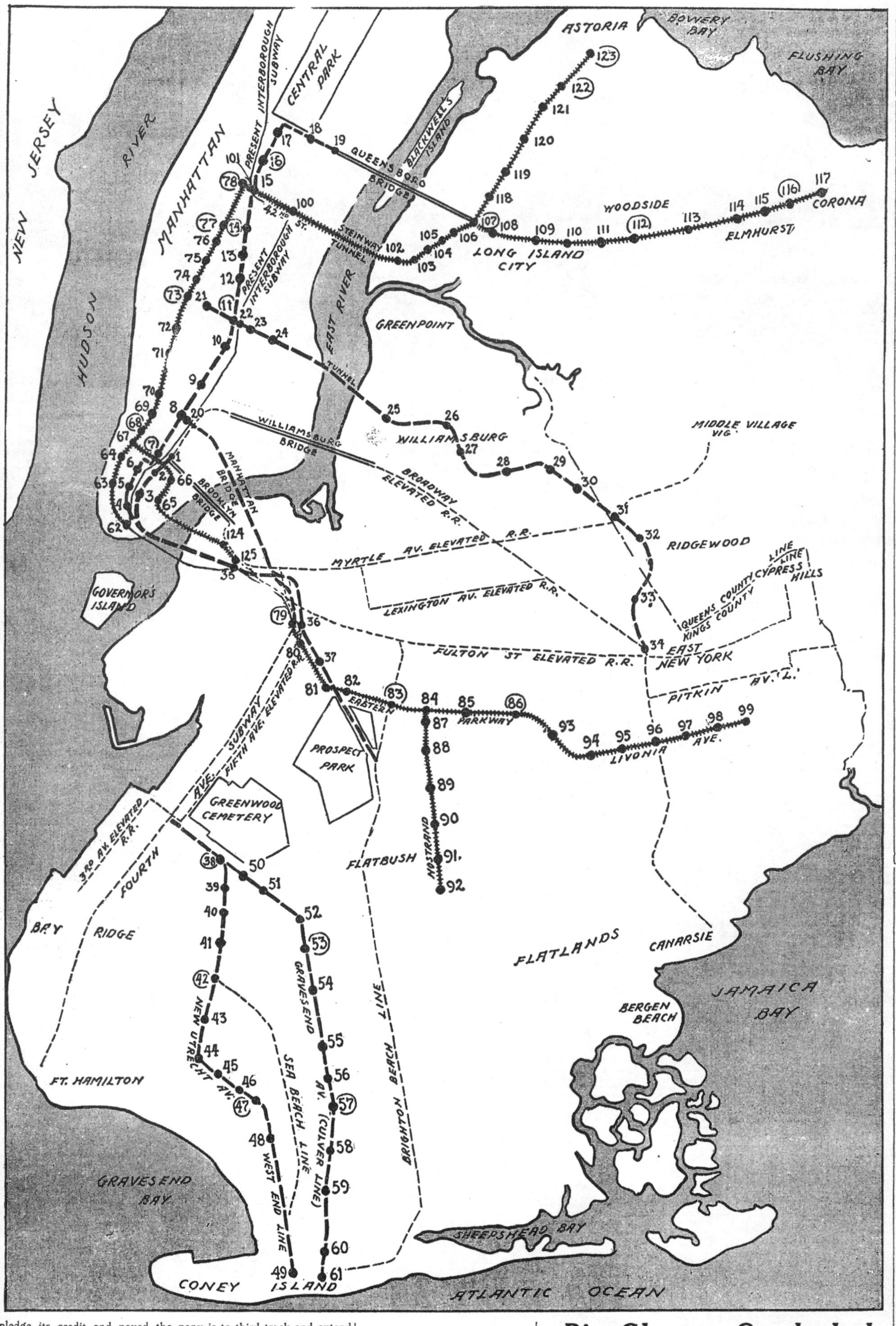

KEY TO MAP OF DUAL SYSTEM

Routes and Stations of the New York Municipal Railway Corporation. On the B. R. T. System:

STATIONS.

NASSAU STREET LINE:
No. 1, Chambers street; No. 2, Fulton street; No. 3, Broad street.

BROADWAY, FIFTY-NINTH STREET LINE:
No. 4, Whitehall street; No. 5, Rector street; No. 6, Cortlandt street; No. 7, City Hall (express); No. 8, Canal street; No. 9, Prince street; No. 10, Eighth street; No. 11, Union Square (express); No. 12, Twenty-third street; No. 13, Twenty-eighth street; No. 14, Thirty-fourth street (express); No. 15, Times Square; No. 16, Forty-ninth street (express); No. 17, Fifty-seventh street; No. 18, Fifth avenue; No. 19, Lexington avenue.

CANAL STREET LINE:
No. 20, Broadway.

FOURTEENTH STREET, UNION SQUARE, EASTERN DISTRICT LINE:
No. 21, Sixth avenue, Manhattan; No. 22, Union Square; No. 23, Third avenue; No. 24, First avenue; No. 25, Bedford avenue; No. 26, Graham avenue; No. 27, Grand street; No. 28, Morgan avenue; No. 29, Flushing avenue; No. 30, De Kalb avenue; No. 31, Ridgewood; No. 32, Halsey street; No. 33, Central avenue; No. 34, Broadway.

MONTAGUE STREET LINE:
No. 35, Court street.

ST. FELIX STREET, FLATBUSH AVENUE LINE:
No. 36, Atlantic avenue; No. 37, Seventh avenue.

NEW UTRECHT AVENUE LINE:
No. 38, Ninth avenue (express); No. 39, Forty-fourth street; No. 40, Forty-ninth street; No. 41, Fifty-fifth street; No. 42, Sixty-second street (express); No. 43, Seventy-first street; No. 44, Seventy-ninth street; No. 45, Eighteenth avenue; No. 46, Twentieth avenue; No. 47, Bay Parkway (express); No. 48, Twenty-fifth avenue; No. 49, Surf avenue.

GRAVESEND AVENUE LINE:
No. 50, Fort Hamilton Parkway; No. 51, Thirteenth avenue; No. 52, Ditmas avenue; No. 53, Eighteenth avenue (express); No. 54, Avenue J; No. 55, Avenue N; No. 56, Avenue P; No. 57, Kings Highway (express); No. 58, Avenue U; No. 59, Avenue X; No. 60, Neptune avenue; No. 61, Surf avenue.

INTERBOROUGH RAPID TRANSIT COMPANY. SEVENTH AVENUE LINE, MANHATTAN:
No. 62, South Ferry; No. 63, Rector street; No. 64, Cortlandt street.

WILLIAMS STREET LINE:
No. 65, Wall street; No. 66, Fulton street; No. 67, Park place; No. 68, Chambers street (express); No. 69, Franklin street; No. 70, Canal street; No. 71, Houston street; No. 72, Christopher street; No. 73, Fourteenth street (express); No. 74, Eighteenth street; No. 75, Twenty-third street; No. 76, Twenty-eighth street; No. 77, Pennsylvania Railroad Station (express); No. 78, Times Square (express).

FLATBUSH AVENUE AND EASTERN PARKWAY LINE:
No. 79, Atlantic avenue (express); No. 80, Bergen street; No. 81, Prospect Park Plaza; No. 82, Underhill avenue; No. 83, Franklin avenue (express); No. 84, Nostrand avenue; No. 85, Kingston avenue; No. 86, Utica avenue (express).

NOSTRAND AVENUE LINE:
No. 87, President street; No. 88, Sterling street; No. 89, Winthrop street; No. 90, Church avenue; No. 91, Beverley road; No. 92, Newkirk avenue.

LIVONIA AVENUE LINE:
No. 93, Sutter avenue; No. 94, Saratoga avenue; No. 95, Rockaway avenue; No. 96, Junius street; No. 97, Georgia avenue; No. 98, Van Sicklen avenue; No. 99, New Lots avenue.

STEINWAY TUNNEL EXTENSION:
No. 100, rGand Central Station; No. 101, Times Square.

STEINWAY TUNNTL. QUEENSBORO BRIDGE PLAZA LINE:
No. 102, Vernon avenue; No. 103, Jack? son avenue; No. 104, Van Alst avenue; No. 105, Ely avenue; No. 106, Twelfth street; No. 107, Queensboro Bridge Plaza (express).

WOODSIDE, CORONA LINE:
No. 108, Rawson street; No. 109, Lowery street; No. 110, Bliss street; No. 111, Lincoln avenue; No. 112, Woodside (express); No. 113, Broadway; No. 114, Twenty-fifth street; No. 115, Elmhurst avenue; No. 116, Junction avenue (express); No. 117, Sycamore avenue.

ASTORIA LINE.
No. 118, Beebe avenue; No. 119, Washington avenue; No. 120, Broadway; No. 121, Grand avenue; No. 122, Hoyt avenue (express); No. 123, Ditmars avenue (express.)

CLARK STREET LINE:
No. 124, Henry street; No. 125, Borough Hall.

WHAT THE DUAL SYSTEM OF SUBWAYS WILL COST.

COST OF CONSTRUCTION.	
I. Interborough system—	
By the city	$59,649,250
By the company	56,000,000
Total	$115,649,250
II. Brooklyn system—	
By the city—new lines	$64,722,950
By the company—city lines	13,000,000
Total	$77,722,950
By city—4th ave.-Centre st. loop	$28,486,000
By company for elevated roads	21,000,000
Total	$127,208,950
III. Combined dual system—	
By city—new lines	$124,372,200
By city—now building	28,486,000
By operating companies	90,000,000
Total	$242,858,200
COST OF EQUIPMENT.	
Interborough Co.	$21,000,000
Brooklyn Co.	26,000,000
Total	$47,000,000
Total construction and equipment	289,858,200
Interborough Co. elevated roads in Manhattan	25,000,000
Grand total	$314,858,200

SPRING BUYING MARKET AT BRIGHTWATERS, L. I.

"While but the slightest evidence of spring are to be seen in the fields, and the chill of winter is still here," said T. B. Ackerson of the Brightwaters Company, "summer residents of Brightwaters are closing their homes in town and are coming here to stay. In the last ten days more than thirty summer houses have been opened in the Brightwaters colony."

The company is completing for spring occupancy a number of bungalows and cottages; among them a handsome stucco bungalow, on harbor front, for Joseph Bishop. Other plans are:

A two-story English Colonial cottage on corner plot in the Oaks for James A. Gray; a two-story Elizabethan Gothic cottage on plot 70x140 for W. H. Corwin; a model seashore cottage on Windsor avenue, plot 75x200, for Mr. and Mrs. James Van Etton Westfall; a pretty Colonial cottage on Bay Way avenue for Paul F. Gebicke on plot 60x140; a very pretentious stucco bungalow on plot 145x138 on Woodland Drive for Charles H. Chambers, assistant auditor of the New York Central lines; a two-story stucco dwelling, corner Woodland Drive and Woodland avenue, for Mr. and Mrs. Alfred J. Worsdell.

Among the recent buyers at Brightwaters are: Joseph F. Fletcher, now living in Laurelton, who will build a substantial bungalow on Plot 4,052, Block 138, in the Oaks; Mrs. Carrie B. Fuller, twelve farm plots; R. F. Brumbaugh, Edward Avila and Mrs. Florence Buchs in the Oaks; Augustin MacHugh in Bay section; Ila Johnston in the Pines and John J. Costello in the Farms.

SENATOR STREET SALE.

Frank A. Seaver has sold the two-story and basement brownstone house at 338 Senator street for John Carboy to a buyer for occupancy.

Big Chances Overlooked

Now Is the Time to Buy—Prices Are Sure to Soar When Subways Come.

(By William C. Demarest.)

THAT the general public is not quick to grasp the import of new movements, especially those which concern local transit improvements, is my opinion.

It has been seen time and again, that the average man pays little or no serious attention to subway construction which is going on right under his eyes. He simply cannot or will not realize what wonderful changes can be brought about almost overnight by the opening of a new subway route. The history of the Bronx boom is too well known to call for any description today, and yet the same conditions which existed in that borough prior to the operation of the subway there are found at this very moment in Brooklyn.

We learn on the best of authority that it is confidently expected that by the early part of 1914 subway trains will be operating from Manhattan over the Manhattan Bridge, up Fourth avenue in Brooklyn, and thence via the Sea Beach Line to Coney Island. The "air line" this route was originally called, and air line it will be when completed, for it is estimated that from downtown Manhattan to the Mapleton Park property in Brooklyn (at about Twenty-second avenue) subway trains will cover the distance of about seven miles in something like 21 minutes. And although the actual completion of this marvelous improvement is not further than twelve months away, there are only a comparatively few people who seem to realize the vast opportunity presented in property values along the new route.

Take the Mapleton Park property, for example. Although I am glad to note that the one-family brick residences which the Alco Building Company have erected there are now bringing $500 more per house than they did last fall (the price now being $6,000, as against $5,500 last October), this increase of $500 is small in comparison to the way prices should soar, and I confidently believe will, once the subway is actually in operation. Incidentally it might be interesting to observe that of fifty dwellings erected on Sixty-seventh street, Mapleton Park, only seven remain unsold; of thirty-two constructed on Sixty-fifth street only two are still for sale; and out of 250 others recently built in this section nearly 150 have been disposed of—and all this has been accomplished in the short period since last August.

WEATHER TO-DAY:
Fair.
Full Report Page 2.

The New York Press

The Press so presents the news that the busy man can read it in the time he has for his morning newspaper.

VOL. XXVIII.—WHOLE NO. 10,020 NEW YORK, SATURDAY, MAY 8, 1915 BC3 PRICE{ ONE CENT within twenty-five miles of City Hall Park; TWO CENTS everywhere else.

FROM 500 TO 1,500 DIE ON LUSITANIA; LINER HIT BY TWO GERMAN TORPEDOES

BRITISH LOSE GUNS ON HILL 60; BATTLE IN EAST INCREASES

Germans Send Several Fresh Army Corps Against Russians in Galicia.

LOSSES MOUNTING RAPIDLY

Allied Fleet Silences Forts at Chanak and Kilid Bahr in the Dardanelles.

Hard battles were reported in both theatres of the war yesterday.

The struggle for the mastery of Hill No. 60 and the desolated country around Ypres continued, and the fighting was violent and the losses of men large.

Berlin reported that repeated attacks by the British failed and that seven machine guns, a mine thrower and a large number of rifles, with ammunition, were captured.

Between the Meuse and the Moselle and in the forest of Ailly there were several sharp encounters, and the Germans assert they maintained their ground.

In Galicia, between the Vistula River and the Carpathians, the Russians and the Teutonic allies were in contact all day yestreday. The losses in the great battle are counting steadily.

Petrograd announced that the Germans have been reinforced by several army corps, but again says the advance of the Austro-Germans has been checked.

The dispatches from German and Austrians sources insist the Russians have been pushed back many miles, first across the Dunajec and then across the Wisloka River, which, in a general way, parallels the Dunajec about fifteen miles to the eastward.

Petrograd and the British military critics still refuse to concede a great victory to the Austro-Germans, but the British newspapers admit a great tentative success has been gained by the Teutonic allies.

The Russians say they are pressing the Austro-Germans closely in region of Mitau, and that they have captured two villages in the direction of Mlawa. They assert also they have repulsed with bayonets attacks in the direction of Mezclaborcz and have won important successes in the valley of Lomnitza.

The bombardment of the Turkish fortifications in the Dardanelles is reported to be proceeding successfully. Some of the forts at Chanak and Kilid Bahr and probably others on both sides of the straits up to the narrows, are said to have been silenced.

Some of the allied warships are shelling the fortifications from the Gulf of Saros and are using inflammable bombs. Maidos is said to have been set on fire.

Three Russian aviators dropped bombs on Constantinople and are reported to have done much damage.

The Russian Black Sea fleet was reported yesterday to have bombarded the Bosporus Wednesday and its shells fell in the suburbs of Constantinople, within ten miles of the city itself.

The date for opening the Italian Parliament was postponed yesterday from May 12, the date originally assigned, to May 20. The situation in Italy grows more tense daily and the Italian press says only a miracle can keep the country out of the war.

The exodus of Germans from Italy is increasing and Austria is making energetic preparations for a possible attack by Italy.

Two more British steamships have been torpedoed off the Irish coast. The crews were saved.

TWO STEAMERS TOPEDOED.

Crews Escape When Submarine Sinks Them Off the Irish Coast.

LONDON, May 7.—The sinking yesterday of two more British steamships, the Centurion and the Candidate, by German submarines off the coast of

(Continued on Page 6, Column 3.)

Warning by German Embassy and Lusitania Sailing on Her Last Voyage

NOTICE!
TRAVELLERS intending to embark on the Atlantic voyage are reminded that a state of war exists between Germany and her allies and Great Britain and her allies; that the zone of war includes the waters adjacent to the British Isles; that, in accordance with formal notice given by the Imperial German Government, vessels flying the flag of Great Britain, or of any of her allies, are liable to destruction in those waters and that travellers sailing in the war zone on ships of Great Britain or her allies do so at their own risk.
IMPERIAL GERMAN EMBASSY.
WASHINGTON, D. C., APRIL 22, 1915

Copyright, 1915, by International News Service.

Big Cunarder as she appeared as she was leaving here on her fateful voyage at noon on May 1; notice at top was published in New York papers for several days previously at the instance of the German Embassy at Washington, warning the American public against sailing on British ships.

PRESIDENT IS STUNNED BY NEWS OF DISASTER

Wilson Leaves White House for Lonely Walk to Consider Situation.

WASHINGTON, May 7.—No action was taken by President Wilson or the State Department to-night regarding the Lusitania, for the reason that the President and his advisers were stunned by the suddenness and the extent of the disaster.

It had been hoped there was no loss of life. Earlier dispatches seemed to indicate this was the fact. The President left the White House alone, and strode for a mile or more through neighboring parks, evidently to think deeply, on his lonely walk, of the situation presented by the latest development of the war.

As he walked, newsboys rushed past crying the extra editions announcing that many lives had been lost. Mr. Wilson halted abruptly and hastened back to the White House to learn the full truth.

Message from U. S. Consul.

The only official communication at hand, however, was a dispatch from Wesley Froest, the American Consul at Queenstown. It read:

"Lusitania sunk at 2.30. Probably many survivors. Rescue work progressing favorably."

The message also asked whether the State Department wished a list of Americans on board the liner. It had been received at 8.30 o'clock, soon after the President left, and was the subject of an anxious consultation among Secretary Bryan and his aids.

Although it was not known how many, if any, of those lost were Americans, the view was general that the most serious situation confronted the American Government since the outbreak of the war in Europe.

Wilson to Consult Congress.

Secretary Bryan, Counsellor Lansing, Senators and Members of the House who were in the city, waited up until a late hour for definite news of the passengers and crew of the ill-fated ship. Earlier in the day they construed the positive announcements from abroad that no lives had been lost is final but later advices dashed their hopes.

Officials said facts and circumstances would have to be obtained by careful investigation during the next few days before any announcements could be made by the American Government.

The disposition among high officials was not to take hasty action, but to await the British Admiralty's reports and results of the investigation of Ambassador Page.

Although Congress is not in session, Chairman Stone of the Senate Foreign Relations Committee, and other members of the committee are now in the city. It is expected they will be consulted by President Wilson before he decided on the policy to be pursued by the United States.

Bryan Cables U. S. Consul.

Immediately on receipt of Consul Froest's message, Secretary Bryan directed that a reply be sent stating that if any of the passengers had been lost to send at once the list of Americans dead.

Torpedoing of the Lusitania aroused official Washington to-day as has no other incident since the outbreak of the war.

The feeling was widespread that the

(Continued on Page 3, Column 1.)

"We Owe It to Humanity and to Our Self-Respect to Act", Says T. R.

SYRACUSE, May 7.—Theodore Roosevelt, after learning details of the sinking of the Lusitania, late to-night, made this statement:

This represents not merely piracy, but piracy on a vaster scale of murder than any old-time pirate ever practiced. This is the warfare which destroyed Louvain and Dinant and hundreds of men, women and children in Belgium.

It is warfare against innocent men, women and children, traveling on the ocean and against our own fellow countrymen and countrywomen, who are among the sufferers.

It seems inconceivable that we can refrain from taking action in this matter, for we owe it not only to humanity, but to our own national self-respect.

Lusitania's Full Passenger List

The following is a list of the first cabin passengers aboard the Lusitania:

ADAMS, Mr. and Mrs. Henry, Boston; Adams, A. H., New York; Adams, W. McM., New York; Allan, Lady, and maid, Montreal; Allan, Miss Anna, Montreal; Allan, Miss Gwen, and maid, Montreal; Alles, N. N., New York; Ayala, Julian de, Cuban Consul General at Liverpool.

BAKER, James, England; Baker, Miss M. A., New York; Barnes, Mr.; Bartlett, Mr. and Mrs. G. W. B., London; Bates, Lindon, Jr.; Battersby, J. J., Stockport, Eng.; Bernard, Oliver, Boston; Bernard, C. P., New York; Bilicke, Mr. and Mrs. Albert C., Los Angeles; Baldwin, Mr. and Mrs. H. B.; Bistis, Leonidas, Atlanta, Ga.; Black, J. J., New York; Bloomfield, Thomas, New York; Bohan, James, Toronto, Can.; Boulton, H., Jr., London; Bowring, Charles W.; Braithwaite, Miss Dorothy, Montreal, Can.; Brandell, Miss Josephine, New York; Brodrick, C. T., Boston; Brodrick-Cloete, W., San Antonio, Tex.; Brooks, J. H., New York; Brown, Mrs. M. C., New York; Bruno, Mr. and Mrs. H. A., Montclair, N. J.; Burnside, Mrs. J. S., and maid, New York; Burnside, Miss Ivis, New York; Byington, A. J., London; Byrne, Michael G., New York; Buswell, P.; Brown, H. H.; Burgess, Henry G.

CAMPBELL-JOHNSTON, Mr. and Mrs. Conway S., London; Campbell, Alexander, London; Chabot, D. L., Montreal, Can.; Chapman, Mrs. W., Toronto, Can.; Charles, J. H., Toronto, Can.; Charles, Miss Doris, Toronto, Can.; Clarke, Rev. Cowley, London; Clarke, A. R., Toronto, Can.; Colebrook, H. G., Toronto, Can.; Conner, Miss Dorothy, New York; Copping, Mr. and Mrs. George R., Toronto, Can.; Crichton, Mrs. William, New York; Crompton, Mr. and Mrs. Paul, infant and nurse, Master Stephen, Master John, Master Romelly, Miss Alberta and Miss Catherine, Philadelphia; Crooks, Robert W., Toronto, Can.; Cross, A. B., F. M. States.

DALY, H. M.; Dearbergh, R. E., New York; Depage, Mrs. A., New York; Dingwall, C. A., Chicago; Dougall, Miss C., Quebec, Can.; Drake, Audley, Detroit; Dredge, Mr. and Mrs. Alan, New York; Dunsmuir, James, Toronto, Can.

EMOND, W. A., Quebec, Can.

FENWICK, John, Switzerland; Fisher, Dr. Howard, New York; Forman, Justus M., New York; Fowles, Mr. and Mrs. Charles, New York; Freeman, Richard R., Jr., Boston; Friedenstein, J., London; Friend, Edwin W., Farmington, Conn.; Frohman, Charles, and valet, New York.

GAUNTLETT, Fred J., New York; Gibson, Mathew; Gilpin, G. A., England; Gorer, Edgar, New York; Grab, Oscar F.; Grant, Mr. and Mrs. Montagu T., Chicago.

HAMMOND, Mr. and Mrs. Frederick S., Toronto, Can.; Hammond, Mr. and Mrs. O. H., New York; Hardwick, C. C., New York; Harper, J. H.; Harris, Dwight C., New York; Hawkins, F. W., Chicago; Hill, C. T., London; Hodges, Mr. and Mrs. William S., and Masters W. S., Jr., and Dean W., Philadelphia; Holt, Master W. R. G., Montreal, Can.; Home, Thomas, New York; Houghston, Dr. J. T.; Hubbard, Mr. and Mrs. Elbert, East Aurora, N. Y.; Hutchinson, Miss P., Orange, N. J.

JEFFERY, C. T., Chicago; Jenkins, Francis B.; Jolivet, Miss Rita; Jones, Miss, New York.

KEEBLE, Mr. and Mrs. W., Toronto, Can.; Kellett, Francis C., Toronto, Can.; Kempson, M., Toronto, Can.; Kenan, Dr. Owen, New York; Kennedy, Mrs. C. Hickson and Miss Katheryn, New York; Keser, Harry J., Philadelphia; Mrs. Keser, Toronto, Can.; King, T. B., New York; Klein, Charles, New York; Knight, Harwood C., and Miss Elaine H., Baltimore; Knox, S. M., Philadelphia.

LANE, Sir Hugh, England; Lassetter, Mrs. H. B., London; Lassetter, F., London; Lauriat, Mrs. Charles E., Jr., London; Learoyd, Mr. and Mrs. C. A., and maid, Sydney, Aus.; Leary, Mrs. James, New York; Leigh, Evan A., Liverpool; Lehmann, Isaac; Levinson, Joseph, J.; Letts, Gerald A., New York; Lewin, F. Guy; Lobb, Mrs. Popham, New York; Lockhart, R. R., Toronto, Can.; Loney, Mr. and Mrs. A. D., and maid, and Miss Loney, New York; Luck, Mrs. A. C., Masters Eldridge C. and Kenneth T., Worcester, Mass.

M'CONNEL, John W., Memphis, Tenn.; McLean, Walter, New York; MacLennan, F. E., New York; McMurray, L., Toronto, Can.; McMurtry, Fred A., New York; Macdona, Mrs. Henry D., New York; Mackworth, Lady, Cardiff, Wales; Mason, Mr. and Mrs. Stewart S., Boston; Mathews, A. T., Montreal Can.; Maturin, Rev. Basil W., Oxford, Eng.; Maurice, George, Toronto, Can.; Medbury, M. B., New York; Miller, Capt. J. B.; Mills, C. V., New York; Mitchell, James D., Philadel-

(Continued on Page 4, Column 2.)

STOCKS SACRIFICED IN AVALANCHE OF SALES

600,000 Shares Change Hands in One Hour of Riotous Trading.

Under an avalanche of selling orders following confirmation of the report of the sinking of the Lusitania, prices in the New York Stock Exchange collapsed yesterday afternoon.

For a time a condition approaching panic prevailed, the excitement equaling in intensity that reported on July 30 last, when values went to pieces on the rush of foreign and domestic liquidation incident to the declaration of war abroad.

And in the last hour of trading, when the downward movement was at its wildest, more shares changed hands than ever before recorded for a single hour in the history of the Stock Exchange, a total in excess of 600,000 shares being reported, with a total for the day of more than 1,100,000.

Prices for a time literally crumbled. Selling was in such volume that in the general list declines of from 10 to 15 points were made, with even greater losses in some of the specialties, as, for instance, Bethlehem Steel, which dropped 29 points from a new high record at 159, and Westinghouse Electric, which went down with a crash to a maximum loss of 21 points.

Enormous Total of Losses.

It was a repetition of the wave of heavy business that swept over the Stock Exchange on April 19, but on that day it was a chorus of hope that brought record breaking operations. It was something akin to despair yesterday that drove holders of margined stocks into the market. Their losses in the issues which recently had been such prominent factors in the upward course of prices aggregated an enormous total.

Liquidation came chiefly from the 100 and 200 share lot bulls, while much of the buying came from the shorts, the latter exercising their best talents to force sales in all parts of the industrial and railroad list.

In the first few minutes of trading following the Lusitania news the market moved as if the future of our international commerce depended upon the fate of this single vessel.

Buying orders for all classes of stocks were quickly canceled by those operators in close touch with the Stock Exchange and, when a flood of selling orders appeared on the receipt at out-of-town points of wire advices regarding the first break in prices there was practically no market in which to sell. Stocks were simply sacrificed.

Leading industrials, tractions and railway stocks shared in a proportionate extent with the so-called war issues, but the greatest losses naturally were sustained by those stocks which had been marked up to extreme high levels because of war contracts and near-war contracts. Brokers having orders to execute paid little attention to prices. For a few minutes almost any price was accepted.

Rally at the Close.

Toward the close the market apparently recovered its reason. In the late dealings heavy buying came from bargain hunters and from interests which refused to believe the intrinsic worth of American securities had been weakened by the loss of the Lusitania, and, in consequence, a rally developed that left last prices far above the low levels.

A governor of the Stock Exchange said:

"Earning power of American corpora-

(Continued on Page 2, Column 7.)

Out of Total of 2,067 Passengers and Crew Only 500 or 600 Known to Be Safe.

GOES DOWN IN 21 MINUTES

Official Reports Say Many Wounded Were Sent to Naval and Military Hospital.

A. G. VANDERBILT REPORTED LOST

Charles Frohman, Charles Klein, Linden Bates, Elbert Hubard and Justus Miles Forman Among Those on Board.

LONDON, May 8—(4.42 A. M.).—The Times's Queenstown correspondent says that some of the survivors who have arrived there report that Alfred Gwynne Vanderbilt was drowned.

The American Ambassador cabled to Washington last night that approximately 700 had been saved.

LONDON, May 8.—With a loss of life estimated variously from 500 to 1,500, the great Cunard liner Lusitania, one of the fastest ships afloat, was torpedoed off the Old Head of Kinsale, Ireland, yesterday afternoon by a German submarine. She sank in twenty-one minutes, after ten of her boats had been swung outboard and loaded with passengers.

Captain W. T. Turner is known to have been saved and landed at Queenstown.

Aboard were 188 Americans, among them men known all over the world. Alfred Gwynne Vanderbilt, Charles Frohman, the theatrical manager; Charles Klein, the playwright, and Elbert Hubbard, the author, probably were the best known among these.

A meagre list of survivors was given out by the Cunard officials to-night. It follows:

George A. Kessler, head of George A. Kessler & Co., importers of wines, with offices at No. 20 Beaver street, Robert Rankin, Samuel Sharp, M. G. Byrne, Miss R Martin, F. J. Gautlett, Miss Loney, John Herris, Miss Holland, Miss Jospehine Brandell, F. K. A. Perry, O. H. Gab, G. G. Mosley, J. H. Broks, A. M. Jeffry, M. Cairns, O. H. Hammond of N. Y. ;Jessie Taft Smith of Braceville, O.; Mrs H. B. Lassetter, wife of General Lassetter, and her son, P. Lassetter, of London; Mr. and Mrs. Cyril Bretherton and their children—Paul, 1, and Elizabeth, 3—of Los Angeles; Irene Payntor of Liverpool and Charles E. Lauriat, Jr., of Boston.

In a calm sea and under a tranquil sky the huge liner, which left New York last Saturday with 1,251 passengers and 816 officers and crew and was due in Liverpool yesterday, was sent to the bottom almost in the twinkling of an eye.

Weather conditions aided in the work of rescue, but the suddenness with which the liner plunged to the bottom of St. George's Channel made it impossible to get off all on board. A steward in the first boat landed at Queenstown said he estimated 900 lives were lost.

TWO TORPEDOES FIRED AT LINER.

Two torpedoes were fired at the Lusitania by the German undersea boat. Passengers were at lunch, and officers, though maintaining the constant vigilance which marked the voyage across, were unaware of danger.

Suddenly the periscope of the lurking submarine broke the smooth surface of the water. Before the commander of the liner, Captain W. T. Turner, could take any action to save his vessel the two torpedoes had been launched at her.

Both took effect, opening great, gaping wounds through which the water rushed in volumes. As the passengers, hastily quitting their meal, tumbled up on deck, shouting that the crisis all had feared and expected had come, Captain Turner set in motion wireless messages for aid and then directed that the utmost haste be made in getting out the boats.

Many of the boats and rafts could not be launched, however. The motorboat Elizabeth, which picked up seventy-nine survivors and then transferred them to a tug

PRICE---Within 25 Miles of City Hall---ONE CENT

WEATHER TO-DAY:
Showers; moderate winds.
Full Report Page 2.

The New York Press

The Press so presents the news that the busy man can read it in the time he has for his morning newspaper.

VOL. XXVIII—WHOLE NO. 10,077 | NEW YORK, SUNDAY, JULY 4, 1915—TWENTY PAGES. | PRICE { ONE CENT within twenty-five miles of City Hall Park; TWO CENTS everywhere else.

CORNELL TEACHER SHOOTS J. P. MORGAN; CONFESSES ATTEMPT TO BLOW UP CAPITOL

Morgan's Assailant in Hands of Constables

Copyright, Underwood & Underwood.
THEODORE CAMPBELL, Constable. — FRANK HOLT. — FRANK MAC CAHILL, Constable.
The picture shows the bandage over the wound made in Holt's head when he was overpowered after the shooting.

Banker Hit in Leg and Severely Wounded in Groin, but Doctors Call His Condition "Excellent."

MRS. MORGAN TRIED TO SAVE HIM

Assailant Tells in Jail How He Set Off Dynamite with Sulphuric Acid in Washington, Then Caught Train Here.

J. P. Morgan was shot twice and seriously wounded yesterday by Frank Holt, a university instructor and German sympathizer, who forced his way into the Morgan summer home near Glen Cove, L. I., carrying two revolvers and a stick of dynamite, when the banker was at breakfast with a party of guests, including Sir Cecil Spring-Rice, the British Ambassador.

Holt confessed last night to Captain Thomas Tunney of the New York Detective Bureau and to Justice of the Peace William E. Luyster that he is the man who set the infernal machine that exploded in the Capitol in Washington Friday night.

Morgan's wounds are considered serious, although a bulletin issued by the physicians in attendance last evening says the wounds did not involve any vital organ. The banker, by latest reports, was resting easily.

Holt asserted that his purpose in going to the Morgan home was to ask the banker, as head of the firm which is the commercial agent in this country for the allies, to put a stop to the shipment of arms and munitions. He insisted that he did not intend to injure the banker.

The encounter between Morgan and his assailant took place at the head of the stairway on the second floor, after Morgan had been warned of his danger by Henry Physick, the butler. Mrs. Morgan threw herself between her husband and Holt, but Morgan quickly pushed her aside just as Holt fired one shot from each revolver.

ONE OF THE BULLETS REMOVED.

One bullet went through Morgan's right leg in the groin. The other entered the right quadrant of the abdomen and lodged near the base of the spine. It was removed several hours afterward by an operation.

Holt was arraigned before Justice Luyster and pleaded not guilty to a charge of assault with intent to kill. He was locked up last night in the Nassau County jail in Mineola.

He was an instructor in German in Columbia University during the last academic year and had accepted a position as professor of French in the Southwestern Methodist University in Dallas, Tex., to take effect next fall.

Holt's own admissions, together with the evidence developed so far by the Glen Cove and New York authorities, show that the attack on Morgan was planned far ahead and with great care. The would-be assassin had familiarized himself with the names of the members of the Morgan family, as was shown by a slip of paper found in his pocket, and he knew the names of all the twenty or more servants on the big estate.

Holt has been seen loitering about Glen Cove for the past two weeks at different times. Last Thursday he walked into the grounds and made a careful survey of the property. Between visits to Glen Cove he made his headquarters in Mills Hotel No. 2, at Thirty-sixth street and Seventh avenue. The clerks there did not remember seeing him on Friday, when the police say he was in Washington.

Carrying a suit case containing sticks of dynamite and many cartridges, Holt took a train for Glen Cove from the Pennsylvania Station at 7.50 o'clock yesterday morning, arriving at Glen Cove at 8.53 o'clock. He hired an automobile from Milton Fred Ford, a garage owner in the village, and gave orders to be taken to the Morgan home, which is about three and one-half miles from the Glen street station.

DRIVER SUSPECTED NO WRONG.

Ford drove the car. He remarked afterward that his fare was a "long, gawky-looking boob," but he suspected nothing wrong. On the way down to the shore the stranger asked several questions about the Morgan household. The automobile fetched up at the Morgan estate about 9.25 o'clock.

The Morgan home stands on a high rise of ground facing the Sound. East Island is separated from the mainland of Long Island by a narrow bridge at the entrance to which is posted a sign warning strangers not to enter. Holt, however, got into the grounds and passed the house of Superintendent McGregor without being challenged.

Leaving his suit case in the automobile, Holt walked to the door and rang. Physick, the butler, responded.

"I want to see Mr. Morgan," said Holt somewhat excitedly.

"What is your business?" the butler demanded. Holt drew

KAISER'S SON GETS A REPULSE; FRENCH GENERAL WOUNDED

Crown Prince, Pushing Drive for Verdun, Has to Yield Ground in Vosges.

GOURAND HAS TO RETIRE

Succeeded at Dardanelles by General Baillond — Russian Armie sStill Retreating.

The German army in the Argonne region of France, under the command of the Crown Prince, with Verdun as its object, renewed its efforts yesterday to break through the French lines.

The Germans charged repeatedly, and with much determination, but each time were beaten back and their losses are reported by Paris to have been great.

The French are said to be using a deadly gas that is even more effective than that employed by the Kaiser's troops.

Berlin admits the Germans have been forced to yield the ground captured by them on the Hilgen ridge of the Vosges Mountains.

General H. J. E. Gouroud, commander of the French expeditionary force at the Dardanells, has been wounded, and is on his way to France. He received his injuries by the explosion of a shell which fell near an ambulance. An official announcement from Paris says the General's wounds are not dangerous.

General Bailloud, former commander of the French troops in Algeria, has taken Gouraud's place provisionally.

The allies continue their offensive in the Dardanelles, and the Turks assert they have beaten back the Anglo-French forces at every point with heavy losses.

It was reported again yesterday that the Germans are moving big forces from the eastern to the western front. The British in Flanders remain remarkably quiet, a fact which is regarded as an indication that an important movement on one side or the other will be made soon.

The armies of Emperor William an. Emperor Francis Joseph continue their impetuous drive against the forces of Emperor Nicholas along a front measuring approximately 150 miles in southern Russian Poland and in Galicia.

Te Austrians and Germans, says the German statement, have gained possession of the lowlands of Labunka, in the Russian Province of Lublin, despite stubborn resistance, and also have advanced in pursuit of the fleeing Russians in the Zlota Lipa section of Galicia.

Petrograd admits the retirement of the Russians across the Gnila, and explains that the Petrograde movement further to the north wes caused by strong flanking operations of the Austro-Germans against the Russian positions in the Tanew region, making them untenable. Russian military experts profess to believe that the Galician campaign now is ended.

In the Italian theatre of operations the Italians say they are making slow but steady gains, though the Austro-Hungarians are increasing their forces and the counter-attacks are said to be becoming more resolute. Unofficial reports say that Tolmino, on the Isonzo River, has been occupied by the Italians.

German submarine activity in the war zone drawn around the British Isles has accounted for five more British steamships and one Belgian vessel, aggregating 19,277 tons gross. The lives of all the members of the crews were saved before the ships were sent to the bottom by torpedoes or shell fire.

A Russian submarine in the Black Sea sank two Turkish steamships and a sailing ship, carrying provisions and coal, and later engaged and drove ashore three armed schooners near the mouth of the Bosphohus.

Berlin admitted yesterday that in the naval fight in the Baltic Sea the mine layer Albatross was run ashore

(Continued on Page 4, Column 3.)

HUERTA IS IN JAIL AFTER NEW ARREST UPON PLOT CHARGE

Ex-Dictator Unable to Get Bail on Accusation of Planning Revolt.

GENERAL OROZCO ESCAPES

Fighter Eludes Six Guards Around His House in El Paso.

EL PASO, July 3.—General Victoriano Huerta, ex-dictator of Mexico, was rearrested here to-day on a Federal warrant issued at San Antonio, charging conspiracy to violate the neutrality laws of the United States by attempting to launch a revolutionary movement in Mexico.

Huerta and five arrested with him failed to secure bonws, and shortly after 5 o'clock were taken to the county jail. A military guard was stationed around the building.

General Huerta is already under $7,500 bail to appear July 12 to answer charges of violating the United States neutrality laws.

Another sensation to-day was the escape of General Pascual Orozco from his house here while six men were guarding it. He is believed to have jumped from a window into the surrounding shrubbery and fled in a moto- car. Juarez is believed to be his destination once he gets over the border. Orozco was under bail to appear at the Huerta hearing July 12.

General Caus J. B. Ratner and Enrique Gorostita were among those arrested to-day. Ratner is confidential associate and interpreter, and Gorostita is a secretary to General Huerta.

Think Case Against Huerta Strong.

WASHINGTON, July 3.— United States Attorney Camp. at San Antonio, has been ordered to El Paso by Attorney General Gregory to take personal charge of the Government's case against General Huerta. The Administration has decided to prosecute Huerta for conspiracy to incite a revolution against a friendly nation.

For the present no effort will be made to deport him as an undesirable alien. If a conviction is not returned, recourse may be had to the immigration laws. Officials here feel the case against Huerta is strong.

Carranza Asks for Huerta.

An application to the United States for formal extradition of Huerta, Felix Diaz, Manuel Mondragon and Areliano Blanquet has been filed with Secretary of State Lansing by Eliseo Arredondo, confidential agent for Carranza.

The application asserts the men are planning another revolution, and asks that they be detained and be sent back to Mexico for trial.

Eliseo Arredondo, General Carranza's agent here, said to-day he based the request for extradition of Huerta and the other Mexican exiles principally on the deaths of President Madero and Vice President Suarez.

General Villa also has asked for the extradition of Huerta in proceedings between the Governor of Chihuahua and the Governor of Texas.

Investigate Orozco Escape.

A rigid investigation of the circumstances surrounding the escape of Pascual Orozco from the surveillance of Government agents at El Paso was ordered to-day by the Department of Justice.

A message to the Carranza agency here received late to-day from the border said General Orozco was at Valentine, Texas, not far from Marfa, Mexico. He intended to cross into Mexico tomorrow, the message said.

LETTER CARRIER INJURED.

Henry Simmons, 71, of No. 160 Bleecker street, a letter carrier, fell on his head from a United States parcels post wagon yesterday at First avenue and Forty-second street. He was unconscious when taken to Flower Hospital. After being revived he was taken home.

MEAD SONS GET $100,000.

The will of Mrs. Lemoine C. Mead, who died June 29 in New Rochelle, leaving an estate of about $100,000, was filed for probate yesterday. The entire estate goes to three sons, John, George and William Walworth, all of New Rochelle.

GIRL'S ANNOYER IS WARNED.

Edward Uher, 17 years old, a student, of No. 305 East Sixty-ninth street, was put on probation for a year by Magistrate House in Yorkville Court yesterday after he had been found guilty of annoying girls in the monkey house in Central Park.

FALL KILLS IRONWORKER.

NEWARK, July 3.—William Heybrook of No. 405 Steinway avenue, Long Island City, an ironworker, fell twenty feet from the new Public Service Railway power house at Point No Point to-day and was killed.

OSBORNE DEFIES FOES, WON'T QUIT SING SING

In Lewisohn's Home, Pleads for Support of Prison Reformers.

Thomas Mott Osborne, Warden of Sing Sing Prison, told the members of the National Committee on Prisons and Prison Labor at the country home of Adolph Lewisohn yesterday afternoon that he has absolutely no intention of resigning as a result of friction with John B. Riley, Superintendent of Prisons:

"I knew I would have to fight for my official life when I took this job," said Osborne, "but I am ready, and the fight is on. I know I have the prisoners behind me.

"I will not resign. I am going to fight. I want you to try and get public opinion back of me to combat the political influence."

Osborne admitted that there was "some truth" in the stories of a near riot at Sing Sing Thursday.

This Fellow Is Crazy, Is Thaw's Comment

Prisoner Is Served with Attachment in Yonkers Lawyer's Fight for $50 Fee.

As Harry K. Thaw was about to demonstrate his prowess as a handball player in Ludlow Street Jail yesterday afternoon he was served with an attachment growing out of a judgment for $50 obtained in the Westchester County Court by William Riley, a Yonkers lawyer. Thaw read the paper carefully and then exclaimed:

"Why, this fellow is crazy!"

Riley alleges that Thaw wrote to him in 1914 asking for an opinion regarding a statement made by Thomas Carmody, Attorney General, and printed in the newspapers. Carmody was quoted as saying that "Thaw is at liberty because his money has triumphed above law." Thaw wrote that he thought this reflected upon a decision which Justice Aldrich was then preparing, and asked Riley, the latter says, what he thought about it.

Riley replied that he thought so, too, and that Carmody was not justified in saying it—and then sent Thaw a bill for $50, to which, he said, Thaw paid no attention.

YACHT CLUB MEMBERS SEE DEATH AND RESCUE

Youth Almost Drowns in Hudson Trying Vainly to Save Best Friend.

Near enough for the smartly gowned women and idling men on the balcony of the clubhouse to see every detail of the tragedy, Frederick W. Dobbeling drowned last evening and Charles Schum all but gave his life trying to save his best friend before the eyes of fellow members of the Hudson River Yacht Club, at Ninety-first street and North River.

Dobbeling was an artist, 28 years old. He lived in No. 304 West Ninety-second street.

Schum is a clerk, 20 years old, and lives in No. 422 West 144th street.

Dobbeling owned an automobile boat, and yesterday afternoon they went swimming from the boat near the club.

Soon a cry for help was heard, and Schum was seen swimming to Dobbeling's aid. Dobbeling seized him, both went down, and Schum a little later was seen to rise alone.

John Carlson rescued Schum. He will recover.

Dobbeling's body was recovered and given to his father, William Dobbeling, a retired contractor.

The price of this newspaper is One Cent in New York City and within twenty-five miles of City Hall. Beyond the twenty-five-mile circuit the price is Two Cents, the same as the weekday issues. Purchasers of The Press, either weekday or Sunday issues, should not pay more.

FRANK A. MUNSEY.

Morgan's Wife Tried to Shield Banker from Assassin's Attack

out a card on which was printed "The Summer Society for Recreation, represented by Thomas S. Lester."

"I am an old friend of Mr. Morgan," he assured Physick.

"Just wait here and I'll ask if Mr. Morgan will see you," the butler responded.

"I must see him at once," insisted Holt.

"You can't see him now."

"Yes, I can, too."

Holt's right hand flashed out, holding a .38 Iver Johnson revolver. He pressed the barrel against the butler's stomach, and without another word walked into the large hallway.

Physick staggered beside the intruder, pretending to be overcome with fright. He thought rapidly.

"Mr. Morgan is in the library," he said, pointing to the curtained doorway at the right side of the hall. Holt ran in the direction indicated, and at the same time the butler rushed to the door of he breakfast room, where Morgan, Mrs. Morgan and several of their guests sat at breakfast.

Warned to Hurry Up Stairs.

"Up stairs, Mr. Morgan, up stairs!" the butler called. There was no mistaking the note of alarm in his voice. Morgan jumped up from the table and, followed by Mrs. Morgan, ran up a stairway in the back of the hall to the second floor. Rosalie McCabe, a nurse, met them at the head of the stairs.

Morgan, not knowing what was wrong, ran from room to room, thinking something had happened up stairs. Meanwhile Holt, having heard the butler's warning cry, ran back into the hall and up the main staircase.

Morgan emerged into the upper hallway just as Holt was reaching the top landing. Holt pulled out a revolver from each coat pocket.

"I've got you, Mr. Morgan; I've got you!" he exclaimed.

As Holt reached the top stair Mrs. Morga nthrew herself on him. An instant later Morgan pushed her aside and grappled with the intruder. At the same time both revolvers went off.

Morgan hurled his full weight against Holt and bore him bodily to the floor. Mrs. Morgan seized one of the intruder's hands and wrenched away the revolver, while Miss McCabe tore away the other. Physick, who had alarmed the other servants, came back just then and hit Holt on the forehead with a huge chunk of coal. Holt collapsed.

Workmen on Estate Summoned.

Ford, who had seen the stranger pull his revolver on the butler, had aroused the superintendent and some of the workmen on the estate. Deputy Sheriff Frank E. McCahill, in Glen Cove, was telephoned for and the county authorities in Mineola notified.

Neither Mrs. Morgan nor any one in the house realized that Morgan was shot until the banker, picking himself up from the floor, calmly walked to a telephone and called up Dr. William H. Zabriskie in Glen Cove, and asked him to come at once to the house.

"I've been hurt—I'm shot," Morgan said over the telephone. Dr. Zabriskie hurried to the house in an automobile and dressed the banker's wounds. Dr. J. M. Markoe of New York city, a friend of Morgan's, and Dr. H. N. N. Lyle, head physician in St. Luke's Hospital, were also summoned. They were taken to East Island in a swift steam-yacht belonging to Hanry P. Davidson, a member of the Morgan firm, who is now in London.

McCahill took Holt over to Glen Cove in an automobile and locked him up in the town jail. Meanwhile Morgan, having been put to bed, had a telephone placed at his bedside and proceeded to reassure his friends and relatives that he was not seroiusly hurt. He first called up his mother, Mrs. J. Pierpont Morgan, in Utica, and told her she would hear reports about his being shot, but not to worry. He also called up William H. Porter, a member of the firm of J. P. Morgan & Co. in the city, and gave similar reassuarances.

When Holt was taken into custody the Glen Cove police found a long stick of dynamite in his rear pocket. In the suitcase, which he had left in Ford's machine, they found two more sticks of dynamite and several boxes of cartridges. In his coat pocket were found several wads of newspaper clippings, consisting chiefly of letters letters written in German to editors of the metropolitan newspapers. There were several clippings of letters signed by himself.

Questioned for an Hour.

Holt at first refused to tell his name, but he soon became talkative. He was brought into Justice Luyster's chambers and questioned for nearly an hour.

"I fired to scare him," was Holt's first sentence. "They tell me I hit him. I hope he isn't badly hurt."

Soon Holt decided that he would write what he had to make public on the matter. He then prepared a statement addressed to Justice Luyster and intended for the newspapers. In this statement he repeated, to great extent, what he had told Mr. Luyster verbally.

Holt signed the communication "F. Holt, Dallas, Tev., and Ithaca." The statement reads as follows:

"My motive in coming here was to try to force Mr. Morgan to use his influence with the manufacturers of munitions in the United States and with the millionaires who are financing the war loans to have an embargo put on shipments of war munitions so ts to relieve the American people from complicity in the death of thousands of our European brothers.

"If Germany should be able to buy munitions here we would, of course, positively refuse to sell to her. The reason that the American people have not as yet stopped the shipments seems to be that we are getting rich out of this traffic; but do we not get enough prosperity out of non-contraband shipments, and would it not be better for us to make what money we can without causing the slaughter of thousands of Europeans?

"I am very sorry that I had to cause the Morgan family this unpleasantness, but I believe that if Mr. Morgan would put his shoulder to the wheel he could accomplish what I have endeavored to. Of course I did not want to injure Mr. Morgan, as I wanted him to do the work I could not do. I hope that he will do his share anyhow. We must stop our participation in the killing of Europeans and God will take care of the rest."

Home in Dallas, Texas.

"My home is in Dallas, Texas. I have a wife and children and am 40 years old. I was born in this country, and so were my father and mother. My ancestors were French and German; it wa sall mixed up. I received a degree of Doctor of Philosophy from Cornell in 1914, but before that I was an instructor in French. I was formerly an instructor in Vanderbilt University.

"I came to New York two weeks ago from Ithaca and put up at the Mills Hotel, at Thirty-sixth street and Seventh avenue. I took no pains to conceal my identity, and registered under my own name.

"About a month ago I conceived the idea to see J. P. Morgan and get him to use his influence in stopping the exportation of arms, which make you and I responsible for the murder which is going on over there.

"I could not go from manufacturer to manufacturer myself, but I thought that Mr. Morgan's banking connections would render it more easy for him to accomplish this.

"I have not been influenced to do this by anybody else. I think President Wilson's notes were fine, but they did not seem to do anytihng to stop the war."

Doctors Probe for Bullet.

While Holt was being questioned in the jail Drs. Lyle and Markoe were probing for the .38 calibre bullet which entered Morgan's abdomen. An operation was necessary to reach it, as it was lodged under the base of the spine. It was extracted about 2 o'clock in the afternoon.

At 3.30 o'clock the physicians issued this bulletin from Morgan's home:

"An examination of Mr. Morgan discloses that there are two bullet wounds in the region of his right hip. There are no unfavorable symptoms and he is resting easily. "H. M. LYLE,
"J. W. MARKOE."

Another statement was issued by the physicians at 6.1 o'clock, and it was said then that no more bulletins would be issued until to-day, as the condition of the patient did not make it necessary. The last bulletin was this:

"A further examination of Mr. Morgan's wounds shows that the bullets did not involve any vital organ. The condition of the patient continues excellent.

(Signed.) "J. W. MARKOE,
"H. H. W. LYLE,

"Time 6.15 p. m."

Justice Luyster, Charles R. Weeks, Assistant District Attorney of Nassau county; Charles N. Wysongs, former District Attorney, and Thomas S. Cheshire, the county clerk, went in an automobile to the Morgan home at 2 o'clock an dtook affidavits concerning the shooting from the butler, from Miss McCabe and from Bernard Stuart, a valet. They returned about 4 o'clock and Justice Luyster had Holt brought into the small courtroom for arraignment.

Holt's sead was bandager and his hair clotted with blood. The coat of his decent gray suit in which he had gone to the Morgan home had been removed, ebing covered with blood, and one of the court attendants had given him a short blue office coat. He was collarless and looked the picture of repection and disarrangement.

Captain of Detectives Thomas Tunney of the New York police and Justice Luyster, after Holt's arraignment, put him through a "third degree" which resulted in his confession that he had set the bomb in the Capitol Friday night. He asserted that his infernal machine would set a new mark in police annals.

Tunney, at the direction of Arthur Woods, Police Commissioner, also sought to learn whether Holt was the man who placed the bomb in front of the home of Andrew Carnegie last week. Holt denied that charge.

In a statement made to Justice Luyster and Captain Tunney, head of the bomb and Anarchist squad of the New York City Detective Bureau, Holt confessed setting the bomb and described it in detail. As a missile of terror, it was said to be unique in the annals of the New York Police Departmentn.

"I made this bomb," Holt is quoted as having said in his confession, "with three sticks of dynamite, some match heads and a bottle of sulphuric acid."

"Pretty slick," commented Captain Tunney. "I don't see how you did it."

"Well, you see," Holt answered, his eyes brightening, "I had experimented on it before. Not once, you know, but many times. I knew just what I was doing and just how to do it. I really didn't take any chances, for all my observations had been checked up and I knew when the bomb would go off, almost to the minute. In fact, I waited in Washington till I heard it go off. Then I hurried away as afst as I could and caught the train for New York. I didn't have much time, so I had to hurry."

"How did you make the bomb?" he was asked.

Acid Ate to Match Heads.

"Well," he answered, "I took three sticks of dynamite and bound them together. Then I took my knife and hollowed out a place in one of the sticks. When I had cleaned it out deep enough I put some match heads inte the hole—three or four, I don't know exactly how many.

"When the match heads were put in the hole I the hole I took a little bottle of sulphuric acid out of my pocket and put a regaltr cork in the neck. I turned the bottle upside down and fastened the cork in the hole in the dynamite, just above the match heads. You see I had timed the sulphuric acid in my tests before, and I knew just how long it would take to eat through the cork and get to the match heads.

"When the acid reached the match heads it set them on fire and caused the explosion. There wasn't any guesswork about it. I knew how much time I had, so I hung around while the acid was eating its way through the cork. I pulled out my watch and said to myself that it ought to be going pretty soon, and sure enough it did go pretty soon. Then I hurried away."

Holt's confession of the Capitol outrage came fast on the heels of his denial to newspaper men of the same charge. Reporters told him the story from Washington, calling his attention to the marked similarity in the language used by him in hs statement and that of the letter relating to the bomb in Washington.

"Don't you know anything about this?" they asked him.

"No, I don't," he asserted. "I wasn't in Washington yesterday at all. I was in New York. I had my breakfast and my luncheon at the Mills Hotel, at Thirty-sixth street and Seventh avenue. So you see I couldn't have been in Washington."

"What were you doing all day?"

Told of Walking Street.

"I was walking around the streets in New York trying to make up my mind to come out here to-day and do my duty. That was all. I was thinking it over."

When Holt was told that the Mills Hotel clerks had not recalled seeing him there Friday he still stuck to his story.

"It does look strange, doesn't it?" he said, after reading the Washington story for the second time. "It seems that the man who did that thought about like I did, oo, doesn't it? It was rather odd that he usel almost the same words as I did. I can't explain it."

When the newspaper reporters left Justice Luyster and Captain Tunny began to question him. They soon obtained his confession, they asserted.

Captain Tunney intimated that so-called third-degree methods were employed when Holt denied the charge, and Justice Luyster said:

"We had to go after him good and strong before he would tell us what he knew."

According to Holt's confession, he went to Washington from New York Friday, arriving there about noon. He went to the Capitol during the afternoon and set the bomb at 4 o'clock. He had timed the explosion at midnight.

After setting the bomb he strolled about Washington for several hours. In the evening he went to the Union station, a short distance from the Capitol and waited several hours for the noise of the explosion, which he knew would soon occur.

"I had two or three sticks of dynamite left over that I didn't need on the Washington job," he explained, "so I brought them along to Glen Cove and intended to use them here if I had to."

"Why did you want to blow up the Capitol?" Captain Tunney asked him.

Explained All in Letter.

"Well,' Holt replied, "I thought that was a good way to bring the attention of the American people to the terrible murders being committed in Europe. But why do you ask me that for? I explained the whole thing in my letter to the editor of the Washington paper. I understand my letter was printed today. Well, my reasons are all in that letter."

PROMINENT MEN CALL.

Immediately after the first official announcement made by J. P. Morgan & Co. regarding the shooting—which was in substance that a man, presumably a crank, had at 9 o'clock visited the home of Mr. Morgan and shot him. The injuries not being serious—many of the most prominent men in the financial district hurried to the firm's offices to inquire as to the banker's condition and express regret.

One of the first to arrive were A. Barton Hepburn, chairman of the board of the Chase National Bank; Stephen Baker, president of the Bank of Manhattan Company; James Alexander, president of the National Bank of Commerce and Jerome J. Hamauer of Kurn, Loeb & Co. Many others called up on the telephone.

Captain Charles Lahey of the Old Slip police station, an acquaintance of Morgan, hurried to the banking house as soon as he had heard the story of the shooting and asked if his services were needed. Later Captain Lahey and several plain clothes men stationed themselves about the building.

There were only two members of the firm in the city when the news was received and one of them, Dwight W. Morrow, immediately went by motor to Glen Cove. William H. Porter, the other member, remained in town to receive reports.

MORGAN'S CAREER.

Has Been Head of Father's Firm Since 1907.

John Pierpont Morgan was born in this city in 1867, the son of the world-famous financier of the same name. He prepared in St. Paul's School and was graduated from Harvard with the degree of B. A. in 1889. Immediately on receiving his diploma he entered the house of Drexel, Morgan & Co., now J. P. Morgan & Co. In 1890 he married Jane Norton Grew.

To learn his father's business thoroughly, Morgan worked as loan clerk and later in the bonding and corresponding clerkships. He was with the firm six years before taken in as junior partner. He devoted most of his banking training to the international business and has become probably the most prominent banking individual in the world.

In 1901 he took charge of the London firm of J. Spencer Morgan & Co. Four years later he returned to America. In 1907 he took over the position of head of the firm of J. P. Morgan & Co. His father, however, dominated the company's activities until his death.

Director of Railroads.

Morgan, like his father, is director of many corporations, notably Astor Trust Company, Harlem River & Portchester Railroad, Hartford & Connecticut Western Railroad, International Mercantile Marine Company, Millbrook Company, National Bank of Commerce, National City Bank of New York, New England Navigation Company, New England Steamship Company, New York & Harlem Railroad, New York Central and Hudson River Railroad, New York, New Haven & Hartford Railroad, Northern Pacific Railway, United States Steel Corporation, West Shore Railroad, Western Union Telegraph Company.

His home is in No. 231 Madison avenue. He is a member of the Metropolitan, Union, University, Racquet and Tennis, The Brook, Harvard and New York Yacht Clubs and the Century Association.

He has four children, Junius Spencer, married recently; Jane Norton, Frances Tracy and Henry Sturgis.

Morgan Like His Father.

Morgan has many characteristics of his father, as well as certain physical resemblances. He has the same fearless and independent judgment, directness and finality of decision that marked the elder Morgan. He is affable, democratic and lacks much of the brusqueness which characterized his father.

Morgan is almost 6 feet in height, weighs 200 pounds, is broad of shoulder and firm in bearing. His broad forehead, facial lines, distinctive nose, firm jaws and strong mouth and deep-set eyes produce a strong likeness to his father.

Adverse criticism has been made here and in England of the arrangement by which the house of Morgan was selected as munitions agent for the British Government. American contractors for supplies have complained they were rivals of the Morgan firm in certain commercial lines. In Parliament it has been asserted that "one reason why more orders are not going to Canada is that the big shadow of an interloper stands between her and the Government."

J. P. Morgan; Man Who Shot Him

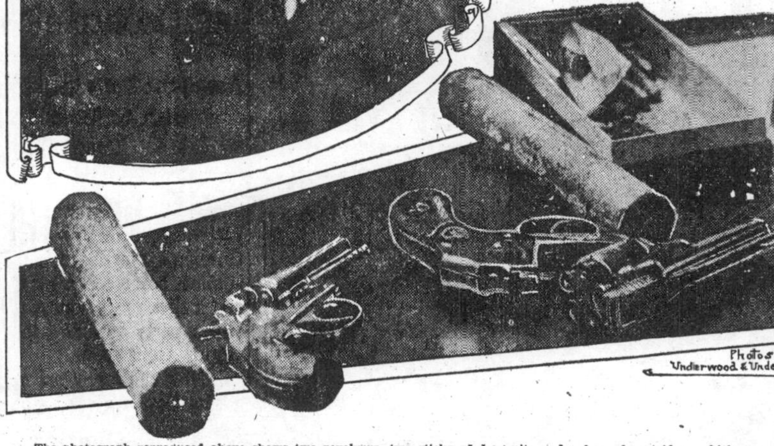

The photograph reproduced above shows two revolvers, two sticks of dynamite and a box of cartridges which were taken in connection with the attack upon Morgan. The revolvers were found in the pockets of the assassin. The dynamite and cartridges were in a dress suit case which belonged to Holt.

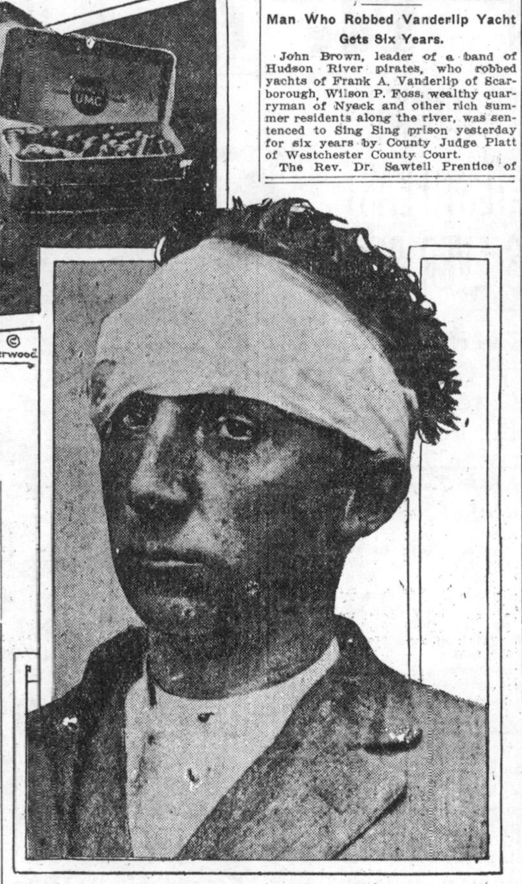

FRANK HOLT, WHO MADE THE MURDEROUS ATTACK UPON MORGAN.

Strong Parallel Between Bomb Note and Statement by Holt

STRIKING similarity between the letter to the Washington Times explaining the Capitol bomb and the statement made by the fanatic who shot J. Pierpont Morgan first led investigators to suspect that either there wa sa widespread plot or that the two deeds were committed by the same man.

Not only the reasoning, but even the phrases, were alike in each case. Excerpts show the startling parallel:

From the letter to the Washington Times:

1. "We would, of course, not sell to the Germans if they could buy here, and since, so far we sold only to the allies, neither side should object if we stopped."
2. "We want prosperity. Yes. But Europe needs enough non-contraband materials to give us prosperity."
3. " 'We will not be a party to this wholesale murder.' Would not that be national spirit? * * * Let us stop this colossal American crime."
4. "Are we also within the moral law, the law of peace, or of love, or of Christ, or whatever else a Christian nation may call it?"

From F. Holt's statement:

1. "If Germany should be able to buy munitions here we would, of course, positively refuse to sell to her."
2. "But do we not get enough prosperity out of non-contraband shipments and would it not be better for us to make what money we can without causing the slaughter of thousands of Europeans?"
3. "So as to relieve the American people from the complicity in the death of thousands of our European brothers."
4. "We must stop our participating in the killing of Europeans and God will take care of us."

PINNED IN WRECK AN HOUR

Two Men on Motor Hurt in Head-On Collision.

Pinned for more than half an hour in a mass of wreckage between two trolley cars, two men were seriously injured at Fifth avenue and Seventy-fourth street, Brooklyn, yesterday when an automobile truck crashed into a northbound car.

Theodore Miller of No. 3111 Canal street, Woodhaven, L. I., was driving the automobile, which belonged to the R. F. Stevens Milk Company of Third avenue and Bergen street, Brooklyn. John Irvine of No. 5410 Fifth avenue, Brooklyn, sat beside him. The machine was behind a southbound Fifth avenue trolley and when the car stopped at the corner of Seventy-fourth street Miller turned to the left to pass it. He ran his machine headlong into a northbound trolley.

Several companies of firemen worked an hour before they could release them. Both were taken to the Norwegian Hospital.

RIVER PIRATE SENTENCED.

Man Who Robbed Vanderlip Yacht Gets Six Years.

John Brown, leader of a band of Hudson River pirates, who robbed yachts of Frank A. Vanderlip of Scarborough, Wilson P. Foss, wealthy quarryman of Nyack and other rich summer residents along the river, was sentenced to Sing Sing prison yesterday for six years by County Judge Platt of Westchester County Court.

The Rev. Dr. Sawtell Prentice of Nyack, a brother-in-law of John D. Rockefeller, Jr., helped to bring about the capture of Brown's gang.

FIGHT BY BOY MILLIONAIRE

Father and Stepfather in Court. Lad Prefers Latter.

William Crossman Lee, only 11 years old and a millionaire, yesterday told Justice A. S. Tompkins in the Supreme Court, White Plains, during the hearing on a writ of habeas corpus, that he would rather remain with his stepfather, William Lee, than go to California with his father, William Mills, Jr., whom he has seen only once during his life.

The boy has inherited more than $1,500,000 from various sources. His mother, who died a short time ago, was originally the wife of Mills, but obtained a divorce from him and married lee. The boy then assumed his stepfather's name.

Mills maintained yesterday that he was financially able to care for his son. Justice Tomkins adjourned the hearing until next Saturday.

IN MEMORY OF A MONKEY.

Handsome Monument Put Up Over the Grave of Humphrey's Pet.

SUMMIT, N. J., July 3.—A handsome monument to the memory of Snookie, a pet monkey belonging to Mr. and Mrs. Frank E. Humphreys, was erected to-day over his grave on the Humphrey estate in Morris avenue, East Summit. The stone is a tall shaft of Vermont granite, with this inscription:

"In loving memory of Snookie, a Brazilian marmoset, died September 28, 1914."

Snookie's funeral was an event last fall. He was buried in a specially made rosewood casket and around his neck was tenderly placed a jeweled collar worth many hundreds of collars.

BOY OF 16 ENDS LIFE.

Police Say Youth Was Distracted by Family Quarrel Due to Drink.

Distracted, according to the Jersey City police, by a quarrel between his father and mother, Albert Harris, 16, shot himself dead yesterday afternoon in front of his home, No. 1684 Boulevard, Jersey City.

The police assert the father had been drinking and that the son had taken the part of his mother in the quarrel. The father ordered his son from the house, and he went out and bought a pistol, returned and shot himself.

LIBERTY BELL GOES WEST TO-MORROW

Revolutionary Relic to Make 10,000-Mile Trip to and from Panama Exposition.

IS ITS EIGHTH JOURNEY

Will Travel in Blaze of Light as It Passes Through Towns at Night.

PHILADELPHIA, July 3.—The Liberty Bell, precious relic of the American Revolution, will start Monday on its eighth and longest journey from Philadelphia since it was first hung in the old State House of the Province of Pennsylvania in 1752. It goes to the Panama-Pacific International Exposition, and before it is returned to its big glass case in Independence Hall next November or December it will have traveled more than 10,000 miles and will have been seen by millions of people.

On its journey to San Francisco the Liberty Bell special train will traverse Pennsylvania, Ohio, Indiana, Illinois, Iowa, Missouri, Kansas, Nebraska, Colorado, Wyoming, Utah, Idaho, Washington, Oregon and California.

Elaborate arrangements have been made for the journey, and everything that will aid in safeguarding the bell from injury has been done. Four policemen from the Philadelphia traffic squad will guard the relic until it is again returned to its home.

At sunrise on Monday workmen will remove the bell from its case and put it on the special hanger which will support it across the country. It will be wheeled on a truck into Independence Square, where patriotic exercises will be held.

At noon the First Brigade, Pennsylvania National Guard, will escort the bell to the West Philadelphia station of the Pennsylvania Railroad, where it will be hoisted on a special car. The First Troop, Philadelphia City Cavalry, which organization escorted George Washington on State functions in Philadelphia, will be the special escort of the bell. At 3 p. m. the bell train, with a party of twenty-six City Councilmen, will start on the journey.

Special Car for Bell.

The train will consist of a baggage car, diner, three sleepers, a special car for the reception of guests en route, and a car for the bell at the rear. This is a specially constructed flat car, with an iron railing at the sides and ends. American Flags will wave from staffs at each corner, and there will be other decorations in American colors.

Even cities traversed in the night will get a glimpse of the relic, a system of illumination having been devised which will throw a blaze of light on the bell as it passes through in the darkness.

Shock absorbers have been installed on the flat car to keep the bell from being jolted. The train crews will be specially picked for their carefulness in starting and stopping trains. The speed limits across the continent will be not less than eighteen miles an hour nor more than thirty-five miles. The schedule will be rigidly observed, so that crowds may not be kept waiting.

Another absolute rule the committee has made is that the bell will not under any circumstances be taken from the car. Many municipalities have been advised to build movable platforms the height of the flat car, with an incline at each end, so that children may go up one incline, pass the bell, touch it if they care to, and then pass down at the other end.

During stops booklets containing the history of the bell, cards with a picture of the relic and buttons, also containing a picture of the bell and the American Flag will be distributed to children. It will take hundreds of thousands of these souvenirs to supply the demand. To the Governors and Mayors the history of the bell in a small bound volume will be presented. Governors have been invited to journey with the bell through their respective States.

Take Own Motion Pictures.

The committee refused to make any concessions to motion picture concerns, virtually every such enterprise in the country having applied for the privilege of sending representatives on the trip. The committee, however, purchased a special motion picture machine for its own use. Pictures will be taken through the journey and films will be furnished to public schools without expense.

The train will arrive in San Francisco Friday night, July 16, and Saturday, July 17, will be Liberty Bell Day at the Exposition. Early in the morning the relic will be conveyed to its place in the Pennsylvania building of the Exposition grounds, where exercises will be held.

The bell will leave San Francisco in November and will return by the Southern route, through Los Angeles, San Diego, Arizona and Texas.

Sending the bell to the Western coast will cost the city of Philadelphia $75,000. The escorting committee of twenty-six Councilmen will pay its own expenses.

The first time the bell left Philadelphia was under different circumstances from those which caused the later pilgrimages from the "Cradle of Liberty." That was when the British army occupied the city of Philadelphia in 1777-1778 and George Washington, with his Continental army, spent the winter at Valley Forge. At the British approached the city in September the bell was taken hurriedly to Allentown, Pa., and was kept in the Zion Lutheran Church of that place until June, 1778, when it was returned to Philadelphia. Its subsequent journeys were:

1885—To the World's Industrial and Cotton Exposition, New Orleans.

1893—World's Columbian Exposition, Chicago.

1895—Cotton States and International Exposition, Atlanta.

1902—Charleston Exposition.

1903—Battle of Bunker Hill celebration, Boston.

1904—Louisiana Purchase Exposition, St. Louis.

LATEST EXTRA

The Evening World.

LATEST EXTRA

"Circulation Books Open to All."

"Circulation Books Open to All."

PRICE ONE CENT in Greater New York and Hudson County, N. J. TWO CENTS elsewhere.

NEW YORK, THURSDAY, AUGUST 30, 1917. 16 PAGES

PRICE ONE CENT in Greater New York and Hudson County, N. J. TWO CENTS elsewhere.

2,500,000 SEE GREAT PARADE OF N. Y. TROOPS OFF TO WAR

SOLDIERS' SEND-OFF DINNER PROVES THE GREATEST FEAST THE NATION HAS EVER SEEN

30,000 Dined and Entertained in Camp and Armory From Van Cortlandt Park to Garden City—Not a Hitch Mars the Festivities.

Evening World Send-Off Dinner Pronounced Unparalleled Success

After making a tour of all the encampments from Mineola to Sheepshead Bay, and from Van Cortlandt Park to Pelham, August Silz, Chairman of the Mayor's Committee of Business Men, said: "It is enough for me and the other members of the committee to hear from the commanders of the regiments that the dinner has been a huge success. For us it has been a duty which we felt we had to perform. If we have performed it as satisfactorily and as successfully as the scenes which we have witnessed indicate, we have reason to be pleased."

Said Mrs. Charles S. Whitman, wife of the Governor: "I am not in the habit of speaking for publication, but on this occasion I am anxious to be quoted. I want the public to know how really wonderful were the scenes that I witnessed."

Thirty thousand New York soldiers were guests last night at the great farewell dinner arranged in their honor under the auspices of the Mayor's Committee and The Evening World. It was a gorgeous success.

Probably never before in the history of the country has a dinner on such a gigantic scale been given for any purpose. The number of men served and the great area covered by the guests in field service made the undertaking one to stagger the imagination of ordinary caterers.

But it was New York's soldier boys who were being honored. They are soon to leave the city in which they have been quartered since the War Department's recent mobilization order. They are New York's favorite sons, and even the most difficult undertaking was easy when New York determined to pay them the honor that was their due; so the serving of the long-distance dinner was no obstacle for the Mayor's Committee and The Evening World.

30,000 MEN "FALL IN" PROMPTLY FOR FEAST.

So accurately had the schedule been arranged that promptly at 5.30 o'clock yesterday mess call sounded in thirty-two camps and armories. Thirty thousand men, making up the Twenty-seventh Division, United States Army, "fell in" with plates, cups, knives, forks and spoons, and with military promptness began filing past cook tents to be served with the big dinner.

This culinary feat would have been worthy of historic mention had it been performed with the thirty thousand diners assembled in one place. As a matter of fact, they were scattered over a territory more than twenty-five miles from end to end.

As an example of the difficulties in the way of success (which, by the way, proved not to be difficulties at all if the success which resulted be taken into consideration) the guests of the Mayor's Committee and The Evening World were at Van Cortlandt Park in the persons of the Seventy-first, Twenty-third and First Infantry, and Squadron A; at Pelham Bay Park the Third Infantry and the divisional ammunition train; at Garden City the One Hundred and Sixty-fifth Infantry. The other guests were

(Continued on Sixth Page.)

LAUD WILSON NOTE AS GIVING VIEWS OF ENTENTE ALLIES

British Newspapers Search for Superlatives in Which to Express Approval.

LONDON, Aug. 30.—British newspapers searched for adjectives and superlatives to-day in which to express admiration and complete approval of President Wilson's reply to the Pope. The only feeble note of difference with the President's doctrine was sounded in the Northcliffe newspapers. They agreed with every other feature of the reply except President Wilson's "acquittal of the German people from any responsibility for the war."

The Northcliffe editorials pointed out this was "incompatible" with the fact that the German people accepted the war enthusiastically and have given their support to it throughout, their representatives continually voting supplies and the press exulting "in the worst atrocities."

Every London newspaper except the Chronicle overlooked the significance of the President's phrase as to "selfish, exclusive, economic leagues." The Chronicle pointed out with evident satisfaction that the President, inferentially at least, had thus condemned the resolutions of the Paris Allied conference and incidentally demonstrated his independence.

GREAT PARADE MOVING DOWN FIFTH AVENUE

AMERICAN CAPTURED 30 GERMANS SINGLE HANDED

St. Louis Boy Who Fought With Foreign Legion at Verdun to Get War Cross.

PARIS, Aug. 30.—Allen, son of Richard Blount of St. Louis, who joined the Foreign Legion in April, has written to his father that he has been proposed for the War Cross with palm for taking thirty prisoners single-handed in the fighting at Verdun. He was wounded slightly in the hand.

Mr. Blount has considerably exceeded the expectations of his father, who said at the time of his boy's enlistment:

"I want my son to account for five Germans."

WILSON AND ROOT CONFER.

WASHINGTON, Aug. 30.—President Wilson again turned his attention to the situation in Russia at a conference to-day with Elihu Root, who headed the American Mission.

Mr. Root and other members of the Mission have been pressing the immediate necessity of material as well as moral assistance to the Provisional Government, and besides the recent $100,000,000 credit, other steps already have been taken toward that end. Further action may follow to-day's conference.

FRANCE TO TAX PROFITS ON WAR UP TO 80 PER CENT.

Also Urges Americans to Aid by Purchasing Their Luxuries From French Factories.

PARIS, Aug. 30.—France proposes to put the cost of the war on those best able to bear it by taxing war profits up to 80 per cent.

Minister of Finance Thierry made this announcement to-day in explaining France's scheme of financing the war. He added a special plea that Americans aid France by purchasing their luxuries from French factories, these industries yielding a large part of France's taxes.

"The French nation is well able to bear the larger share of war expenses. To date she has contributed $13,000,000,000. But this is hardly a fifth of the total war cost. New taxes will add a billion of State revenues to this.

President Gets Absolute Control in Trading With Enemy Act.

WASHINGTON, Aug. 30.—Because Secretaries McAdoo and Redfield could not agree on what powers would be conferred on them by the Trading With the Enemy act, now pending in Congress, the measure was amended to-day by the Senate Commerce Committee so that all powers would be placed with the President.

TEARS OF MOTHERS MINGLE WITH THE CHEERS AS 30,000 MARCH DOWN FIFTH AVE.

Seventh Regiment Sets Crowds Wild With Applause—Roosevelt Leads Ovation as Column Passes Stand—Many Women Faint.

[illegible] Fifth Avenue to say good-bye to the [illegible]gest War[illegible] of [illegible] York, now starting for the battlefields of F[illegible] way [illegible] the southern training camp, but it was more than tribute to the Twenty-seventh Division of the army. To-day brought to this city for the first time realization of what a serious job the nation has on its hands and the celebration was almost a rite.

Police officers who have seen all the great parades in the past quarter of a century say they never witnessed anything like Fifth Avenue during the parade to-day. In the first place the 26,000 odd former militiamen and the 4,000 members of the Coast Artillery and Coast Defense forces formed the largest military body that has ever marched through the streets of the city. And the crowd that viewed the parade was the largest that ever assembled in Fifth Avenue between One Hundred and Tenth Street and Washington Square.

Those who had anticipated that the young soldiers of New York would march down Fifth Avenue to the accompaniment of tumultuous cheering found themselves treated to a lesson in the psychology of crowds. There was an unexpected solemnity about to-day's affair.

The officers were cheered. Major Gen. John F. O'Ryan and his staff, at the head of the line, were greeted enthusiastically, but when the boys came along carrying their packs and their guns the cheering died away. There were too many in the crowds jamming the sidewalks who had personal interest in the soldiers passing by to permit the cheers and good-natured chaffing that generally characterizes a parade.

The strange silence of the crowds was puzzling until one trailed along with the parade for a time and observed what the spectators were doing. Every few feet there was a weeping woman—sometimes an elderly woman, sometimes a young woman, but always a weeping woman.

"There goes my boy," a woman would cry with a brave effort to voice the exultation she felt, and the boy would hear her and shoot a glance in her direction, and the woman would begin to cry and all the women around her would begin to weep, and all the men around her would pull out their handkerchiefs and mop their faces and eyes and pretend to be suffering from hay fever. With something like this happening every few seconds there wasn't much time for cheering.

TROOPS ARE CHEERED FROM THE SKYSCRAPERS.

It was not until the troops got away downtown among the skyscrapers that there was a great deal of cheering. The reception there was more impersonal. Tens of thousands of people in the windows of the towering buildings viewing the soldiers as a marching body and not as an aggregation of personalities applauded and waved flags, but even down there the weeping women had their influence on the crowds.

Kipling's comparison of the colonel's lady to Judy O'Grady held good to-day in at least one incident which was witnessed by thousands. As Col. Cornelius Vanderbilt, at the head of the Twenty-second Engineers, passed his home at No. 677 Fifth Avenue he smilingly saluted his wife, who was at a window with a party of friends.

A stout little woman on the sidewalk called "Eddie!" as the first privates of the engineers passed by and a bronzed youth nodded his head. Then the private's mother on the sidewalk and the Colonel's wife in the mansion window broke down and wept and were not ashamed.

The first really great demonstration of enthusiasm occurred as the head of the marching column reached the reviewing stand at the Union League Club at 11.20 o'clock. Gov. Whitman and Mayor Mitchel suddenly pushed ex-President Theodore Roosevelt to the front of the platform.

The Colonel took off his hat and emitted a yell that was heard a couple of blocks away. Then everybody joined in and the Colonel, plainly experiencing one of the happiest experiences of his crowded life, just naturally constituted himself cheer leader and whooped it up as each unit swept along.

ROOSEVELT IS ENTHUSIASTICALLY HAILED AS "TEDDY."

Gov. Whitman, Mayor Mitchel and Col. Roosevelt, with a police and military escort, moved from the Union League Club grandstand to the larger grand stand in front of the Public Library at noon. As the Colonel appeared in the van of the escorting party he was enthusiastically hailed

ALL MERCHANDISE ADVERTISED IN THE TRIBUNE IS *GUARANTEED*

New York Tribune

First to Last—the Truth: News - Editorials - Advertisements

WEATHER
Overcast and rising temperatures to-day; unsettled to-morrow; moderate south winds.
Full Report on Page 10

VOL. LXXVIII No. 26,350 [Copyright, 1919, New York Tribune Inc.] TUESDAY, JANUARY 7, 1919 * * * TWO CENTS {In Greater New York and within commuting distance | THREE CENTS Elsewhere

Roosevelt Dies Suddenly in Sleep; Nation Mourns Loss of Ex-President

Italians Hail Wilson As 'Apostle'

Turin, Last Stop on His Triumphal Tour Hears World Peace Plea

Great Ovations Stir President

Thousands Vainly Crowd to Kiss Hand of Executive; In Paris To-day

By Frederick Moore
New York Tribune Special Cable Service

(Copyright, 1919, New York Tribune Inc.)

TURIN, Jan. 6.—After an all-night ride, President Wilson and party arrived, at 9 o'clock this morning, at Turin, Northern Italy's most modern city, noted for its advanced political views.

The Mayor of Turin, in greeting the President, called him "the new apostle of liberty."

Despite the drizzling rain, great crowds stood thick in the streets behind the lines of soldiers. The Presidential procession, in closed motor cars and bearing Italian and American flags, traversed Via Roma and Via Garibaldi to the Palazzo di Cita, where, after receiving Turin's official welcome, the President appeared on the palace balcony, standing bareheaded in the rain, and briefly addressed the people packed in the small, open square before him.

He concluded his address with the Italian phrase, proclaimed so vigorously and clearly as to reach the walls of the majestic buildings incuosing the quaint open square, "Viva Italia!"

After lunch with several hundred of Turin's leading citizens at the San Carlo Philharmonic Hall, a private palace of great beauty, the Wilsons bade farewell to Italy this afternoon and started for Paris.

Doctrine of Brotherhood

With relentless energy President Wilson, in his pilgrimage through Italy, preached his doctrine of brotherhood among the peoples.

Speaking before great audiences, special delegations, small groups of supporters and individual statesmen, he declared to all that the old order of rival armaments must pass and a league of nations must be inaugurated.

In a pouring rain he drove through the streets of Genoa yesterday morning to make known at the Ducal Palace, which is now the City Hall, his project for world peace. He came as the prophet of the New World to the birthplace of Christopher Columbus, its discoverer, and was received with all the ancient ceremony of that city and with the customary acclamations and shouts of support for his new creed.

Not only the people and the newspapers acclaimed him, but the acclamations were displayed on the walls of the norrow streets, and wide-open places of the ancient Mediterranean city bristled with posters carrying such inscriptions as "Woodrow Wilson—Defender," "Wilson—Knight of Humanity," "Wilson—Leader of Liberty."

The royal train, bearing the President and his party, was greeted at every important station between Genoa and Milan by guards of honor, among whom British officers and American Red Cross workers were conspicuous.

Milan received him with a display only second to Rome's. The route from the station through the principal streets was lined with Italian veterans, behind whom were crowded masses of people.

Crowds Cheer President

In the great square before Milan's magnificent cathedral and royal palace a vast crowd assembled, including delegates of ancient and civic orders, carrying historical banners and making a mediæval picture against the gray walls of the cathedral and the palace. As an American travelling with the President said, it was one of the most inspirng scenes he had seen in Europe.

At Milan the President made the significant statement that the whole social structure of the world rested upon the working classes, and intimat-

Continued on page eleven

Wilson Will Return To Address Congress

PARIS, Jan. 6.—President Wilson will return to the United States to attend the closing sessions of the present Congress, leaving Europe about Feb. 12, and will come back to France for the later sittings of the peace congress, according to present plans.

The President not only intends to be in Washington before Congress closes, but to deliver several addresses concerning the settlement of the war and the establishment of a peace which it is hoped will be durable.

He is expected to return to France soon after March 4.

Deportations To Curb 'Red' Menace in U. S.

Nation-Wide Arrests Also Are Promised in Federal Crusade on Bolsheviki

Deportations and a series of nation-wide arrests to curb the growing menace of Bolshevism were promised yesterday by officials of the Department of Justice, who asserted that the "Reds" are more dangerous now to the safety of the country than the Teutonic propaganda and espionage rings were when the United States entered the war.

Evidence that the Bolshevik propaganda in this country is being financed by Lenine and Trotzky and that effort is being made to break up the American Federation of Labor, has been gathered by the Department of Justice. Special Attorney General Alfred L. Becker, who has been investigating enemy propaganda, said yesterday that a huge sum had been sent here from Russia for propaganda. This money went from Siberia to Japan and was later transferred to San Francisco. It is now being held by a man in New York who is suspected of being Trotzky's personal representative. Mr. Becker said he understood that about $400,000 had already been sent to America.

The I. W. W., various anarchist groups and radical Socialists have joined forces with the Bolsheviki, according to the Department of Justice. In addition they are said to be getting aid from the Socialist Labor party and the Workers' International Industrial Union, and are enlisting recruits from the radical elements in all labor organizations.

Two Bolshevik Organs

Department of Justice officials say the Bolsheviki have two official organs in this country devoted exclusively to the dissemination of "Red" propaganda —"The Novy Mir" in New York and "The Revolutionary Age," published at 885 Washington Street, Boston. Gregory Weinstein and Nicholas Horowitz edit "The Novy Mir" and the Boston paper is edited by Louis Frania. Among the contributing editors of "The Revolutionary Age" are John Reed, Edmond McAlpine, Gregory Weinstein, Nicholas Horowitz, Scott Nearing and Sautere Nuorteva, a Finn.

Tons of propaganda books designed to sway the masses to Bolshevism have been sent out. This propaganda is against the use of American soldiers in Russia. It attacks the Mooney prosecution and demands the immediate release of so-called political prisoners, among whom are Alexander Berkman, Emma Goldman and Roger Baldwin.

The Federal authorities, in pointing out the growing menace, say that they have files on more than 2,000 leaders and assert that there are more than half a million Bolsheviki or sympathizers in the New York district alone. They point out that the leaders are aliens and can be deported and that 85 per cent of the members are foreign born.

Meetings Held Nightly

"Meetings are being held every night, some in secret and some in public," said a high Federal official. "The highbrow radicals are doing everything in their power to have the espionage act repealed. They are the teachers, editors and professional pacifists who, when they saw their game beaten when we entered the war and defeated Germany, threw their strength to the Bolsheviki."

This official also said that the League for Amnesty of Political Prisoners and the Workers' Defence Union have been coöperating with the Bolsheviki. He said the New York Bolsheviki are divided into two classes, the Russian workers and the anarchists, and that they operate in five groups, which have been commissioned to form soviets in the shops and factories. So far this work has not been very satis-

Continued on page eight

Berlin at War With Red Russia

Diplomatic Hostilities Exist and Military Measures Are to Follow Soon

Spartacides Start Revolt in Germany

Radicals Seize Five Newspapers and Attempt to Operate Government

LONDON, Jan. 6.—Germany has taken diplomatic and is about to take military measures against the Bolshevik government of Russia, according to a German official statement received here by wireless to-day.

The message says:

"The advance of the Bolsheviki and the presence in Berlin of M. Radek (a Bolshevik emissary) have brought about a diplomatic state of war with Russia and a military state of war almost has intervened. Germany, faced with the necessity, not for the purpose of pleasing the Entente, but of protecting her own interests, must intervene energetically by taking diplomatic and military measures."

AMSTERDAM, Jan. 6.—There was an attempt at a coup d'état in Berlin yesterday, it is believed here, on the basis of advices from the German capital.

Attempt to Seize Power

The Spartacus group made an effort to seize the reins of power.

The offices of the "Tageblatt," "Vossische Zeitung," "Lokal Anzeiger," "Vorwaerts" and "Morgenpost" were occupied by the Spartacides, according to a telegram from Berlin. It is added that the newspapers will not appear Monday, with the exception of the "Vorwaerts," which will be issued by a committee of revolutionary workingmen.

The office of the Wolff Bureau has been closed by the Spartacides, and the news agency has ceased operations.

There had been intimations that an overturn of some sort in the German capital was expected Saturday.

The officers of the Wolff Bureau and the leading newspapers are concentrated in a small area south of Unter den Linden, which is accessible from Oranienburg, a workingmen's quarter. This is one of the strongholds of the Spartacides, who previously seized newspaper offices, but were unable to gain control of the city.

Germany Expects to Unite With Allies To Repel Bolsheviki

By Joseph G. Saxe
(By Wireless)

(Copyright, 1919, New York Tribune Inc.)

BERLIN, Jan. 3.—Great excitement has been caused throughout Germany by recent events in the Baltic provinces. The situation appears to be puzzling indeed. It is difficult to foretell to what strange developments it may yet lead.

Reports are coming of common action by German and Entente troops against the Bolshevik forces.

The facts appear to be that the newly established democratic republics of Esthonia and Livonia have applied to the Entente for help against strong forces of Bolsheviki, which are steadily advancing. The Entente hesitated to comply, and merely sent small naval forces, but, being desirous of blocking the Soviet government's road to the west and keeping the Baltic provinces, with their ports and railways, under its control, the Entente ordered the German occupation authorities to keep German troops in the country until further notice for the purpose of repelling the Bolsheviki.

Based on Armistice

In justification of this demand the Entente officials referred to Section 12 of the armistice convention, about which important correspondence has passed between the Allied supreme command and the German armistice commission.

Section 12 sets forth that all German troops now in former Russian territory must retire behind the original German frontiers as soon as the Allies think it opportune, having regard for the internal condition of those areas.

Marshal Foch, it is said here, interpreted this provision as meaning that German troops must remain in Russia

Continued on page nine

Roosevelt's Death Stirs Washington

Congress Adjourns Out of Respect to Memory of the Former President

Baker and Daniels Praise His Career

Supreme Court Sets Precedent by Adjourning Immediately on News

New York Tribune Washington Bureau

WASHINGTON, Jan. 6.—The national capital was shocked beyond measure by the news of Colonel Roosevelt's death. It came with a suddenness that staggered officials of the government and members of Congress. Everywhere surprise was succeeded by expressions of profound and universal regret. Democrats joined with Republicans in eulogies of the former President. Flags at halfmast were ordered over all buildings of the government.

Both houses of Congress adjourned out of respect, and all committee meetings and hearings immediately were called off for the day. The Supreme Court of the United States did the unprecedented thing of adjourning immediately after it met without attempting to dispose of any business.

The State Department, on being informed of the Colonel's death, at once flashed a message to President Wilson, advising him of the fact. At a late hour this evening the department was without information that the message had been received. It rests with the President to decide whether the War Department shall arrange for a military funeral. The thought among his advisers here is that he will first communicate his condolences to Mrs. Roosevelt, and consult her wishes in the matter.

Baker Shocked by News

"If the family desires representation from the army and navy at Colonel Roosevelt's funeral," said Secretary of War Baker, "the arrangements will be made by Major General J. Franklin Bell, commander of the Eastern Department."

"I did not know that Colonel Roosevelt's illness was so grave," the Secretary of War added, "and I am greatly shocked at his sudden death. During his long and brilliant career he touched the public life of America in more ways than any other of our public men. His relations to the navy and to the army are, of course, a part of the history of these two services, and during his terms as President he brought his powerful personality and great energy to bear upon economic problems of the greatest moment.

"I do not know of any career which combined so many diversified and intensively pursued activities—frontiersman, explorer, naturalist, seaman, soldier, executive and publicist. In each of those relations he was conspicuous and left his mark. Taken all in all, it is the close of a great career, typically American and marked at every point by loyalty to American ideals, as well as by resistless energy and determination."

Naval vessels and naval stations in all parts of the world were ordered to fly flags at halfmast. Following is the order sent out by Secretary of the Navy Daniels:

"Ex-President Roosevelt died this morning. Colors are to be halfmasted until sunset this evening."

Daniels Praises Career

Later Secretary Daniels issued the following statement:

"The death of ex-President Roosevelt removes one of the ablest of the dynamic forces this country has produced. He has blazed new paths and refused to be fettered by conventions that other distinguished men recognized. Original, forceful, courageous, he was the monitor of millions of his fellow countrymen, who will miss his inspiring leadership. I knew him first when he was chairman of the Civil Service Commission in Cleveland's last administration. Always he was a virile leader, inviting contests and dealing heavy blows to those with whom he did not agree. His personality was dominant and compelling. He was interested in everything that concerned his country and the world. He was ready with his remedy for every ill and supremely confident that his remedy was the best. Believing in himself and the cause he espoused, he threw himself into every conflict with

Continued on page six

Theodore Roosevelt

DRAWN FROM © PHOTO BY UNDERWOOD & UNDERWOOD

The full story of
Colonel Roosevelt's Career
On pages 12 and 13

T.R. Famous as Phrase Maker

COLONEL ROOSEVELT'S alert mind and trenchant phraseology enabled him to put his views before the public in memorable fashion. The following excerpts from his speeches, letters and statements show the manner of man he was:

"I don't care a hang for the law! I want that canal built."—*To Colonel George W. Goethals during the régime of the first Canal Zone Commission.*

"After you have learned to fight you can be as peaceful as you want to."—*Aug. 25, 1913.*

"I wish to smite the enemy. I wish to strike with the sword of the Lord and of Gideon. I wish to hew Ammon hip and thigh."—*Speech to Progressive leaders, Aug. 6, 1914.*

"I haven't got a bit of use for a bully, but, on the other hand, I haven't got the least use for a softy."—*Dec. 22, 1916.*

"When the war with Spain was through it was through. But peace still continues to rage as furiously as ever in Mexico." —*Aug. 31, 1916.*

"The most important thing that a nation can save is its own soul."—*Sept. 23, 1916.*

"And more than that, don't you do it if you expect me to pussy-foot on any single issue I have raised."—*To a Republican delegate at Oyster Bay, April 5, 1916.*

"Almost without exception these fine words have had the meaning weaselled out of them by other words."—*Battle Creek (Mich.) address on Wilson's Mexican policy, Sept. 30, 1916.*

"I was wise before the event, they were wise after the event."—*Discussion of the Administration's naval programme, Oct. 10, 1916.*

"Instead of speaking softly and carrying a big stick, President Wilson spoke bombastically and carried a dishrag."—*Address at Louisville, Ky., Oct. 18, 1916.*

"A good motto for us all, my friends, is never to hit unless it is necesary, but when you do hit, hit hard."—*Address at Phoenix, Ariz., Oct. 21, 1916.*

"It is worthless to make promises about the future unless in the present we keep those we have already made."—*Jan. 22, 1917.*

"Let us wage war on Germany with all our energy and courage and regain the right to look the whole world in the eyes without flinching."—*March 19, 1917.*

"It now rests with the people of the country to see that we strike as hard, as soon and as effectively as possible."—*April 3, 1917.*

"We Americans are the children of the crucible."—*Sept. 9, 1917.*

"In this country now there is no room for 50-50 men who are half German and half American."—*Oyster Bay, August 10, 1917.*

"Any man who says he loves the country from which he came as well as this country is no better than the man who loves another woman as well as he loves his wife."—*Trinity College, June 16, 1918.*

Taft Mourns Death As Personal Loss

HARRISBURG, Pa., Jan. 6.—Commenting on the death of Mr. Roosevelt, William H. Taft said to-day:

"I am deeply shocked by the death of Colonel Roosevelt. I saw him in the hospital six weeks ago, and he seemed to be very vigorous. He was suffering from rheumatism, but his voice was strong, his personality was as vigorous as ever, and his interest in questions of the day as tense and acute as always.

"I mourn his loss personally, and I greatly regret it for the sake of his country."

Asked if he thought Colonel Roosevelt's death would affect the international future of the nation, Mr. Taft replied:

"That's a difficult question to answer. His influence and advice were important. His patriotic Americanism will be missed, of course. I am very, very sorry."

Bryan Pays Tribute to Colonel's Rare Qualities

"Picturesque Career Will Form Fascinating Chapter of Nation's History"

BALTIMORE, Jan. 6.—William Jennings Bryan, who is staying in Baltimore while his wife is undergoing treatment at Johns Hopkins Hospital, paid the following tribute to Colonel Roosevelt:

"The rare qualities that won for Colonel Roosevelt a multitude of devoted followers naturally arrayed against him a host of opponents, but his death puts an end to controversy and he will be mourned by foe as well as by friend.

"He was a great American and made a profound impression on the thought of his generation. His picturesque career will form a fascinating chapter in our nation's history."

Blood Clot Ends Career Of Colonel At His Home

Simple Funeral Service, for Close Friends Only, To Be Held in Oyster Bay To-morrow Noon

Family Scattered Over 2 Continents

Only Servant at Bedside as Statesman Breathes Last; Had Complained of Feeling Depression

Theodore Roosevelt, twenty-sixth President of the United States, died at 4:15 yesterday morning in his home on Sagamore Hill, Oyster Bay.

The man who had filled sixty years with "strenuous life"; who had been author, naturalist, explorer, rancher, historian, publicist, statesman and, above all, patriot, died peacefully in his sleep.

Only a negro servant, James Amos, witnessed his passing. Two of the four sons he had given to the nation's service are still abroad. His two daughters were away. His wife sat by his bedside until 2 o'clock and had then gone to bed, little thinking he was in danger.

The end came quietly and painlessly. Amos suddenly realized that his employer had stopped breathing. That was all.

America is mourning the loss of him whom statesmen yesterday united in terming one of her greatest sons. Throughout the country flags on all public buildings fluttered at halfmast.

Senator Lodge Breaks Down

In Washington the Senate and House adjourned upon receiving the news. Senator Lodge, a lifelong friend of the Colonel, broke down during the brief tribute he was speaking. The Supreme Court of the United States, on motion of Attorney General Gregory, also adjourned. Ships of the navy have been ordered to halfmast their ensigns in memory of their former commander in chief.

When the State Legislature meets to-morrow night it is probable that it, too, will adjourn. Governor Smith's first official proclamation since he took office was to order the flags placed at halfmast on all state buildings.

The immediate cause of Colonel Roosevelt's death, in non-technical language, was a blood clot in the lungs. In the language of the medical profession, as expressed in the death certificate signed by Dr. George W. Faller, the cause of death was "pulmonary embolus."

Colonel Roosevelt's death was as unexpected as it was painless. He had retired at 11 o'clock Sunday night after an evening spent in dictating a letter to his son Kermit, a captain in the army now in Germany, and in correcting the proof of an editorial for the "Metropolitan Magazine."

Complained of Depression

During the day he had been about the house, apparently in better condition than usual, except that just before retiring he had complained of a sensation of depression about the chest. Because of this, Dr. Faller, who had been at the house early in the evening, as has been his wont since Colonel Roosevelt returned home on Christmas Day from Roosevelt Hospital, was called. Dr. Faller examined him carefully, found no indication of anything wrong with heart and lungs, and after giving him a slight stimulant, left him.

Immediately the physician had gone, the colonel was assisted to bed by Amos, his negro man servant, who had been with him since White House days.

It took him but a moment to settle between the sheets and almost immediately after a cheery "Please put out the light, James," he was sound asleep.

Finds Colonel Dying

In his report to the family Amos said that in the adjoining room he could hear the Colonel breathing softly until just after 4 o'clock, when he was aroused from a half slumber by absolute quiet in the Colonel's room. He hurried in and found him breathing irregularly, but softly, though his temperature seemed normal and his brow was dry. He immediately called Miss Alice Thoms, a nurse, who had been engaged to assist in caring for the colonel on Saturday. She called Mrs.

"It matters not how long you live, but how well"—*Publius Syrus*

Cardinal Mercier's Own Story On Page 8

The Boston Post

THE GREAT Breakfast Table Paper OF NEW ENGLAND

TWENTY-TWO PAGES—TWO CENTS | *Established 1831* | TUESDAY, JANUARY 6, 1920 ** | *Copyright, 1920, by Post Publishing Co.* | TWENTY-TWO PAGES—TWO CENTS

BABE RUTH SOLD TO THE YANKEES

Frazee Disposes of Mighty Slugger for Cash—Price Is Said to Be $125,000—Greatest Sum Ever Paid for a Baseball Player in the Game's History

Ruth Termed a Handicap and Not an Asset by the Red Sox President

Purchase Price Is Pledged to Secure New Stars for the Boston Club

HUGGINS ANNOUNCES THAT RUTH HAS SIGNED

LOS ANGELES, Cal., Jan. 5.—Miller Huggins, manager of the New York Americans, tonight announced he had signed "Babe" Ruth, champion home run hitter, to play with the Yankees next season. Papers were exchanged here late today, Huggins said. He refused to state what salary Ruth was to receive.

BY PAUL H. SHANNON

George (Babe) Ruth, greatest home run swatter of all time, will drive out home runs for the Boston Red Sox no more. Yesterday afternoon the home run record king passed into the possession of the New York Yankees, the deal being closed over the telephone by Colonel Huston of the New York club and President Harry Frazee, the Red Sox magnate.

Continued on Page 15—First Col.

REDS WILL BATTLE TO STAY HERE

Many Have Retained Counsel to Fight Deportation

PRISONERS TO GET SPEEDY HEARINGS

City Appropriates $15,000 to Stay Radicals

RAID ON "REDS" IS RESUMED IN GOTHAM

NEW YORK, Jan. 5.—The sweeping raids against "Reds" by federal agents, which netted nearly 700 prisoners last Friday night, were resumed at 7:30 tonight when 10 large automobiles and two army transport wagons left the local headquarters of the Department of Justice to round up Communists and other sedition mongers, who escaped the first dragnet. Twenty-five houses had been raided and about 75 persons arrested up to midnight.

More than half of the 413 men and women radicals now at Deer Island as a result of the nation-wide Red raid of last Friday have engaged counsel and are going to make a desperate legal fight to remain in this country. Their battle against deportation will be carried to the Supreme Court if necessary.

It became known yesterday that those arrested on deportation warrants will be charged with various offences, each of which is often regard-

Continued on Page 11—Fourth Col.

WOMAN SAVED FROM DEATH

Mrs. Conroy Burned and Ankle Broken

Mrs. Ellen Conroy, 72-year-old invalid of 4 Pleasant street, Dorchester, was saved from burning to death in her home early last night by Mrs. Margaret Hyland, a tenant in the same house, who rushed to the woman's assistance after she had been enveloped in flames while sitting in her kitchen. The woman's shawl caught fire while she was lighting a gas jet.

Mrs. Hyland extinguished the flames on the woman's clothes as well as on the table at which she was sitting.

Leaving Mrs. Conroy alone in the house while she went to the street, Mrs. Hyland again heard groans, and found that the woman had toppled down the stairs in trying to leave the house, breaking her ankle. An ambulance removed her to the City Hospital, where her name was placed on the danger list.

"WETS" LOSE, BUT TO START NEW BATTLE

Supreme Court, 5 to 4 Against 2.75 War-Time Beer—New Fight to Be Under the Constitutional Amendment

THE WAGON'S LATEST RECRUIT.

WASHINGTON, Jan. 5.—By a margin of one vote the Supreme Court today upheld the right of Congress to define intoxicating liquors, insofar as applied to war-time prohibition. The "wets" will now make their fight for 2.75 per cent beer under the constitutional amendment, and they are hopeful of better success.

In a five to four opinion rendered by Associate Justice Brandeis, the court today sustained the constitutionality of provisions in the Volstead prohibition enforcement act prohibiting the manufacture and sale of beverages containing one-half of 1 per cent or more of alcohol. Associate Justices Day, Vandevanter, McReynolds and Clarke dissented.

DECISION IS SWEEPING

Validity of the federal prohibition constitutional amendment and of portions of the Volstead act affecting its enforcement was not involved in the proceedings, but the opinion was regarded as so sweeping as to leave little hope among "wet" adherents.

Wayne B. Wheeler, general counsel for the Anti-Saloon League of America, hailed it as "a sweeping victory," and in a statement tonight said the

Continued on Page 22—Second Col.

COOLIDGE NOT TO SEEK PRESIDENCY

Says Office Must Seek the Man—Runs Strong in Poll of the Roosevelt Club

BY ROBERT T. BRADY

A poll participated in by a little more than half of the members of the Roosevelt Club, announced by Vice-President Robert M. Washburn last night, showed Leonard Wood a favorite for the Republican nomination for President, with Governor

Continued on Page 11—Second Col.

PLANS FLIGHT OVER PACIFIC

VANCOUVER, B. C., Jan. 5.—Major D. A. Yarnold, British Royal Flying Corps ace, who is credited with 83 German airplanes, announced today that he intends to leave tomorrow for England to make arrangements for an attempted flight across the Pacific from Australia to San Francisco.

A special Vickers-Viking machine will be built at Waybridge, England, for the flight, he said. He must secure permission to make the flight, he said, from the British war office.

GALLI-CURCI WINS HER DIVORCE SUIT

Case Goes Practically by Default—Husband Withdraws Spicy Answer to Suit

CHICAGO, Jan. 5.—Mme. Amelita Galli-Curci today won a divorce from Luigi Curci, artist. Judge Charles A. McDonald in the Superior Court indicated he would sign a decree.

The hearing, which ended a year of brief drawing, deposition taking and detailed evidence seeking, was a disappointment to several hundred court fans, who had expected a bitter legal battle extending over several days. The case went practically by default, the spicy answer to Mme. Galli-Curci's bill being withdrawn at the last moment.

HUSBAND NOT IN COURT

Nevertheless, the diva was there, and she offered a bit of bright testimony and told tales of Luigi Curci's "other loves." Two pictures of those loves were introduced.

Luigi Curci was not in court. His attorney, Roy D. Keehn, declined to cross-examine the witnesses. When Mme. Galli-Curci heard Judge McDonald say "that's all," she sighed and smiled and declared that her thoughts in the future would be far from matrimony.

The charge against Luigi Curci was infidelity. The girl named was one Melissa Brown of Flischman's. In a deposition Miss Brown admitted that Curci had made love to her in a motor car on a lonely moonlit road.

On Girl's Admission

It is upon that deposition, Attorney Joseph B. Fleming said, that the divorce will be granted. Mr. Fleming represented Mme. Galli-Curci.

Continued on Page 4—Second Col.

MME. AMELITA GALLI-CURCI, Noted opera singer, who yesterday secured a divorce.

MORE SHOTS IN PHOENIX PARK

Mysterious Affair at Irish Viceroy's Lodge

LONDON, Jan. 5.—"There was another mysterious affair in Phoenix Park shortly after Sunday midnight," says a Central News despatch from Dublin. "A volley of shots was heard in the park. Then all was quiet for 25 minutes, when a fusillade started and lasted for several minutes. It apparently came from the direction of the magazine of the fort near the viceregal lodge.

"It is also stated that from then until dawn the park was scoured by armored cars with bright searchlights. No official explanation has yet been made."

DIES OF BURNS

Mrs. John Cooper of 16 Burridge place, Malden, died at the Malden Hospital last night as the result of burns received when her dress caught fire from a gas stove.

WILSON WILL GREET LEADERS

To Send 'Important Word' to Jackson Banquet

WASHINGTON, Jan. 5.—Announcement from the White House that President Wilson plans to send "an important word of greeting" to the Democratic dinner here on Jackson Day, Jan. 8, aroused great interest among Democratic leaders arriving today to attend the love feast and the quadrennial meeting of the party's national committee, both of which are to be held Thursday.

Prominent Democrats said they had no information as to the message of the President beyond the brief announcement from the White House, and there was wide speculation as to whether the "word of greeting" would take up the question of a third term or would outline the President's views on party policies.

HIGH TIDE TODAY

A. M. 11:21 — P. M. 11:56

SUN Rises 7:13. Sets 4:27. **MOON** Rises at 5:51 p. m.

Light all vehicles tonight at 4:57.

TODAY'S ANNIVERSARIES, ETC.

Twelfth Day or twelfth tide.

Russia annihilated Turkish army corps at Sarryramysh, 1915.

Fire in New York subway killed one and affected 200 others, 1915.

One year ago today—Theodore Roosevelt died.—President Wilson returned to Paris.

FAIR—WARMER

Forecast for Boston and vicinity: Fair and warmer Tuesday and Wednesday; moderate shifting winds, becoming southerly.

WASHINGTON, Jan. 5.—Forecast for New England: Fair and warmer Tuesday; Wednesday partly cloudy and warmer.

Winds off Atlantic coast—North of Sandy Hook, moderate to fresh, shifting, becoming south, fair; Sandy Hook to Hatteras, fresh northeast, except variable, becoming south, off New Jersey coast, fair.

In the middle Atlantic States and New England fair weather will prevail Tuesday and Wednesday.

Temperatures will rise slowly.

YESTERDAY'S TEMPERATURE

Reported by Thompson's Spa.

	'19	'20		'19	'20
3 a. m.	18	9	3 p. m.	25	27
6 a. m.	17	9	6 p. m.	25	27
9 a. m.	18	18	9 p. m.	21	19
12 m.	23	23	12 mid.	21	18

Average temperature yesterday, 17 18-24.
Average temperature one year ago, 20 22-24.

TEACHERS' PAY RAISE IN EFFECT

Three-Fourths of the Force Get $384 Increase

The salary schedule for teachers, members of the supervisory force and other employees of the Boston school department—all of which embody the recent increases authorized by the Legislature—were passed by the school committee last night.

An order was passed also making the salaries of the assistant superintendents $6000. This was opposed by Michael H. Corcoran, but he was outvoted four to one. The same order authorized the pay of the business agent and the secretary at $5496, and that of the schoolhouse custodian at $3300. All the increases take effect on Jan. 1 of this year.

GREATEST TO MISS ABORN

Practically three-fourths of the teachers get the benefit of the $384 increase which was embodied in the committee's bill passed by the Legislature.

The one person in the entire school department getting the biggest increase, according to the schedule, is Miss Caroline D. Aborn, the present director of kindergartens. She receives a $480 minimum increase. Under the old schedule her minimum salary was $1620. It is now $2100.

The next highest increases go to three assistant directors of the Mechanic Arts High School. They get a raise of $408 as a maximum.

The smallest increase goes to the masters. They will draw a $72 raise.

According to a statement submitted by Secretary Apollonio, the number of pupils in the schools who were savings bank depositors on Oct. 31, 1919, was 5590, with deposits of $15,916. This shows a decrease from a year ago. Then 6564 pupils had on deposit $21,143.

PERSHING AIDS TO FIGHT FIRE

Directs Battle With Flames at Camp Grant

ROCKFORD, Ill., Jan. 5.—Fire broke out in one of the buildings at Camp Grant soon after the arrival of General Pershing today and he directed the work of the camp firemen in fighting the flames, which were quickly extinguished. General Pershing inspected the camp this morning and was the guest of Rockford this afternoon. Ten thousand school children paraded for him.

$6,000 GEM ROBBERY REVEALED

THE WISCONSIN NEWS

AN INDEPENDENT NEWSPAPER

5 O'CLOCK

The Evening Wisconsin, Est. 1847
The Milwaukee Daily News, Est. 1885

MILWAUKEE, THURSDAY, EMBER 16, 1920

PRICE 2 CENTS EVERYWHERE.

BLAST ROCKS NEW YORK!

S Today

Be 1,000,000 to 1.
assenger Service.
Week to Live.
ers and Heroes.

By Arthur Brisbane

In Wall street the betting is 5 to 1 on Harding. The question is, What generous soul is putting up the one without the slightest chance of getting it back?

The issue in this election is the war League of Nations, which would take from the United States the independence that it won in 1776 and hand it back to a group of foreign nations controlled by England. That the people of the United States will not vote to give up their independence is a 1,000,000 to 1, not a 5 to 1 bet.

Thanks to Mr. Burleson, government ownership of passenger service has begun in a small way, it is true, but in the right place. Contracts have been let to a Chicago firm and flying cars with wicker chairs, inclosed in glass and steel, will carry passengers as well as mail, and the United States will be the owner of the transportation.

As soon as the thing is a success "private ownership" will step in and kindly explain that the government is not able to do anything well. It is to be hoped that those soon to be in charge of the government will have the energy, once started, to keep on.

The most weak-kneed thing ever heard of was done by the Democratic administration, handing back railroads to private owners, after spending billions of the people's money rebuilding and re-equipping the roads and paying the highest profit to the private owners.

Mayor MacSwiney has gone without food for thirty-four days. His mental courage and interest in the fight that he is making may keep him alive ten days more. He probably cannot live longer than that.

He probably will die in the course of the coming week if England's attitude does not change. Meanwhile, the Irish correspondent of the London Times, owned by the son of an Irishwoman, says that if MacSwiney dies it will make it impossible for the Irish and English difficulty to be successfully arranged or compromised.

That, undoubtedly, is true. Every Irishman feels toward MacSwiney now as though he were his own son or brother. When he dies every Irishman will feel that he has been murdered.

The harm that will be done to England, and to English representatives in Ireland, should MacSwiney die, is clear to everybody. What good England hopes to achieve by allowing him to die is not clear here. There must exist an undercurrent of hatred in England, not understood in this country.

"News," so called, from Russia, tells of serious rioting against the Bolshevik government at Petrograd and "six of the Bolshevist commissioners" drowned. This is a variation in news of that kind. Usually Lenin kills Trotsky, or Trotsky kills Lenin. Neither has done that for some months.

Another kind of news, representing facts more closely, says the Russians are getting together an army of four and three-quarter millions and that Gen. Wrangle, who was supposed to restore ancient conditions and force payment of Russian bonds, has again been kicked out of the place where he most recently was.

All of this does not affect the United States much, as long as we keep our men out of Siberia and our country out of the League of Nations.

But when you read about that Russian army of four and three-quarter millions, you understand how glad other countries would be if they could trap old Uncle Sam in the League of Nations, and make it his business to take care of that Bolshevik crowd and finance that war.

...wo more flying men in the government mail service are killed, ...ed to death. This fills with hor... ...hose that learned to read quite ...ily about death in war.

Friends of the dead flyers have the satisfaction of knowing that they were soldiers and heroes in the truest sense, men fighting to achieve progress for all time, not fighting against other men, in quarrels to be renewed indefinitely.

Every tunnel built, almost every great building, means one to a hundred workmen's deaths. Perhaps an occasional dramatic death, in the flying service, will cause the public to appreciate the heroes of industry ...lled every week in blast furnaces, ...nels, railroad construction, with ...ands playing and no newspapers ...ise them.

...t Milwaukee

...'s Slogan.
"Milwauk... Have a $10,000,000 ...Dock."
Tomorr... Slogan.
"Milwaukee ...ls Nation in To...king."

$6,000 GEM ROBBERY EXPOSED

Two Upper East Side Homes Entered; Posed as Meter Inspector.

Information now in the hands of Shorewood police and deputy sheriffs, points plainly that the "screen burglar," who has successfully looted more than a score of homes during the last month, is working with a "set of books" which contain valuable data, pertaining to homes which will be entered.

The homes entered on the upper East Side a month ago are: A. L. Frisch, 555 Wahl av., and Byron H. Abert, 936 Shepard av. The amount of jewelry taken from both is placed at $3,000 each.

Entrance to the homes were made by the ruse that the robber was connected with the Electric company and wanted to inspect the meters.

HOME IS GUARDED.

As a result of this discovery a Frederick av. home, one of the most exclusive residential streets in the city, is being carefully guarded by authorities on the theory that it is marked for a visit by the robber within the next 24 hours.

The clew which the investigators have obtained comes in the form of a scrap of paper bearing a name and address on Frederick av., which they refuse to give out. The scrap of paper was found in the eave trough of the A. E. Jackson home, 1547 Farwell av., an hour after that home had been visited by the robber early today.

The attempt to loot the Jackson home was unsuccessful. Members of the family, awakened by a loud crash of breaking wood, ran out on the porch of the home and saw a man fleeing across the yard in the dark.

Searching the yard, Mr. Jackson discovered a box standing near the corner of the porch. The top of the box had been broken by the robber, evidently while letting himself down from the roof of the porch.

POLICE FIND PAPER.

Police of Shorewood were called to the scene and the investigation of the ground and roof of the porch resulted in the finding of the paper.

Outside of the name and address

(Turn to Page 9, Column 4)

DOUBLE FUNERAL FOR BROTHER AND SISTER

PORTAGE, Wis.—James Sweaney, aged 75, and his sister, Miss Elizabeth Sweaney, aged 65, died a few hours apart on their farm in Fort Winnebago, near here. Both had been ill for several weeks of erysipelas. A double funeral was held yesterday from St. Mary's church in Portage, the Rev. J. J. Nicholas being assisted in the service by the Rev. Thomas Cosgrove of Fond du Lac and the Rev. McCarthy of Briggsville. The brother and sister had lived together for a great many years on the farm near Portage.

BOSTON STORE TO CLOSE FOR A. L. STONE FUNERAL

The Boston store will be closed all day Friday in tribute to its late vice president, Abraham L. Stone, who will be buried in Chicago tomorrow. Mr. Stone died Wednesday, after an illness of several weeks. He was a brother of Nat Stone, head of the Herzfeld-Phillipson company, which own the Boston store. The late Mr Stone was vice president and treasurer of the company, with which his son, Stanley, is also identified. Mr. Stone was 62 years old and was born in St. Louis.

"The Great Redeemer" Is Viewed by Clergymen

"The Great Redeemer," a photoplay with religious motive as its reason for existence, was viewed today at a private exhibition at the Strand theater.

The audience was composed of about 200 Milwaukee ministers, their wives, Christian Scientists, and leading exponents of the Catholic faith who had been invited by Manager Frank Cook to view the film and give their opinions of it. By this "acid test" Mr. Cook will determine whether or not he will book the photoplay for the Strand. Written criticisms will be sent by the guests to their host, Mr. Cook.

Maurice Tourneur is the producer of "The Great Redeemer;" Marjorie Daw and House Peters play the leading roles. The photoplay is founded on a story by H. H. Van Loan and released through Metro.

THINK BRENNER LEAPED TO DEATH

That Herbert Brenner, 19 year old chauffeur, who left a bundle of clothing and a note, in which he expressed his intention of ending his life, at the foot of Cherry st. bridge, actually leaped to his death in the river, was practically established today.

Mrs. Sarah Stein, 55 years old, 673 East Water st., reported to the police that early Tuesday morning, as she was returning from the public market at Fifth and Poplar sts., she saw a young man, coatless and hatless, standing at the north end of the bridge. A moment after she first caught sight of him, the man shouted, "Shoot me, shoot me," and leaped into the water, according to Mrs. Stein.

"I ran to the spot, but could see nothing of him. Meantime, I had cried out for help and a number of persons came running up. Then we discovered the bundle of clothing and cap, with the note, at the end of the bridge, just at the spot where I had seen the fellow standing. I was about 200 feet away when he leaped into the water."

If Brenner's body is in the water it probably has been carried out into the lake by the strong current, police say. Brenner was awaiting trial on a charge of operating an automobile without the owner's consent. Friends say he brooded over this fact.

LOST WILL COPY BRINGS HUSBAND $30,000 LOSS

The admission of a copy of the lost will of the late Anna K. Binder to probate today by County Judge M. S. Sheridan resulted in the loss of a $30,000 estate to Joseph Binder, widower and second husband of Mrs. Binder, and a distribution of the estate among her brothers, sisters, nieces and nephews.

At the time of her death, June 1, 1920, no will was found. There being no children, the estate according to probate law would go to her second husband, Joseph. A sister of Mrs. Binder objected, producing what was purported to be a copy of a lost will.

The lost will provided that the estate be divided between Charles F. Kargl, 553 Reed st.; Joseph Kargl, 552 Reed st., and Mrs. Mary Vogel, 553 Reed st., brothers and sister of the deceased. No provision was made for the widower, Joseph. A number of bequests were made to nieces and nephews.

MERRILL'S POPULATION REPORTED DECREASED

WASHINGTON—The 1920 population of Merrill was announced today as 8,068, a decrease of 7.1 per cent since 1910 or 621.

Richland Center, Wis., gained 28.5 per cent, having a population of 3,409.

RENT QUIZ TO COVER COUNTY

Bender Says Check Will Be Kept on Operations of All Landlords.

The rent bureau plans to investigate profits of all landlords in the county, it was announced today by Administrator Walter H. Bender, who has returned from a conference with the railroad rate commission at Madison.

Mr. Bender said that he was convinced that heretofore the bureau has only been scratching the surface and that, while relief has been granted in many cases, the great majority of tenants fear to make complaint because of the landlord's power to force them to move.

This condition has been unfair to the honest landlord, Mr. Bender pointed out, because scores of those who have been collecting exorbitant rents have thus far been unmolested.

REVIEW ALL PROFITS.

"We expect to have on file within a short time a card index system including every landlord in our county," said Mr. Bender, "together with the profits he is realizing. "We shall compile our lists from the office of the tax commissioner, the building inspector and other sources.

"All rents and profits will be reviewed and we will initiate action without a complaint from the tenant in those cases where the rents appear exorbitant.

"Scores of persons have been coming into the office to seek advice on purely hypothetical cases. They have refused to give the name of the landlord and put in a formal complaint. A close study of the situation has convinced me that we have been traveling only around the edges of the siuation and that something further ought to be done. We have had our hands full with the present staff but expect to increase it.

PROTECTION TO LANDLORDS.

"It should be understood that the rent bureau does not intend to adopt an inquisitorial and drastic attitude toward the landlords. The information we desire is not very detailed and can be easily given. We intend to protect the honest landlord as well as compel reductions where raises have been exorbitant.

"It is not fair that scores of landlords should be pursuing an equitable policy and others permitted to go on collecting excessive sums.

"Every landlord in our files will have to give us notification of proposed raises and each case will be reviewed. We feel that this in itself will make

(Turn to Page 9, Column 3)

PERCIVAL ROBERTS JR. REPORTED ASHORE

MACKINAW CITY, Mich. — The steamer Percival Roberts, Jr. of the Pittsburgh Steamship company, from Lake Superior to Lake Michigan with cargo of ore, is ashore on the north side of Round island. The wrecking tug Favorite is pulling on the stranded vessel. The small barge Snyder and consort are ashore on the south side of Mackinac island. Strong westerly winds, rain and fog when vessels went ashore.

OPEN FIGHT TO OBTAIN BAIL FOR CHAS. ROWAN

A fight to obtain bail for Charles Rowan, held for trial in federal court on a charge of using the mails to defraud, has been opened by his attorneys. Judge Geiger refused to grant Rowan bail when he was recaptured after jumping a bond of $10,000. A writ of habeas corpus, returnable next Wednesday, has been obtained at which time arguments will be heard. Rowan is charged with having obtained $100,000 from persons to whom he sold rabbits and guinea pigs on presentation that he would buy their offspring. This he failed to do, it is alleged.

30 DEAD, 200 HURT AT MORGAN'S OFFICE

NEW YORK—A mysterious explosion, disastrous in its effect, occurred at noon today in Wall st., killing 30 persons and injuring approximately 200.

Office workers were just hurrying into the street for their noon day meal when a jet of black smoke and flame rose from the center of the world's great street of finance.

MORGAN'S SON NEAR DEATH IN BLAST

JUNIUS SPENCER MORGAN.

THOMAS W. LAMONT.

HENRY W. DAVISON.

Above is shown Junius Spencer Morgan, son of the noted financier, who was in the Morgan firm's offices when the explosion occurred and was cut by flying glass.

Below are Thomas W. Lamont and Henry W. Davison, members of the firm. Both were in the office when it was wrecked by the explosion, but escaped injury.

Then came a blast. A moment later scores of men, women and children were lying, blood-covered on the pavements.

Two minutes later nearly all the exchanges had closed. Men had turned from barter to an errand or mercy.

While the police toiled for hours seeking the dead and injured, trained investigators were trying in vain to determine definitely whether the explosion had occurred from a bomb dropped in front of the office of J. P. Morgan & Co. or whether an automobile dashing into a wagon loaded with explosives had taken its toll.

Police announce they have found enough evidence to justify belief that the Morgan explosion was caused by a huge T. N. T. bomb, timed to explode at 12:01 p. m.

COLLISION THEORY.

Frank Francisco, one of the most able investigators of the department of justice, declared after arriving on the scene that it was his opinion that not a bomb plot but a collision had been responsible for the blast which rocked skyscrapers, tore the fronts from office buildings for blocks around and scattered deadly missiles in all directions.

The wall of the Morgan building on the Wall st. side is pitted with holes as if it had been bombarded by light caliber artillery.

Word reached here that William J. Flynn, chief of the United States secret service, was speeding to New York upon a special train to take charge of the federal end of the investigation.

The Broad st. hospital announced at 2 o'clock that it had treated nearly 200 people, mostly men, for injuries due to the explosion.

GIRLS AMONG DEAD.

According to a clerk in the Morgan offices at the time of the explosion three men and one girl employe of the Morgan house were killed. A number of the employes of the Equitable Trust company were injured and have been taken to the Broad st. hospital.

FIND WRECKED AUTO.

The first thing that occupied the attention of the investigators were wrecks of a truck and automobile at the spot from which the blast was believed to have come. From the wreckage were taken a New Jersey automobile license whose reported number corresponded with that issued to Dunham Beedon, a Newark pharmacist, who was reported this morning to have come to Wall Street on business.

Beedon later was found safe in an accountant's office at 52 Wall street. He said he had parked his car, which contained no explosive, in front of the building and behind another machine. He added that he knew no more of the explosion.

Federal investigators, soon to be headed by William J. Flynn, chief of the department of justice bureau of investigation, summoned from Washington, centered their attention on these wrecks.

Some advanced the theory that the automobile had collided with a powder wagon, and the Du Pont company was asked to find out whether any of its vehicles had been in the vicinity at the time.

Other investigators sought to run down reports that a bomb had been exploded in front of the Morgan building.

HOLD TO BOMB THEORY.

Assistant District Attorney Tally after visiting the scene, announced his belief that the explosion could not have been due to an accident.

He announced that his staff would question all witnesses of

(Turn to Page 2, Column 1.)

BIG NEWS

Two series of games starting today in the National and American leagues probably will decide definitely the two teams that will meet in the World's Series. These games will be between the New York and Chicago teams, American league, and the Brooklyn and Cincinnati teams, National league. By special arrangement THE WISCONSIN NEWS will carry the stories of these two important series play by play as they are made. This extraordinary news service starts today in the Sporting Extra editions. This is a reading "treat" no one can afford to miss.

Baseball, Football, Golf, Tennis, Track, Boxing, Turf and Amateur Sports expertly reported by the best sporting writers in the West

CHARACTER QUALITY AMERICA FIRST ENTERPRISE ACCURACY

Los Angeles Examiner Sports

AN AMERICAN PAPER FOR THE AMERICAN PEOPLE — THE GREAT NEWSPAPER OF THE GREAT SOUTHWEST

The Examiner carries the most complete Daily Sports Section of any newspaper west of New York

THURSDAY, OCTOBER 11, 1923 — SECTION III—PAGE 1

GIANTS WIN; STENGEL HERO

WHATNOTS More What Than Not

Negro vs. Indian
Some Ancient History
Old Time Stars
White Race, Beware!
—By Mark Kelly—

Maurice Webb, a student of football, has the floor for the day. What the young man has to say is interesting:

* * *

HOW'D you like to see a game between an All Star Indian team and the eleven greatest Negroes? Who do you think would win? Naturally your mind would leap to the great teams put out by Pop Warner at Carlisle and you would say the Indians. But just wait till you hear this array of dusky-hued warriors.

Starting at the ends we'd have Robeson, unanimously chosen All American in 1917 and 1918. Standing six feet three, shoeless and scaling two hundred and thirty pounds on the hoof, this Rutgers blackbird was the terror of every team he faced and the plays that gained around his end could be counted on the fingers of the left hand of a right-handed blind butcher. At the other terminal we station one Mistah Williams, End Extraordinary. A place had to be reserved for him on the All Eastern and frequently the All A during the years he cavorted on the gridiron for Brown University.

* * *

AT tackle, Duke Slater, Iowa, the sensation of Middle Western football for three years. Picked by Camp regularly. As his running mate, G. E. Smith from the Michigan Aggies probably not so well known, but one of the greatest all round linemen in the history of the game. Can you imagine a tackle being pulled out of the line to run back punts? That was one of this tarbaby's regular jobs. Walt Gordon, now assistant coach at California. His ability is well known to Pacific Coast football fans.

Johnson, Columbia guard, who was also one of the finest basketball players ever turned out in the East. Turner, who centered for a Chicago High School and later played tackle for Northwestern is another wonder. Charley West, W. and J.'s quarter this year, is a running fool. Took Eastern Pentathlon honors in last year's track season. Try and find somebody who hasn't heard of Fred Pollard, that wonderful little Brown halfback. Sol Butler, Olympic games satellite, more famous for his deeds on the cinder path than at half, but only because he hails from a comparatively obscure college, Dubuque.

* * *

SHELBURNE at full is probably the best man who has played that position for the Green of Dartmouth in recent years. Some lineup. Six All American and the rest picked for their respective sectional teams. Even with such an imposing muster roll of names the Indians would probably bring home the kinky scalps.

Perform a little tuning, get the old radio all set and listen in on this bunch of Redskins. Ends: Pete Calac, All-A fullback at Carlisle and later end at West Virginia Wesleyan. If there ever was a man who hit the line any harder or tacked a runner more viciously than this wild man, he's still in Borneo. Evans, a little papoose from Haskell, who, barring Weaver of Center, is the topnotch converter of goals from touchdowns for all time, and the kind of fellow who took passes off his left ear. Missed one goal from touchdown in four years and was so broken up about it he quit the team and joined the army.

* * *

PLAYING one of the tackles we would have Joe Guyon, Jim Thorpe's twin brother. Why amplify that statement? Cooper, Louisiana State tackle for many moons and one of the finest linemen ever put out in the Sunny South where football players bloom like apple blossoms in Normandy.

Elmer Busch, another of Warner's wonder men and receiving the selection in '12 and '13. Busch was generally conceded to be the greatest guard at leading interference since the year one and was the man responsible for many of Thorpe, Guyon, et al's long runs. Bergie, a marvelous center, is switched to guard on account of the presence of Pete Garlow, who could not be ousted from the pivot position save by a precious few centers of recent years.

* * *

NOW for the backfield. Gustave Welch, absolutely the trickiest quarter that ever callled a signal. The only time opponents ever knew where the ball was when this gentleman was playing was when they saw it planted behind the goal posts for another touchdown. Welch's pet individual specialty was eighty and ninety-yard runs from scrimmage. Jim Thorpe. Plenty spoken. We will not talk foolish. A worthy comrade for this superman was Arcasa. As a runner pure and simple the great "Jeems" himself had little on him.

Finally, we come to Murdock, Haskell famous fullback. 'Tis said this guy could hit a dime at fifty yards with a football. Probably a slight exaggeration, but unquestionably some passer. A runaway mallet would do but little more damage to an opposing line. Well, there they are. A couple of teams like that would pack the coliseum and leave a mob standing outside.

* * *

IN case there wasn't enough color in this battle to suit everybody, we might inject Sammie Kai Kee, California's Chinese halfback of several seasons back; and "Sneeze" Achiu, yellow flash now playing at the University of Dayton. To even things up we'd give the other side Brash, one of the greatest players ever attending the University of Hawaii. Hawaii left a dark brown taste in Pomona's mouth last year, you know. Old timers will recall "Sonny" Cunha, the smiling Hawaiian lineman, who was such a sensation at Yale years ago.

The white footballers had better watch their step, or the boys of color will be stealing their thunder.

Yankees Display Genius; Giant Win Proves It

—By Ring W. Lardner—

YANKEE STADIUM, N. Y., Oct. 10.—Well, boys, they have started again and it looks maybe we would be out of the trenches by Saturday night. At the conclusion of this battle the general consensus of opinion among us half-witted newspaper men that it was a game that could of been lost by only one team in the world, namely, the Yankees.

It takes real genius to get beat in a ball game like this one, and it don't seem hardly possible that the Giants can lose any of the rest of them, no matter how hard they try.

The only thing might save the American League champs would be to have last year's umpires re-engaged, so that some game might be called while it was still a tie.

However, it might help a little if Manager Huggins would change his tactics and every time one of his boys gets on base, send in somebody to run for him. The Yanks made a whole lot of runs this season, and in order to make runs they must of visited different bases, but today they acted like it was their first trip away from home. This ain't knocking the Giants, who played their regular worlds' serious baseball and deserved to win. And personly I am glad it was Casey, mighty Casey, that busted it up, though I don't suppose he care whether I like him or not. Well, to begin at the beginning. On the way from the subway to the press gate the writer must of passed at least 50 policemens but was neither recognized nor hit over the head. Outside the gate I run into the high commissioner of baseball, who asked the newspaper boys the other day to kindly keep his name out of the paper on the grounds that the people was not interested. The Judge helped me get away with a couple of Harry Stevens' hot roast beef sandwiches which was so good that I took some of the juice home on my coat to show the wife and kiddies.

At 1 o'clock Judge L——s went out on the field and decided it was light enough to play. The clients was then entertained by a novelty in the way of batting and fielding practice, which is usually held in secret before a big game. Messrs. Altrock and Schacht staged their imitation of the misunderstanding between our champion and the Wild Bull and it was voted the best baseball's star comics has ever put on. Personly I would of enjoyed it and the ball game more if the boys had not given me a press seat that was not only made for Jackie Coogan, but was bounded on the front by the largest steel pillar in The Bronx. If the serious goes over 3 games it will be called on acct. of cramps as far as I am conserned.

The gent that announced the batteries in the press box said that Hurt would pitch for the Yankees. This is what they call him in Brooklyn. Amongst the prominent experts present was Jack Hendricks and Clarence Rowland. Jack is covering the serious for Jim Jam Jems and Clarence for the Encyclopedia. When Mr. Watson was named as the Giant pitcher, Nick, lately of Boston, said that McGraw was probably sending him in as punishment for not obeying the training rules. He was released on parole after two nervous innings. Mr. Hurt got bumped off in the next innings and I practically decided to nick name the game a air-tight pitchers' battle. It took one hour and 5 minutes to get the first three innings over and Judge L——s gave the gathering gloom a couple of dirty looks.

During the long and tedious progress of the third inning I sought an interview with Mrs. Caroline Dorsey of Travers City, Mich. Mrs. Dorsey is the lady who stood in line in front of the general admission ticket window since May 14, hoping against hope that she would get a ticket.

At 10 o'clock this morning she received the coveted pasteboard and picked out a choice seat under the score board.

"Mrs. Dorsey," I said to her, "what do you think of the game?"

She did not hear me the first time, on account of being so far away, so I had to put the query once more.

"Mrs. Dorsey," I said, "what do you think of the game?"

She did not hear me this time either, and when the game was over I asked some of the people who had sat near her if they had heard her say what she had thought of the game, but I could get no information that sounded reliable.

The pastime speeded up after Bush and Ryan took what is called the helm. With the sun under cover, the Giants was unable to see Mr. Bush's fast ball until he got in the hole to Mr. Stengel in the ninth, when Casey ran an exhibition circuit of the bases. He had been scheduled to run this race against Papyrus before the game, but the horse failed to leave his stall. Plenty of Yanks got on base, but once there they seemed to be overcome by nausea.

The disease was contagious and Yankee fans all had it leaving the park.

"BUGS" BAER SAYS

Yanks Curl Up Like Bed Spring.
Take Flop After Getting Three-Run Jump on the Giants.

THE Giants pasted their usual label on the Yanks in New York's annual baseball convention. he series has been here so often it starts to look like an old-home week for Casey Stengel. Casey looked up his contract in the ninth and decided that his bonus clause called for no overtime.

SO he broadcast one of Bush's wave lengths and came home while the Yanks' outfield buckle brigade was passing the ball to one another.

BY THE time Witt got the ball to Meusel it was't a ball any more. It was a souvenir. For Casey was back in the covered wagon by that time.

THE Yanks got a three-run jump on the Giants, but curled up like a bedspring when the Giants started to ask Hoyt questions with their bats.

JUDGE LANDIS was there to see that everything was on the up and up. He started the series wrong by faking a throw for the photographers.

M'GRAW crossed everybody and himself by starting Mule Watson.

HOYT lasted long enough to tell his folks he was in the series.

THE Yanks were hitting everything that came across until Watson started to fool them with wild pitches.

EVANS, O'Day, Hart and Nallin were the four umpires of the Apocalppse.

EACH one of the first three innings was a world series in itself. The Yanks' three run lead looked like Turkey in the oven. But it never reached the dining room.

THE Giants came back in the third and started to figure out the population of the United States in base runners. They scored four times and the bell boy showed Mr. Hoyt to his room.

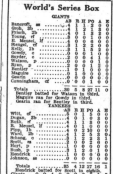

BABE RUTH knocked himself for a foul when he bumped into Frank Snyder at the plate in the fifth. Babah hit a three-bagger but was out at the platel n a right-of-way collision with Snyder.

RYAN and Bush took charge of the shooting gallery when Watson and Hoyt were paged by their managers. The Yanks tied it up in the seventh with a three-bagger that Joe Dugan had been asving ever since he left Philadelphia.

RYAN pitched golf style. Always trying to get himself into a hole.

KELLY'S throw on Dugan in the fifth was like a beard at a House of David banquet. Right over the plate.

* * *

CASEY STENGEL kept on gishing until he laid the lumber against Bush in the ninth. Casey whacked one loose to the fence and ran like he was going to meet Papyrus next week.

* * *

IT was the longest hit of the game, and Casey could have crawled around on all fours. The old boy stalls all summer, but he certainly takes charge of the series.

RENAULT WINS AGAIN.

MONTREAL, Oct. 10. — Jack Renault, heavyweight champion of Canada, was awarded the decision over Soldier Jones of Toronto tonight at the end of their ten-round match.

Casey at the Bat!

Oh! Somewhere in this favored land the sun is shining bright,
The band is playing somewhere, and somewhere hearts are light;
And somewhere men are laughing, and somewhere children shout,
But there is no joy in Yankville—after mighty Casey's clout!
—With apologies to Thayer.

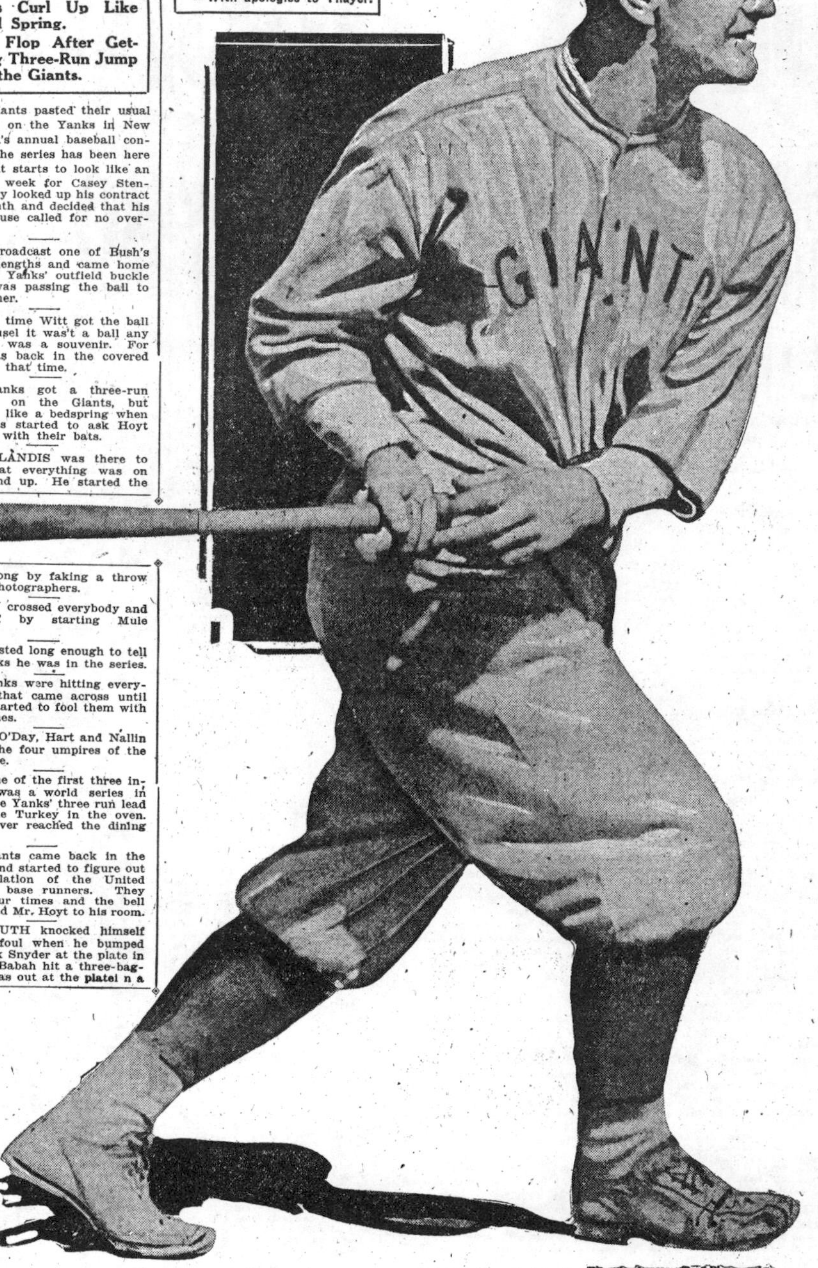

CASEY STENGEL

Photo by American Staff Photographer

HOME RUN IN NINTH BREAKS UP 4 TO 4 TIE

Hoyt Batted Out in Third; Ryan Relieves Watson and Pitches Effectively

By DAMON RUNYON
Staff Correspondent Universal Service

YANKEE STADIUM, NEW YORK, Oct. 10.—This is the way old "Casey" Stengel ran this afternoon, running his home-run home.

This is the way old "Casey" Stengel ran, running his home-run home to a Giant victory over the Yankees by a score of 5 to 4 in the first game of the World's Series of 1923.

This is the way old "Casey" Stengel ran, running his home-run home, when two were out in the ninth inning and the score was tied, and the ball was still bounding inside the Yankee yard.

This is the way:

His mouth wide open—

His warped-out legs bending beneath him at every stride—

His arms flying back and forth, like those of a man swimming with a crawl stroke—

His flanks heaving, his breath whistling, his head far back.

Yankee infielders, passed by old "Casey" Stengel as he was running his home-run home, say "Casey" was muttering to himself, adjuring himself to greater speed, as a jockey mutters to his horse in a race, that he was saying:

"Go on, Casey."

People generally laugh when they see old "Casey" Stengel run, but they were not laughing while he was running his home-run home this afternoon. People—sixty thousand of 'em—men and women, were standing in the Yankee stands and bleachers up there in the Bronx roaring sympathetically, whether they were for or against the the Giants:

"Come on, Casey."

The warped old legs, twisted and bent by many a year of baseball campaigning, just barely held out until "Casey" Stengel reached the plate, running his home-run home.

Then they collapsed.

They gave not inwardly, as legs often do, but outwardly, so that old "Casey" Stengel fell sprawling, all spread out over the plate, with Schang, the catcher of the Yankees, futilely reaching for him with the ball.

He suggested a huge crab spread out down there, his arms and legs wiggling in all directions, with Billy Evans, the American League umpire, poised over him in a set pose, his right thumb jerked backwards to indicate that old "Casey" was safe.

Half a dozen Giants rushed forward to help old "Casey" to his feet, to hammer him on his feet, to bawl congratulations in his ear as he limped unsteadily, still panting furiously, to the bench, where John J. McGraw, chief of the Giants, relaxed his stern features in a smile for the man who had won the game.

"Casey" Stengel's warped old legs, one of them broken not so long ago, wouldn't carry him out for the next inning, when the Yankees made a dying effort to undo the damage done by "Casey." His place in centerfield was taken by young Bill Cunningham, whose legs are still unwarped, and "Casey" sat on the bench with John J. McGraw.

Not Much Expected

No one expected much of "Casey" Stengel when he appeared at the plate in the Giants' side of the ninth inning, the score a tie at 4 to 4.

Ross Young and "Irish" Meusel, stout, dependable hitters, had been quickly disposed of by the superb pitching of "Bullet Joe" Bush.

No one expected Stengel to accomplish anything where they had failed. Bush, pitching as only Bush can pitch in an emergency, soon had two strikes and three balls on "Casey." He was at the plate so long that many fans were fidgeting nervously, wondering why he didn't hurry up and get put out, so the game could go on.

"Casey" Stengel is not an imposing figure at bat, not an imposing figure under any circumstances. Those warped old legs have something to do with it. A man with

(Continued on Page 2, Column 1)

Papyrus' Jockey Given Ovation as He Leaves

LONDON, Oct. 10.

STEVE DONAGHUE, England's champion jockey, who will ride Papyrus in his race against Zev at Belmont Park, October 20, had an enthusiastic send off at Waterloo station today when he left for Southampton to embark on the liner Olympic for New York. Crowds on their way to business assembled outside the platform barrier and shouted the familiar race course slogan, "Come on Steve," as the little jockey made his way to the train.

"Papyrus is a generous, game horse, as I well know and I hope I shall win," he said.

Jockey Dillon Boxes Tonight

Jockey Joe Dillon, holder of the New York boxing commission's junior flyweight champi nship belt, makes his bow to Southern California glove patrons in the main event of the C. P. O. club's weekly boxing show at San Pedro this Thursday night.

Matchmaker Luke Lucas of the harbor club has dug up the toughest sort of opposition for Jockey Joe. Art Springer, one of the busiest and best bantams in this section, will do the glove flinging for the other side. If Dillon can best Springer he will be in demand.

Lucas has Larry Murphy and Georgie Siddon boxing the semi-windup at 126 pounds. Dean Hood of the Union Tool Company and Bert Meyers, a San Francisco boy, will appear in the special event at 155 pounds.

World's Series Box

GIANTS

	AB	R	H	PO	A	E
Bancroft, ss	4	1	1	2	0	0
Groh, 3b	4	1	2	1	3	0
Frisch, 2b	4	0	1	3	2	0
Young, rf	3	0	0	1	0	0
E. Meusel, lf	4	0	0	6	0	0
Stengel, cf	3	1	2	2	0	0
Kelly, 1b	3	1	1	5	2	0
Gowdy, c	0	0	0	1	0	0
Snyder, c	2	0	0	4	1	0
Watson, p	0	0	0	0	1	0
Ryan, p	2	0	0	1	2	0
Bentley	1	0	1	0	0	0
Maguire	0	1	0	0	0	0
Gearin	0	0	0	0	0	0
Cunningham, cf	0	0	0	1	0	0
Totals	30	5	8	27	11	0

Bentley batted for Watson in third.
Maguire ran for Gowdy in third.
Gearin ran for Bentley in third.

YANKEES

	AB	R	H	PO	A	E
Witt, cf	5	0	1	5	0	0
Dugan, 3b	4	0	1	0	3	0
Ruth, rf	4	1	1	3	0	0
R. Meusel, lf	4	0	1	0	0	0
Pipp, 1b	4	0	2	10	0	0
Ward, 2b	4	1	2	5	3	0
Schang, c	3	1	2	2	3	1
Scott, ss	2	0	0	2	6	0
Hoyt, p	1	0	0	0	0	0
Bush, p	3	1	2	0	1	0
Hendrick	1	0	0	0	0	0
Johnson, ss	0	0	0	0	0	0
Totals	35	4	12	27	16	1

Hendrick batted for Scott in eighth.

Giants	0	0	4	0	0	0	0	0	1	—5
Yankees	1	2	0	0	0	0	1	0	0	—4

Earned runs—Giants, 5; Yankees, 4. Two-base hits—R. Meusel, Bush, Schang. Three-base hits—Groh, Dugan, Ruth. Home run—Stengel. Bases on balls—Off Bush, 2; Ryan, 1; Watson, 1. Struck out—By Watson, 1 (Hoyt); by Ryan, 1 (Scott); by Bush, 2 (Ryan and Snyder). Left on bases—Giants, 2; Yankees, 6. Double plays—Scott to Ward to Pipp, 2; Frisch to Snyder. Stolen base—Bancroft. Sacrifice hit—Scott. Wild pitch—Ryan. Three runs, 4 hits off Watson in two innings; 4 runs, 4 hits off Hoyt in 2 1-3 innings. Losing pitcher—Bush. Winning pitcher—Ryan. Time—2:05.

Records Fall As Fans File Into Stadium

NEW YORK, Oct. 10.

ATTENDANCE and receipts for the first world series game today broke all previous records. Total attendance was 55,307; total receipts $181,912. Of the total sum, the players will get $92,775.12; each club will get $30,925.05; the baseball commission will get $27,286.80.

Sherman Battles Layman to Draw

GEORGE SHERMAN and Joe Layman battled to a hard fought draw last night in the main event at the San Fernando arena. In the semi-windup "Pewee Nolan, substituting for Benny Diaz, won the decision over Frankie Layman in a fast affair. Following are the remaining bouts and results:

"Peanuts" Jensen won over Red Howard.
Billy Blake was knocked out by Young Lotti.
Young Richie won over Joe Carroll.
Mike Downey won over Walter Williams.

Cubs Defeat White Sox in Opening Game

CHICAGO, Oct. 10.—The National League drew first blood in the Chicago city series today when the Cubs defeated the American League White Sox, 8 to 4. Charley Robertson, the Sox starting pitcher, paved the way to the Cub victory with a bad throw to the plate in the fourth inning, which allowed two of the four Cubs' runs of the inning to score.

Score:

WHITE SOX	AB	H	O	A	E	CUBS	AB	H	O	A	E
Mostil, cf.	5	1	1	0	0	Statz, cf..	3	3	2	0	0
Hooper, rf	5	1	1	0	0	Adams, ss	4	4	3	7	0
Collins, 2b	3	2	2	1	0	Grntm, 2b	5	0	4	8	3
Sheely, 1b	4	0	12	1	0	Grimes, 1b	3	1	12	1	1
Falk, lf...	4	0	0	0	0	Fribrg, 3b	2	1	0	2	0
Kamm, 3b	4	1	1	2	0	Miller, lf.	4	1	0	0	0
M'Clan, ss	4	3	2	2	0	Hethte, rf	4	0	1	0	0
Schalk, c.	4	1	4	2	0	Hartnet, c	2	1	5	1	0
Robtson, p	2	1	1	1	1	Alexndr, p	3	0	0	0	0
Lyons, p..	1	0	0	4	0						
Strunk...	1	1	0	0	0						
Totals..	37	11	24	13	1	Totals..	30	11	27	19	4

White Sox.....	0	0	1	0	2	1	0	0	0	—4
Cubs.........	0	0	2	4	0	1	0	1	*	—8

Cubs Strunk batted for Lyons in ninth.

Two base hits—Statz, Adams (2), McClellan. Three base hit—Adams. Home run—Collins. Stolen bases—Collins, Adams. Bases on balls—Off Robertson, 2; Alexander, 3; Lyons, 2. Struck out—By Alexander, 4; Robertson, 1; Lyons, 1. Losing pitcher—Robertson. Umpires—Klem, Holmes, Quigley and Ormsby.

22,000 Tickets to Bear-Trojan Battle on Sale

THE public sale of tickets for the California-U. S. C. game, to be played November 10 at the Los Angeles Coliseum, will start today. Graduate Manager Gwynne Wilson of the Trojan institution yesterday sent 22,000 choice seats to the five sporting goods stores. These will be sold to the public and represent the best of the remaining seats. There are no box seats for sale, as the allotment is oversubscribed. San Francisco has requested 15,000 seats.

Hope Wins Over Adams at Venice

WILLIE HOPE won the decision over Johnny Adams, San Bernardino lightweight, last night at the Venice boxing show. In the semi-windup Marty Burman scored a knockout over Red Burke in the first round.

5:30 P. M.

SPORTING EXTRA

The Evening Bulletin.

5:30 P. M.

VOLUME LXI. NO. 242. TUESDAY: Fair. PROVIDENCE, MONDAY, OCTOBER 15, 1923 32 PAGES TWO CENTS 14 Cents Per Week Delivered by Carrier.

YANKS WIN WORLD'S BASEBALL CHAMPIONSHIP

"BOB" MEUSEL

Yankee Outfielder Who Won World Series for His Team To-day When He Drove Tieing and Winning Runs Across in the Eighth

COMPLETE BOX SCORE OF SIXTH WORLD SERIES GAME

YANKEES	AB	R	H	PO	A	E
Witt, m......	3	0	0	3	1	0
Haines, m....	0	1	0	0	0	0
Dugan, 3......	3	1	0	2	1	0
Ruth, r.......	3	1	1	1	0	0
R.Meusel, l ...	4	0	1	1	0	0
Pipp, 1b......	4	0	0	12	0	0
Ward, 2......	4	0	1	0	7	0
Schang, c	4	1	1	7	0	0
Scott, s......	4	1	1	1	2	0
Pennock, p ...	2	0	0	0	1	0
*Hofman, ...	0	0	0	0	0	0
‡Bush, ...	0	0	0	0	0	0
xJohnson, ...	0	1	0	0	0	0
Jones, p......	0	0	0	0	1	0
Totals.....	31	6	5	27	13	0

GIANTS	AB	R	H	PO	A	E
Bancroft, s ...	4	0	0	1	7	0
Groh, 3	4	1	1	1	2	0
Frisch, 2......	4	2	3	0	6	0
Young, r	4	0	2	0	0	0
E. Meusel, l...	4	0	1	1	0	0
Cun'gham, m .	3	0	1	0	0	1
Stengel, m....	1	0	0	0	0	0
Kelly, 1b.....	4	0	0	20	0	0
Snyder, c.....	4	1	2	4	0	0
Nehf, p	3	0	0	0	5	0
Ryan, p	0	0	0	0	0	0
†Bentley ...	1	0	0	0	0	0
Totals.....	36	4	10	27	20	1

INNINGS	1	2	3	4	5	6	7	8	9	R	H	E
YANKEES	1	0	0	0	0	0	0	5	0	6	5	0
GIANTS	1	0	0	1	1	0	1	0	0	4	10	1

Hits—Off Nehf 4 in 7 1-3 innings; off Pennock 9 in 7 innings.
Three base hit—Frisch.
Home runs—Ruth, Snyder.
Double plays—Nehf to Bancroft to Kelly.
Struck Out—By Nehf 3, by Pennock 5, by Ryan 1.
Bases on Balls—Off Nehf 3, off Ryan 1.
Left on bases—Yankees 2, Giants 4.
Time of game—2h. 8m.
Umpires — Evans, Nallin, Hart, O'Day.

*Hofmann batted for Pennock in seventh.
†Bentley batted for Ryan in ninth.
‡Bush batted for Witt in seventh.
xJohnson ran for Bush in seventh.

GEORGE "BABE" RUTH

The Mighty Bambino, Who Created New World Series Record To-day When He Got a Home Run in the First Inning, Making Three Circuit Clouts for the Series.

TWELVE INDICTED HERE ON GAMBLING CHARGES

Nearly Score of Secret Bills Are Also Returned as Grand Jury Reports in Superior Court

The crusade against gamblers which has been conducted in different sections of the State hit Providence County to-day when the September grand jury, which has been in session the past few weeks in the Superior Court building, returned indictments against the following:

George B. Briggs of Warwick, charged with being a common gambler in Cranston and Pawtuxet Valley.

Joseph Payan, alleged manager of the Pilgrim Club in Cranston, charged with being a common gambler and with maintaining a nuisance.

John F. Hennessey of East Providence, charged with being a common gambler and with maintaining a nuisance.

James Cianci, alleged proprietor of the Silver Lake Hotel in Cranston, which recently burned, charged with being a common gambler and with maintaining a nuisance.

William Riley of North Providence, charged with being a common gambler.

Joseph Lizard of North Providence, alleged to be in the employ of William Riley, charged with being a common gambler.

Bessie Cook, alias Ramsey, alleged proprietor of the Admiral Inn, Cumberland, which was raided Friday night by Sheriff Jonathan Andrews and Deputy Thomas, charged with being a common gambler and with maintaining a nuisance.

Briggs, Riley and Lizard are alleged to be the owners or operators of slot machines.

Bertha Koch of Foster, two indictments, alleging maintaining gambling nuisances.

Jacob Kulze, alleged proprietor of the Sunnyside Hotel, Johnston, maintaining common gambling nuisance.

James P. Cahill, Foster, alleged proprietor of the Hartford Pike House, two indictments, alleging common gambler and maintaining gambling unisance.

Joseph George, alias Blind Joe, Woonsocket, maintaining common nuisance.

Cornelius Keating, alleged proprietor of the St. Cloud Hotel, Johnston, maintaining nuisance.

Nineteen secret indictments were also returned, a large number of which were said to be the result of the crusade of the Attorney General's office against gambling.

The report of the grand jury shows that thus far 26 gambling indictments have been filed against 12 different persons, in addition to the secret indictments.

No indictments were found against the following: James E. Spelman, charged

Continued on Page 2, Col. 5.

SIX, TRAPPED IN ATTIC, BURN TO DEATH IN BROOKLYN

Firemen Find Charred Bodies in Ruins Two Hours After Blaze is Discovered.—Investigation of Cause Ordered.

[By the Associated Press]

New York, Oct. 15.—Six persons were trapped in an attic and burned to death, and a seventh, a woman, suffered grave injuries in leaping from the flames in a fire which early to-day destroyed a frame three-story dwelling in the Bensonhurst section of Brooklyn.

The dead are:

Mrs. Lillian Andrews, her nephew, Charles, and niece, Margaret.

George Kyne, playwright.

Francis Poncho Fowler.

Miss Roberta Wigert.

Mrs. Anna Andrews, who was trapped with the others in the attic of the building, leaped through a window, sustaining internal injuries which may prove fatal.

Neighbors, seeing smoke rolling from the basement of the dwelling house, rushed to the spot just in time to see Mrs. Anna Andrews leap from a window of the attic apartment. Two hours later firemen found the charred bodies of the six victims. They apparently had been overcome after escape had been cut off by the flames.

The body of Charles Andrews, 19-year-old athlete and student at Polytechnic Institute, Brooklyn, lay just inside of a rear window. Near him lay his aunt, Mrs. Lillian Andrews. The body of 12-year-old Margaret was found clasped in the arms of Miss Wigert, a maid, in an adjoining room.

The ruins of a third bedroom disclosed the body of Fowler. Kyne had been trapped in the bathroom in an attempt to reach a window. They were roomers in the Andrews home.

A dozen occupants of the first and second floor apartments of the burned building were awakened and led through the flames to safety by Dr. Thomas McNickle, a dentist, and his brother, whose four nieces were among the rescued.

Heads of the fire department have ordered an investigation to determine the origin of the fire.

TWO CIVILIANS KILLED IN MEININGEN, GERMANY

Troops Aid Police in Clearing Streets of Rioters.

[By the Associated Press]

Berlin, Oct. 15.—Two civilians are reported to have been killed and several others injured at Meiningen Saturday night when the Reichswehr was called upon to help the police clear the streets of rioters.

Three persons were injured in a food riot at Frankfort-on-Main on Saturday.

NO IDLENESS IN FRANCE, LABOR STATISTICS SHOW

Only 66 in All Paris Out of Work; 1275 in Whole Country.

[By the Associated Press]

Paris, Oct. 15.—The French Government has no unemployment problem on its hands. Statistics compiled by the Ministry of Labor show that only 1275 persons are out of work in all France, of whom 66 are in Paris, whereas in March, 1921, the number of unemployed was 91,225. Of this number 45,100 were in Paris.

Series Results

FIRST GAME
GIANTS 5—YANKEES 4

SECOND GAME
YANKEES 4—GIANTS 2

THIRD GAME
GIANTS 1—YANKEES 0

FOURTH GAME
YANKEES 8—GIANTS 4

FIFTH GAME
YANKEES 8—GIANTS 1

SIXTH GAME
YANKEES 6—GIANTS 4

4 MEN SEIZED WITH LIQUOR-LADEN CARS FAIL TO RAISE BAIL

Quartet Apprehended Early Yesterday Morning in East Providence is Jailed.—464 Bottles of Whiskey Found in Two Machines Are Valued at $5000.

Four alleged rum runners, piloting two liquor-laden touring cars, fell victims to the vigilance of Patrolmen Frederick Hancock and John Estes of the East Providence police after an exciting chase at 3 o'clock yesterday morning. The haul aggregated 464 bottles of Scotch whiskey, valued at $5000, and the prisoners, W. B. Bradley and Bertram M. Armstrong of Albany, King Johnson of Riverside and Alex Carron, formerly of East Providence, arraigned before Judge Malcolm D. Champlin in the Seventh District Court, East Providence, yesterday forenoon, were jailed in default of bail. Trial was set for next Saturday.

All entered not guilty pleas. Bradley was charged with carrying a concealed weapon and transporting liquor. Bail was set at $500 on the first charge and $1000 on the second.

Armstrong's case was similarly disposed of. Johnson and Carron were charged with transporting liquor only. Their bail was $1000 each.

Signal Unheeded

Hancock, on duty in Riverside, signalled a touring car to stop when he saw it speeding into Turner avenue. The big automobile hurtled on, unheeding, how-

Continued on Page 3, Col. 4.

NEW PRESIDENT OF CHINA IS TENDERED RECEPTION

Pekin, Oct. 15.—(By the Associated Press))—The entire diplomatic body attended the reception this morning to Marshal Tsao Kun, the new President of China.

BABE RUTH GETS THIRD HOME RUN, NEW RECORD

Mighty Swatsmith Sets Mark That May Stand for All Time

Special to the Evening Bulletin.

Polo Grounds, New York, Oct. 15.—All hail the Yankees, new baseball champions of the world. After two years of dismal failure the American League crew under Miller Huggins came into its own to-day. The result of to-day's final set-to of the 1923 struggle was:

Yankees 6, Giants 4

Starters in the blue ribbon classic of baseball the past three years, each year against "Jawn" McGraw and his Giants, the Yankees landed the bacon this year for the first time. Two years ago the Yankees obtained an early lead and it looked as though there was nothing to it but the American Leaguers. Then, in one of the most sensational rallies ever witnessed in the fall classic, the Giants took three straight and the series, making monkeys out of Babe Ruth and the other big sticks of the Yankee crew.

Last year the Yanks made their punkiest showing, falling down miserably in five games, the best they could do being to tie the Giants in one of the games and losing the other four. But this year it was a different story. Losing the first game, the Yankees came back in the second and evened the series. Casey Stengel gave the Giants a 2 to 1 lead in the third game when his home run was the only run scored in the set-to.

But in the fourth battle the Yankees unlimbered their heavy artillery and when the smoke of battle had cleared away they were out on the long end of an 8 to 4 score, the clan of Huggins having crushed to a pulp the Giant firing squad. Hit after hit of every description rolled off the bats of the American Leaguers. Yesterday it was almost a repetition of the day before, Babe Ruth et al., taking kindly to everything

RED MAGIC SECTION
Edited by The World Famous HOUDINI
The World
Copyright, (New York World), Press Publishing Co. 1924.
EDUCATION as well as ENTERTAINMENT

Vol. 1 NEW YORK, SUNDAY, DECEMBER 21, 1924. No. 6

HELP HOUDINI OUT OF THE HANDCUFFS

Harry Houdini can escape from real handcuffs, straitjackets or prison cells as easily as you or I would walk out of the room; but we have put him in paper handcuffs here so tight that he can't get away. You can help him escape by following directions:

As many as you please can play the game. Hang this page on the wall, at about the height of your eyes. Then stand about ten feet away from the picture with a pencil in your hand; take a good look at it, close your eyes and walk toward it; when you have reached it without opening your eyes make three marks in where you think three of the handcuffs are. Then let some one else try. You had better each decide on a special mark—say, one a cross, another a circle, a third a triangle, and so on. The first to get his mark in three of the handcuffs sets Houdini free and wins the game.

SAVE YOUR RED MAGIC SECTIONS EACH WEEK

ANSWERS NEXT SUNDAY

The World

OFFICIAL WEATHER FORECAST
Increasing cloudiness to-day; to-morrow, rain, with rising temperature; moderate to fresh northeast winds to-day.

TEMPERATURE YESTERDAY
Highest 50, 12.01 A. M.; lowest 39, 9 P.M.

VOL. LXVII. NO. 23,971—DAILY. Copyright Press Publishing Company (New York World) 1927 NEW YORK, FRIDAY, APRIL 8, 1927. Entered as Second-Class Matter Post Office, New York, N. Y. ** TWO CENTS In Greater New York | THREE CENTS Within 200 Miles | FOUR CENTS Elsewhere

GOV. SMITH SIGNS BILL TO PADLOCK DIRTY THEATRES

Justifies Approval of Wales Licensing Measure by Citing Banton; Vetoes 70 Bills and Leaves Albany for Vacation

APPROVES VETO POWER ON PORT AUTHORITY ACTS

Kills Gas Cut-Off Repealer—O. K.'s City Permit for Sewage Plant on Ward's Island

By Frank L. Hopkins
Staff Correspondent of The World
Special Despatch to The World

ALBANY, April 7.—Gov. Smith to-day wrote finis on the 1927 legislative session.

In a whirlwind wind-up of thirty-day bills, the earliest made by any recent Governor, he this morning affixed his signature to fifty bills, wrote the executive disapproval across seventy others, including omnibus vetoes of sixty-four acts, and departed for a vacation which will begin in New York City and continue with several rounds of golf next week at the Seaview Club, Absecon, N. J.

Year's Closing Provided

One of the Governor's final acts was to approve the Wales Theatre Padlock Bill, vesting in the Commissioner of Licenses the power to close for a year any showhouse permitting on its stage an act or a scene which may be convicted of indecency.

The Knight bill, giving the Governor the power of veto over the acts of the New York Commissioners of the Port Authority, was signed, thereby placing this State on a par with New Jersey in respect to control of port development and bridge building.

Other important bills signed included the act permitting New York City to erect a sewage disposal plant on Ward's Island, several salary increase bills for county and judicial officials, a measure which at last will permit Assemblyman Louis Cuvillier to try out in the Court of Claims his plea for reimbursement for expenses incurred in defending the Enright libel suit, and the New York City Retirement Bill, permitting allowances to be based on the last five years instead of the last ten years of service.

No Opinion on Gas Cut-Off Law

But the Governor killed a half dozen other retirement bills, including the one which would have reduced the age to fifty-five years and thereby permitted former Mayor Hylan and several of the latter's friends to receive pensions. He also killed the Thayer bill, designed to repeal a New York City ordinance passed during the Hylan Administration, requiring installation of automatic cut-off valves in gas mains in buildings more than five stories in height. The Governor held that not only was the Thayer measure too broad, but that the place to seek a repeal was in the body which gave the city the original enactment. As it stands now, the cut-off must be installed.

Other important measures to be slaughtered included the Jenks bill to permit osteopaths to administer anaesthetics and perform certain minor surgical operations, the Berg bill to permit optometrists to use the title of doctor, the Love bill to permit the Montauk Riding and Driving Club to erect a special apartment house not in conformity with the Tenement House Law, the Stone Spanish-American War

(Continued on Fourth Page)

Television Now Fact; Talkers 200 Miles Off Shown on Telephone

A. T. & T. HEAD Who Supervises Successful Television Test

WALTER S. GIFFORD
© by Underwood & Underwood

Group in New York Watches Hoover Speak in Washington—Both Wires and Radio Used

Man won a new faculty from nature yesterday. Television was pulled out of the dictionary and into the world of fact. For the first time men sat in New York and looked 200 miles over a telephone wire at other men in Washington, D. C.

"Hello, General, you're looking fine," said Walter S. Gifford. "I see you've got your glasses on. You screen well, Gen. Carty."

J. J. Carty's bass voice boomed out of the cabinet as if he were gigantically imprisoned inside the black box: "Does it—ah—does it flatter me?"

"An Improvement"

Mr. Gifford studied the luminous screen where electrons, just trained to this new trick, painted a living, flickering, changing image of the man at the far end:

"Yes," he said by and by. "I think it's an improvement."

And out of the obscurity behind Mr. Gifford, in the auditorium on top of the Bell Telephone laboratory at West and Bethune Streets, came the chuckle of fifty newspaper men who were witnessing the opening demonstration.

Years of Research Work

What was being seen was the upshot of years of research work. Tons of apparatus ranged the walls. Technicians hurried here and there in the darkened room. The visitors sat spellbound in pews arranged for the occasion as if they were votaries at some strange, new religious spectacle. Lilliputian red and purple lamps glimmered and glowed here and there upon the panels of the instruments.

And through the maze of wires and coils and humming motors the millions of electrons, newly yoked by man, invisibly threaded their mazy way in a tremendous dance so that men might see "beyond eyeshot." Alexander Graham Bell gave to men an electric ear. Now in the laboratories which bear his name, and in whose museum reposes still Bell's first contraption, man was being given his new electric eye.

An Interruption

The visitors, who included Gerard Swope, President of the General Electric Company, saw by radio as well as wire. In Washington an address was read into a telephone transmitter by Secretary of Commerce Herbert Hoover and the group in the New York laboratory saw as well as heard him. Various others present in the capital came to the phone and were telephoned and televised by those in New York.

Then the vision that had come reeling by wire across Maryland and Pennsylvania and New Jersey and tumbled out upon the glowing screen was interrupted and over in Whippany, N. J., radio station 3XN came on the air.

Instantly those awed spectators in West Street saw the shimmering screen break and darken, scatter in a blur, then suddenly re-form to show a placard being waved before it—"Station 3XN." E. L. Nelson, technician in charge at Whippany, came on and talked. He was forty miles away, but his countenance was plain and his voice boomed into the auditorium with

(Continued on Second Page)

U. S. to Fingerprint New Dry Agents in Drastic Merit Test

From The World's Bureau
Special Despatch to The World

WASHINGTON, April 7.—"Practical" competitive examinations for 2,500 jobs in the Bureau of Prohibition and subsequent fingerprinting of all successful candidates will be conducted by the United States Civil Service Commission in 600 cities as soon as recruits can be obtained.

The situations classified under the act of March 3 last are:

One chief of field division, $6,000 a year; 5 zone supervisors, $5,200; 24 administrators, $4,000 to $6,000; 24 assistant administrators (enforcement work), $3,300 to $5,200; 24 assistant administrators (permissive work), $3,300 to $5,200; 50 deputy administrators, $3,000 to $4,600; 2 field office inspectors, $3,800 to $3,900; 4 associate field office inspectors, $3,000 to $3,600; 18 senior investigators, $3,800; 109 investigators, $3,000; 53 junior investigators, $2,400; 228 agents, $2,400; 1,260 junior agents, $1,860; 102 watchmen, $1,140 to $1,800, and 74 attorneys, $1,860 to $5,200.

"A searching oral test and a rigid character investigation" will be made of all applicants, according to the announcement.

"The commission feels," it goes on, "that any person worthy of appointment will not object to the most searching investigation into his past life."

HORSE HOLDS ON IN FRANCE

PARIS, April 7 (A. P.)—The horse shows no signs of disappearing from France. In 1802 there were 1,332,112 horses. The number increased to 2,859,000 in 1862, despite the inroads of trains. In 1906, when automobiles began appearing, there were 3,170,000 horses, and, despite heavy war losses, 2,859,000 remained in 1924.

WHY THE KING WALKED HOME

MADRID, April 7 (A. P.)—King Alfonso was out motoring to-day when he met a youth on horseback. The horse became frightened and threw his rider. The King stopped, got out and ordered the boy put in the car and sent to the Royal Infirmary. Then the King walked home.

White House Roof Long in Danger Of Serious Crash, Repairs Reveal

From The World's Bureau
Special Despatch to The World

WASHINGTON, April 7.—Repair work at the White House has revealed the danger under which President Coolidge, his recent predecessors and their families lived, owing to a poorly supported roof that might have dropped at any time.

The hazard was disclosed when the N. P. Severin Company, Chicago contractors, ripped off the old roof. This work has just been completed. Mr. Severin reported that reconstruction of the upper portion of the Executive Mansion and the roofing had not been started any too soon.

The outer walls were supposed to carry most of the roof weight, but virtually all the load was resting on the interior walls.

Army engineers examined the building some time ago and recommended the reconstruction, explaining that any unusual strain, such as a heavy snow, might bring the roof in on the President and his family. Some wonder is now being expressed that the roof stood under the heavy snow that crashed in the Knickerbocker Theatre six years ago. When the weakness was first discovered a 2,000-gallon water tank, weighing eight tons, was removed, relieving part of the strain.

The White House attic had not been changed since the mansion was rebuilt after its burning by the British in the War of 1812. The lower floors were renovated and made fireproof under President Roosevelt.

TARDY JUDGE FINES HIMSELF

Special Despatch to The World

DANVILLE, Va., April 7.—Judge A. B. Dabney of Charlottesville fined himself $5 to-day for being twenty minutes late in convening the Corporation Court. He said his car had broken down. H. T. Williams, an attorney, moved for remittance of the fine, saying it was the unanimous desire of the Danville bar, but Judge Dabney said he intended to pay and wouldn't make an exception of himself when he fined others for being tardy.

CAN'T WIN STRIKE WITHOUT GRAFT, FUR MEN SAID

Police Paid in Other Walkouts, Frayne Testifies Leaders Told—Counsel for Communists Tries by Queries to Discredit A. F. L. Inquiry

INDUSTRIAL SQUAD OFFICER CONFIDENT OF VINDICATION

Receipts for Cops' Money Said to Have Been Marked "X"; Auditor Saw Only Two

By John J. Leary Jr.

Receipts for money paid to police for protection were marked with an "X," Samuel Liebowitz of the Communist-controlled fur strike committee, testified at St. Augustine, Fla., before the American Federation of Labor Commission which investigated the walkout. Miss Henrietta Holden, stenographer to the commission, who read her record taken at the inquiry in Florida, so told Magistrate Joseph E. Corrigan at the John Doe inquiry yesterday.

"We charged money paid to the police to incidentals,'" she quoted him as saying. "We marked them with an 'X.' The 'X' meant the money went to the police. I can identify the receipts for money given to police."

Herman Volk, an auditor employed by the commission, following Miss Holden, said he recalled only two receipts so marked in the partial examination he and Walter M. Cook were permitted to make.

"So, out of 300 receipts you saw," Assistant District Attorney George N. Brothers asked, "you saw but two marked with an 'X.'?"

"That is my recollection," the witness replied.

The name of only one policeman appeared in yesterday's testimony—that of Capt. John Lyons, in charge of the police at Carnegie Hall when an organized Communist demonstration prevented Hugh Frayne and other representatives of the American Federation of Labor speaking.

Mr. Frayne, testifying yesterday, gave Capt. Lyons a clean bill of health, saying he had no doubt Lyons did his full duty as he saw it that day.

No one testifying before the commission, he said, had named individual policemen as profiting through the strike, a statement corroborated by other witnesses.

Beside the auditors and Miss Holden, only two witnesses were examined yesterday—Hugh Frayne and Joseph P. Ryan, of the Federation's investigating commission.

Mr. Frayne's testimony, like that of

(Continued on Sixth Page)

WHITE HOUSE "Envoy Paramount" to Nicaragua

HENRY L. STIMSON
© Henry Miller

STIMSON TO SEEK NICARAGUA PEACE

Coolidge Sends Him There to Iron Out Affairs Annoying Administration

1928 CAMPAIGN INVOLVED

"Boys Out of the Trenches by Christmas," Is Slogan

From The World's Bureau
Special Despatch to The World

WASHINGTON, April 7.—Henry L. Stimson, Secretary of War under President Taft, starts for Nicaragua Saturday by order of President Coolidge to settle the affairs of that distracted country.

The State Department makes mystery of the purpose of the mission, but it is literally to "get the boys out of the trenches by Christmas."

He goes with ample authority to treat with Diaz and Sacasa, and the probable process will be by getting them to agree to an election. Diaz wants the election at the expiration of his term in 1929. Sacasa wants it now.

Recent despatches from down there indicate the revolutionists are discouraged. Wherever they have opportunity for an effective attack on the Government forces the American marines get in the way. This process and the "neutral zone" proclaimed by Admiral Latimer, make it impossible that the insurgent Vice President can attain the capital, and the theory of the Stimson expedition is that Sacasa may be discouraged sufficiently to listen to some compromise proposal.

The Coolidge Administration is worried at the idea of the troubles in Nicaragua running into the coming Presidential campaign. It is obvious that when Congress convenes in December there will be a lot of criticism and demands that the marines be brought home. It will be urged against

(Continued on Sixth Page)

Physician's Killer Is Guilty Of Murder in First Degree

Jury Finds Premeditation in Attack of Francesco Caruso When Boy Died—Deliberated 6 Hours and 10 Minutes—Prisoner Takes Verdict Calmly

Francesco Caruso, thirty-five, Brooklyn laborer, killer of Dr. Casper S. Pendola, was found guilty of murder in the first degree at 11.51 o'clock last night by a jury before Kings County Judge McLaughlin. The jurors had deliberated six hours and ten minutes. Sentence will be imposed April 18. Caruso accepted the verdict calmly.

The jury received the case at 5.30 o'clock in the afternoon. Their first ballot was indicated as seven to five for first degree murder, the minority holding out for a lesser degree. The second ballot was reported as ten to two for a first degree murder verdict, and it was believed deliberation would continue many hours.

At 7.30 o'clock, with the vote unchanged, County Judge McLaughlin recessed court until 9 o'clock, permitting the jurors to go out for dinner under guard. A few minutes after 9 o'clock deliberation was resumed. At 10.25 the jurors returned to the courtroom for instructions as to the proportion of guilt required for a first or second degree murder verdict. Judge McLaughlin defined the degrees and the jurors resumed deliberation.

At 10.40 the jurors again returned to the courtroom for instructions as to the charge of premeditated murder. By the time the jurors had been instructed the members of the Caruso and Pendola families had left for their homes.

The preponderate vote reported for a first degree verdict came as somewhat of a surprise to Caruso's defense counsel. George W. Voss, directing the defense, had predicted a quick verdict of second degree murder or less.

The jurors voting for the harsher verdict, which carries with it death in the electric chair, argued that the stained knife, which had been waved under their noses by Assistant District Attorney Gallagher in his summation, was strong evidence of premeditation. Caruso has admitted plunging the knife into the throat of Dr. Pendola after he had already choked him into helplessness.

It is believed that it is on the point as to whether or not the murder was premeditated that the jurors debated. On their third visit to the court room at 11 o'clock they had asked Judg McLaughlin to read to them that part of the charge specifying deliberation and premeditation.

At that time it was believed the jurors had agreed upon th guilt of the defendant but had been unabl to fix the degree. As th hours passed, the courtroom gradually became empy of spectators. Only a score were on hand early this morning. Caruso, slumped deep in his chair, wept silently through the day as the trial approached its close.

TWO BOYS KILLED, 3 HURT, AS TRUCK SMASHES COUPE

Big Machine Crashes Into Smaller After Youngsters Had Climbed on Running Boards to Get Ride Home From School

ONE DIES UNDER WHEELS, OTHER ON WAY TO HOSPITAL

Victims of Brooklyn Accident Were Members of Confirmation Class

Two schoolboys were killed and three were seriously injured yesterday afternoon when a small coupe they were boarding was struck and overturned by a five-ton motor truck at Rugby and Beverly Roads, Brooklyn. Two of the boys were hurled under the wheels of the truck and one was instantly killed. The other died on the way to a hospital.

The dead are Lawrence Moen, eleven, of No. 360 East Seventh Street, and Caesar Sauva, ten, of No. 698 Coney Island Avenue, both Brooklyn.

Three boys taken to Kings County Hospital were John Tedeschi, thirteen, of No. 260 East Ninth Street; Nicholas De Marinis, thirteen, of No. 239 East Ninth Street, and Timothy Barlow, eleven, of No. 240 East Ninth Street, Brooklyn. Tedeschi and Barlow suffered cuts and possible internal injuries. De Marinis's left leg was broken and he was internally injured.

Preparing for Confirmation

The victims of the accident, with four other boys, all about the same age, pupils of Holy Innocents Parochial School, East 17th Street and Beverly Road, were walking through Beverly Road on their way home from Holy Innocents Church, where they were preparing for confirmation to-morrow morning, when they met the coupe, occupied by Stephen Collins, thirty, a contractor, of No. 1042 Flatbush Avenue, Brooklyn, and his wife, Marian.

One of the lads, William Conavery, eleven, of No. 618 Coney Island Avenue, called to Collins and asked for a lift. Collins, who was well acquainted with William, took him aboard. He told the other youngsters there was no room for them.

Others Decide to Ride

With William sitting on Mrs. Collins's lap, the coupe was just getting under way, a few minutes later, when the other youngsters decided to scramble to the running boards. Several managed to get aboard. Just who they were police were unable to determine.

The youngsters were yelling when the motor truck, coming through Beverly Road, with Frank Whelan of No. 647 74th Street, Brooklyn, at the steering wheel, struck the coupe in the rear, tore off the back wheels and hurled the car over on its side at the curbing. The front wheels of the truck passed over Moen and Sauva. The other boys, flung to the sidewalk, lay in a tangled heap, moaning or screaming.

Whelan's truck plowed toward the sidewalk, where other boys were standing, but he gained control before further damage was done. The occupants of the coupe, extricated by passersby,

(Continued on Fourth Page)

Boston Scurrying to Speculators For Seats at Dry Debate To-Night

Special Despatch to The World

BOSTON, April 7.—The wet-dry debate to-morrow night between President Nicholas Murray Butler of Columbia University and Senator William E. Borah (R., Ida.) is becoming almost as great an attraction as a successful musical comedy or a championship fight.

Twenty dollars a seat is being offered to speculators for the opportunity to hear the leading Prohibitionist among Republican Senators and one of the outstanding Republican wets argue the question: "Resolved, That the Republican National Convention of 1928 should advocate the repeal of the Eighteenth Amendment."

Dr. Butler will debate the affirmative for forty-five minutes, Senator Borah will answer for an hour, and Dr. Butler will then have twelve minutes of rebuttal.

The tickets were withdrawn from public sale because of the great demand for them by members of the Roosevelt Club, which organized the debate and has taken Symphony Hall to hold it in. Even standing room has already been bespoken, and though handsome offers were made to speculators, few had any tickets to sell.

The Roosevelt Club now has over 1,000 members, whereas last summer it had but 350, and realization that only members would get tickets for the debate is said to have been partly responsible for the increase. Robert M. Washburn, President of the club, and former Senator William M. Butler, Chairman of the Republican National Committee, will be the only persons on the platform with the speaker.

"Liquor is the first political question of the hour," declared Mr. Washburn. "The Symphony Hall meeting is planned in the hope that the Republican Party can be stimulated to recognize that it can no longer be ignored."

The speeches will be broadcast by WNAC of Boston on a 430-metre wave length and by WEAN of Providence on 367 metres, beginning at 8 o'clock.

Soviet Consulate Under Guard of Shanghai Police

No One Permitted to Enter or Depart—Chinese Commissioner Refused Admission Unless He Submitted to Search

REMOVAL OF EMBASSY FROM PEKING FORECAST

Anti-Foreign Agitation Steadily Grows—Evacuation of Foreigners Rushed

Following are chief developments of the day in China:

AFTER A RAID on the Soviet Embassy in Peking Wednesday, the Soviet Consulate in Shanghai was surrounded by police. The Soviet Consul warned the Diplomatic Corps of the serious situation and said the Soviet Embassy may be moved to Hankow.

ANTI-FOREIGN agitation in Hankow continues and plans are being made for removing the few foreigners remaining there.

PREMIER WELLINGTON KOO in Peking resigned and is expected to be succeeded by Gen Yang Yu Ting, Chief Adviser to Marshal Chang Tso Lin.

SHANGHAI, April 7 (A. P.)—Police assisted by White Russian volunteer late to-day surrounded the Soviet consulate in the international settlement with orders to prevent any one from entering or leaving the premises.

No reason for this action was given but it was stated that there were no present intention to raid the consulate.

Among the visitors whom the police held up was the Chinese Commissioner of Foreign Affairs, who was informed he would not be allowed to enter unless he consented to be searched. The Commissioner refused to permit this and departed.

No Change in Relations

The relations between the Northern Government and Soviet Russia as a result of yesterday's raid under direction of Northern soldiers and police on buildings attached to the Soviet Embassy in Peking to-night apparently had undergone no official hcange. Although no official action appears to have been taken as yet by Russia, severance of relations between Peking and Moscow was regarded as a possibility.

The situation, however, was further complicated by the resignation of Dr. V. K. Wellington Koo as Acting Premier to Marshal Chang Tso Lin. Reports were circulated that Gen. Yang Yu Ting, chief adviser to the Manchurian war lord, would become premier.

Koo a Wu Sympathizer

Although no explanation for the resignation was received from Peking it was believed little change nl the political situation in North China was to be expected. Mr. Koo was known to be a sympathizer of Gen. Wu Pei-Fu, who is a bitter enecy of Chang Tso-Lin, who is now considered to be the real power behind both the military and political affairs of the Peking Government.

Before the resignation of Dr. Koo was announced, it was learned that acting at Chang Tsolin's request, he had drafted a protest to the Soviet Charge d'Affairs, accusing the Soviet Embassy of sheltering criminal plotters, who were seeking to undermine the authority o fthe Northern Government.

May Remove Embassy

Possibility of the removal of the Soviet Embassy at Peking to Hankow, the seat of the Cantonese, or Nationalist Government, was suggested by Wilhelm F. Linde, Soviet Consul here.

Mr. Linde said such a removal was not impossible in discussing the incident after he had called upon the Norwegian Consul General, dean of the Diplomatic Corps in Shanghai, to announce he would hold the consular body responsible if the Soviet Consulate here were raided also.

While interest continued to centre here on the international possibilities of the Peking raid insofar as it may cause serious repercussions in Moscow, foreigners in various sections of China were steadily evacuating the areas where anti-foreign agitation has been spreading.

Hankow, scene of a growing tenseness, was the centre of riotous foreign outbreaks over last wee

RESIGNS POST as Premier Following Raid on Soviet Consulate

WELLINGTON KOO
© by Underwood & Underwood

MILLARD TO WRITE ARTICLES ON CHINA

Noted Authority on Problems of Orient to Interpret Situation for The World

FIRST TO APPEAR MONDAY

Unofficial Adviser at Geneva and Versailles

Thomas F. Millard has returned to the staff of The World. Beginning Monday he will write a weekly review of events in China, lending to them the weight of the experience that has made him perhaps the foremost authority of to-day on the affairs of the Far East.

Mr. Millard is not only an exceptionally able reporter but he has lived in China for so long that it is possible for him to speak with an understanding few other men possess. His relations with the leaders of thought and activity in the republic are intimate, but he is wholly without partisanship and his presentations long have been conspicuous for their objectivity. It has been said of him that he is neither conservative nor liberal; neither pro-China nor anti-China; neither pro-British nor anti-British; nothing but pro-truth and anti-lies.

China is in the midst of the greatest political and social changes of our generation, perhaps. Much of the "news" that has been coming from there, however, has been unsatisfactory, even when it has been without bias. It has been superficial and unrelated to the underlying implications of events. It is just this interpretation that Mr. Millard will offer in the weekly articles that will begin in The World Monday, and appear regularly on that day thereafter so long as the situation justifies.

Mr. Millard has been in active news-

(Continued on Second Page)

ılting in further plans for a rapid ·arture of the comparatively few re- ıining foreigners. "Situation grow- ıg worse steadily," was a wireless mes- sage received from there to-day.

With lawlessness in the city apparently increasing, the commander of the United States Yangtse river patrol is urging Americans still in the city to depart as soon as possible. Japanese are leaving the city in increasing numbers, while German and Russian Nationals are preparing to go soon.

Dr. C. P. Triberg of St. Peter, Minn., a member of the Augustana Synod Mission of the American Lutheran Church, was reported missing to-day and it is feared he has been captured by bandits. All the members of the mission, which was centred in the province of Honan, are leaving China, fifty-four of the ninety-four members sailing to-morrow on the President Pierce.

In line with the decision to bring all British gunboats out of the Upper Yangtse areas, the British consuls and the remainder of the British communities at Chungking, Ichang, Changsha and Changling have been removed to Hankow.

A report received several days ago that Gen. Pi Shu Chen, Shantungese commander in Shanghai at the time of its capture by the Cantonese, had been executed, was confirmed in advices reaching here to-day.

The messages indicated that although Gen. Chang Tsung Chang, the Shantungese Commander in Chief, was inclined to condone the loss of Shanghai, on account of which Pi had been accused of treachery, Chu Yu Pu, Military Governor of Chihli Province, had insisted upon the death penalty.

Dr. Koo became Premier and Foreign Minister Oct. 1, 1926. He assumed office in a reorganization effected by Chang Tso Lin, who is credited with having directed the Peking Government since last April.

Dr. Koo formerly was Minister to the United States and to Great Britain. He is widely known in the United States, where he spent some years.

Dr. Koo holds the degree of doctor of philosophy from Columbia University and doctor of laws from both Columbia and Yale. He is a member of Phi Beta Kappa.

He was a delegate to the Paris Peace Conference, later Chinese representative on the League of Nations Council, and delegate to the Washington Conference in 1921.

Police Search Soviet Buildings With French Consent

TIENTSIN, April 7 (A. P.)—Chinese police this afternoon entered the French concession, with permission of the Consul, and searched the Dahl Bank and various Soviet trade missions. The Chinese detained all persons pending the search and removed documents for examination. French police took no direct part in the raid but maintained order outside.

Moscow Indignant, Blaming Legations for Raid

MOSCOW, April 7 (A. P.)—Great in- ·gnation exists in official quarters ·er the raid yesterday on buildings at- ·ched to the Soviet Embassy in Peking. ·tails of the raid thus far have been ·thheld from the public.

Bitter feeling exists here toward Mar- ·al Chang Tso Lin, Northern commander, whose troops are understood to have executed the raid and with whom the Soviet Government has clashed ·equently. But even more resentment expressed toward the foreign lega- ·ions in Peking which are reported to ·ve permitted the entry of the ·ldiers.

Soviet officials remark that for a time there has been a rule pro- ·ing entry of Chinese into the le- ·ation quarter of Peking when armed or in considerable numbers. Therefore the raid is being described here as unwarranted and unprecedented.

The course of the Soviet Government with regard to the raid has not been stated, but the question of what representations to make already is under discussion. Up to noon to-day no report on the raid had been received from the Peking Embassy nor had Tass, the official news agency, received advices from its Peking correspondent. These circumstances were interpreted at the Foreign Office as indicating that a censorship is operating in China.

Much anxiety is expressed over the fate of the Russian personnel reported arrested in the raid. It is denied, however, that any of the documents seized are of a compromising character.

Transport Sails for China With Marine Regiment

SAN DIEGO., Cal., April 7 (A. P.)—Bound for Shanghai with 1,550 officers and men of the Sixth Regiment, United States Marine Corps, the navy transport Henderson sailed to-day from San Diego. She is scheduled to go to Honolulu and thence to Chinese waters, arriving at Shanghai in about twenty-two days. The regiment was aboard at midnight last night with all supplies and equipment.

TEST FLIGHT POSTPONED

Unfavorable Weather Delays Start of Fifty-Hour Attempt

Unfavorable weather forecasts for today and to-morrow will delay the start of the proposed fifty-hour duration flight by Clarence D. Chamberlain and Leigh Wade, Charles A. Levine of the Columbia Aircraft Corporation, owners of the Wright-Bellanca monoplane in which the attempt will be made, announced yesterday. He said the hop off would be made on the first suitable day.

The flight is scheduled to be made about Manhattan with frequent trips to Mitchel Field, L. I., where messages will be dropped.

CLASSIFIED ADVERTISING INDEX

RUSH EVACUATION OF YANGTSE AREA

Increasing Anti-American Agitation Causes Consuls to Hasten Departure

BOYCOTT ON AT CHANGSHA

General Exodus From Hankow Also Is Reported

From The World's Bureau
Special Despatch to The World

WASHINGTON, April 7.—Increasing anti-American and anti-foreign agitation is hastening withdrawal of American Consuls and evacuation of American citizens still remaining in the upper Yangtse River districts

John Carter Vincent, Consul at Changsha, who had planned to depart April 17, sailed yesterday. In a message to the State Department dated April 4, Mr. Adams said the enforced strike of employees of both American companies and the American Consulate, together with a boycott of Americans and a strong anti-American agitation, developed suddenly on that date. This caused him to advance the date of his departure and to advise all Americans to evacuate. Most of these, who have homes in West Honan, withdrew with the Consul.

Standard Oil Shops Closed

Consul Vincent added that the shops of the Standard Oil Company at Changsha were closed April 4 by the labor union. The office and the installation of the company had been occupied by pickets. The American Business Community moved aboard the steamship Meiyun, a Standard Oil ship.

Walter A. Adams, Consul at Chungking, advised the Department Tuesday that he and Vice Consul Paul W. Meyer would sail on that date. Consul Adams added that he left on friendly terms with local Chinese authorities.

A message from Consul General Lockhart at Hankow states that at 2 P. M. yesterday a strong naval force was lying in the Yangtse at that port. There were eight Japanese naval vessels, six British, four American, two French and one Italian. Within forty-eight hours after the anti-Japanese riots on April 3 four Japanese destroyers arrived to strengthen Nippon's naval force there.

A half-day strike was called at Hankow yesterday to protest against the incident of April 3. Large crowds gathered in the former German concession which adjoins the Japanese concession.

Mr. Lockhart added that the general exodus of Japanese and other foreigners from Hankow continues steadily. A number of Russians who are affiliated with the Nationalist movement also have departed for down the river. All precautions have been taken to insure the evacuation of remaining Americans should an acute emergency arise.

In view of published reports to the effect that Dr. John E. Williams, the American killed in the Nanking outrages March 24, had a gun in his hand when attacked, Consul General Gauss in a despatch to the State Department from Shanghai, gives a summary of the facts as established by the sworn affidavits of eye witnesses taken by Consul John K. Davis at Nanking and by Mr. Gauss at Shanghai. The summary follows:

"On March 24, about 8 P. M. a group of six or seven Americans of Nanking University, including Dr. Williams, who was on his way to chapel met a group of seven or eight Chinese soldiers. At first these were thought to be of the Northern forces and were advised to flee since the city was in the possession of the Southern forces.

Stripped of Valuables

"The soldiers, however, declared to the Americans that they belonged to the Southern forces. It was then that they were identified as such by their insignia, cap and the usual Nationalist neckerchiefs. The soldiers then fired shots around the group of Americans and started to search them for arms, stripping them, however, of all valuables.

"The Americans were wholly unarmed and no resistance was made by them whatever. While one of the soldiers was taking a watch from him, Dr. Williams, without resisting or touching either the soldier or the watch, stated that the watch belonged to his mother and that the soldiers would not want it. At that point another of the soldiers shot Dr. Williams and killed him. Two other soldiers looted his dead body. They then walked away unconcernedly."

Minister MacMurray confirmed reports of the search of the Dahl Bank and the Chinese Eastern Railway offices yesterday by Chinese police and Northern troops. Permission was given by the senior Minister (Dutch) in behalf of the diplomatic quarter for the search of these buildings, which are private property, on the declaration of the Chinese authorities that they were known to be headquarters of subversive Soviet agitation.

Mr. MacMurray states the Chinese apparently went beyond the authorization and raided also the compound of the former Russian Legation guard.

A leading American trans-Pacific shipping company reports that shipments to and out of China continue as usual. There are no indications of any disruption of communications between Shanghai and foreign ports.

At the Navy Department it was said that in the event additional marines are sent to China within the next month they will travel on commercial vessels.

Figures in Television and Where New Miracle of Science Traveled

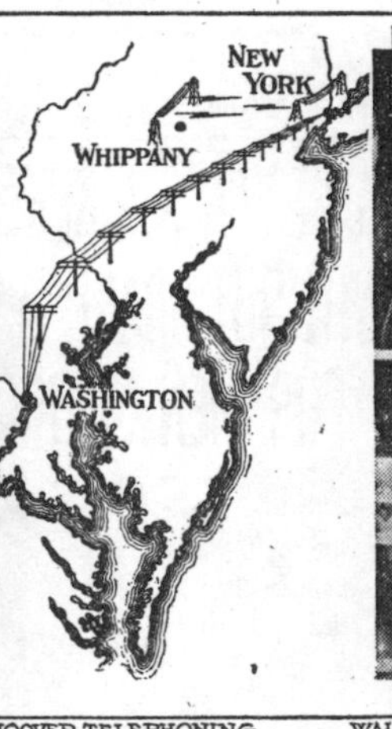

Standing, L to R.- A. E. BERRY and J. J. CARTY. Secretary HOOVER TELEPHONING — WALTER S. GIFFORD TELEPHONING and Dr. HERBERT E. IVES

SOVIET HINTS ARMS MAY CURB CHINESE

Consul General Declares Raids on Consulates "Violate Every Code Extant"

CALLS SITUATION GRAVE

Charges Opium Smugglers Are Responsible

By Lawrence Wilson
Special Cable to The World

SHANGHAI, April 8.—Possibility of armed intervention in China to prevent violation of Russia's diplomatic privileges was suggested to-day in a statement by Wilhelm Linde, Soviet Consul General, following placing of an armed guard about the Soviet Consulate here.

In an exclusive statement to the correspondent of The World and the North American Newspaper Alliance, Linde characterized the Peking and Shanghai incidents as unheard of and violations of every code extant, and said he already had protested to Moscow.

"I cannot say whether war will result," he said, "but the situation is one of extreme gravity."

"The incident at Peking has been used by irresponsible people here to create a political demonstration to embarrass and intimidate us. The dean of the consular corps has disclaimed all knowledge of the municipal council's action and later said that Fessenden, the Chairman of the municipal council, had been informed and would be held responsible for this action and for any further incidents.

Vice Consul Held Up

"It is most surprising that the ruffians of the Shantung army should be redecorated in volunteer corps uniforms and permitted to surround the consulate. We protested the incorporation of these brigands in the volunteer corps six weeks ago. Although they have not penetrated the consulate, yet they to-day refused the Vice Consul permission to leave the building without a search, in violation of every code extant. A Consul or his employees can be stopped only for the violation of criminal—not political—laws.

"According to international law, every Consul has a right to such literature and flags as he chooses to have.

Blames Opium Smugglers

"I believe the action is due to certain opium smugglers, who have heeded the irresponsible cries of the North China Daily News, which urged a raid on the consulate in an editorial this morning."

Tai Chi, Chinese Commissioner of Foreign Affairs, in an exclusive interview with this correspondent, also said he would protest the action.

"It is wholly without legal basis," he said. "The British Consul and the United States Consul have denied any knowledge of the affair, which proves that is was engineered by local authorities. Such actions tend to embitter the Chinese people against the foreign nations, due to the actions of a few local officials who violate the privileges of embassies."

(Copyright, 1927, in all countries by the North American Newspaper Alliance.)

ALABAMA MURDERER TO BE FIRST TO DIE THERE IN CHAIR

BIRMINGHAM, Ala., April 7 (A. P.)—Horace De Vaughn, Negro, will be executed early to-morrow for the murder last January of A. B. Moore and Mrs. Ruby Thornton, who were found shot to death on a suburban road. The execution will mark the first use of the electric chair in Alabama.

TELEVISION SHOWN A SUCCESS IN TEST

(Continued From First Page)

greater strength than had he been actually on the platform.

He announced a studio program. Songs and readings and blackface comedians. A new noise was in the ether and if those Hertzian vibrations yesterday escaped this globe and went washing out to other shores, there must have been some puzzled minds somewhere in the universe.

Mr. Gifford, President of the American Telephone and Telegraph Company, began the program before he spoke with the company's Vice President, Gen. Carty.

"To-day," said Mr. Gifford, "we are to witness another milestone in the conquest of nature by science. We shall see the fruition of years of study on the problem of seeing at a distance and as though face to face.

"The principles underlying television, which are related to the principles involved in electrical transmission of speech, have been known for a long time, but to-day we shall demonstrate its successful achievement. The elaborateness of the equipment required by the very nature of the undertaking precludes any present possibility of television being available in homes and offices generally.

"What its practical use may be I shall leave to your imagination. I am confident, however, that in many ways and in due time it will be found to add substantially to human comfort and happiness."

Television's Relative Progress

Dr. Frank B. Jewett, Vice President of the A. T. and T., spoke after Mr. Gifford and said in part:

"To-day we are relatively farther along in our work on television than we were on transoceanic telephony in 1915 when the American Telephone and Telegraph Company conducted the first successful test from Washington to Paris and Honolulu. Just what the ultimate field of television is to be can, as Mr. Gifford has said, be left to your imagination."

Dr. Jewett gave the floor over to Dr. Herbert E. Ives, a past President of the Optical Society of America and the man who directed the years of research which solved the problems of television.

Dr. Ives arose softly, like some medievalist potent in black magic, and as he spoke softly and precisely the colored, dim lights of mysterious tubes gleamed mystically from his glasses and polished skull and ran along the point of his beard, which shone like a bundle of fine copper wires.

The man seemed from another world telling to children a new fairy story of new giants and dragons and flying horses and magicians in black gardens. Indeed, he dealt in the mysteries of time and space more bewilderingly than the brothers Grimm dealt in fairies.

Like the Human Eye

The simplest television, he said, was that of the human eye.

"In this light is reflected from an object and falls upon the lens of the eye, which focuses it upon a screen which is called the retina. From this screen a million separate nerve fibres lead to the brain, and this bundle of nerve fibres we call the optic nerve. The impulses which they carry from the retinal screen are interpreted by the brain as sight or vision.

"But in man the optic nerve is but a couple of inches long. The problem is more difficult when we go outside the human body."

He displayed a great electric eye which had been made by his men, a honeycomb of lights with 2,500 cells, and each one had its separate copper wire. Their bundle—a great optic nerve—made an armful of conductors.

An Extra Dimension

The problem of television is akin to that of telephony, only more intricate. In telephony the sound viabrations of the voice must be converted into variations of an electric current and at the receiving end the varying electric current reconverted into sound viabrations. In short, the problem is to convey facsimiles in altering forms of energy.

In television the problem is to convert light shadings into electric variations and at the receiving end to translate them back into their original form. The difficulty arises from the entrance into the problem of an extra dimension. That is, the "image" must flow over a wire which, theoretically, has the sole dimension of length and at the receiving end must be converted into an image of length and breadth, like the image on any motion picture screen.

Continuous Motion Picture

In reality, that is what the television equipment provides, a continuous motion picture of the person who is talking at the other end of the line.

This extra dimension is obtained by what is called "scanning." A spot of light the size of a dime is made, by a mechanical contrivance, to streak across the face of the person who is talking so that the whole surface is covered in an eighteenth of a second.

This is accomplished by revolving a perforated disk in front of a neon tube, the red glow of which shines through the successive holes upon the person in front. The holes are so arranged in a spiral which moves toward the centre of the disk that the light spot or beam moves downward at each successive streak until the bottom level is reached, when instantly it starts from the top downward again, this whole operation being continuously performed eighteen times a second, which is the speed of the disk's rotation.

The spot thus covers the transmission area in successive streaks, much as the eye of a fast reader scans a page of print. And it is the light reflected from this spot which produces a varying electric current which may be sent out as "sight." When the spot strikes a dark eyebrow, for example, little light is reflected and but a feeble current is released by the photoelectric cell which actualy sends out the current. When the spot reaches the forehead or some other highlight then much light is reflected and the photoelectric cell transmits a strong current. These variations in the current strength go out at the rate of 20,000 per second.

Mileage Makes No Difference

The swiftly varying current is transmitted by wire or radio, a hundred or a thousand miles, it makes no difference, and at the receiving end the operation is reversed. There another disk, running exactly "in step" with the transmitting disk, revolves in front of a glowing red neon tube, the brightness of which alters in exact sympathy with the varying incoming current. It is this fast-flickering light which falls through the perforations of the receiving disk upon a small screen which reproduces the image ot the remote transmitter.

In short, the whole process is a continuously shifting painting performed by a slender beam of light.

"The energy amplication," explained Dr. Ives, "is enormous, there being an amplification of 5,000,000,000,000,000 times from the photo-electric cells, where the image starts, to the antenna, where it is finally sent out."

On wire transmission from Washington two channels or circuits were used, one for vision and one for a synchronizing current which kept the transmitting and receiving disks in step. Dr. Ives said it would be possible to put both these operations, plus the additional one of telephony, upon a single channel.

On the radio circuit, vision was sent on a wave length of 191 metres, accompanying speech at 270 metres, and the snychrsnizing frequency was 1,600 metres. The image in the receiver, when on the small screen, two by two and a half inches, was very distinct, like an old daguerreotype printed in fiery red. On the large screen, two feet square, the image was more blurry and identification of individuals became difficult.

Hoover Pictures Approach of New Era in Scientific Discovery

Special Despatch to The World

WASHINGTON, April 7.—Although Washington did not share equally with New York in the first demonstration of "television," the achievement touched the imagination of the capital.

A small group consisting largely of newspaper correspondents gathered at the demonstration room of the telephone company and heard Secretary Hoover deliver the address heard in New York by the group that also saw the Secretary as he spoke. The New York audience could not be seen in Washington.

Mr. Hoover read his speech into the telephone mouthpiece, as follows:

"It is a matter of just pride to have a part in this historic occasion. We have long been familiar with the electrical transmission of sound. To-day we have in a sense the transmission of sight for the first time in the world's history.

"Human genius has now destroyed the impediment of distance in a new respect and in a manner hitherto unknown. What its uses may finally be no one can tell, any more than man could foresee in past years the modern development of the telegraph or the telephone. All we can say to-day is that there has been created a marvelous agency for whatever use the future may find, with the full realization that every great and fundamental discovery of the past has been followed by use far beyond the vision of its creator.

"This invention again emphasizes a new era in approach to important scientific discovery, of which we have already within the last two months seen another great exhibit—the trans-Atlantic telephone."

CAR PORTER WITH REAL STUFF

SPRINGFIELD, Mass., April 7 (A. P.)—Houston S. Butler, Montreal, a Pullman porter, was arrested in the Boston and Maine Railroad yards here to-day after Federal and railroad officers had found thirty-six bottles of Canadian liquor in the linen closet of his car.

MILLARD TO WRITE ARTICLES ON CHINA

(Continued From First Page)

paper work for more than thirty years, starting in St. Louis after leaving the University of Missouri. He served as a correspondent during the Spanish War, and was the only one present at the well-remembered action at Matanzas, as well as at other more important engagements. He served as a correspondent in the Greco-Turkish and Boer Wars. His first visit to China was during the Boxer uprising of 1900. He represented The World in Manchuria during the Russo-Japanese War. He has represented, besides The World, Scribner's Magazine, the New York Herald and the London Daily Mail. For some time in China he represented the New York Times.

Since 1911 Mr. Millard has been a resident of China. He founded the China Press at Shanghai in that year, and continued its publication until 1917, when he established Millard's Review. During the Peace Conference at Versailles he was an unofficial adviser to the Chinese delegation, as he was at the 1920, 1921 and 1922 sessions of the League of Nations. In a like capacity he attended the Conference on Pacific Ocean and Far Eastern Questions at Washington.

Books that have come from the pen of Mr. Millard in the last twenty years include "The New Far East," "America and the Far Eastern Question," "Our Eastern Question," "Democracy and the Eastern Question" and "Conflict of Policies in Asia."

Mr. Millard's articles will appear exclusively in The World in New York.

NEGRO NOT BARRED IN ARMY TRAINING

War Department Explains Camps Are Provided for Classes of Fifty

ERROR IN BARNELL'S CASE

Adjutant General's Order Issued in 1923 Is Cited

From The World's Bureau
Special Despatch to The World

WASHINGTON, April 7.—The War Department denied to-day that Marsden B. Barnell, a Negro, had been barred from the Citizens' Military Training Camps on account of race.

On Jan. 17, 1923, the Adjutant General of the army issued instructions to the corps area commanders governing Negro units in C. M. T. camps. These instructions have not been changed. Where as many as fifty qualified colored applicants express a desire for training the commanding officer is directed to organize a separate unit in the camp, with separate barracks and separate mess, handling the unit just as Negro units are handled in the Regular Army.

Last year additional instructions were given that separate camps for Negro trainers might be provided where 100 or more applicants qualified.

It was pointed out at the department that fifty men constitute a platoon, and this is the minimum number that can be effectively organized into a unit for training. However, the instructions provide if a smaller number than fifty should appear for training after a separate unit has been organized, the training would continue.

At least one month in advance, however, fifty or more colored applicants must have qualified in order to have a unit established for them in any camp. Barnell can get training provided a sufficient number of other colored men qualify, and not otherwise.

In this connection it was stated that reports that the 2d Corps Area C. M. T. C. officers who advised Barnell to apply to the 4th Corps Area commander apparently overlooked the Adjutant General's instructions of Jan. 17, 1923, and should have informed him he could be accommodated provided as many as forty-nine other colored men qualified for training.

DENY CANADIAN PROPOSAL

Both Nations Scout Report of New Reciprocity Compact

Special Despatch to The World

WASHINGTON, April 7.—Both the State Department and the Canadian Legation to-day denied a published report that the Dominion Government has submitted to the United States a proposed new reciprocity compact covering both tariff questions and development of the St. Lawrence waterway project.

The reciprocity issue came to fruition during the Taft Administration, only to be rejected by Canada.

At the State Department is was stated that nothing was known of the matter beyond what has appeared in the newspapers. Responsible officials apparently are not looking for affirmative developments at present.

STRIKE LOSS SMASHES UNION

Special Despatch to The World

ONECO, Conn., April 7.—The complete surrender of the cotton mill strikers in Woonsocket, R. I., and their return to work has called away several hundred hands that have been working in various Eastern Connecticut mills. The return of the help at Woonsocet has practically disrupted the union.

NEW DOHENY-FALL ARGUMENT TO-DAY

Justice Hitz to Pass on Demurrer to Second Trial, This Time for $100,000 Bribe

BOTH MEN REPORTED ILL

They Base Plea on Invalidity of Naval Oil Leases

From The World's Bureau
Special Despatch to The World

WASHINGTON, April 7.—Whether Edward L. Doheny and Albert B. Fall are to be tried here on the pending bribery indictments against them hinges on the outcome of the demurrer which is to be argued to-morrow before Justice Hitz of the District Supreme Court.

Since the millionaire oil man and the former Secretary of the Interior were acquitted by a jury on the indictment alleging conspiracy to defraud the Government in the lease of the Elk Hills naval oil reserve, the United States Supreme Court, in the civil suit to recover the oil lands, has pronounced the Elk Hills transaction illegal and corrupt.

Another jury now will pass upon the facts in the case if the demurrer fails. There are two bribery indictments, one accusing Doheny of offering and the other accusing Fall of accepting a bribe—otherwise the $100,000 of cash in the famous brown satchel which figured prominently in the conspiracy trial as well as in the civil suit.

The defense bases its demurrer mainly on the contention that as President Harding's Executive order empowering Fall to make the oil leases was invalid, as contended by the Government in all the prosecutions so far, there is no foundation for a bribery indictment. The defense argues that, under the law and the rulings of the courts, an official can not be bribed to do what he has no legal power to do.

The prosecution will contend that for all practical purposes Fall possessed the power, that he actually did negotiate the leases, and that the $100,000 was in fact a bribe.

Both Fall and Doheny are reported to be ill. If the demurrer is not sustained the bribery trials will be held as soon as possible after the conspiracy trial of Fall and Harry F. Sinclair, which is set for April 25. In the bribery caese Fall and Doheny would be tried separately.

SALMON RIGHTS GO UP

New York Club Pays $21,000 for Leases in New Brunswick

FREDERICTON, N. B., April 7 (A. P.)—Exclusive salmon angling rights on the Restigouche, Patapedia and Kedgewick Rivers brought a record annual rental of $75,000 at the auction sale of five-year leases to-day.

This represents an increase of $58,700 yearly in revenue for the province, the annual rental obtained in the sale five years ago being $16,800. The total amount realized was $22,750 in excess of the upset prices asked for the seven stretches into which the waters were divided.

B. W. Boyle of Leominster, Mass., acting for the du Pont interests, paid the highest price for a single lease. He bid $12,800 for a stretch in the Kedgewick River.

The Restigouche Salmon Club of New York paid $21,000 for its leases, but lost two important stretches of water formerly held.

GRETNA GREEN LID DOWN

Special Despatch to The World

GREENWICH, Conn., April 7.—A bill has been signed by Gov. Trumbull requiring residents of Connecticut to file applications for marriage licenses five days prior to the issuance of such licenses, just as non-residents have had to do for several years past. The bill becomes effective July 1.

Fourteen Pages Lindy Pictures!

WEATHER Probably showers; easterly winds.	DAILY MIRROR NEW YORK'S *BEST* PICTURE NEWSPAPER	NEWS EDITION

Vol. III. No. 305. Copyright, 1927, by the Public Press Corporation. Registered U. S. Pat. Off. New York, Tuesday, June 14, 1927 Entered as second class matter, Post Office, New York, N. Y. 2 Cents IN CITY LIMITS | 3 CENTS Elsewhere

LINDBERGH'S GLORY

Story on Page 3

LINDY'S FAMOUS SMILE THANKS NEW YORK FOR WORLD'S GREATEST WELCOME

Here's the boy! What do you think of him? This, we believe, is the best photograph ever taken of Col. Charles A. Lindbergh, the quiet kid who hopped the Atlantic as nonchalantly as most of us would cross the street to buy a pat of butter. There's the never to be forgotten little twist of a smile that 4,300,000 persons, according to official police estimates, saw for the first time yesterday. And this is "Lindy" telling quite a few more millions of radio listeners what he thinks of it all.

FOURTEEN PAGES OF LINDY PICTURES ON PAGES 4, 10, 11, 14, 16, 17, 20, 21, 24, 25, 27, 31, BACK PAGE

DEMPSEY WINS

THE BALTIMORE NEWS

PRICE 2 CENTS - PAY NO MORE

EXTRA

VOL. CXI.—NO. 66. THURSDAY EVENING, JULY 21, 1927 Daily Average NET PAID Circulation for June, 148,241

ROUND BY ROUND

(By ASSOCIATED PRESS)

ROUND 1—Dempsey came out in a crouch and fell into a clinch, hammering five short rights to the body as Sharkey missed a left hook. Dempsey bored in again, drilling hard smashes to the ribs. Jack hooked two lefts to Dempsey's head. Sharkey socked Dempsey with a left to the head. Dempsey bored in again. Sharkey looked tired. A left hook shook Sharkey's head back. He sent two uppercuts . Dempsey, reeling and groggy, woved about the ring under a fussilade. Sharkey smashed him again with rights. Dempsey was groggy as Sharkey used a long right. Dempsey went to his corner very tired.

ROUND 2 — Jack came out slowly and Sharkey missed a left. Sharkey drove Dempsey to the ropes with a right to the jaw. Dempsey fought fiercely at Sharkey's body. In close, they cwapped jolts to the ribs. Dempsey held as Sharkey clubbed him to the body. Sharkey nailed Dempsey with a left to the head and drove Dempsey to the ropes with short rights to the jaw They slugged in the center of the ring as Dempsey nailed Sharkey with two hooks to the chin.

ROUND 3—Dempsey's left eye was cut by Sharkey's jab. Dempsey drove a long left to the stomach and then took a left and right uppercut as he swayed to close quarters. Dempsey missed a left to the head, but landed two right jolts on Sharkey's chin. Jack Dempsey shuffled in, in apparently stronger, crowding Sharkey with a body attack. Dempsey whipped over a right uppercut. Sharkey caught Dempsey with a wicked right to the chin. Sharkey slipped and went down in his own corner, but was up without a count.

ROUND 4—Sharkey was less confident as he missed a wild right. Dempsey drove Sharkey around the ring with fierce punches to the body. Dempsey nailed a left to the chin and a right to the ribs. Sharkey left-jabbed Dempsey and hooked both hands to the face. Dempsey sent a short right to the body and lifted Sharkey's head with a right uppercut. Sharkey took three jolts from Dempsey's left, driving the sailor into a crouch.

ROUND 5—Dempsey skimmed Sharkey's chin with a left. Sharkey split blood as Dempsey charged into a body attack. Dempsey threw rights to the body taking Sharkey's left four times to the head. Dempsey hooked a solid left to Sharkey's head.

ROUND 6—Sharkey began playing a waiting game. He let Dempsey rush him. Sharkey was all elbows on defense. Sharkey slapped a right to Dempsey's face. Dempsey's head shot back from a terrific right uppercut to the jaw. Dempsey caught the sailor coming out with three smashes to the head.

ROUND 7—Dempsey was weaving in again and Sharkey held as the fire grew hot about his body.

Dempsey knocked Sharkey down with a right to the jaw. Sharkey got to his knees at the count of nine, swayed and fell flat, and got up. Dempsey suddenly whipped his left into Sharkey's stomach and followed with a straight right hand smash to the jaw.

DEMPSEY WINS KNOCKOUT, ROUND SEVEN

DRYS SEIZE HOME BREW ON TRUCK HERE

Dry agents seized a truck loaded with 20 cases of alleed home brew on Pennsylvania avenue late today, and arrested Harry Goodman, 601 South Fremont street, driver. At 5 Maryland avenue, Westport, aents seized a 150-allon still and 2500 gallons of mash.

ORIOLES DEFEAT INSECTS

JER. CITY	r	h	o	a	e	BALTIMORE	r	h	o	a	e
Moore, lf...	0	1	3	0	0	Fewster, 2b	1	2	4	4	0
Gaudette, rf.	0	1	3	0	0	Brower, rf..	0	0	2	1	0
Sheehan, ss.	1	2	2	2	1	Porter, cf..	2	3	6	0	0
Whitman, 2b.	1	2	2	1	0	Poole, 1b..	1	2	7	0	0
Nietze, cf...	1	2	3	0	0	Sheedy, lf..	0	2	2	0	0
Monahan, 1b	0	1	5	1	0	Urbanski, 3b	1	1	2	2	0
Radwan, 3b.	0	0	1	0	1	Scott, ss...	0	0	2	3	1
Daly, c.....	0	1	3	0	0	Lake, c....	0	1	1	0	0
Williams, p..	1	2	2	1	0	Ogden, p...	0	0	1	0	0
Shannon...	0	0	0	0	0	Earnshaw, p	0	0	0	0	0
....	0	0	0	0	0	Vincent, p..	1	1	0	0	1
Totals...	4	12	24	5	2	Totals...	6	12	27	10	2

SCORE BY INNINGS

Jersey City........	0	0	0	2	1	0	0	0	1	—4
Baltimore	0	0	0	1	1	4	0	0	x	—6

Two base hits—Williams, Sheehan. Three-base hits—Nietzke, Porter. Home runs—Poole. Stolen Bases Sheehan, Lake. Sacrifices—Radwan, Fewster. Left on bases—Jersey City, 13. Baltimore, 12. Base on balls—off Oden, 1; off Vincent, 1; off Williams, 4. Hit by pitcher—Nietzke. Struck out—by Williams, 2. Umpires—Carroll and Solodor.

Wins Right to Box Tunney

JACK DEMPSEY

THE thirty-two-year-old ring veteran in defeating Jack Sharkey of Boston tonight at the Yankee Stadium in New York, not only won the right to face Gene Tunney for the world's heavyweight championship in September, but upset the old adage "They Never Comeback." Dempsey's comeback tonight was the biggest pugilistic upset of modern times.

VICTOR WILL MEET GENE TUNNEY FOR TITLE

YANKEE STADIUM, N. Y., July 21.—Jack Dempsey, former heavyweight champion of the world, staged the most spectacular comeback in pugilistic history here tonight when he defeated Jack Sharkey of Boston. As a result of tonight's victory, Dempsey is now in line for a championship bout with Gene Tunney, the title-holder, in September.

(For blow-by-blow story of fight see red box.)

A crowd, which numbered in the neighborhood of 80,000, and which paid over $1,000,000 into Promoter Tex Rickard's box office, witnessed the spectacular glove engagement. At the end they rose as one man and gave Dempsey a salvo of cheers that probably could be heard clear over in Brooklyn and surrounding territory.

Ex-Champ Returns

No heavyweight of the modern ring has accomplished what Dempsey did here tonight. Many defeated heavyweights have tried to climb back to the championship heights and failed. After more than a dozen years of fighting, Dempsey defied tradition and whipped the ex-sailor, who entered the ring tonight a favorite in the wagering.

The majority of those in attendance tonight were drawn solely to see Dempsey's return quest for the laurels he lost in the Sesqui ring to Gene Tunney in a ten-round bout to a decision last year in Philadelphia. The ex-champion did not disappoint the vast throng, and his victory means another million-dollar gate when he meets Gene Tunney for the championship.

BITTERLY CONTESTED

Tonight's battle was a bitterly fought one; in fact, old-timers at the ringside said it was the hardest-fought heavyweight mill in recent years. The two Jacks lost little time in swinging into action when the opening gong clanged, and from then until the close it was a give-and-take affair, with Dempsey keeping in front at all time.

Sharkey, although seeing his chances for a titular go with Tunney being dimmed for the time being, was not disgraced. The big youngster from Boston fought one of the best fights of his spectacular career, but it was simply a case of his meeting a superior gloveman.

At times tonight Dempsey flashed impressions of the young killer who crashed down the giant Willard in the sun-baked ring at Toledo eight years ago. At other moments he looked like the Dempsey who flayed the gorgeous Orchid Man of France, Carpentier, into submission at Boyle's Thirty Acres, and the enraged Dempsey who crawled back into the ring at the Polo Grounds and stilled his tormentor, Firpo, the Wild Bull of the Pampas.

SET NEW RECORD

Tonight's fight set a new gate receipt record for a non-championship fight. The best previous record was $462,850 when Harry Wills fought Luis Firpo in Jersey City, but tonight's receipts more than doubled those figures.

Jack Sharkey was the first of the main-go principals to reach the Stadium dressing room. He was accompanied by his handlers and seemed in his usual confident spirits.

YANKEE STADIUM, New York, July 21—(A. P.).—Under a blue sky that apparently held some threat of rain, early arrivals by the thousands were pouring into the Yankee Stadium two hours before Jack Dempsey and Jack Sharkey were scheduled to enter the ring to decide if the experience of

Continued on Page 17, Column 1.

BIRDS DEFEAT INSECTS, 6 TO 4

ORIOLE PARK, July 21.—Jack Dunn's Orioles returned home from a poor round trip and defeated the Jersey City Insects, 6 to 4.

Jack Ogden, who started on the mound for the ultimate winners, was driven to cover in the fifth

Continued on Page 19, Column 1.

EMPIRE CITY RACE CHARTS

WEATHER CLEAR. TRACK FAST.

FIRST RACE—FIVE AND ONE-HALF FURLONGS. FOR TWO-YEAR-OLDS. Claiming. Purse $1000. Value to winner $700, second $200, third $100. Went to post at 2.33. Off at 2.35. Start good. Won driving, place same. Owned by MRS. J. ZOELLER. Trained by J. ZOELLER. Time .23, .47 1-5, 1.08 2-5.

Equipment—W, Whip; S, Spurs; B, Blinkers.

Starters	Wt.	Post	St.	¼	½	Str.	Fin.	Jockeys	O.	C.	P.	S.
aPhilene	106	11	1	$1^{1½}$	1^{1}	1^{1}	1^{h}	Catrone	2	5-2	1	1-2
Philip's First .wb	103	5	3	2^{h}	$2^{1½}$	$2^{1½}$	2^{1}	Zoeller	4	5	2	1
Discovered	101	9	10	8^{h}	5^{1}	4½	3^{1}	Goodwin	4	7-2	7-5	7-10
Noon Joy .wb	108½	10	5	3^{1}	7^{h}	$5^{1½}$	4^{6}	Robbins	4	9-2	8-5	4-5
Wrackeen .wb	112½	4	3	4½	3^{2}	3^{h}	5^{1}	Kum'er	15	15	6	3
Flood Gate	109	2	7	$10^{1½}$	10^{1}	10½	6^{1}	Heupel	15	15	6	3
Brahman .all	109	3	2	5^{n}	7^{h}	6^{1}	7^{1}	A'brose	15	15	6	3
Mob Law .wb	109	1	6	$6^{1½}$	$6^{1½}$	7^{h}	8^{h}	Richard	15	25	10	5
Stella May	106	6	9	7½	8½	11	9^{h}	Craig'e	30	40	15	8
Riquette	107½	7	11	9^{1}	9½	9^{h}	10^{1}	Kelsay	15	20	8	4
Frank .wb	110½	8	8	11	11	8^{1}	11	McTagu	20	10	4	2

aDisqualified.

Philene broke rapidly from the outside displayed high early speed and outlasted Philip's First in the final drive. He was disqualified for bearing over after the start. The latter raced in close quarters nearing the final quarter pole and was forced to take back. He finished strong at the end. Discovered worked her way up steadily came through on the inside entering the stretch and finished fast. Noon Joy was outrun the first part Wrackeen went well. Flood Gate came to the outside entering the stretch. Brahman was kept in the deep going rounding the turn. Frank was caught in a jam shortly after the break and almost went down.

Results at Other Tracks on Sports Page

SECOND RACE—FIVE AND ONE-HALF FURLONGS. FOR THREE-YEAR-OLDS AND UP. Purse $1000. Value to winner $700, second $200, third $100. Went to post at 3.05. Off at 3.08. Start poor. Won driving, place same. Owned by F. W. BARLOW. Trained by C. TURNER. Time .23, .48 3-5, 1.08.

Starters	Wt.	Post	St.	¼	½	Str.	Fin.	Jockeys	O.	C.	P.	S.
Pheasant .wb	111	11	12	8½	6½	3^{1}	1^{n}	Rose	5-2	13-5	1	1-2
Durie M	105	3	1	2½	1^{h}	1^{1}	2^{h}	Stevens	10	12	5	5-2
Ensign .wb	116	5	5	5^{8}	5^{1}	2^{n}	3^{6}	Allen	30	30	12	6
Dry Toast	110	12	10	7^{1}	7^{1}	6½	4^{h}	Craig'e	30	30	20	10
Forget Me Not .wb	106	8	4	3^{h}	4½	5^{h}	5^{h}	Zoeller	8	10	4	2
La Ferte	106	7	6	4^{2}	2^{n}	4½	6^{h}	O'Hara	50	50	20	10
Martha Martin .wb	106	6	8	6^{h}	8½	7^{2}	7^{6}	Force	10	12	5	5-2
Everglade .wb	116	10	11	10^{n}	10^{8}	10^{1}	8^{1}	Weiner	10	6	5-2	6-5
Fourteen-Sixty	112	2	7	9^{h}	9½	9½	9^{h}	Collins	20	20	8	4
Doubloon .wb	110	4	2	$1^{1½}$	$3^{1½}$	8^{1}	10^{h}	Fields	6	7-2	8-5	4-5
Manweh .wb	110	1	9	11	11	11	11	Catrone	8	12	5	5-2
Santrock .wb	110	9	3	ran	oou			Callahan	5-2	5-2	1	1-2

Pheasant was as good as left, worked his way up on the outside and closing on his own courage wore down the leaders in the final strides. Durie M. away rapidly raced Doubloon into defeat and had no excuses. Ensign moved up stoutly entering the stretch and had no excuses. thereafter. Dry Toast closed fast on the outside. Forget Me Not broke slowly and was rushed into contention. La Ferte showed a good effort. Santrock ran out nearing the far turn and was eased up.

Continued on Page 2, Column 4

HEIRESS LEAPS TO DEATH

ATLANTIC CITY, N. J., July 21. Plunging seven stories from the window of her suite in the President Hotel, Miss Lillian Jaeger, twenty-six, New York heiress, was found dead, a crumpled heap on the Boardwalk early today.

Atlantic City police said the girl had committed suicide.

Miss Jaeger was the daughter of the late Otto J. Jaeger, millionaire

Continued on Page 2, Column 7.

THE WEATHER

Fair tonight. Friday partly cloudy. Little change in temperature. Gentle winds.

TOMORROW'S SUN AND TIDES.

Sun Rises	4.58 A.M.	High Tide	12.56 A.M.
Sun Sets	7.27 P.M.	Low Tide	7.22 P.M.

TODAY'S HOME RUNS

Goslin, Senators, 8th inning.
Schulte, Cardinals, 7th inning.

BALTIMORE FANS BATTLE ON TRAIN

By International News Service.

PHILADELPHIA, July 21. — A Baltimore and Ohio Railroad "fight special" bearing more than a hundred Baltimore fight fans to New York to witness the Dempsey-Sharkey encounter tonight, lived up to its name so well that when the train arrived here police reserves were called to restore peace.

Police found the embattled fans congregated in one car and all members of the train crew in another car, with the platforms between the cars a veritable "no man's land."

The fight started, according to participants, when a special officer on the train objected to fans mixing drinks.

Other fans went to the support of the drink mixers, and members of the train crew supported the special officer, with the result that the majority of the passengers and crew soon were embroiled.

After police had re-established peace the fight special continued to New York.

RAID 3 INNS HERE; END DRY CLEAN-UP

Striking almost simultaneously, squads of prohibition agents today raided five places, three of them inns, in the drive to dry up Baltimore.

The raids today, according to the agents, brought the number of places to fall in the dry onslaught to 42 and the number of persons arrested or cited to 60.

Meanwhile dry officials called an armistice in the drive and an-

Continued on Page 7, Column 8.

WOMAN SHOOTS U. S. JUDGE ON BENCH

91 St. Louis Tornado Dead

NIGHT EDITION

AMERICAN LEAGUE

At New York— R. H. E.
Washington ....0 0 0 2 0 0 0 0 0—2 5 0
New York ....0 0 0 1 0 1 0 2 x—4 9 1
Batteries—Zachary and Ruel; Pipgras, Pennock and Bengough.

At Chicago (first game, 13 innings)— R. H. E.
Detroit ....0 0 0 0 1 2 0 1 0 0 0 0 0—4 9 2
Chicago ....0 0 0 0 3 1 0 0 0 0 0 0 1—5 9 0
Batteries—Gibson and Bassler; Thomas and McCurdy.

At Chicago (2nd game, called, darkness)— R. H. E.
Detroit ....0 0 0 1 0 0. —1 6 0
Chicago ....0 0 3 0 1 x —4 7 0
Batteries—Stoner and Woodall; Faber and Crouse.

At St. Louis (first game)— R. H. E.
Cleveland ....0 0 0 0 0 2 2 0 1—5 8 1
St. Louis ....1 0 0 1 0 2 0 0 0—4 10 0
Batteries—Hudlin and Sewell; Blaeholder and Schang.

At St. Louis (second game)— R. H. E.
Cleveland ....4 0 0 0 0 0 0 0 0—4 5 1
St. Louis ....2 2 0 4 0 0 1 0 x—9 12 2
Batteries—Underhill, McKain and Myatt; Wright and Dixon.

NATIONAL LEAGUE

At Cincinnati— R. H. E.
Pittsburg ....0 0 0 0 0 0 0 1 0—1 5 0
Cincinnati ....0 0 0 0 0 1 1 0 x—2 8 0
Batteries—Aldridge, Miljus and Gooch, Spencer; Lucas and Pleinich, Hargrave.

At Brooklyn— R. H. E.
New York ....2 1 0 0 0 0 1 0 1—5 6 1
Brooklyn ....0 0 0 0 4 0 6 0 x—10 9 5
Batteries—Henry, Barnes, Fitzsimmons and Cummings, Taylor; Vance and Deberry.

At Boston— R. H. E.
Philadelphia ....1 0 0 0 1 0 0 0 0—2 6 0
Boston ....3 4 0 1 0 3 1 0 x—12 18 0
Batteries—Taber, Scott and Jonnard, O'Donnell; Genewich and Hogan.

LITTLE WORLD SERIES

At Toledo— R. H. E.
Buffalo ....0 0 0 1 0 0 0 1 0—2 5 2
Toledo ....0 2 3 0 0 0 0 0 x—5 7 1
Batteries—Mangum, Stryker and Devins; Barnes and O'Neill.

EASTERN BALL SCORES

THREE CENTS

LOS ANGELES EVENING HERALD
AN INDEPENDENT NEWSPAPER

Reg. U. S. Patent Office. Copyright, 1927, by Evening Herald Publishing Company
The Evening Herald Grows Just Like Los Angeles

VOL. LII THREE CENTS Hotels and Trains Five Cents FRIDAY, SEPTEMBER 30, 1927 Hotels and Trains Five Cents THREE CENTS NO. 286

RUTH HITS 60TH HOME RUN

WIDOW FIRES FOUR SHOTS AT JURIST IN COURT

SALT LAKE CITY, Sept. 30.—After brooding over a decision against her in a damage suit, Mrs. Eliza Simmons, a widow, shot and wounded Judge Tilman F. Johnson in the federal district court here today.

Mrs. Simmons walked into the courtroom with other spectators before the opening of the morning session and took a seat in the front row next to the bailiff.

FIRES FOUR SHOTS

When Judge Johnson entered and mounted the bench Mrs. Simmons stepped quickly forward and fired four times at him before court attendants could reach her.

A bailiff finally wrested the gun from her and she was placed under arrest. She made no attempt to escape and gave no reason for her act.

Court records showed Judge Johnson had rendered a decision against Mrs. Simmons in 1925 in her suit to collect $10,000 damages from the Utah Copper Co. for the death of her husband.

BROODED OVER SUIT

Following affirmation of this decision by the circuit court of appeals, court costs were collected from Mrs. Simmons a short time ago.

Since then, acquaintances said she had brooded over the case and been extremely despondent. She has four children.

Judge Johnson, 65 years of age, was appointed to the federal bench in 1912 by President Wilson. He made his home in Ogden and had been a prominent member of the Utah bar for many years.

Big Boulder Keeps Ship From Sinking As It Runs Aground

SAN DIEGO, Sept. 30.—A huge boulder that stuck in the hull of the freight Circinus when it grounded 17 miles south of the border was all that kept the ship from sinking, a diver discovered here yesterday.

The ship was floated Wednesday and brought here for temporary repairs. The diver found that the rock had punctured both bottoms of the ship and was embedded firmly. Mattresses were placed around the boulder from the inside of the ship and last night the ship left under tow for Los Angeles harbor, where it will go into dry dock.

GIRLS BODIES FOUND; OVER 1000 HURT IN STORM

ST. LOUIS, Sept. 30.—The death toll of the tornado which wrecked buildings over an area of six square miles here yesterday, reached 91 this afternoon with recovery of three more bodies of girl students from the ruins of Central high school.

Two other bodies of girls were taken out yesterday from the school building debris, where three floors caved in from pressure of the 80-mile-an-hour wind. Two of the three bodies brought out this afternoon were identified as those of Alice Berner, 15, and Eois Shaw, 14.

INJURED TOLL GROWS

The toll of injured also grew through the day, totaling somewhere between 1000 and 1500, many seriously hurt.

More than 25,000 were homeless.

Thirteen were known missing and unaccounted for.

Property damage could not be accurately estimated, but was variously placed by officials at between $50,000,000 and $100,000,000.

With relatives of the missing wandering hysterically among the ruins searching for their loved ones, city officials acted promptly to halt any possible outbreak of disorders Every available city and county officer was on continuous duty in the stricken areas and the entire Missouri National guard was called out to reinforce them under orders to shoot to kill anyone caught looting.

Despite the widespread destruction, Mayor Victor Miller today announced St. Louis would not need outside help.

APPEAL IS MET

He declared his appeal for funds had been met so bountifully by St. Louis citizens that adequate money was available for relief work. He stated the local Red Cross and other relief agencies were meeting the situation heroically and fully.

Mayor Miller received word today that the 1000 regular army soldiers at Jefferson barracks would be dispatched to the city by the federal government to aid in guard work.

Food stations using war department supplies were today sent into the wrecked areas, and food was dispensed to the homeless from rolling army canteens.

Fully six square miles of buildings and streets on the west side were devastated by the tornado, which hurtled into the city shortly after 1 o'clock yesterday afternoon.

The storm gained in intensity as it tore through Manchester and

(CONTINUED ON PAGE TWENTY)

Top photo shows the globe-girdling plane Pride of Detroit landing at Vail field, Los Angeles, today, after a flight from San Francisco. Below, the world flight companions in adventure, Edward F. Schlee, left, and William S. Brock are pictured just as they stepped from the plane. Brock asked for a light for his cigaret and somebody gave him a carton of matches.

Awards in Quake At Santa Barbara Upheld by Court

By Pacific Coast News Service

SAN FRANCISCO, Sept., 30.—Rumblings of the earthquake in Santa Barbara two years ago were heard again in the state supreme court here today when the higher tribunal upheld two industrial commission awards growing out of the disaster.

The first award was to Louisa Mosteiro, whose husband, Segismondo, was killed during the quake while employed in a building as a janitor. Mrs. Mosteiro was awarded $5000.

The second award was to William D. Wilson, dairyman, who was injured during the quake when bricks from a building fell on his head.

Zasu Pitts' Mate Flies from L. A. to Mother's Bedside

By International News Service

CHICAGO, Sept. 30.—Tom Gallery, motion picture actor and husband of Zasu Pitts, is winging across the continent from his home in Beverly Hills, Cal., to the bedside of his mother here. Mrs. Gallery is critically ill and has not yet been told that her son is expected to be here tomorrow morning.

The husky 6-foot young actor is known to Chicagoans as the son of Police Captain Mike Gallery.

"Tom left Los Angeles in a plane that had been used in an aviation picture," the captain said this afternoon. "He and the pilot took off as soon as the last scene was shot and they're due here early tomorrow."

Weather Bureau Forecasts Clear Skies for So. Cal.

Clear skies were promised for tonight and tomorrow throughout Southern California by Col. H. B. Hersey today in the official weather bureau forecast.

Moderate temperature will continue, Colonel Hersey said. The thermometer stood at 58 early today, rising to 63 just before noon.

3 PARTIALLY IDENTIFY SUSPECT

Three employes of the Los Angeles department of water and power today partially identified a picture of Joseph C. Senellan, 33, held in the county jail at Ventura, as one of the two men who bound them and gagged them with rubber balls during the $73,600 payroll robbery at the bureau last Monday, according to police.

Detective Lieutenants Evans and Tomasen, who brought the picture of Senellan to Los Angeles, immediately returned to Ventura to bring Senellan back to Los Angeles Police said he would be confronted by the three bureau employes, S. F. Arthurs, Glenn Brockway and George Pessill.

CAUGHT IN CHASE

A too desperate attempt to escape arrest on a speeding charge and a scar on his face led to the examination of Senellan as a suspect in connection with the payroll holdup.

Senellan bears a scar on his nose and cheek. One of the bandits wore a piece of tape, as if to conceal a scar, in the same place.

Senellan first came to the attention of police when he shot an auto through Santa Barbara at a high rate of speed. State Motorcycle Police Inspector J. Blackwell started after him, sounding his siren as he went.

CAR TURNS OVER

Down the coast highway the pair raced. As they passed through hamlets motorcycle policemen and police cars joined the chase. A stream of shots was directed at the fleeing car and although lead pierced the body and windshield, the driver kept ahead of his pursuers.

Turns at high speed and wild careening to avoid tourist cars added thrills to the chase. One state officer was thrown from his motorcycle and the machine burst into flames.

One mile north of Malibu junc-

(CONTINUED ON PAGE EIGHTEEN)

BERLENBACH TO FIGHT MICKEY WALKER HERE

By United Press

NEW YORK, Sept. 30.—Mickey Walker, middleweight champion of the world, and Paul Berlenbach, who is attempting a "come-back," were signed this afternoon to fight 10 rounds in Los Angeles for the middleweight title.

Dick Donald, promoter, signed the two fighters.

The fight will take place this fall, the exact date to be announced later.

MILK POISONS IOWANS

OSAGE, Ia., Sept. 30.—Mrs. Elmer Morris, McIntire, near here, and several other persons were poisoned by milk from a cow that had been bitten by a rattlesnake. All are recovering.

WORLD FLIERS HERE, PLAN TO TRY AGAIN

That they probably will start out again on a 'round-the-world flight, completing their flight next time by flying from Japan to Hawaii and then to California, was the declaration here today of William S. Brock and Edward F. Schlee, 'round-the-world fliers.

This was the word of the two fearless aviators when they alighted at Vail field at 12:19 p. m. from San Francisco on their return flight to Detroit, their home city, in the monoplane Pride of Detroit.

Brock and Schlee made a perfect landing at the Western Air Express field on Telegraph road and were met by a small crowd of persons who knew approximately when the fliers were expected. It was not

(CONTINUED ON PAGE EIGHTEEN)

Stars 8, Indians 7

INDIANS—	Ab	R	H	Po	A	E
Callaghan, cf	5	0	0	5	0	0
Ellsworth, 2b	5	3	2	5	2	1
Easterling, lf	3	1	3	3	1	0
Huft, rf	4	1	1	2	0	0
Hudgens, 1b	5	0	1	3	0	0
Sherlock, ss	4	0	0	2	1	1
Kimmick, 3b	4	1	1	2	2	0
Borreani, c	4	1	1	3	1	0
Nance, p	3	0	0	1	0	1
Guilland, p	1	0	1	0	0	0
Totals	38	7	10	26	7	3

STARS—	Ab	R	H	Po	A	E
Lee, ss	3	1	1	0	2	1
Bouton, 3b	2	2	0	2	0	0
Twombly, lf	3	0	0	6	0	0
McNulty, cf	4	1	2	3	0	0
Lowell, 1b	4	2	1	7	0	0
Frederick, rf	4	1	1	3	0	0
Kerr, 2b	3	1	2	2	1	0
Cook, c	3	0	1	6	1	1
Agnew, c	1	0	1	0	0	0
McCabe, p	3	0	0	0	0	0
Teachout, p	0	0	0	0	0	0
Heath	1	0	0	0	0	0
Totals	31	8	9	27	4	2

Seattle......102 010 021 —7
Hollywood...400 100 021 —8

Ninth Inning Rally Wins For Stars

At Sacramento— R. H. E.
ANGELS 0 1 0 2
SOLONS 0 0 0 7
Batteries—Cunningham and Hannah; Keefe and Severeid.

At Oakland— R. H. E.
SEALS 0 0 2 0 0
OAKS 1 0 2 0 3
Batteries—Ferguson and Jolley; Delaney and Read.

At San Francisco— R. H. E.
REAVERS ..3 0 0 0
BELLS 0 0 1 0
Batteries—Hughes and Yelle; Pillette and Baldwin.

Scoring one run in the last half of the ninth inning gave Hollywlod a 8 to 7 victory over Seattle in the fourth game of the local series at Wrigley field this afternoon.

FIRST INNING

INDIANS—Callaghan flied to Frederick. Ellsworth popped to Lowell and was safe

(CONTIN'D ON PAGE TWENTY-TWO)

SWAT KING SETS NEW WORLD'S RECORD

YANKEE STADIUM, NEW YORK, Sept. 30.—Babe Ruth, baseball's master slugger, today broke the record of 59 home runs in a single season that he set six years ago.

In the eighth inning of the next to last game of the regular schedule Ruth's bat met squarely a ball thrown by Pitcher Tom Zachary of the Washington Senators and propelled it into the right-field bleachers.

It was the sixtieth homer Ruth has hit since the season's first game in mid-April and the four hundred and sixteenth he has hit since he first came to the major leagues with the Boston Red Sox in 1915.

SCORES KOENIG

Koenig, who had tripled, scored ahead of Ruth.

Ruth had been up three times before. Once he walked and twice he singled. The Yankees and the Senators were tied at two-all in the eighth when Ruth came to the plate.

One ball.

One strike.

Then the southpaw let fly with one just to Ruth's liking.

The climax of the king of clout's greatest season came after a brilliant performance yesterday, when he knocked two homers, tying his previous best performance for a season.

New York won the game, 4 to 2.

Pipgras and Pennock hurled for the Yankees, allowing only five hits. Zachary for the Senators yielded nine safeties.

BAN JOHNSON HITS AT JUDGE LANDIS IN FIERY STATEMENT

CHICAGO, Sept. 30.—Byron Bancroft Johnson, founder of the American league and pilot of that organization through a stormy quarter century, today fired a parting shot at his two most bitter enemies, Baseball Commissioner K. M. Landis and Charles Comiskey, owner of the Chicago White Sox.

Johnson, who resigned under pressure in July with the provision that he be given time to "set his house in order," is expected to retire from baseball within a few days, although he refused today to set a definite date.

Judge Landis laughed when he

(CONTINUED ON PAGE TWENTY-TWO)

EXTRA

YANKS CHAMPS

WORLD EXTRA SERIES

THE SAN FRANCISCO CALL AND POST
AN INDEPENDENT NEWSPAPER

5 CENTS
A Clean Wholesome Paper for California Homes

CALL AND POST, VOL. 122, NO. 77
SAN FRANCISCO CALL, Vol. 142, No. 77
THIRTY-EIGHT PAGE[S] [SAN] FRANCISCO, SATURDAY, OCTOBER 8, 1927
5c DELIVERED BY CARRIER 75c a Month

70,000 AT U. C. TILT

BOX SCORE

PITTSBURGH

Player—	AB	R	H	PO	A	E
L. Waner, center field	4	1	3	0	0	1
Barnhart, left field	5	0	1	2	0	0
P. Waner, right field	4	0	1	0	0	0
Wright, shortstop	4	0	1	1	6	0
Traynor, third base	4	0	0	1	4	0
Grantham, second base	4	0	2	0	2	0
Harris, first base	4	0	2	13	0	0
Smith, catcher	3	0	0	6	0	0
Hill, pitcher	1	0	0	0	0	0
Yde	0	1	0	0	0	0
Brickell	1	1	0	0	0	0
Miljus, pitcher	1	0	0	0	0	1
Gooch, catcher	0	0	0	3	0	0
Totals	36	3	10	*26	12	2

Brickell batted for Hill in seventh.
Yde ran for Smith in seventh.
Two out when winning run was scored.

NEW YORK

Player—	AB	R	H	PO	A	E
Combs, center field	4	3	2	2	0	0
Koenig, shortstop	5	0	3	0	3	0
Ruth, right field	4	1	2	1	0	0
Gehrig, first base	5	0	0	14	2	0
Meusel, left field	5	0	0	2	0	0
Lazzeri, second base	3	0	0	5	3	1
Dugan, third base	4	0	1	1	5	0
Collins, catcher	3	0	3	2	1	0
Moore, pitcher	4	0	1	0	3	1
Totals	37	4	12	27	17	2

										R.	H.	E.
Pirates	1	0	0	0	0	0	2	0	0—	3	10	1
Yankees	1	0	0	0	2	0	0	0	1—	4	12	2

SUMMARY

Home run—Ruth. Two-base hit—Collins. Sacrifice hits—L. Waner, P. Waner. Stolen base—Ruth. Double plays—Dugan to Lazzeri to Gehrig; Lazzeri to Gehrig; Traynor, Wright, Harris. Struck out—By Hill 6, by Miljus 2; by Moore 2. Bases on balls—Off Hill 0, off Miljus 3; off Moore 3. Wild pitch—Miljus. Losing pitcher—Miljus.

PLAY-BY-PLAY

By Associated Press

The following play by play description of the world's series is by Carl S. Brandebury (Associated Press sports writer):

FIRST INNING

Pirates—There was a big cheer as the Yanks trotted out to their positions. Wilcy Moore tossed up a few to Collins. L. Waner up. L. Waner beat out a hit to short. The Yankees kicked. Barnhart up. Stri: 1, called. This was a fast ball. Koenig threw out Barnhart at first, L. Waner going to second. P. Waner up. Ball 1, low, inside. Dugan threw out P. Waner at first, L. Waner holding second. Wright up. L. Waner scored on Wright's single to right. Wright went to second on Ruth's throw to the plate. Traynor up. Dugan took Traynor's hot smash and touched out Wright. One run, two hits, no errors, one left.

Yankees — Combs up. Strike 1, called. Ball 1, outside. Combs singled into right. Grantham made a hard try for it, but could not reach the ball. Koenig up. Foul, strike 1. Koenig singled into right, Combs halting at second. Smith went down to talk to Hill. Ruth up. Ball 1, inside. Foul, strike 1. Combs scored on Ruth's single to right, Koenig going to third. Gehrig up. Ball 1, wide. Foul, strike 1. Strike 2, swung. Ball 2, inside. Gehrig struck out, swinging for the third strike. Meusel up. Strike 1, called. Strike 2, swung. Ruth stole second. Meusel fanned, taking a third called strike. Lazzeri up. Ball 1, outside. Strike 1, swung. Hill halted the play until he could wipe his spectacles. Strike 2, called. Lazzeri struck out, taking a

Con. on Page Nineteen, Column Two.

Registered? Tonight's Last Chance

HAVE YOU REGISTERED? If not, you have only until 9 o'clock tonight to do so, and qualify for voting at the November election.

Registration for any election closes thirty days prior to that election. But anyone who voted in any election held since the first of January, 1926, may vote in this one—unless, of course, he has since moved, or otherwise lost his registration.

The November election will be one of the most keenly contested political fights yet held in San Francisco, and registration for it will exceed all previous records by at least 15,000, J. Harry Zemansky, registrar, predicted today. So, if you have not registered, and are not yet qualified to vote—obey that impulse—do it NOW!

YANKS GRAB SERIES WITH 4 TO 3 WIN

Ruth Knocks Homer in Fifth Inning, Putting N. Y. Ahead

YANKEE STADIUM, NEW YORK, Oct. 8 (AP).—The New York Yankees won the world baseball championship today by defeating the Pittsburgh Pirates for the fourth straight time. The score was 4 to 3.

It was the first time since 1914, when the Boston Braves beat the Athletics four in a row, that a world series has been decided in four straight games.

59,909 WATCH

The official attendance today was 59,909, nearly capacity, in spite of the bad weather, and the total receipts $208,097.

The final game developed many tense situations, and although played under lowering clouds, with a light drizzle at intervals, was the most exciting of the series.

Wilcy Moore, who won fame as a great relief pitcher in his first season in the major leagues, went the whole way for the Yankees, and although he permitted ten hits, the Pirates' heaviest attack of the series, he was effective after the first inning, when he gave two hits and a run.

MILJUS RELIEVES HILL

Miljus entered the game as a relief pitcher for the Pirates, Carmen Hill, the starting choice of Manager Bush, being taken out in the seventh for a pinch hitter. Hill pitched well in four of his six innings of duty, although Ruth hit him for a terrific home run in the fifth inning with one on the bases, to shove the Yankees out in front.

Combs scored the winning run in the ninth inning, when Miljus made a wild pitch with the bases full.

The end of the game was an anticlimax. Miljus had seen the bases filled with none out and

Cont'd on Page Nineteen, Col. Four

Frayne Quizzes Arthur Brisbane On Sports Page

Arthur Brisbane, the Hearst writer who can say more about one certain thing in less words than any editor in America, has a message for sports readers in The Call today. Turn to the first page of The Call's sporting section where you will find an exclusive interview on athletics obtained by Pat Frayne, sporting editor of The Call.

"There Once Were Bold Pirates---

—who tried to plunder us Yanks," said George Herman, who today biffed No. 62 after telling Kid Gotham the bad, bad story of a gang of Buccaneers who terrorized the National League. He then went on to tell the Manhattan youngster ab-ut the way the big Bambino sneaked u-on the terrible fellows with the big throat slicers and when one of their lesser terrorists was on guard rammed out a sock that made the Pirates walk their own plank.

COURT DENIES FIGHT FILM RELEASE

Federal Judge Frank H. Kerrigan today refused to release from federal custody the motion picture films of the Dempsey-Tunney fight, which were seized last week after exhibition at the Capitol Theater. At the same time the court refused to grant an order restraining federal agents from making further seizures.

REFUSED TO BAN ARRESTS

Judge Kerrigan took the position that possession of the films is evidence of the existence of a conspiracy to violate the law, even though the law had not been violated. This point, Kerrigan said, must be set

Con. on Page Nineteen, Col. Seven

Results of Games on Many Gridirons

EASTERN

At Durham, N. H.—Bowdoin 12, New Hampshire 7.

At Philadelphia—Pennsylvania 14, Brown 6.

At Philadelphia (pro)—Frankford Yellow Jackets 0, Dayton Triangles 0.

At Syracuse—Syracuse 21, Johns Hopkins 6.

At Philadelphia—Temple University 58, Juanita College 0.

At Providence—Providence College 7, Norwich 7.

At New York—New York University 65, Alfred 0.

At New York—Columbia 28, Wesleyan 0.

At State College, Pa.—Penn State 13, Bucknell 7.

At Hamilton, N. Y.—Virginia Poly

Continued on Page 19, Column 8

CARDS EXPECT EASY PREY IN NEVADA

By "NIP" M'HOSE

STANFORD STADIUM, PALO ALTO, Oct. 8.—"Pop" Warner went to a football game this afternoon while his own Cardinal aggregation disported in the oval here preparatory to tackling the Wolf Pack from the University of Nevada.

"Pop" went down to Los Angeles to "scout" the University of Southern California squad in its skirmish with the Oregon Aggies.

MANY THOUSAND FANS

A throng of many thousands of fans filled the stands here when the game began, despite the bigger at-

Cont'd on Page Nineteen, Col. Seven

Three Students' Sought in Death Believed Murder

Suspicion that Erhardt Kamper, 18, 1458 Third street, Berkeley, was murdered, led police today to begin a thorough investigation of the events leading up to his death Thursday night in the Alameda County Hospital.

Kamper, a tanner, died of a fractured skull suffered in a fall, it was believed.

Today, George Sdravkivich, Kamper's roommate, told the police that on September 23 Kamper returned from Emeryville, claiming that he had been slugged and robbed by "three

Betty Blythe Has Minor Operation

HOLLYWOOD, Oct. 8.—The hospital list of the film colony for this week was raised to three today when it was learned that Betty Blythe, picture actress, underwent a minor operation yesterday. She is recovering rapidly.

Mrs. Wright Free On Mail Charge

MADISON, Wis., Oct. 8.—Miriam Noel Wright was freed of a charge of misuse of the mails here today when her divorced husband, Frank Lloyd Wright, noted architect, refused to appear against her.

Irish Cardinal Ill

BELFAST, Oct. 8 (AP). — Patrick Cardinal O'Donnell, primate of Ireland, who has been spending a vacation at Carlingford, County Louth, is suffering from an attack of pleurisy. He was reported this morning to be "not too well, but sleeping."

BEARS, GAELS LINE UP IN CRUCIAL TEST

St. Mary's Big Favorite as Biggest Mid-Season Crowd Gathers

By PAT FRAYNE

California and St. Mary's this afternoon played to a crowd of 70,000 people, the greatest crowd ever to witness any but a California and Stanford football game at Berkeley.

The huge stadium was packed with humanity and men sitting under the warm California sun in their shirtsleeves and women forming a multicolored background of every hue.

First on the field was the California band playing "Fight for California." The California band was followed by the Golden Bear varsity.

The greatest traffic tieup in the history of Berkeley was causing fire hazards and blocking ersidents in their homes this afternoon as more than 30,000 cars were held in the vicinity of the California Memorial Stadium, with little hope of extrication before night fall.

AT STANFORD STADIUM—Stanford, 0; Nevada, 0; 1st period.
Santa Clara Freshmen beat Stanford Freshmen, 7 to 0.

AT MEMORIAL STADIUM—Cal., 6; St. Mary's 0; 1st period.
California Freshmen defeated St. Mary's freshmen, 14 to 6.

AT EWING FIELD—Cogswell High, 7; Commerce, 0; final.

ONE HURT IN EWING FIELD CRASH

On Ewing Field during a high school football game today, the old baseball score board in the south end of the field collapsed, carrying a score of youths to the ground with it and seriously injuring Leo Maynard, 13, 119 Crescent street.

TWO HURT IN OAKLAND CRASH

Scores of passengers were shaken up shortly after noon today when a College avenue car, inbound, crashed into an outbound Telegraph avenue car at 30th street and Broadway, Oakland. Two persons were injured.

GRASS FIRE MENACES SUTRO FOREST

A grass fire brkoe out near the city's reservoir on Twin Peaks this afternoon and climbed rapidly toward Sutro Forest, causing two alarms to be turned in.

Passing the Woolworth Tower

P. & A. PHOTO

Park Ave. Gin-Jazz Love Drama Bared in Millionaires' Death Duel

How Death Stalked Park Ave. Party

Held for homicide in slaying of his friend after quarrel over woman, Samuel E. Bell is shown (right) in Yorkville court with detective at arraignment.

DEATH and love were the two mystery guests that attended with men and women, the sumptuous party of the $7,000,000 heiress, Mrs. Robert H. Schuette, in the Hotel Marguery, 270 Park ave., on Wednesday evening. Thereafter the tragedy developed as follows:

At 2:15 a. m. Thursday, Arthur M. Smith, wealthy Cleveland manufacturer, fell mortally hurt under the hotel's proud canopy.

At 3:30 a. m. Smith was pronounced suffering from "acute alcoholism."

At 10:10 a. m. Friday Smith was given a suspended sentence be- cause a magistrate noted he was ill rather than drunk.

At 2 p. m. . . . Smith was dead, following convulsions.

At 6 p. m. Saturday . . . Samuel E. Bell, rich oil man, accused of punching Smith and killing him, arrested in connection with the jazz-and-dry-age drama.

Mrs. Robert T. Brown, a matron of the racy Lexington, Ky., so- cial set, was named as the woman in the case over whom Smith and Bell fought.

Mrs. Robert H. Schuette, society woman who inherited $7,000,000 as the widow of Harry S. Harkness, was revealed as the hostess at a gay and speedy champagne party after which Bell and Smith are said to have quarreled over Mrs. Brown with the ardor of schoolboys.

Rich Women to Face Banton Today

By JOHN O'DONNELL.

THE majestic canopy that awes the passerby before the exclusive Hotel Marguery was rolled aside yesterday to reveal a fatal love drama sweeping from the fragrant blue grass of Kentucky to denouement in the gin-and-jazz atmosphere of Park avenue's gold-screened night life.

Beneath that canopy, it is charged, violent death stalked in the wake of a drinking party attended by fifteen fashionable folk in the luxurious apartment of Mrs. Robert H. Schuette, who inherited $7,000,000 from the vast Standard Oil estate of her first husband, the late Harry S. Harkness.

With the ardor of schoolboys in love, Samuel E. Bell, a Chesterfieldian oil promoter who cut a wide swath in Kentucky society during the 1917 boom, and Arthur Morgan Smith, rich, married manufacturer of Cleveland, fought over the right to escort a 39-year-old Lexington, Ky., matron to her hotel.

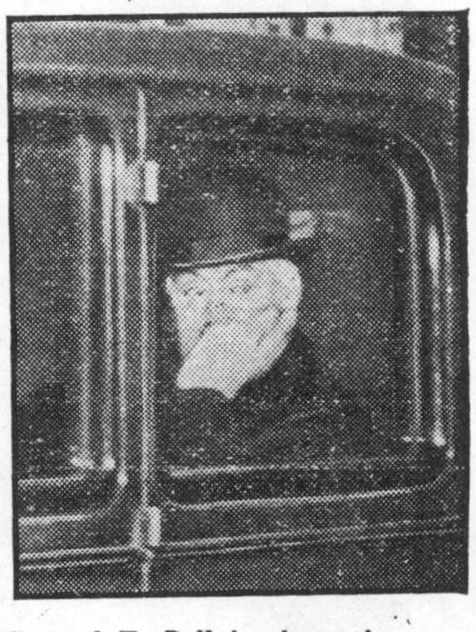

Samuel E. Bell is shown in car as he left East 51st st. police station after arrest.

Witnesses say it happened like this:

Smith was drunk. He wanted to enter a cab with Bell and the Blue Grass belle, Mrs. Robert T. Brown, comely wife of a bond salesman. Bell punched Smith. The Clevelander was picked up as a "plain drunk." Twelve hours after he was found in the gutter—at 2 a. m. last Thursday morning—Smith died of injuries he received in the battle, complicated by his generally poor physical condition.

Haughty and nonchalant in the manner of a man who has been in jams before and knows how to take care of himself, the silver haired Bell, konwn as "old Sam Bell" to hundreds who met him during his de luxe oil barnstorming, revealed the tale when he was jailed on a homicide charge yesterday.

Goes Back to Blue Grass.

The story of the death of Smith after a gay drinking party begins in the atmosphere of sleepy tradition and romance peculiar to Lexington, Ky., one of the few places in the world where aristocracy of man and beast still is determined by blood alone.

Sam Bell, considered a millionaire oil man, met the then young and lovely Bessie McGann Brown, daughter of William McGann, a Lexington capitalist, and wife of Robert T. Brown, a bond salesman, who remains in the background throughout.

There at the Brown's, beneath the magnolia blossoms of somnolent 3rd st. in Lexington, Bell attended many parties. He and the Browns also visited Mrs. Schuette, then the second wife of Harkness, at Walnut Hall, the famous estate of the $100,000,000 Standard Oil king.

Bessie McGann Brown, whose husband earned a modest income, tasted the life of the very wealthy in all its refinements there. To Sam Bell, the coast-to-coast promoter, it was an old story.

It was for a reunion, then, that Bell, now a Baltimore financier, telephoned Mrs. Brown at her room in the Hotel Plaza last Thursday.

She had just seen her sub-deb daughter, Martha Lawson, at Goucher college in Baltimore and had come on to New York to taste the gilded life of the oil folk of Park ave.

Bell and Mrs. Brown dined quietly together in the Hotel Plaza. Then they jorneyed to the Mar-

(Continued on page 4, col. 1)

Test Campbell Today to Link Torch Slayings

By ARTHUR MEFFORD.

A grey fedora hat—a scrawling signature—the memory of a hotel man—

With these threads of evidence police of Elizabeth, N. J., hope to

Mrs. Henry C. Campbell Henry Colin Campbell

Present wife and confessed slayer.

weave a pattern today that will depict Henry Colin Campbell, confessed flame-slayer of Mildred Mowry, as the inventor of a monstrous mode of murder that he first tried out more than a year ago on Miss Margaret Brown.

Two days after the incinerated body of Miss Brown, a Park ave. governess, was found smoldering behind a hot dog stand near Bernardsville, N. J., on Feb. 21, 1928,

(Continued on page 25)

Bambino Swats Report He'll Wed Claire Today

By GRACE ROBINSON.

Close friends of Babe Ruth became highly excited last night over a report that the big hero of baseball was to be married here early today.

The young woman nominated for the honor was Mrs. Claire Hodgson, a former Follies girl, whose close friendship with the Sultan of Swat has often been commented on both here and in the Florida training camps.

Questioned at Ebbets field, where the Yankees played yesterday, Ruth steadfastly denied any intention of marrying Mrs. Hodgson, or anybody else.

"If I'm getting married, it's news to me," said the Babe, wrinkling his broad forehead. "But everybody knows more about my life than I do myself. No, I'm not getting married tomorrow, nor any time this week, or any time, ever, that I know of.

"But then maybe you know something I don't. No, I haven't seen Mrs. Hodgson. I don't know where she's living. I don't know if she's even in New York."

Mrs. Hodgson is the young woman whose name has been linked with Ruth's since long before the tragic death of his wife in Watertown, Mass., last winter. It was well known that the Babe wanted a divorce, but according to one friend, Mrs. Ruth demanded $100,000 as the price of his freedom.

Claire Hodgson was formerly Clara Merritt, daughter of Joe M. Merritt, a lawyer, of Athens, Ga. The family was not prosperous. Mrs. Merritt kept a boarding house.

To Wed Babe?

Claire Hodgson

4 P. M. Ticker Prices---Closing Bid and Asked

COMPLETE FINAL ★★★★★★

Temperature—Min., 38; Max., 49. (Detailed weather report on page 25.)

The Sun

Copyright, 1929, by The Sun Printing and Publishing Association.

COMPLETE FINAL ★★★★★★

United States Official Weather Forecast: Rain tonight or tomorrow; continued cool.

VOL. XCVII.—NO. 49—DAILY. NEW YORK, TUESDAY, OCTOBER 29, 1929. PRICE THREE CENTS.

STOCKS OFF IN 16 MILLION SHARE DAY

SAYS EXAMINERS OF FERRARI BANK WERE VERY LAX

Warder Defense Witness Bolsters Attempt to Shift Responsibility.

WAS HIMSELF CHIEF EXAMINER

Tompkins, From Bench, Asserts Superintendent Is Primarily Accountable in Situation.

Startling laxity in the examinations of the City Trust Company by State bank examiners, as testified to today by Samuel Rauch and a statement from Justice Arthur S. Tompkins that "the State Banking Superintendent is primarily responsible for the examinations of banks under his care" featured today's session of the trial of Frank H. Warder, former State Superintendent of Banks, who is under indictment for receiving more than $100,000 in bribes and gratuities from Francesco M. Ferrari, president of the looted City Trust Company. The conditions of laxity were admitted today by Rauch under cross-examination by Chief Assistant District Attorney Ferdinand Pecora, who interrogated the witnesses placed on the stand by the defense.

The statement from the bench as to Warder's responsibility was drawn by an appeal on the part of James I. Cuff, chief defense counsel, for an instruction to the jury that Warder was not on trial for the failure of his former subordinates to do their duty. In this connection the court said that such an instruction might be included in the charge to the jury.

Start of the Day's Testimony.

Samuel W. Rauch, who was deputized chief examiner for the purpose of examining the Atlantic State Bank and the Harlem Bank of Commerce and later the City Trust Company after the two Ferrari banks

Continued on Third Page.

U. S. STEEL EARNS $5.62 ON COMMON

Third Quarter Earnings Are $51,575,350.

Consolidated net earnings of the United States Steel Corporation for the September quarter were $70,173,713, the company announced today after the regular quarterly dividend meeting of the board of directors. The directors declared the usual quarterly dividends of $1.75 a share on both the preferred and the common stocks.

The directors declared an extra dividend of $1 a share.

Net earnings for the September quarter compared with net of $71,995,461 earned in the June quarter and with $52,148,476 net earned in the September quarter of 1928.

The balance available for dividends at the end of September was $51,575,350. That compared with a balance of $53,825,843 reported for the June quarter and with a balance of $29,886,259 reported for the September quarter, 1928.

The balance for the September quarter was equivalent to $5.62 a share on 8,056,827 common shares which the directors announced are outstanding today, after allowance for preferred dividends.

Net for the June quarter available for dividends was equivalent to $5.91 a share on 8,030,304 common shares outstanding at the end of the June quarter. The difference in shares outstanding since that time is due to the fact that certain stockholders

Continued on Forty-second Page.

In The Sun Today

CALVARY PASTOR DIES.

The Rev. Dr. John Roach Straton.

DR. STRATON DIES OF HEART ATTACK

Breakdown Reported Due to Church Overwork.

CLIFTON SPRINGS, N. Y., Oct. 29.—The Rev. Dr. John Roach Straton, pastor of the Calvary Baptist Church of New York for the last ten years and a noted militant fundamentalist Baptist preacher, died at a sanitarium here today. He was 54 years old.

Death came unexpectedly at 5:50 A. M. after a heart attack. Dr. Straton had been in the sanitarium about two weeks, suffering from a

Continued on Third Page.

LAKE SHIP SINKS IN FIERCE GALE, 15 MAY BE LOST

About Sixty Are Rescued as Captain Goes Down With His Vessel.

WAVES GOOD-BY TO HIS CREW

Thirty-Foot Rollers Send Old Craft Under Water in a Few Hours.

KENOSHA, Wis., Oct. 29 (A. P.).—Between ten and fifteen men went down with the lake steamship Wisconsin in a severe storm off the Kenosha shore early today.

More than three-score were saved, many of them maddened and some near death from the horror and the exposure of hours in the wind-whipped sea. The three passengers aboard wer rescued.

Capt. Dougal Morrison, bound to his duty and true to the tradition of the sea, remained aboard his ship to the last and went down with a score of shipmates. His body was picked up later by coast guard crews.

Chief Engineer Judas Buschmann of Manitowoc, Wis., clung to a life raft as the steamer upended, rolled over and sank. Rescuers tried to haul him from the water but, crazed by his plight, he fought them off and died.

Set Off in Lifeboats.

For five hours the twin coast guard crews from Racine and Kenosha and the crew of the tug Chambers Brothers battled grimly with the 30-foot waves and the driving northerly gale

Continued on Second Page.

Walker Reassures the Public

Says Basic Industries Are Sound and There Is No Change in Fundamentals.

Mayor Walker made a special plea to the public today not to become excited and lose confidence in the business and prosperity of the country because of the drop in the stock market.

Addressing 150 motion picture men, nearly all of whom he has known personally for years, the Mayor added his note of optimism to the situation. The occasion was a luncheon at the Astor Hotel.

"The basic industries of the nation are sound and secure," the Mayor said. "More automobiles are being manufactured than ever before, and there is greater demand for luxuries. There is nothing in the general tone of American business to justify any fundamental reason for a big decline in values.

"This is no time for the public to lose confidence. If that should happen it might be that many boys would be called home from college and the standard of living might be lowered in many homes.

"Undoubtedly these are gloomy days. Nearly every one seems to have lost money. I hear it every time I enter an elevator or go about in public. The public in general gave over hard-earned savings to brokers and received scraps of paper which they expected would give them profits. Now they have the scraps of paper left and cannot understand what has become of their savings.

"I appeal to the motion picture industry to help cheer up the people. It is a great opportunity for the picture industry to do a good public service.

"Sound a new note of confidence in the picture houses; give the people a good laugh; show them stories of courage and bravery, and help them to forget their troubles."

R-101 Is Ready to Fly Again.

CARDINGTON, England, Oct. 29 (A. P.).—Britain's great new dirigible R-101 is ready to resume her trial flights as soon as weather conditions are favorable. The defect in one of her auxiliary engines has been remedied.

Sports

Results of this afternoon's Racing and other late Sporting News will be found on Page 38.

HEAD OF WEBSTER, EISENLOHR KILLED

Anthony Schneider Tumbles From Hotel Window.

While leaning out of the window today to fix the aerial of his radio Anthony Schneider, 60 years old, president of Webster, Eisenlohr, Inc., of 511 Fifth avenue, a cigar concern, lost his balance and fell five stories from his apartment in the fashionable Beverly Hotel at Fiftieth street and Lexington avenue. He fell to the roof of the Lexington Theater and was killed instantly.

Louis Morell, a waiter, of 322 East Thirty-third street, was in the room when Schneider fell. He was placing the cigar manufacturer's breakfast on the table and heard him scream as he lost his balance and began to fall. Morell dropped his tray and dashed to Schneider's assistance, reaching the window just in time to make a snatch for his foot.

The body was taken to the Fifty-first street police station for an autopsy. Schneider, who was unmarried, had lived in the hotel since February 1.

John L. Rogers, a vice-president of Webster, Eisenlohr, Inc., will act as president of the company pending a meeting of the board of directors, it was announced today. Mr. Schneider had been connected with the firm in an executive capacity since the April of 1928.

Webster, Eisenlohr was quoted on the Stock Exchange, as having sold at $6 a share today, after having sold at as high as $113 a share since the beginning of 1929.

Captain of Tanker Lost at Sea.

MANILA, Oct. 29 (A. P.).—Capt. I. Anderson, captain of the Standard Oil tanker Yankee Arrow for the last eight years, disappeared from the ship a week ago while 1,400 miles from this city, it was learned here today. The captain was not missed until at least an hour and a half after he went overboard. Two letters he left indicated he was despondent.

Bid & Asked

CLOSING.

Closing Prices and Fluctuations of Leading Stocks

DURING TODAY'S TRADING ON THE STOCK EXCHANGE

The accompanying table is a compilation of stock prices showing the fluctuations at half hourly intervals during trading today and giving closing prices. The prices are those of leading issues as sent out from the New York Stock Exchange on the bond ticker:

	Yest'd'y Close	Open	10:30	11:00	11:30	12	12:30	1:00	1:30	2:00	2:30	Close	Net Ch'ge
American Can	136	130¼	133	125¼	120	118½	115	110	119	119½	119	120	—16
Am & For Power	77½	68	68	64½	51	50⅛	56	53	57	53	52½	55	—22½
Am Smelting	90	81	82	84	84	84	84	84	84	84	84	84	— 6
Am Tel & Tel	232	225	225	219	220	211½	214½	212	215	216	214	204	—28
Anaconda	93½	82	85	84½	83½	81	80	77	80	80½	81	85	— 8½
Atlantic Refining	40⅝	30	37	35¼	..	32	34	34	35⅛	36½	36¾	35	— 5⅝
Baltimore & Ohio	115¼	115¼	115¼	115⅛	114½	112¼	114¾	113	115½	117	116	114½	— ¾
Barnsdall	22⅛	22	..	22	22⅛	22	22	21½	20⅞	20⅞	20⅞	20⅞	— 1¼
Beth Steel	94⅛	90¼	90	88	88	88	80	80	85	84⅞	83¼	84	—10⅛
Canadian Pacific	203	200	198⅛	197⅛	195	195	191¼	191⅛	198	195	193½	192	—11
Chrysler	40	33	32	33¾	32	30¼	29¼	29½	30⅜	33⅜	32	33½	— 6½
Columbia G & E	70¾	66	69	61¾	60	58	58¼	57¾	62	65	67½	63	— 7¾
Col Graphophone	26¾	20½	22½	22	20½	20	20⅛	21	20¼	21⅞	20⅝	19¼	— 7½
Comm & Southern	15	13⅛	..	11½	10	10½	11	11	11¼	12¾	12⅛	12¼	— 2¾
Consolidated Gas	97¼	95¼	96¼	96	96	93½	93½	93½	92¾	91½	91½	91½	— 5¾
Erie	55	50	52¾	50½	50	44¼	46½	45	44	46	45⅞	45¼	— 9¾
Gen Foods	48⅛	42¼	46	42⅛	42	35	40	38	40	40¾	41⅞	40	— 8⅛
Gen Electric	250	245	243	232	217	215½	216	210	220	223	226	222	—28
Gen Motors	47½	45¼	45	43⅝	35	36½	37	40	40	40	40⅛	40	— 7½
Gold Dust	40	35	38½	36	33	33	33	33	32⅞	33¾	32½	32⅞	— 7⅛
Johns-Manville	132	128	134	124½	124¼	121	113	109	120	120	119½	115	—17
Kennecott	70⅝	69⅛	69⅛	68⅛	67⅛	66	65	65¼	66½	66⅝	67⅝	65¾	— 4⅞
Montgomery Ward	59½	52	53½	51½	50¾	50¼	50	51	52	54	54½	53¾	— 5¾
Nat Cash Reg	75	72	73	72⅞	71	71	69¾	67	67¼	70	70⅛	76	+ 1
Nat Dairy Prod	50½	40¼	47	45	45	40	40	37	37¾	39¾	40⅞	40	—10½
N Y Central	186	184	188	184	183	180½	176	175	183	184½	187¼	189½	+ 3½
Paramount	49¼	37	42	42	41	39½	37	38¼	40	41	41	40	— 9¼
Radio	40¼	30	36	34	30½	32½	32	31½	38½	38⅛	38	38½	— 1¾
Sears Roebuck	111¼	107½	108	102¼	100	95⅜	99	99	95⅜	99	97	95	—16¼
Std Oil of N J	64¾	57	61⅞	58¼	55¾	54	52	56	57½	58	53	57¾	— 7
Union Carbide	84	70¼	80	75⅛	71	70	66¼	68	70¼	77½	76	73	—11
Union Pacific	240	231¼	240	246	240	240	240	240	240	240	239	239⅞	— ⅛
United Aircraft	60⅛	51	57½	46¼	43	40¼	40	42	43	40¼	42	41	—19⅛
United Corp	33½	26	29	27	25¾	25⅛	25¼	24½	25½	26	26¾	25¾	— 7¾
U S Steel	186	185¾	187	181	178½	177	173½	170	180	175	176	174	—12
Westinghouse	145	130½	135	132	125	111	117	119	121	124	123	126	—19
Woolworth	80	75	..	75	75	75	75	75	75	75	75	75	— 5

PRICES SLUMP FROM 10 TO OVER 30 POINTS

Sales on Curb Reach More Than 7,000,000 Shares During Session.

INVESTMENT BUYING APPARENT

New York Central Closes at Net Gain of 3½ Points—Tickers Running Far Behind.

A day of record volume and further drastic breaks in values in the stock market ended this afternoon in a manner indicating that liquidation had been fairly well absorbed.

Losses of ten, twenty, thirty points or more, piled on top of the unprecedented breaks of yesterday, were forced by the tremendous quantity of stocks dumped on the market at the opening and throughout the day. Bankers played only a small part in promoting occasional rallies. Investment buying, however, came in from many sources.

Sales on the Stock Exchange totaled 16,410,030 shares, a new high record, compared with the previous peak of 12,894,600, set last Thursday. Curb sales were 7,096,300 shares, also a new record.

A bullish development after the close tonight was the declaration of an extra dividend of $1 on Steel common.

Of Stock Exchange sales General Motors accounted for 971,300 shares.

Despite the heavy volume the tickers were better able to keep up with the market than in recent sessions, for sales came in large blocks. The Stock Exchange ticker at 2:50 was an hour and 29 minutes late. The Curb Exchange ticker at 3 o'clock was 2 hours and 35 minutes behind.

Preliminary averages of Dow, Jones & Co. showed a loss of 30.62 points on 30 industrials and 6.35 points on 20 rails.

Steel Down Near 170.

United States Steel, the rallying point of the constructive forces, opened at 185¾, a net loss of ¼, was carried up to 192, broke to 181⅛,

Continued on Second Page.

Mayor of East Rockaway Sues Commissioner

Trouble between Ossian E. Weig, Mayor of East Rockaway, L. I., and Clarence A. Nordine, honorary Police Commissioner of the town, has resulted in a civil suit being filed against Nordine by Weig. It is understood that slander is one of the allegations in the case. Summonses have been served by the Nassau county Supreme Court and a complaint is expected to be filed shortly.

Max Eigg of 280 Broadway is the attorney for Mayor Weig. He refused to comment on the case today, saying he does not want to "try the case in the newspapers," but he intimated there would be plenty to say and plenty of action in East Rockaway when the complaint is filed.

Joshua Egelson Made Assistant Prosecutor

District Attorney Joab H. Banton announced today the appointment of Joshua Egelson of 416 Fort Washington avenue to be an Assistant District Attorney.

Mr. Egelson is 41 years old, and came to New York from Rochester three years ago. He is a graduate of the New York University Law School, and was highly recommended, Mr. Banton said, by District Attorney William F. Love and Surrogate Joseph Feeley of Rochester.

W

	Bid	Asked		Bid	Asked
Wabash	—	—	Weston E	32¼	34
Wab pf A	—	—	West E A	—	—
Wab pf B	—	—	WestvacoC.	—	39¾
Waldorf	23½	23¾	WextarkRS	—	—
Walgreen pf	99	100	Wheel&LE.	100	120
Walworth	22	25	Wh &LE pf	100	130
WardBak B	5	6½	White Eag.	23	25
Ward Bak p.	—	69	White Mot.	33	35
Warner BP.	25	45	White Rock	—	—
WarnrBP p	20	40	White S M.	5½	10
WarnrQuin.	16	18	Wh S M pf.	32	36¾

BANKERS' GROUP MEETS AGAIN IN MORGAN OFFICES

Owen Young Joins Heads of 5 of City's Largest Banks in Conference.

Heads of the five strongest banks in the city and Owen D. Young at noon today held the second bankers' conference in twenty-four hours at the offices of J. P. Morgan & Co. The session ended shortly after 1 o'clock when Thomas W. Lamont, of the Morgan firm, met the newspaper men present only to say that he had no statement to make at that time. Mr. Lamont said that another conference would be held in the late afternoon, following which he would have something to say.

While Mr. Lamont declined to make any formal statement he did say in reply to a question that the bankers' pool, formed to give support to the market, has functioned continuously since it was created and was continuing to function.

One of the bankers who attended the conference answering a suggestion that the pool's support was not in evidence in halting the break, asked in reply whether the price of anything had ever been successfully "pegged." He intimated that the bankers were not endeavoring to peg the market, but were simply taking stocks as they were liquidated in order to stabilize the market.

Another banker who was present ventured the prediction that today's break would witness the end of the collapse. He expressed the view that stock prices in many instances had reached levels where adequate buying will be attracted into the market.

A third member of the group which is striving to stabilize the market intimated his belief that the public had lost its mind. He went on to state that he was urging various interests with which he was associated, such as insurance companies and investment trusts, to purchase stocks. He added that he knew of a great deal of investment buying which was going on from those sources. In his opinion, he continued, stocks bought at current prices represent real bargains. He thought that market conditions were getting better and predicted that a turn was near.

The bankers present were Thomas W. Lamont and George Whitney, representing J. P. Morgan & Co.; Charles E. Mitchell, chairman of the National City Bank; William C. Potter, president of the Guaranty Trust Company; Seward Prosser, chairman of the Bankers Trust Company; Albert H. Wiggin, chairman of the Chase National Bank, and George F. Baker, Jr., vice-chairman of the First National Bank.

FAILURE OF CURB HOUSE ANNOUNCED

John J. Bell & Co. Unable to Meet Commitments.

The only failure of a financial house in the present reaction was announced this morning at 11 o'clock by the Curb Exchange. John J. Bell & Co., having announced its failure to meet its engagements, was suspended from regular membership on the Curb.

John J. Bell, head of the firm, was admitted to the Curb Exchange on June 24, 1921. Mr. Bell was an individual trader on the Curb. His obligations are reported to be small, and he will be sold out, under the rules of the Curb, it was learned.

BRUNS IN PARIS FEARS HE'S BROKE

Veteran on Stock Exchange Sailing for U. S.

PARIS, Oct. 29 (U. P.).—Many Americans with stock market interests were hurriedly engaging passage to New York in an attempt to return from European travels in time to salvage fortunes lost in the Stock Exchange crash.

United States Consular offices were besieged by broke or "nearly broke" Americans demanding the Consolate guaranty for C. O. D. cable messages, it was learned.

Among the tourists at the Consular office today was Edwin G. Bruns, who had been on the Stock Exchange for forty years.

"Yesterday broke me," he said. "I don't know if I have anything left."

Bruns said he had intended to return to the United States in the most expensive suite in the liner Bremen November 7. Today, however, he bought a cheap ticket on the Ile de France and will sail November 1.

"My ticket merely insures my passage," he said. "I may have to sleep in the steerage."

He said he was leaving his wife here until he is able to determine whether any of his fortune is left.

"If I still have some money left I would buy now certainly to recoup," he said.

Mr. Bruns, who is close to 60, was 21 years old when he purchased his seat and began trading on the floor of the Stock Exchange December 31, 1891. His father had already been, for many years, a prominent member of the Exchange. In 1921, Edwin G. Bruns, Jr., was admitted to membership, joining his father with the firm of A. J. Johnson & Co.

Throughout his long career as a member of the Exchange Mr. Bruns was known as an exceptionally shrewd and successful trader. He successfully weathered several panics and near-panics that wiped others out of business.

He is a member of the New York Yacht Club, the New York Athletic Club, the Friars Club and the Deal

Stocks Off in 16 Million Day

Continued from First Page.

rallied, and then tumbled to around 170, at which level determined efforts to steady the market were successful. Steel was boosted to 186 quickly before settling into the high 170s.

From there it broke again in the last hour to around 167 before the final rally carried it to close at 174, a net loss of 12 points for the day.

Other losses at the close, which were considerably less than at the low points for the day, included the following: Hudson Motors, 45, off 15; Consolidated Gas, 91½, off 5¾; American Can, 120, off 16; Studebaker, 46, off 7; United Corporation, 25¾, off 7¾; Standard Oil of New Jersey, 57¾, off 7.

American Telephone, 204, off 28; Radio, 38½, off 1¾; Anaconda, 85, off 8½; General Motors, 40, off 7⅛; General Electric, 222, off 28; Chrysler, 33½, off 6½; Bethlehem Steel, 84, off 10⅛; Montgomery Ward, 53¾, off 5¾; American & Foreign Power, 55, off 22½; Columbia Gas, 63, off 7¾; Kennecott, 65¾, off 4⅞; American Smelting, 84, off 6.

Cities Service closed at 22½, off 5, with a total turnover of 1,105,900 shares; Electric Bond & Share 59½, off 25½; Goldman Sachs 35⅛, off 14⅞; American Superpower 19, off 6⅛; Blue Ridge 7⅜, off 5; Electric Investors 85, off 40; Allied Power 31¾, off 11⅞; Lehman Corporation 82, off 10; Shenandoah 11, off 6; Midwest Utilities old 190, off 85; United Gas 18½, off 6½.

New York Central, after selling down around 175, closed at 189½ for a net gain of 3½ points. National Cash Register came up from 67 to 76 to close up 1 from last night's price.

American Can, on which directors declared an extra dividend of $1 today, rallied from 110 to 120.

Westinghouse rebounded from 111 to 126, closing there with a loss of 19 points.

City Bond Sale Postponed.

Effects of the market break on financing plans of corporations and others were evident today.

The sale of the $60,000,000 fifty-year 4 per cent. bonds of the city of New York scheduled for tomorrow has been postponed indefinitely by Comptroller Berry.

The Cities Service Company, which has been offering rights to stockholders to purchase additional shares, today called a meeting of directors for tomorrow to withdraw the offering. The common stock sold today around 20, compared with the price of $45 at which it was offering rights.

Continued unloading of impaired accounts, especially those of large operators, forced today's crash in spite of favorable developments overnight and during the morning. Bankers last night were in a more cheerful frame of mind than in recent days, and indicated that tremendous buying power was ready to come into the market for stocks at attractive levels.

The firm of J. P. Morgan & Co. stated at 11:15 A. M. today that many leading banks, including Morgan, National City Bank, First National Bank, Chase National Bank, Bankers' Trust Company and Bank of America, are requiring from their customers the maintenance of only 25 per cent. margin on their Street demand loans.

Similar notice was given earlier by one Stock Exchange firm to its customers, with the explanation that the reduction in margin requirements was warranted by the present level of stocks.

The Board of Governors of the Stock Exchange, meeting this morning to discuss the conditions of trading, announced that the Exchange would not close early today. Another meeting was called for 6 P. M.

One brokerage failure was announced—that of the firm of John J. Bell & Co., members of the Curb Exchange. The default was not expected to have any repercussion among other firms. Mr. Bell was an individual trader.

Trans-America Corporation provided one of the sensations of a crowded day. The stock was suspended on the San Francisco Exchange for fifty minutes to allow bookkeepers to handle the enormous volume of selling orders, and the New York Curb specialist refused to open the stock before the San Francisco opening. On the Pacific coast the stock broke 32¾ points on an opening sale of 17,500 shares. On the New York Curb it opened off 42¼ on the sale of 25,000 shares at 20¼ soon after 12 o'clock.

The wide break in Trans America followed announcement by A. P. Giannini that the corporation would not support its own stock in the face of a worldwide break in security prices.

United States Steel opened 10,000 shares at 185¾, off ¼, and then rallied a point or so.

Some of the large blocks on initial sales, with net declines, follow: Westinghouse, 25,000 at 130¼, off 14½; Anaconda, 45,000 at 8, off 11¼; International Nickel, 47,000 at 30, off 8; United Corporation, 50,000 at 26, off 7½; Kennecott, 25,000 at 69⅛, off 1½; Allied Chemical, 5,500 at 205, off 40; American International, 15,000, off 30; Kroger, 16,000 at 47¼, off 12½; Erie, 20,000 at 50, off 5; Columbia Graphophone, 35,000 at 20½, off 6¾; Sinclair, 20,000 at 26 1-8, off 1¼; General Electric, 8,500 at 245, off 5; American & Foreign Power, 10,000 at 68, off 9½; Montgomery Ward, 20,000 at 52, off 7½; Union Carbide, 25,000 at 70¼, off 13¾; Chrysler, 50,000 at 33, off 7; Canadian Pacific, 10,000 at 200, off 3; Radio, 30,000 at 30, off 10¼; American Telephone, 15,000 at 225, off 7.

New Low for Cities Service.

Cities Service opened with a block of 117,000 at 24⅞, a new low. Electric Investors opened at 75, a loss of 50 points; Electric Bond & Share, 50,000 at 50¼, off 35¼; American Superpower, 54,000 at 17½, off 8; Goldman Sachs Trading, 45⅛, off 24⅞.

A quick rally which ensued was attributed to an appeal by Mr. Giannini to his friends and stockholders to buy the stock on its investment character, which he said was unimpaired by the market cataclysm.

The break in Transamerica stock on the Curb from 62½ to 20 sliced about $900,000,000 off the market value of this company alone, but about half of this was regained in an immediate rally of more than 100 per

of Transamerica and about 200,000 stockholders. The corporation, by offering 2,000,000 shares to its stockholders and others around 60 a share planned to raise $115,000,000 new money by next January 4, when the rights expire.

On the first twenty-six blocks of stock at the opening on the Stock Exchange more than 630,000 shares were turned over.

Precedents were broken in Wall Street when the Stock Exchange ticker a few minutes before the opening of the market printed the announcement that call money would renew at 5 per cent. This was the second time this month and this year that the renewal has been 5 per cent., but the surprise element was in announcing the money rate prior to the opening of the market. The rate for renewals is not usually announced until 10:40 o'clock. Observers of this incident saw it as a part of the general effort being made to allay fears and instil new confidence.

Rates on acceptances were lowered again today to 4¾ bid on ninety day bills. Possibilities of a cut in the rediscount rate of the New York Federal Reserve Bank this Thursday from 6 per cent. were discussed more confidently than ever today in the financial district, although it was agreed that the cut would have little psychological effect now. Brokers' loans to be announced Thursday afternoon will show a tremendous reduction, guesses in the Street running as high as one billion dollars.

The New York Federal Reserve Bank confirmed the report that the bank was today a heavy buyer of Government securities in the open market. Such buying usually precedes a reduction in the discount rate.

A more immediate effect is to increase the reserves of the member banks and thereby put them in funds which they are now using, it is understood, to replace in the call money market the withdrawals by corporations.

Investment trusts and other corporations were heavy buyers of stocks today, using funds heretofore employed in the call market.

The Chicago wheat market today suffered from the same headlong selling that prevailed in stocks. Initial prices were off 2½ to 6⅝ cents before good support was uncovered.

Banks and brokers today acted to aid investors in stocks to the extent they legitimately could by modifying requirements for loans and margins. With prices of stocks thoroughly deflated banks lending on stock collateral felt more sure of the essential value of such stocks and were willing to loan a larger percentage of market value upon them. It was believed that this action on the part of banks added about 25 per cent. more to the loanable value of standard stocks than recent customs would lead borrowers to expect.

Margin Limit Reduced.

Leading brokerage firms in the financial district held special meetings of partners and considered the margin situation. One firm, F. B. Keech & Co., announced that present prices of listed stocks justified a reduction in margin requirements, and that they had accordingly reduced such requirements to 25 per cent. so long as prices remained at present levels.

In several brokerage firms which have good clienteles, but not the vast numbers of customers such as the big wire houses have, it was learned that measures had been taken to protect the customers. These measures in some instances amounted to virtually "carrying" the customer on a margin reduced to the size of a shoe string. "We feel we can safely do this," the partner of one firm declared, "because we have faith in the essential soundness of the situation and no fear of the ultimate value of the securities held by the customers."

Margin requirements in Wall Street are not uniform. They range from 25 to 50 per cent., according to the type of customer, type of firm and type of securities traded in. Few Curb stocks are carried on margin.

So far as the banks are concerned, now that the decline they have been worrying about for months has occurred, they look with more favor upon stock values and are not, in their own opinion, assuming as great a risk in loaning liberally upon present values as they did loaning conservatively upon the old inflated values.

The break yesterday, carrying down even the premier investment securities of the country from twenty to fifty points, undoubtedly ended, at least for some time, the speculative activities of thousands of individuals.

One of the largest Stock Exchange houses was reported to have closed out about 980 accounts yesterday alone and another large house more than 800 accounts.

More Margin Calls Out.

Margin calls went out again to thousands of traders who had believed their position still sound when quiet irregularity succeeded Thursday's day of panic and record-breaking volume. Rich men and poor men alike were sufferers, though yesterday's was a rich men's market.

There was little sleep for brokerage house employees, buried under the load of 36,467,700 shares on the Stock Exchange alone during the last six trading days. Stock Clearing House business was being pushed through in a manner reflecting credit on the efficiency of Exchange machinery, but there was a good deal of talk of the possibility of an extra holiday soon to permit a final cleanup of error accounts and books. In addition to day-to-day records, clerical forces will have the monthly statements to cope with this week.

The time for delivery of securities was advanced again today from 2:15 to 3 P. M.

Many reassuring statements came from investment trusts and bankers during the day.

Finds Investments Cheap.

Louis H. Seagrave, president of the United Founders Corporation and American Founders Corporation, two of the largest investment trusts, stated that his group had more than $48,000,000 cash, and in the last [illegible] days had been buying care[illegible] lected American stocks. [illegible] have near- other affiliated compa[illegible]

Founders group has more than $61,000,000 invested in bonds.

Robert S. Binkerd, president of the United States Shares Financial Corporation, issued the following statement: "Our studies of the real worth of securities indicated that at the prices obtaining today many of the fine investment stocks of this country were cheap. Accordingly we have been substantial purchasers in today's market. Among the issues which we purchased were American Telephone, Atchison, Topeka & Santa Fe; Atlantic Coast Line, American Can, American Smelting & Refining, Baltimore & Ohio, Chicago & Northwestern, Chesapeake & Ohio, Delaware & Hudson, Electric Bond & Share, General Railway Signal, International Harvester, Montgomery Ward, New York Central, Northern Pacific, Pepperell Manufacturing Company, Southern Pacific, Southern Railway, Standard Oil of New Jersey, Trico Products, Union Carbide and Westinghouse Electric."

Insurance Presidents Meet.

Albert Conway, Superintendent of Insurance of New York State, expressed the opinion that there has been such a drastic readjustment of prices of leading common stocks of the country that he felt justified in recommending to leading insurance companies the investment of a substantial amount of their assets in such leading stocks.

A meeting of life insurance company presidents was held in his office this afternoon.

R. W. McNeel, director of a financial service, stated that "this is the time to buy stocks. Within a few days there is likely to be a bear panic rather than a bull panic. Many of the low price made as a result of this hysterical selling are not likely to be reached again in many years."

A. P. Giannini, president of the Transamerica Corporation, remarked:

"This is a period that calls for clear heads and bold hearts:

LONDON, Oct. 29 (A. P.).—Considerable excitement prevailed in Throgmorton street today to see what effect the Wall Street slump would have on various sections.

Those stocks in which America is interested opened lower than on yesterday. Hydros were 5 points down, Brazil Traction 11 points down, and International Nickels and Graphophones correspondingly weak, but selling was not pronounced and at noontime slight recoveries set in.

The speculative section recorded general losses and stocks in which America is interested declined. There was no panic, however, and the chief fear seemed to be whether there would be further falls on Wall Street with sales of investment securities to meet losses on speculative issues.

AMSTERDAM, Holland, Oct. 29 (A. P.).—Large selling took place on the unofficial exchange here today in consequence of yesterday's break in Wall Street. The support of certain banks failed to check declines which were especially noticeable in Phillips Lamps, which were 40 lower at 428, following yesterday's fall of 80 points.

Royal Dutch declined 25 points to 365 and several other shares also were weak.

Break Badly in Montreal.

MONTREAL, Que., Oct. 29 (A. P.).—The Montreal Stock Exchange was rocked to its foundations this morning, when yesterday's violent collapse of values was followed by a further wide open break, and prominent issues suffered losses ranging up to 13 points.

Brazilian Traction slipped down $10 at the opening, but rallied to $46 for a net loss of $3.50 after the first hour. The rally also brought International Nickel up to $33 after having touched $30. At the higher figure the stock was $5 lower than yesterday's close.

Dominion Bridge was the greatest loser, selling off $13 to $69. Montreal Power added to its heavy loss of yesterday by selling down to $137 for a net loss of $10.

National Breweries was off $4, Shawinigan off $8, Power Corporation off $7, Winnipeg Electric off $3, Smelters off $3, Steel of Canada off $2.50, Quebec Power off $2, British Columbia Power A off $2.50, General Steel Wares off $22, Famous Players off $4 at $43.

Massey Harris was firm, selling unchanged at $39.50.

Tumbling in Pittsburgh.

PITTSBURGH, Pa., Oct. 29 (U. P.).—The Pittsburgh Stock Exchange prices continued to tumble today with virtually every issue selling lower than at yesterday's close.

Within a short time after the opening 19,000 shares of Pittsburgh Screw & Bolt sold at 20, off ⅛ from yesterday's close. Blaw-Knox & Lone Star Gas, usually strong local leaders, were selling at 59⅞ and 34, off 3¼ and 6¼ respectively.

Prices Down in St. Louis.

ST. LOUIS, Mo., Oct. 29 (U. P.).—The St. Louis stock market opened lower today, with leading issues off from two to three points from yesterday's close.

International Shoe common opened at 62⅛, off 36; Wagner Electric 29, off 3; National City 24, off 2.

Heavy Sales in Detroit.

DETROIT, Mich., Oct. 29 (U. P.).—Stocks sagged again today on the Detroit Stock Exchange, but comparatively few sales were made despite heavy offerings.

Hall Lamp sold at 14, off 4; Parke Davis 47, off 5; Wilcox Rich B 16, off 6, and Third National Investors 32, off 12, at the opening.

Cleveland Is Bullish.

CLEVELAND, Oct. 29 (U. P.).—While a few issues listed both on the New York Stock Exchange and the local board met severe reverses today, the rank and file gave ground grudgingly and on the bullish statement of Arthur Reynolds of the Continental Illinois Trust Company, started to recover.

Richman Brothers broke 14 points before powerful banking interests could get into action, but when they did, it came back with a heavy volume of buying. Standard industrial stocks dropped a point to three points during the morning, but came back for net gains in some instances later in the day.

It was pointed out that the local market being a cash market, there was no forced liquidation to protect accounts and what selling came into the market was to raise funds to support accounts in New York and Chicago.

Some Support at Toronto.

TORONTO, Ont., Oct. 29 (A. P.).—With the appearance of some buying support half way through the session, prices on the Toronto Stock Exchange this morning rallied slightly. However, the battle for control between the bears and the bulls was still in favor of the former. The rally was very slight and just enough to allow some of the leading stocks to stage recoveries from a fraction to more than one point, which compared with losses of one to ten points at the opening half hour.

Owing to the volume of sales it was impossible to keep up withr the trend of the market, as the ticker was approximately thirty minutes behind.

International Nickel rallied to 31¼ after hitting a new low of 30, Brazilian Traction opened at 49, hit a low of 40, and later said at 41½.

The oils also showed fractional improvement, Imperial snapped back to 31 after touching 30. British American was selling at 41½, as compared with 40 at the opening. Service stations regained one point of its two point loss at 54.

Opening Sales Of Leading Stocks

Blocks of 20,000 to 50,000 shares and losses of five to fifty points were registered at the opening of the Stock Exchange today.

Some of the large opening transactions, with net losses from last night's prices, follow:

Stock.	Sales.	Open.	Net Chge.
Alleghany Corp.	50,000	24¼	— 4⅞
Am International	15,000	30	—14
Am Smelting	12,000	81	— 9
Am Foreign	10,000	68	— 9½
Am Radiator	25,000	30	+ 2
Am Power Light	18,400	75¼	— 3—
Anaconda	45,000	82	—11½
Am Tel & Tel	15,000	225	— 7
Am Can	10,000	130¼	— 5¾
Atlantic Refining	25,000	30	—10⅝
Bendix	20,000	38⅛	— 3⅞
Briggs	11,000	12⅛	— 3½
Can Pacific	10,000	200	— 3
Chi, M & St P pf	20,000	34½	— 7½
Chrysler	50,000	33	— 7
Col Graphophone	35,000	20½	— 6¾
Com Credit	10,700	28½	— 1½
Com Solvents	13,000	22½	—12
Con Gas N Y	45,000	95¼	— 2
Col Gas	20,000	66	— 4¾
Congoleum	25,000	12¼	— 1½
Continental Motors	10,000	8¼	— ¾
Coty	11,000	21	—11
Curtiss Wright	45,000	11⅝	— 1¼
Du Pont	20,000	138	—12⅛
Elec Auto	10,000	75	—20
Elec Pow & Lt	15,000	34	— 1⅜
Erie	20,000	50	— 5
Fox Film	10,000	50	—18
Gen Motors	50,000	45¼	— 2¼
Gen Foods	20,000	42¼	— 5⅞
Glidden	10,000	30½	— 5½
Gold Dust	30,000	35	— 5
Goodyear	10,000	61	—16
Hudson Motors	12,000	52	— 8
Int Tel & Tel	50,000	71	—17
Kennecott	25,000	69⅛	— 1½
Kreuger Toll	20,000	28½	— 1⅝
Kroger Groc	16,000	47¼	—12½
Loft	11,000	4⅝	— ⅞
Mex Seaboard	10,000	14	— 3
Mid Cont Pete	15,000	26¼	— 2⅛
Miss Kansas	10,000	36¼	+ 1¼
Mont Ward	20,000	52	— 7½
Nat Dairy	30,000	40¼	—10¼
Nat Power	30,000	28¾	— 3⅛
Nevada Cop	10,000	31½	— 3½
N Y Central	12,000	184	— 2
Packard	50,000	16⅛	— 1⅛
Pan Am Pete B	15,000	55	— 3
Paramount	30,000	37	—12¼
Pathe	10,000	4	— 6
Penn R R	10,000	86	— 4
Phillips Pete	20,000	33½	— 2⅝
Pub Ser, N J	15,000	80⅛	— 7⅝
Pure Oil	13,000	22½	— 1⅛
Purity Bak	11,000	70	—29½
Radio	30,000	30	—10¼
Radio Keith	20,000	15¼	— 4¾
Reynolds Tob B	23,000	50⅛	— 2
Sears Roebuck	15,000	107½	— 3¾
Sinclair	20,000	26⅛	— 1¼
Stand Brands	40,000	26	— 1
Stand Oil Cal	13,000	64½	— 1
Stand Oil N J	50,000	57	— 7¾
Stand Oil N Y	27,000	35½	— 1⅝
Stewart Warner	16,000	31	—16
Texas Corp	30,000	50⅝	— 4¼
Timken Roller	25,000	70¼	—19¾
Union Carbide	25,000	70¼	—13¾
United Corp	50,000	26	— 7½
U. S. Steel	10,000	185¾	— ¼
U. S. Rubber	10,000	30⅝	— 8⅛
Westinghouse	25,000	130½	—14½
Woolworth	15,000	75	— 5
Yellow Truck	10,000	12⅛	— 2⅞

Senator Brookhart Fears Bank Failures

WASHINGTON, Oct. 29 (A. P.).—Senator Brookhart, Republican of Iowa, predicted today that if the severe decline of stock prices in Wall Street continued, "banks all over the country would go into bankruptcy."

LAKE STEAMSHIP SINKS IN A STORM

Continued from First Page.

to take off the luckless passengers and crew.

Unable to take aboard a line from the rescuers, most of the crew set off in five lifeboats and were transferred to the coast guard ships.

The Racine and Kenosha crews and the Chambers tug were fighting their way to the ship again when it foundered. A score of men were taken from the two life rafts that floated free of the wreck.

Four hours after the Wisconsin went down there were nine known dead, while sixty-six had been accounted for, eight of the dead had been identified.

The Dead.

MORRISON, Capt. DOUGAL, Chicago.
BURT, JOSEPH, third cook.
BUSCHMANN, JULIUS, chief engineer, Manitowoc, Wis.
ESTES, VICTOR, seaman, Chicago.
RYAN, WALTER, deck hand.
CASSEGAS, de L. H., Chicago.
JOE, third cook.
METZ, JOE, deck hand.
Unidentified deck hand.

In addition to the nine known dead, four others were missing. They were believed to be drowned. Nineteen were in hospitals.

Fifteen men who clung to a life raft aboard the Wisconsin as it sank were rescued by the Chambers Brothers fishing tug and were brought ashore.

No women were aboard the ship when it left Chicago last night with a cargo of merchandise for Milwaukee. A cabin maid, Mrs. Davidson of Chicago, had missed the boat.

Pounding waves played an obligato to their conversation as crew and passengers from the Wisconsin told the story of the "nightmare cruise" only one degree removed from tragedy for most of them.

Dazed and chilled by exposure to the force of a storm as bad as that in which three Great Lakes boats went down last week, their refrain was at first, "Where's a stove?" "Where's a cigarette?" "Who's got something hot to drink?" Later, as they huddled around a huge stove in the Kenosha coast guard station, they related how Lake Michigan had proved too strong for the passenger-freight boat which had weathered many fiercer blows.

Hardly a minute after the Wisconsin poked her nose out of Chicago harbor, she was caught up in the storm. Pitching and rocking like "a big swing," one sailor said, she struggled up the Wisconsin shore toward Milwaukee.

Begins to Take Water.

Then she began to take water in her bunkers. It came cascading in on the stokers working desperately in the engine room. The pumps were falling behind. Soon five feet of water had flooded the floor. Just about 1 A. M. the water reached the fires and the stokers had to leave to save their lives.

Above, the radio operator clung to his post, sending first "We are in distress" and then the S O S, "We are in a sinking condition." On the deck, in sharp relief from the red light of flares, the captain, crew and passengers were calmly working to lower lifeboats.

The lifeboats rocked as they were lowered and one pitched two men overboard. Fred Trubera of Milwaukee was in that boat, but he made no outcry when his arm was crushed and broken against the steamer's side. Jokingly he watched while mates manned the oars and waited for a coast guard launch to pick them up.

Three times the launch cruised back and forth, riding the crest of the waves. There still were between twelve to seventeen men aboard when the last lifeboat left the sinking ship.

The crew looked back and saw through the spray Capt. Dougal Morrison waving good-by. Then mist and the waves blotted him from sight.

Eight life rafts and one of the six lifeboats were still on board when the stern of the ship was seen to sink. The boat rolled heavily on its side and settled beneath the waves.

There was fifteen feet of water in the vessel at 5 A. M., when the last of the rescued left the ship. They had left their shipmates huddled on the deck, clinging to life rafts, shivering and soaked by the huge waves whipped up by the second violent storm in a week. The Wisconsin had ridden out the gale of a week ago.

Several survivors were unconscious when the rescue boats landed them here. Fred Trueber, the lookout, suffered a broken arm. Others were soaked to the skin, chilled and weakened.

The two passengers rescued were Sanders Grant of Sycamore, Ill., and Frank Cabbowski, Chicago.

Elmer Ross of Muskegon, Mich., an oiler, said the crew acted with coolness and obedience throughout the exciting hours preceding the sending of the S O S. The only confusion developed, Ross said, was when three lifeboats were launched, the crews having difficulty in handling them in the high seas.

The men in the lifeboats were picked up by the coast guard craft and the lifeboats turned adrift.

There was some speculation that the Wisconsin may have struck the hull of the car ferry Milwaukee, which sank in the storm of a week ago with its crew of forty-eight. The car ferry went down at about the same place the Wisconsin was abandoned today.

... ...49
... ...67
Mean average 10 years, same date......55
Complete Report on Page 19.

BROOKLYN DAILY EAGLE

WALL STREET CLOSING PRICES ★★★★

90th YEAR—No. 120. ★ NEW YORK CITY, FRIDAY, MAY 1, 1931. ★ 40 PAGES THREE CENTS

Reveal No Clue To Mrs. Driggs, Missing 2 Days

Society Woman's Safety Deposit Boxes Opened by Police in Search

Twenty detectives, under Deputy Chief Inspector Sweeney, today pushed the search for Mrs. Josephine Driggs, Brooklyn society woman, who disappeared last Wednesday, leaving no trace.

Several safe-deposit boxes owned by the missing woman are to be opened in the hope of obtaining a clue, according to Edmund F. Driggs, her lawyer but not a relative.

According to the lawyer, a visit to the boxes was made today. Cards on file showed that the missing woman, who is 56 years old, had not called there for the past several weeks. He said he had received a call from her within the last two weeks, but it had not been on business matters.

A search of hospitals and morgues in the city, instituted by the police in the belief that she may have been the victim of an automobile accident, amnesia or a stroke, has proved without results, Lieutenant Goldman of the Atlantic Ave. Precinct said today.

She was last seen about noon Wednesday in a grocery store at Nostrand Ave. and St. Mark's Ave., a short distance from her home at 780 St. Mark's Ave.

On Business Trip

A few minutes before she had left her home, telling her daughter, Miss Mary Driggs, that she intended stopping at the grocer's and later going downtown to transact some business.

She gave no clue to the nature of the business, the daughter told Detective Schmitt of the Atlantic Ave. precinct.

Her mother said she might go to the theater before returning home, according to Miss Driggs. She had asked the daughter to accompany her, but the latter pleaded illness. She returned from a hospital only a few days ago.

According to the daughter, the missing woman carried only $10 or $15 in a black handbag at the time of her disappearance.

She was wearing a black, close-fitting straw hat with a feather on the right side, a black georgette dress trimmed with velvet, black suede oxfords, black kid gloves and a black coat with fur around the neck and a white pearl necklace.

Miss Driggs could think of no reason why her mother should drop from sight unless she was the victim of an accident, she told police.

The missing woman was an active member of the Brooklyn Woman's Club, the Colony House Club and the Mundell Choral Society. Her husband, the late Elliott F. Driggs, was proprietor of Brooklyn Storage Warehouse. He died about 18 months ago.

Mrs. Driggs before her marriage was Miss Josephine Glover, a member of a wealthy New Orleans, La., family.

The daughter did not notify police until Thursday morning. When her mother failed to return for dinner Wednesday she assumed she was visiting friends or had gone to the ..., she said.

Later in the evening she called friends of the missing woman on the telephone without learning anything of her whereabouts. Thursday morning she was still absent and the daughter notified police, who spent yesterday questioning friends and associates, unsuccessfully.

Stocks Irregular; Lose Early Gains

Stocks were unable to hold further gains scored in many instances in the first half of today's session, when more active selling appeared in the afternoon.

U. S. Steel, after running up to 121, dropped to the 118 level by delivery time. Similar gains and losses were scored by New York Central, Standard Gas, Case, American Telephone and a long list of speculative favorites. Pullman and a few others dropped to new low prices for the year.

The reaction represented some bear pressure designed to test out the strength of the rally, a profit taking and liquidation which had been held up waiting a better market. News was somewhat mixed and generally not sufficiently cheerful to make for much large-scale buying. The Street was somewhat more cheerful, but not inclined to place much faith in the rally, which was regarded as largely technical.

Stock Table on Page 37

Hawaii Statehood Bill Vetoed by Governor

Honolulu, May 1 (AP)—Governor Lawrence M. Judd has vetoed a measure of the Territorial Legislature asking Congress to authorize statehood for Hawaii.

He returned the bill yesterday. Action upon the veto is considered unlikely in the 30 days remaining of the session.

THE EAGLE INDEX

Lockwood's Suit Hit as Threat To Unification

B. M. T. Considers It Hostile Move and Certain to Delay Program—Transit Commission Reported at Loggerheads Over Issue—No Papers Have Yet Been Filed

Transit Commissioner Charles C. Lockwood's insistence on a suit against the B. M. T. to settle the deferred preferential dispute threatens to wreck unification negotiations under the Downing-Steingut bill.

The B. M. T. regards the action as hostile. It is refusing to accept the explanation that the suit is "friendly" and designed merely as an expeditious way to adjudicate the $6,000,000 difference.

The company insists it has been ready and is now willing to settle the matter by negotiation as part of the unification plan.

B. M. T. Cites Contracts

It takes the stand that the contracts provide for arbitration as the orderly method of procedure and that launching of a suit plunges the subject into mazes of litigation that will delay agreement upon price.

Lockwood, in reply, says repeated efforts to get W. S. Menden, president of the B. M. T., to take up the matter brought forth nothing but promises.

It is understood the matter has been the subject of some heated discussion in the recent secret transit conferences and is one of the things engendering bad feeling. Considerable mystery veils the whole matter. Rumors of rows are spreading but official statements are withheld.

The Lockwood report, it develops, was kept a secret nearly two weeks. It was adopted April 14 but did not appear on the calendar of the board for that week. It was withheld from publication until April 27.

Papers Not Prepared

And now, despite its provision for the institution of a suit by Samuel Untermyer, as the commission's special counsel, no orders to prepare papers for such action have been given. No suit can be started until

Please Turn to Page 3

CALLED CRUEL

Los Angeles, May 1 (AP)—Charging Pauline Starke, screen actress, with kicking him in the face, calling him names and otherwise abusing him, Jack White, film producer, filed suit for a divorce here yesterday.

Miss Starke was unduly jealous, he alleged, discharging his nurse at a hospital and wrongfully accusing him of associating with other women.

The actress filed suit April 13, asking division of $100,000 in community property.

MARTIN LOSES TO CITY TRUST

LATE NEWS BULLETIN

County Judge George W. Martin and Thomas J. Buckley owe the defunct City Trust Company $24,000.

This was the decision this afternoon of Supreme Court Justice Faber in the bank receiver's suit against the men which was tried last week.

Two notes of the Buckmoran Realty Company and the Fabin Realty Corporation aggregating this sum had been endorsed by Judge Martin and Buckley and discounted at the bank.

McCooey Holds 7 Judgeships In Palm of Hand

Silent on Selections as Aspirants Wage Personal Campaigns

Behind the grim silence of the political leaders on the subject of a deal to divide the 12 new Supreme Court justiceships, eager aspirants are waging individual campaigns on the basis of mutual nominations.

Other leaders have deemed it safer to remain publicly silent, following the examples of John H. McCooey, Brooklyn Democratic boss, and Frederick J. H. Kracke, Brooklyn Republican leader.

Privately, however, they said today that their "guess" is there will be but 12 new nominees for Supreme Court justice, all told, throughout the whole second judicial district.

This embraces Kings, Queens, Nassau, Suffolk and Richmond.

This fall's election will be, as of old, throughout the whole judicial district as it exists now.

And McCooey holds such a large control over the situation that his decision will be final.

The calculations for new jobs do not include Presiding Justice Edward Lazansky of the Appellate Division and Lewis L. Fawcett of the Supreme Court, both Kings County men, whose terms expire at the end of this year.

Leaders and aspirants are not taking those two jobs into account, for they confidently expect, a lot of them said today, that both Lazansky and Fawcett will be renominated by both parties.

Lazansky is a Democrat, Fawcett a Republican with an exceedingly

Please Turn to Page 15

9 Young Reds Seized in May Day Disorders

Held as School Strike Agitators—Police Guard Union Square Displays

Barcelona, Lisbon Riots Injure Many

Barcelona, Spain, May 1 (AP)—One policeman was killed, two were wounded and 15 civilians were shot today during a May Day clash.

Francisco Macia, president of the Catalonian State, helped to restore order by speaking from a balcony.

He blamed the outbreak on the refusal of the provisional government at Madrid to "grant Catalonia all the political liberty she is entitled to."

Lisbon, Portugal, May 1 (AP)—Several thousand May Day demonstrators rioted today, fighting off the police until they were reinforced by soldiers. A score or more were injured.

May Day opened quietly in New York with the exception of a minor disturbance on the part of eight juvenile radicals nea a Coney Island school and the arrest of a girl at another Brooklyn school.

Five youths and three girls were taken into custody charged with disorderly conduct when they attempted to harangue a group of children on their way to Public School 100, Sea Breeze Ave. and W. 3d St., urging them not to attend classes today.

The boos and yells of derision of the school children drew the attention of the school custodian, John Esposito. When he attempted to drive the sextet away they set upon him and pummeled him about.

The cries of the school children, who by now had formed a milling group of over 200, were heard by Patrolmen John Reddy and Edward Eder of the Coney Island station.

At the station house they gave their names as Ethel Zamos, 14, of 291 Neptune Ave.; Jack Kliede, 19, 2994 W. 27th St., Coney Island; Leo Demzeloss, 17, of 2119 68th St.; Solomon Leofrowitz, 13, of 3024 Coney Island Ave.; David Perisky, 17, of 3171 Coney Island Ave., and Jacob Cohen, 16, of 2011 Lafatine Ave., the Bronx.

When they were arraigned, later, in Coney Island Court, Magistrate Steers held Kliede and Demzeloss in $500 bail and paroled Cohen and Perisky for hearings on May 5. The

Please Turn to Page 15

Dr. Brady on Bad Plumbing—Page 18
Debate Birth Control Question Here—Page 21

Empire State, World's Highest Building, Opens

President, in Capital, Starts Lights—Smith and Roosevelt March

A Governor and a former Governor today formally opened the Empire State Building, tallest in the world, and they were aided by the President of the United States in Washington.

Governor Roosevelt was one of a long list of celebrities who attended the opening of the tall tower of steel and stone at 5th Ave. and 34th St., Manhattan, on the site of the historic old Waldorf-Astoria Hotel. With him was former Gov. Alfred E. Smith, head of the Empire State Building Corporation.

There was a parade, led by Arthur Smith Jr., 4½, and Miss Mary Adams Warner, 4, grandchildren of Governor Smith. There were music and packed crowds.

The Parade Starts

At 11:15 a.m. Smith placed a red, white and blue ribbon on the 33d St. entrance and a few minutes later the parade started, while bands played.

At 11:30, President Hoover in the White House, pressed a button, and throughout the 102 stories of the Empire State Building electric lights flashed on, in competition with the light of a brilliant sun. The building, towering 1,248 feet from the street level, has two stories below

Please Turn to Page 2

ILL IN PARIS

Stricken with influenza, Mrs. James Delano Roosevelt, 76, the Governor's mother, was reported resting comfortably at the American Hospital in Paris today. Her condition is described as not serious.

With receipt of this word Governor Roosevelt had indefinitely postponed his departure for Warm Springs, Ga., for a vacation. He may even go to Paris, it was said, if his mother's condition grows serious. The Governor is in constant telephonic communication with his mother's bedside.

Mrs. Roosevelt, with Mrs. D. D. Forbes, the Governor's aunt, sailed April 10 for a European tour.

2 Try to Escape From Welfare Island and Fail

John Sprint, Burglar, Caught in River Dash—Another Saws Bars

Two attempted escapes from the Welfare Island Penitentiary were made today. Both failed.

In one case a bar had been sawed. This was discovered in time to redouble guards and avert a break. In the other case a prisoner sough freedom perilously by diving in the East River. The fugitive was taken out of the water while swimming strongly toward Manhattan.

No arrests were made in connection with the sawing of the bars.

Sprint Sprints for Home

Appropriately, the prisoner who attempted to swim to freedom was named John Sprint. He is a former burglar who violated his parole. His home was at 424 E. 13th St., Manhattan.

Sprint was working with the house gang in the South prison. At noon, as the line formed for the march to the mess hall, Sprint sprinted for the sea wall, outdistancing Keeper Arthur Joyce. He was overtaken in the water by a tugboat and removed to the penitentiary hospital.

Harvard Club Fire Mostly Excitement

Fire in a flue of the Harvard Club, 27 W. 44th St., Manhattan, about 11:30 o'clock this morning, caused considerable excitement but did practically no damage. The excitement centered in 45th St.

The crowd was so large that vehicular traffic was shut off in that block for almost half an hour. The fire was confined to the flue.

Marine Park Plan Fought by Citizens Union

Action on Architect Lay Referred to Committee of the Whole

The Citizens Union stepped in today as an added opponent of Park Commissioner James J. Browne's plan to release $1,000,000, already appropriated, for the development of Marine Park.

The plan involves retaining Charles Downing Lay of 11 Cranberry St. as landscape architect to furnish designs for the projected 1,500-acre park on the Brooklyn water front between Floyd Benett Field and Sheepshead Bay.

He is to be paid $45,000 for the blueprints and Commissioner Browne has also suggested that he be retained at an annual salary of $18,000 to put the plans into effect.

Goes Over to Tuesday

For the first time today, the proposal came up before the Board of Estimate. At the instance of the Park Commissioer, it was referred to the Committee of the Whole for its action next Tuesday instead of the Tuesday following.

Though it was thus rushed, without argument, through the Board of Estimate, it was not done without a formal expression of opposition. Letters from the New York Park Association and the City Club of New York were read, expressing the previously announced stand of those organizations against the Browne plan and in favor of another that involves spending $50,000 in a prize competition for the "best landscape architects in the world" to plan the park.

And in addition came the opposition of the Citizens Union, in the form of a letter from R. E. McGahen, executive secretary. It read "The creation of a park of this

Please Turn to Page 3

Trouble in India, Hunger in Lyons

By GUY HICKOK — Eagle Bureau, 53 Rue Cambon.

Paris, April 22—Trouble in India . . . 20,000 highly specialized workers in gold textiles unemployed in Lyons and an industry dating from the Saracen invasions of Europe in danger of death. For centuries the wealthy Hindus of Madras have taken the bulk of the output of this little de luxe industry of Lyons. Now, for the first time, the market is gone.

A rod of silver in a tube of gold is pulled through a hole in a plate of steel. It comes out longer and thinner. The process is continued until the rod is a gossamer thread, still a core of silver in a sheath of gold. Of this glistening thread, wound in long skeins, the rich Hindus made their wedding gowns.

Both bride and groom wore wedding gowns, or near gowns, which made the market better.

Needed for Uniforms

With the Hindu wedding trousseau trade as a basis, the curious little home industry in Lyons went on and made the thread for most of the gold braid used on the world's uniforms.

Officers shoulder straps, braid on the uniforms of admirals, generals and even police and fire chiefs all over the world could be traced back to the 20,000 gold wire drawers beside the River Rhone.

Finest of the thread went to the Hindus. They demanded a high percentage of fine gold and silver, insisted that it be wound in skeins, not on spools, and that it be sealed, with a ticket stating the exact purity of the metal used.

For the world's uniforms the specifications were not so rigid. The gentlemen wanted something shiny and reasonably durable; but wanted it as cheaply as they could get it.

Competition Came

Competition came in the military and semi-military trade. Germans found false gold that shone and was reasonably durable and much cheaper. They made it by machinery, and Nuremberg became the great competitor against the Lyons hand-drawn gold thread of quality.

Still the Lyons people did not worry. Did they not have the monopoly of the India trade, where quality alone counted and where competition was totally unknown, where the demand was so constant that the thread could be made almost on a cost-plus basis and sold as long as marriage remained a Hindu institution?

Now that is gone. The ancient wooden drawing benches, precisely like those of the middle ages exhibited in the Cluny Museum, are gathering dust. And the wire-drawers and their families are growing thin.

Trouble in India, hunger in Lyons.

RIGID INVESTIGATION OF GEOGHAN'S OFFICE SLATED BY SEABURY

Carol and His Wife Talk at Son's Bedside

He Breaks Long Silence to Warn Her of Diphtheria Contagion—'What Is Life to Me?' She Answers—Prince Runs Fever

Bucharest, May 1 (AP)—While estranged father and mother stared coldly at each other from opposite sides of his sick bed, Michael, the boy who was king, today lay suffering with diphtheria, dread disease of childhood.

Two injections of serum administered by the royal physicians were believed to have averted serious danger of death, although it was said that anxiety must continue. The Crown Prince, who carries the title Grand Voivode of Alba Julia, was running a high temperature.

The physicians warned Queen Helen, mother of Michael, that she must not endanger her own life or run the risks of contagion by too constant attendance upon the patient, who is 9 years old.

Helen looked at King Carol, who was standing near her in the sick room, and answered:

"What is life to me? I have only one child. I shall never have another. My place is at his side!"

Carol Pleads With Her

Carol, breaking a near silence of months, in which he is said to have spoken to her only from over his shoulder, reiterated the physician's warning and assured her that Michael had trustworthy nurses and attendants. But Helen only shook her head.

It is the second time this year that Michael has been ill, he having suffered from a chill and influenza in January. Some concern was felt by the royal family last year at his tendency to obesity. Recently King Carol instructed attendants to teach him everything about automobile mechanics.

Carol, called to the bedside of Michael at Helen's quarters in the Sinaia Palace, was having his political troubles at the same time.

Premier Jorga dissolved Parliament and called new elections for next month against widespread popular protests. Crowds, which shouted "Long live the King" in answer to the shouts of other crowds which cheered the new Spanish republic, ranged the streets of Bucharest during the night.

A SICK PRINCE

Prince Michael

Richard P. Ganly, Vice Policeman, Gets 4 to 8 Years

Sentenced for Perjury in Framing of Woman on False Affidavit

Richard P. Ganly, 33, of 8 W. 13th St., former vice squad patrolman, who was convicted April 17 of perjury in making a false affidavit in Women's Court in January, 1929, was sentenced today to from four to eight years in Sing Sing.

Ganly was convicted of arraigning Mme. Nina Artska on a vice charge of which she was later exonerated. He was sentenced by Judge Charles C. Nott Jr., in General Sessions.

Jacob Shientag, counsel for Ganly, had asked for leniency. Judge Knott replied that his investigation had showed that the complainant was a "respectable woman of good character" and that a stool pigeon had been used in the case.

"I don't know of any more serious situation arising than when a citizen of this town can be locked up in a situation of this kind," said Judge Knott. "I see absolutely no extenuating circumstance in this case."

Jamaica Results

FIRST RACE—Uncovered, 120 (G. Rose), 16-5, 6-5, 3-5, first; Whisking, 110 (T. Malley), 2-1, 1-1, second; Jillion, 110 (C. Greenwood), 2-1, third. Time, 1:00 2-5. Lida G., Jane Mc., Trust, All Stakes, Sea Saint, Azenby, Stefan Jr., Dun Rode, How, Brandon Prince, Polygamize, Agnes N. and Solar Blaze also ran.

Little Lie About Love No Annulment Cause

The Appellate Division of the Supreme Court, by a 3 to 2 vote, decided today that as a matter of law a husband can not get an annulment of marriage on the ground of fraud where the ground consists solely of misrepresentation of love.

The question arose in a suit brought by Max Feig of 1038 Freeman St., the Bronx, against his bride of three weeks, Regina Roza Feig, whom he married in Rumania on July 8, 1928.

Feig contended that his consent to the marriage was obtained by his wife's fraudulent representations of love for him and that these representations were prompted by her desire to gain admission to the United States in avoidance of the immigration laws of this country.

Seabury Finds Slot Machines Paying Racket

Each Showed Profit of From $15 to $40 Day—Agents Did Fast Work

Referee Seabury delved today into the slot machine racket.

He found it to be expertly organized, all the way down to bondsmen and lawyers to "take care of" clients harassed by police.

He found it to be a well-paying racket, too. Individual machines were pictured as coining from $15 to $40 a day.

The revelations came as the referee resumed public hearings in the magistrates' courts inquiry, after a lapse of several weeks.

Harry E. McKay, proprietor of a stationery store at 1533 Lexington Ave., Manhattan, told of a machine being put in his store last December.

"Who did the machine belong to?" Irving Ben Cooper, counsel, asked the witness.

"The Star Amusement Company," McKay declared.

The shopkeeper related that the machine was put in by an "agent" whose name he did not know. The machine vended cheap mints—and an occasional few slugs for merchandise. The agreement was for McKay and the company to split the profits fifty-fifty.

"If I got in trouble," the witness related, "he said they would bail me out and pay the fine."

McKay was arrested a week later. He phoned the company.

"The bondsman was in the police

Please Turn to Page 3

To Renew License Of Raided Phila. Club

Philadelphia, May 1 (AP)—Mayor Harry A. Mackey announced today that the Philadelphia Cricket Club, whose dance license had not been renewed because of a liquor raid there a year ago, would be granted a renewal of its permit if an officer of the club made the application.

Smith, Kirkwood In London Crash

London, May 1 (AP)—Horton Smith and Joe Kirkwood, American golf professionals, narrowly escaped injury today when a taxi in which they were riding was in collision with a truck.

Billingsley Cleared By Appellate Court

The conviction of Logan Billingsley, president of the Bronx Chamber of Commerce, for contempt of court was unanimously reversed today by the Appellate Division.

Ford Buys Mansion In Essex, England

Chelmsford, Essex, Eng., May 1 (AP)—Announcement was made here today that Henry Ford had purchased Boreham House, a handsome Eighteenth Century mansion, which stands near this town. He probably will reside there from time to time.

Probe Similar to Crain Inquiry Planned for All Boroughs—Moley to Prepare Figures Record in Manhattan 'Worst in 25 Years'

Samuel Seabury's city-wide investigation will train the spotlight on the district attorneys' offices of the city.

This decision is the result of the amazing breakdown of the Manhattan Prosecutor's office under District Attorney Crain as shown by Dr. Raymond C. Moley's analysis.

The Seabury probe, it was learned, plans to subject the Prosecutors' offices in Brooklyn, Queens, Bronx and Richmond to the same searching study.

The examination, it was stated, will be the first of its breadth to be made of the Brooklyn District Attorney's office.

To Start With Cropsey

Dr. Moley, according to plans, will conduct the analysis of the Brooklyn prosecutor's office and in the same manner as his explorations into Crain's office were made.

This means that the administrations of Supreme Court Justices Cropsey and Lewis in the Brooklyn prosecutor's office will be the starting point. Their records will be carefully ascertained. To be compared with them will be the records of the Dodd, Brower and Geoghan administrations.

District Attorney Geoghan commented:

"I will be very glad to welcome the investigators. Our records are open to any one who wants to look at them."

It was reported at Geoghan's office that in the event of an inquiry Geoghan would insist that Dr. Moley make an analysis of cases handled by the Brooklyn office since Geoghan succeeded District Attorney Brower.

Meanwhile, Dr. Moley's surveys were regarded today as having scored the strongest point made so far in the case against Crain.

The analyst, internationally known crime consultant and professor of law at Columbia University, depicted the breakdown of Crain's office on a dozen charts. But his analysis went much deeper than into Crain's record, and the question before Seabury as to whether or not he will recommend the removal of the Manhattan prosecutor.

Crain Record Called Worst

The Moley tables, charts and figures purported to show that the efficiency of the Manhattan district attorney's office has sagged downward steadily under Tammany's domination, reaching the low point under Crain.

Conversely, the Moley charts showed that under Tammany and Crain, the Manhattan office has gone up steadily as a political patronage tree.

The Jerome and Whitman administrations, independent of Tammany, were shown by Dr. Moley's study to have arrived at the highest points of efficiency with appropriations running from $300,000 to $500,000. The Crain "worst in 25 years record" was accomplished on a 1930 appropriation of $333,000.

Manhattan's population and crime figures, meanwhile, did not advance materially.

Dr. Moley's charts reveal that the Crain administration has been notably less successful in securing convictions than were its predecessors.

Lesser Pleas Increase

They also showed that "bargain day"—the accepting from offenders of pleas of guilty to lesser offenses—has reached its high point under the Crain administration.

The Jerome administration, 25 years ago, recorded only 27.8 percent of its convictions for misdemeanors. The figure was the same for the Whitman regime. The percentage of misdemeanor convictions grew to 42 percent, while the percentage of felony convictions shrank, when Tammany captured the prosecutor's office and the Swann regime went in office in 1918.

The Banton administration lowered this figure to 40.3 percent. The Crain regime so far has recorded 50 percent of its convictions on misdemeanor charges.

Walker, Berry Clash; Subway Bonds Passed

$52,000,000 Voted—Sheehan, Hylan Aide, Hits McKee on Buses

The Board of Estimate today authorized the sale of $52,000,000 four-year rapid transit corporate stock to finance city subway construction. This brought the total amount of stock sold or authorized for building the new city-owned subway system to $260,000,000.

The Sinking Fund Commission earlier fixed the maximum interest on the new issue at 4 percent.

The authorization was voted by the board after a three-cornered clash in which the participants were Mayor Walker, Controller Berry and Cornelius M. Sheehan, deputy water commissioner in the Hylan administration.

Sheehan Starts Clash

The clash was precipitated by Sheehan, who said:

"In view of the fact that no one has decided how the lines are going to be operated, this board should go slow.

"If the city is to operate the lines, the issue will be a good one. If they are to be handed over to a private corporation to operate, it is equivalent to a $260,000,000 gift."

The Mayor replied: "These lines haven't been built yet. You're talking about the part that already has been built. This has nothing to do with those."

Controller Berry chimed in: "This money already has been spent and this issue merely takes up scrip which is maturing."

Mayor Retorts Hotly

The Mayor's face flushed and he retorted hotly: "These are roads which haven't been finished yet. That's what I mean. I know what I am talking about."

Controller Berry replied: "The only question is whether the issue shall be for 50 or for four years. Haste is necessary to take advantage of the present bond market."

Apparently mollified, the Mayor agreed: "Yes, that's right."

The authorization then was voted.

Chairman Delaney of the Board of Transportation pointed out that no increase in the budget will be required for the interest charges and amortization on this issue, since the last installment of the $52,000,000 stock issue voted in 1927 will be paid this year.

Alternate Bids

Controller Berry said that on the issue investors for the first time will have an opportunity to submit alternate bids on city securities. They can, he explained, bid an amount above par, or they can bid on the rate of interest.

Protests of property owners on W. 6th St. from 65th St. to Avenue P against a paving assessment drew sympathy from the board. The board listened to a delegation headed by N. I. Helfgott. Then Herman H. Smith, chief engineer of the board, was directed to investigate the possibility of placing the tax burden on the borough instead of the local area. He is to report next week.

Helfgott said the property owners couldn't pay the assessment, which averages about $500 for each.

Buses Start Fireworks

Verbal fireworks were set off when the board came to the question of the Brooklyn bus franchise.

Before it confirmed the proposal made by the Committee of the While last Tuesday, that the franchise eb granted to the Brooklyn Bus Corporation, and set May 29 for a public hearing, Aldermanic President Joseph V. McKee and Mr. Sheehan exchanged acrimonious remarks.

The flareup occurred when Sheehan declared the Committee of the Whole had "slipped one over on the public" in making this decision.

To this McKee, who was presiding, although Mayor Walker was sitting in the room, replied:

"I really should not dignify your charge with an answer. There is too much venom in your remarks. Your statement, implying something underhanded in the actions of the Committee of the Whole, is unworthy of a man appearing before this board Evil minds conceive a lot of evil implications."

Indignant, Sheehan leaped to his feet:

"I can stand that. I had a long course in hard knocks."

Walker Wisecracks

Mayor Walker, who had taken no hand in the argument, could not resist this opportunity for a wisecrack and interrupted with:

"And that's all you know—knocks. Let's stop this blatherskiting and get on with the meeting."

Other bus companies appearing to oppose the granting of the franchise to the Brooklyn Bur Corporation were the Sheepshead Bay Bus Corporation and the Kings Coach Company.

John Flannary, who represented the former, offered to lay $200,00 on the table if his company was given the franchise. This $200,000 offer was duplicated later when Murray Kouz spoke for the Kings Voach Company.

After the Sinking Fund Commission had held a special meeting and voted to issue $52,000,000 in corporate stock it was sent to the Board of Estimate and this body immediately gave its approval. This sum is needed for the city's subway program.

The rate of interest was set at 4 percent, but Controller Berry declared he believed it would be sold below this figure.

TWO SMALL FOLK BRING STEEL GIANT TO LIFE

Little Jack killed a giant, but Mary Adams Warner (3) and Alfred Smith Jr. (4), grandchildren of former Gov. Alfred E. Smith, reversed his role and brought that giant of steel and stone, the Empire State Building, to life. After President Hoover in Washington pressed an electric button, the children cut away the ribbons in front of the doors and the world's tallest building was officially open. At the right of Mary and Arthur are the former Governor (2) and Mrs. Smith (1).

Payroll Robbers Get $2,300 Cash In Water St. Raid

Three Loot Office as Fourth Sits at Wheel of Waiting Motorcar

First of theu sual weekend payroll holdups occurred shortly before 2 o'clock this afternoon.

Three armed robbers appeared at the office of the John RJobertson Company on the second floor of 133 Water St., where N. F. Robertson, president; Allen Harrgie, treasurer, and a bookkeeper were making up a $2,300 payroll.

While one of the men stood guard at the door the other two hastily scooped up the envelopes of money and fled.

Waiting a minute for his companions to escape, the third man dashed down the stairs and leaped into the waiting car in which a fourth man had remained at the wheel.

Inspector George Bishop and detectives from the Poplar St. station arrived, but failed to obtain anything except a good description of the holdup men.

Park Miniature Golf Course to Open

A miniature golf course in Prospect Park will be open to the public tomorrow. Park Commissioner Browne said today that much work had been done on these greens last fall and this Spring. The courses comprise two cages for practicing drives and nine regulation greens for practicing holing out. Permits may be obtained at the office of the Park Department in Prospect Park. The price is $1 for each permit.

Dean Brown Assumes Office of Bishop

Harrisburg, Pa., May 1 (AP) — In the presence of several hundred Church dignitaries and lay readers, the Very Rev. Wyatt Brown, former dean of St. Paul's Cathedral, Buffalo, today was consecrated bishop of the Harrisburg diocese of the Protestant Episcopal Church.

He succeeds the late Bishop James Henry Darlington, formerly of Brooklyn, who helped found the diocese about 25 years ago.

Robber Slays Youth After Kidnaping Him

Jackson, Mich., May 1 (AP)—Local and State police today were searching for a man who kidnaped and killed David Foy Jr., 26, son of a prominent Jackson family. After he and two companions were robbed of 018, an unidentified man compelled Foy to drive him away in his machine. Near Michigan Center, a village six miles out of town, the car is thought to have run out of gas. The robber shot Foy through the heart and fled.

Empire State Building Opens

Continued from Page 1

ground and 86 above, plus 16 in the mooring mast tower.

The "Highest" Luncheon

A luncheon followed on the 86th floor, just beneath the dirigible mooring mast that tops it off, said to be the highest luncheon so far in the world, not counting mountain picnics and dining by plane.

Fifth Ave. was packed tight with humanity, eager to watch the opening. So were 33d and 34th Sts. Two hundred policemen kept the crowd in order. From the tall buildings nearby—shrunk to pigmy size by comparison with their new neighbor—flags fluttered in celebration.

Among the celebrities present were Lt. Gov. Herbert H. Lehman, William F. Kenny, Arthur Brisbane, Mrs. Smith and Mr. and Mrs. Alfred E. Smith Jr.

Smith at 'Mike'

Smiling, Governor Smith acted as announcer over the N. B. C. and Columbia hookups which broadcast the formal opening services after the luncheon.

He had praise for everybody. Everyone praised him.

Paul Starrett of Starrett Brothers & Eken, Inc., builders, spoke first, congratulated the former Governor. Robert H. Shreve of Shreve, Lamb & Harmon, architects, was next.

Then Governor Roosevelt, who said he would be around to see Al Smith when he finished public life, to rent some floor space. Governor Smith explained this was a "rather busy day," but he would be "in the renting office first thing in the morning."

Monument to Smith

Towering as it does majestically, supreme, the Empire State Building, said Governor Roosevelt, typifies the "splendid accomplishments" of Mr. Smith, and represents a "continuance of his splendid service to the State."

This project, too, represents the "vision and faith of Governor Smith," said Mr. Roosevelt. He closed his brief talk by saying that Mr. Smith had kept faith with his public and his promise when he said the Empire State would be opened just a year from the day of the start of construction, which day this is.

Mayor Walker stepped up to the microphone next and wisecracked.

Mayor Wisecracks

"Perhaps Governor Smith has built this building so high that some of our public officials can get away and hide sometime," he opened.

More serious then, the Mayor talked of the rapid growth of the mid-town section, gave the assurance that despite difficulties, the 6th Ave. subway would be built and paid a tribute to Mr Smith.

Between 2 and 6 p.m. the 2,000 invited guests will be taken on a general inspection tour of this huge work from the first floor lobby to the higher of the two observation towers.

At 10:30 p.m. the R. K. O. Theater of the Air will broadcast over an N. B. C. hookup from the 82d floor tower, Governor Smith will be guest speaker.

"A supper in the 86th floor observation tower" will follow at 11 p.m.

The building will be opened for inspection of the public at 9 a.m. tomorrow.

Celebrities Attend

Before the luncheon the guests, some 200 of them, strolled about the observation tower, and looked out upon New York.

Among them were the men who run New York—names to conjure with in Mayor Walker's "imperial city."

There were Merlin H. Aylesworth, president of the National Broadcasting Company; Vincent Astor, Represetative William W. Cohen, Tammany Leader John J. Curry and J. Herbert Case, governor of the Federal Reserve Bank of New York. There also were:

Howard S. Cullman, commissioner of the Port of New York Authority; Pierre S. duPont, the Rev. Francis P. Duffy, Frederick Ecker, president of the Metropolitan Life Insurance Company; Surrogate James A. Foley, Secretary of State Edward J. Flynn.

Also the Rev. Dr. Harry Emerson Fosdick, Charles Dana Gibson, August Heckscher, E. F. Hutton, Roy Howard, Queens Borough President George U. Harvey, Rabbi Nathan Krass, Louis G. Kaufman, president of the Chathame Phenix National Bank & Trust Company; Albert Kobler, publisher of the Mirror; Borough President Samuel Levy of Manhattan, Henry Morgenthau Jr., Adolph S. Ochs, publisher of the New York Times; Capt. William J. Pedrick, vice president of the Fifth Avenue Association; Seward Prosser, president of the Bankers' Trust Company; Percy Straus, president of R. H. Macy & Co.; Franklin Simon, Walter P. Chrysler, Louis D. Wiley, William H. Woodin, president of the American Car & Foundry Company; Grover Whalen and Owen D. Young.

Tells of Light Term Promised On Guilty Plea

Spiegel Asks Writ Staying Severe Sentence He Had Hoped to Dodge

In an effort to wriggle out of the ten-year sentence imposed by County Judge McLaughlin, Max Spiegel, stickup man, told Justice Dunne in Supreme Court today that Assistant District Attorney Bernard J. Becker had promised him a very much lighter penalty.

Pleaded After Promise

Spiegel said he relied on that promise and pleaded guilty when called for trial in County Court He asked Justice Dunne for a certificate of reasonable doubt, which would release him in bail until the higher courts can decide if he should to allowed to withdraw his guilty plea.

Assistant District Attorney Henry J. Walsh told Justice Dunne Spiegel's story was "bunk" and showed a long statement that Spiegel made in the District Attorney's office to Becker, who handled his case throughout.

Becker Make Denial

Becker, in an affidavit, denied emphatically that he had made promises o fany sort. He said Spiegel voluntarily told all the details o fthe job for which he and Emil Varelli were arrested.

At 3 a.m. Nov. 15 they engaged a taxi at Prospect Park and robbed the driver of his money at E. 3d St. and Neck Road, it was charged. Varelli also pleaded guilty and was sentenced to penitentiary. Spiegel ha da record, having spent most of 1918 in prison for larceny. Decision was reserved.

Permission Given To I.R.T. to Appeal 5-Cent Fare Case

Applications Granted by Appellate Division Involving Two Decisions

Applications of the Interborough Rapid Transit Company for permission to appeal to the Court of Appeals from the decision upholding the 5-cent fare were granted today by the Appellate Division of the Supreme Court.

The decision was made in two suits, one by the city acting for the Transit Commission against the Interborough to sustain the 5-cent fare on subway trains, and the other being a certiorari proceeding brought by the Interborough against the Transit Commission for permission to establish a 10-cent fare on the elevated lines.

France Is Cold To British Plan For Naval Pact

Not Inclined to Put Off Until 1935 the Things She Thinks Immediate

Paris, May 1 (AP)—It was stated unofficially today that France will not accept Great Britain's proposals for ironing out the difficulties in the drafting of the Franco-Italian naval agreement.

Great Britain suggested, it is understood, that France and Italy sign the treaty on a limited naval building program which was announced on March 1, leaving the way open for France to outline her replacement needs at a naval conference in 1935.

France's Position

Such a proposal, it is asserted here, would place France in the position of asking permission in 1935 for what she considers now to be her right of replacement. It is not believed that such a suggestion would be acceptable.

If the Italian note, when it is received, supports the British position, the French course, it is declared unofficially, would be to propose an exchange of letters between Rome and Paris making an interim agreement extending to 1934 on the building figures announced on March 1.

England as Go-Between

[The Franco-Italian naval agreement was reached on March 1, with England acting as go-between. Subsequently it became obvious that the French thought the treaty meant one thing, thee Italians another, in regard to France's right to replace obsolete ships.

[Lack of agreement between France and Italy may cause building between those two Powers at such a rate that England will be obliged to put the esculator clause of the London Treaty into effect to keep pace with France. This would mean the United States and Japan also would be free to exceed the limits which they placed on themselves a year ago.—Ed.]

State Will End Its Fiscal Year 'Out of the Red'

Despite Income, Bank Tax Drops, Other Revenues Will Make Up

Albany, May 1 (AP)—Although the State's revenues will be reduced sharply by the slump in returns from income and stock taxes, the Associated Press was reliably inother special taxes probably will make up the shortage before the end of the fiscal year, uJne 30.

The State's share in the income and stock tax drop is about $34,000,000.

Against this decrease there was an increase in the inheritance tax for the first nine months of 15,000,000. The increase in bank taxes was $2,500,000. Other increases were in gasoline tax, $3,000,000; corporation tax, $2,000,000 and franchise tax, $4,500,00, a total increase of $27,000,000.

The budget officer expects to enter the new fiscal year July 1 with a surplus of $10,000,000 to $11,000,000.

FourCourse Captures 1,000 Guineas Stakes

Newmarket, England, May 1 (AP)—Lord Ellesmere's Four Course today won he One Thousand Guineas. The race is at one mile for three-year-old fillies. M. H. Benson's Lady Marjorie was second and Helen McCalmont's Lindos Ojos, favored by many, third.

Four Course, despite her record of three important stakes as a two-year-old, paid off at 100 to 9. John Hay (Jock) Whitney's Kingswoman and Mrs. Corlette Glorney's Carola also ran.

General Food Relief Will End on May 31

General distribution of food in Brooklyn and Queens by the Mayor's Committee will terminate May 31.

After that relief work will be continued on a small scale in isolated cases. This was announced today by A. R. McDonald, in charge of the food distribution, as the 22d general distribution in the two boroughs took place.

New Queens Park Purchase Confirmed

The Board of Estimate today confirmed action of its committee of the whole in purchasing the Clearview Golf Club property for a new Queens park near Whitestone. The site has considerable waterfront, a pier, bathing houses and an 18-hole golf links. The purchase at $940,000 was recommended by Controller Berry, who negotiated it by private sale.

Scientists 'Monkey' With Smoke Problem

St. Louis, May 1 (AP)—Scientists here are "monkeying" with the smoke problem. Under the direction of Dr. L. W. Dean of Washington University Medical School, a group of monkeys will breathe artificially purified air while another group will be exposed to the smoke-laden air of St. Louis. A comparison will be made at the end of a year to determine exactly the deleterious effects of smoke on living organisms.

Women Urge School to Train Police—Just Like Lawyers

The New York City Federation of Women's Clubs today unanimously adopted suggestions calling for equal culpability of men and women in vice cases.

It also urged that uniforms be furnished new policemen to avoid the incurring of debt at the beginning of service, and the passage of Federal laws regulating the purchase of firearms.

A more definite stand than a mere "suggestion" was taken with respect to the standards for entry into the police department.

The Federation recommended that a school for the training of men who wish to take the examination for the police department be established, either as a public or private institution, and that young men be trained for the "police profession" as they are for the bar.

These suggestions and the recommendation were incorporated in the report of the committee of women lawyers of the Federation and read at the 85th convention of the organization in the Hotel Astor, Manhattan.

Contest for Babies Howling Success; 3 Winners Picked

27 Voice Protest Against Judges in Colony House—2 Tie for First Place

Better babies have better lungs, to judge by the lusty protests of 27 of the youngest generation as they were being examined today at Colony House, 297 Dean St., as part of the Child Health Day program.

Amid lively howls which even in power could not decied the better, two young hopefuls tied for first place in the contest which is a feature of the Annual Health Conference for babies up to 3 years.

Neither the golden curls of Muriel Donlon, daughter of Mr. and Mrs. George Donlon of 257 Hoyt St., nor the rosy cheeks of George O'Reilly Jr., son of Mr. and Mrs. George O'Reilly, 256 Hoyt St., could bring the doctors to a decision.

Both were given silver cups and announced as winners in the group from 15 months to 3 years.

In the younger group, Angela Zahner, daughter of Mr. and Mrs. John Zahner of 11 St. Mark's Place, was awerded the silver spoon of the winner.

New Subway Car Experiment Will Cost City $21,000

Four-Door Trains Will Be Run in B. M. T. Tubes as Test of Their Worth

It will cost the city $21,000 to find out if its four-door subway cars are practical in operation.

A contract between the city and the B. M. T. to cover experimental use of 20 of the cars has been drawn by the Board of Transportation. It will be submitted to the Board of Estimate and Apportionment.

The 20 cars are designed for operation in the city-owned subway system now under construction. The city wants to see how they work before deciding whether to buy 300 more.

Therefore the B. M. T. will have the cars leased to it. It will be paid on a mileage basis, getting $21,000 for six months. It will be insured by the city against any loss or damage that may occur if one of the cars breaks down.

The necessity for the experiment lies in the four doors. The ordinary subway car has three doors. The theory of the four-door car is that it will load and unload quickly at stations.

The cars are now at the city's 207th St. yards, Manhattan. If the Board of Estimate approves the contract, the cars will be carried on floats to Brooklyn and run into the B. M. T. cut near 65th St.

Betty Nuthall Loses To French Net Ace

Bournemouth, England, May 1 (AP)—Betty Nuthall, the English girl who is women's tennis champion of the United States, today was defeated by Mme. Mathieu, France's ranking player, in the seim-finals of the National Hard Court Championships.

The victory was achieved in straight sets, 8—6, 6—. In the other semi-final another champion fell. Signorina Valerio of Italy, best in her country, was defeated by Mary Heeley, former English junior champion, 5—7, 6—4, 6—4.

Miss Heeley and Mme. Mathieu will met in the finals tomorrow.

Joan Fry won the title last year.

Negro Talks in 'Mike' And Court Gets Laugh

The newly installed amplifier in Judge Algeron R. Nova's courtroom caused a laugh this morning following the testimony of Jadie Johnson, Negro, who gave his address as "Georgia."

He had testified, in a clear voice, into the michrophone which is set in front of the witness box and was then excused.

As he resumed his seat his soto voice conversation to a friend came distinctly over the amplifier—and promptly threw the court into laughter. It was:

"What station was that? I sho' hope mah fowks down in Gawgia was listen' in."

May Harriman Will Proved Over Contest

Newport, R. I., May 1 (AP)—The will of May Brady Harriman, disposing of a $750,000 estate, was proved today at an adjourned session of the Probate Court by Judge Walter Curry. A sister, Mrs. Katherine Harris, who is left only $5,000, sought to contest the will.

MRS. ANNIE G. O'KEEFE, widow of Patrick O'Keefe, died Friday at her home, 111 Congress St. Born in Brooklyn, she was a lifelong parishioner of St. Peter's Church. The funeral will be held from the funeral chapel at Henry and Warren Sts., Monday, at 9:30 a.m., with a solemn requiem mass in St. Peter's R. C. Church. Interment will be in Holy Cross Cemetery.

Liquor Sentences Show It's Safer To Use a Truck

Two Who Did So Get Six Months, While Pair in Boat Get Year Each

Liquor law violations afloat are twice as serious as ashore, according to Brooklyn Federal Court sentences imposed today.

Two men pleaded guilty before Judge Campbell to transporting 100 cases of liquor in a speedboat off Jones Beach last Washington's Birthday. Each received one year and a day in prison.

Two pleaded guilty before Judge Inch to transporting 100 cases in a truck on the highway near Montauk Point the night of Feb. 25 last. They received six months imprisonment each.

Andrew Nelson of Bedell St. and Perc Boyden of Stillwell Place, both Freeport, were sentenced by Judge Campbell.

The lesser penalties were imposed by Judge Inch on George Larson and Kirby Spaulding of Montauk Point, while suspended sentences were given to two other men who also rode the truck and today pleaded guilty to possession. The fortunate pair were Michael Kelly of 502 W. 47th St., Manhattan, and John Benson of Montauk Point.

Assistant Federal Attorney William T. Cowin described the truck as a "sacrifice." He said it was the "tail" of a convoy and had attained its intended end in delaying pursuit while advance, larger trucks made good their escape. The seizure was by a night road patrol of Coast Guardsmen.

L. I. Crossing Work Crippled for Year, Godley Declares

Blames Legislature's Failure to Vote Fund—Atlantic Ave. Included

At the end of the final hearing on the proposed Grant City-New Dorp grade crossing elimination on the Staten Island Rapid Transit Railway Company route, Transit Commissioner Leon G. Godley announced today that he doubted whether there would be any ruling by the commission on the form of elimination for a year.

Mr. Godley explained that the failure of the Legislature at its recent session to appropriate $31,000,000 to be added to the $76,000,000 already appropriated to bear the State's burden would probably delay grade crossing elimination projects that have not yet been started.

He indicated that approximately 40 crossings on Staten Island and Long Island would be tied up, including the score or so along the Atlantic Ave. division of the Long Island Railroad. The city pays 1 percent of the cost, the State 49 percent and the railroad 50 percent.

Nannery Extradicted By New York State

Trenton, May 1 (AP)—Officers from Sing Sing Prison obtained extradition today of James Nannery, escaped convict and alleged gangster and slayer, held in the Morris County jail since his capture Sunday. He was wanted as a suspect in robberies in north Jersey.

Governor Larson signed the warrant permitting the man's removal from the State. John J. Shuhy, principal keeper of Sing Sing, was accompanied by three guards. He said they would probably take Nannery back to New York by automobile.

Bull Kills a Man; Woman Routs It

Marlton, N. J., May 1 (AP)—Henry Evans, 76, a farmhand at Kresson, near here, died in a Camden hospital today from a fractured skull, received when he was attacked by a bull yesterday. Evans was repairing a fence when the bull, owned by Srank Tusca, a neighboring farmer, broke loose. Mrs. Joseph Gibbs, 35, wife of the owner of the farm on which Evans was employed, armed herself with a pitchfork and drove off the animal.

Cobbler Comes Back; Customers Relieved

Customers of Jacob Miller, who disappeared from his shoe repair shop at 2620 Newkirk Ave. seven weeks ago, were set to play their trump trick today.

They had persuaded Mrs. Hattie Wolff, owner of the building, to obtain a dispossess writ and force their shoes out of the shop, but it was not necessary.

Miller showed up at the last moment and promised to pay. He made no explanation of his absence.

World Fliers Off For Port au Prince

Miami, Fla., May 1 (AP)—Clyde Pangborn and Hugh Herndon Jr. hopped off from here at 7:25 a.m. E. S. T. today for Port au Prince on a leisurely flight from New York to Porto Rico in preparation for a proposed around-the-world airplane trip.

Stone Resents 'Unfair' Attacks On Farm Board

Tells U. S. Chamber to Get Information Before Criticizing

Atlantic City, May 1 (AP)—Advice to American business men by James C. Stone, chairman of the Federal Farm Board, not to criticize the Farm Board too strenuously without full information was given today. He gave it to the United States Chamber of Commerce in remarks interpolated in his set address by the Farm Board chairman.

Mr. Stone said emergency stabilization activities of the board cannot cope successfully with continuous overproduction. They can be resorted to only as temporary remedies, he said.

The board, Stone asserted, believes its stabilization operations in cotton and wheat "have been fully justified by the serious emergency that faced agriculture" as a result of the stock market crash in 1929.

Losses that may be sustained by the revolving fund, he said, "will be inconsequential compared to the benefits."

He told more than 2,500 delegates to the 19th annual meeting of the chamber that the "gradually growing" antagonism between farmers and industry was largely due "to a lack of understanding." The Farm Board, he said, was attempting to lessen this breach.

Answering criticism of the lending of money by the Farm Board, Mr. Stone said such loans were absolutely necessary because of the difficulty co-operative associations experience in obtaining necessary credits.

Immediately at the conclusion of Mr. Stone's address Julius H. Barnes, chairman of the Chamber's board, rose and pledged the support of the Chamber to the Farm Board's activities, "up to the point where those activities do not infringe" on the economic interests of private business.

Mr. Barnes' statement was generally interpreted as meaning the Chamber could not recognize the grain and cotton market activities of the Farm Board.

Wants Ore Stabilized

W. R. Boyd Jr., secretary of the American Petroleum Institute, made a plea for approval of appointment of a committee to inquire into the feasibility of establishment of an agency to interpret the needs of industry to Congress and plan for stabilization of industries.

F. E. Murphy, publisher of the Minneapolis Tribune, told the convention that "a new agriculture is born" when farmers and businessmen "really get together," which happened in the Northwest. Farmers have learned, he asserted, that no act of Congress or price-fixing schemes "can ever restore fertility to wheatsick soils or raise sagging wheat yields one bushel."

After hearing Harper Sibly, farming expert and manager of estates in several States, the delegates were scheduled to consider aviation at a round-table conference to be addressed by Charles L. Lawrance, president of the Aeronautical Chamber of Commerce of America.

Humbert Miele Not L. I. Rum Defendant

The name of Humbert Miele was erroneously included with those of the defendants in a report yesterday in The Eagle of the arraignment of eight Long Beach police officers and a Long Beach civilian on a Federal charge of smuggling liquor. Miele, a contractor, posted a realty deed as bond for the appearance of the officers in Brooklyn Federal Court on May 19.

The one civilian defendant in the case was Frank Barberi, 502 Jackson Boulevard, alleged contact man between the police and rumrunners who the authorities assert landed liquor at Long Beach. Yesterday's arraignment charge is based on the same alleged transactions whereon the defendants were unsuccessfully prosecuted by the Nassau County authorities in Mineola the day before.

HOME EDITION

TEMPERATURES.
Min., 52 Max., 57.
(Detailed weather report on page 14.)

SCHOOL NEWS ON PAGE 26

The Sun

Copyright, 1931, by The Sun Printing and Publishing Association.

HOME EDITION

United States Official Weather Forecast:
Fair today, little change in temperature;
tomorrow showers.

SCHOOL NEWS ON PAGE 26

VOL. XCIX.—NO. 46—DAILY. NEW YORK, SATURDAY, OCTOBER 24, 1931. PRICE THREE CENTS.

TWO STATES OPEN HUDSON SPAN TODAY

Copyrighted by William Frange, 1931.

DECISION AWAITED ON PUTTING INQUIRY OFF TILL ELECTION

Democrats Favor Adjourning and Republicans Make No Comment.

With the Democratic members of the Hofstadter legislative committee frankly favoring an adjournment until after election time and the Republicans a bit reticent on the subject, speculation continued today as to whether or not Judge Samuel Seabury expected to delay his inquiry on the bipartisan judicial deal.

Following the appearance on the stand yesterday of Edgar F. Hazleton, former Municipal Court Justice, who testified that Warren B. Ashmead, the Republican leader in Queens had intimated that the successful candidate in the Second district would be expected to contribute $5,000 to the campaign fund, it was generally believed that Mr. Seabury needed time to prepare further evidence.

The Democratic members have urged that further public hearings be postponed until after election. No definite decision has been reached, but the next public hearing will not be held until Wednesday.

Damper on Bench Inquiry.

If the hearings are adjourned for a longer time it will put something of a quietus on the general discussion of the bipartisan deal whereby twelve Supreme Court justiceships were parceled out. At least until after election.

The interval between now and Monday may give Mr. Seabury sufficient time to prepare further evidence, but whether he will continue with this line of inquiry remains to be seen. If he does the names of John McCooey, leader in Kings county, and W. Kingsland Macy, State Republican leader, may be brought into the picture. McCooey's 32-year-old son is one of the bench candidates who will benefit by a fourteen-year term at a $25,000 annual salary.

In the meantime Mr. Seabury has before him for consideration the challenge of Col. Edward S. Carrington, Republican candidate for Borough President of Manhattan, that United States Senator Robert F. Wagner be called as a witness.

Cosgrove's Land Offered.

Col. Carrington testified Wednesday that some real estate owned by

Continued on Second Page.

In The Sun Today

Army-Yale Game Tops the List

Navy-Princeton and N. Y. U.-Colgate Matches Also on Today's Football Program.

The two service teams are headliners in the East's football program today with New York city having an added attraction in the N. Y. U.-Colgate game at the Yankee Stadium.

West Point against Yale is outstanding, and the Bowl at New Haven undoubtedly will be filled for the parade of the Cadet regiment and the sixty minutes of football which follow. The game itself is an even bet. It is a rare year when the score is one-sided, and last week's events cast their shadow on today's. Army had a severe afternoon with Harvard and two of its best halfbacks, Stecker and Sebastian, are out. Yale, on the other hand, showed up surprisingly well against a weak Chicago eleven and is rated an even choice against the Army.

The Navy meets Princeton in Palmer Stadium and here it is a case of two elevens which have been floundering through the early season, failing to absorb new systems of play. One or the other or both must find themselves to make a showing on the season.

Gives Test for N. Y. U.

New York University appears to be headed for its first severe test. Colgate won last year's game by the margin of a point after touchdown, and its 1931 eleven is rated as the equal of the one which defeated the New York boys. N. Y. U. has run roughshod over all opposition so far and appears as one of those teams which will not be stopped until it runs into an opponent with a great defense.

Columbia should have no great trouble with Williams at Baker Field, but she has had some difficulty with these little fellows in the

Continued on Thirty-second Page.

Important Football Games East, South and West

LOCAL.

N. Y. U. vs. Colgate, at Yankee Stadium, 2:20 P. M.
Fordham vs. Drake, at Polo Grounds, 2:30 P. M.
Columbia vs Williams, at Baker Field, 2:30 P. M.

EAST.

Yale vs. Army, at New Haven.
Harvard vs. Texas, at Cambridge.
Princeton vs. Navy, at Princeton.
Penn vs. Wisconsin, at Philadelphia.
Carnegie Tech vs. Purdue, at Pittsburgh.
Syracuse vs. Penn State.
Lafayette vs. W. & J., at Easton.
C. C. N. Y. vs. Drexel, at Philadelphia.
Holy Cross vs. Rutgers, at Worcester.
Brown vs. Lehigh, at Providence.

WEST.

Notre Dame vs. Pittsburgh, at South Bend.
Illinois vs. Michigan, at Champaign.
Ohio State vs. Northwestern, at Columbus,
Minnesota vs. Iowa, at Minneapolis.

SOUTH.

Tulane vs. Georgia Tech, at New Orleans.
Georgia vs. Vanderbilt, at Athens.
Florida vs. Auburn, at Jacksonville.

FAR WEST.

California vs Southern California, at Berkeley.
Washington vs. Stanford, at Seattle.
Montana vs. Washington State, at Missoula.

3 PEDESTRIANS HIT

Acting Police Inspector Hurt by Heedless Motorist.

Three persons, one of them Acting Police Inspector Richard O'Connor, are suffering from injuries received in motor accidents in the city last night.

Acting Inspector O'Connor, 59 years old, in command of the Second Traffic district, was injured when he was struck by an automobile while attempting to cross Pelham Parkway at Southern Boulevard in the Bronx. After being attended at Fordham Hospital he went to his home at 81 East 208th street, the Bronx.

John Jay Cunningham, 48 years old, of 28 East Sixty-fourth street, an associate of M. Knoedler Co., art dealers at 14 East Fifty-seventh street, was taken to Bellevue Hospital last night suffering from injuries received when he was struck by an automobile driven by John Cappola of 9730 Farragut Road, Brooklyn, in First avenue, between Fifty-fourth and Fifty-fifth streets.

Joseph Hill, 10 years old, of 1443 Madison avenue, was severely injured last night when he was struck by an automobile driven by Harry Hirschfield of 200 West Eighty-sixth street, at Ninety-seventh street and the Transverse Road, in Central Park, two hundred feet west of Fifth avenue. Hirschfield took the boy to Mount Sinai Hospital.

Graf Returning From Brazil.

RECIFE, Brazil, Oct. 24 (U. P.).—The Graf Zeppelin was en route to Friedrichshafen today on the return journey of a commercial flight to South America. The ship left here at 12:15 A. M. today.

OLD LOWRY HOTEL SWEPT BY FLAMES

Vacant Brooklyn Structure Burned to Ground.

The old Lowry Hotel at the foot of Seventeenth avenue, Brooklyn, was destroyed last night by flames which were visible from Coney Island and Staten Island across the Narrows.

When the walls of the long untenanted structure collapsed two firemen were injured. A third fireman and a policeman who went to their rescue also suffered minor injuries.

Four alarms were sent in and apparatus from the entire southern portion of Brooklyn responded. The men caught in the collapse were Capt. Edward Williams of 1738 Seventy-seventh street, who suffered a dislocated shoulder, and Firemen Joseph McAuliffe of 1730 Stewart street, Brooklyn, whose leg was injured. They were removed to Harbor Hospital.

A crowd of about 50,000 persons gathered. In the excitement James Horan, 65 years old, of 2807 Glenwood avenue, Brooklyn, a retired fireman, collapsed and was dead when he arrived at Harbor Hospital.

HOOVER AND LAVAL SAY ONLY POLICIES ARE BEING DEBATED

Joint Statement Denies Any 'Demands' or 'Terms' Are Under Discussion.

WASHINGTON, Oct. 24 (A. P.).—President Hoover and Premier Laval of France have agreed that their conversations here deal "solely" with policies that their Governments can develop to expedite world economic recovery.

In their first joint expression they wrote an emphatic "no" across any implication that the discussions had to do with subjects which might be classified as "demands" or calls for "terms of settlement."

"Happily," a statement issued yesterday through the White House said, "there are no controversies to be settled between France and America. None such exists."

With Secretary Stimson, Under Secretary Mills of the Treasury and Jacques Bizot, a French financial expert, present the two men conversed for three hours before the statement was issued. They continued their talk for four more hours before the lights were turned out after midnight in the quiet Lincoln study on the second floor of the White House. The Premier then went to rest in the Lincoln bedroom.

Hoover Calls Mills.

Today President Hoover summoned Mr. Mills for a conference directly after breakfast before going into further detail with the Premier, as to just what policies their Governments were willing to follow in "the promotion of constructive progress in the world."

After the issuing of the White House statement the opinion was prevalent that the question of French security had not been broached. There was also some question as to whether they had reached a stage where disarmament could be discussed in any detail.

The whole question of world armament is one that President Hoover has close to his heart. He has repeatedly said that one of the great barriers to world economic recovery was excessive expenditure for military establishments.

On the other hand Premier Laval has stressed French unwillingness to

Continued on Second Page.

DIES IN TERRACE FALL

Lawyer Drops From Penthouse of 19-Story Hotel.

Benjamin F. Feiner, a partner in the law firm of Feiner & Skutch of 37 Wall street, fell or plunged to his death last night from the terrace of his penthouse on top of the nineteen-story Hotel Lombardy at 111 East Fifty-sixth street. He was 53 years old, and had been in ill health for several months.

Last night he went for a walk on the terrace while his wife and a nurse remained inside. His body was found on the roof of a two-story extension.

Store Increases Wages.

OMAHA, Oct. 24 (A. P.).—A 5 per cent. increase in the wages of all employees, described as an indication of confidence in the future, was announced last night by officials of Ruedy's department store here. The store has eighty-six employees and the pay roll is about $2,600 weekly.

Text of Statement By Hoover and Laval

WASHINGTON, Oct. 24.—The following statement regarding the nature of the conversations of the President and Premier Laval was issued last night at the White House:

"Both the President and Premier Laval wish it made clear that the conversations upon which they are engaged are solely in respect of such policies as each of the two governments can develop to expedite recovery from the world economic depression.

"There is no remote basis whatever for statements as to "demands," "terms of settlement" or any other like discussions.

"Happily there are no controversies to be settled between France and America. None such exist.

"The sole purpose of these conversations is the earnest, frank exchange of views with a view to finding common ground for helpful action in the promotion of constructive progress in the world."

FOG EARLY TODAY DELAYS FERRIES

Accidents in Harbor Are Narrowly Avoided.

A heavy fog delayed traffic in the harbor early today, and in several instances accidents narrowly were avoided. The fog settled over the harbor and lower bay at dawn and did not begin to lift until shortly before 9 o'clock. Ferry service was impaired; two incoming ocean steamships were delayed in reaching their piers, and all traffic was hampered.

Ferry service between Cortlandt street and Weehawken was suspended at 6 30 A. M., to await the lifting of the mist. Other ferry boats in operation ran from fgifteen to twenty minutes behind schedule.

The municipal ferryboat Richmond, plying between St. George, Staten Island, and the Battery, left her slip at St. George at 6:30 A. M. and did not arrive at the Battery until 7:40—seventy minutes for a trip that ordinarily requires only twenty-five.

During the trip the Richmond grazed a coast guard cutter and a tug, brushed a pier and barely avoided a head on collision with two other boats.

A. J. Cook, Mine Leader, Near Death in London

LONDON, Oct. 24.—A. J. (Emperor) Cook, secretary of the Miners Federation, was reported near death in a hospital today.

Mr. Cook suffered an injury to his leg this year following rioting at a miners' meeting protesting against delay in settling a labor dispute. Later the leg was amputated.

30 Motor Boats Burned In Ontario Storage Yard

PENETANG, Ont., Oct. 24 (A. P.).—Thirty motor cruisers and a storage building were destroyed by fire in the Gidley Boat Company's plant across the bay from here yesterday. Harry Warnock, manager, estimated the loss at between $100,000 and $200,000.

The boats were owned by residents of New York, Chicago, Detroit and Canadian cities who spent vacations here.

JAPANESE REJECT LEAGUE DEMAND TO WITHDRAW TROOPS

Submit Counter Proposals for Direct Negotiations With Chinese.

GENEVA, Oct. 24 (U. P.).—Japan rejected today the League of Nations formula for settlement of the Manchurian dispute with China.

Kenkichi Yoshizawa, Japanese delegate told the league council that his Government was unable to accept the council's draft resolution.

The league council adjourned until 4 P. M. without voting on either the council's resolution or the Japanese counter proposals.

The resolution recommended that China and Japan appoint representatives to arrange details of evacuation of Japanese troops to within the treaty zone in Manchuria and that they begin direct negotiations as soon as evacuation was completed. It also suggested the creation of a permanent Sino-Japanese conciliatory committee.

Salvador de Madariaga, Spanish Ambassador to Washington, insisted that Japan accept a solemn pledge before the entire council that general negotiations would begin the day evacuation was completed.

Council Still Hopeful.

GENEVA, Oct. 24 (A. P.).—On the point of overriding Japanese opposition and fixing November 16 as the time limit for complete evacuation of Japanese troops from Manchuria, the League of Nations council adjourned a morning session today until late in the afternoon in the hope that some way might be found to remove the opposition.

With Viscount Cecil, British representative, and Salvador de Madariaga of Spain leading a strong drive against the objections of Kenkichi Yoshizawa, Japanese delegate, the line-up was clearly drawn, 13 to 1, in favor of the council's proposal when Aristide Briand, acting chairman, closed the session until 4 P. M.

Lord Cecil besought the Japanese Ambassador to learn what Japan meant by "certain fundamental principles" that she considered essential as a preliminary to an agreement between herself and China.

M. Yoshizawa replied that these principles concerned "a certain number of questions" on which there must be an agreement with China before withdrawal of troops could be effected. His Government did not authorize him to give further explanations, he said.

Dangerous Situation Seen.

"We face an extremely dangerous situation," warned Senor De Madariaga. "Japan," he continued, "herself assumes responsibility for the security of the invaded areas in moving her troops out of the railway zone." He wanted to know why the Japanese Minister preferred the phrase "in the spirit of the covenant" to the council's expression "according to the terms of the covenant" in defining Japan's intentions in Manchuria.

"If I understand the Japanese po-

Continued on Second Page.

Radio Section Today.

The regular Saturday Radio Section of The Sun will be found today on Pages 20, 21, 22 and 23. Week-end radio programs, advance information on radio features and technical information are carried on those pages.

$60,000,000 George Washington Span Dedicated Today by Officials of New York and Jersey.

The George Washington Bridge, longest span in the world, which reaches across the Hudson from 178th street to Fort Lee in New Jersey, will be formally dedicated today.

At 5 A. M. tomorrow the bridge will be opened to motor traffic. The first toll will be paid, the first car will speed across the long, wide lanes over the bridge that cost $60,000,000.

When the sun rose today its light caught the bright colors of flying banners and streamers and great arrays of bunting, a blaze of decoration that Fort Lee—bursting with pride—and Washington Heights, no less prideful, had arranged for the great day.

The program for the dedication begins when the guests of the Port Authority assemble at the armory at West 168th street and Fort Washington avenue. Boy Scouts will escort the group to the New York plaza, where, at noon, the New York Police Department band will give a concert.

The Port Authority members and their guests will then proceed to the middle of the bridge, where they will be met by the New Jersey officials near the grand stand which has been built for the occasion.

Will Cut Ribbons.

John J. Galvin, chairman of the Port Authority, will be the first speaker, and, when his speech is done, the Governors of New York and New Jersey will simultaneously cut ribbons of white silk that will be stretched across the center of the bridge. At this moment several war vessels, at anchor in the Hudson, will fire a salute.

Speaking at the center of the bridge is scheduled to begin at 3 P. M. It will be broadcast by two radio stations. Secretary of the Navy Adams will be one of the speakers. Mayor Walker and the Governors of New Jersey and New York also will speak.

The bridge will be open to pedestrians from 6 P. M. to 11 o'clock tonight free of charge. The automobile traffic, however, will not be admitted until tomorrow morning, when a toll of 50 cents a car and 10 cents per person for pedestrians will go into effect.

Fort Lee did not wait until today for its observance of the completion of the bridge. Its officials, supported by several hundred townsmen, gathered yesterday afternoon at the toll gates on the Jersey side and held a little ribbon-cutting of its own.

Freeholders Present.

Among those present were the Bergen County Board of Freeholders, the county Chamber of Commerce, and scores of other officials of the State of New Jersey, including the State Highway Department

Continued on Third Page.

ANTISMOKE DRIVE SEEN AS GAINING

1400 Cases Reach Trial Board in First Year.

In the first twelve months of its operation, beginning October 2, 1930, the trial board of the Health Department for smoke offenders has heard 1,400 cases. Inspectors of the smoke squad investigated 10,790 complaints.

According to Samuel Sergeant, head of the smoke squad and one of the three members of the trial board, the campaign has resulted in a great improvement in conditions in the city. He estimated that the smoke evil has been reduced 60 per cent.

Eighty-nine cases were taken to court during the year, and of this number only three were dismissed. Defendants in 75 per cent. of the cases received suspended sentences, while the remainder paid fines of from $5 to $100.

At present twenty-six court cases are pending, twenty-one of which are alleged violations by boat owners in the harbor.

Mr. Sargeant said that complaints against apartment houses, power houses, factories, steamships and tugboats usually were investigated on the same day they were received by a staff of ten inspectors. Under the rules of the Health Department the names of any persons complaining against smoke nuisance are not disclosed by the investigators. This has resulted in greater public support in the campaign to abate smoke.

New York Women Hurt In Penn Bus Crash

ALLENTOWN, Pa., Oct. 24 (A. P.).—A Quakertown man was critically injured and two New York city women were severely hurt last night when a Reading Transportation Company Shamokin-bound bus and a truck were in collision here.

Harry D. Swartz, 47 years old, is in a serious condition at the Allentown Hospital with a possible fractre of the skull. The injured women were Mae McBride of 2800 Bailey avenue, the Bronx, and Anna Smyth, 633 Fairmont avenue, Brooklyn. Miss McBride has a possible fracture of the knee and lacerations, while Miss Smyth suffered cuts of the face and body.

Paraguayan Delegate Coming for Boundary Case

MEXICO CITY, Oct. 24 (A. P.).—Juan Jose Soler, Paraguay Minister to Mexico, will leave tomorrow night for Washington to represent his Government on the Paraguay-Bolivia Boundary Commission, which will meet there to attempt to settle the Gran Chaco boundary dispute.

The first duty of the commission, Soler said, was to fix a neutral zone and put an end to the bloody disputes that have taken place in the area.

Seven Reported Killed In Peruvian Plot

LIMA, Peru, Oct. 24 (U. P.).—Reports reaching here today said seven persons were killed, including two women, and twenty-five wounded in a clash between police and residents of the village of Pariamarca.

The citizens held a mass meeting protesting against the methods of a subprefect of police and rioting followed.

BORAH'S VIEWS GOOD COPY FOR FRENCH SCRIBES

Correspondents Kept Busy as Senator Gives Them Half Hour Interview.

PROPOSES TREATY REVISION

Favors Debt Cancellation Only if Allies Cancel German Reparations.

WASHINGTON, Oct. 24 (A. P.).—Indirectly, but none the less emphatically, Senator Borah has stretched before President Hoover and Premier Laval International questions absent from their Agenda.

In an interview with French newspaper correspondents who accompanied the French Premier to Washington, he said revision of the Versailles treaty is necessary to the peace and reconstruction of the world.

He told the mhe would favor America cancelling war debts owed by her former allies if they would cancel Germany's reparations payment.

He told them the time for any extension of the moratorium of intergovernment debts had passed.

He scoffed at the idea of providing "teeth" for the Kellogg-Briand pact for outlawing war.

President Hoover and the French Premier were in the midst of their duscissions at the White House when the chairman of the Senate Foreign Relations Committee spoke. What he said was relayed to them.

Tonight M. Laval and Senator Borah will meet, at the request of the former, for a conference at the home of Secretary Stimson.

Not New to Americans.

Much of what the Senator said to the French correspondents was not news to the American public, which knows well the views of the Senator against American-European political alliances.

To the Frenchmen it was different. Pencils scurried busily while Senator Borah answered their questions "frankly, if not diplomatically," as he put it. At times the half-hour meeting developed into something nearer a debate over Anglo-French principles than an interview. Senator Borah's face reddened more once, but he kept his smile and replied.

He warned that unless the Versailles treaty is revised peacefully forcible revision will probably eventuate.

"I don't think you are going to get any disarmament in Europe so long as certain conditions which arise out of the Versailles treaty continue to exist," he said.

Wants Russia Recognized.

It is up to france, he added, to determine for herself the limit of disarmament. On the same subject, he contended that American recognition of Russia is necessary for world disarmament.

He expressed opposition to international intervention of any kind or under any circumstances, contended that economic pressure against a nation is the same as war and asserted that American economic interests are intertwined with Europe's and the world's.

"Teeth in peace pacts are meaningless," he said, adding:

"You people had plenty to teeth the other day in the covenant of the league, but you did not dare to show your teeth with reference to Japan. . . . If we have not reached the stage where nations are willing to reason out disputes, to meet and discuss in a peaceful way and settle their controversies in a peaceful way, we have not reached the time when we may expect disarmament."

NEW HUDSON BRIDGE TO BE OPENED TODAY

Continued from First Page.

and the various commissioners.

Major.-Gen. Hugh L. Scott, chairman of the New Jersey State Highway Commission, cut the ribbon. Gen. Scott is the famous Indian fighter. He was assisted in yesterday's ceremony by two pretty five-year-old girls, one of them his granddaughter. They held the white ribbon up while the white-haired General poised the scissors over the band of silk until the photographers were satisfied. Then he cut it—and one of the little girls, with a very sober expression on her face, carefully wrapped the ribbon and put a good part of it into her pocket.

350 Feet Wide.

A large number of cars then took the officials and their guests over the new roads that will carry the Jersey traffic to and from the bridge.

The cars passed over the Jersey routes that converge at the Fort Lee Plaza of th Washington Bridge. The thoroughfare, at its greatest limit, is 350 feet wide. Yesterday a row of automobiles, thirty-five in number, lined up in that space. The road, moreover, is classed as a "super-roadway" in New Jersey because it is entirely free of all railroad grade crossings, intersecting streets and heavy grades and curvatures.

All of the work planned by the New Jersey State Highway Commission to accommodate the thousands of cars in the traffic that starts tomorrow over the new bridge will entail an expenditure of $15,000,000. One mile of the roadway, beginning at the bridgehead, has cost more than $1,500,000.

Completing Highways.

Despite the preparation of many new roads on the Jersey side of the river, it is expected that the flow of automobile traffic tomorrow will overtax the transportation facilities. Much congestion is expected there because several of the routes are not yet completed.

Traffic from the bridge can proceed as far as Grand avenue, Englewood, on Route 4, and as far as Broad avenue, Palisades Park, on Route 6. For Route 1, it will be necessary to detour from Lemoine avenue to Hudson Terrace.

Large crews of men were at work today on many of the supplementary highways and completion of the work is expected within the next three months.

New York Police to Aid.

One of the features of today's ceremony will be the appearance of the special corps of police recruited and trained for the operation and care of the bridge. They were chosen from 3,000 applicants by a board headed by Cornelius F. Cohalane, a tormer inspector of the New York Police Department.

He is now consultant for the Port Authority and is director of the Holland Tunnel police. From the tunnel police many of the men were chosen to take higher places in the bridge force.

The bridge police will be assisted today and tomorrow by hundreds of New York patrolmen. On the Jersey side, the traffic problems will be in the hands of the Fort Lee police, the Bergen county police and State troopers.

Span Is 3,500 Feet Long.

There are plenty of awe-inspiring statistics about the 3,500-foot span.

Its two giant towers are 635 feet high; 40,000 tons of steel and 1,000,000 rivets went into their construction.

A block of masonry weighing 260,000 tons forms the anchorage for the cables on the New York side, while across the river the engineers found a natural anchorage in the Palisades.

The bridge is suspended 250 feet above the river so all ocean-going ships may clear it.

The bridge has been constructed so that the number of lanes may be increased to eight, the sidewalks to four, and a lower deck added for four rapid transit tracks.

The toll fees will be: 50 cents for passenger cars; 25 for bicycles and motorcycles; 10 cents for pedestrians 75 and up for trucks and $1 and up for buses.

Construction of the bridge was begun four and one-half years ago.

The opening of the bridge has been marked by a new activity in real estate on the Jersey side. Yesterday it was revealed that hundreds of thousands of dollars had been spent in the last few years by a group of real estate operators, or an individual, in the purchase of tracts along the Palisades, starting at Fort Lee.

Some estimates of the tracts purchased place the value of the land at $25,000,000. Another estimate was $40,000,000. The purchases have been going on for the past four years and includes lots of land extending from Fort Lee to points far up the Jersey side of the Hudson River.

Conflicting reports have been made concerning the identity of the purchasers. One is that representatives of the Rockefeller family had made the purchases in the interest of a plan to preserve the Palisades as a public reservation.

The Russell Sage Foundation and Columbia University were also mentioned as having bought the land with a similar object in mind. However, representatives of all these interests denied that they had any connection with the purchases.

LOOKING OVER THE NEW HUDSON BRIDGE TOWARD JERSEY

Fairchild Aerial Surveys, Inc., Photo.

The George Washington span crosses the Hudson River from West 179th street, Manhattan, to Fort Lee, N. J.

Figures That Are Eloquent

Statistics of Washington Memorial Bridge

Cost	$60,000,000
Time in building	Four and a half years
Length of main span	3,500 feet
Length between anchorages	4,760 feet
Width of main structure, over all	120 feet
Number of cables	Four
Diameter of cables	36 inches
Number of wires in each cable	26,474
Length of all wire used	107,000 miles
Diameter of wire	0.196 inches
Specified minimum strength of wire	220,000 lbs. per. sq. inch
Weight of main bridge steel	73,000 tons
Masonry at New York tower	165,000 cubic yards
Masonry at New Jersey tower	37,500 cubic yards

Lindberghs Rest at Englewood

Arrive at Morrow Estatè at 10:40 P. M. After Transcontinental Flight.

Col. and Mrs. Charles A. Lindbergh were resting today at the Morrow estate at Englewood, following their return from the aerial trip to the Orient, which was interrupted in China by the death of Senator Dwight W. Morrow, Mrs. Lindbergh's father. They had been away from home since July.

The Lindberghs arrived at the Newark Airport at 9:22 o'clock last night, having flown from Victoria, B. C., where they landed from the liner President Jefferson on Thursday. Their actual flying time from Victoria to Newark was 19 hours 9 minutes. They covered the last lap of the flight from Cleveland to Newark in 3 hours 1 minute.

Both the Colonel and his wife appeared unfatigued, although they had spent more than twelve hours in the air yesterday. A crowd of about 150 persons greeted them at the airport, where they were welcomed officially by Peter J. O'Toole, City Clerk of Newark. Col. Lindbergh said they were eager to hurry home and asked reporters to defer their questions about the trip to some other time.

First Mishap of Trip.

The first mishap since they landed at Victoria occurred as they were leaving to drive to Englewood. One of the tires of their car blew out, forcing them to change to a smaller machine which already was loaded with six pieces of baggage. The Colonel declined a formal police escort, but his car was escorted until it reached the main highway to Englewood. They reached the Morrow home at 10:40 P. M.

Mrs. Lindbergh said the trip across the continent had been very pleasant. She also expressed her thanks for the many expressions of sympathy that had reached her at the death of her father.

Both Mrs. Lindbergh and her husband expressed their eagerness to see Charles Augustus, Jr., whom they last saw at the Morrow summer home at North Haven, Me., July 30, the day they took off for the long flight to Japan and China.

"When we left home he was just starting to walk," Mrs. Lindbergh said. "We can't wait to see him."

No Flight Plans at Present.

The Colonel was hatless, as usual, and wore a gray business suit. His wife wore a blue skirt with white dots, a white blouse and blue hat. They said they had no plans for any other flights in the immediate future.

The plane in which the Lindberghs flew from Victoria was loaned to them by the Detroit Aircraft Corporation. Their own Lockheed-Sirius was damaged when it was overturned by the current in the Yangtze River and is being shipped to the United States.

After flying to Japan by way of Arctic Canada and Alaska, and thence to China, it had been the intention of Col. and Mrs. Lindbergh to fly home by easy stages. They were aboard the British aircraft carrier Hermes when news of Senator Morrow's death reached them October 6 and immediately landed at Shanghai. They sailed for home four days later.

W. H. Lawrence Heads Laundrymen

LOUISVILLE, Oct. 24 (A. P.).—W. H. Lawrence, Minneapolis, has been elected president of the Laundrymen's National Association, to succeed Frank J. Huebsch, San Francisco, at the final session of the annual convention here yesterday. The directors will decide later whether to hold next year's convention in Miami or New Orleans.

Legions Hail Duce at Naples

Mussolini Returns in Splendor to City Where He Ordered March on Rome.

NAPLES, Italy, Oct. 24 (A. P.).—Premier Mussolini, dictator of Italy, came back in splendor today to Maddaloni Hall, where, nine years ago, almost to the hour, he stood as a young Deputy before the Fascist leaders and ordered the famous "march on Rome."

Four days after that memorable occasion the young deputy stepped into the supreme power and began the Fascist experiment of a "benevolent state."

He came today surrounded by lieutenants and their lieutenants. As he entered the harbor in his yacht the guns boomed in salute. Mount Vesuvious, far to the right, lazily emitted its usual column of smoke, but below the peak in letters 900 feet high, was the illuminated word: "DUX."

Impressive Salute.

The piers and streets, as far as they were visible, were filled with black-shirted Fascist legions and brilliantly dressed Neopolitans. With a motion that spread like ripples on a sea, nearly a million arms swung up in the Fascist salute and the arm of Il Duce snapped to salute in acknowledgement.

As he entered an open car he passed ranks of militia backed by masses of people shouting "Duce! Duce!"

Shrouding his movements with the customary secrecy, he sailed last night from Gaeta instead of Civita Vecchia, as had been announced.

His yacht came into the bay here past the Italian fleet, which fired a 21-gun salute.

This was the Premier's first visit to Naples since 1924, although he had promised to come more than a year ago. The visit was kept secret until almost the last moment in order to prevent preparation of any hostile act. Naples has been regarded as least enthusiastic toward Fascism among the big cities.

Renew Their Oath.

Later all the Fascist forces of Naples and vicinity gathered in the Plazza Plebiscito. The Duce appeared at a balcony overlooking the square, was met with tremendous applause and the Fascists shouted a renewal of their oath of allegiance to the regime.

At Mussolini's side stood the three members still alive of the quadrumvirate who led the march on Rome—Gen. Balbo, Minister of Aeronautics; Signor Del Bono, Minister of the Colonies, and Count De Vecchi, Ambassador to the Vatican.

Under the direction of the Premier the Fascist directorate prepared a message to the nation outlining the party's program for the tenth year of the regime, to culminate in a gigantic celebration next year on October 28.

Mrs. Judd Admits Double Killing

Trunk Slayer, Composed and Defiant, Says She Murdered in Self-Defense.

LOS ANGELES, Oct. 24 (U. P.).—Composed and defiant, Winnie Ruth Judd, comely blonde, was held today on a charge that she murdered two former roommates in Phoenix, Ariz.

Selecting a funeral parlor for the scene, she voluntarily surrendered last night to peace officers who had sought her almost 100 hours while she stayed "here and there in downtown Los Angeles."

She told them that she shot Miss Hedvig Samuelson, 27 years old, and Mrs. Agnes Le Roi, 35, in self-defense.

She exhibited a bullet in her left hand to support her contention that the killings were acts of self-defense.

Chief of Detectives Joe Taylor said she admitted dissecting the body of Miss Samuelson and then packing and shipping both bodies from Phoenix to Los Angeles as luggage.

Taylor said she claimed she had no accomplice.

The twenty-seven-year-old woman was questioned at great length by Arizona and California officials, but she stuck to her story.

Refuses to Explain.

She refused to answer many questions. She declined to explain her motive. She said she herself started the fatal argument when she made an uncomplimentary remark about Mrs. Le Roi while visiting the two girls Friday night.

"I killed them after Miss Samuelson shot me in the hand during the quarrel," she was quoted by Taylor as saying.

"I scuffled with Miss Samuelson and the gun dropped to the floor. Mrs. Le Roi hit me on the head with an ironing board. I fell to the floor. I picked up Miss Samuelson's gun. Then I shot them both."

Despite Taylor's statements Mrs. Judd's attorney, Richard Cantillon, said she made "no statement of legal standing," "And she will make none until she goes to trial," he added.

Following her surrender Mrs. Judd was taken to the Georgia Street Receiving Hospital, where a .25 caliber bullet was removed from her left hand. Bullets of the same size killed Miss Samuelson and Mrs. Leroi.

Hand Badly Infected.

Fearful of detection if she appeared at a physisian's office or a hospital, Mrs. Judd had suffered the painful wound for a week with only applications of "home remedies." Police surgeons said the hand was badly infected. Antitoxin was administered to guard against gangrene or lockjaw.

Mrs. Judd's surrender was as unusual as it was dramatic.

Knowing that her husband, Dr. William C. Judd, Santa Monica physician, had engaged attorneys to represent her, she telephoned him several times during the day.

She disapproved of each suggested meeting place, until Cantillon finally mentioned a funeral parlor operated by an old and close friend of his.

"I think that will be all right," she said over the telephone. "Send some one to meet me at Fifth and Olive street—in front of the Biltmore Hotel."

This location is one of the busiest in Los Angeles and in view of hundreds of passers by and policemen looking for her. She kept the appointment with David Malloy, employee of Gus Alvarez, funeral parlor owner.

Hand Hurting Her.

"I'm a little nervous," she told Malloy as she entered the automobile that took her to the funeral parlors. "My hand is hurting me dreadfully."

A wake was in progress in the mortuary when a dozen authorities and fifty newspaper men descended upon it. One mortuary attendant was knocked down when he attempted to prevent Detective Inspector David Davidson from entering the upstairs room where Mrs. Judd was secluded.

Mrs. Judd finally came down to go to headquarters.

She was supported by her two attorneys and followed by Dr. Judd, her brother, B. J. McKinnell, and the dozen police officials.

Mrs. Judd was wearing a green sports outfit, and a fur trimmed black coat. She wore no stockings or hat and carried no handbag.

Even the lack of make-up, an occasional tear and the fact that her hair curled over her eyes could not hide her attractiveness. Her hand was swathed in an ungainly white bandage.

"Look up, Ruth. Look up!" a photographer called.

Said She Felt Ill.

She did, then winced as a dozen flashbulbs exploded. As relatives and police crowded in to get in camera range, Mrs. Judd appeared the most composed person in the room.

"My God, but I feel sick," the woman, a tubercular, said.

"How long since you've eaten?" a reporter asked.

"She's had one meal in four days," Dr. Judd answered for her. "You see she had very little money."

Mrs. Judd was taken from the mortuary to the hospital and there, on the operating table, she showed her first sign of nerves.

She screamed when a photographer dropped a flash bulb on the floor and she babbled a bit to her husband when she took gas.

"I've told them everything," she said to her husband. "Don't let them question me any more and please make them stop taking pictures."

From the hospital she was taken to the Detective Bureau. Hours later detectives admitted Mrs. Judd "almost defied questioning."

Attorney Obtains Writ.

LOS ANGELES, Oct. 24 (U. P.).—A fight over the extradition of Mrs. Winnie Ruth Judd developed immediately on her arrest here last night. County Attorney Lloyd Andrews of Phoenix asked for extradition papers, but Attorney Cantillon obtained a writ of habeas corpus, returnable November 3, and preventing her from being taken from Los Angeles county until after arguments then.

Arizona officials bitterly assailed Mrs. Judd's story.

They said they did not believe her story of self-defense, nor her claim that she had no accomplice.

As the prosecution and defense girded for the bitter legal struggle to come, Mrs. Judd's relatives declared they would stand by her.

"We are glad to end the suspense of a week," said the Rev. W. H. McKinnell, aged father of the prisoner. The retired minister was quoted as saying that he and his invalid wife would sell their home in Darlington, Ind., and come to Los Angeles to aid their daughter.

Mrs. Judd's husband and her student brother made similar statements. Both said they would stand by her to the end.

Known in Mexico.

MAZATLAN, Mexico, Oct. 24 (U. P.).—Dr. and Mrs. William Judd were formerly employed at the Heart Mines in Durango, Mexico, according to information received here, but left Mexico about a year ago because Mrs. Judd was subject to uncontrollable temper and hysteria.

QUEEN'S NIECE WEDS TODAY

Fotegrams, N. Y.

Lady May Cambridge.

Associated Press Photo.

Jennifer Bevan, who will be one of the bridesmaids at the marriage of Lady May Cambridge, niece of Queen Mary of England to Capt. Abel Smith in London.

Capone Sentence To Come Today

CHICAGO, Oct. 24 (A. P.).—Al Capone, convicted income tax dodger, may learn his fate today.

Judge James H. Wilkerson ordered that the case be disposed of at 10 o'clock this morning, and unless he grants a motion for arrest of judgment sentence may be pronounced at once.

Capone, overlord of the city's racketeering, bootlegging and vice for ten years, may go to the penitentiary in a few days if Judge Wilkerson denies a supersedeas bond.

The maximumb punishment under his conviction on five counts, three of which are for felony, is fifteen years in the penitentiary, two years in jail and fines totaling $50,000.

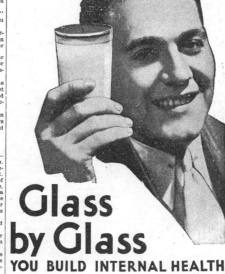

WEE PRINCESS'S DEBUT

Little Elizabeth Bridesmaid in Silver Slippers Today.

BALCOMBE, England, Oct. 24 (A. P.).—In tiny silver slippers and a quaint blue velvet dress, little Princess Elizabeth, granddaughter of King George and Queen Mary, is making her first bow to society here today as one of the bridesmaids at the wedding of the Queen's niece, Lady May Cambridge, to Capt. Henry Abel Smith.

The princess is only 5½ years old and she is rather excited about the day.

She is in line for the throne under present circumstances and is a favorite of the public. Any appearance draws hundreds to see her and the crowds that throng this Sussex village came as much to see her as the wedding.

The little princess, blue-eyed and golden-haired, is one of four girls who will be dressed alike. They have had specially made silver slippers and blue velvet gowns of empire design specially selected for them by the bride.

Calles's Daughter En Route Here With Husband

DALLAS, Oct. 24 (A. P.).—Dr. Joseph J. Eller of New York and his bride, the former Artemisa Calles, plan to leave for New York by air tomorrow.

The "flying honeymooners" arrived here from San Antonio late today. They will continue the trip East by plane. They plan to sail for Europe on the steamship Europa, October 31. The couple were married at the home of the bride's father, former President Plutarco Elias Calles, in Mexico City.

Kerrymen's Festival On Tonight.

At least 5,000 persons are expected at the annual autumn festival and dance of the Kerrymen's P. and B. Association at the Star Casino, 101 East 107th street, this evening. Delegates will attend from every one of the thirty-two Irish societies in New York.

THE WEATHER
By U. S. Weather Bureau
PARTLY CLOUDY TONIGHT AND TOMORROW; MODERATE TEMPERATURE
Temperature, 12 M. 40
Year ago (clear) 40
Mean average 10 years, same date....35
Complete Report on Page 21

BROOKLYN DAILY EAGLE

WALL STREET CLOSING PRICES ★ ★ ★ ★

91st YEAR—No. 349 ★ NEW YORK CITY, FRIDAY, DECEMBER 18, 1931 ★ 42 PAGES THREE CENTS

DIAMOND IS SLAIN AFTER ACQUITTAL

DOYLE UPHELD IN DEFIANCE OF SEABURY PROBE

Appellate Court O.K.'s Justice Dore's Purging Former Horse Doctor of Contempt—Seabury to Appeal Decision

Dr. William F. Doyle gained the upper hand over Samuel Seabury for the first time today and Seabury promptly announced he will attempt to carry the fight to the Court of Appeals.

The Manhattan Appellate Division, in a unanimous decision and without opinion, sustained the contention of the $2,000,000 horse doctor that he had purged himself of contempt of the Hofstadter Committee in denying he had bribed any public officials.

The Appellate Division upheld the findings of Supreme Court Justice Dore, who had ruled in favor of Doyle in the latter's six months battle to keep the secrets of his fee splits and zoning victories safe from the Hofstadter probers.

Seabury to Fight

As soon as Seabury was informed at the headquarters of the Hofstadter Committee of the Doyle victory, he announced he would ask the Appellate Division at the January term for the right to appeal to the Court of Appeals at Albany.

The principal issue before the court was Seabury's contention that Doyle had "perjured, not purged" himself before the committee when he denied having bribed officials or politicians out of the proceeds of his Board of Standards and Appeals fees.

Second Major Reversal

The Doyle legal battery argued that "perjury had not been proved and that, even if it had, Doyle had obeyed the court order when he answered questions.

Seabury's principal victory in the Doyle case was the confining of the erstwhile horse doctor to jail for 18 days as a defiant witness.

The defeat was the second major reversal suffered by Seabury this week. Clarence J. Shearn, Appellate Division referee, recently cleared 13 of the 14 Women's Court lawyers whose disbarment Seabury sought.

Sherwood Case Put Over

Hearing on Seabury's application to have the missing Russell T. Sherwood fined $100,000 for failure to heed the published call of the probers was today put over until

Please Turn to Page 2

WHAT A GIFT!

Washington, Dec. 18 (AP)—Edward B. McLean, publisher of the Washington Post, was cited for contempt of court today for sending a daintily wrapped Christmas box to his home containing a summons for his estranged wife to appear in a Latvian Court as a defendant in divorce proceedings.

Leaders Pledge Quick Passage Of Moratorium

Chiefs of Both Parties at Hoover Breakfast—McFadden Is Snubbed

Colorado Building.

Washington, Dec. 18—President Hoover breakfasted this morning with Republican and Democratic House leaders and received the following assurances:

1. The debt moratorium bill will be taken up by the House today and passed before adjournment tomorrow night.

2. The farm loan bank legislation will be passed before the holiday recess Tuesday.

3. The reconstruction finance corporation legislation will be taken up immediately after the holidays.

As the White House sees it, these pledges given by the leaders of the two parties are absolutely without qualification. The President, it was authoritatively asserted, was given to understand that there would be no hitches. No "ifs," "ands" or "buts" accompanied the pledges, it was stated.

McFadden Ignored

Those at the breakfast were Speaker Garner, Republican Floor Leader Snell, James W. Collier, chairman of the Ways and Means Committee; Henry B. Steagall, chairman of the Banking and Currency Committee; Charles R. Crisp,

Please Turn to Page 3

Stocks and Bonds Advance Rapidly

The security markets got over their fright today and rallied briskly. There was a close race between bonds and stocks, with the breadth of gains the objective. Many stocks were up two to five points, many bonds as much. Trading was fairly active, notably on the advance. Wheat recovered a cent or more.

By mid-afternoon American Telephone had recovered three points to 118. U. S. Steel as much to above 40, while Auburn was up seven points or so to above 131. Gains of three and four points were seen in New York Central, American Can, Chesapeake & Ohio, Woolworth, Consolidated Gas, D. & H., Northern Pacific and others.

An assuring statement by Thomas W. Lamont in Washington to the Senate Finance Committee to the effect that German short term credits were no menace to American banking, higher prices for copper and the meeting of rail men here to discuss rail wage cuts tended to help the markets upward.

Stock Table on Page 39

S. B. Chapin Jr. Injured by Car

Simeon B. Chapin Jr., socially prominent member of the brokerage and banking firm of S. B. Chapin & Co., 111 Broadway, Manhattan, was injured critically by an automobile shortly before 1:30 o'clock this morning at 74th St. and Park Avenue.

The operator of the automobile, Louis Slater of 600 W. 111th St., took the injured man to Lenox Hill Hospital, where it was found he was suffering from a fracture of the skull and a compound fracture of the left leg.

German Woman Flier Reported Missing

Basra, Irak, Dec. 18 (AP)—Fraulein Elli Beinhorn, German woman flier, was reported missing today somewhere in Irak or Persia.

She left Bagdad yesterday and has not been heard from since. Radio inquiries were made over all the territory she planned to cover but they failed to bring forth any information.

THE EAGLE INDEX

Asks Jury Quiz On Short Sales

Washington, Dec. 18 (AP)—Investigation by both the Administration and the Senate into short selling operations on the Stock Exchanges was asked today by Senator Thomas, Democrat, of Oklahoma.

He blamed the declines in prices of securities on "bear raids" in the market brought about through selling stocks short.

One resolution would have the Senate request President Hoover to direct Attorney General Mitchell to summon a grand jury to inquire into short sales.

Lamont Calls Reich Credits In U. S. Heavy

Cumbersome, but Do Not Endanger Banks, He Informs Senators

Washington, Dec. 18 (AP)—A member of J. P. Morgan & Co. said today there had been a cumbersome amount of German short term credit in this country, but that it did not endanger American banks.

He was Thomas W. Lamont, testifying before the Senate Finance Committee. He said probably 90 percent of American banks engaged in the process.

"The largest holding of such credits by any one bank is $70,000,000, and that institution is so large that it is not a matter of danger or even of comment," he added.

Lamont told how his company had handled $300,000,000 of loans for France and $208,250,000 for Germany. He added that all but $131,000,000 of the French loans had been repaid.

House Vote Due Tonight

As the committee recessed for lunch the House took up the moratorium measure with the expectation of ratifying it before adjournment, which may be deferred until late tonight.

"The banks are not loaded up with German bonds to the extent the people believe," stated Lamont.

"Yes," interrupted Senator Gore, Democrat, Oklahoma, "it is Tom, Dick and Harry who have taken the losses."

"It is true that upon the great investing public has fallen the brunt of the declines and not upon the banks," Lamont replied.

Lamont had said the first German loan issue bore 7 and the second 5½ percent interest.

He told the committee he was "a little mortified" to tell of the small commission that firm had received from floating foreign bonds in this country.

"I am afraid it will make the sympathy and pity of the committee too much," he said.

Lamont enumerated numerous bond issues the firm handled for Argentina, Canada, Austria and Belgium. The committee was making the study at the request of

Please Turn to Page 2

Laval Defeated In Chamber Vote

Paris, Dec. 18 (AP)—Premier Laval's government was defeated by a vote of 292 to 281 in the Chamber of Deputies today but a question of confidence was not involved. The vote was on the Government's motion to set a date for closing of debate on unemployment.

Duce Gets New Publicity Agent

Rome, Dec. 18 (AP)—Lando Serretti, chief of the Government Press Bureau and as such the most powerful factor in the dissemination of news in Italy, was reported to have resigned today, and it was said the announcement would be made after tomorrow's cabinet meeting.

Gaetano Polverelli, editor of Premier Mussolini's newspaper, Popolo D'Italia, a member of the Chamber of Deputies, was said to be in line to succeed him. The change was described as merely an item in the Premier's policy of a periodical turnover.

Smuts Warns Party To Prepare for Vote

Johannesburg, S. A., Dec. 18 (AP)—Gen. Jan. Christian Smuts, former South African Prime Minister, warned the South African party to prepare for an early general election.

He launched another vigorous attack against remaining on the gold standard.

HOOVER HOST TO GANNETT

Washington, Dec. 18 (AP)—Frank E. Gannett, Rochester, N. Y., newspaper publisher, was a luncheon guest of President Hoover today at the White House

Schoolboy's Death Laid To Classroom Prank

East Orange, N. J., Dec. 18—Earl McQuillan, 15, of 19 Eaton Place, a freshman at East Orange High School, died today in Orange Memorial Hospital of blood poisoning which physicians said resulted from an intestinal injury received when he sat upon a lead pencil in school, Dec. 11.

John Meeker, 13, of 105 N. Arlington Ave., a classmate, was holding the pencil on the seat at the time, according to police. School authorities and police, however, decided the injury was accidental.

John McQuillan, father of the dead boy, said: "I hope his death will be a lesson to all boys and that it will teach them the seriousness of such pranks."

Rich Woman Is Freed By Kansas City Gang; Fail to Get Ransom

Mrs. Donnelly and Chauffeur Left at Bridge by Kidnapers—Tells How She Fought and Screamed as Cars Streamed By

Kansas City, Dec. 18 (AP)—Nervous but unharmed after almost 36 hours in the "filthy" rendezvous of three kidnapers, Mrs. Nelly Donnelly, wealthy founder of a Kansas City garment company, and George Blair, her Negro chauffeur, were freed by their captors early today.

They were released from a car near the Kansas Ave. bridge on the Kansas side of the city and soon were back at the Donnelly home. Their return marked the end of a period of anxious waiting by her husband, Paul Donnelly, and his attorneys, who were at a loss as to how to get in touch with the abductors for the delivery of $75,000 in ransom, demanded under a threat of death to Blair and blindness for the woman.

Anonymous Call

James A. Reed, neighbor and counsel to Donnelly, said today no ransom had been paid for the release of his wife, Mrs. Nelly Donnelly.

"We did not arrange the matter. It happened. That is all."

He was referring to the most heavily insured woman in Kansas City. Mrs. Donnelly carries life insurance of approximately $750,000, much of which is in favor of her company and her employes.

"It's wonderful," said Reed, who had spent a sleepless night. "Now

Please Turn to Page 18

FREED

Mrs. Nelly Donnelly

5 Million Home Aid Is Voted; Berry Objects

Prial, Speaking for Controller, Voices His Fear of Scandal

The $5,000,000 home relief resolution the Board of Estimate has been considering three weeks was passed this afternoon after a discussion lasting two hours.

This appropriation is in addition to the $15,000,000 unemployment fund the city already has voted and is to be used exclusively for destitute and needy families not eligible for the benefits of the other appropriation.

Considerable surprise was registered when Deputy Controller Prial stated that, on orders of Controller Berry, he would vote against the resolution.

Berry Fears Scandal

Prial said that Berry believed that "at best home relief plans presented a danger because of scandals in the past in the distribution of public money."

He said Berry also told him to state that he was in sympathy with the needy, but that he believed some restrictions should be placed on the expenditure of this money.

At the word "scandal" Mayor Walker interrupted and stated vehemently that there never had been

Please Turn to Page 2

2 Scientists to Get Rewards for Labors

Washington, Dec. 18 (AP)—Two scientists will be honored tonight by the Smithsonian Institution.

Dr. Andrew E. Douglass of Tucson, Ariz., and Dr. Ernst Antevs of the University of Stockholm will receive awards of $2,500 each.

Dr. Douglass developed the "tree-ring" method of prehistoric chronology. Dr. Antevs worked out a similar chronology based on the annual layers of clay left in the wake of melting glaciers.

Jury at Odds In Ewald Case

The jury in the Federal Court, Manhattan, deadlocked over the fate of former Magistrate George F. Ewald and three others, resumed deliberation this afternoon after being taken to a hotel for lunch.

The jurors debated all night without reaching a decision on the alleged guilt of Ewald, Dr. Francis M. Schirp, Harry C. Cotter and Frank E. Mitterlechner, accused of fraudulent promotion of stock in the Cotter Butte Mines Company.

Winston Churchill Rests Comfortably

Winston Churchill, British statesman, spent a very comfortable night, it was reported this morning at Lenox Hill Hospital, Manhattan, where he is recovering from injuries received last Sunday when he was struck by a taxicab. Mr. Churchill slept soundly through the night.

Needy Cases Benefit From Eagle Dinner

Entire Proceeds of Employes' Fete at Guild Contributed to Fund—Dealers Donate Food and Prizes

By JANE CORBY

All promises of a good time were fulfilled at The Eagle's annual "50 Neediest Cases" party last night, held by Eagle employes at the Home Guild. The festivities began with a six-course duck dinner at 6 o'clock and continued with dancing and games, with substantial rewards for the winners. Through the courtesy of many manufacturers and retailers all proceeds of the affair are to be turned over to the Neediest Cases Fund.

Everything at the party was donated, from the services of the orchestra, Addy Amor and his Villanovans, to the last item in the menu. Mr. Amor's 10-piece collegiate orchestra, which had its origin in Villanova College, Philadelphia, is well known on the radio and is a feature at the Hotel Piccadilly Sunday nights. The piano was loaned by the Lester Company. Thanks are also due the Silver Key Orchestra for their services.

Hoffman's Beverages were sold at their booth and the proceeds donated to the cause.

Groceries as Prizes

The feature prizes included 25 baskets of groceries donated by the

Please Turn to Page 19

Contributions Today

J. F. C.	$100.00
A Friend	10.00
H. F. Quinn	10.00
W. C. Taggard	10.00
S. M. M.	10.00
In Memory of J. A. H.	10.00
Thomas L. Driscoll	10.00
Mme. Geraldine	5.00
Mrs. Agnes B. Kellogg	5.00
Mrs. Edward J. Aylward	5.00
Anonymous	5.00
Fred A. Ebert	5.00
In Memory of Mother	5.00
Miss E. W.	5.00
In Memory of Frances Wells Speck	5.00
Alpha Kappa Sorority	5.00
Vivien F. Gallagher	5.00
Henry Siedenburg	5.00
Henry E. Sloan	5.00
C. E. Edwards	5.00
R. F. Forshaw	5.00
A. Adelaide Bahrenburg	5.00
A Friend	5.00
In Memory of E. M. B.	5.00
Grace Boeckel	2.00
A Friend	2.00
G. M. Jr.	2.00
A Friend	2.00
E. E. Simey	2.00
Emeline R. Kendall	2.00
M. A. M.	1.00
Mrs. E. L. Kane	1.00
Mrs. M. K. H.	1.00
Mari	1.00
Today's total	$310.50
Previously reported	[illegible]
Total	$8,084.4[illegible]

BEFORE GANGLAND 'RUBBED HIM OUT'

Jack (Legs) Diamond, right, with his counsel, Daniel A. Prior, shown yesterday after his acquittal in Troy of kidnaping.

IN RE POCKETS

How to replace man's customary 13 or more pockets in the costume of the woman legislator has been solved by Representative Ruth Bryan Owen (Dem.) of Florida. Her invention is a handbag slung from one shoulder. She contends the lawmaker's hands must be free for handling bills and briefs, without mentioning oratorical gestures. All the necessaries go in the handbag.

Obregon's Daughter Wedded to Engineer

Paris, Dec. 18 (AP)—Senorita Serafina Obregon, daughter of the former Mexican President, was married yesterday at Passy in the Church of Notre Dame de Grace to Pierre Lakhovski, son of a prominent French engineer.

Benefit Review Tonight

The 105th Artillery review for the 50 Neediest Cases takes place at the armory, 171 Clermont Ave., this evening. See Page 19.

U. S. Warning Sent to Japan On Manchuria

Nanking Ousts Student Rioters—Tokio Plans New Bandit Campaign

Washington, Dec. 18 (AP)—A new expression of concern over the Manchurian situation, in friendly but positive terms, has been communicated to Japan by the American Government.

Ambassador Forbes in Tokio, on instructions of Secretary Stimson, has again emphasized to the Japanese Foreign Office American solicitude that obligations under the Nine-Power and Kellogg-Briand treaties be respected.

Readiness to show correspondence on Manchuria to the Senate was indicated this afternoon by Stimson. The Senate has asked it.

The Secretary indicated, however, there were some documents he would be unable to give the Senate for publication and would have to show them to individual Senators in confidence.

Nanking Expels Students

Nanking, Dec. 18 (AP)—The government moved today, with troops, to terminate the student demonstrations which have bordered on a reign of terror here for more than two weeks.

Without advance notice but with sharp precision large units of soldiers were sent out to round up the students, who were then escorted to waiting trains which immediately left for the youths' homes in north China cities and Shanghai.

As a result of the cleanup the capital breathed easier this afternoon and the belief was expressed

Please Turn to Page 2

Pola Negri Facing Crisis in 72 Hours

Santa Monica, Cal., Dec. 18 (AP)—A rising temperature marked the condition of Pola Negri, film actress, today, but her physicians were not alarmed.

They said it was a reaction to an operation for removal of an intestinal obstruction she underwent Wednesday.

A crisis is expected within 72 hours.

Coast Guard Speeds Woman To Her Dying Father's Side

Mrs. John J. Mealey was at the bedside of her dying father, George Mancuso of 1080 78th St., today through the good offices of the United States Coast Guard and the Massachusetts State police.

On Monday afternoon Mrs. Mealey, who was with her husband on Nantucket Island, received word that her father had suffered a stroke, and was seriously ill. She appealed to authorities for aid in getting off the island. A Coast Guard patrol rushed her and Mr. Mealey through the four-hour trip from Nantucket to Woods Hole.

There State troopers met them and drove them to New Bedford, where they caught a train for New York. They arrived home yesterday, where Mrs. Mealey's mother, three sisters and brothers awaited her.

Mr. Mancuso is a retired importer. It was said that he was "very low" today.

Tipsy After Party, Trapped In Albany Room

One Holds 'Legs' Down on Bed as the Other Pumps Lead Into Him

Eagle Bureau, Capitol Building.

Albany, Dec. 18—Cornered like a rat in his own bedroom, Jack (Legs) Diamond was shot and killed in a lodging house here at 4:45 a.m. today.

While one of two men who had followed the slightly intoxicated gangster from a speakeasy where he had been celebrating his kidnaping acquittal yesterday held him on the bed, the other pumped three bullets into his head.

"Oh, hell, that's enough!" Mrs. Laura Woods, proprietor of the rooming house, heard one of them exclaim after the third shot.

She looked out of a front window in time to see two men climb into a motorcar and speed away.

Carefully Planned

The murder gun and a flashlight, carefully wrapped in a handkerchief, found on a vacant lot a block away, are the only tangible clues in the hands of the police.

They were investigating a report current in New York City that two gunmen had been hired by a Manhattan gambler to "get" Diamond.

The motive, according to this report, was that the gambler suspected the racketeer of being involved in a plot to extort $25,000 from him.

Several New York City detectives attended the kidnaping trial but the State took no special precautions to guard Diamond in the courtroom.

A brief investigation convinced the authorities that the killing was a carefully planned underworld crime. They were not notified of the shooting until two hours after it occurred.

Meanwhile, newspapers and press associations in Albany received long distance telephone inquiries from unidentified persons in Chicago, Cleveland and New York City, asking if it were true that Diamond had been shot.

Three former Diamond gangsters, who attended his trial and the subsequent celebration tour of speakeasies are being sought in New York City.

Near State Capitol

The lodging house in which the shooting occurred is at 67 Dove St., not far from the State Capitol. Diamond had the front room on the second floor. His sister-in-law, Mrs. Eddie Diamond, and her 5-year-old son had engaged a rear room on the same floor but were not in the house when the shooting occurred.

So far as the police have been able to learn, Diamond, after his acquittal in Troy yesterday, came to Albany with his wife, his sister-in-law, Daniel Prior, his counsel, and Mrs. Prior.

The celebration began in a speakeasy on Broadway. Who the celebrators were other than "Legs," his wife and his sister-in-law the police have not learned. Diamond left about midnight to continue the celebration in another speakeasy on Pembroke St. Mrs. Diamond remained at the Broadway place and was there when notified of the shooting.

Fired From Front

Diamond's chauffeur said he drove her to the Dove St. house after she had been told her husband had been wounded.

Contrary to earlier reports, all three of the bullets that tore through Diamond's head had been fired from the front and slightly to one side. The first report was that one of the bullets had been fired into the back of his skull.

He was befuddled with liquor and unsteady on his feet when he summoned a taxicab to go to his lodging house.

come in somewhere around 4:30 a.m. She did not hear his assailants

Please Turn to Page 3

Christmas CHURCH NUMBER

ALL of Brooklyn's churches will celebrate Christmas with their most beautiful services of the year. And the Christmas Church Number of The Eagle, out tomorrow, will publish complete details of special programs and sermons for the guidance of its readers. This is an annual editorial feature and the largest newspaper church section in the entire country.

TOMORROW in Saturday's EAGLE

Finds Hoover Delay Cause of Debt Tangle

Say President Should Have Called Special Session on Ratification

Eagle Bureau, Colorado Building.

By HENRY SUYDAM

Washington, Dec. 18—Criticism of Congress for not ratifying the moratorium before Dec. 15, when an installment on the war debts fell due, fails to take into account some of the most obvious facts.

The ill-temper of the moratorium debate is open to criticism, but Congress cannot be blamed for want of speed.

It required more than two weeks for President Hoover to get the consent of France last Summer. Congress has had the moratorium before it for just a week.

At the time when the moratorium was initiated the President was warned that an extra session of Congress was advisable if ratification was to be assured before Dec. 15. In view of the apparent subsequent change in American public opinion, which is now in large degree hostile, the President would have been well advised to have summoned Congress forthwith. The moratorium iron was hot in midsummer; it is cold now. It does seem reasonable that Mr. Hoover should have called Congress not later than Nov. 15.

The President was well aware that if Congress didn't meet until the regular date, Dec. 7, ratification before Dec. 15 was out of the question. The President didn't submit the moratorium until Thursday, Dec. 10. Yet he seems to have hoped that Congress would act before the following Tuesday, Dec. 15.

Must Have Known Conditions

Mr. Hoover must have realized that a fight seemed probable on the Speakership, that if control of the House of Representatives passed to the Democrats there would be certain difficulties in organization, that the moratorium itself would have to go to the appropriate committees of both houses, be reported out, and pass through the various legislative stages common to the usual transaction of business at the Capitol.

Newspapers and public men who have criticized Congress for want of speed, under these circumstances, exhibit complete ignorance of legislative procedure. The Democrats took control of the House, elected a Speaker and organized with great dispatch. Congress has moved faster on the moratorium than it moves under normal circumstances on other bills. Members of all opinions are anxious to dispose of the question.

If the process is cumbersome this is inevitable in a Legislature composed of 531 members, where the rules have been devised as a safeguard against snap judgment on issues of large public importance.

If there is blame because the moratorium was not ratified before Dec. 15 and if the European debtors are in unquestionable technical default the cause of this situation is to be sought at the White House, where the President, for reasons sufficient unto himself, preferred to take a chance on prompt ratification rather than summon Congress to meet two or three weeks earlier. As William E. Borah said on the floor of the Senate, it is probable that Congress would not be in session even now if the Constitution did not compel it.

Added Debt Board Issue

In requesting the consent of Congress to the one-year moratorium which expires on June 30 next Mr. Hoover recommended the recreation of the World War Debt Funding Commission, with the object of still further reducing the European debts—a suphemism for further cancellation.

The idea that Congress should not consider this project at some length is a strange one. The idea that committees of Congress should hold no hearings, seek no information, and exercise no independent judgment is even more strange. The strangest of all these phenomena is the evident disinclination of the President to take Congress into his confidence.

The French debt installment due on Dec. 15 was less than $20,000,000. The French Government realizes that if "capacity to pay" is the American standard, then there can be no hope of the French installments being cut. If, on the other hand, the French installments are to be reduced in proportion to the cut in the French share of German reparations, the picture would be different.

This important phase of the issue has almost escaped the attention of Congress. The White House has said not a word about it. Representative Louis T. McFadden blurted it out in the course of his ill-considered attack on the President. Yet on the basis of half-facts or no facts at all Congress is being asked to rush through the entire Hoover program.

Research Council Elects Officers

Dr. Robert T. Crane, professor of political science in the University of Michigan, has been appointed permanent secretary of the Social Science Research Council with headquarters at 230 Park Ave., Manhattan, it was announced today. Dr. Crane succeeds Dr. Robert S. Lynd, who has resigned to become professor of sociology in Columbia University.

Upon the retirement as president Feb. 1, 1932, of Prof. Robert S. Woodworth of Columbia, Dr. Crane will become executive head of the council.

Prof. Arthur M. Schlessinger of Harvard has been re-elected chairman of the council. Prof. William F. Ogburn of the University of Chicago will again be vice chairman. Dr. R. H. Coats, Dominion statistician for Canada, succeeds Dean Henry M. Fates of the University of Michigan as secretary.

DEAD GANG LEADER'S MOUNTAIN RUM HEADQUARTERS

Headquarters of Legs Diamond's beer gang at Cairo, Greene County, N. Y., known as Villa Pedro, where $5,000 worth of booze was found last May while Federal and State officials were probing the gang leader's activities. Insets show (above) Legs in natural pose, (below) when his face registers trouble.

Diamond Slain After Acquittal

Continued from Page 1

enter, she told the police. But it was only 10 minutes after she heard Diamond come in and go up the stairs that she heard three shots and the exclamation of one of the gunmen.

The police believe the men followed Diamond from the speakeasy and entered almost directly behind him, waiting in the hall outside his room for the most favorable opportunity to burst in and take him unawares.

There was no indication that Diamond had an opportunity to put up the slightest struggle. Everything in the room was in perfect order. Diamond's trousers, which he had removed, were neatly folded over the back of a chair.

The slain gangster was 33 years old.

Six persons are being questioned by the police: Mrs. Diamond, Jack Storey, his chauffeur; Mrs. Woods, and three roomers in the lodging house.

Mrs. Diamond became hysterical under the police questioning:

"I didn't do it; I don't know anything about it," she shrieked.

When her husband was acquitted yesterday she almost climbed over the courtroom rail in her eagerness to hug and kiss him.

Mysterious Calls

Chief of Police David Smurl attributed the killing to rival gangsters. He said that while the investigation had not developed a concrete motive, there were perhaps dozens of reasons why underworld characters might desire his death.

Smurl attached great significance to the long-distance telephone calls from out of town inquiring if Diamond had been "rubbed out."

"The police," he said, "were first notified by a mysterious phone call at 6:55 a.m. I do not know who called."

But Dr. Thomas H. Holmes, who treated Diamond the last time he was the target for gangster bullets, was summoned at 6 a.m. He did not reach the house, however, until an hour later. He found the body still warm.

One of the bullets had ripped through the base of Diamond's skull and the other two were fired into the side of the head near the right ear. Diamond's face was twisted and distorted as though he had died in great agony.

Question Roomer

Smurl declined to reveal the address on Broadway where the slain man's wife and Mrs. Eddie Diamond spent the night. He also said he knew nothing of the whereabouts of Diamond's chorus girl friend, Marion (Kiki) Roberts.

Prior appeared at the police station soon after District Attorney John L. Delaney began questioning the first of the six persons held.

He said he would represent Mrs. Diamond as counsel but would make no attempt to obtain her release from custody until the authorities had had ample time to question her thoroughly.

One of the roomers who was questioned was Patrick Delaney. He agreed with Mrs. Woods that the shots were fired about 4:30. They woke him up, he said. He jumped out of bed and looked out of a window. He said he saw a man, about 5 feet 7 inches, enter an automobile which immediately drove off. Neither he nor Mrs. Woods was able to note the license number.

After the two Mrs. Diamonds, Mrs. Woods and the chauffeur had been questoned, two of the women were taken from the police station by a rear exit and whisked away in a motorcar with detectives. Which of the women were taken or what their destination was was kept secret.

Planned on Trip

Reporters and photographers were barred from the police station and also from the house where the shooting took place. At the rooming house one photographer who attempted to enter was arrested and

Please Turn to Page 26

Legs Called 'Gangland King' and 'Cheap Mug'

Began Criminal Career as Package Thief When Boy—Ostrich-Like Limbs Gave Him Speed and Name—Survived Other Shootings

Jack (Legs) Diamond, whose real name was John Nolan, was a product of Manhattan's lower east side.

Sentimentalists and sensationalists alike have been in the habit of referring to him as a "king of the underworld."

But 20 years ago, when his name first appeared in a memorandum filed by the criminal identification clerk at Police Headquarters, his classification was:

"Cheap mug; package thief."

In spite of the Diamond legends which have grown up since that time, Commissioner Mulrooney believes Diamond never was much more than a cheap mug, a hoodlum, a "rat." He was not a "big shot."

Called Thief as Boy

As a boy, he was a thief, according to a New York detective who was his playmate when both wore knee pants. It was in those very early years that he was given the nickname Legs.

"Ever since I can remember him," said this detective, "Legs was a thief. As a kid he was a catch thief. He grabbed goods on display outside of stores. He picked stuff off trucks and delivery wagons.

"To us boys, at the time, it seemed like more or less of a bold, bad boy's prank, but as time went on he went at it in a serious way. He thought nothing of taking a crate of seltzer bottles off a truck.

"Diamond's legs seemed to start up around his Adam's apple. They were as much out of proportion as a giraffe's neck. Run? He ran like an ostrich, with a stride twice as long as that of a normally framed man.

"He got away with his package thieving by 'legging it.' Hence the nickname. It was his legs that gave him his brazen confidence that he could get away with anything—including murder."

Arrested 23 Times

Such was the beginning of the criminal career of the man who successively became known as a "wagon bouncer," small-time chiseler, labor terrorizer, Rothstein bodyguard and a robber, murder, torture and narcotic smuggler suspect, and leader of a "mob" in the liquor traffic.

He was arrested 23 times, five times on homicide charges. But only twice did he see the inside of a prison, once on a burglary charge and once for deserting from an army post. On the other 21 charges he was dismissed for "lack of evidence."

It is a matter of official record that Diamond was shot four times before the last fatal attempt upon his life. The police say, however,

Please Turn to Page 26

Leaders Pledge Quick Passage

Continued from Page 1

ranking Democrat on the Ways and Means Committee; Willis C. Hawley, ranking Republican on the same committee; Robert Luce and James G. Strong, Republican members of the Banking and Currency Committee, and Charles H. Brand, ranking Democrat, on the same committee.

Conspicuous by his absence was Louis T. McFadden, last year's chairman of the Banking and Currency Committee and now ranking Republican member of the committee.

He was purposely ignored because of his sensational attack alleging that President Hoover had "sold out" on the question of debt postponement.

Congressman Bachrach, New Jersey Republican, was absent from the breakfast because he was at his home in Atlantic City. He is one of the leading Republicans on the Ways and Means Committee.

This is, by all odds, the most important "harmony breakfast" yet held by Mr. Hoover, according to observers. Through it he feels he has an expeditious working program on his major economic policies, taxation included.

Before the House Banking Committee, Governor Meyer of the Federal Reserve Board put in a good word for the Strong bill to create a half billion dollar corporation to advance cash to needy industries.

Speaking extemporaneously in the crowded and smoked-filled committee room, Meyer said "lack of confidence and fear" were largely responsible for the tight credit situation and the existing economic conditions.

"I believe a bill of this kind would restore confidence in many areas and that alone would be commendable," he said.

"I do not want to predict, however, as to price levels."

In emergency the Government can afford "to depart from its ordinary rules and principles," he said.

"The political and financial disorders in Europe are important factors in our condition," in his opinion.

Turning to the growth of the real estate business in this country, Meyer said the development was carried on too long and the financial arrangements became "dangerous" with "dangerous valuations."

Through the reconstruction finance corporation, Meyer said, the "weak could be sustained and the strong would be better able to go along."

Meyer explained the measure.

With a capital of $500,000,000 furnished by the Government, the corporation would be authorized to issue bonds not exceeding $1,500,000,000.

Directors would be the treasury secretary, governor of the Reserve Board, the farm loan commissioner and two presidential appointees, each to serve 5 years and be approved by the Senate.

The corporation would be authorized to make loans on terms and conditions it may determine to any bank, banker, savings bank, trust company, clearing house, building and loan association and insurance and other financial institutions.

Loans also may be made to railroads for temporary financing. The treasury would be finally responsible for all debts of the corporations.

Bad Mood Sends Him To Cell for 30 Years

Being in a bad mood cost Eugene Washington, 32-year-old Negro, 30 years of freedom.

July 20, in Fort Greene Park, Washington resented Milton Vincent's request for a match. Instead of reaching for a match he drew a gun and killed Vincent. A jury found him guilty of manslaughter, first degree. Today County Judge Taylor sentenced him to Sing Sing for 30 years.

Edward Cluff Dies In Montclair, N. J.

Edward Cluff, 86, a former resident of Brooklyn for 40 years, died yesterday at his home, 289 Claremont Ave., Montclair, N. J., after a long illness. He was formerly in the insurance business and at one time was president of the Union Casualty & Surety Company of St. Louis. He retired eight years ago. Three sons, Frederick H., Edward R. and Warren Cluff, survive. Services will be held tonight and interment will be in Greenwood Cemetery tomorrow.

Principal Felter Back at His Desk

Principal William L. Felter is back at his desk at Girls High School, following a slight attack of pneumonia which has kept him out for the past three weeks.

Legs' Murder Laid to Bronx Beer Runners

Gangster Was Recently Warned His Territory Was to Be Invaded

Eagle Bureau, Capitol Building.

By CLINTON L. MOSHER

Albany, Dec. 18—Beer runners from the Bronx, musceling into the territory from the Bronx line to Albany, rubbed out the much-shot-at Jack Diamond, in the opinion of investigators for the Attorney General's office.

Attorney General John J. Bennett, whose office twice tried Diamond and twice failed to get a verdict of guilty, has been informed that a week and a half ago, certain gangsters from the upper end of New York City sent word up the Hudson that they were taking over the remains of the Diamond business and that any opposition would be answered with gun fire.

The theory here is that Diamond, all puffed up over his second acquittal, talked out of turn and boasted about reviving the beer-running racket he had developed with headquarters in Catskill.

Shot Near Capitol

The Dove St. rooming house in which Diamond was put on the spot is in the residential section on the hill behind the State Capitol, a half dozen blocks from what was Diamond's favorite speakeasy hangout.

The liquor emporium was located on Hawks St. four doors from the side entrance to the Capitol. Word reached the Governor's office that the number one gangster was hanging out there and the next day the local police cleaned out the place, booze, bottles and bar.

Bennett, who left here last night to prosecute a bank failure in Binghampton, was notified by telephone this morning of the murder. He made no comment, but it is understood he instructed his deputies in Albany to give the police every possible aid.

Gang Leaders to Be Grilled

Because of the exhaustive study they made of Diamond and his habits in preparation for his torture and kidnaping trials, it is expected that the Attorney General's men can be of great assistance to the police in worming out of the underworld the story of Diamond's murder.

All the well-known figures in gangland will be brought in for questioning, according to the present plan, and among them will be Ciro Terranova, who pretended to be nothing more than a dealer in artichokes in the Harlem Market.

Steinberg Case Echo Seen

In the tangled skein of motives which might lie behind the slaying of Legs Diamond, the local police are not overlooking the possibility that it is the final echo of the mysterious disappearance of Leo Steinberg, Brooklyn rum runner who vanished at Long Beach, L. I., in October of last year.

Ask any detective who worked on that case and he'll shrug his shoulders and reply, "Ask Vannie Higgins."

Following the disappearance of Steinberg, Diamond is known to have stepped into the picture and shaken down friends and relatives of Steinberg to the tune of $25,000.

Capt. John P. Ryan, in charge of the 10th District, who probably knows more about the activities of Higgins and Diamond in Brooklyn than any other officer, does not think it far-fetched that this shakedown was the real motive for rubbing Diamond out.

Believed Thrown Overboard

"Up to a little more than a year ago," Captain Ryan said today, "Vannie and Legs worked together in supplying local speakeasies with beer. Then Steinberg, whose motorboats Vannie used to land rum at Long Beach, disappeared and he has never been seen since. While there is no proof, the best bet is that he was dropped overboard from one of his own boats."

DUKE AND ACTRESS SAY 'I DO'

Probate Judge William C. Rungee of Greenwich, Conn., marrying Miss Kathleen Ethel Dawes, former actress of London, and the Duke of Manchester, in law office at Greenwich in civil ceremony.

Brannon Comment On Bridge Battle Unfair, Says Huske

Eagle Expert Points Out That Neither Team Has Escaped His Criticism

As the long-distance Contract Bridge tournament continues, it becomes more and more a verbal war as well as a pasteboard tournament.

Nerves are getting frayed—and that includes the nerves of the expert kibitzers as well as the players.

Yesterday F. D Courtenay, president of Bridge Headquarters, Inc. (which sponsors the Official System), said all the players were "making monkeys of themselves" and weren't bidding according to their systems. He blamed the referees for not doing their duty and throwing out most of the hands played.

Today Mr. Courtenay explained that he didn't really mean Sidney S. Lenz was not playing the Official System, but he stood by what he had said of Ely Culbertson and the referees.

And today, also, came a counter-attack from William J. Huske, associate editor of the Bridge World and a Culbertson protagonist.

In a letter to The Eagle Mr. Huske wrote that Robert M. Brannon, in his bridge articles, in The Eagle, has been interpreting the match in a manner far from nonpartisan.

Brannon Answers Critic

His criticisms of it, in general more or less like those of Courtenay's, have had, Huske wrote, "gross deviations from fair interpretation or fair criticism in them." And he added:

"Perhaps this may be explained by the fact that Mr. Brannon is a paid employe of Bridge Headquarters" which "is engaged in a campaign to discredit this match, not only because of extreme unfriendliness toward Mr. Culbertson but also of strained relations with Mr. Lenz."

To that Mr. Brannon replied that he has criticised Lenz and Oswald Jacoby quite as sharply as Culbertson and that his editorial connection with Bridge Headquarters has not influenced his articles in The Eagle, with which Bridge Headquarters "is in no way acquainted."

The criticism of the referees for failing to take extreme action was met by Lt. Alfred M. Gruenther, the chief referee, who said today that, according to the term of the contract under which the tournament is being played, the referees can take no such action except after passing on a complaint submitted in writing by one side or the other—and there have been no such complaints.

Lieutenant Gruenther declined to say whether he thought the players actually were or were not bidding according to their respective systems.

"If I gave my opinion now," he said, "and written complaint were to be made later and it appeared that Dec 18 I had said the players had not strayed from their systems, why I would be in the position of having already committed myself on something I would have to pass on after investigating the hands played."

Lightner Defends Players

Theodore A. Lightner, who joined the ranks of the players only last night as substitute for Mrs. Culbertson, had no such hesitancy in committing himself.

All the contestants, said he, have been playing their systems, but with divergences. Which, however, said he, is all right.

"According to a strict interpretation of the rules," he explained, "a certain bid could not be made. But owing to the fact that it is the best choice in a given situation, the requirement for the bid should be stretched to cover the particular case. The result is shaded bid, which must be used, exceptionally, because the circumstances are exceptional."

Lawyer Disbarred, Another Censured

The Appellate Division in Manhattan today disbarred one lawyer and censured another.

Max S. Rebarber was disbarred for misappropriating about $3,000 of a client's money and for giving two bad checks to clients for $15 each.

Francis P. Burns was censured because, after he had been instructed by the court to pay $100 to Herbert O'Burden, an attorney substituted for in a divorce action, he gave Burden a bad check and failed to make good until seven months later when Burden brought an action in magistrate's court.

Two Hands Show Differences Of Lenz-Culbertson Systems

Jacoby in Contract of 7 Hearts, Founded on Psychic Bid

By WILLIAM J. HUSKE

Associate Editor of the Bridge World

(Named by Mr. Culbertson to comment on match for The Eagle)

Perhaps as a counterblast to some of the statements of commentators on the match the bidding of the hands in last night's session of the contract bridge battle between Ely Culbertson and Sidney Lenz furnished two dramatic hands illustrating the differences between the systems.

William J. Huske

The first hand was played by Mr. Jacoby in a contract of seven hearts, which had as its foundation a psychic opening heart bid made with only 1½ honor tricks. The hand

Please Turn to Page 27

STUART McKENZIE DIES

Stuart McKenzie, 63, of 17 Lawson St., Hempstead, L. I., died of a heart attack yesterday afternoon in the offices of the Lawyers' Management Company at 1912 Arthur Ave., the Bronx, where he was employed as a title searcher.

Discovers What Average Citizen Thinks of Match

By WILLIAM WEER

I picked half a dozen citizens at random. Not too much at random, you understand, for there must be some logic and order in the world. But moderately at random. And each in turn I asked:

"What do you think of the great contract bridge tournament now raging between the Culbertsons and the Lenz-Jacobies or Jacoby-Lenzes?"

For I wanted to find out, if the truth be told, what the ordinary citizen thought about it all. Not the participants, who had had their say, nor the experts, who have been saying so much. But the man-you-catch-at-the-other-end-of-the-telephone-wire or the woman ditto.

I asked my question first of a rising young citizen who now and then sits down at a bridge table when there is nothing else to do. And he said:

It's a Good Thing

"It's a good thing. I think it's a very good thing. It takes people's minds off their troubles. I was up-State the other day in a small town, Utica, and I was amazed—I found bridge books on display in the book stores.

"People everywhere, in Utica and in the trains going and coming back, talking bridge, arguing about the Culbertson system and the official

Please Turn to Page 27

Broun Referees on Assurance Job Is Mostly Sitting

By SIDNEY S. LENZ

Our total loss last night was 4,555 points, which put us 4,965 points minus on the entire match up to date. We lost the first five rubbers, and finally succeeded in breaking through by winning the sixth.

Last night's session was again delayed by a short conference. A number of newspapers had published in the afternoon a statement by F. D. Courtenay in regard to the match, which apparently did not meet with his approval. As soon as I heard of this I telephoned to Mr. Courtenay, who denied absolutely having made the remarks imputed to him by the newspapers concerning the 1-2-3 system, and to which I had taken exception. Because of this denial, the conference was of no consequence.

Sidney S. Lenz

No Easier Task

Theodore A. Lightner, Ely's usual partner in tournaments, took Mrs. Culbertson's place last night. She will return during the latter part of the match. Lightner is a great stu-

Please Turn to Page 27

Reich Railways Unable to Meet 1932 Payments

Young Plan Experts Find Non-Postponable Debt Default Needed

Basel, Switzerland, Dec. 18 (AP)—The Young Plan committee of experts decided today by unanimous vote that the German railways will be unable to meet their nonpostponable reparations payments next year.

The experts committee accepted a subcommittee's report which contained the statement that it will be impossible for the railways to balance their budget in 1932, even though the unconditional payments which the Young Plan places upon them, should be turned back to them now through the Hoover plan.

This disclosure was accepted as the first official indication that the experts' final report would contain a recommendation for a moratorium on conditional payments rather than for cancellation.

As soon as Germany gets back to normal, the subcommittee report said, "the railways may be expected to attain net earnings comparable to those of the railways in other countries."

The commission reported that the 1930 profits dropped to 480,000,000 marks, a decrease of 13 percent, and that by December, 1931, receipts had fallen by 28 percent.

The German members of the Young Plan advisory committee expressed pleasure today over the publication last night by the experts committee of statistics showing a deficit in Germany's balance payments of from 1,300,000,000 reichsmarks to 1,450,000,000.

The German members said this publication admitted the validity of the Reich's plea of inability to pay its reparations annuities.

Frank B. Robinson, Steel Leader, Dies

Frank B. Robinson, founder of the Carbon Steel Company of Pittsburgh, died at the Engineers Club yesterday afternoon, it was learned today. He is survived by one daughter, Mrs. E. G. Robinson of 76 Irving Place, Manhattan.

Before engaging in the steel business Mr. Robinson was a prominent member of the New York Stock Exchange, heading a corps of brokers identified with the security market operations of H. O. Mills. Closely related with the Pennsylvania Steel Company, Mr. Robinson furnished the steel work for the Brooklyn Bridge, and later from his own works the steel for the Manhattan Bridge.

Further Relief Aid Pledged by Hoover

President Hoover, who recently donated $5,000 to the Professional Engineers Committee on Unemployment, has expressed his willingness to be of further help to the committee in its relief activities, H. DeB. Parsons, general chairman, announced today. Acknowledging a letter from Mr. Parsons, expressing the thanks of the engineers for his assistance, Mr. Hoover replied:

"It is very kind of you to write your letter of Dec. 10. I am indeed glad to be of help and will be glad to be of further help in any other way you may suggest."

Leaps to His Death Under Subway Train

William Le Grand, 42, of 1044 Wyckoff Ave., committed suicide shortly before 4 o'clock this morning by jumping in front of a southbound train at the 72d St. station, Manhattan, of the west side subway. Traffic on the southbound tracks was tied up for 11 minutes and northbound traffic for five minutes while members of a police emergency squad extricated the body from under the front trucks of the second car. No money was found in the pockets of the suicide. The train was in charge of Motorman John Lence.

THE WEATHER
Today: Generally fair and cooler
Tomorrow: Mostly cloudy with probable showers
Temperatures Yesterday: Max., 87; Min., 71
Detailed report on Page 29

NEW YORK
Herald Tribune

NEW YORK HERALD TRIBUNE Established March 19, 1924
NEW YORK HERALD Founded May 6, 1835
NEW YORK TRIBUNE

VOL. XCII No. 31,337 (Copyright, 1932, New York Tribune Inc.) FRIDAY, SEPTEMBER 2, 1932 ** TWO CENTS In Greater New York | THREE CENTS Within 200 Miles | FOUR CENTS Elsewhere

Mayor Walker Resigns Office and Will Run Again; Announcement Is Made at City Hall at 10:20 P. M.

Paris Rebuffs Armed Reich; U. S. May Get Bid to Confer

Washington Would Be Invited to Scan Berlin Appeal if Ex-Allies Call Kellogg Pact the Issue

Herriot and Briton Deem Plea Unwise

Germany Asks 300,000 Conscripted Soldiers; Air Force and Modern Fleet Reported Sought

From the Herald Tribune Bureau
Copyright, 1932, New York Tribune Inc.

PARIS, Sept. 1.—Meeting in an atmosphere supercharged with excitement, the French Cabinet decided this afternoon to reject Germany's bid for bilateral negotiations regarding reorganization of the Reichswehr (German army), holding that any question which affects the Treaty of Versailles must be a matter, not for negotiation between two parties, but for consideration by all the former allied powers.

Premier Edouard Herriot returned to Paris from the Channel Isles this morning and went straight to the Foreign Office, where he conferred with Joseph Paul-Boncour, Minister of War, and Joseph Paganon, Under Secretary for Foreign Affairs, regarding the German aide memoire, which was communicated to him on Tuesday. The Premier then received Ronald Campbell, the British Charge d'Affaires, who, it is understood, assured M. Herriot that the British government was in accord with the French in considering the whole incident "unfortunate," and also agreed with the view that the ex-Allies, as a body, were concerned with any attempt to retouch the arms clauses of the Versailles Treaty.

France May Consult United States

There are indications that France not only will consult her ex-Allies but, if it is found that the German proposals are in any way likely to affect the Briand-Kellogg pact outlawing war, will consult also her ex-associated power, the United States.

More than anything else, it was asserted, the French Foreign Office is concerned today about the "blunt" manner in which the German demarche was launched. It was contended that, by making what was described as a public demarche, Germany only was complicating negotiations on a matter already delicate enough. It was added that the "clearly calculated coincidence" of this official gesture with the newspaper interview given yesterday by General Kurt von Schleicher, the Reichswehr Minister, made it exceedingly difficult for France to do anything except refuse to proceed farther.

French officials said they considered the German aide memoire almost an ultimatum, since the implication behind it was felt to be that if no reply was received before the scheduled meeting of disarmament conference bureau on September 19, the Germans would withdraw from the conference.

French Plan Consultations

An impression gathered in well-informed circles this evening was that Premier Herriot considered that Germany could not bluff France into taking on the responsibility of single-handed negotiations on such a ticklish subject. The French, it was said, were in no hurry, and would undertake thorough consultations among juridical and military experts before making their next move.

In some quarters it was suggested that the most logical position would be for France to remind Germany that the Reich, along with other nations,

(Continued on last page—page 32)

Opens Work-Sharing Drive

Blank & Stoller photo
Walter C. Teagle

Teagle Begins National Drive To Share Work

Jersey Standard Oil Head Opens Office Here to Carry Out President's Idea

Walter C. Teagle, president of the Standard Oil Company of New Jersey, who was appointed by President Hoover's Economic Conference last week to head the "Share-the-Work" movement, opened headquarters yesterday in the Federal Reserve Bank Building, 33 Liberty Street, and began a campaign to persuade the nation's employers to increase the number of their employees through fixing a shorter working week for those now hired. While no definite objective was set, it was learned that Mr. Teagle and his associates believe the movement should result in the early placing on pay rolls of from 1,000,000 to 2,000,000 persons now idle.

The movement will be undertaken in the twelve Federal Reserve districts under direction of the Banking and Industrial Committee of each district. One member from each district committee will compose a co-ordination committee, with Mr. Teagle as its head, and L. C. Walker, president of the Shaw Walker Company, as vice-chairman. Mr. Teagle, who has taken a leave of absence from the oil industry to give full time to the relief project, explained the plan yesterday.

"The purpose of this endeavor," he said, "is to spread the available jobs among as many workers as possible. There is less work to be done today than there was before the depression

(Continued on page eight)

R. F. C. Ready To Lend on Raw Staples

Textile Industry Delegation, Seeking Loan to Buy Wool and Cotton, Will Be Heard Today

Triborough Span Advance Likely

Hovey Named to Supervise Farm Credit Chain; Pennsylvania Asks Loan

From the Herald Tribune Bureau

WASHINGTON, Sept. 1.—The Reconstruction Finance Corporation, it was indicated today, is about ready to move in several directions under the new provisions of the emergency relief act to carry out its part in President Hoover's program for business recovery and relief of unemployment. The plan of the corporation as revealed by the developments includes:

Assistance to industry, particularly the producer and manufacturer of staple raw materials, in the form of loans for the carrying and marketing of commodities. The members of the board of directors, it was learned, will receive a delegation from the textile industry tomorrow, proposing a loan for the purchase of wool and cotton. The move is in addition to the program of the commodities' credit organization recently formed as the result of conferences in New York between Eugene Meyer, governor of the Federal Reserve Board, and interests concerned with the commodity buying project.

Early organization of the new chain of government-aided agricultural credit corporations was foreseen as the Finance Corporation announced the appointment of Frank Hovey, Omaha banker, to supervise the system. Mr. Hovey reached Washington today to assume his new post and Wilson McCarthy, Finance Corporation director, who handles the agricultural matters, said the personnel of the regional corporations would be announced within a few days.

The Pennsylvania Railroad today filed application with the Interstate Commerce Commission for approval of a loan of $2,000,000 by the Finance Corporation for the purchase of new equipment, the first step in the program of the roads to utilize the provisions of the Emergency Relief act which authorizes railroad loans for repairs, maintenance-of-way work and equipment acquirement to provide employment. Announcement has been

(Continued on page eight)

Summary of Today's News

Mayor Who Resigns and His Successor

James J. Walker

Joseph V. McKee

War 'Disabled' Win Police and Fire Pay Rises

Civil Service Reformers Assail Preference Law Use by Able Pensioners

Hundreds of active members of the New York police and fire departments are augmenting their salaries by drawing compensation from the Federal treasury as disabled war veterans, it was learned yesterday, in a controversy as to abuses of the state law which grants preferences to these men in appointment and promotion.

The policemen and firemen who have obtained the preferences are not noticeably disabled. In fact, they have passed the strict physical and mental tests required in their departments and, to the casual eye they appear as able-bodied as fellow officers over whose heads they are promoted. Some of the non-disabled men have been unkind enough to suggest that the disabilities are exaggerated. A movement to halt the abuses of the preference law has been started by H. Eliot Kaplan, secretary of the Civil Service Reform Association, of 521 Fifth Avenue.

Police Commissioner Edward P. Mulrooney explained that the state law makes it mandatory upon him to give preference to ex-service men who are classified as disabled by the United States Veterans' Bureau, even though police surgeons find no serious disabilities.

"Some of the men may not even have dandruff," Commissioner Mulrooney remarked.

The Police Department, with its 19,000 men, has approximately 3,000

(Continued on page fourteen)

Gronau Is Off for Japan Over 800 Miles of Sea

German Plane Quits Aleutians for the Kuriles

ST. PAUL ISLAND, Alaska, Sept. 1 (AP).—Captain Wolfgang von Gronau, German aviator who has flown the North Atlantic three times, and his three companions, circling the globe in their seaplane Groenland Wal, took off from Attu Island, westernmost of the Aleutians, for Paramushir Island, northernmost of the Kuriles, at 12:10 p. m. today. Pacific standard time (4:10 p. m., New York daylight saving time), said a wireless message received at the United States Naval station here.

Route to Berlin Charted

Attu Island is American territory and Paramushir belongs to Japan. Between them lies nearly 800 miles of the open Pacific.

From Paramushir, Captain von Gronau expects to fly southward to Japan, then back to Berlin over the long coastal route via Shanghai, Hongkong, Singapore and India. He may touch at Manila.

Captain von Gronau's plane left Germany on July 21 and has made stops, among other places, at Iceland, Greenland, Labrador, Montreal, Detroit, Chicago, Prince Rupert, B. C., and Alaskan towns. The German flyer is seeking to demonstrate the practicability of a mail and passenger air route from Europe to Japan by way of Canada.

Text of Walker Statement

STATEMENT BY JAMES J. WALKER,
Mayor of the City of New York.

September 1, 1932.

A letter from my counsel, Mr. John J. Curtin, received today, has caused me to make a momentous decision—that is, whether or not I shall refuse to go again to Albany to further subject myself to an un-American, unfair proceeding conducted by Governor Roosevelt against me.

Three weeks ago I went to Albany with my counsel, confident that we would be accorded a fair hearing, conducted in accordance with the rules established under our principles of government.

My counsel, Mr. Curtin, demanded at the opening of the hearing that the Governor summon those witnesses upon whose testimony Mr. Seabury or the Governor made the so-called charges against me, in order that I might face them and that my counsel might have an opportunity to cross-examine them. This was denied by the Governor. At no time was Mr. Seabury even called upon by the Governor to name those witnesses, much less to summon them. As soon as this ruling was made I protested, but without avail.

Day after day during the course of the proceedings it became more and more apparent that I was being subjected to an extraordinary inquisition. I was not accorded even the elementary rights guaranteed to any defendant in a court of law. Instead of an impartial hearing, the proceedings before the Governor developed into a travesty, a mock trial, a proceeding in comparison to which even the practice of a drumhead court martial seemed liberal.

Upon my counsel's insistence, the conduct of this proceeding was submitted to the Supreme Court in order that the validity of the objections of my counsel might be impartially adjudicated. The court decided on Monday of this week that the Governor proceeded in excess of his jurisdiction and without warrant of law:

(1) By denying me the right to which I am entitled under the Constitution and the law to confront accusing witnesses and cross-examine them and by his treating accusations as self-proven without supporting evidence.

(2) By considering as charges, upon which he might act adversely, a group of accusations more than two-thirds of the total number of charges involving no wrong-doing in fact, and which concerned alleged incidents occurring prior to my second election, over which he has no jurisdiction under the Constitution, the Statutes, the decisions of the courts, and the rulings of prior Executives, including Governors Charles E. Hughes, David B. Hill and Theodore Roosevelt.

(3) By considering as charges, upon which he might act adversely, certain incidents involving no element of wrong-doing on my part, relating not only to my official conduct but to my private affairs and the private affairs of others having no official relation with the City of New York.

The Supreme Court also held that it was without power to restrain the Governor or prevent the invasion by him of my legal rights, which legal rights have been accorded without hesitancy by all prior Governors when requested by officials under scrutiny.

The Supreme Court says that this lack of power results from the Governor invoking a technicality—by making a "special appearance" and refusing to yield jurisdiction to the Courts. The Court says this leaves me at the mercy of the Governor and his avowed determination to subject me to an unlawful and unconstitutional exercise of power—a perversion of executive power—a usurpation of power without color of authority under any statutory or constitutional provision or any judicial or executive decision. All this in order that he may accomplish a wrongful and unlawful end.

I am told that the Governors of numerous states, and even in England the King, yielded to the Courts in order that no one may suffer from an unjust or illegal act of the Executive or the Crown.

I am also told that, so far as the courts are concerned at present, I must submit to being outraged by the unlawful acts of the Governor. I do not believe that in this day and age any man in this country would assert the right to act above the law, to exercise arbitrary and unlawful power, while conceding he did not in law possess arbitrary power.

The Governor announced that he would not yield jurisdiction to the courts, which might restrain him from doing illegal acts leveled at me, unlawful under long settled prior decisions, even before the pronouncement of Justice Staley. The Governor has announced that he will persist in his illegal course. He has so announced at a time when I am informed that if the rights which he denies to me were accorded, the alleged charges would have to be dismissed. But I am told that I am without remedy at the present time in the courts because the Governor asserts and stands on an immunity from the process of the courts which has not been asserted even in England since the time of George III, whose assertions of arbitrary power provoked the Amreican Revolutionary War.

I am told that I am without remedy at the present time in the courts although the conceded and substantial unlawful invasion of my rights is

(Continued on page two)

City Clerk Cruise Gets Formal Word

His Action, Effective Immediately, Accompanied by Statement Attacking Hearings Before Governor

Joseph V. McKee Succeeds Him; Election This Fall Is in Doubt

Executive, Ill and Haggard at Funeral of Brother, Appears Late in Evening; Directs Reporters to City Hall

CITY OF NEW YORK.
Office of the Mayor,

Sept. 1, 1932.

Hon. Michael J. Cruise,
City Clerk of the City of New York,
Municipal Building, New York.

Dear Sir:

I hereby resign as Mayor of the City of New York, the resignation to take effect immediately. Very truly yours,

JAMES J. WALKER, Mayor.

Mayor James J. Walker's resignation from office was announced last night at 10:20 o'clock.

Mr. Walker's intention is to run again for Mayor, presumably at the next general election, November 8. This he could not do if Governor Roosevelt were to remove him. His term normally would expire December 31, 1933.

The Mayor's announcement was made at City Hall, where City Clerk Michael J. Cruise announced he had received it.

The resignation ended the Mayor's hearing in removal proceedings brought by Samuel Seabury, which was to have entered its thirteenth day this afternoon before Governor Roosevelt at Albany.

By the resignation, Joseph V. McKee, President of the Board of Aldermen, automatically becomes Mayor. Dennis J. Ahearn succeeds him as President of the Aldermen.

Mayor Walker, who had been absent and unaccounted for since 2:30 in the afternoon, when he left his apartment at Mayfair House, returned there at 10 p. m. and told waiting reporters that an announcement would be forthcoming at City Hall.

The reporters, who had been given to understand that he was undergoing a physical examination to determine whether he would return to Albany for the hearing today, asked how the Mayor felt.

Feels "Great," He Says

"Great!" he declared, and got into the elevator with his assistant, Charles F. Kerrigan.

A few minutes later the announcement came from City Hall, in a si[x]-page statement declaring that th[e] Mayor was submitting his case to th[e] people of New York by offering him[-]self as a candidate for re-election.

The declaration was made in th[e] form of an answer to a long letter [of] advice addressed to the Mayor [by] John J. Curtin, his counsel in the proceedings before the Governor.

On Hearst's Advice

The Mayor's action was in accord with the advice offered to him yesterday morning by William Randolph Hearst, his one journalistic supporter in New York City, in a signed editorial in "The New York American."

Although the Mayor did not specifically say he would run again, he declared he was taking a "change of venue" to the forum of the people.

With the decision of Supreme Court Justice Ellis J. Staley that the Governor had power to remove the Mayor and that the courts had no power to dictate how he should do it, hope had gone out of the Mayor's camp, so far as avoiding removal was concerned.

The tactics of the Walker defense at Albany had been directed toward the hope of stopping the Go[vernor] or of forcing him to go thro[ugh a pro]cedure analogous to a l[egal] trial, and of trying to pu[t him in the] position of an unjust j[udge rather] than to answer the spec[ific charges] made by Samuel Seabury fro[m] evidence before the Hofstadter le[gis]lative committee.

His statement, which accompanied his resignation, went through the same complaints made at Albany, especially dwelling upon the procedure of accepting the Hofstadter committee testimony as evidence before the Governor and not calling the wit-

Walker's Act Not Surprising To Roosevelt

Governor Gets Word in Midst of Finance Parley, but Defers His Comment

By a Staff Correspondent

ALBANY, Sept. 1.—Governor Roosevelt, informed tonight of the resignation of Mayor Walker, whose trial on charges was to be resumed before the Governor tomorrow afternoon, declined to make any comment. He said he would have to read and digest first the correspondence between Mayor Walker and his counsel.

The Governor was in conference with leaders of his party when the message came that Mayor Walker had sent in his resignation on the ground that he was not getting a fair hearing from the Governor on the charges against him. James A. Farley, national campaign manager for Governor Roosevelt; Frank C. Walker, treasurer of the National Democratic Committee; Arthur Mullen, national committeeman from Nebraska, and Basil O'Connor, the Governor's law partner, were with him. They were discussing the financial affairs of the Democratic party.

No intimation of Mayor Walker's intention of resigning had reached Governor Roosevelt either from the Mayor or from his attorney, but the news of his resignation did not come as a complete surprise, by any means. Governor Roosevelt had been reading newspaper reports for two days which intimated that the Mayor might resign tomorrow, and all day today there was a succession of calls from newspapers and news agencies which wanted to know what Governor Roosevelt knew of the Mayor's intentions.

All inquirers were informed that the Governor knew nothing at all about them.

Although not taken by surprise therefore by the announcement of the Mayor's resignation, it is believed that Governor Roosevelt was shocked by the reiterated statements of the Mayor and his counsel that they had been treated unfairly in the hearings at Albany.

The Governor has felt from the beginning that he was treating Mayor Walker with the utmost fairness throughout the hearings. It is believed that contrary statements will rankle

(Continued on page two)

Section III — SPORTS — NEW YORK Herald Tribune — SPORTS — Section III

TWELVE PAGES — SUNDAY, OCTOBER 2, 1932 — **** — TWELVE PAGES

Miss Van Wie Routs Mrs. Vare For U.S. Golf Crown, 10 and 8, 73 on First 18 Shattering Par

Chicago Star, 13 and 12 Victim in '28, Crushes Five-Time Champion in Their Third Final

Victor 8 Up at Noon, One Over Men's Par

Ex-Titleholder, Even on Drives, Bows to Deadly Spoons, Chips Unequaled in History of Tourney

By Kerr N. Petrie

SALEM, Mass., Oct. 1.—Cutting loose with a game that in its devastating power carried all the relentless sweep of a tornado, Miss Virginia Van Wie, of Chicago, crowned years of defeat and discouragement today at the Salem Country Club by overwhelming Mrs. Glenna Collett Vare, of Philadelphia, in the thirty-six-holes final of the women's national championship, 10 and 8. Four years ago at Hot Springs, Va., Mrs. Vare triumphed over Miss Van Wie by 13 and 12. The Chicago girl could not match that record in her triumph this afternoon, but she came closer to the mark than any one ever believed was humanly possible.

The game which Miss Van Wie tossed against her conqueror of former years, victor in five of these championship finals and loser in only one, has never been equaled for sheer mechanical precision and brilliance in the last round of the national championship. It is doubtful if it has ever been approximated in women's golf save perhaps in the epic match which Mrs. Vare and Miss Joyce Wethered flashed last year in the British classic.

Victor Makes One Error

Miss Van Wie this morning played a round of golf that contained one mistake. There in itself is one for the book. That single error kept her from equaling men's par for the heavily trapped, testing Salem lay-out carved from the heart of the woods. She decimated women's par completely.

With two approximations, neither too liberal, Miss Van Wie played a 73 on her march to the title, which after she had taken two final-round beatings of 13 and 12 and 6 and 5 from Mrs. Vare, she must have begun to believe was to be denied her forever. But this time a gasping, gaping gallery saw the tables completely turned. Familiar as they are with the game's eccentricities and uncertainties, they scarcely expected to see Mrs. Vare smothered as she was. Some favored this one of the finalists, some the other, but none looked for such a rout as transpired, least of all did they ever dream that anything of the kind should fall upon the shoulders of the five-time champion.

Mrs. Vare did not play up to the form of which she is capable. That must be admitted. Even so it would have taken her best, her very best, to come anything like close to stopping the Chicagoan. Mrs. Vare was 8 down at noon, an amazing position for one so skilled and experienced.

Mrs. Vare's Task Hopeless

Even the most sanguine had little hope after that of seeing Mrs. Vare shake off defeat. Miss Van Wie resumed not quite as brilliantly as she had begun in the morning, but it was not long before her relentless attack had brought her advantage to double figures.

On the second round Mrs. Vare went out in 40, two over women's par. Even with this she lost ground. The end would have come at the ninth in all probability had Miss Van Wie not found her ball down in a patch of rough following her tee shot. With an iron she endeavored to tear the ball out and send it over the pond, but the water hazard had the last word, and Mrs. Vare was enabled to continue the match after standing 10 down with 10 to play.

The concluding hole was the counterpart of many others. Miss Van Wie did not outpoint her opponent with the driver, but she made the better spoon second and the better chip. From below the plateau green she chipped a dozen feet short. Miss Van Wie had played her second to the right of the green. Her chip was four feet strong but she was not asked to try it. Missing the putt, Mrs. Vare stepped up and conceded defeat, the official margin being announced as 10 and 8, although had Miss Van Wie putted and missed the advantage would have been only 9 up. One hole at that stage made little difference either way.

Victor Over Miss Glutting

Miss Van Wie's final victory rounded out a week of consistent golf. In both medal and match play she showed her complete mastery of her clubs. The fact that she tied for the qualifying prize at 77 with Miss Maureen Orcutt removes whatever possibility there might have remained for any one's entering a claim that Miss Van Wie only came onto her game in time to catch a somewhat faltering former champion.

The Chicago girl did not play through the harder half of the draw, but in every match she played solid, consistent golf, rising to the heights whenever she happened to be facing an opponent who appeared to demand special atttention.

This was particularly true of Miss Van Wie's handling of the Charlotte Glutting situation. Fired by her march to the semi-finals over such formidable opponents as Miss Mary K. Browne, Miss Bernice Wall and the British titleholder of the last two years, Miss Enid Wilson, Miss Glutting would have been difficult for any but the most expert and most experienced to subdue. Miss Van Wie handled the task perfectly.

And so today against Mrs. Vare the

(Continued on page five)

Her Perseverance Finally Is Rewarded

Miss Virginia Van Wie, of Chicago, who won the national women's golf championship yesterday by defeating Mrs. Glenna Collett Vare in the final at West Peabody, 10 and 8. Miss Van Wie had been beaten by Mrs. Vare, then Miss Glenna Collett, twice before in the final round

Equipoise Easy Victor, Adds $21,250 to Earnings

C. V. Whitney Ace, With Twenty Grand Scratched, Takes Havre de Grace Handicap by Galloping Mile and Furlong Ahead of Gallant Sir, Tred Avon

Special to the Herald Tribune

HAVRE DE GRACE, Md., Oct. 1.—Equipoise, son of Pennant, redeemed himself for his disappointing race a week ago when he ran unplaced behind Pairbypair, by galloping to easy victory in the twenty-first running of the Havre de Grace Handicap here this afternoon. It was a striking performance, and bore out the fact that when in running humor there is none to take his measure. Mrs. Payne Whitney's Twenty Grand, champion three-year-old of last season, was scratched so that the much-looked for duel between these two horses was denied the big crowd.

Equipoise, however, did not lack for competition. Thirteen of the best handicap horses in training faced the starter, but none could fully extend him through the last furlong, as he drew out to win by a comfortable margin. In spite of his doleful race recently, he went to the post favorite, around even money, and by one of those freaks of the mutuel machines he also paid even money for third. In truth, he paid slightly more to run second than to win, the mutuel prices being $4.10, $4.40 and $4.00.

Carries 128 Pounds

The race was at one mile and a furlong and the good horse ran the distance in 1:50 1-5, one-fifth of a second behind the track record. If Sonny Workman, who had the mount, had been forced to ride him out, a new track record would have been established. He carried 128 pounds, which made his performance the more praiseworthy.

The Northway Stable's Gallant Sir, Western three-year-old, finished second, while Tred Avon was three lengths back in third place. White Clover II, the English horse which won the Suburban Handicap at Belmont Park last Spring, came next, while George D. Widener's Jack High finished fifth.

Mr. and Mrs. C. V. Whitney were on hand with 20,000 others to see their good horse race to one of his most impressive victories of the year. Mr. Whitney accepted the trophy which went with the race, and was among the first to compliment Workman for his capable ride.

Equipoise earned $21,250 and so brought his earnings for the season to $104,870 and his total earnings over three seasons of racing to $264,710.

Equipoise's Tenth Victory

The son of Pennant-Swinging has won ten out of twelve starts this year, including such stakes as the Toboggan, the Metropolitan, the Stars and Stripes, the Arlington Gold Cup, the Wilson and the Whitney. He also ran second to Plucky Play in the rich Arlington Handicap, beaten a short neck. His only poor race this season came a week ago, when he behaved badly and to

(Continued on page six)

William-Mary Upsets Navy, 6-0, On End Run in Third Quarter

Middies Outrushed Throughout; Long Pass in 4th Fails in Effort to Tie

Special to the Herald Tribune

ANNAPOLIS, Md., Oct. 1.—A generously disappointed Navy contingent and some thousands of others looked on at Farragut Field this afternoon as the Naval Academy football team lost to William and Mary, 6 to 0. It was the seventh attempt for victory by the Indians, who made a strong effort last year, and their followers were elated.

The visitors clearly deserved the verdict, having the edge in first downs made, yards gained by rushing, and kicking. The Navy offense flashed rarely.

Walkup made the best showing of the Navy backs in the first half, and Chung-Hoon played well in the second, making repeated gains off tackle and passing accurately to erratic receivers.

The visitors scored in the third quarter when Becht fumbled and Halligan recovered on Navy's 30-yard line. Two plays by Palese took the ball across the goal line. One was a sprint around Navy's right end for eleven yards and the other around the other flank for nineteen. Halligan failed on the placement attempt.

Navy's great effort came in the fourth quarter, when, with the ball on William and Mary's 35-yard line, Chung-Hoon heaved a pass to the far right corner. Samuels, five yards from a score, got his arms around the ball, but it bounced off his chest.

Navy had a slight advantage at the start when Palese received Erck's punt and Halligan kicked back to Navy's 45-yard line. Chung-Hoon ran twenty yards into the visitors' territory, but Navy lost the ball when Becht missed an easy pass from Chung-Hoon.

Walkup retired in the third quarter with a bad ankle, and Harbold, center, who played well on defense, went out with the same injury in the final quarter. During the game, Baumberger, Slack, Clark and Samuels were used in the backfield, in addition to the starting group. William and Marys had several effective backs, including Palese, Slade and Lacroix.

The line-up:

Pos.	William and Mary (6)	Navy (0)
L. E.	Sorensen	Murray
L. T.	Stewart	Brooks
L. G.	Anderson	Reedy
C.	Bridges	Harbold
R. G.	Meade	Burns
R. T.	Quirk	Kane
R. E.	Halligan	Pray
Q. B.	Shade	Becht
L. H.	Palese	Chung Hoon
R. H.	Lacroix	Walkup
F. B.	Spack	Erck

SCORE BY PERIODS

Williams and Mary	0	0	6	0	—6
Navy	0	0	0	0	—0

Substitutions — Navy: Heileman for Brooks, Dornin for Pray, Slack for Becht, Becht for Slack, W. C. Clark for Chung Hoon, Chung Hoon for W. C. Clark, Baumberger for Chung Hoon, W. C. Clark for Baumberger, Chung Hoon for W. C. Clark, Samuels for Walkup, Waybright for Erck, Campbell for Waybright, Ruble for Burns, Dawson for Harbold. William and Mary: Yakavonas for Sorensen, Sorensen for Yakavonas, Darden for Anderson, Anderson for Darden, Darden for Anderson, Wilson for Bridges, Bridges for Wilson, Wilson for Bridges, Cholko for Shade, Smith for Palese, Giles for Lacroix, Smith for Giles, Lacroix for Smith, Worrell for Lacroix, Young for Spack.

Touchdown—Palese.

Referee—P. P. Magoffin, University of Michigan. Umpire—C. G. Eckles, Washington and Jefferson. Linesman—M. J. Thompson, Georgetown. Field Judge—E. E. Miller, Penn State. Time of quarters—15 minutes.

Bates Holds Yale to 0-0 Opening Tie

Pricher's Triple Threat Attack Twice Nearly Scores as Maine Team Outrushes Blue Line

Elis Halted at End On One-Yard Line

Belated Drive by Heim and Pony Backfield Is Futile in Short Contest

Special to the Herald Tribune

NEW HAVEN, Conn., Oct. 1.—Little Bates College of Lewiston, Me., scored a major upset in the Yale Bowl today by holding Yale's eleven to a scoreless tie. Yale's pony backfield almost saved the day in the last minutes of play, but failed after marching sixty-six yards to Bates's 1-yard line. These lightweights had first down on the Scarlet's 1-yard stripe, but time permitted only two fast plays, and Bates broke through the Blue wall to toss Charley Heim for two successive losses.

Heim, the little flash who startled Yale fans two years ago with his deeds when Albie Booth was injured, and who has not had much of a break since that time, went into the game in the final minutes and might have saved Yale had there been sufficient time. He and Clem Williamson did all the carrying for sixty yards and a penalty put the ball near the visitors' goal line.

Eleven-Minute Periods

While Yale might have scored if it had one more minute, the Eli forces, apparently confident of an overwhelming victory, had agreed upon four eleven-minute periods, cutting the game sixteen minutes short of a regulation contest. Yale was wishing for some of that wasted time tonight.

That one march was the only real threat made by the Elis. Bob Lassiter, the Blue's left halfback, was out of action because of a leg injury suffered in yesterday's practice. The backfield, without Lassiter, was comparatively helpless as far as consistent advancing was concerned, although Big Joe Crowley did more than his share. Del Marting and Eddie King, substitutes for Lassiter, failed to click.

Yale might well have been beaten and was fortunate in holding Bates to a tie for the visitors brought to the Bowl a triple threat star who menaced the Eli defense repeatedly and paved the way for a possible Bates touchdown which failed to materialize. Late in the first period Billy Pritcher, of Brooklyn, climaxed a series of fine gains by dashing sixteen yards to Yale's 15-yard line. Bates failed to make good, Stone's place kick on fourth down going wide by yards.

In the fourth period Pricher again dashed dangerously near the Yale goal line, reeling off a 38-yard run, the longest of the day, around Yale's left end, and was stopped at the Blue's 28-yard line. This threat was dashed when Joe Crowley came out of nowhere to intercept McClusky's pass which otherwise might have resulted in a touchdown.

Yale Threatens Twice

Only twice prior to the final rush did Yale appear on its way to a score and both times the Blue failed.

In the second period Yale marched 35 yards from mid-field only to lose the ball on downs when two forward passes failed, and in the third period the Blue gained three first downs in a row and appeared to have made a

(Continued on page two)

Colum[bia ...] Lehi[gh ...]

Reserves' F[...] Near Fini[...] ning, 233 [...]

Lehigh determi[...] at Baker Field yest[...] eleven under the t[...] watched the Blue a[...]

Columbia score[...] peak in the second, five yards from ano[...]

In so far as actual[...] cerned, it mattered [...] sity or reserves wer[...] Columbia. Each gr[...] three touchdowns [...] everything Lehigh h[...] buttal except for th[...]

[...] Rivero smashed through for the first score. Brominski place kicked the extra point and the rout was on.

Another twenty-six-yard Montgomery-Matal toss moved the ball into scoring territory just before the period ended, and one of twenty yards early in the second quarter got it down to where Montgomery could punch through for number two.

Frank Chippendale relieved Schwartz and Joe Linehan took Brominski's place at this juncture. The former's plunging and Linehan's running and pass receiving produced a third touch-

(Continued on page seven)

College Football Res[ults]

Local

Brooklyn College	0	Arnold	0
Catholic U.	47	C. C. N. Y.	0
Columbia	41	Lehigh	6
Fordham	69	Baltimore	0
Manhattan	32	St. Joseph's	2
N. Y. U.	33	Hobart	0

East

Army	13	Furman	0
Boston College	20	Loyola (Md.)	0
Boston University	13	New Hampshire	6
Bowdoin	20	Mass. State	6
Brown	19	Rhode Island	0
Bethany	0	Marietta	0
*Bluefield College	14	Campbell	0
Cornell	7	Niagara	0
Clarkson	31	Hamilton	0
Colby	19	Trinity	7
Carnegie Tech	7	Geneva	0
Colgate	27	Case	0
Cortland Tchrs	6	Mansfield Tchrs	6
Drexel	18	Westchester Tchrs.	6
Delaware	11	La Salle (Phila.)	6
Dartmouth	32	Vermont	6
Davis-Elkins	7	W. Liberty Tchrs	6
Georgetown	26	Mt. St. Mary's	0
Harvard	66	Buffalo	0
Holy Cross	26	Providence	6
Hillsdale	31	Jackson Jr.	0
Juniata	3	Gettysburg	2
Johns Hopkins	21	Wash. College	0
Lafayette	6	Muhlenberg	0
Lowell Textile	19	St. Michael's	0
Maine	33	Conn. State	6
Morgan	38	Cheyney Tchrs	0
Montpelier Sem.	53	Norwich J. V.	0
National Farm	27	Hartwick	0
Penn	38	F. and M.	0
Penn State	27	Lebanon Valley	0
Pittsburgh	40	West Virginia	0
Princeton	22	Amherst	0
Rochester	8	Alfred	6
Rutgers	20	P. M. C.	6
R. P. I.	7	Williams	6
*Syracuse	51	St. Lawrence	0
St. Bonaventure	39	Ithaca College	6
St. John's (Md.)	19	N. Y. Normal	6
Susquehanna	12	Moravian	7
South Carolina	7	Villanova	6
Shepherdstown	3	Shippensburg Tchrs	0
Springfield	20	E. Stroudsburg	0
Tufts	9	Middlebury	0
Upsala	35	Cooper Union	0
West Maryland	35	St. Thomas	6
Worcester Poly	6	Coast Gd. Acad.	0
W. and J.	20	W. Va. Wesleyan	0
W. and M.	6	Navy	0
Wesleyan	16	Union	6
Waynesburg	19	Slippery Rock	0
Yale	0	Bates	0

GAMES CANCELED

At Collegeville, Pa.—Haverford vs. Ursinus.

West

Aurora	0	Concordia	0
Ball State Tchrs.	26	Earlham	6
Beloit	32	Dubuque	0
Bluffton	6	Ohio Northern	6
Bowling Green	7	Mt. Union	6
*Cincinnati	22	Georgetown (Ky.)	12
Concordia	20	Moorehead Tchrs	6
*Creighton	6	Haskell	0
Dayton Reserves	13	Wilmington	6
Heidelberg	0	Findlay	0
Hope	0	Kalamazoo	0
Indiana	7	Ohio U.	6
Illinois	20	Miami	7
		(first game)	
Illinois	13	Coe	0
		(second game)	
Iowa	31	Bradley Tech	7
Iowa State	32	Morningside	0
Iowa St. Tchrs	14	Penn College	0
Ill. Normal	8	Dekalb Tchrs	7
Kent	6	Hiram	0
Lawrence	0	St. Norbert	0
Lake Forest	27	Northwestern Coll.	13
Lacrosse Tchrs	6	Columbia College	0
Michigan	26	Michigan State	0
Michigan B.	0	Mount Pleasant	0
Mich. Min. Tchrs.	6	Amer. Legion	0
Manchester	7	De Pauw	6
Minnesota	12	South Dakota	0

We[st]

Monmouth	27
Notre Dame	91
Northwestern	27
Nebraska	56
Oshkosh Normal	13
Ohio State	34
Otterbein	18
Purdue	29
River Falls Tchrs.	13
Rio Grande	14
St. John's (Minn)	19
Spearfish Tchrs.	7
St. Thomas (Minn.)	7
Toledo	18
Valparaiso	33
Virginia Jr. Coll.	32
Wisconsin	7
Western Reserve	6
Wooster	12
Wabash	0
Wilberforce	53
*Wash'gton (St.L.)	6

So[uth]

Alabama	53
Auburn	77
Baylor	6
Bowling Gr. Tchrs.	27
Centenary	13
Chattanooga	45
Davidson	7
Duke	44
*Emory-Henry	16
Georgia Tech	32
Georgia St.	40
Hampton	19
Hampden-Sidney	42
Kentucky	18
Knoxville	13
Langley Field	43
Mercer	21
Missouri Mines	20
Miss. College	32
M'freesboro Tchrs	18
N. C. State	9
Newberry	9
Oklahoma	7
Parris Is. Mar.	19
Piedmont	19
Presbyterian	9
Rice	10
Randolph-Macon	12
*Roanoke	19
St. Paul	9
Tennessee	33
Tennessee Tech	13
Texas Christian	55
Texas Mines	38
*Texas Tech	6
Tulane	26
Tusculum	
Union (Ky.)	32
Virginia State	7
Vanderbilt	39
V. P. I.	7
Virginia	7
Wofford	34

Far

Brigham Young	38		
Colorado	31		
California	22		
Idaho (S. B.)	18		
New Mexico Nor.	13	New Mexico Mines	0
Oregon	7	Santa Clara	0
So. Calif.	20	Wash. State	0
Stanford	27	Oregon State	0
St. Mary's	35	Nevada	0
Utah	54	Colorado College	6
Utah Aggies	26	Montana State	0
Wyoming	28	Chadron Normal	6
Washington	26	Montana	13

Freshman

Allbright '36	0	Allentown Prep	0
Bucknell '36	33	Shenandoah	0
Blair Acad	25	Penn State '36	18
California '36	63	Oneonta M. A.	0
Compton	19	So. Calif. '36	0
Exeter	14	New Hamp. '36	6
Pitt '36	9	Wyoming Sem	0
Syracuse '36	21	Manlius	0

*Night game.

Yankee Home Runs Crush Cubs, 7 to 5, Ruth and Gehrig Smashing Two Apiece In Third Straight World Series Victory

Ruth Scoring the First of Two Homers Against Cubs

The Babe about to cross the plate after his first inning blow, which also scored Combs and Sewell. Those in the picture are Van Graflan, umpire, at right; Sewell, No. 21; Gehrig, No. 4, next up, and Hartnett, No. 7, Cubs catcher. Ruth hit another homer in the fifth followed by Gehrig's second, his first coming in the third inning

Associated Press telephoto

4 Drives, All Off Root, Score 6 Runs; 2 on Successive Pitches in 5th Snap Tie, Rout Hurler

Babe Cracks First With Two on Bases

Pipgras Removed in 9th, Pennock Turning Back Last Three; N. Y. Is One Game From 4th Crown

By Richards Vidmer

CHICAGO, Oct. 1.—The Cubs threw caution to the winds today and the third game of the World Series with it, the Yankees winning, 7 to 5.

Stung with the thought that too many bases on balls might have cost them the first two contests, the Cubs went out determined to pitch to the batters and make them hit, but they never realized what hitting Babe Ruth and Lou Gehrig were capable of producing.

The mighty Ruth twice drove the ball into the bleachers and out of the park for home runs and Gehrig sounded a Ruthian echo after each. Between them they drove in six runs by sheer power, and the Cubs were conquered for the third successive time.

Home Runs Silence Jeers

With a capacity crowd of 51,000 looking on, Ruth cast a spell of awe over the throng with one of his greatest World Series performances. On two other occasions in his glamorous career he has hit three home runs in the course of a single World Series game, but never with the arrogance and the supershowmanship he displayed today.

Surrounded by a hostile crowd which booed him vigorously at the start, facing the combined taunts of the Cubs, the Babe turned the jeers to cheers and silenced the sneers, leaving an awed audience staring wide-eyed through the sunshine as he lifted two balls against the blue of the skies.

The very first time he came to bat, in the opening inning, there was confidence in his manner as he stepped up to the plate. He paused to jest with the raging Cubs, pointed to the right-field bleachers and grinned.

Two men were on the bases, as Jurges had thrown Combs's grounder over Grimm's head and Sewell had walked. Charley Root stood in the box under instructions to pitch to the batters and issue no unnecessary passes. But the Cubs couldn't have done worse if that order never had been issued.

First Three Romp Across

With a step forward, a lurch of his massive shoulders and a sweep of his celebrated bat, Ruth drove the ball high into the temporary bleachers that had been erected beyond the right field fence. Upward and onward the ball flew, a white streak was outlined against the bright blue sky, and the first three Yankee runs romped home.

But this was only the beginning. After the Babe had backed Cuyler to the fence to catch his line drive in to catch his whistling line drive in the second inning, Gehrig opened the third with another homer, his second of the series. It wasn't as high nor as far as Ruth's, and it came with nobody on the bases, but it was just as effective in throwing fear into the hearts of the Cubs.

Perhaps at this point the thought may have occurred to some of the Chicago players that pitching to Ruth and Gehrig wasn't such a great idea after all, but it took one more turn to convince them.

Cubs Tie in Fourth

Before it came the Cubs had tied the score. A pass to Herman and a double by Cuyler gave them one run in the first, a home run by Cuyler, a single by Stephenson and a double by Grimm gave them two more in the third, and a double by Jurges followed by an error sent the tying tally across the plate in the fourth.

The crowd was in an uproar when the fifth inning started. Their Cubs at last had an even chance of winning. Root had struck out the last two men in the fourth and seemed to have the Yankees under control. The players showed a new dash as they ran out to their positions and whipped the ball about the infield.

When Sewell was retired on a grounder to shortstop, a third of another inning was safely passed. But there still were Ruth and Gehrig.

As the Babe moved toward the plate, swinging three bats over his shoulder, a concerted shout of derision broke in the stands. There was a bellowing of boos, hisses and jeers. There were cries of encouragement for the pitcher and from the Cubs' dugout came a storm of abuse leveled at the Babe.

They Do It Again

But Ruth grinned in the face of the hostile greeting. He laughed back at the Cubs and took his plac supremely confident. A strike whistled over the plate and joyous outcries filled the air, but the Babe held up one finger as though to say: "That's only one, though. Just wait."

Two balls went by, then another strike. The stands rocked with delight. The Chicago players hurled their laughter at the great man, but Ruth held up two fingers and still grinned, the super-showman.

On the next pitch the Babe swung. There was a resounding report like the explosion of a gun. Straight for the center-field fence the ball soared on a line. Johnny Moore went racing back with some vague idea of catching it, then suddenly stopped short and stared as the ball sailed on, clearing the farthest corner of the barrier and dropping out into the street, 436 feet from home plate.

Before Ruth left the plate and started his swing around the bases he paused to laugh at the Chicago players, suddenly silent in their dugout. As he rounded first he flung a remark at Grimm, as he turned second he tossed a jest at Herman and his shoulders shook with satisfaction as he trotted on.

The Yankee players tumbled out of

(Continued on page three)

Home Runs Silence Jeers

With a capacity crowd of 51,000 looking on, Ruth cast a spell of awe over the throng with one of his greatest World Series performances. On two other occasions in his glamorous career he has hit three home runs in the course of a single World Series game, but never with the arrogance and the supershowmanship he displayed today.

Surrounded by a hostile crowd which booed him vigorously at the start, facing the combined taunts of the Cubs, the Babe turned the jeers to cheers and silenced the sneers, leaving an awed audience staring wide-eyed through the sunshine as he lifted two balls against the blue of the skies.

The very first time he came to bat, in the opening inning, there was confidence in his manner as he stepped up to the plate. He paused to jest with the raging Cubs, pointed to the right-field bleachers and grinned.

They Do It Again

But Ruth grinned in the face of the hostile greeting. He laughed back at the Cubs and took his plac supremely confident. A strike whistled over the plate and joyous outcries filled the air, but the Babe held up one finger as though to say: "That's only one, though. Just wait."

Two balls went by, then another strike. The stands rocked with delight. The Chicago players hurled their laughter at the great man, but Ruth held up two fingers and still grinned, the super-showman.

On the next pitch the Babe swung. There was a resounding report like the explosion of a gun. Straight for the center-field fence the ball soared on a line. Johnny Moore went racing back with some vague idea of catching it, then suddenly stopped short and stared as the ball sailed on, clearing the farthest corner of the barrier and dropping out into the street, 436 feet from home plate.

[...] Errors [...]inceton [...]mherst

[O]pening Game, [O]nly One Tally [...]m Real Drive

[...] Woodward

[...], Oct. 1.—The re[...]ball team, taking [...] coaching regime of [...] serious afternoon [...]oday. A big, hard-[...]am, almost devoid [...]d and grudging on [...]e Tiger solidly. [...] materially by er[...] by the boys from [...]ceton won, 22 to 0. [...] Tiger touchdowns [...] of anything like a [...] that culminated in [...] game on the first [...] period, when Jack [...]ck, broke through [...] Amherst line and [...]rds across the goal

[...] again in the third [...] Kalbaugh, the [...] poor pass from the [...]hind the Amherst [...] poor pass gave the [...] the fourth quar[ter ...]s completed when [...]twenty yards with[...]es, Tom Johnston, [...]acking a grudging [...]en Amherst suc[...]is plunges, Millard [...]end for the touch[...]so made the break [...] the score by inter[...]ass.

[...] 1-Yard Line

[...]s development, the [...] for downs on its [...] four plays that [...]rd line. Johnston [...] this unaccepted [...]run the free kick [...]ety back sixty-five [...]30-yard line. Only [...] tackle by English, [...] had stopped him [...]

[...]nd Millard Draudt [...]ing backs for the [...] attack, evolving [...]ota shift, at times [...] the Purple and [...]onally got Draudt [...]here was nothing [...] process, however, [...]in- the Tiger was [...]layed 6-2-2-1 de[...]en though stalled

[... o]n page two)

[Seri]es Results, [an]d Schedule

[...]d summaries of [...]played thus far, [...]ors and batteries.

[FIRST G]AME

	R.	H.	E.
[...]0 2 2 0—	6	10	1
[...]3 3 1 x—12	8	2	

[...]rimes, Smith and [...]d Dickey.

[SECOND] GAME

	R.	H.	E.
[...]0 0 0 0 0—2	9	0	
[...]1 0 0 0 x—5	10	1	

[...] and Hartnett.

[THIRD G]AME

		R.	H.	E.
N. Y. (A.L.)	3 0 1 0 2 0 0 0 1—7	8	1	
Chi. (N.L.)	1 0 2 1 0 0 0 0 1—5	9	4	

Batteries—Pipgras, Pennock and Dickey; Root, Malone, May, Tinning and Hartnett.

STANDING OF THE CLUBS

	Won.	Lost.	Pct.
New York	3	0	1.000
Chicago	0	3	.000

SCHEDULE

Fourth game at Wrigley Field, Chicago, today at 1:30 p. m. (2:30 p. m., New York time).

Fifth game, if necessary, tomorrow at Wrigley Field.

Sixth and seventh games, if necessary, Yankee Stadium, October 5 and 6.

Yankee Homers Crush Cubs, 7-5, Ruth and Gehrig Hitting Two Apiece in 3d Straight

All Four Made Off Root, Bring Six Runs Over

Chicago Hurler Blasted Out in 5th as Sluggers Hit for Circuit in Succession

(Continued from page one)

their dugout and danced with glee. They rushed forward to shake Ruth's hand and pound him on the back, but the celebration had hardly subsided before another report rang out from the plate and Gehrig started off on the same course Ruth had just covered. He hit the first ball Root pitched and away it went into the right-field bleachers, putting the Yankees two runs ahead.

The crowd sat stunned at the feats of these two master maulers. The Cubs might catch up, they might stop the rest of the Yankee hitters, but what was the use—there always were Ruth and Gehrig to contend with. Each had come to bat three times and each had driven out two home runs.

Back in the lead once more, hoisted there by the herculean efforts of the mighty Babe and the powerful Lou, George Pipgras, the Yankee pitcher, held the Cubs in check. He allowed just one hit through the next four innings and faced only twelve men. Pat Malone, who relieved Root after Gehrig's second homer, also managed to keep the Yankees from further scoring, although he passed three of the first four men he faced, but Malone was lifted for a pinch hitter and Jackie May came on the scene in the eighth.

Fumbles Send May Out

May's arrival indicated the desperation to which the Cubs had been driven. A failure through the season, he was the only left-hander on the Chicago staff and Grimm probably felt he might as well use him. He had tried every means of stopping the Yanks without success, and a left-hander might survive.

As a matter of fact, May wouldn't have been scored on except for two glaring muffs of pop flies in the ninth inning. Hartnett went into the middle of the diamond for one that Lazzeri lifted and let it bounce out of his glove. Herman went back for one that Dickey raised and dropped it. Then Chapman stung a double down the left field foul line and the Yankees' seventh run was scored. Lyle Tinning finished the game, relieving May.

When Hartnett hit a home run to start the ninth and Jurges singled to left a spark of hope was kindled in the hearts of the crowd, but Joe McCarthy wasn't taking any chances. In spite of the fact that Pipgras had pitched brilliantly, allowing only seven hits up to the ninth, Herb Pennock was beckoned from the bullpen, where he had been warming up through the game.

Pennock Quells Rally

With the arrival of Pennock the Cubs' last hope dwindled and died. He struck out Hemsley, who batted for Tinning, tossed out Herman and forced English to roll weakly to Gehrig for the final out of the game.

For the third time in three games the Cubs outhit the Yankees in the matter of mere numbers, getting nine safe blows to eight for the New Yorkers, but the savage swats of Ruth and Gehrig were worth innumerable singles. After each had hit two homers the pitchers' orders to cast caution to the winds must have been rescinded, for the next time Ruth came to bat Malone threw four balls right at him and let him walk.

Gehrig was called out on a third strike in his next appearance, and the crowd found some solace in that sight, but they would have liked it so much more if only it had been the arrogant, self-confident, swaggering Ruth, who had laughed at them hostilely and jolted them into glum silence with the power of his bat.

McCarthy announced tonight that he would send Johnny Allen, who led the American League in his first season as a major leaguer, against the Cubs tomorrow with the hope of ending the series. Grimm is going back to his first selection, Black Guy Bush, who was beaten, 12 to 6, in the opening encounter. The Cubs have small hope of winning the series and they probably would consider just one victory a triumph worth celebrating.

Box Score of Third Game of World Series

NEW YORK (A. L.)

	ab	r	h	po	a	e
Combs cf	5	1	0	1	0	0
Sewell, 3b	2	1	0	2	2	0
Ruth lf	4	2	2	2	0	0
Gehrig, 1b	5	2	2	13	1	0
Lazzeri, 2b	4	1	0	3	4	1
Dickey, c	4	0	1	2	1	0
Chapman, rf	4	0	2	0	0	0
Crosetti, ss	4	0	1	4	4	0
PIPGRAS, p	5	0	0	0	0	0
PENNOCK, p	0	0	0	0	1	0
Totals	37	7	8	27	13	1

CHICAGO (N. L.)

	ab	r	h	po	a	e
Herman, 2b	4	1	0	1	2	1
English, 3b	4	0	0	0	3	0
Cuyler, rf	4	1	3	1	0	0
Stephenson, lf	4	0	1	1	0	0
J. Moore, cf	3	1	0	3	0	0
Grimm, 1b	4	0	1	8	0	0
Hartnett, c	4	1	1	10	1	1
Jurges ss	4	1	3	3	3	2
ROOT, p	2	0	0	0	0	0
MALONE, p	0	0	0	0	0	0
*Gudat	1	0	0	0	0	0
MAY, p	0	0	0	0	0	0
TINNING p	0	0	0	0	0	0
†Koenig	0	0	0	0	0	0
‡Hemsley	1	0	0	0	0	0
Totals	35	5	9	27	9	4

*Batted for Malone in seventh inning.

†Batted for Tinning in ninth inning.

‡Batted for Koenig in ninth inning.

New York..3 0 1 0 2 0 0 0 1—7
Chicago ...1 0 2 1 0 0 0 0 1—5

Runs batted in—Ruth (4), Cuyler (2), Gehrig (2), Grimm, Chapman, Hartnett. Two-base hits—Cuyler, Grimm, Jurges, Chapman. Home runs—Ruth (2), Gehrig (2), Cuyler, Hartnett. Stolen base—Jurges. Double plays—Sewell, Lazzeri and Gehrig; Herman, Jurges and Grimm. Left on bases—New York, 11; Chicago, 6. Bases on balls—Off Root, 3 (Sewell, 2; Chapman); off Malone, 4 (Lazzeri, Dickey, Crosetti, Ruth); off Pipgras, 3 (Herman, Moore, English). Struck out—By Root, 4 (Lazzeri, Pipgras, 2; Combs); by Malone, 4; (Pipgras, 2; Ruth, Chapman); by May, 1 (Combs); by Tinning, 1 (Pipgras); by Pipgras, 1 (Root); by Pennock, 1 (Hemsley). Hits and runs—Off Root, 6 hits, 6 runs in 4 1-3 innings; off Malone, 1 hit, 0 runs in 2 2-3; off May, 1 hit, 1 run in 1 1-3; off Tinning, 0 hits, 0 runs in 2-3; off Pipgras, 9 hits, 5 runs in 8 (none out in 9th); off Pennock, 0 runs, 0 hits in 1. Hit by pitcher—By May (Sewell). Winning pitcher—Pipgras. Losing pitcher—Root. Umpires—Van Graflan (A. L.), plate; Magerkurth (N. L.), first base; Dinneen (A. L.), second base; Klem (N. L.), third base. Time—2:11.

Jurges Sliding Home With the Run That Tied the Score

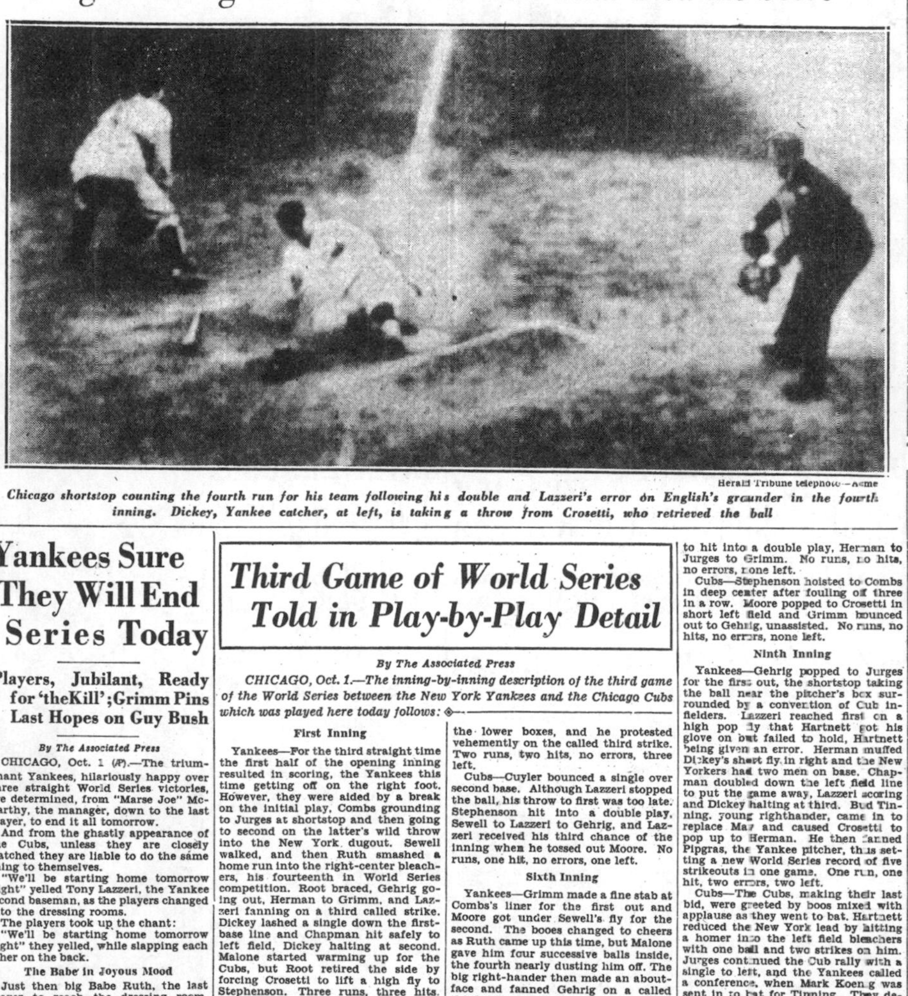

Herald Tribune telephoto—Acme

Chicago shortstop counting the fourth run for his team following his double and Lazzeri's error on English's grounder in the fourth inning. Dickey, Yankee catcher, at left, is taking a throw from Crosetti, who retrieved the ball

Yankees Sure They Will End Series Today

Players, Jubilant, Ready for 'the Kill'; Grimm Pins Last Hopes on Guy Bush

By The Associated Press

CHICAGO, Oct. 1 (AP).—The triumphant Yankees, hilariously happy over three straight World Series victories, are determined, from "Marse Joe" McCarthy, the manager, down to the last player, to end it all tomorrow.

And from the ghastly appearance of the Cubs, unless they are closely watched they are liable to do the same thing to themselves.

"We'll be starting home tomorrow night" yelled Tony Lazzeri, the Yankee second baseman, as the players changed into the dressing rooms.

The players took up the chant:

"We'll be starting home tomorrow night" they yelled, while slapping each other on the back.

The Babe in Joyous Mood

Just then big Babe Ruth, the last player to reach the dressing room, shoved his 230-pound frame through the door. The Babe, who belted two of the longest home runs ever made in Wrigley Field, today was gloriously happy. He first asked questions and answered them himself with a big grin on his face.

"Did Mr. Ruth chase those guys back in the dugout?" he asked.

Then he responded:

"I'll say Mr. Ruth did."

Ruth was referring to the time he was at bat in the fifth inning, just before he slammed that last home run out to the flagpole in center field. That clout went exactly 450 feet.

Before he connected for that blow, there were two strikes on him, and the Cub players, yelling from their dugout, were making uncomplimentary remarks. The Babe waved them back to their dugout, raising his two fingers to tell them that there were two strikes on him and to watch out. He connected with the next ball for his second homer and the Cubs crawled farther back in their dugout.

McCarthy sat as if in a trance. Players spoke to him, but he did not reply. He stared out the open window as if he believed it could hardly be true that he had conquered his former players three games in a row.

Then he suddenly blurted out:

"I'm going to try to end it tomorrow night. Johnny Allen will be my pitching selection."

Grimm Counts on Bush

The Cubs' dressing room wasn't exactly like a funeral establishment, but it was the next thing to it. The players filed in sober-faced and went about the task of changing their clothes without much comment.

"Too much Ruth and Gehrig," said Charley Grimm, the manager, in summing up the defeat.

"But we're not licked yet," he snapped. "They have got to beat us tomorrow, and then we'll be whipped. I haven't quit, neither have my men, and we'll be out there fighting tomorrow.

Grimm said he would rely on Guy Bush to stop the Yankees tomorrow, if there is any way of stopping them.

Charley Root, pitching at the time Ruth made his two homers, declared the big Babe wasn't human.

"The first one Babe hit," Root said, "was a fast ball going outside. The second one was a change of pace breaking slowly on the outside. If I had it to do over again, I'd throw the same kind of ball to Ruth and then duck."

Portland Wins Coast Pennant

PORTLAND, Ore., Oct. 1 (AP).—Portland has won the 1932 Pacific Coast League pennant just two days before the end of the season. The standing:

	W.	L.	Pct.		W.	L.	Pct.
Portland	109	77	.586	Los Ang.	94	92	.505
Hollywood	105	81	.565	Seattle	89	93	.489
Sac'mento	100	87	.535	Oakland	79	106	.427
San Fran.	94	89	.514	Missions	70	115	.378

Lazzeri and Girl Fan Divide Fielding Glory

By a Staff Correspondent

CHICAGO, Oct. 1.—Tony Lazzeri was mixed up in three of the five fielding features today. He made a sparkling catch in short centerfield of a high twisting fly hit by English in the fourth, and he glided gracefully over behind second to grab a grounder by Jurges, whom he tossed out, in the sixth.

Then he made possible the most sensational catch of all when he hit a foul into the upper grandstand. A young woman speared the ball with one upflung hand and held it. This catch drew the greatest applause of the day.

Grimm and Cuyler provided the other standout defensive plays. The Cub manager made a shoe-string catch of a hard hit liner from Combs's bat in the sixth and Kiki backed up against the right field screen to haul down Ruth's drive in the second.

Third Game of World Series Told in Play-by-Play Detail

By The Associated Press

CHICAGO, Oct. 1.—The inning-by-inning description of the third game of the World Series between the New York Yankees and the Chicago Cubs which was played here today follows:

First Inning

Yankees—For the third straight time the first half of the opening inning resulted in scoring, the Yankees this time getting off on the right foot. However, they were aided by a break on the initial play, Combs grounding to Jurges at shortstop and then going to second on the latter's wild throw into the New York dugout. Sewell walked, and then Ruth smashed a home run into the right-center bleachers, his fourteenth in World Series competition. Root braced, Gehrig going out, Herman to Grimm, and Lazzeri fanning on a third called strike. Dickey lashed a single down the first-base line and Chapman hit safely to left field, Dickey halting at second. Malone started warming up for the Cubs, but Root retired the side by forcing Crosetti to lift a high fly to Stephenson. Three runs, three hits, one error, two left.

Cubs—Pipgras, unsteady, walked Herman, and pitched three successive balls to English before the Cub batter took a called strike. After taking another called strike and fouling one off he flied out to Ruth. Cuyler batted a liner against the right-field screen for two bases, Herman scoring, and Stephenson grounded out, Crosetti to Herman, Cuyler holding second. Moore walked on four successive pitches, but Grimm failed to answer the plaints of the crowd, and bounced out, Crosetti to Gehrig. One run, one hit, no errors, two left.

Second Inning

Yankees—Root improved in this inning, only four men facing him. Pipgras struck out, Combs hoisted a long fly to Moore, who took it near the bleachers in left center, Sewell walked and Ruth flied out to Cuyler in right field after the count reached three and two. No runs, no hits, no errors, one left.

Cubs—Hartnett was out, Crosetti to Gehrig, but Jurges got one past Crosetti for a single. Root came to bat and received a big hand, but struck out swinging, although the Cubs protested that he moved his bat on the third strike merely to get out of the way of the pitch. With one and one on Herman, Jurges stole second. Herman ended the inning by flying out to Ruth near the foul line. No runs, one hit, no errors, one left.

Third Inning

Yankees—On the first pitched ball Gehrig clouted a home run high into the right field bleachers, his second of the series. Lazzeri was tossed out, Jurges to Grimm, the manager making a nice pick-up of the shortstop's low throw. Dickey lifted a high fly to Moore, and Chapman walked. Then, with Crosetti up, Chapman attempted to steal, but Jurges nailed him after a fine throw by Hartnett. One run, one hit, no errors, none left.

Cubs—English was out, Crosetti to Gehrig, but the Cubs kept in the ball game when Cuyler drove a homer into the right field bleachers. Stephenson dropped a Texas Leaguer into short right center. The Yankees had a chance to pull a double play when Moore grounded to Gehrig, who tossed to Crosetti in time to get Stephenson at second, but Moore beat the relay back to first. Grimm lashed a double through Chapman's legs, scoring Sewell. Two runs, three hits, no errors, one left.

Fourth Inning

Yankees—Root was close to his best in this stretch, retiring Pipgras and Combs on called third strikes after Crosetti bounced out, English to Grimm, for the first out. No runs, no hits, no errors, none left.

Cubs—The Cubs, fighting back hard, tied the score. Jurges hit to left field and reached second base as Ruth dashed in for a shoestring catch and came up only with the shoestring. It was scored as a double. Root grounded out, Sewell to Gehrig, Jurges holding second. Lazzeri made a spectacular catch over his shoulder of Herman's pop fly in short center field and on the next play he fumbled English's bounce, Jurges scoring and English reaching first. With two strikes and one ball on Cuyler, English was thrown out trying to steal second, Dickey to Lazzeri. One run, one hit, one error, none left.

Fifth Inning

Yankees—With the top of the batting order coming up, the New Yorkers relentlessly began an attack on Root that sent him to the showers. Sewell bounced out, Jurges to Grimm, and Ruth came up paying no attention to the boos of the crowd. With the count two and two, the Babe hit a high drive for a home run, the ball clearing the wire fence in deep center. Gehrig gave Root no rest, hitting the first pitch for another homer, the ball striking the flag pole a few feet inside the right field line. Malone replaced Root and after getting the first two balls over as strikes on Lazzeri, he issued four balls in a row. Dickey likewise walked after the count was three and two, and Chapman was tossed out, English to Grimm, each runner advancing a base. Grimm ordered Crosetti purposely passed and the bases were filled. Pipgras was called out on strikes. This spectacle afforded the crowd laughs on two occasions, for he broke his bat hitting a foul into the lower boxes, and he protested vehemently on the called third strike. Two runs, two hits, no errors, three left.

Cubs—Cuyler bounced a single over second base. Although Lazzeri stopped the ball, his throw to first was too late. Stephenson hit into a double play, Sewell to Lazzeri to Gehrig, and Lazzeri received his third chance of the inning when he tossed out Moore. No runs, one hit, no errors, one left.

Sixth Inning

Yankees—Grimm made a fine stab at Combs's liner for the first out and Moore got under Sewell's fly for the second. The booes changed to cheers as Ruth came up this time, but Malone gave him four successive balls inside, the fourth nearly dusting him off. The big right-hander then made an about-face and fanned Gehrig on a called third strike that cut the outside corner. No runs, no hits, no errors, one left.

Cubs—Grimm grounded out, Lazzeri to Gehrig. Hartnett popped up to Sewell in foul territory, and Jurges bounced over Pipgras's head and was called out on a close play, Lazzeri to Gehrig. Umpire Magerkurth reversed himself after momentarily calling Jurges safe. No runs, no hits, no errors, none left.

Seventh Inning

Yankees—Lazzeri bounced to English for the first out, and Dickey was safe at first when Grimm was pulled off the bag by Jurges's wide throw after fielding a grounder. Chapman fanned, swinging, after lacing a ball down the left-field line that was inches from being an extra-base blow. Crosetti smashed a single past English, Dickey stopped at second, but the Yankee rally halted as Pipgras fanned for the fourth time and tied the World Series record. No runs, one hit, one error, two left.

Cubs—Marvin Gudat entered the scene at this point as a pinch hitter for Malone, but he could do no better than pop to Crosetti. Gehrig retired Herman, unassisted, but English walked. Cuyler grounded to Crosetti, who picked up the ball after momentarily fumbling and stepped on second for the force-out. No runs, no hits, no errors, one left.

Eighth Inning

Yankees—Jakie May, southpaw, took up the twirling for the Cubs and struck out Combs. However, he hit Sewell with a pitched ball and caused Ruth to hit into a double play, Herman to Jurges to Grimm. No runs, no hits, no errors, none left.

Cubs—Stephenson hoisted to Combs in deep center after fouling off three in a row. Moore popped to Crosetti in short left field and Grimm bounced out to Gehrig, unassisted. No runs, no hits, no errors, none left.

Ninth Inning

Yankees—Gehrig popped to Jurges for the first out, the shortstop taking the ball near the pitcher's box surrounded by a convention of Cub infielders. Lazzeri reached first on a high pop fly that Hartnett got his glove on but failed to hold, Hartnett being given an error. Herman muffed Dickey's short fly in right and the New Yorkers had two men on base. Chapman doubled down the left field line to put the game away, Lazzeri scoring and Dickey halting at third. Bud Tinning, young righthander, came in to replace May and caused Crosetti to pop up to Herman. He then fanned Pipgras, the Yankee pitcher, thus setting a new World Series record of five strikeouts in one game. One run, one hit, two errors, two left.

Cubs—The Cubs, making their last bid, were greeted by boos mixed with applause as they went to bat. Hartnett reduced the New York lead by hitting a homer into the left field bleachers with one ball and two strikes on him. Jurges continued the Cub rally with a single to left, and the Yankees called a conference, when Mark Koenig was sent in to bat for Tinning. They decided to take out Pipgras and sent in Pennock, a southpaw, and this caused the Cubs to shift their strategy once more. Hemsley, a righthanded hitter, batted in place of Koenig and went out on strikes, two of them slow balls. Herman bounced out, Pennock to Gehrig, Jurges reaching second. English came up and on the first strike Jurges went to third unmolested. With the count two and two English grounded out to Gehrig, unassisted, to end the game. One run, two hits, no errors, one left.

Official Series Figures For First Three Games

The official figures for the third game of the World Series between the New York Yankees and the Chicago Cubs and the totals for the three games, compared with the same figures last year, follow:

THIRD GAME TOTALS

	1932	1931
Attend'ce (pd).	49,986	32,295
Receipts	$211,912.00	$152,735.00
Players' share.	108,075.12	77,894.85
Clubs' share	18,012.52	25,964.95
Leagues' share.	18,012.52	25,964.95
Advisory council's share	31,786.80	22,910.25

TOTALS FOR THREE GAMES

	1932	1931
Attend'ce (pd.)	142,154	106,771
Receipts	$501,324.00	$475,311.00
Players' share.	255,675.24	242,468.61
Clubs' share	121,250.10	80,867.87
Leagues' share.	121,250.10	80,867.87
Advisory council's share	75,198.60	71,296.65

Composite Score of First Three Games

Chicago Cubs

	G.	AB.	R.	H.	2B.	3B.	HR.	SH.	SB.	BB.	SO.	Bat. aver.	PO.	A.	E.	Field. aver.
Herman, 2b	3	13	4	3	1	0	0	0	0	1	2	.231	3	10	1	.923
English, 3b	3	12	1	2	0	0	0	0	0	2	2	.167	2	4	1	.857
Cuyler, rf	3	13	2	5	1	1	1	0	1	0	2	.385	4	0	0	1.000
Stephenson, lf	3	13	1	6	1	0	0	0	0	0	[illegible]	.462	3	0	0	1.000
J. Moore, cf	2	7	1	0	0	0	0	0	0	2	1	.000	4	0	0	1.000
Demaree, cf	1	4	0	1	0	0	0	0	0	0	[illegible]	.250	1	0	0	1.000
Grimm, 1b	3	11	0	3	1	0	0	0	0	2	2	.273	24	1	0	1.000
Hartnett, c	3	12	2	4	2	0	1	0	0	1	3	.333	23	5	1	.966
*Koenig, ss	2	4	1	1	0	1	0	0	0	1	[illegible]	.250	4	3	0	1.000
Jurges, ss	2	7	1	3	1	0	0	1	1	0	[illegible]	.429	7	6	2	.867
Bush, p	1	1	0	0	0	0	0	0	0	1	[illegible]	.000	0	2	0	1.000
Grimes, p	1	1	0	0	0	0	0	0	0	0	1	.000	0	0	0	.000
Smith, p	1	0	0	0	0	0	0	0	0	0	[illegible]	.000	0	0	0	.000
Warneke, p	1	3	0	0	0	0	0	0	0	0	3	.000	0	2	0	1.000
Root, p	1	2	0	0	0	0	0	0	0	0	1	.000	0	0	0	.000
Malone, p	1	0	0	0	0	0	0	0	0	0	[illegible]	.000	0	0	0	.000
May, p	1	0	0	0	0	0	0	0	0	0	[illegible]	.000	0	0	0	.000
Tinning, p	1	0	0	0	0	0	0	0	0	0	[illegible]	.000	0	0	0	.000
*Gudat	2	2	0	0	0	0	0	0	0	0	1	.000	0	0	0	.000
*Hemsley	2	2	0	0	0	0	0	0	0	0	2	.000	0	0	0	.000
Totals		107	13	28	7	2	2	1	2	10	[illegible]	.271	75	33	5	.956

*Pinch hitter.

New York Yankees

	G.	AB.	R.	H.	2B.	3B.	HR.	SH.	SB.	BB.	SO.	Bat. aver.	PO.	A.	E.	Field. aver.
Combs, cf	3	12	4	3	1	0	0	0	0	2	[illegible]	.250	8	0	0	1.000
Sewell, 3b	3	9	3	2	0	0	0	0	0	4	[illegible]	.222	4	4	0	1.000
Ruth, rf, lf	3	10	6	4	0	0	2	0	0	4	[illegible]	.400	6	0	1	.857
Gehrig, 1b	3	13	7	7	0	0	3	0	0	1	[illegible]	.538	25	2	0	1.000
Lazzeri, 2b	3	12	2	2	0	0	0	0	0	1	[illegible]	.167	7	7	1	.933
Dickey, c	3	10	0	4	0	0	0	0	0	2	[illegible]	.400	21	1	0	1.000
Chapman, lf, rf	3	12	1	3	1	0	0	0	0	1	4	.250	2	1	0	1.000
Crosetti, ss	3	9	1	1	0	0	0	1	0	2	[illegible]	.111	7	7	2	.875
Ruffing, p	1	4	0	0	0	0	0	0	0	0	1	.000	1	3	0	1.000
Gomez, p	1	3	0	0	0	0	0	0	0	0	[illegible]	.000	0	3	0	1.000
Pipgras, p	1	5	0	0	0	0	0	0	0	0	5	.000	0	0	0	.000
Pennock, p	1	0	0	0	0	0	0	0	0	0	[illegible]	.000	0	1	0	1.000
Totals		99	24	26	2	0	5	1	0	17	20	.263	81	29	4	.965

Runs batted in—Stephenson (4), Dickey (4), Chapman (5), Gehrig (5), Combs (2), Ruth (5), Lazzeri, Koenig, Herman, Sewell, Demaree, Cuyler (2), Grimm, Hartnett.

Double plays—Herman, Koenig and Grimm; Herman, Jurges and Grimm (3); Warneke, Hartnett and Jurges; Hartnett and Herman; Sewell, Lazzeri and Gehrig.

Left on bases—Chicago, 24; New York, 20.

Pitching Records

	G.	Ins.	Hits off	Runs off	BB.	SO.	WP.	HB.	W.	L.	Pct.
Bush	1	5 1-3	3	8	5	2	0	0	0	1	.000
Grimes	1	1 2-3	3	3	1	0	1	0	0	0	.000
Smith	1	1	3	3	1	0	1	1	0	0	.000
Warneke	1	8	10	5	4	7	0	0	0	1	.000
Root	1	4 1-3	6	6	3	4	0	0	0	1	.000
Malone	1	2 2-3	1	0	4	4	0	0	0	0	.000
May	1	1 1-3	1	1	0	1	0	1	0	0	.000
Tinning	1	2-3	0	0	0	1	0	0	0	0	.000
Ruffing	1	9	10	6	6	10	0	0	1	0	1.000
Gomez	1	9	9	2	1	8	0	0	1	0	1.000
Pipgras	1	8	9	5	3	1	0	0	1	0	1.000
Pennock	1	1	0	0	0	1	0	0	0	0	.000

Umpires—Dinneen and Van Graflan (American League); Klem and Magerkurth (National League).

Time of games—2:31 (first game), 1:46 (second game), 2:11 (third game)

Gov. Roosevelt Forgotten Man In Hit Landslide

Nominee Is Welcomed by 51,000, but Bandwagon Follows Ruth and Gehrig

CHICAGO, Oct. 1.—A Presidential nominee couldn't compete with the twin thrillers, Babe Ruth and Lou Gehrig, in the matter of popularity here today. Governor Franklin D. Roosevelt of New York attended the third game of the World Series, but the eyes of 51,000 spectators were not for him.

Only when he made his entrance, during the fielding practice, did he hold the spotlight. Necks turned and eyes peered as he made his way slowly to a box near the Yankees' dugout, but once the game was under way he was the Forgotten Man.

Through the nine innings he watched the performance before him with eager interest, following the play and half rising in his seat as Ruth hit his second home run of the day. His face was wreathed in smiles.

Whether the Democratic nominee was completely a Yankee fan because he governed the State of New York or whether he was simply one of the millions who have been won over to the cause of Babe Ruth couldn't be determined, but when the game was over and the crowd dispersed he departed with the appearance of having enjoyed what he had seen anyway.

Not only the weather but the wind was perfect—at least for the Yankee heavy artillery. A brisk breeze blew from the plate toward right field and the temporary seats that extended out into the street were an easy target.

Some of the fans who sat in the bleachers had been sitting in the streets since Wednesday night and weren't sure whether it was worth waiting for after all.

They said through the season that the Cubs were a great team because they won close ones, but the Yanks have found a remedy for that—they just don't make 'em close.

The crowd of 51,000 jammed every available seat in Wrigley Field, while a crowd of 51,000 just rattled around loose in the Yankee stadium on Thursday.

Only the entrance of Governor Franklin D. Roosevelt, surrounded by a bodyguard in blue, distracted the fans' attention from the master maulers.

There was the usual band, bunting and babble.

The parade to the flagpole was made over a long, roundabout route, but the Yankees have become accustomed to walking. Bush and Warneke gave them plenty of practice.

Kiki Cuyler's West Point training asserted itself during the parade. He was the only ball player who marched in time to the music.

As a lead-off man Billy Herman has a perfect record in this series. He has been on base his first time at bat in each game, first with a single, next with a double and today with a pass.

The Yankees didn't let the fans linger long in ignorance of what they looked like. Eight of 'em appeared at the plate in the first inning.

When Sewell walked in the first inning and scored on Ruth's first homer eleven Yankees had been passed in the series and ten of them had tallied, showing again that "He also serves who only stands and waits."

Some morbid-minded fan came loaded with a pocketful of lemons and pelted the players with childish glee. In his delirium he didn't seem to know against which team he wanted to vent his wrath, for he hit Charley Root in the back with one heave and hurled another at Babe Ruth.

Chapman made his first attempt to steal a base after walking with two out in the third. He was barely nipped by a perfect throw from Hartnett to Jurges.

The Cubs gave Koenig only half a cut on the World Series money, but they didn't even give him that much of a cut at the plate in the ninth. He went to the plate to bat for Tinning, but when Pennock appeared from the bullpen, relieving Pipgras, Hemsley was sent up to bat instead. He fanned.

Not a soul left the park until the last man was out. Maybe it was the memory of all the Cubs' ninth-inning victories that made them linger or maybe they just wanted to get their money's worth.

RICHARDS VIDMER.

Bears' Trunks Pushed Off Express by Illegal Rider

PHILADELPHIA, Oct. 1 (AP).—Somewhere in the Middle West the Newark baseball team of the International League is speeding on toward Minneapolis and the fourth game of the little world series, probably wondering what it is going to do for uniforms.

Four trunks, containing the team's uniforms, were found early today along the Pennsylvania Railroad tracks at Deans, N. J., and W. J. Chipman, of New York, is held here on the charge of illegal train riding after telling police he pushed the trunks off the train which carried the ball club West.

Chipman said he boarded the train in Newark, seeking a place to rest in the baggage car. He failed to find sufficient space for himself, police said he told them so he pushed four of the trunks off the train as it speeded on toward Trenton. He was arrested when the train arrived here.

Chipman was held in $400 bail for a further hearing October 7. One of the trunks, containing bats, balls and gloves, was sent West by airplane from Newark. Another with uniforms was shipped from North Philadelphia on an express train to Chicago.

Batting Order in 4th Game of World Series

CHICAGO, Oct. 1 (AP).—The probable batting order of the fourth game of the World Series at Wrigley Field tomorrow follows:

YANKEES (A. L.)	CUBS (N. L.)
Combs, cf.	Herman, 2b.
Sewell, 3b.	English, 3b.
Ruth, lf.	Cuyler, rf.
Gehrig, 1b.	Stephenson, lf.
Lazzeri, 2b.	Moore, cf.
Dickey, c.	Grimm, 1b.
Chapman, rf.	Hartnett, c.
Crosetti, ss.	Jurges, ss.
ALLEN, p.	BUSH, p.

Umpires—Magerkurth (N. L.), plate; Dinneen (A. L.), first base; Klem (N. L.), second base; Van Graflan (A. L.), third base. Time of game, 1:30 (2:30 Eastern standard).

Major League Averages

American League

CLUB BATTING

Club.	G.	AB.	R.	H.	RBI.	SB.	Pct.
Phila'phia	154	5536	981	1606	905	38	.290
New York	156	5477	992	1575	943	77	.288
Wash'gton	154	5501	840	1566	771	71	.285
Cleveland	153	5414	845	1453	772	53	.285
St. Louis	154	5442	735	1504	679	69	.276
Detroit	153	5416	799	1489	720	105	.275
Chicago	152	5327	667	1425	602	86	.268
Boston	154	5293	561	1330	530	48	.251

CLUB FIELDING

Club.	G.	PO.	A.	E.	DP.	Pct.
Washington	154	4251	1742	125	155	.980
Philadelphia	154	4167	1720	125	143	.979
New York	156	4223	1615	188	130	.969
Cleveland	153	4105	1801	190	129	.969
Detroit	153	4085	1776	187	153	.969
St. Louis	154	4134	1788	194	153	.968
Boston	154	4063	1966	230	157	.963
Chicago	152	4043	1899	268	174	.957

INDIVIDUAL BATTING

Player, club.	G.	AB.	R.	H.	RBI.	SB.	Pct.
Alexander, Det., Bos.	124	392	59	144	60	4	.367
Foxx, Phila	154	585	150	213	167	4	.364
Hoag, N. Y.	46	53	18	19	7	1	.358
Hebert, St. L.	35	34	5	12	1	0	.353
Kingdon, Wash	18	34	10	12	3	3	.353
Gehrig, N. Y.	156	595	138	208	151	4	.350
Manush, Wash.	149	624	125	214	114	7	.343
Ruth, N. Y.	133	459	120	157	136	2	.342
Coleman, Phila.	26	73	13	25	12	1	.342
Cramer, Phila.	92	385	73	129	43	3	.335
Harris, Wash.	81	157	26	51	29	4	.325
Simmons, Phil.	154	668	145	216	148	4	.323
Walker, Det.	127	480	72	155	77	28	.323
Combs, N. Y.	144	590	142	190	65	3	.322
Rice, Wash.	106	287	59	92	31	8	.321
Cronin, Wash.	143	555	95	177	120	7	.319
Ferrell, St. L.	126	438	67	139	63	5	.317
English, Chi.	24	63	7	20	8	0	.317
Cissell, Cl., Chi.	143	586	86	185	96	18	.316
Jolley, Chi., Bos.	149	573	60	181	109	1	.316
Sullivan, Chi.	93	307	31	97	44	1	.316
Kimsey, St. L., Chi.	41	19	2	6	1	0	.316
Averill, Cleve.	153	631	116	198	123	5	.314
Vosmik, Cleve.	153	621	105	195	97	3	.314
Dickey, N. Y.	108	424	67	131	83	2	.309
Scharein, St. L.	81	301	43	92	43	4	.306
Ruffing, N. Y.	55	124	20	38	20	0	.306
Burns, St. L.	149	613	109	187	69	17	.305
Haas, Phila.	143	558	90	170	63	2	.305
R'ynolds, Wash.	102	406	54	124	63	9	.305
Porter, Cleve.	146	628	106	191	58	2	.304
Lazzeri, N. Y.	142	511	78	154	111	10	.302
Rommel, Phila.	17	20	5	6	1	0	.300
Chapman, N.Y.	151	583	101	174	108	38	.299
Stone, Det.	145	582	105	174	105	2	.299
Goslin, St. L.	150	572	88	171	102	12	.299
Burnett, Cleve.	129	512	81	153	51	2	.299
Maple, Wash.	44	47	9	14	7	0	.298
Gehringer, Det.	152	618	94	183	100	10	.296
Morgan, Cleve.	144	533	96	157	66	7	.295
Cochrane, Phil.	139	516	118	152	109	0	.295
F. Schulte, St. L.	146	565	107	166	73	5	.294
Fothergill, Chi.	116	347	36	102	50	4	.294
Goldstein, Det.	16	17	3	5	3	0	.294
Miller, Phila.	95	307	40	90	58	9	.293
Hayworth, Det.	109	340	41	99	46	1	.291
Berry, Bos., Chi.	82	258	33	75	40	3	.291
Jenkins, St. L.	25	62	5	18	5	0	.290
Kuhel, Wash.	101	349	52	101	52	6	.289
West, Wash.	146	552	88	159	80	3	.288
Seeds, Cl., Chi.	118	438	53	126	43	5	.288
Byrd, N. Y.	104	215	48	62	30	1	.288
Weaver, Wash.	44	94	13	27	13	0	.287
Spognarti, Bos.	17	35	9	10	1	0	.286
Campbell, Chi., St. L.	147	608	86	173	86	7	.285
M'Nair, Phila.	135	554	89	158	92	4	.285
Kamm, Cleve.	148	522	75	149	82	6	.285
Webb, Bs., Det.	140	531	72	151	78	1	.284
Garms, St. L.	34	134	20	38	8	4	.284
Selph, Chi.	116	396	50	112	49	7	.283
Earnshaw, Phil.	36	92	10	26	9	0	.283
Levey, St. L.	152	569	59	160	61	6	.281
Johnson, Det., Bos.	153	545	102	153	66	21	.281
Grube, Chi.	93	278	36	78	30	6	.281
Rhiel, Det.	85	250	30	70	37	2	.280
Myer, Wash.	143	577	120	161	56	12	.279
Appling, Chi.	139	485	66	134	63	9	.276
Sewell, N. Y.	125	503	96	138	68	0	.274
Hadley, Chi., St. L.	43	84	4	23	6	0	.274
Kress, St. L., Ch.	149	567	83	155	65	6	.273
Kerr, Wash.	52	132	14	36	16	3	.273
Heving, Phila.	33	77	14	21	10	0	.273
Davis, Det.	141	592	92	159	76	11	.269
Dykes, Phila.	153	558	70	150	90	8	.269
Rogell, Det.	144	557	88	150	60	15	.269
Schuble, Det.	102	340	58	90	51	14	.265
White, Det.	80	280	26	55	23	6	.265
Judge, Wash.	83	290	44	76	30	4	.262
Pickering, Bos.	132	456	46	119	41	3	.261
Hayes, Chi.	117	475	51	123	53	5	.260
Lyons, Chi.	48	73	12	19	9	0	.260
Bluege, Wash.	149	510	63	132	62	8	.259
Oliver, Bos.	122	455	40	118	37	1	.259
Funk, Chi.	122	441	59	114	41	17	.259
Storti, St. L.	53	193	18	50	28	1	.259
Hogsett, Det.	47	55	11	14	4	0	.255
Russell, Bs., Cle.	31	51	3	13	6	0	.255
Watwood, Chi., Bos.	108	315	31	80	31	7	.254
Bishop, Phila.	114	407	89	103	36	2	.253
Sewell, Cleve.	87	301	36	76	50	4	.253
Bengough, St. L.	54	139	13	35	15	0	.252
Brown, Cleve.	39	100	13	25	17	0	.250
Blue, Chi.	112	373	51	93	43	18	.248
Williams, Phil.	63	218	30	54	26	0	.248
Olson, Bos.	114	405	57	100	25	1	.247
Myatt, Cleve.	82	251	45	62	44	2	.247
M'tague, Cleve.	67	192	29	47	23	3	.245
Fischer, Wash., St. L.	36	49	4	12	0	0	.245
Whitehill, Det.	33	90	3	22	7	0	.244
Welch, Bos.	23	37	5	9	3	0	.243
Ferrell, Cleve.	55	128	14	31	18	0	.242

PITCHING RECORDS

Pitcher, club.	G.	H.	BB.	SO.	W.	L.	Pct.
McAfee, Wash.	8	47	22	9	6	1	.857
Allen, N. Y.	33	164	74	108	17	4	.810
Krause, Phila.	20	68	23	15	4	1	.800
Gomez, N. Y.	37	266	105	174	24	7	.774
Ruffing, N. Y.	35	219	115	190	18	7	.720
Grove, Phila.	44	269	79	188	25	10	.714
Brown, N. Y.	19	58	29	32	5	2	.714
Freitas, Phila.	23	150	47	28	12	5	.706
Weaver, Wash.	43	234	112	80	22	10	.688
Crowder, Wash.	50	319	77	99	26	13	.667
Marberry, Wash.	53	201	72	67	8	4	.667
Pennock, N. Y.	22	191	38	49	9	5	.643
Pipgras, N. Y.	32	237	86	110	16	9	.640
Ferrell, Cleve.	38	299	103	104	23	13	.639
Walberg, Phila.	41	295	193	94	17	10	.630
Kimsey, St. L., Chi.	40	94	39	20	5	3	.625
Gregory, Chi.	33	125	51	39	5	3	.625
Hudlin, Cleve.	33	200	55	62	12	8	.600
Goldstein, Det.	16	63	41	14	3	2	.600
Earnshaw, Phila.	36	261	94	112	19	13	.594
Connally, Cleve.	35	122	41	39	8	6	.571
Hildebrand, Clev.	27	127	62	48	8	6	.571
Brown, Cleve.	37	298	53	55	15	12	.556
Brown, Wash.	46	238	51	51	15	12	.556
Hogsett, Det.	47	202	64	57	11	9	.550
Bridges, Det.	34	178	120	112	14	12	.538
Harder, Cleve.	39	277	70	99	15	13	.536
Andrews, N. Y., Bos.	29	162	62	38	9	8	.529
Thomas, Chi., Wh.	31	176	61	48	11	10	.524
Blaeholder, St. L.	42	300	76	69	14	14	.500
Sorrell, Det.	32	233	77	78	14	14	.500
Mahaffey, Phila.	37	243	95	94	13	13	.500
Uhle, Det.	34	142	43	52	6	6	.500
Wells, N. Y.	22	40	12	13	3	3	.500
Kline, Bos.	45	203	76	31	11	13	.458
Cain, Phila.	10	42	28	23	3	4	.429
Stewart, St. L.	41	270	97	87	14	19	.424
Wyatt, Det.	43	228	101	80	9	13	.409
Hadley, Chi., St. L.	43	259	170	143	14	21	.400
Jones, Chi.	30	216	74	61	10	15	.400
Lyons, Chi.	33	244	72	57	10	15	.400
Gray, St. L.	52	248	60	77	8	12	.400
Fischer, Wash., St. L.	35	176	73	60	6	9	.400
Coffman, St. L., Wh.	31	159	51	31	6	9	.400
Moore, Bos., N. Y.	46	127	49	38	6	9	.400
Welch, Bos.	20	90	38	26	4	6	.400
MacFayden, Bos., N. Y.	29	228	70	64	8	15	.348
Burke, Wash.	22	98	44	32	3	6	.333
Daglia, Chi.	12	67	20	15	2	4	.333
Durham, Bos.	33	180	47	51	6	13	.316
Russell, Bos., Cle.	29	205	42	36	6	14	.300
Gaston, Chi.	28	183	71	45	7	17	.292
Marrow, Det.	18	70	30	30	2	5	.286
Weiland, Bos.	43	233	97	64	6	16	.273
Carway, Chi.	19	81	37	14	2	6	.250
Frasier, Chi.	29	180	71	34	3	13	.188
Rhodes, N.Y., Bos.	22	107	52	34	2	10	.167
Faber, Chi.	42	122	36	21	2	11	.154
Michaels, Bos.	28	101	27	16	1	6	.143
Hebert, St. L.	35	145	44	31	1	12	.077

National League

CLUB BATTING

Club.	G.	AB.	R.	H.	RBI.	SB.	Pct.
Phila'phia	154	5509	844	1606	776	74	.292
Pittsburgh	154	5430	701	1543	649	73	.284
Brooklyn	154	5432	752	1535	703	62	.283
Chicago	154	5463	715	1519	666	49	.278
New York	154	5544	755	1527	713	29	.275
St. Louis	156	5448	684	1466	619	92	.269
Boston	155	5504	645	1465	589	37	.266
Cincinnati	155	5447	575	1427	541	33	.262

CLUB FIELDING

Club.	G.	PO.	A.	E.	DP.	Pct.
Boston	155	4243	1900	156	150	.975
Chicago	154	4199	1942	174	149	.972
Cincinnati	155	4138	1835	175	122	.972
Brooklyn	154	4151	1961	185	164	.971
St. Louis	156	4178	1741	176	150	.971
New York	154	4123	1903	192	141	.969
Phila'phia	154	4117	1829	196	132	.968
Pittsburgh	154	4098	1630	187	130	.968

Triple plays—Boston and Brooklyn.

INDIVIDUAL BATTING

Player, Club.	G.	AB.	R.	H.	RBI.	SB.	Pct.
O'Doul, Bklyn.	148	595	119	218	92	12	.366
Rosenfeld, Bkn.	35	39	8	14	7	2	.359
Koenig, Chi.	33	102	15	36	11	0	.353
Terry, N. Y.	154	644	124	225	116	4	.349
Medwick, St. L.	26	106	13	37	12	3	.349
Klein, Phila.	154	650	154	225	134	20	.346
Hafey, Cin.	83	254	34	87	35	4	.343
P. Waner, Pitts.	154	630	109	215	78	13	.341
Hurst, Phila.	150	589	108	197	141	10	.340
V. Davis, Phil.	125	401	45	135	71	2	.337
Orsatti, St. L.	101	374	43	126	42	5	.337
L. Waner, Pitts.	134	565	90	188	38	6	.333
Brickell, Phila.	45	66	9	22	2	2	.333
Traynor, Pitts.	135	512	74	169	67	6	.330
Herman, Cin.	148	577	87	188	89	7	.326
Stephen'n, Chi.	147	582	86	188	87	8	.323
Jordan, Bos.	49	212	27	68	28	1	.321
Ott, N. Y.	154	565	119	180	122	6	.319
Taylor, Ch., Bkn.	121	317	87	133	50	14	.319
Vaughan, Pitts.	129	497	69	158	61	9	.318
Herman, Chi.	154	655	101	204	52	14	.311
Watkins, St. L.	127	458	68	142	63	17	.310
G. Davis, Phi.	137	576	101	178	57	17	.309
Grimm, Chi.	149	569	66	176	79	2	.309
Bartell, Phila.	154	615	115	189	54	7	.307
Berger, Bos.	145	602	91	185	72	5	.307
Clancy, Bklyn.	53	196	14	60	15	0	.306
Lombardi, Cin.	118	413	44	126	69	0	.305
J. Moore, N. Y.	86	361	53	110	26	3	.305
Hen'k, St. L., Cin.	122	470	63	143	45	4	.304
Worthin'n, Bos.	105	434	61	132	61	1	.304
Thurston, Bkn.	29	56	7	17	5	0	.304
Stripp, Bklyn.	138	534	94	162	64	14	.303
Moore, Chi.	119	443	59	134	63	4	.303
Lee, Phila.	149	596	75	180	83	6	.302
Fred'k, Bklyn.	118	384	54	115	57	1	.299
Bottomley, St. L.	91	311	45	93	47	2	.299
Whitney, Phila.	154	625	92	186	122	8	.298
Fullis, N. Y.	96	235	35	70	21	1	.298
Wilson, Bkln.	135	481	78	143	122	2	.297
Holland, Bos.	39	156	15	46	8	1	.295
Moore, Bos.	107	351	41	103	41	1	.294
Frisch, St. L.	115	486	58	142	59	18	.292
Leslie, N. Y.	77	76	6	22	16	0	.289
Grantham, Cin.	126	493	81	144	37	8	.292
Cuyler, Chi.	110	445	59	130	77	9	.292
Hogan, N. Y.	140	502	36	144	74	0	.287
Lucas, Cin.	78	150	13	43	18	0	.287
Comorosky, Pit.	118	371	54	106	47	7	.286
Dudley, Phila.	23	14	5	4	2	0	.286
Piet, Pitts.	154	573	65	162	82	20	.283
Mancuso, St. L.	103	309	25	87	43	0	.282
Cuccinello, Bk.	154	596	73	167	77	4	.280
Roettger, Cin.	106	348	27	97	43	0	.279
Collins, St. L.	149	550	82	153	91	4	.278
Puccinelli, St. L.	31	108	17	30	12	1	.278
Critz, N. Y.	151	659	90	182	49	3	.276
Adams, St. L.	31	127	22	35	13	0	.276
Wright, Bklyn.	127	447	50	122	61	4	.273
Grace, Pitts.	115	392	41	107	56	8	.273
Zachary, Bos.	33	77	5	21	7	0	.273
Urbanski, Bos.	136	562	80	153	45	7	.272
Crabtree, Cin.	109	402	38	109	30	2	.271
Lindstr'm, N.Y.	144	596	83	161	91	6	.270
Hartnett, Chi.	121	408	52	110	54	0	.270
Spohrer, Bos.	104	333	31	90	34	2	.270
English, Chi.	127	522	70	140	47	5	.268
Gelbert, St. L.	122	455	61	122	44	8	.268
Ford, St. L.-Bos.	41	97	9	26	6	0	.268
Lopez, Bklyn.	126	404	44	108	43	4	.267
Moore, N. Y.	36	86	9	23	5	1	.267
Reese, St. L.	90	130	38	82	24	4	.265
Collins, Phila.	43	68	9	18	6	0	.265
Rixey, Cin.	25	34	2	9	1	0	.265
Suhr, Pitts.	154	581	79	153	81	7	.263
Vergez, N. Y.	118	373	42	98	45	1	.263
Hargrave, Bos.	82	217	20	57	33	1	.263
Padden, Pitts.	47	118	12	31	9	0	.263
Schulm'h, Bos.	119	405	47	106	58	5	.262
Heath'e, Cin. Ph.	38	42	10	11	5	0	.262
Cantwell, Bos.	37	50	3	13	4	0	.260
Dean, St. L.	47	97	10	25	12	0	.258
Hellmann, Cin.	15	31	3	8	6	0	.258
Barbee, Pitts.	97	327	37	84	57	1	.257
Richbourg, Chi.	44	148	22	38	20	0	.257
Picinich, Bklyn.	41	70	8	18	11	0	.257
Jackson, N. Y.	52	195	23	50	39	4	.256
Flowers, St. L.	67	147	35	63	17	7	.255
Koenecke, N. Y.	42	137	32	35	14	2	.255
Gudat, Chi.	60	94	15	24	15	0	.255
Mallon, Phila.	103	354	45	90	31	1	.254
Jurges, Chi.	115	396	40	100	53	1	.253
Marshall, N. Y.	68	226	18	57	28	1	.252
Akers, Bos.	37	96	8	24	17	0	.250
Demaree, Chi.	23	56	4	14	6	0	.250
Gibson, N. Y.	41	20	1	5	1	0	.250
J. Wilson, St. L.	92	274	36	68	27	9	.248
Leach, Bos.	84	222	21	55	29	1	.248
Pepper, St. L.	21	57	3	14	5	1	.246
Kelly, Bklyn.	64	201	23	49	22	0	.244
Grimes, Chi.	30	45	4	11	5	1	.244
Clark, Bos.	50	45	11	11	4	1	.244
O'Farrell, N. Y.	51	66	7	16	8	0	.242
Knothe, Bos.	88	341	45	82	34	6	.241
Slade, Bklyn.	79	249	23	60	20	3	.241
Hubbell, N. Y.	40	108	11	26	6	0	.241

PITCHING RECORDS

Pitcher, Club	G.	H.	BB.	SO.	W.	L.	Pct.
Warneke, Chi.	35	248	64	110	22	6	.786
Heimach, Bkn.	36	293	28	30	9	4	.692
Brown, Bos.	36	184	106	108	14	7	.667
Bell, N. Y.	35	132	16	25	8	4	.667
Swetonic, Pitts.	24	134	55	39	11	6	.647
Chagnon, Pitts.	30	141	34	53	5	5	.643
Bush, Chi.	40	259	71	71	19	11	.633
Hallahan, St. L.	25	169	69	108	12	7	.632
Clark, Bklyn.	40	282	49	99	20	12	.625
Rhem, St. L.-Ph.	32	225	59	53	15	9	.625
Tinning, Chi.	24	90	24	30	5	3	.625
Hubbell, N. Y.	40	259	40	138	18	11	.621
Root, Chi.	39	214	57	95	15	10	.600
Thurston, Bkln.	28	174	38	35	12	8	.600
Swift, Pitts.	39	206	30	64	14	10	.583
Meine, Pitts.	28	193	45	33	12	9	.571
Smith, Chi.	34	148	35	34	4	3	.571
Kremer, Pitts.	11	61	16	6	4	3	.571
Dean, St. L.	46	280	102	191	18	15	.545
Mungo, Bklyn.	39	224	116	106	13	11	.542
Cantwell, Bos.	37	133	33	33	13	11	.542
Betts, Bos.	31	228	36	33	13	11	.542
Collins, Phila.	43	230	63	64	14	12	.538
French, Pitts.	47	304	61	72	18	16	.529
Harris, Pitts.	37	178	38	62	10	9	.526
J. Elliott, Phila.	39	204	53	60	11	10	.524
Vance, Bklyn.	27	171	58	103	12	11	.522
Zachary, Bos.	32	231	55	68	12	11	.522
Benge, Phila.	41	247	58	88	13	12	.520
Brandt, Bos.	35	272	53	78	16	16	.500
Fitzsim'ns, N.Y.	35	277	83	67	11	11	.500
Hansen, Phila.	39	234	50	54	10	11	.500
Shaute, Bklyn.	34	145	21	32	7	7	.500
Frank'se, Bos.	27	112	35	35	5	5	.500
Rixey, Cin.	25	108	16	13	5	5	.500
Lindsey, St. L.	33	94	38	29	3	3	.500
Malone, Chi.	37	222	73	124	15	17	.469
Johnson, Cin.	42	246	54	92	13	15	.464
Holley, Phila.	34	246	56	87	12	14	.462
Luque, N. Y.	38	128	32	32	6	7	.462
Schum'er, N. Y.	27	115	39	38	5	6	.455
Stout, St. L.	36	87	28	32	4	5	.444
Phelps, Bklyn.	20	101	27	21	4	5	.444
Derringer, St. L.	39	297	66	76	11	14	.440
Carleton, St. L.	44	197	70	112	10	13	.435
Lucas, Cin.	31	260	36	62	13	17	.433
Walker, N. Y.	31	186	55	74	8	12	.400
Grimes, Chi.	30	175	51	35	6	10	.375
Kolp, Cin.	32	165	27	42	6	10	.375
Mooney, N. Y.	29	154	42	36	6	10	.375
Hoyt, Bk.-N. Y.	26	140	37	36	6	10	.375
Haines, St. L.	20	116	16	27	3	5	.375
Carroll, Cin.	32	245	46	55	10	19	.345
Spencer, Pitts.	39	166	43	33	4	8	.333
Gibson, N. Y.	41	110	29	39	4	8	.333
H. Elliott, Phil.	15	66	30	13	2	4	.333
Benton, Cin.	35	200	28	34	6	13	.316
Quinn, Bklyn.	42	101	24	27	3	7	.300
Johnson, St. L.	32	190	38	84	5	14	.263
Frey, St. L.-Cin.	33	162	32	26	4	12	.250
Seibold, Bos.	28	172	40	32	3	11	.231
Pruett, Bos.	13	77	30	27	1	5	.167

Ruth Sets Nine Records In 3d Game of Series

CHICAGO, Oct. 1 (AP).—The third game of the World Series today between the Cubs and the Yankees was marked by an even dozen record performances, in nine of which Babe Ruth's exploits were involved. Ten series records were broken and two others equaled as the Yankees made it three in a row.

Altogether, in three games so far, fifteen records, including eleven by Ruth, have been broken or equaled.

1.—Most consecutive victories, total series, 11, by Yankees.
2.—Most home runs, two clubs, one game, 6, in third game.
3.—Most home runs, one inning, one club, two in succession, third game by Ruth and Gehrig, equaling former mark.
4.—Most home runs, total series, 15, by Ruth.
5.—Most total bases, total series, 95, by Ruth.
6.—Most long hits, total series, 22, by Ruth.
7.—Most extra bases, total series, long hits, 54, by Ruth.
8.—Most bases on balls, total series, 33, by Ruth.
9.—Most strikeouts, total series, 28, by Ruth.
10.—Most strikeouts, one game, 5, by George Pipgras, of Yankees, third game.
11.—Largest score, both clubs, one game, 18 runs, first game.
12.—Most series played, 10, by Ruth.
13.—Most runs, total series, 37, by Ruth.
14.—Most runs batted in, total series, 32, by Ruth.
15.—Most runs batted in, one game, 4, by Ruth, third game equaling record formerly held by himself and five others.

Today! Post Starts New Contest. $10,000 1st Prize! Page 20

BASEBALL FINAL ★★★★★★★ Late Racing Results

New York Post

THREE 3 CENTS 12 FOUNDED 1801. VOL. 134, NO. 167. MONDAY, JUNE 3, 1935 MEMBER OF THE ASSOCIATED PRESS THREE 3 CENTS

NORMANDIE SETS RECORD; 100,000 HERE CHEER ARRIVAL

Post airplane photo by Ben Leider.

Crossing the finish line in record time! The Normandie, France's seagoing skyscraper, shows her speed as she steams past Ambrose Lightship at the conclusion of her maiden transatlantic crossing.

Yanks, Athletics Score; Lazzeri Clouts Triple

TONY'S SMASH SCORES 2 RUNS

Crosetti's Double Tallies Selkirk–Moses Homers –DeShong Hurls

The Lineup

ATHLETICS	YANKEES
Moses, rf.	Combs, lf.
Cramer, cf.	Rolfe, 3b.
Johnson, lf.	Chapman, cf.
Foxx, 1b.	Gehrig, 1b
Higgins, 3b.	Lazzeri, 2b
McNair, ss.	Dickey, c.
Warstler, 2b.	Selkirk, rf.
Richards, c.	Crosetti, ss.
Blaeholder, p.	DeShong, p.

Umpires: Moriarty and Owens.
Attendance: 5,00.

YANKEE STADIUM, June 3 (AP). —The Yankees, who have won fifteen of their last twenty games and were enjoying a two-game grip on first place, opened their last series at the Stadium before setting off into the West again on Thursday night when they faced the Philadelphia Athletics in the first of a four-game set here today.

Jimmy Deshong, youthful right-hander, who pitched a one-hit game against the Mackmen last year, was sent to the mound by Manager Joe McCarthy with the hope that his effectiveness over the A's was still intact. It was Deshong's first start of the current season.

As his opponent he drew the A's recent acquisition from the St. Louis Browns, the seasoned right-hander, George Blaeholder. It was Blaeholder's fourth start for the Mackmen since joining them, and he sought to keep the Philadelphia winning streak, which stood at four straight, moving ahead while breaking into the winning column for the first time himself. He lost all of his previous starts in a Philly uniform.

Several members of the New York Giants, enjoying an off-day before opening a series with the Phillies in Philadelphia tomorrow, were among the 5,000 spectators present when the game started. In addition there were several thousand school children in the left-field stands as guests of the Yankees.

First Inning

ATHLETICS—Moses dropped a single in short center, but was out trying to stretch it, Lazzeri to Rolfe, who covered second base. DeShong tossed out Cramer. Johnson popped to Rolfe. One hit.

YANKEES—Combs singled over second. Higgins threw out Rolfe, Combs going to second. Chapman walked. Gehrig hit in front of the plate and was thrown out by Richards, Combs and Chapman advancing. Lazzeri tripled over Cramer's head, Combs and Chapman scoring.

Continued on Page 16, Col. 4

Phila. (A)	0	1	1	0	0	0	0		
Yankees	2	1	0	0	0	3			

Blaeholder and Richards; De Shong and Dickey.

St. L. (N)	0	0	0	0
Chi. (N)	0	0	1	

Heusser and Davis; Root and Hartnett.

Cleveland
St. L. (A).

INTERNATIONAL LEAGUE

Buffalo	0	0	3	0	0	0	0	0
Montreal	1	1	1	0	0	0	0	0

Ash and Crouse; Myllykangas and Tate.
Only Games Scheduled

LATEST RACING RESULTS

BELMONT PARK — Off

4—Gold Foam 10-1 4-1 8-5; Silversmith 1-2 1-5; G. Prince 1-1. 4:06
5—Coequel 9-2 8-5 7-10; Ind. Runner 4-5 out; Bonanba out. 4:32½

ROCKINGHAM

5—Pantoufle 10.60 6.90 3.30; B. Brook 6.60 3.50; F. Fiber 2.40. 4:33½

THORNCLFFE

3—Meloy 5.60 3.60 2.80; Exhibition 7.50 3.80; Your Flag 6.65. 3:51¼

LATONIA

4—Bustanybody 7.80 7.00 3.00; C. Nadi 8.40 3.80; Morlute 3.00 4:18½

WASHINGTON PARK

3—Flight of Gold 8.06 4.50 3.28; Spicate 7.50 4.82; Cheerus 7.56. 4:13

DETROIT

2—Piping Hot 7.80 4.80 3.60; My Peter 7.20 5.00; Neon 8.60. 4:05
3—Be Big 9.40 4.20 3.20; C. Queen 4.40 4.20; C. W. Hay 3.60. 4:30½

Race Charts, Other Results, Scratches on Page 17

VERMONT BANS SCANTILY-CLAD THESPIANS

BRATTLEBORO, Vt., June 3 (AP).—The Repertory Playhouse Associates of New York, a theatrical group which was denied the use of the community center at Putney this summer because of the scanty garb worn by its members, will locate in Keene, N. H., their counsel announced today.

JOBLESS JERSEYITE KILLS SELF

MONTICELLO, N. Y., June 3 (AP).—Deputy Sheriff Francis Huff and Under-Sheriff Fred Stratton made a formal report today that Edward Muth, twenty-seven, an unemployed plumber of Palisades Park, N. J., had shot and killed himself in a summer cottage at Southwood, four miles east of Monticello, Friday night.

11 ARE RESCUED AFTER TRAWLER BURNS

CHATHAM, Mass., June 3 (AP).—The Captain and crew of the fishing trawler Milton, which sank last night off here after being swept by fire, were brought into port today, uninjured. The freighter Gypsum Express picked them up in their dories.

CORBIN NAMED RACKET PROBER; GETS FREE HAND

Chosen by Dodge From List Offered by Grand Jury

CONFUSION ATTENDS THE FINAL SELECTION

By WILLARD WIENER

Harold Corbin was appointed today to be special prosecutor for the vice, policy and bail bond racket investigations with a pledge of a free hand.

Mr. Corbin was chosen by District Attorney Dodge from a list of lawyers recommended by the Grand Jury. It started as a list of six, but grew to nine before an acceptable prosecutor who was willing to take the job could be found.

The new prosecutor will serve as a Deputy Assistant District Attorney—the lowest salaried post which carries the right to appear before the Grand Jury and conduct prosecutions.

Admitted to Bar in 1911

Mr. Corbin is a partner in former Governor Miller's law firm, Hornblower, Miller & Owens.

He was admitted to the bar in 1911, and practiced at first in Saratoga, where he was associated with the late Senator Edgar T. Brackett. In 1917 he served as counsel for the whitney Committee, a joint legislative group which investigated narcotic traffic in the Etate.

In 1925 he came to New York City as a partner of Max D. Steuer, and later moved to the Miller firm.

"He is an able trial lawyer and investigator," District Attorney Dodge said. "He has a free hand and can undertake action on anything pending before the Grand Jury."

Jury Proposed Name

It was the jury, the District Attorney insisted, which first proposed the name.

From other sources it was learned

Continued on Page 3, Col. 5

CLEVELAND EDITOR DIES DURING CRUISE

Morocco Consul Sends Cable to Plain Dealer

CLEVELAND, June 3 (AP).—The Plain Dealer received a cablegram today from George D. Hopper, American Consul in Rabat, Morocco, telling of the death of Carl T. Robertson, fifty-nine, associate editor of the Cleveland newspaper.

The message said Robertson died unexpectedly. Mr. and Mrs. Robertson were on a summer cruise. They left Cleveland two weeks ago.

U. S. Sets Trap To Seize Gang With Ransom

Banks Get Numbers of Bills Paid for Boy's Release

Copyright, 1935, by the Associated Press

TACOMA, June 3.—Department of Justice agents today began distributing pamphlets listing the numbers of 20,000 bills which made up the $200,000 ransom paid for the return of nine-year-old George Weyerhaeuser.

The bulletin describing the ransom money listed the numbers of nine United States notes and 19,991 Federal notes. The Federal Reserve notes are all of the L series, but are not in sequence. Thus it takes fifty-five booksize pages to list the bills, starting with L00000034A and L0000-3778* and ending with L35643933A and L35979275A.

The lists were being distributed to banks and all other places where large amounts of money are handled.

Operatives refused to comment on published reports that the kidnapers were paid the ransom money by George's uncle, F. Rodman Titcomb, on Thursday.

Uncle's Car Stolen

In that report the Seattle Post-Intelligencer today said the abductors then stole Titcomb's car—the machine which was the "kidnap car" recovered here. The paper said the ransom was paid in the foothills of the Cascades, about fifty miles east of the Issaquah, where George was released Saturday. It said Titcomb was picked up by his associate in the Weyerhaeuser Timber Company, Charles Ingram, after the kidnapers left him afoot.

William Cole, State patrol chief, commented that the car recovered in Seattle was stolen some time ago and the license plates stolen from a Tacoma machine, but he did not remember the owner.

The boy was released early Saturday and as soon as he was safe at home the Federal agents went into

Continued on Page 2, Col. 1

F. D. R. PUTS OFF ANSWER TO BORAH

Statement on NIRA Not Expected Before Wednesday —Byrns at White House

See Today's Editorial: "The Supreme Court Is Not Above Criticism."

By KENNETH CRAWFORD
Staff Correspondent New York Post

WASHINGTON, June 3. — President Roosevelt will not immediately accept the challenge of Senator Borah of Idaho to propose a constitutional amendment broadening Federal authority to cope with the present emergency.

It was made plain at the White House today that the next statement issued by the President would deal with measures necessary to comply with the Supreme Court's decision in the Schechter poultry case.

Like his announcement Saturday night that all pending NRA prosecutions would be dropped, the forthcoming statement will deal with changes in immediate plans necessitated by the decision.

Indications were that a comprehensive announcement of the Presi-

Continued on Page 2, Col. 2

U. S. WINS BATTLE FOR MELLON DATA

Subpena Orders Union Trust to Submit Records

WASHINGTON, June 3 (AP).—A long fight to subpena records of the Union Trust Company of Pittsburgh in connection with Andrew W. Mellon's income tax case was won today by the Government.

Robert H. Jackson, chief of Government counsel, disclosed that the subdivision of the Board of Tax Appeals hearing evidence in the case had reconsidered its previous refusal.

Twenty-four items were listed in the subpena on which the Union Trust Company was ordered to submit all its data, many of them referring to the organization of the company and the position held by the late R. B. Mellon, brother of the former Secretary of the Treasury.

GAY WELCOME GIVEN FRANCE'S NEW SEA QUEEN

Harbor Clamor Recalls Fetes of Walker Era to Visiting Heroes

BIGGEST SHIP CUTS REX'S TIME 2 HOURS

By MALCOLM LOGAN

It was like Jimmy Walker's New York today—the old, buoyant New York that gave such lavish receptions to arriving heroes—when the Normandie came in.

There were crowds running into hundreds of thousands. There were official welcoming committees. There were fireboats spouting streams of water and harbor craft whistling. There was even a shower of ticker tape and scraps of paper.

From the welcome given the French Line's new flagship as she ended a triumphant maiden voyage on which she captured the Atlantic speed record, any one might have thought it was an American ship bringing the supremacy of the ocean to the city.

Proves Speed Claim

It has been many years since any single ship has received such a welcome, though perhaps when the United States fleet came in last year there was an even greater crowd and a more deafening din of whistles.

But the Normandie had proved herself worthy of all the superlatives that the French Line's publicity men had heaped on her.

She is indisputably the biggest and most luxurious ocean liner ever built. And on her maiden voyage she had proved that she is also the fastest.

And so the city gave her the welcome that she had won by clipping more than two hours off the record crossing made by the Italian liner Rex almost two years ago.

Crosses Finish Line

It was 10:53 A. M. when three blasts from the whistle of the Ambrose Lightship announced that the Normandie had passed, crossing the finish line.

At 2:45 she was at her pier, and at 3:25 she was docked by a dozen tugs, her maiden voyage over.

When the liner swept past the lightship, her commander, Captain Rene Pugnet, commodore of the line, announced that her elapsed time from Southampton Nab was four days, eleven hours and thirty-three minutes.

Not only had the Normandie bettered the Rex's best time. She had also covered a longer distance in setting her record.

Boats of all descriptions swarmed out to meet her—excursion boats, speedboats, outboard motorboats. They whistled at her in every note of the scale, from rumbling bass to shrill soprano, and were joined in this welcome by ferries, tramps, rival passenger vessels, Coast Guard cutters and fireboats which arched streams of water high in the air.

Welcoming parties of French and American officials, representatives of the city, and the press went down the bay and boarded her at Quarantine.

Secretary of State Cordell Hull sent a welcome along a beam of light from the torch of the Statue of Liberty, France's gift to the United States.

These, however, were formal greetings.

Great Outpouring Along Piers

More impressive was the great outpouring of New Yorkers to places along the waterfront to see France's supreme achievement in shipbuilding.

Well over a hundred thousand watched from the Battery, from the Coney Island boardwalk, from Shore Road in Brooklyn and from points along the North River as the Normandie, leaving Quarantine at 1:38, moved slowly toward her pier at Forty-eighth Street.

Many more craned their necks from the wndows, obserevation towers of skyscrapers and the roofs of North River piers.

The Normandie in establishing her

Continued on Page 3, Col. 1

THE WEATHER

Showers and thunderstorm tonight; tomorrow fair and cooler.

Temperature at Each Hour

8	9	10	11	12	1	2	3	4	5
63	64	69	73	74	71	72	77	74	72

Sweeps Net 7 Million In Profits From U. S.

3,000,000 Americans Play, With One Chance in About 350,000 for Each Ticket to Win Top Prize

By JOSEPH COOKMAN

Hello, sucker!

So you're hoping that your number will come up in the next sweeps draw?

That's swell. I'm hoping, too.

In fact, there will be more than 3,000,000 of us American suckers hoping hard.

We're a determined and optimistic bunch, and for us the moon is a bright and shining target.

And if we don't get a hit next time we can be counted on to be in there trying with new tickets for some race still later in the year—piling up a profit of around $7,000,000 a year for smart fellows from abroad.

Taking one with another of us we haven't got much money — not enough to go gunning in Wall Street.

But between the lot of us we've got so much that we're getting to be quite a problem to our Uncle Sam. Also to those unofficial aids of his that we always have with us and who want to keep us from spending our money foolishly while indulging our reprehensible human traits.

A Billion a Year—Maybe

What with postal inspectors busily feeling envelopes to find tickets and money, what with professional tut-tutters pointing out how foolish and even unpatriotic it is, we ought to have a different attitude toward this illegal gamble.

But—remember prohibition!

It's true, of course, that we do

Continued on Page 22, Col. 4

6 WIN $30,000 HERE IN SWEEPS

Girl, 10, to Get Full Residual Prize—Boy, 3½, Wins Half Share

Gambling children came into their own in today's drawings of residual winners in the Irish Hospital Trust sweepstakes.

Of six residual prizes won by New York tickets, all of one goes to a ten-year-old girl and half of another to a boy three and a half. The prizes are worth about $30,000 each.

A seventh residual prize was won by a Seattle, Wash., woman, and only three went to other countries.

In addition, Americans won $440,900 in consolation prizes of approximately $500 each. Out of 1,100 consolations drawn, 457 came to this

Continued on Page 22, Col. 1

HEUSSER OPPOSES ROOT ON MOUND

St. Louis Cards Seek Clean Sweep in Finale of Series With Cubs

The Lineup

CARDINALS	CUBS
Martin, 3b.	Galan, lf.
Rothrock, rf.	Herman, 2b.
Frisch, 2b.	Hack, 3b.
Medwick, lf.	Hartnett, c.
J. Collins, 1b.	Klein, rf.
Davis, c.	Cavarretta, 1b.
Moore, cf.	Cuyler, cf.
Durocher, ss.	Jurgess, s.
Heusser, p.	Root, p.

Umpires—Reardon, Stewart and Sears.
Attendance, 1,500.

WRIGLEY FIELD, Chicago, Ill., June 3 (AP).—The spurting St. Louis Cardinals, in second place with six straight victories to their credit, and the slumping Cubs, who lost their four preceding games, met here this afternoon in the final game of their series of four.

Ed Heuser, young rookie right-hander, who has yet to pitch a complete big league game, but who has a relief win over Pittsburgh to his credit, started on the mound for the Cardinals.

First Inning

CARDINALS—Martin struck out. Rothrock walked. Frisch popped

Continued on Page 16, Col. 5

RUTH MAY RETURN AS BRAVES' BOSS

Boston Reports Judge Fuchs Will Quit, Babe to Be Made Manager

By JERRY MITCHELL

He was to return to New York town some time today, a tired and sadly disillusioned old fellow, eager to rest bones that are weary and worn and a head that aches, he says, from the cross and double cross.

He's nobody's baby now. He returns a man without a ball club, and yet the idea seems to be that George Herman Ruth acted wisely and not a moment too soon.

He was fast becoming a comic-strip ball player on a burlesque ball club. He was endangering a personal popularity achieved through many glamorous baseball years by exhibiting himself like a side-show freak in order that the more desperate half of a business concern divided against itself could earn enough dollars to pay up back debts and pay off the other side.

He was played out, crippled and

Continued on Page 13, Col. 8

Normandie Clips Speed Record in Maiden Voyage to N. Y.

LESSER VESSELS SHRIEK WELCOME TO GREAT LINER

Largest Vessel Afloat Crosses Atlantic in Four Days Eleven Hours

100,000 IN BATTERY PARK TO SEE BIG SHIP COME IN

Continued from Page One

record traveled 3,192 miles at an average speed of 29.68 knots. The Rex's record was 3,181 miles in four days, thirteen hours and fifty-eight minutes, at an average of 28.92 knots.

In the twenty-four hours ending yesterday noon the Normandie made a record run of 748 nautical miles, beating by four miles her own record established on her first day at se.. and topping the best day's run of the Rex by twelve miles.

The Rex made its record between Gibraltar and Ambrose Light. The best record before today for the northern route which the Normandie took was four days, fourteen hours, twenty-seven minutes, established by the Bremen from Cherbourg breakwater to Ambrose Light.

At 11:34 A. M. the Normandie reached Sandy Hook and turned into the Narrows.

The pilot boat Sandy Hook tooted a welcome. A number of speedboats followed the huge liner like minnows chasing a whale.

Six Planes in Group

Six airplanes appeared in a group, one towing a sign: "New York Welcomes Normandie." As she approached Quarantine, the Normandie was puffing smoke from the middle of her three vast stacks and some of the planes swooped low through this dark plume.

Approaching the Narrows, the Normandie participated in a tableau representing the old and new in shipping. A full-rigged schooner, with all sails set, passed close under the towering bows of the liner which is the last word in de luxe ocean travel.

At Fort Hamilton and along the Shore Road in Brooklyn at least 10,000 persons waited for a glimpse of the new queen of the Atlantic. At 11:45 some one cried, "There she Is!" and there was a stampede to the sea wall.

The great liner loomed up clear off the Highlands, her dazzling white superstructure set off by the black hull. A police boat led the way for her.

Speedboats, launches, outboard motor boats and larger craft made all the noise they could, but the crowd on the sea wall paid tribute to her size and beauty by its silence.

Long Wait at Quarantine

The liner dropped her seventeen-ton anchors at Quarantine at 12:03 and then there was a long wait before she resumed the trip to her North River pier at Forty-eighth Street.

Two official welcoming parties boarded the Normandie. One was headed by the French Ambassador, Andre Lefebvre de LaBoulaye, and included Mme. LaBoulaye, Richard Southgate of the State Department, Henri Morin de Lindays, the French Consul General, and Charles de Ferry de Fontnouvelle, general manager of the French Line in the United States and Canada.

The other included a number of city officials and Mrs. Fiorello H. LaGuardia, who presented flowers to Mme. Lebrun, wife of the President of France, a passenger in one of the Normandie's two suites that have their own private terraces.

"Marseillaise" From Air

More airplanes were added to the ship's escort when she left Quarantine at 1:38. One of them carried a loud speaker, which blared out the "Marseillaise." Another announced in stentorian tones to the crowds among the waterfront that the ship will be open to the public tomorrow.

By the time the Normandie came within sight of the Battery a crowd which police estimated at 100,000 was waiting there, jamming every inch of the walk for half a mile from the Barge Office to Pier A.

Many carried French flags, and except for an occasional Italian who resented the loss of the Rex's Atlantic record, the spectators of all nationalities were Francophiles for the day.

Barkers circulated, announcing in fog-horn voices that the Normandie would pass close to the Statue of Liberty. The Hook Mountain took 3,000 persons—three times its day's average—to Bedloe's Island.

About 4,000 others paid to board the Mayflower, Mandalay, Americana and Berkshire of the Hudson River Line, which went down near Quarantine and joined in the procession up to the pier. Handkerchiefs and hats waved from the excursion boats' decks as they approached the Normandie.

Fireboat Aids Welcome

It was a proud day for Lieutenant Arthur Bracconier, commander of the fireboat John J. Harvey, flagship of the Fire Department fleet. The lieutenant is a good American, but he is of French descent and he was acutely aware of it when he was assigned to participate in the water display.

His men were aware of it, too, for he kept them busy all morning polishing the already blinding brightwork and generally making the John J. Harvey fittingly spotless.

"There She Comes!"

To Lieutenant Bracconier fell the honor of announcing the Normandie to the crowd at the Battery.

With his eyes shielded by his hand, he watched until at 1.45 he cried, "There she comes!"

The crowd pushed forward and took up the cry, and the lieutenant ordered the boat out into the arbor, where it arched streams of water from its eight standpipes as the Normandie and its escort came into plainer view.

Before she reached the Battery, the Normandie abreast of the Statue of Liberty received Secretary Hull's message.

Voice in Liberty's Torch

Mr. Hull in Washington spoke into a microphone which carried his voice by direct wire to the statue where, in the huge torch, engineers had set up an elaborate equipment for relaying his words over a bea mof light.

It required special apparatus on the ship to receive this talking light beam—a concave mirror which converged the light rays on an "electric eye' which converted the light rays back into radio waves.

A public address system on the ship amplified Mr. Hull's voice, while a short wave set sent it to the RCA Building. Thence it went to Schenectady, where it was broadcast on the station's regular wave length to the United States and by short wave to France.

Rumble Replies to Din

As the liner came closer to the Battery and then swung into the North River, a din of whistles, foghorns and bells followed her. She responded at intervals with three long whistle blasts.

The Normandie's voice is a deep bass rumble, like the growl of distant thunder—the sort of voice one would expect from a ship of her great bulk.

As soon as she had passed the Battery the crowd there broke up, many persons following up West Street on foot, walking in the street.

All the way up the river the tugs, launches and other boats escorting the Normandie kept their whistles blowing, and liners and freighters at the piers responded. Ticker tape was flung from the windows of some downtown buildings.

Sea Scouts Wig-wag Greeting

Windows and towers of skyscrapers were crowded. When the Normandie passed the Woolworth Building, Whitney Rogovay, a mate in the Manhattan Sea Scouts, wigwagged a message of greeting.

But he and the other scouts had forgotten to bring field glasses, so if the Normandie sent any answer, they never knew it.

Alice Jayne McHenry, the girl who put upside-down stomachs on the first pages of the newspapers, was to have been there when the message was sent.

But, motoring down from Fall River, Mass., she did not arrive until after the Normandie had reached her pier, a long distance away from the Woolworth Building.

Crowd Lines Jersey Shore

The Jersey shore, as well as the Manhattan water front, was lined with spectators. Near the pier there was a crowd of 15,000 in Twelfth Avenue when the Normandie reached the dock at 2:45. Some had come as early as 7 o'clock this morning.

No one was allowed to approach within half a block of the dock, but below this restricted area the crowd was thick by early afternoon.

Hundreds stood on the east side of Twelfth Avenue, some sat on boxes, many carried their lunches. Hundreds of automobile owners parked their cars under the express highway and sat down on the roofs, whence they had an excellent view of the pier.

Deputy Chief Inspector David J. McAuliffe was in command of 300 policemen at the pier. No persons except members of the official welcoming party were allowed on it.

The 1,100-foot pier, costing the city $4,275,500, was loud with the activity of a thousand workmen, who stayed until the last possible minute.

The pier from Twelfth Avenue looked finished, for the facade was completed and hung with French and American flags and bunting, not to mention a sign with the names of Mayor LaGuardia and Dock Commissioner McKenzie in large and prominent letters.

Bare Girders Obtrude

But behind this false front was a alf-finished structure with no walls, with bare girders obtruding in many places, with the floor of the upper level, on which most of the passengers were to disembark, only half laid.

This incompleteness was to some extent disguised by a line of flags and tri-color bunting in the form of huge semi-circles hung from the ceiling down the length of the dock.

The construction of the liner was interrupted by labor trouble and only police diplomacy prevented more labor trouble which would have delayed her docking.

At 1 o'clock more than a thousand longshoremen marched on the pier in a body to apply for 250 jobs handling the liner's baggage and freight.

Deputy Inspector Michael J. Wall stopped them at the pier entrance. He finally settled the question of how the 250 would be chosen by having a union official throw the 250 work checks into the crowd.

There was a great scramble for the precious tickets and a lot of grumbling from those who did not get any, but the crowd was quieted.

Another Labor Row

A little later officials of Local 3 of the International Brotherhood of Electrical Workers demanded that five newsreel crews leave the pier because they were not members of the local.

They threatened to call off the electricians on the pier, which would have left no none to operate the gangplanks and the unloading machinery.

Inspector McAuliffe persuaded them to stay when they admitted that the local could not replace the newsreel crews if the latter were ordered from the pier.

Peace Restored

Everything was peaceful when the Normandie arrived off the pier at 2:45.

Twelve tugboats, headed by the veteran Alice M. Moran, swarmed out to her. They pushed and hauled and finally at 3:25 had her made fast to the side of the pier. The gangplanks were lowered. Passengers swarmed ashore.

The Normandie had finished a maiden voyage which left her owners nothing to desire and New York had enjoyed one of its biggest in a long time.

The Army engineers co-operated in the reception by working continuously from Friday night until today dredging out the channel over the bore of the midtown vehicular tunnel to a depth of forty feet.

Work on the tunnel had pushed up ridges of mud six to eight feet high at various points and as the Normandie draws thirty-five feet, these constituted a danger. They were all removed before she reached Quarantine.

Reception at Waldorf-Astoria

This afternoon Mme. Lebrun, Ambassador Laboulaye and other celebrities will be guests at a reception at the Waldorf-Astoria. Tonight a formal dinner will be given there by Mayor LaGuardia.

Tomorrow from 10:30 A. M. to 3 P. M. the public will be permitted its first closeup view of the ship. No passes will be issued but a 50-cent fee will be charged for the French and American Seamen's Fund. Visiting hours Wednesday will be 1 to 3 P. M.

The Normandie will be in port five days. There will be a round of dinners, dances and other functions.

Mme. Lebrun will go to Washington tomorrow to call on President Roosevelt and on Thursday will go to his home at Hyde Park.

Here Comes the Queen of the Seas!

This picture, taken from a plane as France's queen of the seas, the Normandie, arrived here today, shows both the great liner and, in the background, the Ambrose Lightship, "finish line" for transatlantic crossings. A speed record was established as the maiden voyage ended. The two white streaks are speed boats buzzing about.

Normandie, Queen of Seas, 22,000 Tons Over Majestic

For those who like their statistics straight, these are the facts about the Normandie:

She is 22,659 tons heavier and 113.5 feet longer than the next largest passenger ship afloat, the Cunarder Majestic.

Her tonnage is 79,280 and her length 1,029 feet.

Her draft is 34 feet 6 inches forward, 35 feet aft.

She has a beam of 119.5 feet.

Her four propellers weigh 23 tons each and are driven by engines of 40,000 horse power each.

She carries a crew of 1,339 and can carry 3,000 passengers.

Even when the Cunarder Queen Mary is launched, she will still be biggest. with a margin of 11 feet in length and 6,000 tons' weight

The Normandie has 1,100 telephones, cabins with private terraces, a formal garden, a theatre, a night club and not one swimming pool, but several.

CHRISTIAN SCIENTISTS NAME BACON AS HEAD

Bostonian Succeeds Dr. Brewer of Harvard

BOSTON, June 3 (AP).—A Barry Bacon of Boston and Marshfield, Mass., today was elected president of the Mother Church, the First Church of Christ, Scientist, Boston, at the annual meeting attended by approximately 6,000 members.

Bacon, a native of Pontiac, Mich., in his address, declared that "when the whole world was struggling under unemployment, lack, want and woe, Christian Science had come to the rescue of many," and that through its application many had been healed of erroneous conditions.

He stressed the fact that "in the midst of this period the building of a new publishing house was wisely undertaken," furnishing employment.

C. C. N. Y. SUSPENDS 2 FOR PEACE RALLY

Students Led Demonstration Against the R. O. T. C.

Two City College students were suspended today by Dean Morton Gottschall for leading a demonstration of 300 undergraduates against the college R. O. T. C. Wednesday afternoon.

The students are Meyer Rangdell and Meyer Schwartz, both juniors. Dean Gottschall ordered their suspensions on complaint of George M. Brett, curator.

The demonstration took place outside Lewisohn Stadium, where the R. O. T. C. was holding its annual review. It had been forbidden by the Board of Higher Education.

Final action on the cases of the suspended undergraduates will be taken Wednesday by the Committee on Student Discipline, of which Professor Morris R. Cohen is chairman.

SOUP KING'S ESTATE LOSES TAX APPEAL

U. S. Court Denies Injuncton on $12,000,000 N. J. Levy

TRENTON, June 3 (AP).—A specially constituted Federal court today denied executors of the estate of the late Dr. John T. Dorrance, Camden soup manufacturer, a preliminiary injunction to restrain New Jersey from collecting an inheritance tax of $12,247,333.

The executors appealed to the court for relief after the New Jersey Supreme Court ruled Dorrance was domiciled in this State and upheld the assessment.

Pennsylvania already has collected a tax of approximately $14,000,000 and the executors sought to prevent a dual assessment.

LONGSHOREMAN STABBED

Michael Miller, forty-eight, a longshoreman, of 448 West Forty-first Street, was stabbed three times last night by unidentified men in Forty-first Street near Tenth Avenue. He was taken to Polyclinic Hospital with wounds in the right hip, right side and left forearm.

CORBIN IS NAMED RACKETS PROBER

Picked by Dodge From List Jury Offered—Confusion Marks Selection

Continued from Page One

that great confusion surrounded the final selection, which has been delayed several weeks.

Mr. Corbin was approached last Wednesday, an dwas reluctant to serve. He specified guarantees on a umber of points, notably appropriations, personnel of staff and quarters. Then he decided he did not wish to serve.

As a result the post was offered to John M'Harlan, former Assistant United States Attorney and partner of former United States Attorney Buckner.

Corbin Reconsidered

Then Mr. Corbin reconsidered and Mr. Dodge announced this morning that a prosecutor had been chosen. He said he could not give out the name pending stranghtening out of technicalities.

The Post was able to announce that the choice lay between Mr. Corbin and Mr. Harlan, and this afternoon Mr. Dodge conceded that Mr. Corbin was the choice.

Mr. Dodge made it plain that he knew Mr. Corbin by reputation only until he started conferences with him after the Grand Jury mentioned the name.

One of the chief difficulties which had to be surmounted was in deciding the exact status of the new prosecutor. When the inquiry began, Samuel Marcus of the Society for the Prevention of Vice was named as a special Assistant District Attorney, but found that in that unpaid capacity he could not have a free hand with the Grand Jury. Mr. Corbin insisted upan a position which would establish beyond dispute his right to serve as an active prosecutor.

The Grand Jury returned ten indictments today, naming eight persons on perjury and subornation of perjury charges, and then recessed until next Monday to give Mr. Corbin an opportunity to get acquainted with the progress of the inquiry.

'Faith in God' Cures Pastor Of Snake Bite

1,000 See Holiness Preacher Handle More Reptiles

ST. CHARLES, Va., June 3 (AP).—Recovering from the poisonous bite of a copperhead snake, received in a "demonstration of faith," and unharmed by three large rattlers he handled before a highly emotional congregation, the Rev. George Hensley, Holiness preacher, today reiterated his claim of immunity to reptile venom through "faith in God."

A crowd estimated at 1,000, which swarmed into a grove of cedar trees at Ramsey last night, watched the revivalist and five others handle rattlesnakes imported from the mountains of Kentucky.

The minister said his prayers prevented the snakes from biting, and cited chapter and verse of the Scriptures as explanation.

Besides Hensley, those who handled the snakes without harm were the Rev. Oscar Hutton of Wise County, the Rev. Connelly White and Bill Edmonds of Evarts, Ky., Told Lawson and Lloyd Scott of St. Charles.

Hensley's left hand was still somewhat swollen from the bite Thursday night of the copperhead.

COLUMNIST SWUNG FIST TO GET STORY

Village Paragrapher Admits Striking Victim in I. R. T. Beating Trial

Special Dispatch to New York Post

MINEOLA, L. I., June 3.—Just a a vigilant columnist in pursuit of a paragraph.

That's the way Harold Wallinsky, thirty-nine, described himself today in defending himself against a charge he helped beat up George Howard in the Times Square I. R. T. subway station last November.

Wallinsky, columnist for a Greenwich Village newspaper, and two subway guards are on trial in Supreme Court here on second-degree assault charges in connection with the alleged beating.

Three Picked by Witnesses

The co-defendants are Frank J. Walsh and John J. Corbett, both I. R. T. employees.

The State contends Howard was taken to the locker room and beaten by the three defendants.

All have denied the charges, but a succession of witnesses testified that they saw Howard beaten and several identified the three defendants as his assailants.

Today Wallinsky said he was going up the stairs of the subway station when he saw Howard run past him, pursued by the two guards. He said Howard fell on the steps and that when he arose blood was flowing from cuts in his face.

Admits Striking Blow

Wallinsky said he followed the guards and Howard into the locker room, thinking he might pick up a story for his column.

He denied Howard was beaten, but he admitted, on questioning, that he struck Howard in the face. He insisted the blow was struck only after Howard had hit him.

He said the exchange of blows came after the guards had asked him to aid in putting handcuffs on Howard's wrists.

BADLANDS SCOURED FOR MISSING ARTIST

Utah Searchers Defy Death—Youth Gone Five Months

SODA SEEPS, Utah, June 3 (AP).—Defying death in a search of hazardous badland country in Southwestern Utah, a band of desert-trained men today continued their hunt for Everett Reuss, young Los Angeles, Cal., artist, who disappeared in the wasttelands five months ago.

The searchers came upon the last known camp of the young artist in Davis Gulch Saturday. The remains of a fire were found in a cave and on the wall the name "Nemo" had been carved with a knife. The date, "1934," also was found on the walls.

HOUSE CRUSHES MOVE TO CURB U. S. JUDGES

Votes 220 to 2 Against Putting Limit on Terms

WASHINGTON, June 3 (AP).—In its first business session since the Supreme Court declared NRA unconstitutional, the House today crushed, 220 to 2, the opening move in an attempt to limit the terms of Federal judges.

The issue arose on a bill by Representative Montague (Dem., Va.) for the appointment of a new Federal judge for the Eastern District of Virginia.

Representative Traux (Dem., Ohio) proposed an amendment to limit the term of the new judge to four years.

"It is high time," he said, "that Congress should limit the terms of all Federal judges, including those on the Supreme Court."

BOY SAVED, MOTHER FIGHTS AND DROWNS

Although witnesses said they saw a twenty-eight-year-old mother fight off the rescuer of her boy before she drowned off Beach Sixty-eighth Street, Arverne, Queens, police today listed her death as accidental.

The woman was Mrs. Luba Benditovitz of 2925 Matthews Avenue, The Bronx. Witnesses told police she had pushed her son, Abraham, three, off a jetty and jumped in after him. Philip Greenberg, thirty, of 175 Beach Sixty-eighth Street, Arverne, jumped in and rescued the boy but said he was prevented from rescuing the woman because she beat him off.

Police, however, said the woman apparently had become panic-stricken.

Special

Taxi Delivery None Too Good for This Hat

CHICAGO, June 3 (AP).—"Deliver this hat box to St. Vincent's Orphanage, please."

Taxicab Driver William Korshak accepted the cardboard box from a woman who had hailed him at a street intersection early today, pocketed $1.50 and set out.

Several blocks away curiosity overcame him. He peeked into the box. Then he laid it carefully in his lap and drove to the Rogers Park police station. There the box was transferred to a squad car and delivered to the Rogers Park Hospital.

"It's a baby boy, not over two hours old and in perfect health," hospital attaches said.

WIDOW GETS ESTATE OF GEORGE T. BROKAW

Trust Fund Settled on His First Wife, Ann Clare

George Tuttle Brokaw, retired lawyer and sportsman, who died last week, left his entire residuary estate of "more than $10,000" to his second wife, Mrs. Frances Seymour Brokaw, his will filed for probate today reveals.

The instrument also reveals that Mr. Brokaw settled a trust fund on his first wife, Mrs. Ann Clare Brokaw, a former editor of Vanity Fair, some time before his death.

His will makes no provision for his daughters, Ann Clare and Frances Devilliers Brokaw, because, it is explained, they were provided for in the will of their grandfather, the late Isaac V. Brokaw, head of the chain of Brokaw Brothers' clothing stores.

NEWS GUILD SPLIT ON A. F. OF L. TIEUP

CLEVELAND, June 3 (AP).—The American Newspaper Guild's convention opened today with delegates from seventy units divided on whether they wanted to remain a semiprofessional group or to affiliate with the American Federation of Labor.

Heywood Broun, president of the organization, who favors affiliation, said the delegates will not vote on the issue until Thursday. Ultimate decision will be by referendum vote of the entire membership.

THEY GOT IN, O.K.; COPS GET 'EM OUT

Burglars Trapped in Store When Unable to Reach Hole Cut in Ceiling

Two burglars gained entrance to a dress shop at 1370 Third Avenue today by sawing a hole through the floor of an empty apartment above. But the entrance was a one-way passage—they had to call on police to get them out.

The trouble was that there were no chairs, ladders or rope by which the pair could get back up through the hole, and front and rear doors of the shop were bolted outside.

Martin Bray, twenty-two, 214 East Eighty-second Street, and Thomas McCormack, twenty-three, 421 East Seventy-eighth Street, tried to break through a panel in the rear door. They succeeded only in arousing neighbors, who called police.

Unable to get in, police cut a hole in the rear door, made the youths strip to their underwear and dragged them out. The pair went to the station wrapped in coats of their captors. They are charged with burglary.

THE WEATHER
Fair, colder; moderate to fresh northwest winds.
High tides at 1:15 a. m. and 1:23 p. m.
Light all vehicles at 5:10 p. m.

DAILY RECORD

Copyright, 1935, by Northeastern Publishing Co., 5 Winthrop Square, Boston.
BOSTON'S HOME PICTURE NEWSPAPER
Entered as second class mail matter at Boston, Mass., under the Acts of March 3, 1879.

FINAL EDITION

Vol. 244, No. 100 32 Pages Boston, Thursday, October 24, 1935 PRICE TWO CENTS

DUTCH SCHULTZ SHOT DOWN!

DYING IN GANG WAR; FIVE PALS WOUNDED

Newark, N. J., Oct. 23 (AP)—Gang guns blazed tonight in a vicious outburst of racketeering rivalry, and Arthur "Dutch Schultz" Flegenheimer and three lieutenants fell on two fronts.

SCHULTZ IN 1925

SCHULTZ IN 1935

International News Photo

Schultz was critically wounded, his lungs punctured and a bullet lodged near the heart, and two henchmen were shot down in a Newark tavern.

A third member of the gang dropped in a hail of bullets that struck a subway barber shop refuge he sought near crowded 47th st. and Seventh ave. in New York at almost the same time.

Police definitely linked the shootings with the Brooklyn hatchet-torch killing early today of Louis "Pretty Louie" Amberg, the seventh to die in recent weeks during a New York gang war over control of petty rackets.

Deputy Chief Inspector Francis J. Kear, commanding detectives in Manhattan, began a hunt for Charles "Lucky Charlie" Luciano, whom he accused of having set a "zero hour" to extirpate the Schultz legions.

Kear said Luciano nominaly owned a chain of cabarets but he described him as "the most powerful gangster in Manhattan."

He said he believed Luciano conceived the

Continued on Page 2, Column 4

DIMAGGIO GETS 3 HITS IN N.Y. DEBUT

SEALS WIN DOUBLE HEADER FROM SACS

'OUR JOE' TAKES OVER N.Y.

Joe Blasts Triple 'Nervous at First'

DERBY HEAT OFF

Louisville Subsides

By JOHN LARDNER

Chronicle Sporting Green
EDITED BY HARRY B. SMITH AND BILL LEISER
FOUNDED 1865 MONDAY, MAY 4, 1936 CCC 21 VOL. CXLVIII, NO. 109

San Francisco Triumphs by 10-3, 10-4

PARD HERO

O'Doul's Club Takes Series, 4 to 3

By ED. R. HUGHES

The Seals finished the series with Sacramento in gallant fashion. They won Saturday afternoon, they copped two games yesterday, morning and afternoon, and they took the long end of the series, four games to three. The scores yesterday were: Seals 10, Sacramento 3, in the morning, and in the afternoon Seals 10, Sacramento 4.

The two victories were welcomed by Manager O'Doul, but, most of all, he was pleased with the pitching and hitting of Pete Daglia, a large, well-fed gentleman from Napa, who has spent the last 10 days getting in shape. Pete looks to be ready now and if he is, he will be a big help, for he can work often.

Old Pard Ballou handled the afternoon game and after the third inning he looked great, for he allowed Sacramento only two hits and no runs. The curve was breaking just right and the Old Pard kept shoving it in there, to the bewilderment of some of the young fellows on the Sacramento club.

O'DOUL SHOWS HIS CONFIDENCE IN BALLOU

Garibaldi opened the afternoon game with a single and scored on a three-bagger by Epps, so things did not look any too bright for the Old Pard right then. But Manager O'Doul had faith larger than a grain of mustard seed and even when Epps scored on an infield out, he did not disturb Old Pard.

The Seals came back with four runs in their half of the first inning and batted Andrews out of the box. Ted Norbert mopped up with a home run, to drive in two of the runs, and as Thomas followed with a single and Barath drew a pass, Andrews was banished and Lyons, a little left-hander, took his place.

Sacramento attacked Old Pard

Continued on Page 24, Col. 8

MEXICO BEATS U. S. ARMY FOUR

MEXICO CITY, May 3 (AP)—The Mexican Olympic polo team defeated the United States Army Eighth Area Corps quartet, 5 to 4, today, scoring the winning goal after a 2-minute overtime period.

PHILLY TAKES SOCCER TITLE

PHILADELPHIA, May 3 (AP)—The German-Americans, of Philadelphia, won the United States open soccer championship today by defeating the St. Louis Shamrocks, 3 to 0, in the second and final game of the national championships.

WITH A GREAT BIG BANG, Joe DiMaggio, once of our own Seals, made his bow as a baseball player in little old New York yesterday. The size of the bang Joe created can be measured only by the storm of approval scribes and fans heaped upon him after his smashing day.

DIMAGGIO COLLECTED three hits in six times at the plate and he handled his only fielding chance perfectly. A triple and two singles were his bit toward the Yankees' 14-5 victory over the St. Louis Browns and his bingles drove in one run and scored 3.

Armstrong Race Victor

Art Armstrong, San Mateo, won the 60-lap auto race on the Oakland speedway's half-mile track in 31 minutes 3 4-5 seconds yesterday.

Fred Agabashian, Berkeley, finished second and "Herk" Edwards, Watsonville, third. "Tex" Peterson Pasadena, heavy pre-race favorite, placed sixth.

Peterson, however, won the three-lap trophy dash and a 10-lap sprint race. He led the main race until he went into a spin, relinquishing his first place to Agabashian. The later whirled at the same spot several laps later and Armstrong took and held the lead to the finish.

Duane Carter, Fresno, and "Bud" Rose, Los Angeles, were winners in 10 and 15-lap events.

U. S. WALKING RECORD SET

NEW YORK, May 3 (AP)—Charles Eschenbach of the New York Athletic Club, claimed a new national record as he won the National Senior A. A. U. 30,000 meter walking championship on Staten Island today in two hours, 33 minutes. No official record for the distance is listed among national or world marks.

HE WANTED GLASSES

Doc Turns Down Monk

Examination Reveals Grid Star's Perfect Pair of Eyes

By WILL CONNOLLY

James Henderson Moscrip, the handsome Monk of Stanford, has a pair of eyes that are as near perfection as it is possible to get without looking like Eddie Cantor.

So Monk concluded he needed glasses.

He went to Dr. H. Gordon Smith of Palo Alto, who tends to the Stanford hypochondriacs, and suggested, maybe, please, could I have glasses for reading?

Dr. Smith, always willing to oblige, made Monk read EFTHGR on a lighted glass panel, which was easy for him, because he is a senior in college. Monk had a minor difficulty trying to pronounce it, though.

Then Dr. Smith put all kinds of testing gadgets on Monk's eyes and at length chased him out of the office.

"Get out of here! Don't be wasting my time," said Dr. Smith with some pique. "Your eyes are pips. Never in my born days have I seen such muscular coordination, such refraction, such depth of perception. You can't have glasses."

Monk was crestfallen to learn he couldn't wear cheaters and his eyes were perhaps the best Dr. Smith had ever come across. It was a great blow to discover there was nothing wrong with them.

BAD NEWS FOR MONK TO TAKE

Dr. Smith further discouraged Monk by telling him he would make a swell aviator. The ocular muscle test he passed with highest honors in his class is given student flyers before they can take a crate off the ground.

We have a prodigy in our midst. Maybe Monk's eyes are the best in the world, like Kitty Gordon's back and Claudette Colbert's legs.

I think Stanford ought to enter Mon kin the national amateur ogling tournament to afford him an opportunity to bring more glory to the old school. He might even get to Berlin and the Olympic googoo eye event, which is stern competition indeed.

Monk's eyes are either gray, sea green or tinted with brown. He isn't sure himself. But they're not blue.

The minute but sturdy muscles

Continued on Page 22, Col. 5

SO THEY'RE PERFECT?

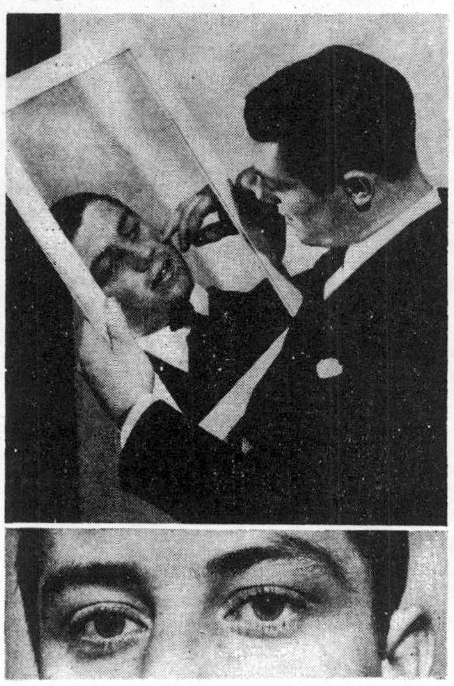

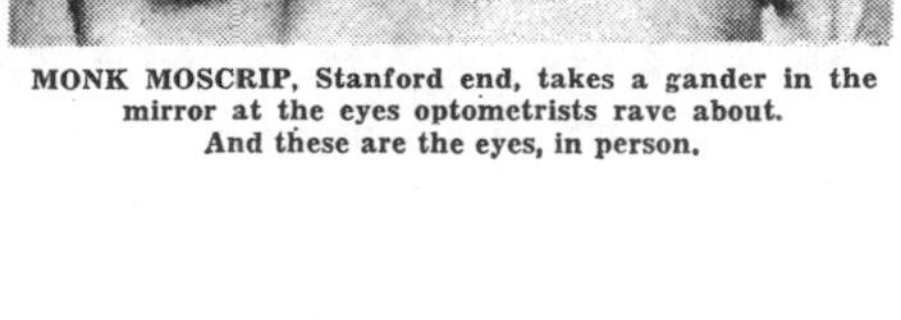

MONK MOSCRIP, Stanford end, takes a gander in the mirror at the eyes optometrists rave about. And these are the eyes, in person.

J. HARRINGTON OF BLUMS DIES

Joe Harrington, prominent in semi pro baseball circles of Northern California, died here yesterday. Joe was former manager of the Blum Sweets in the Golden Gate Valley League. He was son of the late Tim Harrington, one-time Fire Department lieutenant and brother of John, Bill and George Harrington. Funeral will be Wednesday from Carew and English.

FRENCH SWEEP DAVIS SERIES

PARIS, May 3 (AP)—France made a clean sweep in its Davis Cup tennis encounter with China with two singles victories today, Boussus defeating Guy Chang and Destremeau defeating Kho Sin Kie.

MONTE CARLO, May 3 (AP) — Holland clinched a berth in the second round of the European zone Davis Cup tennis competition today

LEVINSKY TO BOX RAMAGE

LOS ANGELES, May 3 (AP)—Joe Waterman, Los Angeles matchmaker, announced today he had signed Lee Ramage, San Diego heavy weight, and King Levinsky, Chicago, for a return bout at the Olympic Auditorium May 26.

2 Outboard Marks Fall

VALLEJO, May 3—Two crackups and two unofficial world records featured today's windup of the Vallejo outboard regatta.

Ernie Lewis, Windcat, an outboard, went amuck and cracked into Watson's barge after the driver had dived overboard. "Pop" Foster of the Sacramento Yacht Club rescued both.

Lou Garibaldi in his Garry III set an unofficial world's mark of 44.7 in the service runabout class while Tommy Eldridge of Oakland in his Flash set an unofficial world's mark of 50.4 in the .151 cubic inch class.

FAMILY RUNABOUT—First, E. S. Hughes, Sacramento; H. Anderson, Oakland, second; H. Brasefield, Oakland, third. Time, 47 mpd.

151 CUBIC INCH—First, Tommy Eldridge, Oakland; Bill Knight, Vallejo second. Time, 50.4 mpd.

225 CUBIC INCH—First, Tommy Eldridge, Oakland; E. S. Hughes, Sacramento, second. Time, 44.4 mpd.

718 CUBIC INCH GOLD CUP CLASS—First, Gene Armstrong; W. H. Sheehan, second. Time, 56.4 mph.

CLASS C SERVICE RUNADOUT—First, Lou Garibaldi; Bud Kehke, second; Sid McMurtrey, all Vallejo. Time, 44.5.

CLASS C HYDROPLANE—Won, Bud Kehke, Vallejo. Time, 45.6.

OUTBOARD FREE FOR ALL—Won by Lou Garibaldi, Vallejo.

HOW DI MAG' DID IT

PLAY-BY-PLAY OF JOE

Special Story Records His Every Move at Bat, in Field

(Special to The Chronicle)

NEW YORK, May 3 — Joe DiMaggio, $25,000 slugging outfielding beauty from the San Francisco Seals made his debut with the New York Yankees today and starred with a vengeance.

Kept out of action for the first three weeks of the season by a burned foot, he took—as advertised—the field against the last-place St. Louis Browns and hit and fielded well to the delight of a sizeable section of New York's vast Italian-American element.

He, certainly not the lowly Hornsby troupe, drew 26,000 to Colonel Jake Ruppert's ball park despite intermittent showers and, spotted in third place in the batting order just ahead of the great Lou Gehrig, pounded out three hits for a total of five bases —one of his blows being a triple— in six turns at bat against four brown hurlers, drove in a run and scored three times himself to aid Joe McCarthy's charges to an easy 14 to 5 victory.

HASN'T THROWN

The youthful appearing newcomer, never off the West Coast until he trained with the Yanks at St. Petersburg this spring, comported himself like a veteran although he had but one fly to handle in his left field position and encountered no real test of his throwing prowess.

After the Browns tallied thrice in their first turn at bat with the aid of Clift's line double to DiMaggio's territory, the Browns' starting pitcher, John Knott, lasted for only one out after New York went to work on him.

Crosetti tripled and Rolfe walked. DiMaggio slapped toward third and when Knott tossed home, a runup ensued, ending in a poor throw by Knott and after Gehrig walked and Caldwell replaced Knott, Chapman's double cleared the filled bases. Chapman tallied later and the Yanks were in front, never to be headed.

In the second inning the Yankees added three more, this time DiMaggio's high fly falling for a hit in the midst of the fireworks and he subsequently scored his number two run.

OOP! FANNED

In the fourth DiMaggio struck out, but his mates added two more counters. After Lefty Gomez was batted out by the Browns in the fifth, and Caldwell went out for a pinch hitter, DiMaggio's triple to left off Hoggsett figured in another four-run scoring jamboree.

DiMaggio flied to right to start the seventh, but the Yanks added another tally in that session. With Van Atta the opposing thrower, DiMaggio once more came to bat in the eighth with two out and singled cleanly—but Gehrig fanned.

New York fandom then and there decided DiMaggio would make the grade.

Ex-Seal Admits Flutter in Opener

SCORES 3

26,000 People Applaud Our Hero

By JACK CUDDY

NEW YORK, May 3 (U.P.)—Joe DiMaggio, most widely publicized rookie of the 1936 season, made a brilliant though belated major league debut with the Yankees today, as the New Yorkers crushed Rogers Hornsby's Browns, 14-5.

Although the weather man played "Gloomy Sunday" and the game was halted temporarily by rain, this slender Italian outfielder from the San Francisco Seals brought plenty of California sunshine to the hearts of New York fans and particularly to Manager Joe McCarthy.

Assigned to left field for his initial performance in the big time, the "$25,000 beauty" lived up to his price tag and played like a polished veteran. He was as cool as a frozen cucumber despite the tremendous pressure that must have come from realization that he was facing one of the toughest assignments ever given any rookie.

He made three hits in six times up, including a screaming triple to the left field wall, for .500 at bat. And he handled his lone fielding try perfectly.

FANS GIVE JOE GREAT BIG HAND

No wonder the 25,430 fans gave the loping fly-hawk a grand ovation in his last turn at bat, and no wonder Yankee veterans swarmed around smiling Joe in the dressing room after the game, pumping his hand and patting his back and offering congratulations.

And no wonder Marse Joe McCarthy told reporters, "Yes sir—he came through like a real money player. He lived up to my expectations. I'm certin Joe will be an important factor in our pennant drive. He'll certainly take up a lot of slack in our club."

Joe modestly disclaimed any great nervousness after the game.

"The only time I felt anything like a flutter around the heart was when I stepped up to bat for the first time," he said. "Guess that was only natural. But after I connected with the ball and got to second on

Continued on Page 24, Col. 4

SEMIPRO HAS NO-HIT GAME

MARYSVILLE, May 3 (AP)—Norman Coad, semi-pro baseball pitcher, hurled a no-hit, no-run game for the Marysville Giants as they defeated Grass Valley, 4 to 0

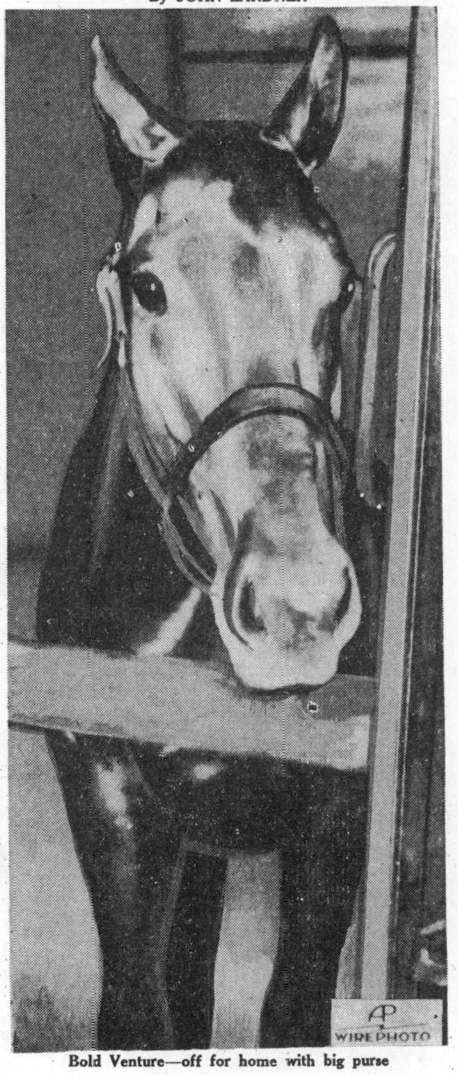

Bold Venture—off for home with big purse

Kentucky Almost Back to Normal After Big Race

By JOHN LARDNER

LOUISVILLE, Ky., May 3—They're saying that Brevity was the best horse in the Kentucky Derby, and Mr. Maxie Hirsch, who trained the winning horse, Bold Venture, does not actually deny it.

"Maybe Brevity was the best horse," said Mr. Hirsch as he swung a leg aboard the eastbound rattler. "Maybe he was. But they hung up my horse's number on the board when the race was over, and that satisfies me."

You know by this time that the sleek chestnut colt named Bold Venture won a most remarkable victory in the sixty-second edition of the Blue Grass and Julep classic. He won by the length of his barrel nose over a beast which was backed so strongly that he would have paid only eighty cents for a dollar's investment had he finished first. Brevity was supported right to the teeth. The crowd loved him. And naturally the crowd was a bit vexed by the manner in which its favorite lost.

JOHN'S IDEA

After twenty-four hours of investigation, I am prepared to give you some idea of the scenario of the race, which resulted in the suspension of three jockeys, including the winning rider. The big jam occurred soon after the start. Bold Venture, anxious to slip through the middle and toward the rail, banged hard against Granville, who promptly threw his rider, Jimmy Stout. Ira Hanford, up on Bold Venture, says he remembers this very well.

"I don't remember which horse it was we bumped against," declares Ira, better known as Babe, "but I know that when he went over I had to swing Bold Venture way to the right to avoid his heels. We lost some ground right there."

BUMPED!

Brevity, the favorite, seems to have been bumped by Mack Garner on Sangreal, though the episode was not seen clearly and Garner drew no suspension. Wayne Wright, Brevity's rider, when he conquered his bitter disappointment sufficiently to talk about it, said that the great Widener colt went almost to his knees, staggered, and lost a number of strides getting back in the race.

"And when you figure that we only lost by one stride," said Mr. Wright, "you can see what might

Continued on Page 22, Col. 7

HONUS WAGNER 'BUSH LANDIS'

WICHITA, Kas., May 3 (AP) — Honus Wagner, a former great shortstop in the National League, today was appointed national high commissioner for the National Semipro Baseball Congress.

CLOUDY
Not much change in temperature; gentle southerly winds. High tides at 7:38 a.m. and 8:03 p.m. Light autos at 8:53. See report on Page 2.

DAILY RECORD
BOSTON'S HOME PICTURE NEWSPAPER

Vol. 250, No. 180 | 36 Pages | Boston, Thursday, June 23, 1938 | PRICE TWO CENTS

6 A.M. FINAL

LOUIS WINS BY K. O. IN FIRST

Story on Page 2

Just Before Taps Were Sounded

Hanging on ropes, his eyes glazed, mouth awry, Max Schmeling awaits coupe de grace from Joe Louis who's ready for "the kill" in first round of Yankee Stadium go last night. An instant after this photo was made, Max hit the deck. Handler threw in towel

(Other Pictures Pages 2, 18, 19, 27, 29 and 36)

WOMEN IN WHITE, a New Series Begins Today on Page 15

SHOWERS TONIGHT
Tomorrow fair and cooler. Details on Page 8.

HOURLY TEMPERATURE (D. S. T.)

8	9	10	11	12	1	2	3	4	5	6
75	75	76	78	80	82	83	82	79	81	

EVENING PUBLIC LEDGER

2 STAR ★★ FINAL
Complete Stocks, Curb—Pages 25-26

VOL. CCV.—NO. 95 | Entered as Second-Class Matter at the Postoffice at Philadelphia, Pa., Under the Act of March 3, 1879. | PHILADELPHIA, THURSDAY, JULY 14, 1938 | Published Daily except Sunday. Copyright, 1938, by Public Ledger, Inc. | PRICE THREE CENTS

HUGHES FLIES AROUND WORLD IN 91 HOURS

Latest Racing Results

HAGERSTOWN—Third—Reigh Tetrarch, $11.70, $6.20, $4.60; Schley Buck, $12.70, $9; Boulder Dam, $6.40. Time, 1:29.

ARLINGTON—Fourth—Inscomira, $8, $4.40, $3; Dusky Maid, $4.60, $2.30; Russia, $3. Time, 1:56 4-5.

ROCKINGHAM—Sixth—Birthday, $6.12, $2.76, $2.40; Barfly, $2.38, $2.12; Landlubber, $2.76. Time, 1:46.

FORT ERIE—Fifth—Bernardine W., $8.20, $4.30, $3.25; Pagan King, $6.10, $3.55; Alwintour, $4. Time, 1:17 2-5.

ITALIAN PLANE FALLS IN SEA 20 LIVES ARE BELIEVED LOST

ROME, July 14.—(AP)—Twenty persons were believed to have lost their lives today when an Ala Littoria Lines seaplane fell into the Tyrrhenian Sea between Italy and the Island of Sardinia. The plane was on a flight from Cagliari, Sardinia, to Rome. Among the passengers on board was a sister of General Giuseppe Valle, Subsecretary of Aviation. Officials of the airline said sixteen passengers and a crew of four were on board.

Hines, Picard Win in P. G. A.

SHAWNEE-ON-DELAWARE, July 14. — Johnny Hines and Henry Picard reached the semifinal round of the P. G. A. tournament today. Hines beat Byron Nelson, 2 and 1. Picard defeated Gene Sarazen, 3 and 2.

Phils Lose First to Cubs, 3-0

CHICAGO........0 5 3 0 1 0 —
ATHLETICS......3 0 2 0 2 —
Whitehead and Sewell; Thomas and Hayes

PHILLIES (1st)...0 0 0 0 0 0 0 0 0—0 3 1
CHICAGO........0 0 0 0 3 0 0 0 X—3 6 0
Passeau and Atwood; Bryant and O'Dea

PHILLIES (2d)...0 0 0 —
CHICAGO........2 0 0 —
Mulcahy and Atwood; Lee and Hartnett

DETROIT (AL)...0 0 0 0 0 0 0 1 0-1 9 0
BOSTON..........0 6 0 0 0 0 2 4 X-12 15 1
Gill and York; Grove and Desautels

ST. LOUIS (AL)...0 0 0 2 0 0 2 —
NEW YORK......2 0 0 0 1 2 —
Newsom and Heath; Pearson and Dickey

CLEVEL'D (AL)..2 0 0 1 0 —
WASHINGTON...0 0 0 0 —
Harder and Pytlak; Leonard and R. Ferrell

NEW YORK (NL).0 0 0 0 0 0 —
CINCINNATI.....1 0 0 0 0 0 —
Gumbert and Mancuso; Walters and Lombardi

BROOKLYN (NL).0 2 0 0 0 0 0 0 0 0 —
PITTSBURGH.......0 0 0 0 0 0 0 0 2 0 —
Fitzsimmons and Shea; Blanton and Todd

BOSTON (NL)....0 —
ST. LOUIS........0 —
Fette and Mueller; Macon and Owen

Navy Asks for New Ship Bids

WASHINGTON, July 14.—(AP)—The navy invited bids from private shipbuilders today for construction of three of the four battleships provided for by the last session of Congress. Bids will be opened here October 5.

Ickes Vetoes N. Y. Tube Project

WASHINGTON, July 14.—(AP)—Secretary Ickes said today the proposed Battery tunnel in New York City was "out of the picture" as a public works project because construction could not meet PWA time limitations.

Must Face Trial as Slayer

EBENSBURG, PA., July 14.—(UP)—Peter Srino, 22, of Pittsburgh, must be extradited to Ohio to face trial on a charge of participating in the murder of George Conn, an Ohio State highway patrolman, Chief Justice Kephart, of the State Supreme Court, ruled this afternoon.

JAPAN DROPS OLYMPICS DUE TO WAR DRAIN

Finds It Impossible to Finance 1940 Games and Stadium

WORLD EXPOSITION ALSO IS ABANDONED

By RELMAN MORIN

Tokio, July 14.—(AP)—For the second time in a generation, war caused cancellation today of plans to hold the Olympic Games in the capital of a warring empire.

The Japanese Government faced with the possibility of two more years of conflict in China and shortage of funds and materials, suddenly abandoned its support of plans to hold the 1940 games in Tokio.

The World War wrecked plans to hold the 1916 Olympics in Berlin, capital of a Germany at war with most of the major powers.

Japan, although at war only with China, has faced a steadily rising tide of criticism and threats of athletic and economic boycotts.

The Japanese Army's opposition to the Games as an influence for internationalism, considered hostile to the orthodox military creed of Japan, also was a powerful factor in the decision to give up the Olympics.

At the same time, the Government announced cancellation of the International Exposition of 1940, planned for more than a decade to celebrate what orthodox Japanese consider the 2500th anniversary of

OLYMPICS
Continued on Page Twenty-seven, Col. Eight

Race Results

By Associated Press

Rockingham

FIRST, purse $800, claiming, 4-year-olds and up, 6 furlongs (chute):
1. Night Raven, 112, Nodarse $28.50 $15.44 $7.92
2. Baby Sweep, 113, Albrecht 28.50 11.74
3. Fumble, 112, Yarberry 15.58

Time, 1:12 3-5. Romney Royal, Hastinola, Ipso Facto, Maebob, Mistract, Bugle Ann, Strange Times, Col. Greenock, Black Thorn also ran.

SECOND, purse $800, maiden 3-year-olds and up, 6 furlongs (chute):
1. Foggy Morn, 102, Evans $41.00 $13.68 $5.56
2. Aethelwold, 112, Laidley .. 7.10 4.10
3. Sport's Heel, 107, Berger 2.64

Time, 1:13 2-5. Billy's Folly, Play by Play, Mag's Choice, Critical Lady, Bowtip and Just An Idea also ran.

Winner selected by A. P. Consensus.

Daily Double—Night Raven and Foggy Morn paid $257.48 for $2.

THIRD, purse $800, conditions, 2-year-old fillies, 5 furlongs:
1. Catechism, 118, Donoso $7.12 $4.32 $2.30
2. War Streak, 112, Lynch.. 11.12 2.58
3. Nellie Bly, 118, Arcaro.......... 2.12

Time, 1:01. Sun Bess, Ellasaw, Honey Maid and Dona Montez also ran.

FOURTH, purse $800, claiming, 3-year-olds, 1 1-16 miles:
1. Weary Flower, 103, F. A. Smith..........$4.64 $3.14 $2.64
2. Brogan, 113, Donoso...... 6.78 3.36
3. Standard Time, 113, Arcaro...... 3.54

Time, 1:47 4-5. Bertillon, Howdoino and Affirmation also ran.

Winner selected by Tack, Noone, A. P. Consensus.

RACE RESULTS
Continued on Page Twenty-eight, Col. Seven

DR. BROOME JOINS STAFF AT TEMPLE

Ex-Superintendent of Schools to Lecture in University Teachers' Course

Dr. Edwin C. Broome, former Superintendent of Schools, has been engaged as a member of the faculty of Temple University Teachers' School, it was reported today.

Six months ago, Dr. Broome obtained a six months' leave of absence and later resigned at the termination of the leave. His place has been taken by Dr. Alexander J. Stoddard, who headed the schools of Denver.

The resignation of Dr. Broome was accepted by the Board of Education "with reluctance" after he explained that the condition of his health forbade continuation of his duties.

Reports said he would take up his duties at Temple at the opening of classes next Fall and that his lectures would consume only two hours a week.

His subjects, it was said, will include problems dealing with educational administration and a survey of contemporary education in the United States.

Dr. Broome's long career as a teacher and educator started in the high school at Pawtucket, R. I. Later he served for eight years as Superintendent of Schools at East Orange, N. J. before coming to Philadelphia, where he held his post for seventeen years.

For some months his health has not been of the best and recently his condition was aggravated by an eye ulcer. Friends have intimated that he has showed signs of continued improvement and might well take over the comparatively lighter duties at Temple.

Mayor La Guardia welcomes tired crew back home — *Associated Press Wirephotos*

Crowd surrounds world plane as it ends flight in New York — *Associated Press Wirephoto*

MAYOR OFFERS CITY AS OLYMPICS SITE

Wilson Makes Bid for 1940 Games; Plan Supported by Kelly

A strong bid was made today to bring the 1940 International Olympic Games to Philadelphia in view of Japan's sudden cancellation of acceptance.

Backed by a number of outstanding athletes, Mayor Wilson sent a telegram to Henry Avery Brundage, president of the American Olympic Association, urging him to consider the facilities of the city from the sportsman's viewpoint.

He said he would continue to go

OLYMPIC BID
Continued on Page Twenty-nine, Col. Five

F. R. on West Coast To Review Fleet

Aboard President Roosevelt's Train En Route to San Francisco, July 14.—(AP)—President Roosevelt pushed through to the Pacific Coast today on a program much to his liking.

Arranging to arrive at Crockett, near San Francisco, this morning, his day's plans included a sightseeing and inspection tour in the San Francisco area, a speech at the exposition grounds, and a review of the United States Fleet.

The fleet review takes the President back to one of his first loves, the Navy. His plans called for him to board the cruiser Houston at Oakland in midafternoon and to stay aboard at least seven hours.

The President will come ashore late tonight to entrain for El Portal, entrance to Yosemite National Park, which the Presidential party will tour tomorrow.

Blames Peculations Of $3500 on 'Horses'

William R. Schmitz, 35, cashier for a coastwise passenger and freight line, was quoted by police today as blaming "horses and family expenses" for the embezzlement of $3500.

Magistrate Costello held him in $1000 bail for the Grand Jury. Schmitz, who lives in Oaklyn, N. J., was arrested yesterday. He was said to have admitted taking small amounts two years ago.

Council Asks State To Finance WPA Jobs

Amid jeers, boos and shouted threats of a sit-down strike in City Hall by several hundred unemployed, City Council passed to the State Government this afternoon the responsibility for finding $2,000,000 necessary to obtain the city's share of Federal WPA and PWA grants.

A resolution introduced by Councilman George Maxman petitioned Governor Earle to transfer the needed sum from funds allocated by the Legislature for direct relief throughout the State.

The resolution was adopted by a vote of 15 to 6. Councilmen Clark, Crossan, Fox, Irvin, Edward A. Kelly and Minehart voted against it.

Time after time Council's debate on the matter was interrupted by jeers and catcalls from the crowded galleries. As the vote was being taken and when it appeared certain the measure had a majority, there were cries of "throw 'em out," and "we are going to sit down here and stay until you find us jobs."

Says City May Provide Money

Bernard Samuel, chairman of the Finance Committee, held out a ray of hope that the city might be able to find the money in the event that the State Government turned a deaf ear to the resolution.

He declared amid shouts from the unemployed that if the State failed to heed the request he would call a special meeting of the Finance Committee to see whether "some or all of the recently authorized $2,000,000 emergency loan could not be used for this purpose."

The tumult in the gallery continued to grow and the noise was such that Councilman George Connell, president of Council, sent for a squad of police and ordered them to clear the balconies. Policemen passed through the throng, ordering them to leave. As they marched out the demonstrators continued to jeer, but otherwise gave the police no opposition.

Crowd Cheers Minehart

Just before the balconies were cleared Councilman Minehart, the lone Democratic member, was loudly cheered when he commented:

"I sincerely hope this is not City Council's final action on this question. If it is, then the chamber has sunk to a new low in intelligence and management of city government. If City Council cannot raise $2,000,000, then it should be turned over to a bankruptcy commission."

Earlier Mayor Wilson sent a special message to the chamber urging an appropriation of not less than $2,000,000 as the city's share in WPA projects. Such an appropriation, he said, would bring more than $20,000,000 worth of "absolutely necessary public improvements to the city."

The vanguard of the unemployed, who had marched 3000 strong from Reyburn Plaza, reached the fourth floor of City Hall shortly after 2 P. M.

Held Back by Ten Policemen

They found two grilled gates and a "thin line" of ten policemen barring their way to City Council Chamber.

As the gates swayed, in momentary danger of falling in, the per-

WPA WORK
Continued on Page Four, Col. Six

JOBLESS HERE TOP NATIONAL AVERAGE

R. P. Brown Sees Phila. Unemployment 45 P. C. Greater Than in U. S. as a Whole

The highest State taxes in the Nation—levied on manufacturing corporations in Pennsylvania — were blamed today for the following situation:

First. Unemployment in Philadelphia is now 45 per cent greater than anywhere else in the United States.

Second. Unemployment in Pennsylvania is 25 per cent greater than in any other State.

This commentary on the industrial plight of a great industrial city and State was made today by Richard P. Brown, of the Brown Instrument Company, in an address

JOBS
Continued on Page Four, Col. Two

Log of Hughes' World Hop

The log of the around-the-world flight of Howard Hughes:

Philadelphia Time

SUNDAY, JULY 10

7:20 P. M.—Took off from Floyd Bennett Field, New York.

11:20 P. M.—Passed Cape Breton Island.

MONDAY, JULY 11

1:30 A. M.—Passed over St. Johns, Newfoundland, last land.

9:30 A. M.—Reached Ireland.

11:55 A. M.—Arrived Paris, covering 3641 miles in 16 hours 35 minutes.

8:24 P. M.—Took off for Moscow after refueling and repairs.

12:15 P. M.—Over Pomorze, Poland.

TUESDAY, JULY 12

4:13 A. M.—Arrived Moscow, covering 1675 miles in 7 hours 49 minutes.

6:25 A. M.—Took off for Omsk, U. S. S. R., after refueling.

8:30 A. M.—Crossed Volga River.

2:00 P. M.—Arrived Omsk, covering 1380 miles in 7 hours 35 minutes.

6:37 P. M.—Took off for Yakutsk, Siberia.

WEDNESDAY, JULY 13

5:08 A. M.—Arrived Yakutsk, covering 2177 miles in 10 hours 31 minutes.

8:01 A. M.—Took off from Yakutsk, Siberia, for Fairbanks, Alaska.

5 P. M.—Left Siberia, heads for Alaska via Bering Strait route.

8:18 P. M.—Arrived Fairbanks, covering hazardous 2456-mile hop in 12 hours 17 minutes.

9:36 P. M.—Took off from Fairbanks.

THURSDAY, JULY 14

1:32 A. M.—Reported 811 miles out from Fairbanks, speeding toward Canadian-American border.

3 A. M.—Encountered electrical storms near Fort Nelson, British Columbia. Crossing rugged Canadian Rockies, rose to 14,500 feet.

9:38 A. M.—Landed at Minneapolis to refuel.

10:11 A. M. — Hopped off at Minneapolis on 1054-mile flight to New York, last leg of trip, after refueling.

11:08 A. M.—Sighted over Stevens Point, Wis.

11:28 A. M.—Flew over Two Rivers, Wis., 740 miles from New York.

12:24 P. M.—Flew over Saginaw, Mich., 560 miles from New York.

12:40 P. M.—Sighted over Camlachie, twelve miles northeast of Sarnia, Ontario. Approximately 480 miles from goal.

1:39 P. M. — Reached Wellsville, N. Y., 235 miles from Floyd Bennett Field.

2 P. M.—Passed over Scranton, Pa., airport, 135 miles to go.

2:37 P. M.—Landed in New York.

30,000 Cheer His Arrival in N. Y.

POST'S TIME IS CUT IN HALF BY FLIGHT

Plane Averaged 206 Miles an Hour for Actual Flying Time

By CHARLES McCANN

Floyd Bennett Field, New York, July 14. — (UP) — Howard Hughes, first man ever to circle the world within the span of four days, landed here at 2:37 P. M. daylight time today in a super-airplane stained with the dust of three continents.

Like a thoroughbred that is fastest on the run down the stretch for home, Hughes and his four companions roared in from Minneapolis on a forty-mile tail wind, hitting at times the highest speed of the entire flight of 14,690 miles.

When the wheels of the big plane bumped on the concrete landing field, Hughes had cut in half the best previous round - the - world record—186 hours 49½ minutes, made by the late Wiley Post in 1933.

The fliers followed virtually the same course as Wiley Post in 1933.

Hughes had crossed three continents and two oceans since leaving this same field at 7:20 P. M. last Sunday. His unofficial round - the - world time was 91 hours and 17 minutes.

His average flying speed was 206.71 miles an hour, and the speed for elapsed time was 161.02 miles an hour.

30,000 Await Him

It was a shining achievement—one of the great triumphs of aviation—for the five bearded, weary men and the stout ship that carried them through the frozen blasts of the Arctic and the hot winds of prairie America between two sunsets.

The end came under gray

HUGHES HOP
Continued on Page Seven, Col. Two

Hepburn Is Linked To Hughes Welcome

Old Saybrook, Conn., July 14. — (UP)—Katharine Hepburn, screen and stage star, whose engagement to Howard Hughes has been reported and denied frequently, left hurriedly today by automobile from the Summer home of her parents at Fenwick Point.

It was assumed she was driving to New York to greet Hughes.

In Today's

Evening Ledger

DANZIG PLEBISCITE PUT UP TO BRITISH

Nazi Leader From Free City Seeks O. K. on Balloting for Return to Reich

By LOUIS P. LOCHNER

Berlin, July 14.—(AP)—Albert Foerster, Nazi district leader in the Free City of Danzig, is in London, it was learned today, to obtain British acquiescence to an Autumn plebiscite as a result of which Danzig's return to Germany would be demanded.

Foerster left Danzig July 7 so secretly that only the smallest official circle knew about the departure.

Before the World War Danzig was the capital of German West Prussia. The Versailles Treaty gave it the status of free city under League of Nations protection with a League high commissioner stationed in the city and with its foreign relations conducted by Poland. Its 1924 population was 385,000, of which 96 per cent were German. Its Government is now Nazi-dominated.

Foerster went to London incognito after visiting Polish Foreign Minister Beck in Warsaw. The Nazi proposed the plebiscite to Beck and promises that the Polish minority always would be conceded two seats in the Danzig Parliament.

Beck was said to have replied he could not recognize Foerster as competent to deal with another Government since he was merely a party leader without a State office.

To the theoretical question whether Poland would agree to a plebiscite in the Fall, Beck was reported to have answered Poland might waive objections provided Great Britain as a League of Nations member also agreed.

Fliers' Wives on Reception Committee

Mrs. Connor (left), wife of Navigator Harry P. McLean Connor; Mrs. Richard Stoddart (center), wife of the radio engineer, and Mrs. Thomas Thurlow (right), whose husband was also a navigator on the Hughes plane, join Grover Whalen and Mayor La Guardia in welcoming "the boys" back home

Associated Press Wirephoto

Hughes Hop

Continued from Page One

skies on a field where 30,000, aroused with admiration, waited to see, listen and cheer.

Hughes' big silver ship appeared over Floyd Bennett Field at 2:34 P. M. There was a ceiling of about 1000 feet, the sun was under clouds and a spatter of rain was falling.

The big ship streaked in fast at about 800 feet and circled from the west. Twice Hughes curved her around the Administration Building at the field. Lower and lower he came. Then he put her nose toward the southeast and set her down on a short runway.

Hughes taxied the ship up to the Administration Building.

Thirty thousand throats smothered him in cheers.

A fire truck's siren wailed a greeting as the big ship's taxi speed slackened.

Hughes at Controls

Twenty-four motorcycle policemen sputtered out toward the ship to form an escort for the fliers. The plane went on through a lane of the policemen, barely moving now.

Hughes brought her home the way he took her out—at the controls himself.

Grover Whalen, head of the New York World Fair, walked out to the ship. Field attendants carried a big bouquet of flowers to the plane.

Mayor La Guardia and Whalen stepped into the plane, and within a few minutes Hughes emerged. Photographers clustered around and the air was bright with exploding flash bulbs.

The four members of the crew, cramped and stiff from their long confinement in the cabin, followed Hughes out of the plane. The ship, glittering like a new half dollar when it left here Sunday, had been turned a dull gray by wind and weather.

Flight Was Wonderful

Some one dragged a loudspeaker up to where the fliers were standing and Mayor La Guardia turned to Hughes and said: "Congratulations."

"The flight was wonderful," Hughes replied.

Then Hughes paid tribute to the four men who helped him girdle the globe.

"This is the best crew in the world," he said.

The man who had braved the wildest flying country in the world then added:

"All I can say is that this crowd has frightened me more than anything else in the last few days."

The crowd surged against a fence and broke it. Police picked up the fence and used it to shove the crowd back into line.

Hughes, wearing the same old brown hat he had on when he left, walked toward a tent on the field where he was scheduled to talk to reporters. His white shirt was soiled and splotched with grease.

Only a few of the 30,000 persons at the field had seen Hughes a half hour after he landed. The crowd was so dense that the fliers were lost in the knot of policemen and newspaper men who surrounded them.

No Danger at Any Time

Inside the tent where he gave the interview to reporters, Hughes said:

"I was in no danger at any time. I feel all right, I guess. I'm a little tired."

He was asked how often he used the robot pilot on the plane, and he replied in a joking voice: "All the time."

"Will you try another world flight?" Hughes was asked.

"Not today, thanks," he said.

"I'm glad it's all over," Hughes added. "I expect to get as much sleep this week as I can possibly absorb."

One of the first persons to enter the plane was a United States customs official who made a routine inspection of the contents of the cabin.

"Let's hurry it up," Hughes suggested to him. "I've been in here long enough."

Tired as he was, Hughes went over to a hangar and saw his plane safely berthed before leaving the field. Then he got into an automobile and headed for Manhattan, looking forward to "a shave, a bath and a massage."

The five fliers, the wives of the three who are married and Mayor La Guardia went to the home of Whalen.

In a soul-trying fight against storms and exhaustion, the five American air conquerors had flown 2483 miles overnight to Minneapolis from Fairbanks, Alaska. There they refueled in thirty-three minutes, to take off at 10:11 A. M., Philadelphia time, for their final 1054-mile flight to New York City.

The flight from Fairbanks to Minneapolis was a test for men of the toughest caliber. Swirling winds tossed the big snub-nosed monoplane as it flew, at higher than 20,000 feet, over the thrusting peaks of the Canadian Rockies.

Then a real fight began. The aviators found themselves headed into a magnetic storm area. Lightning played in the air. At 3:05 A. M. the plane reported its position as over the Northwest Alberta Province, Canada. Then there was silence.

Plane Silent Six Hours

Then for more than six anxious hours there was no word from the plane—by far the longest time it had been silent during the entire flight. The radio antenna had gone bad; the transmitter was balky. Stresses all over the plane, struggling like a racehorse over the finish stretch of its course of more than 14,000 miles began to signal danger to the five exhausted men in the plane.

Instead of stopping at Winnipeg, where the fliers at first intended to land, the plane streaked toward the airport at Minneapolis. One hundred persons, all the crowd there was at the airport—for the fliers were expected to land 400 miles away—stood tense as Hughes, at the controls, brought his plane in.

The silver plane glinted in the morning sun as it came down between the thinly scattered clouds and headed for a landing against the twelve-mile northwest wind that had aided it to its landing place. There had been headwinds against it almost all the way.

Steps Out Like Old Man

The plane came down on the wide concrete-surfaced runway and Hughes taxied it to the apron, where gasoline trucks were waiting. Gasoline trucks were waiting, too, at a dozen other airports in the United States and Canada, for nobody knew where the plane would land.

Hughes stepped from the plane like an old man. He was stiff with exhaustion.

"It was about as hard as any leg of the flight," he said. "We bucked bad weather two-thirds of the way."

He paused a moment and said:

"We're going to give it all we've got the rest of the way."

"We're Going On"

As 750 gallons of gasoline were put into the plane's tanks—and one and a half gallons of oil taken out—Hughes chatted:

"A lot of little things are wrong with her . . we won't stop to repair them here . . she's ready for the flight, and we're going on."

The refueling crew gave the all-ready signal. Hughes took the controls. He waved, the little crowd—500 people now—cheered, and he gave his plane the gun. It lifted easily after a short run of about 750 feet. It cleared the airport fence like a steeplechaser and, flying low still, swung due east and disappeared.

Hughes was at the controls for the takeoff from Minneapolis, as he had been for the landing. He waved cheerily to the crowd just before gunning the ship.

Morale at High Level

Hughes said the morale of the crew was at high level.

"We're tired, of course," he said, "but it's been a great trip so far, and we're going to give it all we've got the rest of the way."

His flying companions, Ed Lund, T. L. Thurlow, Richard Stoddart and Harry P. McL. Connor, echoed his sentiments.

Hughes said the reason the ship had been unreported for six hours was that the radio transmitter had failed after leaving Fairbanks. He said they had experienced intermittent trouble with the transmitter ever since leaving Paris.

Airman's Fiancee Collapses Under Strain of Waiting

MISS ELINOR HOAGLAND

Floyd Bennett Airport, New York, July 14.—(UP)—Thousands jammed Floyd Bennett Field to welcome Howard Hughes and his crew home, but one who wanted most to be there fainted before the triumphal hour arrived and was taken away.

The one whose nerves couldn't stand the days and nights of waiting and the excitement of final hours was Elinor Hoagland, 19-year-old Brooklyn girl who is engaged to Ed Lund, flight engineer on the Hughes flight.

She had been staying at the field ever since the flight began on Sunday, sleeping on a cot in a hangar. Last night she couldn't sleep at all. As the time for arrival approached she grew more and more nervous and fainted. Friends decided it would be best to take her home, to greet her sweetheart later.

'Hello,' Says Wife To Flier as Crowd Ties Her Tongue

New York, July 14.—(AP)—The anxious wives of three members of the Hughes around-the-world flight crew were mere spectators for a time today as the fliers landed at Floyd Bennett Field.

The wives—Mrs. Thomas L. Thurlow, Mrs. Harry P. McL. Connor and Mrs. Richard Stoddart — were momentarily held back in the press of the vast crowd when the plane landed, in spite of the efforts of a special squad of policemen.

As the great silver plane circled overhead Mrs. Stoddart yelled:

"Hurray, boys!"

Mrs. Connor smiled.

"Aren't you proud?" she said to her companions. "Isn't it wonderful? It's all like a dream."

Mrs. Thurlow thought it was "the best-looking ship I've ever seen."

Mrs. Stoddart tried to light a cigarette. Her hands shook. She finally got the light and smoked nervously.

When at last they got through to greet their husbands, this was what they said:

Mrs. Connor (too excited for more): "Oh, hello."

Mrs. Stoddart (with a kiss): "Thank God you're back!"

Mrs. Thurlow (kiss and embrace): "Tommy!"

Margiotti Here To Talk Politics

Former Attorney General Margiotti today paid a surprise visit to Philadelphia, presumably to discuss politics before making public whom he intends to support in the November Gubernatorial election.

Margiotti was accompanied by Edward Friedman, a former Deputy Attorney General and his law partner, and N. L. Wynard, who also served as a Deputy Attorney General until Margiotti broke with Governor Earle, just before the primary.

"I have several engagements to talk over the political situation during the day, but at this time that's all I want to say," Margiotti declared when asked whom he intends to see.

It was reported, however, that Margiotti expected to get in touch with Mayor Wilson and possibly both Democratic and Republican leaders.

Bandit Car Found

Chester, July 14.—Police of Linwood, five miles southwest of here, today at noon recovered the car which was used yesterday morning by three bandits in the armed robbery of a $2700 payroll from the A. H. Wirz Manufacturing Company, Fourth and Townsend Streets. The machine was stolen in West Philadelphia July 11.

3 Police Promotions Ordered Certified

Mayor Wilson today ordered the certification of three acting police commanders to permanent rank. The move was interpreted as an attempt by the Mayor to make peace with the Civil Service Commission.

Inspector Thomas Burns, who has been acting inspector in the Northeast section, has been made inspector in charge of the radio police service. His place will be taken by Captain Reuben F. Reynolds, who has been commanding the Seventh and Carpenter Streets station. Sergeant John F. Driscoll, who has been acting inspector in South Philadelphia, has been elevated to a full inspectorship.

Pertinent Data On Hughes Plane And Equipment

New York, July 14.—(AP)—Here is a thumbnail sketch of the Hughes plane, cost, flight stops and other pertinent data:

Plane

Lockheed 14, monoplane, dual Wright cyclone motors developing 1100 horsepower each.

The plane has a wing span of 65 feet 6 inches and is 44 feet 4 inches in length. Its fuel capacity is 1750 gallons, of which 1200 gallons are in the main storage tanks. Its flight range, at cruising speed, is 4700 miles.

The cost, with special equipment, has been estimated at $200,000.

Equipment

Both motors are equipped with Hamilton-standard hydromatic propellers with variable pitch. A Sperry gyroscope, three radios with range from 333 to 22,080 kilocycles and a voice broadcasting radio are included in the special apparatus.

Emergency equipment includes two rubber liferafts each capable of keeping afloat the crew of five men, five parachutes each containing an emergency ration pack sufficient for thirty days, plus fishing tackle, hunting knife and first-aid kit. Oxygen tanks are carried as are flares and in the nose of the ship are two powerful searchlights behind flexiglass.

Flight Cost

Flight headquarters estimates the cost of the flight at $300,000.

Fuel

Gasoline consumption is figured at the rate of seventy-two gallons per hour.

Tennis Queen Weds Scottish Doctor

London, July 14.—(AP) — Anita Lizana, Chilean holder of the United States singles tennis championship, was married today to Ronald Ellis, Scottish doctor.

Senorita Lizana, who stands 4 feet 10 in her tennis slippers, employed three-inch heels and an eight-inch white Spanish comb to bring herself to her husband's height.

Average net paid circulation for September exceeded
Daily---1,800,000
Sunday-3,150,000

DAILY NEWS

NEW YORK'S PICTURE NEWSPAPER

FINAL

Vol. 20. No. 109 | New York, Monday, October 31, 1938★ | 48 Pages | 2 Cents IN CITY LIMITS | 3 CENTS Elsewhere

Entered as 2nd class matter, Post Office, New York, N. Y.

FAKE RADIO 'WAR' STIRS TERROR THROUGH U.S.

Story on Page 2

Love Notes

Mrs. Myrl Alderman, suing Ruth Etting (above) for theft of husband's love, yesterday asserted she'll produce torchy letters written by Ruth to Alderman. —*Story on page 3.*

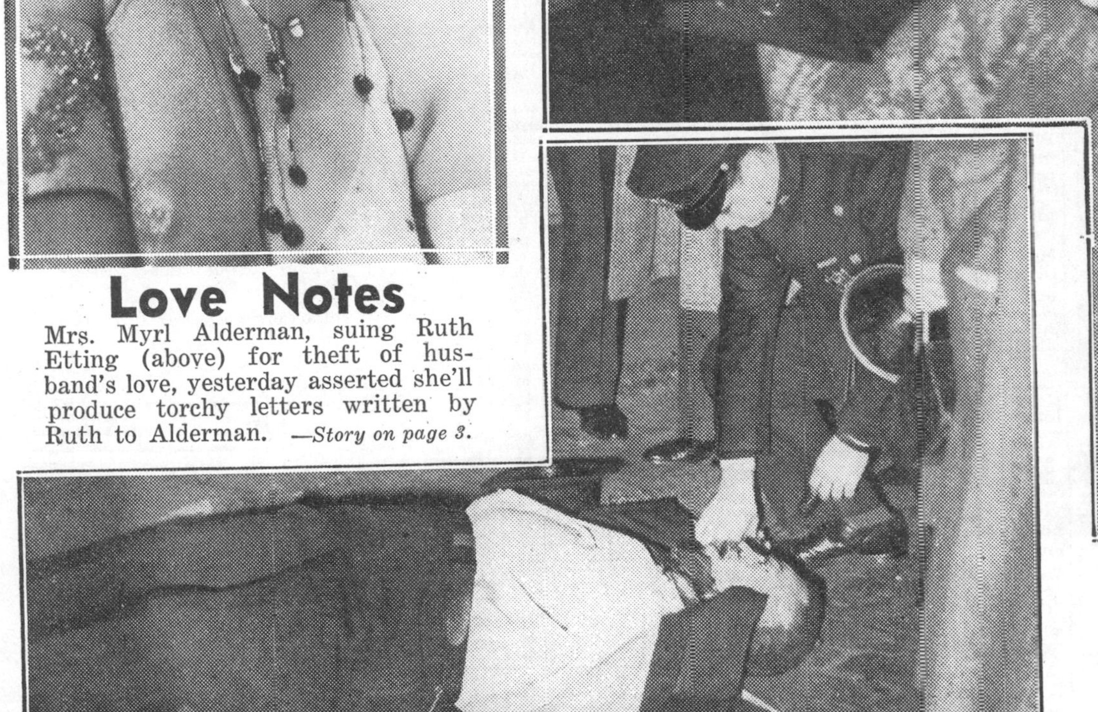

(NEWS fotos)

Murder on the Street

Mrs. Rose Tejada struggles hysterically in grasp of detective to reach body of husband, Peter, shown at left after he was shot yesterday by unknown assailants at Adams and High Sts., Brooklyn. Life-long friend of slain man, who was Puerto Rican colony leader, is wanted for questioning. —*Story p. 10*

Fake Radio Air Attack Throws U. S. Into Panic

By GEORGE DIXON.

A radio dramatization of H. G. Wells' "War of the Worlds"—which thousands of people misunderstood as a news broadcast of a current catastrophe in New Jersey—created almost unbelievable scenes of terror in New York, New Jersey, the South and even west to San Francisco between 8 and 9 o'clock last night.

The panic started when an announcer suddenly interrupted the program of a dance orchestra—which was part of the dramatization—to "flash" an imaginary bulletin that a mysterious "meteor" had struck New Jersey, lighting the heavens for miles around.

A few seconds later, the announcer "flashed" the tidings that weird monsters were swarming out of the mass of metal—which was not a meteor but a tube-like car from Mars—and were destroying thousands of people with fire.

Thousands Flee.

Without waiting for further details, thousands of persons rushed from their homes in New York and New Jersey, many with towels across their faces to protect themselves from the "gas" which the meteor was supposed to be giving forth.

Simultaneously, thousands more in states that stretched west to California and south to the Gulf of Mexico rushed to their telephones to inquire of newspapers, the police, switchboard operators, and electric companies what they should do to protect themselves.

Occupants of Park Ave. apartment houses flocked to the street.

Churches Filled.

In Harlem excited crowds shouted that President Roosevelt's voice had warned them to "pack up and move north because the machines are coming from Mars." The dramatization of Wells' novel had featured a fictitious speech from "the Governor of New Jersey," assuring the public that the National Guard had been mobilized to fight the "Martian monsters" and the Harlem residents had confused the mythical "Governor" with the President.

Churches in both New York and New Jersey were filled suddenly

(Continued on page 6, col. 1)

Senator Maps Bill on Radio 'Abuses'

Des Moines, Oct. 30 (AP).—Senator Clyde L. Herring (Dem., Iowa) said tonight he planned to introduce a bill in the next session of Congress "controlling just such abuses as was heard over the radio tonight." He said the bill would propose a censorship board to which all radio programs must be submitted.

Frank R. McNinch, chairman of the Federal Communications Commission, in Washington said that an investigation would be held at once by the FCC. He would not predict what action might be taken, but said a thorough probe would be made.

'End of World' Shock to U. S.

The radio's "end of the world," as some listeners understood it, produced repercussions throughout the United States. Samples, as reported by the Associated Press, follow:

Wants to Fight Mars

San Francisco.—An offer to volunteer in stopping an invasion from Mars came among hundreds of telephone inquiries to police and newspapers tonight during the radio dramatization of the H. G. Wells' story. One excited man called Oakland police and shouted: "My God! Where can I volunteer my services? We've got to stop this awful thing!"

Church Lets Out

Indianapolis.—A woman ran into a church screaming: "New York destroyed; it's the end of the world. You might as well go home to die. I just heard it on the radio." Services were dismissed immediately.

College Boys Faint

Brevard, N. C.—Five Brevard College students fainted and panic gripped the campus for a half hour with many students fighting for telephones to inform their parents to come and get them.

It's a Massacre

Providence, R. I., weeping and hysterical women swamped the switchboard of the Providence Journal for details of the "massacre". The electric company received scores of calls urging it to turn off all lights so that the city would be safe from the "enemy."

She Sees "the Fire"

Boston.—One woman declared she could "see the fire" an dtold the oBston Globe she and many others in her neighborhood were "getting out of here."

"Where Is It Safe?"

Kansas City.—One telephone informant said he had loaded all his children into his car, had filled it with gasoline, and was going somewhere. "Where is it safe?" He wanted to know. The Assocated Press bureau received queries on the "meteors" from Los Angeles, Salt Lake City, Beaumont, Tex., and St. Joseph, Mo.

Prayrs in Richmond

Richmond, Va.—The Times-Dispatch, reported some of its telephone calls came from persons who said they were praying.

Atlanta's "Monsters"

Atlanta—Listeners throughout the Southeast called newspapers reporting that "a planet struck in New Jersey, with monsters and almost everything, and anywhere from 40 to 7,000 people were killed." Editors said responsible persons, known to them, were among the anxious information seekers.

Carolina Weeps

Fayetteville, N. C.—Persons with relatives in New Jersey went to a newspaper office in tears, seeking information.

Minneapolis Scared

Minneapolis.—Police switchboards were swamped with calls from frightened people.

Dewey's City Gain Clips Foe's Poll

By ROGER DAKIN

Gov. Lehman's hairline lead in the state-wide results of The News Gubernatorial Straw Poll—now only 1.2 per cent. over District Attorney Dewey—has been steadily reduced in the last few days' polling by a falling away of Democratic support in what was expected to be the Governor's stronghold, New York City.

Dewey's strength upstate, which will be 6.61 per cent. better than the showing made by the Republican candidate for Governor in 1936, according to the straws thus far, was expected by both parties.

Democrats Upset.

The Democrats, however, have declared that Dewey, far from picking up new strength in the city, actually would make a worse race than his Republican predecessor, William F. Bleakley, who, in 1936, got only 32.7 per cent. of the vote in the five boroughs, against 67.3 per cent. for Lehman.

But the straws thus far show that it will be Lehman who will run behind 1936.

Lehman has lost strength in every borough polled to date, according to the straws. He has lost the most in Brooklyn, the least in the Bronx. Altogether he dropped 8.01 per cent., comparing this year's

(Continued on page 22, col. 1)

How They Stand to Date.

LEHMAN	DEWEY
50.6%	49.4%

DAILY ALMANAC

MONDAY, OCT. 31, 1938.
(Eastern Standard Time)

Fair.

Tomorrow partly cloudy and warmer.

THE MOON

Oct. 31-Nov. 6 First Q.
Nov. 7-13 Full
Nov. 14-20 Last Q.
Nov. 21-28 New

THE NEWS BAROMETER

Sunrise, 6:24 A. M. sunset, 4:55 P. M. Moon rises, 12:54 P. M.; sets, 11:54 P. M. Morning star, Mars; evening star, Venus.

TEMPERATURES IN NEW YORK

MAXIMUM, 1:10 P. M.——56
MINIMUM, 6:00 A. M.——47
Highest this date, 73 in 1918
Lowest this date, 31 in 1928

1 a. m.	54	10 a. m.	49	6 p. m.	53
2 a. m.	52	11 a. m.	52	7 p. m.	51
3 a. m.	52	Noon	54	8 p. m.	51
4 a. m.	50	1 p. m.	55	9 p. m.	50
5 a. m.	48	1:10 p. m.	56	10 p. m.	50
6 a. m.	47	2 p. m.	55	Unofficial	
7 a. m.	47	3 p. m.	54	11 p. m.	50
8 a. m.	48	4 p. m.	55	Midnight	49
9 a. m.	50	5 p. m.	55	1 a. m.	

For twenty-four hours ended at 7:30 P. M., Oct. 30:

Mean temperature, 52; normal 51; excess since Jan. 1, 606 degrees; excess since Oct. 1, 75 degrees.

Precipitation, none; excess since Jan. 1, 4.54 inches; deficiency since Oct. 1, 1.80 inches.

	5 A. M. 7:30 A.M.	5 P. M. 7:30 P.M.
Barometer	30.03	30.10
Humidity	81	65
Wind—direction	N	N
Wind—velocity	21	16

TIME OF TIDES

	Sandy Hook A.M.	Sandy Hook P.M.	Gov. Is. A.M.	Gov. Is. P.M.	Hell Gate A.M.	Hell Gate P.M.
High water	12:49	1:10	1:56	2:02	3:56	4:02
Low water	7:04	7:48	8:13	8:49	10:13	10:49

RECORDS IN AMERICAN CITIES.

Observations at United States Weather Bureau stations taken at 7:30 P. M.

Cities	Temperature Last 24 Hrs. High	Low	Bar.	Precipitation Last 24 Hrs.	Weather
Albany	52	42	30.22	—	Clear
Bismarck	74	48	29.66	—	P.Cl'dy
Boston	52	50	30.14	.01	Cloudy
Buffalo	44	42	30.30	—	Clear
Chicago	48	48	30.22	—	Clear
Cincinnati	62	38	30.20	—	Clear
Dallas	80	54	29.96	—	Clear
Denver	72	48	29.70	—	Cloudy
Kansas City	75	42	30.02	—	Clear
Los Angeles	64	58	29.94	*	Cloudy
Miami	78	58	29.98	—	Clear
Minneapolis	62	—	30.02	—	Cloudy
New Orleans	78	60	30.02	—	Clear
New York	56	47	30.10	—	Clear
Portland, Me.	54	46	30.22	—	P.Cl'dy
Seattle	54	52	29.68	—	Clear
St. Louis	70	48	30,10	—	Clear
Wash'ton, D. C.	64	50	30.10	—	Clear

*Trace—Rainfall less than .01 inch.

1938 OCTOBER 1938

SUNDAY	MONDAY	TUESDAY	WED'DAY	TH'SDAY	FRIDAY	SAT'DAY
30	31					

1938 NOVEMBER 1938

SUNDAY	MONDAY	TUESDAY	WED'DAY	TH'SDAY	FRIDAY	SAT'DAY
		1	2	3	4	5
6	7		9	10		12
13	14	15	16	17	18	19
20	21	22	23		25	26

The NEWS in TABLOID

AND INDEX

INDEX TO FEATURES

Fake Radio Air Raid Casts U. S. Into Panic

(Continued from page 2)

with persons seeking protection, and who found them, providentially, as they thought, open. In Providence, R. I., terror-stricken citizens pleaded with the electric company to turn off the street lights to "blackout" the city.

At St. Michaels Hospital, in Newark, fifteen persons were treated for shock.

In New York, police and fire departments and the newspapers were swamped with telephone calls from people, apparently frightened half out of their wits.

The telephone company also was deluged. The thing finally assumed such serious proportions that the Columbia Broadcasting System put bulletins on the air explaining that the "meteor" broadcast was part of a play and that nothing untoward had happened.

'Halloween Prank.'

The broadcasting company added that the whole thing had been somewhat in the nature of a Halloween prank. The program, which came over station WABC from 8 to 9 P. M., was presented by Orson Welles' "Mercury Theatre of the Air."

"The War of the Worlds" was a typical H. G. Wells shocker. It described the bombardment of England by huge "space capsules" carrying warriors from Mars. These inhuman, gigantic warriors laid waste to England and killed hundreds of thousands of people. Finally, they were killed by germs and infections—because they came from a planet which had no disease and thus were susceptible to every disease. In Wells' book, there was no mention of the United States.

Doctors Offer Help.

In its dramatization last night the radio station changed the locale to America.

Within a couple of minutes of the first death and destruction bulletin the telephone calls began pouring in. Many of the callers seemed on the point of hysteria. One woman said she had relatives in the "stricken" section of New Jersey and wanted to know if their names were on the casualty lists.

The New York City Department of Health was among the first to call The News. The department wanted to know what assistance it could lend to the maimed and dying.

Hundreds of physicians and nurses were among the callers. Many of them said they were prepared to rush at once into the devastated area to aid in caring for their victims.

Scores of motorists traveling through Jersey heard the broadcast and immediately detoured so as not to pass through the supposedly doomed region. Police in many small Jersey towns and villages called State Police Headquarters to offer assistance.

The trouble was that thousands who were listening to the program rushed out immediately — or at least stopped listening—the moment they heard about the meteor.

In Watchung, N. J., an excited policeman on desk duty—notified by horrified citizens that a meteor struck somewhere near by, sent squad cars out to look for injured.

Among the flood of calls to CBS offices was one from Mayor Barlow, of Plainfield, N. J., asking that the radio station broadcast an announcement to listeners in this community that Plainfield had not been struck by the meteor.

Pleas of "What can we do? Where can we go to save ourselves?" flooded New Jersey police switchboards from Hoboken to Cape May. In Newark alone two patrolmen handled more than 2,000 calls from hysterical persons terrified by the fake news bulletin.

Families Flee House.

Harrassed Newark police, trying to reassure thousands of panicky citizens, received a call about a gas explosion in a six-family house at 145 Hedden Terrace. Emergency trucks raced to the scene to find that more than thirty people, occupants of the house, were on the street, holding their clothes and bedding.

An investigation disclosed that Louis Celowitz and his wife, Esther, tuned in on the program just as a news bulletin announced that 600 persons were killed in a gas attack.

"We got nervous," said Celowitz, "and notified every one in the house." All the other tenants then rushed out, taking with them whatever they could grab.

Church Is Thronged.

In Irvington, N. J., hundreds of motorists who heard the announcement of the meteor and the gas attack shouted warnings to each other in the streets.

"Drive like hell into the country; we're being bombed by enemies", drivers shouted to one another. Motorcycle police, astounded by the sudden bursts of speed by motorists, rushed to call boxes to inquire from headquarters about the supposed raids.

In the Sacred Heart Church in Elizabeth priests were amazed by a sudden influx of panicky persons who rushed inside, fell on their knees and began to pray. A phone call to police soon brought an explanation.

State police at Morristown said that dozens of calls from irate radio listeners demanded that authorities obtain indictments against broadcast company officials.

Orson Welles
He started something.

WABC Explains

At 10 P. M., WABC sent out the following explanation of its "War of the Worlds" broadcast:

"For those listeners who tuned in to Orson Welles' Mercury Theatre on the Air broadcast from 8 to 9 P. M. tonight, and did not realize that the program was merely a radio adaptation of H. G. Wells' famous novel, 'War of the Worlds,' we are repeating the fact, which was made clear four times on the program, that the entire content of the play was entirely fictitious."

NBC Says 'Ouch!'

The CBS broadcast of H. G. Wells' "War of the Worlds" created a minor panic at the transmitter station of WJZ, a member of the rival NBC network, last night. WJZ's transmitters are at Bound Brook, N. J., in the heart of the zone where a fictitious news bulletin said that thousands were dead. Someone there tuned in on WABC. A frantic wire flashed in to the NBC offices a few minutes later: "Please tell us what is happening." NBC reassured its men that nothing was happening—except a startling radio broadcast.

Wells Play Reaction Stuns Orson Welles

The reaction of the public seemed almost as fantastic as the play itself to Orson Welles, who adapted the script from the Wells book and portrayed the principal character.

"We've been putting on all sorts of things from the most realistic situations to the wildest fantasy," Welles said, "but nobody ever bothered to get serious about them before. We just can't understand why this should have had such an amazing reaction.

"Four times during the hour—at the beginning, twice during the show and at the end—we explained that it was all a play and that none of it actually was happening. H. G. Wells' book is written about a suburb of London. That seemed so remote that we changed it to a suburb of New York.

Interrupted by Bulletins.

"It started off with music and then I made a speech, supposedly in 1939, saying that as I looked back I never dreamed that such things existed as had actually come before my sight. Then there was a jazz band playing and it was interrupted by bulletins announcing the arrival of the Martians—huge creatures that crawled around shooting death rays and so forth.

"For the next few minutes the program was devoted to special broadcasts, bulletins and so forth announcing the progress of the invasion of the Martians.

"Things seemed to be in a bad way, all right, but just then we broke in for station announcements and disclosed once again that it was all just a huge make-believe.

Described Scenes of 1939.

"After that we dropped the convention of the news bulletins, and I began to talk as if I were describing what I saw in 1939 . . . people lying dead in the streets and near by the Martians—dead, too. They had succumbed to disease germs.

"It's too bad that so many people got excited, but after all, we kept reminding them that it wasn't really true. You can't do much more and hope to keep up any impression of suspense when you're putting on a play."

Get your Horoscope from Wynn, News Astrologer, 220 E. 42d St., New York. Send 5 cents and self-addressed, stamped envelope, giving name, date of birth, birthplace and hour of birth, if possible.

The New York Times
APRIL 30, 1939
SECTION 8
THE FAIR and THE CITY

AN ASSORTMENT OF FAIR MARVELS

THE FAIR, an ancient institution, dates back to the fifth century, but no exposition in history has cost as much, offered as much or made accommodations for as many visitors as the New York World's Fair. The current show is, in a manner of speaking, a library of Time, Space, History, Industry, Art and High Jinks—the universe in full color with a wide perspective on the future to boot. The fair-goer can see and do incredible things.

* * *

A SIGHTSEER with good wind, and the inclination, can journey around 90 per cent of the earth's inhabited surface, take a flight into interstellar space and return; stand in Yesterday, Today and Tomorrow—all within two hours and within the boundaries of the Fair's 1,216 acres.

* * *

SIX BABIES were born at Chicago's Century of Progress. New York's Fair, unless the actuaries have slipped up in their arithmetic, should be the birthplace of twelve to eighteen babies. The Fair's medical staff is prepared to handle at least that many.

* * *

THE TOTAL paved area at the Fair is equivalent to sixty miles of two-lane highways.

* * *

MOUNTAINS WERE moved to prepare the Fair site. The exposition stands on a primeval bog that had been used for many years as a city dump. One heap of ashes 100 feet high, locally known as Mount Corona, was moved to make way for the Fair.

* * *

TO REMOVE the ashes for the Fair site 30,000 men worked 190 days. They removed 7,000,000 cubic yards of fill, used 800,000 cubic yards of top soil and built two great artificial lakes. The ash removal job alone cost $2,200,000.

* * *

MORE THAN 15,000,000 hot dogs and 15,000,000 hamburgers, as exposition statisticans figure it, will be sold no the grounds. These, strung necklace fashion, would reach from New York to London. Rolls to match would pave all the city streets.

* * *

FIVE HUNDRED motion pictures will be run off daily in fifty auditoria. There will be full-length Hollywood features, animated cartoons, educational, scenic and industrial films, many in color.

* * *

MORE THAN a quarter-million people can be fed in the Fair's eighty restaurants in a single night. Statisticians estimate that the restaurants should peddle $18,000,000 worth of victuals, refreshment stands and bars about $4,647,000 worth.

* * *

THE 300 buildings on the grounds cost between $40,000,000 and $50,000,000. Building contracts, in many cases, provide for destruction of these edifices as soon as the Fair ends. World of Here-Today-Gone-Tomorrow.

* * *

IN THE Time and Space Auditorium the sight-seer can outdo Buck Rogers; soar into celestial vastness at 480,000,000,000,000,000,000 miles an hour, through meteoric showers, see Earth drop away and vanish; get a close-up of a solar eclipse and intimate glimpses of Venus, the Moon, Saturn and Mars without taxing his blood pressure or disturbing his hair.

* * *

THE JOB of preparing the Fair was equivalent to building an entirely new city of 800,000 population on an uninhabited spot.

* * *

MURDER WILL be committed at the Fair several times each day with the help of the police.

Hugh Ferriss.

Looking down the Mall.

The murders will be immediately solved, though, through fingerprints and scientific scrutiny of clues at the police laboratory. It's part of the New York City Police Exhibit.

* * *

THE BEAM on the Star Trylon is equivalent to 1,000,000 100-*watt lamps.*

* * *

A MANUFACTURER of playing cards will show the world's most complete collection of "Devil's picture books," including a deck made 300 years ago from human scalps. You can pass this hand, if you like.

* * *

THE GREATEST migration of living trees, some of them fifty-five and sixty feet high, was accomplished to give the Fair natural shade and decoration. The trees were carted an average of sixty miles from Maryland, Pennsylvania, Connecticut, New Jersey and upper New York State in specially designed trucks. A total of 10,000 trees was brought in, some of them up to twenty-five to thirty tons each.

* * *

IN ADDITION to planting 10,000 live trees, Fair gardeners planted 1,000,000 bulbs (gift from Holland), 274,000 beddings plants, 400,000 pansies, 500,000 hedge plants, 250 acres of greensward. One workman sat up all night with an ailing chestnut tree and begged for more fertilizer for it. As a boy he had known the tree in his home town.

* * *

MORE THAN $12,000,000 was spent for underground improvements, much of which the visitor will never see—for thirteen miles of gas mains, fifteen miles of water mains, thirty miles of sewers and fifteen miles of electric cable housing.

* * *

GEORGE GERSHWIN, who wrote the music for the Fair's theme song, "Dawn of a New Day," never heard the lyric. Ira Gershwin, his brother, wrote it after George Gershwin's death.

* * *

ELEVEN ENTRANCE gates will admit 160,000 *visitors an hour, at peak hours.*

* * *

FROM REVOLVING balconies in the 200-foot Perisphere you can look down, as from an altitude of two miles, on a metropolis of 250,000 souls; see dawn, dusk, noon and night and how they affect the whole scene—all within six minutes, real as life.

* * *

WITHOUT a sneeze you can step from a snow-covered ski jump in Sun Valley, Idaho, into Southern Rhodesia; trek by day and night through jungle damp and a tropical storm with real lightning; see and hear Victoria Falls pouring 60,000 gallons of water over its spillway every minute. The water's real, the roar of the Falls a sound effect.

* * *

IN THE amusement zone visitors can jump 250 feet from a parachute tower and be sure of a safe landing. Wire guides make it fool-proof.

* * *

AN ENTIRE forest was destroyed to convert the Flushing marsh into solid foundation. Seven hundred and fifty-eight miles of piling were driven into the ground. The Trylon and Perisphere combined weigh 13,500,000 pounds and rest on 1,000 timber piles.

* * *

IRELAND'S EXHIBIT, in a shamrock-shaped building, has transplanted chunks of "the ould sod" for its lawns and gardens, and water from the River Shannon and the Lakes of Killarney for miniature versions of those places.

* * *

EACH DAY at noon, in the Polish exhibit, a trumpeter will sound the "heynal," a tribute to a bugler who sounded the call 700 years ago when Genghis Khan marched on Cracow.

* * *

TWENTY-SIX Eastern railroads invested over $3,000,000 for their exhibit. For the outdoor display 3,600 feet of track were laid out and 200,000 square feet of exhibit space were required for the indoor, or roundhouse stuff. The model railroad, 160 feet wide and 40 feet deep, is the world's largest; it is part of a diorama including 500 pieces of rolling stock, with 300,000 feet of wire in the signal and control system.

* * *

TWO HUNDRED tons of paint were used on Fair buildings.

* * *

LIVING ACTORS in a universe all their own, magnified to 2,000 times normal size, will cavort on a five-foot screen for the edification of visitors. It's done with the micro-vivarium, a combination microscope and projection lantern in the Westinghouse exhibit. The actors are inhabitants of a drop of water.

* * *

FAIR DOCTORS (forty of them aided by seventy nurses) will handle more than 40,000 cases of one kind or another, according to aches-and-pains statisticians.

* * *

IN THE New York Zoology Society building electric eels will ring bells and light lamps—unless they get temperamental and refuse to do their stuff.

* * *

THE WORLD'S largest steam locomotive, 130 feet long, weighing 519 tons, built for the Pennsylvania Railroad will keep running at seventy-five miles an hour at the Fair—on friction bearings. Actually it won't move one inch; just mark time at high speed.

* * *

GENTLEMEN INCLINED to see things after the first or second round are advised to keep out of the Men's Apparel Quality Guild exhibition. The ceiling there is an aquarium alive with goldfish.

* * *

TWIN PROWS in the Hall of Marine Transportation are each thirty feet higher than the nose of the Normandie.

* * *

THE PARKING zone, covering 215 acres, has room for 43,000 cars.

* * *

EVERY THREE days a fresh cargo of orchids plucked out of Venezuelan jungles will be flown to the Fair for exhibition.

* * *

ONE BILLION dollars (if the statisticians are borne out) will be spent in Greater New York during the Fair, as follows: $250,000,000 for entertainment; $200,000,000 for housing; $250,000,000 for food and liquor; $100,000,000 for transportation; $50,000,000 for personal service; $10,000,000 for communication; $140,000,000 for merchandise.

* * *

THE FORECOURT of the Government Building in the Federal Exhibit Area has room for 50,000 parading troops.

* * *

THE FAIR police force will include 1,000 patrolmen, 30 sergeants, 3 captains. G-men, city detectives and special details of New York's "finest" will swell the force on special occasions to as much as 3,000 and more.

* * *

A MATURE orange grove, just so much orange juice on the hoof, was transported all the way from Florida for that State's exhibit.

* * *

MORE THAN 300,000 persons at one time can see the 231 shows in the Amusement Zone. This zone covers two square miles.

* * *

A REAL skeleton in the Hall of Man, Medical and Health Building moves his joints—and explains each action to the audience. It's done with a recording device.

THE FAIR'S HUGE EXHIBIT AREA

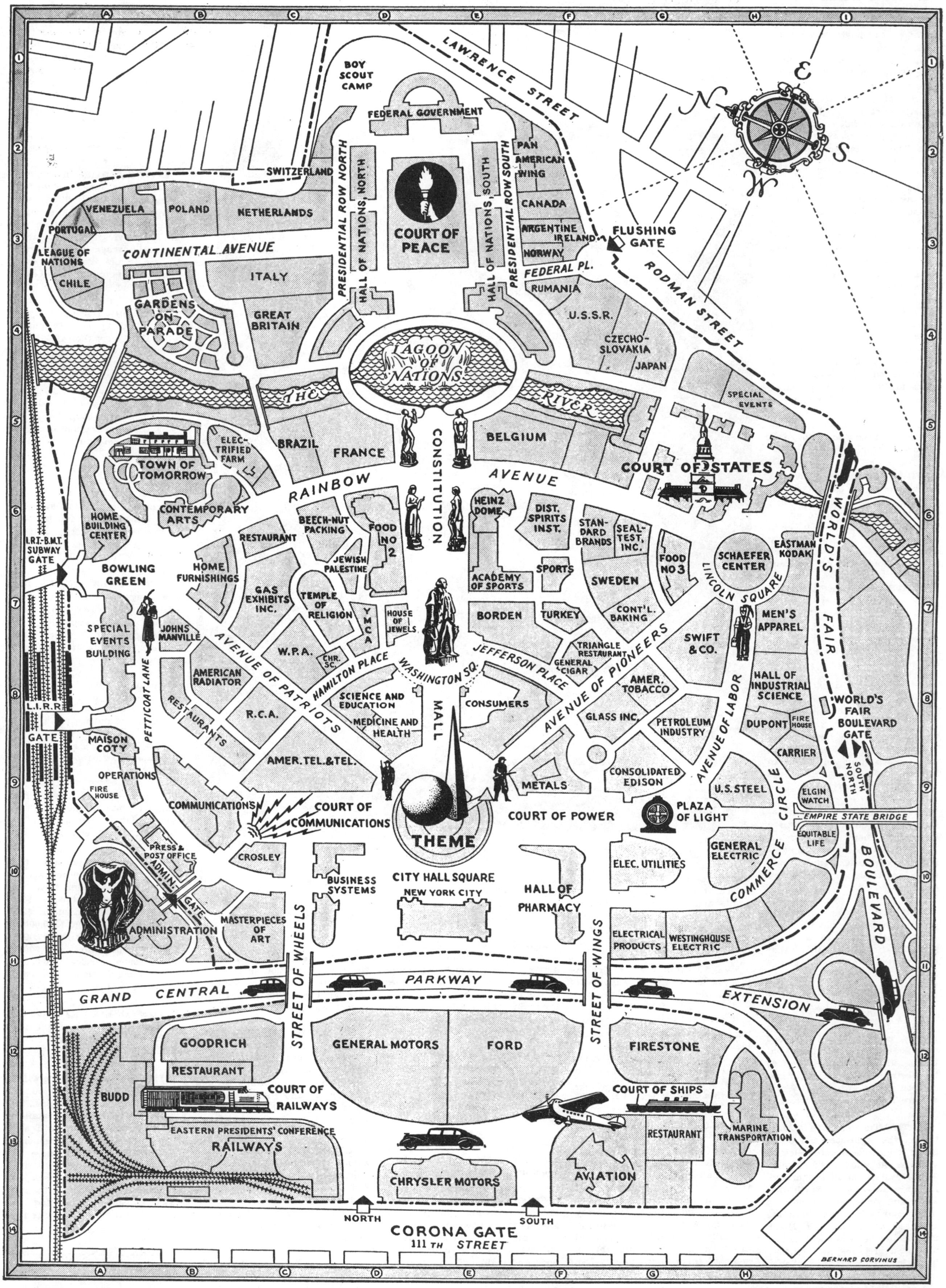

In the Exhibit Area there are about 200 separate buildings. The Fair statisticians haven't figured out what those buildings and their contents represent in cash—but the total is well over $100,000,000. The foremost of the world's designers have labored to present in the hundreds of exhibits the stories of industry, government, science and the arts. Their aim was to be informative without being dull—to interest as well as to educate. They have achieved that aim.

Letters and numbers on the margin of the map will assist in locating the exhibits described on the following pages. A key reference to the position of each building will be found in each descriptive paragraph.

STAGE PLAYS IN NEW YORK

First Tarkington Play In 8 Years Listed for Summer Playhouse

Booth Tarkington's first play since 1931—a script which has been written almost in secret and will arrive on its first stage with no fuss whatever—is scheduled for Kennebunkport, Maine, Aug. 1. It's called "Karabash" and is described as a "pro-American comedy." Kennebunkport has been the 70-year-old Tarkington's Summer home for years.

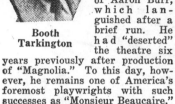

The Summer theatre Garrick Players will cast Diana Cheswick and Harry Townes in leading roles and will launch a Booth Tarkington Drama Festival with the comedy.

Booth Tarkington

Tarkington's last local play was "Colonel Satan," a romantic comedy of Aaron Burr, which languished after a brief run. He had "deserted" the theatre six years previously after production of "Magnolia." To this day, however, he remains one of America's foremost playwrights with such successes as "Monsieur Beaucaire," "The Man From Home," "Cameo Kirby," "Your Humble Servant," "Clarence," "The Country Cousin" and "Mister Antonio" to his credit.

He is perhaps most widely known for his novels and stories of "Penrod" and "Seventeen." Tarkington won the Pulitzer Prize in 1919 with "The Magnificent Ambersons" and in 1922 with "Alice Adams."

WPA Theatre Rally.

A mass rally of Broadway actors, directors, producers and theatrical celebrities was listed yesterday for 11:30 Monday night at the Majestic. Purpose: to devise ways and means to save the Federal Theatre from abandonment. Speakers will include Tallulah Bankhead, Herman Shumlin, Blanche Yurka, Heywood Broun and Donald Ogden Stewart.

Top matinee price for "From Vienna" at the Music Box will be $1.65 . . . Jean Sablon, French singer in "The Streets of Paris" has recorded two of the show tunes . . . And Charles "Think-a-Drink" Hoffman, who pours any sort of a cocktail from apparently empty shakers, has been made honorary member of twenty-three bartenders' union since the opening.

Open Air Opera

Alfredo Salmaggi will produce two grand operas at Tri-Boro Stadium (Randalls Island), July 15 and 16. Ann Roselle and Sydney Raynor will sing "Aida" July 15. The second opera will be "Carmen."

Stands 'Em Up

Katharine Hepburn and "The Philadelphia Story" played to 117 standees at the Shubert Theatre yesterday afternoon, a new record for the comedy.

'Kiss the Boys' Cast in Barn

With most of the original cast intact, "Kiss the Boys Goodbye" will open Bela Blau's theatre at Harrison, Me., July 10th. Helen Claire, Sheldon Leonard, Millard Mitchell, Philip Ober, Ollie Burgoyne and Frank Wilson have their old roles. Phillips Holmes plays "Journey's End" in Great Neck, next week. Glenda Farrell and Nance O'Neill do "Anna Christie" at Westport July 3. Mildred Natwick joines Douglas Montgomery in "Autumn Crocus" at Marblehead, Mass., July 31. Equity won't let the Stony Creek, Conn., company play Sunday night shows.

Helen Claire

$200,000 Radium to Move, Guarded

Picked detectives will guard four grams of radium—worth $200,000—when it is moved at 9:30 A. M. today from the old Memorial Hospital for Cancer and Allied Diseases, 106th St. and Central Park West, to the institution's new quarters at 444 E. 68th St.

Casa Vs. Rose

Jack Shapiro and Louis Blumenthal, owners of the Casa Manana (former Earl Carroll Theatre) yesterday said they are instituting legal proceedings against Billy Rose for rent due under the terms of Rose's lease. The owners claim that Rose has been dispossessed for non-payment of rent. Rose wired newspapers that he forfeited $20,000 when he abandoned the big cabaret and that the sum more than covered his obligation under a short term lease.

Schwartz' Next

Sholem Asch's "Salvation" will be Maurice Schwartz' next production at the Yiddish Art Theatre, opening Sept. 18. Aaron Zeitlin's "Esterke" has been postponed.

Rejoins Class

FRAYE GILBERT, who toured for thirty-two weeks with the Road company of "What A Life," has returned to her old classes in the original production of the high school comedy which has passed the 500-performance mark at the Mansfield.

Berle Does Book; Shields Returning

Milton Berle, young comedy headliner at the International Casino, has sold his novel on the theatre and stage folk, "Laughingly Yours," for publication in September, by Samuel French. The manuscript is also being considered for a film which would star the comic . . . Arthur Shields, Abbey Theatre stalwart, arrives tomorrow on the new Mauretania en route to Hollywood . . . Fred Keating, past president of the Actors Federation of America, yesterday attacked the "one or ones" who are using Sophie Tucker as a "shield" in the current actors union melee . . . Vera Zorina and husband George Balanchine will vacation in Norway this Summer at the completion of the dancer's film chore . . . It's July 6 and the Lobero Theatre, Santa Barbara, for the premiere of Helen Hayes, Herbert Marshall and "Ladies and Gentlemen."

Milton Berle

Eunice Kennedy Has Gala London Debut

London, June 22.—Thousands of cheering Britons clamoring in London's West End made Eunice Kennedy's party tonight doubly exciting because papa Joe, with ambassadorial foresight, had picked the day of the royal homecoming for his daughter's debut.

Cheers from the Palace reechoed inside the Embassy, where 250 Mayfair socialites shook hands with Mrs. Kennedy and her daughter, Eunice, in the lily and rose decorated entrance hall.

Eunice's sisters, Rosemary and Kathleen, and her brothers, Jack and Joe Jr., completed the family party. The other young members of the large Kennedy brood were unable to get leave of absence from their schools to attend the party.

The festivities went on until early morning. The Kennedy boys danced with such London belles as debutante Sarah Spencer Churchill, daughter of the half-American Duke of Marlborough; with Sir Oswald Mosley's daughter, Vivian; with Lady Mary Stuart and with Valerie Cole, niece of Chamberlain.

Eunice Kennedy
Makes London debut.

Antoinette Donnelly's Beauty Leaflets are free at The News Information Bureau.

Sunday Is 'Young Citizenship Day'

Sunday will be set aside as "Young Citizenship Day," in recognition of New York youths "who are becoming and will become for the first time American citizens," according to a proclamation of Mayor LaGuardia yesterday. The Mayor, though in Washington, ordered the proclamation made from Summer City Hall and directed that "fitting and dignified ceremonies" be held to mark the occasion on Sunday.

AMUSEMENTS

AMUSEMENTS

HOTELS AND RESTAURANTS

AMUSEMENTS *AMUSEMENTS*